BASEBALL GUIDE

2001 EDITION

Editors

CRAIG CARTER

DAVE SLOAN

EXPLANATION OF STATISTICAL ABBREVIATIONS

A: assists. **AB:** at-bats. **Avg.:** batting average (hits divided by at-bats). **BB:** bases on balls. **Bk.:** balks. **CG:** complete games. **CS:** caught stealing. **E:** errors. **ER:** earned runs. **ERA:** earned-run average (earned runs times nine divided by innings pitched). **G:** games. **GB:** games behind. **GF:** games finished. **GDP:** grounding into double plays. **GS:** games started. **H:** hits. **HB:** hit batsmen. **HP:** hit by pitches. **HR:** home runs. **IBB:** intentional bases on balls. **IP:** innings pitched. **L:** losses. **OBP:** on-base percentage (hits plus bases on balls plus hit by pitches divided by at-bats plus bases on balls plus hit by pitches plus sacrifice flies). **PO:** putouts. **Pos.:** position. **R:** runs. **RBI:** runs batted in. **SB:** stolen bases. **SF:** sacrifice flies (run-scoring flyouts). **SH:** sacrifice hits (bunts that advance one or more runners but result in the batter being retired at first base or reaching first on an error). **ShO:** shutouts. **Slg.:** slugging percentage (total bases divided by at-bats). **SO:** strikeouts. **Sv.:** saves. **TB:** total bases (hits plus doubles plus two times the number of triples plus three times the number of home runs). **TBF:** total batters faced. **TC:** total chances (putouts plus assists plus errors). **TPA:** total plate appearances (at-bats plus bases on balls plus sacrifice hits plus sacrifice flies plus hit by pitches plus times reaching base on catcher's interference). **W:** wins. **WP:** wild pitches. **2B:** doubles. **3B:** triples.

World Series, A.L. Championship Series, N.L. Championship Series, A.L. Division Series, N.L. Division Series and All-Star Game highlights written by Jared Hoffman and Ron Smith of THE SPORTING NEWS.

Major league statistics compiled by STATS, Inc., Lincolnwood, Ill.

Minor league statistics compiled by SportsTicker Enterprises, L.P., Boston.

Copyright ©2001 by The Sporting News, a division of Vulcan Print Media, Inc.,
10176 Corporate Square Drive, Suite 200, St. Louis, MO 63132. All rights reserved. Printed in the U.S.A.

No part of the *Baseball Guide* may be reproduced or transmitted in any form or by any means, electronic or mechanical, including photocopy, recording or any information storage and retrieval system now known or to be invented, without permission in writing from the publisher, except by a reviewer who wishes to quote brief passages in connection with a review written for inclusion in a magazine, newspaper or broadcast.

THE SPORTING NEWS is a registered trademark of The Sporting News.

ISBN: 0-89204-644-9

10 9 8 7 6 5 4 3 2 1

CONTENTS

ON THE COVER: Mike Piazza. (Large photo by Bob Leverone/THE SPORTING NEWS, small photo by John Dunn for THE SPORTING NEWS.)

Spine photo of Derek Jeter by Albert Dickson/THE SPORTING NEWS.

Back photo of the New York Yankees by John Dunn for THE SPORTING NEWS.

2001 SEASON

Major League Baseball directories

Team by team

MAJOR LEAGUE BASEBALL

Address
245 Park Avenue
New York, NY 10167
Telephone
212-931-7800
FAX
212-949-5654
Website
www.mlb.com
Commissioner of baseball
Allan H. "Bud" Selig
President & chief operating officer
Paul Beeston
Executive v.p., baseball operations
Richard "Sandy" Alderson
Executive v.p., administration
Robert A. DuPuy
Exec. vice president, labor relations and human resources
Robert D. Manfred Jr.
Executive vice president, business
Timothy Brosnan
Sr. vice president, public relations
Richard Levin

Sr. v.p., security and facilities
Kevin Hallinan
Sr. v.p. and general counsel
Thomas J. Ostertag
Sr. vice president, baseball operations
Jimmie Lee Solomon
Sr. v.p. and chief financial officer
Jeffrey White
Sr. vice president, team services
Mark Gorris
V.p., club relations and scheduling
Katy Feeney
Vice president, club relations
Phyllis Merhige
Vice president, on field operations
Frank Robinson
Vice president, umpiring
Ralph Nelson
Vice president, international baseball operations and security liaison
Louis Melendez
Vice president, marketing
Kathleen Francis

Vice president, broadcasting
Leslie Sullivan
Vice president, human resources and office services
Wendy L. Lewis
V.p. & general counsel, labor relations
Frank Coonelly
Vice president and general counsel, legal business affairs
Ethan G. Orlinsky
V.p., accounting and treasurer
Robert Clark
V.p., international business operations
Paul Archey
Vice president, licensing
Howard Smith
Vice president, business affairs
Christopher Tully
Vice president, special events
Marla Miller
Vice president, programming and sales
James Scott
V.p. and exec. producer, productions
Dave Gavant

OTHER ORGANIZATIONS

LABOR RELATIONS COMMITTEE
Address
245 Park Avenue
New York, NY 10167
Telephone
212-931-7401
212-949-5690 (FAX)
Exec. vice president, labor relations and human resources
Robert D. Manfred Jr.
V.p. & general counsel, labor relations
Francis Coonelly
Associate counsels
Derek Jackson
Paul Mifsud
System administration
John Ricco
Deputy general counsel
Jennifer Gefsky

NATIONAL ASSOCIATION OF PROFESSIONAL BASEBALL LEAGUES
Address
P.O. Box A
St. Petersburg, FL 33731
Telephone
727-822-6937
727-821-5819 (FAX)
President
Mike Moore
Vice president/administration
Pat O'Conner
Executive director of special operations
Misann Ellmaker

General counsel
Scott Poley
Director/licensing
Brian Earle
Director/media relations
Jim Ferguson
Director of baseball operations
Tim Brunswick
Director of marketing
Rod Meadows
Director of business/finance
Eric Krupa
Director of Professional Baseball Umpire Corporation
Mike Fitzpatrick
Director of Professional Baseball Employment Opportunities
Ann Perkins

BASEBALL ASSISTANCE TEAM INC.
Address
245 Park Avenue
New York, NY 10167
Telephone
212-931-7821
Chairman
Ralph Branca
President
Earl Wilson
President emeritus
Joe Garagiola
Vice presidents
Joe Black
Bob Gibson
Ed Stack
Frank Torre

Executive director
James J. Martin
Secretary
Thomas J. Ostertag
Treasurer
Jeffrey White

ASSOCIATION OF PROFESSIONAL BASEBALL PLAYERS OF AMERICA
Address
1820 W. Orangewood Ave., Suite 206
Orange, CA 92868
Telephone
714-935-9993
714-935-0431 (FAX)
President
John J. McHale
Vice presidents
Roland Hemond
Robert Kennedy
Secretary/treasurer
Dick Beverage

NATIONAL BASEBALL HALL OF FAME AND MUSEUM
Address
P.O. Box 590
Cooperstown, NY 13326
Telephone
607-547-7200
607-547-2044 (FAX)
Hall of Fame board of directors chairman
Jane Forbes Clark
President
Dale Petroskey

V.p. of business and administration
Bill Haase

V.p. and chief curator
William T. Spencer Jr.

Curator of collections
Peter P. Clark

Executive director of retail marketing
Barbara Shinn

Controller
Frances L. Althiser

Librarian
James L. Gates

V.p. of communications and education
Jeff Idelson

MAJOR LEAGUE SCOUTING BUREAU

Address
3500 Porsche Way, Suite 100
Ontario, CA 91764

Telephone
909-980-1881
909-980-7794 (FAX)

Director
Frank Marcos

MAJOR LEAGUE BASEBALL PLAYERS ASSOCIATION

Address
12 E. 49th St., 24th Floor
New York, NY 10017

Telephone
212-826-0808
212-752-3649 (FAX)

Executive director and general counsel
Donald M. Fehr

Special assistants
Tony Bernazard
Phil Bradley
Steve Rogers

Associate general counsel
Eugene D. Orza

Assistant general counsel
Doyle R. Pryor
Michael Weiner

Counsel
Robert Leneghan

Director of licensing
Judy Heeter

Director of communications
Greg Bouris

MAJOR LEAGUE BASEBALL PLAYERS ALUMNI ASSOC.

Address
1631 Mesa Ave., Suite C
Colorado Springs, CO 80906

Telephone
719-477-1870
719-477-1875 (FAX)

President
Brooks Robinson

Vice presidents
Bob Boone
George Brett
Mike Hegan
Chuck Hinton
Al Kaline
Carl Erskine
Rusty Staub
Robin Yount

Vice chairman
Fred Valentine

WORLD UMPIRES ASSOCIATION

Address
P.O. Box 760
Cocoa, FL 32923-0760

Telephone
321-637-3471
321-633-7018 (FAX)

President
John Hirschbeck

Vice president
Joe Brinkman

Secretary/treasurer
Tim Welke

Labor counsel
Joel Smith

BASEBALL WRITERS' ASSOCIATION OF AMERICA

President
Ian MacDonald, Montreal Gazette

Vice president
Bill Center, San Diego Union Tribune

Secretary/treasurer
Jack O'Connell, Hartford Courant

ELIAS SPORTS BUREAU

Address
500 Fifth Ave.
New York, NY 10110

Telephone
212-869-1530
212-354-0980 (FAX)

General manager
Seymour Siwoff

SPORTSTICKER ENTERPRISES, L.P.

Address
Harborside Financial Center
800 Plaza Two
Jersey City, NJ 07311

Boston office
Boston Fish Pier
West Building No. 1
Boston, MA 02210

Telephone
201-309-1200
201-860-9742 (FAX)

Boston office
617-951-0070
617-737-9960 (FAX)

General manager
Jim Morganthaler

Director, special projects
Jay Virshbo

Director, minor league operations
Jim Keller

ANAHEIM ANGELS
AMERICAN LEAGUE WEST DIVISION

Angels
2001 SCHEDULE
Home games shaded; D—Day game (games starting before 5 p.m.)
*—All-Star Game at Safeco Field (Seattle)

APRIL

SUN	MON	TUE	WED	THU	FRI	SAT
1	2	3 D TEX	4 TEX	5 TEX	6 OAK	7 D OAK
8 OAK	D 9	10 TEX	11 TEX	12 TEX	13 SEA	14 SEA
15 SEA	16 OAK	17 OAK	18 OAK	19 SEA	20 SEA	21 D SEA
22 D SEA	23	24 CLE	25 CLE	26 CLE	27 TOR	28 D TOR
29 D TOR	30					

MAY

SUN	MON	TUE	WED	THU	FRI	SAT
		1 CWS	2 CWS	3 CWS	4 DET	5 DET
6 D DET	7	8 CWS	9 CWS	10 CWS	11 DET	12 D DET
13 DET	14	15 TOR	16 TOR	17 TOR	18 CLE	19 CLE
20 CLE	21	22 BAL	23 D BAL	24	25 TB	26 D TB
27 D TB	28 D TB	29 MIN	30 MIN	31 MIN		

JUNE

SUN	MON	TUE	WED	THU	FRI	SAT
					1 KC	2 KC
3 KC	4	5 OAK	6 OAK	7 OAK	8 LA	9 D LA
10 LA	D 11	12 SF	13 SF	14 D SF	15 LA	16 LA
17 LA	D 18	19 TEX	20 TEX	21 TEX	22 SEA	23 SEA
24 D SEA	25 TEX	26 TEX	27 TEX	28 TEX	29 SEA	30 D SEA

JULY

SUN	MON	TUE	WED	THU	FRI	SAT
1 SEA	2 OAK	3 OAK	4 OAK	5 D OAK	6 D COL	7 COL
8 COL	D 9	10	* 11	12 ARI	13 ARI	14 ARI
15 SD	16 SD	17 D SD	18 TB	19 TB	20 BAL	21 D BAL
22 BAL	23 D BAL	24 TB	25 TB	26 TB	27 BAL	28 BAL
29 BAL	30	31 BOS				

AUGUST

SUN	MON	TUE	WED	THU	FRI	SAT
			1 BOS	2 BOS	3 NYY	4 D NYY
5 D NYY	D 6 NYY	D 7 NYY	8 CWS	9 CWS	10 TOR	11 TOR
12 TOR	13	14 DET	15 DET	16 D DET	17 CLE	18 D CLE
19 CLE	D 20 BOS	21 BOS	22 BOS	23 NYY	24 NYY	25 D NYY
26 NYY	27	28 KC	29 KC	30 KC	31 MIN	

SEPTEMBER

SUN	MON	TUE	WED	THU	FRI	SAT
						1 MIN
2 MIN	D 3	4 KC	5 KC	6 KC	7 MIN	8 MIN
9 MIN	D 10	11 SEA	12 SEA	13 OAK	14 OAK	15 D OAK
16 OAK	17	18 SEA	19 SEA	20 D SEA	21 TEX	22 TEX
23 TEX	D 24	25 OAK	26 OAK	27 D OAK	28 TEX	29 TEX
30 D TEX						

2001 SEASON
CLUB DIRECTORY

Owner
The Walt Disney Company
Chairman and CEO, The Walt Disney Co.
Michael Eisner
President
Tony Tavares
Vice president and general manager
Bill Stoneman
Vice president of finance/administation
Andy Roundtree
V.p., advertising sales and broadcasting
John Covarrubias
V.p., sales, marketing and operations
Kevin Uhlich
Vice president, communications
Tim Mead
V.p., business and legal affairs
Rick Schlesinger
Assistant general manager
Ken Forsch
Special assistant to general manager
Preston Gomez
Legal counsel/contract negotiations
Mark Rosenthal
Director, scouting
Donny Rowland
Director, player development
Darrell Miller
Manager, baseball operations
Tony Reagins
Equipment manager
Ken Higdon
Visiting clubhouse manager
Brian Harkins
Senior video coordinator
Diego Lopez
Manager, baseball information
Larry Babcock
Manager, media services
Nancy Mazmanian
Manager, publications
Doug Ward

Manager, community relations
Matt Bennett
Media services/travel coordinator
Tom Taylor
Director, marketing
Robert Alvarado
Manager, ticket operations
Sheila Brazelton
Medical director
Dr. Lewis Yocum
Team physician
Dr. Craig Milhouse
Head athletic trainer
Ned Bergert
International supervisor
Clay Daniel
Eastern supervisor
Guy Mader
Western supervisor
Tom Davis
Midwestern supervisor
Ron Marigny
National cross-checkers
Rick Ingalls, Hank Sargent
Major league scouts
Jay Hankins, Jon Niederer, Rich Schlenker, Moose Stubing, Dale Sutherland, Gary Sutherland, John Van Ornum
Scouts
Don Archer, Todd Blyleven, Brian Bridges, Jon Bunnell, John Burden, Tom Burns, Todd Claus, Tim Corcoran, Jeff Crane, David Crowson, Bobby Dejardin, Kevin Ham, Al Hammell, Tom Kotchman, Dan Lynch, Chris McAlpin, Mike Powers, Marc Russo, Jeff Scholzen, Jack Uhey
International scouts
Amador Arias, Arnold Cochrane, Luis Cuevas, Felipe Gutierrez, Mario Mendoza, Tak Kawamoto, Leo Perez, Carlos Porte, Takanori Takeuchi, Grant Weir

MINOR LEAGUE AFFILIATES

Class	Team	League	Manager
AAA	Salt Lake	Pacific Coast	Garry Templeton
AA	Arkansas	Texas	Mike Brumley
A	Cedar Rapids	Midwest	Tyrone Boykin
A	Rancho Cucamonga	California	Tim Wallach
Rookie	Mesa Angels	Arizona	Brian Harper
Rookie	Provo	Pioneer	Tom Kotchman

BROADCAST INFORMATION

Radio: KLAC-AM (570).
TV: KCAL-TV (Channel 9).
Cable TV: Fox Sports West.

SPRING TRAINING

Ballpark (city): Tempe Diablo Stadium (Tempe, Ariz.).
Ticket information: 602-254-3300, 800-326-0331.

Follow the Angels all season at: www.sportingnews.com/baseball/teams/angels/

Manager—Mike Scioscia (14).
Coaches—Bud Black (24), Alfredo Griffin (4), Mickey Hatcher (7), Joe Madden (70), Orlando Mercado (88), Bobby Ramos (13), Ron Roenicke (12).

No.	PITCHERS	B/T	Ht./Wt.	Born	2000 clubs
18	Alvarez, Juan	L/L	6-0/175	8-9-73	Edmonton, Anaheim
45	Cooper, Brian	R/R	6-1/185	10-22-76	Edmonton, Anaheim, Lake Elsinore
47	Espina, Rendy	L/L	6-0/180	5-11-78	Tennessee
27	Fyhrie, Michael	R/R	6-2/203	12-9-69	Anaheim, Edmonton
68	Green, Steve	R/R	6-2/195	1-26-78	Erie, Edmonton
21	Hasegawa, Shigetoshi	R/R	5-11/178	8-1-68	Anaheim
65	Holtz, Mike	L/L	5-9/188	10-10-72	Edmonton, Anaheim
43	Levine, Al	R/R	6-3/198	5-22-68	Anaheim, Erie
33	Lukasiewicz, Mark	L/L	6-7/240	3-8-73	Syracuse, Tennessee
66	Miadich, Bart	R/R	6-4/205	2-3-76	Erie, Edmonton
59	Nina, Elvin	R/R	6-0/185	11-25-75	Erie, Edmonton
36	Ortiz, Ramon	R/R	6-0/175	5-23-76	Anaheim, Lake Elsinore, Edmonton
40	Percival, Troy	R/R	6-3/236	8-9-69	Anaheim, Lake Elsinore
58	Pote, Lou	R/R	6-3/208	8-27-71	Anaheim, Edmonton
34	Rapp, Pat	R/R	6-3/215	7-13-67	Baltimore
60	Schoeneweis, Scott	L/L	6-0/186	10-2-73	Anaheim, Lake Elsinore, Edmonton
62	Shields, Scot	R/R	6-1/175	7-22-75	Edmonton
54	Turnbow, Derrick	R/R	6-3/180	1-25-78	Anaheim
	Valdes, Ismael	R/R	6-4/225	8-21-73	Chicago N.L., Los Angeles
56	Washburn, Jarrod	L/L	6-1/198	8-13-74	Lake Elsinore, Edmonton, Anaheim
57	Weber, Ben	R/R	6-4/180	11-17-69	San Francisco, Fresno, Erie, Anaheim
32	Wise, Matt	R/R	6-4/190	11-18-75	Edmonton, Anaheim

No.	CATCHERS	B/T	Ht./Wt.	Born	2000 clubs
6	Fabregas, Jorge	L/R	6-3/215	3-13-70	Omaha, Kansas City
1	Molina, Bengie	R/R	5-11/207	7-20-74	Anaheim
44	Wooten, Shawn	R/R	5-10/205	7-24-72	Erie, Edmonton, Anaheim

No.	INFIELDERS	B/T	Ht./Wt.	Born	2000 clubs
37	Barnes, Larry	L/L	6-1/195	7-23-74	Edmonton
38	Caceres, Wilmy	B/R	6-0/165	10-2-78	Chattanooga
9	DiSarcina, Gary	R/R	6-2/195	11-19-67	Anaheim
22	Eckstein, David	R/R	5-8/165	1-20-75	Pawtucket, Edmonton
10	Gil, Benji	R/R	6-2/190	10-6-72	Anaheim
25	Glaus, Troy	R/R	6-5/229	8-3-76	Anaheim
2	Kennedy, Adam	L/R	6-1/180	1-10-76	Anaheim
23	Spiezio, Scott	B/R	6-2/225	9-21-72	Anaheim
42	Vaughn, Mo	L/R	6-1/268	12-15-67	Anaheim

No.	OUTFIELDERS	B/T	Ht./Wt.	Born	2000 clubs
16	Anderson, Garret	L/L	6-3/220	6-30-72	Anaheim
46	Bartee, Kimera	R/R	6-0/200	7-21-72	Louisville, Cincinnati
17	Erstad, Darin	L/L	6-2/212	6-4-74	Anaheim
48	Guzman, Elpidio	L/L	6-0/165	2-24-79	Lake Elsinore
53	Haynes, Nathan	L/L	5-9/170	9-7-79	Erie
3	Palmeiro, Orlando	L/L	5-11/175	1-19-69	Anaheim
15	Salmon, Tim	R/R	6-3/231	8-24-68	Anaheim

BALLPARK INFORMATION

Ballpark (capacity, surface)
Edison International Field of Anaheim (45,050, grass)
Address
2000 Gene Autry Way
Anaheim, CA 92806
Official website
www.angelsbaseball.com
Business phone
714-940-2000
Ticket information
714-634-2000
Ticket prices
$24 (terrace MVP)
$22 (club loge, field box)
$20 (terrace box)
$15 (lower view MVP)
$12 (lower view box)
$10 (view)
$8 (RF pavilion-adult)
$7 (LF pavilion-adult)
$6 (RF pavilion-child)
$4 (LF pavilion-child)
Field dimensions (from home plate)
To left field at foul line, 330 feet
To center field, 400 feet
To right field at foul line, 330 feet
First game played
April 19, 1966 (White Sox 3, Angels 1)

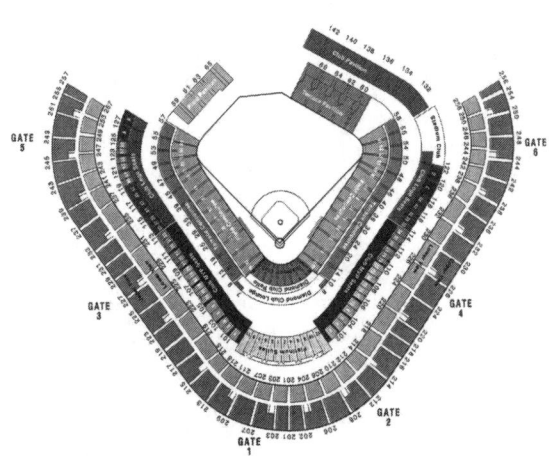

2000 REVIEW
DAY BY DAY

Date	Opp.	Res.	Score	(inn.*)	Hits	Opp. hits	Winning pitcher	Losing pitcher	Save	Record	Pos.	GB
4-3	N.Y.	L	2-3		10	6	Hernandez	Hill	Rivera	0-1	T2nd	1.0
4-4	N.Y.	L	3-5		10	9	Mendoza	Percival	Rivera	0-2	T3rd	2.0
4-5	N.Y.	W	12-6		12	13	Schoeneweis	Cone		1-2	4th	1.0
4-7	Bos.	W	7-3		9	6	Dickson	Schourek		2-2	T3rd	1.0
4-8	Bos.	W	7-5		13	7	Hill	Rose	Percival	3-2	T1st	...
4-9	Bos.	L	2-5		7	9	P. Martinez	Bottenfield		3-3	T3rd	...
4-10	Tor.	W	6-0		7	3	Schoeneweis	Carpenter		4-3	T2nd	0.5
4-11	Tor.	W	5-4		8	10	Ortiz	Escobar	Percival	5-3	1st	+0.5
4-12	Tor.	L	2-6		9	13	Borbon	Petkovsek		5-4	2nd	0.5
4-14	At Chi.	L	4-9		12	12	Sirotka	Hill		5-5	T2nd	1.0
4-15	At Chi.	W	3-1		7	7	Bottenfield	Wells	Percival	6-5	T2nd	1.0
4-16	At Chi.	W	3-1		13	3	Schoeneweis	Parque	Percival	7-5	2nd	1.0
4-17	At Tor.	L	1-7		8	10	Escobar	Ortiz		7-6	2nd	1.5
4-18	At Tor.	W	16-10		19	17	Dickson	Castillo		8-6	2nd	1.0
4-19	At Tor.	L	4-12		8	17	Wells	Hill		8-7	2nd	0.5
4-20	At Tor.	L	11-12		19	14	Halladay	Bottenfield	Koch	8-8	2nd	1.0
4-21	At T.B.	W	9-6		12	8	Petkovsek	Hernandez	Percival	9-8	2nd	1.0
4-22	At T.B.	L	9-11	(10)	10	12	Lopez	Mercker		9-9	2nd	2.0
4-23	At T.B.	L	0-1		4	5	Eiland	Dickson	Hernandez	9-10	2nd	3.0
4-24	Det.	W	10-4		14	13	Hill	Mlicki		10-10	2nd	2.0
4-25	Det.	L	2-4		8	10	Poole	Bottenfield	Jones	10-11	2nd	3.0
4-26	Det.	W	6-1		11	5	Schoeneweis	Nitkowski		11-11	2nd	2.0
4-27	T.B.	L	3-7		6	12	Gooden	Ortiz		11-12	2nd	2.5
4-28	T.B.	L	2-11		7	19	Yan	Dickson		11-13	2nd	2.5
4-29	T.B.	W	7-6	(13)	13	16	Levine	Sparks		12-13	2nd	2.5
4-30	T.B.	W	5-2		9	7	Bottenfield	Trachsel	Percival	13-13	2nd	1.5
5-2	At Bal.	L	6-7		11	9	Trombley	Percival		13-14	T2nd	2.5
5-3	At Bal.	W	6-5		9	8	Ortiz	Johnson	Percival	14-14	T2nd	1.5
5-4	At Bal.	W	8-5		11	9	Hill	Mussina	Hasegawa	15-14	2nd	1.0
5-5	At Sea.	W	6-5		11	11	Bottenfield	Sele	Percival	16-14	2nd	...
5-6	At Sea.	L	0-1		2	7	Sasaki	Holtz		16-15	2nd	1.0
5-7	At Sea.	L	2-8		7	7	Halama	Schoeneweis		16-16	2nd	2.0
5-8	Oak.	W	9-8		17	10	Petkovsek	Mathews	Percival	17-16	2nd	1.0
5-9	Oak.	L	2-5		9	9	Heredia	Hill	Isringhausen	17-17	2nd	2.0
5-10	Oak.	L	4-7		9	13	Isringhausen	Petkovsek		17-18	3rd	2.0
5-11	Tex.	W	3-2		10	8	Hasegawa	Rogers	Percival	18-18	3rd	1.0
5-12	Tex.	L	11-13		14	14	Davis	Schoeneweis	Wetteland	18-19	3rd	1.5
5-13	Tex.	L	5-6		7	9	Helling	Washburn	Wetteland	18-20	3rd	2.0
5-14	Tex.	W	7-6		8	8	Hasegawa	Cordero		19-20	3rd	1.5
5-16	Bal.	L	3-4		9	7	Erickson	Bottenfield	Timlin	19-21	4th	2.5
5-17	Bal.	W	8-7		11	12	Percival	Timlin		20-21	4th	2.5
5-19	K.C.	W	6-4		12	10	Washburn	Suppan	Percival	21-21	3rd	2.5
5-20	K.C.	W	9-8		11	12	Hasegawa	Reichert	Percival	22-21	3rd	1.5
5-21	K.C.	L	6-10		7	14	Santiago	Bottenfield		22-22	3rd	2.5
5-23	At Min.	W	7-4		12	7	Cooper	Mays	Percival	23-22	3rd	1.5
5-24	At Min.	W	6-5	(10)	18	7	Percival	Wells	Levine	24-22	3rd	0.5
5-25	At Min.	W	3-1		9	7	Schoeneweis	Radke	Percival	25-22	2nd	0.5
5-26	At K.C.	L	4-9		6	14	Fussell	Weaver	Bottalico	25-23	3rd	0.5
5-27	At K.C.	L	5-6	(10)	9	8	Reichert	Weaver		25-24	3rd	1.5
5-28	At K.C.	W	8-4		13	10	Cooper	Batista	Hasegawa	26-24	2nd	0.5
5-29	At Cle.	W	3-2	(10)	4	5	Hasegawa	Karsay	Percival	27-24	2nd	0.5
5-30	At Cle.	L	1-6		9	9	Burba	Schoeneweis		27-25	2nd	0.5
5-31	At Cle.	L	3-7		14	10	Finley	Etherton	Karsay	27-26	T3rd	0.5
6-2	L.A.	W	12-5		18	11	Bottenfield	Dreifort		28-26	T2nd	0.5
6-3	L.A.	L	3-8		12	9	Park	Cooper		28-27	4th	1.0
6-4	L.A.	W	8-7		9	11	Percival	Osuna		29-27	T3rd	0.5
6-5	S.F.	L	4-5	(11)	14	10	Fultz	Hasegawa		29-28	4th	1.5
6-6	S.F.	W	6-5		10	9	Percival	Nen		30-28	4th	1.5
6-7	S.F.	W	10-9		13	15	Hasegawa	Embree		31-28	3rd	1.0
6-9	At Ari.	L	1-4		5	8	Johnson	Cooper	Kim	31-29	3rd	2.0
6-10	At Ari.	W	10-3		13	7	Washburn	Daal		32-29	3rd	1.0
6-11	At Ari.	L	2-3		8	6	Plesac	Schoeneweis	Kim	32-30	3rd	2.0
6-13	At T.B.	W	5-3		10	7	Etherton	Rekar	Percival	33-30	3rd	2.0
6-14	At T.B.	L	2-3		7	8	Lopez	Percival		33-31	3rd	2.5
6-15	At T.B.	L	1-2		6	5	Trachsel	Hasegawa		33-32	3rd	3.0
6-16	At Bal.	L	3-4		9	7	Mussina	Schoeneweis	Timlin	33-33	3rd	4.0
6-17	At Bal.	W	8-3		9	10	Belcher	Johnson		34-33	3rd	4.0
6-18	At Bal.	W	8-6		14	7	Etherton	Erickson	Percival	35-33	3rd	4.0
6-20	K.C.	L	6-8		5	17	Santiago	Percival	Bottalico	35-34	3rd	5.5
6-21	K.C.	W	3-1		6	5	Washburn	Suzuki	Percival	36-34	3rd	5.5
6-22	K.C.	W	4-3		10	3	Belcher	Witasick	Petkovsek	37-34	3rd	5.0
6-23	Min.	W	8-3		11	8	Etherton	Ryan	Levine	38-34	3rd	5.0
6-24	Min.	L	5-11		11	16	Milton	Bottenfield		38-35	3rd	5.0
6-25	Min.	W	7-6	(11)	10	11	Hasegawa	Guardado		39-35	3rd	5.0

Date	Opp.	Res.	Score	(inn.*)	Opp. Hits	Winning hits	Winning pitcher	Losing pitcher	Save	Record	Pos.	GB
6-26	Min.	L	6-10		11	13	Radke	Washburn		39-36	3rd	5.5
6-27	At Sea.	L	3-5		5	8	Sele	Belcher	Sasaki	39-37	3rd	6.5
6-28	At Sea.	W	3-2		8	6	Hill	Moyer	Percival	40-37	3rd	5.5
6-29	At Sea.	L	2-7		7	8	Paniagua	Bottenfield		40-38	3rd	6.0
6-30	Oak.	W	7-0		12	3	Cooper	Mulder		41-38	3rd	5.0
7-1	Oak.	W	7-2		8	3	Washburn	Prieto		42-38	3rd	5.0
7-2	Oak.	L	3-10		8	12	Hudson	Belcher		42-39	3rd	6.0
7-3	Sea.	L	6-8		13	13	Moyer	Hill	Sasaki	42-40	3rd	7.0
7-4	Sea.	W	7-6		8	8	Petkovsek	Mesa	Percival	43-40	3rd	6.0
7-5	Sea.	L	4-6		10	11	Halama	Cooper	Sasaki	43-41	3rd	7.0
7-6	Sea.	W	5-1		5	8	Washburn	Abbott		44-41	3rd	6.0
7-7	Col.	W	12-4		13	7	Ortiz	Jarvis		45-41	3rd	5.0
7-8	Col.	W	6-2		11	9	Hill	Bohanon		46-41	3rd	5.0
7-9	Col.	W	10-4		13	10	Bottenfield	Yoshii		47-41	3rd	5.0
7-13	At L.A.	L	3-4	(10)	9	8	Osuna	Levine		47-42	3rd	5.0
7-14	At L.A.	W	5-3		11	3	Bottenfield	Brown	Percival	48-42	3rd	5.0
7-15	At L.A.	W	6-2		10	6	Etherton	Park		49-42	3rd	4.0
7-16	At S.D.	L	5-6	(10)	13	11	Wall	Levine		49-43	3rd	5.0
7-17	At S.D.	W	3-2		6	4	Cooper	Clement	Percival	50-43	3rd	4.0
7-18	At S.D.	W	3-2	(11)	7	8	Levine	Hoffman		51-43	3rd	4.0
7-19	Tex.	L	2-3		13	10	Rogers	Bottenfield	Wetteland	51-44	T2nd	5.0
7-20	Tex.	W	6-1		9	7	Etherton	Oliver	Hasegawa	52-44	3rd	4.0
7-21	At Oak.	W	12-3		16	8	Washburn	Hudson		53-44	2nd	4.0
7-22	At Oak.	L	3-10		5	18	Zito	Cooper		53-45	T2nd	5.0
7-23	At Oak.	L	0-5		6	11	Mulder	Hill		53-46	3rd	5.0
7-24	At Tex.	W	6-5	(12)	11	11	Hasegawa	Crabtree	Percival	54-46	3rd	5.0
7-25	At Tex.	L	6-9		10	10	Davis	Holtz	Wetteland	54-47	3rd	5.0
7-26	At Tex.	L	5-6		7	12	Wetteland	Levine		54-48	3rd	5.0
7-27	Chi.	L	5-6		9	18	Garland	Cooper	Foulke	54-49	3rd	5.0
7-28	Chi.	W	10-7		10	13	Holtz	Beirne	Percival	55-49	3rd	5.0
7-29	Chi.	W	6-5		11	9	Bottenfield	Barcelo	Percival	56-49	3rd	5.0
7-30	Chi.	L	7-11	(10)	12	18	Foulke	Levine		56-50	3rd	6.0
7-31	Det.	W	5-4		7	10	Petkovsek	Jones		57-50	3rd	5.0
8-1	Det.	L	3-6		8	10	Cruz	Cooper	Jones	57-51	3rd	6.0
8-2	Det.	L	3-5		9	9	Moehler	Hill	Jones	57-52	3rd	6.0
8-4	At Cle.	L	10-11		13	13	Wickman	Percival		57-53	3rd	6.0
8-5	At Cle.	L	3-6		6	16	Speier	Schoeneweis		57-54	3rd	7.0
8-6	At Cle.	L	2-5		7	10	Colon	Cooper	Wickman	57-55	3rd	8.0
8-7	Bos.	W	4-1		10	5	Washburn	Ohka	Hasegawa	58-55	3rd	8.0
8-8	Bos.	W	2-1		3	2	Ortiz	P. Martinez		59-55	3rd	8.5
8-9	Bos.	L	2-4		6	8	Fassero	Wise	Lowe	59-56	3rd	8.5
8-11	N.Y.	W	8-3		10	11	Schoeneweis	Hernandez		60-56	3rd	9.0
8-12	N.Y.	W	9-6		12	10	Pote	Neagle	Hasegawa	61-56	3rd	8.0
8-13	N.Y.	L	1-4		4	5	Clemens	Ortiz	Rivera	61-57	3rd	8.0
8-15	At Tor.	W	8-4		12	8	Wise	Wells		62-57	3rd	6.5
8-16	At Tor.	L	6-8		11	10	Koch	Pote		62-58	3rd	6.5
8-17	At N.Y.	L	1-6		11	6	Neagle	Mercker		62-59	3rd	7.0
8-18	At N.Y.	W	9-8	(11)	15	13	Hasegawa	Stanton		63-59	3rd	6.0
8-19	At N.Y.	L	1-9		5	11	Pettitte	Cooper		63-60	3rd	6.0
8-20	At N.Y.	W	5-4		6	9	Wise	Nelson	Hasegawa	64-60	3rd	5.0
8-21	At Bos.	L	6-7	(11)	8	8	Lowe	Hasegawa		64-61	3rd	5.5
8-22	At Bos.	W	11-4		14	9	Mercker	Wakefield		65-61	3rd	5.5
8-23	At Bos.	L	1-3		8	5	Ohka	Ortiz	Lowe	65-62	3rd	5.5
8-25	Cle.	W	4-1		9	4	Wise	Burba	Hasegawa	66-62	3rd	4.0
8-26	Cle.	L	5-9		9	12	Bere	Schoeneweis		66-63	3rd	5.0
8-27	Cle.	W	10-9		16	14	Levine	Finley	Hasegawa	67-63	3rd	4.0
8-28	Tor.	L	2-4		7	5	Loaiza	Ortiz	Koch	67-64	3rd	4.0
8-29	Tor.	W	9-4		12	11	Holtz	Carpenter		68-64	3rd	4.0
8-30	Tor.	L	2-11		9	19	Wells	Wise		68-65	3rd	4.0
9-1	At Chi.	L	8-9		10	14	Ginter	Hasegawa	Foulke	68-66	3rd	4.0
9-2	At Chi.	L	6-13		5	14	Parque	Mercker		68-67	3rd	5.0
9-3	At Chi.	L	12-13		11	15	Wunsch	Hasegawa	Foulke	68-68	3rd	6.0
9-4	At Det.	L	0-5		5	11	Nomo	Karl		68-69	3rd	6.0
9-5	At Det.	L	5-7		10	10	Moehler	Wise	Jones	68-70	3rd	7.0
9-6	At Det.	W	1-0		9	2	Schoeneweis	Sparks	Percival	69-70	3rd	6.0
9-7	At Det.	W	6-4		11	9	Belcher	Mlicki	Hasegawa	70-70	3rd	6.0
9-8	Bal.	W	2-1		7	3	Ortiz	Rapp	Percival	71-70	3rd	5.0
9-9	Bal.	L	3-10		8	14	Mercedes	Karl		71-71	3rd	6.0
9-10	Bal.	W	2-1		5	7	Hasegawa	Mussina	Percival	72-71	3rd	6.0
9-11	Bal.	L	1-3		8	9	Ponson	Schoeneweis		72-72	3rd	6.0
9-12	T.B.	W	5-2		8	5	Belcher	Rekar	Percival	73-72	3rd	6.0
9-13	T.B.	W	8-4		10	7	Ortiz	Lidle		74-72	3rd	6.0
9-15	At Min.	W	16-5		21	9	Karl	Kinney		75-72	3rd	6.0
9-16	At Min.	W	7-6		13	8	Hasegawa	Hawkins	Percival	76-72	3rd	6.0
9-17	At Min.	L	0-1		8	5	Radke	Belcher		76-73	3rd	7.0
9-19	At K.C.	L	1-5		3	10	Stein	Ortiz		76-74	3rd	8.5
9-20	At K.C.	W	7-4	(10)	14	10	Percival	Santiago	Petkovsek	77-74	3rd	8.5
9-21	At K.C.	L	3-8		6	16	Suppan	Schoeneweis		77-75	3rd	8.5

Date	Opp.	Res.	Score	(inn.*)	Hits	Opp. hits	Winning pitcher	Losing pitcher	Save	Record	Pos.	GB
9-22	At Tex.	W	2-1		9	8	Weber	Oliver	Percival	78-75	3rd	7.5
9-23	At Tex.	W	15-4		18	4	Karl	Helling		79-75	3rd	6.5
9-24	At Tex.	W	9-2		5	5	Ortiz	Johnson		80-75	3rd	6.5
9-25	At Oak.	L	5-7		11	10	Zito	Belcher		80-76	3rd	7.0
9-26	At Oak.	L	3-10		7	8	Hudson	Schoeneweis		80-77	3rd	8.0
9-27	At Oak.	L	7-9		13	10	D. Jones	Holtz	Isringhausen	80-78	3rd	9.0
9-28	At Oak.	W	6-3	(14)	12	8	Holtz	Service	Percival	81-78	3rd	8.0
9-29	Sea.	W	9-3		10	5	Ortiz	Abbott	Pote	82-78	3rd	7.5
9-30	Sea.	L	9-21		12	22	Halama	Belcher		82-79	3rd	8.5
10-1	Sea.	L	2-5		7	12	Rhodes	Hasegawa	Sasaki	82-80	3rd	9.5

Monthly records: April (13-13), May (14-13), June (14-12), July (16-12), August (11-15), September (14-14), October (0-1).
*Innings, if other than nine.

HIGHLIGHTS

High point: A 10-3 stretch in July, including a three-game sweep of the Rockies, pushed the Angels' record to a season-best nine games over .500 (53-44). Starting pitching fueled the run, temporarily alleviating the burden on an overworked bullpen, and the Angels pulled to within four games of first-place Seattle.
Low point: Trailing the Mariners by four after games of August 29, the Angels lost six straight to Toronto, Chicago and Detroit, their longest skid of the season, and fell out of contention. A devastating 13-12 loss to the White Sox, a game in which the Angels erased a 9-4 first-inning deficit and took a 12-10 lead, might have sealed their fate.
Turning point: Within a three-day period from August 5-7, the Angels lost starting pitchers Jarrod Washburn and Seth Etherton to season-ending injuries. The two youngsters had combined for a 12-3 record before the injuries and their performance was instrumental in the decision to trade veteran righthander Kent Bottenfield.
Most valuable player: Darin Erstad emerged as one of baseball's most exciting young players, amassing a major league-leading 240 hits, batting .355 and setting an all-time record for leadoff hitters with 100 RBIs. The left fielder also won a Gold Glove, hit 25 home runs and stole 28 bases in a breakthrough season after a .253 performance in 1999.
Most valuable pitcher: Japanese righthander Shigetoshi Hasegawa filled a variety of relief roles and excelled in all, going 10-6 with a 3.57 ERA and nine saves in 66 appearances. Hasegawa was virtually untouchable from July 13-August 29, throwing 27 1/3 consecutive scoreless innings.
Most improved player: In his second full season, third baseman Troy Glaus led the A.L. with 47 home runs and set a franchise record with 85 extra-base hits. Glaus hit .284, 44 points higher than his 1999 average, and avoided the prolonged slumps that plagued him in the past.
Most pleasant surprise: The emergence of rookie catcher Bengie Molina. He handled a diverse pitching staff, threw out 33 percent (34-of-104) of would-be basestealers and batted .281 with 14 homers, 20 doubles and 71 RBIs.

Key injuries: Shortstop Gary DiSarcina (torn rotator cuff) and pitchers Tim Belcher (elbow injury) and Jason Dickson (shoulder tendinitis) missed most of the season. ... Ken Hill (strained rib cage, arthritic elbow) made only 16 starts before being released in August. ... Washburn (stress fracture in shoulder) and Etherton (shoulder tendinitis) missed the final two months.
Notable: The Angels hit a franchise-record 236 home runs, 44 more than the previous mark set in 1996. Sixty-two percent of them (147) came with the bases empty. ... The Angels became the first team in A.L. history to have four players hit 30 or more home runs. Glaus hit 47, Mo Vaughn 36, Garret Anderson 35 and Tim Salmon 34.

—MIKE DiGIOVANNA

RECORDS

2000 regular-season record: 82-80 (3rd in A.L. West); 46-35 at home; 36-45 on road; 28-27 vs. East; 25-26 vs. Central; 29-27 vs. West; 21-25 vs. lefthanded starters; 61-55 vs. righthanded starters; 73-71 on grass; 9-9 on turf; 18-24 in daytime; 64-56 at night; 32-23 in one-run games; 9-7 in extra-inning games; 0-0 in doubleheaders.
Team record past five years: 391-418 (.483, ranks 10th in league in that span).

TEAM LEADERS

Batting average: Darin Erstad (.355).
At-bats: Darin Erstad (676).
Runs: Darin Erstad (121).
Hits: Darin Erstad (240).
Total Bases: Darin Erstad (366).
Doubles: Garret Anderson (40).
Triples: Adam Kennedy (11).
Home runs: Troy Glaus (47).
Runs batted in: Garret Anderson, Mo Vaughn (117).
Stolen bases: Darin Erstad (28).
Slugging percentage: Troy Glaus (.604).
On-base percentage: Darin Erstad (.409).
Wins: Shigetoshi Hasegawa (10).
Earned-run average: Scott Schoeneweis (5.45).
Complete games: Ramon Ortiz (2).

Shutouts: Brian Cooper, Scott Schoeneweis (1).
Saves: Troy Percival (32).
Innings pitched: Scott Schoeneweis (170.0).
Strikeouts: Scott Schoeneweis (78).

GAMES BY POSITION

Catcher: Ben Molina 127, Matt Walbeck 44, Shawn Wooten 4.
First base: Mo Vaughn 147, Scott Spiezio 29, Darin Erstad 3, Benji Gil 3, Keith Johnson 3, Shawn Wooten 3, Matt Walbeck 2, Garret Anderson 1.
Second base: Adam Kennedy 155, Benji Gil 7, Justin Baughman 5, Keith Luuloa 3, Keith Johnson 2, Scott Spiezio 2, Trent Durrington 1.
Third base: Troy Glaus 156, Scott Spiezio 15.
Shortstop: Benji Gil 94, Kevin Stocker 69, Gary DiSarcina 12, Troy Glaus 6, Justin Baughman 5, Keith Luuloa 4, Keith Johnson 1.
Outfield: Garret Anderson 148, Darin Erstad 136, Tim Salmon 124, Orlando Palmeiro 72, Edgard Clemente 32, Ron Gant 21, Scott Spiezio 10, Mo Vaughn 1.
Designated hitter: Scott Spiezio 50, Tim Salmon 33, Darin Erstad 20, Orlando Palmeiro 19, Mo Vaughn 14, Ron Gant 12, Edgard Clemente 11, Garret Anderson 10, Benji Gil 6, Justin Baughman 4, Troy Glaus 4, Ben Molina 2, Matt Walbeck 1.

TOP DRAFT CHOICES

1a. **Joe Torres,** LHP, Gateway H.S., Kissimmee, Fla.
1b. **Chris Bootcheck,** RHP, Auburn U.
2. **Jared Abruzzo,** C, El Capitan H.S. La Mesa, Calif.
3. **Tommy Murphy,** SS, Fla. Atlantic U.
4. **Charlie Thames,** RHP, U. of Texas.
5. **Bobby Jenks,** RHP, Inglemoor H.S., Spirit Lake, Ida.
6. **Brandon O'Neal,** RHP, U. of Kansas.
7. **Aaron Hill,** SS, Redwood H.S., Visalia, Calif.
8. **Adam Pace,** LHP, Dominican (N.Y.) College.
9. **Jason Coulie,** OF, Bates (Me.) College.
10. **Matt Hensley,** RHP, Grossmont (Calif.) J.C.

BALTIMORE ORIOLES
AMERICAN LEAGUE EAST DIVISION

Orioles
2001 SCHEDULE
Home games shaded; D—Day game (games starting before 5 p.m.)
*—All-Star Game at Safeco Field (Seattle)

APRIL

SUN	MON	TUE	WED	THU	FRI	SAT
1	2 D BOS	3	4 BOS	5 BOS	6 CLE	7 D CLE
8 D CLE	9	10 BOS	11 BOS	12 BOS	13 TB	14 D TB
15 D TB	16	17 CLE	18 CLE	19 D CLE	20 TB	21 D TB
22 TB	23	24 DET	25 DET	26 D DET	27 MIN	28 MIN
29 MIN	30 TB					

MAY

SUN	MON	TUE	WED	THU	FRI	SAT
		1 TB	2 TB	3 NYY	4 NYY	5 D NYY
6 NYY	7	8 TB	9 TB	10 TB	11 NYY	12 D NYY
13 D NYY	14	15 DET	16 DET	17 DET	18 MIN	19 D MIN
20 D MIN	21	22 ANA	23 ANA	24 D	25 TEX	26 D TEX
27 D TEX	28 TEX	29 SEA	30 SEA	31 SEA		

JUNE

SUN	MON	TUE	WED	THU	FRI	SAT
					1 OAK	2 D OAK
3 D OAK	4	5 NYY	6 NYY	7 NYY	8 MON	9 D MON
10 D MON	11	12 NYM	13 NYM	14 NYM	15 PHI	16 PHI
17 D PHI	18 TOR	19 TOR	20 TOR	21 CWS	22 CWS	23 D CWS
24 D CWS	25 TOR	26 TOR	27 TOR	28 D TOR	29 CWS	30 CWS

JULY

SUN	MON	TUE	WED	THU	FRI	SAT
1 D CWS	2	3 NYY	4 D NYY	5 NYY	6 PHI	7 D PHI
8 PHI	9	10	*11	12 ATL	13 ATL	14 ATL
15 D FLA	16 FLA	17 FLA	18 TEX	19 TEX	20 ANA	21 D ANA
22 D ANA	23 D TEX	24 TEX	25 TEX	26 TEX	27 ANA	28 ANA
29 ANA	30	31 TB				

AUGUST

SUN	MON	TUE	WED	THU	FRI	SAT
			1 TB	2 TB	3 TOR	4 D TOR
5 TOR	6 D KC	7 KC	8 KC	9 KC	10 BOS	11 D BOS
12 BOS	13	14 KC	15 KC	16 KC	17 BOS	18 BOS
19 D BOS	20	21 TB	22 TB	23 TB	24 TOR	25 D TOR
26 D TOR	27	28 OAK	29 OAK	30 OAK	31 SEA	

SEPTEMBER

SUN	MON	TUE	WED	THU	FRI	SAT
						1 D SEA
2 D SEA	3 OAK	4 OAK	5 OAK	6 D	7 SEA	8 SEA
9 D SEA	10	11 TOR	12 TOR	13 TOR	14 BOS	15 D BOS
16 BOS	17	18 TOR	19 TOR	20 TOR	21 NYY	22 D NYY
23 NYY	24 BOS	25 BOS	26 BOS	27 BOS	28 NYY	29 D NYY
30 D NYY						

2001 SEASON
CLUB DIRECTORY

Chairman/chief executive officer
Peter Angelos

Vice chairman, chief operating officer
Joe Foss

Executive vice president
John Angelos

Vice president/chief financial officer
Robert Ames

Vice president, baseball operations
Syd Thrift

Director, minor league operations
Don Buford

Director of scouting
Tony DeMacio

Assistant dir., minor league operations
Tripp Norton

Special assistants to the v.p., baseball operations
Ed Kenney Jr., Bob Schaeffer, Danny Garcia

Traveling secretary
Philip Itzoe

Director, public relations
Bill Stetka

Manager, baseball information
Kevin Behan

Director, ballpark operations
Roger Hayden

Director, community relations
Julie Wagner

Director, computer services
James Kline

Director, publishing and advertising
Jessica Fisher

Director, fan and ticket services
Donald Grove

Director, sales
Matthew Dryer

Head athletic trainer
Richard Bancells

Assistant athletic trainer
Brian Ebel

Strength and conditioning
Tim Bishop

Advance scout
Deacon Jones

Professional scouts
Danny Garcia, Curt Motton, Tim Thompson, Fred Uhlman Sr.

National cross-checkers
Mike Ledna, Shawn Pender

Regional cross-checkers
Dean Decillis, Deron Rombach, Logan White

Full-time scouts
Joe Almaraz, Dean Decillis, Ralph Garr Jr., John Gillette, Troy Hoerner, Jim Howard, Dave Jennings, Ray Kraczyk, Gil Kubski, Jeff Morris, Lamar North, Nick Presto, Harry Shelton, Ed Sprague, Marc Tramuta, Mike Tullier, Dominic Viola, Marc Ziegler

Director, Latin American scouting
Carlos Bernhardt

Caribbean & S. American supervisor
Jesus Halabi

International scouts
Ubaldo Heredia, Salvator Ramirez, Arturo Sanchez, Brett Ward

MINOR LEAGUE AFFILIATES

Class	Team	League	Manager
AAA	Rochester	International	Andy Etchebarren
AA	Bowie	Eastern	Dave Machemer
A	Frederick	Carolina	Dave Cash
A	Delmarva	South Atlantic	Joe Ferguson
Rookie	Bluefield	Appalachian	Joe Almaraz
Rookie	Gulf Coast Orioles	Gulf Coast	Jesus Alfaro

BROADCAST INFORMATION

Radio: WBAL-AM (1090).
TV: WJZ (Channel 13), WNUV (Channel 54), WFTY (Channel 50).
Cable TV: Home Team Sports.

SPRING TRAINING

Ballpark (city): Ft. Lauderdale Stadium (Ft. Lauderdale, Fla.).
Ticket information: 954-523-3309, 305-358-5885.

Follow the Orioles all season at: www.sportingnews.com/baseball/teams/orioles/

SPRING TRAINING ROSTER

Manager—Mike Hargrove (21).
Coaches—Terry Crowley (48), Elrod Hendricks (44), Eddie Murray (33), Sam Perlozzo (2), Tom Trebelhorn, Mark Wiley.

No.	PITCHERS	B/T	Ht./Wt.	Born	2000 clubs
	Bale, John	L/L	6-4/205	5-22-74	Syracuse, Toronto
	Douglass, Sean	R/R	6-6/200	4-28-79	Bowie
19	Erickson, Scott	R/R	6-4/230	2-2-68	Frederick, Bowie, Baltimore
51	Falkenborg, Brian	R/R	6-6/195	1-18-78	DID NOT PLAY
	Figueroa, Juan	R/R	6-3/150	6-24-79	Winston-Salem, Birmingham, Bowie
27	Groom, Buddy	L/L	6-2/207	7-10-65	Baltimore
57	Guzman, Juan	R/R	6-2/184	3-4-78	Bowie, Frederick
	Hamilton, Jimmy	L/L	6-3/190	8-1-75	Rochester, Bowie
	Hentgen, Pat	R/R	6-2/195	11-13-68	St. Louis
41	Johnson, Jason	R/R	6-6/235	10-27-73	Rochester, Baltimore
50	Kohlmeier, Ryan	R/R	6-2/195	6-25-77	Rochester, Baltimore
47	McElroy, Chuck	L/L	6-0/205	10-1-67	Baltimore
31	Mercedes, Jose	R/R	6-1/180	3-5-71	Baltimore
75	Mills, Alan	R/R	6-1/195	10-18-66	Los Angeles, Baltimore, Frederick
	Nussbeck, Mark	R/L	6-4/180	5-25-74	Memphis, Rochester
53	Parrish, John	L/L	5-11/180	11-26-77	Bowie, Rochester, Baltimore
43	Ponson, Sidney	R/R	6-1/225	11-2-76	Baltimore
	Riley, Matt	L/L	6-1/201	8-2-79	Rochester, Bowie
60	Rivera, Luis	R/R	6-3/163	6-21-78	Atlanta, Richmond, Gulf Coast Braves, Rochester, Baltimore
52	Ryan, B.J.	L/L	6-6/230	12-28-75	Baltimore, Rochester
29	Spurgeon, Jay	R/R	6-6/210	7-5-76	Frederick, Bowie, Rochester, Baltimore
	Towers, Josh	R/R	6-1/165	2-26-77	Rochester
28	Trombley, Mike	R/R	6-2/204	4-14-67	Baltimore

No.	CATCHERS	B/T	Ht./Wt.	Born	2000 clubs
26	Fordyce, Brook	R/R	6-0/190	5-7-70	Charlotte, Chicago A.L., Baltimore
51	Lunar, Fernando	R/R	6-1/190	5-25-77	Greenville, Atlanta, Bowie, Baltimore
37	Myers, Greg	L/R	6-2/225	4-14-66	Baltimore

No.	INFIELDERS	B/T	Ht./Wt.	Born	2000 clubs
14	Bordick, Mike	R/R	5-11/175	7-21-65	Baltimore, New York N.L.
13	Coffie, Ivanon	L/R	6-1/192	5-16-77	Bowie, Baltimore, Rochester
18	Conine, Jeff	R/R	6-1/220	6-27-66	Baltimore
11	DeShields, Delino	L/R	6-1/175	1-15-69	Baltimore
	Gibbons, Jay	L/L	6-0/200	3-2-77	Tennessee
15	Hairston, Jerry	R/R	5-10/175	5-29-76	Baltimore, Rochester, Gulf Coast Orioles, Frederick
39	Kinkade, Mike	R/R	6-1/210	5-6-73	Binghamton, New York N.L., Bowie, Rochester, Baltimore
38	Richard, Chris	L/L	6-2/185	6-7-74	Memphis, St. Louis, Baltimore
8	Ripken, Cal	R/R	6-4/220	8-24-60	Baltimore
	Segui, David	B/L	6-1/202	7-19-66	Texas, Cleveland

No.	OUTFIELDERS	B/T	Ht./Wt.	Born	2000 clubs
9	Anderson, Brady	L/L	6-1/202	1-18-64	Baltimore
88	Belle, Albert	R/R	6-2/225	8-25-66	Baltimore
40	Kingsale, Gene	B/R	6-3/194	8-20-76	Gulf Coast Orioles, Frederick, Bowie, Rochester, Baltimore
32	Matos, Luis	R/R	6-0/179	10-30-78	Baltimore
6	Mora, Melvin	R/R	5-10/180	2-2-72	New York N.L., Norfolk, Baltimore

BALLPARK INFORMATION

Ballpark (capacity, surface)
Oriole Park at Camden Yards (48,876, grass)
Address
333 W. Camden St.
Baltimore, MD 21201
Official website
www.theorioles.com
Business phone
410-685-9800
Ticket information
410-685-9800
Ticket prices
$35 (club box sec. 204-270), $30 (field box sec. 20-54)
$27 (field box sec. 14-18, 56-58)
$23 (terrace box sec. 19-53)
$22 (LF club sec. 272-288; lower box sec. 6-12, 60-64)
$20 (terrace box sec. 1-17, 55-65)
$18 (LF lower box sec. 66-86; upper box sec. 306-372)
$16 (LF upper box sec. 374-388; lower res. sec. 19-53)
$13 (upper res., sec. 306-372; lower res. sec. 4, 7-17, 55-87)
$11 (LF upper res., sec. 374-388)
$9 (bleachers sec. 90-98), $7 (standing room)
Field dimensions (from home plate)
To left field at foul line, 333 feet
To center field, 400 feet
To right field at foul line, 318
First game played
April 6, 1992 (Orioles 2, Indians 0)

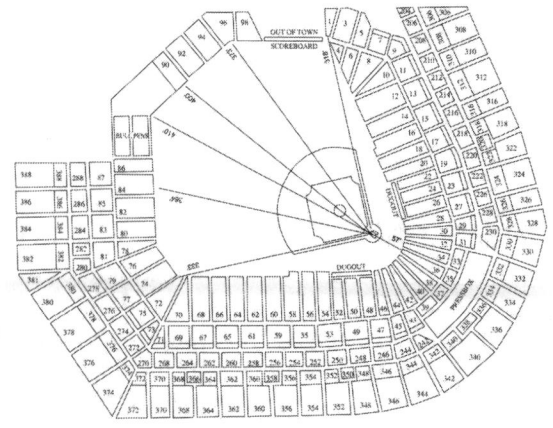

DAY BY DAY

2001 SEASON *Baltimore Orioles*

Date	Opp.	Res.	Score	(inn.*)	Hits	Opp. hits	Winning pitcher	Losing pitcher	Save	Record	Pos.	GB
4-3	Cle.	L	1-4		6	6	Colon	Mussina	Karsay	0-1	T4th	1.0
4-5	Cle.	W	11-7		12	10	Ryan	Kamieniecki		1-1	T3rd	0.5
4-6	Cle.	W	6-2		10	6	Rapp	Nagy	Groom	2-1	T1st	...
4-7	Det.	W	14-10		13	14	Worrell	Mlicki		3-1	1st	+1.0
4-8	Det.	W	2-1	(10)	8	10	Reyes	Brocail		4-1	1st	+1.0
4-9	Det.	W	11-6		16	10	Mercedes	Nitkowski		5-1	1st	+2.0
4-11	At K.C.	L	5-7	(12)	11	11	Santiago	Worrell		5-2	1st	+1.5
4-12	At K.C.	L	6-7		8	8	Santiago	Trombley		5-3	1st	+0.5
4-13	At K.C.	L	5-6		12	12	Bottalico	Ryan		5-4	T2nd	0.5
4-14	At Min.	L	9-10		16	12	Redman	Groom	Guardado	5-5	T2nd	1.5
4-15	At Min.	W	6-4		15	9	Worrell	Miller	Trombley	6-5	T2nd	1.5
4-16	At Min.	W	5-0		8	4	Ponson	Mays		7-5	T2nd	1.5
4-19	T.B.	W	3-2		7	7	Trombley	Mecir		8-5	2nd	2.5
4-20	T.B.	W	8-4		8	7	Rapp	Rupe		9-5	2nd	2.0
4-21	At Oak.	W	11-9		15	11	Ponson	Olivares	Timlin	10-5	2nd	1.0
4-22	At Oak.	W	4-3		10	9	Mercedes	Heredia	Groom	11-5	T1st	...
4-23	At Oak.	L	2-3	(11)	7	7	Isringhausen	Worrell		11-6	2nd	1.0
4-24	At Chi.	L	2-8		2	9	Eldred	Mussina		11-7	2nd	1.0
4-25	At Chi.	W	12-6		12	11	Rapp	Sirotka		12-7	T1st	...
4-26	At Chi.	L	6-11		10	10	Wells	Ponson		12-8	3rd	1.0
4-27	At Chi.	L	4-13		9	13	Parque	Mercedes		12-9	3rd	1.5
4-28	Tex.	W	4-3		8	9	Groom	Zimmerman		13-9	2nd	1.5
4-29	Tex.	W	3-1		6	9	Mussina	Oliver		14-9	2nd	0.5
4-30	Tex.	L	4-8		9	14	Rogers	Rapp		14-10	2nd	1.5
5-2	Ana.	W	7-6		9	11	Trombley	Percival		15-10	2nd	2.0
5-3	Ana.	L	5-6		8	9	Ortiz	Johnson	Percival	15-11	3rd	3.0
5-4	Ana.	L	5-8		9	11	Hill	Mussina	Hasegawa	15-12	3rd	3.5
5-5	At N.Y.	L	10-12		14	16	Nelson	Ryan		15-13	3rd	4.5
5-6	At N.Y.	L	1-3		6	6	Clemens	Rapp	Rivera	15-14	3rd	5.5
5-7	At N.Y.	W	7-6		12	10	Groom	Rivera	Timlin	16-14	3rd	4.5
5-8	At Tor.	L	5-6		14	12	Escobar	Johnson	Koch	16-15	3rd	5.5
5-9	At Tor.	L	4-6		10	12	Wells	Mussina	Koch	16-16	4th	6.5
5-10	At Tor.	L	2-7		5	14	Painter	Erickson	Quantrill	16-17	4th	7.0
5-11	Bos.	L	4-11		8	16	Cormier	Mercedes		16-18	4th	7.0
5-12	Bos.	L	0-9		2	16	P. Martinez	Ponson		16-19	4th	7.0
5-13	Bos.	L	1-5		11	6	Garces	Trombley		16-20	4th	7.0
5-14	Bos.	L	1-10		6	12	Rose	Mussina		16-21	4th	7.5
5-16	At Ana.	W	4-3		7	9	Erickson	Bottenfield	Timlin	17-21	4th	7.0
5-17	At Ana.	L	7-8		12	11	Percival	Timlin		17-22	4th	8.0
5-18	At Tex.	L	7-8		11	13	Helling	Ryan	Wetteland	17-23	4th	8.5
5-20	At Tex.	L	1-2		7	6	Loaiza	Mussina	Wetteland	17-24	4th	9.0
5-21	At Tex.	L	5-6		14	7	Venafro	Groom	Wetteland	17-25	4th	9.0
5-23	Sea.	W	4-2		6	8	Timlin	Mesa		18-25	4th	8.0
5-24	Sea.	W	4-3		8	7	Groom	Sasaki		19-25	4th	8.0
5-25	Sea.	W	5-1		9	5	Mussina	Rodriguez		20-25	4th	7.0
5-26	Oak.	W	8-3		13	6	Erickson	Mulder		21-25	4th	7.0
5-27	Oak.	L	0-4		2	11	Hudson	Johnson		21-26	4th	7.0
5-29	At T.B.	W	5-1		9	13	Rapp	Trachsel		22-26	4th	7.0
5-30	At T.B.	W	8-7		12	14	Ponson	Yan	Timlin	23-26	4th	7.0
5-31	At T.B.	L	3-4		9	6	Mecir	Groom	Hernandez	23-27	4th	7.0
6-1	At T.B.	L	1-2		6	8	Rekar	Erickson	Hernandez	23-28	4th	7.0
6-2	At Mon.	L	3-5		9	9	Pavano	Johnson	Kline	23-29	4th	7.0
6-3	At Mon.	L	4-7		9	12	Lira	Rapp	Kline	23-30	4th	8.0
6-4	At Mon.	L	0-1		3	6	Armas	Ponson	Kline	23-31	4th	8.0
6-5	At N.Y. (NL)	W	4-2		10	6	Mussina	Hampton	Timlin	24-31	4th	7.0
6-7	At N.Y. (NL)	L	3-11		12	12	Mahomes	Erickson		24-32	4th	8.5
6-8	At N.Y. (NL)	L	7-8	(10)	13	11	Cook	Mercedes		24-33	4th	9.0
6-9	Phi.	L	5-9		9	10	Wolf	Rapp		24-34	4th	9.0
6-10	Phi.	W	11-4		12	6	Ponson	Schilling		25-34	4th	9.0
6-11	Phi.	W	7-2		12	5	Mussina	Ashby		26-34	4th	8.5
6-13	Tex.	W	3-2		6	6	Erickson	Helling	Timlin	27-34	4th	7.5
6-14	Tex.	W	11-10		12	10	Timlin	Crabtree		28-34	4th	7.5
6-15	Tex.	W	10-1		8	5	McElroy	Loaiza		29-34	4th	6.5
6-16	Ana.	W	4-3		7	9	Mussina	Schoeneweis	Timlin	30-34	4th	6.0
6-17	Ana.	L	3-8		10	9	Belcher	Johnson		30-35	4th	6.0
6-18	Ana.	L	6-8		7	14	Etherton	Erickson	Percival	30-36	4th	6.0
6-19	At Oak.	L	12-13	(10)	16	14	Tam	Timlin		30-37	4th	6.5
6-20	At Oak.	L	5-8		9	9	Hudson	Ponson	Isringhausen	30-38	4th	7.5
6-21	At Oak.	L	3-10		8	15	Prieto	Mussina		30-39	4th	7.5
6-22	At Sea.	L	4-11		8	14	Moyer	Johnson		30-40	4th	8.0
6-23	At Sea.	L	3-8		10	11	Meche	Erickson		30-41	4th	8.5
6-24	At Sea.	L	1-2		7	4	Halama	Rapp	Sasaki	30-42	T4th	9.5
6-25	At Sea.	L	2-4		4	4	Rhodes	Timlin	Sasaki	30-43	T4th	10.5
6-27	At Bos.	W	6-3	(10)	11	10	Trombley	Lowe	Groom	31-43	T4th	9.5

2001 SEASON Baltimore Orioles

Date	Opp.	Res.	Score	(inn.*)	Hits	Opp. hits	Winning pitcher	Losing pitcher	Save	Record	Pos.	GB
6-28	At Bos.	W	8-7	(11)	16	11	Mercedes	Florie	Groom	32-43	4th	9.5
6-29	At Bos.	L	4-12		12	16	Wakefield	Erickson		32-44	4th	10.5
6-30	Tor.	W	8-3		11	7	Rapp	Halladay		33-44	4th	9.5
7-1	Tor.	W	12-5		13	8	Ponson	Carpenter		34-44	4th	8.5
7-2	Tor.	W	3-2		7	8	Trombley	Quantrill	Mills	35-44	4th	7.5
7-3	Tor.	L	4-6		11	6	Wells	Johnson	Koch	35-45	4th	8.5
7-4	At N.Y.	W	7-6		7	10	Erickson	Cone	Trombley	36-45	4th	7.5
7-5	At N.Y.	L	6-12		10	13	Pettitte	Rapp		36-46	4th	7.5
7-6	At N.Y.	L	9-13		11	10	Stanton	Johnson		36-47	4th	8.5
7-7	At Phi.	W	2-1		7	8	Mussina	Schilling	Timlin	37-47	4th	8.0
7-8	At Phi.	L	4-13		9	15	Ashby	Mercedes		37-48	4th	9.5
7-9	At Phi.	W	5-4		12	8	Mills	Brantley	Timlin	38-48	4th	8.5
7-13	Atl.	L	3-6		8	6	Maddux	Mussina	Kamieniecki	38-49	4th	8.5
7-14	Atl.	L	1-4		7	10	Ashby	Ponson		38-50	4th	9.5
7-15	Atl.	L	3-7		8	11	Glavine	Erickson		38-51	4th	10.0
7-16	Fla.	W	9-5		16	11	Mills	Darensbourg	Timlin	39-51	4th	10.0
7-17	Fla.	W	5-3		8	8	Mercedes	Cornelius	Timlin	40-51	4th	9.0
7-18	Fla.	L	0-7		8	13	Sanchez	Mussina		40-52	4th	10.0
7-20†	Bos.	L	7-11		11	17	R. Martinez	Ponson		40-53		
7-20‡	Bos.	W	9-4		14	4	Erickson	Schourek		41-53	4th	10.0
7-21	At Tor.	W	9-5		16	9	Rapp	Halladay		42-53	4th	10.0
7-22	At Tor.	W	8-2		13	9	Mercedes	Loaiza		43-53	4th	9.0
7-23	At Tor.	L	1-4		5	8	Castillo	Mussina	Koch	43-54	4th	10.0
7-24	N.Y.	L	3-4		6	5	Clemens	Parrish	Rivera	43-55	4th	11.0
7-25	N.Y.	L	1-19		9	20	Pettitte	Erickson		43-56	4th	12.0
7-26	N.Y.	L	1-4		8	8	Gooden	Ponson	Rivera	43-57	4th	13.0
7-29†	Cle.	L	3-14		9	20	Bere	Rapp		43-58		
7-29‡	Cle.	W	4-0		8	10	Mercedes	Woodard		44-58	4th	12.5
7-30	Cle.	W	10-7		12	9	Parrish	Finley		45-58	4th	12.5
7-31	Min.	W	6-5		9	9	Ponson	Romero	Trombley	46-58	4th	12.0
8-1	Min.	W	10-0		13	1	Mussina	Redman		47-58	4th	12.0
8-2	Min.	L	6-10		12	14	Radke	Rapp		47-59	4th	12.0
8-4	At T.B.	W	10-9	(15)	17	12	Johnson	Yan		48-59	4th	12.5
8-5	At T.B.	L	4-5	(10)	6	9	Hernandez	Trombley		48-60	4th	12.5
8-6	At T.B.	L	4-7		10	10	Rupe	Mussina	Hernandez	48-61	4th	12.5
8-7	At Det.	W	4-3		7	11	Groom	Brocail	Kohlmeier	49-61	4th	11.5
8-8	At Det.	L	1-4		8	7	Moehler	Rapp		49-62	4th	12.5
8-9	At Det.	W	5-2		11	7	Mercedes	Blair	Kohlmeier	50-62	4th	12.5
8-10	At Det.	L	3-14		6	14	Sparks	Ponson		50-63	T4th	13.5
8-11	At K.C.	L	6-7		8	11	Reichert	Mussina	Bottalico	50-64	T4th	13.5
8-12	At K.C.	W	12-11		11	14	Groom	Bottalico	Kohlmeier	51-64	4th	12.5
8-13	At K.C.	L	5-10		12	14	Suzuki	Brea		51-65	T4th	13.5
8-14	Chi.	W	8-2		11	10	Mercedes	Sirotka		52-65	4th	13.5
8-15	Chi.	L	4-14		8	16	Biddle	Johnson		52-66	T4th	14.5
8-16	Chi.	L	3-7		5	9	Parque	Mussina		52-67	T4th	14.5
8-17	Chi.	W	5-3		10	4	Parrish	Baldwin		53-67	4th	14.5
8-18	K.C.	L	1-4		8	4	Stein	Rapp		53-68	4th	14.5
8-19	K.C.	L	0-7		4	11	Suzuki	Mercedes		53-69	4th	15.5
8-20	K.C.	W	2-1		9	6	Ponson	Wilson	Kohlmeier	54-69	4th	14.5
8-21	K.C.	W	2-1		7	8	Mussina	Meadows	Kohlmeier	55-69	4th	14.5
8-23	At Chi.	L	4-8		8	7	Barcelo	Parrish		55-70	T4th	15.0
8-24	At Chi.	W	8-5		10	9	Mercedes	Hill		56-70	4th	15.0
8-25	T.B.	W	4-3		7	10	Ryan	Taylor	Kohlmeier	57-70	4th	14.0
8-26†	T.B.	L	1-4		7	7	Eiland	Ponson	Hernandez	57-71		
8-26‡	T.B.	W	2-0		7	4	Groom	Lidle	Trombley	58-71	4th	14.5
8-27	T.B.	W	3-2		10	10	Spurgeon	Rupe	Kohlmeier	59-71	4th	14.5
8-29	Det.	L	2-12		7	16	Weaver	Parrish		59-72	4th	15.0
8-30	Det.	W	5-1		11	2	Mercedes	Nomo		60-72	4th	15.0
8-31	Det.	L	1-6		5	11	Patterson	Trombley		60-73	4th	15.5
9-1	At Cle.	L	2-5		7	11	Finley	Ponson	Wickman	60-74	4th	16.5
9-2	At Cle.	W	8-6		13	9	Rapp	Karsay	Kohlmeier	61-74	4th	16.5
9-3	At Cle.	L	11-12	(13)	16	18	Cairncross	Trombley		61-75	4th	16.5
9-4	At Min.	W	3-2		9	10	Mercedes	Redman	Kohlmeier	62-75	4th	16.5
9-5	At Min.	W	6-5		10	14	Mussina	Romero	Kohlmeier	63-75	4th	16.5
9-6	At Min.	L	1-4		6	9	Radke	Ponson		63-76	4th	16.5
9-8	At Ana.	L	1-2		3	7	Ortiz	Rapp	Percival	63-77	4th	18.0
9-9	At Ana.	W	10-3		14	8	Mercedes	Karl		64-77	4th	18.0
9-10	At Ana.	L	1-2		7	5	Hasegawa	Mussina	Percival	64-78	4th	19.0
9-11	At Ana.	W	3-1		9	8	Ponson	Schoeneweis		65-78	4th	18.0
9-12†	At Tex.	L	1-9		3	16	Helling	Parrish		65-79		
9-12‡	At Tex.	L	5-6		8	5	Rogers	Spurgeon	Wetteland	65-80	4th	19.5
9-13	At Tex.	W	9-4		14	6	Rapp	Glynn		66-80	4th	19.5
9-15	Sea.	L	2-10		8	10	Sele	Mercedes		66-81	4th	19.0
9-16	Sea.	L	0-14		3	16	Moyer	Mussina		66-82	4th	20.0
9-17	Sea.	L	2-3		7	7	Garcia	Ponson	Sasaki	66-83	4th	20.0
9-18	Oak.	L	3-12		8	17	Appier	Rapp		66-84	4th	20.0
9-19	Oak.	L	4-7		13	8	Mecir	Johnson	Isringhausen	66-85	4th	20.0
9-20†	Oak.	W	2-0		4	4	McElroy	Zito	Kohlmeier	67-85		

Date	Opp.	Res.	Score	(inn.*)	Hits	Opp. hits	Winning pitcher	Losing pitcher	Save	Record	Pos.	GB
9-20‡	Oak.	L	0-4		9	10	Heredia	Mercedes		67-86	4th	19.5
9-22	At Bos.	W	3-1		6	4	Ponson	R. Martinez		68-86	4th	18.0
9-23	At Bos.	L	7-8	(10)	13	12	Carrasco	Kohlmeier		68-87	4th	19.0
9-24	At Bos.	W	1-0		4	8	Mussina	Ohka	Kohlmeier	69-87	4th	19.0
9-26	Tor.	W	2-1		7	5	Mercedes	Wells	Kohlmeier	70-87	4th	17.5
9-27	Tor.	L	0-4		4	7	Castillo	Ponson		70-88	4th	17.5
9-28	Tor.	W	23-1		23	2	Rapp	Carpenter		71-88	4th	16.5
9-29	N.Y.	W	13-2		13	6	McElroy	Pettitte		72-88	4th	15.5
9-30	N.Y.	W	9-1		12	7	Mussina	Cone		73-88	4th	14.5
10-1	N.Y.	W	7-3		10	9	Mercedes	Hernandez		74-88	4th	13.5

Monthly records: April (14-10), May (9-17), June (10-17), July (13-14), August (14-15), September (13-15), October (1-0).
*Innings, if other than nine. †First game of a doubleheader. ‡Second game of a doubleheader.

HIGHLIGHTS

High point: The Orioles ended their difficult season with a three-game sweep of the New York Yankees. The positive finish was punctuated by a 7-3 win and the sight of a sellout crowd, clearly having bought into the team's youth movement, standing and chanting, "Let's go, Orioles!"

Low point: On July 25, with the inevitability of a salary purge sinking in, the Orioles were embarrassed 19-1 at Camden Yards by the Yankees. Worse than the score was the realization that many voices in the sellout crowd apparently belonged to Yankees fans.

Turning point: On July 28, the Orioles traded shortstop Mike Bordick to the New York Mets for Melvin Mora and three prospects—the first of five trades and a series of callups that would transform the roster and change the way the team played the rest of the season.

Most valuable player: Only a handful of players were with the Orioles the entire season and Delino DeShields was the most productive. His average hovered around .300 for most of the season and he finished third in the league with 37 stolen bases. He also made a relatively seamless transition from second base to left field when the Orioles called up second base prospect Jerry Hairston.

Most valuable pitcher: Although Mike Mussina's 11-15 record was the worst of his career, his other numbers were right in line—3.80 ERA, 237 innings, 210 strikeouts. If the Orioles had given him any support, he would have won many more games.

Most improved player: Shortstop Bordick was enjoying a career offensive season when the Orioles traded him to the Mets. Always known for his defense, the 35-year-old Bordick earned his first All-Star berth and hit 16 home runs in 100 games.

Most pleasant surprise: Jose Mercedes, who had been released by three different organizations in 1999, led the team with 14 wins and secured a spot in the front half of the rotation. Mercedes was successful despite being shuttled from the rotation to the bullpen.

Key injuries: Pitchers Scott Erickson and Matt Riley both underwent Tommy John surgery and will miss most of the 2001 season. ... Third baseman Cal Ripken went on the disabled list with a bad back

for the third time in two seasons and played only 83 games. ... Right fielder Albert Belle, slowed by a degenerative hip condition during much of the second half, probably will be limited to designated hitter duty in 2001.

Notable: Ripken joined the 3,000-hit club with a single during an April 15 game at Minneapolis. ... Lefthander Buddy Groom set an A.L. record by making 70 appearances for a fifth straight season. ... Rookie first baseman Chris Richard homered 13 times in his 56 games with the Orioles, surpassing the four-month production of Will Clark before he was traded. ... Ripken made his first career appearance as a designated hitter on May 9 at Toronto.

—DAVE SHEININ

RECORDS

2000 regular-season record: 74-88 (4th in A.L. East); 44-37 at home; 30-51 on road; 32-36 vs. East; 24-24 vs. Central; 18-28 vs. West; 23-24 vs. lefthanded starters; 51-64 vs. righthanded starters; 63-74 on grass; 11-14 on turf; 25-30 in daytime; 49-58 at night; 29-25 in one-run games; 4-7 in extra-inning games; 0-1-4 in doubleheaders.

Team record past five years: 417-393 (.515, ranks 6th in league in that span).

TEAM LEADERS

Batting average: Delino DeShields (.296).
At-bats: Delino DeShields (561).
Runs: Brady Anderson (89).
Hits: Delino DeShields (166).
Total Bases: Albert Belle (265).
Doubles: Delino DeShields (43).
Triples: Delino DeShields (5).
Home runs: Albert Belle (23).
Runs batted in: Albert Belle (103).
Stolen bases: Delino DeShields (37).
Slugging percentage: Albert Belle (.474).
On-base percentage: Brady Anderson (.375).
Wins: Jose Mercedes (14).
Earned-run average: Mike Mussina (3.79).
Complete games: Mike Mussina, Sidney Ponson (6).
Shutouts: Mike Mussina, Sidney Ponson (1).

Saves: Ryan Kohlmeier (13).
Innings pitched: Mike Mussina (237.2).
Strikeouts: Mike Mussina (210).

GAMES BY POSITION

Catcher: Charles Johnson 83, Brook Fordyce 52, Greg Myers 28, Fernando Lunar 9, Willie Morales 3.
First base: Will Clark 72, Chris Richard 53, Jeff Conine 39, Ryan Minor 5, Rich Amaral 1, Mike Kinkade 1.
Second base: Delino DeShields 96, Jerry Hairston Jr. 49, Mark Lewis 21, Jesse Garcia 6, Melvin Mora 1.
Third base: Cal Ripken Jr. 73, Jeff Conine 44, Mark Lewis 29, Ryan Minor 26, Ivanon Coffie 15.
Shortstop: Mike Bordick 100, Melvin Mora 52, Mark Lewis 14, Jesse Garcia 5, Ivanon Coffie 4.
Outfield: Brady Anderson 127, Albert Belle 110, B.J. Surhoff 102, Luis Matos 69, Delino DeShields 41, Trenidad Hubbard 24, Gene Kingsale 24, Rich Amaral 19, Jeff Conine 19, Karim Garcia 2, Chris Richard 1.
Designated hitter: Harold Baines 62, Albert Belle 31, Jeff Conine 20, Brady Anderson 11, Delino DeShields 10, Cal Ripken Jr. 10, Greg Myers 9, Will Clark 6, Trenidad Hubbard 6, Rich Amaral 5, Karim Garcia 4, Mark Lewis 4, Luis Matos 3, Carlos Casimiro 2, Mike Kinkade 2, Ivanon Coffie 1, Charles Johnson 1, Gene Kingsale 1, Chris Richard 1, B.J. Surhoff 1.

TOP DRAFT CHOICES

1a. **Beau Hale,** RHP, U. of Texas.
1b. **Tripper Johnson,** RHP, Newport H.S., Bellevue, Wash.
2. None.
3a. **Richard Bartlett,** RHP, Kamiakin H.S., Kennewick, Wash.
3b. **Tommy Arko,** C, Cooper H.S., Abilene, Tex.
4. **Jon Skaggs,** RHP, Rice University.
5. **Doug Gredvig,** 1B, Sacramento C.C.
6. **Brandon Spillers,** RHP, Tattnall Square Academy, Roberta, Ga.
7. **B.J. Littleton,** OF, Lamar University.
8. **Jayme Sperring,** RHP, Rice University.
9. **Mike Russell,** C, Bothell (Wash.) H.S.
10. **Casey Cahill,** RHP, Immaculata H.S., New Brunswick, N.J.

BOSTON RED SOX
AMERICAN LEAGUE EAST DIVISION

Red Sox
2001 SCHEDULE
Home games shaded; D—Day game (games starting before 5 p.m.)
*—All-Star Game at Safeco Field (Seattle)

APRIL
SUN	MON	TUE	WED	THU	FRI	SAT
1	2 BAL	D 3	4 BAL	5 BAL	6 D TB	7 TB
8 TB	9	10 BAL	11 BAL	12 BAL	13 NYY	14 D NYY
15 NYY	D 16 NYY	17 TB	18 TB	19 TB	20 NYY	21 D NYY
22 NYY	23	24 MIN	25 MIN	26 MIN	27 KC	28 D KC
29 KC	D 30					

MAY
SUN	MON	TUE	WED	THU	FRI	SAT
		1 SEA	2 SEA	3 SEA	4 OAK	5 D OAK
6 OAK	7	8 SEA	9 SEA	10 SEA	11 OAK	12 D OAK
13 OAK	D 14	15 MIN	16 MIN	17 D MIN	18 KC	19 KC
20 KC	D 21	22 NYY	23 NYY	24 D NYY	25 TOR	26 TOR
27 TOR	D 28 NYY	29	30 NYY	31 TOR		

JUNE
SUN	MON	TUE	WED	THU	FRI	SAT
					1 TOR	2 D TOR
3 D TOR	4	5 DET	6 DET	7 DET	8 PHI	9 D PHI
10 PHI	D 11	12 FLA	13 FLA	14 FLA	15 ATL	16 ATL
17 ATL	D 18	19 TB	20 TB	21 TB	22 TOR	23 TOR
24 TOR	D 25 TB	26 TB	27 TB	28 TB	29 TOR	30 TOR

JULY
SUN	MON	TUE	WED	THU	FRI	SAT
1 TOR	2 TOR	D 3 CLE	4 CLE	D 5 CLE	6 ATL	7 ATL
8 ATL	9	10	* 11	12 NYM	13 NYM	14 D NYM
15 MON	16 MON	17 MON	18 TOR	19 TOR	20 CWS	21 D CWS
22 CWS	D 23	24 TOR	25 TOR	26 TOR	27 CWS	28 CWS
29 CWS	D 30	31 ANA				

AUGUST
SUN	MON	TUE	WED	THU	FRI	SAT
		1 ANA	2 ANA	3 TEX	4 D TEX	
5 TEX	D 6 TEX	7 OAK	8 OAK	9 D OAK	10 BAL	11 D BAL
12 BAL	D 13	14 SEA	15 SEA	16 SEA	17 BAL	18 BAL
19 BAL	D 20 ANA	21 ANA	22 ANA	23 ANA	24 TEX	25 TEX
26 TEX	27	28 CLE	29 CLE	30 CLE	31 NYY	

SEPTEMBER
SUN	MON	TUE	WED	THU	FRI	SAT
						1 D NYY
2 NYY	D 3	4 CLE	5 CLE	6 NYY	7 NYY	8 D NYY
9 NYY	D 10 NYY	11 TB	12 TB	13 BAL	14 BAL	15 D NYY
16 BAL	D 17	18 TB	19 TB	20 TB	21 DET	22 DET
23 DET	D 24 BAL	25 BAL	26 BAL	27 BAL	28 DET	29 DET
30 D DET						

2001 SEASON
CLUB DIRECTORY

Chief executive officer
John L. Harrington

Exec. v.p. and general manager
Daniel F. Duquette

Executive vice president, administration
John S. Buckley

V.p. and chief financial officer
Robert C. Furbush

Vice president, baseball operations
Michael D. Port

V.p., broadcasting and technology
James P. Healey

Vice president, public affairs
Richard L. Bresciani

Vice president, sales and marketing
Lawrence C. Cancro

Vice president, stadium operations
Joseph F. McDermott

Vice president, assistant g.m. and legal counsel
Elaine W. Steward

Special assistants to the general manager
Lee Thomas, Carlton E. Fisk

Dir. of communications and baseball information
Kevin J. Shea

Dir. of human resources and office management
Michele Julian

Vice president, scouting
W. Wayne Britton

Executive director of int'l baseball operations
R. Ray Poitevint

Director of player development
Kent A. Qualls

Minor league field coordinator
David P. Jauss

Coordinator of Florida operations
Ryan Richeal

Traveling secretary
John F. McCormick

Major league scout
Frank J. Malzone

Major league special assignment scout
G. Edwin Haas

Baseball administration coordinator
Marci S. Blacker

Assistant scouting director
Thomas L. Moore

Information technology manager
Clay N. Rendon

Director of sales
Michael D. Schetzel

Group sales manager
Corey Bowdre

Season ticket manager
Joseph F. Matthews

Telephone sales managers
Sean Carragher, Marcell Saporita

Property maintenance manager
John M. Caron

600 Club and suites manager
Daniel E. Lyons

Medical director
Arthur M. Pappas, M.D.

Team physician
William J. Morgan, M.D.

Head trainer
James W. Rowe Jr.

Assistant trainer/rehabilitation coordinator
Christopher T. Correnti

Assistant trainer/strength and conditioning
Merle V. "B.J." Baker III

Baseball information coordinator
Glenn Wilburn

Instructors
Theodore S. Williams, Carl M. Yastrzemski, Jim Rice

Special assignment instructors
John M. Pesky, Edward J. Popowski, Charles T. Wagner

Executive administrative assistant
Lorraine Leong

Equipment manager and clubhouse operations
J. Joseph Cochran

Controller
Stanley H. Tran

Director of advertising and sponsorships
Jeffrey E. Goldenberg

Director of facilities management
Thomas L. Queenan Jr.

Director of 600 Club
Patricia T. Flanagan

Director of ticket operations
Joseph P. Helyar

Executive consultant, public affairs
James "Lou" Gorman

Superintendent of grounds and maintenance
Joseph P. Mooney

Ticket office manager
Richard J. Beaton Jr.

Broadcasting manager
James E. Shannahan

Community relations manager
Ronald E. Burton Jr.

Customer relations manager
Ann Marie C. Starzyk

Public affairs manager
Fred Seymour Jr.

Ground crew manager
Casey Erven

Promotions and special events manager
Marcita E. Thompson

Publications manager
Debra A. Matson

Director of Latin American scouting
Levy Ochoa

Scouts
Walter "Chet" Atkins, Raymond Boone, Buzz Bowers, Kevin Burrell, Ben Cherington, Edwin Correa, Ray Crone jr., George Digby, Johnny DiPuglia, Danny Doyle, William Enos, Ray Fagnant, Steve Flores, Eddie Haas, Matt Haas, Ernie Jacobs, Wally Komatsubara, Chuck Koney, Kenneth "Jack" Lee, Don Lenhardt, Frank Malzone, Joe Mason, Steve McAllister, Tom Mooney, Gary Rajsich, Eddie Robinson, Jim Robinson, Ed Roebuck, Edward Scott, Mathew Sczesny, Harry Smith, Dick Sorkin, Jerry Stephenson, Joseph Stephenson, Lee Thomas, Fay Thompson, Charles T. Wagner, Jeffrey Zona

International scouts
Mark Garcia, Jon Kodama, Ray Poitevint, Lee Sigman

Latin American scouts
Robinson Garcia, Sebastian Martinez, Jose Maza, Levy Ochoa, Carlos Ramirez, Michael Victoria

MINOR LEAGUE AFFILIATES

Class	Team	League	Manager
AAA	Pawtucket	International	Gary Jones
AA	Trenton	Eastern	Billy Gardner Jr.
A	Augusta	South Atlantic	Mike Boulanger
A	Lowell	New York-Pennsylvania	Arnie Beyeler
A	Sarasota	Florida State	Ron Johnson
Rookie	Gulf Coast Red Sox	Gulf Coast	John Sanders

BROADCAST INFORMATION
Radio: WEEI-AM (680).
TV: WFXT-TV (Fox 25).
Cable TV: New England Sports Network.

SPRING TRAINING
Ballpark (city): City of Palms Park (Fort Myers, Fla.).
Ticket information: 941-334-4700.

Follow the Red Sox all season at: www.sportingnews.com/baseball/teams/redsox/

2001 SEASON *Boston Red Sox*

Manager—Jimy Williams (22).
Coaches—John Cumberland (52), Rick Down, Tommy Harper (35), Joe Kerrigan (16), Gene Lamont, Nelson Norman, Dana LeVangie (60).

No.	PITCHERS	B/T	Ht./Wt.	Born	2000 clubs
44	Arrojo, Rolando	R/R	6-4/220	7-18-68	Colorado, Boston
47	Beck, Rod	R/R	6-1/235	8-3-68	Pawtucket, Boston
	Castillo, Frank	R/R	6-1/200	4-1-69	Toronto
	Cho, Jin Ho	R/R	6-3/220	8-16-75	Sarasota, Trenton, Pawtucket
	Cone, David	L/R	6-1/200	1-2-63	New York A.L.
63	Crawford, Paxton	R/R	6-3/205	8-4-77	Trenton, Pawtucket, Boston
55	Croushore, Rick	R/R	6-4/210	8-7-70	Colorado Springs, Colorado, Pawtucket, Boston
39	Florie, Bryce	R/R	5-11/192	5-21-70	Boston, Sarasota, Trenton
34	Garces, Richard	R/R	6-0/215	5-18-71	Boston
40	Lee, Sang	L/L	6-1/190	3-11-71	Pawtucket, Boston
32	Lowe, Derek	R/R	6-6/200	6-1-73	Boston
45	Martinez, Pedro	R/R	5-11/170	10-25-71	Boston
	Nomo, Hideo	R/R	6-2/230	8-31-68	Detroit
53	Ohka, Tomo	R/R	6-1/179	3-18-76	Pawtucket, Boston
38	Pena, Jesus	L/L	6-0/170	3-8-75	Charlotte, Chicago A.L., Birmingham, Boston
	Pena, Juan	R/R	6-5/215	6-27-77	DID NOT PLAY
35	Pichardo, Hipolito	R/R	6-1/195	8-22-69	Pawtucket, Sarasota, Boston
17	Saberhagen, Bret	R/R	6-1/200	4-11-64	Sarasota, Lowell, Pawtucket, Trenton
49	Wakefield, Tim	R/R	6-2/210	8-2-66	Boston

No.	CATCHERS	B/T	Ht./Wt.	Born	2000 clubs
10	Hatteberg, Scott	L/R	6-1/205	12-14-69	Boston
	Hillenbrand, Shea	R/R	6-1/200	7-27-75	Trenton
	Lomasney, Steve	R/R	6-0/195	8-29-77	Trenton, Gulf Coast Red Sox
33	Varitek, Jason	B/R	6-2/220	4-11-72	Boston

No.	INFIELDERS	B/T	Ht./Wt.	Born	2000 clubs
54	Burkhart, Morgan	B/L	5-11/225	1-29-72	Pawtucket, Boston
23	Daubach, Brian	L/R	6-1/201	2-11-72	Boston
	Diaz, Juan	R/R	6-2/228	2-19-76	Sarasota, Trenton, Pawtucket
5	Garciaparra, Nomar	R/R	6-0/180	7-23-73	Boston
3	Lansing, Mike	R/R	6-0/195	4-3-68	Colorado, Boston
26	Merloni, Lou	R/R	5-10/195	4-6-71	Pawtucket, Boston
30	Offerman, Jose	B/R	6-0/190	11-8-68	Boston
	Stenson, Dernell	L/L	6-1/230	6-17-78	Pawtucket
	Stynes, Chris	R/R	5-10/185	1-19-73	Cincinnati
13	Valentin, John	R/R	6-0/185	2-18-67	Boston
	Veras, Wilton	R/R	6-2/198	1-19-78	Pawtucket, Boston

No.	OUTFIELDERS	B/T	Ht./Wt.	Born	2000 clubs
19	Bichette, Dante	R/R	6-2/235	11-18-63	Cincinnati, Boston
2	Everett, Carl	B/R	6-0/215	6-3-71	Boston
20	Lewis, Darren	R/R	6-0/190	8-28-67	Boston, Gulf Coast Red Sox
7	Nixon, Trot	L/L	6-2/200	4-11-74	Boston, Gulf Coast Red Sox
25	O'Leary, Troy	L/L	6-0/200	8-4-69	Boston, Gulf Coast Red Sox
24	Ramirez, Manny	R/R	6-0/205	5-30-72	Cleveland, Akron, Buffalo

BALLPARK INFORMATION

Ballpark (capacity, surface)
Fenway Park (33,991; grass)
Address
4 Yawkey Way
Boston, MA 02215-3496
Official website
www.redsox.com
Business phone
617-267-9440
Ticket information
617-267-1700, 617-482-4769
Ticket prices
$55 (field box, loge box and infield roof)
$40 (reserved grandstand)
$30 (right-field boxes and right-field roof)
$25 (outfield grandstand)
$20 (lower bleachers)
$18 (upper bleachers)
Field dimensions (from home plate)
To left field at foul line, 310 feet
To center field, 420 feet
To right field at foul line, 302 feet
First game played
April 20, 1912
(Red Sox 7, New York Highlanders 6)

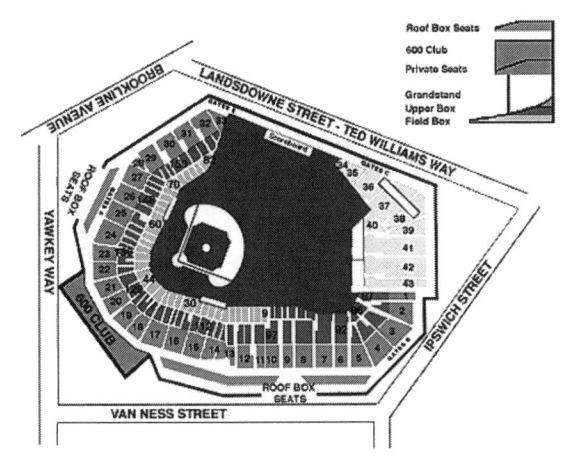

2000 REVIEW
DAY BY DAY

Date	Opp.	Res.	Score	(inn.*)	Hits	Opp. hits	Winning pitcher	Losing pitcher	Save	Record	Pos.	GB
4-4	At Sea.	W	2-0		7	2	P. Martinez	Moyer	Lowe	1-0	T1st	0.5
4-5	At Sea.	L	3-9		9	9	Garcia	R. Martinez		1-1	T3rd	0.5
4-6	At Sea.	L	2-5		8	7	Mesa	Florie	Sasaki	1-2	5th	1.0
4-7	At Ana.	L	3-7		6	9	Dickson	Schourek		1-3	5th	2.0
4-8	At Ana.	L	5-7		7	13	Hill	Rose	Percival	1-4	5th	3.0
4-9	At Ana.	W	5-2		9	7	P. Martinez	Bottenfield		2-4	4th	3.0
4-11	Min.	W	13-4		16	9	R. Martinez	Mays		3-4	3rd	2.0
4-12	Min.	W	7-3		10	9	Fassero	Santana		4-4	3rd	1.0
4-13	Min.	W	4-3		7	7	Wakefield	Wells	Lowe	5-4	T2nd	0.5
4-14	Oak.	L	6-13		12	11	Appier	Rose		5-5	T2nd	1.5
4-15	Oak.	W	14-2		13	6	P. Martinez	Hudson		6-5	T2nd	1.5
4-16	Oak.	W	5-4		9	10	Lowe	Mathews		7-5	T2nd	1.5
4-17	Oak.	L	0-1		4	10	Heredia	Fassero	Isringhausen	7-6	3rd	2.5
4-18	At Det.	W	7-0		10	6	Schourek	Mlicki	Lowe	8-6	3rd	2.5
4-19	At Det.	W	10-0		15	6	Rose	Nomo		9-6	3rd	2.5
4-24	At Tex.	L	4-5		9	7	Rogers	Wakefield	Wetteland	9-7	3rd	2.0
4-25	At Tex.	W	6-3		9	6	P. Martinez	Helling	Lowe	10-7	3rd	1.0
4-26	At Tex.	W	14-4		21	10	Fassero	Clark		11-7	2nd	1.0
4-28	At Cle.	L	3-4		7	8	Burba	Schourek	Karsay	11-8	3rd	2.0
4-29	At Cle.	L	2-3		5	5	Finley	R. Martinez	Karsay	11-9	3rd	2.0
4-30	At Cle.	W	2-1		7	6	P. Martinez	Nagy	Lowe	12-9	3rd	2.0
5-1	Det.	W	10-6		11	11	Fassero	Nitkowski		13-9	2nd	2.0
5-2	Det.	L	6-7	(12)	10	18	Blair	Wakefield	Jones	13-10	3rd	3.0
5-3	Det.	W	4-2		7	6	Lowe	Weaver		14-10	3rd	3.0
5-5	T.B.	W	5-3		10	8	R. Martinez	Eiland	Lowe	15-10	2nd	3.0
5-6	T.B.	L	0-1		3	6	Trachsel	P. Martinez		15-11	2nd	4.0
5-7	T.B.	W	9-7		12	13	Fassero	Rekar	Lowe	16-11	2nd	3.0
5-8	Chi.	W	3-2		8	8	Rose	Sturtze	Lowe	17-11	2nd	3.0
5-9	Chi.	L	0-6		3	10	Baldwin	Schourek		17-12	2nd	4.0
5-10	Chi.	W	5-3	(7)	7	7	R. Martinez	Eldred	Garces	18-12	2nd	3.5
5-11	At Bal.	W	11-4		16	8	Cormier	Mercedes		19-12	2nd	2.5
5-12	At Bal.	W	9-0		16	2	P. Martinez	Ponson		20-12	2nd	1.5
5-13	At Bal.	W	5-1		6	11	Garces	Trombley		21-12	2nd	0.5
5-14	At Bal.	W	10-1		12	6	Rose	Mussina		22-12	1st	+0.5
5-15	At Tor.	W	8-1		13	6	Schourek	Castillo		23-12	1st	+1.0
5-16	At Tor.	L	6-7		11	14	Munro	Lowe		23-13	1st	+1.0
5-17	At Tor.	W	8-0		15	4	P. Martinez	Carpenter		24-13	1st	+1.0
5-19	Det.	W	3-0		7	5	Fassero	Moehler	Lowe	25-13	1st	+1.0
5-20	Det.	L	1-2		6	9	Mlicki	Wakefield	Jones	25-14	1st	+1.0
5-21	Det.	L	5-7		12	11	Nomo	R. Martinez	Jones	25-15	1st	+1.0
5-23	Tor.	L	2-3		9	7	Carpenter	P. Martinez	Koch	25-16	1st	+1.0
5-24	Tor.	W	6-3	(11)	9	10	Cormier	Frascatore		26-16	1st	+1.0
5-25	Tor.	L	6-11		13	17	Wells	Schourek		26-17	T1st	...
5-26	At N.Y.	W	4-1		8	8	R. Martinez	Cone	Lowe	27-17	1st	+1.0
5-27	At N.Y.	L	3-8		9	11	Stanton	Wasdin		27-18	T1st	...
5-28	At N.Y.	W	2-0		5	4	P. Martinez	Clemens		28-18	1st	+1.0
5-30	K.C.	W	8-2		12	8	Fassero	Suppan		29-18	1st	+1.5
5-31	K.C.	L	7-9		12	14	Suzuki	Schourek	Spradlin	29-19	1st	+1.5
6-1	K.C.	L	11-13		12	19	Santiago	Lowe	Reichert	29-20	1st	+1.0
6-2	At Phi.	L	1-2	(11)	9	9	Brantley	Wasdin		29-21	T1st	...
6-3	At Phi.	L	3-9		3	10	Wolf	Wakefield		29-22	T1st	...
6-4	At Phi.	L	5-6	(12)	8	12	Schrenk	Cormier		29-23	2nd	1.0
6-5	At Fla.	W	3-2		9	6	Wakefield	Bones	Lowe	30-23	T1st	...
6-6	At Fla.	W	4-3		10	9	R. Martinez	Sanchez	Lowe	31-23	T1st	...
6-7	At Fla.	L	2-6		10	5	Darensbourg	Rose		31-24	2nd	1.0
6-8	Cle.	W	3-0		9	2	P. Martinez	Colon	Lowe	32-24	2nd	0.5
6-9	At Atl.	L	4-6		8	9	Maddux	Fassero	Seanez	32-25	2nd	0.5
6-10	At Atl.	L	0-6		5	9	Mulholland	Schourek		32-26	2nd	1.5
6-11	At Atl.	W	5-3		8	7	Garces	Seanez	Lowe	33-26	2nd	1.0
6-13	At N.Y.	W	5-3		10	6	Pichardo	Hernandez	Lowe	34-26	2nd	...
6-14	At N.Y.	L	1-2		10	8	Grimsley	Wakefield	Rivera	34-27	2nd	1.0
6-16	Tor.	W	7-4		12	11	Pichardo	Escobar	Lowe	35-27	1st	+0.5
6-17	Tor.	L	10-11		13	14	Wells	R. Martinez	Koch	35-28	1st	+0.5
6-18	Tor.	L	1-5		6	9	Castillo	Fassero	Koch	35-29	1st	+0.5
6-19	N.Y.	L	1-22		6	19	Mendoza	Rose		35-30	2nd	0.5
6-20	N.Y.	L	0-3		6	5	Pettitte	P. Martinez	Rivera	35-31	2nd	1.5
6-21	N.Y.	W	9-7		11	10	Garces	Grimsley		36-31	2nd	0.5
6-22	N.Y.	W	4-2		8	5	R. Martinez	Westbrook	Lowe	37-31	1st	+0.5
6-23	At Tor.	L	4-5		7	9	Castillo	Wasdin	Koch	37-32	2nd	0.5
6-24	At Tor.	L	4-6		7	9	Halladay	Rose	Koch	37-33	3rd	1.5
6-25	At Tor.	L	5-6	(13)	15	10	DeWitt	Florie		37-34	3rd	2.5
6-27	Bal.	L	3-6	(10)	10	11	Trombley	Lowe	Groom	37-35	3rd	2.5
6-28	Bal.	L	7-8	(11)	11	16	Mercedes	Florie	Groom	37-36	3rd	3.5

Date	Opp.	Res.	Score	(inn.*)	Hits	Opp. hits	Winning pitcher	Losing pitcher	Save	Record	Pos.	GB
6-29	Bal.	W	12-4		16	12	Wakefield	Erickson		38-36	3rd	3.5
6-30	At Chi.	L	4-10		11	13	Parque	Pichardo		38-37	3rd	3.5
7-1	At Chi.	L	2-7		6	5	Sirotka	Crawford		38-38	3rd	3.5
7-2	At Chi.	L	2-8		6	11	Baldwin	Schourek		38-39	3rd	3.5
7-3	At Min.	W	11-8		15	13	Pichardo	Lincoln	Lowe	39-39	3rd	3.5
7-4	At Min.	W	14-4		18	10	Wakefield	Milton	Florie	40-39	3rd	2.5
7-5	At Min.	W	11-8		12	10	Wasdin	Redman	Lowe	41-39	3rd	1.5
7-6	At Min.	W	8-7		8	12	Crawford	Radke		42-39	3rd	1.5
7-7	Atl.	L	3-5		7	11	Glavine	Schourek	Ligtenberg	42-40	3rd	2.0
7-8	Atl.	L	1-5		7	10	Mulholland	R. Martinez		42-41	3rd	3.5
7-9	Atl.	W	7-2		14	6	Wakefield	Millwood		43-41	3rd	2.5
7-13	N.Y. (NL)	W	4-3		8	8	Garces	Benitez		44-41	3rd	1.5
7-14	N.Y. (NL)	L	4-6		12	12	Mahomes	Lowe	Benitez	44-42	3rd	2.5
7-15	N.Y. (NL)	W	6-4		9	10	R. Martinez	Hampton	Lowe	45-42	3rd	2.0
7-16	Mon.	W	5-2		8	4	Wakefield	Johnson	Wasdin	46-42	3rd	2.0
7-17	Mon.	W	7-3		9	7	Pichardo	Telford		47-42	3rd	1.0
7-18	Mon.	W	3-1		9	6	P. Martinez	Vazquez	Lowe	48-42	2nd	1.0
7-20†	At Bal.	W	11-7		17	11	R. Martinez	Ponson		49-42		
7-20‡	At Bal.	L	4-9		4	14	Erickson	Schourek		49-43	3rd	1.0
7-21	Chi.	L	5-8		11	15	Simas	Pichardo	Howry	49-44	3rd	2.0
7-22	Chi.	W	8-6		11	10	Fassero	Garland		50-44	2nd	1.0
7-23	Chi.	W	1-0		5	6	P. Martinez	Sirotka		51-44	2nd	1.0
7-24	Min.	L	2-4		6	14	Milton	Ohka		51-45	2nd	2.0
7-25	Min.	L	2-4		8	8	Mays	R. Martinez	Guardado	51-46	2nd	3.0
7-27	At Oak.	W	5-4	(10)	8	10	Garces	Tam	Lowe	52-46	3rd	2.5
7-28	At Oak.	W	4-1		7	5	P. Martinez	Mulder	Lowe	53-46	2nd	2.5
7-29	At Oak.	L	1-12		7	11	Appier	Fassero		53-47	2nd	2.5
7-30	At Oak.	L	2-5		6	3	Heredia	Arrojo	Isringhausen	53-48	2nd	3.5
7-31	At Sea.	W	8-5		11	3	Garces	Mesa	Pichardo	54-48	2nd	3.0
8-1	At Sea.	L	4-5	(19)	12	12	Sasaki	Fassero		54-49	2nd	4.0
8-2	At Sea.	W	5-2		8	5	P. Martinez	Garcia		55-49	2nd	3.0
8-4	K.C.	W	5-4		11	8	Garces	Larkin	Lowe	56-49	2nd	3.5
8-5	K.C.	L	5-7		8	13	Meadows	Cormier	Bottalico	56-50	2nd	3.5
8-6	K.C.	L	1-3		10	8	Reichert	Wakefield	Bottalico	56-51	2nd	3.5
8-7	At Ana.	L	1-4		5	10	Washburn	Ohka	Hasegawa	56-52	2nd	3.5
8-8	At Ana.	L	1-2		2	3	Ortiz	P. Martinez		56-53	2nd	4.5
8-9	At Ana.	W	4-2		8	6	Fassero	Wise	Lowe	57-53	2nd	4.5
8-11	At Tex.	W	7-3		11	7	Arrojo	Glynn		58-53	2nd	4.0
8-12	At Tex.	L	3-6		6	6	Helling	Wakefield		58-54	2nd	4.0
8-13	At Tex.	W	4-2		7	6	Ohka	Rogers	Lowe	59-54	2nd	4.0
8-14	T.B.	W	7-3		9	11	Lowe	Taylor		60-54	2nd	4.0
8-15	T.B.	L	1-3		9	11	Sturtze	Fassero	Hernandez	60-55	2nd	5.0
8-16	T.B.	W	4-3		11	7	Arrojo	Wilson	Lowe	61-55	2nd	4.0
8-17	Tex.	W	8-7		18	12	Garces	Wetteland		62-55	2nd	4.0
8-18	Tex.	W	6-4		11	8	Ohka	Rogers	Lowe	63-55	2nd	3.0
8-19	Tex.	W	9-0		11	5	P. Martinez	Perisho		64-55	2nd	3.0
8-20	Tex.	L	2-6		9	9	Davis	Fassero		64-56	2nd	3.0
8-21	Ana.	W	7-6	(11)	8	8	Lowe	Hasegawa		65-56	2nd	3.0
8-22	Ana.	L	4-11		9	14	Mercker	Wakefield		65-57	2nd	3.0
8-23	Ana.	W	3-1		5	8	Ohka	Ortiz	Lowe	66-57	2nd	3.0
8-24	At K.C.	W	9-7	(10)	12	11	Pichardo	Larkin	Lowe	67-57	2nd	3.0
8-25	At K.C.	L	2-6		5	13	Suppan	Florie		67-58	2nd	3.0
8-26	At K.C.	W	5-3		14	9	Arrojo	Meadows	Lowe	68-58	2nd	3.0
8-27	At K.C.	L	7-11		11	10	Reichert	Wakefield		68-59	2nd	4.0
8-28	At T.B.	L	2-5		8	9	Rekar	Pichardo	Hernandez	68-60	2nd	5.0
8-29	At T.B.	W	8-0		12	1	P. Martinez	Eiland		69-60	2nd	4.0
8-30	At T.B.	L	1-3		4	11	Lopez	Fassero	Hernandez	69-61	2nd	5.0
9-1	Sea.	W	6-2		14	6	Arrojo	Halama		70-61	2nd	5.0
9-2	Sea.	L	1-4		3	7	Garcia	Garces	Sasaki	70-62	2nd	6.0
9-3	Sea.	L	0-5		1	9	Abbott	Ohka	Paniagua	70-63	2nd	6.0
9-4	Sea.	W	5-1		7	7	P. Martinez	Moyer		71-63	2nd	6.0
9-5	Oak.	W	10-3		12	6	Schourek	Appier		72-63	2nd	6.0
9-6	Oak.	L	4-6		9	13	Mulder	Arrojo	Mecir	72-64	2nd	6.0
9-7	Min.	W	11-6		16	9	R. Martinez	Milton		73-64	2nd	6.0
9-8	N.Y.	L	0-4		5	8	Clemens	Ohka		73-65	2nd	7.0
9-9	N.Y.	L	3-5		9	7	Pettitte	P. Martinez		73-66	2nd	8.0
9-10	N.Y.	L	2-6		7	11	Keisler	Schourek	Gooden	73-67	3rd	9.0
9-11	At N.Y.	W	4-0		7	5	Arrojo	Hernandez	Lowe	74-67	2nd	8.0
9-12	At Cle.	W	8-6		12	7	R. Martinez	Finley	Lowe	75-67	2nd	8.0
9-13	At Cle.	L	3-10		6	12	Colon	Ohka		75-68	2nd	9.0
9-14	At Cle.	W	7-4		10	7	P. Martinez	Nagy	Lowe	76-68	2nd	8.0
9-15	At Det.	W	7-6		12	9	Beck	Cruz	Lowe	77-68	2nd	7.0
9-16†	At Det.	W	8-5		13	11	Pichardo	Anderson	Lowe	77-68		
9-16‡	At Det.	L	2-12		8	13	Nomo	Ontiveros		78-69	2nd	7.5
9-17	At Det.	L	4-5		8	9	Mlicki	R. Martinez	Jones	78-70	2nd	7.5
9-19	Cle.	W	7-4		12	11	Beck	Nagy	Lowe	79-70	2nd	6.0
9-20†	Cle.	L	1-2		6	7	Woodard	P. Martinez	Wickman	79-71		
9-20‡	Cle.	L	4-5		10	10	Karsay	Cormier	Wickman	79-72	3rd	6.5

Date	Opp.	Res.	Score	(inn.*)	Hits	Opp. hits	Winning pitcher	Losing pitcher	Save	Record	Pos.	GB
9-21†	Cle.	W	9-8		12	12	Ontiveros	Speier	Lowe	80-72		
9-21‡	Cle.	L	5-8		12	15	Finley	Wakefield		80-73	3rd	6.0
9-22	Bal.	L	1-3		4	6	Ponson	R. Martinez		80-74	3rd	6.0
9-23	Bal.	W	8-7	(10)	12	13	Carrasco	Kohlmeier		81-74	3rd	6.0
9-24	Bal.	L	0-1		8	4	Mussina	Ohka	Kohlmeier	81-75	3rd	7.0
9-26	At Chi.	W	4-3		6	5	P. Martinez	Beirne	Lowe	82-75	T2nd	5.5
9-27	At Chi.	W	2-1		7	5	Crawford	Baldwin	Lowe	83-75	T2nd	4.5
9-28	At Chi.	W	7-6		9	8	Beck	Simas	Lowe	84-75	2nd	3.5
9-29	At T.B.	L	6-8		11	11	Yan	Carrasco	Hernandez	84-76	2nd	3.5
9-30	At T.B.	W	4-2		11	5	Cormier	Hernandez	Lowe	85-76	2nd	2.5
10-1	At T.B.	L	2-3	(10)	9	10	Wheeler	Croushore		85-77	2nd	2.5

Monthly records: April (12-9), May (17-10), June (9-18), July (16-11), August (15-13), September (16-15), October (0-1).
*Innings, if other than nine. †First game of a doubleheader. ‡Second game of a doubleheader.

HIGHLIGHTS

High point: When Pedro Martinez and Roger Clemens hooked up at Yankee Stadium on May 28, both pitched eight shutout innings before the Red Sox prevailed in the ninth, 2-0. At the time, all was rosy for the Red Sox: They were in first place in the A.L. East, Martinez looked phenomenal and new acquisition Carl Everett was playing like an MVP candidate.
Low point: A line drive off the bat of Yankee Ryan Thompson hit Red Sox reliever Bryce Florie squarely in the right eye, horrifying a September 8 crowd at Fenway Park and threatening Florie's career. The fading Red Sox lost that game 4-0 and were swept in the three-game weekend series, falling into third place, nine games behind the Yankees.
Turning point: Carl Everett's July 15 tantrum, during which he bumped the home plate umpire in an argument over where his feet were in the batter's box, cast a distasteful pall over the team. Everett's unpredictable behavior and an inability to find chemistry on a changing roster kept the Red Sox from generating any momentum.
Most valuable player: There's no question about the best player on this team. Shortstop Nomar Garciaparra won his second straight batting title (.372) and ranks among the most dangerous bats in the league.
Most valuable pitcher: Martinez. His astounding 1.74 ERA was nearly two runs lower than the next closest (Roger Clemens, 3.70) in the league and he is fast approaching the mystique of Hall of Famers Sandy Koufax, Steve Carlton and Bob Gibson.
Most improved player: Young right-hander Tomo Ohka began showing more aggressiveness to go with his good stuff and excellent control. His 3.12 ERA in 13 appearances bodes well for the future.
Most pleasant surprise: When Martinez went on the disabled list near mid-season, Paxton Crawford jumped from Class AA and made two superb starts. He returned in September and finished 2-1 with a 3.41 ERA in six appearances.
Key injuries: Third baseman John Valentin went down with a serious knee injury in early May. ... Second baseman Jose Offerman (groin, knee) went on the D.L. twice and Martinez was sidelined in late June with a strained side muscle. ... Left fielder Troy O'Leary missed a couple weeks in June to attend to personal issues. ... Right fielder Trot Nixon strained a hamstring in late June and never returned to form. ... Reliever Rod Beck (neck) missed the first few months and righthanders Juan Pena (elbow) and Bret Saberhagen (shoulder) never pitched an inning.
Notable: The club set a single-season franchise record for attendance with 2.58 million. ... Martinez became the first unanimous A.L. Cy Young winner in consecutive years. ... Garciaparra became the first righthanded hitter to win back-to-back A.L. batting titles since Joe DiMaggio in 1939-40. ... The club won the league ERA title (4.23) in consecutive seasons for the first time since 1902-04. ... Derek Lowe's 42 saves tied for the league lead.

—MICHAEL SILVERMAN

RECORDS

2000 regular-season record: 85-77 (2nd in A.L. East); 42-39 at home; 43-38 on road; 32-35 vs. East; 32-24 vs. Central; 21-18 vs. West; 20-22 vs. lefthanded starters; 65-55 vs. righthanded starters; 77-66 on grass; 8-11 on turf; 22-24 in daytime; 63-53 at night; 20-23 in one-run games; 5-8 in extra-inning games; 0-1-3 in doubleheaders.
Team record past five years: 434-376 (.536, ranks 3rd in league in that span).

TEAM LEADERS

Batting average: Nomar Garciaparra (.372).
At-bats: Nomar Garciaparra (529).
Runs: Nomar Garciaparra (104).
Hits: Nomar Garciaparra (197).
Total Bases: Nomar Garciaparra (317).
Doubles: Nomar Garciaparra (51).
Triples: Trot Nixon (8).
Home runs: Carl Everett (34).
Runs batted in: Carl Everett (108).
Stolen bases: Carl Everett (11).
Slugging percentage: Nomar Garciaparra (.599).
On-base percentage: Nomar Garciaparra (.434).
Wins: Pedro Martinez (18).
Earned-run average: Pedro Martinez (1.74).
Complete games: Pedro Martinez (7).
Shutouts: Pedro Martinez (4).
Saves: Derek Lowe (42).
Innings pitched: Pedro Martinez (217.0).
Strikeouts: Pedro Martinez (284).

GAMES BY POSITION

Catcher: Jason Varitek 128, Scott Hatteberg 48.
First base: Brian Daubach 83, Jose Offerman 39, Mike Stanley 39, Rico Brogna 37, Israel Alcantara 5, Morgan Burkhart 5, Ed Sprague 3, Andy Sheets 1.
Second base: Jose Offerman 80, Jeff Frye 53, Mike Lansing 49, Donnie Sadler 12, Manny Alexander 7.
Third base: Manny Alexander 63, Wilton Veras 49, Lou Merloni 40, Ed Sprague 31, John Valentin 10, Jeff Frye 3, Donnie Sadler 3, Sean Berry 1, Brian Daubach 1, Scott Hatteberg 1, Mike Lansing 1.
Shortstop: Nomar Garciaparra 136, Manny Alexander 20, Donnie Sadler 19, Andy Sheets 1.
Outfield: Troy O'Leary 137, Carl Everett 126, Trot Nixon 118, Darren Lewis 89, Bernard Gilkey 22, Curtis Pride 9, Israel Alcantara 8, Brian Daubach 8, Midre Cummings 4, Morgan Burkhart 1.
Designated hitter: Brian Daubach 41, Dante Bichette 30, Scott Hatteberg 20, Morgan Burkhart 19, Mike Stanley 18, Jose Offerman 9, Israel Alcantara 8, Bernard Gilkey 8, Carl Everett 5, Gary Gaetti 5, Darren Lewis 5, Manny Alexander 3, Jeff Frye 3, Rico Brogna 2, Donnie Sadler 2, Andy Sheets 2, Midre Cummings 1, Nomar Garciaparra 1, Trot Nixon 1, Curtis Pride 1, Ed Sprague 1, Jason Varitek 1.

TOP DRAFT CHOICES

1. **Phil Dumatrait,** LHP, Bakersfield (Calif.) J.C.
2. **Manny Delcarmen,** RHP, West Roxbury H.S., Hyde Park, Mass.
3. **Matt Cooper,** 1B, Ripley H.S., Stillwater, Okla.
4. **Brandon Mims,** LHP, Prattville (Ala.) H.S.
5. **Brian Esposito,** C, U. of Connecticut.
6. **Kenny Perez,** SS, S. Miami (Fla.) H.S.
7. **Tony Fontana,** RHP, Bowling Green State University.
8. **Brian Adams,** LHP, Liberty University.
9. **Patrick Johnson,** OF, William Carey (Miss.) College.
10. **Eric Doble,** RHP, Arizona State Univ.

CHICAGO WHITE SOX
AMERICAN LEAGUE CENTRAL DIVISION

White Sox
2001 SCHEDULE
Home games shaded; D—Day game (games starting before 5 p.m.)
*—All-Star Game at Safeco Field (Seattle)

APRIL

SUN	MON	TUE	WED	THU	FRI	SAT
1	2 D CLE	3	4 CLE	5	6 D DET	7 D DET
8 DET	9 D CLE	10 CLE	11 D CLE	12	13 MIN	14 MIN
15 MIN	16 D	17 DET	18 DET	19 DET	20 D MIN	21 D MIN
22 MIN	23 D	24 OAK	25 OAK	26 OAK	27 SEA	28 SEA
29 SEA	30 D					

MAY

SUN	MON	TUE	WED	THU	FRI	SAT
		1 ANA	2 ANA	3 ANA	4 TEX	5 TEX
6 D TEX	7	8 ANA	9 ANA	10 ANA	11 TEX	12 TEX
13 D TEX	14	15 SEA	16 SEA	17 SEA	18 D OAK	19 D OAK
20 D OAK	21 D TOR	22	23 TOR	24 TOR	25 DET	26 DET
27 DET	28 TOR	29 TOR	30 TOR	31 DET		

JUNE

SUN	MON	TUE	WED	THU	FRI	SAT
					1 DET	2 DET
3 DET	4 D	5 KC	6 KC	7 KC	8 CUB	9 CUB
10 CUB	11 D	12 CIN	13 CIN	14 CIN	15 STL	16 D STL
17 STL	18 D KC	19 KC	20 D KC	21 D BAL	22 BAL	23 D BAL
24 BAL	25 D	26 MIN	27 MIN	28 D MIN	29 BAL	30 BAL

JULY

SUN	MON	TUE	WED	THU	FRI	SAT
1 BAL	2 D MIN	3 MIN	4 MIN	5 MIN	6 PIT	7 PIT
8 D PIT	9	10	11 *	12 D CUB	13 D CUB	14 D CUB
15 MIL	16 MIL	17 MIL	18 D CLE	19 CLE	20 BOS	21 D BOS
22 BOS	23 CLE	24 CLE	25 CLE	26 CLE	27 BOS	28 BOS
29 BOS	30 D	31 KC				

AUGUST

SUN	MON	TUE	WED	THU	FRI	SAT
			1 KC	2 KC	3 TB	4 TB
5 TB	6 D TB	7 D ANA	8 ANA	9 ANA	10 SEA	11 SEA
12 SEA	13	14 TEX	15 TEX	16 TEX	17 D OAK	18 D OAK
19 D OAK	20 D KC	21 KC	22 KC	23 KC	24 TB	25 D TB
26 TB	27 DET	28 DET	29 DET	30 DET	31 CLE	

SEPTEMBER

SUN	MON	TUE	WED	THU	FRI	SAT
						1 CLE
2 CLE	3 D CLE	4 DET	5 DET	6 D DET	7 D CLE	8 D CLE
9 CLE	10 D CLE	11 NYY	12 NYY	13 NYY	14 MIN	15 D MIN
16 MIN	17 D	18 NYY	19 NYY	20 NYY	21 KC	22 KC
23 D KC	24	25 MIN	26 MIN	27 MIN	28 KC	29 KC
30 D KC						

2001 SEASON
CLUB DIRECTORY

Chairman
Jerry Reinsdorf
Vice chairman
Eddie Einhorn
Executive vice president
Howard Pizer
Senior vice president, general manager
Ken Williams
Sr. v.p., marketing and broadcasting
Rob Gallas
Senior vice president, baseball
Jack Gould
Senior vice president and special advisor to Jerry Reinsdorf
Ron Schueler
V.p., administration and finance
Tim Buzard
Vice president, stadium operations
Terry Savarise
Vice president, free agent and major league scouting
Larry Monroe
Special assistant to Jerry Reinsdorf
Dennis Gilbert
Special assistants to Ken Williams
George Bradley
Dave Yoakum
Executive advisor to Ken Williams
Roland Hemond
Special assignment
Bryan Little
Senior director of scouting
Duane Shaffer
Director of scouting
Doug Laumann
Director of player development
Bob Fontaine Jr.
Director of major league administration
Rick Hahn
Director of minor league administration
Grace Guerrero Zwit
Director of baseball operations systems
Daniel Fabian
Director of minor league instruction
Jim Snyder
Manager of team travel
Ed Cassin
Asst. dir. of baseball operations systems
Andrew Pinter

Director of broadcasting and marketing
Bob Grim
Director of community relations
Christine Makowski
Director of sales
Jim Muno
Director of ticket operations
Bob DeVoy
Dir. of management information services
Don Brown
Director of human resources
Moira Foy
Controller
Bill Waters
Director of public relations
Scott Reifert
Trainers
Herm Schneider
Brian Ball
Director of conditioning
Steve Odgers
Team physicians
Dr. James Boscardin, Dr. Hugo Cuadros, Dr. Bernard Feldman, Dr. David Orth, Dr. Scott Price, Dr. Lowell Scott Weil
Scouting national cross-checker
Ed Pebley
Scouting supervisors
Joe Butler, Ken Stauffer
Professional scouts
Larry Massie, Gary Pellant, Bill Young
Full-time scouts
Herman Cortes, Alex Cosmidis, Nathan Durst, Roberto Espinoza, Alex Flaugherty, Denny Gonzalez, Larry Grefer, Matt Hattabaugh, Warren Hughes, Miguel Ibarra, George Kachigian, John Kazanas, Jose Ortega, Paul Provas, Mark Salas, Alex Slattery, John Tumminia
Part-time scouts
Tommy Butler, Javier Centeno, Jaime Correa, Curt Daniels, Mike Davenport, Mariano DeLeon, John Doldoorian, James Ellison, Chuck Fox, Joe Ingalls, Jack Jolly, Robert Jones, Dario Lodigiani, Don Metzger, Glenn Murdock, Paul Murphy, Al Otto, Wuarnner Rincones, Tony Rodriguez, Oswaldo Salazar, Mike Shireley, Keith Staab, Fermin Urbi, Adam Virchis

MINOR LEAGUE AFFILIATES

Class	Team	League	Manager
AAA	Charlotte	International	Nick Leyva
AA	Birmingham	Southern	Nick Capra
A	Kannapolis	South Atlantic	To be announced
A	Winston-Salem	Carolina	To be announced
Rookie	Bristol	Appalachian	R.J. Reynolds
Rookie	Tucson	Arizona	Jerry Hairston

BROADCAST INFORMATION

Radio: ESPN-AM (1000).
TV: WGN-TV (Channel 9).
Cable TV: Fox Sports Chicago.

SPRING TRAINING

Ballpark (city): Tucson Electric Park (Tucson, Ariz.).
Ticket information: 520-434-1111.

Follow the White Sox all season at: www.sportingnews.com/baseball/teams/whitesox/

SPRING TRAINING ROSTER

Manager—Jerry Manuel (7).
Coaches—Nardi Contreras (54), Wallace Johnson (18), Von Joshua (48), Art Kusnyer (53), Mansoo Lee (59), Joe Nossek (23), Gary Pettis (20).

No.	PITCHERS	B/T	Ht./Wt.	Born	2000 clubs
37	Baldwin, James	R/R	6-3/210	7-15-71	Chicago A.L.
49	Barcelo, Lorenzo	R/R	6-4/220	8-10-77	Charlotte, Chicago A.L.
60	Biddle, Rocky	R/R	6-3/230	5-21-76	Birmingham, Chicago A.L.
56	Buehrle, Mark	L/L	6-2/200	3-23-79	Birmingham, Chicago A.L.
21	Eldred, Cal	R/R	6-4/237	11-24-67	Chicago A.L., Charlotte
	Fogg, Josh	R/R	6-2/205	12-13-76	Birmingham
29	Foulke, Keith	R/R	6-0/200	10-19-72	Chicago A.L.
52	Garland, Jon	R/R	6-6/205	9-27-79	Charlotte, Chicago A.L., Birmingham
70	Ginter, Matt	R/R	6-1/215	12-24-77	Birmingham, Chicago A.L.
	Glover, Gary	R/R	6-5/205	12-3-76	Syracuse
46	Howry, Bobby	L/R	6-5/215	8-4-73	Chicago A.L.
50	Lowe, Sean	R/R	6-2/205	3-29-71	Chicago A.L., Charlotte
40	Parque, Jim	L/L	5-11/165	2-8-76	Chicago A.L.
41	Simas, Bill	L/R	6-3/235	11-28-71	Chicago A.L.
	Vining, Ken	L/L	6-0/180	12-5-74	Birmingham
	Wells, David	L/L	6-4/235	5-20-63	Toronto
32	Wells, Kip	R/R	6-3/196	4-21-77	Chicago A.L., Charlotte
65	Wunsch, Kelly	L/L	6-5/220	7-12-72	Chicago A.L.

No.	CATCHERS	B/T	Ht./Wt.	Born	2000 clubs
10	Johnson, Mark	L/R	6-0/185	9-12-75	Chicago A.L.
15	Paul, Josh	R/R	6-1/185	5-19-75	Chicago A.L., Charlotte

No.	INFIELDERS	B/T	Ht./Wt.	Born	2000 clubs
	Clayton, Royce	R/R	6-0/183	1-2-70	Texas
24	Crede, Joe	R/R	6-3/195	4-26-78	Birmingham, Chicago A.L.
34	Dellaero, Jason	B/R	6-2/195	12-17-76	Birmingham
5	Durham, Ray	B/R	5-8/180	11-30-71	Chicago A.L.
	Garcia, Amaury	R/R	5-10/160	5-20-75	Calgary
47	Graffanino, Tony	R/R	6-1/195	6-6-72	Tampa Bay, Durham, Chicago A.L.
14	Konerko, Paul	R/R	6-3/211	3-5-76	Chicago A.L.
43	Perry, Herbert	R/R	6-2/220	9-15-69	Tampa Bay, Chicago A.L.
35	Thomas, Frank	R/R	6-5/270	5-27-68	Chicago A.L.
22	Valentin, Jose	L/R	5-10/190	10-12-69	Chicago A.L.

No.	OUTFIELDERS	B/T	Ht./Wt.	Born	2000 clubs
26	Christensen, McKay	L/L	5-11/180	8-14-75	Chicago A.L., Charlotte
45	Lee, Carlos	R/R	6-2/220	6-20-76	Chicago A.L.
39	Liefer, Jeff	L/R	6-3/195	8-17-74	Chicago A.L., Charlotte
30	Ordonez, Magglio	R/R	6-0/200	1-28-74	Chicago A.L.
	Ramirez, Julio	R/R	5-11/170	8-10-77	Calgary
66	Rowand, Aaron	R/R	6-1/200	8-29-77	Birmingham
12	Singleton, Chris	L/L	6-2/195	8-15-72	Chicago A.L.

BALLPARK INFORMATION

Ballpark (capacity, surface)
Comiskey Park (45,887, grass)

Address
333 W. 35th St.
Chicago, IL 60616

Official website
www.whitesox.com

Business phone
312-674-1000

Ticket information
312-674-1000

Ticket prices
$26 (lower deck box, club level)
$20 (lower deck reserved)
$18 (upper deck box, bleacher reserved)
$12 (upper deck reserved)

Field dimensions (from home plate)
To left field at foul line, 330 feet
To center field, 400 feet
To right field at foul line, 335 feet

First game played
April 18, 1991 (Tigers 16, White Sox 0)

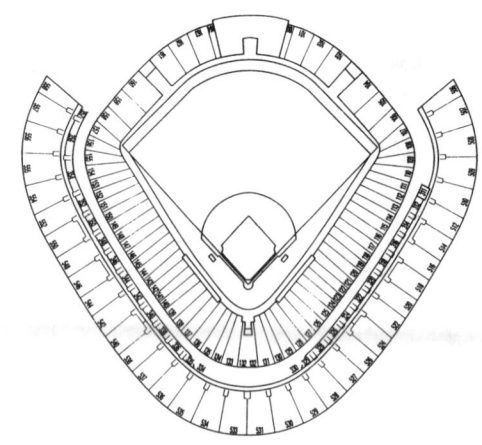

Chicago White Sox

2001 SEASON

Date	Opp.	Res.	Score	(inn.*)	Hits	Opp. hits	Winning pitcher	Losing pitcher	Save	Record	Pos.	GB
4-3	At Tex.	L	4-10		10	11	Rogers	Sirotka		0-1	T3rd	1.0
4-4	At Tex.	L	8-12		14	12	Cordero	Simas		0-2	T4th	1.5
4-5	At Tex.	W	12-8		15	13	Foulke	Zimmerman		1-2	T3rd	1.0
4-6	At Tex.	W	6-2		11	6	Baldwin	Loaiza		2-2	T1st	...
4-7	At Oak.	W	7-6		9	6	Eyre	Magnante	Foulke	3-2	T1st	...
4-8	At Oak.	W	7-3		13	7	Sirotka	Mahay		4-2	T1st	...
4-9	At Oak.	L	2-14		9	9	Appier	Wells		4-3	T2nd	0.5
4-11	At T.B.	W	13-6		18	10	Parque	Yan		5-3	3rd	1.0
4-12	At T.B.	W	7-1		15	7	Baldwin	Wheeler		6-3	3rd	1.0
4-13	At T.B.	L	5-6	(12)	8	11	Mecir	Sturtze		6-4	3rd	1.5
4-14	Ana.	W	9-4		12	12	Sirotka	Hill		7-4	3rd	0.5
4-15	Ana.	L	1-3		7	7	Bottenfield	Wells	Percival	7-5	3rd	0.5
4-16	Ana.	L	1-3		3	13	Schoeneweis	Parque	Percival	7-6	3rd	1.5
4-18	Sea.	W	18-11		19	13	Sturtze	Sele		8-6	2nd	0.5
4-19	Sea.	W	5-2		6	8	Lowe	Meche	Howry	9-6	1st	+0.5
4-21	Det.	W	7-2		8	8	Wells	Nitkowski		10-6	1st	+0.5
4-22	Det.	W	14-6		14	6	Parque	Weaver		11-6	1st	+1.0
4-23	Det.	W	9-4		9	9	Baldwin	Borkowski		12-6	1st	+1.5
4-24	Bal.	W	8-2		9	2	Eldred	Mussina		13-6	1st	+1.5
4-25	Bal.	L	6-12		11	12	Rapp	Sirotka		13-7	1st	+1.5
4-26	Bal.	W	11-6		10	10	Wells	Ponson		14-7	1st	+1.5
4-27	Bal.	W	13-4		13	9	Parque	Mercedes		15-7	1st	+2.0
4-28	At Det.	W	3-2		10	6	Baldwin	Weaver	Foulke	16-7	1st	+2.0
4-29	At Det.	W	2-1		5	6	Eldred	Mlicki	Foulke	17-7	1st	+2.0
4-30	At Det.	L	3-4	(12)	10	15	Anderson	Eyre		17-8	1st	+2.0
5-1	Tor.	L	3-5		6	9	Carpenter	Wells	Koch	17-9	1st	+2.0
5-2	Tor.	L	1-4		5	7	Castillo	Wunsch	Koch	17-10	1st	+2.0
5-3	Tor.	W	7-3		8	5	Baldwin	Escobar	Foulke	18-10	1st	+3.0
5-5	At K.C.	L	1-5		8	10	Fussell	Eldred		18-11	1st	+3.5
5-6	At K.C.	L	5-11		10	18	Spradlin	Sirotka		18-12	1st	+2.5
5-7	At K.C.	L	8-12		13	13	Bottalico	Wunsch		18-13	1st	+1.5
5-8	At Bos.	L	2-3		8	8	Rose	Sturtze	Lowe	18-14	1st	+0.5
5-9	At Bos.	W	6-0		10	3	Baldwin	Schourek		19-14	1st	+1.5
5-10	At Bos.	L	3-5	(7)	7	7	R. Martinez	Eldred	Garces	19-15	1st	+0.5
5-12	Min.	L	3-4	(10)	9	12	Miller	Lowe	Carrasco	19-16	2nd	...
5-13	Min.	W	4-3		8	8	Wunsch	Wells		20-16	2nd	...
5-14	Min.	W	5-3		10	8	Wunsch	Radke	Foulke	21-16	1st	+1.0
5-16	At N.Y.	W	4-0		7	3	Eldred	Hernandez		22-16	1st	+1.0
5-17	At N.Y.	L	4-9		7	15	Clemens	Parque		22-17	2nd	...
5-19	At Tor.	W	5-3		5	11	Sirotka	Escobar	Foulke	23-17	1st	+1.0
5-20	At Tor.	W	6-2		12	7	Baldwin	Wells		24-17	1st	+1.0
5-21	At Tor.	W	2-1		1	6	Eldred	Castillo	Foulke	25-17	1st	+1.0
5-22	At Tor.	L	3-4		6	11	Koch	Howry		25-18	1st	+0.5
5-23	N.Y.	W	8-2		11	9	Wells	Clemens		26-18	1st	+1.5
5-24	N.Y.	L	4-12		7	18	Pettitte	Sirotka		26-19	1st	+1.5
5-25	N.Y.	L	0-7		4	12	Mendoza	Baldwin		26-20	1st	+0.5
5-26	Cle.	W	5-3		6	8	Eldred	Finley	Foulke	27-20	1st	+1.5
5-27	Cle.	W	14-3		16	9	Parque	Wright		28-20	1st	+2.5
5-28	Cle.	L	3-12		7	15	Colon	Wells		28-21	1st	+1.5
5-29	At Sea.	L	4-5		7	6	Halama	Sirotka	Sasaki	28-22	1st	+1.5
5-30	At Sea.	W	2-1		4	5	Baldwin	Abbott	Foulke	29-22	1st	+1.5
5-31	At Sea.	W	4-3		6	6	Howry	Sasaki	Foulke	30-22	1st	+1.5
6-2	At Hou.	W	7-4		9	10	Parque	Reynolds	Foulke	31-22	1st	+2.5
6-3	At Hou.	L	1-6		8	10	Holt	Wells		31-23	1st	+1.5
6-4	At Hou.	W	7-3		13	5	Sirotka	Dotel		32-23	1st	+1.5
6-5	At Cin.	W	4-3		7	10	Baldwin	Parris	Foulke	33-23	1st	+1.5
6-6	At Cin.	W	17-12		19	12	Eldred	Villone		34-23	1st	+1.5
6-7	At Cin.	W	6-4		11	8	Parque	Bell	Foulke	35-23	1st	+1.5
6-9	Chi. (NL)	W	6-5	(14)	15	8	Pena	Van Poppel		36-23	1st	+2.0
6-10	Chi. (NL)	W	4-3		5	7	Sirotka	Wood	Foulke	37-23	1st	+2.0
6-11	Chi. (NL)	L	5-6		10	8	Van Poppel	Pena	Aguilera	37-24	1st	+2.0
6-12	At Cle.	W	8-7		14	13	Eldred	Rigdon	Foulke	38-24	1st	+3.0
6-13	At Cle.	W	4-3	(10)	8	8	Simas	Speier	Howry	39-24	1st	+4.0
6-14	At Cle.	W	11-4		12	5	Beirne	Brower		40-24	1st	+5.0
6-15	At N.Y.	W	12-3		16	12	Sirotka	Pettitte		41-24	1st	+5.5
6-16	At N.Y.	W	3-1		9	6	Baldwin	Stanton	Howry	42-24	1st	+6.5
6-17	At N.Y.	W	10-9		15	15	Eldred	Westbrook	Foulke	43-24	1st	+7.5
6-18	At N.Y.	W	17-4		18	10	Parque	Hernandez		44-24	1st	+7.5
6-19	Cle.	W	6-1		13	5	Wells	Colon		45-24	1st	+8.5
6-20	Cle.	L	1-4		7	9	Brower	Sirotka	Karsay	45-25	1st	+7.5
6-21	Cle.	L	6-8		14	12	Burba	Baldwin	Karsay	45-26	1st	+6.5
6-22	Cle.	W	6-0		11	7	Eldred	Finley		46-26	1st	+7.5

Date	Opp.	Res.	Score	(inn.*)	Hits	Opp. hits	Winning pitcher	Losing pitcher	Save	Record	Pos.	GB
6-23	N.Y.	W	4-3		8	11	Lowe	Rivera		47-26	1st	+8.5
6-24	N.Y.	L	8-12		13	16	Mendoza	Wells	Rivera	47-27	1st	+8.0
6-25	N.Y.	W	8-7		13	10	Sirotka	Pettitte	Howry	48-27	1st	+8.5
6-27	Min.	L	4-7		9	12	Mays	Baldwin	Wells	48-28	1st	+7.5
6-28	Min.	W	7-3		14	4	Eldred	Lincoln		49-28	1st	+8.5
6-29	Min.	L	1-10		6	15	Milton	Wells		49-29	1st	+8.5
6-30	Bos.	W	10-4		13	11	Parque	Pichardo		50-29	1st	+9.5
7-1	Bos.	W	7-2		5	6	Sirotka	Crawford		51-29	1st	+10.5
7-2	Bos.	W	8-2		11	6	Baldwin	Schourek		52-29	1st	+10.5
7-3	At K.C.	W	14-10		22	10	Pena	Santiago		53-29	1st	+11.0
7-4	At K.C.	L	7-10		14	12	Spradlin	Garland		53-30	1st	+10.0
7-5	At K.C.	W	6-3	(13)	13	17	Wunsch	Bochtler		54-30	1st	+10.0
7-7	At Chi. (NL)	W	4-2	(12)	11	6	Lowe	Van Poppel	Pena	55-30	1st	+11.5
7-8	At Chi. (NL)	L	2-9		5	14	Lieber	Baldwin		55-31	1st	+11.5
7-9	At Chi. (NL)	L	6-9		8	11	Tapani	Simas	Worrell	55-32	1st	+10.5
7-13	StL.	L	5-13		11	14	An. Benes	Sirotka		55-33	1st	+9.5
7-14	StL.	L	4-9		8	11	Stephenson	Wunsch		55-34	1st	+8.5
7-15	StL.	W	15-7		15	13	Parque	Kile		56-34	1st	+8.5
7-16	Mil.	W	11-5		16	9	Baldwin	Snyder		57-34	1st	+9.5
7-17	Mil.	W	11-2		13	4	Garland	Bere		58-34	1st	+9.5
7-18	Mil.	W	7-5		10	9	Sirotka	Wright	Wunsch	59-34	1st	+9.5
7-19	At Min.	W	3-2		9	8	Buehrle	Milton	Foulke	60-34	1st	+10.5
7-20	At Min.	L	1-5		6	12	Mays	Parque		60-35	1st	+10.5
7-21	At Bos.	W	8-5		15	11	Simas	Pichardo	Howry	61-35	1st	+11.5
7-22	At Bos.	L	6-8		10	11	Fassero	Garland		61-36	1st	+11.5
7-23	At Bos.	L	0-1		6	5	P. Martinez	Sirotka		61-37	1st	+10.5
7-24	K.C.	W	7-6		9	14	Wunsch	Suzuki	Foulke	62-37	1st	+11.0
7-25	K.C.	L	1-6		4	8	Suppan	Parque		62-38	1st	+10.0
7-26	K.C.	L	6-7		9	10	Spradlin	Howry	Bottalico	62-39	1st	+10.0
7-27	At Ana.	W	6-5		18	9	Garland	Cooper	Foulke	63-39	1st	+10.5
7-28	At Ana.	L	7-10		13	10	Holtz	Beirne	Percival	63-40	1st	+10.0
7-29	At Ana.	L	5-6		9	11	Bottenfield	Barcelo	Percival	63-41	1st	+9.5
7-30	At Ana.	W	11-7	(10)	18	12	Foulke	Levine		64-41	1st	+10.5
8-1	At Tex.	W	4-3		12	7	Howry	Wetteland		65-41	1st	+11.5
8-2	At Tex.	L	2-7		4	13	Helling	Garland	Crabtree	65-42	1st	+10.5
8-4	Oak.	L	3-5		8	8	Appier	Sirotka	Isringhausen	65-43	1st	+9.0
8-5	Oak.	W	4-3	(10)	9	7	Foulke	Mathews		66-43	1st	+9.0
8-6	Oak.	W	13-0		15	5	Baldwin	Hudson		67-43	1st	+9.0
8-8†	Sea.	L	4-12		10	17	Pineiro	Garland	Tomko	67-44		
8-8‡	Sea.	L	5-7		8	9	Garcia	Buehrle	Sasaki	67-45	1st	+8.0
8-9	Sea.	W	19-3		24	8	Sirotka	Moyer		68-45	1st	+8.0
8-10	Sea.	L	3-6		11	9	Sele	Biddle	Sasaki	68-46	1st	+7.5
8-11	At T.B.	W	6-5		8	6	Buehrle	Wilson	Foulke	69-46	1st	+8.5
8-12	At T.B.	W	5-4	(10)	11	10	Buehrle	Hernandez	Foulke	70-46	1st	+8.5
8-13	At T.B.	L	3-5		5	8	Lopez	Howry		70-47	1st	+7.5
8-14	At Bal.	L	2-8		10	11	Mercedes	Sirotka		70-48	1st	+7.5
8-15	At Bal.	W	14-4		16	8	Biddle	Johnson		71-48	1st	+8.5
8-16	At Bal.	W	7-3		9	5	Parque	Mussina		72-48	1st	+9.5
8-17	At Bal.	L	3-5		4	10	Parrish	Baldwin		72-49	1st	+9.0
8-18	T.B.	W	5-2		9	7	Garland	Rekar	Foulke	73-49	1st	+9.0
8-19	T.B.	W	7-0		11	3	Sirotka	Lopez		74-49	1st	+9.0
8-20	T.B.	L	11-12		15	15	Yan	Foulke	Hernandez	74-50	1st	+8.0
8-21	T.B.	L	4-11		8	10	Sturtze	Parque		74-51	1st	+7.5
8-23	Bal.	W	8-4		7	8	Barcelo	Parrish		75-51	1st	+7.0
8-24	Bal.	L	5-8		9	10	Mercedes	Hill		75-52	1st	+7.0
8-25	At Sea.	W	4-1		10	4	Sirotka	Sele	Foulke	76-52	1st	+8.0
8-26	At Sea.	L	5-11		8	12	Halama	Biddle		76-53	1st	+7.0
8-27	At Sea.	W	2-1		6	4	Barcelo	Garcia	Foulke	77-53	1st	+8.0
8-28	At Oak.	L	0-3		1	6	Hudson	Parque		77-54	1st	+7.0
8-29	At Oak.	W	3-0		7	5	Baldwin	Zito	Foulke	78-54	1st	+7.0
8-30	At Oak.	W	8-3		11	9	Sirotka	Appier	Howry	79-54	1st	+7.0
9-1	Ana.	W	9-8		14	10	Ginter	Hasegawa	Foulke	80-54	1st	+7.5
9-2	Ana.	W	13-6		14	5	Parque	Mercker		81-54	1st	+8.5
9-3	Ana.	W	13-12		15	11	Wunsch	Hasegawa	Foulke	82-54	1st	+8.5
9-4	Tex.	L	4-5		11	13	Davis	Garland	Wetteland	82-55	1st	+7.5
9-5	Tex.	L	1-2		8	10	Johnson	Howry	Wetteland	82-56	1st	+6.5
9-6	Tex.	W	13-1		13	4	Wells	Helling		83-56	1st	+6.5
9-7	Tex.	W	10-6		12	12	Barcelo	Zimmerman	Foulke	84-56	1st	+7.5
9-8	At Cle.	W	5-4		10	9	Buehrle	Woodard	Foulke	85-56	1st	+8.5
9-9	At Cle.	L	3-9		7	12	Burba	Garland		85-57	1st	+7.5
9-11	Det.	W	10-3		12	7	Sirotka	Moehler	Howry	86-57	1st	+8.0
9-12	Det.	L	3-10		4	11	Mlicki	Wells		86-58	1st	+8.0
9-13	Det.	W	1-0		4	5	Parque	Weaver	Foulke	87-58	1st	+8.5
9-15	Tor.	L	5-6		11	6	Escobar	Garland	Koch	87-59	1st	+7.5
9-16	Tor.	W	6-3		8	11	Wunsch	Escobar	Foulke	88-59	1st	+8.5
9-17	Tor.	L	1-14		6	15	Painter	Wells		88-60	1st	+7.5

Date	Opp.	Res.	Score	(inn.*)	Hits	Opp. hits	Winning pitcher	Losing pitcher	Save	Record	Pos.	GB
9-18	At Det.	L	2-5		3	12	Weaver	Barcelo	Jones	88-61	1st	+6.5
9-19	At Det.	W	6-2		13	7	Lowe	Sparks		89-61	1st	+7.5
9-20	At Det.	W	13-6		15	10	Garland	Moehler		90-61	1st	+7.0
9-21	At Min.	W	9-4		11	11	Sirotka	Santana		91-61	1st	+7.5
9-22	At Min.	W	5-4		10	12	Barcelo	Wells	Foulke	92-61	1st	+8.5
9-23	At Min.	W	5-3		8	8	Parque	Milton	Foulke	93-61	1st	+8.5
9-24	At Min.	L	5-6	(10)	12	10	Guardado	Beirne		93-62	1st	+8.5
9-25	At Cle.	L	2-9		8	13	Burba	Garland		93-63	1st	+7.5
9-26	Bos.	L	3-4		5	6	P. Martinez	Beirne		93-64	1st	+7.0
9-27	Bos.	L	1-2		5	5	Crawford	Baldwin	Lowe	93-65	1st	+6.0
9-28	Bos.	L	6-7		8	9	Beck	Simas	Lowe	93-66	1st	+6.0
9-29	K.C.	W	6-4		9	14	Bradford	Reichert	Foulke	94-66	1st	+6.0
9-30	K.C.	W	9-1		11	6	Wells	Stein		95-66	1st	+6.0
10-1	K.C.	L	2-6		8	10	Fussell	Baldwin		95-67	1st	+5.0

Monthly records: April (17-8), May (13-14), June (20-7), July (14-12), August (15-13), September (16-12), October (0-1).
*Innings, if other than nine. †First game of a doubleheader. ‡Second game of a doubleheader.

HIGHLIGHTS

High point: There were two. One came on a mid-June romp through Cleveland and New York, when the young White Sox won seven straight games and took control of the A.L. Central Division. The other came September 24 when the Sox, despite a loss at Minnesota, clinched their first division title since 1993 and ended Cleveland's five-year reign.

Low point: The White Sox entered the playoffs with the best record in the A.L. and high hopes. But a Division Series sweep by the Mariners sent them back to the drawing board. The Sox scored only seven runs on 17 hits in the series—single-game totals in many regular-season games.

Turning point: During an April 22 game against the Tigers at Comiskey Park, two separate brawls resulted in the suspension of seven Sox players and manager Jerry Manuel. The team pulled together after the fracas and finished April with a sizzling 17-8 record.

Most valuable player: Frank Thomas was the best player on the league's best team. After two sluggish seasons, Thomas bounced back with a .328 average and reached career highs in home runs (43) and RBIs (143).

Most valuable pitcher: While James Baldwin and Cal Eldred (elbow) battled late-season injuries, lefty Mike Sirotka quietly put up solid numbers—a career-high 15 wins and a 3.79 ERA that ranked third in the A.L. In nine starts against the Yankees, A's and Mariners, Sirotka was 6-3 with a 3.08 ERA.

Most improved player: Jim Parque bounced back from an 0-9, 6.95 ERA second half of 1999 to post a 13-6 record and 4.28 ERA. The White Sox gave him plenty of opportunity to win by averaging 8.6 runs for every nine innings he pitched.

Most pleasant surprise: Herbert Perry, an undistinguished role player with Tampa Bay and Cleveland, started 98 games at third base and delivered nicely. He batted .308, hit 12 homers and drove in 61 runs in 109 games.

Key injuries: Starters Cal Eldred and James Baldwin combined for a 21-6

record in the first half, but injuries took their toll. Baldwin (shoulder) was 3-3 and Eldred (elbow) failed to win a game after the All-Star break. ...Shortstop Jose Valentin stayed in the lineup, even though he was bothered by an inflamed muscle in his pelvic region for much of the second half. ... Center fielder Chris Singleton was a different player after dislocating his right index finger in mid-May. Prior to the injury, Singleton was batting .285. He finished at .254.

Notable: The White Sox reeled off 11 straight road wins in June, the longest streak in the major leagues since 1984. Ten of those wins were over teams with .500-plus records. ... Baldwin has had 10 or more wins and at least 100 strikeouts in each of his first five full seasons. ... Seven pitchers made their major league debuts in 2000 and eight rookies won their first game in the big leagues.

—SCOT GREGOR

RECORDS

2000 regular-season record: 95-67 (1st in A.L. Central); 46-35 at home; 49-32 on road; 30-24 vs. East; 41-26 vs. Central; 24-17 vs. West; 21-10 vs. lefthanded starters; 74-57 vs. righthanded starters; 81-62 on grass; 14-5 on turf; 26-30 in daytime; 69-37 at night; 28-18 in one-run games; 7-4 in extra-inning games; 0-1-0 in doubleheaders.

Team record past five years: 415-393 (.514; ranks 7th in league in that span).

TEAM LEADERS

Batting average: Frank Thomas (.328).
At-bats: Ray Durham (614).
Runs: Ray Durham (121).
Hits: Frank Thomas (191).
Total Bases: Frank Thomas (364).
Doubles: Frank Thomas (44).
Triples: Ray Durham (9).
Home runs: Frank Thomas (43).
Runs batted in: Frank Thomas (143).
Stolen bases: Ray Durham (25).
Slugging percentage: Frank Thomas (.625).

On-base percentage: Frank Thomas (.436).
Wins: Mike Sirotka (15).
Earned-run average: Mike Sirotka (3.79).
Complete games: James Baldwin, Cal Eldred (2).
Shutouts: James Baldwin, Cal Eldred (1).
Saves: Keith Foulke (34).
Innings pitched: Mike Sirotka (197.0).
Strikeouts: Mike Sirotka (128).

GAMES BY POSITION

Catcher: Mark L. Johnson 74, Charles Johnson 43, Brook Fordyce 40, Josh Paul 34.
First base: Paul Konerko 122, Frank Thomas 30, Greg Norton 17, Herbert Perry 3, Jeff Liefer 1.
Second base: Ray Durham 151, Tony Graffanino 19, Craig Wilson 4.
Third base: Herbert Perry 104, Greg Norton 47, Tony Graffanino 12, Paul Konerko 7, Joe Crede 6.
Shortstop: Jose Valentin 141, Tony Graffanino 21, Craig Wilson 10.
Outfield: Magglio Ordonez 152, Carlos Lee 149, Chris Singleton 145, Jeff Abbott 65, McKay Christensen 29, Jeff Liefer 5, Josh Paul 1, Jose Valentin 1.
Designated hitter: Frank Thomas 127, Harold Baines 16, Jeff Abbott 7, Paul Konerko 7, Tony Graffanino 3, Greg Norton 3, Herbert Perry 3, Carlos Lee 2, Joe Crede 1, Mark L. Johnson 1, Chris Singleton 1.

TOP DRAFT CHOICES

1. **Joe Borchard**, OF, Stanford University.
2. **Tim Hummel**, SS, Old Dominion U.
3. **Mike Morse**, SS, Nova H.S., Plantation, Fla.
4. **Alvin Jones**, RHP, Seguin (Tex.) H.S.
5. **Tony Richie**, C, Bishop Kenny H.S., Jacksonville.
6. **Bjorn Ivy**, OF, Shannon (Miss.) H.S.
7. **Eddie Young**, OF, Jones County H.S., Macon, Ga.
8. **Chris Amador**, SS, Luis-Felipe Crespo H.S., Camuy, P.R.
9. **Jason Aspito**, OF, Loyola Marymount University.
10. **Heath Phillips**, LHP-1B, Central H.S., Evansville, Ind.

CLEVELAND INDIANS
AMERICAN LEAGUE CENTRAL DIVISION

Indians
2001 SCHEDULE
Home games shaded; D—Day game (games starting before 5 p.m.)
*—All-Star Game at Safeco Field (Seattle)

APRIL
SUN	MON	TUE	WED	THU	FRI	SAT
1	2 D CWS	3	4 D CWS	5	6 BAL	7 D BAL
8 D BAL	9 CWS	10 CWS	11 D CWS	12 DET	13 DET	14 DET
15 D DET	16	17 BAL	18 BAL	19 D BAL	20 DET	21 D DET
22 D DET	23 D	24 ANA	25 ANA	26 ANA	27 TEX	28 TEX
29 TEX	30 D					

MAY
SUN	MON	TUE	WED	THU	FRI	SAT
		1 KC	2 KC	3 KC	4 D TB	5 D TB
6 TB	7 D	8 KC	9 KC	10 KC	11 TB	12 TB
13 D TB	14	15 TEX	16 TEX	17 TEX	18 D ANA	19 ANA
20 ANA	21	22 DET	23 DET	24 DET	25 NYY	26 D NYY
27 D NYY	28 D DET	29 DET	30 DET	31		

JUNE
SUN	MON	TUE	WED	THU	FRI	SAT
					1 NYY	2 D NYY
3 D NYY	4 D MIN	5 MIN	6 MIN	7 MIN	8 CIN	9 D CIN
10 CIN	11 D	12 MIL	13 MIL	14 MIL	15 PIT	16 PIT
17 PIT	18 D	19 MIN	20 MIN	21 MIN	22 KC	23 KC
24 D KC	25 D NYY	26 NYY	27 NYY	28	29 KC	30 KC

JULY
SUN	MON	TUE	WED	THU	FRI	SAT
1 D KC	2 D KC	3 D BOS	4 D BOS	5 BOS	6 STL	7 STL
8 D STL	9 D	10 *	11	12 CIN	13 CIN	14 D CIN
15 D HOU	16 D HOU	17 HOU	18 CWS	19 CWS	20 DET	21 D DET
22 DET	23 D CWS	24 CWS	25 CWS	26 CWS	27 DET	28 DET
29 DET	30 D	31 OAK				

AUGUST
SUN	MON	TUE	WED	THU	FRI	SAT
			1 OAK	2 OAK	3 SEA	4 SEA
5 SEA	6 D SEA	7 MIN	8 MIN	9 D MIN	10 TEX	11 TEX
12 TEX	13	14 MIN	15 MIN	16 MIN	17 ANA	18 D ANA
19 ANA	20 D OAK	21 OAK	22 OAK	23 D OAK	24 SEA	25 D SEA
26 SEA	27 D	28 BOS	29 BOS	30 BOS	31 CWS	

SEPTEMBER
SUN	MON	TUE	WED	THU	FRI	SAT
						1 CWS
2 D CWS	3 D CWS	4 BOS	5 BOS	6 BOS	7 CWS	8 D CWS
9 D CWS	10 D CWS	11 KC	12 KC	13 D KC	14 TOR	15 D TOR
16 TOR	17 D	18 KC	19 KC	20 KC	21 MIN	22 MIN
23 MIN	24 D TOR	25 TOR	26 TOR	27	28 MIN	29 D MIN
30 D MIN						

2001 SEASON
CLUB DIRECTORY

President and chief executive officer
Lawrence J. Dolan
Executive vice president, general manager
John Hart
Executive vice president, business
Dennis Lehman
Vice president, public relations
Bob DiBiasio
Vice president and general counsel
Paul J. Dolan
V.p., marketing and communications
Jeff Overton
Vice president of baseball operations/asst. general manager
Mark Shapiro
Vice president, finance
Ken Stefanov
Director, team travel
Mike Seghi
Director, player development
Neal Huntington
Director, scouting
John Mirabelli
Assistant director, scouting
Brad Grant
Director, media relations
Bart Swain
Manager, media relations, administration & credentials
Susie Giuliano

Manager, media relations
Curtis Danburg
Coordinator, media relations
Jeff Sibel
Head trainer
Paul Spicuzza
Assistant trainer
Jim Warfield
Clubhouse manager
Ted Walsh
Visiting clubhouse
Cy Buynak
Groundskeeper
Brandon Koehnke
National cross-checker, West Coast supervisor
Jesse Flores
National cross-checker, East Coast supervisor
Jerry Jordan
Midwest supervisor
Bob Mayer
Full-time scouts
Steve Abney, Doug Baker, Keith Boeck, Jim Bretz, Paul Cogan, Henry Cruz, Dan Durst, Jim Gabella, Chris Jefts, Tim Kissner, Chad MacDonald, Scott Meaney, Dave Miller, Les Parari, Chuck Ricci, Phil Rossi, Bill Schudlich, Jason Smith, Shawn Whalen

MINOR LEAGUE AFFILIATES

Class	Team	League	Manager
AAA	Buffalo	International	Eric Wedge
AA	Akron	Eastern	Willie Upshaw
A	Columbus	South Atlantic	Ted Kubiak
A	Kinston	Carolina	Brad Komminsk
A	Mahoning Valley	New York-Pennsylvania	Chris Bando
Rookie	Burlington	Appalachian	Dave Turgeon

BROADCAST INFORMATION

Radio: WTAM-AM (1100).
TV: WUAB-TV (Channel 43).
Cable TV: Fox Sports Net Ohio.

SPRING TRAINING

Ballpark (city): Chain Of Lakes (Winter Haven, Fla.).
Ticket information: 813-287-8844.

Follow the Indians all season at: www.sportingnews.com/baseball/teams/indians/

SPRING TRAINING ROSTER

Manager—Charlie Manuel (32).
Coaches—Luis Isaac (4), Clarence Jones (28), Grady Little (9), Dick Pole (38), Joel Skinner, Ted Uhlaender (11), Dan Williams (43).

No.	PITCHERS	B/T	Ht./Wt.	Born	2000 clubs
55	Baez, Danys	R/R	6-3/225	9-10-77	Kinston, Akron
	Vargas, Martin	R/R	6-0/155	2-22-78	Akron
64	Brammer, J.D.	R/R	6-4/235	1-30-75	Akron, Buffalo
49	Brown, Jamie	R/R	6-2/205	3-31-77	Akron
34	Burba, Dave	R/R	6-4/240	7-7-66	Cleveland
	Cairncross, Cameron	L/L	6-0/195	5-11-72	Akron, Cleveland, Buffalo
40	Colon, Bartolo	R/R	6-0/230	5-24-75	Cleveland, Buffalo
	Day, Zach	R/R	6-4/185	6-15-78	Greensboro, Tampa, Akron
56	DePaula, Sean	R/R	6-4/215	11-7-73	Buffalo, Cleveland, Akron
	Drese, Ryan	R/R	6-3/220	4-5-76	Kinston
	Drew, Tim	R/R	6-1/195	8-31-78	Akron, Cleveland, Buffalo
73	Rincon, Ricky	L/L	5-10/187	4-13-70	Cleveland
31	Finley, Chuck	L/L	6-6/225	11-26-62	Cleveland
20	Karsay, Steve	R/R	6-3/215	3-24-72	Cleveland
41	Nagy, Charles	L/R	6-3/200	5-5-67	Cleveland, Buffalo, Akron
39	Reed, Steve	R/R	6-2/212	3-11-66	Cleveland
54	Riske, Dave	R/R	6-2/180	10-23-76	Buffalo, Akron
53	Shuey, Paul	R/R	6-3/215	9-16-70	Cleveland, Akron
46	Speier, Justin	R/R	6-4/205	11-6-73	Buffalo, Cleveland
78	Westbrook, Jake	R/R	6-3/185	9-29-77	Columbus, New York A.L.
27	Wickman, Bob	R/R	6-1/234	2-6-69	Milwaukee, Cleveland
37	Woodard, Steve	L/R	6-4/217	5-15-75	Milwaukee, Cleveland
27	Wright, Jaret	R/R	6-2/230	12-29-75	Cleveland, Buffalo, Akron

No.	CATCHERS	B/T	Ht./Wt.	Born	2000 clubs
2	Diaz, Einar	R/R	5-10/185	12-28-72	Cleveland
10	Taubensee, Eddie	L/R	6-3/230	10-31-68	Cincinnati

No.	INFIELDERS	B/T	Ht./Wt.	Born	2000 clubs
12	Alomar, Roberto	B/R	6-0/185	2-5-68	Cleveland
33	Branyan, Russell	L/R	6-3/195	12-19-75	Buffalo, Cleveland
6	Cabrera, Jolbert	R/R	6-0/177	12-8-72	Buffalo, Cleveland
12	Cordero, Wil	R/R	6-2/200	10-3-71	Pittsburgh, Cleveland
17	Fryman, Travis	R/R	6-1/195	3-25-69	Cleveland
72	McDonald, John	R/R	5-11/175	9-24-74	Buffalo, Mahoning Valley, Cleveland, Kinston
25	Thome, Jim	L/R	6-4/240	8-27-70	Cleveland
13	Vizquel, Omar	B/R	5-9/185	4-24-67	Cleveland

No.	OUTFIELDERS	B/T	Ht./Wt.	Born	2000 clubs
23	Burks, Ellis	R/R	6-2/205	9-11-64	San Francisco
51	Cruz, Jacob	L/L	6-0/215	1-28-73	Cleveland
	Gonzalez, Juan	R/R	6-3/220	10-16-69	Detroit
7	Lofton, Kenny	L/L	6-0/190	5-31-67	Cleveland
70	Padilla, Roy	L/L	6-5/227	8-4-75	Kinston, Akron
65	Peoples, Danny	R/R	6-1/207	1-20-75	Buffalo
10	Roberts, Dave	L/L	5-10/175	5-31-72	Buffalo, Cleveland

BALLPARK INFORMATION

Ballpark (capacity, surface)
Jacobs Field (43,863, grass)
Address
2401 Ontario St.
Cleveland, OH 44115
Official website
www.indians.com
Business phone
216-420-4200
Ticket information
216-420-4200
Ticket prices
$40 (field box)
$27 (baseline box, IF lower box, view box)
$25 (lower box), $21 (IF upper box)
$20 (lower reserved, mezzanine, upper box)
$19 (field bleachers), $17 (bleachers)
$12 (upper reserved)
$7 (upper reserved general admission)
$6 (standing room)
Field dimensions (from home plate)
To left field at foul line, 325 feet
To center field, 405 feet
To right field at foul line, 325 feet
First game played
April 4, 1994 (Indians 4, Mariners 3, 11 innings)

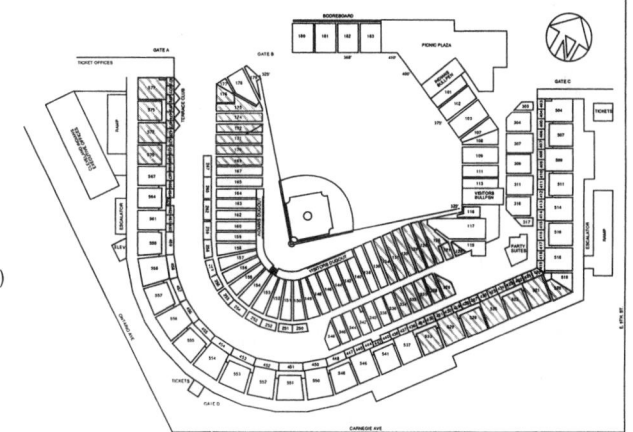

2000 REVIEW
DAY BY DAY

Date	Opp.	Res.	Score	(inn.*)	Hits	Opp. hits	Winning pitcher	Losing pitcher	Save	Record	Pos.	GB
4-3	At Bal.	W	4-1		6	6	Colon	Mussina	Karsay	1-0	T1st	...
4-5	At Bal.	L	7-11		10	12	Ryan	Kamieniecki		1-1	2nd	0.5
4-6	At Bal.	L	2-6		6	10	Rapp	Nagy	Groom	1-2	T4th	0.5
4-7	At T.B.	W	14-5		15	10	Wright	Guzman		2-2	3rd	0.5
4-8	At T.B.	W	6-4		11	10	Burba	Trachsel	Karsay	3-2	3rd	0.5
4-9	At T.B.	W	17-4		16	11	Colon	Rupe		4-2	1st	+0.5
4-10	At Oak.	W	9-4		14	9	Kamieniecki	Tam		5-2	1st	+0.5
4-11	At Oak.	W	5-1		7	4	Nagy	Olivares		6-2	1st	+0.5
4-12	At Oak.	W	5-0		8	5	Wright	Heredia		7-2	1st	+0.5
4-14	Tex.	L	2-7		4	14	Helling	Burba		7-3	1st	...
4-15	Tex.	L	4-6		6	11	Clark	Colon	Wetteland	7-4	1st	...
4-16	Tex.	W	2-1		4	5	Finley	Wetteland		8-4	1st	+1.0
4-18	Oak.	L	5-8		9	9	Mulder	Nagy	Isringhausen	8-5	1st	0.5
4-19	Oak.	L	5-10		12	12	Appier	Wright		8-6	2nd	0.5
4-20	Oak.	W	9-5		14	15	Burba	Hudson		9-6	T1st	...
4-24	At Sea.	W	6-0		9	2	Finley	Meche		10-6	2nd	1.5
4-25	At Sea.	L	5-8		11	9	Halama	Nagy		10-7	2nd	1.5
4-26	At Sea.	W	5-3	(10)	13	5	Shuey	Rhodes		11-7	2nd	1.5
4-28	Bos.	W	4-3		8	7	Burba	Schourek	Karsay	12-7	2nd	2.0
4-29	Bos.	W	3-2		5	5	Finley	R. Martinez	Karsay	13-7	2nd	2.0
4-30	Bos.	L	1-2		6	7	P. Martinez	Nagy	Lowe	13-8	2nd	2.0
5-1	N.Y.	L	1-2		7	8	Mendoza	Wright	Rivera	13-9	2nd	2.0
5-2	N.Y.	L	2-4		6	10	Pettitte	Witt	Rivera	13-10	2nd	2.0
5-3	N.Y.	L	5-6		10	9	Grimsley	Karsay	Rivera	13-11	2nd	3.0
5-4	At Tor.	L	1-8		7	10	Wells	Finley		13-12	2nd	3.5
5-5	At Tor.	L	10-11		20	13	Koch	Shuey		13-13	2nd	3.5
5-6	At Tor.	W	8-6		11	10	Rincon	Quantrill	Karsay	14-13	2nd	2.5
5-7	At Tor.	W	10-8	(12)	14	16	Shuey	Gunderson	Karsay	15-13	2nd	1.5
5-8	At Min.	W	3-2	(10)	10	9	Rincon	Wells	Karsay	16-13	2nd	0.5
5-9	At Min.	L	5-6		13	6	Hawkins	Finley	Miller	16-14	2nd	1.5
5-10	At Min.	L	9-10		14	13	Guardado	Karsay		16-15	3rd	1.5
5-11	K.C.	W	16-0		22	5	Wright	Durbin		17-15	2nd	1.0
5-12	K.C.	W	7-3		9	5	Colon	Batista		18-15	1st	...
5-13	K.C.	W	7-6	(12)	12	9	Reed	Reichert		19-15	1st	...
5-14	K.C.	L	4-5		7	8	Suzuki	Finley	Spradlin	19-16	2nd	1.0
5-16	Det.	W	11-9		14	15	Nagy	Nomo	Karsay	20-16	2nd	1.0
5-17	Det.	W	7-2		16	6	Colon	Nitkowski		21-16	1st	...
5-19	N.Y.	L	7-11		9	14	Mendoza	Kamieniecki		21-17	2nd	1.0
5-20	N.Y.	W	3-2		7	9	Shuey	Nelson		22-17	2nd	1.0
5-21	N.Y.	W	6-1		11	4	Rigdon	Hernandez		23-17	2nd	1.0
5-23	At Det.	L	4-10		11	16	Blair	Colon		23-18	2nd	1.5
5-24	At Det.	L	9-10		16	12	Patterson	Watson	Jones	23-19	2nd	1.5
5-25	At Det.	W	4-1		9	5	Burba	Moehler	Karsay	24-19	2nd	0.5
5-26	At Chi.	L	3-5		8	6	Eldred	Finley	Foulke	24-20	2nd	1.5
5-27	At Chi.	L	3-14		9	16	Parque	Wright		24-21	2nd	2.5
5-28	At Chi.	W	12-3		15	7	Colon	Wells		25-21	2nd	1.5
5-29	Ana.	L	2-3	(10)	5	4	Hasegawa	Karsay	Percival	25-22	2nd	1.5
5-30	Ana.	W	6-1		9	9	Burba	Schoeneweis		26-22	2nd	1.5
5-31	Ana.	W	7-3		10	14	Finley	Etherton	Karsay	27-22	2nd	1.5
6-2	At StL.	L	1-5		3	8	Kile	Wright		27-23	2nd	2.5
6-3	At StL.	W	4-2		8	4	Colon	Stephenson	Karsay	28-23	2nd	1.5
6-4	At StL.	W	3-2		7	6	Martin	Morris	Karsay	29-23	2nd	1.5
6-5	At Mil.	W	8-4		9	8	Burba	D'Amico		30-23	2nd	1.5
6-6	At Mil.	W	4-2		7	7	Finley	Snyder		31-23	2nd	1.5
6-7	At Mil.	W	9-5		10	10	Brewington	Bere		32-23	2nd	1.5
6-8	At Bos.	L	0-3		2	9	P. Martinez	Colon	Lowe	32-24	2nd	2.0
6-9	Cin.	W	7-4		12	8	Brower	Neagle	Karsay	33-24	2nd	2.0
6-10	Cin.	W	6-5		12	8	Burba	Parris	Karsay	34-24	2nd	2.0
6-11	Cin.	L	5-7	(13)	14	9	Aybar	Kamieniecki		34-25	2nd	2.0
6-12	Chi.	L	7-8		13	14	Eldred	Rigdon	Foulke	34-26	2nd	3.0
6-13	Chi.	L	3-4	(10)	8	8	Simas	Speier	Howry	34-27	2nd	4.0
6-14	Chi.	L	4-11		5	12	Beirne	Brower		34-28	2nd	5.0
6-16	At Det.	L	2-5		6	8	Moehler	Burba	Jones	34-29	2nd	6.5
6-17	At Det.	L	6-8		6	10	Brocail	Karsay		34-30	2nd	7.5
6-18	At Det.	W	9-4		13	8	Speier	Patterson		35-30	2nd	7.5
6-19	At Chi.	L	1-6		5	13	Wells	Colon		35-31	2nd	8.5
6-20	At Chi.	W	4-1		9	7	Brower	Sirotka	Karsay	36-31	2nd	7.5
6-21	At Chi.	W	8-6		12	14	Burba	Baldwin	Karsay	37-31	2nd	6.5
6-22	At Chi.	L	0-6		7	11	Eldred	Finley		37-32	2nd	7.5
6-23	Det.	L	6-7		9	16	Blair	Navarro	Jones	37-33	2nd	8.5
6-24†	Det.	W	8-1		10	4	Colon	Sparks		38-33		
6-24‡	Det.	L	8-14		12	16	Nitkowski	Mohler		38-34	2nd	8.0
6-25	Det.	W	2-1		9	6	Karsay	Anderson		39-34	2nd	8.0
6-26	Det.	L	2-13		11	16	Moehler	Burba		39-35	2nd	8.5

Date	Opp.	Res.	Score	(inn.*)	Hits	Opp. hits	Winning pitcher	Losing pitcher	Save	Record	Pos.	GB
6-27	At K.C.	W	12-1		13	6	Finley	Suzuki		40-35	2nd	7.5
6-28	At K.C.	L	1-8		4	9	Witasick	Davis		40-36	2nd	8.5
6-29	At K.C.	L	1-6		5	4	Durbin	Colon		40-37	2nd	8.5
6-30	Min.	L	2-7		7	16	Redman	Brower	Hawkins	40-38	2nd	9.5
7-1	Min.	L	3-4	(10)	8	9	Guardado	Karsay	Wells	40-39	2nd	10.5
7-2	Min.	W	7-1		11	6	Finley	Mays		41-39	2nd	10.5
7-4	Tor.	W	9-4		9	9	Colon	Frascatore		42-39	2nd	10.0
7-5	Tor.	W	15-7		16	12	Brewington	Quantrill		43-39	2nd	10.5
7-6	Tor.	L	6-9		15	15	Carpenter	Burba	Koch	43-40	2nd	10.5
7-7	At Cin.	L	1-2		8	7	Neagle	Finley	Graves	43-41	2nd	11.5
7-8	At Cin.	L	5-14		9	17	Parris	Davis		43-42	2nd	11.5
7-9	At Cin.	W	5-3		6	7	Colon	Williamson	Karsay	44-42	2nd	10.5
7-13	Pit.	W	4-3	(10)	10	8	Karsay	Sauerbeck		45-42	2nd	9.5
7-14	Pit.	W	9-3		11	8	Finley	Benson		46-42	2nd	8.5
7-15	Pit.	W	6-4		10	10	Brewington	Silva	Karsay	47-42	2nd	8.5
7-16	Hou.	L	1-5		7	9	Elarton	Colon		47-43	2nd	9.5
7-17	Hou.	W	8-6		9	8	Drew	Miller	Karsay	48-43	2nd	9.5
7-18	Hou.	W	8-2		8	11	Burba	Reynolds		49-43	2nd	9.5
7-19	K.C.	L	5-10		13	12	Suzuki	Finley	Spradlin	49-44	2nd	10.5
7-20	K.C.	L	6-10		11	17	Suppan	Brower		49-45	2nd	10.5
7-21	At Min.	L	1-2		8	8	Redman	Colon	Hawkins	49-46	2nd	11.5
7-22	At Min.	L	6-10		10	18	Santana	Davis	Wells	49-47	2nd	11.5
7-23	At Min.	W	8-3		12	7	Burba	Radke		50-47	2nd	10.5
7-25	At Tor.	W	10-3		10	9	Finley	Escobar		51-47	2nd	10.0
7-26	At Tor.	L	1-8		5	9	Wells	Colon		51-48	2nd	10.0
7-29†	At Bal.	W	14-3		20	8	Bere	Rapp		52-48		
7-29‡	At Bal.	L	0-4		10	8	Mercedes	Woodard		52-49	2nd	9.5
7-30	At Bal.	L	7-10		9	12	Parrish	Finley		52-50	2nd	10.5
8-1	At T.B.	L	5-6		10	7	Creek	Wickman		52-51	2nd	11.5
8-2	At T.B.	W	5-3		12	5	Karsay	Creek	Wickman	53-51	2nd	10.5
8-3	At T.B.	W	5-1		9	6	Bere	Lopez		54-51	2nd	10.0
8-4	Ana.	W	11-10		13	13	Wickman	Percival		55-51	2nd	9.0
8-5	Ana.	W	6-3		16	6	Speier	Schoeneweis		56-51	2nd	9.0
8-6	Ana.	W	5-2		10	7	Colon	Cooper	Wickman	57-51	2nd	9.0
8-7	Tex.	W	2-0		7	5	Reed	Helling	Wickman	58-51	2nd	8.5
8-8	Tex.	L	2-11		9	18	Rogers	Bere		58-52	2nd	8.0
8-9	Tex.	W	6-4		8	7	Speier	Perisho	Wickman	59-52	2nd	8.0
8-11	At Sea.	L	1-7		6	10	Abbott	Finley	Paniagua	59-53	2nd	8.5
8-12	At Sea.	W	5-4		7	7	Colon	Halama	Wickman	60-53	2nd	8.5
8-13	At Sea.	W	10-4		11	8	Speier	Garcia		61-53	2nd	7.5
8-14	At Oak.	L	1-8		8	13	Appier	Bere		61-54	2nd	7.5
8-15	At Oak.	L	3-5		10	6	Mulder	Burba	Isringhausen	61-55	2nd	8.5
8-16	At Oak.	L	6-7		9	12	D. Jones	Wickman		61-56	2nd	9.5
8-18	Sea.	W	9-8		10	14	Karsay	Rhodes		62-56	2nd	9.0
8-19	Sea.	W	10-4		11	8	Bere	Moyer		63-56	2nd	9.0
8-20	Sea.	W	12-4		15	11	Burba	Sele		64-56	2nd	8.0
8-22	Oak.	W	14-6		16	12	Finley	Heredia		65-56	2nd	7.0
8-23	Oak.	W	7-5		12	10	Shuey	Hudson	Wickman	66-56	2nd	7.0
8-24	Oak.	L	7-11		11	12	Zito	Woodard	Mecir	66-57	2nd	7.0
8-25	At Ana.	L	1-4		4	9	Wise	Burba	Hasegawa	66-58	2nd	8.0
8-26	At Ana.	W	9-5		12	9	Bere	Schoeneweis		67-58	2nd	7.0
8-27	At Ana.	L	9-10		14	16	Levine	Finley	Hasegawa	67-59	2nd	8.0
8-28	At Tex.	W	5-2		11	6	Colon	Rogers	Wickman	68-59	2nd	7.0
8-29	At Tex.	W	12-1		14	6	Woodard	Glynn		69-59	2nd	7.0
8-30	At Tex.	W	5-3		13	7	Burba	Davis	Wickman	70-59	2nd	7.0
8-31	At Tex.	L	7-14		14	21	Venafro	Karsay		70-60	2nd	7.5
9-1	Bal.	W	5-2		11	7	Finley	Ponson	Wickman	71-60	2nd	7.5
9-2	Bal.	L	6-8		9	13	Rapp	Karsay	Kohlmeier	71-61	2nd	8.5
9-3	Bal.	W	12-11	(13)	18	16	Cairncross	Trombley		72-61	2nd	8.5
9-4	T.B.	W	5-1		13	7	Burba	Lopez		73-61	2nd	7.5
9-5	T.B.	W	7-4		9	5	Bere	Fiore	Wickman	74-61	2nd	6.5
9-6	T.B.	W	6-2		11	4	Finley	Harper		75-61	2nd	6.5
9-7	T.B.	L	3-4		7	15	Rekar	Karsay	Hernandez	75-62	2nd	7.5
9-8	Chi.	L	4-5		9	10	Buehrle	Woodard	Foulke	75-63	2nd	8.5
9-9	Chi.	W	9-3		12	7	Burba	Garland		76-63	2nd	7.5
9-12	Bos.	L	6-8		7	12	R. Martinez	Finley	Lowe	76-64	2nd	8.0
9-13	Bos.	W	10-3		12	6	Colon	Ohka		77-64	2nd	8.0
9-14	Bos.	L	4-7		7	10	P. Martinez	Nagy	Lowe	77-65	2nd	8.5
9-15	At N.Y.	W	11-1		15	4	Burba	Cone		78-65	2nd	7.5
9-16	At N.Y.	L	3-6		4	12	Hernandez	Bere		78-66	2nd	8.5
9-17	At N.Y.	W	15-4		15	5	Finley	Neagle		79-66	2nd	7.5
9-18	At N.Y.	W	2-0		7	1	Colon	Clemens		80-66	2nd	6.5
9-19	At Bos.	L	4-7		11	12	Beck	Nagy	Lowe	80-67	2nd	7.5
9-20†	At Bos.	W	2-1		7	6	Woodard	P. Martinez	Wickman	81-67		
9-20‡	At Bos.	W	5-4		10	10	Karsay	Cormier	Wickman	82-67	2nd	7.0
9-21†	At Bos.	L	8-9		12	12	Ontiveros	Speier	Lowe	82-68		
9-21‡	At Bos.	W	8-5		15	12	Finley	Wakefield		83-68	2nd	7.5
9-22	At K.C.	L	2-3		10	10	Bottalico	Karsay		83-69	2nd	8.5

Date	Opp.	Res.	Score	(inn.*)	Hits	Opp. hits	Winning pitcher	Losing pitcher	Save	Record	Pos.	GB
9-23	At K.C.	W	11-1		16	4	Colon	Reichert		84-69	2nd	8.5
9-24	At K.C.	L	0-9		6	12	Stein	Nagy		84-70	2nd	8.5
9-25	Chi.	W	9-2		13	8	Burba	Garland		85-70	2nd	7.5
9-25	Min.	L	3-4		11	10	Miller	Shuey	Hawkins	85-71	2nd	8.0
9-26	Min.	W	4-2		8	8	Finley	Romero	Wickman	86-71	2nd	7.0
9-27	Min.	W	8-2		13	7	Bere	Radke		87-71	2nd	6.0
9-28	Min.	L	3-4	(10)	9	7	Guardado	Wickman	Hawkins	87-72	2nd	6.0
9-29	Tor.	W	8-4		9	5	Speier	Trachsel	Karsay	88-72	2nd	6.0
9-30	Tor.	W	6-5		11	10	Finley	Loaiza	Wickman	89-72	2nd	6.0
10-1	Tor.	W	11-4		12	8	Woodard	Wells		90-72	2nd	5.0

Monthly records: April (13-8), May (14-14), June (13-16), July (12-12), August (18-10), September (19-12), October (1-0).
*Innings, if other than nine. †First game of a doubleheader. ‡Second game of a doubleheader.

HIGHLIGHTS

High point: A September 20 pitching matchup between Steve Woodard and Boston's Pedro Martinez looked like a mismatch. But Woodard, the sacrificial lamb, threw six shutout innings and Kenny Lofton's ninth-inning home run was the difference in a 2-1 victory. The loss was the first for Martinez in 10 lifetime decisions against Cleveland.

Low point: When the Indians were swept by the young White Sox in a three-game series from June 12-14, the five-time defending-champion Indians fell five games behind in the A.L. Central. The sweep sent the Indians into a skid that lasted two months and they never made a serious run at the Sox the rest of the season.

Turning point: With the Indians fighting desperately to stay in the wild-card race, G.M. John Hart added pitchers Bob Wickman, Jason Bere and Woodard, first baseman David Segui and left fielder Wil Cordero at the trade deadline. The Indians' playoff drive came up one game short, but the season would have been over much earlier without the deals.

Most valuable player: When right fielder Manny Ramirez was out from May 30 to July 12 with a pulled hamstring, the Indians went 19-20. When he returned, they vaulted back into the playoff hunt. Despite playing only 118 games, he batted .351 with 38 homers and 122 RBIs. His numbers after coming off the D.L. were even more impressive: .371, 25 homers and 75 RBIs in 71 games.

Most valuable pitcher: Righthander Dave Burba was steady all season. His 16 wins were a career high and he was 8-2 over the second half—4-0 in September and a 5-0 over his last seven starts.

Most improved player: Third baseman Travis Fryman, a .274 career hitter entering the season, batted .321 with 106 RBIs and 184 hits, all career highs. Fryman also won his first Gold Glove.

Most pleasant surprise: Reliever Justin Speier, not even in the Indians' plans at the beginning of the season, came to the aid of a ravaged staff and compiled a 5-2 record and 3.29 ERA in 47 games as a setup man. Speier struck out 69 batters in 68 1/3 innings and held hitters to a .226 average.

Key injuries: Righthander Bartolo Colon was on the disabled from April 16 to May 12 with a pulled rib cage muscle. ... Catcher Sandy Alomar Jr. missed three

weeks with a pulled hamstring. ... Center fielder Kenny Lofton was on the D.L. with a strained biceps and outfielder Jacob Cruz missed most of the season with a knee injury. ... Righthander Charles Nagy underwent elbow surgery in May and did not return until September 14. He made three starts and returned to the D.L. for the rest of the season. ... Righthander Jaret Wright missed most of the season with shoulder problems. ... Righthander Ricardo Rincon missed more than three months with an elbow injury. ... Ramirez missed 39 games with his hamstring problem.

Notable: The Indians played host to the Chicago White Sox and Minnesota Twins in a day-night doubleheader on September 25. It was the first time a team had played two full games against two different teams in the same day since 1951.

—STEVE HERRICK

RECORDS

2000 regular-season record: 90-72 (2nd in A.L. Central); 48-33 at home; 42-39 on road; 31-22 vs. East; 34-35 vs. Central; 25-15 vs. West; 17-21 vs. lefthanded starters; 73-51 vs. righthanded starters; 79-62 on grass; 11-10 on turf; 37-15 in daytime; 53-57 at night; 17-24 in one-run games; 6-5 in extra-inning games; 1-0-3 in doubleheaders.
Team record past five years: 461-347 (.571, ranks 2nd in league in that span).

TEAM LEADERS

Batting average: Manny Ramirez (.351).
At-bats: Omar Vizquel (613).
Runs: Roberto Alomar (111).
Hits: Roberto Alomar (189).
Total Bases: Manny Ramirez (306).
Doubles: Roberto Alomar (40).
Triples: Kenny Lofton (5).
Home runs: Manny Ramirez (38).
Runs batted in: Manny Ramirez (122).
Stolen bases: Roberto Alomar (39).
Slugging percentage: Manny Ramirez (.697).
On-base percentage: Manny Ramirez (.457).
Wins: Dave Burba, Chuck Finley (16).
Earned-run average: Bartolo Colon (3.88).
Complete games: Chuck Finley (3).

Shutouts: Bartolo Colon, Jaret Wright (1).
Saves: Steve Karsay (20).
Innings pitched: Chuck Finley (218.0).
Strikeouts: Bartolo Colon (212).

GAMES BY POSITION

Catcher: Sandy Alomar Jr. 95, Einar Diaz 74.
First base: Jim Thome 107, David Segui 35, Richie Sexson 27, Travis Fryman 1, Chan Perry 1.
Second base: Roberto Alomar 155, Jolbert Cabrera 19, Enrique Wilson 7, Bill Selby 6, John McDonald 2.
Third base: Travis Fryman 154, Enrique Wilson 12, Bill Selby 4, Russ Branyan 1, Einar Diaz 1.
Shortstop: Omar Vizquel 156, Jolbert Cabrera 8, John McDonald 7, Enrique Wilson 7.
Outfield: Kenny Lofton 135, Manny Ramirez 93, Jolbert Cabrera 74, Richie Sexson 58, David Justice 47, Wil Cordero 38, Russ Branyan 33, Alex Ramirez 31, Ricky Ledee 17, Dave Roberts 17, Bill Selby 7, Jacob Cruz 7, Chan Perry 7, David Segui 7, Mark Whiten 5.
Designated hitter: Jim Thome 49, Manny Ramirez 25, Russ Branyan 23, David Justice 20, David Segui 15, Richie Sexson 10, Enrique Wilson 8, Alex Ramirez 6, Bill Selby 6, Chan Perry 4, Jolbert Cabrera 2, Jacob Cruz 2, Sandy Alomar Jr. 1, Travis Fryman 1, Kenny Lofton 1.

TOP DRAFT CHOICES

1a. **Corey Smith**, SS, Piscataway (N.J.) H.S.
1b. **Derek Thompson**, LHP, Land O'Lakes (Fla.) H.S.
2a. **Brian Tallet**, LHP, Louisiana State U.
2b. **Mark Folsom**, OF, West Orange H.S., Winter Garden, Fla.
3. **Sean Swedlow**, C, San Dimas (Calif.) H.S.
4. **Adam Cox**, OF, Darton (Ga.) College.
5. **Rashad Eldridge**, OF, First Presbyterian H.S., Macon, Ga.
6. **Kyle Evans**, RHP, Baylor University.
7. **Victor Kleine**, LHP, John A. Logan (Ky.) College
8. **Joe Inglett**, OF, Univ. of Nevada.
9. **Scott Tolbert**, RHP, Madison County H.S., Danielsville, Ga.
10. **Tom Canale**, RHP, California Lutheran University.

DETROIT TIGERS
AMERICAN LEAGUE CENTRAL DIVISION

Tigers
2001 SCHEDULE
Home games shaded; D—Day game (games starting before 5 p.m.)
*—All-Star Game at Safeco Field (Seattle)

APRIL

SUN	MON	TUE	WED	THU	FRI	SAT
1	2	3 D	4	5 D MIN	6 D CWS	7 D CWS
8 D CWS	9 MIN	10 MIN	11 MIN	12 CLE	13 CLE	14 D CLE
15 D CLE	16	17 CWS	18 CWS	19 CWS	20 CLE	21 D CLE
22 CLE	23	24 BAL	25 BAL	26 BAL	27 TB	28 D TB
29 D TB	30					

MAY

SUN	MON	TUE	WED	THU	FRI	SAT
		1 TEX	2 TEX	3 D TEX	4 ANA	5 ANA
6 D ANA	7	8 TEX	9 TEX	10 D TEX	11 ANA	12 D ANA
13 D ANA	14	15 BAL	16 BAL	17 BAL	18 TB	19 D TB
20 D TB	21	22 CLE	23 CLE	24 CLE	25 CWS	26 CWS
27 CWS	28 CLE	29 D CLE	30 CLE	31 CWS		

JUNE

SUN	MON	TUE	WED	THU	FRI	SAT
					1 CWS	2 CWS
3 D CWS	4	5 BOS	6 BOS	7 BOS	8 MIL	9 MIL
10 D MIL	11	12 PIT	13 PIT	14 PIT	15 ARI	16 ARI
17 D ARI	18	19 NYY	20 NYY	21 NYY	22 MIN	23 MIN
24 D MIN	25 D MIN	26 KC	27 KC	28 D KC	29 MIN	30 MIN

JULY

SUN	MON	TUE	WED	THU	FRI	SAT
1 MIN	2 D	3 KC	4 KC	5 KC	6 CUB	7 CUB
8 D CUB	9	10 *	11	12 STL	13 STL	14 D STL
15 D CIN	16 CIN	17 CIN	18 NYY	19 NYY	20 CLE	21 D CLE
22 D CLE	23	24 NYY	25 NYY	26 NYY	27 CLE	28 CLE
29 D CLE	30	31 SEA				

AUGUST

SUN	MON	TUE	WED	THU	FRI	SAT
			SEA	1 SEA	2 OAK	3 OAK
5 OAK	6 D OAK	7 D TEX	7 TEX	8 TEX	9 KC	10 KC
12 D KC	13	14 ANA	15 ANA	16 ANA	17 KC	18 KC
19 D KC	20 SEA	21 SEA	22 SEA	23 SEA	24 OAK	25 D OAK
26 OAK	27	28 CWS	29 CWS	30 CWS	31 TOR	

SEPTEMBER

SUN	MON	TUE	WED	THU	FRI	SAT
						1 D TOR
2 TOR	3 D	4 CWS	5 CWS	6 D CWS	7 TOR	8 TOR
9 D TOR	10 MIN	11 MIN	12 MIN	13 D MIN	14 KC	15 KC
16 D KC	17	18 MIN	19 MIN	20 D MIN	21 BOS	22 BOS
23 BOS	24 KC	25 KC	26 KC	27 KC	28 D BOS	29 BOS
30 D BOS						

2001 SEASON
CLUB DIRECTORY

Owner
Michael Ilitch
President, chief executive officer
John McHale Jr.
Vice president, baseball operations/g.m.
Randy Smith
Vice president, business operations
David H. Glazier
Assistant general manager
Steve Lubratich
Assistants to baseball operations
Ricky Bennett, Hiroshi Yoshimura
Asst., bb operations, foreign affairs
Ramon Pena
Special assistants to the g.m.
Al Hargesheimer, Randy Johnson
Director of scouting
Greg Smith
Latin American liaison
Luis Mayoral
Director minor league operations
Dave Miller
Traveling secretary
Bill Brown
Sr. dir., marketing and communications
Tyler Barnes
Manager of public relations
Jim Anderson
Manager, community relations
Celia Bobrowsky
Coordinator, community relations
Fred Feliciano
Coordinator, public relations
Brian Britten
Coordinator, public relations
Melanie Waters
Coordinator, community relations
Masico Brown
Marketing manager
Ellen Hill

Vice president, ballpark operations
Tom Folk
Special assistant to the president
Gary Vitto
Director of corporate sales
Dan Sinagoga
Director of finance
Jennifer Orow
Director of ticket services
Ken Marchetti
Director of ticket sales
Barry Gibson
Director of merchandise
Kayla French
Manager, home clubhouse
Jim Schmakel
Assistant manager, visiting clubhouse
John Nelson
Team physicians
David J. Collon, M.D., Terry Lock, M.D., Louis Saco, M.D., Michael Workings, M.D.
Medical director/head trainer
Russ Miller
Assistant trainer
Steve Carter
Strength and conditioning coach
Dennie Taft
Scouts
Scott Bream, Bill Buck, Jerome Cochran, Tim Grieve, Rob Guzik, Jack Hays, Mike Herbert, Joe Hodges, Lou Laslo, Dennis Lieberthal, Jeff Malinoff, Mark Monahan, Pat Murtaugh, Steve Nichols, Frank Paine, Derrick Ross, Steve Taylor, Clyde Weir, Jeff Wetherby, Rob Wilfong, Ellis Williams, Steve Williams, Gary York, Harold Zonder

MINOR LEAGUE AFFILIATES

Class	Team	League	Manager
AAA	Toledo	International	Bruce Fields
AA	Erie	Eastern	To be announced
A	Lakeland	Florida State	Skeeter Barnes
A	Oneonta	New York-Pennsylvania	Gary Green
A	West Michigan	Midwest	Kevin Bradshaw
Rookie	Gulf Coast Tigers	Gulf Coast	Howard Bushong

BROADCAST INFORMATION

Radio: WXYT-AM (1270).
TV: WKBD (Channel 50).
Cable TV: FOX Sports Detroit.

SPRING TRAINING

Ballpark (city): Marchant Stadium (Lakeland, Fla.).
Ticket information: 941-603-6278 or 941-603-6279.

Follow the Tigers all season at: www.sportingnews.com/baseball/teams/tigers/

SPRING TRAINING ROSTER

Manager—Phil Garner (33).
Coaches—Bill Madlock (48), Doug Mansolino (32), Ed Ott, Lance Parrish (13), Juan Samuel (10), Dan Warthen (31), Dennie Taft (00).

No.	PITCHERS	B/T	Ht./Wt.	Born	2000 clubs
14	Anderson, Matt	R/R	6-4/200	8-17-76	Detroit
49	Bernero, Adam	R/R	6-4/205	11-28-76	Jacksonville, Toledo, Detroit
	Borkowski, Dave	R/R	6-1/200	2-7-77	Toledo, Detroit, Gulf Coast Tigers, Lakeland
50	Greisinger, Seth	R/R	6-3/200	7-29-75	DID NOT PLAY
	Heams, Shane	R/R	6-1/175	9-29-75	Jacksonville, Toledo
	Holt, Chris	R/R	6-4/205	9-18-71	Houston
59	Jones, Todd	R/R	6-3/230	4-24-68	Detroit
	Keller, Kris	R/R	6-2/225	3-1-78	Jacksonville
	Loux, Shane	R/R	6-2/205	8-13-79	Lakeland, Jacksonville
	Maroth, Mike	L/L	6-0/180	8-17-77	Jacksonville
	Miller, Matt	L/L	6-3/175	8-2-74	Jacksonville
30	Milcki, Dave	R/R	6-4/205	6-8-68	Detroit, West Michigan, Toledo
38	Moehler, Brian	R/R	6-3/235	12-31-71	Detroit, West Michigan
27	Nitkowski, C.J.	L/L	6-3/205	3-9-73	Detroit
28	Patterson, Danny	R/R	6-0/185	2-17-71	Detroit
	Perisho, Matt	L/L	6-0/205	6-8-75	Texas
	Pettyjohn, Adam	L/R	6-3/190	6-11-77	Jacksonville, Toledo
	Pineda, Luis	R/R	6-1/160	6-10-78	Lakeland
37	Sparks, Steve	R/R	6-0/180	7-2-65	Toledo, Detroit
36	Weaver, Jeff	R/R	6-5/210	8-22-76	Toledo, Detroit

No.	CATCHERS	B/T	Ht./Wt.	Born	2000 clubs
53	Cardona, Javier	R/R	6-1/185	9-15-75	Toledo, Detroit
18	Fick, Robert	L/R	6-1/189	3-15-74	Detroit, Toledo
	Inge, Brandon	B/R	5-11/185	5-19-77	Jacksonville, Toledo
	Meluskey, Mitch	B/R	6-0/185	9-18-73	Houston
17	Munson, Eric	L/R	6-3/220	10-3-77	Jacksonville, Detroit

No.	INFIELDERS	B/T	Ht./Wt.	Born	2000 clubs
	Clark, Jermaine	L/R	5-10/175	9-29-76	New Haven
44	Clark, Tony	B/R	6-7/245	6-15-72	Detroit, Toledo
8	Cruz, Deivi	R/R	6-0/184	11-6-75	Detroit
9	Easley, Damion	R/R	5-11/185	11-11-69	Detroit, Toledo
17	Halter, Shane	R/R	6-0/180	11-8-69	Detroit
33	Macias, Jose	B/R	5-10/173	1-25-74	Toledo, Detroit
7	Palmer, Dean	R/R	6-1/210	12-27-68	Detroit
	Santana, Pedro	R/R	5-11/160	9-21-76	Jacksonville

No.	OUTFIELDERS	B/T	Ht./Wt.	Born	2000 clubs
	Cedeno, Roger	B/R	6-1/205	8-16-74	Houston, New Orleans
34	Encarnacion, Juan	R/R	6-3/187	3-8-76	Detroit
4	Higginson, Bobby	L/R	5-11/195	8-18-70	Detroit
29	Magee, Wendell	R/R	6-0/220	8-3-72	Detroit, Toledo
43	McMillon, Billy	L/L	5-11/179	11-17-71	Toledo, Detroit
	Torres, Andres	B/R	5-10/175	1-26-78	Lakeland, Jacksonville
	Wakeland, Chris	L/L	6-0/185	6-15-74	Toledo

BALLPARK INFORMATION

Ballpark (capacity, surface)
Comerica Park (40,120, grass)

Address
2100 Woodward
Detroit, MI 48201

Official website
www.detroittigers.com

Business phone
313-471-2000

Ticket information
313-471-BALL

Ticket prices
$60 (Tiger Den)
$35 (terrace, club)
$30 (infield box)
$25 & $15 (outfield box)
$20 (upper box)
$15 (mezzanine)
$14 (pavilion)
$12 (upper reserved)
$8 (bleachers)

Field dimensions (from home plate)
To left field at foul line, 345 feet
To center field, 420 feet
To right field at foul line, 330 feet

First game played
April 11, 2000 (Tigers 5, Mariners 2)

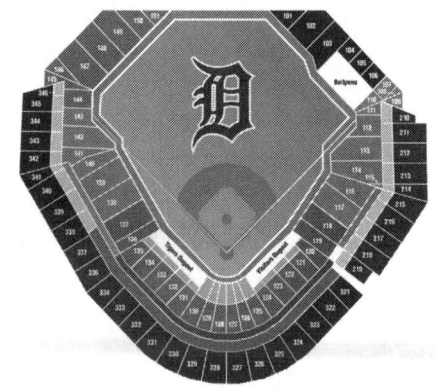

Detroit Tigers

2001 SEASON

Date	Opp.	Res.	Score	(inn.*)	Hits	Opp. hits	Winning pitcher	Losing pitcher	Save	Record	Pos.	GB
4-3	At Oak.	W	7-4		11	4	Nomo	Appier	Jones	1-0	T1st	...
4-4	At Oak.	L	1-3		2	5	Hudson	Nitkowski	Isringhausen	1-1	T2nd	0.5
4-5	At Oak.	L	2-8		6	10	Olivares	Moehler		1-2	T3rd	1.0
4-7	At Bal.	L	10-14		14	13	Worrell	Mlicki		1-3	5th	1.5
4-8	At Bal.	L	1-2	(10)	10	8	Reyes	Brocail		1-4	5th	2.5
4-9	At Bal.	L	6-11		10	16	Mercedes	Nitkowski		1-5	5th	3.0
4-11	Sea.	W	5-2		8	12	Moehler	Garcia	Jones	2-5	5th	3.5
4-12	Sea.	L	0-4		3	9	Sele	Mlicki		2-6	5th	4.5
4-13	Sea.	W	2-0		9	9	Brocail	Rhodes	Jones	3-6	4th	4.0
4-14	T.B.	W	10-5		11	14	Nitkowski	Rupe		4-6	4th	3.0
4-15	T.B.	L	0-7		6	11	Gooden	Weaver		4-7	4th	3.0
4-16	T.B.	L	6-7		8	16	Hernandez	Jones		4-8	4th	4.0
4-18	Bos.	L	0-7		6	10	Schourek	Mlicki	Lowe	4-9	5th	4.0
4-19	Bos.	L	0-10		6	15	Rose	Nomo		4-10	5th	4.5
4-21	At Chi.	L	2-7		8	8	Wells	Nitkowski		4-11	5th	5.5
4-22	At Chi.	L	6-14		6	14	Parque	Weaver		4-12	5th	6.5
4-23	At Chi.	L	4-9		9	9	Baldwin	Borkowski		4-13	5th	7.5
4-24	At Ana.	L	4-10		13	14	Hill	Mlicki		4-14	5th	8.5
4-25	At Ana.	W	4-2		10	8	Poole	Bottenfield	Jones	5-14	5th	7.5
4-26	At Ana.	L	1-6		5	11	Schoeneweis	Nitkowski		5-15	5th	8.5
4-28	Chi.	L	2-3		6	10	Baldwin	Weaver	Foulke	5-16	5th	10.0
4-29	Chi.	L	1-2		6	5	Eldred	Mlicki	Foulke	5-17	5th	11.0
4-30	Chi.	W	4-3	(12)	15	10	Anderson	Eyre		6-17	5th	10.0
5-1	At Bos.	L	6-10		11	11	Fassero	Nitkowski		6-18	5th	10.0
5-2	At Bos.	W	7-6	(12)	18	10	Blair	Wakefield	Jones	7-18	5th	9.0
5-3	At Bos.	L	2-4		6	7	Lowe	Weaver		7-19	5th	10.0
5-4	At Min.	W	8-6	(11)	10	12	Anderson	Wells	Jones	8-19	5th	9.5
5-5	At Min.	W	10-8		14	11	Patterson	Carrasco	Jones	9-19	5th	8.5
5-6	At Min.	L	1-6		10	8	Redman	Nitkowski		9-20	5th	8.5
5-7	At Min.	L	0-4		5	6	Mays	Johnson		9-21	5th	8.5
5-8	K.C.	L	1-4	(11)	3	8	Santiago	Brocail		9-22	5th	8.5
5-10	K.C.	L	0-6		4	9	Fussell	Nomo		9-23	5th	9.0
5-12	N.Y.	W	9-7		16	12	Nitkowski	Clemens	Jones	10-23	5th	8.0
5-13	N.Y.	W	6-3		13	8	Weaver	Pettitte	Jones	11-23	5th	8.0
5-14	N.Y.	W	2-1		8	5	Mlicki	Cone	Jones	12-23	5th	8.0
5-16	At Cle.	L	9-11		15	14	Nagy	Nomo	Karsay	12-24	5th	9.0
5-17	At Cle.	L	2-7		6	16	Colon	Nitkowski		12-25	5th	9.0
5-19	At Bos.	L	0-3		5	7	Fassero	Moehler	Lowe	12-26	5th	10.0
5-20	At Bos.	W	2-1		9	6	Mlicki	Wakefield	Jones	13-26	5th	10.0
5-21	At Bos.	W	7-5		11	12	Nomo	R. Martinez	Jones	14-26	5th	10.0
5-23	Cle.	W	10-4		16	11	Blair	Colon		15-26	5th	9.5
5-24	Cle.	W	10-9		12	16	Patterson	Watson	Jones	16-26	5th	8.5
5-25	Cle.	L	1-4		5	9	Burba	Moehler	Karsay	16-27	5th	8.5
5-26	Tor.	L	2-8		7	12	Frascatore	Brocail		16-28	5th	9.5
5-27	Tor.	W	4-3		7	7	Brocail	Quantrill		17-28	5th	9.5
5-28	Tor.	L	7-12		11	15	Andrews	Blair		17-29	5th	9.5
5-29	Tex.	L	2-3		11	7	Rogers	Weaver	Wetteland	17-30	5th	9.5
5-30	Tex.	W	7-4		13	9	Moehler	Loaiza	Jones	18-30	5th	9.5
5-31	Tex.	L	5-13		11	16	Oliver	Mlicki		18-31	5th	10.5
6-2	At Chi. (NL)	L	0-2		8	5	Downs	Nomo	Aguilera	18-32	5th	11.5
6-3	At Chi. (NL)	W	5-3		7	6	Weaver	Wood	Jones	19-32	5th	10.5
6-4	At Chi. (NL)	W	3-2	(12)	7	9	Anderson	Van Poppel	Jones	20-32	5th	10.5
6-5	At Pit.	L	1-5		7	9	Cordova	Mlicki		20-33	5th	11.5
6-6	At Pit.	W	2-1		5	11	Nitkowski	Anderson	Jones	21-33	5th	11.5
6-7	At Pit.	L	3-4		8	9	Ritchie	Nomo	Williams	21-34	5th	12.5
6-9	StL.	W	4-2		7	4	Weaver	Stephenson	Jones	22-34	5th	12.5
6-10	StL.	W	10-1		13	7	Moehler	Ankiel		23-34	5th	12.5
6-11	StL.	L	3-7		6	11	Hentgen	Mlicki		23-35	5th	12.5
6-12	Tor.	L	2-4		8	10	Castillo	Nomo	Koch	23-36	5th	13.5
6-13	Tor.	W	16-3		21	9	Blair	Andrews		24-36	5th	13.5
6-14	Tor.	L	1-8		9	9	Carpenter	Weaver		24-37	5th	14.5
6-16	Cle.	W	5-2		8	6	Moehler	Burba	Jones	25-37	5th	15.0
6-17	Cle.	W	8-6		10	6	Brocail	Karsay		26-37	5th	15.0
6-18	Cle.	L	4-9		8	13	Speier	Patterson		26-38	5th	16.0
6-20	At Tor.	W	18-6		18	8	Weaver	Carpenter		27-38	5th	15.5
6-21	At Tor.	L	0-6		4	12	Escobar	Moehler		27-39	5th	15.5
6-22	At Tor.	L	4-7		8	8	Wells	Nomo		27-40	5th	16.5
6-23	At Cle.	W	7-6		16	9	Blair	Navarro	Jones	28-40	5th	16.5
6-24†	At Cle.	L	1-8		4	10	Colon	Sparks		28-41		
6-24‡	At Cle.	W	14-8		16	12	Nitkowski	Mohler		29-41	5th	16.0
6-25	At Cle.	L	1-2		6	9	Karsay	Anderson		29-42	5th	17.0
6-26	At Cle.	W	13-2		16	11	Moehler	Burba		30-42	5th	16.5
6-27	N.Y.	W	7-6	(11)	17	15	Cruz	Rivera		31-42	5th	15.5
6-28	N.Y.	W	13-6		12	11	Blair	Ford	Sparks	32-42	4th	15.5

Date	Opp.	Res.	Score	(inn.*)	Hits	Opp. hits	Winning pitcher	Losing pitcher	Save	Record	Pos.	GB
6-29	N.Y.	L	0-8		6	14	Pettitte	Mlicki		32-43	5th	15.5
6-30	At K.C.	W	3-1		5	7	Weaver	Reichert	Jones	33-43	5th	15.5
7-1	At K.C.	W	8-7		15	14	Brocail	Bottalico	Jones	34-43	5th	15.5
7-2	At K.C.	W	2-0		6	3	Nomo	Suzuki	Jones	35-43	4th	15.5
7-3	At T.B.	W	5-4	(10)	11	7	Patterson	Hernandez	Jones	36-43	4th	15.5
7-4	At T.B.	W	11-0		12	9	Mlicki	Lidle		37-43	4th	14.5
7-5	At T.B.	L	1-4		8	9	Rekar	Weaver	Hernandez	37-44	4th	15.5
7-7	At Mil.	L	3-4		6	9	Haynes	Moehler	Wickman	37-45	4th	16.5
7-8	At Mil.	W	4-2	(15)	12	15	Cruz	de los Santos		38-45	4th	15.5
7-9	At Mil.	L	3-10		10	13	Bere	Blair		38-46	4th	15.5
7-13	Hou.	W	8-2		12	11	Moehler	Reynolds		39-46	3rd	14.5
7-14	Hou.	L	4-9		10	13	Holt	Nomo		39-47	3rd	14.5
7-15	Hou.	W	11-6		15	11	Patterson	Henry		40-47	3rd	14.5
7-16	Cin.	W	6-2		10	10	Weaver	Parris		41-47	3rd	14.5
7-17	Cin.	W	3-1		8	10	Mlicki	Luebbers	Jones	42-47	3rd	14.5
7-18	Cin.	L	4-5		10	15	Dessens	Moehler	Graves	42-48	3rd	15.5
7-19	At N.Y.	L	1-9		6	11	Clemens	Nomo		42-49	3rd	16.5
7-20	At N.Y.	W	5-3		8	8	Blair	Pettitte	Jones	43-49	3rd	15.5
7-21	K.C.	L	0-4		6	9	Reichert	Weaver		43-50	4th	16.5
7-22†	K.C.	L	5-8		9	11	Witasick	Mlicki	Bottalico	43-51		
7-22‡	K.C.	W	10-6		14	8	Cruz	Bochtler		44-51	4th	16.0
7-23	K.C.	W	12-9		14	13	Brocail	Byrdak	Jones	45-51	3rd	15.0
7-24	T.B.	L	2-4		5	10	Lopez	Nomo	Hernandez	45-52	3rd	16.0
7-25	T.B.	W	6-4		10	9	Blair	Trachsel	Jones	46-52	3rd	15.0
7-26	T.B.	L	2-6		5	10	Yan	Weaver	Hernandez	46-53	3rd	15.0
7-27	At Tex.	L	3-7		4	11	Glynn	Sparks	Zimmerman	46-54	4th	16.0
7-28	At Tex.	L	5-11		8	14	Helling	Moehler		46-55	4th	16.0
7-29	At Tex.	W	10-2		15	7	Nomo	Rogers		47-55	3rd	15.0
7-30	At Tex.	W	8-7		11	12	Blair	Oliver	Jones	48-55	3rd	15.0
7-31	At Ana.	L	4-5		10	7	Petkovsek	Jones		48-56	3rd	15.5
8-1	At Ana.	W	6-3		10	8	Cruz	Cooper	Jones	49-56	3rd	15.5
8-2	At Ana.	W	5-3		9	9	Moehler	Hill	Jones	50-56	3rd	14.5
8-4	Min.	L	1-3		4	10	Milton	Nitkowski	Wells	50-57	3rd	14.5
8-5	Min.	W	4-3		6	9	Sparks	Mays	Jones	51-57	3rd	14.5
8-6	Min.	L	3-7		10	10	Romero	Weaver		51-58	3rd	15.5
8-7	Bal.	L	3-4		11	7	Groom	Brocail	Kohlmeier	51-59	3rd	16.0
8-8	Bal.	W	4-1		7	8	Moehler	Rapp		52-59	3rd	14.5
8-9	Bal.	L	2-5		7	11	Mercedes	Blair	Kohlmeier	52-60	3rd	15.5
8-10	Bal.	W	14-3		14	6	Sparks	Ponson		53-60	3rd	14.5
8-11	At Oak.	W	11-4		15	9	Weaver	Heredia		54-60	3rd	14.5
8-12	At Oak.	L	5-9		9	11	Hudson	Bernero		54-61	3rd	15.5
8-13	At Oak.	W	5-3		11	10	Moehler	Zito	Jones	55-61	3rd	14.5
8-14	At Sea.	W	15-4		18	12	Blair	Moyer		56-61	3rd	13.5
8-15	At Sea.	W	9-0		17	5	Sparks	Sele		57-61	3rd	13.5
8-16	At Sea.	W	12-8		16	10	Weaver	Tomko		58-61	3rd	13.5
8-18	Oak.	W	10-1		17	3	Nomo	Hudson		59-61	3rd	13.0
8-19	Oak.	W	4-3		9	10	Moehler	Zito	Jones	60-61	3rd	13.0
8-20	Oak.	L	4-5	(11)	10	14	Isringhausen	Cruz	Tam	60-62	3rd	13.0
8-21	Oak.	W	3-1		8	5	Sparks	Mulder	Jones	61-62	3rd	12.0
8-22	Sea.	L	4-8		6	10	Paniagua	Weaver	Sasaki	61-63	3rd	12.5
8-23	Sea.	W	6-5		11	11	Cruz	Rhodes	Jones	62-63	3rd	12.5
8-24	Sea.	W	10-3		12	8	Moehler	Moyer		63-63	3rd	11.5
8-25	At Min.	L	3-8		7	10	Radke	Blair	Wells	63-64	3rd	12.5
8-26	At Min.	W	8-2		11	5	Sparks	Milton		64-64	3rd	11.5
8-27	At Min.	L	6-7	(10)	9	11	Carrasco	Jones		64-65	3rd	12.0
8-29	At Bal.	W	12-2		16	7	Weaver	Parrish		65-65	3rd	12.0
8-30	At Bal.	L	1-5		2	11	Mercedes	Nomo		65-66	3rd	13.0
8-31	At Bal.	W	6-1		11	5	Patterson	Trombley		66-66	3rd	12.5
9-1	Tex.	W	7-5		10	11	Sparks	Helling	Jones	67-66	3rd	12.5
9-2	Tex.	W	5-3		10	10	Blair	Rogers	Anderson	68-66	3rd	12.5
9-3	Tex.	L	1-4		7	11	Glynn	Weaver	Wetteland	68-67	3rd	13.5
9-4	Ana.	W	5-0		11	5	Nomo	Karl		69-67	3rd	12.5
9-5	Ana.	W	7-5		10	10	Moehler	Wise	Jones	70-67	3rd	11.5
9-6	Ana.	L	0-1		2	9	Schoeneweis	Sparks	Percival	70-68	3rd	12.5
9-7	Ana.	L	4-6		9	11	Belcher	Mlicki	Hasegawa	70-69	3rd	13.5
9-8	At Tor.	L	0-3		5	7	Loaiza	Weaver		70-70	3rd	14.5
9-9	At Tor.	L	5-6		10	8	Koch	Nitkowski		70-71	3rd	14.5
9-10	At Tor.	L	2-6		8	7	Carpenter	Sparks	Escobar	70-72	3rd	15.0
9-11	At Chi.	L	3-10		7	12	Sirotka	Moehler	Howry	70-73	3rd	16.0
9-12	At Chi.	W	10-3		11	4	Mlicki	Wells		71-73	3rd	15.0
9-13	At Chi.	L	0-1		5	4	Parque	Weaver	Foulke	71-74	3rd	16.0
9-15	Bos.	L	6-7		9	12	Beck	Cruz	Lowe	71-75	3rd	16.0
9-16†	Bos.	L	5-8		11	13	Pichardo	Anderson	Lowe	71-76		
9-16‡	Bos.	W	12-2		13	8	Nomo	Ontiveros		72-76	3rd	16.5
9-17	Bos.	W	5-4		9	8	Mlicki	R. Martinez	Jones	73-76	3rd	15.5
9-18	Chi.	W	5-2		12	3	Weaver	Barcelo	Jones	74-76	3rd	14.5
9-19	Chi.	L	2-6		7	13	Lowe	Sparks		74-77	3rd	15.5
9-20	Chi.	L	6-13		10	15	Garland	Moehler		74-78	3rd	16.5

Date	Opp.	Res.	Score	(inn.*)	Hits	Opp. hits	Winning pitcher	Losing pitcher	Save	Record	Pos.	GB
9-22	At N.Y.	W	9-6		10	9	Nomo	Neagle	Jones	75-78	3rd	17.0
9-23	At N.Y.	L	8-13		8	18	Nelson	Blair	Rivera	75-79	3rd	18.0
9-24	At N.Y.	L	3-6		7	10	Pettitte	Weaver	Rivera	75-80	3rd	18.0
9-25	At N.Y.	W	15-4		18	11	Sparks	Gooden		76-80	3rd	17.0
9-26	At K.C.	L	6-7		9	10	Bottalico	Blair		76-81	3rd	17.0
9-27	At K.C.	L	0-3		6	9	Suppan	Nomo		76-82	3rd	17.0
9-28	At K.C.	L	5-8		12	12	Santiago	Jones	Bottalico	76-83	T3rd	17.0
9-29	Min.	W	1-0		7	7	Weaver	Mays	Jones	77-83	3rd	17.0
9-30	Min.	W	6-5	(11)	13	13	Jones	Hawkins		78-83	3rd	17.0
10-1	Min.	W	12-11		19	15	Jones	Guardado		79-83	3rd	16.0

Monthly records: April (6-17), May (12-14), June (15-12), July (15-13), August (18-10), September (12-17), October (1-0).
*Innings, if other than nine. †First game of a doubleheader. ‡Second game of a doubleheader.

HIGHLIGHTS

High point: The Tigers capped a 61-44 run with a 7-5 win over the Angels September 5, pushing their record a season-high three games over .500 (70-67). That eased the pain of a horrible start and put the club on the fringes of the wild-card chase before it suffered a late collapse.

Low point: The team bottomed out at 9-23 with a 6-0 loss to Kansas City on May 10. It marked the sixth shutout against the Tigers in 32 games as the team struggled to adjust to the vast dimensions of new Comerica Park.

Turning point: A three-game sweep of the defending World Series-champion Yankees at Comerica May 12-14 seemed to provide a major psychological boost. Playing with a new confidence, the Tigers suddenly began winning low-scoring games, especially on their home turf.

Most valuable player: Left fielder Bobby Higginson bounced back from two subpar seasons and hit .300 with 30 homers, 102 RBIs, 104 runs and 15 steals. He also led both leagues with 19 assists and made several sensational catches.

Most valuable pitcher: Aided by the addition of a slider and changeup, All-Star closer Todd Jones set a franchise record with 42 saves. He allowed only two earned runs in 31 appearances from May 2 through July 29.

Most improved player: Righthander Jeff Weaver began looking like a future ace as he rebounded from the terrible second half that spoiled his rookie 1999 season. Weaver won 11 times and would have had four or five more wins with decent support. He posted a staff-leading 200 innings.

Most pleasant surprise: Steve Sparks wasn't doing much at Class AAA Toledo when he was recalled to patch up an injury-plagued rotation. The 35-year-old knuckleballer went 5-0 in August and won six straight starts overall, during which he allowed 10 earned runs.

Key injuries: Right fielder Juan Gonzalez missed 47 games because of hamstring, foot and back problems. ... First baseman Tony Clark had three stints on the disabled list and played only 60 games. ... Second baseman Damion Easley missed 31 of the team's first 49 games with various injuries. ... Third baseman Dean Palmer played the entire season with a painful throwing shoulder. ... Setup man Doug Brocail missed most of September with a sore elbow. ... Righthander Dave Mlicki missed two months with a sinus problem that required surgery. ... Righthander Seth Greisinger, a rotation candidate, missed virtually the whole season with arm problems. ... Backup catcher Robert Fick missed eight weeks with a separated shoulder.

Notable: The team was shut out a major league-leading 15 times. ... The pitching staff walked 496 batters, the lowest total in the league and a big accomplishment in the wake of pitching failures in recent years. ... After an April 22 brawl at Comiskey Park, regulars Dean Palmer, Bobby Higginson and Juan Encarnacion were among those who received staggered suspensions, adding another headache to the horrid start.

—REID CREAGER

RECORDS

2000 regular-season record: 79-83 (3rd in A.L. Central); 43-38 at home; 36-45 on road; 24-31 vs. East; 32-36 vs. Central; 23-16 vs. West; 24-21 vs. lefthanded starters; 55-62 vs. righthanded starters; 72-71 on grass; 7-12 on turf; 21-28 in daytime; 58-55 at night; 20-18 in one-run games; 8-4 in extra-inning games; 0-0-3 in doubleheaders.

Team record past five years: 345-464 (.426, ranks 13th in league in that span).

TEAM LEADERS

Batting average: Deivi Cruz (.302).
At-bats: Bobby Higginson (597).
Runs: Bobby Higginson (104).
Hits: Bobby Higginson (179).
Total Bases: Bobby Higginson (321).
Doubles: Deivi Cruz (46).
Triples: Juan Encarnacion (6).
Home runs: Bobby Higginson (30).
Runs batted in: Bobby Higginson, Dean Palmer (102).
Stolen bases: Juan Encarnacion (16).
Slugging percentage: Bobby Higginson (.538).
On-base percentage: Bobby Higginson (.377).
Wins: Brian Moehler (12).
Earned-run average: Jeff Weaver (4.32).

Complete games: Brian Moehler, Jeff Weaver (2).
Shutouts: Steve Sparks (1).
Saves: Todd Jones (42).
Innings pitched: Jeff Weaver (200.0).
Strikeouts: Hideo Nomo (181).

GAMES BY POSITION

Catcher: Brad Ausmus 150, Javier Cardona 26, Robert Fick 16, Shane Halter 2.
First base: Tony Clark 58, Hal Morris 38, Robert Fick 34, Shane Halter 29, Gregg Jefferies 20, Dean Palmer 20, Dusty Allen 17, Eric Munson 3, Brad Ausmus 1.
Second base: Damion Easley 125, Jose Macias 39, Gregg Jefferies 14, Shane Halter 10, Brad Ausmus 1.
Third base: Dean Palmer 115, Shane Halter 55, Jose Macias 26, Gregg Jefferies 6, Dusty Allen 1, Brad Ausmus 1.
Shortstop: Deivi Cruz 156, Shane Halter 17, Jose Macias 1.
Outfield: Bobby Higginson 145, Juan Encarnacion 141, Rich Becker 80, Wendell Magee 76, Juan Gonzalez 66, Luis Polonia 27, Billy McMillon 15, Shane Halter 8, Karim Garcia 7, Rod Lindsey 7, Jose Macias 3, Dusty Allen 1, Gregg Jefferies 1, Hal Morris 1.
Designated hitter: Juan Gonzalez 48, Luis Polonia 44, Billy McMillon 24, Dean Palmer 14, Robert Fick 12, Bobby Higginson 10, Wendell Magee 6, Rich Becker 4, Gregg Jefferies 2, Gabe Alvarez 1, Tony Clark 1, Karim Garcia 1, Jose Macias 1.

TOP DRAFT CHOICES

1. **Matt Wheatland,** RHP, Rancho Bernardo H.S., San Diego.
2. **Chad Petty,** LHP, Chalker H.S., West Farmington, Ohio.
3. **Exavier Logan,** SS, Copiah-Lincoln (Miss.) C.C.
4. **Mark Woodyard,** RHP, Bethune-Cookman College.
5. **Miles Durham,** OF, Texas Tech.
6. **Matt Parris,** RHP, Highland H.S., Palmdale, Calif.
7. **Ron Merrill,** SS, University of Tampa.
8. **Andy Warren,** RHP, Sam Houston State U.
9. **Steven Hofius,** 1B, Lakewood (Calif.) H.S.
10. **Lee Rodney,** RHP, Kennesaw (Ga.) State University.

KANSAS CITY ROYALS
AMERICAN LEAGUE CENTRAL DIVISION

Royals 2001 SCHEDULE
Home games shaded; D—Day game (games starting before 5 p.m.)
*—All-Star Game at Safeco Field (Seattle)

APRIL

SUN	MON	TUE	WED	THU	FRI	SAT
1	2 D NYY	3	4 NYY	5 D NYY	6 D MIN	7 D MIN
8 MIN	9 D NYY	10 NYY	11 D NYY	12 TOR	13 D TOR	14 D TOR
15 D TOR	16 MIN	17 MIN	18 D MIN	19	20 TOR	21 TOR
22 D TOR	23	24 TB	25 TB	26 D TB	27 BOS	28 D BOS
29 D BOS	30					

MAY

SUN	MON	TUE	WED	THU	FRI	SAT
		1 CLE	2 CLE	3 D CLE	4 D MIN	5 MIN
6 MIN	7 D	8 CLE	9 CLE	10 MIN	11 MIN	12 MIN
13 D MIN	14 TB	15 TB	16 TB	17 TB	18 BOS	19 BOS
20 BOS	21	22 OAK	23 OAK	24	25 SEA	26 SEA
27 SEA	28 D SEA	29 TEX	30 TEX	31 D TEX		

JUNE

SUN	MON	TUE	WED	THU	FRI	SAT
					1 ANA	2 ANA
3 D ANA	4	5 CWS	6 CWS	7 CWS	8 ARI	9 ARI
10 ARI	11	12 STL	13 STL	14 STL	15 MIL	16 MIL
17 MIL	18 CWS	19 CWS	20 D CWS	21	22 CLE	23 CLE
24 D CLE	25	26 DET	27 DET	28 DET	29 CLE	30 CLE

JULY

SUN	MON	TUE	WED	THU	FRI	SAT
1 CLE	2 CLE	3 DET	4 DET	5 D DET	6 HOU	7 HOU
8 HOU	9 D	10 *	11	12 PIT	13 PIT	14 D PIT
15 D CUB	16 CUB	17 D CUB	18 SEA	19 SEA	20 OAK	21 OAK
22 OAK	23 OAK	24 SEA	25 SEA	26 SEA	27 OAK	28 D OAK
29 OAK	30	31 CWS				

AUGUST

SUN	MON	TUE	WED	THU	FRI	SAT
		1 CWS	2 CWS	3 MIN	4 MIN	
5 MIN	6 D	7 BAL	8 BAL	9 BAL	10 DET	11 DET
12 D DET	13	14 BAL	15 BAL	16 D BAL	17 DET	18 DET
19 DET	20 CWS	21 CWS	22 CWS	23 CWS	24 MIN	25 MIN
26 D MIN	27	28 ANA	29 ANA	30 ANA	31 TEX	

SEPTEMBER

SUN	MON	TUE	WED	THU	FRI	SAT
						1 TEX
2 D TEX	3	4 ANA	5 ANA	6 ANA	7 TEX	8 TEX
9 D TEX	10	11 CLE	12 CLE	13 D CLE	14 D DET	15 DET
16 D DET	17	18 CLE	19 CLE	20 CLE	21 CWS	22 CWS
23 CWS	24 DET	25 DET	26 DET	27 DET	28 CWS	29 CWS
30 D CWS						

2001 SEASON
CLUB DIRECTORY

Board of directors
David Glass, Dan Glass, Ruth Glass, Don Glass, Dayna Glass, Julia Irene Kauffman, Herk Robinson

Chairman of the board & owner
David Glass

President
Dan Glass

Exec. v.p. and chief operating officer
Herk Robinson

Sr. v.p., business operations & admin.
Art Chaudry

V.p. and general manager, baseball operations
Allard Baird

Vice president, baseball operations
George Brett

Vice president, operations
Jay Hinrichs

V.p., marketing and communications
Mike Levy

V.p., finance & information services
Dale Rohr

Asst. general manager, baseball operations
Muzzy Jackson

Sr. advisor to the general manager
Art Stewart

Assistant to the general manager
Brian Murphy

Special assistant to the general manager
Pat Jones

Manager of major league operations
Karol Kyte

Senior director, scouting
Deric Ladnier

Senior director, minor league operations
Bob Hegman

Manager of team travel
Jeff Davenport

Director of community relations
Shani Tate

Director of human resources
Sylvia Patillo

Director of Lancer program
Rick Amos

Director, season ticket services
Joe Grigoli

Senior director/controller
John Luther

Director, payroll and benefits accounting
Tom Pfannenstiel

Senior director, information systems
Jim Edwards

Dir., broadcast services & Royals alumni
Fred White

Senior director, media relations
David Witty

Director, corporate sponsorship sales
Kevin Battle

Director, group sales
Michele Kammerer

Director, marketing
Tonya Mangels

Dir., event ops. & revenue development
Chris Richardson

Dir., groundskeeping & landscaping
Trevor Vance

Director, stadium operations
Rodney Lewallen

Director, ticket operations
Lance Buckley

Team physician
Dr. Steve Joyce

Athletic trainer
Nick Swartz

Assistant athletic trainer
Lee Kuntz

Strength & conditioning coordinator
Tim Maxey

Equipment manager
Mike Burkhalter

Visiting clubhouse manager
Chuck Hawke

Professional scouts
Rod Fridley, Louie Medina, Earl Winn

Special assignment scout
John Wathan

Regional cross-checkers
Jeff McKay, Dennis Woody

Latin American scouting coordinator
Albert Gonzalez

Dominican scouting coordinator
Luis Silverio

Territorial scouts
Bob Bishop, Mike Brown, Jason Bryans, Albert Gonzalez, Dave Herrera, Keith Hughes, Phil Huttman, Gary Johnson, Cliff Pastornicky, Johnny Ramos, Sean Rooney, Max Semler, Chet Sergo, Greg Smith, Gerald Turner, Brad Vaughn, Junior Vizcaino, Mark Willoughby

MINOR LEAGUE AFFILIATES

Class	Team	League	Manager
AAA	Omaha	Pacific Coast	John Mizerock
AA	Wichita	Texas	Keith Bodie
A	Burlington	Midwest	Joe Szekely
A	Spokane	Northwest	Tom Poquette
A	Wilmington	Carolina	Jeff Garber
Rookie	Gulf Coast Royals	Gulf Coast	Lino Diaz

BROADCAST INFORMATION

Radio: KMBZ-AM (980).
TV: KMBC (Channel 9), KCWB (Channel 29).
Cable TV: Fox Sports Net.

SPRING TRAINING

Ballpark (city): Baseball City Stadium (Davenport, Fla.).
Ticket information: 941-424-2500.

Follow the Royals all season at: www.sportingnews.com/baseball/teams/royals/

SPRING TRAINING ROSTER

Manager—Tony Muser (40).
Coaches—Rich Dauer (25), Tom Gamboa, Lamar Johnson (23), Jamie Quirk (9), Brent Strom (30), Frank White (20).

No.	PITCHERS	B/T	Ht./Wt.	Born	2000 clubs
	Affeldt, Jeremy	L/L	6-4/185	6-5-79	Wilmington
33	Durbin, Chad	R/R	6-2/200	12-3-77	Kansas City, Omaha
49	Fussell, Chris	R/R	6-2/200	5-19-76	Kansas City, Omaha, Gulf Coast Royals
	Guerrero, Junior	R/R	6-2/175	8-21-79	Wichita
	Henry, Doug	R/R	6-4/205	12-10-63	Houston, San Francisco
	Hernandez, Roberto	R/R	6-4/250	11-11-64	Tampa Bay
32	Laxton, Brett	L/R	6-1/210	10-5-73	Omaha, Kansas City
59	Meadows, Brian	R/R	6-4/220	11-21-75	San Diego, Kansas City
45	Moreno, Orber	R/R	6-3/200	4-27-77	DID NOT PLAY
57	Mullen, Scott	R/L	6-2/190	1-17-75	Wichita, Omaha, Kansas City
36	Murray, Dan	R/R	6-1/195	11-21-73	Omaha, Kansas City
41	Reichert, Dan	R/R	6-3/175	7-12-76	Kansas City
50	Rosado, Jose	L/L	6-0/185	11-9-74	Kansas City
46	Santiago, Jose	R/R	6-3/215	11-5-74	Kansas City, Omaha
	Sonnier, Shawn	R/R	6-5/210	7-5-76	Wichita
34	Stein, Blake	R/R	6-7/240	8-3-73	Wilmington, Wichita, Omaha, Kansas City
37	Suppan, Jeff	R/R	6-2/210	1-2-75	Kansas City
17	Suzuki, Mac	R/R	6-3/205	5-31-75	Kansas City
51	Wilson, Kris	R/R	6-3/225	8-6-76	Kansas City

No.	CATCHERS	B/T	Ht./Wt.	Born	2000 clubs
	Hinch, A.J.	R/R	6-1/207	5-15-74	Sacramento, Oakland
22	Ortiz, Hector	R/R	6-0/205	10-14-69	Omaha, Kansas City
	Phillips, Paul	R/R	5-11/180	4-15-77	Wichita
44	Zaun, Gregg	B/R	5-10/190	4-14-71	Kansas City, Omaha

No.	INFIELDERS	B/T	Ht./Wt.	Born	2000 clubs
19	Delgado, Wilson	B/R	5-11/165	7-15-75	New York A.L., Kansas City
3	Febles, Carlos	R/R	5-11/185	5-24-76	Kansas City, Gulf Coast Royals, Wichita, Omaha
8	Ordaz, Luis	R/R	5-11/170	8-12-75	Kansas City
16	Randa, Joe	R/R	5-11/190	12-18-69	Kansas City
1	Sanchez, Rey	R/R	5-9/175	10-5-67	Kansas City
29	Sweeney, Mike	R/R	6-3/225	7-22-73	American, Kansas City

No.	OUTFIELDERS	B/T	Ht./Wt.	Born	2000 clubs
15	Beltran, Carlos	B/R	6-1/190	4-24-77	Kansas City, Gulf Coast Royals, Wilmington, Omaha
27	Brown, Dee	L/R	6-0/215	3-27-78	Omaha, Kansas City
	Chavez, Endy	L/L	6-0/150	2-7-78	St. Lucie
24	Dye, Jermaine	R/R	6-5/220	1-28-74	Kansas City
	Gomez, Alexis	L/L	6-2/160	8-6-80	Wilmington
6	McCarty, Dave	R/L	6-5/215	11-23-69	Kansas City
14	Quinn, Mark	R/R	6-1/195	5-21-74	Kansas City, Omaha

BALLPARK INFORMATION

Ballpark (capacity, surface)
Kauffman Stadium (40,529, grass)

Address
P.O. Box 419969
Kansas City, MO 64141-6969

Official website
www.kcroyals.com

Business phone
816-921-8000

Ticket information
816-921-8000

Ticket prices
$19 (club box)
$17 (field box)
$15 (plaza reserved)
$12 (view upper box)
$11 (view upper reserved)
$7 (general admission)
$5.50 (Royal nights)

Field dimensions (from home plate)
To left field at foul line, 330 feet
To center field, 400 feet
To right field at foul line, 330 feet

First game played
April 10, 1973 (Royals 12, Rangers 1)

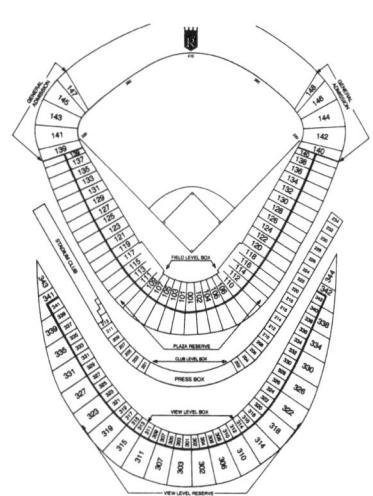

2000 REVIEW
DAY BY DAY

Date	Opp.	Res.	Score	(inn.*)	Hits	Opp. hits	Winning pitcher	Losing pitcher	Save	Record	Pos.	GB
4-3	At Tor.	L	4-5		9	8	Koch	Spradlin		0-1	T3rd	1.0
4-4	At Tor.	L	3-6		7	7	Halladay	Witasick	Koch	0-2	T4th	1.5
4-5	At Tor.	W	4-3		7	5	Rosado	Carpenter	Bottalico	1-2	T3rd	1.0
4-6	At Tor.	W	9-3		17	5	Durbin	Escobar	Rigby	2-2	T1st	...
4-7	Min.	W	10-6		15	12	Fussell	Miller		3-2	T1st	...
4-8	Min.	W	5-2		10	6	Suppan	Radke	Santiago	4-2	T1st	...
4-9	Min.	L	7-13		9	16	Milton	Witasick		4-3	T2nd	0.5
4-10	Min.	W	6-5		14	8	Bottalico	Hawkins		5-3	2nd	0.5
4-11	Bal.	W	7-5	(12)	11	11	Santiago	Worrell		6-3	2nd	0.5
4-12	Bal.	W	7-6		8	8	Santiago	Trombley		7-3	2nd	0.5
4-13	Bal.	W	6-5		12	12	Bottalico	Ryan		8-3	2nd	...
4-14	At N.Y.	L	5-7		9	10	Clemens	Witasick	Rivera	8-4	2nd	...
4-15	At N.Y.	L	1-7		2	11	Mendoza	Rosado		8-5	2nd	...
4-16	At N.Y.	L	4-8		9	10	Nelson	Fussell		8-6	2nd	1.0
4-18	At Min.	L	1-3		6	7	Radke	Suppan	Wells	8-7	3rd	1.0
4-19	At Min.	L	6-7		10	9	Carrasco	Santiago		8-8	3rd	1.5
4-20	At Min.	L	7-9		12	13	Bergman	Rosado	Wells	8-9	3rd	2.0
4-21	At Sea.	L	2-10		8	10	Rodriguez	Durbin		8-10	T3rd	3.0
4-22	At Sea.	L	2-4		6	7	Tomko	Witasick	Sasaki	8-11	T3rd	4.0
4-23	At Sea.	L	5-8		10	7	Rhodes	Bottalico		8-12	4th	5.0
4-25	T.B.	W	7-6		13	10	Reichert	Lopez		9-12	4th	4.5
4-26	T.B.	W	7-6		12	8	Bottalico	Lopez		10-12	4th	4.5
4-28	Sea.	W	8-5		12	9	Batista	Tomko	Bottalico	11-12	3rd	5.0
4-29	Sea.	L	3-11		10	17	Sele	Suppan		11-13	3rd	6.0
4-30	Sea.	W	6-3		10	7	Rosado	Meche	Bottalico	12-13	3rd	5.0
5-1	Oak.	L	5-7		9	7	Olivares	Reichert	Isringhausen	12-14	3rd	5.0
5-2	Oak.	W	8-7	(10)	14	10	Rakers	Isringhausen		13-14	3rd	4.0
5-3	Oak.	L	5-14		15	20	Heredia	Suppan		13-15	3rd	5.0
5-5	Chi.	W	5-1		10	8	Fussell	Eldred		14-15	3rd	4.0
5-6	Chi.	W	11-5		18	10	Spradlin	Sirotka		15-15	3rd	3.0
5-7	Chi.	W	12-8		13	13	Bottalico	Wunsch		16-15	3rd	2.0
5-8	At Det.	W	4-1	(11)	8	3	Santiago	Brocail		17-15	3rd	1.0
5-10	At Det.	W	6-0		9	4	Fussell	Nomo		18-15	2nd	0.5
5-11	At Cle.	L	0-16		5	22	Wright	Durbin		18-16	3rd	1.0
5-12	At Cle.	L	3-7		5	9	Colon	Batista		18-17	3rd	1.0
5-13	At Cle.	L	6-7	(12)	9	12	Reed	Reichert		18-18	3rd	2.0
5-14	At Cle.	W	5-4		8	7	Suzuki	Finley	Spradlin	19-18	3rd	2.0
5-15	At Oak.	L	3-6		7	7	Mulder	Fussell	Isringhausen	19-19	3rd	2.5
5-16	At Oak.	W	8-7		11	11	Reichert	D. Jones	Spradlin	20-19	3rd	2.5
5-17	At Oak.	W	4-3		8	3	Batista	Olivares	Spradlin	21-19	3rd	1.5
5-19	At Ana.	L	4-6		10	12	Washburn	Suppan	Percival	21-20	3rd	2.5
5-20	At Ana.	L	8-9		12	11	Hasegawa	Reichert	Percival	21-21	3rd	3.5
5-21	At Ana.	W	10-6		14	7	Santiago	Bottenfield		22-21	3rd	3.5
5-23	Tex.	L	3-4		9	7	Helling	Batista	Wetteland	22-22	3rd	4.0
5-24	Tex.	W	3-0		8	6	Suppan	Rogers	Spradlin	23-22	3rd	3.0
5-25	Tex.	L	3-5		10	8	Loaiza	Santiago	Wetteland	23-23	3rd	3.0
5-26	Ana.	W	9-4		14	6	Fussell	Weaver	Bottalico	24-23	3rd	3.0
5-27	Ana.	W	6-5	(10)	8	9	Reichert	Weaver		25-23	3rd	3.0
5-28	Ana.	L	4-8		10	13	Cooper	Batista	Hasegawa	25-24	3rd	3.0
5-30	At Bos.	L	2-8		8	12	Fassero	Suppan		25-25	3rd	3.5
5-31	At Bos.	W	9-7		14	12	Suzuki	Schourek	Spradlin	26-25	3rd	3.5
6-1	At Bos.	W	13-11		19	12	Santiago	Lowe	Reichert	27-25	3rd	3.0
6-2	At Pit.	L	3-9		4	8	Ritchie	Batista		27-26	3rd	4.0
6-3	At Pit.	W	16-3		18	8	Witasick	Schmidt		28-26	3rd	3.0
6-4	At Pit.	W	7-5	(11)	9	9	Rakers	Christiansen	Reichert	29-26	3rd	3.0
6-5	At StL.	W	7-4		10	6	Suzuki	Hentgen	Spradlin	30-26	3rd	3.0
6-6	At StL.	L	4-5		10	7	An. Benes	Witasick	Veres	30-27	3rd	4.0
6-7	At StL.	L	2-4		7	10	Kile	Batista		30-28	3rd	5.0
6-9	Pit.	W	6-5	(10)	13	9	Spradlin	Christiansen		31-28	3rd	5.0
6-10	Pit.	W	2-1	(12)	10	13	Bottalico	Silva		32-28	3rd	5.0
6-11	Pit.	L	6-10	(10)	11	18	Sauerbeck	Spradlin		32-29	3rd	5.0
6-12	Sea.	L	3-5		7	7	Moyer	Batista	Sasaki	32-30	3rd	6.0
6-13	Sea.	L	0-7	(6)	1	10	Meche	Laxton		32-31	3rd	7.0
6-14	Sea.	W	5-4		11	9	Bottalico	Sasaki		33-31	3rd	7.0
6-16	Oak.	L	3-8		8	11	D. Jones	Reichert	Tam	33-32	3rd	8.5
6-17	Oak.	L	4-10		7	13	Appier	Witasick		33-33	3rd	9.5
6-18	Oak.	L	3-21		8	21	Heredia	D'Amico		33-34	3rd	10.5
6-20	At Ana.	W	8-6		17	5	Santiago	Percival	Bottalico	34-34	3rd	10.0
6-21	At Ana.	L	1-3		5	6	Washburn	Suzuki	Percival	34-35	3rd	10.0
6-22	At Ana.	L	3-4		3	10	Belcher	Witasick	Petkovsek	34-36	3rd	11.0
6-23	At Oak.	L	6-10		12	13	Appier	Durbin		34-37	3rd	12.0
6-24	At Oak.	W	8-3		13	9	Bottalico	Heredia		35-37	3rd	11.0
6-25	At Oak.	L	3-4		7	9	Mulder	Suppan	Isringhausen	35-38	3rd	12.0

Kansas City Royals

2001 SEASON

Date	Opp.	Res.	Score	(inn.*)	Hits	Opp. hits	Winning pitcher	Losing pitcher	Save	Record	Pos.	GB
6-27	Cle.	L	1-12		6	13	Finley	Suzuki		35-39	3rd	12.0
6-28	Cle.	W	8-1		9	4	Witasick	Davis		36-39	3rd	12.0
6-29	Cle.	W	6-1		4	5	Durbin	Colon		37-39	3rd	11.0
6-30	Det.	L	1-3		7	5	Weaver	Reichert	Jones	37-40	3rd	12.0
7-1	Det.	L	7-8		14	15	Brocail	Bottalico	Jones	37-41	3rd	13.0
7-2	Det.	L	0-2		3	6	Nomo	Suzuki	Jones	37-42	3rd	14.0
7-3	Chi.	L	10-14		10	22	Pena	Santiago		37-43	3rd	15.0
7-4	Chi.	W	10-7		12	14	Spradlin	Garland		38-43	3rd	14.0
7-5	Chi.	L	3-6	(13)	17	13	Wunsch	Bochtler		38-44	3rd	15.0
7-7	At Hou.	L	5-9		6	10	Elarton	Stein		38-45	3rd	16.0
7-8	At Hou.	W	5-2		13	9	Suzuki	Miller		39-45	3rd	15.0
7-9	At Hou.	L	6-9		10	13	Lima	Witasick	Dotel	39-46	3rd	15.0
7-13	Mil.	L	2-5		10	8	Wright	Stein	Wickman	39-47	4th	15.0
7-14	Mil.	L	0-4		4	12	D'Amico	Suzuki		39-48	4th	15.0
7-15	Mil.	W	7-4		11	11	Suppan	Haynes	Bottalico	40-48	4th	15.0
7-16	Chi. (NL)	L	7-10		14	10	Wood	Reichert	Aguilera	40-49	4th	16.0
7-17	Chi. (NL)	L	1-3		7	8	Downs	Durbin	Aguilera	40-50	4th	17.0
7-18	Chi. (NL)	W	12-4		20	8	Stein	Valdes		41-50	4th	17.0
7-19	At Cle.	W	10-5		12	13	Suzuki	Finley	Spradlin	42-50	4th	17.0
7-20	At Cle.	W	10-6		17	11	Suppan	Brower		43-50	4th	16.0
7-21	At Det.	W	4-0		9	6	Reichert	Weaver		44-50	3rd	16.0
7-22†	At Det.	W	8-5		11	9	Witasick	Mlicki	Bottalico	45-50		
7-22‡	At Det.	L	6-10		8	14	Cruz	Bochtler		45-51	3rd	15.5
7-23	At Det.	L	9-12		13	14	Brocail	Byrdak	Jones	45-52	4th	15.5
7-24	At Chi.	L	6-7		14	9	Wunsch	Suzuki	Foulke	45-53	4th	16.5
7-25	At Chi.	W	6-1		8	4	Suppan	Parque		46-53	4th	15.5
7-26	At Chi.	W	7-6		10	9	Spradlin	Howry	Bottalico	47-53	3rd	14.5
7-27	T.B.	L	5-8		14	10	Rupe	Durbin	Hernandez	47-54	3rd	15.5
7-28	T.B.	L	3-10		8	12	Rekar	Stein		47-55	3rd	15.5
7-29	T.B.	L	1-2		7	4	Lopez	Suzuki	Hernandez	47-56	4th	15.5
7-30	T.B.	L	6-7	(10)	12	12	Sturtze	Spradlin	Hernandez	47-57	4th	16.5
8-1	At N.Y.	L	4-5		6	9	Nelson	Bottalico	Rivera	47-58	4th	17.5
8-2	At N.Y.	W	4-1		11	2	Stein	Neagle	Bottalico	48-58	4th	16.5
8-3	At N.Y.	L	2-3		5	6	Rivera	Spradlin		48-59	4th	17.0
8-4	At Bos.	L	4-5		8	11	Garces	Larkin	Lowe	48-60	5th	17.0
8-5	At Bos.	W	7-5		13	8	Meadows	Cormier	Bottalico	49-60	4th	17.0
8-6	At Bos.	W	3-1		8	10	Reichert	Wakefield	Bottalico	50-60	4th	17.0
8-7	Tor.	W	8-7		14	14	Stein	Loaiza	Bottalico	51-60	4th	16.5
8-8	Tor.	L	1-6		4	14	Castillo	Suzuki		51-61	4th	16.0
8-9	Tor.	W	5-3		10	11	Suppan	Trachsel	Larkin	52-61	4th	16.0
8-10	Tor.	L	7-15		14	17	Carpenter	Fussell		52-62	4th	16.0
8-11	Bal.	W	7-6		11	8	Reichert	Mussina	Bottalico	53-62	4th	16.0
8-12	Bal.	L	11-12		14	11	Groom	Bottalico	Kohlmeier	53-63	4th	17.0
8-13	Bal.	W	10-5		14	12	Suzuki	Brea		54-63	4th	16.0
8-15	At Min.	L	2-6		5	11	Milton	Suppan	Wells	54-64	4th	16.5
8-16	At Min.	W	9-3		16	7	Meadows	Romero		55-64	4th	16.5
8-17	At Min.	W	8-4		15	9	Reichert	Redman		56-64	4th	15.5
8-18	At Bal.	W	4-1		4	8	Stein	Rapp		57-64	4th	15.5
8-19	At Bal.	W	7-0		11	4	Suzuki	Mercedes		58-64	4th	15.5
8-20	At Bal.	L	1-2		6	9	Ponson	Wilson	Kohlmeier	58-65	4th	15.5
8-21	At Bal.	L	1-2		8	7	Mussina	Meadows	Kohlmeier	58-66	4th	15.5
8-22	At Tor.	L	5-7		11	10	Escobar	Santiago	Koch	58-67	4th	16.0
8-23	At Tor.	L	8-9		11	13	Escobar	Larkin	Koch	58-68	4th	17.0
8-24	Bos.	L	7-9	(10)	11	12	Pichardo	Larkin	Lowe	58-69	4th	17.0
8-25	Bos.	W	6-2		13	5	Suppan	Florie		59-69	4th	17.0
8-26	Bos.	L	3-5		9	14	Arrojo	Meadows	Lowe	59-70	4th	17.0
8-27	Bos.	W	11-7		10	11	Reichert	Wakefield		60-70	4th	17.0
8-29	Min.	W	7-3		10	5	Stein	Romero		61-70	4th	16.5
8-30	Min.	W	8-7		14	17	Suzuki	Redman	Bottalico	62-70	4th	16.5
8-31	At T.B.	L	1-2		6	7	Fiore	Suppan	Hernandez	62-71	4th	17.0
9-1	At T.B.	W	9-5		15	8	Meadows	Rupe		63-71	4th	17.0
9-2	At T.B.	W	7-5		8	8	Santiago	Hernandez	Bottalico	64-71	4th	17.0
9-3	At T.B.	W	8-2		10	6	Stein	Eiland		65-71	4th	17.0
9-4	N.Y.	L	3-4		12	8	Pettitte	Suzuki	Rivera	65-72	4th	17.0
9-5	N.Y.	L	5-10		10	17	Gooden	Suppan		65-73	4th	17.0
9-6	N.Y.	W	3-2		12	9	Meadows	Stanton		66-73	4th	17.0
9-7	N.Y.	L	3-7		8	7	Neagle	Bottalico	Rivera	66-74	4th	18.0
9-8	Tex.	L	5-6		12	12	Glynn	Stein	Wetteland	66-75	4th	19.0
9-9	Tex.	L	5-6		10	11	Zimmerman	Suzuki	Wetteland	66-76	4th	19.0
9-10	Tex.	W	13-8		14	16	Suppan	Oliver		67-76	4th	18.5
9-11	At Sea.	W	6-3		15	7	Meadows	Halama	Santiago	68-76	4th	18.5
9-12	At Sea.	L	3-11		9	15	Garcia	Reichert		68-77	4th	18.5
9-13	At Sea.	L	1-2	(11)	8	6	Mesa	Bottalico		68-78	4th	19.5
9-14	At Tex.	L	1-8		4	9	Davis	Suzuki	Crabtree	68-79	4th	20.0
9-15	At Tex.	L	11-12	(10)	18	15	Wetteland	Santiago		68-80	4th	20.0
9-16	At Tex.	W	8-5		8	10	Meadows	Sikorski		69-80	4th	20.0

Date	Opp.	Res.	Score	(inn.*)	Hits	Opp. hits	Winning pitcher	Losing pitcher	Save	Record	Pos.	GB
9-17	At Tex.	L	5-6		12	11	Rogers	Reichert	Wetteland	69-81	4th	20.0
9-19	Ana.	W	5-1		10	3	Stein	Ortiz		70-81	4th	19.5
9-20	Ana.	L	4-7	(10)	10	14	Percival	Santiago	Petkovsek	70-82	4th	20.5
9-21	Ana.	W	8-3		16	6	Suppan	Schoeneweis		71-82	4th	20.5
9-22	Cle.	W	3-2		10	10	Bottalico	Karsay		72-82	4th	20.5
9-23	Cle.	L	1-11		4	16	Colon	Reichert		72-83	4th	21.5
9-24	Cle.	W	9-0		12	6	Stein	Nagy		73-83	4th	20.5
9-26	Det.	W	7-6		10	9	Bottalico	Blair		74-83	4th	19.0
9-27	Det.	W	3-0		9	6	Suppan	Nomo		75-83	4th	18.0
9-28	Det.	W	8-5		12	12	Santiago	Jones	Bottalico	76-83	T3rd	17.0
9-29	At Chi.	L	4-6		14	9	Bradford	Reichert	Foulke	76-84	4th	18.0
9-30	At Chi.	L	1-9		6	11	Wells	Stein		76-85	4th	19.0
10-1	At Chi.	W	6-2		10	8	Fussell	Baldwin		77-85	4th	18.0

Monthly records: April (12-13), May (14-12), June (11-15), July (10-17), August (15-14), September (14-14), October (1-0).
*Innings, if other than nine. †First game of a doubleheader. ‡Second game of a doubleheader.

HIGHLIGHTS

High point: The Royals plowed through an improbable early season stretch in which the club won six straight home games in its final at-bat. That April magic set a positive tone for the season and the Royals proved adept at fighting back from deficits and staying in every game.

Low point: The icy relationship between the Royals and outfielder Carlos Beltran, the 1999 Rookie of the Year who was suspended in August for defying team orders to rehabilitate an injured knee at the club's facility in Florida. That led to nasty words from both sides and an arbitration hearing that still hadn't been resolved by the end of the year.

Turning point: The Royals played themselves out of contention in the first month of the season, going 0-9 on a trip from April 14-23. The team never led in any of those nine games.

Most valuable player: First baseman Mike Sweeney edged Jermaine Dye and Johnny Damon. Sweeney batted .333 and drove in a franchise-record 144 runs. He was disciplined, striking out only 67 times, and led the A.L. with a .385 average with runners in scoring position.

Most valuable pitcher: Righthander Jeff Suppan gets the nod by default. He led the club with a modest 10 victories and chewed up more innings (217) than any other pitcher while compiling a 4.94 ERA. Righthanders Brian Meadows and Blake Stein pitched far better than Suppan, but Stein was injured for most of the first half and Meadows didn't join the team until August.

Most improved player: Mac Suzuki, who came perilously close to losing his job in 1999, made slight alterations in his delivery and wound up being one of the club's most consistent pitchers. He led the team in strikeouts (135) while compiling the best ERA (4.34) among all starters. He was just 8-10 overall, but lost a lot of close games.

Most pleasant surprise: The Royals expected outfielder Mark Quinn to hold his own against big-league pitching, but not to make a run at Rookie of the Year honors. He batted .294 with 20 home runs and 78 RBIs while displaying uncanny patience for a rookie. He also reined in a brash attitude during a short exile in the minors and enjoyed a productive finish.

Key injuries: Nothing hurt more than the shoulder injury that robbed lefthander Jose Rosado of almost the entire season. He pitched only 27 2/3 innings before finally having shoulder surgery to repair the posterior labrum. ... Righthander Blake Stein, who suffered a cracked bone in his forearm, missed most of the first half. ... Beltran's nagging knee injury limited him to 98 games. ... Various injuries to second baseman Carlos Febles (shoulder, ankle) limited him to 100.

Notable: The Royals, for the second year in a row, established a franchise record for runs scored with 879. ... Three players, Sweeney (144), Jermaine Dye (118) and Joe Randa (106), topped 100 RBIs, matching the feat accomplished by the 1999 team.

—STEVE ROCK

RECORDS

2000 regular-season record: 77-85 (4th in A.L. Central); 42-39 at home; 35-46 on road; 24-26 vs. East; 36-30 vs. Central; 17-29 vs. West; 18-24 vs. lefthanded starters; 59-61 vs. righthanded starters; 68-75 on grass; 9-10 on turf; 29-19 in daytime; 48-66 at night; 21-26 in one-run games; 7-8 in extra-inning games; 0-0-1 in doubleheaders.

Team record past five years: 355-451 (.440, ranks 11th in league in that span).

TEAM LEADERS

Batting average: Mike Sweeney (.333).
At-bats: Johnny Damon (655).
Runs: Johnny Damon (136).
Hits: Johnny Damon (214).
Total Bases: Jermaine Dye (337).
Doubles: Johnny Damon (42).
Triples: Johnny Damon (10).
Home runs: Jermaine Dye (33).
Runs batted in: Mike Sweeney (144).
Stolen bases: Johnny Damon (46).
Slugging percentage: Jermaine Dye (.561).
On-base percentage: Mike Sweeney (.407).
Wins: Jeff Suppan (10).
Earned-run average: Makoto Suzuki (4.34).
Complete games: Jeff Suppan (3).
Shutouts: Dan Reichert, Jeff Suppan, Makoto Suzuki (1).
Saves: Ricky Bottalico (16).
Innings pitched: Jeff Suppan (217.0).
Strikeouts: Makoto Suzuki (135).

GAMES BY POSITION

Catcher: Gregg Zaun 76, Jorge Fabregas 39, Brian Johnson 37, Hector Ortiz 26.
First base: Mike Sweeney 114, Dave McCarty 63, Gregg Zaun 1.
Second base: Carlos Febles 99, Jeff Reboulet 50, Luis Ordaz 22, Wilson Delgado 19, Ray Holbert 1, Gregg Zaun 1.
Third base: Joe Randa 156, Jeff Reboulet 11, Wilson Delgado 3, Ray Holbert 1.
Shortstop: Rey Sanchez 143, Luis Ordaz 38, Wilson Delgado 12, Jeff Reboulet 5, Ray Holbert 1.
Outfield: Jermaine Dye 146, Johnny Damon 133, Carlos Beltran 88, Mark Quinn 81, Todd Dunwoody 40, Dave McCarty 11, Scott Pose 11, Dee Brown 5.
Designated hitter: Mark Quinn 48, Mike Sweeney 45, Johnny Damon 25, Todd Dunwoody 11, Jermaine Dye 10, Carlos Beltran 7, Dave McCarty 7, Scott Pose 4, Jorge Fabregas 1, Joe Randa 1, Jeff Reboulet 1.

TOP DRAFT CHOICES

1. **Mike Stodolka,** LHP, Centennial H.S., Corona, Calif.
2. **Mike Tonis,** C, University of California.
3. **Scott Walter,** C, Loyola Marymount U.
4. **David DeJesus,** OF, Rutgers Univ.
5. **Zach McClellan,** RHP, U. of Indiana.
6. **Brian Bass,** RHP, Robert E. Lee H.S., Montgomery, Ala.
7. **Jason Kaanoi,** RHP, Kamehameha H.S., Kaneohe, Hi.
8. **Luis Cotto,** SS, Instituto Cumbre, Carolina, P.R.
9. **Luis Escobar,** C, Fernando Callejo H.S., Manati, P.R.
10. **Jason Fingers,** RHP, Arizona State U.

MINNESOTA TWINS
AMERICAN LEAGUE CENTRAL DIVISION

Twins
2001 SCHEDULE
Home games shaded; D—Day game (games starting before 5 p.m.)
*—All-Star Game at Safeco Field (Seattle)

APRIL
SUN	MON	TUE	WED	THU	FRI	SAT
1	2	3 D DET	4	5 D DET	6 D KC	7 D KC
8 D KC	9 DET	10 DET	11 DET	12	13 CWS	14 CWS
15 D CWS	16 KC	17 KC	18 D KC	19	20 CWS	21 D CWS
22 D CWS	23	24 BOS	25 BOS	26 BOS	27 BAL	28 BAL
29 BAL	30 NYY					

MAY
SUN	MON	TUE	WED	THU	FRI	SAT
		1 NYY	2 NYY	3	4 KC	5 KC
6 D KC	7	8 NYY	9 NYY	10 NYY	11 KC	12 KC
13 D KC	14 KC	15 BOS	16 BOS	17 D BOS	18 BAL	19 D BAL
20 D BAL	21	22 SEA	23 D SEA	24	25 OAK	26 DH OAK
27 OAK	28	29 ANA	30 ANA	31 ANA		

JUNE
SUN	MON	TUE	WED	THU	FRI	SAT
					1 TEX	2 TEX
3 TEX	4 CLE	5 CLE	6 CLE	7 CLE	8 PIT	9 PIT
10 D PIT	11	12 HOU	13 HOU	14 HOU	15 D CUB	16 D CUB
17 D CUB	18	19 CLE	20 CLE	21 CLE	22 DET	23 DET
24 D DET	25 D DET	26 CWS	27 CWS	28 CWS	29 DET	30 DET

JULY
SUN	MON	TUE	WED	THU	FRI	SAT
1 D DET	2 CWS	3 CWS	4 CWS	5 CWS	6 CIN	7 CIN
8 D CIN	9	10	11 *	12 MIL	13 MIL	14 MIL
15 D STL	16 STL	17 STL	18 OAK	19 OAK	20 SEA	21 SEA
22 D SEA	23 SEA	24 OAK	25 OAK	26 OAK	27 D SEA	28 D SEA
29 SEA	30	31 TOR				

AUGUST
SUN	MON	TUE	WED	THU	FRI	SAT
			1 TOR	2 D TOR	3 D KC	4 KC
5 D KC	6	7 CLE	8 CLE	9 D CLE	10 TB	11 D TB
12 D TB	13 D TB	14 CLE	15 CLE	16 CLE	17 TB	18 TB
19 D TB	20 TOR	21 TOR	22 TOR	23 D TOR	24 KC	25 KC
26 D KC	27	28 TEX	29 TEX	30 TEX	31 ANA	

SEPTEMBER
SUN	MON	TUE	WED	THU	FRI	SAT
						1 ANA
2 D ANA	3	4 TEX	5 TEX	6 ANA	7 ANA	8 ANA
9 D DET	10 DET	11 DET	12 DET	13 D CWS	14 CWS	15 D CWS
16 D CWS	17	18 DET	19 DET	20 D CLE	21 CLE	22 CLE
23 D CLE	24	25 CWS	26 CWS	27 D CWS	28 CLE	29 D CLE
30 D CLE						

2001 SEASON
CLUB DIRECTORY

Owner
Carl R. Pohlad
President
Jerry Bell
Chairman of executive committee
Howard Fox
Directors
Carl R. Pohlad
Eloise Pohlad
James O. Pohlad
Robert C. Pohlad
William M. Pohlad
T. Geron (Jerry) Bell
Kirby Puckett
Chris Clouser
Senior vice president, business affairs
Dave St. Peter
Vice president, general manager
Terry Ryan
Vice president, asst. general manager
Bill Smith
Assistant general manager
Wayne Krivsky
Executive vice president, baseball
Kirby Puckett
Vice president, operations
Matt Hoy
Director of minor leagues
Jim Rantz
Director of scouting
Mike Radcliff
Director of baseball operations
Rob Antony
Traveling secretary
Remzi Kiratli
Manager, media relations
Sean Harlin

Club physicians
Dr. Dan Buss
Dr. VeeJay Eyunni
Dr. John Hallberg
Dr. Tom Jetzer
Dr. John Steubs
Scouts
Kevin Bootay
Ellsworth Brown
Larry Corrigan
Cal Ermer
Marty Esposito
Vern Followell (pro scouting supervisor)
Earl Frishman (east supervisor)
Bill Harford
Deron Johnson (west supervisor)
John Leavitt
Joel Lepel (midwest supervisor)
Bill Lohr
Lee MacPhail
Bill Mele
Gregg Miller
Bill Milos
Tim O'Neil
Hector Otero
Mark Quimuyog
Mike Ruth (midwest supervisor)
Ricky Taylor
Jay Weitzel
Brad Weitzel
John Wilson
Mark Wilson
International scouts
David Kim
Jose Leon
Joe McIlvaine
Howard Norsetter
Yoshi Okamoto
Johnny Sierra
Frank Valdez

MINOR LEAGUE AFFILIATES

Class	Team	League	Manager
AAA	Edmonton	Pacific Coast	John Russell
AA	New Britain	Eastern	Stan Cliburn
A	Fort Myers	Florida State	Jose Marzan
A	Quad City	Midwest	Jeff Carter
Rookie	Elizabethton	Appalachian	Rudy Hernandez
Rookie	Gulf Coast Twins	Gulf Coast	Al Newman

BROADCAST INFORMATION

Radio: WCCO-AM (830).
TV: KMSP-TV (Channel 9).
Cable TV: Midwest Sports Channel.

SPRING TRAINING

Ballpark (city): Lee County Sports Complex (Fort Myers, Fla.).
Ticket information: 800-33-TWINS.

Follow the Twins all season at: www.sportingnews.com/baseball/teams/twins/

SPRING TRAINING ROSTER

Manager—Tom Kelly (10).
Coaches—Ron Gardenhire (35), Paul Molitor (4), Rick Stelmaszek (43), Dick Such (44), Scott Ullger (45), Jerry White (13).

No.	PITCHERS	B/T	Ht./Wt.	Born	2000 clubs
	Balfour, Grant	R/R	6-2/170	12-30-77	Fort Myers
59	Cressend, Jack	R/R	6-1/185	5-13-75	Salt Lake, Minnesota
18	Guardado, Eddie	R/L	6-0/194	10-2-70	Minnesota
32	Hawkins, LaTroy	R/R	6-5/204	12-21-72	Minnesota
51	Kinney, Matt	R/R	6-5/220	12-16-76	New Britain, Salt Lake, Minnesota
	Knight, Brandon	L/R	6-0/170	10-1-75	Columbus
	Lohse, Kyle	R/R	6-2/190	10-4-78	New Britain
	Martinez, Willie	R/R	6-2/180	1-4-78	Buffalo, Cleveland
53	Mays, Joe	B/R	6-1/185	12-10-75	Minnesota, Salt Lake
20	Miller, Travis	R/L	6-3/215	11-2-72	Minnesota
	Mills, Ryan	L/R	6-5/205	7-21-77	Quad City, New Britain
21	Milton, Eric	L/L	6-3/220	8-4-75	Minnesota
52	Mota, Danny	R/R	6-0/170	10-9-75	Fort Myers, New Britain, Salt Lake, Minnesota
22	Radke, Brad	R/R	6-2/188	10-27-72	Minnesota
55	Redman, Mark	L/L	6-5/220	1-5-74	Minnesota
	Rincon, Juan	R/R	5-11/190	1-23-79	Fort Myers, New Britain
	Rivera, Saul	R/R	5-11/155	12-7-77	Fort Myers, New Britain
33	Romero, J.C.	B/L	5-11/195	6-4-76	Minnesota, Fort Myers, Salt Lake
57	Santana, Johan	L/L	6-0/195	3-13-79	Minnesota
	Thomas, Brad	L/L	6-3/205	10-22-77	Fort Myers, New Britain
46	Wells, Bob	R/R	6-0/200	11-1-66	Minnesota

No.	CATCHERS	B/T	Ht./Wt.	Born	2000 clubs
12	Ardoin, Danny	R/R	6-0/218	7-8-74	Sacramento, Modesto, Salt Lake, Minnesota
24	LeCroy, Matt	R/R	6-2/225	12-13-75	Minnesota, New Britain, Salt Lake
39	Moeller, Chad	R/R	6-3/210	2-18-75	Salt Lake, Minnesota
9	Pierzynski, A.J.	L/R	6-3/220	12-30-76	New Britain, Salt Lake, Minnesota

No.	INFIELDERS	B/T	Ht./Wt.	Born	2000 clubs
28	Blake, Casey	R/R	6-2/200	8-23-73	Syracuse, Salt Lake, Minnesota
1	Canizaro, Jay	R/R	5-9/178	7-4-73	Salt Lake, Minnesota
15	Guzman, Cristian	B/R	6-0/195	3-21-78	Minnesota
7	Hocking, Denny	B/R	5-10/183	4-2-70	Minnesota
47	Koskie, Corey	L/R	6-3/217	6-28-73	Minnesota
25	Mientkiewicz, Doug	L/R	6-2/200	6-19-74	Salt Lake, Minnesota
27	Ortiz, David	L/L	6-4/230	11-18-75	Minnesota
1	Rivas, Luis	R/R	5-11/175	8-30-79	New Britain, Salt Lake, Minnesota
	Sears, Todd	R/R	6-1/185	10-23-75	Carolina, New Britain, Salt Lake

No.	OUTFIELDERS	B/T	Ht./Wt.	Born	2000 clubs
31	Allen, Chad	R/R	6-1/195	2-6-75	Salt Lake, Minnesota
40	Barnes, John	R/R	6-2/205	4-24-76	Salt Lake, Minnesota
30	Buchanan, Brian	R/R	6-4/230	7-21-73	Salt Lake, Minnesota
48	Hunter, Torii	R/R	6-2/205	7-18-75	Minnesota
11	Jones, Jacque	L/L	5-10/176	4-25-75	Minnesota
50	Lawton, Matt	L/R	5-10/186	11-3-71	Minnesota

BALLPARK INFORMATION

Ballpark (capacity, surface)
Hubert H. Humphrey Metrodome (48,678, artificial)

Address
34 Kirby Puckett Place
Minneapolis, MN 55415

Official website
www.twinsbaseball.com

Business phone
612-375-1366

Ticket information
1-800-338-9467

Ticket prices
$25 (lower deck club level)
$23 (Diamond View level)
$15 (lower deck reserved)
$10 (upper deck club level; g.a., lower LF)
$5 (g.a., upper deck)

Field dimensions (from home plate)
To left field at foul line, 343 feet
To center field, 408 feet
To right field at foul line, 327 feet

First game played
April 6, 1982 (Mariners 11, Twins 7)

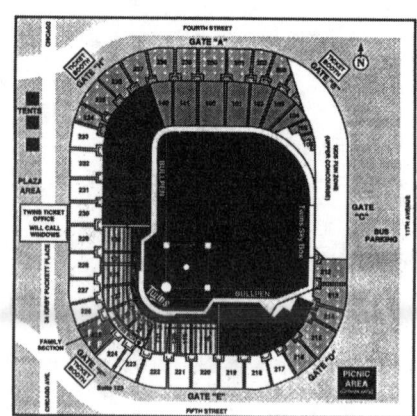

2001 SEASON *Minnesota Twins*

Date	Opp.	Res.	Score	(inn.*)	Hits	Opp. hits	Winning pitcher	Losing pitcher	Save	Record	Pos.	GB
4-3	T.B.	L	0-7		8	14	Trachsel	Radke		0-1	T3rd	1.0
4-4	T.B.	W	6-5		11	9	Carrasco	Hernandez		1-1	T2nd	0.5
4-5	T.B.	W	10-7		12	13	Guardado	White		2-1	1st	+0.5
4-6	T.B.	L	6-7		13	10	Mecir	Carrasco	Hernandez	2-2	T1st	...
4-7	At K.C.	L	6-10		12	15	Fussell	Miller		2-3	4th	1.0
4-8	At K.C.	L	2-5		6	10	Suppan	Radke	Santiago	2-4	4th	2.0
4-9	At K.C.	W	13-7		16	9	Milton	Witasick		3-4	4th	1.5
4-10	At K.C.	L	5-6		8	14	Bottalico	Hawkins		3-5	4th	2.5
4-11	At Bos.	L	4-13		9	16	R. Martinez	Mays		3-6	4th	3.5
4-12	At Bos.	L	3-7		9	10	Fassero	Santana		3-7	4th	4.5
4-13	At Bos.	L	3-4		7	7	Wakefield	Wells		3-8	5th	5.0
4-14	Bal.	W	10-9		12	16	Redman	Groom	Guardado	4-8	5th	4.0
4-15	Bal.	L	4-6		9	15	Worrell	Miller	Trombley	4-9	5th	4.0
4-16	Bal.	L	0-5		4	8	Ponson	Mays		4-10	5th	5.0
4-18	K.C.	W	3-1		7	6	Radke	Suppan	Wells	5-10	4th	4.0
4-19	K.C.	W	7-6		9	10	Carrasco	Santiago		6-10	4th	3.5
4-20	K.C.	W	9-7		13	12	Bergman	Rosado	Wells	7-10	4th	3.0
4-21	At Tex.	W	10-5		12	15	Carrasco	Clark		8-10	T3rd	3.0
4-22	At Tex.	L	3-8		11	11	Loaiza	Santana		8-11	T3rd	4.0
4-23	At Tex.	W	5-4		13	11	Radke	Oliver	Wells	9-11	3rd	4.0
4-24	At N.Y.	W	7-3		6	5	Milton	Clemens		10-11	3rd	4.0
4-25	At N.Y.	W	6-1		10	7	Bergman	Mendoza		11-11	3rd	3.0
4-26	At N.Y.	L	0-2		5	6	Nelson	Mays	Rivera	11-12	3rd	4.0
4-28	Oak.	L	2-5		7	6	Heredia	Radke	Isringhausen	11-13	4th	5.5
4-29	Oak.	L	2-6	(10)	10	7	Mathews	Guardado		11-14	4th	6.5
4-30	Oak.	L	2-8		7	14	Hudson	Bergman		11-15	4th	6.5
5-2	Sea.	L	4-5		10	9	Halama	Mays	Sasaki	11-16	4th	6.0
5-3	Sea.	W	5-4	(10)	10	12	Guardado	Mesa		12-16	4th	6.0
5-4	Det.	L	6-8	(11)	12	10	Anderson	Wells	Jones	12-17	4th	6.5
5-5	Det.	L	8-10		11	14	Patterson	Carrasco	Jones	12-18	4th	6.5
5-6	Det.	W	6-1		8	10	Redman	Nitkowski		13-18	4th	5.5
5-7	Det.	W	4-0		6	5	Mays	Johnson		14-18	4th	4.5
5-8	Cle.	L	2-3	(10)	9	10	Rincon	Wells	Karsay	14-19	4th	4.5
5-9	Cle.	W	6-5		6	13	Hawkins	Finley	Miller	15-19	4th	4.5
5-10	Cle.	W	10-9		13	14	Guardado	Karsay		16-19	4th	3.5
5-12	At Chi.	W	4-3	(10)	12	9	Miller	Lowe	Carrasco	17-19	4th	2.5
5-13	At Chi.	L	3-4		8	8	Wunsch	Wells		17-20	4th	3.5
5-14	At Chi.	L	3-5		8	10	Wunsch	Radke	Foulke	17-21	4th	4.5
5-15	At Sea.	L	0-14		2	16	Sele	Milton		17-22	4th	5.0
5-16	At Sea.	L	5-9		10	9	Meche	Bergman		17-23	4th	6.0
5-17	At Sea.	L	0-4		4	6	Halama	Mays		17-24	4th	6.0
5-18	At Oak.	W	10-5		18	7	Redman	Vizcaino		18-24	4th	5.5
5-19	At Oak.	W	3-2		9	3	Radke	Heredia		19-24	4th	5.5
5-20	At Oak.	W	3-0		9	3	Milton	Mulder	Guardado	20-24	4th	5.5
5-21	At Oak.	L	4-13		11	15	Hudson	Bergman		20-25	4th	6.5
5-23	Ana.	L	4-7		7	12	Cooper	Mays	Percival	20-26	4th	7.0
5-24	Ana.	L	5-6	(10)	7	18	Percival	Wells	Levine	20-27	4th	7.0
5-25	Ana.	L	1-3		7	9	Schoeneweis	Radke	Percival	20-28	4th	7.0
5-26	Tex.	W	10-2		16	5	Milton	Oliver		21-28	4th	7.0
5-27	Tex.	W	10-5		10	8	Mays	Clark		22-28	4th	7.0
5-28	Tex.	W	4-3		7	8	Bergman	Helling	Hawkins	23-28	4th	6.0
5-30	At Tor.	W	4-1		10	5	Redman	Escobar	Hawkins	24-28	4th	5.5
5-31	At Tor.	L	2-4		9	6	Wells	Radke	Koch	24-29	4th	6.5
6-1	At Tor.	W	5-1		6	6	Milton	Castillo		25-29	4th	6.0
6-2	At Cin.	L	3-4		7	10	Bell	Mays	Graves	25-30	4th	7.0
6-3	At Cin.	L	3-9		4	8	Neagle	Bergman		25-31	4th	7.0
6-4	At Cin.	L	2-3	(10)	9	9	Graves	Hawkins		25-32	4th	8.0
6-5	At Hou.	L	2-8		8	11	Elarton	Radke		25-33	4th	9.0
6-6	At Hou.	W	3-1		6	6	Santana	Lima	Guardado	26-33	4th	9.0
6-7	At Hou.	W	2-0		9	6	Mays	Reynolds	Guardado	27-33	4th	9.0
6-9	Mil.	W	9-6		10	10	Bergman	Wright		28-33	4th	9.0
6-10	Mil.	L	3-5		7	13	Haynes	Redman	Wickman	28-34	4th	10.0
6-11	Mil.	L	3-5		10	13	Snyder	Radke	Wickman	28-35	4th	10.0
6-12	Oak.	W	7-2		8	9	Milton	Heredia		29-35	4th	10.0
6-13	Oak.	L	5-6		12	13	Mulder	Mays	Isringhausen	29-36	4th	11.0
6-14	Oak.	L	6-9		8	16	Hudson	Bergman		29-37	4th	12.0
6-15	Sea.	L	5-12		8	18	Ramsay	Redman		29-38	4th	13.0
6-16	Sea.	W	7-2		12	4	Radke	Sele		30-38	4th	13.0
6-17	Sea.	L	3-12		7	17	Moyer	Milton		30-39	4th	14.0
6-18	Sea.	L	2-10		6	12	Meche	Mays		30-40	4th	15.0
6-20	At Tex.	L	2-5		5	13	Rogers	Redman	Wetteland	30-41	4th	15.5
6-21	At Tex.	L	5-7		12	11	Loaiza	Radke	Wetteland	30-42	4th	15.5
6-22	At Tex.	W	3-2		6	9	Hawkins	Crabtree	Wells	31-42	4th	15.5
6-23	At Ana.	L	3-8		8	11	Etherton	Ryan	Levine	31-43	4th	16.5

Date	Opp.	Res.	Score	(inn.*)	Hits	Opp. hits	Winning pitcher	Losing pitcher	Save	Record	Pos.	GB
6-24	At Ana.	W	11-5		16	11	Milton	Bottenfield		32-43	4th	15.5
6-25	At Ana.	L	6-7	(11)	11	10	Hasegawa	Guardado		32-44	4th	16.5
6-26	At Ana.	W	10-6		13	11	Radke	Washburn		33-44	4th	16.0
6-27	At Chi.	W	7-4		12	9	Mays	Baldwin	Wells	34-44	4th	15.0
6-28	At Chi.	L	3-7		4	14	Eldred	Lincoln		34-45	5th	16.0
6-29	At Chi.	W	10-1		15	6	Milton	Wells		35-45	5th	15.0
6-30	At Cle.	W	7-2		16	7	Redman	Brower	Hawkins	36-45	4th	15.0
7-1	At Cle.	W	4-3	(10)	9	8	Guardado	Karsay	Wells	37-45	4th	15.0
7-2	At Cle.	L	1-7		6	11	Finley	Mays		37-46	5th	16.0
7-3	Bos.	L	8-11		13	15	Pichardo	Lincoln	Lowe	37-47	5th	17.0
7-4	Bos.	L	4-14		10	18	Wakefield	Milton	Florie	37-48	5th	17.0
7-5	Bos.	L	8-11		10	12	Wasdin	Redman	Lowe	37-49	5th	18.0
7-6	Bos.	L	7-8		12	8	Crawford	Radke		37-50	5th	18.5
7-7	At Pit.	L	6-8		9	13	Christiansen	Wells	Williams	37-51	5th	19.5
7-8	At Pit.	L	1-4		5	8	Benson	Milton	Williams	37-52	5th	19.5
7-9	At Pit.	W	3-2		8	8	Redman	Silva	Hawkins	38-52	5th	18.5
7-13	Chi. (NL)	W	5-1		11	6	Radke	Valdes	Hawkins	39-52	5th	17.5
7-14	Chi. (NL)	L	2-6		8	12	Lieber	Milton		39-53	5th	17.5
7-15	Chi. (NL)	L	4-8		13	13	Tapani	Mays		39-54	5th	18.5
7-16	StL.	W	5-2		10	6	Redman	Ankiel	Guardado	40-54	5th	18.5
7-17	StL.	L	3-8		11	13	Hentgen	Lincoln		40-55	5th	19.5
7-18	StL.	W	3-2		7	9	Radke	An. Benes	Hawkins	41-55	5th	19.5
7-19	Chi.	L	2-3		8	9	Buehrle	Milton	Foulke	41-56	5th	20.5
7-20	Chi.	W	5-1		12	6	Mays	Parque		42-56	5th	19.5
7-21	Cle.	W	2-1		8	8	Redman	Colon	Hawkins	43-56	5th	19.5
7-22	Cle.	W	10-6		18	10	Santana	Davis	Wells	44-56	5th	18.5
7-23	Cle.	L	3-8		7	12	Burba	Radke		44-57	5th	18.5
7-24	At Bos.	W	4-2		14	6	Milton	Ohka		45-57	5th	18.5
7-25	At Bos.	W	4-2		8	8	Mays	R. Martinez	Guardado	46-57	5th	17.5
7-27	N.Y.	W	9-3		12	9	Redman	Cone		47-57	5th	17.0
7-28	N.Y.	L	5-9		5	17	Rivera	Guardado		47-58	5th	17.0
7-29	N.Y.	W	6-2		8	2	Milton	Mendoza		48-58	5th	16.0
7-30	N.Y.	L	4-7		9	12	Pettitte	Mays		48-59	5th	17.0
7-31	At Bal.	L	5-6		9	9	Ponson	Romero	Trombley	48-60	5th	17.5
8-1	At Bal.	L	0-10		1	13	Mussina	Redman		48-61	5th	18.5
8-2	At Bal.	W	10-6		14	12	Radke	Rapp		49-61	5th	17.5
8-4	At Det.	W	3-1		10	4	Milton	Nitkowski	Wells	50-61	4th	16.5
8-5	At Det.	L	3-4		9	6	Sparks	Mays	Jones	50-62	5th	17.5
8-6	At Det.	W	7-3		10	10	Romero	Weaver		51-62	5th	17.5
8-7	At T.B.	W	4-2		9	6	Redman	Rekar	Guardado	52-62	5th	17.0
8-8	At T.B.	L	0-5		4	10	Lopez	Radke		52-63	5th	16.5
8-9	At T.B.	L	4-5	(10)	13	11	Taylor	Hawkins		52-64	5th	17.5
8-10	At T.B.	L	4-10		9	7	Sturtze	Mays		52-65	5th	17.5
8-11	Tor.	W	9-4		13	8	Romero	Escobar		53-65	5th	17.5
8-12	Tor.	W	6-3		13	10	Redman	Loaiza	Hawkins	54-65	5th	17.5
8-13	Tor.	L	3-13		8	20	Carpenter	Radke		54-66	5th	17.5
8-15	K.C.	W	6-2		11	5	Milton	Suppan	Wells	55-66	5th	17.0
8-16	K.C.	L	3-9		7	16	Meadows	Romero		55-67	5th	18.0
8-17	K.C.	L	4-8		9	15	Reichert	Redman		55-68	5th	18.0
8-18	At Tor.	L	2-3		8	8	Loaiza	Kinney	Koch	55-69	5th	19.0
8-19	At Tor.	W	5-1		8	8	Radke	Guthrie	Guardado	56-69	5th	19.0
8-20	At Tor.	L	3-6		9	10	Wells	Carrasco		56-70	5th	19.0
8-22	T.B.	L	2-3		5	5	Rupe	Romero	Hernandez	56-71	5th	19.0
8-23	T.B.	W	8-2		13	5	Redman	Rekar	Hawkins	57-71	5th	19.0
8-25	Det.	W	8-3		10	7	Radke	Blair	Wells	58-71	5th	18.5
8-26	Det.	L	2-8		5	11	Sparks	Milton		58-72	5th	18.5
8-27	Det.	W	7-6	(10)	11	9	Carrasco	Jones		59-72	5th	18.5
8-29	At K.C.	L	3-7		5	10	Stein	Romero		59-73	5th	19.0
8-30	At K.C.	L	7-8		17	14	Suzuki	Redman	Bottalico	59-74	5th	20.0
9-1	At N.Y.	L	2-4		6	10	Hernandez	Radke	Rivera	59-75	5th	21.0
9-2	At N.Y.	L	4-13	(8)	10	11	Neagle	Milton	Grimsley	59-76	5th	22.0
9-3	At N.Y.	W	2-1	(10)	4	5	Guardado	Rivera	Hawkins	60-76	5th	22.0
9-4	Bal.	L	2-3		10	9	Mercedes	Redman	Kohlmeier	60-77	5th	22.0
9-5	Bal.	L	5-6		14	10	Mussina	Romero	Kohlmeier	60-78	5th	22.0
9-6	Bal.	W	4-1		9	6	Radke	Ponson		61-78	5th	22.0
9-7	At Bos.	L	6-11		9	16	R. Martinez	Milton		61-79	5th	23.0
9-8	At Sea.	W	4-2		10	6	Kinney	Abbott	Hawkins	62-79	5th	23.0
9-9	At Sea.	L	2-7		5	10	Moyer	Redman		62-80	5th	23.0
9-10	At Sea.	L	1-8		7	8	Sele	Romero		62-81	5th	23.5
9-12	At Oak.	L	3-5		6	10	Mulder	Radke	Isringhausen	62-82	5th	24.0
9-13	At Oak.	W	7-6		17	9	Milton	Heredia	Hawkins	63-82	5th	24.0
9-15	Ana.	L	5-16		9	21	Karl	Kinney		63-83	5th	24.0
9-16	Ana.	L	6-7		8	13	Hasegawa	Hawkins	Percival	63-84	5th	25.0
9-17	Ana.	W	1-0		5	8	Radke	Belcher		64-84	5th	24.0
9-18	Tex.	W	3-1		7	10	Mays	Helling	Guardado	65-84	5th	23.0
9-19	Tex.	W	15-7		20	10	Kinney	Glynn		66-84	5th	23.0
9-20	Tex.	L	4-6	(12)	11	10	Wetteland	Miller	Venafro	66-85	5th	24.0
9-21	Chi.	L	4-9		11	11	Sirotka	Santana		66-86	5th	25.0

Date	Opp.	Res.	Score	(inn.*)	Hits	Opp. hits	Winning pitcher	Losing pitcher	Save	Record	Pos.	GB
9-22	Chi.	L	4-5		12	10	Barcelo	Wells	Foulke	66-87	5th	26.0
9-23	Chi.	L	3-5		8	8	Parque	Milton	Foulke	66-88	5th	27.0
9-24	Chi.	W	6-5	(10)	10	12	Guardado	Beirne		67-88	5th	26.0
9-25	At Cle.	W	4-3		10	11	Miller	Shuey	Hawkins	68-88	5th	25.0
9-26	At Cle.	L	2-4		8	8	Finley	Romero	Wickman	68-89	5th	25.0
9-27	At Cle.	L	2-8		7	13	Bere	Radke		68-90	5th	25.0
9-28	At Cle.	W	4-3	(10)	7	9	Guardado	Wickman	Hawkins	69-90	5th	24.0
9-29	At Det.	L	0-1		7	7	Weaver	Mays	Jones	69-91	5th	25.0
9-30	At Det.	L	5-6	(11)	13	13	Jones	Hawkins		69-92	5th	26.0
10-1	At Det.	L	11-12		15	19	Jones	Guardado		69-93	5th	26.0

Monthly records: April (11-15), May (13-14), June (12-16), July (12-15), August (11-14), September (10-18), October (0-1).
*Innings, if other than nine. †First game of a doubleheader. ‡Second game of a doubleheader.

HIGHLIGHTS

High point: On July 3, the Twins signed pitcher Brad Radke to a $36 million contract extension that could keep him with the club through the 2004 season. That move provided unusual hope for a team that played the 2000 season with a $16.5 million payroll. Radke's signing and the subsequent long-term extension signed by shortstop Cristian Guzman appear to be the first steps toward keeping together a corps of young players that also includes Eric Milton, Corey Koskie, Jacque Jones and Matt Lawton.

Low point: When Todd Walker was optioned to the minors on May 4, the former No. 1 draft pick fired some parting shots at manager Tom Kelly. Walker ripped Kelly's handling of young players—and several other former Twins echoed his criticism. The jabs hurt worse when Walker was traded to Colorado and batted .316 over the final two months.

Turning point: Opening day, when the Twins were blanked 7-0 by Tampa Bay before 43,830 fans at the Metrodome. It only got worse as the Twins suffered through their eighth straight losing season.

Most valuable player: Matt Lawton, the team's only All-Star representative, led the Twins in batting (.305), hits (171), doubles (44), RBIs (88), walks (91) and multi-hit games (46). Lawton's numbers could have been better if not for a severely bruised toe that bothered him over the final two months.

Most valuable pitcher: After a dismal spring and first three weeks of the season, LaTroy Hawkins righted himself and emerged as a leading candidate to become the team's future closer. The righthander finished with a 3.41 ERA, 66 relief appearances and a perfect 14-of-14 mark in save opportunities.

Most improved player: After seeing his average dip to .190 after his recall in late July, Torii Hunter caught fire, providing hope that the organization had found its everyday center fielder. Hunter batted .355 with five homers and 33 RBIs over the final 49 games to raise his average to a respectable .280.

Most pleasant surprise: Mark Redman didn't get his first start until May 6, but the lefthander won 12 of his first 18 and finished with a 12-9 record. Only a season-ending knee injury kept him from making a serious run for Rookie of the Year honors.

Key injuries: The Twins were one of the healthiest teams in baseball. Lawton suffered his toe injury in late July when he crashed into an outfield fence in Baltimore and did not start the next six games. Redman and Eric Milton both suffered September knee injuries, neither of which required surgery.

Notable: Kelly managed the 1,000th victory of his career May 7 against Detroit. ... The Twins finished last in the major leagues with 116 home runs—34 fewer than Kansas City's next-lowest total in the American League. ... The Twins have played 17 rookies in each of the last two seasons. ... Shortstop Guzman tied a franchise record with 20 triples.

—DENNIS BRACKIN

RECORDS

2000 regular-season record: 69-93 (5th in A.L. Central); 36-45 at home; 33-48 on road; 19-29 vs. East; 31-37 vs. Central; 19-27 vs. West; 11-29 vs. lefthanded starters; 58-64 vs. righthanded starters; 28-37 on grass; 41-56 on turf; 22-27 in daytime; 47-66 at night; 22-26 in one-run games; 7-9 in extra-inning games; 0-0 in doubleheaders.
Team record past five years: 348-460 (.431, ranks 12th in league in that span).

TEAM LEADERS

Batting average: Matt Lawton (.305).
At-bats: Cristian Guzman (631).
Runs: Cristian Guzman (89).
Hits: Matt Lawton (171).
Total Bases: Matt Lawton (258).
Doubles: Matt Lawton (44).
Triples: Cristian Guzman (20).
Home runs: Jacque Jones (19).
Runs batted in: Matt Lawton (88).
Stolen bases: Cristian Guzman (28).
Slugging percentage: Jacque Jones (.463).
On-base percentage: Matt Lawton (.405).
Wins: Eric Milton (13).
Earned-run average: Brad Radke (4.45).
Complete games: Brad Radke (4).

Shutouts: Joe Mays, Brad Radke (1).
Saves: LaTroy Hawkins (14).
Innings pitched: Brad Radke (226.2).
Strikeouts: Eric Milton (160).

GAMES BY POSITION

Catcher: Marcus Jensen 49, Matt LeCroy 49, Chad Moeller 48, A.J. Pierzynski 32, Danny Ardoin 15.
First base: Ron Coomer 124, David Ortiz 27, Denny Hocking 12, Butch Huskey 9, Matt LeCroy 3, Doug Mientkiewicz 3, Casey Blake 1.
Second base: Jay Canizaro 90, Denny Hocking 47, Jason Maxwell 30, Todd Walker 19, Luis Rivas 14.
Third base: Corey Koskie 139, Jason Maxwell 19, Denny Hocking 16, Casey Blake 5, Ron Coomer 1.
Shortstop: Cristian Guzman 151, Denny Hocking 15, Jason Maxwell 5, Luis Rivas 2.
Outfield: Jacque Jones 147, Matt Lawton 143, Torii Hunter 99, Denny Hocking 51, Midre Cummings 40, Brian Buchanan 25, Chad Allen 15, Butch Huskey 15, John Barnes 11, Jason Maxwell 2.
Designated hitter: David Ortiz 88, Butch Huskey 39, Midre Cummings 15, Ron Coomer 9, Matt Lawton 9, Jason Maxwell 7, Matt LeCroy 3, Brian Buchanan 2, Jay Canizaro 2, Denny Hocking 2, Todd Walker 2, Casey Blake 1, Cristian Guzman 1, Marcus Jensen 1, Corey Koskie 1.

TOP DRAFT CHOICES

1a. **Adam Johnson,** RHP, Cal State Fullerton.
1b. **Aaron Heilman,** RHP, U. of Notre Dame.
2a. **Taggert Bozied,** 1B, U. of San Francisco.
2b. **J.D. Durbin,** RHP, Coronado H.S., Scottsdale, Ariz.
3. **Colby Miller,** RHP, Weatherford (Okla.) H.S.
4. **Jason Miller,** LHP, Sarasota (Fla.) H.S.
5. **Edgardo LeBron,** SS, Ramon Power, H.S., Las Piedras, P.R.
6. **Ron Corona,** RHP, Cal State Fullerton.
7. **James Tomlin,** OF, St. Bernard H.S., Los Angeles.
8. **Henry Bonilla,** RHP, Tulane University.
9. **Ken Holubec,** LHP, U. of Louisiana-Monroe.
10. **Kelly Gulledge,** C, U. of Alabama.

NEW YORK YANKEES
AMERICAN LEAGUE EAST DIVISION

Yankees
2001 SCHEDULE
Home games shaded; D—Day game (games starting before 5 p.m.)
*—All-Star Game at Safeco Field (Seattle)

APRIL
SUN	MON	TUE	WED	THU	FRI	SAT
1	2 D KC	3	4 KC	5 D KC	6 D TOR	7 D TOR
8 D TOR	9 KC	10 KC	11 D KC	12	13 BOS	14 D BOS
15 D BOS	16 D BOS	17 TOR	18 TOR	19 TOR	20 BOS	21 D BOS
22 BOS	23	24 SEA	25 SEA	26 SEA	27 OAK	28 D OAK
29 OAK	30 MIN					

MAY
SUN	MON	TUE	WED	THU	FRI	SAT
		1 MIN	2 MIN	3 BAL	4 BAL	5 D BAL
6 D BAL	7	8 MIN	9 MIN	10 MIN	11 BAL	12 D BAL
13 D BAL	14	15 OAK	16 OAK	17 D OAK	18 SEA	19 D SEA
20 D SEA	21	22 BOS	23 BOS	24 D BOS	25 CLE	26 D CLE
27 CLE	28 BOS	29	30 BOS	31		

JUNE
SUN	MON	TUE	WED	THU	FRI	SAT
					1 CLE	2 D CLE
3 CLE	4	5 BAL	6 BAL	7 BAL	8 ATL	9 D ATL
10 ATL	11	12 MON	13 MON	14 MON	15 NYM	16 D NYM
17 NYM	18 DET	19 DET	20 DET	21 DET	22 TB	23 D TB
24 TB	25 CLE	26 CLE	27 CLE	28	29 TB	30 D TB

JULY
SUN	MON	TUE	WED	THU	FRI	SAT
1 TB	2 D BAL	3 D BAL	4 BAL	5 D BAL	6 NYM	7 D NYM
8 NYM	9	10 *	11	12 FLA	13 FLA	14 D FLA
15 D PHI	16 PHI	17 PHI	18 DET	19 DET	20 TOR	21 D TOR
22 D TOR	23 TOR	24 DET	25 DET	26 DET	27 TOR	28 D TOR
29 TOR	30	31 TEX				

AUGUST
SUN	MON	TUE	WED	THU	FRI	SAT
			1 TEX	2 D TEX	3 D ANA	4 D ANA
5 D ANA	6 D ANA	7 TB	8 TB	9 TB	10 OAK	11 D OAK
12 D OAK	13	14 TB	15 TB	16 TB	17 SEA	18 D SEA
19 D SEA	20 TEX	21 TEX	22 TEX	23 TEX	24 ANA	25 D ANA
26 ANA	27	28 TOR	29 TOR	30 D TOR	31 BOS	

SEPTEMBER
SUN	MON	TUE	WED	THU	FRI	SAT
						1 D BOS
2 BOS	3 D TOR	4 D TOR	5 TOR	6	7 BOS	8 D BOS
9 D BOS	10 CWS	11 CWS	12 CWS	13 TB	14 TB	15 D TB
16 D TB	17 CWS	18 CWS	19 CWS	20 CWS	21 BAL	22 D BAL
23 D BAL	24 TB	25 TB	26	27	28 BAL	29 D BAL
30 D BAL						

2001 SEASON
CLUB DIRECTORY

Principal owner
George M. Steinbrenner III
General partners
Hal Z. Steinbrenner, Henry C. Steinbrenner, Steven W. Swindal
President
Randy Levine
Chief operating officer
Lonn A. Trost
Vice president, chief financial officer
Martin Greenspun
Vice president, ticket operations
Frank Swaine
Vice president
Ed Weaver
Vice president, marketing
Deborah A. Tymon
Vice president, administration
Sonny Hight
Special advisors
Yogi Berra, Reggie Jackson, Clyde King, Don Mattingly, Al Rosen, Dick Williams
Vice president, general manager
Brian Cashman
Vice president, baseball operations
Mark Newman
Assistant general manager
Kim Ng
Vice president, major league scouting
Gene Michael
Vice president, international and professional scouting
Gordon Blakeley
Vice president, scouting
Lin Garrett
Vice president, player personnel
Billy Connors
Special assistant to the general manager
Stump Merrill
Director of player development
Rob Thomson
Director of player personnel
Damon Oppenheimer
Director of baseball operations
Dan Matheson
Assistant directors of baseball operations
Rigo Garcia, Tommy Larsen
Traveling secretary
David Szen
Equipment manager
Rob Cucuzza
Visiting clubhouse manager
Lou Cucuzza Jr.
Assistant, video operations
Leo Astacio
Controller
Robert Brown
Director of stadium operations
Kirk Randazzo
Assistant director of stadium operations
Doug Behar
Stadium superintendent
Pete Pullara
Manager, information services
Kris Zocco
Head groundskeeper
Dan Cunningham
Director of media relations & publicity
Rick Cerrone

Assistant director of media relations & publicity
Jason Zillo
Senior advisor
Arthur Richman
Assistants, media relations
Rikki Dileo, Chris Romano
Director of concessions & hospitality
Joel White
Director of sponsorship services
Michael Tustani
Special assistant
Joe Pepitone
Assistant director of concessions & hospitality
David M. Bernstein
Sponsorship development manager
Kristin Costello
Scoreboard & broadcasting manager
Joe Pullia
Scoreboard & broadcasting assistant manager
Mike Bonner
Senior coordinator, sponsorship services
Bill O'Sullivan
Coordinator, concessions & hospitality
Jacqueline Feinberg
Coordinator, promotions and special events
Jonathan Hopkins
Coordinator, sponsorship services
Cliff Rowley
Director of publications and multimedia
Dan Cahalane
Editor-in-chief, Yankees publications
Dan Cahalane
Special assistant to George M. Steinbrenner/director of community relations
Brian Smith
Assistant director of community relations
Jason Feneque
Team physician
Dr. Stuart Hershon
Head trainer
Gene Monahan
Assistant trainer
Steve Donohue
Strength & conditioning coach
Jeff Mangold
Regional cross-checkers
Joe Arnold, Tim Kelly, Greg Orr
Pro scouts
Joe Caro, Bill Emslie, Mick Kelleher, Bob Miske, Mike Naples
Scouts
Mike Baker, Mark Batchko, Steve Boros, Bobby Dejardin, Dick Groch, Steve Lemke, Abe Martinez, Bob Miske, Scott Pleis, Cesar Presbott, Gus Quattlebaum, Joe Robison, Phil Rossi, Steve Swail, Leon Wurth, Bill Young
Coordinator of Pacific rim scouting
John Cox
Coordinator of Latin American scouting
Carlos Rios
Foreign scouts
Manuel Duran, Ricardo Finol, Karl Heron, Ricardo Heron, Rudy Jabalera, Victor Mata, Jim Patterson, Jose Quintero, Edgar Rodriguez, Arquimedes Rojas, Freddy Tiburcio
Special assignment scouts
Stump Merrill, Ket Barber

MINOR LEAGUE AFFILIATES

Class	Team	League	Manager
AAA	Columbus	International	Trey Hillman
AA	Norwich	Eastern	Dan Radison
A	Greensboro	South Atlantic	Stan Hough
A	Staten Island	New York-Pennsylvania	Joe Arnold
A	Tampa	Florida State	Tom Nieto
Rookie	Tampa	Gulf Coast	Derek Shelton

BROADCAST INFORMATION

Radio: WABC-AM (770).
TV: WNYW-TV (Channel 5).
Cable TV: Madison Square Garden Network.

SPRING TRAINING

Ballpark (city): Legends Field (Tampa, Fla.).
Ticket information: 813-879-2244, 813-287-8844.

Follow the Yankees all season at: www.sportingnews.com/baseball/teams/yankees/

Manager—Joe Torre (6).
Coaches—Tony Cloninger (40), Billy Connors (57), Lee Mazzilli (54), Willie Randolph (30), Mel Stottlemyre (34), Don Zimmer (52).

No.	PITCHERS	B/T	Ht./Wt.	Born	2000 clubs
37	Boehringer, Brian	B/R	6-2/190	1-8-70	San Diego, Rancho Cucamonga
	Bradley, Ryan	R/R	6-4/226	10-26-75	Columbus
	Choate, Randy	L/L	6-3/180	9-5-75	Columbus, New York A.L.
22	Clemens, Roger	R/R	6-4/238	8-4-62	New York A.L.
64	De Los Santos, Luis	R/R	6-2/216	11-1-77	Gulf Coast Yankees
57	Einertson, Darrell	R/R	6-2/196	9-4-72	Columbus, New York A.L.
26	Hernandez, Orlando	R/R	6-2/220	10-11-65	New York A.L., Tampa
	Keisler, Randy	L/L	6-3/190	2-24-76	Norwich, Columbus, New York A.L.
	Lee, David	R/R	6-1/202	3-12-73	Colorado, Colorado Springs
	Lilly, Ted	L/L	6-0/185	1-4-76	Tampa, Columbus, New York A.L.
55	Mendoza, Ramiro	R/R	6-2/195	6-15-72	New York A.L., Tampa
35	Mussina, Mike	R/R	6-2/185	12-8-68	Baltimore
83	Noel, Ted	R/R	6-4/225	9-28-78	Tampa
	Parker, Christian	R/R	6-1/200	7-3-75	Norwich
46	Pettitte, Andy	L/L	6-5/225	6-15-72	New York A.L.
42	Rivera, Mariano	R/R	6-2/185	11-29-69	New York A.L.
	Rogers, Brian	R/R	6-6/200	2-13-77	Norwich
29	Stanton, Mike	L/L	6-1/215	6-2-67	New York A.L.
27	Watson, Allen	L/L	6-1/224	11-18-70	New York A.L., Columbus, Tampa, Gulf Coast Yankees

No.	CATCHERS	B/T	Ht./Wt.	Born	2000 clubs
9	Oliver, Joe	R/R	6-3/220	7-24-65	Seattle, Tacoma
20	Posada, Jorge	B/R	6-2/200	8-17-71	New York A.L.

No.	INFIELDERS	B/T	Ht./Wt.	Born	2000 clubs
	Almonte, Erick	R/R	6-2/180	2-1-78	Norwich
15	Bellinger, Clay	R/R	6-3/215	11-18-68	New York A.L., Columbus
18	Brosius, Scott	R/R	6-1/202	8-15-66	New York A.L., Tampa
2	Jeter, Derek	R/R	6-3/195	6-26-74	New York A.L., Tampa
68	Jimenez, D'Angelo	R/R	6-0/194	12-21-77	Gulf Coast Yankees, Tampa, Columbus
70	Johnson, Nick	L/L	6-3/224	9-19-78	DID NOT PLAY
11	Knoblauch, Chuck	R/R	5-9/175	7-7-68	New York A.L., Tampa
24	Martinez, Tino	L/R	6-2/210	12-7-67	New York A.L.
	Seabol, Scott	R/R	6-4/200	5-17-75	Norwich
14	Sojo, Luis	R/R	5-11/185	1-3-66	Pittsburgh, New York A.L.
58	Soriano, Alfonso	R/R	6-1/160	1-7-78	New York A.L., Columbus

No.	OUTFIELDERS	B/T	Ht./Wt.	Born	2000 clubs
61	Frank, Mike	L/L	6-2/195	1-14-75	Louisville, Chattanooga, Columbus
31	Hill, Glenallen	R/R	6-3/230	3-22-65	Chicago N.L., New York A.L.
28	Justice, David	L/L	6-3/200	4-14-66	Cleveland, New York A.L.
84	McDonald, Donzell	B/R	5-11/180	2-20-75	Columbus, Norwich
21	O'Neill, Paul	L/L	6-4/215	2-25-63	New York A.L.
81	Pena, Wily	R/R	6-3/215	1-23-82	Greensboro, Staten Island
47	Spencer, Shane	R/R	5-11/225	2-20-72	New York A.L.
51	Williams, Bernie	B/R	6-2/205	9-13-68	New York A.L.

BALLPARK INFORMATION

Ballpark (capacity, surface)
Yankee Stadium (57,530, grass)

Address
Yankee Stadium
E. 161 St. and River Ave.
Bronx, NY 10451

Official website
www.yankees.com

Business phone
718-293-4300

Ticket information
212-307-1212, 718-293-6013

Ticket prices
$65 (Championship Seat, loge)
$55 (Championship Seat, main box)
$47 (main box MVP)
$42 (field box & loge box MVP)
$37 (main reserved MVP)
$37 (main & loge box)
$33 (tier box), $33 (main reserved)
$17 (tier reserved), $15 (tier reserved value)
$8 (bleachers)

Field dimensions (from home plate)
To left field at foul line, 318 feet
To center field, 408 feet
To right field at foul line, 314 feet

First game played
April 18, 1923 (Yankees 4, Red Sox 1)

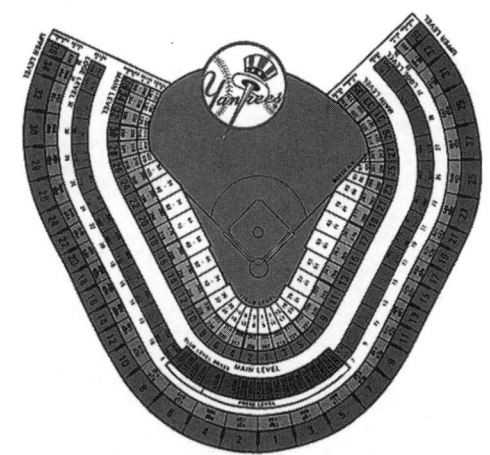

2000 REVIEW
DAY BY DAY

Date	Opp.	Res.	Score	(inn.*)	Hits	Opp. hits	Winning pitcher	Losing pitcher	Save	Record	Pos.	GB
4-3	At Ana.	W	3-2		6	10	Hernandez	Hill	Rivera	1-0	T1st	...
4-4	At Ana.	W	5-3		9	10	Mendoza	Percival	Rivera	2-0	T1st	...
4-5	At Ana.	L	6-12		13	12	Schoeneweis	Cone		2-1	T1st	...
4-7	At Sea.	L	5-7		9	12	Halama	Pettitte	Sasaki	2-2	2nd	1.0
4-8	At Sea.	W	3-2		10	5	Nelson	Mesa	Rivera	3-2	2nd	1.0
4-9	At Sea.	L	3-9		3	9	Moyer	Clemens		3-3	2nd	2.0
4-12	Tex.	W	8-6		13	10	Nelson	Munoz	Rivera	4-3	2nd	0.5
4-13	Tex.	W	5-1		8	4	Hernandez	Rogers		5-3	1st	+0.5
4-14	K.C.	W	7-5		10	9	Clemens	Witasick	Rivera	6-3	1st	+1.5
4-15	K.C.	W	7-1		11	2	Mendoza	Rosado		7-3	1st	+1.5
4-16	K.C.	W	8-4		10	9	Nelson	Fussell		8-3	1st	+1.5
4-17	At Tex.	W	5-4	(11)	8	11	Rivera	Crabtree	Erdos	9-3	1st	+2.0
4-18	At Tex.	W	6-3		11	8	Hernandez	Rogers		10-3	1st	+2.5
4-19	At Tex.	W	5-4	(10)	12	7	Rivera	Zimmerman		11-3	1st	+2.5
4-21	At Tor.	L	3-8		5	12	Carpenter	Mendoza		11-4	1st	+1.0
4-22	At Tor.	L	2-8		9	10	Escobar	Cone		11-5	T1st	...
4-23	At Tor.	W	10-7		15	8	Hernandez	Andrews	Rivera	12-5	1st	+1.0
4-24	Min.	L	3-7		5	6	Milton	Clemens		12-6	1st	+1.0
4-25	Min.	L	1-6		7	10	Bergman	Mendoza		12-7	T1st	...
4-26	Min.	W	2-0		6	5	Nelson	Mays	Rivera	13-7	1st	+1.0
4-28	Tor.	W	6-0		8	3	Cone	Escobar		14-7	1st	+1.5
4-29	Tor.	L	2-6		11	14	Wells	Hernandez	Koch	14-8	1st	+0.5
4-30	Tor.	W	7-1		12	9	Clemens	Halladay		15-8	1st	+1.5
5-1	At Cle.	W	2-1		8	7	Mendoza	Wright	Rivera	16-8	1st	+2.0
5-2	At Cle.	W	4-2		10	6	Pettitte	Witt	Rivera	17-8	1st	+2.0
5-3	At Cle.	W	6-5		9	10	Grimsley	Karsay	Rivera	18-8	1st	+3.0
5-5	Bal.	W	12-10		16	14	Nelson	Ryan		19-8	1st	+3.0
5-6	Bal.	W	3-1		6	6	Clemens	Rapp	Rivera	20-8	1st	+4.0
5-7	Bal.	L	6-7		10	12	Groom	Rivera	Timlin	20-9	1st	+3.0
5-8	T.B.	W	6-3		8	9	Pettitte	Gooden	Rivera	21-9	1st	+3.0
5-9	T.B.	W	4-3	(10)	7	8	Nelson	White		22-9	1st	+4.0
5-11	T.B.	L	0-1		4	7	Trachsel	Hernandez	Lopez	22-10	1st	+2.5
5-12	At Det.	L	7-9		12	16	Nitkowski	Clemens	Jones	22-11	1st	+1.5
5-13	At Det.	L	3-6		8	13	Weaver	Pettitte	Jones	22-12	1st	+0.5
5-14	At Det.	L	1-2		5	8	Mlicki	Cone	Jones	22-13	2nd	0.5
5-16	Chi.	L	0-4		3	7	Eldred	Hernandez		22-14	2nd	1.0
5-17	Chi.	W	9-4		15	7	Clemens	Parque		23-14	2nd	1.0
5-19	At Cle.	W	11-7		14	9	Mendoza	Kamieniecki		24-14	2nd	1.0
5-20	At Cle.	L	2-3		9	7	Shuey	Nelson		24-15	2nd	1.0
5-21	At Cle.	L	1-6		4	11	Rigdon	Hernandez		24-16	2nd	1.0
5-23	At Chi.	L	2-8		9	11	Wells	Clemens		24-17	2nd	1.0
5-24	At Chi.	W	12-4		18	7	Pettitte	Sirotka		25-17	2nd	1.0
5-25	At Chi.	W	7-0		12	4	Mendoza	Baldwin		26-17	T1st	...
5-26	Bos.	L	1-4		8	8	R. Martinez	Cone	Lowe	26-18	2nd	1.0
5-27	Bos.	W	8-3		11	9	Stanton	Wasdin		27-18	T1st	...
5-28	Bos.	L	0-2		4	5	P. Martinez	Clemens		27-19	2nd	1.0
5-29	Oak.	W	4-1		6	2	Pettitte	Olivares		28-19	2nd	0.5
5-30	Oak.	L	4-7		10	11	Appier	Mendoza	Isringhausen	28-20	2nd	1.5
5-31	Oak.	L	7-8		11	9	Heredia	Cone	Isringhausen	28-21	2nd	1.5
6-2	At Atl.	W	5-2		10	5	Hernandez	Millwood	Rivera	29-21	T1st	...
6-3	At Atl.	L	7-11		13	11	Remlinger	Grimsley		29-22	T1st	...
6-4	At Atl.	W	7-6		16	12	Pettitte	Mulholland	Rivera	30-22	T1st	+1.0
6-5	At Mon.	L	4-6		13	8	Johnson	Cone	Kline	30-23	T1st	...
6-6	At Mon.	W	8-1		13	3	Grimsley	Vazquez		31-23	T1st	...
6-7	At Mon.	W	7-2		9	4	Hernandez	Pavano		32-23	1st	+1.0
6-9	N.Y. (NL)	L	2-12		8	15	Leiter	Clemens		32-24	1st	+0.5
6-10	N.Y. (NL)	W	13-5		17	8	Pettitte	B.J. Jones		33-24	1st	+1.5
6-13	Bos.	L	3-5		6	10	Pichardo	Hernandez	Lowe	33-25	1st	...
6-14	Bos.	W	2-1		8	10	Grimsley	Wakefield	Rivera	34-25	1st	+1.0
6-15	Chi.	L	3-12		12	16	Sirotka	Pettitte		34-26	1st	+0.5
6-16	Chi.	L	1-3		6	9	Baldwin	Stanton	Howry	34-27	2nd	0.5
6-17	Chi.	L	9-10		15	15	Eldred	Westbrook	Foulke	34-28	2nd	0.5
6-18	Chi.	L	4-17		10	18	Parque	Hernandez		34-29	2nd	0.5
6-19	At Bos.	W	22-1		19	6	Mendoza	Rose		35-29	1st	+0.5
6-20	At Bos.	W	3-0		5	6	Pettitte	P. Martinez	Rivera	36-29	1st	+1.5
6-21	At Bos.	L	7-9		10	11	Garces	Grimsley		36-30	1st	+0.5
6-22	At Bos.	L	2-4		5	8	R. Martinez	Westbrook	Lowe	36-31	2nd	0.5
6-23	At Chi.	L	3-4		11	8	Lowe	Rivera		36-32	3rd	1.0
6-24	At Chi.	W	12-8		16	13	Mendoza	Wells	Rivera	37-32	2nd	1.0
6-25	At Chi.	L	7-8		10	13	Sirotka	Pettitte	Howry	37-33	2nd	2.0
6-27	At Det.	L	6-7	(11)	15	17	Cruz	Rivera		37-34	2nd	2.0
6-28	At Det.	L	6-13		11	12	Blair	Ford	Sparks	37-35	2nd	3.0
6-29	At Det.	W	8-0		14	6	Pettitte	Mlicki		38-35	2nd	3.0
6-30	At T.B.	L	4-6		7	12	Mecir	Nelson	Hernandez	38-36	2nd	3.0

Date	Opp.	Res.	Score	(inn.*)	Hits	Opp. hits	Winning pitcher	Losing pitcher	Save	Record	Pos.	GB
7-1	At T.B.	W	6-1		12	5	Hernandez	Lopez		39-36	2nd	2.0
7-2	At T.B.	W	5-2		10	4	Clemens	Trachsel	Rivera	40-36	2nd	1.0
7-4	Bal.	L	6-7		10	7	Erickson	Cone	Trombley	40-37	2nd	1.5
7-5	Bal.	W	12-6		13	10	Pettitte	Rapp		41-37	2nd	0.5
7-6	Bal.	W	13-9		10	11	Stanton	Johnson		42-37	2nd	0.5
7-7	At N.Y. (NL)	W	2-1		6	6	Hernandez	Leiter	Rivera	43-37	1st	+0.5
7-8†	At N.Y. (NL)	W	4-2		6	6	Gooden	B.J. Jones	Rivera	44-37		
7-8‡	N.Y. (NL)	W	4-2		5	7	Clemens	Rusch	Rivera	45-37	1st	+1.0
7-9	At N.Y. (NL)	L	0-2		7	6	Hampton	Pettitte	Benitez	45-38	1st	...
7-13	Fla.	L	9-11		12	14	Penny	Hernandez	Alfonseca	45-39	1st	...
7-14	Fla.	W	6-2		9	7	Clemens	Dempster		46-39	1st	...
7-16	Phi.	W	9-8	(10)	13	14	Rivera	Brantley		47-39	1st	+0.5
7-17	Phi.	L	8-10		12	9	Coggin	Cone	Brock	47-40	1st	+0.5
7-18	Phi.	W	3-1		4	5	Neagle	Schilling	Rivera	48-40	1st	+1.0
7-19	Det.	W	9-1		11	6	Clemens	Nomo		49-40	1st	+1.5
7-20	Det.	L	3-5		8	8	Blair	Pettitte	Jones	49-41	1st	+0.5
7-21	T.B.	W	11-1		17	10	Gooden	Yan		50-41	1st	+1.5
7-22	T.B.	L	4-12		12	14	Rupe	Cone		50-42	1st	+1.0
7-23	T.B.	W	5-1		7	4	Neagle	Rekar		51-42	1st	+1.0
7-24	At Bal.	W	4-3		5	6	Clemens	Parrish	Rivera	52-42	1st	+2.0
7-25	At Bal.	W	19-1		20	9	Pettitte	Erickson		53-42	1st	+3.0
7-26	At Bal.	W	4-1		8	8	Gooden	Ponson	Rivera	54-42	1st	+3.0
7-27	At Min.	L	3-9		9	12	Redman	Cone		54-43	1st	+2.0
7-28	At Min.	W	9-5		17	5	Rivera	Guardado		55-43	1st	+2.5
7-29	At Min.	L	2-6		2	8	Milton	Mendoza		55-44	1st	+2.5
7-30	At Min.	W	7-4		12	9	Pettitte	Mays		56-44	1st	+3.5
8-1	K.C.	W	5-4		9	6	Nelson	Bottalico	Rivera	57-44	1st	+4.0
8-2	K.C.	L	1-4		2	11	Stein	Neagle	Bottalico	57-45	1st	+3.0
8-3	K.C.	W	3-2		6	5	Rivera	Spradlin		58-45	1st	+3.5
8-4	Sea.	W	13-6		16	15	Pettitte	Moyer		59-45	1st	+3.5
8-5	Sea.	L	5-6		10	11	Tomko	Gooden	Sasaki	59-46	1st	+3.5
8-6	Sea.	L	1-11		8	16	Abbott	Hernandez		59-47	1st	+3.5
8-7	Sea.	L	5-8		11	13	Halama	Neagle		59-48	1st	+3.5
8-8	Oak.	W	4-3		6	7	Rivera	Isringhausen		60-48	1st	+4.5
8-9	Oak.	W	12-1		12	9	Pettitte	Appier		61-48	1st	+4.5
8-10	Oak.	W	12-6		15	13	Cone	Mulder		62-48	1st	+5.0
8-11	At Ana.	L	3-8		11	10	Schoeneweis	Hernandez		62-49	1st	+4.0
8-12	At Ana.	L	6-9		10	12	Pote	Neagle	Hasegawa	62-50	1st	+4.0
8-13	At Ana.	W	4-1		5	4	Clemens	Ortiz	Rivera	63-50	1st	+4.0
8-14	At Tex.	W	7-3		9	7	Pettitte	Perisho		64-50	1st	+4.0
8-15	At Tex.	W	10-2		17	8	Cone	Davis	Gooden	65-50	1st	+5.0
8-16	At Tex.	L	0-5		4	8	Sikorski	Hernandez		65-51	1st	+4.0
8-17	Ana.	W	6-1		6	11	Neagle	Mercker		66-51	1st	+4.0
8-18	Ana.	L	8-9	(11)	13	15	Hasegawa	Stanton		66-52	1st	+3.0
8-19	Ana.	W	9-1		11	5	Pettitte	Cooper		67-52	1st	+3.0
8-20	Tex.	W	4-5		9	6	Wise	Nelson	Hasegawa	67-53	1st	+3.0
8-21	Tex.	W	12-3		13	8	Hernandez	Sikorski		68-53	1st	+3.0
8-22	Tex.	L	4-5		6	8	Crabtree	Neagle	Wetteland	68-54	1st	+3.0
8-23	Tex.	W	10-9		17	11	Rivera	Crabtree		69-54	1st	+3.0
8-24	Tex.	W	8-7		12	11	Pettitte	Perisho	Rivera	70-54	1st	+3.0
8-25	At Oak.	L	1-8		5	8	Appier	Cone		70-55	1st	+3.0
8-26	At Oak.	W	10-6		14	10	Hernandez	Mulder	Rivera	71-55	1st	+3.0
8-27	At Oak.	W	7-5		10	6	Neagle	Mecir	Rivera	72-55	1st	+4.0
8-28	At Sea.	W	9-1		10	5	Clemens	Abbott		73-55	1st	+5.0
8-29	At Sea.	L	3-5		8	8	Tomko	Pettitte	Sasaki	73-56	1st	+4.0
8-30	At Sea.	W	5-4		10	8	Cone	Sele	Rivera	74-56	1st	+5.0
9-1	Min.	W	4-2		10	6	Hernandez	Radke	Rivera	75-56	1st	+5.0
9-2	Min.	W	13-4	(8)	11	10	Neagle	Milton	Grimsley	76-56	1st	+6.0
9-3	Min.	L	1-2	(10)	5	4	Guardado	Rivera	Hawkins	76-57	1st	+6.0
9-4	At K.C.	W	4-3		8	12	Pettitte	Suzuki	Rivera	77-57	1st	+6.0
9-5	At K.C.	W	10-5		17	10	Gooden	Suppan		78-57	1st	+6.0
9-6	At K.C.	L	2-3		9	12	Meadows	Stanton		78-58	1st	+6.0
9-7	At K.C.	W	7-3		7	8	Neagle	Bottalico	Rivera	79-58	1st	+6.0
9-8	At Bos.	W	4-0		8	5	Clemens	Ohka		80-58	1st	+7.0
9-9	At Bos.	W	5-3		7	9	Pettitte	P. Martinez		81-58	1st	+8.0
9-10	At Bos.	W	6-2		11	7	Keisler	Schourek	Gooden	82-58	1st	+8.5
9-11	Bos.	L	0-4		5	7	Arrojo	Hernandez	Lowe	82-59	1st	+8.0
9-12	Tor.	W	10-2		11	8	Neagle	Hamilton		83-59	1st	+8.0
9-13	Tor.	W	3-2		7	11	Clemens	Loaiza	Rivera	84-59	1st	+9.0
9-14	Tor.	L	2-3	(11)	11	6	Koch	Choate	Escobar	84-60	1st	+8.0
9-15	Cle.	L	1-11		4	15	Burba	Cone		84-61	1st	+7.0
9-16	Cle.	L	6-3		12	4	Hernandez	Bere		85-61	1st	+7.5
9-17	Cle.	L	4-15		5	15	Finley	Neagle		85-62	1st	+7.5
9-18	Cle.	L	0-2		1	7	Colon	Clemens		85-63	1st	+7.0
9-19	At Tor.	L	3-16		4	19	Trachsel	Pettitte		85-64	1st	+6.0
9-20	At Tor.	L	2-7		9	10	Loaiza	Cone		85-65	1st	+5.5
9-21	At Tor.	L	1-3		5	9	Wells	Hernandez		85-66	1st	+4.5
9-22	Det.	L	6-9		9	10	Nomo	Neagle	Jones	85-67	1st	+4.5
9-23	Det.	W	13-8		18	8	Nelson	Blair	Rivera	86-67	1st	+4.5

Date	Opp.	Res.	Score	(inn.*)	Hits	Opp. hits	Winning pitcher	Losing pitcher	Save	Record	Pos.	GB
9-24	Det.	W	6-3	10	7	Pettitte	Weaver	Rivera		87-67	1st	+5.5
9-25	Det.	L	4-15		11	18	Sparks	Gooden		87-68	1st	+5.5
9-26	At T.B.	L	1-2		8	3	Hernandez	Nelson		87-69	1st	+5.5
9-27	At T.B.	L	1-11		7	9	Lidle	Neagle		87-70	1st	+4.5
9-28	At T.B.	L	3-11		10	15	Rekar	Clemens		87-71	1st	+3.5
9-29	At Bal.	L	2-13		6	13	McElroy	Pettitte		87-72	1st	+3.5
9-30	At Bal.	L	1-9		7	12	Mussina	Cone		87-73	1st	+2.5
10-1	At Bal.	L	3-7		9	10	Mercedes	Hernandez		87-74	1st	+2.5

Monthly records: April (15-8), May (13-13), June (10-15), July (18-8), August (18-12), September (13-17), October (0-1).
*Innings, if other than nine. †First game of a doubleheader. ‡Second game of a doubleheader.

HIGHLIGHTS

High point: Mike Piazza's fly ball to deep center field, caught by Bernie Williams, in World Series Game 5 at Shea Stadium. With that out, the Yankees had a third straight World Series crown and distinction as baseball's first three-peaters since the 1972-74 Oakland A's. They also became the first team to win four titles in five years since the 1949-53 Yankees won five in a row.

Low point: A 17-4 loss to Chicago at Yankee Stadium on June 18. The Bombers were embarrassed at home, getting swept in four games by the upstart White Sox, and starter Orlando Hernandez lasted just two-thirds of an inning before leaving with elbow problems. The team was falling apart, trade discussions were swirling and everyone was getting testy.

Turning point: Three positives happened in one weekend: David Justice arrived from Cleveland June 30, ending rampant trade speculation; El Duque pitched well the next day after sitting out 13 days with an injury, and Roger Clemens followed that with a good outing after sitting out with a groin injury. Clemens and Justice became second-half keys.

Most valuable player: Justice. He came through with numerous big hits, both in the regular season and the postseason, and the team played infinitely better with him around.

Most valuable pitcher: A tie between the two setup men, righthander Jeff Nelson and lefty Mike Stanton. They pitched brilliantly in the early going, when the Yanks jumped out to a 22-9 record, before tiring in the second half. After resting in September, both contributed strong postseasons.

Most improved player: In the wake of a disappointing 1999 season as a part-time player, Jorge Posada took over full-time catching duties and was fantastic. He woke up at the plate (28 homers, 86 RBIs), rediscovered his cannon arm (nailing 34-of-104 basestealers) and became adept at calling a game.

Most pleasant surprise: Glenallen Hill, acquired to provide righthanded bench power, batted .411 with 10 homers and 19 RBIs in a blazing August. He gave the Yanks far more than anyone could have hoped when they got him from the Cubs.

Key injuries: Third baseman Scott Brosius bruised his rib cage on the second day of the season and missed 25 games. ... 19-game winner Andy Pettitte

missed most of April with a strained muscle in his back. ... Hernandez endured two separate respites in an effort to heal his elbow and back. ... Clemens missed time with a groin injury in June. ... Outfielder Shane Spencer tore the ACL in his right knee in July and missed the entire second half. ... Second baseman Chuck Knoblauch injured his elbow and wrist and played in just 102 games. ... Righthander Ramiro Mendoza went down in June with weakness in his shoulder and he wound up needing season-ending surgery. ... Outfielder Bernie Williams missed chunks of August and September while coping with a strained rib cage. ... Outfielder Paul O'Neill was hampered late by a hip pointer. ... Righthander David Cone, after finally showing signs of turning around his miserable season, dislocated his left shoulder in September.

Notable: Shortstop Derek Jeter, in just his fifth season, reached the 1,000-hit milestone. ... Williams established career highs with 30 homers and 121 RBIs. ...The Yankees' bullpen, mostly reliable, coughed up five potential Clemens victories.

—KEN DAVIDOFF

RECORDS

2000 regular-season record: 87-74 (1st in A.L. East); 44-36 at home; 43-38 on road; 36-30 vs. East; 26-28 vs. Central; 25-16 vs. West; 22-24 vs. lefthanded starters; 65-50 vs. righthanded starters; 80-62 on grass; 7-12 on turf; 34-25 in daytime; 53-49 at night; 20-18 in one-run games; 4-4 in extra-inning games; 0-0 in doubleheaders.

Team record past five years: 487-322 (.602, ranks 1st in league in that span).

TEAM LEADERS

Batting average: Derek Jeter (.339).
At-bats: Derek Jeter (593).
Runs: Derek Jeter (119).
Hits: Derek Jeter (201).
Total Bases: Bernie Williams (304).
Doubles: Tino Martinez, Bernie Williams (37).
Triples: Bernie Williams (6).
Home runs: Bernie Williams (30).
Runs batted in: Bernie Williams (121).
Stolen bases: Derek Jeter (22).
Slugging percentage: Bernie Williams (.566).

On-base percentage: Jorge Posada (.417).
Wins: Andy Pettitte (19).
Earned-run average: Roger Clemens (3.70).
Complete games: Orlando Hernandez, Andy Pettitte (3).
Shutouts: Ramiro Mendoza, Andy Pettitte (1).
Saves: Mariano Rivera (36).
Innings pitched: Andy Pettitte (204.2).
Strikeouts: Roger Clemens (188).

GAMES BY POSITION

Catcher: Jorge Posada 142, Chris Turner 36, Jim Leyritz 2.
First base: Tino Martinez 154, Jorge Posada 12, Clay Bellinger 10, Luis Sojo 7, Scott Brosius 2, Jim Leyritz 1, Chris Turner 1.
Second base: Chuck Knoblauch 82, Jose Vizcaino 62, Luis Sojo 25, Clay Bellinger 21, Wilson Delgado 14, Alfonso Soriano 1.
Third base: Scott Brosius 134, Clay Bellinger 18, Luis Sojo 10, Alfonso Soriano 10, Jose Vizcaino 6, Wilson Delgado 5.
Shortstop: Derek Jeter 148, Wilson Delgado 11, Alfonso Soriano 9, Clay Bellinger 6, Luis Sojo 2, Jose Vizcaino 2.
Outfield: Paul O'Neill 140, Bernie Williams 137, David Justice 60, Ricky Ledee 49, Clay Bellinger 46, Shane Spencer 40, Ryan Thompson 31, Luis Polonia 28, Felix Jose 14, Glenallen Hill 12, Roberto Kelly 10, Jose Canseco 5, Lance Johnson 4, Scott Brosius 3.
Designated hitter: Shane Spencer 33, Jose Canseco 26, Glenallen Hill 24, Chuck Knoblauch 20, David Justice 18, Jim Leyritz 15, Ricky Ledee 10, Luis Polonia 7, Jorge Posada 4, Jose Vizcaino 4, Bernie Williams 4, Lance Johnson 3, Felix Jose 2, Paul O'Neill 2, Scott Brosius 1, Alfonso Soriano 1.

TOP DRAFT CHOICES

1. **David Parrish**, C, U. of Michigan.
2. **Danny Borrell**, LHP, Wake Forest U.
3. **Jason Grove**, OF, Washington State U.
4. **Matt Smith**, LHP, Oklahoma State U.
5. **Andy Beal**, LHP, Vanderbilt University.
6. **Jeremy King**, RHP, DeSoto H.S., Nocatee, Fla.
7. **Mitch Jones**, OF, Arizona State U.
8. **Sam Bozanich**, 2B, U. of Alabama.
9. **Eric Reynolds**, LHP, Itawamba (Miss.) J.C.
10. **Jason Anderson**, RHP, U. of Illinois.

OAKLAND ATHLETICS
AMERICAN LEAGUE WEST DIVISION

Athletics
2001 SCHEDULE
Home games shaded; D—Day game (games starting before 5 p.m.)
*—All-Star Game at Safeco Field (Seattle)

APRIL
SUN	MON	TUE	WED	THU	FRI	SAT
1	2 SEA	3 SEA	4 SEA	5	6 ANA	7 ANA
8 ANA	9 D	10 SEA	11 SEA	12 SEA	13 TEX	14 TEX
15 TEX	16	17 ANA	18 ANA	19 TEX	20 TEX	21 TEX
22 TEX	23 D	24 CWS	25 CWS	26 CWS	27 NYY	28 NYY
29 NYY	30					

MAY
SUN	MON	TUE	WED	THU	FRI	SAT
		1 TOR	2 TOR	3 TOR	4 D BOS	5 D BOS
6 BOS	7	8 TOR	9 TOR	10 TOR	11 BOS	12 D BOS
13 D BOS	14	15 NYY	16 NYY	17 D NYY	18 CWS	19 D CWS
20 D CWS	21	22 KC	23 KC	24	25 MIN	26 DH MIN
27 D MIN	28	29 TB	30 TB	31 D TB		

JUNE
SUN	MON	TUE	WED	THU	FRI	SAT
					1 BAL	2 D BAL
3 D BAL	4	5 ANA	6 ANA	7 ANA	8 SF	9 D SF
10 D SF	11	12 SD	13 SD	14 D SD	15 SF	16 D SF
17 D SF	18 SEA	19 SEA	20 SEA	21 D SEA	22 SEA	23 D TEX
24 D TEX	25	26 SEA	27 SEA	28 D SEA	29 TEX	30 TEX

JULY
SUN	MON	TUE	WED	THU	FRI	SAT
1 TEX	2 ANA	3 ANA	4 D ANA	5	6 ARI	7 ARI
8 ARI	9	10 *	11	12 LA	13 LA	14 D LA
15 COL	16 D COL	17 COL	18 MIN	19 MIN	20 KC	21 KC
22 KC	23	24 MIN	25 MIN	26 MIN	27 KC	28 KC
29 KC	30	31 CLE				

AUGUST
SUN	MON	TUE	WED	THU	FRI	SAT
			1 CLE	2 CLE	3 D DET	4 DET
5 D DET	6 D	7 BOS	8 BOS	9 BOS	10 D NYY	11 NYY
12 D NYY	13	14 TOR	15 TOR	16 D TOR	17 CWS	18 D CWS
19 CWS	20	21 CLE	22 CLE	23 D CLE	24 DET	25 D DET
26 DET	27	28 BAL	29 BAL	30 BAL	31 TB	

SEPTEMBER
SUN	MON	TUE	WED	THU	FRI	SAT
						1 D TB
2 TB	3 BAL	4 BAL	5 BAL	6	7 TB	8 D TB
9 TB	10 TEX	11 TEX	12 D TEX	13 ANA	14 ANA	15 D ANA
16 ANA	17	18 TEX	19 TEX	20 TEX	21 SEA	22 D SEA
23 SEA	24	25 ANA	26 ANA	27 ANA	28 SEA	29 SEA
30 D SEA						

2001 SEASON
CLUB DIRECTORY

Owners
Stephen C. Schott
Ken Hofmann
President
Michael P. Crowley
Vice president and general manager
Billy Beane
Assistant general manager
Paul DePodesta
Special assistant to general manager
Bill Rigney
Director of player development
Keith Lieppman
Director of player personnel
J.P. Ricciardi
Director of scouting
Grady Fuson
Director of minor league operations
Ted Polakowski
Director of baseball administration
Pam Pitts
Traveling secretary
Mickey Morabito
Scouting and player dev. coordinator
Danny McCormack
Baseball operations assistant
Dave Forst
V.p., broadcasting and communications
Ken Pries
Director of public relations
Jim Young
Baseball information manager
Mike Selleck
Broadcasting manager
Robert Buan
Vice president, stadium operations
David Rinetti
Vice president, sales and marketing
David Alioto
Director of corporate sales
Franklin Lowe

Dir. of promotions and special events
Susan Weiglein
Director of ticket sales
Steve Fanelli
Director of business services
David Lozow
Executive assistant
Carolyn Jones
Exec. assistant, baseball operations
Betty Shinoda
Team physician
Dr. Allan Pont
Team orthopedist
Dr. Jerrald Goldman
Trainers
Larry Davis
Steven Sayles
Equipment manager
Steve Vucinich
Visiting clubhouse manager
Mike Thalblum
Special assignment scout
Dick Bogard
National cross-checkers
Ron Hopkins
Chris Pittaro
Major League advance scout
Bob Johnson
Supervisor of international scouting
Eric Kubota
Scouts
Steve Bowden, Tom Clark, Ruben Escalera, Kelly Heath, Tim Holt, John Kuehl, Rick Magnante, Gary McGraw, Kelsey Mucker, Billy Owens, John Poloni, Jim Pransky, Will Shock, Rich Sparks, Ron Vaughn

MINOR LEAGUE AFFILIATES

Class	Team	League	Manager
AAA	Sacramento	Pacific Coast	Bob Geren
AA	Midland	Texas	Tony DeFrancesco
A	Modesto	California	Greg Sparks
A	Vancouver	Northwest	Dave Joppie
A	Visalia	California	Juan Navarette
Rookie	Scottsdale A's	Arizona	John Kuehl

BROADCAST INFORMATION
Radio: KABL-AM (960).
TV: KICU-TV (Channel 36).
Cable TV: Fox Sports Bay Area.

SPRING TRAINING
Ballpark (city): Phoenix Municipal Stadium (Phoenix, Ariz.).
Ticket information: 602-392-0074.

Follow the Athletics all season at: www.sportingnews.com/baseball/teams/athletics/

SPRING TRAINING ROSTER

Manager—Art Howe (18).
Coaches—Thad Bosley (41), Brad Fischer (35), Ken Macha (39), Rick Peterson (47), Mike Quade (45), Ron Washington (38).

No.	PITCHERS	B/T	Ht./Wt.	Born	2000 clubs
36	Belitz, Todd	L/L	6-3/200	10-23-75	Durham, Sacramento, Oakland
	Bradford, Chad	R/R	6-5/205	9-14-74	Charlotte, Chicago A.L.
49	Enochs, Chris	R/R	6-3/225	10-11-75	Visalia
	Guthrie, Mark	R/L	6-4/215	9-22-65	Chicago N.L., Tampa Bay, Toronto
32	Harville, Chad	R/R	5-9/180	9-16-76	Sacramento
31	Heredia, Gil	R/R	6-1/221	10-26-65	Oakland
15	Hudson, Tim	R/R	6-0/160	7-14-75	Oakland
58	Ireland, Eric	R/R	6-1/170	3-11-77	Round Rock
44	Isringhausen, Jason	R/R	6-3/210	9-7-72	Oakland
	Lidle, Cory	R/R	5-11/180	3-22-72	Durham, Tampa Bay
52	Magnante, Mike	L/L	6-1/185	6-17-65	Oakland, Sacramento
33	Mathews, T.J.	R/R	6-1/214	1-19-70	Oakland, Sacramento
45	Mecir, Jim	B/R	6-1/210	5-16-70	Tampa Bay, Oakland
59	Miller, Justin	R/R	6-2/195	8-27-77	Midland, Sacramento
20	Mulder, Mark	L/L	6-6/200	8-5-77	Sacramento, Oakland
40	Olivares, Omar	R/R	6-1/205	7-6-67	Oakland, Modesto, Sacramento
57	Pena, Juan	L/L	6-3/165	6-4-79	Modesto
53	Snow, Bert	R/R	6-1/190	3-23-77	Sacramento, Midland
29	Tam, Jeff	R/R	6-1/202	8-19-70	Oakland
54	Vasquez, Leo	L/L	6-4/193	7-1-73	Midland
51	Vizcaino, Luis	R/R	5-11/169	6-1-77	Oakland, Sacramento
75	Zito, Barry	L/L	6-4/205	5-13-78	Sacramento, Oakland

No.	CATCHERS	B/T	Ht./Wt.	Born	2000 clubs
13	Fasano, Sal	R/R	6-2/230	8-10-71	Oakland
55	Hernandez, Ramon	R/R	6-0/227	5-20-76	Oakland

No.	INFIELDERS	B/T	Ht./Wt.	Born	2000 clubs
49	Bellhorn, Mark	B/R	6-4/214	8-23-74	Sacramento, Oakland
3	Chavez, Eric	L/R	6-0/204	12-7-77	Oakland
16	Giambi, Jason	L/R	6-3/235	1-8-71	Oakland
7	Giambi, Jeremy	L/L	6-0/200	9-30-74	Oakland, Sacramento
37	Hart, Jason	R/R	6-3/225	9-5-77	Midland, Sacramento
5	Jaha, John	R/R	6-1/217	5-27-66	Oakland, Sacramento, Modesto
11	Menechino, Frank	R/R	5-9/175	1-7-71	Oakland, Sacramento
2	Ortiz, Jose	R/R	5-9/177	6-13-77	Sacramento, Oakland
5	Piatt, Adam	R/R	6-2/195	2-8-76	Sacramento, Oakland
9	Saenz, Olmedo	R/R	6-0/185	10-8-70	Oakland, Sacramento
21	Salazar, Oscar	R/R	6-0/155	6-27-78	Sacramento, Midland
4	Tejada, Miguel	R/R	5-9/188	5-25-76	Oakland
50	Valdez, Mario	L/R	6-1/210	11-19-74	Salt Lake, Sacramento, Visalia, Oakland

No.	OUTFIELDERS	B/T	Ht./Wt.	Born	2000 clubs
22	Byrnes, Eric	R/R	6-2/205	2-16-76	Midland, Sacramento, Oakland
28	Christenson, Ryan	R/R	6-0/210	3-28-74	Oakland
	Damon, Johnny	L/L	6-2/190	11-5-73	Kansas City
24	Encarnacion, Mario	R/R	6-2/205	9-24-77	Sacramento, Modesto
12	Long, Terrence	L/L	6-1/190	2-29-76	Sacramento, Oakland

BALLPARK INFORMATION

Ballpark (capacity, surface)
Network Associates Coliseum (43,662, grass)

Address
Oakland Athletics
7677 Oakport St., Suite 200
Oakland, CA 94621

Official website
www.oaklandathletics.com

Business phone
510-638-4900

Ticket information
510-638-4627

Ticket prices
$30 (plaza club)
$25 (MVP infield)
$19 (field level-infield)
$18 (field level, plaza-infield)
$16 (plaza)
$8 (upper reserved)
$6 (bleachers)

Field dimensions (from home plate)
To left field at foul line, 330 feet
To center field, 400 feet
To right field at foul line, 330 feet

First game played
April 17, 1968 (Orioles 4, Athletics 1)

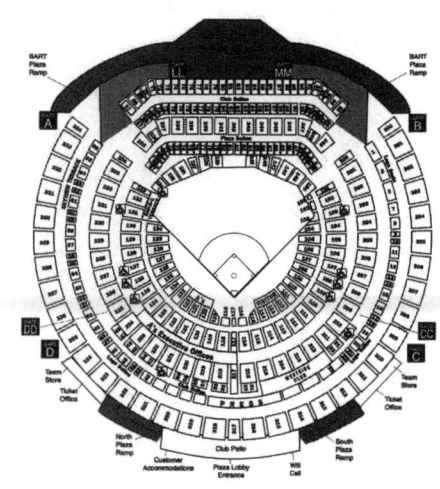

Date	Opp.	Res.	Score	(inn.*)	Hits	Opp. hits	Winning pitcher	Losing pitcher	Save	Record	Pos.	GB
4-3	Det.	L	4-7		4	11	Nomo	Appier	Jones	0-1	T2nd	1.0
4-4	Det.	W	3-1		5	2	Hudson	Nitkowski	Isringhausen	1-1	2nd	1.0
4-5	Det.	W	8-2		10	6	Olivares	Moehler		2-1	T1st	...
4-7	Chi.	L	6-7		6	9	Eyre	Magnante	Foulke	2-2	T3rd	1.0
4-8	Chi.	L	3-7		7	13	Sirotka	Mahay		2-3	4th	1.0
4-9	Chi.	W	14-2		9	9	Appier	Wells		3-3	T3rd	1.0
4-10	Cle.	L	4-9		8	14	Kamieniecki	Tam		3-4	4th	1.5
4-11	Cle.	L	1-5		4	7	Nagy	Olivares		3-5	4th	2.0
4-12	Cle.	L	0-5		5	8	Wright	Heredia		3-6	4th	2.5
4-14	At Bos.	W	13-6		11	12	Appier	Rose		4-6	4th	2.0
4-15	At Bos.	L	2-14		6	13	P. Martinez	Hudson		4-7	4th	3.0
4-16	At Bos.	L	4-5		10	9	Lowe	Mathews		4-8	4th	4.0
4-17	At Bos.	W	1-0		10	4	Heredia	Fassero	Isringhausen	5-8	4th	3.5
4-18	At Cle.	W	8-5		9	9	Mulder	Nagy	Isringhausen	6-8	T3rd	2.5
4-19	At Cle.	W	10-5		12	12	Appier	Wright		7-8	3rd	1.5
4-20	At Cle.	L	5-9		15	14	Burba	Hudson		7-9	3rd	2.0
4-21	Bal.	L	9-11		11	15	Ponson	Olivares	Timlin	7-10	3rd	3.0
4-22	Bal.	L	3-4		9	10	Mercedes	Heredia	Groom	7-11	4th	4.0
4-23	Bal.	W	3-2	(11)	7	7	Isringhausen	Worrell		8-11	3rd	4.0
4-24	Tor.	L	2-3		10	7	Wells	Appier	Koch	8-12	4th	4.0
4-25	Tor.	W	11-2		12	4	Hudson	Halladay		9-12	3rd	4.0
4-26	Tor.	L	2-4		6	9	Carpenter	Olivares	Koch	9-13	3rd	4.0
4-28	At Min.	W	5-2		6	7	Heredia	Radke	Isringhausen	10-13	3rd	3.0
4-29	At Min.	W	6-2	(10)	7	10	Mathews	Guardado		11-13	3rd	3.0
4-30	At Min.	W	8-2		14	7	Hudson	Bergman		12-13	3rd	2.0
5-1	At K.C.	W	7-5		7	9	Olivares	Reichert	Isringhausen	13-13	T2nd	1.5
5-2	At K.C.	L	7-8	(10)	10	14	Rakers	Isringhausen		13-14	T2nd	2.5
5-3	At K.C.	W	14-5		20	15	Heredia	Suppan		14-14	T2nd	1.5
5-5	At Tex.	L	16-17		16	21	Wetteland	Tam		14-15	3rd	1.5
5-6	At Tex.	L	10-11		14	17	Wetteland	Isringhausen		14-16	3rd	2.5
5-7	At Tex.	W	7-6		9	12	Olivares	Davis	Jones	15-16	3rd	2.5
5-8	At Ana.	L	8-9		10	17	Petkovsek	Mathews	Percival	15-17	3rd	2.5
5-9	At Ana.	W	5-2		9	9	Heredia	Hill	Isringhausen	16-17	3rd	2.5
5-10	At Ana.	W	7-4		13	9	Isringhausen	Petkovsek		17-17	2nd	1.5
5-11	Sea.	W	7-6		10	8	Hudson	Meche	Isringhausen	18-17	2nd	0.5
5-12	Sea.	W	9-7		6	10	Mathews	Sasaki		19-17	1st	+0.5
5-13	Sea.	L	4-6		8	6	Tomko	Appier	Mesa	19-18	2nd	0.5
5-14	Sea.	W	7-2		6	10	Heredia	Abbott		20-18	1st	+0.5
5-15	K.C.	W	6-3		7	7	Mulder	Fussell	Isringhausen	21-18	1st	+0.5
5-16	K.C.	L	7-8		11	11	Reichert	D. Jones	Spradlin	21-19	2nd	0.5
5-17	K.C.	L	3-4		3	8	Batista	Olivares	Spradlin	21-20	2nd	1.5
5-18	Min.	L	5-10		7	18	Redman	Vizcaino		21-21	3rd	2.0
5-19	Min.	L	2-3		3	9	Radke	Heredia		21-22	4th	3.0
5-20	Min.	L	0-3		3	9	Milton	Mulder	Guardado	21-23	4th	3.0
5-21	Min.	W	13-4		15	11	Hudson	Bergman		22-23	4th	3.0
5-23	At T.B.	L	4-6		10	11	Rekar	Olivares	Hernandez	22-24	4th	3.0
5-24	At T.B.	W	9-2		12	6	Appier	Gooden	Tam	23-24	4th	2.0
5-25	At T.B.	W	6-3		8	8	Heredia	Yan	Isringhausen	24-24	4th	2.0
5-26	At Bal.	L	3-8		6	13	Erickson	Mulder		24-25	4th	2.0
5-27	At Bal.	W	4-0		11	2	Hudson	Johnson		25-25	4th	2.0
5-29	At N.Y.	L	1-4		2	6	Pettitte	Olivares		25-26	4th	2.5
5-30	At N.Y.	W	7-4		11	10	Appier	Mendoza	Isringhausen	26-26	4th	1.5
5-31	At N.Y.	W	8-7		9	11	Heredia	Cone	Isringhausen	27-26	T3rd	0.5
6-2	S.F.	W	5-4		8	10	Mulder	Ortiz	Isringhausen	28-26	T2nd	0.5
6-3	S.F.	W	9-7		11	9	D. Jones	Embree	Isringhausen	29-26	1st	+0.5
6-4	S.F.	L	2-18		7	19	Estes	Olivares		29-27	T3rd	0.5
6-5	S.D.	W	3-2	(10)	5	4	Isringhausen	Almanzar		30-27	3rd	0.5
6-6	S.D.	W	5-4		7	7	Heredia	Lopez	Isringhausen	31-27	2nd	0.5
6-7	S.D.	W	10-4		13	10	Service	Clement	Jones	32-27	1st	+0.5
6-9	At L.A.	W	3-1		4	5	Tam	Osuna	Isringhausen	33-27	1st	+1.5
6-10	At L.A.	L	2-7		7	13	Brown	Olivares		33-28	1st	+0.5
6-11	At L.A.	W	6-0		7	7	Appier	Gagne		34-28	1st	+0.5
6-12	At Min.	L	2-7		9	8	Milton	Heredia		34-29	2nd	0.5
6-13	At Min.	W	6-5		13	12	Mulder	Mays	Isringhausen	35-29	2nd	0.5
6-14	At Min.	W	9-6		16	8	Hudson	Bergman		36-29	1st	+0.5
6-16	At K.C.	W	8-3		11	8	D. Jones	Reichert	Tam	37-29	1st	+1.0
6-17	At K.C.	W	10-4		13	7	Appier	Witasick		38-29	1st	+1.0
6-18	At K.C.	W	21-3		21	8	Heredia	D'Amico		39-29	1st	+1.0
6-19	Bal.	W	13-12	(10)	14	16	Tam	Timlin		40-29	1st	+2.0
6-20	Bal.	W	8-5		9	9	Hudson	Ponson	Isringhausen	41-29	1st	+2.0
6-21	Bal.	W	10-3		15	8	Prieto	Mussina		42-29	1st	+2.0
6-23	K.C.	W	10-6		13	12	Appier	Durbin		43-29	1st	+1.5
6-24	K.C.	L	3-8		9	13	Bottalico	Heredia		43-30	1st	+0.5

Date	Opp.	Res.	Score	(inn.*)	Hits	Opp. hits	Winning pitcher	Losing pitcher	Save	Record	Pos.	GB
6-25	K.C.	W	4-3		9	7	Mulder	Suppan	Isringhausen	44-30	1st	+0.5
6-27	Tex.	W	7-6		10	10	Hudson	Perisho	Isringhausen	45-30	1st	+0.5
6-28	Tex.	L	3-5		6	10	Helling	Appier	Wetteland	45-31	1st	+0.5
6-29	Tex.	L	1-3		8	9	Loaiza	Heredia	Wetteland	45-32	2nd	0.5
6-30	At Ana.	L	0-7		3	12	Cooper	Mulder		45-33	2nd	0.5
7-1	At Ana.	L	2-7		3	8	Washburn	Prieto		45-34	2nd	1.5
7-2	At Ana.	W	10-3		12	8	Hudson	Belcher		46-34	2nd	1.5
7-3	At Tex.	L	3-8		9	9	Helling	Appier		46-35	2nd	2.5
7-4	At Tex.	L	7-10		11	13	Davis	Service	Wetteland	46-36	2nd	2.5
7-5	At Tex.	L	4-9		11	17	Rogers	Mulder		46-37	2nd	3.5
7-7	Ari.	W	5-4	(11)	11	9	Tam	Daal		47-37	2nd	2.0
7-8	Ari.	W	8-7	(10)	13	9	Isringhausen	Swindell		48-37	2nd	2.0
7-9	Ari.	L	2-4		6	13	Johnson	Heredia	Mantei	48-38	2nd	3.0
7-13	At S.F.	L	2-4		7	6	Ortiz	Mulder	Nen	48-39	2nd	3.0
7-14	At S.F.	L	2-4		5	10	Gardner	Appier	Nen	48-40	2nd	4.0
7-15	At S.F.	W	6-2		16	9	Heredia	Rueter		49-40	2nd	3.0
7-17†	At Col.	W	11-10		13	12	Magnante	White	Isringhausen	50-40		
7-17‡	At Col.	L	9-10	(10)	12	15	DeJean	Isringhausen		50-41		3.0
7-18	At Col.	L	3-18		8	21	Astacio	Mulder		50-42	2nd	4.0
7-19	Sea.	L	3-6		7	10	Moyer	Appier	Sasaki	50-43	T2nd	5.0
7-20	Sea.	W	5-4		5	9	Heredia	Sele	Isringhausen	51-43	2nd	4.0
7-21	Ana.	L	3-12		8	16	Washburn	Hudson		51-44	3rd	5.0
7-22	Ana.	W	10-3		18	5	Zito	Cooper		52-44	T2nd	5.0
7-23	Ana.	W	5-0		11	6	Mulder	Hill		53-44	2nd	4.0
7-24	At Sea.	L	4-6		9	11	Moyer	Appier	Sasaki	53-45	2nd	5.0
7-25	At Sea.	W	8-7		11	11	Heredia	Sele	Isringhausen	54-45	2nd	4.0
7-26	At Sea.	W	6-1		5	8	Hudson	Abbott		55-45	2nd	3.0
7-27	Bos.	L	4-5	(10)	10	8	Garces	Tam	Lowe	55-46	2nd	3.0
7-28	Bos.	L	1-4		5	7	P. Martinez	Mulder	Lowe	55-47	2nd	4.0
7-29	Bos.	W	12-1		11	7	Appier	Fassero		56-47	2nd	4.0
7-30	Bos.	W	5-2		3	6	Heredia	Arrojo	Isringhausen	57-47	2nd	4.0
7-31	Tor.	W	6-1		12	4	Hudson	Wells		58-47	2nd	3.0
8-1	Tor.	W	3-1	(10)	6	7	Isringhausen	Koch		59-47	2nd	3.0
8-2	Tor.	W	5-4		12	10	Mecir	Guthrie	Isringhausen	60-47	2nd	2.0
8-4	At Chi.	W	5-3		8	8	Appier	Sirotka	Isringhausen	61-47	2nd	1.0
8-5	At Chi.	L	3-4	(10)	7	9	Foulke	Mathews		61-48	2nd	2.0
8-6	At Chi.	L	0-13		5	15	Baldwin	Hudson		61-49	2nd	3.0
8-8	At N.Y.	L	3-4		7	6	Rivera	Isringhausen		61-50	2nd	5.0
8-9	At N.Y.	L	1-12		9	12	Pettitte	Appier		61-51	2nd	5.0
8-10	At N.Y.	L	6-12		13	15	Cone	Mulder		61-52	2nd	6.0
8-11	Det.	L	4-11		9	15	Weaver	Heredia		61-53	2nd	7.0
8-12	Det.	W	9-5		11	9	Hudson	Bernero		62-53	2nd	6.0
8-13	Det.	L	3-5		10	11	Moehler	Zito	Jones	62-54	2nd	6.0
8-14	Cle.	W	8-1		13	8	Appier	Bere		63-54	2nd	5.0
8-15	Cle.	W	5-3		6	10	Mulder	Burba	Isringhausen	64-54	2nd	4.0
8-16	Cle.	W	7-6		12	9	D. Jones	Wickman		65-54	2nd	3.0
8-18	At Det.	L	1-10		3	17	Nomo	Hudson		65-55	2nd	3.0
8-19	At Det.	L	3-4		10	9	Moehler	Zito	Jones	65-56	2nd	3.0
8-20	At Det.	W	5-4	(11)	14	10	Isringhausen	Cruz	Tam	66-56	2nd	2.0
8-21	At Det.	L	1-3		5	8	Sparks	Mulder	Jones	66-57	2nd	2.5
8-22	At Cle.	L	6-14		12	16	Finley	Heredia		66-58	2nd	3.5
8-23	At Cle.	L	5-7		10	12	Shuey	Hudson	Wickman	66-59	2nd	3.5
8-24	At Cle.	W	11-7		12	11	Zito	Woodard	Mecir	67-59	2nd	2.5
8-25	N.Y.	W	8-1		8	5	Appier	Cone		68-59	2nd	1.5
8-26	N.Y.	L	6-10		10	14	Hernandez	Mulder	Rivera	68-60	2nd	2.5
8-27	N.Y.	L	5-7		6	10	Neagle	Mecir	Rivera	68-61	2nd	2.5
8-28	Chi.	W	3-0		6	1	Hudson	Parque		69-61	2nd	1.5
8-29	Chi.	L	0-3		5	7	Baldwin	Zito	Foulke	69-62	2nd	2.5
8-30	Chi.	L	3-8		9	11	Sirotka	Appier	Howry	69-63	2nd	2.5
9-1	At Tor.	L	3-4		10	14	Frascatore	D. Jones		69-64	2nd	2.5
9-2	At Tor.	W	8-0		9	5	Heredia	Trachsel	Mecir	70-64	2nd	2.5
9-3	At Tor.	W	4-3		7	8	Hudson	Loaiza	Mecir	71-64	2nd	2.5
9-4	At Tor.	W	10-0		19	2	Zito	Wells		72-64	2nd	1.5
9-5	At Bos.	L	3-10		6	12	Schourek	Appier		72-65	2nd	2.5
9-6	At Bos.	W	6-4		13	9	Mulder	Arrojo	Mecir	73-65	2nd	1.5
9-8	T.B.	L	0-4		2	5	Lidle	Heredia	Creek	73-66	2nd	2.0
9-9	T.B.	W	10-0		14	2	Hudson	Lopez		74-66	2nd	2.0
9-10	T.B.	W	11-0		12	5	Zito	Wilson		75-66	2nd	2.0
9-11	T.B.	W	5-1		7	6	Appier	Creek		76-66	2nd	1.0
9-12	Min.	W	5-3		10	6	Mulder	Radke	Isringhausen	77-66	2nd	1.0
9-13	Min.	L	6-7		9	17	Milton	Heredia	Hawkins	77-67	2nd	2.0
9-15	At T.B.	W	17-3		20	4	Zito	Lopez		78-67	2nd	2.0
9-16	At T.B.	W	5-2		8	8	Hudson	Wilson	Isringhausen	79-67	2nd	2.0
9-18	At Bal.	W	12-3		17	8	Appier	Rapp		80-67	2nd	2.5
9-19	At Bal.	W	7-4		8	13	Mecir	Johnson	Isringhausen	81-67	2nd	2.5
9-20†	At Bal.	L	0-2		4	4	McElroy	Zito	Kohlmeier	81-68		
9-20‡	At Bal.	W	4-0		10	9	Heredia	Mercedes		82-68	2nd	3.0

Date	Opp.	Res.	Score	(inn.*)	Hits	Opp. hits	Winning pitcher	Losing pitcher	Save	Record	Pos.	GB
9-21	At Sea.	W	5-2		6	5	Hudson	Moyer	Isringhausen	83-68	2nd	2.0
9-22	At Sea.	W	8-3		9	7	Olivares	Garcia	Service	84-68	2nd	1.0
9-23	At Sea.	W	8-2		10	2	Appier	Rhodes		85-68	1st	...
9-24	At Sea.	L	2-3		8	6	Halama	Prieto	Sasaki	85-69	2nd	1.0
9-25	Ana.	W	7-5		10	11	Zito	Belcher		86-69	2nd	0.5
9-26	Ana.	W	10-3		8	7	Hudson	Schoeneweis		87-69	2nd	0.5
9-27	Ana.	W	9-7		10	13	D. Jones	Holtz	Isringhausen	88-69	2nd	0.5
9-28	Ana.	L	3-6	(14)	8	12	Holtz	Service	Percival	88-70	2nd	0.5
9-29	Tex.	W	7-5		8	12	Mecir	Cordero	Isringhausen	89-70	1st	+0.5
9-30	Tex.	W	23-2		24	9	Zito	Oliver		90-70	1st	+0.5
10-1	Tex.	W	3-0		8	6	Hudson	Glynn	Isringhausen	91-70	1st	+0.5

Monthly records: April (12-13), May (15-13), June (18-7), July (13-14), August (11-16), September (21-7), October (1-0).
*Innings, if other than nine. †First game of a doubleheader. ‡Second game of a doubleheader.

HIGHLIGHTS

High point: The A's won their first division title since 1992 by beating Texas 3-0 on the final day. Adding spice to the celebration were Tim Hudson's 20th victory and Jason Isringhausen's 33rd save. With the win, Oakland finished a half game ahead of wild-card winner Seattle and avoided having to travel to Tampa for a season-extending makeup game.

Low point: After being swept at New York, the A's lost 11-4 to the Tigers on August 11 and lost 11-4 to the Tigers—Oakland's season-high sixth consecutive defeat. The loss pushed the A's seven games behind the first-place Mariners.

Turning point: After missing eight of 13 games with a shoulder injury, Jason Giambi returned to action September 2 and the A's took off. Giambi hit .400 the rest of the way (38-for-95) with 13 homers and 32 RBIs and Oakland finished on a 22-6 tear.

Most valuable player: Giambi, the league's MVP, continued his amazing rise up the star charts. The first baseman established career highs in average (.333), homers (43) and RBIs (137) and his 137 walks and .474 on-base percentage led both leagues.

Most valuable pitcher: In less than two full seasons, Hudson has established himself as one of the league's elite. An All-Star at age 24, Hudson tied for the league lead in wins (20) and raised his career record to 31-8. Opponents batted only .227 against him, second lowest in the league.

Most improved player: Miguel Tejada is being compared to the Big Three of shortstops—Alex Rodriguez, Nomar Garciaparra and Derek Jeter. Tejada has cut back on mental errors and his defense is spectacular. So is his bat, which produced 30 homers and 115 RBIs.

Most pleasant surprise: Minor league free-agent pickup Jeff Tam finished with a 2.63 ERA out of the bullpen. The 30-year-old sinkerballer allowed just three homers in 85 2/3 innings.

Key injuries: The A's lost designated hitter John Jaha, their cleanup hitter, to season-ending shoulder surgery. That took a much-needed righthanded threat out of the lefty-heavy Oakland lineup and left Jason Giambi without much protection. ... Olmedo Saenz, who took over as the A's top righthanded slugger, missed nearly two months with a hamstring injury late in the season.

Notable: The A's set record with 91 games, an improvement of four over 1999, and spent 26 days in sole possession of first place in the A.L. West. Most of those days were in June. From June 29 until September 29, the A's were in first only once, a brief one-day tie with Seattle. ... The A's set a major league record with 14 grand slams, two more than Atlanta hit in 1997. Jason Giambi had four. ... The A's set Oakland records for average (.270), runs (947), hits (1.501) and RBIs (908). ... Jason Giambi won the A.L. MVP and the A's had the runners-up in each of the other award categories. Art Howe was second in Manager of the Year voting, Hudson was second in Cy Young balloting and center fielder Terrence Long was second in Rookie of the Year voting

—SUSAN SLUSSER

RECORDS

2000 regular-season record: 91-70 (1st in A.L. West); 47-34 at home; 44-36 on road; 30-20 vs. East; 28-27 vs. Central; 33-23 vs. West; 21-26 vs. lefthanded starters; 70-44 vs. righthanded starters; 79-67 on grass; 12-3 on turf; 35-25 in daytime; 56-45 at night; 21-19 in one-run games; 8-5 in extra-inning games; 0-0-2 in doubleheaders.
Team record past five years: 395-414 (.488, ranks 9th in league in that span).

TEAM LEADERS

Batting average: Jason Giambi (.333).
At-bats: Miguel Tejada (607).
Runs: Jason Giambi (108).
Hits: Jason Giambi (170).
Total Bases: Jason Giambi (330).
Doubles: Ben Grieve (40).
Triples: Adam Piatt (5).
Home runs: Jason Giambi (43).
Runs batted in: Jason Giambi (137).
Stolen bases: Randy Velarde (9).
Slugging percentage: Jason Giambi (.647).

On-base percentage: Jason Giambi (.476).
Wins: Tim Hudson (20).
Earned-run average: Gil Heredia (4.12).
Complete games: Gil Heredia, Tim Hudson (2).
Shutouts: Tim Hudson (2).
Saves: Jason Isringhausen (33).
Innings pitched: Tim Hudson (202.1).
Strikeouts: Tim Hudson (169).

GAMES BY POSITION

Catcher: Ramon Hernandez 142, Sal Fasano 52, A.J. Hinch 5.
First base: Jason Giambi 124, Mike Stanley 19, Olmedo Saenz 17, Jeremy Giambi 15, Mario Valdez 4, Adam Piatt 3, Matt Stairs 1.
Second base: Randy Velarde 122, Frank Menechino 51, Jorge Velandia 14, Jose Ortiz 3, Mark Bellhorn 2.
Third base: Eric Chavez 146, Olmedo Saenz 18, Adam Piatt 13, Frank Menechino 2, Mark Bellhorn 2.
Shortstop: Miguel Tejada 160, Frank Menechino 5, Jorge Velandia 4, Eric Chavez 2, Mark Bellhorn 1.
Outfield: Ben Grieve 144, Terrence Long 137, Ryan Christenson 114, Matt Stairs 103, Jeremy Giambi 55, Adam Piatt 29, Rich Becker 19, Bo Porter 16, Eric Byrnes 4.
Designated hitter: Matt Stairs 37, John Jaha 30, Olmedo Saenz 27, Jason Giambi 24, Jeremy Giambi 21, Adam Piatt 13, Ben Grieve 12, Mike Stanley 8, Frank Menechino 2, Jose Ortiz 4, Rich Becker 2, Eric Byrnes 2, Eric Chavez 1, A.J. Hinch 1, Tim Hudson 1, Ron Mahay 1.

TOP DRAFT CHOICES

1. None.
2. **Freddie Bynum,** SS, Pitt County (N.C.) C.C.
3. **Daylan Holt,** OF, Texas A&M Univ.
4. **Kevin McGerry,** RHP, St. John's U.
5. **Kenny Baugh,** RHP, Rice University.
6. **Beau Craig,** C, U. of So. California.
7. **Marcus Gwyn,** RHP, Rice University.
8. **Kyle Crowell,** RHP, U. of Houston.
9. **Marshall McDougall,** 3B, Florida State University.
10. **Derell McCall,** RHP, Tate H.S., Gonzalez, Fla.

SEATTLE MARINERS
AMERICAN LEAGUE WEST DIVISION

Mariners
2001 SCHEDULE
Home games shaded; D—Day game (games starting before 5 p.m.)
*—All-Star Game at Safeco Field (Seattle)

APRIL
SUN	MON	TUE	WED	THU	FRI	SAT
1	2 OAK	3 OAK	4 OAK	5 D	6 TEX	7 TEX
8 D TEX	9	10 OAK	11 OAK	12 D OAK	13 ANA	14 ANA
15 D ANA	16 TEX	17 TEX	18 TEX	19 ANA	20 ANA	21 D ANA
22 D ANA	23	24 NYY	25 NYY	26 NYY	27 CWS	28 CWS
29 CWS	30 D					

MAY
SUN	MON	TUE	WED	THU	FRI	SAT
		1 BOS	2 BOS	3 BOS	4 TOR	5 D TOR
6 TOR	7 D	8 BOS	9 BOS	10 BOS	11 TOR	12 D TOR
13 D TOR	14	15 CWS	16 CWS	17 D CWS	18 NYY	19 D NYY
20 D NYY	21	22 MIN	23 D MIN	24	25 KC	26 KC
27 KC	28 D KC	29 BAL	30 BAL	31 BAL		

JUNE
SUN	MON	TUE	WED	THU	FRI	SAT
					1 TB	2 TB
3 D TB	4 TEX	5 TEX	6 TEX	7	8 SD	9 SD
10 SD	11	12 COL	13 COL	14 D COL	15 SD	16 SD
17 SD	18 OAK	19 OAK	20 OAK	21 D OAK	22 ANA	23 ANA
24 ANA	25	26 OAK	27 OAK	28 D OAK	29 ANA	30 ANA

JULY
SUN	MON	TUE	WED	THU	FRI	SAT
1 ANA	2 TEX	3 TEX	4 TEX	5 TEX	6 LA	7 D LA
8 D LA	9	10	*11	12 SF	13 SF	14 D SF
15 D ARI	16 ARI	17 D ARI	18 KC	19 KC	20 MIN	21 MIN
22 D MIN	23 MIN	24 KC	25 KC	26 KC	27 MIN	28 D MIN
29 MIN	30	31 DET				

AUGUST
SUN	MON	TUE	WED	THU	FRI	SAT
			1 DET	2 DET	3 CLE	4 CLE
5 CLE	6 D CLE	7 TOR	8 TOR	9 TOR	10 CWS	11 CWS
12 D CWS	13	14 BOS	15 BOS	16 BOS	17 NYY	18 D NYY
19 D NYY	20 DET	21 DET	22 DET	23 D CLE	24 CLE	25 D CLE
26 CLE	27	28 TB	29 TB	30 D TB	31 BAL	

SEPTEMBER
SUN	MON	TUE	WED	THU	FRI	SAT
						1 D BAL
2 BAL	3 D TB	4 TB	5 TB	6	7 BAL	8 D BAL
9 BAL	10 ANA	11 ANA	12 ANA	13 TEX	14 TEX	15 D TEX
16 TEX	17	18 ANA	19 ANA	20 D ANA	21 OAK	22 D OAK
23 OAK	24 TEX	25 TEX	26 TEX	27	28 OAK	29 OAK
30 D OAK						

2001 SEASON
CLUB DIRECTORY

Chairman & chief executive officer
Howard Lincoln
Board of directors
Howard Lincoln, chairman; John Ellis, chairman emeritus; Minoru Arakawa; Chris Larson; John McCaw; Frank Shrontz; Craig Watjen
President and chief operating officer
Chuck Armstrong
Executive v.p., baseball operations
Pat Gillick
Executive v.p., business operations
Bob Aylward
Exec. v.p., finance and ballpark ops.
Kevin Mather
Vice president, baseball administration
Lee Pelekoudas
V.p., scouting and player development
Roger Jongewaard
Vice president, communications
Randy Adamack
Vice president, ballpark operations
Neil Campbell
Controller
Tim Kornegay
Supervisor, Pacific rim scouting
Ted Heid
Director, player development
Benny Looper
Director, professional scouting
Ken Compton
Director, scouting
Frank Mattox
Director, team travel
Ron Spellecy
Director, baseball information
Tim Hevly
Director, public information
Rebecca Hale
Special assignment
Woody Woodward
Coord. of baseball technical information
Mike Kuharich
Coordinator of minor league instruction
Mike Goff
Home clubhouse manager
Scott Gilbert

Visiting clubhouse manager
Henry Genzale
Medical director
Dr. Larry Pedegana
Trainers
Rick Griffin, Tom Newberg, Ken Roll
Team physician
Dr. Mitchel Storey
Team dentist
Dr. Robert Hughes
Video coordinator
Carl Hamilton
Strength and conditioning coach
Allen Wirtala
Head groundskeeper
Bob Christopherson
Assistant groundskeeper
To be announced
Senior advisor
Bob Engle
Advance scout
Stan Williams
National cross-checker
Steve Jongewaard
Major League scouts
Bob Harrison, Bill Kearns, Steve Pope
Scouting supervisors
Curtis Dishman, Ken Madeja, John McMichen, Carroll Sembera
Scouts
Dave Alexander, Pedro Avila, Craig Bell, Emilio Carrasquel, Rodney Davis, Sam Eldridge, Luis Fuenmayor, Phil Geisler, Pedro Grifol, Patrick Guerrero, Ron Hafner, Des Hamilton, Jae Lee, Stan Lewis, Mark Lummus, Ken Madejia, John Martin, Emiliano Martinez, David May, Mauro Mazzotti, John McMitchen, Julio Molina, Luis Molina, Joe Moreno, Omer Munoz Sr., Wayne Norton, Dana Papasedero, Myron Pines, Phil Pote, Carlos Ramirez, Steve Rath, Eric Robinson, Carroll Sembera, Scott Smith, Jamie Storvick, Harry Stricklett, Derek Valenzuela, Ray Vince, Curtis Wallace, Karl Williams

MINOR LEAGUE AFFILIATES

Class	Team	League	Manager
AAA	Tacoma	Pacific Coast	Dan Rohn
AA	San Antonio	Texas	Dave Brundage
A	Everett	Northwest	Terry Pollreisz
A	San Bernardino	California	To be announced
A	Wisconsin	Midwest	Gary Thurman
Rookie	Peoria Mariners	Arizona	Omer Munoz Jr.

BROADCAST INFORMATION

Radio: KIRO-AM (710).
TV: Fox Sports Net Northwest.
Cable TV: Fox Sports Net Northwest.

SPRING TRAINING

Ballpark: Peoria Stadium (Peoria, Ariz.).
Ticket information: 480-784-4444.

Follow the Mariners all season at: www.sportingnews.com/baseball/teams/mariners/

SPRING TRAINING ROSTER

Manager—Lou Piniella (14).
Coaches—John McLaren (7), John Moses (12), Dave Myers (1), Gerald Perry (29), Bryan Price (35), Matt Sinatro (15).

No.	PITCHERS	B/T	Ht./Wt.	Born	2000 clubs
48	Abbott, Paul	R/R	6-3/195	9-15-67	Seattle
	Franklin, Ryan	R/R	6-3/165	3-5-73	Tacoma
	Fuentes, Brian	L/L	6-4/220	8-9-75	New Haven
34	Garcia, Freddy	R/R	6-4/235	10-6-76	Seattle, Tacoma, Everett
54	Halama, John	L/L	6-5/210	2-22-72	Seattle
58	Hodges, Kevin	R/R	6-4/200	6-24-73	Tacoma, Seattle
	Kaye, Justin	R/R	6-4/185	6-9-76	New Haven
55	Meche, Gil	R/R	6-3/200	9-8-78	Seattle, Tacoma, Wisconsin, Everett
	Meyer, Jake	R/R	6-1/195	1-7-75	New Haven, Arizona Mariners, Tacoma
50	Moyer, Jamie	L/L	6-0/175	11-18-62	Seattle
43	Nelson, Jeff	R/R	6-8/235	11-17-66	New York A.L.
36	Paniagua, Jose	R/R	6-2/190	8-20-73	Seattle
38	Pineiro, Joel	R/R	6-1/180	9-25-78	New Haven, Tacoma, Seattle
37	Ramsay, Robert	L/L	6-5/215	12-3-73	Tacoma, Seattle, Everett
53	Rhodes, Arthur	L/L	6-2/205	10-24-69	Seattle
33	Rodriguez, Frankie	R/R	6-0/210	12-11-72	Seattle, Tacoma
22	Sasaki, Kazuhiro	R/R	6-4/209	2-22-68	Seattle
30	Sele, Aaron	R/R	6-5/215	6-25-70	Seattle
	Soriano, Rafael	R/R	6-1/175	12-19-79	Wisconsin Rapids
	Stark, Dennis	R/R	6-2/210	10-27-74	New Haven
40	Tomko, Brett	R/R	6-4/215	4-7-73	Tacoma, Seattle
	Watson, Mark	R/L	6-4/215	1-23-74	Buffalo, Cleveland, Tacoma
	Wooten, Greg	R/R	6-7/210	3-30-74	New Haven
	Zimmerman, Jordan	R/L	6-0/200	4-28-75	Arizona Mariners, Tacoma, Lancaster

No.	CATCHERS	B/T	Ht./Wt.	Born	2000 clubs
17	Lampkin, Tom	L/R	5-11/195	3-4-64	Tacoma, Seattle
16	Widger, Chris	R/R	6-2/215	5-21-71	Montreal, Seattle
6	Wilson, Dan	R/R	6-3/202	3-25-69	Seattle, Everett, Tacoma

No.	INFIELDERS	B/T	Ht./Wt.	Born	2000 clubs
25	Bell, David	R/R	5-10/190	9-14-72	Seattle
	Boone, Bret	R/R	5-10/180	4-6-69	San Diego
	Caruso, Mike	L/R	6-1/175	5-27-77	Charlotte
	Grabowski, Jason	L/R	6-3/200	5-24-76	Tulsa
8	Guillen, Carlos	B/R	6-1/180	9-30-75	Seattle, Tacoma
11	Martinez, Edgar	R/R	5-11/210	1-2-63	Seattle
4	McLemore, Mark	B/R	5-11/207	10-4-64	Seattle
5	Olerud, John	L/L	6-5/220	8-5-68	Seattle

No.	OUTFIELDERS	B/T	Ht./Wt.	Born	2000 clubs
19	Buhner, Jay	R/R	6-3/210	8-13-64	Seattle
9	Cameron, Mike	R/R	6-6/190	1-8-73	Seattle
1	Gipson, Charles	R/R	6-2/180	12-16-72	Seattle, Tacoma
16	Javier, Stan	B/R	6-0/200	1-9-64	Seattle
18	Martin, Al	L/L	6-2/214	11-24-67	San Diego, Seattle
	Sanders, Anthony	R/R	6-2/200	3-2-74	Tacoma, Seattle
51	Suzuki, Ichiro	L/R	5-9/156	10-22-73	Orix (Japan)

BALLPARK INFORMATION

Ballpark (capacity, surface)
Safeco Field (47,116, grass).

Address
1250 First Avenue South
Seattle, WA 98104

Official website
www.seattlemariners.com

Business phone
206-346-4000

Ticket information
206-346-4001

Ticket prices
$37 (terrace club infield)
$32 (lower box)
$29 (terrace club outfield)
$27 (field)
$18 (view box, lower outfield reserved)
$14 (view reserved)
$9 (left field bleachers)
$5 (center field bleachers)

Field dimensions (from home plate)
To left field at foul line, 331 feet
To center field, 405 feet
To right field at foul line, 326 feet

First game played
July 15, 1999 (Padres 3, Mariners 2)

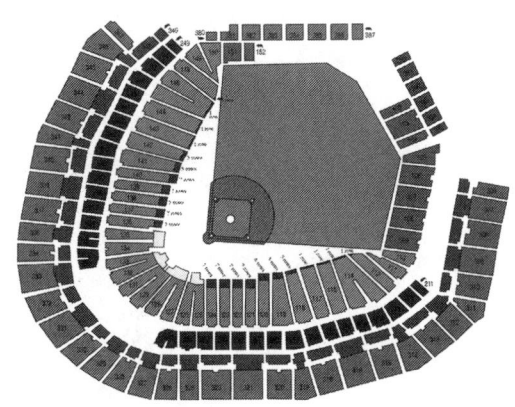

Date	Opp.	Res.	Score	(inn.*)	Hits	Opp. hits	Winning pitcher	Losing pitcher	Save	Record	Pos.	GB
4-4	Bos.	L	0-2		2	7	P. Martinez	Moyer	Lowe	0-1	T3rd	1.5
4-5	Bos.	W	9-3		9	9	Garcia	R. Martinez		1-1	3rd	0.5
4-6	Bos.	W	5-2		7	8	Mesa	Florie	Sasaki	2-1	1st	...
4-7	N.Y.	W	7-5		12	9	Halama	Pettitte	Sasaki	3-1	1st	+0.5
4-8	N.Y.	L	2-3		5	10	Nelson	Mesa	Rivera	3-2	T1st	...
4-9	N.Y.	W	9-3		9	3	Moyer	Clemens		4-2	1st	+0.5
4-11	At Det.	L	2-5		12	8	Moehler	Garcia	Jones	4-3	T2nd	0.5
4-12	At Det.	W	4-0		9	3	Sele	Mlicki		5-3	1st	+0.5
4-13	At Det.	L	0-2		9	9	Brocail	Rhodes	Jones	5-4	T1st	...
4-14	At Tor.	W	11-9		12	16	Moyer	Wells		6-4	1st	+1.0
4-15	At Tor.	W	17-6		16	10	Rodriguez	Halladay	Paniagua	7-4	1st	+1.0
4-16	At Tor.	W	19-7		22	13	Garcia	Carpenter		8-4	1st	+1.0
4-18	At Chi.	L	11-18		13	19	Sturtze	Sele		8-5	1st	+0.5
4-19	At Chi.	L	2-5		8	6	Lowe	Meche	Howry	8-6	1st	+0.5
4-21	K.C.	W	10-2		10	8	Rodriguez	Durbin		9-6	1st	+1.0
4-22	K.C.	W	4-2		7	6	Tomko	Witasick	Sasaki	10-6	1st	+2.0
4-23	K.C.	W	8-5		7	10	Rhodes	Bottalico		11-6	1st	+3.0
4-24	Cle.	L	0-6		2	9	Finley	Meche		11-7	1st	+2.0
4-25	Cle.	W	8-5		9	11	Halama	Nagy		12-7	1st	+3.0
4-26	Cle.	L	3-5	(10)	5	13	Shuey	Rhodes		12-8	1st	+2.0
4-28	At K.C.	L	5-8		9	12	Batista	Tomko	Bottalico	12-9	1st	+2.5
4-29	At K.C.	W	11-3		17	10	Sele	Suppan		13-9	1st	+2.5
4-30	At K.C.	L	3-6		7	10	Rosado	Meche	Bottalico	13-10	1st	+1.5
5-2	At Min.	W	5-4		9	10	Halama	Mays	Sasaki	14-10	1st	+2.5
5-3	At Min.	L	4-5	(10)	12	10	Guardado	Mesa		14-11	1st	+1.5
5-5	Ana.	L	5-6		11	11	Bottenfield	Sele	Percival	14-12	1st	...
5-6	Ana.	W	1-0		7	2	Sasaki	Holtz		15-12	1st	+1.0
5-7	Ana.	W	8-2		7	7	Halama	Schoeneweis		16-12	1st	+2.0
5-8	At Tex.	L	1-10		5	14	Helling	Tomko		16-13	1st	+1.0
5-9	At Tex.	W	13-3		19	6	Abbott	Loaiza		17-13	1st	+2.0
5-10	At Tex.	L	6-7		12	13	Wetteland	Sasaki		17-14	1st	+1.5
5-11	At Oak.	L	6-7		8	10	Hudson	Meche	Isringhausen	17-15	1st	+0.5
5-12	At Oak.	L	7-9		10	6	Mathews	Sasaki		17-16	2nd	0.5
5-13	At Oak.	W	6-4		6	8	Tomko	Appier	Mesa	18-16	2nd	+0.5
5-14	At Oak.	L	2-7		10	6	Heredia	Abbott		18-17	2nd	0.5
5-15	Min.	W	14-0		16	2	Sele	Milton		19-17	2nd	0.5
5-16	Min.	W	9-5		9	10	Meche	Bergman		20-17	1st	+0.5
5-17	Min.	W	4-0		6	4	Halama	Mays		21-17	1st	+1.5
5-19	T.B.	W	7-6		13	7	Mesa	Taylor	Sasaki	22-17	1st	+2.0
5-20	T.B.	L	3-4		8	8	Yan	Ramsay	Hernandez	22-18	1st	+1.0
5-21	T.B.	W	8-4		16	10	Sele	Trachsel		23-18	1st	+1.0
5-23	At Bal.	L	2-4		8	6	Timlin	Mesa		23-19	1st	...
5-24	At Bal.	L	3-4		7	8	Groom	Sasaki		23-20	1st	...
5-25	At Bal.	L	1-5		5	9	Mussina	Rodriguez		23-21	3rd	1.0
5-26	At T.B.	W	11-4		15	9	Sele	Trachsel		24-21	1st	...
5-27	At T.B.	W	6-3		11	4	Tomko	Rekar	Sasaki	25-21	1st	+1.0
5-28	At T.B.	L	4-14		5	20	Mecir	Mesa		25-22	1st	+0.5
5-29	Chi.	W	5-4		6	7	Halama	Sirotka	Sasaki	26-22	1st	+0.5
5-30	Chi.	L	1-2		5	4	Baldwin	Abbott	Foulke	26-23	1st	+0.5
5-31	Chi.	L	3-4		6	6	Howry	Sasaki	Foulke	26-24	1st	...
6-2	S.D.	W	7-4		7	8	Moyer	Clement	Sasaki	27-24	1st	+0.5
6-3	S.D.	L	4-7		7	10	Spencer	Halama	Hoffman	27-25	2nd	0.5
6-4	S.D.	W	6-4		5	10	Abbott	Meadows		28-25	1st	...
6-5	Col.	W	6-2		10	6	Sele	Yoshii		29-25	1st	...
6-6	Col.	W	4-1		7	8	Tomko	Bohanon	Sasaki	30-25	1st	+0.5
6-7	Col.	L	1-6		5	13	Arrojo	Moyer		30-26	2nd	0.5
6-9	At S.F.	L	2-9		8	16	Rueter	Halama		30-27	2nd	1.5
6-10	At S.F.	W	5-2		12	6	Abbott	Estes		31-27	2nd	0.5
6-11	At S.F.	W	9-2		13	7	Sele	Hernandez		32-27	2nd	0.5
6-12	At K.C.	W	5-3		7	7	Moyer	Batista	Sasaki	33-27	1st	+0.5
6-13	At K.C.	W	7-0	(6)	10	1	Meche	Laxton		34-27	1st	+0.5
6-14	At K.C.	L	4-5		9	11	Bottalico	Sasaki		34-28	2nd	0.5
6-15	At Min.	W	12-5		18	8	Ramsay	Redman		35-28	1st	...
6-16	At Min.	L	2-7		4	12	Radke	Sele		35-29	2nd	1.0
6-17	At Min.	W	12-3		17	7	Moyer	Milton		36-29	2nd	1.0
6-18	At Min.	W	10-2		12	6	Meche	Mays		37-29	2nd	1.0
6-19	T.B.	L	3-10		7	14	Lopez	Halama		37-30	2nd	2.0
6-20	T.B.	W	4-3		5	6	Abbott	Trachsel	Sasaki	38-30	2nd	2.0
6-21	T.B.	W	8-5		7	7	Sele	Yan	Sasaki	39-30	2nd	2.0
6-22	Bal.	W	11-4		14	8	Moyer	Johnson		40-30	2nd	1.5
6-23	Bal.	W	8-3		11	10	Meche	Erickson		41-30	2nd	1.5
6-24	Bal.	W	2-1		4	7	Halama	Rapp	Sasaki	42-30	2nd	0.5
6-25	Bal.	W	4-2		4	4	Rhodes	Timlin	Sasaki	43-30	2nd	0.5
6-27	Ana.	W	5-3		8	5	Sele	Belcher	Sasaki	44-30	2nd	0.5

Date	Opp.	Res.	Score	(inn.*)	Hits	Opp. hits	Winning pitcher	Losing pitcher	Save	Record	Pos.	GB
6-28	Ana.	L	2-3		6	8	Hill	Moyer	Percival	44-31	2nd	0.5
6-29	Ana.	W	7-2		8	7	Paniagua	Bottenfield		45-31	1st	+0.5
6-30	At Tex.	L	3-13		8	18	Rogers	Halama		45-32	1st	+0.5
7-1	At Tex.	W	6-3		8	8	Abbott	Clark	Sasaki	46-32	1st	+1.5
7-2	At Tex.	W	11-4		11	10	Sele	Perisho		47-32	1st	+1.5
7-3	At Ana.	W	8-6		13	13	Moyer	Hill	Sasaki	48-32	1st	+2.5
7-4	At Ana.	L	6-7		8	8	Petkovsek	Mesa	Percival	48-33	1st	+2.5
7-5	At Ana.	W	6-4		11	10	Halama	Cooper	Sasaki	49-33	1st	+3.5
7-6	At Ana.	L	1-5		8	5	Washburn	Abbott		49-34	1st	+3.0
7-7	L.A.	L	2-3	(11)	12	5	Herges	Rhodes	Fetters	49-35	1st	+2.0
7-8	L.A.	W	11-0		10	5	Sele	Gagne		50-35	1st	+2.0
7-9	L.A.	W	2-0		4	7	Moyer	Park	Sasaki	51-35	1st	+3.0
7-13	At S.D.	L	1-2	(10)	6	5	Hoffman	Tomko		51-36	1st	+3.0
7-14	At S.D.	W	7-5		12	9	Moyer	Meadows	Sasaki	52-36	1st	+4.0
7-15	At S.D.	L	1-4		4	9	Williams	Sele	Hoffman	52-37	1st	+3.0
7-16	At Ari.	W	6-3		9	8	Mesa	Springer	Sasaki	53-37	1st	+3.5
7-17	At Ari.	L	0-7		5	13	Guzman	Halama		53-38	1st	+4.0
7-18	At Ari.	W	5-2		11	6	Rhodes	Padilla	Sasaki	54-38	1st	+4.0
7-19	At Oak.	W	6-3		10	7	Moyer	Appier	Sasaki	55-38	1st	+5.0
7-20	At Oak.	L	4-5		9	5	Heredia	Sele	Isringhausen	55-39	1st	+4.0
7-21	Tex.	W	12-3		11	8	Abbott	Perisho		56-39	1st	+4.0
7-22	Tex.	W	13-5		14	9	Halama	Glynn		57-39	1st	+5.0
7-23	Tex.	L	2-3		8	9	Helling	Rhodes	Wetteland	57-40	1st	+4.0
7-24	Oak.	W	6-4		11	9	Moyer	Appier	Sasaki	58-40	1st	+5.0
7-25	Oak.	L	7-8		11	11	Heredia	Sele	Isringhausen	58-41	1st	+4.0
7-26	Oak.	L	1-6		8	5	Hudson	Abbott		58-42	1st	+3.0
7-27	Tor.	L	2-7		7	16	Loaiza	Rhodes		58-43	1st	+3.0
7-28	Tor.	W	7-4		9	6	Garcia	Carpenter	Sasaki	59-43	1st	+4.0
7-29	Tor.	W	6-5	(13)	16	9	Tomko	Halladay		60-43	1st	+4.0
7-30	Tor.	W	10-6		5	10	Sele	Escobar	Paniagua	61-43	1st	+4.0
7-31	Bos.	L	5-8		3	11	Garces	Mesa	Pichardo	61-44	1st	+3.0
8-1	Bos.	W	5-4	(19)	12	12	Sasaki	Fassero		62-44	1st	+3.0
8-2	Bos.	L	2-5		5	8	P. Martinez	Garcia		62-45	1st	+2.0
8-4	At N.Y.	L	6-13		15	16	Pettitte	Moyer		62-46	1st	+1.0
8-5	At N.Y.	W	6-5		11	10	Tomko	Gooden	Sasaki	63-46	1st	+2.0
8-6	At N.Y.	W	11-1		16	8	Abbott	Hernandez		64-46	1st	+3.0
8-7	At N.Y.	W	8-5		13	11	Halama	Neagle		65-46	1st	+3.5
8-8†	At Chi.	W	12-4		17	10	Pineiro	Garland	Tomko	66-46		
8-8‡	At Chi.	W	7-5		9	8	Garcia	Buehrle	Sasaki	67-46	1st	+5.0
8-9	At Chi.	L	3-19		8	24	Sirotka	Moyer		67-47	1st	+5.0
8-10	At Chi.	W	6-3		9	11	Sele	Biddle	Sasaki	68-47	1st	+6.0
8-11	Cle.	W	7-1		10	6	Abbott	Finley	Paniagua	69-47	1st	+7.0
8-12	Cle.	L	4-5		7	7	Colon	Halama	Wickman	69-48	1st	+6.0
8-13	Cle.	L	4-10		8	11	Speier	Garcia		69-49	1st	+6.0
8-14	Det.	L	4-15		12	18	Blair	Moyer		69-50	1st	+5.0
8-15	Det.	L	0-9		5	17	Sparks	Sele		69-51	1st	+4.0
8-16	Det.	L	8-12		10	16	Weaver	Tomko		69-52	1st	+3.0
8-18	At Cle.	L	8-9		14	10	Karsay	Rhodes		69-53	1st	+3.0
8-19	At Cle.	L	4-10		8	11	Bere	Moyer		69-54	1st	+3.0
8-20	At Cle.	L	4-12		11	15	Burba	Sele		69-55	1st	+2.0
8-22	At Det.	W	8-4		10	6	Paniagua	Weaver	Sasaki	70-55	1st	+3.5
8-23	At Det.	L	5-6		11	11	Cruz	Rhodes	Jones	70-56	1st	+3.5
8-24	At Det.	L	3-10		8	12	Moehler	Moyer		70-57	1st	+2.5
8-25	Chi.	L	1-4		4	10	Sirotka	Sele	Foulke	70-58	1st	+1.5
8-26	Chi.	W	11-5		12	8	Halama	Biddle		71-58	1st	+2.5
8-27	Chi.	L	1-2		4	6	Barcelo	Garcia	Foulke	71-59	1st	+2.5
8-28	N.Y.	L	1-9		5	10	Clemens	Abbott		71-60	1st	+1.5
8-29	N.Y.	W	5-3		8	8	Tomko	Pettitte	Sasaki	72-60	1st	+2.5
8-30	N.Y.	L	4-5		8	10	Cone	Sele	Rivera	72-61	1st	+2.5
9-1	At Bos.	L	2-6		6	14	Arrojo	Halama		72-62	1st	+2.5
9-2	At Bos.	W	4-1		7	3	Garcia	Garces	Sasaki	73-62	1st	+2.5
9-3	At Bos.	W	5-0		9	1	Abbott	Ohka	Paniagua	74-62	1st	+2.5
9-4	At Bos.	L	1-5		7	7	P. Martinez	Moyer		74-63	1st	+1.5
9-5	At Tor.	W	4-3		7	6	Rhodes	Escobar	Sasaki	75-63	1st	+2.5
9-6	At Tor.	L	3-7		6	12	Hamilton	Halama		75-64	1st	+1.5
9-7	At Tor.	W	8-1		12	3	Garcia	Trachsel		76-64	1st	+2.0
9-8	Min.	L	2-4		6	10	Kinney	Abbott	Hawkins	76-65	1st	+2.0
9-9	Min.	W	7-2		10	5	Moyer	Redman		77-65	1st	+2.0
9-10	Min.	W	8-1		8	7	Sele	Romero		78-65	1st	+2.0
9-11	K.C.	L	3-6		7	15	Meadows	Halama	Santiago	78-66	1st	+1.0
9-12	K.C.	W	11-3		15	9	Garcia	Reichert		79-66	1st	+1.0
9-13	K.C.	W	2-1	(11)	6	8	Mesa	Bottalico		80-66	1st	+2.0
9-15	At Bal.	W	10-2		10	8	Sele	Mercedes		81-66	1st	+2.0
9-16	At Bal.	W	14-0		16	3	Moyer	Mussina		82-66	1st	+2.0
9-17	At Bal.	W	3-2		7	7	Garcia	Ponson	Sasaki	83-66	1st	+2.5
9-18	At T.B.	W	4-3		10	7	Paniagua	Hernandez		84-66	1st	+2.5
9-19	At T.B.	W	5-2		6	6	Halama	Harper	Paniagua	85-66	1st	+2.5
9-20	At T.B.	W	5-4		10	10	Sele	Lopez	Sasaki	86-66	1st	+3.0

Date	Opp.	Res.	Score	(inn.*)	Hits	Opp. hits	Winning pitcher	Losing pitcher	Save	Record	Pos.	GB
9-21	Oak.	L	2-5		5	6	Hudson	Moyer	Isringhausen	86-67	1st	+2.0
9-22	Oak.	L	3-8		7	9	Olivares	Garcia	Service	86-68	1st	+1.0
9-23	Oak.	L	2-8		2	10	Appier	Rhodes		86-69	2nd	...
9-24	Oak.	W	3-2		6	8	Halama	Prieto	Sasaki	87-69	1st	+1.0
9-26	Tex.	W	5-0		10	6	Sele	Glynn		88-69	1st	+0.5
9-27	Tex.	W	6-4		11	9	Garcia	Davis	Sasaki	89-69	1st	+0.5
9-28	Tex.	L	6-13		9	15	Helling	Tomko		89-70	1st	+0.5
9-29	At Ana.	L	3-9		5	10	Ortiz	Abbott	Pote	89-71	2nd	0.5
9-30	At Ana.	W	21-9		22	12	Halama	Belcher		90-71	2nd	0.5
10-1	At Ana.	W	5-2		12	7	Rhodes	Hasegawa	Sasaki	91-71	2nd	0.5

Monthly records: April (13-10), May (13-14), June (19-8), July (16-12), August (11-17), September (18-10), October (1-0).
*Innings, if other than nine. †First game of a doubleheader. ‡Second game of a doubleheader.

HIGHLIGHTS

High point: After a sluggish start, the Mariners vaulted to the top of the A.L. West Division with a 35-20 record in June and July. They took over first by beating Anaheim on June 29 and held that position until the last week of the season.

Low point: After August 11, when the Mariners held a seven-game lead over second-place Oakland and rested 22 games above .500 for the first time in franchise history, the bottom nearly fell out. The Mariners lost eight straight games and 15-of-18 while watching their lead shrink to 2½.

Turning point: The final day of the regular season, when the Mariners earned their third postseason berth with a do-or-die 5-2 win at Anaheim. They failed to win the division title, but the victory gave them the A.L.'s wild-card position.

Most valuable player: Shortstop Alex Rodriguez had another superb season, but 37-year-old designated hitter Edgar Martinez was even better. Martinez, playing his 14th season with Seattle, set career highs with 37 home runs and an A.L.-leading 145 RBIs while batting .324. Four of those 37 homers were grand slams.

Most valuable pitcher: A rookie at age 32, closer Kazuhiro Sasaki made the difficult transition from Japanese baseball and stabilized the Mariners' shaky bullpen. After losing four games in May, Sasaki went on to post 37 saves and blew only three opportunities, the best mark in the A.L. His 0.73 ERA in September was punctuated by a save in the wild-card-clinching season finale.

Most improved player: Manager Lou Piniella talked Jay Buhner out of retirement and the injury-plagued outfielder rewarded him with 26 home runs and 82 RBIs in a part-time role. Buhner had managed only 29 homers and 83 RBIs in the previous two seasons combined.

Most pleasant surprise: Asked to succeed Ken Griffey Jr. in center field, newcomer Mike Cameron turned in a spectacular year defensively and became one of the Mariners' best clutch hitters. An athletic combination of power, speed and grace, Cameron quickly became a fan favorite at Safeco Field.

Key injuries: Opening-night starter Jamie Moyer pulled a muscle in his left shoulder and was on the disabled list from April 21 to June 1. ... Righthander Freddy Garcia, the team's No. 2 starter, missed 2½ months with a stress fracture in his leg. ... Righthander Gil Meche was slowed by injuries early and never pitched after July. ... Catcher Tom Lampkin, one of the few lefthanded hitters on the roster, began the season recovering from knee surgery and then was lost for the year on June 28 when he tore a ligament in his elbow. ... Rodriguez missed two weeks in July with a concussion and sprained knee.

Notable: Just one season after using a club-record 28 different pitchers, the Mariners used 15 in 2000—nine as starters. The staff's final 4.49 ERA was second in the A.L. only to Boston. ... The Mariners matched the franchise record with 11 grand slams. ... The Mariners finished 20 games over .500, but they were just 19-19 against A.L. West competition. They were 15-20 against the other three A.L. playoff qualifiers. ... The Mariners finished second in the A.L. behind Baltimore with 122 steals.

—LARRY LaRUE

RECORDS

2000 regular-season record: 91-71 (2nd in A.L. West); 47-34 at home; 44-37 on road; 35-17 vs. East; 26-28 vs. Central; 30-26 vs. West; 20-11 vs. lefthanded starters; 71-60 vs. righthanded starters; 77-67 on grass; 14-4 on turf; 32-24 in daytime; 59-47 at night; 15-22 in one-run games; 3-4 in extra-inning games; 1-0-0 in doubleheaders.

Team record past five years: 421-387 (.521, ranks 4th in league in that span).

TEAM LEADERS

Batting average: Edgar Martinez (.324).
At-bats: John Olerud (565).
Runs: Alex Rodriguez (134).
Hits: Edgar Martinez (180).
Total Bases: Alex Rodriguez (336).
Doubles: John Olerud (45).
Triples: Stan Javier (5).
Home runs: Alex Rodriguez (41).
Runs batted in: Edgar Martinez (145).
Stolen bases: Rickey Henderson (31).

Slugging percentage: Alex Rodriguez (.606).
On-base percentage: Edgar Martinez (.423).
Wins: Aaron Sele (17).
Earned-run average: Paul Abbott (4.22).
Complete games: Aaron Sele (2).
Shutouts: Aaron Sele (2).
Saves: Kazuhiro Sasaki (37).
Innings pitched: Aaron Sele (211.2).
Strikeouts: Aaron Sele (137).

GAMES BY POSITION

Catcher: Dan Wilson 88, Joe Oliver 66, Tom Lampkin 28, Robert Machado 8, Chris Widger 6.

First base: John Olerud 158, Brian Lesher 4, Raul Ibanez 3, Stan Javier 3, John Mabry 3, David Bell 2, Edgar Martinez 2, Chris Widger 2, Joe Oliver 1, Dan Wilson 1.

Second base: Mark McLemore 129, David Bell 48.

Third base: David Bell 93, Carlos Guillen 68, Charles Gipson 5, Carlos E. Hernandez 2, Dan Wilson 1.

Shortstop: Alex Rodriguez 148, Carlos Guillen 23, Charles Gipson 5, David Bell 1.

Outfield: Mike Cameron 155, Jay Buhner 104, Rickey Henderson 88, Stan Javier 88, Raul Ibanez 76, Charles Gipson 48, Al Martin 35, John Mabry 19, Mark McLemore 14, Anthony Sanders 1, Chris Widger 1.

Designated hitter: Edgar Martinez 146, John Mabry 5, Raul Ibanez 4, Stan Javier 4, Tom Lampkin 3, Rickey Henderson 2, Al Martin 2, Chris Widger 2, David Bell 1, Jay Buhner 1, Charles Gipson 1, Brian Lesher 1, Joe Oliver 1.

TOP DRAFT CHOICES

1. None.
2. None.
3. None.
4. **Sam Hays,** LHP, Waco (Tex.) H.S.
5. **Derrick Vandusen,** LHP, Riverside (Calif.) C.C.
6. **Jamal Strong,** OF, Univ. of Nebraska.
7. **Jaime Bubela,** OF, Baylor University.
8. **Rett Johnson,** RHP, Coastal Carolina University.
9. **Charlie Manning,** LHP, U. of Tampa.
10. **Ryan Ketchner,** LHP, John Leonard H.S., Lantana, Fla.

Devil Rays 2001 SCHEDULE

Home games shaded; D—Day game (games starting before 5 p.m.)
*—All-Star Game at Safeco Field (Seattle)

APRIL

SUN	MON	TUE	WED	THU	FRI	SAT
1	2	3 TOR	4 TOR	5 D TOR	6 D BOS	7 BOS
8 D BOS	9 TOR	10 TOR	11 TOR	12	13 BAL	14 D BAL
15 D BAL	16 BAL	17 TOR	18 BOS	19 BOS	20 BAL	21 D BAL
22 D BAL	23	24 KC	25 KC	26 D KC	27 DET	28 D DET
29 D DET	30 BAL					

MAY

SUN	MON	TUE	WED	THU	FRI	SAT
		1 BAL	2 BAL	3	4 CLE	5 D CLE
6 CLE	7	8 BAL	9 BAL	10 BAL	11 CLE	12 CLE
13 D CLE	14 KC	15 KC	16 KC	17 KC	18 DET	19 D DET
20 D DET	21 TEX	22 TEX	23 TEX	24 TEX	25 ANA	26 D ANA
27 ANA	28 D ANA	29 D OAK	30 D OAK	31 D OAK		

JUNE

SUN	MON	TUE	WED	THU	FRI	SAT
					1 SEA	2 SEA
3 D SEA	4	5 TOR	6 TOR	7 D TOR	8 NYM	9 D NYM
10 D NYM	11	12 PHI	13 PHI	14 D PHI	15 FLA	16 FLA
17 D FLA	18	19 BOS	20 BOS	21 BOS	22 NYY	23 D NYY
24 D NYY	25 BOS	26 BOS	27 BOS	28 BOS	29 NYY	30 D NYY

JULY

SUN	MON	TUE	WED	THU	FRI	SAT
1 D NYY	2 D NYY	3 D TOR	4 TOR	5 D TOR	6 D FLA	7 D FLA
8 D FLA	9 D	10	11 MON	12 MON	13 MON	14 D MON
15 ATL	16 ATL	17 ATL	18 ANA	19 D ANA	20 TEX	21 D TEX
22 D TEX	23 ANA	24 ANA	25 ANA	26 ANA	27 TEX	28 TEX
29 TEX	30	31 BAL				

AUGUST

SUN	MON	TUE	WED	THU	FRI	SAT
		1 BAL	2 BAL	3 CWS	4 CWS	
5 CWS	6 D CWS	7 D NYY	8 NYY	9 NYY	10 MIN	11 D MIN
12 D MIN	13 D NYY	14 NYY	15 NYY	16 MIN	17 MIN	18 MIN
19 MIN	20 BAL	21 BAL	22 BAL	23 CWS	24 CWS	25 D CWS
26 D CWS	27 SEA	28 SEA	29 SEA	30 OAK	31	

SEPTEMBER

SUN	MON	TUE	WED	THU	FRI	SAT
						1 D OAK
2 D OAK	3 SEA	4 SEA	5 SEA	6	7 OAK	8 D OAK
9 D OAK	10 BOS	11 BOS	12 BOS	13 NYY	14 NYY	15 D NYY
16 D NYY	17 BOS	18 BOS	19 BOS	20 TOR	21 TOR	22 TOR
23 TOR	24 NYY	25 NYY	26 TOR	27 TOR	28 TOR	29 D TOR
30 D TOR						

2001 SEASON CLUB DIRECTORY

Managing general partner/CEO
Vincent J. Naimoli

Sr. v.p.baseball operations/g.m.
Chuck LaMar

Sr. v.p.-admin. & general counsel
John P. Higgins

Vice president of sales & marketing
John Browne

Vice president of public relations
Rick Vaughn

Vice president of operations/facilities
Rick Nafe

Asst. general manager-baseball operations
Bart Braun

Assistant general manager-administration
Scott Proefrock

Special assistants to the general manager
Eddie Bane, Bill Livesey

Director of scouting
Dan Jennings

Senior advisor for baseball operations
Frank Howard

Field coordinator
Tom Foley

Assistant to player development
Mitch Lukevics

Traveling secretary
Jeffrey Ziegler

Controller
Patrick Smith

Director of human resources
Louise "Jeep" Weber

Director of business administration
Bill Wiener Jr.

Sr. director of corporate sales & broadcasting
Larry McCabe

Manager of broadcast operations
Joe Ciaravino

Managers of sponsorship coordination
Kelly Davis, Sean McHale, Lauren Miller

Manager of promotions & special events
Christopher Dean

Director of ticket operations
Robert Bennett

Assistant director of ticket operations
Ken Mallory

Assistant to the v.p. of public relations
Carmen Molina

Director of publications
Matt Lorenz

Director of media relations
Chris Costello

Assistant media relations manager
Greg Landy

Manager of community relations
Liz-Beth Lauck

Director of event productions & entertainment
John Franzone

Video producer
Jason Rundle

Video coordinator
Chris Fernandez

Head trainer
Jamie Reed

Assistant head trainer
Ken Crenshaw

Strength & conditioning coordinator
To be announced

Medical team physician
Dr. Michael Reilly

Orthopaedic team physician
Dr. Koco Eaton

Clubhouse operations-home
Carlos Ledezma

Clubhouse operations-visitor
Guy Gallagher

Major League scouts
Jerry Gardner, Bart Johnson, Matt Keough, Al LaMacchia, Don Lindeberg, Don Williams

Crosscheckers
Jack Gillis, R.J. Harrison, Dave Roberts, Mac Seibert

Area scouts
Jonathan Bonifay, James Bonnici, Skip Bundy, Rickey Drexler, Kevin Elfering, Milt Hill, Hank King, Paul Kirsch, Benny Latino, Fred Repke, Joe Robinson Jr., Edwin Rodriguez, Scott Sealy, Dale Tilleman, Craig F. Weissmann, Doug Witt, Mike Zimmerman

Part-time scouts
Philip Elhage, Jose Perez, Juan Pringle, Junior Ramirez, Gustavo Rodriguez, Ron Stinnett, Freddy Torres, Mel Zitter

MINOR LEAGUE AFFILIATES

Class	Team	League	Manager
AAA	Durham	International	Bill Evers
AA	Orlando	Southern	Mike Ramsey
A	Bakersfield	California	To be announced
A	Charleston (S.C.)	South Atlantic	Buddy Biancalana
A	Hudson Valley	New York-Pennsylvania	To be announced
Rookie	Princeton	Appalachian	Edwin Rodriguez

BROADCAST INFORMATION

Radio: WFLA-AM (970).
TV: MORE-TV (Channel 32); WTSP (Channel 10).
Cable TV: Fox Sports Net.

SPRING TRAINING

Ballpark (city): Florida Power Park Home of Al Lang Field (St. Petersburg, Fla.).
Ticket information: 727-825-3250.

Follow the Devil Rays all season at: www.sportingnews.com/baseball/teams/devilrays/

SPRING TRAINING ROSTER

Manager—Larry Rothschild (11).
Coaches—Wade Boggs (12), Jose Cardenal (7), Terry Collins, Bill Fischer (56), Billy Hatcher (22), Hal McRae, Darren Daulton.

No.	PITCHERS	B/T	Ht./Wt.	Born	2000 clubs
40	Alvarez, Wilson	L/L	6-1/245	3-24-70	St. Petersburg
	Colome, Jesus	R/R	6-4/170	6-2-80	Midland, Orlando
38	Creek, Doug	L/L	6-0/200	3-1-69	Durham, Tampa Bay
57	Guzman, Juan	R/R	5-11/195	10-28-66	Tampa Bay, St. Petersburg, Orlando, Durham
58	Harper, Travis	L/R	6-4/195	5-21-76	Orlando, Durham, Tampa Bay
	James, Delvin	R/R	6-4/222	1-3-78	St. Petersburg, Orlando
32	Lopez, Albie	R/R	6-2/240	8-18-71	Tampa Bay, Princeton
	Phelps, Travis	R/R	6-2/195	7-25-77	Orlando, Durham
35	Rekar, Bryan	R/R	6-3/220	6-3-72	Tampa Bay, Durham
24	Rupe, Ryan	R/R	6-5/230	3-31-75	Tampa Bay, Durham
	Seay, Bobby	L/L	6-2/221	6-20-78	Orlando
	Standridge, Jason	R/R	6-4/217	11-9-78	St. Petersburg, Orlando
49	Sturtze, Tanyon	R/R	6-5/205	10-12-70	Chicago A.L., Tampa Bay
34	Wheeler, Dan	R/R	6-3/222	12-10-77	Tampa Bay, Durham
	White, Matt	R/R	6-5/230	7-13-78	Orlando, Durham
41	Wilson, Paul	R/R	6-5/235	3-28-73	St. Lucie, Norfolk, Tampa Bay
43	Yan, Esteban	R/R	6-4/230	6-22-74	Tampa Bay

No.	CATCHERS	B/T	Ht./Wt.	Born	2000 clubs
8	Difelice, Mike	R/R	6-2/205	5-28-69	Tampa Bay
6	Flaherty, John	R/R	6-1/200	10-21-67	Tampa Bay
81	Hall, Toby	R/R	6-3/205	10-21-75	Orlando, Durham, Tampa Bay

No.	INFIELDERS	B/T	Ht./Wt.	Born	2000 clubs
	Abernathy, Brent	R/R	6-1/185	9-23-77	Syracuse, Durham
	Brewer, Jace	R/R	6-0/170	8-6-79	Charleston, S.C.
9	Castilla, Vinny	R/R	6-1/205	7-4-67	Tampa Bay, Durham
28	Cox, Steve	L/L	6-4/222	10-31-74	Tampa Bay
21	Huff, Aubrey	L/R	6-4/221	12-20-76	Durham, Tampa Bay
10	Johnson, Russ	R/R	5-10/180	2-22-73	Houston, Tampa Bay
16	Martinez, Felix	B/R	6-0/180	5-18-74	Durham, Tampa Bay
29	McGriff, Fred	L/L	6-3/215	10-31-63	Tampa Bay
71	Rolls, Damian	R/R	6-2/205	9-15-77	Tampa Bay, St. Petersburg, Orlando
	Sandberg, Jared	R/R	6-3/212	3-2-78	Orlando, Durham
20	Smith, Bobby	R/R	6-3/190	5-10-74	Durham, Tampa Bay

No.	OUTFIELDERS	B/T	Ht./Wt.	Born	2000 clubs
	Grieve, Ben	L/R	6-4/230	5-4-76	Oakland
30	Guillen, Jose	R/R	5-11/195	5-17-76	Durham, Tampa Bay
15	Kelly, Kenny	R/R	6-2/180	1-26-79	Orlando, Tampa Bay
	Sanchez, Alex	L/L	5-10/180	8-26-76	Durham, Orlando
14	Tyner, Jason	L/L	6-1/170	4-23-77	Norfolk, New York N.L., Tampa Bay
23	Vaughn, Greg	R/R	6-0/202	7-3-65	Tampa Bay
4	Williams, Gerald	R/R	6-2/187	8-10-66	Tampa Bay
2	Winn, Randy	B/R	6-2/193	6-9-74	Durham, Tampa Bay

BALLPARK INFORMATION

Ballpark (capacity, surface)
Tropicana Field (43,370, artificial)

Address
One Tropicana Drive
St. Petersburg, FL 33607

Official website
www.devilray.com

Business phone
727-825-3242

Ticket information
727-825-3250

Ticket prices
$195 (home plate box)
$75 (field box)
$40 (lower club box)
$35 (diamond club box, diamond club reserved)
$30 (lower box)
$23 (lower reserved, terrace box)
$19 (upper box)
$14 (terrace reserved, outfield)
$10 (the beach, upper reserved)
$8 (upper general admission)

Field dimensions (from home plate)
To left field at foul line, 315 feet
To center field, 404 feet
To right field at foul line, 322 feet

First game played
March 31, 1998 (Tigers 11, Devil Rays 6)

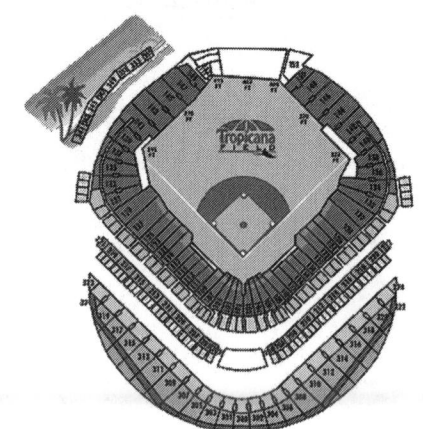

2001 SEASON *Tampa Bay Devil Rays*

Date	Opp.	Res.	Score	(inn.*)	Hits	Opp. hits	Winning pitcher	Losing pitcher	Save	Record	Pos.	GB
4-3	At Min.	W	7-0		14	8	Trachsel	Radke		1-0	T1st	...
4-4	At Min.	L	5-6		9	11	Carrasco	Hernandez		1-1	4th	1.0
4-5	At Min.	L	7-10		13	12	Guardado	White		1-2	5th	1.0
4-6	At Min.	W	7-6		10	13	Mecir	Carrasco	Hernandez	2-2	T3rd	0.5
4-7	Cle.	L	5-14		10	15	Wright	Guzman		2-3	T3rd	1.5
4-8	Cle.	L	4-6		10	11	Burba	Trachsel	Karsay	2-4	4th	2.5
4-9	Cle.	L	4-17		11	16	Colon	Rupe		2-5	5th	3.5
4-11	Chi.	L	6-13		10	18	Parque	Yan		2-6	5th	3.5
4-12	Chi.	L	1-7		7	15	Baldwin	Wheeler		2-7	5th	3.5
4-13	Chi.	W	6-5	(12)	11	8	Mecir	Sturtze		3-7	5th	3.0
4-14	At Det.	L	5-10		14	11	Nitkowski	Rupe		3-8	5th	4.0
4-15	At Det.	W	7-0		11	6	Gooden	Weaver		4-8	T4th	4.0
4-16	At Det.	W	7-6		16	8	Hernandez	Jones		5-8	4th	4.0
4-19	At Bal.	L	2-3		7	7	Trombley	Mecir		5-9	5th	6.0
4-20	At Bal.	L	4-8		7	8	Rapp	Rupe		5-10	5th	6.5
4-21	Ana.	L	6-9		8	12	Petkovsek	Hernandez	Percival	5-11	5th	6.5
4-22	Ana.	W	11-9	(10)	12	10	Lopez	Mercker		6-11	5th	5.5
4-23	Ana.	W	1-0		5	4	Eiland	Dickson	Hernandez	7-11	5th	5.5
4-25	At K.C.	L	6-7		10	13	Reichert	Lopez		7-12	5th	5.0
4-26	At K.C.	L	6-7		8	12	Bottalico	Lopez		7-13	5th	6.0
4-27	At Ana.	W	7-3		12	6	Gooden	Ortiz		8-13	5th	5.5
4-28	At Ana.	W	11-2		19	7	Yan	Dickson		9-13	5th	5.5
4-29	At Ana.	L	6-7	(13)	16	13	Levine	Sparks		9-14	5th	5.5
4-30	At Ana.	L	2-5		7	9	Bottenfield	Trachsel	Percival	9-15	5th	6.5
5-2	Tex.	L	1-8		2	12	Helling	Rupe		9-16	5th	8.0
5-3	Tex.	L	1-5		11	11	Clark	Gooden	Wetteland	9-17	5th	9.0
5-4	Tex.	W	8-7	(11)	12	12	Lopez	Zimmerman		10-17	5th	8.5
5-5	At Bos.	L	3-5		8	10	R. Martinez	Eiland	Lowe	10-18	5th	9.5
5-6	At Bos.	W	1-0		6	3	Trachsel	P. Martinez		11-18	5th	9.5
5-7	At Bos.	L	7-9		13	12	Fassero	Rekar	Lowe	11-19	5th	9.5
5-8	At N.Y.	L	3-6		9	8	Pettitte	Gooden	Rivera	11-20	5th	10.5
5-9	At N.Y.	L	3-4	(10)	8	7	Nelson	White		11-21	5th	11.5
5-11	At N.Y.	W	1-0		7	4	Trachsel	Hernandez	Lopez	12-21	5th	10.5
5-12	Tor.	W	4-3		8	10	White	Carpenter	Lopez	13-21	5th	9.5
5-13	Tor.	L	4-8		5	12	Escobar	Lidle		13-22	5th	9.5
5-14	Tor.	L	2-3		7	8	Wells	Lopez		13-23	5th	11.0
5-15	At Tex.	L	5-6		6	10	Oliver	White	Wetteland	13-24	5th	11.0
5-16	At Tex.	L	7-9		11	12	Zimmerman	Lopez	Wetteland	13-25	5th	11.0
5-17	At Tex.	L	6-11		8	16	Crabtree	Rekar		13-26	5th	12.0
5-19	At Sea.	L	6-7		7	13	Mesa	Taylor	Sasaki	13-27	5th	13.0
5-20	At Sea.	W	4-3		8	8	Yan	Ramsay	Hernandez	14-27	5th	12.0
5-21	At Sea.	L	4-8		10	16	Sele	Trachsel		14-28	5th	12.0
5-23	Oak.	W	6-4		11	10	Rekar	Olivares	Hernandez	15-28	5th	11.0
5-24	Oak.	L	2-9		6	12	Appier	Gooden	Tam	15-29	5th	12.0
5-25	Oak.	L	3-6		8	8	Heredia	Yan	Isringhausen	15-30	5th	12.0
5-26	Sea.	L	4-11		9	15	Sele	Trachsel		15-31	5th	13.0
5-27	Sea.	L	3-6		4	11	Tomko	Rekar	Sasaki	15-32	5th	13.0
5-28	Sea.	W	14-4		20	5	Mecir	Mesa		16-32	5th	13.0
5-29	Bal.	L	1-5		13	9	Rapp	Trachsel		16-33	5th	13.5
5-30	Bal.	L	7-8		14	12	Ponson	Yan	Timlin	16-34	5th	14.5
5-31	Bal.	W	4-3		6	9	Mecir	Groom	Hernandez	17-34	5th	13.5
6-1	Bal.	W	2-1		8	6	Rekar	Erickson	Hernandez	18-34	5th	12.5
6-2	At N.Y. (NL)	L	3-5		7	5	Rusch	White	Benitez	18-35	5th	12.5
6-3	At N.Y. (NL)	L	0-1		5	6	Leiter	Trachsel	Benitez	18-36	5th	12.5
6-4	At N.Y. (NL)	W	15-5		14	9	Yan	B.J. Jones		19-36	5th	12.5
6-5	At Phi.	W	5-3	(12)	9	5	Guthrie	Boyd	White	20-36	5th	11.5
6-6	At Phi.	W	5-3	(10)	9	8	Hernandez	Brantley	White	21-36	5th	11.5
6-7	At Phi.	L	4-5		8	10	Brock	Guthrie	Brantley	21-37	5th	12.5
6-9	Fla.	W	6-4		9	7	Trachsel	Dempster	Hernandez	22-37	5th	11.5
6-10	Fla.	L	1-5		3	10	Cornelius	Yan	Alfonseca	22-38	5th	12.5
6-11	Fla.	W	7-6		13	13	Mecir	Bones	Hernandez	23-38	5th	12.0
6-13	Ana.	L	3-5		7	10	Etherton	Rekar	Percival	23-39	5th	12.0
6-14	Ana.	W	3-2		8	7	Lopez	Percival		24-39	5th	12.0
6-15	Ana.	W	2-1		5	6	Trachsel	Hasegawa		25-39	5th	11.0
6-16	Tex.	W	9-2		13	8	Yan	Oliver		26-39	5th	10.5
6-17	Tex.	L	0-5		3	13	Perisho	Lidle		26-40	5th	10.5
6-18	Tex.	W	6-1		9	9	White	Helling		27-40	5th	9.5
6-19	At Sea.	W	10-3		14	7	Lopez	Halama		28-40	5th	9.0
6-20	At Sea.	L	3-4		6	5	Abbott	Trachsel	Sasaki	28-41	5th	10.0
6-21	At Sea.	L	5-8		7	7	Sele	Yan	Sasaki	28-42	5th	10.0
6-23	At Tex.	W	7-4		13	9	Lidle	Helling	Hernandez	29-42	5th	9.5
6-24	At Tex.	W	9-7		18	13	White	Crabtree	Hernandez	30-42	T4th	9.5
6-25	At Tex.	L	5-9		10	14	Rogers	Lopez	Loaiza	30-43	T4th	10.5

Date	Opp.	Res.	Score	(inn.*)	Hits	Opp. hits	Winning pitcher	Losing pitcher	Save	Record	Pos.	GB
6-27	Tor.	W	11-1		13	9	Trachsel	Escobar		31-43	T4th	9.5
6-28	Tor.	L	2-5		5	7	Wells	Yan		31-44	5th	10.5
6-29	Tor.	L	3-12		10	14	Castillo	Lidle		31-45	5th	11.5
6-30	N.Y.	W	6-4		12	7	Mecir	Nelson	Hernandez	32-45	5th	10.5
7-1	N.Y.	L	1-6		5	12	Hernandez	Lopez		32-46	5th	10.5
7-2	N.Y.	L	2-5		4	10	Clemens	Trachsel	Rivera	32-47	5th	10.5
7-3	Det.	L	4-5	(10)	7	11	Patterson	Hernandez	Jones	32-48	5th	11.5
7-4	Det.	L	0-11		9	12	Mlicki	Lidle		32-49	5th	11.5
7-5	Det.	W	4-1		9	8	Rekar	Weaver	Hernandez	33-49	5th	10.5
7-7	At Fla.	W	8-3		11	7	Lopez	Dempster	Mecir	34-49	5th	10.5
7-8	At Fla.	L	5-6		11	13	Looper	White	Alfonseca	34-50	5th	12.0
7-9	At Fla.	L	9-10		11	14	Sanchez	Creek	Alfonseca	34-51	5th	12.0
7-13	Mon.	W	6-4		14	8	Mecir	Lira	Hernandez	35-51	5th	11.0
7-14	Mon.	W	8-5		11	12	Lopez	Armas	Hernandez	36-51	5th	11.0
7-15	Mon.	L	1-4		9	13	Hermanson	Trachsel	Kline	36-52	5th	11.5
7-16	Atl.	L	4-6		5	8	Kamieniecki	Mecir		36-53	5th	12.5
7-17	Atl.	W	8-6		12	10	Rupe	Mulholland	Hernandez	37-53	5th	11.5
7-18	Atl.	L	2-8		7	10	Maddux	Rekar		37-54	5th	12.5
7-19	At Tor.	L	2-5		2	9	Escobar	Lopez	Koch	37-55	5th	13.5
7-20	At Tor.	L	5-6		7	10	Quantrill	White	Koch	37-56	5th	13.5
7-21	At N.Y.	L	1-11		10	17	Gooden	Yan		37-57	5th	14.5
7-22	At N.Y.	W	12-4		14	12	Rupe	Cone		38-57	5th	13.5
7-23	At N.Y.	L	1-5		4	7	Neagle	Rekar		38-58	5th	14.5
7-24	At Det.	W	4-2		10	5	Lopez	Nomo	Hernandez	39-58	5th	14.5
7-25	At Det.	L	4-6		9	10	Blair	Trachsel	Jones	39-59	5th	15.5
7-26	At Det.	W	6-2		10	5	Yan	Weaver	Hernandez	40-59	5th	15.5
7-27	At K.C.	W	8-5		10	14	Rupe	Durbin	Hernandez	41-59	5th	14.5
7-28	At K.C.	W	10-3		12	8	Rekar	Stein		42-59	5th	14.5
7-29	At K.C.	W	2-1		4	7	Lopez	Suzuki	Hernandez	43-59	5th	13.5
7-30	At K.C.	W	7-6	(10)	12	12	Sturtze	Spradlin	Hernandez	44-59	5th	13.5
8-1	Cle.	W	6-5		7	10	Creek	Wickman		45-59	5th	13.5
8-2	Cle.	L	3-5		5	12	Karsay	Creek	Wickman	45-60	5th	13.5
8-3	Cle.	L	1-5		6	9	Bere	Lopez		45-61	5th	14.5
8-4	Bal.	L	9-10	(15)	12	17	Johnson	Yan		45-62	5th	15.5
8-5	Bal.	W	5-4	(10)	9	6	Hernandez	Trombley		46-62	5th	14.5
8-6	Bal.	W	7-4		10	10	Rupe	Mussina	Hernandez	47-62	5th	13.5
8-7	Min.	L	2-4		6	9	Redman	Rekar	Guardado	47-63	5th	13.5
8-8	Min.	W	5-0		10	4	Lopez	Radke		48-63	5th	13.5
8-9	Min.	W	5-4	(10)	11	13	Taylor	Hawkins		49-63	5th	13.5
8-10	Min.	W	10-4		7	9	Sturtze	Mays		50-63	T4th	13.5
8-11	Chi.	L	5-6		6	8	Buehrle	Wilson	Foulke	50-64	5th	13.5
8-12	Chi.	L	4-5	(10)	10	11	Buehrle	Hernandez	Foulke	50-65	5th	13.5
8-13	Chi.	W	5-3		8	5	Lopez	Howry		51-65	T4th	13.5
8-14	At Bos.	L	3-7		11	9	Lowe	Taylor		51-66	5th	14.5
8-15	At Bos.	W	3-1		11	9	Sturtze	Fassero	Hernandez	52-66	T4th	14.5
8-16	At Bos.	L	3-4		7	11	Arrojo	Wilson	Lowe	52-67	T4th	14.5
8-18	At Chi.	L	2-5		7	9	Garland	Rekar	Foulke	52-68	5th	15.0
8-19	At Chi.	L	0-7		3	11	Sirotka	Lopez		52-69	5th	16.0
8-20	At Chi.	W	12-11		15	15	Yan	Foulke	Hernandez	53-69	5th	15.0
8-21	At Chi.	W	11-4		10	8	Sturtze	Parque		54-69	5th	15.0
8-22	At Min.	W	3-2		5	5	Rupe	Romero	Hernandez	55-69	T4th	14.0
8-23	At Min.	L	2-8		5	13	Redman	Rekar	Hawkins	55-70	T4th	15.0
8-25	At Bal.	L	3-4		10	7	Ryan	Taylor	Kohlmeier	55-71		15.5
8-26†	At Bal.	W	4-1		7	7	Eiland	Ponson	Hernandez	56-71		
8-26‡	At Bal.	L	0-2		4	7	Groom	Lidle	Trombley	56-72	5th	16.0
8-27	At Bal.	L	2-3		10	10	Spurgeon	Rupe	Kohlmeier	56-73	5th	17.0
8-28	Bos.	W	5-2		9	8	Rekar	Pichardo	Hernandez	57-73	5th	17.0
8-29	Bos.	L	0-8		1	12	P. Martinez	Eiland		57-74	5th	17.0
8-30	Bos.	W	3-1		11	4	Lopez	Fassero	Hernandez	58-74	5th	17.0
8-31	K.C.	W	2-1		7	6	Fiore	Suppan	Hernandez	59-74	5th	16.5
9-1	K.C.	L	5-9		8	15	Meadows	Rupe		59-75	5th	17.5
9-2	K.C.	L	5-7		8	8	Santiago	Hernandez	Bottalico	59-76	5th	18.5
9-3	K.C.	L	2-8		6	10	Stein	Eiland		59-77	5th	18.5
9-4	At Cle.	L	1-5		7	13	Burba	Lopez		59-78	5th	19.5
9-5	At Cle.	L	4-7		5	9	Bere	Fiore	Wickman	59-79	5th	20.5
9-6	At Cle.	L	2-6		4	11	Finley	Harper		59-80	5th	20.5
9-7	At Cle.	W	4-3		15	7	Rekar	Karsay	Hernandez	60-80	5th	20.5
9-8	At Oak.	W	4-0		5	4	Lidle	Heredia	Creek	61-80	5th	20.5
9-9	At Oak.	L	0-10		2	14	Hudson	Lopez		61-81	5th	21.5
9-10	At Oak.	L	0-11		5	12	Zito	Wilson		61-82	5th	22.5
9-11	At Oak.	L	1-5		6	5	Appier	Creek		61-83	5th	22.5
9-12	At Ana.	L	2-5		5	8	Belcher	Rekar	Percival	61-84	5th	23.5
9-13	At Ana.	L	4-8		7	10	Ortiz	Lidle		61-85	5th	24.5
9-15	Oak.	L	3-17		4	20	Zito	Lopez		61-86	5th	24.0
9-16	Oak.	L	2-5		8	8	Hudson	Wilson	Isringhausen	61-87	5th	25.0
9-18	Sea.	L	3-4		7	10	Paniagua	Hernandez		61-88	5th	24.5
9-19	Sea.	L	2-5		6	6	Halama	Harper	Paniagua	61-89	5th	24.5

Date	Opp.	Res.	Score	(inn.*)	Hits	Opp. hits	Winning pitcher	Losing pitcher	Save	Record	Pos.	GB
9-20	Sea.	L	4-5		10	10	Sele	Lopez	Sasaki	61-90	5th	24.5
9-22	At Tor.	W	3-2	10	10	7	Lidle	Frascatore	Hernandez	62-90	5th	23.0
9-23	At Tor.	L	6-7		9	13	Koch	Enders		62-91	5th	24.0
9-24	At Tor.	W	6-0		13	2	Harper	Trachsel		63-91	5th	24.0
9-25	At Tor.	W	5-1		10	5	Wilson	Loaiza	Hernandez	64-91	5th	23.0
9-26	N.Y.	W	2-1		3	8	Hernandez	Nelson		65-91	5th	22.0
9-27	N.Y.	W	11-1		9	7	Lidle	Neagle		66-91	5th	21.0
9-28	N.Y.	W	11-3		15	10	Rekar	Clemens		67-91	5th	20.0
9-29	Bos.	W	8-6		11	11	Yan	Carrasco	Hernandez	68-91	5th	19.0
9-30	Bos.	L	2-4		5	11	Cormier	Hernandez	Lowe	68-92	5th	19.0
10-1	Bos.	W	3-2	(10)	10	9	Wheeler	Croushore		69-92	5th	18.0

Monthly records: April (9-15), May (8-19), June (15-11), July (12-14), August (15-15), September (9-18), October (1-0).
*Innings, if other than nine. †First game of a doubleheader. ‡Second game of a doubleheader.

HIGHLIGHTS

High point: The Devil Rays finished with an 8-2 run against playoff contenders Toronto, New York and Boston. It's probably inaccurate to say that the hot finish saved manager Larry Rothschild's job, but it didn't hurt.

Low point: When the team opened September with a 2-16 collapse (including losing streaks of six and 10 games), it was the low point of the franchise's three-year existence. Left fielder Greg Vaughn called the team's play embarrassing and first baseman Fred McGriff complained the franchise was moving backward. The atmosphere in the clubhouse was as dark as it has ever been.

Turning point: It came early, when left-hander Wilson Alvarez went down with a shoulder injury in spring training and righthander Juan Guzman went down after one regular-season start. Minus its top two starters, the rotation couldn't get back in sync until June.

Most valuable player: Center fielder Gerald Williams hit the first pitch of the season for a home run and went on to hit .274 with 21 homers and 89 RBIs. He became only the seventh player to hit at least 20 homers and drive in 80 runs from the leadoff spot. Defensively, he was solid.

Most valuable pitcher: Albie Lopez moved from the bullpen to the rotation and became a No. 1 starter. His 11-13 record and 4.13 ERA were impressive for a team that finished 69-92.

Most improved player: Clearly overmatched in his first major league start on August 4 against Baltimore, Travis Harper went to the minors and returned a month later to better reviews. In his fifth major league start, he raised eyebrows with a complete-game, two-hit shutout of Toronto. Harper retired 17 of the last 18 batters in that game.

Most pleasant surprise: The starting performance turned in by Lopez, who was being groomed as a closer.

Key injuries: Alvarez and Guzman were lost for the year with shoulder injuries. ... Ryan Rupe ended the year on the disabled list after a blood clot was discovered in September. ... Righthander

Tanyon Sturtze missed the final month with a muscle injury. ... Tony Saunders broke his left arm for the second time in 15 months and retired from baseball. ... Third baseman Vinny Castilla made three appearances on the D.L. and hit just six homers in a disappointing season. ... Before being claimed by the Yankees on August 7, designated hitter Jose Canseco missed 46 games with a sore heel. ... Vaughn missed 19 games with a hamstring injury and struggled late with a sore shoulder.

Notable: McGriff hit his 400th career homer, recorded his 2,000th career hit and played in his 2,000th career game. He also became the second player to hit at least 200 homers in both leagues. ... Tampa Bay's 4.43 team ERA after June 1 ranked third in the A.L. ... Tampa Bay was the only A.L. East team to improve its winning percentage from 1999.

—CHRIS ANDERSON

RECORDS

2000 regular-season record: 69-92 (5th in A.L. East); 36-44 at home; 33-48 on road; 31-36 vs. East; 22-27 vs. Central; 16-29 vs. West; 11-25 vs. lefthanded starters; 58-67 vs. righthanded starters; 25-41 on grass; 44-51 on turf; 22-30 in daytime; 47-62 at night; 26-26 in one-run games; 9-5 in extra-inning games; 0-0-1 in doubleheaders.

Team record past five years: 201-284 in three years (.414, ranks 14th in league in that span).

TEAM LEADERS

Batting average: Fred McGriff (.277).
At-bats: Gerald Williams (632).
Runs: Gerald Williams (87).
Hits: Gerald Williams (173).
Total Bases: Gerald Williams (270).
Doubles: Gerald Williams (30).
Triples: Jose Guillen (5).
Home runs: Greg Vaughn (28).
Runs batted in: Fred McGriff (106).
Stolen bases: Miguel Cairo (28).
Slugging percentage: Greg Vaughn (.499).

On-base percentage: Fred McGriff (.373).
Wins: Albie Lopez (11).
Earned-run average: Albie Lopez (4.13).
Complete games: Albie Lopez (4).
Shutouts: Travis Harper, Albie Lopez, Steve Trachsel (1).
Saves: Roberto Hernandez (32).
Innings pitched: Albie Lopez (185.1).
Strikeouts: Esteban Yan (111).

GAMES BY POSITION

Catcher: John Flaherty 108, Mike DiFelice 59, Toby Hall 4.
First base: Fred McGriff 144, Steve Cox 24, Ozzie Guillen 5, Herbert Perry 1.
Second base: Miguel Cairo 108, Bobby Smith 45, Russ Johnson 18, Tony Graffanino 6, Ozzie Guillen 2.
Third base: Vinny Castilla 83, Russ Johnson 49, Aubrey Huff 37, Ozzie Guillen 11, Herbert Perry 7, Bobby Smith 5, Tony Graffanino 3, Damian Rolls 1.
Shortstop: Felix Martinez 106, Ozzie Guillen 42, Kevin Stocker 40, Russ Johnson 11, Tony Graffanino 1.
Outfield: Gerald Williams 138, Jose Guillen 99, Greg Vaughn 72, Steve Cox 56, Bubba Trammell 48, Randy Winn 47, Jason Tyner 31, Dave Martinez 28, Quinton McCracken 11, Ozzie Timmons 9.
Designated hitter: Jose Canseco 60, Greg Vaughn 52, Steve Cox 17, Fred McGriff 10, Bubba Trammell 9, Gerald Williams 7, Miguel Cairo 2, Kenny Kelly 1, Damian Rolls 1, Ozzie Timmons 1, Jason Tyner 1, Randy Winn 1.

TOP DRAFT CHOICES

1. **Rocco Baldelli**, OF, Bishop Hendriken H.S., Warwick, R.I.
2. None.
3. None.
4. None.
5. **Jace Brewer**, SS, Baylor University.
6. **Dan Massiatte**, C, University of Louisiana-Lafayette.
7. **Mike Krga**, SS, St. Ignatius H.S., Chicago.
8. **Mark Malaska**, LHP, Akron University.
9. **John Dischiavo**, RHP, Las Vegas (Nev.) H.S.
10. **John Benedetti**, RHP, Augustana (Ill.) College.

TEXAS RANGERS
AMERICAN LEAGUE WEST DIVISION

Rangers
2001 SCHEDULE
Home games shaded; D—Day game (games starting before 5 p.m.)
*—All-Star Game at Safeco Field (Seattle) † Game played in San Juan, Puerto Rico.

APRIL

SUN	MON	TUE	WED	THU	FRI	SAT
1 TOR	†2	3 ANA	D 4 ANA	5 ANA	6 SEA	7 SEA
8 SEA	D 9	10 ANA	11 ANA	12 ANA	13 OAK	14 D OAK
15 OAK	16 SEA	17 SEA	18 SEA	19 OAK	20 OAK	21 OAK
22 OAK	D 23	24 TOR	25 TOR	26	27 CLE	28 CLE
29 CLE	D 30					

MAY

SUN	MON	TUE	WED	THU	FRI	SAT
		1 DET	2 DET	3 DET	4 CWS	5 CWS
6 CWS	D 7	8 DET	9 DET	10 D DET	11 CWS	12 CWS
13 CWS	D 14	15 CLE	16 CLE	17 CLE	18 TOR	19 TOR
20 TOR	D 21	22 TB	23 TB	24 TB	25 BAL	26 D BAL
27 BAL	D 28 BAL	29 KC	30 KC	31 KC		

JUNE

SUN	MON	TUE	WED	THU	FRI	SAT
					1 MIN	2 MIN
3 MIN	D 4 SEA	5 SEA	6 SEA	7	8 HOU	9 HOU
10 HOU	11 LA	12 LA	13 LA	14	15 HOU	16 D HOU
17 HOU	D 18	19 ANA	20 ANA	21 ANA	22 OAK	23 D OAK
24 OAK	D 25 ANA	26 ANA	27 ANA	28 ANA	29 OAK	30 OAK

JULY

SUN	MON	TUE	WED	THU	FRI	SAT
1 OAK	2 SEA	3 SEA	4 SEA	5 SEA	6 SD	7 D SD
8 SD	D 9	10	11	12 COL	13 COL	14 COL
15 SF	16 SF	17 SF	18 BAL	19 BAL	20 TOR	21 D TOR
22 TB	D 23	24 BAL	25 BAL	26 BAL	27 TB	28 TB
29 TB	30	31 NYY				

AUGUST

SUN	MON	TUE	WED	THU	FRI	SAT
		1 NYY	2 NYY	3 BOS	D 4 BOS	
5 BOS	D 6 BOS	7 DET	8 DET	9 DET	10 CLE	11 CLE
12 CLE	13	14 CWS	15 CWS	16 CWS	17 TOR	18 D TOR
19 TOR	D 20 NYY	21 NYY	22 NYY	23 NYY	24 BOS	25 BOS
26 BOS	27	28 MIN	29 MIN	30 MIN	31 KC	

SEPTEMBER

SUN	MON	TUE	WED	THU	FRI	SAT
						1 KC
2 KC	D 3	4 MIN	5 MIN	6 MIN	7 KC	8 KC
9 KC	D 10 OAK	11 OAK	12 D OAK	13 SEA	14 SEA	15 D SEA
16 SEA	D 17	18 OAK	19 OAK	20 OAK	21 ANA	22 ANA
23 ANA	D 24 SEA	25 SEA	26 SEA	27	28 ANA	29 ANA
30 ANA	D					

2001 SEASON
CLUB DIRECTORY

Chairman of the board and owner
Thomas O. Hicks
President
James R. Lites
Exec. v.p., general manager
Doug Melvin
Exec. v.p., business operations
John McMichael
Exec. v.p., broadcasting and sales
Bill Strong
Exec. v.p., marketing and communications
Jeff Cogen
Sr. vice president, communications
John Blake
Sr. vice president, strategic planning
Rick McLaughlin
V.p., community development/relations
Norm Lyons
Vice president, facilities and construction
Billy Ray Johnson
Vice president, information technology
Steve McNeill
Vice president, business operations
Geoff Moore
Vice president, event operations
Tim Murphy
Vice president, merchandising
Steve Shilts
Vice president, corporate sales
Charlie Seraphin
Vice president, advertising sales
Tom Comerford
Director, human resources
Terry Turner
Corporate counsel
Casey Coffman
Assistant vice president, ticket sales
Brian Byrnes
Asst. vice president, corporate services
Jill Cogen
Asst. vice president, ticket operations
Augie Manfredo
Assistant vice president, marketing
Christy Martinez
Assistant v.p., suites & new media sales
Brad Alberts
Assistant vice president, sponsorship sales
Tom Fireoved
Controller
Kellie Fischer
Assistant general manager
Dan O'Brien
Director, Major League administration
Judy Johns

Director, scouting
Tim Hallgren
Assistant director, scouting
Russ Ardolina
Director, player development
Reid Nichols
Asst. dir., professional and int'l scouting
Monty Clegg
Assistant to director of scouting
Debbie Bent
Asst. to director of player development
Debbie Bent
Director of travel
Chris Lyngos
Director, medical services
Dr. John Conway
Director, community relations
Taunee Paur Taylor
Director, community development
Rhonda Houston
Assistant director, communications
Dana Wilcox
Assistant director, media relations
Amy Gunter
Media relations assistant
Rich Rice
Senior director, events
Lee Gleiser
Senior director, entertainment
Chuck Morgan
Senior director, graphic design
Rainer Uhlir
Head trainer
Danny Wheat
Visiting clubhouse manager
Kelly Terrell
Equipment and home clubhouse manager
Zack Minasian
National cross-checkers
Kip Fagg
David Klipstein
Jeff Taylor
Latin coordinator
Manny Batista
Scouts
Dave Birecki, Ted Brzenk, Carl Cassell, Jim Cuthbert, Jay Eddings, Jim Fairey, Tim Fortugno, Mark Giegler, Joel Grampietro, Mike Grouse, Todd Guggiana, Doug Harris, Mark Harris, Zackary Hoyrst, Ray Jackson, Jim Lentine, Dennis Meeks, Gary Neibauer, Mike Paustian, Javier Rodriguez, Rick Schroeder, Randy Taylor, Aris Tirado, Ron Toenjes, Greg Whitworth, Jeff Wren

MINOR LEAGUE AFFILIATES

Class	Team	League	Manager
AAA	Oklahoma	Pacific Coast	DeMarlo Hale
AA	Tulsa	Texas	Paul Carey
A	Charlotte	Florida State	Darryl Kennedy
A	Savannah	South Atlantic	To be announced
Rookie	Gulf Coast Rangers	Gulf Coast	Carlos Subero
Rookie	Pulaski	Appalachian	Bruce Crabbe

BROADCAST INFORMATION

Radio: KRLD-AM (1080); KESS (1270), Spanish.
TV: KDFI-TV (Channel 27).
Cable TV: Fox Sports Net.

SPRING TRAINING

Ballpark (city): Charlotte County Stadium (Port Charlotte, Fla.).
Ticket information: 941-625-9500.

Follow the Rangers all season at: www.sportingnews.com/baseball/teams/rangers/

SPRING TRAINING ROSTER

Manager—Johnny Oates (26).
Coaches—Bobby Cuellar, Bucky Dent (20), Larry Hardy (48), Rudy Jaramillo (8), Bobby Jones (31), Jerry Narron (5).

No.	PITCHERS	B/T	Ht./Wt.	Born	2000 clubs
53	Benoit, Joaquin	R/R	6-3/205	7-26-79	Tulsa
	Cedeno, Jovanny	R/R	6-0/160	10-25-79	Savannah
30	Cordero, Francisco	R/R	6-2/200	8-11-77	Texas, Oklahoma
35	Crabtree, Tim	R/R	6-4/220	10-13-69	Texas
41	Cubillan, Darwin	R/R	6-2/170	11-15-74	Syracuse, Toronto, Oklahoma, Texas
46	Davis, Doug	R/L	6-3/190	9-21-75	Texas, Oklahoma
47	Elder, David	R/R	6-0/180	9-23-75	Tulsa
38	Glynn, Ryan	R/R	6-3/195	11-1-74	Oklahoma, Texas
32	Helling, Rick	R/R	6-3/220	12-15-70	Texas
50	Johnson, Jonathan	R/R	6-0/180	7-16-74	Oklahoma, Texas
52	Kolb, Danny	R/R	6-4/215	3-29-75	Oklahoma, Texas
	Myette, Aaron	R/R	6-4/195	9-26-77	Birmingham, Charlotte, Chicago A.L.
28	Oliver, Darren	R/L	6-2/210	10-6-70	Texas, Oklahoma, Tulsa
45	Petkovsek, Mark	R/R	6-0/198	11-18-65	Anaheim, Lake Elsinore
37	Rogers, Kenny	L/L	6-1/217	11-10-64	Texas
49	Sikorski, Brian	R/R	6-1/190	7-27-74	Oklahoma, Texas
22	Thompson, Justin	L/L	6-4/215	3-8-73	Charlotte, Tulsa, Oklahoma
43	Venafro, Mike	L/L	5-10/180	8-2-73	Texas
59	Zimmerman, Jeff	R/R	6-1/200	8-9-72	Texas

No.	CATCHERS	B/T	Ht./Wt.	Born	2000 clubs
33	Haselman, Bill	R/R	6-3/225	5-25-66	Texas
7	Rodriguez, Ivan	R/R	5-9/205	11-30-71	Texas

No.	INFIELDERS	B/T	Ht./Wt.	Born	2000 clubs
11	Caminiti, Ken	B/R	6-0/200	4-21-63	Houston
27	Catalanotto, Frank	L/R	6-0/195	4-27-74	Texas, Oklahoma
44	Dransfeldt, Kelly	R/R	6-2/195	4-16-75	Oklahoma, Texas
14	Galarraga, Andres	R/R	6-3/235	6-18-61	Atlanta
	Hafner, Travis	L/L	6-3/215	6-3-77	Charlotte
13	Lamb, Mike	L/R	6-1/195	8-9-75	Oklahoma, Texas
25	Palmeiro, Rafael	L/L	6-0/190	9-24-64	Texas
	Pena, Carlos	L/L	6-2/210	5-17-78	Tulsa
3	Rodriguez, Alex	R/R	6-3/210	7-27-75	Seattle
	Romano, Jason	R/R	6-0/185	6-24-79	Tulsa
4	Sheldon, Scott	R/R	6-3/215	11-20-68	Texas
18	Velarde, Randy	R/R	6-0/200	11-24-62	Oakland, Midland, Sacramento
2	Young, Mike	R/R	6-0/185	10-19-76	Tennessee, Tulsa, Texas

No.	OUTFIELDERS	B/T	Ht./Wt.	Born	2000 clubs
9	Curtis, Chad	R/R	5-10/185	11-6-68	Texas
29	Greer, Rusty	L/L	6-0/195	1-21-69	Texas, Tulsa
19	Kapler, Gabe	R/R	6-2/208	8-31-75	Texas, Oklahoma, Tulsa
12	Ledee, Ricky	L/L	6-1/200	11-22-73	New York A.L., Cleveland, Texas
21	Mateo, Ruben	R/R	6-0/185	2-10-78	Texas
	Porter, Bo	R/R	6-2/195	7-5-72	Sacramento, Oakland

BALLPARK INFORMATION

Ballpark (capacity, surface)
The Ballpark in Arlington (49,200, grass)

Address
1000 Ballpark Way
Arlington, TX 76011

Official website
www.texasrangers.com

Business phone
817-273-5222

Ticket information
817-273-5100

Ticket prices
$40 (lower box, club box)
$32.50 (club reserved)
$28 (corner box)
$22 (terrace club box)
$20 (left field, lower home run porch)
$16 (upper box)
$13 (upper home run porch)
$12 (upper reserved, bleachers)
$6 (grandstand reserved)
$5 (grandstand)

Field dimensions (from home plate)
To left field at foul line, 334 feet
To center field, 400 feet
To right field at foul line, 325 feet

First game played
April 11, 1994 (Brewers 4, Rangers 3)

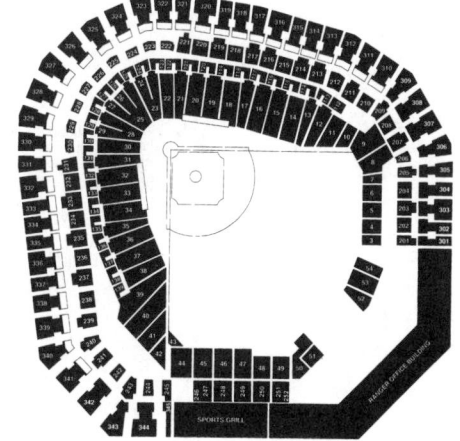

2001 SEASON *Texas Rangers*

Date	Opp.	Res.	Score	(inn.*)	Hits	Opp. hits	Winning pitcher	Losing pitcher	Save	Record	Pos.	GB
4-3	Chi.	W	10-4		11	10	Rogers	Sirotka		1-0	1st	+0.5
4-4	Chi.	W	12-8		12	14	Cordero	Simas		2-0	1st	+1.0
4-5	Chi.	L	8-12		13	15	Foulke	Zimmerman		2-1	T1st	...
4-6	Chi.	L	2-6		6	11	Baldwin	Loaiza		2-2	3rd	0.5
4-7	Tor.	W	11-5		11	11	Clark	Castillo		3-2	2nd	0.5
4-8	Tor.	L	0-4		9	10	Wells	Rogers		3-3	3rd	0.5
4-9	Tor.	W	7-5		9	7	Helling	Halladay		4-3	2nd	0.5
4-12	At N.Y.	L	6-8		10	13	Nelson	Munoz	Rivera	4-4	3rd	1.0
4-13	At N.Y.	L	1-5		4	8	Hernandez	Rogers		4-5	3rd	1.0
4-14	At Cle.	W	7-2		14	4	Helling	Burba		5-5	T2nd	1.0
4-15	At Cle.	W	6-4		11	6	Clark	Colon	Wetteland	6-5	T2nd	1.0
4-16	At Cle.	L	1-2		5	4	Finley	Wetteland		6-6	3rd	2.0
4-17	N.Y.	L	4-5	(11)	11	8	Rivera	Crabtree	Erdos	6-7	3rd	2.5
4-18	N.Y.	L	3-6		8	11	Hernandez	Rogers		6-8	T3rd	2.5
4-19	N.Y.	L	4-5	(10)	7	12	Rivera	Zimmerman		6-9	4th	2.5
4-21	Min.	L	5-10		15	12	Carrasco	Clark		6-10	4th	3.5
4-22	Min.	W	8-3		11	11	Loaiza	Santana		7-10	3rd	3.5
4-23	Min.	L	4-5		11	13	Radke	Oliver	Wells	7-11	4th	4.5
4-24	Bos.	W	5-4		7	9	Rogers	Wakefield	Wetteland	8-11	3rd	3.5
4-25	Bos.	L	3-6		6	9	P. Martinez	Helling	Lowe	8-12	4th	4.5
4-26	Bos.	L	4-14		10	21	Fassero	Clark		8-13	4th	4.5
4-28	At Bal.	L	3-4		9	8	Groom	Zimmerman		8-14	4th	4.5
4-29	At Bal.	L	1-3		9	6	Mussina	Oliver		8-15	4th	5.5
4-30	At Bal.	W	8-4		14	9	Rogers	Rapp		9-15	4th	4.5
5-2	At T.B.	W	8-1		12	2	Helling	Rupe		10-15	4th	4.5
5-3	At T.B.	W	5-1		11	11	Clark	Gooden	Wetteland	11-15	4th	3.5
5-4	At T.B.	L	7-8	(11)	12	12	Lopez	Zimmerman		11-16	4th	4.0
5-5	Oak.	W	17-16		21	16	Wetteland	Tam		12-16	4th	3.0
5-6	Oak.	W	11-10		17	14	Wetteland	Isringhausen		13-16	4th	3.0
5-7	Oak.	L	6-7		12	9	Olivares	Davis	Jones	13-17	4th	4.0
5-8	Sea.	W	10-1		14	5	Helling	Tomko		14-17	4th	3.0
5-9	Sea.	L	3-13		6	19	Abbott	Loaiza		14-18	4th	4.0
5-10	Sea.	W	7-6		13	12	Wetteland	Sasaki		15-18	4th	3.0
5-11	At Ana.	L	2-3		8	10	Hasegawa	Rogers	Percival	15-19	4th	3.0
5-12	At Ana.	W	13-11		14	14	Davis	Schoeneweis	Wetteland	16-19	4th	2.5
5-13	At Ana.	W	6-5		9	7	Helling	Washburn	Wetteland	17-19	4th	2.0
5-14	At Ana.	L	6-7		8	8	Hasegawa	Cordero		17-20	4th	2.5
5-15	T.B.	W	6-5		10	6	Oliver	White	Wetteland	18-20	4th	2.5
5-16	T.B.	W	9-7		12	11	Zimmerman	Lopez	Wetteland	19-20	3rd	2.0
5-17	T.B.	W	11-6		16	8	Crabtree	Rekar		20-20	3rd	2.0
5-18	Bal.	W	8-7		13	11	Helling	Ryan	Wetteland	21-20	2nd	1.5
5-20	Bal.	W	2-1		6	7	Loaiza	Mussina	Wetteland	22-20	2nd	1.0
5-21	Bal.	W	6-5		7	14	Venafro	Groom	Wetteland	23-20	2nd	1.0
5-23	At K.C.	W	4-3		7	9	Helling	Batista	Wetteland	24-20	2nd	...
5-24	At K.C.	L	0-3		6	8	Suppan	Rogers	Spradlin	24-21	2nd	...
5-25	At K.C.	W	5-3		8	10	Loaiza	Santiago	Wetteland	25-21	1st	+0.5
5-26	At Min.	L	2-10		5	16	Milton	Oliver		25-22	2nd	...
5-27	At Min.	L	5-10		8	10	Mays	Clark		25-23	2nd	1.0
5-28	At Min.	L	3-4		8	7	Bergman	Helling	Hawkins	25-24	3rd	1.0
5-29	At Det.	W	3-2		7	11	Rogers	Weaver	Wetteland	26-24	3rd	1.0
5-30	At Det.	L	4-7		9	13	Moehler	Loaiza	Jones	26-25	3rd	1.0
5-31	At Det.	W	13-5		16	11	Oliver	Mlicki		27-25	2nd	...
6-2	Ari.	L	4-5		7	13	Anderson	Helling	Mantei	27-26	4th	1.0
6-3	Ari.	W	4-3		9	7	Rogers	Figueroa	Wetteland	28-26	3rd	0.5
6-4	Ari.	W	7-6		10	14	Perisho	Kim	Wetteland	29-26	2nd	...
6-5	L.A.	W	2-0		5	2	Glynn	Brown	Wetteland	30-26	2nd	...
6-6	L.A.	L	1-7		6	14	Gagne	Clark		30-27	3rd	1.0
6-7	L.A.	L	6-11		12	15	Dreifort	Helling		30-28	4th	1.5
6-9	At Col.	L	2-3	(12)	10	8	Tavarez	Wetteland		30-29	4th	2.5
6-10	At Col.	L	6-12		11	15	Karl	Loaiza		30-30	4th	2.5
6-11	At Col.	L	8-9		18	13	DeJean	Crabtree	Jimenez	30-31	4th	3.5
6-13	At Bal.	L	2-3		6	6	Erickson	Helling	Timlin	30-32	4th	4.5
6-14	At Bal.	L	10-11		10	12	Timlin	Crabtree		30-33	4th	5.0
6-15	At Bal.	L	1-10		5	8	McElroy	Loaiza		30-34	4th	5.5
6-16	At T.B.	L	2-9		8	13	Yan	Oliver		30-35	4th	6.5
6-17	At T.B.	W	5-0		13	3	Perisho	Lidle		31-35	4th	6.5
6-18	At T.B.	L	1-6		9	9	White	Helling		31-36	4th	7.5
6-20	Min.	W	5-2		13	5	Rogers	Redman	Wetteland	32-36	4th	8.0
6-21	Min.	W	7-5		11	12	Loaiza	Radke	Wetteland	33-36	4th	8.0
6-22	Min.	L	2-3		9	6	Hawkins	Crabtree	Wells	33-37	4th	8.5
6-23	T.B.	L	4-7		9	13	Lidle	Helling	Hernandez	33-38	4th	9.5
6-24	T.B.	L	7-9		13	18	White	Crabtree	Hernandez	33-39	4th	9.5
6-25	T.B.	W	9-5		14	10	Rogers	Lopez	Loaiza	34-39	4th	9.5
6-27	At Oak.	L	6-7		10	10	Hudson	Perisho	Isringhausen	34-40	4th	10.5

Date	Opp.	Res.	Score	(inn.*)	Hits	Opp. hits	Winning pitcher	Losing pitcher	Save	Record	Pos.	GB
6-28	At Oak.	W	5-3		10	6	Helling	Appier	Wetteland	35-40	4th	9.5
6-29	At Oak.	W	3-1		9	8	Loaiza	Heredia	Wetteland	36-40	4th	9.0
6-30	Sea.	W	13-3		18	8	Rogers	Halama		37-40	4th	8.0
7-1	Sea.	L	3-6		8	8	Abbott	Clark	Sasaki	37-41	4th	9.0
7-2	Sea.	L	4-11		10	11	Sele	Perisho		37-42	4th	10.0
7-3	Oak.	W	8-3		9	9	Helling	Appier		38-42	4th	10.0
7-4	Oak.	W	10-7		13	11	Davis	Service	Wetteland	39-42	4th	9.0
7-5	Oak.	W	9-4		17	11	Rogers	Mulder		40-42	4th	9.0
7-7	S.D.	W	5-4	(10)	9	6	Davis	Whiteside		41-42	4th	7.5
7-8	S.D.	W	8-1		12	3	Helling	Eaton		42-42	4th	7.5
7-9	S.D.	L	3-4		8	13	Clement	Rogers	Hoffman	42-43	4th	8.5
7-13	At Ari.	W	6-4		7	11	Zimmerman	Kim	Wetteland	43-43	4th	7.5
7-14	At Ari.	L	1-6		6	10	Reynoso	Rogers		43-44	4th	8.5
7-15	At Ari.	W	6-5	(11)	10	13	Zimmerman	Swindell	Wetteland	44-44	4th	7.5
7-16	At S.F.	L	4-6		8	11	Estes	Loaiza	Nen	44-45	4th	8.5
7-17	At S.F.	L	8-10		12	13	Hernandez	Davis	Nen	44-46	4th	8.5
7-18	At S.F.	L	3-5		11	10	Fultz	Wetteland		44-47	4th	9.5
7-19	At Ana.	W	3-2		10	13	Rogers	Bottenfield	Wetteland	45-47	4th	9.5
7-20	At Ana.	L	1-6		7	9	Etherton	Oliver	Hasegawa	45-48	4th	9.5
7-21	At Sea.	L	3-12		8	11	Abbott	Perisho		45-49	4th	10.5
7-22	At Sea.	L	5-13		9	14	Halama	Glynn		45-50	4th	11.5
7-23	At Sea.	W	3-2		9	8	Helling	Rhodes	Wetteland	46-50	4th	10.5
7-24	Ana.	L	5-6	(12)	11	11	Hasegawa	Crabtree	Percival	46-51	4th	11.5
7-25	Ana.	W	9-6		10	10	Davis	Holtz	Wetteland	47-51	4th	10.5
7-26	Ana.	W	6-5		12	7	Wetteland	Levine		48-51	4th	9.5
7-27	Det.	W	7-3		11	4	Glynn	Sparks	Zimmerman	49-51	4th	8.5
7-28	Det.	W	11-5		14	8	Helling	Moehler		50-51	4th	8.5
7-29	Det.	L	2-10		7	15	Nomo	Rogers		50-52	4th	9.5
7-30	Det.	L	7-8		12	11	Blair	Oliver	Jones	50-53	4th	10.5
8-1	Chi.	L	3-4		7	12	Howry	Wetteland		50-54	4th	11.0
8-2	Chi.	W	7-2		13	4	Helling	Garland	Crabtree	51-54	4th	10.0
8-3	At Tor.	L	1-3		4	12	Castillo	Rogers	Koch	51-55	4th	10.5
8-4	At Tor.	L	8-10		10	14	Quantrill	Venafro	Koch	51-56	4th	10.5
8-5	At Tor.	L	5-8		11	12	Wells	Davis	Koch	51-57	4th	11.5
8-6	At Tor.	W	11-6		16	10	Glynn	Escobar		52-57	4th	11.5
8-7	At Cle.	L	0-2		5	7	Reed	Helling	Wickman	52-58	4th	12.5
8-8	At Cle.	W	11-2		18	9	Rogers	Bere		53-58	4th	13.0
8-9	At Cle.	L	4-6		7	8	Speier	Perisho	Wickman	53-59	4th	13.0
8-11	Bos.	L	3-7		7	11	Arrojo	Glynn		53-60	4th	14.5
8-12	Bos.	W	6-3		6	6	Helling	Wakefield		54-60	4th	13.5
8-13	Bos.	L	2-4		6	7	Ohka	Rogers	Lowe	54-61	4th	13.5
8-14	N.Y.	L	3-7		7	9	Pettitte	Perisho		54-62	4th	13.5
8-15	N.Y.	L	2-10		8	17	Cone	Davis	Gooden	54-63	4th	13.5
8-16	N.Y.	W	5-0		8	4	Sikorski	Hernandez		55-63	4th	12.5
8-17	At Bos.	L	7-8		12	18	Garces	Wetteland		55-64	4th	13.0
8-18	At Bos.	L	4-6		8	11	Ohka	Rogers	Lowe	55-65	4th	13.0
8-19	At Bos.	L	0-9		5	11	P. Martinez	Perisho		55-66	4th	13.0
8-20	At Bos.	W	6-2		9	9	Davis	Fassero		56-66	4th	12.0
8-21	At N.Y.	L	3-12		8	13	Hernandez	Sikorski		56-67	4th	12.5
8-22	At N.Y.	W	5-4		8	6	Crabtree	Neagle	Wetteland	57-67	4th	12.5
8-23	At N.Y.	L	9-10		11	17	Rivera	Crabtree		57-68	4th	12.5
8-24	At N.Y.	L	7-8		11	12	Pettitte	Perisho	Rivera	57-69	4th	12.5
8-25	Tor.	W	1-0	(11)	13	5	Venafro	Koch		58-69	4th	11.5
8-26	Tor.	L	3-9		6	17	Hamilton	Sikorski	Borbon	58-70	4th	12.5
8-27	Tor.	L	4-6		8	14	Trachsel	Helling	Koch	58-71	4th	12.5
8-28	Cle.	L	2-5		6	11	Colon	Rogers	Wickman	58-72	4th	12.5
8-29	Cle.	L	1-12		6	14	Woodard	Glynn		58-73	4th	13.5
8-30	Cle.	L	3-5		7	13	Burba	Davis	Wickman	58-74	4th	13.5
8-31	Cle.	W	14-7		21	14	Venafro	Karsay		59-74	4th	13.0
9-1	At Det.	L	5-7		11	10	Sparks	Helling	Jones	59-75	4th	13.0
9-2	At Det.	L	3-5		10	10	Blair	Rogers	Anderson	59-76	4th	14.0
9-3	At Det.	W	4-1		11	7	Glynn	Weaver	Wetteland	60-76	4th	14.0
9-4	At Chi.	W	5-4		13	11	Davis	Garland	Wetteland	61-76	4th	13.0
9-5	At Chi.	W	2-1		10	8	Johnson	Howry	Wetteland	62-76	4th	13.0
9-6	At Chi.	L	1-13		4	13	Wells	Helling		62-77	4th	13.0
9-7	At Chi.	L	6-10		12	12	Barcelo	Zimmerman	Foulke	62-78	4th	14.0
9-8	At K.C.	W	6-5		12	12	Glynn	Stein	Wetteland	63-78	4th	13.0
9-9	At K.C.	W	6-5		11	10	Zimmerman	Suzuki	Wetteland	64-78	4th	13.0
9-10	At K.C.	L	8-13		16	14	Suppan	Oliver		64-79	4th	14.0
9-12†	Bal.	W	9-1		16	3	Helling	Parrish		65-79		
9-12‡	Bal.	W	6-5		5	8	Rogers	Spurgeon	Wetteland	66-79	4th	13.0
9-13	Bal.	L	4-9		6	14	Rapp	Glynn		66-80	4th	14.0
9-14	K.C.	W	8-1		9	4	Davis	Suzuki	Crabtree	67-80	4th	13.5
9-15	K.C.	W	12-11	(10)	15	18	Wetteland	Santiago		68-80	4th	13.5
9-16	K.C.	L	5-8		10	8	Meadows	Sikorski		68-81	4th	14.5
9-17	K.C.	W	6-5		11	12	Rogers	Reichert	Wetteland	69-81	4th	14.5
9-18	At Min.	L	1-3		10	7	Mays	Helling	Guardado	69-82	4th	15.5
9-19	At Min.	L	7-15		10	20	Kinney	Glynn		69-83	4th	16.5

Date	Opp.	Res.	Score	(inn.*)	Hits	Opp. hits	Winning pitcher	Losing pitcher	Save	Record	Pos.	GB
9-20	At Min.	W	6-4	(12)	10	11	Wetteland	Miller	Venafro	70-83	4th	16.5
9-22	Ana.	L	1-2		8	9	Weber	Oliver	Percival	70-84	4th	16.0
9-23	Ana.	L	4-15		4	18	Karl	Helling		70-85	4th	16.0
9-24	Ana.	L	2-9		5	5	Ortiz	Johnson		70-86	4th	17.0
9-26	At Sea.	L	0-5		6	10	Sele	Glynn		70-87	4th	18.0
9-27	At Sea.	L	4-6		9	11	Garcia	Davis	Sasaki	70-88	4th	19.0
9-28	At Sea.	W	13-6		15	9	Helling	Tomko		71-88	4th	18.0
9-29	At Oak.	L	5-7		12	8	Mecir	Cordero	Isringhausen	71-89	4th	18.5
9-30	At Oak.	L	2-23		9	24	Zito	Oliver		71-90	4th	19.5
10-1	At Oak.	L	0-3		6	8	Hudson	Glynn	Isringhausen	71-91	4th	20.5

Monthly records: April (9-15), May (18-10), June (10-15), July (13-13), August (9-21), September (12-16), October (0-1).
*Innings, if other than nine. †First game of a doubleheader. ‡Second game of a doubleheader.

HIGHLIGHTS

High point: The blockbuster deal that sent Juan Gonzalez to the Tigers didn't work out the way either team expected, but the second-half surge of outfielder Gabe Kapler gave the Rangers reason for optimism. Kapler batted .328 over the final 92 games and put together a franchise-record 28-game hitting streak. That produced the only suspenseful moments after the All-Star Game.

Low point: On the next-to-last day, the Rangers hit rock bottom in a 23-2 loss at Oakland—their 90th defeat of the season. In one fell swoop they allowed the most runs and suffered the worst defeat in club history.

Turning point: The Rangers began June tied for first in the A.L. West. But it was all downhill from there. On June 2, dynamic rookie Ruben Mateo broke his leg in a game against Arizona and the Rangers lost 10 of the next 13, including nine in a row from June 6-16.

Most valuable player: Rafael Palmeiro. Although there were more peaks and valleys than usual, the numbers all added up. He hit 39 home runs, including career No. 400, and drove in 120. Palmeiro also walked a career-high 103 times.

Most valuable pitcher: Rick Helling finished with a 16-13 record and 4.48 ERA, but only after wearing down during a horrid September. Helling entered the final month 14-9 and among the A.L. leaders in ERA.

Most improved player: In 1999, righthander Ryan Glynn was a jittery young pitcher with a hurry-up delivery that compromised his command. He was much more poised and relaxed in 2000 and, despite a September struggle, made a favorable impression with the Rangers.

Most pleasant surprise: When the veteran rotation sprung leaks, 24-year-old lefty Doug Davis stepped in and kept the team from jumping into the overpriced free-agent market. Davis unexpectedly made 13 starts and finished 7-6.

Key injuries: Lefthander Justin Thompson (shoulder surgery) did not pitch all season after reinjuring himself during rehabilitation. ... All-Star catcher Ivan Rodriguez (broken thumb) missed the final two months. ... Center fielder Mateo (broken leg) missed the final four months. ... Catcher Bill Haselman (torn rotator cuff) missed the final two weeks.

... Kapler (quadriceps, shoulder) missed six weeks. ... Outfielder Rusty Greer (ankle) missed nearly nine weeks.

Notable: The Rangers suffered their first 90-loss season since 1988. They also became the fourth team in history to sink from first place to last in consecutive seasons. ... The Rangers made 135 errors, the most in the A.L., and allowed a major league-worst 98 unearned runs. The Rangers also ranked last in the A.L. in fielding percentage at .978. ... Righthander John Wetteland topped the 300-save plateau in May. ... Outfielder Scarborough Green set a club record with five stolen bases in a game at Seattle on September 28, the Rangers' last win of the season.

—EVAN GRANT

RECORDS

2000 regular-season record: 71-91 (4th in A.L. West); 42-39 at home; 29-52 on road; 22-34 vs. East; 25-27 vs. Central; 24-30 vs. West; 19-15 vs. lefthanded starters; 52-76 vs. righthanded starters; 66-80 on grass; 5-11 on turf; 16-23 in daytime; 55-68 at night; 27-25 in one-run games; 5-5 in extra-inning games; 1-0 in doubleheaders.

Team record past five years: 421-389 (.520, ranks 5th in league in that span).

TEAM LEADERS

Batting average: Luis Alicea (.294).
At-bats: Rafael Palmeiro (565).
Runs: Rafael Palmeiro (102).
Hits: Rafael Palmeiro (163).
Total Bases: Rafael Palmeiro (315).
Doubles: Rusty Greer (34).
Triples: Luis Alicea (8).
Home runs: Rafael Palmeiro (39).
Runs batted in: Rafael Palmeiro (120).
Stolen bases: Royce Clayton (11).
Slugging percentage: Rafael Palmeiro (.558).
On-base percentage: Rafael Palmeiro (.397).
Wins: Rick Helling (16).
Earned-run average: Rick Helling (4.48).
Complete games: Kenny Rogers (2).
Shutouts: None.
Saves: John Wetteland (34).
Innings pitched: Kenny Rogers (227.1).
Strikeouts: Rick Helling (146).

GAMES BY POSITION

Catcher: Ivan Rodriguez 87, Bill Haselman 62, B.J. Waszgis 23, Randy Knorr 15, Scott Sheldon 3.
First base: Rafael Palmeiro 108, David Segui 38, Frank Catalanotto 17, Scott Sheldon 10, Dave Martinez 4, B.J. Waszgis 3, Tom Evans 1.
Second base: Luis Alicea 130, Frank Catalanotto 49, Scott Sheldon 12, Kelly Dransfeldt 2, Mike Young 1.
Third base: Mike Lamb 135, Tom Evans 21, Scott Sheldon 15, Luis Alicea 8.
Shortstop: Royce Clayton 148, Scott Sheldon 22, Kelly Dransfeldt 14, Luis Alicea 2.
Outfield: Gabe Kapler 116, Rusty Greer 97, Chad Curtis 80, Scarborough Green 65, Ricky Ledee 57, Ruben Mateo 52, Dave Martinez 35, Jason McDonald 32, Pedro Valdes 14, Scott Sheldon 2, Frank Catalanotto 1.
Designated hitter: David Segui 52, Rafael Palmeiro 46, Frank Catalanotto 19, Chad Curtis 16, Ruben Sierra 14, Scarborough Green 6, Luis Alicea 5, Pedro Valdes 3, Rusty Greer 2, Mike Lamb 2, Tom Evans 1, Jason McDonald 1, Ivan Rodriguez 1, Scott Sheldon 1.

TOP DRAFT CHOICES

1a. None.
1b. **Scott Heard,** C, Rancho Bernardo H.S., San Diego.
1c. **Tyrell Godwin,** OF, University of North Carolina.
1d. **Chad Hawkins,** RHP, Baylor University.
2a. **Jason Bourgeois,** SS, Forest Brook H.S., Houston.
2b. **Randy Truselo,** RHP, Delcastle Tech, Wilmington, Del.
3. **Chris Russ,** LHP, Towson University.
4. **Laynce Nix,** OF, Midland (Tex.) H.S.
5. **Greg Runser,** RHP, Univ. of Houston.
6. **Matt Meisenheimer,** RHP, Greenville (Tex.) H.S.
7. **Virgil Vasquez,** RHP, Santa Barbara (Calif.) H.S.
8. **Nick Masset,** RHP, Pinellas Park H.S., Largo, Fla.
9. **Edwin Encarnacion,** 3B, Manuela Toro H.S., Caguas, P.R.
10. **Billy Montgomery,** OF, San Diego State University.

TORONTO BLUE JAYS
AMERICAN LEAGUE EAST DIVISION

Blue Jays
2001 SCHEDULE
Home games shaded; D—Day game (games starting before 5 p.m.)
*—All-Star Game at Safeco Field (Seattle) † Game played in San Juan, Puerto Rico.

APRIL

SUN	MON	TUE	WED	THU	FRI	SAT
1 TEX	†2	3 TB	4 TB	5 D TB	6 NYY	7 D NYY
8 D NYY	9 TB	10 TB	11 TB	12 KC	13 KC	14 D KC
15 KC	D 16	17 NYY	18 NYY	19 NYY	20 KC	21 KC
22 D KC	23	24 TEX	25 TEX	26	27 ANA	28 D ANA
29 ANA	D 30					

MAY

SUN	MON	TUE	WED	THU	FRI	SAT
		1 OAK	2 OAK	3 D OAK	4 SEA	5 D SEA
6 D SEA	7	8 OAK	9 OAK	10 OAK	11 SEA	12 D SEA
13 SEA	D 14	15 ANA	16 ANA	17 ANA	18 TEX	19 TEX
20 D TEX	21 D CWS	22	23 CWS	24 CWS	25 BOS	26 BOS
27 D BOS	28 CWS	29 CWS	30 CWS	31 BOS		

JUNE

SUN	MON	TUE	WED	THU	FRI	SAT
					1 BOS	2 D BOS
3 BOS	D 4	5 TB	6 TB	7 TB	8 FLA	9 D FLA
10 FLA	D 11 ATL	12 ATL	13 ATL	14	15 MON	16 MON
17 D MON	D 18 BAL	19 BAL	20 BAL	21	22 BOS	23 BOS
24 D BOS	D 25 BAL	26 BAL	27 BAL	28 BAL	29 BOS	30 BOS

JULY

SUN	MON	TUE	WED	THU	FRI	SAT
1 D BOS	D 2 BOS	3 TB	4 D TB	5 TB	6 MON	7 D MON
8 D MON	D 9	10	* 11	12 PHI	13 PHI	14 D PHI
15 NYM	D 16 NYM	17 NYM	18 BOS	19 BOS	20 NYY	21 D NYY
22 NYY	23 NYY	24 BOS	25 BOS	26 BOS	27 NYY	28 D NYY
29 NYY	D 30	31 MIN				

AUGUST

SUN	MON	TUE	WED	THU	FRI	SAT
		1 MIN	2 MIN	3 D BAL	4 D BAL	
5 D BAL	6	7 SEA	8 SEA	9 ANA	10 ANA	11 ANA
12 ANA	13	14 OAK	15 OAK	16 OAK	D 17 TEX	18 D TEX
19 D TEX	20 MIN	21 MIN	22 MIN	23 D BAL	24 BAL	25 D BAL
26 BAL	D 27	28 NYY	29 NYY	30 D NYY	31 DET	

SEPTEMBER

SUN	MON	TUE	WED	THU	FRI	SAT
						1 D DET
2 DET	D 3 NYY	D 4 NYY	5 NYY	6	7 DET	8 D DET
9 DET	D 10	11 BAL	12 BAL	13 BAL	14 CLE	15 D CLE
16 CLE	D 17	18 BAL	19 BAL	20 BAL	21 TB	22 TB
23 TB	D 24 CLE	25 CLE	26 CLE	27 TB	28 TB	29 D TB
30 D TB						

Follow the Blue Jays all season at: www.sportingnews.com/baseball/teams/bluejays/

2001 SEASON
CLUB DIRECTORY

President and chief executive officer
Paul Godfrey
President, baseball & general manager
Gord Ash
Sr. v.p., finance and operations
Stu Hutcheson
Sr. v.p., sales and marketing
Paul Allamby
Vice president, baseball
Bob Mattick
Vice president, baseball
Tim Wilken
V.p., baseball ops. and asst. g.m.
Tim McCleary
Asst. g.m. and dir. of player personnel
Dave Stewart
Special asst. to pres., baseball and g.m.
Al Widmar
Special asst. to pres., baseball and g.m./dir. international scouting
Wayne Morgan
Vice president, media relations
Howard Starkman
Vice president, sales
Greg McNamara
V.p., finance and administration
Susan Quigley
V.p., corp. partnerships & bus. dev.
Mark Lemmon
Director, scouting
Chris Buckley
Assistant director, scouting
Mark Snipp
Director, player development
Jim Hoff
Director, minor leagues
Bob Nelson

Director, Florida operations
Ken Carson
Director, marketing
Peter Cosentino
Director, operations
Mario Coutinho
General manager, TBJ merchandising
Michael Andrejak
Manager, team travel
John Brioux
Trainers
George Poulis, Scott Shannon
Strength and conditioning coordinator
Jeff Krushell
Team physicians
Dr. Allan Gross, Dr. Steve Mirabello, Dr. Ron Taylor
Advance scout
Sal Butera
Special assignment scouts
Chris Bourjos, Duane Larson, Ted Lekas
Special assignment/nat. cross-checker
Mike Mangan
Southeast regional supervisor
Mike Cadahia
Northwest regional supervisor
Ron Tostenson
Dir., Canadian/Northeast reg. supervisor
Bill Byckowski
Scouts
Charles Aliano, Tony Arias, Jaymie Bayne, Andy Beene, Dave Blume, Rick Cerrone, Joey Davis, Ellis Dungan, Joe Ford, Tom Hinkle, Tim Huff, Jim Hughes, Edwin Lawrence, Marty Miller, Ty Nichols, Andy Pienovi, Demerius Pittman, Jorge Rivera, Jim Rooney, Joe Siers, Gerry Sobeck

MINOR LEAGUE AFFILIATES

Class	Team	League	Manager
AAA	Syracuse	International	Omar Malave
AA	Tennessee	Southern	Rocket Wheeler
A	Auburn	New York-Penn	To be announced
A	Charleston (WV)	South Atlantic	Rolando Pino
A	Dunedin	Florida State	Marty Pevey
Rookie	Medicine Hat	Pioneer	To be announced

BROADCAST INFORMATION

Radio: CHUM-AM (1050).
TV: CBC-TV.
Cable TV: The Sports Network, CTV SportsNet.

SPRING TRAINING

Ballpark (city): Dunedin Stadium at Grant Field (Dunedin, Fla.).
Ticket information: 800-707-8269; 727-733-0429.

SPRING TRAINING ROSTER

Manager—Buck Martinez (13).
Coaches—Terry Bevington (35), Mark Connor (53), Cito Gaston (41), Garth Iorg (16), Gil Patterson (47), Cookie Rojas (1).

No.	PITCHERS	B/T	Ht./Wt.	Born	2000 clubs
	Beirne, Kevin	L/R	6-4/210	1-1-74	Charlotte, Chicago A.L.
51	Borbon, Pedro	L/L	6-1/224	11-15-67	Toronto
26	Carpenter, Chris	R/R	6-6/225	4-27-75	Toronto
38	Coco, Pasqual	R/R	6-1/185	9-24-77	Tennessee, Toronto
45	Escobar, Kelvim	R/R	6-1/210	4-11-76	Toronto
29	Eyre, Scott	L/L	6-1/200	5-30-72	Chicago A.L., Charlotte
36	File, Bob	R/R	6-4/210	1-28-77	Tennessee, Syracuse
52	Frascatore, John	R/R	6-1/223	2-4-70	Toronto
32	Halladay, Roy	R/R	6-6/230	5-14-77	Toronto, Syracuse
50	Hamilton, Joey	R/R	6-4/240	9-9-70	Syracuse, Toronto
44	Koch, Billy	R/R	6-3/215	12-14-74	Toronto
21	Loaiza, Esteban	R/R	6-3/205	12-31-71	Texas, Toronto
28	Painter, Lance	L/L	6-1/200	7-21-67	Toronto, Dunedin
39	Parris, Steve	R/R	6-0/195	12-17-67	Cincinnati
54	Perez, George	R/R	6-4/220	3-20-79	Queens
19	Plesac, Dan	L/L	6-5/217	2-4-62	Arizona
48	Quantrill, Paul	L/R	6-1/195	11-3-68	Toronto
	Sirotka, Mike	L/L	6-1/200	5-13-71	Chicago A.L.
49	Woodards, Orlando	R/R	6-2/200	1-2-78	Dunedin

No.	CATCHERS	B/T	Ht./Wt.	Born	2000 clubs
30	Castillo, Alberto	R/R	6-0/200	2-10-70	Toronto
9	Fletcher, Darrin	L/R	6-2/205	10-3-66	Toronto
6	Lawrence, Joe	R/R	6-2/190	2-13-77	Dunedin, Tennessee
17	Phelps, Josh	R/R	6-3/220	5-12-78	Tennessee, Toronto, Dunedin
64	Werth, Jayson	R/R	6-5/190	5-20-79	Bowie, Frederick

No.	INFIELDERS	B/T	Ht./Wt.	Born	2000 clubs
7	Batista, Tony	R/R	6-0/205	12-9-73	Toronto
18	Bush, Homer	R/R	5-10/208	11-12-72	Toronto
25	Delgado, Carlos	L/R	6-3/230	6-25-72	Toronto
3	Frye, Jeff	R/R	5-9/160	8-31-66	Boston, Colorado
20	Fullmer, Brad	L/R	6-0/215	1-17-75	Toronto
8	Gonzalez, Alex	R/R	6-0/195	4-8-73	Toronto, Syracuse
3	Izturis, Cesar	B/R	5-9/175	2-10-80	Syracuse
5	Woodward, Chris	R/R	6-0/185	6-27-76	Toronto, Syracuse

No.	OUTFIELDERS	B/T	Ht./Wt.	Born	2000 clubs
23	Cruz, Jose	B/R	6-0/200	4-19-74	Toronto
12	Freel, Ryan	R/R	5-10/185	3-8-76	Tennessee, Dunedin, Syracuse
27	Greene, Todd	R/R	5-10/208	5-8-71	Syracuse, Toronto, Dunedin
43	Mondesi, Raul	R/R	5-11/230	3-12-71	Toronto
	Simmons, Brian	B/R	6-2/190	9-4-73	DID NOT PLAY
24	Stewart, Shannon	R/R	6-1/205	2-25-74	Toronto, Dunedin
15	Thompson, Andy	R/R	6-3/220	10-8-75	Syracuse, Toronto
10	Wells, Vernon	R/R	6-1/215	12-8-78	Syracuse, Toronto
11	Wise, DeWayne	L/L	6-1/180	2-24-78	Toronto

BALLPARK INFORMATION

Ballpark (capacity, surface)
SkyDome (45,100, artificial)

Address
One Blue Jays Way
Suite 3200
Toronto, Ontario M5V 1J1

Official website
www.bluejays.com

Business phone
416-341-1000

Ticket information
416-341-1234 and 1-888-OK GO JAY

Ticket prices
$44 (premium dugout level)
$41 (field level-infield)
$35 (field level-bases)
$29 (field level-baselines)
$23 (100 & 200 level-outfield; SkyDeck-infield)
$16 (SkyDeck-bases)
$7 (Skydeck-baselines)

Field dimensions (from home plate)
To left field at foul line, 330 feet
To center field, 400 feet
To right field at foul line, 330 feet

First game played
June 5, 1989 (Brewers 5, Blue Jays 3)

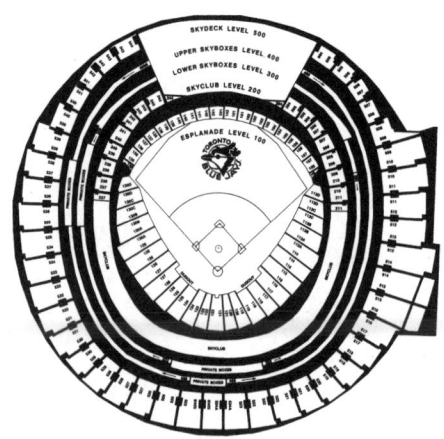

Date	Opp.	Res.	Score	(inn.*)	Hits	Opp. hits	Winning pitcher	Losing pitcher	Save	Record	Pos.	GB
4-3	K.C.	W	5-4		8	9	Koch	Spradlin		1-0	T1st	...
4-4	K.C.	W	6-3		7	7	Halladay	Witasick	Koch	2-0	T1st	...
4-5	K.C.	L	3-4		5	7	Rosado	Carpenter	Bottalico	2-1	T1st	...
4-6	K.C.	L	3-9		5	17	Durbin	Escobar	Rigby	2-2	T3rd	0.5
4-7	At Tex.	L	5-11		11	11	Clark	Castillo		2-3	T3rd	1.5
4-8	At Tex.	W	4-0		10	9	Wells	Rogers		3-3	3rd	1.5
4-9	At Tex.	L	5-7		7	9	Helling	Halladay		3-4	3rd	2.5
4-10	At Ana.	L	0-6		3	7	Schoeneweis	Carpenter		3-5	3rd	3.0
4-11	At Ana.	L	4-5		10	8	Ortiz	Escobar	Percival	3-6	4th	3.0
4-12	At Ana.	W	6-2		13	9	Borbon	Petkovsek		4-6	4th	2.0
4-14	Sea.	L	9-11		16	12	Moyer	Wells		4-7	4th	3.0
4-15	Sea.	L	6-17		10	16	Rodriguez	Halladay	Paniagua	4-8	T4th	4.0
4-16	Sea.	L	7-19		13	22	Garcia	Carpenter		4-9	5th	5.0
4-17	Ana.	W	7-1		10	8	Escobar	Ortiz		5-9	5th	5.0
4-18	Ana.	L	10-16		17	19	Dickson	Castillo		5-10	5th	6.0
4-19	Ana.	W	12-4		17	8	Wells	Hill		6-10	4th	6.0
4-20	Ana.	W	12-11		14	19	Halladay	Bottenfield	Koch	7-10	4th	5.5
4-21	N.Y.	W	8-3		12	5	Carpenter	Mendoza		8-10	4th	4.5
4-22	N.Y.	W	8-2		10	9	Escobar	Cone		9-10	4th	3.5
4-23	N.Y.	L	7-10		8	15	Hernandez	Andrews	Rivera	9-11	4th	4.5
4-24	At Oak.	W	3-2		7	10	Wells	Appier	Koch	10-11	4th	3.5
4-25	At Oak.	L	2-11		4	12	Hudson	Halladay		10-12	4th	3.5
4-26	At Oak.	W	4-2		9	6	Carpenter	Olivares	Koch	11-12	4th	3.5
4-28	At N.Y.	L	0-6		3	8	Cone	Escobar		11-13	4th	4.5
4-29	At N.Y.	W	6-2		14	11	Wells	Hernandez	Koch	12-13	4th	3.5
4-30	At N.Y.	L	1-7		9	12	Clemens	Halladay		12-14	4th	4.5
5-1	At Chi.	W	5-3		9	6	Carpenter	Wells	Koch	13-14	4th	4.5
5-2	At Chi.	W	4-1		7	5	Castillo	Wunsch	Koch	14-14	4th	4.5
5-3	At Chi.	L	3-7		5	8	Baldwin	Escobar	Foulke	14-15	4th	5.5
5-4	Cle.	W	8-1		10	7	Wells	Finley		15-15	4th	5.0
5-5	Cle.	W	11-10		13	20	Koch	Shuey		16-15	4th	5.0
5-6	Cle.	L	6-8		10	11	Rincon	Quantrill	Karsay	16-16	4th	6.0
5-7	Cle.	L	8-10	(12)	16	14	Shuey	Gunderson	Karsay	16-17	4th	6.0
5-8	Bal.	W	6-5		12	14	Escobar	Johnson	Koch	17-17	4th	6.0
5-9	Bal.	W	6-4		12	10	Wells	Mussina	Koch	18-17	3rd	6.0
5-10	Bal.	W	7-2		14	5	Painter	Erickson	Quantrill	19-17	3rd	5.5
5-12	At T.B.	L	3-4		10	8	White	Carpenter	Lopez	19-18	3rd	5.0
5-13	At T.B.	W	8-4		12	5	Escobar	Lidle		20-18	3rd	4.0
5-14	At T.B.	W	3-2		8	7	Wells	Lopez		21-18	3rd	3.5
5-15	Bos.	L	1-8		6	13	Schourek	Castillo		21-19	3rd	4.5
5-16	Bos.	W	7-6		14	11	Munro	Lowe		22-19	3rd	3.5
5-17	Bos.	L	0-8		4	15	P. Martinez	Carpenter		22-20	3rd	4.5
5-19	Chi.	L	3-5		11	5	Sirotka	Escobar	Foulke	22-21	3rd	5.5
5-20	Chi.	L	2-6		7	12	Baldwin	Wells		22-22	3rd	5.5
5-21	Chi.	L	1-2		6	1	Eldred	Castillo	Foulke	22-23	3rd	5.5
5-22	Chi.	W	4-3		11	6	Koch	Howry		23-23	3rd	5.0
5-23	At Bos.	W	3-2		7	9	Carpenter	P. Martinez	Koch	24-23	3rd	4.0
5-24	At Bos.	L	3-6	(11)	10	9	Cormier	Frascatore		24-24	3rd	5.0
5-25	At Bos.	W	11-6		17	13	Wells	Schourek		25-24	3rd	4.0
5-26	At Det.	W	8-2		12	7	Frascatore	Brocail		26-24	3rd	4.0
5-27	At Det.	L	3-4		7	7	Brocail	Quantrill		26-25	3rd	4.0
5-28	At Det.	W	12-7		15	11	Andrews	Blair		27-25	3rd	4.0
5-30	Min.	L	1-4		5	10	Redman	Escobar	Hawkins	27-26	3rd	5.0
5-31	Min.	W	4-2		6	9	Wells	Radke	Koch	28-26	3rd	4.0
6-1	Min.	L	1-5		6	6	Milton	Castillo		28-27	3rd	4.0
6-2	At Fla.	L	10-11		15	15	Bones	Munro	Alfonseca	28-28	3rd	4.0
6-3	At Fla.	L	1-2		5	7	Looper	Koch	Alfonseca	28-29	3rd	4.0
6-4	At Fla.	W	7-2		12	8	Escobar	Nunez		29-29	3rd	4.0
6-5	At Atl.	W	9-3		12	9	Wells	Burkett		30-29	3rd	3.0
6-6	At Atl.	L	6-7		10	11	Remlinger	Frascatore		30-30	3rd	4.0
6-7	At Atl.	W	12-8		9	16	Cubillan	Millwood	Koch	31-30	3rd	4.0
6-9	Mon.	W	13-3		16	8	Carpenter	Tucker		32-30	3rd	3.0
6-10	Mon.	L	2-11		6	14	Armas	Escobar		32-31	3rd	4.0
6-11	Mon.	W	8-3		9	13	Koch	Mota		33-31	3rd	3.5
6-12	At Det.	W	4-2		10	8	Castillo	Nomo	Koch	34-31	3rd	3.0
6-13	At Det.	L	3-16		8	21	Blair	Andrews		34-32	3rd	3.0
6-14	At Det.	W	8-1		9	9	Carpenter	Weaver		35-32	3rd	3.0
6-16	At Bos.	L	4-7		11	12	Pichardo	Escobar	Lowe	35-33	3rd	3.0
6-17	At Bos.	W	11-10		14	13	Wells	R. Martinez	Koch	36-33	3rd	2.0
6-18	At Bos.	W	5-1		9	6	Castillo	Fassero	Koch	37-33	3rd	1.0
6-20	Det.	L	6-18		8	18	Weaver	Carpenter		37-34	3rd	2.0
6-21	Det.	W	6-0		12	4	Escobar	Moehler		38-34	3rd	1.0
6-22	Det.	W	7-4		8	8	Wells	Nomo		39-34	3rd	0.5
6-23	Bos.	W	5-4		9	7	Castillo	Wasdin	Koch	40-34	1st	+0.5

Date	Opp.	Res.	Score	(inn.*)	Hits	Opp. hits	Winning pitcher	Losing pitcher	Save	Record	Pos.	GB
6-24	Bos.	W	6-4		9	7	Halladay	Rose	Koch	41-34	1st	+1.0
6-25	Bos.	W	6-5	(13)	10	15	DeWitt	Florie		42-34	1st	+2.0
6-27	At T.B.	L	1-11		9	13	Trachsel	Escobar		42-35	1st	+2.0
6-28	At T.B.	W	5-2		7	5	Wells	Yan		43-35	1st	+3.0
6-29	At T.B.	W	12-3		14	10	Castillo	Lidle		44-35	1st	+3.0
6-30	At Bal.	L	3-8		7	11	Rapp	Halladay		44-36	1st	+3.0
7-1	At Bal.	L	5-12		8	13	Ponson	Carpenter		44-37	1st	+2.0
7-2	At Bal.	L	2-3		8	7	Trombley	Quantrill	Mills	44-38	1st	+1.0
7-3	At Bal.	W	6-4		6	11	Wells	Johnson	Koch	45-38	1st	+1.5
7-4	At Cle.	L	4-9		9	9	Colon	Frascatore		45-39	1st	+1.5
7-5	At Cle.	L	7-15		12	16	Brewington	Quantrill		45-40	1st	+0.5
7-6	At Cle.	W	9-6		15	15	Carpenter	Burba	Koch	46-40	1st	+0.5
7-7	At Mon.	L	5-10		10	12	Lira	Quantrill		46-41	2nd	0.5
7-8	At Mon.	W	6-3		7	6	Wells	Armas	Koch	47-41	2nd	1.0
7-9	At Mon.	W	13-3		18	8	Castillo	Hermanson		48-41	2nd	...
7-13	Phi.	L	5-8		7	11	Schilling	Carpenter	Brantley	48-42	2nd	...
7-14	Phi.	W	3-2		13	6	Koch	Brantley		49-42	2nd	...
7-15	Phi.	L	3-7		5	11	Chen	Wells		49-43	2nd	0.5
7-16	N.Y. (NL)	W	7-3		8	10	Halladay	Leiter	Koch	50-43	2nd	0.5
7-17	N.Y. (NL)	L	5-7	(11)	5	11	Franco	Borbon	Benitez	50-44	2nd	0.5
7-18	N.Y. (NL)	L	7-11		13	12	B.J. Jones	Carpenter		50-45	3rd	1.5
7-19	T.B.	W	5-2		9	2	Escobar	Lopez	Koch	51-45	3rd	1.5
7-20	T.B.	W	6-5		10	7	Quantrill	White	Koch	52-45	2nd	0.5
7-21	Bal.	L	5-9		9	16	Rapp	Halladay		52-46	2nd	1.5
7-22	Bal.	L	2-8		9	13	Mercedes	Loaiza		52-47	3rd	1.5
7-23	Bal.	W	4-1		8	5	Castillo	Mussina	Koch	53-47	3rd	1.5
7-25	Cle.	L	3-10		9	10	Finley	Escobar		53-48	3rd	3.0
7-26	Cle.	W	8-1		9	5	Wells	Colon		54-48	2nd	3.0
7-27	At Sea.	W	7-2		16	7	Loaiza	Rhodes		55-48	2nd	2.0
7-28	At Sea.	L	4-7		6	9	Garcia	Carpenter	Sasaki	55-49	3rd	3.0
7-29	At Sea.	L	5-6	(13)	9	16	Tomko	Halladay		55-50	3rd	3.0
7-30	At Sea.	L	6-10		10	13	Sele	Escobar	Paniagua	55-51	3rd	4.0
7-31	At Oak.	L	1-6		4	12	Hudson	Wells		55-52	3rd	4.5
8-1	At Oak.	L	1-3	(10)	7	6	Isringhausen	Koch		55-53	3rd	5.5
8-2	At Oak.	L	4-5		10	12	Mecir	Guthrie	Isringhausen	55-54	3rd	5.5
8-3	Tex.	W	3-1		12	4	Castillo	Rogers	Koch	56-54	3rd	5.5
8-4	Tex.	W	10-8		14	10	Quantrill	Venafro	Koch	57-54	3rd	5.5
8-5	Tex.	W	8-5		12	11	Wells	Davis	Koch	58-54	3rd	4.5
8-6	Tex.	L	6-11		10	16	Glynn	Escobar		58-55	3rd	4.5
8-7	At K.C.	L	7-8		14	14	Stein	Loaiza	Bottalico	58-56	3rd	4.5
8-8	At K.C.	W	6-1		14	4	Castillo	Suzuki		59-56	3rd	4.5
8-9	At K.C.	L	3-5		11	10	Suppan	Trachsel	Larkin	59-57	3rd	5.5
8-10	At K.C.	W	15-7		17	14	Carpenter	Fussell		60-57	3rd	5.5
8-11	At Min.	L	4-9		8	13	Romero	Escobar		60-58	3rd	5.5
8-12	At Min.	L	3-6		10	13	Redman	Loaiza	Hawkins	60-59	3rd	5.5
8-13	At Min.	W	13-3		20	8	Carpenter	Radke		61-59	3rd	5.5
8-15	Ana.	L	4-8		8	12	Wise	Wells		61-60	3rd	7.0
8-16	Ana.	W	8-6		10	11	Koch	Pote		62-60	3rd	6.0
8-18	Min.	W	3-2		8	8	Loaiza	Kinney	Koch	63-60	3rd	5.5
8-19	Min.	L	1-5		8	8	Radke	Guthrie	Guardado	63-61	3rd	6.5
8-20	Min.	W	6-3		10	9	Wells	Carrasco		64-61	3rd	5.5
8-22	K.C.	W	7-5		10	11	Escobar	Santiago	Koch	65-61	3rd	5.0
8-23	K.C.	W	9-8		13	11	Escobar	Larkin	Koch	66-61	3rd	5.0
8-25	At Tex.	L	0-1	(11)	5	13	Venafro	Koch		66-62	3rd	5.5
8-26	At Tex.	W	9-3		17	6	Hamilton	Sikorski	Borbon	67-62	3rd	5.5
8-27	At Tex.	W	6-4		14	8	Trachsel	Helling	Koch	68-62	3rd	5.5
8-28	At Ana.	W	4-2		5	7	Loaiza	Ortiz	Koch	69-62	3rd	5.5
8-29	At Ana.	L	4-9		11	12	Holtz	Carpenter		69-63	3rd	5.5
8-30	At Ana.	W	11-2		19	9	Wells	Wise		70-63	3rd	5.5
9-1	Oak.	W	4-3		14	10	Frascatore	D. Jones		71-63	3rd	5.5
9-2	Oak.	L	0-8		5	9	Heredia	Trachsel	Mecir	71-64	3rd	6.5
9-3	Oak.	L	3-4		8	7	Hudson	Loaiza	Mecir	71-65	3rd	6.5
9-4	Oak.	L	0-10		2	19	Zito	Wells		71-66	3rd	7.5
9-5	Sea.	L	3-4		6	7	Rhodes	Escobar	Sasaki	71-67	3rd	8.5
9-6	Sea.	W	7-3		12	6	Hamilton	Halama		72-67	3rd	7.5
9-7	Sea.	L	1-8		3	12	Garcia	Trachsel		72-68	3rd	8.5
9-8	Det.	W	3-0		7	5	Loaiza	Weaver		73-68	3rd	8.5
9-9	Det.	W	6-5		8	10	Koch	Nitkowski		74-68	3rd	8.5
9-10	Det.	W	6-2		7	8	Carpenter	Sparks	Escobar	75-68	2nd	8.5
9-12	At N.Y.	L	2-10		8	11	Neagle	Hamilton		75-69	3rd	9.0
9-13	At N.Y.	L	2-3		11	7	Clemens	Loaiza	Rivera	75-70	3rd	10.0
9-14	At N.Y.	W	3-2	(11)	6	11	Koch	Choate	Escobar	76-70	3rd	9.0
9-15	At Chi.	W	6-5		6	11	Escobar	Garland	Koch	77-70	3rd	8.0
9-16	At Chi.	L	3-6		11	8	Wunsch	Escobar	Foulke	77-71	3rd	9.0
9-17	At Chi.	W	14-1		15	6	Painter	Wells		78-71	3rd	8.0
9-19	N.Y.	W	16-3		19	4	Trachsel	Pettitte		79-71	3rd	6.5
9-20	N.Y.	W	7-2		10	9	Loaiza	Cone		80-71	2nd	5.5
9-21	N.Y.	W	3-1		9	5	Wells	Hernandez		81-71	2nd	4.5

Date	Opp.	Res.	Score	(inn.*)	Hits	Opp. hits	Winning pitcher	Losing pitcher	Save	Record	Pos.	GB
9-22	T.B.	L	2-3		7	10	Lidle	Frascatore	Hernandez	81-72	2nd	4.5
9-23	T.B.	W	7-6	13	9		Koch	Enders		82-72	2nd	4.5
9-24	T.B.	L	0-6		2	13	Harper	Trachsel		82-73	2nd	5.5
9-25	T.B.	L	1-5		5	10	Wilson	Loaiza	Hernandez	82-74	2nd	5.5
9-26	At Bal.	L	1-2		5	7	Mercedes	Wells	Kohlmeier	82-75	T2nd	5.5
9-27	At Bal.	W	4-0		7	4	Castillo	Ponson		83-75	T2nd	4.5
9-28	At Bal.	L	1-23		2	23	Rapp	Carpenter		83-76	3rd	4.5
9-29	At Cle.	L	4-8		5	9	Speier	Trachsel	Karsay	83-77	3rd	4.5
9-30	At Cle.	L	5-6	10	10	11	Finley	Loaiza	Wickman	83-78	3rd	4.5
10-1	At Cle.	L	4-11		8	12	Woodard	Wells		83-79	3rd	4.5

Monthly records: April (12-14), May (16-12), June (16-10), July (11-16), August (15-11), September (13-15), October (0-1).
*Innings, if other than nine. †First game of a doubleheader. ‡Second game of a doubleheader.

HIGHLIGHTS

High point: A three-game sweep of the Red Sox in late June propelled the Blue Jays into the A.L. East Division lead. It would expand briefly to three games.
Low point: Still within striking distance of the first-place Yankees entering September, the Jays opened a 10-game homestand by losing three of four to Oakland and two of three to Seattle, getting outscored 40-18.
Turning point: On July 22, when right fielder and No. 3 hitter Raul Mondesi was placed on the disabled list with an elbow injury—effectively ending his season. Five days later, the club started a 1-6 trip to Seattle and Oakland, after which they never again got closer to first than 4½ games.
Most valuable player: Carlos Delgado made a strong run at the A.L.'s first triple crown since 1967. Batting cleanup, he established career highs with a .344 average, 115 runs, 196 hits, 57 doubles, 137 RBIs, 99 extra-base hits, 123 walks and a 22-game hitting streak.
Most valuable pitcher: David Wells led the A.L. with 15 wins at the All-Star break and went on to record the fifth 20-win season in club history. Wells did not walk a batter in 16 of his 35 starts and his strikeout-to-walk ratio of 5.35 set a club record.
Most improved player: Center fielder Jose Cruz Jr., who batted .241 and showed spotty power in 106 games in 1999, broke through with career highs in doubles, triples, homers, hits and stolen bases while playing all 162 games in the field.
Most pleasant surprise: Veteran Frank Castillo, perilously close to losing his roster spot, rediscovered his control and posted a 10-5 record, one win shy of his 1995 career high. Castillo, who held opponents to a .220 average, reeled off nine straight wins starting June 12.
Key injuries: Righthanded starter Joey Hamilton missed the first 4½ months while recovering from 1999 shoulder surgery. ... Castillo missed a month with a sprained right forearm. ... Reliever Lance Painter spent three weeks on the disabled list with a strained elbow. ... Mondesi missed 66 games and shortstop Alex Gonzalez (groin) and outfielder Shannon Stewart (hamstring) missed

two weeks. ... Second baseman Homer Bush missed time early with a hip injury and broke his hand July 30, ending his season. ... Catcher Darrin Fletcher missed three weeks with a tear in his rotator cuff.
Notable: The Blue Jays hit a franchise-record 244 home runs and put together a club-record 23-game homer streak. ... The Jays posted winning records against the top two teams in the East—7-5 vs. the Yankees and 8-4 vs. the Red Sox. But they were 5-15 against the two West Division playoff teams—Seattle and Oakland. ... In an April series against Seattle, the Jays scored 22 runs and lost all three games. Seattle piled up 47 runs. ... Manager Jim Fregosi was fired after compiling a 167-157 record and directing consecutive third-place finishes in two seasons. ... The final home attendance of 1,819,886 marked the first time the club failed to draw 2 million fans since the SkyDome opened in 1989.
—TOM MALONEY

RECORDS

2000 regular-season record: 83-79 (3rd in A.L. East); 45-36 at home; 38-43 on road; 37-30 vs. East; 28-25 vs. Central; 18-24 vs. West; 19-24 vs. lefthanded starters; 64-55 vs. righthanded starters; 31-38 on grass; 52-41 on turf; 28-28 in daytime; 55-51 at night; 21-19 in one-run games; 2-6 in extra-inning games; 0-0 in doubleheaders.
Team record past five years: 405-405 (.500, ranks 8th in league in that span).

TEAM LEADERS

Batting average: Carlos Delgado (.344).
At-bats: Tony Batista (620).
Runs: Carlos Delgado (115).
Hits: Carlos Delgado (196).
Total Bases: Carlos Delgado (378).
Doubles: Carlos Delgado (57).
Triples: Jose Cruz, Shannon Stewart (5).
Home runs: Tony Batista, Carlos Delgado (41).
Runs batted in: Carlos Delgado (137).
Stolen bases: Raul Mondesi (22).
Slugging percentage: Carlos Delgado (.664).

On-base percentage: Carlos Delgado (.470).
Wins: David Wells (20).
Earned-run average: David Wells (4.11).
Complete games: David Wells (9).
Shutouts: Kelvim Escobar, Esteban Loaiza, David Wells (1).
Saves: Billy Koch (33).
Innings pitched: David Wells (229.2).
Strikeouts: David Wells (166).

GAMES BY POSITION

Catcher: Darrin Fletcher 117, Alberto Castillo 66, Charlie Greene 3, Todd Greene 2, Josh Phelps 1.
First base: Carlos Delgado 162, Chris Woodward 3, Brad Fullmer 1.
Second base: Homer Bush 75, Craig Grebeck 56, Mickey Morandini 35, Chris Woodward 3.
Third base: Tony Batista 154, Chris Woodward 9.
Shortstop: Alex S. Gonzalez 141, Chris Woodward 22, Craig Grebeck 8.
Outfield: Jose Cruz 162, Shannon Stewart 136, Raul Mondesi 96, Dave Martinez 47, Marty Cordova 41, Dewayne Wise 18, Rob Ducey 3, Chad Mottola 3, Vernon Wells 3, Andy Thompson 2, Todd Greene 1.
Designated hitter: Brad Fullmer 129, Todd Greene 23, Marty Cordova 15, Darrin Fletcher 2, Dewayne Wise 2.

TOP DRAFT CHOICES

1a. **Miguel Negron,** OF, Manuela Toro H.S., Caguas, P.R.
1b. **Dustin McGowan,** RHP, Long County H.S., Ludowici, Ga.
2a. **Peter Bauer,** RHP, University of South Carolina.
2b. **Dominic Rich,** 2B, Auburn Univ.
3. **Morrin Davis,** OF, Hillsborough H.S., Tampa, Fla.
4. **Raul Tablado,** SS, Southridge H.S., Miami.
5. **Mike Smith,** RHP, U. of Richmond.
6. **Rich Thompson,** OF, James Madison University.
7. **Aaron Sisk,** 3B, U. of New Mexico.
8. **Dave Abbott,** RHP, Univ. of Arizona.
9. **Nom Siriveaw,** 3B-OF, Oklahoma State University.
10. **Jerrod Payne,** RHP, University of North Florida.

ARIZONA DIAMONDBACKS
NATIONAL LEAGUE WEST DIVISION

Diamondbacks
2001 SCHEDULE
Home games shaded; D—Day game (games starting before 5 p.m.)
*—All-Star Game at Safeco Field (Seattle)

APRIL

SUN	MON	TUE	WED	THU	FRI	SAT
1	2	3 LA	4 LA	5 LA	6 STL	7 D STL
8 D STL	9	10 LA	11 LA	12 LA	13 COL	14 D COL
15 D COL	16 STL	17 STL	18 STL	19	20 COL	21 COL
22 D COL	23 FLA	24 FLA	25 FLA	26 ATL	27 ATL	28 ATL
29 ATL	30					

MAY

SUN	MON	TUE	WED	THU	FRI	SAT
		1 MON	2 MON	3 MON	4 NYM	5 D NYM
6 NYM	7 D CIN	8 CIN	9 CIN	10	11 PHI	12 PHI
13 D PHI	14	15 CIN	16 CIN	17 D CIN	18 D CUB	19 D CUB
20 D CUB	21 SF	22 SF	23 SF	24 D SD	25 SD	26 SD
27 D SD	28 D SF	29 SF	30 SF	31		

JUNE

SUN	MON	TUE	WED	THU	FRI	SAT
					1 SD	2 SD
3 D SD	4 LA	5 LA	6 LA	7 LA	8 KC	9 KC
10 KC	11	12 CUB	13 CUB	14 D CUB	15 DET	16 DET
17 D DET	18	19 LA	20 LA	21 COL	22 COL	23 D COL
24 COL	25 D HOU	26 HOU	27 HOU	28	29 COL	30 COL

JULY

SUN	MON	TUE	WED	THU	FRI	SAT
1 COL	2	3 HOU	4 HOU	5 HOU	6 OAK	7 OAK
8 OAK	9 D	10	11 *	12 ANA	13 ANA	14 ANA
15 SEA	16 SEA	17 D SEA	18 SD	19 SD	20 SF	21 D SF
22 D SF	23 SD	24 SD	25 SD	26 SF	27 SF	28 SF
29 D SF	30	31 MON				

AUGUST

SUN	MON	TUE	WED	THU	FRI	SAT
			1 MON	2 MON	3 NYM	4 D NYM
5 NYM	6	7 FLA	8 FLA	9 D FLA	10 ATL	11 D ATL
12 ATL	13 PIT	14 PIT	15 PIT	16	17 CUB	18 CUB
19 CUB	20	21 PIT	22 PIT	23 PIT	24 PHI	25 D PHI
26 PHI	27 D PHI	28 SF	29 SF	30 SF	31 SD	

SEPTEMBER

SUN	MON	TUE	WED	THU	FRI	SAT
						1 SD
2 SD	3	4 SF	5 SF	6 SF	7 D SD	8 D SD
9 D SD	10 SD	11 COL	12 COL	13 COL	14 MIL	15 MIL
16 MIL	17 COL	18 COL	19 D COL	20 LA	21 LA	22 LA
23 LA	24	25 MIL	26 MIL	27 MIL	28 LA	29 LA
30 D LA						

2001 SEASON
CLUB DIRECTORY

Managing general partner
Jerry Colangelo
President
Richard Dozer
Vice president and general manager
Joe Garagiola Jr.
Sr. vice president, sales and marketing
Scott Brubaker
Vice president, finance
Thomas Harris
V.p., tickets and special services
Dianne Aguilar
Vice president, sales
Blake Edwards
Vice president, community affairs
Mark Fernandez
Assistant general manager
Sandy Johnson
Director of Hispanic marketing
Richard Saenz
Director of Tucson operations
Rich Tomey
Director of public relations
Mike Swanson
Director of ballpark services
Russ Amaral
Director of suite services
Diney Mahoney
Director of team travel
Roger Riley
Director of minor league operations
Tommy Jones
Director of Pacific Rim operations
Jim Marshall

Director of scouting
Mike Rizzo
Assistant director of scouting
Bob Miller
Trainer
Paul Lessard
Assistant trainer
Dave Edwards
Club physician
Dr. Michael Lee
National scouting supervisor
Kendall Carter
Regional supervisors
Mark Baca, Ed Durkin, Kris Kline, Charles Scott
Scouting coordinators
Derek Bryant, Junior Noboa
Professional scouts
Bill Earnhart, Mike Piatnik
Major League and advance scouts
Mack Babitt, Jim Marshall, Phil Rizzo, Dick Scott
Special assignment scout
Bryan Lambe
Scouts
Ray Blanco, Ray Corbett, Mike Daughtry, Doug Gassaway, Jason Goligoski, Scott Jaster, Steve Kmetko, Hal Kurtzman, Greg Lonigro, Howard McCullough, Matt Merullo, Bob Steinkamp, Mike Valarezo, Luke Wren

MINOR LEAGUE AFFILIATES

Class	Team	League	Manager
AAA	Tucson	Pacific Coast	Tom Spencer
AA	El Paso	Texas	Al Pedrique
A	Lancaster	California	Scott Coolbaugh
A	South Bend	Midwest	Steve Scarsone
A	Yakima	Northwest	Greg Lonigro
Rookie	Missoula	Pioneer	Chip Hale

BROADCAST INFORMATION

Radio: KTAR-AM (620).
TV: KTVK (Channel 3)
Cable TV: Fox Sports Net Arizona.

SPRING TRAINING

Ballpark (city): Tucson Electric Park (Tucson, Ariz.).
Ticket information: 800-638-4253, 520-434-1111.

Follow the Diamondbacks all season at:
www.sportingnews.com/baseball/teams/diamondbacks/

SPRING TRAINING ROSTER

Manager—Bob Brenly (15).
Coaches—Bob Melvin (3), Eddie Rodriguez (14), Chris Speier (16), Dwayne Murphy (21), Glenn Sherlock (53), Bob Welch.

No.	PITCHERS	B/T	Ht./Wt.	Born	2000 clubs
34	Anderson, Brian	B/L	6-1/183	4-26-72	Arizona
43	Batista, Miguel	R/R	6-0/190	2-19-71	Montreal, Kansas City, Omaha
47	Bierbroldt, Nick	L/L	6-5/185	5-16-78	Tucson, Arizona Diamondbacks, El Paso
50	Guzman, Geraldo	R/R	6-2/180	11-28-73	Tucson, Arizona, El Paso
	Jacome, Jason	L/L	6-1/185	11-24-70	Yakult (Japan)
51	Johnson, Randy	R/L	6-10/230	9-10-63	Arizona
49	Kim, Byung-Hyun	R/R	5-11/176	1-21-79	Arizona, Tucson
31	Mantei, Matt	R/R	6-1/190	7-7-73	Tucson, Arizona
36	Morgan, Mike	R/R	6-2/220	10-8-59	Arizona
24	Patterson, John	R/R	6-5/183	1-30-78	Tucson
65	Prinz, Bret	R/R	6-3/185	6-15-77	South Bend, El Paso
27	Reynoso, Armando	R/R	6-0/204	5-1-66	Arizona
66	Sanchez, Duaner	R/R	6-0/160	11-14-79	South Bend
38	Schilling, Curt	R/R	6-4/231	11-14-66	Philadelphia, Arizona
36	Springer, Russ	R/R	6-4/205	11-7-68	Arizona
30	Stottlemyre, Todd	L/R	6-3/215	5-20-65	Arizona, Arizona Diamondbacks
22	Swindell, Greg	L/L	6-3/230	1-2-65	Arizona

No.	CATCHERS	B/T	Ht./Wt.	Born	2000 clubs
48	Barajas, Rod	R/R	6-2/220	9-5-75	Tucson, Arizona
45	Huckaby, Ken	R/R	6-1/205	1-27-71	Tucson
26	Miller, Damian	R/R	6-2/212	10-13-69	Arizona

No.	INFIELDERS	B/T	Ht./Wt.	Born	2000 clubs
33	Bell, Jay	R/R	6-0/184	12-11-65	Arizona
44	Durazo, Erubiel	L/L	6-3/225	1-23-74	Arizona
64	Cintron, Alexander	B/R	6-1/170	12-17-78	El Paso
28	Colbrunn, Greg	R/R	6-0/205	7-26-69	Arizona
4	Counsell, Craig	L/R	6-0/175	8-21-70	Tucson, Arizona
2	Frias, Hanley	B/R	6-0/173	12-5-73	Arizona
17	Grace, Mark	L/L	6-2/200	6-28-64	Chicago N.L.
7	Klassen, Danny	R/R	6-0/175	9-22-75	Tucson, Arizona
63	Spivey, Junior	R/R	6-0/185	1-28-75	Tucson, El Paso
9	Williams, Matt	R/R	6-2/214	11-28-65	El Paso, Arizona, High Desert
5	Womack, Tony	L/R	5-9/159	9-25-69	Arizona

No.	OUTFIELDERS	B/T	Ht./Wt.	Born	2000 clubs
29	Bautista, Danny	R/R	5-11/170	5-24-72	Florida, Arizona
6	Conti, Jason	L/R	5-11/180	1-27-75	Tucson, Arizona
	Cummings, Midre	L/R	6-0/195	10-14-71	Minnesota, Boston
61	Cust, Jack	L/R	6-1/205	1-16-79	El Paso
25	Dellucci, David	L/L	5-11/198	10-31-73	Arizona, Tucson, Arizona Diamondbacks, South Bend
12	Finley, Steve	L/L	6-2/180	3-12-65	Arizona
20	Gonzalez, Luis	L/R	6-2/190	9-2-67	Arizona
8	Ryan, Rob	L/L	5-11/190	6-24-73	Tucson, Arizona
	Sanders, Reggie	R/R	6-1/185	12-1-67	Atlanta

BALLPARK INFORMATION

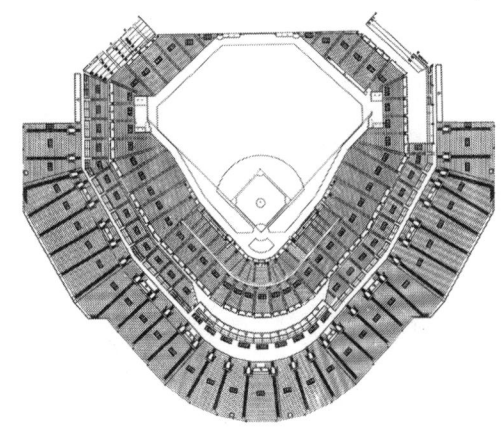

Ballpark (capacity, surface)
Bank One Ballpark (49,033, grass)

Address
401 East Jefferson
Phoenix, AZ 85004

Official website
www.azdiamondbacks.com

Business phone
602-462-6500

Ticket information
602-514-8400

Ticket prices
$11 to $26 (lower level)
$1 to $17 (upper level)
$43 to $70 (lower level premium seats)
$29 and $36 (Infiniti Diamond level)

Field dimensions (from home plate)
To left field at foul line, 330 feet
To center field, 407 feet
To right field at foul line, 334 feet

First game played
March 31, 1998 (Rockies 9, Diamondbacks 2)

2000 REVIEW
DAY BY DAY

Date	Opp.	Res.	Score	(inn.*)	Hits	Opp. hits	Winning pitcher	Losing pitcher	Save	Record	Pos.	GB
4-4	Phi.	W	6-4		10	6	Johnson	Ashby	Holmes	1-0	T1st	0.5
4-5	Phi.	W	11-3		12	9	Stottlemyre	Byrd	Morgan	2-0	1st	+0.5
4-6	Phi.	W	3-2	(11)	7	8	Springer	Schrenk		3-0	1st	+1.0
4-7	Pit.	L	2-7		7	12	Christiansen	Reynoso		3-1	T1st	...
4-8	Pit.	W	6-5		12	12	Swindell	Christiansen		4-1	1st	+1.0
4-9	Pit.	W	1-0		4	5	Johnson	Schmidt		5-1	1st	+2.0
4-10	At S.D.	W	8-4		12	11	Stottlemyre	Williams	Morgan	6-1	1st	+2.5
4-11	At S.D.	L	2-3	(13)	7	9	Whisenant	Springer		6-2	1st	+1.5
4-12	At S.D.	L	2-4		6	6	Meadows	Reynoso	Hoffman	6-3	1st	+1.0
4-13	At S.D.	W	5-4		9	10	Anderson	Hitchcock	Morgan	7-3	1st	+0.5
4-14	At S.F	W	3-1		8	5	Johnson	Hernandez		8-3	1st	+0.5
4-15	At S.F	W	7-4		9	8	Stottlemyre	Ortiz	Swindell	9-3	1st	+1.5
4-17	Col.	L	1-9		8	15	Yoshii	Daal		9-4	1st	+1.5
4-18	Col.	W	7-1		12	4	Reynoso	Karl		10-4	1st	+1.5
4-19	Col.	W	8-7		13	12	Morgan	Tavarez	Kim	11-4	1st	+2.5
4-20	Col.	W	3-0		5	4	Johnson	Arrojo		12-4	1st	+3.0
4-21	S.F	L	5-11		12	16	Ortiz	Stottlemyre		12-5	1st	+2.0
4-22	S.F	L	6-8		7	7	Rueter	Daal	Nen	12-6	1st	+1.0
4-23	S.F	L	7-12		11	14	Nathan	Reynoso		12-7	2nd	...
4-25	At Phi.	W	10-2		10	5	Johnson	Brock		13-7	1st	+1.5
4-26	At Phi.	W	10-4		9	6	Stottlemyre	Ashby		14-7	1st	+2.5
4-27	At Phi.	L	4-5		6	10	Gomes	Kim		14-8	1st	+2.5
4-28	At Chi.	L	5-6		7	10	Tapani	Springer	Aguilera	14-9	1st	+1.5
4-29	At Chi.	W	7-4	(10)	10	9	Mantei	Guthrie	Morgan	15-9	1st	+1.5
4-30	At Chi.	W	6-0		12	6	Johnson	Lorraine		16-9	1st	+1.5
5-2	At Mil.	W	5-1		9	4	Stottlemyre	Haynes		17-9	1st	+3.0
5-3	At Mil.	L	1-4		4	10	Estrada	Daal	Wickman	17-10	1st	+2.0
5-4	At Mil.	W	6-2		10	4	Reynoso	Stull	Kim	18-10	1st	+2.5
5-5	S.D.	W	5-3		8	5	Johnson	Hitchcock		19-10	1st	+2.5
5-6	S.D.	W	10-5		12	8	Anderson	Lopez		20-10	1st	+2.5
5-7	S.D.	W	8-1		11	8	Stottlemyre	Clement		21-10	1st	+3.5
5-8	L.A.	W	15-7		20	7	Daal	Park		22-10	1st	+4.0
5-9	L.A.	W	11-7	(12)	15	15	Padilla	Hershiser		23-10	1st	+5.0
5-10	L.A.	W	2-1		9	9	Kim	Adams		24-10	1st	+5.0
5-12	At S.D.	W	6-4		8	9	Anderson	Clement	Kim	25-10	1st	+6.0
5-13	At S.D.	W	6-2		9	9	Stottlemyre	Spencer	Morgan	26-10	1st	+6.5
5-14	At S.D.	L	1-3		2	5	Meadows	Daal	Hoffman	26-11	1st	+6.5
5-16	At Mon.	L	0-2		5	5	Vazquez	Johnson	Hermanson	26-12	1st	+5.5
5-17	At Mon.	L	2-10		6	14	Pavano	Reynoso		26-13	1st	+4.5
5-18	At Mon.	W	8-6		10	8	Kim	Telford		27-13	1st	+5.0
5-19	At N.Y.	L	3-4		9	8	B.J. Jones	Stottlemyre	Benitez	27-14	1st	+4.0
5-20	At N.Y.	L	7-8		13	11	Hampton	Daal	Benitez	27-15	1st	+3.0
5-21	At N.Y.	L	6-7		10	10	Wendell	Kim		27-16	1st	+2.0
5-23	Pit.	W	6-1		11	8	Anderson	Anderson		28-16	1st	+2.5
5-24	Pit.	W	6-5		9	8	Stottlemyre	Schmidt	Kim	29-16	1st	+3.5
5-25	Pit.	W	7-5		12	9	Daal	Benson	Mantei	30-16	1st	+4.0
5-26	Mil.	W	9-2		9	6	Johnson	Snyder		31-16	1st	+4.0
5-27	Mil.	W	7-3		14	6	Reynoso	Acevedo	Kim	32-16	1st	+5.0
5-28	Mil.	L	3-4	(11)	8	11	Wickman	Swindell		32-17	1st	+5.0
5-29	StL.	L	0-3		6	5	Stephenson	Stottlemyre		32-18	1st	+4.0
5-30	StL.	L	1-6		5	10	Ankiel	Daal	Morris	32-19	1st	+4.0
5-31	StL.	W	6-2		8	10	Johnson	Hentgen	Kim	33-19	1st	+4.0
6-1	StL.	W	4-0		7	4	Reynoso	An. Benes		34-19	1st	+4.5
6-2	At Tex.	W	5-4		13	7	Anderson	Helling	Mantei	35-19	1st	+4.5
6-3	At Tex.	L	3-4		7	9	Rogers	Figueroa	Wetteland	35-20	1st	+4.5
6-4	At Tex.	L	6-7	(10)	14	10	Perisho	Kim	Wetteland	35-21	1st	+3.5
6-5	At Chi.	L	3-4	(10)	8	10	Heredia	Mantei		35-22	1st	+3.5
6-6	At Chi.	L	1-4		5	8	Tapani	Reynoso		35-23	1st	+3.5
6-7	At Chi.	L	4-9		11	11	Downs	Anderson	Van Poppel	35-24	1st	+2.5
6-9	Ana.	W	4-1		8	5	Johnson	Cooper	Kim	36-24	1st	+2.5
6-10	Ana.	L	3-10		7	13	Washburn	Daal		36-25	1st	+1.5
6-11	Ana.	W	3-2		6	8	Plesac	Schoeneweis	Kim	37-25	1st	+1.5
6-12	At L.A.	W	4-2		5	8	Anderson	Dreifort	Kim	38-25	1st	+2.0
6-13	At L.A.	L	1-6		5	10	Park	Morgan		38-26	1st	+2.0
6-14	At L.A.	W	5-1		11	6	Johnson	Perez		39-26	1st	+3.0
6-15	At L.A.	L	0-4		4	8	Brown	Stottlemyre		39-27	1st	+2.0
6-17	At Col.	L	5-14		8	17	Bohanon	Anderson		39-28	1st	+1.0
6-18	At Col.	L	2-19		8	23	Yoshii	Reynoso		39-29	2nd	...
6-19	S.D.	W	3-2		7	6	Padilla	Kolb		40-29	1st	+0.5
6-20	S.D.	L	1-3		2	7	Tollberg	Stottlemyre	Hoffman	40-30	1st	+0.5
6-21	S.D.	W	11-8		16	8	Morgan	Reyes		41-30	1st	+0.5
6-23	Col.	W	2-0		5	2	Anderson	Bohanon	Kim	42-30	1st	+2.0
6-24	Col.	L	0-4		7	6	Yoshii	Johnson		42-31	1st	+1.0
6-25	Col.	W	8-3		14	8	Morgan	Astacio		43-31	1st	+2.0

Date	Opp.	Res.	Score	(inn.*)	Hits	Opp. hits	Winning pitcher	Losing pitcher	Save	Record	Pos.	GB
6-26	Hou.	W	6-1		8	5	Reynoso	Dotel	Kim	44-31	1st	+2.0
6-27	Hou.	L	4-12		8	13	Elarton	Daal		44-32	1st	+2.0
6-28	Hou.	W	6-2		10	8	Anderson	Lima	Kim	45-32	1st	+2.0
6-29	Hou.	W	7-1		10	5	Johnson	Reynolds		46-32	1st	+2.0
6-30	Cin.	L	4-5		7	11	Harnisch	Morgan	Graves	46-33	1st	+1.0
7-1	Cin.	W	9-6		12	6	Springer	Fernandez	Kim	47-33	1st	+2.0
7-2	Cin.	L	2-14		9	20	Neagle	Daal		47-34	1st	+1.0
7-3	Cin.	L	2-3		9	8	Parris	Anderson	Graves	47-35	2nd	...
7-4	At Hou.	W	10-4		11	6	Johnson	Lima		48-35	1st	+1.5
7-5	At Hou.	W	12-9		16	10	Morgan	Valdes	Kim	49-35	1st	+2.5
7-6	At Hou.	W	2-1		4	4	Guzman	Holt	Mantei	50-35	1st	+3.5
7-7	At Oak.	L	4-5	(11)	9	11	Tam	Daal		50-36	1st	+3.5
7-8	At Oak.	L	7-8	(10)	9	13	Isringhausen	Swindell		50-37	1st	+2.5
7-9	At Oak.	W	4-2		13	6	Johnson	Heredia	Mantei	51-37	1st	+3.5
7-13	Tex.	L	4-6		11	7	Zimmerman	Kim	Wetteland	51-38	1st	+2.5
7-14	Tex.	W	6-1		10	6	Reynoso	Rogers		52-38	1st	+2.5
7-15	Tex.	L	5-6	(11)	13	10	Zimmerman	Swindell	Wetteland	52-39	1st	+2.5
7-16	Sea.	L	3-6		8	9	Mesa	Springer	Sasaki	52-40	1st	+1.5
7-17	Sea.	W	7-0		13	5	Guzman	Halama		53-40	1st	+1.5
7-18	Sea.	L	2-5		6	11	Rhodes	Padilla	Sasaki	53-41	1st	+0.5
7-19	StL.	W	4-3		9	6	Reynoso	Stephenson	Mantei	54-41	1st	+1.5
7-20	StL.	W	3-2		4	6	Johnson	Veres		55-41	1st	+1.5
7-21	At Cin.	W	5-4		14	11	Swindell	Sullivan	Mantei	56-41	1st	+2.5
7-22	At Cin.	L	3-7		8	14	Villone	Guzman		56-42	1st	+1.5
7-23	At Cin.	L	3-5		9	10	Dessens	Anderson	Graves	56-43	1st	+1.5
7-25	At StL.	L	3-7		5	7	Stephenson	Johnson		56-44	1st	+1.0
7-26	At StL.	L	4-8		10	11	Kile	Reynoso		56-45	2nd	...
7-27	At StL.	W	17-5		19	10	Guzman	Ankiel		57-45	1st	+0.5
7-28	At Fla.	W	4-1		6	6	Schilling	Cornelius	Mantei	58-45	1st	+0.5
7-29	At Fla.	L	2-4		2	7	Miceli	Kim	Alfonseca	58-46	1st	+0.5
7-30	At Fla.	L	3-4		6	10	Almanza	Morgan	Alfonseca	58-47	1st	+0.5
8-1	Atl.	L	2-4		2	8	Millwood	Swindell	Remlinger	58-48	2nd	1.0
8-2	Atl.	W	2-0		6	6	Schilling	Maddux		59-48	2nd	...
8-3	Atl.	W	8-4		11	10	Anderson	Ashby		60-48	2nd	...
8-4	N.Y.	L	1-6		6	11	Reed	Johnson	Cook	60-49	2nd	1.0
8-5	N.Y.	L	2-6		11	14	B.J. Jones	Guzman	White	60-50	2nd	1.0
8-6	N.Y.	W	9-5		12	13	Reynoso	Rusch	Mantei	61-50	2nd	1.0
8-7	Mon.	W	5-2		9	8	Schilling	Moore		62-50	2nd	1.0
8-8	Mon.	L	3-9		9	16	Lira	Anderson		62-51	2nd	2.0
8-9	Mon.	L	3-4		8	15	Strickland	Guzman	Telford	62-52	2nd	3.0
8-11	At Pit.	W	6-1		10	4	Reynoso	Serafini		63-52	2nd	2.0
8-12	At Pit.	L	6-9		10	11	Sauerbeck	Schilling		63-53	2nd	2.0
8-13	At Pit.	W	7-6		14	12	Morgan	Arroyo	Mantei	64-53	2nd	1.0
8-14	At Phi.	W	4-3	(11)	7	6	Plesac	Brantley	Mantei	65-53	2nd	1.0
8-15	At Phi.	W	11-6		16	13	Kim	Gomes		66-53	2nd	1.0
8-16	At Phi.	W	5-1		10	7	Reynoso	Chen		67-53	2nd	1.0
8-18	Chi.	W	11-2		12	6	Schilling	Quevedo		68-53	2nd	1.5
8-19	Chi.	W	11-3		15	7	Anderson	Lieber		69-53	2nd	1.5
8-20	Chi.	W	5-4		10	4	Johnson	Rain		70-53	2nd	0.5
8-21	Mil.	L	8-16		13	19	Stull	Reynoso		70-54	2nd	1.5
8-22	Mil.	L	3-4		8	8	D'Amico	Guzman	Leskanic	70-55	2nd	1.5
8-23	Mil.	L	5-8		11	9	Haynes	Schilling	Leskanic	70-56	2nd	2.5
8-25	At N.Y.	L	3-13		6	16	Reed	Johnson		70-57	2nd	3.5
8-26	At N.Y.	W	5-1	(10)	11	5	Plesac	White		71-57	2nd	2.5
8-27	At N.Y.	L	1-2		3	4	Hampton	Reynoso	Benitez	71-58	2nd	2.5
8-28	At Mon.	L	5-9		9	14	Thurman	Schilling	Telford	71-59	2nd	3.5
8-29	At Mon.	W	8-7		8	12	Plesac	Forster	Mantei	72-59	2nd	2.5
8-30	At Mon.	W	7-0		10	5	Johnson	Lira		73-59	2nd	2.5
9-1	Fla.	L	7-8	(11)	13	15	Darensbourg	Swindell	Alfonseca	73-60	2nd	4.0
9-2	Fla.	L	1-10		9	17	Dempster	Schilling		73-61	2nd	5.0
9-3	Fla.	W	10-5		18	11	Kim	Burnett		74-61	2nd	5.0
9-5	At Atl.	L	2-5		7	6	Glavine	Johnson	Rocker	74-62	2nd	6.5
9-6	At Atl.	L	1-7		6	7	Millwood	Reynoso		74-63	2nd	7.5
9-7	At Atl.	L	0-4		4	12	Maddux	Schilling		74-64	2nd	8.5
9-8	At Fla.	W	2-1		8	6	Kim	Bones	Mantei	75-64	2nd	7.5
9-9	At Fla.	W	4-1		9	5	Stottlemyre	Burnett	Mantei	76-64	2nd	6.5
9-10	At Fla.	L	3-4	(12)	4	9	Looper	Springer		76-65	2nd	7.5
9-11	L.A.	L	3-6		6	11	Gagne	Reynoso		76-66	2nd	8.5
9-12	L.A.	W	5-4		8	7	Kim	Masaoka	Mantei	77-66	2nd	8.5
9-13	L.A.	W	3-2		9	5	Plesac	Adams		78-66	2nd	8.5
9-15	Atl.	W	2-1		8	7	Johnson	Glavine	Mantei	79-66	2nd	7.5
9-16	Atl.	L	10-12		14	14	Burkett	Stottlemyre	Rocker	79-67	2nd	8.5
9-17	Atl.	L	1-7		4	16	Millwood	Schilling		79-68	2nd	9.5
9-18	At L.A.	L	1-2		9	6	Shaw	Swindell		79-69	2nd	9.5
9-19	At L.A.	L	0-1		6	7	Park	Anderson	Shaw	79-70	2nd	10.5
9-20	At L.A.	L	0-1		9	7	Herges	Kim		79-71	3rd	11.5
9-21	At S.F	L	7-8		9	9	Henry	Morgan	Nen	79-72	3rd	12.5
9-22	At S.F	W	7-1		11	4	Schilling	Gardner		80-72	2nd	11.5

Date	Opp.	Res.	Score	(inn.*)	Hits	Opp. hits	Winning pitcher	Losing pitcher	Save	Record	Pos.	GB
9-23†	At S.F	W	7-5		9	8	Guzman	Estes	Mantei	81-72		
9-23‡	At S.F	L	5-9		9	10	del Toro	Reynoso		81-73	3rd	11.5
9-24	At S.F	W	8-3	10		7	Anderson	Hernandez		82-73	3rd	10.5
9-25	At Col.	W	6-4	13		10	Johnson	Rose		83-73	T2nd	10.0
9-26	At Col.	L	6-7	7		10	Chouinard	Morgan	Mantei	83-74	3rd	10.0
9-27	At Col.	L	4-6	6		14	White	Plesac	Jimenez	83-75	3rd	11.0
9-28	At Col.	W	12-3	13		7	Reynoso	Wasdin	Jimenez	84-75	T2nd	11.0
9-29	S.F	L	3-4	9		7	Hernandez	Anderson		84-76	3rd	12.0
9-30	S.F	W	5-1	11		5	Guzman	Embree	Nen	85-76	3rd	11.0
10-1	S.F	L	4-11	8		12	Ortiz	Johnson		85-77	3rd	12.0

Monthly records: April (16-9), May (17-10), June (13-14), July (12-14), August (15-12), September (12-17), October (0-1).
*Innings, if other than nine. †First game of a doubleheader. ‡Second game of a doubleheader.

HIGHLIGHTS

High point: On May 13, the Diamondbacks recorded their team-record ninth straight victory, a 6-2 decision over San Diego. That lifted their major league-best mark to 26-10 and gave them a 6½-game lead over the Dodgers in the N.L. West.

Low point: Having fallen out of contention for a division title, the Diamondbacks watched their wild-card hopes evaporate during a six-game losing streak in mid-September. The final loss was a tough one to take. The Giants' 8-7 win at San Francisco on September 21 clinched the N.L. West title.

Turning point: Milwaukee's three-game sweep at Bank One Ballpark from August 21-23 dropped Arizona from a half-game behind the Giants to 2½ games back, a deficit that would only grow. In the opener, the Diamondbacks cut an 8-0 deficit to 8-7 before losing 16-8. In the third game, Arizona trailed 5-4 after seven innings, but the bullpen gave up key insurance runs.

Most valuable player: Steve Finley carried the club over the first half, hitting 27 homers and driving in 75 runs by July 21. He finished with a career-best 35 homers and only late injuries kept his RBI total (96) below 100.

Most valuable pitcher: Randy Johnson won his second straight Cy Young, improving in many ways on his remarkable 1999 season. He went 19-7 with a 2.64 ERA, second best in the N.L., and struck out a major league-high 347 batters. Johnson, dominating over the first half, entered the break with a 15-2 record and 2.01 ERA.

Most improved player: Lefthander Brian Anderson compiled a so-so 11-7 record and 4.05 ERA, but those numbers were deceptive. He made 10 starts in which he allowed two or fewer earned runs but did not win, and led the N.L. with 14 no-decisions. Anderson set a career high with 213⅓ innings and finished second in the league in walks per nine innings (1.6).

Most pleasant surprise: Veteran Greg Colbrunn, who was supposed to be a part-time player and pinch hitter, was pressed into duty as the regular first baseman and, with Matt Williams strug-gling, the cleanup hitter. Over his final 50 starts, Colbrunn batted .349 with nine homers and 38 RBIs.

Key injuries: Third baseman Matt Williams missed half the season with a broken foot and strained quadriceps and played the other half with a sore foot. ... First baseman Erubiel Durazo had two operations on his wrist. ... Righthander Todd Stottlemyre missed a third of the season with elbow tendinitis. ... Shortstop Tony Womack was hampered by a sore knee. ... Closer Matt Mantei was bothered by biceps tendinitis and shoulder trouble.

Notable: Johnson's three Cy Young Awards leave him second among left-handers to Steve Carlton (four). ... Luis Gonzalez, the only National Leaguer to start all 162 games, became the first Arizona batter to hit for the cycle. He did it July 5 at Houston. ... Arizona became the first team to fall from 100 or more wins to fewer than 90 since the 1991 Athletics, who followed their 1990 A.L. pennant (103-59) by going 84-78.

—ED PRICE

RECORDS

2000 regular-season record: 85-77 (3rd in N.L. West); 47-34 at home; 38-43 on road; 21-24 vs. East; 29-21 vs. Central; 35-32 vs. West; 23-17 vs. lefthanded starters; 62-60 vs. righthanded starters; 74-70 on grass; 11-7 on turf; 22-24 in daytime; 63-53 at night; 22-27 in one-run games; 5-8 in extra-inning games; 0-0-1 in doubleheaders.

Team record past five years: 250-236 in three years (.514, ranks 6th in league in that span).

TEAM LEADERS

Batting average: Luis Gonzalez (.311).
At-bats: Luis Gonzalez (618).
Runs: Luis Gonzalez (106).
Hits: Luis Gonzalez (192).
Total Bases: Luis Gonzalez (336).
Doubles: Luis Gonzalez (47).
Triples: Tony Womack (14).
Home runs: Steve Finley (35).
Runs batted in: Luis Gonzalez (114).
Stolen bases: Tony Womack (45).

Slugging percentage: Luis Gonzalez (.544).
On-base percentage: Luis Gonzalez (.392).
Wins: Randy Johnson (19).
Earned-run average: Randy Johnson (2.64).
Complete games: Randy Johnson (8).
Shutouts: Randy Johnson (3).
Saves: Matt Mantei (17).
Innings pitched: Randy Johnson (248.2).
Strikeouts: Randy Johnson (347).

GAMES BY POSITION

Catcher: Damian Miller 97, Kelly Stinnett 74, Rod Barajas 37.
First base: Greg Colbrunn 99, Erubiel Durazo 60, Travis Lee 23, Alex Cabrera 15, Damian Miller 2, Andy Fox 1.
Second base: Jay Bell 145, Craig Counsell 25, Hanley Frias 15.
Third base: Matt Williams 94, Danny Klassen 25, Craig Counsell 23, Andy Fox 20, Lenny Harris 20, Hanley Frias 7, Greg Colbrunn 1.
Shortstop: Tony Womack 143, Hanley Frias 21, Craig Counsell 6, Danny Klassen 3.
Outfield: Luis Gonzalez 162, Steve Finley 148, Danny Bautista 82, Travis Lee 55, Jason Conti 35, Bernard Gilkey 17, Turner Ward 15, Alex Cabrera 12, David Dellucci 12, Andy Fox 6, Lenny Harris 3, Rob Ryan 2, Tony Womack 2, Matt Mieske 1.
Designated hitter: Greg Colbrunn 2, Steve Finley 2, Jay Bell 1, Rob Ryan 1, Matt Williams 1.

TOP DRAFT CHOICES

1. None.
2. **Mike Schultz,** RHP, Loyola Marymount University.
3. **Bill White,** LHP, Jacksonville State U.
4. **Josh Kroeger,** OF, Scripps Ranch H.S., San Diego.
5. **Brad Cresse,** C, Louisiana State U.
6. **Scott Barber,** RHP, University of South Carolina.
7. **Tim Olson,** OF, University of Florida.
8. **Brandon Webb,** RHP, U. of Kentucky.
9. **Tanner Eriksen,** RHP, U. of Southern California.
10. **Cedrick Harris,** OF, Louisiana State U.

ATLANTA BRAVES
NATIONAL LEAGUE EAST DIVISION

Braves
2001 SCHEDULE
Home games shaded; D—Day game (games starting before 5 p.m.)
*—All-Star Game at Safeco Field (Seattle)

APRIL

SUN	MON	TUE	WED	THU	FRI	SAT
1	2 D	3 D	4	5	6	7
	CIN	NYM	NYM	NYM	FLA	FLA
8 D	9	10	11	12	13	14
FLA	NYM		NYM	NYM	PHI	PHI
15 D	16	17	18 D	19	20	21
PHI	FLA	FLA	FLA		PHI	PHI
22 D	23	24	25	26	27	28
PHI	HOU	HOU	HOU	ARI	ARI	ARI
29	30					
ARI						

MAY

SUN	MON	TUE	WED	THU	FRI	SAT
		1	2	3	4	5
		MIL	MIL	MIL	STL	STL
6 D	7	8	9	10 D	11	12
STL		SD	SD	SD	LA	LA
13 D	14	15	16 D	17	18	19
LA		COL	COL	COL	SF	SF
20 D	21	22	23	24	25	26
SF	FLA	FLA	FLA		PIT	PIT
27 D	28	29	30 D	31		
PIT	MON	MON	MON			

JUNE

SUN	MON	TUE	WED	THU	FRI	SAT
					1	2
					PIT	PIT
3 D	4	5	6	7	8	9 D
PIT		MON	MON	MON	NYY	NYY
10	11	12	13	14	15	16
NYY	TOR	TOR	TOR		BOS	BOS
17 D	18	19	20	21 D	22	23 D
BOS	FLA	FLA	FLA	FLA	NYM	NYM
24 D	25	26	27 D	28	29	30 D
NYM	PHI	PHI	PHI		NYM	NYM

JULY

SUN	MON	TUE	WED	THU	FRI	SAT
1	2	3	4	5	6	7
NYM		PHI	PHI	PHI	BOS	BOS
8 D	9	10	* 11	12	13	14
BOS				BAL	BAL	BAL
15 D	16	17	18	19 D	20	21
TB	TB	TB	CIN	CIN	MON	MON
22 D	23	24	25 D	26	27	28
MON	CIN	CIN	CIN	MON	MON	MON
29 D	30	31				
MON		STL				

AUGUST

SUN	MON	TUE	WED	THU	FRI	SAT
		1	2	3	4 D	
		STL	STL	MIL	MIL	
5 D	6	7	8	9	10	11 D
MIL		HOU	HOU	HOU	ARI	ARI
12 D	13	14	15	16	17	18 D
ARI		COL	COL	COL	SF	SF
19 D	20	21	22	23	24	25
SF		SD	SD	SD	LA	LA
26 D	27	28	29	30	31	
LA		LA	MON	MON	MON	CUB

SEPTEMBER

SUN	MON	TUE	WED	THU	FRI	SAT
						1 D
						CUB
2 D	3 D	4 D	5	6	7 D	8 D
CUB	MON	MON	MON		CUB	CUB
9 D	10	11	12 D	13	14	15
CUB		PHI	PHI	PHI	FLA	FLA
16 D	17	18	19	20	21	22
FLA	PHI	PHI	PHI	PHI	NYM	NYM
23 D	24	25	26	27		29
NYM	FLA	FLA	FLA		NYM	NYM
30 D						
NYM						

2001 SEASON
CLUB DIRECTORY

Owner
R.E. Turner III
Chairman of the board of directors
William C. Bartholomay
President
Stanley H. Kasten
Executive vice president and general manager
John Schuerholz
Senior v.p. and assistant to the president
Henry L. Aaron
Senior vice president, administration
Bob Wolfe
Vice president, assistant general manager
Frank Wren
V.p., director of marketing and broadcasting
Wayne Long
Vice president
Lee Douglas
Vice president of development
Janet Marie Smith
Vice president of human resources
Michelle Thomas
Special assistants to general manager
Jim Fregosi, Paul Snyder, Scott Nethery, Chuck McMichael
Special assistant to g.m./player development
Jose Martinez
Director of team travel, equipment manager
Bill Acree
Director of player development
Dick Balderson
Director of scouting
Roy Clark
Dir. of international and professional scouting
Dayton Moore
Senior director of promotions and civic affairs
Miles McRea
Vice president/Controller
Chip Moore
Director of ticket sales
Paul Adams
Director of minor league business operations
Bruce Baldwin
Director of stadium operations and security
Larry Bowman
Field director
Ed Mangan
Director of ticket operations
Ed Newman
Team counsel
David Payne
Director of community relations
Cara Maglione

Director of audio video operations
Jennifer Berger
Director of corporate sales
Jim Allen
Director of public relations
Jim Schultz
Media relations manager
Glen Serra
Public relations assistants
Adam Lieberman, Meagan Swingle
Head trainer
Dave Pursley
Assistant trainer
Jeff Porter
Club physician
Dr. David T. Watson
Associate physicians
Dr. William Barber, Dr. John Cantwell, Dr. Norman Elliott
Major league scout
Bobby Wine
National supervisors
Tim Conroy, John Flannery
Regional supervisors
Harold Cronin, Paul Faulk, Bob Wadsworth
Area supervisors
Mike Baker, Dan Bates, Tyrone Brooks, Stu Cann, Rob English, Ralph Garr, John Hagemann, "J" Harrison, Kurt Kemp, Marco Paddy, J.J. Picollo, Donnie Poplin, Willie Powell, John Ramey, John Stewart, Don Thomas, Terry Tripp
Scouts
Robert Aquino, Nez Balelo, Neil Burke, Joe Caputo, Todd Cook, Matt Dodd, Edgar Fernandez, Jose Figueroa, Pedro Flores, Bill Froberg, Ruben Garcia, Diego Herrera, Luis Herrera, Nick Hostetler, Bob Isabelle, Rafael Josela, James Kane, Dewayne Kitts, Al Kubski, David Latham, Duk Jung Lee, Jose Leon, Robert Lucas, William Marcot, Giorgio Moretti, Jose Mota, Ernie Pedersen, Elvis Pineda, Ubaldo Salinas, Charlie Smith, Miguel Teren, Raymond Tew, Ted Thornton, Marv Throneberry, Carlos Torres, Bo Trumbo, Jerry Turner, Rip Tutor, Murray Zuk
International supervisors
Phil Dale, Rene Francisco, Julian Perez
International scouts
Armando Dinzey, Felix Francisco, Gil Garrido, Jason Lee, Andres Lopez, Hirouki Oya, Rolando Petit, Fernando Villescusa
Professional scouts
Rod Gilbreath, Tim Martz, Gene Watson

MINOR LEAGUE AFFILIATES

Class	Team	League	Manager
AAA	Richmond	International	Carlos Tosca
AA	Greenville	Southern	Paul Runge
A	Myrtle Beach	Carolina	Brian Snitker
A	Macon	South Atlantic	Randy Ingle
A	Jamestown	New York-Pennsylvania	Jim Saul
Rookie	Danville	Appalachian	Ralph Henriquez
Rookie	Gulf Coast Braves	Gulf Coast	Rick Albert

BROADCAST INFORMATION

Radio: WSB-AM (750).
TV: TBS-TV (Channel 17).
Cable TV: Fox Sports Net, Turner South.

SPRING TRAINING

Ballpark (city): Disney's Wide World of Sports Baseball Stadium (Kissimmee, Fla.).
Ticket information: 407-839-3900, 407-939-4263.

Follow the Braves all season at: www.sportingnews.com/baseball/teams/braves/

SPRING TRAINING ROSTER

Manager—Bobby Cox (6).
Coaches—Pat Corrales (39), Bobby Dews (52), Glenn Hubbard (17), Leo Mazzone (54), Merv Rettenmund (28), Ned Yost (5).

No.	PITCHERS	B/T	Ht./Wt.	Born	2000 clubs
74	Abreu, Winston	R/R	6-2/155	4-5-77	Macon, Greenville, Gulf Coast Braves, Richmond
19	Burkett, John	R/R	6-3/215	11-28-64	Atlanta
47	Glavine, Tom	L/L	6-0/185	3-25-66	Atlanta
	Lewis, Derrick	R/R	6-5/215	5-7-76	Greenville
46	Ligtenberg, Kerry	R/R	6-2/215	5-11-71	Atlanta, Richmond
31	Maddux, Greg	R/R	6-0/185	4-14-66	Atlanta
51	Marquis, Jason	L/R	6-1/185	8-21-78	Greenville, Atlanta, Richmond
30	McGlinchy, Kevin	R/R	6-5/220	6-28-77	Atlanta, Greenville, Richmond, Gulf Coast Braves
34	Millwood, Kevin	R/R	6-4/220	12-24-74	Atlanta
	Moore, Trey	L/L	6-0/190	10-2-72	Ottawa, Montreal
61	Moss, Damian	R/L	6-0/187	11-24-76	Richmond
43	Perez, Odalis	L/L	6-0/150	6-7-78	DID NOT PLAY
	Ramirez, Horacio	L/L	6-1/170	11-24-79	Myrtle Beach
37	Remlinger, Mike	L/L	6-1/210	3-23-66	Atlanta
49	Rocker, John	R/L	6-4/225	10-17-74	Atlanta, Richmond
58	Seelbach, Chris	R/R	6-4/180	12-18-72	Richmond, Atlanta
29	Smoltz, John	R/R	6-3/220	5-15-67	DID NOT PLAY
	Sobkowiak, Scott	R/R	6-5/230	10-26-77	Greenville
	Sylvester, Billy	R/R	6-5/220	10-1-76	Myrtle Beach
	Voyles, Brad	R/R	6-0/195	12-30-76	Myrtle Beach

No.	CATCHERS	B/T	Ht./Wt.	Born	2000 clubs
9	Bako, Paul	L/R	6-2/205	6-20-72	Houston, Florida, Atlanta
8	Lopez, Javy	R/R	6-3/200	11-5-70	Atlanta
12	Perez, Eddie	R/R	6-1/185	5-4-68	Atlanta

No.	INFIELDERS	B/T	Ht./Wt.	Born	2000 clubs
	Betemit, Wilson	B/R	6-2/155	7-28-80	Jamestown
	Brogna, Rico	L/L	6-2/203	4-18-70	Philadelphia, Clearwater, Boston
2	DeRosa, Mark	R/R	6-1/195	2-2-75	Richmond, Atlanta
1	Furcal, Rafael	B/R	5-10/165	8-24-80	Greenville, Atlanta
	Garcia, Jesse	R/R	5-10/171	9-24-73	Baltimore, Rochester
	Giles, Marcus	R/R	5-8/180	5-18-78	Greenville
18	Helms, Wes	R/R	6-4/230	5-12-76	Richmond, Atlanta
10	Jones, Chipper	B/R	6-4/210	4-24-72	Atlanta
7	Lockhart, Keith	L/R	5-10/170	11-10-64	Atlanta
4	Veras, Quilvio	B/R	5-10/183	4-3-71	Atlanta

No.	OUTFIELDERS	B/T	Ht./Wt.	Born	2000 clubs
	Aldridge, Cory	L/R	6-0/210	6-13-79	Myrtle Beach
25	Jones, Andruw	R/R	6-1/210	4-23-77	Atlanta
33	Jordan, Brian	R/R	6-1/205	3-29-67	Atlanta
26	Lombard, George	L/R	6-0/202	9-14-75	Richmond, Atlanta
	Martinez, Dave	L/L	5-10/190	9-26-64	Tampa Bay, Chicago N.L., Texas, Toronto
15	Surhoff, B.J.	L/R	6-1/200	8-4-64	Baltimore, Atlanta

BALLPARK INFORMATION

Ballpark (capacity, surface)
Turner Field (50,091, grass)

Address
P.O. Box 4064
Atlanta, GA 30302

Official website
www.atlantabraves.com

Business phone
404-522-7630

Ticket information
404-249-6400 or 800-326-4000

Ticket prices
$40 (dugout level)
$32 (club level)
$27 (field level, terrace level)
$18 (field pavilion, terrace pavilion)
$12 (upper level)
$5 (upper pavilion)
$1 (skyline)

Field dimensions (from home plate)
To left field at foul line, 335 feet
To center field, 401 feet
To right field at foul line, 330 feet

First game played
April 4, 1997 (Braves 5, Cubs 4)

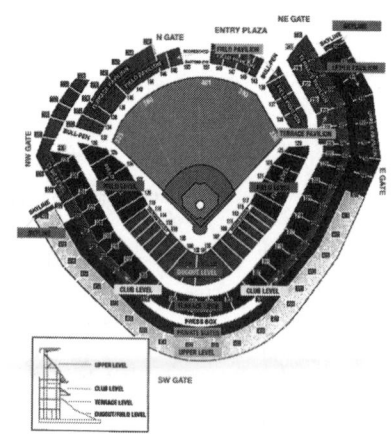

2001 SEASON *Atlanta Braves*

Date	Opp.	Res.	Score	(inn.*)	Hits	Opp. hits	Winning pitcher	Losing pitcher	Save	Record	Pos.	GB
4-3	Col.	W	2-0		7	6	Maddux	Astacio	Remlinger	1-0	T1st	...
4-4	Col.	L	3-5		6	11	Tavarez	Burkett	Jimenez	1-1	T2nd	0.5
4-5	Col.	W	9-6		12	9	Chen	Aybar	Ligtenberg	2-1	1st	+0.5
4-7	S.F	L	2-6		10	8	Gardner	Mulholland		2-2	T2nd	0.5
4-8	S.F	W	7-5		11	10	Maddux	Hernandez	Ligtenberg	3-2	1st	+0.5
4-9	S.F	W	9-3		12	7	Glavine	Ortiz		4-2	1st	+0.5
4-10	At Chi.	L	3-4		7	10	Guthrie	Ligtenberg		4-3	T1st	...
4-12	At Chi.	L	4-11		6	12	Farnsworth	Mulholland		4-4	T3rd	0.5
4-13	At Chi.	L	2-3		8	7	Guthrie	Remlinger		4-5	T3rd	0.5
4-14	At Mil.	W	6-3		14	7	Glavine	Woodard	Remlinger	5-5	3rd	0.5
4-15	At Mil.	L	3-6		5	9	Weathers	Burkett	Wickman	5-6	3rd	1.0
4-16	At Mil.	W	2-1		6	8	Mulholland	Stull	Remlinger	6-6	T2nd	0.5
4-18	Phi.	W	4-3	(12)	9	9	Rivera	Reyes		7-6	T2nd	1.0
4-19	Phi.	W	10-1		12	4	Glavine	Wolf		8-6	T1st	...
4-20	Phi.	W	6-4		8	8	Millwood	Aldred	Rocker	9-6	1st	...
4-21	Pit.	W	6-2		12	8	Mulholland	Garcia		10-6	1st	+1.0
4-22	Pit.	W	4-2		9	9	Chen	Benson	Rocker	11-6	1st	+0.5
4-23	Pit.	W	5-3		7	7	Maddux	Cordova	Rocker	12-6	1st	+0.5
4-25	L.A.	W	1-0		6	3	Glavine	Brown		13-6	1st	...
4-26	L.A.	W	5-1		9	5	Millwood	Gagne		14-6	1st	+1.0
4-27	L.A.	W	6-3		9	9	Mulholland	Park	Rocker	15-6	1st	+2.0
4-28	At S.D.	W	7-2		7	8	Maddux	Meadows	Remlinger	16-6	1st	+2.5
4-29	At S.D.	W	7-4	(12)	10	10	Chen	Palacios	Rocker	17-6	1st	+3.0
4-30	At S.D.	W	7-4		8	6	Glavine	Hitchcock		18-6	1st	+3.0
5-1	At L.A.	W	2-1		6	6	Millwood	Gagne	Rocker	19-6	1st	+4.0
5-2	At L.A.	W	5-3		6	11	Chen	Adams	Rocker	20-6	1st	+5.0
5-3	At L.A.	L	4-6		6	9	Perez	Maddux	Shaw	20-7	1st	+5.0
5-5	Phi.	W	6-5		9	9	Seanez	Gomes		21-7	1st	+5.5
5-6	Phi.	L	0-6		11	13	Schilling	Millwood		21-8	1st	+4.5
5-7	Phi.	L	4-7		11	14	Ashby	Mulholland	Gomes	21-9	1st	+4.5
5-8	At Fla.	L	2-3		7	9	Miceli	Seanez		21-10	1st	+4.0
5-9	At Fla.	W	10-5		12	9	Burkett	Penny		22-10	1st	+4.0
5-10	At Fla.	L	3-5		10	9	Sanchez	Glavine	Alfonseca	22-11	1st	+4.0
5-11	At Fla.	L	4-5		12	8	Grilli	Millwood	Alfonseca	22-12	1st	+4.0
5-12	At Phi.	W	8-7		12	9	Ligtenberg	Gomes	Rocker	23-12	1st	+4.0
5-13	At Phi.	W	3-2	(10)	8	6	Seanez	Aldred	Rocker	24-12	1st	+4.0
5-14	At Phi.	W	11-2		16	8	Burkett	Byrd		25-12	1st	+5.0
5-16	S.F	W	9-7		15	14	Glavine	Ortiz	Mulholland	26-12	1st	+5.0
5-17	S.F	W	5-4		12	7	Millwood	Rueter	Seanez	27-12	1st	+5.0
5-18	S.F	W	3-2		10	7	Maddux	Estes	Rocker	28-12	1st	+6.0
5-19	S.D.	L	7-11		15	12	Whiteside	Mulholland	Hoffman	28-13	1st	+5.0
5-20	S.D.	W	10-6		10	13	Burkett	Cunnane		29-13	1st	+5.0
5-21	S.D.	W	12-6		16	11	Glavine	Hitchcock		30-13	1st	+5.0
5-23	At Mil.	L	6-7		5	7	Wright	Millwood	Wickman	30-14	1st	+4.0
5-24	At Mil.	W	11-2		17	5	Maddux	Haynes		31-14	1st	+5.0
5-25	At Mil.	W	7-3		12	6	Mulholland	D'Amico		32-14	1st	+6.0
5-26	At Hou.	L	4-5	(10)	11	10	Henry	Seanez		32-15	1st	+6.0
5-27	At Hou.	W	6-5		9	10	Burkett	Reynolds	Ligtenberg	33-15	1st	+6.5
5-28	At Hou.	L	3-4		8	5	Valdes	Seanez	Wagner	33-16	1st	+5.5
5-29	At Chi.	W	1-0		2	6	Maddux	Lieber		34-16	1st	+6.5
5-30	At Chi.	W	5-2		9	9	Mulholland	Quevedo	Remlinger	35-16	1st	+6.5
6-1	At Chi.	L	3-5		6	9	Tapani	Glavine	Aguilera	35-17	1st	+6.5
6-2	N.Y. (AL)	L	2-5		5	10	Hernandez	Millwood	Rivera	35-18	1st	+5.5
6-3	N.Y. (AL)	W	11-7		11	13	Remlinger	Grimsley		36-18	1st	+5.5
6-4	N.Y. (AL)	L	6-7		12	16	Pettitte	Mulholland	Rivera	36-19	1st	+5.0
6-5	Tor.	L	3-9		9	12	Wells	Burkett		36-20	1st	+4.0
6-6	Tor.	W	7-6		11	10	Remlinger	Frascatore		37-20	1st	+5.0
6-7	Tor.	L	8-12		16	9	Cubillan	Millwood	Koch	37-21	1st	+5.0
6-9	Bos.	W	6-4		9	8	Maddux	Fassero	Seanez	38-21	1st	+4.5
6-10	Bos.	W	6-0		9	5	Mulholland	Schourek		39-21	1st	+5.5
6-11	Bos.	L	3-5		7	8	Garces	Seanez	Lowe	39-22	1st	+5.0
6-12	At Pit.	W	10-8		13	9	Ligtenberg	Christiansen	Remlinger	40-22	1st	+5.5
6-13	At Pit.	L	6-7	(10)	14	10	Silva	Wengert		40-23	1st	+5.5
6-14	At Pit.	W	8-4		7	9	Maddux	Anderson	Ligtenberg	41-23	1st	+5.5
6-15	At Pit.	L	0-2		6	7	Benson	Millwood		41-24	1st	+5.0
6-16	At Phi.	L	1-2		5	4	Schilling	Glavine	Brantley	41-25	1st	+4.0
6-17	At Phi.	L	3-9		7	16	Politte	Mulholland		41-26	1st	+4.0
6-18	At Phi.	W	5-3		8	6	Burkett	Schrenk	Rocker	42-26	1st	+4.0
6-19	At Phi.	L	2-5		5	8	Brock	Remlinger	Brantley	42-27	1st	+3.5
6-20	Chi.	W	11-4		14	9	Millwood	Tapani		43-27	1st	+4.5
6-21	Chi.	L	1-8		5	11	Wood	Glavine		43-28	1st	+4.5
6-22	Chi.	W	6-4		11	14	Mulholland	Downs	Remlinger	44-28	1st	+4.5
6-23	Mil.	W	3-2		6	7	Marquis	Weathers	Rocker	45-28	1st	+4.5
6-24	Mil.	L	1-2		5	6	Wright	Maddux	Wickman	45-29	1st	+3.5

– 85 –

Date	Opp.	Res.	Score	(inn.*)	Hits	Opp. hits	Winning pitcher	Losing pitcher	Save	Record	Pos.	GB
6-25	Mil.	W	5-4		4	8	Rocker	Leskanic		46-29	1st	+3.5
6-27	At Mon.	L	4-6		5	9	Armas	Glavine	Kline	46-30	1st	+2.0
6-28	At Mon.	W	7-4		10	12	Mulholland	Hermanson	Ligtenberg	47-30	1st	+2.0
6-29	At N.Y.	W	6-4		11	7	Burkett	Reed	Ligtenberg	48-30	1st	+3.0
6-30	At N.Y.	L	8-11		11	12	Benitez	Mulholland		48-31	1st	+2.0
7-1	At N.Y.	L	1-9		6	11	Leiter	Maddux		48-32	1st	+1.0
7-2	At N.Y.	W	10-2		17	5	Glavine	Rusch		49-32	1st	+2.0
7-3	Mon.	L	1-17		6	18	Armas	Mulholland		49-33	1st	+2.0
7-4	Mon.	W	7-3		10	7	Maddux	Hermanson		50-33	1st	+3.0
7-5	Mon.	L	5-6		10	13	Vazquez	Millwood	Kline	50-34	1st	+2.0
7-6	Mon.	L	2-4		6	14	Johnson	Burkett	Kline	50-35	1st	+1.5
7-7	At Bos.	W	5-3		11	7	Glavine	Schourek	Ligtenberg	51-35	1st	+2.5
7-8	At Bos.	W	5-1		10	7	Mulholland	R. Martinez		52-35	1st	+4.0
7-9	At Bos.	L	2-7		6	14	Wakefield	Millwood		52-36	1st	+3.0
7-13	At Bal.	W	6-3		6	8	Maddux	Mussina	Kamieniecki	53-36	1st	+4.0
7-14	At Bal.	W	4-1		10	7	Ashby	Ponson		54-36	1st	+4.0
7-15	At Bal.	W	7-3		11	8	Glavine	Erickson		55-36	1st	+5.0
7-16	At T.B.	W	6-4		8	5	Kamieniecki	Mecir		56-36	1st	+6.0
7-17	At T.B.	L	6-8		10	12	Rupe	Mulholland	Hernandez	56-37	1st	+5.0
7-18	At T.B.	W	8-2		10	7	Maddux	Rekar		57-37	1st	+5.0
7-20†	At Fla.	W	5-3		9	10	Glavine	Dempster	Ligtenberg	58-37		
7-20‡	At Fla.	L	1-6		3	8	Burnett	Kamieniecki		58-38	1st	+5.0
7-21	N.Y.	W	6-3		7	7	Burkett	Leiter	Remlinger	59-38	1st	+6.0
7-22	N.Y.	L	0-4		4	5	Reed	Maddux		59-39	1st	+5.0
7-23	N.Y.	W	1-0		7	4	Ashby	B.J. Jones		60-39	1st	+6.0
7-25	Fla.	W	6-5		6	15	Glavine	Dempster	Ligtenberg	61-39	1st	+6.0
7-26	Fla.	W	6-3		10	9	Millwood	Burnett	Rocker	62-39	1st	+6.5
7-27	Fla.	L	4-12		8	15	Smith	Maddux		62-40	1st	+5.0
7-28	Hou.	W	5-2		8	7	Ashby	Miller	Rocker	63-40	1st	+5.0
7-29	Hou.	W	13-5		14	12	Burkett	Reynolds		64-40	1st	+5.0
7-30	Hou.	W	6-3		10	8	Glavine	Holt	Remlinger	65-40	1st	+5.0
8-1	At Ari.	W	4-2		8	2	Millwood	Swindell	Remlinger	66-40	1st	+5.5
8-2	At Ari.	L	0-2		6	6	Schilling	Maddux		66-41	1st	+4.5
8-3	At Ari.	L	4-8		10	11	Anderson	Ashby		66-42	1st	+4.0
8-4	At StL.	W	6-4		10	10	Glavine	An. Benes	Kamieniecki	67-42	1st	+4.0
8-5	At StL.	L	0-5		5	8	Stephenson	Burkett		67-43	1st	+3.0
8-6	At StL.	W	6-4		10	9	Remlinger	Kile	Ligtenberg	68-43	1st	+4.0
8-7	At Cin.	L	2-3	(10)	12	11	Sullivan	Ligtenberg		68-44	1st	+3.0
8-8	At Cin.	W	5-4		11	9	Ashby	Dessens	Remlinger	69-44	1st	+4.0
8-9	At Cin.	L	6-10		9	12	Harnisch	Glavine		69-45	1st	+3.0
8-11	L.A.	W	7-2		12	5	Remlinger	Adams		70-45	1st	+2.5
8-12	L.A.	W	4-1		6	7	Maddux	Valdes	Ligtenberg	71-45	1st	+2.5
8-13	L.A.	L	2-7		14	11	Dreifort	Ashby		71-46	1st	+1.5
8-14	S.D.	W	9-2		14	6	Glavine	Witasick		72-46	1st	+2.5
8-15	S.D.	W	3-1		7	7	Remlinger	Williams	Rocker	73-46	1st	+2.0
8-16	S.D.	W	4-1		5	5	Kamieniecki	Walker	Rocker	74-46	1st	+3.0
8-18	At S.F	L	0-2		4	7	Hernandez	Maddux		74-47	1st	+1.5
8-19	At S.F	L	3-12		8	12	Ortiz	Ashby		74-48	1st	+1.5
8-20	At S.F	W	8-5		15	4	Glavine	Rueter		75-48	1st	+1.5
8-21	At Col.	W	7-4		13	10	Millwood	Bohanon	Rocker	76-48	1st	+2.5
8-22	At Col.	L	6-7	(12)	14	16	Mayne	Rocker		76-49	1st	+2.5
8-23	At Col.	W	5-2		10	8	Maddux	Rose	Remlinger	77-49	1st	+2.5
8-24	StL.	L	5-12		9	13	Hentgen	Ashby		77-50	1st	+2.0
8-25	StL.	W	7-4		9	8	Glavine	Timlin	Ligtenberg	78-50	1st	+2.0
8-26	StL.	L	3-6		10	10	Stephenson	Millwood		78-51	1st	+2.0
8-27	StL.	L	2-7		8	9	Kile	Ligtenberg		78-52	1st	+1.0
8-28	Cin.	L	3-6		5	11	Villone	Maddux		78-53	T1st	...
8-29	Cin.	L	2-4		9	11	Parris	Remlinger	Graves	78-54	T1st	...
8-30	Cin.	W	5-2		14	3	Glavine	Dessens		79-54	T1st	...
8-31	Cin.	L	3-4		4	8	Riedling	Millwood	Graves	79-55	2nd	0.5
9-1	At Hou.	L	2-3		7	6	Lima	Burkett	Dotel	79-56	2nd	0.5
9-2	At Hou.	W	8-6		10	10	Maddux	Elarton	Rocker	80-56	1st	+0.5
9-3	At Hou.	L	3-9		11	15	Miller	Ashby		80-57	1st	+0.5
9-5	Ari.	W	5-2		6	7	Glavine	Johnson	Rocker	81-57	1st	+1.0
9-6	Ari.	W	7-1		7	6	Millwood	Reynoso		82-57	1st	+2.0
9-7	Ari.	W	4-0		12	4	Maddux	Schilling		83-57	1st	+2.5
9-8	Mon.	W	3-2		9	10	Ashby	Moore	Rocker	84-57	1st	+3.5
9-9	Mon.	L	5-7	(12)	15	14	Santana	Seelbach		84-58	1st	+3.5
9-10	Mon.	L	0-4		6	7	Vazquez	Glavine		84-59	1st	+2.5
9-12	Fla.	L	4-5		12	11	Sanchez	Millwood	Alfonseca	84-60	1st	+2.0
9-13	Fla.	W	4-0		8	4	Maddux	Dempster		85-60	1st	+2.0
9-14	Fla.	W	5-3		10	8	Ashby	Cornelius	Rocker	86-60	1st	+2.0
9-15	At Ari.	L	1-2		7	8	Johnson	Glavine	Mantei	86-61	1st	+2.0
9-16	At Ari.	W	12-10		14	14	Burkett	Stottlemyre	Rocker	87-61	1st	+2.0
9-17	At Ari.	W	7-1		16	4	Millwood	Schilling		88-61	1st	+3.0
9-18	N.Y.	W	6-3		7	9	Maddux	Hampton	Rocker	89-61	1st	+4.0
9-19	N.Y.	W	12-4		13	7	Ashby	Rusch		90-61	1st	+5.0
9-20	N.Y.	L	3-6		6	9	Leiter	Glavine	Benitez	90-62	1st	+4.0

Date	Opp.	Res.	Score	(inn.*)	Hits	Opp. hits	Winning pitcher	Losing pitcher	Save	Record	Pos.	GB
9-22	At Mon.	L	4-6		6	9	Armas	Millwood	Strickland	90-63	1st	+3.5
9-23	At Mon.	W	10-0		9	5	Maddux	Lira		91-63	1st	+3.5
9-24	At Mon.	W	14-5		21	10	Ashby	Thurman		92-63	1st	+3.5
9-25	At Mon.	W	6-0		12	8	Glavine	Vazquez		93-63	1st	+4.0
9-26	At N.Y.	W	7-1		9	7	Burkett	Leiter		94-63	1st	+5.0
9-27	At N.Y.	L	2-6		6	9	Reed	Millwood		94-64	1st	+4.0
9-28	At N.Y.	L	2-8		7	10	B.J. Jones	Maddux		94-65	1st	+3.0
9-29	Col.	L	2-4		6	6	Bohanon	Ashby	Jimenez	94-66	1st	+2.0
9-30	Col.	W	5-2		8	6	Glavine	Rose	Rocker	95-66	1st	+2.0
10-1	Col.	L	5-10		7	17	Tavarez	Rocker		95-67	1st	+1.0

Monthly records: April (18-6), May (17-10), June (13-15), July (17-9), August (14-15), September (16-11), October (0-1).
*Innings, if other than nine. †First game of a doubleheader. ‡Second game of a doubleheader.

HIGHLIGHTS

High point: The Braves beat the Mets 7-1 on September 26 at Shea Stadium to clinch their ninth straight division championship. They didn't even know they had secured the title until the next day when they were informed of a tie-breaker advantage over the Mets.

Low point: After blowing a two-run lead in the seventh inning of an August 29 loss to Cincinnati, the Braves were locked in a first-place tie with the Mets. The loss was their season-high fourth straight.

Turning point: On September 18, the Braves opened a pivotal series against the second-place Mets in Atlanta with a 6-3 win, upping their division lead to four games with 12 remaining.

Most valuable player: Rafael Furcal. The rookie shortstop made the jump from Class A to the majors look easy, hitting .294 and stealing 40 bases. Furcal took over the leadoff job in July and ignited the offense, compiling a .382 on-base percentage while leading N.L. rookies in runs (87) and walks (73).

Most valuable pitcher: Tom Glavine. In addition to recording his 200th victory, he reached 20 wins for the fifth time and pitched a career-high 241 innings. He was clearly the club's clutch pitcher, going 10-2 following Atlanta losses.

Most improved player: Andruw Jones. In his fourth full season, Jones blossomed into a legitimate slugger, reaching career-highs in average (.303), home runs (36), RBIs (103), runs (122) and hits (199). He became just the second Braves player (Hank Aaron was the other) to post three straight 20-20 seasons and the fifth-fastest player in major league history to reach 100 home runs.

Most pleasant surprise: Andres Galarraga. After missing all of the 1999 season while recovering from cancer, Galarraga made a remarkable comeback at age 39, hitting .302 and driving in 100 runs. Galarraga's importance was demonstrated by the club's 24-3 record in games in which he homered.

Key injuries: The Braves were devastated by the March loss of John Smoltz to Tommy John surgery, which eventually forced the club to trade for Andy Ashby. ... Backup catcher Eddie Perez was diagnosed with a torn rotator cuff in May and missed the remainder of the season. ... Second baseman Quilvio Veras suffered a torn ACL in July and missed the rest of the season. ... The bullpen was depleted by the losses of relievers Greg McMichael (shoulder surgery) and Rudy Seanez (elbow surgery).

Notable: The Braves became only the third team in major league history to post 90-plus wins in nine straight full seasons. ... Greg Maddux hurled 39 1/3 consecutive scoreless innings, the third-longest streak in the majors since Orel Hershiser set the record with 59 shutout innings in 1988. ... Glavine became only the 33rd pitcher since 1900 to win 20 games five times. ... Chipper Jones became only the second third baseman in major league history to post five straight 100-RBI seasons. ...Furcal's 40 steals set an Atlanta rookie record.

—BILL ZACK

RECORDS

2000 regular-season record: 95-67 (1st in N.L. East); 51-30 at home; 44-37 on road; 38-31 vs. East; 25-23 vs. Central; 32-13 vs. West; 21-14 vs. lefthanded starters; 74-53 vs. righthanded starters; 82-57 on grass; 13-10 on turf; 30-20 in daytime; 65-47 at night; 18-18 in one-run games; 3-5 in extra-inning games; 0-0-1 in doubleheaders.

Team record past five years: 501-309 (.619, ranks 1st in league in that span).

TEAM LEADERS

Batting average: Chipper Jones (.311).
At-bats: Andruw Jones (656).
Runs: Andruw Jones (122).
Hits: Andruw Jones (199).
Total Bases: Andruw Jones (355).
Doubles: Chipper Jones (38).
Triples: Andruw Jones (6).
Home runs: Andruw Jones, Chipper Jones (36).
Runs batted in: Chipper Jones (111).
Stolen bases: Rafael Furcal (40).
Slugging percentage: Chipper Jones (.566).
On-base percentage: Chipper Jones (.404).
Wins: Tom Glavine (21).
Earned-run average: Greg Maddux (3.00).
Complete games: Greg Maddux (6).
Shutouts: Greg Maddux (3).
Saves: John Rocker (24).
Innings pitched: Greg Maddux (249.1).
Strikeouts: Greg Maddux (190).

GAMES BY POSITION

Catcher: Javy Lopez 132, Paul Bako 23, Fernando Lunar 22, Eddie Perez 7, Mike Hubbard 1.
First base: Andres Galarraga 132, Wally Joyner 55, Tim Unroe 2, Paul Bako 1.
Second base: Quilvio Veras 82, Keith Lockhart 74, Rafael Furcal 31, Steve Sisco 5.
Third base: Chipper Jones 152, Keith Lockhart 18, Wes Helms 5, Steve Sisco 2, Bobby Bonilla 1.
Shortstop: Rafael Furcal 110, Walt Weiss 69, Mark DeRosa 10, Chipper Jones 6.
Outfield: Andruw Jones 161, Brian Jordan 130, Reggie Sanders 96, Bobby Bonilla 64, Trinidad Hubbard 43, B.J. Surhoff 32, George Lombard 15, Steve Sisco 6, Pedro Swann 3, Tim Unroe 1.
Designated hitter: Wally Joyner 7, Bobby Bonilla 1, Andres Galarraga 1, Steve Sisco 1.

TOP DRAFT CHOICES

1a. **Adam Wainwright,** RHP, Glynn Academy, St. Simons, Ga.
1b. **Scott Thorman,** 3B, Preston H.S., Cambridge, Ontario.
1c. **Kelly Johnson,** SS, Westwood H.S., Austin, Tex.
1d. **Aaron Herr,** SS, Hempfield H.S., Lancaster, Pa.
2a. **Kenny Nelson,** RHP, Riverdale Baptist H.S., Fort Washington, Md.
2b. **Bryan Digby,** RHP, McIntosh H.S., Peachtree City, Ga.
3. **Blaine Boyer,** RHP, Walton H.S., Marietta, Ga.
4a. **Zach Miner,** RHP, Palm Beach Gardens (Fla.) H.S.
4b. **Brian Montalbo,** RHP, Dimond H.S., Anchorage, Aka.
5. **Chris Waters,** RHP, South Florida C.C.
6. **Matt Merricks,** LHP, Oxnard (Calif.) H.S.
7. **Brian Almeida,** RHP, Lemon Bay H.S., Englewood, Fla.
8. **Robert Perkins,** C, Modesto (Calif.) J.C.
9. **Ahmad Woods,** OF, Redan H.S., Stone Mountain, Ga.
10. **Rodric Douglas,** RHP, Colmesneil (Tex.) H.S.

CHICAGO CUBS
NATIONAL LEAGUE CENTRAL DIVISION

Cubs 2001 SCHEDULE
Home games shaded; D—Day game (games starting before 5 p.m.)
*—All-Star Game at Safeco Field (Seattle)

APRIL

SUN	MON	TUE	WED	THU	FRI	SAT
1	2 D MON	3	4 D MON	5 D MON	6 D PHI	7 D PHI
8 PHI	9 D MON	10 MON	11 D MON	12	13 D PIT	14 D PIT
15 D PIT	16 D PHI	17 D PHI	18 D PHI	19	20 PIT	21 D PIT
22 D PIT	23	24 COL	25 COL	26 D COL	27 SF	28 SF
29 SF	30					

MAY

SUN	MON	TUE	WED	THU	FRI	SAT
		1 SD	2 SD	3 D SD	4 D LA	5 D LA
6 LA	7 MIL	8 MIL	9 MIL	10 D MIL	11 STL	12 D STL
13 D STL	14	15 HOU	16 HOU	17 D HOU	18 ARI	19 D ARI
20 D ARI	21	22 CIN	23 D CIN	24 CIN	25 D MIL	26 D MIL
27 MIL	28 D CIN	29 CIN	30 CIN	31		

JUNE

SUN	MON	TUE	WED	THU	FRI	SAT
					1 MIL	2 MIL
3 D MIL	4	5 STL	6 STL	7 D STL	8 CWS	9 D CWS
10 D CWS	11	12 ARI	13 ARI	14 ARI	15 D MIN	16 D MIN
17 D MIN	18 STL	19 STL	20 STL	21 D STL	22 MIL	23 D MIL
24 D MIL	25 NYM	26 NYM	27 NYM	28 CIN	29 CIN	30 D CIN

JULY

SUN	MON	TUE	WED	THU	FRI	SAT
1 CIN	2 D	3 NYM	4 NYM	5 NYM	6 DET	7 DET
8 DET	9 D	10 *	11 D CWS	12 CWS	13 D CWS	14 D CWS
15 D KC	16 KC	17 KC	18 PIT	19 PIT	20 HOU	21 HOU
22 HOU	23 HOU	24 PIT	25 D PIT	26 D STL	27 D STL	28 STL
29 STL	30	31 SD				

AUGUST

SUN	MON	TUE	WED	THU	FRI	SAT
			1 D SD	2 SD	3 D LA	4 D LA
5 LA	6	7 COL	8 COL	9 D COL	10 SF	11 D SF
12 SF	13 HOU	14 HOU	15 HOU	16	17 ARI	18 ARI
19 D ARI	20 MIL	21 MIL	22 D MIL	23 D MIL	24 STL	25 D STL
26 STL	27	28 FLA	29 FLA	30 FLA	31 ATL	

SEPTEMBER

SUN	MON	TUE	WED	THU	FRI	SAT
						1 D ATL
2 ATL	3 D FLA	4 FLA	5 FLA	6	7 ATL	8 D ATL
9 ATL	10 D CIN	11 CIN	12 CIN	13 D CIN	14 PIT	15 D PIT
16 PIT	17	18 CIN	19 CIN	20 D CIN	21 HOU	22 HOU
23 HOU	24 PIT	25 PIT	26 PIT	27 HOU	28 HOU	29 D HOU
30 D HOU						

2001 SEASON
CLUB DIRECTORY

Board of directors
Dennis FitzSimons
Andrew B. MacPhail
Andrew McKenna

President and chief executive officer
Andrew B. MacPhail

Assistant general manager
Jim Hendry

Director, baseball operations
Scott Nelson

Special assistants to the g.m.
Keith Champion
Larry Himes
Ken Kravec

Director of scouting
John Stockstill

Director of player development
Oneri Fleita

Major league advance scout
Brad Mills

Traveling secretary
Jimmy Bank

Executive v.p., business operations
Mark McGuire

Manager, information systems
Carl Rice

Sr. legal counsel/corporate secretary
Crane Kenney

Controller
Jodi Norman

Director, human resources
Jenifer Surma

V.p., marketing and broadcasting
John McDonough

Director, promotions and advertising
Jay Blunk

Director, publications
Lena McDonagh

Manager, publications
Jim McArdle

Director, stadium operations
Paul Rathje

Manager, event operations/security
Mike Hill

Head groundskeeper
Roger Baird

Director, ticket operations
Frank Maloney

Director, media relations
Sharon Pannozzo

Manager, media information
Chuck Wasserstrom

Team physician
Michael Schafer, M.D.

Head athletic trainer
David Tumbas

Assistant athletic trainer
Sandy Krum

Strength and conditioning coordinator
Mark Wilbert

Home clubhouse manager, emeritus
Yosh Kawano

Home clubhouse manager
Tom Hellmann

Visiting clubhouse manager
Dana Noeltner

Pacific Rim coordinator
Leon Lee

Regional scouting supervisors
Joe Housey, Brad Kelley, Jim Olander, Mike Soper

Scouts
Mark Adair, Billy Blitzer, Jim Crawford, Steve Fuller, Al Geddes, John Gracio, Bob Hale, Gene Handley, Bill Harford, Steve Hinton, Sam Hughes, Spider Jorgensen, Scott May, Brian Milner, Hector Ortega, Fred Peterson, Tad Powers, Steve Riha, Jose Serra, Mark Servais, Tom Shafer, Mike Soper, Billy Swoope, Jose Trujillo, Glen Van Proyen, Harry Von Suskil

MINOR LEAGUE AFFILIATES

Class	Team	League	Manager
AAA	Iowa	Pacific Coast	Bruce Kimm
AA	West Tenn	Southern	Dave Bialas
A	Boise	Northwest	Steve McFarland
A	Daytona	Florida State	Dave Trembley
A	Lansing	Midwest	Julio Garcia
Rookie	Mesa Cubs	Arizona	Carmelo Martinez

BROADCAST INFORMATION

Radio: WGN-AM (720).
TV: WGN-TV (Channel 9); WCIU-TV (Channel 26).
Cable TV: Fox Sports Net Chicago.

SPRING TRAINING

Ballpark (city): HoHoKam Park (Mesa, Ariz.).
Ticket information: 800-638-4253.

Follow the Cubs all season at: www.sportingnews.com/baseball/teams/cubs/

SPRING TRAINING ROSTER

Manager—Don Baylor (25).
Coaches—Oscar Acosta (8), Sandy Alomar Sr. (2), Gene Glynn (3), Rene Lachemann (5), Jeff Pentland (4), Billy Williams (26).

No.	PITCHERS	B/T	Ht./Wt.	Born	2000 clubs
46	Bere, Jason	R/R	6-3/215	5-26-71	Milwaukee, Cleveland
	Chiasson, Scott	R/R	6-2/185	8-14-77	Visalia
59	Duncan, Courtney	L/R	6-0/180	10-9-74	West Tenn
44	Farnsworth, Kyle	R/R	6-4/215	4-14-76	Chicago N.L., Iowa
13	Fassero, Jeff	L/L	6-1/195	1-5-63	Boston
31	Gissell, Chris	R/R	6-5/200	1-4-78	West Tenn
54	Gonzalez, Jeremi	R/R	6-2/215	1-8-75	Arizona Cubs, Lansing
45	Gordon, Tom	R/R	5-9/190	11-18-67	DID NOT PLAY
49	Heredia, Felix	L/L	6-0/180	6-18-76	Chicago N.L.
32	Lieber, Jon	L/R	6-3/225	4-2-70	Chicago N.L.
33	McNichol, Brian	L/L	6-5/225	5-20-74	Iowa
43	Meyers, Mike	R/R	6-2/210	10-18-77	West Tenn, Iowa
52	Nation, Joey	L/L	6-2/205	9-28-78	West Tenn, Chicago N.L.
35	Ohman, Will	L/L	6-2/195	8-13-77	West Tenn, Chicago N.L.
48	Quevedo, Ruben	R/R	6-1/230	1-5-79	Iowa, Chicago N.L.
36	Tapani, Kevin	R/R	6-1/190	2-18-64	Chicago N.L.
50	Tavarez, Julian	L/R	6-2/190	5-22-73	Colorado
	Teut, Nathan	R/L	6-7/215	3-11-76	West Tenn
47	Van Poppel, Todd	R/R	6-5/235	12-9-71	Iowa, Chicago N.L.
34	Wood, Kerry	R/R	6-5/230	6-16-77	Daytona, Iowa, Chicago N.L.
	Yennaco, Jay	R/R	6-2/225	11-17-75	West Tenn

No.	CATCHERS	B/T	Ht./Wt.	Born	2000 clubs
27	Girardi, Joe	R/R	5-11/200	10-14-64	Chicago N.L.
	Hundley, Todd	B/R	5-11/199	5-27-69	Los Angeles, Albuquerque

No.	INFIELDERS	B/T	Ht./Wt.	Born	2000 clubs
	Coomer, Ron	R/R	5-11/206	11-18-66	Minnesota
56	Frese, Nate	R/R	6-3/200	7-10-77	Daytona
	Gload, Ross	L/L	6-0/185	4-5-76	Portland, Iowa, Chicago N.L.
12	Gutierrez, Ricky	R/R	6-1/195	5-23-70	Chicago N.L., Daytona
	Hinske, Eric	L/R	6-2/225	8-5-77	West Tenn
20	Meyers, Chad	R/R	6-0/190	8-8-75	Chicago N.L., Iowa
33	Mueller, Bill	B/R	5-10/180	3-17-71	San Francisco
11	Nieves, Jose	R/R	6-0/180	6-16-75	Chicago N.L., Daytona, West Tenn, Iowa
57	Ojeda, Augie	B/R	5-9/170	12-20-74	Iowa, Chicago N.L.
	Smith, Jason	L/R	6-3/190	7-24-77	West Tenn
7	Young, Eric	R/R	5-8/175	5-18-67	Chicago N.L.
15	Zuleta, Julio	R/R	6-5/235	3-28-75	Chicago N.L., Iowa

No.	OUTFIELDERS	B/T	Ht./Wt.	Born	2000 clubs
28	Brown, Roosevelt	L/R	5-11/195	8-3-75	Chicago N.L., Iowa
9	Buford, Damon	R/R	5-10/180	6-12-70	Chicago N.L.
51	Matthews, Gary	B/R	6-3/200	8-25-74	Iowa, Chicago N.L.
20	Patterson, Corey	L/R	5-10/180	8-13-79	West Tenn, Chicago N.L.
	Randolph, Jaisen	B/R	6-0/180	1-19-79	West Tenn
21	Sosa, Sammy	R/R	6-0/220	11-12-68	Chicago N.L.
22	White, Rondell	R/R	6-1/210	2-23-72	Montreal, Chicago N.L.

BALLPARK INFORMATION

Ballpark (capacity, surface)
Wrigley Field (39,059, grass)

Address
1060 W. Addison St.
Chicago, IL 60613-4397

Official website
www.cubs.com

Business phone
773-404-2827

Ticket information
773-404-2827

Ticket prices
$30 (club box)
$28 (field box)
$23 (upper deck box, terrace box, family section)
$20 (bleachers)
$18 (terrace reserved)

Field dimensions (from home plate)
To left field at foul line, 355 feet
To center field, 400 feet
To right field at foul line, 353 feet

First game played
April 20, 1916 (Cubs 7, Reds 6)

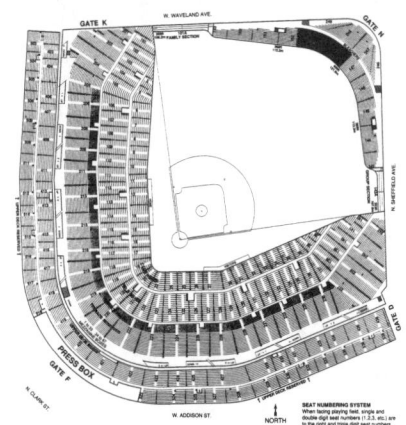

2000 REVIEW
DAY BY DAY

Date	Opp.	Res.	Score	(inn.*)	Hits	Opp. hits	Winning pitcher	Losing pitcher	Save	Record	Pos.	GB
3-29	At N.Y.§	W	5-3		12	7	Lieber	Hampton	Aguilera	1-0	1st	+0.5
3-30	N.Y.§	L	1-5	(11)	5	6	Cook	Young		1-1	1st	...
4-3	At StL.	L	1-7		3	10	Kile	Tapani		1-2	2nd	1.0
4-5	At StL.	L	4-10		9	12	Hentgen	Lieber		1-3	4th	2.0
4-6	At StL.	L	3-13		6	11	Stephenson	Farnsworth		1-4	6th	3.0
4-7	At Cin.	W	10-6		8	8	Lorraine	Harnisch	Aguilera	2-4	5th	2.0
4-8	At Cin.	L	3-4	(11)	4	11	Graves	Guthrie		2-5	6th	3.0
4-9	At Cin.	L	7-8	(11)	13	9	Graves	Karchner		2-6	6th	4.0
4-10	Atl.	W	4-3		10	7	Guthrie	Ligtenberg		3-6	T5th	4.0
4-12	Atl.	W	11-4		12	6	Farnsworth	Mulholland		4-6	5th	3.5
4-13	Atl.	W	3-2		7	8	Guthrie	Remlinger		5-6	3rd	2.5
4-14	Fla.	L	4-9		8	10	Fernandez	Lorraine		5-7	4th	2.5
4-15	Fla.	W	4-2		6	4	Downs	Dempster	Aguilera	6-7	3rd	2.0
4-16	Fla.	L	5-6	(10)	10	8	Miceli	Quevedo	Alfonseca	6-8	4th	2.5
4-17	Fla.	L	5-6		6	12	Sanchez	Farnsworth	Alfonseca	6-9	6th	3.0
4-18	At Mon.	L	3-4		7	9	Strickland	Tapani	Urbina	6-10	6th	4.0
4-19	At Mon.	L	3-7		7	11	Pavano	Quevedo		6-11	6th	5.0
4-20	At Mon.	W	10-6		10	13	Williams	Blank		7-11	6th	5.0
4-22†	At N.Y.	L	3-8		8	12	Rusch	Lieber		7-12		
4-22‡	At N.Y.	L	6-7		11	10	Cook	Farnsworth	Benitez	7-13	6th	5.0
4-23	At N.Y.	L	8-15		10	18	Hampton	Tapani		7-14	T5th	6.0
4-25	At Hou.	L	7-11		10	16	Reynolds	Downs		7-15	6th	7.0
4-26	At Hou.	W	13-8		16	11	Karchner	Maddux	Aguilera	8-15	6th	7.0
4-27	At Hou.	W	12-3		14	5	Lieber	Lima		9-15	5th	6.0
4-28	Ari.	W	6-5		10	7	Tapani	Springer	Aguilera	10-15	4th	6.0
4-29	Ari.	L	4-7	(10)	9	10	Mantei	Guthrie	Morgan	10-16	5th	7.0
4-30	Ari.	L	0-6		6	12	Johnson	Lorraine		10-17	6th	8.0
5-2	Hou.	W	11-1		16	4	Wood	Lima	Williams	11-17	5th	7.0
5-3	Hou.	W	4-3		7	8	Lieber	Holt	Aguilera	12-17	4th	6.0
5-4	Hou.	L	2-6		9	9	Elarton	Valdes	Wagner	12-18	5th	7.0
5-5	Pit.	L	2-4		8	7	Ritchie	Tapani	Williams	12-19	5th	7.0
5-6	Pit.	L	9-11		16	16	Wallace	Farnsworth	Williams	12-20	5th	8.0
5-7	Pit.	L	3-11		9	13	Schmidt	Wood		12-21	5th	8.0
5-8	Mil.	W	12-11	(10)	16	13	Heredia	Wickman		13-21	5th	7.0
5-9	Mil.	L	3-4		5	8	D'Amico	Guthrie	Weathers	13-22	5th	8.0
5-10	Mil.	W	9-8	(11)	10	9	Aguilera	de los Santos		14-22	5th	7.0
5-11	Mil.	L	8-14		17	18	Woodard	Williams		14-23	5th	7.5
5-12	At Mon.	L	3-8		7	10	Thurman	Wood	Hermanson	14-24	6th	7.5
5-13	At Mon.	W	2-1		6	8	Lieber	Armas		15-24	5th	7.0
5-14	At Mon.	L	15-16		21	16	Hermanson	Aguilera		15-25	5th	7.5
5-16	L.A.	L	5-6		7	9	Mills	Tapani	Shaw	15-26	6th	8.5
5-17	L.A.	L	6-8		7	9	Mills	Heredia	Shaw	15-27	6th	8.5
5-19	Cin.	W	4-1		7	6	Valdes	Parris	Van Poppel	16-27	6th	8.0
5-20	Cin.	L	3-5		10	8	Villone	Lieber	Graves	16-28	6th	9.0
5-21	Cin.	W	4-2		5	10	Tapani	Bell	Heredia	17-28	5th	9.0
5-23	At Col.	L	7-10		9	10	Bohanon	Garibay		17-29	5th	10.0
5-24	At Col.	L	4-9		12	8	Astacio	Farnsworth	Jimenez	17-30	5th	11.0
5-25	At Col.	W	6-5		9	10	Lieber	DeJean	Aguilera	18-30	5th	11.0
5-26	At S.F	L	3-5		8	10	Gardner	Tapani		18-31	6th	11.0
5-27	At S.F	W	3-2	(11)	4	9	Garibay	Fultz	Aguilera	19-31	5th	10.0
5-28	At S.F	W	4-1		8	5	Wood	Rueter	Aguilera	20-31	5th	9.0
5-29	Atl.	L	0-1		6	2	Maddux	Lieber		20-32	5th	10.0
5-30	Atl.	L	2-5		9	9	Mulholland	Quevedo	Remlinger	20-33	5th	11.0
6-1	Atl.	W	5-3		9	6	Tapani	Glavine	Aguilera	21-33	5th	9.5
6-2	Det.	W	2-0		5	8	Downs	Nomo	Aguilera	22-33	5th	9.5
6-3	Det.	L	3-5		6	7	Weaver	Wood	Jones	22-34	5th	9.5
6-4	Det.	L	2-3	(12)	9	7	Anderson	Van Poppel	Jones	22-35	5th	10.0
6-5	Ari.	W	4-3	(10)	10	8	Heredia	Mantei		23-35	5th	9.0
6-6	Ari.	W	4-1		8	5	Tapani	Reynoso		24-35	4th	8.5
6-7	Ari.	W	9-4		11	11	Downs	Anderson	Van Poppel	25-35	4th	8.5
6-9	At Chi. (AL)	L	5-6	(14)	8	15	Pena	Van Poppel		25-36	4th	8.5
6-10	At Chi. (AL)	L	3-4		7	5	Sirotka	Wood	Foulke	25-37	4th	8.5
6-11	At Chi. (AL)	W	6-5		8	10	Van Poppel	Pena	Aguilera	26-37	4th	8.5
6-13	N.Y.	W	4-3		11	5	Heredia	Franco	Aguilera	27-37	4th	9.0
6-14	N.Y.	L	8-10		14	14	Rusch	Garibay	Benitez	27-38	T4th	10.0
6-16	Mon.	W	9-8		9	8	Van Poppel	Armas	Aguilera	28-38	4th	10.0
6-17	Mon.	W	1-0		4	8	Rain	Hermanson	Aguilera	29-38	4th	10.0
6-18	Mon.	L	3-4	(11)	9	9	Telford	Garibay	Rigby	29-39	4th	10.0
6-20	At Atl.	L	4-11		9	14	Millwood	Tapani		29-40	4th	11.0
6-21	At Atl.	W	8-1		11	5	Wood	Glavine		30-40	4th	10.0
6-22	At Atl.	L	4-6		14	11	Mulholland	Downs	Remlinger	30-41	4th	11.0
6-23	At Fla.	L	1-6		8	12	Penny	Lieber		30-42	4th	12.0
6-24	At Fla.	L	4-7		12	9	Strong	Heredia	Alfonseca	30-43	5th	13.0

Date	Opp.	Res.	Score	(inn.*)	Hits	Opp. hits	Winning pitcher	Losing pitcher	Save	Record	Pos.	GB
6-25	At Fla.	L	7-8	(10)	9	10	Alfonseca	Heredia		30-44	5th	14.0
6-27	At Pit.	L	0-6		3	5	Ritchie	Wood		30-45	5th	14.5
6-28	At Pit.	W	5-4		8	9	Lieber	Cordova	Aguilera	31-45	4th	13.5
6-29	At Pit.	L	4-5	(10)	7	7	Wilkins	Worrell		31-46	5th	14.5
6-30	At Mil.	W	7-4	(15)	13	12	Garibay	Levrault	Aguilera	32-46	4th	14.5
7-1	At Mil.	L	0-4		2	11	D'Amico	Valdes		32-47	5th	15.5
7-2	At Mil.	L	2-4		6	7	Haynes	Wood	Wickman	32-48	5th	15.5
7-3	Pit.	W	3-0		9	2	Lieber	Cordova		33-48	5th	15.0
7-4	Pit.	W	4-10		8	12	Wilkins	Aguilera		33-49	5th	16.0
7-5	Pit.	L	6-9		10	12	Anderson	Downs		33-50	5th	17.0
7-7	Chi. (AL)	L	2-4	(12)	6	11	Lowe	Van Poppel	Pena	33-51	5th	16.5
7-8	Chi. (AL)	W	9-2		14	5	Lieber	Baldwin		34-51	5th	15.5
7-9	Chi. (AL)	W	9-6		11	8	Tapani	Simas	Worrell	35-51	5th	15.5
7-13	At Min.	L	1-5		6	11	Radke	Valdes	Hawkins	35-52	5th	16.5
7-14	At Min.	W	6-2		12	8	Lieber	Milton		36-52	5th	16.5
7-15	At Min.	W	8-4		13	13	Tapani	Mays		37-52	5th	15.5
7-16	At K.C.	W	10-7		10	14	Wood	Reichert	Aguilera	38-52	T4th	14.5
7-17	At K.C.	W	3-1		8	7	Downs	Durbin	Aguilera	39-52	3rd	14.5
7-18	At K.C.	L	4-12		8	20	Stein	Valdes		39-53	T3rd	14.5
7-19	Phi.	W	5-4		10	9	Heredia	Holzemer		40-53	3rd	13.5
7-20	Phi.	L	2-3		8	6	Brownson	Tapani	Brantley	40-54	T3rd	13.5
7-21	Mil.	W	4-2		7	5	Wood	Snyder	Aguilera	41-54	T3rd	13.5
7-22	Mil.	W	3-2	(13)	7	10	Heredia	Woodard		42-54	T3rd	12.5
7-23	Mil.	W	5-4		4	7	Valdes	Wright	Aguilera	43-54	3rd	11.5
7-25	At Phi.	W	8-7		7	14	Worrell	Brock	Aguilera	44-54	3rd	11.5
7-26	At Phi.	W	14-9		14	9	Heredia	Byrd		45-54	3rd	11.5
7-27	At Phi.	W	4-1		12	7	Rain	Padilla	Aguilera	46-54	3rd	10.5
7-28	S.F	L	0-2		7	5	Hernandez	Worrell	Nen	46-55	3rd	10.5
7-29	S.F	W	8-1		13	6	Wood	Ortiz	Farnsworth	47-55	3rd	9.5
7-30	S.F	W	3-1		10	4	Lieber	Rueter		48-55	3rd	8.5
7-31	Col.	W	2-0		8	4	Tapani	Bohanon	Aguilera	49-55	3rd	8.5
8-1	Col.	L	1-2		2	7	Astacio	Farnsworth	White	49-56	3rd	8.5
8-2	Col.	W	3-2		8	4	Rain	Wasdin	Aguilera	50-56	3rd	8.5
8-3	At S.D.	L	5-6		10	8	Walker	Worrell	Hoffman	50-57	3rd	9.0
8-4	At S.D.	L	9-11		13	13	Almanzar	Rain	Hoffman	50-58	3rd	9.0
8-5	At S.D.	W	6-3		10	8	Tapani	Williams	Aguilera	51-58	3rd	9.0
8-6	At S.D.	L	6-8		12	11	Eaton	Garibay	Hoffman	51-59	3rd	9.0
8-7	At L.A.	W	7-3		10	7	Quevedo	Herges		52-59	3rd	9.0
8-8	At L.A.	L	5-7		8	13	Dreifort	Norton	Shaw	52-60	3rd	9.0
8-9	At L.A.	W	5-4	(10)	10	8	Worrell	Osuna	Aguilera	53-60	3rd	8.0
8-11	Cin.	L	4-6		6	11	Wohlers	Rain	Graves	53-61	3rd	8.5
8-12	Cin.	L	0-3		5	7	Williamson	Garibay	Graves	53-62	3rd	9.5
8-13	Cin.	L	0-3		7	6	Parris	Quevedo	Sullivan	53-63	3rd	10.5
8-14	StL.	W	7-3		11	8	Lieber	An. Benes		54-63	3rd	9.5
8-15	StL.	L	2-4		7	11	Stephenson	Arnold	Veres	54-64	3rd	10.5
8-16	StL.	L	1-5		6	9	Kile	Tapani		54-65	3rd	11.5
8-18	At Ari.	L	2-11		6	12	Schilling	Quevedo		54-66	3rd	12.5
8-19	At Ari.	L	3-11		7	15	Anderson	Lieber		54-67	3rd	13.5
8-20	At Ari.	L	4-5		4	9	Johnson	Rain		54-68	3rd	13.5
8-21	At Hou.	L	4-5		8	6	Elarton	Tapani	Slusarski	54-69	3rd	14.5
8-22	At Hou.	L	7-10		8	9	Valdes	Farnsworth	Cabrera	54-70	3rd	14.5
8-23	At Hou.	W	15-5		19	4	Quevedo	Miller		55-70	3rd	14.5
8-25†	L.A.	L	3-5		10	13	Osuna	Lieber	Shaw	55-71		
8-25‡	L.A.	L	1-3		9	5	Perez	Garibay	Shaw	55-72	T3rd	15.5
8-26	L.A.	W	6-4		8	9	Worrell	Olson	Aguilera	56-72	T3rd	15.5
8-27	L.A.	L	6-7	(10)	13	9	Fetters	Van Poppel	Shaw	56-73	T3rd	16.5
8-28	S.D.	L	2-8		3	11	Clement	Quevedo		56-74	T3rd	17.5
8-29	S.D.	W	7-6	(13)	10	10	Heredia	Hoffman		57-74	3rd	16.5
8-30	S.D.	W	5-1		10	4	Lieber	Tollberg		58-74	3rd	16.5
8-31	S.D.	L	5-11		8	16	Witasick	Tapani		58-75	T3rd	17.0
9-1	At S.F	L	2-7		6	10	Gardner	Wood		58-76	T3rd	18.0
9-2	At S.F	L	2-13		8	10	Estes	Quevedo		58-77	4th	19.0
9-3	At S.F	L	2-5		5	13	Hernandez	Garibay	Nen	58-78	4th	20.0
9-4	At Col.	L	2-6		8	12	Rose	Lieber		58-79	4th	21.0
9-5	At Col.	L	2-10		4	13	Tavarez	Arnold		58-80	T5th	22.0
9-6	At Col.	W	8-5	(11)	13	11	Van Poppel	White	Aguilera	59-80	T5th	21.0
9-8	Hou.	L	10-13		10	20	Miller	Tapani	Dotel	59-81	6th	21.5
9-9	Hou.	L	4-14		9	19	Holt	Quevedo		59-82	6th	22.5
9-10	Hou.	L	6-7		13	10	McKnight	Lieber	Dotel	59-83	6th	22.5
9-11	At Cin.	L	6-7		14	9	Harnisch	Garibay	Graves	59-84	6th	23.5
9-12	At Cin.	W	2-1		6	4	Wood	Fernandez		60-84	6th	23.5
9-13	At Cin.	L	3-13		6	16	Bell	Arnold		60-85	6th	24.5
9-14	At StL.	L	0-4		3	5	Hentgen	Quevedo		60-86	6th	25.5
9-15	At StL.	L	2-3		6	4	James	Lieber	Veres	60-87	6th	26.5
9-16	At StL.	L	6-7		11	10	Timlin	Spradlin	Veres	60-88	6th	27.5
9-17	At StL.	L	2-4		7	4	Kile	Worrell	Morris	60-89	6th	28.5
9-18	At Mil.	L	1-2		4	5	D'Amico	Van Poppel	Leskanic	60-90	6th	29.0
9-19	At Mil.	L	8-9		7	9	King	Farnsworth		60-91	6th	29.0

Date	Opp.	Res.	Score	(inn.*)	Hits	Opp. hits	Winning pitcher	Losing pitcher	Save	Record	Pos.	GB
9-20	At Mil.	L	2-3	(10)	8	9	Leskanic	Farnsworth		60-92	6th	30.0
9-22	StL.	W	5-4		10	5	Ohman	Veres		61-92	6th	28.5
9-23	StL.	L	5-6		7	10	Reames	Nation	Morris	61-93	6th	29.5
9-24	StL.	W	10-5		12	8	Van Poppel	Hentgen	Heredia	62-93	6th	28.5
9-25	Phi.	W	4-3		4	8	Quevedo	Person	Worrell	63-93	6th	28.0
9-26	Phi.	L	4-10		14	14	Daal	Lieber		63-94	6th	29.0
9-27	Phi.	W	1-0		6	8	Wood	Wolf	Worrell	64-94	6th	29.0
9-28	Phi.	L	2-4		7	7	Politte	Nation	Padilla	64-95	6th	30.0
9-29	At Pit.	L	4-8		10	13	Wilkins	Rain		64-96	6th	30.0
9-30	At Pit.	L	2-4		11	7	Ritchie	Quevedo	Williams	64-97	6th	30.0
10-1	At Pit.	W	10-9		12	14	Farnsworth	Sauerbeck	Arnold	65-97	6th	30.0

Monthly records: March (1-1), April (9-16), May (10-16), June (12-13), July (17-9), August (9-20), September (6-22), October (1-0). *Innings, if other than nine. †First game of a doubleheader. ‡Second game of a doubleheader. §Game played in Tokyo, Japan.

HIGHLIGHTS

High point: The season highlight came before the Cubs even played a game in North America. They opened with a two-game series against the Mets in Tokyo and won the opener, accounting for their only above-.500 record of the year. The series was the first in the regular season featuring major league teams outside North America.

Low point: Before the Cubs played Arizona on June 6, right fielder Sammy Sosa ripped manager Don Baylor for "lack of respect," touching off a month-long trade watch. Baylor had publicly suggested that Sosa needed to concentrate on baserunning and defense, as well as home runs. The two men eventually mended fences and Sosa did indeed enjoy a "complete season."

Turning point: The Cubs, 18 games below .500 at the All-Star break, were 53-60 when Cincinnati came to Wrigley Field August 11. Reliever Steve Rain, trying to protect Kevin Tapani's 4-0 eighth-inning lead, surrendered a three-run homer to Ken Griffey Jr., a two-run shot to Dmitri Young and a solo homer to Pokey Reese in a stunning 6-4 loss. The Reds would go on to a three-game sweep.

Most valuable player: Sosa won his first home run crown with 50 and enjoyed his best all-around year at the plate. He batted a career-best .320 and would have reached the 200-hit mark if not for a late-season back injury. Sosa finished with 193 hits, 138 RBIs and a career-high 91 walks.

Most valuable pitcher: Jon Lieber led the N.L. in innings pitched (251) and starts (35) and finished third with six complete games. With a good team, his record probably would have been much better than 12-11.

Most improved player: Former pitching phenom Todd Van Poppel didn't make the club out of spring training, but he came up May 12 and enjoyed the best year of his career. He pitched in 51 games, compiling a 4-5 record and 3.75 ERA, and excelled as a middle-to-late-inning reliever.

Most pleasant surprise: The Cubs found unexpected shortstop stability from Ricky Gutierrez, a free-agent pickup from Houston. Gutierrez batted .276 and posted career bests in home runs (11) and

RBIs (56) and led both leagues with 16 sacrifice bunts.

Key injuries: Mark Grace broke the middle finger of his right hand in spring training and it affected his swing. Grace also missed three weeks with a hamstring injury. ... Tapani had his second straight season cut short, this time with a knee problem that required surgery. ... Rondell White dislocated his shoulder August 26 and missed the rest of the season. ... Third baseman Shane Andrews missed three months because of surgery to remove a herniated disk in his lower back. ... Closer Rick Aguilera suffered a small fracture in his thumb and missed the final three weeks.

Notable: The Cubs finished in last place for the third time in four seasons and posted back-to-back 95-plus-loss seasons for the first time in their history. ... The Cubs played 22 extra-inning games, just one short of the club record. They were 9-13 in extra innings. ... Sosa finished with a club-record 179 home runs over three seasons. ... Eric Young's 54 steals were the fourth-highest club total since 1900.

—BRUCE MILES

RECORDS

2000 regular-season record: 65-97 (6th in N.L. Central); 38-43 at home; 27-54 on road; 18-23 vs. East; 29-48 vs. Central; 18-26 vs. West; 14-21 vs. lefthanded starters; 51-76 vs. righthanded starters; 53-83 on grass; 12-14 on turf; 36-56 in daytime; 29-41 at night; 27-30 in one-run games; 9-13 in extra-inning games; 0-2-0 in doubleheaders.

Team record past five years: 366-445 (.451, ranks 15th in league in that span).

TEAM LEADERS

Batting average: Sammy Sosa (.320).
At-bats: Eric Young (607).
Runs: Sammy Sosa (106).
Hits: Sammy Sosa (193).
Total Bases: Sammy Sosa (383).
Doubles: Mark Grace (41).
Triples: Damon Buford, Jose Nieves (3).
Home runs: Sammy Sosa (50).
Runs batted in: Sammy Sosa (138).

Stolen bases: Eric Young (54).
Slugging percentage: Sammy Sosa (.634).
On-base percentage: Sammy Sosa (.406).
Wins: Jon Lieber (12).
Earned-run average: Jon Lieber (4.41).
Complete games: Jon Lieber (6).
Shutouts: Jon Lieber (1).
Saves: Rick Aguilera (29).
Innings pitched: Jon Lieber (251.0).
Strikeouts: Jon Lieber (192).

GAMES BY POSITION

Catcher: Joe Girardi 103, Jeff Reed 71, Mike Mahoney 4.
First base: Mark Grace 140, Julio Zuleta 14, Dave Martinez 9, Brant Brown 7, Shane Andrews 6, Ross Gload 2, Jeff Huson 1.
Second base: Eric Young 150, Jeff Huson 17, Chad Meyers 8, Jose Nieves 7, Augie Ojeda 4.
Third base: Willie Greene 90, Shane Andrews 58, Jose Nieves 39, Jeff Huson 18, Chad Meyers 8.
Shortstop: Ricky Gutierrez 121, Augie Ojeda 25, Jose Nieves 24, Jeff Huson 17.
Outfield: Sammy Sosa 156, Damon Buford 148, Henry Rodriguez 70, Gary Matthews Jr. 61, Glenallen Hill 29, Brant Brown 28, Roosevelt Brown 28, Rondell White 18, Corey Patterson 11, Tarrik Brock 10, Dave Martinez 10, Ross Gload 8, Julio Zuleta 6, Raul Gonzalez 2.
Designated hitter: Glenallen Hill 9.

TOP DRAFT CHOICES

1. **Luis Montanez,** SS, Coral Park H.S., Miami.
2. **Bobby Hill,** SS, Newark (Atlantic League).
3a. **Aaron Krawiec,** LHP, Villanova Univ.
3b. **Nic Jackson,** OF, U. of Richmond.
4. **Todd Wellemeyer,** RHP, Bellarmine (Ky.) College.
5. **Gary Banks,** SS, Southern Choctaw H.S., Gilbertown, Ala.
6. **J.J. Johnson,** SS, Grianbrier H.S., Appling, Ga.
7. **Ryan Jorgensen,** C, Louisiana State U.
8. **Dontrelle Willis,** LHP, Encinal H.S., Alameda, Calif.
9. **Mark Freed,** LHP, Mississippi State U.
10. **Blake Blasi,** 2B, Wichita State Univ.

CINCINNATI REDS
NATIONAL LEAGUE CENTRAL DIVISION

Reds
2001 SCHEDULE
Home games shaded; D—Day game (games starting before 5 p.m.)
'—All-Star Game at Safeco Field (Seattle)

APRIL
SUN	MON	TUE	WED	THU	FRI	SAT
1	2 D	3	4 D	5 D	6	7 D
	ATL	PIT	PIT	PIT	MIL	MIL
8 D	9 D	10	11	12	13	14 D
MIL	PIT		PIT	PIT	NYM	NYM
15 D	16	17	18	19	20	21 D
NYM		MIL	MIL		NYM	NYM
22 D	23	24	25	26 D	27	28 D
NYM		SF	SF	SF	COL	COL
29 D	30					
COL						

MAY
SUN	MON	TUE	WED	THU	FRI	SAT
		1	2	3	4	5 D
		LA	LA	LA	SD	SD
6 D	7	8	9	10	11	12
SD	ARI	ARI	ARI		HOU	HOU
13	14	15	16	17 D	18	19 D
HOU	HOU	ARI	ARI	ARI	HOU	HOU
20 D	21	22	23 D	24 D	25	26
HOU		CUB	CUB	CUB	STL	STL
27 D	28 D	29	30	31		
STL	CUB	CUB	CUB			

JUNE
SUN	MON	TUE	WED	THU	FRI	SAT
					1	2 D
					STL	STL
3	4	5	6	7	8	9 D
STL	STL	MIL	MIL		CLE	CLE
10 D	11	12	13	14	15	16
CLE		CWS	CWS	CWS	COL	COL
17 D	18	19	20	21	22	23
COL	MIL	MIL	MIL		HOU	HOU
24 D	25	26	27	28	29	30 D
HOU		STL	STL	CUB	CUB	CUB

JULY
SUN	MON	TUE	WED	THU	FRI	SAT
1 D	2	3	4 D	5 D	6	7
CUB	PIT	PIT	PIT	PIT	MIN	MIN
8 D	9	10 *	11		12	13 D	14 D
MIN		CLE		CLE	CLE	
15 D	16	17	18	19 D	20	21
DET	DET	DET	DET	ATL	ATL	FLA
22 D	23	24	25 D	26	27	28
FLA	ATL	ATL	ATL		FLA	FLA
29 D	30	31				
FLA		LA				

AUGUST
SUN	MON	TUE	WED	THU	FRI	SAT
		1	2	3	4	5
		LA	LA	SD	SD	
5 D	6	7	8	9	10	11
SD		SF	SF	SF	COL	COL
12 D	13	14	15	16	17	18
COL	STL	STL	STL	STL	MIL	MIL
19 D	20 D	21	22	23 D	24	25
MIL	STL	STL	STL	STL	MON	MON
26 D	27	28	29	30 D	31	
MON		HOU	HOU	HOU	PIT	

SEPTEMBER
SUN	MON	TUE	WED	THU	FRI	SAT
						1
						PIT
2 D	3 D	4	5 D	6	7	8
PIT	HOU	HOU	HOU	PIT	PIT	PIT
9 D	10	11	12 D	13 D	14	15 D
PIT	CUB	CUB	CUB		PHI	PHI
16 D	17	18	19	20 D	21	22
PHI		CUB	CUB	CUB	MIL	MIL
23 D	24	25	26	27	28	29 D
MIL		PHI	PHI	PHI	MON	MON
30 D						
MON						

2001 SEASON
CLUB DIRECTORY

Chief executive officer
Carl H. Lindner
Chief operating officer
John Allen
General manager
Jim Bowden
Assistant general manager
Darrell "Doc" Rodgers
Director of player personnel
Leland Maddox
Special asst. to the g.m./advance scout
Gene Bennett
Special assistants to the g.m.
Larry Barton Jr., Johnny Bench, Al Goldis, Gary Hughes
Director of baseball administration
Brad Kullman
Director of scouting
Kasey McKeon
Assistant director of scouting
Johnny Almaraz
Executive assistant to the g.m.
Lois Schneider
Senior advisor, player development
Sheldon "Chief" Bender
Admin. assistant, player development
Lois Hudson
Senior advisor, scouting
Bob Zuk
Director of scouting administration
Wilma Mann
Traveling secretary
Gary Wahoff
Director of media relations
Rob Butcher
Public relations assistant
Larry Herms
Controller
Anthony Ward
Director, stadium operations
Dellan Mullin
Director, ticket department
John O'Brien
Director of season/group sales
Pat McCaffrey
Director of communications
Mike Ringering
Assistant director of communications
Ralph Mitchell
Director of new stadium development
Jenny Gardner
Marketing consultant
Cal Levy

Legal counsel
Robert C. Martin
Director, group sales
Brad Blettner
Assistant director, media relations
Michael Vassallo
Exec. assistant to chief operating officer
Joyce Pfarr
Business and broadcast administrator
Ginny Kamp
Head trainer
Greg Lynn
Assistant trainer
Mark Mann
Conditioning coordinator
Lance Sewell
Field superintendent
Jeff Guilkey
Sr. clubhouse & equipment manager
Bernie Stowe
Reds clubhouse & equipment manager
Rick Stowe
Visiting clubhouse & equip. manager
Mark Stowe
Major League scout/national cross-checker
Jeff Barton
Major League scout
De Jon Watson
Assistant, scouting
Paul Pierson
Assistant, video operations
Joe Harkins
Cross-checkers
Butch Baccala, John Castleberry, Alvin Rittman, Bill Scherrer
Director of international scouting
Jorge Oquendo
Scouting supervisors
Terry Abbott, Howard Bowens, John Brickley, Mark Corey, Rex De La Nuez, Robert Filotei, Jerry Flowers, Jimmy Gonzales, Robert Koontz, Craig Kornfeld, Steve Kring, Tom LeVasseur, Brian Mejia, Cotton Nye, Tom Severtson, Perry Smith, Brian Wilson, Greg Zunino
Scouts
Oswaldo Alvarez, John Bellino, George Blackburn, Fred Blair, Kevin Carcamo, Keith Chapman, Edwin Daub, Felix Delgado, Orlando Granda, Jim Grief, Don Gust, Frank Henderson, Don Hill, Thomas Herrera, Juan Linares, Victor Mateo, Denny Nagel, Rafael Nava, Everett Renteria, Glenn Serviente, Marlon Styles, Lee Toole, Ruben Vargas, Mike Wallace, John Walsh, Nathan Ware, Roger Weberg

MINOR LEAGUE AFFILIATES

Class	Team	League	Manager
AAA	Louisville	International	Dave Miley
AA	Chattanooga	Southern	Phil Wellman
A	Dayton	Midwest	Donnie Scott
A	Mudville	California	Len Dykstra
Rookie	Billings	Pioneer	To be announced
Rookie	Gulf Coast Reds	Gulf Coast	Edgar Caceres

BROADCAST INFORMATION

Radio: WLW-AM (700).
Cable TV: Fox Sports Net.

SPRING TRAINING

Ballpark (city): Ed Smith Stadium (Sarasota, Fla.).
Ticket information: 941-954-4101.

Follow the Reds all season at: www.sportingnews.com/baseball/teams/reds/

SPRING TRAINING ROSTER

Manager—Bob Boone (9).
Coaches—Bill Doran (19), Tim Foli (10), Ken Griffey Sr. (33), Don Gullett (35), Tom Hume (47), Ron Oester (16).

No.	PITCHERS	B/T	Ht./Wt.	Born	2000 clubs
57	Andrews, Clayton	R/L	6-0/175	5-15-78	Syracuse, Toronto
61	Atchley, Justin	L/L	6-3/215	9-5-73	Louisville
29	Bell, Rob	R/R	6-5/225	1-17-77	Cincinnati, Louisville
52	Brower, Jim	R/R	6-2/205	12-29-72	Buffalo, Cleveland
68	Estrella, Leo	R/R	6-1/185	2-20-75	Tennessee, Syracuse, Toronto
40	Etherton, Seth	R/R	6-1/200	10-17-76	Edmonton, Anaheim
43	Fernandez, Osvaldo	R/R	6-2/193	11-4-68	Chattanooga, Louisville, Cincinnati
59	Glauber, Keith	R/R	6-2/190	1-18-72	Chattanooga, Louisville, Cincinnati
32	Graves, Danny	R/R	5-11/185	8-7-73	Cincinnati
38	Harnisch, Pete	R/R	6-0/228	9-23-66	Cincinnati, Louisville
45	Dessens, Elmer	R/R	6-0/187	1-13-72	Louisville, Cincinnati
39	Mercado, Hector	L/L	6-3/235	4-29-74	Louisville, Cincinnati
54	Reith, Brian	R/R	6-5/190	2-28-78	Tampa, Dayton, Chattanooga
53	Reitsma, Chris	R/R	6-5/214	12-31-77	Trenton, Sarasota
49	Reyes, Dennys	R/L	6-3/246	4-19-77	Cincinnati
46	Riedling, John	R/R	5-11/190	8-29-75	Louisville, Cincinnati
56	Sullivan, Scott	R/R	6-3/210	3-13-71	Cincinnati
48	Williamson, Scott	R/R	6-0/185	2-17-76	Cincinnati
51	Wohlers, Mark	R/R	6-4/207	1-23-70	Dayton, Louisville, Cincinnati
41	Yarnall, Ed	L/L	6-3/234	12-4-75	Louisville, New York A.L., Columbus

No.	CATCHERS	B/T	Ht./Wt.	Born	2000 clubs
2	LaRue, Jason	R/R	5-11/200	3-19-74	Louisville, Cincinnati
50	Sardinha, Dane	R/R	5-11/205	4-8-79	DID NOT PLAY
	Stinnett, Kelly	R/R	5-11/225	2-4-70	Arizona

No.	INFIELDERS	B/T	Ht./Wt.	Born	2000 clubs
17	Boone, Aaron	R/R	6-2/200	3-9-73	Cincinnati
21	Casey, Sean	L/R	6-4/225	7-2-74	Cincinnati
12	Castro, Juan	R/R	5-10/187	6-20-72	Louisville, Cincinnati
6	Dawkins, Gookie	R/R	6-1/180	5-12-79	Cincinnati, Chattanooga
79	Espinosa, David	B/R	6-1/170	12-16-81	DID NOT PLAY
11	Larkin, Barry	R/R	6-0/185	4-28-64	Cincinnati
28	Larson, Brandon	R/R	6-0/210	5-24-76	Chattanooga, Louisville
3	Reese, Pokey	R/R	5-11/180	6-10-73	Cincinnati
16	Sadler, Donnie	R/R	5-6/175	6-17-75	Pawtucket, Boston

No.	OUTFIELDERS	B/T	Ht./Wt.	Born	2000 clubs
22	Clark, Brady	R/R	6-2/195	4-18-73	Louisville, Cincinnati
4	Coleman, Michael	R/R	5-11/215	8-16-75	Pawtucket
77	Dunn, Adam	L/R	6-6/235	11-9-79	Dayton
30	Griffey, Ken	L/L	6-3/205	11-21-69	Cincinnati
	Guerrero, Wilton	B/R	6-0/175	10-24-74	Montreal
76	Melian, Jackson	R/R	6-2/190	1-7-80	Norwich, Chattanooga
7	Ochoa, Alex	R/R	6-0/195	3-29-72	Cincinnati, Chattanooga
34	Tucker, Michael	L/R	6-2/185	6-25-71	Cincinnati
25	Young, Dmitri	B/R	6-2/235	10-11-73	Cincinnati

BALLPARK INFORMATION

Ballpark (capacity, surface)
Cinergy Field (39,000, grass)

Address
100 Cinergy Field
Cincinnati, OH 45202

Official website
www.cincinnatireds.com

Business phone
513-421-4510

Ticket information
513-421-7337, 1-800-829-5353

Ticket prices
$28, $21 (blue level box seats)
$21, $16 (green level box seats)
$15 (yellow level box seats)
$14 (red level box seats)
$9 (red level reserved seats)
$5 ("top six" reserved seats)

Field dimensions (from home plate)
To left field at foul line, 330 feet
To center field, 404 feet
To right field at foul line, 330 feet

First game played
June 30, 1970 (Braves 8, Reds 2)

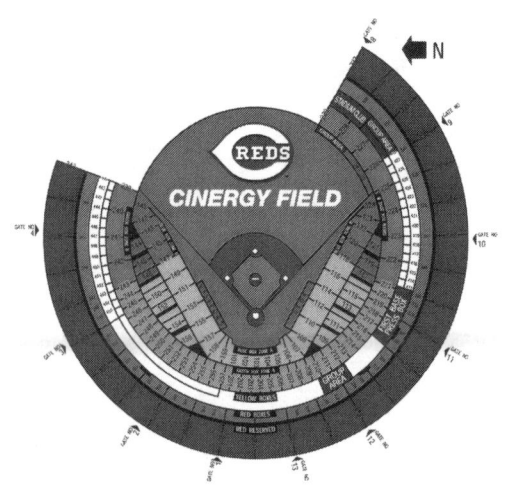

DAY BY DAY

Date	Opp.	Res.	Score	(inn.*)	Hits	Opp. hits	Winning pitcher	Losing pitcher	Save	Record	Pos.	GB
4-3	Mil.	T	3-3	(6)	5	7				0-0	T3rd	0.5
4-4	Mil.	L	1-5		4	10	Bruske	Williamson		0-1	T5th	1.0
4-5	Mil.	L	5-8		13	10	Haynes	Parris	Wickman	0-2	T5th	2.0
4-6	Mil.	W	5-1		7	8	Villone	Navarro		1-2	T4th	2.0
4-7	Chi.	L	6-10		8	8	Lorraine	Harnisch	Aguilera	1-3	6th	2.0
4-8	Chi.	W	4-3	(11)	11	4	Graves	Guthrie		2-3	T4th	2.0
4-9	Chi.	W	8-7	(11)	9	13	Graves	Karchner		3-3	T2nd	2.0
4-10	At Col.	L	5-7		10	13	Arrojo	Parris	Belinda	3-4	T3rd	3.0
4-11	At Col.	W	10-3		14	6	Villone	Bohanon		4-4	3rd	3.0
4-12	At Col.	L	5-7		9	9	Jimenez	Reyes	Tavarez	4-5	T3rd	3.0
4-14	At L.A.	L	1-8		9	9	Hershiser	Bell		4-6	T5th	2.5
4-15	At L.A.	W	5-4		8	7	Williamson	Mills	Graves	5-6	T4th	2.0
4-16	At L.A.	W	5-3		7	6	Parris	Park	Graves	6-6	T2nd	1.5
4-18	S.F	L	9-13		8	16	Rueter	Williamson		6-7	T2nd	2.5
4-19	S.F	W	5-4		9	8	Bell	Estes	Graves	7-7	2nd	2.5
4-20	S.F	W	11-1		15	6	Neagle	Hernandez		8-7	2nd	2.5
4-21	L.A.	L	2-9		10	11	Herges	Parris	Adams	8-8	2nd	2.5
4-22	L.A.	L	2-16		5	15	Park	Harnisch	Mills	8-9	2nd	2.5
4-23	L.A.	L	3-11		13	11	Perez	Villone		8-10	2nd	3.5
4-25	At N.Y.	L	5-6		8	8	Wendell	Sullivan	Benitez	8-11	2nd	4.5
4-26	At N.Y.	L	12-1		18	4	Neagle	Springer		9-11	2nd	4.5
4-27	At N.Y.	W	2-1	(12)	8	6	Graves	Benitez	Sullivan	10-11	2nd	3.5
4-28	At Pit.	L	1-2		5	6	Benson	Harnisch	Williams	10-12	2nd	4.5
4-29	At Pit.	W	6-5		8	8	Williamson	Christiansen	Graves	11-12	2nd	4.5
4-30	At Pit.	W	6-2		10	6	Bell	Ritchie	Williamson	12-12	2nd	4.5
5-2	At Phi.	W	7-0		12	3	Neagle	Ashby	Sullivan	13-12	2nd	3.5
5-3	At Phi.	L	2-5		4	9	Byrd	Parris		13-13	2nd	3.5
5-4	At Phi.	L	1-14		7	21	Person	Harnisch		13-14	2nd	4.5
5-5	StL.	W	3-2		8	7	Villone	Benes	Williamson	14-14	2nd	3.5
5-6	StL.	L	1-3		6	5	Kile	Bell	Veres	14-15	2nd	4.5
5-7	StL.	W	9-7		8	10	Neagle	Holmes	Williamson	15-15	2nd	3.5
5-9	S.D.	W	2-0		7	8	Parris	Meadows	Graves	16-15	2nd	3.0
5-10	S.D.	W	5-1		8	6	Villone	Hitchcock	Williamson	17-15	2nd	2.0
5-11	S.D.	W	11-9		16	11	Graves	Whisenant		18-15	2nd	1.5
5-12	At Hou.	W	7-3	(11)	10	9	Graves	Maddux		19-15	2nd	0.5
5-13	At Hou.	W	8-7		12	10	Reyes	Wagner	Williamson	20-15	1st	+0.5
5-14	At Hou.	L	3-10		6	13	Elarton	Parris		20-16	2nd	0.5
5-15	At Hou.	W	4-3		9	4	Villone	Lima	Graves	21-16	T1st	...
5-16	Pit.	W	6-2		12	9	Bell	Ritchie		22-16	T1st	...
5-17	Pit.	L	6-9		12	13	Silva	Sullivan		22-17	T1st	...
5-18	Pit.	W	4-3	(10)	9	10	Graves	Garcia		23-17	T1st	...
5-19	At Chi.	L	1-4		6	7	Valdes	Parris	Van Poppel	23-18	T1st	...
5-20	At Chi.	W	5-3		8	10	Villone	Lieber	Graves	24-18	T1st	...
5-21	At Chi.	L	2-4		10	5	Tapani	Bell	Heredia	24-19	2nd	1.0
5-22	At L.A.	L	3-4	(14)	10	9	Herges	Aybar		24-20	2nd	1.5
5-23	At L.A.	W	3-1		7	3	Fernandez	Gagne	Graves	25-20	2nd	1.5
5-24	At L.A.	W	10-3		11	7	Sullivan	Park		26-20	2nd	1.5
5-26	Fla.	W	3-2		8	8	Graves	Miceli		27-20	2nd	1.0
5-27	Fla.	L	6-8	(10)	8	12	Alfonseca	Williamson		27-21	2nd	1.0
5-28	Fla.	L	1-3		10	8	Dempster	Sullivan	Alfonseca	27-22	2nd	1.0
5-30	Mon.	W	4-2		5	3	Fernandez	Armas	Williamson	28-22	2nd	1.5
5-31	Mon.	L	4-10		6	16	Johnson	Parris		28-23	2nd	1.5
6-1	Mon.	L	7-9		16	17	Vazquez	Villone	Kline	28-24	2nd	1.5
6-2	Min.	W	4-3		10	7	Bell	Mays	Graves	29-24	2nd	1.5
6-3	Min.	W	9-3		8	4	Neagle	Bergman		30-24	2nd	0.5
6-4	Min.	W	3-2	(10)	9	9	Graves	Hawkins		31-24	1st	+0.5
6-5	Chi. (AL)	L	3-4		10	7	Baldwin	Parris	Foulke	31-25	1st	+0.5
6-6	Chi. (AL)	L	12-17		12	19	Eldred	Villone		31-26	2nd	0.5
6-7	Chi. (AL)	L	4-6		8	11	Parque	Bell	Foulke	31-27	2nd	1.5
6-9	At Cle.	L	4-7		8	12	Brower	Neagle	Karsay	31-28	2nd	1.5
6-10	At Cle.	L	5-6		8	12	Burba	Parris	Karsay	31-29	2nd	1.5
6-11	At Cle.	W	7-5	(13)	9	14	Aybar	Kamieniecki		32-29	2nd	1.5
6-12	At S.F	L	3-10		9	11	Nathan	Bell		32-30	2nd	2.5
6-13	At S.F	L	2-3		8	7	Nen	Graves		32-31	2nd	3.5
6-14	At S.F	L	2-6		8	12	Rueter	Neagle	Rodriguez	32-32	2nd	4.5
6-16	At S.D.	L	5-8		10	11	Reyes	Parris	Hoffman	32-33	2nd	5.5
6-17	At S.D.	L	1-3		5	6	Walker	Villone	Hoffman	32-34	2nd	6.5
6-18	At S.D.	L	7-8		11	8	Clement	Bell	Hoffman	32-35	2nd	6.5
6-20	Col.	W	3-2		11	7	Graves	Astacio		33-35	2nd	6.5
6-21	Col.	L	4-6		8	11	Tavarez	Williamson	Jimenez	33-36	2nd	6.5
6-22	Col.	W	5-3		10	6	Parris	Jarvis	Graves	34-36	2nd	6.5
6-23	S.D.	L	7-10	(10)	14	12	Hoffman	Williamson	Reyes	34-37	2nd	7.5
6-24	S.D.	W	11-5		15	14	Villone	Clement	Dessens	35-37	2nd	7.5
6-25	S.D.	L	4-5		12	7	Tollberg	Fernandez	Hoffman	35-38	2nd	8.5

Date	Opp.	Res.	Score	(inn.*)	Hits	Opp. hits	Winning pitcher	Losing pitcher	Save	Record	Pos.	GB
6-26	StL.	W	3-2		10	7	Neagle	Stephenson	Graves	36-38	2nd	7.5
6-27	StL.	L	3-4	11	9	7	Kile	Parris	Veres	36-39	2nd	8.5
6-28	StL.	W	7-3		8	7	Reyes	Al. Benes		37-39	2nd	7.5
6-29	StL.	L	3-12		4	15	An. Benes	Villone		37-40	2nd	8.5
6-30	At Ari.	W	5-4		11	8	Harnisch	Morgan	Graves	38-40	2nd	8.5
7-1	At Ari.	L	6-9		6	12	Springer	Fernandez	Kim	38-41	2nd	9.5
7-2	At Ari.	W	14-2		20	9	Neagle	Daal		39-41	2nd	8.5
7-3	At Ari.	W	3-2		8	9	Parris	Anderson	Graves	40-41	2nd	8.0
7-4	At StL.	L	3-14		9	13	An. Benes	Villone		40-42	2nd	9.0
7-5	At StL.	L	3-4		6	5	Hentgen	Harnisch	Veres	40-43	2nd	10.0
7-6	At StL.	W	12-6		13	13	Dessens	Ankiel		41-43	2nd	9.0
7-7	Cle.	W	2-1		7	8	Neagle	Finley	Graves	42-43	2nd	8.0
7-8	Cle.	W	14-5		17	9	Parris	Davis		43-43	2nd	7.0
7-9	Cle.	L	3-5		7	6	Colon	Williamson	Karsay	43-44	2nd	8.0
7-13	At Col.	W	15-6		13	9	Dessens	Astacio		44-44	2nd	8.0
7-14	At Col.	W	9-2		14	5	Harnisch	Arrojo		45-44	2nd	8.0
7-15	At Col.	W	7-4		12	8	Williamson	Yoshii	Graves	46-44	2nd	7.0
7-16	At Det.	L	2-6		10	10	Weaver	Parris		46-45	2nd	7.0
7-17	At Det.	L	1-3		10	8	Mlicki	Luebbers	Jones	46-46	2nd	7.0
7-18	At Det.	W	5-4		15	10	Dessens	Moehler	Graves	47-46	2nd	7.0
7-19	At Hou.	W	4-0		7	4	Harnisch	Holt		48-46	2nd	6.0
7-20	At Hou.	L	2-6		8	8	Lima	Williamson		48-47	2nd	6.0
7-21	Ari.	L	4-5		11	14	Swindell	Sullivan	Mantei	48-48	2nd	7.0
7-22	Ari.	W	7-3		14	8	Villone	Guzman		49-48	2nd	6.0
7-23	Ari.	W	5-3		10	9	Dessens	Anderson	Graves	50-48	2nd	5.0
7-24	Hou.	L	5-7	(10)	7	15	Dotel	Graves		50-49	2nd	5.5
7-25	Hou.	L	4-7		6	12	Valdes	Villone		50-50	2nd	6.5
7-26	Hou.	L	2-3		6	11	Elarton	Parris	Dotel	50-51	2nd	7.5
7-28	At Mon.	W	8-3		12	8	Dessens	Johnson		51-51	2nd	6.0
7-29	At Mon.	W	4-3	(11)	11	11	Graves	Santana		52-51	2nd	5.0
7-30	At Mon.	W	7-4		11	8	Bell	Hermanson	Graves	53-51	2nd	4.0
7-31	At N.Y.	W	6-0		10	8	Williamson	Rusch	Luebbers	54-51	2nd	4.0
8-1	At N.Y.	L	2-3		9	9	Hampton	Parris	Benitez	54-52	2nd	4.0
8-2	At N.Y.	L	1-2		5	7	Leiter	Dessens	Benitez	54-53	2nd	5.0
8-4	Fla.	L	1-2		8	10	Dempster	Harnisch	Alfonseca	54-54	2nd	5.0
8-5	Fla.	L	5-10	(11)	15	13	Alfonseca	Wohlers		54-55	2nd	6.0
8-6	Fla.	L	6-9		12	9	Aybar	Graves	Looper	54-56	2nd	6.0
8-7	Atl.	W	3-2	(10)	11	12	Sullivan	Ligtenberg		55-56	2nd	6.0
8-8	Atl.	L	4-5		9	11	Ashby	Dessens	Remlinger	55-57	2nd	6.0
8-9	Atl.	W	10-6		12	9	Harnisch	Glavine		56-57	2nd	5.0
8-11	At Chi.	W	6-4		11	6	Wohlers	Rain	Graves	57-57	2nd	4.5
8-12	At Chi.	W	3-0		7	5	Williamson	Garibay	Graves	58-57	2nd	4.5
8-13	At Chi.	W	3-0		6	7	Parris	Quevedo	Sullivan	59-57	2nd	4.5
8-14	At Mil.	L	3-4		8	8	Rigdon	Dessens	Leskanic	59-58	2nd	4.5
8-15	At Mil.	L	1-2	(10)	5	7	Leskanic	Wohlers		59-59	2nd	5.5
8-16	At Mil.	L	1-5		9	9	D'Amico	Bell		59-60	2nd	6.5
8-18	Pit.	L	3-6		6	11	Ritchie	Sullivan	Williams	59-61	2nd	7.5
8-19	Pit.	W	7-1		7	8	Parris	Anderson		60-61	2nd	7.5
8-20	Pit.	L	3-7		9	8	Silva	Dessens		60-62	2nd	7.5
8-21	Phi.	W	7-4		13	11	Harnisch	Wolf	Graves	61-62	2nd	7.5
8-22	Phi.	L	4-5		6	9	Padilla	Luebbers	Brantley	61-63	2nd	7.5
8-23	Phi.	L	3-4		5	7	Brock	Graves	Padilla	61-64	2nd	8.5
8-24	Phi.	W	8-3		11	11	Parris	Daal		62-64	2nd	8.5
8-25	At Fla.	W	6-0		13	6	Dessens	Cornelius		63-64	2nd	7.5
8-26	At Fla.	W	3-2		5	9	Harnisch	Darensbourg	Graves	64-64	2nd	7.5
8-27	At Fla.	L	6-7		13	10	Miceli	Graves		64-65	2nd	8.5
8-28	At Atl.	W	6-3		11	5	Villone	Maddux		65-65	2nd	8.5
8-29	At Atl.	W	4-2		11	9	Parris	Remlinger	Graves	66-65	2nd	7.5
8-30	At Atl.	L	2-5		3	14	Glavine	Dessens		66-66	2nd	8.5
8-31	At Atl.	W	4-3		8	4	Riedling	Millwood	Graves	67-66	2nd	8.0
9-1	Mon.	W	8-2		10	7	Bell	Hermanson		68-66	2nd	8.0
9-2	Mon.	L	5-9		6	12	Lira	Villone		68-67	2nd	9.0
9-3	Mon.	W	8-1		12	11	Parris	Thurman		69-67	2nd	9.0
9-4	N.Y.	W	6-2		8	6	Dessens	Leiter		70-67	2nd	9.0
9-5	N.Y.	L	2-3	(10)	8	6	Wendell	Sullivan	Benitez	70-68	2nd	10.0
9-6	N.Y.	W	11-8		13	6	Riedling	Franco	Graves	71-68	2nd	9.0
9-8†	At Pit.	L	3-7		7	11	Ritchie	Williamson		71-69		
9-8‡	At Pit.	L	1-3		9	6	Wilkins	Villone	Williams	71-70	2nd	10.0
9-9	At Pit.	W	6-4		14	9	Parris	Benson	Graves	72-70	2nd	10.0
9-10	At Pit.	W	6-4		8	6	Dessens	Anderson	Graves	73-70	2nd	9.0
9-11	Chi.	W	7-6		9	14	Harnisch	Garibay	Graves	74-70	2nd	9.0
9-12	Chi.	L	1-2		4	6	Wood	Fernandez		74-71	2nd	10.0
9-13	Chi.	W	13-3		16	6	Bell	Arnold		75-71	2nd	10.0
9-14	Mil.	L	4-6		12	8	Haynes	Villone	Leskanic	75-72	2nd	11.0
9-15	Mil.	W	6-4		11	7	Parris	Wright	Graves	76-72	2nd	11.0
9-16	Mil.	W	7-3		9	10	Dessens	Rigdon	Riedling	77-72	2nd	11.0
9-17	Mil.	W	8-4		7	5	Harnisch	Snyder		78-72	2nd	11.0
9-18	At S.F	W	7-1		12	4	Fernandez	Estes		79-72	2nd	10.5

Date	Opp.	Res.	Score	(inn.*)	Hits	Opp. hits	Winning pitcher	Losing pitcher	Save	Record	Pos.	GB
9-19	At S.F	L	3-7		7	14	Hernandez	Bell		79-73	2nd	10.5
9-20	At S.F	L	2-4		4	5	Ortiz	Parris	Nen	79-74	2nd	11.5
9-22	Hou.	W	12-5		14	12	Dessens	Lima		80-74	2nd	10.0
9-23	Hou.	W	6-4		12	11	Riedling	Slusarski	Graves	81-74	2nd	10.0
9-24	Hou.	W	4-3		7	6	Sullivan	Dotel		82-74	2nd	9.0
9-26	At Mil.	L	4-7		9	13	Wright	Parris	Leskanic	82-75	2nd	10.0
9-27	At Mil.	L	6-10		11	8	de los Santos	Riedling		82-76	2nd	11.0
9-28	At Mil.	W	8-1		14	2	Dessens	D'Amico		83-76	2nd	11.0
9-29	At StL.	W	8-1		15	2	Villone	Stephenson		84-76	2nd	10.0
9-30	At StL.	W	8-4		12	9	Fernandez	Hentgen		85-76	2nd	9.0
10-1	At StL.	L	2-6		8	8	An. Benes	Parris		85-77	2nd	10.0

Monthly records: April (12-12), May (16-11), June (10-17), July (16-11), August (13-15), September (18-10), October (0-1).
*Innings, if other than nine. †First game of a doubleheader. ‡Second game of a doubleheader.

HIGHLIGHTS

High point: June 4. Pokey Reese's one-out, 10th-inning single drove in the winning run in a 3-2 win over Minnesota and completed a three-game sweep at Cinergy Field. The win gave the Reds a half game lead over the Cardinals in the Central Division and closer Danny Graves an 8-0 record.

Low point: August 16. The Brewers completed their first-ever sweep of the Reds and put a serious damper on Cincinnati's playoff hopes. The Reds, fresh off five wins in six games against Atlanta and the Cubs, fell one game below .500 and 6 1/2 behind St. Louis.

Turning point: When the Reds were swept out of first place by the White Sox in a June 5-7 series at Cinergy Field—the beginning of a serious tailspin. In one game, Reds pitchers surrendered 17 runs. In another, the team blew a 3-0 lead. The series started a 12-game stretch in which the Reds lost 11 times.

Most valuable player: Switch-hitting Dmitri Young batted a solid .303 and led the team with 166 hits and 37 doubles. He was second with 88 RBIs and third with 18 home runs, both of which were career highs. Young also hit .336 with runners in scoring position.

Most valuable pitcher: Veteran righthander Pete Harnisch struggled early when weakness in his rotator cuff contributed to an 0-4 start. After a stint on the disabled list, he made 16 starts, recording an 8-2 record and 3.49 ERA. The team was 43-44 in the first half when Harnisch was ineffective and out of action, 42-33 in the second half when he was healthy.

Most improved player: Juan Castro came from the Dodgers with a good-field, no-hit reputation. He lived up to it as a slick glove man at short and second, but his .241 average and four home runs over 82 games was much better than expected.

Most pleasant surprise: Journeyman righthander Elmer Dessens moved into the rotation spot vacated by the mid-season trade of Denny Neagle and proceeded to post 11 wins in 16 starts. He was 5-0 with a 2.55 ERA in September.

Key injuries: The broken thumb suffered by Sean Casey in the last exhibition game before Opening Day cost the first baseman 28 games but plagued him through a difficult first half. ... Harnisch's weak rotator cuff left the Reds without an ace for the first half. ... Aaron Boone's torn anterior cruciate ligament forced utility-man Chris Stynes into the lineup and hurt the Reds' bench strength for much of the second half.

Notable: The Reds became only the second team to go through an entire season without being shut out. ... Reds pitchers set a major league record with 96 wild pitches, led by Scott Williamson's club-record 21. ... Not coincidentally, Reds pitchers also handed out a club-record 659 walks. ... Cincinnati became the first team to reach the 3 million mark in road attendance (3,016,074). ... Shortstop Barry Larkin became the fourth player in Reds history to collect 2,000 career hits. He joined Pete Rose, Dave Concepcion and Johnny Bench.

—MARK SCHMETZER

RECORDS

2000 regular-season record: 85-77 (2nd in N.L. Central); 43-38 at home; 42-39 on road; 22-19 vs. East; 41-37 vs. Central; 22-21 vs. West; 25-12 vs. lefthanded starters; 60-65 vs. righthanded starters; 34-34 on grass; 51-43 on turf; 35-27 in daytime; 50-50 at night; 25-23 in one-run games; 9-7 in extra-inning games; 0-1-0 in doubleheaders.

Team record past five years: 415-396 (.512, ranks 9th in league in that span).

TEAM LEADERS

Batting average: Sean Casey (.315).
At-bats: Dmitri Young (548).
Runs: Ken Griffey Jr. (100).
Hits: Dmitri Young (166).
Total Bases: Ken Griffey Jr. (289).
Doubles: Dmitri Young (37).
Triples: Pokey Reese, Dmitri Young (6).
Home runs: Ken Griffey Jr. (40).
Runs batted in: Ken Griffey Jr. (118).
Stolen bases: Pokey Reese (29).
Slugging percentage: Ken Griffey Jr. (.556).

On-base percentage: Ken Griffey Jr. (.387).
Wins: Steve Parris (12).
Earned-run average: Steve Parris (4.81).
Complete games: Pete Harnisch (3).
Shutouts: Pete Harnisch (1).
Saves: Danny Graves (30).
Innings pitched: Steve Parris (192.2).
Strikeouts: Scott Williamson (136).

GAMES BY POSITION

Catcher: Benito Santiago 84, Eddie Taubensee 76, Jason LaRue 31.
First base: Sean Casey 129, Dmitri Young 36, Hal Morris 16, D.T. Cromer 13, Brooks Kieschnick 1.
Second base: Pokey Reese 133, Juan Castro 21, Chris Stynes 15, Chris Sexton 12, Michael Tucker 1.
Third base: Aaron Boone 84, Chris Stynes 77, Mike Bell 13, Juan Castro 7, Mark Lewis 5, Chris Sexton 3.
Shortstop: Barry Larkin 102, Juan Castro 57, Gookie Dawkins 14, Chris Sexton 14, Aaron Boone 2.
Outfield: Ken Griffey Jr. 141, Dante Bichette 121, Michael Tucker 120, Dmitri Young 111, Alex Ochoa 95, Brian L. Hunter 25, Chris Stynes 8, Brady Clark 5, Kimera Bartee 3, Hal Morris 1.
Designated hitter: Dmitri Young 4, Barry Larkin 1, Hal Morris 1.

TOP DRAFT CHOICES

1a. **David Espinosa**, SS, Gulliver Prep, Miami.
1b. **Dustin Moseley**, RHP, Arkansas H.S., Texarkana, Ark.
2a. **Dane Sardinha**, C, Pepperdine Univ.
2b. **Ryan Snare**, LHP, University of North Carolina.
3. **David Gil**, RHP, University of Miami.
4. **Marc Kaiser**, RHP, Reno (Nev.) H.S.
5. **Roydell Williams**, OF, East St. John H.S., LaPlace, La.
6. **Ryan Mottl**, RHP, Clemson University.
7. **Daniel Fletcher**, RHP, Bridge City (Tex.) H.S.
8. **Daniel Gooris**, LHP, Creighton Univ.
9. **Bryan Edwards**, RHP, Newark (Atlantic League).
10. **Gary Varner**, 3B, St. Catharine (Ky.) J.C.

COLORADO ROCKIES
NATIONAL LEAGUE WEST DIVISION

Rockies
2001 SCHEDULE
Home games shaded; D—Day game (games starting before 5 pm).
*—All-Star Game at Safeco Field (Seattle)

APRIL
SUN	MON	TUE	WED	THU	FRI	SAT
1	2 D	3	4 STL	5 STL	6 SD	7 D SD
8 D SD	9 STL	D 10	11 STL	12 STL	13 D ARI	14 ARI
15 ARI	16	17 SD	18 SD	19 SD	20 D ARI	21 ARI
22 ARI	D 23	24 CUB	25 CUB	26 D CUB	27 CIN	28 D CIN
29 CIN	D 30					

MAY
SUN	MON	TUE	WED	THU	FRI	SAT
		1 PHI	2 PHI	3 D PHI	4 PIT	5 PIT
6 PIT	D 7 PIT	8 NYM	9 NYM	10 D NYM	11 MON	12 D MON
13 MON	14	15 ATL	16 D ATL	17 ATL	18 FLA	19 FLA
20 D FLA	21 LA	22 LA	23 D LA	24 SF	25 SF	26 D SF
27 D SF	28 D LA	29 LA	30 LA	31		

JUNE
SUN	MON	TUE	WED	THU	FRI	SAT
					1 SF	2 D SF
3 SF	D 4	5 HOU	6 HOU	7 HOU	8 STL	9 STL
10 D STL	11	12 SEA	13 SEA	14 D SEA	15 CIN	16 CIN
17 CIN	D 18 HOU	19 HOU	20 HOU	21 ARI	22 ARI	23 D ARI
24 ARI	D 25 SD	26 SD	27 SD	28	29 ARI	30 ARI

JULY
SUN	MON	TUE	WED	THU	FRI	SAT
1 ARI	D 2	3 SD	4 SD	5 SD	D 6	7 ANA
6 D 9 ANA		10 *	11	12 TEX	13 TEX	14 TEX
15 OAK	D 16 OAK	17 OAK	18 SF	19 SF	20 LA	21 D LA
22 LA	D 23 SF	24 SF	25 SF	D 26 LA	27 LA	28 D LA
29 LA	30	31 PHI				

AUGUST
SUN	MON	TUE	WED	THU	FRI	SAT
			1 PHI	2 PHI	3 D PIT	4 PIT
5 PIT	D 6	7 CUB	8 CUB	D 9 CUB	D 10 CIN	11 CIN
12 CIN	D 13	14 ATL	15 ATL	16 ATL	17 FLA	18 FLA
19 D FLA	D 20	21 NYM	22 NYM	23 NYM	24 MIL	25 MIL
26 MIL	D 27	28 LA	29 LA	30 LA	31 SF	

SEPTEMBER
SUN	MON	TUE	WED	THU	FRI	SAT
						1 D SF
2 SF	D 3 SF	D 4 LA	5 LA	6 LA	7 SF	8 D SF
9 SF	D 10	11 ARI	12 ARI	13 ARI	14 SD	15 SD
16 SD	17 ARI	18 ARI	19 ARI	20 MON	21 MON	22 MON
23 MON	24 SD	25 SD	26 D SD	27 D MIL	28 MIL	29 D MIL
30 D MIL						

2001 SEASON
CLUB DIRECTORY

Chairman, president and CEO
Jerry McMorris
Vice chairmen
Charles Monfort
Richard Monfort
Executive v.p., business operations
Keli McGregor
Executive v.p., general manager
Dan O'Dowd
Senior v.p., chief financial officer
Hal Roth
Vice president, finance
Michael Kent
Vice president, sales and marketing
Greg Feasel
V.p., ticket operations & sales
Sue Ann McClaren
Sr. dir., baseball ops. and asst. g.m.
Josh Byrnes
Special assistant to the g.m.
Pat Daugherty
Sr. dir., public rel. & communications
Jay Alves
Senior director, Coors Field operations
Kevin Kahn
Sr. director, personnel & administration
Liz Stecklein
Sr. director, corporate sales
Marcy English Glasser
Director, player personnel
Bill Geivett
Director, player development
Michael Hill
Director, major league operations
Paul Egins
Director, scouting
Bill Schmidt
Manager, broadcasting
Jim Fairchild
Director, community affairs
Roger Kinney

Director, information systems
Bill Stephani
Director, merchandising
Jim Kellogg
Dir., promotions and special events
Alan Bossart
Director, ticket sales
Jill Roberts
Dir., ticket services & spring training business operations
Chuck Javernick
Head groundskeeper
Mark Razum
Coordinator of instruction
Rick Mathews
Special assignment scout
Dave Holliday
Regional supervisors
Jay Darnell
Danny Montgomery
Major league scouts
Pat Daugherty, Jim Fregosi Jr., Dave Garcia, Will George
Professional scouts
Joe McDonald, Art Pontarelli, Steve Schryver
Scouts
John Cedarburg, Ty Coslow, Dar Cox, Mike Day, Mike Ericson, Abe Flores, Mike Garlatti, Orsino Hill, Bert Holt, Greg Hopkins, Bill Hughes, Damon Iannelli, Eric Johnson, Bill Mackenzie, Jay Matthews, Lance Nichols, Sean O'Connor, Ed Santa, Tom Wheeler
International scouts
Phil Allen, Dario Arias, Kent Blasingame, Francisco Cartaya, Cristobal A. Giron, Alexander Marquez, Brian McRobie, Atanacio Mendez, Jorge Moreno, Ramon Pena, Jorge Posada, Reed Spencer, Ron Steele

MINOR LEAGUE AFFILIATES

Class	Team	League	Manager
AAA	Colorado Springs	Pacific Coast	Chris Cron
AA	Carolina	Southern	Ron Gideon
A	Asheville	South Atlantic	Joe Mikulik
A	Salem	Carolina	Dave Collins
A	Tri-Cities	Northwest	Billy White
Rookie	Casper	Pioneer	P.J. Carey

BROADCAST INFORMATION
Radio: KOA-AM (850), KCUV-AM (1150).
TV: KWGN-TV (Channel 2).
Cable TV: Fox Sports Rocky Mountain.

SPRING TRAINING
Ballpark (city): Hi Corbett Field (Tucson, Ariz.).
Ticket information: 1-800-388-ROCK.

Follow the Rockies all season at: www.sportingnews.com/baseball/teams/rockies/

Manager—Buddy Bell (25).
Coaches—Rich Donnelly (26), Toby Harrah (11), Clint Hurdle (13), Fred Kendall (16), Marcel Lachemann (53), Dallas Williams (20).

No.	PITCHERS	B/T	Ht./Wt.	Born	2000 clubs
34	Astacio, Pedro	R/R	6-2/210	11-28-69	Colorado
73	Averette, Robert	R/R	6-2/195	9-30-76	Chattanooga, Louisville, Carolina
41	Bohanon, Brian	L/L	6-2/240	8-1-68	Colorado
56	Chacon, Shawn	R/R	6-3/212	12-23-77	Carolina
43	Chouinard, Bobby	R/R	6-1/190	5-1-72	Colorado Springs, Colorado
50	Christman, Tim	L/L	6-0/195	3-31-75	Carolina
70	Cook, Aaron	R/R	6-3/175	2-8-79	Asheville, Salem
18	DeJean, Mike	R/R	6-2/212	9-28-70	Colorado Springs, Colorado
45	Dipoto, Jerry	R/R	6-2/205	5-24-68	Colorado Springs, Colorado
68	Dorame, Randey	L/L	6-2/205	1-23-79	Vero Beach, San Antonio, Carolina
10	Hampton, Mike	R/L	5-10/180	9-9-72	New York N.L.
48	House, Craig	R/R	6-2/210	7-8-77	Salem, Carolina, Colorado Springs, Colorado
74	Hudson, Luke	R/R	6-3/195	5-2-77	Salem
49	Jimenez, Jose	R/R	6-3/228	7-7-73	Colorado
60	Kalinowski, Josh	L/L	6-2/190	12-12-76	Carolina
28	Myers, Mike	L/L	6-4/214	6-26-69	Colorado
15	Neagle, Denny	L/L	6-3/225	9-13-68	Cincinnati, New York A.L.
40	Rose, Brian	R/R	6-3/215	2-13-76	Boston, Pawtucket, Colorado
52	Thomson, John	R/R	6-3/187	10-1-73	Arizona Rockies, Portland
29	Villone, Ron	L/L	6-3/237	1-16-70	Cincinnati
46	Wasdin, John	R/R	6-2/195	8-5-72	Boston, Pawtucket, Colorado
36	White, Gabe	L/L	6-2/200	11-20-71	Cincinnati, Colorado
21	Yoshii, Masato	R/R	6-2/210	4-20-65	Colorado

No.	CATCHERS	B/T	Ht./Wt.	Born	2000 clubs
8	Mayne, Brent	L/R	6-1/192	4-19-68	Colorado
15	Petrick, Ben	R/R	6-0/205	4-7-77	Colorado Springs, Colorado

No.	INFIELDERS	B/T	Ht./Wt.	Born	2000 clubs
2	Butler, Brent	R/R	6-0/180	2-11-78	Colorado Springs
7	Cirillo, Jeff	R/R	6-1/195	9-23-69	Colorado
17	Helton, Todd	L/L	6-2/206	8-20-73	Colorado
	Norton, Greg	B/R	6-1/205	7-6-72	Chicago A.L., Charlotte
23	Pena, Elvis	B/R	5-11/155	9-15-76	Colorado, Carolina
5	Perez, Neifi	B/R	6-0/175	6-2-75	Colorado
22	Shumpert, Terry	R/R	6-0/200	8-16-66	Colorado
	Sosa, Juan	R/R	6-1/175	8-19-75	Colorado Springs
51	Uribe, Juan	R/R	5-11/175	7-22-80	Salem
14	Walker, Todd	L/R	6-0/181	5-25-73	Minnesota, Salt Lake, Colorado

No.	OUTFIELDERS	B/T	Ht./Wt.	Born	2000 clubs
	Gant, Ron	R/R	6-0/196	3-2-65	Philadelphia, Anaheim
27	Hollandsworth, Todd	L/L	6-2/215	4-20-73	Los Angeles, Colorado
9	Pierre, Juan	L/L	6-0/170	8-14-77	Carolina, Colorado Springs, Colorado
33	Walker, Larry	L/R	6-3/237	12-1-66	Colorado

Ballpark (capacity, surface)
Coors Field (50,445, grass)
Address
2001 Blake St.
Denver, CO 80205-2000
Official website
www.coloradorockies.com
Business phone
303-292-0200
Ticket information
800-388-7625
Ticket prices
$32 (club level, infield), $30 (club level, outfield)
$27 (infield box), $21.50 (outfield box)
$16 (lower reserved, infield)
$13 (lower reserved, outfield)
$12 (upper reserved infield, RF box)
$11 (lower reserved corner)
$10 (RF mezzanine)
$9 (upper reserved, outfield; lower pavilion)
$8 (lower pavilion)
$7 (upper reserved corner)
$6 (lower RF reserved), $5 (upper RF reserved)
$4 (rockpile), $1 (rockpile)
Field dimensions (from home plate)
To left field at foul line, 347 feet
To center field, 415 feet
To right field at foul line, 350
First game played
April 26, 1995 (Rockies 11, Mets 9, 14 innings)

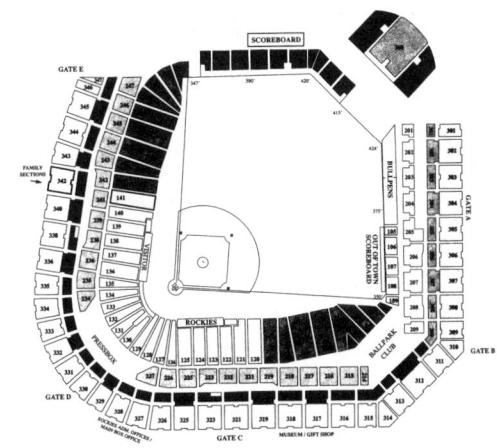

2001 SEASON *Colorado Rockies*

Date	Opp.	Res.	Score	(inn.*)	Hits	Opp. hits	Winning pitcher	Losing pitcher	Save	Record	Pos.	GB
4-3	At Atl.	L	0-2		6	7	Maddux	Astacio	Remlinger	0-1	T2nd	1.0
4-4	At Atl.	W	5-3		11	6	Tavarez	Burkett	Jimenez	1-1	T3rd	1.0
4-5	At Atl.	L	6-9		9	12	Chen	Aybar	Ligtenberg	1-2	5th	1.5
4-7	At Fla.	L	3-4		7	5	Penny	Yoshii	Alfonseca	1-3	5th	2.0
4-8	At Fla.	W	4-2		10	9	Jimenez	Fernandez	Lee	2-3	5th	2.0
4-9	At Fla.	L	6-7		10	9	Dempster	Astacio	Alfonseca	2-4	5th	3.0
4-10	Cin.	W	7-5		13	10	Arrojo	Parris	Belinda	3-4	T3rd	3.0
4-11	Cin.	L	3-10		6	14	Villone	Bohanon		3-5	T4th	3.0
4-12	Cin.	W	7-5		9	9	Jimenez	Reyes	Tavarez	4-5	4th	2.0
4-13	StL.	W	12-6		14	11	Croushore	Kile		5-5	T3rd	2.0
4-14	StL.	W	6-2		9	6	Astacio	Ankiel		6-5	3rd	2.0
4-16†	StL.	L	3-9		9	11	Hentgen	Arrojo		6-6		
4-16‡	StL.	W	14-13		15	17	Jimenez	Mohler	White	7-6	T3rd	2.5
4-17	At Ari.	W	9-1		15	8	Yoshii	Daal		8-6	3rd	1.5
4-18	At Ari.	L	1-7		4	12	Reynoso	Karl		8-7	3rd	2.5
4-19	At Ari.	L	7-8		12	13	Morgan	Tavarez	Kim	8-8	3rd	3.5
4-20	At Ari.	L	0-3		4	5	Johnson	Arrojo		8-9	3rd	4.5
4-21	At StL.	W	6-4		10	12	Jarvis	Hentgen	Jimenez	9-9	3rd	3.5
4-22	At StL.	W	7-6		11	6	Croushore	James	Jimenez	10-9	3rd	2.5
4-23	At StL.	L	3-6	(7)	4	8	An. Benes	Karl	Slocumb	10-10	4th	2.5
4-25	At Mon.	L	4-10		11	14	Pavano	Bohanon		10-11	4th	3.5
4-26	At Mon.	L	2-9		5	12	Hermanson	Jarvis	Urbina	10-12	4th	4.5
4-28	N.Y.	W	12-5		14	12	Astacio	Hampton		11-12	T3rd	3.0
4-29	N.Y.	L	6-13		10	23	Reed	Yoshii		11-13	T3rd	4.0
4-30	N.Y.	L	11-14		10	15	Leiter	Bohanon		11-14	T3rd	5.0
5-1	Mon.	W	15-8		18	15	White	Hermanson		12-14	3rd	4.5
5-2	Mon.	W	12-6		13	11	Karl	Powell		13-14	3rd	4.5
5-3	Mon.	W	16-7		24	12	Astacio	Irabu		14-14	T3rd	3.5
5-5	At S.F	L	0-5		3	6	Nathan	Yoshii		14-15	4th	5.0
5-6	At S.F	L	0-6		9	9	Estes	Arrojo		14-16	4th	6.0
5-8	At Hou.	W	3-1		6	3	Astacio	Holt		15-16	4th	6.5
5-9	At Hou.	L	8-13		10	11	Perez	Tavarez		15-17	4th	7.5
5-10	At Hou.	L	1-5		5	7	Reynolds	Yoshii		15-18	4th	8.5
5-12	S.F	W	15-7		15	10	Bohanon	Nathan		16-18	4th	8.5
5-13	S.F	W	10-9		15	10	White	Johnstone	Jimenez	17-18	4th	8.5
5-14	S.F	W	11-7		15	13	White	Hernandez		18-18	4th	7.5
5-16	At N.Y.	W	4-3	(11)	9	12	Tavarez	Wendell	Jimenez	19-18	3rd	6.5
5-17	At N.Y.	L	2-4		5	10	Leiter	Arrojo	Franco	19-19	3rd	6.5
5-19	At Phi.	W	10-2		14	6	Astacio	Ashby		20-19	3rd	6.0
5-20	At Phi.	W	4-3		6	2	Tavarez	Brock	Jimenez	21-19	3rd	5.0
5-21	At Phi.	L	3-4		7	6	Person	Yoshii	Brantley	21-20	3rd	5.0
5-23	Chi.	W	10-7		10	9	Bohanon	Garibay		22-20	3rd	5.0
5-24	Chi.	W	9-4		8	12	Astacio	Farnsworth	Jimenez	23-20	3rd	5.0
5-25	Chi.	L	5-6		10	9	Lieber	DeJean	Aguilera	23-21	3rd	6.0
5-26	Pit.	L	1-2		6	8	Cordova	Yoshii	Williams	23-22	3rd	7.0
5-27	Pit.	W	7-6		10	12	White	Christiansen		24-22	3rd	7.0
5-28	Pit.	W	11-2		17	7	Arrojo	Anderson		25-22	3rd	6.0
5-29	Hou.	W	8-7		15	12	White	Cabrera	Jimenez	26-22	3rd	5.0
5-30	Hou.	W	10-7		12	12	Belinda	Valdes	Jimenez	27-22	T2nd	4.0
5-31	Hou.	W	8-6		12	14	White	Slusarski	Jimenez	28-22	T2nd	4.0
6-2	At Mil.	W	8-6		12	9	Arrojo	Bere	Myers	29-22	2nd	4.5
6-3	At Mil.	L	1-2	(12)	3	6	de los Santos	Belinda		29-23	T2nd	4.5
6-4	At Mil.	W	7-1		12	5	Jarvis	Haynes		30-23	2nd	3.5
6-5	At Sea.	L	2-6		6	10	Sele	Yoshii		30-24	2nd	3.5
6-6	At Sea.	L	1-4		8	7	Tomko	Bohanon	Sasaki	30-25	T2nd	3.5
6-7	At Sea.	W	6-1		13	5	Arrojo	Moyer		31-25	T2nd	2.5
6-9	Tex.	W	3-2	(12)	8	10	Tavarez	Wetteland		32-25	2nd	2.5
6-10	Tex.	W	12-6		15	11	Karl	Loaiza		33-25	2nd	1.5
6-11	Tex.	W	9-8		13	18	DeJean	Crabtree	Jimenez	34-25	2nd	1.5
6-13	Hou.	L	3-6		10	15	Reynolds	Arrojo	Wagner	34-26	2nd	2.0
6-14	Hou.	L	4-8		8	11	Slusarski	Astacio		34-27	2nd	3.0
6-15	Hou.	W	5-4		8	10	Jimenez	Wagner		35-27	2nd	2.0
6-17	Ari.	W	14-5		17	8	Bohanon	Anderson		36-27	2nd	1.0
6-18	Ari.	W	19-2		23	8	Yoshii	Reynoso		37-27	1st	...
6-20	At Cin.	L	2-3		7	11	Graves	Astacio		37-28	2nd	0.5
6-21	At Cin.	W	6-4		11	8	Tavarez	Williamson	Jimenez	38-28	2nd	0.5
6-22	At Cin.	L	3-5		6	10	Parris	Jarvis	Graves	38-29	2nd	1.0
6-23	At Ari.	L	0-2		2	5	Anderson	Bohanon	Kim	38-30	2nd	2.0
6-24	At Ari.	W	4-0		6	7	Yoshii	Johnson		39-30	2nd	1.0
6-25	At Ari.	L	3-8		8	14	Morgan	Astacio		39-31	2nd	2.0
6-26	S.F	W	15-6		16	9	Arrojo	Gardner		40-31	2nd	2.0
6-27	S.F	L	7-12		9	15	Estes	Jarvis		40-32	2nd	2.0
6-28	S.F	W	17-13		17	13	DeJean	Johnstone		41-32	2nd	2.0

Date	Opp.	Res.	Score	(inn.*)	Hits	Opp. hits	Winning pitcher	Losing pitcher	Save	Record	Pos.	GB
6-29	S.F	W	11-4		15	13	Yoshii	Nathan		42-32	2nd	2.0
6-30	At S.D.	W	5-4		10	7	Astacio	Almanzar	Jimenez	43-32	2nd	1.0
7-1	At S.D.	L	3-5		9	7	Meadows	Arrojo	Hoffman	43-33	2nd	2.0
7-2	At S.D.	W	3-2	(10)	10	7	DeJean	Hoffman	Jimenez	44-33	2nd	1.0
7-3	At S.D.	W	3-1		4	4	Bohanon	Montgomery	Jimenez	45-33	1st	...
7-4†	At S.F	L	1-4		4	9	Hernandez	Yoshii	Nen	45-34		
7-4‡	At S.F	L	0-3		6	7	Gardner	Karl	Nen	45-35	2nd	1.5
7-5	At S.F	L	2-4		7	9	Nathan	Belinda	Rodriguez	45-36	2nd	2.5
7-6	At S.F	L	5-6		7	12	Nen	Myers		45-37	2nd	3.5
7-7	At Ana.	L	4-12		7	13	Ortiz	Jarvis		45-38	T2nd	3.5
7-8	At Ana.	L	2-6		9	11	Hill	Bohanon		45-39	3rd	3.5
7-9	At Ana.	L	4-10		10	13	Bottenfield	Yoshii		45-40	3rd	4.5
7-13	Cin.	L	6-15		9	13	Dessens	Astacio		45-41	3rd	4.5
7-14	Cin.	L	2-9		5	14	Harnisch	Arrojo		45-42	3rd	5.5
7-15	Cin.	L	4-7		8	12	Williamson	Yoshii	Graves	45-43	3rd	5.5
7-17†	Oak.	L	10-11		12	13	Magnante	White	Isringhausen	45-44		
7-17‡	Oak.	W	10-9	(10)	15	12	DeJean	Isringhausen		46-44	4th	5.5
7-18	Oak.	W	18-3		21	8	Astacio	Mulder		47-44	3rd	4.5
7-19	At L.A.	L	1-9		1	9	Brown	Arrojo		47-45	4th	5.5
7-20	At L.A.	L	3-6		5	10	Park	Yoshii	Fetters	47-46	4th	6.5
7-21	S.D.	L	1-5		7	12	Eaton	Bohanon		47-47	4th	7.5
7-22	S.D.	W	9-4		16	11	White	Clement		48-47	4th	6.5
7-23	S.D.	L	4-6	(10)	7	11	Hoffman	Belinda	Wall	48-48	4th	6.5
7-24	L.A.	L	1-4		5	11	Brown	Arrojo	Fetters	48-49	4th	7.0
7-25	L.A.	L	4-6		11	8	Park	Chouinard	Shaw	48-50	4th	7.0
7-26	L.A.	W	11-4		14	6	Bohanon	Perez		49-50	4th	6.0
7-27	L.A.	L	11-16		15	20	Masaoka	Carrara		49-51	4th	7.0
7-28	At Mil.	L	0-5		8	8	Wright	Astacio		49-52	4th	8.0
7-29	At Mil.	W	10-2		14	6	Tavarez	Rigdon		50-52	4th	7.0
7-30	At Mil.	L	2-3		7	5	D'Amico	Yoshii	Leskanic	50-53	4th	7.0
7-31	At Chi.	L	0-2		4	8	Tapani	Bohanon	Aguilera	50-54	4th	7.5
8-1	At Chi.	W	2-1		7	2	Astacio	Farnsworth	White	51-54	4th	7.5
8-2	At Chi.	L	2-3		4	8	Rain	Wasdin	Aguilera	51-55	4th	7.5
8-4	Phi.	W	8-1		13	7	Tavarez	Bottenfield		52-55	4th	8.0
8-5	Phi.	W	7-6		15	9	Jimenez	Brantley		53-55	4th	7.0
8-6	Phi.	L	9-10		16	13	Chen	Astacio		53-56	4th	8.0
8-7	Pit.	L	7-8		12	13	Sauerbeck	Jimenez	Williams	53-57	4th	9.0
8-8	Pit.	W	6-1		15	10	Rose	Silva		54-57	4th	9.0
8-9	Pit.	W	4-3		7	7	White	Williams		55-57	4th	9.0
8-10	At StL.	L	4-5		10	12	Timlin	Jimenez		55-58	4th	9.5
8-11	At Mon.	W	10-3		13	11	Bohanon	Hermanson		56-58	4th	8.5
8-12	At Mon.	W	14-2		22	6	Yoshii	Moore		57-58	4th	7.5
8-13	At Mon.	W	5-3		12	7	Chouinard	Strickland	White	58-58	4th	6.5
8-14	At Mon.	W	4-3		12	10	House	Strickland	Jimenez	59-58	4th	6.5
8-15†	At N.Y.	L	5-7		9	9	Cook	House	Benitez	59-59		
8-15‡	At N.Y.	L	3-4		4	10	B.J. Jones	Chouinard	Benitez	59-60	4th	8.0
8-16	At N.Y.	W	7-5		11	8	Bohanon	Rusch	White	60-60	4th	8.0
8-17	At N.Y.	L	2-13		4	15	Wendell	Yoshii		60-61	4th	9.0
8-18	Fla.	L	8-9		18	12	Smith	Rose	Alfonseca	60-62	4th	10.0
8-19	Fla.	W	10-3		10	10	Tavarez	Cornelius		61-62	4th	10.0
8-20	Fla.	W	13-4		14	8	Astacio	Sanchez		62-62	4th	9.0
8-21	Atl.	L	4-7		10	13	Millwood	Bohanon	Rocker	62-63	4th	10.0
8-22	Atl.	W	7-6	(12)	16	14	Mayne	Rocker		63-63	4th	9.0
8-23	Atl.	L	2-5		8	10	Maddux	Rose	Remlinger	63-64	4th	10.0
8-25	At Pit.	W	6-3		13	9	Tavarez	Anderson		64-64	4th	10.0
8-26	At Pit.	W	11-4		19	10	Astacio	Silva		65-64	4th	9.0
8-27	At Pit.	W	9-2		16	4	Bohanon	Serafini		66-64	4th	8.0
8-28	At Phi.	L	2-3		8	8	Person	Yoshii	Brantley	66-65	4th	9.0
8-29	At Phi.	W	2-1		9	3	Rose	Daal	Jimenez	67-65	4th	8.0
8-30	At Phi.	W	5-4	(11)	7	10	White	Gomes	Jimenez	68-65	4th	8.0
9-1	Mil.	W	5-3		11	7	Astacio	Snyder	White	69-65	4th	8.5
9-2	Mil.	L	3-8		10	14	D'Amico	DeJean		69-66	4th	9.5
9-3	Mil.	L	4-6	(11)	8	13	Acevedo	DeJean	Leskanic	69-67	4th	10.5
9-4	Chi.	W	6-2		12	8	Rose	Lieber		70-67	4th	10.5
9-5	Chi.	W	10-2		13	4	Tavarez	Arnold		71-67	4th	10.5
9-6	Chi.	L	5-8	(11)	11	13	Van Poppel	White	Aguilera	71-68	4th	11.5
9-8	L.A.	W	8-5		14	9	Bohanon	Brown		72-68	4th	11.0
9-9	L.A.	W	7-6		13	7	White	Park	Jimenez	73-68	3rd	10.0
9-10	L.A.	L	1-12		5	12	Dreifort	Astacio	Herges	73-69	4th	11.0
9-11	At S.D.	L	2-7		6	10	Williams	Tavarez		73-70	4th	12.0
9-12	At S.D.	W	6-3		12	6	Yoshii	Clement	Jimenez	74-70	4th	12.0
9-13	At S.D.	W	11-0		16	9	Bohanon	Eaton		75-70	3rd	12.0
9-14	At L.A.	W	5-4		9	8	Rose	Park	Jimenez	76-70	3rd	11.5
9-15	At L.A.	W	3-4	(10)	5	5	Herges	DeJean		76-71	3rd	11.5
9-16	At L.A.	L	4-5		13	14	Gagne	Tavarez	Shaw	76-72	4th	12.5
9-17	At L.A.	L	6-12		11	12	Prokopec	Yoshii		76-73	4th	13.5
9-19	S.D.	L	2-7		6	12	Clement	Bohanon		76-74	4th	14.0
9-20	S.D.	L	11-15		11	15	Eaton	Rose	Hoffman	76-75	4th	15.0

Date	Opp.	Res.	Score	(inn.*)	Hits	Opp. hits	Winning pitcher	Losing pitcher	Save	Record	Pos.	GB
9-21	S.D.	W	13-4		17	4	Jarvis	Tollberg		77-75	4th	15.0
9-22	Fla.	L	4-8		7	13	Penny	Tavarez		77-76	4th	15.0
9-23	Fla.	L	1-3	(7)	4	6	Smith	Wasdin		77-77	4th	15.5
9-24	Fla.	W	9-3		14	8	Bohanon	Sanchez		78-77	4th	14.5
9-25	Ari.	L	4-6		10	13	Johnson	Rose	Mantei	78-78	4th	15.0
9-26	Ari.	W	7-6		10	7	Chouinard	Morgan	Jimenez	79-78	4th	14.0
9-27	Ari.	W	6-4		14	6	White	Plesac	Jimenez	80-78	4th	14.0
9-28	Ari.	L	3-12		7	13	Reynoso	Wasdin		80-79	4th	15.0
9-29	At Atl.	W	4-2		6	6	Bohanon	Ashby	Jimenez	81-79	4th	15.0
9-30	At Atl.	L	2-5		6	8	Glavine	Rose	Rocker	81-80	4th	15.0
10-1	At Atl.	W	10-5		17	7	Tavarez	Rocker		82-80	4th	15.0

Monthly records: April (11-14), May (17-8), June (15-10), July (7-22), August (18-11), September (13-15), October (1-0).
*Innings, if other than nine. †First game of a doubleheader. ‡Second game of a doubleheader.

HIGHLIGHTS

High point: July 3. After Jeffrey Hammonds delivered a 3-1 victory at San Diego with a two-run, eighth-inning home run, the Rockies stood a season-best 12 games over .500 (45-33) and in sole possession of first place in the N.L. West. It would only go downhill from there.

Low point: Most of the month of July. From July 4-31, the Rockies were locked in a 5-21 slide that destroyed any playoff hopes. Eleven of those losses came in quick succession and nine in the thin air of Coors Field.

Turning point: The 11-game losing streak, which started at San Francisco and wrapped around the All-Star break. Not only did the four-game San Francisco series send the Rockies spiraling out of contention, it propelled the struggling Giants toward an N.L. West title—and the best record in the N.L.

Most valuable player: First baseman Todd Helton was a one-man wrecking machine. Helton led the league with his .372 average and 147 RBIs and he led the N.L. in numerous other offensive category while ranking seventh with 42 home runs. Helton even flirted with .400, lifting his average to .397 as late as August 28—the team's 131st game.

Most valuable pitcher: Righthander Julian Tavarez opened the season in the bullpen and finished as the team's most dependable starter, compiling an 11-5 record and 4.43 ERA. Tavarez, who made 12 starts and worked a career-high 120 innings, enjoyed one four-month stretch in which he was 9-0 with a 3.22 ERA.

Most improved player: Hammonds, who has struggled throughout an inconsistent career with injuries, enjoyed a breakout season. He batted .335 with 20 homers and 106 RBIs in 122 games. The left fielder added serious punch to the middle of the Rockies' lineup.

Most pleasant surprise: Reliever Gabe White, a journeyman pickup, pitched in 67 games and compiled an 11-2 record and 2.17 ERA. His 2.36 relief ERA ranked second in the N.L.

Key injuries: The most significant shot down right fielder Larry Walker, who played only 87 games because of a problem with his throwing elbow. The injury visibly affected Walker's swing when he did play, forcing him to settle for opposite-field singles and dropping him from 37 to 9 home runs. ... Hammonds missed 17 of the first 18 games with a hamstring injury and the final 12 games with a shoulder problem. ... Staff ace Pedro Astacio and No. 4 starter Masato Yoshii both missed their last three starts. Astacio suffered a strained oblique muscle and Yoshii needed season-ending surgery on his elbow.

Notable: Helton (59) and Jeff Cirillo (53) finished 1-2 in the N.L. in doubles. ... Helton led the N.L. with a club-record .463 on-base percentage. His road batting average of .353 ranked third in the N.L., behind only Mike Piazza (.377) and Moises Alou (.362). ... Recovering slowly from offseason elbow surgery, Brian Bohanon was 0-3 with a 9.67 ERA in April. From June 6, when he was inserted into the rotation, he was 10-7 with a 4.08 ERA. He had the best road ERA in the league as his 2.789 ERA edged the 2.793 ERA by Cy Young winner Randy Johnson.

—MIKE KLIS

RECORDS

2000 regular-season record: 82-80 (4th in N.L. West); 48-33 at home; 34-47 on road; 24-21 vs. East; 29-24 vs. Central; 29-35 vs. West; 24-13 vs. lefthanded starters; 58-67 vs. righthanded starters; 70-74 on grass; 12-6 on turf; 27-30 in daytime; 55-50 at night; 23-20 in one-run games; 6-5 in extra-inning games; 0-2 in doubleheaders.

Team record past five years: 397-413 (.490, ranks 10th in league in that span).

TEAM LEADERS

Batting average: Todd Helton (.372).
At-bats: Neifi Perez (651).
Runs: Todd Helton (138).
Hits: Todd Helton (216).
Total Bases: Todd Helton (405).
Doubles: Todd Helton (59).
Triples: Neifi Perez (11).
Home runs: Todd Helton (42).
Runs batted in: Todd Helton (147).

Stolen bases: Tom Goodwin (39).
Slugging percentage: Todd Helton (.698).
On-base percentage: Todd Helton (.463).
Wins: Pedro Astacio, Brian Bohanon (12).
Earned-run average: Brian Bohanon (4.68).
Complete games: Pedro Astacio (3).
Shutouts: Brian Bohanon (1).
Saves: Jose Jimenez (24).
Innings pitched: Pedro Astacio (196.1).
Strikeouts: Pedro Astacio (193).

GAMES BY POSITION

Catcher: Brent Mayne 106, Ben Petrick 48, Scott Servais 32, Adam Melhuse 1.
First base: Todd Helton 160, Butch Huskey 8, Terry Shumpert 6, Aaron Ledesma 3, Adam Melhuse 3, Angel Echevarria 2, Jeff Manto 1.
Second base: Mike Lansing 88, Todd Walker 52, Jeff Frye 27, Terry Shumpert 23, Elvis Pena 1.
Third base: Jeff Cirillo 155, Terry Shumpert 15, Aaron Ledesma 5, Jeff Frye 1, Jeff Manto 1.
Shortstop: Neifi Perez 162, Terry Shumpert 7, Elvis Pena 4.
Outfield: Jeffrey Hammonds 118, Tom Goodwin 88, Larry Walker 83, Brian L. Hunter 63, Juan Pierre 50, Todd Hollandsworth 48, Darren Bragg 43, Terry Shumpert 40, Butch Huskey 23, Bubba Carpenter 6, Carlos Mendoza 3, Angel Echevarria 1, Adam Melhuse 1.
Designated hitter: Larry Walker 3, Bubba Carpenter 2, Terry Shumpert 1.

TOP DRAFT CHOICES

1. **Matt Harrington**, RHP, Palmdale (Calif.) H.S.
2. **Jason Young**, RHP, Stanford Univ.
3. **Chris Buglovsky**, RHP, College of New Jersey.
4. **Cory Vance**, LHP, Georgia Tech.
5. **Garrett Atkins**, 1B, UCLA.
6. **Scott Dohmann**, RHP, University of Louisiana-Lafayette.
7. **Edmund Muth**, OF, Stanford Univ.
8. **Dan Conway**, C, Wake Forest Univ.
9. **Nick Webb**, LHP, University of Louisiana-Lafayette.
10. **Clint Barmes**, SS, Indiana State U.

FLORIDA MARLINS
NATIONAL LEAGUE EAST DIVISION

Marlins 2001 SCHEDULE
Home games shaded; D—Day game (games starting before 5 p.m.)
*—All-Star Game at Safeco Field (Seattle)

APRIL

SUN	MON	TUE	WED	THU	FRI	SAT
1	2 PHI	D 3 PHI	4 PHI	5	6 ATL	7 ATL
8 ATL	D 9 PHI	10 PHI	11 PHI	12	13 MON	14 MON
15 MON	D 16 ATL	17 ATL	18 D ATL	19 MON	20 MON	21 ATL
22 D MON	D 23 ARI	24 ARI	25 ARI	26	27 HOU	28 D HOU
29 HOU	D 30					

MAY

SUN	MON	TUE	WED	THU	FRI	SAT
		1 STL	2 STL	3 STL	4 MIL	5 MIL
6 D MIL	7 LA	8 LA	9 LA	10 LA	11 SD	12 SD
13 D SD	14	15 SF	16 SF	17 SF	18 COL	19 COL
20 COL	D 21 ATL	22 ATL	23 ATL	24 NYM	25 NYM	26 D NYM
27 D NYM	28 PIT	29 PIT	30 PIT	31 NYM		

JUNE

SUN	MON	TUE	WED	THU	FRI	SAT
					1 NYM	2 NYM
3 D NYM	4	5 PIT	6 PIT	7 PIT	8 TOR	9 TOR
10 D TOR	11	12 BOS	13 BOS	14 TB	15 TB	16 TB
17 D TB	18 ATL	19 ATL	20 ATL	21 PHI	22 PHI	23 PHI
24 D PHI	D 25 MON	26 MON	27 MON	28 PHI	29 PHI	30 PHI

JULY

SUN	MON	TUE	WED	THU	FRI	SAT
1 D PHI	D 2	3 MON	4 MON	5 MON	6 TB	7 TB
8 D TB	D 9	10 *	11	12 NYY	13 NYY	14 D NYY
15 D BAL	16 BAL	17 BAL	18 NYM	19 NYM	20 D CIN	21 CIN
22 D CIN	D 23 NYM	24 NYM	25 NYM	26	27 CIN	28 CIN
29 CIN	30 MIL	31 MIL				

AUGUST

SUN	MON	TUE	WED	THU	FRI	SAT
			1 MIL	2 MIL	3 STL	4 STL
5 D STL	D 6	7 ARI	8 ARI	9 ARI	10 HOU	11 HOU
12 D HOU	13	14 SF	15 SF	16 SF	17 COL	18 COL
19 D COL	20	21 LA	22 LA	23 LA	24 SD	25 SD
26 D SD	D 27 SD	28 CUB	29 CUB	30 CUB	31 NYM	

SEPTEMBER

SUN	MON	TUE	WED	THU	FRI	SAT
						1 NYM
2 NYM	D 3 CUB	D 4 CUB	5 CUB	6	7 NYM	8 NYM
9 D NYM	10	11 MON	12 MON	13 MON	14 ATL	15 ATL
16 ATL	D 17 MON	18 MON	19 MON	20	21 PHI	22 PHI
23 D PHI	D 24 ATL	25 ATL	26 ATL	27	28 PHI	29 PHI
30 D PHI						

2001 SEASON
CLUB DIRECTORY

Owner/chairman
John W. Henry
Vice chairman
David Ginsberg
President and general manager
David Dombrowski
Vice president and assistant general manager
Dave Littlefield
V.p. and assistant to the general manager
Scott Reid
Vice president, baseball legal counsel
John Westhoff
Exec. v.p., sales, marketing & communication
Julio G. Rebull Jr.
V.p., communications & broadcasting
Ron Colangelo
Vice president, scouting
Al Avila
Vice president, finance
Susan Jaison
Vice president, legal affairs/ballpark
Lucinda Treat
Vice president, administration/corporate counsel
Michael Whittle
Director of team travel
Bill Beck
Sr. advisor & special assistant to general manager
Whitey Lockman
Special assistants to the g.m.
Andre Dawson, Orrin Freeman, Tony Perez
Director, Major League operations
Dan Lunetta
Director, minor league operations
Rick Williams
Manager, minor league operations
Mike Parkinson
Manager, minor league administration
Kim-Lee Carkeek Luchs
Manager, scouting administration
Cheryl Evans
Director of media relations
Steve Copses
Media relations coordinator
Jonathan Jensen
Hispanic media coordinator
Susu Rodriguez
Media information coordinator
Andrew Feirstein
Manager, broadcasting
Sandra van Meek
Manager, community affairs
Israel Negron
Director, marketing
Susan Budd
Manager, Marlins en Miami store
Juan Martinez
Director, marketing partnerships
Jim Frevola

Director, creative services & in-game
Leslie Riguero
Director, season & group sales
Pat McNamara
Manager, customer service
Jeff Tanzer
Director, team security
Dan Newhoff
Executive director, foundation
Nancy Olson
Manager, baseball information systems
David Kuan
MLB advanced media site editor
Lindsay Reid
Team physician
Dr. Dan Kanell
Head athletic trainer
Larry Starr
Strength and conditioning director
Rick Slate
Equipment manager
Mike Wallace
Visiting clubhouse manager
Matt Rosenthal
National cross-checker
Murray Cook
Regional cross-checkers
David Chadd, Mike Russell, Tim Schmidt
Coordinator, Latin-American Scouting
Louie Eljaua
Master scouts
Ed Bockman, Kelvin Bowles, Al Diez, Lou Fitzgerald, Dr. Demi Mainieri, Charlie Silvera
Scouting supervisors
John Booher, Ty Brown, Brad DelBarba, Jon Deeble, David Finley, Larry Keller, Bob Laurie, Steve Minor, Steve Mondile, Cucho Rodriguez, Doug Rogalski, Jim Rough, Dennis Sheehan, Keith Snider, Doug Strange, Mike Tosar, Stan Zielinski
Consulting scouts
Tom Evans, Fred Long, Dave McQueen, Dave Mumper, John Nilmeyer, Terry Sullivan, Dick Wilson
Part-time scouts
Pedro Cintron, Dick Smith
Director, Dominican Republic operations
Jesus Alou
Dominican Republic scouts
Pablo Lantigua, Cesar Santiago
Panamanian scout
Ramon Webster
Colombian scout
Alvaro Blanco
Nicaraguan scout
Hubert Silva
Supervisor, Venezuela
Miguel Angel Garcia
Venezuelan scouts
Ernesto Gomez, Jesus Laya, Jorge Rengel, German Robles, Oscar Sarmiento

MINOR LEAGUE AFFILIATES

Class	Team	League	Manager
AAA	Calgary	Pacific Coast	Chris Chambliss
AA	Portland	Eastern	Rick Renteria
A	Brevard County	Florida State	Dave Huppert
A	Kane County	Midwest	Russ Morman
A	Utica	New York-Pennsylvania	Kevin Boles
Rookie	Gulf Coast Marlins	Gulf Coast	Jon Deeble

BROADCAST INFORMATION

Radio: WQAM-AM (560); WQBA-AM (1140, Spanish language).
TV: WAMI-TV (Channel 69).
Cable TV: Fox Sports Net.

SPRING TRAINING

Ballpark (city): Space Coast Stadium (Melbourne, Fla.).
Ticket information: 321-633-9200.

Follow the Marlins all season at: www.sportingnews.com/baseball/teams/marlins/

SPRING TRAINING ROSTER

Manager—John Boles (13).
Coaches—Joe Breeden (12), Rich Dubee (31), Fredi Gonzalez (33), Lynn Jones (35), Jack Maloof (16), Tony Taylor (8).

No.	PITCHERS	B/T	Ht./Wt.	Born	2000 clubs
57	Alfonseca, Antonio	R/R	6-5/235	4-16-72	Florida
55	Almanza, Armando	L/L	6-3/220	10-26-72	Florida
59	Almonte, Hector	R/R	6-2/190	10-17-75	Calgary, Brevard County, Portland, Gulf Coast Marlins
64	Anderson, Wes	R/R	6-4/175	9-10-79	Brevard County
27	Aybar, Manny	R/R	6-1/177	11-28-69	Colorado, Cincinnati, Louisville, Florida
61	Beckett, Josh	R/R	6-4/190	5-15-80	Kane County
29	Bones, Ricky	R/R	6-0/202	4-7-69	Florida
43	Burnett, A.J.	R/R	6-5/205	1-3-77	Florida, Brevard County, Calgary
38	Cornelius, Reid	R/R	6-2/200	6-2-70	Calgary, Florida
22	Darensbourg, Vic	L/L	5-10/165	11-13-70	Florida
46	Dempster, Ryan	R/R	6-1/201	5-3-77	Florida
32	Fernandez, Alex	R/R	6-1/225	8-13-69	Florida
54	Goetz, Geoff	L/L	5-11/165	3-3-79	Brevard County, Portland
37	Grilli, Jason	R/R	6-4/185	11-11-76	Calgary, Florida
56	Knotts, Gary	R/R	6-4/200	2-12-77	Portland
53	Lara, Nelson	R/R	6-4/185	7-15-78	Portland, Brevard County
41	Looper, Braden	R/R	6-5/225	10-28-74	Florida
34	Miceli, Dan	R/R	6-0/225	9-9-70	Florida, Gulf Coast Marlins, Brevard County
53	Neal, Blaine	R/L	6-5/205	4-6-78	Brevard County
36	Nunez, Vladimir	R/R	6-4/224	3-15-75	Florida, Calgary
28	Penny, Brad	R/R	6-4/200	5-24-78	Florida, Brevard County, Calgary
21	Sanchez, Jesus	L/L	5-10/155	10-11-74	Florida
45	Smith, Chuck	R/R	6-1/185	10-21-69	Oklahoma, Florida
58	Tejera, Michael	L/L	5-9/175	10-18-76	DID NOT PLAY
47	Vargas, Claudio	R/R	6-3/210	5-19-79	Brevard County, Portland

No.	CATCHERS	B/T	Ht./Wt.	Born	2000 clubs
17	Castro, Ramon	R/R	6-3/225	3-1-76	Calgary, Florida
23	Johnson, Charles	R/R	6-2/220	7-20-71	Baltimore, Chicago A.L.
52	Redmond, Mike	R/R	6-1/185	5-5-71	Florida

No.	INFIELDERS	B/T	Ht./Wt.	Born	2000 clubs
10	Berg, David	R/R	5-11/196	9-3-70	Brevard County, Florida
1	Castillo, Luis	B/R	5-11/196	9-12-75	Florida, Calgary
6	Fox, Andy	L/R	6-4/202	1-12-71	El Paso, Tucson, Arizona, Florida
11	Gonzalez, Alex	R/R	6-0/170	2-15-77	Florida, Brevard County
25	Lee, Derrek	R/R	6-5/242	9-6-75	Florida
19	Lowell, Mike	R/R	6-4/205	2-24-74	Florida
15	Millar, Kevin	R/R	6-0/210	9-24-71	Florida
3	Ozuna, Pablo	R/R	6-0/160	8-25-78	Portland, Florida
26	Rolison, Nate	L/R	6-6/240	3-27-77	Calgary, Florida

No.	OUTFIELDERS	B/T	Ht./Wt.	Born	2000 clubs
18	Abbott, Jeff	R/L	6-2/200	8-17-72	Chicago A.L.
30	Floyd, Cliff	L/R	6-4/240	12-5-72	Florida
7	Kotsay, Mark	L/L	6-0/201	12-2-75	Florida
	Mottola, Chad	R/R	6-3/225	10-15-71	Syracuse, Toronto
14	Nunez, Abraham	R/R	6-2/185	2-5-80	Portland, Brevard County
44	Wilson, Preston	R/R	6-2/208	7-19-74	Florida

BALLPARK INFORMATION

Ballpark (capacity, surface)
Pro Player Stadium (36,331, grass)
Address
2267 N.W. 199th St.
Miami, Fla. 33056
Official website
www.floridamarlins.com
Business phone
305-626-7400
Ticket information
305-350-5050
Ticket prices
$55 (founders club), $32 (club level section A)
$25 (infield box), $18 (power alley section C)
$15 (terrace box, mezzanine box)
$12 (club level sections B & C-senior citizens)
$10 (OF reserved, adult), $9 (mezzanine reserved, adult)
$5 (OF reserved, children), $4 (fish tank-last three rows, adult)
$3 (mezzanine reserved, children)
$2 (fish tank-last three rows, children)
Field dimensions (from home plate)
To left field at foul line, 330 feet
To center field, 434 feet
To right field at foul line, 345 feet
First game played
April 5, 1993 (Marlins 6, Dodgers 3)

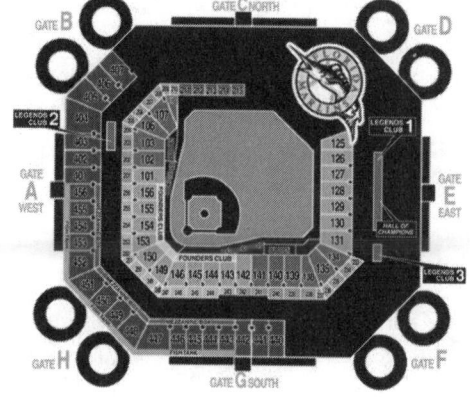

Date	Opp.	Res.	Score	(inn.*)	Hits	Opp. hits	Winning pitcher	Losing pitcher	Save	Record	Pos.	GB
4-3	S.F	W	6-4		12	10	Fernandez	Hernandez	Alfonseca	1-0	T1st	...
4-4	S.F	L	0-3		4	7	Ortiz	Dempster	Nen	1-1	T2nd	0.5
4-5	S.F	L	9-11		12	15	Johnstone	Alfonseca	Nen	1-2	T3rd	1.0
4-6	S.F	W	5-4		8	7	Miceli	Johnstone		2-2	T2nd	0.5
4-7	Col.	W	4-3		5	7	Penny	Yoshii		3-2	1st	+0.5
4-8	Col.	L	2-4		9	10	Jimenez	Fernandez	Lee	3-3	T2nd	0.5
4-9	Col.	W	7-6		9	10	Dempster	Astacio	Alfonseca	4-3	T2nd	0.5
4-10	At Mil.	L	3-4		9	6	Haynes	Nunez	Wickman	4-4	T2nd	0.5
4-12	At Mil.	W	11-4		11	8	Sanchez	Navarro		5-4	T1st	...
4-13	At Mil.	L	0-4		4	6	Bere	Penny		5-5	T1st	...
4-14	At Chi.	W	9-4		10	8	Fernandez	Lorraine		6-5	T1st	...
4-15	At Chi.	L	2-4		4	6	Downs	Dempster	Aguilera	6-6	2nd	0.5
4-16	At Chi.	W	6-5	(10)	8	10	Miceli	Quevedo	Alfonseca	7-6	1st	+0.5
4-17	At Chi.	W	6-5		12	6	Sanchez	Farnsworth	Alfonseca	8-6	1st	+1.0
4-18	Pit.	W	12-5		17	10	Penny	Cordova		9-6	1st	+1.0
4-19	Pit.	L	1-5		8	8	Ritchie	Fernandez		9-7	3rd	...
4-20	Pit.	W	3-2	(14)	10	11	Darensbourg	Williams		10-7	2nd	...
4-21	Phi.	L	3-4		7	8	Ashby	Nunez		10-8	4th	1.0
4-22	Phi.	W	4-2		6	8	Sanchez	Byrd	Alfonseca	11-8	3rd	1.0
4-23	Phi.	W	5-2		5	6	Penny	Person	Alfonseca	12-8	3rd	1.0
4-24	Phi.	W	3-1		7	7	Fernandez	Wolf	Alfonseca	13-8	3rd	0.5
4-25	S.F	L	4-6	(11)	7	13	Gardner	Miceli		13-9	3rd	1.5
4-26	S.F	L	7-8	(12)	16	11	Fultz	Alfonseca		13-10	4th	2.5
4-28	At L.A.	L	3-5		7	9	Adams	Penny	Shaw	13-11	4th	4.0
4-29	At L.A.	L	12-13		12	17	Shaw	Alfonseca		13-12	4th	5.0
4-30	At L.A.	L	1-7		3	9	Brown	Fernandez		13-13	4th	6.0
5-1	At S.D.	W	5-2		9	8	Dempster	Williams	Alfonseca	14-13	4th	6.0
5-2	At S.D.	L	3-8		6	11	Clement	Nunez		14-14	4th	7.0
5-3	At S.D.	L	1-3		5	5	Meadows	Penny	Hoffman	14-15	4th	7.0
5-5	N.Y.	L	1-4		4	5	Leiter	Sanchez	Franco	14-16	4th	8.0
5-6	N.Y.	W	9-1		12	8	Fernandez	Pulsipher		15-16	4th	7.0
5-7	N.Y.	W	3-0		9	1	Dempster	Rusch		16-16	4th	6.0
5-8	Atl.	W	3-2		9	7	Miceli	Seanez		17-16	T3rd	5.0
5-9	Atl.	L	5-10		9	12	Burkett	Penny		17-17	4th	6.0
5-10	Atl.	W	5-3		9	10	Sanchez	Glavine	Alfonseca	18-17	T3rd	5.0
5-11	Atl.	W	5-4		8	12	Grilli	Millwood	Alfonseca	19-17	T3rd	4.0
5-12	At N.Y.	W	6-4		12	10	Dempster	Rusch	Alfonseca	20-17	3rd	4.0
5-13	At N.Y.	W	7-6		8	12	Mahay	Cook	Alfonseca	21-17	2nd	4.0
5-14	At N.Y.	L	1-5		8	5	Hampton	Penny		21-18	3rd	5.0
5-16	S.D.	L	3-7		7	9	Hitchcock	Sanchez		21-19	3rd	6.0
5-17	S.D.	W	4-2		9	8	Dempster	Clement	Alfonseca	22-19	3rd	6.0
5-18	S.D.	L	2-6		6	15	Spencer	Fernandez		22-20	3rd	7.0
5-19	L.A.	L	3-5		7	8	Herges	Looper	Shaw	22-21	4th	7.0
5-20	L.A.	L	6-12		14	15	Perez	Penny		22-22	4th	8.0
5-21	L.A.	L	3-12		7	17	Brown	Sanchez		22-23	4th	9.0
5-23	At StL.	L	3-10		5	13	Kile	Dempster		22-24	4th	9.0
5-24	At StL.	L	1-5		5	11	Stephenson	Nunez		22-25	4th	10.0
5-25	At StL.	L	6-7		11	9	Ankiel	Cornelius	Veres	22-26	4th	11.0
5-26	At Cin.	L	2-3		8	8	Graves	Miceli		22-27	4th	11.0
5-27	At Cin.	W	8-6	(10)	12	8	Alfonseca	Williamson		23-27	4th	11.0
5-28	At Cin.	W	3-1		8	10	Dempster	Sullivan	Alfonseca	24-27	4th	10.0
5-29	At Pit.	L	4-10		11	13	Schmidt	Nunez		24-28	4th	11.0
5-30	At Pit.	L	2-3	(10)	5	11	Williams	Alfonseca		24-29	4th	12.0
5-31	At Pit.	L	2-5		12	5	Cordova	Sanchez	Williams	24-30	4th	12.5
6-2	Tor.	W	11-10		15	15	Bones	Munro	Alfonseca	25-30	4th	11.0
6-3	Tor.	W	2-1		7	5	Looper	Koch	Alfonseca	26-30	4th	11.0
6-4	Tor.	L	2-7		8	12	Escobar	Nunez		26-31	4th	11.0
6-5	Bos.	L	2-3		6	9	Wakefield	Bones	Lowe	26-32	4th	11.0
6-6	Bos.	L	3-4		9	10	R. Martinez	Sanchez	Lowe	26-33	4th	12.0
6-7	Bos.	W	6-2		5	10	Darensbourg	Rose		27-33	4th	11.0
6-9	At T.B.	L	4-6		7	9	Trachsel	Dempster	Hernandez	27-34	4th	12.0
6-10	At T.B.	W	5-1		10	3	Cornelius	Yan	Alfonseca	28-34	4th	12.0
6-11	At T.B.	L	6-7		13	13	Mecir	Bones	Hernandez	28-35	4th	12.0
6-12	At Phi.	W	5-2		10	6	Darensbourg	Politte	Alfonseca	29-35	4th	12.0
6-13	At Phi.	L	3-4		9	10	Gomes	Strong	Brantley	29-36	4th	12.0
6-14	At Phi.	W	8-1		13	4	Dempster	Wolf		30-36	4th	12.0
6-16	At Pit.	W	8-3		10	8	Cornelius	Cordova	Looper	31-36	4th	10.5
6-17	At Pit.	W	4-3	(11)	10	12	Alfonseca	Loiselle	Strong	32-36	4th	9.5
6-18	At Pit.	W	5-4		10	8	Bones	Christiansen	Alfonseca	33-36	4th	9.5
6-19	Mil.	L	0-2		3	5	Wright	Smith	Wickman	33-37	4th	9.5
6-20	Mil.	W	8-2		13	5	Dempster	Woodard		34-37	4th	9.5
6-21	Mil.	W	5-4		9	11	Looper	Haynes	Alfonseca	35-37	4th	8.5
6-22	Mil.	L	1-6		6	10	Snyder	Sanchez		35-38	4th	9.5

Date	Opp.	Res.	Score	(inn.*)	Hits	Opp. hits	Winning pitcher	Losing pitcher	Save	Record	Pos.	GB
6-23	Chi.	W	6-1		12	8	Penny	Lieber		36-38	4th	9.5
6-24	Chi.	W	7-4		9	12	Strong	Heredia	Alfonseca	37-38	4th	8.5
6-25	Chi.	W	8-7	(10)	10	9	Alfonseca	Heredia		38-38	4th	8.5
6-26	At N.Y.	L	5-10		11	12	Leiter	Cornelius		38-39	4th	9.0
6-27	At N.Y.	L	2-5		6	7	Rusch	Sanchez	Benitez	38-40	4th	9.0
6-28	At N.Y.	L	5-6		10	13	B.J. Jones	Penny	Franco	38-41	4th	10.0
6-30	At Mon.	W	5-4		12	7	Almanza	Kline	Alfonseca	39-41	4th	9.5
7-1	At Mon.	W	6-5		10	13	Dempster	Johnson	Alfonseca	40-41	4th	8.5
7-2	At Mon.	W	2-1		5	4	Cornelius	Santana	Alfonseca	41-41	3rd	8.5
7-3	N.Y.	W	2-0		6	4	Almanza	Wendell		42-41	3rd	7.5
7-4	N.Y.	W	9-8		10	9	Darensbourg	B.M. Jones	Alfonseca	43-41	3rd	7.5
7-5	N.Y.	L	2-11		6	15	Hampton	Smith		43-42	3rd	7.5
7-7	T.B.	L	3-8		7	11	Lopez	Dempster	Mecir	43-43	4th	8.0
7-8	T.B.	W	6-5		13	11	Looper	White	Alfonseca	44-43	T3rd	8.0
7-9	T.B.	W	10-9		14	11	Sanchez	Creek	Alfonseca	45-43	3rd	7.0
7-13	At N.Y. (AL)	W	11-9		14	12	Penny	Hernandez	Alfonseca	46-43	3rd	7.0
7-14	At N.Y. (AL)	L	2-6		7	9	Clemens	Dempster		46-44	3rd	8.0
7-16	At Bal.	L	5-9		11	16	Mills	Darensbourg	Timlin	46-45	3rd	9.5
7-17	At Bal.	L	3-5		8	8	Mercedes	Cornelius	Timlin	46-46	3rd	9.5
7-18	At Bal.	W	7-0		13	8	Sanchez	Mussina		47-46	3rd	9.5
7-20†	Atl.	L	3-5		10	9	Glavine	Dempster	Ligtenberg	47-47		
7-20‡	Atl.	W	6-1		8	3	Burnett	Kamieniecki		48-47	3rd	9.5
7-21	Mon.	L	3-7		8	9	Thurman	Smith		48-48	3rd	10.5
7-22	Mon.	L	7-17		7	19	Johnson	Cornelius		48-49	3rd	10.5
7-23	Mon.	L	6-7		11	17	Vazquez	Sanchez	Strickland	48-50	4th	11.5
7-25	At Atl.	L	5-6		15	6	Glavine	Dempster	Ligtenberg	48-51	4th	12.5
7-26	At Atl.	L	3-6		9	10	Millwood	Burnett	Rocker	48-52	4th	13.5
7-27	At Atl.	W	12-4		15	8	Smith	Maddux		49-52	3rd	12.5
7-28	Ari.	L	1-4		6	6	Schilling	Cornelius	Mantei	49-53	3rd	13.5
7-29	Ari.	W	4-2		7	2	Miceli	Kim	Alfonseca	50-53	3rd	13.5
7-30	Ari.	W	4-3		10	6	Almanza	Morgan	Alfonseca	51-53	3rd	13.5
7-31	Hou.	L	2-4		9	8	Lima	Burnett	Dotel	51-54	3rd	14.0
8-1	Hou.	L	3-4		6	2	Elarton	Smith	Dotel	51-55	3rd	15.0
8-2	Hou.	W	5-4		8	11	Miceli	Valdes		52-55	3rd	14.0
8-3	Hou.	W	4-3		11	6	Looper	Slusarski	Alfonseca	53-55	3rd	14.0
8-4	At Cin.	W	2-1		10	8	Dempster	Harnisch	Alfonseca	54-55	3rd	13.0
8-5	At Cin.	W	10-5	(11)	13	15	Alfonseca	Wohlers		55-55	3rd	13.0
8-6	At Cin.	W	9-6		9	12	Aybar	Graves	Looper	56-55	3rd	12.0
8-7	At StL.	L	1-2	(11)	4	9	Timlin	Darensbourg		56-56	3rd	12.0
8-8	At StL.	W	7-0		10	6	Sanchez	Hentgen		57-56	3rd	12.0
8-9	At StL.	W	5-3		7	11	Almanza	Morris	Alfonseca	58-56	3rd	11.0
8-11	S.D.	L	0-3		7	5	Eaton	Burnett	Hoffman	58-57	3rd	12.0
8-12	S.D.	L	1-2	(10)	5	9	Walker	Alfonseca	Hoffman	58-58	3rd	13.0
8-13	S.D.	L	3-7		11	8	Walker	Almanza	Hoffman	58-59	3rd	13.0
8-14	L.A.	W	11-2		12	10	Sanchez	Brown		59-59	3rd	13.0
8-15	L.A.	W	7-3		12	6	Dempster	Herges		60-59	3rd	13.0
8-16	L.A.	L	4-10		13	11	Adams	Miceli		60-60	3rd	14.0
8-18	At Col.	W	9-8		12	18	Smith	Rose	Alfonseca	61-60	3rd	13.0
8-19	At Col.	L	3-10		10	10	Tavarez	Cornelius		61-61	3rd	13.0
8-20	At Col.	L	4-13		8	14	Astacio	Sanchez		61-62	3rd	14.0
8-21	At S.F	L	0-6		6	10	Gardner	Dempster		61-63	3rd	15.0
8-22	At S.F	W	7-5		13	8	Burnett	Estes	Alfonseca	62-63	3rd	14.0
8-23	At S.F	L	0-5		4	7	Hernandez	Smith		62-64	3rd	15.0
8-25	Cin.	L	0-6		8	13	Dessens	Cornelius		62-65	3rd	15.5
8-26	Cin.	L	2-3		9	5	Harnisch	Darensbourg	Graves	62-66	3rd	15.5
8-27	Cin.	W	7-6		10	13	Miceli	Graves		63-66	3rd	14.5
8-28	StL.	L	2-5		5	12	James	Almanza	Veres	63-67	3rd	14.5
8-29	StL.	W	3-1		7	4	Smith	Hentgen	Alfonseca	64-67	3rd	13.5
8-30	StL.	L	2-4		8	7	Morris	Alfonseca	Veres	64-68	3rd	14.5
9-1	At Ari.	W	8-7	(11)	15	13	Darensbourg	Swindell	Alfonseca	65-68	3rd	13.5
9-2	At Ari.	W	10-1		17	9	Dempster	Schilling		66-68	3rd	13.0
9-3	At Ari.	L	5-10		11	18	Kim	Burnett		66-69	3rd	13.0
9-4	At Hou.	W	5-2		11	5	Smith	Holt	Alfonseca	67-69	3rd	12.5
9-5	At Hou.	L	5-9		9	15	McKnight	Cornelius		67-70	3rd	13.5
9-6	At Hou.	L	5-13		7	14	Lima	Sanchez		67-71	3rd	14.5
9-7	At Hou.	L	3-7		7	9	Elarton	Miceli		67-72	3rd	15.5
9-8	Ari.	L	1-2		6	8	Kim	Bones	Mantei	67-73	3rd	16.5
9-9	Ari.	L	1-4		5	9	Stottlemyre	Burnett	Mantei	67-74	3rd	16.5
9-10	Ari.	W	4-3	(12)	9	4	Looper	Springer		68-74	3rd	15.5
9-12	At Atl.	W	5-4		11	12	Sanchez	Millwood	Alfonseca	69-74	3rd	14.5
9-13	At Atl.	L	0-4		4	8	Maddux	Dempster		69-75	3rd	15.5
9-14	At Atl.	L	3-5		8	10	Ashby	Cornelius	Rocker	69-76	3rd	16.5
9-15	At Phi.	L	4-7		7	8	Person	Burnett		69-77	3rd	16.5
9-16	At Phi.	W	3-2		7	4	Penny	Daal	Alfonseca	70-77	3rd	16.5
9-17	At Phi.	L	5-6		10	9	Wolf	Smith	Jacquez	70-78	3rd	17.5
9-18	At Mon.	L	4-11		6	9	Lira	Sanchez		70-79	3rd	18.5
9-19	At Mon.	W	3-1		7	5	Dempster	Thurman	Alfonseca	71-79	3rd	18.5

Date	Opp.	Res.	Score	(inn.*)	Hits	Opp. hits	Winning pitcher	Losing pitcher	Save	Record	Pos.	GB
9-20	At Mon.	L	2-4		9	9	Vazquez	Cornelius	Strickland	71-80	3rd	18.5
9-21	At Mon.	L	3-10		7	14	Hermanson	Burnett		71-81	3rd	19.0
9-22	At Col.	W	8-4		13	7	Penny	Tavarez		72-81	3rd	18.0
9-23	At Col.	W	3-1	(7)	6	4	Smith	Wasdin		73-81	3rd	18.0
9-24	At Col.	L	3-9		8	14	Bohanon	Sanchez		73-82	3rd	19.0
9-26	Mon.	W	5-4	(10)	8	8	Alfonseca	Kline		74-82	3rd	19.5
9-27	Mon.	W	6-3		9	5	Burnett	Armas	Alfonseca	75-82	3rd	18.5
9-28	Mon.	W	7-4		9	8	Penny	Lira	Alfonseca	76-82	3rd	17.5
9-29	Phi.	W	7-1		10	4	Smith	Chen		77-82	3rd	16.5
9-30	Phi.	W	11-5		17	10	Cornelius	Person		78-82	3rd	16.5
10-1	Phi.	W	7-5		11	9	Dempster	Telemaco	Alfonseca	79-82	3rd	15.5

Monthly records: April (13-13), May (11-17), June (15-11), July (12-13), August (13-14), September (14-14), October (1-0).
*Innings, if other than nine. †First game of a doubleheader. ‡Second game of a doubleheader.

HIGHLIGHTS

High point: After a 5-11 finish in July, the Marlins needed a confidence boost. They got it during a six-game swing through Cincinnati and St. Louis that produced five wins—the last a come-from-behind triumph that was sealed by Mike Lowell's three-run, eighth-inning home run. The Marlins played the rest of the season with a bit of a swagger.

Low point: The Marlins hit bottom shortly after the All-Star break when they fell under .500 with three ugly losses to the Expos—7-3, 17-7 and 7-6. The next day, they committed five errors in the first of two straight losses to the Braves. Gone was the premature talk of a surprising Marlins team contending for the playoffs. After the Expos finale, usually optimistic manager John Boles snapped: "We were pathetic for three games. Anybody want to talk about the wild card?"

Turning point: Can it occur at the end of a season? A six-game season-ending winning streak was important for the young Marlins, who exceeded expectations with their third-place finish in the N.L. East, recorded a 15-win improvement over 1999 and set a positive tone for the future.

Most valuable player: Luis Castillo, a scrappy little second baseman, was the undisputed spark in the lineup. He set five club records—average (.334), hits (180), singles (158), multi-hit games (55) and stolen bases (62). His steals total was the best in baseball and his defense wasn't far behind.

Most valuable pitcher: Ryan Dempster was the undisputed ace of the staff, but the most valuable pitcher was closer Antonio Alfonseca. The big righthander saved a major league-high 45 games and won five, meaning he figured in 63.3 percent of the team's 79 wins.

Most improved player: After batting .206 in 70 games in 1999, Derrek Lee lost the starting first base job to Kevin Millar in the spring. By mid-April, Lee was back in the lineup and he more than made the most of his opportunity. He batted .281 with 28 homers and 70 RBIs in the No. 6 slot.

Most pleasant surprise: Chuck Smith, a 30-year-old journeyman minor leaguer, arrived as a trade throw-in and helped stabilize the rotation. His 6-6 record was deceiving, but not the 3.23 ERA or the 118 batters he struck out in 122$\frac{2}{3}$ innings.

Key injuries: The biggest loss was righthander Alex Fernandez, the expected staff ace who was 4-4 when he finally shut it down in May because of a sore shoulder and elbow. ... Righthander Brian Edmondson, the workhorse of the 1999 bullpen, missed the entire 2000 season with a bad shoulder... Righthanders Dan Miceli and Brad Penny missed action with sore arms. ... Expectations were high for lefty Michael Tejera, but he missed the season with a torn ligament in his elbow.

Notable: The 79-82 Marlins became just the second N.L. team in 50 years to post a 10-win improvement in back-to-back seasons. ... By hitting 31 homers and stealing 36 bases, center fielder Preston Wilson joined a select club. He became the 23rd player in history to accomplish the feat and the first for the Marlins. ... Dempster broke Kevin Brown's club record for strikeouts with 209.

—JOE CAPOZZI

RECORDS

2000 regular-season record: 79-82 (3rd in N.L. East); 43-38 at home; 36-44 on road; 36-31 vs. East; 26-23 vs. Central; 17-28 vs. West; 17-22 vs. lefthanded starters; 62-60 vs. righthanded starters; 63-70 on grass; 16-12 on turf; 25-21 in daytime; 54-61 at night; 32-20 in one-run games; 9-5 in extra-inning games; 0-1 in doubleheaders.

Team record past five years: 369-440 (.456, ranks 12th in league in that span).

TEAM LEADERS

Batting average: Luis Castillo (.334).
At-bats: Preston Wilson (605).
Runs: Luis Castillo (101).
Hits: Luis Castillo (180).
Total Bases: Preston Wilson (294).
Doubles: Mike Lowell (38).
Triples: Mark Kotsay (5).
Home runs: Preston Wilson (31).

Runs batted in: Preston Wilson (121).
Stolen bases: Luis Castillo (62).
Slugging percentage: Derrek Lee (.507).
On-base percentage: Luis Castillo (.418).
Wins: Ryan Dempster (14).
Earned-run average: Ryan Dempster (3.66).
Complete games: Ryan Dempster, Jesus Sanchez (2).
Shutouts: Jesus Sanchez (2).
Saves: Antonio Alfonseca (45).
Innings pitched: Ryan Dempster (226.1).
Strikeouts: Ryan Dempster (209).

GAMES BY POSITION

Catcher: Mike Redmond 85, Paul Bako 56, Ramon Castro 50, Sandy Martinez 9.
First base: Derrek Lee 147, Kevin Millar 34, Brant Brown 5, Nate Rolison 4, Mark Kotsay 2.
Second base: Luis Castillo 136, Chris Clapinski 14, Dave Berg 11, Pablo Ozuna 7, Andy Fox 2.
Third base: Mike Lowell 136, Dave Berg 13, Kevin Millar 13, Andy Fox 12, Chris Clapinski 3.
Shortstop: Alex Gonzalez 104, Dave Berg 49, Andy Fox 33, Chris Clapinski 1.
Outfield: Preston Wilson 158, Mark Kotsay 142, Cliff Floyd 108, Mark Smith 49, Danny Bautista 38, Henry Rodriguez 29, Kevin Millar 18, Andy Fox 14, Brant Brown 13, Chris Clapinski 3.
Designated hitter: Kevin Millar 6, Cliff Floyd 1, Mark Smith 1.

TOP DRAFT CHOICES

1. **Adrian Gonzalez**, 1B, Lakeside H.S., Chula Vista, Calif.
2. **Jason Stokes**, 1B, Coppell (Tex.) H.S.
3. **Rob Henkel**, LHP, UCLA.
4. **Anthony Brewer**, OF, Simeon H.S., Chicago.
5. **Jim Kavourias**, OF, Univ. of Tampa.
6. **Will Smith**, OF, Palo Verde H.S., Tucson.
7. **Brandon Sloan**, RHP, Wichita State U.
8. **Matt Massingale**, RHP, University of Washington.
9. **Jesse Kozlowski**, RHP, Westlake H.S., Thousand Oaks, Calif.
10. **Bill Clayton**, RHP, Glenwood H.S., Chatham, Ill.

HOUSTON ASTROS
NATIONAL LEAGUE CENTRAL DIVISION

Astros 2001 SCHEDULE
Home games shaded; D—Day game (games starting before 5 p.m.)
*—All-Star Game at Safeco Field (Seattle)

APRIL

SUN	MON	TUE	WED	THU	FRI	SAT
1	2	3	4 D MIL	5 MIL	6 PIT	7 D PIT
8 PIT	9 D	10 MIL	11 MIL	12 D MIL	13 STL	14 D STL
15 STL	16 D PIT	17 PIT	18 PIT	19	20 STL	21 D STL
22 STL	23 ATL	24 ATL	25 ATL	26	27 FLA	28 D FLA
29 FLA	30 NYM					

MAY

SUN	MON	TUE	WED	THU	FRI	SAT
		1 NYM	2 NYM	3	4 MON	5 MON
6 MON	7 D PHI	8 PHI	9 PHI	10	11 CIN	12 CIN
13 CIN	14 CIN	15 CUB	16 CUB	17 D CUB	18 CIN	19 D CIN
20 CIN	21 D SD	22 SD	23 SD	24	25 LA	26 LA
27 D LA	28	29 SD	30 SD	31 D SD		

JUNE

SUN	MON	TUE	WED	THU	FRI	SAT
					1 LA	2 D LA
3 LA	4 D	5 COL	6 COL	7 COL	8 TEX	9 TEX
10 TEX	11	12 MIN	13 MIN	14 MIN	15 TEX	16 D TEX
17 TEX	18 D CIN	19 COL	20 COL	21 CIN	22 CIN	23 CIN
24 CIN	25 D ARI	26 ARI	27 ARI	28	29 MIL	30 MIL

JULY

SUN	MON	TUE	WED	THU	FRI	SAT
1 MIL	2 D	3 ARI	4 ARI	5 ARI	6 KC	7 KC
8 KC	9 D	10 *	11	12 SD	13 SD	14 SD
15 CLE	16 D CLE	17 CLE	18 STL	19 STL	20 CUB	21 CUB
22 CUB	23 D CUB	24 STL	25 D STL	26 PIT	27 PIT	28 PIT
29 D PIT	30	31 NYM				

AUGUST

SUN	MON	TUE	WED	THU	FRI	SAT
			1 NYM	2 NYM	3 MON	4 MON
5 MON	6 D	7 ATL	8 ATL	9 ATL	10 FLA	11 FLA
12 FLA	13 CUB	14 CUB	15 CUB	16 PIT	17 PIT	18 D PIT
19 PIT	20	21 PHI	22 PHI	23 PHI	24 PIT	25 PIT
26 PIT	27	28 CIN	29 CIN	30 D MIL	31 MIL	

SEPTEMBER

SUN	MON	TUE	WED	THU	FRI	SAT
						1 MIL
2 MIL	3 D CIN	4 D CIN	5 CIN	6 D	7 MIL	8 MIL
9 MIL	10	11 SF	12 SF	13 SF	14 STL	15 STL
16 STL	17 D SF	18 SF	19 SF	20 D SF	21 CUB	22 CUB
23 CUB	24 D STL	25 STL	26 STL	27 CUB	28 CUB	29 D CUB
30 D CUB						

2001 SEASON
CLUB DIRECTORY

Chairman and chief executive officer
Drayton McLane Jr.

President, baseball operations
Tal Smith

President, business operations
Bob McClaren

General manager
Gerry Hunsicker

Assistant general manager
Tim Purpura

Director of baseball administration
Barry Waters

Director of scouting
David Lakey

Special asst. to the g.m. for international scouting and development
Andres Reiner

Sr. v.p., ops. and communications
Rob Matwick

Sr. v.p., finance and administration
Teresa Pelanne

Vice president, human resources
Mike Anders

V.p., security and traffic operations
Don Collins

V.p., community development
Marian Harper

Vice president, market development
Rosi Hernandez

Vice president, sales and broadcasting
Jamie Hildreth

Vice president, engineering
Bert Pope

Vice president, marketing
Garry Sawka

Vice president, special events
Kala Sorenson

V.p., ticket sales and services
John Sorrentino

Director of media relations
Warren Miller

Assistant director of media relations
Todd Fedewa

Professional scouts
Kimball Crossley, Gene DeBoer, Leo Labossiere, Joe Pittman, Tom Romenesko, Scipio Spinks

Major league scouts
Stan Benjamin, Bill Kelso, Jack Lind, Walt Matthews, Paul Weaver

Full-time scouts
Bob Blair, Joe Bogar, Ralph Bratton, Chuck Carlson, Andrew Cotner, Gerry Craft, Doug Deutsch, James Farrar, David Henderson, Dan Huston, Marc Johnson, Brian Keegan, Mike Maggart, Jerry Marik, Tom McCormack, Mel Nelson, Rusty Pendergrass, Bob Poole, Joe Robinson, Tad Slowik, Frankie Thon, Tim Tolman, Nick Venuto, Danny Watkins, Gene Wellman

Foreign scouts
Ricardo Aponte, Jesus Aristimuno, Sergio A. Beltre, Rafael Cariel, Arnold Elles, Orlando Fernandez, Mario Gonzalez, Julio Linares, Rodney Linares, Omar Lopez, Carlos Maldonado, Ramon Morales, Oscar Padron, Guillermo Ramirez, Rafael Ramirez, Wolfgang Ramos, Anibal Reluz, Adriano Rodriguez, Dr. Lester Storey, Alejandro Tavares, Pablo Torrealba, Calixto Vargas, Mark Van Zanten

MINOR LEAGUE AFFILIATES

Class	Team	League	Manager
AAA	New Orleans	Pacific Coast	Tony Pena
AA	Round Rock	Texas	Jackie Moore
A	Lexington	South Atlantic	J.J. Cannon
A	Michigan	Midwest	John Massarelli
A	Pittsfield	New York-Pennsylvania	Ivan DeJesus
Rookie	Martinsville	Appalachian	Jorge Orta

BROADCAST INFORMATION

Radio: KTRH-AM (740); KXYZ-AM (1320, Spanish language).
TV: KNWS-TV (Channel 51).
Cable TV: Fox Sports Southwest.

SPRING TRAINING

Ballpark (city): Osceola County Stadium (Kissimmee, Fla.).
Ticket information: 407-839-3900.

Follow the Astros all season at: www.sportingnews.com/baseball/teams/astros/

Manager—Larry Dierker (49).
Coaches—Jose Cruz (25), Mike Cubbage (24), Matt Galante (8), Harry Spilman (12), Burt Hooton (48), John Tamargo (30).

No.	PITCHERS	B/T	Ht./Wt.	Born	2000 clubs
	Bottenfield, Kent	R/R	6-3/240	11-14-68	Anaheim, Philadelphia
	Brocail, Doug	L/R	6-5/235	5-16-67	Detroit
51	Cabrera, Jose	R/R	6-0/180	3-24-72	Houston, New Orleans
	Cruz, Nelson	R/R	6-1/185	9-13-72	Toledo, Detroit
41	Dotel, Octavio	R/R	6-0/175	11-25-75	Houston
50	Elarton, Scott	R/R	6-7/240	2-23-76	Houston, New Orleans, Round Rock
53	Franklin, Wayne	L/L	6-2/195	3-9-74	New Orleans, Houston
	Hernandez, Carlos	L/L	5-10/145	4-22-80	Michigan
	Jackson, Mike	R/R	6-2/225	12-22-64	DID NOT PLAY
	Kessel, Kyle	L/L	6-0/190	6-2-76	Kissimmee, Round Rock
	Lidge, Brad	R/R	6-5/200	12-23-76	Kissimmee
42	Lima, Jose	R/R	6-2/205	9-30-72	Houston
36	Linebrink, Scott	R/R	6-3/185	8-4-76	Fresno, San Francisco, Houston, New Orleans
59	McKnight, Tony	R/R	6-5/205	6-29-77	Round Rock, New Orleans, Houston
	Miller, Greg	L/L	6-5/215	9-30-79	Kissimmee, Round Rock
52	Miller, Wade	R/R	6-2/185	9-13-76	New Orleans, Houston
	Oswalt, Roy	R/R	6-0/170	8-29-77	Kissimmee, Round Rock
39	Powell, Jay	R/R	6-4/225	1-9-72	Houston, New Orleans, Round Rock
	Redding, Tim	R/R	6-0/180	2-12-78	Kissimmee, Round Rock
37	Reynolds, Shane	R/R	6-3/210	3-26-68	Houston
66	Rodriguez, Wilfredo	L/L	6-3/180	3-20-79	Round Rock, Kissimmee
13	Wagner, Billy	L/L	5-11/180	7-25-71	Houston

No.	CATCHERS	B/T	Ht./Wt.	Born	2000 clubs
	Ausmus, Brad	R/R	5-11/195	4-14-69	Detroit
20	Eusebio, Tony	R/R	6-2/210	4-27-67	Houston
	Maldonado, Carlos	R/R	6-2/185	1-3-79	Round Rock

No.	INFIELDERS	B/T	Ht./Wt.	Born	2000 clubs
5	Bagwell, Jeff	R/R	6-0/195	5-27-68	Houston
7	Biggio, Craig	R/R	5-11/180	12-14-65	Houston
2	Ensberg, Morgan	R/R	6-2/210	8-26-75	Round Rock, Houston
3	Everett, Adam	R/R	6-0/156	2-2-77	New Orleans
1	Ginter, Keith	R/R	5-10/190	5-5-76	Round Rock, Houston
	Hayes, Charlie	R/R	6-0/215	5-29-65	Milwaukee
4	Lugo, Julio	R/R	6-2/165	11-16-75	Houston
62	McNeal, Aaron	R/R	6-3/230	4-28-78	Round Rock
28	Spiers, Bill	L/R	6-2/190	6-5-66	Houston
6	Truby, Chris	R/R	6-2/190	12-9-73	Houston, New Orleans
	Vizcaino, Jose	B/R	6-1/180	3-26-68	Los Angeles, New York A.L.
31	Ward, Daryle	L/L	6-2/230	6-27-75	Houston

No.	OUTFIELDERS	B/T	Ht./Wt.	Born	2000 clubs
18	Alou, Moises	R/R	6-3/195	7-3-66	Houston
29	Barker, Glen	R/R	5-10/180	5-10-71	Houston, New Orleans
17	Berkman, Lance	B/L	6-1/205	2-10-76	New Orleans, Houston
15	Hidalgo, Richard	R/R	6-3/190	7-2-75	Houston

BALLPARK INFORMATION

Ballpark (capacity, surface)
Enron Field (40,950, grass)

Address
P.O. Box 288
Houston, TX 77001-0288

Official website
www.astros.com

Business phone
713-259-8000

Ticket information
713-259-8500; 1-800-ASTROS-2

Ticket prices
$29 (dugout)
$28 (club)
$25 (field box)
$24 (club)
$17 (Crawford box)
$15 (bullpen box)
$12 (mezzanine, terrace deck)
$10 (upper deck)
$5-$1 (outfield deck)

Field dimensions (from home plate)
To left field at foul line, 315 feet
To center field, 435 feet
To right field at foul line, 326 feet

First game played
April 7, 2000 (Phillies 4, Astros 1)

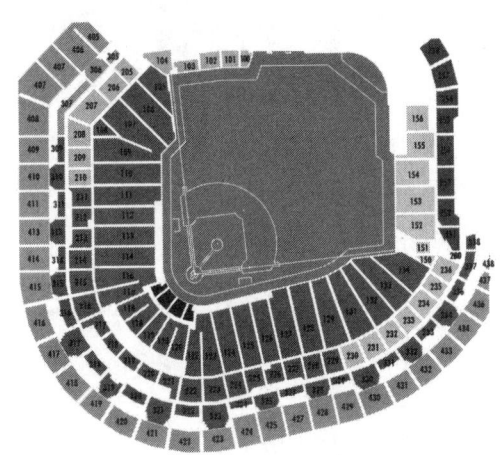

2001 SEASON *Houston Astros*

Date	Opp.	Res.	Score	(inn.*)	Hits	Opp. hits	Winning pitcher	Losing pitcher	Save	Record	Pos.	GB
4-4	At Pit.	W	5-2		5	6	Reynolds	Schmidt	Wagner	1-0	T1st	...
4-5	At Pit.	W	11-2		10	9	Lima	Benson		2-0	T1st	...
4-6	At Pit.	L	1-10		2	16	Cordova	Holt		2-1	T3rd	1.0
4-7	Phi.	L	1-4		5	6	Wolf	Dotel	Gomes	2-2	T3rd	1.0
4-8	Phi.	W	8-5		11	11	Maddux	Brock	Wagner	3-2	T2nd	1.0
4-9	Phi.	L	2-3		5	7	Schrenk	J. Powell	Gomes	3-3	T2nd	2.0
4-10	StL.	L	7-8		7	13	Hentgen	Lima	Veres	3-4	T3rd	3.0
4-11	StL.	L	6-10		8	9	Stephenson	Holt		3-5	4th	4.0
4-12	StL.	W	7-5		9	9	Perez	Wainhouse	Wagner	4-5	T3rd	3.0
4-14	At S.D.	W	10-4		11	13	Reynolds	Boehringer		5-5	T2nd	1.5
4-15	At S.D.	L	3-5		7	9	Williams	Lima	Hoffman	5-6	T4th	2.0
4-16	At S.D.	L	3-13		8	18	Clement	Holt		5-7	T5th	2.5
4-18	At L.A.	L	3-5		5	8	Dreifort	Dotel	Shaw	5-8	T4th	3.5
4-19	At L.A.	W	10-3		14	7	Reynolds	Hershiser		6-8	T3rd	3.5
4-21	S.D.	L	2-7		6	11	Williams	Lima		6-9	3rd	4.0
4-22	S.D.	L	6-8	(10)	6	14	Cunnane	Perez	Hoffman	6-10	4th	4.0
4-23	S.D.	L	10-11		10	14	Whisenant	Wagner	Hoffman	6-11	4th	5.0
4-25	Chi.	W	11-7		16	10	Reynolds	Downs		7-11	3rd	5.0
4-26	Chi.	L	8-13		11	16	Karchner	Maddux	Aguilera	7-12	4th	6.0
4-27	Chi.	L	3-12		5	14	Lieber	Lima		7-13	6th	6.0
4-28	At Mil.	W	7-0		8	1	Holt	Navarro		8-13	5th	6.0
4-29	At Mil.	W	10-3		5	7	Maddux	Stull		9-13	3rd	6.0
4-30	At Mil.	L	3-4		7	7	Weathers	Henry		9-14	3rd	7.0
5-1	At Mil.	W	5-0		11	2	Dotel	Woodard		10-14	3rd	6.5
5-2	At Chi.	L	1-11		4	16	Wood	Lima	Williams	10-15	T3rd	6.5
5-3	At Chi.	L	3-4		8	7	Lieber	Holt	Aguilera	10-16	5th	6.5
5-4	At Chi.	W	6-2		9	9	Elarton	Valdes	Wagner	11-16	T3rd	6.5
5-5	At L.A.	L	2-3		4	9	Shaw	Henry		11-17	4th	6.5
5-6	At L.A.	L	6-9		12	7	Dreifort	Dotel		11-18	4th	7.5
5-7	At L.A.	W	14-8	(10)	17	12	Wagner	Shaw		12-18	4th	6.5
5-8	Col.	L	1-3		3	6	Astacio	Holt		12-19	4th	6.5
5-9	Col.	W	13-8		11	10	Perez	Tavarez		13-19	4th	6.5
5-10	Col.	W	5-1		7	5	Reynolds	Yoshii		14-19	4th	5.5
5-12	Cin.	L	3-7	(11)	9	10	Graves	Maddux		14-20	4th	5.5
5-13	Cin.	L	7-8		10	12	Reyes	Wagner	Williamson	14-21	4th	6.0
5-14	Cin.	W	10-3		13	6	Elarton	Parris		15-21	4th	5.5
5-15	Cin.	L	3-4		4	9	Villone	Lima	Graves	15-22	4th	6.0
5-16	At Mil.	L	5-6	(16)	14	11	Estrada	Holt		15-23	4th	7.0
5-19	At Mon.	L	2-3	(10)	8	8	Hermanson	Slusarski		15-24	5th	7.0
5-20	At Mon.	L	7-8		10	15	Irabu	Elarton	Hermanson	15-25	5th	8.0
5-21	At Mon.	L	3-8		7	11	Vazquez	Lima		15-26	6th	9.0
5-22†	At Mil.	L	9-10	(10)	13	14	Weathers	Slusarski		15-27		
5-22‡	At Mil.	L	1-6		7	8	Bere	Gross		15-28	6th	10.0
5-23	Phi.	W	10-2		13	8	Holt	Wolf		16-28	6th	10.0
5-24	Phi.	L	7-9		9	13	Gomes	Wagner	Brantley	16-29	6th	11.0
5-25	Phi.	W	10-6		11	8	Elarton	Ashby	Slusarski	17-29	6th	11.0
5-26	Atl.	W	5-4	(10)	10	11	Henry	Seanez		18-29	5th	10.0
5-27	Atl.	L	5-6		10	9	Burkett	Reynolds	Ligtenberg	18-30	6th	10.0
5-28	Atl.	W	4-3		5	8	Valdes	Seanez	Wagner	19-30	6th	9.0
5-29	At Col.	L	7-8		12	15	White	Cabrera	Jimenez	19-31	6th	10.0
5-30	At Col.	L	7-10		12	12	Belinda	Valdes	Jimenez	19-32	6th	11.0
5-31	At Col.	L	6-8		14	12	White	Slusarski	Jimenez	19-33	6th	11.0
6-2	Chi. (AL)	L	4-7		10	9	Parque	Reynolds	Foulke	19-34	6th	11.5
6-3	Chi. (AL)	W	6-1		10	8	Holt	Wells		20-34	6th	10.5
6-4	Chi. (AL)	L	3-7		5	13	Sirotka	Dotel		20-35	6th	11.0
6-5	Min.	W	8-2		11	8	Elarton	Radke		21-35	6th	10.0
6-6	Min.	L	1-3		6	6	Santana	Lima	Guardado	21-36	6th	10.5
6-7	Min.	L	0-2		6	9	Mays	Reynolds	Guardado	21-37	6th	11.5
6-8	At L.A.	L	2-5		6	9	Park	Holt	Fetters	21-38	6th	12.0
6-9	At S.D.	W	7-6		10	11	Wagner	Hoffman		22-38	6th	11.0
6-10	At S.D.	L	3-13		12	12	Meadows	Elarton		22-39	6th	11.0
6-11	At S.D.	L	1-4		4	11	Walker	Lima	Hoffman	22-40	6th	12.0
6-13	At Col.	W	6-3		15	10	Reynolds	Arrojo	Wagner	23-40	6th	12.5
6-14	At Col.	W	8-4		11	8	Slusarski	Astacio		24-40	6th	12.5
6-15	At Col.	L	4-5		10	8	Jimenez	Wagner		24-41	6th	13.0
6-16	At S.F	L	4-7		9	12	Estes	Elarton	Nen	24-42	6th	14.0
6-17	At S.F	L	4-6		10	8	Hernandez	Lima	Nen	24-43	6th	15.0
6-18	At S.F	W	4-2	(11)	6	6	J. Powell	Nen	Henry	25-43	6th	14.0
6-20	L.A.	L	6-9	(10)	13	18	Herges	Slusarski		25-44	6th	15.0
6-21	L.A.	L	6-7		7	13	Herges	Cabrera		25-45	6th	15.0
6-22	L.A.	W	6-3		7	6	Elarton	Dreifort	Valdes	26-45	6th	15.0
6-23	S.F	L	3-10		10	14	Hernandez	Lima		26-46	6th	16.0
6-24	S.F	L	4-13		12	22	Nathan	Reynolds		26-47	6th	17.0
6-25	S.F	L	2-4		8	14	Ortiz	Holt	Nen	26-48	6th	18.0

Date	Opp.	Res.	Score	(inn.*)	Hits	Opp. hits	Winning pitcher	Losing pitcher	Save	Record	Pos.	GB
6-26	At Ari.	L	1-6		5	8	Reynoso	Dotel	Kim	26-49	6th	18.0
6-27	At Ari.	W	12-4		13	8	Elarton	Daal		27-49	6th	18.0
6-28	At Ari.	L	2-6		8	10	Anderson	Lima	Kim	27-50	6th	18.0
6-29	At Ari.	L	1-7		5	10	Johnson	Reynolds		27-51	6th	19.0
6-30	At StL.	L	4-5		6	13	Al. Benes	Holt	Veres	27-52	6th	20.0
7-1	At StL.	L	9-10		15	11	Thompson	Slusarski	Veres	27-53	6th	21.0
7-2	At StL.	W	6-3		10	8	Elarton	Kile	Valdes	28-53	6th	20.0
7-4	Ari.	L	4-10		6	11	Johnson	Lima		28-54	6th	21.0
7-5	Ari.	L	9-12		10	16	Morgan	Valdes	Kim	28-55	6th	22.0
7-6	Ari.	L	1-2		4	4	Guzman	Holt	Mantei	28-56	6th	22.0
7-7	K.C.	W	9-5		10	6	Elarton	Stein		29-56	6th	21.0
7-8	K.C.	L	2-5		9	13	Suzuki	Miller		29-57	6th	21.0
7-9	K.C.	W	9-6		13	10	Lima	Witasick	Dotel	30-57	6th	21.0
7-13	At Det.	L	2-8		11	12	Moehler	Reynolds		30-58	6th	22.0
7-14	At Det.	W	9-4		13	10	Holt	Nomo		31-58	6th	22.0
7-15	At Det.	L	6-11		11	15	Patterson	Henry		31-59	6th	22.0
7-16	At Cle.	W	5-1		9	7	Elarton	Colon		32-59	6th	21.0
7-17	At Cle.	L	6-8		8	9	Drew	Miller	Karsay	32-60	6th	22.0
7-18	At Cle.	L	2-8		11	8	Burba	Reynolds		32-61	6th	22.0
7-19	Cin.	L	0-4		4	7	Harnisch	Holt		32-62	6th	22.0
7-20	Cin.	W	6-2		8	8	Lima	Williamson		33-62	6th	21.0
7-21	StL.	L	1-12		6	16	Ankiel	Elarton		33-63	6th	22.0
7-22	StL.	W	10-5		17	6	Miller	Hentgen		34-63	6th	21.0
7-23	StL.	W	15-7		14	10	Reynolds	An. Benes		35-63	6th	20.0
7-24	At Cin.	W	7-5	(10)	15	7	Dotel	Graves		36-63	6th	19.5
7-25	At Cin.	W	7-4		12	6	Valdes	Villone		37-63	6th	19.5
7-26	At Cin.	W	3-2		11	6	Elarton	Parris	Dotel	38-63	6th	19.5
7-28	At Atl.	L	2-5		7	8	Ashby	Miller	Rocker	38-64	6th	19.0
7-29	At Atl.	L	5-13		12	14	Burkett	Reynolds		38-65	6th	19.0
7-30	At Atl.	L	3-6		8	10	Glavine	Holt	Remlinger	38-66	6th	19.0
7-31	At Fla.	W	4-2		8	9	Lima	Burnett	Dotel	39-66	6th	18.0
8-1	At Fla.	W	4-3		2	6	Elarton	Smith	Dotel	40-66	6th	18.0
8-2	At Fla.	L	4-5		11	8	Miceli	Valdes		40-67	6th	19.0
8-3	At Fla.	L	3-4		6	11	Looper	Slusarski	Alfonseca	40-68	6th	19.5
8-4	Mon.	W	7-6		12	14	Green	Kline	Dotel	41-68	6th	18.5
8-5	Mon.	L	9-10	(10)	15	14	Strickland	Valdes	Kline	41-69	6th	19.5
8-6	Mon.	W	8-1		12	4	Elarton	Thurman		42-69	6th	18.5
8-7	N.Y.	L	5-6	(11)	12	8	Benitez	Green		42-70	6th	19.5
8-8	N.Y.	W	9-3		10	11	B. Powell	Leiter		43-70	6th	18.5
8-9	N.Y.	L	5-12		9	16	Reed	Lima		43-71	6th	19.5
8-10	N.Y.	L	3-10		12	14	B.J. Jones	McKnight		43-72	6th	19.5
8-11	At Phi.	W	7-2		12	7	Valdes	Padilla		44-72	6th	18.5
8-12	At Phi.	L	2-3		7	6	Person	Miller	Brantley	44-73	6th	19.5
8-13	At Phi.	W	14-7		19	8	Cabrera	Daal		45-73	6th	19.5
8-14	Pit.	W	16-2		19	5	Holt	Silva		46-73	6th	18.5
8-15	Pit.	W	5-4		7	9	Lima	Benson	Dotel	47-73	6th	18.5
8-16	Pit.	W	11-10		9	12	Elarton	Serafini	Dotel	48-73	6th	18.5
8-18	Mil.	W	5-4		12	6	Miller	Haynes	Dotel	49-73	6th	18.5
8-19	Mil.	W	10-8		11	8	Cabrera	Acevedo	Dotel	50-73	6th	18.5
8-20	Mil.	L	5-6		7	14	Leskanic	Cabrera		50-74	6th	18.5
8-21	Chi.	W	5-4		6	8	Elarton	Tapani	Slusarski	51-74	6th	18.5
8-22	Chi.	W	10-7		9	8	Valdes	Farnsworth	Cabrera	52-74	6th	17.5
8-23	Chi.	L	5-15		4	19	Quevedo	Miller		52-75	6th	18.5
8-25	At Mon.	W	3-1		7	8	Holt	Lira	Dotel	53-75	5th	18.0
8-26	At Mon.	L	4-5		10	9	Hermanson	Lima	Kline	53-76	5th	19.0
8-27	At Mon.	W	7-3		10	6	Elarton	Moore		54-76	5th	19.0
8-28	At N.Y.	L	2-4		8	6	Rusch	B. Powell	Wendell	54-77	5th	20.0
8-29	At N.Y.	W	11-1		16	5	Miller	Leiter		55-77	5th	19.0
8-30	At N.Y.	L	0-1		3	9	Reed	Holt	Benitez	55-78	5th	20.0
9-1	Atl.	W	3-2		6	7	Lima	Burkett	Dotel	56-78	5th	20.0
9-2	Atl.	L	6-8		10	10	Maddux	Elarton	Rocker	56-79	5th	21.0
9-3	Atl.	W	9-3		15	11	Miller	Ashby		57-79	5th	21.0
9-4	Fla.	L	2-5		5	11	Smith	Holt	Alfonseca	57-80	6th	22.0
9-5	Fla.	W	9-5		15	9	McKnight	Cornelius		58-80	T5th	22.0
9-6	Fla.	W	13-5		14	7	Lima	Sanchez		59-80	T5th	21.0
9-7	Fla.	W	7-3		9	7	Elarton	Miceli		60-80	4th	21.0
9-8	At Chi.	W	13-10		20	10	Miller	Tapani	Dotel	61-80	5th	20.0
9-9	At Chi.	W	14-4		19	9	Holt	Quevedo		62-80	3rd	20.0
9-10	At Chi.	W	7-6		10	13	McKnight	Lieber	Dotel	63-80	3rd	19.0
9-11	S.F	L	7-8	(10)	9	12	Nen	Valdes		63-81	4th	20.0
9-12	S.F	L	5-9		11	12	Estes	Elarton		63-82	4th	21.0
9-13	S.F	L	2-3		8	9	Hernandez	Miller	Nen	64-83	4th	22.0
9-14	Pit.	W	8-7		11	12	Slusarski	Skrmetta		65-83	3rd	22.0
9-15	Pit.	W	16-7		19	12	B. Powell	Skrmetta	Slusarski	66-83	3rd	22.0
9-16	Pit.	W	10-9	(10)	9	16	Valdes	Sauerbeck		67-83	3rd	22.0
9-17	Pit.	W	5-3		9	8	Elarton	Serafini	Dotel	68-83	3rd	22.0
9-19	At StL.	W	8-6	(10)	13	8	Dotel	Al. Benes	Cabrera	68-83	3rd	21.0
9-20	At StL.	L	6-11		9	11	Ankiel	Holt		68-84	3rd	22.0

Date	Opp.	Res.	Score	(inn.*)	Hits	Opp. hits	Winning pitcher	Losing pitcher	Save	Record	Pos.	GB
9-21	At StL.	W	7-5		12	11	McKnight	An. Benes	Dotel	69-84	3rd	21.0
9-22	At Cin.	L	5-12		12	14	Dessens	Lima		69-85	3rd	21.0
9-23	At Cin.	L	4-6		11	12	Riedling	Slusarski	Graves	69-86	T3rd	22.0
9-24	At Cin.	L	3-4		6	7	Sullivan	Dotel		69-87	4th	22.0
9-26	At Pit.	L	4-9		7	10	Benson	Holt		69-88	4th	23.0
9-27	At Pit.	W	10-1		10	4	McKnight	Anderson		70-88	4th	23.0
9-28	At Pit.	L	2-3		10	3	Silva	Dotel		70-89	4th	24.0
9-29	Mil.	L	3-13		7	15	Estrada	Elarton		70-90	4th	24.0
9-30	Mil.	W	7-6		11	11	Miller	Haynes	Dotel	71-90	4th	23.0
10-1	Mil.	W	6-1		8	7	Holt	Wright		72-90	4th	23.0

Monthly records: April (9-14), May (10-19), June (8-19), July (12-14), August (16-12), September (16-12), October (1-0).
*Innings, if other than nine. †First game of a doubleheader. ‡Second game of a doubleheader.

HIGHLIGHTS

High point: The Astros won five straight games in mid-August and went on to complete a 7-2 homestand—their first serious home winning streak of the year. Suddenly the 315-foot left field fence and the monster power alleys didn't seem so adversarial at new Enron Field.

Low point: A 9-7 May 24 loss to the Phillies in which the Astros blew a seven-run lead. The game marked Billy Wagner's fourth straight blown save and dropped the team's record to 16-29. Three weeks later, Wagner was diagnosed with a partially torn flexor muscle in his elbow and eventually submitted to season-ending surgery.

Turning point: September 1-3, when the Astros took two of three from the Braves, kicking off a 17-12 final month and raising hopes for a 2001 rebound.

Most valuable player: Jeff Bagwell batted .310 with 132 RBIs and posted club records for home runs (47) and runs scored (152). More importantly, Bagwell hit .331 with 68 RBIs after the All-Star break, triggering the team's late resurgence.

Most valuable pitcher: Scott Elarton's 17-7 record was remarkable for a team that finished 18 games below .500. Elarton struck out 131 batters in 192 $\frac{2}{3}$ innings, his top numbers as a major leaguer. Elarton won 11 of 12 decisions in one midseason stretch.

Most improved player: Richard Hidalgo, a .259 hitter in three partial seasons, skied to a .314 average with 44 homers and 122 RBIs. His move from right field to center was an important reason for the Astros' second-half defensive improvement.

Most pleasant surprise: Backup catcher Tony Eusebio stepped in for injured starter Mitch Meluskey and put together a club-record 24-game hitting streak in late August and September. Eusebio's sterling relief duty was a big factor in the Astros' second-half rebound.

Key injuries: The struggles and loss of Wagner constituted the biggest blow. The once-dominant lefthanded closer blew nine saves in 15 opportunities before admitting to his elbow problem and opting for the season-ending surgery. ... Third baseman Ken Caminiti, who was hitting .303 with 45 RBIs, went down for the season after 208 at-bats with a rup-tured tendon in his wrist. ... Reliever Jay Powell spent two stints on the disabled list before having shoulder surgery that ended his season in August. ... Second baseman Craig Biggio missed the last 56 games because of knee surgery, his first time ever on the disabled list. ... Outfielder Roger Cedeno missed 75 games with a broken hand. ... Righthander Shane Reynolds missed the last six weeks with back problems.

Notable: For the first time in Larry Dierker's four years as manager, the team did not win the Central Division. ... Jose Lima allowed an N.L.-record 48 home runs, beating his old club record of 34 by mid-July. Lima, who finished 7-16, also set a club mark with 13 straight losses. ... Bagwell (47) and Hidalgo (44) both broke Bagwell's former franchise record of 43 home runs in a season. ... The team's 249 home runs were an N.L. record, topping Colorado's 239 in 1997. And it wasn't all Enron Field. The team hit 114 homers on the road. ... The Astros set a major league record by hitting six or more homers five times. ... In their first season at Enron, the Astros topped three million in attendance—a season record for any sports franchise in Texas.

—JIM CARLEY

RECORDS

2000 regular-season record: 72-90 (4th in N.L. Central); 39-42 at home; 33-48 on road; 20-22 vs. East; 41-36 vs. Central; 11-32 vs. West; 15-21 vs. lefthanded starters; 57-69 vs. righthanded starters; 62-79 on grass; 10-11 on turf; 22-31 in daytime; 50-59 at night; 15-31 in one-run games; 6-9 in extra-inning games; 0-1-0 in doubleheaders.
Team record past five years: 437-373 (.540, ranks 3rd in league in that span).

TEAM LEADERS

Batting average: Moises Alou (.355).
At-bats: Jeff Bagwell (590).
Runs: Jeff Bagwell (152).
Hits: Jeff Bagwell (183).
Total Bases: Jeff Bagwell (363).
Doubles: Richard Hidalgo (42).
Triples: Craig Biggio, Roger Cedeno, Julio Lugo (5).
Home runs: Jeff Bagwell (47).
Runs batted in: Jeff Bagwell (132).
Stolen bases: Roger Cedeno (25).
Slugging percentage: Richard Hidalgo (.636).
On-base percentage: Jeff Bagwell (.424).
Wins: Scott Elarton (17).
Earned-run average: Scott Elarton (4.81).
Complete games: Chris Holt (3).
Shutouts: Chris Holt (1).
Saves: Octavio Dotel (16).
Innings pitched: Chris Holt (207.0).
Strikeouts: Octavio Dotel (142).

GAMES BY POSITION

Catcher: Mitch Meluskey 103, Tony Eusebio 68, Raul Chavez 14, Paul Bako 1, Frank Charles 1.
First base: Jeff Bagwell 158, Daryle Ward 19, Lance Berkman 2.
Second base: Craig Biggio 100, Julio Lugo 45, Bill Spiers 26, Russ Johnson 3, Tim Bogar 2, Keith Ginter 2, Tripp Cromer 1.
Third base: Chris Truby 74, Ken Caminiti 58, Bill Spiers 51, Russ Johnson 4, Tripp Cromer 2, Tim Bogar 1, Morgan Ensberg 1, Mitch Meluskey 1.
Shortstop: Tim Bogar 95, Julio Lugo 60, Bill Spiers 27, Russ Johnson 5, Tripp Cromer 1.
Outfield: Richard Hidalgo 151, Moises Alou 121, Lance Berkman 96, Glen Barker 69, Roger Cedeno 67, Daryle Ward 47, Matt Mieske 18, Bill Spiers 10, Julio Lugo 6.
Designated hitter: Daryle Ward 4, Moises Alou 1, Jeff Bagwell 1.

TOP DRAFT CHOICES

1. **Robert Stiehl**, RHP, El Camino (Calif.) J.C.
2. **Chad Qualls**, RHP, Univ. of Nevada.
3. **Anthony Pluta**, RHP, Las Vegas (Nev.) H.S.
4. **Eric Keefner**, 3B, De la Salle H.S., Bridgeview, Ill.
5. **Jake Whitesides**, OF, Hickman H.S., Columbia, Mo.
6. **Tommy Whiteman**, SS, University of Oklahoma.
7. **Joe Lydic**, 3B, Univ. of Pittsburgh.
8. **Cory Doyne**, RHP, Land O'Lakes, H.S., Lutz, Fla.
9. **Eric Bruntlett**, SS, Stanford University.
10. **Nate Nelson**, 3B, University of Louisiana-Lafayette.

LOS ANGELES DODGERS
NATIONAL LEAGUE WEST DIVISION

Dodgers 2001 SCHEDULE
Home games shaded; D—Day game (games starting before 5 p.m.)
*—All-Star Game at Safeco Field (Seattle)

APRIL

SUN	MON	TUE	WED	THU	FRI	SAT
1	2 MIL	3 ARI	4 ARI	5 ARI	6 SF	7 SF
8 SF	9	10 ARI	11 ARI	12 ARI	13 SD	14 SD
15 SD	D 16	17 SF	18 SF	19 SF	20 SD	21 SD
22 SD	D 23	24 PIT	25 PIT	26 PIT	27 PHI	28 PHI
29 PHI	D 30					

MAY

SUN	MON	TUE	WED	THU	FRI	SAT
		1 CIN	2 CIN	3 CIN	4 CUB	D 5 CUB
6 CUB	D 7 FLA	8 FLA	9 FLA	10 FLA	11 ATL	12 ATL
13 ATL	D 14	15 MON	16 MON	17 MON	18 NYM	19 NYM D
20 NYM	D 21 COL	22 COL	23 COL D	24	25 HOU	26 HOU
27 HOU	D 28 COL	D 29 COL	30 COL	31		

JUNE

SUN	MON	TUE	WED	THU	FRI	SAT
					1 HOU	2 HOU D
3 HOU D	4 ARI	5 ARI	6 ARI	7 ARI D	8 ANA	9 ANA D
10 ANA	11 TEX	12 TEX	13 TEX	14	15 ANA	16 ANA
17 ANA	D 18	19 ARI	20 ARI	21	22 SD	23 SD
24 SD	D 25 SF	26 SF	27 SF	D 28 SD	29 SD	30 SD

JULY

SUN	MON	TUE	WED	THU	FRI	SAT
1 SD	D 2 SF	3 SF	4 SF	5 SF	6 SEA	7 SEA D
8 SEA	9	10 *	11	12 OAK	13 OAK	14 OAK D
15 PIT	16 PIT	17 PIT	18 MIL	19 MIL	20 COL	21 COL D
22 COL	D 23 MIL	24 MIL	25 MIL D	26 COL	27 COL	28 COL
29 COL	30	31 CIN				

AUGUST

SUN	MON	TUE	WED	THU	FRI	SAT
			1 CIN	2 CIN	3 CUB	4 CUB D
5 CUB	6	7 PIT	8 PIT	9 PIT	10 PHI	11 PHI
12 PHI	D 13	14 MON	15 MON	16 MON D	17 NYM	18 NYM
19 NYM	D 20	21 FLA	22 FLA	23 FLA	24 ATL	25 ATL
26 ATL	D 27 ATL	28 COL	29 COL	30 COL	31 STL	

SEPTEMBER

SUN	MON	TUE	WED	THU	FRI	SAT
						1 STL
2 STL	3	4 COL	5 COL	6 COL	7 STL	8 STL D
9 STL	10	11 SD	12 SD	13 SD D	14 SF	15 SF D
16 SF	D 17 SD	18 SD	19 SD	20 SD	21 ARI	22 ARI
23 ARI	D 24 SF	25 SF	26 SF	27	28 ARI	29 ARI
30 ARI	D					

2001 SEASON
CLUB DIRECTORY

President and CEO
Bob Graziano

Board of directors
Chase Carey, Peter Chernin, Peter O'Malley, Bob Graziano, Sam Fernandez

Executive vice president and g.m.
Kevin Malone

Executive vice president and CMO
Kris Rone

Senior vice president, communications
Derrick Hall

Senior vice president
Tommy Lasorda

Vice president, external affairs
Tommy Hawkins

Traveling secretary
Billy DeLury

Sr. vice president and general counsel
Santiago Fernandez

Vice president, spring training/minor league facilities
Craig Callan

Director of player development
Jerry Weinstein

Director, finance and CFO
Christine Hurley

Dir. of management info. services
Mike Mularky

Director of sales and marketing
Sergio Del Prado

Director, public relations
John Olguin

Assistant director, team travel
Shaun Rachau

Dir., broadcasting and new media
Brent Shyer

Director, community relations
Don Newcombe

Vice president, stadium operations
Doug Duennes

Director, ticket operations
Billy Hunter

Assistant to the g.m., scouting
Ed Creech

Director, scouting operations
Matt Slater

Head trainer
Stan Johnston

Assistant trainer
Matt Wilson

Physical therapist
Pat Screnar

Strength and conditioning
Todd Clausen

Club physicians
Dr. Frank Jobe, Dr. Michael Mellman, Dr. Herndon Harding

Special asst. to the general manager
Jeff Schugel

Senior scouting advisor
Don Welke

Pro scouts
Dan Freed, Carl Loewenstine, Vance Lovelace, Claude Osteen, Terry Reynolds, Ron Rizzi, Mark Weidemaier

Full-time scouts
John Barr, Gib Bodet, Mike Brito, Doug Carpenter, James Chapman, Bobby Darwin, Joseph Ferrone, Scott Groot, Michael Hankins, Clarence Johns, Hank Jones, Lon Joyce, Pat Kelly, John Kosciak, Marty Lamb, Jimmy Lester, Michael Leuzinger, James Merriweather, Camilio Pascual, Pablo Peguero, Bill Pleis, Scott Sharp, Mark Sheehy, Chris Smith, Bob Szymkowski, Thomas Thomas, Mitch Webster

---

MINOR LEAGUE AFFILIATES

Class	Team	League	Manager
AAA	Las Vegas	Pacific Coast	Rick Sofield
AA	Jacksonville	Southern	John Shoemaker
A	Vero Beach	Florida State	Dino Ebel
A	Wilmington	South Atlantic	To be announced
Rookie	Great Falls	Pioneer	Dave Silvestri
Rookie	Gulf Coast Dodgers	Gulf Coast	Juan Bustabad

BROADCAST INFORMATION

Radio: XTRA-AM (1150); KWKW-AM (1330, Spanish language).
TV: KTLA-TV (Channel 5)
Cable TV: Fox Sports West 2.

SPRING TRAINING

Ballpark (city): Holman Stadium (Vero Beach, Fla.).
Ticket information: 561-569-6858.

Follow the Dodgers all season at: www.sportingnews.com/baseball/teams/dodgers/

2001 SEASON *Los Angeles Dodgers*

Manager—Jim Tracy (12).
Coaches—Jack Clark (44), Jim Colborn (45), Glenn Hoffman (35), Jim Lett (17), Manny Mota (5), Jim Riggleman (5), John Shelby (31).

No.	PITCHERS	B/T	Ht./Wt.	Born	2000 clubs
51	Adams, Terry	R/R	6-3/215	3-6-73	Los Angeles
43	Ashby, Andy	R/R	6-1/202	7-11-67	Philadelphia, Atlanta
27	Brown, Kevin	R/R	6-4/200	3-14-65	Los Angeles
60	Burnside, Adrian	R/L	6-3/168	3-15-77	San Antonio
37	Dreifort, Darren	R/R	6-2/211	5-3-72	Los Angeles
56	Fetters, Mike	R/R	6-4/226	12-19-64	Los Angeles
67	Foster, Kris	R/R	6-1/200	6-30-74	San Bernardino
48	Gagne, Eric	R/R	6-2/195	1-7-76	Albuquerque, Los Angeles
49	Herges, Matt	L/R	6-0/200	4-1-70	Los Angeles
60	Judd, Mike	R/R	6-1/217	6-30-75	Albuquerque, Los Angeles
	Martinez, Ramon	R/R	6-4/184	3-22-68	Boston
40	Masaoka, Onan	R/L	6-0/188	10-27-77	Los Angeles, Albuquerque
	Nunez, Jose	L/L	6-2/175	3-14-79	Columbia
30	Olson, Gregg	R/R	6-4/208	10-11-66	Los Angeles, San Bernardino, Albuquerque
13	Osuna, Antonio	R/R	5-11/206	4-12-73	Los Angeles, San Bernardino, Albuquerque
61	Park, Chan Ho	R/R	6-2/204	6-30-73	Los Angeles
33	Perez, Carlos	L/L	6-3/210	1-14-71	Los Angeles
	Prokopec, Luke	L/R	5-11/166	2-23-78	San Antonio, Los Angeles
32	Reyes, Al	R/R	6-1/206	4-10-71	Rochester, Baltimore, Albuquerque, Los Angeles
63	Ricketts, Chad	R/R	6-5/225	2-12-75	Albuquerque
41	Shaw, Jeff	R/R	6-2/200	7-7-66	Los Angeles
54	Williams, Jeff	R/L	6-0/185	6-6-72	Albuquerque, Los Angeles

No.	CATCHERS	B/T	Ht./Wt.	Born	2000 clubs
21	Kreuter, Chad	B/R	6-2/200	8-26-64	Los Angeles
16	LoDuca, Paul	R/R	5-10/185	4-12-72	Albuquerque, Los Angeles
36	Pena, Angel	R/R	5-10/228	2-16-75	Albuquerque

No.	INFIELDERS	B/T	Ht./Wt.	Born	2000 clubs
	Allen, Luke	L/R	6-2/208	8-4-78	San Antonio
29	Beltre, Adrian	R/R	5-11/170	4-7-79	Los Angeles
66	Bocachica, Hiram	R/R	5-11/165	3-4-76	Albuquerque, Los Angeles
3	Cora, Alex	L/R	6-0/180	10-18-75	Albuquerque, Los Angeles
3	Donnels, Chris	L/R	6-0/185	4-21-66	Albuquerque, Los Angeles
8	Grudzielanek, Mark	R/R	6-1/185	6-30-70	Los Angeles
25	Hansen, Dave	L/R	6-0/195	11-24-68	Los Angeles
23	Karros, Eric	R/R	6-4/226	11-4-67	Los Angeles

No.	OUTFIELDERS	B/T	Ht./Wt.	Born	2000 clubs
37	Aven, Bruce	R/R	5-9/180	3-4-72	Pittsburgh, Nashville, Albuquerque, Los Angeles
24	Goodwin, Tom	L/R	6-1/175	7-27-68	Colorado, Los Angeles
15	Green, Shawn	L/L	6-4/200	11-10-72	Los Angeles
14	Santangelo, F.P.	B/R	5-10/190	10-24-67	Los Angeles, San Bernardino
10	Sheffield, Gary	R/R	5-11/205	11-18-68	Los Angeles
22	White, Devon	B/R	6-2/190	12-29-62	Los Angeles, San Bernardino

BALLPARK INFORMATION

Ballpark (capacity, surface)
Dodger Stadium (56,000, grass)
Address
1000 Elysian Park Ave.
Los Angeles, CA 90012
Official website
www.dodgers.com
Business phone
323-224-1500
Ticket information
323-224-1448
Ticket prices
$17 (field box)
$15 (inner reserve)
$13 (loge box)
$10 (outer reserve)
$6 (top deck, left and right pavilion)
Field dimensions (from home plate)
To left field at foul line, 330 feet
To center field, 395 feet
To right field at foul line, 330 feet
First game played
April 10, 1962 (Reds 6, Dodgers 3)

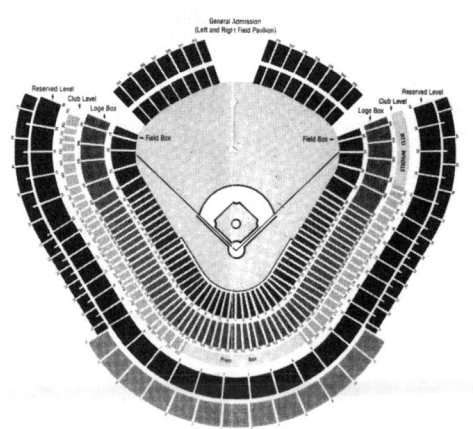

2001 SEASON *Los Angeles Dodgers*

Date	Opp.	Res.	Score	(inn.*)	Hits	Opp. hits	Winning pitcher	Losing pitcher	Save	Record	Pos.	GB
4-3	At Mon.	W	10-4		9	9	Brown	Hermanson	Adams	1-0	1st	+0.5
4-4	At Mon.	W	10-4		17	6	Park	Irabu		2-0	T1st	+0.5
4-5	At Mon.	L	5-6		12	10	Telford	Shaw		2-1	T2nd	0.5
4-6	At Mon.	L	3-11		6	14	Pavano	Perez		2-2	T3rd	1.5
4-7	At N.Y.	L	1-2		4	2	Reed	Dreifort	Benitez	2-3	4th	1.5
4-8	At N.Y.	W	6-5	(10)	9	11	Fetters	Benitez	Shaw	3-3	T3rd	1.5
4-11	At S.F	W	6-5		12	8	Park	Rueter	Shaw	4-3	2nd	1.5
4-12	At S.F	W	6-5		8	7	Adams	Weber	Shaw	5-3	2nd	1.0
4-13	At S.F	W	11-7		13	11	Perez	Gardner	Shaw	6-3	2nd	0.5
4-14	Cin.	W	8-1		9	9	Hershiser	Bell		7-3	2nd	0.5
4-15	Cin.	L	4-5		7	8	Williamson	Mills	Graves	7-4	2nd	1.5
4-16	Cin.	L	3-5		6	7	Parris	Park	Graves	7-5	2nd	2.0
4-18	Hou.	W	5-3		8	5	Dreifort	Dotel	Shaw	8-5	2nd	1.5
4-19	Hou.	L	3-10		7	14	Reynolds	Hershiser		8-6	2nd	2.5
4-21	At Cin.	W	9-2		11	10	Herges	Parris	Adams	9-6	2nd	2.0
4-22	At Cin.	W	16-2		15	5	Park	Harnisch	Mills	10-6	2nd	1.0
4-23	At Cin.	W	11-3		11	13	Perez	Villone		11-6	1st	...
4-24	At N.Y.	L	0-1		3	8	Benitez	Adams		11-7	2nd	0.5
4-25	At Atl.	L	0-1		3	6	Glavine	Brown		11-8	2nd	1.5
4-26	At Atl.	L	1-5		5	9	Millwood	Gagne		11-9	2nd	2.5
4-27	At Atl.	L	3-6		9	9	Mulholland	Park	Rocker	11-10	2nd	2.5
4-28	Fla.	W	5-3		9	7	Adams	Penny	Shaw	12-10	2nd	1.5
4-29	Fla.	W	13-12		17	12	Shaw	Alfonseca		13-10	2nd	1.5
4-30	Fla.	W	7-1		9	3	Brown	Fernandez		14-10	2nd	1.5
5-1	Atl.	L	1-2		6	6	Millwood	Gagne	Rocker	14-11	2nd	2.0
5-2	Atl.	L	3-5		11	6	Chen	Adams	Rocker	14-12	2nd	3.0
5-3	Atl.	W	6-4		9	6	Perez	Maddux	Shaw	15-12	2nd	2.0
5-5	Hou.	W	3-2		9	4	Shaw	Henry		16-12	2nd	2.5
5-6	Hou.	W	9-6		7	12	Dreifort	Dotel		17-12	2nd	2.5
5-7	Hou.	L	8-14	(10)	12	17	Wagner	Shaw		17-13	2nd	3.5
5-8	At Ari.	L	7-15		7	20	Daal	Park		17-14	3rd	4.5
5-9	At Ari.	L	7-11	(12)	15	15	Padilla	Hershiser		17-15	3rd	5.5
5-10	At Ari.	L	1-2		9	9	Kim	Adams		17-16	3rd	6.5
5-12	At StL.	W	13-0		13	2	Dreifort	Kile		18-16	3rd	6.5
5-13	At StL.	W	3-1		7	3	Park	Veres	Shaw	19-16	3rd	6.5
5-14	At StL.	L	10-12		11	17	Slocumb	Perez	Veres	19-17	2nd	6.5
5-16	At Chi.	W	6-5		9	7	Mills	Tapani	Shaw	20-17	2nd	5.5
5-17	At Chi.	W	8-6		9	7	Mills	Heredia	Shaw	21-17	2nd	4.5
5-19	At Fla.	W	5-3		8	7	Herges	Looper	Shaw	22-17	2nd	4.0
5-20	At Fla.	W	12-6		15	14	Perez	Penny		23-17	2nd	3.0
5-21	At Fla.	W	12-3		17	7	Brown	Sanchez		24-17	2nd	2.0
5-22	Cin.	W	4-3	(14)	9	10	Herges	Aybar		25-17	2nd	1.5
5-23	Cin.	L	1-3		3	7	Fernandez	Gagne	Graves	25-18	2nd	2.5
5-24	Cin.	L	3-10		7	11	Sullivan	Park		25-19	2nd	3.5
5-26	Phi.	W	11-4		10	8	Brown	Byrd		26-19	2nd	4.0
5-27	Phi.	L	6-7		10	9	Person	Dreifort	Brantley	26-20	2nd	5.0
5-28	Phi.	L	2-4		6	12	Wolf	Osuna		26-21	2nd	5.0
5-29	N.Y.	W	4-1		8	4	Park	Leiter		27-21	2nd	4.0
5-30	N.Y.	L	5-10		13	13	Franco	Shaw		27-22	T2nd	4.0
5-31	N.Y.	W	4-3		6	8	Fetters	Wendell		28-22	T2nd	4.0
6-2	At Ana.	L	5-12		11	18	Bottenfield	Dreifort		28-23	3rd	5.5
6-3	At Ana.	W	8-3		9	12	Park	Cooper		29-23	T2nd	4.5
6-4	At Ana.	L	7-8		11	9	Percival	Osuna		29-24	3rd	4.5
6-5	At Tex.	L	0-2		2	5	Glynn	Brown	Wetteland	29-25	3rd	4.5
6-6	At Tex.	W	7-1		14	6	Gagne	Clark		30-25	T2nd	3.5
6-7	At Tex.	W	11-6		15	12	Dreifort	Helling		31-25	T2nd	2.5
6-8	Hou.	W	5-2		9	6	Park	Holt	Fetters	32-25	2nd	2.0
6-9	Oak.	L	1-3		5	4	Tam	Osuna	Isringhausen	32-26	3rd	3.0
6-10	Oak.	W	7-2		13	7	Brown	Olivares		33-26	3rd	2.0
6-11	Oak.	L	0-6		7	7	Appier	Gagne		33-27	3rd	3.0
6-12	Ari.	L	2-4		8	5	Anderson	Dreifort	Kim	33-28	3rd	4.0
6-13	Ari.	W	6-1		10	5	Park	Morgan		34-28	3rd	3.0
6-14	Ari.	L	1-5		6	11	Johnson	Perez		34-29	3rd	4.0
6-15	Ari.	W	4-0		8	4	Brown	Stottlemyre		35-29	3rd	3.0
6-16	StL.	L	3-6		7	9	Hentgen	Hershiser	Veres	35-30	3rd	3.5
6-17	StL.	L	3-4		8	13	An. Benes	Dreifort	Veres	35-31	3rd	3.5
6-18	StL.	W	6-3		8	7	Park	Kile	Shaw	36-31	3rd	2.5
6-20	At Hou.	W	9-6	(10)	18	13	Herges	Slusarski		37-31	3rd	2.0
6-21	At Hou.	W	7-6		13	7	Herges	Cabrera		38-31	3rd	2.0
6-22	At Hou.	L	3-6		6	7	Elarton	Dreifort	Valdes	38-32	3rd	2.5
6-23	At StL.	L	6-9	(12)	10	9	Stechschulte	Shaw		38-33	3rd	3.5
6-24	At StL.	L	1-6		6	9	Al. Benes	Hershiser		38-34	3rd	3.5
6-25	At StL.	L	1-2		6	6	Slocumb	Osuna		38-35	4th	4.5
6-26	S.D.	L	5-9		7	9	Meadows	Hershiser		38-36	4th	5.5

Date	Opp.	Res.	Score	(inn.*)	Hits	Opp. hits	Winning pitcher	Losing pitcher	Save	Record	Pos.	GB
6-27	S.D.	W	5-4	(10)	10	7	Fetters	Whiteside		39-36	T3rd	4.5
6-28	S.D.	W	5-4		7	6	Adams	Montgomery		40-36	3rd	4.5
6-29	S.D.	L	4-5		6	7	Clement	Dreifort	Hoffman	40-37	3rd	5.5
6-30	At S.F	W	9-2		13	6	Brown	Ortiz		41-37	3rd	4.5
7-1	At S.F	L	1-4		9	10	Rueter	Perez	Nen	41-38	3rd	5.5
7-2	At S.F	L	5-6		13	10	Nen	Fetters		41-39	4th	5.5
7-4	At S.D.	L	2-7		4	9	Clement	Park		41-40	4th	6.0
7-5	At S.D.	W	7-5		11	11	Osuna	Whiteside	Fetters	42-40	4th	6.0
7-6	At S.D.	W	9-3		14	5	Brown	Meadows		43-40	4th	6.0
7-7	At Sea.	W	3-2	(11)	5	12	Herges	Rhodes	Fetters	44-40	4th	5.0
7-8	At Sea.	L	0-11		5	10	Sele	Gagne		44-41	4th	6.0
7-9	At Sea.	L	0-2		7	4	Moyer	Park	Sasaki	44-42	4th	6.0
7-13	Ana.	W	4-3	(10)	8	9	Osuna	Levine		45-42	4th	5.0
7-14	Ana.	L	3-5		8	11	Bottenfield	Brown	Percival	45-43	4th	6.0
7-15	Ana.	L	2-6		6	10	Etherton	Park		45-44	4th	6.0
7-16	Pit.	W	7-3		8	7	Adams	Williams		46-44	T3rd	5.0
7-17	Pit.	W	9-6		12	10	Dreifort	Arroyo	Shaw	47-44	3rd	5.0
7-18	Pit.	L	6-8		12	8	Manzanillo	Judd	Williams	47-45	4th	5.0
7-19	Col.	W	9-1		9	1	Brown	Arrojo		48-45	3rd	5.0
7-20	Col.	W	6-3		10	5	Park	Yoshii	Fetters	49-45	3rd	5.0
7-21	S.F	W	6-5		7	11	Herges	Rodriguez	Shaw	50-45	3rd	5.0
7-22	S.F	L	2-5		5	6	Hernandez	Gagne	Nen	50-46	3rd	5.0
7-23	S.F	W	5-0		10	2	Dreifort	Ortiz		51-46	3rd	4.0
7-24	At Col.	W	4-1		11	5	Brown	Arrojo	Fetters	52-46	3rd	3.5
7-25	At Col.	W	6-4		8	11	Park	Chouinard	Shaw	53-46	3rd	2.5
7-26	At Col.	L	4-11		6	14	Bohanon	Perez		53-47	3rd	2.5
7-27	At Col.	W	16-11		20	15	Masaoka	Carrara		54-47	3rd	2.5
7-28	At Phi.	W	2-0		7	2	Dreifort	Daal	Shaw	55-47	3rd	2.5
7-29	At Phi.	L	0-3		6	7	Politte	Brown	Brantley	55-48	3rd	2.5
7-30	At Phi.	L	2-3		4	9	Wolf	Park	Brantley	55-49	3rd	2.5
8-1†	At Pit.	L	0-6		6	12	Anderson	Perez		55-50		
8-1‡	At Pit.	W	5-3		7	8	Herges	Wilkins	Shaw	56-50	3rd	3.0
8-2	At Pit.	W	11-5		11	10	Dreifort	Silva		57-50	3rd	2.0
8-4	Mil.	W	2-1		7	6	Fetters	Acevedo		58-50	3rd	2.5
8-5	Mil.	L	2-4	(10)	7	10	Acevedo	Fetters	Leskanic	58-51	3rd	2.5
8-6	Mil.	L	6-9		12	15	Haynes	Valdes	Leskanic	58-52	3rd	3.5
8-7	Chi.	L	3-7		7	10	Quevedo	Herges		58-53	3rd	4.5
8-8	Chi.	W	7-5		13	8	Dreifort	Norton	Shaw	59-53	3rd	4.5
8-9	Chi.	L	4-5	(10)	8	10	Worrell	Osuna	Aguilera	59-54	3rd	5.5
8-11	At Atl.	L	2-7		5	12	Remlinger	Adams		59-55	3rd	5.5
8-12	At Atl.	L	1-4		7	6	Maddux	Valdes	Ligtenberg	59-56	3rd	5.5
8-13	At Atl.	W	7-2		11	14	Dreifort	Ashby		60-56	3rd	4.5
8-14	At Fla.	L	2-11		10	12	Sanchez	Brown		60-57	3rd	5.5
8-15	At Fla.	L	3-7		6	12	Dempster	Herges		60-58	3rd	6.5
8-16	At Fla.	W	10-4		11	13	Adams	Miceli		61-58	3rd	6.5
8-18	N.Y.	L	3-5		8	10	White	Adams	Benitez	61-59	3rd	8.0
8-19	N.Y.	W	4-1		9	4	Park	Reed		62-59	3rd	8.0
8-20	N.Y.	L	6-9		11	10	Wendell	Adams	Benitez	62-60	3rd	8.0
8-21	Mon.	L	1-4		8	9	Hermanson	Herges	Strickland	62-61	3rd	9.0
8-22	Mon.	W	14-6		16	13	Adams	Santana		63-61	3rd	8.0
8-23	Mon.	W	5-1		6	4	Brown	Thurman		64-61	3rd	8.0
8-24	Mon.	W	7-0		11	5	Park	Vazquez		65-61	3rd	7.5
8-25†	At Chi.	W	5-3		13	10	Osuna	Lieber	Shaw	66-61		
8-25‡	At Chi.	W	3-1		5	9	Perez	Garibay	Shaw	67-61	3rd	7.0
8-26	At Chi.	L	4-6		9	8	Worrell	Olson	Aguilera	67-62	3rd	7.0
8-27	At Chi.	W	7-6	(10)	9	13	Fetters	Van Poppel	Shaw	68-62	3rd	6.0
8-28	At Mil.	W	5-3		10	7	Brown	D'Amico	Shaw	69-62	3rd	6.0
8-29	At Mil.	W	7-2		8	1	Park	Haynes		70-62	3rd	5.0
8-30	At Mil.	L	2-3		6	6	King	Adams		70-63	3rd	6.0
8-31	At Mil.	L	2-8		8	14	Rigdon	Perez		70-64	3rd	7.0
9-1	Phi.	W	2-1		7	4	Fetters	Brock	Shaw	71-64	3rd	7.0
9-2	Phi.	W	1-0	(10)	6	6	Herges	Padilla		72-64	3rd	7.0
9-3	Phi.	W	6-1		9	4	Park	Person	Shaw	73-64	3rd	7.0
9-4	Pit.	L	1-12		10	13	Anderson	Dreifort		73-65	3rd	8.0
9-5	Pit.	L	0-8		6	15	Silva	Perez		73-66	3rd	9.0
9-6	Pit.	L	3-8		6	12	Serafini	Valdes		73-67	3rd	10.0
9-8	At Col.	L	5-8		9	14	Bohanon	Brown		73-68	3rd	10.5
9-9	At Col.	L	6-7		7	13	White	Park	Jimenez	73-69	4th	10.5
9-10	At Col.	W	12-1		12	5	Dreifort	Astacio	Herges	74-69	3rd	10.5
9-11	At Ari.	W	6-3		11	6	Gagne	Reynoso		75-69	3rd	10.5
9-12	At Ari.	L	4-5		7	8	Kim	Masaoka	Mantei	75-70	3rd	11.5
9-13	At Ari.	L	2-3		5	9	Plesac	Adams		75-71	4th	12.5
9-14	Col.	L	4-5		8	9	Rose	Park	Jimenez	75-72	4th	13.0
9-15	Col.	W	4-3	(10)	5	5	Herges	DeJean		76-72	4th	12.0
9-16	Col.	W	5-4		7	13	Gagne	Tavarez	Shaw	77-72	3rd	12.0
9-17	Col.	W	12-6		12	11	Prokopec	Yoshii		78-72	3rd	12.0
9-18	Ari.	W	2-1		6	9	Shaw	Swindell		79-72	3rd	11.0
9-19	Ari.	W	1-0		7	6	Park	Anderson	Shaw	80-72	3rd	11.0

Date	Opp.	Res.	Score	(inn.*)	Hits	Opp. hits	Winning pitcher	Losing pitcher	Save	Record	Pos.	GB
										81-72	2nd	11.0
9-20	Ari.	W	1-0		7	9	Herges	Kim		81-73	3rd	11.5
9-22	S.D.	L	2-3		8	7	Maurer	Osuna	Hoffman	82-73	2nd	11.0
9-23	S.D.	W	2-1		5	2	Brown	Williams		83-73	2nd	10.0
9-24	S.D.	W	1-0		3	2	Park	Clement	Shaw	84-73	2nd	9.0
9-26	S.F	W	9-0		9	2	Dreifort	Ortiz		84-74	2nd	10.0
9-27	S.F	L	0-4		6	5	Rueter	Prokopec		84-75	T2nd	11.0
9-28	S.F	L	3-5		5	10	Fultz	Adams	Nen	85-75	2nd	11.0
9-29	At S.D.	W	3-0		6	2	Park	Williams		86-75	2nd	10.0
9-30	At S.D.	W	10-2		9	6	Gagne	Clement				
10-1	At S.D.	L	0-4		7	7	Eaton	Dreifort	Hoffman	86-76	2nd	11.0

Monthly records: April (14-10), May (14-12), June (13-15), July (14-12), August (15-15), September (16-11), October (0-1).
*Innings, if other than nine. †First game of a doubleheader. ‡Second game of a doubleheader.

HIGHLIGHTS

High point: A six-game winning streak put the Dodgers a season-high eight games above .500 (25-17) on May 22. The rotation, bullpen, everyday lineup and bench were productive, providing fans with hope after several disappointing seasons. It wouldn't last long.

Low point: After going 2-8, including losing streaks of five and three games, the Dodgers dropped to fourth place (a season-high 13 games out of first) on September 14. They also were out of the wild-card race and the season couldn't end soon enough.

Turning point: Chairman Bob Daly criticized Davey Johnson in the *Los Angeles Times* at the All-Star break, eroding whatever team confidence remained for the embattled manager. From that point, the focus was taken off the field and put on Johnson, who was fired after the season.

Most valuable player: Left fielder Gary Sheffield. The six-time All-Star became the first player in franchise history to twice bat at least .300 with 30 home runs, 100 runs batted in, 100 runs and 100 walks. Sheffield's consistency was impressive.

Most valuable pitcher: Kevin Brown. Don't be fooled by the righthander's seemingly mediocre 13-6 record. Brown led the N. L. with a 2.58 earned-run average. He gave up three or fewer earned runs in 28 of 33 starts, and one or less in 14.

Most improved player: Chan Ho Park. The hard-throwing righthander had a breakthrough season, going 18-10 with a 3.27 ERA and 217 strikeouts in 226 innings. He benefited greatly from the tutelage of veteran catcher Chad Kreuter.

Most pleasant surprise: Matt Herges. The 30-year-old rookie reliever was 11-3 with a 3.17 ERA, pitching 110 2/3 innings in 59 appearances. Herges won his first eight decisions, the best start by a Dodger since Fernando Valenzuela won his first eight in 1981.

Key injuries: Pitcher Kevin Brown was on the disabled list 15 days in April because of a broken pinky finger. ... Catcher Todd Hundley played in only 90 games because of a strained oblique muscle and broken thumb. ... Lefthander

Carlos Perez underwent arthroscopic surgery on his pitching shoulder in September. ... Closer Jeff Shaw went on the disabled list (elbow tendinitis) for the first time in his career.

Notable: Sheffield hit 43 home runs, setting a Los Angeles record and matching Duke Snider's single-season franchise mark. ... First baseman Eric Karros became the all-time Los Angeles franchise leader with 242 homers, eclipsing Ron Cey's previous mark of 228. ... Infielder Dave Hansen broke baseball's single-season pinch-hit home run record with seven. ... The bullpen had a 3.76 ERA—the lowest in the majors. ... The Dodgers were 42-39 on the road. Only the Atlanta Braves and St. Louis Cardinals had more road wins in the N.L.

—JASON REID

RECORDS

2000 regular-season record: 86-76 (2nd in N.L. West); 44-37 at home; 42-39 on road; 23-21 vs. East; 27-25 vs. Central; 36-30 vs. West; 19-25 vs. lefthanded starters; 67-51 vs. righthanded starters; 78-71 on grass; 8-5 on turf; 23-22 in daytime; 63-54 at night; 25-21 in one-run games; 9-5 in extra-inning games; 1-0-1 in doubleheaders.

Team record past five years: 424-386 (.523, ranks 5th in league in that span).

TEAM LEADERS

Batting average: Gary Sheffield (.325).
At-bats: Mark Grudzielanek (617).
Runs: Gary Sheffield (105).
Hits: Mark Grudzielanek (172).
Total Bases: Gary Sheffield (322).
Doubles: Shawn Green (44).
Triples: Alex Cora, Mark Grudzielanek (6).
Home runs: Gary Sheffield (43).
Runs batted in: Gary Sheffield (109).
Stolen bases: Shawn Green (24).
Slugging percentage: Gary Sheffield (.643).
On-base percentage: Gary Sheffield (.438).
Wins: Chan Ho Park (18).
Earned-run average: Kevin Brown (2.58).
Complete games: Kevin Brown (5).

Shutouts: Kevin Brown, Darren Dreifort, Chan Ho Park (1).
Saves: Jeff Shaw (27).
Innings pitched: Kevin Brown (230.0).
Strikeouts: Chan Ho Park (217).

GAMES BY POSITION

Catcher: Todd Hundley 84, Chad Kreuter 78, Paul LoDuca 20, Jim Leyritz 3.
First base: Eric Karros 153, Dave Hansen 16, Jim Leyritz 8, Chris Donnels 4, Geronimo Berroa 2, Kevin Elster 1, Jose Vizcaino 1.
Second base: Mark Grudzielanek 148, Alex Cora 8, F.P. Santangelo 7, Jeff Branson 3, Jose Vizcaino 3, Hiram Bocachica 2, Chris Donnels 1, Mike Metcalfe 1.
Third base: Adrian Beltre 138, Dave Hansen 16, Jose Vizcaino 12, Kevin Elster 8, Jeff Branson 3, Chris Donnels 2, Paul LoDuca 1.
Shortstop: Alex Cora 101, Kevin Elster 55, Jose Vizcaino 19, Jeff Branson 7, Adrian Beltre 1, Mark Grudzielanek 1.
Outfield: Shawn Green 161, Gary Sheffield 139, Todd Hundley 77, Tom Goodwin 50, F.P. Santangelo 50, Devon White 41, Shawn Gilbert 14, Bruce Aven 9, Paul LoDuca 8, Geronimo Berroa 6, Chris Donnels 6, Jim Leyritz 6, Mike Metcalfe 4, Dave Hansen 3.
Designated hitter: Dave Hansen 5, Gary Sheffield 2, Todd Hundley 1, Eric Karros 1, Jose Vizcaino 1.

TOP DRAFT CHOICES

1. **Ben Diggins**, RHP, Univ. of Arizona.
2. **Joel Hanrahan**, RHP, Norwalk (Iowa) Community H.S.
3. **Jeff Tibbs**, RHP, Davis H.S., Farmington, Utah.
4. **Koyie Hill**, C/3B, Wichita State Univ.
5. **Heath Totten**, RHP, Lamar University.
6. **Greg Withelder**, LHP, Wilmington (Del.) College.
7. **Jared Price**, C, Minico H.S., Rupert, Ida.
8. **Jason Hickman**, LHP, Ball State Univ.
9. **Humberto Sanchez**, RHP, South Bronx (N.Y.) H.S.
10. **Andy Toussaint**, C, Centennial H.S., Los Angeles.

MILWAUKEE BREWERS
NATIONAL LEAGUE CENTRAL DIVISION

Brewers
2001 SCHEDULE
Home games shaded; D—Day game (games starting before 5 p.m.)
*—All-Star Game at Safeco Field (Seattle)

APRIL

SUN	MON	TUE	WED	THU	FRI	SAT
1	2 D	3 D LA	4 HOU	5 D HOU	6 CIN	7 D CIN
8 D CIN	9	10 HOU	11 HOU	12 D HOU	13 SF	14 SF
15 SF	16	17 CIN	18 CIN	19	20 SF	21 D SF
22 SF	23	24 NYM	25 NYM	26 D NYM	27 MON	28 D MON
29 MON	30					

MAY

SUN	MON	TUE	WED	THU	FRI	SAT
		1 ATL	2 ATL	3 ATL	4 FLA	5 FLA
6 FLA	7 CUB	8 CUB	9 CUB	10 D CUB	11 PIT	12 PIT
13 PIT	14 D PIT	15 D PHI	16 PHI	17 PHI	18 PIT	19 PIT
20 PIT	21	22 STL	23 STL	24 D STL	25 D CUB	26 D CUB
27 CUB	28 D STL	29 STL	30 STL	31 STL		

JUNE

SUN	MON	TUE	WED	THU	FRI	SAT
					1 CUB	2 CUB
3 CUB	4 D	5 CIN	6 CIN	7	8 DET	9 DET
10 DET	11 D	12 CLE	13 CLE	14 CLE	15 KC	16 KC
17 KC	18 CIN	19 CIN	20 CIN	21	22 D CUB	23 CUB
24 D CUB	25 PIT	26 PIT	27 PIT	28 D PIT	29 HOU	30 HOU

JULY

SUN	MON	TUE	WED	THU	FRI	SAT
	D 2 HOU	3 D STL	4 D STL	5 D STL	6 SF	7 D SF
8 D SF	D 9	10	* 11	12 MIN	13 MIN	14 MIN
15 CWS	D 16 CWS	17 CWS	18 LA	19 D LA	20 SD	21 SD
22 D LA	23 LA	24 LA	25 D	26	27 SD	28 SD
29 SD	D 30	31 FLA				

AUGUST

SUN	MON	TUE	WED	THU	FRI	SAT
			1 FLA	2 D FLA	3 ATL	4 D ATL
5 ATL	D 6	7 NYM	8 NYM	9 NYM	10 MON	11 MON
12 D MON	D 13	14 PHI	15 PHI	16 D PHI	17 CIN	18 CIN
19 CIN	D 20 CUB	21 CUB	22 D CUB	23 CUB	24 COL	25 COL
26 COL	D 27 PIT	28 PIT	29 PIT	30	31 HOU	

SEPTEMBER

SUN	MON	TUE	WED	THU	FRI	SAT
						1 HOU
2 D HOU	3 PIT	4 PIT	5 PIT	6 HOU	7 HOU	8 HOU
9 D HOU	10 STL	11 STL	12 STL	13 D STL	14 ARI	15 ARI
16 ARI	17 STL	18 STL	19 D STL	20	21 CIN	22 CIN
23 D CIN	24	25 ARI	26 ARI	27 ARI	28 COL	29 D COL
30 D COL						

2001 SEASON
CLUB DIRECTORY

President and chief executive officer
Wendy Selig-Prieb
Sr. vice president and general manager
Dean Taylor
Vice president & general counsel
Tom Gausden
Assistant general counsel
Eugene (Pepi) Randolph
Special assistant to the president
Sal Bando
Vice president, community and governmental affairs
Lynn Sprangers
Vice president, corporate sales
Dean Rennicke
Vice president, finance
Paul Baniel
Vice president, marketing
Laurel Prieb
V.p., new ballpark development
Michael Bucek
Vice president, player personnel
David Wilder
Vice president, stadium operations
Scott Jenkins
Vice president, ticket sales
Bob Voight
Director, community relations
Michael Downs
Director, event services
Steve Ethier
Director, grounds
Gary Vanden Berg
Director, media relations
Jon Greenberg
Director, player development
Greg Riddoch
Director, Brewers Gold Club & Baseball for Wisconsin
Mike Harlan
Director of publications
Mario Ziino
Director of ticket operations
John Barnes

Director, scouting
Jack Zduriencik
Director, clubhouse operations
Tony Migliaccio
Traveling secretary
Dan Larrea
Trainers
John Adam
Roger Caplinger
Strength and conditioning coach
Phil Falco
Team physician
Dr. Angelo Mattalino
National cross-checker
Larry Doughty
Southwest supervisor
Ric Wilson
Midwest supervisor
Tom Allison
International supervisor
Epy Guerrero
East coast supervisor
Bobby Heck
Professional scouts
Hank Allen, Carl Blando, Dick Hager, Alan Regier, Daranka Shaheed
Major League scouts
Russ Bove, Ken Califano, Larry Haney, Bill Lajoie, Al Monchak, Chuck Tanner, Elanis Westbrooks, Dick Wiencek
Scouts
Larry Aaron, Fred Beane, Jeff Brookens, Felix Delgado, Mike Farrell, Edward Fastaia, Dick Foster, Mike Gibbons, Manolo Hernandez, Brian Johnson, Chris Knabenshue, Harvey Kuenn Jr., John Logan, Justin McCray, Tom McNamara, Brandon Newell, Larry Pardo, Douglas Reynolds, Corey Rodriguez, Bruce Seid, Jonathan Story, Tom Tanous, Andy Tomberlin, John Viney, Walter Youse

MINOR LEAGUE AFFILIATES

Class	Team	League	Manager
AAA	Indianapolis	International	Wendell Kim
AA	Huntsville	Southern	Ed Romero
A	Beloit	Midwest	Don Money
A	High Desert	California	Frank Kremblas
Rookie	Maryvale	Arizona	Carlos Lezcano
Rookie	Ogden	Pioneer	Ed Sedar

BROADCAST INFORMATION

Radio: WTMJ-AM (620).
TV: WCGV-TV (Channel 24).
Cable TV: Midwest Sports Channel.

SPRING TRAINING

Ballpark (city): Maryvale Baseball Park (Phoenix, Ariz.).
Ticket information: 623-245-5500.

Follow the Brewers all season at: www.sportingnews.com/baseball/teams/brewers/

Manager—Davey Lopes (30).
Coaches—Gary Allenson (45), Bob Apodaca (36), Rod Carew (29), Bill Castro (35), Jerry Royster (3), Luis Salazar (43).

No.	PITCHERS	B/T	Ht./Wt.	Born	2000 clubs
53	Acevedo, Juan	R/R	6-2/243	5-5-70	Milwaukee, Indianapolis
65	Altman, Gene	R/R	6-7/235	9-1-78	Dayton, Beloit
47	Buddie, Mike	R/R	6-3/219	12-12-70	Columbus, Indianapolis, Milwaukee
50	Chantres, Carlos	R/R	6-3/175	4-1-76	Charlotte
60	Childers, Matt	R/R	6-5/195	12-3-78	Beloit, Mudville
33	Cunnane, Will	R/R	6-2/200	4-24-74	San Diego, Las Vegas
13	D'Amico, Jeff	R/R	6-7/250	12-27-75	Indianapolis, Milwaukee
37	Davis, Kane	R/R	6-3/194	6-25-75	Akron, Buffalo, Cleveland, Milwaukee, Indianapolis
28	De Los Santos, Valerio	L/L	6-2/206	10-6-75	Milwaukee
48	Estrada, Horacio	L/L	6-0/192	10-19-75	Indianapolis, Milwaukee
56	Garcia, Jose	R/R	6-3/195	4-29-78	Huntsville
51	Haynes, Jimmy	R/R	6-4/214	9-5-72	Milwaukee
46	King, Ray	L/L	6-1/240	1-15-74	Iowa, Indianapolis, Milwaukee
38	Kolb, Brandon	R/R	6-1/190	11-20-73	Las Vegas, San Diego
39	Leskanic, Curtis	R/R	6-0/196	4-2-68	Milwaukee
55	Levrault, Allen	R/R	6-3/230	8-15-77	Indianapolis, Milwaukee
	Mieses, Jose	R/R	6-1/165	10-14-79	Beloit, Mudville
	Penney, Mike	R/R	6-1/190	3-29-77	Mudville, Huntsville, Indianapolis
26	Peterson, Kyle	L/R	6-3/220	4-9-76	Beloit, Huntsville
31	Rigdon, Paul	R/R	6-5/242	11-2-75	Buffalo, Cleveland, Milwaukee
52	Roque, Rafael	L/L	6-4/201	10-27-73	Indianapolis, Milwaukee
59	Snyder, John	R/R	6-3/206	8-16-74	Huntsville, Indianapolis, Milwaukee
41	Stull, Everett	R/R	6-3/206	8-24-71	Indianapolis, Milwaukee
49	Weathers, Dave	R/R	6-3/233	9-25-69	Milwaukee
21	Wright, Jamey	R/R	6-5/236	12-24-74	Huntsville, Indianapolis, Milwaukee

No.	CATCHERS	B/T	Ht./Wt.	Born	2000 clubs
12	Blanco, Henry	R/R	5-11/224	8-29-71	Milwaukee, Indianapolis
27	Brown, Kevin	R/R	6-2/224	4-21-73	Syracuse, Indianapolis, Milwaukee

No.	INFIELDERS	B/T	Ht./Wt.	Born	2000 clubs
22	Barker, Kevin	R/R	6-3/205	7-26-75	Milwaukee, Indianapolis
10	Belliard, Ron	R/R	5-8/190	7-4-76	Milwaukee
16	Collier, Lou	R/R	5-10/182	8-21-73	Indianapolis, Huntsville, Milwaukee
18	Hernandez, Jose	R/R	6-1/186	7-14-69	Milwaukee, Indianapolis
2	Houston, Tyler	L/R	6-1/218	1-17-71	Milwaukee
1	Lopez, Luis	B/R	5-11/170	9-4-70	Milwaukee
8	Loretta, Mark	R/R	6-0/189	8-14-71	Milwaukee, Indianapolis
11	Sexson, Richie	R/R	6-8/215	12-29-74	Cleveland, Milwaukee

No.	OUTFIELDERS	B/T	Ht./Wt.	Born	2000 clubs
20	Burnitz, Jeromy	L/R	6-0/213	4-15-69	Milwaukee
39	Echevarria, Angel	R/R	6-3/230	5-25-71	Colorado Springs, Colorado, Milwaukee
9	Grissom, Marquis	R/R	5-11/190	4-17-67	Milwaukee
6	Hammonds, Jeffrey	R/R	6-0/200	3-5-71	Colorado
5	Jenkins, Geoff	L/R	6-1/206	7-21-74	Milwaukee

Ballpark (capacity, surface)
Miller Park (To be announced, grass)
Address
One Brewers Way
Milwaukee, WI 53214-3652
Official website
www.milwaukeebrewers.com
Business phone
414-902-4400
Ticket information
414-902-4000
Ticket prices
$50 (field diamond box)
$32 (field IF box, club IF box)
$27 (field OF box, loge diamond box)
$24 (club OF box), $23 (loge IF box)
$20 (loge OF box), $16 (terrace IF box)
$14 (terrace OF box)
$10 (terrace reserved, field bleachers)
$6 (loge bleachers, club bleachers)
$5 (terrace bleachers)
Field dimensions (from home plate)
To left field at foul line, 342 feet
To center field, 400 feet
To right field at foul line, 345 feet
First game played
Scheduled for April 6, 2001 vs. Cincinnati

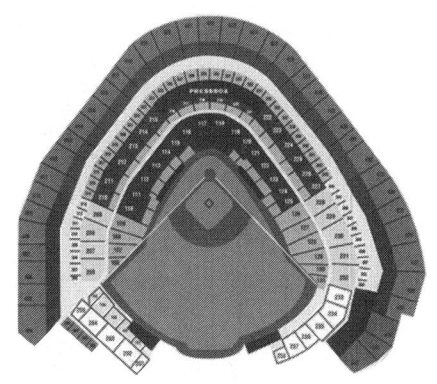

2001 SEASON *Milwaukee Brewers*

Date	Opp.	Res.	Score	(inn.*)	Hits	Opp. hits	Winning pitcher	Losing pitcher	Save	Record	Pos.	GB
4-3	At Cin.	T	3-3	(6)	7	5				0-0	T3rd	0.5
4-4	At Cin.	W	5-1		10	4	Bruske	Williamson		1-0	T1st	...
4-5	At Cin.	W	8-5		10	13	Haynes	Parris	Wickman	2-0	T1st	...
4-6	At Cin.	L	1-5		8	7	Villone	Navarro		2-1	T2nd	1.0
4-7	At StL.	W	9-1		11	6	Bere	An. Benes		3-1	T1st	...
4-8	At StL.	L	8-10		9	15	Kile	Woodard	Veres	3-2	T2nd	1.0
4-9	At StL.	L	2-11		6	16	Ankiel	de los Santos		3-3	T2nd	2.0
4-10	Fla.	W	4-3		6	9	Haynes	Nunez	Wickman	4-3	2nd	2.0
4-12	Fla.	L	4-11		8	11	Sanchez	Navarro		4-4	2nd	2.5
4-13	Fla.	W	4-0		6	4	Bere	Penny		5-4	2nd	1.5
4-14	Atl.	L	3-6		7	14	Glavine	Woodard	Remlinger	5-5	T2nd	1.5
4-15	Atl.	W	6-3		9	5	Weathers	Burkett	Wickman	6-5	2nd	1.0
4-16	Atl.	L	1-2		8	6	Mulholland	Stull	Remlinger	6-6	T2nd	1.5
4-18	At N.Y.	L	7-10		9	11	Hampton	Navarro	Benitez	6-7	T2nd	2.5
4-19	At N.Y.	L	1-3		8	8	Reed	Bere	Benitez	6-8	T3rd	3.5
4-20	At N.Y.	L	4-5	(10)	9	7	Wendell	Leskanic		6-9	T4th	4.5
4-21	At Mon.	L	1-5		8	8	Hermanson	Haynes	Urbina	6-10	T5th	4.5
4-22	At Mon.	W	7-3		15	5	Stull	Irabu		7-10	3rd	3.5
4-23	At Mon.	L	4-6		7	10	Vazquez	Navarro	Urbina	7-11	3rd	4.5
4-25	At StL.	L	2-7		7	10	Kile	Bere		7-12	T4th	5.5
4-26	At StL.	L	0-7		4	9	Ankiel	Woodard		7-13	5th	6.5
4-27	At StL.	W	8-4		10	6	Haynes	Hentgen		8-13	T3rd	5.5
4-28	Hou.	L	0-7		1	8	Holt	Navarro		8-14	6th	6.5
4-29	Hou.	L	3-10		7	5	Maddux	Stull		8-15	6th	7.5
4-30	Hou.	W	4-3		7	7	Weathers	Henry		9-15	T4th	7.5
5-1	Hou.	L	0-5		2	11	Dotel	Woodard		9-16	6th	8.0
5-2	Ari.	L	1-5		4	9	Stottlemyre	Haynes		9-17	6th	8.0
5-3	Ari.	W	4-1		10	4	Estrada	Daal	Wickman	10-17	6th	7.0
5-4	Ari.	L	2-6		4	10	Reynoso	Stull	Kim	10-18	6th	8.0
5-5	Mon.	L	2-10		7	14	Vazquez	Bere		10-19	6th	8.0
5-6	Mon.	L	2-3		4	11	Telford	Weathers	Urbina	10-20	6th	9.0
5-7	Mon.	W	9-4		13	8	Haynes	Hermanson		11-20	6th	8.0
5-8	At Chi.	L	11-12	(10)	13	16	Heredia	Wickman		11-21	6th	8.0
5-9	At Chi.	W	4-3		8	5	D'Amico	Guthrie	Weathers	12-21	6th	8.0
5-10	At Chi.	L	8-9	(11)	9	10	Aguilera	de los Santos		12-22	6th	8.0
5-11	At Chi.	W	14-8		18	17	Woodard	Williams		13-22	6th	7.5
5-12	At Pit.	W	6-1		11	4	Haynes	Schmidt		14-22	5th	6.5
5-13	At Pit.	L	8-11		10	16	Sauerbeck	Acevedo	Williams	14-23	6th	7.0
5-14	At Pit.	L	0-3		4	7	Benson	D'Amico	Christiansen	14-24	6th	7.5
5-16	Hou.	W	6-5	(16)	11	14	Estrada	Holt		15-24	5th	7.5
5-19	S.F	W	11-10	(10)	11	15	Wickman	Nen		16-24	4th	6.5
5-20	S.F	W	7-0		6	4	D'Amico	Gardner		17-24	4th	6.5
5-21	S.F	L	10-16		9	20	Ortiz	Ramirez		17-25	4th	7.5
5-22†	Hou.	W	10-9	(10)	14	13	Weathers	Slusarski		18-25		
5-22‡	Hou.	W	6-1		8	7	Bere	Gross		19-25	4th	6.5
5-23	Atl.	W	7-6		7	5	Wright	Millwood	Wickman	20-25	3rd	6.5
5-24	Atl.	L	2-11		5	17	Maddux	Haynes		20-26	3rd	7.5
5-25	Atl.	L	3-7		6	12	Mulholland	D'Amico		20-27	3rd	8.5
5-26	At Ari.	L	2-9		6	9	Johnson	Snyder		20-28	4th	8.5
5-27	At Ari.	L	3-7		6	14	Reynoso	Acevedo	Kim	20-29	4th	8.5
5-28	At Ari.	W	4-3	(11)	11	8	Wickman	Swindell		21-29	3rd	7.5
5-29	At S.D.	W	8-3		10	8	Haynes	Meadows		22-29	3rd	7.5
5-30	At S.D.	L	3-6		9	11	Eaton	D'Amico	Hoffman	22-30	4th	8.5
5-31	At S.D.	L	5-9		10	9	Almanzar	Weathers		22-31	4th	8.5
6-2	Col.	L	6-8		9	12	Arrojo	Bere	Myers	22-32	4th	9.0
6-3	Col.	W	2-1	(12)	6	3	de los Santos	Belinda		23-32	4th	8.0
6-4	Col.	L	1-7		5	12	Jarvis	Haynes		23-33	4th	8.5
6-5	Cle.	L	4-8		8	9	Burba	D'Amico		23-34	4th	8.5
6-6	Cle.	L	2-4		7	7	Finley	Snyder		23-35	5th	9.0
6-7	Cle.	L	5-9		10	10	Brewington	Bere		23-36	5th	10.0
6-9	At Min.	L	6-9		10	10	Bergman	Wright		23-37	5th	10.0
6-10	At Min.	W	5-3		13	7	Haynes	Redman	Wickman	24-37	5th	9.0
6-11	At Min.	W	5-3		13	10	Snyder	Radke	Wickman	25-37	5th	9.0
6-12	Mon.	W	8-1		12	5	Bere	Vazquez		26-37	T4th	9.0
6-13	Mon.	L	4-9		10	12	Pavano	Woodard		26-38	5th	10.0
6-14	Mon.	W	11-2		12	8	Wright	Johnson		27-38	T4th	10.0
6-16	N.Y.	L	1-7		3	15	Leiter	Haynes		27-39	5th	11.0
6-17	N.Y.	W	3-2		4	9	Snyder	Rusch	Wickman	28-39	5th	11.0
6-18	N.Y.	L	3-7		7	10	Reed	Bere		28-40	5th	11.0
6-19	At Fla.	W	2-0		5	3	Wright	Smith	Wickman	29-40	5th	10.5
6-20	At Fla.	L	2-8		5	13	Dempster	Woodard		29-41	5th	11.5
6-21	At Fla.	L	4-5		11	9	Looper	Haynes	Alfonseca	29-42	5th	11.5
6-22	At Fla.	W	6-1		10	6	Snyder	Sanchez		30-42	5th	11.5
6-23	At Atl.	L	2-3		7	6	Marquis	Weathers	Rocker	30-43	5th	12.5

Date	Opp.	Res.	Score	(inn.*)	Hits	Opp. hits	Winning pitcher	Losing pitcher	Save	Record	Pos.	GB
6-24	At Atl.	W	2-1		6	5	Wright	Maddux	Wickman	31-43	4th	12.5
6-25	At Atl.	L	4-5		8	4	Rocker	Leskanic		31-44	4th	13.5
6-27	At Phi.	L	0-7		6	8	Schilling	Haynes		31-45	4th	14.0
6-28	At Phi.	L	7-9		11	13	Brock	Acevedo	Brantley	31-46	5th	14.0
6-29	At Phi.	W	8-6		12	10	Bere	Schrenk	Leskanic	32-46	4th	14.0
6-30	Chi.	L	4-7	(15)	12	13	Garibay	Levrault	Aguilera	32-47	5th	15.0
7-1	Chi.	W	4-0		11	2	D'Amico	Valdes		33-47	4th	15.0
7-2	Chi.	W	4-2		7	6	Haynes	Wood	Wickman	34-47	4th	14.0
7-3	Phi.	L	3-5		6	10	Ashby	Snyder	Brantley	34-48	4th	14.5
7-4	Phi.	L	4-7		10	11	Brock	Wickman	Brantley	34-49	4th	15.5
7-5	Phi.	L	2-5		7	12	Wolf	Wright	Gomes	34-50	4th	16.5
7-6	Phi.	W	4-2		8	11	D'Amico	Byrd	Wickman	35-50	4th	15.5
7-7	Det.	W	4-3		9	6	Haynes	Moehler	Wickman	36-50	4th	14.5
7-8	Det.	L	2-4	(15)	15	12	Cruz	de los Santos		36-51	4th	14.5
7-9	Det.	W	10-3		13	10	Bere	Blair		37-51	4th	14.5
7-13	At K.C.	W	5-2		8	10	Wright	Stein	Wickman	38-51	4th	14.5
7-14	At K.C.	W	4-0		12	4	D'Amico	Suzuki		39-51	3rd	14.5
7-15	At K.C.	L	4-7		11	11	Suppan	Haynes	Bottalico	39-52	3rd	14.5
7-16	At Chi. (AL)	L	5-11		9	16	Baldwin	Snyder		39-53	3rd	14.5
7-17	At Chi. (AL)	L	2-11		4	13	Garland	Bere		39-54	4th	15.5
7-18	At Chi. (AL)	L	5-7		9	10	Sirotka	Wright	Wunsch	39-55	5th	15.5
7-19	Pit.	W	6-0		5	5	D'Amico	Benson		40-55	4th	14.5
7-20	Pit.	L	2-9		5	12	Silva	Haynes		40-56	5th	14.5
7-21	At Chi.	L	2-4		5	7	Wood	Snyder	Aguilera	40-57	5th	15.5
7-22	At Chi.	L	2-3	(13)	10	7	Heredia	Woodard		40-58	5th	15.5
7-23	At Chi.	L	4-5		7	4	Valdes	Wright	Aguilera	40-59	5th	15.5
7-25	At Pit.	W	4-1	(11)	10	6	Leskanic	Christiansen	Wickman	41-59	5th	15.5
7-26	At Pit.	L	4-5		8	10	Silva	Haynes	Williams	41-60	5th	16.5
7-27	At Pit.	W	4-3		9	7	Leskanic	Manzanillo	Wickman	42-60	5th	15.5
7-28	Col.	W	5-0		8	8	Wright	Astacio		43-60	5th	14.5
7-29	Col.	L	2-10		6	14	Tavarez	Rigdon		43-61	5th	14.5
7-30	Col.	W	3-2		5	7	D'Amico	Yoshii	Leskanic	44-61	5th	13.5
7-31	S.F	L	3-4	(11)	4	5	Rodriguez	Weathers	Nen	44-62	5th	14.5
8-1	S.F	L	8-13		10	17	Henry	King		44-63	5th	14.5
8-2	S.F	W	6-4		8	6	Acevedo	Hernandez	Leskanic	45-63	5th	14.5
8-4	At L.A.	L	1-2		6	7	Fetters	Acevedo		45-64	5th	14.5
8-5	At L.A.	W	4-2	(10)	10	7	Acevedo	Fetters	Leskanic	46-64	5th	14.5
8-6	At L.A.	W	9-6		15	12	Haynes	Valdes	Leskanic	47-64	5th	13.5
8-7	At S.F	L	1-8		9	8	Hernandez	Snyder		47-65	5th	14.5
8-8	At S.F	L	0-1		2	6	Ortiz	Wright	Nen	47-66	5th	14.5
8-9	At S.F	L	3-9		6	13	Rueter	Rigdon		47-67	5th	14.5
8-11	StL.	W	6-2		8	7	D'Amico	Kile		48-67	5th	14.0
8-12	StL.	L	1-2	(12)	7	9	Morris	Leskanic	James	48-68	5th	15.0
8-13	StL.	L	4-6		8	13	Hentgen	Wright	Veres	48-69	5th	16.0
8-14	Cin.	W	4-3		8	8	Rigdon	Dessens	Leskanic	49-69	5th	15.0
8-15	Cin.	W	2-1	(10)	7	5	Leskanic	Wohlers		50-69	4th	15.0
8-16	Cin.	W	5-1		9	9	D'Amico	Bell		51-69	4th	15.0
8-18	At Hou.	L	4-5		6	12	Miller	Haynes	Dotel	51-70	4th	16.0
8-19	At Hou.	L	8-10		8	11	Cabrera	Acevedo	Dotel	51-71	4th	17.0
8-20	At Hou.	W	6-5		14	7	Leskanic	Cabrera		52-71	4th	16.0
8-21	At Ari.	W	16-8		19	13	Stull	Reynoso		53-71	4th	16.0
8-22	At Ari.	W	4-3		8	8	D'Amico	Guzman	Leskanic	54-71	4th	15.0
8-23	At Ari.	W	8-5		9	11	Haynes	Schilling	Leskanic	55-71	4th	15.0
8-25	S.D.	L	0-4		6	12	Tollberg	Wright		55-72	T3rd	15.5
8-26	S.D.	W	6-5	(10)	8	14	Leskanic	Hoffman		56-72	T3rd	15.5
8-27	S.D.	L	1-2		8	7	Williams	Weathers	Hoffman	56-73	T3rd	16.5
8-28	L.A.	L	3-5		7	10	Brown	D'Amico	Shaw	56-74	T3rd	17.5
8-29	L.A.	L	2-7		1	8	Park	Haynes		56-75	4th	17.5
8-30	L.A.	W	3-2		6	6	King	Adams		57-75	4th	17.5
8-31	L.A.	W	8-2		14	8	Rigdon	Perez		58-75	T3rd	17.0
9-1	At Col.	L	3-5		7	11	Astacio	Snyder	White	58-76	T3rd	18.0
9-2	At Col.	W	8-3		14	10	D'Amico	DeJean		59-76	3rd	18.0
9-3	At Col.	W	6-4	(11)	13	8	Acevedo	DeJean	Leskanic	60-76	3rd	18.0
9-4	At S.D.	L	3-4		5	7	Davey	King	Hoffman	60-77	3rd	19.0
9-5	At S.D.	L	1-3		3	5	Witasick	Rigdon	Hoffman	60-78	3rd	20.0
9-6	At S.D.	L	6-7		9	11	Williams	Snyder	Hoffman	60-79	3rd	20.0
9-8	StL.	W	6-5		12	8	Leskanic	Veres		61-79	T3rd	19.5
9-9	StL.	L	6-7		12	15	Veres	Acevedo		61-80	T4th	20.5
9-10	StL.	W	4-3	(10)	9	8	King	An. Benes		62-80	4th	19.5
9-11	At N.Y.	W	8-2		12	7	Rigdon	Reed		63-80	3rd	19.5
9-12	At N.Y.	L	2-10		7	13	B.J. Jones	Snyder		63-81	3rd	20.5
9-13	At N.Y.	L	1-4	(10)	5	9	Benitez	Acevedo		63-82	3rd	21.5
9-14	At Cin.	W	6-4		8	12	Haynes	Villone	Leskanic	64-82	3rd	21.5
9-15	At Cin.	L	4-6		7	11	Parris	Wright	Graves	64-83	4th	22.5
9-16	At Cin.	L	3-7		10	9	Dessens	Rigdon	Riedling	64-84	4th	23.5
9-17	At Cin.	L	4-8		5	7	Harnisch	Snyder		64-85	4th	24.5
9-18	Chi.	W	2-1		5	4	D'Amico	Van Poppel	Leskanic	65-85	4th	24.0
9-19	Chi.	W	9-8		9	7	King	Farnsworth		66-85	4th	23.0

Date	Opp.	Res.	Score	(inn.*)	Hits	Opp. hits	Winning pitcher	Losing pitcher	Save	Record	Pos.	GB
9-20	Chi.	W	3-2	(10)	9	8	Leskanic	Farnsworth		67-85	4th	23.0
9-21	Pit.	W	12-2		14	5	Rigdon	Anderson		68-85	4th	22.0
9-23†	Pit.	L	2-4		5	14	Silva	D'Amico	Williams	68-86		
9-23‡	Pit.	W	5-4	(10)	8	10	Leskanic	Arroyo		69-86	T3rd	22.0
9-24	Pit.	W	8-5		9	6	Leskanic	Williams		70-86	3rd	21.0
9-26	Cin.	W	7-4		13	9	Wright	Parris	Leskanic	71-86	3rd	21.0
9-27	Cin.	W	10-6		8	11	de los Santos	Riedling		72-86	3rd	21.0
9-28	Cin.	L	1-8		2	14	Dessens	D'Amico		72-87	3rd	22.0
9-29	At Hou.	W	13-3		15	7	Estrada	Elarton		73-87	3rd	21.0
9-30	At Hou.	L	6-7		11	11	Miller	Haynes	Dotel	73-88	3rd	21.0
10-1	At Hou.	L	1-6		7	8	Holt	Wright		73-89	3rd	22.0

Monthly records: April (9-15), May (13-16), June (10-16), July (12-15), August (14-13), September (15-13), October (0-1).
*Innings, if other than nine. †First game of a doubleheader. ‡Second game of a doubleheader.

HIGHLIGHTS

High point: The Brewers were 8-2 during County Stadium's final homestand and that late spurt against Central Division rivals secured a third-place finish. That completed a respectable August and September that gave the team something to build on.

Low point: The Brewers lost eight of nine games in mid-July and were on pace to set a team record for losses when the month ended. Their frustration compounded when Jeromy Burnitz halted contract negotiations because he didn't think the Brewers would change their losing ways while he was still in his prime.

Turning point: On July 28, the Brewers acquired first baseman Richie Sexson from Cleveland and the entire season outlook changed. It was uncanny how much Sexson's bat meant to the middle of the lineup. Hitting in between Geoff Jenkins and Burnitz, Sexson batted .296 with 14 home runs and 47 RBIs over the final two months.

Most valuable player: Jenkins, despite missing three weeks with a broken finger, was a consistent run producer. He hit .303 with 34 home runs and 94 RBIs even though he played the second half of the season in pain.

Most valuable pitcher: Jeff D'Amico. After missing almost two entire seasons with shoulder problems, D'Amico wasn't just the best pitcher on the staff, he was one of the most consistent in the N.L. D'Amico, who didn't even win a rotation spot until May, finished 12-7 with a 2.66 ERA that ranked third in the league.

Most improved player: After going 6-2 with a 5.08 ERA for Colorado in 1999, Curtis Leskanic developed into one of the top setup men in the league. When Bob Wickman was traded to Cleveland in late July, Leskanic inherited the closer's job and finished 9-3, converting 12 of 13 save opportunities. He allowed just eight earned runs after the break and opponents batted .195 against him.

Biggest surprise: Lefty Ray King, recalled from the minor leagues for the third time on July 6, became a dominant setup man over the second half of the season. King finished with a 1.26 ERA and held opponents to a .180 average. The former Cubs farmhand didn't give up a run in his last 23 appearances.

Key injuries: Shortstop Mark Loretta missed more than two months with a broken foot. ... Jenkins missed three weeks with his broken finger. ... Jamey Wright, counted on as the team's No. 2 starter, suffered a partial tear of his rotator cuff and didn't pitch until June. ... Righthander John Snyder missed the first two months with a strained muscle. ... Catcher Henry Blanco missed most of September with a sore throwing shoulder.

Notable: Brewers pitchers set a club record for walks with 728. ... Sexson (30), Jenkins (34) and Burnitz (31) became the first Brewers' trio to finish the season with 30 or more home runs since Gorman Thomas, Ben Oglivie and Cecil Cooper accomplished the feat in 1982. Sexson hit 16 homers for Cleveland and 14 for Milwaukee. ... Burnitz topped 30 home runs for the third straight year, despite hitting just .232. Burnitz has averaged 34 home runs over the last four seasons.

—EMMETT PROSSER

RECORDS

2000 regular-season record: 73-89 (3rd in N.L. Central); 42-39 at home; 31-50 on road; 15-26 vs. East; 39-39 vs. Central; 19-24 vs. West; 14-21 vs. lefthanded starters; 59-68 vs. righthanded starters; 63-77 on grass; 10-12 on turf; 21-29 in daytime; 52-60 at night; 26-21 in one-run games; 13-9 in extra-inning games; 1-0-1 in doubleheaders.

Team record past five years: 379-429 (.469, ranks 11th in league in that span).

TEAM LEADERS

Batting average: Geoff Jenkins (.303).
At-bats: Marquis Grissom (595).
Runs: Geoff Jenkins (100).
Hits: Geoff Jenkins (155).
Total Bases: Geoff Jenkins (301).
Doubles: Geoff Jenkins (36).
Triples: Ron Belliard (9).
Home runs: Geoff Jenkins (34).
Runs batted in: Jeromy Burnitz (98).
Stolen bases: Marquis Grissom (20).
Slugging percentage: Geoff Jenkins (.588).

On-base percentage: Geoff Jenkins (.360).
Wins: Jeff D'Amico, Jimmy Haynes (12).
Earned-run average: Jeff D'Amico (2.66).
Complete games: Jeff D'Amico, Steve Woodard (1).
Shutouts: Jeff D'Amico (1).
Saves: Bob Wickman (16).
Innings pitched: Jimmy Haynes (199.1).
Strikeouts: Jeff D'Amico (101).

GAMES BY POSITION

Catcher: Henry Blanco 88, Raul Casanova 72, Tyler Houston 23, Kevin L. Brown 5.
First base: Charlie Hayes 57, Richie Sexson 57, Tyler Houston 35, Kevin Barker 32, Angel Echevarria 9, Mark Sweeney 2.
Second base: Ron Belliard 151, Luis Lopez 22, Mark Loretta 1.
Third base: Jose Hernandez 95, Charlie Hayes 59, Tyler Houston 28, Sean Berry 9, Luis Lopez 6, Lou Collier 1.
Shortstop: Mark Loretta 90, Luis Lopez 45, Jose Hernandez 37, Santiago Perez 20.
Outfield: Jeromy Burnitz 158, Marquis Grissom 142, Geoff Jenkins 131, James Mouton 46, Lyle Mouton 27, Lou Collier 10, Angel Echevarria 5, Mark Sweeney 3, Jose Hernandez 2, Chris Jones 2.
Designated hitter: Mark Sweeney 4, Raul Casanova 3, Jeromy Burnitz 1, Charlie Hayes 1.

TOP DRAFT CHOICES

1. **David Krynzel,** OF, Green Valley H.S., Henderson, Nev.
2. None.
3. **Dane Artman,** LHP, Westminster Academy, Ft. Lauderdale, Fla.
4. **Eric Henderson,** LHP, University of North Carolina.
5. **Jason Belcher,** C, Walnut Ridge (Ark.) H.S.
6. **Bryan Hicks,** OF, Natchitoches (La.) Central H.S.
7. **Gerard Oakes,** RHP, Archbishop Carroll H.S., Upper Darby, Pa.
8. **Bill Scott,** OF, UCLA.
9. **Ryan Miller,** RHP, Univ. of Evansville.
10. **Brian Nielsen,** LHP, Seminole H.S., Sanford, Fla.

MONTREAL EXPOS
NATIONAL LEAGUE EAST DIVISION

Expos
2001 SCHEDULE
Home games shaded; D—Day game (games starting before 5 p.m.)
*—All-Star Game at Safeco Field (Seattle)

APRIL

SUN	MON	TUE	WED	THU	FRI	SAT
1	2 D CUB	3	4 D CUB	5 D CUB	6 NYM	7 D NYM
8 D NYM	9 D CUB	10 CUB	11 CUB	12	13 FLA	14 FLA
15 FLA	16 NYM	17 NYM	18 D NYM	19 FLA	20 FLA	21 FLA
22 D FLA	23	24 STL	25 STL	26 STL	27 MIL	28 D MIL
29 MIL	30					

MAY

SUN	MON	TUE	WED	THU	FRI	SAT
		1 ARI	2 ARI	3 ARI	4 HOU	5 HOU
6 D HOU	7 SF	8 SF	9 SF	10 D COL	11 COL	12 D COL
13 D COL	14	15 LA	16 LA	17 LA	18 SD	19 SD
20 D SD	21 NYM	22 NYM	23 NYM	24	25 PHI	26 PHI
27 D PHI	28 ATL	29 ATL	30 D ATL	31 PHI		

JUNE

SUN	MON	TUE	WED	THU	FRI	SAT
					1 PHI	2 PHI
3 D PHI	4	5 ATL	6 ATL	7 ATL	8 BAL	9 D BAL
10 D BAL	11	12 NYY	13 NYY	14 NYY	15 TOR	16 TOR
17 D TOR	18 NYM	19 NYM	20 NYM	21 NYM	22 PIT	23 PIT
24 D PIT	25 FLA	26 FLA	27 FLA	28	29 PIT	30 PIT

JULY

SUN	MON	TUE	WED	THU	FRI	SAT
1 PIT	2	3 FLA	4 FLA	5 FLA	6 D TOR	7 TOR
8 D TOR	9	10	* 11	12 TB	13 TB	14 D TB
15 BOS	16 BOS	17 BOS	18 PHI	19 PHI	20 D ATL	21 ATL
22 ATL	23 PHI	24 PHI	25 D PHI	26 ATL	27 ATL	28 ATL
29 D ATL	30	31 ARI				

AUGUST

SUN	MON	TUE	WED	THU	FRI	SAT
			1 ARI	2 ARI	3 HOU	4 HOU
5 HOU	6 D	7 STL	8 STL	9 STL	10 MIL	11 MIL
12 D MIL	13	14 LA	15 LA	16 LA	17 SD	18 SD
19 SD	20 D	21 SF	22 SF	23 SF	24 CIN	25 CIN
26 CIN	27 D	28 ATL	29 ATL	30 ATL	31 PHI	

SEPTEMBER

SUN	MON	TUE	WED	THU	FRI	SAT
						1 PHI
2 D PHI	3 D ATL	4 ATL	5 ATL	6 PHI	7 PHI	8 PHI
9 D PHI	10	11 FLA	12 FLA	13 D FLA	14 NYM	15 NYM
16 NYM	17 D FLA	18 FLA	19 FLA	20 COL	21 COL	22 COL
23 D COL	24	25 NYM	26 NYM	27 NYM	28 CIN	29 D CIN
30 D CIN						

2001 SEASON
CLUB DIRECTORY

Chairman, CEO & managing general partner
Jeffrey H. Loria

Executive vice president
David P. Samson

Vice president and general manager
Jim Beattie

V.p., dir. of international operations
Fred Ferreira

Assistant general manager
Larry Beinfest

Assistants to the general manager
Mike Berger, Don Reynolds

Director, scouting
Jim Fleming

Director, player development
Tony LaCava

Assistant director, scouting
Gregg Leonard

Assistant director, player development
Adam Wogan

Assistant dir., international scouting
Randy Kierce

Coord., conditioning & team travel
Sean Cunningham

Assistant, baseball operations
Mike Wickham

Vice president & CFO
Michel Bussiere

Vice president, stadium operations
Claude Delorme

Director, media relations
P.J. Loyello

Director, media services
Monique Giroux

Director, advertising sales
Hubert Richard

Director, broadcast activities & web site editor
Marc Griffin

Director, promotions & special events
Gina Hackl

Director, ticket sales
John Di Terlizzi

Dir., administration, sales & marketing
Chantal Dalpe

Dir., management information systems
Yves Poulin

Team orthopedist
Dr. Larry Coughlin

Team physician
Dr. Mike Thomassin

Strength, condit. & rehab coordinator
Paul Fournier

Major league scouts
Mike Berger, Bob Cluck, Joe Moeller, Donnie Reynolds, Tommy Thompson

Scouts
Alex Agostino, Matt Anderson, Carlos Berroa, Dennis Cardoza, Dave Dangler, Marc DelPiano, Scot Engler, Scott Goldby, John Hughes, Joe Jordan, Mark Leavitt, Joel Matthews, Stan Meek, Bob Oldis, Steve Payne, Pat Puccinelli, Joel Smith, Scott Stanley

MINOR LEAGUE AFFILIATES

Class	Team	League	Manager
AAA	Ottawa	International	Stan Hough
AA	Harrisburg	Eastern	Luis Dorante
A	Clinton	Midwest	Steve Phillips
A	Jupiter	Florida State	Tim Leiper
A	Vermont	New York-Pennsylvania	Tony Barbone
Rookie	Gulf Coast Expos	Gulf Coast	Dave Dangler

BROADCAST INFORMATION

Radio: To be announced.
TV: To be announced.
Cable TV: TSN, RDS (French).

SPRING TRAINING

Ballpark (city): Roger Dean Stadium (Jupiter, Fla.).
Ticket information: 561-775-1818.

Follow the Expos all season at: www.sportingnews.com/baseball/teams/expos/

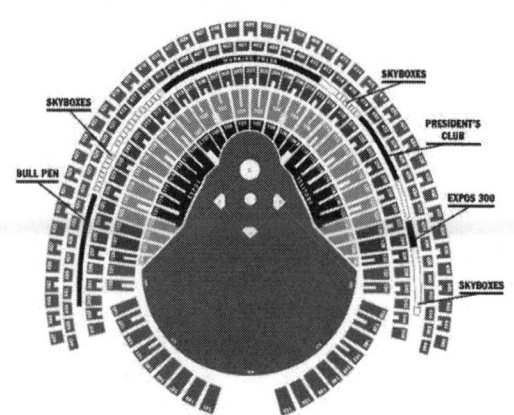

2001 SEASON Montreal Expos

SPRING TRAINING ROSTER

Manager—Felipe Alou (17).
Coaches—Brad Arnsberg (38), Pierre Arsenault (67), Jeff Cox (26), Perry Hill (7), Pat Roessler (6).

No.	PITCHERS	B/T	Ht./Wt.	Born	2000 clubs
36	Armas, Tony	R/R	6-4/205	4-29-78	Jupiter, Ottawa, Montreal
48	Billingsley, Brent	L/L	6-2/200	4-19-75	Ottawa
50	Blank, Matt	L/L	6-2/195	4-5-76	Montreal
	Bridges, Donnie	R/R	6-4/195	12-10-78	Harrisburg, Jupiter
33	Burrows, Terry	L/L	6-1/185	11-28-68	Sacramento
48	Downs, Scott	L/L	6-2/190	3-17-76	Chicago N.L., Montreal
14	Irabu, Hideki	R/R	6-4/240	5-5-69	Montreal
47	Johnson, Mike	L/R	6-2/170	10-3-75	Ottawa, Montreal
43	Lira, Felipe	R/R	6-0/170	4-26-72	Ottawa, Montreal
37	Lloyd, Graeme	L/L	6-7/225	4-9-67	DID NOT PLAY
	Mattes, Troy	R/R	6-7/185	8-26-75	Harrisburg
40	Mota, Guillermo	R/R	6-4/205	7-25-73	Ottawa, Montreal
32	Munoz, Bobby	R/R	6-7/237	3-3-68	Louisville
45	Pavano, Carl	R/R	6-5/230	1-8-76	Montreal
68	Reames, Britt	R/R	5-11/170	8-19-73	Arkansas, Memphis, St. Louis
50	Scanlan, Bob	R/R	6-8/215	8-9-66	Indianapolis, Milwaukee
56	Smart, J.D.	R/R	6-2/180	11-12-73	Ottawa
53	Spencer, Sean	L/L	5-11/185	5-29-75	Tacoma, Ottawa, Montreal
20	Strickland, Scott	R/R	5-11/180	4-26-76	Montreal, Ottawa
32	Telford, Anthony	R/R	6-0/195	3-6-66	Montreal
35	Thurman, Mike	R/R	6-5/210	7-22-73	Jupiter, Ottawa, Montreal, Harrisburg
52	Tucker, T.J.	R/R	6-3/245	8-20-78	Harrisburg, Montreal
41	Urbina, Ugueth	R/R	6-0/205	2-15-74	Montreal
23	Vazquez, Javier	R/R	6-2/195	7-25-76	Montreal

No.	CATCHERS	B/T	Ht./Wt.	Born	2000 clubs
13	Henley, Bob	R/R	6-2/205	1-30-73	DID NOT PLAY
14	Martinez, Sandy	L/R	6-2/215	10-3-72	Florida, Calgary
39	Schneider, Brian	L/R	6-1/180	11-26-76	Ottawa, Montreal

No.	INFIELDERS	B/T	Ht./Wt.	Born	2000 clubs
5	Barrett, Michael	R/R	6-2/200	10-22-76	Montreal
11	Blum, Geoff	B/R	6-3/195	4-26-73	Montreal
18	Cabrera, Orlando	R/R	5-10/175	11-2-74	Montreal, Ottawa
2	De La Rosa, Tomas	R/R	5-10/165	1-28-78	Ottawa, Montreal
	Hodges, Scott	L/R	6-0/185	12-26-78	Jupiter, Harrisburg
	Mateo, Henry	B/R	5-11/170	10-14-76	Harrisburg
25	Minor, Ryan	R/R	6-7/245	1-5-74	Rochester, Baltimore, Frederick, Gulf Coast Orioles
12	Mordecai, Mike	R/R	5-10/185	12-13-67	Montreal
56	Nunnari, Talmadge	L/L	6-1/200	4-9-75	Ottawa, Harrisburg, Montreal
1	Sasser, Rob	R/R	6-3/205	3-9-75	Toledo
19	Seguignol, Fernando	B/R	6-5/230	1-19-75	Ottawa, Montreal
9	Stevens, Lee	L/L	6-4/219	7-10-67	Montreal
23	Tatis, Fernando	R/R	5-10/180	1-1-75	St. Louis, Memphis
46	Tracy, Andy	L/L	6-3/220	12-11-73	Ottawa, Montreal
3	Vidro, Jose	B/R	5-11/190	8-27-74	Montreal

No.	OUTFIELDERS	B/T	Ht./Wt.	Born	2000 clubs
33	Bergeron, Peter	L/R	6-0/185	11-9-77	Montreal
24	Bradley, Milton	B/R	6-0/170	4-15-78	Ottawa, Montreal
27	Guerrero, Vladimir	R/R	6-3/205	2-9-76	Montreal
1	Jones, Terry	B/R	5-10/160	2-15-71	Montreal
11	Pride, Curtis	L/R	5-11/195	12-17-68	Norfolk, Pawtucket, Boston, Albuquerque
30	Raines, Tim	B/R	5-8/186	9-16-59	DID NOT PLAY
	Ruan, Wilken	R/R	6-0/170	11-18-79	Cape Fear

BALLPARK INFORMATION

Ballpark (capacity, surface)
Olympic Stadium (46,500, artificial)
Address
P.O. Box 500, Station M
Montreal, Que. H1V 3P2
Official website
www.montrealexpos.com
Business phone
514-253-3434
Ticket information
800-GO-EXPOS
Ticket prices
$36 (VIP box seats)
$26 (box seats)
$16 (terrace)
$8 (general admission)
Field dimensions (from home plate)
To left field at foul line, 325 feet
To center field, 404 feet
To right field at foul line, 325 feet
First game played
April 15, 1977 (Phillies 7, Expos 2)

DAY BY DAY

Date	Opp.	Res.	Score	(inn.*)	Hits	Opp. hits	Winning pitcher	Losing pitcher	Save	Record	Pos.	GB
4-3	L.A.	L	4-10		9	9	Brown	Hermanson	Adams	0-1	T4th	1.0
4-4	L.A.	L	4-10		6	17	Park	Irabu		0-2	T4th	1.5
4-5	L.A.	W	6-5		10	12	Telford	Shaw		1-2	T3rd	1.0
4-6	L.A.	W	11-3		14	6	Pavano	Perez		2-2	T2nd	0.5
4-7	S.D.	L	5-10		12	13	Meadows	Powell		2-3	4th	1.0
4-8	S.D.	W	10-9		11	11	Telford	Wall	Urbina	3-3	T2nd	0.5
4-9	S.D.	W	2-1		4	7	Irabu	Boehringer	Urbina	4-3	T2nd	0.5
4-11	At Pit.	W	7-3		9	4	Vazquez	Benson	Kline	5-3	1st	+0.5
4-12	At Pit.	L	4-6		7	10	Silva	Batista	Williams	5-4	T1st	...
4-13	At Pit.	L	3-4		8	10	Silva	Urbina		5-5	T1st	...
4-14	At Phi.	W	4-0		9	6	Hermanson	Brock		6-5	T1st	...
4-16	At Phi.	L	4-5		7	9	Aldred	Telford		6-6	T2nd	0.5
4-18	Chi.	W	4-3		9	7	Strickland	Tapani	Urbina	7-6	T2nd	1.0
4-19	Chi.	W	7-3		11	7	Pavano	Quevedo		8-6	T1st	...
4-20	Chi.	L	6-10		13	10	Williams	Blank		8-7	4th	1.0
4-21	Mil.	W	5-1		8	8	Hermanson	Haynes	Urbina	9-7	T2nd	1.0
4-22	Mil.	L	3-7		5	15	Stull	Irabu		9-8	4th	2.0
4-23	Mil.	W	6-4		10	7	Vazquez	Navarro	Urbina	10-8	4th	2.0
4-25	Col.	W	10-4		14	11	Pavano	Bohanon		11-8	4th	2.0
4-26	Col.	W	9-2		12	5	Hermanson	Jarvis	Urbina	12-8	3rd	2.0
4-28	At S.F	W	9-3		8	11	Telford	Ortiz		13-8	2nd	2.5
4-29	At S.F	L	1-2		3	9	Johnstone	Telford	Nen	13-9	3rd	3.5
4-30	At S.F	W	4-3		6	6	Strickland	Johnstone	Urbina	14-9	3rd	3.5
5-1	At Col.	L	8-15		15	18	White	Hermanson		14-10	3rd	4.5
5-2	At Col.	L	6-12		11	13	Karl	Powell		14-11	3rd	5.5
5-3	At Col.	L	7-16		12	24	Astacio	Irabu		14-12	3rd	5.5
5-5	At Mil.	W	10-2		14	7	Vazquez	Bere		15-12	2nd	5.5
5-6	At Mil.	W	3-2		11	4	Telford	Weathers	Urbina	16-12	2nd	4.5
5-7	At Mil.	L	4-9		8	13	Haynes	Hermanson		16-13	2nd	4.5
5-9	Phi.	W	3-2		8	6	Kline	Gomes		17-13	2nd	4.0
5-10	Phi.	L	0-8		4	13	Person	Vazquez		17-14	2nd	4.0
5-11	Phi.	L	4-6		8	8	Wolf	Pavano	Gomes	17-15	2nd	4.0
5-12	Chi.	W	8-3		10	7	Thurman	Wood	Hermanson	18-15	2nd	4.0
5-13	Chi.	L	1-2		8	6	Lieber	Armas		18-16	3rd	5.0
5-14	Chi.	W	16-15		16	21	Hermanson	Aguilera		19-16	2nd	5.0
5-16	Ari.	W	2-0		5	5	Vazquez	Johnson	Hermanson	20-16	2nd	5.0
5-17	Ari.	W	10-2		14	6	Pavano	Reynoso		21-16	2nd	5.0
5-18	Ari.	L	6-8		8	10	Kim	Telford		21-17	2nd	6.0
5-19	Hou.	W	3-2	(10)	8	8	Hermanson	Slusarski		22-17	2nd	5.0
5-20	Hou.	W	8-7		15	10	Irabu	Elarton	Hermanson	23-17	2nd	5.0
5-21	Hou.	W	8-3		11	7	Vazquez	Lima		24-17	2nd	5.0
5-23	At S.F	W	3-2		11	8	Pavano	Rueter	Hermanson	25-17	2nd	4.0
5-24	At S.F	L	0-18		7	18	Estes	Thurman		25-18	2nd	5.0
5-25	At S.F	L	1-4		6	9	Hernandez	Armas	Nen	25-19	2nd	6.0
5-26	At S.D.	L	2-6		6	11	Whiteside	Irabu		25-20	2nd	6.0
5-27	At S.D.	L	2-4		7	10	Wall	Kline	Hoffman	25-21	3rd	7.0
5-28	At S.D.	L	3-4		8	6	Walker	Pavano	Hoffman	25-22	3rd	7.0
5-30	At Cin.	L	2-4		3	5	Fernandez	Armas	Williamson	25-23	3rd	8.5
5-31	At Cin.	W	10-4		16	6	Johnson	Parris		26-23	3rd	8.0
6-1	At Cin.	W	9-7		17	16	Vazquez	Villone	Kline	27-23	3rd	7.0
6-2	Bal.	W	5-3		9	9	Pavano	Johnson	Kline	28-23	3rd	6.0
6-3	Bal.	W	7-4		12	9	Lira	Rapp	Kline	29-23	3rd	6.0
6-4	Bal.	W	1-0		6	3	Armas	Ponson	Kline	30-23	2nd	5.0
6-5	N.Y. (AL)	W	6-4		8	13	Johnson	Cone	Kline	31-23	2nd	4.0
6-6	N.Y. (AL)	L	1-8		3	13	Grimsley	Vazquez		31-24	2nd	5.0
6-7	N.Y. (AL)	L	2-7		4	9	Hernandez	Pavano		31-25	2nd	5.0
6-9	At Tor.	L	3-13		8	16	Carpenter	Tucker		31-26	3rd	6.0
6-10	At Tor.	W	11-2		14	6	Armas	Escobar		32-26	3rd	6.0
6-11	At Tor.	L	3-8		13	9	Koch	Mota		32-27	3rd	6.0
6-12	At Mil.	L	1-8		5	12	Bere	Vazquez		32-28	3rd	7.0
6-13	At Mil.	W	9-4		12	10	Pavano	Woodard		33-28	3rd	6.0
6-14	At Mil.	L	2-11		8	12	Wright	Johnson		33-29	3rd	7.0
6-16	At Chi.	L	8-9		8	9	Van Poppel	Armas	Aguilera	33-30	3rd	6.5
6-17	At Chi.	L	0-1		8	4	Rain	Hermanson	Aguilera	33-31	3rd	6.5
6-18	At Chi.	W	4-3	(11)	9	9	Telford	Garibay	Rigby	34-31	3rd	6.5
6-19	Pit.	W	2-1		7	6	Pavano	Loiselle	Kline	35-31	3rd	5.5
6-20	Pit.	L	1-2		6	4	Benson	Johnson	Williams	35-32	3rd	6.5
6-21	Pit.	L	3-8		9	10	Cordova	Armas	Peters	35-33	3rd	6.5
6-22	Pit.	W	6-5		8	11	Hermanson	Ritchie	Telford	36-33	3rd	6.5
6-23	Phi.	L	6-13		9	17	Coggin	Vazquez		36-34	3rd	7.5
6-24	Phi.	L	1-8		7	11	Wolf	Pavano		36-35	3rd	7.5
6-25	Phi.	W	3-1		9	8	Johnson	Byrd	Kline	37-35	3rd	7.5
6-27	Atl.	W	6-4		9	5	Armas	Glavine	Kline	38-35	3rd	6.5

Date	Opp.	Res.	Score	(inn.*)	Hits	Opp. hits	Winning pitcher	Losing pitcher	Save	Record	Pos.	GB
6-28	Atl.	L	4-7		12	10	Mulholland	Hermanson	Ligtenberg	38-36	3rd	7.5
6-30	Fla.	L	4-5		7	12	Almanza	Kline	Alfonseca	38-37	3rd	8.0
7-1	Fla.	L	5-6		13	10	Dempster	Johnson	Alfonseca	38-38	3rd	8.0
7-2	Fla.	L	1-2		4	5	Cornelius	Santana	Alfonseca	38-39	4th	9.0
7-3	At Atl.	W	17-1		18	6	Armas	Mulholland		39-39	4th	8.0
7-4	At Atl.	L	3-7		7	10	Maddux	Hermanson		39-40	4th	9.0
7-5	At Atl.	W	6-5		13	10	Vazquez	Millwood	Kline	40-40	4th	8.0
7-6	At Atl.	W	4-2		14	6	Johnson	Burkett	Kline	41-40	T3rd	7.0
7-7	Tor.	W	10-5		12	10	Lira	Quantrill		42-40	3rd	7.0
7-8	Tor.	L	3-6		6	7	Wells	Armas	Koch	42-41	T3rd	8.0
7-9	Tor.	L	3-13		8	18	Castillo	Hermanson		42-42	4th	8.0
7-13	At T.B.	L	4-6		8	14	Mecir	Lira	Hernandez	42-43	4th	9.0
7-14	At T.B.	L	5-8		12	11	Lopez	Armas	Hernandez	42-44	4th	10.0
7-15	At T.B.	W	4-1		13	9	Hermanson	Trachsel	Kline	43-44	4th	10.0
7-16	At Bos.	L	2-5		4	8	Wakefield	Johnson	Wasdin	43-45	4th	11.0
7-17	At Bos.	L	3-7		7	9	Pichardo	Telford		43-46	4th	11.0
7-18	At Bos.	L	1-3		6	9	P. Martinez	Vazquez	Lowe	43-47	4th	12.0
7-19	N.Y.	L	3-5		9	11	Mahomes	Kline	Benitez	43-48	4th	12.5
7-20	N.Y.	W	4-1		8	7	Hermanson	Hampton	Strickland	44-48	4th	12.0
7-21	At Fla.	W	7-3		9	8	Thurman	Smith		45-48	4th	12.0
7-22	At Fla.	W	17-7		19	7	Johnson	Cornelius		46-48	4th	11.0
7-23	At Fla.	W	7-6		17	11	Vazquez	Sanchez	Strickland	47-48	3rd	11.0
7-25	At N.Y.	L	0-5		5	12	Rusch	Hermanson		47-49	3rd	12.0
7-27†	At N.Y.	L	8-9		9	15	Franco	Strickland	Benitez	47-50		
7-27‡	At N.Y.	L	3-4		7	7	Hampton	Irabu		47-51	4th	13.0
7-28	Cin.	L	3-8		8	12	Dessens	Johnson		47-52	4th	14.0
7-29	Cin.	L	3-4	(11)	11	11	Graves	Santana		47-53	4th	15.0
7-30	Cin.	L	4-7		8	11	Bell	Hermanson	Graves	47-54	4th	16.0
7-31	StL.	L	0-4		6	10	Kile	Thurman		47-55	4th	16.5
8-1	StL.	W	4-0		9	5	Moore	Ankiel		48-55	4th	16.5
8-2	StL.	L	7-10		11	11	Hentgen	Johnson		48-56	4th	16.5
8-4	At Hou.	L	6-7		14	12	Green	Kline	Dotel	48-57	4th	17.0
8-5	At Hou.	W	10-9	(10)	14	15	Strickland	Valdes	Kline	49-57	4th	16.0
8-6	At Hou.	L	1-8		4	12	Elarton	Thurman		49-58	4th	17.0
8-7	At Ari.	L	2-5		8	9	Schilling	Moore		49-59	4th	17.0
8-8	At Ari.	W	9-3		16	9	Lira	Anderson		50-59	4th	17.0
8-9	At Ari.	W	4-3		15	8	Strickland	Guzman	Telford	51-59	4th	16.0
8-11	Col.	L	3-10		11	13	Bohanon	Hermanson		51-60	4th	17.0
8-12	Col.	L	2-14		6	22	Yoshii	Moore		51-61	4th	18.0
8-13	Col.	L	3-5		7	12	Chouinard	Strickland	White	51-62	4th	18.0
8-14	Col.	L	3-4		10	12	House	Strickland	Jimenez	51-63	4th	19.0
8-15	S.F	L	7-9		9	11	del Toro	Lira	Nen	51-64	4th	20.0
8-16	S.F	L	1-4		8	7	Gardner	Hermanson	Nen	51-65	4th	21.0
8-17	S.F	L	4-5		7	11	Estes	Moore	Rodriguez	51-66	4th	21.5
8-18	At S.D.	W	6-3		11	7	Thurman	Clement	Strickland	52-66	4th	20.5
8-19	At S.D.	L	3-4	(11)	8	12	Walker	Santana		52-67	4th	20.5
8-20	At S.D.	L	4-5		10	7	Witasick	Lira	Hoffman	52-68	4th	21.5
8-21	At L.A.	W	4-1		9	8	Hermanson	Herges	Strickland	53-68	4th	21.5
8-22	At L.A.	L	6-14		13	16	Adams	Santana		53-69	4th	21.5
8-23	At L.A.	L	1-5		4	6	Brown	Thurman		53-70	4th	22.5
8-24	At L.A.	L	0-7		5	11	Park	Vazquez		53-71	4th	22.5
8-25	Hou.	L	1-3		8	7	Holt	Lira	Dotel	53-72	4th	23.5
8-26	Hou.	W	5-4		9	10	Hermanson	Lima	Kline	54-72	4th	22.5
8-27	Hou.	L	3-7		6	10	Elarton	Moore		54-73	4th	22.5
8-28	Ari.	W	9-5		14	9	Thurman	Schilling	Telford	55-73	5th	21.5
8-29	Ari.	L	7-8		12	8	Plesac	Forster	Mantei	55-74	5th	21.5
8-30	Ari.	L	0-7		5	10	Johnson	Lira		55-75	5th	22.5
9-1	At Cin.	L	2-8		7	10	Bell	Hermanson		55-76	5th	22.5
9-2	At Cin.	W	9-5		12	6	Lira	Villone		56-76	4th	22.0
9-3	At Cin.	L	1-8		11	12	Parris	Thurman		56-77	4th	22.0
9-4	At StL.	L	2-4		9	6	Hentgen	Vazquez	Veres	56-78	4th	22.5
9-5	At StL.	L	6-7		4	7	Reames	Santana	Timlin	56-79	4th	23.5
9-6	At StL.	W	7-2		12	8	Hermanson	Stephenson		57-79	4th	23.5
9-7	At StL.	L	1-6		5	11	Kile	Armas		57-80	4th	24.5
9-8	At Atl.	L	2-3		10	9	Ashby	Moore	Rocker	57-81	4th	25.5
9-9	At Atl.	W	7-5	(12)	14	15	Santana	Seelbach		58-81	4th	24.5
9-10	At Atl.	W	4-0		7	6	Vazquez	Glavine		59-81	4th	23.5
9-11†	At Phi.	L	2-5		7	8	Politte	Hermanson	Brantley	59-82		
9-11‡	At Phi.	W	7-6		12	10	Mota	Padilla	Strickland	60-82	4th	23.5
9-12	At Phi.	W	1-0		3	3	Armas	Telemaco	Strickland	61-82	4th	22.5
9-13	At Phi.	L	5-15		8	19	Chen	Lira		61-83	4th	23.5
9-14	N.Y.	L	4-10		10	12	Rusch	Thurman		61-84	4th	24.5
9-15	N.Y.	W	4-3		10	9	Vazquez	Wendell	Strickland	62-84	4th	23.5
9-16	N.Y.	L	4-10		11	14	Reed	Hermanson		62-85	4th	24.5
9-17	N.Y.	W	5-0		7	4	Armas	B.J. Jones		63-85	4th	24.5
9-18	Fla.	W	11-4		9	6	Lira	Sanchez		64-85	4th	24.5
9-19	Fla.	L	1-3		5	7	Dempster	Thurman	Alfonseca	64-86	4th	25.5
9-20	Fla.	W	4-2		9	9	Vazquez	Cornelius	Strickland	65-86	4th	24.5

Date	Opp.	Res.	Score	(inn.*)	Hits	Opp. hits	Winning pitcher	Losing pitcher	Save	Record	Pos.	GB
9-21	Fla.	W	10-3		14	7	Hermanson	Burnett		66-86	4th	24.0
9-22	Atl.	W	6-4		9	6	Armas	Millwood	Strickland	67-86	4th	23.0
9-23	Atl.	L	0-10		5	9	Maddux	Lira		67-87	4th	24.0
9-24	Atl.	L	5-14		10	21	Ashby	Thurman		67-88	4th	25.0
9-25	Atl.	L	0-6		8	12	Glavine	Vazquez		67-89	4th	26.0
9-26	At Fla.	L	4-5	(10)	8	8	Alfonseca	Kline		67-90	4th	27.0
9-27	At Fla.	L	3-6		5	9	Burnett	Armas	Alfonseca	67-91	4th	27.0
9-28	At Fla.	L	4-7		8	9	Penny	Lira	Alfonseca	67-92	4th	27.0
9-29	At N.Y.	L	2-11		7	11	Hampton	Thurman		67-93	4th	27.0
9-30	At N.Y.	L	2-4		4	7	Wendell	Vazquez	Benitez	67-94	4th	28.0
10-1	At N.Y.	L	2-3	(13)	9	9	Mahomes	Powell		67-95	4th	28.0

Monthly records: April (14-9), May (12-14), June (12-14), July (9-18), August (8-20), September (12-19), October (0-1).
*Innings, if other than nine. †First game of a doubleheader. ‡Second game of a doubleheader.

HIGHLIGHTS

High point: Having dropped below .500 for the first time since the opening week of the season, the Expos went to Atlanta and posted a surprising 17-1 victory behind young Tony Armas Jr. After losing Game 2 of the series to Greg Maddux, the Expos rebounded to win the next two and lift their head above .500 for the last time.

Low point: Only one win away from matching its 1999 win total (68), the Expos lost their final nine games and faded quietly into the sunset. The final six defeats were administered on the road by the Marlins and the Mets—the finale ending in the 13th inning after the Expos failed to score with the bases loaded in the 10th and 11th.

Turning point: The club was eight games over .500 after beating the Yankees on June 5 at Olympic Stadium. But the roof began caving in on a promising season the next day when the Yanks battered the Montreal bullpen for six runs in the eighth inning of an 8-1 loss. It was all downhill after that.

Most valuable player: Vladimir Guerrero continued to rewrite the club's record book as he batted .345 with 44 home runs and 123 RBIs. Guerrero joined Joe DiMaggio, Ted Williams and Jimmie Foxx as the only players to bat .300 with 35 homers and 100 RBIs in three straight seasons before age 25.

Most valuable pitcher: In the absence of a bona fide No. 1 starter, 24-year-old righthander Javier Vazquez emerged as the defacto leader of the rotation. Vazquez, who led the team in wins (11), innings (217 2/3), strikeouts (196), ERA (4.05) and starts (33), was dominant for extended periods and pushed himself to go deeper and deeper into games as the season progressed.

Most improved player: Second baseman Jose Vidro, shaking off the challenge of free-agent veteran Mickey Morandini, set unexpectedly high marks for homers (24), runs (101) and RBIs (97) in addition to batting .331.

Most pleasant surprise: Pitching through a suspected rotator cuff tear, 24-year-old Scott Strickland enjoyed a breakout second half and became the late-season closer, converting 9 of 12 save opportunities and finishing with a scoreless streak of 15 2/3 innings. A September MRI showed no tear in his shoulder.

Key injuries: Starters Carl Pavano (tri-ceps), Mike Thurman (elbow), Armas (elbow, shoulder) and Hideki Irabu (elbow, knee) all went down for extended periods. ... Closer Ugueth Urbina (elbow) appeared in only 13 games. ... Newly acquired lefty specialist Graeme Lloyd (shoulder) didn't throw a pitch for his new team after May surgery. ... Workhorse reliever Anthony Telford (rotator cuff) didn't appear in a game after September 8.

Notable: Vladimir Guerrero set team records in eight categories and finished in the top five in nine N.L. categories. He led both leagues in intentional walks with 23. ... Vladimir Guerrero and Vidro combined for 397 hits, a team record for two hitters combined. ... Armas was dominant against the Braves, going 3-0 with a 2.95 ERA. ... Steve Kline's 83 appearances tied Chicago White Sox reliever Kelly Wunsch for the major league lead. He has a two-year total of 165. Kline recorded five saves in consecutive games from June 1-5 after replacing the injured Urbina as the team's closer.

—STEPHANIE MYLES

RECORDS

2000 regular-season record: 67-95 (4th in N.L. East); 37-44 at home; 30-51 on road; 28-40 vs. East; 23-27 vs. Central; 16-28 vs. West; 19-24 vs. lefthanded starters; 48-71 vs. righthanded starters; 21-39 on grass; 46-56 on turf; 18-29 in daytime; 49-66 at night; 23-24 in one-run games; 4-4 in extra-inning games; 0-1-1 in doubleheaders.

Team record past five years: 366-444 (.452, ranks 14th in league in that span).

TEAM LEADERS

Batting average: Vladimir Guerrero (.345).
At-bats: Jose Vidro (606).
Runs: Vladimir Guerrero, Jose Vidro (101).
Hits: Jose Vidro (200).
Total Bases: Vladimir Guerrero (379).
Doubles: Jose Vidro (51).
Triples: Vladimir Guerrero (11).
Home runs: Vladimir Guerrero (44).
Runs batted in: Vladimir Guerrero (123).
Stolen bases: Peter Bergeron (11).
Slugging percentage: Vladimir Guerrero (.664).

On-base percentage: Vladimir Guerrero (.410).
Wins: Dustin Hermanson (12).
Earned-run average: Javier Vazquez (4.05).
Complete games: Dustin Hermanson, Javier Vazquez (2).
Shutouts: Dustin Hermanson, Javier Vazquez (1).
Saves: Steve Kline (14).
Innings pitched: Javier Vazquez (217.2).
Strikeouts: Javier Vazquez (196).

GAMES BY POSITION

Catcher: Chris Widger 85, Brian Schneider 43, Lenny Webster 32, Michael Barrett 28, Charlie O'Brien 9, Yohanny Valera 7.
First base: Lee Stevens 123, Fernando Seguignol 30, Andy Tracy 28, Talmadge Nunnari 14, Geoff Blum 11, Mike Mordecai 3.
Second base: Jose Vidro 153, Geoff Blum 13, Mike Mordecai 9, Trace Coquillette 8, Orlando Cabrera 1, Wilton Guerrero 1.
Third base: Mike Mordecai 58, Michael Barrett 55, Geoff Blum 55, Andy Tracy 34, Trace Coquillette 19.
Shortstop: Orlando Cabrera 124, Geoff Blum 44, Tomas de la Rosa 29, Mike Mordecai 10.
Outfield: Vladimir Guerrero 151, Peter Bergeron 146, Terry Jones 78, Wilton Guerrero 75, Rondell White 74, Milton Bradley 41, Fernando Seguignol 31, Trace Coquillette 2.
Designated hitter: Wilton Guerrero 6, Vladimir Guerrero 2, Tomas de la Rosa 1, Fernando Seguignol 1.

TOP DRAFT CHOICES

1. **Justin Wayne,** RHP, Stanford Univ.
2. None.
3. **Grady Sizemore,** OF, Cascade H.S., Mill Creek, Wash.
4. **Cliff Lee,** LHP, University of Arkansas.
5. **Thomas Mitchell,** RHP, Bladenboro (N.C.) H.S.
6. **Shawn Hill,** RHP, Bishop Reding H.S., Georgetown, Ontario.
7. **Wes Littleton,** RHP, Vista H.S., Oceanside, Calif.
8. **Phil Seibel,** LHP, University of Texas.
9. **Benji DeQuin,** LHP, Gavilan (Calif.) J.C.
10. **Darryl Jenkins,** SS, Plainfield (Ill.) H.S.

NEW YORK METS
NATIONAL LEAGUE EAST DIVISION

Mets
2001 SCHEDULE
Home games shaded; D—Day game (games starting before 5 p.m.)
*—All-Star Game at Safeco Field (Seattle)

APRIL
SUN	MON	TUE	WED	THU	FRI	SAT
1	2	3 D ATL	4 ATL	5 ATL	6 MON	7 D MON
8 MON	9 D ATL	10 D	11 ATL	12 ATL	13 CIN	14 D CIN
15 D CIN	16 D MON	17 MON	18 D MON	19	20 CIN	21 D CIN
22 D CIN	23	24 MIL	25 MIL	26 D MIL	27 STL	28 D STL
29 STL	30 D HOU					

MAY
SUN	MON	TUE	WED	THU	FRI	SAT
		1 HOU	2 HOU	3	4 ARI	5 D ARI
6 ARI	7 D COL	8 COL	9 COL	10 D COL	11 SF	12 D SF
13 D SF	14	15 SD	16 SD	17 SD	18 LA	19 D LA
20 LA	21 D MON	22 MON	23 MON	24 FLA	25 FLA	26 D FLA
27 FLA	28 D PHI	29 PHI	30 D PHI	31 FLA		

JUNE
SUN	MON	TUE	WED	THU	FRI	SAT
					1 FLA	2 FLA
3 D FLA	4	5 PHI	6 PHI	7 PHI	8 TB	9 D TB
10 D TB	11	12 BAL	13 BAL	14 BAL	15 NYY	16 D NYY
17 NYY	18 MON	19 MON	20 MON	21 MON	22 ATL	23 D ATL
24 ATL	25 CUB	26 D CUB	27 D CUB	28 ATL	29 ATL	30 D ATL

JULY
SUN	MON	TUE	WED	THU	FRI	SAT
1 ATL	2 D	3 CUB	4 D CUB	5 D CUB	6 NYY	7 D NYY
8 D NYY	9	10 *	11 *	12 BOS	13 BOS	14 D BOS
15 D TOR	16 TOR	17 TOR	18 FLA	19 D FLA	20 PHI	21 PHI
22 D PHI	23 FLA	24 FLA	25 FLA	26 PHI	27 PHI	28 D PHI
29 D PHI	30	31 HOU				

AUGUST
SUN	MON	TUE	WED	THU	FRI	SAT
			1 HOU	2 HOU	3 ARI	4 D ARI
5 D ARI	6	7 MIL	8 MIL	9 D MIL	10 STL	11 D STL
12 D STL	13	14 SD	15 SD	16 D SD	17 LA	18 LA
19 D LA	20	21 COL	22 COL	23 COL	24 SF	25 SF
26 D SF	27 D SF	28 D PHI	29 PHI	30 PHI	31 FLA	

SEPTEMBER
SUN	MON	TUE	WED	THU	FRI	SAT
						1 FLA
2 D FLA	3 D PHI	4 D PHI	5 PHI	6	7 FLA	8 FLA
9 FLA	10 D	11 PIT	12 PIT	13 PIT	14 MON	15 MON
16 D MON	17 D PIT	18 PIT	19 PIT	20	21 ATL	22 ATL
23 ATL	24 D	25 MON	26 MON	27 MON	28 ATL	29 ATL
30 ATL	D					

2001 SEASON
CLUB DIRECTORY

Chairman of the board
Nelson Doubleday
President and chief executive officer
Fred Wilpon
Directors
Nelson Doubleday, Fred Wilpon, Saul B. Katz, Steve Phillips, Marvin B. Tepper
Special advisor to the board of directors
Richard Cummins
Senior v.p., general manager
Steve Phillips
Sr. asst. g.m./international scouting dir.
Omar Minaya
Sr. assistant g.m./player personnel
Jim Duquette
Assistant g.m./amateur scouting
Gary LaRocque
Assistant g.m./professional scouting
Carmen Fusco
Assistant directors of amateur scouting
Jack Bowen, Fred Wright
Assistant director of player personnel
Kevin Morgan
Senior v.p. and treasurer
Harold W. O'Shaughnessy
Senior v.p. of business & legal affairs
David Howard
Vice president, marketing
To be announced
V.p., purchasing and special projects
Bob Mandt
V.p., ticket sales and services
Bill Ianniciello
Senior v.p. and consultant
J. Frank Cashen
Director of marketing
To be announced
Director of marketing production
Tim Gunkel
Director of human resources
Shez Jackson
General counsel
David Cohen

Dir., admin. and data processing
To be announced
Director, community outreach
Jill Knee
Director of corporate sales
Paul Danforth
Controller
Lennie Labita
Director of media relations
Jay Horwitz
Director, ticket operations
Dan DeMato
Manager, customer relations
Joann Galardy
Director of stadium operations
Kevin McCarthy
Director of minor league operations
Kevin Morgan
Club physicians
Dr. David Altchek
Club psychologist/E.A.P.
Dr. Allan Lans
Team trainers
Fred Hina, Scott Lawrenson
Advance scouts
Bruce Benedict, Mike Toomey
Professional scouts
Bruce Benedict, Edwin Bryant, Harry Dunlop, Dick Gernert, Roland Johnson, Buddy Kerr, Bill Latham, Harry Minor, Tim Teufel, Mike Toomey
Regional scouting supervisors
Paul Fryer, Gene Kerns, Terry Tripp
Scouting supervisors
Kevin Blankenship, Quincy Boyd, Larry Chase, Joe DelliCarri, Kevin Frady, Chuck Hensley Jr., Dave Lottsfeldt, Fred Mazuca, Marlin McPhail, Randy Milligan, Bob Minor, Greg Morhardt, Joe Morlan, Joe Nigro, Jim Reeves, Junior Roman, Bob Rossi, Joe Salermo, Greg Tubbs

MINOR LEAGUE AFFILIATES

Class	Team	League	Manager
AAA	Norfolk	International	John Gibbons
AA	Binghamton	Eastern	Howie Freiling
A	Brooklyn	New York-Pennsylvania	Edgar Alfonzo
A	Capital City	South Atlantic	To be announced
A	St. Lucie	Florida State	To be announced
Rookie	Kingsport	Appalachian	Joey Cora

BROADCAST INFORMATION

Radio: WFAN-AM (660).
TV: WPIX-TV (Channel 11).
Cable TV: Fox Sports New York.

SPRING TRAINING

Ballpark (city): Thomas J. White Stadium (Port St. Lucie, Fla.).
Ticket information: 561-871-2115.

Follow the Mets all season at: www.sportingnews.com/baseball/teams/mets/

2001 SEASON *New York Mets*

Manager—Bobby Valentine (2).
Coaches—Dave Engle (53), Bobby Floyd (55), Charlie Hough (54), Randy Niemann (52), John Stearns (12), Mookie Wilson (1).

No.	PITCHERS	B/T	Ht./Wt.	Born	2000 clubs
17	Appier, Kevin	R/R	6-2/200	12-6-67	Oakland
49	Benitez, Armando	R/R	6-4/229	11-3-72	New York N.L.
26	Cammack, Eric	R/R	6-1/180	8-14-75	Norfolk, New York N.L.
27	Cook, Dennis	L/L	6-3/190	10-4-62	New York N.L.
45	Franco, John	L/L	5-10/185	9-17-60	New York N.L.
66	Gonzalez, Dicky	R/R	5-11/170	10-21-78	Binghamton
21	Jones, Bobby	R/L	6-0/178	4-11-72	Norfolk, New York N.L.
22	Leiter, Al	L/L	6-3/220	10-23-65	New York N.L.
61	Maness, Nick	R/R	6-4/210	10-17-78	St. Lucie, Binghamton
	Martin, Tom	L/L	6-1/200	5-21-70	Cleveland, Buffalo
35	Reed, Rick	R/R	6-1/195	8-16-65	New York N.L.
34	Riggan, Jerrod	R/R	6-3/200	5-16-74	Binghamton, New York N.L.
36	Roberts, Grant	R/R	6-3/205	9-13-77	Norfolk, New York N.L.
46	Rodriguez, Rich	L/L	6-0/205	3-1-63	New York N.L., Norfolk
48	Rusch, Glendon	L/L	6-1/200	11-7-74	New York N.L.
39	Santana, Julio	R/R	6-0/225	1-20-74	Pawtucket, Montreal
63	Seo, Jae	R/R	6-1/215	5-24-77	DID NOT PLAY
29	Trachsel, Steve	R/R	6-4/205	10-31-70	Tampa Bay, Toronto
	Walker, Tyler	R/R	6-3/255	5-15-76	Binghamton, Norfolk
33	Wall, Donne	R/R	6-1/205	7-11-67	San Diego, Las Vegas
99	Wendell, Turk	L/R	6-2/205	5-19-67	New York N.L.
51	White, Rick	R/R	6-4/230	12-23-68	Tampa Bay, New York N.L.

No.	CATCHERS	B/T	Ht./Wt.	Born	2000 clubs
31	Piazza, Mike	R/R	6-3/215	9-4-68	New York N.L.
7	Pratt, Todd	R/R	6-3/230	2-9-67	New York N.L.
3	Wilson, Vance	R/R	5-11/190	3-17-73	Norfolk, New York N.L.

No.	INFIELDERS	B/T	Ht./Wt.	Born	2000 clubs
13	Alfonzo, Edgardo	R/R	5-11/187	11-8-73	New York N.L.
19	Harris, Lenny	L/R	5-10/220	10-28-64	Arizona, New York N.L.
47	McEwing, Joe	R/R	5-11/170	10-19-72	Norfolk, New York N.L.
10	Ordonez, Rey	R/R	5-9/159	11-11-72	New York N.L.
8	Relaford, Desi	B/R	5-9/174	9-16-73	Philadelphia, San Diego
30	Toca, Jorge	R/R	6-3/220	1-7-75	Norfolk, Binghamton, New York N.L.
4	Ventura, Robin	L/R	6-1/198	7-14-67	New York N.L.
9	Zeile, Todd	R/R	6-1/200	9-9-65	New York N.L.

No.	OUTFIELDERS	B/T	Ht./Wt.	Born	2000 clubs
50	Agbayani, Benny	R/R	6-0/225	12-28-71	New York N.L.
60	Cole, Brian	R/R	5-9/170	9-28-78	St. Lucie, Binghamton
25	Escobar, Alex	R/R	6-1/180	9-6-78	Binghamton
18	Hamilton, Darryl	L/R	6-1/192	12-3-64	New York N.L., St. Lucie, Norfolk
44	Payton, Jay	R/R	5-10/185	11-22-72	New York N.L.
6	Perez, Timo	L/L	5-9/165	4-8-77	St. Lucie, Norfolk, New York N.L.

BALLPARK INFORMATION

Ballpark (capacity, surface)
Shea Stadium (56,516, grass)

Address
123-01 Roosevelt Ave.
Flushing, NY 11368

Official website
www.mets.com

Business phone
718-507-METS

Ticket information
718-507-TIXX

Ticket prices
$64 (Metropolitan Club gold, inner baseline box)
$60 (Metropolitan Club)
$43 (inner field box, inner loge box, outer baseline box)
$38 (middle field box)
$33 (outer field box, outer loge box, mezzanine box)
$29 (loge reserved)
$23 (mezzanine reserved, upper box)
$12 (upper reserved, back rows loge and mezzanine)

Field dimensions (from home plate)
To left field at foul line, 338 feet
To center field, 410 feet
To right field at foul line, 338 feet

First game played
April 17, 1964 (Pirates 4, Mets 3)

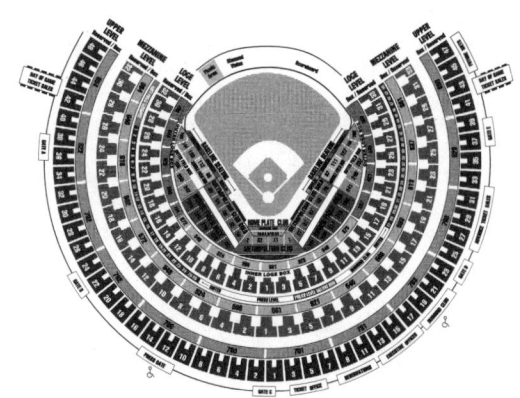

2001 SEASON *New York Mets*

Date	Opp.	Res.	Score	(inn.*)	Hits	Opp. hits	Winning pitcher	Losing pitcher	Save	Record	Pos.	GB
3-29	Chi.§	L	3-5		7	12	Lieber	Hampton	Aguilera	0-1	T1st	0.5
3-30	At Chi.§	W	5-1	(11)	6	5	Cook	Young		1-1	1st	...
4-3	S.D.	W	2-1		4	5	Leiter	Wall	Benitez	2-1	3rd	...
4-5	S.D.	L	0-4		7	11	Williams	B.J. Jones		2-2	2nd	0.5
4-6	S.D.	L	5-8		8	10	Clement	Hampton		2-3	4th	1.0
4-7	L.A.	W	2-1		2	4	Reed	Dreifort	Benitez	3-3	T2nd	0.5
4-8	L.A.	L	5-6	(10)	11	9	Fetters	Benitez	Shaw	3-4	4th	1.0
4-10	At Phi.	L	7-9		9	9	Telemaco	Rodriguez	Gomes	3-5	5th	1.5
4-12	At Phi.	L	5-8		7	12	Person	Hampton	Gomes	3-6	5th	2.0
4-13	At Phi.	W	2-1		8	5	Cook	Aldred	Benitez	4-6	5th	1.0
4-14	At Pit.	W	8-5	(12)	20	11	Franco	Silva		5-6	4th	1.0
4-15	At Pit.	L	0-2		5	4	Anderson	Rusch	Williams	5-7	4th	1.5
4-16	At Pit.	W	12-9		15	11	Mahomes	Peters	Benitez	6-7	4th	1.0
4-18	Mil.	W	10-7		11	9	Hampton	Navarro	Benitez	7-7	4th	1.5
4-19	Mil.	W	3-1		8	8	Reed	Bere	Benitez	8-7	4th	0.5
4-20	Mil.	W	5-4	(10)	7	9	Wendell	Leskanic		9-7	3rd	0.5
4-22†	Chi.	W	8-3		12	8	Rusch	Lieber		10-7		
4-22‡	Chi.	W	7-6		10	11	Cook	Farnsworth	Benitez	11-7	2nd	0.5
4-23	Chi.	W	15-8		18	10	Hampton	Tapani		12-7	2nd	0.5
4-24	L.A.	W	1-0		8	3	Benitez	Adams		13-7	2nd	...
4-25	Cin.	W	6-5		8	8	Wendell	Sullivan	Benitez	14-7	2nd	...
4-26	Cin.	L	1-12		4	18	Neagle	Springer		14-8	2nd	1.0
4-27	Cin.	L	1-2	(12)	6	8	Graves	Benitez	Sullivan	14-9	2nd	2.0
4-28	At Col.	L	5-12		12	14	Astacio	Hampton		14-10	3rd	3.0
4-29	At Col.	W	13-6		23	10	Reed	Yoshii		15-10	2nd	3.0
4-30	At Col.	W	14-11		15	10	Leiter	Bohanon		16-10	2nd	3.0
5-1	At S.F	L	3-10		7	11	Estes	Pulsipher		16-11	2nd	4.0
5-2	At S.F	L	1-7		8	11	Hernandez	Rusch		16-12	2nd	5.0
5-3	At S.F	L	5-8	(11)	14	12	Rodriguez	Wendell		16-13	2nd	5.0
5-4	At S.F	L	2-7		4	7	Rodriguez	Reed		16-14	3rd	5.5
5-5	At Fla.	W	4-1		5	4	Leiter	Sanchez	Franco	17-14	3rd	5.5
5-6	At Fla.	L	1-9		8	12	Fernandez	Pulsipher		17-15	3rd	5.5
5-7	At Fla.	L	0-3		1	9	Dempster	Rusch		17-16	3rd	5.5
5-9	At Pit.	W	2-0		8	6	Hampton	Benson	Benitez	18-16	3rd	5.0
5-10	At Pit.	L	9-13		13	20	Silva	Cook		18-17	T3rd	5.0
5-11	At Pit.	W	3-2		6	8	Leiter	Anderson		19-17	T3rd	4.0
5-12	Fla.	L	4-6		10	12	Dempster	Rusch	Alfonseca	19-18	4th	5.0
5-13	Fla.	L	6-7		12	8	Mahay	Cook	Alfonseca	19-19	4th	6.0
5-14	Fla.	W	5-1		5	8	Hampton	Penny		20-19	4th	6.0
5-16	Col.	L	3-4	(11)	12	9	Tavarez	Wendell	Jimenez	20-20	4th	7.0
5-17	Col.	W	4-2		10	5	Leiter	Arrojo	Franco	21-20	4th	7.0
5-19	Ari.	W	4-3		8	9	B.J. Jones	Stottlemyre	Benitez	22-20	3rd	6.5
5-20	Ari.	W	8-7		11	13	Hampton	Daal	Benitez	23-20	3rd	6.5
5-21	Ari.	W	7-6		10	10	Wendell	Kim		24-20	3rd	6.5
5-22	At S.D.	L	0-1		5	5	Clement	Franco	Hoffman	24-21	3rd	7.0
5-23	At S.D.	W	5-3	(10)	6	7	Wendell	Hoffman	Benitez	25-21	3rd	6.0
5-24	At S.D.	L	4-5		7	11	Wall	Mahomes	Hoffman	25-22	3rd	7.0
5-26	At StL.	W	5-2		9	9	Hampton	Thompson	Benitez	26-22	3rd	6.5
5-27	At StL.	W	12-8		15	11	Cook	Veres		27-22	2nd	6.5
5-28	At StL.	W	6-2		11	6	Rusch	Kile		28-22	2nd	5.5
5-29	At L.A.	L	1-4		4	8	Park	Leiter		28-23	2nd	6.5
5-30	At L.A.	W	10-5		13	13	Franco	Shaw		29-23	2nd	6.5
5-31	At L.A.	L	3-4		8	6	Fetters	Wendell		29-24	2nd	7.0
6-2	T.B.	W	5-3		5	7	Rusch	White	Benitez	30-24	2nd	5.5
6-3	T.B.	W	1-0		6	5	Leiter	Trachsel	Benitez	31-24	2nd	5.5
6-4	T.B.	L	5-15		9	14	Yan	B.J. Jones		31-25	3rd	5.5
6-5	Bal.	L	2-4		6	10	Mussina	Hampton	Timlin	31-26	3rd	5.5
6-7	Bal.	W	11-3		12	12	Mahomes	Erickson		32-26	3rd	5.0
6-8	Bal.	W	8-7	(10)	11	13	Cook	Mercedes		33-26	2nd	4.5
6-9	At N.Y. (AL)	W	12-2		15	8	Leiter	Clemens		34-26	2nd	4.5
6-10	At N.Y. (AL)	L	5-13		8	17	Pettitte	B.J. Jones		34-27	2nd	5.5
6-13	At Chi.	L	3-4		5	11	Heredia	Franco	Aguilera	34-28	2nd	5.5
6-14	At Chi.	W	10-8		14	14	Rusch	Garibay	Benitez	35-28	2nd	5.5
6-16	At Mil.	W	7-1		15	3	Leiter	Haynes		36-28	2nd	4.0
6-17	At Mil.	L	2-3		9	4	Snyder	Rusch	Wickman	36-29	2nd	4.0
6-18	At Mil.	W	7-3		10	7	Reed	Bere		37-29	2nd	4.0
6-20	Phi.	L	2-3	(10)	7	7	Brock	Benitez	Brantley	37-30	2nd	4.5
6-21	Phi.	L	5-10		10	12	Gomes	Franco		37-31	2nd	4.5
6-22	Phi.	W	5-4		7	8	Rusch	Politte	Cook	38-31	2nd	4.5
6-23	Pit.	W	12-2		14	7	B.J. Jones	Arroyo		39-31	2nd	4.5
6-24	Pit.	W	10-8		12	15	Franco	Loiselle	Benitez	40-31	2nd	3.5
6-25	Pit.	W	9-0		12	5	Hampton	Benson		41-31	2nd	3.5
6-26	Fla.	W	10-5		12	11	Leiter	Cornelius		42-31	2nd	3.0

Date	Opp.	Res.	Score	(inn.*)	Hits	Opp. hits	Winning pitcher	Losing pitcher	Save	Record	Pos.	GB
6-27	Fla.	W	5-2		7	6	Rusch	Sanchez	Benitez	43-31	2nd	2.0
6-28	Fla.	W	6-5		13	10	B.J. Jones	Penny	Franco	44-31	2nd	2.0
6-29	Atl.	L	4-6		7	11	Burkett	Reed	Ligtenberg	44-32	2nd	3.0
6-30	Atl.	W	11-8		12	11	Benitez	Mulholland		45-32	2nd	2.0
7-1	Atl.	W	9-1		11	6	Leiter	Maddux		46-32	2nd	1.0
7-2	Atl.	L	2-10		5	17	Glavine	Rusch		46-33	2nd	2.0
7-3	At Fla.	L	0-2		4	6	Almanza	Wendell		46-34	2nd	2.0
7-4	At Fla.	L	8-9		9	10	Darensbourg	B.M. Jones	Alfonseca	46-35	2nd	3.0
7-5	At Fla.	W	11-2		15	6	Hampton	Smith		47-35	2nd	2.0
7-7	N.Y. (AL)	L	1-2		6	6	Hernandez	Leiter	Rivera	47-36	2nd	2.5
7-8†	N.Y. (AL)	L	2-4		6	6	Gooden	B.J. Jones	Rivera	47-37		
7-8‡	At N.Y. (AL)	L	2-4		7	5	Clemens	Rusch	Rivera	47-38	2nd	4.0
7-9	N.Y. (AL)	W	2-0		6	7	Hampton	Pettitte	Benitez	48-38	2nd	3.0
7-13	At Bos.	L	3-4		8	8	Garces	Benitez		48-39	2nd	4.0
7-14	At Bos.	W	6-4		12	12	Mahomes	Lowe	Benitez	49-39	2nd	4.0
7-15	At Bos.	L	4-6		10	9	R. Martinez	Hampton	Lowe	49-40	2nd	5.0
7-16	At Tor.	L	3-7		10	8	Halladay	Leiter	Koch	49-41	2nd	6.0
7-17	At Tor.	W	7-5	(11)	11	5	Franco	Borbon	Benitez	50-41	2nd	5.0
7-18	At Tor.	W	11-7		12	13	B.J. Jones	Carpenter		51-41	2nd	5.0
7-19	At Mon.	W	5-3		11	9	Mahomes	Kline	Benitez	52-41	2nd	4.5
7-20	At Mon.	L	1-4		7	8	Hermanson	Hampton	Strickland	52-42	2nd	5.0
7-21	At Atl.	L	3-6		7	7	Burkett	Leiter	Remlinger	52-43	2nd	6.0
7-22	At Atl.	W	4-0		5	4	Reed	Maddux		53-43	2nd	5.0
7-23	At Atl.	L	0-1		4	7	Ashby	B.J. Jones		53-44	2nd	6.0
7-25	Mon.	W	5-0		12	5	Rusch	Hermanson		54-44	2nd	6.0
7-27†	Mon.	W	9-8		15	9	Franco	Strickland	Benitez	55-44		
7-27‡	Mon.	W	4-3		7	7	Hampton	Irabu		56-44	2nd	5.0
7-28	StL.	W	3-2		9	5	Leiter	Hentgen	Benitez	57-44	2nd	5.0
7-29	StL.	W	4-3		5	7	White	James	Benitez	58-44	2nd	5.0
7-30	StL.	W	4-2		7	4	B.J. Jones	Stephenson		59-44	2nd	5.0
7-31	Cin.	L	0-6		8	10	Williamson	Rusch	Luebbers	59-45	2nd	5.5
8-1	Cin.	W	3-2		9	9	Hampton	Parris	Benitez	60-45	2nd	5.5
8-2	Cin.	W	2-1		7	5	Leiter	Dessens	Benitez	61-45	2nd	4.5
8-4	At Ari.	W	6-1		11	6	Reed	Johnson	Cook	62-45	2nd	4.0
8-5	At Ari.	W	6-2		14	11	B.J. Jones	Guzman	White	63-45	2nd	3.0
8-6	At Ari.	L	5-9		13	12	Reynoso	Rusch	Mantei	63-46	2nd	4.0
8-7	At Hou.	W	6-5	(11)	8	12	Benitez	Green		64-46	2nd	3.0
8-8	At Hou.	L	3-9		11	10	B. Powell	Leiter		64-47	2nd	4.0
8-9	At Hou.	W	12-5		16	9	Reed	Lima		65-47	2nd	3.0
8-10	At Hou.	W	10-3		14	12	B.J. Jones	McKnight		66-47	2nd	2.5
8-11	S.F	W	4-1		7	5	Rusch	Gardner	Benitez	67-47	2nd	2.5
8-12	S.F	W	3-2		6	6	Hampton	Rodriguez	Benitez	68-47	2nd	2.5
8-13	S.F	W	2-0		7	2	Leiter	Hernandez	Franco	69-47	2nd	1.5
8-14	S.F	L	1-11		2	14	Ortiz	Reed		69-48	2nd	2.5
8-15†	Col.	W	7-5		9	9	Cook	House	Benitez	70-48		
8-15‡	Col.	W	4-3		10	4	B.J. Jones	Chouinard	Benitez	71-48	2nd	2.0
8-16	Col.	L	5-7		8	11	Bohanon	Rusch	White	71-49	2nd	3.0
8-17	Col.	W	13-2		15	4	Wendell	Yoshii		72-49	2nd	2.5
8-18	At L.A.	W	5-3		10	8	White	Adams	Benitez	73-49	2nd	1.5
8-19	At L.A.	L	1-4		4	9	Park	Reed		73-50	2nd	1.5
8-20	At L.A.	W	9-6		10	11	Wendell	Adams	Benitez	74-50	2nd	1.5
8-21	At S.D.	L	4-5	(10)	10	8	Hoffman	Cook		74-51	2nd	2.5
8-22	At S.D.	L	1-16		7	12	Eaton	Mahomes	Erdos	74-52	2nd	2.5
8-23	At S.D.	W	4-1		7	3	Leiter	Clement	Benitez	75-52	2nd	2.5
8-25	Ari.	W	13-3		16	6	Reed	Johnson		76-52	2nd	2.0
8-26	Ari.	L	1-5	(10)	5	11	Plesac	White	Benitez	76-53	2nd	2.0
8-27	Ari.	W	2-1		4	3	Hampton	Reynoso	Benitez	77-53	2nd	1.0
8-28	Hou.	W	4-2		6	8	Rusch	B. Powell	Wendell	78-53	T1st	...
8-29	Hou.	L	1-11		5	16	Miller	Leiter		78-54	T1st	...
8-30	Hou.	W	1-0		9	3	Reed	Holt	Benitez	79-54	T1st	...
9-1	At StL.	L	5-6		9	11	Veres	Mahomes		79-55	1st	+0.5
9-2	At StL.	L	1-2		5	9	Kile	Hampton		79-56	2nd	0.5
9-3	At StL.	L	3-4	(11)	5	7	Morris	White		79-57	2nd	0.5
9-4	At Cin.	L	2-6		6	8	Dessens	Leiter		79-58	2nd	1.0
9-5	At Cin.	W	3-2	(10)	6	8	Wendell	Sullivan	Benitez	80-58	2nd	1.0
9-6	At Cin.	L	8-11		6	13	Riedling	Franco	Graves	80-59	2nd	2.0
9-8	Phi.	L	0-2		9	4	Padilla	Hampton	Brantley	80-60	2nd	3.5
9-9	Phi.	L	3-6		6	13	Person	Wendell		80-61	2nd	3.5
9-10	Phi.	W	3-0		6	5	Leiter	Daal		81-61	2nd	2.5
9-11	Mil.	L	2-8		7	12	Rigdon	Reed		81-62	2nd	3.0
9-12	Mil.	W	10-2		13	7	B.J. Jones	Snyder		82-62	2nd	2.0
9-13	Mil.	W	4-1	(10)	9	5	Benitez	Acevedo		83-62	2nd	2.0
9-14	At Mon.	W	10-4		12	10	Rusch	Thurman		84-62	2nd	2.0
9-15	At Mon.	L	3-4		9	10	Vazquez	Wendell	Strickland	84-63	2nd	2.0
9-16	At Mon.	W	10-4		14	11	Reed	Hermanson		85-63	2nd	2.0
9-17	At Mon.	L	0-5		4	7	Armas	B.J. Jones		85-64	2nd	3.0
9-18	At Atl.	L	3-6		9	7	Maddux	Hampton	Rocker	85-65	2nd	4.0
9-19	At Atl.	L	4-12		7	13	Ashby	Rusch		85-66	2nd	5.0

Date	Opp.	Res.	Score	(inn.*)	Hits	Opp. hits	Winning pitcher	Losing pitcher	Save	Record	Pos.	GB
9-20	At Atl.	W	6-3		9	6	Leiter	Glavine	Benitez	86-66	2nd	4.0
9-21	At Phi.	L	5-6		11	12	Brantley	White		86-67	2nd	4.5
9-22	At Phi.	W	9-6		8	8	B.J. Jones	Wolf	Benitez	87-67	2nd	3.5
9-23	At Phi.	W	7-3		10	6	Hampton	Politte		88-67	2nd	3.5
9-24	At Phi.	W	3-2		4	7	Rusch	Chen	Benitez	89-67	2nd	3.5
9-26	Atl.	L	1-7		7	9	Burkett	Leiter		89-68	2nd	5.0
9-27	Atl.	W	6-2		9	6	Reed	Millwood		90-68	2nd	4.0
9-28	Atl.	W	8-2		10	7	B.J. Jones	Maddux		91-68	2nd	3.0
9-29	Mon.	W	11-2		11	7	Hampton	Thurman		92-68	2nd	2.0
9-30	Mon.	W	4-2		7	4	Wendell	Vazquez	Benitez	93-68	2nd	2.0
10-1	Mon.	W	3-2	(13)	9	9	Mahomes	Powell		94-68	2nd	1.0

Monthly records: March (1-1), April (15-9), May (13-14), June (16-8), July (14-13), August (20-9), September (14-14), October (1-0).
*Innings, if other than nine. †First game of a doubleheader. ‡Second game of a doubleheader. §Game played in Tokyo, Japan.

HIGHLIGHTS

High point: One day after watching Atlanta players celebrate their clinching of the N.L. East Division title at Shea Stadium, the Mets clinched a wild-card berth with a 6-2 September 27 win over the Braves. Tired of playing second fiddle to the Braves, the Mets would get the last laugh in the playoffs.

Low point: Following a sloppy 12-4 loss at Atlanta on September 19, manager Bobby Valentine ripped into his club. "We're a great team, a playoff team. And we need to show it," Valentine said. The loss seriously damaged the Mets' hope of finally wresting the N.L. East title from the Braves.

Turning point: On September 20 in Atlanta, Al Leiter beat the Braves, 6-3, to salvage the final game of a critical three-game series. The win over Tom Glavine—the Mets' first September win in Atlanta over the last three years—provided a boost to the club's psyche and it went on to win nine of its final 11 regular-season games.

Most valuable player: Mike Piazza (.324, 38 homers, 113 RBIs) was the league's MVP until he hit a September slide—and the Mets slid right with him. Second baseman Edgardo Alfonzo was the club's all-around best player, but Piazza's game-affecting presence made him the most valuable to a lineup short on offensive threats.

Most valuable pitcher: Al Leiter and Mike Hampton provided a dominant one-two punch, but time and again Leiter won the meaningful games. The Mets were 21-10 in Leiter's starts and the 34-year-old lefty posted the league's fifth-best ERA (3.20).

Most improved player: With two major elbow surgeries robbing him of about 700 minor league at-bats, Payton was forced to learn on the job. He learned well, batting .291 with 17 homers and 62 RBIs while rising from 25th on the Mets' roster to third in Rookie of the Year balloting.

Most pleasant surprise: The emergence of speedy outfielder Timo Perez in September and October helped the Mets claim their fourth N.L. pennant. But an honorable mention has to go to lefty Glendon Rusch, who rose from a murky pool of fifth starters to stabilize the back of the rotation.

Key injuries: Rey Ordonez broke his left forearm in Los Angeles May 29, costing him the rest of the season. ... Darryl Hamilton had a second operation on an arthritic big toe and was out from April until August 10. He still played in pain. ... Derek Bell sprained his ankle in Division Series Game 1 and was lost for the year.

Notable: When the Mets claimed sole possession of first place on August 31, it marked the latest date they had been atop the N.L. East standings since 1988. Their first-place stay lasted two days. ... By winning their second-straight wild-card, the Mets earned consecutive post-season bids for the first time in club history .... The Mets had five starters with double-digit wins, the first time that has happened since 1988: Leiter (16), Hampton (15), Rusch (11), Rick Reed (11) and Bobby J. Jones (11). ... Native New Yorker John Franco, pitching in his first World Series at age 40, earned the Mets' only Subway Series victory over the Yankees in Game 3 at Shea.

—PETE CALDERA

RECORDS

2000 regular-season record: 94-68 (2nd in N.L. East); 55-26 at home; 39-42 on road; 36-32 vs. East; 34-16 vs. Central; 24-20 vs. West; 18-13 vs. lefthanded starters; 76-55 vs. righthanded starters; 79-56 on grass; 15-12 on turf; 33-24 in daytime; 61-44 at night; 29-20 in one-run games; 10-8 in extra-inning games; 3-0-0 in doubleheaders.

Team record past five years: 438-373 (.540, ranks 2nd in league in that span).

TEAM LEADERS

Batting average: Mike Piazza (.324).
At-bats: Derek Bell (546).
Runs: Edgardo Alfonzo (109).
Hits: Edgardo Alfonzo (176).
Total Bases: Mike Piazza (296).
Doubles: Edgardo Alfonzo (40).
Triples: Lenny Harris, Todd Zeile (3).
Home runs: Mike Piazza (38).
Runs batted in: Mike Piazza (113).
Stolen bases: Derek Bell, Lenny Harris (8).
Slugging percentage: Mike Piazza (.614).
On-base percentage: Edgardo Alfonzo (.425).
Wins: Al Leiter (16).
Earned-run average: Mike Hampton (3.14).

Complete games: Mike Hampton (3).
Shutouts: Mike Hampton, Al Leiter (1).
Saves: Armando Benitez (41).
Innings pitched: Mike Hampton (217.2).
Strikeouts: Al Leiter (200).

GAMES BY POSITION

Catcher: Mike Piazza 124, Todd Pratt 71, Vance Wilson 3.
First base: Todd Zeile 151, Matt Franco 28, Lenny Harris 10, Jorge Toca 5, Mark P. Johnson 4, Robin Ventura 1.
Second base: Edgardo Alfonzo 146, Kurt Abbott 23, Joe McEwing 16, Jorge Velandia 8, Melvin Mora 4, Lenny Harris 3, David Lamb 2, Matt Franco 1.
Third base: Robin Ventura 137, Matt Franco 22, Joe McEwing 19, Lenny Harris 16, Melvin Mora 4, David Lamb 3, Jorge Velandia 3, Kurt Abbott 2.
Shortstop: Mike Bordick 56, Melvin Mora 44, Rey Ordonez 44, Kurt Abbott 39, Jorge Velandia 7, Joe McEwing 4, David Lamb 2.
Outfield: Jay Payton 146, Derek Bell 143, Benny Agbayani 110, Joe McEwing 52, Jon Nunnally 34, Darryl Hamilton 31, Rickey Henderson 29, Melvin Mora 28, Bubba Trammell 25, Timoniel Perez 19, Jason Tyner 12, Lenny Harris 11, Matt Franco 3, Kurt Abbott 2, Mark P. Johnson 1, Mike Kinkade 1, Ryan McGuire 1, Jorge Toca 1.
Designated hitter: Mike Piazza 5, Edgardo Alfonzo 2, Matt Franco 2, Benny Agbayani 1, Lenny Harris 1, Mark P. Johnson 1, Todd Pratt 1.

TOP DRAFT CHOICES

1a. **Billy Traber,** LHP, Loyola Marymount.
1b. None
1c. **Bob Keppel,** RHP, DeSmet H.S., Chesterfield, Mo.
2. **Matt Peterson,** RHP, Rapides H.S., Alexandria, La.
3. **Josh Reynolds,** RHP, Central Missouri State University.
4. **Brandon Wilson,** C, Christian Life Academy, Baton Rouge, La.
5. **Quenten Patterson,** RHP, Oklahoma State University.
6. **Craig Basak,** SS, University of Illinois.
7. **Jeff Duncan,** OF, Arizona State Univ.
8. **Chad Bowen,** RHP, Gallatin (Tenn.) H.S.
9. **Nick Mattioni,** RHP, Florida Atlantic U.
10. **Travis Veracka,** LHP, University of Massachusetts.

PHILADELPHIA PHILLIES
NATIONAL LEAGUE EAST DIVISION

Phillies
2001 SCHEDULE
Home games shaded; D—Day game (games starting before 5 p.m.)
*—All-Star Game at Safeco Field (Seattle)

APRIL

SUN	MON	TUE	WED	THU	FRI	SAT
1	2 D FLA	3 D FLA	4 FLA	5	6 D CUB	7 D CUB
8 CUB	9 FLA	10 FLA	11 FLA	12	13 ATL	14 ATL
15 D ATL	16 CUB	17 D CUB	18 D CUB	19	20 ATL	21 ATL
22 ATL	23 D SD	24 SD	25 SD	26 D SD	27 LA	28 LA
29 LA	30					

MAY

SUN	MON	TUE	WED	THU	FRI	SAT
		1 COL	2 COL	3 D COL	4 SF	5 SF
6 SF	7 HOU	8 HOU	9 HOU	10	11 ARI	12 ARI
13 D ARI	14	15 MIL	16 MIL	17 MIL	18 STL	19 STL
20 D STL	21	22 PIT	23 PIT	24 PIT	25 MON	26 MON
27 D MON	28 D NYM	29 NYM	30 NYM	31 MON		

JUNE

SUN	MON	TUE	WED	THU	FRI	SAT
					1 MON	2 MON
3 D MON	4	5 NYM	6 NYM	7 NYM	8 BOS	9 D BOS
10 D BOS	11	12 TB	13 TB	14 D TB	15 BAL	16 BAL
17 D BAL	18	19 PIT	20 PIT	21 PIT	22 FLA	23 FLA
24 D FLA	25 ATL	26 ATL	27 ATL	28 FLA	29 FLA	30 FLA

JULY

SUN	MON	TUE	WED	THU	FRI	SAT
1 D FLA	2	3 ATL	4 ATL	5 ATL	6 BAL	7 D BAL
8 D BAL	9	10 TOR	11 *	12 TOR	13 D TOR	14 D TOR
15 NYY	16 NYY	17 NYY	18 MON	19 MON	20 D NYM	21 NYM
22 NYM	23 D MON	24 MON	25 D MON	26 NYM	27 NYM	28 D NYM
29 NYM	30 NYM	31 COL				

AUGUST

SUN	MON	TUE	WED	THU	FRI	SAT
			1 COL	2 D COL	3 SF	4 D SF
5 D SF	6	7 SD	8 SD	9 D SD	10 D LA	11 LA
12 D LA	13	14 MIL	15 MIL	16 D MIL	17 STL	18 STL
19 D STL	20	21 HOU	22 HOU	23 HOU	24 ARI	25 D ARI
26 ARI	27 ARI	28 NYM	29 NYM	30 NYM	31 MON	

SEPTEMBER

SUN	MON	TUE	WED	THU	FRI	SAT
						1 MON
2 MON	3 D NYM	4 NYM	5 NYM	6 MON	7 MON	8 MON
9 MON	10	11 ATL	12 D ATL	13 ATL	14 CIN	15 D CIN
16 CIN	17 D ATL	18 ATL	19 ATL	20 ATL	21 FLA	22 FLA
23 D FLA	24	25 CIN	26 CIN	27 CIN	28 FLA	29 FLA
30 D FLA						

2001 SEASON
CLUB DIRECTORY

General partner, president, CEO
David Montgomery
Chairman
Bill Giles
Partners
Claire S. Betz, Tri-Play Associates (Alexander K. Buck, J. Mahlon Buck Jr., William C. Buck), Double Play, Inc. (John Middleton, chairman), Giles Limited Partnership (Bill Giles)
V.p., general counsel and secretary
Bill Webb
Senior vice president, CFO
Jerry Clothier
Special assistant to the president
Sharon Swainson
Director, business development
Joe Giles
Vice president and general manager
Ed Wade
Assistant general manager
Ruben Amaro Jr.
Controller
John Fusco
Director, minor leagues and scouting
Mike Arbuckle
Senior advisors to general manager
Dallas Green, Paul Owens
Director, minor league operations
Steve Noworyta
Executive asst. to the general manager
Susan Ingersoll
Vice president, public relations
Larry Shenk
Manager, media relations
Leigh Tobin
Director, community relations
Gene Dias
Vice president, advertising sales
Dave Buck
Director, information systems
Brian Lamoreaux
Vice president, ticket operations
Richard Deats

Director, ticket department
Dan Goroff
Director, sales
John Weber
Dir., broadcasting and video services
Rory McNeil
Director, stadium operations
Mike DiMuzio
Club physician
Dr. Michael Ciccotti
Club trainers
Jeff Cooper, Mark Andersen
Mgr., equipment and team travel
Frank Coppenbarger
Manager, visiting clubhouse
Kevin Steinhour
National supervisors
Marti Wolever, Sonny Bowers
Director, Florida operations
John Timberlake
Director, Latin American operations
Sal Artiaga
Director, Major League scouts
Gordon Lakey
Major League scout
Jimmy Stewart
Advance scout, Major Leagues
Hank King
Special assignment scout
Dean Jongewaard
Coordinator, professional coverage
Dick Lawlor
Cross-checkers
Scott Trcka, Brian Kohlscheen, Mitch Sokol
Regular scouts
Sal Agostinelli, Emil Belich, Darrell Connor, Steve Gillispie, Ken Hultzapple, Marlon Jones, Tim Kissner, Jerry Lafferty, Matt Lundin, Miguel Machado, Lloyd Merritt, Venice Murray, Dave Owen, Scott Ramsay, Paul Scott, Doug Takaragawa, Roy Tanner

MINOR LEAGUE AFFILIATES

Class	Team	League	Manager
AAA	Scranton/Wilkes-Barre	International	Marc Bombard
AA	Reading	Eastern	Gary Varsho
A	Batavia	New York-Pennsylvania	Frank Klebe
A	Clearwater	Florida State	Ramon Aviles
A	Lakewood	South Atlantic	Greg Legg
Rookie	Gulf Coast Phillies	Gulf Coast	Roly de Armas

BROADCAST INFORMATION

Radio: WPHT-AM (1210).
TV: UPN 57.
Cable TV: Comcast SportsNet.

SPRING TRAINING

Ballpark (city): Jack Russell Stadium (Clearwater, Fla.).
Ticket information: 215-463-1000 or 727-442-8496.

Follow the Phillies all season at: www.sportingnews.com/baseball/teams/phillies/

2001 SEASON *Philadelphia Phillies*

Manager—Larry Bowa (10).
Coaches—Greg Gross (25), Richie Hebner (7), Ramon Henderson (59), Vern Ruhle (46), Tony Scott (15), John Vukovich (18).

No.	PITCHERS	B/T	Ht./Wt.	Born	2000 clubs
27	Bottalico, Ricky	L/R	6-1/215	8-26-69	Kansas City
41	Boyd, Jason	R/R	6-3/173	2-23-73	Clearwater, Scranton/Wilkes-Barre, Philadelphia
62	Brester, Jason	L/L	6-3/190	12-7-76	Reading
45	Brock, Chris	R/R	6-0/185	2-5-70	Philadelphia
39	Chen, Bruce	L/L	6-2/210	6-19-77	Atlanta, Richmond, Philadelphia
48	Coggin, Dave	R/R	6-4/205	10-30-76	Clearwater, Reading, Scranton/Wilkes-Barre, Philadelphia
33	Cormier, Rheal	L/L	5-10/187	4-23-67	Boston
37	Daal, Omar	L/L	6-3/195	3-1-72	Arizona, Philadelphia
62	Duckworth, Brandon	B/R	6-2/185	1-23-76	Reading
53	Eaton, Adam	R/R	6-2/190	11-23-77	Mobile, San Diego
57	Figueroa, Nelson	B/R	6-1/155	5-18-74	Tucson, Arizona, Scranton/Wilkes-Barre
61	Gomes, Wayne	R/R	6-2/227	1-15-73	Philadelphia, Scranton/Wilkes-Barre
72	Jacquez, Tom	L/L	6-2/195	12-29-75	Reading, Scranton/Wilkes-Barre, Philadelphia
49	Mesa, Jose	R/R	6-3/225	5-22-66	Seattle
51	Nickle, Doug	R/R	6-4/210	10-2-74	Reading, Philadelphia
73	Nunez, Franklin	R/R	6-0/175	1-18-77	Clearwater
58	Osting, Jimmy	R/L	6-5/180	4-7-77	Myrtle Beach, Greenville, Richmond, Reading
44	Padilla, Vicente	R/R	6-2/200	9-27-77	Tucson, Arizona, Philadelphia
31	Person, Robert	R/R	6-0/194	10-6-69	Philadelphia, Clearwater, Reading
35	Politte, Cliff	R/R	5-11/185	2-27-74	Scranton/Wilkes-Barre, Philadelphia
68	Silva, Carlos	R/R	6-4/225	4-23-79	Clearwater
47	Telemaco, Amaury	R/R	6-3/222	1-19-74	Philadelphia, Scranton/Wilkes-Barre
70	Thomas, Evan	R/R	5-10/170	6-14-74	Scranton/Wilkes-Barre
43	Wolf, Randy	L/L	6-0/194	8-22-76	Philadelphia

No.	CATCHERS	B/T	Ht./Wt.	Born	2000 clubs
4	Bennett, Gary	R/R	6-0/208	4-17-72	Scranton/Wilkes-Barre, Philadelphia
76	Estrada, Johnny	B/R	5-11/210	6-27-76	Reading
24	Lieberthal, Mike	R/R	6-0/190	1-18-72	Philadelphia

No.	INFIELDERS	B/T	Ht./Wt.	Born	2000 clubs
8	Anderson, Marlon	L/R	5-11/198	1-6-74	Scranton/Wilkes-Barre, Philadelphia
13	Perez, Tomas	B/R	5-11/177	12-29-73	Reading, Philadelphia, Scranton/Wilkes-Barre
75	Punto, Nick	R/R	5-9/170	11-8-77	Reading
17	Rolen, Scott	R/R	6-4/226	4-4-75	Philadelphia
29	Rollins, Jimmy	B/R	5-8/165	11-27-78	Scranton/Wilkes-Barre, Philadelphia

No.	OUTFIELDERS	B/T	Ht./Wt.	Born	2000 clubs
53	Abreu, Bobby	L/R	6-0/197	3-11-74	Philadelphia
5	Burrell, Pat	R/R	6-4/225	10-10-76	Scranton/Wilkes-Barre, Philadelphia
2	Ducey, Rob	L/R	6-2/183	5-24-65	Philadelphia, Toronto
6	Glanville, Doug	R/R	6-2/172	8-25-70	Philadelphia
	Hunter, Brian L.	R/R	6-3/180	3-5-71	Colorado, Cincinnati
64	Perez, Josue	B/R	6-0/180	8-12-77	Clearwater, Reading
16	Lee, Travis	L/L	6-3/214	5-26-75	Arizona, El Paso, Tucson, Philadelphia
67	Michaels, Jason	R/R	6-0/205	5-4-76	Reading
28	Taylor, Reggie	L/R	6-1/178	1-12-77	Scranton/Wilkes-Barre, Philadelphia
71	Valent, Eric	L/L	6-0/190	4-4-77	Reading

BALLPARK INFORMATION

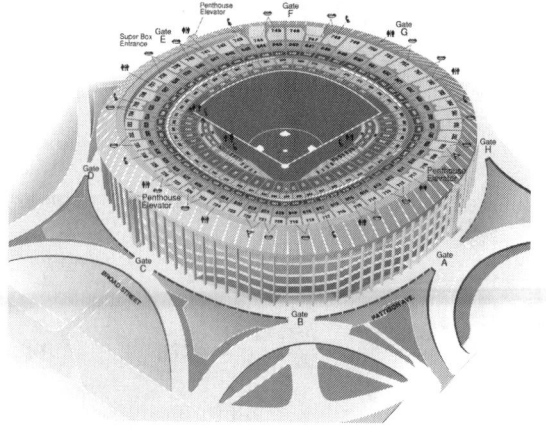

Ballpark (capacity, surface)
Veterans Stadium (62,418, artificial)

Address
P.O. Box 7575
Philadelphia, PA 19101

Official website
www.phillies.com

Business phone
215-463-6000

Ticket information
215-463-1000

Ticket prices
$24 (field box)
$20 (sections 258-201, terrace box)
$18 (loge box)
$14 (reserved, 600 level)
$8 (reserved, 700 level, adult gen. admission)
$5 (children's general admission)

Field dimensions (from home plate)
To left field at foul line, 330 feet
To center field, 408 feet
To right field at foul line, 330 feet

First game played
April 10, 1971 (Phillies 4, Expos 1)

DAY BY DAY

Philadelphia Phillies

2001 SEASON

Date	Opp.	Res.	Score	(inn.*)	Hits	Opp. hits	Winning pitcher	Losing pitcher	Save	Record	Pos.	GB
4-4	At Ari.	L	4-6		6	10	Johnson	Ashby	Holmes	0-1	T4th	1.0
4-5	At Ari.	L	3-11		9	12	Stottlemyre	Byrd	Morgan	0-2	5th	1.5
4-6	At Ari.	L	2-3	(11)	8	7	Springer	Schrenk		0-3	5th	2.0
4-7	At Hou.	W	4-1		6	5	Wolf	Dotel	Gomes	1-3	5th	1.5
4-8	At Hou.	L	5-8		11	11	Maddux	Brock	Wagner	1-4	5th	2.0
4-9	At Hou.	W	3-2		7	5	Schrenk	J. Powell	Gomes	2-4	5th	2.0
4-10	N.Y.	W	9-7		9	9	Telemaco	Rodriguez	Gomes	3-4	4th	1.0
4-12	N.Y.	W	8-5		12	7	Person	Hampton	Gomes	4-4	T3rd	0.5
4-13	N.Y.	L	1-2		5	8	Cook	Aldred	Benitez	4-5	T3rd	0.5
4-14	Mon.	L	0-4		6	9	Hermanson	Brock		4-6	5th	1.5
4-16	Mon.	W	5-4		9	7	Aldred	Telford		5-6	5th	1.0
4-18	At Atl.	L	3-4	(12)	9	9	Rivera	Reyes		5-7	5th	2.5
4-19	At Atl.	L	1-10		4	12	Glavine	Wolf		5-8	5th	2.5
4-20	At Atl.	L	4-6		8	8	Millwood	Aldred	Rocker	5-9	5th	3.5
4-21	At Fla.	W	4-3		8	7	Ashby	Nunez		6-9	5th	3.5
4-22	At Fla.	L	2-4		8	6	Sanchez	Byrd	Alfonseca	6-10	5th	4.5
4-23	At Fla.	L	2-5		6	5	Penny	Person	Alfonseca	6-11	5th	5.5
4-24	At Fla.	L	1-3		7	7	Fernandez	Wolf	Alfonseca	6-12	5th	6.0
4-25	Ari.	L	2-10		5	10	Johnson	Brock		6-13	5th	7.0
4-26	Ari.	L	4-10		6	9	Stottlemyre	Ashby		6-14	5th	8.0
4-27	Ari.	W	5-4		10	6	Gomes	Kim		7-14	5th	8.0
4-28	StL.	L	4-7		9	10	Stephenson	Reyes	Veres	7-15	5th	9.0
4-29	StL.	L	6-7	(10)	10	9	Mohler	Gomes		7-16	5th	10.0
4-30	StL.	L	3-4		8	9	Kile	Schilling	James	7-17	5th	11.0
5-2	Cin.	L	0-7		3	12	Neagle	Ashby	Sullivan	7-18	5th	12.5
5-3	Cin.	W	5-2		9	4	Byrd	Parris		8-18	5th	11.5
5-4	Cin.	W	14-1		21	7	Person	Harnisch		9-18	5th	11.0
5-5	At Atl.	L	5-6		9	9	Seanez	Gomes		9-19	5th	12.0
5-6	At Atl.	W	6-0		13	11	Schilling	Millwood		10-19	5th	11.0
5-7	At Atl.	W	7-4		14	11	Ashby	Mulholland	Gomes	11-19	5th	10.0
5-9	At Mon.	L	2-3		6	8	Kline	Gomes		11-20	5th	10.5
5-10	At Mon.	W	8-0		13	4	Person	Vazquez		12-20	5th	9.5
5-11	At Mon.	W	6-4		8	8	Wolf	Pavano	Gomes	13-20	5th	8.5
5-12	Atl.	L	7-8		9	12	Ligtenberg	Gomes	Rocker	13-21	5th	9.5
5-13	Atl.	L	2-3	(10)	6	8	Seanez	Aldred	Rocker	13-22	5th	10.5
5-14	Atl.	L	2-11		8	16	Burkett	Byrd		13-23	5th	11.5
5-16	StL.	L	2-8		10	9	An. Benes	Person		13-24	5th	12.5
5-17	StL.	W	5-4		11	9	Wolf	Slocumb	Brantley	14-24	5th	12.5
5-18	StL.	L	2-7		10	13	Stephenson	Schilling		14-25	5th	13.5
5-19	Col.	L	2-10		6	14	Astacio	Ashby		14-26	5th	13.5
5-20	Col.	L	3-4		2	6	Tavarez	Brock	Jimenez	14-27	5th	14.5
5-21	Col.	W	4-3		6	7	Person	Yoshii	Brantley	15-27	5th	14.5
5-23	At Hou.	L	2-10		8	13	Holt	Wolf		15-28	5th	14.5
5-24	At Hou.	W	9-7		13	9	Gomes	Wagner	Brantley	16-28	5th	14.5
5-25	At Hou.	L	6-10		8	11	Elarton	Ashby	Slusarski	16-29	5th	15.5
5-26	At L.A.	L	4-11		8	10	Brown	Byrd		16-30	5th	15.5
5-27	At L.A.	W	7-6		9	10	Person	Dreifort	Brantley	17-30	5th	15.5
5-28	At L.A.	W	4-2		12	6	Wolf	Osuna		18-30	5th	14.5
5-29	At S.F	L	2-7		4	13	Estes	Schilling	Embree	18-31	5th	15.5
5-30	At S.F	L	3-7		8	12	Hernandez	Ashby	Nen	18-32	5th	16.5
5-31	At S.F	L	4-10		9	14	Gardner	Byrd		18-33	5th	17.0
6-2	Bos.	W	2-1	(11)	9	9	Brantley	Wasdin		19-33	5th	15.5
6-3	Bos.	W	9-3		10	3	Wolf	Wakefield		20-33	5th	15.5
6-4	Bos.	W	6-5	(12)	12	8	Schrenk	Cormier		21-33	5th	14.5
6-5	T.B.	L	3-5	(12)	5	9	Guthrie	Boyd	White	21-34	5th	14.5
6-6	T.B.	L	3-5	(10)	8	9	Hernandez	Brantley	White	21-35	5th	15.5
6-7	T.B.	W	5-4		10	8	Brock	Guthrie	Brantley	22-35	5th	14.5
6-9	At Bal.	W	9-5		10	9	Wolf	Rapp		23-35	5th	14.5
6-10	At Bal.	L	4-11		6	12	Ponson	Schilling		23-36	5th	15.5
6-11	At Bal.	L	2-7		5	12	Mussina	Ashby		23-37	5th	15.5
6-12	Fla.	L	2-5		6	10	Darensbourg	Politte	Alfonseca	23-38	5th	16.5
6-13	Fla.	W	4-3		10	9	Gomes	Strong	Brantley	24-38	5th	15.5
6-14	Fla.	L	1-8		4	13	Dempster	Wolf		24-39	5th	16.5
6-16	Atl.	W	2-1		4	5	Schilling	Glavine	Brantley	25-39	5th	15.0
6-17	Atl.	W	9-3		16	7	Politte	Mulholland		26-39	5th	14.0
6-18	Atl.	L	3-5		6	8	Burkett	Schrenk	Rocker	26-40	5th	15.0
6-19	Atl.	W	5-2		8	5	Brock	Remlinger	Brantley	27-40	5th	14.0
6-20	At N.Y.	W	3-2	(10)	7	7	Brock	Benitez	Brantley	28-40	5th	14.0
6-21	At N.Y.	W	10-5		12	10	Gomes	Franco		29-40	5th	13.0
6-22	At N.Y.	L	4-5		8	7	Rusch	Politte	Cook	29-41	5th	14.0
6-23	At Mon.	W	13-6		17	9	Coggin	Vazquez		30-41	5th	14.0
6-24	At Mon.	W	8-1		11	7	Wolf	Pavano		31-41	5th	13.0
6-25	At Mon.	L	1-3		8	9	Johnson	Byrd	Kline	31-42	5th	14.0
6-27	Mil.	W	7-0		8	6	Schilling	Haynes		32-42	5th	13.0

Date	Opp.	Res.	Score	(inn.*)	Hits	Opp. hits	Winning pitcher	Losing pitcher	Save	Record	Pos.	GB
6-28	Mil.	W	9-7		13	11	Brock	Acevedo	Brantley	33-42	5th	13.0
6-29	Mil.	L	6-8		10	12	Bere	Schrenk	Leskanic	33-43	5th	14.0
6-30	Pit.	L	3-8		11	13	Benson	Wolf		33-44	5th	14.0
7-1	Pit.	W	4-3		10	5	Byrd	Arroyo	Brantley	34-44	5th	13.0
7-2	Pit.	W	9-1		15	9	Schilling	Ritchie		35-44	5th	13.0
7-3	At Mil.	W	5-3		10	6	Ashby	Snyder	Brantley	36-44	5th	12.0
7-4	At Mil.	W	7-4		11	10	Brock	Wickman	Brantley	37-44	5th	12.0
7-5	At Mil.	W	5-2		12	7	Wolf	Wright	Gomes	38-44	5th	11.0
7-6	At Mil.	L	2-4		11	8	D'Amico	Byrd	Wickman	38-45	5th	11.0
7-7	Bal.	L	1-2		8	7	Mussina	Schilling	Timlin	38-46	5th	12.0
7-8	Bal.	W	13-4		15	9	Ashby	Mercedes		39-46	5th	12.0
7-9	Bal.	L	4-5		8	12	Mills	Brantley	Timlin	39-47	5th	12.0
7-13	At Tor.	W	8-5		11	7	Schilling	Carpenter	Brantley	40-47	5th	12.0
7-14	At Tor.	L	2-3		6	13	Koch	Brantley		40-48	5th	13.0
7-15	At Tor.	W	7-3		11	5	Chen	Wells		41-48	5th	13.0
7-16	At N.Y. (AL)	L	8-9	(10)	14	13	Rivera	Brantley		41-49	5th	14.0
7-17	At N.Y. (AL)	W	10-8		9	12	Coggin	Cone	Brock	42-49	5th	13.0
7-18	At N.Y. (AL)	L	1-3		5	4	Neagle	Schilling	Rivera	42-50	5th	14.0
7-19	At Chi.	L	4-5		9	10	Heredia	Holzemer		42-51	5th	14.5
7-20	At Chi.	W	3-2		6	8	Brownson	Tapani	Brantley	43-51	5th	14.0
7-21	At Pit.	L	2-9		4	11	Anderson	Byrd		43-52	5th	15.0
7-22	At Pit.	L	1-2		4	5	Arroyo	Person	Williams	43-53	5th	15.0
7-23	At Pit.	W	4-1		7	3	Schilling	Ritchie		44-53	5th	15.0
7-25	Chi.	L	7-8		14	7	Worrell	Brock	Aguilera	44-54	5th	16.0
7-26	Chi.	L	9-14		9	14	Heredia	Byrd		44-55	5th	17.0
7-27	Chi.	L	1-4		7	12	Rain	Padilla	Aguilera	44-56	5th	17.0
7-28	L.A.	L	0-2		2	7	Dreifort	Daal	Shaw	44-57	5th	18.0
7-29	L.A.	W	3-0		7	6	Politte	Brown	Brantley	45-57	5th	18.0
7-30	L.A.	W	3-2		9	4	Wolf	Park	Brantley	46-57	5th	18.0
7-31	At S.D.	L	1-4		4	7	Williams	Chen		46-58	5th	18.5
8-1	At S.D.	L	9-10	(10)	11	13	Almanzar	Brantley		46-59	5th	19.5
8-2	At S.D.	L	2-5		8	9	Clement	Daal	Hoffman	46-60	5th	19.5
8-4	At Col.	L	1-8		7	13	Tavarez	Bottenfield		46-61	5th	20.0
8-5	At Col.	L	6-7		9	15	Jimenez	Brantley		46-62	5th	20.0
8-6	At Col.	W	10-9		13	16	Chen	Astacio		47-62	5th	20.0
8-7	S.D.	L	4-6		11	8	Clement	Person	Hoffman	47-63	5th	20.0
8-8	S.D.	W	10-4		14	8	Daal	Tollberg		48-63	5th	20.0
8-9	S.D.	W	3-2		9	6	Brock	Slocumb		49-63	5th	19.0
8-10	S.D.	L	3-15		8	19	Williams	Wolf		49-64	5th	19.5
8-11	Hou.	L	2-7		7	12	Valdes	Padilla		49-65	5th	20.5
8-12	Hou.	W	3-2		6	7	Person	Miller	Brantley	50-65	5th	20.5
8-13	Hou.	L	7-14		8	19	Cabrera	Daal		50-66	5th	20.5
8-14	Ari.	L	3-4	(11)	6	7	Plesac	Brantley	Mantei	50-67	5th	21.5
8-15	Ari.	L	6-11		13	16	Kim	Gomes		50-68	5th	22.5
8-16	Ari.	L	1-5		7	10	Reynoso	Chen		50-69	5th	23.5
8-18	At StL.	L	6-7		7	7	Christiansen	Brock		50-70	5th	23.5
8-19	At StL.	L	3-6		7	9	Hentgen	Daal		50-71	5th	23.5
8-20	At StL.	W	6-0		10	5	Bottenfield	Reames		51-71	5th	23.5
8-21	At Cin.	L	4-7		11	13	Harnisch	Wolf	Graves	51-72	5th	24.5
8-22	At Cin.	W	5-4		9	6	Padilla	Luebbers	Brantley	52-72	5th	23.5
8-23	At Cin.	W	4-3		7	5	Brock	Graves	Padilla	53-72	5th	23.5
8-24	At Cin.	L	3-8		11	11	Parris	Daal		53-73	5th	23.5
8-25	S.F	L	3-16		11	21	Ortiz	Bottenfield		53-74	5th	24.5
8-26	S.F	W	5-2		11	8	Wolf	Rueter	Brantley	54-74	5th	23.5
8-27	S.F	W	2-1	(10)	7	3	Vosberg	Fultz		55-74	4th	22.5
8-28	Col.	W	3-2		8	8	Person	Yoshii	Brantley	56-74	4th	21.5
8-29	Col.	L	1-2		3	9	Rose	Daal	Jimenez	56-75	4th	21.5
8-30	Col.	L	4-5	(11)	10	7	White	Gomes	Jimenez	56-76	4th	22.5
9-1	At L.A.	L	1-2		4	7	Fetters	Brock	Shaw	56-77	4th	22.5
9-2	At L.A.	L	0-1	(10)	6	6	Herges	Padilla		56-78	5th	23.0
9-3	At L.A.	L	1-6		4	9	Park	Person	Shaw	56-79	5th	23.5
9-4	At S.F	L	0-3		4	5	Ortiz	Daal	Nen	56-80	5th	23.5
9-5	At S.F	L	5-8		8	11	Johnstone	Vosberg	Nen	56-81	5th	24.5
9-6	At S.F	L	4-5		11	6	Fultz	Padilla	Embree	56-82	5th	25.5
9-8	At N.Y.	W	2-0		4	9	Padilla	Hampton	Brantley	57-82	5th	26.0
9-9	At N.Y.	W	6-3		13	6	Person	Wendell		58-82	5th	25.0
9-10	At N.Y.	L	0-3		5	6	Leiter	Daal		58-83	5th	25.0
9-11†	Mon.	W	5-2		8	7	Politte	Hermanson	Brantley	59-83		
9-11‡	Mon.	L	6-7		10	12	Mota	Padilla	Strickland	59-84	5th	25.0
9-12	Mon.	L	0-1		3	3	Armas	Telemaco	Strickland	59-85	5th	25.0
9-13	Mon.	W	15-5		19	8	Chen	Lira		60-85	5th	25.0
9-15	Fla.	W	7-4		8	7	Person	Burnett		61-85	5th	24.5
9-16	Fla.	L	2-3		4	7	Penny	Daal	Alfonseca	61-86	5th	25.5
9-17	Fla.	W	6-5		9	10	Wolf	Smith	Jacquez	62-86	5th	25.5
9-18	Pit.	L	5-6		10	11	Loiselle	Padilla	Williams	62-87	5th	26.5
9-19	Pit.	L	8-12		6	13	Skrmetta	Telemaco	Williams	62-88	5th	27.5
9-20	Pit.	L	6-7	(10)	7	12	Loiselle	Brock	Williams	62-89	5th	27.5
9-21	N.Y.	W	6-5		12	11	Brantley	White		63-89	5th	27.0

Date	Opp.	Res.	Score	(inn.*)	Hits	Opp. hits	Winning pitcher	Losing pitcher	Save	Record	Pos.	GB
9-22	N.Y.	L	6-9		8	8	B.J. Jones	Wolf	Benitez	63-90	5th	27.0
9-23	N.Y.	L	3-7		6	10	Hampton	Politte		63-91	5th	28.0
9-24	N.Y.	L	2-3		7	4	Rusch	Chen	Benitez	63-92	5th	29.0
9-25	At Chi.	L	3-4		8	4	Quevedo	Person	Worrell	63-93	5th	30.0
9-26	At Chi.	W	10-4		14	14	Daal	Lieber		64-93	5th	30.0
9-27	At Chi.	L	0-1		8	6	Wood	Wolf	Worrell	64-94	5th	30.0
9-28	At Chi.	W	4-2		7	7	Politte	Nation	Padilla	65-94	5th	29.0
9-29	At Fla.	L	1-7		4	10	Smith	Chen		65-95	5th	29.0
9-30	At Fla.	L	5-11		10	17	Cornelius	Person		65-96	5th	30.0
10-1	At Fla.	L	5-7		9	11	Dempster	Telemaco	Alfonseca	65-97	5th	30.0

Monthly records: April (7-17), May (11-16), June (15-11), July (13-14), August (10-18), September (9-20), October (0-1).
*Innings, if other than nine. †First game of a doubleheader. ‡Second game of a doubleheader.

HIGHLIGHTS

High point: A 10-5 victory over the eventual N.L. champion Mets on June 21 at Shea Stadium provided one of the few highs in a down season. The game was decided on a ninth-inning grand slam by rookie first baseman Pat Burrell off Mets closer Armando Benitez. Burrell hit five of his 18 home runs in the ninth inning.
Low point: The season's most crushing defeat, a 9-8 setback in 10 innings, took place July 16 before 53,131 fans at Yankee Stadium. Paul Byrd, in his best outing of the season, limited the champions to one run over 6 2/3 innings, but the Yankees scored five runs in the bottom of the ninth to force extra innings. After the Phillies took an 8-6 lead against Mariano Rivera in the 10th, closer Jeff Brantley recorded just one out before the Yankees scored three runs to win.
Turning point: Free-agent closer Mike Jackson reported stiffness in his throwing shoulder while warming up in the third game of the season. Unable to battle through the pain, the talented veteran underwent season-ending shoulder surgery and watched the bullpen blow 20-of-55 save opportunities.
Most valuable player: Right fielder Bobby Abreu. The 26-year-old Venezuelan batted .316, scored 103 runs and was the only National Leaguer to reach double figures in doubles, triples, homers and stolen bases. He also became the first Phillie since Mike Schmidt (1982-83) to draw more than 100 walks and score 100 runs in back-to-back seasons.
Most valuable pitcher: After nearly losing his rotation spot during spring training, lefthander Randy Wolf enjoyed an impressive sophomore season. Wolf made every scheduled start, pitched a team-high 206 1/3 innings and compiled an 11-9 record that suffered from poor run support.
Most improved player: Righthander Cliff Politte added a changeup to his fastball/slider repertoire and made a valuable contribution as a spot starter. Politte was 4-3 with a 3.66 ERA in 12 games.
Most pleasant surprise: Unable to crack Atlanta's rotation, lefty Bruce Chen was acquired in a three-player trade July 12 and made 15 starts, going 3-4 with a 3.63 ERA. Chen allowed only 81 hits in

94 1/3 innings and posted a team-best 20 2/3-inning scoreless streak.
Key injuries: Jackson was one of five significant pitchers to experience shoulder problems. Curt Schilling did not return to the rotation until late April as he rehabilitated from arthroscopic surgery. Lefthander Scott Aldred (season-ending surgery in June), righthander Robert Person (one month on the D.L.) and Byrd (season-ending surgery in August) all missed major chunks of time. ... First baseman Rico Brogna suffered a broken wrist May 10 in Montreal and was never the same. ... Catcher Mike Lieberthal had his season interrupted by a sprained ankle July 17.
Notable: The team used a franchise-record 27 pitchers ... The Phillies were 12-31 against N.L. West opposition (a .279 winning percentage). ... After scoring 841 runs in 1999, the club tailed off to 708 and batted .207 with two outs and runners in scoring position. ... The team's .983 fielding percentage tied for third in the N.L. and the Phillies matched their 1999 record-low of 100 errors. ... Outfielder Rob Ducey led the N.L. with 81 pinch-hit appearances. ... At age 25, third baseman Scott Rolen came within one hit of his first .300 season and became the second-youngest Phillies player to reach 100 career homers (behind Del Ennis).

—CHRIS EDWARDS

RECORDS

2000 regular-season record: 65-97 (5th in N.L. East); 34-47 at home; 31-50 on road; 32-37 vs. East; 21-29 vs. Central; 12-31 vs. West; 14-22 vs. lefthanded starters; 51-75 vs. righthanded starters; 22-43 on grass; 43-54 on turf; 21-20 in daytime; 44-77 at night; 25-35 in one-run games; 4-12 in extra-inning games; 0-0-1 in doubleheaders.
Team record past five years: 352-458 (.435, ranks 16th in league in that span).

TEAM LEADERS

Batting average: Bobby Abreu (.316).
At-bats: Doug Glanville (637).
Runs: Bobby Abreu (103).
Hits: Bobby Abreu (182).
Total Bases: Bobby Abreu (319).

Doubles: Bobby Abreu (42).
Triples: Bobby Abreu (10).
Home runs: Scott Rolen (26).
Runs batted in: Scott Rolen (89).
Stolen bases: Doug Glanville (31).
Slugging percentage: Bobby Abreu (.554).
On-base percentage: Bobby Abreu (.416).
Wins: Randy Wolf (11).
Earned-run average: Robert Person (3.63).
Complete games: Curt Schilling (4).
Shutouts: Kent Bottenfield, Robert Person, Curt Schilling (1).
Saves: Jeff Brantley (23).
Innings pitched: Randy Wolf (206.1).
Strikeouts: Robert Person (164).

GAMES BY POSITION

Catcher: Mike Lieberthal 106, Tom Prince 46, Gary Bennett 31, Clemente Alvarez 2.
First base: Pat Burrell 58, Travis Lee 47, Brian Hunter 40, Rico Brogna 34, Kevin Jordan 9, Chris Pritchett 3.
Second base: Mickey Morandini 85, Kevin Jordan 47, Marlon Anderson 41, David Newhan 3, Alex Arias 1.
Third base: Scott Rolen 128, Kevin Jordan 39, Alex Arias 10.
Shortstop: Desi Relaford 81, Tomas Perez 44, Alex Arias 39, Jimmy Rollins 13.
Outfield: Bobby Abreu 152, Doug Glanville 150, Ron Gant 84, Kevin Sefcik 50, Pat Burrell 48, Rob Ducey 33, Travis Lee 10, Brian Hunter 9, Reggie Taylor 3.
Designated hitter: Rob Ducey 5, Pat Burrell 4, Brian Hunter 1, Kevin Sefcik 1.

TOP DRAFT CHOICES

1. **Chase Utley**, 2B, UCLA.
2. None.
3. **Keith Bucktrot**, RHP, Claremore (Okla.) H.S.
4. **Danny Gonzalez**, SS, Florida Air Academy, Melbourne, Fla.
5. **Matt Riethmaier**, RHP, U. of Arkansas.
6. **Taylor Buchholz**, RHP, Springfield (Pa.) H.S.
7. **Tony Cancio**, 1B, Plant H.S., Tampa, Fla.
8. **Ryan Carter**, LHP, UCLA.
9. **Felix Ortega**, C, Medardo Carazo H.S., Trujillo Alto, P.R.
10. **Scott Youngbauer**, SS, Georgia State University.

PITTSBURGH PIRATES
NATIONAL LEAGUE CENTRAL DIVISION

Pirates 2001 SCHEDULE

Home games shaded; D—Day game (games starting before 5 p.m.).
*—All-Star Game at Safeco Field (Seattle).

APRIL

SUN	MON	TUE	WED	THU	FRI	SAT
1	2	3 CIN	4 CIN	5 CIN	D 6 HOU	7 D HOU
8 D HOU	9 D CIN	D 10	11 CIN	12 CIN	13 D CUB	14 D CUB
15 CUB	16 D HOU	17 HOU	18 HOU	19	20 CUB	21 D CUB
22 CUB	D 23	24 LA	25 LA	26 LA	27 SD	28 SD
29 SD	D 30					

MAY

SUN	MON	TUE	WED	THU	FRI	SAT
		1 SF	2 SF	3 SF	4 COL	5 COL
6 COL	D 7 STL	8 STL	9 STL	10 D STL	11 MIL	12 MIL
13 MIL	D 14 STL	D 15 STL	16 STL	17 STL	18 MIL	19 MIL
20 D 21		22 PHI	23 PHI	24 PHI	25 ATL	26 ATL
27 ATL	D 28 FLA	29 FLA	30 FLA	31		

JUNE

SUN	MON	TUE	WED	THU	FRI	SAT
					1 D ATL	2 ATL
3 ATL	D 4	5 FLA	6 FLA	7 FLA	D 8 MIN	9 MIN
10 MIN	D 11	12 DET	13 DET	14 DET	15 CLE	16 CLE
17 CLE	D 18	19 PHI	20 PHI	21 PHI	22 MON	23 MON
24 MON	D 25	26 MIL	27 MIL	28 D MIL	29 MON	30 MON

JULY

SUN	MON	TUE	WED	THU	FRI	SAT
1 MON	2 CIN	3 CIN	4 CIN	5 CIN	D 6	7 CWS
8 CWS	9	10 *	11	12 KC	13 KC	14 D KC
15 LA	16 LA	17 STL	18 CUB	19 CUB	20 STL	21 STL
22 STL	D 23	24 CUB	25 D CUB	26 HOU	27 HOU	28 HOU
29 HOU	D 30	31 SF				

AUGUST

SUN	MON	TUE	WED	THU	FRI	SAT
			1 SF	2 SF	D 3 COL	4 COL
5 COL	D 6	7 LA	8 LA	9 LA	10 SD	11 SD
12 SD	13 ARI	14 ARI	15 ARI	16 HOU	17 HOU	18 D HOU
19 HOU	D 20	21 ARI	22 ARI	23 ARI	24 HOU	25 HOU
26 HOU	D 27 MIL	28 MIL	29 MIL	30	31 CIN	

SEPTEMBER

SUN	MON	TUE	WED	THU	FRI	SAT
						1 CIN
2 CIN	D 3 MIL	4 MIL	5 MIL	6 CIN	7 CIN	8 CIN
9 CIN	D 10	11 NYM	12 NYM	13 D NYM	14 CUB	15 D CUB
16 CUB	17 NYM	18 NYM	19 NYM	20 STL	21 STL	22 STL
23 STL	D 24 CUB	25 CUB	26 CUB	27	28 STL	29 D STL
30 STL	D					

2001 SEASON
CLUB DIRECTORY

General partner
Kevin S. McClatchy
Board of directors
William B. Allen
Donald Beaver
Frank Brenner
Chip Ganassi
Kevin S. McClatchy
Mayor Tom Murphy
G. Ogden Nutting
William E. Springer
Chief operating officer
Dick Freeman
Sr. v.p. and general manager
Cam Bonifay
Assistant g.m./baseball operations
John Sirignano
Assistant g.m./player personnel
Roy Smith
Sr. advisor/player personnel
Lenny Yochim
Special assistants to the g.m.
John Mercurio, Chet Montgomery, Ken Parker, Willie Stargell
V.p., finance and administration
Jim Plake
V.p., broadcasting and marketing
Vic Gregovits
V.p., communications and new ballpark dev.
Steven N. Greenberg
Vice president, operations
Dennis DaPra
Vice president, special events
Nellie Briles
Assistant vice president, communications and new ballpark development
Patty Paytas
Controller
David Bowman
Director of finance
Patti Mistick
Traveling secretary
Greg Johnson
Dir. of corporate sales
Mark Ferraco

Director of community development
Rod Scott
Director of Florida baseball operations
Mike Kennedy
Director of community services and sales
Al Gordon
Director of information systems
Terry Zeigler
Director of media relations
Jim Trdinich
Director of merchandising
Joe Billetdeaux
Director of player development
Paul Tinnell
Dir. of community & player relations
Kathy Guy
Dir. of promotions and advertising
Rick Orienza
Director of sales
Jim Alexander
Club physician
Dr. Joseph Coroso
Team orthopedist
Dr. Jack Failla
Head trainer
Kent Biggerstaff
Equipment manager
Roger Wilson
Director of scouting
Mickey White
Scouting coordinators
Tom Barnard, Dana Brown, Mark McKnight
Special assignment scout
Jim Guinn
Latin America coordinators
Pablo Cruz (advisor), Jose Luna
Scouting supervisors
Jason Angel, Russell Bowen, Grant Brittain, Dan Durst, Duane Gustavson, James House, Mike Kendall, Jose Luna, Greg McClain, John Mercurio, Jack Powell, Everett Russell, Delvy Santiago, Rob Sidwell, Charlie Sullivan, Mike Williams, Ted Williams

MINOR LEAGUE AFFILIATES

Class	Team	League	Manager
AAA	Nashville	Pacific Coast	Marty Brown
AA	Altoona	Eastern	Dale Sveum
A	Hickory	South Atlantic	To be announced
A	Lynchburg	Carolina	Curtis Wilkerson
A	Williamsport	New York-Pennsylvania	Tony Beasley
Rookie	Gulf Coast Pirates	Gulf Coast	Woody Huyke

BROADCAST INFORMATION

Radio: KDKA-AM (1020).
Cable TV: Fox Sports Pittsburgh.

SPRING TRAINING

Ballpark (city): McKechnie Field (Bradenton, Fla.).
Ticket information: 941-748-4610.

Follow the Pirates all season at: www.sportingnews.com/baseball/teams/pirates/

SPRING TRAINING ROSTER

Manager—Lloyd McClendon (23).
Coaches—Dave Clark (35), Trent Jewett (44), Tommy Sandt (37), Bruce Tanner (52), Bill Virdon (19), Spin Williams (54).

No.	PITCHERS	B/T	Ht./Wt.	Born	2000 clubs
55	Anderson, Jimmy	L/L	6-1/215	1-22-76	Nashville, Pittsburgh, Altoona
69	Arroyo, Bronson	R/R	6-5/181	2-24-77	Nashville, Pittsburgh, Lynchburg
53	Beimel, Joe	L/L	6-2/200	4-19-77	Lynchburg, Altoona
34	Benson, Kris	R/R	6-4/195	11-7-74	Pittsburgh
32	Cordova, Francisco	R/R	6-1/204	4-26-72	Pittsburgh
39	Grabow, John	L/L	6-2/190	11-4-78	Altoona
46	Guzman, Wilson	L/L	5-9/200	7-14-77	Altoona, Lynchburg
51	Loiselle, Rich	R/R	6-5/245	1-12-72	Altoona, Pittsburgh, Gulf Coast Pirates, Nashville
49	Manzanillo, Josias	R/R	6-0/205	10-16-67	Nashville, Pittsburgh
45	Mulholland, Terry	R/L	6-3/220	3-9-63	Atlanta
41	O'Connor, Brian	L/L	6-2/195	1-4-77	Altoona, Pittsburgh, Nashville
53	Pena, Alex	R/R	6-2/205	9-9-77	Hickory
48	Ritchie, Todd	R/R	6-3/220	11-7-71	Pittsburgh
47	Sauerbeck, Scott	R/L	6-3/197	11-9-71	Pittsburgh, Nashville
22	Schmidt, Jason	R/R	6-5/220	1-29-73	Pittsburgh, Gulf Coast Pirates
38	Serafini, Daniel	B/L	6-1/195	1-25-74	San Diego, Las Vegas, Pittsburgh, Nashville
56	Silva, Jose	R/R	6-5/235	12-19-73	Pittsburgh
50	Spurling, Chris	R/R	6-6/240	6-28-77	Tampa, Lynchburg
58	Williams, David	L/L	6-2/205	3-12-79	Hickory, Lynchburg
43	Williams, Mike	R/R	6-2/200	7-29-68	Pittsburgh

No.	CATCHERS	B/T	Ht./Wt.	Born	2000 clubs
11	Cota, Humberto	R/R	6-0/175	2-7-79	Altoona
7	Haad, Yamid	R/R	6-2/204	9-2-77	Altoona, Lynchburg
18	Kendall, Jason	R/R	6-0/195	6-26-74	Pittsburgh
15	Osik, Keith	R/R	6-0/195	10-22-68	Pittsburgh
36	Wilson, Craig	R/R	6-2/217	11-30-76	Nashville

No.	INFIELDERS	B/T	Ht./Wt.	Born	2000 clubs
10	Nunez, Abraham	B/R	5-11/185	3-16-76	Pittsburgh
6	Benjamin, Mike	R/R	6-0/175	11-22-65	Pittsburgh
2	Meares, Pat	R/R	6-0/187	9-6-68	Pittsburgh
30	Morris, Warren	L/R	5-11/180	1-11-74	Pittsburgh
16	Ramirez, Aramis	R/R	6-1/219	6-25-78	Pittsburgh, Nashville
25	Wilson, Enrique	B/R	5-11/195	7-27-75	Cleveland, Nashville, Pittsburgh
12	Wilson, Jack	R/R	6-0/175	12-29-77	Potomac, Arkansas, Altoona
29	Young, Kevin	R/R	6-3/225	6-16-69	Pittsburgh

No.	OUTFIELDERS	B/T	Ht./Wt.	Born	2000 clubs
14	Bell, Derek	R/R	6-2/215	12-11-68	New York N.L.
13	Brown, Adrian	B/R	6-0/185	2-7-74	Pittsburgh, Altoona, Nashville
17	Brown, Emil	R/R	6-2/193	12-29-74	Nashville, Pittsburgh
26	Davis, J.J.	R/R	6-4/250	10-25-78	Lynchburg
3	Hermansen, Chad	R/R	6-2/185	9-10-77	Pittsburgh, Nashville
27	Hernandez, Alex	L/L	6-4/190	5-28-77	Altoona, Nashville, Pittsburgh
5	Redman, Tike	L/L	5-11/166	3-10-77	Nashville, Pittsburgh
28	Vander Wal, John	L/L	6-1/197	4-29-66	Pittsburgh

BALLPARK INFORMATION

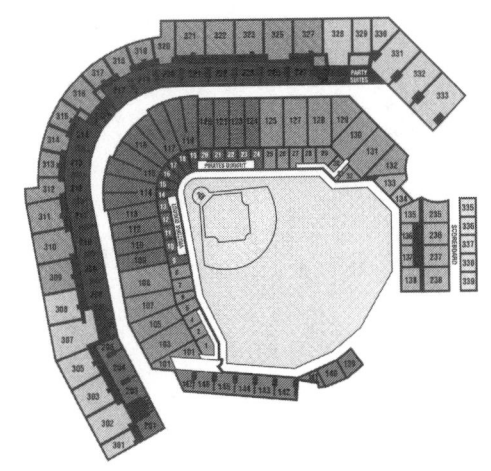

Ballpark (capacity, surface)
PNC Park (38,000, grass)

Address
PNC Park at North Shore
115 Federal Street
Pittsburgh, PA 15212

Official website
www.pittsburghpirates.com

Business phone
412-323-5000

Ticket information
800-BUY-BUCS

Ticket prices
$35 (dugout boxes)
$25 (baseline and IF boxes, club level-group seating)
$23 (LF/RF boxes)
$16 (OF reserved, deck seating, grandstand)
$12 (bleachers)
$9 (LF/RF grandstand)

Field dimensions (from home plate)
To left field at foul line, 325 feet
To center field, 399 feet
To right field at foul line, 320 feet

First game played
Scheduled for April 9, 2001 vs. Cincinnati

2000 REVIEW
DAY BY DAY

Date	Opp.	Res.	Score	(inn.*)	Hits	Opp. hits	Winning pitcher	Losing pitcher	Save	Record	Pos.	GB
4-4	Hou.	L	2-5		6	5	Reynolds	Schmidt	Wagner	0-1	T5th	1.0
4-5	Hou.	L	2-11		9	10	Lima	Benson		0-2	T5th	2.0
4-6	Hou.	W	10-1		16	2	Cordova	Holt		1-2	T4th	2.0
4-7	At Ari.	W	7-2		12	7	Christiansen	Reynoso		2-2	T3rd	1.0
4-8	At Ari.	L	5-6		12	12	Swindell	Christiansen		2-3	T4th	2.0
4-9	At Ari.	L	0-1		5	4	Johnson	Schmidt		2-4	5th	3.0
4-11	Mon.	L	3-7		4	9	Vazquez	Benson	Kline	2-5	6th	4.5
4-12	Mon.	W	6-4		10	7	Silva	Batista	Williams	3-5	6th	3.5
4-13	Mon.	W	4-3		10	8	Silva	Urbina		4-5	T4th	2.5
4-14	N.Y.	L	5-8	(12)	11	20	Franco	Silva		4-6	T5th	2.5
4-15	N.Y.	W	2-0		4	5	Anderson	Rusch	Williams	5-6	T4th	2.0
4-16	N.Y.	L	9-12		11	15	Mahomes	Peters	Benitez	5-7	T5th	2.5
4-18	At Fla.	L	5-12		10	17	Penny	Cordova		5-8	T4th	3.5
4-19	At Fla.	W	5-1		8	8	Ritchie	Fernandez		6-8	T3rd	3.5
4-20	At Fla.	L	2-3	(14)	11	10	Darensbourg	Williams		6-9	T4th	4.5
4-21	At Atl.	L	2-6		8	12	Mulholland	Garcia		6-10	T5th	4.5
4-22	At Atl.	L	2-4		9	9	Chen	Benson	Rocker	6-11	5th	4.5
4-23	At Atl.	L	3-5		7	7	Maddux	Cordova	Rocker	6-12	T5th	5.5
4-25	S.D.	W	4-3	(11)	9	13	Sauerbeck	Almanzar		7-12	T4th	5.5
4-26	S.D.	W	9-8		12	10	Williams	Whisenant		8-12	3rd	5.5
4-27	S.D.	L	4-12		4	15	Clement	Parra		8-13	T3rd	5.5
4-28	Cin.	W	2-1		6	5	Benson	Harnisch	Williams	9-13	3rd	5.5
4-29	Cin.	L	5-6		8	8	Williamson	Christiansen	Graves	9-14	4th	6.5
4-30	Cin.	L	2-6		6	10	Bell	Ritchie	Williamson	9-15	T4th	7.5
5-2	At StL.	W	10-7		13	9	Wallace	Slocumb		10-15	T3rd	6.5
5-3	At StL.	W	8-2		13	5	Benson	Hentgen		11-15	3rd	5.5
5-4	At StL.	L	0-5		4	9	Stephenson	Cordova		11-16	T3rd	6.5
5-5	At Chi.	W	4-2		7	8	Ritchie	Tapani	Williams	12-16	3rd	5.5
5-6	At Chi.	W	11-9		16	16	Wallace	Farnsworth	Williams	13-16	3rd	5.5
5-7	At Chi.	W	11-3		13	9	Schmidt	Wood		14-16	3rd	4.5
5-9	N.Y.	L	0-2		6	8	Hampton	Benson	Benitez	14-17	3rd	5.0
5-10	N.Y.	W	13-9		20	13	Silva	Cook		15-17	3rd	4.0
5-11	N.Y.	L	2-3		8	6	Leiter	Anderson		15-18	3rd	4.5
5-12	Mil.	L	1-6		4	11	Haynes	Schmidt		15-19	3rd	4.5
5-13	Mil.	W	11-8		16	10	Sauerbeck	Acevedo	Williams	16-19	3rd	4.0
5-14	Mil.	W	3-0		7	4	Benson	D'Amico	Christiansen	17-19	3rd	3.5
5-16	At Cin.	L	2-6		9	12	Bell	Ritchie		17-20	3rd	4.5
5-17	At Cin.	W	9-6		13	12	Silva	Sullivan		18-20	3rd	3.5
5-18	At Cin.	L	3-4	(10)	10	9	Graves	Garcia		18-21	3rd	4.5
5-19	StL.	W	13-1		15	3	Benson	Ankiel		19-21	3rd	3.5
5-20	StL.	L	4-19		9	19	Hentgen	Cordova		19-22	3rd	4.5
5-21	StL.	L	5-7		9	10	An. Benes	Ritchie	Veres	19-23	3rd	5.5
5-23	At Ari.	L	1-6		8	11	Anderson	Anderson		19-24	4th	6.5
5-24	At Ari.	L	5-6		8	9	Stottlemyre	Schmidt	Kim	19-25	4th	7.5
5-25	At Ari.	L	5-7		9	12	Daal	Benson	Mantei	19-26	4th	8.5
5-26	At Col.	W	2-1		8	6	Cordova	Yoshii	Williams	20-26	3rd	7.5
5-27	At Col.	L	6-7		12	10	White	Christiansen		20-27	3rd	7.5
5-28	At Col.	L	2-11		7	17	Arrojo	Anderson		20-28	4th	7.5
5-29	Fla.	W	10-4		13	11	Schmidt	Nunez		21-28	4th	7.5
5-30	Fla.	W	3-2	(10)	11	5	Williams	Alfonseca		22-28	3rd	7.5
5-31	Fla.	W	5-2		5	12	Cordova	Sanchez	Williams	23-28	3rd	6.5
6-2	K.C.	W	9-3		8	4	Ritchie	Batista		24-28	3rd	6.0
6-3	K.C.	L	3-16		8	18	Witasick	Schmidt		24-29	3rd	6.0
6-4	K.C.	L	5-7	(11)	9	9	Rakers	Christiansen	Reichert	24-30	3rd	6.5
6-5	Det.	W	5-1		9	7	Cordova	Mlicki		25-30	3rd	5.5
6-6	Det.	L	1-2		11	5	Nitkowski	Anderson	Jones	25-31	3rd	6.0
6-7	Det.	W	4-3		9	8	Ritchie	Nomo	Williams	26-31	3rd	6.0
6-9	At K.C.	L	5-6	(10)	9	13	Spradlin	Christiansen		26-32	3rd	6.0
6-10	At K.C.	L	1-2	(12)	13	10	Bottalico	Silva		26-33	3rd	6.0
6-11	At K.C.	W	10-6	(10)	18	11	Sauerbeck	Spradlin		27-33	3rd	6.0
6-12	Atl.	L	8-10		9	13	Ligtenberg	Christiansen	Remlinger	27-34	3rd	7.0
6-13	Atl.	W	7-6	(10)	10	14	Silva	Wengert		28-34	3rd	7.0
6-14	Atl.	L	4-8		9	7	Maddux	Anderson	Ligtenberg	28-35	3rd	8.0
6-15	Atl.	W	2-0		7	6	Benson	Millwood		29-35	3rd	7.5
6-16	Fla.	L	3-8		8	10	Cornelius	Cordova	Looper	29-36	3rd	8.5
6-17	Fla.	L	3-4	(11)	12	10	Alfonseca	Loiselle	Strong	29-37	3rd	9.5
6-18	Fla.	L	4-5		8	10	Bones	Christiansen	Alfonseca	29-38	3rd	9.5
6-19	At Mon.	L	1-2		6	7	Pavano	Loiselle	Kline	29-39	T3rd	10.0
6-20	At Mon.	W	2-1		4	6	Benson	Johnson	Williams	30-39	3rd	10.0
6-21	At Mon.	W	8-3		10	9	Cordova	Armas	Peters	31-39	3rd	9.0
6-22	At Mon.	L	5-6		11	8	Hermanson	Ritchie	Telford	31-40	3rd	10.0
6-23	At N.Y.	L	2-12		7	14	B.J. Jones	Arroyo		31-41	3rd	11.0

Date	Opp.	Res.	Score	(inn.*)	Hits	Opp. hits	Winning pitcher	Losing pitcher	Save	Record	Pos.	GB
6-24	At N.Y.	L	8-10		15	12	Franco	Loiselle	Benitez	31-42	3rd	12.0
6-25	At N.Y.	L	0-9		5	12	Hampton	Benson		31-43	3rd	13.0
6-27	Chi.	W	6-0		5	3	Ritchie	Wood		32-43	3rd	12.5
6-28	Chi.	L	4-5		9	8	Lieber	Cordova	Aguilera	32-44	3rd	12.5
6-29	Chi.	W	5-4	(10)	7	7	Wilkins	Worrell		33-44	3rd	12.5
6-30	At Phi.	W	8-3		13	11	Benson	Wolf		34-44	3rd	12.5
7-1	At Phi.	L	3-4		5	10	Byrd	Arroyo	Brantley	34-45	3rd	13.5
7-2	At Phi.	L	1-9		9	15	Schilling	Ritchie		34-46	3rd	13.5
7-3	At Chi.	L	0-3		2	9	Lieber	Cordova		34-47	3rd	14.0
7-4	At Chi.	W	10-4		12	8	Wilkins	Aguilera		35-47	3rd	14.0
7-5	At Chi.	W	9-6		12	10	Anderson	Downs		36-47	3rd	14.0
7-7	Min.	W	8-6		13	9	Christiansen	Wells	Williams	37-47	3rd	12.5
7-8	Min.	W	4-1		8	5	Benson	Milton	Williams	38-47	3rd	11.5
7-9	Min.	L	2-3		8	8	Redman	Silva	Hawkins	38-48	3rd	12.5
7-13	At Cle.	L	3-4	(10)	8	10	Karsay	Sauerbeck		38-49	3rd	13.5
7-14	At Cle.	L	3-9		8	11	Finley	Benson		38-50	4th	14.5
7-15	At Cle.	L	4-6		10	10	Brewington	Silva	Karsay	38-51	4th	14.5
7-16	At L.A.	L	3-7		7	8	Adams	Williams		38-52	T4th	14.5
7-17	At L.A.	L	6-9		10	12	Dreifort	Arroyo	Shaw	38-53	5th	15.5
7-18	At L.A.	W	8-6		8	12	Manzanillo	Judd	Williams	39-53	5th	14.5
7-19	At Mil.	L	0-6		5	5	D'Amico	Benson		39-54	5th	14.5
7-20	At Mil.	W	9-2		12	5	Silva	Haynes		40-54	T3rd	13.5
7-21	Phi.	W	9-2		11	4	Anderson	Byrd		41-54	T3rd	13.5
7-22	Phi.	W	2-1		5	4	Arroyo	Person	Williams	42-54	T3rd	12.5
7-23	Phi.	L	1-4		3	7	Schilling	Ritchie		42-55	4th	12.5
7-25	Mil.	L	1-4	(11)	6	10	Leskanic	Christiansen	Wickman	42-56	4th	13.5
7-26	Mil.	W	5-4		10	8	Silva	Haynes	Williams	43-56	4th	13.5
7-27	Mil.	L	3-4		7	9	Leskanic	Manzanillo	Wickman	43-57	4th	13.5
7-28	S.D.	W	16-5		14	9	Arroyo	Clement		44-57	4th	12.5
7-29	S.D.	W	10-2		16	6	Cordova	Tollberg		45-57	4th	11.5
7-30	S.D.	L	8-9		13	14	Wall	Wilkins	Hoffman	45-58	4th	11.5
8-1†	L.A.	W	6-0		12	6	Anderson	Perez		46-58		
8-1‡	L.A.	L	3-5		8	7	Herges	Wilkins	Shaw	46-59	4th	11.5
8-2	L.A.	L	5-11		10	11	Dreifort	Silva		46-60	4th	12.5
8-3	At S.F	L	2-10		7	12	Ortiz	Cordova		46-61	4th	13.0
8-4	At S.F	L	3-5		11	10	Henry	Benson	Nen	46-62	4th	13.0
8-5	At S.F	W	7-2		13	9	Serafini	Gardner		47-62	4th	13.0
8-6	At S.F	L	1-7		10	9	Estes	Arroyo		47-63	4th	13.0
8-7	At Col.	W	8-7		13	12	Sauerbeck	Jimenez	Williams	48-63	4th	13.0
8-8	At Col.	L	1-6		10	15	Rose	Silva		48-64	4th	13.0
8-9	At Col.	L	3-4		7	7	White	Williams		48-65	4th	13.0
8-11	Ari.	L	1-6		4	10	Reynoso	Serafini		48-66	4th	13.5
8-12	Ari.	W	9-6		11	10	Sauerbeck	Schilling		49-66	4th	13.5
8-13	Ari.	L	6-7		12	14	Morgan	Arroyo	Mantei	49-67	4th	14.5
8-14	At Hou.	L	2-16		5	19	Holt	Silva		49-68	4th	14.5
8-15	At Hou.	L	4-5		9	7	Lima	Benson	Dotel	49-69	5th	15.5
8-16	At Hou.	L	10-11		12	9	Elarton	Serafini	Dotel	49-70	5th	16.5
8-18	At Cin.	W	6-3		11	6	Ritchie	Sullivan	Williams	50-70	5th	16.5
8-19	At Cin.	L	1-7		8	7	Parris	Anderson		50-71	5th	17.5
8-20	At Cin.	W	7-3		8	9	Silva	Dessens		51-71	5th	16.5
8-21	At StL.	L	4-7		6	8	Stephenson	Benson	Veres	51-72	5th	17.5
8-22	At StL.	W	6-2		11	10	Manzanillo	Kile		52-72	5th	16.5
8-23	At StL.	L	2-5		8	10	Ankiel	Ritchie	Veres	52-73	5th	17.5
8-25	Col.	L	3-6		9	13	Tavarez	Anderson		52-74	6th	18.0
8-26	Col.	L	4-11		10	19	Astacio	Silva		52-75	6th	19.0
8-27	Col.	L	2-9		4	16	Bohanon	Serafini		52-76	6th	20.0
8-28	S.F	L	4-5		6	8	Embree	Sauerbeck	Nen	52-77	6th	21.0
8-29	S.F	W	8-0		10	1	Benson	Hernandez		53-77	6th	20.0
8-30	S.F	L	0-2		4	5	Ortiz	Anderson	Nen	53-78	6th	21.0
8-31	S.F	L	2-10		10	13	Rueter	Silva		53-79	6th	21.5
9-1	At S.D.	W	3-2	(10)	10	6	Williams	Hoffman		54-79	6th	21.5
9-2	At S.D.	W	6-3		8	8	Ritchie	Clement	Sauerbeck	55-79	6th	21.5
9-3	At S.D.	W	8-6	(13)	11	16	Skrmetta	Almanzar	Williams	56-79	5th	21.5
9-4	At L.A.	W	12-1		13	10	Anderson	Dreifort		57-79	5th	21.5
9-5	At L.A.	W	8-0		15	6	Silva	Perez		58-79	4th	21.5
9-6	At L.A.	W	8-3		12	6	Serafini	Valdes		59-79	4th	20.5
9-8†	Cin.	W	7-3		11	7	Ritchie	Williamson		60-79		
9-8‡	Cin.	W	3-1		6	9	Wilkins	Villone	Williams	61-79	T3rd	19.5
9-9	Cin.	L	4-6		9	14	Parris	Benson	Graves	61-80	T4th	20.5
9-10	Cin.	L	4-6		6	8	Dessens	Anderson	Graves	61-81	5th	20.5
9-11	StL.	L	4-8		7	12	Stephenson	Manzanillo		61-82	5th	21.5
9-12	StL.	L	1-11		7	16	Kile	Serafini		61-83	5th	22.5
9-13	StL.	L	5-9		10	13	Ankiel	Ritchie		61-84	5th	23.5
9-14	At Hou.	L	7-8		12	11	Slusarski	Skrmetta		61-85	5th	24.5
9-15	At Hou.	L	7-16		12	19	B. Powell	Skrmetta	Slusarski	61-86	5th	25.5
9-16	At Hou.	L	9-10	(10)	16	9	Valdes	Sauerbeck		61-87	5th	26.5

Date	Opp.	Res.	Score	(inn.*)	Hits	Opp. hits	Winning pitcher	Losing pitcher	Save	Record	Pos.	GB
9-17	At Hou.	L	3-5		8	9	Elarton	Serafini	Dotel	61-88	5th	27.5
9-18	At Phi.	W	6-5		11	10	Loiselle	Padilla	Williams	62-88	5th	27.0
9-19	At Phi.	W	12-8		13	6	Skrmetta	Telemaco	Williams	63-88	5th	26.0
9-20	At Phi.	W	7-6	(10)	12	7	Loiselle	Brock	Williams	64-88	5th	26.0
9-21	At Mil.	L	2-12		5	14	Rigdon	Anderson		64-89	5th	26.0
9-23†	At Mil.	W	4-2		14	5	Silva	D'Amico	Williams	65-89		
9-23‡	At Mil.	L	4-5	(10)	10	8	Leskanic	Arroyo		65-90	5th	26.0
9-24	At Mil.	L	5-8		6	9	Leskanic	Williams		65-91	5th	26.0
9-26	Hou.	W	9-4		10	7	Benson	Holt		66-91	5th	26.0
9-27	Hou.	L	1-10		4	10	McKnight	Anderson		66-92	5th	27.0
9-28	Hou.	W	3-2		3	10	Silva	Dotel		67-92	5th	27.0
9-29	Chi.	W	8-4		13	10	Wilkins	Rain		68-92	5th	26.0
9-30	Chi.	W	4-2		7	11	Ritchie	Quevedo	Williams	69-92	5th	25.0
10-1	Chi.	L	9-10		14	12	Farnsworth	Sauerbeck	Arnold	69-93	5th	26.0

Monthly records: April (9-15), May (14-13), June (11-16), July (11-14), August (8-21), September (16-13), October (0-1).
*Innings, if other than nine. †First game of a doubleheader. ‡Second game of a doubleheader.

HIGHLIGHTS

High point: An eight-game winning streak to open September offered hope that the team was getting better and would finish strong. But it was another false alarm. That streak was preceded by a 2-7 fade and followed by a nine-game losing skid.

Low point: An 8-21 August doomed the team to its eighth straight losing season and probably sealed the fate of manager Gene Lamont, whose contract was not renewed after four seasons with the team.

Turning point: Jason Schmidt went on the disabled list June 10 with inflammation in his shoulder. The condition eventually required surgery and Schmidt, the team's opening night starter, had his season end after just 11 starts. Schmidt's injury, combined with Francisco Cordova's ongoing elbow problems, was an irreparable blow to the starting staff.

Most valuable player: Brian Giles was indispensable, especially after he moved back to left field. Giles matched his 1999 average (.315) and improved on his RBI total (123) despite hitting four fewer home runs (35) and drawing a team-high 114 walks.

Most valuable pitcher: With Schmidt and Cordova injured, the No. 1 starter job fell to second-year man Kris Benson. It was still a learning experience, but Benson provided some consistency and missed posting a winning record (10-12) only because of weak offensive and defensive support.

Most improved player: Adrian Brown started as the sixth outfielder and finished as the starting center fielder. Brown, a switch-hitter, improved his upper-body strength and spent hours in the cage working on his lefthanded swing. He has transformed himself from a lightly regarded prospect into a valuable leadoff man.

Most pleasant surprise: The Pirates knew they were acquiring a premier pinch hitter when they traded for John Vander Wal. But the 34-year-old veteran forced his way into the lineup and batted .299 with 24 home runs and 94 RBIs.

Key injuries: Schmidt didn't appear in a game after June 9 and Cordova made one appearance over the last two months. Their absences blew a hole in a rotation that had been overappraised by management. ... Adrian Brown was sidelined six weeks with a recurring hamstring injury.

Notable: Pittsburgh's last streak of eight losing seasons occurred from 1949-57. ... The team ERA of 4.94 was the highest since 1953, when the Pirates checked in at 5.22. ... Giles became the franchise's first player to top .300 with 30 home runs and 100 RBIs in consecutive seasons. ... Pitchers issued a team-record 711 walks.

—JOHN MEHNO

RECORDS

2000 regular-season record: 69-93 (5th in N.L. Central); 37-44 at home; 32-49 on road; 18-23 vs. East; 33-44 vs. Central; 18-26 vs. West; 15-22 vs. lefthanded starters; 54-71 vs. righthanded starters; 23-42 on grass; 46-51 on turf; 15-33 in daytime; 54-60 at night; 17-30 in one-run games; 8-11 in extra-inning games; 1-0-2 in doubleheaders.

Team record past five years: 368-441 (.455, ranks 13th in league in that span).

TEAM LEADERS

Batting average: Jason Kendall (.320).
At-bats: Jason Kendall (579).
Runs: Jason Kendall (112).
Hits: Jason Kendall (185).
Total Bases: Brian Giles (332).
Doubles: Brian Giles (37).
Triples: Brian Giles (7).
Home runs: Brian Giles (35).
Runs batted in: Brian Giles (123).
Stolen bases: Jason Kendall (22).
Slugging percentage: Brian Giles (.594).
On-base percentage: Brian Giles (.432).

Wins: Jose Silva (11).
Earned-run average: Kris Benson (3.85).
Complete games: Kris Benson (2).
Shutouts: Kris Benson, Todd Ritchie (1).
Saves: Mike Williams (24).
Innings pitched: Kris Benson (217.2).
Strikeouts: Kris Benson (184).

GAMES BY POSITION

Catcher: Jason Kendall 147, Keith Osik 26.
First base: Kevin Young 129, John Vander Wal 33, Alex Hernandez 12, Keith Osik 5, Mike Benjamin 1, Ivan Cruz 1, Alex Ramirez 1.
Second base: Warren Morris 134, Mike Benjamin 27, Enrique Wilson 11, Abraham Nunez 6, Luis Sojo 1.
Third base: Aramis Ramirez 72, Luis Sojo 50, Mike Benjamin 34, John Wehner 16, Enrique Wilson 16, Keith Osik 12.
Shortstop: Pat Meares 126, Mike Benjamin 30, Abraham Nunez 21, Enrique Wilson 8.
Outfield: Brian Giles 155, Adrian Brown 92, Wil Cordero 85, John Vander Wal 78, Bruce Aven 41, Emil Brown 38, Chad Hermansen 31, Alex Ramirez 31, Tike Redman 6, Alex Hernandez 5, Adam Hyzdu 5, John Wehner 1.
Designated hitter: John Vander Wal 3, Wil Cordero 1, Keith Osik 1, Kevin Young 1.

TOP DRAFT CHOICES

1. **Sean Burnett,** LHP, Wellington (Fla.) Community H.S.
2. **David Beigh,** RHP, Harrison H.S., Battle Ground, Ind.
3. **Chris Young,** RHP, Princeton Univ.
4. **Patrick Boyd,** OF, Clemson University.
5. **Jason Sharber,** RHP, Oakland H.S., Murfreesboro, Tenn.
6. **Josh Shortslef,** LHP, Hannibal Central H.S., Sterling, N.Y.
7. **Cole Burzynski,** RHP, Navasota (Tex.) H.S.
8. **Kurt Shafer,** RHP, Land O'Lakes (Fla.) H.S.
9. **Chris Bass,** SS, Madison (Ind.) H.S.
10. **Brandon Chaves,** SS, University of Hawaii-Hilo.

ST. LOUIS CARDINALS
NATIONAL LEAGUE CENTRAL DIVISION

Cardinals 2001 SCHEDULE
Home games shaded; D—Day game (games starting before 5 p.m.)
*—All-Star Game at Safeco Field (Seattle)

APRIL
SUN	MON	TUE	WED	THU	FRI	SAT
1	2 COL	3 D	4 COL	5 COL	6 ARI	7 D ARI
8 ARI	9 D COL	10	11 COL	12 D COL	13 HOU	14 D HOU
15 HOU	16 ARI	17 ARI	18 HOU	19	20 HOU	21 D HOU
22 HOU	23	24 MON	25 MON	26 D MON	27 NYM	28 D NYM
29 NYM	30					

MAY
SUN	MON	TUE	WED	THU	FRI	SAT
		1 FLA	2 FLA	3 FLA	4 ATL	5 ATL
6 D ATL	7 PIT	8 PIT	9 PIT	10 D PIT	11 CUB	12 D CUB
13 CUB	14	15 PIT	16 PIT	17 PIT	18 PHI	19 PHI
20 D PHI	21	22 MIL	23 MIL	24 D MIL	25 CIN	26 CIN
27 D CIN	28 MIL	29 MIL	30 MIL	31 MIL		

JUNE
SUN	MON	TUE	WED	THU	FRI	SAT
					1 CIN	2 D CIN
3 CIN	4 CIN	5 CUB	6 CUB	7 D CUB	8 COL	9 COL
10 D COL	11	12 KC	13 KC	14 KC	15 CWS	16 CWS
17 CWS	18 CUB	19 CUB	20 CUB	21 D CUB	22 SF	23 SF
24 SF	25	26 CIN	27 CIN	28	29 SF	30 D SF

JULY
SUN	MON	TUE	WED	THU	FRI	SAT
1 D SF	2	3 MIL	4 D MIL	5 MIL	6 CLE	7 D CLE
8 D CLE	9	10 *	11	12 DET	13 DET	14 D DET
15 D MIN	16 MIN	17 MIN	18 HOU	19 HOU	20 PIT	21 PIT
22 D PIT	23	24 HOU	25 HOU	26 D CUB	27 CUB	28 D CUB
29 CUB	30	31 ATL				

AUGUST
SUN	MON	TUE	WED	THU	FRI	SAT
			1 ATL	2 ATL	3 FLA	4 FLA
5 FLA	6	7 MON	8 MON	9 MON	10 NYM	11 D NYM
12 NYM	13 CIN	14 CIN	15 CIN	16 CIN	17 PHI	18 PHI
19 D PHI	20 CIN	21 CIN	22 CIN	23 CIN	24 D CUB	25 D CUB
26 CUB	27	28 SD	29 SD	30 SD	31 LA	

SEPTEMBER
SUN	MON	TUE	WED	THU	FRI	SAT
						1 LA
2 LA	3 SD	4 SD	5 SD	6	7 LA	8 D LA
9 D MIL	10 MIL	11 MIL	12 MIL	13 MIL	14 HOU	15 HOU
16 HOU	17 MIL	18 MIL	19 MIL	20 PIT	21 PIT	22 PIT
23 PIT	24 HOU	25 HOU	26 HOU	27	28 PIT	29 D PIT
30 PIT						

2001 SEASON
CLUB DIRECTORY

Chairman of the board/general partner
William O. DeWitt Jr.
Chairman
Frederick O. Hanser
Secretary-treasurer
Andrew N. Baur
President
Mark C. Lamping
Vice president, general manager
Walt Jocketty
Admin. assistant to the president
Julie Laningham
Sr. exec. asst. to v.p., general manager
Judy Carpenter-Barada
Vice president/player personnel
Jerry Walker
Special asst. to the general manager
Bob Gebhard
Senior v.p., sales and marketing
Dan Farrell
Vice president, controller
Brad Wood
Vice president, community relations
Marty Hendin
Vice president, business development
Bill DeWitt III
Vice president, stadium operations
Joe Abernathy
Vice president, ticket operations
Josie Arnold
Vice president, sales
Kevin Wade
Director, group sales
Joe Strohm
Manager, ticket sales
Mark Murray
Director, corporate sales/marketing
Thane van Breusegen
Group director, community outreach/ Cardinals Care
Tim Hanser
Director, target marketing
Ted Savage
Director, media relations
Brian Bartow
Mgr., media relations & publications
Steve Zesch

Assistant to director, media relations
Brad Hainje
Traveling secretary
C.J. Cherre
Director, player development
Mike Jorgensen
Director, international operations
Jeff Scott
Director, baseball operations
John Mozeliak
Director, minor league operations
Scott Smulczenski
Director, player procurement
Marty Maier
Director, professional scouting
Marteese Robinson
Mgr., baseball info./player dev.
John Vuch
Major league trainer
Barry Weinberg
Assistant major league trainer
Brad Henderson
Medical/rehabilitation coordinator
Mark O'Neal
Equipment manager
Buddy Bates
Assistant equipment manager
Rip Rowan
Special assignment scouts
Bing Devine, Jim Leyland, Fred McAlister, Joe Sparks (advance scout), Mike Squires
Professional scouts
Clark Crist, Marty Keough, Joe Rigoli
National cross-checkers
Mike Roberts, Chuck Fick
Scouts
Randy Benson, Ben Galante, Steve Gossett, Steve Grilli, Manny Guerra, Dave Karaff, Scott Melvin, Scott Nichols, Jay North, Dan Ontiveros, Tommy Shields, Roger Smith, Steve Turco, Dane Walker
International scouts
Jorge Brito, Domingo Carrasquel, Bobby Diaz

MINOR LEAGUE AFFILIATES

Class	Team	League	Manager
AAA	Memphis	Pacific Coast	Gaylen Pitts
AA	New Haven	Eastern	Dan Sheaffer
A	New Jersey	New York-Pennsylvania	Brian Rupp
A	Peoria	Midwest	Joe Hall
A	Potomac	Carolina	Joe Cunningham
Rookie	Johnson City	Appalachian	Chris Maloney

BROADCAST INFORMATION

Radio: KMOX-AM (1120).
TV: KPLR-TV (Channel 11).
Cable TV: Fox Sports Midwest.

SPRING TRAINING

Ballpark (city): Roger Dean Stadium (Jupiter, Fla.).
Ticket information: 561-966-3309.

Follow the Cardinals all season at: www.sportingnews.com/baseball/teams/cardinals/

SPRING TRAINING ROSTER

Manager—Tony La Russa (10).
Coaches—Mark DeJohn (34), Dave Duncan (18), Mike Easler (19), Marty Mason (38), Dave McKay (39), Jose Oquendo (11).

No.	PITCHERS	B/T	Ht./Wt.	Born	2000 clubs
66	Ankiel, Rick	L/L	6-1/210	7-19-79	St. Louis
31	Benes, Alan	R/R	6-5/235	1-21-72	Memphis, St. Louis
40	Benes, Andy	R/R	6-6/245	8-20-67	St. Louis
56	Brunette, Justin	L/L	6-1/200	10-7-75	Arkansas, St. Louis, Memphis
48	Christiansen, Jason	R/L	6-5/241	9-21-69	Pittsburgh, St. Louis
63	Hackman, Luther	R/R	6-4/195	10-10-74	Memphis, St. Louis
30	Hermanson, Dustin	R/R	6-2/200	12-21-72	Montreal
65	Hutchinson, Chad	R/R	6-5/230	2-21-77	Memphis, Arkansas
49	James, Mike	R/R	6-3/180	8-15-67	Memphis, St. Louis
	Karnuth, Jason	R/R	6-2/190	5-15-76	Arkansas, Memphis
57	Kile, Darryl	R/R	6-5/212	12-2-68	St. Louis
44	Kline, Steve	B/L	6-1/215	8-22-72	Montreal
50	Matthews, Mike	L/L	6-2/180	10-24-73	Memphis, St. Louis
35	Morris, Matt	R/R	6-5/210	8-9-74	Arkansas, Memphis, St. Louis
67	Stechschulte, Gene	R/R	6-5/210	8-12-73	Memphis, St. Louis, Arkansas
55	Stephenson, Garrett	R/R	6-5/208	1-2-72	St. Louis
50	Timlin, Mike	R/R	6-4/210	3-10-66	Baltimore, St. Louis
43	Veres, Dave	R/R	6-2/220	10-19-66	St. Louis
	Walrond, Les	L/L	6-0/195	11-7-76	Potomac
	Weibl, Clint	R/R	6-3/180	3-17-75	Memphis, Arkansas

No.	CATCHERS	B/T	Ht./Wt.	Born	2000 clubs
13	Figga, Mike	R/R	6-0/185	7-31-70	Pawtucket, Trenton, Albuquerque, San Antonio
8	Hernandez, Carlos	R/R	5-11/215	5-24-67	San Diego, St. Louis
26	Marrero, Eli	R/R	6-1/180	11-17-73	St. Louis, Memphis
44	Matheny, Mike	R/R	6-3/205	9-22-70	St. Louis
32	McDonald, Keith	R/R	6-2/215	2-8-73	Memphis, St. Louis
	Stefanski, Mike	R/R	6-2/190	9-12-69	Louisville

No.	INFIELDERS	B/T	Ht./Wt.	Born	2000 clubs
	Haas, Chris	L/R	6-2/210	10-15-76	Memphis, Arkansas
	Lucca, Lou	R/R	5-11/210	10-13-70	Memphis
25	McGwire, Mark	R/R	6-5/250	10-1-63	St. Louis
21	Paquette, Craig	R/R	6-0/190	3-28-69	St. Louis
27	Polanco, Placido	R/R	5-10/168	10-10-75	St. Louis
3	Renteria, Edgar	R/R	6-1/180	8-7-75	St. Louis
28	Sutton, Larry	L/L	6-0/185	5-14-70	Memphis, St. Louis
4	Vina, Fernando	L/R	5-9/174	4-16-69	St. Louis

No.	OUTFIELDERS	B/T	Ht./Wt.	Born	2000 clubs
	Bonilla, Bobby	B/R	6-3/240	2-23-63	Atlanta
7	Drew, J.D.	L/R	6-1/195	11-20-75	St. Louis
15	Edmonds, Jim	L/L	6-1/212	6-27-70	St. Louis
16	Lankford, Ray	L/L	5-11/200	6-5-67	St. Louis
	McCracken, Quinton	B/R	5-7/173	3-16-70	Tampa Bay, Durham
	Ortega, Bill	R/R	6-4/205	7-24-75	Arkansas
13	Saturria, Luis	R/R	6-2/165	7-21-76	Arkansas, St. Louis
	Snead, Esix	B/R	5-10/175	6-7-76	Potomac

BALLPARK INFORMATION

Ballpark (capacity, surface)
Busch Stadium (49,779, grass)

Address
250 Stadium Plaza
St. Louis, MO 63102

Official website
www.stlcardinals.com

Business phone
314-421-3060

Ticket information
314-421-2400

Ticket prices
$36 (field boxes-IF), $33 (loge boxes-IF)
$31 (field boxes-OF), $27 (loge boxes-OF)
$24 (loge reserved-IF), $22 (terrace boxes-IF)
$20 (terrace boxes-OF, loge reserved-OF)
$17 (terrace reserved-adults), $10 (bleachers)
$9 (upper terrace-OF-adults)
$8 (terrace reserved-children)
$4 (upper terrace reserved-children)

Field dimensions (from home plate)
To left field at foul line, 330 feet
To center field, 402 feet
To right field at foul line, 330 feet

First game played
May 12, 1966 (Cardinals 4, Braves 3)

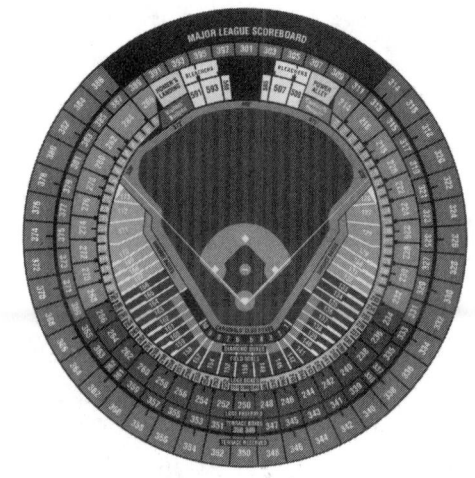

2001 SEASON St. Louis Cardinals

Date	Opp.	Res.	Score	(inn.*)	Hits	Opp. hits	Winning pitcher	Losing pitcher	Save	Record	Pos.	GB
4-3	Chi.	W	7-1		10	3	Kile	Tapani		1-0	1st	+1.0
4-5	Chi.	W	10-4		12	9	Hentgen	Lieber		2-0	T1st	...
4-6	Chi.	W	13-3		11	6	Stephenson	Farnsworth		3-0	1st	+1.0
4-7	Mil.	L	1-9		6	11	Bere	An. Benes		3-1	T1st	...
4-8	Mil.	W	10-8		15	9	Kile	Woodard	Veres	4-1	1st	+1.0
4-9	Mil.	W	11-2		16	6	Ankiel	de los Santos		5-1	1st	+2.0
4-10	At Hou.	W	8-7		13	7	Hentgen	Lima	Veres	6-1	1st	+2.0
4-11	At Hou.	W	10-6		9	8	Stephenson	Holt		7-1	1st	+2.5
4-12	At Hou.	L	5-7		9	9	Perez	Wainhouse	Wagner	7-2	1st	+2.5
4-13	At Col.	L	6-12		11	14	Croushore	Kile		7-3	1st	+1.5
4-14	At Col.	L	2-6		6	9	Astacio	Ankiel		7-4	1st	+1.5
4-16†	At Col.	W	9-3		11	9	Hentgen	Arrojo		8-4		
4-16‡	At Col.	L	13-14		17	15	Jimenez	Mohler	White	8-5	1st	+1.5
4-18	S.D.	W	5-4		10	9	An. Benes	Meadows	Veres	9-5	1st	+2.5
4-19	S.D.	W	4-3		9	6	Kile	Hitchcock	Veres	10-5	1st	+2.5
4-20	S.D.	W	14-1		14	6	Ankiel	Boehringer		11-5	1st	+2.5
4-21	Col.	L	4-6		12	10	Jarvis	Hentgen	Jimenez	11-6	1st	+2.5
4-22	Col.	L	6-7		6	11	Croushore	James	Jimenez	11-7	1st	+2.5
4-23	Col.	W	6-3	(7)	8	4	An. Benes	Karl	Slocumb	12-7	1st	+3.5
4-25	Mil.	W	7-2		10	7	Kile	Bere		13-7	1st	+4.5
4-26	Mil.	W	7-0		9	4	Ankiel	Woodard		14-7	1st	+4.5
4-27	Mil.	L	4-8		6	10	Haynes	Hentgen		14-8	1st	+3.5
4-28	At Phi.	W	7-4		10	9	Stephenson	Reyes	Veres	15-8	1st	+4.5
4-29	At Phi.	W	7-6	(10)	9	10	Mohler	Gomes		16-8	1st	+4.5
4-30	At Phi.	W	4-3		9	8	Kile	Schilling	James	17-8	1st	+4.5
5-2	Pit.	L	7-10		9	13	Wallace	Slocumb		17-9	1st	+3.5
5-3	Pit.	L	2-8		5	13	Benson	Hentgen		17-10	1st	+3.5
5-4	Pit.	W	5-0		9	4	Stephenson	Cordova		18-10	1st	+4.5
5-5	At Cin.	L	2-3		7	8	Villone	An. Benes	Williamson	18-11	1st	+3.5
5-6	At Cin.	W	3-1		5	6	Kile	Bell	Veres	19-11	1st	+4.5
5-7	At Cin.	L	7-9		10	8	Neagle	Holmes	Williamson	19-12	1st	+3.5
5-8	At S.F	L	4-6		9	8	Hernandez	Hentgen	Nen	19-13	1st	+3.0
5-9	At S.F	W	13-6		15	11	Stephenson	Ortiz		20-13	1st	+3.0
5-10	At S.F	L	3-4		7	7	Rodriguez	Slocumb	Nen	20-14	1st	+2.0
5-12	L.A.	L	0-13		2	13	Dreifort	Kile		20-15	1st	+0.5
5-13	L.A.	L	1-3		3	7	Park	Veres	Shaw	20-16	2nd	0.5
5-14	L.A.	W	12-10		17	11	Slocumb	Perez	Veres	21-16	1st	+0.5
5-16	At Phi.	W	8-2		9	10	An. Benes	Person		22-16	T1st	...
5-17	At Phi.	L	4-5		9	11	Wolf	Slocumb	Brantley	22-17	T1st	...
5-18	At Phi.	W	7-2		13	10	Stephenson	Schilling		23-17	T1st	...
5-19	At Pit.	L	1-13		3	15	Benson	Ankiel		23-18	T1st	...
5-20	At Pit.	W	19-4		19	9	Hentgen	Cordova		24-18	T1st	...
5-21	At Pit.	W	7-5		10	9	An. Benes	Ritchie	Veres	25-18	1st	+1.0
5-23	Fla.	W	10-3		13	5	Kile	Dempster		26-18	1st	+1.5
5-24	Fla.	W	5-1		11	5	Stephenson	Nunez		27-18	1st	+1.5
5-25	Fla.	W	7-6		9	11	Ankiel	Cornelius	Veres	28-18	1st	+2.0
5-26	N.Y.	L	2-5		9	9	Hampton	Thompson	Benitez	28-19	1st	+1.0
5-27	N.Y.	L	8-12		11	15	Cook	Veres		28-20	1st	+1.0
5-28	N.Y.	L	2-6		6	11	Rusch	Kile		28-21	1st	+1.0
5-29	At Ari.	W	3-0		5	6	Stephenson	Stottlemyre		29-21	1st	+1.5
5-30	At Ari.	W	6-1		10	5	Ankiel	Daal	Morris	30-21	1st	+1.5
5-31	At Ari.	L	2-6		10	8	Johnson	Hentgen	Kim	30-22	1st	+1.5
6-1	At Ari.	L	0-4		4	7	Reynoso	An. Benes		30-23	1st	+1.5
6-2	Cle.	W	5-1		8	3	Kile	Wright		31-23	1st	+1.5
6-3	Cle.	L	2-4		4	8	Colon	Stephenson	Karsay	31-24	1st	+0.5
6-4	Cle.	L	2-3		6	7	Martin	Morris	Karsay	31-25	2nd	0.5
6-5	K.C.	L	4-7		6	10	Suzuki	Hentgen	Spradlin	31-26	2nd	0.5
6-6	K.C.	W	5-4		7	10	An. Benes	Witasick	Veres	32-26	1st	+0.5
6-7	K.C.	W	4-2		10	7	Kile	Batista		33-26	1st	+1.5
6-9	At Det.	L	2-4		4	7	Weaver	Stephenson	Jones	33-27	1st	+1.5
6-10	At Det.	L	1-10		7	13	Moehler	Ankiel		33-28	1st	+1.5
6-11	At Det.	W	7-3		11	6	Hentgen	Mlicki		34-28	1st	+1.5
6-12	At S.D.	W	7-3		10	8	An. Benes	Clement		35-28	1st	+2.5
6-13	At S.D.	W	8-3		16	11	Kile	Lopez	Veres	36-28	1st	+3.5
6-14	At S.D.	W	3-1		7	6	Stephenson	Spencer	Morris	37-28	1st	+4.5
6-16	At L.A.	W	6-3		9	7	Hentgen	Hershiser	Veres	38-28	1st	+5.5
6-17	At L.A.	W	4-3		13	8	An. Benes	Dreifort	Veres	39-28	1st	+6.5
6-18	At L.A.	L	3-6		7	8	Park	Kile	Shaw	39-29	1st	+6.5
6-20	S.F	W	7-2		8	4	Ankiel	Ortiz		40-29	1st	+6.5
6-21	S.F	L	1-4		5	7	Rueter	Stephenson	Nen	40-30	1st	+6.5
6-22	S.F	W	11-10		12	15	Veres	Gardner		41-30	1st	+6.5
6-23	L.A.	W	9-6	(12)	9	10	Stechschulte	Shaw		42-30	1st	+7.5
6-24	L.A.	W	6-1		9	6	Al. Benes	Hershiser		43-30	1st	+7.5
6-25	L.A.	W	2-1		6	6	Slocumb	Osuna		44-30	1st	+8.5

Date	Opp.	Res.	Score	(inn.*)	Hits	Opp. hits	Winning pitcher	Losing pitcher	Save	Record	Pos.	GB
6-26	At Cin.	L	2-3		7	10	Neagle	Stephenson	Graves	44-31	1st	+7.5
6-27	At Cin.	W	4-3		9	11	Kile	Parris	Veres	45-31	1st	+8.5
6-28	At Cin.	L	3-7		7	8	Reyes	Al. Benes		45-32	1st	+7.5
6-29	At Cin.	W	12-3		15	4	An. Benes	Villone		46-32	1st	+8.5
6-30	Hou.	W	5-4		13	6	Al. Benes	Holt	Veres	47-32	1st	+8.5
7-1	Hou.	W	10-9		11	15	Thompson	Slusarski	Veres	48-32	1st	+9.5
7-2	Hou.	L	3-6		8	10	Elarton	Kile	Valdes	48-33	1st	+8.5
7-4	Cin.	W	14-3		13	9	An. Benes	Villone		49-33	1st	+9.0
7-5	Cin.	W	4-3		5	6	Hentgen	Harnisch	Veres	50-33	1st	+10.0
7-6	Cin.	L	6-12		13	13	Dessens	Ankiel		50-34	1st	+9.0
7-7	S.F	L	2-4		9	9	Embree	Morris	Nen	50-35	1st	+8.0
7-8	S.F	L	6-7		14	11	Estes	Stephenson	Nen	50-36	1st	+7.0
7-9	S.F	W	8-7		10	8	Hentgen	Hernandez	Veres	51-36	1st	+8.0
7-13	At Chi. (AL)	W	13-5		14	11	An. Benes	Sirotka		52-36	1st	+8.0
7-14	At Chi. (AL)	W	9-4		11	8	Stephenson	Wunsch		53-36	1st	+8.0
7-15	At Chi. (AL)	L	7-15		13	15	Parque	Kile		53-37	1st	+7.0
7-16	At Min.	L	2-5		6	10	Redman	Ankiel	Guardado	53-38	1st	+7.0
7-17	At Min.	W	8-3		13	11	Hentgen	Lincoln		54-38	1st	+8.0
7-18	At Min.	L	2-3		9	7	Radke	An. Benes	Hawkins	54-39	1st	+7.0
7-19	At Ari.	L	3-4		6	9	Reynoso	Stephenson	Mantei	54-40	1st	+6.0
7-20	At Ari.	L	2-3		6	4	Johnson	Veres		54-41	1st	+6.0
7-21	At Hou.	W	12-1		16	6	Ankiel	Elarton		55-41	1st	+7.0
7-22	At Hou.	L	5-10		6	17	Miller	Hentgen		55-42	1st	+6.0
7-23	At Hou.	L	7-15		10	14	Reynolds	An. Benes		55-43	1st	+5.0
7-25	Ari.	W	7-3		7	5	Stephenson	Johnson		56-43	1st	+6.5
7-26	Ari.	W	8-4		11	10	Kile	Reynoso		57-43	1st	+7.5
7-27	Ari.	L	5-17		10	19	Guzman	Ankiel		57-44	1st	+7.0
7-28	At N.Y.	L	2-3		5	9	Leiter	Hentgen	Benitez	57-45	1st	+6.0
7-29	At N.Y.	L	3-4		7	5	White	James	Benitez	57-46	1st	+5.0
7-30	At N.Y.	L	2-4		4	7	B.J. Jones	Stephenson		57-47	1st	+4.0
7-31	At Mon.	W	4-0		10	6	Kile	Thurman		58-47	1st	+4.0
8-1	At Mon.	L	0-4		5	9	Moore	Ankiel		58-48	1st	+4.0
8-2	At Mon.	W	10-7		11	11	Hentgen	Johnson		59-48	1st	+5.0
8-4	Atl.	L	4-6		10	10	Glavine	An. Benes	Kamienicki	59-49	1st	+5.0
8-5	Atl.	W	5-0		8	5	Stephenson	Burkett		60-49	1st	+6.0
8-6	Atl.	L	4-6		9	10	Remlinger	Kile	Ligtenberg	60-50	1st	+6.0
8-7	Fla.	W	2-1	(11)	9	4	Timlin	Darensbourg		61-50	1st	+6.0
8-8	Fla.	L	0-7		6	10	Sanchez	Hentgen		61-51	1st	+6.0
8-9	Fla.	L	3-5		11	7	Almanza	Morris	Alfonseca	61-52	1st	+5.0
8-10	Col.	W	5-4		12	10	Timlin	Jimenez		62-52	1st	+5.5
8-11	At Mil.	L	2-6		7	8	D'Amico	Kile		62-53	1st	+4.5
8-12	At Mil.	W	2-1	(12)	9	7	Morris	Leskanic	James	63-53	1st	+4.5
8-13	At Mil.	W	6-4		13	8	Hentgen	Wright	Veres	64-53	1st	+4.5
8-14	At Chi.	L	3-7		8	11	Lieber	An. Benes		64-54	1st	+4.5
8-15	At Chi.	W	4-2		11	7	Stephenson	Arnold	Veres	65-54	1st	+5.5
8-16	At Chi.	W	5-1		9	6	Kile	Tapani		66-54	1st	+6.5
8-18	Phi.	W	7-6		7	7	Christiansen	Brock		67-54	1st	+7.5
8-19	Phi.	W	6-3		9	7	Hentgen	Daal		68-54	1st	+7.5
8-20	Phi.	L	0-6		5	10	Bottenfield	Reames		68-55	1st	+7.5
8-21	Pit.	W	7-4		8	6	Stephenson	Benson	Veres	69-55	1st	+7.5
8-22	Pit.	L	2-6		10	11	Manzanillo	Kile		69-56	1st	+7.5
8-23	Pit.	W	5-2		10	8	Ankiel	Ritchie	Veres	70-56	1st	+8.5
8-24	At Atl.	W	12-5		13	9	Hentgen	Ashby		71-56	1st	+8.5
8-25	At Atl.	L	4-7		8	9	Glavine	Timlin	Ligtenberg	71-57	1st	+7.5
8-26	At Atl.	W	6-3		10	10	Stephenson	Millwood		72-57	1st	+7.5
8-27	At Atl.	W	7-2		9	8	Kile	Ligtenberg		73-57	1st	+8.5
8-28	At Fla.	W	5-2		12	5	James	Almanza	Veres	74-57	1st	+8.5
8-29	At Fla.	L	1-3		4	7	Smith	Hentgen	Alfonseca	74-58	1st	+7.5
8-30	At Fla.	W	4-2		7	8	Morris	Alfonseca	Veres	75-58	1st	+8.5
9-1	N.Y.	W	6-5		11	9	Veres	Mahomes		76-58	1st	+8.0
9-2	N.Y.	W	2-1		9	5	Kile	Hampton		77-58	1st	+9.0
9-3	N.Y.	W	4-3	(11)	7	5	Morris	White		78-58	1st	+9.0
9-4	Mon.	W	4-2		6	9	Hentgen	Vazquez	Veres	79-58	1st	+9.0
9-5	Mon.	W	7-6		7	4	Reames	Santana	Timlin	80-58	1st	+10.0
9-6	Mon.	L	2-7		8	12	Hermanson	Stephenson		80-59	1st	+9.0
9-7	Mon.	W	6-1		11	5	Kile	Armas		81-59	1st	+9.5
9-8	At Mil.	L	5-6		8	12	Leskanic	Veres		81-60	1st	+10.0
9-9	At Mil.	W	7-6		15	12	Veres	Acevedo		82-60	1st	+10.0
9-10	At Mil.	L	3-4	(10)	8	9	King	An. Benes		82-61	1st	+9.0
9-11	At Pit.	W	8-4		12	7	Stephenson	Manzanillo		83-61	1st	+9.0
9-12	At Pit.	W	11-1		16	7	Kile	Serafini		84-61	1st	+10.0
9-13	At Pit.	W	9-5		13	10	Ankiel	Ritchie		85-61	1st	+10.0
9-14	Chi.	W	4-0		5	3	Hentgen	Quevedo		86-61	1st	+11.0
9-15	Chi.	W	3-2		4	6	James	Lieber	Veres	87-61	1st	+11.0
9-16	Chi.	W	7-6		10	11	Timlin	Spradlin	Veres	88-61	1st	+11.0
9-17	Chi.	W	4-2		4	7	Kile	Worrell	Morris	89-61	1st	+11.0
9-19	Hou.	L	6-8	(10)	8	13	Dotel	Al. Benes	Cabrera	89-62	1st	+10.5
9-20	Hou.	W	11-6		11	9	Ankiel	Holt		90-62	1st	+11.5

Date	Opp.	Res.	Score	(inn.*)	Hits	Opp. hits	Winning pitcher	Losing pitcher	Save	Record	Pos.	GB
9-21	Hou.	L	5-7		11	12	McKnight	An. Benes	Dotel	90-63	1st	+11.0
9-22	At Chi.	L	4-5		5	10	Ohman	Veres		90-64	1st	+10.0
9-23	At Chi.	W	6-5	10	10	7	Reames	Nation	Morris	91-64	1st	+10.0
9-24	At Chi.	L	5-10		8	12	Van Poppel	Hentgen	Heredia	91-65	1st	+9.0
9-26	At S.D.	W	7-1		11	6	An. Benes	Eaton		92-65	1st	+10.0
9-27	At S.D.	W	3-0		7	7	Ankiel	Tollberg	Veres	93-65	1st	+11.0
9-28	At S.D.	W	7-6		8	7	Kile	Davey	Veres	94-65	1st	+11.0
9-29	Cin.	L	1-8		2	15	Villone	Stephenson		94-66	1st	+10.0
9-30	Cin.	L	4-8		9	12	Fernandez	Hentgen		94-67	1st	+9.0
10-1	Cin.	W	6-2		8	8	An. Benes	Parris		95-67	1st	+10.0

Monthly records: April (17-8), May (13-14), June (17-10), July (11-15), August (17-11), September (19-9), October (1-0).
*Innings, if other than nine. †First game of a doubleheader. ‡Second game of a doubleheader.

HIGHLIGHTS

High point: After beating the Atlanta Braves three times in a four-game late August showdown, the Cardinals swept the Braves in the Division Series, never trailing after any complete inning. They won that series even though only one of their three starting pitchers lasted past the fourth inning.

Low point: After their impressive romp past the Braves, the Cardinals dropped four of five games to the New York Mets in the N.L. Championship Series. The Cardinals played shorthanded against the Mets, one starting pitcher (Garrett Stephenson) lost to injury and another (Rick Ankiel) rendered ineffective because of wildness.

Turning point: The Cardinals fought off their biggest challenger and extended their N.L. Central lead by taking four of seven games from Cincinnati over an 11-day span in late June and early July. Their lead never dipped below four games the rest of the way.

Most valuable player: It's hard to ignore the 167 strikeouts, but center fielder Jim Edmonds still posted career highs in home runs (42) and runs batted in (108) while playing Gold Glove defense in his first St. Louis season.

Most valuable pitcher: Having posted 21 wins over his previous two seasons in Colorado, Darryl Kile became a 20-game winner in his first season with the Cardinals. And he never missed a turn in the rotation.

Most improved player: Utility infielder Placido Polanco might have been the most improved player in major league baseball. Polanco batted .316 and played in stellar, sometimes even spectacular, fashion at second base, shortstop and third.

Most pleasant surprise: Stephenson, who never had won in double figures as a major leaguer, finished second behind Kile with 16 wins. He made good in his first big-league shot as a rotation regular.

Key injuries: Mark McGwire missed virtually the entire second half with tendinitis in his knee and hit only two home runs after the All-Star break. ... Third baseman Fernando Tatis missed two months early in the season because of a torn groin muscle and he never regained top form, hitting only .204 after the break. ... Andy Benes missed almost a month because of torn cartilage in his knee but still won 12 games. ... Gold Glove catcher Mike Matheny missed all of the postseason after slashing a finger in a freak home accident. ... Lefthanded relievers Scott Radinsky and Jesse Orosco made only cameo appearances as they battled elbow problems that required surgery.

Notable: The Cardinals were in first place for all but four days, one of which was the result of a Chicago Cubs victory before they played their first game. The Cardinals' biggest lead was 11½ games on September 20 and their peak of 28 games over .500 was reached four times in September. ... Despite the absence of McGwire for half a season, the Cardinals set a team record with 235 home runs, 12 more than they hit during Big Mac's record-breaking 1998 season. ... Ankiel, despite his playoff problems, completed his rookie season with an 11-7 record and impressive 3.50 ERA.

—RICK HUMMEL

RECORDS

2000 regular-season record: 95-67 (1st in N.L. Central); 50-31 at home; 45-36 on road; 25-16 vs. East; 44-33 vs. Central; 26-18 vs. West; 17-23 vs. lefthanded starters; 78-44 vs. righthanded starters; 79-58 on grass; 16-9 on turf; 38-20 in daytime; 57-47 at night; 28-16 in one-run games; 5-2 in extra-inning games; 0-1 in doubleheaders.
Team record past five years: 414-395 (.512, ranks 8th in league in that span).

TEAM LEADERS

Batting average: Fernando Vina (.300).
At-bats: Edgar Renteria (562).
Runs: Jim Edmonds (129).
Hits: Edgar Renteria (156).
Total Bases: Jim Edmonds (306).
Doubles: Edgar Renteria (32).
Triples: Fernando Vina (6).
Home runs: Jim Edmonds (42).
Runs batted in: Jim Edmonds (108).
Stolen bases: Edgar Renteria (21).
Slugging percentage: Jim Edmonds (.583).

On-base percentage: Jim Edmonds (.411).
Wins: Darryl Kile (20).
Earned-run average: Rick Ankiel (3.50).
Complete games: Darryl Kile (5).
Shutouts: Garrett Stephenson (2).
Saves: Dave Veres (29).
Innings pitched: Darryl Kile (232.1).
Strikeouts: Rick Ankiel (194).

GAMES BY POSITION

Catcher: Mike Matheny 124, Eli Marrero 38, Carlos Hernandez 16, Keith McDonald 4, Rick Wilkins 3.
First base: Mark McGwire 70, Will Clark 50, Craig Paquette 28, Eduardo Perez 24, Mike Matheny 8, Eli Marrero 7, Shawon Dunston 6, Jim Edmonds 6, Larry Sutton 6, Chris Richard 2, Thomas Howard 1, Placido Polanco 1, Fernando Tatis 1.
Second base: Fernando Vina 122, Placido Polanco 51, Craig Paquette 13.
Third base: Fernando Tatis 91, Craig Paquette 86, Placido Polanco 35, Shawon Dunston 5, Eduardo Perez 2.
Shortstop: Edgar Renteria 149, Placido Polanco 29, Shawon Dunston 8.
Outfield: Jim Edmonds 146, J.D. Drew 127, Ray Lankford 117, Eric Davis 69, Shawon Dunston 58, Craig Paquette 31, Thomas Howard 27, Luis Saturria 9, Eduardo Perez 4, Larry Sutton 4, Chris Richard 3.
Designated hitter: Eric Davis 4, Thomas Howard 3, Fernando Tatis 2, Shawon Dunston 1, Ray Lankford 1.

TOP DRAFT CHOICES

1a. **Shaun Boyd,** OF, Vista H.S., Oceanside, Calif.
1b. **Blake Williams,** RHP, Southwest Texas State University.
2. **Chris Narveson,** LHP, T.C. Roberson H.S., Arden, N.C.
3. **Chase Voshell,** SS, Wake Forest Univ.
4. **Yedeal Molina,** C, Maestro Ladi H.S., Vega Alta, P.R.
5. **Josh Axelson,** RHP, Michigan State U.
6. **Justin Woodrow,** OF, Knoch H.S., Saxonburg, Pa.
7. **Shaun Stokes,** RHP, William Paterson (N.J.) University.
8. **Dan Moylan,** C, U. of North Carolina.
9. **John Novinsky,** RHP, Iona (N.Y.) College.
10. **Carmen Cali,** LHP, Florida Atlantic U.

SAN DIEGO PADRES
NATIONAL LEAGUE WEST DIVISION

Padres
2001 SCHEDULE
Home games shaded; D—Day game (games starting before 5 p.m.)
*—All-Star Game at Safeco Field (Seattle)

APRIL
SUN	MON	TUE	WED	THU	FRI	SAT
1	2 D SF	D 3	4 SF	5 SF	6 D COL	7 D COL
8 COL	D 9	10 SF	D 11 SF	12 D SF	13 D LA	14 LA
15 LA	D 16	17 COL	18 COL	19 D COL	20 LA	21 LA
22 D LA	23 PHI	24 PHI	25 PHI	26 D PHI	D 27 PIT	28 PIT
29 PIT	D 30					

MAY
SUN	MON	TUE	WED	THU	FRI	SAT
		1 CUB	2 CUB	3 D CUB	D 4 CIN	5 D CIN
6 D CIN	7	8 ATL	9 ATL	10 D ATL	11 FLA	12 FLA
13 D FLA	14	15 NYM	16 NYM	17 NYM	18 MON	19 MON
20 D MON	21 HOU	22 HOU	23 HOU	24 D ARI	25 ARI	26 ARI
27 D ARI	28	29 HOU	30 HOU	31 D HOU		

JUNE
SUN	MON	TUE	WED	THU	FRI	SAT
					1 ARI	2 ARI
3 D ARI	4	5 SF	6 SF	7 D SF	8 SEA	9 SEA
10 D SEA	11	12 OAK	13 OAK	14 D OAK	15 SEA	16 SEA
17 D SEA	18	19 SF	20 SF	21 D SF	22 LA	23 LA
24 D LA	25 COL	26 COL	27 COL	28 LA	29 LA	30 LA

JULY
SUN	MON	TUE	WED	THU	FRI	SAT
1 LA	D 2	3 COL	4 COL	5 D COL	6 D TEX	7 D TEX
8 D TEX	9	* 10	11	12 HOU	13 HOU	14 HOU
15 ANA	16 ANA	17 D ANA	18 ARI	19 D ARI	20 MIL	21 MIL
22 D MIL	23 ARI	24 ARI	25 ARI	26	27 MIL	28 MIL
29 MIL	D 30	31 CUB				

AUGUST
SUN	MON	TUE	WED	THU	FRI	SAT
			1 CUB	2 CUB	3 D CIN	4 CIN
5 D CIN	6	7 PHI	8 PHI	9 D PHI	10 PIT	11 PIT
12 D PIT	13	14 NYM	15 NYM	16 D NYM	17 MON	18 MON
19 D MON	20	21 ATL	22 ATL	23 ATL	24 FLA	25 FLA
26 D FLA	27 FLA	28 STL	29 STL	30 D STL	31 ARI	

SEPTEMBER
SUN	MON	TUE	WED	THU	FRI	SAT
						1 ARI
2 ARI	3 STL	4 STL	5 STL	6	7 ARI	8 D ARI
9 D ARI	10 LA	11 LA	12 LA	13	14 COL	15 COL
16 D COL	17 LA	18 LA	19 LA	20	21 SF	22 SF
23 D SF	24 COL	25 COL	26 COL	27 COL	28 SF	29 D SF
30 D SF						

2001 SEASON
CLUB DIRECTORY

Chairman
John Moores

President and chief executive officer
Larry Lucchino

Executive vice president, public affairs
Charles Steinberg

Exec. v.p., baseball ops. and g.m.
Kevin Towers

Sr. v.p., corporate marketing
Michael Dee

Sr. vice president, general counsel
Bob Vizas

V.p., scouting and player development
Ted Simmons

Vice president, community relations
Michele Anderson

V.p., Hispanic & international mktg.
Enrique Morones

Assistant general manager
Fred Uhlman Jr.

Director, merchandising
Michael Babida

Controller
Steve Fitch

Director, administrative services
Lucy Freeman

Exec. dir., ticket ops. and services
Dave Gilmore

Director, sales
Mark Tilson

Director, entertainment
George Stieren

Director, ballpark planning
Erik Judson

Director, baseball operations
Theo Epstein

Director, Padres Foundation
Sue Botos

Director, corporate development
Sam Kennedy

Director, video production
Tom Catlin

Director, military marketing
Captain Jack Ensch (Ret.)

Director, stadium operations
Mark Guglielmo

Director, player development
Tye Waller

Director, minor league operations
Priscilla Oppenheimer

Director, team travel
Brian Prilaman

Director, public relations
Glenn Geffner

Director, fan services
Tim Katzman

Director, scouting
Bill "Chief" Gayton

Trainer
Todd Hutcheson

Assistant trainer
Jim Daniel

Strength and conditioning coordinator
Bill Henry

Club physicians
Cliff Colwell
Jan Fronek
Paul Hirshman
Blaine Phillips

Major league scouts
Ken Bracey, Ray Crone Sr., Moose Johnson

Director of professional scouting
Gary Nickels

Advance scout
Jeff Gardner

International scouting supervisor
Bill Clark

Professional scouts
Brandy Davis, Mal Fichman, Ben McLure, Gary Roenicke, Craig Shipley, Van Smith

Full-time scouts
Joe Bochy, Rich Bordi, Bob Cummings, Takeo Daigo, Lane Decker, Jimmy Dreyer, Ronquito Garcia, Chris Gwynn, Don "Trip" Keister, Don Lyle, Tim McWilliam, Billy Merkel, Darryl Milne, Rene Mons, Mike Rickard, Mark Wasinger, Jim Woodward

MINOR LEAGUE AFFILIATES

Class	Team	League	Manager
AAA	Portland	Pacific Coast	Rick Sweet
AA	Mobile	Southern	Tracy Woodson
A	Eugene	Northwest	Randy Whisler
A	Fort Wayne	Midwest	To be announced
A	Lake Elsinore	California	Craig Colbert
Rookie	Idaho Falls	Pioneer	Don Werner

BROADCAST INFORMATION

Radio: KOGO-AM (600), KURS-AM (1040, Spanish).
TV: KUSI (Channel 9).
Cable TV: Channel 4 Padres.

SPRING TRAINING

Ballpark (city): Peoria Stadium (Peoria, Ariz.).
Ticket information: 623-878-4337, 800-409-1511.

Follow the Padres all season at: www.sportingnews.com/baseball/teams/padres/

2001 SEASON *San Diego Padres*

Manager—Bruce Bochy (15).
Coaches—Greg Booker (38), Duane Espy (52), Tim Flannery (11), Rob Picciolo (5), Dave Smith (45), Alan Trammell (3).

No.	PITCHERS	B/T	Ht./Wt.	Born	2000 clubs
40	Almanzar, Carlos	R/R	6-2/200	11-6-73	San Diego, Las Vegas
21	Clement, Matt	R/R	6-3/195	8-12-74	San Diego
44	Davey, Tom	R/R	6-7/230	9-11-73	Tacoma, Las Vegas, San Diego
59	Herndon, Harry	R/R	6-1/190	9-11-78	Las Vegas
41	Hitchcock, Sterling	L/L	6-0/205	4-29-71	San Diego
51	Hoffman, Trevor	R/R	6-0/205	10-13-67	San Diego
	Jarvis, Kevin	L/R	6-2/200	8-1-69	Colorado Springs, Colorado
29	Karl, Scott	L/L	6-2/209	8-9-71	Colorado, Colorado Springs, Lake Elsinore, Anaheim
57	Lawrence, Brian	R/R	6-0/195	5-14-76	Mobile, Las Vegas
46	Loewer, Carlton	R/R	6-6/211	9-24-73	Las Vegas, Rancho Cucamonga
60	Lopez, Rodrigo	R/R	6-1/180	12-14-75	Las Vegas, San Diego
54	Maurer, David	R/L	6-2/205	2-23-75	Mobile, Las Vegas, San Diego
48	Myers, Randy	L/L	6-1/210	9-19-62	DID NOT PLAY
66	Myers, Rodney	R/R	6-1/215	6-26-69	San Diego, Rancho Cucamonga
64	Serrano, Wascar	R/R	6-2/178	6-2-78	Mobile, Las Vegas
55	Tollberg, Brian	R/R	6-3/195	9-16-72	Las Vegas, San Diego
56	Walker, Kevin	L/L	6-4/190	9-20-76	Mobile, San Diego
49	Watkins, Steve	R/R	6-4/190	7-19-78	Rancho Cucamonga
18	Williams, Woody	R/R	6-0/195	8-19-66	San Diego, Rancho Cucamonga, Las Vegas
34	Witasick, Jay	R/R	6-4/235	8-28-72	Kansas City, San Diego

No.	CATCHERS	B/T	Ht./Wt.	Born	2000 clubs
13	Davis, Ben	B/R	6-4/215	3-10-77	Las Vegas, San Diego
7	Gonzalez, Wiki	R/R	5-11/203	5-17-74	San Diego

No.	INFIELDERS	B/T	Ht./Wt.	Born	2000 clubs
9	Arias, Alex	R/R	6-3/202	11-20-67	Philadelphia
63	Eberwein, Kevin	R/R	6-4/200	3-30-77	Mobile
10	Gomez, Chris	R/R	6-1/195	6-16-71	San Diego
2	Jackson, Damian	R/R	5-11/185	8-6-73	San Diego
30	Klesko, Ryan	L/L	6-3/220	6-12-71	San Diego
	Magadan, Dave	L/R	6-4/215	9-30-62	San Diego
17	Mendez, Donaldo	R/R	6-1/155	6-7-78	Michigan
22	Nady, Xavier	R/R	6-2/205	11-14-78	San Diego
23	Nevin, Phil	R/R	6-2/231	1-19-71	San Diego
16	Nicholson, Kevin	B/R	5-10/190	3-29-76	Las Vegas, San Diego
1	Perez, Santiago	B/R	6-2/150	12-30-75	Indianapolis, Milwaukee

No.	OUTFIELDERS	B/T	Ht./Wt.	Born	2000 clubs
60	Colangelo, Mike	R/R	6-1/185	10-22-76	DID NOT PLAY
26	Darr, Mike	L/R	6-3/205	3-21-76	Las Vegas, San Diego
25	DeHaan, Kory	L/R	6-2/187	7-16-76	Rancho Cucamonga, Las Vegas, San Diego
	Green, Chad	B/R	5-10/180	6-28-75	Huntsville, Indianapolis
19	Gwynn, Tony	L/L	5-11/225	5-9-60	San Diego
8	Owens, Eric	R/R	6-0/198	2-3-71	San Diego
61	Owens, Jeremy	R/R	6-1/200	12-9-76	Rancho Cucamonga
28	Rivera, Ruben	R/R	6-3/208	11-14-73	San Diego, Las Vegas
27	Trammell, Bubba	R/R	6-2/220	11-6-71	Tampa Bay, New York N.L.

BALLPARK INFORMATION

Ballpark (capacity, surface)
Qualcomm Stadium (66,307, grass)

Address
P.O. Box 2000
San Diego, CA 92112-2000

Official website
www.padres.com

Business phone
619-881-6500

Ticket information
888-697-2373

Ticket prices
$26 (field level/IF), $24 (club level/IF)
$22 (field level/OF, plaza level/IF, club level/OF)
$20 (plaza level/OF), $18 (loge level/IF)
$16 (loge level/OF), $14 (press level)
$9 (grandstand/plaza level, view level/lower IF)
$8 (grandstand/club level, view level/IF)
$7 (view level/OF), $5 (outfield bleachers)

Field dimensions (from home plate)
To left field at foul line, 327 feet
To center field, 405 feet
To right field at foul line, 330 feet

First game played
April 8, 1969 (Padres 2, Astros 1)

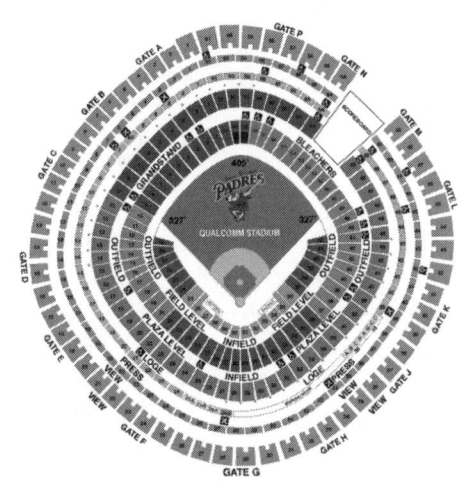

2000 REVIEW
DAY BY DAY

Date	Opp.	Res.	Score	(inn.*)	Hits	Opp. hits	Winning pitcher	Losing pitcher	Save	Record	Pos.	GB
4-3	At N.Y.	L	1-2		5	4	Leiter	Wall	Benitez	0-1	T2nd	1.0
4-5	At N.Y.	W	4-0		11	7	Williams	B.J. Jones		1-1	4th	1.0
4-6	At N.Y.	W	8-5		10	8	Clement	Hampton		2-1	2nd	1.0
4-7	At Mon.	W	10-5		13	12	Meadows	Powell		3-1	T1st	...
4-8	At Mon.	L	9-10		11	11	Telford	Wall	Urbina	3-2	2nd	1.0
4-9	At Mon.	L	1-2		7	4	Irabu	Boehringer	Urbina	3-3	T2nd	2.0
4-10	Ari.	L	4-8		11	12	Stottlemyre	Williams	Morgan	3-4	T3rd	3.0
4-11	Ari.	W	3-2	(13)	9	7	Whisenant	Springer		4-4	3rd	2.0
4-12	Ari.	W	4-2		6	6	Meadows	Reynoso	Hoffman	5-4	3rd	1.0
4-13	Ari.	L	4-5		10	9	Anderson	Hitchcock	Morgan	5-5	T3rd	2.0
4-14	Hou.	L	4-10		13	11	Reynolds	Boehringer		5-6	4th	3.0
4-15	Hou.	W	5-3		9	7	Williams	Lima	Hoffman	6-6	4th	3.0
4-16	Hou.	W	13-3		18	8	Clement	Holt		7-6	T3rd	2.5
4-18	At StL.	L	4-5		9	10	An. Benes	Meadows	Veres	7-7	4th	3.0
4-19	At StL.	L	3-4		6	9	Kile	Hitchcock	Veres	7-8	4th	4.0
4-20	At StL.	L	1-14		6	14	Ankiel	Boehringer		7-9	4th	5.0
4-21	At Hou.	W	7-2		11	6	Williams	Lima		8-9	4th	4.0
4-22	At Hou.	W	8-6	(10)	14	6	Cunnane	Perez	Hoffman	9-9	4th	3.0
4-23	At Hou.	W	11-10		14	10	Whisenant	Wagner	Hoffman	10-9	3rd	2.0
4-25	At Pit.	L	3-4	(11)	13	9	Sauerbeck	Almanzar		10-10	3rd	3.0
4-26	At Pit.	L	8-9		10	12	Williams	Whisenant		10-11	4th	3.0
4-27	At Pit.	W	12-4		15	4	Clement	Parra		11-11	3rd	3.0
4-28	Atl.	L	2-7		8	7	Maddux	Meadows	Remlinger	11-12	T3rd	3.0
4-29	Atl.	L	4-7	(12)	10	10	Chen	Palacios	Rocker	11-13	T3rd	4.0
4-30	Atl.	L	4-7		6	8	Glavine	Hitchcock		11-14	T3rd	5.0
5-1	Fla.	L	2-5		8	9	Dempster	Williams	Alfonseca	11-15	5th	5.5
5-2	Fla.	W	8-3		11	6	Clement	Nunez		12-15	5th	5.5
5-3	Fla.	W	3-1		5	5	Meadows	Penny	Hoffman	13-15	5th	4.5
5-5	At Ari.	L	3-5		5	8	Johnson	Hitchcock		13-16	5th	6.0
5-6	At Ari.	L	5-10		8	12	Anderson	Lopez		13-17	5th	7.0
5-7	At Ari.	L	1-8		8	11	Stottlemyre	Clement		13-18	5th	8.0
5-9	At Cin.	L	0-2		8	7	Parris	Meadows	Graves	13-19	5th	9.5
5-10	At Cin.	L	1-5		6	8	Villone	Hitchcock	Williamson	13-20	5th	10.5
5-11	At Cin.	L	9-11		11	16	Graves	Whisenant		13-21	5th	11.0
5-12	Ari.	L	4-6		9	8	Anderson	Clement	Kim	13-22	5th	12.0
5-13	Ari.	L	2-6		9	9	Stottlemyre	Spencer	Morgan	13-23	5th	13.0
5-14	Ari.	W	3-1		5	2	Meadows	Daal	Hoffman	14-23	5th	12.0
5-16	At Fla.	W	7-3		9	7	Hitchcock	Sanchez		15-23	5th	11.0
5-17	At Fla.	L	2-4		8	9	Dempster	Clement	Alfonseca	15-24	5th	11.0
5-18	At Fla.	W	6-2		15	6	Spencer	Fernandez		16-24	5th	11.0
5-19	At Atl.	W	11-7		12	15	Whiteside	Mulholland	Hoffman	17-24	5th	10.0
5-20	At Atl.	L	6-10		13	10	Burkett	Cunnane		17-25	5th	10.0
5-21	At Atl.	L	6-12		11	16	Glavine	Hitchcock		17-26	5th	10.0
5-22	N.Y.	W	1-0		5	5	Clement	Franco	Hoffman	18-26	5th	9.5
5-23	N.Y.	L	3-5	(10)	7	6	Wendell	Hoffman	Benitez	18-27	5th	10.5
5-24	N.Y.	W	5-4		11	7	Wall	Mahomes	Hoffman	19-27	5th	10.5
5-26	Mon.	W	6-2		11	6	Whiteside	Irabu		20-27	5th	11.0
5-27	Mon.	W	4-2		10	7	Wall	Kline	Hoffman	21-27	5th	11.0
5-28	Mon.	W	4-3		6	8	Walker	Pavano	Hoffman	22-27	5th	10.0
5-29	Mil.	L	3-8		8	10	Haynes	Meadows		22-28	5th	10.0
5-30	Mil.	W	6-3		11	9	Eaton	D'Amico	Hoffman	23-28	5th	9.0
5-31	Mil.	W	9-5		9	10	Almanzar	Weathers		24-28	5th	9.0
6-2	At Sea.	L	4-7		8	7	Moyer	Clement	Sasaki	24-29	5th	10.5
6-3	At Sea.	W	7-4		10	7	Spencer	Halama	Hoffman	25-29	5th	9.5
6-4	At Sea.	L	4-6		10	5	Abbott	Meadows		25-30	5th	9.5
6-5	At Oak.	L	2-3	(10)	4	5	Isringhausen	Almanzar		25-31	5th	9.5
6-6	At Oak.	L	4-5		7	7	Heredia	Lopez	Isringhausen	25-32	5th	9.5
6-7	At Oak.	L	4-10		10	13	Service	Clement	Jones	25-33	5th	9.5
6-9	Hou.	L	6-7		11	10	Wagner	Hoffman		25-34	5th	10.5
6-10	Hou.	W	13-3		12	12	Meadows	Elarton		26-34	5th	9.5
6-11	Hou.	W	4-1		11	4	Walker	Lima	Hoffman	27-34	5th	9.5
6-12	StL.	L	3-7		8	10	An. Benes	Clement		27-35	5th	10.5
6-13	StL.	L	3-8		11	16	Kile	Lopez	Veres	27-36	5th	10.5
6-14	StL.	L	1-3		6	7	Stephenson	Spencer	Morris	27-37	5th	11.5
6-16	Cin.	W	8-5		11	10	Reyes	Parris	Hoffman	28-37	5th	10.5
6-17	Cin.	W	3-1		6	5	Walker	Villone	Hoffman	29-37	5th	9.5
6-18	Cin.	W	8-7		8	11	Clement	Bell	Hoffman	30-37	5th	8.5
6-19	At Ari.	L	2-3		6	7	Padilla	Kolb		30-38	5th	9.5
6-20	At Ari.	W	3-1		7	2	Tollberg	Stottlemyre	Hoffman	31-38	5th	8.5
6-21	At Ari.	L	8-11		8	16	Morgan	Reyes		31-39	5th	9.5
6-23	At Cin.	W	10-7	(10)	12	14	Hoffman	Williamson	Reyes	32-39	5th	9.5
6-24	At Cin.	L	5-11		14	15	Villone	Clement	Dessens	32-40	5th	9.5
6-25	At Cin.	W	5-4		7	12	Tollberg	Fernandez	Hoffman	33-40	5th	9.5
6-26	At L.A.	W	9-5		9	7	Meadows	Hershiser		34-40	5th	9.5

Date	Opp.	Res.	Score	(inn.*)	Hits	Opp. hits	Winning pitcher	Losing pitcher	Save	Record	Pos.	GB
6-27	At L.A.	L	4-5	(10)	7	10	Fetters	Whiteside		34-41	5th	9.5
6-28	At L.A.	L	4-5		6	7	Adams	Montgomery		34-42	5th	10.5
6-29	At L.A.	W	5-4		7	6	Clement	Dreifort	Hoffman	35-42	5th	10.5
6-30	Col.	L	4-5		7	10	Astacio	Almanzar	Jimenez	35-43	5th	10.5
7-1	Col.	W	5-3		7	9	Meadows	Arrojo	Hoffman	36-43	5th	10.5
7-2	Col.	L	2-3	(10)	7	10	DeJean	Hoffman	Jimenez	36-44	5th	10.5
7-3	Col.	L	1-3		4	4	Bohanon	Montgomery	Jimenez	36-45	5th	10.5
7-4	L.A.	W	7-2		9	4	Clement	Park		37-45	5th	10.5
7-5	L.A.	L	5-7		11	11	Osuna	Whiteside	Fetters	37-46	5th	11.5
7-6	L.A.	L	3-9		5	14	Brown	Meadows		37-47	5th	12.5
7-7	At Tex.	L	4-5	(10)	6	9	Davis	Whiteside		37-48	5th	12.5
7-8	At Tex.	L	1-8		3	12	Helling	Eaton		37-49	5th	12.5
7-9	At Tex.	W	4-3		13	8	Clement	Rogers	Hoffman	38-49	5th	12.5
7-13	Sea.	W	2-1	(10)	5	6	Hoffman	Tomko		39-49	5th	11.5
7-14	Sea.	L	5-7		9	12	Moyer	Meadows	Sasaki	39-50	5th	12.5
7-15	Sea.	W	4-1		6	4	Williams	Sele	Hoffman	40-50	5th	11.5
7-16	Ana.	W	6-5	(10)	11	13	Wall	Levine		41-50	5th	10.5
7-17	Ana.	L	2-3		4	6	Cooper	Clement	Percival	41-51	5th	11.5
7-18	Ana.	L	2-3	(11)	8	7	Levine	Hoffman		41-52	5th	11.5
7-19	At S.F	W	4-3	(10)	13	10	Wall	Embree		42-52	5th	11.5
7-20	At S.F	L	3-7		5	8	Rueter	Williams	Fultz	42-53	5th	12.5
7-21	At Col.	W	5-1		12	7	Eaton	Bohanon		43-53	5th	12.5
7-22	At Col.	L	4-9		11	16	White	Clement		43-54	5th	12.5
7-23	At Col.	W	6-4	(10)	11	7	Hoffman	Belinda	Wall	44-54	5th	11.5
7-24	S.F	L	0-3		6	6	Gardner	Meadows	Nen	44-55	5th	12.0
7-25	S.F	W	3-2		10	7	Williams	Rueter	Hoffman	45-55	5th	11.0
7-26	S.F	L	1-3		5	5	Estes	Eaton	Nen	45-56	5th	11.0
7-28	At Pit.	L	5-16		9	14	Arroyo	Clement		45-57	5th	12.5
7-29	At Pit.	L	2-10		6	16	Cordova	Tollberg		45-58	5th	12.5
7-30	At Pit.	W	9-8		14	13	Wall	Wilkins	Hoffman	46-58	5th	11.5
7-31	Phi.	W	4-1		7	4	Williams	Chen		47-58	5th	11.0
8-1	Phi.	W	10-9	(10)	13	11	Almanzar	Brantley		48-58	5th	11.0
8-2	Phi.	W	5-2		9	8	Clement	Daal	Hoffman	49-58	5th	10.0
8-3	Chi.	W	6-5		8	10	Walker	Worrell	Hoffman	50-58	5th	10.0
8-4	Chi.	W	11-9		13	13	Almanzar	Rain	Hoffman	51-58	5th	10.0
8-5	Chi.	L	3-6		8	10	Tapani	Williams	Aguilera	51-59	5th	10.0
8-6	Chi.	W	8-6		11	12	Eaton	Garibay	Hoffman	52-59	5th	10.0
8-7	At Phi.	W	6-4		8	11	Clement	Person	Hoffman	53-59	5th	10.0
8-8	At Phi.	L	4-10		8	14	Daal	Tollberg		53-60	5th	11.0
8-9	At Phi.	L	2-3		6	9	Brock	Slocumb		53-61	5th	12.0
8-10	At Phi.	W	15-3		19	8	Williams	Wolf		54-61	5th	11.5
8-11	At Fla.	W	3-0		5	7	Eaton	Burnett	Hoffman	55-61	5th	10.5
8-12	At Fla.	W	2-1	(10)	9	5	Walker	Alfonseca	Hoffman	56-61	5th	9.5
8-13	At Fla.	W	7-3		8	11	Walker	Almanza	Hoffman	57-61	5th	8.5
8-14	At Atl.	L	2-9		6	14	Glavine	Witasick		57-62	5th	9.5
8-15	At Atl.	L	1-3		7	7	Remlinger	Williams	Rocker	57-63	5th	10.5
8-16	At Atl.	L	1-4		5	5	Kamieniecki	Walker	Rocker	57-64	5th	11.5
8-18	Mon.	L	3-6		7	11	Thurman	Clement	Strickland	57-65	5th	13.0
8-19	Mon.	W	4-3	(11)	12	8	Walker	Santana		58-65	5th	13.0
8-20	Mon.	W	5-4		7	10	Witasick	Lira	Hoffman	59-65	5th	12.0
8-21	N.Y.	W	5-4	(10)	8	10	Hoffman	Cook		60-65	5th	12.0
8-22	N.Y.	W	16-1		12	7	Eaton	Mahomes	Erdos	61-65	5th	11.0
8-23	N.Y.	L	1-4		3	7	Leiter	Clement	Benitez	61-66	5th	12.0
8-25	At Mil.	W	4-0		12	6	Tollberg	Wright		62-66	5th	12.0
8-26	At Mil.	L	5-6	(10)	14	8	Leskanic	Hoffman		62-67	5th	12.0
8-27	At Mil.	W	2-1		7	8	Williams	Weathers	Hoffman	63-67	5th	11.0
8-28	At Chi.	W	8-2		11	3	Clement	Quevedo		64-67	5th	11.0
8-29	At Chi.	L	6-7	(13)	10	10	Heredia	Hoffman		64-68	5th	11.0
8-30	At Chi.	L	1-5		4	10	Lieber	Tollberg		64-69	5th	12.0
8-31	At Chi.	W	11-5		16	8	Witasick	Tapani		65-69	5th	12.0
9-1	Pit.	L	2-3	(10)	6	10	Williams	Hoffman		65-70	5th	13.0
9-2	Pit.	L	3-6		8	8	Ritchie	Clement	Sauerbeck	65-71	5th	14.0
9-3	Pit.	L	6-8	(13)	16	11	Skrmetta	Almanzar	Williams	65-72	5th	15.0
9-4	Mil.	W	4-3		7	5	Davey	King	Hoffman	66-72	5th	15.0
9-5	Mil.	W	3-1		5	3	Witasick	Rigdon	Hoffman	67-72	5th	15.0
9-6	Mil.	W	7-6		11	9	Williams	Snyder	Hoffman	68-72	5th	15.0
9-7	At S.F.	L	0-13		5	16	Estes	Clement		68-73	5th	16.0
9-8	At S.F.	W	10-7		16	13	Almanzar	Embree	Hoffman	69-73	5th	15.0
9-9	At S.F.	W	7-3		8	11	Tollberg	Ortiz		70-73	5th	14.0
9-10	At S.F.	L	2-10		5	10	Rueter	Witasick		70-74	5th	15.0
9-11	Col.	W	7-2		10	6	Williams	Tavarez		71-74	5th	15.0
9-12	Col.	L	3-6		6	12	Yoshii	Clement	Jimenez	71-75	5th	16.0
9-13	Col.	L	0-11		9	16	Bohanon	Eaton		71-76	5th	17.0
9-15	S.F	W	5-4		9	9	Davey	Henry	Hoffman	72-76	5th	16.0
9-16	S.F	L	3-4	(13)	10	16	Embree	Almanzar	Nen	72-77	5th	17.0
9-17	S.F	L	1-5		5	9	Gardner	Williams		72-78	5th	18.0
9-19	At Col.	W	7-2		12	6	Clement	Bohanon		73-78	5th	17.5
9-20	At Col.	W	15-11		15	11	Eaton	Rose	Hoffman	74-78	5th	17.5

Date	Opp.	Res.	Score	(inn.*)	Hits	Opp. hits	Winning pitcher	Losing pitcher	Save	Record	Pos.	GB
9-21	At Col.	L	4-13		4	17	Jarvis	Tollberg		74-79	5th	18.5
9-22	At L.A.	W	3-2		7	8	Maurer	Osuna	Hoffman	75-79	5th	17.5
9-23	At L.A.	L	1-2		2	5	Brown	Williams		75-80	5th	18.0
9-24	At L.A.	L	0-1		2	3	Park	Clement	Shaw	75-81	5th	18.0
9-26	StL.	L	1-7		6	11	An. Benes	Eaton		75-82	5th	18.0
9-27	StL.	L	0-3		7	7	Ankiel	Tollberg	Veres	75-83	5th	19.0
9-28	StL.	L	6-7		7	8	Kile	Davey	Veres	75-84	5th	20.0
9-29	L.A.	L	0-3		2	6	Park	Williams		75-85	5th	21.0
9-30	L.A.	L	2-10		6	9	Gagne	Clement		75-86	5th	21.0
10-1	L.A.	W	4-0		7	7	Eaton	Dreifort	Hoffman	76-86	5th	21.0

Monthly records: April (11-14), May (13-14), June (11-15), July (12-15), August (18-11), September (10-17), October (1-0).
*Innings, if other than nine. †First game of a doubleheader. ‡Second game of a doubleheader.

HIGHLIGHTS

High point: Rookie reliever Kevin Walker improved his record to 6-0 August 13 in a 7-3 victory over Florida at Pro Player Stadium. The win completed the franchise's first three-game sweep in Florida and brought the Padres to within four games of .500 for the first time since June 3.

Low point: The Padres rolled into Atlanta after their Marlins sweep and lost three straight to the Braves. They fell into the basement of the N.L. West Division, 11 1/2 games out of first place, and remained there the rest of the season.

Turning point: The Padres were 13-15 in early May when they embarked on a six-game trip to Arizona and Cincinnati. They lost all six games and returned to San Diego 11 games out of first.

Most valuable player: Cleanup man Phil Nevin led the team in home runs (31), doubles (34) and RBIs (107). He batted .394 with nine home runs and 29 RBIs in 104 August at-bats.

Most valuable pitcher: Trevor Hoffman stabilized a bullpen that suffered from inconsistent set-up work over several prolonged stretches. The veteran righthander totaled 43 saves, pitched in 70 games and served as mentor to several young teammates.

Most improved player: Speedy Damian Jackson blossomed after replacing injured Bret Boone at second base. Jackson made huge strides at the plate, where he learned to hit the ball to all fields.

Most pleasant surprise: Walker, who started the season at the Class AA level, became the most reliable lefthanded reliever in Bruce Bochy's six seasons as manager. The 24-year-old Texan, who appeared in 70 games, was more resilient and poised than many veteran teammates.

Key injuries: Projected No. 1 starter Sterling Hitchcock underwent reconstructive elbow surgery after making 11 starts. ... A knee ailment that required surgery in June limited right fielder Tony Gwynn to 36 games. The eight-time batting champion finished at .323, topping .300 for the 18th consecutive season. ... Randy Myers, a $13.6-million addition from August 1998, has missed the 1999 and 2000 seasons. ... Chris Gomez, who led

N.L. shortstops in fielding percentage in 1998, suffered through another injury-marred season. ... Starter Woody Williams inspired fans, teammates and officials when he returned to the mound July 2 to face the Rockies after being sidelined for two months by an aneurysm. Williams went on to win 10 games and post a 3.75 ERA over 168 innings.

Notable: Rookie Adam Eaton came up from Class AA and showed why the club views him as a future staff ace. Over his first 16 starts, Eaton posted a 2.89 ERA. ... The club led both leagues in errors (141). ... Center fielder Ruben Rivera, touted as a future star, batted .208—an improvement over his .195 average in 1999. Rivera's 137 strikeouts led the club. ... The Padres lost all nine of their games against the N.L. Central-champion Cardinals, and eight of nine games to East-champion Atlanta.

—TOM KRASOVIC

RECORDS

2000 regular-season record: 76-86 (5th in N.L. West); 41-40 at home; 35-46 on road; 25-18 vs. East; 26-27 vs. Central; 25-41 vs. West; 19-30 vs. lefthanded starters; 57-56 vs. righthanded starters; 69-74 on grass; 7-12 on turf; 23-26 in daytime; 53-60 at night; 25-27 in one-run games; 11-13 in extra-inning games; 0-0-0 in doubleheaders.

Team record past five years: 415-395 (.512, ranks 7th in league in that span).

TEAM LEADERS

Batting average: Phil Nevin (.303).
At-bats: Eric Owens (583).
Runs: Ryan Klesko (88).
Hits: Eric Owens (171).
Total Bases: Phil Nevin (292).
Doubles: Phil Nevin (34).
Triples: Eric Owens (7).
Home runs: Phil Nevin (31).
Runs batted in: Phil Nevin (107).
Stolen bases: Eric Owens (29).
Slugging percentage: Phil Nevin (.543).
On-base percentage: Ryan Klesko (.393).
Wins: Matt Clement (13).
Earned-run average: Woody Williams (3.75).

Complete games: Woody Williams (4).
Shutouts: None.
Saves: Trevor Hoffman (43).
Innings pitched: Matt Clement (205.0).
Strikeouts: Matt Clement (170).

GAMES BY POSITION

Catcher: Wiki Gonzalez 87, Carlos Hernandez 54, Ben Davis 38, George Williams 6.
First base: Ryan Klesko 136, Ed Sprague 25, Joe Vitiello 17, Dave Magadan 8, John Mabry 2, John Roskos 2, Dusty Allen 1, Carlos Hernandez 1.
Second base: Bret Boone 126, Damian Jackson 36, Kevin Nicholson 4, Chris Gomez 3, David Newhan 3, Greg LaRocca 2, Eric Owens 1, Ed Sprague 1.
Third base: Phil Nevin 142, Dave Magadan 29, Ed Sprague 10, Greg LaRocca 8, Gabe Alvarez 3, David Newhan 2.
Shortstop: Damian Jackson 88, Desi Relaford 45, Kevin Nicholson 30, Chris Gomez 17, Greg LaRocca 4, Dave Magadan 2.
Outfield: Eric Owens 144, Ruben Rivera 133, Al Martin 89, Kory DeHaan 60, Mike Darr 57, John Mabry 32, Tony Gwynn 26, Damian Jackson 17, Ed Sprague 8, John Roskos 6, David Newhan 5, Ryan Klesko 4, Dusty Allen 2, Gabe Alvarez 2, Joe Vitiello 2.
Designated hitter: Tony Gwynn 6, Dave Magadan 2, Dusty Allen 1, Ben Davis 1, Kory DeHaan 1.

TOP DRAFT CHOICES

1. **Mark Phillips,** LHP, Hanover (Pa.) H.S.
2. **Xavier Nady,** 3B, Univ. of California.
3. **Omar Falcon,** C, Southridge H.S., Miami.
4. **Mewelde Moore,** OF, Belaire H.S., Baton Rouge, La.
5. **Jon Huber,** RHP, North Fort Myers (Fla.) H.S.
6. **Ryan Earey,** RHP, University of North Carolina.
7. **Lee McCool,** SS, U. of North Florida.
8. **David Georgis,** OF, Rancho Bernardo H.S., San Diego.
9. **J.K. Scott,** RHP, Ramona (Calif.) H.S.
10. **Kevin Nulton,** SS, El Capitan H.S., Lakeside, Calif.

SAN FRANCISCO GIANTS
NATIONAL LEAGUE WEST DIVISION

Giants
2001 SCHEDULE
Home games shaded; D—Day game (games starting before 5 p.m.)
*—All-Star Game at Safeco Field (Seattle)

APRIL

SUN	MON	TUE	WED	THU	FRI	SAT
1	2 D SD	3	4 SD	5 D SD	6 LA	7 LA
8 LA	9	10 SD	11 SD	12 D SD	13 MIL	14 MIL
15 D MIL	16	17 LA	18 LA	19 LA	20 MIL	21 D MIL
22 D MIL	23	24 CIN	25 CIN	26 D CIN	27 CUB	28 CUB
29 CUB	30					

MAY

SUN	MON	TUE	WED	THU	FRI	SAT
		1 PIT	2 PIT	3 D PIT	4 PHI	5 PHI
6 D PHI	7 MON	8 MON	9 MON	10 D MON	11 NYM	12 D NYM
13 D NYM	14	15 FLA	16 FLA	17 FLA	18 ATL	19 ATL
20 D ATL	21 ARI	22 ARI	23 ARI	24 COL	25 D COL	26 D COL
27 COL	28 D ARI	29 D ARI	30 ARI	31		

JUNE

SUN	MON	TUE	WED	THU	FRI	SAT
					1 COL	2 D COL
3 COL	4 D SD	5 SD	6 SD	7 D SD	8 OAK	9 OAK
10 D OAK	11	12 ANA	13 ANA	14 D ANA	15 OAK	16 D OAK
17 D OAK	18	19 SD	20 SD	21 D SD	22 STL	23 STL
24 STL	25 LA	26 LA	27 D LA	28	29 STL	30 D STL

JULY

SUN	MON	TUE	WED	THU	FRI	SAT
1 STL	2 D LA	3 LA	4 LA	5 LA	6 MIL	7 D MIL
8 MIL	9	10	11 *	12 SEA	13 SEA	14 D SEA
15 TEX	16 TEX	17 TEX	18 COL	19 COL	20 ARI	21 D ARI
22 ARI	23 COL	24 COL	25 COL	26 D ARI	27 ARI	28 ARI
29 ARI	30 D	31 PIT				

AUGUST

SUN	MON	TUE	WED	THU	FRI	SAT
		1 PIT	2 PIT	3 D PHI	4 D PHI	
5 D PHI	6	7 CIN	8 CIN	9 CIN	10 D CUB	11 D CUB
12 D CUB	13	14 FLA	15 FLA	16 FLA	17 D ATL	18 D ATL
19 D ATL	20	21 MON	22 MON	23 MON	24 NYM	25 NYM
26 D NYM	27 D NYM	28 ARI	29 ARI	30 COL	31 COL	

SEPTEMBER

SUN	MON	TUE	WED	THU	FRI	SAT
						1 D COL
2 COL	3 D COL	4 D ARI	5 ARI	6 D ARI	7 COL	8 D COL
9 COL	10 D	11 HOU	12 HOU	13 HOU	14 LA	15 D LA
16 LA	17 D	18 HOU	19 HOU	20 D HOU	21 SD	22 SD
23 SD	24 D LA	25 LA	26 LA	27	28 SD	29 D SD
30 SD	D					

2001 SEASON
CLUB DIRECTORY

President and managing general partner
Peter A. Magowan

Executive vice president/COO
Larry Baer

Senior v.p. and general manager
Brian Sabean

Vice president and assistant g.m.
Ned Colletti

Vice president of player personnel
Dick Tidrow

Special assistant to the general manager
Ron Perranoski

Director of player development
Jack Hiatt

Coordinator of international operations
Rick Ragazzo

Sr. v.p. and chief financial officer
John Yee

Sr. v.p., ballpark operations/security
Jorge Costa

Vice president, communications
Bob Rose

Sr. vice president, corporate marketing
Mario Alioto

Sr. v.p., consumer marketing
Tom McDonald

General manager, retail
Connie Kullberg

Director of ballpark operations
Gene Telucci

Vice president, ticket services
Russ Stanley

Director of travel
Reggie Younger Jr.

Sr. vice president and general counsel
Jack Bair

Media relations manager
Jim Moorehead

Western regional cross-checker
Doug Mapson

Eastern regional cross-checker
Alan Marr

West Coast cross-checker
Darren Wittcke

East Coast cross-checker
Bobby Myrick

Canadian cross-checker
Steve Arnieri

Major league scouts
Joe DiCarlo, Stan Saleski, Paul Turco,
Randy Waddill, Tom Zimmer

Major league advance scout
Pat Dobson

Special assignment scouts
Dick Cole, Bo Osborne

Scouts
Mateo Alou, Jose Cassino, Pedro
Chavez, John DiCarlo, Lee Elder,
Charlie Gonzalez, Tom Korenek,
Doug McMillan, Luis Pena, John
Shafer, Jesus Stephens, Joe Strain,
Todd Thomas, Alex Torres, Glenn
Tufts, Paul Turco Jr., Ciro Villalobos,
Cal Webster

MINOR LEAGUE AFFILIATES

Class	Team	League	Manager
AAA	Fresno	Pacific Coast	Shane Turner
AA	Shreveport	Texas	Bill Russell
A	Hagerstown	South Atlantic	Bill Hayes
A	San Jose	California	Lenn Sakata
Rookie	Salem-Keizer	Northwest	Fred Stanley
Rookie	Giants	Arizona	Keith Comstock

BROADCAST INFORMATION

Radio: KNBR-AM (680).
TV: KTVU-TV (Channel 2).
Cable TV: FOX Sports Net.

SPRING TRAINING

Ballpark (city): Scottsdale Stadium
(Scottsdale, Ariz.).
Ticket information: 602-990-7972.

Follow the Giants all season at: www.sportingnews.com/baseball/teams/giants/

SPRING TRAINING ROSTER

Manager—Dusty Baker (12).
Coaches—Gene Clines (18), Sonny Jackson (16), Juan Lopez (59), Dave Righetti (19), Robby Thompson (5), Ron Wotus (10).

No.	PITCHERS	B/T	Ht./Wt.	Born	2000 clubs
51	Andra, Jeff	L/L	6-5/210	9-9-75	Shreveport, Fresno
58	Brous, David	L/L	6-2/195	3-9-80	San Jose
56	Embree, Alan	L/L	6-2/190	1-23-70	San Francisco
55	Estes, Shawn	R/L	6-2/195	2-18-73	Fresno, San Jose, San Francisco
38	Fultz, Aaron	L/L	6-0/196	9-4-73	San Francisco
26	Gardner, Mark	R/R	6-1/220	3-1-62	San Francisco
61	Hernandez, Livan	R/R	6-2/222	2-20-75	San Francisco
43	Jensen, Ryan	R/R	6-0/205	9-17-75	Fresno
49	Johnstone, John	R/R	6-3/210	11-25-68	San Francisco, San Jose, Arizona Giants, Fresno
50	Joseph, Kevin	R/R	6-4/200	8-1-76	Shreveport
36	Nathan, Joe	R/R	6-4/195	11-22-74	San Francisco, San Jose, Bakersfield, Fresno
31	Nen, Robb	R/R	6-5/215	11-28-69	San Francisco
48	Ortiz, Russ	R/R	6-1/210	6-5-74	San Francisco
47	Rodriguez, Felix	R/R	6-1/190	12-5-72	San Francisco
46	Rueter, Kirk	L/L	6-3/205	12-1-70	San Francisco
40	Urban, Jeff	L/R	6-8/215	1-25-77	DID NOT PLAY
14	Vogelsong, Ryan	R/R	6-3/195	7-22-77	Shreveport, San Francisco
45	Worrell, Tim	R/R	6-4/231	7-5-67	Baltimore, Iowa, Chicago N.L.
41	Zerbe, Chad	L/L	6-0/190	3-27-72	Shreveport, Fresno, San Francisco

No.	CATCHERS	B/T	Ht./Wt.	Born	2000 clubs
33	Chiaramonte, Giuseppe	R/R	6-0/200	2-19-76	Fresno
29	Estalella, Bobby	R/R	6-1/205	8-23-74	San Francisco
15	Mirabelli, Doug	R/R	6-1/218	10-18-70	San Francisco
9	Torrealba, Yorvit	R/R	5-11/190	7-19-78	Shreveport

No.	INFIELDERS	B/T	Ht./Wt.	Born	2000 clubs
35	Aurilia, Rich	R/R	6-1/185	9-2-71	San Francisco
28	Castro, Nelson	R/R	5-10/190	6-4-76	Bakersfield, Fresno
52	Crespo, Felipe	B/R	5-11/200	3-5-73	San Francisco
18	Davis, Russ	R/R	6-0/195	9-13-69	San Francisco
39	Feliz, Pedro	R/R	6-1/195	4-27-77	Fresno, San Francisco
2	Guzman, Edwards	L/R	5-11/205	9-11-76	Fresno
21	Kent, Jeff	R/R	6-1/205	3-7-68	San Francisco
34	Martinez, Ramon	R/R	6-1/187	10-10-72	San Francisco
22	Minor, Damon	L/L	6-7/230	1-9-75	Fresno, San Francisco
23	Ransom, Cody	R/R	6-2/190	2-17-76	Shreveport
6	Snow, J.T.	L/L	6-2/205	2-26-68	San Francisco

No.	OUTFIELDERS	B/T	Ht./Wt.	Born	2000 clubs
7	Benard, Marvin	L/L	5-9/185	1-20-70	San Francisco
25	Bonds, Barry	L/L	6-2/210	7-24-64	San Francisco
	Davis, Eric	R/R	6-3/200	5-29-62	St. Louis
	Dunston, Shawon	R/R	6-1/180	3-21-63	St. Louis
8	Murray, Calvin	R/R	5-11/190	7-30-71	San Francisco
1	Rios, Armando	L/L	5-9/185	9-13-71	San Francisco
53	Valderrama, Carlos	R/R	6-3/186	11-30-77	Bakersfield

BALLPARK INFORMATION

Ballpark (capacity, surface)
Pacific Bell Park (40,800, grass)
Address
24 Willie Mays Plaza
San Francisco, CA 94107
Official website
www.sfgiants.com
Business phone
415-972-2000
Ticket information
415-972-2000
Ticket prices
$26 (lower box)
$20 (view box, arcade)
$16 (view reserved)
$10 (bleachers)
Field dimensions (from home plate)
To left field at foul line, 339 feet
To center field, 399 feet
To right field at foul line, 309 feet
First game played
April 11, 2000 (Dodgers 6, Giants 5)

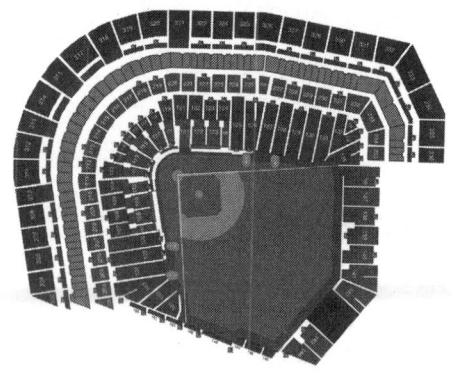

Date	Opp.	Res.	Score	(inn.*)	Hits	Opp. hits	Winning pitcher	Losing pitcher	Save	Record	Pos.	GB
4-3	At Fla.	L	4-6		10	12	Fernandez	Hernandez	Alfonseca	0-1	T2nd	1.0
4-4	At Fla.	W	3-0		7	4	Ortiz	Dempster	Nen	1-1	T3rd	1.0
4-5	At Fla.	W	11-9		15	12	Johnstone	Alfonseca	Nen	2-1	T2nd	0.5
4-6	At Fla.	L	4-5		7	8	Miceli	Johnstone		2-2	T3rd	1.5
4-7	At Atl.	W	6-2		8	10	Gardner	Mulholland		3-2	3rd	0.5
4-8	At Atl.	L	5-7		10	11	Maddux	Hernandez	Ligtenberg	3-3	T3rd	1.5
4-9	At Atl.	L	3-9		7	12	Glavine	Ortiz		3-4	4th	2.5
4-11	L.A.	L	5-6		8	12	Park	Rueter	Shaw	3-5	T4th	3.0
4-12	L.A.	L	5-6		7	8	Adams	Weber	Shaw	3-6	5th	2.5
4-13	L.A.	L	7-11		11	13	Perez	Gardner	Shaw	3-7	5th	4.0
4-14	Ari.	L	1-3		5	8	Johnson	Hernandez		3-8	5th	5.0
4-15	Ari.	L	4-7		8	9	Stottlemyre	Ortiz	Swindell	3-9	5th	6.0
4-18	At Cin.	W	13-9		16	8	Rueter	Williamson		4-9	5th	5.5
4-19	At Cin.	L	4-5		8	9	Bell	Estes	Graves	4-10	5th	6.5
4-20	At Cin.	L	1-11		6	15	Neagle	Hernandez		4-11	5th	7.5
4-21	At Ari.	W	11-5		16	12	Ortiz	Stottlemyre		5-11	5th	6.5
4-22	At Ari.	W	8-6		7	7	Rueter	Daal	Nen	6-11	5th	5.5
4-23	At Ari.	W	12-7		14	11	Nathan	Reynoso		7-11	5th	4.5
4-25	At Fla.	W	6-4	(11)	13	7	Gardner	Miceli		8-11	5th	4.5
4-26	At Fla.	W	8-7	(12)	11	16	Fultz	Alfonseca		9-11	5th	4.5
4-28	Mon.	L	3-9		11	8	Telford	Ortiz		9-12	5th	4.0
4-29	Mon.	W	2-1		9	3	Johnstone	Telford	Nen	10-12	5th	4.0
4-30	Mon.	L	3-4		6	6	Strickland	Johnstone	Urbina	10-13	5th	5.0
5-1	N.Y.	W	10-3		11	7	Estes	Pulsipher		11-13	4th	4.5
5-2	N.Y.	W	7-1		11	8	Hernandez	Rusch		12-13	4th	4.5
5-3	N.Y.	W	8-5	(11)	12	14	Rodriguez	Wendell		13-13	T3rd	3.5
5-4	N.Y.	W	7-2		7	4	Rodriguez	Reed		14-13	3rd	3.5
5-5	Col.	W	5-0		6	3	Nathan	Yoshii		15-13	3rd	3.5
5-6	Col.	W	6-0		9	9	Estes	Arrojo		16-13	3rd	3.5
5-8	StL.	W	6-4		8	9	Hernandez	Hentgen	Nen	17-13	2nd	4.0
5-9	StL.	L	6-13		11	15	Stephenson	Ortiz		17-14	2nd	5.0
5-10	StL.	W	4-3		7	7	Rodriguez	Slocumb	Nen	18-14	2nd	5.0
5-12	At Col.	L	7-15		10	15	Bohanon	Nathan		18-15	2nd	6.0
5-13	At Col.	L	9-10		10	15	White	Johnstone	Jimenez	18-16	3rd	7.0
5-14	At Col.	L	7-11		13	15	White	Hernandez		18-17	3rd	7.0
5-16	At Atl.	L	7-9		14	15	Glavine	Ortiz	Mulholland	18-18	4th	7.0
5-17	At Atl.	L	4-5		7	12	Millwood	Rueter	Seanez	18-19	4th	7.0
5-18	At Atl.	L	2-3		7	10	Maddux	Estes	Rocker	18-20	4th	8.0
5-19	At Mil.	L	10-11	(10)	15	11	Wickman	Nen		18-21	4th	8.0
5-20	At Mil.	L	0-7		4	6	D'Amico	Gardner		18-22	4th	8.0
5-21	At Mil.	W	16-10		20	9	Ortiz	Ramirez		19-22	4th	7.0
5-23	Mon.	L	2-3		8	11	Pavano	Rueter	Hermanson	19-23	4th	8.0
5-24	Mon.	W	18-0		18	7	Estes	Thurman		20-23	4th	8.0
5-25	Mon.	W	4-1		9	6	Hernandez	Armas	Nen	21-23	4th	8.0
5-26	Chi.	W	5-3		10	8	Gardner	Tapani		22-23	4th	8.0
5-27	Chi.	L	2-3	(11)	9	4	Garibay	Fultz	Aguilera	22-24	4th	9.0
5-28	Chi.	L	1-4		5	8	Wood	Rueter	Aguilera	22-25	4th	9.0
5-29	Phi.	W	7-2		13	4	Estes	Schilling	Embree	23-25	4th	8.0
5-30	Phi.	W	7-3		12	8	Hernandez	Ashby	Nen	24-25	4th	7.0
5-31	Phi.	W	10-4		14	9	Gardner	Byrd		25-25	4th	7.0
6-2	At Oak.	L	4-5		10	8	Mulder	Ortiz	Isringhausen	25-26	4th	8.5
6-3	At Oak.	L	7-9		9	11	D. Jones	Embree	Isringhausen	25-27	4th	8.5
6-4	At Oak.	W	18-2		19	7	Estes	Olivares		26-27	4th	7.5
6-5	At Ana.	W	5-4	(11)	10	14	Fultz	Hasegawa		27-27	4th	6.5
6-6	At Ana.	L	5-6		9	10	Percival	Nen		27-28	4th	6.5
6-7	At Ana.	L	9-10		15	13	Hasegawa	Embree		27-29	4th	6.5
6-9	Sea.	W	9-2		16	8	Rueter	Halama		28-29	4th	6.5
6-10	Sea.	L	2-5		6	12	Abbott	Estes		28-30	4th	6.5
6-11	Sea.	L	2-9		7	13	Sele	Hernandez		28-31	4th	7.5
6-12	Cin.	W	10-3		11	9	Nathan	Bell		29-31	4th	7.5
6-13	Cin.	W	3-2		7	8	Nen	Graves		30-31	4th	6.5
6-14	Cin.	W	6-2		12	8	Rueter	Neagle	Rodriguez	31-31	4th	6.5
6-16	Hou.	W	7-4		12	9	Estes	Elarton	Nen	32-31	4th	5.5
6-17	Hou.	W	6-4		8	10	Hernandez	Lima	Nen	33-31	4th	4.5
6-18	Hou.	L	2-4	(11)	6	6	J. Powell	Nen	Henry	33-32	4th	4.5
6-20	At StL.	L	2-7		4	8	Ankiel	Ortiz		33-33	4th	5.0
6-21	At StL.	W	4-1		7	5	Rueter	Stephenson	Nen	34-33	4th	5.0
6-22	At StL.	L	10-11		15	12	Veres	Gardner		34-34	4th	5.5
6-23	At Hou.	W	10-3		14	10	Hernandez	Lima		35-34	4th	5.5
6-24	At Hou.	W	13-4		22	12	Nathan	Reynolds		36-34	4th	4.5
6-25	At Hou.	W	4-2		14	8	Ortiz	Holt	Nen	37-34	3rd	4.5
6-26	At Col.	L	6-15		9	16	Arrojo	Gardner		37-35	3rd	5.5

Date	Opp.	Res.	Score	(inn.*)	Hits	Opp. hits	Winning pitcher	Losing pitcher	Save	Record	Pos.	GB
6-27	At Col.	W	12-7		15	9	Estes	Jarvis		38-35	T3rd	4.5
6-28	At Col.	L	13-17		13	17	DeJean	Johnstone		38-36	4th	5.5
6-29	At Col.	L	4-11		13	15	Yoshii	Nathan		38-37	4th	6.5
6-30	L.A.	L	2-9		6	13	Brown	Ortiz		38-38	4th	6.5
7-1	L.A.	W	4-1		10	9	Rueter	Perez	Nen	39-38	4th	6.5
7-2	L.A.	W	6-5		10	13	Nen	Fetters		40-38	3rd	5.5
7-4†	Col.	W	4-1		9	4	Hernandez	Yoshii	Nen	41-38		
7-4‡	Col.	W	3-0		7	6	Gardner	Karl	Nen	42-38	3rd	4.5
7-5	Col.	W	4-2		9	7	Nathan	Belinda	Rodriguez	43-38	3rd	4.5
7-6	Col.	W	6-5		12	7	Nen	Myers		44-38	3rd	4.5
7-7	At StL.	W	4-2		9	9	Embree	Morris	Nen	45-38	T2nd	3.5
7-8	At StL.	W	7-6		11	14	Estes	Stephenson	Nen	46-38	2nd	2.5
7-9	At StL.	L	7-8		8	10	Hentgen	Hernandez	Veres	46-39	2nd	3.5
7-13	Oak.	W	4-2		6	7	Ortiz	Mulder	Nen	47-39	2nd	2.5
7-14	Oak.	W	4-2		10	5	Gardner	Appier	Nen	48-39	2nd	2.5
7-15	Oak.	L	2-6		9	16	Heredia	Rueter		48-40	2nd	2.5
7-16	Tex.	W	6-4		11	8	Estes	Loaiza	Nen	49-40	2nd	1.5
7-17	Tex.	W	10-8		13	12	Hernandez	Davis	Nen	50-40	2nd	1.5
7-18	Tex.	W	5-3		10	11	Fultz	Wetteland		51-40	2nd	0.5
7-19	S.D.	L	3-4	(10)	10	13	Wall	Embree		51-41	2nd	1.5
7-20	S.D.	W	7-3		8	5	Rueter	Williams	Fultz	52-41	2nd	1.5
7-21	At L.A.	L	5-6		11	7	Herges	Rodriguez	Shaw	52-42	2nd	2.5
7-22	At L.A.	W	5-2		6	5	Hernandez	Gagne	Nen	53-42	2nd	1.5
7-23	At L.A.	L	0-5		2	10	Dreifort	Ortiz		53-43	2nd	1.5
7-24	At S.D.	W	3-0		6	6	Gardner	Meadows	Nen	54-43	2nd	1.0
7-25	At S.D.	L	2-3		7	10	Williams	Rueter	Hoffman	54-44	2nd	1.0
7-26	At S.D.	W	3-1		5	5	Estes	Eaton	Nen	55-44	1st	...
7-28	At Chi.	W	2-0		5	7	Hernandez	Worrell	Nen	56-44	2nd	0.5
7-29	At Chi.	L	1-8		6	13	Wood	Ortiz	Farnsworth	56-45	2nd	0.5
7-30	At Chi.	L	1-3		4	10	Lieber	Rueter		56-46	2nd	0.5
7-31	At Mil.	W	4-3	(11)	5	4	Rodriguez	Weathers	Nen	57-46	1st	...
8-1	At Mil.	W	13-8		17	10	Henry	King		58-46	1st	+1.0
8-2	At Mil.	L	4-6		6	8	Acevedo	Hernandez	Leskanic	58-47	1st	...
8-3	Pit.	W	10-2		12	7	Ortiz	Cordova		59-47	1st	...
8-4	Pit.	W	5-3		10	11	Henry	Benson	Nen	60-47	1st	+1.0
8-5	Pit.	L	2-7		9	13	Serafini	Gardner		60-48	1st	+1.0
8-6	Pit.	W	7-1		9	10	Estes	Arroyo		61-48	1st	+1.0
8-7	Mil.	W	8-1		8	9	Hernandez	Snyder		62-48	1st	+1.0
8-8	Mil.	W	1-0		6	2	Ortiz	Wright	Nen	63-48	1st	+2.0
8-9	Mil.	W	9-3		13	6	Rueter	Rigdon		64-48	1st	+3.0
8-11	At N.Y.	L	1-4		5	7	Rusch	Gardner	Benitez	64-49	1st	+2.0
8-12	At N.Y.	L	2-3		6	6	Hampton	Rodriguez	Benitez	64-50	1st	+2.0
8-13	At N.Y.	L	0-2		2	7	Leiter	Hernandez	Franco	64-51	1st	+1.0
8-14	At N.Y.	W	11-1		14	2	Ortiz	Reed		65-51	1st	+1.0
8-15	At Mon.	W	9-7		11	9	del Toro	Lira	Nen	66-51	1st	+1.0
8-16	At Mon.	W	4-1		7	8	Gardner	Hermanson	Nen	67-51	1st	+1.5
8-17	At Mon.	W	5-4		11	7	Estes	Moore	Rodriguez	68-51	1st	+1.5
8-18	Atl.	W	2-0		7	4	Hernandez	Maddux	Nen	69-51	1st	+1.5
8-19	Atl.	W	12-3		12	8	Ortiz	Ashby		70-51	1st	+1.5
8-20	Atl.	L	5-8		4	15	Glavine	Rueter		70-52	1st	+0.5
8-21	Fla.	W	6-0		10	6	Gardner	Dempster		71-52	1st	+1.5
8-22	Fla.	L	5-7		8	13	Burnett	Estes	Alfonseca	71-53	1st	+1.5
8-23	Fla.	W	5-0		7	4	Hernandez	Smith		72-53	1st	+2.5
8-25	At Phi.	W	16-3		21	11	Ortiz	Bottenfield		73-53	1st	+3.5
8-26	At Phi.	L	2-5		8	11	Wolf	Rueter	Brantley	73-54	1st	+2.5
8-27	At Phi.	L	1-2	(10)	3	7	Vosberg	Fultz		73-55	1st	+2.5
8-28	At Pit.	W	5-4		8	6	Embree	Sauerbeck	Nen	74-55	1st	+3.5
8-29	At Pit.	L	0-8		1	10	Benson	Hernandez		74-56	1st	+2.5
8-30	At Pit.	W	2-0		5	4	Ortiz	Anderson	Nen	75-56	1st	+2.5
8-31	At Pit.	W	10-2		13	10	Rueter	Silva		76-56	1st	+3.0
9-1	Chi.	W	7-2		10	6	Gardner	Wood		77-56	1st	+4.0
9-2	Chi.	W	13-2		10	8	Estes	Quevedo		78-56	1st	+5.0
9-3	Chi.	W	5-2		13	5	Hernandez	Garibay	Nen	79-56	1st	+5.0
9-4	Phi.	W	3-0		5	4	Ortiz	Daal	Nen	80-56	1st	+6.5
9-5	Phi.	W	8-5		11	8	Johnstone	Vosberg	Nen	81-56	1st	+6.5
9-6	Phi.	W	5-4		6	11	Fultz	Padilla	Embree	82-56	1st	+7.5
9-7	S.D.	W	13-0		16	5	Estes	Clement		83-56	1st	+8.5
9-8	S.D.	L	7-10		13	16	Almanzar	Embree	Hoffman	83-57	1st	+7.5
9-9	S.D.	L	3-7		11	8	Tollberg	Ortiz		83-58	1st	+6.5
9-10	S.D.	W	10-2		10	5	Rueter	Witasick		84-58	1st	+7.5
9-11	At Hou.	W	8-7	(10)	12	9	Nen	Valdes		85-58	1st	+8.5
9-12	At Hou.	W	9-5		12	11	Estes	Elarton		86-58	1st	+8.5
9-13	At Hou.	W	3-2		9	8	Hernandez	Miller	Nen	87-58	1st	+8.5
9-15	At S.D.	L	4-5		9	9	Davey	Henry	Hoffman	87-59	1st	+7.5
9-16	At S.D.	W	4-3	(13)	16	10	Embree	Almanzar	Nen	88-59	1st	+8.5
9-17	At S.D.	W	5-1		9	5	Gardner	Williams		89-59	1st	+9.5

Date	Opp.	Res.	Score	(inn.*)	Hits	Opp. hits	Winning pitcher	Losing pitcher	Save	Record	Pos.	GB
9-18	Cin.	L	1-7		4	12	Fernandez	Estes		89-60	1st	+9.5
9-19	Cin.	W	7-3		14	7	Hernandez	Bell		90-60	1st	+10.5
9-20	Cin.	W	4-2		5	4	Ortiz	Parris	Nen	91-60	1st	+11.0
9-21	Ari.	W	8-7		9	9	Henry	Morgan	Nen	92-60	1st	+11.5
9-22	Ari.	L	1-7		4	11	Schilling	Gardner		92-61	1st	+11.5
9-23†	Ari.	L	5-7		8	9	Guzman	Estes	Mantei	92-62		
9-23‡	Ari.	W	9-5		10	9	del Toro	Reynoso		93-62	1st	+11.0
9-24	Ari.	L	3-8		7	10	Anderson	Hernandez		93-63	1st	+10.0
9-26	At L.A.	L	0-9		2	9	Dreifort	Ortiz		93-64	1st	+9.0
9-27	At L.A.	W	4-0		5	6	Rueter	Prokopec		94-64	1st	+11.0
9-28	At L.A.	W	5-3		10	5	Fultz	Adams	Nen	95-64	1st	+11.0
9-29	At Ari.	W	4-3		7	9	Hernandez	Anderson	Nen	96-64	1st	+11.0
9-30	At Ari.	L	1-5		5	11	Guzman	Embree		96-65	1st	+10.0
10-1	At Ari.	W	11-4		12	8	Ortiz	Johnson		97-65	1st	+11.0

Monthly records: April (10-13), May (15-12), June (13-13), July (19-8), August (19-10), September (20-9), October (1-0).
*Innings, if other than nine. †First game of a doubleheader. ‡Second game of a doubleheader.

HIGHLIGHTS

High point: On September 21, the Giants beat Arizona, 8-7, to clinch their second N.L. West Division title in four years. It was a joyous conclusion to a celebratory season that began with the opening of Pacific Bell Park.

Low point: On April 20, the Giants suffered a taxing 11-1 loss at Cincnnati, dropping their record to 4-11—an unexpected and horrifying start that included five straight losses in their new ballpark. Some fans were only half joking when they called for a return to 3Com Park.

Turning point: On May 4, the Giants beat the New York Mets, 7-2, and concluded a four-game sweep that asserted their superiority at Pac Bell and catapulted them back into the N.L. West race. The Giants would go on to finish 55-26 in their home park.

Most valuable player: Not only was second baseman Jeff Kent the team's MVP, he also was the league MVP after hitting .334 with 33 homers and 125 RBIs—his fourth straight season with at least 100 runs batted in. His clutch first-half hitting helped the Giants overcome their terrible start and he continued in his clutch role throughout the season.

Most valuable pitcher: Livan Hernandez was touted as the staff ace before the season and he did not disappoint. Hernandez won 17 games (he was 12-3 at home) and set the tone for a rotation that rated among the best in baseball.

Most improved player: At age 38, Mark Gardner rebounded from offseason shoulder surgery and posted an 11-7 record—a vast improvement over his 5-11 mark of 1999. Gardner also bailed out the Giants when heralded youngster Joe Nathan spent most of the second half on the disabled list.

Most pleasant surprise: Reliever Felix Rodriguez stepped in for injured John Johnstone and became one of the most reliable setup men in the majors. He appeared in 76 games and struck out 95 batters while setting the stage for closer Robb Nen.

Key injuries: Nathan spent 56 days on the disabled list with a shoulder injury that would require postseason surgery. ... Johnstone needed postseason surgery to repair a bad back. Although he did not go on the disabled list until mid-July, Johnstone clearly was affected and struggled through a lost season.

Notable: The Giants finished with baseball's best record for the first time since 1962. ... The team's season run total of 925 was second in franchise history only to the 959 scored by the New York Giants in 1930. ... Kent's total of 475 RBIs from 1997 to 2000 is the most ever by a second baseman over a four-year span. ... Barry Bonds finished the season with 494 home runs, 17th on baseball's all-time list.

—HENRY SCHULMAN

RECORDS

2000 regular-season record: 97-65 (1st in N.L. West); 55-26 at home; 42-39 on road; 27-17 vs. East; 36-17 vs. Central; 34-31 vs. West; 19-20 vs. lefthanded starters; 78-45 vs. righthanded starters; 89-60 on grass; 8-5 on turf; 37-29 in daytime; 60-36 at night; 18-22 in one-run games; 7-5 in extra-inning games; 1-0-1 in doubleheaders.

Team record past five years: 430-381 (.530, ranks 4th in league in that span).

TEAM LEADERS

Batting average: Jeff Kent (.334).
At-bats: Jeff Kent (587).
Runs: Barry Bonds (129).
Hits: Jeff Kent (196).
Total Bases: Jeff Kent (350).
Doubles: Jeff Kent (41).
Triples: Jeff Kent (7).
Home runs: Barry Bonds (49).
Runs batted in: Jeff Kent (125).
Stolen bases: Marvin Benard (22).
Slugging percentage: Barry Bonds (.688).
On-base percentage: Barry Bonds (.440).

Wins: Livan Hernandez (17).
Earned-run average: Livan Hernandez (3.75).
Complete games: Livan Hernandez (5).
Shutouts: Shawn Estes, Livan Hernandez (2).
Saves: Robb Nen (41).
Innings pitched: Livan Hernandez (240.0).
Strikeouts: Russ Ortiz (167).

GAMES BY POSITION

Catcher: Bobby Estalella 106, Doug Mirabelli 80, Scott Servais 6.
First base: J.T. Snow 153, Jeff Kent 16, Felipe Crespo 11, Russ Davis 6, Damon Minor 4, Ramon E. Martinez 2, Armando Rios 1.
Second base: Jeff Kent 150, Ramon E. Martinez 32, Felipe Crespo 7, Juan Melo 6, Bill Mueller 2.
Third base: Bill Mueller 145, Russ Davis 43, Pedro Feliz 4, Ramon E. Martinez 2.
Shortstop: Rich Aurilia 140, Ramon E. Martinez 44.
Outfield: Marvin Benard 141, Barry Bonds 141, Ellis Burks 108, Calvin Murray 106, Armando Rios 93, Felipe Crespo 26, Terrell Lowery 20.
Designated hitter: Russ Davis 3, Ellis Burks 2, Felipe Crespo 1, Terrell Lowery 1.

TOP DRAFT CHOICES

1. **Boof Bonser,** RHP, Gibbs H.S., Pinellas Park, Fla.
2. **Lance Niekro,** 3B, Florida Southern College.
3. **Brion Treadway,** RHP, UNC Charlotte.
4. **Ryan Hannaman,** LHP, Murphy H.S., Mobile, Ala.
5. **Kyle Gross,** RHP, Cuesta (Calif.) J.C.
6. **Chad Ashlock,** RHP, Southern Nazarene (Okla.) University.
7. **Eric Threets,** LHP, Modesto (Calif.) J.C.
8. **Nick Wilfong,** OF, Univ. of Missouri.
9. **Edwin Maldonado,** SS, Oklahoma Christian University.
10. **Adam Shabala,** OF, U. of Nebraska.

2000 REVIEW

Year in review

American League Division Series

National League Division Series

American League Championship Series

National League Championship Series

World Series

All-Star Game

Notable Performances

Transactions

Award Winners

Miscellaneous

Necrology

YEAR IN REVIEW

By STEVE GIETSCHIER

TSN Senior Managing Editor

The 2000 season provided a potpourri of highlights that captured the attention of fans and casual observers alike. On the field, what began as yet another attack on home run records settled instead into a spectacular year for Boston Red Sox pitcher Pedro Martinez, one of the game's outstanding, albeit controversial, stars. Competition for playoff spots, especially for the wild card in the American League, proved intense with several unexpected teams advancing to postseason play. The New York Yankees, despite playing terribly in September, repeated as division champions and moved on to face the New York Mets in the World Series for the first time, thus reviving the phrase "Subway Series" that had been in mothballs since 1956. The Yankees emerged victorious, capturing their third consecutive Series, their fourth in five years and their 26th overall. Yet, the Yankees' iterative triumph and the Mets' rise to challenge them gave further ammunition to those who believe that the competitive balance that should exist between teams has been corrupted by a business structure in need of repair.

Off the field, Major League Baseball continued its administrative restructuring by merging most of the functions of the American and National leagues and strengthening the powers of the commissioner. MLB also signed a collective bargaining agreement with a new umpires union, revamped its disciplinary system, investigated the performance characteristics of major league baseballs and received the report from a task force commissioned to study the game's economics. Underlying these events was this widely-held perception: That the popularity of the game on the field and its viability as a business have been compromised by a nexus of unfortunate but correctable developments. The charges bolstering this contention include the following: That watching today's players hit home runs in record numbers is fun, but that the balls they are hitting may be too lively or "juiced"; That expansion, last effected in 1998, has decimated the quality of major league pitching; That umpires are too strident and that they do not call balls and strikes according to the rule book; That games are too long; That players' salaries are too high, due partly to salary arbitration; That salaries exert upward pressure on ticket prices, now so high that ordinary families cannot attend games on a regular basis; That the current schedule and alignment of teams make little sense; And that the economic disparities between so-called large-market teams and small-market teams are so great that many teams are inevitably doomed to open each season with no hope of advancing to postseason play.

Despite this gloomy scenario, baseball enjoyed a season that some would call both competitive and prosperous. For the first time in modern baseball history, no team finished with a winning percentage below .400 or above .600. Teams with the highest payrolls qualified for the playoffs, but so did teams near the bottom. Two low-revenue teams, the San Francisco Giants and Chicago White Sox, won their divisions and also finished with the best records in their leagues. Both Western Division champions, the Giants and the Oakland Athletics, had the lowest payrolls in their divisions. And the Yankees, the team most often identified as the poster child for competitive imbalance, finished with the majors' ninth best record, 3 1/2 games worse than any other postseason qualifier.

In addition, major league baseball set an all-time attendance record, and at the annual winter meetings in December, teams committed roughly a billion dollars to the year's crop of free agents. Pitcher Mike Hampton left the Mets to sign for eight years with the Colorado Rockies for $121 million, the largest contract in baseball history, only to be trumped three days later when shortstop Alex Rodriguez signed a 10-year deal with the Texas Rangers for $252 million.

MAJOR LEAGUE CONSTITUTION

On January 19, owners renamed the Major League Agreement, the document that governed the two leagues, the Major League Constitution, incorporating in it a new administrative framework to be run by Sandy Alderson, Executive Vice President for Baseball Operations, and new authority for Commissioner Allan H. (Bud) Selig. It included expanded power, under the "best interests of baseball" clause, to block trades, levy fines on clubs, negotiate an extension of the collective bargaining agreement with the Major League Baseball Players Association and take action to restore long-term competitive balance, such as mandating increased revenue sharing. Selig was also granted control of each club's internet rights, both audio and video.

ROBINSON NAMED DISCIPLINARIAN

Pursuant to this reorganization, MLB hired Hall of Fame member Frank Robinson to be Vice President of On-Field Operations on February 25 and assigned him to be in charge of player discipline, uniform policies, stadium configuration and speeding up games. Robinson's approach to discipline was generally regarded as quite harsh. The first major penalties he imposed followed two bench-clearing brawls in the April 22 game between the Detroit Tigers and the White Sox. Robinson suspended both managers, a coach and 13 players for a total of 82 games and fined nine others. In May he suspended 19 members of the Chicago Cubs and Los Angeles Dodgers a total of 84 games and levied fines totaling $77,000 for their part in a brawl that involved some fans at Wrigley Field. He also suspended Pedro Martinez for five games and fined him an undisclosed amount for hitting Roberto Alomar of the Cleveland Indians after he had been warned not to retaliate.

JOHN ROCKER

Much attention in the preseason focused on John Rocker, the Atlanta Braves relief pitcher who, during the 1999 postseason, taunted Mets fans and then, in a December Sports Illustrated article, expressed his disdain for New Yorkers and a host of minority groups, including immigrants and gays. Rocker later apologized for these remarks and for calling an African-American teammate "a fat monkey," saying that his competitive zeal made him say things he didn't mean. Braves players and management disassociated themselves from these comments, and Selig called them "inappropriate and offensive."

In early January, Selig ordered Rocker to undergo psychological testing prior to being disciplined and then, on January 31, suspended him until May 1, fined him $20,000 and required him to attend sensitivity training. The Players Association filed a grievance on Rocker's behalf on February 1, and the case was assigned to the sport's new independent arbitrator, Shaym Das. He heard testimony on February 9 and 10 and ruled on March 1. His decision cut the suspension to the first 14 days of the regular season, allowing Rocker to report to spring training, and reduced the fine to $500.

Once Rocker returned to the Braves bullpen and began to enter games in various ballparks, he was greeted by combinations of cheers and jeers that affected his performance and saw him optioned to the minors for a time. Still, he regained his role as a closer and led the team in saves (24) for the second consecutive season.

ECONOMIC STUDY COMMISSION

On July 14, MLB released "The Report of the Independent Members of the Commissioner's Blue Ribbon Panel on Baseball Economics." The panel, appointed on January 13, 1999, had four members who were not club officials: Yale President Richard C. Levin, former Federal Reserve Chairman Paul Volcker, former U.S. Senator George Mitchell and columnist George Will. The report presented data to support the contention that baseball is suffering from "chronic competitive imbalance" and urged baseball to adopt a series of measures, including a steeper luxury tax on large payrolls, increased revenue sharing, overhauling the amateur draft, relocating franchises and increasing domestic and international promotion. Selig repeated much of this argument in testimony before a Senate subcommittee in November.

Players Association Executive Director Donald M. Fehr dismissed the report as a predictable prelude to the next round of collective bargaining and declined to testify before the subcommittee. On August 28, the union exercised its option to extend the existing agreement through October 31, 2001.

NEW UMPIRES UNION SIGNS CONTRACT

On August 31, MLB reached agreement on a labor contract with the World Umpires Association, the new union certified to replace the Major League Umpires Association. The contract, ratified by the union on September 14 by a vote of 40-2 and approved by the owners on October 31, runs through 2004. It calls for a salary range of $81,704 to $260,545 in 2000 and a range of $85,716 to $340,705 in 2004, bonuses excluded.

This agreement marked the end of a prolonged period of acrimony highlighted by a mass resignation of 55 umpires announced in July 1999. This negotiating strategy designed by Richie Phillips, general counsel of the MLUA since 1978, backfired. MLB accepted some of the resignations, and 22 umpires lost their jobs. In addition, Phillips' ploy exposed dissension in the union's ranks that led to a November decertification election administered by the National Labor Relations Board.

The MLUA appealed the results of the election, and David Leach, an NLRB hearing officer, heard the appeal in January. Phillips claimed that owners had illegally conspired with the dissidents who prevailed in the election. He cited telephone records showing calls between Selig's office and the home of A.L. umpire John Hirshbeck, head of the Major League Umpires Independent Organizing Committee, and introduced other testimony alleging improper inducements to the dissidents. On January 21, Leach denied the appeal, saying that there were no grounds to overturn the election. The MLUA appealed to the full NLRB on February 4, but on February 24, that appeal was denied. Thus, the NLRB certified the results of the November election and established the WUA as the umpires' collective bargaining representative.

Simultaneously, another case proceeded to determine the legality of MLB's decision to accept the resignation of the 22 umpires, in effect firing them. The two sides had agreed in September to have the MLUA's grievance submitted to arbitrator Alan Symonette. He heard testimony in December 1999, and then periodically throughout 2000, but at year's end had not announced a decision.

On February 28, the WUA elected John Hirschbeck president, Joe Brinkman vice-president and Tim Welke secretary-treasurer. On March 20, the union reached an interim agreement with MLB to replace the last MLUA contract that had expired on December 31 and insure an orderly start to the season. Under its terms, in effect until a permanent agreement could be reached, umpires became employees of MLB instead of the two leagues, and crews were subsequently assigned to both A.L. and N.L. games without distinction. After additional bargaining, during which Jerry Crawford, the last MLUA president, joined the WUA's negotiating team, the two sides reached agreement on a five-year contract. In addition to higher salaries, the contract grants tenure to umpires after three years instead of five; gives the umpires a seat on the official Playing Rules Committee; grants 91 days' pay in the event of a work stoppage instead of 75; and binds the owners to consult with the union before implementing any new policies or directives, such as the dimensions of the strike zone or ways to speed up the game. The union did not win the right to independent arbitration for grievances which will instead be processed by an independent fact-finder who will report to the Commissioner.

During negotiations, MLB, urged by the WUA, offered to rehire 13 of the dismissed umpires, retire five others and buy out the remaining four. The

MLUA rejected this proposal, opting instead to continue its grievance proceeding.

SEASON OPENER IN JAPAN

MLB continued to expand its international presence by opening the 2000 season in Japan. After exhibition contests against the Yomiuri Giants and the Seibu Lions, the Mets and Cubs played a two-game series at the Tokyo Dome. The Cubs beat the Mets, 5-3, on March 29, and the Mets returned the favor, 5-1, in 11 innings, the next day. Neither team played again until April 3 in the United States.

The 2001 season will open on April 1 with the Toronto Blue Jays playing the Rangers in San Juan, Puerto Rico.

THREE BALLPARKS OPEN; TWO CLOSE

The Giants, Tigers and Houston Astros opened new parks at the start of the year. On April 7, the Astros began play at Enron Field, losing to the Philadelphia Phillies, 4-1, before a sellout crowd of 41,583. Enron soon proved to be a pitchers' nightmare. On April 11, the Giants lost to the Dodgers before a standing-room-only crowd of 40,930 at Pacific Bell Park. Barry Bonds hit two home runs for the Giants, and J.T. Snow hit one, but Kevin Elster hit three for the Dodgers. San Francisco lost its next five home games, but finished the season tied with the Mets for best home record in the majors, 55-26. Also on April 11, the Tigers opened Comerica Park on a cold, blustery day, beating the Seattle Mariners, 5-2, with 39,168 in attendance. Gregg Jefferies and Bobby Higginson each drove in two runs.

As the season came to an end, the Milwaukee Brewers and Pittsburgh Pirates closed their ballparks in anticipation of opening the 2001 campaign in new homes. The Brewers lost to the Cincinnati Reds, 8-1, on September 28, before a crowd of 56,354 at Milwaukee County Stadium, their home since the club moved from Seattle for the 1970 season and, before that, home to the Milwaukee Braves. The Brewers planned to open 2001 in Miller Park, construction of which was delayed following an accident on July 14, 1999, that took three lives. The Pirates closed Three Rivers Stadium, their home since 1970, on October 1, losing to the Cubs, 10-9. They will open PNC Park in 2001.

INTERLEAGUE PLAY IN FOURTH YEAR

Regular-season games between A.L. and N.L. clubs continued for the fourth consecutive year with each team once again playing its interleague games against the teams in the corresponding division of the other league. The 2000 schedule called for two periods of interleague play: June 2-11 and July 7-18, surrounding the All-Star break. All A.L. teams and teams in the N.L. East played 18 games. All others played 15, except for the Rockies who played 12.

Overall, A.L. teams won 136 interleague games and lost 115. Cleveland compiled the best interleague record among A.L. teams (13-5) while three teams (the Baltimore Orioles, Minnesota Twins and Texas) won only seven games. In the N.L., only the Braves won more interleague games than they lost (11-7). The San Diego Padres finished worst at 5-10. One game between the Yankees and Florida Marlins

was postponed by rain and not made up. Attendance at interleague games averaged 33,213, down slightly from 1999's 33,482, but 14.4 percent higher than the average for intraleague games played prior to the interleague periods.

REALIGNMENT POSTPONED

Attempting to solve baseball's scheduling problems through realignment has been a high priority for the commissioner, but to date, only the Brewers have changed leagues. Selig wanted to use provisions in the agreements that added the Arizona Diamondbacks to the N.L. and the Tampa Bay Devil Rays to the A.L. in 1998 that would allow these teams to be moved to other divisions or leagues after 2000 as a jumping-off point for further action.

Thus, in April, Selig advanced a plan to move Arizona to the A.L. West, Tampa Bay to the N.L. and the Rangers to the A.L. Central. The N.L. would have four four-team divisions with no wild-card entrant in postseason play, and the A.L. would have four teams each in the East and West and six teams in its Central Division. Under this plan, each N.L. team would play 20 games against other teams in its division, A.L. East and A.L. West teams would play 18 such games and A.L. Central teams would play 15 games against two division foes and 14 against the other three. The balance of the 162-game schedule would be filled out with interdivision and interleague games.

The Players Association advanced a counterproposal in June. In this much simpler scheme, the Astros would move from the N.L. Central to the A.L. West, thus creating two 15-team leagues and giving Texas a division opponent in its time zone. Each league would still have three division winners and a wild card, and interleague play would have to occur nearly every day. A further suggestion by the union broached the possibility of moving Seattle to the N.L. West and either Arizona or Colorado to the A.L. West.

Reports from the July 14 owners meeting suggested that a majority of clubs supported Selig's plan, but that the White Sox, Kansas City Royals and Minnesota objected to being placed in a six-team division. Thus, realignment was postponed until at least 2002, and owners opted instead to adopt an unbalanced schedule for 2001, something the A.L. had abandoned in 1977 and the N.L. in 1993. Clubs in the four five-team divisions will play 19 games against division foes, A.L. West clubs will play 19 or 20 and N.L. Central teams will play 16 or 17. Interleague play will occur as it did in 2000 with an exception that will allow the Astros and the Rangers to play each other for the first time.

MARTINEZ'S SEASON

Major league teams hit a record 5,693 home runs, bettering 1999's mark by 165. N.L. batters also set a league record, 3,005, far above the previous season's 2,893. Both leagues also set records for grand slams, 89 in the A.L. and 87 in the N.L. Even though the season commenced with a rash of homers—including a record 57 on April 7 and 262 during the first week—the pace slackened in the second half, and the drama associated with assaults on individual home run marks did not materialize. Only Sammy Sosa of the Cubs hit the 50 mark, and just 15 other players, up slightly from 1999's 13, hit 40 or more.

In reaction to this multi-season barrage, MLB officials toured the Rawlings baseball factory in Turrialba, Costa Rica, and the Rawlings testing facility in Missouri, looking for evidence of "juiced" baseballs. They found none, but a study done by the Baseball Research Center, University of Massachusetts-Lowell, showed that 1999 baseballs and 2000 baseballs performed near the upper limits of performance standards. Looking for some way to restrain offense and simultaneously to speed up games, MLB brought umpires and managers together near the end of the year to discuss calling strikes strictly according to the rule book, that is, from the "hollow beneath the kneecap" up to "the midpoint between the top of the shoulders and the top of the uniform pants."

What could have been the "Year of the Home Run" thus ended up as the "Year of Pedro Martinez," who put together a spectacular season. He won his third Cy Young Award in four years and was named TSN's A.L. Pitcher of the Year. In a truly dominant fashion, he went 18-6 and led the league in strikeouts (284), shutouts (4) and ERA (1.74), an incredible 1.96 earned runs better than runner-up Roger Clemens and 3.17 ahead of the league average. He pitched a one-hitter against Tampa Bay on August 29 and a two-hitter against Baltimore on May 12. In that game as well as against the White Sox on July 23, he struck out 15. Moreover, he set a modern major league record for lowest on-base average against, .213 (the league average was .349), and an all-time major league record for lowest batting average against, .167 (the league average was .276).

ATLANTA WINS DIVISION AGAIN

The Braves won the N.L. East title for the sixth year in a row. Leaving aside the incomplete 1994 season, Atlanta has now won an unprecedented nine straight division titles. The Mets challenged the Braves for the second consecutive year but came up a game short. Atlanta used a 15-game winning streak to build a five-game lead over New York on May 2, but saw it dwindle to three games at the All-Star break. The Mets tied for first place on August 28 and took a half-game lead three days later, but the Braves regained first place on September 2 and were not headed again. They clinched the division on September 26 with a 7-1 win over New York.

The Braves' offense was led by Chipper Jones, who hit .311 with 36 home runs and 111 RBIs, and Andruw Jones, who hit .303 with 36 homers and 104 RBIs. Andres Galarraga, TSN's N.L. Comeback Player of the Year, hit 28 home runs and drove in 100 runs, and Javy Lopez drove in 89 runs before being injured. TSN's N.L. Rookie Player of the Year, infielder Rafael Furcal, hit .295.

Atlanta's pitching staff led the league in ERA (4.05) and was tied for third in batting-average-against (.258). Tom Glavine, TSN's N.L. Pitcher of the Year, won 21 games, tops in the league, and Greg Maddux won 19, tied for third. Maddux also finished third in ERA (3.00). Kerry Ligtenberg and Mike Remlinger each had 12 saves.

NEW YORK WINS WILD CARD

The Mets qualified as the N.L. wild card for the second year in a row. They battled the Braves closely for most of the second half of the season, but held first place alone for only one day. With Atlanta going

16-12 after August 31, the Mets managed to finish only 15-14. They clinched the wild card on September 27, beating the Braves, 6-2.

Mike Piazza hit .324 with 38 home runs and 113 RBIs. Edgardo Alfonzo (.324, 25, 94), Robin Ventura (24 homers) and Todd Zeile (22 homers) added to the attack. Al Leiter won 16 games, and Hampton won 15. New York's pitchers finished second in the league in strikeouts and third in ERA. Armando Benitez recorded 41 saves, tied for third in the league.

CARDINALS WIN N.L. CENTRAL TITLE

St. Louis unseated the Astros, winners of the last three Central Division titles, to capture its first division crown since 1996. The Cardinals held first place for all but three days of the season and were never headed after June 6. They built an eight-game lead at the All-Star break and clinched the pennant on September 20 by beating Houston, 11-6. Cincinnati finished in second place, 10 games behind.

The Cardinals set a club record for most home runs in a season (235) and a league record for most strikeouts in a season (1,253). Mark McGwire, St. Louis' most feared batter, started just 70 games at first base because of back spasms at the beginning of the season and patella tendinitis that flared up in July. Still, he hit 32 homers and drove in 73 runs. Jim Edmonds hit .295 with 42 homers, 108 RBIs and 167 strikeouts (third in the league). Ray Lankford added 26 home runs and struck out 148 times (fourth in the league). Will Clark, acquired on July 31, hit 12 homers in 51 games.

St. Louis used only five starting pitchers through its first 122 games and just six in all. Darryl Kile won 20 games, second in the league, and struck out 192 batters. Garrett Stephenson won 16 games, Pat Hentgen added 15 and TSN's N.L. Rookie Pitcher of the Year, Rick Ankiel, had 11 along with 194 strikeouts. Dave Veres saved 29 games.

SAN FRANCISCO WINS N.L. WEST FLAG

The Giants won their second N.L. West division title in four years, finishing 11 games ahead of the Dodgers. The Giants reached first place briefly on July 26, regained the division lead on July 31 and clinched the pennant on September 21 by beating the Diamondbacks, 8-7. Dusty Baker was named TSN's N.L. Manager of the Year.

In winning 97 games, San Francisco scored 925 runs (third in the league) and hit a franchise record 226 home runs (also third in the league). Jeff Kent and Bonds led the offensive barrage. Kent batted .334 with 33 homers, 114 runs and 125 RBIs. Bonds hit .306 and scored 129 runs with 49 homers (second in the league) and 106 RBIs. Ellis Burks added 24 home runs, and both he and Snow had 96 RBIs.

Giants pitching finished fourth in the league in ERA (4.21) and led the league with 15 shutouts. All five starters won 11 or more games. Livan Hernandez won 17, Shawn Estes added 15 and Russ Ortiz 14. Robb Nen saved 41 games, tied for third in the league.

NEW YORK WINS A.L. EAST

In the A.L.'s 100th season, the Yankees won their third straight A.L. East title and fourth in five seasons. Even though New York dropped as low at third place for only one day and held first place from July 7 on, the team did not dominate the division as it had in previous years. The Yankees went 13-18 in September, lost their last seven games and nearly squandered a nine-game lead. In seven of those 18 losses, they gave up 11 or more runs.

New York featured a balanced offense led by Bernie Williams, who hit .307 with 30 home runs and 121 RBIs. Derek Jeter had 201 hits and batted .339 (fifth in the league), while David Justice hit 41 home runs (tied for fourth in the league) and drove in 118 runs. Jorge Posada added 28 homers, and Paul O'Neill had 100 RBIs.

Andy Pettitte won 19 games (third in the league), and Clemens added 13 wins and 188 strikeouts (fifth in the league). Mariano Rivera saved 36 games (fourth in the league).

CHICAGO TAKES A.L. CENTRAL CROWN

The White Sox bested the Indians by five games to win their first division title since 1993, not counting the shortened 1994 season, and end Cleveland's five-year reign as Central Division champs. Having grabbed first place for good on April 19, the White Sox led by 10 1/2 games at the All-Star break and seven games at the end of August. They clinched the division on September 24 when the Indians lost to Minnesota. Jerry Manuel was named TSN's A.L. Manager of the Year.

Chicago's robust offense, leading the league in runs scored, was led by Frank Thomas, TSN's A.L. Comeback Player of the Year. He hit .328 and set career marks for hits (191), home runs (43), RBIs (143), extra-base hits (87) and runs (115). Magglio Ordonez (.315, 32, 126), Carlos Lee (.301, 24, 92), Paul Konerko (.298, 21, 97), Ray Durham (.280, 17, 75) and Jose Valentin (.273, 25, 92) balanced the White Sox attack.

Mike Sirotka won 15 games, James Baldwin won 14 and Jim Parque added 13 for a pitching staff that finished fourth in the league in ERA (4.66). Keith Foulke recorded 34 saves, tied for fifth in the league.

A's NIP M's FOR A.L. WEST FLAG

Oakland won its first division title since 1992, taking over first place on the last Friday of the season and finishing a half-game ahead of Seattle. The Mariners and the Athletics had taken turns at the top during the first half of the year, but the M's moved in front on June 29 and built a lead that grew to seven games. Oakland chipped away steadily at this margin, but did not tie the Mariners until September 23. After losing to Seattle the next day, the A's won six of their remaining seven games while the Mariners won four of six. The A's played only 161 games, but were awarded first place by a tie-breaker.

The A's finished third in the league in runs scored and second in home runs. Jason Giambi hit .333 with 43 homers (tied for third) and 137 RBIs (tied for fourth). Miguel Tejada hit 30 home runs, and Ben Grieve and Eric Chavez added 27 and 26, respectively. Tejada drove in 115 runs, and Grieve 104.

Oakland's pitchers finished third in the league in ERA (4.58). Tim Hudson won 20 games, to tie for the league lead. Kevin Appier and Gil Heredia had 15 each. Jason Isringhausen recorded 33 saves.

SEATTLE TAKES WILD CARD

The Mariners survived baseball's most hectic wild-card race yet, a battle that had four teams within three games of wild-card leader Cleveland with two weeks to go in the season. Seattle lost the A.L. West on the season's last day, but edged out the Indians for the wild card with a victory over the Anaheim Angels. Seattle was led offensively by Edgar Martinez, who hit .324 with 37 homers and a league-leading 145 RBIs, and Rodriguez (.316, 41, 132). John Olerud added 103 RBIs. Aaron Sele won 17 games, John Halama 14 and Jamie Moyer 13. Kazuhiro Sasaki had 37 saves (third in the league and a major league record for a rookie).

DIVISION SERIES WINNERS

For the third season in a row, the teams qualifying for the best-of-five Division Series were seeded to determine their opponents. In the N.L., the Giants earned home-field advantage and the right to face the wild-card Mets, but New York, after losing the first game, took the next three. The Cardinals swept the Braves, and in the A.L., Seattle swept the White Sox. The Yankees and the As went to five games with the Yankees prevailing, 7-5, in the decider.

METS OUST CARDS IN FIVE

In the N.L. Championship Series, the Mets surprised the Cardinals by winning the first two games in St. Louis, 6-2 and 6-5, as New York's lefthanded pitchers, Hampton and Leiter, shackled St. Louis's lefthanded batters. In Game 1, the Mets pounced on Kile for two runs in the first and put the game away with three runs in the ninth. In Game 2, the Cardinals were victimized by starter Ankiel, who replicated the wildness he showed in his Division Series outing. Here, he walked three and threw two wild pitches in 2/3 of an inning. His teammates committed three errors, one of which led to the winning run in the ninth.

When the series shifted to New York, Andy Benes halted the Mets' momentum in Game 3, 8-2. The Cardinals collected eight hits off starter Rick Reed and turned two key double plays to stifle New York rallies. The Mets took a commanding lead in the series by winning Game 4, 10-6, behind six doubles and a Piazza home run. Back in St. Louis, the Mets closed the Cardinals out by taking Game 5, 7-0, jumping on Hentgen for three runs in the first and another three in the fourth. Hampton pitched a three-hitter to send his team to the World Series for the first time since 1986. New Yorkers looking for the first so-called Subway Series in 44 years had one piece of the puzzle in place.

YANKEES DEFEAT MARINERS IN SIX

The Yankees and the Mariners split the first two games of the A.L. Championship Series in New York. The Mariners won Game 1, 2-0, behind starter Freddy Garcia and three relievers with Rodriguez hitting a sixth-inning home run. The M's were ahead in Game 2 as well, until the Yankees scored seven runs on eight hits in the eighth inning to win, 7-1.

When the series moved to Seattle, New York took Games 3 and 4, 8-2 and 5-0. Pettitte and Clemens, who pitched a one-hitter, earned the wins. In Game 3, Tino Martinez and Williams homered, and Justice drove in three runs. In Game 4, Clemens tied an LCS record with 15 strikeouts, and Justice and Jeter each hit home runs. Seattle bounced back in Game 5, 6-2, as Garcia defeated Denny Neagle for the second time. Rodriguez, Martinez and Olerud each drove in a pair of runs.

Back in New York, the Yankees completed the Subway Series puzzle by coming from behind to win Game 6, 9-7. They spotted Seattle a four-run lead but scored three in the fourth and six in the seventh. Justice and O'Neill each had three RBIs. New York thus returned to the World Series for the third consecutive season.

YANKEES TAKE SERIES IN FIVE

The much-ballyhooed Subway Series opened at Yankee Stadium with the longest game by time in Series history. After 4 hours, 51 minutes, the Yankees emerged victorious, 4-3, in 12 innings. The Mets hurt themselves with several baserunning blunders, but still managed to score three runs in the seventh to lead by one. The Yankees tied the game in the ninth on a Chuck Knoblauch sacrifice fly, and Jose Vizcaino drove in the winning run with a single to left, scoring Martinez. The Mets also came up short in Game 2, losing 6-5 and scoring all their runs in the ninth inning. The game was marred by a most unusual incident involving Piazza and Clemens, who had hit the Mets catcher in the head during the regular season. In the first inning, Piazza hit a foul ball that splintered his bat into three pieces, and he instinctively took a few steps toward first base. Clemens, perhaps also instinctively, picked up one piece of the bat that had landed near him and hurled it in Piazza's general direction. Piazza stopped short in wonderment and both benches cleared, but there was no physical confrontation. Clemens was fined $50,000 for his action. He appealed the fine, but at year's end, a decision had not been rendered.

In Game 3 at Shea Stadium, the Mets prevailed, 4-2, thereby snapping the Yankees' 14-game winning streak in Series play. The game was tied, 2-2, until the Mets pulled ahead in the eighth inning on three hits and a sacrifice fly. The following night, the Yankees won Game 4, 3-2, as leadoff man Jeter hit a first-pitch home run. The Mets scored a pair of runs off starter Neagle, but then could manage only two hits against four relievers. The Yankees closed the Series out in Game 5, winning 4-2. They mounted a two-out rally in the top of the ninth, and the lead run scored on a single by Luis Sojo.

The Yankees voted 34 full World Series shares, each worth $294,783.41, 69 partial shares and two cash awards. The Mets voted 37 full shares, each worth $238,653.80, 26 partial shares and 40 cash awards. Television ratings for the World Series, televised by Fox, hit an all-time low. They fell 22.5 percent from 1999 and were 12 percent below the previous low when the Yankees swept the Padres in 1998.

OTHER FEATS AND EVENTS

Todd Helton of the Rockies led the N.L. in batting with a .372 average. He flirted with the .400 mark throughout the season, reaching the hallowed standard for the last time on August 21. By also leading the league in on-base percentage (.463) and slug-

ging percentage (.698), he became the second Rockie in two years, following Larry Walker, to win the "percentage triple crown." Helton also led the N.L. in runs batted in (147), hits (216), extra-base hits (103), doubles (59), multi-hit games (63) and total bases (405). Florida's Luis Castillo led the league in stolen bases with 62. Pitching leaders included Randy Johnson of Arizona with 347 strikeouts, the Dodgers' Kevin Brown with an ERA of 2.58 and Florida's Antonio Alfonseca with 45 saves.

The A.L.'s leading batter was Boston's Nomar Garciaparra, who hit .372. Troy Glaus of the Angels hit 47 home runs, and his teammate, Darin Erstad, had 240 hits. Johnny Damon of the Royals led the league in runs (136) and stolen bases (46). Toronto's David Wells tied for the league lead in wins with 20. Oakland second baseman Randy Velarde became the 11th player to record an unassisted triple play, performing the feat in the sixth inning of a May 29 game in New York. Baltimore's Cal Ripken became the 24th member of the 3,000-hit club on April 15, singling off the Twins' Hector Carrasco in the seventh inning of a game in Minnesota. On September 6, Scott Sheldon of the Rangers became the third player to play all nine positions in one game. The Tigers' Shane Halter became the fourth on October 1.

The average length of a nine-inning game rose five minutes to 2:58, an all-time high. The average length of an N.L. game was 2:55 and in the A.L. an even 3:00. On May 11, the Brewers and the Cubs played a game lasting 4:22, tying the major league record for the longest nine-inning game. In October, Selig pledged new initiatives in to shorten games. "The pace of the game, I believe, can be corrected by a myriad of things, including enforcement of our rules," he said.

FOX TELEVISION CONTRACT

On September 27, MLB and Fox Television reached agreement on a comprehensive over-the-air and cable television rights package. Fox will pay $2.5 billion for a six-year deal (2001-2006) that gives it exclusive rights to the All-Star Game, all Division Series, both League Championship Series, the World Series, a Saturday game-of-the-week package and two night games each week.

Negotiations for this contract, the value of which will be about 50 percent higher than the previous five-year contracts in which Fox and NBC split these television rights, followed an outright refusal by those two networks to triple their rights fees.

ATTENDANCE RECORD

Major league baseball drew an all-time record 72,748,970 fans, up 3.7 percent over 1999. Average attendance, 30,099, topped the 30,000 mark for the first time since the 1994-95 work stoppage. The 16 N.L. teams drew 39,851,427 to their home games while the 14 A.L. teams attracted 32,897,543 to theirs.

Ten teams drew more than three million fans: Cleveland (which led both leagues with 3,456,278, exceeding the three-million mark for the fifth consecutive year), Baltimore, New York and Seattle in the A.L., and St. Louis, San Francisco, Colorado (over three million for a record eighth consecutive year), Atlanta, Houston and Los Angeles in the N.L.

Nine other clubs exceeded the two-million mark, and all other clubs except Montreal drew at least one million.

The Giants showed the greatest increase, up 1,236,931, to 3,315,330, while the Blue Jays declined the most, 343,578 to 1,819,886.

EIGHT MANAGERIAL CHANGES

Nearly the entire season passed without a manager being fired, but the Phillies dismissed Terry Francona on October 1, the season's last day, as Philadelphia was about to finish last in the N.L. East. Francona was allowed to manage his team for its final game, a loss which put the Phillies' record at 65-97, tied with the Cubs for worst in either league. Philadelphia hired former infielder and former Padres manager Larry Bowa on November 1.

On the day following the end of the season, the Pirates fired Gene Lamont, the Diamondbacks fired Buck Showalter and the Reds fired Jack McKeon. Lamont managed Pittsburgh for four seasons and finished 2000 in fifth place in the N.L. Central. The Pirates named hitting coach Lloyd McClendon as his replacement on October 23. Showalter was Arizona's first manager and had led the team to the N.L. West title in 1999, only its second year of play, but the Diamondbacks faded to third place in 2000. Arizona named broadcaster and former catcher Bob Brenly to succeed Showalter on October 30. McKeon, who replaced Ray Knight on July 25, 1997, led the Reds to second place in the N.L. Central after narrowly missing the playoffs in 1999. On November 3, Cincinnati hired Bob Boone, who had been Special Assistant to General Manager Jim Bowden.

The Dodgers fired Davey Johnson on October 6 after the team finished second in the N.L. West and replaced him with bench coach Jim Tracy on November 1. Toronto fired Jim Fregosi on October 10 after the Blue Jays finished third in the A.L. East and named broadcaster and former catcher John (Buck) Martinez as his replacement on November 2.

FINAL LUXURY TAX PAYMENTS

Clubs received their bills in January for the final year of the three-year luxury tax on salaries adopted as part of the settlement to the 1994-1995 work stoppage. Under this plan, teams with the five highest payrolls paid a 34 percent tax on the difference between their payrolls and the midpoint between the fifth and sixth highest payrolls.

For 1999, the Yankees were assessed the highest tax, $4,804,081, followed by the Orioles ($3,475,048), the Dodgers ($2,663,079) and the Mets ($1,137,992). Over the three years of the tax, Baltimore paid the most, a total of $10,643,897. The monies collected went to baseball's industry growth fund to be distributed to the sport's lower-revenue franchises.

LEAGUES AND OWNERS

As part of MLB's restructuring, league presidents Eugene Budig and Leonard Coleman resigned their positions and were each named Senior Advisor to the Commissioner.

On January 19, owners approved the sale of the Indians from Richard Jacobs to Larry Dolan and his family trusts for $320 million, a record price for a major league franchise, topping the 1998 sale price

for the Dodgers by $9 million. The team's public shareholders, who bought four million shares at $15 each in June 1998, later approved the deal and received $22.66 per share. On the same day, owners also approved a transfer in operating control of the Dodgers from the Fox Group to Bob Daly, hired on October 28, 1999, as chairman, chief executive officer and managing partner. Daly also bought a small interest in the club.

On April 17, owners approved the sale of the Royals to David Glass for $96 million. Glass, chairman of the team since shortly after the death of Ewing Kauffman in September 1993, came forward as a potential owner in December 1999, following rejection of a bid from attorney Miles Prentice.

On October 6, the Jean R. Yawkey Trust, majority owner of the Red Sox, announced that the team was for sale for the first time since 1933.

On December 3, owned approved the purchase of 80 percent of the Blue Jays for $112 million by Rogers Communications from Interbrew SA which retained 20 percent of the club. The Canadian Imperial Bank of Commerce sold its 10 percent stake to Rogers for about $12 million.

TEN ARBITRATION CASES

Ninety-one players filed for salary arbitration, but only 10 cases proceeded through the hearing and decision stage. A total of 52 players exchanged figures with their teams. Bobby Abreu, who settled with the Phillies before exchanging figures, won the year's largest salary increase, 1,088 percent. He signed a three-year contract for $14.25 million after earning $400,000 in 1999. Close behind was Andruw Jones, who signed with the Braves for $3.7 million after making $330,000 in 1999, a raise of 1,021 percent.

Four players (Karim Garcia, Brian L. Hunter, C.J. Nitkowski and Scott Sullivan) won their cases, while six (Jason Dickson, Charles Johnson, Steve Parris, Ariel Prieto, Mariano Rivera and Lee Stevens) lost theirs. These decisions gave the owners a 242-185 record since arbitration began in 1974, but the players who filed still earned an average increase of 124 percent. Their average annual salary rose from $906,091 in 1999 to $2,031,917 in 2000, according to the Associated Press. Rivera asked for $9.25 million, lost his case and accepted the Yankees' offer of $7.25 million, thereby setting a record for salary received after a hearing.

Derek Jeter got the highest salary among those who filed, signing a one-year contract for $10 million before a hearing. In all, 57 players doubled their salaries, 27 tripled theirs, 11 got fivefold increases and 8 got sixfold increases. None of those who filed took a pay cut, but seven wound up with the same salaries they had in 1999.

SALARIES RISE

According to figures compiled by the Players Association and released by the Associated Press in December, the average major league salary rose 17.5 percent in 2000 to $1,895,630. (Salary figures, it should be noted, differ slightly, depending on what factors are included.) The Yankees had the highest average salary for the second consecutive year, $3,656,542, and the Twins had the lowest, $601,680.

FREE AGENTS

Several prominent players signed contract extensions while others moved to teams as free agents. During the season, the Yankees extended the contract of Roger Clemens (two years, $30.9 million), and the Braves extended Chipper Jones' contract (six years, $90 million). After the season, the Blue Jays signed Carlos Delgado (four years, $68 million), and the Astros extended Jeff Bagwell's contract (five years, $85 million). Besides Hampton and Rodriguez, free agents who signed large deals included Mike Mussina with the Yankees (six years, $88.5 million), Denny Neagle with the Rockies (five years, $51.5 million), Kevin Appier with the Mets (four years, $42 million) and Manny Ramirez with the Red Sox (eight years, $160 million).

CONCLUSION

Commenting on the total amount of money clubs spent for free agents, Smith College economist Andrew Zimbalist, sometimes a consultant to the Players Association, said, "The imbalance must be dealt with. These signings have raised the premium on figuring out some way to level the playing field. It puts a great deal of pressure on upcoming negotiations." However prophetic this analysis proves to be, here is how the game on the field ended up in 2000:

FINAL STANDINGS

AMERICAN LEAGUE

EAST DIVISION

Team	N.Y.	Bos.	Tor.	Bal.	T.B.	Chi.	Cle.	Det.	K.C.	Min.	Oak.	Sea.	Ana.	Tex.	Atl.	N.Y.	Fla.	Mon.	Phi.	W	L	Pct.	GB
New York	....	7	5	7	6	4	5	4	8	5	6	4	5	10	2-1	4-2	1-1	2-1	2-1	87	74	.540	....
Boston	6	....	4	7	6	7	6	7	4	8	5	5	4	7	2-4	2-1	2-1	3-0	0-3	85	77	.525	2.5
Toronto	7	8	....	6	7	5	4	9	6	4	3	2	7	6	2-1	1-2	1-2	4-2	1-2	83	79	.512	4.5
Baltimore	5	5	7	....	8	4	5	6	3	6	4	3	5	6	0-3	1-2	2-1	0-3	4-2	74	88	.457	13.5
Tampa Bay	6	6	5	5	....	4	2	5	5	6	2	3	6	5	1-2	1-2	3-3	2-1	2-1	69	92	.429	18.0

CENTRAL DIVISION

Team	Chi.	Cle.	Det.	K.C.	Min.	N.Y.	Bos.	Tor.	Bal.	T.B.	Oak.	Sea.	Ana.	Tex.	St.L.	Cin.	Mil.	Hou.	Pit.	Chi.	W	L	Pct.	GB
Chicago	....	8	9	5	7	8	5	5	6	8	6	7	6	5	1-2	3-0	3-0	2-1	....	3-3	95	67	.586	....
Cleveland	5	....	6	5	5	5	6	8	4	8	6	7	6	6	2-1	3-3	3-0	2-1	3-0	....	90	72	.556	5.0
Detroit	3	7	....	5	7	8	5	3	4	4	6	7	5	5	2-1	2-1	1-2	2-1	1-2	2-1	79	83	.488	16.0
Kansas City	7	7	7	....	7	2	6	4	7	5	4	4	6	3	1-2	....	1-2	2-1	1-2	2-1	77	85	.475	18.0
Minnesota	5	8	6	5	....	5	2	5	3	4	5	3	3	8	2-1	0-3	1-2	2-1	1-2	1-2	69	93	.426	26.0

WEST DIVISION

Team	Oak.	Sea.	Ana.	Tex.	N.Y.	Bos.	Tor.	Bal.	T.B.	Chi.	Cle.	Det.	K.C.	Min.	S.F.	L.A.	Ari.	Col.	S.D.	W	L	Pct.	GB
Oakland	....	9	8	5	3	5	7	8	7	3	6	4	8	7	3-3	2-1	2-1	1-2	3-0	91	70	.565	....
Seattle	4	....	8	7	6	5	8	7	9	5	2	2	8	9	2-1	2-1	2-1	2-1	3-3	91	71	.562	0.5
Anaheim	5	5	....	7	5	5	5	7	6	4	3	5	6	7	2-1	4-2	1-2	3-0	2-1	82	80	.506	9.5
Texas	7	5	5	....	2	3	4	6	7	5	4	5	7	4	0-3	1-2	4-2	0-3	2-1	71	91	.438	20.5

NOTE: Read across for wins, down for losses.

Clinching dates: New York (East)—September 29; Chicago (Central)—September 24; Oakland (West)—October 1; Seattle (wild card)—October 1.

NATIONAL LEAGUE

EAST DIVISION

Team	Atl.	N.Y.	Fla.	Mon.	Phi.	St.L.	Cin.	Mil.	Hou.	Pit.	Chi.	S.F.	L.A.	Ari.	Col.	S.D.	N.Y.	Bos.	Tor.	Bal.	T.B.	W	L	Pct.	GB
Atlanta	....	7	6	6	8	3	2	6	5	4	6	7	6	5	8		1-2	4-2	1-2	3-0	2-1	95	67	.586	....
New York	6	....	6	9	6	4	7	5	7	5	3	5	7	6	3		2-4	1-2	2-1	2-1	2-1	94	68	.580	1.0
Florida	6	6	....	7	9	3	6	3	3	5	6	3	2	5	5	2	1-1	1-2	2-1	1-2	3-3	79	82	.491	15.5
Montreal	7	3	6	....	5	2	3	5	5	3	5	3	5	2	3		1-2	0-3	2-4	3-0	1-2	67	95	.414	28.0
Philadelphia	5	7	4	7	....	2	4	5	4	3	3	2	4	1	3	2	1-2	3-0	2-1	2-4	1-2	65	97	.401	30.0

CENTRAL DIVISION

Team	St.L.	Cin.	Mil.	Hou.	Pit.	Chi.	Atl.	N.Y.	Fla.	Mon.	Phi.	S.F.	L.A.	Ari.	Col.	S.D.	Chi.	Cle.	Det.	K.C.	Min.	W	L	Pct.	GB
St. Louis	....	6	7	6	8	10	4	3	6	5	7	4	6	4	3	9	2-1	1-2	1-2	2-1	1-2	95	67	.586	....
Cincinnati	7	....	5	7	7	8	5	5	3	6	3	3	4	5	6	4	0-3	3-3	1-2		3-0	85	77	.525	10.0
Milwaukee	5	8	....	6	7	7	3	2	4	4	2	3	4	5	5	2	0-3	0-3	2-1	2-1	2-1	73	89	.451	22.0
Houston	6	5	7	....	10	7	4	2	5	4	5	1	3	1	4	2	1-2	1-2	1-2	2-1	1-2	72	90	.444	23.0
Pittsburgh	4	6	5	3	....	9	2	2	4	4	6	2	5	2	2	7	....	0-3	2-1	2-4	2-1	69	93	.426	26.0
Chicago	3	4	6	5	3	....	5	2	1	4	6	4	3	4	4	3	3-3	....	1-2	2-1	2-1	65	97	.401	30.0

WEST DIVISION

Team	S.F.	L.A.	Ari.	Col.	S.D.	Atl.	N.Y.	Fla.	Mon.	Phi.	St.L.	Cin.	Mil.	Hou.	Pit.	Chi.	Oak.	Sea.	Ana.	Tex.	W	L	Pct.	GB
San Francisco	....	5	7	7	7	3	5	6	6	7	5	6	6	8	6	5	3-3	1-2	1-2	3-0	97	65	.599	....
Los Angeles	7	....	6	9	8	2	4	7	5	5	3	5	3	6	4	6	1-2	1-2	2-4	2-1	86	76	.531	11.0
Arizona	6	7	....	7	9	3	2	4	4	8	5	2	4	6	7	5	1-2	1-2	2-1	2-4	85	77	.525	12.0
Colorado	6	4	6	....	7	4	3	4	7	6	5	3	4	5	7	5	2-1	1-2	0-3	3-0	82	80	.506	15.0
San Diego	5	5	4	6	....	1	6	7	6	5	0	5	7	7	2	5	0-3	3-3	1-2	1-2	76	86	.469	21.0

NOTE: Read across for wins, down for losses.

Tie game—Milwaukee at Cincinnati, April 3 (5 innings).

Clinching dates: Atlanta (East)—September 26; St. Louis (Central)—September 20; San Francisco (West)—September 21; New York (wild card)—September 27.

2000 REVIEW Year in review

A.L. DIVISION SERIES
SEATTLE VS. CHICAGO

The bottom line: The A.L. Central Division-champion Chicago White Sox, unable to get key hits from the middle of its lineup or solve Seattle's bullpen, were swept out of their first postseason appearance since 1993 and denied a shot at their first World Series appearance since 1959. The wild-card Mariners, who didn't clinch a playoff berth until the final day of the regular season, outpitched, outhit and outplayed the American League's winningest team while claiming the second ALCS berth in franchise history. Seattle's surprising success was achieved in the first season after longtime star Ken Griffey Jr. was traded to Cincinnati and the clincher was recorded, appropriately, in the first playoff game at Safeco Field.

Why the Mariners won: Pitching, defense and timely hitting—baseball's traditional winning mix. Seattle pitchers limited the highest scoring team in the major leagues to seven runs and 17 hits over three games and held Chicago's Big Four offensive guns—Frank Thomas, Magglio Ordonez, Carlos Lee and Paul Konerko—to a dismal 3-for-40, two-RBI performance. The Mariners' starting pitching was solid, but their bullpen—Brett Tomko, Jose Paniagua, Arthur Rhodes, Jose Mesa and Kazuhiro Sasaki—was spectacular, working 11 $2/3$ scoreless innings and allowing the team to post two last-at-bat victories. The first two wins came at Chicago's Comiskey Park and continued a late-season trend—the Mariners won eight of the final nine road games while fighting for a playoff spot.

The turning points:

Game 1: The Mariners took control of the series in the 10th inning, a rally set up by former White Sox center fielder Mike Cameron. After singling home the tying run in the seventh, Cameron led off the 10th with a single off Chicago closer Keith Foulke. When Alex Rodriguez popped out, Cameron began stretching his lead, drawing Foulke into a cat-and-mouse pickoff game that finally ended with a stolen base. Obviously distracted, Foulke fired a pitch that Edgar Martinez pounded over the left field wall to give the Mariners a 6-4 lead and John Olerud hit his next pitch over the center field fence for the final 7-4 margin. When Sasaki shut down the White Sox in the bottom of the inning, he completed 6 $2/3$ scoreless innings for the bullpen and a win for Mesa. The loss was particularly difficult for the White Sox, who had rallied from a 3-0 deficit to a 4-3 advantage on a home run by Ray Durham and RBI triples by Ordonez and Chris Singleton.

Game 2: The bottom of the first inning provided a microcosm of the frustration the White Sox would experience in this series. Chicago leadoff man Durham doubled over center fielder Cameron's head and scored when No. 2 hitter Jose Valentin doubled into the right field corner. Valentin set the White Sox up for more when he stole third base off pitcher Paul Abbott. But just as they had in Game 1, Chicago's top offensive guns misfired. Thomas, who hit 43 homers and drove in 143 runs during an outstanding regular season, hit a fly ball to shallow left field as Valentin held. Ordonez walked, but Abbott retired Lee on a popup and Konerko on a soft grounder back to the mound. Having escaped with minimal damage, the Mariners scored twice in the top of the second on third baseman David Bell's single and catcher Dan Wilson's sacrifice fly and took the lead for good on Jay Buhner's fourth-inning home run off loser Mike Sirotka. Seattle's 5-2 victory also featured a superb run-saving defensive play by second baseman Mark McLemore and another $3^1/3$ scoreless innings by the Mariners bullpen.

Game 3: The game—and the series—ended in an unlikely manner with one out in the bottom of the ninth inning when pinch hitter Carlos Guillen successfully squeezed home the winning run in a 2-1 Seattle victory. The White Sox's surprising season came to a sudden halt when Guillen, with Rickey Henderson stationed at third, dragged a hard safety squeeze bunt that eluded diving first baseman Thomas. Henderson was pinch running for Olerud, who had opened the inning by lining a ball off the stomach of pitcher Kelly Wunsch and moved to second when Wunsch made a wild throw. Henderson was sacrificed to third by Stan Javier before Bell drew a four-pitch walk from closer Foulke. Guillen's hit ended a tense battle that opened with Chicago's James Baldwin and Seattle's Aaron Sele matching pitches and ended after yeoman work by both bullpens. Sele, Rhodes and Paniagua, the winner, stopped the White Sox on three hits and stretched Thomas' frustration in an 0-for-9 postseason.

Notable:

White Sox: Before surrendering the two 10th-inning home runs to Seattle in Game 1, relief ace Foulke had been on a roll. The righthander, who saved 34 games, had allowed only one run in his final $14^2/3$ regular-season innings. ... The Game 2 loss at Comiskey Park stretched the White Sox's postseason home losing streak to nine games. The last home playoff victory came in Game 1 of the 1959 World Series against Los Angeles. ... After losing the first two games, the White Sox were understandably optimistic about their comeback chances in Seattle. Chicago recorded a major league-best 49-32 road record in 2000.

Mariners: Seattle claimed its second ALCS appearance in its third postseason venture. The Mariners defeated the New York Yankees in the 1995 Division Series before losing to the Indians in the ALCS. They lost a Division Series to Baltimore in 1997. ... Five players picked up in the trades for Randy Johnson and Ken Griffey Jr. played key roles in the Mariners' regular-season and postseason success. Guillen and Cameron provided key hits during the season and in the series against the White Sox. Freddy Garcia and John Halama were members of the rotation and Tomko worked successfully out of the bullpen. ... Temporary bleachers were added to Safeco Field for the playoffs and 48,010 attended the first postseason game in the stadium's history.

Quotable:

White Sox: Thomas, lamenting his first-inning failure in Game 2: "A guy on third with less than two out. I've got to get him home. That's what I get paid for. That's what I've made my living doing." ... Manager Jerry Manuel after watching his Sox lose their third straight game: "We played good baseball. They played magnificent baseball. It took that kind of effort to beat us. They pitched extremely well; they played great defense. They did everything you have to do to win."

Mariners: Cameron, referring to the surprise visit he received from manager Lou Piniella after he was almost picked off three times by Foulke in the 10th inning of Game 1: "I didn't know what he was going to say to me. The only time you see something like that is in Little League. I can't tell you what he said. It's a baseball secret we keep under the sheets." ... Piniella, when assessing the Mariners' 2-1 Game 3-clinching win: "This was a trademark game for us. We pitched well, we played really good defense."

GAME 1 BOX SCORE

SEATTLE 7, CHICAGO 4 (10 INNINGS)

TUESDAY, OCTOBER 3, AT CHICAGO

Seattle	AB	R	H	RBI	PO	A
Henderson, lf	3	1	1	0	1	0
Javier, ph-lf	2	0	0	0	3	0
Cameron, cf	4	2	2	1	4	0
Rodriguez, ss	5	0	3	1	1	2
Martinez, dh	5	1	2	2	0	0
Olerud, 1b	5	1	1	2	8	0
Buhner, rf	1	0	0	0	2	0
Ibanez, pr-rf	2	1	1	0	1	0
Bell, 3b	4	0	1	0	0	3
Oliver, c	2	1	1	1	3	0
Martin, ph	1	0	0	0	0	0
Wilson, c	2	0	0	0	4	0
McLemore, 2b	3	0	1	0	3	3
Garcia, p	0	0	0	0	0	2
Tomko, p	0	0	0	0	0	0
Paniagua, p	0	0	0	0	0	0
Rhodes, p	0	0	0	0	0	1
Mesa, p	0	0	0	0	0	0
Sasaki, p	0	0	0	0	0	0
Totals	39	7	13	7	30	11

Chicago	AB	R	H	RBI	PO	A
Durham, 2b	3	1	1	1	4	4
Valentin, ss	4	1	1	0	5	6
Thomas, dh	3	0	0	0	0	0
Ordonez, rf	5	0	1	1	4	1
Lee, lf	5	0	1	0	2	0
Konerko, 1b	4	1	0	0	6	0
Perry, 3b	4	0	1	0	1	1
Singleton, cf	5	1	1	1	2	0
Johnson, c	4	0	3	0	5	1
Paul, pr-c	0	0	0	0	1	0
Parque, p	0	0	0	0	0	0
Howry, p	0	0	0	0	0	0
Bradford, p	0	0	0	0	0	0
Wunsch, p	0	0	0	0	0	0
Simas, p	0	0	0	0	0	0
Foulke, p	0	0	0	0	0	0
Totals	37	4	9	3	30	13

Seattle	2	1	0	0	0	0	1	0	0	3—7
Chicago	0	2	2	0	0	0	0	0	0	0—4

Seattle	IP	H	R	ER	BB	SO
Garcia	3.1	6	4	4	3	2
Tomko	2.2	1	0	0	1	0
Paniagua	*2.0	1	0	0	1	2
Rhodes	0.2	0	0	0	0	0
Mesa (W)	0.1	0	0	0	1	0
Sasaki (S)	1.0	1	0	0	0	2

Chicago	IP	H	R	ER	BB	SO
Parque	6.0	6	3	3	1	2
Howry	0.2	1	1	1	2	1
Bradford	0.2	2	0	0	0	0
Wunsch	0.1	1	0	0	0	0
Simas	0.1	0	0	0	0	0
Foulke (L)	2.0	3	3	3	1	2

*Pitched to one batter in ninth.

DP—Seattle 1, Chicago 2. LOB—Seattle 7, Chicago 10. 2B—Bell, Valentin, Lee. 3B—Singleton, Ordonez. HR—Olerud, Martinez, Durham, Oliver. SH—Durham. SB—Cameron, Valentin. CS—Rodriguez. HBP—By Parque (Cameron). WP—Garcia, Tomko. T—4:12. A—45,290. U—Reliford, plate; Danley, first; Reilly, second; Winters, third; Reed, left field; Eddings, right field.

GAME 2 BOX SCORE

SEATTLE 5, CHICAGO 2

WEDNESDAY, OCTOBER 4, AT CHICAGO

Seattle	AB	R	H	RBI	PO	A
Henderson, lf	2	1	1	0	1	0
Ibanez, lf-rf	2	0	1	0	2	0
Cameron, cf	4	0	1	1	2	0
Rodriguez, ss	5	0	1	1	4	4
Martinez, dh	3	1	1	0	0	0
Olerud, 1b	3	1	1	0	7	0
Buhner, rf	4	1	1	1	2	0
Oliver, c	0	0	0	0	5	0
Bell, 3b	4	0	2	1	1	1
Wilson, c	1	0	0	1	1	0
Javier, lf	1	0	0	0	0	0
McLemore, 2b	3	1	0	0	2	3
P. Abbott, p	0	0	0	0	0	1
Rhodes, p	0	0	0	0	0	0
Mesa, p	0	0	0	0	0	1
Sasaki, p	0	0	0	0	0	0
Totals	32	5	9	5	27	10

Chicago	AB	R	H	RBI	PO	A
Durham, 2b	4	1	1	0	4	1
Valentin, ss	3	1	2	1	4	7
Thomas, dh	4	0	0	0	0	0
Ordonez, rf	2	0	0	0	1	0
Lee, lf	3	0	0	1	1	0
Konerko, 1b	4	0	0	0	11	1
Perry, 3b	4	0	2	0	1	4

Chicago	AB	R	H	RBI	PO	A
Singleton, cf	2	0	0	0	1	0
J. Abbott, ph-cf	1	0	0	0	1	0
Baines, ph	1	0	0	0	0	0
Johnson, c	2	0	0	0	3	1
Sirotka, p	0	0	0	0	0	1
Barcelo, p	0	0	0	0	0	0
Wunsch, p	0	0	0	0	0	0
Simas, p	0	0	0	0	0	0
Buehrle, p	0	0	0	0	0	0
Totals	30	2	5	2	27	15

Seattle								
Seattle	0	2	0	1	1	0	0	0	1—5
Chicago	1	0	1	0	0	0	0	0	0—2

Seattle	IP	H	R	ER	BB	SO
P. Abbott (W)	5.2	5	2	1	3	1
Rhodes	0.2	0	0	0	2	0
Mesa	1.2	0	0	0	0	2
Sasaki (S)	1.0	0	0	0	0	3

Chicago	IP	H	R	ER	BB	SO
Sirotka (L)	5.2	7	4	3	2	0
Barcelo	1.2	0	0	0	1	0
Wunsch	0.1	0	0	0	0	0
Simas	1.0	0	1	1	1	2
Buehrle	0.1	0	0	0	0	1

E—Wilson, Valentin. DP—Seattle 1, Chicago 3. LOB—Seattle 7, Chicago 8. 2B—Martinez, Durham, Valentin, Perry. HR—Buhner. SH—Cameron. SF—Wilson, Lee. SB—Henderson, Valentin 2, Ordonez. HBP—By P. Abbott (Johnson), by Sirotka (Olerud). T—3:16. A—45,383. U—Danley, plate; Reilly, first; Winters, second; Reed, third; Eddings, left field; Reliford, right field.

GAME 3 BOX SCORE

SEATTLE 2, CHICAGO 1

FRIDAY, OCTOBER 6, AT SEATTLE

Chicago	AB	R	H	RBI	PO	A
Durham, 2b	3	0	0	0	2	1
Valentin, ss	3	0	0	0	1	4
Thomas, 1b	2	0	0	0	8	0
Ordonez, rf	4	0	1	0	3	0
Baines, dh	3	1	1	0	0	0
Johnson, c	3	0	0	0	5	0
Perry, 3b	1	0	1	1	3	2
Graffanino, pr-3b	0	0	0	0	0	1

Chicago	AB	R	H	RBI	PO	A
Lee, lf	3	0	0	0	3	0
Singleton, cf	2	0	0	0	0	0
Konerko, ph	1	0	0	0	0	0
Christensen, cf	0	0	0	0	0	0
Baldwin, p	0	0	0	0	0	1
Howry, p	0	0	0	0	0	1
Wunsch, p	0	0	0	0	0	0
Foulke, p	0	0	0	0	0	0
Totals	25	1	3	1	25	10

Seattle	AB	R	H	RBI	PO	A
Cameron, cf	4	0	0	0	6	0
Ibanez, rf	4	1	1	0	1	0
Rodriguez, ss	3	0	0	0	3	3
Martinez, dh	3	0	1	0	0	0
Olerud, 1b	2	0	1	0	10	0
Henderson, pr	0	1	0	0	0	0
Javier, lf	3	0	1	1	1	0
Bell, 3b	3	0	1	0	1	0
Oliver, c	2	0	0	0	4	0
Guillen, ph	1	0	1	1	0	0
McLemore, 2b	3	0	0	0	1	3
Sele, p	0	0	0	0	0	1
Rhodes, p	0	0	0	0	0	0
Paniagua, p	0	0	0	0	0	0
Totals	28	2	6	2	27	7

Chicago	0	1	0	0	0	0	0	0	0—1
Seattle	0	0	0	1	0	0	0	0	1—2

One out when winning run scored.

Chicago	IP	H	R	ER	BB	SO
Baldwin	6.0	3	1	1	3	2
Howry	2.0	1	0	0	0	3
Wunsch (L)	*0.0	1	1	0	0	0
Foulke	0.1	1	0	0	1	0

Seattle	IP	H	R	ER	BB	SO
Sele	7.1	3	1	1	3	1
Rhodes	1.1	0	0	0	0	2
Paniagua (W)	0.1	0	0	0	1	1

*Pitched to one batter in ninth.

E—Wunsch. DP—Seattle 3. LOB—Chicago 3, Seattle 8. 2B—Baines. SH—Valentin, Rodriguez, Javier, Oliver. SF—Perry. T—2:40. A—48,010. U—McClelland, plate; Schrieber, first; Clark, second; Nelson, third; Welke, left field; Meriwether, right field.

STATISTICS

SEATTLE MARINERS' BATTING AND FIELDING AVERAGES

Player, position	G	AB	R	H	TB	2B	3B	HR	RBI	BB	IBB	SO	Avg.	PO	A	E	Avg.
Guillen, ph	1	1	0	1	1	0	0	0	1	0	0	0	1.000	0	0	0	.000
Henderson, lf-pr	3	5	3	2	2	0	0	0	0	1	0	0	.400	2	0	0	1.000
Ibanez, pr-rf-lf	3	8	2	3	3	0	0	0	0	0	0	0	.375	4	0	0	1.000
Bell, 3b	3	11	0	4	5	1	0	0	1	2	0	2	.364	2	4	0	1.000
Martinez, dh	3	11	2	4	8	1	0	1	2	2	0	1	.364	0	0	0	.000
Rodriguez, ss	3	13	0	4	4	0	0	0	2	0	0	2	.308	8	9	0	1.000
Olerud, 1b	3	10	2	3	6	0	0	1	2	2	0	1	.300	25	0	0	1.000
Cameron, cf	3	12	2	3	3	0	0	0	2	0	0	0	.250	12	0	0	1.000
Oliver, c	3	4	1	1	4	0	0	1	1	0	0	1	.250	12	0	0	1.000
Buhner, rf	2	5	1	1	4	0	0	1	1	1	2	0	.200	4	0	0	1.000
Javier, ph-lf	3	6	0	1	1	0	0	0	1	0	0	3	.167	4	0	0	1.000
McLemore, 2b	3	9	1	1	1	0	0	0	0	2	0	1	.111	6	9	0	1.000
P. Abbott, p	1	0	0	0	0	0	0	0	0	0	0	0	.000	0	1	0	1.000
Garcia, p	1	0	0	0	0	0	0	0	0	0	0	0	.000	0	2	0	1.000
Mesa, p	2	0	0	0	0	0	0	0	0	0	0	0	.000	0	1	0	1.000
Paniagua, p	2	0	0	0	0	0	0	0	0	0	0	0	.000	0	0	0	.000
Rhodes, p	3	0	0	0	0	0	0	0	0	0	0	0	.000	0	1	0	1.000
Sasaki, p	2	0	0	0	0	0	0	0	0	0	0	0	.000	0	0	0	.000
Sele, p	1	0	0	0	0	0	0	0	0	0	0	0	.000	0	1	0	1.000
Tomko, p	1	0	0	0	0	0	0	0	0	0	0	0	.000	0	0	0	.000

Player, position	G	AB	R	H	TB	2B	3B	HR	RBI	BB	IBB	SO	Avg.	PO	A	E	Avg.
Martin, ph	1	0	0	0	0	0	0	0	0	0	0	0	.000	0	0	0	.000
Wilson, c	2	3	0	0	0	0	0	0	1	1	0	2	.000	5	0	1	.833
Totals	3	99	14	28	42	2	0	4	14	12	0	13	.283	84	28	1	.991

CHICAGO WHITE SOX'S BATTING AND FIELDING AVERAGES

Player, position	G	AB	R	H	TB	2B	3B	HR	RBI	BB	IBB	SO	Avg.	PO	A	E	Avg.
Perry, 3b	3	9	0	4	5	1	0	0	1	2	0	2	.444	5	7	0	1.000
Johnson, c	3	9	0	3	3	0	0	0	0	1	0	1	.333	13	2	0	1.000
Valentin, ss	3	10	2	3	5	2	0	0	1	2	0	2	.300	10	17	1	.964
Baines, ph-dh	2	4	1	1	2	1	0	0	0	0	0	1	.250	0	0	0	.000
Durham, 2b	3	10	2	2	6	1	0	1	1	3	0	3	.200	10	6	0	1.000
Ordonez, rf	3	11	0	2	4	0	1	0	1	2	0	2	.182	8	1	0	1.000
Singleton, cf	3	9	1	1	3	0	1	0	1	0	0	2	.111	3	0	0	1.000
Lee, lf	3	11	0	1	2	1	0	0	1	0	0	2	.091	6	0	0	1.000
Baldwin, p	1	0	0	0	0	0	0	0	0	0	0	0	.000	0	1	0	1.000
Barcelo, p	1	0	0	0	0	0	0	0	0	0	0	0	.000	0	0	0	.000
Bradford, p	1	0	0	0	0	0	0	0	0	0	0	0	.000	0	0	0	.000
Buehrle, p	1	0	0	0	0	0	0	0	0	0	0	0	.000	0	0	0	.000
Christensen, cf	1	0	0	0	0	0	0	0	0	0	0	0	.000	0	0	0	.000
Foulke, p	2	0	0	0	0	0	0	0	0	0	0	0	.000	0	1	0	1.000
Graffanino, pr-3b	1	0	0	0	0	0	0	0	0	0	0	0	.000	0	1	0	1.000
Howry, p	2	0	0	0	0	0	0	0	0	0	0	0	.000	0	0	0	.000
Parque, p	1	0	0	0	0	0	0	0	0	0	0	0	.000	1	0	0	1.000
Paul, pr-c	1	0	0	0	0	0	0	0	0	0	0	0	.000	0	0	0	.000
Simas, p	2	0	0	0	0	0	0	0	0	0	0	0	.000	0	1	0	1.000
Sirotka, p	1	0	0	0	0	0	0	0	0	0	0	0	.000	0	0	1	.000
Wunsch, p	3	0	0	0	0	0	0	0	0	0	0	0	.000	1	0	0	1.000
J. Abbott, ph-cf	1	1	0	0	0	0	0	0	0	0	0	0	.000	1	0	0	1.000
Konerko, 1b-ph	3	9	1	0	0	0	0	0	0	1	0	1	.000	17	1	0	1.000
Thomas, dh-1b	3	9	0	0	0	0	0	0	0	4	1	0	.000	8	0	0	.000
Totals	3	92	7	17	30	6	2	1	6	15	1	16	.185	82	38	2	.984

SEATTLE MARINERS' PITCHING RECORDS

Pitcher	G	GS	CG	IP	H	R	ER	HR	BB	IBB	SO	HB	WP	W	L	Pct.	ERA
Rhodes	3	0	0	2.2	0	0	0	0	2	0	2	0	0	0	0	.000	0.00
Tomko	1	0	0	2.2	1	0	0	0	1	0	0	0	1	0	0	.000	0.00
Paniagua	2	0	0	2.1	1	0	0	0	2	0	3	0	0	1	0	1.000	0.00
Mesa	2	0	0	2.0	0	0	0	0	1	1	2	0	0	1	0	1.000	0.00
Sasaki	2	0	0	2.0	1	0	0	0	0	0	5	0	0	0	0	.000	0.00
Sele	1	1	0	7.1	3	1	1	0	3	0	1	0	0	0	0	.000	1.23
P. Abbott	1	1	0	5.2	5	2	1	0	3	0	1	1	0	1	0	1.000	1.59
Garcia	1	1	0	3.1	6	4	4	1	3	0	2	0	1	0	0	.000	10.80
Totals	3	3	0	28.0	17	7	6	1	15	1	16	1	2	3	0	1.000	1.93

No shutouts. Saves—Sasaki 2.

CHICAGO WHITE SOX'S PITCHING RECORDS

Pitcher	G	GS	CG	IP	H	R	ER	HR	BB	IBB	SO	HB	WP	W	L	Pct.	ERA
Barcelo	1	0	0	1.2	0	0	0	0	1	0	0	0	0	0	0	.000	0.00
Bradford	1	0	0	0.2	2	0	0	0	0	0	0	0	0	0	0	.000	0.00
Wunsch	3	0	0	0.2	2	1	0	0	0	0	0	0	0	0	1	.000	0.00
Buehrle	1	0	0	0.1	2	0	0	0	0	1	0	0	0	0	0	.000	0.00
Baldwin	1	1	0	6.0	3	1	1	0	3	0	2	0	0	0	0	.000	1.50
Howry	2	0	0	2.2	2	1	1	0	2	0	4	0	0	0	0	.000	3.38
Parque	1	1	0	6.0	6	3	3	1	1	0	2	1	0	0	0	.000	4.50
Sirotka	1	1	0	5.2	7	4	3	1	2	0	0	1	0	0	1	.000	4.76
Simas	2	0	0	1.1	0	1	1	0	1	0	2	0	0	0	0	.000	6.75
Foulke	2	0	0	2.1	4	3	3	2	2	0	2	0	0	0	1	.000	11.57
Totals	3	3	0	27.1	28	14	12	4	12	0	13	2	0	0	3	.000	3.95

No shutouts or saves.

SCORE BY INNINGS

Seattle	2	3	0	2	1	0	1	0	2	3—14
Chicago	1	3	3	0	0	0	0	0	0	0— 7

MISCELLANEOUS STATISTICS

Sacrifice hit—Cameron, Durham, Javier, Oliver, Rodriguez, Valentin.
Sacrifice flies—Lee, Perry, Wilson.
Stolen bases—Valentin 3, Cameron, Henderson, Ordonez.

Caught stealing—Rodriguez.
Double plays—McLemore, Rodriguez and Olerud 2; Durham, Valentin and Konerko 2; Johnson, Valentin and Konerko; McLemore and Olerud; Rodriguez, McLemore and Olerud; Sele, Rodriguez and Olerud; Sirotka, Valentin and Konerko; Valentin and Konerko.
Left on bases—Seattle 7, 7, 8—22; Chicago 10, 8, 3—21.
Hit by pitcher—By P. Abbott (Johnson), by Parque (Cameron), by Sirotka (Olerud).
Passed balls—None.
Balks—None.
Time of games—First game, 4:12; second game, 3:16; third game, 2:40.
Attendance—First game, 45,290; second game, 45,383; third game, 48,010.
Umpires—Reliford, Danley, Reilly, Winters, Reed, Eddings, McClelland, Schrieber, Clark, Nelson, Welke and Meriwether.
Official scorers—Terry Mosher, Bob Rosenberg.

NEW YORK VS. OAKLAND

HIGHLIGHTS

The bottom line: The "too old, too tired, inconsistent" New York Yankees, looking for their third straight World Series title and fourth in five years, slipped past the young and restless Oakland Athletics in a tough five-game Division Series that seriously tested their championship resolve. After ending the regular season with seven straight losses and 15 in 18 games, the Yankees lost the series opener to Oakland and seemed to be reeling. But lefthander Andy Pettitte righted the ship with a Game 2 shutout and the A.L. East Division champions came up with big plays and rallies every time they needed them. The A.L. West-champion A's, making their first postseason appearance since 1992, pushed the Yankees to the brink before falling into a 6-0 Game 5 hole they couldn't climb out of. The win completed a Bay Area sweep for New York teams—the Yankees beating the A's a few hours after the Mets had dispatched the Giants.

Why the Yankees won: Because of experience, their ability to turn on a sputtering offense and the Game 5 rescue work of their much-maligned bullpen. Pettitte was outstanding in a must-win Game 2 and Orlando Hernandez followed his lead in Game 3. The Yankees showed old offensive flashes throughout the series and they took control of Game 5 with a six-run, first-inning outburst that shocked the A's and quieted 41,170 fired-up Oakland fans. When the relentless A's kept coming, the bullpen stepped up to deliver 5 1/3 scoreless innings and a 7-5 victory.

The turning points:

Game 1: After being dominated for four innings by Yankees starter Roger Clemens, the A's broke through for four runs in the fifth and sixth innings and went on to record a 5-3 win at Network Associates Coliseum. Clemens, who allowed only one hit and struck out five through four innings, carried a 2-0 lead into the fifth, thanks to back-to-back RBI doubles by Luis Sojo and Scott Brosius in the second. But the A's struck for three runs on RBI singles by Ramon Hernandez and Randy Velarde and a wild pitch by Clemens, and broke a 3-3 deadlock in the sixth on a run-scoring double by Hernandez.

The Yankees, who lost for the eighth straight game and 16th in 19 outings, managed only three hits over the last seven innings off winning pitcher Gil Heredia and relievers Jeff Tam, Jim Mecir and Jason Isringhausen.

Game 2: With their backs planted firmly against the wall and their hopes for a third straight World Series championship at stake, the Yankees turned to Pettitte and snapped their eight-game losing streak. The 19-game winner shut down the free-swinging A's, allowing five hits over 7 2/3 innings en route to a 4-0 victory that evened the Division Series at a game apiece. Pettitte, who was helped by double plays in the first and seventh innings, kept Oakland at bay until the Yankees could get their offense going in the top of the sixth against Kevin Appier. The A's righthander was cruising with two out and a runner on second when manager Art Howe ordered slumping Paul O'Neill, a lefthanded hitter, to be walked intentionally. Righthander Glenallen Hill spoiled the strategy with an RBI single and Sojo's double scored two more. Pettitte left with two out and two runners on base in the eighth and Yankees closer Mariano Rivera finished for his 14th postseason save.

Game 3: The A's inability to handle struggling Orlando Hernandez, combined with a popgun Yankees attack, lifted New York to within one win of the ALCS. El Duque needed 130 pitches to get through seven innings, allowing only four hits but walking five and allowing two runs. He was aided by good defensive plays by left fielder David Justice and second baseman Sojo en route to his sixth win in as many postseason decisions. Playing before a roaring Yankee Stadium crowd of 55,606, the young A's committed two errors and made several more defensive lapses that contributed to Yankee runs. Two scored in the second on infield choppers by Hill and Derek Jeter and another came home in the fourth on Jeter's groundout after a throwing error by catcher Ramon Hernandez. That was all the support needed by Orlando Hernandez and Rivera, who earned his record-tying 15th postseason save. One of the A's runs came on a fifth-inning home run by Terrence Long—the first homer in the series.

Game 4: The A's, facing elimination at pressure-packed Yankee Stadium, delivered a first-inning message that this series was far from over. The unlikely messenger was backup DH Olmedo Saenz, who pounded the first Clemens pitch he saw over the left field fence after the big righthander had walked Long and Jason Giambi. The 3-0 advantage held up until the sixth, when the A's struck for three more runs, two on a single by Ben Grieve, en route to an 11-1 win. While the 38-year-old Clemens, a five-time Cy Young winner, was faltering, 22-year-old A's rookie lefthander Barry Zito was slamming the door on the Yankees, working 5²/₃ innings in his post-season debut. The win forced the series back to Oakland and put the Yankees on the brink of elimination for the first time since their 1997 Division Series loss to Cleveland.

Game 5: As if shooing away an annoying fly, the Yankees jumped on Oakland starter Gil Heredia for six first-inning runs en route to a 7-5 Division Series-clinching victory. But what should have been easy turned into a tense struggle before the two-time defending World Series champs could claim their fourth ALCS berth in five years. Chuck Knoblauch singled twice, stole a base, scored a run and drove in another in the big first inning that featured a bases-loaded triple by first baseman Tino Martinez. But Pettitte, unable to match his Game 2 performance, surrendered 10 hits and five runs over 3²/₃ spotty innings. Only a solo home run by Justice—the Yankees' only homer of the series—and outstanding work by Mike Stanton, Jeff Nelson, Hernandez and Rivera kept the A's from wiping out their deficit and ending the Yankees' postseason series win streak at six. Rivera's 16th postseason save broke the record he had shared with Dennis Eckersley since Game 3.

Notable:
Athletics: The A's, unlike the Yankees, entered the playoff series on a high, having won eight of their last 10 regular-season games to overtake Seattle for the A.L. West title. ... The A's win in Game 1 was the first postseason managerial victory for Art Howe. ... Game 2 starter Kevin Appier, making his first postseason appearance in 12 major league seasons, allowed three runs on six hits over 6¹/₃ innings. ... In Oakland's Game 3 loss to Orlando Hernandez, the A's Nos. 2-7 hitters were a combined 0-for-19. ... That Game 3 loss marked the first time since September 1 that the A's had lost two games in a row. ... After the A's Game 4 win at New York, both teams made the long flight to Oakland, arriving about 4 a.m.—13 hours before game time.

Yankees: Entering the series, the Yankees had won 18 of the last 19 postseason games and 22 of 25. ... When the Yankees took a 2-0 lead in Game 1, it broke a streak of 63 innings in which they trailed or were tied. ... Justice set a major league record in Game 1 when he appeared in his 78th postseason game, breaking a tie with Reggie Jackson. ... Rivera stretched his postseason scoreless-innings streak to

30²/₃ over 21 appearances, moving him within range of Whitey Ford's major league record of 33. ... The six-run first in Game 5 was the Yankees' biggest inning since September 7, when they scored seven in the ninth at Kansas City.

Quotable:
Athletics: First baseman Jason Giambi, after the A's had routed the Yankees in Game 4 to force the series back to Oakland: "Shoot, we won the division on the last day of the season, we are going to a fifth game. They make movies about this stuff. We are in the middle of a 'Rocky' movie right now."... Game 4 starter Zito, after his first postseason win: "It was an awesome experience. The crowd was great. The fans were loud. I just tried not to get caught up in the hype and throw my pitches. My stuff was working pretty well today."... Manager Howe, after the Game 5 loss: "We let them get a running start on us tonight, that's the difference in the ballgame."

Yankees: Pettitte, after his Game 2 shutout: "We've been down. We've been on a terrible skid. I hope this will get us going. This is a big game for us, obviously. We've really been struggling."... Justice, after watching the young A's self-destruct in Game 3: "We knew we were coming home to our crowd and our crowd could be very overwhelming to the opposing team. I don't think they're afraid. I think they just made a couple of misplays that we took advantage of."... Jeter, after the Game 5 clincher: "A lot of people were trying to say that our run was over, but you're not going to beat us that easily. We're still the champs until someone beats us."

GAME 1 BOX SCORE

OAKLAND 5, NEW YORK 3

TUESDAY, OCTOBER 3, AT OAKLAND

New York	AB	R	H	RBI	PO	A
Knoblauch, dh	4	0	1	0	0	0
Jeter, ss	3	0	0	0	2	3
O'Neill, rf	4	0	0	0	1	1
Williams, cf	4	1	2	0	2	0
Justice, lf	4	0	0	0	2	0
Martinez, 1b	3	0	1	1	7	1
Posada, c	3	1	1	0	6	0
Sojo, 2b	3	1	1	1	2	4
Hill, ph	1	0	0	0	0	0
Brosius, 3b	4	0	1	1	3	1
Clemens, p	0	0	0	0	1	0
Stanton, p	0	0	0	0	0	0
Nelson, p	0	0	0	0	0	0
Totals	33	3	7	3	24	10
Oakland	**AB**	**R**	**H**	**RBI**	**PO**	**A**
Long, cf	4	0	1	0	2	0
Velarde, 2b	3	0	1	1	3	3
Ja. Giambi, 1b	2	0	1	0	9	0
Grieve, lf	3	0	0	0	2	0
Christenson, lf	0	0	0	0	0	0
Tejada, ss	4	1	1	0	1	3
Stairs, rf	4	0	0	0	3	0
Chavez, 3b	4	2	3	1	0	1
Je. Giambi, dh	2	1	1	0	0	0
Saenz, ph-dh	1	0	0	0	0	0
R. Hernandez, c	4	1	2	2	7	0
Heredia, p	0	0	0	0	0	0

Oakland	AB	R	H	RBI	PO	A
Tam, p	0	0	0	0	0	0
Mecir, p	0	0	0	0	0	0
Isringhausen, p	0	0	0	0	0	0
Totals	31	5	10	4	27	7

New York	0	2	0	0	0	1	0 0 0—3
Oakland	0	0	0	0	3	1	0 1 x—5

New York	IP	H	R	ER	BB	SO
Clemens (L)	6.0	7	4	4	4	5
Stanton	1.1	3	1	1	1	0
Nelson	0.2	0	0	0	0	0

Oakland	IP	H	R	ER	BB	SO
Heredia (W)	6.0	7	3	3	1	3
Tam	0.2	0	0	0	0	1
Mecir	1.1	0	0	0	0	1
Isringhausen (S)	1.0	0	0	0	0	2

E—Long, Velarde. DP—New York 2, Oakland 1. LOB—New York 6, Oakland 7. 2B—Williams, Sojo, Brosius, R. Hernandez. SF—Martinez. SB—Velarde, Ja. Giambi. HBP—By Heredia (Jeter). WP—Clemens, Stanton. T—3:16. A—47,360. U—Welke, plate; Meriwether, first; McClelland, second; Schrieber, third; Clark, left field; Nelson, right field.

GAME 2 BOX SCORE

NEW YORK 4, OAKLAND 0

WEDNESDAY, OCTOBER 4, AT OAKLAND

New York	AB	R	H	RBI	PO	A
Jeter, ss	5	0	0	0	0	5
Posada, c	3	0	1	0	3	0
Justice, lf	3	0	0	0	1	0
Bellinger, lf	1	0	1	1	0	0
Williams, cf	5	1	2	0	2	0
Martinez, 1b	4	0	2	0	16	1
O'Neill, rf	2	1	0	0	1	0
Hill, dh	4	1	1	1	0	0
Sojo, 2b	3	0	1	2	3	4
Vizcaino, pr-2b	0	1	0	0	0	1
Brosius, 3b	3	0	0	0	0	5
Pettitte, p	0	0	0	0	0	1
Rivera, p	0	0	0	0	1	0
Totals	33	4	8	4	27	17

Oakland	AB	R	H	RBI	PO	A
Long, cf	4	0	0	0	1	0
Velarde, 2b	3	0	0	0	0	4
Ja. Giambi, 1b	4	0	2	0	12	0
Saenz, dh	4	0	0	0	0	0
Tejada, ss	4	0	2	0	3	2
Grieve, lf	4	0	0	0	0	0
Piatt, rf	3	0	0	0	3	0
Chavez, 3b	3	0	1	0	1	3
R. Hernandez, c	3	0	1	0	7	2
Appier, p	0	0	0	0	0	0
Magnante, p	0	0	0	0	0	0
Tam, p	0	0	0	0	0	0
Jones, p	0	0	0	0	0	0
Totals	32	0	6	0	27	11

New York	0	0	0	0	0	3	0 0 1—4
Oakland	0	0	0	0	0	0	0 0 0—0

New York	IP	H	R	ER	BB	SO
Pettitte (W)	7.2	5	0	0	1	3
Rivera (S)	1.1	1	0	0	0	0

Oakland	IP	H	R	ER	BB	SO
Appier (L)	6.1	6	3	3	5	7
Magnante	1.2	1	0	0	1	1
Tam	0.2	1	1	1	0	0
Jones	0.1	0	0	0	0	0

E—Sojo, Ja. Giambi. DP—New York 2, Oakland 1. LOB—New York 9, Oakland 6. 2B—Posada, Bellinger, Williams, Sojo, Tejada, Chavez, R. Hernandez. SH—Brosius. CS—Williams. T—3:15. A—47,860. U—Meriwether, plate; McClelland, first; Schrieber, second; Clark, third; Nelson, left field; Welke, right field.

GAME 3 BOX SCORE

NEW YORK 4, OAKLAND 2

FRIDAY, OCTOBER 6, AT NEW YORK

Oakland	AB	R	H	RBI	PO	A
Long, cf	4	1	2	1	3	1
Velarde, 2b	4	0	0	0	3	3
Ja. Giambi, 1b	2	0	0	0	7	0
Chavez, 3b	4	0	0	0	1	2
Tejada, ss	3	1	0	0	2	5
Stairs, rf	4	0	0	0	3	0
Grieve, lf	2	0	0	0	0	0
Je. Giambi, dh	4	0	1	1	0	0
R. Hernandez, c	3	0	1	0	5	1
Hudson, p	0	0	0	0	0	1
Totals	30	2	4	2	24	13

New York	AB	R	H	RBI	PO	A
Jeter, ss	4	0	1	2	2	3
Posada, c	4	0	0	0	6	1
Justice, lf	4	0	1	0	3	0
Williams, cf	4	1	1	0	2	0
Martinez, 1b	3	1	1	0	7	0
O'Neill, rf	4	1	1	0	3	0
Hill, dh	3	0	0	1	0	0
Knoblauch, pr-dh	0	0	0	0	0	0
Sojo, 2b	3	1	1	1	2	3
Brosius, 3b	2	0	0	0	2	0
O. Hernandez, p	0	0	0	0	0	0
Rivera, p	0	0	0	0	0	0
Totals	31	4	6	4	27	7

Oakland	0	1	0	0	1	0	0 0 0—2
New York	0	2	0	1	0	0	0 1 x—4

Oakland	IP	H	R	ER	BB	SO
Hudson (L)	8.0	6	4	3	4	5

New York	IP	H	R	ER	BB	SO
O. Hernandez (W)	7.0	4	2	2	5	4
Rivera (S)	2.0	0	0	0	0	1

E—Velarde, R. Hernandez, Martinez. DP—New York 2. LOB—Oakland 6, New York 7. 2B—Williams. HR—Long. CS—Jeter. T—3:12. A—56,606. U—Reilly, plate; Winters, first; Reed, second; Eddings, third; Reliford, left field; Danley, right field.

GAME 4 BOX SCORE

OAKLAND 11, NEW YORK 1

SATURDAY, OCTOBER 7, AT NEW YORK

Oakland	AB	R	H	RBI	PO	A
Long, cf	4	0	0	0	2	0
Velarde, 2b	5	2	1	0	3	2
Menechino, 2b	0	0	0	0	2	0
Ja. Giambi, 1b	2	2	0	0	4	0
Saenz, dh	4	1	2	3	0	0
Piatt, pr-dh	0	1	0	0	0	0
Chavez, 3b	5	2	2	2	0	1
Tejada, ss	4	2	1	1	2	2
Grieve, lf	4	1	2	2	2	0
Porter, rf	1	0	1	1	1	0
Je. Giambi, rf	2	0	1	0	1	0
Christenson, pr-rf-lf	2	0	1	1	2	0
R. Hernandez, c	3	0	0	1	7	0
Zito, p	0	0	0	0	0	0
Mecir, p	0	0	0	0	1	0
Magnante, p	0	0	0	0	0	0
Jones, p	0	0	0	0	0	0
Totals	36	11	11	11	27	5

New York	AB	R	H	RBI	PO	A
Jeter, ss	3	0	2	0	1	2
Sojo, 2b	4	0	0	0	4	7
O'Neill, rf	4	1	1	0	1	0
Williams, cf	3	0	0	0	2	0
Justice, lf	4	0	2	0	1	0
Hill, dh	4	0	0	0	0	0
Posada, c	3	0	1	1	8	0

2000 REVIEW A.L. Division Series

New York	AB	R	H	RBI	PO	A
Polonia, ph	1	0	1	0	0	0
Martinez, 1b	4	0	1	0	8	2
Brosius, 3b	4	0	0	0	0	2
Clemens, p	0	0	0	0	0	2
Stanton, p	0	0	0	0	1	0
Choate, p	0	0	0	0	1	0
Gooden, p	0	0	0	0	0	0
Totals	34	1	8	1	27	15

Oakland 3 0 0 | 0 0 3 | 0 1 4—11
New York 0 0 0 | 0 0 1 | 0 0 0—1

Oakland	IP	H	R	ER	BB	SO
Zito (W)	5.2	7	1	1	2	5
Mecir	1.0	0	0	0	0	0
Magnante	1.1	0	0	0	0	1
Jones	1.0	1	0	0	0	1

New York	IP	H	R	ER	BB	SO
Clemens (L)	*5.0	6	6	6	4	5
Stanton	1.0	1	0	0	0	0
Choate	1.1	0	1	1	1	1
Gooden	1.2	4	4	4	1	1

*Pitched to three batters in sixth.
DP—Oakland 1, New York 1. LOB—Oakland 7, New York 8. 2B—Velarde, Chavez, Tejada, Posada. HR—Saenz. SH—R. Hernandez. SB—Tejada. HBP—By Gooden (Saenz, R. Hernandez). T—3:42. A—56,915. U—Winters, plate; Reed, first; Eddings, second; Reliford, third; Danley, left field; Reilly, right field.

GAME 5 BOX SCORE

NEW YORK 7, OAKLAND 5

SUNDAY, OCTOBER 8, AT OAKLAND

New York	AB	R	H	RBI	PO	A
Knoblauch, dh	5	1	2	1	0	0
Jeter, ss	4	1	1	0	1	2
O'Neill, rf	5	1	2	0	2	0
Williams, cf	4	0	0	1	2	0
Justice, lf	3	2	1	1	3	0
Bellinger, lf	0	0	0	0	0	0
Martinez, 1b	5	1	3	3	7	1
Posada, c	4	1	1	0	11	0
Sojo, 2b	3	0	0	1	0	4
Brosius, 3b	4	0	2	0	0	0
Pettitte, p	0	0	0	0	0	0

New York	AB	R	H	RBI	PO	A
Stanton, p	0	0	0	0	1	0
Nelson, p	0	0	0	0	0	0
O. Hernandez, p	0	0	0	0	0	0
Rivera, p	0	0	0	0	0	0
Totals	37	7	12	7	27	7

Oakland	AB	R	H	RBI	PO	A
Long, cf	3	1	0	0	3	0
Fasano, c	0	0	0	0	1	0
Velarde, 2b	5	0	3	2	0	2
Ja. Giambi, 1b	4	0	1	1	8	0
Saenz, dh	4	0	1	1	0	0
Tejada, ss	5	1	3	0	0	2
Chavez, 3b	5	0	1	1	2	1
Piatt, rf	3	1	1	0	2	0
Je. Giambi, ph-rf	1	0	0	0	0	0
Grieve, lf	4	0	0	0	3	0
R. Hernandez, c	3	2	2	0	8	0
Stairs, ph	1	0	1	0	0	0
Porter, pr-cf	0	0	0	0	0	0
Heredia, p	0	0	0	0	0	0
Tam, p	0	0	0	0	0	0
Appier, p	0	0	0	0	0	1
Mecir, p	0	0	0	0	0	0
Isringhausen, p	0	0	0	0	0	0
Totals	38	5	13	5	27	6

New York 6 0 0 | 1 0 0 | 0 0 0—7
Oakland 0 2 1 | 2 0 0 | 0 0 0—5

New York	IP	H	R	ER	BB	SO
Pettitte	3.2	10	5	5	2	4
Stanton (W)	2.0	1	0	0	0	3
Nelson	1.1	0	0	0	0	2
O. Hernandez	0.1	1	0	0	0	1
Rivera (S)	1.2	1	0	0	0	1

Oakland	IP	H	R	ER	BB	SO
Heredia (L)	0.1	4	6	6	2	0
Tam	0.2	2	0	0	0	0
Appier	4.0	4	1	1	1	6
Mecir	3.0	1	0	0	0	1
Isringhausen	1.0	1	0	0	0	1

LOB—New York 8, Oakland 10. 2B—O'Neill, Martinez 2, Chavez, Stairs. HR—Justice. SF—Williams, Sojo, Ja. Giambi, Saenz. SB—Knoblauch. T—3:50. A—41,170. U—Reed, plate; Eddings, first; Reliford, second; Danley, third; Reilly, left field; Winters, right field.

STATISTICS

NEW YORK YANKEES' BATTING AND FIELDING AVERAGES

Player, position	G	AB	R	H	TB	2B	3B	HR	RBI	BB	IBB	SO	Avg.	PO	A	E	Avg.
Bellinger, lf	2	1	0	1	2	1	0	0	1	0	0	0	1.000	0	0	0	.000
Polonia, ph	1	1	0	1	1	0	0	0	0	0	0	0	1.000	0	0	0	.000
Martinez, 1b	5	19	2	8	10	2	0	0	4	1	0	3	.421	45	5	1	.980
Knoblauch, dh-pr	3	9	1	3	3	0	0	0	1	0	0	2	.333	0	0	0	.000
Williams, cf	5	20	3	5	8	3	0	0	1	1	0	4	.250	10	0	0	1.000
Posada, c	5	17	2	4	6	2	0	0	1	3	1	5	.235	34	1	0	1.000
Justice, lf	5	18	2	4	7	0	0	1	3	3	0	4	.222	10	0	0	1.000
Jeter, ss	5	19	1	4	4	0	0	0	2	2	0	3	.211	6	15	0	1.000
O'Neill, rf	5	19	4	4	5	1	0	0	0	2	1	4	.211	8	1	0	1.000
Sojo, 2b	5	16	2	3	5	2	0	0	5	2	0	1	.188	9	22	1	.969
Brosius, 3b	5	17	0	3	4	1	0	0	1	1	0	4	.176	5	8	0	1.000
Hill, ph-dh	4	12	1	1	1	0	0	0	0	2	1	5	.083	0	0	0	.000
Choate, p	1	0	0	0	0	0	0	0	0	0	0	0	.000	1	0	0	1.000
Clemens, p	2	0	0	0	0	0	0	0	0	0	0	0	.000	1	2	0	1.000
Gooden, p	1	0	0	0	0	0	0	0	0	0	0	0	.000	0	0	0	.000
O. Hernandez, p	2	0	0	0	0	0	0	0	0	0	0	0	.000	0	0	0	.000
Nelson, p	2	0	0	0	0	0	0	0	0	0	0	0	.000	0	0	0	.000
Pettitte, p	2	0	0	0	0	0	0	0	0	0	0	0	.000	0	1	0	1.000
Rivera, p	3	0	0	0	0	0	0	0	0	0	0	0	.000	1	0	0	1.000
Stanton, p	3	0	0	0	0	0	0	0	0	0	0	0	.000	2	0	0	1.000
Vizcaino, pr-2b	1	0	1	0	0	0	0	0	0	0	0	0	.000	0	1	0	1.000
Totals	5	168	19	41	56	12	0	1	19	16	2	35	.244	132	56	2	.989

OAKLAND ATHLETICS' BATTING AND FIELDING AVERAGES

Player, position	G	AB	R	H	TB	2B	3B	HR	RBI	BB	IBB	SO	Avg.	PO	A	E	Avg.
Porter, rf-pr-cf	2	1	0	1	1	0	0	0	1	0	0	0	1.000	1	0	0	1.000
Christenson, lf-pr-rf	2	2	0	1	1	0	0	0	1	0	0	1	.500	2	0	0	1.000
R. Hernandez, c	5	16	3	6	8	2	0	0	3	0	0	3	.375	34	3	1	.974
Tejada, ss	5	20	5	7	9	2	0	0	1	2	0	2	.350	8	14	0	1.000
Chavez, 3b	5	21	4	7	10	3	0	0	4	0	0	5	.333	4	8	0	1.000
Je. Giambi, dh-rf-ph	4	9	1	3	3	0	0	0	1	2	0	2	.333	1	0	0	1.000
Ja. Giambi, 1b	5	14	2	4	4	0	0	0	1	7	1	2	.286	40	0	1	.976
Velarde, 2b	5	20	2	5	6	1	0	0	3	2	0	3	.250	9	14	2	.920
Saenz, ph-dh	4	13	1	3	6	0	0	1	4	0	0	2	.231	0	0	0	.000
Piatt, rf-pr-dh	3	6	2	1	1	0	0	0	0	0	0	1	.167	5	0	0	1.000
Long, cf	5	19	2	3	6	0	0	1	1	3	0	2	.158	11	1	1	.923
Grieve, lf	5	17	1	2	2	0	0	0	2	3	0	7	.118	7	0	0	1.000
Stairs, rf-ph	3	9	0	1	2	1	0	0	0	0	0	1	.111	6	0	0	1.000
Appier, p	2	0	0	0	0	0	0	0	0	0	0	0	.000	0	0	0	.000
Fasano, c	1	0	0	0	0	0	0	0	0	0	0	0	.000	1	0	0	1.000
Heredia, p	2	0	0	0	0	0	0	0	0	0	0	0	.000	0	0	0	.000
Hudson, p	1	0	0	0	0	0	0	0	0	0	0	0	.000	0	1	0	1.000
Isringhausen, p	2	0	0	0	0	0	0	0	0	0	0	0	.000	0	0	0	.000
Jones, p	2	0	0	0	0	0	0	0	0	0	0	0	.000	0	0	0	.000
Magnante, p	2	0	0	0	0	0	0	0	0	0	0	0	.000	0	0	0	.000
Mecir, p	3	0	0	0	0	0	0	0	0	0	0	0	.000	1	1	0	1.000
Menechino, 2b	1	0	0	0	0	0	0	0	0	0	0	0	.000	2	0	0	1.000
Tam, p	3	0	0	0	0	0	0	0	0	0	0	0	.000	0	0	0	.000
Zito, p	1	0	0	0	0	0	0	0	0	0	0	0	.000	0	0	0	.000
Totals	5	167	23	44	59	9	0	2	22	19	1	31	.263	132	42	5	.972

NEW YORK YANKEES' PITCHING RECORDS

Pitcher	G	GS	CG	IP	H	R	ER	HR	BB	IBB	SO	HB	WP	W	L	Pct.	ERA
Rivera	3	0	0	5.0	2	0	0	0	0	0	2	0	0	0	0	.000	0.00
Nelson	2	0	0	2.0	0	0	0	0	0	0	2	0	0	0	0	.000	0.00
Stanton	3	0	0	4.1	5	1	1	0	1	0	3	0	1	1	0	1.000	2.08
O. Hernandez	2	1	0	7.1	5	2	2	1	5	0	5	0	0	1	0	1.000	2.45
Pettitte	2	2	0	11.1	15	5	5	0	3	0	7	0	0	1	0	1.000	3.97
Choate	1	0	0	1.1	0	1	1	0	1	0	1	0	0	0	0	.000	6.75
Clemens	2	2	0	11.0	13	10	10	1	8	1	10	0	1	0	2	.000	8.18
Gooden	1	0	0	1.2	4	4	4	0	1	0	1	2	0	0	0	.000	21.60
Totals	5	5	0	44.0	44	23	23	2	19	1	31	2	2	3	2	.600	4.70

Shutouts—Pettitte and Rivera (combined). Saves—Rivera 3.

OAKLAND ATHLETICS' PITCHING RECORDS

Pitcher	G	GS	CG	IP	H	R	ER	HR	BB	IBB	SO	HB	WP	W	L	Pct.	ERA
Mecir	3	0	0	5.1	1	0	0	0	0	0	2	0	0	0	0	.000	0.00
Magnante	2	0	0	3.0	1	0	0	0	0	0	2	0	0	0	0	.000	0.00
Isringhausen	2	0	0	2.0	1	0	0	0	0	0	3	0	0	0	0	.000	0.00
Tam	3	0	0	2.0	3	1	0	0	1	1	1	0	0	0	0	.000	0.00
Jones	2	0	0	1.1	1	0	0	0	0	0	1	0	0	0	0	.000	0.00
Zito	1	1	0	5.2	7	1	1	0	2	0	5	0	0	1	0	1.000	1.59
Hudson	1	1	1	8.0	6	4	3	0	4	0	5	0	0	0	1	.000	3.38
Appier	2	1	0	10.1	10	4	4	1	6	1	13	0	0	0	1	.000	3.48
Heredia	2	2	0	6.1	11	9	9	0	3	0	3	1	0	1	1	.500	12.79
Totals	5	5	1	44.0	41	19	17	1	16	2	35	1	0	2	3	.400	3.48

No shutouts. Save—Isringhausen.

SCORE BY INNINGS

New York	6	4	0	2	0	5	0	1	1—19
Oakland	3	3	1	2	4	4	0	2	4—23

MISCELLANEOUS STATISTICS

Sacrifice hits—Brosius, R. Hernandez.
Sacrifice flies—Ja. Giambi, Martinez, Saenz, Sojo, Williams.
Stolen bases—Ja. Giambi, Knoblauch, Tejada, Velarde.
Caught stealing—Jeter, Williams.
Double plays—Sojo, Jeter and Martinez 3; Brosius, Sojo and Martinez 2; Tejada, Velarde and Ja. Giambi 2; Brosius (unassisted); Jeter, Sojo and Martinez; Velarde, Tejada and Ja. Giambi.
Left on bases—New York 6, 9, 7, 8, 8—38; Oakland 7, 6, 6, 7, 10—36.
Hit by pitcher—By Gooden 2 (R. Hernandez, Saenz), by Heredia (Jeter).
Passed balls—None.
Balks—None.
Time of games—First game, 3:16; second game, 3:15; third game, 3:12; fourth game, 3:42; fifth game, 3:50.
Attendance—First game, 47,360; second game, 47,860; third game, 56,606; fourth game, 56,915; fifth game, 41,170.
Umpires—Welke, Meriwether, McClelland, Schrieber, Clark, Nelson, Reilly, Winters, Reed, Eddings, Reliford and Danley.
Official scorers—Chuck Dybdal, Red Foley, Bill Shannon.

N.L. DIVISION SERIES
NEW YORK VS. SAN FRANCISCO

The bottom line: The New York Mets, looking for their fourth World Series appearance and third championship, advanced to the National League Championship Series for the first time since 1986 with a surprising three-games-to-one win over the San Francisco Giants. The wild-card Mets dispatched baseball's best regular-season team in dramatic fashion, surviving a ninth-inning Giants rally for a 10-inning win in Game 2 at Pacific Bell Park and prevailing in a 13-inning Game 3 marathon at New York's Shea Stadium. After falling quietly in the first game, the Mets rebounded to hand the Giants their first three-game losing streak since early August and end hopes for their first N.L. pennant since 1989.

Why the Mets won: Pitching and timely hitting were the difference after a 5-1 Game 1 loss. Showing the ability to overcome adversity, the Mets shrugged off a three-run, game-tying, ninth-inning home run by J.T. Snow in Game 3 and prevailed in the 10th on Jay Payton's clutch hit. Then they fought valiantly to win Game 3 on a 13th-inning home run by Benny Agbayani. Over the series' final 18 innings, the Mets bullpen combined with starters Rick Reed and Bobby J. Jones to shut out the high-scoring Giants; over the final two games, the Giants' Big Three of Barry Bonds, Jeff Kent and Ellis Burks were a combined 3-for-15 with no RBIs and one run scored.

The turning points:

Game 1: Any hope the Mets had of winning the first playoff game at new Pac Bell Park was shot down in a long third inning in which the Giants scored four times. Bill Mueller triggered the rally with a two-out single off Mets lefthander Mike Hampton and Bonds, who entered the series with a history of postseason failure, followed with a ground-ball triple into the right field corner, breaking a 1-1 deadlock. Suddenly trailing, Hampton was forced to wait about five minutes as manager Bobby Valentine and the trainer examined right fielder Derek Bell, who sprained his ankle while chasing Bonds' hit. Then, after walking Kent, he had to wait again as Darryl Hamilton replaced Bell. When Burks followed with a line drive off the left field foul pole for a three-run homer, Giants ace Livan Hernandez had all the support he needed to improve his playoff record to 5-0. The Cuban righthander worked 7 2/3 innings and allowed only five hits before turning matters over to Felix Rodriguez and Robb Nen. The 5-1 win was the first in the postseason for Baker, and Hampton suffered his first career loss to the Giants after nine victories.

Game 2: The Mets showed their character in the 10th inning of a critical game, after the Giants had risen from the dead with a shocking game-tying rally in the ninth inning off closer Armando Benitez. Facing the prospect of going down two-games-to-none with no momentum, the New Yorkers scored a 10th-inning run on a two-out double by Hamilton and a run-scoring single by rookie center fielder Jay Payton to claim a 5-4 victory. The Mets had carried a 2-1 lead into the ninth behind the pitching of left-hander Al Leiter and they stretched their margin on Edgardo Alfonzo's two-run homer. But the Giants sent the Pac Bell Park faithful into a towel-waving frenzy in the bottom of the ninth when they tied the game on a shocking three-run homer by Snow—his first career pinch-hit home run. After the Mets had regained the lead in the top of the 10th, veteran lefty John Franco came on to record his first career post-season save in the bottom of the inning.

Game 3: If Game 2 was the momentum shifter, this one was the backbreaker. The Mets treated 56,270 Shea Stadium fans to an exhausting and emotional 3-2 victory in a game that lasted 5 hours and 22 minutes before left fielder Agbayani drove an Aaron Fultz pitch over the left-center field fence in the bottom of the 13th inning. The Mets' second straight dramatic win was made possible by the outstanding work of starter Rick Reed, who allowed two runs in six innings, and five relievers, who allowed only four hits over seven shutout frames. After the Mets had tied the game in the eighth on Alfonzo's RBI double off dependable Giants closer Nen, both teams squandered good scoring opportunities before the Mets finally broke through. The Giants' leadoff hitter reached base in the ninth, 10th and 12th innings; the Mets had runners in scoring position in the ninth and 11th. The Giants missed on a chance in the top of the 13th when winning pitcher Rick White retired Bonds on a popup with two runners on base. Agbayani, 0-for-5 before the home run, ended the marathon moments later against Fultz, the Giants' sixth pitcher.

Game 4: This one belonged to Bobby J. Jones—and a raucous Shea Stadium crowd that cheered every pitch of his 4-0 Division Series masterpiece. Jones, confusing the Giants with his 84-mph fastballs and big-breaking curves, pitched the first one-hit shutout in postseason play since 1967 and gave the Mets a berth in the NLCS opposite the St. Louis Cardinals. Jones, who had been demoted to Class AAA Tidewater earlier in the season, retired the Giants in eight of his nine innings and allowed only a fifth-inning double by Kent—a line drive that ticked the top of leaping third baseman Robin

Ventura's glove. That fifth inning was Jones' moment of truth as he retired opposing pitcher Mark Gardner on a popup with the bases loaded after surrendering Kent's hit and two walks. The Mets gave Jones all the support he needed with Ventura's two-run homer in the first and a two-run, fifth-inning double by Alfonzo.

Notable:

Giants: After bashing their way through the regular season with a San Francisco-record 925 runs and a franchise-record 226 home runs, the Giants managed only 11 runs and two homers against the Mets. ... Bonds continued his disappointing play with a .176 series average and one RBI. Kent batted .375, but he, too, drove in only one run. ... To add insult to injury, Bonds made the final out in all three Mets wins. ... Before Game 1, two-time Manager of the Year Dusty Baker had never managed a post-season victory. His 1997 Giants were swept in the Division Series by the eventual World Series-champion Florida Marlins.

Mets: The Mets became only the second N.L. team in the six years of Division Series play to lose the first game and still advance to the NLCS. ... In Game 1, the Giants threesome of Bonds, Kent and Burks were 4-for-9 with five RBIs. They combined for eight hits and one RBI in the other three games. ... In his three starts after taking over in right field for the injured Bell, Timo Perez collected five hits and drove in three runs from the leadoff spot in the Mets lineup. He also played well defensively. ... Jones' one-hit series clincher came on the 44th anniversary of Don Larsen's World Series perfect game at Yankee Stadium.

Quotable:

Giants: Bonds, after watching Hernandez post his Game 1 win: "Livan was phenomenal. He's been doing it for us now for quite awhile. You've got to go with your big dog in the big games, and that's him.".... Baker, on his controversial Game 4 decision not to pinch hit for pitcher Gardner with the bases loaded and the Mets leading 2-0 in the fifth inning: "I don't regret the decision. We were short on pitching and it was only the fifth inning. It was too early to pinch hit. I figured we'd get some more runs."

Mets: Backup outfielder Hamilton, after the Mets had coughed up a ninth-inning Game 2 lead and recovered in the 10th for a dramatic win: "Stuff like this seems to happen to the Mets. Last year, you always wondered what crazy thing was going to happen next. It's hard on the fans and it's hard on us, (but) it's great when we win." ... Valentine, after the 13th-inning win in Game 3: "Brilliant finish, gutted it out. Everyone did their little parts.".... Catcher Mike Piazza on Jones in Game 4: "Just textbook pitching. He really knew how to work the hitters. As the game wore on, he just got tougher and tougher."

GAME 1 BOX SCORE

SAN FRANCISCO 5, NEW YORK 1

WEDNESDAY, OCTOBER 4, AT SAN FRANCISCO

New York	AB	R	H	RBI	PO	A
Agbayani, lf	3	0	1	0	3	0
Cook, p	0	0	0	0	0	0
White, p	0	0	0	0	0	1
McEwing, lf	0	0	0	0	0	0
Harris, ph	1	0	0	0	0	0
Payton, cf	3	0	0	1	0	0
Alfonzo, 2b	4	0	1	0	1	3
Piazza, c	3	0	0	0	7	0
Ventura, 3b	4	0	0	0	1	1
Zeile, 1b	3	0	1	0	7	2
Bell, rf	1	0	0	0	0	0
Hamilton, rf-lf	2	0	0	0	0	0
Rusch, p	0	0	0	0	0	0
Bordick, ss	3	1	1	0	2	3
Hampton, p	2	0	1	0	3	0
Wendell, p	0	0	0	0	0	0
Perez, ph-rf	2	0	0	0	0	0
Totals	31	1	5	1	24	10

San Francisco	AB	R	H	RBI	PO	A
Benard, cf	4	0	0	0	5	0
Davis, ph	1	0	0	0	0	0
Nen, p	0	0	0	0	0	0
Mueller, 3b	5	2	2	0	2	0
Bonds, lf	3	1	2	1	3	0
Kent, 2b	3	1	1	1	2	2
Burks, rf	3	1	1	3	2	0
Aurilia, ss	4	0	2	0	2	2
Snow, 1b	3	0	1	0	5	0
Estalella, c	4	0	0	0	6	0
Hernandez, p	3	0	0	0	0	0
Rodriguez, p	0	0	0	0	0	0
Crespo, ph	1	0	1	0	0	0
Murray, cf	0	0	0	0	0	0
Totals	34	5	10	5	27	4

New York	0	0 1		0 0 0		0 0	0—1
San Francisco	1	0 4		0 0 0		0 0	x—5

New York	IP	H	R	ER	BB	SO
Hampton (L)	5.1	6	5	5	3	2
Wendell	0.2	0	0	0	0	2
Cook	0.2	0	0	0	1	1
White	0.2	4	0	0	1	0
Rusch	0.2	0	0	0	0	2

San Francisco	IP	H	R	ER	BB	SO
Hernandez (W)	7.2	5	1	1	5	5
Rodriguez	0.1	0	0	0	0	1
Nen	1.0	0	0	0	0	0

LOB—New York 9, San Francisco 9. 2B—Zeile, Mueller, Aurilia. 3B—Bonds. HR—Burks. SF—Payton. SB—Bonds. T—3:06. A—40,430. U—Kellogg, home; Cederstrom, first; Montague, second; Morrison, third; Young, left field; Barrett, right field.

GAME 2 BOX SCORE

NEW YORK 5, SAN FRANCISCO 4 (10 INNINGS)

THURSDAY, OCTOBER 5, AT SAN FRANCISCO

New York	AB	R	H	RBI	PO	A
Perez, rf	5	1	3	2	2	0
Alfonzo, 2b	5	1	1	2	2	0
Piazza, c	4	0	2	0	8	0
Zeile, 1b	5	0	0	0	5	0
Ventura, 3b	3	0	0	0	5	1
Agbayani, lf	2	0	1	0	3	0
McEwing, pr-lf	0	0	0	0	0	0
Hamilton, ph-lf	1	1	1	0	0	0
Payton, cf	5	1	1	1	2	0
Bordick, ss	4	1	1	0	3	4
Leiter, p	4	0	0	0	0	1
Benitez, p	0	0	0	0	0	0
J. Franco, p	0	0	0	0	0	1
Totals	38	5	10	5	30	7

San Francisco	AB	R	H	RBI	PO	A
Murray, cf	4	0	1	0	3	0
Benard, ph	0	0	0	0	0	0
Mueller, 3b	5	0	1	0	0	3
Bonds, lf	5	1	1	0	1	0
Kent, 1b-2b	4	2	2	0	6	3
Burks, rf	3	0	1	1	2	0
Martinez, 2b	3	0	0	0	3	5
Snow, ph-1b	1	1	1	3	1	0
Aurilia, ss	4	0	0	0	3	3
Estalella, c	4	0	0	0	9	1
Estes, p	0	0	0	0	1	0
Rueter, p	0	0	0	0	1	0
Henry, p	0	0	0	0	0	0
Crespo, ph	1	0	0	0	0	0
Rodriguez, p	0	0	0	0	0	0
Rios, ph	1	0	1	0	0	0
Totals	35	4	8	4	30	15

New York	0	2	0		0	0	0		0	0	2	1—5
San Francisco	0	1	0		0	0	0		0	0	3	0—4

New York	IP	H	R	ER	BB	SO
Leiter	*8.0	5	2	2	3	6
Benitez (W)	†1.0	3	2	2	0	0
J. Franco (S)	1.0	0	0	0	0	1

San Francisco	IP	H	R	ER	BB	SO
Estes	3.0	3	2	2	3	3
Rueter	4.1	3	0	0	1	1
Henry	0.2	0	0	0	1	0
Rodriguez (L)	2.0	4	3	3	0	3

*Pitched to one batter in ninth.
†Pitched to one batter in 10th.
DP—New York 1, San Francisco 2. LOB—New York 9, San Francisco 5. 2B—Piazza, Hamilton, Bonds, Burks. HR—Snow, Alfonzo. SH—Benard. SB—Kent. HBP—By Estes (Ventura). T—3:41. A—40,430. U—Cederstrom, plate; Montague, first; Morrison, second; Young, third; Barrett, left field; Kellogg, right field.

GAME 3 BOX SCORE

NEW YORK 3, SAN FRANCISCO 2 (13 INNINGS)

SATURDAY, OCTOBER 7, AT NEW YORK

San Francisco	AB	R	H	RBI	PO	A
Benard, cf-rf	6	0	1	1	4	0
Mueller, 3b	6	0	2	0	0	1
Bonds, lf	5	0	0	0	4	0
Kent, 2b	6	0	2	0	1	6
Burks, rf	4	1	1	0	5	0
Fultz, p	0	0	0	0	0	0
Snow, 1b	4	0	2	0	9	0
Aurilia, ss	4	0	0	0	4	4
Nen, p	0	0	0	0	0	0
Rios, ph	1	0	0	0	0	0
Mirabelli, c	1	0	0	0	2	0
Estalella, c	4	1	1	1	8	1
Crespo, ph	1	0	0	0	0	0
Rodriguez, p	0	0	0	0	0	0
Murray, cf	1	0	0	0	0	0
Ortiz, p	3	0	0	0	0	0
Embree, p	0	0	0	0	0	0
Henry, p	0	0	0	0	0	0
Martinez, ss	3	0	2	0	0	2
Totals	49	2	11	2	37	14

New York	AB	R	H	RBI	PO	A
Perez, rf	6	0	1	1	5	0
Alfonzo, 2b	5	0	2	1	2	0
Piazza, c	4	0	1	0	12	1
McEwing, pr-3b	1	0	1	0	0	0
Ventura, 3b-1b	5	0	1	0	1	3
Agbayani, lf	6	1	1	1	2	0
Payton, cf	5	0	1	0	4	0
Zeile, 1b	3	0	0	0	7	1
White, p	0	0	0	0	0	0
Bordick, ss	2	1	0	0	2	2
Benitez, p	0	0	0	0	0	0
Pratt, ph-c	1	0	0	0	4	0
Reed, p	1	0	0	0	0	1
Hamilton, ph	1	0	1	0	0	0
Cook, p	0	0	0	0	0	0

New York	AB	R	H	RBI	PO	A
Wendell, p	0	0	0	0	0	0
Harris, ph	1	1	0	0	0	0
J. Franco, p	0	0	0	0	0	0
Abbott, ss	2	0	0	0	0	0
Totals	43	3	9	3	39	8

San Francisco	0	0	0		2	0	0		0	0	0	0	0	0—2
New York	0	0	0		0	0	1		0	1	0	0	0	1—3

One out when winning run scored.

San Francisco	IP	H	R	ER	BB	SO
Ortiz	5.1	2	1	1	4	4
Embree	0.2	0	0	0	0	0
Henry	1.2	0	1	1	0	1
Nen	1.1	2	0	0	1	3
Rodriguez	2.0	2	0	0	1	2
Fultz (L)	1.1	3	1	1	0	0

New York	IP	H	R	ER	BB	SO
Reed	6.0	7	2	2	2	6
Cook	0.2	0	0	0	1	0
Wendell	1.1	0	0	0	1	3
J. Franco	1.0	1	0	0	0	1
Benitez	2.0	1	0	0	1	3
White (W)	2.0	2	0	0	0	0

DP—San Francisco 2. LOB—San Francisco 16, New York 10. 2B—Mueller, Alfonzo. HR—Agbayani. SH—Mueller. SB—Payton, Harris. CS—Alfonzo. HBP—By Henry (Bordick). T—5:22. A—56,270. U—Crawford, plate; Gorman, first; Roe, second; DiMuro, third; Rieker, left field; Craft, right field.

GAME 4 BOX SCORE

NEW YORK 4, SAN FRANCISCO 0

SUNDAY, OCTOBER 8, AT NEW YORK

San Francisco	AB	R	H	RBI	PO	A
Benard, cf	4	0	0	0	3	0
Mueller, 3b	4	0	0	0	1	1
Bonds, lf	4	0	0	0	2	0
Kent, 2b	3	0	1	0	0	2
Burks, rf	3	0	0	0	3	0
Snow, 1b	2	0	0	0	8	0
Aurilia, ss	3	0	0	0	1	2
Mirabelli, c	1	0	0	0	4	1
Crespo, ph	1	0	0	0	0	0
Del Toro, p	0	0	0	0	0	0
Gardner, p	2	0	0	0	0	1
Henry, p	0	0	0	0	0	0
Embree, p	0	0	0	0	0	0
Davis, p	0	0	0	0	0	0
Estalella, c	0	0	0	0	2	0
Totals	28	0	1	0	24	7

New York	AB	R	H	RBI	PO	A
Perez, rf	4	1	1	0	3	0
Alfonzo, 2b	4	0	1	2	1	4
Piazza, c	3	1	0	0	5	1
Ventura, 3b	2	1	1	2	0	1
Agbayani, lf	4	0	2	0	2	0
McEwing, pr-lf	0	0	0	0	0	0
Payton, cf	4	0	1	0	4	0
Zeile, 1b	3	0	0	0	11	0
Bordick, ss	3	0	0	0	0	1
B.J. Jones, p	4	1	0	0	1	0
Totals	31	4	6	4	27	8

San Francisco	0	0	0		0	0	0		0	0	0—0
New York	2	0	0		0	2	0		0	0	x—4

San Francisco	IP	H	R	ER	BB	SO
Gardner (L)	4.1	4	4	4	2	5
Henry	1.2	1	0	0	2	0
Embree	1.0	0	0	0	0	0
Del Toro	1.0	1	0	0	0	2

New York	IP	H	R	ER	BB	SO
B.J. Jones (W)	9.0	1	0	0	2	5

E—Aurilia. LOB—San Francisco 3, New York 8. 2B—Kent, Perez, Alfonzo, Agbayani. HR—Ventura. SB—Perez. CS—Payton. HBP—By Del Toro (Bordick). WP—Gardner. T—2:48. A—52,888. U—Gorman, plate; Roe, first; DiMuro, second; Rieker, third; Craft, left field; Crawford, right field.

NEW YORK METS' BATTING AND FIELDING AVERAGES

Player, position	G	AB	R	H	TB	2B	3B	HR	RBI	BB	IBB	SO	Avg.	PO	A	E	Avg.
McEwing, lf-pr-3b	4	1	0	1	1	0	0	0	0	0	0	0	1.000	0	0	0	.000
Hamilton, rf-lf-ph	3	4	1	2	3	1	0	0	0	1	0	1	.500	0	0	0	.000
Hampton, p	1	2	0	1	1	0	0	0	0	0	0	1	.500	3	0	0	1.000
Agbayani, lf	4	15	1	5	9	1	0	1	1	3	0	3	.333	10	0	0	1.000
Perez, ph-rf	4	17	2	5	6	1	0	0	3	0	0	2	.294	10	0	0	1.000
Alfonzo, 2b	4	18	1	5	10	2	0	1	5	1	0	2	.278	6	7	0	1.000
Piazza, c	4	14	1	3	4	1	0	0	0	4	1	3	.214	32	2	0	1.000
Payton, cf	4	17	1	3	3	0	0	0	2	0	0	4	.176	10	0	0	1.000
Bordick, ss	4	12	3	2	2	0	0	0	0	3	0	4	.167	7	10	0	1.000
Ventura, 3b-1b	4	14	1	2	5	0	0	1	2	4	1	1	.143	7	6	0	1.000
Zeile, 1b	4	14	0	1	2	1	0	0	0	4	0	3	.071	30	4	0	1.000
Benitez, p	2	0	0	0	0	0	0	0	0	0	0	0	.000	0	0	0	.000
Cook, p	2	0	0	0	0	0	0	0	0	0	0	0	.000	0	0	0	.000
J. Franco, p	2	0	0	0	0	0	0	0	0	0	0	0	.000	0	1	0	1.000
Rusch, p	1	0	0	0	0	0	0	0	0	0	0	0	.000	0	0	0	.000
Wendell, p	2	0	0	0	0	0	0	0	0	0	0	0	.000	0	0	0	.000
White, p	2	0	0	0	0	0	0	0	0	0	0	0	.000	0	1	0	1.000
Bell, rf	1	1	0	0	0	0	0	0	0	0	0	0	.000	0	0	0	.000
Pratt, ph-c	1	1	0	0	0	0	0	0	0	0	0	0	.000	4	0	0	1.000
Reed, p	1	1	0	0	0	0	0	0	0	0	0	0	.000	0	1	0	1.000
Abbott, ss	1	2	0	0	0	0	0	0	0	0	0	1	.000	0	0	0	.000
Harris, ph	2	2	1	0	0	0	0	0	0	0	0	0	.000	0	0	0	.000
B.J. Jones, p	1	4	1	0	0	0	0	0	0	0	0	3	.000	1	0	0	1.000
Leiter, p	1	4	0	0	0	0	0	0	0	0	0	2	.000	0	1	0	1.000
Totals	4	143	13	30	46	7	0	3	13	20	2	30	.210	120	33	0	1.000

SAN FRANCISCO GIANTS' BATTING AND FIELDING AVERAGES

Player, position	G	AB	R	H	TB	2B	3B	HR	RBI	BB	IBB	SO	Avg.	PO	A	E	Avg.
Rios, ph	2	2	0	1	1	0	0	0	0	0	0	0	.500	0	0	0	.000
Snow, 1b-ph	4	10	1	4	7	0	0	1	3	4	2	1	.400	23	0	0	1.000
Kent, 2b-1b	4	16	3	6	7	1	0	0	1	1	0	3	.375	9	13	0	1.000
Martinez, 2b-ss	2	6	0	2	2	0	0	0	0	0	0	2	.333	3	7	0	1.000
Mueller, 3b	4	20	2	5	7	2	0	0	0	0	0	4	.250	3	5	0	1.000
Crespo, ph	4	4	0	1	1	0	0	0	0	0	0	0	.250	0	0	0	.000
Burks, rf	4	13	2	3	7	1	0	1	4	4	0	2	.231	12	0	0	1.000
Murray, cf	3	5	0	1	1	0	0	0	0	0	0	3	.200	3	0	0	1.000
Bonds, lf	4	17	2	3	6	1	1	0	1	3	1	4	.176	10	0	0	1.000
Aurilia, ss	4	15	0	2	3	1	0	0	0	0	0	3	.133	10	11	1	.955
Estalella, c	4	12	1	1	1	0	0	0	1	0	0	2	.083	25	2	0	1.000
Benard, cf-ph-rf	4	14	0	1	1	0	0	0	1	1	0	7	.071	12	0	0	1.000
Del Toro, p	1	0	0	0	0	0	0	0	0	0	0	0	.000	0	0	0	.000
Embree, p	2	0	0	0	0	0	0	0	0	0	0	0	.000	0	0	0	.000
Estes, p	1	0	0	0	0	0	0	0	0	1	0	0	.000	1	0	0	1.000
Fultz, p	1	0	0	0	0	0	0	0	0	0	0	0	.000	0	0	0	.000
Henry, p	3	0	0	0	0	0	0	0	0	0	0	0	.000	0	0	0	.000
Nen, p	2	0	0	0	0	0	0	0	0	0	0	0	.000	0	0	0	.000
Rodriguez, p	3	0	0	0	0	0	0	0	0	0	0	0	.000	0	0	0	.000
Rueter, p	1	0	0	0	0	0	0	0	0	1	0	0	.000	1	0	0	1.000
Davis, ph	2	2	0	0	0	0	0	0	0	0	0	1	.000	0	0	0	.000
Mirabelli, c	2	2	0	0	0	0	0	0	0	1	0	1	.000	6	1	0	1.000
Gardner, p	1	2	0	0	0	0	0	0	0	0	0	1	.000	0	1	0	1.000
Hernandez, p	1	3	0	0	0	0	0	0	0	0	0	1	.000	0	0	0	.000
Ortiz, p	1	3	0	0	0	0	0	0	0	0	0	1	.000	0	0	0	.000
Totals	4	146	11	30	44	6	1	2	11	16	3	36	.205	118	40	1	.994

NEW YORK METS' PITCHING RECORDS

Pitcher	G	GS	CG	IP	H	R	ER	HR	BB	IBB	SO	HB	WP	W	L	Pct.	ERA
B.J. Jones	1	1	1	9.0	1	0	0	0	2	0	5	0	0	1	0	1.000	0.00
White	2	0	0	2.2	6	0	0	0	2	0	4	0	0	1	0	1.000	0.00
J. Franco	2	0	0	2.0	1	0	0	0	0	0	2	0	0	0	0	.000	0.00
Wendell	2	0	0	2.0	0	0	0	0	1	0	5	0	0	0	0	.000	0.00
Cook	2	0	0	1.1	0	0	0	0	2	0	1	0	0	0	0	.000	0.00

Pitcher	G	GS	CG	IP	H	R	ER	HR	BB	IBB	SO	HB	WP	W	L	Pct.	ERA
Rusch	1	0	0	0.2	0	0	0	0	0	0	2	0	0	0	0	.000	0.00
Leiter	1	1	0	8.0	5	2	2	0	3	0	6	0	0	0	0	.000	2.25
Reed	1	1	0	6.0	7	2	2	0	2	1	6	0	0	0	0	.000	3.00
Benitez	2	0	0	3.0	4	2	2	1	1	1	3	0	0	1	0	1.000	6.00
Hampton	1	1	0	5.1	6	5	5	1	3	1	2	0	0	0	1	.000	8.44
Totals	4	4	1	40.0	30	11	11	2	16	3	36	0	0	3	1	.750	2.48

Shutout—B.J. Jones. Save—J. Franco.

SAN FRANCISCO GIANTS' PITCHING RECORDS

Pitcher	G	GS	CG	IP	H	R	ER	HR	BB	IBB	SO	HB	WP	W	L	Pct.	ERA
Rueter	1	0	0	4.1	3	0	0	1	0	1	1	0	0	0	0	.000	0.00
Nen	2	0	0	2.1	2	0	0	1	0	0	3	0	0	0	0	.000	0.00
Embree	2	0	0	1.2	0	0	0	0	0	0	0	0	0	0	0	.000	0.00
Del Toro	1	0	0	1.0	1	0	0	0	0	0	2	1	0	0	0	.000	0.00
Hernandez	1	1	0	7.2	5	1	1	0	5	0	5	0	0	1	0	1.000	1.17
Ortiz	1	1	0	5.1	2	1	1	0	4	1	4	0	0	0	0	.000	1.69
Henry	3	0	0	4.0	1	1	1	0	3	1	1	1	0	0	0	.000	2.25
Estes	1	1	0	3.0	3	2	2	0	3	0	3	1	0	0	0	.000	6.00
Rodriguez	3	0	0	4.1	6	3	3	1	1	0	6	0	0	0	1	.000	6.23
Fultz	1	0	0	1.1	3	1	1	1	0	0	0	0	0	0	1	.000	6.75
Gardner	1	1	0	4.1	4	4	4	1	2	0	5	0	1	0	1	.000	8.31
Totals	4	4	0	39.1	30	13	13	3	20	2	30	3	1	1	3	.250	2.97

No shutouts or saves.

SCORE BY INNINGS

New York	2	2	1		0	2	1		0	1	2		1	0	0	1—13
San Francisco	1	1	4		2	0	0		0	0	3		0	0	0	0—11

MISCELLANEOUS STATISTICS

Sacrifice hits—Benard, Mueller.
Sacrifice fly—Payton.
Stolen bases—Bonds, Harris, Kent, Payton, Perez.
Caught stealing—Alfonzo, Payton.
Double plays—Bordick and Zeile; Estalella and Aurilia; Estalella, Aurilia and Martinez; Kent, Aurilia and Snow; Martinez, Aurilia and Kent.
Left on bases—New York 9, 9, 10, 8—36; San Francisco 9, 5, 16, 3—33.
Hit by pitcher—By Del Toro (Bordick), by Estes (Ventura) by Henry (Bordick).
Passed balls—None.
Balks—None.
Time of games—First game, 3:06; second game, 3:41; third game, 5:22; fourth game, 2:48.
Attendance—First game, 40,430; second game, 40,430; third game, 56,270; fourth game, 52,888.
Umpires—Kellogg, Cederstrom, Montague, Morrison, Young, Barrett, Crawford, Gorman, Roe, DiMuro, Rieker and Craft.
Official scorers—Joe Donnelly, Dick O'Connor.

ST. LOUIS VS. ATLANTA

HIGHLIGHTS

The bottom line: In a shocking reversal of form, the St. Louis Cardinals swept past the "Team of the '90s" and snapped the Braves' unprecedented string of NLCS appearances at eight. The opportunistic Cardinals dominated their playoff-seasoned opponents in a three-game blitz that rocked one of the game's outstanding pitching staffs for 24 runs and avenged a 1996 NLCS loss to the Braves. The Cardinals pounded away with the big bat of center fielder Jim Edmonds, who was 8-of-14 with two home runs, seven RBIs and a Division Series-record four doubles, and they kept Atlanta hitters at bay with a sterling effort from their normally suspect bullpen. The Braves, who compiled a 15-2 Division Series record and made five World Series appearances in the 1990s, saw their playoff losing streak stretch to seven games—four straight to the Yankees in the 1999 fall classic and three to the Cardinals.

Why the Cardinals won: They showed a quick-strike ability that put two of the game's top pitchers in a hole from which they could not recover. Righthander Greg Maddux, a four-time Cy Young Award winner who posted a 19-9 regular-season record, was rocked for six first-inning runs in the opener at Busch Stadium and 21-game winner Tom Glavine, a two-time Cy Young winner, surrendered seven runs over the first three innings of Game 2. While Edmonds and his Cardinals teammates were pounding the Braves with their bats, relievers Britt Reames, Mike James, Matt Morris and Dave Veres were providing timely interference in relief of shaky Cardinals starters.

The turning points:

Game 1: The opener was decided in the first inning on five singles, two Braves errors and a misplayed fly ball. Before Maddux could even catch his breath, the Braves were trailing 6-0 and the series pattern had been set. An error by third baseman Chipper Jones on Ray Lankford's grounder and a throwing error by catcher Paul Bako contributed to the onslaught, which was a lot worse than it should have been. The Cardinals were thankful for the generosity when 21-year-old Rick Ankiel, a surprise Game 1 starter, self-destructed and allowed the Braves to crawl back into the game. Ankiel, a left-hander who was 3-0 with a 1.65 ERA over his last five regular-season starts, gave up four third-inning runs while walking four batters and throwing a modern major league-record five wild pitches in a bizarre breakdown that gave new meaning to the term "wild." Not only did Ankiel start missing the strike zone, he bounced several pitches past catcher Carlos Hernandez and fired others well over his head, off the backstop. Ankiel was replaced by James, who combined with Mike Timlin, Reames and Veres to allow only one run over the final 6⅓ innings. The Cardinals' 7-5 victory was punctuated by Edmonds' fourth-inning home run off Maddux.

Game 2: This, too, was decided in the bottom of the first inning. The Braves, shaken by their first-game collapse, jumped on 20-game winner Darryl Kile for two quick runs on Chipper Jones' RBI single and a groundout by Brian Jordan, temporarily quieting the expectant Busch Stadium crowd. But the Cardinals responded in the bottom of the inning on Fernando Vina's leadoff single, a walk to Edmonds and a dramatic home run by first baseman Will Clark. Having surrendered his early advantage, Glavine surrendered a solo home run to catcher Hernandez in the second and a two-run double to Lankford in a three-run third. When Glavine was relieved by Andy Ashby with one out in the third, it marked his shortest outing since 1993 and his worst postseason start since the 1992 NLCS against Pittsburgh. Kile did not surrender another run while working seven innings in the Cardinals' eventual 10-4 win and Mark McGwire, relegated to pinch-hit duty because of a sore knee, provided the coup de grace with an eighth-inning homer that sent the crowd into ecstasy. Edmonds continued his torrid assault with three doubles, a Division Series single-game record.

Game 3: The turning point for the Cardinals was as easy as 1-2-3. Second baseman Vina, the setup man for St. Louis' offense, provided the "1" on the game's second pitch when he muscled up on a Kevin Millwood fastball and hit a shocking home run. Edmonds took care of the "2" in the third inning, launching a pitch from Millwood 418 feet over the right field wall for a two-run homer, breaking a 1-1 tie. Vina's two-run single highlighted a three-run sixth inning that destroyed any hopes for a Braves comeback. Again the Cardinals' bullpen stepped front and center in relief of Garrett Stephenson, who had to leave the game in the fourth inning with a

stiff elbow. Reames, James, Morris and Veres finished off a three-hitter that left long-spoiled Atlanta fans scratching their heads.

Notable:

Braves: Payback was not so sweet for the Braves, many of whom could remember their comeback from a three-games-to-one deficit to beat the Cardinals in the 1996 NLCS. Atlanta outscored St. Louis, 32-1, over the final three games of that series. ... After five straight Division Series wins, the Braves failed to reach the NLCS for the first time since 1990. ... Atlanta's playoff failure was a continuation of a late regular-season collapse. The Braves lost four of their last five games and a season-ending ninth-inning loss to Colorado cost them home-field advantage in the first round of the playoffs. ... A less-than-capacity crowd of 49,898 in Game 3, the only contest at Turner Field, included many red-clad Cardinals fans. ... The one bright spot for Millwood was his success against Clark, who struck out and popped up against him in Game 3. Entering the game, Clark was 5-for-8 with four career home runs against the righthander.

Cardinals: The underdog Cardinals outscored the Braves 24-10, outhit them .275-.189 and out-homered them 6-1. ... The Cardinals have never lost a game in a best-of-five series, sweeping the Braves in 1982, the Padres in 1996 and the Braves in 2000. ... The Cardinals were 6-for-12 against Game 2 starter Tom Glavine, who had finished the regular season with 14 consecutive scoreless innings. ... Edmonds punctuated his Game 2 performance with a spectacular over-the-shoulder warning-track catch on a drive hit by Braves shortstop Rafael Furcal. ... The Cardinals committed only one error in the three-game series. The Braves committed five.

Quotable:

Braves: Chipper Jones, on the error-filled first inning that allowed the Cardinals to take a 6-0 lead in Game 1: "I'd like to get a do-over on that first inning. We were like the Bad News Bears out there. We have nobody to blame but ourselves for this loss." ... Pitching coach Leo Mazzone, after watching Maddux and Glavine get manhandled in Games 1 and 2: "It's hard to believe what you're seeing with the way these two games have gone. We're so spoiled with the great pitching we've had over the years."

Cardinals: Catcher Hernandez, when asked if he could have caught any of Ankiel's wild pitches in Game 1: "A couple of them were too high. If I'm Superman, maybe. But I don't think I can fly." ... Clark, on the Cardinals' in-your-face offensive approach: "It was awesome. It was a special series because we took it to 'em. There was no fear, there was no hesitation. We took it to 'em and beat 'em."

GAME 1 BOX SCORE

ST. LOUIS 7, ATLANTA 5

TUESDAY, OCTOBER 3, AT ST. LOUIS

Atlanta	AB	R	H	RBI	PO	A
Furcal, 2b-ss	5	0	1	0	1	1
A. Jones, cf	2	2	0	0	2	0
C. Jones, 3b	4	0	1	0	2	2
Galarraga, 1b	2	1	0	0	8	1
Jordan, rf	4	1	3	2	3	0
Sanders, lf	4	0	0	0	3	0
Weiss, ss	3	0	2	2	2	1
Bonilla, ph	1	0	0	0	0	0
Lockhart, 2b	1	0	0	0	0	1
Bako, c	0	0	0	0	0	0
Lopez, ph-c	4	0	0	0	3	0
Maddux, p	1	1	0	0	0	2
Remlinger, p	0	0	0	0	0	0
Joyner, ph	1	0	1	0	0	0
Mulholland, p	0	0	0	0	0	0
Surhoff, ph	1	0	0	0	0	0
Rocker, p	0	0	0	0	0	0
Ligtenberg, p	0	0	0	0	0	0
Totals	33	5	8	4	24	8

St. Louis	AB	R	H	RBI	PO	A
Vina, 2b	5	1	1	0	3	4
Drew, rf	4	1	1	0	0	0
Edmonds, cf	5	2	3	2	1	0
Clark, 1b	5	1	1	1	8	2
Lankford, lf	3	1	0	1	1	0
Reames, p	0	0	0	0	2	0
McGwire, ph	0	0	0	0	0	0
Kile, pr	0	0	0	0	0	0
Veres, p	0	0	0	0	0	0
Renteria, ss	2	0	0	0	3	2
Hernandez, c	3	1	1	0	7	2
Polanco, 3b	4	0	3	2	0	1
Ankiel, p	1	0	0	0	0	0
James, p	1	0	0	0	1	0
Dunston, ph	1	0	1	0	0	0
Timlin, p	0	0	0	0	0	0
Paquette, lf	1	0	0	0	0	0
Totals	35	7	11	6	27	11

Atlanta	0	0	4	0	0	0	0	0	1	—5
St. Louis	6	0	0	1	0	0	0	0	x	—7

Atlanta	IP	H	R	ER	BB	SO
Maddux (L)	4.0	9	7	5	3	2
Remlinger	1.0	2	0	0	0	1
Mulholland	2.0	0	0	0	1	0
Rocker	0.2	0	0	0	1	0
Ligtenberg	0.1	0	0	0	1	0

St. Louis	IP	H	R	ER	BB	SO
Ankiel	2.2	4	4	4	6	3
James (W)	2.1	1	0	0	1	0
Timlin	*1.0	2	0	0	1	1
Reames	2.0	0	0	0	1	0
Veres (S)	1.0	1	1	0	0	2

*Pitched to two batters in seventh.

E—C. Jones, Bako, Rocker, Renteria. DP—St. Louis 1. LOB—Atlanta 11, St. Louis 11. 2B—Jordan, Weiss, Joyner. HR—Edmonds. SH—Renteria. SB—Drew, Edmonds. CS—Furcal, A. Jones. HBP—By Veres (Galarraga). WP—Ankiel 5. T—3:34. A—52,378. U—Rieker, plate; Craft, first; Crawford, second; Gorman, third; Roe, left field; DiMuro, right field.

GAME 2 BOX SCORE

ST. LOUIS 10, ATLANTA 4

THURSDAY, OCTOBER 5, AT ST. LOUIS

Atlanta	AB	R	H	RBI	PO	A
Furcal, ss	4	1	0	0	1	5
A. Jones, cf	3	1	1	1	3	0
C. Jones, 3b	4	2	2	1	0	1
Galarraga, 1b	4	0	1	0	11	0
Jordan, rf	4	0	1	2	1	0
Lopez, c	4	0	0	0	7	0
Sanders, lf	4	0	0	0	0	0
Lockhart, 2b	4	0	1	0	1	4
Glavine, p	1	0	0	0	0	0
Ashby, p	0	0	0	0	0	0
Surhoff, ph	1	0	1	0	0	0
Maddux, pr	0	0	0	0	0	0
Burkett, p	0	0	0	0	0	0
Mulholland, p	0	0	0	0	0	0
Joyner, ph	1	0	0	0	0	0
Ligtenberg, p	0	0	0	0	0	0
Remlinger, p	0	0	0	0	0	0
Bonilla, ph	0	0	0	0	0	0
Totals	34	4	7	4	24	11

St. Louis	AB	R	H	RBI	PO	A
Vina, 2b	4	1	0	0	1	6
Renteria, ss	4	3	1	0	1	0
Edmonds, cf	4	2	3	3	4	0
Clark, 1b	2	2	1	3	10	0
Davis, rf	3	0	0	1	0	0
Lankford, lf	4	0	1	2	4	0
Hernandez, c	4	1	1	1	7	0
Polanco, 3b	3	0	0	0	0	3
Kile, p	3	0	0	0	0	1
Christiansen, p	0	0	0	0	0	0
Timlin, p	0	0	0	0	0	0
McGwire, ph	1	1	1	1	0	0
Morris, p	0	0	0	0	0	0
Totals	32	10	9	10	27	10

Atlanta	2	0	0	0	0	0	0	2	0	—4
St. Louis	3	1	3	1	0	1	0	1	x	—10

Atlanta	IP	H	R	ER	BB	SO
Glavine (L)	2.1	6	7	7	1	2
Ashby	1.2	1	1	1	3	2
Burkett	1.1	1	1	1	0	0
Mulholland	0.2	0	0	0	0	0
Ligtenberg	1.0	0	0	0	0	2
Remlinger	1.0	1	1	1	0	1

St. Louis	IP	H	R	ER	BB	SO
Kile (W)	7.0	4	2	2	2	6
Christiansen	0.1	0	0	0	0	0
Timlin	0.2	3	2	2	0	1
Morris	1.0	0	0	0	0	1

E—Furcal. LOB—Atlanta 6, St. Louis 5. 2B—C. Jones, Galarraga, Edmonds 3, Lankford, Clark. HR—McGwire, A. Jones, Hernandez, Clark. SF—Davis. SB—Renteria. HBP—By Burkett (Vina), by Glavine (Clark). WP—Ashby. T—3:02. A—52,389. U—Craft, plate; Crawford, first; Gorman, second; Roe, third; DiMuro, left field; Rieker, right field.

GAME 3 BOX SCORE

ST. LOUIS 7, ATLANTA 1

SATURDAY, OCTOBER 7, AT ATLANTA

St. Louis	AB	R	H	RBI	PO	A
Vina, 2b	4	1	2	3	3	3
Renteria, ss	4	2	1	0	2	2
Edmonds, cf	5	1	2	3	2	0
Clark, 1b	5	0	1	0	8	0
Lankford, lf	3	1	1	0	3	0
Hernandez, c	4	1	1	0	6	2
Drew, rf	2	0	0	0	2	0
Polanco, 3b	3	1	0	1	1	1
Paquette, 3b	1	0	0	0	0	0
Stephenson, p	1	0	0	0	0	0
Reames, p	1	0	0	0	0	0
Davis, ph	1	0	0	0	0	0
James, p	0	0	0	0	0	0
McGwire, ph	1	0	0	0	0	0
Morris, p	0	0	0	0	0	0
Veres, p	0	0	0	0	0	0
Totals	35	7	8	7	27	8

Atlanta	AB	R	H	RBI	PO	A
Furcal, ss	2	1	0	0	1	5
A. Jones, cf	4	0	0	0	3	0
C. Jones, 3b	4	0	1	0	1	2
Galarraga, 1b	4	0	1	1	7	0
Lopez, c	3	0	1	0	5	1
Bako, c	1	0	0	0	4	0

Atlanta	AB	R	H	RBI	PO	A
Jordan, rf	3	0	0	0	2	0
Sanders, lf	1	0	0	0	1	0
Mulholland, p	0	0	0	0	0	0
Ligtenberg, p	0	0	0	0	0	0
Remlinger, p	0	0	0	0	0	0
Joyner, ph	1	0	0	0	0	0
Ashby, p	0	0	0	0	0	0
Lockhart, 2b	3	0	0	0	3	1
Millwood, p	1	0	0	0	0	0
Bonilla, lf	1	0	0	0	0	0
Totals	28	1	3	1	27	9

St. Louis	1	0 2	0 1 3	0 0	0—7
Atlanta	1	0 0	0 0 0	0 0	0—1

St. Louis	IP	H	R	ER	BB	SO
Stephenson	3.2	3	1	1	2	2
Reames (W)	1.1	0	0	0	2	1
James	2.0	0	0	0	0	1
Morris	1.0	0	0	0	0	0
Veres	1.0	0	0	0	0	2

Atlanta	IP	H	R	ER	BB	SO
Millwood (L)	4.2	4	4	4	3	3
Mulholland	0.2	2	2	2	1	1
Ligtenberg	0.1	0	1	1	0	1
Remlinger	1.1	3	0	0	0	1
Ashby	2.0	0	0	0	0	3

E—C. Jones. DP—St. Louis 2. LOB—St. Louis 6, Atlanta 4. 2B—Edmonds. HR—Vina, Edmonds. SH—Drew. SB—Renteria, Drew, Polanco, Furcal. CS—Vina, Lopez. Balk—Millwood. T—3:09. A—49,898. U—Montague, plate; Morrison, first; Young, second; Barrett, third; Kellogg, left field; Cederstrom, right field.

STATISTICS

ST. LOUIS CARDINALS' BATTING AND FIELDING AVERAGES

Player, position	G	AB	R	H	TB	2B	3B	HR	RBI	BB	IBB	SO	Avg.	PO	A	E	Avg.
Dunston, ph	1	1	0	1	1	0	0	0	0	0	0	0	1.000	0	0	0	.000
Edmonds, cf	3	14	5	8	18	4	0	2	7	1	0	2	.571	7	0	0	1.000
McGwire, ph	3	2	1	1	4	0	0	1	1	1	1	0	.500	0	0	0	.000
Vina, 2b	3	13	3	4	7	0	0	1	3	1	0	1	.308	7	13	0	1.000
Polanco, 3b	3	10	1	3	3	0	0	0	3	1	0	0	.300	1	5	0	1.000
Hernandez, c	3	11	3	3	6	0	0	1	1	1	1	2	.273	20	4	0	1.000
Clark, 1b	3	12	3	3	6	0	0	1	4	1	1	3	.250	26	2	0	1.000
Lankford, lf	3	10	2	2	3	1	0	0	3	2	1	5	.200	8	0	0	1.000
Renteria, ss	3	10	5	2	2	0	0	0	0	4	0	1	.200	6	4	1	.909
Drew, rf	2	6	1	1	1	0	0	0	0	2	0	1	.167	2	0	0	1.000
Christiansen, p	1	0	0	0	0	0	0	0	0	0	0	0	.000	0	0	0	.000
Morris, p	2	0	0	0	0	0	0	0	0	0	0	0	.000	0	0	0	.000
Timlin, p	2	0	0	0	0	0	0	0	0	0	0	0	.000	0	0	0	.000
Veres, p	2	0	0	0	0	0	0	0	0	0	0	0	.000	0	0	0	.000
Ankiel, p	1	1	0	0	0	0	0	0	0	0	0	0	.000	0	0	0	.000
James, p	2	1	0	0	0	0	0	0	0	0	0	1	.000	0	0	0	.000
Reames, p	2	1	0	0	0	0	0	0	0	0	0	0	.000	2	0	0	1.000
Stephenson, p	1	1	0	0	0	0	0	0	0	0	0	0	.000	0	0	0	.000
Paquette, lf-3b	2	2	0	0	0	0	0	0	0	0	0	0	.000	2	0	0	1.000
Kile, pr-p	2	3	0	0	0	0	0	0	0	0	0	1	.000	0	1	0	1.000
Davis, rf-ph	2	4	0	0	0	0	0	0	1	0	0	2	.000	0	0	0	.000
Totals	3	102	24	28	51	5	0	6	23	14	5	19	.275	81	29	1	.991

ATLANTA BRAVES' BATTING AND FIELDING AVERAGES

Player, position	G	AB	R	H	TB	2B	3B	HR	RBI	BB	IBB	SO	Avg.	PO	A	E	Avg.
Weiss, ss	1	3	0	2	3	1	0	0	2	0	0	0	.667	2	1	0	1.000
Surhoff, ph	2	2	0	1	1	0	0	0	0	0	0	0	.500	0	0	0	.000
Jordan, rf	3	11	1	4	5	1	0	0	4	1	0	1	.364	6	0	0	1.000
C. Jones, 3b	3	12	2	4	5	1	0	0	1	1	0	4	.333	3	5	2	.800
Joyner, ph	3	3	0	1	2	1	0	0	0	0	0	0	.333	0	0	0	.000
Galarraga, 1b	3	10	1	2	3	1	0	0	1	2	0	4	.200	26	1	0	1.000
Lockhart, 2b	3	8	0	1	1	0	0	0	0	0	0	1	.125	4	6	0	1.000
A. Jones, cf	3	9	3	1	4	0	0	1	1	4	0	1	.111	8	0	0	1.000
Furcal, 2b-ss	3	11	2	1	1	0	0	0	0	3	0	0	.091	3	11	1	.933
Lopez, ph-c	3	11	0	1	1	0	0	0	0	0	0	1	.091	15	2	0	1.000
Ashby, p	2	0	0	0	0	0	0	0	0	0	0	0	.000	0	0	0	.000
Burkett, p	1	0	0	0	0	0	0	0	0	0	0	0	.000	0	0	0	.000
Ligtenberg, p	3	0	0	0	0	0	0	0	0	0	0	0	.000	0	0	0	.000
Mulholland, p	3	0	0	0	0	0	0	0	0	0	0	0	.000	0	0	0	.000
Remlinger, p	3	0	0	0	0	0	0	0	0	0	0	0	.000	0	0	0	.000
Rocker, p	1	0	0	0	0	0	0	0	0	0	0	0	.000	0	0	1	.000
Bako, c	2	1	0	0	0	0	0	0	0	0	0	1	.000	4	0	1	.800
Glavine, p	1	1	0	0	0	0	0	0	0	0	0	1	.000	0	0	0	.000
Maddux, p-pr	2	1	1	0	0	0	0	0	0	1	0	0	.000	0	2	0	1.000
Millwood, p	1	1	0	0	0	0	0	0	0	0	0	1	.000	0	0	0	.000
Bonilla, ph-lf	3	2	0	0	0	0	0	0	0	2	0	0	.000	0	0	0	.000
Sanders, lf	3	9	0	0	0	0	0	0	0	2	0	5	.000	4	0	0	1.000
Totals	3	95	10	18	26	5	0	1	9	16	0	20	.189	75	28	5	.954

ST. LOUIS CARDINALS' PITCHING RECORDS

Pitcher	G	GS	CG	IP	H	R	ER	HR	BB	IBB	SO	HB	WP	W	L	Pct.	ERA
James	2	0	0	4.1	1	0	0	0	1	0	1	0	0	1	0	1.000	0.00
Reames	2	0	0	3.1	0	0	0	0	3	0	2	0	0	1	0	1.000	0.00
Morris	2	0	0	2.0	0	0	0	0	1	0	0	0	0	0	0	.000	0.00
Veres	2	0	0	2.0	1	1	0	0	0	0	4	1	0	0	0	.000	0.00
Christiansen	1	0	0	0.1	0	0	0	0	0	0	0	0	0	0	0	.000	0.00
Stephenson	1	1	0	3.2	3	1	1	0	2	0	2	0	0	0	0	.000	2.45
Kile	1	1	0	7.0	4	2	2	0	2	0	6	0	0	1	0	1.000	2.57
Timlin	2	0	0	1.2	5	2	2	1	1	0	2	0	0	0	0	.000	10.80
Ankiel	1	1	0	2.2	4	4	4	0	6	0	3	0	5	0	0	.000	13.50
Totals	3	3	0	27.0	18	10	9	1	16	0	20	1	5	3	0	1.000	3.00

No shutouts. Save—Veres.

ATLANTA BRAVES' PITCHING RECORDS

Pitcher	G	GS	CG	IP	H	R	ER	HR	BB	IBB	SO	HB	WP	W	L	Pct.	ERA
Rocker	1	0	0	0.2	0	0	0	0	1	0	0	0	0	0	0	.000	0.00
Ashby	2	0	0	3.2	1	1	1	0	3	2	5	0	1	0	0	.000	2.45
Remlinger	3	0	0	3.1	6	1	1	1	0	0	3	0	0	0	0	.000	2.70
Mulholland	3	0	0	3.1	1	2	2	0	2	0	1	0	0	0	0	.000	5.40
Ligtenberg	3	0	0	1.2	0	1	1	0	1	1	3	0	0	0	0	.000	5.40
Burkett	1	0	0	1.1	1	1	1	0	0	0	0	1	0	0	0	.000	6.75
Millwood	1	1	0	4.2	4	4	4	2	3	0	3	0	0	0	1	.000	7.71
Maddux	1	1	0	4.0	9	7	5	1	3	2	2	0	0	0	1	.000	11.25
Glavine	1	1	0	2.1	6	7	7	2	1	0	2	1	0	0	1	.000	27.00
Totals	3	3	0	25.0	28	24	22	6	14	5	19	2	1	0	3	.000	7.92

No shutouts or saves.

SCORE BY INNINGS

St. Louis	10	1	5		2	1	4		0	2	3—24
Atlanta	3	0	4		0	0	0		0	2	1—10

MISCELLANEOUS STATISTICS

Sacrifice hits—Drew, Renteria.
Sacrifice fly—Davis.
Stolen bases—Drew 2, Renteria 2, Edmonds, Furcal, Polanco.
Caught stealing—Furcal, A. Jones, Lopez, Vina.
Double plays—Hernandez and Vina; Renteria and Vina; Vina and Clark.
Left on bases—St. Louis 11, 5, 6—22; Atlanta 11, 6, 4—21.
Hit by pitcher—By Burkett (Vina), by Glavine (Clark), by Veres (Galarraga).
Passed balls—None.
Balk—Millwood.
Time of games—First game, 3:34; second game, 3:02; third game, 3:09.
Attendance—First game, 52,378; second game, 52,389; third game, 49,898.
Umpires—Rieker, Craft, Crawford, Gorman, Roe, DiMuro, Montague, Morrison, Young, Barrett, Kellogg and Cederstrom.
Official scorers—Jeff Durbin, Mike Stamus.

2000 REVIEW N.L. Division Series

A.L. CHAMPIONSHIP SERIES

HIGHLIGHTS

The bottom line: The Yankees, shaking off the cobwebs of a late-season slump, claimed their third straight A.L. pennant and joined the cross-town Mets in an all-New York World Series—the first Subway Series in 44 years. The six-game ALCS win over the Seattle Mariners gave New York a fall classic monopoly for the first time since 1956, when the Yankees defeated the Brooklyn Dodgers. The Bronx Bombers became the first team since the 1988-90 Oakland Athletics to win three straight pennants and they extended their record pennant total to 37. The Mariners were trying to win their first pennant in their third postseason appearance. If they had succeeded, baseball would have had its first wild-card World Series—the Mariners vs. the Mets—and a trans-continental nightmare.

Why the Yankees won: Because of starting pitchers Orlando Hernandez, Andy Pettitte and Roger Clemens, who revived the Yankees after a Game 1 loss at Yankee Stadium. That trio held the hot-hitting Mariners to three runs over the next three games as the New Yorkers took control with 7-1, 8-2 and 5-0 wins—two of them at Seattle's Safeco Field. The Yankees also brushed off their late-season doldrums (15 losses in the last 18 games; seven straight losses to end the season) and showed the character that had allowed them to win 22 of their last 25 postseason games entering the 2000 playoffs. As the suddenly-rejuvenated offense began delivering in clutch situations, the Yankees began looking more and more like a baseball machine rolling toward a third consecutive championship.

The turning points:

Game 1: For Freddy Garcia, the moment of truth came in the sixth inning when he was faced with a two-on, nobody-out situation while protecting a 2-0 lead. Manager Lou Piniella trudged to the mound and the sellout Yankee Stadium crowd braced for a pitching change. But Piniella decided to stay with his 24-year-old righthander and he wasn't sorry. Garcia struck out Paul O'Neill and Bernie Williams and retired David Justice on a long fly ball. Garcia went on to work 6²/₃ innings of three-hit ball and relievers Jose Paniagua, Arthur Rhodes and Kazuhiro Sasaki held the Yankees scoreless the rest of the way. It was deja vu for the veteran Yankees, who continued their late-season funk with an 0-for-8 effort with runners in scoring position. The Mariners touched tough-luck loser Denny Neagle for Rickey Henderson's RBI single in the fifth and Alex Rodriguez's solo home run an inning later.

Game 2: Trailing 1-0 entering the bottom of the eighth and in danger of going down two games to none, the Yankees' dormant offense finally exploded. Justice greeted reliever Rhodes with a leadoff double, setting the stage for cleanup hitter Bernie Williams. The Yankees were 0-for-5 in the game and 0-for-13 in the series with runners in scoring position when Williams slapped a single to center, scoring Justice and tying the game. The Yankees would go on to collect eight consecutive hits (an LCS single-inning record) and score seven runs—two on Derek Jeter's home run. As the crowd of 55,317 roared, Mariano Rivera came out of the bullpen to close out Hernandez's seventh straight postseason victory. El Duque, pitching on his birthday, worked eight six-hit innings, allowing only one run on Stan Javier's third-inning single. The Mariners wasted a six-inning scoreless outing by New York-born left-hander John Halama.

Game 3: The Yankees took control of the series in the second inning of this game, when Bernie Williams and Tino Martinez hit back-to-back solo home runs to wipe out a 1-0 deficit. Suddenly that old Yankee strut was back—and so was the sense that the Bronx Bombers' title ship was back on course. Pettitte, who lifted his postseason record to 8-4, wasn't exactly overpowering in the 8-2 victory, but he spread out nine hits over 6²/₃ innings and limited the Mariners to solo runs in the first and fifth. Jeff Nelson and Rivera were perfect in relief. Of special note for the Yankees were a sixth-inning RBI single by O'Neill, who had been 0-for-8 in the series and 4-for-27 without an RBI in the postseason, and the continued hot hitting of Justice, who drove in three runs with a double and single.

Game 4: Unsuccessful through most of his postseason career, Clemens blew away the Mariners in one of the most dominating playoff performances in history. Attacking hitters relentlessly with his 97 mph fastball, The Rocket allowed only one hit, struck out 15 and posted a 5-0 victory that lifted the Yankees to within one win of the pennant. And he did it with his usual menacing edge. After retiring the first two Mariners in the first inning, Clemens buzzed Seattle star Rodriguez with two chin-high fastballs that angered the Mariners dugout and prompted Seattle starter Paul Abbott to respond with a second-inning pitch near the head of Yankees catcher Jorge Posada. Clemens walked Rodriguez and the only hit was Al Martin's line-drive double in the seventh inning—a ball that tipped off the glove of leaping first baseman Tino Martinez. The Yankees got a three-run, fifth-inning homer from Jeter and a two-run, eighth-inning shot from Justice to account for all the scoring.

Game 5: Trailing 2-1 in the fifth inning and facing elimination, the Mariners blitzed Yankees starter

Denny Neagle and reliever Nelson for five runs and went on to record a 6-2 victory that forced the series back to New York. The uprising started with a Mark McLemore bunt single and Neagle departed with runners on second and third with one out. Rodriguez greeted Nelson with a two-run single and Edgar Martinez and John Olerud followed with home runs. The beneficiary of the uprising was Garcia, who worked five strong innings to earn his second win of the series.

Game 6: Down 4-3 in the seventh inning and facing the prospect of having to play a seventh game, the Yankees got a dramatic three-run homer from Justice in a six-run outburst that keyed a 9-7 pennant-clinching victory. Yankee Stadium went into a delirious frenzy when Justice drove a Rhodes pitch high into the upper-deck and the celebration really started moments later when O'Neill added a two-run single and Jose Vizcaino added a sacrifice fly. Orlando Hernandez was far from his usual playoff self, but he struggled through seven innings and became the first pitcher to go 8-0 in the postseason. The Mariners scored two first-inning runs off El Duque and stretched their lead to 4-0 in the fourth on Carlos Guillen's upper-deck home run, but the Yankees fought back with three in the fourth and broke it open in the seventh. Rodriguez, possibly playing his final game in a Mariners uniform, collected four hits, including a solo eighth-inning home run.

Notable:

Mariners: When the Yankees broke through for seven eighth-inning runs in Game 2, they snapped a string of 15 scoreless innings by the Seattle bullpen in the playoffs. ... Game 3 loser Aaron Sele saw his postseason record drop to 0-3. ... Entering the playoffs, the Mariners had lost to Clemens 21 times—his most wins over any team. The 15 strikeouts Clemens recorded in Game 4 were a nine-inning LCS record. ... Before scoring five runs in the fifth inning of Game 5, the Mariners were batting .180 against Yankee pitching in the series. ... Dan Wilson's single to right in the fifth inning of Game 6 snapped a record 42-at-bat postseason hitless streak.

Yankees: Before erupting for seven runs in the eighth inning of Game 2, the Yankees had suffered through a 21-inning postseason scoreless streak. ... When closer Mariano Rivera worked 1 2/3 innings to save Game 3, he broke the consecutive-innings postseason record held by former Yankee Whitey Ford. Rivera lifted his streak to 33 1/3 innings, one-third more than Ford. Rivera's streak was snapped in Game 6. ... The Yankees stranded an ALCS-record 15 runners in Game 5. ... Before Game 6, Hernandez had never allowed more than three earned runs in a postseason game.

Quotable:

Mariners: Rodriguez, after the Mariners had defeated the Yankees in Game 1: "We have to attack them, attack them early and be ready to go to war. They're going to come out real hungry and be ready to go to war tomorrow."... Piniella, after his Mariners had forced a Game 6 at New York: "All of the pressure is on them. They are supposed to win and they are going home. The onus is on them."... McLemore, when asked how he felt when the Mariners had a 4-0 Game 6 lead: "The bottom line is they scored more runs than we did. It doesn't matter if we started off 15-0."

Yankees: Nelson, after watching Garcia and three relievers stop the Yankees 2-0 in Game 1: "If they pitch like they pitched tonight, then we're not going to win the series."... Manager Joe Torre, after watching his team snap a scoring slump with seven eighth-inning runs in Game 2: "It was just a great relief for us to score the runs. I just sense we relieved a lot of pressure today."... Clemens, after his Game 4 masterpiece: "Tonight was special. The ball was jumping out of my hand."... Justice, after his Game 6 home run: "It was magical. It was unbelievable when I rounded the bases, to see this place erupt."

GAME 1 BOX SCORE

SEATTLE 2, NEW YORK 0

TUESDAY, OCTOBER 10, AT NEW YORK

Seattle	AB	R	H	RBI	PO	A
Henderson, lf	2	0	1	1	0	0
Ibanez, lf-rf	1	0	0	0	1	0
Cameron, cf	4	0	0	0	5	0
Rodriguez, ss	3	1	1	1	1	1
E. Martinez, dh	4	0	0	0	0	0
Olerud, 1b	4	0	0	0	6	1
Buhner, rf	3	0	0	0	0	0
Gipson, lf	0	0	0	0	0	0
Oliver, c	3	0	0	0	13	0
Bell, 3b	4	0	2	0	0	2
McLemore, 2b	4	1	1	0	0	3
Garcia, p	0	0	0	0	1	1
Paniagua, p	0	0	0	0	0	0
Rhodes, p	0	0	0	0	0	0
Sasaki, p	0	0	0	0	0	0
Totals	32	2	5	2	27	8

New York	AB	R	H	RBI	PO	A
Knoblauch, dh	4	0	2	0	0	0
Jeter, ss	3	0	0	0	2	2
O'Neill, rf	3	0	0	0	1	0
Hill, ph	1	0	0	0	0	0
Bellinger, lf	0	0	0	0	0	0
Williams, cf	4	0	1	0	3	0
Justice, lf-rf	4	0	0	0	2	0
T. Martinez, 1b	4	0	1	0	5	0
Vizcaino, pr	0	0	0	0	0	0
Posada, c	2	0	0	0	10	1
Sojo, 2b	4	0	2	0	4	3
Brosius, 3b	3	0	0	0	0	0
Neagle, p	0	0	0	0	0	1
Nelson, p	0	0	0	0	0	0
Choate, p	0	0	0	0	0	0
Grimsley, p	0	0	0	0	0	0
Totals	32	0	6	0	27	7

Seattle	0	0	0		0	1	1		0	0	0—2
New York	0	0	0		0	0	0		0	0	0—0

Seattle	IP	H	R	ER	BB	SO
Garcia (W)	6.2	3	0	0	2	8
Paniagua	1.0	1	0	0	0	3
Rhodes	0.1	0	0	0	0	1
Sasaki (S)	1.0	2	0	0	0	1

New York	IP	H	R	ER	BB	SO
Neagle (L)	5.2	3	2	2	3	3
Nelson	2.1	1	0	0	0	4
Choate	0.1	0	0	0	0	1
Grimsley	0.2	1	0	0	0	1

E—Brosius. DP—Seattle 1, New York 1. LOB—Seattle 7, New York 8. 2B—McLemore, Knoblauch. HR—Rodriguez. CS—Henderson. HBP—by Garcia (Posada). T—3:45. A—54,481. U—J. Hirschbeck, plate; Hernandez, first; Bell, second; M. Hirschbeck, third; Davis, left field; Marsh, right field.

GAME 2 BOX SCORE

NEW YORK 7, SEATTLE 1

WEDNESDAY, OCTOBER 11, AT NEW YORK

Seattle	AB	R	H	RBI	PO	A
Cameron, cf	3	1	0	0	3	0
Javier, rf	4	0	1	1	1	0
Rodriguez, ss	4	0	1	0	0	1
E. Martinez, dh	3	0	1	0	0	0
Olerud, 1b	4	0	2	0	11	1
Martin, lf	3	0	1	0	2	0
Bell, 3b	4	0	0	0	1	2
Wilson, c	3	0	0	0	4	3
Ibanez, ph	1	0	0	0	0	0
McLemore, 2b	3	0	1	0	1	4
Halama, p	0	0	0	0	1	2
Paniagua, p	0	0	0	0	0	0
Rhodes, p	0	0	0	0	0	0
Mesa, p	0	0	0	0	0	0
Totals	32	1	7	1	24	13

New York	AB	R	H	RBI	PO	A
Knoblauch, dh	4	1	2	1	0	0
Jeter, ss	4	1	2	2	2	2
Justice, lf	4	1	1	0	2	0
Williams, cf	4	1	1	1	2	0
T. Martinez, 1b	4	1	3	0	8	1
Posada, c	4	0	1	1	8	0
O'Neill, rf	3	0	0	1	2	0
Sojo, 2b-3b	4	1	1	0	0	2
Brosius, 3b	3	0	2	0	1	1
Vizcaino, pr-2b	1	1	1	1	0	1
Hernandez, p	0	0	0	0	1	1
Rivera, p	0	0	0	0	1	1
Totals	35	7	14	7	27	9

Seattle	0 0 1	0 0 0	0 0 0—1
New York	0 0 0	0 0 0	0 7 x—7

Seattle	IP	H	R	ER	BB	SO
Halama	6.0	5	0	0	3	2
Paniagua	1.0	1	0	0	0	1
Rhodes (L)	0.1	4	3	3	0	0
Mesa	0.2	4	4	4	0	0

New York	IP	H	R	ER	BB	SO
Hernandez (W)	8.0	6	1	1	3	7
Rivera	1.0	1	0	0	0	0

E—McLemore, Wilson. DP—Seattle 1, New York 2. LOB—Seattle 7, New York 8). 2B—Olerud, Martin, McLemore, Knoblauch, Justice, Vizcaino. HR—Jeter. SF—O'Neill. SB—Cameron, Vizcaino. CS—Posada. PB—Wilson. T—3:36. A—55,317. U—Hernandez, plate; Bell, first; M. Hirschbeck, second; Davis, third; Marsh, left field; J. Hirschbeck, right field.

GAME 3 BOX SCORE

NEW YORK 8, SEATTLE 2

FRIDAY, OCTOBER 13, AT SEATTLE

New York	AB	R	H	RBI	PO	A
Knoblauch, dh	5	1	2	1	0	0
Jeter, ss	4	2	1	0	3	3
Justice, lf	5	0	2	3	2	0
Bellinger, pr-lf	0	0	0	0	0	0
Williams, cf	4	2	3	2	3	0
T. Martinez, 1b	5	1	2	1	12	0
Posada, c	4	0	0	0	4	1
O'Neill, rf	4	0	1	1	1	0
Sojo, 2b	4	0	1	0	1	2
Vizcaino, pr-2b	0	1	0	0	0	1
Brosius, 3b	3	1	1	0	1	3
Pettitte, p	0	0	0	0	0	1
Nelson, p	0	0	0	0	0	0
Rivera, p	0	0	0	0	0	0
Totals	38	8	13	8	27	11

Seattle	AB	R	H	RBI	PO	A
Henderson, lf	4	1	1	0	2	0
Cameron, cf	4	1	2	1	1	0
Rodriguez, ss	4	0	2	0	3	2
E. Martinez, dh	4	0	2	1	0	0
Buhner, rf	3	0	0	0	4	0
Javier, ph-rf	1	0	0	0	0	0
Olerud, 1b	4	0	1	0	6	3
Bell, 3b	3	0	1	0	1	0
Martin, ph	1	0	0	0	0	0
Oliver, c	3	0	1	0	7	1
Ibanez, ph	1	0	0	0	0	0
McLemore, 2b	2	0	0	0	1	5
Sele, p	0	0	0	0	0	0
Tomko, p	0	0	0	0	2	0
Ramsay, p	0	0	0	0	0	0
Totals	34	2	10	2	27	11

New York	0 2 1	0 0 1	0 0 4—8
Seattle	1 0 0	0 1 0	0 0 0—2

New York	IP	H	R	ER	BB	SO
Pettitte (W)	6.2	9	2	2	1	2
Nelson	0.2	1	0	0	0	2
Rivera (S)	1.2	0	0	0	0	0

Seattle	IP	H	R	ER	BB	SO
Sele (L)	*6.0	9	4	4	0	4
Tomko	2.1	3	4	4	2	3
Ramsay	0.2	1	0	0	0	0

*Pitched to one batter in seventh.

E—McLemore. DP—New York 1, Seattle 1. LOB—New York 6, Seattle 7. 2B—Justice, Henderson. HR—Williams, T. Martinez. SH—McLemore. SF—Williams. SB—Vizcaino, Rodriguez. CS—Brosius. WP—Tomko. T—3:35. A—47,827. U—M. Hirschbeck, plate; Bell, first; Davis, second; J. Hirschbeck, third; Hernandez, left field; Culbreth, right field.

GAME 4 BOX SCORE

NEW YORK 5, SEATTLE 0

SATURDAY, OCTOBER 14, AT SEATTLE

New York	AB	R	H	RBI	PO	A
Knoblauch, dh	3	1	0	0	0	0
Jeter, ss	3	2	1	3	1	3
Justice, lf	3	1	1	2	1	0
Bellinger, lf	0	0	0	0	1	0
Williams, cf	4	0	1	0	0	0
T. Martinez, 1b	4	0	0	0	4	2
Posada, c	3	0	0	0	15	0
O'Neill, rf	4	0	1	0	1	0
Sojo, 2b	4	0	0	0	1	0
Brosius, 3b	4	1	1	0	1	0
Clemens, p	0	0	0	0	2	0
Totals	32	5	5	5	27	5

Seattle	AB	R	H	RBI	PO	A
Javier, rf	4	0	0	0	2	0
Martin, lf	4	0	1	0	6	0
Rodriguez, ss	3	0	0	0	3	0
E. Martinez, dh	3	0	0	0	0	0
Olerud, 1b	2	0	0	0	5	0
Cameron, cf	3	0	0	0	5	0
Guillen, 3b	3	0	0	0	0	2
Bell, 2b	3	0	0	0	2	2
Wilson, c	2	0	0	0	4	0
Ibanez, ph	1	0	0	0	0	0
Oliver, c	0	0	0	0	0	1
Abbott, p	0	0	0	0	0	0
Ramsay, p	0	0	0	0	0	0
Mesa, p	0	0	0	0	0	0
Paniagua, p	0	0	0	0	0	0
Totals	28	0	1	0	27	5

New York	0 0 0	0 3 0	0 2 0—5
Seattle	0 0 0	0 0 0	0 0 0—0

New York	IP	H	R	ER	BB	SO
Clemens (W)	9.0	1	0	0	2	15

Seattle	IP	H	R	ER	BB	SO
Abbott (L)	5.0	3	3	3	3	3
Ramsay	1.0	0	0	0	0	1
Mesa	2.0	1	2	2	1	0
Paniagua	1.0	0	0	0	0	0

LOB—New York 4, Seattle 3. 2B—Martin. HR—Jeter, Justice. SB—Williams. T—2:59. A—47,803. U—Bell, plate; Davis, first; J. Hirschbeck, second; Hernandez, third; Culbreth, left field; M. Hirschbeck, right field.

GAME 5 BOX SCORE

SEATTLE 6, NEW YORK 2

SUNDAY, OCTOBER 15, AT SEATTLE

New York	AB	R	H	RBI	PO	A
Knoblauch, dh	4	0	0	0	0	0
Jeter, ss	4	0	2	0	0	2
Justice, lf-rf	5	0	0	0	0	0
Williams, cf	3	0	1	0	4	0
T. Martinez, 1b	4	1	1	0	11	1
Posada, c	3	1	1	0	5	0
O'Neill, rf	2	0	0	0	1	0
Hill, ph	1	0	0	0	0	0
Bellinger, lf	1	0	0	0	0	0
Sojo, 2b	5	0	2	2	3	6
Brosius, 3b	3	0	0	0	0	2
Neagle, p	0	0	0	0	0	0
Nelson, p	0	0	0	0	0	0
Grimsley, p	0	0	0	0	0	0
Gooden, p	0	0	0	0	0	0
Cone, p	0	0	0	0	0	0
Totals	35	2	8	2	24	11

Seattle	AB	R	H	RBI	PO	A
Henderson, lf	3	1	0	0	0	0
Ibanez, lf	1	0	0	0	0	0
Cameron, cf	3	1	0	0	1	0
Rodriguez, ss	3	1	1	2	1	5
E. Martinez, dh	3	1	1	2	0	0
Olerud, 1b	3	1	2	2	12	1
Buhner, rf	4	0	2	0	0	0
Gipson, rf	0	0	0	0	0	0
Bell, 3b	4	0	1	0	1	3
Wilson, c	3	0	0	0	9	0
McLemore, 2b	3	1	1	0	2	4
Garcia, p	0	0	0	0	1	0
Paniagua, p	0	0	0	0	0	0
Rhodes, p	0	0	0	0	0	0
Sasaki, p	0	0	0	0	0	0
Totals	30	6	8	6	27	13

New York	0	0	0	2	0	0	0	0—2
Seattle	1	0	0	0	5	0	0	x—6

New York	IP	H	R	ER	BB	SO
Neagle (L)	4.1	3	3	3	4	4
Nelson	*0.0	3	3	3	0	0
Grimsley	0.1	1	0	0	2	0
Gooden	2.1	1	0	0	0	1
Cone	1.0	0	0	0	0	0

Seattle	IP	H	R	ER	BB	SO
Garcia (W)	5.0	7	2	2	2	3
Paniagua	†1.0	0	0	0	1	0
Rhodes	1.1	0	0	0	3	4
Sasaki	1.2	1	0	0	1	2

*Pitched to three batters in fifth.
†Pitched to one batter in seventh.
LOB—New York 15, Seattle 8. 2B—Williams, T. Martinez, Sojo. HR—E. Martinez, Olerud. SH—Cameron. SF—Olerud. SB—Olerud. HBP—By Garcia (Knoblauch), by Sasaki (Williams). WP—Grimsley, Sasaki. T—4:14. A—47,802. U—Davis, plate; J. Hirschbeck, first; Hernandez, second; Culbreth, third; M. Hirschbeck, left field; Bell, right field.

GAME 6 BOX SCORE

NEW YORK 9, SEATTLE 7

TUESDAY, OCTOBER 17, AT NEW YORK

Seattle	AB	R	H	RBI	PO	A
Javier, cf-lf	5	0	0	0	1	0
Martin, lf	3	1	0	0	1	0
Cameron, cf	1	0	0	0	1	0
Rodriguez, ss	5	2	4	2	1	2
E. Martinez, dh	4	1	1	1	0	0
Olerud, 1b	3	2	2	0	5	1
Ibanez, rf	4	0	0	0	5	0
Guillen, 3b	2	1	1	2	1	1
McLemore, 2b	4	0	1	2	2	2
Wilson, c	3	0	1	0	3	1
Buhner, ph	1	0	0	0	0	0
Oliver, c	0	0	0	0	2	0
Halama, p	0	0	0	0	0	1
Tomko, p	0	0	0	0	2	0
Paniagua, p	0	0	0	0	0	0
Rhodes, p	0	0	0	0	0	0
Mesa, p	0	0	0	0	0	0
Totals	35	7	10	7	24	8

New York	AB	R	H	RBI	PO	A
Knoblauch, dh	3	0	0	0	0	0
Jeter, ss	4	1	1	0	1	4
Justice, lf	5	2	2	3	2	0
Bellinger, lf	0	0	0	0	0	0
Williams, cf	4	2	3	0	2	0
T. Martinez, 1b	4	2	1	0	7	2
Posada, c	3	1	1	2	9	1
O'Neill, rf	4	0	2	3	2	0
Sojo, 2b-3b	2	0	0	0	1	2
Brosius, 3b	2	0	0	0	1	1
Vizcaino, ph-2b	1	1	1	1	0	0
Hernandez, p	0	0	0	0	1	0
Rivera, p	0	0	0	0	1	1
Totals	32	9	11	9	27	11

Seattle	2	0	0	2	0	0	0	3	0—7
New York	0	0	0	3	0	0	6	0	x—9

Seattle	IP	H	R	ER	BB	SO
Halama	3.1	5	3	3	2	1
Tomko	2.2	0	0	0	2	1
Paniagua (L)	0.1	2	2	2	0	0
Rhodes	0.0	4	4	4	1	0
Mesa	1.2	0	0	0	2	3

New York	IP	H	R	ER	BB	SO
Hernandez (W)	*7.0	7	6	6	5	7
Rivera	2.0	3	1	1	0	1

*Pitched to two batters in eighth.
DP—Seattle 1, New York 1. LOB—Seattle 6, New York 8. 2B—Rodriguez 2, Olerud 2, E. Martinez, McLemore, T. Martinez, Posada. HR—Rodriguez, Guillen, Justice. SH—Knoblauch. SF—Vizcaino. SB—Jeter. CS—Guillen. T—4:03. A—56,598. U—J. Hirschbeck, plate; Hernandez, first; Culbreth, second; M. Hirschbeck, third; Bell, left field; Davis, right field.

STATISTICS

NEW YORK YANKEES' BATTING AND FIELDING AVERAGES

					BATTING								FIELDING		
Player, position	G	AB	R	H	TB	2B	3B	HR	RBI	BB	IBB	SO	Avg.	PO	A	E	Avg.
Vizcaino, pr-2b	4	2	3	2	3	1	0	0	2	0	0	0	1.000	0	2	0	1.000
Williams, cf	6	23	5	10	14	1	0	1	3	2	1	3	.435	14	0	0	1.000
T. Martinez, 1b	6	25	5	8	13	2	0	1	1	2	0	4	.320	47	6	0	1.000
Jeter, ss	6	22	6	7	13	0	0	2	5	6	0	7	.318	9	16	0	1.000
Knoblauch, dh	6	23	3	6	8	2	0	0	2	3	0	4	.261	0	0	0	.000
Sojo, 2b-3b	6	23	1	6	7	1	0	0	2	2	0	3	.261	10	15	0	1.000
O'Neill, rf	6	20	0	5	5	0	0	0	5	1	0	2	.250	8	0	0	1.000
Justice, lf-rf	6	26	4	6	14	2	0	2	8	2	0	7	.231	9	0	0	1.000
Brosius, 3b	6	18	2	4	4	0	0	0	0	2	0	3	.222	4	7	1	.917
Posada, c	6	19	2	3	4	1	0	0	3	5	1	5	.158	51	3	0	1.000

Player, position	G	AB	R	H	TB	2B	3B	HR	RBI	BB	IBB	SO	Avg.	PO	A	E	Avg.
Choate, p	1	0	0	0	0	0	0	0	0	0	0	0	.000	0	0	0	.000
Clemens, p	1	0	0	0	0	0	0	0	0	0	0	0	.000	2	0	0	1.000
Cone, p	1	0	0	0	0	0	0	0	0	0	0	0	.000	0	0	0	.000
Gooden, p	1	0	0	0	0	0	0	0	0	0	0	0	.000	0	0	0	.000
Grimsley, p	2	0	0	0	0	0	0	0	0	0	0	0	.000	0	0	0	.000
Hernandez, p	2	0	0	0	0	0	0	0	0	0	0	0	.000	2	1	0	1.000
Neagle, p	2	0	0	0	0	0	0	0	0	0	0	0	.000	0	1	0	1.000
Nelson, p	3	0	0	0	0	0	0	0	0	0	0	0	.000	0	0	0	.000
Pettitte, p	1	0	0	0	0	0	0	0	0	0	0	0	.000	0	1	0	1.000
Rivera, p	3	0	0	0	0	0	0	0	0	0	0	0	.000	2	2	0	1.000
Bellinger, lf-pr	5	1	0	0	0	0	0	0	0	0	0	1	.000	1	0	0	1.000
Hill, ph	2	2	0	0	0	0	0	0	0	0	0	2	.000	0	0	0	.000
Totals	6	204	31	57	85	10	0	6	31	25	2	41	.279	159	54	1	.995

SEATTLE MARINERS' BATTING AND FIELDING AVERAGES

Player, position	G	AB	R	H	TB	2B	3B	HR	RBI	BB	IBB	SO	Avg.	PO	A	E	Avg.
Rodriguez, ss	6	22	4	9	17	2	0	2	5	3	0	8	.409	9	11	0	1.000
Olerud, 1b	6	20	3	7	13	3	0	1	2	2	1	2	.350	45	7	0	1.000
McLemore, 2b	5	16	2	4	7	3	0	0	2	2	0	1	.250	6	18	2	.923
E. Martinez, dh	6	21	2	5	9	1	0	1	4	3	0	5	.238	0	0	0	.000
Bell, 3b	5	18	0	4	4	0	0	0	0	0	0	0	.222	5	9	0	1.000
Henderson, lf	3	9	2	2	3	1	0	0	1	2	0	2	.222	2	0	0	1.000
Guillen, 3b	2	5	1	1	4	0	0	1	2	2	0	2	.200	1	3	0	1.000
Buhner, rf-ph	4	11	0	2	2	0	0	0	0	1	0	6	.182	4	0	0	1.000
Martin, lf-ph	4	11	1	2	4	2	0	0	0	2	1	3	.182	9	0	0	1.000
Oliver, c	4	6	0	1	1	0	0	0	0	1	0	1	.167	22	1	0	1.000
Cameron, cf	6	18	3	2	2	0	0	0	1	2	0	7	.111	16	0	0	1.000
Wilson, c	4	11	0	1	1	0	0	0	0	1	0	5	.091	20	4	1	.960
Javier, rf-ph-cf-lf	4	14	0	1	1	0	0	0	1	0	0	4	.071	4	0	0	1.000
Abbott, p	1	0	0	0	0	0	0	0	0	0	0	0	.000	0	1	0	1.000
Garcia, p	2	0	0	0	0	0	0	0	0	0	0	0	.000	2	1	0	1.000
Gipson, lf	2	0	0	0	0	0	0	0	0	0	0	0	.000	0	0	0	.000
Halama, p	2	0	0	0	0	0	0	0	0	0	0	0	.000	1	3	0	1.000
Mesa, p	3	0	0	0	0	0	0	0	0	0	0	0	.000	0	0	0	.000
Paniagua, p	5	0	0	0	0	0	0	0	0	0	0	0	.000	0	0	0	.000
Ramsay, p	2	0	0	0	0	0	0	0	0	0	0	0	.000	0	0	0	.000
Rhodes, p	4	0	0	0	0	0	0	0	0	0	0	0	.000	0	0	0	.000
Sasaki, p	2	0	0	0	0	0	0	0	0	0	0	0	.000	0	0	0	.000
Sele, p	1	0	0	0	0	0	0	0	0	0	0	0	.000	0	0	0	.000
Tomko, p	2	0	0	0	0	0	0	0	0	0	0	0	.000	4	0	0	1.000
Ibanez, lf-rf-ph	6	9	0	0	0	0	0	0	0	0	0	2	.000	6	0	0	1.000
Totals	6	191	18	41	68	12	0	5	18	21	2	48	.215	156	58	3	.986

NEW YORK YANKEES' PITCHING RECORDS

Pitcher	G	GS	CG	IP	H	R	ER	HR	BB	IBB	SO	HB	WP	W	L	Pct.	ERA
Clemens	1	1	1	9.0	1	0	0	0	2	0	15	0	0	1	0	1.000	0.00
Gooden	1	0	0	2.1	1	0	0	0	0	0	1	0	0	0	0	.000	0.00
Cone	1	0	0	1.0	0	0	0	0	0	0	0	0	0	0	0	.000	0.00
Grimsley	2	0	0	1.0	2	0	0	0	3	0	1	0	1	0	0	.000	0.00
Choate	1	0	0	0.1	0	0	0	0	0	0	1	0	0	0	0	.000	0.00
Rivera	3	0	0	4.2	4	1	1	0	0	0	1	0	0	0	0	.000	1.93
Pettitte	1	1	0	6.2	9	2	2	0	1	0	2	0	0	1	0	1.000	2.70
Hernandez	2	2	0	15.0	13	7	7	2	8	2	14	0	0	2	0	1.000	4.20
Neagle	2	2	0	10.0	6	5	5	1	7	0	7	0	0	0	2	.000	4.50
Nelson	3	0	0	3.0	5	3	3	2	0	0	6	0	0	0	0	.000	9.00
Totals	6	6	1	53.0	41	18	18	5	21	2	48	0	1	4	2	.667	3.06

Shutout—Clemens. Save—Rivera.

SEATTLE MARINERS' PITCHING RECORDS

Pitcher	G	GS	CG	IP	H	R	ER	HR	BB	IBB	SO	HB	WP	W	L	Pct.	ERA
Sasaki	2	0	0	2.2	3	0	0	0	1	0	3	1	1	0	0	.000	0.00
Ramsay	2	0	0	1.2	2	0	0	0	0	0	1	0	0	0	0	.000	0.00
Garcia	2	2	0	11.2	10	2	2	0	4	0	11	2	0	2	0	1.000	1.54
Halama	2	2	0	9.1	10	3	3	0	5	0	3	0	0	0	0	.000	2.89
Paniagua	5	0	0	4.1	4	2	2	0	1	0	4	0	0	0	1	.000	4.15
Abbott	1	1	0	5.0	3	3	3	1	3	0	3	0	0	0	1	.000	5.40
Sele	1	1	0	6.0	9	4	4	2	0	0	4	0	0	0	1	.000	6.00

Pitcher	G	GS	CG	IP	H	R	ER	HR	BB	IBB	SO	HB	WP	W	L	Pct.	ERA
Tomko	2	0	0	5.0	3	4	4	0	4	1	4	0	1	0	0	.000	7.20
Mesa	3	0	0	4.1	5	6	6	2	3	0	3	0	0	0	0	.000	12.46
Rhodes	4	0	0	2.0	8	7	7	1	4	1	5	0	0	0	1	.000	31.50
Totals	6	6	0	52.0	57	31	31	6	25	2	41	3	2	2	4	.333	5.37

Shutout—Garcia, Paniagua, Rhodes and Sasaki (combined). Save—Sasaki.

SCORE BY INNINGS

New York	0	2	1		5	3	1		6	9	4—31
Seattle	4	0	1		2	7	1		0	3	0—18

MISCELLANEOUS STATISTICS

Sacrifice hits—Cameron, Knoblauch, McLemore.
Sacrifice flies—Olerud, O'Neill, Vizcaino, Williams.
Stolen bases—Vizcaino 2, Cameron, Jeter, Olerud, Rodriguez, Williams.
Caught stealing—Brosius, Guillen, Henderson, Posada.
Double plays—Sojo, Jeter and T. Martinez 2; Garcia, McLemore, Rodriguez and Olerud; Hernandez and Jeter; Jeter and T. Martinez; McLemore, Rodriguez and Olerud; Olerud and Rodriguez; Posada, Sojo and T. Martinez; Wilson and Olerud.
Left on bases—New York 8, 8, 6, 4, 15, 8—49; Seattle 7, 7, 7, 3, 8, 6—38.
Hit by pitcher—By Garcia 2 (Knoblauch, Posada), by Sasaki (Williams).
Passed ball—Wilson.
Balks—None.
Time of games—First game, 3:45; second game, 3:36; third game, 3:35; fourth game, 2:59; fifth game, 4:14; sixth game, 4:03.
Attendance—First game, 54,481; second game, 55,317; third game, 47,827; fourth game, 47,803; fifth game, 47,802; sixth game, 56,598.
Umpires—J. Hirschbeck, Hernandez, Bell, M. Hirschbeck, Davis, Marsh and Culbreth.
Official scorers—Joe Donnelly, Howie Karpin, Bill Shannon, Jim Street.

N.L. CHAMPIONSHIP SERIES

HIGHLIGHTS

The bottom line: The New York Mets, fulfilling their half of the all-New York World Series equation, posted a surprisingly easy five-game NLCS win over the St. Louis Cardinals and claimed their first pennant since 1986. With the victory, New York joined the 1997 Florida Marlins as the only wild-card teams to reach the World Series and denied the N.L. Central Division-champion Cardinals their first fall classic appearance since 1987. The Mets showed their superiority in every facet of the game, winning Games 1 and 2 in St. Louis and closing out the series with consecutive wins at Shea Stadium after the Cardinals had rebounded in Game 3. The Cardinals did not even resemble the team that had rolled over the defending N.L.-champion Atlanta Braves in a shocking Division Series.

Why the Mets won: Because their lefthanded starters, Mike Hampton and Al Leiter, were able to shut down the Cardinals' lefty-dominated lineup. Hampton worked seven shutout innings in Game 1 and fired a three-hit shutout in Game 5, striking out Jim Edmonds three times in the clincher. Leiter worked seven solid innings in a Game 2 Mets win that was decided in the ninth inning. The Mets also were able to avoid critical game situations in which they would have to deal with super pinch hitter Mark McGwire, who was forced into that role by a knee injury. Cardinals starting pitchers other than Game 3 winner Andy Benes worked just 14 1/3 innings with a whopping 11.30 ERA and the normally reliable St. Louis defense collapsed at inopportune moments.

The turning points:

Game 1: The first inning provided a double lift for the Mets, who stormed past the Cardinals, 6-2, before 52,225 red-clad fans at Busch Stadium. First, the Mets' sometimes-sluggish offense got a boost when top gun Mike Piazza, a career .211 postseason hitter, broke out of a slump with a double off Darryl Kile that keyed a two-run outburst. Then Hampton, a failure in four previous postseason starts, escaped a bases-loaded jam by getting Carlos Hernandez on a ground ball. Piazza signaled his return to prominence with a 2-for-4 performance and Hampton worked seven shutout innings en route to his first postseason victory. Hampton's biggest scare came in the seventh when, with the Mets leading 3-0, Edmonds drove left fielder Benny Agbayani to the left-center field fence with two men on base. The Mets secured victory by scoring three ninth-inning runs on a solo home run by Todd Zeile and a two-run shot by Jay Payton.

Game 2: The Mets took control of the series when center fielder Payton delivered his second game-winning hit of the postseason—a run-scoring, ninth-inning single that produced a 6-5 win and a two-games-to-none lead. Payton's winner was set up when normally sure-handed Cardinals first baseman Will Clark booted Robin Ventura's ground ball. The Mets, who got a solo home run from Piazza, needed Payton's heroics because they blew a pair of two-run leads. The Cardinals struck for two runs off Leiter in the fifth to tie the game at 3-3 and two more in the eighth off John Franco after the Mets had scored twice in the top of the inning. The Mets broke on top with two first-inning runs, courtesy of Rick Ankiel's wildness. The 21-year-old Cardinals rookie, bringing back memories of his five-wild pitch-inning in a Division Series start against Atlanta, walked three batters, threw two wild pitches and fired several more pitches to the backstop before being relieved with two out by Britt Reames.

Game 3: After falling behind 2-0 before they even batted in Games 1 and 2, the Cardinals turned the tables and went on to claim a face-saving 8-2 victory before a hostile crowd at Shea Stadium. Fernando Vina opened the game with a single and Edgar Renteria reached on an error by third baseman Ventura. Before Rick Reed could record his first out, Edmonds lined a two-run double to left. Starter Andy Benes, pitching for the first time in 13 days because of knee problems, escaped a first-inning jam with one run and went on to work eight six-hit innings. The Cardinals supported him with 14 hits and put the game away by scoring six runs in the third, fourth and fifth innings.

Game 4: Trying to duplicate their Game 2 victory formula, the Cardinals broke on top on Edmonds' two-run, first-inning home run off Bobby J. Jones. But this time the Mets answered back in record-setting fashion and went on to claim a 10-6 victory that put them within one win of an N.L. pennant. Cardinals ace Darryl Kile, working on three days rest, felt the brunt of a New York offensive explosion that produced a 7-2 lead after two innings. The Mets scored four first-inning runs on an LCS-record five doubles and added three runs in the second, two on Zeile's double. The Cardinals knocked out Jones after four innings and fought back to 8-6, but they could never catch up. Piazza contributed a solo home run to the nine-hit Mets attack.

Game 5: The Mets gave Hampton another first-inning boost and he turned the fifth game into one long Shea Stadium victory celebration. The three-run first was a combination of timely New York hitting and shoddy St. Louis defense and the result was a hole out of which the Cardinals could not climb.

Edgardo Alfonzo and Ventura delivered RBI hits off starter Pat Hentgen; catcher Carlos Hernandez and first baseman Clark contributed costly errors. Zeile's three-run, fourth-inning double was icing for Hampton, who completed his NLCS scoreless-innings streak at 16 innings and walked away with MVP honors.

Notable:

Cardinals: After going 3-for-28 with runners in scoring position at St. Louis, the Cardinals were 7-for-16 in their Game 3 victory over the Mets. ... The ability of lefties Hampton, Leiter, Franco and Glendon Rusch to shut down the Cardinals was not surprising. During the regular season, St. Louis was 17-23 against lefthanders. ... After outscoring the Braves 10-3 in their Division Series sweep, the Cardinals were outscored in the first inning by the Mets 12-4. ... Much of the Cardinals' first-inning woes could be traced to Mets right fielder Timo Perez, who replaced injured Derek Bell in right field. Perez scored an LCS-tying eight runs from his leadoff spot in the lineup.

Mets: When the Mets won both games in St. Louis, they had to feel good about their chances of winning the series. No team in LCS play has ever come back to win after dropping the first two games at home. ... Second baseman Alfonzo singled twice in the Game 5 finale, extending his postseason hitting streak to 11 games. ... The NLCS win gave Franco his first World Series opportunity at age 40. ... Center fielder Payton was hit on the helmet by a Dave Veres pitch in the eighth inning of Game 5, but order was quickly restored after both benches emptied. Payton seemed to accept Veres' assurance that the beaning was unintentional.

Quotable:

Cardinals: Will Clark, on his ninth-inning error in Game 2: "It's a shame. I misplayed a ball and it caused us to lose the game."... Kile, referring to those who blamed the short rest on his Game 4 collapse: "That has nothing to do with it. If you make good pitches, it doesn't matter if you're pitching on one day rest. I didn't make good pitches."... McGwire, on why the Cardinals lost: "In a short series, it comes down to pitching. They shut us down."

Mets: Hampton, recalling Edmonds' deep seventh-inning Game 1 drive that came within a few feet of tying the game: "I didn't breathe, I'll tell you that. I was going to breathe, but I thought I might push the ball over the fence."... Zeile, on the prospects of a Subway Series after the Mets had finished off the Cardinals: "I'm rooting for the Yankees, to be perfectly honest. I'd love to see a Subway Series. We have some unfinished business with the Yankees."... Mets manager Bobby Valentine on Hampton's Game 5 performance: "He did a fabulous job. He pitched the game of his life—and mine."

NEW YORK 6, ST. LOUIS 2

WEDNESDAY, OCTOBER 11, AT ST. LOUIS

New York	AB	R	H	RBI	PO	A
Perez, rf	5	1	1	0	2	0
Alfonzo, 2b	3	1	1	1	0	4
Piazza, c	4	0	2	1	5	0
Ventura, 3b	2	0	0	1	0	2
Zeile, 1b	4	1	1	1	11	1
Agbayani, lf	4	0	1	0	2	0
McEwing, pr-lf	0	1	0	0	1	0
Payton, cf	4	1	1	2	2	0
Bordick, ss	3	0	0	0	3	4
Abbott, pr-ss	0	0	0	0	0	0
Hampton, p	3	1	1	0	1	0
J. Franco, p	0	0	0	0	0	0
Hamilton, ph	0	0	0	0	0	0
Trammell, ph	1	0	0	0	0	0
Benitez, p	0	0	0	0	0	0
Totals	33	6	8	6	27	11

St. Louis	AB	R	H	RBI	PO	A
Vina, 2b	4	0	1	0	2	2
Renteria, ss	5	1	1	0	1	3
Edmonds, cf	5	0	2	0	2	0
Davis, rf	5	0	1	0	4	0
Clark, 1b	3	0	1	0	10	1
Hernandez, c	4	0	1	0	3	0
Marrero, pr-c	0	0	0	0	1	0
Drew, lf	3	0	0	0	2	0
Dunston, ph-lf	1	0	0	0	0	0
Polanco, 3b	3	0	1	0	0	4
James, p	0	0	0	0	1	0
Christiansen, p	0	0	0	0	0	1
Lankford, ph	1	1	1	0	0	0
Kile, p	1	0	0	0	1	3
Tatis, ph-3b	2	0	0	0	0	0
Totals	37	2	9	0	27	14

New York	2	0	0	0	1	0	0	0	3—6
St. Louis	0	0	0	0	0	0	0	0	2—2

New York	IP	H	R	ER	BB	SO
Hampton (W)	7.0	6	0	0	3	4
J. Franco	1.0	1	0	0	0	1
Benitez	1.0	2	2	0	0	0

St. Louis	IP	H	R	ER	BB	SO
Kile (L)	7.0	5	3	3	2	1
James	*1.0	3	3	3	0	0
Christiansen	1.0	0	0	0	0	1

*Pitched to four batters in ninth.

E—Agbayani, Abbott, Perez. DP—St. Louis 1. LOB—New York 4, St. Louis 11. 2B—Perez, Piazza, Clark, Lankford. HR—Zeile, Payton. SF—Ventura. HBP—By James (Bordick). WP—Hampton, Kile. T—3:08. A—52,255. U—Froemming, plate; Tschida, first; Rapuano, second; Scott, third; DeMuth, left field; Rippley, right field.

NEW YORK 6, ST. LOUIS 5

THURSDAY, OCTOBER 12, AT ST. LOUIS

New York	AB	R	H	RBI	PO	A
Perez, rf	5	1	1	0	4	0
Alfonzo, 2b	3	2	2	1	4	1
Piazza, c	2	2	1	1	11	0
Zeile, 1b	3	0	2	2	3	0
J. Franco, p	0	0	0	0	0	0
Wendell, p	0	0	0	0	0	0
Benitez, p	0	0	0	0	0	0
Ventura, 3b	4	0	1	0	0	2
McEwing, pr-3b	0	1	0	0	0	0
Agbayani, lf	4	0	1	1	2	0
Payton, cf	4	0	1	1	3	0
Abbott, ss	3	0	0	0	1	0
M. Franco, ph-1b	2	0	0	0	2	0
Leiter, p	3	0	0	0	0	0
Hamilton, ph	1	0	0	0	0	0
Bordick, ss	1	0	0	0	1	0
Totals	35	6	9	6	27	3

St. Louis	AB	R	H	RBI	PO	A
Vina, 2b	5	1	1	0	3	4
Renteria, ss	5	1	3	1	0	4
Edmonds, cf	4	0	0	0	2	0
Tatis, 3b	3	0	1	1	3	0
Morris, p	0	0	0	0	0	0
Hernandez, c	1	1	0	0	0	0
Clark, 1b	4	1	2	0	7	1
Dunston, rf-lf	3	1	1	0	1	0
Lankford, lf	3	0	1	0	2	1
Polanco, ph	0	0	0	0	0	0
Drew, ph-rf	1	0	1	1	0	0
Marrero, c	3	0	0	1	9	0
Veres, p	0	0	0	0	0	0
McGwire, ph	0	0	0	0	0	0
Kile, pr	0	0	0	0	0	0
Timlin, p	0	0	0	0	0	0
Ankiel, p	0	0	0	0	0	0
Reames, p	1	0	0	0	0	0
Davis, ph	1	0	0	0	0	0
Paquette, 3b	2	0	0	0	0	1
Totals	36	5	10	4	27	11

New York	2	0	1	0	0	0	0	2	1—6
St. Louis	0	1	0	0	2	0	0	2	0—5

New York	IP	H	R	ER	BB	SO
Leiter	7.0	8	3	3	0	9
J. Franco	0.2	1	2	2	1	0
Wendell (W)	0.1	1	0	0	1	1
Benitez (S)	1.0	0	0	0	1	1

St. Louis	IP	H	R	ER	BB	SO
Ankiel	0.2	1	2	2	3	1
Reames	4.1	3	1	1	3	6
Morris	3.0	3	2	2	2	2
Veres	0.0	1	0	0	0	0
Timlin (L)	1.0	1	1	0	0	0

E—Vina, Clark, Edmonds. LOB—New York 12, St. Louis 8. 2B—Zeile, Agbayani, Renteria, Tatis, Clark, Dunston, Drew. 3B—Alfonzo. HR—Piazza. SH—Agbayani, Dunston. SF—Zeile. SB—Renteria 3. WP—J. Franco, Ankiel 2. PB—Marrero. T—3:59. A—52,250. U—Tschida, plate; Rapuano, first; Scott, second; DeMuth, third; Rippley, left field; Froemming, right field.

GAME 3 BOX SCORE

ST. LOUIS 8, NEW YORK 2

SATURDAY, OCTOBER 14, AT NEW YORK

St. Louis	AB	R	H	RBI	PO	A
Vina, 2b	5	1	2	1	3	2
Renteria, ss	4	2	2	2	0	1
Edmonds, cf	5	0	1	2	4	0
Clark, 1b	3	1	2	0	7	0
Lankford, lf	2	0	1	1	2	0
McGwire, ph	1	0	0	0	0	0
Paquette, lf	2	0	1	0	1	0
Tatis, 3b	3	1	1	1	0	1
Drew, rf	5	1	2	0	1	0
Hernandez, c	5	1	1	1	8	0
Benes, p	3	1	1	0	1	0
Wilkins, ph	1	0	0	0	0	0
James, p	0	0	0	0	0	0
Veres, p	0	0	0	0	0	0
Totals	39	8	14	8	27	4

New York	AB	R	H	RBI	PO	A
Perez, rf	4	1	1	0	3	1
Alfonzo, 2b	4	0	2	0	1	1
Piazza, c	4	0	1	0	11	0
Ventura, 3b	3	1	0	0	1	2
Zeile, 1b	4	0	2	0	6	0
Agbayani, lf	3	0	0	0	2	0
Payton, cf	3	0	0	0	1	0
Bordick, ss	2	0	0	0	2	4
M. Franco, ph	1	0	0	0	0	0
Reed, p	1	0	0	0	0	0
Rusch, p	0	0	0	0	0	0
Hamilton, ph	1	0	0	0	0	0
White, p	0	0	0	0	0	0
Harris, ph	1	0	0	0	0	0
Cook, p	0	0	0	0	0	0
Wendell, p	0	0	0	0	0	0
Trammell, ph	1	0	1	0	0	0
Totals	32	2	7	0	27	8

St. Louis	2	0	2	1	3	0	0	0	0—8
New York	1	0	0	1	0	0	0	0	0—2

St. Louis	IP	H	R	ER	BB	SO
Benes (W)	8.0	6	2	2	3	5
James	*0.0	1	0	0	1	0
Veres	1.0	0	0	0	0	3

New York	IP	H	R	ER	BB	SO
Reed (L)	3.1	8	5	4	1	4
Rusch	0.2	0	0	0	0	1
White	3.0	5	3	3	1	1
Cook	1.0	1	0	0	0	2
Wendell	1.0	0	0	0	0	1

*Pitched to two batters in ninth.

E—Ventura. DP—St. Louis 2. LOB—St. Louis 10, New York 7. 2B—Edmonds, Tatis. SH—Renteria, Benes. SF—Tatis. HBP—By Rusch (Clark). T—3:23. A—55,693. U—Rapuano, plate; Scott, first; DeMuth, second; Rippley, third; Froemming, left field; Tschida, right field.

GAME 4 BOX SCORE

NEW YORK 10, ST. LOUIS 6

SUNDAY, OCTOBER 15, AT NEW YORK

St. Louis	AB	R	H	RBI	PO	A
Vina, 2b	5	1	1	0	3	1
Renteria, ss	3	0	0	1	0	2
Edmonds, cf	5	0	2	3	3	1
Clark, 1b	4	1	1	1	10	0
Lankford, lf	3	0	0	0	2	0
Tatis, 3b	4	0	1	0	0	4
Drew, rf	3	1	1	0	3	0
Paquette, ph-rf	1	0	0	0	1	0
Hernandez, c	4	1	2	0	2	2
Marrero, pr	0	0	0	0	0	0
Kile, p	1	0	0	0	0	1
James, p	0	0	0	0	0	0
Davis, ph	1	1	1	0	0	0
Timlin, p	0	0	0	0	0	2
Dunston, ph	1	0	1	0	0	0
Morris, p	0	0	0	0	0	0
Christiansen, p	0	0	0	0	0	0
Polanco, ph	0	0	0	0	0	0
Totals	35	6	11	6	24	13

New York	AB	R	H	RBI	PO	A
Perez, rf	4	3	2	0	5	1
Alfonzo, 2b	4	1	1	1	1	1
Piazza, c	3	3	2	2	6	0
Ventura, 3b	2	2	1	3	0	2
Zeile, 1b	4	0	1	2	6	0
Agbayani, lf	4	0	2	2	3	0
McEwing, lf	0	0	0	0	0	0
Payton, cf	4	0	0	0	3	0
Bordick, ss	3	1	0	0	3	1
B.J. Jones, p	2	0	0	0	0	1
Rusch, p	0	0	0	0	0	0
J. Franco, p	0	0	0	0	0	0
Harris, ph	0	0	0	0	0	0
Trammell, ph	1	0	0	0	0	0
Benitez, p	0	0	0	0	0	0
Totals	31	10	9	10	27	6

St. Louis	2	0	0	1	3	0	0	0	0—6
New York	4	3	0	1	0	2	0	0	x—10

St. Louis	IP	H	R	ER	BB	SO
Kile (L)	*3.0	8	7	7	3	2
James	1.0	1	1	1	0	0
Timlin	2.0	0	2	0	1	0
Morris	1.0	0	0	0	0	0
Christiansen	1.0	0	0	0	0	0

New York	IP	H	R	ER	BB	SO
B.J. Jones	†4.0	6	6	6	0	2
Rusch (W)	3.0	3	0	0	0	2
J. Franco	1.0	1	0	0	1	1
Benitez	1.0	1	0	0	1	1

*Pitched to one batter in fourth.
†Pitched to three batters in fifth.

E—Tatis 2. DP—New York 1. LOB—St. Louis 6, New York 4. 2B—Vina, Davis, Perez, Alfonzo, Piazza, Ventura, Zeile, Agbayani. HR—Edmonds, Clark, Piazza. SH—Renteria, Rusch. SF—Renteria, Ventura. SB—Perez. CS—Perez. HBP—By Timlin (Alfonzo). T—3:14. A—55,665. U—Scott, plate; DeMuth, first; Rippley, second; Froemming, third; Tschida, left field; Rapuano, right field.

GAME 5 BOX SCORE

NEW YORK 7, ST. LOUIS 0

MONDAY, OCTOBER 16, AT NEW YORK

St. Louis	AB	R	H	RBI	PO	A
Vina, 2b	4	0	1	0	3	1
Polanco, 3b	2	0	0	0	2	0
Paquette, ph	1	0	0	0	0	0
Edmonds, cf	3	0	0	0	2	0
McGwire, ph	1	0	0	0	0	0
Davis, rf	3	0	0	0	1	0
Drew, rf	0	0	0	0	1	0
Wilkins, ph	1	0	0	0	0	0
Clark, 1b	3	0	1	0	4	2
Renteria, ss	3	0	0	0	4	2
Lankford, lf	3	0	0	0	4	0
Hernandez, c	2	0	0	0	2	0
Marrero, c	1	0	0	0	1	0
Hentgen, p	1	0	1	0	0	1
Timlin, p	0	0	0	0	0	0
Tatis, ph	1	0	0	0	0	0
Reames, p	0	0	0	0	0	1
Ankiel, p	0	0	0	0	0	0
James, p	0	0	0	0	0	0
Dunston, ph	1	0	0	0	0	0
Veres, p	0	0	0	0	0	0
Totals	30	0	3	0	24	7

New York	AB	R	H	RBI	PO	A
Perez, rf-cf	5	2	2	0	2	0
Alfonzo, 2b	4	1	2	1	0	3
Piazza, c	4	2	1	0	7	1
Ventura, 3b	3	1	1	1	1	5
Zeile, 1b	4	0	1	3	12	0
Agbayani, lf	2	0	1	0	2	0
Payton, cf	4	0	1	0	1	0
McEwing, pr-rf	0	0	0	0	0	0
Bordick, ss	4	1	1	0	2	2
Hampton, p	3	0	0	0	0	0
Totals	33	7	10	5	27	11

St. Louis	0	0	0	0	0	0	0	0	0—0
New York	3	0	0	3	0	0	1	0	x—7

St. Louis	IP	H	R	ER	BB	SO
Hentgen (L)	3.2	7	6	6	5	2
Timlin	0.1	0	0	0	1	0
Reames	2.0	2	0	0	1	0
Ankiel	0.2	0	1	1	2	1
James	0.1	0	0	0	0	0
Veres	1.0	1	0	0	0	0

New York	IP	H	R	ER	BB	SO
Hampton (W)	9.0	3	0	0	1	8

E—Hernandez, Clark. LOB—St. Louis 4, New York 13. 2B—Piazza, Zeile. SH—Hampton. HBP—By Veres (Payton). WP—Ankiel 2. T—3:17. A—55,695. U—DeMuth, plate; Rippley, first; Froemming, second; Tschida, third; Rapuano, left field; Scott, right field.

STATISTICS

NEW YORK METS' BATTING AND FIELDING AVERAGES

Player, position	G	AB	R	H	TB	2B	3B	HR	RBI	BB	IBB	SO	Avg.	PO	A	E	Avg.
Alfonzo, 2b	5	18	5	8	11	1	1	0	4	4	0	1	.444	3	10	0	1.000
Piazza, c	5	17	7	7	16	3	0	2	4	5	3	0	.412	40	1	0	.000
Zeile, 1b	5	19	1	7	13	3	0	1	8	2	0	4	.368	38	1	0	1.000
Agbayani, lf	5	17	0	6	8	2	0	0	3	4	0	1	.353	11	0	1	.917
Perez, rf-cf	5	23	8	7	9	2	0	0	0	1	0	3	.304	16	2	1	.947
Ventura, 3b	5	14	4	3	4	1	0	0	5	6	0	0	.214	2	13	1	.938
Hampton, p	2	6	1	1	1	0	0	0	0	0	0	1	.167	1	0	0	1.000
Payton, cf	5	19	1	3	6	0	0	1	3	2	0	5	.158	10	0	0	1.000
Bordick, ss	5	13	2	1	1	0	0	0	0	3	0	1	.077	10	11	0	1.000
Benitez, p	3	0	0	0	0	0	0	0	0	0	0	0	.000	0	0	0	.000
Cook, p	1	0	0	0	0	0	0	0	0	0	0	0	.000	0	0	0	.000
J. Franco, p	3	0	0	0	0	0	0	0	0	0	0	0	.000	0	0	0	.000
McEwing, pr-lf-3b-rf	4	0	2	0	0	0	0	0	0	0	0	0	.000	1	0	0	1.000
Rusch, p	2	0	0	0	0	0	0	0	0	0	0	0	.000	0	0	0	.000
Wendell, p	2	0	0	0	0	0	0	0	0	0	0	0	.000	0	0	0	.000
White, p	1	0	0	0	0	0	0	0	0	0	0	0	.000	0	0	0	.000
Harris, ph	2	1	0	0	0	0	0	0	0	0	0	1	.000	0	0	0	.000
Reed, p	1	1	0	0	0	0	0	0	0	0	0	0	.000	0	0	0	.000
Hamilton, ph	3	2	0	0	0	0	0	0	0	0	0	0	.000	0	0	0	.000
B.J. Jones, p	1	2	0	0	0	0	0	0	0	0	0	1	.000	0	1	0	1.000
Abbott, pr-ss	2	3	0	0	0	0	0	0	0	0	0	2	.000	1	0	1	.500
M. Franco, ph-1b	2	3	0	0	0	0	0	0	0	0	0	1	.000	2	0	0	1.000
Leiter, p	1	3	0	0	0	0	0	0	0	0	0	2	.000	0	0	0	.000
Trammell, ph	3	3	0	0	0	0	0	0	0	0	0	2	.000	0	0	0	.000
Totals	5	164	31	43	69	12	1	4	27	27	3	24	.262	135	39	4	.978

ST. LOUIS CARDINALS' BATTING AND FIELDING AVERAGES

Player, position	G	AB	R	H	TB	2B	3B	HR	RBI	BB	IBB	SO	Avg.	PO	A	E	Avg.
Hentgen, p	1	1	0	1	1	0	0	0	0	0	0	0	1.000	0	1	0	1.000
Clark, 1b	5	17	3	7	12	2	0	1	1	2	0	1	.412	38	4	2	.955
Drew, lf-ph-rf	5	12	2	4	5	1	0	0	1	0	0	3	.333	7	0	0	1.000
Lankford, ph-lf	5	12	1	4	5	1	0	0	1	1	0	5	.333	10	1	0	1.000
Dunston, ph-lf-rf	4	6	1	2	3	1	0	0	0	0	0	0	.333	1	0	0	1.000
An. Benes, p	1	3	1	1	1	0	0	0	0	0	0	2	.333	1	0	0	1.000
Renteria, ss	5	20	4	6	7	1	0	0	4	0	0	2	.300	5	12	0	1.000
Vina, 2b	5	23	3	6	7	1	0	0	1	1	0	4	.261	14	10	1	.960
Hernandez, c	5	16	3	4	4	0	0	0	2	1	0	1	.250	15	2	1	.944
Tatis, ph-3b	5	13	1	3	5	2	0	0	2	1	0	5	.231	3	5	2	.800

Player, position	G	AB	R	H	TB	2B	3B	HR	RBI	BB	IBB	SO	Avg.	PO	A	E	Avg.
Edmonds, cf	5	22	1	5	9	1	0	1	5	1	0	9	.227	13	1	1	.933
Davis, rf-ph	4	10	1	2	3	1	0	0	1	0	0	2	.200	5	0	0	1.000
Polanco, 3b-ph	4	5	0	1	1	0	0	0	0	2	0	1	.200	2	4	0	1.000
Paquette, 3b-lf-ph-rf	4	6	0	1	1	0	0	0	0	0	0	2	.167	2	1	0	1.000
James, p	4	0	0	0	0	0	0	0	0	0	0	0	.000	1	0	0	1.000
Ankiel, p	2	0	0	0	0	0	0	0	0	0	0	0	.000	0	0	0	.000
Christiansen, p	2	0	0	0	0	0	0	0	0	0	0	0	.000	0	1	0	1.000
Morris, p	2	0	0	0	0	0	0	0	0	0	0	0	.000	0	0	0	.000
Timlin, p	3	0	0	0	0	0	0	0	0	0	0	0	.000	0	2	0	1.000
Veres, p	3	0	0	0	0	0	0	0	0	0	0	0	.000	0	0	0	.000
Reames, p	2	1	0	0	0	0	0	0	0	0	0	1	.000	0	1	0	1.000
McGwire, ph	3	2	0	0	0	0	0	0	0	1	1	0	.000	0	0	0	.000
Wilkins, ph	2	2	0	0	0	0	0	0	0	0	0	0	.000	0	0	0	.000
Kile, p-pr	3	2	0	0	0	0	0	0	0	1	0	0	.000	1	4	0	1.000
Marrero, pr-c	4	4	0	0	0	0	0	0	1	0	0	1	.000	11	0	0	1.000
Totals	5	177	21	47	64	11	0	2	18	11	1	39	.266	129	49	7	.962

NEW YORK METS' PITCHING RECORDS

Pitcher	G	GS	CG	IP	H	R	ER	HR	BB	IBB	SO	HB	WP	W	L	Pct.	ERA
Hampton	2	2	1	16.0	9	0	0	0	4	0	12	0	1	2	0	1.000	0.00
Rusch	2	0	0	3.2	3	0	0	0	0	0	3	1	0	1	0	1.000	0.00
Benitez	3	0	0	3.0	3	2	0	0	2	0	2	0	0	0	0	.000	0.00
Wendell	2	0	0	1.1	1	0	0	0	1	1	2	0	0	1	0	1.000	0.00
Cook	1	0	0	1.0	1	0	0	0	0	0	2	0	0	0	0	.000	0.00
Leiter	1	1	0	7.0	8	3	3	0	0	0	9	0	0	0	0	.000	3.86
J. Franco	3	0	0	2.2	3	2	2	0	2	0	2	0	1	0	0	.000	6.75
White	1	0	0	3.0	5	3	3	0	1	0	1	0	0	0	0	.000	9.00
Reed	1	1	0	3.1	8	5	4	0	1	0	4	0	0	0	1	.000	10.80
B.J. Jones	1	1	0	4.0	6	6	6	2	0	0	2	0	0	0	0	.000	13.50
Totals	5	5	1	45.0	47	21	18	2	11	1	39	1	2	4	1	.800	3.60

Shutout—Hampton. Save—Benitez.

ST. LOUIS CARDINALS' PITCHING RECORDS

Pitcher	G	GS	CG	IP	H	R	ER	HR	BB	IBB	SO	HB	WP	W	L	Pct.	ERA
Timlin	3	0	0	3.1	1	3	0	0	2	0	0	1	0	0	1	.000	0.00
Veres	3	0	0	2.1	2	0	0	0	0	0	3	1	0	0	0	.000	0.00
Christiansen	2	0	0	2.0	0	0	0	0	0	0	1	0	0	0	0	.000	0.00
Reames	2	0	0	6.1	5	1	1	1	4	1	6	0	0	0	0	.000	1.42
An. Benes	1	1	0	8.0	6	2	2	0	3	0	5	0	1	1	0	1.000	2.25
Morris	2	0	0	3.2	3	2	2	0	2	1	2	0	0	0	0	.000	4.91
Kile	2	2	0	10.0	13	10	10	0	5	1	3	0	1	0	2	.000	9.00
Hentgen	1	1	0	3.2	7	6	6	0	5	0	2	0	0	0	1	.000	14.73
James	4	0	0	2.1	5	4	4	3	1	0	0	1	0	0	0	.000	15.43
Ankiel	2	1	0	1.1	1	3	3	0	5	0	2	0	4	0	0	.000	20.25
Totals	5	5	0	43.0	43	31	28	4	27	3	24	3	5	1	4	.200	5.86

No shutouts or saves.

SCORE BY INNINGS

New York	12	3	1		5	1	2		1	2	4—31
St. Louis	4	1	2		2	8	0		0	2	2—21

MISCELLANEOUS STATISTICS

Sacrifice hits—Renteria 2, Agbayani, An. Benes, Dunston, Hampton, Rusch.
Sacrifice flies—Ventura 2, Renteria, Tatis, Zeile.
Stolen bases—Renteria 3, Perez 2.
Caught stealing—Perez.
Double plays—Christiansen, Renteria and Clark; Perez and Bordick; Tatis, Vina and Clark 2.
Left on bases—New York 4, 12, 7, 4, 13—40; St. Louis 11, 8, 10, 6, 4—39.
Hit by pitcher—By James (Bordick), by Rusch (Clark), by Timlin (Alfonzo), by Veres (Payton).
Passed ball—Marrero.
Balks—None.
Time of games—First game, 3:08; second game, 3:59; third game, 3:23; fourth game, 3:14; fifth game, 3:17.
Attendance—First game, 52,255; second game, 52,250; third game, 55,693; fourth game, 55,665; fifth game, 55,695.
Umpires—Froemming, Tschida, Rapuano, Scott, DeMuth and Rippley.
Official scorers—Gary Mueller, Bill Shannon.

WORLD SERIES

YANKEES 4, METS 3 (12 INNINGS)

Why the Yankees won: Jose Vizcaino, making his first start of the postseason, went 4-for-6 and singled home the winning run with two outs in the 12th inning. Yankees manager Joe Torre started Vizcaino because he was 10-for-19 (.526) against Mets left-handed starter Al Leiter. However, Vizcaino's biggest hits came in the ninth against righthander reliever Armando Benitez when the Yankees rallied to tie the game, and in the 12th, when he knocked in the game-winning run off Turk Wendell.

Why the Mets lost: Timo Perez was thrown out at home in the sixth inning when he slowed to a jog before reaching second because he thought a ball hit by Todd Zeile would go for a home run. Instead, the ball hit off the top of the left-field wall for a double. If Perez had run hard, he would have scored easily and given New York a 1-0 lead. And perhaps this game never would have gone into extra innings.

The turning point: Benitez, who was 41-for-46 in save opportunities during the regular season, couldn't preserve a 3-2 lead in the ninth against the bottom of the Yankees' order. He walked Paul O'Neill with one out and then allowed singles to Luis Polonia and Vizcaino to load the bases. Chuck Knoblauch tied the game with a sacrifice fly.

Notable: The victory was the Yankees' record 13th straight in World Series play. They lost the first two games of the 1996 World Series before winning the next four. They then swept the Series in both 1998 and 1999. ... It was the longest World Series game by time at 4 hours and 51 minutes. ... The Yankees' bullpen pitched 5 1/3 scoreless innings. ... The Yankees had only two hits—a pair of second-inning singles—in the first five innings against Leiter. ... The Yankees had a great chance to win the game in the 10th with runners at first and third and nobody out. However, Tino Martinez popped out and O'Neill grounded into a double play. ... Benitez blew his sixth postseason save—the most in baseball history—and dropped to 3-for-9 in postseason save opportunities. ... No Met reached base after the ninth inning. ... Leiter and Andy Pettitte became the first two lefthanders to start World Series Game 1 since October 17, 1987, when Minnesota's Frank Viola beat St. Louis' Joe Magrane.

Quotable: Mets manager Bobby Valentine: "We came in with very little World Series experience and got a lot in one night." . ... Zeile, on his double that just missed being a homer: "We needed Jeffrey Maier. Where was he when we needed him?" Maier was the 12-year-old boy who got the Yankees a taint-

ed homer against Baltimore in the 1996 ALCS by reaching over the wall at Yankee Stadium to catch a ball that replays indicated would not have gotten over the wall. Zeile was a member of that Orioles team. ... Vizcaino, on his game-winning hit off Wendell in the 12th: "I knew what was coming. His best pitch is the fastball. I knew he was going to come with the fastball." . ... Torre, on what he said to Vizcaino after the game: "I kissed him on the cheek and said, 'Thanks for making me look smart.' "

BOX SCORE

SATURDAY, OCTOBER 21, AT YANKEE STADIUM, N.Y.

New York Mets	AB	R	H	RBI	PO	A
Perez, rf	6	0	1	0	3	0
Alfonzo, 2b	6	0	1	1	1	3
Piazza, dh	5	0	1	0	0	0
Zeile, 1b	5	0	2	0	9	1
Ventura, 3b	5	0	0	0	0	3
Agbayani, lf	4	1	2	0	2	0
McEwing, lf	1	0	0	0	2	0
Payton, cf	5	1	1	0	5	0
Pratt, c	2	1	0	0	10	0
Bordick, ss	1	0	0	0	2	2
†Trammell, ph	1	0	1	2	0	0
Abbott, ss	2	0	1	0	1	1
Leiter, p	0	0	0	0	0	2
J. Franco, p	0	0	0	0	0	0
Benitez, p	0	0	0	0	0	0
Cook, p	0	0	0	0	0	0
Rusch, p	0	0	0	0	0	0
Wendell, p	0	0	0	0	0	0
Totals	43	3	10	3	35	12

New York Yankees	AB	R	H	RBI	PO	A
Knoblauch, dh	4	1	0	1	0	0
Jeter, ss	4	1	1	0	1	2
Justice, lf	4	0	1	2	0	1
§Bellinger, pr-lf	0	0	0	0	0	0
∞Hill, ph-lf	1	0	0	0	0	0
Williams, cf	4	0	0	0	6	0
Martinez, 1b	6	1	2	0	8	1
Posada, c	5	0	1	0	13	0
O'Neill, rf	4	1	1	0	4	0
Brosius, 3b	3	0	1	0	1	1
‡Polonia, ph	1	0	1	0	0	0
Sojo, 3b	2	0	0	0	0	1
Vizcaino, 2b	6	0	4	1	3	2
Pettitte, p	0	0	0	0	0	4
Nelson, p	0	0	0	0	0	0
Rivera, p	0	0	0	0	0	0
Stanton, p	0	0	0	0	0	0
Totals	44	4	12	4	36	12

New York Mets	0 0 0	0 0 0	3 0 0	0—3
New York Yankees	0 0 0	0 0 2	0 0 1	0 0 1—4

New York Mets	IP	H	R	ER	BB	SO
Leiter	7.0	5	2	2	3	7
J. Franco	1.0	1	0	0	0	0
Benitez	1.0	2	1	1	1	1
Cook	*0.0	0	0	0	2	0
Rusch	1.2	1	0	0	2	0
Wendell (L)	1.0	3	1	1	1	0

New York Yankees	IP	H	R	ER	BB	SO
Pettitte	6.2	8	3	3	1	4
Nelson	1.1	1	0	0	0	0
Rivera	2.0	1	0	0	0	3
Stanton (W)	2.0	0	0	0	0	3

*Pitched to two batters in 10th.

Bases on balls—Off Leiter 3 (Knoblauch, Jeter, Williams), off Benitez 1 (O'Neill), off Cook 2 (Justice, Williams), off Rusch 2 (Posada, Jeter), off Wendell 1 (O'Neill), off Pettitte 1 (Pratt).

Strikeouts—ByLeiter 7 (Jeter, Vizcaino, Williams, Martinez, Posada, O'Neill, Knoblauch), by Benitez 1 (Jeter), by Pettitte 4 (Ventura, Agbayani, Pratt, Bordick), by Rivera 3 (Alfonzo, Piazza, Zeile), by Stanton 3 (Pratt, Perez, Alfonzo).

†Singled for Bordick in seventh. ‡Singled for Brosius in ninth. §Ran for Justice in 10th. ∞Flied out for Bellinger in 11th.

DP—Mets 1. LOB—Mets 8, Yankees 15. 2B—Zeile, Agbayani, Abbott, Justice, Posada. SH—Bordick. SF—Knoblauch. CS—Piazza, Knoblauch. HBP—By Pettitte (Pratt), by Rivera (Pratt). WP—Rusch 2. T—4:51. A—55,913. U—Montague, plate; Reliford, first; Kellogg, second; Welke, third; McClelland, left field; Crawford, right field.

PLAY BY PLAY

FIRST INNING

Mets—Perez grounded out, Vizcaino to Martinez. Alfonzo lined to O'Neill. Piazza flied to O'Neill.

Yankees—Knoblauch flied to Payton. Jeter struck out. Justice flied to Agbayani.

SECOND INNING

Mets—Zeile singled to left. Ventura and Agbayani struck out. Payton flied to Williams.

Yankees—Williams grounded out, Bordick to Zeile. Martinez singled to center. Posada forced Martinez at second, Ventura to Alfonzo. O'Neill singled to center as Posada advanced to third. Brosius grounded out to Zeile.

THIRD INNING

Mets—Pratt hit by a pitch. Bordick sacrificed Pratt to second. Bordick was out on the play, Pettitte to Martinez. Perez popped to Brosius. Alfonzo grounded out, Jeter to Martinez.

Yankees—Vizcaino struck out. Knoblauch walked. Knoblauch caught attempting to steal, Leiter to Zeile to Bordick. Jeter grounded out, Ventura to Zeile.

FOURTH INNING

Mets—Piazza singled to left-center. Piazza caught attempting to steal, Pettitte to Martinez to Jeter. Zeile grounded out, Brosius to Martinez. Ventura grounded out, Pettitte to Martinez.

Yankees—Justice flied to Perez. Williams and Martinez struck out.

FIFTH INNING

Mets—Agbayani doubled to left. Payton grounded out to Posada, unassisted. Pratt and Bordick struck out.

Yankees—Posada struck out. O'Neill flied to Agbayani. Brosius grounded out, Bordick to Zeile.

SIXTH INNING

Mets—Perez singled to center. Alfonzo popped to Vizcaino. Piazza flied to Williams. Zeile doubled to left, but Perez was tagged out at home on the play, Justice to Jeter to Posada.

Yankees—Vizcaino singled to left. Knoblauch forced Vizcaino at second, Leiter to Bordick. Jeter walked. Justice doubled to left-center, scoring Knoblauch and Jeter. Williams was intentionally walked. Martinez grounded to Zeile as Justice advanced to third and Williams to second. Posada flied to Payton. **Yankees 2, Mets 0.**

SEVENTH INNING

Mets—Ventura popped to Vizcaino. Agbayani singled to right. Payton singled to center as Agbayani advanced to second. Pratt walked. Trammell, pinch-hitting for Bordick, singled to left, scoring Agbayani and Payton as Pratt advanced to second. Perez grounded out, Pettitte to Martinez, as Pratt advanced to third and Trammell to second. Nelson now pitching. Alfonzo singled to third, scoring Pratt as Trammell advanced to third. Piazza flied to Williams. **Mets 3, Yankees 2.**

Yankees—Abbott now at shortstop. O'Neill struck out. Brosius singled to center. Vizcaino grounded out, Ventura to Zeile, as Brosius advanced to second. Knoblauch struck out.

EIGHTH INNING

Mets—Zeile popped to Vizcaino. Ventura fouled to Posada. Agbayani flied to O'Neill.

Yankees—J. Franco now pitching and McEwing in left field. Jeter singled to center. Justice flied to Payton. Williams flied to Perez. Martinez flied to Payton.

NINTH INNING

Mets—Rivera now pitching. Payton flied to O'Neill. Pratt hit by a pitch. Abbott doubled to right as Pratt advanced to third. Perez grounded out, Vizcaino to Martinez. Alfonzo struck out.

Yankees—Benitez now pitching. Posada flied to Payton. O'Neill walked. Polonia, pinch-hitting for Brosius, singled to right as O'Neill advanced to second. Vizcaino singled to left as O'Neill advanced to third and Polonia to second. Knoblauch hit a sacrifice fly to McEwing, scoring O'Neill. Jeter struck out. **Mets 3, Yankees 3.**

TENTH INNING

Mets—Sojo now at third base. Piazza and Zeile struck out. Ventura flied to Williams.

Yankees—Cook now pitching. Justice and Williams walked. Bellinger now pinch-running for Justice. Rusch now pitching. Bellinger advanced to third and Williams to second on a wild pitch. Martinez flied to McEwing. Posada was intentionally walked. O'Neill grounded into a double play, Alfonzo to Abbott to Zeile.

ELEVENTH INNING

Mets—Stanton now pitching and Bellinger in left field. McEwing flied to Williams. Payton grounded out, Sojo to Martinez. Pratt struck out.

Yankees—Sojo grounded out, Alfonzo to Zeile. Vizcaino singled to right-center. Knoblauch forced Jeter. Jeter walked on a wild pitch and advanced to second as Vizcaino advanced to third. Wendell now pitching. Hill, pinch-hitting for Bellinger, flied to Perez.

TWELFTH INNING

Mets—Hill now in left field. Abbott flied to Williams. Perez and Alfonzo struck out.

Yankees—Williams grounded out, Alfonzo to Zeile. Martinez singled to right-center. Posada doubled to right-center as Martinez advanced to third. O'Neill was intentionally walked. Sojo fouled to Pratt. Vizcaino singled to left, scoring Martinez and O'Neill to second. **Final score: Yankees 4, Mets 3.**

GAME 2

HIGHLIGHTS

YANKEES 6, METS 5

Why the Yankees won: Roger Clemens, making his first start since throwing a one-hitter against Seattle in the ALCS, was magnificent. He pitched eight scoreless innings and allowed only two singles. He walked none and struck out nine. The Yankees got to Mets lefthander Mike Hampton early, scoring twice in the first and once in the second. The Yankees built a 6-0 lead and needed every run as the Mets rallied for five runs in the ninth.

Why the Mets lost: They needed a great start from Hampton—who pitched 15 scoreless innings in the NLCS—and didn't get it. Hampton struggled with his control early and fell behind in the count to the first six hitters. He retired the first two batters but then walked two and gave up hits to Tino Martinez and Jorge Posada. Hampton allowed four runs in six innings and the bullpen gave up two more. The Mets made a great rally in the ninth but came up short.

The turning point: This game might have been over as soon as the Yankees scored two runs in the first because it was clear Clemens had his best stuff. The Mets got a single in the second and didn't get another hit until one out in the seventh. The Mets had only one runner reach second against Clemens and that was because he granted permission to advance from first via a wild pitch. Of Clemens' 112, pitches, 78 were for strikes. In the ninth, when the Mets had closed the gap to 6-2, Todd Zeile hit a ball over the left-field wall that Clay Bellinger, who was brought into the game for his defense, brought back for an out. It was a huge catch as the Mets' rally fell one run short.

Notable: Most of the headlines stemming from this game concerned the first inning, when Clemens faced Mike Piazza. Piazza hit a foul ball and shattered his bat. Not knowing the ball was foul, Piazza ran toward first and Clemens then tossed the barrel of the bat toward Piazza, with the jagged piece of lumber cartwheeling dangerously close to the Mets catcher. Piazza glared at Clemens, and the two players exchanged words as both benches cleared. Clemens later was fined $50,000 for his actions. ... It was the Yankees' 14th consecutive World Series victory. ... Hampton threw 124 pitches but only 65 strikes. ... Yankees reliever Jeff Nelson faced three batters in the ninth and allowed all three to reach base. ... Mariano Rivera allowed two runs in the ninth inning, snapping a streak of 14 1/3 scoreless innings in World Series competition. ... Yankees shortstop Derek Jeter went 3-for-5 to extend his World Series hitting streak to 11 games. He had reached base in 53 of 58 career postseason games. ... Benny Agbayani singled in the ninth inning for the Mets to hit safely in all 11 of their postseason games. ... Clemens improved to 2-0 with a 1.67 ERA in four career World Series starts. ... In the first two games of the Series the Yankees left a combined 27 men on base.

Quotable: Clemens, on the bat-throwing incident: "There was no intent. I was fired up and emotional and flung the bat toward the on-deck circle where the batboy was. I had no idea that Mike was running." Piazza: "If he (Clemens) says anything that was, like, derogatory or obscene to me, that would have been a problem. But he seemed extremely apologetic and unsure and confused and unstable." . ... Piazza, on why he wouldn't be seeking an apology from Clemens: "An apology is only as good as the source it comes from." . ... Hampton on his performance: "It took a while to settle in. They're a great team. If you make a mistake they capitalize on it." . ... Yankees left fielder David Justice, on the media coverage of the bat-throwing incident: "They've made this into a freak show. Roger threw a two-hitter, one of best playoff performances I've ever seen, and all anyone's talking about is him tossing the end of a bat."

BOX SCORE

SUNDAY, OCTOBER 22, AT YANKEE STADIUM, N.Y.

New York Mets	AB	R	H	RBI	PO	A
Perez, rf	4	0	0	0	1	1
Alfonzo, 2b	3	1	1	0	1	5
Piazza, c	4	1	1	2	6	1
Ventura, 3b	4	0	1	0	0	2
Zeile, 1b	4	0	2	0	9	0
Agbayani, lf	4	1	1	0	0	0
Harris, dh	4	1	0	0	0	0
Payton, cf	4	1	1	3	5	0
Bordick, ss	2	0	0	0	1	3
†Hamilton, ph	1	0	0	0	0	0
Abbott, ss	1	0	0	0	1	1
Hampton, p	0	0	0	0	0	0
Rusch, p	0	0	0	0	0	0
White, p	0	0	0	0	0	0
Cook, p	0	0	0	0	0	0
Totals	35	5	7	5	24	13

New York Yankees	AB	R	H	RBI	PO	A
Knoblauch, dh	4	0	0	0	0	0
Jeter, ss	5	1	3	0	1	4
Justice, lf	3	1	0	0	2	0
Bellinger, lf	0	0	0	0	1	0
Williams, cf	3	1	0	0	1	0
Martinez, 1b	5	1	3	2	11	0
Posada, c	3	1	2	1	10	1
O'Neill, rf	4	0	3	1	0	0
Brosius, 3b	3	1	1	2	0	2
Vizcaino, 2b	4	0	0	0	1	2
Clemens, p	0	0	0	0	0	2
Nelson, p	0	0	0	0	0	0
Rivera, p	0	0	0	0	0	1
Totals	34	6	12	6	27	12

New York Mets	0	0	0	0	0	0	0	0	5—5
New York Yankees	2	1	0	0	1	0	1	1	x—6

New York Mets	IP	H	R	ER	BB	SO
Hampton (L)	6.0	8	4	4	5	4
Rusch	0.1	2	1	1	0	0
White	1.1	1	1	1	1	1
Cook	0.1	1	0	0	0	0

New York Yankees	IP	H	R	ER	BB	SO
Clemens (W)	8.0	2	0	0	0	9
Nelson	*0.0	3	3	3	0	0
Rivera	1.0	2	2	2	0	1

*Pitched to three batters in ninth.

Bases on balls—Off Hampton 5 (Justice, Williams, Knoblauch, Posada 2), off White 1 (Williams).

Strikeouts—By Hampton 4 (Jeter, O'Neill, Brosius, Justice), by White 1 (Vizcaino), by Clemens 9 (Perez, Alfonzo, Agbayani 2, Harris, Payton, Ventura, Bordick, Hamilton), by Rivera 1 (Abbott).

†Struck out for Bordick in eighth.

E—Payton, Bordick, Perez, Clemens. LOB—Mets 4, Yankees 12. 2B—Jeter 2, Martinez, Posada. HR—Piazza, Payton, Brosius. SF—Brosius. CS—Vizcaino. HBP—By Hampton (Justice), by Clemens (Alfonzo). WP—Clemens. PB—Posada. T—3:30. A—56,059. U—Reliford, plate; Kellogg, first; Welke, second; McClelland, third; Crawford, left field; Montague, right field.

PLAY BY PLAY

FIRST INNING

Mets—Perez struck out. Alfonzo struck out and was put out at first after a dropped third strike, Posada to Martinez. Piazza grounded out, Vizcaino to Martinez.

Yankees—Knoblauch lined to Payton. Jeter struck out. Justice walked. Martinez singled to left, scoring Justice as Williams advanced to second. Posada singled to center and reached second on a fielding error by Payton as Williams scored and Martinez advanced to third. O'Neill struck out. Yankees 2, Mets 0.

SECOND INNING

Mets—Ventura grounded out, Clemens to Martinez. Zeile singled to center. Agbayani and Harris struck out.

Yankees—Brosius homered to left. Vizcaino reached first on a fielding error by Bordick. Vizcaino caught attempting to steal second, Piazza to Bordick. Knoblauch walked. Jeter singled to right and reached second on a fielding error by Perez. On the play, Knoblauch was tagged out at home, Perez to Alfonzo to Piazza. Justice grounded out, Alfonzo to Zeile. **Yankees 3, Mets 0.**

THIRD INNING

Mets—Payton struck out. Bordick popped to Jeter. Perez grounded to Martinez.

Yankees—Williams flied to Payton. Martinez grounded out, Alfonzo to Zeile. Posada walked. O'Neill singled to center as Posada advanced to second. Brosius struck out.

FOURTH INNING

Mets—Alfonzo hit by a pitch. Piazza fouled to Martinez. Ventura struck out. Zeile forced Alfonzo at second, Jeter to Vizcaino.

Yankees—Vizcaino grounded out, Bordick to Zeile. Knoblauch flied to Payton. Jeter grounded out, Ventura to Zeile.

FIFTH INNING

Mets—Agbayani grounded out, Jeter to Martinez. Harris and Payton grounded out, Brosius to Martinez.

Yankees—Justice struck out. Williams grounded out, Bordick to Zeile. Martinez doubled to right-center. Posada was intentionally walked. O'Neill singled to right, scoring Martinez as Posada advanced to third. Brosius popped to Alfonzo. **Yankees 4, Mets 0.**

SIXTH INNING

Mets—Bordick struck out. Perez bunted and reached first on a throwing error by Clemens. Alfonzo flied to Williams. Piazza flied to Justice.

Yankees—Vizcaino grounded out, Ventura to Zeile. Knoblauch flied to Payton. Jeter doubled to left-center. Justice was hit by a pitch. Williams flied to Payton.

SEVENTH INNING

Mets—Ventura flied to Justice. Zeile singled to left. Zeile advanced to second on a wild pitch. Agbayani struck out and was put out at first after a dropped third strike, Posada to Martinez. Harris grounded out, Clemens to Martinez.

Yankees—Rusch now pitching. Martinez grounded out, Bordick to Zeile. Posada singled to right-center. O'Neill doubled to right as Posada advanced to third.

White now pitching. Brosius hit a sacrifice fly to Perez, scoring Posada as O'Neill advanced to third. Vizcaino struck out. **Yankees 5, Mets 0.**

EIGHTH INNING

Mets—Payton grounded out, Vizcaino to Martinez. Hamilton, pinch-hitting for Bordick, struck out. Perez grounded out, Jeter to Martinez.

Yankees—Abbott now at shortstop. Knoblauch grounded out, Alfonzo to Zeile. Jeter doubled to right. Justice grounded out, Abbott to Zeile. Williams was intentionally walked. Cook now pitching. Martinez singled to left, scoring Jeter as Williams advanced to second. Posada forced Martinez at second, Alfonzo to Abbott. **Yankees 6, Mets 0.**

NINTH INNING

Mets—Nelson now pitching and Bellinger in left field. Alfonzo singled to left-center. Piazza homered, scoring Alfonzo. Ventura singled to center. Rivera now pitching. Zeile flied to Bellinger. Agbayani singled to left as Ventura advanced to second. Ventura advanced to third and Agbayani to second on a passed ball. Harris reached first on a fielder's choice as Ventura was tagged out at the plate, Rivera to Jeter to Posada. Agbayani advanced to third on the play. Harris advanced to second on defensive indifference. Payton homered to right, scoring Agbayani and Harris. Abbott struck out. **Final score: Yankees 6, Mets 5.**

METS 4, YANKEES 2

Why the Mets won: They got some clutch hits for the first time in the Series. With the game tied 2-2 in the eighth, the Mets got an RBI double from Benny Agbayani to take the lead, and Bubba Trammell added another run with a sacrifice fly to center. The Mets bullpen, which had been scored upon in each of the first two games, pitched three scoreless innings and Armando Benitez picked up the save.

Why the Yankees lost: They were too patient at the plate against Mets starter Rick Reed, who walked only 34 batters in 30 regular season starts. Five Yankees struck out looking in the first four innings alone. The Bronx Bombers never got going on offense. They had only three hits after the fifth inning and for the game went 0-for-5 with runners in scoring position. The top four spots in the Yankee order went 3-for-16 (.188).

The turning point: With the Yankees leading 2-1 in the sixth, the Mets had runners at first and second, nobody out and Todd Zeile at the plate. Mets manager Bobby Valentine had Zeile bunting despite the fact Zeile had no sacrifice bunts all season and only seven in his 12-year career. After one miserable attempt by Zeile, Valentine had Zeile swing away. Zeile came through with an RBI double to tie the game.

Notable: Yankees starter Orlando Hernandez struck out the side in each of the first two innings. His 12 strikeouts for the game were the most by a Yankee in a World Series game, breaking Bob Turley's mark of 11 set in 1956. ... Hernandez suffered his first postseason loss. He entered the game with a postseason record of 8-0 and a 1.90 ERA. ... Mets reliever John Franco, 40, picked up the victory in relief, becoming the second-oldest pitcher to win a World Series game. Dolph Luque was 43 when he won a World Series game for the Giants against the Senators in 1933. ... The Mets' victory snapped the Yankees' 14-game World Series winning streak. ... Yankees right fielder Paul O'Neill doubled and tripled in his first two at-bats to give him five consecutive hits—two short of the Series record of seven set by Cincinnati's Billy Hatcher in 1990. O'Neill grounded out in his next at-bat. ... The Mets had the bases loaded and nobody out in the sixth but failed to score.

Quotable: Franco, noting that the win was the Mets' first in World Series play at Shea Stadium since Game 7 of the 1986 series: "Our fans have been waiting 14 years for this. They're very loud, and we just love being in this ballpark because of the noise." . ... Yankees manager Joe Torre, on why he left Hernandez in the game with the go-ahead run at the plate in the eighth: "He deserved the right to get a decision in this one. I thought he was great.". ... Agbayani, on the end of Hernandez's streak: "All we ever heard was how he won all those games and had never lost. There's the first time for everyone." . ... Valentine: "We were a couple of swings and a couple of pitches away from winning the first two games in Yankee Stadium. We got the swings and we got the pitches this time. We played the same game, minus a couple of mistakes. You know, it seems light years of difference between 0-3 and 1-2, and it's 1-2."

BOX SCORE

TUESDAY, OCTOBER 24, AT SHEA STADIUM, N.Y.

New York Yankees	AB	R	H	RBI	PO	A
Vizcaino, 2b	4	0	0	0	3	0
▼Polonia, ph	1	0	0	0	0	0
Jeter, ss	4	1	2	0	0	1
Justice, lf	3	0	1	1	3	0
Williams, cf	4	0	0	0	1	0
Martinez, 1b	3	1	1	0	2	1
Posada, c	4	0	0	0	14	0
O'Neill, rf	4	0	3	1	1	0
Brosius, 3b	2	0	0	0	0	1
‡Hill, ph	1	0	0	0	0	0
Sojo, 3b	0	0	0	0	0	0
Hernandez, p	2	0	0	0	0	0
Stanton, p	0	0	0	0	0	0
■Knoblauch, ph	1	0	1	0	0	0
Totals	**33**	**2**	**8**	**2**	**24**	**3**

New York Mets	AB	R	H	RBI	PO	A
Perez, rf	3	0	0	0	2	0
Alfonzo, 2b	4	0	0	0	4	3
Piazza, c	4	1	1	0	12	0
Ventura, 3b	3	1	2	1	0	1
Zeile, 1b	4	1	2	1	5	0
Agbayani, lf	3	0	1	1	1	0
§McEwing, pr-lf	0	1	0	0	0	0
Payton, cf	4	0	1	0	3	0
Bordick, ss	3	0	1	0	0	1
∞Harris, ph	0	0	0	0	0	0
▲Trammell, ph	0	0	0	1	0	0
Benitez, p	0	0	0	0	0	0
Reed, p	1	0	1	0	0	1
†Hamilton, ph	1	0	0	0	0	0
Wendell, p	0	0	0	0	0	0
Cook, p	0	0	0	0	0	0
J. Franco, p	0	0	0	0	0	0
◆Abbott, ph-ss	1	0	0	0	0	0
Totals	**31**	**4**	**9**	**4**	**27**	**6**

New York Yankees	0	0 1	1 0 0	0 0	0—2
New York Mets	0	1 0	0 0 1	0 2	x—4

New York Yankees	IP	H	R	ER	BB	SO
Hernandez (L)	7.1	9	4	4	3	12
Stanton	0.2	0	0	0	0	1

New York Mets	IP	H	R	ER	BB	SO
Reed	6.0	6	2	2	1	8
Wendell	0.2	0	0	0	1	2
Cook	*0.1	0	0	0	1	1
J. Franco (W)	1.0	1	0	0	0	0
Benitez (S)	1.0	1	0	0	0	1

*Pitched to one batter in eighth.

Bases on balls—Off Hernandez 3 (Perez, Ventura, Agbayani), off Reed 1 (Justice), off Wendell 1 (Jeter), off Cook 1 (Martinez).

Strikeouts—By Hernandez 12 (Perez, Alfonzo 2, Piazza 2, Zeile 2, Agbayani, Payton 2, Bordick, Ventura), by Stanton 1 (Abbott), by Reed 8 (Jeter, Williams, Martinez, Posada 2, Brosius, Hernandez, Vizcaino), by Wendell 2 (Hernandez, Vizcaino), by Cook 1 (Williams), by Benitez 1 (Jeter).

†Reached on a fielder's choice for Reed in sixth. ‡Flied out for Brosius in eighth. §Ran for Agbayani in eighth. ∞Announced for Bordick in eighth.

▲Hit sacrifice fly for Harris in eighth. ◆Struck out for J. Franco in eighth. ■Singled for Stanton in ninth. ▼Flied out for Vizcaino in ninth.

DP—Mets 1. LOB—Yankees 10, Mets 8. 2B—Justice, O'Neill, Piazza, Ventura, Zeile, Agbayani. 3B—O'Neill. HR—Ventura. SH—Hernandez, Reed. SF—Trammell. HBP—By Reed (Brosius), by Cook (Justice). T—3:39. A—55,299. U—Kellogg, plate; Welke, first; McClelland, second; Crawford, third; Montague, left field; Reliford, right field.

PLAY BY PLAY

FIRST INNING

Yankees—Vizcaino flied to Perez, Jeter struck out. Justice walked. Williams struck out.

Mets—Perez, Alfonzo and Piazza struck out.

SECOND INNING

Yankees—Martinez and Posada struck out. O'Neill doubled to left. Brosius struck out.

Mets—Ventura homered to right-center. Zeile, Agbayani and Payton struck out. **Mets 1, Yankees 0.**

THIRD INNING

Yankees—Hernandez struck out. Vizcaino grounded out, Bordick to Zeile. Jeter singled to left-center. Justice doubled to right, scoring Jeter, and Justice advanced to third on the throw from the outfield. Williams grounded out, Alfonzo to Zeile. **Mets 1, Yankees 1.**

Mets—Bordick flied to Justice. Reed singled to left. Perez flied to Justice. Alfonzo popped to Vizcaino.

FOURTH INNING

Yankees—Martinez singled to right. Posada struck out. O'Neill tripled to right-center, scoring Martinez. Brosius was hit by a pitch. Hernandez sacrificed Brosius to second. Hernandez was out on the play, Reed to Alfonzo, covering first. Vizcaino struck out. **Yankees 2, Mets 1.**

Mets—Piazza struck out. Ventura doubled to right. Zeile struck out Agbayani flied to O'Neill.

FIFTH INNING

Yankees—Jeter singled to short. Justice flied to Payton. Williams grounded to Zeile as Jeter advanced to second. Martinez flied to Payton.

Mets—Payton fouled to Posada. Bordick singled to center. Reed sacrificed Bordick to second. Reed was out on the play, Martinez to Vizcaino, covering first. Perez walked. Alfonzo struck out.

SIXTH INNING

Yankees—Posada flied to Agbayani. O'Neill grounded out, Alfonzo to Zeile. Brosius popped to Alfonzo.

Mets—Piazza doubled to left. Ventura walked. Zeile doubled to left, scoring Piazza as Ventura advanced to third. Agbayani walked. Payton and Bordick struck out. Hamilton, pinch-hitting for Reed, forced Agbayani at second, Jeter to Vizcaino. **Yankees 2, Mets 2.**

SEVENTH INNING

Yankees—Wendell now pitching. Hernandez and Vizcaino struck out. Jeter walked. Cook now pitching. Justice was hit by a pitch. Williams struck out.

Mets—Perez flied to Justice. Alfonzo grounded out, Brosius to Martinez. Piazza popped to Martinez.

EIGHTH INNING

Yankees—Martinez walked. J. Franco now pitching. Posada grounded into a double play, Ventura to Alfonzo to Zeile. O'Neill singled to center. Hill, pinch-hitting for Brosius, flied to Perez.

Mets—Sojo now at third base. Ventura struck out. Zeile singled to left-center. Agbayani doubled to left-center, scoring Zeile. McEwing now pinch-running for Agbayani. Payton singled to second as McEwing advanced to third. Harris now pinch-hitting for Bordick. Stanton now pitching. Trammell, pinch-hitting for Harris, hit a sacrifice fly to Williams, scoring McEwing. Abbott, pinch-hitting for J. Franco, struck out. **Mets 4, Yankees 2.**

Yankees—Benitez now pitching, McEwing in left field and Abbott at shortstop. Knoblauch, pinch-hitting for Stanton, singled to center. Polonia, pinch-hitting for Vizcaino, flied to Payton. Jeter struck out. Knoblauch advanced to second on defensive indifference. Justice popped to Alfonzo. **Final score: Mets 4, Yankees 2.**

GAME 4
HIGHLIGHTS

YANKEES 3, METS 2

Why the Yankees won: They made the most of their scoring opportunities to build an early 3—0 lead. When the Mets cut it to 3-2, the bullpen came in and pitched 4 1/3 scoreless innings, allowing only two hits. The Yankees got a home run from Derek Jeter on the first pitch of the game, a sacrifice fly by Scott Brosius in the second and an RBI groundout by Luis Sojo in the third. Through three innings, the Yankees had three runs on only three hits, but it was all they would need.

Why the Mets lost: Despite having runners on base in every inning except for the fifth and the ninth, their only runs came on a two-run homer by Mike Piazza in the third. Edgardo Alfonzo, the Mets' No. 2 hitter, was held hitless for a second consecutive game, and No. 5 hitter Robin Ventura went 0-for-4. The bottom three spots in the Mets' order went 3-for-14 (.214).

The turning point: Jeter hit in the leadoff spot for the first time in the Series and quickly quieted the crowd by homering on the first pitch from Mets righthander Bobby Jones. Jeter led off the third with a triple to right center and scored on a RBI ground-out. In the fifth, Piazza, who had homered off Denny Neagle in the third, came up to the plate with two outs and nobody on. Torre didn't want Neagle to face Piazza so he took him out and brought in David Cone, who got Piazza to pop out to end the inning.

Notable: Jeter's homer and triple in his first two at-bats put him in a position to become the first player to hit for the cycle in World Series history. However, in his next three at-bats, he struck out, grounded out and reached on a error. ... Paul O'Neill tripled in the second, his second consecutive game with a triple. Before the World Series, O'Neill hadn't hit a triple since July 23, 1999. ... Yankees center fielder Bernie Williams went 0-for-4 to remain hitless in the Series (0-for-15) and lower his career World Series average to .118 (8-for-68). ... Mets left fielder Benny Agbayani went 0-for-3, failing to get a hit for the first time in his team's 13 postseason games. ... By pulling Neagle in the fifth with the Yankees up 3-2, manager Joe Torre prevented him from getting the victory. After the game, Torre admitted Neagle was upset when he went to take him out of the game. ... The Yankees had runners on in every inning after the third but never got one past second base. The 2-3-4 hitters in the Yankees' lineup went 1-for-11.

Quotable: Jeter, on his leadoff homer: "I've been known to swing at the first pitch. When you play games like this, you want to score early. I got a good pitch to hit, and I hit it well." . . . Jones, in his first pitch to Jeter: "I wasn't expecting him to swing." . ... Mets manager Bobby Valentine, whose team fell behind in the series three games to one: "It's not frustrating. We're giving everything we have out there. They're giving just a little extra." . . . Torre on why he took Neagle out of the game when Piazza came to the plate in the fifth: "Denny did a terrific job for us, but when you're managing in a short series, you have to do what you think is right at that moment to get you out of the situation. Mike had two pretty good swings against Denny, and I wouldn't have been able to forgive myself if something bad would have happened there."

BOX SCORE

WEDNESDAY, OCTOBER 25, AT SHEA STADIUM, N.Y.

New York Yankees	AB	R	H	RBI	PO	A
Jeter, ss	5	2	2	1	1	3
Sojo, 2b	4	0	1	1	4	0
Justice, lf	5	0	0	0	2	0
Bellinger, lf	0	0	0	0	1	0
Williams, cf	4	0	0	0	1	0
Martinez, 1b	4	0	2	0	7	0
O'Neill, rf	4	1	2	0	3	0
Posada, c	3	0	0	0	8	0
Brosius, 3b	1	0	1	1	0	1
Neagle, p	2	0	0	0	0	0
Cone, p	0	0	0	0	0	0
†Canseco, ph	1	0	0	0	0	0
Nelson, p	0	0	0	0	1	1
Stanton, p	0	0	0	0	0	0
Rivera, p	1	0	0	0	0	0
Totals	34	3	8	3	27	5

New York Mets	AB	R	H	RBI	PO	A
Perez, rf	3	1	1	0	2	0
▲Abbott, ph-ss	1	0	0	0	1	1
Alfonzo, 2b	3	0	0	0	1	5
Piazza, c	4	1	1	2	6	0
Zeile, 1b	4	0	2	0	6	1
◆McEwing, pr	0	0	0	0	0	0
Benitez, p	0	0	0	0	0	0
Ventura, 3b	4	0	0	0	0	2
Agbayani, lf	3	0	0	0	1	0
Payton, cf	4	0	2	0	4	0
Bordick, ss	2	0	0	0	1	1
‡Harris, ph	1	0	0	0	0	0
J. Franco, p	0	0	0	0	1	0
M. Franco, 1b	1	0	0	0	1	0
B.J. Jones, p	2	0	0	0	1	0
Rusch, p	0	0	0	0	0	0
§Hamilton, ph	0	0	0	0	0	0
∞Trammell, ph-rf	1	0	0	0	2	0
Totals	32	2	6	2	27	10

New York Yankees	1	1	1	0	0	0	0	0	0—3
New York Mets	0	0	2	0	0	0	0	0	0—2

New York Yankees	IP	H	R	ER	BB	SO
Neagle	4.2	4	2	2	2	3
Cone	0.1	0	0	0	0	0
Nelson (W)	1.1	1	0	0	1	1
Stanton	0.2	0	0	0	0	2
Rivera (S)	2.0	1	0	0	0	2

New York Mets	IP	H	R	ER	BB	SO
B.J. Jones (L).........................	5.0	4	3	3	3	3
Rusch....................................	2.0	3	0	0	0	2
J. Franco	1.0	1	0	0	0	1
Benitez.................................	1.0	0	0	0	1	0

Bases on balls—Off Neagle 2 (Alfonzo, Agbayani), off Nelson 1 (Harris), off B.J. Jones 3 (Posada, Brosius, Sojo), off Benitez 1 (Brosius).

Strikeouts—By Neagle 3 (Perez, Piazza, B.J. Jones), by Nelson 1 (Payton), by Stanton 2 (Trammell, Abbott), by Rivera 2 (Agbayani, M. Franco), by B.J. Jones 3 (Martinez, Neagle, Jeter), by Rusch 2 (Canseco, Williams), by J. Franco (Posada).

†Struck out for Cone in sixth. ‡Walked for Bordick in seventh. §Announced for Rusch in seventh. ∞Struck out for Hamilton in seventh. ▲Struck out for Perez in seventh. ◆Ran for Zeile in eighth.

E—Trammell. DP—Yankees 1, Mets 1. LOB—Yankees 9, Mets 6. 3B—Jeter, Jeter. HR—Jeter, Piazza. SF—Brosius. SB—Sojo. T—3:20. A—55,290. U—Welke, plate; McClelland, first; Crawford, second; Montague, third; Reliford, left field; Kellogg, right field.

PLAY BY PLAY

FIRST INNING

Yankees—Jeter homered to left. Sojo grounded out, Ventura to Zeile. Justice flied to Perez. Williams lined to Payton. **Yankees 1, Mets 0.**

Mets—Perez struck out. Alfonzo walked. Piazza struck out. Zeile forced Alfonzo at second, Jeter to Sojo.

SECOND INNING

Yankees—Martinez struck out. O'Neill tripled to right. Posada was intentionally walked. Brosius hit a sacrifice fly to Payton, scoring O'Neill. Neagle struck out. **Yankees 2, Mets 0.**

Mets—Ventura grounded out, Jeter to Martinez. Agbayani walked. Payton singled to right as Agbayani advanced to second. Bordick popped to Sojo. B.J. Jones popped to Martinez.

THIRD INNING

Yankees—Jeter tripled to right-center. Sojo grounded out, Alfonzo to Zeile, as Jeter scored. Justice grounded to Zeile. Williams flied to Payton. **Yankees 3, Mets 0.**

Mets—Perez singled to center. Alfonzo grounded out, Brosius to Martinez, as Perez advanced to second. Piazza homered to left, scoring Perez. Zeile popped to Sojo. Ventura grounded to Martinez. **Yankees 3, Mets 2.**

FOURTH INNING

Yankees—Martinez singled to right-center. O'Neill forced Martinez at second, Ventura to Alfonzo. Posada grounded out, Alfonzo to B.J. Jones, as O'Neill advanced to second. Brosius was intentionally walked. Neagle flied to Perez.

Mets—Agbayani fouled to Martinez. Payton singled to center. Bordick flied to Justice. B.J. Jones struck out.

FIFTH INNING

Yankees—Jeter struck out. Sojo walked. Justice grounded out, Alfonzo to Zeile, as Sojo advanced to second. Williams lined to Bordick.

Mets—Perez and Alfonzo flied to O'Neill. Cone now pitching. Piazza popped to Sojo.

SIXTH INNING

Yankees—Rusch now pitching. Martinez grounded out, Bordick to Zeile. O'Neill singled to center. Posada flied to Agbayani. Brosius singled to left as O'Neill advanced to second. Canseco, pinch-hitting for Cone, struck out.

Mets—Nelson now pitching. Zeile singled to center. Ventura flied to Justice. Agbayani lined into a double play, Nelson to Martinez.

SEVENTH INNING

Yankees—Jeter grounded out, Alfonzo to Zeile. Sojo singled to right. Justice lined to Payton. Sojo stole second. Williams struck out.

Mets—Payton struck out. Harris, pinch-hitting for Bordick, walked. Hamilton now pinch-hitting for Rusch. Stanton now pitching. Trammell, pinch-hitting for Hamilton, struck out. Abbott, pinch-hitting for Perez, struck out.

EIGHTH INNING

Yankees—J. Franco now pitching, Abbott at shortstop and Trammell in right field. Martinez singled to right. O'Neill grounded into a double play, Zeile to Abbott to J. Franco. Posada struck out.

Mets—Rivera now pitching. Alfonzo flied to O'Neill. Piazza grounded out, Jeter to Martinez. Zeile singled to center. McEwing now pinch-running for Zeile. Ventura popped to Jeter.

NINTH INNING

Yankees—Benitez now pitching and M. Franco at first base. Brosius walked. Rivera flied to Trammell. Jeter reached first on Trammell's fielding error as Brosius advanced to second. Sojo grounded out, Alfonzo to M. Franco, as Brosius advanced to third and Jeter to second. Justice flied to Trammell.

Mets—Bellinger now in left field. Agbayani struck out. Payton flied to Bellinger. M. Franco struck out. **Final score: Yankees 3, Mets 2.**

GAME 5

HIGHLIGHTS

YANKEES 4, METS 2

Why the Yankees won: Bernie Williams, hitless in his last 22 World Series at-bats, got his first hit of the 2000 Series in the second inning with a solo homer down the left field line to give the Yankees a 1-0 lead. With the game tied 2-2 in the top of the ninth, the Yankees scored two runs with the bottom of the order doing most of the damage. The big hit was delivered by No. 9 hitter Luis Sojo, whose two-out single scored two runs.

Why the Mets lost: Once again, they couldn't get the big hit. The Mets had runners on base in seven of the nine innings but were just 1-for-7 with runners in scoring position. The top five spots in the order went 3-for-21. Also, manager Bobby Valentine may have stuck with his starter, Al Leiter, too long. The pitch Sojo smacked for the decisive hit was Leiter's 142nd of the game.

The turning point: The Mets scored both their runs thanks to poor defense by the Yankees. Leiter came up with runners at second and third and two outs and hit a dribbler to first baseman Tino Martinez. Pitcher Andy Pettitte, who was covering first, dropped the throw for an error to hand the Mets their first run. The next batter, Benny Agbayani, hit a grounder to third that Scott Brosius unsuccessfully tried to grab with his bare hand. It was ruled a RBI single but was a play Brosius normally makes. In the fourth with the Mets up 2-1 and a chance to extend their lead, Kurt Abbott walked to put runners at first and second and only one out, but then he got picked off.

Notable: The Yankees became the first team since the Oakland A's (1972-74) to win three consecutive World Series. ... Yankees manager Joe Torre improved his World Series record to 16-3. His .842

winning percentage is the highest of any manager. ... Derek Jeter, who hit .409 (9-for-22) with two doubles, one triple, two homers and six runs, was named World Series MVP. Jeter joined Frank Robinson (1966) as the only players to be named All-Star MVP and World Series MVP in the same season. ... When Jeter homered in the sixth to tie the game 2-2, he also extended his World Series hitting streak to 14 games. ... Leiter retired 16 of the first 19 hitters he faced. Before the ninth the only two Yankees to get past second were Jeter and Williams on the solo homers. ... Mariano Rivera pitched a scoreless ninth for the save, the 18th consecutive postseason save opportunity he successfully converted. ... The Yankees set a five-game World Series record by leaving 52 men on base, easily shattering the previous record of 42 set by the 1941 Yankees. ... Leiter's 8²/₃ innings in Game 5 was the longest start by a pitcher in a World Series game since Atlanta's Greg Maddux pitched a nine-inning complete game in Game 1 of the 1995 Series against Cleveland. Leiter's record dropped to 0-3 in 11 postseason starts, the most starts in postseason history without a win. ... Despite being ousted in five games, the Mets were only outscored 19-16 in the Series. ... It was the Yankees' 26th World Series championship. No other franchise has more than nine.

Quotable: Paul O'Neill, on the Yankees winning the World Series after losing 13 of their last 15 regular season games, many by lopsided scores: "Whether you like us or not, we're winners. Everybody was ready for the collapse. Everybody was waiting for us to lose." . ... Torre: "We may not have the greatest players, but we have the greatest team." . ... Jeter, on the Mets: "In my opinion, the Mets were the toughest team we have played in my five years here. Every one of these games could have gone either way. They could have given up after (losing) the first two games, but they never quit. You can't say enough about the New York Mets." . . . Mets reliever Turk Wendell on Leiter's performance: "Al deserved to win this game. In many ways, he deserved to be out there to lose this game, too. It doesn't even need to be questioned. Al deserved to be the deciding factor." . ... Valentine, with a touch of sarcasm lacing his comments when asked why he left Leiter in the game: "It was the wrong decision, obviously. If I brought somebody else in, they definitely would have gotten the guy out, and we'd still be playing."

BOX SCORE

THURSDAY, OCTOBER 26, AT SHEA STADIUM, N.Y.

New York Yankees	AB	R	H	RBI	PO	A
Vizcaino, 2b	3	0	0	0	2	2
†Knoblauch, ph	1	0	0	0	0	0
Stanton, p	0	0	0	0	0	0
‡Hill, ph	1	0	0	0	0	0
Rivera, p	0	0	0	0	0	0
Jeter, ss	4	1	1	1	2	5
Justice, lf	4	0	1	0	1	0
Bellinger, lf	0	0	0	0	0	0
Williams, cf	3	1	2	1	2	0
Martinez, 1b	4	0	0	0	11	2
O'Neill, rf	3	0	0	0	2	0
Posada, c	3	1	1	0	7	0
Brosius, 3b	4	1	1	0	0	4
Pettitte, p	3	0	0	0	0	1
Sojo, 2b	1	0	1	1	0	0
Totals	34	4	7	3	27	14

New York Mets	AB	R	H	RBI	PO	A
Agbayani, lf	4	0	1	1	5	0
Alfonzo, 2b	5	0	1	0	0	3
Piazza, c	5	0	2	0	10	0
Zeile, 1b	3	0	0	0	10	0
Ventura, 3b	4	0	0	0	1	0
Trammell, rf	3	1	1	0	1	0
Perez, rf	0	0	0	0	0	0
Payton, cf	4	1	2	0	0	0
Abbott, ss	3	0	1	0	0	2
Leiter, p	2	0	0	0	0	1
J. Franco, p	0	0	0	0	0	0
§Hamilton, ph	1	0	0	0	0	0
Totals	34	2	8	1	27	6

New York Yankees	0	1	0	0	0	1	0	0	2—4
New York Mets	0	2	0	0	0	0	0	0	0—2

New York Yankees	IP	H	R	ER	BB	SO
Pettitte	7.0	8	2	0	3	5
Stanton (W)	1.0	0	0	0	0	1
Rivera (S)	1.0	0	0	0	1	1

New York Mets	IP	H	R	ER	BB	SO
Leiter (L)	8.2	7	4	3	3	9
J. Franco	0.1	0	0	0	0	0

Bases on balls—Off Pettitte 3 (Trammell, Abbott, Zeile), off Rivera 1 (Agbayani), off Leiter 3 (Williams, O'Neill, Posada).

Strikeouts—By Pettitte 5 (Ventura 2, Zeile 2, Agbayani), by Stanton 1 (Payton), by Rivera 1 (Hamilton), by Leiter 9 (Jeter 2, O'Neill 2, Pettitte, Vizcaino, Justice, Williams, Martinez).

†Fouled out for Vizcaino in eighth. ‡Flied out for Stanton in ninth. §Struck out for J. Franco in ninth.

E—Pettitte, Payton. LOB—Yankees 6, Mets 10. 2B—Piazza. HR—Jeter, Williams. SH—Leiter. T—3:32. A—55,292. U—McClelland, plate; Crawford, first; Montague, second; Reliford, third; Kellogg, left field; Welke, right field.

PLAY BY PLAY

FIRST INNING

Yankees—Vizcaino grounded out, Alfonzo to Zeile. Jeter struck out. Justice grounded to Zeile.

Mets—Agbayani and Alfonzo grounded out, Brosius to Martinez. Piazza singled to center. Zeile forced Piazza at second, Jeter, unassisted.

SECOND INNING

Yankees—Williams homered to left. Martinez flied to Agbayani. O'Neill struck out. Posada grounded out, Alfonzo to Zeile. **Yankees 1, Mets 0.**

Mets—Ventura struck out. Trammell walked. Payton singled to right-center as Trammell advanced to second. Abbott grounded out, Jeter to Martinez, as Trammell advanced to third and Payton to second. Leiter reached first base on Pettitte's fielding error (assist by Martinez), scoring Trammell as Payton advanced to third. Agbayani singled to third, scoring Payton as Leiter advanced to second. Alfonzo popped to Vizcaino. **Mets 2, Yankees 1.**

THIRD INNING

Yankees—Brosius fouled to Zeile. Pettitte and Vizcaino struck out.

Mets—Piazza grounded out, Brosius to Martinez. Zeile struck out. Ventura grounded out, Vizcaino to Martinez.

FOURTH INNING

Yankees—Jeter and Justice flied to Agbayani. Williams singled to left. Martinez fouled to Ventura.

Mets—Trammell singled to right. Payton forced Trammell at second, Vizcaino to Jeter. Abbott walked. Abbott picked off first base, Pettitte to Martinez. Leiter grounded out, Jeter to Martinez.

FIFTH INNING

Yankees—ONeill grounded out, Abbott to Zeile. Posada singled to left. Brosius grounded to Zeile as Posada advanced to second. Pettitte grounded out, Alfonzo to Zeile.

Mets—Agbayani struck out. Alfonzo grounded out, Jeter to Martinez. Piazza doubled to left-center. Zeile was intentionally walked. Ventura flied to Justice.

SIXTH INNING

Yankees—Vizcaino grounded out, Leiter to Zeile. Jeter homered to left. Justice struck out. Williams walked. Martinez grounded out, Abbott to Zeile. **Mets 2, Yankees 2.**

Mets—Trammell grounded out, Jeter to Martinez. Payton singled to third. Abbott singled to center as Payton advanced to second. Leiter sacrificed Payton to third and Abbott to second. Leiter was out on the play, Martinez to Vizcaino, covering first. Agbayani grounded out, Jeter to Martinez.

SEVENTH INNING

Yankees—O'Neill walked. Posada flied out to Agbayani. Brosius flied to Trammell. Pettitte grounded to Zeile.

Mets—Alfonzo singled to left. Piazza flied to Williams. Zeile and Ventura struck out.

EIGHTH INNING

Yankees—Knoblauch, pinch-hitting for Vizcaino, fouled to Piazza. Jeter struck out. Justice singled to short. Williams struck out.

Mets—Stanton now pitching and Sojo at second base. Trammell grounded out, Brosius to Martinez. Payton struck out. Abbott flied to O'Neill.

NINTH INNING

Yankees—Perez now in right field. Martinez and O'Neill struck out. Posada walked. Brosius singled to left as Posada advanced to second. Sojo singled to center, scoring Posada. During the play, Sojo advanced to second on the throw in from the outfield and reached third and then scored on Payton's throwing error. Hill now pinch-hitting for Stanton. J. Franco now pitching. Hill flied to Agbayani. **Yankees 4, Mets 2.**

Mets—Rivera now pitching and Bellinger in left field. Hamilton, pinch-hitting for J. Franco, struck out. Agbayani walked. Agbayani advanced to second on defensive indifference. Alfonzo flied to O'Neill as Agbayani advanced to third. Piazza flied to Williams. **Final score: Yankees 4, Mets 2.**

STATISTICS

NEW YORK YANKEES' BATTING AND FIELDING AVERAGES

Player, position	G	AB	R	H	TB	2B	3B	HR	RBI	BB	IBB	SO	Avg.	PO	A	E	Avg.
Polonia, ph	2	2	0	1	1	0	0	0	0	0	0	0	.500	0	0	0	.000
O'Neill, rf	5	19	2	9	15	2	2	0	2	3	1	4	.474	10	0	0	1.000
Jeter, ss	5	22	6	9	19	2	1	2	2	3	0	8	.409	5	15	0	1.000
Martinez, 1b	5	22	3	8	9	1	0	0	2	1	0	4	.364	39	4	0	1.000
Brosius, 3b	5	13	2	4	7	0	0	1	3	2	1	2	.308	1	9	0	1.000
Sojo, 3b-2b	4	7	0	2	2	0	0	0	2	1	0	0	.286	4	1	0	1.000
Vizcaino, 2b	4	17	0	4	4	0	0	0	1	0	0	5	.235	9	6	0	1.000
Posada, c	5	18	2	4	5	1	0	0	1	5	3	4	.222	52	1	0	1.000
Justice, lf	5	19	1	3	5	2	0	0	3	3	0	2	.158	8	1	0	1.000
Williams, cf	5	18	2	2	5	0	0	1	1	5	2	5	.111	10	0	0	1.000
Knoblauch, dh-ph	4	10	1	1	1	0	0	0	1	2	0	1	.100	0	0	0	.000
Bellinger, pr-lf	4	0	0	0	0	0	0	0	0	0	0	0	.000	2	0	0	1.000
Clemens, p	1	0	0	0	0	0	0	0	0	0	0	0	.000	0	2	1	.667
Cone, p	1	0	0	0	0	0	0	0	0	0	0	0	.000	0	0	0	.000
Nelson, p	3	0	0	0	0	0	0	0	0	0	0	0	.000	1	1	0	1.000
Stanton, p	4	0	0	0	0	0	0	0	0	0	0	0	.000	0	0	0	.000
Canseco, ph	1	1	0	0	0	0	0	0	0	0	0	1	.000	0	0	0	.000
Rivera, p	2	0	0	0	0	0	0	0	0	0	0	0	.000	0	1	0	1.000
Hernandez, p	1	2	0	0	0	0	0	0	0	0	0	2	.000	0	0	0	.000
Neagle, p	1	2	0	0	0	0	0	0	0	0	0	1	.000	0	0	0	.000
Hill, ph-lf	3	3	0	0	0	0	0	0	0	0	0	1	.000	0	5	1	.833
Pettitte, p	2	3	0	0	0	0	0	0	0	0	0	0	.000	0	0	0	.000
Totals	5	179	19	47	73	8	3	4	18	25	7	40	.263	141	46	2	.989

NEW YORK METS' BATTING AND FIELDING AVERAGES

Player, position	G	AB	R	H	TB	2B	3B	HR	RBI	BB	IBB	SO	Avg.	PO	A	E	Avg.
Reed, p	1	1	0	1	1	0	0	0	0	0	0	0	1.000	0	1	0	1.000
Zeile, 1b	5	20	1	8	10	2	0	0	1	1	1	5	.400	39	2	0	1.000
Trammell, ph-rf	4	5	1	2	2	0	0	0	3	1	0	1	.400	3	0	1	.750
Payton, cf	5	21	3	7	10	0	0	1	3	0	0	5	.333	17	0	2	.895
Agbayani, lf	5	18	2	5	7	2	0	0	2	3	0	6	.278	9	0	0	1.000
Piazza, dh-c	5	22	3	6	14	2	0	2	4	0	0	4	.273	34	1	0	1.000
Abbott, ss-ph	5	8	0	2	3	1	0	0	0	1	0	3	.250	3	5	0	1.000
Ventura, 3b	5	20	1	3	7	1	0	1	1	1	0	5	.150	1	8	0	1.000
Alfonzo, 2b	5	21	1	3	3	0	0	0	1	1	0	5	.143	7	19	0	1.000
Perez, rf	5	16	1	2	2	0	0	0	0	1	0	4	.125	8	1	1	.900
Bordick, ss	4	8	0	1	1	0	0	0	0	0	0	3	.125	4	7	1	.917

Player, position	G	AB	R	H	TB	2B	3B	HR	RBI	BB	IBB	SO	Avg.	PO	A	E	Avg.
						BATTING									FIELDING		
Benitez, p	3	0	0	0	0	0	0	0	0	0	0	0	.000	0	0	0	.000
Cook, p	3	0	0	0	0	0	0	0	0	0	0	0	.000	0	0	0	.000
Hampton, p	1	0	0	0	0	0	0	0	0	0	0	0	.000	0	0	0	.000
J. Franco, p	4	0	0	0	0	0	0	0	0	0	0	0	.000	1	0	0	1.000
Rusch, p	3	0	0	0	0	0	0	0	0	0	0	0	.000	0	0	0	.000
Wendell p	2	0	0	0	0	0	0	0	0	0	0	0	.000	0	0	0	.000
White, p	1	0	0	0	0	0	0	0	0	0	0	0	.000	0	0	0	.000
M. Franco, 1b	1	1	0	0	0	0	0	0	0	0	0	1	.000	1	0	0	1.000
McEwing, lf-pr	3	1	1	0	0	0	0	0	0	0	0	0	.000	2	0	0	1.000
B.J. Jones, p	1	2	0	0	0	0	0	0	0	0	0	1	.000	1	0	0	1.000
Leiter, p	2	2	0	0	0	0	0	0	0	0	0	0	.000	0	3	0	1.000
Pratt, c	1	2	1	0	0	0	0	0	0	1	0	2	.000	10	0	0	1.000
Hamilton, ph	4	3	0	0	0	0	0	0	0	0	0	2	.000	0	0	0	.000
Harris, dh-ph	3	4	1	0	0	0	0	0	0	1	0	1	.000	0	0	0	.000
Totals	5	175	16	40	60	8	0	4	15	11	1	48	.229	140	47	5	.974

NEW YORK YANKEES' PITCHING RECORDS

Pitcher	G	GS	CG	IP	H	R	ER	HR	BB	IBB	SO	HB	WP	W	L	Pct.	ERA
Clemens	1	1	0	8.0	2	0	0	0	0	0	9	1	1	1	0	1.000	0.00
Stanton	4	0	0	4.1	0	0	0	0	0	0	7	0	0	2	0	1.000	0.00
Cone	1	0	0	0.1	0	0	0	0	0	0	0	0	0	0	0	.000	0.00
Pettitte	2	2	0	13.2	16	5	3	0	4	1	9	1	0	0	0	.000	1.98
Rivera	4	0	0	6.0	4	2	2	1	1	0	7	1	0	0	0	.000	3.00
Neagle	1	1	0	4.2	4	2	2	1	2	0	3	0	0	0	0	.000	3.86
Hernandez	1	1	0	7.1	9	4	4	1	3	0	12	0	0	0	1	.000	4.91
Nelson	3	0	0	2.2	5	3	3	1	1	0	1	0	0	1	0	1.000	10.13
Totals	5	5	0	47.0	40	16	14	4	11	1	48	3	1	4	1	.800	2.68

No shutouts. Saves—Rivera 2.

NEW YORK METS' PITCHING RECORDS

Pitcher	G	GS	CG	IP	H	R	ER	HR	BB	IBB	SO	HB	WP	W	L	Pct.	ERA
J. Franco	4	0	0	3.1	3	0	0	0	0	0	1	0	0	1	0	1.000	0.00
Cook	3	0	0	0.2	1	0	0	0	3	0	1	1	0	0	0	.000	0.00
Rusch	3	0	0	4.0	6	1	1	0	2	1	2	0	2	0	0	.000	2.25
Leiter	2	2	0	15.2	12	6	5	2	6	1	16	0	0	0	1	.000	2.87
Reed	1	1	0	6.0	6	2	2	0	1	0	8	1	0	0	0	.000	3.00
Benitez	3	0	0	3.0	3	1	1	0	2	0	2	0	0	0	0	.000	3.00
B.J. Jones	1	1	0	5.0	4	3	3	1	3	2	3	0	0	0	1	.000	5.40
Wendell	2	0	0	1.2	3	1	1	0	2	1	2	0	0	0	1	.000	5.40
Hampton	1	1	0	6.0	8	4	4	1	5	1	4	1	0	0	1	.000	6.00
White	1	0	0	1.1	1	1	1	0	1	1	1	0	0	0	0	.000	6.75
Totals	5	5	0	46.2	47	19	18	4	25	7	40	3	2	1	4	.200	3.47

No shutouts. Save—Benitez.

SCORE BY INNINGS

New York Yankees	3	3	2	1	1	3	1	1	3	0	0	1—19
New York Mets	0	3	2	0	0	1	3	2	5	0	0	0—16

MISCELLANEOUS STATISTICS

Sacrifice hit—Bordick, Hernandez, Leiter, Reed.
Sacrifice flies—Brosius 2, Knoblauch, Trammell.
Stolen base—Sojo.
Caught stealing—Knoblauch, Piazza, Vizcaino.
Double plays—Alfonzo, Abbott and Zeile; Nelson and Martinez; Ventura, Alfonzo and Zeile; Zeile, Abbott and J. Franco.
Left on bases—Yankees 15, 12, 10, 9, 6—52; Mets 8, 4, 8, 6, 10—36.
Hit by pitcher—By Clemens (Alfonzo), by Cook (Justice), by Hampton (Justice), by Pettitte (Pratt), by Reed (Brosius), by Rivera (Pratt).
Passed ball—Posada.
Balks—None.
Time of games—First game, 4:51; second game, 3:30; third game, 3:39; fourth game, 3:20; fifth game, 3:32.
Attendance—First game, 55,913; second game, 56,059; third game, 55,299; fourth game, 55,290; fifth game, 55,292.
Umpires—Montague, Reliford, Kellogg, Welke, McClelland and Crawford.
Official scorers—Joe Donnelly, Red Foley, Howie Karpin, Charles Scoggins, Bill Shannon.

ALL-STAR GAME

HIGHLIGHTS

AMERICAN LEAGUE 6, NATIONAL LEAGUE 3

Why the American League won: A combination of timely hitting, clutch pitching and poor N.L. defense lifted the Americans to their fourth straight All-Star victory and 10th in 13 games. The A.L., dominating the midsummer classic in the era of power baseball, won without the aid of a home run against eight N.L. pitchers. Much of the damage was perpetrated by Yankees shortstop Derek Jeter, who collected three hits, drove in two runs and scored another en route to MVP honors.

Why the National League lost: The N.L. stars managed nine hits off eight A.L. hurlers, but they couldn't break through in key situations. Defensively, they contributed to their own downfall with two errors and a difficult third inning during which Dodgers righthander Kevin Brown walked three batters. One bright spot for the National Leaguers was the hitting of Atlanta's Jones boys, Chipper and Andruw, who combined for four hits and two RBIs before their home fans at Turner Field.

The turning points:

1. The Americans broke on top in the third inning when Brown inexplicably lost his control, walking Roberto Alomar, surrendering a single to Jeter and walking Jason Giambi and Carl Everett to force in a run. The damage would have been worse if not for a twisting, back-to-the-infield catch by N.L. center fielder Jim Edmonds on a drive hit by Mike Bordick.

2. After Chipper Jones had hit a pitch by Chicago White Sox righthander James Baldwin over the left-center field fence to tie the game in the bottom of the third, the Americans came right back in the fourth. Jermaine Dye drew a walk off Al Leiter and Travis Fryman singled to center. Shortstop Barry Larkin's error on a Mike Sweeney grounder loaded the bases and set the stage for the opportunistic Jeter. After Alomar had popped out, the Yankee shortstop stepped in against the Mets lefthander and won the New York matchup by driving a two-run single to center.

3. Leading only 3-2 after a fifth-inning RBI single by Andruw Jones, the A.L. put the game away with three runs in the ninth. Singles by Ray Durham, Nomar Garciaparra and Matt Lawton produced one run and a sacrifice fly by Chicago's Magglio Ordonez netted another. The finale crossed the plate on second baseman Jose Vidro's error.

Notable: The game opened without seven of the players voted to starting lineups by the fans.

Missing from the lineups were such names as Mark McGwire, Ken Griffey Jr., Barry Bonds and Mike Piazza. Pitchers Pedro Martinez and Greg Maddux also were unavailable because of injury. ... Jeter's All-Star MVP award was the first ever earned by a New York Yankee. The talented shortstop had struck out in his previous two All-Star at-bats. ... With the victory, the A.L. cut its overall deficit to 40-30-1. ... Yankee boss Joe Torre joined Tony La Russa and Tommy Lasorda as the only managers to win their first three All-Star Games. ... Chipper Jones became the 13th player to hit an All-Star home run in his home ballpark.

Quotable: Jeter, when informed he was the first Yankee ever to win an All-Star MVP: "You have to play for a lot of years before you can be considered a Yankee great. I've only played four years. This is my fifth. Hopefully, I can play for a few more years, then start that debate."... Chipper Jones, commenting on the performance of Jeter, who had worn out the Braves in the 1996 and 1999 World Series: "That really is a shocker. Derek Jeter stealing all the headlines. It's good to see no one else in the National League can get him out, either."... Braves first baseman Andres Galarraga, the recovered cancer patient who received a rousing ovation from his home fans: "Probably no words to explain how happy, how excited I am feeling."

BOX SCORE

American League	AB	R	H	RBI	PO	A
R. Alomar, 2b (Indians)..........	2	0	0	0	3	1
Durham, 2b (White Sox)........	2	1	1	0	1	3
Jeter, ss (Yankees)................	3	1	3	2	0	1
Garciaparra, ss (Red Sox)......	2	1	1	0	2	2
Williams, cf (Yankees)	3	0	0	0	0	0
Lawton, cf (Twins)	2	1	1	1	0	0
Ja. Giambi, 1b (Athletics)	2	0	0	0	2	0
Sele, p (Mariners)................	0	0	0	0	0	0
Ordonez, rf (White Sox)........	1	0	1	1	1	0
Everett, lf (Red Sox)	2	0	0	1	1	0
Erstad, lf (Angels)	2	0	0	1	0	0
Rodriguez, c (Rangers).........	3	0	1	0	3	0
Posada, c (Yankees)	2	0	0	0	2	0
Dye, rf (Royals)	2	1	0	0	1	0
Isringhausen, p (Athletics).....	0	0	0	0	0	0
Lowe, p (Red Sox)................	0	0	0	0	0	0
McGriff, 1b (Devil Rays)	2	0	0	0	5	0
Fryman, 3b (Indians)	2	1	1	0	0	0
Glaus, 3b (Angels)	1	0	0	0	2	0
∞Batista, ph-3b (Blue Jays)...	1	0	0	0	0	0
Wells, p (Blue Jays).............	0	0	0	0	0	0
*Bordick, ph (Orioles)	1	0	0	0	0	0
Baldwin, p (White Sox)	0	0	0	0	0	0
‡Sweeney, ph (Royals)	1	0	0	0	0	0
Delgado, 1b (Blue Jays)........	1	0	1	0	4	0
T. Jones, p (Tigers)..............	0	0	0	0	0	0
▲Martinez, ph (Mariners)	1	0	0	0	0	0
Hudson, p (Athletics)...........	0	0	0	0	0	0
Rivera, p (Yankees).............	0	0	0	0	0	1
Totals................	38	6	10	6	27	8
National League	**AB**	**R**	**H**	**RBI**	**PO**	**A**
Larkin, ss (Reds)	3	0	0	0	0	2
Renteria, ss (Cardinals)	2	0	0	0	0	2
C. Jones, 3b (Braves)	3	1	3	1	1	0

2000 REVIEW All-Star Game

National League	AB	R	H	RBI	PO	A
Cirillo, 3b (Rockies)	1	0	0	0	2	1
V. Guerrero, lf (Expos)	2	0	1	0	1	0
Leiter, p (Mets)	0	0	0	0	0	0
A. Jones, cf (Braves)	2	0	1	1	2	0
Sosa, rf (Cubs)	3	0	0	0	1	0
Kile, p (Cardinals)	0	0	0	0	0	1
Wickman, p (Brewers)	0	0	0	0	0	0
◆Vidro, ph-2b (Expos)	1	0	0	0	0	0
Kent, 2b (Giants)	2	0	0	0	0	0
Alfonzo, 2b (Mets)	2	0	0	0	0	1
Hoffman, p (Padres)	0	0	0	0	0	0
Galarraga, 1b (Braves)	2	0	1	0	4	0
§Helton, pr-1b (Rockies)	2	0	0	0	5	0
Edmonds, cf (Cardinals)	2	0	1	0	3	0
Lieberthal, c (Phillies)	2	1	1	0	4	0
Kendall, c (Pirates)	2	0	0	0	3	1
Glavine, p (Braves)	0	0	0	0	0	0
Giles, rf (Pirates)	2	0	0	0	0	0
Johnson, p (Diamondbacks)	0	0	0	0	0	0
Graves, p (Reds)	0	0	0	0	0	0
Brown, p (Dodgers)	0	0	0	0	0	0
†Hammonds, ph (Rockies)	1	0	0	0	0	0
Sheffield, lf (Dodgers)	1	1	0	0	1	0
S. Finley, lf (Diamondbacks)	1	0	1	1	0	0
Totals	36	3	9	3	27	8

American League	0	0	1		2	0	0		0	0	3—6
National League	0	0	1		0	1	0		0	0	1—3

American League	IP	H	R	ER	BB	SO
Wells (Blue Jays)	2.0	2	0	0	0	2
Baldwin (White Sox) (W)	1.0	2	1	1	0	1
Sele (Mariners)	1.0	1	0	0	0	0
Isringhausen (Athletics)	1.0	2	1	1	1	0
Lowe (Red Sox)	1.0	0	0	0	0	0
T. Jones (Tigers)	1.0	0	0	0	0	1
Hudson (Athletics)	1.0	0	0	0	0	1
Rivera (Yankees)	1.0	2	1	0	0	0

National League	IP	H	R	ER	BB	SO
Johnson (Diamondbacks)	1.0	1	0	0	0	1
Graves (Reds)	1.0	1	0	0	0	1
Brown (Dodgers)	1.0	1	1	1	3	1
Leiter (Mets) (L)	1.0	2	2	1	1	1
Glavine (Braves)	1.0	0	0	0	0	1
Kile (Cardinals)	2.0	2	0	0	0	0
Wickman (Brewers)	1.0	0	0	0	0	1
Hoffman (Padres)	1.0	3	3	3	0	2

Bases on balls—Off Isringhausen 1 (Sheffield), off Brown 3 (R. Alomar, Ja. Giambi, Everett), off Leiter 1 (Dye).

Strikeouts—By Wells 2 (Sosa, Kendall), by T. Jones 1 (A. Jones), by Hudson 1 (Alfonzo), by Johnson 1 (Ja. Giambi), by Graves 1 (Fryman), by Leiter 1 (Ja. Giambi), by Glavine 1 (Dye), by Wickman 1 (Batista), by Hoffman 2 (Posada, McGriff).

*Flied out for Wells in third. †Flied out for Brown in third. ‡Reached on a fielder's choice for Baldwin in the 4th. §Ran for Galarraga in fourth. ∞Struck out for Glaus in eighth. ▲Lined out for T. Jones in eighth. ◆Popped out for Wickman in eighth. E—Garciaparra 2, Larkin, Vidro. DP—A.L. 1. LOB—A.L. 10, N.L. 7. 2B—Delgado, Ordonez. HR—C. Jones. SB—Lawton. SF—Ordonez. T—2:56. A—51,323. U—Reilly, plate; M. Hirschbeck, first; Ford, second; Schrieber, third; O'Nora, left field; Diaz, right field. Official scorers—Mark Frederickson, Charlie Scoggins and Bill Zack.

Players listed on rosters but not used: A.L.—C. Finley (Indians); N.L.—Dempster (Marlins); Girardi (Cubs); Reynolds (Astros).

PLAY BY PLAY

FIRST INNING

A.L.—R. Alomar grounded out, Larkin to Galarraga. Jeter doubled to left. Williams grounded out, Larkin to Galarraga. Giambi struck out.

N.L.—Larkin popped to Giambi. C. Jones singled to center. V. Guerrero lined to R. Alomar. Sosa struck out.

SECOND INNING

A.L.—Graves now pitching. Everett flied to Edmonds. Rodriguez singled to right. Dye flied to Guerrero. Fryman struck out.

N.L.—Kent grounded out to Giambi, unassisted. Galarraga lined to Everett. Edmonds singled to right. Kendall struck out.

THIRD INNING

A.L.—Bordick pinch hit for Wells. Brown now pitching. Bordick flied to Edmonds. R. Alomar walked. Jeter singled to cen-

ter as R. Alomar advanced to second. Williams forced R. Alomar at third, C. Jones, unassisted, as Jeter advanced to second. Giambi walked. Everett walked, scoring Jeter. Rodriguez lined to Edmonds. **A.L. 1, N.L. 0.**

N.L.—Baldwin now pitching. Hammonds pinch-hitting for Brown, flied to Dye. Larkin popped to R. Alomar. C. Jones homered to left. Guerrero singled to left. Sosa popped to R. Alomar. **A.L. 1, N.L. 1.**

FOURTH INNING

A.L.—Sheffield now in left and Leiter pitching. Dye walked. Fryman singled to center as Dye advanced to second. Sweeney pinch hit for Baldwin. Sweeney forced Fryman at second, but Fryman was safe on Larkin's error. R. Alomar popped to Galarraga. Jeter singled to left, scoring Dye and Fryman as Sweeney advanced to third and Jeter to second. Giambi struck out. **A.L. 3, N.L. 1.**

N.L.—Glaus now at third, Delgado at first and Sele pitching. Kent grounded out, R. Alomar to Delgado. Galarraga singled to center. Helton now pinch-running for Galarraga. Edmonds popped to Glaus in foul territory. Kendal grounded out, Jeter to Delgado.

FIFTH INNING

A.L.—A. Jones now in center, Alfonzo at second, Helton at first, Lieberthal catching and Glavine pitching. Everett grounded out, Alfonzo to Helton. Rodriguez flied to Sosa. Dye struck out.

N.L.—Durham now at second, Garciaparra at shortstop, Ordonez in right, Erstad in left and Isringhausen pitching. Sheffield walked. Larking popped top Rodriguez in foul territory. C. Jones singled to right as Sheffield advanced to second. A. Jones singled to center, scoring Sheffield as C. Jones advanced to second. Sosa flied to Ordonez as C. Jones advanced to third. Alfonzo popped to Delgado in foul territory. **A.L. 3, N.L. 2.**

SIXTH INNING

A.L.—Renteria now at short, Cirillo at third, Giles in right and Kile pitching. Glaus grounded out, Renteria to Helton. Delgado doubled to right. Durham popped to Cirillo in foul territory. Garciaparra lined to Sheffield.

N.L.—Lawton now in center, Posada catching and Lowe pitching. Helton lined to Garciaparra. Lieberthal popped to Glaus in foul territory. Giles reached first on an error by Garciaparra. Sheffield grounded out, Garciaparra to Delgado.

SEVENTH INNING

A.L.—S. Finley now in left. Lawton grounded out, Kile to Helton. Ordonez doubled to right. Erstad grounded out, Renteria to Helton, as Ordonez advanced to third. Posada grounded out, Cirillo to Helton.

N.L.—McGriff now at first and T. Jones pitching. Renteria grounded out, Durham to McGriff. Cirillo popped to McGriff in foul territory. A. Jones struck out.

EIGHTH INNING

A.L.—Wickman now pitching. McGriff popped to Cirillo in foul territory. Batista, pinch-hitting for Glaus, struck out. Martinez, pinch-hitting for T. Jones, lined to A. Jones.

N.L.—Batista now at third and Hudson pitching. Vidro, pinch-hitting for Wickman, popped to Garciaparra. Alfonzo struck out. Helton grounded out, Durham to McGriff.

NINTH INNING

A.L.—Vidro now at second and Hoffman pitching. Durham singled to right. Garciaparra singled to left as Durham advanced to third. Lawton singled to right, scoring Durham as Garciaparra advanced to third. Lawton stole second. Ordonez hit a sacrifice fly to A. Jones, scoring Garciaparra as Lawton advanced to third. Erstad reached first on Vidro's error as Lawton scored. Posada and McGriff struck out. **A.L. 6, N.L. 2.**

N.L.—Rivera now pitching. Lieberthal singled to short and advanced to second on a wild-throw error by Garciaparra. Giles grounded out, Rivera to McGriff. S. Finley singled to center, scoring Lieberthal. Renteria grounded into a double play, Garciaparra to Durham to McGriff. **Final score: A.L. 6, N.L. 3.**

NOTABLE PERFORMANCES

LOW-HIT GAMES

AMERICAN LEAGUE

ONE-HIT GAMES

Date **Pitcher(s), Team, Opponent, Result—Player with hit**

5-21 Frank Castillo (7 inn.), Pedro Borbon (1 inn.) and Billy Koch (1 inn.), Toronto vs. Chicago, L 1-2—Mark L. Johnson (single in third)

6-13 Gil Meche, Seattle at Kansas City, W 7-0—Mike Sweeney (double in first)

8-1 Mike Mussina, Baltimore vs. Minnesota, W 10-0—Ron Coomer (single in seventh)

8-28 Tim Hudson, Oakland vs. Chicago, W 3-0—Frank Thomas (single in fourth)

8-29 Pedro Martinez, Boston at Tampa Bay, W 8-0—John Flaherty (single in ninth)

9-3 Paul Abbott (7 2/3 innings) and Jose Paniagua (1.1 inn.), Seattle at Boston, W 5-0—Rico Brogna (single in eighth)

9-18 Bartolo Colon, Cleveland at New York, W 2-0—Luis Polonia (single in eighth)

TWO-HIT GAMES

Date **Pitcher(s), Team, Opponent, Result—Player(s) with hit(s)**

4-4 Pedro Martinez (7 inn.) and Derek Lowe (2 inn.), Boston at Seattle, W 2-0—John Olerud (single in fourth), Carlos Guillen (single in third)

4-4 Tim Hudson (7 inn.), T.J. Mathews (1 inn.) and Jason Isringhausen (1 inn.), Oakland vs. Detroit, W 3-1—Tony Clark (double in seventh and single in ninth)

4-15 Ramiro Mendoza (6.2 inn.), Darrell Einertson (1.1 inn.) and Allen Watson (1 inn.), New York vs. Kansas City, W 7-1—Carlos Febles (single in seventh), Jermaine Dye (double in seventh)

4-24 Cal Eldred, Chicago vs. Baltimore, W 8-2—Delino DeShields (double in first), Charles Johnson (home run in sixth)

4-24 Chuck Finley (8 inn.) and Steve Karsay (1 inn.), Cleveland at Seattle, W 6-0—Dan Wilson (single in fifth), Charles Gipson (single in eighth)

5-2 Rick Helling (7.1 inn.), Mike Venafro (0.1 inn.) and Tim Crabtree (1.1 inn.), Texas at Tampa Bay, W 8-1—Fred McGriff (single in sixth), Steve Cox (single in ninth)

5-6 Gil Meche (7 inn.), Arthur Rhodes (1 inn.) and Kazuhiro Sasaki (1 inn.), Seattle vs. Anaheim, W 1-0—Tim Salmon (single in second), Garret Anderson (single in fourth)

5-12 Pedro Martinez, Boston at Baltimore, W 9-0—Albert Belle (single in fifth), Jeff Conine (single in fifth)

5-15 Aaron Sele (7 inn.), Kazuhiro Sasaki (1 inn.) and Jose Paniagua (1 inn.), Seattle vs. Minnesota, W 14-0—Corey Koskie (single in second), Matt LeCroy (single in fifth)

5-27 Tim Hudson (7.1 inn.) and Jeff Tam (1.2 inn.), Oakland at Baltimore, W 4-0—Will Clark (single in fifth), Mike Bordick (single in eighth)

5-29 Andy Pettitte, New York vs. Oakland, W 4-1—Randy Velarde (home run in ninth), Jason Giambi (double in first)

6-5 Ryan Glynn (8 inn.) and John Wetteland (1 inn.), Texas vs. Los Angeles N.L., W 2-0—F.P. Santangelo (single in sixth), Mark Grudzielanek (single in sixth)

6-8 Pedro Martinez (8 inn.) and Derek Lowe (1 inn.), Boston vs. Cleveland, W 3-0—Russ Branyan (double in fifth), Enrique Wilson (single in ninth)

7-19 Kelvim Escobar (8 inn.) and Billy Koch (1 inn.), Toronto vs. Tampa Bay, W 5-2—Jose Canseco (home run in fourth), Miguel Cairo (single in third)

7-29 Eric Milton (8 inn.) and LaTroy Hawkins (1 inn.), Minnesota vs. New York, W 6-2—Jose Vizcaino (single in sixth), Derek Jeter (single in sixth)

8-2 Blake Stein (8 inn.) and Ricky Bottalico (1 inn.), Kansas City at New York, W 4-1—Chuck Knoblauch (single in third), Derek Jeter (single in eighth)

8-8 Ramon Ortiz, Anaheim vs. Boston, W 2-1—Troy O'Leary (double in fifth), Mike Lansing (single in third)

8-30 Jose Mercedes, Baltimore vs. Detroit, W 5-1—Damion Easley (single in second), Brad Ausmus (home run in eighth)

9-4 Barry Zito (6.2 inn.), Jeff Tam (0.2 inn.), Todd Belitz (0 inni.) T.J. Mathews (0.2 inn.) and Jason Isringhausen (1 inn.), Oakland at Toronto, W 10-0—Dave Martinez (single in fourth), Craig Grebeck (single in seventh)

9-6 Scott Schoeneweis (8 inn.) and Troy Percival (1 inn.), Anaheim at Detroit, W 1-0—Bobby Higginson (single in seventh), Brad Ausmus (single in third)

9-8 Cory Lidle (7 inn.) and Doug Creek (2 inn.), Tampa Bay at Oakland, W 4-0—Jason Giambi (double in fourth and single in sixth)

9-9 Tim Hudson, Oakland vs. Tampa Bay, W 10-0—Gerald Williams (single in sixth), John Flaherty (single in third)

9-23 Kevin Appier (7 inn.), Jeff Tam (1 inn.) and Doug Jones (1 inn.), Oakland at Seattle, W 8-2—Edgar Martinez (home run in fourth), David Bell (single in eighth)

9-24 Travis Harper, Tampa Bay at Toronto, W 6-0—Tony Batista (double in seventh), Darrin Fletcher (single in third)

9-28 Pat Rapp (7 inn.), Jay Spurgeon (1 inn.), Buddy Groom (0.1 inn.) and Leslie Brea (0.2 inn.), Baltimore vs. Toronto, W 23-1—Shannon Stewart (single in fourth), Darrin Fletcher (home run in fifth)

NATIONAL LEAGUE

ONE-HIT GAMES

Date **Pitcher(s), Team, Opponent, Result—Player with hit**

4-28 Chris Holt, Houston at Milwaukee, W 7-0—Ron Belliard (single in second)

5-7 Ryan Dempster, Florida vs. New York, W 3-0—Mike Piazza (double in sixth)

7-19 Kevin Brown (8 inn.) and Mike Fetters (1 inn.), Los Angeles vs. Colorado, W 9-1—Larry Walker (single in first)

8-29 Kris Benson (8 inn.) and Josias Manzanillo (1 inn.), Pittsburgh vs. San Francisco, W 8-0—Barry Bonds (single in first)

8-29 Chan Ho Park (8 inn.) and Mike Fetters (1 inn.), Los Angeles at Milwaukee, W 7-2—James Mouton (home run in sixth)

TWO-HIT GAMES

Date | **Pitcher(s), Team, Opponent, Result—Player(s) with hit(s)**

4-6 Francisco Cordova (8 inn.) and Jose Silva (1 inn.), Pittsburgh vs. Houston, W 10-1—Mitch Meluskey (double in eighth), Tim Bogar (double in eighth)

4-7 Darren Dreifort (5 inn.), Matt Herges (2 inn.) and Terry Adams (1 inn.), Los Angeles at New York, L 1-2—Mike Piazza (double in first), Rick Reed (single in fourth)

5-1 Octavio Dotel (5 inn.), Mike Maddux (2 inn.), Jay Powell (1 inn.) and Billy Wagner (1 inn.), Houston at Milwaukee, W 5-0—Tyler Houston (single in fifth and double in seventh)

5-12 Darren Dreifort, Los Angeles at St. Louis, W 13-0—Fernando Vina (single in sixth), Eric Davis (double in first)

5-14 Brian Meadows (8 inn.) and Trevor Hoffman (1 inn.), San Diego vs. Arizona, W 3-1—Tony Womack (home run in first), Steve Finley (single in first)

5-20 Kevin Jarvis (6 inn.), Julian Tavarez (1 inn.), Mike DeJean (1 inn.), Mike Myers (0.1 inn.) and Jose Jimenez (0.2 inn.), Colorado at Philadelphia, W 4-3—Doug Glanville (home run in sixth), Bobby Abreu (home run in sixth)

5-29 Jon Lieber (8 inn.) and Todd Van Poppel (1 inn.), Chicago vs. Atlanta, L 0-1—Andres Galarraga (home run in seventh), Rafael Furcal (single in eighth)

6-20 Brian Tollberg (7 inn.), Kevin Walker (1 inn.) and Trevor Hoffman (1 inn.), San Diego at Arizona, W 3-1—Luis Gonzalez (double in ninth), Steve Finley (single in fourth)

6-23 Brian Anderson (8 inn.) and Byung-Hyun Kim (1 inn.), Arizona vs. Colorado, W 2-0—Larry Walker (single in seventh), Jeffrey Hammonds (single in fifth)

7-1 Jeff D'Amico (8 inn.) and Curtis Leskanic (1 inn.), Milwaukee vs. Chicago, W 4-0—Eric Young (single in sixth), Willie Greene (single in seventh)

7-3 Jon Lieber, Chicago vs. Pittsburgh, W 3-0—Warren Morris (single in sixth), Kevin Young (single in second)

7-23 Darren Dreifort (7 inn.), Terry Adams (1.2 inn.) and Jeff Shaw (0.1 inn.), Los Angeles vs. San Francisco, W 5-0—Barry Bonds (single in fourth), Bobby Estalella (double in fifth)

7-28 Darren Dreifort (7 inn.), Mike Fetters (1 inn.) and Jeff Shaw (1 inn.), Los Angeles at Philadelphia, W 2-0—Mickey Morandini (double in sixth), Scott Rolen (single in seventh)

7-29 Jesus Sanchez (7 inn.), Dan Miceli (1 inn.) and Antonio Alfonseca (1 inn.), Florida vs. Arizona, W 4-2—Damian Miller (home run in fourth), Brian Anderson (double in fourth)

8-1 Pedro Astacio (7 inn.) and Gabe White (2 inn.), Colorado at Chicago, W 2-1—Eric Young (double in first and single in sixth)

8-1 Kevin Millwood (7 inn.), Kerry Ligtenberg (1 inn.), John Rocker (0.1 inn.) and Mike Remlinger (0.2 inn.), Atlanta at Arizona, W 4-2—Luis Gonzalez (double in seventh), Steve Finley (single in fifth)

8-1 Chuck Smith (7 inn.), Manny Aybar (1 inn.) and Vic Darensbourg (1 inn.), Florida vs. Houston, L 3-4—Moises Alou (single in sixth), Raul Chavez (single in sixth)

8-8 Russ Ortiz (7 inn.), Felix Rodriguez (1 inn.) and Robb Nen (1 inn.), San Francisco vs. Milwaukee, W 1-0—Richie Sexson (double in fifth), Jamey Wright (single in sixth)

8-13 Al Leiter (8 inn.) and John Franco (1 inn.), New York vs. San Francisco, W 2-0—Ramon E. Martinez (single in first), Jeff Kent (single in seventh)

8-14 Russ Ortiz (7 inn.), Aaron Fultz (1 inn.) and Robb Nen (1 inn.), San Francisco at New York, W 11-1—Jay Payton (home run in eighth), Mike Bordick (single in sixth)

9-23 Kevin Brown, Los Angeles vs. San Diego, W 2-1—Damian Jackson (double in ninth), Ryan Klesko (single in fourth)

9-24 Chan Ho Park (8 inn.) and Jeff Shaw (1 inn.), Los Angeles vs. San Diego, W 1-0—John Mabry (single in fourth), Ruben Rivera (triple in fifth)

9-26 Darren Dreifort (7 inn.), Mike Fetters (1 inn.) and Terry Adams (1 inn.), Los Angeles vs. San Francisco, W 9-0—Barry Bonds (single in first), Ellis Burks (single in fourth)

9-28 Elmer Dessens, Cincinnati at Milwaukee, W 8-1—Raul Casanova (single in third and triple in sixth)

9-29 Chan Ho Park, Los Angeles at San Diego, W 3-0—Phil Nevin (single in fourth), Greg LaRocca (single in fifth)

9-29 Ron Villone, Cincinnati at St. Louis, W 8-1—Fernando Vina (triple in eighth), Eric Davis (single in second)

15-STRIKEOUT GAMES

AMERICAN LEAGUE

Date	Pitcher, Team, Opponent	IP	H	R	ER	BB	SO	Result
5-6	Pedro Martinez, Boston vs. Tampa Bay	9	6	1	1	1	17	L 0-1
5-12	Pedro Martinez, Boston at Baltimore	9	2	0	0	0	15	W 9-0
7-23	Pedro Martinez, Boston vs. Chicago	9	6	0	0	0	15	W 1-0
8-1	Mike Mussina, Baltimore vs. Minnesota	9	1	0	0	2	15	W 10-0
9-24	Mike Mussina, Baltimore at Boston	7	5	0	0	0	15	W 1-0

NATIONAL LEAGUE

Date	Pitcher, Team, Opponent	IP	H	R	ER	BB	SO	Result
9-29	Ron Villone, Cincinnati at St. Louis	9	2	1	0	5	16	W 8-1

10-STRIKEOUT GAMES

AMERICAN LEAGUE

Team	No.	Pitchers
Boston	16	Pedro Martinez 15, Jeff Fassero 1.
Cleveland	10	Bartolo Colon 6, Chuck Finley 3, Dave Burba 1.
Baltimore	6	Mike Mussina 4, Sidney Ponson 2.
Toronto	5	David Wells 3, Esteban Loaiza 1, Kelvim Escobar 1.

Team	No.	Pitchers
New York	4	Roger Clemens 2, Andy Pettitte 1, Orlando Hernandez 1.
Chicago	3	Cal Eldred 1, James Baldwin 1, Mike Sirotka 1.
Oakland	3	Tim Hudson 2, Barry Zito 1.
Minnesota	2	Eric Milton 2.
Detroit	1	Jeff Weaver 1.

Team	No.	Pitchers
Seattle	1	Aaron Sele 1.
Texas	1	Esteban Loaiza 1.
Tampa Bay	1	Steve Trachsel 1.
Anaheim	0	None.
Kansas City	0	None.

NATIONAL LEAGUE

Team	No.	Pitchers
Arizona	26	Randy Johnson 23, Curt Schilling 2, Todd Stottlemyre 1.
St. Louis	14	Rick Ankiel 6, Darryl Kile 5, Andy Benes 3.
Los Angeles	10	Chan Ho Park 5, Kevin Brown 4, Darren Dreifort 1.
Colorado	8	Pedro Astacio 7, John Wasdin 1.

Team	No.	Pitchers
Chicago	7	Jon Lieber 4, Kerry Wood 2, Kevin Tapani 1.
Philadelphia	6	Robert Person 3, Curt Schilling 2, Chris Brock 1.
San Francisco	6	Russ Ortiz 4, Shawn Estes 1, Livan Hernandez 1.
Montreal	5	Javier Vazquez 5.
New York	5	Al Leiter 3, Rick Reed 1, Glendon Rusch 1.
Florida	5	Chuck Smith 3, Ryan Dempster 1, A.J. Burnett 1.
Atlanta	3	Greg Maddux 2, Kevin Millwood 1.
Pittsburgh	3	Kris Benson 3.
San Diego	3	Sterling Hitchcock 1, Jay Witasick 1, Adam Eaton 1.
Milwaukee	2	Jason Bere 1, Jeff D'Amico 1.
Houston	2	Octavio Dotel 2.
Cincinnati	1	Ron Villone 1.

1-0 GAMES
AMERICAN LEAGUE

Date	Winner	Loser	Inn.*	Site
4-17	†Gil Heredia, Oakland	†Jeff Fassero, Boston	6	Boston
4-23	†Dave Eiland, Tampa Bay	†Jason Dickson, Anaheim	5	Tampa Bay
5-6	Steve Trachsel, Tampa Bay	Pedro Martinez, Boston	8	Boston
5-6	†Kazuhiro Sasaki, Seattle	†Mike Holtz, Anaheim	9	Seattle
5-11	†Steve Trachsel, Tampa Bay	Orlando Hernandez, New York	7	New York
6-3	†Al Leiter, New York	†Steve Trachsel, Tampa Bay	4	New York
6-4	†Tony Armas Jr., Montreal	Sidney Ponson, Baltimore	8	Montreal
7-23	Pedro Martinez, Boston	Mike Sirotka, Chicago	4	Boston
8-25	†Mike Venafro, Texas	†Billy Koch, Toronto	11	Texas
9-6	†Scott Schoeneweis, Anaheim	†Steve W. Sparks, Detroit	3	Detroit
9-13	†Jim Parque, Chicago	†Jeff Weaver, Detroit	1	Chicago
9-17	Brad Radke, Minnesota	Tim Belcher, Anaheim	1	Minnesota
9-24	†Mike Mussina, Baltimore	†Tomokazu Ohka, Boston	8	Boston
9-29	†Jeff Weaver, Detroit	Joe Mays, Minnesota	1	Detroit

PLAYERS HITTING HOME RUNS IN 1-0 GAMES: 5-11--Fred McGriff, Tampa Bay.

*Inning in which run scored. †Did not pitch complete game. Note: Interleague 1-0 games are listed in the winning club's league.

NATIONAL LEAGUE

Date	Winner	Loser	Inn.*	Site
4-9	Randy Johnson, Arizona	†Jason Schmidt, Pittsburgh	7	Arizona
4-24	†Armando Benitez, New York	†Terry Adams, Los Angeles	9	New York
4-25	Tom Glavine, Atlanta	†Kevin Brown, Los Angeles	5	Atlanta
5-22	†Matt Clement, San Diego	†John Franco, New York	8	San Diego
5-29	Greg Maddux, Atlanta	†Jon Lieber, Chicago	7	Chicago
6-3	†Al Leiter, New York	†Steve Trachsel, Tampa Bay	4	New York
6-4	†Tony Armas Jr., Montreal	Sidney Ponson, Baltimore	8	Montreal
6-17	†Steve Rain, Chicago	†Dustin Hermanson, Montreal	2	Chicago
7-23	Andy Ashby, Atlanta	†Bobby J. Jones, New York	6	Atlanta
8-8	†Russ Ortiz, San Francisco	†Jamey Wright, Milwaukee	5	San Francisco
8-30	†Rick Reed, New York	†Chris Holt, Houston	1	New York
9-2	†Matt Herges, Los Angeles	†Vicente Padilla, Philadelphia	10	Los Angeles
9-12	†Tony Armas Jr., Montreal	†Amaury Telemaco, Philadelphia	8	Philadelphia
9-19	†Chan Ho Park, Los Angeles	Brian Anderson, Arizona	8	Los Angeles
9-20	†Matt Herges, Los Angeles	†Byung-Hyun Kim, Arizona	9	Los Angeles
9-24	†Chan Ho Park, Los Angeles	†Matt Clement, San Diego	4	Los Angeles
9-27	†Kerry Wood, Chicago	†Randy Wolf, Philadelphia	3	Chicago

PLAYERS HITTING HOME RUNS IN 1-0 GAMES: 5-29--Andres Galarraga, Atlanta; 9-12--Jose Vidro, Montreal; 9-20--Eric Karros, Los Angeles.

*Inning in which run scored. †Did not pitch complete game. Note: Interleague 1-0 games are listed in the winning club's league.

FOUR OR MORE HITS IN ONE GAME
AMERICAN LEAGUE

Team	No.	Hitters
Kansas City	28	Johnny Damon 9, Mike Sweeney 8, Joe Randa 3, Jermaine Dye 2, Todd Dunwoody 2, Rey Sanchez 1, Dave McCarty 1, Carlos Febles 1, Mark Quinn 1.
Anaheim	21	Darin Erstad 5, Tim Salmon 3, Garret Anderson 3, Ben Molina 3, Orlando Palmeiro 2, Troy Glaus 2, Adam Kennedy 2, Mo Vaughn 1.
New York	20	Derek Jeter 5, Jorge Posada 4, Scott Brosius 3, Paul O'Neill 2, Jose Vizcaino 2, Bernie Williams 2, Lance Johnson 1, Tino Martinez 1.

Team	No.	Hitters
Chicago	16	Magglio Ordonez 4, Carlos Lee 4, Paul Konerko 3, Chris Singleton 2, Frank Thomas 1, Jose Valentin 1, Ray Durham 1.
Seattle	16	John Olerud 4, Alex Rodriguez 4, Edgar Martinez 3, Stan Javier 1, Jay Buhner 1, Al Martin 1, Mike Cameron 1, Carlos Guillen 1.
Minnesota	15	Cristian Guzman 3, Denny Hocking 2, Corey Koskie 2, Ron Coomer 1, Matt Lawton 1, Jay Canizaro 1, Torii Hunter 1, David Ortiz 1, A.J. Pierzynski 1, Jacque Jones 1, Luis Rivas 1.
Cleveland	14	Roberto Alomar 4, Sandy Alomar Jr. 2, Travis Fryman 2, Kenny Lofton 2, Jolbert Cabrera 2, Omar Vizquel 1, Jim Thome 1, Wil Cordero 1, Einar Diaz 1.
Texas	14	Luis Alicea 4, Ivan Rodriguez 2, Rusty Greer 2, Frank Catalanotto 2, Rafael Palmeiro 1, David Segui 1, Royce Clayton 1, Chad Curtis 1.
Toronto	14	Shannon Stewart 6, Darrin Fletcher 3, Tony Batista 2, Craig Grebeck 1, Marty Cordova 1, Brad Fullmer 1.
Oakland	13	Jason Giambi 2, Ben Grieve 2, Terrence Long 2, Mike Stanley 1, Matt Stairs 1, Miguel Tejada 1, Jeremy Giambi 1, Eric Chavez 1, Ramon Hernandez 1, Adam Piatt 1.
Detroit	12	Bobby Higginson 3, Shane Halter 2, Juan Encarnacion 2, Juan Gonzalez 1, Dean Palmer 1, Brad Ausmus 1, Wendell Magee 1, Deivi Cruz 1.
Boston	11	Carl Everett 3, Nomar Garciaparra 2, Brian Daubach 2, Mike Stanley 1, Jose Offerman 1, Troy O'Leary 1, Trot Nixon 1.
Baltimore	9	B.J. Surhoff 3, Harold Baines 1, Cal Ripken Jr. 1, Delino DeShields 1, Brook Fordyce 1, Melvin Mora 1, Chris Richard 1.
Tampa Bay	6	Greg Vaughn 2, Fred McGriff 1, Gerald Williams 1, Felix Martinez 1, Steve Cox 1.

NATIONAL LEAGUE

Team	No.	Hitters
Colorado	31	Jeff Cirillo 6, Todd Helton 6, Larry Walker 3, Jeffrey Hammonds 3, Neifi Perez 3, Brent Mayne 2, Juan Pierre 2, Tom Goodwin 1, Jeff Frye 1, Mike Lansing 1, Brian L. Hunter 1, Todd Hollandsworth 1, Todd Walker 1.
Cincinnati	21	Eddie Taubensee 3, Dmitri Young 3, Pokey Reese 3, Barry Larkin 2, Dante Bichette 2, Chris Stynes 2, Alex Ochoa 2, Sean Casey 2, Benito Santiago 1, Ken Griffey Jr. 1.
Chicago	19	Eric Young 4, Mark Grace 3, Sammy Sosa 3, Damon Buford 3, Joe Girardi 2, Jeff Huson 1, Henry Rodriguez 1, Willie Greene 1, Rondell White 1.
Pittsburgh	16	Jason Kendall 4, Warren Morris 4, Brian Giles 3, Kevin Young 2, John Vander Wal 1, Wil Cordero 1, Adrian Brown 1.
Houston	15	Moises Alou 3, Jeff Bagwell 3, Tim Bogar 2, Roger Cedeno 2, Ken Caminiti 1, Tony Eusebio 1, Richard Hidalgo 1, Mitch Meluskey 1, Julio Lugo 1.
New York	12	Derek Bell 3, Edgardo Alfonzo 3, Mike Piazza 2, Todd Pratt 1, Jay Payton 1, Benny Agbayani 1, Melvin Mora 1.
San Francisco	12	Marvin Benard 4, Jeff Kent 2, J.T. Snow 2, Barry Bonds 1, Ellis Burks 1, Doug Mirabelli 1, Terrell Lowery 1.
Arizona	11	Luis Gonzalez 3, Greg Colbrunn 2, Jay Bell 1, Steve Finley 1, Tony Womack 1, Craig Counsell 1, Andy Fox 1, Damian Miller 1.
Atlanta	10	Andres Galarraga 2, Chipper Jones 2, Quilvio Veras 2, Andruw Jones 2, Walt Weiss 1, Brian Jordan 1.
Los Angeles	10	Mark Grudzielanek 3, Adrian Beltre 2, Devon White 1, Gary Sheffield 1, Tom Goodwin 1, Eric Karros 1, Alex Cora 1.
Philadelphia	10	Bobby Abreu 3, Doug Glanville 2, Ron Gant 1, Tom Prince 1, Mike Lieberthal 1, Travis Lee 1, Pat Burrell 1.
Montreal	9	Lee Stevens 2, Rondell White 2, Vladimir Guerrero 2, Jose Vidro 1, Orlando Cabrera 1, Peter Bergeron 1.
Milwaukee	8	Ron Belliard 2, Geoff Jenkins 2, Marquis Grissom 1, Luis Lopez 1, James Mouton 1, Mark Loretta 1.
Florida	8	Mark Kotsay 3, Cliff Floyd 2, Luis Castillo 2, Kevin Millar 1.
St. Louis	7	Fernando Vina 2, Eric Davis 1, Craig Paquette 1, Jim Edmonds 1, Placido Polanco 1, J.D. Drew 1.
San Diego	6	Eric Owens 2, Ed Sprague 1, Al Martin 1, Phil Nevin 1, Damian Jackson 1.

FIVE OR MORE HITS IN ONE GAME
AMERICAN LEAGUE

Date	Player, Team, Opponent	AB	R	H	2B	3B	HR	RBI	Result
4-22	Chris Singleton, Chicago vs. Detroit	5	3	5	1	0	1	5	W 14- 6
5-5	Einar Diaz, Cleveland at Toronto	5	2	5	3	0	0	2	L 10- 11
5-17	Frank Catalanotto, Texas vs. Tampa Bay	5	1	5	0	0	0	1	W 11- 6
5-18	Denny Hocking, Minnesota at Oakland	6	2	5	2	0	1	3	W 10- 5
5-24	Mo Vaughn, Anaheim at Minnesota	5	1	5	2	0	0	2	W 6- 5
6-28	B.J. Surhoff, Baltimore at Boston	6	2	5	2	0	0	1	W 8- 7
7-18	Johnny Damon, Kansas City vs. Chicago N.L.	6	1	5	4	0	0	2	W 12- 4
7-29†	Jolbert Cabrera, Cleveland at Baltimore	5	1	5	1	0	0	1	W 14- 3
8-6	Stan Javier, Seattle at New York	6	2	5	1	0	0	2	W 11- 1
8-31	Rusty Greer, Texas vs. Cleveland	6	3	5	0	0	0	4	W 14- 7
9-4	Mike Stanley, Oakland at Toronto	5	2	5	1	0	1	5	W 10- 0
9-11	Johnny Damon, Kansas City at Seattle	5	2	5	2	0	1	2	W 6- 3

† First game of doubleheader
‡ Second game of doubleheader

NATIONAL LEAGUE

Date	Player, Team, Opponent	AB	R	H	2B	3B	HR	RBI	Result
4-6	Brian Giles, Pittsburgh vs. Houston	5	3	5	0	1	2	4	W 10- 1
4-14	Mike Piazza, New York at Pittsburgh	6	2	5	1	0	2	4	W 8- 5
4-16‡	Fernando Vina, St. Louis at Colorado	5	4	5	1	0	0	0	L 13- 14
4-20	Pokey Reese, Cincinnati vs. San Francisco	5	2	5	1	0	0	3	W 11- 1
5-3	Todd Helton, Colorado vs. Montreal	5	2	5	0	0	0	2	W 16- 7
5-4	Doug Glanville, Philadelphia vs. Cincinnati	5	3	5	1	0	0	1	W 14- 1
5-7	Mitch Meluskey, Houston at Los Angeles	6	2	5	1	0	0	2	W 14- 8
5-10	Wil Cordero, Pittsburgh vs. New York	5	3	5	1	0	1	4	W 13- 9
5-11	Mark Loretta, Milwaukee at Chicago	5	1	5	0	0	0	0	W 14- 8
5-12	Roger Cedeno, Houston vs. Cincinnati	6	1	5	0	0	0	2	L 3- 7
5-14	Sammy Sosa, Chicago at Montreal	6	3	5	1	0	0	5	L 15- 16
5-14	Craig Paquette, St. Louis vs. Los Angeles	5	2	5	0	0	1	4	W 12- 10
5-16	Ken Caminiti, Houston at Milwaukee	7	1	5	2	0	0	0	L 5- 6
5-21	Terrell Lowery, San Francisco at Milwaukee	6	3	5	3	0	0	1	W 16- 10
5-21	Andres Galarraga, Atlanta vs. San Diego	5	3	5	1	0	0	2	W 12- 6
5-24	Dante Bichette, Cincinnati at Los Angeles	6	1	5	1	0	0	4	W 10- 3
6-10	Warren Morris, Pittsburgh at Kansas City A.L.	6	0	5	0	0	0	0	L 1- 2
6-18	Jeff Cirillo, Colorado vs. Arizona	6	2	5	0	0	1	4	W 19- 2
6-24	Barry Larkin, Cincinnati vs. San Diego	5	4	5	0	0	2	4	W 11- 5
6-24	Doug Mirabelli, San Francisco at Houston	6	3	5	3	0	1	3	W 13- 4
7-8	Chris Stynes, Cincinnati vs. Cleveland A.L.	6	4	5	1	0	1	2	W 14- 5
7-15	Eric Davis, St. Louis at Chicago A.L.	5	0	5	0	0	0	2	L 7- 15
7-29	Brian Giles, Pittsburgh vs. San Diego	5	2	5	2	0	0	2	W 10- 2
8-6	Mark Grace, Chicago at San Diego	5	3	5	2	0	1	2	L 6- 8
9-4	Juan Pierre, Colorado vs. Chicago	5	1	5	0	0	0	1	W 6- 2
9-8	Julio Lugo, Houston at Chicago	6	1	5	0	0	0	0	W 13- 10

HITTING STREAKS OF 15 OR MORE GAMES

AMERICAN LEAGUE

G	Player, Team	Span of streak
28	Gabe Kapler, Texas	July 17-Aug. 15
22	Carlos Delgado, Toronto	June 4-June 29
21	B.J. Surhoff, Baltimore	June 5-June 28
	Dave Martinez, Toronto	Aug. 6-Sept. 1
20	Manny Ramirez, Cleveland	Aug. 15-Sept. 5
	Nomar Garciaparra, Boston	Sept. 10-Sept. 29
19	Juan Encarnacion, Detroit	Apr. 16-May 7
18	Roberto Alomar, Cleveland	Sept. 17-Oct. 1
17	Roberto Alomar, Cleveland	May 5-May 25
	Alex Rodriguez, Seattle	May 5-May 23
	Terrence Long, Oakland	June 10-June 29
	Bernie Williams, New York	June 19-July 7
	Dante Bichette, Cincinnati	June 30-July 23
	Tim Salmon, Anaheim	July 23-Aug. 9
16	Matt Lawton, Minnesota	Apr. 13-Apr. 30
	Johnny Damon, Kansas City	Aug. 5-Aug. 21
	Mike Sweeney, Kansas City	Aug. 13-Aug. 30
15	Carlos Febles, Kansas City	Apr. 6-Apr. 21
	Wil Cordero, Pittsburgh	Apr. 29-May 23
	Eric Chavez, Oakland	May 27-June 18
	Alex S. Gonzalez, Toronto	Aug. 2-Aug. 18

NATIONAL LEAGUE

G	Player, Team	Span of streak
24	Tony Womack, Arizona	May 2-May 29
	Tony Eusebio, Houston	July 9-Aug. 28
21	B.J. Surhoff, Baltimore	June 5-June 28
	Mike Piazza, New York	June 7-July 3
	Sean Casey, Cincinnati	July 4-July 30
19	Chipper Jones, Atlanta	June 1-June 21
	Luis Castillo, Florida	July 3-July 28
18	Dmitri Young, Cincinnati	Apr. 20-May 13
	Jeffrey Hammonds, Colorado	May 29-June 21
	Jeff Bagwell, Houston	Aug. 2-Aug. 20
17	Dante Bichette, Cincinnati	June 30-July 23
	Fernando Vina, St. Louis	Aug. 8-Aug. 25
16	Craig Biggio, Houston	Apr. 5-Apr. 26
	Juan Pierre, Colorado	Aug. 8-Aug. 23
	Mike Lowell, Florida	Aug. 18-Sept. 5
	John Vander Wal, Pittsburgh	Aug. 29-Sept. 16
15	Jeff Cirillo, Colorado	Apr. 21-May 9
	Wil Cordero, Pittsburgh	Apr. 29-May 23
	Bill Mueller, San Francisco	May 1-May 19
	Sammy Sosa, Chicago	July 4-July 22
	Danny Bautista, Arizona	Aug. 13-Sept. 1
	Richard Hidalgo, Houston	Aug. 28-Sept. 13
	Juan Pierre, Colorado	Sept. 6-Sept. 22

MULTI-HOMER GAMES
AMERICAN LEAGUE

Team	No.	Hitters
Cleveland	22	Jim Thome 4, Manny Ramirez 4, Roberto Alomar 3, Russ Branyan 3, David Justice 2, Travis Fryman 2, Richie Sexson 2, Omar Vizquel 1, Kenny Lofton 1.
Anaheim	20	Troy Glaus 6, Mo Vaughn 4, Darin Erstad 3, Scott Spiezio 2, Ron Gant 1, Tim Salmon 1, Garret Anderson 1, Ben Molina 1, Adam Kennedy 1.
Toronto	16	Carlos Delgado 5, Tony Batista 4, Raul Mondesi 2, Brad Fullmer 2, Darrin Fletcher 1, Shannon Stewart 1, Jose Cruz 1.
Chicago	14	Frank Thomas 4, Magglio Ordonez 4, Jose Valentin 3, Charles Johnson 1, Brook Fordyce 1, Carlos Lee 1.

Team	No.	Hitters
Kansas City	10	Jermaine Dye 3, Mike Sweeney 2, Mark Quinn 2, Joe Randa 1, Johnny Damon 1, Carlos Beltran 1.
Baltimore	9	Chris Richard 3, Albert Belle 2, Charles Johnson 2, Harold Baines 1, Brook Fordyce 1.
Boston	9	Carl Everett 3, Nomar Garciaparra 2, Brian Daubach 2, Jose Offerman 1, Troy O'Leary 1.
New York	9	David Justice 3, Bernie Williams 2, Jorge Posada 2, Glenallen Hill 1, Tino Martinez 1.
Detroit	7	Bobby Higginson 3, Juan Gonzalez 1, Dean Palmer 1, Tony Clark 1, Billy McMillon 1.
Oakland	7	Jason Giambi 5, Sal Fasano 1, Miguel Tejada 1.
Seattle	7	Alex Rodriguez 3, John Olerud 2, Jay Buhner 1, Edgar Martinez 1.
Texas	7	Ivan Rodriguez 4, Rafael Palmeiro 1, Royce Clayton 1, Gabe Kapler 1.
Tampa Bay	6	Fred McGriff 3, Greg Vaughn 3.
Minnesota	3	Ron Coomer 2, Matt Lawton 1.

NATIONAL LEAGUE

Team	No.	Hitters
Houston	20	Jeff Bagwell 4, Richard Hidalgo 4, Moises Alou 3, Lance Berkman 3, Ken Caminiti 1, Bill Spiers 1, Tim Bogar 1, Daryle Ward 1, Mitch Meluskey 1, Chris Truby 1.
Los Angeles	18	Gary Sheffield 6, Eric Karros 3, Todd Hundley 2, Shawn Green 2, Kevin Elster 1, Darren Dreifort 1, Bruce Aven 1, Alex Cora 1, Adrian Beltre 1.
St. Louis	18	Ray Lankford 4, Jim Edmonds 4, Mark McGwire 2, Fernando Tatis 2, J.D. Drew 2, Shawon Dunston 1, Will Clark 1, Craig Paquette 1, Eli Marrero 1.
Atlanta	15	Chipper Jones 6, Brian Jordan 3, Andruw Jones 3, Andres Galarraga 1, Reggie Sanders 1, Javy Lopez 1.
Montreal	15	Vladimir Guerrero 8, Lee Stevens 2, Jose Vidro 2, Rondell White 1, Chris Widger 1, Orlando Cabrera 1.
Colorado	14	Todd Helton 8, Jeffrey Hammonds 3, Mike Lansing 1, Jeff Cirillo 1, Todd Hollandsworth 1.
San Francisco	13	Barry Bonds 4, Ellis Burks 2, Jeff Kent 2, J.T. Snow 2, Doug Mirabelli 1, Bobby Estalella 1, Armando Rios 1.
Arizona	12	Steve Finley 3, Jay Bell 2, Luis Gonzalez 2, Kelly Stinnett 2, Danny Bautista 1, Damian Miller 1, Erubiel Durazo 1.
Cincinnati	10	Ken Griffey Jr. 5, Barry Larkin 1, Dante Bichette 1, Eddie Taubensee 1, Sean Casey 1, Jason LaRue 1.
Chicago	9	Sammy Sosa 5, Henry Rodriguez 2, Rondell White 1, Shane Andrews 1.
Philadelphia	9	Bobby Abreu 2, Pat Burrell 2, Rob Ducey 1, Ron Gant 1, Tom Prince 1, Mike Lieberthal 1, Scott Rolen 1.
San Diego	9	Bret Boone 3, Ed Sprague 2, Ryan Klesko 2, Phil Nevin 2.
Florida	9	Derrek Lee 3, Preston Wilson 2, Cliff Floyd 1, Mark Smith 1, Alex Gonzalez 1, Mike Lowell 1.
Milwaukee	7	Jeromy Burnitz 3, Tyler Houston 2, Geoff Jenkins 2.
New York	7	Mike Piazza 3, Benny Agbayani 2, Todd Zeile 1, Robin Ventura 1.
Pittsburgh	7	Brian Giles 2, John Vander Wal 1, Kevin Young 1, Wil Cordero 1, Bruce Aven 1, Aramis Ramirez 1.

THREE-HOMER GAMES
AMERICAN LEAGUE

Date	Player, Team, Opponent	AB	R	H	2B	3B	HR	RBI	Result
4-16	Alex Rodriguez, Seattle at Toronto	5	5	4	0	0	3	7	W 19-7
6-24 †	Bobby Higginson, Detroit at Cleveland	5	3	3	0	0	3	6	W 14-8
8-27	Darrin Fletcher, Toronto at Texas	4	3	3	0	0	3	3	W 6-4

† Second game of doubleheader.

NATIONAL LEAGUE

Date	Player, Team, Opponent	AB	R	H	2B	3B	HR	RBI	Result
4-11	Kevin Elster, Los Angeles at San Francisco	3	3	3	0	0	3	4	W 6-5
5-1	Todd Helton, Colorado vs. Montreal	5	4	4	0	0	3	5	W 15-8
5-18	Mark McGwire, St. Louis at Philadelphia	4	3	3	0	0	3	7	W 7-2
6-23	Bret Boone, San Diego at Cincinnati	4	4	3	0	0	3	6	W 10-7
6-28	Jeff Cirillo, Colorado vs. San Francisco	5	5	4	1	0	3	6	W 17-13
7-9	Tyler Houston, Milwaukee vs. Detroit	4	3	3	0	0	3	6	W 10-3

GRAND SLAMS
AMERICAN LEAGUE

Date	Batter, Team	Pitcher, Team	Inn.*	Site
4-3	Fred McGriff, Tampa Bay	Brad Radke, Minnesota	5	Minnesota
4-7	Omar Vizquel, Cleveland	Juan Guzman, Tampa Bay	2	Tampa Bay
4-9	Jason Giambi, Oakland	Tanyon Sturtze, Chicago	7	Oakland
4-14	Eric Chavez, Oakland	Brian Rose, Boston	1	Boston
4-15	Edgar Martinez, Seattle	Pedro Borbon, Toronto	6	Toronto
4-16	Alex Rodriguez, Seattle	Pedro Borbon, Toronto	8	Toronto

Date	Batter, Team	Pitcher, Team	Inn.*	Site
4-17	Brad Fullmer, Toronto	Lou Pote, Anaheim	8	Toronto
4-18	Adam Kennedy, Anaheim	Frank Castillo, Toronto	4	Toronto
4-19	Miguel Tejada, Oakland	Sean DePaula, Cleveland	5	Cleveland
4-19	Trot Nixon, Boston	Jim Poole, Detroit	6	Detroit
4-20	Darrin Fletcher, Toronto	Kent Mercker, Anaheim	4	Toronto
4-26	Frank Thomas, Chicago	Sidney Ponson, Baltimore	4	Chicago
4-26	Jermaine Dye, Kansas City	Ryan Rupe, Tampa Bay	1	Kansas City
4-29	Ben Grieve, Oakland	Eddie Guardado, Minnesota	10	Minnesota
5-7	Scott Brosius, New York	Mike Trombley, Baltimore	8	New York
5-8	Darrin Fletcher, Toronto	Jason Johnson, Baltimore	4	Toronto
5-11	Manny Ramirez, Cleveland	Chad Durbin, Kansas City	1	Cleveland
5-12	Royce Clayton, Texas	Scott Schoeneweis, Anaheim	6	Anaheim
5-17	Bernie Williams, New York	Tanyon Sturtze, Chicago	5	New York
5-17	Fred McGriff, Tampa Bay	Doug Davis, Texas	5	Texas
5-21	Garret Anderson, Anaheim	Chris Fussell, Kansas City	3	Anaheim
5-21	Jason Giambi, Oakland	Sean Bergman, Minnesota	2	Oakland
5-26	Darrin Fletcher, Toronto	Doug Brocail, Detroit	8	Detroit
6-1	Carl Everett, Boston	Chris Fussell, Kansas City	3	Boston
6-6	Matt Stairs, Oakland	Rodrigo Lopez, San Diego N.L.	1	Oakland
6-7	Jason Giambi, Oakland	Matt Clement, San Diego N.L.	4	Oakland
6-7	Carlos Delgado, Toronto	Kevin Millwood, Atlanta N.L.	5	Atlanta N.L.
6-11	Tony Batista, Toronto	Felipe Lira, Montreal N.L.	8	Toronto
6-14	Albert Belle, Baltimore	Kenny Rogers, Texas	1	Baltimore
6-15	Albert Belle, Baltimore	Mark Clark, Texas	8	Baltimore
6-15	Mike Cameron, Seattle	Mark Redman, Minnesota	2	Minnesota
6-17	Russ Branyan, Cleveland	Hideo Nomo, Detroit	4	Detroit
6-18	Jose Valentin, Chicago	Orlando Hernandez, New York	1	New York
6-20	Tim Salmon, Anaheim	Jeff Suppan, Kansas City	3	Anaheim
6-22	Edgar Martinez, Seattle	Buddy Groom, Baltimore	8	Seattle
6-25	Tom Lampkin, Seattle	Mike Timlin, Baltimore	8	Seattle
6-25	Jose Guillen, Tampa Bay	Kenny Rogers, Texas	6	Texas
6-27	Dean Palmer, Detroit	David Cone, New York	5	Detroit
6-27	Steve Cox, Tampa Bay	Kelvim Escobar, Toronto	4	Tampa Bay
7-3	Tony Batista, Toronto	Jason Johnson, Baltimore	3	Baltimore
7-3	Jorge Fabregas, Kansas City	Kevin Beirne, Chicago	3	Kansas City
7-7	Ben Molina, Anaheim	Scott Karl, Colorado N.L.	5	Anaheim
7-7	Ivan Rodriguez, Texas	Woody Williams, San Diego N.L.	1	Texas
7-8	Jeremy Giambi, Oakland	Dan Plesac, Arizona N.L.	8	Oakland
7-16	Magglio Ordonez, Chicago	Juan Acevedo, Milwaukee N.L.	6	Chicago
7-16	Marty Cordova, Toronto	Al Leiter, New York N.L.	6	Toronto
7-19	Dave McCarty, Kansas City	Chuck Finley, Cleveland	6	Cleveland
7-20 †	Will Clark, Baltimore	Ramon Martinez, Boston	1	Baltimore
7-22	Richie Sexson, Cleveland	Mike Lincoln, Minnesota	4	Minnesota
7-22	Ben Grieve, Oakland	Brian Cooper, Anaheim	4	Oakland
7-22	Joe Oliver, Seattle	Ryan Glynn, Texas	5	Seattle
7-22 ‡	Jose Macias, Detroit	Tim Byrdak, Kansas City	7	Detroit
7-25	Bernie Williams, New York	Chuck McElroy, Baltimore	7	Baltimore
7-28	Glenallen Hill, New York	Bob Wells, Minnesota	9	Minnesota
7-29 †	Manny Ramirez, Cleveland	Pat Rapp, Baltimore	2	Baltimore
7-30	David Segui, Cleveland	John Parrish, Baltimore	6	Baltimore
7-30	Sal Fasano, Oakland	Rolando Arrojo, Boston	2	Oakland
7-31	Jay Buhner, Seattle	Ramon Martinez, Boston	1	Seattle
8-7	Carlos Guillen, Seattle	Denny Neagle, New York	6	New York
8-8 †	Edgar Martinez, Seattle	Bill Simas, Chicago	8	Chicago
8-8 †	Jay Buhner, Seattle	Jon Garland, Chicago	1	Chicago
8-9	Tony Graffanino, Chicago	Rob Ramsay, Seattle	6	Chicago
8-9	Tino Martinez, New York	Kevin Appier, Oakland	3	New York
8-12	Troy Glaus, Anaheim	Denny Neagle, New York	2	Anaheim
8-12	Ricky Ledee, Texas	Tim Wakefield, Boston	4	Texas
8-14	Rico Brogna, Boston	Billy Taylor, Tampa Bay	9	Boston
8-19	Manny Ramirez, Cleveland	Jamie Moyer, Seattle	6	Cleveland
8-20	Kenny Lofton, Cleveland	Aaron Sele, Seattle	2	Cleveland
8-24	Terrence Long, Oakland	Steve Woodard, Cleveland	2	Cleveland
8-25	Jay Canizaro, Minnesota	Willie Blair, Detroit	4	Minnesota
8-27	Roberto Alomar, Cleveland	Mark Petkovsek, Anaheim	7	Anaheim
8-29	Edgar Martinez, Seattle	Jeff Nelson, New York	8	Seattle
9-1	Mo Vaughn, Anaheim	Lorenzo Barcelo, Chicago	5	Chicago
9-1	Jermaine Dye, Kansas City	Ryan Rupe, Tampa Bay	4	Tampa Bay
9-3	Mark Quinn, Kansas City	Dave Eiland, Tampa Bay	3	Tampa Bay
9-5	Manny Alexander, Boston	Kevin Appier, Oakland	1	Boston
9-5	Scott Brosius, New York	Andy Larkin, Kansas City	8	Kansas City
9-7	David Ortiz, Minnesota	Ramon Martinez, Boston	1	Boston

Date	Batter, Team	Pitcher, Team	Inn.*	Site
9-10	Frank Catalanotto, Texas	Andy Larkin, Kansas City	9	Kansas City
9-11	Frank Thomas, Chicago	Nelson Cruz, Detroit	8	Chicago
9-15	David Segui, Cleveland	Jason Grimsley, New York	6	New York
9-15	Johnny Damon, Kansas City	Jeff Zimmerman, Texas	6	Texas
9-15	Jason Giambi, Oakland	Albie Lopez, Tampa Bay	3	Tampa Bay
9-17	Carlos Delgado, Toronto	Jesus Pena, Chicago	6	Chicago
9-20	Ray Durham, Chicago	Matt Anderson, Detroit	8	Detroit
9-23	Billy McMillon, Detroit	Roger Clemens, New York	5	New York
9-23	Ben Grieve, Oakland	Jose Paniagua, Seattle	7	Seattle
9-24	Mo Vaughn, Anaheim	Mike Venafro, Texas	8	Texas
9-30	Miguel Tejada, Oakland	Francisco Cordero, Texas	5	Oakland

*Inning in which grand slam was hit. †First game of doubleheader. ‡Second game of doubleheader.

NATIONAL LEAGUE

Date	Batter, Team	Pitcher, Team	Inn.*	Site
3-30	Benny Agbayani, New York	Danny Young, Chicago	11	Chicago
4-3	Eric Karros, Los Angeles	Scott Strickland, Montreal	7	Montreal
4-4	Richard Hidalgo, Houston	Jason Schmidt, Pittsburgh	6	Pittsburgh
4-5	Lenny Harris, Arizona	Paul Byrd, Philadelphia	1	Arizona
4-6	J.D. Drew, St. Louis	Brian Williams, Chicago	4	St. Louis
4-8	Andres Galarraga, Atlanta	Livan Hernandez, San Francisco	5	Atlanta
4-11	Thomas Howard, St. Louis	Chris Holt, Houston	7	Houston
4-11	Ken Griffey Jr., Cincinnati	Gabe White, Colorado	4	Colorado
4-14	Jeff Bagwell, Houston	Kevin Walker, San Diego	6	San Diego
4-18	Robin Ventura, New York	Jaime Navarro, Milwaukee	4	New York
4-20	Sammy Sosa, Chicago	Miguel Batista, Montreal	6	Montreal
4-20	Eli Marrero, St. Louis	Brian Boehringer, San Diego	1	St. Louis
4-21	Kevin Elster, Los Angeles	Norm Charlton, Cincinnati	9	Cincinnati
4-23	Placido Polanco, St. Louis	Scott Karl, Colorado	2	St. Louis
4-26	Pat Meares, Pittsburgh	Woody Williams, San Diego	6	Pittsburgh
4-27	Henry Rodriguez, Chicago	Jose Lima, Houston	4	Houston
4-27	John Vander Wal, Pittsburgh	Matt Clement, San Diego	5	Pittsburgh
4-30	Tom Goodwin, Colorado	Dennis Cook, New York	8	Colorado
5-2	Bobby Estalella, San Francisco	Glendon Rusch, New York	4	San Francisco
5-2	Jeffrey Hammonds, Colorado	Jeremy Powell, Montreal	1	Colorado
5-6	Todd Hundley, Los Angeles	Octavio Dotel, Houston	3	Los Angeles
5-6	Preston Wilson, Florida	Armando Benitez, New York	8	Florida
5-7	Eric Davis, St. Louis	Denny Neagle, Cincinnati	5	Cincinnati
5-9	Ken Caminiti, Houston	Scott Karl, Colorado	5	Houston
5-9	Javy Lopez, Atlanta	Brad Penny, Florida	1	Florida
5-9	Damian Miller, Arizona	Orel Hershiser, Los Angeles	12	Arizona
5-12	Scott Rolen, Philadelphia	Rudy Seanez, Atlanta	7	Philadelphia
5-12	Henry Blanco, Milwaukee	Jason Schmidt, Pittsburgh	2	Pittsburgh
5-14	Mike Piazza, New York	Brad Penny, Florida	6	New York
5-19	Phil Nevin, San Diego	Kevin McGlinchy, Atlanta	7	Atlanta
5-20	Jose Hernandez, Milwaukee	Mark Gardner, San Francisco	1	Milwaukee
5-20	Gary Sheffield, Los Angeles	Joe Strong, Florida	7	Florida
5-21	J.T. Snow, San Francisco	Valerio de los Santos, Milwaukee	6	Milwaukee
5-21	Brian Hunter, Philadelphia	Masato Yoshii, Colorado	4	Philadelphia
5-21	Shawn Green, Los Angeles	Antonio Alfonseca, Florida	9	Florida
5-21	Adrian Beltre, Los Angeles	Jesus Sanchez, Florida	5	Florida
5-23	Jose Hernandez, Milwaukee	Kevin Millwood, Atlanta	3	Milwaukee
5-24	Shawn Estes, San Francisco	Mike Johnson, Montreal	5	San Francisco
5-27	Todd Zeile, New York	Dave Veres, St. Louis	8	St. Louis
5-29	Shawn Green, Los Angeles	Al Leiter, New York	6	Los Angeles
5-30	Todd Pratt, New York	Terry Adams, Los Angeles	9	Los Angeles
5-30	Shawon Dunston, St. Louis	Omar Daal, Arizona	6	Arizona
6-6	Dante Bichette, Cincinnati	Jesus Pena, Chicago A.L.	9	Cincinnati
6-9	Mike Piazza, New York	Roger Clemens, New York A.L.	3	New York A.L.
6-10	Bret Boone, San Diego	Scott Elarton, Houston	1	San Diego
6-13	Raul Casanova, Milwaukee	Steve Kline, Montreal	8	Milwaukee
6-16	Derrek Lee, Florida	Francisco Cordova, Pittsburgh	5	Pittsburgh
6-21	John Vander Wal, Pittsburgh	Tony Armas Jr., Montreal	3	Montreal
6-21	Pat Burrell, Philadelphia	Armando Benitez, New York	9	New York
6-21	Mark Kotsay, Florida	Valerio de los Santos, Milwaukee	7	Florida
7-13	Shawon Dunston, St. Louis	Jesus Pena, Chicago A.L.	7	Chicago A.L.
7-14	Eduardo Perez, St. Louis	Bob Howry, Chicago A.L.	8	Chicago A.L.
7-17	Bobby Abreu, Philadelphia	Jason Grimsley, New York A.L.	7	New York A.L.
7-17 ‡	Tom Goodwin, Colorado	Mike Magnante, Oakland A.L.	7	Colorado
7-18	Mike Piazza, New York	Chris Carpenter, Toronto A.L.	5	Toronto A.L.
7-22	Andy Tracy, Montreal	Reid Cornelius, Florida	3	Florida

Date	Batter, Team	Pitcher, Team	Inn.*	Site
7-23	Bill Spiers, Houston	Heathcliff Slocumb, St. Louis	7	Houston
7-25	Fernando Tatis, St. Louis	Russ Springer, Arizona	6	St. Louis
7-26	Mark Grace, Chicago	Paul Byrd, Philadelphia	9	Philadelphia
7-27	Mike Lowell, Florida	Jason Marquis, Atlanta	8	Atlanta
7-27	Adrian Beltre, Los Angeles	Kevin Jarvis, Colorado	3	Colorado
7-28	Ken Griffey Jr., Cincinnati	Mike Johnson, Montreal	2	Montreal
7-28	Aramis Ramirez, Pittsburgh	Matt Clement, San Diego	1	Pittsburgh
7-30	Ruben Rivera, San Diego	Josias Manzanillo, Pittsburgh	7	Pittsburgh
8-6	Chris Truby, Houston	Mike Thurman, Montreal	3	Houston
8-8	Pat Burrell, Philadelphia	Kevin Walker, San Diego	8	Philadelphia
8-9	Jeff Kent, San Francisco	Paul Rigdon, Milwaukee	2	San Francisco
8-11	Larry Walker, Colorado	Scott Forster, Montreal	6	Montreal
8-12	Aramis Ramirez, Pittsburgh	Johnny Ruffin, Arizona	8	Pittsburgh
8-15	J.T. Snow, San Francisco	Mike Johnson, Montreal	1	Montreal
8-21	Dmitri Young, Cincinnati	Randy Wolf, Philadelphia	3	Cincinnati
8-21	Russ Davis, San Francisco	Armando Almanza, Florida	8	San Francisco
8-22	Alex Ochoa, Cincinnati	Bruce Chen, Philadelphia	1	Cincinnati
8-22	Damian Jackson, San Diego	Pat Mahomes, New York	2	San Diego
9-4	Brian Giles, Pittsburgh	Darren Dreifort, Los Angeles	2	Los Angeles
9-6	Benito Santiago, Cincinnati	Armando Benitez, New York	8	Cincinnati
9-13	Todd Hollandsworth, Colorado	Adam Eaton, San Diego	1	San Diego
9-16	Fernando Tatis, St. Louis	Daniel Garibay, Chicago	3	St. Louis
9-19	Roosevelt Brown, Chicago	Juan Acevedo, Milwaukee	6	Milwaukee
9-20	Jim Edmonds, St. Louis	Chris Holt, Houston	3	St. Louis
9-24	Will Clark, St. Louis	Todd Van Poppel, Chicago	5	Chicago
9-24	Matt Williams, Arizona	Livan Hernandez, San Francisco	2	San Francisco
9-27	Raul Casanova, Milwaukee	Danny Graves, Cincinnati	8	Milwaukee
9-29	Jay Payton, New York	Mike Thurman, Montreal	1	New York
9-30	Todd Hundley, Los Angeles	Matt Clement, San Diego	1	San Diego
9-30	Cliff Floyd, Florida	Tom Jacquez, Philadelphia	6	Florida
10-1	Calvin Murray, San Francisco	Randy Johnson, Arizona	4	Arizona

*Inning in which grand slam was hit. ‡Second game of doubleheader.

2000 REVIEW *Notable performances*

TRANSACTIONS

JANUARY 1, 2000-DECEMBER 31, 2000

JANUARY 3

Orioles organization signed P Jose Mercedes.
Astros organization signed P Travis Driskill, P Rick Huisman, P Brad Kaufman, P Rusty Meacham, P Joe Slusarski, P Bryan Wolff, P Eric Plantenberg and OF Marc Sagmoen.
Mets released OF Bobby Bonilla.

JANUARY 4

Twins organization signed C Marcus Jensen.

JANUARY 5

Angels organization signed P Greg Cadaret.
Astros organization signed C Raul Chavez, 1B Mike Robertson and P Don Wengert.
Dodgers signed P Gregg Olson.
Mets organization signed IF Domingo Cedeno.

JANUARY 6

Dodgers traded OF Terry Jones to Yankees for a player to be named.
Rangers organization signed IF Jon Shave.
Astros organization signed P Dwight Gooden.

JANUARY 7

Angels signed 2B Scott Spiezio, 2B Pat Kelly and 2B Jason Bates.
Devil Rays signed P Juan Guzman and P Norm Chartlon.
Blue Jays signed P Pedro Borbon.
Braves organization signed P Bobby St. Pierre.
Cubs signed P Brian Williams.
Dodgers signed OF-IF F.P. Santangelo.
Cardinals signed P Andy Benes.

JANUARY 8

Indians organization signed P Chris Haney.

JANUARY 10

Indians organization signed C Matt Nokes.
Tigers organization signed OF Billy McMillon.
Mariners signed P Aaron Sele.
Rangers organization signed OF Jason McDonald and IF Luis Ortiz.
Giants signed P John Johnstone.

JANUARY 11

Padres organization signed P Nobuaki Yoshida.

JANUARY 12

Royals organization signed C Jorge Fabregas.
Rangers signed P Darren Oliver.
White Sox traded P Jaime Navarro and P John Snyder to Brewers for P Cal Eldred and IF Jose Valentin.

JANUARY 13

White Sox organization signed IF Esteban Beltre, OF Yamil Benitez, OF Steve Gibralter and P Kelly Wunsch.
Indians organization signed OF Lance Johnson and C Jesse Levis.
Devil Rays signed P Steve Trachsel.

JANUARY 14

Royals signed P Ricky Bottalico.
Twins organization signed P Bobby Ayala.
Devil Rays organization signed IF Dave Hollins, C John Marzano and 1B-OF Ryan Jackson.
Diamondbacks organization signed P Mike Morgan.
Cubs organization signed IF Jeff Huson.
Brewers traded OF Alex Ochoa to Reds for OF Mark Sweeney and a player to be named; Reds sent P Gene Altman to complete deal (May 15).
Mets traded P Masato Yoshii to Rockies for P Bobby M. Jones and P Lariel Gonzalez.

JANUARY 17

Devil Rays organization signed P John Burkett.
Brewers signed C Tyler Houston.
Padres organization signed IF Jed Hansen.

JANUARY 19

Angels organization signed IF Archi Cianfrocco and P Brett Hinchliffe.
Red Sox organization signed OF Marty Cordova.
Indians organization signed P Bobby Witt.
Mariners signed C Joe Oliver.
Cubs signed 3B-OF Willie Greene.
Mets organization signed 3B Charlie Hayes.
Pirates organization signed IF Luis Sojo.
Cardinals organization signed P Jim Dougherty, P John Hudek, C Steve Bieser, C Henry Mercedes, C Marc Ronan, IF Casey Candaele, IF Luis Garcia and OF Ernie Young.

JANUARY 20

Devil Rays organization signed P Terry Mathews.
Braves organization signed OF Trenidad Hubbard.
Reds organization signed OF Deion Sanders, P Mark Portugal and P Johnny Ruffin.
Dodgers organization signed C Chad Kreuter.
Mets organization signed OF Curtis Pride.

JANUARY 21

Tigers signed P Hideo Nomo.
Mets traded IF Luis Lopez to Brewers for P Bill Pulsipher and signed P Rich Rodriguez.
Pirates organization signed P John Smiley.

JANUARY 24

Angels organization signed P Tom Candiotti and P Steve Mintz.
Rockies signed P Billy Taylor.
Giants organization signed 3B Russ Davis.

JANUARY 25

Astros organization signed C Frank Charles and C Pedro Lopez.

JANUARY 26

Angels organization signed P Kent Mercker and P Eric Weaver.
Indians organization signed P Alan Newman, P Curtis King and P Steve Falteisek.
Royals organization signed 1B Paul Sorrento.
Mets organization signed IF Kurt Abbott.

JANUARY 27

Indians organization signed P Scott Sanders.
Devil Rays organization signed C Pat Borders.
Expos organization signed 2B Mickey Morandini.

JANUARY 28

Orioles signed P Pat Rapp.
Devil Rays signed P Steve Trachsel.
Braves organization signed OF Bobby Bonilla.
Reds organization signed P Mark Wohlers.
Padres organization signed P Danny Tartabull.

JANUARY 31

Angels organization signed IF Carlos Garcia.
Twins organization signed OF Butch Huskey.
Yankees organization signed P Mike Grace.

FEBRUARY 1

Angels organization signed IF Benji Gil.
Yankees organization signed OF Tim Raines.
Devil Rays organization signed P Doug Creek.
Reds organization signed P Javier Martinez and P Willis Roberts.
Astros organization signed P Mike Maddux and P Kip Gross.
Dodgers organization signed OF Geronimo Berroa.

FEBRUARY 2

Red Sox organization signed P Julio Santana.
Yankees organization signed IF Rafael Bournigal.
Diamondbacks released P Bobby Chouinard.
Rockies signed OF Darren Bragg.
Phillies organization signed P Steve Sparks.

FEBRUARY 3

Royals organization signed P Edwin Hurtado.
Cardinals organization signed IF-OF Shawon Dunston, OF Brian McRae, 1B Eduardo Perez and C Rick Wilkins.
Padres organization signed 3B Ed Sprague.

FEBRUARY 4

Orioles organization signed P Tim Worrell and P Rick Krivda.
Rangers organization signed OF Scarborough Green.
Braves organization signed P Paul Assenmacher.
Expos organization signed C Charlie O'Brien.
Mets organization signed P Dennis Springer.

FEBRUARY 7

Mets claimed IF David Lamb on waivers from Devil Rays.

FEBRUARY 8

Indians organization signed P Chris Nichting, P Marc Pisciotta, P Mike Bovee, C Matt Curtis, C Cesar Devarez, IF Kelcey Mucker, IF Jeff Patzke and OF Andy Tomberlin.
Yankees organization signed OF Luke Wilcox.
Cubs organization signed P Greg McMichael.

FEBRUARY 9

Pirates organization signed P Mark Leiter, P Danilo Leon, P Josias Manzanillo and P Dave Stevens.

FEBRUARY 10

Mariners traded OF Ken Griffey Jr. to Reds for P Brett Tomko, OF Mike Cameron, IF Antonio Perez and P Jake Meyer.

FEBRUARY 14

Cubs released P Andy Larkin.

FEBRUARY 15

Reds organization signed P Osvaldo Fernandez.

FEBRUARY 16

Red Sox organization signed P Hipolito Pichardo.
Athletics organization signed P Doug Johns.
Blue Jays organization signed P Eric Gunderson.
Expos organization signed OF Patrick Lennon and P Felipe Lira.

FEBRUARY 18

Indians organization signed OF Mark Whiten.
Royals traded OF Jeremy Giambi to Athletics for P Brett Laxton.
Diamondbacks released P Al Garcia.

FEBRUARY 19

Diamondbacks organization signed OF Turner Ward and P Jim Corsi.
Brewers organization signed P Jim Bruske.

FEBRUARY 22

Braves organization signed P Steve Avery.
Mets organization signed 1B Mark Johnson.

FEBRUARY 23

Pirates traded OF Al Martin and cash to Padres for OF-1B John Vander Wal, P Geraldo Padua and P James Sak.

FEBRUARY 24

Devil Rays organization signed IF Carlos Baerga.
Reds organization signed C Benito Santiago.
Rockies announced retirement of P Roger Pavlik.

MARCH 1

Pirates released P Pep Harris.

MARCH 6

Tigers released OF Marc Newfield.

MARCH 7

Tigers traded C Gregg Zaun to Royals for a player to be named or cash.
Yankees released P Jeff Juden.
Devil Rays released OF Danny Clyburn.

MARCH 9

Mets released IF Shane Halter.

MARCH 10

Phillies traded OF Wendell Magee Jr. to Tigers for P Bobby Sismondo.

MARCH 11

Tigers released P Mike Oquist.
Royals released P Carl Dale.

MARCH 13

Indians released P Brian Barber.
Braves traded IF-OF Freddy Garcia to Reds for P Dennis Russo.
Mets organization signed P Rene Arocha.

MARCH 15

Red Sox released OF Jermaine Allensworth.
Tigers released P Ramon Tatis.

MARCH 16

Angels released P Greg Cadaret.
Rangers traded IF Lee Stevens to Expos, Expos traded 1B Brad Fullmer to Blue Jays, Blue Jays traded 1B David Segui and cash to Rangers.

MARCH 17

Angels released IF Archi Cianfrocco and IF Carlos Garcia.
Diamondbacks organization signed IF Craig Counsell.
Mets organization signed OF Timoniel Perez.

MARCH 18

Indians announced retirement of P Mark Langston and released OF Ruben Sierra.
Mets traded P Jesse Orosco to Cardinals for IF-OF Joe McEwing.

MARCH 20

Braves released P Everett Stull.
Mets released IF Charlie Hayes.

MARCH 21

Yankees released P Mike Grace.
Mariners traded C Carlos Maldonado to Astros for IF Carlos Hernandez.

MARCH 22

Angels announced retirement of IF Pat Kelly and released IF Jason Bates.
Brewers organization signed IF Charlie Hayes.
Mets traded IF Jersen Perez to Blue Jays to keep the rights to P Jim Mann.

MARCH 23

Angels traded OF Jim Edmonds to Cardinals for P Kent Bottenfield and 2B Adam Kennedy.
Yankees announced retirement of OF Tim Raines and traded IF Juan Melo to Giants for IF Wilson Delgado.
Cubs released P Greg McMichael.
Rockies released P Billy Taylor.
Pirates released P Mark Leiter.
Cubs traded P Rodney Myers to Padres for OF Gary Matthews Jr.

MARCH 24

Athletics traded 1B-OF David McCarty to Royals for cash.
Yankees organization signed IF Carlos Garcia.
Marlins claimed Derrick Gibson on waivers from Rockies.
Rockies released C Raul Casanova.

MARCH 25

Red Sox released OF Marty Cordova.
Yankees released IF Rafael Bournigal.
Braves organization signed P Greg McMichael.

MARCH 27

Indians traded SS Jose Olmeda to White Sox for future consid-
erations and traded P Steve Falteisek to Marlins for SS Victor
Rodriguez.
Twins released P Bobby Ayala.
Mariners released OF Brian L. Hunter.
Blue Jays organization signed OF Marty Cordova.
Rockies released IF David Howard.

MARCH 28

Indians organization signed P Clint Sodowsky, P Joe Roa and P
Brian Looney.
Royals released P Ken Ryan and P Billy Brewer.
Brewers released C Bobby Hughes and C Brian Banks.
Expos traded IF Mickey Morandini to the Phillies for cash.
Mets claimed P Nerio Rodriguez on waivers from Blue Jays.

MARCH 29

Angels released C-DH Todd Greene.
White Sox released P Carlos Castillo.
Indians released P Scott Sanders.
Yankees released catcher Tom Pagnozzi.
Devil Rays released C Mike Figga, P John Burkett and P Chad
Ogea and signed IF Rafael Bournigal.
Blue Jays claimed P Mike Kusiewicz on waivers from Minnesota.
Diamondbacks released P Brad Clontz.
Braves released 1B Randall Simon and P Rafael Medina and
signed P John Burkett.
Reds released P Mark Portugal.
Rockies traded OF Edgard Clemente to Anaheim for OF Norm
Hutchins and C Jason Dewey.
Astros traded P Trever Miller to Phillies for P Yorkis Perez.
Brewers claimed P Jason Boyd on waivers from Pirates.
Pirates released P Pete Schourek.
Giants released IF Jay Canizaro.

MARCH 30

Indians released OF Lance Johnson.
Royals traded C Sal Fasano to Athletics for cash.
Mariners organization signed C Alberto Hernandez.
Devil Rays organization signed P Julio Cesar Villalon.
Braves organization signed OF Nataniel Reinoso.
Rockies signed OF Brian L. Hunter.
Cardinals released OF Brian McRae.

MARCH 31

Yankees organization signed OF Lance Johnson.
Mariners claimed OF Anthony Sanders on waivers from Blue Jays.
Braves released SS Ozzie Guillen and P Paul Assenmacher.

APRIL 1

Angels released P Tom Candiotti.
Indians organization signed P Scott Sanders.
Yankees released OF Ryan Thompson and IF Jason Bates.
Dodgers traded IF Juan Castro to Reds for a player to be named.
Expos claimed OF Terry Jones on waivers from Yankees.

APRIL 3

Red Sox signed P Pete Schourek.
Indians organization signed C Bobby Hughes.
Royals organization signed P Paul Spoljaric and 3B Kevin Orie.
Diamondbacks organization signed P Jim Corsi.

APRIL 4

Cubs organization signed P Bobby Ayala.

APRIL 5

Royals claimed IF Luis Ordaz on waivers from Diamondbacks.
Devil Rays signed SS Ozzie Guillen.
Rangers organization signed OF Monty Lee and IF Matt Halloran.

APRIL 6

Rangers organization signed P Terry Mathews.
Mets claimed P Radhames Dykhoff on waivers from Orioles.
Pirates organization signed P Brad Clontz.
Padres signed 1B Young-Jin Jung.

APRIL 7

Athletics organization signed OF Bo Porter.
Reds traded P Gabe White to Rockies for P Manny Aybar.

APRIL 8

Reds organization signed P Norm Charlton.

APRIL 11

Astros traded C Paul Bako to Marlins for cash and a player to be
named.
Mets organization signed IF Rafael Bournigal.

APRIL 12

Indians organization signed P Chad Ogea.
Mets claimed P Anthony Shumaker on waivers from Phillies.

APRIL 13

Astros traded P Dwight Gooden to Devil Rays for cash.
Cubs traded C Pat Cline to Brewers for a player to be named.

APRIL 14

Red Sox announced retirement of 3B Gary Gaetti.

APRIL 19

Red Sox organization signed IF Freddy Garcia. Diamondbacks
traded OF Garry Maddox Jr. to Red Sox for IF Javier Fuentes.

APRIL 20

Indians traded OF Dan McKinley to Expos for OF Scott Hunter.

APRIL 21

White Sox claimed 3B Herbert Perry on waivers from Devil
Rays.
Mariners released OF Shane Monahan.
Phillies claimed OF Brian R. Hunter on waivers from Braves.

APRIL 25

Red Sox organization signed P Mel Rojas and C Mike Figga.
Expos traded P Miguel Batista to Royals for P Brad Rigby.

APRIL 26

Orioles claimed IF Mark Lewis on waivers from Reds.

APRIL 27

Mets traded OF Curtis Pride to Red Sox for a player to be
named.

APRIL 28

Angels claimed OF Scott Morgan on waivers from Indians.
Reds released P Norm Charlton.
Brewers organization signed C Mark Dalesandro.

APRIL 29

Indians signed IF-OF Jeff Manto.
Yankees signed OF-DH Felix Jose.
Brewers released P Jamie Navarro.

MAY 3

Orioles released P Tim Worrell.
Rangers organization signed IF Scott Livingstone.

MAY 4

Cardinals signed P Darren Holmes.

MAY 8

Cubs organization signed P Tim Worrell and released RHP
Bobby Ayala.

MAY 10

Tigers signed OF Rich Becker.
Phillies claimed C Cesar King on waivers from Rangers.

MAY 12

Cubs traded P Mark Guthrie and cash to Devil Rays for 1B-OF Dave Martinez.

MAY 13

Mets released OF Rickey Henderson.

MAY 17

Indians signed P Jason Davis.
Tigers released P Jim Poole.
Mariners signed OF Rickey Henderson.

MAY 18

Indians released P Bobby Witt.

MAY 19

Braves organization signed C Brayan Pena.
Dodgers claimed P Trever Miller on waivers from Phillies.

MAY 22

Mets traded P Richie Lewis to Indians for a player to be named.
Cubs released P Andrew Lorraine.
Padres organization signed P Carlos Reyes.

MAY 24

Mets organization signed IF Jed Hansen.
Phillies signed OF Lawrence Alexander.

MAY 25

Devil Rays released SS Kevin Stocker and P Dwight Gooden.

MAY 26

Cubs released P Brian Williams.

MAY 27

Astros traded IF Russ Johnson to Devil Rays for P Marc Valdes.

MAY 30

Angels signed IF Kevin Stocker.

MAY 31

Angels released P Cody Salter.
White Sox traded P Tanyon Sturtze to Devil Rays for IF Tony Graffanino.
Diamondbacks released P Doug Kohl and OF Justin Graham.

JUNE 1

Blue Jays signed P Brandon Lyon.

JUNE 2

Diamondbacks traded OF-IF Lenny Harris to Mets for P Bill Pulsipher.

JUNE 5

Indians signed P Brian Williams and P Tyler Green.

JUNE 7

White Sox signed P Kevin Zaug.
Expos released P Jim Poole.

JUNE 8

Tigers sold P Masao Kida to Orix of the Japanese Pacific League.
Mets sold OF Jon Nunnally to Orix of the Japanese Pacific League.

JUNE 9

Indians organization signed P Jim Poole.
Rangers traded P Chuck Smith to Marlins, Marlins traded OF Brant Brown to Cubs, Cubs traded OF Dave Martinez to Texas.
Diamondbacks traded IF Andy Fox to Marlins for OF Danny Bautista.

JUNE 10

Yankees organization signed P Dwight Gooden.

JUNE 12

Tigers traded OF Karim Garcia to Orioles for future considerations.

JUNE 13

Orioles traded P Al Reyes to Dodgers for P Alan Mills and cash.

JUNE 14

Rangers claimed P Scott Randall on waivers from Twins.

JUNE 15

Rockies released P Jaime Navarro.
Indians signed P Jaime Navarro.

JUNE 16

Rangers claimed P Jared Camp on waivers from Indians.

JUNE 17

Marlins organization signed pitcher Scott Sanders.
Dodgers traded C Adam Melhuse to Rockies for a player to be named.

JUNE 19

Blue Jays organization signed P Mark Eichhorn.

JUNE 20

Twins released P Sean Bergman.
Yankees traded DH Jim Leyritz to Dodgers for IF Jose Vizcaino and cash.

JUNE 22

Expos released C Charlie O'Brien.

JUNE 23

Mariners claimed P Mark Watson on waivers from Indians.

JUNE 27

Dodgers released P Orel Hershiser.

JUNE 28

Cardinals traded P Darren Holmes to Orioles for future considerations.
Rockies traded P Ed Vosberg to Phillies for a player to be named.

JUNE 29

Yankees traded OF Ricky Ledee and two players to be named to Indians for OF David Justice; Yankees sent P Jake Westbrook and Zach Day to complete deal (July 25).

JUNE 30

Padres traded 3B Ed Sprague to Red Sox for P Dennis Tankersley and IF Cesar Saba.

JULY 3

Rangers released P Mark Clark.

JULY 4

Red Sox signed OF Bernard Gilkey.

JULY 5

Braves signed P Scott Kamieniecki.
Astros released P Mike Maddux.

JULY 7

Reds claimed P Jason Sekany on waivers from Red Sox.

JULY 12

Reds traded P Denny Neagle and OF Mike Frank to Yankees for 3B Drew Henson, OF Jackson Melian, P Brian Reith and P Ed Yarnall.
Mets organization signed P Willie Banks and P Oscar Henriquez.
Phillies traded P Andy Ashby to Braves for P Bruce Chen and P Jim Osting.
Padres claimed P Todd Erdos on waivers from Yankees.

JULY 13

Orioles organization signed 3B Dave Hollins.

JULY 15

Rockies traded 1B Todd Sears and cash to Twins for 2B Todd Walker and OF Butch Huskey.

JULY 17

Tigers traded IF Gabe Alvarez to Padres for 1B-OF Dusty Allen.
Rangers released P Jared Camp.

JULY 18

Reds traded 1B Hal Morris to Tigers for cash.

JULY 19

Orioles released P Darren Holmes.
Royals claimed P Andy Larkin on waivers from Reds.
Rangers traded P Esteban Loaiza to Blue Jays for P Darwin Dubillan and IF Mike Young.
Brewers claimed OF Angel Echevarria on waivers from Rockies.

JULY 21

Braves claimed C Paul Bako on waivers from Marlins.
Cubs traded OF Glenallen Hill to Yankees for P Ben Ford and P Ozwaldo Mairena.

JULY 22

Astros released P Yorkis Perez.

JULY 25

Blue Jays traded C Kevin Brown to Brewers for OF Alvin Morrow.

JULY 26

Phillies traded P Curt Schilling to Diamondbacks for 1B-OF Travis Lee, P Omar Daal, P Vicente Padilla and P Nelson Figueroa.
Reds traded P Manny Aybar to Marlins for P Jorge Cordova.
Rockies released OF Darren Bragg.
Cubs traded P Ismael Valdes to Dodgers for P Jamie Arnold, OF Jorge Piedra and cash considerations.
Phillies traded OF Rob Ducey to Blue Jays for a player to be named; Blue Jays sent P John Sneed to complete deal (July 31).

JULY 27

Rockies traded P Rolando Arrojo, P Rick Croushore, IF Mike Lansing and cash to Red Sox for P Brian Rose, P John Wasdin, P Jeff Taglienti and IF Jeff Frye.

JULY 28

Angels traded P Brett Hinchcliffe and IF Keith Luuloa to Cubs for OF Chris Hatcher, P Mike Heathcott and IF Brett King.
Brewers traded P Bob Wickman, P Steve Woodard and P Jason Bere to Indians for OF Richie Sexson, P Paul Rigdon, P Kane Davis and a player to be named; Indians sent 2B Marcos Scutaro to complete deal (August 30).
Indians traded OF Alex Ramirez and IF Enrique Wilson to Pirates for OF Wil Cordero.
Devil Rays traded P Jim Mecir and P Todd Belitz to Athletics for P Jesus Colome and a player to be named later.
Rangers traded 1B David Segui to Indians for OF Ricky Ledee.
Orioles traded SS Mike Bordick to Mets for IF Melvin Mora, IF Mike Kinkade, P Lesli Brea and P Pat Gorman.
Mets traded OF Jason Tyner and P Paul Wilson to Devil Rays for P Rick White and OF Bubba Trammell.

JULY 29

Orioles traded C Charles Johnson and DH Harold Baines to White Sox for C Brook Fordyce, P Miguel Felix, P Juan Figueroa and P Jason Lakman.
Cardinals traded 1B Chris Richard and P Mark Nussbeck to Orioles for P Mike Timlin and cash.
Braves signed P Stan Belinda.
Astros traded P Doug Henry to Giants for P Scott Linebrink.
Phillies traded OF Ron Gant to Angels for P Kent Bottenfield.
Pirates traded P Jason Christiansen to Cardinals for SS Jack Wilson.

JULY 31

Orioles traded OF B.J. Surhoff and P Gabe Molina to Braves for OF Trenidad Hubbard, C Fernando Lunar and P Luis Rivera.
Cardinals traded 3B Jose Leon to Orioles for 1B Will Clark and cash.
Tigers released OF Luis Polonia.
Royals traded P Jay Witasick to Padres for P Brian Meadows.
Twins traded 1B Mario Valdez to Athletics for C Danny Ardoin.
Mariners traded 1B-OF John Mabry and P Tom Davey to Padres for OF Al Martin.
Devil Rays traded P Steve Trachsel and P Mark Guthrie to Blue Jays for 2B Brent Abernathy and a player to be named.

Cubs traded OF Henry Rodriguez to Marlins for 1B-OF Ross Gload and P Dave Noyce. Montreal traded OF Rondell White to Cubs for P Scott Downs.
Dodgers traded OF Todd Hollandsworth, OF Kevin Gibbs and P Randey Dorame to Rockies for OF Tom Goodwin and cash.
Orioles traded P Juan Aracena to Mets for P Anthony Shumaker.
Cardinals traded P Heathcliff Slocumb and OF Ben Johnson to Padres for C Carlos Hernandez and IF-OF Nate Tebbs.

AUGUST 3

Red Sox claimed 1B Rico Brogna on waivers from Phillies.
Yankees signed OF Luis Polonia.

AUGUST 4

Athletics signed DH-1B Mike Stanley.
Rangers traded OF Dave Martinez to Blue Jays for a player to be named; Blue Jays sent P Pete Munro to complete deal (August 8).
Marlins organization signed P Jack Armstrong.
Phillies traded SS Desi Relaford to Padres for a player to be named; Padres sent IF David Newhan to complete deal (August 7).

AUGUST 5

Reds traded P Robert Averette to Rockies for OF Brian L. Hunter.
Phillies traded 2B Mickey Morandini to Blue Jays for a player to be named; Blue Jays sent Rob Ducey to complete deal (August 7).
Pirates traded OF Bruce Aven to Dodgers for a player to be named.

AUGUST 7

Angels released pitcher Ken Hill.
Yankees claimed OF-DH Jose Canseco off waivers from Devil Rays.
Pirates traded IF Luis Sojo to Yankees for P Chris Spurling.
Marlins organization signed IF-OF Casey Candaele.
Padres claimed IF David Newhan on waivers.

AUGUST 8

Expos traded C Chris Widger to Mariners for a player to be named; Mariners sent to OF Terrmel Sledge to complete deal (September 28).

AUGUST 11

Indians organization signed 3B Dave Hollins.
Yankees traded IF Wilson Delgado to Royals for SS Nick Ortiz.

AUGUST 16

Angels organization signed P Bryan Ward and claimed 2B David Eckstein on waivers from Red Sox.

AUGUST 18

White Sox organization signed P Ken Hill.
Astros released OF Matt Mieske.

AUGUST 22

Rockies traded P Scott Karl and cash to Angels for a player to be named.

AUGUST 23

Blue Jays claimed P Pat Daneker on waivers from White Sox.

AUGUST 24

Indians organization signed IF Sean Berry.
Tigers organization signed C Brad Wise.

AUGUST 25

Braves organization signed OF Rich Amaral.

AUGUST 30

Angels claimed P Ben Weber on waivers from Giants.
White Sox released P Ken Hill.
Royals released P Jerry Spradlin.
Athletics traded IF Jorge Velandia to Tigers for OF Nelson Cruz.

AUGUST 31

Twins traded OF Midre Cummings to Red Sox for IF Hector De Los Santos.

Reds traded OF Dante Bichette to Red Sox for P Chris Reitsma and P John Curtice.
Giants claimed C Scott Servais on waivers from Rockies.

SEPTEMBER 8
Indians claimed P Eric Dubose on waivers from Athletics.
Cubs signed P Jerry Spradlin.

SEPTEMBER 9
Red Sox traded OF Lew Ford to Twins for P Hector Carrasco.

SEPTEMBER 11
Red Sox signed P Steve Ontiveros.
Athletics released IF Joey Espada.

SEPTEMBER 20
White Sox traded P Jesus Pena to Red Sox for a player to be named.

SEPTEMBER 22
Tigers claimed P Eric DuBose on waivers from Indians.

OCTOBER 3
Blue Jays claimed P John Sneed on waivers from Phillies.

OCTOBER 5
Orioles released OF Trenidad Hubbard.
Mets claimed P Jason Middlebrook on waivers from Padres.

OCTOBER 11
Angels claimed P Mark Lukasiewicz on waivers from Blue Jays.
Indians released P Chris Haney.
Rangers claimed OF Bo Porter on waivers from Athletics.
Pirates released P Brad Clontz.

OCTOBER 12
Mets claimed SS Desi Relaford on waivers from Padres.
Padres organization signed IF Greg LaRocca, IF John Roskos and IF Joe Vitiello.

OCTOBER 13
Athletics claimed P Marc Wilkins on waivers from Pirates.
Diamondbacks organization signed P Kennie Steenstra.
Rockies claimed P Jason Green on waivers from Astros.

OCTOBER 17
Padres claimed OF Mike Colangelo on waivers from Diamondbacks.

OCTOBER 19
Mariners organization signed P Kenny Rayborn and OF Chad Alexander.

OCTOBER 24
Tigers organization signed P Sean Runyan.

NOVEMBER 2
Tigers released P Hideo Nomo.
Devil Rays organization signed P Bill Pulsipher, OF Norm Hutchins and P Juan Rosario.
Diamondbacks signed C Ken Huckaby.
Cardinals announced retirement of 1B Will Clark.

NOVEMBER 6
Rangers signed C Mike Hubbard.
Expos organization signed P Scott Stewart.

NOVEMBER 7
Blue Jays traded P Gary Glover to White Sox for P Scott Eyre.
White Sox released IF Craig Wilson.

NOVEMBER 8
Reds traded P Ron Villone to Rockies for two players to be named.

NOVEMBER 10
Devil Rays organization signed 1B-OF Chris Hatcher and 1B Ron Wright.

NOVEMBER 13
Rangers organization signed P Jayson Durocher.
Blue Jays organization signed P Jason Dickson.

NOVEMBER 15
Indians organization signed IF Ralph Milliard and P Dan Smith.
Yankees released OF Ryan Thompson.
Devil Rays organization signed IF Andy Sheets, P Jim Pittsley and C Yohanny Valera.
Diamondbacks signed P Miguel Batista.
Phillies signed P Joel Adamson, IF P.J. Forbes, P Eddie Oropesa, IF Pete Rose Jr., 1B Gene Schall and OF Ken Woods.
Cardinals organization signed IF Lou Lucca, C Mike Stefanski, C Mike Figga and SS Kevin Polkovich.

NOVEMBER 16
Orioles organization signed P Willis Roberts.
Reds traded C Eddie Taubensee to Indians for P Jim Brower and P Robert Purgmire.
Mariners released P Todd Williams and 1B Brian Lesher.
Cubs signed P Julian Tavarez.
Reds traded IF Chris Stynes to Red Sox for OF Michael Coleman and IF Donnie Sadler.

NOVEMBER 17
Angels signed C Jorge Fabregas.
Athletics traded 2B Randy Velarde to Rangers for P Ryan Cullen and P Aaron Harang.
Rangers released OF Scarborough Green.
Expos organization signed P Felipe Lira, P Pat Flury, P Scott Stewart, C Randy Knorr, C Sandy Martinez, 3B Rob Sasser and OF Mark Smith and released P J.D. Smart.
Mets organization signed P Nerio Rodriguez, P Manny Barrios and OF Ray Montgomery.
Phillies signed P Jose Mesa.

NOVEMBER 18
Indians signed OF Ellis Burks.
Mariners signed OF Ichiro Suzuki.
Cubs traded P Tim Worrell to Giants for 3B Bill Mueller.

NOVEMBER 20
Yankees released P Jason Grimsley.
Cubs claimed P Eric Ireland on waivers from Astros.
Athletics traded OF Matt Stairs to Cubs for P Eric Ireland.
Astros signed IF Jose Vizcaino.
Padres organization signed P Bryan Corey, P Matt Miller, P Ron Mahay, OF Ernie Young, IF Keith Luuloa and C Charlie Greene.

NOVEMBER 21
Yankees signed C Joe Oliver and released C Chris Turner.
Marlins organization signed C Matt Treanor, C B.J. Waszgis and P Pat Ahearne.

NOVEMBER 22
Devil Rays organization signed P Sean Bergman, P Dwayne Jacobs, IF Ray Holbert and IF Mike Metcalfe.
Reds traded P Steve Parris to Blue Jays for P Clayton Andrews and P Leo Estrella.
Padres claimed P Jason Middlebrook on waivers from Mets.

NOVEMBER 24
Expos signed P Luis Herrera and P Lenin Aragon.

NOVEMBER 27
Devil Rays released P Jim Morris, P Jeff Sparks, IF Miguel Cairo, OF Quinton McCracken and OF Ozzie Timmons.
Cubs released P Ben Ford and P Jerry Spradlin.
Marlins traded IF Amaury Garcia to White Sox for a player to be named; White Sox sent P Mark Roberts to complete deal (December 11).
Brewers released OF Lyle Mouton.

NOVEMBER 28
Brewers signed P Curtis Leskanic.

NOVEMBER 29

Phillies signed P Rheal Cormier.

NOVEMBER 30

Yankees signed P Mike Mussina.
Phillies organization signed P Brian R. Hunter.

DECEMBER 1

Reds claimed P Jeff Wallace on waivers from Pirates and released OF Kimera Bartee.
Padres traded P Brandon Kolb to Brewers for SS Santiago Perez and a player to be named or cash and signed P Scott Karl.

DECEMBER 4

Mariners signed P Jeff Nelson.
Braves claimed P Trey Moore on waivers from Expos.
Rockies signed P Denny Neagle.

DECEMBER 5

Mets organization signed IF-OF David Howard, P Brett Hinchliffe, P Joe Crawford and SS Kevin Baez.

DECEMBER 6

Athletics organization signed P Dave Eiland, P Eric Hiljus, P Frank Lankford, P Jon Ratliff, P Steve Schrenk and C Tom Wilson.
Blue Jays organization signed 2B Mickey Morandini.
Diamondbacks signed P Armando Reynoso.
Dodgers signed P Andy Ashby.

DECEMBER 7

Red Sox signed P Frank Castillo and P Pete Schourek.
White Sox traded P Chad Bradford to Athletics for a player to be named; Athletics sent C Miguel Olivo to complete deal (December 13).
Diamondbacks signed P Jason Jacome and sold the contract of 1B Alex Cabrera to Seibu of the Japanese Pacific League.
Brewers signed OF James Mouton.
Mets organization signed P Scott Forster.

DECEMBER 8

Rangers signed 1B Andres Galarraga.
Blue Jays signed P Dan Plesac.
Diamondbacks signed 1B Mark Grace.
Cubs signed P Jeff Fassero.
Mets signed OF Bubba Carpenter.
Giants signed OF-IF Shawon Dunston.

DECEMBER 9

Reds traded SS Wilmy Caceres to Angels for P Seth Etherton.
Rangers signed 3B Ken Caminiti and P Mark Petkovsek.
Braves signed OF Dave Martinez.
Reds signed P Dennys Reyes.
Rockies signed P Mike Hampton and OF Ron Gant.
Marlins traded OF Julio Ramirez to White Sox for OF Jeff Abbott.
Pirates signed P Terry Mulholland and OF Derek Bell.

DECEMBER 11

Angels signed P Pat Rapp and OF Kimera Bartee.
Orioles traded C Jayson Werth to Blue Jays for P John Bale.
Tigers traded C Brad Ausmus, P Doug Brocail and P Nelson Cruz to Astros for OF Roger Cedeno, C Mitch Meluskey and P Chris Holt.
Royals signed P Doug Henry.
Twins released P Jason Ryan.
Rangers signed SS Alex Rodriguez.
Blue Jays signed IF Jeff Frye.
Mets signed P Kevin Appier, P Steve Trachsel and OF Tsuyoshi Shinjo.
Padres traded P Donne Wall to Mets for OF Bubba Trammell.

DECEMBER 13

Red Sox signed OF Manny Ramirez.

DECEMBER (cont.)

Blue Jays organization signed P Jaime Navarro, OF Ryan Thompson, C Izzy Molina, IF Aaron Holbert, OF Chris Latham and P Chris Michalak.
Rangers organization signed P Kevin Foster, P Mike Munoz and OF Ruben Sierra.
Braves signed IF Rico Brogna and IF Kurt Abbott.
Cubs signed C Todd Hundley, OF Scarborough Green, C Brian Banks, C Robert Machado, IF Chris Snopek, IF Trace Coquillette, P Rob Stanifer, P Dave Wainhouse and P Brian Barkley.
Padres signed 3B Alex Arias.

DECEMBER 14

Yankees organization signed P Brian Boehringer.
Mariners claimed IF Mike Caruso on waivers from White Sox.
Rangers traded SS Royce Clayton to White Sox for P Aaron Myette and P Brian Schmack.
Cubs signed P Tom Gordon and P Jason Bere.
Astros signed P Mike Jackson.
Dodgers organization signed P Jim Morris and P Matt Whisenant.
Cardinals traded 3B Fernando Tatis and P Britt Reames to Expos for P Dustin Hermanson and P Steve Kline.

DECEMBER 15

Red Sox signed P Hideo Nomo.
Rangers traded P Matt Perisho to Tigers for P Kevin Mobley and P Brandon Villafuerte.
Athletics released P Marc Wilkins.
Diamondbacks signed OF Midre Cummings.
Expos organization signed P Bobby Munoz and P Terry Burrows.
Phillies signed P Ricky Bottalico.
Padres organization signed OF-1B Kevin Witt, 2B Adam Riggs and P Jeremy Powell.

DECEMBER 18

Braves traded 3B Steve Sisco to Orioles for INF Jesse Garcia.
White Sox signed C Sandy Alomar Jr.
Cubs signed P Jason Bere.
Marlins signed C Charles Johnson.
Dodgers organization signed P Eddie Priest, P Todd Rizzo, IF Keith Johnson, OF Jeff Barry.

DECEMBER 19

Orioles signed P Pat Hentgen.
Twins organization signed C Tom Prince and IF Edwin Diaz.
Mariners organization signed P Norm Charlton.

DECEMBER 20

Orioles signed SS Mike Bordick.
Red Sox released OF Izzy Alcantara.
Indians organization signed P Scott Aldred, P Eric Gunderson, C Tim Laker, P Tim Kubinski, OF Marty Cordova and OF Scott Krause.
Phillies organization signed P Edwin Hurtado, P Rigo Beltran, IF Kevin Orie, P Eddie Oropesa, C Eric Schreimann, P Clint Sodowsky and OF Turner Ward.

DECEMBER 21

Orioles signed 1B David Segui.
Expos organization signed OF Tim Raines, OF Curtis Pride and P Bob Scanlan.

DECEMBER 22

Expos traded P Jorge Julio to Orioles for 3B Ryan Minor.
Indians organization signed OF Karim Garcia.
Mariners signed 2B Bret Boone.
Brewers signed OF Jeffrey Hammonds.
Cardinals signed OF Quinton McCracken.

DECEMBER 23

Indians organization signed P Tim Byrdak.

AWARD WINNERS

THE SPORTING NEWS

AMERICAN LEAGUE

Pitcher of the Year: Pedro Martinez, Boston
Rookie Player of the Year: Mark Quinn, Kansas City, OF-DH
Rookie Pitcher of the Year: Kazuhiro Sasaki, Seattle
Fireman of the Year: Todd Jones, Detroit
Comeback Player of the Year: Frank Thomas, Chicago
Manager of the Year: Jerry Manuel, Chicago

NATIONAL LEAGUE

Pitcher of the Year: Tom Glavine, Atlanta
Rookie Player of the Year: Rafael Furcal, Atlanta, 2B-SS
Rookie Pitcher of the Year: Rick Ankiel, St. Louis
Fireman of the Year: Antonio Alfonseca, Florida
Comeback Player of the Year: Andres Galarraga, Atlanta
Manager of the Year: Dusty Baker, San Francisco

MAJOR LEAGUE

Player of the Year: Carlos Delgado, Toronto
Executive of the Year: Walt Jocketty, St. Louis

MINOR LEAGUE

Player of the Year: John Rauch, Winston-Salem, Carolina; Birmingham, Southern
Manager of the Year: Joel Skinner, Buffalo, International
Executive of the Year: Art Savage, Sacramento, Pacific Coast

BASEBALL WRITERS' ASSOCIATION OF AMERICA

AMERICAN LEAGUE

MOST VALUABLE PLAYER

Player, Team	1	2	3	4	5	6	7	8	9	10	Pts.
Jason Giambi, Oakland	14	11	2	-	1	-	-	-	-	-	317
Frank Thomas, Chicago	10	7	7	2	2	-	-	-	-	-	285
Alex Rodriguez, Seattle	4	4	6	7	3	1	1	-	1	-	218
Carlos Delgado, Toronto	-	4	10	9	2	3	-	-	-	-	206
Pedro Martinez, Boston	-	1	1	6	1	5	1	2	-	3	103
Manny Ramirez, Cleveland	-	-	1	-	7	3	4	2	4	2	97
Edgar Martinez, Seattle	-	-	-	-	5	5	3	7	4	1	97
Darin Erstad, Anaheim	-	1	1	1	4	4	3	2	3	2	94
Nomar Garciaparra, Boston	-	-	-	2	-	4	3	3	4	3	66
Derek Jeter, New York	-	-	-	-	-	1	5	4	2	3	44
Mike Sweeney, Kansas City	-	-	-	-	1	-	1	2	5	7	33
Magglio Ordonez, Chicago	-	-	-	-	-	2	1	3	2	1	28
David Justice, Cleveland-New York	-	-	-	1	1	-	1	2	-	-	23
Bernie Williams, New York	-	-	-	-	-	1	3	1	1	-	23
Tim Hudson, Oakland	-	-	-	-	-	-	1	-	1	2	8
Miguel Tejada, Oakland	-	-	-	-	-	-	1	-	-	1	5
Travis Fryman, Cleveland	-	-	-	-	-	-	-	-	1	-	2
David Wells, Toronto	-	-	-	-	-	-	-	-	-	2	2
Johnny Damon, Kansas City	-	-	-	-	-	-	-	-	-	1	1

Fourteen points awarded for a first-place vote, nine for second and down to one for 10th.

ROOKIE OF THE YEAR

Player, Team	1	2	3	Pts.
Kazuhiro Sasaki, Seattle	17	5	4	104
Terrence Long, Oakland	7	15	3	83
Mark Quinn, Kansas City	4	8	12	56
Bengie Molina, Anaheim	-	-	3	3
Kelly Wunsch, Chicago	-	-	2	2
Steve Cox, Tampa Bay	-	-	1	1
Adam Kennedy, Anaheim	-	-	1	1
Mark Redman, Minnesota	-	-	1	1
Barry Zito, Oakland	-	-	1	1

Five points awarded for a first-place vote, three for second and one for third.

CY YOUNG AWARD

Pitcher, Team	1	2	3	Pts.
Pedro Martinez, Boston	28	-	-	140
Tim Hudson, Oakland	-	16	6	54
David Wells, Toronto	-	12	10	46
Andy Pettitte, New York	-	-	7	7
Todd Jones, Detroit	-	-	3	3
Roger Clemens, New York	-	-	1	1
Mike Mussina, Baltimore	-	-	1	1

Five points awarded for a first-place vote, three for second and one for third.

MANAGER OF THE YEAR

Manager, Team	1	2	3	Pts.
Jerry Manuel, Chicago	25	3	-	134
Art Howe, Oakland	2	20	4	74
Lou Piniella, Seattle	1	3	14	28
Mike Scioscia, Anaheim	-	1	5	8
Joe Torre, New York	-	1	2	5
Phil Garner, Detroit	-	-	2	2
Jimy Williams, Boston	-	-	1	1

Five points awarded for a first-place vote, three for second and one for third.

MOST VALUABLE PLAYER

Player, Team	1	2	3	4	5	6	7	8	9	10	Pts.
Jeff Kent, San Francisco	22	5	4	1	-	-	-	-	-	-	392
Barry Bonds, San Francisco	6	8	8	6	1	1	1	-	1	-	279
Mike Piazza, New York	3	10	11	5	1	2	-	-	-	-	271
Jim Edmonds, St. Louis	-	6	7	5	9	1	-	-	2	-	208
Todd Helton, Colorado	1	3	1	12	5	4	2	2	-	1	198
Vladimir Guerrero, Montreal	-	-	-	1	4	7	7	2	7	3	117
Jeff Bagwell, Houston	-	-	-	-	1	6	8	8	4	2	102
Andruw Jones, Atlanta	-	-	-	1	8	3	-	5	4	2	95
Sammy Sosa, Chicago	-	-	-	1	1	3	3	5	5	6	71
Gary Sheffield, Los Angeles	-	-	-	-	-	2	8	6	4	3	71
Chipper Jones, Atlanta	-	-	1	-	1	-	-	1	2	2	23
Greg Maddux, Atlanta	-	-	-	-	-	2	-	-	1	-	12
Robb Nen, San Francisco	-	-	-	-	-	-	1	2	-	2	12
Tom Glavine, Atlanta	-	-	-	-	-	-	1	-	1	2	8
Ellis Burks, San Francisco	-	-	-	-	1	-	-	-	-	-	6
Edgardo Alfonzo, New York	-	-	-	-	-	1	-	-	-	1	6
Randy Johnson, Arizona	-	-	-	-	-	-	-	1	-	2	5
Darryl Kile, St. Louis	-	-	-	-	-	-	1	-	-	-	4
Brian Giles, Pittsburgh	-	-	-	-	-	-	-	-	-	3	3
Moises Alou, Houston	-	-	-	-	-	-	-	-	1	-	2
Richard Hidalgo, Houston	-	-	-	-	-	-	-	-	-	2	2
Antonio Alfonseca, Florida	-	-	-	-	-	-	-	-	-	1	1

Fourteen points awarded for a first-place vote, nine for second and down to one for 10th.

MANAGER OF THE YEAR

Manager, Team	1	2	3	Pts.
Dusty Baker, San Francisco	30	1	1	154
Tony La Russa, St. Louis	1	16	6	59
Bobby Cox, Atlanta	1	8	12	41
Bobby Valentine, New York	-	4	4	16
John Boles, Florida	-	3	6	15
Buddy Bell, Colorado	-	-	2	2
Felipe Alou, Montreal	-	-	1	1

Five points awarded for a first-place vote, three for second and one for third.

CY YOUNG AWARD

Pitcher, Team	1	2	3	Pts.
Randy Johnson, Arizona	22	7	2	133
Tom Glavine, Atlanta	4	12	8	64
Greg Maddux, Atlanta	3	10	14	59
Robb Nen, San Francisco	2	2	4	20
Darryl Kile, St. Louis	1	-	3	8
Kevin Brown, Los Angeles	-	1	1	4

Five points awarded for a first-place vote, three for second and one for third.

ROOKIE OF THE YEAR

Player, Team	1	2	3	Pts.
Rafael Furcal, Atlanta	25	6	1	144
Rick Ankiel, St. Louis	6	17	6	87
Jay Payton, New York	1	7	11	37
Pat Burrell, Philadelphia	-	1	7	10
Mitch Meluskey, Houston	-	1	4	7
Lance Berkman, Houston	-	-	1	1
Juan Pierre, Colorado	-	-	1	1
Chuck Smith, Florida	-	-	1	1

Five points awarded for a first-place vote, three for second and one for third.

2000 REVIEW *Award winners*

MISCELLANEOUS

ATTENDANCE

AMERICAN LEAGUE

	Home	Road
Cleveland	3,456,278	2,377,993
Baltimore	3,295,128	2,014,809
New York	3,227,657	2,876,506
Seattle	3,148,317	2,208,974
Texas	2,800,147	2,406,986
Boston	2,586,032	2,524,776
Detroit	2,533,752	2,110,536
Anaheim	2,066,977	2,272,015
Chicago	1,947,799	2,353,137
Toronto	1,819,886	2,207,931
Oakland	1,728,888	2,466,594
Kansas City	1,677,915	2,323,443
Tampa Bay	1,549,052	2,223,268
Minnesota	1,059,715	2,332,786
Totals	32,897,543	32,699,754

NATIONAL LEAGUE

	Home	Road
St. Louis	3,336,493	2,723,861
San Francisco	3,315,330	2,595,222
Colorado	3,285,710	2,232,144
Atlanta	3,234,301	2,533,903
Houston	3,056,139	2,446,596
Los Angeles	3,010,819	2,678,742
Arizona	2,942,516	2,420,700
New York	2,800,221	2,575,263
Chicago	2,789,511	2,764,792
Cincinnati	2,577,351	3,016,074
San Diego	2,423,149	2,414,741
Pittsburgh	1,748,908	2,453,147
Philadelphia	1,612,769	2,467,356
Milwaukee	1,573,621	2,200,757
Florida	1,218,326	2,306,371
Montreal	926,263	2,219,547
Totals	39,851,427	40,049,216

DEBUTS

Player	Pos.	Team	Birth date	Birthplace	Debut
Alcantara, Israel Cristostomo	RF	Boston	5-6-73	Santo Domingo, Dominican Republic	6-25
Allen, Dustin R.	PH	San Diego	8-9-72	Oklahoma City, Oklahoma	7-1
Alvarez, Clemente Rafael	PH	Philadelphia	5-18-68	Anzoategui, Venezuela	9-19
Andrews, Clayton John	P	Toronto	5-15-78	Dunedin, Florida	4-16
Ardoin, Daniel Wayne	C	Minnesota	7-8-74	Mamou, Louisiana	8-2
Arroyo, Bronson Anthony	PH	Pittsburgh	2-24-77	Key West, Florida	6-12
Barcelo, Lorenzo A.	P	Chicago A.L.	8-10-77	San Pedro de Macoris, D.R.	7-22
Barnes, John Delbert	CF	Minnesota	4-24-76	San Diego, California	9-16
Beirne, Kevin P.	P	Chicago A.L.	1-1-74	Houston, Texas	5-17
Belitz, Todd Stephen	P	Oakland	10-23-75	Des Moines, Iowa	9-4
Bell, Michael John	PH	Cincinnati	12-7-74	Cincinnati, Ohio	7-20
Bell, Robert Allen	P	Cincinnati	1-17-77	Newburgh, New York	4-8
Bernero, Adam G.	P	Detroit	11-28-76	San Jose, California	8-1
Biddle, Lee F.	P	Chicago A.L.	5-21-76	Las Vegas, Nevada	8-10
Blank, Matthew Clarence	P	Montreal	4-5-76	Texarkana, Texas	4-3
Bocachica, Hiram Colon	PR	Los Angeles	3-4-76	Ponce, Puerto Rico	9-13
Bradley, Milton Obelle	CF	Montreal	4-15-78	Harbor City, Florida	7-19
Brea, Lesli Guillermo	P	Baltimore	10-12-78	San Pedro de Macoris, D.R.	8-13
Brock, Tarrik Jumaan	LF	Chicago N.L.	12-25-73	Goleta, California	3-29
Brunette, Justin Thomas	P	St. Louis	10-7-75	Los Alamitos, California	4-13
Buchanan, Brian James	RF	Minnesota	7-21-73	Miami, Florida	5-19
Buehrle, Mark A.	P	Chicago A.L.	3-23-79	St. Charles, Missouri	7-16
Burkhart, Morgan	DH	Boston	1-29-72	St. Louis, Missouri	6-27
Burrell, Patrick B.	1B	Philadelphia	10-10-76	Eureka Springs, Arkansas	5-24
Byrnes, Eric James	DH	Oakland	2-16-76	Redwood City, California	8-22
Cabrera, Alexander Alberto	PH	Arizona	12-24-71	Caripito, Venezuela	6-26
Cairncross, Cameron	P	Cleveland	5-11-72	Queensland, Australia	7-20
Cammack, Eric Wade	P	New York N.L.	8-14-75	Nederland, Texas	4-28
Cardona, Javier Peterson	C	Detroit	9-15-75	Santurce, Puerto Rico	5-31
Carpenter, Charles Sydney	PH	Colorado	7-23-68	Dallas, Texas	5-13
Casimiro, Carlos Rafael	PH	Baltimore	11-8-76	San Pedro de Macoris, D.R.	7-31
Charles, Franklin Scott	PH	Houston	2-23-69	Fontana, California	9-5
Choate, Randol Doyle	P	New York A.L.	9-5-75	San Antonio, Texas	7-1
Clark, Brady William	PH	Cincinnati	4-18-73	Portland, Oregon	9-3
Coco, Pasqual Reynoso	P	Toronto	9-24-77	Santo Domingo, D.R.	7-17
Coffie, Ivanon Angelo	PR	Baltimore	5-16-77	Klein, Curacao	7-15
Coggin, David Raymond	P	Philadelphia	10-30-76	Covina, California	6-23
Conti, Stanley Jason	PH	Arizona	1-27-75	Pittsburgh, Pennsylvania	6-29
Crawford, Paxton Keith	P	Boston	8-4-77	Little Rock, Arkansas	7-1
Crede, Joseph	3B	Chicago A.L.	4-26-78	Jefferson City, Missouri	9-12
Cressend, John Baptiste	P	Minnesota	5-13-75	New Orleans, Louisiana	8-26
Cromer, David Thomas	PH	Cincinnati	3-19-71	Lake City, South Carolina	4-5
Cubillan, Darwin Harrikson Salom	P	Toronto	11-15-74	Bobure, Venezuela	5-20

Player	Pos.	Team	Birth date	Birthplace	Debut
D'Amico, Jeffrey Michael	P	Kansas City	11-9-74	Inglewood, California	6-3
Davis, Kane Thomas	P	Cleveland	6-25-75	Ripley, West Virginia	6-12
DeHaan, Korwin Jay	PH	San Diego	7-16-76	Pella, Iowa	4-25
de la Rosa, Tomas Agramonte	SS	Montreal	1-28-78	La Victoria, Sierra Leone	7-17
DeWitt, Matthew Brian	P	Toronto	9-4-77	San Bernardino, California	6-20
Dingman, Craig Allen	P	New York A.L.	3-12-74	Wichita, Kansas	6-30
Downs, Scott Jeremy	P	Chicago N.L.	3-17-76	Louisville, Kentucky	4-9
Drew, Timothy A.	P	Cleveland	8-31-78	Valdosta, Georgia	5-24
Eaton, Adam Thomas	P	San Diego	11-23-77	Seattle, Washington	5-30
Einertson, Darrell Lee	P	New York A.L.	9-4-72	Rhinelander, Wisconsin	4-15
Enders, Trevor	P	Tampa Bay	12-22-74	Milwaukee, Wisconsin	9-2
Ensberg, Morgan P.	PH	Houston	8-26-75	Redondo Beach, California	9-20
Estrella, Leoncio Ramirez	P	Toronto	2-20-75	Puerto Plata, Dominican Republic	7-18
Etherton, Seth	P	Anaheim	10-17-76	Laguna Beach, California	5-26
Feliz, Pedro Julio	PH	San Francisco	4-27-77	Azua, Dominican Republic	9-5
Figueroa, Nelson Walter	P	Arizona	5-18-74	Brooklyn, New York	6-3
Fiore, Anthony	P	Tampa Bay	10-12-71	Oak Park, Illinois	8-27
Forster, Scott Christian	P	Montreal	10-27-71	Philadelphia, Pennsylvania	6-18
Franklin, Gary Wayne	P	Houston	3-9-74	Wilmington, Delaware	7-24
Fultz, Richard Aaron	P	San Francisco	9-4-73	Memphis, Tennessee	4-5
Furcal, Rafael Antoni	SS	Atlanta	8-24-80	Loma de Cabrera, D.R.	4-4
Garibay, Daniel	P	Chicago N.L.	2-14-73	Maneadero, Mexico	4-9
Garland, Jon Steven	P	Chicago A.L.	9-27-79	Valencia, California	7-4
Ginter, Keith Michael	PH	Houston	5-5-76	Norwalk, California	9-20
Ginter, Matthew Shane	P	Chicago A.L.	12-24-77	Lexington, Kentucky	9-1
Gload, Ross P.	LF	Chicago N.L.	4-5-76	Brooklyn, New York	8-31
Gonzalez, Victor Raul	PH	Chicago N.L.	12-27-73	Santurce, Puerto Rico	5-25
Green, David Jason	P	Houston	6-5-75	Port Hope, Canada	7-23
Grilli, Jason Michael	P	Florida	11-11-76	Royal Oak, Michigan	5-11
Guzman, Geraldo Moreno	P	Arizona	11-28-72	Arroyo Seco Tenares, D.R.	7-6
Hall, Toby Jason	C	Tampa Bay	10-21-75	Tacoma, Washington	9-15
Harper, Travis Boyd	P	Tampa Bay	5-21-76	Harrisonburg, Virginia	8-4
Hernandez, Alexander	1B	Pittsburgh	5-28-77	San Juan, Puerto Rico	9-1
Hodges, Kevin Jon	P	Seattle	6-24-73	Houston, Texas	4-24
House, Craig Michael	P	Colorado	7-8-77	Okinawa, Japan	8-6
Huff, Aubrey L.	3B	Tampa Bay	12-20-76	Marion, Ohio	8-2
Hyzdu, Adam David	LF	Pittsburgh	12-6-71	San Jose, California	9-8
Jacquez, Thomas Patrick	P	Philadelphia	12-29-75	Stockton, California	9-9
Johnson, Keith	PR	Anaheim	4-17-71	Hanford, California	4-17
Johnson, Mark	P	Detroit	5-2-75	Dayton, Ohio	4-7
Jones, Marcus Ray	P	Oakland	3-29-75	Bellflower, California	7-17
Keisler, Randy Dean	P	New York A.L.	2-24-76	Richards, Texas	9-10
Kelly, Kenneth Alphonso	PR	Tampa Bay	1-26-79	Plant City, Florida	9-7
Kinney, Matthew John	P	Minnesota	12-16-76	Bangor, Maine	8-18
Kohlmeier, Ryan Lyle	P	Baltimore	6-25-77	Salina, Kansas	7-29
Kolb, Brandon Charles	P	San Diego	11-20-73	Oakland, California	5-12
Lamb, Michael Robert	3B	Texas	8-9-75	West Covina, California	4-23
Lara, Yovanny B.	P	Montreal	9-20-75	San Cristobal, Dominican Republic	6-28
LaRocca, Gregory Mark	3B	San Diego	11-10-72	Oswego, New York	9-7
LeCroy, Matthew Hanks	C	Minnesota	12-13-75	Belton, South Carolina	4-3
Lee, Sang-Hoon	P	Boston	3-11-71	Seoul, South Korea	6-29
Levrault, Allen Harry	P	Milwaukee	8-15-77	Fall River, Massachusetts	6-13
Lindsey, Rodney Lee	PR	Detroit	1-28-76	Opelika, Alabama	9-2
Linebrink, Scott Cameron	P	San Francisco	8-4-76	Austin, Texas	4-15
Lopez, Rodrigo Munoz	P	San Diego	12-14-75	Tlalnepantla, Mexico	4-29
Lugo, Julio	PR	Houston	11-16-75	Barahona, Dominican Republic	4-15
Lunar, Fernando Jose	C	Atlanta	5-25-77	Cantanura, Venezuela	5-8
Luuloa, Keith H.M.	PR	Anaheim	12-24-74	Honolulu, Hawaii	5-17
Mahoney, Michael John	C	Chicago N.L.	12-5-72	Des Moines, Iowa	9-8
Mairena, Oswaldo Antonio	P	Chicago N.L.	7-30-75	Chinandega, Nicaragua	9-5
Mann, James Joseph	P	New York N.L.	11-17-74	Brockton, Massachusetts	5-29
Marquis, Jason Scott	P	Atlanta	8-21-78	Manhasset, New York	6-6
Martinez, William Jose	P	Cleveland	1-4-78	Barquisimeto, Venezuela	6-14
Matos, Luis D	CF	Baltimore	10-30-78	Bayamon, Puerto Rico	6-19
Matthews, Michael Scott	P	St. Louis	10-24-73	Fredericksburg, Virginia	5-31
Maurer, David Charles	P	San Diego	2-23-75	Minneapolis, Minnesota	7-22
McDonald, William Keith	PH	St. Louis	2-8-73	Yokosuka, Japan	7-4
McKnight, Tony Mark	P	Houston	6-29-77	Texarkana, Arkansas	8-10
Melhuse, Adam Michael	PH	Los Angeles	3-27-72	Santa Clara, California	6-16
Melo, Juan Esteban	PH	San Francisco	11-5-76	Bani, Dominican Republic	9-2
Mercado, Hector Luis	P	Cincinnati	4-29-74	Catano, Puerto Rico	4-4
Minor, Damon Reed	PH	San Francisco	1-5-74	Canton, Ohio	9-2

Player	Pos.	Team	Birth date	Birthplace	Debut
Moeller, Chad Edward	C	Minnesota	2-18-75	Upland, California	6-20
Moraga, David Michael	P	Montreal	7-8-75	Torrance, California	6-11
Morales, William Anthony	C	Baltimore	9-7-72	Tucson, Arizona	4-9
Mota, Daniel Avila	P	Minnesota	10-9-75	Seybol, Dominican Republic	9-15
Mulder, Mark Alan	P	Oakland	8-5-77	South Holland, Illinois	4-18
Mullen, Kenneth Scott	P	Kansas City	1-17-75	San Benito, Texas	8-31
Munson, Eric Walter	1B	Detroit	10-3-77	San Diego, California	7-18
Nady, Xavier C.	PH	San Diego	11-14-78	Salinas, California	9-30
Nation, Joseph Paul	P	Chicago N.L.	9-28-78	Oklahoma City, Oklahoma	9-23
Nicholson, Kevin Ronald	SS	San Diego	3-29-76	Vancouver, Canada	6-23
Nickle, Douglas Alan	P	Philadelphia	10-2-74	Sonoma, California	9-18
Norton, Phillip Douglas	P	Chicago N.L.	2-1-76	Texarkana, Texas	8-3
Nunnari, Talmadge Raphael	1B	Montreal	4-9-75	Pensacola, Florida	9-7
O'Connor, Brian Michael	P	Pittsburgh	1-4-77	Cincinnati, Ohio	5-13
Ohman, William McDaniel	P	Chicago N.L.	8-13-77	Frankfurt, West Germany	9-19
Ojeda, Octavio Augie	SS	Chicago N.L.	12-20-74	Eldorado Culican, Mexico	6-4
Ortiz, Jose Daniel	PH	Oakland	6-13-77	Santo Domingo, D.R.	9-15
Ozuna, Pablo Jose	2B	Florida	8-25-78	Santo Domingo, D.R.	4-23
Parrish, John Henry, Jr.	P	Baltimore	11-26-77	Lancaster, Pennsylvania	7-24
Patterson, Donald Corey	PH	Chicago N.L.	8-13-79	Atlanta, Georgia	9-18
Pena, Elvis	PH	Colorado	9-15-76	San Pedro de Macoris, D.R.	9-2
Penny, Bradley Wayne	P	Florida	5-24-78	Broken Arrow, Oklahoma	4-7
Perez, Santiago Alberto	PH	Milwaukee	12-30-75	Santo Domingo, D.R.	6-3
Perez, Timoniel	PH	New York N.L.	4-8-77	Bani, Dominican Republic	9-1
Perry, Chan Everett	RF	Cleveland	9-13-72	Live Oak, Florida	8-5
Phelps, Joshua Lee	C	Toronto	5-12-78	Anchorage, Alaska	6-13
Piatt, Adam David	DH	Oakland	2-8-76	Chicago, Illinois	4-24
Pierre, Juan D'Vaughn	PR	Colorado	8-14-77	Mobile, Alabama	8-7
Pineiro, Joel Alberto	P	Seattle	9-25-78	Rio Pedres, Puerto Rico	8-8
Prokopec, Kenneth Luke	P	Los Angeles	2-23-78	Blackwood, Australia	9-4
Quevedo, Ruben Eduardo	P	Chicago N.L.	1-5-79	Valencia Carabobo, Venezuela	4-14
Ratliff, Jon Charles	P	Oakland	12-22-71	Syracuse, New York	9-15
Reames, William B.	P	St. Louis	8-19-73	Seneca, South Carolina	8-20
Redman, Julian Jawonn	RF	Pittsburgh	3-10-77	Tuscaloosa, Alabama	6-30
Richard, Christopher Robert	LF	St. Louis	6-7-74	San Diego, California	7-17
Riedling, John Richard	P	Cincinnati	8-29-75	Fort Lauderdale, Florida	8-30
Rigdon, Paul David	P	Cleveland	11-2-75	Jacksonville, Florida	5-21
Riggan, Jerrod Ashley	P	New York N.L.	5-16-74	Brewster, Washington	8-29
Rivas, Luis Wilfredo	2B	Minnesota	8-30-79	La Guaira, Venezuela	9-16
Rivera, Luis Gutierrez	P	Atlanta	6-21-78	Chihuahua, Mexico	4-4
Roberts, Grant William	P	New York N.L.	9-13-77	El Cajon, California	7-27
Rodriguez, Jose I.	P	St. Louis	12-18-74	Cayey, Puerto Rico	5-18
Rolison, Nathan Mardis	1B	Florida	3-27-77	Hattiesburg, Mississippi	9-5
Rollins, James Calvin	SS	Philadelphia	11-27-78	Oakland, California	9-17
Rolls, Damian Michael	PH	Tampa Bay	9-15-77	Manhattan, Kansas	9-3
Santana, Johan Alexander	P	Minnesota	3-13-79	Tovar Merida, Venezuela	4-3
Sasaki, Kazuhiro	P	Seattle	2-22-68	Sendai, Japan	4-5
Saturria, Luis Arturo	PR	St. Louis	7-21-76	San Pedro de Macoris, D.R.	9-11
Schneider, Brian Duncan	C	Montreal	11-26-76	Jacksonville, Florida	5-26
Seelbach, Christopher Don	P	Atlanta	12-18-72	Lufkin, Texas	9-9
Sikorski, Brian Patrick	P	Texas	7-27-74	Detroit, Michigan	8-16
Sisco, Steve Michael	PH	Atlanta	12-2-69	Thousand Oaks, California	5-6
Skrmetta, Matthew Leland	P	Montreal	11-6-72	Biloxi, Mississippi	6-6
Smith, Charles Edward	P	Florida	10-21-69	Memphis, Tennessee	6-13
Smith, Randall Brian	P	Pittsburgh	9-17-72	Salisbury, North Carolina	9-11
Sparks, Stephen Lanier	P	Pittsburgh	3-28-75	Mobile, Alabama	7-19
Spurgeon, Jay Aaron	P	Baltimore	7-5-76	West Covina, California	8-15
Stechschulte, Eugene Urban	P	St. Louis	8-12-73	Lima, Ohio	4-20
Strong, Joseph Benjamin	P	Florida	9-9-62	Fairfield, California	5-11
Swann, Pedro	PH	Atlanta	10-27-70	Wilmington, Delaware	9-9
Taylor, Reginald Tremain	CF	Philadelphia	1-12-77	Newberry, South Carolina	9-17
Thompson, Andrew John	LF	Toronto	10-8-75	Oconomowoc, Wisconsin	5-2
Tolar, Kevin	P	Detroit	1-28-71	Panama City, Florida	9-11
Tollberg, Brian Patrick	P	San Diego	9-16-72	Tampa, Florida	6-20
Tracy, Andrew	PH	Montreal	12-11-73	Bowling Green, Ohio	4-25
Truby, Christopher John	3B	Houston	12-9-73	Palm Springs, California	6-16
Tucker, Thomas J.	P	Montreal	8-20-78	Clearwater, Florida	6-3
Turnbow, Thomas Derrick	P	Anaheim	1-25-78	Union City, Tennessee	4-17
Tyner, Jason Renyt	LF	New York N.L.	4-23-77	Beaumont, Texas	6-5
Valera, Yohanny	C	Montreal	8-17-76	Santo Domingo, D.R.	9-13
Villafuerte, Brandon Paul	P	Detroit	12-17-75	Hilo, Hawaii	5-23
Villegas, Ismael	P	Atlanta	8-12-76	Rio Piedras, Puerto Rico	7-3

Player	Pos.	Team	Birth date	Birthplace	Debut
Vogelsong, Ryan Andrew	P	San Francisco	7-22-77	Charlotte, North Carolina	9-2
Walker, Kevin Michael	P	San Diego	9-20-76	Irving, Texas	4-14
Waszgis, Robert Michael, Jr.	C	Texas	8-24-70	Omaha, Nebraska	7-29
Watson, Mark Bradford	P	Cleveland	1-23-74	Atlanta, Georgia	5-19
Weber, Benjamin Edward	P	San Francisco	11-17-69	Port Arthur, Texas	4-3
Westbrook, Jacob Cauthen	P	New York A.L.	9-29-77	Athens, Georgia	6-17
Williams, Matthew Taylor	P	Milwaukee	4-12-71	Virginia Beach, Virginia	4-5
Wilson, Kristopher Kyle	P	Kansas City	8-6-76	Washington, District of Columbia	7-28
Wise, Larry Dewayne	CF	Toronto	2-24-78	Columbia, South Carolina	4-6
Wise, Matthew John	P	Anaheim	11-18-75	Montclair, California	8-2
Wooten, Shawn	C	Anaheim	7-24-72	Glendora, California	8-19
Wunsch, Kelly Douglas	P	Chicago A.L.	7-12-72	Houston, Texas	4-3
Young, Daniel Bracey	P	Chicago N.L.	11-3-71	Smyrna, Tennessee	3-30
Young, Michael B.	PR	Texas	10-19-76	Covina, California	9-29
Zerbe, William Chad	P	San Francisco	4-27-72	Findlay, Ohio	9-18
Zito, Barry William	P	Oakland	5-13-78	Las Vegas, Nevada	7-22
Zuleta, Julio Ernesto	PH	Chicago N.L.	3-28-75	Panama City, Panama	4-6

SALARY ARBITRATION RESULTS

WINNERS

Player, Team	Salary awarded	Team's offer
Brian L. Hunter, Seattle	$2,450,000	$1,750,000
Scott Sullivan, Cincinnati	$1,100,000	$775,000
C.J. Nitkowski, Detroit	$950,000	$600,000
Karim Garcia, Detroit	$700,000	$475,000

LOSERS

Player, Team	Salary awarded	Player's request
Mariano Rivera, New York A.L.	$7,250,000	$9,250,000
Charles Johnson, Baltimore	$4,600,000	$5,100,000
Lee Stevens, Texas	$3,500,000	$4,700,000
Steve Parris, Cincinnati	$1,400,000	$1,825,000
Jason Dickson, Anaheim	$375,000	$600,000
Ariel Prieto, Oakland	$300,000	$500,000

2000 FREE-AGENT FILINGS

AMERICAN LEAGUE

Anaheim: Tim Belcher, Gary DiSarcina, Ron Gant, Kent Mercker, Mark Petkovsek, Kevin Stocker, Matt Walbeck.
Baltimore: Mark Lewis, Mike Mussina, Pat Rapp.
Boston: Manny Alexander, Rico Brogna, Hector Carrasco, Rheal Cormier, Jeff Fassero, Bernard Gilkey, Tom Gordon, Ramon Martinez, Steve Ontiveros, Peter Schourek, Tim Wakefield.
Chicago: Harold Baines, Cal Eldred, Charles Johnson, Jose Valentin.
Cleveland: Sandy Alomar Jr., Jason Bere, Manny Ramirez, David Segui.
Detroit: Rich Becker, Willie Blair, Juan Gonzalez, Gregg Jefferies, Hal Morris.
Kansas City: Ricky Bottalico, Jorge Fabregas, Jeff Reboulet.
Minnesota: None.
New York: Jose Canseco, David Cone, Dwight Gooden, Roberto Kelly, Denny Neagle, Jeff Nelson, Paul O'Neill, Luis Polonia, Darryl Strawberry, Luis Sojo, Jose Vizcaino.
Oakland: Kevin Appier, Doug Jones, Mike Stanley.
Seattle: Jay Buhner, Rickey Henderson, Tom Lampkin, Jose Mesa, Joe Oliver, Alex Rodriguez.
Tampa Bay: Ozzie Guillen.
Texas: Luis Alicea, Mike Munoz, Ruben Sierra, Mike Simms, John Wetteland.
Toronto: Frank Castillo, Alex Gonzalez, Craig Grebeck, Mark Guthrie, Dave Martinez, Mickey Morandini, Steve Trachsel.

NATIONAL LEAGUE

Arizona: Matt Mieske, Dan Plesac, Armando Reynoso.
Atlanta: Andy Ashby, Bobby Bonilla, John Burkett, Andres Galarraga, Wally Joyner, Scott Kamieniecki, Greg McMichael, Terry Mulholland, Reggie Sanders, Rudy Seanez, Walt Weiss.
Chicago: Rick Aguilera, Shane Andrews, Mark Grace, Jeff Huson, Jeff Reed.
Cincinnati: Deion Sanders, Benito Santiago, Mark Wohlers.
Colorado: Jeff Frye, Jeffrey Hammonds, Todd Hollandsworth, Julian Tavarez.
Florida: Henry Rodriguez.
Houston: Tim Bogar, Ken Caminiti.
Los Angeles: Darren Dreifort, Todd Hundley, Jim Leyritz, Ismael Valdes.
Milwaukee: Charlie Hayes, James Mouton.
Montreal: Lenny Webster.
New York: Kurt Abbott, Derek Bell, Mike Bordick, John Franco, Mike Hampton, Bobby J. Jones, Rick Reed, Turk Wendell.
Philadelphia: Alex Arias, Kent Bottenfield, Jeff Brantley, Brian R. Hunter.
Pittsburgh: None.
St. Louis: Eric Davis, Shawon Dunston, Pat Hentgen, Thomas Howard, Jesse Orosco, Scott Radinsky, Rick Wilkins.
San Diego: Bret Boone, Tony Gwynn, John Mabry, Dave Magadan, Randy Myers, Ed Sprague.
San Francisco: Ellis Burks, Mark Gardner, Doug Henry, Scott Servais.

MAJOR LEAGUE RULE 5 DRAFT

(Listed in order of selection)

Player	Pos.	Drafted by	Drafted from (major league organization)
Scott Chiasson	P	Chicago N.L.	Sacramento, Pacific Coast League (Athletics)
Brandon Knight	P	Minnesota	Columbus, International League (Yankees)
Ted Rose	P	Montreal	Louisville, International League (Reds)
Jay Gibbons	1B	Baltimore	Syracuse, International League (Blue Jays)
Endy Chavez Meza	OF	Kansas City	Norfolk, International League (Mets)
Jermaine Clark	2B	Detroit	Tacoma, Pacific Coast League (Mariners)
Donaldo Mendez	SS	San Diego	New Orleans, Pacific Coast League (Astros)
Rendy Espina	P	Anaheim	Syracuse, International League (Blue Jays)
Jose Antonio Nunez	P	Los Angeles	Norfolk, International League (Mets)
Julio Santana	P	New York N.L.	Fresno, Pacific Coast League (Giants)

NECROLOGY

Hugh Alexander, 83, at Oklahoma City on November 25. Alexander was an acclaimed major league scout for more than 60 years. A promising outfielder (he played seven games for the Indians in 1937 at age 20), Alexander turned to scouting after losing a hand in an off-season accident.

Bob Barthelson, 75, at Branford, Conn., on April 14. Righthander Barthelson compiled a 1-1 record in seven games for the 1944 Giants.

Larry Bearnarth, 58, at St. Petersburg, Fla., on January 1. Bearnarth made 56 relief appearances for the Mets in 1963 and pitched in 173 games over five major league seasons. He was the first pitching coach in Rockies history, serving from 1993 through 1995.

Frenchy Bordagaray, 90, at Ventura, Calif., on April 13. A reserve player for most of his 11-season major league career, outfielder/third baseman Bordagaray played for five clubs and batted .283 in 930 games. He appeared in the 1939 World Series for the Reds and the 1941 Series for the Yankees.

Harry Bright, 70, at Sacramento on March 13. An eight-year major leaguer, the first baseman/third baseman saw his most extensive duty in 1962, when he had 392 at-bats for the Senators and hit .273 with 17 home runs. As a reserve player for the Yankees, he appeared in two games of the 1963 World Series.

Clarence "Soup" Campbell, 84, at Sparta, Va., on February 16. Outfielder Campbell played 104 of his 139 big-league games for the 1941 Indians and batted .250 in 328 at-bats.

Andujar Cedeno, 31, in an automobile accident in the Dominican Republic on October 28. Shortstop Cedeno spent seven seasons in the majors and played for the Astros (two stints), Padres and Tigers. In 1993, he batted .283 for Houston with 11 home runs and 56 RBIs.

Ed Chapman, 94, at Clarksdale, Miss., on May 3. Chapman pitched in six games for the 1933 Senators.

Ellis Clary, 83, at Valdosta, Ga., on June 2. Clary was a big-league scout for more than three decades. As a wartime major leaguer, he spent 2½ seasons with the Browns and 1½ years with the Senators. An infielder, he made one pinch-hitting appearance for the Browns in the 1944 World Series.

Eddie Collins Jr., 83, at Kennett Square, Pa., on November 2. Son of a Hall of Famer, he was a reserve outfielder for the Athletics in 1939, 1941 and 1942.

Harry Dorish, 79, at Wilkes-Barre, Pa., on December 31. Dorish was a righthander who compiled a 45-43 record pitching for the Red Sox, Browns, White Sox and Orioles from 1947-56.

Len Gabrielson, 85, at Stanford, Calif., on November 14. A first baseman, Gabrielson appeared in five games for the 1939 Phillies. He was the father of a major league outfielder of the same name.

Ted Gullic, 93, at West Plains, Mo., on January 28. Gullic was a Browns outfielder/infielder in 1930 and 1933, batting .247 in 196 games.

Ken Heintzelman, 84, at St. Peters, Mo., on August 14. Lefthander Heintzelman, who won 17 games and posted a 3.02 ERA for the Phillies in 1949, was 77-98 in 13 seasons in the majors. He started Game 3 of the 1950 World Series for the Phils, limiting the Yankees to four hits and two runs (one earned) in 7⅔ innings. The Phillies wound up losing that game in the ninth inning and were swept in the Series. Heintzelman's son Tom played in the majors in the 1970s.

Ron Herbel, 62, at Tacoma, Wash., on January 20. Primarily a reliever, the righthander pitched in the majors from 1963 through 1971 and compiled a 42-37 record. Herbel spent seven seasons with San Francisco, winning 12 games for the Giants in 1965, and he appeared in an N.L.-leading 76 games in 1970, a year in which he pitched for the Padres and Mets.

Frank "Lefty" Hoerst, 82, at Maple Shade, N.J., on February 18. Hoerst went 10-33 in five seasons with the Phillies in the 1940s.

Don Johnson, 88, at Laguna Beach, Calif., on April 6. Johnson was the second baseman on the Cubs' last World Series team, the 1945 club. Johnson batted .302 for the Cubs in the '45 regular season, but he was only 5-for-29 in the Series, which the Cubs lost to Detroit in seven games.

Russ Kerns, 79, at Placerville, Calif., on August 21. The catcher's major league career consisted of one failed pinch-hitting appearance for the 1945 Tigers.

Doyle Lade, 79, at Lincoln, Neb., on May 18. Lade pitched all five of his big-league seasons for the Cubs. The righthander's best year was 1947, when he finished 11-10.

James "Lefty" LaMarque, 80, at Kansas City on January 15. LaMarque was a standout Negro leagues pitcher in the late 1940s.

Gene Lambert, 78, at Germantown, Tenn., on February 10. Righthander Lambert pitched in two games for the 1941 Phillies and made one appearance for the 1942 Phils.

Brooks Lawrence, 75, at Springfield, Ohio, on April 27. Righthander Lawrence, who reached the majors at age 29, went 15-6 for the Cardinals in his rookie season of 1954. Two years later, he won his first 13 decisions for the Reds on the way to a 19-10 record. Lawrence another big season in 1957, winning 16 games for Cincinnati.

Bob Lemon, 79, at Long Beach, Calif., on January 11. Lemon compiled a 207-128 record in a Hall of Fame career that spanned 13 seasons. Pitching exclusively for Cleveland, he won 20 or more games seven times in a nine-year span ending in 1956. He won two games in the 1948 World Series, including decisive Game 6. Thirty years later, he succeeded Billy Martin as Yankees manager in July and led the club to the World Series championship. Those '78 Yanks overcame a 14-game deficit and defeated Boston in an A.L. East playoff.

John Leovich, 81, at Lincoln City, Ore., on February 3. Catcher Leovich appeared in one big-league game—for the A's vs. the Indians on May 1, 1941—and went 1-for-2 against Bob Feller. Leovich's hit was a double.

Don Liddle, 75, at Mount Carmel, Ill., on June 5. Lefthander Liddle was a key member of the 1954 World Series champion Giants. He posted a 9-4 regular-season record in '54, then was the starting and winning pitcher in Game 4 of the Giants' Series sweep of Cleveland. In Game 1, he was pitching when the Indians' Vic Wertz smashed a long drive that Willie Mays—in one of the most memorable plays in Series history—ran down in deep center field. Liddle was 10-4 for the '55 Giants, but he wound up pitching only four seasons overall in the majors.

Bob Mahoney, 72, at Lincoln, Neb., on August 27. The righthander pitched in 36 major league games—33 of them for the St. Louis Browns in 1951 and 1952. His career record: 2-5.

Georges Maranda, 68, at Levis, Quebec, on July 14. The Canadian righthander went 1-4 for the 1960 Giants and 1-3 for the 1962 Twins.

Willard Marshall, 79, at Norwood, N.J., on November 5. A fixture in the New York Giants' outfield for five seasons in the 1940s and later a member of the Braves, Reds and White Sox, Marshall stood out in '47 when he hit 36 home runs and drove in 107 runs for the Giants.

Merrill "Pinky" May, 89, at Corydon, Ind., on September 4. May spent five years (1939 through 1943) in the majors and was the Phillies' No. 1 third baseman all of those seasons. He hit .293 in 1940 and played in the All-Star Game that year. May, father of longtime major league catcher Milt May, also was a longtime minor league manager.

Jack Merson, 78, at Elkridge, Md., on April 28. Merson played 81 games at second base and appeared in 111 games overall for a 1952 Pirates team that won only 42 games. He hit 20 doubles and batted .246.

Hank Miklos, 89, at Adrian, Mich., on March 29. Miklos made two relief appearances for the 1944 Cubs.

John Milner, 50, at East Point, Ga., on January 4. First baseman/outfielder Milner, who played 12 seasons in the majors, hit 23 home runs for the 1973 Mets and started all seven games for that club in the team's World Series loss to Oakland. In 1979, he contributed 16 homers and 60 RBIs for the World Series-winning Pirates.

Blas Monaco, 84, at San Antonio on February 10. Infielder Monaco appeared in five games for Cleveland in 1937 and 12 games for the Indians in 1946.

Danny Musser, 94, at Upper Sandusky, Ohio, on March 2. Infielder Musser appeared in one major league game—for the Senators in 1932.

George Myatt, 86, at Altamonte Springs, Fla., on September 14. Primarily a second baseman, Myatt was a regular in the Senators' lineup in 1944 and 1945 and hit .284 and .296 in those seasons. In addition to a seven-year playing career in the majors, he was a big-league coach for 23 seasons.

Lynn Myers, 85, at Harrisburg, Pa., on January 19. Shortstop Myers played in 70 games for the 1938 Cardinals and 74 for the 1939 Cards.

Willard Nixon, 72, at Rome, Ga., on December 10. Righthander Nixon was a key member of the Red Sox's rotation in the mid-1950s, reaching double-digit victory totals in 1954, 1955 and 1957.

Frankie Pack, 71, at Hendersonville, N.C., on January 26. Outfielder Pack struck out in his only major league at-bat, which came as a pinch hitter for the 1949 St. Louis Browns.

Roy Partee, 83, at Eureka, Calif., on December 26. Partee was a major league catcher for five seasons in the 1940s. He was behind the plate for the Red Sox in Game 7 of the 1946 World Series when St. Louis' Enos Slaughter made his decisive "mad dash" from first base to home.

John Perkovich, 76, at Little Rock, Ark., on September 16. He relieved in one game for the 1950 White Sox.

Lou Polli, 99, at Berlin., Vt., on December 19. Polli made five relief appearances for the 1932 Browns and 19 for the 1944 Giants.

Bob Ramazzotti, 83, at Altoona, Pa., on February 15. Ramazzotti was a utility player for the Dodgers (1946, 1948-49) and Cubs ('49 through '53).

Culley Rikard, 85, at Memphis on February 25. After brief duty with the Pirates in 1941 and 1942, outfielder Rikard had 324 at-bats for Pittsburgh in 1947, a year in which he batted .287.

Jack Robinson, 79, at Ormond Beach, Fla., on March 2. Robinson pitched in three games for the 1949 Red Sox.

Aurelio Rodriguez, 52, at Detroit on September 23 when he was struck by a car. Possessor of an exceptional arm, he was the Tigers' third baseman for most of the 1970s and had a 17-year career in the big leagues. Rodriguez, a Gold Glove winner in 1976, played in four League Championship Series (one with Detroit, two with the Yankees and one with the White Sox). In his only World Series, he went 5-for-12 for the Yanks against the Dodgers in 1981.

Hank Ruszkowski, 74, at Cleveland on May 31. A catcher, he appeared in a total of 40 games for the Indians in 1944, 1945 and 1947. In '47, three of his seven hits were home runs.

Byrum "By" Saam, 85, at Devon, Pa., on January 16. Saam called A's and Phillies games for nearly four decades in a Philadelphia broadcasting career that began in the late 1930s. He was elected to the broadcasting wing of baseball's Hall of Fame in 1990.

Chico Salmon, 59, at Bocas del Toro, Panama, on September 17. Salmon played all four infield positions and the outfield in a nine-season major league career with the Indians and Orioles (with whom he appeared in the 1969 and 1970 World Series).

Jack Sanford, 70, at Beckley, W.Va., on March 7. Sanford won N.L. Rookie of the Year honors at age 28 when he compiled a 19-8 record for the 1957 Phillies. Traded to the Giants after the 1958 season, he tossed six shutouts for San Francisco in 1960 and then went 24-7

(with 16 consecutive victories) for the pennant-winning Giants in 1962. He was 137-101 in his 12-season major league career.

Bill Schweppe, 86, at Anaheim on July 31. He was the Dodgers' farm director from 1967 through 1987 and worked for the club for more than four decades.

Joe Soares, 85, at Fort Lauderdale, Fla., on February 3. Soares was the Yankees' trainer from 1962 through 1972.

Bud Stewart, 84, at Palo Alto, Calif., on June 21. Outfielder Stewart played for the Pirates, Yankees, Senators and White Sox in a 773-game major league career. He saw steady duty in the Senators' outfield in 1948, 1949 and 1950, hitting a career-high .284 in '49.

Jim Suchecki, 72, at Crofton, Md., on July 20. The righthander pitched in 38 big-league games—29 of them for the 1951 St. Louis Browns. His career record: 0-6.

Clyde Sukeforth, 98, at Waldoboro, Maine, on September 3. Sukeforth was the scout dispatched by Branch Rickey to make the Dodgers' initial contact with Jackie Robinson in 1945—and he was Brooklyn's acting manager on April 15, 1947, when Robinson broke the majors' modern color barrier.

Harry Taylor, 81, at Terre Haute, Ind., on November 5. Taylor, who went 19-21 in six big-league seasons, had a notable year in 1947. A rookie in '47, the righthander compiled a 10-5 record for the N.L. champion Dodgers and started Game 4 of the World Series against the Yankees. Taylor pitched to only four batters in that game before being relieved; his opponent, Bill Bevens, pitched 8⅔ innings of no-hit ball before losing his no-hitter and the game to Brooklyn.

Bob Tiefenauer, 70, at Desloge, Mo., on June 13. A longtime minor leaguer, reliever Tiefenauer appeared in 179 games in a 10-season major league career. His best year was 1964, when he had a 3.21 ERA for the Braves in 46 games.

Bob Tillman, 63, at Gallatin, Tenn., on June 23. Tillman caught for the Red Sox, Yankees and Braves in a nine-year major league career that began in 1962. In 1964, he batted .278 for the Red Sox and hit 17 home runs.

Cecil "Turkey" Tyson, 85, at Elm City, N.C., on February 17. Tyson, a first baseman, appeared in one big-league game—as an unsuccessful pinch hitter for the Phillies in 1944.

Al Vincent, 93, at Beaumont, Texas, on December 14. A longtime minor league player and manager, he was a major league coach (Tigers, Orioles, Phillies and Athletics) for 12 seasons. His first coaching job came in 1943, his last in 1967.

Dewey Williams, 84, at Williston, N.D., on March 19. Williams was a backup catcher on the Cubs' 1945 World Series team.

Hank Wyse, 82, at Pryor, Okla., on October 22. Righthander Wyse was a key member of the N.L. champion Cubs in '45, going 22-10 with a 2.68 ERA. He was 0-1 in three World Series games (one start) that year. Overall, he was 79-70 in eight major league seasons.

Butch Yatkeman, 91, at St. Louis on January 22. Yatkeman was the Cardinals' equipment manager for nearly six decades, spanning the time frame from Rogers Hornsby in the 1920s to Ozzie Smith in the 1980s.

2000 A.L. STATISTICS

Batting

Designated hitting

Pinch-hitting

Pitching

Fielding

Miscellaneous

BATTING

TEAM

Team	Avg.	G	TPA	AB	R	H	TB	2B	3B	HR	RBI	SH	SF	HP	BB	IBB	SO	SB	CS	GDP	LOB	ShO	Slg.	OBP
Cleveland	.288	162	6512	5683	950	1639	2672	310	30	221	889	41	52	51	685	27	1057	113	34	134	1260	4	.470	.367
Kansas City	.288	162	6394	5709	879	1644	2429	281	27	150	831	56	70	48	511	28	840	121	35	139	1184	4	.425	.348
Chicago	.286	162	6406	5646	978	1615	2654	325	33	216	926	55	61	53	591	28	960	119	42	140	1127	3	.470	.356
Texas	.283	162	6363	5648	848	1601	2520	330	35	173	806	48	48	39	580	39	922	69	47	161	1198	6	.446	.352
Anaheim	.280	162	6373	5628	864	1574	2659	309	34	236	837	47	43	47	608	43	1024	93	52	126	1173	5	.472	.352
New York	.277	161	6310	5556	871	1541	2500	294	25	205	833	16	50	57	631	42	1007	99	48	134	1189	7	.450	.354
Detroit	.275	162	6340	5644	823	1553	2473	307	41	177	785	42	49	43	562	22	982	83	38	142	1185	15	.438	.343
Toronto	.275	162	6326	5677	861	1562	2664	328	21	244	826	29	34	60	526	32	1026	89	34	130	1152	7	.469	.341
Baltimore	.272	162	6237	5549	794	1508	2414	310	22	184	750	27	54	49	558	34	900	126	65	148	1129	8	.435	.341
Minnesota	.270	162	6281	5615	748	1516	2287	325	49	116	711	24	51	35	556	31	1021	90	45	143	1198	8	.407	.337
Oakland	.270	161	6432	5560	947	1501	2545	281	23	239	908	26	44	52	750	32	1159	40	15	147	1210	7	.458	.360
Seattle	.269	162	6444	5497	907	1481	2427	300	26	198	869	63	61	48	775	34	1073	122	56	129	1247	5	.442	.361
Boston	.267	162	6371	5630	792	1503	2384	316	32	167	755	40	48	42	611	40	1019	43	30	115	1226	5	.423	.341
Tampa Bay	.257	161	6206	5505	733	1414	2197	253	22	162	692	52	40	51	558	25	1022	90	46	126	1140	8	.399	.329
Totals	.276	1133	88995	78547	11995	21652	34825	4269	420	2688	11418	566	705	675	8502	457	14012	1297	587	1914	16618	95	.443	.349

INDIVIDUAL

TOP QUALIFIERS FOR BATTING CHAMPIONSHIP

Minimum 502 plate appearances. *Lefthanded batter. †Switch-hitter.

Player, Team	Avg.	G	TPA	AB	R	H	TB	2B	3B	HR	RBI	SH	SF	HP	BB	IBB	SO	SB	CS	GDP	Slg.	OBP
Garciaparra, Nomar, Bos.	.372	140	599	529	104	197	317	51	3	21	96	0	7	2	61	20	50	5	2	8	.599	.434
Erstad, Darin, Ana.*	.355	157	747	676	121	240	366	39	6	25	100	2	4	1	64	9	82	28	8	8	.541	.409
Ramirez, Manny, Cle.	.351	118	532	439	92	154	306	34	2	38	122	0	4	3	86	9	117	1	1	9	.697	.457
Delgado, Carlos, Tor.*	.344	162	711	569	115	196	378	57	1	41	137	0	4	15	123	18	104	0	1	12	.664	.470
Jeter, Derek, N.Y.	.339	148	679	593	119	201	285	31	4	15	73	3	3	12	68	4	99	22	4	14	.481	.416
Segui, David, Tex.-Cle.†	.334	150	674	574	93	192	293	42	1	19	103	0	6	1	53	2	84	0	1	20	.510	.388
Sweeney, Mike, K.C.	.333	159	717	618	105	206	323	30	0	29	144	0	13	15	71	5	67	8	3	15	.523	.407
Giambi, Jason, Oak.*	.333	152	664	510	108	170	330	29	1	43	137	0	8	9	137	6	96	2	0	9	.647	.476
Thomas, Frank, Chi.	.328	159	707	582	115	191	364	44	0	43	143	0	5	5	112	18	94	1	3	13	.625	.436
Damon, Johnny, K.C.*	.327	159	741	655	136	214	324	42	10	16	88	8	12	1	65	4	60	46	9	7	.495	.382
Martinez, Edgar, Sea.	.324	153	665	556	100	180	322	31	0	37	145	0	8	5	96	8	95	3	0	13	.579	.423
Fryman, Travis, Cle.	.321	155	658	574	93	184	296	38	4	22	106	0	10	1	73	2	111	1	1	15	.516	.392
Dye, Jermaine, K.C.	.321	157	679	601	107	193	337	41	2	33	118	0	6	3	69	6	99	0	1	12	.561	.390
Stewart, Shannon, Tor.	.319	136	631	583	107	186	302	43	5	21	69	1	4	6	37	1	79	20	5	12	.518	.363
Rodriguez, Alex, Sea.	.316	148	672	554	134	175	336	34	2	41	132	0	11	7	100	5	121	15	4	10	.606	.420

DEPARTMENTAL LEADERS: G—Cruz, Tor., Delgado, Tor., 162; AB—Erstad, Ana., 676; R—Damon, K.C., 136; H—Erstad, Ana., 240; TB—Delgado, Tor., 378; 1B—Erstad, Ana., 170; 2B—Delgado, Tor., 57; 3B—Guzman, Min., 20; HR—Glaus, Ana., 47; RBI—Martinez, Sea., 145; SH—Gonzalez, Tor., 16; SF—Ordonez, Chi., 15; HP—Delgado, Tor., Sweeney, K.C., 15; BB—Ja. Giambi, Oak., 137; IBB—Garciaparra, Bos., 20; SO—Vaughn, Ana., 181; SB—Damon, K.C., 46; CS—McLemore, Sea., 14; GIDP—Grieve, Oak., 32; Slg. Pct.—M. Ramirez, Cle., .697; OB. Pct.—Ja. Giambi, Oak., .476.

ALL PLAYERS

*Lefthanded batter. †Switch-hitter.

Player, Team	Avg.	G	TPA	AB	R	H	TB	2B	3B	HR	RBI	SH	SF	HP	BB	IBB	SO	SB	CS	GDP	Slg.	OBP
Abbott, Jeff, Chi.	.274	80	241	215	31	59	85	15	1	3	29	2	1	2	21	1	38	2	1	2	.395	.343
Abbott, Paul, Sea.	.400	35	6	5	1	2	3	1	0	0	1	0	0	0	0	0	1	0	0	0	.600	.400
Alcantara, Israel, Bos.	.289	21	48	45	9	13	26	1	0	4	7	0	0	0	3	0	7	0	0	0	.578	.333
Alexander, Manny, Bos.	.211	101	209	194	30	41	63	4	3	4	19	2	0	0	13	0	41	2	0	0	.325	.261
Alicea, Luis, Tex.†	.294	139	618	540	85	159	218	25	8	6	63	7	7	5	59	1	75	1	3	13	.404	.365
Allen, Dusty, Det.	.438	18	18	16	5	7	15	2	0	2	2	0	0	0	2	0	7	0	0	0	.938	.500
Allen, Chad, Min.	.300	15	55	50	2	15	18	3	0	0	7	0	1	1	3	0	14	0	2	1	.360	.345
Alomar, Roberto, Cle.†	.310	155	697	610	111	189	290	40	2	19	89	11	6	6	64	4	82	39	4	19	.475	.378
Alomar, Sandy Jr., Cle.	.289	97	384	356	44	103	144	16	2	7	42	4	4	4	16	1	41	2	2	7	.404	.324
Alvarez, Gabe, Det.	.000	1	3	1	0	0	0	0	0	0	0	0	0	0	2	0	1	0	1	0	.000	.667
Amaral, Rich, Bal.	.217	30	67	60	10	13	16	1	1	0	6	0	0	0	7	0	8	6	2	2	.267	.299
Anderson, Brady, Bal.*	.257	141	618	506	89	130	213	26	0	19	50	5	7	8	92	5	103	16	9	4	.421	.375
Anderson, Garret, Ana.*	.286	159	681	647	92	185	336	40	3	35	117	1	9	0	24	5	87	7	6	21	.519	.307
Andrews, Clayton, Tor.	.000	8	3	3	0	0	0	0	0	0	0	0	0	0	0	0	2	0	0	0	.000	.000
Appier, Kevin, Oak.	.167	31	6	6	0	1	1	0	0	0	0	0	0	0	0	0	3	0	0	0	.167	.167
Ardoin, Danny, Min.	.125	15	40	32	4	4	8	1	0	1	5	0	0	0	8	0	10	0	0	0	.250	.300
Ausmus, Brad, Det.	.266	150	604	523	75	139	191	25	3	7	51	4	2	6	69	0	79	11	5	19	.365	.351
Baines, Harold, Bal.-Chi.*	.254	96	320	283	26	72	118	13	0	11	39	0	1	0	36	7	50	0	0	6	.417	.338
Baldwin, James, Chi.	.000	29	5	4	0	0	0	0	0	0	0	0	1	0	0	0	2	0	0	0	.000	.000
Barnes, John, Min.	.351	11	41	37	5	13	17	4	0	0	2	0	0	2	2	0	6	0	1	3	.459	.415
Batista, Miguel, K.C.	.000	14	3	3	0	0	0	0	0	0	0	0	0	0	0	0	3	0	0	0	.000	.000
Batista, Tony, Tor.	.263	154	664	620	96	163	322	32	2	41	114	0	3	6	35	1	121	5	4	15	.519	.307
Baughman, Justin, Ana.	.227	16	23	22	4	5	7	2	0	0	0	0	0	0	1	0	2	3	0	0	.318	.261
Becker, Rich, Oak.-Det.*	.242	115	357	285	59	69	107	14	0	8	39	0	4	1	67	0	87	2	2	1	.375	.384
Bell, David, Sea.	.247	133	512	454	57	112	173	24	2	11	47	6	6	4	42	0	66	2	3	11	.381	.316
Belle, Albert, Bal.	.281	141	622	559	71	157	265	37	1	23	103	0	7	4	52	11	68	0	5	17	.474	.342
Bellhorn, Mark, Oak.†	.154	9	15	13	2	2	2	0	0	0	0	0	0	0	2	0	7	0	0	0	.154	.267
Bellinger, Clay, N.Y.	.207	98	209	184	33	38	68	8	2	6	21	1	2	5	17	1	48	5	0	1	.370	.288

Player, Team	Avg.	G	TPA	AB	R	H	TB	2B	3B	HR	RBI	SH	SF	HP	BB	IBB	SO	SB	CS	GDP	Slg.	OBP
Beltran, Carlos, K.C.†	.247	98	413	372	49	92	136	15	4	7	44	2	4	0	35	2	69	13	0	12	.366	.309
Bergman, Sean, Min.	.500	15	2	2	0	1	2	1	0	0	0	0	0	0	0	0	1	0	0	0	1.000	.500
Berry, Sean, Bos.	.000	1	4	4	0	0	0	0	0	0	0	0	0	0	0	0	2	0	0	0	.000	.000
Bichette, Dante, Bos.	.289	30	122	114	13	33	59	5	0	7	14	0	0	0	8	0	22	0	0	3	.518	.336
Blair, Willie, Det.	.333	47	3	3	0	1	1	0	0	0	0	0	0	0	0	0	2	0	0	0	.333	.333
Blake, Casey, Min.	.188	7	21	16	1	3	5	2	0	0	1	0	1	1	3	0	7	0	0	1	.313	.333
Bordick, Mike, Bal.	.297	100	433	391	70	116	188	22	1	16	59	2	5	1	34	0	71	6	5	12	.481	.350
Bottenfield, Kent, Ana.	.667	21	3	3	1	2	2	0	0	0	0	0	0	0	0	0	1	0	0	0	.667	.667
Branyan, Russell, Cle.*	.238	67	220	193	32	46	105	7	2	16	38	0	1	4	22	1	76	0	0	2	.544	.327
Brewington, Jamie, Cle.	.000	26	2	1	1	0	0	0	0	0	0	0	0	0	1	0	0	0	0	0	.000	.500
Brogna, Rico, Bos.*	.196	43	60	56	8	11	17	3	0	1	8	1	0	0	3	0	13	0	0	1	.304	.237
Brosius, Scott, N.Y.	.230	135	519	470	57	108	176	20	0	16	64	0	2	2	45	1	73	0	3	17	.374	.299
Brower, Jim, Cle.	.000	17	3	3	0	0	0	0	0	0	0	0	0	0	0	0	2	0	0	0	.000	.000
Brown, Dee, K.C.*	.160	15	28	25	4	4	5	1	0	0	4	0	0	0	3	0	9	0	0	0	.200	.250
Buchanan, Brian, Min.	.232	30	93	82	10	19	25	3	0	1	8	0	2	1	8	0	22	0	2	3	.305	.301
Buhner, Jay, Sea.	.253	112	430	364	50	92	190	20	0	26	82	1	2	4	59	3	98	0	2	10	.522	.361
Burba, Dave, Cle.	.000	32	3	1	0	0	0	0	0	0	0	2	0	0	0	0	1	0	0	0	.000	.000
Burkhart, Morgan, Bos.†	.288	25	95	73	16	21	36	3	0	4	18	0	1	4	17	1	25	0	0	1	.493	.442
Bush, Homer, Tor.	.215	76	325	297	38	64	75	8	0	1	18	4	1	5	18	0	60	9	4	10	.253	.271
Byrnes, Eric, Oak.	.300	10	11	10	5	3	3	0	0	0	0	0	0	1	0	0	1	2	1	0	.300	.364
Cabrera, Jolbert, Cle.	.251	100	187	175	27	44	55	3	1	2	15	1	1	2	8	0	15	6	4	1	.314	.290
Cairo, Miguel, T.B.	.261	119	417	375	49	98	123	18	2	1	34	6	5	2	29	0	34	28	7	7	.328	.314
Cameron, Mike, Sea.	.267	155	643	543	96	145	238	28	4	19	78	7	6	9	78	0	133	24	7	10	.438	.365
Canizaro, Jay, Min.	.269	102	371	346	43	93	137	21	1	7	40	0	0	1	24	0	57	4	2	8	.396	.318
Canseco, Jose, T.B.-N.Y.	.252	98	401	329	47	83	146	18	0	15	49	0	4	4	64	2	102	2	0	7	.444	.377
Cardona, Javier, Det.	.175	26	42	40	1	7	11	1	0	1	2	0	1	1	0	0	9	0	0	1	.275	.190
Carpenter, Chris, Tor.	.000	34	2	2	0	0	0	0	0	0	0	0	0	0	0	0	1	0	0	0	.000	.000
Casimiro, Carlos, Bal.	.125	2	8	8	0	1	2	1	0	0	3	0	0	0	0	0	2	0	0	0	.250	.125
Castilla, Vinny, T.B.	.221	85	354	331	22	73	102	9	1	6	42	0	6	3	14	3	41	1	2	9	.308	.254
Castillo, Alberto, Tor.	.211	66	211	185	14	39	49	7	0	1	16	2	3	0	21	0	36	0	0	3	.265	.287
Castillo, Frank, Tor.	.143	25	7	7	0	1	1	0	0	0	0	0	0	0	0	0	3	0	0	1	.143	.143
Catalanotto, Frank, Tex.*	.291	103	326	282	55	82	129	13	2	10	42	3	2	6	33	0	36	6	2	5	.457	.375
Chavez, Eric, Oak.*	.277	153	569	501	89	139	248	23	4	26	86	0	5	1	62	8	94	2	2	9	.495	.355
Christensen, McKay, Chi.*	.105	32	22	19	4	2	2	0	0	0	1	0	0	1	2	0	6	1	1	0	.105	.227
Christenson, Ryan, Oak.	.248	121	153	129	31	32	50	2	2	4	18	4	0	1	19	0	33	1	2	1	.388	.349
Clark, Tony, Det.†	.274	60	232	208	32	57	110	14	0	13	37	0	0	0	24	2	51	0	0	10	.529	.349
Clark, Will, Bal.*	.301	79	310	256	49	77	121	15	1	9	28	0	3	4	47	3	45	4	2	4	.473	.413
Clayton, Royce, Tex.	.242	148	573	513	70	124	197	21	5	14	54	12	3	4	42	1	92	11	7	21	.384	.301
Clemens, Roger, N.Y.	.000	32	3	3	0	0	0	0	0	0	0	0	0	0	0	0	1	0	0	0	.000	.000
Clemente, Edgard, Ana.	.218	46	80	78	4	17	19	2	0	0	5	1	0	1	0	0	27	0	1	0	.244	.228
Coffie, Ivanon, Bal.*	.217	23	67	60	6	13	19	4	1	0	6	0	1	1	5	0	11	1	0	3	.317	.284
Colon, Bartolo, Cle.	.000	30	5	5	0	0	0	0	0	0	0	0	0	0	0	0	5	0	0	0	.000	.000
Cone, David, N.Y.*	.333	30	3	3	0	1	1	0	0	0	0	0	0	0	0	0	1	0	0	0	.333	.333
Conine, Jeff, Bal.	.284	119	451	409	53	116	179	20	2	13	46	0	4	2	36	1	53	4	3	14	.438	.341
Coomer, Ron, Min.	.270	140	589	544	64	147	226	29	1	16	82	0	5	4	36	2	50	2	0	25	.415	.317
Cooper, Brian, Ana.	.000	15	4	4	0	0	0	0	0	0	0	0	0	0	0	0	3	0	0	0	.000	.000
Cordero, Wil, Cle.	.264	38	158	148	18	39	54	11	2	0	17	0	0	3	7	0	18	0	0	7	.365	.310
Cordova, Marty, Tor.	.245	62	221	200	23	49	68	7	0	4	18	0	0	3	18	0	35	3	2	6	.340	.317
Cox, Steve, T.B.*	.283	116	369	318	44	90	144	19	1	11	35	0	1	5	45	2	47	1	2	9	.453	.379
Crede, Joe, Chi.	.357	7	15	14	2	5	6	1	0	0	3	0	1	0	0	0	3	0	0	0	.429	.333
Cruz, Deivi, Det.	.302	156	615	583	68	176	262	46	5	10	82	8	7	4	13	2	43	1	4	25	.449	.318
Cruz, Jacob, Cle.*	.241	11	36	29	3	7	10	3	0	0	5	0	1	1	5	0	4	1	0	0	.345	.361
Cruz, Jose Jr., Tor.†	.242	162	681	603	91	146	281	32	5	31	76	2	3	2	71	3	129	15	5	11	.466	.323
Cruz, Nelson, Det.	.000	27	1	1	0	0	0	0	0	0	0	0	0	0	0	0	0	0	0	0	.000	.000
Cubillan, Darwin, Tor.-Tex.	.000	20	1	1	0	0	0	0	0	0	0	0	0	0	0	0	0	0	0	0	.000	.000
Cummings, Midre, Min.-Bos.*	.277	98	227	206	29	57	79	10	0	4	24	1	0	3	17	1	28	0	0	5	.383	.341
Curtis, Chad, Tex.	.272	108	381	335	48	91	142	25	1	8	48	5	3	1	37	0	71	3	3	12	.424	.343
Damon, Johnny, K.C.*	.327	159	741	655	136	214	324	42	10	16	88	8	12	1	65	4	60	46	9	7	.495	.382
Daubach, Brian, Bos.*	.248	142	549	495	55	123	222	32	2	21	76	0	4	6	44	2	130	1	1	6	.448	.315
Davis, Kane, Cle.	.000	5	1	1	0	0	0	0	0	0	0	0	0	0	0	0	1	0	0	0	.000	.000
Delgado, Carlos, Tor.*	.344	162	711	569	115	196	378	57	1	41	137	0	4	15	123	18	104	0	1	12	.664	.470
Delgado, Wilson, N.Y.-K.C.†	.258	64	141	128	21	33	38	2	0	1	11	0	2	0	11	0	26	2	1	2	.297	.312
DeShields, Delino, Bal.*	.296	151	643	561	84	166	249	43	5	10	86	3	9	1	69	2	82	37	10	16	.444	.369
Diaz, Einar, Cle.	.272	75	275	250	29	68	98	14	2	4	25	6	0	8	11	0	29	4	2	7	.392	.323
DiFelice, Mike, T.B.	.240	60	233	204	23	49	82	13	1	6	19	5	2	0	12	0	40	0	0	8	.402	.280
DiSarcina, Gary, Ana.	.395	12	42	38	6	15	20	2	0	1	11	2	0	1	1	0	3	0	1	1	.526	.425
Dransfeldt, Kelly, Tex.	.115	16	27	26	2	3	5	2	0	0	2	0	0	0	1	0	14	0	0	0	.192	.148
Ducey, Rob, Tor.*	.154	5	15	13	2	2	3	1	0	0	1	0	0	0	2	0	2	0	0	0	.231	.267
Dunwoody, Todd, K.C.*	.208	61	195	178	12	37	49	9	0	1	23	2	6	1	8	0	42	3	0	4	.275	.238
Durham, Ray, Chi.†	.280	151	709	614	121	172	276	35	9	17	75	5	8	7	75	0	105	25	13	13	.450	.361
Durrington, Trent, Ana.	.000	4	3	3	0	0	0	0	0	0	0	0	0	0	0	0	1	0	0	0	.000	.000
Dye, Jermaine, K.C.	.321	157	679	601	107	193	337	41	2	33	118	0	6	3	69	6	99	0	1	12	.561	.390
Easley, Damion, Det.	.259	126	535	464	76	120	193	27	2	14	58	4	1	11	55	1	79	13	4	11	.416	.350
Eldred, Cal, Chi.	.250	20	6	4	3	1	1	0	0	0	0	0	0	0	2	0	1	0	0	0	.250	.500
Encarnacion, Juan, Det.	.289	141	590	547	75	158	237	25	6	14	72	3	4	7	29	1	90	16	4	15	.433	.330
Erdos, Todd, N.Y.	.000	14	1	1	0	0	0	0	0	0	0	0	0	0	0	0	0	0	0	0	.000	.000
Erickson, Scott, Bal.	.400	17	5	5	2	2	3	1	0	0	1	0	0	0	0	0	0	0	0	1	.600	.400
Erstad, Darin, Ana.*	.355	157	747	676	121	240	366	39	6	25	100	2	4	1	64	9	82	28	8	8	.541	.409
Escobar, Kelvim, Tor.	.000	43	7	7	0	0	0	0	0	0	0	0	0	0	0	0	4	0	0	0	.000	.000
Etherton, Seth, Ana.	.000	11	3	2	1	0	0	0	0	0	0	1	0	0	0	0	1	0	0	0	.000	.333
Evans, Tom, Tex.	.278	23	67	54	10	15	19	4	0	0	5	1	1	1	10	0	13	0	3	1	.352	.394
Everett, Carl, Bos.†	.300	137	561	496	82	149	291	32	4	34	108	0	5	8	52	5	113	11	4	4	.587	.373

Player, Team	Avg.	G	TPA	AB	R	H	TB	2B	3B	HR	RBI	SH	SF	HP	BB	IBB	SO	SB	CS	GDP	Slg.	OBP
Fabregas, Jorge, K.C.*	.282	43	152	142	13	40	53	4	0	3	17	2	0	0	8	1	11	1	0	1	.373	.320
Fasano, Sal, Oak.	.214	52	144	126	21	27	54	6	0	7	19	0	1	3	14	0	47	0	0	3	.429	.306
Fassero, Jeff, Bos.*	.000	38	3	2	1	0	0	0	0	0	0	1	0	0	0	0	2	0	0	0	.000	.000
Febles, Carlos, K.C.	.257	100	399	339	59	87	107	12	1	2	29	13	1	10	36	1	48	17	6	10	.316	.345
Fick, Robert, Det.*	.252	66	188	163	18	41	61	7	2	3	22	0	2	1	22	2	39	2	1	4	.374	.340
Finley, Chuck, Cle.*	.000	34	7	7	0	0	0	0	0	0	0	0	0	0	0	0	4	0	0	0	.000	.000
Flaherty, John, T.B.	.261	109	418	394	36	103	148	15	0	10	39	2	2	0	20	2	57	0	0	11	.376	.296
Fletcher, Darrin, Tor.*	.320	122	445	416	43	133	214	19	1	20	58	0	4	5	20	3	45	1	0	8	.514	.355
Fordyce, Brook, Chi.-Bal.	.301	93	330	302	41	91	153	18	1	14	49	2	5	4	17	0	50	0	0	4	.507	.341
Frye, Jeff, Bos.	.289	69	273	239	35	69	85	13	0	1	13	4	1	1	28	0	38	1	3	5	.356	.364
Fryman, Travis, Cle.	.321	155	658	574	93	184	296	38	4	22	106	0	10	1	73	2	111	1	1	15	.516	.392
Fullmer, Brad, Tor.*	.295	133	524	482	76	142	269	29	1	32	104	0	6	6	30	3	68	3	1	14	.558	.340
Fussell, Chris, K.C.	.000	20	2	2	0	0	0	0	0	0	0	0	0	0	0	0	2	0	0	0	.000	.000
Gaetti, Gary, Bos.	.000	5	11	10	0	0	0	0	0	0	1	0	1	0	0	0	3	0	0	0	.000	.000
Gant, Ron, Ana.	.232	34	103	82	15	19	42	3	1	6	16	0	1	0	20	0	18	1	2	0	.512	.379
Garcia, Freddy, Sea.	.667	21	6	3	0	2	2	0	0	0	0	3	0	0	0	0	0	0	0	0	.667	.667
Garcia, Jesse, Bal.	.059	14	19	17	2	1	1	0	0	0	0	0	0	0	2	0	2	0	0	0	.059	.158
Garcia, Karim, Det.-Bal.*	.091	16	33	33	1	3	3	0	0	0	0	0	0	0	0	0	10	0	0	1	.091	.091
Garciaparra, Nomar, Bos.	.372	140	599	529	104	197	317	51	3	21	96	0	7	2	61	20	50	5	2	8	.599	.434
Giambi, Jason, Oak.*	.333	152	664	510	108	170	330	29	1	43	137	0	8	9	137	6	96	2	0	9	.647	.476
Giambi, Jeremy, Oak.*	.254	104	302	260	42	66	110	10	2	10	50	3	4	3	32	2	61	0	0	7	.423	.338
Gil, Benji, Ana.	.239	110	343	301	28	72	106	14	1	6	23	5	2	5	30	0	59	10	6	7	.352	.317
Gilkey, Bernard, Bos.	.231	36	104	91	11	21	31	5	1	1	9	0	0	3	10	0	12	0	0	5	.341	.322
Gipson, Charles, Sea.	.310	59	33	29	7	9	12	1	1	0	3	0	0	0	4	0	9	2	3	0	.414	.394
Glaus, Troy, Ana.	.284	159	678	563	120	160	340	37	1	47	102	0	1	2	112	6	163	14	11	14	.604	.404
Glynn, Ryan, Tex.	.000	16	2	2	0	0	0	0	0	0	0	0	0	0	0	0	1	0	0	0	.000	.000
Gonzalez, Alex S., Tor.	.252	141	591	527	68	133	213	31	2	15	69	16	1	4	43	0	113	4	4	14	.404	.313
Gonzalez, Juan, Det.	.289	115	496	461	69	133	233	30	2	22	67	0	1	2	32	3	84	1	2	13	.505	.337
Gooden, Dwight, T.B.-N.Y.	.000	26	2	2	0	0	0	0	0	0	0	0	0	0	0	0	1	0	0	0	.000	.000
Graffanino, Tony, T.B.-Chi.	.274	70	194	168	33	46	60	6	1	2	17	1	1	2	22	0	27	7	4	2	.357	.363
Grebeck, Craig, Tor.	.295	66	270	241	38	71	99	19	0	3	23	1	1	2	25	0	33	0	0	7	.411	.364
Green, Scarborough, Tex.†	.234	79	139	124	21	29	32	1	1	0	9	5	0	0	10	0	26	10	6	3	.258	.291
Greene, Charlie, Tor.	.111	3	9	9	0	1	1	0	0	0	0	0	0	0	0	0	5	0	0	0	.111	.111
Greene, Todd, Tor.	.235	34	90	85	11	20	37	2	0	5	10	0	0	0	5	0	18	0	0	4	.435	.278
Greer, Rusty, Tex.*	.297	105	453	394	65	117	181	34	3	8	65	0	5	3	51	1	61	4	1	14	.459	.377
Grieve, Ben, Oak.*	.279	158	675	594	92	166	289	40	1	27	104	0	5	3	73	2	130	3	0	32	.487	.359
Grimsley, Jason, N.Y.	.000	63	3	1	0	0	0	0	0	0	0	0	0	0	2	0	1	0	0	0	.000	.667
Guillen, Carlos, Sea.†	.257	90	328	288	45	74	114	15	2	7	42	7	3	2	28	0	53	1	3	6	.396	.324
Guillen, Jose, T.B.	.253	105	349	316	40	80	136	16	5	10	41	2	0	13	18	1	65	3	1	6	.430	.320
Guillen, Ozzie, T.B.*	.243	63	114	107	22	26	36	4	0	2	12	1	0	0	6	0	7	1	0	1	.336	.283
Guzman, Cristian, Min.†	.247	156	690	631	89	156	245	25	20	8	54	7	4	2	46	1	101	28	10	5	.388	.299
Hairston, Jerry Jr., Bal.	.256	49	212	180	27	46	66	5	0	5	19	5	0	6	21	0	22	8	5	8	.367	.353
Halama, John, Sea.*	.500	30	3	2	0	1	1	0	0	0	0	1	0	0	0	0	1	0	0	0	.500	.500
Hall, Toby, T.B.	.167	4	13	12	1	2	5	0	0	1	1	0	0	1	0	0	1	0	0	0	.417	.231
Halter, Shane, Det.	.261	105	265	238	26	62	87	12	2	3	27	10	2	1	14	0	49	5	2	5	.366	.302
Hasegawa, Shigetoshi, Ana.	.000	66	1	1	0	0	0	0	0	0	0	0	0	0	0	0	0	0	0	0	.000	.000
Haselman, Bill, Tex.	.275	62	210	193	23	53	89	18	0	6	26	0	1	1	15	0	36	0	1	1	.461	.329
Hatteberg, Scott, Bos.*	.265	92	271	230	21	61	100	15	0	8	36	1	2	0	38	3	39	0	1	8	.435	.367
Hawkins, LaTroy, Min.	.000	66	1	1	0	0	0	0	0	0	0	0	0	0	0	0	1	0	0	0	.000	.000
Helling, Rick, Tex.	.000	35	5	5	0	0	0	0	0	0	0	0	0	0	0	0	2	0	0	0	.000	.000
Henderson, Rickey, Sea.	.238	92	395	324	58	77	106	13	2	4	30	3	3	2	63	0	55	31	9	9	.327	.362
Heredia, Gil, Oak.	.500	32	3	2	0	1	1	0	0	0	0	0	1	0	0	0	0	0	0	0	.500	.500
Hernandez, Carlos E., Sea.	.000	2	1	1	0	0	0	0	0	0	0	0	0	0	0	0	1	0	1	0	.000	.000
Hernandez, Orlando, N.Y.	.000	29	10	9	0	0	0	0	0	0	0	1	0	0	0	0	7	0	0	0	.000	.000
Hernandez, Ramon, Oak.	.241	143	479	419	52	101	162	19	0	14	62	10	5	7	38	1	64	1	0	14	.387	.311
Higginson, Bobby, Det.*	.300	154	678	597	104	179	321	44	4	30	102	2	3	2	74	6	99	15	3	5	.538	.377
Hill, Glenallen, N.Y.	.333	40	143	132	22	44	97	5	0	16	29	0	1	1	9	0	33	0	0	1	.735	.378
Hill, Ken, Ana.-Chi.	.333	18	4	3	0	1	1	0	0	0	0	1	0	0	0	0	0	0	0	0	.333	.333
Hinch, A.J., Oak.	.250	6	9	8	1	2	2	0	0	0	0	0	0	0	1	0	1	0	0	0	.250	.333
Hocking, Denny, Min.†	.298	134	433	373	52	111	155	24	4	4	47	7	5	0	48	1	77	7	5	2	.416	.373
Holbert, Ray, K.C.	.250	3	4	4	0	1	1	0	0	0	0	0	0	0	0	0	2	0	0	0	.250	.250
Hubbard, Trenidad, Bal.	.185	31	27	27	3	5	7	0	1	0	0	0	0	0	0	0	3	2	1	2	.259	.185
Hudson, Tim, Oak.	.000	33	3	3	0	0	0	0	0	0	0	0	0	0	0	0	1	0	0	0	.000	.000
Huff, Aubrey, T.B.*	.287	39	129	122	12	35	54	7	0	4	14	0	1	1	5	1	18	0	0	6	.443	.318
Hunter, Torii, Min.	.280	99	358	336	44	94	137	14	7	5	44	0	2	2	18	2	68	4	3	13	.408	.318
Huskey, Butch, Min.	.223	64	245	215	22	48	76	13	0	5	27	0	3	2	25	1	49	0	2	5	.353	.306
Ibanez, Raul, Sea.*	.229	92	156	140	21	32	46	8	0	2	15	0	1	1	14	1	25	2	0	1	.329	.301
Jaha, John, Oak.	.175	33	133	97	14	17	21	1	0	1	5	0	0	3	33	0	38	1	0	4	.216	.390
Javier, Stan, Sea.†	.275	105	392	342	61	94	137	18	5	5	40	4	4	0	42	2	64	4	3	7	.401	.351
Jefferies, Gregg, Det.†	.275	41	160	142	18	39	53	8	0	2	14	0	2	0	16	1	10	0	2	7	.373	.344
Jensen, Marcus, Min.†	.209	52	164	139	16	29	47	7	1	3	14	1	0	0	24	0	36	0	1	3	.338	.325
Jeter, Derek, N.Y.	.339	148	679	593	119	201	285	31	4	15	73	3	3	12	68	4	99	22	4	14	.481	.416
Johnson, Brian, K.C.	.208	37	132	125	9	26	44	6	0	4	18	1	2	0	4	0	28	0	0	4	.352	.229
Johnson, Charles, Chi.-Bal.	.304	128	478	421	76	128	245	24	0	31	91	1	3	1	52	0	106	2	0	8	.582	.379
Johnson, Jason, Bal.	.000	25	5	3	0	0	0	0	0	0	0	2	0	0	0	0	0	0	0	0	.000	.000
Johnson, Keith, Ana.	.500	6	7	4	2	2	2	0	0	0	0	1	0	0	2	0	0	0	0	0	.500	.667
Johnson, Lance, N.Y.*	.300	18	30	30	6	9	10	1	0	0	2	0	0	0	0	0	7	2	0	1	.333	.300
Johnson, Mark L., Chi.*	.225	75	251	213	29	48	68	11	0	3	23	10	0	1	27	0	40	3	2	3	.319	.315
Johnson, Russ, T.B.	.254	74	215	185	28	47	61	8	0	2	17	3	1	1	25	0	30	4	1	4	.330	.344
Jones, Jacque, Min.*	.285	154	550	523	66	149	242	26	5	19	76	1	0	0	26	4	111	7	5	17	.463	.319
Jones, Marcus, Oak.	.000	1	2	2	0	0	0	0	0	0	0	0	0	0	0	0	0	0	0	0	.000	.000
Jose, Felix, N.Y.†	.241	20	32	29	4	7	10	0	0	1	5	0	1	0	2	0	9	0	1	1	.345	.281

Player, Team	Avg.	G	TPA	AB	R	H	TB	2B	3B	HR	RBI	SH	SF	HP	BB	IBB	SO	SB	CS	GDP	Slg.	OBP
Justice, David, Cle.-N.Y.*	.286	146	605	524	89	150	306	31	1	41	118	0	3	1	77	3	91	2	1	13	.584	.377
Kapler, Gabe, Tex.	.302	116	491	444	59	134	210	32	1	14	66	2	3	0	42	2	57	8	4	12	.473	.360
Karsay, Steve, Cle.	.000	72	1	1	0	0	0	0	0	0	0	0	0	0	0	0	0	0	0	0	.000	.000
Kelly, Kenny, T.B.	.000	2	1	1	0	0	0	0	0	0	0	0	0	0	0	0	0	0	0	0	.000	.000
Kelly, Roberto, N.Y.	.120	10	27	25	4	3	7	1	0	1	1	0	0	1	1	0	6	0	0	0	.280	.185
Kennedy, Adam, Ana.*	.266	156	641	598	82	159	241	33	11	9	72	8	4	3	28	5	73	22	8	10	.403	.300
Kingsale, Eugene, Bal.†	.239	26	91	88	13	21	25	2	1	0	9	0	1	0	2	0	14	1	2	4	.284	.253
Kinkade, Mike, Bal.	.429	3	8	7	0	3	4	1	0	0	1	0	0	1	0	0	0	0	0	0	.571	.500
Knoblauch, Chuck, N.Y.	.283	102	457	400	75	113	154	22	2	5	26	1	2	8	46	0	45	15	7	6	.385	.366
Knorr, Randy, Tex.	.294	15	37	34	5	10	18	2	0	2	2	3	0	0	0	0	3	0	0	0	.529	.294
Koch, Billy, Tor.	.000	68	1	1	0	0	0	0	0	0	0	0	0	0	0	0	1	0	0	0	.000	.000
Konerko, Paul, Chi.	.298	143	586	524	84	156	252	31	1	21	97	0	5	10	47	0	72	1	0	22	.481	.363
Koskie, Corey, Min.*	.300	146	559	474	79	142	209	32	4	9	65	1	3	4	77	7	104	5	4	11	.441	.400
Lamb, Mike, Tex.*	.278	138	538	493	65	137	184	25	2	6	47	5	2	4	34	6	60	0	2	10	.373	.328
Lampkin, Tom, Sea.*	.252	36	117	103	15	26	55	6	1	7	23	0	2	3	9	1	17	0	0	7	.534	.325
Lansing, Mike, Bos.	.194	49	148	139	10	27	31	4	0	0	13	0	2	0	7	1	26	0	0	7	.223	.230
Lawton, Matt, Min.*	.305	156	664	561	84	171	258	44	2	13	88	0	5	7	91	8	63	23	7	10	.460	.405
LeCroy, Matthew, Min.	.174	56	190	167	18	29	54	10	0	5	17	1	3	2	17	2	38	0	0	6	.323	.254
Ledee, Ricky, N.Y.-Cle.-Tex.*	.236	137	531	467	59	110	178	19	5	13	77	0	3	2	59	4	98	13	6	17	.381	.322
Lee, Carlos, Chi.	.301	152	619	572	107	172	277	29	2	24	92	1	5	3	38	1	94	13	4	17	.484	.345
Lesher, Brian, Sea.	.800	5	6	5	1	4	7	1	1	0	3	0	0	0	1	0	0	1	0	0	1.400	.833
Lewis, Darren, Bos.	.241	97	303	270	44	65	83	12	0	2	17	8	0	3	22	0	34	10	5	2	.307	.305
Lewis, Mark, Bal.	.270	71	178	163	19	44	67	17	0	2	21	1	1	1	12	0	31	7	2	5	.411	.322
Leyritz, Jim, N.Y.	.218	24	63	55	2	12	15	0	0	1	4	0	0	1	7	0	14	0	0	2	.273	.317
Lidle, Cory, T.B.	.000	31	2	2	0	0	0	0	0	0	0	0	0	0	0	0	0	0	0	0	.000	.000
Liefer, Jeff, Chi.*	.182	5	11	11	0	2	2	0	0	0	0	0	0	0	0	0	4	0	0	0	.182	.182
Lindsey, Rodney, Det.	.333	11	5	3	6	1	2	1	0	0	0	1	0	1	0	0	1	2	1	0	.667	.500
Loaiza, Esteban, Tex.-Tor.	.000	34	3	3	0	0	0	0	0	0	0	0	0	0	0	0	0	0	0	0	.000	.000
Lofton, Kenny, Cle.*	.278	137	640	543	107	151	229	23	5	15	73	6	8	4	79	3	72	30	7	11	.422	.369
Long, Terrence, Oak.*	.288	138	631	584	104	168	264	34	4	18	80	0	3	1	43	1	77	5	0	18	.452	.336
Lopez, Albie, T.B.	.000	45	7	6	0	0	0	0	0	0	0	1	0	0	0	0	5	0	0	0	.000	.000
Lowe, Derek, Bos.	.000	74	1	1	0	0	0	0	0	0	0	0	0	0	0	0	1	0	0	0	.000	.000
Lunar, Fernando, Bal.	.125	9	17	16	0	2	2	0	0	0	1	0	1	0	0	0	4	0	0	0	.125	.176
Luuloa, Keith, Ana.	.333	6	19	18	3	6	6	0	0	0	0	0	0	1	0	0	1	0	0	0	.333	.368
Mabry, John, Sea.*	.243	48	115	103	18	25	33	5	0	1	7	0	0	2	10	0	31	0	1	1	.320	.322
Machado, Robert, Sea.	.214	8	15	14	2	3	6	0	0	1	1	0	0	1	0	0	4	0	0	0	.429	.267
Macias, Jose, Det.†	.254	73	196	173	25	44	63	3	5	2	24	4	0	1	18	0	24	2	0	3	.364	.333
Magee, Wendell Jr., Det.	.274	91	197	186	31	51	80	4	2	7	31	0	1	0	10	0	28	1	0	7	.430	.310
Magnante, Mike, Oak.*	.000	55	1	1	0	0	0	0	0	0	0	0	0	0	0	0	0	0	0	0	.000	.000
Martin, Al, Sea.*	.231	42	145	134	19	31	53	2	4	4	9	0	1	2	8	0	31	4	1	1	.396	.283
Martinez, Tino, N.Y.*	.258	155	632	569	69	147	240	37	4	16	91	0	3	8	52	9	74	4	1	16	.422	.328
Martinez, Dave, T.B.-Tex.-Tor.*	.285	114	457	403	55	115	156	18	4	5	46	1	3	2	48	3	65	7	7	12	.387	.362
Martinez, Edgar, Sea.	.324	153	665	556	100	180	322	31	0	37	145	0	8	5	96	8	93	0	3	13	.579	.423
Martinez, Felix, T.B.†	.214	106	353	299	42	64	89	11	4	2	17	12	2	8	32	0	68	9	3	4	.298	.305
Martinez, Ramon J., Bos.*	.200	27	5	5	1	1	1	0	0	0	0	0	0	0	0	0	1	0	0	0	.200	.200
Mateo, Ruben, Tex.	.291	52	222	206	32	60	92	11	0	7	19	1	0	5	10	1	34	6	0	5	.447	.339
Mathews, T.J., Oak.	.000	50	1	0	0	0	0	0	0	0	0	0	0	0	1	0	0	0	0	0	.000	1.000
Matos, Luis, Bal.	.225	72	201	182	21	41	56	6	3	1	17	2	2	3	12	0	30	13	4	7	.308	.281
Maxwell, Jason, Min.	.243	64	124	111	14	27	36	6	0	1	11	0	3	1	9	0	32	2	1	2	.324	.298
Mays, Joe, Min.†	.400	31	6	5	1	2	3	1	0	0	0	1·	0	0	0	0	2	0	0	0	.600	.400
McCarty, David, K.C.	.278	103	295	270	34	75	129	14	2	12	53	0	3	0	22	1	68	0	0	6	.478	.329
McCracken, Quinton, T.B.†	.129	15	37	31	5	4	4	0	0	0	2	0	0	0	6	0	4	0	1	3	.129	.270
McDonald, Jason, Tex.†	.234	38	114	94	15	22	36	5	0	3	13	2	0	1	17	0	25	4	4	2	.383	.357
McDonald, John, Cle.	.444	9	9	9	0	4	4	0	0	0	0	0	0	0	0	0	1	0	0	0	.444	.444
McGriff, Fred, T.B.*	.277	158	664	566	82	157	256	18	0	27	106	0	7	0	91	10	120	2	0	16	.452	.373
McLemore, Mark, Sea.†	.245	138	578	481	72	118	152	23	1	3	46	11	4	1	81	0	78	30	14	12	.316	.353
McMillon, Billy, Det.*	.301	46	149	123	20	37	58	7	1	4	24	2	4	1	19	0	19	1	0	2	.472	.388
Menechino, Frank, Oak.	.255	66	169	145	31	37	66	9	1	6	26	1	2	1	20	0	45	1	4	1	.455	.345
Mercedes, Jose, Bal.	.000	36	1	1	0	0	0	0	0	0	0	0	0	0	0	0	0	0	0	0	.000	.000
Merloni, Lou, Bos.	.320	40	139	128	10	41	56	11	2	0	18	4	2	1	4	1	22	1	0	8	.438	.341
Mientkiewicz, Doug, Min.*	.429	3	15	14	0	6	6	0	0	0	4	0	1	0	0	0	0	0	0	0	.429	.400
Milton, Eric, Min.*	.000	33	2	2	0	0	0	0	0	0	0	0	0	0	0	0	0	0	0	0	.000	.000
Minor, Ryan, Bal.	.131	32	88	84	4	11	12	1	0	0	3	0	0	1	3	0	20	0	0	1	.143	.170
Mlicki, Dave, Det.	.000	24	2	2	0	0	0	0	0	0	0	0	0	0	0	0	1	0	0	0	.000	.000
Moehler, Brian, Det.	.000	29	4	4	0	0	0	0	0	0	0	0	0	0	0	0	1	0	0	0	.000	.000
Moeller, Chad, Min.	.211	48	139	128	13	27	35	3	1	1	9	1	1	0	9	0	33	1	0	4	.273	.261
Molina, Bengie, Ana.	.281	130	513	473	59	133	199	20	2	14	71	4	7	6	23	0	33	1	0	17	.421	.318
Mondesi, Raul, Tor.	.271	96	426	388	78	105	203	22	2	24	67	0	3	3	32	0	73	22	6	8	.523	.329
Mora, Melvin, Bal.	.291	53	222	199	25	58	79	9	3	2	17	2	0	4	17	0	32	5	8	2	.397	.359
Morales, Willie, Bal.	.273	3	11	11	1	3	4	1	0	0	0	0	0	0	0	0	3	0	0	0	.364	.273
Morandini, Mickey, Tor.*	.271	35	116	107	10	29	33	2	1	0	7	2	0	0	7	0	23	1	0	2	.308	.316
Morris, Hal, Det.*	.311	40	126	106	15	33	43	7	0	1	8	1	0	0	19	1	16	0	0	3	.406	.416
Mottola, Chad, Tor.	.222	3	10	9	1	2	2	0	0	0	2	0	0	1	0	0	4	0	0	0	.222	.300
Moyer, Jamie, Sea.*	.000	26	2	2	0	0	0	0	0	0	0	0	0	0	0	0	0	0	0	0	.000	.000
Mulder, Mark, Oak.*	.000	27	4	4	0	0	0	0	0	0	0	0	0	0	0	0	3	0	0	1	.000	.000
Munro, Peter, Tor.	.000	9	1	1	0	0	0	0	0	0	0	0	0	0	0	0	1	0	0	0	.000	.000
Munson, Eric, Det.*	.000	3	5	5	0	0	0	0	0	0	0	0	0	0	0	0	1	0	0	0	.000	.000
Mussina, Mike, Bal.*	.000	34	6	6	0	0	0	0	0	0	0	0	0	0	0	0	1	0	0	0	.000	.000
Myers, Greg, Bal.*	.224	43	134	125	9	28	43	6	0	3	12	1	0	0	9	2	29	0	0	7	.344	.271
Nelson, Jeff, N.Y.	.000	73	1	1	0	0	0	0	0	0	0	0	0	0	0	0	0	0	0	0	.000	.000
Nixon, Trot, Bos.*	.276	123	502	427	66	118	197	27	8	12	60	5	5	2	63	2	85	8	1	11	.461	.368
Nomo, Hideo, Det.	.000	32	6	6	0	0	0	0	0	0	0	0	0	0	0	0	2	0	0	0	.000	.000

Player, Team	Avg.	G	TPA	AB	R	H	TB	2B	3B	HR	RBI	SH	SF	HP	BB	IBB	SO	SB	CS	GDP	Slg.	OBP
Norton, Greg, Chi.†	.244	71	231	201	25	49	75	6	1	6	28	0	2	2	26	0	47	1	0	2	.373	.333
Offerman, Jose, Bos.†	.255	116	527	451	73	115	162	14	3	9	41	2	3	1	70	0	70	0	8	9	.359	.354
O'Leary, Troy, Bos.*	.261	138	563	513	68	134	211	30	4	13	70	0	4	2	44	2	76	0	2	12	.411	.320
Olerud, John, Sea.*	.285	159	683	565	84	161	248	45	0	14	103	2	10	4	102	11	96	0	2	17	.439	.392
Olivares, Omar, Oak.	1.000	21	1	1	0	1	1	0	0	0	0	0	0	0	0	0	0	0	0	0	1.000	1.000
Oliver, Darren, Tex.	.000	21	3	2	0	0	0	0	0	0	0	0	0	1	0	0	1	0	0	0	.000	.333
Oliver, Joe, Sea.	.265	69	219	200	33	53	98	13	1	10	35	5	0	0	14	1	38	2	1	6	.490	.334
O'Neill, Paul, N.Y.*	.283	142	628	566	79	160	240	26	0	18	100	0	11	0	51	2	90	14	9	17	.424	.336
Ordaz, Luis, K.C.	.221	65	117	104	17	23	25	2	0	0	11	4	3	1	5	0	10	4	2	6	.240	.257
Ordonez, Magglio, Chi.	.315	153	665	588	102	185	321	34	3	32	126	0	15	2	60	3	64	18	4	28	.546	.371
Ortiz, David, Min.*	.282	130	478	415	59	117	185	36	1	10	63	0	6	0	57	2	81	1	0	13	.446	.364
Ortiz, Hector, K.C.	.386	26	99	88	15	34	40	6	0	0	5	2	0	1	8	1	8	0	0	0	.455	.443
Ortiz, Jose, Oak.	.182	7	13	11	4	2	2	0	0	0	1	0	0	0	2	0	3	0	0	0	.182	.308
Palmeiro, Orlando, Ana.*	.300	108	296	243	38	73	97	20	2	0	25	10	3	2	38	0	20	4	1	4	.399	.395
Palmeiro, Rafael, Tex.*	.288	158	678	565	102	163	315	29	3	39	120	0	7	3	103	17	77	2	1	14	.558	.397
Palmer, Dean, Det.	.256	145	604	524	73	134	247	22	2	29	102	0	10	4	66	2	146	4	2	9	.471	.338
Paniagua, Jose, Sea.	.000	69	1	1	0	0	0	0	0	0	0	0	0	0	0	0	1	0	0	0	.000	.000
Parque, Jim, Chi.*	.000	33	4	3	0	0	0	0	0	0	0	1	0	0	0	0	3	0	0	0	.000	.000
Paul, Josh, Chi.	.282	36	79	71	15	20	30	3	2	1	8	2	0	1	5	0	17	1	0	3	.423	.338
Perisho, Matt, Tex.*	.000	34	4	4	0	0	0	0	0	0	0	0	0	0	0	0	4	0	0	0	.000	.000
Perry, Chan, Cle.	.071	13	14	14	1	1	1	0	0	0	0	0	0	0	0	0	5	0	0	1	.071	.071
Perry, Herbert, T.B.-Chi.	.302	116	450	411	71	124	192	30	1	12	62	2	4	9	24	1	75	4	1	13	.467	.350
Pettitte, Andy, N.Y.*	.000	32	5	5	0	0	0	0	0	0	0	0	0	0	0	0	2	0	0	0	.000	.000
Phelps, Josh, Tor.	.000	1	1	1	0	0	0	0	0	0	0	0	0	0	0	0	1	0	0	0	.000	.000
Piatt, Adam, Oak.	.299	60	182	157	24	47	77	5	5	5	23	1	0	1	23	0	44	0	1	1	.490	.392
Pichardo, Hipolito, Bos.	.000	38	1	1	0	0	0	0	0	0	0	0	0	0	0	0	0	0	0	0	.000	.000
Pierzynski, A.J., Min.*	.307	33	96	88	12	27	40	5	1	2	11	0	1	2	5	0	14	1	0	1	.455	.354
Polonia, Luis, Det.-N.Y.*	.276	117	383	344	48	95	140	14	5	7	30	3	6	1	29	1	32	12	7	4	.407	.329
Ponson, Sidney, Bal.	.000	32	3	1	0	0	0	0	0	0	0	2	0	0	0	0	1	0	0	0	.000	.000
Porter, Bo, Oak.	.154	17	15	13	3	2	5	0	0	1	2	0	0	0	2	0	5	0	0	0	.385	.267
Posada, Jorge, N.Y.†	.287	151	624	505	92	145	266	35	1	28	86	0	4	8	107	10	151	2	2	11	.527	.417
Pose, Scott, K.C.*	.188	47	54	48	6	9	9	0	0	1	0	1	0	0	6	0	13	0	1	1	.188	.278
Pride, Curtis, Bos.*	.250	9	21	20	4	5	6	1	0	0	0	0	0	0	1	0	7	0	0	0	.300	.286
Prieto, Ariel, Oak.	.000	8	2	2	0	0	0	0	0	0	0	0	0	0	0	0	1	0	0	0	.000	.000
Quantrill, Paul, Tor.*	.000	68	1	0	0	0	0	0	0	0	0	0	0	0	1	0	0	0	0	0	.000	1.000
Quinn, Mark, K.C.	.294	135	544	500	76	147	244	33	2	20	78	3	3	3	35	1	91	5	2	11	.488	.342
Radke, Brad, Min.	.000	34	2	2	0	0	0	0	0	0	0	0	0	0	0	0	2	0	0	0	.000	.000
Ramirez, Alex, Cle.	.286	41	117	112	13	32	54	5	1	5	12	0	0	0	5	0	17	1	0	3	.482	.316
Ramirez, Manny, Cle.	.351	118	532	439	92	154	306	34	2	38	122	0	4	3	86	9	117	1	1	9	.697	.457
Randa, Joe, K.C.	.304	158	665	612	88	186	268	29	4	15	106	1	10	6	36	3	66	6	3	19	.438	.343
Rapp, Pat, Bal.	.000	31	3	3	0	0	0	0	0	0	0	0	0	0	0	0	0	0	0	0	.000	.000
Reboulet, Jeff, K.C.	.242	66	212	182	29	44	51	7	0	0	14	6	1	0	23	0	32	3	1	8	.280	.325
Redman, Mark, Min.*	.000	32	5	4	0	0	0	0	0	0	0	1	0	0	0	0	3	0	0	0	.000	.000
Reichert, Dan, K.C.	.000	44	1	1	0	0	0	0	0	0	0	0	0	0	0	0	0	0	0	0	.000	.000
Rekar, Bryan, T.B.	.333	30	3	3	0	1	2	1	0	0	1	0	0	0	0	0	1	0	0	0	.667	.333
Richard, Chris, Bal.*	.276	56	221	199	38	55	112	14	2	13	36	0	3	4	15	3	38	7	5	5	.563	.335
Ripken, Cal, Bal.	.256	83	339	309	43	79	140	16	0	15	56	0	4	3	23	0	37	0	0	10	.453	.310
Rivas, Luis, Min.	.310	16	64	58	8	18	24	4	1	0	6	2	2	0	2	0	4	2	0	2	.414	.323
Roberts, Dave, Cle.*	.200	19	13	10	1	2	2	0	0	0	1	1	0	0	2	0	2	1	1	0	.200	.333
Rodriguez, Alex, Sea.	.316	148	672	554	134	175	336	34	2	41	132	0	11	7	100	5	121	15	4	10	.606	.420
Rodriguez, Frankie, Sea.	.000	23	1	1	0	0	0	0	0	0	0	0	0	0	0	0	1	0	0	0	.000	.000
Rodriguez, Ivan, Tex.	.347	91	389	363	66	126	242	27	4	27	83	0	6	1	19	5	48	5	5	17	.667	.375
Rogers, Kenny, Tex.*	.500	34	5	4	0	2	2	0	0	0	0	0	0	0	1	0	1	0	0	0	.500	.500
Rolls, Damian, T.B.	.333	4	3	3	0	1	1	0	0	0	0	0	0	0	0	0	0	0	0	0	.333	.333
Rose, Brian, Min.	.000	15	4	3	0	0	0	0	0	0	0	0	0	0	1	0	1	0	0	0	.000	.250
Rupe, Ryan, T.B.	.000	18	1	1	0	0	0	0	0	0	0	0	0	0	0	0	0	0	0	0	.000	.000
Sadler, Donnie, Bos.	.222	49	112	99	14	22	30	5	0	1	10	5	2	1	5	0	18	3	1	1	.303	.262
Saenz, Olmedo, Oak.	.313	76	247	214	40	67	110	12	2	9	33	0	1	7	25	2	40	1	0	6	.514	.401
Salmon, Tim, Ana.	.290	158	680	568	108	165	307	36	2	34	97	0	2	6	104	5	139	0	2	14	.540	.404
Sanchez, Rey, K.C.	.273	143	555	509	68	139	164	18	2	1	38	11	3	4	28	0	55	7	3	17	.322	.314
Sanders, Anthony, Sea.	1.000	1	1	1	1	1	1	0	0	0	0	0	0	0	0	0	0	0	0	0	1.000	1.000
Santana, Johan, Min.*	.000	30	1	1	0	0	0	0	0	0	0	0	0	0	0	0	0	0	0	0	.000	.000
Schoeneweis, Scott, Ana.*	.333	27	3	3	0	1	1	0	0	0	1	0	0	0	0	0	1	0	0	0	.333	.333
Schourek, Pete, Bos.*	.500	22	4	4	0	2	2	0	0	0	0	0	0	0	0	0	1	0	0	0	.500	.500
Segui, David, Tex.-Cle.†	.334	150	634	574	93	192	293	42	1	19	103	0	6	1	53	2	84	0	1	20	.510	.388
Selby, Bill, Cle.*	.239	30	48	46	8	11	12	1	0	0	4	0	1	1	1	0	9	0	0	1	.261	.271
Sele, Aaron, Sea.	.000	34	4	3	0	0	0	0	0	0	0	1	0	0	0	0	0	0	0	0	.000	.000
Sexson, Richie, Cle.	.256	91	356	324	45	83	149	16	1	16	44	0	3	4	25	0	96	1	0	8	.460	.315
Sheets, Andy, Bos.	.095	12	21	21	1	2	2	0	0	0	1	0	0	0	0	0	3	0	0	1	.095	.095
Sheldon, Scott, Tex.	.282	58	138	124	21	35	58	11	0	4	19	1	2	1	10	0	37	0	0	2	.468	.336
Sierra, Ruben, Tex.†	.233	20	64	60	5	14	17	0	0	1	7	0	0	0	4	0	9	1	0	1	.283	.281
Singleton, Chris, Chi.*	.254	147	563	511	83	130	195	22	5	11	62	12	4	1	35	2	85	22	7	6	.382	.301
Sirotka, Mike, Chi.*	.000	32	5	4	0	0	0	0	0	0	0	1	0	0	1	0	2	0	0	0	.000	.200
Smith, Bobby, T.B.	.234	49	191	175	21	41	67	8	0	6	26	0	1	1	14	1	59	2	2	6	.383	.293
Sojo, Luis, N.Y.	.288	34	134	125	19	36	51	7	1	2	17	3	0	0	6	0	6	1	0	5	.408	.321
Soriano, Alfonso, N.Y.	.180	22	53	50	5	9	18	3	0	2	3	2	0	1	0	0	15	2	0	0	.360	.196
Speier, Justin, Cle.	.500	47	2	2	0	1	1	0	0	0	0	0	0	0	0	0	1	0	0	0	.500	.500
Spencer, Shane, N.Y.	.282	73	276	248	33	70	114	11	3	9	40	0	7	2	19	0	45	1	2	4	.460	.330
Spiezio, Scott, Ana.†	.242	123	345	297	47	72	138	11	2	17	49	1	4	3	40	2	56	1	2	5	.465	.334
Sprague, Ed Jr., Bos.	.216	33	123	111	11	24	34	4	0	2	9	0	0	0	12	0	18	0	0	2	.306	.293
Stairs, Matt, Oak.*	.227	143	562	476	74	108	197	26	0	21	81	1	6	1	78	4	122	5	2	7	.414	.333
Stanley, Mike, Bos.-Oak.	.238	90	331	282	33	67	121	12	0	14	46	1	3	1	44	0	65	0	0	4	.429	.339

Player, Team	Avg.	G	TPA	AB	R	H	TB	2B	3B	HR	RBI	SH	SF	HP	BB	IBB	SO	SB	CS	GDP	Slg.	OBP
Stanton, Mike, N.Y.*	1.000	69	1	1	1	1	1	0	0	0	0	0	0	0	0	0	0	0	0	0	1.000	1.000
Stein, Blake, K.C.	.000	17	2	2	0	0	0	0	0	0	0	0	0	0	0	0	2	0	0	0	.000	.000
Stewart, Shannon, Tor.	.319	136	631	583	107	186	302	43	5	21	69	1	4	6	37	1	79	20	5	12	.518	.363
Stocker, Kevin, T.B.-Ana.†	.219	110	409	343	41	75	109	20	4	2	24	10	1	4	51	0	81	1	5	11	.318	.326
Suppan, Jeff, K.C.	.000	35	3	3	0	0	0	0	0	0	0	0	0	0	0	0	0	0	0	0	.000	.000
Surhoff, B.J., Bal.*	.292	103	444	411	56	120	186	27	0	13	57	1	1	2	29	3	46	7	2	5	.453	.341
Suzuki, Mac, K.C.	.200	32	6	5	1	1	1	0	0	0	0	1	0	0	0	0	2	0	0	0	.200	.200
Sweeney, Mike, K.C.	.333	159	717	618	105	206	323	30	0	29	144	0	13	15	71	5	67	8	3	15	.523	.407
Tejada, Miguel, Oak.	.275	160	681	607	105	167	291	32	1	30	115	2	2	4	66	6	102	6	0	15	.479	.349
Thomas, Frank, Chi.	.328	159	707	582	115	191	364	44	0	43	143	0	8	5	112	18	94	1	3	13	.625	.436
Thome, Jim, Cle.*	.269	158	684	557	106	150	296	33	1	37	106	0	5	4	118	4	171	1	0	8	.531	.398
Thompson, Andy, Tor.	.167	2	9	6	2	1	1	0	0	0	1	0	0	0	3	0	2	0	0	0	.167	.444
Thompson, Ryan, N.Y.	.260	33	56	50	12	13	25	3	0	3	14	0	1	0	5	0	12	0	1	0	.500	.339
Timmons, Ozzie, T.B.	.341	12	42	41	9	14	29	3	0	4	13	0	0	0	1	0	7	0	0	2	.707	.357
Trachsel, Steve, T.B.-Tor.	.250	34	5	4	0	1	1	0	0	0	0	0	0	0	1	0	1	0	0	0	.250	.400
Trammell, Bubba, T.B.	.275	66	213	189	19	52	88	11	2	7	33	0	1	2	21	0	30	3	0	5	.466	.352
Trombley, Mike, Bal.	.000	75	1	1	0	0	0	0	0	0	0	0	0	0	0	0	1	0	0	0	.000	.000
Turner, Chris, N.Y.	.236	37	102	89	9	21	27	3	0	1	7	2	0	1	10	0	21	0	1	2	.303	.320
Tyner, Jason, T.B.*	.241	37	94	83	6	20	22	2	0	0	8	5	1	1	4	0	12	6	1	1	.265	.281
Valdes, Pedro, Tex.*	.278	30	60	54	4	15	23	5	0	1	5	0	0	0	6	0	7	0	0	0	.426	.350
Valdez, Mario, Oak.*	.000	5	12	12	0	0	0	0	0	0	0	0	0	0	0	0	3	0	0	0	.000	.000
Valentin, John, Bos.	.257	10	38	35	6	9	16	1	0	2	2	1	0	0	2	0	5	0	1	1	.457	.297
Valentin, Jose, Chi.†	.273	144	648	568	107	155	279	37	6	25	92	13	4	4	59	1	106	19	2	11	.491	.343
Varitek, Jason, Bos.†	.248	139	519	448	55	111	174	31	1	10	65	1	4	6	60	3	84	1	1	16	.388	.342
Vaughn, Greg, T.B.	.254	127	545	461	83	117	230	27	1	28	74	0	2	2	80	3	128	8	1	10	.499	.365
Vaughn, Mo, Ana.*	.272	161	712	614	93	167	306	31	0	36	117	0	5	14	79	11	181	2	0	14	.498	.365
Velandia, Jorge, Oak.	.125	18	25	24	1	3	4	1	0	0	2	0	0	1	0	0	6	0	0	0	.167	.160
Velarde, Randy, Oak.	.278	122	546	485	82	135	194	23	0	12	41	3	1	3	54	0	95	9	3	15	.400	.354
Veras, Wilton, Bos.	.244	49	179	164	21	40	49	7	1	0	14	3	3	2	7	0	20	0	0	2	.299	.278
Vizcaino, Jose, N.Y.†	.276	73	191	174	23	48	58	8	1	0	10	3	2	0	12	0	28	5	7	3	.333	.319
Vizquel, Omar, Cle.†	.287	156	717	613	101	176	230	27	3	7	66	7	5	5	87	0	72	22	10	13	.375	.377
Wakefield, Tim, Bos.	.000	52	3	2	0	0	0	0	0	0	0	0	0	0	0	0	2	0	0	0	.000	.000
Walbeck, Matt, Ana.†	.199	47	155	146	17	29	52	5	0	6	12	1	0	1	7	0	22	0	1	2	.356	.240
Walker, Todd, Min.*	.234	23	87	77	14	18	25	1	0	2	8	3	0	7	0	10	3	0	3	.325	.287
Washburn, Jarrod, Ana.*	.333	14	6	3	0	1	1	0	0	0	2	2	0	1	0	0	0	0	0	.333	.500
Waszgis, B.J., Tex.	.222	24	51	45	6	10	11	1	0	0	4	0	1	1	4	0	10	0	0	1	.244	.294
Weaver, Jeff, Det.	.000	31	3	3	0	0	0	0	0	0	0	0	0	0	0	0	0	0	0	0	.000	.000
Wells, David, Tor.*	.167	35	6	6	0	1	1	0	0	0	0	0	0	0	0	0	2	0	0	0	.167	.167
Wells, Kip, Chi.	.000	20	2	2	0	0	0	0	0	0	0	0	0	0	0	0	0	0	0	0	.000	.000
Wells, Vernon, Tor.	.000	3	2	2	0	0	0	0	0	0	0	0	0	0	0	0	0	0	0	0	.000	.000
Whiten, Mark, Cle.†	.286	6	10	7	2	2	3	1	0	0	1	0	0	0	3	0	2	0	0	0	.429	.500
Widger, Chris, Sea.	.091	10	12	11	1	1	4	0	0	1	1	0	0	0	1	0	2	0	0	0	.364	.167
Williams, Bernie, N.Y.†	.307	141	616	537	108	165	304	37	6	30	121	0	3	5	71	11	84	13	5	15	.566	.391
Williams, Gerald, T.B.	.274	146	682	632	87	173	270	30	2	21	89	9	4	3	34	0	103	12	12	6	.427	.312
Wilson, Craig, Chi.	.260	28	83	73	12	19	22	3	0	0	4	4	0	1	5	0	11	1	0	5	.301	.316
Wilson, Dan, Sea.	.235	90	303	268	31	63	90	12	0	5	27	11	2	0	22	0	51	1	2	8	.336	.291
Wilson, Enrique, Cle.†	.325	40	127	117	16	38	53	9	0	2	12	2	1	0	7	0	11	2	1	2	.453	.360
Winn, Randy, T.B.†	.252	51	190	159	28	40	48	5	0	1	16	2	1	2	26	0	25	6	7	2	.302	.362
Wise, Dewayne, Tor.*	.136	28	24	22	3	3	3	0	0	0	0	0	0	1	1	0	5	1	0	0	.136	.208
Witasick, Jay, K.C.	.000	22	4	4	0	0	0	0	0	0	0	0	0	0	0	0	2	0	0	0	.000	.000
Woodward, Chris, Tor.	.183	37	115	104	16	19	35	7	0	3	14	1	0	0	10	3	28	1	0	1	.337	.254
Wooten, Shawn, Ana.	.556	7	9	9	2	5	6	1	0	0	1	0	0	0	0	0	0	0	0	0	.667	.556
Wright, Jaret, Cle.	.000	9	2	1	0	0	0	0	0	0	0	0	0	0	0	0	1	0	0	0	.000	.000
Yan, Esteban, T.B.	1.000	43	2	1	1	1	4	0	0	1	1	1	0	0	0	0	0	0	0	0	4.000	1.000
Young, Mike B., Tex.	.000	2	2	2	0	0	0	0	0	0	0	0	0	0	0	0	0	0	0	0	.000	.000
Zaun, Gregg, K.C.†	.274	83	282	234	36	64	96	11	0	7	33	0	2	3	43	3	34	7	3	4	.410	.390

AWARDED FIRST BASE ON OBSTRUCTION OR CATCHER'S INTERFERENCE—Singleton, Chicago 3 (Girardi, Molina, DiFelice); Jones, Minnesota 2 (Ausmus 2); Abbott, Chicago (Hernandez); Alicea, Texas (Erickson); Conine, Baltimore (Varitek); Higginson, Detroit (LeCroy); Justice, Cle.-N.Y. (DiFelice); Magee, Detroit (LeCroy); McMillon, Detroit (Fordyce).

PLAYERS WITH TWO OR MORE TEAMS

Player, Team	Avg.	G	TPA	AB	R	H	TB	2B	3B	HR	RBI	SH	SF	HP	BB	IBB	SO	SB	CS	GDP	Slg.	OBP
Baines, Harold, Bal.*	.266	72	252	222	24	59	97	8	0	10	30	0	1	0	29	6	39	0	0	6	.437	.349
Baines, Harold, Chi.*	.213	24	68	61	2	13	21	5	0	1	9	0	0	0	7	1	11	0	0	0	.344	.294
Becker, Rich, Oak.*	.234	23	59	47	11	11	16	2	0	1	5	0	0	1	11	0	17	1	0	1	.340	.390
Becker, Rich, Det.*	.244	92	298	238	48	58	91	12	0	7	34	0	4	0	56	0	70	1	2	0	.382	.383
Canseco, Jose, T.B.	.257	61	264	218	31	56	98	15	0	9	30	0	1	4	41	1	65	2	0	5	.450	.383
Canseco, Jose, N.Y.	.243	37	137	111	16	27	48	3	0	6	19	0	3	0	23	1	37	0	0	2	.432	.365
Cummings, Midre, Min.*	.276	77	196	181	28	50	72	10	0	4	22	1	0	3	11	1	25	0	0	4	.398	.328
Cummings, Midre, Bos.*	.280	21	31	25	1	7	7	0	0	0	2	0	0	0	6	0	3	0	0	1	.280	.419
Delgado, Wilson, N.Y.†	.244	31	51	45	6	11	15	1	0	1	4	0	1	0	5	0	9	1	1	1	.333	.314
Delgado, Wilson, K.C.†	.265	33	90	83	15	22	23	1	0	0	7	0	1	0	6	0	17	1	1	1	.277	.311
Fordyce, Brook, Chi.	.272	40	136	125	18	34	58	7	1	5	21	2	1	2	6	0	23	0	0	1	.464	.313
Fordyce, Brook, Bal.	.322	53	194	177	23	57	95	11	0	9	28	0	4	2	11	0	27	0	0	3	.537	.361
Garcia, Karim, Det.*	.176	8	17	17	1	3	3	0	0	0	0	0	0	0	0	0	4	0	0	1	.176	.176
Garcia, Karim, Bal.*	.000	8	16	16	0	0	0	0	0	0	0	0	0	0	0	0	6	0	0	0	.000	.000
Graffanino, Tony, T.B.	.300	13	22	20	8	6	7	1	0	0	1	0	1	1	0	0	2	0	1	1	.350	.364
Graffanino, Tony, Chi.	.270	57	172	148	25	40	53	5	1	2	16	1	1	1	21	0	25	7	4	1	.358	.363
Johnson, Charles, Bal.	.294	84	320	286	52	84	163	16	0	21	55	1	1	0	32	0	69	2	0	8	.570	.364
Johnson, Charles, Chi.	.326	44	158	135	24	44	82	8	0	10	36	0	2	1	20	0	37	0	0	0	.607	.411

Player, Team	Avg.	G	TPA	AB	R	H	TB	2B	3B	HR	RBI	SH	SF	HP	BB	IBB	SO	SB	CS	GDP	Slg.	OBP
Justice, David, Cle.*	.265	68	288	249	46	66	145	14	1	21	58	0	1	0	38	2	49	1	1	7	.582	.361
Justice, David, N.Y.*	.305	78	317	275	43	84	161	17	0	20	60	0	2	1	39	1	42	1	0	6	.585	.391
Ledee, Ricky, N.Y.*	.241	62	220	191	23	46	80	11	1	7	31	0	2	1	26	2	39	7	3	7	.419	.332
Ledee, Ricky, Cle.*	.222	17	71	63	13	14	24	2	1	2	8	0	0	0	8	0	9	0	0	3	.381	.310
Ledee, Ricky, Tex.*	.235	58	240	213	23	50	74	6	3	4	38	0	1	1	25	2	50	6	3	7	.347	.317
Martinez, Dave, T.B.*	.260	29	117	104	12	27	38	4	2	1	12	1	2	0	10	1	17	1	4	1	.365	.319
Martinez, Dave, Tex.*	.269	38	134	119	14	32	44	4	1	2	12	0	0	1	14	2	20	2	1	8	.370	.351
Martinez, Dave, Tor.*	.311	47	206	180	29	56	74	10	1	2	22	0	1	1	24	0	28	4	2	3	.411	.393
Perry, Herbert, T.B.	.214	7	30	28	2	6	7	1	0	0	1	0	0	0	2	0	7	0	0	0	.250	.267
Perry, Herbert, Chi.	.308	109	420	383	69	118	185	29	1	12	61	2	4	9	22	1	68	4	1	13	.483	.356
Polonia, Luis, Det.*	.273	80	298	267	37	73	111	10	5	6	25	3	5	1	22	1	25	8	5	2	.416	.325
Polonia, Luis, N.Y.*	.286	37	85	77	11	22	29	4	0	1	5	0	1	0	7	0	7	4	2	2	.377	.341
Segui, David, Tex.†	.336	93	389	351	52	118	182	29	1	11	57	0	4	0	34	1	51	0	1	12	.519	.391
Segui, David, Cle.†	.332	57	245	223	41	74	111	13	0	8	46	0	2	1	19	1	33	0	0	8	.498	.384
Stanley, Mike, Bos.	.222	58	218	185	22	41	76	5	0	10	28	1	2	0	30	0	44	0	0	1	.411	.327
Stanley, Mike, Oak.	.268	32	113	97	11	26	45	7	0	4	18	0	1	1	14	0	21	0	0	3	.464	.363
Stocker, Kevin, T.B.†	.263	40	137	114	20	30	45	7	1	2	8	2	0	2	19	0	27	1	2	3	.395	.378
Stocker, Kevin, Ana.†	.197	70	272	229	21	45	64	13	3	0	16	8	1	2	32	0	54	0	3	8	.279	.299

DESIGNATED HITTING

TEAM

Team	Avg.	G	TPA	AB	R	H	TB	2B	3B	HR	RBI	SH	SF	HP	BB	IBB	SO	SB	CS	GDP	Slg.	OBP
Seattle	.324	153	690	577	110	187	333	32	0	38	149	0	7	5	101	8	101	5	1	13	.577	.425
Chicago	.296	153	695	581	99	172	311	43	0	32	117	0	6	4	104	16	101	1	2	12	.535	.403
Detroit	.293	153	683	598	89	175	267	34	5	16	91	2	10	1	72	4	87	10	5	12	.446	.364
Texas	.288	153	681	607	92	175	275	33	2	21	88	2	5	3	64	5	86	4	1	13	.453	.356
Toronto	.285	153	656	606	92	173	325	33	1	39	120	0	6	6	38	3	93	3	2	18	.536	.331
Kansas City	.283	153	677	600	91	170	262	35	0	19	101	3	10	6	58	1	93	12	3	15	.437	.347
Anaheim	.275	153	674	579	93	159	264	27	0	26	81	1	1	7	86	3	96	8	5	11	.456	.374
New York	.274	152	652	588	88	153	248	23	3	22	71	1	8	6	79	1	132	10	5	10	.444	.366
Minnesota	.269	153	663	588	79	158	232	35	0	13	85	1	11	5	58	2	116	3	3	23	.395	.334
Cleveland	.266	153	675	579	103	154	313	30	0	43	117	1	2	5	88	4	153	0	1	11	.541	.366
Baltimore	.261	153	655	586	71	153	231	32	2	14	72	0	3	3	63	12	101	6	3	15	.394	.334
Tampa Bay	.260	152	663	565	86	147	258	36	0	25	89	1	3	5	89	4	145	4	2	9	.457	.364
Boston	.242	153	671	591	72	143	260	28	1	29	94	2	8	6	64	3	151	0	1	11	.440	.318
Oakland	.242	152	682	563	95	136	213	23	3	16	67	3	3	10	103	3	153	5	2	12	.378	.367
Totals	.276	2454	9417	8178	1260	2255	3792	444	17	353	1342	17	83	72	1067	69	1608	71	36	185	.464	.361

TOP DESIGNATED HITTERS

Minimum 100 at-bats. *Lefthanded batter. †Switch-hitter.

Player, Team	Avg.	G	TPA	AB	R	H	TB	2B	3B	HR	RBI	SH	SF	HP	BB	IBB	SO	SB	CS	GDP	Slg.	OBP
Segui, David, Tex.-Cle.†	.331	68	288	263	38	87	133	19	0	9	39	0	2	0	23	0	40	0	1	11	.506	.382
Damon, Johnny, K.C.*	.330	25	116	106	20	35	46	11	0	0	10	1	2	0	7	0	15	8	2	2	.434	.365
Martinez, Edgar, Sea.	.323	146	652	545	100	176	317	30	0	37	143	0	7	5	95	8	94	3	0	13	.582	.423
Thomas, Frank, Chi.	.321	127	573	467	88	150	274	34	0	30	102	0	6	3	97	15	81	1	2	8	.587	.436
Gonzalez, Juan, Det.	.305	48	216	200	26	61	91	13	1	5	26	0	1	0	15	2	37	1	1	5	.455	.352
Belle, Albert, Bal.	.303	31	135	122	11	37	48	8	0	1	12	0	1	0	12	5	19	0	1	2	.393	.363
Ortiz, David, Min.*	.303	88	354	310	50	94	148	27	0	9	50	0	6	0	38	1	62	1	0	13	.477	.373
Sweeney, Mike, K.C.	.301	45	209	183	37	55	93	11	0	9	41	0	2	6	18	0	25	3	0	4	.508	.378
Fullmer, Brad, Tor.*	.295	129	520	478	75	141	268	29	1	32	104	0	6		30	3	68	3	1	14	.561	.340
Justice, David, Cle.-N.Y.*	.291	38	163	141	22	41	82	11	0	10	32	0	0	0	22	1	24	0	0	6	.582	.387
Polonia, Luis, Det.-N.Y.*	.290	51	210	193	25	56	81	8	4	3	19	1	4	0	12	0	17	8	3	3	.420	.325
Bichette, Dante, Bos.	.289	30	122	114	13	33	59	5	0	7	14	0	0	0	8	0	22	0	0	3	.518	.336
Salmon, Tim, Ana.	.287	33	145	115	23	33	55	7	0	5	15	0	0	2	28	0	18	0	0	3	.478	.434
Palmeiro, Rafael, Tex.*	.266	46	203	173	28	46	85	8	2	9	34	0	2	1	27	5	20	0	0	3	.491	.365
Canseco, Jose, T.B.-N.Y.	.258	86	374	306	46	79	139	18	0	14	46	0	4	4	60	2	93	2	0	6	.454	.382

ALL DESIGNATED HITTERS

*Lefthanded batter. †Switch-hitter.

Player, Team	Avg.	G	TPA	AB	R	H	TB	2B	3B	HR	RBI	SH	SF	HP	BB	IBB	SO	SB	CS	GDP	Slg.	OBP
Abbott, Jeff, Chi.	.286	7	14	14	2	4	6	2	0	0	2	0	0	0	0	0	3	0	0	0	.429	.286
Alcantara, Israel, Bos.	.217	8	23	23	5	5	12	1	0	2	5	0	0	0	0	0	5	0	0	0	.522	.217
Alexander, Manny, Bos.	.000	3	4	4	2	0	0	0	0	0	0	0	0	0	0	0	2	0	0	0	.000	.000
Alicea, Luis, Tex.†	.231	4	17	13	1	3	3	0	0	0	2	0	0	0	4	0	1	0	0	1	.231	.412
Alomar, Sandy Jr., Cle.	.000	1	1	1	0	0	0	0	0	0	0	0	0	0	0	0	0	0	0	0	.000	.000
Alvarez, Gabe, Det.	.000	1	3	1	0	0	0	0	0	0	0	0	0	0	2	0	1	0	1	0	.000	.667
Amaral, Rich, Bal.	.000	5	2	1	1	0	0	0	0	0	0	0	0	0	1	0	1	1	1	0	.000	.500
Anderson, Brady, Bal.*	.207	11	37	29	6	6	10	4	0	0	2	0	0	0	8	1	6	1	0	0	.345	.378
Anderson, Garret, Ana.*	.300	10	41	40	4	12	20	2	0	2	10	0	0	0	1	0	5	0	0	1	.500	.317
Baines, Harold, Bal.-Chi.*	.256	78	303	270	26	69	115	13	0	11	39	0	1	0	32	6	43	0	0	6	.426	.333
Baughman, Justin, Ana.	.000	4	2	2	1	0	0	0	0	0	0	0	0	0	0	0	0	1	0	0	.000	.000
Becker, Rich, Oak.-Det.*	.429	6	9	7	3	3	4	1	0	0	0	0	0	0	2	0	1	0	0	0	.571	.556
Bell, David, Sea.	.000	1	0	0	0	0	0	0	0	0	0	0	0	0	0	0	0	0	0	0	.000	.000
Belle, Albert, Bal.	.303	31	135	122	11	37	48	8	0	1	12	0	1	0	12	5	19	0	1	2	.393	.363
Beltran, Carlos, K.C.†	.273	7	29	22	0	6	6	0	0	0	6	0	2	0	5	0	3	0	0	2	.273	.379
Bichette, Dante, Bos.	.289	30	122	114	13	33	59	5	0	7	14	0	0	0	8	0	22	0	0	3	.518	.336
Blake, Casey, Min.	.000	1	3	1	1	0	0	0	0	0	0	1	0	1	0	0	0	0	0	0	.000	.333
Branyan, Russell, Cle.*	.244	23	90	78	17	19	52	3	0	10	20	0	0	3	9	0	32	0	0	0	.667	.344
Brogna, Rico, Bos.*	.000	2	1	1	0	0	0	0	0	0	0	0	0	0	0	0	0	0	0	0	.000	.000
Brosius, Scott, N.Y.	.000	1	1	1	0	0	0	0	0	0	1	0	0	0	0	0	0	0	0	0	.000	.000
Buchanan, Brian, Min.	.000	2	1	0	0	0	0	0	0	0	0	1	0	0	0	0	1	0	0	0	.000	.000
Buhner, Jay, Sea.	.500	1	4	2	0	1	1	0	0	0	1	0	0	0	2	0	0	0	0	0	.500	.750
Burkhart, Morgan, Bos.†	.274	19	79	62	11	17	31	2	0	4	16	0	1	4	12	1	22	0	0	1	.500	.418
Byrnes, Eric, Oak.	.500	2	5	4	3	2	2	0	0	0	0	0	0	0	1	0	0	2	0	0	.500	.600
Cabrera, Jolbert, Cle.	.000	2	1	1	1	0	0	0	0	0	0	0	0	0	0	0	0	0	0	0	.000	.000
Cairo, Miguel, T.B.	.200	2	5	5	0	1	1	0	0	0	1	0	0	0	0	0	1	0	0	0	.200	.200
Canizaro, Jay, Min.	.250	2	4	4	0	1	1	0	0	0	0	0	0	0	0	0	1	0	0	0	.250	.250
Canseco, Jose, T.B.-N.Y.	.258	86	374	306	46	79	139	18	0	14	46	0	4	4	60	2	93	2	0	6	.454	.382
Casimiro, Carlos, Bal.	.125	2	8	8	0	1	2	1	0	0	3	0	0	0	0	0	2	0	0	0	.250	.125
Catalanotto, Frank, Tex.*	.307	20	85	75	18	23	37	5	0	3	11	1	1	1	7	0	9	1	0	1	.493	.369
Chavez, Eric, Oak.*	.000	1	0	0	0	0	0	0	0	0	0	0	0	0	0	0	0	0	0	0	.000	.000
Clark, Tony, Det.†	.000	1	4	4	1	0	0	0	0	0	0	0	0	0	0	0	0	0	0	0	.000	.000
Clark, Will, Bal.*	.278	6	24	18	4	5	7	2	0	0	3	0	1	0	5	0	5	0	0	0	.389	.417
Clemente, Edgard, Ana.	.143	11	21	21	0	3	3	0	0	0	1	0	0	0	0	0	9	0	0	0	.143	.143

Player, Team	Avg.	G	TPA	AB	R	H	TB	2B	3B	HR	RBI	SH	SF	HP	BB	IBB	SO	SB	CS	GDP	Slg.	OBP
Coffie, Ivanon, Bal.*	.000	1	1	1	0	0	0	0	0	0	0	0	0	0	0	0	0	0	0	0	.000	.000
Conine, Jeff, Bal.	.214	20	62	56	5	12	19	2	1	1	5	0	0	1	5	1	9	0	0	3	.339	.290
Coomer, Ron, Min.	.308	9	41	39	6	12	15	0	0	1	5	0	0	1	1	0	2	0	0	3	.385	.341
Cordova, Marty, Tor.	.292	15	51	48	5	14	20	3	0	1	6	0	0	0	3	0	6	0	1	0	.417	.333
Cox, Steve, T.B.*	.365	17	66	63	9	23	33	4	0	2	7	0	0	0	3	0	10	0	1	0	.524	.394
Crede, Joe, Chi.	.000	1	0	0	1	0	0	0	0	0	0	0	0	0	0	0	0	0	0	0	.000	.000
Cruz, Jacob, Cle.*	.500	2	5	4	1	2	3	1	0	0	0	0	0	0	1	0	1	0	0	0	.750	.600
Cummings, Midre, Min.-Bos.*	.318	16	48	44	5	14	19	2	0	1	6	1	0	2	1	0	7	0	0	4	.432	.362
Curtis, Chad, Tex.	.357	16	59	56	6	20	28	5	0	1	7	1	0	1	1	0	12	0	0	0	.500	.379
Damon, Johnny, K.C.*	.330	25	116	106	20	35	46	11	0	0	10	1	2	0	7	0	15	8	2	2	.434	.365
Daubach, Brian, Bos.*	.220	41	164	150	13	33	63	7	1	7	22	0	3	0	11	1	49	0	0	1	.420	.268
DeShields, Delino, Bal.*	.349	10	44	43	7	15	20	3	1	0	6	0	0	0	1	0	7	1	0	1	.465	.364
Dunwoody, Todd, K.C.*	.256	11	45	39	3	10	13	3	0	0	7	0	2	0	4	0	7	1	0	2	.333	.311
Dye, Jermaine, K.C.	.325	10	45	40	4	13	21	2	0	2	8	0	0	0	5	0	6	0	0	0	.525	.400
Erstad, Darin, Ana.*	.407	20	97	91	19	37	56	4	0	5	18	0	0	0	6	1	8	5	2	3	.615	.443
Evans, Tom, Tex.	.000	1	0	0	1	0	0	0	0	0	0	0	0	0	0	0	0	0	0	0	.000	.000
Everett, Carl, Bos.†	.474	5	22	19	6	9	15	3	0	1	9	0	1	0	2	0	5	0	1	1	.789	.500
Fabregas, Jorge, K.C.*	1.000	1	1	1	0	1	1	0	0	0	0	0	0	0	0	0	0	0	0	0	1.000	1.000
Fick, Robert, Det.*	.263	12	43	38	4	10	14	1	0	1	5	0	1	0	4	1	6	0	0	1	.368	.326
Fletcher, Darrin, Tor.*	.333	2	6	6	2	2	5	0	0	1	1	0	0	0	0	0	1	0	0	0	.833	.333
Frye, Jeff, Bos.	.333	3	5	3	1	1	1	0	0	0	0	0	0	1	1	0	0	0	0	0	.333	.600
Fryman, Travis, Cle.	.000	1	4	4	0	0	0	0	0	0	0	0	0	0	0	0	2	0	0	0	.000	.000
Fullmer, Brad, Tor.*	.295	129	520	478	75	141	268	29	1	32	104	0	6	6	30	3	68	3	1	14	.561	.340
Gaetti, Gary, Bos.	.000	5	11	10	0	0	0	0	0	0	1	0	1	0	0	0	3	0	0	0	.000	.000
Gant, Ron, Ana.	.346	12	33	26	6	9	21	3	0	3	5	0	0	7	0	5	0	2	0	.808	.485
Garcia, Karim, Det.-Bal.*	.000	5	12	12	1	0	0	0	0	0	0	0	0	0	0	0	5	0	0	0	.000	.000
Garciaparra, Nomar, Bos.	.000	1	4	3	0	0	0	0	0	0	0	0	0	0	1	0	0	0	0	0	.000	.250
Giambi, Jason, Oak.*	.259	24	106	85	14	22	43	6	0	5	15	0	1	2	18	1	20	0	0	0	.506	.396
Giambi, Jeremy, Oak.*	.194	21	70	62	12	12	21	1	1	2	6	1	1	1	5	0	11	0	0	1	.339	.261
Gil, Benji, Ana.	.333	6	6	6	2	2	5	0	0	1	1	0	0	0	0	0	0	0	0	1	.833	.333
Gilkey, Bernard, Bos.	.200	8	28	25	1	5	8	3	0	0	2	0	0	1	2	0	1	0	0	0	.320	.286
Gipson, Charles, Sea.	.000	1	0	0	0	0	0	0	0	0	0	0	0	0	0	0	0	0	1	0	.000	.000
Glaus, Troy, Ana.	.444	4	12	9	5	4	7	0	0	1	1	0	0	0	3	0	2	1	0	0	.778	.583
Gonzalez, Juan, Det.	.305	48	216	200	26	61	91	13	1	5	26	0	1	0	15	2	37	1	1	5	.455	.352
Graffanino, Tony, T.B.-Chi.	.000	3	1	1	1	0	0	0	0	0	0	0	0	0	0	0	0	0	0	0	.000	.000
Green, Scarborough, Tex.†	.000	6	1	1	2	0	0	0	0	0	0	0	0	0	0	0	1	1	0	0	.000	.000
Greene, Todd, Tor.	.216	23	79	74	10	16	32	1	0	5	9	0	0	0	5	0	18	0	0	4	.432	.266
Greer, Rusty, Tex.*	.250	2	10	8	2	2	2	0	0	0	0	0	0	0	2	0	3	1	0	0	.250	.400
Grieve, Ben, Oak.*	.262	12	48	42	6	11	16	5	0	0	2	0	0	0	6	0	11	0	0	0	.381	.354
Guzman, Cristian, Min.†	.000	1	0	0	0	0	0	0	0	0	0	0	0	0	0	0	0	0	1	0	.000	.000
Hatteberg, Scott, Bos.*	.232	20	74	56	6	13	26	4	0	3	10	1	1	0	16	1	9	0	0	2	.464	.397
Henderson, Rickey, Sea.	.000	2	0	0	0	0	0	0	0	0	0	0	0	0	0	0	0	0	0	0	.000	.000
Higginson, Bobby, Det.*	.412	10	43	34	11	14	23	3	0	2	10	0	0	0	9	1	6	1	0	0	.676	.535
Hill, Glenallen, N.Y.	.314	24	95	86	14	27	58	4	0	9	14	0	1	1	7	0	24	0	0	0	.674	.368
Hinch, A.J., Oak.	.000	1	1	1	0	0	0	0	0	0	0	0	0	0	0	0	1	0	0	0	.000	.000
Hocking, Denny, Min.†	.333	2	3	3	0	1	1	0	0	0	2	0	0	0	0	0	1	0	0	0	.333	.333
Hubbard, Trenidad, Bal.	.000	6	2	2	3	0	0	0	0	0	0	0	0	0	0	0	1	2	1	0	.000	.000
Hudson, Tim, Oak.	.000	1	0	0	0	0	0	0	0	0	0	0	0	0	0	0	0	0	0	0	.000	.000
Huskey, Butch, Min.	.194	39	151	134	11	26	36	4	0	2	16	0	3	1	13	0	32	0	2	3	.269	.265
Ibanez, Raul, Sea.*	.000	4	1	1	0	0	0	0	0	0	0	0	0	0	0	0	0	0	0	0	.000	.000
Jaha, John, Oak.	.177	30	130	96	14	17	21	1	0	1	5	0	0	2	32	0	38	1	0	4	.219	.392
Javier, Stan, Sea.†	.333	4	14	12	2	4	5	1	0	0	0	0	0	0	2	0	1	1	0	0	.417	.429
Jefferies, Gregg, Det.†	.333	2	6	3	1	1	1	0	0	0	0	0	0	0	3	0	1	0	0	0	.333	.667
Jensen, Marcus, Min.†	.000	1	4	4	0	0	0	0	0	0	0	0	0	0	0	0	2	0	0	1	.000	.000
Johnson, Charles, Bal.-Chi.	.000	1	1	1	0	0	0	0	0	0	0	0	0	0	0	0	1	0	0	0	.000	.000
Johnson, Lance, N.Y.*	.400	3	10	10	2	4	5	1	0	0	1	0	0	0	0	0	2	2	0	1	.500	.400
Johnson, Mark T., Chi.*	.000	1	1	1	0	0	0	0	0	0	0	0	0	0	0	0	0	0	0	0	.000	.000
Jose, Felix, N.Y.†	1.000	2	2	2	0	2	2	0	0	0	0	0	0	0	0	0	0	0	1	0	1.000	1.000
Justice, David, Cle.-N.Y.*	.291	38	163	141	22	41	82	11	0	10	32	0	0	0	22	1	24	0	0	6	.582	.387
Kelly, Kenny, T.B.	.000	1	1	1	0	0	0	0	0	0	0	0	0	0	0	0	0	0	0	0	.000	.000
Kingsale, Eugene, Bal.†	.000	1	2	2	0	0	0	0	0	0	0	0	0	0	0	0	0	0	0	0	.000	.000
Kinkade, Mike, Bal.	.500	2	7	6	0	3	4	1	0	0	1	0	0	0	1	0	0	0	0	0	.667	.571
Knoblauch, Chuck, N.Y.	.333	20	92	72	24	24	27	3	0	0	6	0	1	4	15	0	11	5	1	2	.375	.467
Konerko, Paul, Chi.	.115	7	27	26	2	3	5	2	0	0	1	0	0	1	0	0	4	0	0	4	.192	.148
Koskie, Corey, Min.*	.250	1	4	4	0	1	1	0	0	0	1	0	0	0	0	0	1	0	0	0	.250	.250
Lamb, Mike, Tex.*	.222	2	9	9	2	2	5	0	0	1	1	0	0	0	0	0	1	0	0	0	.556	.222
Lampkin, Tom, Sea.*	.455	3	11	11	2	5	9	1	0	1	4	0	0	0	0	0	1	0	0	0	.818	.455
Lawton, Matt, Min.*	.182	9	37	33	2	6	7	1	0	0	2	0	0	0	4	0	5	0	0	0	.212	.270
LeCroy, Matthew, Min.	.250	3	8	8	1	2	3	1	0	0	1	0	0	0	0	0	2	0	0	0	.375	.250
Ledee, Ricky, N.Y.-Cle.-Tex.*	.038	10	30	26	0	1	1	0	0	0	0	0	0	0	4	0	8	0	0	0	.038	.167
Lee, Carlos, Chi.	.250	2	8	8	1	2	5	0	0	1	3	0	0	0	0	0	3	0	0	0	.625	.250
Lesher, Brian, Sea.	.000	1	0	0	0	0	0	0	0	0	0	0	0	0	0	0	0	0	0	0	.000	.000
Lewis, Darren, Bos.	.000	5	0	0	2	0	0	0	0	0	0	0	0	0	0	0	0	0	0	0	.000	.000
Lewis, Mark, Bal.	.000	4	2	2	0	0	0	0	0	0	0	0	0	0	0	0	0	0	0	0	.000	.000
Leyritz, Jim, N.Y.	.250	15	49	44	1	11	11	0	0	0	3	0	0	0	5	0	13	0	0	1	.250	.327
Lofton, Kenny, Cle.*	.250	1	4	4	0	1	1	0	0	0	0	0	0	0	0	0	0	0	0	0	.250	.250
Mabry, John, Sea.*	.200	5	7	5	4	1	1	0	0	0	1	0	0	0	2	0	4	0	0	0	.200	.429
Macias, Jose, Det.†	.000	1	1	1	0	0	0	0	0	0	0	0	0	0	0	0	0	0	0	0	.000	.000
Magee, Wendell Jr., Det.	.286	6	7	7	1	2	2	0	0	0	0	0	0	0	0	0	1	0	0	1	.286	.286
Mahay, Ron, Oak.*	.000	1	0	0	0	0	0	0	0	0	0	0	0	0	0	0	0	0	0	0	.000	.000
Martin, Al, Sea.*	.000	2	0	0	2	0	0	0	0	0	0	0	0	0	0	0	0	1	0	0	.000	.000
Martinez, Edgar, Sea.	.323	146	652	545	100	176	317	30	0	37	143	0	7	5	95	8	94	3	0	13	.582	.423

Player, Team	Avg.	G	TPA	AB	R	H	TB	2B	3B	HR	RBI	SH	SF	HP	BB	IBB	SO	SB	CS	GDP	Slg.	OBP
Matos, Luis, Bal.	.000	3	0	0	1	0	0	0	0	0	0	0	0	0	0	0	0	0	0	0	.000	.000
Maxwell, Jason, Min.	.000	7	2	2	2	0	0	0	0	0	0	0	0	0	0	0	0	0	0	0	.000	.000
McCarty, David, K.C.	.217	7	24	23	2	5	11	0	0	2	6	0	0	0	1	0	5	0	0	1	.478	.250
McDonald, Jason, Tex.†	.000	1	0	0	0	0	0	0	0	0	0	0	0	0	0	0	0	0	0	0	.000	.000
McGriff, Fred, T.B.*	.282	10	44	39	8	11	16	2	0	1	7	0	0	0	5	1	10	0	0	1	.410	.364
McMillon, Billy, Det.*	.273	24	97	77	13	21	35	5	0	3	17	1	3	1	15	0	12	1	0	1	.455	.385
Menechino, Frank, Oak.	.000	4	0	0	2	0	0	0	0	0	0	0	0	0	0	0	0	0	0	0	.000	.000
Molina, Bengie, Ana.	.167	2	8	6	1	1	4	0	0	1	1	0	0	0	2	0	1	0	0	1	.667	.375
Myers, Greg, Bal.*	.208	9	25	24	2	5	11	0	0	2	4	0	0	0	1	0	4	0	0	1	.458	.240
Nixon, Trot, Bos.*	.000	1	1	1	0	0	0	0	0	0	0	0	0	0	0	0	0	0	0	0	.000	.000
Norton, Greg, Chi.†	.167	3	6	6	0	1	1	0	0	0	0	0	0	0	0	0	2	0	0	0	.167	.167
O'Neill, Paul, N.Y.*	.500	2	10	8	4	4	8	1	0	1	3	0	0	0	2	0	1	0	0	0	1.000	.600
Offerman, Jose, Bos.†	.205	9	44	39	2	8	9	1	0	0	1	1	0	0	4	0	8	0	0	2	.231	.279
Oliver, Joe, Sea.	.000	1	1	1	0	0	0	0	0	0	0	0	0	0	0	0	1	0	0	0	.000	.000
Ortiz, David, Min.*	.303	88	354	310	50	94	148	27	0	9	50	0	6	0	38	1	62	1	0	13	.477	.373
Ortiz, Jose, Oak.	.250	4	4	4	3	1	1	0	0	0	1	0	0	0	0	0	1	0	0	0	.250	.250
Palmeiro, Orlando, Ana.*	.180	19	57	50	4	9	9	0	0	0	4	1	0	1	5	0	3	0	0	1	.180	.268
Palmeiro, Rafael, Tex.*	.266	46	203	173	28	46	85	8	2	9	34	0	2	1	27	5	20	0	0	3	.491	.365
Palmer, Dean, Det.	.239	14	57	46	6	11	21	4	0	2	14	0	1	0	10	0	9	1	0	2	.457	.368
Perry, Chan, Cle.	.000	4	4	4	1	0	0	0	0	0	0	0	0	0	0	0	0	0	0	0	.000	.000
Perry, Herbert, T.B.-Chi.	.000	3	5	3	2	0	0	0	0	0	0	0	0	0	2	0	1	0	0	0	.000	.400
Piatt, Adam, Oak.	.250	13	40	36	3	9	17	1	2	1	6	1	0	1	2	0	14	0	0	0	.472	.308
Polonia, Luis, Det.-N.Y.*	.290	51	210	193	25	56	81	8	4	3	19	1	4	0	12	0	17	8	3	3	.420	.325
Posada, Jorge, N.Y.†	.182	4	14	11	0	2	2	0	0	0	0	0	0	1	2	0	6	0	0	0	.182	.357
Pose, Scott, K.C.*	.000	4	6	5	0	0	0	0	0	0	0	0	0	0	1	0	0	0	1	1	.000	.167
Pride, Curtis, Bos.*	.000	1	0	0	1	0	0	0	0	0	0	0	0	0	0	0	0	0	0	0	.000	.000
Quinn, Mark, K.C.	.243	48	198	177	24	43	68	7	0	6	21	2	2	0	17	1	32	0	0	3	.384	.306
Ramirez, Alex, Cle.	.067	6	18	15	0	1	1	0	0	0	1	0	0	0	3	0	1	0	0	0	.067	.222
Ramirez, Manny, Cle.	.326	25	109	89	21	29	66	4	0	11	28	0	1	0	19	2	25	0	0	1	.742	.440
Randa, Joe, K.C.	.500	1	4	4	0	2	3	1	0	0	2	0	0	0	0	0	0	0	0	0	.750	.500
Reboulet, Jeff, K.C.	.000	1	0	0	1	0	0	0	0	0	0	0	0	0	0	0	0	0	0	0	.000	.000
Richard, Chris, Bal.*	.000	1	4	3	0	0	0	0	0	0	0	0	0	1	0	0	1	0	0	0	.000	.250
Ripken, Cal, Bal.	.289	10	40	38	4	11	14	3	0	0	6	0	0	0	2	0	4	0	0	2	.368	.325
Rodriguez, Ivan, Tex.	.000	1	4	4	0	0	0	0	0	0	0	0	0	0	0	0	2	0	0	0	.000	.000
Rolls, Damian, T.B.	1.000	1	1	1	0	1	1	0	0	0	0	0	0	0	0	0	0	0	0	0	1.000	1.000
Sadler, Donnie, Bos.	.000	2	0	0	1	0	0	0	0	0	0	0	0	0	0	0	0	0	0	0	.000	.000
Saenz, Olmedo, Oak.	.310	27	100	84	18	26	34	2	0	2	10	0	3	13	0	14	1	0	2	.405	.420
Salmon, Tim, Ana.	.287	33	145	115	23	33	55	7	0	5	15	0	2	28	0	18	0	0	3	.478	.434
Segui, David, Tex.-Cle.†	.331	68	288	263	38	87	133	19	0	9	39	0	2	0	23	0	40	0	1	11	.506	.382
Selby, Bill, Cle.*	.400	6	5	5	3	2	2	0	0	0	3	0	0	0	0	0	0	0	0	1	.400	.400
Sexson, Richie, Cle.	.206	10	38	34	4	7	11	1	0	1	1	0	0	1	3	0	12	0	0	1	.324	.289
Sheets, Andy, Bos.	.000	2	2	2	0	0	0	0	0	0	0	0	0	0	0	0	1	0	0	0	.000	.000
Sheldon, Scott, Tex.	.000	1	1	1	1	0	0	0	0	0	0	0	0	0	0	0	0	0	0	0	.000	.000
Sierra, Ruben, Tex.†	.241	14	58	54	5	13	16	0	0	1	6	0	0	0	4	0	8	1	0	0	.296	.293
Singleton, Chris, Chi.*	.000	1	0	0	0	0	0	0	0	0	0	0	0	0	0	0	0	0	0	0	.000	.000
Soriano, Alfonso, N.Y.	.000	1	1	1	0	0	0	0	0	0	0	1	0	0	0	0	1	0	0	0	.000	.000
Spencer, Shane, N.Y.	.233	33	131	116	15	27	49	4	3	4	12	0	3	0	12	0	23	1	1	2	.422	.298
Spiezio, Scott, Ana.†	.224	50	192	161	19	36	61	7	0	6	16	0	1	3	27	2	27	1	1	1	.379	.344
Sprague, Ed Jr., Bos.	.000	1	6	6	0	0	0	0	0	0	0	0	0	0	0	0	2	0	0	0	.000	.000
Stairs, Matt, Oak.*	.226	37	148	124	16	28	44	7	0	3	18	1	0	0	23	2	36	1	2	3	.355	.347
Stanley, Mike, Bos.-Oak.	.286	26	104	91	11	26	49	2	0	7	17	0	2	0	11	0	26	0	0	2	.538	.356
Surhoff, B.J., Bal.*	.333	1	4	3	1	1	1	0	0	0	0	0	0	0	1	0	0	1	0	0	.333	.500
Sweeney, Mike, K.C.	.301	45	209	183	37	55	93	11	0	9	41	0	2	6	18	0	25	3	0	4	.508	.378
Thomas, Frank, Chi.	.321	127	573	467	88	150	274	34	0	30	102	0	6	3	97	15	81	1	2	8	.587	.436
Thome, Jim, Cle.*	.232	48	217	181	25	42	74	8	0	8	29	0	1	1	34	1	51	0	0	2	.409	.355
Timmons, Ozzie, T.B.	.500	1	4	4	3	2	5	0	0	1	3	0	0	0	0	0	0	0	0	0	1.250	.500
Trammell, Bubba, T.B.	.263	9	24	19	1	5	6	1	0	0	3	0	1	0	4	0	4	0	0	0	.316	.375
Tyner, Jason, T.B.*	.000	1	1	1	0	0	0	0	0	0	0	0	0	0	0	0	1	0	0	0	.000	.000
Valdes, Pedro, Tex.*	.250	4	12	12	0	3	3	0	0	0	0	0	0	0	0	0	3	0	0	0	.250	.250
Varitek, Jason, Bos.†	.200	1	5	5	0	1	1	0	0	0	0	0	0	0	0	0	0	0	0	0	.200	.200
Vaughn, Greg, T.B.	.212	52	220	184	31	39	83	11	0	11	32	0	1	1	34	2	51	2	1	3	.451	.336
Vaughn, Mo, Ana.*	.260	14	58	50	9	13	23	4	0	2	9	0	0	1	7	0	17	0	0	0	.460	.362
Vizcaino, Jose, N.Y.†	.000	4	1	1	1	0	0	0	0	0	0	0	0	0	0	0	0	0	0	0	.000	.000
Walbeck, Matt, Ana.†	.000	1	2	2	0	0	0	0	0	0	0	0	0	0	0	0	1	0	0	0	.000	.000
Walker, Todd, Min.*	.333	2	4	3	1	1	1	0	0	0	0	0	0	0	1	0	2	2	0	0	.333	.500
Widger, Chris, Sea.	.000	2	0	0	0	0	0	0	0	0	0	0	0	0	0	0	0	0	0	0	.000	.000
Williams, Bernie, N.Y.†	.267	4	18	15	3	4	10	3	0	1	3	0	0	0	3	0	1	0	0	0	.667	.389
Williams, Gerald, T.B.	.290	7	33	31	3	9	15	3	0	1	6	0	0	0	2	0	5	0	0	0	.484	.333
Wilson, Enrique, Cle.†	.286	8	25	21	3	6	13	1	0	2	3	1	0	0	3	0	1	0	1	0	.619	.375
Winn, Randy, T.B.†	.000	1	1	0	0	0	0	0	0	0	0	0	1	0	0	0	0	0	0	0	.000	.000
Wise, Dewayne, Tor.*	.000	2	0	0	0	0	0	0	0	0	0	0	0	0	0	0	0	0	0	0	.000	.000

DESIGNATED HITTERS WITH TWO OR MORE TEAMS

Player, Team	Avg.	G	TPA	AB	R	H	TB	2B	3B	HR	RBI	SH	SF	HP	BB	IBB	SO	SB	CS	GDP	Slg.	OBP
Baines, Bal.*	.265	62	243	215	24	57	95	8	0	10	30	0	1	0	27	5	36	0	0	6	.442	.346
Baines, Chi.*	.218	16	60	55	2	12	20	5	0	1	9	0	0	0	5	1	7	0	0	0	.364	.283
Becker, Det.*	.500	4	8	6	2	3	4	1	0	0	0	0	0	0	2	0	0	0	0	0	.667	.625
Becker, Oak.*	.000	2	1	1	1	0	0	0	0	0	0	0	0	0	0	0	1	0	0	0	.000	.000
Canseco, N.Y.	.258	26	111	89	15	23	41	3	0	5	16	0	3	0	19	1	29	0	0	1	.461	.378
Canseco, T.B.	.258	60	263	217	31	56	98	15	0	9	30	0	1	4	41	1	64	2	0	5	.452	.384

Player, Team	Avg.	G	TPA	AB	R	H	TB	2B	3B	HR	RBI	SH	SF	HP	BB	IBB	SO	SB	CS	GDP	Slg.	OBP
Cummings, Bos.*	.000	1	1	1	0	0	0	0	0	0	0	0	0	0	0	0	0	0	0	1	.000	.000
Cummings, Min.*	.326	15	47	43	5	14	19	2	0	1	6	1	0	2	1	0	7	0	0	3	.442	.370
Garcia, Det.*	.000	1	0	0	1	0	0	0	0	0	0	0	0	0	0	0	0	0	0	0	.000	.000
Garcia, Bal.*	.000	4	12	12	0	0	0	0	0	0	0	0	0	0	0	0	5	0	0	0	.000	.000
Justice, Cle.*	.276	20	88	76	15	21	53	8	0	8	20	0	0	0	12	1	13	0	0	4	.697	.375
Justice, N.Y.*	.308	18	75	65	7	20	29	3	0	2	12	0	0	0	10	0	11	0	0	2	.446	.400
Polonia, Det.*	.287	44	198	181	23	52	76	7	4	3	19	1	4	0	12	0	14	6	3	2	.420	.325
Polonia, N.Y.*	.333	7	12	12	2	4	5	1	0	0	0	0	0	0	0	0	3	2	0	1	.417	.333
Segui, Cle.†	.387	16	66	62	12	24	37	4	0	3	12	0	0	0	4	0	12	0	0	3	.597	.424
Segui, Tex.†	.313	52	222	201	26	63	96	15	0	6	27	0	2	0	19	0	28	0	1	8	.478	.369
Stanley, Bos.	.269	18	75	67	8	18	35	2	0	5	13	0	1	0	7	0	20	0	0	0	.522	.333
Stanley, Oak.	.333	8	29	24	3	8	14	0	0	2	4	0	1	0	4	0	6	0	0	2	.583	.414

The following designated hitters, each of whom appeared in at least one game, had no plate appearances, runs scored or stolen base attempts: Henderson, Rickey, Seattle (2); Widger, Chris, Seattle (2); Wise, Dewayne, Toronto (2); Bell, David, Seattle; Chavez, Eric, Oakland; Hudson, Tim, Oakland; Lesher, Brian, Seattle; Mahay, Ron, Oakland; McDonald, Jason, Texas; Singleton, Chris, Chicago; Stocker, Kevin, Tampa Bay.

PINCH-HITTING

TEAM

Team	Avg.	G	TPA	AB	R	H	TB	2B	3B	HR	RBI	SH	SF	HP	BB	IBB	SO	SB	CS	GDP	Slg.	OBP
Texas	.340	82	121	103	13	35	59	8	2	4	22	1	0	1	16	1	16	1	0	1	.573	.433
Toronto	.333	42	59	51	6	17	20	3	0	0	8	1	1	0	6	1	7	1	0	2	.392	.397
Detroit	.299	87	125	107	15	32	46	3	1	3	19	2	1	1	14	0	22	1	1	1	.430	.382
Tampa Bay	.265	82	113	98	8	26	38	1	1	3	18	3	0	1	11	3	19	0	0	3	.388	.345
Boston	.256	83	155	133	10	34	47	4	0	3	19	1	1	0	20	2	32	0	2	3	.353	.351
Minnesota	.253	95	177	146	14	37	48	6	1	1	25	1	3	0	27	2	39	2	1	4	.329	.364
Kansas City	.250	82	134	120	13	30	33	0	0	1	18	0	3	0	11	0	26	2	0	1	.275	.306
New York	.237	65	85	76	10	18	32	2	0	4	15	0	1	1	7	0	23	2	0	1	.421	.306
Anaheim	.232	78	109	82	12	19	28	3	0	2	11	2	2	1	22	0	19	1	1	1	.341	.393
Cleveland	.231	52	72	65	5	15	21	3	0	1	5	0	1	0	6	0	17	0	0	2	.323	.292
Baltimore	.213	58	73	61	5	13	22	6	0	1	9	0	1	1	10	3	17	0	0	2	.361	.329
Oakland	.212	96	162	137	14	29	38	3	0	2	20	0	1	3	21	3	41	0	0	3	.277	.327
Seattle	.202	75	108	94	10	19	24	3	1	0	12	0	2	1	11	2	26	1	1	1	.255	.287
Chicago	.192	62	82	73	7	14	26	1	1	3	16	0	0	0	9	1	19	0	0	0	.356	.280
Totals	.251	1039	1575	1346	142	338	482	46	7	28	217	11	17	10	191	18	323	11	6	25	.358	.345

TOP PINCH-HITTERS

Minimum 20 at-bats. *Lefthanded batter. †Switch-hitter.

Player, Team	Avg.	G	TPA	AB	R	H	TB	2B	3B	HR	RBI	SH	SF	HP	BB	IBB	SO	SB	CS	GDP	Slg.	OBP
Saenz, Olmedo, Oak.	.400	24	24	20	2	8	12	1	0	1	4	0	0	1	3	1	4	0	0	1	.600	.500
McCarty, David, K.C.	.391	28	28	23	3	9	12	0	0	1	9	0	2	0	3	0	3	0	0	0	.522	.429
Magee, Wendell Jr., Det.	.385	27	26	26	2	10	13	0	0	1	5	0	0	0	0	0	3	0	0	0	.500	.385
Catalanotto, Frank, Tex.*	.357	32	32	28	4	10	13	1	1	0	4	0	0	1	3	0	5	1	0	0	.464	.438
Cox, Steve, T.B.*	.333	25	25	21	1	7	8	1	0	0	2	0	0	0	4	0	2	0	0	2	.381	.440
Hocking, Denny, Min.†	.333	33	33	24	3	8	8	0	0	0	3	1	1	0	7	0	9	1	0	0	.333	.469
Cummings, Midre, Min.-Bos.*	.319	54	52	47	2	15	18	3	0	0	12	0	0	0	5	0	5	0	0	1	.383	.385
Hatteberg, Scott, Bos.*	.292	28	28	24	2	7	13	0	0	2	5	0	0	0	4	0	3	0	0	0	.542	.393
Spiezio, Scott, Ana.†	.286	36	36	28	5	8	14	0	0	2	8	0	2	1	5	0	5	0	0	1	.500	.389
Becker, Rich, Oak.-Det.*	.269	31	31	26	6	7	10	0	0	1	4	0	0	0	5	0	10	0	1	0	.385	.387
Giambi, Jeremy, Oak.*	.250	26	26	24	1	6	6	0	0	0	3	0	1	0	1	0	11	0	0	0	.250	.269
Palmeiro, Orlando, Ana.*	.250	31	30	20	4	5	6	1	0	0	1	2	0	0	8	0	4	1	0	0	.300	.464
Pose, Scott, K.C.*	.222	30	30	27	4	6	6	0	0	0	1	0	0	0	3	0	7	0	0	1	.222	.300
Javier, Stan, Sea.†	.200	23	23	20	4	4	6	2	0	0	5	0	0	0	3	1	4	0	1	0	.300	.304

ALL PINCH-HITTERS

*Lefthanded batter. †Switch-hitter.

Player, Team	Avg.	G	TPA	AB	R	H	TB	2B	3B	HR	RBI	SH	SF	HP	BB	IBB	SO	SB	CS	GDP	Slg.	OBP
Abbott, Jeff, Chi.	.133	18	17	15	2	2	6	1	0	1	3	0	0	0	2	1	5	0	0	0	.400	.235
Alcantara, Israel, Bos.	.143	8	8	7	0	1	1	0	0	0	0	0	0	0	1	0	1	0	0	0	.143	.250
Alexander, Manny, Bos.	.000	4	4	4	0	0	0	0	0	0	0	0	0	0	0	0	0	0	0	0	.000	.000
Alicea, Luis, Tex.†	.333	4	4	3	1	1	1	0	0	0	0	0	0	0	1	0	1	0	0	0	.333	.500
Allen, Dusty, Det.	1.000	1	1	1	0	1	1	0	0	0	0	0	0	0	0	0	0	0	0	1	1.000	1.000
Alomar, Sandy Jr., Cle.	.000	3	3	3	0	0	0	0	0	0	0	0	0	0	0	0	0	0	0	0	.000	.000
Amaral, Rich, Bal.	.000	4	4	4	0	0	0	0	0	0	0	0	0	0	0	0	1	0	0	1	.000	.000
Anderson, Brady, Bal.*	.000	6	6	4	0	0	0	0	0	0	0	0	0	0	2	1	0	0	0	0	.000	.333
Anderson, Garret, Ana.*	.000	1	1	1	0	0	0	0	0	0	0	0	0	0	0	0	0	0	0	0	.000	.000
Ausmus, Brad, Det.	.500	3	3	2	1	1	1	0	0	0	0	0	0	0	1	0	0	0	0	0	.500	.667
Baines, Harold, Bal.-Chi.*	.267	20	19	15	0	4	4	0	0	0	0	0	0	0	4	1	7	0	0	0	.267	.421
Baughman, Justin, Ana.	.000	1	1	0	0	0	0	0	0	0	0	0	0	0	1	0	0	0	0	0	.000	1.000
Becker, Rich, Oak.-Det.*	.269	31	31	26	6	7	10	0	0	1	4	0	0	0	5	0	10	0	1	0	.385	.387
Bell, David, Sea.	.000	4	4	4	0	0	0	0	0	0	0	0	0	0	0	0	2	0	0	0	.000	.000
Bellhorn, Mark, Oak.†	.000	6	6	4	0	0	0	0	0	0	0	0	0	0	2	0	0	0	0	0	.000	.333
Bellinger, Clay, N.Y.	.333	6	6	6	1	2	5	0	0	1	1	0	0	0	0	0	2	0	0	0	.833	.333
Beltran, Carlos, K.C.†	.000	3	3	3	0	0	0	0	0	0	0	0	0	0	0	0	1	0	0	0	.000	.000
Bichette, Dante, Bos.	1.000	2	2	1	0	1	1	0	0	0	0	0	0	0	1	0	0	0	0	1	1.000	1.000
Blake, Casey, Min.	.000	2	2	0	0	0	0	0	0	0	1	0	1	0	1	0	0	0	0	0	.000	.500
Branyan, Russell, Cle.*	.100	11	11	10	0	1	2	1	0	0	1	0	0	0	1	0	4	0	0	1	.200	.182
Brogna, Rico, Bos.*	.000	5	5	5	0	0	0	0	0	0	0	0	0	0	0	0	1	0	0	0	.000	.000
Brosius, Scott, N.Y.	.000	1	1	1	0	0	0	0	0	0	1	0	0	0	0	0	0	0	0	0	.000	.000
Brown, Dee, K.C.*	.273	11	11	11	2	3	3	0	0	0	4	0	0	0	0	0	3	0	0	0	.273	.273
Buchanan, Brian, Min.	.000	4	4	2	1	0	0	0	0	0	0	0	1	0	1	0	1	0	0	0	.000	.250
Buhner, Jay, Sea.	.250	10	10	8	0	2	2	0	0	0	1	0	0	0	2	1	3	0	0	0	.250	.400
Burkhart, Morgan, Bos.†	.000	3	3	3	0	0	0	0	0	0	0	0	0	0	0	0	2	0	0	0	.000	.000
Byrnes, Eric, Oak.	.333	3	3	3	1	1	1	0	0	0	0	0	0	0	0	0	0	0	0	0	.333	.333
Cabrera, Jolbert, Cle.	.000	5	5	5	0	0	0	0	0	0	0	0	0	0	0	0	1	0	0	0	.000	.000
Cairo, Miguel, T.B.	.286	9	9	7	1	2	2	0	0	0	0	1	0	0	1	0	2	0	0	0	.286	.375
Cameron, Mike, Sea.	.333	4	4	3	2	1	2	1	0	0	2	0	0	1	0	0	2	0	0	0	.667	.500
Canizaro, Jay, Min.	.200	12	12	10	0	2	3	1	0	0	1	0	0	0	2	0	3	0	0	1	.300	.333
Canseco, Jose, T.B.-N.Y.	.125	8	8	8	0	1	1	0	0	0	0	0	0	0	0	0	3	0	0	0	.125	.125
Cardona, Javier, Det.	.000	2	2	1	0	0	0	0	0	0	0	0	0	1	0	0	0	0	0	0	.000	.500
Casimiro, Carlos, Bal.	1.000	1	1	1	0	1	2	1	0	0	2	0	0	0	0	0	0	0	0	0	2.000	1.000
Castilla, Vinny, T.B.	.000	2	2	1	0	0	0	0	0	0	0	0	0	0	1	1	0	0	0	0	.000	.500

Player, Team	Avg.	G	TPA	AB	R	H	TB	2B	3B	HR	RBI	SH	SF	HP	BB	IBB	SO	SB	CS	GDP	Slg.	OBP
Catalanotto, Frank, Tex.*	.357	32	32	28	4	10	13	1	1	0	4	0	0	1	3	0	5	1	0	0	.464	.438
Chavez, Eric, Oak.*	.200	10	10	10	1	2	3	1	0	0	1	0	0	0	0	0	3	0	0	1	.300	.200
Christensen, McKay, Chi.*	.000	1	1	1	0	0	0	0	0	0	0	0	0	0	0	0	0	0	0	0	.000	.000
Christenson, Ryan, Oak.	.500	5	5	4	1	2	2	0	0	0	1	0	0	1	0	1	0	0	0	0	.500	.600
Clark, Tony, Det.†	1.000	1	1	1	0	1	1	0	0	0	0	0	0	0	0	0	0	0	0	0	1.000	1.000
Clark, Will, Bal.*	.000	2	2	1	0	0	0	0	0	0	1	0	1	0	0	0	0	0	0	0	.000	.000
Clemente, Edgard, Ana.	.125	8	8	8	0	1	1	0	0	0	0	0	0	0	0	0	4	0	1	0	.125	.125
Coffie, Ivanon, Bal.*	.667	4	4	3	1	2	2	0	0	0	0	0	0	1	0	0	1	0	0	0	.667	.750
Conine, Jeff, Bal.	.333	10	10	9	1	3	8	2	0	1	3	0	0	0	1	1	1	0	0	0	.889	.400
Coomer, Ron, Min.	.250	4	4	4	0	1	1	0	0	0	0	0	0	0	0	0	1	0	0	1	.250	.250
Cordova, Marty, Tor.	.333	7	7	6	1	2	2	0	0	0	1	0	0	0	1	0	2	0	0	0	.333	.429
Cox, Steve, T.B.*	.333	25	25	21	1	7	8	1	0	0	2	0	0	0	4	0	2	0	0	2	.381	.440
Cruz, Jacob, Cle.*	1.000	1	1	1	0	1	2	1	0	0	0	0	0	0	0	0	0	0	0	0	2.000	1.000
Cummings, Midre, Min.-Bos.*	.319	54	52	47	2	15	18	3	0	0	12	0	0	0	5	0	5	0	0	1	.383	.385
Curtis, Chad, Tex.	.389	28	26	18	2	7	11	1	0	1	4	1	0	0	7	0	5	0	0	0	.611	.560
Damon, Johnny, K.C.*	.000	1	1	0	0	0	0	0	0	0	0	0	0	0	1	0	0	0	0	0	.000	1.000
Daubach, Brian, Bos.*	.111	14	13	9	1	1	4	0	0	1	5	0	1	0	3	1	3	0	0	0	.444	.308
Delgado, Wilson, N.Y.-K.C.†	.143	7	7	7	0	1	1	0	0	0	0	0	0	0	0	0	1	0	0	0	.143	.143
DeShields, Delino, Bal.*	.000	7	7	5	1	0	0	0	0	0	0	0	0	0	2	0	0	0	0	0	.000	.286
Diaz, Einar, Cle.	1.000	1	1	1	0	1	1	0	0	0	0	0	0	0	0	0	0	0	0	0	1.000	1.000
DiFelice, Mike, T.B.	.000	1	1	1	0	0	0	0	0	0	0	0	0	0	0	0	0	0	0	0	.000	.000
Dransfeldt, Kelly, Tex.	.500	2	2	2	0	1	2	1	0	0	1	0	0	0	0	0	0	0	0	0	1.000	.500
Ducey, Rob, Tor.*	.000	2	2	2	0	0	0	0	0	0	0	0	0	0	0	0	0	0	0	0	.000	.000
Dunwoody, Todd, K.C.*	.071	15	15	14	0	1	1	0	0	0	0	0	0	0	1	0	6	0	0	0	.071	.133
Durham, Ray, Chi.†	.000	2	2	2	0	0	0	0	0	0	0	0	0	0	0	0	0	0	0	0	.000	.000
Dye, Jermaine, K.C.	1.000	1	1	1	0	1	1	0	0	0	0	0	0	0	0	0	0	0	0	0	1.000	1.000
Erstad, Darin, Ana.*	1.000	1	1	1	0	1	1	0	0	0	0	0	0	0	0	0	0	0	0	0	1.000	1.000
Evans, Tom, Tex.	.000	1	1	1	0	0	0	0	0	0	0	0	0	0	0	0	0	0	0	0	.000	.000
Everett, Carl, Bos.†	.250	10	10	8	1	2	2	0	0	0	1	0	0	0	2	0	2	0	1	0	.250	.400
Fabregas, Jorge, K.C.*	.250	4	4	4	0	1	1	0	0	0	0	0	0	0	0	0	1	0	0	0	.250	.250
Fasano, Sal, Oak.	.000	1	1	1	0	0	0	0	0	0	0	0	0	0	0	0	1	0	0	0	.000	.000
Fick, Robert, Det.*	.250	14	14	12	0	3	4	1	0	0	4	0	1	0	1	0	4	1	0	0	.333	.286
Flaherty, John, T.B.	.500	2	2	2	0	1	1	0	0	0	1	0	0	0	0	0	0	0	0	0	.500	.500
Fletcher, Darrin, Tor.*	.308	15	14	13	1	4	5	1	0	0	2	0	0	1	0	0	2	0	0	0	.385	.357
Fordyce, Brook, Chi.-Bal.	.200	5	5	5	0	1	1	0	0	0	2	0	0	0	0	0	1	0	0	1	.200	.200
Frye, Jeff, Bos.	.400	5	5	5	1	2	2	0	0	0	0	0	0	0	0	0	1	0	1	0	.400	.400
Fullmer, Brad, Tor.*	.214	17	17	14	1	3	3	0	0	0	1	0	1	0	2	1	3	0	0	1	.214	.294
Gaetti, Gary, Bos.	.000	3	3	3	0	0	0	0	0	0	0	0	0	0	0	0	2	0	0	0	.000	.000
Gant, Ron, Ana.	.111	13	13	9	1	1	2	1	0	0	2	0	0	0	4	0	2	0	0	0	.222	.385
Garcia, Jesse, Bal.	.000	1	1	1	0	0	0	0	0	0	0	0	0	0	1	0	0	0	0	0	.000	1.000
Garcia, Karim, Det.-Bal.*	.000	3	3	3	0	0	0	0	0	0	0	0	0	0	0	0	0	0	0	0	.000	.000
Garciaparra, Nomar, Bos.	.667	3	3	3	0	2	2	0	0	0	1	0	0	0	0	0	0	0	0	0	.667	.667
Giambi, Jason, Oak.*	.333	4	4	3	0	1	1	0	0	0	1	0	0	0	1	1	1	0	0	0	.333	.500
Giambi, Jeremy, Oak.*	.250	26	26	24	1	6	6	0	0	0	3	0	1	0	1	0	11	0	0	0	.250	.250
Gil, Benji, Ana.	.500	2	2	2	1	1	1	0	0	0	0	0	0	0	0	0	0	0	0	0	.500	.500
Gilkey, Bernard, Bos.	.182	11	11	11	1	2	2	0	0	0	0	0	0	0	0	0	3	0	0	1	.182	.182
Gipson, Charles, Sea.	1.000	1	1	1	0	1	1	0	0	0	0	0	0	0	0	0	0	0	0	0	1.000	1.000
Glaus, Troy, Ana.	.000	1	1	0	0	0	0	0	0	0	0	0	0	0	1	0	0	0	0	0	.000	1.000
Gonzalez, Juan, Det.	.000	1	1	1	0	0	0	0	0	0	0	0	0	0	0	0	0	0	0	1	.000	.000
Graffanino, Tony, T.B.-Chi.	.167	8	7	6	2	1	3	0	1	0	1	0	0	0	1	0	0	0	0	0	.500	.286
Grebeck, Craig, Tor.	.500	4	4	2	1	1	2	1	0	0	1	0	0	0	2	0	0	0	0	0	1.000	.750
Green, Scarborough, Tex.†	.000	3	3	3	0	0	0	0	0	0	0	0	0	0	0	0	1	0	0	0	.000	.000
Greene, Todd, Tor.	.400	10	10	10	2	4	5	1	0	0	3	0	0	0	0	0	0	0	0	1	.500	.400
Greer, Rusty, Tex.*	.333	6	6	6	0	2	4	2	0	0	1	0	0	0	0	0	1	0	0	0	.667	.333
Grieve, Ben, Oak.*	.500	3	3	2	1	1	1	0	0	0	1	0	0	0	1	0	0	0	0	0	.500	.667
Guillen, Carlos, Sea.†	.200	5	5	5	0	1	1	0	0	0	0	0	0	0	0	0	2	0	0	0	.200	.200
Guillen, Jose, T.B.	.375	9	9	8	1	3	5	0	1	0	3	0	0	1	0	0	2	0	0	0	.625	.444
Guillen, Ozzie, T.B.*	.000	5	5	4	0	0	0	0	0	0	0	1	0	0	0	0	0	0	0	0	.000	.000
Guzman, Cristian, Min.†	.200	7	7	5	1	1	1	0	0	0	0	0	0	0	2	1	2	0	0	1	.200	.429
Halter, Shane, Det.	.000	3	3	3	0	0	0	0	0	0	0	0	0	0	0	0	2	0	0	0	.000	.000
Hatteberg, Scott, Bos.*	.292	28	28	24	2	7	13	0	0	2	5	0	0	0	4	0	3	0	0	0	.542	.393
Hernandez, Carlos E., Sea.	.000	1	1	1	0	0	0	0	0	0	0	0	0	0	0	0	1	0	0	0	.000	.000
Hernandez, Ramon, Oak.	.143	16	16	14	2	2	5	0	0	1	3	0	0	0	2	0	3	0	0	0	.357	.250
Hill, Glenallen, N.Y.	.333	6	6	6	2	2	8	0	0	2	5	0	0	0	0	0	0	0	0	1	1.333	.333
Hinch, A.J., Oak.	.000	2	2	1	0	0	0	0	0	0	0	0	0	1	0	0	1	0	0	0	.000	.000
Hocking, Denny, Min.†	.333	33	33	24	3	8	8	0	0	0	3	1	1	0	7	0	9	1	0	0	.333	.469
Hubbard, Trenidad, Bal.	.000	2	1	1	0	0	0	0	0	0	0	0	0	1	0	0	0	0	0	0	.000	.000
Huff, Aubrey, T.B.*	.667	3	3	3	0	2	2	0	0	0	1	0	0	0	0	0	0	0	0	0	.667	.667
Hunter, Torii, Min.	.500	2	2	2	1	1	3	0	1	0	0	0	0	0	0	0	1	0	0	0	1.500	.500
Huskey, Butch, Min.	.000	5	5	5	0	0	0	0	0	0	2	0	0	0	1	0	0	0	0	0	.000	.400
Ibanez, Raul, Sea.*	.133	17	17	15	1	2	2	0	0	0	1	0	1	0	1	0	3	0	0	0	.133	.176
Jaha, John, Oak.	.000	3	3	1	0	0	0	0	0	0	0	0	0	0	1	0	0	0	0	0	.000	.667
Javier, Stan, Sea.†	.200	23	23	20	4	4	6	2	0	0	5	0	0	0	3	1	4	0	0	1	.300	.304
Jefferies, Gregg, Det.†	.500	4	4	2	1	1	2	1	0	0	1	0	0	0	2	0	1	0	0	0	1.000	.750
Jensen, Marcus, Min.†	.000	8	8	7	0	0	0	0	0	0	0	0	0	0	1	0	3	0	0	1	.000	.125
Johnson, Charles, Bal.-Chi.	.000	2	2	2	0	0	0	0	0	0	0	0	0	0	0	0	2	0	0	0	.000	.000
Johnson, Lance, N.Y.*	.214	14	14	14	2	3	3	0	0	0	1	0	0	0	0	0	4	0	0	1	.214	.214
Johnson, Mark L., Chi.*	.000	1	1	1	0	0	0	0	0	0	0	0	0	0	0	0	0	0	0	0	.000	.000
Johnson, Russ, T.B.	.417	12	12	12	1	5	5	0	0	0	2	0	0	0	0	0	2	0	0	0	.417	.417
Jones, Jacque, Min.*	.308	15	14	13	2	4	5	1	0	0	3	0	0	1	0	0	4	0	0	0	.385	.357
Jose, Felix, N.Y.†	.000	6	6	6	0	0	0	0	0	0	0	0	0	0	0	0	2	0	0	0	.000	.000
Justice, David, Cle.-N.Y.*	.000	4	3	2	0	0	0	0	0	0	0	0	0	0	1	0	1	0	0	0	.000	.333

Player, Team	Avg.	G	TPA	AB	R	H	TB	2B	3B	HR	RBI	SH	SF	HP	BB	IBB	SO	SB	CS	GDP	Slg.	OBP
Kapler, Gabe, Tex.	.000	1	1	1	0	0	0	0	0	0	0	0	0	0	0	0	0	0	0	0	.000	.000
Kelly, Kenny, T.B.	.000	1	1	1	0	0	0	0	0	0	0	0	0	0	0	0	0	0	0	0	.000	.000
Kennedy, Adam, Ana.*	.143	7	7	7	1	1	2	1	0	0	0	0	0	0	0	0	0	0	0	0	.286	.143
Kingsale, Eugene, Bal.†	.000	3	3	3	0	0	0	0	0	0	0	0	0	0	0	0	0	0	0	0	.000	.000
Kinkade, Mike, Bal.	.000	1	1	1	0	0	0	0	0	0	0	0	0	0	0	0	0	0	0	0	.000	.000
Konerko, Paul, Chi.	.500	10	10	10	0	5	5	0	0	0	5	0	0	0	0	0	0	0	0	0	.500	.500
Koskie, Corey, Min.*	.500	10	10	6	3	3	3	0	0	0	0	0	0	0	4	0	1	0	1	0	.500	.700
Lamb, Mike, Tex.*	.667	3	3	3	0	2	2	0	0	0	2	0	0	0	0	0	0	0	0	0	.667	.667
Lampkin, Tom, Sea.*	.000	7	6	5	0	0	0	0	0	0	0	0	0	0	1	0	1	0	0	0	.000	.167
Lansing, Mike, Bos.	1.000	1	1	1	1	1	2	1	0	0	2	0	0	0	0	0	0	0	0	0	2.000	1.000
Lawton, Matt, Min.*	.143	7	7	7	0	1	1	0	0	0	2	0	0	0	0	0	1	0	0	0	.143	.143
LeCroy, Matthew, Min.	.000	2	1	1	0	0	0	0	0	0	0	0	0	0	0	0	0	0	0	0	.000	.000
Ledee, Ricky, N.Y.-Cle.-Tex.*	.250	8	8	8	1	2	5	0	0	1	4	0	0	0	0	0	2	1	0	0	.625	.250
Lee, Carlos, Chi.	.000	2	2	2	0	0	0	0	0	0	0	0	0	0	0	0	1	0	0	0	.000	.000
Lesher, Brian, Sea.	.667	4	4	3	0	2	4	0	1	0	1	0	0	0	1	0	0	0	0	0	1.333	.750
Lewis, Darren, Bos.	.333	4	4	3	1	1	2	1	0	0	0	0	0	0	1	0	2	0	0	0	.667	.500
Lewis, Mark, Bal.	.500	5	3	2	0	1	2	1	0	0	0	0	0	0	1	0	1	0	0	0	1.000	.667
Leyritz, Jim, N.Y.	.200	9	8	5	0	1	1	0	0	0	0	0	0	1	2	0	1	0	0	0	.200	.500
Liefer, Jeff, Chi.*	1.000	1	1	1	0	1	1	0	0	0	0	0	0	0	0	0	0	0	0	0	1.000	1.000
Lofton, Kenny, Cle.*	.000	1	1	1	0	0	0	0	0	0	0	0	0	0	0	0	0	0	0	0	.000	.000
Long, Terrence, Oak.*	.250	4	4	4	1	1	1	0	0	0	0	0	0	0	0	0	0	0	0	0	.250	.250
Mabry, John, Sea.*	.125	9	9	8	0	1	1	0	0	0	1	0	0	0	1	0	3	0	0	0	.125	.222
Macias, Jose, Det.†	.071	15	15	14	1	1	3	0	1	0	3	0	0	0	1	0	3	0	0	0	.214	.133
Magee, Wendell Jr., Det.	.385	27	26	26	2	10	13	0	0	1	5	0	0	0	0	0	3	0	0	0	.500	.385
Martin, Al, Sea.*	.500	5	5	4	0	2	2	0	0	0	0	0	0	0	1	0	1	0	0	0	.500	.600
Martinez, Dave, T.B.-Tex.-Tor.*	.250	5	5	4	0	1	1	0	0	0	0	0	0	0	1	0	0	0	0	0	.250	.400
Martinez, Edgar, Sea.	.250	5	5	4	0	1	1	0	0	0	1	0	1	0	0	0	1	0	0	0	.250	.200
Martinez, Tino, N.Y.*	.400	6	6	5	2	2	3	1	0	0	0	0	0	0	1	0	2	1	0	0	.600	.500
Matos, Luis, Bal.	.000	1	1	1	0	0	0	0	0	0	0	0	0	0	0	0	0	0	0	0	.000	.000
Maxwell, Jason, Min.	.111	9	9	9	0	1	1	0	0	0	0	0	0	0	0	0	4	0	0	0	.111	.111
McCarty, David, K.C.	.391	28	28	23	3	9	12	0	0	1	9	0	2	0	3	0	3	0	0	0	.522	.429
McCracken, Quinton, T.B.†	.250	5	5	4	0	1	1	0	0	0	0	0	0	0	1	0	0	0	0	1	.250	.400
McDonald, Jason, Tex.†	.000	2	2	2	0	0	0	0	0	0	0	0	0	0	0	0	1	0	0	0	.000	.000
McDonald, John, Cle.	1.000	2	2	2	0	2	2	0	0	0	0	0	0	0	0	0	0	0	0	0	1.000	1.000
McGriff, Fred, T.B.*	.000	4	4	2	0	0	0	0	0	0	1	0	0	0	2	2	0	0	0	0	.000	.500
McLemore, Mark, Sea.†	.333	4	4	3	2	1	1	0	0	0	0	0	0	0	1	0	1	1	0	0	.333	.500
McMillon, Billy, Det.*	.714	10	10	7	1	5	6	1	0	0	2	0	0	0	3	0	1	0	0	0	.857	.800
Menechino, Frank, Oak.	.000	4	4	4	0	0	0	0	0	0	1	0	0	0	0	0	1	0	0	0	.000	.000
Minor, Ryan, Bal.	.500	2	2	2	0	1	1	0	0	0	1	0	0	0	0	0	0	0	0	0	.500	.500
Moeller, Chad, Min.	.000	1	1	1	0	0	0	0	0	0	0	0	0	0	0	0	0	0	0	0	.000	.000
Molina, Bengie, Ana.	.000	2	2	1	0	0	0	0	0	0	0	0	0	0	1	0	1	0	0	0	.000	.500
Mondesi, Raul, Tor.	.000	1	1	1	0	0	0	0	0	0	0	0	0	0	0	0	0	0	0	0	.000	.000
Morandini, Mickey, Tor.*	1.000	2	2	1	0	1	1	0	0	0	0	1	0	0	0	0	0	0	0	0	1.000	1.000
Morris, Hal, Det.*	.250	4	4	4	0	1	1	0	0	0	1	0	0	0	0	0	0	0	0	0	.250	.250
Myers, Greg, Bal.*	.222	9	9	9	0	2	4	2	0	0	2	0	0	0	0	0	5	0	0	0	.444	.222
Nixon, Trot, Bos.*	.111	12	11	9	0	1	2	1	0	0	0	0	0	0	2	1	4	0	0	0	.222	.273
Norton, Greg, Chi.†	.000	11	11	10	0	0	0	0	0	0	0	0	0	0	1	0	6	0	0	0	.000	.091
O'Leary, Troy, Bos.*	.000	1	1	1	0	0	0	0	0	0	0	0	0	0	0	0	0	0	0	0	.000	.000
O'Neill, Paul, N.Y.*	.000	1	1	0	0	0	0	0	0	0	0	0	0	0	1	0	0	0	0	0	.000	1.000
Offerman, Jose, Bos.†	.000	1	1	1	0	0	0	0	0	0	0	0	0	0	0	0	1	0	0	0	.000	.000
Olerud, John, Sea.*	.000	2	2	2	0	0	0	0	0	0	0	0	0	0	0	0	0	0	0	1	.000	.000
Oliver, Joe, Sea.	.000	3	3	3	0	0	0	0	0	0	0	0	0	0	0	0	0	0	0	0	.000	.000
Ordaz, Luis, K.C.	.286	7	7	7	2	2	2	0	0	0	0	0	0	0	0	0	1	0	0	0	.286	.286
Ordonez, Magglio, Chi.	.000	1	1	1	0	0	0	0	0	0	0	0	0	0	0	0	0	0	0	0	.000	.000
Ortiz, David, Min.*	.188	21	19	16	1	3	6	0	0	1	4	0	0	0	3	0	5	1	0	0	.375	.316
Ortiz, Jose, Oak.	.000	2	2	2	0	0	0	0	0	0	0	0	0	0	0	0	0	0	0	0	.000	.000
Palmeiro, Orlando, Ana.*	.250	31	30	20	4	5	6	1	0	0	1	2	0	0	8	0	4	1	0	0	.300	.464
Palmeiro, Rafael, Tex.*	.500	4	4	2	0	1	1	0	0	0	2	0	0	0	2	1	1	0	0	0	.500	.750
Palmer, Dean, Det.	.000	3	3	2	1	0	0	0	0	0	0	0	0	0	1	0	0	0	0	0	.000	.333
Perry, Chan, Cle.	.000	5	5	5	0	0	0	0	0	0	0	0	0	0	0	0	3	0	0	0	.000	.000
Perry, Herbert, T.B.-Chi.	.000	6	6	3	1	0	0	0	0	0	0	0	0	0	3	0	0	0	0	0	.000	.500
Piatt, Adam, Oak.	.100	14	14	10	1	1	1	0	0	0	1	0	0	0	4	0	6	0	0	1	.100	.357
Pierzynski, A.J., Min.*	1.000	1	1	1	0	1	2	1	0	0	0	0	0	0	0	0	0	0	0	0	2.000	1.000
Polonia, Luis, Det.-N.Y.*	.250	19	19	16	4	4	7	0	0	1	2	2	1	0	0	0	2	0	0	0	.438	.235
Porter, Bo, Oak.	.000	3	3	2	1	0	0	0	0	0	0	0	0	0	1	0	1	0	0	0	.000	.333
Posada, Jorge, N.Y.†	.500	4	4	4	1	2	2	0	0	0	0	0	0	0	0	0	1	0	0	0	.500	.500
Pose, Scott, K.C.*	.222	30	30	27	4	6	6	0	0	0	1	0	0	0	3	0	7	0	0	1	.222	.300
Quinn, Mark, K.C.	.200	7	7	5	0	1	1	0	0	0	2	0	1	0	1	0	1	0	0	0	.200	.286
Ramirez, Alex, Cle.	.333	6	6	6	1	2	2	0	0	0	0	0	0	0	0	0	1	0	0	1	.333	.333
Randa, Joe, K.C.	.000	1	1	1	0	0	0	0	0	0	0	0	0	0	0	0	0	0	0	0	.000	.000
Reboulet, Jeff, K.C.	.000	3	3	3	0	0	0	0	0	0	0	0	0	0	0	0	0	0	0	0	.000	.000
Richard, Chris, Bal.*	.000	1	1	0	1	0	0	0	0	0	0	0	0	0	1	0	0	0	0	0	.000	1.000
Roberts, Dave, Cle.*	.000	1	1	0	0	0	0	0	0	0	0	0	0	0	1	0	0	0	0	0	.000	1.000
Rodriguez, Ivan, Tex.	.750	4	4	4	2	3	10	1	0	2	3	0	0	0	0	0	0	0	0	0	2.500	.750
Rolls, Damian, T.B.	.333	3	3	3	0	1	1	0	0	0	0	0	0	0	0	0	1	0	0	0	.333	.333
Saenz, Olmedo, Oak.	.400	24	24	20	2	8	12	1	0	1	4	0	0	1	3	1	4	0	0	1	.600	.500
Salmon, Tim, Ana.	1.000	1	1	1	0	1	1	0	0	0	0	0	0	0	0	0	0	0	0	0	1.000	1.000
Sanchez, Rey, K.C.	.000	1	1	1	0	0	0	0	0	0	0	0	0	0	0	0	0	0	0	0	.000	.000
Sanders, Anthony, Sea.	1.000	1	1	1	1	1	1	0	0	0	0	0	0	0	0	0	0	0	0	0	1.000	1.000
Schourek, Pete, Bos.*	1.000	1	1	1	0	1	1	0	0	0	0	0	0	0	0	0	0	0	0	0	1.000	1.000
Segui, David, Tex.-Cle.†	.600	5	5	5	1	3	6	1	1	0	3	0	0	0	0	0	0	0	0	0	1.200	.600
Selby, Bill, Cle.*	.500	8	8	8	1	4	4	0	0	0	1	0	0	0	0	0	1	0	0	0	.500	.500

Player, Team	Avg.	G	TPA	AB	R	H	TB	2B	3B	HR	RBI	SH	SF	HP	BB	IBB	SO	SB	CS	GDP	Slg.	OBP
Sexson, Richie, Cle.	.400	7	7	5	2	2	6	1	0	1	3	0	1	0	1	0	3	0	0	0	1.200	.429
Sheldon, Scott, Tex.	.500	3	3	2	1	1	4	0	0	1	1	0	0	0	1	0	0	0	0	0	2.000	.667
Sierra, Ruben, Tex.†	.250	8	8	8	1	2	2	0	0	0	1	0	0	0	0	0	1	0	0	1	.250	.250
Singleton, Chris, Chi.*	.000	1	1	1	0	0	0	0	0	0	0	0	0	0	0	0	0	0	0	0	.000	.000
Smith, Bobby, T.B.	.000	1	1	1	0	0	0	0	0	0	0	0	0	0	0	0	1	0	0	0	.000	.000
Soriano, Alfonso, N.Y.	.000	1	1	1	0	0	0	0	0	0	0	0	0	0	0	0	0	0	0	0	.000	.000
Spiezio, Scott, Ana.†	.286	36	36	28	5	8	14	0	0	2	8	0	2	1	5	0	5	0	0	1	.500	.389
Sprague, Ed Jr., Bos.	1.000	1	1	1	1	1	1	0	0	0	0	0	0	0	0	0	0	0	0	0	1.000	1.000
Stairs, Matt, Oak.*	.100	12	12	10	1	1	2	1	0	0	3	0	0	0	2	1	1	0	0	0	.200	.250
Stanley, Mike, Bos.-Oak.	.300	11	11	10	0	3	3	0	0	0	1	0	0	0	1	0	2	0	0	0	.300	.364
Stocker, Kevin, T.B.-Ana.†	.000	4	4	2	0	0	0	0	0	0	0	0	0	0	2	0	2	0	0	0	.000	.500
Tejada, Miguel, Oak.	1.000	1	1	1	0	1	1	0	0	0	0	0	0	0	0	0	0	0	0	0	1.000	1.000
Thomas, Frank, Chi.	.500	2	2	2	1	1	4	0	0	1	2	0	0	0	0	0	0	0	0	0	2.000	.500
Thome, Jim, Cle.*	.000	4	4	4	0	0	0	0	0	0	0	0	0	0	0	0	2	0	0	0	.000	.000
Thompson, Ryan, N.Y.	.333	3	3	3	0	1	2	1	0	0	0	0	0	0	0	0	1	0	0	0	.667	.333
Timmons, Ozzie, T.B.	.000	2	2	2	0	0	0	0	0	0	0	0	0	0	0	0	1	0	0	0	.000	.000
Trammell, Bubba, T.B.	.286	15	15	14	3	4	13	0	0	3	7	0	0	0	1	0	2	0	0	0	.929	.333
Turner, Chris, N.Y.	.000	3	3	2	0	0	0	0	0	0	0	0	0	0	1	0	2	0	0	0	.000	.333
Tyner, Jason, T.B.*	.000	1	1	1	0	0	0	0	0	0	0	0	0	0	0	0	0	0	0	0	.000	.000
Valdes, Pedro, Tex.*	.214	15	15	14	2	3	4	1	0	0	0	0	0	0	1	0	0	0	0	0	.286	.267
Valdez, Mario, Oak.*	.000	1	1	1	0	0	0	0	0	0	0	0	0	0	0	0	1	0	0	0	.000	.000
Valentin, Jose, Chi.†	.400	5	5	5	1	2	5	0	0	1	3	0	0	0	0	0	0	0	0	0	1.000	.400
Varitek, Jason, Bos.†	.286	18	18	14	1	4	5	1	0	0	2	0	0	0	4	0	3	0	0	1	.357	.444
Vaughn, Greg, T.B.	.000	3	3	3	0	0	0	0	0	0	0	0	0	0	0	0	3	0	0	0	.000	.000
Vaughn, Mo, Ana.*	.000	1	1	1	0	0	0	0	0	0	0	0	0	0	0	0	1	0	0	0	.000	.000
Velandia, Jorge, Oak.	.000	5	5	4	0	0	0	0	0	0	0	0	0	1	0	0	2	0	0	0	.000	.200
Vizcaino, Jose, N.Y.†	.333	4	4	3	0	1	1	0	0	0	1	0	0	0	1	0	1	0	0	0	.333	.500
Vizquel, Omar, Cle.†	.000	1	1	1	0	0	0	0	0	0	0	0	0	0	0	0	0	0	0	0	.000	.000
Wakefield, Tim, Bos.	.000	1	1	0	0	0	0	0	0	0	0	1	0	0	0	0	0	0	0	0	.000	.000
Walbeck, Matt, Ana.†	.000	1	1	1	0	0	0	0	0	0	0	0	0	0	0	0	1	0	0	0	.000	.000
Walker, Todd, Min.*	.000	2	2	2	0	0	0	0	0	0	0	0	0	0	0	0	1	0	0	0	.000	.000
Whiten, Mark, Cle.†	1.000	3	3	1	0	1	1	0	0	0	0	0	0	0	2	0	0	0	0	0	1.000	1.000
Williams, Bernie, N.Y.†	.000	1	1	1	0	0	0	0	0	0	1	0	0	0	0	0	0	0	0	0	.000	.000
Williams, Gerald, T.B.	.000	1	1	1	0	0	0	0	0	0	0	0	0	0	0	0	1	0	0	0	.000	.000
Wilson, Craig, Chi.	.000	4	4	4	0	0	0	0	0	0	0	0	0	0	0	0	0	0	0	0	.000	.000
Wilson, Dan, Sea.	.000	4	4	4	0	0	0	0	0	0	0	0	0	0	0	0	0	0	0	0	.000	.000
Wilson, Enrique, Cle.†	.000	10	10	9	0	0	0	0	0	0	0	0	0	0	1	0	2	0	0	0	.000	.100
Winn, Randy, T.B.†	.000	5	5	3	1	0	0	0	0	0	0	0	1	0	1	0	1	0	0	0	.000	.250
Wise, Dewayne, Tor.*	1.000	1	1	1	0	1	1	0	0	0	0	0	0	0	0	0	0	1	0	0	1.000	1.000
Zaun, Gregg, K.C.†	.357	16	16	14	2	5	5	0	0	0	2	0	0	0	2	0	2	2	0	0	.357	.438

PINCH-HITTERS WITH TWO OR MORE TEAMS

Player, Team	Avg.	G	TPA	AB	R	H	TB	2B	3B	HR	RBI	SH	SF	HP	BB	IBB	SO	SB	CS	GDP	Slg.	OBP
Baines, Harold, Bal.*	.375	11	10	8	0	3	3	0	0	0	0	0	0	0	2	1	3	0	0	0	.375	.500
Baines, Harold, Chi.*	.143	9	9	7	0	1	1	0	0	0	0	0	0	0	2	0	4	0	0	0	.143	.333
Becker, Rich, Oak.*	.286	7	7	7	1	2	2	0	0	0	1	0	0	0	0	0	3	0	0	0	.286	.286
Becker, Rich, Det.*	.263	24	24	19	5	5	8	0	0	1	3	0	0	0	5	0	7	0	1	0	.421	.417
Canseco, Jose, T.B.	.000	2	2	2	0	0	0	0	0	0	0	0	0	0	0	0	1	0	0	0	.000	.000
Canseco, Jose, N.Y.	.167	6	6	6	0	1	1	0	0	0	0	0	0	0	0	0	2	0	0	0	.167	.167
Cummings, Midre, Min.*	.333	37	36	33	2	11	14	3	0	0	10	0	0	0	3	0	3	0	0	0	.424	.389
Cummings, Midre, Bos.*	.286	17	16	14	0	4	4	0	0	0	2	0	0	0	2	0	2	0	0	1	.286	.375
Delgado, Wilson, N.Y.†	.000	1	1	1	0	0	0	0	0	0	0	0	0	0	0	0	0	0	0	0	.000	.000
Delgado, Wilson, K.C.†	.167	6	6	6	0	1	1	0	0	0	0	0	0	0	0	0	1	0	0	0	.167	.167
Fordyce, Brook, Chi.	.500	2	2	2	0	1	1	0	0	0	2	0	0	0	0	0	0	0	0	0	.500	.500
Fordyce, Brook, Bal.	.000	3	3	3	0	0	0	0	0	0	0	0	0	0	0	0	1	0	0	1	.000	.000
Graffanino, Tony, T.B.	.000	1	1	1	0	0	0	0	0	0	0	0	0	0	0	0	0	0	0	0	.000	.000
Graffanino, Tony, Chi.	.200	7	6	5	2	1	3	0	1	0	1	0	0	0	1	0	0	0	0	0	.600	.333
Johnson, Charles, Bal.	.000	1	1	1	0	0	0	0	0	0	0	0	0	0	0	0	1	0	0	0	.000	.000
Johnson, Charles, Chi.	.000	1	1	1	0	0	0	0	0	0	0	0	0	0	0	0	0	0	0	0	.000	.000
Justice, David, Cle.*	.000	2	1	1	0	0	0	0	0	0	0	0	0	0	0	0	0	0	0	0	.000	.000
Justice, David, N.Y.*	.000	2	2	1	0	0	0	0	0	0	0	0	0	0	1	0	1	0	0	0	.000	.500
Ledee, Ricky, N.Y.*	.286	7	7	7	1	2	5	0	0	1	4	0	0	0	0	0	2	1	0	0	.714	.286
Ledee, Ricky, Tex.*	.000	1	1	1	0	0	0	0	0	0	0	0	0	0	0	0	0	0	0	0	.000	.000
Martinez, Dave, T.B.*	.000	1	1	1	0	0	0	0	0	0	0	0	0	0	0	0	0	0	0	0	.000	.000
Martinez, Dave, Tex.*	.000	3	3	2	0	0	0	0	0	0	0	0	0	0	1	0	0	0	0	0	.000	.333
Martinez, Dave, Tor.*	1.000	1	1	1	0	1	1	0	0	0	0	0	0	0	0	0	0	0	0	0	1.000	1.000
Polonia, Luis, Det.*	.250	14	14	12	3	3	6	0	0	1	1	2	0	0	0	0	1	0	0	0	.500	.250
Polonia, Luis, N.Y.*	.250	5	5	4	1	1	1	0	0	0	1	0	1	0	0	0	1	0	0	0	.250	.200
Segui, David, Tex.†	.667	3	3	3	0	2	5	1	1	0	3	0	0	0	0	0	0	0	0	0	1.667	.667
Segui, David, Cle.†	.500	2	2	2	1	1	1	0	0	0	0	0	0	0	0	0	0	0	0	0	.500	.500
Stanley, Mike, Bos.	.600	5	5	5	0	3	3	0	0	0	1	0	0	0	0	0	1	0	0	0	.600	.600
Stanley, Mike, Oak.	.000	6	6	5	0	0	0	0	0	0	0	0	0	0	1	0	1	0	0	0	.000	.167

PITCHING

TEAM

Team	W	L	Pct.	ERA	G	ShO	Rel.	Sv.	IP	H	TBF	R	ER	HR	SH	SF	HB	BB	IBB	SO	WP	Bk.
Boston	85	77	.525	4.23	162	12	425	46	1452.2	1433	6225	745	683	173	46	49	58	498	40	1121	33	2
Seattle	91	71	.562	4.49	162	10	383	44	1441.2	1442	6269	780	720	167	39	55	38	634	37	998	43	6
Oakland	91	70	.565	4.58	161	11	381	43	1435.1	1535	6355	813	730	158	35	51	48	615	57	963	46	1
Chicago	95	67	.586	4.66	162	7	466	43	1450.1	1509	6337	839	751	195	39	49	54	614	27	1037	43	8
Detroit	79	83	.488	4.71	162	6	429	44	1443.1	1583	6295	827	755	177	33	63	47	496	22	978	51	5
New York	87	74	.540	4.76	161	6	382	40	1424.1	1458	6286	814	753	177	45	48	52	577	23	1040	49	6
Cleveland	90	72	.556	4.84	162	5	462	34	1442.1	1511	6380	816	775	173	34	42	42	666	45	1213	50	3
Tampa Bay	69	92	.429	4.86	161	8	401	38	1431.1	1553	6283	842	773	198	42	45	66	533	33	955	57	3
Anaheim	82	80	.506	5.00	162	3	441	46	1448.0	1534	6401	869	805	228	40	53	36	662	44	846	47	10
Toronto	83	79	.512	5.14	162	4	388	37	1437.1	1615	6377	908	821	195	44	40	64	560	19	978	37	3
Minnesota	69	93	.426	5.14	162	4	412	35	1432.2	1634	6336	880	819	212	41	46	35	516	12	1042	68	4
Baltimore	74	88	.457	5.37	162	6	396	33	1433.1	1547	6433	913	855	202	48	57	36	665	32	1017	51	1
Kansas City	77	85	.475	5.48	162	6	329	29	1439.1	1585	6443	930	876	239	39	45	42	693	35	927	77	5
Texas	71	91	.438	5.52	162	4	415	39	1429.0	1683	6559	974	876	202	42	62	63	661	40	918	40	6
Totals	1143	1122	.505	4.91	1133	92	5710	551	20141.0	21622	88949	11950	10992	2696	567	705	681	8390	466	14033	692	63

NOTE—Totals for earned runs for several clubs do not agree with composite total for all pitchers of each respective club due to instances in which provisions of Section 10.18(i) of the Scoring Rules were applied. The following differences are to be noted: Boston pitchers add to 684; Seattle pitchers add to 726; Chicago pitchers add to 752; Detroit pitchers add to 759; Anaheim pitchers add to 807; Toronto pitchers add to 826; Minnesota pitchers add to 821; Kansas City pitchers add to 877.

INDIVIDUAL

TOP QUALIFIERS FOR EARNED-RUN AVERAGE TITLE

Minimum 162 innings. *Throws lefthanded.

Pitcher, Team	W	L	Pct.	ERA	G	GS	CG	ShO	GF	Sv.	IP	H	TBF	R	ER	HR	SH	SF	HB	BB	IBB	SO	WP	Bk.
Martinez, Pedro, Bos.	18	6	.750	1.74	29	29	7	4	0	0	217.0	128	817	44	42	17	2	1	14	32	0	284	1	0
Clemens, Roger, N.Y.	13	8	.619	3.70	32	32	1	0	0	0	204.1	184	878	96	84	26	1	2	10	84	0	188	2	1
Mussina, Mike, Bal.	11	15	.423	3.79	34	34	6	1	0	0	237.2	236	987	105	100	28	8	6	3	46	0	210	3	0
Sirotka, Mike, Chi.*	15	10	.600	3.79	32	32	1	1	0	0	197.0	203	832	101	83	23	4	3	1	69	1	128	8	2
Colon, Bartolo, Cle.	15	8	.652	3.88	30	30	2	1	0	0	188.0	163	807	86	81	21	2	3	4	98	4	212	4	0
Wells, David, Tor.*	20	8	.714	4.11	35	35	9	1	0	0	229.2	266	972	115	105	23	6	7	8	31	0	166	9	1
Heredia, Gil, Oak.	15	11	.577	4.12	32	32	2	0	0	0	198.2	214	860	106	91	24	4	6	4	66	5	101	3	0
Lopez, Albie, T.B.	11	13	.458	4.13	45	24	4	1	10	2	185.1	199	798	95	85	24	6	3	1	70	3	96	4	1
Hudson, Tim, Oak.	20	6	.769	4.14	32	32	2	2	0	0	202.1	169	847	100	93	24	5	7	7	82	5	169	7	0
Finley, Chuck, Cle.*	16	11	.593	4.17	34	34	3	0	0	0	218.0	211	936	108	101	23	5	4	2	101	3	189	9	0
Abbott, Paul, Sea.	9	7	.563	4.22	35	27	0	0	2	0	179.0	164	766	89	84	23	1	4	5	80	4	100	3	0
Parque, Jim, Chi.*	13	6	.684	4.28	33	32	0	0	0	0	187.0	208	828	105	89	21	5	5	11	71	1	111	2	5
Weaver, Jeff, Det.	11	15	.423	4.32	31	30	2	0	0	0	200.0	205	849	102	96	26	3	9	15	52	2	136	3	2
Suzuki, Mac, K.C.	8	10	.444	4.34	32	29	1	1	0	0	188.2	195	839	100	91	26	2	3	3	94	6	135	11	0
Pettitte, Andy, N.Y.*	19	9	.679	4.35	32	32	3	1	0	0	204.2	219	903	111	99	17	7	4	4	80	4	125	2	3

DEPARTMENTAL LEADERS: W—Hudson, Oak, Wells, Tor., 20; L—Radke, Min., 16; G—Wunsch, Chi., 83; GS—Helling, Tex., Wells, Tor., 35; CG—Wells, Tor., 9; ShO—P. Martinez, Bos., 4; GF—Lowe, Bos., 64; Sv.—Jones, Det., Lowe, Bos., 42; IP—Mussina, Bal., 237.2; H—Wells, Tor., 266; TBF—Rogers, Tex., 998; R—Carpenter, Tor., 130; ER—Carpenter, Tor., 122; HR—Suppan, K.C., 36; SH—Carrasco, Min.-Bos., Mussina, Bal., 8; SF—Helling, Tex., Rekar, T.B., Weaver, Det., 9; HB—Weaver, Det., 15; TBB—Appier, Oak., 102; IBB—Appier, Oak., 10; SO—P. Martinez, Bos., 284; WP—Reichert, K.C., 18; BK—Parque, Chi., 5.

ALL PITCHERS

*Throws lefthanded.

Pitcher, Team	W	L	Pct.	ERA	G	GS	CG	ShO	GF	Sv.	IP	H	TBF	R	ER	HR	SH	SF	HB	BB	IBB	SO	WP	Bk.
Abbott, Paul, Sea.	9	7	.563	4.22	35	27	0	0	2	0	179.0	164	766	89	84	23	1	4	5	80	4	100	3	0
Alvarez, Juan, Ana.*	0	0	.000	13.50	11	0	0	0	3	0	6.0	14	38	9	9	3	0	1	0	7	1	2	1	0
Anderson, Matt, Det.	3	2	.600	4.72	69	0	0	0	27	1	74.1	61	324	44	39	8	2	6	3	45	4	71	4	0
Andrews, Clayton, Tor.*	1	2	.333	10.02	8	2	0	0	1	0	20.2	34	102	23	23	6	1	1	0	9	0	12	0	1
Appier, Kevin, Oak.	15	11	.577	4.52	31	31	1	1	0	0	195.1	200	884	109	98	23	5	6	9	102	10	129	6	0
Arrojo, Rolando, Bos.	5	2	.714	5.05	13	13	0	0	0	0	71.1	67	301	41	40	10	1	0	4	22	0	44	3	0
Baldwin, James, Chi.	14	7	.667	4.65	29	28	2	1	0	0	178.0	185	758	96	92	34	6	5	9	53	3	116	4	1
Bale, John, Tor.*	0	0	.000	14.73	2	0	0	0	0	0	3.2	5	22	7	6	1	0	1	2	3	0	6	0	0
Barcelo, Lorenzo, Chi.	4	2	.667	3.69	22	1	0	0	5	0	39.0	34	157	17	16	5	0	1	0	9	1	26	1	0
Batista, Miguel, K.C.	2	6	.250	7.14	14	9	0	0	2	0	57.0	66	261	54	49	17	0	1	0	34	2	30	4	0
Beck, Rod, Bos.	3	0	1.000	3.10	34	0	0	0	8	0	40.2	34	169	15	14	2	2	0	2	12	1	35	1	0
Beirne, Kevin, Chi.	1	3	.250	6.70	29	1	0	0	8	0	49.2	50	220	41	37	9	1	5	4	20	1	41	1	0
Belcher, Tim, Ana.	4	5	.444	6.86	9	9	1	0	0	0	40.2	45	186	31	31	8	1	1	2	22	1	22	1	1
Belitz, Todd, Oak.*	0	0	.000	2.70	5	0	0	0	3	0	3.1	4	19	2	1	0	0	0	0	4	0	3	1	0
Bere, Jason, Cle.	6	3	.667	6.63	11	11	0	0	0	0	54.1	65	252	41	40	6	0	3	4	26	0	44	2	0
Bergman, Sean, Min.	4	5	.444	9.66	15	14	0	0	0	0	68.0	111	337	76	73	18	2	3	3	33	1	35	2	0
Bernero, Adam, Det.	0	1	.000	4.19	12	4	0	0	4	0	34.1	33	141	18	16	3	2	3	1	13	1	20	1	0
Biddle, Rocky, Chi.	1	2	.333	8.34	4	4	0	0	0	0	22.2	31	105	25	21	5	0	2	0	8	0	7	2	0
Blair, Willie, Det.	10	6	.625	4.88	47	17	0	0	8	0	156.2	185	671	89	85	20	1	7	2	35	0	74	2	0
Bochtler, Doug, K.C.	0	2	.000	6.48	6	0	0	0	2	0	8.1	13	46	6	6	2	1	0	0	10	4	4	1	0
Borbon, Pedro Jr., Tor.*	1	1	.500	6.48	59	0	0	0	6	1	41.2	45	213	37	30	5	2	7	5	38	5	29	0	0
Borkowski, Dave, Det.	0	1	.000	21.94	2	1	0	0	0	0	5.1	11	34	13	13	2	0	1	0	7	1	1	0	0
Bottalico, Ricky, K.C.	9	6	.600	4.83	62	0	0	0	50	16	72.2	65	319	40	39	12	3	1	2	41	3	56	5	1
Bottenfield, Kent, Ana.	7	8	.467	5.71	21	21	0	0	0	0	127.2	144	571	82	81	25	2	5	3	56	4	75	1	0
Bradford, Chad, Chi.	1	0	1.000	1.98	12	0	0	0	5	0	13.2	13	52	4	3	0	0	0	0	1	1	9	0	0

2000 A.L. STATISTICS — Pitching

Pitcher, Team	W	L	Pct.	ERA	G	GS	CG	ShO	GF	Sv.	IP	H	TBF	R	ER	HR	SH	SF	HB	BB	IBB	SO	WP	Bk.
Brea, Leslie, Bal.	0	1	.000	11.00	6	1	0	0	3	0	9.0	12	49	11	11	1	0	1	1	10	0	5	1	0
Brewington, Jamie, Cle.	3	0	1.000	5.36	26	0	0	0	10	0	45.1	56	205	28	27	3	2	2	2	19	0	34	1	0
Brocail, Doug, Det.	5	4	.556	4.09	49	0	0	0	10	0	50.2	57	221	25	23	5	3	3	1	14	2	41	1	1
Brower, Jim, Cle.	2	3	.400	6.24	17	11	0	0	1	0	62.0	80	293	45	43	11	1	0	2	31	1	32	3	0
Buehrle, Mark, Chi.*	4	1	.800	4.21	28	3	0	0	6	0	51.1	55	225	27	24	5	1	0	3	19	1	37	0	0
Burba, Dave, Cle.	16	6	.727	4.47	32	32	0	0	0	0	191.1	199	848	99	95	19	5	5	2	91	2	180	7	0
Byrdak, Tim, K.C.*	0	1	.000	11.37	12	0	0	0	1	0	6.1	11	34	8	8	3	0	0	0	4	0	8	1	0
Cairncross, Cameron, Cle.*	1	0	1.000	3.86	15	0	0	0	2	0	9.1	11	40	4	4	1	0	1	0	3	1	8	0	0
Carpenter, Chris, Tor.	10	12	.455	6.26	34	27	2	0	1	0	175.1	204	795	130	122	30	3	1	5	83	1	113	3	0
Carrasco, Hector, Min.-Bos.	5	4	.556	4.69	69	1	0	0	20	1	78.2	90	364	46	41	8	8	4	4	38	1	64	14	1
Castillo, Frank, Tor.	10	5	.667	3.59	25	24	0	0	1	0	138.0	112	576	58	55	18	5	2	5	56	0	104	0	1
Choate, Randy, N.Y.*	0	1	.000	4.76	22	0	0	0	6	0	17.0	14	75	10	9	3	0	1	1	8	0	12	1	0
Clark, Mark, Tex.	3	5	.375	7.98	12	8	0	0	1	0	44.0	66	220	42	39	10	1	2	3	24	2	16	1	0
Clemens, Roger, N.Y.	13	8	.619	3.70	32	32	1	0	0	0	204.1	184	878	96	84	26	1	2	10	84	0	188	2	1
Coco, Pasqual, Tor.	0	0	.000	9.00	1	1	0	0	0	0	4.0	5	23	4	4	1	0	0	1	5	0	2	1	0
Colon, Bartolo, Cle.	15	8	.652	3.88	30	30	2	1	0	0	188.0	163	807	86	81	21	2	3	4	98	4	212	4	0
Cone, David, N.Y.	4	14	.222	6.91	30	29	0	0	0	0	155.0	192	733	124	119	25	6	8	9	82	3	120	11	0
Cooper, Brian, Ana.	4	8	.333	5.90	15	15	1	1	0	0	87.0	105	396	66	57	18	4	4	2	35	1	36	1	0
Cordero, Francisco, Tex.	1	2	.333	5.35	56	0	0	0	13	0	77.1	87	365	51	46	11	2	6	4	48	3	49	7	0
Cormier, Rheal, Bos.*	3	3	.500	4.61	64	0	0	0	12	0	68.1	74	293	40	35	7	5	2	0	17	2	43	1	0
Crabtree, Tim, Tex.	2	7	.222	5.15	68	0	0	0	28	2	80.1	86	352	52	46	7	1	4	2	31	6	54	4	0
Crawford, Paxton, Bos.	2	1	.667	3.41	7	4	0	0	2	0	29.0	25	123	15	11	0	0	4	2	13	2	17	0	0
Creek, Doug, T.B.*	1	3	.250	4.60	45	0	0	0	8	1	60.2	49	265	33	31	10	2	3	2	39	3	73	3	0
Cressend, Jack, Min.	0	0	.000	5.27	11	0	0	0	4	0	13.2	20	61	8	8	0	0	0	0	6	0	6	0	0
Croushore, Rick, Bos.	0	1	.000	5.79	5	0	0	0	3	0	4.2	4	24	3	3	0	1	1	1	5	1	3	1	0
Cruz, Nelson, Det.	5	2	.714	3.07	27	0	0	0	12	0	41.0	39	172	14	14	4	0	2	3	13	3	34	2	0
Cubillan, Darwin, Tor.-Tex.	0	1	.000	9.45	20	0	0	0	6	0	33.1	52	172	36	35	9	0	3	1	25	0	27	1	0
D'Amico, Jeff M., K.C.	0	1	.000	9.22	7	1	0	0	1	0	13.2	19	71	14	14	2	1	0	0	15	1	9	1	2
Davis, Doug, Tex.*	7	6	.538	5.38	30	13	1	0	4	0	98.2	109	450	61	59	14	6	4	3	58	3	66	5	1
Davis, Kane, Cle.	0	3	.000	14.73	5	2	0	0	0	0	11.0	20	61	21	18	3	0	1	0	8	0	2	0	1
DePaula, Sean, Cle.	0	0	.000	5.94	13	0	0	0	3	0	16.2	13	83	11	11	3	0	1	0	14	2	16	0	0
DeWitt, Matt, Tor.	1	0	1.000	8.56	8	0	0	0	4	0	13.2	20	68	13	13	4	0	0	2	9	0	6	1	0
Dickson, Jason, Ana.	2	2	.500	6.11	6	6	0	0	0	0	28.0	39	125	20	19	5	1	0	1	7	0	18	0	0
Dingman, Craig, N.Y.	0	0	.000	6.55	10	0	0	0	4	0	11.0	18	51	8	8	1	0	0	3	8	0	8	0	0
Drew, Tim, Cle.	1	0	1.000	10.00	3	3	0	0	0	0	9.0	17	51	12	10	1	0	2	1	8	0	5	0	0
Durbin, Chad, K.C.	2	5	.286	8.21	16	16	0	0	0	0	72.1	91	349	71	66	14	1	3	0	43	1	37	7	0
Duvall, Mike, T.B.*	0	0	.000	7.71	2	0	0	0	0	0	2.1	5	12	2	2	0	0	0	1	0	0	0	0	0
Eiland, Dave, T.B.	2	3	.400	7.24	17	10	0	0	1	0	54.2	77	260	46	44	8	0	2	4	18	0	17	1	0
Einertson, Darrell, N.Y.	0	0	.000	3.55	11	0	0	0	4	0	12.2	16	58	9	5	1	1	0	0	4	0	3	0	0
Eldred, Cal, Chi.	10	2	.833	4.58	20	20	2	1	0	0	112.0	103	492	61	57	12	3	2	5	59	0	97	4	0
Enders, Trevor, T.B.*	0	1	.000	10.61	9	0	0	0	4	0	9.1	14	46	13	11	2	2	0	5	5	0	6	1	0
Erdos, Todd, N.Y.	0	0	.000	5.04	14	0	0	0	6	1	25.0	31	114	14	14	2	0	0	1	11	0	18	1	0
Erickson, Scott, Bal.	5	8	.385	7.87	16	16	1	0	0	0	92.1	127	446	81	81	14	3	5	5	48	0	41	3	0
Escobar, Kelvim, Tor.	10	15	.400	5.35	43	24	3	1	8	2	180.0	186	794	118	107	26	5	4	3	85	3	142	4	0
Estrella, Leo, Tor.	0	0	.000	5.79	2	0	0	0	0	0	4.2	9	21	3	3	1	0	1	0	0	0	3	0	0
Etherton, Seth, Ana.	5	1	.833	5.52	11	11	0	0	0	0	60.1	68	270	38	37	16	1	1	1	22	0	32	2	0
Eyre, Scott, Chi.*	1	1	.500	6.63	13	1	0	0	3	0	19.0	29	93	15	14	3	0	2	1	12	0	16	0	0
Fassero, Jeff, Bos.*	8	8	.500	4.78	38	23	0	0	4	0	130.0	153	577	72	69	16	7	2	1	50	2	97	2	0
Finley, Chuck, Cle.*	16	11	.593	4.17	34	34	3	0	0	0	218.0	211	936	108	101	23	5	4	2	101	3	189	9	0
Fiore, Tony, T.B.	1	1	.500	8.40	11	0	0	0	3	0	15.0	21	74	16	14	3	0	0	2	9	2	8	1	0
Florie, Bryce, Bos.	0	4	.000	4.56	29	0	0	0	14	1	49.1	57	223	30	25	5	6	3	1	19	6	34	0	0
Ford, Ben, N.Y.	0	1	.000	9.00	4	2	0	0	0	0	11.0	14	52	11	11	1	0	0	3	7	0	5	0	0
Foulke, Keith, Chi.	3	1	.750	2.97	72	0	0	0	58	34	88.0	66	350	31	29	9	5	2	2	22	2	91	1	0
Frascatore, John, Tor.	2	4	.333	5.42	60	0	0	0	15	0	73.0	87	335	51	44	14	2	4	7	33	2	30	3	0
Fussell, Chris, K.C.	5	3	.625	6.30	20	9	0	0	2	0	70.0	76	320	52	49	18	3	5	2	44	2	46	3	0
Fyhrie, Mike, Ana.	0	0	.000	2.39	32	0	0	0	7	0	52.2	54	220	14	14	4	1	3	0	15	4	43	0	0
Garces, Rich, Bos.	8	1	.889	3.25	64	0	0	0	9	1	74.2	64	309	28	27	7	1	4	1	23	5	69	3	0
Garcia, Freddy, Sea.	9	5	.643	3.91	21	20	0	0	0	0	124.1	112	538	62	54	16	6	1	2	64	4	79	4	2
Garland, Jon, Chi.	4	8	.333	6.46	15	13	0	0	1	0	69.2	82	324	55	50	10	0	2	1	40	0	42	4	0
Ginter, Matt, Chi.	1	0	1.000	13.50	7	0	0	0	3	0	9.1	18	52	14	14	5	0	1	0	7	0	6	1	0
Glynn, Ryan, Tex.	5	7	.417	5.58	16	16	0	0	0	0	88.2	107	412	65	55	15	3	0	3	41	2	33	3	0
Gooden, Dwight, T.B.-N.Y.	6	5	.545	4.54	26	13	0	0	3	2	101.0	113	447	60	51	22	4	2	3	41	3	54	3	0
Grimsley, Jason, N.Y.	3	2	.600	5.04	63	4	0	0	18	1	96.1	100	428	58	54	10	2	6	5	42	1	53	16	0
Groom, Buddy, Bal.*	6	3	.667	4.85	70	0	0	0	14	4	59.1	63	260	37	32	5	5	5	0	21	2	44	1	0
Guardado, Eddie, Min.*	7	4	.636	3.94	70	0	0	0	36	9	61.2	55	262	27	27	14	3	2	1	25	3	52	1	1
Gunderson, Eric, Tor.*	0	1	.000	7.11	6	0	0	0	4	0	6.1	15	37	6	5	0	0	1	1	2	1	2	0	0
Guthrie, Mark, T.B.-Tor.*	1	3	.250	4.61	57	0	0	0	12	0	52.2	53	233	30	27	7	2	1	1	27	5	46	9	0
Guzman, Juan, T.B.	0	1	.000	43.20	1	1	0	0	0	0	1.2	7	14	8	8	2	1	0	0	2	0	3	0	0
Halama, John, Sea.*	14	9	.609	5.08	30	30	1	1	0	0	166.2	206	736	108	94	19	4	6	2	56	0	87	4	1
Halladay, Roy, Tor.	4	7	.364	10.64	19	13	0	0	4	0	67.2	107	349	87	80	14	2	3	2	42	0	44	6	1
Halter, Shane, Det.	0	0	.000	---	1	0	0	0	0	0	.0	0	1	0	0	0	0	0	0	1	0	0	0	0
Hamilton, Joey, Tor.	2	1	.667	3.55	6	6	0	0	0	0	33.0	28	135	13	13	3	0	1	2	12	0	15	0	0
Haney, Chris, Cle.*	0	0	.000	9.00	1	0	0	0	1	0	1.0	1	5	1	1	0	0	0	0	1	0	0	0	0
Harper, Travis, T.B.	1	2	.333	4.78	6	5	1	1	0	0	32.0	30	141	17	17	5	1	1	1	15	0	14	1	0
Hasegawa, Shigetoshi, Ana.	10	5	.667	3.48	66	0	0	0	26	9	95.2	100	415	42	37	11	2	3	2	38	6	59	2	1
Hawkins, LaTroy, Min.	2	5	.286	3.39	66	0	0	0	38	14	87.2	85	370	34	33	7	4	1	1	32	1	59	6	0
Helling, Rick, Tex.	16	13	.552	4.48	35	35	0	0	0	0	217.0	212	963	122	108	29	4	9	9	99	2	146	2	0
Heredia, Gil, Oak.	15	11	.577	4.12	32	32	2	0	0	0	198.2	214	860	106	91	24	4	6	4	66	5	101	3	0
Hernandez, Orlando, N.Y.	12	13	.480	4.51	29	29	3	0	0	0	195.2	186	820	104	98	34	4	5	12	51	2	141	1	0
Hernandez, Roberto, T.B.	4	7	.364	3.19	68	0	0	0	58	32	73.1	76	315	33	26	9	7	3	3	23	1	61	2	1
Hiljus, Erik, Det.	0	0	.000	7.36	3	0	0	0	2	0	3.2	5	16	3	3	1	0	0	0	1	0	2	0	0
Hill, Ken, Ana.-Chi.	5	8	.385	7.16	18	17	0	0	0	0	81.2	107	399	67	65	16	3	8	2	59	1	50	6	0

Pitcher, Team	W	L	Pct.	ERA	G	GS	CG	ShO	GF	Sv.	IP	H	TBF	R	ER	HR	SH	SF	HB	BB	IBB	SO	WP	Bk.
Hinchliffe, Brett, Ana.	0	0	.000	5.40	2	0	0	0	0	0	1.2	1	7	1	1	0	0	0	0	1	0	0	0	0
Hodges, Kevin, Sea.	0	0	.000	5.19	13	0	0	0	7	0	17.1	18	73	10	10	4	0	1	2	12	0	7	1	0
Holmes, Darren, Bal.	0	0	.000	25.07	5	0	0	0	0	0	4.2	13	32	13	13	3	0	0	0	5	0	6	0	0
Holtz, Mike, Ana.*	3	4	.429	5.05	61	0	0	0	6	0	41.0	37	176	26	23	4	4	3	2	18	2	40	1	0
Howry, Bob, Chi.	2	4	.333	3.17	65	0	0	0	29	7	71.0	54	289	26	25	6	2	4	4	29	2	60	2	0
Hudson, Tim, Oak.	20	6	.769	4.14	32	32	2	2	0	0	202.1	169	847	100	93	24	5	7	7	82	5	169	7	0
Isringhausen, Jason, Oak.	6	4	.600	3.78	66	0	0	0	57	33	69.0	67	304	34	29	6	2	1	3	32	5	57	5	1
Johnson, Jason, Bal.	1	10	.091	7.02	25	13	0	0	3	0	107.2	119	501	95	84	21	3	5	4	61	2	79	3	0
Johnson, Jonathan, Tex.	1	1	.500	6.21	15	0	0	0	3	0	29.0	34	144	23	20	3	0	2	6	19	2	23	2	0
Johnson, Mark J., Det.	0	1	.000	7.50	9	3	0	0	3	0	24.0	25	116	23	20	3	1	4	1	16	1	11	2	0
Jones, Doug, Oak.	4	2	.667	3.93	54	0	0	0	22	2	73.1	86	319	34	32	6	2	2	2	18	4	54	1	0
Jones, Marcus, Oak.	0	0	.000	15.43	1	1	0	0	0	0	2.1	5	15	4	4	1	0	0	0	3	0	1	0	0
Jones, Todd, Det.	2	4	.333	3.52	67	0	0	0	60	42	64.0	67	271	28	25	6	1	1	1	25	1	67	2	0
Kamieniecki, Scott, Cle.	1	3	.250	5.67	26	1	0	0	7	0	33.1	42	157	22	21	6	1	0	1	20	5	29	3	0
Karl, Scott, Ana.*	2	2	.500	6.65	6	4	0	0	0	0	21.2	31	105	21	16	2	1	0	0	12	0	9	2	0
Karsay, Steve, Cle.	5	9	.357	3.76	72	0	0	0	46	20	76.2	79	329	33	32	5	2	2	3	25	4	66	0	0
Keisler, Randy, N.Y.*	1	0	1.000	11.81	4	1	0	0	0	0	10.2	16	52	14	14	1	0	0	0	8	0	6	0	0
Kida, Masao, Det.	0	0	.000	10.13	2	0	0	0	0	0	2.2	5	13	3	3	1	0	0	0	0	0	0	0	0
Kinney, Matt, Min.	2	2	.500	5.10	8	8	0	0	0	0	42.1	41	186	26	24	7	0	4	0	25	1	24	4	0
Koch, Billy, Tor.	9	3	.750	2.63	68	0	0	0	62	33	78.2	78	326	28	23	6	4	0	2	18	4	60	1	0
Kohlmeier, Ryan, Bal.	0	1	.000	2.39	25	0	0	0	22	13	26.1	30	120	9	7	1	1	1	0	15	2	17	0	0
Kolb, Danny, Tex.	0	0	.000	67.50	1	0	0	0	0	0	.2	5	9	5	5	0	0	1	0	2	0	0	0	0
Larkin, Andy, K.C.	0	3	.000	8.84	18	0	0	0	9	1	19.1	29	97	20	19	5	2	1	0	11	2	17	2	0
Laxton, Brett, K.C.	0	1	.000	8.10	6	1	0	0	1	0	16.2	23	79	15	15	0	1	0	2	10	1	14	1	0
Lee, Sang-Hoon, Bos.*	0	0	.000	3.09	9	0	0	0	1	0	11.2	11	49	4	4	2	0	1	2	4	0	6	0	0
Levine, Al, Ana.	3	4	.429	3.87	51	5	0	0	12	2	95.1	98	426	44	41	10	3	3	2	49	5	42	1	0
Lidle, Cory, T.B.	4	6	.400	5.03	31	11	0	0	5	0	96.2	114	424	61	54	13	3	1	3	29	3	62	6	0
Lilly, Ted, N.Y.*	0	0	.000	5.63	7	0	0	0	1	0	8.0	8	39	6	5	1	0	0	0	5	0	11	1	1
Lincoln, Mike, Min.	0	3	.000	10.89	8	4	0	0	1	0	20.2	36	109	25	25	10	0	0	2	13	0	15	1	0
Loaiza, Esteban, Tex.-Tor.	10	13	.435	4.56	34	31	1	1	2	1	199.1	228	871	112	101	29	4	5	13	57	1	137	1	0
Lopez, Albie, T.B.	11	13	.458	4.13	45	24	4	1	10	2	185.1	199	798	95	85	24	6	3	1	70	3	96	4	1
Lorraine, Andrew, Cle.*	0	0	.000	3.86	10	0	0	0	3	0	9.1	8	41	4	4	1	0	0	0	5	0	5	0	0
Lowe, Derek, Bos.	4	4	.500	2.56	74	0	0	0	64	42	91.1	90	379	27	26	6	4	1	2	22	5	79	2	1
Lowe, Sean, Chi.	4	1	.800	5.48	50	5	0	0	8	0	70.2	78	325	47	43	10	4	1	6	39	3	53	3	0
Mabry, John, Sea.	0	0	.000	27.00	1	0	0	0	1	0	.2	3	6	2	2	0	0	0	0	1	0	0	0	0
Maduro, Calvin, Bal.	0	0	.000	9.64	15	2	0	0	6	0	23.1	29	113	25	25	8	1	2	2	16	1	18	1	0
Magnante, Mike, Oak.*	1	1	.500	4.31	55	0	0	0	6	0	39.2	50	189	22	19	3	6	0	2	19	7	17	1	0
Mahay, Ron, Oak.*	0	1	.000	9.00	5	2	0	0	1	0	16.0	26	82	18	16	4	1	1	0	9	0	5	2	0
Martin, Tom, Cle.*	1	0	1.000	4.05	31	0	0	0	7	0	33.1	32	143	16	15	3	0	1	1	15	2	21	1	0
Martinez, Pedro, Bos.	18	6	.750	1.74	29	29	7	4	0	0	217.0	128	817	44	42	17	2	1	14	32	0	284	1	0
Martinez, Ramon J., Bos.	10	8	.556	6.13	27	27	0	0	0	0	127.2	143	590	94	87	16	2	7	9	67	3	89	0	0
Martinez, Willie J., Cle.	0	0	.000	3.00	1	0	0	0	0	0	3.0	1	11	1	1	0	1	0	1	0	1	0	0	0
Mathews, T.J., Oak.	2	3	.400	6.03	50	0	0	0	19	0	59.2	73	273	40	40	10	1	4	2	25	5	42	2	0
Mays, Joe, Min.	7	15	.318	5.56	31	28	2	1	1	0	160.1	193	723	105	99	20	3	5	2	67	1	102	11	0
McDill, Allen, Det.*	0	0	.000	7.20	13	0	0	0	1	0	10.0	10	43	9	8	2	0	0	1	1	0	7	1	0
McElroy, Chuck, Bal.*	3	0	1.000	4.69	43	2	0	0	16	0	63.1	60	282	36	33	6	0	3	2	34	2	50	6	0
Meadows, Brian, K.C.	6	2	.750	4.77	11	10	2	0	0	0	71.2	84	304	39	38	8	0	3	0	14	0	26	0	0
Meche, Gil, Sea.	4	4	.500	3.78	15	15	1	1	0	0	85.2	75	363	37	36	7	5	4	1	40	0	60	2	0
Mecir, Jim, T.B.-Oak.	10	3	.769	2.96	63	0	0	0	17	5	85.0	70	352	31	28	4	1	2	2	36	2	70	2	0
Mendoza, Ramiro, N.Y.	7	4	.636	4.25	14	9	1	1	0	0	65.2	66	281	32	31	9	1	2	4	20	1	30	0	0
Menechino, Frank, Oak.	0	0	.000	36.00	1	0	0	0	1	0	1.0	6	8	4	4	1	0	0	0	0	0	0	0	0
Mercedes, Jose, Bal.	14	7	.667	4.02	36	20	1	0	7	0	145.2	150	636	71	65	15	7	7	3	64	1	70	3	0
Mercker, Kent, Ana.*	1	3	.250	6.52	21	7	0	0	2	0	48.1	57	225	35	35	12	3	1	2	29	3	30	2	0
Mesa, Jose, Sea.	4	6	.400	5.36	66	0	0	0	29	1	80.2	89	372	48	48	11	2	6	5	41	0	84	3	0
Miller, Travis, Min.*	2	3	.400	3.90	67	0	0	0	12	1	67.0	83	316	35	29	4	1	3	1	32	2	62	2	0
Mills, Alan, Bal.	2	0	1.000	6.46	23	0	0	0	3	1	23.2	25	115	17	17	6	0	0	1	19	1	18	3	0
Milton, Eric, Min.*	13	10	.565	4.86	33	33	0	0	0	0	200.0	205	849	123	108	35	4	6	7	44	0	160	5	0
Mlicki, Dave, Det.	6	11	.353	5.58	24	21	0	0	1	0	119.1	143	547	79	74	17	3	6	3	44	1	57	4	0
Moehler, Brian, Det.	12	9	.571	4.50	29	29	2	0	0	0	178.0	222	776	99	89	20	3	4	2	40	0	103	2	1
Mohler, Mike, Cle.*	0	1	.000	9.00	2	0	0	0	0	0	1.0	1	4	1	1	1	0	0	0	0	0	2	0	0
Molina, Gabe, Bal.	0	0	.000	9.00	9	0	0	0	3	0	13.0	25	74	14	13	2	0	2	0	9	0	8	0	0
Morris, Jim, T.B.*	0	0	.000	4.35	16	0	0	0	3	0	10.1	10	48	9	5	1	0	0	0	7	1	10	1	0
Mota, Danny, Min.	0	0	.000	8.44	4	0	0	0	3	0	5.1	10	28	5	5	1	0	0	0	1	0	3	1	0
Moyer, Jamie, Sea.*	13	10	.565	5.49	26	26	0	0	0	0	154.0	173	678	103	94	22	3	3	3	53	2	98	4	1
Mulder, Mark, Oak.*	9	10	.474	5.44	27	27	0	0	0	0	154.0	191	705	106	93	22	3	8	4	69	3	88	6	0
Mullen, Scott, K.C.*	0	0	.000	4.35	11	0	0	0	5	0	10.1	10	44	5	5	2	0	0	0	3	0	7	0	0
Munoz, Mike, Tex.*	0	1	.000	13.50	7	0	0	0	2	0	4.0	11	25	6	6	1	1	0	3	1	1	0	0	0
Munro, Peter, Tor.	1	1	.500	5.96	9	3	0	0	2	0	25.2	38	127	22	17	1	1	0	3	16	0	16	1	0
Murray, Dan, K.C.	0	0	.000	4.66	10	0	0	0	3	0	19.1	20	86	10	10	7	2	1	1	10	0	16	2	0
Mussina, Mike, Bal.	11	15	.423	3.79	34	34	6	1	0	0	237.2	236	987	105	100	28	8	6	3	46	0	210	3	0
Myette, Aaron, Chi.	0	0	.000	0.00	2	0	0	0	1	0	2.2	0	12	0	0	0	0	0	0	4	0	1	0	0
Nagy, Charles, Cle.	2	7	.222	8.21	11	11	0	0	0	0	57.0	71	267	53	52	15	5	2	2	21	2	41	1	0
Navarro, Jaime, Cle.	0	1	.000	7.98	7	2	0	0	1	0	14.2	20	69	13	13	3	0	2	1	5	0	9	0	0
Neagle, Denny, N.Y.*	7	7	.500	5.81	16	15	1	0	0	0	91.1	99	400	61	59	16	6	5	2	31	1	58	4	1
Nelson, Jeff, N.Y.	8	4	.667	2.45	73	0	0	0	13	0	69.2	44	296	24	19	2	6	2	2	45	1	71	4	0
Newman, Alan, Cle.*	0	0	.000	20.25	1	0	0	0	1	0	1.1	6	10	3	3	1	0	0	0	1	0	0	0	0
Nichting, Chris, Cle.	0	0	.000	7.00	7	0	0	0	1	0	9.0	13	46	7	7	0	0	1	2	5	1	7	1	0
Nitkowski, C.J., Det.*	4	9	.308	5.25	67	11	0	0	7	0	109.2	124	497	79	64	13	3	8	4	49	3	81	3	1
Nomo, Hideo, Det.	8	12	.400	4.74	32	31	1	0	0	0	190.0	191	828	102	100	31	6	3	3	89	1	181	16	1
Ohka, Tomo, Bos.	3	6	.333	3.12	13	12	0	0	1	0	69.1	70	297	25	24	7	1	2	2	26	0	40	3	0
Olivares, Omar, Oak.	4	8	.333	6.75	21	16	1	0	1	0	108.0	134	508	86	81	10	0	7	7	60	0	57	4	0
Oliver, Darren, Tex.*	2	9	.182	7.42	21	21	0	0	0	0	108.0	151	501	95	89	16	5	4	4	42	3	49	4	1

Pitcher, Team	W	L	Pct.	ERA	G	GS	CG	ShO	GF	Sv.	IP	H	TBF	R	ER	HR	SH	SF	HB	BB	IBB	SO	WP	Bk.
Ontiveros, Steve, Bos.	1	1	.500	10.13	3	1	0	0	0	0	5.1	9	28	6	6	1	0	0	6	4	0	1	2	0
Ortiz, Ramon, Ana.	8	6	.571	5.09	18	18	2	0	0	0	111.1	96	472	69	63	18	4	4	2	55	0	73	7	4
Painter, Lance, Tor.*	2	0	1.000	4.73	42	2	0	0	11	0	66.2	69	285	37	35	9	5	1	2	22	1	53	4	0
Paniagua, Jose, Sea.	3	0	1.000	3.47	69	0	0	0	26	5	80.1	68	344	31	31	6	3	5	7	38	3	71	4	1
Parque, Jim, Chi.*	13	6	.684	4.28	33	32	0	0	0	0	187.0	208	828	105	89	21	5	5	11	71	1	111	2	5
Parrish, John, Bal.*	2	4	.333	7.18	8	8	0	0	0	0	36.1	40	180	32	29	6	1	4	1	35	0	28	1	0
Patterson, Danny, Det.	5	1	.833	3.97	58	0	0	0	12	0	56.2	69	244	26	25	4	3	2	2	14	2	29	1	0
Pena, Jesus, Chi.-Bos.*	2	1	.667	5.13	22	0	0	0	7	1	26.1	28	123	19	15	7	0	2	1	19	0	20	1	0
Percival, Troy, Ana.	5	5	.500	4.50	54	0	0	0	45	32	50.0	42	221	27	25	7	3	2	2	30	4	49	1	0
Perisho, Matt, Tex.*	2	7	.222	7.37	34	13	0	0	4	0	105.0	136	515	99	86	20	6	5	6	67	3	74	4	0
Petkovsek, Mark, Ana.	4	2	.667	4.33	64	1	0	0	21	2	81.0	86	341	40	39	8	4	1	3	23	6	31	3	0
Pettitte, Andy, N.Y.*	19	9	.679	4.35	32	32	3	1	0	0	204.2	219	903	111	99	17	7	4	4	80	4	125	2	3
Pichardo, Hipolito, Bos.	6	3	.667	3.46	38	1	0	0	5	1	65.0	63	275	29	25	1	2	2	3	26	2	37	2	0
Pineiro, Joel, Sea.	1	0	1.000	5.59	8	1	0	0	5	0	19.1	25	94	13	12	3	0	2	0	13	0	10	0	0
Ponson, Sidney, Bal.	9	13	.409	4.82	32	32	6	1	0	0	222.0	223	953	125	119	30	3	3	1	83	0	152	5	0
Poole, Jim Ri., Det.*	1	0	1.000	7.27	18	0	0	0	1	0	8.2	13	41	8	7	4	1	2	1	1	0	5	0	0
Pote, Lou, Ana.	1	1	.500	3.40	32	1	0	0	12	1	50.1	52	214	23	19	4	1	1	0	17	1	44	3	0
Prieto, Ariel, Oak.	1	2	.333	5.12	8	6	0	0	2	0	31.2	42	148	21	18	3	2	1	1	13	0	19	0	0
Quantrill, Paul, Tor.	2	5	.286	4.52	68	0	0	0	24	1	83.2	100	367	45	42	7	1	3	2	25	1	47	1	0
Radke, Brad, Min.	12	16	.429	4.45	34	34	4	1	0	0	226.2	261	978	119	112	27	7	4	5	51	1	141	5	0
Rakers, Jason, K.C.	2	0	1.000	9.14	11	0	0	0	3	0	21.2	33	102	22	22	5	0	1	0	7	0	16	3	0
Ramsay, Rob, Sea.*	1	1	.500	3.40	37	1	0	0	6	0	50.1	43	230	22	19	3	2	3	1	40	3	32	4	0
Rapp, Pat, Bal.	9	12	.429	5.90	31	30	0	0	0	0	174.0	203	798	125	114	18	1	7	5	83	5	106	8	0
Ratliff, Jon, Oak.	0	0	.000	0.00	1	0	0	0	1	0	1.0	0	3	0	0	0	0	0	0	0	0	0	0	0
Redman, Mark, Min.*	12	9	.571	4.76	32	24	0	0	3	0	151.1	168	651	81	80	22	3	2	3	45	0	117	6	0
Reed, Steve, Cle.	2	0	1.000	4.34	57	0	0	0	16	0	56.0	58	243	30	27	7	4	1	1	21	4	39	2	1
Reichert, Dan, K.C.	8	10	.444	4.70	44	18	1	1	11	2	153.1	157	690	92	80	15	5	7	7	91	1	94	18	0
Rekar, Bryan, T.B.	7	10	.412	4.41	30	27	2	0	2	0	173.1	200	743	92	85	22	3	9	4	39	0	95	5	0
Reyes, Al, Bal.	1	0	1.000	6.92	13	0	0	0	2	0	13.0	13	62	10	10	2	1	2	0	11	1	10	0	0
Rhodes, Arthur, Sea.*	5	8	.385	4.28	72	0	0	0	9	0	69.1	51	281	34	33	6	1	2	0	29	3	77	4	0
Rigby, Brad, K.C.	0	0	.000	16.20	4	0	0	0	1	0	8.1	19	51	16	15	6	0	0	1	5	0	3	0	0
Rigdon, Paul, Cle.	1	1	.500	7.64	5	4	0	0	0	0	17.2	21	79	15	15	4	0	0	0	9	1	15	0	0
Rincon, Ricardo, Cle.*	2	0	1.000	2.70	35	0	0	0	4	0	20.0	17	90	7	6	1	0	0	1	13	1	20	1	0
Rivera, Luis, Bal.	0	0	.000	0.00	1	0	0	0	0	0	.2	1	4	0	0	0	0	0	0	1	0	0	0	0
Rivera, Mariano, N.Y.	7	4	.636	2.85	66	0	0	0	61	36	75.2	58	311	26	24	4	5	2	0	25	3	58	2	0
Rodriguez, Frankie, Sea.	2	1	.667	6.27	23	0	0	0	5	0	47.1	60	214	33	33	8	0	3	0	22	2	19	3	0
Rogers, Kenny, Tex.*	13	13	.500	4.55	34	34	0	0	0	0	227.1	257	998	126	115	20	3	4	11	78	2	127	1	1
Romero, J.C., Min.*	2	7	.222	7.02	12	11	0	0	0	0	57.2	72	268	51	45	8	4	2	1	30	0	50	2	1
Rosado, Jose, K.C.*	2	2	.500	5.86	5	5	0	0	0	0	27.2	29	122	18	18	4	1	1	4	9	0	15	0	1
Rose, Brian, Bos.	3	5	.375	6.11	15	12	0	0	1	0	53.0	58	239	37	36	11	1	2	3	21	3	24	2	0
Runyan, Sean, Det.*	0	0	.000	6.00	3	0	0	0	1	0	3.0	2	12	2	2	0	0	1	0	2	0	1	0	0
Rupe, Ryan, T.B.	5	6	.455	6.92	18	18	0	0	0	0	91.0	121	425	75	70	19	2	6	9	31	3	61	4	0
Ryan, Jay, Min.	0	1	.000	7.62	16	1	0	0	6	0	26.0	37	125	24	22	8	0	2	1	10	0	19	2	0
Ryan, B.J., Bal.*	2	3	.400	5.91	42	0	0	0	9	0	42.2	36	193	29	28	7	1	1	0	31	1	41	2	1
Santana, Johan, Min.*	2	3	.400	6.49	30	5	0	0	9	0	86.0	102	398	64	62	11	3	2	54	0	64	5	2
Santiago, Jose, K.C.	8	6	.571	3.91	45	0	0	0	20	2	69.0	70	302	33	30	7	1	3	26	3	44	0	0
Sasaki, Kazuhiro, Sea.	2	5	.286	3.16	63	0	0	0	58	37	62.2	42	265	25	22	10	2	2	2	31	5	78	1	0
Sauveur, Rich, Oak.*	0	0	.000	4.35	10	0	0	0	4	0	10.1	13	43	5	5	3	0	0	0	1	0	7	0	0
Schoeneweis, Scott, Ana.*	7	10	.412	5.45	27	27	1	1	0	0	170.0	183	742	112	103	21	2	5	3	67	2	78	4	3
Schourek, Pete, Bos.*	3	10	.231	5.11	21	21	0	0	0	0	107.1	116	464	67	61	17	4	1	3	38	2	63	5	0
Sele, Aaron, Sea.	17	10	.630	4.51	34	34	2	2	0	0	211.2	221	908	110	106	17	5	8	5	74	7	137	5	0
Service, Scott, Oak.	1	2	.333	6.38	20	0	0	0	6	1	36.2	45	172	31	26	5	1	2	1	19	1	35	0	0
Sheldon, Scott, Tex.	0	0	.000	0.00	1	0	0	0	0	0	.1	0	1	0	0	0	0	0	0	0	0	1	0	0
Shuey, Paul, Cle.	4	2	.667	3.39	57	0	0	0	12	0	63.2	51	270	25	24	4	1	3	3	30	3	69	0	0
Sikorski, Brian, Tex.	1	3	.250	5.73	10	5	0	0	2	0	37.2	46	187	31	24	9	0	1	1	25	1	32	1	0
Simas, Bill, Chi.	2	3	.400	3.46	60	0	0	0	9	0	67.2	69	283	27	26	9	6	4	1	22	6	49	1	0
Sirotka, Mike, Chi.*	15	10	.600	3.79	32	32	1	0	0	0	197.0	203	832	101	83	23	4	3	1	69	1	128	8	2
Smith, Dan, Bos.	0	0	.000	8.10	2	0	0	0	0	0	3.1	2	15	3	3	1	0	3	0	1	0	0	0	0
Sparks, Jeff, T.B.	0	1	.000	3.54	15	0	0	0	4	0	20.1	13	90	8	8	2	0	0	2	18	1	24	3	0
Sparks, Steve W., Det.	7	5	.583	4.07	20	15	1	1	5	1	104.0	108	446	55	47	7	1	1	4	29	0	53	6	0
Speier, Justin, Cle.	5	2	.714	3.29	47	0	0	0	12	0	68.1	57	290	27	25	9	2	4	4	28	3	69	7	1
Spoljaric, Paul, K.C.*	0	0	.000	6.52	13	0	0	0	4	0	9.2	9	40	7	7	4	1	0	0	5	0	6	0	0
Spradlin, Jerry, K.C.	4	4	.500	5.52	50	0	0	0	30	7	75.0	81	320	49	46	9	3	1	3	27	2	54	1	0
Spurgeon, Jay, Bal.	1	1	.500	6.00	7	4	0	0	1	0	24.0	26	110	16	16	5	1	0	2	15	0	11	3	0
Stanifer, Rob, Bos.	0	0	.000	7.62	8	0	0	0	3	0	13.0	22	66	19	11	3	0	0	0	4	1	3	0	0
Stanton, Mike, N.Y.*	2	3	.400	4.10	69	0	0	0	20	0	68.0	68	291	32	31	5	2	4	2	24	2	75	1	0
Stein, Blake, K.C.	8	5	.615	4.68	17	17	1	0	0	0	107.2	98	464	57	56	19	3	4	3	57	1	78	7	0
Sturtze, Tanyon, Chi.-T.B.	5	2	.714	4.74	29	6	0	0	9	0	68.1	72	300	39	36	8	1	2	3	29	1	44	2	0
Suppan, Jeff, K.C.	10	9	.526	4.94	35	33	3	1	0	0	217.0	240	948	121	119	36	5	6	7	84	3	128	7	1
Suzuki, Mac, K.C.	8	10	.444	4.34	32	29	1	1	0	0	188.2	195	839	100	91	26	2	3	3	94	6	135	11	0
Tam, Jeff, Oak.	3	3	.500	2.63	72	0	0	0	23	3	85.2	86	351	30	25	3	2	4	1	23	8	46	3	0
Taylor, Billy, T.B.	1	3	.250	8.56	17	0	0	0	7	0	13.2	13	62	13	13	2	0	2	9	2	13	0	0
Tessmer, Jay, N.Y.	0	0	.000	6.75	7	0	0	0	5	0	6.2	9	31	6	5	3	0	0	0	1	1	5	0	0
Timlin, Mike, Bal.	2	3	.400	4.89	37	0	0	0	31	11	35.0	37	157	22	19	6	1	1	2	15	3	26	0	0
Tolar, Kevin, Det.*	0	0	.000	3.00	5	0	0	0	1	0	3.0	1	12	1	1	0	0	0	0	1	0	3	0	0
Tomko, Brett, Sea.	7	5	.583	4.68	32	8	0	0	10	1	92.1	92	401	53	48	12	5	5	3	40	4	59	1	1
Trachsel, Steve, T.B.-Tor.	8	15	.348	4.80	34	34	3	1	0	0	200.2	232	882	116	107	26	6	6	6	74	2	110	4	0
Trombley, Mike, Bal.	4	5	.444	4.13	75	0	0	0	32	4	72.0	67	322	34	33	11	5	7	2	43	8	72	8	0
Turnbow, Derrick, Ana.	0	0	.000	4.74	24	1	0	0	16	0	38.0	36	181	21	20	7	0	1	2	36	0	25	3	1
Venafro, Mike, Tex.*	3	1	.750	3.83	77	0	0	0	21	1	56.1	64	248	27	24	2	4	4	21	4	32	1	0
Villafuerte, Brandon, Det.	0	0	.000	10.38	3	0	0	0	2	0	4.1	4	20	5	5	0	0	0	4	0	1	1	0
Vizcaino, Luis, Oak.	0	1	.000	7.45	12	0	0	0	1	0	19.1	25	96	17	16	2	0	1	2	11	0	18	1	0

Pitcher, Team	W	L	Pct.	ERA	G	GS	CG	ShO	GF	Sv.	IP	H	TBF	R	ER	HR	SH	SF	HB	BB	IBB	SO	WP	Bk.
Wakefield, Tim, Bos.	6	10	.375	5.48	51	17	0	0	13	0	159.1	170	706	107	97	31	4	8	4	65	3	102	4	0
Ward, Bryan, Ana.*	0	0	.000	5.63	7	0	0	0	2	0	8.0	8	36	6	5	1	0	0	0	2	0	3	2	0
Wasdin, John, Bos.	1	3	.250	5.04	25	1	0	0	10	1	44.2	48	198	25	25	8	0	5	2	15	1	36	1	0
Washburn, Jarrod, Ana.*	7	2	.778	3.74	14	14	0	0	0	0	84.1	64	340	38	35	16	1	3	1	37	0	49	1	0
Watson, Allen, N.Y.*	0	0	.000	10.23	17	0	0	0	9	0	22.0	30	115	25	25	6	2	2	2	18	0	20	2	0
Watson, Mark, Cle.*	0	1	.000	8.53	6	0	0	0	1	0	6.1	12	33	7	6	0	0	0	1	2	0	4	0	0
Weaver, Eric, Ana.	0	2	.000	6.87	17	0	0	0	4	0	18.1	20	92	16	14	5	0	1	0	16	1	8	1	0
Weaver, Jeff, Det.	11	15	.423	4.32	31	30	2	0	0	0	200.0	205	849	102	96	26	3	9	15	52	2	136	3	2
Weber, Ben, Ana.	1	0	1.000	1.84	10	0	0	0	1	0	14.2	12	59	6	3	0	0	1	2	1	0	8	1	0
Wells, David, Tor.*	20	8	.714	4.11	35	35	9	1	0	0	229.2	266	972	115	105	23	6	7	8	31	0	166	9	1
Wells, Kip, Chi.	6	9	.400	6.02	20	20	0	0	0	0	98.2	126	468	76	66	15	1	3	2	58	4	71	7	0
Wells, Bob, Min.	0	7	.000	3.65	76	0	0	0	25	10	86.1	80	351	39	35	14	3	5	4	15	2	76	1	0
Westbrook, Jake, N.Y.	0	2	.000	13.50	3	2	0	0	1	0	6.2	15	38	10	10	1	0	2	0	4	1	1	0	0
Wetteland, John, Tex.	6	5	.545	4.20	62	0	0	0	57	34	60.0	67	269	35	28	10	4	4	2	24	2	53	0	0
Wheeler, Dan, T.B.	1	1	.500	5.48	11	2	0	0	6	0	23.0	29	111	14	14	2	1	1	2	11	2	17	2	0
White, Rick, T.B.	3	6	.333	3.41	44	0	0	0	8	2	71.1	57	293	30	27	7	1	2	5	26	3	47	3	0
Wickman, Bob, Cle.	1	3	.250	3.38	26	0	0	0	24	14	26.2	27	115	12	10	0	3	0	0	12	3	11	0	0
Williams, Brian, Cle.	0	0	.000	4.00	7	0	0	0	1	0	18.0	23	81	9	8	2	0	1	1	8	1	6	1	0
Wilson, Kris, K.C.	0	1	.000	4.19	20	0	0	0	5	0	34.1	38	145	16	16	3	1	1	0	11	3	17	0	0
Wilson, Paul, T.B.	1	4	.200	3.35	11	7	0	0	0	0	51.0	38	206	20	19	1	2	2	4	16	2	40	1	0
Wise, Matt, Ana.	3	3	.500	5.54	8	6	0	0	0	0	37.1	40	163	23	23	7	0	2	1	13	1	20	1	0
Witasick, Jay, K.C.	3	8	.273	5.94	22	14	2	0	2	0	89.1	109	410	65	59	15	3	3	4	38	0	67	3	0
Witt, Bobby, Cle.	0	1	.000	7.63	7	2	0	0	2	0	15.1	28	77	13	13	4	0	0	0	6	1	6	2	0
Woodard, Steve, Cle.	3	3	.500	5.67	13	11	0	0	1	0	54.0	57	227	35	34	10	1	1	2	11	1	35	3	0
Worrell, Tim, Bal.	2	2	.500	7.36	5	0	0	0	2	0	7.1	12	39	6	6	3	0	0	5	3	5	0	0
Wright, Jaret, Cle.	3	4	.429	4.70	9	9	1	1	0	0	51.2	44	217	27	27	6	0	1	1	28	0	36	2	0
Wunsch, Kelly, Chi.*	6	3	.667	2.93	83	0	0	0	12	1	61.1	50	259	22	20	4	0	2	2	29	1	51	0	0
Yan, Esteban, T.B.	7	8	.467	6.21	43	20	0	0	8	0	137.2	158	618	98	95	26	4	6	11	42	0	111	7	1
Yarnall, Ed, N.Y.*	0	0	.000	15.00	2	1	0	0	1	0	3.0	5	16	5	5	1	0	0	1	3	0	1	0	0
Young, Tim, Bos.*	0	0	.000	6.43	8	0	0	0	3	0	7.0	7	29	5	5	3	0	1	2	0	6	0	0
Zimmerman, Jeff, Tex.	4	5	.444	5.30	65	0	0	0	17	1	69.2	80	323	45	41	10	2	5	2	34	3	74	3	3
Zito, Barry, Oak.*	7	4	.636	2.72	14	14	1	1	0	0	92.2	64	376	30	28	6	1	0	2	45	2	78	2	0

COMBINATION SHUTOUTS: **Anaheim (1)**—Schoeneweis and Percival. **Baltimore (4)**—Mercedes, Groom, Mills and Trombley; Mussina, Groom and Trombley; Mussina, Groom and Trombley; McElroy, Rivera, Ryan, Trombley and Kohlmeier; Mussina, Trombley, Groom and Kohlmeier. **Boston (8)**—P. Martinez and Lowe (2); Schourek and Lowe; Rose, Garces, Stanifer and Wasdin; P. Martinez, Rose and Young; Fassero, Garces and Lowe; P. Martinez and Florie; Arrojo and Lowe. **Chicago (5)**—Eldred, Howry and Foulke; Baldwin and Buehrle; Sirotka, Simas, Wunsch and Barcelo; Baldwin, Buehrle and Foulke; Parque, Howry and Foulke. **Cleveland (3)**—Finley and Karsay; Wright and Reed; Woodard, Martin, Reed, Karsay and Wickman. **Detroit (5)**—Nomo, Poole, Patterson, Brocail and Jones; Nomo, Brocail and Jones; Mlicki, Nitkowski and Sparks; Nomo and Patterson; Weaver and Jones. **Kansas City (3)**—Fussell, Spradlin and Witasick; Suppan and Spradlin; Stein and Santiago. **Minnesota (2)**—Milton and Guardado; Mays, Miller, Hawkins and Guardado. **New York (4)**—Pettitte, Nelson, Stanton and Rivera; Cone, Nelson and Stanton; Pettitte and Rivera; Clemens and Rivera. **Oakland (7)**—Heredia, D. Jones and Isringhausen; Hudson and Tam; Mulder, Magnante and Isringhausen; Heredia and Mecir; Zito, Tam, Belitz, Mathews and Isringhausen; Heredia, Magnante and Tam; Hudson and Isringhausen. **Seattle (6)**—Meche, Rhodes and Sasaki; Sele, Sasaki and Paniagua; Sele and Tomko; Moyer, Paniagua and Sasaki; Abbott and Paniagua; Moyer, Ramsay and Hodges. **Tampa Bay (5)**—Trachsel, White and Morris; Gooden, Mecir and Sparks; Eiland, Sparks and Hernandez; Trachsel and Lopez; Lidle and Creek. **Texas (4)**—Glynn and Wetteland; Perisho, Crabtree and Wetteland; Sikorski and Venafro; Davis, Wetteland and Venafro. **Toronto (1)**—F. Castillo, Escobar and Koch.

PITCHERS WITH TWO OR MORE TEAMS

Pitcher, Team	W	L	Pct.	ERA	G	GS	CG	ShO	GF	Sv.	IP	H	TBF	R	ER	HR	SH	SF	HB	BB	IBB	SO	WP	Bk.
Carrasco, Hector, Min.	4	3	.571	4.25	61	0	0	0	18	1	72.0	75	324	38	34	6	6	4	3	33	0	57	14	0
Carrasco, Hector, Bos.	1	1	.500	9.45	8	1	0	0	2	0	6.2	15	40	8	7	2	2	0	1	5	1	7	0	1
Cubillan, Darwin, Tor.	1	0	1.000	8.04	7	0	0	0	1	0	15.2	20	75	14	14	5	0	0	1	11	0	14	0	0
Cubillan, Darwin, Tex.	0	0	.000	10.70	13	0	0	0	5	0	17.2	32	97	22	21	4	0	3	0	14	0	13	1	0
Gooden, Dwight, T.B.	2	3	.400	6.63	8	8	0	0	0	0	36.2	47	173	32	27	14	1	0	3	20	0	23	2	0
Gooden, Dwight, N.Y.	4	2	.667	3.36	18	5	0	0	3	2	64.1	66	274	28	24	8	3	2	0	21	3	31	1	0
Guthrie, Mark, T.B.*	1	1	.500	4.50	34	0	0	0	7	0	32.0	33	145	18	16	4	1	0	18	5	26	7	0
Guthrie, Mark, Tor.*	0	2	.000	4.79	23	0	0	0	5	0	20.2	20	88	12	11	3	1	1	1	9	0	20	2	0
Hill, Ken, Ana.	5	7	.417	6.52	16	16	0	0	0	0	78.2	102	380	59	57	16	2	7	2	53	1	50	6	0
Hill, Ken, Chi.	0	1	.000	24.00	2	1	0	0	0	0	3.0	5	19	8	8	0	1	1	0	6	0	0	0	0
Loaiza, Esteban, Tex.	5	6	.455	5.37	20	17	0	0	2	1	107.1	133	480	67	64	21	2	4	3	31	1	75	1	0
Loaiza, Esteban, Tor.	5	7	.417	3.62	14	14	1	1	0	0	92.0	95	391	45	37	8	2	1	10	26	0	62	0	0
Mecir, Jim, T.B.	7	2	.778	3.08	38	0	0	0	10	1	49.2	35	199	17	17	2	1	1	1	22	0	33	0	0
Mecir, Jim, Oak.	3	1	.750	2.80	25	0	0	0	7	4	35.1	35	153	14	11	2	0	1	1	14	2	37	2	0
Pena, Jesus, Chi.*	2	1	.667	5.40	20	0	0	0	7	1	23.1	25	109	18	14	6	0	2	1	16	0	19	1	0
Pena, Jesus, Bos.*	0	0	.000	3.00	2	0	0	0	0	0	3.0	3	14	1	1	1	0	0	3	0	1	0	0
Sturtze, Tanyon, Chi.	1	2	.333	12.06	10	1	0	0	2	0	15.2	25	85	23	21	4	0	2	15	0	6	1	0
Sturtze, Tanyon, T.B.	4	0	1.000	2.56	19	5	0	0	7	0	52.2	47	215	16	15	4	1	0	1	14	1	38	1	0
Trachsel, Steve, T.B.	6	10	.375	4.58	23	23	3	1	0	0	137.2	160	606	76	70	16	2	5	6	49	1	78	3	0
Trachsel, Steve, Tor.	2	5	.286	5.29	11	11	0	0	0	0	63.0	72	276	40	37	10	4	1	0	25	1	32	1	0

FIELDING

TEAM

Team	Pct.	G	PO	A	E	TC	DP	TP	PB
Cleveland	.988	162	4327	1665	72	6064	147	0	10
Seattle	.984	162	4325	1629	99	6053	176	0	8
Toronto	.984	162	4312	1679	100	6091	176	0	11
Kansas City	.983	162	4318	1751	102	6171	185	0	7
Detroit	.983	162	4330	1754	105	6189	171	0	7
Minnesota	.983	162	4298	1526	102	5926	155	0	13
Boston	.982	162	4358	1647	109	6114	120	0	26
New York	.981	161	4273	1487	109	5869	132	0	13
Tampa Bay	.981	161	4294	1814	118	6226	169	0	14
Baltimore	.981	162	4300	1578	116	5994	151	1	6
Anaheim	.978	162	4344	1746	134	6224	182	0	6
Chicago	.978	162	4351	1686	133	6170	190	0	13
Oakland	.978	161	4306	1726	134	6166	164	1	8
Texas	.978	162	4287	1594	135	6016	162	0	8
Totals	.982	1133	60423	23282	1568	85273	2280	2	150

INDIVIDUAL

FIRST BASEMEN

NOTE: All caps denotes fielding-percentage leader based on 81 games for catchers, 108 for all other non-pitchers and 162 innings for pitchers. *Throws lefthanded.

Player, Team	Pct.	G	PO	A	E	TC	DP
Alcantara, Israel, Bos.	1.000	5	9	0	0	9	1
Allen, Dusty, Det.	1.000	17	45	1	0	46	5
Amaral, Rich, Bal.	1.000	1	5	4	0	9	4
Ausmus, Brad, Det.	1.000	1	2	0	0	2	1
Bell, David, Sea.	1.000	2	4	0	0	4	0
Bellinger, Clay, N.Y.	1.000	10	29	1	0	30	3
Blake, Casey, Min.	1.000	1	5	0	0	5	1
Brogna, Rico, Bos.*	.983	37	165	9	3	177	13
Brosius, Scott, N.Y.	1.000	2	3	0	0	3	0
Burkhart, Morgan, Bos.*	.964	5	26	1	1	28	1
Catalanotto, Frank, Tex.	.973	17	100	7	3	110	12
Clark, Tony, Det.	.993	58	488	45	4	537	49
Clark, Will, Bal.*	.991	72	583	44	6	633	58
Conine, Jeff, Bal.	.985	39	304	31	5	340	27
Coomer, Ron, Min.	.995	124	1020	67	5	1092	102
Cox, Steve, T.B.*	.988	24	160	10	2	172	12
Daubach, Brian, Bos.	.996	83	642	51	3	696	49
Delgado, Carlos, Tor.	.991	162	1416	82	13	1511	157
Erstad, Darin, Ana.*	1.000	3	5	0	0	5	0
Evans, Tom, Tex.	1.000	1	1	2	0	3	0
Fick, Robert, Det.	.984	34	222	18	4	244	19
Fryman, Travis, Cle.	1.000	1	4	0	0	4	1
Fullmer, Brad, Tor.	1.000	1	2	1	0	3	0
Giambi, Jason, Oak.	.995	124	1161	59	6	1226	114
Giambi, Jeremy, Oak.*	1.000	15	55	5	0	60	5
Gil, Benji, Ana.	1.000	3	4	0	0	4	0
Guillen, Ozzie, T.B.	1.000	5	7	1	0	8	0
Halter, Shane, Det.	.995	29	172	14	1	187	21
Hocking, Denny, Min.	1.000	12	35	5	0	40	6
Huskey, Butch, Min.	.971	9	61	5	2	68	2
Ibanez, Raul, Sea.	1.000	3	13	0	0	13	2
Javier, Stan, Sea.	1.000	3	21	1	0	22	2
Jefferies, Gregg, Det.	.994	20	163	15	1	179	18
Johnson, Keith, Ana.	1.000	3	3	0	0	3	0
Kinkade, Mike, Bal.	1.000	1	1	0	0	1	0
Konerko, Paul, Chi.	.991	122	1051	67	10	1128	118
LeCroy, Matt, Min.	1.000	3	13	0	0	13	1
Lesher, Brian, Sea.*	1.000	4	4	1	0	5	0
Leyritz, Jim, N.Y.	1.000	1	2	0	0	2	0
Liefer, Jeff, Chi.	.875	1	6	1	1	8	1
Mabry, John, Sea.	1.000	3	8	1	0	9	1
Martinez, Dave, Tex.*	1.000	4	11	0	0	11	0
Martinez, Edgar, Sea.	1.000	2	12	1	0	13	3
Martinez, Tino, N.Y.	.994	154	1154	88	7	1249	110
McCarty, Dave, K.C.*	.992	63	463	59	4	526	62
McGriff, Fred, T.B.*	.993	144	1300	82	10	1392	137
Mientkiewicz, Doug, Min.	1.000	3	22	0	0	22	3
Minor, Ryan, Bal.	1.000	5	26	3	0	29	1
Morris, Hal, Det.*	.990	38	263	23	3	289	27
Munson, Eric, Det.	.941	3	16	0	1	17	2
Norton, Greg, Chi.	.990	17	94	10	1	105	12
Offerman, Jose, Bos.	.986	38	253	29	4	286	19
OLERUD, John, Sea.*	.996	158	1271	132	5	1408	154
Oliver, Joe, Sea.	1.000	1	5	0	0	5	1
Ortiz, David, Min.*	.996	27	210	12	1	223	17
Palmeiro, Rafael, Tex.*	.995	108	820	56	4	880	86
Palmer, Dean, Det.	.984	20	122	5	2	129	13
Perry, Chan, Cle.	1.000	1	3	0	0	3	0
Perry, Herbert, T.B.-Chi.	1.000	4	12	0	0	12	1
Piatt, Adam, Oak.	1.000	3	5	0	0	5	0
Posada, Jorge, N.Y.	.986	12	63	8	1	72	6
Richard, Chris, Bal.*	.989	53	439	18	5	462	52
Saenz, Olmedo, Oak.	.993	17	126	8	1	135	14
Segui, David, Tex.-Cle.*	1.000	73	556	61	0	617	59
Sexson, Richie, Cle.	.996	27	198	25	1	224	11
Sheets, Andy, Bos.	1.000	1	0	1	0	1	0
Sheldon, Scott, Tex.	1.000	10	42	2	0	44	6
Sojo, Luis, N.Y.	.960	7	20	4	1	25	0
Spiezio, Scott, Ana.	.993	29	141	4	1	146	12
Sprague, Ed, Bos.	1.000	3	17	4	0	21	1
Stairs, Matt, Oak.	1.000	1	2	0	0	2	0
Stanley, Mike, Bos.-Oak.	.993	58	410	44	3	457	44
Sweeney, Mike, K.C.	.991	114	960	88	9	1057	107
Thomas, Frank, Chi.	.996	30	267	15	1	283	38
Thome, Jim, Cle.	.995	107	834	91	5	930	101
Turner, Chris, N.Y.	1.000	1	1	0	0	1	0
Valdez, Mario, Oak.	1.000	4	26	2	0	28	2
Vaughn, Mo, Ana.	.990	147	1257	69	14	1340	156
Walbeck, Matt, Ana.	1.000	2	1	0	0	1	0
Waszgis, B.J., Tex.	1.000	3	4	0	0	4	1
Widger, Chris, Sea.	1.000	2	9	0	0	9	2
Wilson, Dan, Sea.	1.000	1	3	0	0	3	0
Woodward, Chris, Tor.	1.000	3	6	1	0	7	1
Wooten, Shawn, Ana.	1.000	3	10	1	0	11	2
Zaun, Gregg, K.C.	1.000	1	1	0	0	1	0

TRIPLE PLAY: Conine, Bal.

FIRST BASEMEN WITH TWO OR MORE TEAMS

Player, Team	Pct.	G	PO	A	E	TC	DP
Perry, Herbert, T.B.	1.000	1	2	0	0	2	0
Perry, Herbert, Chi.	1.000	3	10	0	0	10	1
Segui, David, Tex.*	1.000	38	295	28	0	323	38
Segui, David, Cle.*	1.000	35	261	33	0	294	21
Stanley, Mike, Bos.	.997	39	264	31	1	296	26
Stanley, Mike, Oak.	.988	19	146	13	2	161	18

SECOND BASEMEN

Player, Team	Pct.	G	PO	A	E	TC	DP
Alexander, Manny, Bos.	1.000	7	5	7	0	12	1
Alicea, Luis, Tex.	.978	129	247	318	13	578	85
Alomar, Roberto, Cle.	.980	155	293	437	15	745	109
Ausmus, Brad, Det.	.000	1	0	0	0	0	0
Baughman, Justin, Ana.	.958	5	8	15	1	24	4
Bell, David, Sea.	.984	48	85	102	3	190	33
Bellhorn, Mark, Oak.	1.000	2	0	1	0	1	0
Bellinger, Clay, N.Y.	1.000	21	19	49	0	68	5
Bush, Homer, Tor.	.986	75	165	246	6	417	68
Cabrera, Jolbert, Cle.	1.000	19	13	19	0	32	7
Cairo, Miguel, T.B.	.983	108	218	302	9	529	76
Canizaro, Jay, Min.	.982	90	120	199	6	325	41
Catalanotto, Frank, Tex.	.966	49	69	103	6	178	21
Delgado, Wilson, N.Y.-K.C.	.986	33	44	92	2	138	18
DeShields, Delino, Bal.	.975	96	171	254	11	436	46
Dransfeldt, Kelly, Tex.	1.000	2	0	1	0	1	0
Durham, Ray, Chi.	.980	151	299	419	15	733	126
Durrington, Trent, Ana.	1.000	1	1	2	0	3	0
EASLEY, Damion, Det.	.990	125	198	411	6	615	98
Febles, Carlos, K.C.	.978	99	165	285	10	460	76
Frye, Jeff, Bos.	.991	52	95	122	2	219	20
Garcia, Jesse, Bal.	1.000	6	5	18	0	23	3

Player, Team	Pct.	G	PO	A	E	TC	DP
Gil, Benji, Ana.	1.000	7	20	19	0	39	10
Graffanino, Tony, T.B.-Chi.	.973	25	39	69	3	111	16
Grebeck, Craig, Tor.	.968	56	100	174	9	283	34
Guillen, Ozzie, T.B.	1.000	2	3	2	0	5	0
Hairston Jr., Jerry, Bal.	.981	49	101	156	5	262	45
Halter, Shane, Det.	1.000	10	12	14	0	26	2
Hocking, Denny, Min.	.978	47	56	75	3	134	19
Holbert, Ray, K.C.	1.000	1	3	1	0	4	1
Jefferies, Gregg, Det.	1.000	14	23	33	0	56	6
Johnson, Keith, Ana.	1.000	2	2	7	0	9	0
Johnson, Russ, T.B.	.976	18	27	55	2	84	9
Kennedy, Adam, Ana.	.976	155	337	425	19	781	106
Knoblauch, Chuck, N.Y.	.958	82	149	190	15	354	42
Lansing, Mike, Bos.	1.000	49	73	106	0	179	12
Lewis, Mark, Bal.	.978	21	37	51	2	90	11
Luuloa, Keith, Ana.	1.000	3	6	9	0	15	3
Macias, Jose, Det.	.976	39	39	85	3	127	19
Maxwell, Jason, Min.	.967	30	28	61	3	92	13
McDonald, John, Cle.	1.000	2	2	2	0	4	0
McLemore, Mark, Sea.	.987	129	262	346	8	616	87
Menechino, Frank, Oak.	.973	51	83	131	6	220	30
Mora, Melvin, Bal.	1.000	1	2	1	0	3	1
Morandini, Mickey, Tor.	.993	35	58	92	1	151	28
Offerman, Jose, Bos.	.981	80	150	202	7	359	43
Ordaz, Luis, K.C.	1.000	22	27	30	0	57	10
Ortiz, Jose, Oak.	.857	3	2	4	1	7	1
Reboulet, Jeff, K.C.	.982	50	71	143	4	218	36
Rivas, Luis, Min.	.983	14	30	28	1	59	8
Sadler, Donnie, Bos.	1.000	12	9	18	0	27	3
Selby, Bill, Cle.	1.000	6	3	2	0	5	0
Sheldon, Scott, Tex.	.931	12	12	15	2	29	2
Smith, Bobby, T.B.	.970	45	84	144	7	235	26
Sojo, Luis, N.Y.	.989	25	33	59	1	93	7
Soriano, Alfonso, N.Y.	.000	1	0	0	1	1	0
Spiezio, Scott, Ana.	.000	2	0	0	0	0	0
Velandia, Jorge, Oak.	1.000	14	15	22	0	37	6
Velarde, Randy, Oak.	.982	122	243	399	12	654	94
Vizcaino, Jose, N.Y.	.990	62	83	120	2	205	28
Walker, Todd, Min.	.946	19	34	36	4	74	12
Wilson, Craig, Chi.	.950	4	11	8	1	20	3
Wilson, Enrique, Cle.	1.000	7	10	12	0	22	2
Woodward, Chris, Tor.	.941	3	5	11	1	17	1
Young, Mike, Tex.	.000	1	0	0	0	0	0
Zaun, Gregg, K.C.	.000	1	0	0	0	0	0

TRIPLE PLAYS: Hairston, Bal.; Velarde, Oak.

SECOND BASEMEN WITH TWO OR MORE TEAMS

Player, Team	Pct.	G	PO	A	E	TC	DP
Delgado, Wilson, N.Y.	.950	14	16	22	2	40	3
Delgado, Wilson, K.C.	1.000	19	28	70	0	98	15
Graffanino, Tony, T.B.	1.000	6	12	16	0	28	4
Graffanino, Tony, Chi.	.964	19	27	53	3	83	12

THIRD BASEMEN

Player, Team	Pct.	G	PO	A	E	TC	DP
Alexander, Manny, Bos.	.944	63	39	79	7	125	5
Alicea, Luis, Tex.	.706	8	5	7	5	17	1
Allen, Dusty, Det.	1.000	1	1	0	0	1	0
Ausmus, Brad, Det.	.000	1	0	0	0	0	0
Batista, Tony, Tor.	.963	154	120	318	17	455	35
Bell, David, Sea.	.944	93	50	151	12	213	14
Bellhorn, Mark, Oak.	1.000	2	0	4	0	4	0
Bellinger, Clay, N.Y.	.921	18	10	25	3	38	4
Berry, Sean, Bos.	.000	1	0	0	0	0	0
Blake, Casey, Min.	1.000	5	2	5	0	7	0
Branyan, Russ, Cle.	.500	1	0	1	1	2	1
Brosius, Scott, N.Y.	.968	134	101	231	11	343	23
Castilla, Vinny, T.B.	.967	83	50	185	8	243	20
Chavez, Eric, Oak.	.951	146	91	256	18	365	17
Coffie, Ivanon, Bal.	.971	15	6	27	1	34	1
Conine, Jeff, Bal.	.932	44	21	75	7	103	10
Coomer, Ron, Min.	1.000	5	3	15	0	18	2
Crede, Joe, Chi.	.933	6	5	9	1	15	1
Daubach, Brian, Bos.	1.000	1	0	1	0	1	0
Delgado, Wilson, N.Y.-K.C.	.800	8	1	3	1	5	0
Diaz, Einar, Cle.	.000	1	0	0	0	0	0
Evans, Tom, Tex.	.909	21	12	38	5	55	5
Frye, Jeff, Bos.	1.000	3	1	2	0	3	0
FRYMAN, Travis, Cle.	.978	154	79	276	8	363	20
Gipson, Charles, Sea.	1.000	5	1	9	0	10	1
Glaus, Troy, Ana.	.933	156	111	349	33	493	33

Player, Team	Pct.	G	PO	A	E	TC	DP
Graffanino, Tony, T.B.-Chi.	1.000	15	12	9	0	21	2
Guillen, Carlos, Sea.	.911	68	57	116	17	190	7
Guillen, Ozzie, T.B.	1.000	11	4	22	0	26	2
Halter, Shane, Det.	.937	55	26	63	6	95	11
Hatteberg, Scott, Bos.	.000	1	0	0	0	0	0
Hernandez, Carlos E., Sea.	1.000	2	1	0	0	1	0
Hocking, Denny, Min.	.958	16	3	20	1	24	2
Holbert, Ray, K.C.	.000	1	0	0	0	0	0
Huff, Aubrey, T.B.	.939	37	24	53	5	82	3
Jefferies, Gregg, Det.	1.000	6	2	4	0	6	1
Johnson, Russ, T.B.	.967	49	14	74	3	91	6
Konerko, Paul, Chi.	.900	7	2	7	1	10	1
Koskie, Corey, Min.	.966	139	96	241	12	349	27
Lamb, Mike, Tex.	.913	135	118	230	33	381	24
Lansing, Mike, Bos.	.000	1	0	0	0	0	0
Lewis, Mark, Bal.	.857	29	8	34	7	49	2
Mabry, John, Sea.	.862	22	6	19	4	29	3
Macias, Jose, Det.	.976	26	11	29	1	41	3
Maxwell, Jason, Min.	.935	19	5	24	2	31	4
Menechino, Frank, Oak.	1.000	4	3	4	0	7	1
Merloni, Lou, Bos.	.928	40	26	64	7	97	3
Minor, Ryan, Bal.	.927	26	19	32	4	55	5
Norton, Greg, Chi.	.926	47	32	56	7	95	5
Palmer, Dean, Det.	.914	115	66	180	23	269	14
Perry, Herbert, T.B.-Chi.	.967	111	87	210	10	307	18
Piatt, Adam, Oak.	1.000	13	4	11	0	15	0
Randa, Joe, K.C.	.957	156	132	293	19	444	30
Reboulet, Jeff, K.C.	.813	11	4	9	3	16	2
Ripken Jr., Cal, Bal.	.974	73	56	134	5	195	17
Rolls, Damian, T.B.	.000	1	0	0	0	0	0
Sadler, Donnie, Bos.	1.000	3	0	3	0	3	1
Saenz, Olmedo, Oak.	.923	18	11	25	3	39	2
Selby, Bill, Cle.	1.000	4	0	1	0	1	1
Sheldon, Scott, Tex.	.975	15	11	28	1	40	6
Smith, Bobby, T.B.	.875	5	0	7	1	8	0
Sojo, Luis, N.Y.	1.000	10	9	10	0	19	0
Soriano, Alfonso, N.Y.	.846	10	11	11	4	26	2
Spiezio, Scott, Ana.	.929	15	9	17	2	28	4
Sprague, Ed, Bos.	.972	30	19	50	2	71	1
Valentin, John, Bos.	1.000	10	6	9	0	15	0
Veras, Wilton, Bos.	.907	49	33	94	13	140	11
Vizcaino, Jose, N.Y.	1.000	6	3	5	0	8	1
Wilson, Craig, Chi.	.938	15	6	24	2	32	2
Wilson, Dan, Sea.	.000	1	0	0	0	0	0
Wilson, Enrique, Cle.	.950	12	2	17	1	20	0
Woodward, Chris, Tor.	1.000	9	5	18	0	23	3

THIRD BASEMEN WITH TWO OR MORE TEAMS

Player, Team	Pct.	G	PO	A	E	TC	DP
Delgado, Wilson, N.Y.	.667	5	1	1	1	3	0
Delgado, Wilson, K.C.	1.000	3	0	2	0	2	0
Graffanino, Tony, T.B.	1.000	3	2	1	0	3	0
Graffanino, Tony, Chi.	1.000	12	10	8	0	18	2
Perry, Herbert, T.B.	.938	7	5	10	1	16	1
Perry, Herbert, Chi.	.969	104	82	200	9	291	17

SHORTSTOPS

Player, Team	Pct.	G	PO	A	E	TC	DP
Alexander, Manny, Bos.	1.000	20	16	33	0	49	7
Alicea, Luis, Tex.	1.000	2	1	3	0	4	0
Baughman, Justin, Ana.	1.000	5	4	2	0	6	0
Bell, David, Sea.	.000	1	0	0	0	0	0
Bellhorn, Mark, Oak.	1.000	1	0	0	0	0	0
Bellinger, Clay, N.Y.	1.000	6	9	11	0	20	1
Bordick, Mike, Bal.	.979	100	161	258	9	428	57
Cabrera, Jolbert, Cle.	1.000	8	7	17	0	24	2
Chavez, Eric, Oak.	1.000	2	1	0	0	1	0
Clayton, Royce, Tex.	.977	148	265	411	16	692	94
Coffie, Ivanon, Bal.	1.000	4	7	5	0	12	1
Cruz, Deivi, Det.	.982	156	222	482	13	717	116
Delgado, Wilson, N.Y.-K.C.	.982	23	16	39	1	56	10
DiSarcina, Gary, Ana.	.934	12	24	47	5	76	12
Dransfeldt, Kelly, Tex.	1.000	14	13	28	0	41	8
Garcia, Jesse, Bal.	1.000	5	4	4	0	8	2
Garciaparra, Nomar, Bos.	.971	136	201	402	18	621	65
Gil, Benji, Ana.	.957	94	140	260	18	418	59
Gipson, Charles, Sea.	1.000	5	0	2	0	2	0
Glaus, Troy, Ana.	1.000	6	1	4	0	5	1
Gonzalez, Alex S., Tor.	.975	141	213	407	16	636	100
Graffanino, Tony, T.B.-Chi.	.967	22	24	63	3	90	16
Grebeck, Craig, Tor.	1.000	8	10	19	0	29	4

2000 A.L. STATISTICS Fielding

Player, Team	Pct.	G	PO	A	E	TC	DP
Guillen, Carlos, Sea.	.947	23	28	44	4	76	14
Guillen, Ozzie, T.B.	.948	42	26	65	5	96	12
Guzman, Cristian, Min.	.967	151	228	413	22	663	96
Halter, Shane, Det.	.981	17	19	33	1	53	8
Hocking, Denny, Min.	.983	15	19	38	1	58	10
Holbert, Ray, K.C.	1.000	1	1	1	0	2	1
Jeter, Derek, N.Y.	.961	148	237	349	24	610	78
Johnson, Keith, Ana.	1.000	1	2	2	0	4	0
Johnson, Russ, T.B.	1.000	11	4	14	0	18	1
Lewis, Mark, Bal.	.975	14	19	20	1	40	5
Luuloa, Keith, Ana.	.833	4	2	3	1	6	1
Macias, Jose, Det.	1.000	1	1	2	0	3	1
Martinez, Felix, T.B.	.976	106	191	368	14	573	80
Maxwell, Jason, Min.	.923	5	2	10	1	13	1
McDonald, John, Cle.	1.000	7	2	6	0	8	1
Menechino, Frank, Oak.	1.000	5	4	4	0	8	0
Mora, Melvin, Bal.	.952	52	78	160	12	250	32
Ordaz, Luis, K.C.	.986	38	37	35	1	73	14
Reboulet, Jeff, K.C.	.923	5	9	15	2	26	3
Rivas, Luis, Min.	1.000	2	1	1	0	2	1
Rodriguez, Alex, Sea.	.986	148	243	438	10	691	123
Sadler, Donnie, Bos.	.958	19	19	50	3	72	7
Sanchez, Rey, K.C.	.994	143	224	446	4	674	106
Sheets, Andy, Bos.	1.000	10	7	17	0	24	4
Sheldon, Scott, Tex.	.970	22	25	40	2	67	6
Sojo, Luis, N.Y.	1.000	2	2	2	0	4	0
Soriano, Alfonso, N.Y.	.875	9	7	7	2	16	1
Stocker, Kevin, T.B.-Ana.	.963	109	141	321	18	480	74
Tejada, Miguel, Oak.	.972	160	233	501	21	755	115
Valentin, Jose, Chi.	.950	141	233	456	36	725	117
Velandia, Jorge, Oak.	1.000	4	2	2	0	4	1
Vizcaino, Jose, N.Y.	1.000	2	2	2	0	4	2
VIZQUEL, Omar, Cle.	.995	156	231	414	3	648	99
Wilson, Craig, Chi.	1.000	10	14	29	0	43	4
Wilson, Enrique, Cle.	1.000	7	8	15	0	23	5
Woodward, Chris, Tor.	.955	22	26	58	4	88	9

TRIPLE PLAY: Mora, Bal.

SHORTSTOPS WITH TWO OR MORE TEAMS

Player, Team	Pct.	G	PO	A	E	TC	DP
Delgado, Wilson, N.Y.	1.000	11	6	14	0	20	2
Delgado, Wilson, K.C.	.972	12	10	25	1	36	8
Graffanino, Tony, T.B.	1.000	1	0	2	0	2	0
Graffanino, Tony, Chi.	.966	21	24	61	3	88	16
Stocker, Kevin, T.B.	.933	40	43	111	11	165	25
Stocker, Kevin, Ana.	.978	69	98	210	7	315	49

OUTFIELDERS

Player, Team	Pct.	G	PO	A	E	TC	DP
Abbott, Jeff, Chi.*	.981	65	101	2	2	105	0
Alcantara, Israel, Bos.*	.889	7	8	0	1	9	0
Allen, Chad, Min.	1.000	15	26	2	0	28	2
Allen, Dusty, Det.	1.000	1	1	0	0	1	0
Amaral, Rich, Bal.	1.000	19	45	1	0	46	0
Anderson, Brady, Bal.*	.997	127	301	1	1	303	1
Anderson, Garret, Ana.*	.990	148	380	5	4	389	0
Barnes, John, Min.	1.000	11	28	2	0	30	2
Becker, Rich, Oak.-Det.*	.954	99	162	5	8	175	5
Belle, Albert, Bal.	.986	110	211	8	3	222	2
Bellinger, Clay, N.Y.	.968	46	60	1	2	63	0
Beltran, Carlos, K.C.	.975	88	231	5	6	242	2
Branyan, Russ, Cle.	.968	33	59	2	2	63	0
Brosius, Scott, N.Y.	.000	2	0	0	0	0	0
Brown, Dee, K.C.	1.000	5	12	0	0	12	0
Buchanan, Brian, Min.	1.000	25	34	1	0	35	0
Buhner, Jay, Sea.	1.000	104	176	4	0	180	0
Burkhart, Morgan, Bos.*	.000	1	0	0	0	0	0
Byrnes, Eric, Oak.	1.000	4	4	0	0	4	0
Cabrera, Jolbert, Cle.	.989	74	89	3	1	93	1
Cameron, Mike, Sea.	.985	155	399	5	6	410	3
Canseco, Jose, N.Y.	.818	5	9	0	2	11	0
Catalanotto, Frank, Tex.	.000	1	0	0	0	0	0
Christensen, McKay, Chi.*	1.000	29	20	1	0	21	0
Christensen, Ryan, Oak.	.951	114	95	2	5	102	1
Clemente, Edgard, Ana.	1.000	32	36	2	0	38	0
Conine, Jeff, Bal.	.930	19	38	2	3	43	1
Cordero, Wil, Cle.	1.000	38	79	2	0	81	0
Cordova, Marty, Tor.	.982	41	55	1	1	57	1
Cox, Steve, T.B.*	.948	56	107	3	6	116	0
Cruz, Jacob, Cle.*	1.000	9	16	1	0	17	1
Cruz, Jose, Tor.	.993	162	405	9	3	417	1
Cummings, Midre, Min.-Bos.	1.000	44	65	4	0	69	2
Curtis, Chad, Tex.	.965	80	135	4	5	144	0
Damon, Johnny, K.C.*	.986	133	334	6	5	345	1
Daubach, Brian, Bos.	1.000	8	20	0	0	20	0
DeShields, Delino, Bal.	.975	41	76	3	2	81	1
Ducey, Rob, Tor.	.889	3	8	0	1	9	0
Dunwoody, Todd, K.C.*	.976	40	81	0	2	83	0
Dye, Jermaine, K.C.	.976	146	277	11	7	295	3
Encarnacion, Juan, Det.	.987	141	363	3	5	371	2
Erstad, Darin, Ana.*	.992	136	350	9	3	362	2
Everett, Carl, Bos.	.980	126	276	11	6	293	4
Frye, Jeff, Bos.	1.000	15	20	0	0	20	0
Gant, Ron, Ana.	.977	21	42	1	1	44	1
Garcia, Karim, Det.-Bal.*	1.000	9	10	0	0	10	0
Giambi, Jeremy, Oak.*	.966	55	81	3	3	87	0
Gilkey, Bernard, Bos.	1.000	22	36	1	0	37	0
Gipson, Charles, Sea.	1.000	48	22	1	0	23	0
Gonzalez, Juan, Det.	.992	66	118	2	1	121	1
Green, Scarborough, Tex.	1.000	65	102	8	0	110	1
Greene, Todd, Tor.	.000	1	0	0	0	0	0
Greer, Rusty, Tex.*	.985	97	194	3	3	200	0
Grieve, Ben, Oak.	.988	144	237	6	3	246	0
Guillen, Jose, T.B.	.978	99	169	7	4	180	3
Halter, Shane, Det.	1.000	8	15	1	0	16	0
Henderson, Rickey, Sea.*	.984	88	181	0	3	184	0
Higginson, Bobby, Det.	.979	145	307	19	7	333	3
Hill, Glenallen, N.Y.	1.000	12	19	0	0	19	0
Hocking, Denny, Min.	1.000	51	70	5	0	75	3
Hubbard, Trenidad, Bal.	.929	24	12	1	1	14	0
Hunter, Torii, Min.	.989	99	270	12	3	285	3
Huskey, Butch, Min.	.975	15	37	2	1	40	0
Ibanez, Raul, Sea.	.978	76	86	1	2	89	1
Javier, Stan, Sea.	.993	88	140	6	1	147	0
Jefferies, Gregg, Det.	.000	1	0	0	0	0	0
Johnson, Lance, N.Y.*	1.000	4	2	0	0	2	0
Jones, Jacque, Min.*	.994	147	334	9	2	345	1
Jose, Felix, N.Y.	.929	14	13	0	1	14	0
Justice, David, Cle.-N.Y.*	.982	107	211	8	4	223	2
Kapler, Gabe, Tex.	.969	116	307	5	10	322	4
Kelly, Roberto, N.Y.	1.000	10	18	0	0	18	0
Kingsale, Gene, Bal.	.954	24	60	2	3	65	0
Lawton, Matt, Min.	.983	143	278	4	5	287	1
Ledee, Ricky, N.Y.-Cle.-Tex.*	.981	123	261	2	5	268	0
Lee, Carlos, Chi.	.990	149	273	10	3	286	0
Lewis, Darren, Bos.	.981	89	152	5	3	160	1
Liefer, Jeff, Chi.	1.000	5	2	0	0	2	0
Lindsey, Rod, Bal.	1.000	7	2	0	0	2	0
Lofton, Kenny, Cle.*	.989	135	348	4	4	356	1
Long, Terrence, Oak.*	.971	137	328	2	10	340	1
Mabry, John, Sea.	1.000	19	23	0	0	23	0
Macias, Jose, Det.	1.000	3	2	0	0	2	0
Magee, Wendell, Det.	1.000	76	86	3	0	89	0
Martin, Al, Sea.*	.963	35	76	3	3	82	0
Martinez, Dave, T.B.-Tex.-Tor.*	.992	110	229	15	2	246	4
Mateo, Ruben, Tex.	.980	52	140	4	3	147	0
Matos, Luis, Bal.	.988	69	168	3	2	173	0
Maxwell, Jason, Min.	1.000	2	2	0	0	2	0
McCarty, Dave, K.C.*	.955	11	19	2	1	22	1
McCracken, Quinton, T.B.	1.000	11	19	0	0	19	0
McDonald, Jason, Tex.	.988	32	75	6	1	82	2
McLemore, Mark, Sea.	1.000	14	24	0	0	24	0
McMillon, Billy, Det.*	.964	15	27	0	1	28	0
Mondesi, Raul, Tor.	.967	96	203	5	7	215	3
Morris, Hal, Det.*	1.000	1	1	0	0	1	0
Mottola, Chad, Tor.	1.000	3	5	0	0	5	0
Nixon, Trot, Bos.*	.991	118	216	8	2	226	4
O'Leary, Troy, Bos.*	.988	137	243	9	3	255	0
O'Neill, Paul, N.Y.*	.993	140	293	5	2	300	3
Ordonez, Magglio, Chi.	.983	152	280	12	5	297	3
Palmeiro, Orlando, Ana.*	.984	72	117	6	2	125	0
Paul, Josh, Chi.	.000	1	0	0	0	0	0
Perry, Chan, Cle.	1.000	7	5	0	0	5	0
Piatt, Adam, Oak.	.950	29	37	1	2	40	0
Polonia, Luis, Det.-N.Y.*	.987	55	76	2	1	79	0
Porter, Bo, Oak.	1.000	16	13	0	0	13	0
Pose, Scott, K.C.	1.000	11	6	0	0	6	0
Pride, Curtis, Bos.	1.000	9	15	0	0	15	0
Quinn, Mark, K.C.	.988	81	158	9	2	169	1
Ramirez, Alex, Cle.	.978	31	44	1	1	46	0
Ramirez, Manny, Cle.	.986	93	134	7	2	143	1
Richard, Chris, Bal.*	1.000	1	3	0	0	3	0
Roberts, Dave, Cle.*	1.000	17	10	0	0	10	0
Sadler, Donnie, Bos.	1.000	17	21	0	0	21	0

Player, Team	Pct.	G	PO	A	E	TC	DP
Salmon, Tim, Ana.	.979	124	274	12	6	292	4
Sanders, Anthony, Sea.	1.000	1	1	0	0	1	0
Segui, David, Cle.*	1.000	7	6	0	0	6	0
Selby, Bill, Cle.	1.000	10	16	0	0	16	0
Sexson, Richie, Cle.	1.000	58	79	3	0	82	0
Sheldon, Scott, Tex.	.000	2	0	0	0	0	0
Singleton, Chris, Chi.*	.992	145	373	9	3	385	0
Spencer, Shane, N.Y.	.989	40	83	3	1	87	1
Spiezio, Scott, Ana.	1.000	10	14	0	0	14	0
Stairs, Matt, Oak.	.979	103	185	5	4	194	1
Stewart, Shannon, Tor.	.993	136	298	5	2	305	2
Surhoff, B.J., Bal.	.987	102	226	5	3	234	1
Thompson, Andy, Tor.	1.000	2	2	0	0	2	0
Thompson, Ryan, N.Y.	1.000	31	33	0	0	33	0
Timmons, Ozzie, T.B.	1.000	9	8	0	0	8	0
Trammell, Bubba, T.B.	1.000	48	66	2	0	68	1
Tyner, Jason, T.B.*	1.000	31	51	4	0	55	0
Valdes, Pedro, Tex.*	1.000	14	17	0	0	17	0
Valentin, Jose, Chi.	.000	1	0	0	0	0	0
Vaughn, Greg, T.B.	.993	72	145	6	1	152	1
Vaughn, Mo, Ana.	.000		.		.		
Wells, Vernon, Tor.	1.000	3	2	0	0	2	0
Whiten, Mark, Cle.	1.000	5	3	0	0	3	0
Widger, Chris, Sea.	.000	1	0	0	0	0	0
WILLIAMS, Bernie, N.Y.	1.000	137	353	2	0	355	1
Williams, Gerald, T.B.	.983	138	349	6	6	361	1
Winn, Randy, T.B.	.990	47	92	4	1	97	1
Wise, Dewayne, Tor.*	1.000	18	20	0	0	20	0

OUTFIELDERS WITH TWO OR MORE TEAMS

Player, Team	Pct.	G	PO	A	E	TC	DP
Becker, Rich, Oak.*	.949	19	35	2	2	39	2
Becker, Rich, Det.*	.956	80	127	3	6	136	3
Cummings, Midre, Min.	1.000	40	58	4	0	62	2
Cummings, Midre, Bos.	1.000	4	7	0	0	7	0
Garcia, Karim, Det.*	1.000	7	8	0	0	8	0
Garcia, Karim, Bal.*	1.000	2	2	0	0	2	0
Justice, David, Cle.*	.977	47	84	2	2	88	1
Justice, David, N.Y.*	.985	60	127	6	2	135	1
Ledee, Ricky, N.Y.*	.979	49	94	1	2	97	0
Ledee, Ricky, Cle.*	1.000	17	39	1	0	40	0
Ledee, Ricky, Tex.*	.977	57	128	0	3	131	0
Martinez, Dave, T.B.*	1.000	28	46	5	0	51	1
Martinez, Dave, Tex.*	1.000	35	82	2	0	84	1
Martinez, Dave, Tor.*	.982	47	101	8	2	111	2
Polonia, Luis, Det.*	1.000	27	44	2	0	46	0
Polonia, Luis, N.Y.*	.970	28	32	0	1	33	0

CATCHERS

Player, Team	Pct.	G	PO	A	E	TC	DP	PB
Alomar Jr., Sandy, Cle.	.989	95	661	42	8	711	6	6
Ardoin, Danny, Min.	.989	15	80	8	1	89	0	3
Ausmus, Brad, Det.	.992	150	898	68	8	974	8	3
Cardona, Javier, Det.	.973	26	66	7	2	75	0	2
Castillo, Alberto, Tor.	.993	66	372	31	3	406	2	5
Diaz, Einar, Cle.	.994	74	579	48	4	631	4	4
DiFelice, Mike, T.B.	.980	59	351	35	8	394	6	10
Fabregas, Jorge, K.C.	.992	39	219	21	2	242	2	1
Fasano, Sal, Oak.	.981	52	231	22	5	258	2	1
Fick, Robert, Det.	.981	16	50	3	1	54	1	2
Flaherty, John, T.B.	.993	108	611	51	5	667	9	4
Fletcher, Darrin, Tor.	.994	117	621	39	4	664	7	6
Fordyce, Brook, Chi.-Bal.	.993	92	564	33	4	601	4	5
Greene, Charlie, Tor.	1.000	3	13	0	0	13	0	0
Greene, Todd, Tor.	1.000	2	2	0	0	2	0	0
Hall, Toby, T.B.	1.000	4	19	2	0	21	0	0
Halter, Shane, Det.	1.000	2	1	0	0	1	0	0
Haselman, Bill, Tex.	.989	62	336	20	4	360	4	1
Hatteberg, Scott, Bos.	.981	48	297	16	6	319	3	12
Hernandez, Ramon, Oak.	.984	142	764	43	13	820	7	7
Hinch, A.J., Oak.	.900	5	9	0	1	10	0	0
Jensen, Marcus, Min.	.993	49	261	13	2	276	3	4
Johnson, Brian, K.C.	.991	37	221	12	2	235	1	4
Johnson, Charles, Bal.-Chi.	.992	126	722	42	6	770	7	5
Johnson, Mark L., Chi.	.992	74	466	27	4	497	4	7
Knorr, Randy, Tex.	.985	15	64	2	1	67	0	1
Lampkin, Tom, Sea.	.987	28	138	13	2	153	2	1
LeCroy, Matt, Min.	.988	49	317	16	4	337	8	4
Leyritz, Jim, N.Y.	1.000	2	13	0	0	13	0	0
Lunar, Fernando, Bal.	1.000	9	43	2	0	45	0	0
Machado, Robert, Sea.	1.000	8	35	2	0	37	1	0
Moeller, Chad, Min.	.979	48	266	13	6	285	0	0
Molina, Ben, Ana.	.991	127	683	61	7	751	9	6
Morales, Willie, Bal.	1.000	3	22	2	0	24	1	0
Myers, Greg, Bal.	1.000	28	166	14	0	180	1	0
Oliver, Joe, Sea.	.995	66	354	18	2	374	1	0
Ortiz, Hector, K.C.	.993	26	130	18	1	149	1	0
Paul, Josh, Chi.	.974	34	130	17	4	151	5	2
Phelps, Josh, Tor.	1.000	1	1	0	0	1	0	0
Pierzynski, A.J., Min.	1.000	32	160	10	0	170	3	2
Posada, Jorge, N.Y.	.993	142	892	56	7	955	7	11
RODRIGUEZ, Ivan, Tex.	.996	87	507	34	2	543	10	2
Sheldon, Scott, Tex.	1.000	3	3	0	0	3	0	0
Turner, Chris, N.Y.	1.000	36	171	5	0	176	0	2
Varitek, Jason, Bos.	.992	128	867	46	7	920	3	14
Walbeck, Matt, Ana.	.991	44	200	16	2	218	0	0
Waszgis, B.J., Tex.	1.000	23	66	2	0	68	1	4
Widger, Chris, Sea.	1.000	6	11	0	0	11	0	1
Wilson, Dan, Sea.	.990	88	482	30	5	517	5	6
Wooten, Shawn, Ana.	1.000	4	5	0	0	5	0	0
Zaun, Gregg, K.C.	.988	76	376	31	5	412	4	2

CATCHERS WITH TWO OR MORE TEAMS

Player, Team	Pct.	G	PO	A	E	TC	DP	PB
Fordyce, Brook, Chi.	1.000	40	251	13	0	264	2	2
Fordyce, Brook, Bal.	.988	52	313	20	4	337	2	3
Johnson, Charles, Bal.	.994	83	498	30	3	531	4	3
Johnson, Charles, Chi.	.987	43	224	12	3	239	3	2

PITCHERS

Player, Team	Pct.	G	PO	A	E	TC	DP
Abbott, Paul, Sea.	.969	35	12	19	1	32	3
Alvarez, Juan, Ana.*	1.000	11	2	0	0	2	1
Anderson, Matt, Det.	1.000	69	4	6	0	10	0
Andrews, Clayton, Tor.*	1.000	8	0	1	0	1	0
Appier, Kevin, Oak.	.957	31	8	14	1	23	1
Arrojo, Rolando, Bos.	1.000	13	6	10	0	16	1
Baldwin, James, Chi.	.952	29	14	26	2	42	2
Bale, John, Tor.*	.000	2	0	0	0	0	0
Barcelo, Lorenzo, Chi.	1.000	22	0	1	0	1	0
Batista, Miguel, K.C.	.875	14	3	4	1	8	0
Beck, Rod, Bos.	1.000	34	0	3	0	3	0
Beirne, Kevin, Chi.	.857	29	2	4	1	7	0
Belcher, Tim, Ana.	1.000	9	1	5	0	6	0
Belitz, Todd, Oak.*	.000	5	0	0	0	0	0
Bere, Jason, Cle.	1.000	11	6	2	0	8	1
Bergman, Sean, Min.	.952	15	8	12	1	21	2
Bernero, Adam, Det.	1.000	12	2	6	0	8	2
Biddle, Rocky, Chi.	.800	4	1	3	1	5	0
Blair, Willie, Det.	1.000	47	4	13	0	17	1
Bochtler, Doug, K.C.	.000	6	0	0	0	0	0
Borbon, Pedro, Tor.*	1.000	59	2	9	0	11	1
Borkowski, Dave, Det.	.000	2	0	0	0	0	0
Bottalico, Ricky, K.C.	.929	62	6	7	1	14	1
Bottenfield, Kent, Ana.	1.000	21	7	18	0	25	1
Bradford, Chad, Chi.	1.000	12	0	2	0	2	0
Brea, Leslie, Bal.	.000	6	0	0	0	0	0
Brewington, Jamie, Cle.	1.000	26	4	4	0	8	1
Brocail, Doug, Det.	.933	49	7	7	1	15	0
Brower, Jim, Cle.	.955	17	9	12	1	22	1
Buehrle, Mark, Chi.*	.909	28	1	9	1	11	2
Burba, Dave, Cle.	1.000	32	10	27	0	37	0
Byrdak, Tim, K.C.*	1.000	12	1	0	0	1	0
Cairncross, Cam, Cle.*	.500	15	0	1	1	2	0
Carpenter, Chris, Tor.	.950	34	7	12	1	20	2
Carrasco, Hector, Min.-Bos.	.933	69	2	12	1	15	0
Castillo, Frank, Tor.	.964	25	8	19	1	28	4
Choate, Randy, N.Y.*	.750	22	0	3	1	4	0
Clark, Mark, Tex.	1.000	12	1	6	0	7	3
Clemens, Roger, N.Y.	.958	32	14	32	2	48	2
Coco, Pasqual, Tor.	.000	1	0	0	0	0	0
Colon, Bartolo, Cle.	.946	30	17	18	2	37	1
Cone, David, N.Y.	.935	30	9	20	2	31	0
Cooper, Brian, Ana.	.882	15	3	12	2	17	1
Cordero, Francisco, Tex.	.900	56	4	5	1	10	0
Cormier, Rheal, Bos.*	1.000	64	1	14	0	15	0
Crabtree, Tim, Tex.	1.000	68	5	11	0	16	3
Crawford, Paxton, Bos.	1.000	7	1	0	0	1	0
Creek, Doug, T.B.*	1.000	45	2	9	0	11	1
Cressend, Jack, Min.	1.000	11	1	0	0	1	0
Croushore, Rick, Bos.	1.000	5	0	1	0	1	0
Cruz, Nelson, Det.	1.000	27	1	6	0	7	1

Player, Team	Pct.	G	PO	A	E	TC	DP
Cubillan, Darwin, Tor.-Tex.	1.000	20	2	4	0	6	1
D'Amico, Jeff M., K.C.	1.000	7	1	1	0	2	0
Davis, Doug, Tex.*	.952	30	3	17	1	21	0
Davis, Kane, Cle.	1.000	5	1	3	0	4	0
DePaula, Sean, Cle.	1.000	13	4	2	0	6	0
DeWitt, Matt, Tor.	1.000	8	2	1	0	3	0
Dickson, Jason, Ana.	1.000	6	3	2	0	5	0
Dingman, Craig, N.Y.	.000	10	0	0	0	0	0
Drew, Tim, Cle.	.800	3	1	3	1	5	0
Durbin, Chad, K.C.	.938	16	8	7	1	16	2
Duvall, Mike, T.B.*	1.000	2	0	1	0	1	0
Eiland, Dave, T.B.	1.000	17	6	15	0	21	0
Einertson, Darrell, N.Y.	1.000	11	0	2	0	2	0
Eldred, Cal, Chi.	1.000	20	8	13	0	21	2
Enders, Trevor, T.B.*	1.000	9	2	2	0	4	0
Erdos, Todd, N.Y.	1.000	14	1	1	0	2	0
Erickson, Scott, Bal.	.800	16	7	5	3	15	0
Escobar, Kelvim, Tor.	.963	43	11	15	1	27	1
Estrella, Leo, Tor.	1.000	2	0	1	0	1	0
Etherton, Seth, Ana.	1.000	11	1	11	0	12	1
Eyre, Scott, Chi.*	1.000	13	0	3	0	3	0
Fassero, Jeff, Bos.*	.967	38	11	18	1	30	3
Finley, Chuck, Cle.*	.886	34	11	20	4	35	1
Fiore, Tony, T.B.	1.000	11	1	1	0	2	0
Florie, Bryce, Bos.	1.000	29	7	12	0	19	1
Ford, Ben, N.Y.	1.000	4	0	1	0	1	0
Foulke, Keith, Chi.	1.000	72	7	3	0	10	1
Frascatore, John, Tor.	.923	60	7	5	1	13	2
Fussell, Chris, K.C.	.929	20	9	4	1	14	0
Fyhrie, Mike, Ana.	1.000	32	1	6	0	7	0
Garces, Rich, Bos.	1.000	64	5	6	0	11	0
Garcia, Freddy, Sea.	.889	21	5	19	3	27	1
Garland, Jon, Chi.	.857	15	2	10	2	14	0
Ginter, Matt, Chi.	1.000	3	0	1	0	1	0
Glynn, Ryan, Tex.	1.000	16	9	12	0	21	1
Gooden, Dwight, T.B.-N.Y.	.952	26	4	16	1	21	3
Grimsley, Jason, N.Y.	.917	63	11	11	2	24	4
Groom, Buddy, Bal.*	.857	70	2	10	2	14	1
Guardado, Eddie, Min.*	1.000	70	0	3	0	3	0
Gunderson, Eric, Tor.*	.667	6	0	2	1	3	0
Guthrie, Mark, T.B.-Tor.*	1.000	57	1	7	0	8	0
Guzman, Juan, T.B.	.000	1	0	0	0	0	0
Halama, John, Sea.*	.912	30	4	27	3	34	3
Halladay, Roy, Tor.	1.000	19	4	7	0	11	0
Halter, Shane, Det.	.000	1	0	0	0	0	0
Hamilton, Joey, Tor.	1.000	6	2	2	0	4	1
Haney, Chris, Cle.*	1.000	1	0	1	0	1	0
Harper, Travis, T.B.	1.000	6	1	3	0	4	0
Hasegawa, Shigetoshi, Ana.	1.000	66	6	10	0	16	1
Hawkins, LaTroy, Min.	.905	66	3	16	2	21	1
Helling, Rick, Tex.	.962	35	8	17	1	26	1
Heredia, Gil, Oak.	.974	32	9	29	1	39	0
Hernandez, Orlando, N.Y.	1.000	29	12	24	0	36	4
Hernandez, Roberto, T.B.	.938	68	4	11	1	16	1
Hiljus, Erik, Det.	.000	3	0	0	0	0	0
Hill, Ken, Ana.-Chi.	.950	18	5	14	1	20	1
Hinchliffe, Brett, Ana.	.000	2	0	0	0	0	0
Hodges, Kevin, Sea.	1.000	13	1	1	0	2	0
Holmes, Darren, Bal.	.000	5	0	0	0	0	0
Holtz, Mike, Ana.*	1.000	61	3	7	0	10	0
Howry, Bob, Chi.	1.000	65	3	6	0	9	1
Hudson, Tim, Oak.	.897	32	15	20	4	39	1
Isringhausen, Jason, Oak.	.923	66	1	11	1	13	0
Johnson, Jason, Bal.	1.000	25	3	4	0	7	0
Johnson, Jonathan, Tex.	1.000	15	1	7	0	8	0
Johnson, Mark, Det.	1.000	9	1	5	0	6	0
Jones, Doug, Oak.	.941	54	6	10	1	17	0
Jones, Marcus, Oak.	.000	1	0	0	0	0	0
Jones, Todd, Det.	1.000	67	3	2	0	5	0
Kamieniecki, Scott, Cle.	.889	26	3	5	1	9	1
Karl, Scott, Ana.*	.500	6	0	1	1	2	0
Karsay, Steve, Cle.	.957	72	9	13	1	23	0
Keisler, Randy, N.Y.*	.000	4	0	0	0	0	0
Kida, Masao, Det.	1.000	2	2	1	0	3	0
Kinney, Matt, Min.	.889	8	3	5	1	9	0
Koch, Billy, Tor.	1.000	68	5	8	0	13	2
Kohlmeier, Ryan, Bal.	1.000	25	2	2	0	4	0
Kolb, Danny, Tex.	.000	1	0	0	0	0	0
Larkin, Andy, K.C.	1.000	18	2	1	0	3	0
Laxton, Brett, K.C.	.000	6	0	0	0	0	0
Lee, Sang-Hoon, Bos.*	1.000	9	0	2	0	2	0
Levine, Al, Ana.	.944	51	4	13	1	18	0
Lidle, Cory, T.B.	.962	31	6	19	1	26	1
Lilly, Ted, N.Y.*	1.000	7	1	1	0	2	0
Lincoln, Mike, Min.	1.000	8	1	2	0	3	0
Loaiza, Esteban, Tex.-Tor.	.932	34	12	29	3	44	4
Lopez, Albie, T.B.	.906	45	12	17	3	32	2
Lorraine, Andrew, Cle.*	1.000	10	1	1	0	2	0
Lowe, Derek, Bos.	1.000	74	8	11	0	19	0
Lowe, Sean, Chi.	.917	50	3	8	1	12	0
Mabry, John, Sea.	.000	1	0	0	0	0	0
Maduro, Calvin, Bal.	1.000	15	1	2	0	3	0
Magnante, Mike, Oak.*	.944	55	3	14	1	18	1
Mahay, Ron, Oak.*	1.000	5	1	2	0	3	0
Martin, Tom, Cle.*	.889	31	5	3	1	9	0
Martinez, Pedro, Bos.	1.000	29	14	28	0	42	2
Martinez, Ramon, Bos.	1.000	27	16	7	0	23	0
Martinez, Willie, Cle.	1.000	1	0	2	0	2	0
Mathews, T.J., Oak.	1.000	50	2	11	0	13	1
Mays, Joe, Min.	.943	31	9	24	2	35	2
McDill, Allen, Det.*	1.000	13	0	1	0	1	0
McElroy, Chuck, Bal.*	.900	43	3	6	1	10	1
Meadows, Brian, K.C.	1.000	11	6	7	0	13	0
Meche, Gil, Sea.	1.000	15	7	7	0	14	0
Mecir, Jim, T.B.-Oak.	1.000	63	3	7	0	10	1
Mendoza, Ramiro, N.Y.	1.000	14	2	8	0	10	0
Menechino, Frank, Oak.	.000	1	0	0	0	0	0
Mercedes, Jose, Bal.	1.000	36	2	16	0	18	0
Mercker, Kent, Ana.*	.857	21	1	5	1	7	1
Mesa, Jose, Sea.	1.000	66	7	8	0	15	0
Miller, Travis, Min.*	1.000	67	2	6	0	8	0
Mills, Alan, Bal.	.800	23	2	2	1	5	0
Milton, Eric, Min.*	.957	33	7	15	1	23	0
Mlicki, Dave, Det.	1.000	24	12	14	0	26	3
Moehler, Brian, Det.	1.000	29	13	30	0	43	5
Mohler, Mike, Cle.*	.000	2	0	0	0	0	0
Molina, Gabe, Bal.	1.000	9	1	1	0	2	0
Morris, Jim, T.B.*	.000	16	0	0	0	0	0
Mota, Danny, Min.	.000	4	0	0	0	0	0
Moyer, Jamie, Sea.*	.974	26	11	27	1	39	1
Mulder, Mark, Oak.*	.906	27	7	22	3	32	1
Mullen, Scott, K.C.*	1.000	11	0	1	0	1	0
Munoz, Mike, Tex.*	.000	7	0	0	0	0	0
Munro, Peter, Tor.	1.000	9	2	3	0	5	2
Murray, Dan, K.C.	1.000	10	4	4	0	8	0
Mussina, Mike, Bal.	.977	34	17	26	1	44	1
Myette, Aaron, Chi.	.000	2	0	0	0	0	0
Nagy, Charles, Cle.	1.000	11	12	13	0	25	0
Navarro, Jaime, Cle.	.000	7	0	0	0	0	0
Neagle, Denny, N.Y.*	.900	16	7	11	2	20	1
Nelson, Jeff, N.Y.	.909	73	0	10	1	11	1
Newman, Alan, Cle.*	.000	1	0	0	0	0	0
Nichting, Chris, Cle.	1.000	7	1	1	0	2	0
Nitkowski, C.J., Det.*	.966	67	7	21	1	29	2
Nomo, Hideo, Det.	.966	32	12	16	1	29	1
Ohka, Tomokazu, Bos.	.938	13	8	7	1	16	1
Olivares, Omar, Oak.	.957	21	6	16	1	23	2
Oliver, Darren, Tex.*	1.000	21	7	15	0	22	0
Ontiveros, Steve, Bos.	.000	3	0	0	0	0	0
Ortiz, Ramon, Ana.	1.000	18	1	12	0	13	1
Painter, Lance, Tor.*	1.000	42	4	17	0	21	2
Paniagua, Jose, Sea.	1.000	69	8	8	0	16	1
Parque, Jim, Chi.*	.900	33	2	25	3	30	0
Parrish, John, Bal.*	.833	8	1	4	1	6	1
Patterson, Danny, Det.	1.000	58	4	8	0	12	0
Pena, Jesus, Chi.-Bos.*	.857	22	0	6	1	7	0
Percival, Troy, Ana.	1.000	54	2	3	0	5	0
Perisho, Matt, Tex.*	.813	34	4	9	3	16	0
Petkovsek, Mark, Ana.	1.000	64	4	12	0	16	0
Pettitte, Andy, N.Y.*	.926	32	17	33	4	54	3
Pichardo, Hipolito, Bos.	.944	38	7	10	1	18	1
Pineiro, Joel, Sea.	1.000	8	1	2	0	3	0
Ponson, Sidney, Bal.	1.000	32	13	22	0	35	0
Poole, Jim, Det.*	1.000	18	0	3	0	3	0
Pote, Lou, Ana.	1.000	32	2	9	0	11	1
Prieto, Ariel, Oak.	.900	8	4	5	1	10	0
Quantrill, Paul, Tor.	1.000	68	3	9	0	12	0
Radke, Brad, Min.	.982	34	29	25	1	55	5
Rakers, Jason, K.C.	1.000	11	1	0	0	1	0
Ramsay, Rob, Sea.*	1.000	37	3	7	0	10	1
Rapp, Pat, Bal.	.967	31	4	25	1	30	2
Ratliff, Jon, Oak.	.000	1	0	0	0	0	0
Redman, Mark, Min.*	.955	32	4	17	1	22	1
Reed, Steve, Cle.	.933	57	6	8	1	15	0

Player, Team	Pct.	G	PO	A	E	TC	DP
Reichert, Dan, K.C.	1.000	44	14	16	0	30	1
Rekar, Bryan, T.B.	.970	30	11	21	1	33	2
Reyes, Al, Bal.	1.000	13	0	3	0	3	0
Rhodes, Arthur, Sea.*	1.000	72	2	8	0	10	1
Rigby, Brad, K.C.	1.000	4	3	0	0	3	0
Rigdon, Paul, Cle.	1.000	5	0	2	0	2	0
Rincon, Ricky, Cle.*	1.000	35	2	3	0	5	0
Rivera, Luis, Bal.	.000	1	0	0	0	0	0
Rivera, Mariano, N.Y.	1.000	66	8	15	0	23	0
Rodriguez, Frank, Sea.	.929	23	6	7	1	14	2
Rogers, Kenny, Tex.*	.970	34	18	46	2	66	6
Romero, J.C., Min.*	1.000	12	6	10	0	16	0
Rosado, Jose, K.C.*	1.000	5	2	4	0	6	0
Rose, Brian, Bos.	.889	15	4	4	1	9	0
Runyan, Sean, Det.*	1.000	3	0	2	0	2	0
Rupe, Ryan, T.B.	1.000	18	2	10	0	12	0
Ryan, B.J., Bal.*	1.000	42	0	4	0	4	0
Ryan, Jason, Min.	.600	16	2	1	2	5	0
Santana, Johan, Min.*	.947	30	5	13	1	19	2
Santiago, Jose, K.C.	.933	45	5	9	1	15	0
Sasaki, Kazuhiro, Sea.	1.000	63	2	3	0	5	0
Sauveur, Rich, Oak.*	1.000	10	0	1	0	1	0
Schoeneweis, Scott, Ana.*	.968	27	5	25	1	31	4
Schourek, Pete, Bos.*	.875	21	3	18	3	24	1
Sele, Aaron, Sea.	.946	34	19	34	3	56	2
Service, Scott, Oak.	.833	20	2	3	1	6	0
Sheldon, Scott, Tex.	.000	1	0	0	0	0	0
Shuey, Paul, Cle.	1.000	57	7	8	0	15	0
Sikorski, Brian, Tex.	.833	10	4	1	1	6	0
Simas, Bill, Chi.	1.000	60	1	8	0	9	0
Sirotka, Mike, Chi.*	.958	32	5	18	1	24	2
Smith, Dan, Bos.	.000	2	0	0	0	0	0
Sparks, Jeff, T.B.	1.000	15	1	0	0	1	0
Sparks, Steve W., Det.	.966	20	11	17	1	29	2
Speier, Justin, Cle.	.875	47	1	6	1	8	0
Spoljaric, Paul, K.C.*	1.000	13	1	4	0	5	1
Spradlin, Jerry, K.C.	.917	50	4	7	1	12	1
Spurgeon, Jay, Bal.	.667	7	0	2	1	3	0
Stanifer, Rob, Bos.	1.000	8	0	2	0	2	0
Stanton, Mike, N.Y.*	1.000	69	3	11	0	14	0
Stein, Blake, K.C.	.941	17	8	8	1	17	0
Sturtze, Tanyon, Chi.-T.B.	1.000	29	6	3	0	9	0
Suppan, Jeff, K.C.	.944	35	14	20	2	36	0
Suzuki, Makoto, K.C.	.972	32	20	15	1	36	2
Tam, Jeff, Oak.	.950	72	3	16	1	20	3
Taylor, Billy, T.B.	1.000	17	1	0	0	1	0
Tessmer, Jay, N.Y.	.000	7	0	0	0	0	0
Timlin, Mike, Bal.	1.000	37	1	10	0	11	1
Tolar, Kevin, Det.*	.000	5	0	0	0	0	0
Tomko, Brett, Sea.	1.000	32	6	6	0	12	1
TRACHSEL, Steve, T.B.-Tor.	1.000	34	20	29	0	49	4
Trombley, Mike, Bal.	1.000	75	3	11	0	14	1
Turnbow, Derrick, Ana.	1.000	24	0	1	0	1	0
Venafro, Mike, Tex.*	.857	77	3	9	2	14	1
Villafuerte, Brandon, Det.	1.000	3	1	0	0	1	0
Vizcaino, Luis, Oak.	1.000	12	1	3	0	4	0
Wakefield, Tim, Bos.	.917	51	11	11	2	24	2
Ward, Bryan, Ana.*	.500	7	1	0	1	2	0
Wasdin, John, Bos.	1.000	25	2	2	0	4	0
Washburn, Jarrod, Ana.*	1.000	14	1	14	0	15	1
Watson, Allen, N.Y.*	1.000	17	1	2	0	3	0
Watson, Mark, Cle.*	1.000	6	1	0	0	1	0
Weaver, Eric, Ana.	1.000	17	1	4	0	5	0
Weaver, Jeff, Det.	.978	31	17	28	1	46	0
Weber, Ben, Ana.	1.000	10	1	1	0	2	0
Wells, Bob, Min.	.846	76	2	9	2	13	2
Wells, David, Tor.*	.897	35	8	18	3	29	1
Wells, Kip, Chi.	.688	20	6	5	5	16	0
Westbrook, Jake, N.Y.	1.000	3	1	0	0	1	0
Wetteland, John, Tex.	1.000	62	2	5	0	7	0
Wheeler, Dan, T.B.	1.000	11	1	4	0	5	1
White, Rick, T.B.	1.000	44	1	7	0	8	1
Wickman, Bob, Cle.	1.000	26	1	5	0	6	0
Williams, Brian, Cle.	1.000	7	2	2	0	4	0
Wilson, Kris, K.C.	.917	20	2	9	1	12	0
Wilson, Paul, T.B.	1.000	11	3	4	0	7	1
Wise, Matt, Ana.	1.000	8	2	5	0	7	0
Witasick, Jay, K.C.	.917	22	5	6	1	12	0
Witt, Bobby, Cle.	1.000	7	0	3	0	3	0
Woodard, Steve, Cle.	1.000	13	7	10	0	17	1
Worrell, Tim, Bal.	1.000	5	1	0	0	1	0
Wright, Jaret, Cle.	1.000	9	5	3	0	8	0
Wunsch, Kelly, Chi.*	1.000	83	3	8	0	11	0
Yan, Esteban, T.B.	.905	43	11	8	2	21	1
Yarnall, Ed, N.Y.*	.000	2	0	0	0	0	0
Young, Tim, Bos.*	1.000	8	1	0	0	1	0
Zimmerman, Jeff, Tex.	.900	65	2	7	1	10	0
Zito, Barry, Oak.*	1.000	14	4	9	0	13	0

PITCHERS WITH TWO OR MORE TEAMS

Player, Team	Pct.	G	PO	A	E	TC	DP
Carrasco, Hector, Min.	1.000	61	2	12	0	14	0
Carrasco, Hector, Bos.	.000	8	0	0	1	1	0
Cubillan, Darwin, Tor.	1.000	7	1	2	0	3	1
Cubillan, Darwin, N.Y.	1.000	13	1	2	0	3	0
Gooden, Dwight, T.B.	.667	8	0	2	1	3	0
Gooden, Dwight, N.Y.	1.000	18	4	14	0	18	3
Guthrie, Mark, T.B.*	1.000	34	1	6	0	7	0
Guthrie, Mark, Tor.*	1.000	23	0	1	0	1	0
Hill, Ken, Ana.	.947	16	5	13	1	19	1
Hill, Ken, Chi.	1.000	2	0	1	0	1	0
Loaiza, Esteban, Tex.	.963	20	8	18	1	27	3
Loaiza, Esteban, Tor.	.882	14	4	11	2	17	1
Mecir, Jim, T.B.	1.000	38	1	4	0	5	1
Mecir, Jim, Oak.	1.000	25	2	3	0	5	0
Pena, Jesus, Chi.*	.857	20	0	6	1	7	0
Pena, Jesus, Bos.*	.000	2	0	0	0	0	0
Sturtze, Tanyon, Chi.	.000	10	0	0	0	0	0
Sturtze, Tanyon, T.B.	1.000	19	6	3	0	9	0
Trachsel, Steve, T.B.	1.000	23	12	18	0	30	4
Trachsel, Steve, Tor.	1.000	11	8	11	0	19	0

MISCELLANEOUS

SHUTOUT GAMES

Read across for wins, down for losses.

Team	Chi.	Sea.	Oak.	Bos.	K.C.	Cle.	TB.	N.Y.	Bal.	Tex.	Ana.	Tor.	Min.	Det.	N.L.	W	L	Pct.
Chicago	..	0	2	1	0	1	1	1	0	0	0	0	0	1	0	7	3	.700
Seattle	0	..	0	1	1	0	0	0	1	1	1	0	2	1	2	10	5	.667
Oakland	1	0	..	1	0	0	2	0	2	1	1	2	0	0	1	11	7	.611
Boston	1	1	0	..	0	1	1	2	1	1	0	1	0	3	0	12	8	.600
Kansas City	0	0	0	0	..	1	0	0	1	1	0	0	0	3	0	6	4	.600
Cleveland	0	1	1	0	1	..	0	1	0	1	0	0	0	0	0	5	4	.556
Tampa Bay	0	0	1	1	0	0	..	1	0	0	1	1	2	1	0	8	8	.500
New York	1	0	0	2	0	0	0	..	0	0	0	1	1	1	0	6	7	.462
Baltimore	0	0	1	1	0	1	1	0	..	0	0	2	0	0	0	6	8	.429
Texas	0	0	0	0	0	0	1	1	0	..	0	1	0	0	1	4	6	.400
Anaheim	0	0	1	0	0	0	0	0	0	0	..	1	0	1	0	3	5	.375
Toronto	0	0	0	0	0	0	0	0	1	1	0	..	0	2	0	4	7	.364
Minnesota	0	0	1	0	0	0	0	0	1	1	0	1	..	1	1	4	8	.333
Detroit	0	2	0	0	1	0	0	1	0	0	0	1	0	..	0	6	15	.286
N.L. Clubs	0	1	0	1	1	0	1	1	2	0	0	0	1	..	..	..	..	..
Lost	3	5	7	8	4	4	8	7	8	6	5	7	8	15	..	92	95	.492

A.L. shutouts vs. N.L. clubs (5): Seattle vs. Los Angeles 2; Minnesota vs. Houston; Oakland vs. Los Angeles; Texas vs. Los Angeles.

HOME RECORD

Read across for home wins, down for road losses.

Team	Cle.	Oak.	Sea.	Ana.	Chi.	Tor.	N.Y.	Bal.	Det.	Bos.	K.C.	Tex.	TB.	Min.	N.L.	W	L	Pct.
Cleveland	..	3	3	5	2	5	2	2	4	3	3	3	3	3	7	48	33	.593
Oakland	3	..	4	5	2	4	1	4	3	2	3	4	3	2	7	47	34	.580
Seattle	2	2	..	4	2	3	3	4	0	3	5	4	4	5	6	47	34	.580
Anaheim	2	3	3	..	2	3	3	3	3	4	4	3	4	2	7	46	35	.568
Chicago	4	2	3	4	..	2	3	5	3	2	2	1	2	7	6	46	35	.568
Toronto	3	1	1	4	2	..	5	4	5	4	4	3	3	3	4	45	36	.556
New York	1	4	1	2	1	4	..	4	3	2	5	5	4	3	5	44	36	.550
Baltimore	4	2	3	2	2	5	3	..	4	1	2	5	5	2	4	44	37	.543
Detroit	4	3	4	2	2	2	5	2	..	2	2	3	2	4	6	43	38	.531
Boston	3	3	2	4	4	2	2	2	2	..	4	4	4	0	6	42	39	.519
Kansas City	4	1	3	4	4	2	1	5	3	2	..	2	2	5	4	42	39	.519
Texas	1	5	3	2	3	3	1	5	2	2	3	..	4	3	5	42	39	.519
Tampa Bay	1	1	1	4	2	2	4	4	1	4	1	3	..	3	5	36	44	.450
Minnesota	4	1	2	1	2	2	2	2	4	0	4	5	3	..	4	36	45	.444
N.L. Clubs	3	5	4	4	3	4	3	6	5	6	5	7	5	6	..	..	..	..
Lost on Road	39	36	37	45	32	43	38	51	45	38	46	52	48	48	..	608	524	.537

HOME RECORDS IN INTERLEAGUE GAMES

Team	Atl.	Fla.	Mon.	N.Y.	Phi.
Baltimore	0-3	2-1	..	..	2-1
Boston	1-2	..	3-0	2-1	..
New York	..	1-1	..	2-1	2-1
Tampa Bay	1-2	2-1	2-1	..	..
Toronto	..	..	2-1	1-2	1-2

Team	Chi.	Cin.	Hou.	Mil.	Pit.	St.L.
Chicago	2-1	..	..	3-0	..	1-2
Cleveland	..	2-1	2-1	..	3-0	..
Detroit	..	2-1	2-1	..	..	2-1
Kansas City	1-2	..	..	1-2	2-1	..
Minnesota	1-2	..	..	1-2	..	2-1

Team	Ariz.	Col.	L.A.	S.D.	S.F.
Anaheim	..	3-0	2-1	..	2-1
Oakland	2-1	..	..	3-0	2-1
Seattle	..	2-1	2-1	2-1	..
Texas	2-1	..	1-2	2-1	..

ROAD RECORD

Read across for road wins, down for home losses.

Team	Chi.	Oak.	Sea.	Bos.	N.Y.	Cle.	Tor.	Ana.	Det.	K.C.	Min.	TB.	Bal.	Tex.	N.L.	W	L	Pct.
Chicago	..	4	4	2	5	4	3	2	4	2	4	4	2	3	6	49	32	.605
Oakland	1	..	5	3	2	3	3	1	5	5	4	4	1	4	3	44	36	.550
Seattle	3	2	..	3	0	5	4	2	3	4	5	3	3	5	2	44	37	.543
Boston	3	2	3	..	4	3	2	2	4	2	4	2	5	4	3	43	38	.531
New York	3	2	3	5	..	4	1	3	1	3	2	2	3	5	6	43	38	.531
Cleveland	3	3	4	3	3	..	3	1	2	2	2	5	2	3	6	42	39	.519
Toronto	4	2	1	4	2	1	..	3	4	2	1	4	2	3	5	38	43	.469
Anaheim	2	2	2	1	2	1	2	..	2	2	5	2	4	4	5	36	45	.444
Detroit	1	3	3	3	3	3	1	3	..	3	3	2	2	2	4	36	45	.444
Kansas City	3	3	1	4	1	3	2	2	4	..	2	3	2	1	4	35	46	.432
Minnesota	3	4	1	2	3	4	3	2	2	1	..	1	1	3	3	33	48	.407
Tampa Bay	2	1	2	2	1	3	2	4	4	3	1	..	2	4	2	33	48	.407
Baltimore	2	2	0	2	4	2	1	2	3	2	1	4	..	1	3	30	47	.370
Texas	2	2	2	1	1	3	1	3	3	4	1	3	1	..	2	29	52	.358
N.L. Clubs	3	2	3	3	3	2	5	2	3	5	5	4	5	4	..	..	..	..
Lost at home	35	34	34	39	36	33	36	35	38	39	45	44	37	39	..	535	598	.472

ANAHEIM—82-80

Pitcher	Bal. W-L	Bos. W-L	Chi. W-L	Cle. W-L	Det. W-L	K.C. W-L	Min. W-L	N.Y. W-L	Oak. W-L	Sea. W-L	T.B. W-L	Tex. W-L	Tor. W-L	N.L. W-L	Total W-L
Alvarez, Juan	0-0	0-0	0-0	0-0	0-0	0-0	0-0	0-0	0-0	0-0	0-0	0-0	0-0	0-0	0-0
Belcher, Tim	1-0	0-0	0-0	0-0	1-0	1-0	0-1	0-0	0-2	0-2	1-0	0-0	0-0	0-0	4-5
Bottenfield, Kent	0-1	0-1	2-0	0-0	0-1	0-1	0-1	0-0	0-0	1-1	0-0	0-1	0-1	3-0	7-8
Cooper, Brian	0-0	0-0	0-1	0-1	0-1	1-0	1-0	0-1	1-1	0-1	0-0	0-0	0-0	1-2	4-8
Dickson, Jason	0-0	1-0	0-0	0-0	0-0	0-0	0-0	0-0	0-0	0-0	0-0	0-0	0-0	0-0	2-2
Etherton, Seth	1-0	0-0	0-0	0-1	0-0	0-0	0-0	0-0	0-0	0-0	1-0	1-0	0-0	1-0	5-1
Fyhrie, Mike	0-0	0-0	0-0	0-0	0-0	0-0	0-0	0-0	0-0	0-0	0-0	0-0	0-0	0-0	0-0
Hasegawa, Shigetoshi	1-0	0-1	0-2	1-0	0-0	1-0	2-0	1-0	0-0	0-1	0-1	3-0	0-0	1-1	10-6
Hill, Ken	1-0	1-0	0-1	0-0	1-1	0-0	0-0	0-0	0-2	1-1	0-0	0-0	0-1	1-0	5-7
Hinchliffe, Brett	0-0	0-0	0-0	0-0	0-0	0-0	0-0	0-0	0-0	0-0	0-0	0-0	0-0	0-0	0-0
Holtz, Mike	0-0	0-0	1-0	0-0	0-0	0-0	0-0	0-0	1-1	0-1	0-0	0-1	1-0	0-0	3-3
Karl, Scott	0-1	0-0	0-0	0-0	0-1	0-0	1-0	0-0	0-0	0-0	0-0	1-0	0-0	0-0	2-2
Levine, Al	0-0	0-0	0-1	1-0	0-0	0-0	0-0	0-0	0-0	0-0	1-0	0-0	0-0	1-2	3-4
Mercker, Kent	0-0	1-0	0-1	0-0	0-0	0-0	0-0	0-1	0-0	0-0	0-1	0-0	0-0	0-0	1-3
Ortiz, Ramon	2-0	1-1	0-0	0-0	0-0	0-1	0-0	0-0	0-0	1-0	1-1	0-0	1-2	1-0	8-6
Percival, Troy	1-1	0-0	0-0	0-1	0-0	1-1	1-0	0-1	0-0	0-0	0-1	0-0	2-0	0-0	5-5
Petkovsek, Mark	0-0	0-0	0-0	0-0	1-0	0-0	0-0	0-0	1-1	1-0	1-0	0-0	0-1	0-0	4-2
Pote, Lou	0-0	0-0	0-0	0-0	0-0	0-0	0-0	1-0	0-0	0-0	0-0	0-0	0-0	0-0	1-1
Schoeneweis, Scott	0-2	0-0	1-0	0-3	2-0	0-1	1-0	2-0	0-1	0-1	0-0	0-1	1-0	0-1	7-10
Turnbow, Derrick	0-0	0-0	0-0	0-0	0-0	0-0	0-0	0-0	0-0	0-0	0-0	0-0	0-0	0-0	0-0
Ward, Bryan	0-0	0-0	0-0	0-0	0-0	0-0	0-0	0-0	0-0	0-0	0-0	0-0	0-0	0-0	0-0
Washburn, Jarrod	0-0	1-0	0-0	0-0	0-0	2-0	0-1	0-0	2-0	1-0	0-0	0-1	0-0	1-0	7-2
Weaver, Eric	0-0	0-0	0-0	0-0	0-0	0-2	0-0	0-0	0-0	0-0	0-0	0-0	0-0	0-0	0-2
Weber, Ben	0-0	0-0	0-0	0-0	0-0	0-0	0-0	0-0	0-0	0-0	0-0	1-0	0-0	0-0	1-0
Wise, Matt	0-0	0-1	0-0	1-0	0-1	0-0	0-0	1-0	0-0	0-0	0-0	0-0	1-1	0-0	3-3
Totals	7-5	5-4	4-6	3-6	5-5	6-6	7-3	5-5	5-8	5-8	6-6	7-5	5-7	12-6	82-80

INTERLEAGUE: Bottenfield 2-0, Percival 1-0, Etherton 1-0, Levine 0-1, Cooper 0-1 vs. Dodgers; Levine 1-1, Cooper 1-0 vs. Padres; Hasegawa 1-1, Percival 1-0 vs. Giants; Ortiz 1-0, Hill 1-0, Bottenfield 1-0 vs. Rockies; Washburn 1-0, Cooper 0-1, Schoeneweis 0-1 vs. Diamondbacks. Total: 12-6.

BALTIMORE—74-88

Pitcher	Ana. W-L	Bos. W-L	Chi. W-L	Cle. W-L	Det. W-L	K.C. W-L	Min. W-L	N.Y. W-L	Oak. W-L	Sea. W-L	T.B. W-L	Tex. W-L	Tor. W-L	N.L. W-L	Total W-L
Brea, Leslie	0-0	0-0	0-0	0-0	0-0	0-1	0-0	0-0	0-0	0-0	0-0	0-0	0-0	0-0	0-1
Erickson, Scott	1-1	1-1	0-0	0-0	0-0	0-0	0-0	1-1	1-0	0-1	0-1	1-0	0-1	0-2	5-8
Groom, Buddy	0-0	0-0	0-0	0-0	1-0	1-0	0-1	1-0	0-0	1-0	1-1	0-0	0-0	0-0	6-3
Holmes, Darren	0-0	0-0	0-0	0-0	0-0	0-0	0-0	0-0	0-0	0-0	0-0	0-0	0-0	0-0	0-0
Johnson, Jason	0-2	0-0	0-1	0-0	0-0	0-0	0-0	0-1	0-2	0-1	1-0	0-0	0-2	0-1	1-10
Kohlmeier, Ryan	0-0	0-1	0-0	0-0	0-0	0-0	0-0	0-0	0-0	0-0	0-0	0-0	0-0	0-0	0-1
Maduro, Calvin	0-0	0-0	0-0	0-0	0-0	0-0	0-0	0-0	0-0	0-0	0-0	0-0	0-0	0-0	0-0
McElroy, Chuck	0-0	0-0	0-0	0-0	0-0	0-0	1-0	1-0	0-0	0-0	1-0	0-0	0-0	0-0	3-0
Mercedes, Jose	1-0	1-1	2-1	1-0	3-0	0-1	1-0	1-0	0-0	0-1	0-0	0-0	2-0	1-2	14-7
Mills, Alan	0-0	0-0	0-0	0-0	0-0	0-0	0-0	0-0	0-0	0-0	0-0	0-0	2-0	0-0	2-0
Molina, Gabe	0-0	0-0	0-0	0-0	0-0	0-0	0-0	0-0	0-0	0-0	0-0	0-0	0-0	0-0	0-0
Mussina, Mike	1-2	1-1	0-2	0-1	0-0	1-1	2-0	1-0	1-1	0-1	1-1	0-1	0-2	3-2	11-15
Parrish, John	0-0	0-0	1-1	0-0	0-1	0-0	0-0	0-1	0-0	0-0	0-1	0-0	0-0	0-0	2-4
Ponson, Sidney	1-0	1-2	0-1	0-1	0-1	1-0	2-1	0-1	1-1	0-1	1-1	0-0	1-1	1-2	9-13
Rapp, Pat	0-1	0-0	1-0	2-1	0-1	0-1	0-1	0-2	0-1	0-1	2-0	1-1	3-0	0-2	9-12
Reyes, Al	0-0	0-0	0-0	0-0	1-0	0-0	0-0	0-0	0-0	0-0	0-0	0-0	0-0	0-0	1-0
Rivera, Luis	0-0	0-0	0-0	0-0	0-0	0-0	0-0	0-0	0-0	0-0	0-0	0-0	0-0	0-0	0-0
Ryan, B.J.	0-0	0-0	0-0	1-0	0-0	0-1	0-0	0-1	0-0	0-0	1-0	0-1	0-0	0-0	2-3
Spurgeon, Jay	0-0	0-0	0-0	0-0	0-0	0-0	0-0	0-0	0-0	0-0	0-0	0-0	0-0	0-0	1-1
Timlin, Mike	0-1	0-0	0-0	0-0	0-0	0-0	0-0	0-0	0-1	1-1	0-0	1-0	0-0	0-0	4-5
Trombley, Mike	1-0	1-1	0-0	0-0	0-0	0-1	1-0	0-0	0-1	0-0	0-0	0-0	0-0	0-0	2-2
Worrell, Tim	0-0	0-0	0-0	0-0	1-0	0-1	1-0	0-0	0-1	0-0	0-0	0-0	0-0	0-0	2-2
Totals	5-7	5-7	4-6	5-4	6-4	3-7	6-3	5-7	4-8	3-7	8-5	6-6	7-6	7-11	74-88

INTERLEAGUE: Mussina 0-1, Ponson 0-1, Erickson 0-1 vs. Braves; Johnson 0-1, Rapp 0-1, Ponson 0-1 vs. Expos; Mussina 1-0, Erickson 0-1, Mercedes 0-1 vs. Mets; Mussina 2-0, Ponson 1-0, Mills 1-0, Rapp 0-1 vs. Phillies; Mills 1-0, Mercedes 1-0, Mussina 0-1 vs. Marlins. Total: 7-11.

BOSTON—85-77

Pitcher	Ana. W-L	Bal. W-L	Chi. W-L	Cle. W-L	Det. W-L	K.C. W-L	Min. W-L	N.Y. W-L	Oak. W-L	Sea. W-L	T.B. W-L	Tex. W-L	Tor. W-L	N.L. W-L	Total W-L
Arrojo, Rolando	0-0	0-0	0-0	0-0	0-0	1-0	0-0	1-0	0-2	1-0	1-0	1-0	0-0	0-0	5-2
Beck, Rod	0-0	0-0	1-0	1-0	1-0	0-0	0-0	0-0	0-0	0-0	0-0	0-0	0-0	0-0	3-0
Carrasco, Hector	0-0	1-0	0-0	0-0	0-0	0-0	0-0	0-0	0-0	0-0	0-1	0-0	0-0	0-0	1-1
Cormier, Rheal	0-0	1-0	0-0	0-1	0-0	0-1	0-0	0-0	0-0	0-0	0-0	0-0	1-0	0-1	3-3
Crawford, Paxton	0-0	0-0	1-1	0-0	0-0	0-0	1-0	0-0	0-0	0-0	0-0	0-0	0-0	0-0	2-1
Croushore, Rick	0-0	0-0	0-0	0-0	0-0	0-0	0-0	0-0	0-0	0-1	0-0	0-0	0-0	0-0	0-1
Fassero, Jeff	1-0	0-0	1-0	0-0	2-0	1-0	1-0	0-0	0-2	0-1	1-2	1-1	0-1	0-1	8-8
Florie, Bryce	0-0	0-1	0-0	0-0	0-0	0-0	0-0	0-0	0-0	0-1	0-0	0-0	0-1	0-0	0-4
Garces, Rich	0-0	1-0	0-0	0-0	0-0	1-0	0-0	1-0	1-1	0-0	1-0	0-0	0-0	2-0	8-1
Lee, Sang-Hoon	0-0	0-0	0-0	0-0	0-0	0-0	0-0	0-0	1-0	0-0	1-0	0-0	0-1	0-1	4-4
Lowe, Derek	1-0	1-0	0-0	1-0	0-0	1-0	0-0	0-0	0-0	0-0	1-0	0-0	0-0	0-0	4-4
Martinez, Pedro	1-1	1-0	2-0	3-1	0-0	0-0	0-0	1-2	2-0	3-0	1-1	2-0	1-1	1-0	18-6
Martinez, Ramon	0-0	1-1	1-0	1-1	0-2	0-0	2-1	2-0	0-0	0-1	1-0	0-0	0-1	2-1	10-8
Ohka, Tomokazu	1-1	0-1	0-0	0-1	0-0	0-1	0-0	0-0	0-0	0-0	0-0	2-0	0-0	0-0	3-6

Pitcher	Ana. W-L	Bal. W-L	Chi. W-L	Cle. W-L	Det. W-L	K.C. W-L	Min. W-L	N.Y. W-L	Oak. W-L	Sea. W-L	T.B. W-L	Tex. W-L	Tor. W-L	N.L. W-L	Total W-L
Ontiveros, Steve	0-0	0-0	0-0	1-0	0-1	0-0	0-0	0-0	0-0	0-0	0-0	0-0	0-0	0-0	1-1
Pena, Jesus	0-0	0-0	0-0	0-0	0-0	0-0	0-0	0-0	0-0	0-0	0-0	0-0	0-0	0-0	0-0
Pichardo, Hipolito	0-0	0-0	0-2	0-0	1-0	1-0	1-0	1-0	0-0	0-0	0-1	0-0	1-0	1-0	6-3
Rose, Brian	0-1	1-0	1-0	0-0	1-0	0-0	0-0	0-1	0-1	0-0	0-0	0-0	0-1	0-1	3-5
Schourek, Pete	0-1	0-1	0-2	0-1	1-0	0-1	0-0	0-1	1-0	0-0	0-0	0-0	1-1	0-2	3-10
Smith, Dan	0-0	0-0	0-0	0-0	0-0	0-0	0-0	0-0	0-0	0-0	0-0	0-0	0-0	0-0	0-0
Stanifer, Rob	0-0	0-0	0-0	0-0	0-0	0-0	0-0	0-0	0-0	0-0	0-0	0-0	0-0	0-0	0-0
Wakefield, Tim	0-1	1-0	0-0	0-1	0-2	0-2	2-0	0-1	0-0	0-0	0-0	0-2	0-0	3-1	6-10
Wasdin, John	0-0	0-0	0-0	0-0	0-0	0-0	1-0	0-1	0-0	0-0	0-0	0-0	0-1	0-1	1-3
Young, Tim	0-0	0-0	0-0	0-0	0-0	0-0	0-0	0-0	0-0	0-0	0-0	0-0	0-0	0-0	0-0
Totals	4-5	7-5	7-5	6-6	7-5	4-6	8-2	6-7	5-5	5-5	6-6	7-3	4-8	9-9	85-77

INTERLEAGUE: Garces 1-0, Wakefield 1-0, Schourek 0-2, Fassero 0-1, R. Martinez 0-1 vs. Braves; Wakefield 1-0, Pichardo 1-0, P. Martinez 1-0 vs. Expos; Garces 1-0, R. Martinez 1-0, Lowe 0-1 vs. Mets; Cormier 0-1, Wasdin 0-1, Wakefield 0-1 vs. Phillies; Wakefield 1-0, R. Martinez 1-0, Rose 0-1 vs. Marlins. Total: 9-9.

CHICAGO—95-67

Pitcher	Ana. W-L	Bal. W-L	Bos. W-L	Cle. W-L	Det. W-L	K.C. W-L	Min. W-L	N.Y. W-L	Oak. W-L	Sea. W-L	T.B. W-L	Tex. W-L	Tor. W-L	N.L. W-L	Total W-L
Baldwin, James	0-0	0-1	2-1	0-1	2-0	0-1	0-1	1-1	2-0	1-0	1-0	1-0	2-0	2-1	14-7
Barcelo, Lorenzo	0-1	1-0	0-0	0-0	0-1	0-0	1-0	0-0	0-0	1-0	0-0	1-0	0-0	0-0	4-2
Beirne, Kevin	0-1	0-0	0-1	1-0	0-0	0-0	0-1	0-0	0-0	0-0	0-0	0-0	0-0	0-0	1-3
Biddle, Rocky	0-0	1-0	0-0	0-0	0-0	0-0	0-0	0-0	0-0	0-2	0-0	0-0	0-0	0-0	1-2
Bradford, Chad	0-0	0-0	0-0	0-0	0-0	1-0	0-0	0-0	0-0	0-0	0-0	0-0	0-0	0-0	1-0
Buehrle, Mark	0-0	0-0	0-0	1-0	0-0	0-0	1-0	0-0	0-1	2-0	0-0	0-0	0-0	0-0	4-1
Eldred, Cal	0-0	1-0	0-1	3-0	1-0	0-1	1-0	2-0	0-0	0-0	0-0	0-0	1-0	1-0	10-2
Eyre, Scott	0-0	0-0	0-0	0-0	0-1	0-0	0-0	0-0	1-0	0-0	0-0	0-0	0-0	0-0	1-1
Foulke, Keith	1-0	0-0	0-0	0-0	0-0	0-0	0-0	1-0	0-0	0-1	1-0	0-0	0-0	0-0	3-1
Garland, Jon	1-0	0-0	0-1	0-2	1-0	0-1	0-0	0-0	0-1	1-0	0-2	0-1	1-0	0-0	4-8
Ginter, Matt	1-0	0-0	0-0	0-0	0-0	0-0	0-1	0-0	0-0	0-0	0-0	0-0	0-0	0-0	1-0
Hill, Ken	0-0	0-1	0-0	0-0	0-0	0-0	0-0	0-0	0-0	0-0	0-0	0-0	0-0	0-0	0-1
Howry, Bob	0-0	0-0	0-0	0-0	0-1	0-0	0-0	0-0	1-0	0-1	1-1	0-0	0-0	0-0	2-4
Lowe, Sean	0-0	0-0	0-0	0-0	1-0	0-0	0-1	1-0	0-0	1-0	0-0	0-1	0-1	1-0	4-1
Myette, Aaron	0-0	0-0	0-0	0-0	0-0	0-0	0-0	0-0	0-0	0-0	0-0	0-0	0-0	0-0	0-0
Parque, Jim	1-1	2-0	1-0	1-0	2-0	0-1	1-1	1-1	0-1	0-0	1-1	0-0	0-0	3-0	13-6
Pena, Jesus	0-0	0-0	0-0	0-0	0-0	0-0	0-0	0-0	0-0	0-0	0-0	0-0	0-1	1-1	2-1
Simas, Bill	0-0	0-0	1-1	1-0	0-0	0-0	0-0	0-0	0-0	0-0	0-1	0-0	0-1	0-1	2-3
Sirotka, Mike	1-0	0-2	1-1	0-1	1-0	0-1	1-0	2-1	2-1	2-1	1-0	0-1	1-0	3-1	15-10
Sturtze, Tanyon	0-0	0-0	0-1	0-0	0-0	0-0	0-0	0-0	0-0	0-0	0-0	0-0	0-0	0-0	0-1
Wells, Kip	0-1	1-0	0-0	1-1	1-1	0-0	0-1	1-1	0-1	0-0	0-0	0-0	0-2	0-1	6-9
Wunsch, Kelly	1-0	0-0	0-0	0-0	0-0	2-1	2-0	0-0	0-1	0-0	0-0	0-0	1-1	0-1	6-3
Totals	6-4	6-4	5-7	8-5	9-3	5-7	7-5	8-4	6-3	7-5	6-4	5-5	5-5	12-6	95-67

INTERLEAGUE: Baldwin 1-0, Garland 1-0, Sirotka 1-0 vs. Brewers; Pena 1-1, Lowe 1-0, Sirotka 1-0, Simas 0-1, Baldwin 0-1 vs. Cubs; Baldwin 1-0, Eldred 1-0, Parque 1-0 vs. Reds; Parque 1-0, Sirotka 0-1, Wells 0-1 vs. Astros; Parque 0-1, Wunsch 0-1 vs. Cardinals. Total: 12-6.

CLEVELAND—90-72

Pitcher	Ana. W-L	Bal. W-L	Bos. W-L	Chi. W-L	Det. W-L	K.C. W-L	Min. W-L	N.Y. W-L	Oak. W-L	Sea. W-L	T.B. W-L	Tex. W-L	Tor. W-L	N.L. W-L	Total W-L
Bere, Jason	1-0	1-0	0-0	0-0	0-0	0-0	1-0	0-1	0-1	1-0	2-0	0-1	0-0	0-0	6-3
Brewington, Jamie	0-0	0-0	0-0	0-0	0-0	0-0	0-0	0-0	0-0	0-0	0-0	0-0	1-0	2-0	3-0
Brower, Jim	0-0	0-0	0-0	1-1	0-0	0-1	0-1	0-0	0-0	0-0	0-0	0-0	0-0	1-0	2-3
Burba, Dave	1-1	0-0	1-0	3-0	1-2	0-0	1-0	1-0	1-1	1-0	2-0	1-1	0-1	3-0	16-6
Cairncross, Cam	0-0	1-0	0-0	0-0	0-0	0-0	0-0	0-0	0-0	0-0	0-0	0-0	0-0	0-0	1-0
Colon, Bartolo	1-0	1-0	1-1	1-1	2-1	2-1	0-1	1-0	0-0	1-0	1-0	1-1	1-1	2-1	15-8
Davis, Kane	0-0	0-0	0-0	0-0	0-1	0-1	0-0	0-0	0-0	0-0	0-0	0-0	0-0	0-1	0-3
DePaula, Sean	0-0	0-0	0-0	0-0	0-0	0-0	0-0	0-0	0-0	0-0	0-0	0-0	0-0	0-0	0-0
Drew, Tim	0-0	0-0	0-0	0-0	0-0	0-0	0-0	0-0	0-0	0-0	0-0	0-0	1-0	0-0	1-0
Finley, Chuck	1-1	1-1	2-1	0-2	0-0	1-2	2-1	1-0	1-0	1-1	1-0	1-0	2-1	2-1	16-11
Haney, Chris	0-0	0-0	0-0	0-0	0-0	0-0	0-0	0-0	0-0	0-0	0-0	0-0	0-0	0-0	0-0
Kamieniecki, Scott	0-0	0-1	0-0	0-0	0-0	0-0	0-1	1-0	0-0	0-0	0-0	0-0	0-1	0-0	1-3
Karsay, Steve	0-1	0-1	1-0	0-0	1-1	0-1	0-2	0-1	0-0	1-0	1-1	0-1	0-0	1-0	5-9
Lorraine, Andrew	0-0	0-0	0-0	0-0	0-0	0-0	0-0	0-0	0-0	0-0	0-0	0-0	0-0	0-0	0-0
Martin, Tom	0-0	0-0	0-0	0-0	0-0	0-0	0-0	0-0	0-0	0-0	0-0	0-0	1-0	0-0	1-0
Martinez, Willie	0-0	0-0	0-0	0-0	0-0	0-0	0-0	0-0	0-0	0-0	0-0	0-0	0-0	0-1	0-1
Mohler, Mike	0-0	0-0	0-0	0-0	0-1	0-0	0-0	0-0	0-0	0-0	0-0	0-0	0-0	0-0	0-1
Nagy, Charles	0-0	0-1	0-3	0-0	1-0	0-1	0-0	0-0	1-1	0-1	0-0	0-0	0-0	0-0	2-7
Navarro, Jaime	0-0	0-0	0-0	0-0	0-1	0-0	0-1	0-0	0-0	0-0	0-0	0-0	0-0	0-1	0-1
Newman, Alan	0-0	0-0	0-0	0-0	0-0	0-0	0-0	0-0	0-0	0-0	0-0	0-0	0-0	0-0	0-0
Nichting, Chris	0-0	0-0	0-0	0-0	0-0	0-0	0-0	0-0	0-0	0-0	0-0	0-0	0-0	0-0	0-0
Reed, Steve	0-0	0-0	0-0	0-0	0-0	1-0	0-0	0-0	0-0	0-0	1-0	0-0	0-0	0-0	2-0
Rigdon, Paul	0-0	0-0	0-0	0-1	0-0	0-0	0-0	1-0	0-0	0-0	0-0	0-0	0-0	0-0	1-1
Rincon, Ricky	0-0	0-0	0-0	0-0	0-0	0-0	1-0	0-0	0-0	0-0	0-0	1-0	0-0	0-0	2-0
Shuey, Paul	0-0	0-0	0-0	0-0	0-0	0-0	0-1	1-0	1-0	0-0	0-0	1-1	0-0	0-0	4-2
Speier, Justin	1-0	0-0	0-1	0-1	1-0	0-0	0-0	0-0	0-0	1-0	0-0	1-0	0-0	0-0	5-2
Watson, Mark	0-0	0-0	0-0	0-0	0-1	0-0	0-0	0-0	0-0	0-0	0-0	0-0	0-0	0-0	0-1
Wickman, Bob	1-0	0-0	0-0	0-0	0-0	0-0	0-1	0-0	0-1	0-0	0-1	0-0	0-0	0-0	1-3
Williams, Brian	0-0	0-0	0-0	0-0	0-0	0-0	0-0	0-0	0-0	0-0	0-0	0-0	0-0	0-0	0-0
Witt, Bobby	0-0	0-0	0-0	0-0	0-0	0-0	0-0	0-0	0-0	0-0	0-0	0-0	0-0	0-0	0-0
Woodard, Steve	0-0	0-1	1-0	0-1	0-1	0-0	0-0	0-1	0-0	0-0	0-0	1-0	1-0	0-0	3-3
Wright, Jaret	0-0	0-0	0-0	0-1	0-0	1-0	0-0	0-1	1-1	0-0	1-0	0-0	0-0	0-1	3-4
Totals	6-3	4-5	6-6	5-8	6-7	5-7	5-8	5-5	6-6	7-2	8-2	6-4	8-4	13-5	90-72

INTERLEAGUE: Burba 1-0, Finley 1-0, Brewington 1-0 vs. Brewers; Brower 1-0, Burba 1-0, Colon 1-0, Kamieniecki 0-1, Finley 0-1, Davis 0-1 vs. Reds; Drew 1-0, Burba 1-0, Colon 0-1 vs. Astros; Karsay 1-0, Finley 1-0, Brewington 1-0 vs. Pirates; Martin 1-0, Colon 1-0, Wright 0-1 vs. Cardinals. Total: 13-5.

DETROIT—79-83

Pitcher	Ana. W-L	Bal. W-L	Bos. W-L	Chi. W-L	Cle. W-L	K.C. W-L	Min. W-L	N.Y. W-L	Oak. W-L	Sea. W-L	T.B. W-L	Tex. W-L	Tor. W-L	N.L. W-L	Total W-L
Anderson, Matt	0-0	0-0	0-1	1-0	0-1	0-0	1-0	0-0	0-0	0-0	0-0	0-0	0-0	1-0	3-2
Bernero, Adam	0-0	0-0	0-0	0-0	0-0	0-0	0-0	0-0	0-1	0-0	0-0	0-0	0-0	0-0	0-1
Blair, Willie	0-0	0-1	1-0	0-0	2-0	0-1	0-1	2-1	0-0	1-0	1-0	2-0	1-1	0-1	10-6
Borkowski, Dave	0-0	0-0	0-0	0-1	0-0	0-0	0-0	0-0	0-0	0-0	0-0	0-0	0-0	0-0	0-1
Brocail, Doug	0-0	0-2	0-0	0-0	1-0	2-1	0-0	0-0	0-0	1-0	0-0	0-0	1-1	0-0	5-4
Cruz, Nelson	1-0	0-0	0-1	0-0	0-0	0-0	0-0	1-0	0-1	1-0	0-0	0-0	0-0	1-0	5-2
Halter, Shane	0-0	0-0	0-0	0-0	0-0	0-0	0-0	0-0	0-0	0-0	0-0	0-0	0-0	0-0	0-0
Hiljus, Erik	0-0	0-0	0-0	0-0	0-0	0-0	0-0	0-0	0-0	0-0	0-0	0-0	0-0	0-0	0-1
Johnson, Mark	0-0	0-0	0-0	0-0	0-0	0-0	0-1	0-0	0-0	0-0	0-0	0-0	0-0	0-0	0-1
Jones, Todd	0-1	0-0	0-0	0-0	0-0	0-1	2-1	0-0	0-0	0-0	0-1	0-0	0-0	0-0	2-4
Kida, Masao	0-0	0-0	0-0	0-0	0-0	0-0	0-0	0-0	0-0	0-0	0-0	0-0	0-0	0-0	0-0
McDill, Allen	0-0	0-0	0-0	0-0	0-0	0-0	0-0	0-0	0-0	0-0	0-0	0-0	0-0	0-0	0-0
Mlicki, Dave	0-2	0-1	2-1	1-1	0-0	0-1	0-0	1-1	0-0	0-1	1-0	0-1	0-0	1-2	6-11
Moehler, Brian	2-0	1-0	0-1	0-2	2-1	0-0	0-0	0-0	2-1	2-0	0-0	1-1	0-1	2-2	12-9
Nitkowski, C.J.	0-1	0-1	0-1	0-1	1-1	0-0	0-2	1-0	0-1	0-0	1-0	0-0	0-1	1-0	4-9
Nomo, Hideo	1-0	0-1	2-1	0-0	0-0	1-2	0-0	1-1	2-0	0-0	1-0	0-0	0-0	1-0	8-12
Patterson, Danny	0-0	1-0	0-0	0-0	1-1	0-0	1-0	0-0	0-0	0-0	0-0	0-0	0-0	1-0	5-1
Poole, Jim	1-0	0-0	0-0	0-0	0-0	0-0	0-0	0-0	0-0	0-0	0-0	0-0	0-0	0-0	1-0
Runyan, Sean	0-0	0-0	0-0	0-0	0-0	0-0	0-0	0-0	0-0	0-0	0-0	0-0	0-0	0-0	0-0
Sparks, Steve W.	0-1	1-0	0-0	0-1	0-1	0-0	2-0	1-0	1-0	1-0	0-0	1-1	0-1	0-0	7-5
Tolar, Kevin	0-0	0-0	0-0	0-0	0-0	0-0	0-0	0-0	0-0	0-0	0-0	0-0	0-0	0-0	0-0
Villafuerte, Brandon	0-0	0-0	0-0	0-0	0-0	0-0	0-0	0-0	0-0	0-0	0-0	0-0	0-0	0-0	0-0
Weaver, Jeff	0-0	1-0	0-1	1-3	0-0	1-1	1-1	1-1	1-0	1-1	0-3	0-2	1-2	3-0	11-15
Totals	5-5	4-6	5-7	3-9	7-6	5-7	7-6	8-4	6-4	7-2	4-5	5-5	3-9	10-8	79-83

INTERLEAGUE: Cruz 1-0, Moehler 0-1, Blair 0-1 vs. Brewers; Weaver 1-0, Anderson 1-0, Nomo 0-1 vs. Cubs; Weaver 1-0, Mlicki 1-0, Moehler 0-1 vs. Reds; Moehler 1-0, Patterson 1-0, Nomo 0-1 vs. Astros; Nitkowski 1-0, Mlicki 0-1, Nomo 0-1 vs. Pirates; Weaver 1-0, Moehler 1-0, Mlicki 0-1 vs. Cardinals. Total: 10-8.

KANSAS CITY—77-85

Pitcher	Ana. W-L	Bal. W-L	Bos. W-L	Chi. W-L	Cle. W-L	Det. W-L	Min. W-L	N.Y. W-L	Oak. W-L	Sea. W-L	T.B. W-L	Tex. W-L	Tor. W-L	N.L. W-L	Total W-L
Batista, Miguel	0-1	0-0	0-0	0-0	0-1	0-0	0-0	0-0	1-0	1-1	0-0	0-1	0-0	0-2	2-6
Bochtler, Doug	0-0	0-0	0-0	0-1	0-0	0-1	0-0	0-0	0-0	0-0	0-0	0-0	0-0	0-0	0-2
Bottalico, Ricky	0-0	1-1	0-0	1-0	1-0	0-2	1-0	0-2	1-0	1-2	1-0	0-0	0-0	1-0	9-6
Byrdak, Tim	0-0	0-0	0-0	0-0	0-0	0-1	0-0	0-0	0-0	0-0	0-0	0-0	0-0	0-0	0-1
D'Amico, Jeff M.	0-0	0-0	0-0	0-0	0-0	0-0	0-0	0-0	0-1	0-0	0-0	0-0	0-0	0-0	0-1
Durbin, Chad	0-0	0-0	0-0	0-0	1-1	0-0	0-0	0-1	0-1	0-1	0-1	0-0	1-0	0-1	2-5
Fussell, Chris	1-0	0-0	0-0	2-0	0-0	1-0	1-0	0-1	0-1	0-0	0-0	0-0	0-1	0-0	5-3
Larkin, Andy	0-0	0-0	0-2	0-0	0-0	0-0	0-0	0-0	0-0	0-0	0-0	0-0	0-1	0-0	0-3
Laxton, Brett	0-0	0-0	0-0	0-0	0-0	0-0	0-0	0-0	0-0	0-0	0-0	0-0	0-0	0-0	0-0
Meadows, Brian	0-0	0-1	1-1	0-0	0-0	0-0	1-0	1-0	0-0	1-0	1-0	1-0	0-0	0-0	6-2
Mullen, Scott	0-0	0-0	0-0	0-0	0-0	0-0	0-0	0-0	0-0	0-0	0-0	0-0	0-0	0-0	0-0
Murray, Dan	0-0	0-0	0-0	0-0	0-0	0-0	0-0	0-0	0-0	0-0	0-0	0-0	0-0	0-0	0-0
Rakers, Jason	0-0	0-0	0-0	0-0	0-0	0-0	0-0	0-0	1-0	0-0	0-0	0-0	0-0	1-0	2-0
Reichert, Dan	1-1	1-0	2-0	0-1	0-2	1-1	1-0	0-0	1-2	0-1	1-0	0-1	0-0	0-1	8-10
Rigby, Brad	0-0	0-0	0-0	0-0	0-0	0-0	0-0	0-0	0-0	0-0	0-0	0-0	0-0	0-0	0-0
Rosado, Jose	0-0	0-0	0-0	0-0	0-0	0-0	0-1	0-1	1-0	0-0	0-0	1-0	0-0	0-0	2-2
Santiago, Jose	2-1	2-0	1-0	0-0	0-0	2-0	0-1	0-0	0-0	0-0	1-0	0-2	0-1	0-0	8-6
Spoljaric, Paul	0-0	0-0	0-0	0-0	0-0	0-0	0-0	0-0	0-0	0-0	0-0	0-0	0-0	0-0	0-0
Spradlin, Jerry	0-0	0-0	0-0	3-0	0-0	0-0	0-0	0-1	0-0	0-0	0-1	0-0	0-1	1-1	4-4
Stein, Blake	1-0	1-0	0-0	0-0	1-0	0-0	1-0	1-0	0-0	0-0	1-1	0-1	1-0	1-2	8-5
Suppan, Jeff	1-1	0-0	1-1	1-0	1-0	1-0	1-2	0-1	0-2	0-1	0-1	2-0	1-0	1-0	10-9
Suzuki, Makoto	0-1	2-0	1-0	0-0	2-1	0-1	1-0	0-1	0-0	0-0	0-1	0-2	0-1	2-1	8-10
Wilson, Kris	0-0	0-1	0-0	0-0	0-0	0-0	0-0	0-0	0-0	0-0	0-0	0-0	0-0	0-0	0-1
Witasick, Jay	0-1	0-0	0-0	0-0	1-0	1-0	0-1	0-1	0-1	0-1	0-0	0-0	0-1	1-2	3-8
Totals	6-6	7-3	6-4	7-5	7-5	7-5	7-5	2-8	4-8	4-8	5-5	3-7	4-6	8-10	77-85

INTERLEAGUE: Suppan 1-0, Stein 0-1, Suzuki 0-1 vs. Brewers; Stein 1-0, Reichert 0-1, Durbin 0-1 vs. Cubs; Suzuki 1-0, Stein 0-1, Witasick 0-1 vs. Astros; Spradlin 1-1, Rakers 1-0, Witasick 1-0, Bottalico 1-0, Batista 0-1 vs. Pirates; Suzuki 0-1, Witasick 0-1, Batista 0-1 vs. Cardinals. Total: 8-10.

MINNESOTA—69-93

Pitcher	Ana. W-L	Bal. W-L	Bos. W-L	Chi. W-L	Cle. W-L	Det. W-L	K.C. W-L	N.Y. W-L	Oak. W-L	Sea. W-L	T.B. W-L	Tex. W-L	Tor. W-L	N.L. W-L	Total W-L
Bergman, Sean	0-0	0-0	0-0	0-0	0-0	0-0	1-0	1-0	0-3	0-1	0-0	1-0	0-0	1-1	4-5
Carrasco, Hector	0-0	0-0	0-0	0-0	0-0	1-1	1-0	0-0	0-0	0-0	1-1	1-0	0-1	0-0	4-3
Cressend, Jack	0-0	0-0	0-0	0-0	0-0	0-0	0-0	0-0	0-0	0-0	0-0	0-0	0-0	0-0	0-0
Guardado, Eddie	0-1	0-0	0-0	1-0	3-0	0-1	0-0	1-1	0-1	1-0	1-0	0-0	0-0	0-0	7-4
Hawkins, LaTroy	0-1	0-0	0-0	0-0	1-0	0-1	0-0	0-0	0-0	1-0	0-0	0-0	0-0	0-0	2-2
Kinney, Matt	0-1	0-0	0-0	0-0	0-0	0-0	0-0	0-0	0-0	0-0	0-0	0-0	0-0	0-1	0-3
Lincoln, Mike	0-0	0-0	0-1	0-1	0-0	0-0	0-0	0-0	0-0	0-0	0-0	0-0	0-0	0-1	0-3
Mays, Joe	0-1	0-1	1-1	2-0	0-1	1-2	0-0	0-2	0-1	0-3	0-1	2-0	0-0	1-2	7-15
Miller, Travis	0-0	0-1	0-0	1-0	1-0	0-0	0-1	0-0	0-0	0-0	0-0	0-0	0-0	0-0	2-3
Milton, Eric	1-0	0-1	1-2	1-2	0-0	1-1	2-0	2-1	3-0	0-2	0-0	1-0	1-0	0-0	13-10
Mota, Danny	0-0	0-0	0-0	0-0	0-0	0-0	0-0	0-0	0-0	0-0	0-0	0-0	0-0	0-0	0-0
Radke, Brad	2-1	2-0	0-1	0-1	0-2	1-0	1-1	0-1	1-2	1-0	0-2	1-1	1-2	2-2	12-16
Redman, Mark	0-0	1-2	0-1	0-0	2-0	1-0	0-2	1-0	1-0	0-2	2-0	0-1	2-0	1-2	12-9

2000 A.L. STATISTICS   Miscellaneous

Pitcher	Ana. W-L	Bal. W-L	Bos. W-L	Chi. W-L	Cle. W-L	Det. W-L	K.C. W-L	N.Y. W-L	Oak. W-L	Sea. W-L	T.B. W-L	Tex. W-L	Tor. W-L	N.L. W-L	Total W-L
Romero, J.C.	0-0	0-2	0-0	0-0	0-1	1-0	0-2	0-0	0-0	0-1	0-1	0-0	1-0	0-0	2-7
Ryan, Jason	0-1	0-0	0-0	0-0	0-0	0-0	0-0	0-0	0-0	0-0	0-0	0-0	0-0	0-0	0-1
Santana, Johan	0-0	0-0	0-1	0-1	1-0	0-0	0-0	0-0	0-0	0-0	0-0	0-0	0-1	1-0	2-3
Wells, Bob	0-1	0-0	0-1	0-2	0-1	0-1	0-0	0-0	0-0	0-0	0-0	0-0	0-0	0-1	0-7
Totals	3-7	3-6	2-8	5-7	8-5	6-7	5-7	5-5	5-7	3-9	4-6	8-4	5-4	7-11	69-93

INTERLEAGUE: Bergman 1-0, Redman 0-1, Radke 0-1 vs. Brewers; Radke 1-0, Milton 0-1, Mays 0-1 vs. Cubs; Mays 0-1, Bergman 0-1, Hawkins 0-1 vs. Reds; Santana 1-0, Mays 1-0, Radke 0-1 vs. Astros; Redman 1-0, Wells 0-1, Milton 0-1 vs. Pirates; Redman 1-0, Radke 1-0, Lincoln 0-1 vs. Cardinals. Total: 7-11.

NEW YORK—87-74

Pitcher	Ana. W-L	Bal. W-L	Bos. W-L	Chi. W-L	Cle. W-L	Det. W-L	K.C. W-L	Min. W-L	Oak. W-L	Sea. W-L	T.B. W-L	Tex. W-L	Tor. W-L	N.L. W-L	Total W-L
Choate, Randy	0-0	0-0	0-0	0-0	0-0	0-0	0-0	0-0	0-0	0-0	0-0	0-0	0-1	0-0	0-1
Clemens, Roger	1-0	2-0	1-1	1-1	0-1	1-1	1-0	0-1	0-0	1-1	1-1	0-0	2-0	2-1	13-8
Cone, David	0-1	0-2	0-1	0-0	0-1	0-0	0-1	1-2	1-0	0-1	1-0	1-2	0-2	0-0	4-14
Dingman, Craig	0-0	0-0	0-0	0-0	0-0	0-0	0-0	0-0	0-0	0-0	0-0	0-0	0-0	0-0	0-0
Einertson, Darrell	0-0	0-0	0-0	0-0	0-0	0-0	0-0	0-0	0-0	0-0	0-0	0-0	0-0	0-0	0-0
Erdos, Todd	0-0	0-0	0-0	0-0	0-0	0-0	0-0	0-0	0-0	0-0	0-0	0-0	0-0	0-0	0-0
Ford, Ben	0-0	0-0	0-0	0-0	0-0	0-0	0-1	0-0	0-0	0-0	0-0	0-0	0-0	0-0	0-1
Gooden, Dwight	0-0	1-0	0-0	0-0	0-0	1-0	0-0	0-0	0-1	1-0	0-0	0-0	0-0	1-0	4-2
Grimsley, Jason	0-0	0-0	1-1	0-0	1-0	0-0	0-0	0-0	0-0	0-0	0-0	0-0	0-0	1-1	3-2
Hernandez, Orlando	1-1	0-1	0-2	0-2	1-1	0-0	0-0	1-0	1-0	0-1	1-1	3-1	1-2	3-1	12-13
Keisler, Randy	0-0	0-0	1-0	0-0	0-0	0-0	0-0	0-0	0-0	0-1	0-0	0-0	0-0	0-0	1-0
Lilly, Ted	0-0	0-0	0-0	0-0	0-0	0-0	0-0	0-0	0-0	0-0	0-0	0-0	0-0	0-0	0-0
Mendoza, Ramiro	1-0	0-0	1-0	2-0	2-0	0-0	1-0	0-2	0-1	0-0	0-0	0-1	0-0	0-0	7-4
Neagle, Denny	1-1	0-0	0-0	0-0	0-1	0-1	1-1	1-0	1-0	0-1	1-1	0-1	1-0	0-0	7-7
Nelson, Jeff	0-1	1-0	0-0	0-0	0-1	1-0	2-0	1-0	0-0	1-0	1-2	0-0	0-0	0-0	8-4
Pettitte, Andy	1-0	2-1	2-0	1-2	1-0	2-2	1-0	1-0	2-0	1-2	1-0	2-0	0-1	0-0	19-9
Rivera, Mariano	0-0	0-1	0-0	0-1	0-0	0-1	1-0	1-1	1-0	0-0	0-0	3-0	0-1	2-1	7-4
Stanton, Mike	0-1	1-0	1-0	0-1	0-0	0-0	0-1	0-0	0-0	0-0	0-0	0-0	0-0	0-0	2-3
Tessmer, Jay	0-0	0-0	0-0	0-0	0-0	0-0	0-0	0-0	0-0	0-0	0-0	0-0	0-0	0-0	0-0
Watson, Allen	0-0	0-0	0-0	0-0	0-0	0-0	0-0	0-0	0-0	0-0	0-0	0-0	0-0	0-0	0-0
Westbrook, Jake	0-0	0-0	0-1	0-1	0-0	0-0	0-0	0-0	0-0	0-0	0-0	0-0	0-0	0-0	0-2
Yarnall, Ed	0-0	0-0	0-0	0-0	0-0	0-0	0-0	0-0	0-0	0-0	0-0	0-0	0-0	0-0	0-0
Totals	5-5	7-5	7-6	4-8	5-5	4-8	8-2	5-5	6-3	4-6	6-6	10-2	5-7	11-6	87-74

INTERLEAGUE: Hernandez 1-0, Pettitte 1-0, Grimsley 0-1 vs. Braves; Grimsley 1-0, Hernandez 1-0, Cone 0-1 vs. Expos; Clemens 1-1, Pettitte 1-1, Hernandez 1-0, Gooden 1-0 vs. Mets; Rivera 1-0, Neagle 1-0, Cone 0-1 vs. Phillies; Clemens 1-0, Hernandez 0-1 vs. Marlins. Total: 11-6.

OAKLAND—91-70

Pitcher	Ana. W-L	Bal. W-L	Bos. W-L	Chi. W-L	Cle. W-L	Det. W-L	K.C. W-L	Min. W-L	N.Y. W-L	Sea. W-L	T.B. W-L	Tex. W-L	Tor. W-L	N.L. W-L	Total W-L
Appier, Kevin	0-0	1-0	2-1	2-1	2-0	0-1	2-0	0-0	2-1	1-3	2-0	0-2	0-1	1-1	15-11
Belitz, Todd	0-0	0-0	0-0	0-0	0-0	0-0	0-0	0-0	0-0	0-0	0-0	0-0	0-0	0-0	0-0
Heredia, Gil	1-0	1-1	2-0	0-0	0-2	0-1	2-1	1-3	1-0	3-0	1-1	0-1	1-0	2-1	15-11
Hudson, Tim	2-1	2-0	0-1	1-1	0-2	2-1	0-0	3-0	0-0	3-0	2-0	2-0	3-0	0-0	20-6
Isringhausen, Jason	1-0	1-0	0-0	0-0	0-0	1-0	0-1	0-0	0-1	0-0	0-1	1-0	0-0	2-1	6-4
Jones, Doug	1-0	0-0	0-0	0-0	1-0	0-0	1-1	0-0	0-0	0-0	0-0	0-0	0-1	1-0	4-2
Jones, Marcus	0-0	0-0	0-0	0-0	0-0	0-0	0-0	0-0	0-0	0-0	0-0	0-0	0-0	0-0	0-0
Magnante, Mike	0-0	0-0	0-0	0-1	0-0	0-0	0-0	0-0	0-0	0-0	0-0	0-0	0-0	1-0	1-1
Mahay, Ron	0-0	0-0	0-0	0-0	0-1	0-0	0-0	0-0	0-0	0-0	0-0	0-0	0-0	0-0	0-1
Mathews, T.J.	0-1	0-0	0-1	0-1	0-0	0-0	0-0	1-0	0-0	1-0	0-0	0-0	0-0	0-0	2-3
Mecir, Jim	0-0	1-0	0-0	0-0	0-0	0-0	0-0	0-0	0-1	0-0	0-0	1-0	1-0	0-0	3-1
Menechino, Frank	0-0	0-0	0-0	0-0	0-0	0-0	0-0	0-0	0-0	0-0	0-0	0-0	0-0	0-0	0-0
Mulder, Mark	1-1	0-1	1-1	0-0	2-0	0-1	2-0	2-1	0-2	0-0	0-0	0-1	0-0	1-2	9-10
Olivares, Omar	0-0	0-1	0-0	0-0	0-1	1-0	1-1	0-0	0-1	0-0	0-1	1-0	0-1	0-2	4-8
Prieto, Ariel	0-1	1-0	0-0	0-0	0-0	0-0	0-0	0-0	0-1	0-0	0-0	0-0	0-0	0-0	1-2
Ratliff, Jon	0-0	0-0	0-0	0-0	0-0	0-0	0-0	0-0	0-0	0-0	0-0	0-0	0-0	0-0	0-0
Sauveur, Rich	0-0	0-0	0-0	0-0	0-0	0-0	0-0	0-0	0-0	0-0	0-0	0-0	0-0	0-0	0-0
Service, Scott	0-1	0-0	0-0	0-0	0-0	0-0	0-0	0-0	0-0	0-0	0-0	0-0	0-0	1-0	1-2
Tam, Jeff	0-0	1-0	0-1	0-0	0-0	0-1	0-0	0-0	0-0	0-0	0-0	0-1	0-0	2-0	3-3
Vizcaino, Luis	0-0	0-0	0-0	0-0	0-0	0-0	0-1	0-0	0-0	0-0	0-0	0-0	0-0	0-0	0-1
Zito, Barry	2-0	0-1	0-0	0-1	1-0	0-2	0-0	0-0	0-0	0-0	2-0	1-0	1-0	0-0	7-4
Totals	8-5	8-4	5-5	3-6	6-6	4-6	8-4	7-5	3-6	9-4	7-2	5-7	7-3	11-7	91-70

INTERLEAGUE: Tam 1-0, Appier 1-0, Olivares 0-1 vs. Dodgers; Isringhausen 1-0, Heredia 1-0, Service 1-0 vs. Padres; Mulder 1-1, Jones 1-0, Heredia 1-0, Olivares 0-1, Appier 0-1 vs. Giants; Magnante 1-0, Isringhausen 0-1, Mulder 0-1 vs. Rockies; Isringhausen 1-0, Tam 1-0, Heredia 0-1 vs. Diamondbacks. Total: 11-7.

SEATTLE—91-71

Pitcher	Ana. W-L	Bal. W-L	Bos. W-L	Chi. W-L	Cle. W-L	Det. W-L	K.C. W-L	Min. W-L	N.Y. W-L	Oak. W-L	T.B. W-L	Tex. W-L	Tor. W-L	N.L. W-L	Total W-L
Abbott, Paul	0-2	0-0	1-0	0-1	1-0	0-0	0-0	0-1	1-1	0-2	1-0	3-0	0-0	2-0	9-7
Garcia, Freddy	0-0	1-0	2-1	1-1	0-1	0-1	1-0	0-0	0-0	0-1	0-0	1-0	3-0	0-0	9-5
Halama, John	3-0	1-0	0-1	2-0	1-1	0-0	0-1	2-0	2-0	1-0	1-1	1-1	0-1	0-3	14-9
Hodges, Kevin	0-0	0-0	0-0	0-0	0-0	0-0	0-0	0-0	0-0	0-0	0-0	0-0	0-0	0-0	0-0
Mabry, John	0-0	0-0	0-0	0-0	0-0	0-0	0-0	0-0	0-0	0-0	0-0	0-0	0-0	0-0	0-0
Meche, Gil	0-0	1-0	0-0	0-1	0-1	0-0	1-1	2-0	0-0	0-1	0-0	0-0	0-0	0-0	4-4
Mesa, Jose	0-1	0-1	1-1	0-0	0-0	0-0	1-0	0-1	0-1	0-0	1-1	0-0	1-0	0-0	4-6
Moyer, Jamie	1-1	2-0	0-2	0-1	1-0	0-2	1-0	2-0	1-1	2-1	0-0	0-0	1-0	3-1	13-10
Paniagua, Jose	1-0	0-0	0-0	0-0	0-0	0-0	0-0	0-0	0-0	1-0	0-0	0-0	0-0	0-0	3-0

SEATTLE — 91-71 (continued)

Pitcher	Ana. W-L	Bal. W-L	Bos. W-L	Chi. W-L	Cle. W-L	Det. W-L	K.C. W-L	Min. W-L	N.Y. W-L	Oak. W-L	T.B. W-L	Tex. W-L	Tor. W-L	N.L. W-L	Total W-L
Pineiro, Joel	0-0	0-0	0-0	1-0	0-0	0-0	0-0	0-0	0-0	0-0	0-0	0-0	0-0	0-0	1-0
Ramsay, Rob	0-0	0-0	0-0	0-0	0-0	0-0	0-0	1-0	0-0	0-0	0-0	0-1	0-0	0-0	1-1
Rhodes, Arthur	1-0	1-0	0-0	0-0	0-2	0-2	1-0	0-0	0-0	0-1	0-0	0-1	1-1	1-1	5-8
Rodriguez, Frank	0-0	0-1	0-0	0-0	0-0	0-0	1-0	0-0	0-0	0-0	0-0	0-0	1-0	0-0	2-1
Sasaki, Kazuhiro	0-0	0-1	1-0	0-1	0-0	0-0	0-1	0-0	0-0	0-1	0-0	0-0	1-0	0-1	2-5
Sele, Aaron	1-1	1-0	0-0	1-2	0-1	1-1	1-0	2-1	0-1	0-2	4-0	2-0	1-0	3-1	17-10
Tomko, Brett	0-0	0-0	0-0	0-0	0-0	0-1	1-1	0-0	2-0	1-0	1-0	0-2	1-0	1-1	7-5
Totals	8-5	7-3	5-5	5-7	2-7	2-7	8-4	9-3	6-4	4-9	9-3	7-5	8-2	11-7	91-71

INTERLEAGUE: Sele 1-0, Moyer 1-0, Rhodes 0-1 vs. Dodgers; Moyer 2-0, Abbott 1-0, Tomko 0-1, Halama 0-1, Sele 0-1 vs. Padres; Abbott 1-0, Sele 1-0, Halama 0-1 vs. Giants; Sele 1-0, Tomko 1-0, Moyer 0-1 vs. Rockies; Mesa 1-0, Rhodes 1-0, Halama 0-1 vs. Diamondbacks. Total: 11-7.

TAMPA BAY — 69-92

Pitcher	Ana. W-L	Bal. W-L	Bos. W-L	Chi. W-L	Cle. W-L	Det. W-L	K.C. W-L	Min. W-L	N.Y. W-L	Oak. W-L	Sea. W-L	Tex. W-L	Tor. W-L	N.L. W-L	Total W-L
Creek, Doug	0-0	0-0	0-0	0-0	1-1	0-0	0-0	0-0	0-0	0-1	0-0	0-0	0-0	0-1	1-3
Duvall, Mike	0-0	0-0	0-0	0-0	0-0	0-0	0-0	0-0	0-0	0-0	0-0	0-0	0-0	0-0	0-0
Eiland, Dave	1-0	1-0	0-2	0-0	0-0	0-0	0-1	0-0	0-0	0-0	0-0	0-0	0-1	0-0	2-3
Enders, Trevor	0-0	0-0	0-0	0-0	0-0	0-0	0-0	0-0	0-0	0-0	0-0	0-0	0-1	0-0	0-1
Fiore, Tony	0-0	0-0	0-0	0-0	0-1	0-0	1-0	0-0	0-0	0-0	0-0	0-0	0-0	0-0	1-1
Gooden, Dwight	1-0	0-0	0-0	0-0	0-0	0-0	0-0	0-1	0-1	0-0	0-0	0-1	0-0	1-1	2-3
Guthrie, Mark	0-0	0-0	0-0	0-0	0-0	0-0	0-0	0-0	0-0	0-0	0-0	0-0	0-0	0-1	0-1
Guzman, Juan	0-0	0-0	0-0	0-0	0-1	0-0	0-0	0-0	0-0	0-0	0-1	0-0	1-0	0-0	1-2
Harper, Travis	0-1	1-0	0-1	0-1	0-0	0-1	0-0	0-0	1-0	0-0	0-1	1-1	1-2	0-0	4-7
Hernandez, Roberto	0-1	1-0	0-1	0-1	0-0	0-1	0-0	0-0	1-0	0-0	0-1	1-1	1-2	0-0	4-6
Lidle, Cory	0-1	0-1	0-0	0-1	0-2	0-1	0-0	0-0	0-1	0-2	1-1	1-2	0-2	2-0	11-13
Lopez, Albie	2-0	0-0	1-0	1-1	0-2	1-0	1-2	1-0	0-1	0-2	1-0	1-0	0-0	0-0	7-2
Mecir, Jim	0-0	1-1	0-0	1-0	0-0	0-0	0-0	1-0	0-0	0-0	0-0	0-0	0-0	0-0	0-0
Morris, Jim	0-2	1-0	1-1	0-1	1-0	1-0	1-0	0-2	1-1	1-0	0-1	0-1	0-0	0-1	7-10
Rekar, Bryan	0-0	1-2	0-0	0-0	0-1	1-0	1-0	1-0	0-0	0-0	0-0	0-0	0-0	0-0	5-6
Rupe, Ryan	0-1	0-0	0-0	0-0	0-0	0-0	0-0	1-0	0-0	0-0	0-0	0-0	0-0	0-0	0-1
Sparks, Jeff	0-0	0-0	1-0	1-0	0-0	0-0	0-0	1-0	0-0	0-0	0-0	0-0	0-0	0-0	4-0
Sturtze, Tanyon	0-0	0-1	0-1	0-0	0-0	0-0	0-0	1-0	0-0	0-0	0-1	0-0	1-0	1-2	6-10
Taylor, Billy	1-1	0-1	0-1	0-0	0-1	0-1	0-0	1-0	1-1	0-0	0-3	0-0	1-0	1-2	1-1
Trachsel, Steve	0-0	0-0	0-0	0-1	0-0	0-0	0-0	0-0	0-0	0-0	0-0	2-1	1-1	0-2	3-6
Wheeler, Dan	0-0	0-0	0-0	0-0	0-0	0-0	0-0	0-0	0-0	0-2	0-0	0-0	1-0	0-0	1-4
White, Rick	1-0	0-2	1-0	1-1	0-0	1-0	1-0	0-2	0-0	0-0	1-1	1-1	0-0	9-9	7-8
Yan, Esteban	—	—	—	—	—	—	—	—	—	—	—	—	—	—	—
Totals	6-6	5-8	6-6	4-6	2-8	5-4	5-5	6-4	6-6	2-7	3-9	5-7	5-7	9-9	69-92

INTERLEAGUE: Rupe 1-0, Mecir 0-1, Rekar 0-1 vs. Braves; Mecir 1-0, Lopez 1-0, Trachsel 0-1 vs. Expos; Yan 1-0, White 0-1, Trachsel 0-1 vs. Mets; Guthrie 1-1, Hernandez 1-0 vs. Phillies; Trachsel 1-0, Mecir 1-0, Lopez 1-0, Yan 0-1, Creek 0-1, White 0-1 vs. Marlins. Total: 9-9.

TEXAS — 71-91

Pitcher	Ana. W-L	Bal. W-L	Bos. W-L	Chi. W-L	Cle. W-L	Det. W-L	K.C. W-L	Min. W-L	N.Y. W-L	Oak. W-L	Sea. W-L	T.B. W-L	Tor. W-L	N.L. W-L	Total W-L
Clark, Mark	0-0	0-0	0-1	0-0	1-0	0-0	0-0	0-2	0-0	0-0	0-1	1-0	1-0	0-0	3-5
Cordero, Francisco	0-1	0-0	0-0	1-0	0-0	0-0	0-0	0-0	0-0	0-1	0-0	0-0	0-0	0-0	1-2
Crabtree, Tim	0-1	0-1	0-0	0-0	0-0	0-0	0-0	0-0	0-1	1-2	0-0	0-0	1-1	0-0	0-1	2-7
Cubillan, Darwin	0-0	0-0	0-0	0-0	0-0	0-0	0-0	0-0	0-0	0-0	0-0	0-0	0-0	0-0	0-0
Davis, Doug	2-0	0-0	1-0	1-0	0-1	0-0	1-0	0-1	0-0	0-1	1-1	0-1	0-0	1-0	1-1	7-6
Glynn, Ryan	0-0	0-1	0-1	0-0	0-1	2-0	1-0	0-1	0-0	0-1	0-1	1-2	1-1	1-2	16-13
Helling, Rick	1-1	2-1	1-1	1-1	1-1	1-1	1-0	0-2	0-0	2-0	3-0	1-2	1-1	1-2	1-1
Johnson, Jonathan	0-1	0-0	0-0	0-0	0-0	0-0	0-0	0-0	0-0	0-0	0-0	0-0	0-0	0-0	1-1
Kolb, Danny	0-0	0-0	0-0	0-0	0-0	0-0	0-0	0-0	0-0	0-1	0-0	0-0	0-0	0-2	5-6
Loaiza, Esteban	0-0	1-1	0-0	0-1	0-0	0-1	1-0	2-0	0-0	1-0	0-0	0-0	0-0	0-1	0-1
Munoz, Mike	0-0	0-0	0-0	0-0	0-0	1-1	0-1	0-2	0-0	0-1	0-2	1-1	1-0	0-0	2-9
Oliver, Darren	0-2	0-1	0-0	0-0	0-0	1-1	0-1	0-2	0-0	0-1	0-2	1-0	1-0	0-2	2-7
Perisho, Matt	0-0	0-0	0-1	0-0	0-1	0-0	0-0	0-0	0-2	0-2	1-0	1-0	1-0	1-0	13-13
Rogers, Kenny	1-1	2-0	1-2	1-0	1-1	1-2	1-1	1-0	0-2	1-0	1-0	0-0	0-0	1-2	0-0
Sheldon, Scott	0-0	0-0	0-0	0-0	0-0	0-0	0-0	0-0	0-0	0-0	0-0	0-0	0-1	0-0	1-3
Sikorski, Brian	0-0	0-0	0-0	0-0	0-0	0-0	0-1	0-0	1-1	0-0	0-0	0-0	1-1	0-0	3-1
Venafro, Mike	0-0	1-0	0-0	0-0	1-0	0-0	0-0	0-2	0-0	2-0	1-0	0-0	0-0	0-0	6-5
Wetteland, John	1-0	0-0	0-1	0-1	0-1	0-0	1-0	0-0	0-0	0-1	0-0	1-1	0-0	2-0	4-5
Zimmerman, Jeff	0-0	0-1	0-1	0-2	0-0	0-0	1-0	0-0	0-0	0-0	0-0	0-0	0-0	2-0	4-5
Totals	5-7	6-6	3-7	5-5	4-6	5-5	7-3	4-8	2-10	7-5	5-7	7-5	4-6	7-11	71-91

INTERLEAGUE: Glynn 1-0, Clark 0-1, Helling 0-1 vs. Dodgers; Davis 1-0, Helling 1-0, Rogers 0-1 vs. Padres; Loaiza 0-1, Davis 0-1, Wetteland 0-1 vs. Giants; Crabtree 0-1, Wetteland 0-1, Loaiza 0-1 vs. Rockies; Zimmerman 2-0, Rogers 1-1, Perisho 1-0, Helling 0-1 vs. Diamondbacks. Total: 7-11.

TORONTO — 83-79

Pitcher	Ana. W-L	Bal. W-L	Bos. W-L	Chi. W-L	Cle. W-L	Det. W-L	K.C. W-L	Min. W-L	N.Y. W-L	Oak. W-L	Sea. W-L	T.B. W-L	Tex. W-L	N.L. W-L	Total W-L
Andrews, Clayton	0-0	0-0	0-0	0-0	0-0	1-1	0-0	0-0	0-1	0-0	0-0	0-0	0-0	0-0	1-2
Bale, John	0-0	0-0	0-0	0-0	0-0	0-0	0-0	0-0	0-0	0-0	0-0	0-0	0-0	0-0	0-0
Borbon, Pedro	1-0	0-0	0-0	0-0	0-0	0-0	0-0	0-0	0-0	0-0	0-0	0-0	0-0	0-1	1-1
Carpenter, Chris	0-2	0-2	1-1	1-0	1-0	2-1	1-1	1-0	1-0	1-0	0-2	0-1	0-0	1-2	10-12
Castillo, Frank	0-1	2-0	2-1	1-1	1-0	1-0	1-0	0-1	0-0	0-0	0-0	1-1	1-1	1-0	10-5
Coco, Pasqual	0-0	0-0	0-0	0-0	0-0	0-0	0-0	0-0	0-0	0-0	0-0	0-0	0-0	0-0	0-0
Cubillan, Darwin	0-0	0-0	0-0	0-0	0-0	0-0	0-0	0-0	0-0	0-0	0-0	0-0	0-0	1-0	1-0
DeWitt, Matt	0-0	0-0	1-0	0-0	0-0	0-0	0-0	0-0	0-0	0-0	0-0	0-0	0-0	0-0	1-0

Pitcher	Ana. W-L	Bal. W-L	Bos. W-L	Chi. W-L	Cle. W-L	Det. W-L	K.C. W-L	Min. W-L	N.Y. W-L	Oak. W-L	Sea. W-L	T.B. W-L	Tex. W-L	N.L. W-L	Total W-L
Escobar, Kelvim	1-1	1-0	0-1	1-3	0-1	1-0	2-1	0-2	1-1	0-0	0-2	2-1	0-1	1-1	10-15
Estrella, Leo	0-0	0-0	0-0	0-0	0-0	0-0	0-0	0-0	0-0	0-0	0-0	0-0	0-0	0-0	0-0
Frascatore, John	0-0	0-0	0-0	0-0	0-0	0-0	0-0	0-0	0-0	0-0	0-0	0-0	0-0	0-1	0-0
Gunderson, Eric	0-0	0-0	0-1	0-0	0-1	1-0	0-0	0-0	0-0	0-0	1-0	0-0	0-1	0-0	2-4
Guthrie, Mark	0-0	0-0	0-0	0-0	0-0	0-0	0-0	0-1	0-0	0-1	0-0	0-0	0-0	0-0	0-2
Halladay, Roy	1-0	0-2	1-0	0-0	0-0	1-0	0-0	0-0	0-1	0-1	0-2	0-0	0-1	1-0	4-7
Hamilton, Joey	0-0	0-0	0-0	0-0	0-0	0-0	0-0	0-0	0-1	0-0	0-0	1-0	0-0	1-0	2-1
Koch, Billy	1-0	0-0	0-0	1-0	1-0	0-0	1-0	0-0	1-0	0-1	0-0	1-0	0-0	2-1	9-3
Loaiza, Esteban	1-0	0-1	0-0	0-0	0-1	0-0	0-1	1-1	1-1	0-1	1-0	0-1	2-1	0-0	5-7
Munro, Peter	0-0	0-0	1-0	0-0	0-0	0-0	0-0	0-0	0-0	0-0	0-0	0-0	0-0	0-1	1-1
Painter, Lance	0-0	1-0	0-0	1-0	0-0	0-0	0-0	0-0	0-0	0-0	0-0	0-0	0-0	0-1	1-1
Quantrill, Paul	0-0	0-1	0-0	0-0	0-2	0-0	0-0	0-0	0-0	0-0	0-0	0-0	0-0	0-1	2-5
Trachsel, Steve	0-0	0-0	0-0	0-0	0-0	0-0	0-0	0-0	0-0	0-0	0-0	1-0	1-0	0-0	2-5
Wells, David	2-1	2-1	2-0	0-1	2-1	1-0	0-1	2-0	2-0	1-2	0-1	2-0	2-0	2-1	20-8
Totals	7-5	6-7	8-4	5-5	4-8	9-3	6-4	4-5	7-5	3-7	2-8	7-5	6-4	9-9	83-79

INTERLEAGUE: Wells 1-0, Cubillan 1-0, Frascatore 0-1 vs. Braves; Carpenter 1-0, Wells 1-0, Koch 1-0, Castillo 1-0, Quantrill 0-1, Escobar 0-1 vs. Expos; Halladay 1-0, Borbon 0-1, Carpenter 0-1 vs. Mets; Koch 1-0, Carpenter 0-1, Wells 0-1 vs. Phillies; Escobar 1-0, Munro 0-1, Koch 0-1 vs. Marlins. Total: 9-9.

HOME RUNS BY PARKS

	At Ana.	At Bal.	At Bos.	At Chi.	At Cle.	At Det.	At K.C.	At Min.	At N.Y.	At Oak.	At Sea.	At T.B.	At Tex.	At Tor.	At N.L. Parks	Totals 2000	Totals 1999	HR Allow.
Anaheim	130	13	2	9	3	3	9	7	6	8	2	10	12	9	13	236	158	228
Baltimore	5	90	7	10	4	2	9	7	11	7	3	12	4	4	9	184	203	202
Boston	8	11	66	7	6	10	3	13	7	5	7	8	7	3	6	167	176	173
Chicago	4	6	3	125	5	7	10	5	8	4	7	9	6	3	14	216	162	195
Cleveland	4	8	1	8	122	12	5	11	6	5	3	12	5	4	15	221	209	173
Detroit	8	12	6	8	14	69	9	7	7	6	6	6	4	6	6	177	212	177
Kansas City	5	3	1	5	4	2	84	9	2	8	3	4	5		13	150	151	239
Minnesota	6	1	4	4	5	1	12	54	1	4	2	3	5	4	6	116	105	212
New York	9	6	14	5	5	2	6	3	117	1	6	4	11	7	9	205	193	177
Oakland	10	8	6	2	7	1	18	8	9	126	6	7	10	9	12	239	235	158
Seattle	13	8	4	11	4	6	6	8	4	1	92	7	9	13	6	198	244	167
Tampa Bay	8	6	5	5	3	3	6	8	4	1	8	76	13	7	8	162	145	198
Texas	10	5	2	2	4	4	7	5	6	2	4	7	104	3	8	173	230	202
Toronto	9	9	11	12	7	7	6	5	1	5	4	10	10	134	12	244	212	195
N.L. clubs	14	10	11	16	16	10	11	9	14	13	6	11	5	12	....	158	142	
2000 Totals	243	196	143	229	209	137	201	160	209	195	164	185	209	226	140	2688	....	2696
1999 Totals	179	199	152	183	219	235	158	186	227	157	212	189				....	2635	....

AT ANAHEIM (243):
Anaheim (130)—Glaus 24, Anderson 20, Vaughn 18, Salmon 17, Erstad 11, Molina 11, Spiezio 10, Kennedy 7, Gant 5, Gil 4, Walbeck 2, DiSarcina 1. **Baltimore (5)**—Richard 2, Belle 1, Bordick 1, Conine 1. **Boston (8)**—O'Leary 2, Everett 2, Alexander 1, Garciaparra 1, Nixon 1, Daubach 1. **Chicago (4)**—Valentin 1, Perry 1, Konerko 1, Singleton 1. **Cleveland (4)**—Alomar 1, Vizquel 1, Fryman 1, Lofton 1. **Colorado (1)**—Shumpert 1. **Detroit (8)**—Gonzalez 2, Encarnacion 2, Easley 1, Higginson 1, D. Cruz 1. **Kansas City (5)**—Beltran 2, McCarty 1, Randa 1, Dye 1. **Los Angeles (7)**—Sheffield 2, Karros 2, Elster 1, Kreuter 1, LoDuca 1. **Minnesota (6)**—Coomer 1, Lawton 1, Canizaro 1, Ortiz 1, Koskie 1, Jones 1. **New York (9)**—Williams 2, Spencer 2, Canseco 1, O'Neill 1, Hill 1, Martinez 1, Brosius 1. **Oakland (10)**—Grieve 2, J. Giambi 2, Stairs 2, Saenz 1, J. Giambi 1, Tejada 1, Christenson 1, Long 1. **San Francisco (6)**—Bonds 2, Kent 1, Aurilia 1, Benard 1, Rios 1. **Seattle (13)**—A. Rodriguez 6, Bell 3, Buhner 1, Martinez 1, Oliver 1, Cameron 1. **Tampa Bay (8)**—Vaughn 4, Castilla 2, McGriff 1, Canseco 1. **Texas (10)**—Rodriguez 3, Clayton 2, Mateo 2, Segui 1, Kapler 1, Lamb 1. **Toronto (9)**—Batista 2, Fullmer 2, Martinez 1, Fletcher 1, Mondesi 1, Delgado 1, Cruz 1.

AT BALTIMORE (196):
Anaheim (13)—Vaughn 3, Glaus 3, Salmon 2, Anderson 2, Gil 1, Walbeck 1, Erstad 1. **Atlanta (3)**—Galarraga 1, Lopez 1, C. Jones 1. **Baltimore (90)**—Belle 14, C. Johnson 12, Anderson 9, Ripken Jr. 8, Clark 6, Surhoff 6, Bordick 6, Conine 6, Fordyce 5, Baines 4, DeShields 4, Richard 4, Hairston Jr. 2, Myers 1, Lewis 1, Mora 1, Matos 1. **Boston (11)**—Everett 2, Hatteberg 2, Daubach 2, Stanley 1, Offerman 1, Lewis 1, Varitek 1, Sadler 1. **Chicago (6)**—Thomas 2, Baines 1, Valentin 1, Graffanino 1, Abbott 1. **Cleveland (8)**—M. Ramirez 3, Alomar 1, Segui 1, Fryman 1, Thome 1, Lofton 1. **Detroit (12)**—Palmer 3, Ausmus 2, Encarnacion 2, Higginson 1, Clark 1, Magee 1, D. Cruz 1, Allen 1. **Florida (2)**—Millar 1, Wilson 1. **Kansas City (3)**—Dye 2, Randa 1. **Minnesota (6)**—Coomer 1. **New York (6)**—O'Neill 1, Hill 1, Williams 1, Thompson 1, Jeter 1, Bellinger 1. **Oakland (8)**—Chavez 3, Stairs 2, J. Giambi 2, Tejada 1, J. Giambi 1. **Philadelphia (5)**—Ducey 1, Lieberthal 1, Glanville 1, Rolen 1, Abreu 1. **Seattle (8)**—A. Rodriguez 2, Buhner 1, Martinez 1, Oliver 1, Olerud 1, Wilson 1, Bell 1. **Tampa Bay (6)**—McGriff 1, Canseco 1, Vaughn 1, Castilla 1, Williams 1, Huff 1. **Texas (5)**—Rodriguez 3, Segui 1, Curtis 1. **Toronto (9)**—Batista 4, Mondesi 2, Fletcher 1, Delgado 1, Stewart 1.

AT BOSTON (143):
Anaheim (2)—Vaughn 1, Kennedy 1. **Atlanta (4)**—Galarraga 1, Jordan 1, A. Jones 1. **Baltimore (7)**—C. Johnson 2, Myers 1, Belle 1, Conine 1, Hairston Jr. 1, Richard 1. **Boston (66)**—Everett 17, Daubach 10, O'Leary 7, Garciaparra 4, Stanley 5, Bichette 4, Nixon 4, Offerman 3, Hatteberg 2, Varitek 2, Sprague 1, Brogna 1, Alexander 1, Burkhart 1, Alcantara 1. **Chicago (3)**—Valentin 1, Fordyce 1, Ordonez 1. **Cleveland (1)**—Lofton 1. **Detroit (6)**—Gonzalez 2, Jefferies 1, Clark 1, Magee 1, Halter 1. **Kansas City (1)**—McCarty 1. **Minnesota (4)**—Coomer 2, Ortiz 1, Koskie 1. **Montreal (2)**—V. Guerrero 1, Seguignol 1. **New York A.L. (14)**—Williams 3, Brosius 3, Jeter 2, Canseco 1, O'Neill 1, Jose 1, Justice 1, Posada 1, Spencer 1. **New York N.L. (5)**—Piazza 3, Payton 1, Mora 1. **Oakland (6)**—J. Giambi 2, Stairs 2, Saenz 1, Chavez 1, Menechino 1. **Seattle (4)**—Martinez 1, A. Rodriguez 1, Cameron 1, Guillen 1. **Tampa Bay (5)**—Canseco 1, Castilla 1, Cairo 1, Trammell 1, Cox 1. **Texas (2)**—Haselman 1, Catalanotto 1. **Toronto (11)**—Mondesi 3, Batista 2, Fullmer 2, Delgado 2, Gonzalez 1, Stewart 1, T. Greene 1.

AT CHICAGO (229):
Anaheim (9)—Anderson 2, Erstad 2, Glaus 2, Vaughn 1, Salmon 1, Spiezio 1. **Baltimore (10)**—Conine 2, Baines 1, Surhoff 1, Anderson 1, DeShields 1, Bordick 1, C. Johnson 1, Hairston Jr. 1, Richard 1. **Boston (7)**—Garciaparra 2, Alcantara 2, Bichette 1, Offerman 1, Hatteberg 1. **Chicago A.L. (125)**—Thomas 30, Ordonez 21, Valentin 16, Lee 12, Konerko 10, Perry 7, C. Johnson 7, Durham 4, Singleton 5, Norton 4, Fordyce 3, M. Johnson 2, Graffanino 1, Abbott 1, Paul 1. **Chicago N.L. (4)**—Hill 1, Grace 1, Sosa 1, B. Brown 1. **Cleveland (8)**—Thome 3, Diaz 2, Alomar 1, Fryman 1, A. Ramirez 1. **Detroit (8)**—Higginson 3, Morris 1, Gonzalez 1, Palmer 1, Magee 1, Encarnacion 1. **Kansas City (5)**—Dye 3, Sweeney 1, Quinn 1. **Milwaukee (4)**—Hayes 2, Houston 1, Jenkins 1. **Minnesota (4)**—Canizaro 1, Koskie 1, Jones 1, LeCroy 1. **New York (5)**—O'Neill 1, Brosius 1, Posada 1, Ledee 1. **Oakland (2)**—J. Giambi 1, Grieve 1. **St. Louis (8)**—Tatis 3, Dunston 1, Perez 1, Edmonds 1, Renteria 1, McDonald 1. **Seattle (11)**—Buhner 2, Martinez 1, A. Rodriguez 2, Cameron 2, Lampkin 1, Oliver 1, Widger 1. **Tampa Bay (5)**—Williams 1, DiFelice 1, F. Martinez 1, Smith 1. **Texas (2)**—Ledee 1, Kapler 1. **Toronto (12)**—Cruz 3, Fletcher 2, Gonzalez 2, Fullmer 2, Mondesi 1, Delgado 1, Cordova 1.

AT CLEVELAND (209):

Anaheim (3)—Salmon 2, Glaus 1. **Baltimore (4)**—Fordyce 2, Richard 2. **Boston (6)**—Stanley 2, Bichette 2, Everett 1, Varitek 1. **Chicago (5)**—Durham 2, Thomas 1, Valentin 1, Konerko 1. **Cincinnati (5)**—Griffey Jr. 2, Tucker 1, Young 1, Reese 1. **Cleveland (122)**—M. Ramirez 22, Thome 21, Branyan 13, Justice 10, Lofton 10, Fryman 9, Alomar 8, Sexson 8, Alomar Jr. 5, Segui 4, A. Ramirez 3, Diaz 2, Ledee 2, Wilson 2, Cabrera 2, Vizquel 1. **Detroit (14)**—Gonzalez 3, Higginson 3, Clark 2, Polonia 1, Jefferies 1, Easley 1, Ausmus 1, Becker 1, Magee 1. **Houston (5)**—Ward 2, Biggio 1, Eusebio 1, Hidalgo 1. **Kansas City (4)**—McCarty 1, Randa 1, Zaun 1, Damon 1. **Minnesota (5)**—Lawton 2, Cummings 1, Coomer 1, Hunter 1. **New York (5)**—Ledee 2, O'Neill 1, Williams 1, Spencer 1. **Oakland (7)**—Stairs 2, J. Giambi 2, Tejada 1, Grieve 1, Long 1. **Pittsburgh (6)**—Young 2, Vander Wal 1, Cordero 1, Kendall 1, Redman 1. **Seattle (4)**—Martinez 1, Martin 1, Wilson 1, Guillen 1. **Tampa Bay (3)**—Cox 2, Vaughn 1. **Texas (4)**—Palmeiro 1, Segui 1, Rodriguez 1, Greer 1. **Toronto (7)**—Gonzalez 2, Batista 2, Stewart 1, T. Greene 1, Cruz 1.

AT DETROIT (137):

Anaheim (3)—Salmon 1, Spiezio 1, Glaus 1. **Baltimore (2)**—Anderson 1, DeShields 1. **Boston (10)**—Nixon 3, Stanley 1, Offerman 1, O'Leary 1, Hatteberg 1, Garciaparra 1, Daubach 1, Alcantara 1. **Chicago (7)**—Konerko 2, Valentin 1, C. Johnson 1, Durham 1, Ordonez 1, Singleton 1. **Cincinnati (1)**—Young 1. **Cleveland (12)**—Thome 3, Alomar 2, Justice 2, Sexson 2, Fryman 1, A. Ramirez 1, Branyan 1. **Detroit (69)**—Palmer 15, Higginson 12, Gonzalez 8, Clark 6, Easley 5, Encarnacion 4, Polonia 3, Ausmus 3, Becker 3, McMillon 3, Magee 2, Macias 2, D. Cruz 1, Cardona 1, Allen 1. **Houston (5)**—Hidalgo 2, Eusebio 1, Meluskey 1, Berkman 1. **Kansas City (2)**—Zaun 1, Sweeney 1. **Minnesota (1)**—Hocking 1. **New York (2)**—O'Neill 1, Williams 1. **Oakland (1)**—Grieve 1. **St. Louis (4)**—McGwire 1, Howard 1, Edmonds 1, Drew 1. **Seattle (4)**—Martinez 1, A. Rodriguez 1, Cameron 1. **Tampa Bay (3)**—Williams 2, Cox 1. **Texas (4)**—Palmeiro 1, Alicea 2. **Toronto (7)**—Delgado 2, Fullmer 2, Fletcher 1, Batista 1, Cruz 1.

AT KANSAS CITY (201):

Anaheim (9)—Anderson 3, Erstad 3, Vaughn 1, Salmon 1, Molina 1. **Baltimore (9)**—Fordyce 2, Richard 2, Ripken Jr. 1, Anderson 1, Belle 1, Bordick 1, Hairston Jr. 1. **Boston (3)**—Daubach 2, Everett 1. **Chicago A.L. (10)**—Thomas 2, Durham 2, Valentin 1, Perry 1, Ordonez 1, Konerko 1, M. Johnson 1, Lee 1. **Chicago N.L. (3)**—Sosa 3. **Cleveland (5)**—Thome 2, Alomar Jr. 1, M. Ramirez 1, Sexson 1. **Detroit (9)**—Higginson 3, Palmer 2, Fick 2, Polonia 1, D. Cruz 1. **Kansas City (84)**—Sweeney 17, Dye 15, Quinn 12, Damon 10, Randa 9, McCarty 6, Beltran 4, Johnson 3, Fabregas 2, Zaun 2, Febles 2, Sanchez 1, Dunwoody 1. **Milwaukee (4)**—Burnitz 2, Grissom 1, Hernandez 1. **Minnesota (12)**—Jones 3, Coomer 2, Lawton 2, Huskey 1, Hocking 1, Walker 1, Koskie 1, LeCroy 1. **New York (6)**—Justice 2, O'Neill 1, Brosius 1, Jeter 1, Bellinger 1. **Oakland (18)**—Tejada 3, Hernandez 3, J. Giambi 2, Grieve 2, Chavez 2, Long 2, Jaha 1, Saenz 1, Fasano 1, Menechino 1. **Pittsburgh (4)**—Giles 3, Young 1. **Seattle (6)**—Martinez 2, A. Rodriguez 2, Cameron 2. **Tampa Bay (6)**—Vaughn 2, Williams 1, Flaherty 1, Stocker 1. **Texas (7)**—Palmeiro 2, Segui 2, Curtis 1, Greer 1, Catalanotto 1. **Toronto (6)**—Stewart 3, Fullmer 2, Batista 1.

AT MINNESOTA (160):

Anaheim (7)—Vaughn 3, Salmon 1, Anderson 1, Erstad 1, Glaus 1. **Baltimore (7)**—Conine 2, Surhoff 1, Anderson 1, DeShields 1, Bordick 1, C. Johnson 1. **Boston (13)**—O'Leary 2, Garciaparra 2, Offerman 1, Gilkey 1, Frye 1, Alexander 1, Everett 1, Hatteberg 1, Varitek 1, Daubach 1, Burkhart 1. **Chicago A.L. (5)**—Valentin 1, Perry 1, C. Johnson 1, Fordyce 1, Konerko 1. **Chicago N.L. (3)**—Sosa 2, Hill 1. **Cleveland (11)**—M. Ramirez 3, Fryman 2, Sexson 2, Alomar 1, Vizquel 1, Justice 1, Thome 1. **Detroit (7)**—Easley 2, Ausmus 1, Higginson 1, D. Cruz 1, Halter 1, Encarnacion 1. **Kansas City (9)**—Quinn 4, Sweeney 2, Dye 2, McCarty 1. **Milwaukee (3)**—Grissom 2, Hernandez 1. **Minnesota (54)**—Jones 11, Lawton 8, Ortiz 7, Huskey 4, Hunter 4, Coomer 3, Guzman 3, Cummings 2, Jensen 2, Canizaro 2, LeCroy 2, Hocking 1, Maxwell 1, Pierzynski 1, Koskie 1, Buchanan 1, Moeller 1. **New York (3)**—Hill 1, Justice 1, Posada 1. **Oakland (8)**—Grieve 3, J. Giambi 2, Stairs 1, Tejada 1, Piatt 1. **St. Louis (3)**—Edmonds 1, Tatis 1, Richard 1. **Seattle (9)**—Lampkin 3, Olerud 2, A. Rodriguez 2, Martinez 1, Cameron 1. **Tampa Bay (8)**—McGriff 2, Vaughn 1, Flaherty 1, Williams 1, Stocker 1, J. Guillen 1, Smith 1. **Texas (5)**—Sheldon 2, Palmeiro 1, Segui 1, Mateo 1. **Toronto (5)**—Delgado 1, Gonzalez 1, Stewart 1, Cruz 1, Fullmer 1.

AT NEW YORK (209):

Anaheim (6)—Salmon 2, Vaughn 1, Erstad 1, Spiezio 1, Glaus 1. **Baltimore (11)**—Baines 2, Ripken Jr. 2, Anderson 2, Surhoff 1, DeShields 1, Bordick 1, Lewis 1, C. Johnson 1. **Boston (7)**—Stanley 1, Offerman 1, Valentin 1, Alexander 1, Garciaparra 1, Nixon 1, Varitek 1. **Chicago (8)**—Ordonez 3, Valentin 1, Norton 1, Konerko 1, Lee 1, Singleton 1. **Cleveland (6)**—M. Ramirez 3, Segui 1, Fryman 1, Branyan 1. **Detroit (7)**—Easley 2, Higginson 2, McMillon 1, Magee 1, D. Cruz 1. **Florida (3)**—Lee 1, Wilson 1, Lowell 1. **Kansas City (2)**—Zaun 1, Sweeney 1. **Minnesota (5)**—Coomer 1, Canizaro 1, Walker 1, Ortiz 1, Guzman 1. **New York A.L. (117)**—Posada 18, Williams 15, Justice 14, Martinez 12, Hill 11, O'Neill 10, Jeter 8, Brosius 7, Knoblauch 5, Spencer 4, Canseco 2, Sojo 2, Thompson 2, Ledee 2, Bellinger 2, Polonia 1, Kelly 1, Leyritz 1. **New York N.L. (5)**—Ventura 1, Bell 1, Piazza 1, Alfonzo 1, Payton 1. **Oakland (9)**—Stairs 2, Chavez 2, Velarde 1, J. Giambi 1, Fasano 1, Long 1, Hernandez 1. **Philadelphia (6)**—Abreu 2, Gant 1, Hunter 1, Lieberthal 1, Burrell 1. **Seattle (6)**—A. Rodriguez 3, Buhner 1, Martinez 1, Guillen 1. **Tampa Bay (4)**—Vaughn 2, McGriff 1, Williams 1. **Texas (6)**—Palmeiro 2, Greer 2, Haselman 1, Ledee 1. **Toronto (1)**—Cruz 1.

AT OAKLAND (195):

Anaheim (8)—Spiezio 2, Glaus 2, Vaughn 1, Walbeck 1, Anderson 1, Erstad 1. **Arizona (1)**—Finley 1. **Baltimore (7)**—Bordick 2, Baines 1, Ripken Jr. 1, Clark 1, Belle 1, C. Johnson 1. **Boston (5)**—Garciaparra 2, Sprague 1, Hatteberg 1, Varitek 1. **Chicago (4)**—Durham 2, Thomas 1, Konerko 1. **Cleveland (5)**—Alomar 2, Fryman 2, Justice 1. **Detroit (6)**—Palmer 2, Gonzalez 1, Becker 1, Halter 1, Encarnacion 1. **Kansas City (2)**—McCarty 1, Quinn 1. **Minnesota (3)**—Jones 1, Hocking 1, Guzman 1. **New York (1)**—Canseco 1. **Oakland (126)**—J. Giambi 23, Tejada 16, Chavez 15, Grieve 13, Velarde 11, Stairs 9, Long 9, Hernandez 7, Fasano 4, Stanley 3, Saenz 3, Christenson 3, J. Giambi 3, Menechino 3, Piatt 3, Becker 1. **San Diego (2)**—Sprague 1, Rivera 1. **San Francisco (10)**—Bonds 3, Kent 3, Burks 1, Davis 1, Mueller 1, Martinez 1. **Seattle (6)**—A. Rodriguez 2, Buhner 1, Martinez 1, Bell 1, Guillen 1. **Tampa Bay (1)**—Vaughn 1. **Texas (2)**—Palmeiro 1, Greer 1. **Toronto (5)**—Fullmer 2, Delgado 1, Gonzalez 1, Batista 1.

AT SEATTLE (164):

Anaheim (2)—Vaughn 1, Salmon 1. **Baltimore (3)**—Baines 1, Conine 1, C. Johnson 1. **Boston (7)**—Daubach 2, Lewis 1, Valentin 1, Garciaparra 1, Nixon 1, Varitek 1. **Chicago (7)**—Lee 3, Durham 1, Ordonez 1, Konerko 1. **Cleveland (3)**—Fryman 2, M. Ramirez 1. **Colorado (2)**—Mayne 1, Hammonds 1. **Detroit (6)**—Gonzalez 2, Palmer 1, Higginson 1, D. Cruz 1, Encarnacion 1. **Kansas City (8)**—Sweeney 3, Damon 2, Dye 2, McCarty 1. **Los Angeles (1)**—Karros 1. **Minnesota (2)**—Coomer 1, Pierzynski 1. **New York (6)**—Soriano 2, Canseco 1, Martinez 1, Jeter 1, Spencer 1. **Oakland (6)**—J. Giambi 3, Tejada 1, Grieve 1, Hernandez 1. **San Diego (3)**—Martin 1, Klesko 1, Nevin 1. **Seattle (92)**—Martinez 19, Buhner 15, A. Rodriguez 13, Olerud 8, Oliver 6, Javier 5, Cameron 5, Bell 4, Lampkin 3, Guillen 3, Henderson 2, McLemore 2, Martin 2, Wilson 2, Ibanez 2, Machado 1. **Tampa Bay (8)**—McGriff 2, Vaughn 2, Williams 2, J. Guillen 1, Smith 1. **Texas (4)**—Sierra 1, Segui 1, Rodriguez 1, Catalanotto 1. **Toronto (4)**—Fletcher 1, T. Greene 1, Cruz 1, Fullmer 1.

AT TAMPA BAY (185):

Anaheim (10)—Vaughn 3, Salmon 2, Molina 2, Glaus 2, Spiezio 1. **Atlanta (5)**—A. Jones 2, Joyner 1, Lopez 1, C. Jones 1. **Baltimore (12)**—Surhoff 2, Anderson 2, Belle 2, Ripken Jr. 1, DeShields 1, Bordick 1, C. Johnson 1, Mora 1, Richard 1. **Boston (8)**—Everett 2, Burkhart 2, O'Leary 1, Nixon 1, Varitek 1, Daubach 1. **Chicago (9)**—Ordonez 2, Konerko 2, Lee 2, Thomas 1, Durham 1, Singleton 1. **Cleveland (12)**—Thome 3, M. Ramirez 3, Justice 2, Alomar 1, Alomar Jr. 1, Vizquel 1, Segui 1. **Detroit (6)**—Palmer 2, Easley 2, Higginson 1, D. Cruz 1. **Florida (3)**—Castillo 1, Lee 1, Lowell 1. **Kansas City (3)**—Sweeney 1, Dye 1, Quinn 1. **Minnesota (3)**—Koskie 1, Guzman 1, Ardoin 1. **Montreal (3)**—Stevens 1, Widger 1, V. Guerrero 1. **New York (4)**—Hill 1, Williams 1, Brosius 1, Posada 1. **Oakland (7)**—Stairs 1, Saenz 1, J. Giambi 1, Tejada 1, J. Giambi 1, Chavez 1, Porter 1. **Seattle (7)**—Cameron 2, Henderson 1, Buhner 1, Martinez 1, Olerud 1, Bell 1. **Tampa Bay (76)**—Vaughn 13, McGriff 10, Flaherty 7, Cox 7, Williams 6, Trammell 5, J. Guillen 5, Canseco 4, DiFelice 4, Timmons 3, Huff 3, Castilla 2, Johnson 2, Smith 2, O. Guillen 1, D. Martinez 1, Winn 1. **Texas (7)**—Palmeiro 1, Rodriguez 1, Clayton 1, Curtis 1, Catalanotto 1, Mateo 1, Lamb 1. **Toronto (10)**—Mondesi 2, Gonzalez 2, Batista 2, Cruz 2, Fullmer 2.

AT TEXAS (209):

Anaheim (12)—Glaus 4, Salmon 3, Anderson 2, Vaughn 1, Erstad 1, Spiezio 1. **Arizona (4)**—Bell 1, Finley 1, Gonzalez 1, Counsell 1. **Baltimore (4)**—Anderson 2, Myers 1, Bordick 1. **Boston (7)**—Everett 4, Offerman 1, Garciaparra 1, Varitek 1. **Chicago (6)**—Lee 2, Thomas 1, C. Johnson 1, Durham 1, Singleton 1. **Cleveland (5)**—Alomar 1, Segui 1, Fryman 1, Thome 1, M. Ramirez 1. **Detroit (4)**—Palmer 2, Gonzalez 1, Encarnacion 1. **Kansas City (4)**—Zaun 1, Damon 1, Dye 1, Beltran 1. **Minnesota (5)**—Coomer 3, Jensen 1, Koskie 1. **New York (11)**—Posada 3, Williams 2, Jeter 2, O'Neill 1, Justice 1, Brosius

1, Bellinger 1. **Oakland (10)**—J. Giambi 2, J. Giambi 2, Stairs 1, Grieve 1, Long 1, Hernandez 1, Menechino 1, Piatt 1. **San Diego (1)**—Boone 1. **Seattle (9)**—Buhner 2, Martinez 2, A. Rodriguez 2, Cameron 2, Bell 1. **Tampa Bay (13)**—McGriff 4, J. Guillen 3, Williams 2, O. Guillen 1, Canseco 1, DiFelice 1, Smith 1. **Texas (104)**—Palmeiro 26, Rodriguez 16, Kapler 11, Clayton 9, Catalanotto 6, Curtis 5, Alicea 4, Segui 4, Lamb 4, Haselman 3, Greer 3, McDonald 3, Mateo 3, Knorr 2, Ledee 2, Martinez 1, Valdes 1, Sheldon 1. **Toronto (10)**—Fletcher 3, Cruz 3, Grebeck 1, Gonzalez 1, Stewart 1, Batista 1.

AT TORONTO (226):

Anaheim (9)—Erstad 2, Glaus 2, Gant 1, Vaughn 1, Walbeck 1, Anderson 1, Kennedy 1. **Baltimore (4)**—Baines 1, Clark 1, Belle 1, DeShields 1. **Boston (3)**—Everett 1, Garciaparra 1, Nixon 1. **Chicago (3)**—Thomas 1, Perry 1, Abbott 1. **Cleveland (4)**—Alomar 1, Justice 1, Thome 1, M. Ramirez 1. **Detroit (9)**—Clark 3, Gonzalez 1, Becker 1, Higginson 1, D. Cruz 1, Encarnacion 1, Fick 1. **Kansas City (5)**—Randa 2, Damon 1, Sweeney 1, Dye 1. **Minnesota (4)**—Guzman 2, Cummings 1, Coomer 1. **Montreal (3)**—Stevens 1, Widger 1, V. Guerrero 1. **New York A.L. (7)**—Williams 3, Posada 2, Hill 1, Justice 1. **New York N.L. (5)**—Harris 1, Bell 1, Pratt 1, Piazza 1, McEwing 1. **Oakland (9)**—Tejada 3, Long 2, Stanley 1, Stairs 1, J. Giambi 1, Grieve 1. **Philadelphia (4)**—Gant 2, Rolen 1, Burrell 1. **Seattle (13)**—A. Rodriguez 4, Buhner 2, Martinez 2, McLemore 1, Martin 1, Wilson 1, Mabry 1, Cameron 1. **Tampa Bay (7)**—McGriff 2, Canseco 1, Flaherty 1, Williams 1, Timmons 1, Hall 1. **Texas (3)**—Palmeiro 1, Haselman 1, Kapler 1. **Toronto (134)**—Delgado 30, Batista 25, Fullmer 16, Cruz 15, Stewart 12, Fletcher 10, Mondesi 10, Gonzalez 5, Cordova 3, Grebeck 2, T. Greene 2, Martinez 1, A. Castillo 1, Bush 1, Woodward 1.

2000 N.L. STATISTICS

Batting

Designated hitting

Pinch-hitting

Pitching

Fielding

Miscellaneous

BATTING

TEAM

Team	Avg.	G	TPA	AB	R	H	TB	2B	3B	HR	RBI	SH	SF	HP	BB	IBB	SO	SB	CS	GDP	LOB	ShO	Slg.	OBP
Colorado	.294	162	6453	5660	968	1664	2573	320	53	161	905	75	75	42	601	64	907	131	61	126	1198	8	.455	.362
San Francisco	.278	162	6418	5519	925	1535	2605	304	44	226	889	73	66	51	709	60	1032	79	39	131	1213	5	.472	.362
Houston	.278	162	6444	5570	938	1547	2655	289	36	249	900	57	61	83	673	57	1129	114	52	154	1171	3	.477	.361
Cincinnati	.274	163	6372	5635	825	1545	2519	302	36	200	794	56	58	64	559	60	995	100	38	137	1189	0	.447	.343
Atlanta	.271	162	6275	5489	810	1490	2353	274	26	179	758	87	45	59	595	38	1010	148	56	127	1192	7	.429	.346
St. Louis	.270	162	6369	5478	887	1481	2495	259	25	235	841	79	53	84	675	33	1253	87	51	116	1214	5	.455	.356
Pittsburgh	.267	162	6369	5643	793	1506	2392	320	31	168	749	59	37	66	564	41	1032	86	40	133	1202	7	.424	.339
Montreal	.266	162	6152	5535	738	1475	2389	310	35	178	705	78	34	29	476	53	1048	58	48	111	1100	9	.432	.326
Arizona	.265	162	6240	5527	792	1466	2373	282	44	179	756	61	58	59	535	37	975	97	44	114	1128	7	.429	.333
New York	.263	162	6327	5486	807	1445	2360	281	20	198	761	70	51	45	675	42	1037	66	46	122	1214	9	.430	.346
Florida	.262	161	6202	5509	731	1441	2253	274	29	160	691	42	51	60	540	39	1184	168	55	100	1168	8	.409	.331
Los Angeles	.257	162	6312	5481	798	1408	2362	265	28	211	756	66	46	51	668	42	1083	95	42	129	1188	11	.431	.341
Chicago	.256	162	6397	5577	764	1426	2293	272	23	183	722	89	45	54	632	50	1120	93	37	114	1215	8	.411	.335
San Diego	.254	162	6290	5560	752	1413	2237	279	37	157	714	39	43	46	602	50	1177	131	53	123	1155	7	.402	.330
Philadelphia	.251	162	6273	5511	708	1384	2202	300	40	144	680	70	37	44	611	40	1117	102	30	115	1209	8	.400	.329
Milwaukee	.246	163	6354	5563	740	1366	2244	297	25	177	708	61	49	61	620	47	1245	72	44	126	1183	7	.403	.325
Totals	.266	1297	101247	88743	12976	23594	38305	4632	532	3005	12317	1062	809	898	9735	753	17344	1627	736	1978	18939	109	.432	.342

INDIVIDUAL
TOP QUALIFIERS FOR BATTING CHAMPIONSHIP

Minimum 502 plate appearances. *Lefthanded batter. †Switch-hitter.

Player, Team	Avg.	G	TPA	AB	R	H	TB	2B	3B	HR	RBI	SH	SF	HP	BB	IBB	SO	SB	CS	GDP	Slg.	OBP
Helton, Todd, Col.*	.372	160	697	580	138	216	405	59	2	42	147	0	10	4	103	22	61	5	3	12	.698	.463
Alou, Moises, Hou.	.355	126	517	454	82	161	283	28	2	30	114	0	9	2	52	4	45	3	3	21	.623	.416
Guerrero, Vladimir, Mon.	.345	154	641	571	101	197	379	28	11	44	123	0	4	8	58	23	74	9	10	15	.664	.410
Hammonds, Jeffrey, Col.	.335	122	511	454	94	152	240	24	2	20	106	2	6	5	44	4	83	14	7	11	.529	.395
Castillo, Luis, Fla.†	.334	136	626	539	101	180	209	17	3	2	17	9	0	0	78	0	86	62	22	11	.388	.418
Kent, Jeff, S.F.	.334	159	695	587	114	196	350	41	7	33	125	0	9	9	90	6	107	12	9	17	.596	.424
Vidro, Jose, Mon.†	.330	153	663	606	101	200	327	51	2	24	97	0	6	2	49	4	69	5	4	17	.540	.379
Cirillo, Jeff, Col.	.326	157	684	598	111	195	285	53	2	11	115	1	12	6	67	4	72	3	4	19	.477	.392
Sheffield, Gary, L.A.	.325	141	612	501	105	163	322	24	3	43	109	0	6	4	101	7	71	4	6	13	.643	.438
Piazza, Mike, N.Y.	.324	136	545	482	90	156	296	26	0	38	113	0	2	3	58	10	69	4	2	15	.614	.398
Alfonzo, Edgardo, N.Y.	.324	150	650	544	109	176	295	40	2	25	94	0	6	5	95	1	70	3	2	12	.542	.425
Sosa, Sammy, Chi.	.320	156	705	604	106	193	383	38	1	50	138	0	8	2	91	19	168	7	4	12	.634	.406
Kendall, Jason, Pit.	.320	152	678	579	112	185	272	33	6	14	58	1	4	15	79	3	79	22	12	13	.470	.412
Abreu, Bobby, Phi.*	.316	154	680	576	103	182	319	42	10	25	79	0	3	1	100	9	116	28	8	12	.554	.416
Giles, Brian S., Pit.*	.315	156	688	559	111	176	332	37	7	35	123	0	8	7	114	13	69	6	0	15	.594	.432

DEPARTMENTAL LEADERS: G—Gonzalez, Ari., Green, L.A., Perez, Col., 162; AB—A. Jones, Atl., 656; R—Bagwell, Hou., 152; H—Helton, Col., 216; TB—Helton, Col., 405; 1B—Castillo, Fla., 158; 2B—Helton, Col., 59; 3B—Womack, Ari., 14; HR—Sosa, Chi., 50; RBI—Helton, Col., 147; SH—Gutierrez, Chi., 16; SF—Snow, S.F., 14; HP—Vina, St.L., 28 BB—Bonds, S.F., 117; IBB—V. Guerrero, Mon., 23; SO—Wilson, Fla., 187; SB—Castillo, Fla., 62; CS—Castillo, Fla., 22; GIDP—Alou, Hou., 21; Slg. Pct.—Helton, Col., .698; OB. Pct.—Helton, Col., .463.

ALL PLAYERS

*Lefthanded batter. †Switch-hitter.

Player, Team	Avg.	G	TPA	AB	R	H	TB	2B	3B	HR	RBI	SH	SF	HP	BB	IBB	SO	SB	CS	GDP	Slg.	OBP
Abbott, Kurt, N.Y.	.217	79	173	157	22	34	61	7	1	6	12	0	1	1	14	2	51	1	1	2	.389	.283
Abreu, Bobby, Phi.*	.316	154	680	576	103	182	319	42	10	25	79	0	3	1	100	9	116	28	8	12	.554	.416
Acevedo, Juan, Mil.	.000	62	2	1	1	0	0	0	0	0	0	1	0	0	0	0	1	0	0	0	.000	.500
Adams, Terry, S.A.	.000	66	3	2	0	0	0	0	0	0	0	1	0	0	0	0	1	0	0	0	.000	.000
Agbayani, Benny, N.Y.	.289	119	414	350	59	101	167	19	1	15	60	0	3	7	54	2	68	5	5	6	.477	.391
Alfonzo, Edgardo, N.Y.	.324	150	650	544	109	176	295	40	2	25	94	0	6	5	95	1	70	3	2	12	.542	.425
Allen, Dusty, S.D.	.000	9	14	12	0	0	0	0	0	0	0	0	0	0	2	0	5	0	0	1	.000	.143
Almanza, Armando, Fla.*	.000	67	2	1	0	0	0	0	0	0	0	0	0	0	0	0	0	0	0	1	.000	.000
Almanzar, Carlos, S.D.	.000	62	3	3	0	0	0	0	0	0	0	0	0	0	0	0	2	0	0	1	.000	.000
Alou, Moises, Hou.	.355	126	517	454	82	161	283	28	2	30	114	0	9	2	52	4	45	3	3	21	.623	.416
Alvarez, Clemente, Phi.	.200	2	5	5	1	1	1	0	0	0	0	0	0	0	0	0	1	0	0	0	.200	.200
Alvarez, Gabe, S.D.	.154	11	14	13	1	2	3	1	0	0	0	0	0	0	1	0	1	0	0	0	.231	.214
Anderson, Brian, Ari.†	.188	37	81	69	4	13	16	3	0	0	4	9	2	0	1	0	10	0	0	1	.232	.194
Anderson, Jimmy, Pit.*	.140	27	54	50	5	7	8	1	0	0	1	4	0	0	0	0	11	0	0	0	.160	.140
Anderson, Marlon, Phi.*	.228	41	174	162	10	37	50	8	1	1	15	0	0	0	12	0	22	2	2	5	.309	.282
Andrews, Shane, Chi.	.229	66	222	192	25	44	91	5	0	14	39	0	1	2	27	1	59	1	1	9	.474	.329
Ankiel, Rick, St.L.*	.250	35	73	68	8	17	26	1	1	2	9	1	0	0	4	0	20	0	0	1	.382	.292
Arias, Alex, Phi.	.187	70	180	155	17	29	44	9	0	2	15	3	3	3	16	2	28	1	0	1	.284	.271
Armas, Tony Jr., Mon.	.038	17	30	26	1	1	1	0	0	0	1	3	0	0	1	0	12	0	0	0	.038	.074
Arnold, Jamie, L.A.-Chi.	.111	14	10	9	0	1	2	1	0	0	0	0	0	0	1	0	3	0	0	0	.222	.200
Arrojo, Rolando, Col.	.107	19	32	28	2	3	4	1	0	0	3	3	0	0	1	0	13	0	0	0	.143	.138
Arroyo, Bronson, Pit.	.143	21	23	21	2	3	5	2	0	0	2	0	0	0	0	0	10	0	0	0	.238	.143
Ashby, Andy, Phi.-Atl.	.148	32	72	61	2	9	9	0	0	0	6	9	0	0	2	0	22	0	0	1	.148	.175
Astacio, Pedro, Col.	.098	32	84	82	2	8	8	0	0	0	6	1	0	0	1	0	25	0	0	1	.098	.108
Aurilia, Rich, S.F.	.271	141	571	509	67	138	226	24	2	20	79	4	4	0	54	2	90	1	2	15	.444	.339
Aven, Bruce, Pit.-L.A.	.250	81	176	168	20	42	74	11	0	7	29	0	0	0	8	0	39	2	3	4	.440	.284

Player, Team	Avg.	G	TPA	AB	R	H	TB	2B	3B	HR	RBI	SH	SF	HP	BB	IBB	SO	SB	CS	GDP	Slg.	OBP
Aybar, Manny, Col.-Cin.-Fla. ..	.000	54	9	6	1	0	0	0	0	0	0	1	0	0	2	0	3	0	0	0	.000	.250
Bagwell, Jeff, Hou.	.310	159	719	590	152	183	363	37	1	47	132	0	7	15	107	11	116	9	6	19	.615	.424
Bako, Paul, Hou.-Fla.-Atl.* ...	.226	81	251	221	18	50	68	10	1	2	20	1	1	1	27	10	64	0	0	6	.308	.312
Barajas, Rod, Ari.	.231	5	13	13	1	3	6	0	1	0	3	0	0	0	0	0	4	0	0	0	.462	.231
Barker, Glen, Hou.	.224	84	77	67	18	15	25	2	1	2	6	2	0	1	7	0	23	9	6	0	.373	.307
Barker, Kevin, Mil.*	.220	40	122	100	14	22	33	5	0	2	9	0	1	1	20	0	21	1	0	1	.330	.352
Barrett, Michael, Mon.	.214	89	297	271	28	58	78	15	1	1	22	1	1	1	23	5	35	0	1	7	.288	.277
Bartee, Kimera, Cin.	.000	11	5	4	2	0	0	0	0	0	0	0	0	1	0	0	2	1	0	0	.000	.000
Batista, Miguel, Mon.*	.000	4	2	1	0	0	0	0	0	0	0	1	0	0	0	0	1	0	0	0	.000	.500
Bautista, Danny, Fla.-Ari.	.285	131	388	351	54	100	167	20	7	11	59	4	5	3	25	4	50	6	2	11	.476	.333
Belinda, Stan, Col.-Atl.	.000	57	1	1	0	0	0	0	0	0	0	0	0	0	0	0	1	0	0	0	.000	.000
Bell, Derek, N.Y.	.266	144	622	546	87	145	232	31	1	18	69	2	3	6	65	0	125	8	4	14	.425	.348
Bell, Jay, Ari.	.267	149	649	565	87	151	247	30	6	18	68	6	5	3	70	0	88	7	3	7	.437	.348
Bell, Mike, Cin.	.222	19	31	27	5	6	12	0	0	2	4	0	0	0	4	0	7	0	0	0	.444	.323
Bell, Rob, Cin.	.067	26	49	45	1	3	4	1	0	0	0	3	0	0	1	0	27	0	0	1	.089	.087
Belliard, Ron, Mil.	.263	152	667	571	83	150	222	30	9	8	54	4	7	3	82	4	84	7	5	12	.389	.354
Beltre, Adrian, L.A.	.290	138	575	510	71	148	242	30	2	20	85	3	4	2	56	2	80	12	5	13	.475	.360
Benard, Marvin, S.F.*	.263	149	633	560	102	147	222	27	6	12	55	2	2	6	63	0	97	22	7	4	.396	.342
Benes, Alan, St.L.	.500	30	4	4	0	2	3	1	0	0	0	0	0	0	0	0	1	0	0	0	.750	.500
Benes, Andy, St.L.	.080	30	60	50	1	4	7	0	0	1	1	6	0	0	4	0	19	0	0	3	.140	.143
Benjamin, Mike, Pit.	.270	93	255	233	28	63	91	18	2	2	19	6	1	3	12	0	45	5	4	4	.391	.313
Bennett, Gary, Phi.	.243	31	89	74	8	18	29	5	0	2	5	0	0	2	13	0	15	0	0	3	.392	.371
Benson, Kris, Pit.	.092	32	79	65	3	6	8	2	0	0	1	9	0	1	4	0	29	0	0	1	.123	.157
Bere, Jason, Mil.	.205	20	40	39	3	8	10	0	1	0	2	1	0	0	0	0	17	0	0	1	.256	.205
Berg, Dave, Fla.	.252	82	245	210	23	53	72	14	1	1	21	1	4	5	25	0	46	3	0	5	.343	.340
Bergeron, Peter, Mon.*	.245	148	592	518	80	127	181	25	7	5	31	14	2	0	58	0	100	11	13	4	.349	.320
Berkman, Lance, Hou.†	.297	114	417	353	76	105	198	28	1	21	67	0	7	1	56	1	73	6	2	6	.561	.388
Berroa, Geronimo, L.A.	.258	24	35	31	2	8	10	0	1	0	5	0	0	0	4	1	8	0	0	2	.323	.343
Berry, Sean, Mil.	.152	32	50	46	1	7	12	2	0	1	2	0	0	0	4	0	13	0	1	1	.261	.220
Bichette, Dante, Cin.	.295	125	514	461	67	136	215	27	2	16	76	1	7	4	41	3	69	5	2	18	.466	.353
Biggio, Craig, Hou.	.268	101	466	377	67	101	148	13	5	8	35	7	5	16	61	3	73	12	2	10	.393	.388
Blanco, Henry, Mil.	.236	93	324	284	29	67	112	24	0	7	31	0	4	0	36	6	60	0	3	9	.394	.318
Blank, Matt, Mon.*	.000	13	1	1	0	0	0	0	0	0	0	0	0	0	0	0	0	0	0	0	.000	.000
Blum, Geoff, Mon.†	.283	124	379	343	40	97	154	20	2	11	45	3	4	3	26	2	60	1	4	4	.449	.335
Bocachica, Hiram, L.A.	.300	8	10	10	2	3	3	0	0	0	0	0	0	0	0	0	2	0	0	0	.300	.300
Boehringer, Brian, S.D.†	.250	7	5	4	0	1	2	1	0	0	2	1	0	0	0	0	1	0	0	0	.500	.250
Bogar, Tim, Hou.	.207	110	351	304	32	63	97	9	2	7	33	5	4	3	35	7	56	1	1	15	.319	.292
Bohanon, Brian, Col.*	.208	35	67	53	6	11	20	3	0	2	11	11	1	0	2	0	14	0	0	0	.377	.232
Bonds, Barry, S.F.*	.306	143	607	480	129	147	330	28	4	49	106	0	7	3	117	22	77	11	3	6	.688	.440
Bones, Ricky, Fla.	.000	56	4	2	1	0	0	0	0	0	0	1	0	1	0	0	1	0	0	0	.000	.250
Bonilla, Bobby, Atl.†	.255	114	278	239	23	61	95	13	3	5	28	0	1	1	37	2	51	0	0	3	.397	.356
Boone, Aaron, Cin.	.285	84	331	291	44	83	137	18	0	12	43	2	4	10	24	1	52	6	1	5	.471	.356
Boone, Bret, S.D.	.251	127	525	463	61	116	195	18	2	19	74	0	7	5	50	7	97	8	4	11	.421	.326
Bordick, Mike, N.Y.	.260	56	211	192	18	50	70	8	0	4	21	2	0	2	15	0	28	3	1	4	.365	.321
Bottenfield, Kent, Phi.	.000	8	17	14	2	0	0	0	0	0	0	3	0	0	0	0	3	0	0	0	.000	.000
Bradley, Milton, Mon.†	.221	42	171	154	20	34	50	8	1	2	15	1	1	1	14	0	32	2	1	3	.325	.288
Bragg, Darren, Col.*	.221	71	169	149	16	33	51	7	1	3	21	0	3	0	17	1	41	4	1	3	.342	.296
Branson, Jeff, L.A.*	.235	18	18	17	3	4	5	1	0	0	0	0	0	0	1	0	6	0	0	1	.294	.278
Brock, Tarrik, Chi.*	.167	13	16	12	1	2	2	0	0	0	0	0	0	0	4	0	4	1	1	0	.167	.375
Brock, Chris, Phi.	.222	63	11	9	1	2	6	1	0	1	2	2	0	0	0	0	2	0	0	0	.667	.222
Brogna, Rico, Phi.*	.248	38	139	129	12	32	49	14	0	1	13	0	1	2	7	1	28	1	0	4	.380	.295
Brown, Adrian, Pit.†	.315	104	340	308	64	97	133	18	3	4	28	2	1	0	29	1	34	13	1	1	.432	.373
Brown, Brant, Fla.-Chi.*	.173	95	178	162	11	28	50	7	0	5	16	1	1	1	13	0	62	3	1	3	.309	.237
Brown, Emil, Pit.	.218	50	135	119	13	26	40	5	0	3	16	1	1	3	11	0	34	3	1	3	.336	.299
Brown, Kevin, L.A.	.076	33	84	66	2	5	5	0	0	0	3	14	0	2	2	0	29	0	0	0	.076	.129
Brown, Kevin L., Mil.	.235	5	18	17	3	4	7	3	0	0	1	0	0	0	1	0	5	0	0	0	.412	.278
Brown, Roosevelt, Chi.*	.352	45	98	91	11	32	49	8	0	3	14	0	2	1	4	0	22	0	1	0	.538	.378
Brownson, Mark, Phi.*	.000	2	1	0	0	0	0	0	0	0	0	0	0	0	1	0	0	0	0	0	.000	1.000
Brunette, Justin, St.L.*	1.000	4	1	1	0	1	1	0	0	0	0	0	0	0	0	0	0	0	0	0	1.000	1.000
Bruske, Jim, Mil.	.000	15	1	1	0	0	0	0	0	0	0	0	0	0	0	0	0	0	0	0	.000	.000
Buford, Damon, Chi.	.251	150	556	495	64	124	193	18	3	15	48	4	2	8	47	3	118	4	6	9	.390	.324
Burkett, John, Atl.	.143	31	51	42	2	6	7	1	0	0	3	6	0	0	3	0	15	0	0	0	.167	.200
Burks, Ellis, S.F.	.344	122	458	393	74	135	238	21	5	24	96	0	8	1	56	5	49	5	1	10	.606	.419
Burnett, A.J., Fla.	.280	13	30	25	3	7	13	1	1	1	3	2	0	0	3	0	10	0	0	2	.520	.357
Burnitz, Jeromy, Mil.*	.232	161	686	564	91	131	257	29	2	31	98	0	9	14	99	10	121	6	4	12	.456	.356
Burrell, Pat, Phi.	.260	111	474	408	57	106	189	27	1	18	79	0	2	1	63	2	139	0	0	5	.463	.359
Byrd, Paul, Phi.	.150	17	24	20	2	3	3	0	0	0	0	2	0	1	1	0	6	0	0	0	.150	.227
Cabrera, Alex, Ari.	.263	31	87	80	10	21	40	2	1	5	14	0	2	1	4	0	21	0	0	3	.500	.299
Cabrera, Jose, Hou.	.000	52	1	1	0	0	0	0	0	0	0	0	0	0	0	0	1	0	0	0	.000	.000
Cabrera, Orlando, Mon.	.237	125	454	422	47	100	166	25	1	13	55	3	3	1	25	3	28	4	4	12	.393	.279
Caminiti, Ken, Hou.†	.303	59	253	208	42	63	121	13	0	15	45	0	2	1	42	8	37	3	0	7	.582	.419
Cammack, Eric, N.Y.	1.000	8	1	1	0	1	3	0	1	0	1	0	0	0	0	0	0	0	0	0	3.000	1.000
Carpenter, Bubba, Col.*	.222	15	31	27	4	6	15	0	0	3	5	0	0	0	4	0	13	0	0	0	.556	.323
Carrara, Giovanni, Col.	.000	8	1	1	0	0	0	0	0	0	0	0	0	0	0	0	1	0	0	0	.000	.000
Casanova, Raul, Mil.†	.247	86	265	231	20	57	94	13	3	6	36	2	2	4	26	1	48	1	2	5	.407	.331
Casey, Sean, Cin.*	.315	133	545	480	69	151	248	33	2	20	85	0	6	7	52	4	80	1	0	16	.517	.385
Castillo, Luis, Fla.†	.334	136	626	539	101	180	209	17	3	2	17	9	0	0	78	0	86	62	22	11	.388	.418
Castro, Juan, Cin.	.241	82	244	224	20	54	82	12	2	4	23	4	2	0	14	1	33	0	2	9	.366	.283
Castro, Ramon, Fla.	.239	50	157	138	10	33	43	4	0	2	14	0	2	1	16	7	36	0	0	1	.312	.318
Cedeno, Roger, Hou.†	.282	74	305	259	54	73	103	2	5	6	26	2	1	0	43	0	47	25	11	6	.398	.383
Charles, Frank, Hou.	.429	4	7	7	1	3	4	1	0	0	2	0	0	0	0	0	2	0	0	0	.571	.429
Chavez, Raul, Hou.	.256	14	47	43	3	11	16	2	0	1	5	0	1	0	3	2	6	0	0	5	.372	.298

Player, Team	Avg.	G	TPA	AB	R	H	TB	2B	3B	HR	RBI	SH	SF	HP	BB	IBB	SO	SB	CS	GDP	Slg.	OBP
Chen, Bruce, Atl.-Phi.*	.033	37	38	30	0	1	1	0	0	0	1	7	0	0	1	0	20	0	0	0	.033	.065
Chouinard, Bobby, Col.	.333	31	3	3	1	1	1	0	0	0	0	0	0	0	0	0	1	0	0	0	.333	.333
Cirillo, Jeff, Col.	.326	157	684	598	111	195	285	53	2	11	115	1	12	6	67	4	72	3	4	19	.477	.392
Clapinski, Chris, Fla.†	.306	34	55	49	12	15	24	4	1	1	7	1	0	0	5	0	7	0	0	1	.490	.370
Clark, Brady, Cin.	.273	11	11	11	1	3	4	1	0	0	2	0	0	0	0	0	2	0	0	1	.364	.273
Clark, Will, St.L.*	.345	51	197	171	29	59	112	15	1	12	42	0	1	3	22	0	24	1	0	3	.655	.426
Clement, Matt, S.D.	.067	34	69	60	3	4	6	0	1	0	2	5	0	0	4	0	33	0	0	0	.100	.125
Clontz, Brad, Pit.	.000	5	1	0	1	0	0	0	0	0	0	1	0	0	0	0	0	0	0	0	.000	1.000
Coggin, David, Phi.	.000	5	8	7	0	0	0	0	0	0	0	1	0	0	0	0	4	0	0	0	.000	.000
Colbrunn, Greg, Ari.	.313	116	385	329	48	103	172	22	1	15	57	0	3	10	43	2	45	0	1	13	.523	.405
Collier, Lou, Mil.	.219	14	39	32	9	7	11	1	0	1	2	0	1	0	6	0	4	0	0	1	.344	.333
Conti, Jason, Ari.*	.231	47	99	91	11	21	34	4	3	1	15	0	1	7	2	30	3	0	2	.374	.293
Cook, Dennis, N.Y.*	.000	68	1	0	0	0	0	0	0	0	0	1	0	0	0	0	0	0	0	0	.000	.000
Coquillette, Trace, Mon.	.203	34	67	59	6	12	19	4	0	1	8	0	1	0	7	0	19	0	0	2	.322	.284
Cora, Alex, L.A.*	.238	109	394	353	39	84	126	18	6	4	32	6	2	7	26	4	53	4	1	6	.357	.302
Cordero, Wil, Pit.	.282	89	378	348	46	98	176	24	3	16	51	0	1	4	25	1	58	1	2	11	.506	.336
Cordova, Francisco, Pit.	.114	18	37	35	0	4	4	0	0	0	3	0	0	0	2	0	15	0	0	1	.114	.162
Cornelius, Reid, Fla.	.135	23	41	37	1	5	7	2	0	0	1	4	0	0	0	0	12	0	0	1	.189	.135
Counsell, Craig, Ari.*	.316	67	176	152	23	48	64	8	1	2	11	1	1	2	20	0	18	3	3	4	.421	.400
Crespo, Felipe, S.F.†	.290	89	150	131	17	38	58	6	1	4	29	2	3	4	10	2	23	3	2	3	.443	.351
Cromer, D.T., Cin.*	.340	35	51	47	7	16	26	4	0	2	8	1	1	1	1	1	14	0	0	0	.553	.360
Cromer, Tripp, Hou.	.125	9	10	8	2	1	1	0	0	0	0	1	0	0	1	0	1	0	0	0	.125	.222
Croushore, Rick, Col.	1.000	6	2	1	0	1	1	0	0	0	0	0	0	0	0	0	0	0	0	0	1.000	1.000
Cruz, Ivan, Pit.*	.091	8	11	11	0	1	1	0	0	0	0	0	0	0	0	0	8	0	0	1	.091	.091
Cunnane, Will, S.D.	.143	27	7	7	0	1	2	1	0	0	0	0	0	0	0	0	3	0	0	0	.286	.143
Daal, Omar, Ari.-Phi.*	.267	32	54	45	3	12	18	3	0	1	6	5	0	0	4	0	8	0	0	1	.400	.327
D'Amico, Jeff C., Mil.	.091	23	54	44	2	4	8	1	0	1	2	6	1	0	3	0	19	0	0	3	.182	.143
Darensbourg, Vic, Fla.*	.250	56	8	8	0	2	2	0	0	0	0	0	0	0	0	0	2	0	0	0	.250	.250
Darr, Mike C., S.D.*	.268	58	228	205	21	55	80	14	4	1	30	0	0	0	23	1	45	9	1	9	.390	.342
Davis, Eric, St.L.	.303	92	293	254	38	77	109	14	0	6	40	0	2	1	36	0	60	1	1	7	.429	.393
Davis, Ben, S.D.†	.223	43	148	130	12	29	44	6	0	3	14	3	1	0	14	1	35	1	1	2	.338	.297
Davis, Russ, S.F.	.261	80	192	180	27	47	79	5	0	9	24	0	1	2	9	0	29	0	3	1	.439	.302
Dawkins, Gookie, Cin.	.220	14	44	41	5	9	11	2	0	0	3	1	0	0	2	1	7	0	0	3	.268	.256
DeHaan, Kory, S.D.*	.204	90	110	103	19	21	34	7	0	2	13	1	1	0	5	0	39	4	2	2	.330	.239
DeJean, Mike, Col.	.000	54	2	2	0	0	0	0	0	0	0	0	0	0	0	0	0	0	0	0	.000	.000
De La Rosa, Tomas, Mon.	.288	32	77	66	7	19	30	3	1	2	9	3	0	1	7	0	11	2	1	2	.455	.365
Dellucci, David, Ari.*	.300	34	54	50	2	15	18	3	0	0	2	0	0	0	4	0	9	0	2	1	.360	.352
De Los Santos, Valerio, Mil.*	.000	66	6	6	0	0	0	0	0	0	0	0	0	0	0	0	3	0	0	0	.000	.000
Del Toro, Miguel, S.F.	.500	9	2	2	1	1	1	0	0	0	2	0	0	0	0	0	0	0	0	0	.500	.500
Dempster, Ryan, Fla.	.078	33	82	77	3	6	8	2	0	0	2	4	0	0	1	0	29	0	0	0	.104	.090
DeRosa, Mark, Atl.	.308	22	15	13	9	4	5	1	0	0	3	0	0	0	2	0	1	0	0	0	.385	.400
Dessens, Elmer, Cin.	.100	40	48	40	6	4	4	0	0	0	0	1	0	0	7	0	16	0	0	0	.100	.234
Dipoto, Jerry, Col.	.000	17	1	1	0	0	0	0	0	0	0	0	0	0	0	0	0	0	0	0	.000	.000
Donnels, Chris, L.A.*	.294	27	41	34	8	10	25	3	0	4	9	0	1	0	6	1	7	0	0	3	.735	.390
Dotel, Octavio, Hou.	.031	50	40	32	1	1	1	0	0	0	0	7	0	0	1	0	16	0	0	0	.031	.061
Downs, Scott, Chi.-Mon.*	.071	19	34	28	2	2	2	0	0	0	1	4	0	0	2	0	10	0	0	0	.071	.133
Dreifort, Darren, L.A.	.162	32	71	68	5	11	23	3	0	3	8	1	0	1	1	0	25	0	0	1	.338	.186
Drew, J.D., St.L.*	.295	135	486	407	73	120	195	17	2	18	57	5	1	6	67	4	99	17	9	3	.479	.401
Ducey, Rob, Phi.*	.197	112	183	152	24	30	54	4	1	6	25	0	2	0	29	1	47	1	0	1	.355	.322
Dunston, Shawon, St.L.	.250	98	231	216	28	54	105	11	2	12	43	4	2	3	6	0	47	3	1	11	.486	.278
Durazo, Erubiel, Ari.*	.265	67	233	196	35	52	87	11	0	8	33	0	2	1	34	2	43	1	0	3	.444	.373
Eaton, Adam, S.D.	.289	23	45	38	6	11	13	2	0	0	4	0	0	1	6	0	10	2	0	1	.342	.400
Echevarria, Angel, Col.-Mil.	.196	41	58	51	3	10	15	2	0	1	6	0	0	0	7	0	11	0	0	1	.294	.293
Edmonds, Jim, St.L.*	.295	152	643	525	129	155	306	25	0	42	108	1	8	6	103	3	167	10	3	5	.583	.411
Elarton, Scott, Hou.	.159	30	72	63	6	10	12	2	0	0	6	6	0	2	1	0	20	0	0	2	.190	.197
Elster, Kevin, L.A.	.227	80	259	220	29	50	100	8	0	14	32	1	0	0	38	5	52	0	0	1	.455	.341
Ensberg, Morgan, Hou.	.286	4	7	7	0	2	2	0	0	0	0	0	0	0	0	0	1	0	0	0	.286	.286
Erdos, Todd, S.D.	.000	22	1	1	0	0	0	0	0	0	0	0	0	0	0	0	0	0	0	0	.000	.000
Estalella, Bobby, S.F.	.234	106	361	299	45	70	140	22	3	14	53	0	3	2	57	9	92	3	0	4	.468	.357
Estes, Shawn, S.F.	.206	32	81	68	4	14	21	4	0	1	10	11	0	0	2	0	28	0	0	2	.309	.229
Estrada, Horacio, Mil.*	.143	7	8	7	1	1	1	0	0	0	1	0	0	0	0	0	2	0	0	0	.143	.143
Eusebio, Tony, Hou.	.280	74	249	218	24	61	100	18	0	7	33	0	2	4	25	2	45	0	0	8	.459	.361
Farnsworth, Kyle, Chi.	.071	46	16	14	0	1	2	1	0	0	0	2	0	0	0	0	6	0	0	0	.143	.071
Feliz, Pedro, S.F.	.286	8	7	7	1	2	2	0	0	0	0	0	0	0	0	0	2	0	0	0	.286	.286
Fernandez, Alex, Fla.	.118	9	20	17	1	2	3	1	0	0	3	0	0	0	3	0	10	0	0	2	.176	.250
Fernandez, Osvaldo, Cin.	.091	15	29	22	0	2	2	0	0	0	1	5	0	0	2	0	10	0	0	0	.091	.167
Figueroa, Nelson, Ari.†	.333	3	4	3	1	1	1	0	0	0	0	1	0	0	0	0	1	0	0	0	.333	.333
Finley, Steve, Ari.*	.280	152	623	539	100	151	293	27	5	35	96	2	9	8	65	7	87	12	6	9	.544	.361
Floyd, Cliff, Fla.*	.300	121	487	420	75	126	222	30	0	22	91	0	9	8	50	5	82	24	3	4	.529	.378
Fox, Andy, Ari.-Fla.*	.232	100	275	250	29	58	82	8	2	4	20	0	3	22	4	53	10	4	2	.328	.302
Franco, John, N.Y.*	.000	62	1	1	0	0	0	0	0	0	0	0	0	0	0	0	1	0	0	0	.000	.000
Franco, Matt, N.Y.	.239	101	157	134	9	32	42	4	0	2	14	1	1	0	21	3	22	0	0	3	.313	.340
Franklin, Wayne, Hou.*	.000	25	2	2	0	0	0	0	0	0	0	0	0	0	0	0	0	0	0	0	.000	.000
Frias, Hanley, Ari.†	.205	75	129	112	18	23	34	5	0	2	6	0	0	0	17	0	18	2	2	3	.304	.310
Frye, Jeff, Col.	.356	37	98	87	14	31	37	6	0	0	3	1	1	1	8	0	16	4	0	3	.425	.412
Fultz, Aaron, S.F.*	.333	58	7	6	0	2	2	0	0	0	0	1	0	0	0	0	1	0	0	2	.333	.333
Furcal, Rafael, Atl.†	.295	131	542	455	87	134	174	20	4	4	37	9	2	3	73	0	80	40	14	2	.382	.394
Gagne, Eric, L.A.	.143	20	34	28	1	4	4	0	0	0	6	0	0	0	0	0	5	0	0	0	.143	.143
Galarraga, Andres, Atl.	.302	141	548	494	67	149	260	25	1	28	100	0	17	36	5	126	3	5	15	.526	.369
Gant, Ron, Phi.	.254	89	384	343	54	87	167	16	2	20	38	1	3	1	36	1	73	5	4	7	.487	.324
Garcia, Mike, Pit.	.333	13	3	3	1	1	1	0	0	0	0	0	0	0	0	0	2	0	0	0	.333	.333
Gardner, Mark, S.F.	.116	30	50	43	1	5	5	0	0	0	0	7	0	0	0	0	22	0	0	0	.116	.116

Player, Team	Avg.	G	TPA	AB	R	H	TB	2B	3B	HR	RBI	SH	SF	HP	BB	IBB	SO	SB	CS	GDP	Slg.	OBP
Garibay, Daniel, Chi.*	.133	30	19	15	1	2	2	0	0	0	1	4	0	0	0	0	6	0	0	0	.133	.133
Gilbert, Shawn, L.A.	.150	15	23	20	5	3	7	1	0	1	3	1	0	0	2	0	7	0	0	0	.350	.227
Giles, Brian S., Pit.*	.315	156	688	559	111	176	332	37	7	35	123	0	8	7	114	13	69	6	0	15	.594	.432
Gilkey, Bernard, Ari.	.110	38	81	73	6	8	15	1	0	2	6	0	1	0	7	2	16	0	0	3	.205	.185
Ginter, Keith, Hou.	.250	5	10	8	3	2	5	0	0	1	3	0	1	0	1	0	3	0	0	0	.625	.300
Girardi, Joe, Chi.	.278	106	407	363	47	101	136	15	1	6	40	6	3	3	32	3	61	1	0	12	.375	.339
Glanville, Doug, Phi.	.275	154	689	637	89	175	238	27	6	8	52	12	7	2	31	1	76	31	8	11	.374	.307
Glauber, Keith, Cin.	.000	4	1	1	0	0	0	0	0	0	0	0	0	0	0	0	1	0	0	0	.000	.000
Glavine, Tom, Atl.*	.147	37	89	68	5	10	11	1	0	0	2	14	0	0	7	0	20	0	0	1	.162	.227
Gload, Ross, Chi.*	.194	18	35	31	4	6	11	0	1	1	3	0	1	0	3	0	10	0	0	1	.355	.257
Gomez, Chris, S.D.	.222	33	63	54	4	12	12	0	0	0	3	1	1	0	7	0	5	0	0	1	.222	.306
Gonzalez, Alex, Fla.	.200	109	407	385	35	77	123	17	4	7	42	5	2	2	13	0	77	7	1	7	.319	.229
Gonzalez, Luis, Ari.*	.311	162	722	618	106	192	336	47	2	31	114	2	12	12	78	6	85	2	4	12	.544	.392
Gonzalez, Raul, Chi.	.000	3	2	2	0	0	0	0	0	0	0	0	0	0	0	0	2	0	0	0	.000	.000
Gonzalez, Wiki, S.D.	.232	95	319	284	25	66	98	15	1	5	30	1	1	3	30	4	31	1	2	5	.345	.311
Gooden, Dwight, Hou.	.000	1	1	1	0	0	0	0	0	0	0	0	0	0	0	0	0	0	0	0	.000	.000
Goodwin, Tom, Col.-L.A.*	.263	147	606	528	94	139	186	11	9	6	58	5	4	1	68	2	117	55	10	7	.352	.346
Grace, Mark, Chi.*	.280	143	621	510	75	143	219	41	1	11	82	2	8	6	95	11	28	1	2	7	.429	.394
Graves, Danny, Cin.	.500	66	3	2	1	1	4	0	0	1	1	0	0	0	1	0	0	0	0	0	2.000	.667
Green, Jason, Hou.	.000	14	1	1	0	0	0	0	0	0	0	0	0	0	0	0	0	0	0	0	.000	.000
Green, Shawn, L.A.*	.269	162	714	610	98	164	288	44	4	24	99	0	6	8	90	9	121	24	5	18	.472	.367
Greene, Willie, Chi.*	.201	105	339	299	34	60	109	15	2	10	37	0	2	2	36	2	69	4	0	5	.365	.289
Griffey, Ken Jr., Cin.*	.271	145	631	520	100	141	289	22	3	40	118	0	8	9	94	17	117	6	4	7	.556	.387
Grilli, Jason, Fla.	.500	1	2	2	0	1	1	0	0	0	1	0	0	0	0	0	0	0	0	0	.500	.500
Grissom, Marquis, Mil.	.244	146	640	595	67	145	209	18	2	14	62	2	4	0	39	2	99	20	10	9	.351	.288
Gross, Kip, Hou.	.000	2	1	1	0	0	0	0	0	0	0	0	0	0	0	0	0	0	0	0	.000	.000
Grudzielanek, Mark, L.A.	.279	148	676	617	101	172	240	35	6	7	49	2	3	9	45	0	81	12	3	16	.389	.335
Guerrero, Vladimir, Mon.*	.345	154	641	571	101	197	379	28	11	44	123	0	4	8	58	23	74	9	10	15	.664	.410
Guerrero, Wilton, Mon.†	.267	127	314	288	30	77	94	7	2	2	23	6	1	0	19	0	41	8	1	6	.326	.312
Guthrie, Mark, Chi.	.000	19	2	2	0	0	0	0	0	0	0	0	0	0	0	0	0	0	0	0	.000	.000
Gutierrez, Ricky, Chi.	.276	125	542	449	73	124	180	19	2	11	56	16	4	7	66	0	58	8	2	10	.401	.375
Guzman, Geraldo, Ari.	.000	13	22	19	0	0	0	0	0	0	0	3	0	0	0	0	13	0	0	0	.000	.000
Gwynn, Tony, S.D.*	.323	36	140	127	17	41	56	12	0	1	17	0	3	1	9	2	4	0	1	4	.441	.364
Hamilton, Darryl, N.Y.*	.276	43	120	105	20	29	38	4	1	1	6	0	1	0	14	0	20	2	0	0	.362	.358
Hammonds, Jeffrey, Col.	.335	122	511	454	94	152	240	24	2	20	106	2	6	5	44	4	83	14	7	11	.529	.395
Hampton, Mike, N.Y.	.274	35	84	73	7	20	20	0	0	0	8	4	2	0	5	0	20	0	1	0	.274	.313
Hansen, Dave, L.A.*	.289	102	147	121	18	35	69	6	2	8	26	0	0	0	26	0	32	0	1	3	.570	.415
Harnisch, Pete, Cin.	.186	24	49	43	4	8	13	2	0	1	8	6	0	0	0	0	14	0	0	1	.302	.186
Harris, Lenny, Ari.-N.Y.*	.260	112	248	223	31	58	85	7	4	4	26	2	3	0	20	2	22	13	1	7	.381	.317
Hayes, Charlie, N.Y.	.251	121	434	370	46	93	137	17	0	9	46	0	6	1	57	4	84	1	1	11	.370	.348
Haynes, Jimmy, Mil.	.125	33	70	64	3	8	12	4	0	0	4	5	0	0	1	0	30	0	0	0	.188	.138
Helms, Wes, Atl.	.200	5	5	5	0	1	1	0	0	0	0	0	0	0	0	0	2	0	0	0	.200	.200
Helton, Todd, Col.*	.372	160	697	580	138	216	405	59	2	42	147	0	10	4	103	22	61	5	3	12	.698	.463
Henderson, Rickey, N.Y.	.219	31	124	96	17	21	22	1	0	0	2	0	1	2	25	1	20	5	2	2	.229	.387
Henry, Doug, Hou.-S.F.	.000	72	1	1	0	0	0	0	0	0	0	0	0	0	0	0	0	0	0	0	.000	.000
Hentgen, Pat, St.L.	.133	33	72	60	4	8	8	0	0	0	0	8	0	0	4	0	17	0	0	1	.133	.188
Heredia, Felix, Chi.*	.000	74	2	2	0	0	0	0	0	0	0	0	0	0	0	0	1	0	0	0	.000	.000
Herges, Matt, L.A.*	.077	59	16	13	0	1	1	0	0	0	0	1	0	0	0	0	8	0	0	3	.077	.077
Hermansen, Chad, Pit.	.185	33	117	108	12	20	32	4	1	2	8	2	1	0	6	0	37	0	0	3	.296	.226
Hermanson, Dustin, Mon.	.145	38	65	55	1	8	10	2	0	0	1	8	0	0	2	0	21	0	0	0	.182	.175
Hernandez, Alex, Pit.*	.200	20	60	60	4	12	18	3	0	1	5	0	0	0	0	0	13	1	1	0	.300	.200
Hernandez, C.A., S.D.-St.L.	.256	95	270	242	23	62	86	15	0	3	35	0	3	4	21	1	35	2	3	4	.355	.322
Hernandez, Livan, S.F.	.236	34	99	89	6	21	27	3	0	1	9	9	0	0	1	0	14	0	0	4	.303	.244
Hernandez, Jose, Mil.	.244	124	496	446	51	109	166	22	1	11	59	0	3	6	41	3	125	3	7	12	.372	.315
Hershiser, Orel, L.A.	.000	10	7	7	0	0	0	0	0	0	0	0	0	0	0	0	2	0	0	0	.000	.000
Hidalgo, Richard, Hou.	.314	153	644	558	118	175	355	42	3	44	122	0	9	21	56	3	110	13	6	13	.636	.391
Hill, Glenallen, Chi.	.262	64	178	168	23	44	83	4	1	11	29	0	0	0	10	2	43	0	1	5	.494	.303
Hitchcock, Sterling, S.D.*	.000	11	23	22	0	0	0	0	0	0	0	1	0	0	0	0	12	0	0	1	.000	.000
Hollandsworth, T., L.A.-Col.*	.269	137	471	428	81	115	192	20	0	19	47	0	1	1	41	3	99	18	7	8	.449	.333
Holmes, Darren, Ari.-St.L.-Ari.	.000	13	1	1	0	0	0	0	0	0	0	0	0	0	0	0	1	0	0	0	.000	.000
Holt, Chris, Hou.	.100	34	70	60	3	6	7	1	0	0	3	5	0	1	4	0	33	0	0	0	.117	.169
Holzemer, Mark, Phi.*	.000	25	1	1	0	0	0	0	0	0	0	0	0	0	0	0	0	0	0	0	.000	.000
Houston, Tyler, Mil.*	.250	101	305	284	30	71	140	15	0	18	43	4	0	0	17	3	72	2	1	13	.493	.292
Howard, Thomas, St.L.†	.211	86	141	133	13	28	52	4	1	6	28	0	0	1	7	0	34	1	0	3	.391	.255
Hubbard, Mike, Atl.	.000	2	1	1	0	0	0	0	0	0	0	0	0	0	0	0	1	0	0	0	.000	.000
Hubbard, Trenidad, Atl.	.185	61	96	81	15	15	22	2	1	1	6	3	0	1	11	0	20	2	1	1	.272	.290
Hundley, Todd, L.A.†	.284	90	353	299	49	85	173	16	0	24	70	1	6	2	45	6	69	0	1	5	.579	.375
Hunter, Brian L., Col.-Cin.	.267	104	274	240	47	64	74	5	1	1	14	5	1	1	27	0	40	20	3	2	.308	.342
Hunter, Brian R., Atl.-Phi.	.214	87	160	140	14	30	59	5	0	8	23	0	0	0	20	1	39	0	1	2	.421	.313
Huskey, Butch, Col.	.348	45	111	92	18	32	52	8	0	4	18	0	3	0	16	1	14	1	1	5	.565	.432
Huson, Jeff, Chi.*	.215	70	144	130	19	28	37	7	1	0	11	1	0	0	13	1	9	2	1	6	.285	.287
Hyzdu, Adam, Pit.	.389	12	18	18	2	7	12	2	0	1	4	0	0	0	0	0	6	0	0	0	.667	.389
Irabu, Hideki, Mon.	.125	11	18	16	1	2	2	0	0	0	1	2	0	0	0	0	7	0	0	1	.125	.125
Jackson, Damian, S.D.	.255	138	541	470	68	120	177	27	6	6	37	4	2	3	62	2	108	28	6	7	.377	.345
James, Mike, St.L.	.000	52	1	1	0	0	0	0	0	0	0	0	0	0	0	0	0	0	0	0	.000	.000
Jarvis, Kevin, Col.*	.088	25	40	34	4	3	4	1	0	0	3	0	1	2	0	0	11	0	0	0	.118	.162
Jenkins, Geoff, Mil.*	.303	135	564	512	100	155	301	36	4	34	94	0	4	15	33	6	135	11	1	9	.588	.360
Jimenez, Jose, Col.	.500	72	5	4	0	2	2	0	0	0	1	1	0	0	0	0	0	0	0	0	.500	.500
Johnson, Mark P., N.Y.*	.182	21	27	22	2	4	7	0	0	1	6	0	0	0	5	0	9	0	0	1	.318	.333
Johnson, Mike, Mon.*	.182	41	26	22	1	4	4	0	0	0	3	0	1	0	1	0	8	0	0	1	.182	.217
Johnson, Randy, Ari.	.157	35	92	83	4	13	15	2	0	0	8	5	0	1	3	0	35	0	0	1	.181	.195
Johnson, Russ, Hou.	.178	26	48	45	4	8	14	0	0	0	3	0	0	0	2	0	10	1	1	3	.178	.213

Player, Team	Avg.	G	TPA	AB	R	H	TB	2B	3B	HR	RBI	SH	SF	HP	BB	IBB	SO	SB	CS	GDP	Slg.	OBP
Johnstone, John, S.F.	.000	47	2	2	0	0	0	0	0	0	0	0	0	0	0	0	2	0	0	0	.000	.000
Jones, Andruw, Atl.	.303	161	729	656	122	199	355	36	6	36	104	0	5	9	59	0	100	21	6	12	.541	.366
Jones, Chris C., Mil.	.188	12	17	16	3	3	5	2	0	0	1	0	0	0	1	0	4	0	0	0	.313	.235
Jones, Chipper, Atl.†	.311	156	686	579	118	180	328	38	1	36	111	0	10	2	95	10	64	14	7	14	.566	.404
Jones, Bobby J., N.Y.	.045	27	55	44	4	2	2	0	0	0	0	7	0	1	3	0	21	0	0	0	.045	.125
Jones, Bobby M., N.Y.	.500	11	4	2	0	1	1	0	0	0	0	1	0	0	1	0	1	0	0	0	.500	.667
Jones, Terry, Mon.†	.250	108	181	168	30	42	54	8	2	0	13	3	0	0	10	1	32	7	2	3	.321	.292
Jordan, Brian, Atl.	.264	133	537	489	71	129	206	26	0	17	77	0	5	5	38	1	80	10	2	12	.421	.320
Jordan, Kevin, Phi.	.220	109	358	337	30	74	109	16	2	5	36	0	3	1	17	0	41	0	1	11	.323	.257
Joyner, Wally, Atl.*	.281	119	260	224	24	63	90	12	0	5	32	0	4	1	31	3	31	0	0	2	.402	.365
Judd, Mike, L.A.	1.000	1	2	1	1	1	1	0	0	0	0	1	0	0	0	0	0	0	0	0	1.000	1.000
Karchner, Matt, Chi.	.000	13	2	0	0	0	0	0	0	0	0	0	0	0	0	0	0	0	0	0	.000	.000
Karl, Scott, Col.*	.286	17	18	14	3	4	4	0	0	0	0	1	0	0	1	0	5	0	1	0	.286	.375
Karros, Eric, L.A.	.250	155	663	584	84	146	268	29	0	31	106	0	12	4	63	2	122	4	3	18	.459	.321
Kendall, Jason, Pit.	.320	152	678	579	112	185	272	33	6	14	58	1	4	15	79	3	79	22	12	13	.470	.412
Kent, Jeff, S.F.	.334	159	695	587	114	196	350	41	7	33	125	0	9	9	90	6	107	12	9	17	.596	.424
Kieschnick, Brooks, Cin.*	.000	14	13	12	0	0	0	0	0	0	0	0	0	0	1	0	5	0	0	0	.000	.077
Kile, Darryl, St.L.	.123	34	91	73	5	9	10	1	0	0	3	8	0	0	10	0	38	0	0	0	.137	.229
Kim, Byung-Hyun, Ari.	.000	61	4	3	0	0	0	0	0	0	0	0	0	0	1	0	2	0	0	0	.000	.250
Kinkade, Mike, N.Y.	.000	2	2	2	0	0	0	0	0	0	0	0	0	0	0	0	1	0	0	0	.000	.000
Klassen, Danny, Ari.	.237	29	87	76	13	18	27	3	0	2	8	2	0	1	8	0	24	1	1	0	.355	.318
Klesko, Ryan, S.D.*	.283	145	590	494	88	140	255	33	2	26	92	0	4	1	91	9	81	23	7	10	.516	.393
Kline, Steve, Mon.†	.000	83	2	2	0	0	0	0	0	0	0	0	0	0	0	0	0	0	0	0	.000	.000
Kolb, Brandon, S.D.	.000	11	1	1	1	0	0	0	0	0	0	0	0	0	0	0	0	0	0	0	.000	.000
Kotsay, Mark, Fla.*	.298	152	578	530	87	158	235	31	5	12	57	2	4	0	42	2	46	19	9	17	.443	.347
Kreuter, Chad, L.A.†	.264	80	271	212	32	56	87	13	0	6	28	2	1	2	54	0	48	1	0	6	.410	.416
Lamb, David, N.Y.†	.200	7	6	5	1	1	1	1	0	0	0	0	0	0	1	0	1	0	0	0	.200	.333
Lankford, Ray, St.L.*	.253	128	472	392	73	99	199	16	3	26	65	0	6	4	70	1	148	5	6	6	.508	.367
Lansing, Mike, Col.	.258	90	400	365	62	94	153	14	6	11	47	3	1	0	31	1	49	8	2	13	.419	.315
Larkin, Andy, Cin.	.000	3	1	1	0	0	0	0	0	0	0	0	0	0	0	0	1	0	0	0	.000	.000
Larkin, Barry, Cin.	.313	102	447	396	71	124	193	26	5	11	41	2	0	1	48	0	31	14	6	10	.487	.389
LaRocca, Greg, S.D.	.222	13	30	27	1	6	8	2	0	0	2	2	0	0	1	0	4	0	0	1	.296	.250
LaRue, Jason, Cin.	.235	31	107	98	12	23	41	3	0	5	12	0	0	4	5	2	19	0	0	1	.418	.299
Ledesma, Aaron, Col.	.225	32	43	40	4	9	11	2	0	0	3	0	0	1	2	0	9	0	0	1	.275	.279
Lee, Derrek, Fla.	.281	158	546	477	70	134	242	18	3	28	70	0	2	4	63	6	123	6	3	14	.507	.368
Lee, Travis, Ari.-Phi.*	.235	128	473	404	53	95	148	24	1	9	54	0	2	2	65	1	79	8	1	12	.366	.342
Leiter, Al, N.Y.*	.052	31	71	58	1	3	3	0	0	0	0	9	0	0	4	0	33	0	0	1	.052	.113
Leskanic, Curtis, Mil.	.000	73	2	2	0	0	0	0	0	0	0	0	0	0	0	0	2	0	0	0	.000	.000
Levrault, Allen, Mil.	.000	5	3	3	0	0	0	0	0	0	0	0	0	0	0	0	2	0	0	0	.000	.000
Lewis, Mark, Cin.	.105	11	20	19	1	2	3	1	0	0	3	0	0	0	1	0	3	0	0	1	.158	.150
Leyritz, Jim, L.A.	.200	41	68	60	3	12	16	1	0	1	8	0	0	1	7	0	12	0	0	2	.267	.294
Lieber, Jon, Chi.*	.220	36	94	82	3	18	22	4	0	0	4	10	0	0	2	0	28	0	0	5	.268	.238
Lieberthal, Mike, Phi.	.278	108	438	389	55	108	183	30	0	15	71	0	3	6	40	3	53	2	0	12	.470	.352
Lima, Jose, Hou.	.167	33	69	60	6	10	12	2	0	0	2	8	0	0	1	0	17	0	0	1	.200	.180
Linebrink, Scott, S.F.-Hou.	1.000	11	1	1	0	1	1	0	0	0	0	0	0	0	0	0	0	0	0	0	1.000	1.000
Liniak, Cole, Chi.	.000	3	3	3	0	0	0	0	0	0	0	0	0	0	0	0	2	0	0	0	.000	.000
Lira, Felipe, Mon.	.211	54	21	19	3	4	10	0	0	2	3	1	1	0	0	0	13	0	0	0	.526	.200
Lockhart, Keith, Atl.*	.265	113	313	275	32	73	97	12	3	2	32	5	4	0	29	7	31	4	1	10	.353	.331
LoDuca, Paul, L.A.	.246	34	75	65	6	16	24	2	0	2	8	2	2	0	6	0	8	0	2	2	.369	.301
Lombard, George, Atl.*	.103	27	41	39	8	4	4	0	0	0	2	0	0	1	1	0	14	4	0	2	.103	.146
Looper, Braden, Fla.	.000	73	2	2	0	0	0	0	0	0	0	0	0	0	0	0	2	0	0	0	.000	.000
Lopez, Javy, Atl.	.287	134	525	481	60	138	233	21	1	24	89	0	5	4	35	3	80	0	0	20	.484	.337
Lopez, Luis M., Mil.†	.264	78	225	201	24	53	85	14	0	6	27	8	2	5	9	1	35	1	2	2	.423	.309
Lopez, Mendy, Fla.	.000	4	4	3	0	0	0	0	0	0	0	0	0	0	1	0	1	0	0	0	.000	.250
Lopez, Rodrigo, S.D.	.111	6	9	9	1	1	1	0	0	0	0	0	0	0	0	0	4	0	0	0	.111	.111
Loretta, Mark, Mil.	.281	91	399	352	49	99	143	21	1	7	40	8	1	1	37	2	38	0	3	9	.406	.350
Lorraine, Andrew, Chi.*	.125	8	11	8	2	1	1	0	0	0	2	2	0	0	1	0	4	0	0	0	.125	.222
Lowell, Mike, Fla.	.270	140	582	508	73	137	241	38	0	22	91	0	11	9	54	4	75	4	0	4	.474	.344
Lowery, Terrell, S.F.	.441	24	42	34	13	15	22	4	0	1	5	0	0	1	7	0	8	1	0	1	.647	.548
Luebbers, Larry, Cin.	.000	14	1	0	0	0	0	0	0	0	0	1	0	0	0	0	0	0	0	0	.000	.000
Lugo, Julio, Hou.	.283	116	465	420	78	119	181	22	5	10	40	3	1	4	37	0	93	22	9	9	.431	.346
Lunar, Fernando, Atl.	.185	22	60	54	5	10	11	1	0	0	5	0	0	3	3	1	15	0	2	2	.204	.267
Mabry, John, S.D.*	.228	48	129	123	17	28	57	8	0	7	25	0	1	0	5	0	38	0	0	3	.463	.256
Maddux, Greg, Atl.	.188	35	90	80	2	15	19	2	1	0	5	7	0	1	2	0	19	0	1	1	.238	.217
Maddux, Mike, Hou.*	.000	21	2	2	0	0	0	0	0	0	0	0	0	0	0	0	2	0	0	0	.000	.000
Magadan, Dave, S.D.*	.273	95	166	132	13	36	49	7	0	2	21	0	2	0	32	1	23	0	0	4	.371	.410
Mahay, Ron, Fla.*	.500	18	4	4	0	2	3	1	0	0	0	0	0	0	0	0	1	0	0	0	.750	.500
Mahomes, Pat, N.Y.	.235	53	20	17	1	4	5	1	0	0	1	2	0	0	1	0	5	0	0	0	.294	.278
Mahoney, Mike, Chi.	.286	4	9	7	1	2	3	1	0	0	1	0	0	1	1	0	0	0	0	0	.429	.444
Manto, Jeff, Col.	.800	7	7	5	2	4	9	2	0	1	4	0	0	0	2	0	0	0	0	0	1.800	.857
Manzanillo, Josias, Pit.	.000	43	4	3	0	0	0	0	0	0	0	0	1	0	0	0	2	0	0	0	.000	.000
Marquis, Jason, Atl.*	.000	15	2	2	0	0	0	0	0	0	0	0	0	0	0	0	2	0	0	0	.000	.000
Marrero, Eli, St.L.	.225	53	116	102	21	23	43	3	1	5	17	0	2	3	9	0	16	5	0	3	.422	.302
Martin, Al, S.D.*	.306	93	378	346	62	106	164	13	6	11	27	0	2	2	28	5	54	6	8	2	.474	.360
Martinez, Sandy, Fla.*	.222	10	18	18	1	4	6	2	0	0	0	0	0	0	0	0	8	0	0	0	.333	.222
Martinez, Dave, Chi.*	.185	18	56	54	5	10	13	1	1	0	1	0	0	0	2	0	8	1	0	0	.241	.214
Martinez, Ramon E., S.F.	.302	88	210	189	30	57	92	13	2	6	25	4	1	1	15	1	22	3	2	6	.487	.354
Matheny, Mike, St.L.	.261	128	464	417	43	109	151	22	1	6	47	7	4	4	32	8	96	0	0	11	.362	.317
Matthews, Gary Jr., Chi.†	.190	80	175	158	24	30	47	1	2	4	14	1	0	1	15	1	28	3	0	2	.297	.264
Mayne, Brent, Col.*	.301	117	395	335	36	101	140	21	0	6	64	4	8	1	47	13	48	1	3	12	.418	.381
McDonald, Keith, St.L.	.429	6	9	7	3	3	12	0	0	3	5	0	0	0	2	0	1	0	0	0	1.714	.556
McEwing, Joe, N.Y.	.222	87	169	153	20	34	56	14	1	2	19	8	2	1	5	0	29	3	1	2	.366	.248

Player, Team	Avg.	G	TPA	AB	R	H	TB	2B	3B	HR	RBI	SH	SF	HP	BB	IBB	SO	SB	CS	GDP	Slg.	OBP
McGuire, Ryan, N.Y.*	.000	1	3	2	0	0	0	0	0	0	0	0	0	0	1	0	0	0	0	1	.000	.333
McGwire, Mark, St.L.	.305	89	321	236	60	72	176	8	0	32	73	0	2	7	76	12	78	1	0	5	.746	.483
McKnight, Tony, Hou.*	.000	6	14	13	1	0	0	0	0	0	0	1	0	0	0	0	6	0	0	0	.000	.000
Meadows, Brian, S.D.	.150	22	44	40	2	6	6	0	0	0	2	4	0	0	0	0	17	0	0	1	.150	.150
Meares, Pat, Pit.	.240	132	514	462	55	111	176	22	2	13	47	5	3	8	36	6	91	1	0	13	.381	.305
Melhuse, Adam, L.A.-Col.†	.167	24	27	24	3	4	6	0	1	0	4	0	0	0	3	0	6	0	0	1	.250	.259
Melo, Juan, S.F.†	.077	11	13	13	0	1	1	0	0	0	1	0	0	0	0	0	5	0	0	0	.077	.077
Meluskey, Mitch, Hou.†	.300	117	400	337	47	101	164	21	0	14	69	1	3	4	55	10	74	1	0	7	.487	.401
Mendoza, Carlos R., Col.*	.100	13	11	10	0	1	1	0	0	0	0	0	0	0	1	0	4	0	1	0	.100	.182
Mercado, Hector, Cin.*	.000	12	1	1	0	0	0	0	0	0	0	0	0	0	0	0	1	0	0	0	.000	.000
Metcalfe, Mike, L.A.	.083	4	13	12	0	1	1	0	0	0	0	0	0	0	1	0	2	0	0	0	.083	.154
Meyers, Chad, Chi.	.173	36	57	52	8	9	11	2	0	0	5	0	1	0	3	0	11	1	0	0	.212	.228
Mieske, Matt, Hou.-Ari.	.180	73	99	89	10	16	27	1	2	2	7	0	1	1	8	0	18	0	0	2	.303	.253
Millar, Kevin, Fla.	.259	123	305	259	36	67	129	14	3	14	42	0	2	8	36	0	47	0	0	5	.498	.354
Miller, Damian, Ari.	.275	100	364	324	43	89	143	24	0	10	44	1	2	1	36	4	74	2	2	6	.441	.347
Miller, Wade, Hou.	.100	16	41	40	1	4	5	1	0	0	3	1	0	0	0	0	16	0	0	1	.125	.100
Mills, Alan, L.A.	.000	18	4	3	0	0	0	0	0	0	1	0	0	0	1	0	2	0	0	0	.000	.250
Millwood, Kevin, Atl.	.119	36	75	59	1	7	9	2	0	0	2	14	0	0	2	0	30	0	0	3	.153	.148
Minor, Damon, S.F.*	.444	10	11	9	3	4	13	0	0	3	6	0	0	0	2	0	1	0	0	0	1.444	.545
Mirabelli, Doug, S.F.	.230	82	273	230	23	53	85	10	2	6	28	3	2	2	36	2	57	1	0	6	.370	.337
Mohler, Mike, St.L.	1.000	22	1	1	0	1	1	0	0	0	0	0	0	0	0	0	0	0	0	0	1.000	1.000
Moore, Trey, Mon.*	.125	8	11	8	0	1	1	0	0	0	0	2	0	0	1	0	2	0	0	0	.125	.222
Mora, Melvin, N.Y.	.260	79	242	215	35	56	91	13	2	6	30	2	5	2	18	3	48	7	3	3	.423	.317
Morandini, Mickey, Phi.*	.252	91	341	302	31	76	95	13	3	0	22	5	1	4	29	1	54	5	2	11	.315	.324
Mordecai, Mike, Mon.	.284	86	183	169	20	48	76	16	0	4	16	1	0	1	12	0	34	2	2	1	.450	.335
Morgan, Mike, Ari.	.438	60	17	16	0	7	7	0	0	0	1	1	0	0	0	0	5	0	0	0	.438	.438
Morris, Matt, St.L.	.333	32	6	3	0	1	1	0	0	0	0	3	0	0	0	0	1	0	0	0	.333	.333
Morris, Warren, Pit.*	.259	144	606	528	68	137	181	31	2	3	43	8	3	2	65	3	78	7	10	7	.343	.341
Morris, Hal, Cin.*	.222	59	78	63	9	14	24	2	1	2	6	1	1	1	12	3	10	0	0	3	.381	.351
Mota, Guillermo, Mon.	.000	29	1	1	0	0	0	0	0	0	0	0	0	0	0	0	0	0	0	0	.000	.000
Mouton, James, Mil.	.233	87	197	159	28	37	52	7	1	2	17	4	1	3	30	0	43	13	4	5	.327	.363
Mouton, Lyle, Mil.	.278	42	109	97	14	27	42	7	1	2	16	0	1	1	10	0	29	1	0	2	.433	.349
Mueller, Bill, S.F.†	.268	153	631	560	97	150	217	29	4	10	55	7	6	6	52	0	62	4	2	16	.388	.333
Mulholland, Terry, Atl.	.250	54	45	36	3	9	12	3	0	0	4	9	0	0	0	0	16	0	0	0	.333	.250
Murray, Calvin, S.F.	.242	108	229	194	35	47	67	12	1	2	22	2	1	3	29	0	33	9	3	0	.345	.348
Nady, Xavier, S.D.	1.000	1	1	1	1	1	1	0	0	0	0	0	0	0	0	0	0	0	0	0	1.000	1.000
Nathan, Joe, S.F.	.156	20	38	32	3	5	13	2	0	2	3	4	1	0	1	0	9	0	0	1	.406	.176
Nation, Joey, Chi.*	.500	2	4	4	0	2	2	0	0	0	0	0	0	0	0	0	1	0	0	0	.500	.500
Navarro, Jaime, Mil.	.000	5	5	5	0	0	0	0	0	0	0	0	0	0	0	0	2	0	0	0	.000	.000
Neagle, Denny, Cin.*	.189	19	46	37	1	7	9	2	0	0	3	7	0	0	2	0	9	0	0	0	.243	.231
Nevin, Phil, S.D.	.303	143	605	538	87	163	292	34	1	31	107	0	4	4	59	9	121	2	0	17	.543	.374
Newhan, David, S.D.-Phi.*	.162	24	45	37	8	6	10	1	0	1	2	0	0	0	8	1	13	0	0	2	.270	.311
Nicholson, Kevin, S.D.†	.216	37	105	97	7	21	32	6	1	1	8	3	0	1	4	0	31	1	0	2	.330	.255
Nieves, Jose, Chi.	.212	82	213	198	17	42	69	6	3	5	24	2	2	0	11	1	43	1	1	8	.348	.251
Norton, Phil, Chi.	.667	2	4	3	1	2	2	0	0	0	1	0	0	0	0	0	0	0	0	0	.667	.667
Nunez, Abraham, Pit.†	.220	40	99	91	10	20	24	1	0	1	8	0	0	0	8	1	14	0	0	3	.264	.283
Nunez, Vladimir, Fla.	.118	17	21	17	2	2	5	0	0	1	3	4	0	0	0	0	5	0	0	0	.294	.118
Nunnally, Jon, N.Y.*	.189	48	92	74	16	14	27	5	1	2	6	0	1	0	17	0	26	3	1	1	.365	.337
Nunnari, Talmadge, Mon.*	.200	18	12	5	2	1	1	0	0	0	1	0	1	0	6	1	2	0	0	0	.200	.583
O'Brien, Charlie, Mon.	.211	9	21	19	1	4	8	1	0	1	2	0	0	0	2	1	7	0	0	0	.421	.286
Ochoa, Alex, Cin.	.316	118	275	244	50	77	143	21	3	13	58	0	4	3	24	3	27	9	4	7	.586	.378
O'Connor, Brian, Pit.*	.500	6	2	2	0	1	1	0	0	0	0	0	0	0	0	0	1	0	0	0	.500	.500
Ojeda, Augie, Chi.†	.221	28	89	77	10	17	28	3	1	2	8	1	1	0	10	1	9	0	1	1	.364	.307
Ordonez, Rey, N.Y.	.188	45	155	133	10	25	30	5	0	0	9	4	1	0	17	2	16	0	0	4	.226	.278
Ortiz, Russ, S.F.	.197	33	75	61	7	12	14	2	0	0	5	6	0	0	8	0	16	0	0	2	.230	.290
Osik, Keith, Pit.	.293	46	143	123	11	36	56	6	1	4	22	1	0	5	14	0	11	3	0	2	.455	.387
Osuna, Antonio, L.A.	.000	46	2	2	0	0	0	0	0	0	0	0	0	0	0	0	1	0	0	1	.000	.000
Owens, Eric, S.D.	.293	145	636	583	87	171	222	19	7	6	51	0	4	4	45	4	63	29	14	16	.381	.346
Ozuna, Pablo, Fla.	.333	14	26	24	2	8	9	1	0	0	2	0	0	0	0	0	2	1	0	0	.375	.333
Padilla, Vicente, Ari.-Phi.	1.000	55	1	1	0	1	1	0	0	0	0	0	0	0	0	0	0	0	0	0	1.000	1.000
Paquette, Craig, St.L.	.245	134	420	384	47	94	167	24	2	15	61	1	6	2	27	1	83	4	3	5	.435	.294
Park, Chan Ho, L.A.	.214	34	78	70	6	15	25	4	0	2	6	6	0	0	2	0	16	0	0	0	.357	.236
Parra, Jose, Pit.	.000	6	2	0	0	0	0	0	0	0	0	0	0	0	2	0	0	0	0	0	.000	1.000
Parris, Steve, Cin.	.127	35	62	55	4	7	9	2	0	0	4	4	1	0	2	0	19	0	1	0	.164	.155
Patterson, Corey, Chi.*	.167	11	47	42	9	7	14	1	0	2	2	1	0	1	3	0	14	1	1	0	.333	.239
Pavano, Carl, Mon.	.143	15	38	35	2	5	6	1	0	0	3	0	0	0	0	0	16	0	0	0	.171	.143
Payton, Jay, N.Y.	.291	149	529	488	63	142	218	23	1	17	62	0	8	3	30	0	60	5	11	9	.447	.331
Pena, Elvis, Col.†	.333	10	10	9	1	3	4	1	0	0	1	0	0	0	1	0	1	1	0	2	.444	.400
Penny, Brad, Fla.	.111	24	46	45	2	5	5	0	0	0	2	1	0	0	0	0	17	0	0	1	.111	.111
Perez, Carlos, L.A.*	.047	32	50	43	0	2	5	1	1	0	3	7	0	0	0	0	15	0	1	1	.116	.047
Perez, Eddie, Atl.	.182	7	22	22	0	4	5	1	0	0	3	0	0	0	0	0	2	0	0	0	.227	.182
Perez, Eduardo, St.L.	.297	35	102	91	9	27	40	4	0	3	10	2	1	3	5	0	19	1	0	2	.440	.350
Perez, Neifi, Col.†	.287	162	699	651	92	187	278	39	11	10	71	7	11	0	30	6	63	3	6	9	.427	.314
Perez, Santiago, Mil.†	.173	24	63	52	8	9	11	2	0	0	2	1	1	1	8	2	9	4	0	1	.212	.290
Perez, Timo, N.Y.*	.286	24	54	49	11	14	23	4	1	1	3	0	1	1	3	0	5	1	1	0	.469	.333
Perez, Tomas, Phi.†	.221	45	152	140	17	31	43	7	1	1	13	1	1	0	11	2	30	1	1	3	.307	.278
Perez, Yorkis, Hou.†	.000	33	1	1	0	0	0	0	0	0	0	0	0	0	0	0	1	0	0	0	.000	.000
Person, Robert, Phi.	.132	28	65	53	1	7	10	3	0	0	2	8	1	0	3	0	29	0	0	0	.189	.175
Peters, Chris, Pit.*	.167	18	6	6	1	1	1	0	0	0	0	0	0	0	0	0	1	0	0	0	.167	.167
Petrick, Ben, Col.	.322	52	173	146	32	47	68	10	1	3	20	1	4	2	20	2	33	1	2	1	.466	.401
Piazza, Mike, N.Y.	.324	136	545	482	90	156	296	26	0	38	113	0	2	3	58	10	69	4	2	15	.614	.398
Pierre, Juan, Col.*	.310	51	219	200	26	62	64	2	0	0	20	4	1	1	13	0	15	7	6	2	.320	.353

Player, Team	Avg.	G	TPA	AB	R	H	TB	2B	3B	HR	RBI	SH	SF	HP	BB	IBB	SO	SB	CS	GDP	Slg.	OBP
Polanco, Placido, St.L.	.316	118	350	323	50	102	135	12	3	5	39	7	3	1	16	0	26	4	4	8	.418	.347
Politte, Cliff, Phi.	.133	12	19	15	1	2	3	1	0	0	2	2	1	0	1	0	4	0	0	0	.200	.176
Powell, Jay, Hou.	.000	30	1	1	0	0	0	0	0	0	0	0	0	0	0	0	1	0	0	0	.000	.000
Powell, Jeremy, Mon.	.600	11	5	5	1	3	4	1	0	0	1	0	0	0	0	0	1	0	0	0	.800	.600
Powell, Brian, Hou.	.222	9	10	9	2	2	3	1	0	0	0	0	0	0	1	0	4	0	0	0	.333	.300
Pratt, Todd, N.Y.	.275	80	190	160	33	44	74	6	0	8	25	2	1	5	22	1	31	0	0	5	.463	.378
Prince, Tom, Phi.	.238	46	140	122	14	29	44	9	0	2	16	3	0	2	13	0	31	1	0	6	.361	.321
Pritchett, Chris, Phi.*	.091	5	12	11	0	1	1	0	0	0	0	0	0	0	1	0	3	0	0	1	.091	.167
Prokopec, Luke, L.A.*	.000	6	6	5	0	0	0	0	0	0	0	1	0	0	0	0	2	0	0	0	.000	.000
Pulsiper, Bill, N.Y.*	.000	2	2	2	0	0	0	0	0	0	0	0	0	0	0	0	1	0	0	0	.000	.000
Quevedo, Ruben, Chi.	.133	21	31	30	1	4	4	0	0	0	0	1	1	0	0	0	10	0	0	1	.133	.133
Rain, Steve, Cin.	.000	37	3	2	0	0	0	0	0	0	0	0	0	0	1	0	2	0	0	0	.000	.333
Ramirez, Alex, Pit.	.209	43	123	115	13	24	44	6	1	4	18	1	0	0	7	2	32	1	0	6	.383	.254
Ramirez, Aramis, Pit.	.256	73	274	254	19	65	102	15	2	6	35	1	4	5	10	0	36	0	0	9	.402	.293
Ramirez, Hector, Mil.	1.000	6	1	1	0	1	1	0	0	0	0	0	0	0	0	0	0	0	0	0	1.000	1.000
Reames, Britt, St.L.	.167	10	13	12	1	2	2	0	0	0	0	1	0	0	0	0	2	0	0	0	.167	.167
Redman, Tike, Pit.*	.333	9	19	18	2	6	10	1	0	1	1	0	0	0	1	0	7	1	0	0	.556	.368
Redmond, Mike, Fla.	.252	87	235	210	17	53	63	8	1	0	15	1	3	8	13	3	19	0	0	5	.300	.316
Reed, Jeff, Chi.*	.214	90	277	229	26	49	71	10	0	4	25	2	1	1	44	2	68	0	1	5	.310	.342
Reed, Rick, N.Y.	.204	30	67	49	6	10	10	0	0	0	2	14	2	1	1	0	11	0	0	0	.204	.226
Reese, Pokey, Cin.	.255	115	577	518	76	132	200	20	6	12	46	3	5	6	45	5	86	29	3	8	.386	.319
Relaford, Desi, Phi.-S.D.†	.215	128	502	410	55	88	123	14	3	5	46	3	2	12	75	7	71	13	0	10	.300	.351
Remlinger, Mike, Atl.*	.000	71	4	3	0	0	0	0	0	0	0	1	0	0	0	0	2	0	0	0	.000	.250
Renteria, Edgar, St.L.	.278	150	643	562	94	156	238	32	1	16	76	8	9	1	63	3	77	21	13	19	.423	.346
Reyes, Carlos, Phi.-S.D.†	.000	22	1	1	0	0	0	0	0	0	0	0	0	0	0	0	0	0	0	0	.000	.000
Reyes, Dennys, Cin.	.000	62	3	2	0	0	0	0	0	0	0	0	0	0	1	0	1	0	0	0	.000	.333
Reynolds, Shane, Hou.	.225	22	46	40	2	9	13	1	0	1	2	4	0	1	1	0	13	0	0	1	.325	.262
Reynoso, Armando, Ari.	.104	31	57	48	0	5	5	0	0	0	0	7	0	0	2	0	24	0	0	0	.104	.140
Richard, Chris, St.L.*	.125	6	18	16	1	2	5	0	0	1	1	0	0	0	2	0	2	0	0	1	.313	.222
Riedling, John, Cin.	.000	13	2	2	0	0	0	0	0	0	0	0	0	0	0	0	2	0	0	0	.000	.000
Rigby, Brad, Mon.	.000	6	1	1	0	0	0	0	0	0	0	0	0	0	0	0	0	0	0	0	.000	.000
Rigdon, Paul, Mil.	.188	12	25	16	3	3	6	0	0	1	1	7	0	0	2	0	6	0	0	1	.375	.278
Rios, Armando, S.F.*	.266	115	269	233	38	62	117	15	5	10	50	1	4	0	31	4	43	3	2	9	.502	.354
Ritchie, Todd, Pit.	.217	31	64	60	4	13	15	2	0	0	2	2	0	0	2	0	22	0	0	1	.250	.242
Rivera, Ruben, S.D.	.208	135	479	423	62	88	169	18	6	17	57	0	2	10	44	1	137	8	4	8	.400	.296
Roberts, Grant, N.Y.	.000	4	1	0	0	0	0	0	0	0	0	0	0	0	0	0	0	0	0	0	.000	.000
Rodriguez, Felix, S.F.	.000	76	4	4	0	0	0	0	0	0	0	0	0	0	0	0	3	0	0	0	.000	.000
Rodriguez, Henry, Chi.-Fla.*	.256	112	410	367	47	94	177	21	1	20	61	0	3	4	36	2	99	1	2	5	.482	.327
Rodriguez, Jose, St.L.*	.000	6	1	1	0	0	0	0	0	0	0	0	0	0	0	0	1	0	0	0	.000	.000
Rodriguez, Rich, N.Y.*	.000	32	1	1	0	0	0	0	0	0	0	0	0	0	0	0	0	0	0	0	.000	.000
Rolen, Scott, Phi.	.298	128	541	483	88	144	266	32	6	26	89	0	2	5	51	9	99	8	1	4	.551	.370
Rolison, Nate, Fla.*	.077	8	16	13	0	1	1	0	0	0	2	0	2	0	1	0	4	0	0	0	.077	.125
Rollins, Jimmy, Phi.†	.321	14	55	53	5	17	20	1	1	0	5	0	0	0	2	0	7	3	0	0	.377	.345
Rose, Brian, Col.	.048	12	24	21	1	1	1	0	0	0	0	3	0	0	0	0	10	0	0	1	.048	.048
Roskos, John, S.D.	.037	14	30	27	0	1	2	1	0	0	1	0	0	0	3	0	7	0	0	1	.074	.133
Rueter, Kirk, S.F.*	.200	34	71	60	5	12	15	3	0	0	5	10	0	0	1	0	11	0	0	2	.250	.213
Rusch, Glendon, N.Y.*	.060	31	57	50	2	3	3	0	0	0	1	4	0	0	3	0	19	0	0	1	.060	.113
Ryan, Rob, Ari.*	.296	27	32	27	4	8	11	1	1	0	2	0	0	1	4	0	7	0	0	0	.407	.406
Sanchez, Jesus, Fla.*	.232	45	60	56	6	13	13	0	0	0	4	3	0	0	1	0	15	0	0	1	.232	.246
Sanders, Reggie, Atl.	.232	103	377	340	43	79	137	23	1	11	37	3	0	2	32	2	78	21	4	9	.403	.302
Santana, Julio, Mon.	.000	36	7	7	0	0	0	0	0	0	0	0	0	0	0	0	4	0	0	0	.000	.000
Santangelo, F.P., L.A.†	.197	81	177	142	19	28	35	4	0	1	9	6	2	6	21	0	33	3	2	5	.246	.322
Santiago, Benito, Cin.	.262	89	277	252	22	66	103	11	1	8	45	0	5	1	19	8	45	2	2	7	.409	.310
Saturria, Luis, St.L.	.000	12	6	5	1	0	0	0	0	0	0	0	0	0	1	0	3	0	0	0	.000	.167
Sauerbeck, Scott, Pit.	.000	75	1	1	0	0	0	0	0	0	0	0	0	0	0	0	0	0	0	0	.000	.000
Schilling, Curt, Phi.-Ari.	.213	29	71	61	2	13	16	3	0	0	4	9	0	0	1	0	15	0	1	0	.262	.226
Schmidt, Jason, Pit.	.000	11	22	19	1	0	0	0	0	0	0	2	0	0	1	0	9	0	0	1	.000	.050
Schneider, Brian, Mon.*	.235	45	123	115	6	27	33	6	0	0	11	0	1	0	7	2	24	0	1	1	.287	.276
Sefcik, Kevin, Phi.	.235	99	171	153	15	36	46	6	2	0	10	1	2	2	13	0	19	4	2	4	.301	.300
Seguignol, Fernando, Mon.†	.278	76	175	162	22	45	83	8	0	10	22	0	1	3	9	0	46	0	1	5	.512	.326
Serafini, Dan, S.D.-Pit.	.083	14	27	24	1	2	2	0	0	0	2	3	0	0	0	0	9	0	0	1	.083	.154
Servais, Scott, Col.-S.F.	.220	40	120	109	7	24	31	4	0	1	13	0	1	1	9	3	17	0	1	1	.284	.283
Sexson, Richie, Mil.	.296	57	251	213	44	63	119	14	0	14	47	0	1	3	34	2	63	1	0	3	.559	.398
Sexton, Chris, Cin.	.210	35	118	100	9	21	25	4	0	0	10	2	1	2	13	1	12	4	2	5	.250	.310
Sheffield, Gary, L.A.	.325	141	612	501	105	163	322	24	3	43	109	0	6	4	101	7	71	4	6	13	.643	.438
Shumpert, Terry, Col.	.259	115	300	263	52	68	120	11	7	9	40	0	3	6	28	1	40	8	4	3	.456	.340
Silva, Jose, Pit.	.176	51	41	34	0	6	6	0	0	0	2	5	0	1	1	0	12	0	0	1	.176	.222
Sisco, Steve, Atl.	.185	25	30	27	4	5	8	0	0	1	2	0	0	0	3	0	4	0	0	1	.296	.267
Skrmetta, Matt, Mon.-Pit.†	.000	14	2	2	0	0	0	0	0	0	0	0	0	0	0	0	0	0	0	0	.000	.000
Slocumb, Heathcliff, St.L.-S.D.	.000	66	1	1	0	0	0	0	0	0	0	0	0	0	0	0	1	0	0	0	.000	.000
Slusarski, Joe, Hou.	.111	54	9	9	1	1	1	0	0	0	1	0	0	0	0	0	5	0	0	0	.111	.111
Smith, Chuck, Fla.	.100	21	41	40	2	4	4	0	0	0	2	1	0	0	0	0	19	0	0	1	.100	.100
Smith, Mark, Fla.	.245	104	213	192	22	47	72	8	1	5	27	0	2	2	17	1	54	2	0	2	.375	.310
Snow, J.T., S.F.*	.284	155	627	536	82	152	246	33	2	19	96	0	14	11	66	6	129	1	3	20	.459	.365
Snyder, John, Mil.	.079	24	42	38	1	3	4	1	0	0	0	1	0	1	2	0	7	0	0	1	.105	.146
Sojo, Luis, Pit.	.284	61	189	176	14	50	76	11	0	5	20	0	1	1	11	3	16	1	0	6	.432	.327
Sosa, Sammy, Chi.	.320	156	705	604	106	193	383	38	1	50	138	0	8	2	91	19	168	7	4	12	.634	.406
Spencer, Stan, S.D.	.333	9	14	12	0	4	5	1	0	0	1	2	0	0	0	0	6	0	0	0	.417	.333
Spiers, Bill, Hou.*	.301	124	409	355	41	107	139	17	3	3	43	2	2	1	49	3	38	7	4	8	.392	.386
Spradlin, Jerry, Chi.†	.000	8	1	1	0	0	0	0	0	0	0	0	0	0	0	0	1	0	0	0	.000	.000
Sprague, Ed Jr., S.D.	.261	73	175	157	19	41	83	12	0	10	27	0	2	3	13	2	40	0	0	1	.529	.326
Springer, Dennis, N.Y.	.000	2	4	4	0	0	0	0	0	0	0	0	0	0	0	0	3	0	0	0	.000	.000

Player, Team	Avg.	G	TPA	AB	R	H	TB	2B	3B	HR	RBI	SH	SF	HP	BB	IBB	SO	SB	CS	GDP	Slg.	OBP
Springer, Russ, Ari.	.200	52	5	5	0	1	1	0	0	0	0	0	0	0	0	0	1	0	0	0	.200	.200
Stephenson, Garrett, St.L.	.051	32	76	59	0	3	3	0	0	0	4	13	0	0	4	0	23	0	0	2	.051	.111
Stevens, Dave, Atl.	.000	2	1	1	0	0	0	0	0	0	0	0	0	0	0	0	0	0	0	0	.000	.000
Stevens, Lee, Mon.*	.265	123	501	449	60	119	216	27	2	22	75	0	2	2	48	6	105	0	0	10	.481	.337
Stinnett, Kelly, Ari.	.217	76	265	240	22	52	83	7	0	8	33	0	0	6	19	4	56	0	1	5	.346	.291
Stottlemyre, Todd, Ari.*	.194	18	37	31	6	6	11	2	0	1	4	3	0	0	3	0	14	0	0	0	.355	.265
Strickland, Scott, Mon.	.000	49	2	2	0	0	0	0	0	0	0	0	0	0	0	0	2	0	0	0	.000	.000
Strong, Joe, Fla.†	.000	18	1	1	0	0	0	0	0	0	0	0	0	0	0	0	1	0	0	0	.000	.000
Stull, Everett, Mil.	.000	20	10	9	0	0	0	0	0	0	0	0	0	0	1	0	9	0	0	0	.000	.100
Stynes, Chris, Cin.	.334	119	420	380	71	127	189	24	1	12	40	3	3	2	32	2	54	5	2	5	.497	.386
Sullivan, Scott, Cin.	.286	80	7	7	0	2	2	0	0	0	0	0	0	0	0	0	2	0	0	0	.286	.286
Surhoff, B.J., Atl.*	.289	44	143	128	13	37	53	9	2	1	11	1	1	1	12	0	12	3	0	5	.414	.352
Sutton, Larry, St.L.*	.320	23	33	25	5	8	11	0	0	1	6	1	2	0	5	0	7	0	0	0	.440	.406
Swann, Pedro, Atl.*	.000	4	2	2	0	0	0	0	0	0	0	0	0	0	0	0	2	0	0	0	.000	.000
Sweeney, Mark, Mil.*	.219	71	87	73	9	16	25	6	0	1	6	1	0	1	12	1	18	0	0	1	.342	.337
Swindell, Greg, Ari.	.000	64	2	1	0	0	0	0	0	0	0	1	0	0	0	0	1	0	0	0	.000	.000
Tapani, Kevin, Chi.	.179	30	68	56	3	10	15	2	0	1	4	9	0	0	3	0	20	0	1	1	.268	.222
Tatis, Fernando, St.L.	.253	96	394	324	59	82	159	21	1	18	64	1	2	10	57	1	94	2	3	13	.491	.379
Taubensee, Eddie, Cin.*	.267	81	291	266	29	71	101	12	0	6	24	1	1	2	21	1	44	0	0	7	.380	.324
Tavarez, Julian, Col.*	.086	51	38	35	1	3	3	0	0	0	0	3	0	0	0	0	14	0	0	0	.086	.086
Taylor, Reggie, Phi.*	.091	9	11	11	1	1	1	0	0	0	0	0	0	0	0	0	8	1	0	0	.091	.091
Telemaco, Amaury, Phi.	.000	13	5	4	0	0	0	0	0	0	0	0	0	0	1	0	1	0	0	0	.000	.200
Telford, Anthony, Mon.	.000	64	3	2	0	0	0	0	0	0	0	1	0	0	0	0	0	0	0	0	.000	.000
Thompson, Mark, St.L.	.000	20	3	3	0	0	0	0	0	0	0	0	0	0	0	0	1	0	0	0	.000	.000
Thurman, Mike, Mon.	.042	17	32	24	3	1	1	0	0	0	0	6	0	0	2	0	17	0	0	0	.042	.115
Toca, Jorge, N.Y.	.429	8	7	7	1	3	4	1	0	0	4	0	0	0	0	0	0	0	0	0	.571	.429
Tollberg, Brian, S.D.	.094	19	38	32	1	3	3	0	0	0	1	6	0	0	0	0	11	0	0	1	.094	.094
Tracy, Andy, Mon.*	.260	83	218	192	29	50	93	8	1	11	32	0	2	2	22	1	61	1	0	3	.484	.339
Trammell, Bubba, N.Y.	.232	36	65	56	9	13	24	2	0	3	12	0	1	0	8	0	19	1	0	3	.429	.323
Truby, Chris, Hou.	.260	78	279	258	28	67	123	15	4	11	59	1	5	5	10	1	56	2	1	4	.477	.295
Tucker, Michael, Cin.*	.267	148	323	270	55	72	138	13	4	15	36	0	2	7	44	1	64	13	6	6	.511	.381
Tucker, T.J., Mon.	1.000	2	1	1	1	1	1	0	0	0	0	0	0	0	0	0	0	0	0	0	1.000	1.000
Tyner, Jason, N.Y.*	.195	13	48	41	3	8	10	2	0	0	5	3	2	1	1	0	4	1	1	1	.244	.222
Unroe, Tim, Atl.	.000	4	7	5	0	0	0	0	0	0	0	0	1	0	1	0	2	0	0	0	.000	.167
Urbina, Ugueth, Mon.	.000	13	1	1	0	0	0	0	0	0	0	0	0	0	0	0	1	0	0	0	.000	.000
Valdes, Ismael, Chi.-L.A.	.200	22	33	25	2	5	10	2	0	1	3	7	0	0	1	0	10	0	0	0	.400	.231
Valdes, Marc, Hou.	.000	53	3	3	0	0	0	0	0	0	0	0	0	0	0	0	2	0	0	0	.000	.000
Valera, Yohanny, Mon.	.000	7	13	10	1	0	0	0	0	0	0	1	1	0	1	1	0	0	0	0	.000	.167
Vander Wal, John, Pit.*	.299	134	461	384	74	115	216	29	0	24	94	0	3	2	72	5	92	11	2	7	.563	.410
Van Poppel, Todd, Chi.	.000	51	11	9	0	0	0	0	0	0	0	2	0	0	0	0	4	0	0	0	.000	.000
Vazquez, Javier, Mon.	.231	33	80	65	4	15	17	2	0	0	1	13	0	0	2	0	15	0	0	0	.262	.254
Velandia, Jorge, N.Y.	.000	28	9	7	1	0	0	0	0	0	0	0	0	0	2	0	2	0	0	0	.000	.222
Ventura, Robin, N.Y.*	.232	141	551	469	61	109	206	23	1	24	84	1	4	2	75	12	91	3	5	14	.439	.338
Veras, Quilvio, Atl.†	.309	84	364	298	56	92	122	15	0	5	37	6	4	5	51	0	50	25	12	8	.409	.413
Veres, Dave, St.L.	.000	71	1	1	0	0	0	0	0	0	0	0	0	0	0	0	0	0	0	0	.000	.000
Vidro, Jose, Mon.†	.330	153	663	606	101	200	327	51	2	24	97	0	6	2	49	4	69	5	4	17	.540	.379
Villegas, Ismael, Atl.	.000	1	1	1	0	0	0	0	0	0	0	0	0	0	0	0	0	0	0	0	.000	.000
Villone, Ron, Cin.*	.163	35	45	43	2	7	8	1	0	0	4	2	0	0	0	0	9	0	0	1	.186	.163
Vina, Fernando, St.L.*	.300	123	554	487	81	146	194	24	6	4	31	2	1	28	36	0	36	10	8	5	.398	.380
Vitiello, Joe, S.D.	.250	39	63	52	7	13	22	3	0	2	8	0	1	0	10	0	9	0	0	1	.423	.365
Vizcaino, Jose, L.A.†	.204	40	106	93	9	19	23	2	1	0	4	2	0	1	10	3	15	1	0	3	.247	.288
Wagner, Billy, Hou.*	.000	28	2	2	0	0	0	0	0	0	0	0	0	0	0	0	2	0	0	0	.000	.000
Walker, Kevin, S.D.*	.250	70	4	4	0	1	1	0	0	0	0	0	0	0	0	0	1	0	0	0	.250	.250
Walker, Larry, Col.*	.309	87	372	314	64	97	159	21	7	9	51	0	3	9	46	4	40	5	5	12	.506	.409
Walker, Todd, Col.*	.316	57	196	171	28	54	93	10	4	7	36	1	3	1	20	0	19	4	1	2	.544	.385
Wall, Donne, S.D.	.000	44	2	1	0	0	0	0	0	0	0	1	0	0	0	0	1	0	0	0	.000	.000
Wallace, Jeff, Pit.*	.000	38	1	1	0	0	0	0	0	0	0	0	0	0	0	0	0	0	0	0	.000	.000
Ward, Daryle, Hou.*	.258	119	281	264	36	68	142	10	2	20	47	0	2	0	15	2	61	0	0	6	.538	.295
Ward, Turner, Ari.†	.173	15	59	52	5	9	13	4	0	0	4	1	1	0	5	0	7	1	1	3	.250	.241
Wasdin, John, Col.	.250	14	9	8	0	2	2	0	0	0	0	1	0	0	0	0	2	0	0	0	.250	.250
Weathers, David, Mil.	.000	69	1	1	0	0	0	0	0	0	0	0	0	0	0	0	1	0	0	0	.000	.000
Webster, Lenny, Mon.	.210	39	87	81	6	17	20	3	0	0	5	0	0	0	6	1	14	0	0	5	.247	.264
Wehner, John, Pit.	.300	21	55	50	10	15	21	3	0	1	9	1	0	0	4	0	6	0	0	1	.420	.352
Weiss, Walt, Atl.†	.260	80	227	192	29	50	60	6	2	0	18	3	3	3	26	1	32	1	1	2	.313	.353
Wendell, Turk, N.Y.*	.250	77	4	4	0	1	1	0	0	0	0	0	0	0	0	0	0	0	0	0	.250	.250
White, Devon, L.A.†	.266	47	168	158	26	42	61	5	1	4	13	0	0	1	9	0	30	3	6	3	.386	.310
White, Gabe, Cin.-Col.*	.222	68	10	9	1	2	5	0	0	1	2	1	0	0	0	0	5	0	0	0	.556	.222
White, Rick, N.Y.	.200	24	5	5	0	1	1	0	0	0	0	0	0	0	0	0	1	0	0	0	.200	.200
White, Rondell, Mon.-Chi.	.311	94	396	357	59	111	176	26	0	13	61	0	2	4	33	0	79	5	3	4	.493	.374
Widger, Chris, Mon.	.238	86	312	281	31	67	124	17	2	12	34	0	1	1	29	3	61	1	2	5	.441	.311
Wilkins, Marc, Pit.	.167	52	6	6	0	1	1	0	0	0	0	0	0	0	0	0	4	0	0	0	.167	.167
Wilkins, Rick, St.L.*	.273	4	13	11	3	3	3	0	0	0	1	0	0	0	2	0	2	0	0	0	.273	.385
Williams, Brian, Chi.	.500	22	2	2	0	1	2	1	0	0	1	0	0	0	0	0	0	0	0	0	1.000	.500
Williams, George, S.D.†	.188	11	17	16	2	3	6	0	0	1	2	0	0	1	0	0	4	0	0	0	.375	.235
Williams, Woody, S.D.	.259	30	66	58	10	15	22	4	0	1	9	1	2	1	4	0	26	0	0	1	.379	.308
Williams, Matt T., Mil.†	.000	11	1	1	0	0	0	0	0	0	0	0	0	0	0	0	1	0	0	0	.000	.000
Williams, Matt, Ari.	.275	96	397	371	43	102	160	18	2	12	47	0	3	3	20	1	51	1	2	11	.431	.315
Williams, Mike, Pit.	.000	72	1	1	0	0	0	0	0	0	0	0	0	0	0	0	0	0	0	0	.000	.000
Williamson, Scott, Cin.	.063	48	22	16	1	1	1	0	0	0	0	4	0	0	2	0	8	0	0	0	.063	.167
Wilson, Enrique, Pit.†	.262	40	136	122	11	32	49	6	1	3	15	2	1	0	11	2	13	0	1	4	.402	.321
Wilson, Preston, Fla.	.264	161	674	605	94	160	294	35	3	31	121	0	6	8	55	1	187	36	14	11	.486	.331
Wilson, Vance, N.Y.	.000	4	4	4	0	0	0	0	0	0	0	0	0	0	0	0	2	0	0	0	.000	.000

Player, Team	Avg.	G	TPA	AB	R	H	TB	2B	3B	HR	RBI	SH	SF	HP	BB	IBB	SO	SB	CS	GDP	Slg.	OBP
Witasick, Jay, S.D.	.136	11	25	22	0	3	3	0	0	0	3	2	0	0	1	0	10	0	0	1	.136	.174
Wolf, Randy, Phi.*	.193	32	71	57	5	11	13	2	0	0	4	10	1	0	3	0	19	0	0	0	.228	.230
Womack, Tony, Ari.*	.271	146	659	617	95	167	237	21	14	7	57	2	5	5	30	0	74	45	11	6	.384	.307
Wood, Kerry, Chi.	.250	25	46	40	6	10	13	0	0	1	4	4	0	0	2	0	10	0	0	0	.325	.264
Woodard, Steve, Mil.*	.045	27	26	22	0	1	1	0	0	0	2	2	0	1	1	0	6	0	0	1	.045	.125
Worrell, Tim, Chi.	.000	54	2	2	0	0	0	0	0	0	0	0	0	0	0	0	1	0	0	0	.000	.000
Wright, Jamey, Mil.	.065	26	50	46	0	3	4	1	0	0	0	4	0	0	0	0	17	0	0	0	.087	.065
Yoshii, Masato, Col.	.180	29	64	50	4	9	13	1	0	1	8	12	0	0	2	0	13	1	0	3	.260	.212
Young, Dmitri, Cin.†	.303	152	593	548	68	166	269	37	6	18	88	1	5	3	36	6	80	0	3	16	.491	.346
Young, Eric, Chi.	.297	153	690	607	98	180	242	40	2	6	47	7	5	8	63	1	39	54	7	12	.399	.367
Young, Kevin, Pit.	.258	132	541	496	77	128	215	27	0	20	88	0	5	8	32	1	96	8	3	15	.433	.311
Zeile, Todd, N.Y.	.268	153	623	544	67	146	254	36	3	22	79	0	3	2	74	4	85	3	4	15	.467	.356
Zosky, Eddie, Hou.	.000	4	4	4	0	0	0	0	0	0	0	0	0	0	0	0	1	0	0	0	.000	.000
Zuleta, Julio, Chi.	.294	30	73	68	13	20	37	8	0	3	12	0	0	3	2	0	19	0	1	2	.544	.342

AWARDED FIRST BASE ON OBSTRUCTION OR CATCHER'S INTERFERENCE—Agbayani, New York (Kreuter); Boone, Cincinnati (Kreuter); Bradley, Montreal (Santiago); Counsell, Arizona (Petrick); Gomez, San Diego (Widger); Hayes, Milwaukee (Meluskey); Lowell, Florida (Meluskey).

PLAYERS WITH TWO OR MORE TEAMS

Player, Team	Avg.	G	TPA	AB	R	H	TB	2B	3B	HR	RBI	SH	SF	HP	BB	IBB	SO	SB	CS	GDP	Slg.	OBP
Arnold, Jamie, L.A.	.000	2	0	0	0	0	0	0	0	0	0	0	0	0	0	0	0	0	0	0	.000	.000
Arnold, Jamie, Chi.	.111	12	10	9	0	1	2	1	0	0	0	0	0	1	0	0	3	0	0	0	.222	.200
Ashby, Andy, Phi.	.179	16	35	28	0	5	5	0	0	0	5	5	0	0	2	0	10	0	0	0	.179	.233
Ashby, Andy, Atl.	.121	16	37	33	2	4	4	0	0	0	1	4	0	0	0	0	12	0	0	1	.121	.121
Aven, Bruce, Pit.	.250	72	153	148	18	37	63	11	0	5	25	0	0	5	0	0	31	2	3	4	.426	.275
Aven, Bruce, L.A.	.250	9	23	20	2	5	11	0	0	2	4	0	0	3	0	0	8	0	0	0	.550	.348
Aybar, Manny, Col.	.000	1	0	0	0	0	0	0	0	0	0	0	0	0	0	0	0	0	0	0	.000	.000
Aybar, Manny, Cin.	.000	32	9	6	1	0	0	0	0	0	0	1	0	0	2	0	3	0	0	0	.000	.250
Aybar, Manny, Fla.	.000	21	0	0	0	0	0	0	0	0	0	0	0	0	0	0	0	0	0	0	.000	.000
Bako, Paul, Hou.*	.000	1	2	2	0	0	0	0	0	0	0	0	0	0	0	0	1	0	0	0	.000	.000
Bako, Paul, Fla.*	.242	56	186	161	10	39	47	6	1	0	14	1	1	1	22	7	48	0	0	4	.292	.335
Bako, Paul, Atl.*	.190	24	63	58	8	11	21	4	0	2	6	0	0	0	5	3	15	0	0	2	.362	.254
Bautista, Danny, Fla.	.191	44	94	89	9	17	33	4	0	4	12	0	0	5	0	0	20	1	0	1	.371	.234
Bautista, Danny, Ari.	.317	87	294	262	45	83	134	16	7	7	47	4	5	3	20	4	30	5	2	10	.511	.366
Belinda, Stan, Col.	.000	47	1	1	0	0	0	0	0	0	0	0	0	0	0	0	1	0	0	0	.000	.000
Belinda, Stan, Atl.	.000	10	0	0	0	0	0	0	0	0	0	0	0	0	0	0	0	0	0	0	.000	.000
Brown, Brant, Fla.*	.192	41	76	73	4	14	26	6	0	2	6	0	0	0	3	0	33	1	0	1	.356	.224
Brown, Brant, Chi.*	.157	54	102	89	7	14	24	1	0	3	10	1	1	1	10	0	29	2	1	2	.270	.248
Chen, Bruce, Atl.*	.000	22	7	5	0	0	0	0	0	0	0	2	0	0	0	0	3	0	0	0	.000	.000
Chen, Bruce, Phi.*	.040	15	31	25	0	1	1	0	0	0	1	5	0	0	1	0	17	0	0	0	.040	.077
Christiansen, Jason, Pit.	.000	44	0	0	0	0	0	0	0	0	0	0	0	0	0	0	0	0	0	0	.000	.000
Christiansen, Jason, St.L.	.000	21	0	0	0	0	0	0	0	0	0	0	0	0	0	0	0	0	0	0	.000	.000
Daal, Omar, Ari.*	.259	20	31	27	2	7	11	1	0	1	4	3	0	0	1	0	3	0	0	1	.407	.286
Daal, Omar, Phi.*	.278	12	23	18	1	5	7	2	0	0	2	2	0	0	3	0	5	0	0	0	.389	.381
Downs, Scott, Chi.*	.077	18	32	26	2	2	2	0	0	0	1	4	0	0	2	0	10	0	0	0	.077	.143
Downs, Scott, Mon.*	.000	1	2	2	0	0	0	0	0	0	0	0	0	0	0	0	0	0	0	0	.000	.000
Echevarria, Angel, Col.	.111	10	9	9	0	1	1	0	0	0	2	0	0	0	0	0	2	0	0	0	.111	.111
Echevarria, Angel, Mil.	.214	31	49	42	3	9	14	2	0	1	4	0	0	0	7	0	9	0	0	1	.333	.327
Fox, Andy, Ari.*	.209	31	90	86	10	18	25	4	0	1	10	0	0	0	4	1	16	2	1	1	.291	.244
Fox, Andy, Fla.*	.244	69	185	164	19	40	57	4	2	3	10	0	0	3	18	3	37	8	3	1	.348	.330
Goodwin, Tom, Col.*	.271	91	377	317	65	86	125	8	8	5	47	5	4	1	50	2	76	39	7	3	.394	.368
Goodwin, Tom, L.A.*	.251	56	229	211	29	53	61	3	1	1	11	0	0	0	18	0	41	16	3	4	.289	.310
Harris, Lenny, Ari.*	.188	36	91	85	9	16	22	1	1	1	13	0	3	0	3	1	5	5	0	3	.259	.209
Harris, Lenny, N.Y.*	.304	76	157	138	22	42	63	6	3	3	13	2	0	0	17	1	17	8	1	4	.457	.381
Henry, Doug, Hou.	.000	45	1	1	0	0	0	0	0	0	0	0	0	0	0	0	0	0	0	0	.000	.000
Henry, Doug, S.F.	.000	27	0	0	0	0	0	0	0	0	0	0	0	0	0	0	0	0	0	0	.000	.000
Hernandez, Carlos A., S.D.	.251	58	212	191	16	48	65	11	0	2	25	0	2	3	16	1	26	1	3	4	.340	.316
Hernandez, Carlos A., St.L.	.275	17	58	51	7	14	21	4	0	1	10	0	1	1	5	0	9	1	0	0	.412	.345
Hollandsworth, Todd, L.A.*	.234	81	293	261	42	61	97	12	6	8	24	0	1	1	30	2	61	11	4	4	.372	.314
Hollandsworth, Todd, Col.*	.323	56	178	167	39	54	95	8	0	11	23	0	0	0	11	1	38	7	3	4	.569	.365
Holmes, Darren, St.L.	.000	5	1	1	0	0	0	0	0	0	0	0	0	0	0	0	1	0	0	0	.000	.000
Holmes, Darren, Ari.	.000	8	0	0	0	0	0	0	0	0	0	0	0	0	0	0	0	0	0	0	.000	.000
Hunter, Brian L., Col.	.275	72	226	200	36	55	64	4	1	1	13	4	0	1	21	0	31	15	3	2	.320	.347
Hunter, Brian L., Cin.	.225	32	48	40	11	9	10	1	0	0	1	1	1	0	6	0	9	5	0	0	.250	.319
Hunter, Brian R., Atl.	.500	2	2	2	1	1	4	0	0	1	1	0	0	0	0	0	0	0	0	0	2.000	.500
Hunter, Brian R., Phi.	.210	85	158	138	13	29	55	5	0	7	22	0	0	0	20	1	39	0	1	2	.399	.310
Lee, Travis, Ari.*	.232	72	250	224	34	52	89	13	0	8	40	0	1	0	25	1	46	5	1	6	.397	.308
Lee, Travis, Phi.*	.239	56	223	180	19	43	59	11	1	1	14	0	1	2	40	0	33	3	0	6	.328	.381
Linebrink, Scott, S.F.	.000	3	0	0	0	0	0	0	0	0	0	0	0	0	0	0	0	0	0	0	.000	.000
Linebrink, Scott, Hou.	1.000	8	1	1	0	1	1	0	0	0	0	0	0	0	0	0	0	0	0	0	1.000	1.000
Melhuse, Adam, L.A.†	.000	1	1	1	0	0	0	0	0	0	0	0	0	0	0	0	1	0	0	0	.000	.000
Melhuse, Adam, Col.†	.174	23	26	23	3	4	6	0	1	0	4	0	0	0	3	0	5	0	0	1	.261	.269
Mieske, Matt, Hou.	.173	62	89	81	7	14	22	1	2	1	5	0	0	1	7	0	17	0	0	2	.272	.247
Mieske, Matt, Ari.	.250	11	10	8	3	2	5	0	0	1	2	0	1	0	1	0	1	0	0	0	.625	.300
Miller, Trever, Phi.	.000	14	0	0	0	0	0	0	0	0	0	0	0	0	0	0	0	0	0	0	.000	.000
Miller, Trever, Hou.	.000	2	0	0	0	0	0	0	0	0	0	0	0	0	0	0	0	0	0	0	.000	.000
Moraga, David, Mon.*	.000	3	0	0	0	0	0	0	0	0	0	0	0	0	0	0	0	0	0	0	.000	.000
Moraga, David, Col.*	.000	1	0	0	0	0	0	0	0	0	0	0	0	0	0	0	0	0	0	0	.000	.000
Newhan, David, S.D.*	.150	14	26	20	5	3	7	1	0	1	2	0	0	0	6	1	7	0	0	0	.350	.346
Newhan, David, Phi.*	.176	10	19	17	3	3	3	0	0	0	0	0	0	0	2	0	6	0	0	2	.176	.263

Player, Team	Avg.	G	TPA	AB	R	H	TB	2B	3B	HR	RBI	SH	SF	HP	BB	IBB	SO	SB	CS	GDP	Slg.	OBP
Padilla, Vicente, Ari.	1.000	27	1	1	0	1	1	0	0	0	0	0	0	0	0	0	0	0	0	0	1.000	1.000
Padilla, Vicente, Phi.	.000	28	0	0	0	0	0	0	0	0	0	0	0	0	0	0	0	0	0	0	.000	.000
Relaford, Desi, Phi.†	.221	83	313	253	29	56	83	12	3	3	30	2	1	9	48	7	45	5	0	7	.328	.363
Relaford, Desi, S.D.†	.204	45	189	157	26	32	40	2	0	2	16	1	1	3	27	0	26	8	0	3	.255	.330
Reyes, Carlos, Phi.†	.000	10	0	0	0	0	0	0	0	0	0	0	0	0	0	0	0	0	0	0	.000	.000
Reyes, Carlos, S.D.†	.000	12	1	1	0	0	0	0	0	0	0	0	0	0	0	0	0	0	0	0	.000	.000
Rodriguez, Henry, Chi.*	.251	76	287	259	37	65	136	15	1	18	51	0	3	3	22	2	76	1	2	4	.525	.314
Rodriguez, Henry, Fla.*	.269	36	123	108	10	29	41	6	0	2	10	0	0	1	14	0	23	0	0	1	.380	.358
Schilling, Curt, Phi.	.167	16	33	30	0	5	6	1	0	0	1	2	0	0	1	0	4	0	0	0	.200	.194
Schilling, Curt, Ari.	.258	13	38	31	2	8	10	2	0	0	3	7	0	0	0	0	11	0	1	0	.323	.258
Serafini, Dan, S.D.	.000	3	0	0	0	0	0	0	0	0	0	0	0	0	0	0	0	0	0	0	.000	.000
Serafini, Dan, Pit.	.083	11	27	24	1	2	2	0	0	0	2	3	0	0	0	0	9	0	0	1	.083	.083
Servais, Scott, Col.	.218	33	110	101	6	22	29	4	0	1	13	0	1	1	7	2	16	0	1	1	.287	.273
Servais, Scott, S.F.	.250	7	10	8	1	2	2	0	0	0	0	0	0	0	2	1	1	0	0	0	.250	.400
Skrmetta, Matt, Mon.†	.000	6	0	0	0	0	0	0	0	0	0	0	0	0	0	0	0	0	0	0	.000	.000
Skrmetta, Matt, Pit.†	.000	8	2	2	0	0	0	0	0	0	0	0	0	0	0	0	1	0	0	0	.000	.000
Slocumb, Heathcliff, St.L.	.000	44	1	1	0	0	0	0	0	0	0	0	0	0	0	0	1	0	0	0	.000	.000
Slocumb, Heathcliff, S.D.	.000	22	0	0	0	0	0	0	0	0	0	0	0	0	0	0	0	0	0	0	.000	.000
Valdes, Ismael, Chi.	.286	13	20	14	1	4	6	2	0	0	2	5	0	0	1	0	3	0	0	0	.429	.333
Valdes, Ismael, L.A.	.091	9	13	11	1	1	4	0	0	1	1	2	0	0	0	0	7	0	0	0	.364	.091
White, Gabe, Cin.*	.000	1	0	0	0	0	0	0	0	0	0	0	0	0	0	0	0	0	0	0	.000	.000
White, Gabe, Col.*	.222	67	10	9	1	2	5	0	0	1	2	1	0	0	0	0	5	0	0	0	.556	.222
White, Rondell, Mon.	.307	75	322	290	52	89	146	24	0	11	54	0	2	2	28	0	67	5	1	4	.503	.370
White, Rondell, Chi.	.328	19	74	67	7	22	30	2	0	2	7	0	0	2	5	0	12	0	2	0	.448	.392

DESIGNATED HITTING

TEAM

Team	Avg.	G	TPA	AB	R	H	TB	2B	3B	HR	RBI	SH	SF	HP	BB	IBB	SO	SB	CS	GDP	Slg.	OBP
Arizona	.429	6	29	28	6	12	15	0	0	1	2	0	0	1	0	0	7	0	0	0	.536	.448
St. Louis	.400	9	40	35	5	14	26	3	0	3	12	0	0	2	3	0	7	0	0	1	.743	.475
Milwaukee	.364	9	38	33	4	12	16	1	0	1	7	0	0	0	5	0	8	0	0	0	.485	.447
Pittsburgh	.333	6	29	27	2	9	12	0	0	1	3	0	0	0	2	0	7	1	1	1	.444	.379
New York	.306	9	41	36	7	11	19	2	0	2	7	0	0	1	4	0	8	0	0	0	.528	.390
San Diego	.303	9	41	33	4	10	11	1	0	0	4	0	0	0	8	2	3	0	0	2	.333	.439
Florida	.300	8	36	30	7	9	16	2	1	1	8	0	0	4	2	0	1	0	0	1	.533	.417
Montreal	.286	9	39	35	3	10	10	0	0	0	3	0	0	0	4	0	5	2	0	1	.286	.359
Cincinnati	.280	6	26	25	4	7	15	2	0	2	4	0	0	0	1	0	2	0	0	0	.600	.308
Atlanta	.278	9	39	36	5	10	12	2	0	0	1	0	0	0	3	0	8	0	1	0	.333	.333
San Francisco	.269	6	27	26	5	7	12	2	0	1	2	0	0	0	1	0	3	1	0	2	.462	.296
Chicago	.262	9	42	42	3	11	18	1	0	2	6	0	0	0	0	0	6	0	0	1	.429	.262
Houston	.261	6	26	23	2	6	10	1	0	1	5	0	0	0	3	0	4	0	0	1	.435	.346
Los Angeles	.233	9	40	30	4	7	9	2	0	0	3	0	0	0	10	0	6	0	2	2	.300	.425
Philadelphia	.125	9	38	32	2	4	4	0	0	0	1	0	0	0	6	0	9	0	0	1	.125	.263
Colorado	.105	6	25	19	1	2	2	0	0	0	0	0	0	1	5	0	7	0	0	0	.105	.320
Totals	.288	140	556	490	64	141	207	19	1	15	66	0	0	9	57	2	91	4	3	13	.422	.372

TOP DESIGNATED HITTERS

Minimum 15 at-bats. *Lefthanded batter. †Switch-hitter.

Player, Team	Avg.	G	TPA	AB	R	H	TB	2B	3B	HR	RBI	SH	SF	HP	BB	IBB	SO	SB	CS	GDP	Slg.	OBP
Young, Dmitri, Cin.†	.400	4	16	15	3	6	14	2	0	2	4	0	0	0	1	0	2	0	0	0	.933	.438
Guerrero, Wilton, Mon.†	.400	6	27	25	3	10	10	0	0	0	3	0	0	0	2	0	2	2	0	1	.400	.444
Gwynn, Tony, S.D.*	.375	6	28	24	3	9	10	1	0	0	2	0	0	0	4	2	0	0	0	1	.417	.464
Piazza, Mike, N.Y.	.333	5	21	18	5	6	13	1	0	2	4	0	0	1	2	0	2	0	0	0	.722	.429
Millar, Kevin, Fla.	.286	6	27	21	5	6	13	2	1	1	7	0	0	4	2	0	1	0	0	1	.619	.444
Joyner, Wally, Atl.*	.267	7	30	30	3	8	9	1	0	0	1	0	0	0	0	0	6	0	0	1	.300	.267
Hansen, Dave, L.A.*	.267	5	20	15	2	4	6	2	0	0	2	0	0	0	5	0	2	0	1	0	.400	.450
Sweeney, Mark, Mil.*	.267	4	17	15	2	4	5	1	0	0	2	0	0	0	2	0	5	0	0	0	.333	.353
Hill, Glenallen, Chi.	.262	9	42	42	3	11	18	1	0	2	6	0	0	0	0	0	6	0	0	1	.429	.262
Ward, Daryle, Hou.*	.250	4	16	16	1	4	7	0	0	1	3	0	0	0	0	0	2	0	0	1	.438	.250

ALL DESIGNATED HITTERS

*Lefthanded batter. †Switch-hitter.

Player, Team	Avg.	G	TPA	AB	R	H	TB	2B	3B	HR	RBI	SH	SF	HP	BB	IBB	SO	SB	CS	GDP	Slg.	OBP
Agbayani, Benny, N.Y.	.000	1	1	1	0	0	0	0	0	0	0	0	0	0	0	0	0	0	0	0	.000	.000
Alfonzo, Edgardo, N.Y.	.429	2	9	7	2	3	4	1	0	0	2	0	0	0	2	0	2	0	0	0	.571	.556
Allen, Dusty, S.D.	.000	1	2	1	0	0	0	0	0	0	0	0	0	0	1	0	1	0	0	0	.000	.500
Alou, Moises, Hou.	.250	1	5	4	0	1	1	0	0	0	2	0	0	0	1	0	1	0	0	0	.250	.400
Bagwell, Jeff, Hou.	.333	1	5	3	1	1	2	1	0	0	0	0	0	0	2	0	1	0	0	0	.667	.600
Bell, Jay, Ari.	.800	1	5	5	2	4	7	0	0	1	1	0	0	0	0	0	0	0	0	0	1.400	.800
Bonilla, Bobby, Atl.†	.500	1	4	2	1	1	2	1	0	0	0	0	0	0	2	0	0	0	0	0	1.000	.750
Burks, Ellis, S.F.	.000	2	9	9	0	0	0	0	0	0	0	0	0	0	0	0	1	0	0	2	.000	.000
Burnitz, Jeromy, Mil.*	.333	1	5	3	0	1	1	0	0	0	1	0	0	0	2	0	1	0	0	0	.333	.600
Burrell, Pat, Phi.	.143	4	17	14	1	2	2	0	0	0	1	0	0	0	3	0	5	0	0	0	.143	.294
Carpenter, Bubba, Col.*	.143	2	8	7	0	1	1	0	0	0	0	0	0	0	1	0	4	0	0	0	.143	.250
Casanova, Raul, Mil.†	.417	3	12	12	1	5	5	0	0	0	2	0	0	0	0	0	1	0	0	0	.417	.417
Colbrunn, Greg, Ari.	.429	2	7	7	1	3	3	0	0	0	0	0	0	0	0	0	2	0	0	0	.429	.429
Cordero, Wil, Pit.	.400	1	5	5	1	2	5	0	0	1	1	0	0	0	0	0	1	0	0	0	1.000	.400
Crespo, Felipe, S.F.†	1.000	1	1	1	0	1	2	1	0	0	0	0	0	0	0	0	0	0	0	0	2.000	1.000
Davis, Ben, S.D.†	.250	1	4	4	1	1	1	0	0	0	0	0	0	0	0	0	0	0	0	0	.250	.250
Davis, Eric, St.L.	.583	4	13	12	1	7	7	0	0	0	4	0	0	0	1	0	2	0	0	0	.583	.615
Davis, Russ, S.F.	.417	3	13	12	4	5	9	1	0	1	2	0	0	0	1	0	2	0	0	0	.750	.462
DeHaan, Kory, S.D.*	.000	1	1	1	0	0	0	0	0	0	0	0	0	0	0	0	1	0	0	0	.000	.000
Ducey, Rob, Phi.*	.000	5	17	14	1	0	0	0	0	0	0	0	0	0	3	0	3	0	0	0	.000	.176
Dunston, Shawon, St.L.	.667	1	5	3	1	2	6	1	0	1	4	0	0	0	2	0	0	0	0	0	2.000	.800
Finley, Steve, Ari.*	.250	2	9	8	2	2	2	0	0	0	1	0	0	0	1	0	1	0	0	0	.250	.333
Floyd, Cliff, Fla.*	.500	1	4	4	1	2	2	0	0	0	1	0	0	0	0	0	0	0	0	0	.500	.500
Franco, Matt, N.Y.*	.333	2	3	3	0	1	1	0	0	0	0	0	0	0	0	0	0	0	0	0	.333	.333
Galarraga, Andres, Atl.	.250	1	4	4	0	1	1	0	0	0	0	0	0	0	0	0	2	0	0	0	.250	.250
Guerrero, Vladimir, Mon.	.000	2	8	6	0	0	0	0	0	0	0	0	0	0	2	0	2	0	0	0	.000	.250
Guerrero, Wilton, Mon.†	.400	6	27	25	3	10	10	0	0	0	3	0	0	0	2	0	2	2	0	1	.400	.444
Gwynn, Tony, S.D.*	.375	6	28	24	3	9	10	1	0	0	2	0	0	0	4	2	0	0	0	1	.417	.464
Hansen, Dave, L.A.*	.267	5	20	15	2	4	6	2	0	0	2	0	0	0	5	0	2	0	0	1	.400	.450
Harris, Lenny, N.Y.*	.000	1	3	3	0	0	0	0	0	0	0	0	0	0	0	0	2	0	0	0	.000	.000
Hayes, Charlie, Mil.	.667	1	4	3	1	2	5	0	0	1	2	0	0	0	1	0	1	0	0	0	1.667	.750
Hill, Glenallen, Chi.	.262	9	42	42	3	11	18	1	0	2	6	0	0	0	0	0	6	0	0	1	.429	.262
Howard, Thomas, St.L.†	.200	3	11	10	1	2	5	0	0	1	2	0	0	1	0	0	3	0	0	1	.500	.273
Hundley, Todd, L.A.†	.333	1	4	3	0	1	1	0	0	0	0	0	0	0	1	0	1	0	0	0	.333	.500
Hunter, Brian, Phi.	.000	1	2	2	0	0	0	0	0	0	0	0	0	0	0	0	1	0	0	0	.000	.000
Johnson, Mark P., N.Y.*	.000	1	2	2	0	0	0	0	0	0	0	0	0	0	0	0	1	0	0	0	.000	.000
Joyner, Wally, Atl.*	.267	7	30	30	3	8	9	1	0	0	1	0	0	0	0	0	6	0	0	1	.300	.267

Player, Team	Avg.	G	TPA	AB	R	H	TB	2B	3B	HR	RBI	SH	SF	HP	BB	IBB	SO	SB	CS	GDP	Slg.	OBP
Karros, Eric, L.A.	.250	1	5	4	0	1	1	0	0	0	1	0	0	0	1	0	0	0	0	1	.250	.400
Lankford, Ray, St.L.*	.500	1	2	2	1	1	2	1	0	0	0	0	0	0	0	0	1	0	0	0	1.000	.500
Larkin, Barry, Cin.	.167	1	6	6	1	1	1	0	0	0	0	0	0	0	0	0	0	0	0	0	.167	.167
Lowery, Terrell, S.F.	.250	1	4	4	1	1	1	0	0	0	0	0	0	0	0	0	0	1	0	0	.250	.250
Magadan, Dave, S.D.*	.000	2	6	3	0	0	0	0	0	0	0	0	0	0	3	0	1	0	0	1	.000	.500
Millar, Kevin, Fla.	.286	6	27	21	5	6	13	2	1	1	7	0	4	2	0	1	0	0	1	.619	.444
Morris, Hal, Cin.*	.000	1	4	4	0	0	0	0	0	0	0	0	0	0	0	0	0	0	0	0	.000	.000
Osik, Keith, Pit.	.667	1	4	3	0	2	2	0	0	0	0	0	0	0	1	0	0	0	0	0	.667	.750
Piazza, Mike, N.Y.	.333	5	21	18	5	6	13	1	0	2	4	0	0	1	2	0	2	0	0	0	.722	.429
Pratt, Todd, N.Y.	.500	1	2	2	0	1	1	0	0	0	1	0	0	0	0	0	1	0	0	0	.500	.500
Ryan, Rob, Ari.*	.333	1	3	3	0	1	1	0	0	0	0	0	0	0	0	0	1	0	0	0	.333	.333
Sefcik, Kevin, Phi.	1.000	1	2	2	0	2	2	0	0	0	0	0	0	0	0	0	0	0	0	0	1.000	1.000
Seguignol, Fernando, Mon.†	.000	1	4	4	0	0	0	0	0	0	0	0	0	0	0	0	1	0	0	0	.000	.000
Sheffield, Gary, L.A.	.143	2	9	7	1	1	1	0	0	0	0	0	0	0	2	0	3	0	1	1	.143	.333
Shumpert, Terry, Col.	.000	1	5	3	1	0	0	0	0	0	0	0	0	0	2	0	1	0	0	0	.000	.400
Sisco, Steve, Atl.	.000	1	1	0	1	0	0	0	0	0	0	0	0	0	1	0	0	0	0	0	.000	1.000
Smith, Mark, Fla.	.200	1	5	5	1	1	1	0	0	0	0	0	0	0	0	0	0	0	0	0	.200	.200
Sweeney, Mark, Mil.*	.267	4	17	15	2	4	5	1	0	0	2	0	0	0	2	0	5	0	0	0	.333	.353
Tatis, Fernando, St.L.	.250	2	9	8	1	2	6	1	0	1	2	0	0	1	0	0	1	0	0	0	.750	.333
Vander Wal, John, Pit.*	.231	3	14	13	1	3	3	0	0	0	1	0	0	0	1	0	6	0	1	0	.231	.286
Vizcaino, Jose, L.A.†	.000	1	2	1	1	0	0	0	0	0	0	0	0	0	1	0	0	0	0	0	.000	.500
Walker, Larry, Col.*	.111	3	12	9	0	1	1	0	0	0	0	0	0	1	2	0	2	0	0	0	.111	.333
Ward, Daryle, Hou.*	.250	4	16	16	1	4	7	0	0	1	3	0	0	0	0	0	2	0	0	1	.438	.250
Williams, Matt, Ari.	.400	1	5	5	1	2	2	0	0	0	0	0	0	0	0	0	2	0	0	0	.400	.400
Young, Dmitri, Cin.†	.400	4	16	15	3	6	14	2	0	2	4	0	0	1	0	0	2	0	0	0	.933	.438
Young, Kevin, Pit.	.333	1	6	6	0	2	2	0	0	0	1	0	0	0	0	0	0	1	0	1	.333	.333

The following designated hitters, each of whom appeared in at least one game, had no plate appearances, runs scored or stolen base attempts: de la Rosa, Tomas, Montreal.

PINCH-HITTING

TEAM

Team	Avg.	G	TPA	AB	R	H	TB	2B	3B	HR	RBI	SH	SF	HP	BB	IBB	SO	SB	CS	GDP	Slg	OBP
Cincinnati	.258	126	267	233	24	60	88	10	0	6	42	3	5	3	23	3	51	0	1	5	.378	.326
Pittsburgh	.246	130	234	211	29	52	89	14	1	7	34	1	0	1	21	4	54	3	1	5	.422	.318
Colorado	.246	137	283	248	35	61	87	7	2	5	36	0	3	4	28	3	54	4	2	4	.351	.329
Montreal	.246	115	210	179	21	44	63	8	1	3	27	2	3	2	24	2	34	4	1	3	.352	.337
New York	.245	137	290	249	32	61	95	11	1	7	37	1	2	2	36	2	68	6	2	9	.382	.343
Atlanta	.236	131	246	216	19	51	72	10	1	3	30	0	2	4	24	2	48	0	0	3	.333	.321
San Francisco	.235	119	232	196	25	46	77	10	0	7	48	1	5	0	30	4	41	0	1	3	.393	.329
Arizona	.234	130	249	214	22	50	64	8	0	2	20	2	1	2	30	0	44	3	0	6	.299	.332
Los Angeles	.233	133	244	206	27	48	89	5	0	12	37	4	0	2	32	3	56	1	1	6	.432	.342
Florida	.230	132	251	217	19	50	78	13	0	5	23	0	3	3	31	1	57	2	0	6	.359	.335
Milwaukee	.224	143	282	232	25	52	73	12	0	3	31	4	1	7	38	4	64	1	0	5	.315	.349
San Diego	.224	136	275	232	23	52	85	12	0	7	43	4	3	0	36	2	65	1	0	3	.366	.325
Philadelphia	.199	144	273	231	22	46	61	5	2	2	19	3	1	2	37	1	63	0	0	5	.264	.311
St. Louis	.199	122	235	206	24	41	76	6	1	9	36	1	2	2	24	1	67	0	0	2	.369	.286
Chicago	.188	132	272	234	32	44	73	3	1	8	38	4	3	4	27	1	68	3	1	9	.312	.280
Houston	.184	135	269	244	20	45	68	10	2	3	20	1	1	1	22	5	67	2	0	2	.279	.254
Totals	.226	2102	4112	3548	399	803	1238	144	12	89	521	31	32	38	463	38	901	30	10	76	.349	.320

INDIVIDUAL
TOP PINCH-HITTERS

Minimum 20 at-bats. *Lefthanded batter. †Switch-hitter.

Player, Team	Avg.	G	TPA	AB	R	H	TB	2B	3B	HR	RBI	SH	SF	HP	BB	IBB	SO	SB	CS	GDP	Slg	OBP
Dellucci, David, Ari.*	.350	23	22	20	1	7	9	2	0	0	2	0	0	0	2	0	4	0	0	0	.450	.409
Vander Wal, John, Pit.*	.348	30	30	23	10	8	19	2	0	3	10	0	0	0	7	1	5	2	0	0	.826	.500
Cromer, D.T., Cin.*	.348	24	23	23	2	8	10	2	0	0	2	0	0	0	0	0	8	0	0	0	.435	.348
Seguignol, Fernando, Mon.†	.348	26	26	23	2	8	17	3	0	2	5	0	0	1	2	0	4	0	0	0	.739	.423
Morris, Hal, Cin.*	.333	44	44	36	7	12	20	2	0	2	6	1	1	1	5	2	4	0	0	1	.556	.419
Shumpert, Terry, Col.	.333	50	50	45	9	15	19	1	0	1	10	0	1	0	4	0	4	2	1	0	.422	.380
Stynes, Chris, Cin.	.318	24	24	22	1	7	10	0	0	1	5	1	1	0	0	0	0	0	0	0	.455	.304
Bonilla, Bobby, Atl.†	.308	48	47	39	3	12	18	4	1	0	10	0	1	1	6	0	9	0	0	1	.462	.404
Spiers, Bill, Hou.*	.303	34	34	33	1	10	13	3	0	0	4	0	0	1	1	1	1	1	0	1	.394	.324
Crespo, Felipe, S.F.†	.294	56	56	51	6	15	20	2	0	1	13	0	2	0	3	2	10	0	0	1	.392	.321
Davis, Eric, St.L	.286	23	23	21	1	6	7	1	0	0	2	0	0	2	0	0	6	0	0	0	.333	.348
Leyritz, Jim, L.A.	.286	27	26	21	1	6	6	0	0	0	5	0	0	1	4	0	2	0	0	0	.286	.423
Guerrero, Wilton, Mon.†	.283	53	53	46	6	13	14	1	0	0	9	1	1	0	5	0	4	2	0	0	.304	.346
Frias, Hanley, Ari.†	.280	31	31	25	3	7	8	1	0	0	2	0	0	0	6	0	6	1	0	0	.320	.419
Hansen, Dave, L.A.*	.273	70	65	55	8	15	37	1	0	7	14	0	0	0	10	0	19	0	0	1	.673	.385

ALL PINCH-HITTERS

*Lefthanded batter. †Switch-hitter.

Player, Team	Avg.	G	TPA	AB	R	H	TB	2B	3B	HR	RBI	SH	SF	HP	BB	IBB	SO	SB	CS	GDP	Slg	OBP
Abbott, Kurt, N.Y.	.286	17	16	14	3	4	6	2	0	0	0	0	0	0	2	0	1	0	0	0	.429	.375
Abreu, Bobby, Phi.*	.333	3	3	3	0	1	1	0	0	0	1	0	0	0	0	0	2	0	0	0	.333	.333
Agbayani, Benny, N.Y.	.444	20	20	18	5	8	15	4	0	1	9	0	0	0	2	0	7	1	0	0	.833	.500
Alfonzo, Edgardo, N.Y.	.000	2	2	2	0	0	0	0	0	0	0	0	0	0	0	0	0	0	0	1	.000	.000
Allen, Dusty, S.D.	.000	6	6	5	0	0	0	0	0	0	0	0	0	0	1	0	2	0	0	0	.000	.167
Alou, Moises, Hou.	.333	5	5	3	0	1	2	1	0	0	2	0	0	1	1	0	1	0	0	0	.667	.600
Alvarez, Clemente, Phi.	.000	1	1	1	0	0	0	0	0	0	0	0	0	0	0	0	0	0	0	0	.000	.000
Alvarez, Gabe, S.D.	.143	8	8	7	1	1	2	1	0	0	0	0	0	0	1	0	1	0	0	0	.286	.250
Anderson, Brian, Ari.†	.000	2	2	1	0	0	0	0	0	0	0	0	0	0	1	0	0	0	0	0	.000	.500
Andrews, Shane, Chi.	.091	14	12	11	1	1	4	0	0	1	3	0	0	1	1	0	5	0	0	1	.364	.167
Ankiel, Rick, St.L*	.000	3	3	3	0	0	0	0	0	0	0	0	0	0	0	0	3	0	0	0	.000	.000
Arias, Alex, Phi.	.286	21	20	14	2	4	5	1	0	0	1	2	0	1	3	0	5	0	0	0	.357	.444
Arroyo, Bronson, Pit.	.000	1	1	1	0	0	0	0	0	0	0	0	0	0	0	0	0	0	0	0	.000	.000
Aurilia, Rich, S.F.	.000	1	1	0	0	0	0	0	0	0	0	0	0	0	1	0	0	0	0	0	.000	1.000
Aven, Bruce, Pit.-L.A.	.111	36	36	36	1	4	5	1	0	0	0	0	0	0	0	0	13	0	1	0	.139	.111
Bako, Paul, Hou.-Fla.-Atl.*	.000	1	1	0	0	0	0	0	0	0	0	0	0	0	1	0	0	0	0	0	.000	1.000
Barker, Glen, Hou.	.000	5	5	5	0	0	0	0	0	0	0	0	0	0	0	0	4	0	0	0	.000	.000
Barker, Kevin, Mil.*	.125	9	9	8	2	1	1	0	0	0	1	0	0	0	1	0	3	0	0	0	.125	.222
Barrett, Michael, Mon.	.286	7	7	7	0	2	3	1	0	0	1	0	0	0	0	0	2	0	0	0	.429	.286
Bartee, Kimera, Cin.	.000	4	4	3	0	0	0	0	0	0	0	0	0	0	1	0	1	0	0	0	.000	.250
Bautista, Danny, Fla.-Ari.	.250	18	18	16	1	4	7	3	0	0	0	0	0	0	2	0	2	0	0	1	.438	.333
Bell, Derek, N.Y.	.000	1	1	1	0	0	0	0	0	0	0	0	0	0	0	0	1	0	0	0	.000	.000
Bell, Jay, Ari.	.000	4	4	3	0	0	0	0	0	0	0	0	0	0	0	0	0	0	0	0	.000	.000
Bell, Mike, Cin.	.250	9	9	8	1	2	5	0	0	1	0	0	0	0	1	0	2	0	0	0	.625	.333
Belliard, Ron, Mil.	1.000	1	1	1	1	1	1	0	0	0	0	0	0	0	0	0	0	0	0	0	1.000	1.000
Beltre, Adrian, L.A.	1.000	1	1	1	1	1	4	0	0	1	3	0	0	0	0	0	0	0	0	0	4.000	1.000
Benard, Marvin, S.F.*	.133	16	16	15	1	2	2	0	0	0	2	0	0	0	1	0	3	0	0	0	.133	.188
Benjamin, Mike, Pit.	.500	9	9	8	2	4	7	3	0	0	0	0	0	0	1	0	1	0	0	0	.875	.556
Bennett, Gary, Phi.	.000	1	1	1	0	0	0	0	0	0	0	0	0	0	0	0	0	0	0	0	.000	.000
Berg, Dave, Fla.	.417	15	15	12	3	5	10	2	0	1	0	0	0	1	2	0	3	0	0	0	.833	.533
Bergeron, Peter, Mon.*	.000	4	4	3	1	0	0	0	0	0	0	0	0	0	1	0	1	0	0	0	.000	.250

Player, Team	Avg.	G	TPA	AB	R	H	TB	2B	3B	HR	RBI	SH	SF	HP	BB	IBB	SO	SB	CS	GDP	Slg.	OBP
Berkman, Lance, Hou.†	.056	20	20	18	2	1	2	1	0	0	0	0	0	0	2	0	11	0	0	0	.111	.150
Berroa, Geronimo, L.A.	.267	18	18	15	1	4	4	0	0	0	4	0	0	0	3	1	5	0	0	1	.267	.389
Berry, Sean, Mil.	.091	24	23	22	0	2	3	1	0	0	0	0	0	0	1	0	6	0	0	1	.136	.130
Bichette, Dante, Cin.	.000	6	6	5	1	0	0	0	0	0	1	0	0	0	1	0	3	0	0	0	.000	.167
Biggio, Craig, Hou.	.000	1	1	1	0	0	0	0	0	0	0	0	0	0	0	0	0	0	0	0	.000	.000
Blanco, Henry, Mil.	.200	6	6	5	0	1	1	0	0	0	0	0	0	0	1	0	3	0	0	0	.200	.333
Blum, Geoff, Mon.†	.143	26	26	21	3	3	4	1	0	0	3	1	1	1	2	0	5	0	0	1	.190	.240
Bocachica, Hiram, L.A.	.333	6	6	6	2	2	2	0	0	0	0	0	0	0	0	0	2	0	0	0	.333	.333
Bogar, Tim, Hou.	.167	13	13	12	1	2	2	0	0	0	0	0	0	0	1	0	4	0	0	0	.167	.231
Bohanon, Brian, Col.*	.000	1	1	1	0	0	0	0	0	0	0	0	0	0	0	0	0	0	0	0	.000	.000
Bonds, Barry, S.F.*	.000	4	3	3	0	0	0	0	0	0	0	0	0	0	0	0	2	0	0	0	.000	.000
Bonilla, Bobby, Atl.†	.308	48	47	39	3	12	18	4	1	0	10	0	1	1	6	0	9	0	0	0	.462	.404
Boone, Aaron, Cin.	.000	1	1	0	0	0	0	0	0	0	0	1	0	0	0	0	0	0	0	0	.000	.000
Boone, Bret, S.D.	.000	1	1	1	0	0	0	0	0	0	0	0	0	0	0	0	1	0	0	0	.000	.000
Bradley, Milton, Mon.†	.000	1	1	0	0	0	0	0	0	0	0	0	0	0	1	0	0	0	0	0	.000	1.000
Bragg, Darren, Col.*	.185	31	31	27	3	5	9	1	0	1	5	0	1	0	3	0	13	0	0	0	.333	.258
Branson, Jeff, L.A.*	.000	4	3	2	1	0	0	0	0	0	0	0	0	0	1	0	1	0	0	0	.000	.333
Brock, Tarrik, Chi.*	.000	2	2	1	0	0	0	0	0	0	0	0	0	0	1	0	1	0	0	0	.000	.500
Brogna, Rico, Phi.*	.200	5	5	5	0	1	1	0	0	0	1	0	0	0	0	0	2	0	0	1	.200	.200
Brown, Adrian, Pit.†	.200	23	23	20	4	4	6	2	0	0	0	0	0	0	3	0	3	0	0	1	.300	.304
Brown, Brant, Fla.-Chi.*	.182	49	47	44	1	8	11	3	0	0	2	0	0	0	3	0	23	2	0	2	.250	.234
Brown, Emil, Pit.	.154	15	15	13	0	2	2	0	0	0	0	0	0	0	2	0	6	0	0	0	.154	.267
Brown, Roosevelt, Chi.*	.286	17	15	14	2	4	8	1	0	1	5	0	0	1	0	0	3	0	0	0	.571	.333
Buford, Damon, Chi.	.000	8	8	6	1	0	0	0	0	0	0	0	1	0	1	0	2	0	0	0	.000	.143
Burks, Ellis, S.F.	.444	12	12	9	2	4	5	1	0	0	3	0	0	0	3	2	2	0	0	0	.556	.583
Burnitz, Jeromy, Mil.*	.000	2	2	1	0	0	0	0	0	0	0	0	0	1	0	0	0	0	0	0	.000	.500
Burrell, Pat, Phi.	.000	1	1	0	0	0	0	0	0	0	0	0	0	0	1	0	0	0	0	0	.000	1.000
Cabrera, Alex, Ari.	.143	8	8	7	1	1	4	0	0	1	2	0	0	0	1	0	1	0	0	0	.571	.250
Cabrera, Orlando, Mon.	.000	3	3	2	0	0	0	0	0	0	0	0	0	0	1	0	1	0	0	0	.000	.333
Caminiti, Ken, Hou.†	.000	3	3	1	2	0	0	0	0	0	0	0	0	0	2	2	0	0	0	0	.000	.667
Carpenter, Bubba, Col.*	.286	7	7	7	1	2	5	0	0	1	1	0	0	0	0	0	3	0	0	0	.714	.286
Casanova, Raul, Mil.†	.417	17	17	12	1	5	7	2	0	0	2	0	0	2	3	0	2	0	0	0	.583	.588
Casey, Sean, Cin.*	.000	4	4	4	0	0	0	0	0	0	0	0	0	0	0	0	1	0	0	1	.000	.000
Cedeno, Roger, Hou.†	.222	9	9	9	0	2	2	0	0	0	0	0	0	0	0	0	4	0	0	0	.222	.222
Charles, Frank, Hou.	.667	3	3	3	1	2	3	1	0	0	0	0	0	0	0	0	0	0	0	0	1.000	.667
Cirillo, Jeff, Col.	.500	3	3	2	0	1	1	0	0	0	0	0	0	0	1	1	0	0	0	0	.500	.667
Clapinski, Chris, Fla.†	.444	9	9	9	3	4	8	1	0	1	4	0	0	0	0	0	2	0	0	0	.889	.444
Clark, Brady, Cin.	.250	8	8	8	1	2	3	1	0	0	0	0	0	0	0	0	2	0	0	0	.375	.250
Clark, Will, St.L*	.000	1	1	1	0	0	0	0	0	0	0	0	0	0	0	0	0	0	0	0	.000	.000
Colbrunn, Greg, Ari.	.250	28	28	24	2	6	7	1	0	0	4	0	0	0	4	0	5	0	0	1	.292	.357
Collier, Lou, Mil.	1.000	1	1	1	0	1	1	0	0	0	0	0	0	0	0	0	0	0	0	0	1.000	1.000
Conti, Jason, Ari.*	.154	15	15	13	1	2	2	0	0	0	2	0	0	0	2	0	6	0	0	0	.154	.267
Coquillette, Trace, Mon.	.333	6	6	6	1	2	4	2	0	0	2	0	0	0	0	0	0	0	0	0	.667	.333
Cora, Alex, L.A.*	1.000	1	1	1	0	1	1	0	0	0	0	0	0	0	0	0	0	0	0	0	1.000	1.000
Cordero, Wil, Pit.	.250	4	4	4	1	1	4	0	0	1	1	0	0	0	0	0	3	0	0	0	1.000	.250
Cornelius, Reid, Fla.	.000	1	1	1	0	0	0	0	0	0	0	0	0	0	0	0	0	0	0	0	.000	.000
Counsell, Craig, Ari.*	.261	26	26	23	1	6	6	0	0	0	1	1	0	0	2	0	2	0	0	1	.261	.320
Crespo, Felipe, S.F.†	.294	56	56	51	6	15	20	2	0	1	13	0	2	0	3	2	10	0	0	1	.392	.321
Cromer, D.T., Cin.*	.348	24	23	23	2	8	10	2	0	0	2	0	0	0	0	0	8	0	0	0	.435	.348
Cromer, Tripp, Hou.	.000	5	5	4	1	0	0	0	0	0	0	0	0	0	1	0	0	0	0	0	.000	.200
Cruz, Ivan, Pit.*	.000	7	7	7	0	0	0	0	0	0	0	0	0	0	0	0	6	0	0	1	.000	.000
Darr, Mike C., S.D.*	.667	3	3	3	1	2	2	0	0	0	2	0	0	0	0	0	1	1	0	0	.667	.667
Davis, Ben, S.D.†	.000	5	5	5	0	0	0	0	0	0	0	0	0	0	0	0	1	0	0	0	.000	.000
Davis, Eric, St.L	.286	23	23	21	1	6	7	1	0	0	2	0	0	0	2	0	6	0	0	0	.333	.348
Davis, Russ, S.F.	.161	33	33	31	2	5	11	0	0	2	6	0	1	0	1	0	7	0	1	1	.355	.182
De La Rosa, Tomas, Mon.	.500	4	3	2	0	1	1	0	0	0	0	0	0	0	1	0	0	1	0	0	.500	.667
DeHaan, Kory, S.D.*	.261	27	25	23	5	6	13	4	0	1	5	0	0	0	2	0	10	0	0	0	.565	.320
Dellucci, David, Ari.*	.350	23	22	20	1	7	9	2	0	0	2	0	0	0	2	0	4	0	1	0	.450	.409
DeRosa, Mark, Atl.	1.000	2	2	2	0	2	3	1	0	0	3	0	0	0	0	0	0	0	0	0	1.500	1.000
Donnels, Chris, L.A.*	.400	17	17	15	3	6	12	3	0	1	3	0	0	0	2	0	3	0	0	1	.800	.471
Drew, J.D., St.L*	.375	11	10	8	1	3	7	2	1	0	1	0	0	0	2	0	3	0	0	0	.875	.500
Ducey, Rob, Phi.*	.203	82	81	69	9	14	19	3	1	0	6	0	1	0	11	0	23	0	0	1	.275	.309
Dunston, Shawon, St.L	.091	35	34	33	2	3	9	0	0	2	3	0	0	0	1	0	14	0	0	0	.273	.118
Durazo, Erubiel, Ari.*	.111	11	11	9	0	1	1	0	0	0	2	0	0	0	2	0	5	1	0	1	.111	.273
Echevarria, Angel, Col.-Mil.	.143	32	31	28	0	4	5	1	0	0	3	0	0	0	3	0	7	0	0	1	.179	.226
Edmonds, Jim, St.L*	.000	4	4	2	2	0	0	0	0	0	0	0	0	0	2	0	2	0	0	0	.000	.500
Elster, Kevin, L.A.	.294	19	19	17	3	5	11	0	0	2	3	0	0	0	2	1	3	0	0	0	.647	.368
Ensberg, Morgan, Hou.	.667	3	3	3	0	2	2	0	0	0	0	0	0	0	0	0	0	0	0	0	.667	.667
Estalella, Bobby, S.F.	.500	2	2	2	0	1	2	1	0	0	3	0	0	0	0	0	0	0	0	0	1.000	.500
Eusebio, Tony, Hou.	.143	7	7	7	0	1	2	1	0	0	0	0	0	0	0	0	3	0	0	0	.286	.143
Feliz, Pedro, S.F.	.000	4	4	4	0	0	0	0	0	0	0	0	0	0	0	0	1	0	0	0	.000	.000
Fernandez, Alex, Fla.	.000	1	1	1	0	0	0	0	0	0	0	0	0	0	0	0	1	0	0	0	.000	.000
Floyd, Cliff, Fla.*	.273	13	13	11	2	3	10	1	0	2	5	0	0	0	2	0	3	0	0	0	.909	.385
Fox, Andy, Ari.-Fla.*	.063	18	18	16	0	1	1	0	0	0	0	0	0	0	2	0	1	1	0	0	.063	.167
Franco, Matt, N.Y.*	.208	61	57	48	2	10	10	0	0	0	5	0	1	0	8	2	8	0	0	1	.208	.316
Frias, Hanley, Ari.†	.280	31	31	25	3	7	8	1	0	0	2	0	0	0	6	0	6	1	0	0	.320	.419
Frye, Jeff, Col.	.500	15	15	14	5	7	9	2	0	0	0	0	0	1	0	0	3	0	0	0	.643	.533
Furcal, Rafael, Atl.†	.000	2	2	1	0	0	0	0	0	0	0	0	0	0	1	0	0	0	0	0	.000	.500
Galarraga, Andres, Atl.	.538	15	15	13	1	7	9	2	0	0	5	0	0	1	1	1	3	0	0	0	.692	.600
Gant, Ron, Phi.	.000	5	5	3	0	0	0	0	0	0	0	0	0	0	2	1	2	0	0	0	.000	.400
Garibay, Daniel, Chi.*	.000	1	1	1	0	0	0	0	0	0	0	0	0	0	0	0	1	0	0	0	.000	.000
Giles, Brian S., Pit.*	.000	1	1	0	0	0	0	0	0	0	0	0	0	0	1	1	0	0	0	0	.000	1.000

Player, Team	Avg.	G	TPA	AB	R	H	TB	2B	3B	HR	RBI	SH	SF	HP	BB	IBB	SO	SB	CS	GDP	Slg.	OBP
Gilkey, Bernard, Ari.	.100	22	22	20	0	2	2	0	0	0	0	0	0	0	2	0	3	0	0	1	.100	.182
Ginter, Keith, Hou.	.000	3	2	1	0	0	0	0	0	0	1	0	1	0	0	0	1	0	0	0	.000	.000
Girardi, Joe, Chi.	.000	4	4	3	0	0	0	0	0	0	0	0	0	0	1	0	1	0	0	0	.000	.250
Glanville, Doug, Phi.	.200	6	6	5	2	1	4	0	0	1	1	0	0	0	1	0	2	0	0	0	.800	.333
Glavine, Tom, Atl.*	.000	2	2	2	0	0	0	0	0	0	0	0	0	0	0	0	0	0	0	0	.000	.000
Gload, Ross, Chi.*	.250	9	9	8	2	2	2	0	0	0	0	0	0	0	1	0	2	0	0	0	.250	.333
Gomez, Chris, S.D.	.625	14	12	8	2	5	5	0	0	0	1	0	1	0	3	0	0	0	0	0	.625	.727
Gonzalez, Alex, Fla.	.500	2	2	2	0	1	1	0	0	0	1	0	0	0	0	0	0	0	0	0	.500	.500
Gonzalez, Raul, Chi.	.000	2	2	2	0	0	0	0	0	0	0	0	0	0	0	0	2	0	0	0	.000	.000
Gonzalez, Wiki, S.D.	.125	9	9	8	0	1	1	0	0	0	1	0	0	0	1	0	2	0	0	0	.125	.222
Goodwin, Tom, Col.-L.A.*	.250	9	9	8	0	2	2	0	0	0	1	0	0	0	1	0	2	1	0	0	.250	.333
Grace, Mark, Chi.*	.333	4	4	3	1	1	1	0	0	0	0	0	0	0	1	0	0	0	0	1	.333	.500
Green, Shawn, L.A.*	.000	1	1	1	0	0	0	0	0	0	0	0	0	0	0	0	1	0	0	0	.000	.000
Greene, Willie, Chi.*	.143	17	17	14	2	2	2	0	0	0	1	0	0	0	3	0	4	0	0	1	.143	.294
Griffey, Ken Jr., Cin.*	.500	4	4	4	1	2	5	0	0	1	1	0	0	0	0	0	1	0	0	0	1.250	.500
Grissom, Marquis, Mil.	.500	4	4	2	1	1	1	0	0	0	2	0	0	0	2	0	1	0	0	0	.500	.750
Grudzielanek, Mark, L.A.	.000	2	2	2	0	0	0	0	0	0	0	0	0	0	0	0	2	0	0	0	.000	.000
Guerrero, Vladimir, Mon.	.000	1	1	1	0	0	0	0	0	0	0	0	0	0	0	0	0	0	0	0	.000	.000
Guerrero, Wilton, Mon.†	.283	53	53	46	6	13	14	1	0	0	9	1	1	0	5	0	4	2	0	0	.304	.346
Gutierrez, Ricky, Chi.	.000	5	5	4	0	0	0	0	0	0	1	0	1	0	0	0	1	0	0	0	.000	.000
Gwynn, Tony, S.D.*	.667	4	4	3	0	2	3	1	0	0	2	0	1	0	0	0	0	0	0	1	1.000	.750
Hamilton, Darryl, N.Y.*	.385	16	16	13	2	5	8	0	0	1	3	0	0	0	3	0	6	1	0	0	.615	.500
Hammonds, Jeffrey, Col.	.200	6	6	5	0	1	1	0	0	0	1	0	0	1	0	0	3	0	0	0	.200	.333
Hampton, Mike, N.Y.	.000	1	1	1	0	0	0	0	0	0	0	0	0	0	0	0	1	0	0	0	.000	.000
Hansen, Dave, L.A.*	.273	70	65	55	8	15	37	1	0	7	14	0	0	0	10	0	19	0	0	1	.673	.385
Harris, Lenny, Ari.-N.Y.*	.268	61	60	56	9	15	17	2	0	0	2	1	0	0	3	0	8	1	0	3	.304	.305
Hayes, Charlie, Mil.	.333	20	20	15	3	5	5	0	0	0	6	0	0	1	4	1	3	0	0	0	.333	.500
Helms, Wes, Atl.	.333	3	3	3	0	1	1	0	0	0	0	0	0	0	0	0	1	0	0	0	.333	.333
Helton, Todd, Col.*	.000	2	2	2	0	0	0	0	0	0	0	0	0	0	0	0	0	0	0	0	.000	.000
Hermansen, Chad, Pit.	.000	2	2	2	0	0	0	0	0	0	0	0	0	0	0	0	1	0	0	0	.000	.000
Hernandez, Alex, Pit.*	.500	5	4	4	1	2	3	1	0	0	0	0	0	0	0	0	0	0	0	0	.750	.500
Hernandez, Carlos, S.D.-St.L.	.667	4	4	3	1	2	5	0	0	1	3	0	1	0	0	0	0	0	0	0	1.667	.500
Hernandez, Jose, Mil.	.000	4	4	4	0	0	0	0	0	0	0	0	0	0	0	0	4	0	0	0	.000	.000
Hernandez, Livan, S.F.	.000	1	1	1	0	0	0	0	0	0	0	0	0	0	0	0	1	0	0	0	.000	.000
Hidalgo, Richard, Hou.	.000	2	2	1	0	0	0	0	0	0	0	0	0	0	1	0	0	0	0	0	.000	.500
Hill, Glenallen, Chi.	.200	28	27	25	3	5	9	1	0	1	5	0	0	0	2	0	9	0	0	2	.360	.259
Hollandsworth, Todd, L.A.-Col.*	.200	28	27	25	4	5	9	1	0	1	3	0	0	1	1	0	8	1	1	1	.360	.259
Houston, Tyler, Mil.*	.200	23	22	20	3	4	7	0	0	1	3	0	0	0	2	1	3	1	0	0	.350	.273
Howard, Thomas, St.L†	.208	60	58	53	5	11	19	2	0	2	11	0	0	0	5	0	14	0	0	1	.358	.276
Hubbard, Mike, Atl.	.000	1	1	1	0	0	0	0	0	0	0	0	0	0	0	0	1	0	0	0	.000	.000
Hubbard, Trenidad, Atl.	.333	12	12	12	0	4	4	0	0	0	1	0	0	0	0	0	5	0	0	0	.333	.333
Hundley, Todd, L.A.†	.000	6	6	6	0	0	0	0	0	0	1	0	0	0	0	0	1	0	0	0	.000	.000
Hunter, Brian L., Col.-Cin.	.167	16	16	12	2	2	2	0	0	0	0	0	0	0	4	0	2	0	0	0	.167	.375
Hunter, Brian R., Atl.-Phi.	.238	50	50	42	3	10	17	1	0	2	5	0	0	0	8	0	11	0	0	0	.405	.360
Huskey, Butch, Col.	.231	18	18	13	0	3	3	0	0	0	2	0	1	0	4	0	1	0	0	0	.231	.389
Huson, Jeff, Chi.*	.158	21	21	19	2	3	4	1	0	0	1	0	0	0	2	0	1	0	1	2	.211	.238
Hyzdu, Adam, Pit.	.375	8	8	8	1	3	6	0	0	1	4	0	0	0	0	0	2	0	0	0	.750	.375
Jackson, Damian, S.D.	.250	4	4	4	1	1	1	0	0	0	0	0	0	0	0	0	1	0	0	0	.250	.250
Jenkins, Geoff, Mil.*	.000	5	5	2	1	0	0	0	0	0	1	0	0	1	2	2	1	0	0	0	.000	.600
Johnson, Mark P., N.Y.*	.250	16	16	12	2	3	6	0	0	1	3	0	0	0	4	0	5	0	0	0	.500	.438
Johnson, Russ, Hou.	.077	14	14	13	1	1	1	0	0	0	1	1	0	0	0	0	2	0	0	1	.077	.077
Jones, Chris C., Mil.	.222	9	9	9	2	2	3	1	0	0	1	0	0	0	0	0	2	0	0	0	.333	.222
Jones, Terry, Mon.†	.250	23	23	20	4	5	5	0	0	0	1	0	0	0	3	1	4	1	1	1	.250	.348
Jordan, Brian, Atl.	.667	4	4	3	2	2	2	0	0	0	0	0	0	1	0	0	0	0	0	0	.667	.750
Jordan, Kevin, Phi.	.167	24	24	24	1	4	4	0	0	0	2	0	0	0	0	0	2	0	0	2	.167	.167
Joyner, Wally, Atl.*	.236	66	65	55	3	13	18	2	0	1	5	0	1	1	8	1	10	0	0	1	.327	.338
Karros, Eric, L.A.	.000	1	1	1	0	0	0	0	0	0	1	0	0	0	0	0	0	0	0	0	.000	.000
Kendall, Jason, Pit.	.400	5	5	5	0	2	2	0	0	0	1	0	0	0	0	0	2	1	0	0	.400	.400
Kent, Jeff, S.F.	.500	2	2	2	1	1	2	1	0	0	3	0	0	0	0	0	0	0	0	1	1.000	.500
Kieschnick, Brooks, Cin.*	.000	13	12	11	0	0	0	0	0	0	0	0	0	0	1	0	5	0	0	0	.000	.083
Kinkade, Mike, N.Y.	.000	1	1	1	0	0	0	0	0	0	0	0	0	0	0	0	1	0	0	0	.000	.000
Klassen, Danny, Ari.	.000	2	2	2	0	0	0	0	0	0	0	0	0	0	0	0	0	0	0	0	.000	.000
Klesko, Ryan, S.D.*	.167	15	15	12	2	2	8	0	0	2	4	0	0	0	3	0	5	0	0	0	.667	.333
Kotsay, Mark, Fla.*	.273	12	11	11	0	3	4	1	0	0	0	0	0	0	0	0	2	0	0	0	.364	.273
Kreuter, Chad, L.A.†	.000	2	2	0	0	0	0	0	0	0	0	0	0	0	2	0	0	0	0	0	.000	1.000
Lamb, David, N.Y.†	.000	2	2	2	0	0	0	0	0	0	0	0	0	0	0	0	1	0	0	0	.000	.000
Lankford, Ray, St.L*	.083	14	14	12	0	1	2	1	0	0	2	0	0	0	2	0	6	0	0	0	.167	.214
Lansing, Mike, Col.	.500	2	2	2	1	1	3	0	1	0	0	0	0	0	0	0	0	0	0	0	1.500	.500
Larkin, Barry, Cin.	.000	1	1	0	1	0	0	0	0	0	0	0	0	0	1	0	0	0	0	0	.000	1.000
LaRocca, Greg, S.D.	.000	3	3	1	0	0	0	0	0	0	0	0	2	0	0	0	0	0	0	0	.000	.000
Ledesma, Aaron, Col.	.217	25	25	23	3	5	6	1	0	0	3	0	0	1	1	0	6	0	0	1	.261	.280
Lee, Derrek, Fla.	.182	13	13	11	3	2	5	0	0	1	1	0	0	0	2	0	3	0	0	2	.455	.308
Lee, Travis, Ari.-Phi.*	.167	7	7	6	1	1	1	0	0	0	0	0	0	0	1	0	1	0	0	0	.167	.286
Lewis, Mark, Cin.	.200	6	6	5	1	1	1	0	0	0	3	0	0	0	1	0	1	0	0	0	.200	.333
Leyritz, Jim, L.A.	.286	27	26	21	1	6	6	0	0	0	5	0	0	1	4	0	2	0	0	0	.286	.423
Lieber, Jon, Chi.*	.000	1	1	0	1	0	0	0	0	0	0	0	0	0	1	0	0	0	0	0	.000	1.000
Lieberthal, Mike, Phi.	.000	5	5	4	0	0	0	0	0	0	0	0	0	0	1	0	1	0	0	1	.000	.200
Liniak, Cole, Chi.	.000	3	3	3	0	0	0	0	0	0	0	0	0	0	0	0	0	0	0	0	.000	.000
Lira, Felipe, Mon.	.000	1	1	1	0	0	0	0	0	0	0	0	0	0	0	0	0	0	0	0	.000	.000
Lockhart, Keith, Atl.*	.040	30	28	25	2	1	1	0	0	0	1	0	0	0	3	0	5	0	0	1	.040	.143
LoDuca, Paul, L.A.	.000	5	5	4	0	0	0	0	0	0	0	1	0	0	0	0	1	0	0	0	.000	.000
Lombard, George, Atl.*	.000	5	5	5	0	0	0	0	0	0	0	0	0	0	0	0	3	0	0	1	.000	.000

Player, Team	Avg.	G	TPA	AB	R	H	TB	2B	3B	HR	RBI	SH	SF	HP	BB	IBB	SO	SB	CS	GDP	Slg.	OBP
Lopez, Javy, Atl.	.167	7	7	6	0	1	2	1	0	0	1	0	0	0	1	0	2	0	0	0	.333	.286
Lopez, Luis M., Mil.†	.300	15	15	10	1	3	6	0	0	1	4	3	1	0	1	0	3	0	0	0	.600	.333
Lopez, Mendy, Fla.	.000	4	4	3	0	0	0	0	0	0	0	0	0	0	1	0	1	0	0	0	.000	.250
Loretta, Mark, Mil.	.500	2	2	2	1	1	2	1	0	0	2	0	0	0	0	0	0	0	0	0	1.000	.500
Lowell, Mike, Fla.	.250	4	4	4	0	1	1	0	0	0	1	0	0	0	0	0	1	0	0	0	.250	.250
Lowery, Terrell, S.F.	.143	9	9	7	0	1	1	0	0	0	0	0	0	0	2	0	3	0	0	0	.143	.333
Lugo, Julio, Hou.	.375	10	9	8	1	3	4	1	0	0	1	0	0	0	1	0	1	1	1	0	.500	.444
Lunar, Fernando, Atl.	.000	1	1	1	0	0	0	0	0	0	0	0	0	0	0	0	1	0	0	0	.000	.000
Mabry, John, S.D.*	.182	16	14	11	1	2	3	1	0	0	2	0	1	0	2	0	2	0	0	0	.273	.286
Magadan, Dave, S.D.*	.200	67	65	55	3	11	16	2	0	1	9	0	0	0	10	0	12	0	0	3	.291	.323
Mahomes, Pat, N.Y.	.000	1	1	1	0	0	0	0	0	0	0	0	0	0	0	0	0	0	0	0	.000	.000
Mahoney, Mike, Chi.	.000	1	1	1	0	0	0	0	0	0	0	0	0	0	0	0	0	0	0	0	.000	.000
Manto, Jeff, Col.	.800	6	6	5	2	4	9	2	0	1	4	0	0	0	1	0	0	0	0	0	1.800	.833
Marrero, Eli, St.L	.000	8	8	6	3	0	0	0	0	0	0	0	0	0	2	0	1	0	0	0	.000	.250
Martin, Al, S.D.*	.333	6	6	6	1	2	5	0	0	1	2	0	0	0	0	0	1	0	0	0	.833	.333
Martinez, Dave, Chi.*	.000	2	2	2	0	0	0	0	0	0	0	0	0	0	0	0	1	0	0	0	.000	.000
Martinez, Ramon E., S.F.	.000	17	17	12	2	0	0	0	0	0	1	1	0	0	4	0	4	0	0	0	.000	.250
Martinez, Sandy, Fla.*	.000	1	1	1	0	0	0	0	0	0	0	0	0	0	0	0	0	0	0	0	.000	.000
Matheny, Mike, St.L	1.000	2	2	1	0	1	1	0	0	0	1	0	0	0	1	0	0	0	0	0	1.000	1.000
Matthews, Gary Jr., Chi.†	.240	27	27	25	7	6	14	0	1	2	3	0	0	0	2	0	4	0	0	0	.560	.296
Mayne, Brent, Col.*	.056	22	22	18	1	1	1	0	0	0	1	0	0	0	4	1	0	0	0	1	.056	.227
McDonald, Keith, St.L	.500	4	4	4	2	2	8	0	0	2	3	0	0	0	0	0	0	0	0	0	2.000	.500
McEwing, Joe, N.Y.	.182	13	13	11	1	2	3	1	0	0	3	0	0	0	2	0	5	1	0	0	.273	.308
McGwire, Mark, St.L	.300	13	13	10	1	3	6	0	0	1	2	0	0	2	1	1	3	0	0	0	.600	.462
Meares, Pat, Pit.	.250	6	6	4	0	1	1	0	0	0	0	1	0	0	1	0	1	0	0	0	.250	.400
Melhuse, Adam, L.A.-Col.†	.200	22	22	20	3	4	6	0	1	0	3	0	0	0	2	0	5	0	0	1	.300	.273
Melo, Juan, S.F.†	.000	4	4	4	0	0	0	0	0	0	0	0	0	0	0	0	1	0	0	0	.000	.000
Meluskey, Mitch, Hou.†	.125	22	22	16	2	2	2	0	0	0	1	0	0	0	6	1	3	0	0	0	.125	.364
Mendoza, Carlos R., Col.*	.125	9	9	8	0	1	1	0	0	0	0	0	0	0	1	0	3	0	1	0	.125	.222
Metcalfe, Mike, L.A.	.000	1	1	1	0	0	0	0	0	0	0	0	0	0	0	0	0	0	0	0	.000	.000
Meyers, Chad, Chi.	.188	17	17	16	1	3	3	0	0	0	2	0	0	0	1	0	2	1	0	0	.188	.235
Mieske, Matt, Hou.-Ari.	.151	59	58	53	4	8	16	0	1	2	7	0	1	0	4	0	13	0	0	3	.302	.207
Millar, Kevin, Fla.	.209	56	56	43	1	9	9	0	0	0	5	0	0	1	12	0	13	0	0	3	.209	.393
Miller, Damian, Ari.	.500	3	3	2	1	1	1	0	0	0	0	0	0	0	1	0	0	0	0	0	.500	.667
Minor, Damon, S.F.*	.429	7	7	7	2	3	9	0	0	2	4	0	0	0	0	0	1	0	0	0	1.286	.429
Mirabelli, Doug, S.F.	.000	2	2	0	0	0	0	0	0	0	0	0	0	0	2	0	0	0	0	0	.000	1.000
Mora, Melvin, N.Y.	.000	6	6	4	0	0	0	0	0	0	1	0	1	1	0	0	1	0	0	0	.000	.167
Morandini, Mickey, Phi.*	.333	6	6	6	2	2	2	0	0	0	0	0	0	0	0	0	1	0	0	0	.333	.333
Mordecai, Mike, Mon.	.143	8	8	7	0	1	1	0	0	0	0	0	0	0	1	0	3	0	0	0	.143	.250
Morris, Hal, Cin.*	.333	44	44	36	7	12	20	2	0	2	6	1	1	1	5	2	4	0	0	1	.556	.419
Morris, Warren, Pit.*	.000	12	12	9	0	0	0	0	0	0	0	0	0	0	3	1	0	0	0	0	.000	.250
Mouton, James, Mil.	.250	31	31	24	1	6	7	1	0	0	3	0	0	1	6	0	9	0	0	0	.292	.419
Mouton, Lyle, Mil.	.250	20	20	16	2	4	6	2	0	0	2	0	0	0	4	0	6	0	0	2	.375	.400
Mueller, Bill, S.F.†	.455	14	14	11	2	5	7	2	0	0	1	0	0	0	3	0	1	0	0	0	.636	.571
Murray, Calvin, S.F.	.375	12	12	8	3	3	7	1	0	1	5	0	0	0	4	0	1	0	0	0	.875	.583
Nady, Xavier, S.D.	1.000	1	1	1	1	1	1	0	0	0	0	0	0	0	0	0	0	0	0	0	1.000	1.000
Neagle, Denny, Cin.*	.000	1	1	1	0	0	0	0	0	0	0	0	0	0	0	0	1	0	0	0	.000	.000
Nevin, Phil, S.D.	.000	1	1	1	0	0	0	0	0	0	0	0	0	0	0	0	0	0	0	0	.000	.000
Newhan, David, S.D.-Phi.*	.143	10	8	7	1	1	1	0	0	0	0	0	0	0	1	0	4	0	0	0	.143	.250
Nicholson, Kevin, S.D.†	.500	3	3	2	0	1	1	0	0	0	0	0	1	0	0	0	1	0	0	0	.500	.500
Nieves, Jose, Chi.	.200	25	24	20	2	4	4	0	0	0	3	1	0	0	3	0	4	0	0	0	.200	.304
Nunez, Abraham, Pit.†	.250	12	12	12	1	3	3	0	0	0	1	0	0	0	0	0	1	0	0	0	.250	.250
Nunnally, Jon, N.Y.*	.211	26	24	19	3	4	7	1	1	0	1	0	0	0	5	0	9	0	0	1	.368	.375
Nunnari, Talmadge, Mon.*	.500	4	4	2	1	1	1	0	0	0	0	0	0	0	2	1	1	0	0	0	.500	.750
Ochoa, Alex, Cin.	.176	39	39	34	3	6	8	2	0	0	4	0	1	1	3	1	6	0	0	0	.235	.256
Ojeda, Augie, Chi.†	.000	1	1	1	0	0	0	0	0	0	0	0	0	0	0	0	0	0	0	0	.000	.000
Osik, Keith, Pit.	.222	10	10	9	0	2	2	0	0	0	1	0	1	0	0	0	1	0	0	0	.222	.300
Owens, Eric, S.D.	.500	2	2	2	0	1	2	1	0	0	0	0	0	0	0	0	1	0	0	0	1.000	.500
Ozuna, Pablo, Fla.	.500	2	2	2	0	1	1	0	0	0	0	0	0	0	0	0	0	0	0	0	.500	.500
Paquette, Craig, St.L	.083	12	12	12	1	1	1	0	0	0	0	0	0	0	0	0	3	0	0	0	.083	.083
Patterson, Corey, Chi.*	.000	1	1	1	0	0	0	0	0	0	0	0	0	0	0	0	0	0	0	0	.000	.000
Payton, Jay, N.Y.	.125	8	8	8	0	1	1	0	0	0	0	0	0	0	0	0	2	0	1	1	.125	.125
Pena, Elvis, Col.†	.250	5	5	4	0	1	1	0	0	0	1	0	0	0	1	0	1	0	0	1	.250	.400
Penny, Brad, Fla.	.000	1	1	1	0	0	0	0	0	0	0	0	0	0	0	0	1	0	0	0	.000	.000
Perez, Carlos, L.A.*	.000	1	1	1	0	0	0	0	0	0	0	0	0	0	0	0	1	0	0	0	.000	.000
Perez, Eduardo, St.L	.143	7	7	7	0	1	1	0	0	0	0	0	0	0	0	0	3	0	0	1	.143	.143
Perez, Neifi, Col.†	1.000	1	1	1	0	1	1	0	0	0	1	0	0	0	0	0	0	0	0	0	1.000	1.000
Perez, Santiago, Mil.†	.333	3	3	3	0	1	1	0	0	0	0	0	0	0	0	0	1	0	0	0	.333	.333
Perez, Timo, N.Y.*	.500	5	5	4	0	2	2	0	0	0	1	0	0	1	0	0	0	1	1	0	.500	.600
Perez, Tomas, Phi.†	.000	1	1	1	0	0	0	0	0	0	0	0	0	0	0	0	0	0	0	0	.000	.000
Petrick, Ben, Col.	.000	4	4	4	0	0	0	0	0	0	0	0	0	0	0	0	2	0	0	0	.000	.000
Piazza, Mike, N.Y.	.500	7	7	6	2	3	7	1	0	1	3	0	0	0	1	0	1	0	0	1	1.167	.571
Pierre, Juan, Col.*	.000	3	3	3	0	0	0	0	0	0	0	0	0	0	0	0	1	0	0	0	.000	.000
Polanco, Placido, St.L	.286	17	17	14	2	4	7	0	0	1	6	1	1	0	1	0	2	0	0	0	.500	.313
Powell, Jay, Hou.	.000	1	1	1	0	0	0	0	0	0	0	0	0	0	0	0	0	0	0	0	.000	.000
Pratt, Todd, N.Y.	.077	14	14	13	2	1	4	0	0	1	4	0	0	0	1	0	3	0	0	0	.308	.143
Prince, Tom, Phi.	.500	2	2	2	1	1	1	0	0	0	1	0	0	0	0	0	1	0	0	0	.500	.500
Pritchett, Chris, Phi.*	.000	2	2	1	0	0	0	0	0	0	0	0	0	0	1	0	1	0	0	0	.000	.500
Ramirez, Alex, Pit.	.308	14	14	13	3	4	11	1	0	2	5	0	0	0	1	1	5	0	0	2	.846	.357
Ramirez, Aramis, Pit.	.500	2	2	2	1	1	2	1	0	0	2	0	0	0	0	0	0	0	0	0	1.000	.500
Redman, Tike, Pit.*	.000	3	3	2	0	0	0	0	0	0	0	0	0	0	1	0	2	0	0	0	.000	.333
Redmond, Mike, Fla.	.000	2	2	2	0	0	0	0	0	0	0	0	0	0	0	0	0	0	0	0	.000	.000

Player, Team	Avg.	G	TPA	AB	R	H	TB	2B	3B	HR	RBI	SH	SF	HP	BB	IBB	SO	SB	CS	GDP	Slg.	OBP
Reed, Jeff, Chi.*	.389	22	22	18	1	7	7	0	0	0	5	0	1	0	3	0	6	0	0	1	.389	.455
Relaford, Desi, Phi.-S.D.†	.000	2	2	0	0	0	0	0	0	0	1	1	0	0	1	0	0	0	0	0	.000	1.000
Renteria, Edgar, St.L	.000	1	1	1	0	0	0	0	0	0	0	0	0	0	0	0	1	0	0	0	.000	.000
Richard, Chris, St.L*	.000	2	1	1	0	0	0	0	0	0	0	0	0	0	0	0	0	0	0	0	.000	.000
Rios, Armando, S.F.*	.174	31	31	23	4	4	9	2	0	1	7	0	2	0	6	0	4	0	0	1	.391	.323
Rivera, Ruben, S.D.	.000	3	3	2	1	0	0	0	0	0	0	0	0	0	1	0	0	0	0	0	.000	.333
Rodriguez, Henry, Chi.-Fla.*	.364	13	12	11	2	4	11	1	0	2	6	0	1	0	0	0	4	0	0	0	1.000	.333
Rolen, Scott, Phi.	.000	1	1	1	0	0	0	0	0	0	0	0	0	0	0	0	0	0	0	0	.000	.000
Rolison, Nate, Fla.*	.000	4	4	4	0	0	0	0	0	0	0	0	0	0	0	0	1	0	0	0	.000	.000
Rollins, Jimmy, Phi.†	.000	1	1	1	0	0	0	0	0	0	0	0	0	0	0	0	0	0	0	0	.000	.000
Roskos, John, S.D.	.000	7	7	6	0	0	0	0	0	0	1	0	0	0	1	0	1	0	0	0	.000	.143
Ryan, Rob, Ari.*	.316	24	24	19	3	6	7	1	0	0	2	0	0	1	4	0	4	0	0	0	.368	.458
Sanders, Reggie, Atl.	.222	9	9	9	1	2	2	0	0	0	0	0	0	0	0	0	2	0	0	0	.222	.222
Santangelo, F.P., L.A.†	.143	29	29	21	4	3	6	0	0	1	3	0	0	5	0	0	7	1	0	1	.286	.308
Santiago, Benito, Cin.	.333	14	14	12	1	4	4	0	0	0	7	0	1	0	1	0	4	0	0	0	.333	.357
Saturria, Luis, St.L	.000	1	1	0	0	0	0	0	0	0	0	0	0	0	1	0	0	0	0	0	.000	1.000
Schneider, Brian, Mon.*	.000	2	2	2	0	0	0	0	0	0	0	0	0	0	0	0	0	0	0	0	.000	.000
Sefcik, Kevin, Phi.	.159	55	53	44	1	7	9	0	1	0	2	0	0	0	9	0	8	0	0	0	.205	.302
Seguignol, Fernando, Mon.†	.348	26	26	23	2	8	17	3	0	2	5	0	0	1	2	0	4	0	0	0	.739	.423
Servais, Scott, Col.-S.F.	.000	3	3	3	0	0	0	0	0	0	0	0	0	0	0	0	1	0	0	0	.000	.000
Sexton, Chris, Cin.	.200	6	6	5	1	1	1	0	0	0	0	1	0	0	0	0	1	0	0	1	.200	.200
Shumpert, Terry, Col.	.333	50	50	45	9	15	19	1	0	1	10	0	1	0	4	0	4	2	1	0	.422	.380
Sisco, Steve, Atl.	.200	18	18	15	4	3	6	0	0	1	2	0	0	3	0	2	0	0	0	0	.400	.333
Smith, Mark, Fla.	.229	57	57	48	6	11	14	3	0	0	4	0	0	1	8	1	8	0	0	0	.292	.351
Snow, J.T., S.F.*	.500	4	4	4	0	2	2	0	0	0	0	0	0	0	0	0	0	0	0	0	.500	.500
Sojo, Luis, Pit.	.500	11	11	10	0	5	6	1	0	0	1	0	0	0	1	0	1	0	0	0	.600	.545
Spencer, Stan, S.D.	.000	1	1	1	0	0	0	0	0	0	0	0	0	0	0	0	1	0	0	0	.000	.000
Spiers, Bill, Hou.*	.303	34	34	33	1	10	13	3	0	0	4	0	0	0	1	1	1	1	0	1	.394	.324
Sprague, Ed Jr., S.D.	.200	39	39	35	1	7	12	2	0	1	8	0	0	0	4	2	12	0	0	0	.343	.282
Stevens, Lee, Mon.*	.000	1	1	1	0	0	0	0	0	0	0	0	0	0	0	0	0	0	0	0	.000	.000
Stinnett, Kelly, Ari.	1.000	2	2	1	1	1	1	0	0	0	0	0	0	1	0	0	0	0	0	0	1.000	1.000
Stynes, Chris, Cin.	.318	24	24	22	1	7	10	0	0	1	5	1	1	0	0	0	0	0	0	0	.455	.304
Surhoff, B.J., Atl.*	.000	12	12	11	0	0	0	0	0	0	0	0	0	0	1	0	1	0	0	1	.000	.083
Sutton, Larry, St.L*	.417	15	15	12	4	5	8	0	0	1	4	0	1	0	2	0	4	0	0	0	.667	.467
Swann, Pedro, Atl.*	.000	1	1	1	0	0	0	0	0	0	0	0	0	0	0	0	1	0	0	0	.000	.000
Sweeney, Mark, Mil.*	.185	65	64	54	6	10	16	3	0	1	3	1	0	1	8	0	12	0	0	1	.296	.302
Tatis, Fernando, St.L	.000	2	2	1	0	0	0	0	0	0	0	0	0	0	1	0	1	0	0	0	.000	.500
Taubensee, Eddie, Cin.*	.300	10	10	10	1	3	3	0	0	0	1	0	0	0	0	0	1	0	0	0	.300	.300
Toca, Jorge, N.Y.	.667	3	3	3	0	2	2	0	0	0	0	0	0	0	0	0	0	0	0	0	.667	.667
Tracy, Andy, Mon.*	.250	32	32	28	2	7	12	0	1	1	5	0	0	0	4	0	8	0	0	0	.429	.344
Trammell, Bubba, N.Y.	.167	22	21	18	4	3	6	0	0	1	1	0	0	0	3	0	6	1	0	2	.333	.286
Truby, Chris, Hou.	.250	4	4	4	1	1	1	0	0	0	0	0	0	0	0	0	1	0	0	0	.250	.250
Tucker, Michael, Cin.*	.231	34	33	26	2	6	10	1	0	1	5	0	0	0	7	0	8	0	1	2	.385	.394
Tyner, Jason, N.Y.*	.000	1	1	1	0	0	0	0	0	0	0	0	0	0	0	0	0	0	0	0	.000	.000
Unroe, Tim, Atl.	.000	2	2	2	0	0	0	0	0	0	0	0	0	0	0	0	1	0	0	0	.000	.000
Valdes, Ismael, Chi.-L.A.	.000	1	1	0	0	0	0	0	0	0	0	1	0	0	0	0	0	0	0	0	.000	.000
Vander Wal, John, Pit.*	.348	30	30	23	10	8	19	2	0	3	10	0	0	0	7	1	5	2	0	0	.826	.500
Ventura, Robin, N.Y.*	.500	5	5	4	1	2	6	1	0	1	2	0	0	0	1	0	2	0	0	0	1.500	.600
Veras, Quilvio, Atl.†	.500	2	2	2	1	1	1	0	0	0	1	0	0	0	0	0	0	0	0	0	.500	.500
Vina, Fernando, St.L*	.000	3	3	2	0	0	0	0	0	0	0	0	0	0	1	0	1	0	0	0	.000	.333
Vitiello, Joe, S.D.	.294	22	22	17	2	5	5	0	0	0	2	0	0	0	5	0	5	0	0	0	.294	.455
Vizcaino, Jose, L.A.†	.273	13	13	11	2	3	3	0	0	0	2	0	0	0	2	1	1	0	0	0	.273	.385
Walker, Larry, Col.*	.000	4	3	1	1	0	0	0	0	0	0	0	0	1	1	1	0	0	0	0	.000	.667
Walker, Todd, Col.*	.300	10	10	10	1	3	3	0	0	0	1	0	0	0	0	0	2	0	0	0	.300	.300
Ward, Daryle, Hou.*	.212	55	55	52	5	11	21	2	1	2	5	0	0	0	3	1	16	0	0	0	.404	.255
Webster, Lenny, Mon.	.167	7	7	6	0	1	1	0	0	0	0	0	0	0	1	0	0	0	0	1	.167	.286
Wehner, John, Pit.	.333	6	6	6	1	2	3	1	0	0	2	0	0	0	0	0	0	0	0	0	.500	.333
Weiss, Walt, Atl.†	.167	7	6	6	1	1	1	0	0	0	0	0	0	0	0	0	1	0	0	0	.167	.167
White, Devon, L.A.†	.000	9	9	9	0	0	0	0	0	0	0	0	0	0	0	0	0	0	0	1	.000	.000
White, Rick, N.Y.	.000	2	2	2	0	0	0	0	0	0	0	0	0	0	0	0	1	0	0	0	.000	.000
White, Rondell, Mon.-Chi.	.000	2	2	1	0	0	0	0	0	0	1	0	1	0	0	0	1	0	0	0	.000	.000
Widger, Chris, Mon.	.000	1	1	1	0	0	0	0	0	0	0	0	0	0	0	0	0	0	0	0	.000	.000
Wilkins, Rick, St.L*	.000	1	1	1	0	0	0	0	0	0	1	0	0	0	0	0	0	0	0	0	.000	.000
Williams, George, S.D.†	.000	6	5	5	0	0	0	0	0	0	0	0	0	0	1	0	1	0	0	0	.000	.167
Williams, Matt, Ari.	.000	1	1	1	0	0	0	0	0	0	0	0	0	0	0	0	0	0	0	0	.000	.000
Williams, Woody, S.D.	.000	3	3	3	0	0	0	0	0	0	0	0	0	0	0	0	2	0	0	0	.000	.000
Wilson, Enrique, Pit.†	.333	9	9	9	2	3	6	1	1	0	2	0	0	0	0	0	1	0	0	1	.667	.333
Wilson, Preston, Fla.	.000	2	2	2	0	0	0	0	0	0	0	0	0	0	0	0	2	0	0	0	.000	.000
Wilson, Vance, N.Y.	.000	1	1	1	0	0	0	0	0	0	0	0	0	0	0	0	0	0	0	0	.000	.000
Womack, Tony, Ari.*	1.000	1	1	1	1	1	1	0	0	0	0	0	0	0	0	0	0	0	0	0	1.000	1.000
Wood, Kerry, Chi.	.000	2	2	1	0	0	0	0	0	0	0	1	0	0	0	0	1	0	0	0	.000	.000
Young, Dmitri, Cin.†	.455	13	13	11	0	5	7	2	0	0	5	0	0	0	2	0	2	0	0	0	.636	.538
Young, Eric, Chi.	.000	2	2	2	0	0	0	0	0	0	0	0	0	0	0	0	1	0	0	0	.000	.000
Young, Kevin, Pit.	.200	5	5	5	1	1	1	0	0	0	0	0	0	0	0	0	1	0	0	0	.200	.200
Zeile, Todd, N.Y.	.000	3	3	2	0	0	0	0	0	0	0	0	0	1	0	1	1	0	0	0	.000	.333
Zosky, Eddie, Hou.	.000	4	4	4	0	0	0	0	0	0	0	0	0	0	0	0	1	0	0	0	.000	.000
Zuleta, Julio, Chi.	.222	13	13	9	4	2	5	0	0	1	2	0	0	3	1	0	4	0	0	0	.556	.462

PINCH-HITTERS WITH TWO OR MORE TEAMS

Player, Team	Avg.	G	TPA	AB	R	H	TB	2B	3B	HR	RBI	SH	SF	HP	BB	IBB	SO	SB	CS	GDP	Slg.	OBP
Aven, Bruce, Pit.	.114	35	35	35	1	4	5	1	0	0	3	0	0	0	0	0	12	0	1	0	.143	.114
Aven, Bruce, L.A.	.000	1	1	1	0	0	0	0	0	0	0	0	0	0	0	0	1	0	0	0	.000	.000
Bautista, Danny, Fla.	.167	7	7	6	0	1	2	1	0	0	0	0	0	0	1	0	0	0	0	0	.333	.286
Bautista, Danny, Ari.	.300	11	11	10	1	3	5	2	0	0	0	0	0	0	1	0	2	0	0	1	.500	.364
Brown, Brant, Fla.*	.231	26	26	26	1	6	9	3	0	0	1	0	0	0	0	0	15	0	0	1	.346	.231
Brown, Brant, Chi.*	.111	23	21	18	0	2	2	0	0	0	1	0	0	0	3	0	8	2	0	1	.111	.238
Echevarria, Angel, Col.	.000	8	7	7	0	0	0	0	0	0	2	0	0	0	0	0	1	0	0	0	.000	.000
Echevarria, Angel, Mil.	.190	24	24	21	0	4	5	1	0	0	1	0	0	0	3	0	6	0	0	1	.238	.292
Fox, Andy, Ari.*	.000	5	5	5	0	0	0	0	0	0	0	0	0	0	0	0	1	0	0	0	.000	.000
Fox, Andy, Fla.*	.091	13	13	11	0	1	1	0	0	0	0	0	0	0	2	0	0	1	0	0	.091	.231
Goodwin, Tom, Col.*	.143	8	8	7	0	1	1	0	0	0	1	0	0	0	1	0	2	1	0	0	.143	.250
Goodwin, Tom, L.A.*	1.000	1	1	1	0	1	1	0	0	0	0	0	0	0	0	0	0	0	0	0	1.000	1.000
Harris, Lenny, Ari.*	.250	16	16	16	4	4	5	1	0	0	1	0	0	0	0	0	2	1	0	1	.313	.250
Harris, Lenny, N.Y.*	.275	45	44	40	5	11	12	1	0	0	1	1	0	0	3	0	6	0	0	2	.300	.326
Hernandez, Carlos A., S.D.	1.000	3	3	2	1	2	5	0	0	1	3	0	1	0	0	0	0	0	0	0	2.500	.667
Hernandez, Carlos A., St.L.	.000	1	1	1	0	0	0	0	0	0	0	0	0	0	0	0	0	0	0	0	.000	.000
Hollandsworth, Todd, L.A.*	.077	16	15	13	1	1	2	1	0	0	0	0	0	1	1	0	5	0	1	1	.154	.200
Hollandsworth, Todd, Col.*	.333	12	12	12	3	4	7	0	0	1	3	0	0	0	0	0	3	1	0	0	.583	.333
Hunter, Brian L., Col.	.143	11	11	7	2	1	1	0	0	0	0	0	0	0	4	0	1	0	0	0	.143	.455
Hunter, Brian L., Cin.	.200	5	5	5	0	1	1	0	0	0	0	0	0	0	0	0	1	0	0	0	.200	.200
Hunter, Brian R., Atl.	.500	2	2	2	1	1	4	0	0	1	1	0	0	0	0	0	0	0	0	0	2.000	.500
Hunter, Brian R., Phi.	.225	48	48	40	2	9	13	1	0	1	4	0	0	0	8	0	11	0	0	0	.325	.354
Lee, Travis, Ari.*	.000	5	5	4	0	0	0	0	0	0	0	0	0	0	1	0	1	0	0	0	.000	.200
Lee, Travis, Phi.*	.500	2	2	2	1	1	1	0	0	0	0	0	0	0	0	0	0	0	0	0	.500	.500
Melhuse, Adam, L.A.†	.000	1	1	1	0	0	0	0	0	0	0	0	0	0	0	0	1	0	0	0	.000	.000
Melhuse, Adam, Col.†	.211	21	21	19	3	4	6	0	1	0	3	0	0	0	2	0	4	0	0	1	.316	.286
Mieske, Matt, Hou.	.133	49	48	45	2	6	11	0	1	1	5	0	0	0	3	0	12	0	0	0	.244	.188
Mieske, Matt, Ari.	.250	10	10	8	2	2	5	0	0	1	2	0	1	0	1	0	1	0	0	0	.625	.300
Newhan, David, S.D.*	.000	5	4	3	0	0	0	0	0	0	0	0	0	0	1	0	1	0	0	0	.000	.250
Newhan, David, Phi.*	.250	5	4	4	1	1	1	0	0	0	0	0	0	0	0	0	3	0	0	0	.250	.250
Relaford, Desi, Phi.†	.000	1	1	0	0	0	0	0	0	0	0	1	0	0	0	0	0	0	0	0	.000	.000
Relaford, Desi, S.D.†	.000	1	1	0	0	0	0	0	0	0	1	0	0	0	1	0	0	0	0	0	.000	1.000
Rodriguez, Henry, Chi.*	.400	6	6	5	2	2	8	0	0	2	6	0	1	0	0	0	2	0	0	0	1.600	.333
Rodriguez, Henry, Fla.*	.333	7	6	6	0	2	3	1	0	0	0	0	0	0	0	0	2	0	0	0	.500	.333
Servais, Scott, Col.	.000	1	1	1	0	0	0	0	0	0	0	0	0	0	0	0	1	0	0	0	.000	.000
Servais, Scott, S.F.	.000	2	2	2	0	0	0	0	0	0	0	0	0	0	0	0	0	0	0	0	.000	.000
White, Rondell, Mon.	.000	1	1	0	0	0	0	0	0	0	1	0	1	0	0	0	0	0	0	0	.000	.000
White, Rondell, Chi.	.000	1	1	1	0	0	0	0	0	0	0	0	0	0	0	0	1	0	0	0	.000	.000

PITCHING

TEAM

Team	W	L	Pct.	ERA	G	ShO	Rel.	Sv.	IP	H	TBF	R	ER	HR	SH	SF	HB	BB	IBB	SO	WP	Bk.
Atlanta	95	67	.586	4.05	162	9	376	53	1440.1	1428	6165	714	648	165	64	37	37	484	52	1093	23	6
Los Angeles	86	76	.531	4.10	162	11	371	36	1445.0	1379	6249	729	659	176	68	30	75	600	22	1154	60	6
New York	94	68	.580	4.16	162	10	411	49	1450.0	1398	6276	738	670	164	56	46	60	574	42	1164	34	7
San Francisco	97	65	.599	4.21	162	15	384	47	1444.1	1452	6270	747	675	151	85	63	41	623	26	1076	43	4
Cincinnati	85	77	.525	4.33	163	7	387	42	1456.1	1446	6362	765	700	190	68	48	43	659	53	1015	96	5
Arizona	85	77	.525	4.35	162	8	390	38	1443.2	1441	6158	754	698	190	72	45	42	500	53	1220	30	10
St. Louis	95	67	.586	4.38	162	7	386	37	1433.2	1403	6200	771	698	196	69	52	62	606	28	1100	49	9
San Diego	76	86	.469	4.52	162	5	443	46	1459.1	1443	6414	815	733	191	59	41	68	649	50	1071	66	7
Florida	79	82	.491	4.59	161	4	429	48	1429.2	1477	6307	797	729	169	68	59	43	650	56	1051	49	10
Milwaukee	73	89	.451	4.63	163	7	433	29	1466.1	1501	6497	826	755	174	67	52	65	728	87	967	60	6
Philadelphia	65	97	.401	4.77	162	6	414	34	1438.2	1458	6314	830	763	201	74	53	42	640	32	1123	54	3
Pittsburgh	69	93	.426	4.94	162	7	466	27	1449.0	1554	6514	888	795	163	70	55	60	711	61	1070	67	6
Montreal	67	95	.414	5.13	162	7	452	39	1424.2	1575	6340	902	812	181	66	58	60	579	40	1011	55	7
Chicago	65	97	.401	5.25	162	5	421	39	1454.2	1505	6451	904	849	231	62	54	62	658	45	1143	45	4
Colorado	82	80	.506	5.26	162	2	479	53	1430.0	1568	6340	897	835	221	53	52	72	588	72	1001	40	5
Houston	72	90	.444	5.42	162	2	410	30	1437.2	1596	6455	944	865	234	60	64	60	598	25	1064	55	3
Totals	1285	1306	.496	4.63	1297	112	6652	627	23103.1	23624	101312	13021	11884	2997	1061	809	892	9847	744	17323	826	98

NOTE—Totals for earned runs for several clubs do not agree with composite total for all pitchers of each respective club due to instances in which provisions of Section 10.18(i) of the Scoring Rules were applied. The following differences are to be noted: Atlanta pitchers add to 649; New York pitchers add to 671; San Francisco pitchers add to 676; Arizona pitchers add to 700; St. Louis pitchers add to 701; Philadelphia pitchers add to 766; Pittsburgh pitchers add to 796; Montreal pitchers add to 814; Chicago pitchers add to 850; Colorado pitchers add to 840.

INDIVIDUAL
TOP QUALIFIERS FOR EARNED-RUN AVERAGE TITLE

Minimum 162 innings. *Throws lefthanded.

Pitcher, Team	W	L	Pct.	ERA	G	GS	CG	ShO	GF	Sv.	IP	H	TBF	R	ER	HR	SH	SF	HB	BB	IBB	SO	WP	Bk.
Brown, Kevin, L.A.	13	6	.684	2.58	33	33	5	1	0	0	230.0	181	921	76	66	21	13	4	9	47	1	216	4	0
Johnson, Randy, Ari.*	19	7	.731	2.64	35	35	8	3	0	0	248.2	202	1001	89	73	23	14	5	6	76	1	347	5	2
D'Amico, Jeff C., Mil.	12	7	.632	2.66	23	23	1	1	0	0	162.1	143	667	55	48	14	10	3	6	46	5	101	5	0
Maddux, Greg, Atl.	19	9	.679	3.00	35	35	6	3	0	0	249.1	225	1012	91	83	19	8	5	10	42	12	190	1	2
Hampton, Mike, N.Y.*	15	10	.600	3.14	33	33	3	1	0	0	217.2	194	929	89	76	10	11	5	8	99	5	151	10	0
Leiter, Al, N.Y.*	16	8	.667	3.20	31	31	2	1	0	0	208.0	176	874	84	74	19	10	6	11	76	1	200	4	1
Park, Chan Ho, L.A.	18	10	.643	3.27	34	34	3	1	0	0	226.0	173	963	92	82	21	12	5	12	124	4	217	13	0
Glavine, Tom, Atl.*	21	9	.700	3.40	35	35	4	2	0	0	241.0	222	992	101	91	24	9	5	4	65	6	152	0	0
Ankiel, Rick, St.L*	11	7	.611	3.50	31	30	0	0	0	0	175.0	137	735	80	68	21	8	6	6	90	2	194	12	2
Person, Robert, Phi.	9	7	.563	3.63	28	28	1	1	0	0	173.1	144	743	73	70	13	4	9	6	95	1	164	10	1
Dempster, Ryan, Fla.	14	10	.583	3.66	33	33	2	1	0	0	226.1	210	974	102	92	30	4	5	5	97	7	209	4	0
Hernandez, Livan, S.F.	17	11	.607	3.75	33	33	5	2	0	0	240.0	254	1030	114	100	22	12	9	4	73	3	165	3	0
Williams, Woody, S.D.	10	8	.556	3.75	23	23	4	0	0	0	168.0	152	700	74	70	23	4	3	3	54	2	111	4	0
Schilling, Curt, Phi.-Ari.	11	12	.478	3.81	29	29	8	2	0	0	210.1	204	862	90	89	27	11	4	1	45	4	168	4	0
Benson, Kris, Pit.	10	12	.455	3.85	32	32	2	1	0	0	217.2	206	936	104	93	24	7	6	10	86	5	184	5	0

DEPARTMENTAL LEADERS: W—Glavine, Atl., 21; L—Daal, Ari.-Phi., 19; G—Kline, Mon., 83; GS—Glavine, Atl., Johnson, Ari., Lieber, Chi., Maddux, Atl., Millwood, Atl., 35; CG—Johnson, Ari., Schilling, Ari.-Phi., 8; ShO—Johnson, Ari., Maddux, Atl., 3; GF—Benitez, N.Y., 68; Sv.—Alfonseca, Fla., 45; IP—Lieber, Chi., 251; H—Hernandez, S.F., 254; TBF—Lieber, Chi., 1047; R—Lima, Hou., 152; ER—Lima, Hou., 145; HR—Lima, Hou., 48; SH—Rueter, S.F., 19; SF—Holt, Hou., Lima, Houl, Sanchez, Fla., 12; HB—Wright, Mil., 18; TBB—Clement, S.D., 125; IBB—Maddux, Atl., 12; SO—Johnson, Ari., 347; WP—Clement, S.D., 23; BK—Cornelius, Fla., 5.

ALL PITCHERS

*Throws lefthanded.

Pitcher, Team	W	L	Pct.	ERA	G	GS	CG	ShO	GF	Sv.	IP	H	TBF	R	ER	HR	SH	SF	HB	BB	IBB	SO	WP	Bk.
Acevedo, Juan, Mil.	3	7	.300	3.81	62	0	0	0	18	0	82.2	77	347	38	35	11	1	1	1	31	9	51	3	2
Adams, Terry, L.A.	6	9	.400	3.52	66	0	0	0	18	2	84.1	80	369	42	33	6	3	0	0	39	0	56	5	0
Aguilera, Rick, Chi.	1	2	.333	4.91	54	0	0	0	44	29	47.2	47	210	28	26	11	1	0	4	18	2	38	1	0
Aldred, Scott, Phi.*	1	3	.250	5.75	23	0	0	0	5	0	20.1	23	95	14	13	3	1	2	1	10	0	21	1	0
Alfonseca, Antonio, Fla.	5	6	.455	4.24	68	0	0	0	62	45	70.0	82	311	35	33	7	3	1	1	24	3	47	0	2
Almanza, Armando, Fla.*	4	2	.667	4.86	67	0	0	0	8	0	46.1	38	216	27	25	3	2	2	2	43	6	46	1	0
Almanzar, Carlos, S.D.	4	5	.444	4.39	62	0	0	0	11	0	69.2	73	308	35	34	12	2	3	4	25	2	56	2	0
Anderson, Brian, Ari.*	11	7	.611	4.05	33	32	2	0	0	0	213.1	226	876	101	96	38	6	6	3	39	7	104	1	4
Anderson, Jimmy, Pit.*	5	11	.313	5.25	27	26	1	0	0	0	144.0	169	648	94	84	13	5	3	7	58	2	73	6	0
Ankiel, Rick, St.L*	11	7	.611	3.50	31	30	0	0	0	0	175.0	137	735	80	68	21	8	6	6	90	2	194	12	2
Armas, Tony Jr., Mon.	7	9	.438	4.36	17	17	0	0	0	0	95.0	74	403	49	46	10	7	3	3	50	2	59	3	0
Arnold, Jamie, L.A.-Chi.	0	3	.000	6.18	14	4	0	0	5	1	39.1	38	181	31	27	1	2	4	4	24	0	16	2	0
Arrojo, Rolando, Col.	5	9	.357	6.04	19	19	0	0	0	0	101.1	120	470	77	68	14	3	7	12	46	6	80	1	2
Arroyo, Bronson, Pit.	2	6	.250	6.40	20	12	0	0	1	0	71.2	88	338	61	51	10	5	2	4	36	6	50	3	1
Ashby, Andy, Phi.-Atl.	12	13	.480	4.92	31	31	3	1	0	0	199.1	216	867	124	109	29	18	10	6	61	9	106	6	1
Astacio, Pedro, Col.	12	9	.571	5.27	32	32	3	0	0	0	196.1	217	875	119	115	32	7	4	15	77	5	193	8	0
Aybar, Manny, Col.-Cin.-Fla.	2	2	.500	4.31	54	0	0	0	20	0	79.1	74	349	42	38	11	5	4	2	35	3	45	7	1
Batista, Miguel, Mon.	0	1	.000	14.04	4	0	0	0	1	0	8.1	19	49	14	13	2	1	1	2	3	0	7	0	0
Belinda, Stan, Col.-Atl.	1	3	.250	7.71	56	0	0	0	17	1	46.2	55	220	44	40	14	4	4	3	22	5	51	2	0
Bell, Derek, N.Y.	0	0	.000	36.00	1	0	0	0	1	0	1.0	3	10	5	4	0	0	0	3	0	0	0	0
Bell, Rob, Cin.	7	8	.467	5.00	26	26	1	0	0	0	140.1	130	618	84	78	32	8	2	1	73	6	112	11	0
Beltran, Rigo, Col.*	0	0	.000	40.50	1	1	0	0	0	0	1.1	6	13	6	6	2	0	0	0	3	0	1	0	0

Pitcher, Team	W	L	Pct.	ERA	G	GS	CG	ShO	GF	Sv.	IP	H	TBF	R	ER	HR	SH	SF	HB	BB	IBB	SO	WP	Bk.
Benes, Alan, St.L	2	2	.500	5.67	30	0	0	0	16	0	46.0	54	214	33	29	7	2	1	2	23	2	26	5	0
Benes, Andy, St.L	12	9	.571	4.88	30	27	1	0	1	0	166.0	174	719	95	90	30	9	8	1	68	0	137	1	0
Benitez, Armando, N.Y.	4	4	.500	2.61	76	0	0	0	68	41	76.0	39	304	24	22	10	2	1	0	38	2	106	0	0
Benson, Kris, Pit.	10	12	.455	3.85	32	32	2	1	0	0	217.2	206	936	104	93	24	7	6	10	86	5	184	5	0
Bere, Jason, Mil.	6	7	.462	4.93	20	20	0	0	0	0	115.0	115	515	66	63	19	12	3	1	63	7	98	3	1
Blank, Matt, Mon.*	0	1	.000	5.14	13	0	0	0	3	0	14.0	12	63	8	8	1	2	1	1	5	1	4	0	0
Boehringer, Brian, S.D.	0	3	.000	5.74	7	3	0	0	1	0	15.2	18	74	15	10	4	0	1	0	10	0	9	0	0
Bogar, Tim, Hou.	0	0	.000	4.50	2	0	0	0	2	0	2.0	2	9	1	1	1	0	0	0	1	0	1	0	0
Bohanon, Brian, Col.*	12	10	.545	4.68	34	26	2	1	0	0	177.0	181	772	101	92	24	4	3	6	79	4	98	2	0
Bones, Ricky, Fla.	2	3	.400	4.54	56	0	0	0	13	0	77.1	94	352	43	39	6	6	6	3	27	8	59	2	1
Bottenfield, Kent, Phi.	1	2	.333	4.50	8	8	1	1	0	0	44.0	41	194	24	22	5	0	2	0	21	0	31	0	0
Boyd, Jason, Phi.	0	1	.000	6.55	30	0	0	0	11	0	34.1	39	161	28	25	2	3	0	1	24	4	32	1	0
Brantley, Jeff, Phi.	2	7	.222	5.86	55	0	0	0	47	23	55.1	64	256	36	36	12	1	2	2	29	0	57	2	0
Brock, Chris, Phi.	7	8	.467	4.34	63	5	0	0	17	1	93.1	85	403	48	45	21	1	2	3	41	0	69	4	1
Brown, Kevin, L.A.	13	6	.684	2.58	33	33	5	1	0	0	230.0	181	921	76	66	21	13	4	9	47	1	216	4	0
Brownson, Mark, Phi.	1	0	1.000	7.20	2	0	0	0	0	0	5.0	7	25	4	4	1	1	0	0	3	0	3	0	0
Brunette, Justin, St.L*	0	0	.000	5.79	4	0	0	0	2	0	4.2	8	27	3	3	0	0	0	0	5	0	2	1	1
Bruske, Jim, Mil.	1	0	1.000	6.48	15	0	0	0	1	0	16.2	22	85	15	12	5	0	1	2	12	1	8	0	0
Buddie, Mike, Mil.	0	0	.000	4.50	5	0	0	0	2	0	6.0	8	27	3	3	0	1	0	0	1	1	5	0	0
Bullinger, Kirk, Phi.	0	0	.000	5.40	3	0	0	0	1	0	3.1	4	14	2	2	0	0	1	0	0	0	4	0	0
Burkett, John, Atl.	10	6	.625	4.89	31	22	0	0	4	0	134.1	162	603	79	73	13	8	5	4	51	2	110	2	0
Burnett, A.J., Fla.	3	7	.300	4.79	13	13	0	0	0	0	82.2	80	364	46	44	8	6	3	2	44	3	57	2	0
Byrd, Paul, Phi.	2	9	.182	6.51	17	15	0	0	0	0	83.0	89	371	67	60	17	3	1	3	35	2	53	1	0
Cabrera, Jose, Hou.	2	3	.400	5.92	52	0	0	0	22	2	59.1	74	266	40	39	10	3	3	3	17	2	41	1	1
Cammack, Eric, N.Y.	0	0	.000	6.30	8	0	0	0	2	0	10.0	7	48	7	7	1	0	1	1	10	1	9	0	0
Carlyle, Buddy, S.D.	0	0	.000	21.00	4	0	0	0	2	0	3.0	6	18	7	7	0	0	0	0	3	0	2	0	0
Carrara, Giovanni, Col.	0	1	.000	12.83	8	0	0	0	2	0	13.1	21	72	19	19	5	0	1	1	11	2	15	0	0
Charlton, Norm, Cin.*	0	0	.000	27.00	2	0	0	0	2	0	3.0	6	20	9	9	1	0	0	0	6	0	1	1	0
Chen, Bruce, Atl.-Phi.*	7	4	.636	3.29	37	15	0	0	4	0	134.0	116	559	54	49	18	8	3	2	46	4	112	4	1
Chouinard, Bobby, Col.	2	2	.500	3.86	31	0	0	0	6	0	32.2	35	140	17	14	4	1	1	1	9	2	23	0	0
Christiansen, Jason, Pit.-St.L*	3	8	.273	5.06	65	0	0	0	19	1	48.0	41	210	29	27	3	4	1	2	27	5	53	3	0
Clement, Matt, S.D.	13	17	.433	5.14	34	34	0	0	0	0	205.0	194	940	131	117	22	12	5	16	125	4	170	23	0
Clontz, Brad, Pit.	0	0	.000	5.14	5	0	0	0	0	0	7.0	7	37	4	4	1	0	0	0	11	2	8	1	0
Coggin, David, Phi.	2	0	1.000	5.33	5	5	0	0	0	0	27.0	35	126	20	16	2	2	0	1	12	0	17	1	0
Cook, Dennis, N.Y.*	6	3	.667	5.34	68	0	0	0	15	2	59.0	63	269	35	35	8	0	0	5	31	4	53	3	2
Cordova, Francisco, Pit.	6	8	.429	5.21	18	17	0	0	0	0	95.0	107	421	63	55	12	3	3	2	38	4	66	3	1
Cornelius, Reid, Fla.	4	10	.286	4.82	22	21	0	0	0	0	125.0	135	547	74	67	19	9	6	4	50	4	50	8	5
Croushore, Rick, Col.	2	0	1.000	8.74	6	0	0	0	1	0	11.1	15	56	11	11	1	0	1	1	6	1	11	1	0
Cunnane, Will, S.D.	1	1	.500	4.23	27	3	0	0	4	0	38.1	35	169	21	18	2	1	1	1	21	0	34	1	0
Daal, Omar, Ari.-Phi.*	4	19	.174	6.14	32	28	0	0	1	0	167.0	208	775	128	114	26	6	6	9	72	11	96	0	2
D'Amico, Jeff C., Mil.	12	7	.632	2.66	23	23	1	1	0	0	162.1	143	667	55	48	14	10	3	6	46	5	101	5	0
Darensbourg, Vic, Fla.*	5	3	.625	4.06	56	0	0	0	17	0	62.0	61	274	32	28	7	3	6	2	28	1	59	1	0
Davey, Tom, S.D.	2	1	.667	0.71	11	0	0	0	2	0	12.2	12	50	1	1	0	0	0	0	2	0	6	1	0
Davis, Kane, Mil.	0	0	.000	6.75	3	0	0	0	1	0	4.0	7	24	3	3	1	0	0	1	5	0	2	0	0
DeJean, Mike, Col.	4	4	.500	4.89	54	0	0	0	15	0	53.1	54	235	31	29	9	3	1	0	30	6	34	5	0
De Los Santos, Valerio, Mil.*	2	3	.400	5.13	66	2	0	0	15	0	73.2	72	320	43	42	15	2	1	1	33	7	70	3	1
Del Toro, Miguel, S.F.	2	0	1.000	5.19	9	1	0	0	4	0	17.1	17	77	10	10	3	1	0	2	6	2	16	2	0
Dempster, Ryan, Fla.	14	10	.583	3.66	33	33	2	1	0	0	226.1	210	974	102	92	30	4	5	5	97	7	209	4	0
Dessens, Elmer, Cin.	11	5	.688	4.28	40	16	1	0	6	1	147.1	170	640	73	70	10	12	7	3	43	7	85	4	0
Dipoto, Jerry, Col.	0	0	.000	3.95	17	0	0	0	7	0	13.2	16	59	6	6	1	1	2	0	5	2	9	0	0
Dotel, Octavio, Hou.	3	7	.300	5.40	50	16	0	0	25	16	125.0	127	563	80	75	26	7	8	7	61	3	142	6	0
Downs, Scott, Chi.-Mon.*	4	3	.571	5.29	19	19	0	0	0	0	97.0	122	442	62	57	13	2	4	5	40	1	63	1	0
Dreifort, Darren, L.A.	12	9	.571	4.16	32	32	1	1	0	0	192.2	175	842	105	89	31	9	0	12	87	1	164	17	3
Eaton, Adam, S.D.	7	4	.636	4.13	22	22	0	0	0	0	135.0	134	583	63	62	14	1	3	2	61	3	90	3	0
Elarton, Scott, Hou.	17	7	.708	4.81	30	30	2	0	0	0	192.2	198	855	117	103	29	5	7	6	84	1	131	8	0
Embree, Alan, S.F.*	3	5	.375	4.95	63	0	0	0	21	2	60.0	62	263	34	33	4	4	5	3	25	2	49	1	0
Erdos, Todd, S.D.	0	0	.000	6.67	22	0	0	0	8	1	29.2	32	146	24	22	5	1	4	6	17	1	16	1	0
Estes, Shawn, S.F.*	15	6	.714	4.26	30	30	4	2	0	0	190.1	194	829	99	90	11	7	6	3	108	1	136	11	0
Estrada, Horacio, Mil.*	3	0	1.000	6.29	7	4	0	0	2	0	24.1	30	123	18	17	5	0	1	2	20	4	13	3	0
Farnsworth, Kyle, Chi.	2	9	.182	6.43	46	5	0	0	8	1	77.0	90	371	58	55	14	4	4	4	50	8	74	3	0
Fernandez, Alex, Fla.	4	4	.500	4.13	8	8	0	0	0	0	52.1	59	222	25	24	7	3	1	0	16	1	27	0	0
Fernandez, Osvaldo, Cin.	4	3	.571	3.62	15	14	1	0	0	0	79.2	69	327	33	32	6	1	3	2	31	2	36	1	1
Fetters, Mike, L.A.	6	2	.750	3.24	51	0	0	0	20	5	50.0	35	201	18	18	7	3	0	2	25	2	40	3	0
Figueroa, Nelson, Ari.	0	1	.000	7.47	3	3	0	0	0	0	15.2	17	68	13	13	4	1	2	0	5	0	7	2	0
Forster, Scott, Mon.*	0	1	.000	7.88	42	0	0	0	10	0	32.0	28	154	31	28	5	2	3	2	25	1	23	2	0
Franco, John, N.Y.*	5	4	.556	3.40	62	0	0	0	14	4	55.2	46	239	24	21	6	3	0	2	26	6	56	2	0
Franklin, Wayne, Hou.*	0	0	.000	5.48	25	0	0	0	4	0	21.1	24	103	14	13	2	0	2	4	12	1	21	0	1
Fultz, Aaron, S.F.*	5	2	.714	4.67	58	0	0	0	18	1	69.1	67	299	38	36	8	7	6	3	28	0	62	0	2
Gagne, Eric, L.A.	4	6	.400	5.15	20	19	0	0	0	0	101.1	106	464	62	58	20	5	3	3	60	1	79	4	0
Garcia, Mike, Pit.	0	2	.000	11.12	13	0	0	0	2	0	11.1	21	59	15	14	1	0	3	0	7	1	9	1	0
Gardner, Mark, S.F.	11	7	.611	4.05	30	20	0	0	3	0	149.0	155	634	72	67	16	6	6	5	42	2	92	2	1
Garibay, Daniel, Chi.*	2	8	.200	6.03	30	8	0	0	6	0	74.2	88	345	54	50	9	5	6	1	39	1	46	4	0
Glauber, Keith, Cin.	0	0	.000	3.68	4	0	0	0	0	0	7.1	5	30	3	3	0	0	0	1	2	0	4	0	0
Glavine, Tom, Atl.*	21	9	.700	3.40	35	35	4	2	0	0	241.0	222	992	101	91	24	9	5	4	65	6	152	0	0
Gomes, Wayne, Phi.	4	6	.400	4.40	65	0	0	0	26	7	73.2	72	324	41	36	6	7	4	3	35	3	49	10	0
Gooden, Dwight, Hou.	0	0	.000	9.00	1	1	0	0	0	0	4.0	6	20	4	4	1	0	0	0	3	0	1	2	0
Graves, Danny, Cin.	10	5	.667	2.56	66	0	0	0	57	30	91.1	81	388	31	26	8	6	4	3	42	7	53	3	1
Green, Jason, Hou.	1	1	.500	6.62	14	0	0	0	1	0	17.2	15	87	16	13	3	2	0	1	20	1	19	0	0
Grilli, Jason, Fla.	1	0	1.000	5.40	1	1	0	0	0	0	6.2	11	35	4	4	0	2	0	2	2	0	3	0	0
Gross, Kip, Hou.	0	1	.000	10.38	2	1	0	0	0	0	4.1	9	23	8	5	2	0	0	0	2	0	3	0	0
Guthrie, Mark, Chi.*	2	3	.400	4.82	19	0	0	0	3	0	18.2	17	82	11	10	1	2	3	1	10	4	17	4	0
Guzman, Domingo, S.D.	0	0	.000	9.00	1	0	0	0	0	0	1.0	1	6	1	1	0	0	0	2	1	0	0	0	0

Pitcher, Team	W	L	Pct.	ERA	G	GS	CG	ShO	GF	Sv.	IP	H	TBF	R	ER	HR	SH	SF	HB	BB	IBB	SO	WP	Bk.
Guzman, Geraldo, Ari.	5	4	.556	5.37	13	10	0	0	0	0	60.1	66	259	36	36	8	3	1	2	22	0	52	3	0
Hackman, Luther, St.L	0	0	.000	10.13	1	0	0	0	0	0	2.2	4	17	3	3	0	2	0	1	4	0	1	0	0
Hampton, Mike, N.Y.*	15	10	.600	3.14	33	33	3	1	0	0	217.2	194	929	89	76	10	11	5	8	99	5	151	10	0
Harnisch, Pete, Cin.	8	6	.571	4.74	22	22	3	1	0	0	131.0	133	562	76	69	23	1	4	1	46	1	71	10	0
Haynes, Jimmy, Mil.	12	13	.480	5.33	33	33	0	0	0	0	199.1	228	897	128	118	21	10	6	7	100	7	88	7	0
Henry, Doug, Hou.-S.F.	4	4	.500	3.79	72	0	0	0	21	5	78.1	57	335	36	33	12	5	2	4	49	3	62	3	0
Hentgen, Pat, St.L	15	12	.556	4.72	33	33	1	1	0	0	194.1	202	846	107	102	24	13	8	3	89	4	118	4	0
Heredia, Felix, Chi.*	7	3	.700	4.76	74	0	0	0	24	2	58.2	46	250	31	31	6	4	2	2	33	4	52	5	0
Herges, Matt, L.A.	11	3	.786	3.17	59	4	0	0	17	1	110.2	100	461	43	39	7	9	4	6	40	5	75	4	0
Hermanson, Dustin, Mon.	12	14	.462	4.77	38	30	2	1	7	4	198.0	226	876	128	105	26	10	9	4	75	5	94	5	0
Hernandez, Livan, S.F.	17	11	.607	3.75	33	33	5	2	0	0	240.0	254	1030	114	100	22	12	9	4	73	3	165	3	0
Hershiser, Orel, L.A.	1	5	.167	13.14	10	6	0	0	1	0	24.2	42	136	36	36	5	0	3	11	14	1	13	2	0
Hitchcock, Sterling, S.D.*	1	6	.143	4.93	11	11	0	0	0	0	65.2	69	292	38	36	12	2	1	5	26	1	61	4	0
Hoffman, Trevor, S.D.	4	7	.364	2.99	70	0	0	0	59	43	72.1	61	291	29	24	7	3	5	0	11	4	85	4	0
Holmes, Darren, Ari.-St.L-Ari.	0	1	.000	9.20	13	0	0	0	4	1	14.2	24	71	15	15	3	0	3	2	4	0	10	0	0
Holt, Chris, Hou.	8	16	.333	5.35	34	32	3	1	1	0	207.0	247	916	131	123	22	7	12	8	75	2	136	10	1
Holzemer, Mark, Phi.*	0	1	.000	7.71	25	0	0	0	9	0	25.2	36	121	23	22	4	5	0	1	8	1	19	2	0
House, Craig, Col.	1	1	.500	7.24	16	0	0	0	3	0	13.2	13	69	11	11	3	0	1	2	17	0	8	0	0
Irabu, Hideki, Mon.	2	5	.286	7.24	11	11	0	0	0	0	54.2	77	247	45	44	9	3	2	1	14	0	42	5	2
Jacquez, Thomas, Phi.*	0	0	.000	11.05	9	0	0	0	2	1	7.1	10	34	9	9	2	0	1	0	3	1	6	0	0
James, Mike, St.L	2	2	.500	3.79	51	0	0	0	10	2	51.1	49	213	22	18	7	2	1	3	24	2	41	2	0
Jarvis, Kevin, Col.	3	4	.429	5.95	24	19	0	0	0	0	115.0	138	505	83	76	26	6	2	4	33	3	60	2	0
Jimenez, Jose, Col.	5	2	.714	3.18	72	0	0	0	55	24	70.2	63	301	27	25	4	4	3	3	28	6	44	5	0
Johnson, Mike, Mon.	5	6	.455	6.39	41	13	0	0	5	0	101.1	107	466	73	72	18	4	2	9	53	1	70	8	0
Johnson, Randy, Ari.*	19	7	.731	2.64	35	35	8	3	0	0	248.2	202	1001	89	73	23	14	5	6	76	1	347	5	2
Johnstone, John, S.F.	3	4	.429	6.30	47	0	0	0	9	0	50.0	64	222	35	35	11	4	4	2	13	2	37	0	0
Jones, Bobby J., N.Y.	11	6	.647	5.06	27	27	1	0	0	0	154.2	171	676	90	87	25	7	6	5	49	3	85	2	1
Jones, Bobby M., N.Y.*	0	0	.000	4.15	11	1	0	0	4	0	21.2	18	99	11	10	2	0	1	3	14	1	20	0	0
Judd, Mike, L.A.	0	1	.000	15.75	1	1	0	0	0	0	4.0	4	20	7	7	2	0	0	1	3	0	5	0	0
Kamienecki, Scott, Atl.	2	1	.667	5.47	26	0	0	0	4	2	24.2	22	114	18	15	3	0	0	0	22	1	17	0	0
Karchner, Matt, Chi.	1	1	.500	6.14	13	0	0	0	5	0	14.2	19	75	11	10	3	2	1	0	11	0	5	2	0
Karl, Scott, Col.*	2	3	.400	7.68	17	9	0	0	1	0	65.2	95	319	56	56	14	3	3	3	33	3	29	3	0
Kile, Darryl, St.L	20	9	.690	3.91	34	34	5	1	0	0	232.1	215	960	109	101	33	11	8	13	58	1	192	8	1
Kim, Byung-Hyun, Ari.	6	6	.500	4.46	61	1	0	0	30	14	70.2	52	320	39	35	9	2	3	9	46	5	111	3	2
King, Ray, Mil.*	3	2	.600	1.26	36	0	0	0	8	0	28.2	18	111	7	4	1	0	1	0	10	1	19	1	0
Kline, Steve, Mon.*	1	5	.167	3.50	83	0	0	0	42	14	82.1	88	349	36	32	8	2	1	3	27	2	64	4	0
Kolb, Brandon, S.D.	0	1	.000	4.50	11	0	0	0	5	0	14.0	16	66	8	7	0	0	1	0	11	1	12	3	0
Lara, Yovanny, Mon.	0	0	.000	6.35	6	0	0	0	2	0	5.2	5	29	4	4	0	0	1	0	8	0	3	0	0
Larkin, Andy, Cin.	0	0	.000	8.31	4	0	0	0	3	0	6.2	6	30	4	4	1	0	0	0	5	0	7	0	0
Lee, David, Col.	0	0	.000	11.12	7	0	0	0	3	1	5.2	10	35	9	7	3	0	1	0	6	0	6	0	0
Leiter, Al, N.Y.*	16	8	.667	3.20	31	31	2	1	0	0	208.0	176	874	84	74	19	10	6	11	76	1	200	4	1
Leskanic, Curtis, Mil.	9	3	.750	2.56	73	0	0	0	39	12	77.1	58	333	23	22	7	1	4	3	51	5	75	5	0
Levrault, Allen, Mil.	0	1	.000	4.50	5	1	0	0	2	0	12.0	10	51	7	6	0	1	1	7	0	9	0	0
Lieber, Jon, Chi.	12	11	.522	4.41	35	35	6	1	0	0	251.0	248	1047	130	123	36	9	7	10	54	3	192	2	2
Ligtenberg, Kerry, Atl.	2	3	.400	3.61	59	0	0	0	19	12	52.1	43	217	21	21	7	2	1	0	24	5	51	0	0
Lima, Jose, Hou.	7	16	.304	6.65	33	33	0	0	0	0	196.1	251	895	152	145	48	12	12	2	68	3	124	3	0
Linebrink, Scott, S.F.-Hou.	0	0	.000	6.00	11	0	0	0	4	0	12.0	18	63	8	8	4	0	3	8	0	6	0	0
Lira, Felipe, Mon.	5	8	.385	5.40	53	7	0	0	8	0	101.2	129	468	71	61	11	3	9	4	36	6	51	2	1
Loiselle, Rich, Pit.	2	3	.400	5.10	40	0	0	0	13	0	42.1	43	203	27	24	5	3	3	3	30	5	32	1	0
Looper, Braden, Fla.	5	1	.833	4.41	73	0	0	0	23	2	67.1	71	311	41	33	3	3	2	5	36	6	29	5	0
Lopez, Rodrigo, S.D.	0	3	.000	8.76	6	6	0	0	0	0	24.2	40	120	24	24	5	0	1	0	13	0	17	0	0
Lorraine, Andrew, Chi.*	1	2	.333	6.47	8	5	0	0	1	0	32.0	36	148	25	23	5	2	2	0	18	1	25	0	1
Luebbers, Larry, Cin.	0	2	.000	6.20	14	1	0	0	4	1	20.1	27	94	15	14	1	1	0	0	12	2	9	1	0
Maddux, Greg, Atl.	19	9	.679	3.00	35	35	6	3	0	0	249.1	225	1012	91	83	19	8	5	10	42	12	190	1	2
Maddux, Mike, Hou.	2	2	.500	6.26	21	0	0	0	6	0	27.1	31	128	20	19	6	3	1	2	12	0	17	0	0
Mahay, Ron, Fla.*	1	0	1.000	6.04	18	0	0	0	6	0	25.1	31	117	17	17	6	0	1	0	16	1	27	2	0
Mahomes, Pat, N.Y.	5	3	.625	5.46	53	5	0	0	12	0	94.0	96	439	63	57	15	3	3	2	66	4	76	5	0
Mairena, Oswaldo, Chi.*	0	0	.000	18.00	2	0	0	0	1	0	2.0	7	14	4	4	1	0	0	0	2	0	0	0	0
Mann, Jim, N.Y.	0	0	.000	10.13	2	0	0	0	2	0	2.2	6	15	3	3	1	0	0	1	0	0	0	0
Mantei, Matt, Ari.	1	1	.500	4.57	47	0	0	0	38	17	45.1	31	200	24	23	4	2	0	2	35	1	53	5	0
Manzanillo, Josias, Pit.	2	2	.500	3.38	43	0	0	0	11	0	58.2	50	246	23	22	6	4	2	0	32	4	39	1	0
Marquis, Jason, Atl.	1	0	1.000	5.01	15	0	0	0	7	0	23.1	23	103	16	13	4	1	1	1	12	1	17	1	0
Masaoka, Onan, L.A.*	1	1	.500	4.00	29	0	0	0	8	0	27.0	23	116	12	12	1	2	0	0	15	1	27	2	0
Matthews, Mike, St.L*	0	0	.000	11.57	14	0	0	0	4	0	9.1	15	54	12	12	2	0	0	1	10	2	8	0	0
Maurer, Dave, S.D.*	1	0	1.000	3.68	14	0	0	0	1	0	14.2	15	64	8	6	2	0	2	5	1	13	1	0
Mayne, Brent, Col.	1	0	1.000	0.00	1	0	0	0	1	0	1.0	1	5	0	0	0	0	0	1	0	0	1	0
McGlinchy, Kevin, Atl.	0	0	.000	2.16	10	0	0	0	6	0	8.1	11	42	4	2	1	1	0	6	1	9	1	0
McKnight, Tony, Hou.	4	1	.800	3.86	6	6	1	0	0	0	35.0	35	156	19	15	4	1	1	0	9	0	23	2	0
McMichael, Greg, Atl.	0	0	.000	4.41	15	0	0	0	3	0	16.1	12	61	8	8	3	0	1	0	4	1	14	1	0
Meacham, Rusty, Hou.	0	0	.000	11.57	5	0	0	0	2	0	4.2	8	23	6	6	3	0	0	0	2	0	3	0	0
Meadows, Brian, S.D.	7	8	.467	5.34	22	22	0	0	0	0	124.2	150	565	80	74	24	7	2	8	50	6	53	3	0
Mercado, Hector, Cin.*	0	0	.000	4.50	12	0	0	0	4	0	14.0	12	60	7	7	2	1	1	0	8	0	13	2	0
Miceli, Dan, Fla.	6	4	.600	4.23	45	0	0	0	9	0	48.2	45	207	23	23	4	1	1	1	18	2	40	3	0
Miller, Trever, Phi.-L.A.*	0	0	.000	10.47	16	0	0	0	2	0	16.1	27	90	22	19	3	1	1	2	12	1	11	1	0
Miller, Wade, Hou.	6	6	.500	5.14	16	16	2	0	0	0	105.0	104	453	66	60	14	3	1	3	42	1	89	1	0
Mills, Alan, L.A.	2	1	.667	4.21	18	0	0	0	9	1	25.2	31	119	12	12	3	0	1	0	16	0	18	1	0
Millwood, Kevin, Atl.	10	13	.435	4.66	36	35	0	0	0	0	212.2	213	903	115	110	26	8	5	3	62	2	168	4	0
Mohler, Mike, St.L*	1	1	.500	9.00	22	0	0	0	7	0	19.0	26	98	20	19	1	0	0	2	15	1	8	2	0
Molina, Gabe, Atl.	0	0	.000	9.00	2	0	0	0	1	0	2.0	3	11	4	2	1	1	0	1	0	1	0	0
Montgomery, Steve L., S.D.	0	2	.000	7.94	7	0	0	0	1	0	5.2	6	27	6	5	3	1	0	4	0	3	0	0
Moore, Trey, Mon.*	1	5	.167	6.62	8	8	0	0	0	0	35.1	55	178	31	26	7	2	0	4	21	1	24	1	1
Moraga, David, Mon.-Col.*	0	0	.000	40.50	4	0	0	0	2	0	2.2	10	22	12	12	1	1	2	1	2	0	2	1	0

Pitcher, Team	W	L	Pct.	ERA	G	GS	CG	ShO	GF	Sv.	IP	H	TBF	R	ER	HR	SH	SF	HB	BB	IBB	SO	WP	Bk.
Morgan, Mike, Ari.	5	5	.500	4.87	60	4	0	0	15	5	101.2	123	448	55	55	10	7	4	1	40	5	56	0	0
Morris, Matt, St.L	3	3	.500	3.57	31	0	0	0	12	4	53.0	53	226	22	21	3	3	1	2	17	1	34	0	0
Mota, Guillermo, Mon.	1	1	.500	6.00	29	0	0	0	7	0	30.0	27	126	21	20	3	1	1	2	12	0	24	1	1
Mulholland, Terry, Atl.*	9	9	.500	5.11	54	20	1	0	14	1	156.2	198	702	96	89	24	10	5	4	41	7	78	3	0
Myers, Mike, Col.*	0	1	.000	1.99	78	0	0	0	22	1	45.1	24	177	10	10	2	1	0	2	24	3	41	1	0
Myers, Rodney L., S.D.	0	0	.000	4.50	3	0	0	0	1	0	2.0	2	8	1	1	0	0	0	0	0	0	3	1	0
Nathan, Joe, S.F.	5	2	.714	5.21	20	15	0	0	0	0	93.1	89	426	63	54	12	5	5	4	63	4	61	5	0
Nation, Joey, Chi.*	0	2	.000	6.94	2	2	0	0	0	0	11.2	12	55	9	9	2	1	1	2	8	0	8	0	0
Navarro, Jaime, Mil.	0	5	.000	12.54	5	5	0	0	0	0	18.2	34	105	31	26	6	2	2	0	18	3	7	1	0
Neagle, Denny, Cin.*	8	2	.800	3.52	18	18	0	0	0	0	117.2	111	506	48	46	15	2	1	3	50	3	88	3	0
Nen, Robb, S.F.	4	3	.571	1.50	68	0	0	0	63	41	66.0	37	256	15	11	4	4	3	2	19	1	92	5	0
Nickle, Douglas, Phi.	0	0	.000	13.50	4	0	0	0	3	0	2.2	5	15	4	4	0	0	0	1	2	0	0	0	0
Norton, Phil, Chi.*	0	1	.000	9.35	2	2	0	0	0	0	8.2	14	47	10	9	5	0	0	0	7	0	6	0	0
Nunez, Vladimir, Fla.	0	6	.000	7.90	17	12	0	0	3	0	68.1	88	322	63	60	12	5	5	2	34	2	45	5	0
O'Connor, Brian, Pit.*	0	0	.000	5.11	6	1	0	0	2	0	12.1	12	62	11	7	2	1	1	1	11	0	7	4	0
Ohman, Will, Chi.*	1	0	1.000	8.10	6	0	0	0	2	0	3.1	4	17	3	3	0	0	0	4	1	2	1	0
Olson, Gregg, L.A.	0	1	.000	5.09	13	0	0	0	9	0	17.2	21	81	11	10	4	1	1	1	7	0	15	0	0
Orosco, Jesse, St.L*	0	0	.000	3.86	6	0	0	0	1	0	2.1	3	16	3	1	1	0	0	2	3	2	4	0	0
Ortiz, Russ, S.F.	14	12	.538	5.01	33	32	0	0	0	0	195.2	192	871	117	109	28	10	6	7	112	1	167	8	0
Osik, Keith, Pit.	0	0	.000	45.00	1	0	0	0	1	0	1.0	5	10	5	5	1	0	0	2	0	0	1	1	0
Osuna, Antonio, L.A.	3	6	.333	3.74	46	0	0	0	16	0	67.1	57	293	30	28	7	4	3	2	35	2	70	1	2
Padilla, Vicente, Ari.-Phi.	4	7	.364	3.72	55	0	0	0	16	2	65.1	72	291	33	27	3	5	3	1	28	7	51	1	0
Palacios, Vicente, S.D.	0	1	.000	6.75	7	0	0	0	2	0	10.2	12	46	10	8	4	1	1	0	5	1	8	0	0
Park, Chan Ho, L.A.	18	10	.643	3.27	34	34	3	1	0	0	226.0	173	963	92	82	21	12	5	12	124	4	217	13	0
Parra, Jose, Pit.	0	1	.000	6.94	6	2	0	0	1	0	11.2	17	57	9	9	3	1	0	1	7	0	9	0	0
Parris, Steve, Cin.	12	17	.414	4.81	33	33	0	0	0	0	192.2	227	861	109	103	30	10	3	4	71	5	117	9	1
Pavano, Carl, Mon.	8	4	.667	3.06	15	15	0	0	0	0	97.0	89	408	40	33	8	4	3	8	34	1	64	1	1
Penny, Brad, Fla.	8	7	.533	4.81	23	22	0	0	0	0	119.2	120	529	70	64	13	6	2	5	60	4	80	4	1
Perez, Carlos, L.A.*	5	8	.385	5.56	30	22	0	0	1	0	144.0	192	641	95	89	25	6	2	8	33	1	64	3	1
Perez, Yorkis, Hou.*	2	1	.667	5.56	33	0	0	0	9	0	22.2	25	111	18	13	4	1	2	0	14	2	21	1	0
Person, Robert, Phi.	9	7	.563	3.63	28	28	1	1	0	0	173.1	144	743	73	70	13	4	9	6	95	1	164	10	1
Peters, Chris, Pit.*	1	0	.000	2.86	18	0	0	0	4	1	28.1	23	121	9	9	2	2	0	1	14	2	16	3	0
Plesac, Dan, Ari.*	5	1	.833	3.15	62	0	0	0	14	0	40.0	34	182	21	14	4	6	1	0	26	2	45	3	0
Politte, Cliff, Phi.	4	3	.571	3.66	12	8	0	0	1	0	59.0	55	251	24	24	8	1	1	0	27	1	50	3	0
Poole, Jim Ri., Mon.*	0	0	.000	27.00	5	0	0	0	1	0	2.0	8	17	6	6	1	0	0	3	1	3	0	0
Powell, Jay, Hou.	1	1	.500	5.67	29	0	0	0	10	0	27.0	29	127	18	17	1	1	0	0	19	1	16	0	0
Powell, Jeremy, Mon.	0	3	.000	7.96	11	4	0	0	6	0	26.0	35	121	27	23	6	2	1	0	9	0	19	1	0
Powell, Brian, Hou.	2	1	.667	5.74	9	5	0	0	1	0	31.1	34	140	21	20	8	2	2	1	13	0	14	0	0
Prokopec, Luke, L.A.	1	1	.500	3.00	5	3	0	0	1	0	21.0	19	88	10	7	2	1	1	2	9	0	12	0	0
Pulsipher, Bill, N.Y.*	0	2	.000	12.15	2	2	0	0	0	0	6.2	12	39	9	9	1	1	0	1	6	0	7	0	0
Quevedo, Ruben, Chi.	3	10	.231	7.47	21	15	1	0	1	0	88.0	96	418	81	73	21	4	3	3	54	4	65	2	0
Radinsky, Scott, St.L*	0	0	.000	0.00	1	0	0	0	0	0	.0	1	1	0	0	0	0	0	0	1	0	0	0	0
Rain, Steve, Chi.	3	4	.429	4.35	37	0	0	0	6	0	49.2	46	214	25	24	10	1	1	1	27	0	54	4	0
Ramirez, Hector, Mil.	0	1	.000	10.00	6	0	0	0	1	0	9.0	11	43	10	10	1	0	0	0	5	0	4	0	0
Reames, Britt, St.L	2	1	.667	2.88	8	7	0	0	0	0	40.2	30	170	17	13	4	0	1	1	23	1	31	2	1
Reed, Rick, N.Y.	11	5	.688	4.11	30	30	0	0	0	0	184.0	192	768	90	84	28	3	5	5	34	3	121	2	1
Remlinger, Mike, Atl.*	5	3	.625	3.47	71	0	0	0	18	12	72.2	55	311	29	28	6	3	2	3	37	1	72	3	0
Reyes, Carlos, Phi.-S.D.	1	3	.250	5.72	22	0	0	0	9	1	28.1	25	121	18	18	7	2	0	1	13	0	17	1	1
Reyes, Dennys, Cin.*	2	1	.667	4.53	62	0	0	0	15	0	43.2	43	200	31	22	5	3	3	1	29	0	36	6	0
Reyes, Al, L.A.	0	0	.000	0.00	6	0	0	0	4	0	6.2	2	24	0	0	0	0	0	1	0	4	0	0
Reynolds, Shane, Hou.	7	8	.467	5.22	22	22	0	0	0	0	131.0	150	588	86	76	20	6	8	6	45	2	93	5	0
Reynoso, Armando, Ari.	11	12	.478	5.27	31	30	2	0	0	0	170.2	179	730	102	100	22	11	5	6	52	5	89	3	0
Riedling, John, Cin.	3	1	.750	2.35	13	0	0	0	5	1	15.1	11	63	7	4	1	1	0	1	8	0	18	1	0
Rigby, Brad, Mon.	0	0	.000	5.06	6	0	0	0	4	1	5.1	8	27	5	3	0	0	0	1	3	0	2	0	0
Rigdon, Paul, Mil.	4	4	.500	4.52	12	12	0	0	0	0	69.2	68	302	37	35	14	3	5	1	26	4	48	2	0
Riggan, Jerrod, N.Y.	0	0	.000	0.00	1	0	0	0	0	0	2.0	3	10	2	0	0	0	0	0	0	0	1	0	0
Ritchie, Todd, Pit.	9	8	.529	4.81	31	31	1	1	0	0	187.0	208	804	111	100	26	8	5	3	51	1	124	5	1
Rivera, Luis, Atl.	1	0	1.000	1.35	5	0	0	0	3	0	6.2	4	28	1	1	0	2	0	0	5	1	6	0	0
Roberts, Grant, N.Y.	0	0	.000	11.57	4	1	0	0	0	0	7.0	11	38	10	9	0	0	2	0	4	1	6	0	0
Rocker, John, Atl.*	1	2	.333	2.89	59	0	0	0	41	24	53.0	42	251	25	17	5	1	0	2	48	4	77	5	2
Rodriguez, Felix, S.F.	4	2	.667	2.64	76	0	0	0	19	3	81.2	65	346	29	24	5	2	3	8	42	2	95	3	1
Rodriguez, Jose, St.L*	0	0	.000	0.00	6	0	0	0	1	0	4.0	2	19	2	0	0	1	1	3	0	2	0	0
Rodriguez, Rich, N.Y.*	0	1	.000	7.78	32	0	0	0	13	0	37.0	59	185	40	32	7	0	5	3	15	0	18	2	1
Roque, Rafael, Mil.*	0	0	.000	10.13	4	0	0	0	1	0	5.1	7	29	6	6	1	1	0	1	7	1	4	0	0
Rose, Brian, Col.	4	5	.444	5.51	12	12	0	0	0	0	63.2	72	293	41	39	10	2	2	3	30	6	40	2	1
Rueter, Kirk, S.F.*	11	9	.550	3.96	32	31	0	0	0	0	184.0	205	799	92	81	23	19	9	2	62	5	71	1	0
Ruffin, Johnny, Atl.	0	0	.000	9.00	5	0	0	0	2	0	9.0	14	43	9	9	4	0	0	1	3	0	4	0	0
Rusch, Glendon, N.Y.*	11	11	.500	4.01	31	30	2	0	0	0	190.2	196	802	91	85	18	10	7	6	44	2	157	2	0
Sanchez, Jesus, Fla.*	9	12	.429	5.34	32	32	2	2	0	0	182.0	197	805	118	108	32	9	12	4	76	4	123	4	0
Santana, Julio, Mon.	1	5	.167	5.42	36	4	0	0	9	0	66.2	69	293	45	42	11	1	2	2	33	2	58	2	0
Sauerbeck, Scott, Pit.*	5	4	.556	4.04	75	0	0	0	13	1	75.2	76	349	36	34	4	3	3	1	61	6	83	9	2
Scanlan, Bob, Mil.	0	0	.000	27.00	2	0	0	0	1	0	1.2	6	13	6	5	0	1	1	1	0	0	1	0	0
Schilling, Curt, Phi.-Ari.	11	12	.478	3.81	29	29	8	2	0	0	210.1	204	862	90	89	27	11	4	1	45	4	168	4	0
Schmidt, Jason, Pit.	5	5	.286	5.40	11	11	0	0	0	0	63.1	71	295	43	38	6	1	2	1	41	2	51	1	0
Schrenk, Steve, Phi.	2	3	.400	7.33	20	0	0	0	8	0	23.1	25	109	20	19	3	1	1	1	13	0	19	0	0
Seanez, Rudy, Atl.	2	4	.333	4.29	23	0	0	0	8	2	21.0	15	89	11	10	3	1	0	1	9	1	20	0	0
Seelbach, Chris, Atl.	0	1	.000	10.80	2	0	0	0	2	0	1.2	3	7	2	2	0	0	1	0	1	0	0	0	0
Serafini, Dan, S.D.-Pit.*	2	5	.286	5.51	14	11	0	0	1	0	65.1	79	300	41	40	11	8	2	4	28	1	35	3	0
Shaw, Jeff, L.A.	3	4	.429	4.24	60	0	0	0	51	27	57.1	61	249	29	27	7	2	0	1	16	3	39	0	0
Silva, Jose, Pit.	11	9	.550	5.56	51	19	1	0	12	0	136.0	178	631	96	84	16	9	5	5	50	7	98	6	1
Skrmetta, Matt, Mon.-Pit.	2	2	.500	11.66	14	0	0	0	3	0	14.2	19	73	22	19	3	1	1	1	9	0	11	3	0
Slocumb, Heathcliff, St.L-S.D.	2	4	.333	4.98	65	0	0	0	17	1	68.2	69	309	43	38	9	4	5	3	37	4	46	1	2

Pitcher, Team	W	L	Pct.	ERA	G	GS	CG	ShO	GF	Sv.	IP	H	TBF	R	ER	HR	SH	SF	HB	BB	IBB	SO	WP	Bk.
Slusarski, Joe, Hou.	2	7	.222	4.21	54	0	0	0	16	3	77.0	80	327	36	36	8	2	3	22	3	54	6	0
Smith, Chuck, Fla.	6	6	.500	3.23	19	19	1	0	0	0	122.2	111	513	53	44	6	4	5	3	54	2	118	6	1
Smith, Brian, Pit.	0	0	.000	10.38	3	0	0	0	1	0	4.1	6	20	5	5	1	1	1	0	2	0	3	0	0
Snyder, John, Mil.	3	10	.231	6.17	23	23	0	0	0	0	127.0	147	596	95	87	8	6	7	9	77	10	69	6	0
Sparks, Steve L., Pit.	0	0	.000	6.75	3	0	0	0	2	0	4.0	4	20	3	3	0	0	0	5	0	2	2	0
Spencer, Sean, Mon.*	0	0	.000	5.40	8	0	0	0	1	0	6.2	7	28	4	4	2	0	1	0	3	0	6	4	0
Spencer, Stan, S.D.	2	2	.500	3.26	8	8	0	0	0	0	49.2	44	208	22	18	7	2	1	2	19	1	40	0	1
Spradlin, Jerry, Chi.	0	1	.000	8.40	8	1	0	0	2	0	15.0	20	70	15	14	2	1	2	1	5	1	13	1	0
Springer, Dennis, N.Y.	0	1	.000	8.74	2	2	0	0	0	0	11.1	20	59	11	11	2	0	1	5	0	5	2	0
Springer, Russ, Ari.	2	4	.333	5.08	52	0	0	0	10	0	62.0	63	282	36	35	11	2	3	2	34	6	59	3	0
Stechschulte, Gene, St.L.	1	0	1.000	6.31	20	0	0	0	7	0	25.2	24	116	22	18	6	0	2	0	17	1	12	2	0
Stephenson, Garrett, St.L.	16	9	.640	4.49	32	31	3	2	0	0	200.1	209	858	105	100	31	6	7	7	63	0	123	2	2
Stevens, Dave, Atl.	0	0	.000	12.00	2	0	0	0	2	0	3.0	5	15	4	4	2	0	1	0	4	0	0	0	0
Stottlemyre, Todd, Ari.	9	6	.600	4.91	18	18	0	0	0	0	95.1	98	408	55	52	18	3	2	2	36	2	76	2	1
Strickland, Scott, Mon.	4	3	.571	3.00	49	0	0	0	20	9	48.0	38	200	18	16	3	3	3	1	16	2	48	2	0
Strong, Joe, Fla.	1	1	.500	7.32	18	0	0	0	5	1	19.2	26	95	16	16	3	1	0	2	12	1	18	2	0
Stull, Everett, Mil.	2	3	.400	5.82	20	4	0	0	3	0	43.1	41	199	30	28	7	2	3	4	30	3	33	5	0
Sullivan, Scott, Cin.	3	6	.333	3.47	79	0	0	0	22	3	106.1	87	439	44	41	14	2	5	9	38	8	96	7	0
Swindell, Greg, Ari.*	2	6	.250	3.20	64	0	0	0	21	1	76.0	71	318	29	27	7	6	3	1	20	5	64	0	0
Tapani, Kevin, Chi.	8	12	.400	5.01	30	30	2	0	0	0	195.2	208	829	113	109	35	4	3	8	47	1	150	1	0
Tavarez, Julian, Col.	11	5	.688	4.43	51	12	1	0	8	1	120.0	124	530	68	59	11	3	4	7	53	9	62	2	1
Telemaco, Amaury, Phi.	1	3	.250	6.66	13	2	0	0	2	0	24.1	25	107	22	18	6	0	2	0	14	0	22	1	0
Telford, Anthony, Mon.	5	4	.556	3.79	64	0	0	0	18	3	78.1	76	330	38	33	10	2	4	5	23	1	68	4	1
Thompson, Mark, St.L.	1	1	.500	5.04	20	0	0	0	4	0	25.0	24	116	21	14	4	1	1	3	15	0	19	3	0
Thurman, Mike, Mon.	4	9	.308	6.42	17	17	0	0	0	0	88.1	112	415	69	63	9	5	6	3	46	4	52	2	0
Timlin, Mike, St.L	3	1	.750	3.34	25	0	0	0	9	1	29.2	30	138	11	11	2	2	1	2	20	3	26	0	0
Tollberg, Brian, S.D.	4	5	.444	3.58	19	19	1	0	0	0	118.0	126	506	58	47	13	6	0	5	35	4	76	2	1
Tucker, T.J., Mon.	0	1	.000	11.57	2	2	0	0	0	0	7.0	11	35	9	9	5	0	0	0	3	0	2	1	0
Urbina, Ugueth, Mon.	0	1	.000	4.05	13	0	0	0	11	8	13.1	11	54	6	6	1	0	0	0	5	0	22	1	0
Valdes, Ismael, Chi.-L.A.	2	7	.222	5.64	21	20	0	0	1	0	107.0	124	469	69	67	22	0	4	3	40	2	74	0	0
Valdes, Marc, Hou.	5	5	.500	5.08	53	0	0	0	20	2	56.2	69	264	41	32	3	3	2	5	25	1	35	1	0
Van Poppel, Todd, Chi.	4	5	.444	3.75	51	2	0	0	13	2	86.1	80	378	38	36	10	4	3	2	48	2	77	4	0
Vazquez, Javier, Mon.	11	9	.550	4.05	33	33	2	1	0	0	217.2	247	945	104	98	24	11	3	5	61	10	196	3	0
Veres, Dave, St.L	5	3	.375	2.85	71	0	0	0	61	29	75.2	65	310	26	24	6	5	2	6	25	2	67	3	1
Villegas, Ismael, Atl.	0	0	.000	13.50	1	0	0	0	0	0	2.2	4	15	4	4	2	0	0	1	2	0	2	0	0
Villone, Ron, Cin.*	10	10	.500	5.43	35	23	0	0	5	0	141.0	154	643	95	85	22	10	8	9	78	3	77	7	0
Vogelsong, Ryan, S.F.	0	0	.000	9.00	4	0	0	0	0	0	6.0	4	24	0	0	0	0	0	0	5	0	4	0	0
Vosberg, Ed, Phi.*	1	1	.500	4.13	31	0	0	0	5	0	24.0	21	106	11	11	4	1	0	0	18	0	23	1	0
Wagner, Billy, Hou.*	2	4	.333	6.18	28	0	0	0	19	6	27.2	28	129	19	19	6	0	0	1	18	0	28	7	0
Wainhouse, David, St.L.	0	0	.000	9.35	9	0	0	0	4	0	8.2	13	44	10	9	2	1	0	2	4	1	5	1	0
Walker, Kevin, S.D.*	7	1	.875	4.19	70	0	0	0	14	0	66.2	49	287	35	31	5	4	2	5	38	6	56	2	1
Walker, Pete, Col.	0	0	.000	17.36	3	0	0	0	1	0	4.2	10	27	9	9	1	0	0	0	4	0	2	0	0
Wall, Donne, S.D.	5	2	.714	3.35	44	0	0	0	14	1	53.2	36	211	20	20	4	3	0	0	21	1	29	1	0
Wallace, Jeff, Pit.*	2	0	1.000	7.07	38	0	0	0	6	0	35.2	42	185	32	28	5	0	2	4	34	1	27	5	0
Ward, Bryan, Phi.*	0	0	.000	2.33	20	0	0	0	8	0	19.1	14	79	5	5	2	1	2	0	8	1	11	1	0
Wasdin, John, Col.	0	1	.000	5.80	14	3	1	0	2	0	35.2	42	154	23	23	6	1	3	9	2	35	2	0
Weathers, David, Mil.	3	5	.375	3.07	69	0	0	0	23	1	76.1	73	320	29	26	7	4	1	2	32	8	50	0	0
Weber, Ben, S.F.	0	1	.000	14.63	9	0	0	0	2	0	8.0	16	44	13	13	0	0	0	4	0	6	1	0
Wendell, Turk, N.Y.	8	6	.571	3.59	77	0	0	0	17	1	82.2	60	346	36	33	9	6	3	5	41	7	73	0	1
Wengert, Don, Atl.	0	1	.000	7.20	10	0	0	0	6	0	10.0	12	47	9	8	2	0	0	5	0	7	0	0
Whisenant, Matt, S.D.*	2	2	.500	3.80	24	0	0	0	12	0	21.1	16	95	12	9	1	1	2	0	17	1	12	5	0
White, Gabe, Cin.-Col.*	11	2	.846	2.36	68	0	0	0	17	5	84.0	64	329	23	22	6	2	6	3	15	2	84	1	0
White, Rick, N.Y.	2	3	.400	3.81	22	0	0	0	6	1	28.1	26	127	14	12	2	0	1	2	12	2	20	0	0
Whiteside, Matt, S.D.	2	3	.400	4.14	28	0	0	0	9	0	37.0	32	159	21	17	6	2	1	1	17	3	27	2	1
Wickman, Bob, Mil.	2	2	.500	2.93	43	0	0	0	36	16	46.0	37	194	18	15	1	0	1	1	20	2	44	2	0
Wilkins, Marc, Pit.	4	2	.667	5.07	52	0	0	0	8	0	60.1	54	277	34	34	4	3	7	6	43	3	37	3	0
Williams, Brian, Chi.	1	1	.500	9.62	22	0	0	0	5	1	24.1	28	122	27	26	4	3	1	3	23	2	14	3	0
Williams, Woody, S.D.	10	8	.556	3.75	23	23	4	0	0	0	168.0	152	700	74	70	23	4	3	4	54	2	111	4	0
Williams, Jeff, L.A.*	0	0	.000	15.88	7	0	0	0	5	0	5.2	12	35	11	10	1	0	1	0	8	0	3	0	0
Williams, Matt T., Mil.*	0	0	.000	7.00	11	0	0	0	1	0	9.0	7	46	7	7	2	0	2	4	0	7	0	0
Williams, Mike, Pit.	3	4	.429	3.50	72	0	0	0	63	24	72.0	56	307	34	28	8	2	4	4	40	3	71	1	0
Williamson, Scott, Cin.	5	8	.385	3.29	48	10	0	0	13	6	112.0	92	495	45	41	7	4	2	3	75	7	136	21	0
Winchester, Scott, Cin.	0	0	.000	3.68	5	0	0	0	1	0	7.1	10	35	4	3	1	0	1	0	2	0	3	0	0
Witasick, Jay, S.D.	3	2	.600	5.64	11	11	0	0	0	0	60.2	69	287	42	38	9	5	1	3	35	5	54	2	1
Wohlers, Mark, Cin.	1	2	.333	4.50	20	0	0	0	7	0	28.0	19	119	14	14	3	2	1	0	17	0	20	2	0
Wolf, Randy, Phi.*	11	9	.550	4.36	32	32	1	0	0	0	206.1	210	889	107	100	25	10	8	8	83	2	160	1	0
Wood, Kerry, Chi.	8	7	.533	4.80	23	23	1	0	0	0	137.0	112	603	70	73	17	7	5	9	87	0	132	5	1
Woodard, Steve, Mil.	1	7	.125	5.96	27	11	1	0	6	0	93.2	125	432	70	62	16	7	3	4	33	4	65	5	0
Worrell, Tim, Chi.	3	4	.429	2.47	54	0	0	0	27	3	62.0	60	268	20	17	7	4	1	1	24	8	52	1	0
Wright, Jamey, Mil.	7	9	.438	4.10	26	25	0	0	1	0	164.2	157	718	81	75	12	4	6	18	88	5	96	9	2
Yoshii, Masato, Col.	6	15	.286	5.86	29	29	0	0	0	0	167.1	201	726	112	109	32	8	7	2	53	6	88	2	1
Young, Danny, Chi.*	0	1	.000	21.00	4	0	0	0	2	0	3.0	5	20	7	7	1	0	0	6	0	0	0	0
Zerbe, Chad, S.F.*	2	0	1.000	4.50	11	0	0	0	2	0	6.0	6	24	3	3	1	0	0	3	0	6	0	0

COMBINATION SHUTOUTS: **Arizona (4)**—Johnson and Morgan; Reynoso, Padilla and Mantei; Anderson and Kim; Guzman and Swindell. **Atlanta (3)**—Maddux and Remlinger; Mulholland, Ligtenberg, Seanez, Wengert and Remlinger; Maddux, Remlinger and McGlinchy. **Chicago (4)**—Downs, Worrell and Aguilera; Valdes, Rain, Heredia, Worrell and Aguilera; Tapani, Heredia, Rain and Aguilera; Wood and Worrell. **Cincinnati (6)**—Neagle and Sullivan; Parris, Williamson and Graves; Williamson and Luebbers; Williamson, Sullivan, Villone and Graves; Parris and Sullivan; Dessens and Villone. **Colorado (1)**—Yoshii, White, Myers and Jimenez; **Florida (1)**—Sanchez, Bones and Almanza. **Houston (1)**—Dotel, Maddux, J. Powell and Wagner. **Los Angeles (8)**—Park and Shaw (2); Dreifort, Adams and Shaw; Dreifort, Fetters and Shaw; Park and Olson; Brown, Osuna, Shaw and Herges; Dreifort, Adams and Herges; Dreifort, Fetters and Adams. **Milwaukee (6)**—Bere, Weathers and Wickman; D'Amico, Ramirez and de los Santos; Wright and Wickman; D'Amico and Leskanic; D'Amico, Leskanic and Acevedo; Wright, King and Weathers. **Montreal (5)**—Vazquez, Kline and Hermanson; Armas Jr. and Kline; Moore, Telford and Kline; Armas Jr., Mota and Strickland; Armas Jr., Mota and Kline. **New York (8)**—Hampton and Benitez

(2); Mahomes, Cook, Wendell and Benitez; Leiter, Cook, J. Franco and Benitez; Reed, J. Franco and Benitez; Rusch, Cook and Mahomes; Leiter and J. Franco; Reed, Wendell and Benitez. **Philadelphia (3)**—Schilling and Holzemer; Politte, Padilla and Brantley; Chen, Padilla, Brock, Vosberg and Brantley. **Pittsburgh (5)**—Anderson and Williams; Benson and Christiansen; Anderson, Sauerbeck and Wilkins; Benson and Manzanillo; Silva, Loiselle and Wilkins. **St. Louis (3)**—Ankiel, Wainhouse and Veres; Stephenson and James; Ankiel, Morris, Christiansen, Timlin and Veres. **San Diego (5)**—W. Williams, Almanzar and Hoffman; Clement and Hoffman; Eaton and Hoffman; Tollberg, Slocumb and Walker; Eaton, Walker, Davey and Hoffman. **San Francisco (11)**—Gardner, Rodriguez and Nen (2); Ortiz, Rodriguez and Nen (2); Ortiz and Nen; Nathan, Johnstone and Embree; Gardner, Embree, Rodriguez and Nen; Hernandez and Nen; Ortiz, Embree, Rodriguez and Nen; Estes, del Toro and Vogelsong; Rueter, Rodriguez and Nen.

PITCHERS WITH TWO OR MORE TEAMS

Pitcher, Team	W	L	Pct.	ERA	G	GS	CG	ShO	GF	Sv.	IP	H	TBF	R	ER	HR	SH	SF	HB	BB	IBB	SO	WP	Bk.
Arnold, Jamie, L.A.	0	0	.000	4.05	2	0	0	0	2	0	6.2	4	30	3	3	0	0	1	1	5	0	3	1	0
Arnold, Jamie, ChiN	0	3	.000	6.61	12	4	0	0	3	1	32.2	34	151	28	24	1	2	3	19	0	13	1	0	
Ashby, Andy, Phi.	4	7	.364	5.68	16	16	1	0	0	0	101.1	113	455	75	64	17	11	9	5	38	5	51	4	0
Ashby, Andy, Atl.	8	6	.571	4.13	15	15	2	1	0	0	98.0	103	412	49	45	12	7	1	1	23	4	55	2	1
Aybar, Manny, Col.	0	1	.000	16.20	1	0	0	0	0	0	1.2	5	10	3	3	1	0	0	0	0	0	0	0	0
Aybar, Manny, Cin.	1	1	.500	4.83	32	0	0	0	10	0	50.1	51	226	31	27	7	4	3	2	22	2	31	7	1
Aybar, Manny, Fla.	1	0	1.000	2.63	21	0	0	0	10	0	27.1	18	113	8	8	3	1	1	0	13	1	14	0	0
Belinda, Stan, Col.	1	3	.250	7.07	46	0	0	0	10	1	35.2	39	166	32	28	10	4	2	2	17	4	40	2	0
Belinda, Stan, Atl.	0	0	.000	9.82	10	0	0	0	7	0	11.0	16	54	12	12	4	0	2	1	5	1	11	0	0
Chen, Bruce, Atl.*	4	0	1.000	2.50	22	0	0	0	4	0	39.2	35	176	15	11	4	3	2	1	19	2	32	0	1
Chen, Bruce, Phi.*	3	4	.429	3.63	15	15	0	0	0	0	94.1	81	383	39	38	14	5	1	1	27	2	80	4	0
Christiansen, Jason, Pit.*	2	8	.200	4.97	44	0	0	0	17	1	38.0	28	164	22	21	2	3	1	0	25	4	41	3	0
Christiansen, Jason, St.L*	1	0	1.000	5.40	21	0	0	0	2	0	10.0	13	46	7	6	1	1	0	2	2	1	12	0	0
Daal, Omar, Ari.*	2	10	.167	7.22	20	16	0	0	1	0	96.0	127	460	88	77	17	3	5	7	42	11	45	0	1
Daal, Omar, Phi.*	2	9	.182	4.69	12	12	0	0	0	0	71.0	81	315	40	37	9	3	1	2	30	0	51	0	1
Downs, Scott, ChiN*	4	3	.571	5.17	18	18	0	0	0	0	94.0	117	426	59	54	13	2	4	5	37	1	63	1	0
Downs, Scott, Mon.*	0	0	.000	9.00	1	1	0	0	0	0	3.0	5	16	3	3	0	0	0	0	3	0	0	0	0
Henry, Doug, Hou.	1	3	.250	4.42	45	0	0	0	13	1	53.0	39	225	26	26	10	2	1	3	28	2	46	2	0
Henry, Doug, S.F.	3	1	.750	2.49	27	0	0	0	8	0	25.1	18	110	10	7	2	3	1	1	21	1	16	1	0
Holmes, Darren, St.L	0	1	.000	9.72	5	0	0	0	1	0	8.1	12	39	9	9	2	0	2	1	3	0	5	0	0
Holmes, Darren, Ari.	0	0	.000	8.53	8	0	0	0	3	1	6.1	12	32	6	6	1	0	1	1	1	0	5	0	0
Linebrink, Scott, S.F.	0	0	.000	11.57	3	0	0	0	1	0	2.1	7	16	3	3	1	0	0	0	2	0	0	0	0
Linebrink, Scott, Hou.	0	0	.000	4.66	8	0	0	0	3	0	9.2	11	47	5	5	3	0	0	3	6	0	6	0	0
Miller, Trever, Hou.*	0	0	.000	8.36	14	0	0	0	2	0	14.0	19	72	16	13	3	1	1	1	9	1	10	1	0
Miller, Trever, L.A.*	0	0	.000	23.14	2	0	0	0	0	0	2.1	8	18	6	6	0	0	0	1	3	0	1	0	0
Moraga, David, Mon.*	0	0	.000	37.80	3	0	0	0	1	0	1.2	6	14	7	7	0	1	1	0	2	0	2	1	0
Moraga, David, Col.*	0	0	.000	45.00	1	0	0	0	1	0	1.0	4	8	5	5	1	0	1	0	1	0	0	0	0
Padilla, Vicente, Ari.	2	1	.667	2.31	27	0	0	0	12	0	35.0	32	143	10	9	0	0	1	0	10	2	30	0	0
Padilla, Vicente, Phi.	2	6	.250	5.34	28	0	0	0	4	2	30.1	40	148	23	18	3	5	2	1	18	5	21	1	0
Reyes, Carlos, Phi.	0	0	.000	5.23	10	0	0	0	5	0	10.1	10	44	6	6	2	2	0	0	5	0	4	1	0
Reyes, Carlos, S.D.	1	1	.500	6.00	12	0	0	0	4	1	18.0	15	77	12	12	5	0	0	1	8	0	13	0	1
Schilling, Curt, Phi.	6	6	.500	3.91	16	16	4	1	0	0	112.2	110	474	49	49	17	5	1	1	32	4	96	4	0
Schilling, Curt, Ari.	5	6	.455	3.69	13	13	4	1	0	0	97.2	94	388	41	40	10	6	3	0	13	0	72	0	0
Serafini, Dan, S.D.*	0	0	.000	18.00	3	0	0	0	1	0	3.0	9	20	6	6	2	0	0	0	2	0	3	1	0
Serafini, Dan, Pit.*	2	5	.286	4.91	11	11	0	0	0	0	62.1	70	280	35	34	9	8	2	4	26	1	32	2	0
Skrmetta, Matt, Mon.	0	0	.000	15.19	6	0	0	0	3	0	5.1	6	29	10	9	1	0	1	0	6	0	4	2	0
Skrmetta, Matt, Pit.	2	2	.500	9.64	8	0	0	0	4	0	9.1	13	44	12	10	2	1	0	1	3	0	7	1	0
Slocumb, Heathcliff, St.L	2	3	.400	5.44	43	0	0	0	11	1	49.2	50	218	32	30	9	3	2	1	24	1	34	1	1
Slocumb, Heathcliff, S.D.	0	1	.000	3.79	22	0	0	0	6	0	19.0	19	91	11	8	0	1	3	2	13	3	12	0	1
Valdes, Ismael, ChiN	4	4	.333	5.37	12	12	0	0	0	0	67.0	71	291	40	40	17	0	2	2	27	3	45	0	0
Valdes, Ismael, L.A.	0	3	.000	6.08	9	8	0	0	1	0	40.0	53	178	29	27	5	0	2	1	13	0	29	0	0
White, Gabe, Cin.*	0	0	.000	18.00	1	0	0	0	0	0	1.0	2	6	2	2	1	0	0	0	1	0	2	0	0
White, Gabe, Col.*	11	2	.846	2.17	67	0	0	0	17	5	83.0	62	323	21	20	5	2	6	3	14	2	82	1	0

FIELDING

TEAM

Team	Pct.	G	PO	A	E	TC	DP	TP	PB
San Francisco ...	.985	162	4333	1644	93	6070	173	0	15
Colorado	.985	162	4290	1727	94	6111	176	0	15
Chicago	.983	162	4364	1574	100	6038	139	0	6
Philadelphia	.983	162	4316	1491	100	5907	136	0	4
Arizona	.982	162	4331	1541	107	5979	138	1	4
Cincinnati	.982	163	4369	1639	111	6119	156	0	12
St. Louis	.981	162	4301	1524	111	5936	148	0	8
Milwaukee	.981	163	4399	1747	118	6264	187	0	12
New York	.980	162	4350	1582	118	6050	121	0	8

Team	Pct.	G	PO	A	E	TC	DP	TP	PB
Florida	.980	161	4289	1710	125	6124	144	0	12
Atlanta	.979	162	4321	1733	129	6183	138	1	9
Pittsburgh	.979	162	4347	1828	132	6307	169	0	12
Montreal	.978	162	4274	1703	132	6109	151	1	19
Los Angeles	.978	162	4335	1717	135	6187	151	0	15
Houston	.978	162	4313	1561	133	6007	149	0	6
San Diego	.977	162	4378	1670	141	6189	155	0	13
Totals	.981	1297	69310	26391	1879	97580	2431	3	170

INDIVIDUAL

FIRST BASEMEN

NOTE: All caps denotes fielding-percentage leader based on 81 games for catchers, 108 for all other non-pitchers and 162 innings for pitchers. *Throws lefthanded.

Player, Team	Pct.	G	PO	A	E	TC	DP
Allen, Dusty, S.D.	.000	1	0	0	0	0	0
Andrews, Shane, Chi.	1.000	6	36	7	0	43	3
Bagwell, Jeff, Hou.	.994	158	1264	116	9	1389	128
Bako, Paul, Atl.	1.000	1	2	0	0	2	1
Barker, Kevin, Mil.*	.993	32	250	15	2	267	24
Benjamin, Mike, Pit.	1.000	1	4	0	0	4	0
Berkman, Lance, Hou.*	1.000	2	2	1	0	3	0
Berroa, Geronimo, L.A.	.929	2	11	2	1	14	3
Blum, Geoff, Mon.	1.000	11	33	2	0	35	2
Brogna, Rico, Phi.*	.996	34	248	17	1	266	22
Brown, Brant, Fla.-Chi.*	.982	12	50	6	1	57	2
Burrell, Pat, Phi.	.988	58	460	22	6	488	37
Cabrera, Alex, Ari.	1.000	15	101	6	0	107	9
Casey, Sean, Cin.	.995	129	1064	60	6	1130	106
Clark, Will, St.L.*	.992	50	364	27	3	394	34
Colbrunn, Greg, Ari.	.989	60	649	52	8	709	60
Crespo, Felipe, S.F.	1.000	11	30	1	0	31	1
Cromer, D.T., Cin.*	.964	13	50	3	2	55	8
Cruz, Ivan, Pit.*	1.000	1	6	0	0	6	0
Davis, Russ, S.F.	.923	6	23	1	2	26	4
Donnels, Chris, L.A.	.950	4	19	0	1	20	2
Dunston, Shawon, St.L.	.955	6	21	0	1	22	3
Durazo, Erubiel, Ari.*	.989	60	422	23	5	450	36
Echevarria, Angel, Col.-Mil.	1.000	11	30	3	0	33	5
Edmonds, Jim, St.L.*	1.000	6	40	4	0	44	6
Elster, Kevin, L.A.	.000	1	0	0	1	1	0
Fox, Andy, Ari.	1.000	1	7	0	0	7	3
Franco, Matt, N.Y.	.990	28	89	8	1	98	10
Galarraga, Andres, Atl.	.988	132	1105	61	14	1180	98
Gload, Ross, Chi.*	1.000	2	6	0	0	6	2
GRACE, Mark, Chi.*	.997	140	1098	103	4	1205	99
Hansen, Dave, L.A.	.980	16	44	5	1	50	5
Harris, Lenny, N.Y.	.955	10	36	6	2	44	3
Hayes, Charlie, Mil.	.991	57	407	30	4	441	57
Helton, Todd, Col.*	.995	160	1326	149	7	1482	143
Hernandez, Alex, Pit.*	.992	12	123	3	1	127	14
Hernandez, Carlos, S.D.	1.000	1	2	0	0	2	0
Houston, Tyler, Mil.	.982	35	257	21	5	283	30
Howard, Thomas, St.L.	1.000	1	4	0	0	4	0
Hunter, Brian, Phi.*	.994	40	159	16	1	176	12
Huskey, Butch, Col.	1.000	8	24	1	0	25	6
Huson, Jeff, Chi.	1.000	1	1	0	0	1	0
Johnson, Mark P., N.Y.*	1.000	4	9	0	0	9	1
Jordan, Kevin, Phi.	.967	9	54	5	2	61	11
Joyner, Wally, Atl.*	.992	55	353	30	3	386	33
Karros, Eric, L.A.	.995	153	1296	138	7	1441	123
Kent, Jeff, S.F.	.973	16	73	0	2	75	10
Kieschnick, Brooks, Cin.	1.000	1	1	0	0	1	0
Klesko, Ryan, S.D.*	.992	136	1028	91	9	1128	104
Kotsay, Mark, Fla.*	1.000	2	1	0	0	1	0
Ledesma, Aaron, Col.	1.000	3	28	4	0	32	6
Lee, Derrek, Fla.	.993	147	1101	102	8	1211	104
Lee, Travis, Ari.-Phi.*	.996	70	449	43	2	494	58
Leyritz, Jim, L.A.	1.000	8	27	2	0	29	3
Mabry, John, S.D.	1.000	2	8	1	0	9	0
Magadan, Dave, S.D.	1.000	8	47	10	0	57	7

Player, Team	Pct.	G	PO	A	E	TC	DP
Manto, Jeff, Col.	1.000	1	1	0	0	1	1
Marrero, Eli, St.L.	1.000	7	16	0	0	16	1
Martinez, Dave, Chi.*	.986	9	65	5	1	71	3
Martinez, Ramon E., S.F.	1.000	2	1	0	0	1	1
Matheny, Mike, St.L.	1.000	8	12	1	0	13	0
McGwire, Mark, St.L.	.998	70	535	23	1	559	49
Melhuse, Adam, Col.	1.000	3	11	1	0	12	1
Millar, Kevin, Fla.	.989	34	233	29	3	265	18
Miller, Damian, Ari.	.667	2	2	0	1	3	0
Minor, Damon, S.F.*	1.000	4	5	0	0	5	0
Mordecai, Mike, Mon.	.875	3	6	1	1	8	3
Morris, Hal, Cin.*	1.000	16	50	12	0	62	6
Nunnari, Talmadge, Mon.*	1.000	14	23	2	0	25	1
Osik, Keith, Pit.	1.000	5	29	0	0	29	3
Paquette, Craig, St.L.	.993	28	129	9	1	139	15
Perez, Eduardo, St.L.	1.000	24	156	13	0	169	18
Polanco, Placido, St.L.	1.000	1	2	1	0	3	0
Pritchett, Chris, Phi.	1.000	3	15	4	0	19	1
Ramirez, Alex, Pit.	.000	1	0	0	0	0	0
Richard, Chris, St.L.*	1.000	2	3	0	0	3	0
Rios, Armando, S.F.*	.000	1	0	0	0	0	0
Rolison, Nate, Fla.	1.000	4	21	2	0	23	1
Roskos, John, S.D.	1.000	2	0	1	0	1	0
Seguignol, Fernando, Mon.	.987	30	144	11	2	157	16
Sexson, Richie, Mil.	.991	57	471	66	5	542	50
Shumpert, Terry, Col.	.818	6	8	1	2	11	2
Snow, J.T., S.F.*	.995	153	1197	91	6	1294	135
Sprague, Ed, S.D.	.965	25	181	10	7	198	14
Stevens, Lee, Mon.*	.991	123	1072	85	11	1168	99
Sutton, Larry, St.L.*	1.000	6	26	2	0	28	2
Sweeney, Mark, Mil.*	1.000	2	3	0	0	3	0
Tatis, Fernando, St.L.	1.000	1	7	1	0	8	2
Toca, Jorge, N.Y.	1.000	5	9	0	0	9	0
Tracy, Andy, Mon.	1.000	27	177	11	0	188	15
Unroe, Tim, Atl.	1.000	2	12	2	0	14	0
Vander Wal, John, Pit.*	.996	33	251	10	1	262	21
Ventura, Robin, N.Y.	1.000	1	1	0	0	1	0
Vitiello, Joe, S.D.	.966	17	77	7	3	87	11
Vizcaino, Jose, L.A.	1.000	1	1	0	0	1	0
Ward, Daryle, Hou.*	1.000	19	55	3	0	58	5
Young, Dmitri, Cin.	.984	36	229	16	4	249	18
Young, Kevin, Pit.	.986	129	1109	59	17	1185	121
Zeile, Todd, N.Y.	.992	151	1205	95	10	1310	88
Zuleta, Julio, Chi.	.966	14	77	8	3	88	9

TRIPLE PLAYS: Galarraga, Atl.; Stevens, Mon.

FIRST BASEMEN WITH TWO OR MORE TEAMS

Player, Team	Pct.	G	PO	A	E	TC	DP
Brown, Brant, Fla.*	1.000	5	30	3	0	33	2
Brown, Brant, Chi.*	.958	7	20	3	1	24	0
Echevarria, Angel, Col.	1.000	2	3	0	0	3	1
Echevarria, Angel, Mil.	1.000	9	27	3	0	30	4
Lee, Travis, Ari.*	.984	23	112	8	2	122	16
Lee, Travis, Phi.*	1.000	47	337	35	0	372	42

SECOND BASEMEN

Player, Team	Pct.	G	PO	A	E	TC	DP
Abbott, Kurt, N.Y.	.981	23	23	29	1	53	3
Alfonzo, Edgardo, N.Y.	.985	146	316	362	10	688	84
Anderson, Marlon, Phi.	.989	41	87	100	2	189	32

Player, Team	Pct.	G	PO	A	E	TC	DP
Arias, Alex, Phi.	1.000	1	2	4	0	6	0
Bell, Jay, Ari.	.988	145	290	345	8	643	85
Belliard, Ron, Mil.	.976	151	336	438	19	793	130
Benjamin, Mike, Pit.	1.000	27	57	71	0	128	18
Berg, Dave, Fla.	1.000	11	17	25	0	42	3
Biggio, Craig, Hou.	.987	100	181	280	6	467	57
Blum, Geoff, Mon.	1.000	13	20	26	0	46	6
Bocachica, Hiram, L.A.	1.000	2	3	9	0	12	2
Bogar, Tim, Hou.	.750	2	1	2	1	4	1
Boone, Bret, S.D.	.977	126	292	334	15	641	83
Branson, Jeff, L.A.	.900	3	3	6	1	10	2
Cabrera, Orlando, Mon.	.000	1	0	0	0	0	0
Castillo, Luis, Fla.	.983	136	282	365	11	658	83
Castro, Juan, Cin.	.989	21	47	46	1	94	13
Clapinski, Chris, Fla.	.933	14	25	31	4	60	5
Coquillette, Trace, Mon.	1.000	8	1	6	0	7	0
Cora, Alex, L.A.	1.000	8	11	13	0	24	5
Counsell, Craig, Ari.	.974	25	32	43	2	77	12
Crespo, Felipe, S.F.	1.000	7	2	3	0	5	0
Cromer, Tripp, Hou.	.000	1	0	0	0	0	0
Donnels, Chris, L.A.	1.000	1	1	0	0	1	0
Fox, Andy, Fla.	1.000	2	4	6	0	10	1
Franco, Matt, N.Y.	.000	1	0	0	0	0	0
Frias, Hanley, Ari.	.960	15	11	13	1	25	3
Frye, Jeff, Col.	.989	27	37	56	1	94	15
Furcal, Rafael, Atl.	.992	31	45	73	1	119	18
Ginter, Keith, Hou.	1.000	2	4	5	0	9	2
Gomez, Chris, S.D.	1.000	3	3	3	0	6	2
Grudzielanek, Mark, L.A.	.976	148	286	414	17	717	97
Guerrero, Wilton, Mon.	.000	1	0	0	0	0	0
Harris, Lenny, N.Y.	1.000	3	2	3	0	5	0
Huson, Jeff, Chi.	.952	17	19	21	2	42	7
Jackson, Damian, S.D.	.972	36	70	104	5	179	24
Johnson, Russ, Hou.	.875	3	5	2	1	8	0
Jordan, Kevin, Phi.	.988	47	67	97	2	166	16
Kent, Jeff, S.F.	.986	150	302	394	10	706	96
Lamb, David, N.Y.	.000	2	0	0	0	0	0
Lansing, Mike, Col.	.983	88	175	221	7	403	57
LaRocca, Greg, S.D.	.818	2	3	6	2	11	0
Lockhart, Keith, Atl.	.979	74	103	177	6	286	32
Lopez, Luis, Mil.	.987	22	31	44	1	76	11
Loretta, Mark, Mil.	1.000	1	1	0	0	1	0
Lugo, Julio, Hou.	.976	45	92	108	5	205	26
Martinez, Ramon E., S.F.	1.000	32	43	35	0	78	11
McEwing, Joe, N.Y.	.939	16	16	15	2	33	4
Melo, Juan, S.F.	1.000	6	3	4	0	7	0
Metcalfe, Mike, L.A.	1.000	1	0	1	0	1	0
Meyers, Chad, Chi.	1.000	8	9	14	0	23	4
Mora, Melvin, N.Y.	1.000	4	3	11	0	14	1
Morandini, Mickey, Phi.	.987	85	179	196	5	380	45
Mordecai, Mike, Mon.	1.000	9	8	6	0	14	2
Morris, Warren, Pit.	.979	134	291	414	15	720	92
Mueller, Bill, S.F.	1.000	2	1	0	0	1	0
Newhan, David, S.D.-Phi.	1.000	8	12	18	0	30	5
Nicholson, Kevin, S.D.	.833	4	2	8	2	12	2
Nieves, Jose, Chi.	1.000	7	2	11	0	13	4
Nunez, Abraham, Pit.	1.000	6	12	8	0	20	4
Ojeda, Augie, Chi.	1.000	4	2	2	0	4	1
Owens, Eric, S.D.	.000	1	0	0	0	0	0
Ozuna, Pablo, Fla.	.967	7	12	17	1	30	3
Paquette, Craig, St.L.	.915	13	19	24	4	47	7
Pena, Elvis, Col.	.000	1	0	0	0	0	0
Polanco, Placido, St.L.	.984	51	80	107	3	190	18
Reese, Pokey, Cin.	.980	133	289	393	14	696	88
Santangelo, F.P., L.A.	.971	7	18	15	1	34	2
Sexton, Chris, Cin.	1.000	12	17	26	0	43	6
Shumpert, Terry, Col.	.971	23	33	35	0	68	10
Sisco, Steve, Atl.	1.000	5	3	4	0	7	2
Sojo, Luis, Pit.	.000	1	0	0	0	0	0
Spiers, Bill, Hou.	.979	26	40	53	2	95	13
Sprague, Ed, S.D.	1.000	1	0	1	0	1	0
Stynes, Chris, Cin.	.978	15	19	25	1	45	9
Tucker, Michael, Cin.	.000	1	0	0	0	0	0
Velandia, Jorge, N.Y.	1.000	7	3	1	0	4	0
Veras, Quilvio, Atl.	.984	82	146	223	6	375	42
Vidro, Jose, Mon.	.986	153	260	442	10	712	102
VINA, Fernando, St.L.	.988	122	261	325	7	593	85
Vizcaino, Jose, L.A.	1.000	3	0	1	0	1	0
Walker, Todd, Col.	.975	52	81	118	5	204	25
Wilson, Enrique, Pit.	.970	11	10	22	1	33	4
Young, Eric, Chi.	.979	150	313	401	15	729	86

TRIPLE PLAY: Veras, Atl.

SECOND BASEMEN WITH TWO OR MORE TEAMS

Player, Team	Pct.	G	PO	A	E	TC	DP
Newhan, David, S.D.	1.000	3	3	3	0	6	0
Newhan, David, Phi.	1.000	5	9	15	0	24	5

THIRD BASEMEN

Player, Team	Pct.	G	PO	A	E	TC	DP
Abbott, Kurt, N.Y.	1.000	2	4	1	0	5	0
Alvarez, Gabe, S.D.	1.000	3	0	1	0	1	0
Andrews, Shane, Chi.	.907	58	23	94	12	129	10
Arias, Alex, Phi.	1.000	10	2	6	0	8	1
Barrett, Michael, Mon.	.891	55	23	83	13	119	10
Bell, Mike, Cin.	.900	13	2	16	2	20	2
Beltre, Adrian, L.A.	.944	138	116	273	23	412	30
Benjamin, Mike, Pit.	.974	34	13	61	2	76	5
Berg, Dave, Fla.	.933	13	2	12	1	15	1
Berry, Sean, Mil.	1.000	9	3	4	0	7	1
Blum, Geoff, Mon.	.952	55	26	93	6	125	6
Bogar, Tim, Hou.	.000	1	0	0	0	0	0
Bonilla, Bobby, Atl.	.000	1	0	0	0	0	0
Boone, Aaron, Cin.	.964	84	62	154	8	224	21
Branson, Jeff, L.A.	1.000	3	0	2	0	2	0
Caminiti, Ken, Hou.	.915	58	37	81	11	129	8
Castro, Juan, Cin.	1.000	7	0	2	0	2	0
Cirillo, Jeff, Col.	.964	155	92	304	15	411	41
Clapinski, Chris, Fla.	1.000	3	2	2	0	4	0
Colbrunn, Greg, Ari.	.000	1	0	0	0	0	0
Collier, Lou, Mil.	1.000	1	0	0	0	0	0
Coquillette, Trace, Mon.	.958	19	2	21	1	24	2
Counsell, Craig, Ari.	.952	23	3	37	2	42	6
Cromer, Tripp, Hou.	.500	2	0	1	1	2	0
Davis, Russ, S.F.	.933	43	14	42	4	60	3
Donnels, Chris, L.A.	1.000	2	1	1	0	2	0
Dunston, Shawon, St.L.	1.000	5	0	3	0	3	1
Elster, Kevin, L.A.	.917	8	6	16	2	24	0
Ensberg, Morgan, Hou.	.667	1	1	1	1	3	0
Feliz, Pedro, S.F.	.000	4	0	0	0	0	0
Fox, Andy, Ari.-Fla.	.957	32	15	51	3	69	7
Franco, Matt, N.Y.	.900	22	9	18	3	30	0
Frias, Hanley, Ari.	1.000	7	0	3	0	3	1
Frye, Jeff, Col.	1.000	1	0	2	0	2	1
Greene, Willie, Chi.	.967	90	46	158	7	211	18
Hansen, Dave, L.A.	.955	16	4	17	1	22	2
Harris, Lenny, Ari.-N.Y.	.880	36	26	55	11	92	3
Hayes, Charlie, Mil.	.976	59	31	89	3	123	6
Helms, Wes, Atl.	.833	5	1	4	1	6	1
Hernandez, Jose, Mil.	.950	95	81	165	13	259	23
Houston, Tyler, Mil.	.939	28	12	50	4	66	6
Huson, Jeff, Chi.	1.000	18	10	16	0	26	1
Johnson, Russ, Hou.	1.000	4	1	4	0	5	0
Jones, Chipper, Atl.	.944	152	90	297	23	410	23
Jordan, Kevin, Phi.	.967	39	26	61	3	90	8
Klassen, Danny, Ari.	.962	25	11	39	2	52	4
Lamb, David, N.Y.	1.000	3	0	1	0	1	0
LaRocca, Greg, S.D.	1.000	8	3	3	0	6	0
Ledesma, Aaron, Col.	1.000	5	0	2	0	2	0
Lewis, Mark, Cin.	.909	5	2	8	1	11	0
Lockhart, Keith, Atl.	.946	18	8	27	2	37	2
LoDuca, Paul, L.A.	1.000	1	0	1	0	1	0
Lopez, Luis, Mil.	1.000	6	2	8	0	10	2
Lowell, Mike, Fla.	.968	136	102	260	12	374	19
Magadan, Dave, S.D.	.952	29	11	29	2	42	2
Manto, Jeff, Col.	1.000	1	0	1	0	1	0
Martinez, Ramon E., S.F.	1.000	2	1	1	0	2	0
McEwing, Joe, N.Y.	.914	19	6	26	3	35	1
Meluskey, Mitch, Hou.	.000	1	0	0	1	1	0
Meyers, Chad, Chi.	.778	8	2	5	2	9	1
Millar, Kevin, Fla.	.944	13	11	23	2	36	1
Mora, Melvin, N.Y.	1.000	4	1	0	0	1	0
Mordecai, Mike, Mon.	.937	58	21	68	6	95	9
MUELLER, Bill, S.F.	.974	145	99	244	9	352	24
Nevin, Phil, S.D.	.929	142	96	242	26	364	22
Newhan, David, S.D.	1.000	2	0	1	0	1	0
Nieves, Jose, Chi.	.949	39	17	58	4	79	2
Osik, Keith, Pit.	.958	12	9	14	1	24	2
Paquette, Craig, St.L.	.942	86	41	88	8	137	9
Perez, Eduardo, St.L.	.000	2	0	0	0	0	0
Polanco, Placido, St.L.	1.000	35	18	41	0	59	8
Ramirez, Aramis, Pit.	.917	72	26	128	14	168	7
Rolen, Scott, Phi.	.971	128	89	245	10	344	14
Sexton, Chris, Cin.	1.000	3	2	4	0	6	0

Player, Team	Pct.	G	PO	A	E	TC	DP
Shumpert, Terry, Col.	1.000	15	8	13	0	21	0
Sisco, Steve, Atl.	1.000	2	1	1	0	2	0
Sojo, Luis, Pit.	.960	50	24	97	5	126	5
Spiers, Bill, Hou.	.959	51	33	85	5	123	8
Sprague, Ed, S.D.	1.000	10	3	9	0	12	1
Stynes, Chris, Cin.	.966	77	53	119	6	178	14
Tatis, Fernando, St.L.	.953	91	35	128	8	171	15
Tracy, Andy, Mon.	.882	34	10	35	6	51	2
Truby, Chris, Hou.	.926	74	51	125	14	190	15
Velandia, Jorge, N.Y.	.800	3	2	2	1	5	0
Ventura, Robin, N.Y.	.954	137	95	261	17	373	27
Vizcaino, Jose, L.A.	.931	12	8	19	2	29	2
Wehner, John, Pit.	.973	16	14	22	1	37	0
Williams, Matt, Ari.	.964	94	68	172	9	249	19
Wilson, Enrique, Pit.	.925	16	7	30	3	40	1

TRIPLE PLAY: C. Jones, Atl.

THIRD BASEMEN WITH TWO OR MORE TEAMS

Player, Team	Pct.	G	PO	A	E	TC	DP
Fox, Andy, Ari.	.952	20	11	29	2	42	3
Fox, Andy, Fla.	.963	12	4	22	1	27	4
Harris, Lenny, Ari.	.909	20	11	29	4	44	1
Harris, Lenny, N.Y.	.854	16	15	26	7	48	2

SHORTSTOPS

Player, Team	Pct.	G	PO	A	E	TC	DP
Abbott, Kurt, N.Y.	.953	39	47	75	6	128	10
Arias, Alex, Phi.	.963	39	41	88	5	134	19
Aurilia, Rich, S.F.	.967	140	218	403	21	642	110
Beltre, Adrian, L.A.	1.000	1	1	0	0	1	0
Benjamin, Mike, Pit.	.981	30	30	74	2	106	13
Berg, Dave, Fla.	.957	49	52	105	7	164	27
Blum, Geoff, Mon.	.978	44	43	89	3	135	22
Bogar, Tim, Hou.	.971	95	120	243	11	374	55
Boone, Aaron, Cin.	1.000	2	1	3	0	4	0
Bordick, Mike, N.Y.	.968	56	71	140	7	218	24
Branson, Jeff, L.A.	1.000	7	5	5	0	10	0
Cabrera, Orlando, Mon.	.981	124	167	339	10	516	77
Castro, Juan, Cin.	.994	57	55	117	1	173	27
Clapinski, Chris, Fla.	.000	1	0	0	0	0	0
Cora, Alex, L.A.	.972	101	152	260	12	424	70
Counsell, Craig, Ari.	.900	6	3	15	2	20	2
Cromer, Tripp, Hou.	1.000	1	0	1	0	1	0
Dawkins, Gookie, Cin.	.965	14	21	34	2	57	13
de la Rosa, Tomas, Mon.	.980	29	40	58	2	100	7
DeRosa, Mark, Atl.	1.000	10	6	7	0	13	2
Dunston, Shawon, St.L.	1.000	8	4	6	0	10	2
Elster, Kevin, L.A.	.946	55	60	133	11	204	25
Fox, Andy, Fla.	.932	33	37	86	9	132	12
Frias, Hanley, Ari.	.938	21	18	43	4	65	12
Furcal, Rafael, Atl.	.950	110	147	289	23	459	54
Gomez, Chris, S.D.	.928	17	24	40	5	69	10
Gonzalez, Alex, Fla.	.957	104	139	288	19	446	63
Grudzielanek, Mark, L.A.	1.000	1	2	2	0	4	1
GUTIERREZ, Ricky, Chi.	.986	121	190	290	7	487	60
Hernandez, Jose, Mil.	.968	37	59	93	5	157	32
Huson, Jeff, Chi.	.982	17	23	33	1	57	7
Jackson, Damian, S.D.	.955	88	144	258	19	421	50
Johnson, Russ, Hou.	1.000	5	5	8	0	13	2
Jones, Chipper, Atl.	.875	6	6	8	2	16	2
Klassen, Danny, Ari.	1.000	3	3	3	0	6	0
Lamb, David, N.Y.	1.000	2	2	2	0	4	0
Larkin, Barry, Cin.	.973	102	153	249	11	413	43
LaRocca, Greg, S.D.	1.000	4	4	3	0	7	1
Lopez, Luis, Mil.	.959	45	68	94	7	169	27
Loretta, Mark, Mil.	.995	90	121	254	2	377	54
Lugo, Julio, Hou.	.951	60	93	141	12	246	30
Magadan, Dave, S.D.	1.000	2	0	2	0	2	1
Martinez, Ramon E., S.F.	.991	44	43	72	1	116	20
McEwing, Joe, N.Y.	1.000	4	3	3	0	6	0
Meares, Pat, Pit.	.967	126	191	401	20	612	99
Mora, Melvin, N.Y.	.958	44	56	104	7	167	16
Mordecai, Mike, Mon.	.952	10	7	13	1	21	2
Nicholson, Kevin, S.D.	.983	30	37	79	2	118	11
Nieves, Jose, Chi.	.984	24	27	34	1	62	10
Nunez, Abraham, Pit.	.978	21	31	57	2	90	10
Ojeda, Augie, Chi.	.989	25	28	63	1	92	13
Ordonez, Rey, N.Y.	.965	44	58	108	6	172	20
Pena, Elvis, Col.	1.000	3	1	2	0	3	1
Perez, Neifi, Col.	.978	162	288	523	18	829	120
Perez, Santiago, Mil.	.917	20	21	45	6	72	11

Player, Team	Pct.	G	PO	A	E	TC	DP
Perez, Tomas, Phi.	.976	44	76	89	4	169	20
Polanco, Placido, St.L.	1.000	29	31	53	0	84	11
Relaford, Desi, Phi.-S.D.	.943	126	189	322	31	542	79
Renteria, Edgar, St.L.	.958	149	231	379	27	637	79
Rollins, Jimmy, Phi.	.978	13	23	22	1	46	9
Sexton, Chris, Cin.	.954	14	25	37	3	65	6
Shumpert, Terry, Col.	1.000	7	4	7	0	11	3
Spiers, Bill, Hou.	.990	27	40	57	1	98	18
Velandia, Jorge, N.Y.	1.000	7	3	2	0	5	0
Vizcaino, Jose, L.A.	1.000	19	15	43	0	58	6
Weiss, Walt, Atl.	.949	69	83	197	15	295	38
Wilson, Enrique, Pit.	.933	8	7	21	2	30	7
Womack, Tony, Ari.	.970	143	217	365	18	600	72

TRIPLE PLAYS: Cabrera, Mon.; Womack, Ari.

SHORTSTOPS WITH TWO OR MORE TEAMS

Player, Team	Pct.	G	PO	A	E	TC	DP
Relaford, Desi, Phi.	.930	81	116	202	24	342	46
Relaford, Desi, S.D.	.965	45	73	120	7	200	33

OUTFIELDERS

Player, Team	Pct.	G	PO	A	E	TC	DP
Abbott, Kurt, N.Y.	.000	2	0	0	0	0	0
Abreu, Bobby, Phi.	.989	152	337	13	4	354	2
Agbayani, Benny, N.Y.	.975	110	155	3	4	162	0
Allen, Dusty, S.D.	1.000	2	2	0	0	2	0
Alou, Moises, Hou.	.970	121	192	5	6	203	0
Alvarez, Gabe, S.D.	.000	2	0	0	0	0	0
Aven, Bruce, Pit.-L.A.	.984	50	61	0	1	62	0
Barker, Glen, Hou.	.985	69	64	1	1	66	0
Bartee, Kimera, Cin.	1.000	3	1	0	0	1	0
Bautista, Danny, Fla.-Ari.	.985	120	188	8	3	199	1
Bell, Derek, N.Y.	.988	143	252	5	3	260	1
Benard, Marvin, S.F.*	.997	141	323	11	1	335	1
Bergeron, Peter, Mon.	.985	146	303	16	5	324	3
Berkman, Lance, Hou.*	.968	96	173	6	6	185	0
Berroa, Geronimo, L.A.	1.000	6	7	0	0	7	0
Bichette, Dante, Cin.	.969	121	235	11	8	254	3
Bonds, Barry, S.F.*	.989	141	255	8	3	266	4
Bonilla, Bobby, Atl.	.927	64	50	1	4	55	0
Bradley, Milton, Mon.	.979	40	88	6	2	96	0
Bragg, Darren, Col.	1.000	43	53	0	0	53	0
Brock, Tarrik, Chi.*	.889	10	8	0	1	9	0
Brown, Adrian, Pit.	.976	92	154	7	4	165	1
Brown, Brant, Fla.-Chi.*	.980	41	50	0	1	51	0
Brown, Emil, Pit.	1.000	38	54	3	0	57	1
Brown, Roosevelt, Chi.	1.000	28	38	1	0	39	0
Buford, Damon, Chi.	.986	148	336	4	5	345	1
Burks, Ellis, S.F.	.982	108	215	4	4	223	1
Burnitz, Jeromy, Mil.	.979	158	317	12	7	336	2
Burrell, Pat, Phi.	.976	48	74	6	2	82	0
Cabrera, Alex, Ari.	.957	12	21	1	1	23	0
Carpenter, Bubba, Col.*	1.000	6	3	0	0	3	0
Cedeno, Roger, Hou.	.978	67	135	1	3	139	0
Clapinski, Chris, Fla.	1.000	3	1	0	0	1	0
Clark, Brady, Cin.	1.000	5	6	0	0	6	0
Collier, Lou, Mil.	1.000	10	16	2	0	18	0
Conti, Jason, Ari.	.983	35	53	4	1	58	2
Coquillette, Trace, Mon.	1.000	2	2	0	0	2	0
Cordero, Wil, Pit.	.983	85	110	3	2	115	0
Crespo, Felipe, S.F.	.962	26	25	0	1	26	0
Darr, Mike, S.D.	1.000	57	124	7	0	131	1
Davis, Eric, St.L.	.968	69	120	1	4	125	0
DeHaan, Kory, S.D.	1.000	60	50	3	0	53	1
Dellucci, David, Ari.*	1.000	12	15	0	0	15	0
Donnels, Chris, L.A.	1.000	6	8	0	0	8	0
Drew, J.D., St.L.	.966	127	248	6	9	263	2
Ducey, Rob, Phi.	.936	33	43	1	3	47	0
Dunston, Shawon, St.L.	.989	58	85	1	1	87	0
Echevarria, Angel, Col.-Mil.	1.000	6	2	1	0	3	0
Edmonds, Jim, St.L.*	.989	146	352	10	4	366	2
Finley, Steve, Ari.*	.992	148	342	10	3	355	2
Floyd, Cliff, Fla.	.951	108	168	7	9	184	0
Fox, Andy, Ari.-Fla.	.909	20	9	1	1	11	0
Franco, Matt, N.Y.	1.000	3	2	0	0	2	0
Gant, Ron, Phi.	.968	84	175	4	6	185	0
Gilbert, Shawn, L.A.	.941	14	15	1	1	17	1
Giles, Brian, Pit.*	.982	155	316	14	6	336	1
Gilkey, Bernard, Ari.	1.000	17	29	1	0	30	0
Glanville, Doug, Phi.	.990	150	380	9	4	393	4
Gload, Ross, Chi.*	1.000	8	9	0	0	9	0

Player, Team	Pct.	G	PO	A	E	TC	DP
Gonzalez, Luis, Ari.	.990	162	293	4	3	300	1
Gonzalez, Raul, Chi.	.000	2	0	0	0	0	0
Goodwin, Tom, Col.-L.A.	.992	143	346	5	3	354	3
Green, Shawn, L.A.*	.980	161	280	9	6	295	3
Griffey Jr., Ken, Cin.*	.987	141	375	9	5	389	3
Grissom, Marquis, Mil.	.992	142	352	3	3	358	1
Guerrero, Vladimir, Mon.	.969	151	299	12	10	321	3
Guerrero, Wilton, Mon.	.967	75	115	4	4	123	1
Gwynn, Tony, S.D.*	1.000	26	31	1	0	32	0
Hamilton, Darryl, N.Y.	1.000	33	41	1	0	42	2
Hammonds, Jeffrey, Col.	.991	118	207	8	2	217	0
Hansen, Dave, L.A.	1.000	3	3	0	0	3	0
Harris, Lenny, Ari.-N.Y.	.882	14	14	1	2	17	0
Henderson, Rickey, N.Y.*	.946	29	35	0	2	37	0
Hermansen, Chad, Pit.	.979	31	44	2	1	47	0
Hernandez, Alex, Pit.*	1.000	5	4	1	0	5	0
Hernandez, Jose, Mil.	.500	2	1	0	1	2	0
Hidalgo, Richard, Hou.	.984	150	425	7	7	439	2
Hill, Glenallen, Chi.	.955	29	39	3	2	44	2
Hollandsworth, Todd, L.A.-Col.	.987	125	217	12	3	232	0
Howard, Thomas, St.L.	.960	27	23	1	1	25	1
Hubbard, Trenidad, Atl.	1.000	44	40	1	0	41	0
Hunter, Brian, Phi.*	1.000	9	8	0	0	8	0
Hunter, Brian L., Col.-Cin.	.979	88	133	7	3	143	0
Huskey, Butch, Col.	1.000	23	36	1	0	37	0
Hyzdu, Adam, Pit.	1.000	5	5	0	0	5	0
Jackson, Damian, S.D.	.952	17	20	0	1	21	0
Jenkins, Geoff, Mil.	.975	131	263	12	7	282	3
Johnson, Mark P., N.Y.*	1.000	1	1	1	0	2	0
Jones, Andruw, Atl.	.996	161	438	9	2	449	2
Jones, Chris, Mil.	1.000	2	6	0	0	6	0
Jones, Terry, Mon.	.970	78	94	4	3	101	0
Jordan, Brian, Atl.	.990	130	287	7	3	297	0
Kinkade, Mike, N.Y.	.000	1	0	0	0	0	0
Klesko, Ryan, S.D.*	1.000	4	2	0	0	2	0
Kotsay, Mark, Fla.*	.990	142	288	14	3	305	3
Lankford, Ray, St.L.*	.973	117	179	4	5	188	3
Lee, Travis, Ari.-Phi.*	.984	65	124	3	2	129	1
Leyritz, Jim, L.A.	1.000	6	4	0	0	4	0
LoDuca, Paul, L.A.	1.000	8	8	0	0	8	0
Lombard, George, Atl.	1.000	15	17	1	0	18	0
Lowery, Terrell, S.F.	.917	20	11	0	1	12	0
Lugo, Julio, Hou.	1.000	6	4	0	0	4	0
Mabry, John, S.D.	.980	32	49	1	1	51	0
Martin, Al, S.D.*	.950	89	128	4	7	139	1
Martinez, Dave, Chi.*	1.000	10	12	0	0	12	0
Matthews Jr., Gary, Chi.	.978	61	84	3	2	89	1
McEwing, Joe, N.Y.	1.000	52	42	1	0	43	0
McGuire, Ryan, N.Y.*	1.000	1	3	0	0	3	0
Melhuse, Adam, Col.	.000	1	0	0	0	0	0
Mendoza, Carlos, Col.*	.000	3	0	0	1	1	0
Metcalfe, Mike, L.A.	1.000	4	5	0	0	5	0
Mieske, Matt, Hou.-Ari.	.941	19	16	0	1	17	0
Millar, Kevin, Fla.	1.000	18	25	0	0	25	0
Mora, Melvin, N.Y.	.967	28	29	0	1	30	0
Morris, Hal, Cin.*	.000	1	0	0	0	0	0
Mouton, James, Mil.	.989	45	84	3	1	88	0
Mouton, Lyle, Mil.	.978	27	41	4	1	46	1
Murray, Calvin, S.F.	.980	106	143	2	3	148	1
Newhan, David, S.D.	1.000	5	6	0	0	6	0
Nunnally, Jon, N.Y.	.977	34	38	4	1	43	2
Ochoa, Alex, Cin.	.977	95	125	4	3	132	0
OWENS, Eric, S.D.	1.000	144	315	6	0	321	2
Paquette, Craig, St.L.	.935	31	27	2	2	31	2
Patterson, Corey, Chi.	.963	11	26	0	1	27	0
Payton, Jay, N.Y.	.981	146	311	7	6	324	2
Perez, Eduardo, St.L.	1.000	4	11	0	0	11	0
Perez, Timoniel, N.Y.*	.970	19	30	2	1	33	0
Pierre, Juan, Col.*	.975	50	115	2	3	120	0
Ramirez, Alex, Pit.	.949	31	55	1	3	59	0
Redman, Tike, Pit.*	1.000	6	12	1	0	13	0
Richard, Chris, St.L.*	1.000	3	7	0	0	7	0
Rios, Armando, S.F.*	.959	93	133	6	6	145	1
Rivera, Ruben, S.D.	.984	132	303	10	5	318	3
Rodriguez, Henry, Chi.-Fla.*	.987	99	150	6	2	158	2
Roskos, John, S.D.	.875	6	7	0	1	8	0
Ryan, Rob, Ari.*	1.000	2	1	0	0	1	0
Sanders, Reggie, Atl.	.964	96	155	7	6	168	1
Santangelo, F.P., L.A.	.983	50	58	0	1	59	0
Saturria, Luis, St.L.	1.000	9	3	0	0	3	0
Sefcik, Kevin, Phi.	1.000	50	74	0	0	74	0
Seguignol, Fernando, Mon.	.857	30	17	1	3	21	0

Player, Team	Pct.	G	PO	A	E	TC	DP
Sheffield, Gary, L.A.	.954	139	203	5	10	218	0
Shumpert, Terry, Col.	.967	40	56	2	2	60	0
Sisco, Steve, Atl.	1.000	6	3	1	0	4	0
Smith, Mark, Fla.	1.000	49	65	4	0	69	1
Sosa, Sammy, Chi.	.970	156	318	3	10	331	1
Spiers, Bill, Hou.	1.000	10	5	1	0	6	0
Sprague, Ed, S.D.	1.000	7	10	1	0	11	0
Stynes, Chris, Cin.	1.000	8	11	1	0	12	0
Surhoff, B.J., Atl.	1.000	32	50	1	0	51	0
Sutton, Larry, St.L.*	1.000	4	5	0	0	5	0
Swann, Pedro, Atl.	.000	3	0	0	0	0	0
Sweeney, Mark, Mil.*	1.000	3	8	0	0	8	0
Taylor, Reggie, Phi.	.800	3	4	0	1	5	0
Toca, Jorge, N.Y.	.000	1	0	0	0	0	0
Trammell, Bubba, N.Y.	.963	25	25	1	1	27	0
Tucker, Michael, Cin.	.969	120	153	5	5	163	0
Tyner, Jason, N.Y.*	.920	12	22	1	2	25	1
Unroe, Tim, Atl.	.000	1	0	0	0	0	0
Vander Wal, John, Pit.*	.965	78	134	2	5	141	0
Vitiello, Joe, S.D.	1.000	1	1	0	0	1	0
Walker, Larry, Col.	.994	83	161	10	1	172	4
Ward, Daryle, Hou.*	.986	47	70	1	1	72	1
Ward, Turner, Ari.	1.000	15	35	0	0	35	0
Wehner, John, Pit.	.000	1	0	0	0	0	0
White, Devon, L.A.	.972	40	68	2	2	72	0
White, Rondell, Mon.-Chi.	.995	92	199	4	1	204	1
Wilson, Preston, Fla.	.988	158	387	9	5	401	2
Womack, Tony, Ari.	1.000	2	1	0	0	1	0
Young, Dmitri, Cin.	.978	111	172	4	4	180	1
Zuleta, Julio, Chi.	1.000	6	6	0	0	6	0

TRIPLE PLAY: Finley, Ari.

OUTFIELDERS WITH TWO OR MORE TEAMS

Player, Team	Pct.	G	PO	A	E	TC	DP
Aven, Bruce, Pit.	.980	41	49	0	1	50	0
Aven, Bruce, L.A.	1.000	9	12	0	0	12	0
Bautista, Danny, Fla.	.980	38	46	2	1	49	1
Bautista, Danny, Ari.	.987	82	142	6	2	150	0
Brown, Brant, Fla.*	.923	13	12	0	1	13	0
Brown, Brant, Chi.*	1.000	28	38	0	0	38	0
Echevarria, Angel, Col.	.000	1	0	0	0	0	0
Echevarria, Angel, Mil.	1.000	5	2	1	0	3	0
Fox, Andy, Ari.	1.000	6	3	0	0	3	0
Fox, Andy, Fla.	.875	14	6	1	1	8	0
Goodwin, Tom, Col.	.986	88	208	3	3	214	1
Goodwin, Tom, L.A.	1.000	55	138	2	0	140	2
Harris, Lenny, Ari.	.000	3	0	0	0	0	0
Harris, Lenny, N.Y.	.882	11	14	1	2	17	0
Hollandsworth, Todd, L.A.*	.987	77	143	6	2	151	0
Hollandsworth, Todd, Col.*	.988	48	74	6	1	81	0
Hunter, Brian L., Col.	.981	63	103	3	2	108	0
Hunter, Brian L., Cin.	.971	25	30	4	1	35	0
Lee, Travis, Ari.*	.983	55	115	3	2	120	1
Lee, Travis, Phi.*	1.000	10	9	0	0	9	0
Mieske, Matt, Hou.	.933	18	14	0	1	15	0
Mieske, Matt, Ari.	1.000	1	2	0	0	2	0
Rodriguez, Henry, Chi.*	.983	70	110	5	2	117	2
Rodriguez, Henry, Fla.*	1.000	29	40	1	0	41	0
White, Rondell, Mon.	.994	74	158	4	1	163	1
White, Rondell, Chi.	1.000	18	41	0	0	41	0

CATCHERS

Player, Team	Pct.	G	PO	A	E	TC	DP	PB
Alvarez, Clemente, Phi.	1.000	2	10	0	0	10	0	0
Bako, Paul, Hou.-Fla.-Atl.	.992	80	436	31	4	471	3	3
Barajas, Rod, Ari.	1.000	5	23	0	0	23	0	0
Barrett, Michael, Mon.	.989	28	163	12	2	177	1	5
Bennett, Gary, Phi.	.995	31	173	11	1	185	2	0
Blanco, Henry, Mil.	.991	88	506	58	5	569	13	5
Brown, Kevin L., Mil.	.957	5	20	2	1	23	0	0
Casanova, Raul, Mil.	.990	72	357	29	4	390	6	3
Castro, Ramon, Fla.	.980	50	274	24	6	304	4	3
Charles, Frank, Hou.	1.000	1	7	2	0	9	1	0
Chavez, Raul, Mon.	.986	14	67	6	1	74	1	0
Davis, Ben, S.D.	.996	38	236	17	1	254	2	3
Estalella, Bobby, S.F.	.993	106	654	49	5	708	14	10
Eusebio, Tony, Hou.	.988	68	411	17	5	433	2	3
Girardi, Joe, Chi.	.993	103	706	43	5	754	5	5
Gonzalez, Wiki, S.D.	.991	87	525	42	5	572	13	7
Hernandez, Carlos, S.D.-St.L.	.982	70	439	42	9	490	3	5
Houston, Tyler, Mil.	.972	23	130	9	4	143	1	4

Player, Team	Pct.	G	PO	A	E	TC	DP	PB
Hubbard, Mike, Atl.	1.000	1	3	0	0	3	0	0
Hundley, Todd, L.A.	.979	84	554	38	13	605	3	8
Kendall, Jason, Pit.	.991	147	990	81	10	1081	12	11
Kreuter, Chad, L.A.	.994	78	483	35	3	521	1	7
LaRue, Jason, Cin.	.991	31	190	22	2	214	3	1
Leyritz, Jim, L.A.	1.000	3	10	1	0	11	0	0
Lieberthal, Mike, Phi.	.993	106	724	40	5	769	4	2
LoDuca, Paul, L.A.	.992	20	114	13	1	128	0	0
Lopez, Javy, Atl.	.993	132	817	62	6	885	6	8
Lunar, Fernando, Atl.	.993	22	125	12	1	138	2	0
Mahoney, Mike, Chi.	1.000	4	9	0	0	9	0	0
Marrero, Eli, St.L.	1.000	38	196	14	0	210	2	2
Martinez, Sandy, Fla.	1.000	9	43	2	0	45	0	0
Matheny, Mike, St.L.	.994	124	803	75	5	883	7	4
Mayne, Brent, Col.	.990	105	582	35	6	623	2	5
McDonald, Keith, St.L.	1.000	4	13	1	0	14	0	0
Melhuse, Adam, Col.	1.000	1	0	1	0	1	0	1
Meluskey, Mitch, Hou.	.982	103	623	31	12	666	6	3
Miller, Damian, Ari.	.992	97	681	47	6	734	4	3
Mirabelli, Doug, S.F.	.985	80	429	38	7	474	4	5
O'Brien, Charlie, Mon.	1.000	9	25	2	0	27	0	0
Osik, Keith, Pit.	.992	26	118	9	1	128	1	1
Perez, Eddie, Atl.	.976	7	39	2	1	42	0	1
Petrick, Ben, Col.	.985	48	248	19	4	271	4	8
PIAZZA, Mike, N.Y.	.997	124	862	38	3	903	10	3
Pratt, Todd, N.Y.	.997	71	314	24	1	339	4	5
Prince, Tom, Phi.	.996	46	250	20	1	271	2	2
Redmond, Mike, Fla.	.996	85	446	40	2	488	9	6
Reed, Jeff, Chi.	.990	71	469	19	5	493	7	3
Santiago, Benito, Cin.	.994	84	428	36	3	467	4	5
Schneider, Brian, Mon.	.974	43	205	19	6	230	2	5
Servais, Scott, Col.-S.F.	.988	38	222	17	3	242	1	1
Stinnett, Kelly, Ari.	.990	74	539	40	6	585	4	1
Taubensee, Eddie, Cin.	.989	76	420	26	5	451	8	6
Valera, Yohanny, Mon.	1.000	7	24	2	0	26	0	1
Webster, Lenny, Mon.	1.000	32	126	9	0	135	1	4
Widger, Chris, Mon.	.985	85	503	38	8	549	4	4
Wilkins, Rick, St.L.	1.000	3	28	3	0	31	0	0
Williams, George, S.D.	1.000	6	16	2	0	18	0	0
Wilson, Vance, N.Y.	1.000	3	14	0	0	14	0	0

TRIPLE PLAYS: Miller, Ari.; Widger, Mon.

CATCHERS WITH TWO OR MORE TEAMS

Player, Team	Pct.	G	PO	A	E	TC	DP	PB
Bako, Paul, Hou.	1.000	1	2	1	0	3	0	0
Bako, Paul, Fla.	.991	56	318	21	3	342	2	3
Bako, Paul, Atl.	.992	23	116	9	1	126	1	0
Hernandez, Carlos, S.D.	.987	54	343	33	5	381	3	3
Hernandez, Carlos, St.L.	.963	16	96	9	4	109	0	2
Servais, Scott, Col.	.987	32	204	17	3	224	1	1
Servais, Scott, S.F.	1.000	6	18	0	0	18	0	0

PITCHERS

Player, Team	Pct.	G	PO	A	E	TC	DP
Acevedo, Juan, Mil.	1.000	62	8	8	0	16	0
Adams, Terry, L.A.	.946	66	14	21	2	37	0
Aguilera, Rick, Chi.	1.000	54	6	7	0	13	0
Aldred, Scott, Phi.*	1.000	23	1	2	0	3	0
Alfonseca, Antonio, Fla.	.938	68	1	14	1	16	1
Almanza, Armando, Fla.*	1.000	67	1	3	0	4	0
Almanzar, Carlos, S.D.	1.000	62	3	11	0	14	0
Anderson, Brian, Ari.*	.984	33	13	47	1	61	4
Anderson, Jimmy, Pit.*	.973	27	5	31	1	37	2
Ankiel, Rick, St.L.*	.759	31	8	14	7	29	2
Armas Jr., Tony, Mon.	1.000	17	7	12	0	19	1
Arnold, Jamie, L.A.-Chi.	1.000	14	1	4	0	5	0
Arrojo, Rolando, Col.	.875	19	10	18	4	32	4
Arroyo, Bronson, Pit.	.889	20	3	5	1	9	0
Ashby, Andy, Phi.-Atl.	.936	31	14	30	3	47	0
Astacio, Pedro, Col.	1.000	32	20	22	0	42	0
Aybar, Manny, Col.-Cin.-Fla.	1.000	54	9	14	0	23	0
Batista, Miguel, Mon.	1.000	4	1	0	0	1	0
Belinda, Stan, Col.-Atl.	.857	56	3	3	1	7	0
Bell, Derek, N.Y.	.000	1	0	0	0	0	0
Bell, Rob, Cin.	.917	26	8	14	2	24	0
Beltran, Rigo, Col.*	.000	1	0	0	0	0	0
Benes, Alan, St.L.	1.000	30	2	4	0	6	0
Benes, Andy, St.L.	1.000	30	4	17	0	21	1
Benitez, Armando, N.Y.	1.000	76	2	2	0	4	0
Benson, Kris, Pit.	.947	32	8	28	2	38	0
Bere, Jason, Mil.	1.000	20	11	17	0	28	1

Player, Team	Pct.	G	PO	A	E	TC	DP
Blank, Matt, Mon.*	1.000	13	1	1	0	2	0
Boehringer, Brian, S.D.	.000	7	0	0	0	0	0
Bogar, Tim, Hou.	.000	2	0	0	0	0	0
Bohanon, Brian, Col.*	.971	34	11	23	1	35	3
Bones, Ricky, Fla.	1.000	56	3	11	0	14	0
Bottenfield, Kent, Phi.	.909	8	2	8	1	11	0
Boyd, Jason, Phi.	1.000	30	2	5	0	7	0
Brantley, Jeff, Phi.	1.000	55	3	2	0	5	0
Brock, Chris, Phi.	1.000	63	4	7	0	11	0
Brown, Kevin, L.A.	.944	33	35	33	4	72	1
Brownson, Mark, Phi.	1.000	2	1	1	0	2	0
Brunette, Justin, St.L.*	1.000	4	0	1	0	1	0
Bruske, Jim, Mil.	1.000	15	1	1	0	2	0
Buddie, Mike, Mil.	.000	5	0	0	0	0	0
Bullinger, Kirk, Phi.	1.000	3	0	1	0	1	0
Burkett, John, Atl.	.962	31	10	15	1	26	1
Burnett, A.J., Fla.	.909	13	2	8	1	11	1
Byrd, Paul, Phi.	.938	17	6	9	1	16	1
Cabrera, Jose, Hou.	1.000	52	4	5	0	9	0
Cammack, Eric, N.Y.	1.000	8	1	1	0	2	0
Carlyle, Buddy, S.D.	1.000	4	1	0	0	1	0
Carrara, Giovanni, Col.	1.000	8	3	0	0	3	0
Charlton, Norm, Cin.*	1.000	2	0	1	0	1	0
Chen, Bruce, Atl.-Phi.*	1.000	37	1	14	0	15	1
Chouinard, Bobby, Col.	1.000	31	2	2	0	4	0
Christiansen, Jason, Pit.-St.L.	1.000	65	1	9	0	10	0
Clement, Matt, S.D.	.929	34	27	25	4	56	4
Clontz, Brad, Pit.	1.000	5	0	1	0	1	0
Coggin, Dave, Phi.	.800	5	0	4	1	5	0
Cook, Dennis, N.Y.*	1.000	68	4	10	0	14	2
Cordova, Francisco, Pit.	.897	18	6	20	3	29	1
Cornelius, Reid, Fla.	1.000	22	8	26	0	34	3
Croushore, Rick, Col.	.000	6	0	0	0	0	0
Cunnane, Will, S.D.	1.000	27	4	4	0	8	0
Daal, Omar, Ari.-Phi.*	.907	32	8	31	4	43	1
D'Amico, Jeff, Mil.	1.000	23	9	13	0	22	1
Darensbourg, Vic, Fla.*	1.000	56	6	12	0	18	1
Davey, Tom, S.D.	1.000	11	1	4	0	5	0
Davis, Kane, Mil.	.000	3	0	0	0	0	0
DeJean, Mike, Col.	1.000	54	2	8	0	10	1
de los Santos, Valerio, Mil.*	1.000	66	4	8	0	12	1
del Toro, Miguel, S.F.	1.000	9	0	3	0	3	0
Dempster, Ryan, Fla.	.909	33	11	29	4	44	2
Dessens, Elmer, Cin.	1.000	40	10	26	0	36	3
Dipoto, Jerry, Col.	1.000	17	0	2	0	2	0
Dotel, Octavio, Hou.	.947	50	4	14	1	19	1
Downs, Scott, Chi.-Mon.*	1.000	19	3	11	0	14	1
Dreifort, Darren, L.A.	.982	32	19	36	1	56	2
Eaton, Adam, S.D.	.962	22	7	18	1	26	2
Elarton, Scott, Hou.	1.000	30	14	21	0	35	4
Embree, Alan, S.F.*	1.000	63	0	9	0	9	3
Erdos, Todd, S.D.	1.000	22	1	4	0	5	0
Estes, Shawn, S.F.*	.964	30	11	43	2	56	7
Estrada, Horacio, Mil.*	.875	7	1	6	1	8	0
Farnsworth, Kyle, Chi.	.833	46	4	6	2	12	1
Fernandez, Alex, Fla.	1.000	8	6	8	0	14	1
Fernandez, Osvaldo, Cin.	.889	15	6	10	2	18	3
Fetters, Mike, L.A.	1.000	51	7	7	0	14	2
Figueroa, Nelson, Ari.	1.000	3	1	2	0	3	0
Forster, Scott, Mon.*	1.000	42	3	5	0	8	0
Franco, John, N.Y.*	.900	62	1	8	1	10	0
Franklin, Wayne, Hou.*	1.000	25	1	1	0	2	0
Fultz, Aaron, S.F.*	1.000	58	5	17	0	22	2
Gagne, Eric, L.A.	1.000	20	6	8	0	14	1
Garcia, Mike, Pit.	1.000	13	0	1	0	1	0
Gardner, Mark, S.F.	.938	30	5	10	1	16	1
Garibay, Daniel, Chi.*	1.000	30	8	19	0	27	0
Glauber, Keith, Cin.	1.000	4	1	0	0	1	1
Glavine, Tom, Atl.*	1.000	35	11	41	0	52	5
Gomes, Wayne, Phi.	.889	65	2	6	1	9	0
Gooden, Dwight, Hou.	1.000	1	0	1	0	1	0
Graves, Danny, Cin.	.967	66	5	24	1	30	4
Green, Jason, Hou.	.500	14	0	2	2	4	0
Grilli, Jason, Fla.	1.000	1	0	1	0	1	0
Gross, Kip, Hou.	.000	2	0	0	1	1	0
Guthrie, Mark, Chi.*	1.000	19	0	2	0	2	0
Guzman, Domingo, S.D.	.000	1	0	0	0	0	0
Guzman, Juan, Ari.	1.000	13	0	3	0	3	0
Hackman, Luther, St.L.	1.000	1	0	1	0	1	0
Hampton, Mike, N.Y.*	.965	33	10	45	2	57	2
Harnisch, Pete, Cin.	1.000	22	6	17	0	23	1
Haynes, Jimmy, Mil.	.962	33	16	34	2	52	5

Player, Team	Pct.	G	PO	A	E	TC	DP
Henry, Doug, Hou.-S.F.	.929	72	4	9	1	14	1
Hentgen, Pat, St.L.	.974	33	14	23	1	38	1
Heredia, Felix, Chi.*	1.000	74	2	4	0	6	0
Herges, Matt, L.A.	.960	59	4	20	1	25	2
Hermanson, Dustin, Mon.	.925	38	10	27	3	40	2
HERNANDEZ, Livan, S.F.	1.000	33	18	44	0	62	4
Hershiser, Orel, L.A.	1.000	10	1	6	0	7	0
Hitchcock, Sterling, S.D.*	1.000	11	0	9	0	9	0
Hoffman, Trevor, S.D.	1.000	70	2	7	0	9	0
Holmes, Darren, Ari.-St.L.	1.000	13	3	0	0	3	0
Holt, Chris, Hou.	.930	34	13	27	3	43	4
Holzemer, Mark, Phi.*	1.000	25	0	4	0	4	0
House, Craig, Col.	1.000	16	0	3	0	3	0
Irabu, Hideki, Mon.	1.000	11	2	6	0	8	0
Jacquez, Tom, Phi.*	1.000	9	1	1	0	2	0
James, Mike, St.L.	1.000	51	2	5	0	7	0
Jarvis, Kevin, Col.	1.000	24	15	11	0	26	4
Jimenez, Jose, Col.	.867	72	5	8	2	15	1
Johnson, Mike, Mon.	.941	41	4	12	1	17	1
Johnson, Randy, Ari.*	.900	35	5	22	3	30	1
Johnstone, John, S.F.	1.000	47	3	6	0	9	1
Jones, Bobby J., N.Y.	.957	27	9	13	1	23	0
Jones, Bobby M., N.Y.*	1.000	11	3	3	0	6	0
Judd, Mike, L.A.	.000	1	0	0	0	0	0
Kamieniecki, Scott, Atl.	1.000	26	0	9	0	9	0
Karchner, Matt, Chi.	1.000	13	2	3	0	5	0
Karl, Scott, Col.*	.941	17	4	12	1	17	2
Kile, Darryl, St.L.	.977	34	12	30	1	43	3
Kim, Byung-Hyun, Ari.	.900	61	2	7	1	10	0
King, Ray, Mil.*	1.000	36	2	6	0	8	0
Kline, Steve, Mon.*	.933	83	4	10	1	15	1
Kolb, Brandon, S.D.	.500	11	0	1	1	2	0
Lara, Yovanny, Mon.	.000	6	0	0	0	0	0
Larkin, Andy, Cin.	1.000	3	1	0	0	1	0
Lee, David, Col.	.000	7	0	0	1	1	0
Leiter, Al, N.Y.*	1.000	31	5	34	0	39	2
Leskanic, Curtis, Mil.	1.000	73	12	11	0	23	0
Levrault, Allen, Mil.	1.000	5	1	0	0	1	0
Lieber, Jon, Chi.	.984	35	30	31	1	62	1
Ligtenberg, Kerry, Atl.	1.000	59	0	4	0	4	1
Lima, Jose, Hou.	.974	33	16	22	1	39	3
Linebrink, Scott, S.F.-Hou.	1.000	11	0	1	0	1	0
Lira, Felipe, Mon.	1.000	53	4	17	0	21	3
Loiselle, Rich, Pit.	.875	40	2	5	1	8	0
Looper, Braden, Fla.	.941	73	6	10	1	17	1
Lopez, Rodrigo, S.D.	1.000	6	4	3	0	7	1
Lorraine, Andrew, Chi.*	1.000	8	0	1	0	1	0
Luebbers, Larry, Cin.	1.000	14	1	6	0	7	0
Maddux, Greg, Atl.	.979	35	25	68	2	95	5
Maddux, Mike, Hou.	1.000	21	1	6	0	7	0
Mahay, Ron, Fla.*	1.000	18	1	4	0	5	0
Mahomes, Pat, N.Y.	1.000	53	9	15	0	24	2
Mairena, Oswaldo, Chi.*	.000	2	0	0	0	0	0
Mann, Jim, N.Y.	.000	2	0	0	0	0	0
Mantei, Matt, Ari.	.857	47	4	2	1	7	1
Manzanillo, Josias, Pit.	1.000	43	2	5	0	7	0
Marquis, Jason, Atl.	1.000	15	1	4	0	5	0
Masaoka, Onan, L.A.*	1.000	29	1	2	0	3	0
Matthews, Mike, St.L.*	1.000	14	0	1	0	1	0
Maurer, Dave, S.D.*	1.000	14	2	0	0	2	0
Mayne, Brent, Col.	1.000	1	0	1	0	1	0
McGlinchy, Kevin, Atl.	1.000	10	0	2	0	2	0
McKnight, Tony, Hou.	1.000	6	1	6	0	7	1
McMichael, Greg, Atl.	1.000	15	1	2	0	3	0
Meacham, Rusty, Hou.	1.000	5	1	0	0	1	1
Meadows, Brian, S.D.	.964	22	9	18	1	28	2
Mercado, Hector, Cin.*	1.000	12	0	1	0	1	0
Miceli, Dan, Fla.	1.000	45	6	1	0	7	0
Miller, Trever, Phi.-L.A.*	1.000	16	3	1	0	4	1
Miller, Wade, Hou.	1.000	16	9	11	0	20	4
Mills, Alan, L.A.	1.000	18	4	2	0	6	0
Millwood, Kevin, Atl.	1.000	36	4	19	0	23	1
Mohler, Mike, St.L.*	1.000	22	1	0	0	1	0
Molina, Gabe, Atl.	.000	2	0	0	0	0	0
Montgomery, Steve, S.D.	1.000	7	0	1	0	1	0
Moore, Trey, Mon.*	.800	8	2	2	1	5	0
Moraga, David, Mon.-Col.*	1.000	4	1	0	0	1	0
Morgan, Mike, Ari.	1.000	60	5	13	0	18	1
Morris, Matt, St.L.	1.000	31	3	3	0	6	1
Mota, Guillermo, Mon.	1.000	29	1	3	0	4	1
Mulholland, Terry, Atl.*	.889	54	6	18	3	27	1
Myers, Mike, Col.*	1.000	78	3	7	0	10	3

Player, Team	Pct.	G	PO	A	E	TC	DP
Myers, Rodney, S.D.	.000	3	0	0	0	0	0
Nathan, Joe, S.F.	1.000	20	8	11	0	19	0
Nation, Joey, Chi.*	1.000	2	0	3	0	3	0
Navarro, Jaime, Mil.	1.000	5	1	0	0	1	0
Neagle, Denny, Cin.*	1.000	18	3	12	0	15	1
Nen, Robb, S.F.	.800	68	2	6	2	10	0
Nickle, Doug, Phi.	1.000	4	1	1	0	2	0
Norton, Phil, Chi.*	1.000	2	1	2	0	3	0
Nunez, Vladimir, Fla.	.909	17	9	11	2	22	0
O'Connor, Brian, Pit.*	.000	6	0	0	0	0	0
Ohman, Will, Chi.*	1.000	6	0	2	0	2	0
Olson, Gregg, L.A.	1.000	13	2	2	0	4	0
Orosco, Jesse, St.L.*	.000	6	0	0	0	0	0
Ortiz, Russ, S.F.	1.000	33	11	33	0	44	4
Osik, Keith, Pit.	.000	1	0	0	0	0	0
Osuna, Antonio, L.A.	.917	46	4	7	1	12	0
Padilla, Vicente, Ari.-Phi.	.929	55	6	7	1	14	0
Palacios, Vicente, S.D.	1.000	7	0	3	0	3	1
Park, Chan Ho, L.A.	.952	34	20	39	3	62	4
Parra, Jose, Pit.	1.000	6	0	3	0	3	0
Parris, Steve, Cin.	.974	33	15	22	1	38	4
Pavano, Carl, Mon.	.909	15	7	13	2	22	1
Penny, Brad, Fla.	.933	23	11	17	2	30	1
Perez, Carlos, L.A.*	.966	30	8	20	1	29	2
Perez, Yorkis, Hou.*	.667	33	0	2	1	3	0
Person, Robert, Phi.	1.000	28	6	11	0	17	1
Peters, Chris, Pit.*	1.000	18	1	5	0	6	0
Plesac, Dan, Ari.*	1.000	62	0	2	0	2	0
Politte, Cliff, Phi.	1.000	12	5	8	0	13	0
Poole, Jim, Mon.*	1.000	5	0	0	1	1	0
Powell, Brian, Hou.	1.000	9	3	2	0	5	0
Powell, Jay, Hou.	1.000	29	4	2	0	6	0
Powell, Jeremy, Mon.	1.000	11	2	3	0	5	0
Prokopec, Luke, L.A.	1.000	5	0	3	0	3	1
Pulsipher, Bill, N.Y.*	1.000	5	2	2	0	4	0
Quevedo, Ruben, Chi.	.938	21	6	9	1	16	2
Radinsky, Scott, St.L.*	.000	1	0	0	0	0	0
Rain, Steve, Chi.	1.000	37	2	2	0	4	0
Ramirez, Hector, Mil.	1.000	6	0	1	0	1	0
Reames, Britt, St.L.	1.000	8	4	4	0	8	2
Reed, Rick, N.Y.	.923	30	8	16	2	26	0
Remlinger, Mike, Atl.*	.909	71	2	8	1	11	1
Reyes, Al, L.A.	1.000	6	0	1	0	1	0
Reyes, Carlos, Phi.-S.D.	1.000	22	1	2	0	3	0
Reyes, Dennys, Cin.*	.900	62	4	5	1	10	0
Reynolds, Shane, Hou.	1.000	22	9	20	0	29	0
Reynoso, Armando, Ari.	.979	31	13	34	1	48	3
Riedling, John, Cin.	.000	13	0	0	0	0	0
Rigby, Brad, Mon.	.000	6	0	0	0	0	0
Rigdon, Paul, Mil.	1.000	12	7	7	0	14	0
Riggan, Jerrod, N.Y.	.000	1	0	0	0	0	0
Ritchie, Todd, Pit.	.977	31	8	35	1	44	2
Rivera, Luis, Atl.	1.000	5	0	1	0	1	0
Roberts, Grant, N.Y.	.000	4	0	0	0	0	0
Rocker, John, Atl.*	1.000	59	1	6	0	7	0
Rodriguez, Felix, S.F.	.750	76	0	3	1	4	0
Rodriguez, Jose, St.L.*	.000	6	0	0	0	0	0
Rodriguez, Rich, N.Y.*	1.000	32	3	5	0	8	1
Roque, Rafael, Mil.*	.000	4	0	0	0	0	0
Rose, Brian, Col.	1.000	12	6	8	0	14	0
Rueter, Kirk, S.F.*	1.000	32	8	44	0	52	4
Ruffin, Johnny, Ari.	1.000	5	1	3	0	4	0
Rusch, Glendon, N.Y.*	1.000	31	5	25	0	30	1
Sanchez, Jesus, Fla.*	.921	32	7	28	3	38	3
Santana, Julio, Mon.	1.000	36	3	10	0	13	1
Sauerbeck, Scott, Pit.*	1.000	75	5	10	0	15	2
Scanlan, Bob, Mil.	.000	2	0	0	1	1	0
Schilling, Curt, Phi.-Ari.	1.000	29	11	19	0	30	0
Schmidt, Jason, Pit.	1.000	11	2	7	0	9	0
Schrenk, Steve, Phi.	1.000	20	2	1	0	3	0
Seanez, Rudy, Atl.	1.000	23	1	1	0	2	0
Seelbach, Chris, Atl.	.000	2	0	0	0	0	0
Serafini, Dan, S.D.-Pit.*	1.000	14	2	6	0	8	0
Shaw, Jeff, L.A.	.947	60	4	14	1	19	2
Silva, Jose, Pit.	.909	51	4	16	2	22	1
Skrmetta, Matt, Mon.-Pit.	.750	14	1	2	1	4	0
Slocumb, Heathcliff, St.L.-S.D.	1.000	65	5	9	0	14	0
Slusarski, Joe, Hou.	1.000	54	5	6	0	11	0
Smith, Brian, Pit.	1.000	3	0	1	0	1	0
Smith, Chuck, Fla.	.926	19	11	14	2	27	1
Snyder, John, Mil.	.938	23	12	18	2	32	0
Sparks, Steve, Pit.	1.000	3	1	1	0	2	1

Player, Team	Pct.	G	PO	A	E	TC	DP
Spencer, Sean, Mon.*	.000	8	0	0	0	0	0
Spencer, Stan, S.D.	1.000	8	5	4	0	9	0
Spradlin, Jerry, Chi.	1.000	8	0	2	0	2	0
Springer, Dennis, N.Y.	1.000	2	1	2	0	3	0
Springer, Russ, Ari.	.833	52	1	4	1	6	1
Stechschulte, Gene, St.L.	1.000	20	1	3	0	4	0
Stephenson, Garrett, St.L.	.975	32	9	30	1	40	0
Stevens, Dave, Atl.	1.000	2	0	1	0	1	0
Stottlemyre, Todd, Ari.	.955	18	4	17	1	22	1
Strickland, Scott, Mon.	.900	49	2	7	1	10	0
Strong, Joe, Fla.	1.000	18	2	4	0	6	0
Stull, Everett, Mil.	1.000	20	1	7	0	8	1
Sullivan, Scott, Cin.	.938	79	5	10	1	16	0
Swindell, Greg, Ari.*	1.000	64	1	12	0	13	0
Tapani, Kevin, Chi.	1.000	30	11	19	0	30	1
Tavarez, Julian, Col.	.974	51	14	23	1	38	1
Telemaco, Amaury, Phi.	1.000	13	2	0	0	2	0
Telford, Anthony, Mon.	1.000	64	5	9	0	14	1
Thompson, Mark, St.L.	1.000	20	2	4	0	6	0
Thurman, Mike, Mon.	.800	17	0	12	3	15	0
Timlin, Mike, St.L.	1.000	25	1	5	0	6	0
Tollberg, Brian, S.D.	.960	19	9	15	1	25	1
Tucker, T.J., Mon.	1.000	2	0	1	0	1	0
Urbina, Ugueth, Mon.	1.000	13	1	0	0	1	0
Valdes, Ismael, Chi.-L.A.	.958	21	10	13	1	24	2
Valdes, Marc, Hou.	1.000	53	6	9	0	15	2
Van Poppel, Todd, Chi.	1.000	51	9	11	0	20	1
Vazquez, Javier, Mon.	.955	33	10	32	2	44	2
Veres, Dave, St.L.	.800	71	3	9	3	15	0
Villegas, Ismael, Atl.	1.000	1	0	1	0	1	0
Villone, Ron, Cin.*	.871	35	4	23	4	31	1
Vogelsong, Ryan, S.F.	.000	4	0	0	0	0	0
Vosberg, Ed, Phi.*	1.000	31	1	8	0	9	0
Wagner, Billy, Hou.*	1.000	28	1	2	0	3	0
Wainhouse, Dave, St.L.	1.000	9	0	2	0	2	0
Walker, Kevin, S.D.*	1.000	70	2	8	0	10	0
Walker, Pete, Col.	1.000	3	0	1	0	1	0
Wall, Donne, S.D.	1.000	44	1	5	0	6	0
Wallace, Jeff, Pit.*	.833	38	2	3	1	6	0
Ward, Bryan, Phi.*	1.000	20	0	3	0	3	0
Wasdin, John, Col.	1.000	14	3	3	0	6	1
Weathers, Dave, Mil.	1.000	69	5	7	0	12	0
Weber, Ben, S.F.	.000	9	0	0	0	0	0
Wendell, Turk, N.Y.	.917	77	12	10	2	24	0
Wengert, Don, Atl.	1.000	10	0	1	0	1	0
Whisenant, Matt, S.D.*	1.000	24	1	3	0	4	0
White, Gabe, Cin.-Col.*	1.000	68	2	6	0	8	1
White, Rick, N.Y.	1.000	22	1	3	0	4	0
Whiteside, Matt, S.D.	.917	28	4	7	1	12	0
Wickman, Bob, Mil.	1.000	43	3	9	0	12	2
Wilkins, Marc, Pit.	1.000	52	2	9	0	11	2
Williams, Brian, Chi.	1.000	22	1	2	0	3	0
Williams, Jeff, L.A.*	.000	7	0	0	0	0	0
Williams, Matt T., Mil.*	1.000	11	0	2	0	2	0
Williams, Mike, Pit.	1.000	72	4	11	0	15	2
Williams, Woody, S.D.	.905	23	7	12	2	21	1
Williamson, Scott, Cin.	1.000	48	4	10	0	14	0

Player, Team	Pct.	G	PO	A	E	TC	DP
Winchester, Scott, Cin.	1.000	5	1	1	0	2	0
Witasick, Jay, S.D.	1.000	11	5	10	0	15	1
Wohlers, Mark, Cin.	.833	20	2	3	1	6	0
Wolf, Randy, Phi.*	.970	32	4	28	1	33	2
Wood, Kerry, Chi.	.917	23	8	14	2	24	1
Woodard, Steve, Mil.	1.000	27	4	15	0	19	0
Worrell, Tim, Chi.	1.000	54	0	6	0	6	0
Wright, Jamey, Mil.	.952	26	17	23	2	42	0
Yoshii, Masato, Col.	1.000	29	16	20	0	36	2
Young, Danny, Chi.*	.000	4	0	0	0	0	0
Zerbe, Chad, S.F.*	1.000	4	1	2	0	3	0

PITCHERS WITH TWO OR MORE TEAMS

Player, Team	Pct.	G	PO	A	E	TC	DP
Arnold, Jamie, L.A.	1.000	2	0	2	0	2	0
Arnold, Jamie, Chi.	1.000	12	1	2	0	3	0
Ashby, Andy, Phi.	.955	16	6	15	1	22	0
Ashby, Andy, Atl.	.920	15	8	15	2	25	0
Aybar, Manny, Col.	.000	1	0	0	0	0	0
Aybar, Manny, Cin.	1.000	32	5	8	0	13	0
Aybar, Manny, Fla.	1.000	21	4	6	0	10	0
Belinda, Stan, Col.	.833	46	3	2	1	6	0
Belinda, Stan, Atl.	1.000	10	0	1	0	1	0
Chen, Bruce, Atl.*	1.000	22	0	3	0	3	1
Chen, Bruce, Phi.*	1.000	15	1	11	0	12	0
Christiansen, Jason, Pit.*	1.000	44	1	8	0	9	0
Christiansen, Jason, St.L.*	1.000	21	0	1	0	1	0
Daal, Omar, Ari.*	.852	20	5	18	4	27	0
Daal, Omar, Phi.*	1.000	12	3	13	0	16	1
Downs, Scott, Chi.*	1.000	18	3	11	0	14	1
Downs, Scott, Mon.*	.000	1	0	0	0	0	0
Henry, Doug, Hou.	1.000	45	4	6	0	10	1
Henry, Doug, S.F.	.750	27	0	3	1	4	0
Holmes, Darren, Ari.	1.000	8	2	0	0	2	0
Holmes, Darren, St.L.	1.000	5	1	0	0	1	0
Linebrink, Scott, S.F.	1.000	3	0	1	0	1	0
Linebrink, Scott, Hou.	.000	8	0	0	0	0	0
Miller, Trever, Phi.*	1.000	14	3	1	0	4	1
Miller, Trever, L.A.*	.000	2	0	0	0	0	0
Moraga, David, Mon.*	.000	3	0	0	0	0	0
Moraga, David, Col.*	1.000	1	1	0	0	1	0
Padilla, Vicente, Ari.	1.000	27	3	3	0	6	0
Padilla, Vicente, Phi.	.875	28	3	4	1	8	0
Reyes, Carlos, Phi.	1.000	10	0	1	0	1	0
Reyes, Carlos, S.D.	1.000	12	1	1	0	2	0
Schilling, Curt, Phi.	1.000	16	6	8	0	14	0
Schilling, Curt, Ari.	1.000	13	5	11	0	16	0
Serafini, Dan, S.D.*	1.000	3	1	0	0	1	0
Serafini, Dan, Pit.*	1.000	11	1	6	0	7	0
Skrmetta, Matt, Mon.	.500	6	0	1	1	2	0
Skrmetta, Matt, Pit.	1.000	8	1	1	0	2	0
Slocumb, Heathcliff, St.L.	1.000	43	3	5	0	8	0
Slocumb, Heathcliff, S.D.	1.000	22	2	4	0	6	0
Valdes, Ismael, Chi.	1.000	12	7	9	0	16	1
Valdes, Ismael, L.A.	.875	9	3	4	1	8	1
White, Gabe, Cin.*	.000	1	0	0	0	0	0
White, Gabe, Col.*	1.000	67	2	6	0	8	1

MISCELLANEOUS

SHUTOUT GAMES

Read across for wins, down for losses.

Team	Cin.	S.F.	St.L.	Atl.	Ari.	N.Y.	L.A.	Mil.	Pit.	Mon.	Phi.	S.D.	Hou.	Chi.	Fla.	Col.	A.L.	W	L	Pct.
Cincinnati	..	0	0	0	0	1	0	0	0	0	1	1	1	2	1	0	0	7	0	1.000
San Francisco	0	..	0	1	0	0	1	1	1	1	1	2	0	1	3	3	0	15	5	.750
St. Louis	0	0	..	1	1	0	0	1	1	1	0	1	0	1	0	0	0	7	5	.583
Atlanta	0	0	0	..	1	1	1	0	0	2	0	0	0	1	1	1	1	9	7	.563
Arizona	0	0	1	1	..	0	0	0	1	1	0	0	0	1	0	2	1	8	7	.533
New York	0	1	0	1	0	..	1	0	2	1	1	0	1	0	0	0	2	10	9	.526
Los Angeles	0	2	1	0	3	0	..	0	0	1	2	2	0	0	0	0	0	11	11	.500
Milwaukee	0	1	0	0	0	0	0	..	1	0	0	0	0	1	2	1	1	7	7	.500
Pittsburgh	0	1	0	1	0	1	2	1	..	0	0	0	0	1	0	0	0	7	7	.500
Montreal	0	0	1	1	1	0	0	0	0	..	0	2	0	0	0	0	1	7	9	.438
Philadelphia	0	0	1	1	0	1	1	1	0	1	..	0	0	0	0	0	0	6	8	.429
San Diego	0	0	0	0	0	2	1	1	0	0	0	..	0	1	0	0	0	5	7	.417
Houston	0	0	0	0	0	0	0	2	0	0	0	0	..	0	1	1	0	2	3	.400
Chicago	0	0	0	0	0	0	0	0	1	1	1	0	0	..	0	1	1	5	8	.385
Florida	0	0	1	0	0	2	0	0	0	0	0	0	0	0	..	0	1	4	8	.333
Colorado	0	0	0	0	1	0	0	0	0	0	0	0	1	0	0	..	0	2	8	.200
A.L. Clubs	0	0	0	0	0	0	4	0	0	0	0	0	1	0	0	0	..	..		
Lost	0	5	5	7	7	9	11	7	7	9	8	7	3	8	8	8	..	112	109	.507

N.L. shutouts vs. A.L. clubs (8): Arizona vs. Seattle; Atlanta vs. Boston; Chicago vs. Detroit; Florida vs. Baltimore; Milwaukee vs. Kansas City; Montreal vs. Baltimore; New York vs. New York A.L.; New York vs. Tampa Bay.

HOME RECORD

Read across for home wins, down for road losses.

Team	N.Y.	S.F.	Atl.	St.L.	Col.	Ari.	L.A.	Cin.	Fla.	Mil.	S.D.	Hou.	Chi.	Mon.	Pit.	Phi.	A.L.	W	L	Pct.
New York	..	3	4	3	4	5	2	3	4	5	1	2	3	6	3	2	5	55	26	.679
San Francisco	4	..	2	2	6	2	2	5	2	3	3	2	4	3	3	6	6	55	26	.679
Atlanta	4	5	..	1	3	3	5	1	4	2	5	3	2	2	3	4	3	51	30	.630
St. Louis	3	3	1	..	2	2	4	3	4	4	3	3	7	3	3	2	3	50	33	.617
Colorado	1	6	1	3	..	4	3	2	3	1	2	4	4	3	4	2	5	47	34	.580
Arizona	1	1	3	4	5	..	5	1	1	2	5	3	3	1	5	3	4	44	37	.543
Los Angeles	3	3	1	1	5	5	..	2	3	1	4	4	1	3	2	4	2	44	37	.543
Cincinnati	2	2	2	4	2	2	0	..	1	4	4	3	4	3	2	6	5	43	38	.531
Florida	4	2	4	1	2	3	2	1	..	2	1	2	3	3	2	6	5	43	38	.531
Milwaukee	1	3	2	3	3	1	2	5	2	..	1	4	5	3	4	1	2	42	39	.519
San Diego	4	2	0	0	2	3	2	3	2	5	..	3	3	0	3	3	4	41	40	.506
Houston	1	0	4	3	2	0	1	2	3	4	0	..	3	2	7	3	4	39	42	.481
Chicago	1	2	4	3	2	4	1	2	1	5	2	2	..	4	2	2	5	38	43	.469
Montreal	3	0	2	1	2	3	2	0	3	2	2	1	0	..	2	2	5	37	44	.457
Pittsburgh	2	1	2	1	0	1	1	3	3	4	3	4	4	2	..	2	5	37	44	.457
Philadelphia	3	2	3	1	2	1	2	3	2	2	1	0	4	7	5	..	5	34	47	.420
A.L. Clubs	5	4	2	5	5	4	5	4	5	5	7	4	4	7	5	5	..	..		
Lost on Road	42	39	37	36	47	43	39	39	44	50	46	48	54	51	49	50	..	704	592	.543

HOME RECORDS IN INTERLEAGUE GAMES

Team	Bal.	Bos.	N.Y.	T.B.	Tor.
Atlanta	..	2-1	1-2	..	1-2
Florida	..	1-2	..	2-1	2-1
Montreal	3-0	..	1-2	..	1-2
New York	2-1	..	1-2	2-1	..
Philadelphia	1-2	3-0	..	1-2	..

Team	Chi.	Cle.	Det.	K.C.	Min.
Chicago	2-1	..	1-2	..	..
Cincinnati	0-3	2-1	..	..	3-0
Houston	1-2	..	..	2-1	1-2
Milwaukee	..	0-3	2-1	..	..
Pittsburgh	..	..	2-1	1-2	2-1
St. Louis	..	1-2	..	2-1	..

Team	Ana.	Oak.	Sea.	Tex.
Arizona	2-1	..	1-2	1-2
Colorado	..	..	2-1	3-0
Los Angeles	1-2	1-2	..	..
San Diego	1-2	..	2-1	..
San Francisco	..	2-1	1-2	3-0

ROAD RECORD

Read across for road wins, down for home losses.

Team	St.L.	Atl.	Cin.	L.A.	S.F.	N.Y.	Ari.	Fla.	S.D.	Col.	Hou.	Pit.	Mil.	Phi.	Mon.	Chi.	A.L.	W	L	Pct.
St. Louis	..	3	3	2	1	0	2	2	6	1	3	5	3	5	2	3	4	45	36	.556
Atlanta	2	..	1	2	1	3	3	2	3	2	2	4	4	4	2	7		44	37	.543
Cincinnati	3	3	..	4	1	3	3	2	0	4	4	4	1	1	3	4	2	42	39	.519
Los Angeles	2	1	3	..	4	1	1	4	4	4	2	2	1	2	5	4	2	42	39	.519
San Francisco	3	1	1	3	..	1	5	4	4	1	6	3	3	1	1	2	2	39	42	.481
New York	3	2	1	3	0	..	2	2	2	2	3	4	2	4	3	2	4	38	43	.469
Arizona	1	0	1	2	5	1	..	3	4	2	3	2	1	5	3	2	2	36	44	.450
Florida	2	2	5	0	1	2	2	..	1	3	1	3	1	3	4	3	3	35	46	.432
San Diego	0	1	2	3	3	2	1	5	..	4	3	2	2	1	2	2	2	34	47	.420
Colorado	2	3	1	1	0	2	2	1	5	..	1	3	3	4	4	1	3	34	47	.420
Houston	3	0	3	2	1	1	1	2	2	2	..	3	3	2	2	4	1	33	48	.407
Pittsburgh	3	0	3	4	1	0	1	1	3	2	0	..	2	4	2	5	1	32	49	.395
Milwaukee	2	1	3	2	0	1	4	2	1	2	2	3	..	1	1	2	4	31	50	.383
Philadelphia	1	2	2	2	0	4	0	1	0	1	3	1	3	..	4	3	4	31	50	.383

Team	St.L.	Atl.	Cin.	L.A.	S.F.	N.Y.	Ari.	Fla.	S.D.	Col.	Hou.	Pit.	Mil.	Phi.	Mon.	Chi.	A.L.	W	L	Pct.
Montreal	1	5	3	1	3	0	2	3	1	0	1	1	3	3		1	2	30	51	.370
Chicago	0	1	2	2	2	1	0	0	1	2	3	2	1	3	2	..	5	27	54	.333
A.L. Clubs	3	5	4	4	3	4	5	4	3	1	5	4	4	4	4	3	..	..	..	..
Lost at home	31	30	38	37	26	26	34	38	40	33	42	44	39	47	44	43	..	581	714	.449

PITCHING AGAINST EACH CLUB

ARIZONA—85-77

Pitcher	Atl. W-L	Chi. W-L	Cin. W-L	Col. W-L	Fla. W-L	Hou. W-L	L.A. W-L	Mil. W-L	Mon. W-L	N.Y. W-L	Phi. W-L	Pit. W-L	S.D. W-L	S.F. W-L	StL. W-L	A.L. W-L	Total W-L
Anderson, B.	1-0	1-1	0-2	1-1	0-0	1-0	1-1	0-0	0-1	0-0	0-0	1-0	3-0	1-1	0-0	1-0	11-7
Daal, Omar	0-0	0-0	0-1	0-1	0-0	0-1	1-0	0-1	0-0	0-1	0-0	1-0	0-1	0-1	0-1	0-2	2-10
Figueroa, N.	0-0	0-0	0-0	0-0	0-0	0-0	0-0	0-0	0-0	0-0	0-0	0-0	0-0	0-0	0-0	0-1	0-1
Guzman, G.	0-0	0-0	0-1	0-0	0-0	1-0	0-0	0-1	0-1	0-1	0-0	0-0	2-0	1-0	1-0	5-4
Holmes, D.	0-0	0-0	0-0	0-0	0-0	0-0	0-0	0-0	0-0	0-0	0-0	0-0	0-0	0-0	0-0	0-0	0-0
Johnson, Randy	1-1	2-0	0-0	2-1	0-0	2-0	1-0	1-0	1-1	0-2	2-0	1-0	1-0	1-1	2-1	2-0	19-7
Kim, Byung-H.	0-0	0-0	0-0	0-0	2-1	0-0	2-1	0-0	1-0	0-1	1-1	0-0	0-0	0-0	0-0	0-2	6-6
Mantei, Matt	0-0	1-1	0-0	0-0	0-0	0-0	0-0	0-0	0-0	0-0	0-0	0-0	0-0	0-0	0-0	0-2	6-6
Morgan, Mike	0-0	0-0	0-1	2-1	0-1	1-0	0-0	0-1	0-0	0-0	0-0	1-0	1-0	0-1	0-0	0-0	5-5
Padilla, Vicente	0-0	0-0	0-0	0-0	0-0	0-0	1-0	0-0	0-0	0-0	0-0	1-0	0-0	0-0	0-0	0-1	2-1
Plesac, Dan	0-0	0-0	0-0	0-1	0-0	0-0	1-0	0-0	1-0	1-0	1-0	0-0	0-0	0-0	0-0	0-0	5-1
Reynoso, A.	0-1	0-1	0-1	2-1	0-0	0-0	0-0	1-0	0-0	0-0	0-0	0-0	0-0	0-0	1-0	1-0	5-1
Ruffin, Johnny	0-0	0-0	0-0	0-0	0-0	0-0	2-1	0-1	1-1	1-0	1-1	0-1	0-2	2-1	1-0	11-12
Schilling, Curt	1-2	1-0	0-0	0-0	1-1	0-0	0-1	1-1	0-0	0-0	0-0	0-0	1-0	0-0	0-0	0-0	0-0
Springer, Russ	0-0	0-1	1-0	0-0	0-1	0-0	0-0	0-0	0-0	1-0	0-0	0-0	0-0	0-0	0-0	5-6
Stottlemyre, Todd	0-1	0-0	0-0	0-0	1-0	0-1	0-1	1-0	0-0	0-1	2-0	1-0	3-1	1-1	0-1	0-0	9-6
Swindell, Greg	0-1	0-0	1-0	0-0	0-1	0-0	0-1	0-1	0-0	0-0	0-0	1-0	0-0	0-0	0-2	2-6
Totals	3-6	5-4	2-5	7-6	4-5	6-1	7-6	4-5	4-5	2-7	8-1	7-2	9-4	6-7	5-4	6-9	85-77

INTERLEAGUE: Johnson 1-0, Swindell 0-1, Daal 0-1 vs. Athletics; Guzman 1-0, Springer 0-1, Padilla 0-1 vs. Mariners; Anderson 1-0, Reynoso 1-0, Kim 0-2, Figueroa 0-1, Swindell 0-1 vs. Rangers; Johnson 1-0, Plesac 0-1, Daal 0-1 vs. Angels. Total: 6-9.

ATLANTA—95-67

Pitcher	Ari. W-L	Chi. W-L	Cin. W-L	Col. W-L	Fla. W-L	Hou. W-L	L.A. W-L	Mil. W-L	Mon. W-L	N.Y. W-L	Phi. W-L	Pit. W-L	S.D. W-L	S.F. W-L	StL. W-L	A.L. W-L	Total W-L
Ashby, Andy	0-1	0-0	1-0	0-1	1-0	1-1	0-1	0-0	2-0	2-0	0-0	0-0	0-0	0-1	0-1	1-0	8-6
Belinda, Stan	0-0	0-0	0-0	0-0	0-0	0-0	0-0	0-0	0-0	0-0	0-0	0-0	0-0	0-0	0-0	0-0	0-0
Burkett, John	1-0	0-0	0-0	0-1	1-0	2-1	0-0	0-1	0-1	3-0	2-0	0-0	1-0	0-0	0-1	0-1	10-6
Chen, Bruce	0-0	0-0	0-0	1-0	0-0	0-0	0-0	0-0	0-0	0-0	1-0	0-0	1-0	0-0	0-0	0-0	4-0
Glavine, Tom	1-1	0-2	1-1	0-0	2-1	1-0	1-0	1-2	1-1	1-1	0-0	3-0	3-0	2-0	2-0	2-0	21-9
Kamieniecki, S.	0-0	0-0	0-0	0-0	0-1	0-0	0-0	0-0	0-0	0-0	1-0	0-0	1-0	0-0	1-0	2-1
Ligtenberg, K.	0-0	0-1	0-1	0-0	0-0	0-0	0-0	0-0	0-0	1-0	1-0	0-0	0-1	0-0	0-0	2-3
Maddux, Greg	1-1	1-0	0-1	2-0	1-1	1-0	1-1	1-1	2-0	1-3	2-0	1-0	2-1	0-0	3-0	19-9
Marquis, J.	0-0	0-0	0-0	0-0	0-0	0-0	1-0	0-0	0-0	0-0	0-0	0-0	0-0	0-0	0-0	1-0
McGlinchy, K.	0-0	0-0	0-0	0-0	0-0	0-0	0-0	0-0	0-0	0-0	0-0	0-0	0-0	0-0	0-0	0-0	0-0
McMichael, G.	0-0	0-0	0-0	0-0	0-0	0-0	0-0	0-0	0-0	0-0	0-0	0-0	0-0	0-0	0-0	0-0	0-0
Millwood, K.	3-0	1-0	0-1	1-0	1-2	0-0	2-0	0-1	0-2	0-1	1-1	0-0	0-0	1-0	0-1	0-3	10-13
Molina, Gabe	0-0	0-0	0-0	0-0	0-0	0-0	0-0	0-0	0-0	0-0	0-0	0-0	0-0	0-0	0-0	0-0	0-0
Mulholland, T.	0-0	2-1	0-0	0-0	0-0	1-0	2-0	1-1	0-1	0-2	1-0	0-1	0-0	0-1	0-0	2-2	9-9
Remlinger, M.	0-0	0-1	0-1	0-0	0-0	1-0	0-0	0-0	0-1	0-0	1-0	0-0	1-0	2-0	5-3
Rivera, Luis	0-0	0-0	0-0	0-0	0-0	0-0	0-0	0-0	1-0	0-0	0-0	0-0	0-0	0-0	1-0
Rocker, John	0-0	0-0	0-0	0-2	0-0	0-0	1-0	0-0	0-0	0-0	0-0	0-0	0-0	0-0	1-2
Seanez, Rudy	0-0	0-0	0-0	0-0	0-1	0-0	0-0	0-0	0-0	2-0	0-0	0-0	0-0	0-0	0-1	2-4
Seelbach, C.	0-0	0-0	0-0	0-0	0-0	0-0	0-0	0-0	0-0	0-0	0-0	0-0	0-0	0-0	0-0	0-1	0-1
Stevens, Dave	0-0	0-0	0-0	0-0	0-0	0-0	0-0	0-0	0-0	0-0	0-0	0-0	0-0	0-0	0-0	0-0	0-0
Villegas, I.	0-0	0-0	0-0	0-0	0-0	0-0	0-0	0-0	0-0	0-0	0-0	0-0	0-0	0-0	0-0	0-0	0-0
Wengert, Don	0-0	0-0	0-0	0-0	0-0	0-0	0-0	0-0	0-0	0-0	0-0	0-0	0-0	0-0	0-1	0-1
Totals	6-3	4-5	2-5	5-4	6-6	5-4	7-2	6-3	6-7	7-6	8-5	5-2	8-1	6-3	3-4	11-7	95-67

INTERLEAGUE: Maddux 1-0, Ashby 1-0, Glavine 1-0 vs. Orioles; Mulholland 2-0, Maddux 1-0, Glavine 1-0, Seanez 0-1, Millwood 0-1 vs. Red Sox; Remlinger 1-0, Millwood 0-1, Mulholland 0-1 vs. Yankees; Remlinger 1-0, Burkett 0-1, Millwood 0-1 vs. Blue Jays; Kamieniecki 1-0, Maddux 1-0, Mulholland 0-1 vs. Devil Rays. Total: 11-7.

CHICAGO—65-97

Pitcher	Ari. W-L	Atl. W-L	Cin. W-L	Col. W-L	Fla. W-L	Hou. W-L	L.A. W-L	Mil. W-L	Mon. W-L	N.Y. W-L	Phi. W-L	Pit. W-L	S.D. W-L	S.F. W-L	StL. W-L	A.L. W-L	Total W-L
Aguilera, Rick	0-0	0-0	0-0	0-0	0-0	0-0	0-0	1-0	0-1	0-0	0-0	0-1	0-0	0-0	0-0	1-2
Arnold, Jamie	0-0	0-0	0-1	0-1	0-0	0-0	0-0	0-0	0-0	0-0	0-0	0-0	0-0	0-1	0-0	0-3
Downs, Scott	1-0	0-1	0-0	0-0	1-0	0-1	0-0	0-0	0-0	0-0	0-1	0-0	0-0	0-0	2-0	4-3
Farnsworth, Kyle	0-0	1-0	0-0	0-2	0-1	0-1	0-0	0-2	0-0	0-1	1-1	0-0	0-0	0-1	0-0	2-9
Garibay, D.	0-0	0-0	0-2	0-1	0-0	0-0	0-1	1-0	0-1	0-1	0-0	0-1	1-1	0-0	0-0	2-8
Guthrie, Mark	0-1	2-0	0-1	0-0	0-0	0-0	0-1	0-0	0-0	0-0	0-0	0-0	0-0	0-0	0-0	2-3
Heredia, Felix	1-0	0-0	0-0	0-0	0-2	0-0	0-1	2-0	0-0	2-0	0-0	1-0	0-0	0-0	0-0	7-3
Karchner, Matt	0-0	0-0	0-1	0-0	0-0	1-0	0-0	0-0	0-0	0-0	0-0	0-0	0-0	0-0	0-0	1-1
Lieber, Jon	0-1	0-1	0-1	1-1	0-1	2-1	0-0	1-0	1-1	0-1	2-0	1-0	1-0	1-2	2-0	12-11
Lorraine, A.	0-1	0-0	0-0	0-1	0-0	0-0	0-0	0-0	0-0	0-0	0-0	0-0	0-0	0-0	0-0	1-2
Mairena, O.	0-0	0-0	0-0	0-0	0-0	0-0	0-0	0-0	0-0	0-0	0-0	0-0	0-0	0-0	0-0	0-0
Nation, Joey	0-0	0-0	0-0	0-0	0-0	0-0	0-0	0-0	0-0	0-1	0-0	0-0	0-0	0-1	0-0	0-0
Norton, Phil	0-0	0-0	0-0	0-0	0-0	0-1	0-0	0-0	0-0	0-0	0-0	0-0	0-0	0-1	0-0	0-0
Ohman, Will	0-0	0-0	0-0	0-0	0-0	0-0	0-0	0-0	0-0	0-0	0-0	0-0	0-0	1-0	0-0	1-0
Quevedo, R.	0-1	0-1	0-1	0-0	1-1	1-0	0-0	0-1	0-0	0-0	1-0	0-1	0-1	0-1	0-0	3-10
Rain, Steve	0-1	0-0	0-1	1-0	0-0	0-0	0-0	0-0	1-0	0-1	0-1	0-1	0-0	0-0	0-0	3-4
Spradlin, J.	0-0	0-0	0-0	0-0	0-0	0-0	0-0	0-0	0-0	0-0	0-0	0-0	0-0	0-1	0-0	0-1

Pitcher	Ari. W-L	Atl. W-L	Cin. W-L	Col. W-L	Fla. W-L	Hou. W-L	L.A. W-L	Mil. W-L	Mon. W-L	N.Y. W-L	Phi. W-L	Pit. W-L	S.D. W-L	S.F. W-L	StL. W-L	A.L. W-L	Total W-L
Tapani, Kevin	2-0	1-1	1-0	1-0	0-0	0-2	0-1	0-0	0-1	0-1	0-1	0-1	1-1	0-1	0-2	2-0	8-12
Valdes, Ismael	0-0	0-0	1-0	0-0	0-0	0-0	0-1	0-0	1-1	0-0	0-0	0-0	0-0	0-0	0-0	0-2	2-4
Van Poppel, T.	0-0	0-0	0-0	0-0	0-0	0-0	0-1	0-1	1-0	0-0	0-0	0-0	0-0	0-0	1-0	1-3	4-5
Williams, B.	0-0	0-0	0-0	0-0	0-0	0-0	0-0	0-1	1-0	0-0	0-0	0-0	0-0	0-0	0-0	0-0	1-1
Wood, Kerry	0-0	1-0	1-0	0-0	0-0	0-0	1-0	0-0	1-1	0-1	0-0	1-0	0-2	0-0	2-1	0-0	8-7
Worrell, Tim	0-0	0-0	0-0	0-0	0-0	0-0	2-0	0-0	0-0	0-0	1-0	0-1	0-1	0-1	0-1	0-0	3-4
Young, Danny	0-0	0-0	0-0	0-0	0-0	0-0	0-0	0-0	0-0	0-0	0-0	0-1	0-0	0-0	0-0	0-0	0-1
Totals	4-5	5-4	4-8	4-5	1-6	5-7	3-6	6-7	4-5	2-5	6-3	3-9	3-5	4-5	3-10	8-7	65-97

INTERLEAGUE: Van Poppel 1-2, Lieber 1-0, Tapani 1-0, Wood 0-1 vs. White Sox; Downs 1-0, Wood 0-1, Van Poppel 0-1 vs. Tigers; Wood 0-1, Downs 1-0, Valdes 0-1 vs. Royals; Lieber 1-0, Tapani 1-0, Valdes 0-1 vs. Twins. Total: 8-7.

CINCINNATI—85-77

Pitcher	Ari. W-L	Atl. W-L	Chi. W-L	Col. W-L	Fla. W-L	Hou. W-L	L.A. W-L	Mil. W-L	Mon. W-L	N.Y. W-L	Phi. W-L	Pit. W-L	S.D. W-L	S.F. W-L	StL. W-L	A.L. W-L	Total W-L
Aybar, Manny	0-0	0-0	0-0	0-0	0-0	0-0	0-1	0-0	0-0	0-0	0-0	0-0	0-0	0-0	0-0	1-0	1-1
Bell, Rob	0-0	0-0	1-1	0-0	0-0	0-0	0-1	0-1	2-0	0-0	0-0	2-0	0-1	1-2	0-1	1-1	7-8
Charlton, N.	0-0	0-0	0-0	0-0	0-0	0-0	0-0	0-0	0-0	0-0	0-0	0-0	0-0	0-0	0-0	0-0	0-0
Dessens, E.	1-0	0-2	0-0	1-0	1-0	1-0	0-0	2-1	1-0	1-1	0-0	1-1	0-0	0-0	1-0	1-0	11-5
Fernandez, O.	0-1	0-0	0-1	0-0	0-0	0-0	1-0	0-0	0-0	0-0	0-0	0-1	1-0	1-0	0-0	0-0	4-3
Glauber, Keith	0-0	0-0	0-0	0-0	0-0	0-0	0-0	0-0	0-0	0-0	0-0	0-0	0-0	0-0	0-0	0-0	0-0
Graves, Danny	0-0	0-0	2-0	1-0	1-2	1-1	0-0	0-0	1-0	1-0	0-0	1-0	1-0	0-1	0-0	1-0	10-5
Harnisch, Pete	1-0	1-0	1-1	1-0	1-1	1-0	0-1	1-0	0-0	0-0	1-1	0-1	0-0	0-0	0-1	0-0	8-6
Larkin, Andy	0-0	0-0	0-0	0-0	0-0	0-0	0-0	0-0	0-0	0-0	0-0	0-0	0-0	0-0	0-0	0-0	0-0
Luebbers, L.	0-0	0-0	0-0	0-0	0-0	0-0	0-0	0-0	0-0	0-1	0-0	0-0	0-0	0-0	0-1	0-0	0-2
Mercado, H.	0-0	0-0	0-0	0-0	0-0	0-0	0-0	0-0	0-0	0-0	0-0	0-0	0-0	0-0	0-0	0-0	0-0
Neagle, Denny	1-0	0-0	0-0	0-0	0-0	0-0	0-0	0-0	1-0	1-0	0-0	0-0	0-0	1-1	2-0	2-1	8-2
Parris, Steve	1-0	1-0	1-1	1-1	0-0	0-2	1-1	1-2	1-1	0-1	1-1	2-0	1-1	0-1	0-2	1-3	12-17
Reyes, D.	0-0	0-0	0-0	0-1	0-0	1-0	0-0	0-0	0-0	0-0	0-0	0-0	0-0	1-0	0-0	0-0	2-1
Riedling, John	0-0	0-0	0-0	0-0	0-0	0-0	0-0	0-1	0-0	1-0	0-0	0-0	0-0	0-0	0-0	0-0	3-1
Sullivan, Scott	0-1	1-0	0-0	0-0	0-1	1-0	1-0	0-0	0-2	0-0	0-2	0-0	0-0	0-0	0-0	0-0	3-6
Villone, Ron	1-0	1-0	1-0	1-0	0-0	1-1	0-1	1-1	0-2	0-0	0-0	0-1	2-1	0-0	2-2	0-1	10-10
White, Gabe	0-0	0-0	0-0	0-0	0-0	0-0	0-0	0-0	0-0	0-0	0-0	0-0	0-0	0-0	0-0	0-0	0-0
Williamson, S.	0-0	0-0	1-0	1-1	0-1	0-0	1-0	0-1	0-0	1-0	0-0	1-1	0-1	0-1	0-0	0-1	5-8
Winchester, S.	0-0	0-0	0-0	0-0	0-0	0-0	0-0	0-0	0-0	0-0	0-0	0-0	0-0	0-0	0-0	0-0	0-0
Wohlers, Mark	0-0	0-0	1-0	0-0	0-1	0-0	0-0	0-1	0-0	0-0	0-0	0-0	0-0	0-0	0-0	0-0	1-2
Totals	5-2	5-2	8-4	6-3	3-6	7-5	4-5	5-8	6-3	5-4	3-4	7-6	4-5	3-6	7-6	7-8	85-77

INTERLEAGUE: Parris 0-1, Villone 0-1, Bell 0-1 vs. White Sox; Neagle 1-1, Parris 1-1, Aybar 1-0, Williamson 0-1 vs. Indians; Dessens 1-0, Parris 0-1, Luebbers 0-1 vs. Tigers; Bell 1-0, Graves 1-0, Neagle 1-0 vs. Twins. Total: 7-8.

COLORADO—82-80

Pitcher	Ari. W-L	Atl. W-L	Chi. W-L	Cin. W-L	Fla. W-L	Hou. W-L	L.A. W-L	Mil. W-L	Mon. W-L	N.Y. W-L	Phi. W-L	Pit. W-L	S.D. W-L	S.F. W-L	StL. W-L	A.L. W-L	Total W-L
Arrojo, R.	0-1	0-0	0-0	1-1	0-0	0-1	0-2	1-0	0-0	0-1	0-0	1-0	0-1	1-1	0-1	1-0	5-9
Astacio, P.	0-1	0-1	2-0	0-2	1-1	1-1	0-1	1-1	1-0	1-1	1-0	1-0	0-0	1-0	1-0	1-0	12-9
Aybar, Manny	0-0	0-1	0-0	0-0	0-0	0-0	0-0	0-0	0-0	0-0	0-0	0-0	0-0	0-0	0-0	0-0	0-1
Belinda, Stan	0-0	0-0	0-0	0-0	0-0	1-0	0-0	0-1	0-0	0-0	0-0	0-0	0-1	0-1	0-0	0-0	1-3
Beltran, Rigo	0-0	0-0	0-0	0-0	0-0	0-0	0-0	0-0	0-0	0-0	0-0	0-0	0-0	0-0	0-0	0-0	0-0
Bohanon, B.	1-1	1-1	1-1	0-1	1-0	0-0	2-0	0-0	1-1	1-1	0-0	1-0	2-2	1-0	0-0	0-2	12-10
Carrara, G.	0-0	0-0	0-0	0-0	0-0	0-0	0-1	0-0	0-0	0-0	0-0	0-0	0-0	0-0	0-0	0-0	0-1
Chouinard, B.	1-0	0-0	0-0	0-0	0-0	0-1	0-0	0-0	1-0	0-1	0-0	0-0	0-0	0-0	0-0	0-0	2-2
Croushore, R.	0-0	0-0	0-1	0-0	0-0	0-0	0-1	0-0	0-0	0-0	0-0	0-0	1-0	1-0	0-0	2-0	2-0
DeJean, Mike	0-0	0-0	0-1	0-0	0-0	0-0	0-1	0-2	0-0	0-0	0-0	0-0	1-0	1-0	0-0	2-0	4-4
Dipoto, Jerry	0-0	0-0	0-0	0-0	0-0	0-0	0-0	1-0	0-1	0-0	0-0	0-0	0-0	0-0	0-0	0-0	1-1
House, Craig	0-0	0-0	0-0	0-0	0-0	0-0	0-0	1-0	0-1	0-0	0-0	0-0	0-0	0-0	0-0	0-0	1-1
Jarvis, Kevin	0-0	0-0	0-0	0-1	0-0	0-0	1-0	0-1	0-0	0-0	0-0	0-0	1-0	0-1	1-0	0-1	3-4
Jimenez, Jose	0-0	0-0	0-0	1-0	1-0	1-0	0-0	0-0	0-0	1-0	0-1	0-0	0-1	0-0	1-1	0-0	5-2
Karl, Scott	0-1	0-0	0-0	0-0	0-0	0-0	0-0	1-0	0-0	0-0	0-0	0-0	0-1	0-1	1-0	0-0	2-3
Lee, David	0-0	0-0	0-0	0-0	0-0	0-0	0-0	0-0	0-0	0-0	0-0	0-0	0-0	0-0	0-0	0-0	1-0
Mayne, Brent	0-0	1-0	0-0	0-0	0-0	0-0	0-0	0-0	0-0	0-0	0-0	0-0	0-0	0-0	0-0	0-0	1-0
Moraga, David	0-0	0-0	0-0	0-0	0-0	0-0	0-0	0-0	0-0	0-0	0-0	0-0	0-1	0-0	0-0	0-0	0-1
Myers, Mike	0-0	0-0	0-0	0-0	0-0	0-0	0-0	0-0	0-0	0-0	0-0	0-0	0-1	0-0	0-0	0-0	0-1
Rose, Brian	0-1	0-2	1-0	0-0	0-1	0-0	1-0	0-0	0-0	1-0	1-0	0-1	0-0	0-0	0-0	0-0	4-5
Tavarez, Julian	0-1	2-0	1-0	1-0	1-1	0-1	1-0	1-0	0-1	2-0	1-0	0-1	0-1	1-0	2-0	0-0	11-5
Walker, Pete	0-0	0-0	0-0	0-0	0-0	0-0	0-0	0-0	0-0	0-0	0-0	0-0	0-0	0-0	0-0	0-0	0-3
Wasdin, John	0-1	0-0	0-1	0-0	0-1	0-0	0-0	1-0	0-0	1-0	0-0	0-0	0-0	0-0	0-1	0-1	1-1
White, Gabe	1-0	0-0	0-1	0-0	0-0	2-0	1-0	0-0	1-0	1-0	2-0	1-2	2-0	0-0	0-1	0-0	6-15
Yoshii, M.	3-0	0-0	0-1	0-0	0-1	0-1	0-2	0-1	1-0	0-2	0-2	0-1	1-0	1-2	0-0	0-1	3-7
Totals	6-7	4-5	5-4	3-6	4-5	5-4	4-9	4-5	7-2	3-6	6-3	7-2	7-6	6-7	5-3	6-6	82-80

INTERLEAGUE: DeJean 1-0, Astacio 1-0, White 0-1 vs. Athletics; Arrojo 1-0, Yoshii 0-1, Bohanon 0-1 vs. Mariners; Tavarez 1-0, Karl 1-0, DeJean 1-0 vs. Rangers; Jarvis 0-1, Bohanon 0-1, Yoshii 0-1 vs. Angels. Total: 6-6.

FLORIDA—79-82

Pitcher	Ari. W-L	Atl. W-L	Chi. W-L	Cin. W-L	Col. W-L	Hou. W-L	L.A. W-L	Mil. W-L	Mon. W-L	N.Y. W-L	Phi. W-L	Pit. W-L	S.D. W-L	S.F. W-L	StL. W-L	A.L. W-L	Total W-L
Alfonseca, A.	0-0	0-0	1-0	2-0	0-0	0-0	0-1	0-0	1-0	0-0	0-0	1-1	0-1	0-2	0-1	0-0	5-6
Almanza, A.	1-0	0-0	0-0	0-0	0-0	0-0	0-0	0-0	1-0	1-0	0-0	0-0	0-1	0-0	1-1	0-0	4-2
Aybar, Manny	0-0	0-0	0-0	1-0	0-0	0-0	0-0	0-0	0-0	0-0	0-0	0-0	0-0	0-0	0-0	0-0	1-0
Bones, Ricky	0-1	0-0	0-0	0-0	0-0	0-0	0-0	0-0	0-0	0-0	1-0	0-0	0-0	0-0	0-0	1-2	2-3
Burnett, A.J.	0-2	1-1	0-0	0-0	0-0	0-1	0-0	0-0	1-1	0-0	0-1	0-0	0-1	1-0	0-0	1-1	4-10
Cornelius, R.	0-1	0-1	0-0	0-1	0-1	0-1	0-0	0-0	1-2	0-1	1-0	1-0	0-0	0-0	0-1	1-1	5-3
Darensbourg, V.	1-0	0-0	0-0	0-1	0-0	0-0	0-0	0-0	1-0	1-0	1-0	0-0	0-0	1-2	0-0	0-1	5-3

Pitcher	Ari. W-L	Atl. W-L	Chi. W-L	Cin. W-L	Col. W-L	Hou. W-L	L.A. W-L	Mil. W-L	Mon. W-L	N.Y. W-L	Phi. W-L	Pit. W-L	S.D. W-L	S.F. W-L	StL. W-L	A.L. W-L	Total W-L
Dempster, Ryan.....	1-0	0-3	0-1	2-0	1-0	0-0	1-0	1-0	2-0	2-0	2-0	0-0	2-0	0-2	0-1	0-3	14-10
Fernandez, A.........	0-0	0-0	1-0	0-0	0-1	0-0	0-1	0-0	0-0	1-0	1-0	0-1	0-1	1-0	0-0	0-0	4-4
Grilli, Jason	0-0	1-0	0-0	0-0	0-0	0-0	0-0	0-0	0-0	0-0	0-0	0-0	0-0	0-0	0-0	0-0	1-0
Looper, B.............	1-0	0-0	0-0	0-0	0-0	1-0	0-1	1-0	0-0	0-0	0-0	0-0	0-0	0-0	0-0	2-0	5-1
Mahay, Ron	0-0	0-0	0-0	0-0	0-0	0-0	0-0	0-0	1-0	0-0	0-0	0-0	0-0	0-0	0-0	0-0	1-0
Miceli, Dan	1-0	1-0	1-0	1-1	0-0	1-1	0-1	0-0	0-0	0-0	0-0	0-0	0-0	1-1	0-0	0-0	6-4
Nunez, V...............	0-0	0-0	0-0	0-0	0-0	0-0	0-1	0-0	0-0	0-1	0-1	0-1	0-0	0-1	0-1	0-0	0-6
Penny, Brad	0-0	0-1	1-0	0-0	2-0	0-0	0-2	0-1	1-0	0-2	2-0	1-0	0-1	0-0	0-0	1-0	8-7
Sanchez, J............	0-0	2-0	1-0	0-0	0-2	0-1	1-1	1-1	0-2	0-2	1-0	0-1	0-1	0-0	1-0	2-1	9-12
Smith, Chuck.........	0-0	1-0	0-0	0-0	0-0	0-0	0-0	0-1	0-1	0-1	1-1	0-0	0-0	0-1	1-0	0-0	6-6
Strong, Joe..........	0-0	0-0	1-0	0-0	0-0	0-0	0-0	0-0	0-0	0-1	0-0	0-0	0-0	0-0	0-0	0-0	1-1
Totals	5-4	6-6	6-1	6-3	5-4	3-5	2-7	3-4	7-6	6-6	9-4	5-4	2-7	3-6	3-6	8-9	79-82

INTERLEAGUE: Sanchez 1-0, Darensbourg 0-1, Cornelius 0-1 vs. Orioles; Darensbourg 1-0, Bones 0-1, Sanchez 0-1 vs. Red Sox; Penny 1-0, Dempster 0-1 vs. Yankees; Bones 1-0, Looper 1-0, Nunez 0-1 vs. Blue Jays; Looper 1-0, Cornelius 1-0, Sanchez 1-0, Dempster 0-2, Bones 0-1 vs. Devil Rays. Total: 8-9.

HOUSTON—72-90

Pitcher	Ari. W-L	Atl. W-L	Chi. W-L	Cin. W-L	Col. W-L	Fla. W-L	L.A. W-L	Mil. W-L	Mon. W-L	N.Y. W-L	Phi. W-L	Pit. W-L	S.D. W-L	S.F. W-L	StL. W-L	A.L. W-L	Total W-L
Bogar, Tim	0-0	0-0	0-0	0-0	0-0	0-0	0-0	0-0	0-0	0-0	0-0	0-0	0-0	0-0	0-0	0-0	0-0
Cabrera, Jose	0-0	0-0	0-0	0-0	0-1	0-0	0-1	1-1	0-0	0-0	1-0	0-0	0-0	0-0	0-0	0-0	2-3
Dotel, Octavio	0-1	0-0	0-0	1-1	0-0	0-0	0-2	1-0	0-0	0-1	0-1	0-0	0-0	1-0	0-1	0-0	3-7
Elarton, Scott........	1-0	0-1	2-0	2-0	0-0	2-0	1-0	0-1	2-1	0-0	1-0	2-0	0-1	0-2	1-1	3-0	17-7
Franklin, W.	0-0	0-0	0-0	0-0	0-0	0-0	0-0	0-0	0-0	0-0	0-0	0-0	0-0	0-0	0-0	0-0	0-0
Gooden, D.	0-0	0-0	0-0	0-0	0-0	0-0	0-0	0-0	0-0	0-0	0-0	0-0	0-0	0-0	0-0	0-0	0-0
Green, Jason	0-0	0-0	0-0	0-0	0-0	0-0	0-0	1-0	0-1	0-0	0-0	0-0	0-0	0-0	0-0	0-0	1-1
Gross, Kip	0-0	0-0	0-0	0-0	0-0	0-0	0-0	0-0	0-0	0-0	0-0	0-0	0-0	0-1	0-0	0-0	0-1
Henry, Doug	0-0	1-0	0-0	0-0	0-0	0-0	0-1	0-1	0-0	0-0	0-0	0-0	0-0	0-0	0-0	0-1	1-3
Holt, Chris	0-1	0-1	1-1	0-1	0-1	0-1	0-1	2-1	1-0	0-1	1-0	1-2	0-1	0-1	0-3	2-0	8-16
Lima, Jose	0-2	1-0	0-2	1-2	0-0	2-0	0-0	0-2	0-1	0-0	2-0	0-3	0-2	0-1	1-1	7-16
Linebrink, S...........	0-0	0-0	0-0	0-0	0-0	0-0	0-0	0-0	0-0	0-0	0-0	0-0	0-0	0-0	0-0	0-0	0-0
Maddux, Mike	0-0	0-0	0-1	0-1	0-0	0-0	0-0	0-0	0-0	0-0	0-0	0-0	0-0	0-0	0-0	0-0	2-2
McKnight, T.	0-0	0-0	1-0	0-0	0-0	1-0	0-0	0-0	0-0	0-0	1-0	0-0	0-0	1-0	0-0	0-0	4-1
Meacham, R.	0-0	0-0	0-0	0-0	0-0	0-0	0-0	0-0	0-0	0-0	0-0	0-0	0-0	0-0	0-0	0-0	0-0
Miller, Wade	0-0	0-1	1-1	0-0	0-0	0-0	0-0	2-0	0-0	1-0	0-1	0-0	0-1	1-0	0-2	6-6
Perez, Yorkis	0-0	0-0	0-0	0-0	0-0	1-0	0-0	0-0	0-0	0-0	0-1	0-0	0-0	1-0	0-0	2-1
Powell, Brian	0-0	0-0	0-0	0-0	0-0	0-0	0-0	0-0	0-0	0-0	1-0	0-0	0-0	0-0	0-0	2-1
Powell, Jay	0-0	0-0	0-0	0-0	0-0	0-0	0-0	0-0	0-1	0-0	1-0	0-0	0-0	0-0	0-0	1-1
Reynolds, Shane ...	0-1	0-2	1-0	0-0	2-0	0-0	1-0	0-0	0-0	0-0	1-0	1-0	0-1	1-0	0-4	7-8
Slusarski, Joe	0-0	0-0	0-0	0-1	1-1	0-1	0-0	0-0	0-1	0-0	0-0	0-0	0-0	0-0	0-0	2-7
Valdes, Marc	0-1	1-0	1-0	0-1	0-1	0-1	0-0	0-1	1-0	0-0	0-1	0-0	0-1	0-0	0-0	5-5
Wagner, Billy	0-0	0-0	0-0	0-1	0-1	0-0	1-0	0-0	0-0	0-1	0-0	1-1	0-0	0-0	0-0	2-4
Totals	1-6	4-5	7-5	5-7	4-5	5-3	3-6	7-6	4-5	2-5	5-4	10-3	2-7	1-8	6-6	6-9	72-90

INTERLEAGUE: Holt 1-0, Reynolds 0-1, Dotel 0-1 vs. White Sox; Elarton 1-0, Miller 0-1, Reynolds 0-1 vs. Indians; Holt 1-0, Reynolds 0-1, Henry 0-1 vs. Tigers; Elarton 1-0, Lima 1-0, Miller 0-1 vs. Royals; Elarton 1-0, Lima 0-1, Reynolds 0-1 vs. Twins. Total: 6-9.

LOS ANGELES—86-76

Pitcher	Ari. W-L	Atl. W-L	Chi. W-L	Cin. W-L	Col. W-L	Fla. W-L	Hou. W-L	Mil. W-L	Mon. W-L	N.Y. W-L	Phi. W-L	Pit. W-L	S.D. W-L	S.F. W-L	StL. W-L	A.L. W-L	Total W-L
Adams, Terry	0-2	0-2	0-0	0-0	0-0	2-0	0-0	0-1	1-0	0-3	0-0	1-0	1-0	1-1	0-0	0-0	6-9
Arnold, Jamie	0-0	0-0	0-0	0-0	0-0	0-0	0-0	0-0	0-0	0-0	0-0	0-0	0-0	0-0	0-0	0-0	0-0
Brown, Kevin	1-0	0-1	0-0	0-0	2-1	2-1	0-0	1-0	2-0	0-0	1-1	0-0	2-0	1-0	0-0	1-2	13-6
Dreifort, Darren	1-0	1-0	1-0	0-0	1-0	0-0	2-1	0-0	0-0	0-1	1-1	2-1	2-0	1-1	1-1	12-9
Fetters, Mike	0-0	0-0	1-0	0-0	0-0	0-0	0-0	1-1	0-0	2-0	0-0	1-0	0-1	0-0	0-0	6-2
Gagne, Eric	1-0	0-2	0-0	0-1	1-0	0-0	0-0	0-0	0-1	0-0	0-0	1-0	0-1	0-0	1-2	4-6
Herges, Matt.........	1-0	0-0	0-1	2-0	1-0	1-1	2-0	0-0	0-1	0-0	1-0	0-0	1-0	0-0	1-0	11-3
Hershiser, Orel.......	0-1	0-0	0-0	1-0	0-0	0-0	0-1	0-0	0-0	0-0	0-0	0-1	0-0	0-2	0-0	1-5
Judd, Mike............	0-0	0-0	0-0	0-0	0-0	0-0	0-0	0-0	0-0	0-0	0-1	0-0	0-0	0-0	0-0	0-1
Masaoka, O.	0-1	0-0	0-0	0-0	1-0	0-0	0-0	0-0	0-0	0-0	0-0	0-0	0-0	0-0	0-0	1-1
Miller, Trever.........	0-0	0-0	2-0	0-1	0-0	0-0	0-0	0-0	0-0	0-0	0-0	0-0	0-0	0-0	0-0	0-0
Mills, Alan	0-0	0-0	0-0	0-0	0-0	0-0	0-0	0-0	0-0	0-0	0-0	0-0	0-0	0-0	0-0	2-1
Olson, Gregg	0-0	0-0	0-0	0-0	0-0	0-0	0-0	0-0	0-0	0-0	0-0	0-0	0-0	0-0	0-0	0-1
Osuna, A..............	0-0	0-0	1-1	0-0	0-0	0-0	0-0	0-0	0-0	0-1	0-0	1-1	0-0	0-1	1-2	3-6
Park, Chan Ho	2-1	0-1	0-0	1-2	2-2	0-0	1-0	2-0	2-0	1-1	0-0	2-1	1-0	2-0	1-2	18-10
Perez, Carlos	0-1	1-0	1-0	1-0	0-1	0-0	0-1	0-1	0-0	0-0	0-2	0-1	1-1	0-1	0-0	5-8
Prokopec, L.	0-0	0-0	0-0	0-0	1-0	0-0	0-0	0-0	0-0	0-0	0-0	0-1	0-0	0-0	0-0	1-1
Reyes, Al	0-0	0-0	0-0	0-0	0-0	0-0	0-0	0-0	0-0	0-0	0-0	0-0	0-0	0-0	0-0	0-0
Shaw, Jeff............	1-0	0-0	0-0	0-0	0-0	1-0	1-1	0-0	0-1	0-1	0-0	0-0	0-0	0-0	0-0	3-4
Valdes, Ismael	0-0	0-1	0-0	0-0	0-0	0-0	0-0	0-0	0-0	0-1	0-0	0-0	0-0	0-0	0-1	0-3
Williams, Jeff.........	0-0	0-0	0-0	0-0	0-0	0-0	0-0	0-0	0-0	0-0	0-0	0-0	0-0	0-0	0-0	0-0
Totals	6-7	2-7	6-3	5-4	9-4	7-2	6-3	3-4	5-3	4-5	5-4	4-5	8-5	7-5	3-6	6-9	86-76

INTERLEAGUE: Brown 1-0, Osuna 0-1, Gagne 0-1 vs. Athletics; Herges 1-0, Gagne 0-1, Park 0-1 vs. Mariners; Gagne 1-0, Dreifort 1-0, Brown 0-1 vs. Rangers; Park 1-1, Osuna 1-1, Dreifort 0-1, Brown 0-1 vs. Angels. Total: 6-9.

MILWAUKEE—73-89

Pitcher	Ari. W-L	Atl. W-L	Chi. W-L	Cin. W-L	Col. W-L	Fla. W-L	Hou. W-L	L.A. W-L	Mon. W-L	N.Y. W-L	Phi. W-L	Pit. W-L	S.D. W-L	S.F. W-L	StL. W-L	A.L. W-L	Total W-L
Acevedo, Juan	0-1	0-0	0-0	0-0	1-0	0-0	0-1	1-1	0-0	0-1	0-1	0-0	1-0	0-1	0-0	3-7
Bere, Jason	0-0	0-0	0-0	0-0	0-1	1-0	1-0	0-0	1-1	0-2	1-0	0-0	0-0	1-0	1-2	6-7
Bruske, Jim	0-0	0-0	0-0	1-0	0-0	0-0	0-0	0-0	0-0	0-0	0-0	0-0	0-0	0-0	0-0	1-0
Buddie, Mike	0-0	0-0	0-0	0-0	0-0	0-0	0-0	0-0	0-0	0-0	0-0	0-0	0-0	0-0	0-0	0-0
D'Amico, Jeff.........	1-0	0-1	3-0	1-1	2-0	0-0	0-1	0-0	0-0	1-0	1-2	0-1	1-0	1-0	1-1	12-7
Davis, Kane	0-0	0-0	0-0	0-0	0-0	0-0	0-0	0-0	0-0	0-0	0-0	0-0	0-0	0-0	0-0	0-0

Pitcher	Ari. W-L	Atl. W-L	Chi. W-L	Cin. W-L	Col. W-L	Fla. W-L	Hou. W-L	L.A. W-L	Mon. W-L	N.Y. W-L	Phi. W-L	Pit. W-L	S.D. W-L	S.F. W-L	StL. W-L	A.L. W-L	Total W-L
de los Santos, V.	0-0	0-0	0-1	1-0	1-0	0-0	0-0	0-0	0-0	0-0	0-0	0-0	0-0	0-0	0-1	0-1	2-3
Estrada, H.	1-0	0-0	0-0	0-0	0-0	0-0	2-0	0-0	0-0	0-0	0-0	0-0	0-0	0-0	0-0	0-0	3-0
Haynes, J.	1-1	0-1	1-0	2-0	0-1	1-1	0-2	1-1	1-1	0-1	0-1	1-2	1-0	0-0	1-0	2-1	12-13
King, Ray	0-0	0-0	1-0	0-0	0-0	0-0	1-0	0-0	0-0	0-0	0-0	0-1	0-1	1-0	0-0	0-0	3-2
Leskanic, C.	0-0	0-1	1-0	1-0	0-0	0-0	1-0	0-0	0-0	0-1	0-0	4-0	1-0	0-0	1-1	0-0	9-3
Levrault, Allen	0-0	0-0	0-1	0-0	0-0	0-0	0-0	0-0	0-0	0-0	0-0	0-0	0-0	0-0	0-0	0-0	0-1
Navarro, J.	0-0	0-0	0-0	0-1	0-0	0-1	0-1	0-0	0-1	0-0	0-0	0-0	0-0	0-0	0-0	0-0	0-5
Ramirez, H.	0-0	0-0	0-0	0-0	0-0	0-0	0-0	0-0	0-0	0-0	0-0	0-0	0-1	0-1	0-0	0-0	0-4
Rigdon, Paul	0-0	0-0	0-0	1-1	0-1	0-0	0-0	1-0	0-0	0-0	1-0	0-1	0-1	0-1	0-0	0-0	4-4
Roque, Rafael	0-0	0-0	0-0	0-0	0-0	0-0	0-0	0-0	0-0	0-0	0-0	0-0	0-0	0-0	0-0	0-0	0-0
Scanlan, Bob	0-0	0-0	0-0	0-0	0-0	0-0	0-0	0-0	0-0	0-0	0-0	0-0	0-0	0-0	0-0	0-0	0-0
Snyder, John	0-1	0-0	0-1	0-0	0-1	1-0	0-0	1-1	0-1	0-0	0-1	0-0	0-1	0-1	0-0	1-2	3-10
Stull, Everett	1-1	0-1	0-0	0-0	0-0	0-0	0-1	1-0	0-0	0-0	0-0	0-0	0-0	0-0	0-0	0-0	2-3
Weathers, D.	0-0	1-1	0-0	0-0	0-0	0-0	2-0	0-1	0-0	0-0	0-0	0-2	0-1	0-0	0-0	0-0	3-5
Wickman, B.	1-0	0-0	0-1	0-0	0-0	0-0	0-0	0-0	0-0	0-0	0-1	0-0	0-0	1-0	0-0	0-0	2-2
Williams, M. T.	0-0	0-0	0-0	0-0	0-0	0-0	0-0	0-0	0-0	0-0	0-0	0-0	0-0	0-0	0-0	0-0	0-0
Woodard, S.	0-0	0-1	1-1	0-0	0-0	0-1	0-1	0-0	0-0	0-0	0-0	0-0	0-0	0-1	0-1	0-2	1-7
Wright, Jamey	0-0	0-0	0-1	1-1	1-0	1-0	0-1	1-0	0-0	0-0	0-1	0-0	0-1	0-1	0-1	1-2	7-9
Totals	**5-4**	**3-6**	**7-6**	**8-5**	**5-4**	**4-3**	**6-7**	**4-3**	**4-5**	**2-7**	**2-5**	**7-5**	**2-7**	**3-6**	**5-7**	**6-9**	**73-89**

INTERLEAGUE: Snyder 0-1, Bere 0-1, Wright 0-1 vs. White Sox; D'Amico 0-1, Snyder 0-1, Bere 0-1 vs. Indians; Haynes 1-0, Bere 1-0, de los Santos 0-1 vs. Tigers; Wright 1-0, D'Amico 1-0, Haynes 0-1 vs. Royals; Haynes 1-0, Snyder 1-0, Wright 0-1 vs. Twins. Total: 6-9.

MONTREAL—67-95

Pitcher	Ari. W-L	Atl. W-L	Chi. W-L	Cin. W-L	Col. W-L	Fla. W-L	Hou. W-L	L.A. W-L	Mil. W-L	N.Y. W-L	Phi. W-L	Pit. W-L	S.D. W-L	S.F. W-L	StL. W-L	A.L. W-L	Total W-L
Armas Jr., T.	0-0	3-0	0-2	0-1	0-0	0-1	0-0	0-0	0-0	1-0	1-0	0-1	0-0	0-1	0-1	2-2	7-9
Batista, M.	0-0	0-0	0-0	0-0	0-0	0-0	0-0	0-0	0-0	0-0	0-0	0-1	0-0	0-0	0-0	0-0	0-1
Blank, Matt	0-0	0-0	0-1	0-0	0-0	0-0	0-0	0-0	0-0	0-0	0-0	0-0	0-0	0-0	0-0	0-0	0-1
Downs, Scott	0-0	0-0	0-0	0-0	0-0	0-0	0-0	0-0	0-0	0-0	0-0	0-0	0-0	0-0	0-0	0-0	0-0
Forster, Scott	0-1	0-0	0-0	0-0	0-0	0-0	0-0	0-0	0-0	0-0	0-0	0-0	0-0	0-0	0-0	0-0	0-1
Hermanson, D.	0-0	0-2	1-1	0-2	1-2	1-0	2-0	1-1	1-1	1-2	1-1	1-0	0-0	0-1	1-0	1-1	12-14
Irabu, Hideki	0-0	0-0	0-0	0-0	0-1	0-0	1-0	0-1	0-1	0-1	0-0	1-1	0-0	0-0	0-1	1-1	2-5
Johnson, Mike	0-0	1-0	0-0	1-1	0-0	1-1	0-0	0-1	0-1	1-0	0-1	0-0	0-0	0-0	0-1	1-1	5-6
Kline, Steve	0-0	0-0	0-0	0-0	0-2	0-1	0-0	0-0	0-1	0-1	0-0	0-0	0-0	0-0	0-0	0-0	1-5
Lara, Yovanny	0-0	0-0	0-0	0-0	0-0	0-0	0-0	0-0	0-0	0-0	0-0	0-0	0-0	0-0	0-0	0-0	0-0
Lira, Felipe	1-1	0-1	0-0	1-0	0-0	1-1	0-1	0-0	0-0	0-1	0-1	0-1	0-1	1-0	0-0	2-1	5-8
Moore, Trey	0-1	0-1	0-0	0-0	0-1	0-0	0-0	0-0	0-0	0-0	0-0	0-0	0-0	1-0	0-0	0-0	1-5
Moraga, David	0-0	0-0	0-0	0-0	0-0	0-0	0-0	0-0	0-0	0-0	0-0	0-0	0-0	0-0	0-0	0-0	0-0
Mota, G.	0-0	0-0	0-0	0-0	0-0	0-0	0-0	0-0	0-0	1-0	0-0	0-0	0-0	0-0	0-0	0-1	1-1
Pavano, Carl	1-0	0-0	1-0	0-0	1-0	0-0	1-0	1-0	0-0	0-2	1-0	0-1	1-0	0-0	0-0	1-1	8-4
Poole, Jim	0-0	0-0	0-0	0-0	0-0	0-0	0-0	0-0	0-0	0-0	0-0	0-0	0-0	0-0	0-0	0-0	0-0
Powell, Jim	0-0	0-0	0-0	0-0	0-1	0-0	0-0	0-0	0-0	0-1	0-0	0-0	0-0	0-0	0-0	0-0	0-3
Rigby, Brad	0-0	0-0	0-0	0-0	0-0	0-0	0-0	0-0	0-0	0-0	0-0	0-0	0-0	0-0	0-0	0-0	0-0
Santana, Julio	0-0	1-0	0-0	0-1	0-0	0-0	0-0	0-1	0-0	0-0	0-0	0-0	0-1	0-0	0-0	0-0	1-5
Skrmetta, M.	0-0	0-0	0-0	0-0	0-0	0-0	0-0	0-0	0-0	0-0	0-0	0-0	0-0	0-0	0-0	0-0	0-0
Spencer, Sean	0-0	0-0	0-0	0-0	0-0	0-0	0-0	0-0	0-0	0-0	0-0	0-0	0-0	1-0	0-0	0-0	4-3
Strickland, S.	1-0	0-0	1-0	0-0	0-2	0-0	1-0	0-0	0-0	0-0	0-0	0-0	0-0	1-0	0-1	0-0	4-3
Telford, A.	0-1	0-0	1-0	0-0	0-0	0-0	1-0	1-0	0-0	0-1	0-0	1-0	1-1	0-0	0-1	0-1	5-4
Thurman, M.	1-0	0-1	1-0	0-1	0-0	1-1	0-1	0-1	0-0	0-0	0-2	0-0	1-0	0-1	0-1	1-0	4-9
Tucker, T.J.	0-0	0-0	0-0	0-0	0-0	0-0	0-0	0-0	0-0	0-0	0-0	0-0	0-0	0-0	0-0	0-1	0-1
Urbina, U.	0-0	0-0	0-0	0-0	0-0	0-0	0-0	0-0	0-0	0-0	0-1	0-0	0-0	0-0	0-0	0-0	0-1
Vazquez, J.	0-0	2-1	0-0	0-1	0-0	2-0	0-1	2-1	1-1	0-1	0-0	0-1	0-0	0-0	0-1	0-2	11-9
Totals	**5-4**	**7-6**	**5-4**	**3-6**	**2-7**	**6-7**	**5-4**	**3-5**	**5-4**	**3-9**	**5-7**	**3-4**	**3-6**	**3-6**	**2-5**	**7-11**	**67-95**

INTERLEAGUE: Pavano 1-0, Lira 1-0, Armas Jr. 1-0 vs. Orioles; Johnson 0-1, Telford 0-1, Vazquez 0-1 vs. Red Sox; Johnson 1-0, Vazquez 0-1, Pavano 0-1 vs. Yankees; Armas Jr. 1-1, Lira 1-0, Tucker 0-1, Hermanson 0-1, Mota 0-1 vs. Blue Jays; Hermanson 1-0, Lira 0-1, Armas Jr. 0-1 vs. Devil Rays. Total: 7-11.

NEW YORK—94-68

Pitcher	Ari. W-L	Atl. W-L	Chi. W-L	Cin. W-L	Col. W-L	Fla. W-L	Hou. W-L	L.A. W-L	Mil. W-L	Mon. W-L	Phi. W-L	Pit. W-L	S.D. W-L	S.F. W-L	StL. W-L	A.L. W-L	Total W-L
Bell, Derek	0-0	0-0	0-0	0-0	0-0	0-0	0-0	0-0	0-0	0-0	0-0	0-0	0-0	0-0	0-0	0-0	0-0
Benitez, A.	0-0	1-0	0-0	0-1	0-0	0-0	1-0	1-1	1-0	0-0	0-1	0-0	0-0	0-0	0-0	0-1	4-4
Cammack, E.	0-0	0-0	0-0	0-0	0-0	0-0	0-0	0-0	0-0	0-0	0-0	0-0	0-0	0-0	0-0	0-0	0-0
Cook, Dennis	0-0	0-0	2-0	0-0	1-0	0-1	0-0	0-0	0-0	1-0	0-1	0-1	0-0	0-0	1-0	1-0	6-3
Franco, John	0-0	0-0	0-1	0-1	0-0	0-0	0-0	1-0	0-1	0-0	0-1	2-0	0-1	0-0	1-0	1-0	15-10
Hampton, M.	2-0	0-1	1-1	1-0	0-1	2-0	1-0	0-0	1-0	2-1	1-2	0-0	2-0	0-0	1-0	1-2	15-10
Jones, B. J.	2-0	1-1	0-0	0-0	1-0	1-0	1-0	1-0	1-0	1-0	1-0	0-0	0-0	0-0	1-0	1-3	11-6
Jones, B. M.	0-0	0-0	0-0	0-0	0-0	0-1	0-0	0-0	0-0	0-0	0-0	0-0	0-0	0-0	0-0	0-0	0-1
Leiter, Al	0-0	2-2	0-0	1-1	2-0	2-0	0-2	0-1	1-0	1-0	1-0	2-0	1-0	1-0	1-0	2-2	16-8
Mahomes, Pat	0-0	0-0	0-0	0-0	0-0	0-0	0-0	0-0	0-0	2-0	1-0	0-2	0-0	0-1	2-0	2-0	5-3
Mann, Jim	0-0	0-0	0-0	0-0	0-0	0-0	0-0	0-0	0-0	0-0	0-0	0-0	0-0	0-0	0-0	0-0	0-0
Pulsipher, Bill	0-0	0-0	0-0	0-0	0-0	0-0	0-0	0-0	0-0	0-0	0-0	0-1	0-1	0-0	0-0	0-0	0-2
Reed, Rick	2-0	2-1	0-0	0-0	1-0	0-0	2-0	1-1	2-1	1-0	0-0	0-0	0-2	0-0	1-0	0-0	11-5
Riggan, Jerrod	0-0	0-0	0-0	0-0	0-0	0-0	0-0	0-0	0-0	0-0	0-0	0-0	0-0	0-0	0-0	0-0	0-0
Roberts, Grant	0-0	0-0	0-0	0-0	0-0	0-0	0-0	0-0	0-0	0-0	0-0	0-0	0-0	0-0	0-0	0-0	0-0
Rodriguez, R.	0-0	0-0	0-0	0-0	0-0	0-0	0-0	0-0	0-0	0-0	0-0	0-1	0-0	0-0	0-0	0-0	0-1
Rusch, G.	0-1	0-2	2-0	0-1	0-1	1-2	1-0	0-0	0-1	2-0	2-0	0-1	0-1	1-1	1-0	1-1	11-11
Springer, D.	0-0	0-0	0-0	0-1	0-0	0-0	0-0	0-0	0-0	0-1	0-0	0-0	0-0	0-0	0-0	0-0	0-1
Wendell, Turk	1-0	0-0	0-0	2-0	1-1	0-1	0-0	1-1	1-1	1-1	0-1	0-0	0-0	1-0	0-0	0-0	8-6
White, Rick	0-0	0-0	0-0	0-0	0-0	0-0	0-0	0-0	1-0	0-1	0-0	0-0	0-0	0-0	1-1	0-0	2-3
Totals	**7-2**	**6-7**	**5-2**	**4-5**	**6-3**	**6-6**	**5-2**	**5-4**	**7-2**	**9-3**	**6-7**	**7-2**	**3-6**	**3-5**	**6-3**	**9-9**	**94-68**

INTERLEAGUE: Cook 1-0, Mahomes 1-0, Hampton 0-1 vs. Orioles; Mahomes 1-0, Benitez 0-1, Hampton 0-1 vs. Red Sox; Leiter 1-1, Hampton 1-0, Jones 0-2, Rusch 0-1 vs. Yankees; Franco 1-0, Jones 1-0, Leiter 0-1 vs. Blue Jays; Rusch 1-0, Leiter 1-0, Jones 0-1 vs. Devil Rays. Total: 9-9.

PHILADELPHIA—65-97

Pitcher	Ari. W-L	Atl. W-L	Chi. W-L	Cin. W-L	Col. W-L	Fla. W-L	Hou. W-L	L.A. W-L	Mil. W-L	Mon. W-L	N.Y. W-L	Pit. W-L	S.D. W-L	S.F. W-L	StL. W-L	A.L. W-L	Total W-L
Aldred, Scott	0-0	0-0	0-0	0-0	0-0	0-0	0-0	0-0	0-0	1-0	0-1	0-0	0-0	0-0	0-0	0-0	1-3
Ashby, Andy	0-2	1-0	0-0	0-1	0-1	1-0	0-1	0-0	1-0	0-0	0-0	0-0	0-0	0-1	0-0	1-1	4-7
Bottenfield, K.	0-0	0-0	0-0	0-0	0-1	0-0	0-0	0-0	0-0	0-0	0-0	0-0	0-0	0-1	1-0	0-0	1-2
Boyd, Jason	0-0	0-0	0-0	0-0	0-0	0-0	0-0	0-0	0-0	0-0	0-0	0-0	0-0	0-0	0-0	0-1	0-1
Brantley, Jeff	0-1	0-0	0-0	0-0	0-1	0-0	0-0	0-0	0-0	0-0	1-0	0-0	0-1	0-0	0-0	1-4	2-7
Brock, Chris	0-1	1-0	0-1	1-0	0-1	0-0	0-1	0-1	2-0	0-1	1-0	0-1	1-0	0-0	0-0	1-0	7-8
Brownson, M.	0-0	0-0	1-0	0-0	0-0	0-0	0-0	0-0	0-0	0-0	0-0	0-0	0-0	0-0	0-0	0-0	1-0
Bullinger, Kirk	0-0	0-0	0-0	0-0	0-0	0-0	0-0	0-0	0-0	0-0	0-0	0-0	0-0	0-0	0-0	0-0	0-0
Byrd, Paul	0-1	0-1	0-1	1-0	0-0	0-1	0-0	0-1	0-1	0-1	0-0	1-1	0-0	0-1	0-0	0-0	2-9
Chen, Bruce	0-1	0-0	0-0	0-0	1-0	0-1	0-0	0-0	0-0	1-0	0-1	0-0	0-1	0-0	0-0	1-0	3-4
Coggin, Dave	0-0	0-0	0-0	0-0	0-0	0-0	0-0	0-0	1-0	0-0	0-0	0-0	0-0	0-0	1-0	0-0	2-0
Daal, Omar	0-0	0-0	1-0	0-1	0-1	0-1	0-1	0-1	0-0	0-1	0-0	1-1	0-1	0-1	0-0	0-0	2-9
Gomes, Wayne	1-1	0-2	0-0	0-0	0-1	1-0	1-0	0-0	0-0	0-1	1-0	0-0	0-0	0-1	0-0	0-0	4-6
Holzemer, M.	0-0	0-0	0-1	0-0	0-0	0-0	0-0	0-0	0-0	0-0	0-0	0-0	0-0	0-0	0-0	0-0	0-1
Jacquez, Tom	0-0	0-0	0-0	0-0	0-0	0-0	0-0	0-0	0-0	0-0	0-0	0-0	0-0	0-0	0-0	0-0	0-0
Miller, Trever	0-0	0-0	0-0	0-0	0-0	0-0	0-0	0-0	0-0	0-0	0-0	0-0	0-0	0-0	0-0	0-0	0-0
Nickle, Doug	0-0	0-0	0-0	0-0	0-0	0-0	0-0	0-0	0-0	0-0	0-0	0-0	0-0	0-0	0-0	0-0	0-0
Padilla, V.	0-0	0-0	0-1	1-0	0-0	0-0	0-1	0-1	0-0	0-1	1-0	0-1	0-0	0-0	0-0	0-0	2-6
Person, R.	0-0	0-0	0-1	1-0	2-0	1-2	1-0	1-1	0-0	1-0	2-0	0-1	0-1	0-0	0-1	0-0	9-7
Politte, Cliff	0-0	1-0	1-0	0-0	0-0	0-1	0-0	0-0	1-0	0-0	1-0	0-2	0-0	0-0	0-0	0-0	4-3
Reyes, Carlos	0-0	0-1	0-0	0-0	0-0	0-0	0-0	0-0	0-0	0-0	0-0	0-0	0-0	0-1	0-0	0-0	0-2
Schilling, Curt	0-0	2-0	0-0	0-0	0-0	0-0	0-0	0-0	1-0	0-0	0-0	2-0	0-0	0-1	0-2	1-3	6-6
Schrenk, S.	0-1	0-1	0-0	0-0	0-0	0-0	1-0	0-0	0-1	0-0	0-0	0-0	0-0	0-0	0-0	1-0	2-3
Telemaco, A.	0-0	0-0	0-0	0-0	0-0	0-1	0-0	0-0	0-0	0-1	1-0	0-1	0-0	0-0	0-0	0-0	1-3
Vosberg, Ed	0-0	0-0	0-0	0-0	0-0	0-0	0-0	0-0	0-0	0-0	0-0	0-0	0-0	1-1	0-0	0-0	1-1
Ward, Bryan	0-0	0-0	0-0	0-0	0-0	0-0	0-0	0-0	0-0	0-0	0-0	0-0	0-0	0-0	0-0	0-0	0-0
Wolf, Randy	0-0	0-1	0-1	0-1	0-0	1-2	1-1	2-0	1-0	2-0	0-1	0-1	0-1	1-0	1-0	2-0	11-9
Totals	1-8	5-8	3-6	4-3	3-6	4-9	4-5	4-5	5-2	7-5	7-6	3-6	2-5	2-7	2-7	9-9	65-97

INTERLEAGUE: Ashby 1-1, Wolf 1-0, Schilling 0-2, Brantley 0-1 vs. Orioles; Brantley 1-0, Wolf 1-0, Schrenk 1-0 vs. Red Sox; Coggin 1-0, Brantley 0-1, Schilling 0-1 vs. Yankees; Schilling 1-0, Chen 1-0, Brantley 0-1 vs. Blue Jays; Brock 1-0, Boyd 0-1, Brantley 0-1 vs. Devil Rays. Total: 9-9.

PITTSBURGH—69-93

Pitcher	Ari. W-L	Atl. W-L	Chi. W-L	Cin. W-L	Col. W-L	Fla. W-L	Hou. W-L	L.A. W-L	Mil. W-L	Mon. W-L	N.Y. W-L	Phi. W-L	S.D. W-L	S.F. W-L	StL. W-L	A.L. W-L	Total W-L
Anderson, J.	0-1	0-1	1-0	0-2	0-2	0-0	0-1	2-0	0-1	0-0	1-1	1-0	0-0	0-1	0-0	0-1	5-11
Arroyo, B.	0-1	0-0	0-0	0-0	0-0	0-0	0-0	0-1	0-1	0-0	0-1	1-1	1-0	0-1	0-0	0-0	2-6
Benson, Kris	1-1	1-1	0-0	1-1	0-0	0-0	1-2	0-0	1-1	1-1	0-2	1-0	0-0	1-1	2-1	1-1	10-12
Christiansen, J.	1-1	0-1	0-0	0-0	0-1	0-1	0-0	0-1	0-0	0-0	0-0	0-0	0-0	0-0	0-0	1-2	2-8
Clontz, Brad	0-0	0-0	0-0	0-0	0-0	0-0	0-0	0-0	0-0	0-0	0-0	0-0	0-0	0-0	0-0	0-0	0-0
Cordova, F.	0-0	0-1	0-2	0-0	1-0	1-2	1-0	0-0	0-0	1-0	0-0	0-0	1-0	0-1	0-2	1-0	6-8
Garcia, Mike	0-0	0-1	0-0	0-1	0-0	0-0	0-0	0-0	0-0	0-0	0-0	0-0	0-0	0-0	0-0	0-0	0-2
Loiselle, Rich	0-0	0-0	0-0	0-0	0-0	0-1	0-0	0-0	0-0	0-1	0-1	2-0	0-0	0-0	0-0	0-0	2-3
Manzanillo, J.	0-0	0-0	0-0	0-0	0-0	0-0	0-0	1-0	0-1	0-0	0-0	0-0	0-0	1-1	0-0	0-0	2-2
O'Connor, B.	0-0	0-0	0-0	0-0	0-0	0-0	0-0	0-0	0-0	0-0	0-0	0-0	0-0	0-0	0-0	0-0	0-0
Osik, Keith	0-0	0-0	0-0	0-0	0-0	0-0	0-0	0-0	0-0	0-0	0-0	0-0	0-0	0-0	0-0	0-0	0-0
Parra, Jose	0-0	0-0	0-0	0-0	0-0	0-0	0-0	0-0	0-0	0-0	0-0	0-0	0-1	0-0	0-0	0-0	0-1
Peters, Chris	0-0	0-0	0-0	0-0	0-0	0-0	0-0	0-0	0-0	0-0	0-1	0-0	0-0	0-0	0-0	0-0	0-1
Ritchie, Todd	0-0	0-0	3-0	2-2	0-0	1-0	0-0	0-0	0-1	0-0	0-2	1-0	1-0	0-0	0-3	2-0	9-8
Sauerbeck, S.	1-0	0-0	0-1	0-0	1-0	0-0	0-1	0-0	1-0	0-0	0-0	1-0	0-1	0-1	0-0	1-1	5-4
Schmidt, J.	0-2	0-0	1-0	0-0	0-0	1-0	0-1	0-0	0-0	0-0	0-0	0-0	0-0	0-0	0-1	0-0	2-5
Serafini, Dan	0-1	0-0	0-0	0-0	0-1	0-0	0-2	1-0	0-0	0-0	0-0	0-0	1-0	0-1	0-0	0-0	2-5
Silva, Jose	0-0	1-0	0-0	0-2	0-2	0-0	1-1	1-1	3-0	2-0	1-1	0-0	0-1	0-0	0-3	0-0	11-9
Skrmetta, M.	0-0	0-0	0-0	0-0	0-0	0-0	0-2	0-0	0-0	0-0	1-0	1-0	0-0	0-0	0-0	0-0	2-2
Smith, Brian	0-0	0-0	0-0	0-0	0-0	0-0	0-0	0-0	0-0	0-0	0-0	0-0	0-0	0-0	0-0	0-0	0-0
Sparks, Steve	0-0	0-0	0-0	0-0	0-0	0-0	0-0	0-0	0-0	0-0	0-0	0-0	0-0	0-0	0-0	0-0	0-0
Wallace, Jeff	0-0	0-0	1-0	0-0	0-0	0-0	0-0	0-0	0-0	0-0	0-0	0-0	0-0	1-0	0-0	0-0	2-0
Wilkins, Marc	0-0	0-0	3-0	1-0	0-0	0-0	0-0	0-1	0-0	0-0	0-0	0-1	0-0	0-0	0-0	0-0	4-2
Williams, M.	0-0	0-0	0-0	0-0	0-1	1-1	0-0	0-1	0-1	0-0	0-0	2-0	0-0	0-0	0-0	0-0	3-4
Totals	2-7	2-5	9-3	6-7	2-7	4-5	3-10	5-4	5-7	4-3	2-7	6-3	7-2	2-6	4-8	6-9	69-93

INTERLEAGUE: Sauerbeck 0-1, Benson 0-1, Silva 0-1 vs. Indians; Cordova 1-0, Ritchie 1-0, Anderson 0-1 vs. Tigers; Ritchie 1-0, Sauerbeck 1-0, Christiansen 0-2, Schmidt 0-1, Silva 0-1 vs. Royals; Christiansen 1-0, Benson 1-0, Silva 0-1 vs. Twins. Total: 6-9.

ST. LOUIS—95-67

Pitcher	Ari. W-L	Atl. W-L	Chi. W-L	Cin. W-L	Col. W-L	Fla. W-L	Hou. W-L	L.A. W-L	Mil. W-L	Mon. W-L	N.Y. W-L	Phi. W-L	Pit. W-L	S.D. W-L	S.F. W-L	A.L. W-L	Total W-L
Ankiel, Rick	1-1	0-0	0-0	0-1	0-1	1-0	2-0	0-0	2-0	0-1	0-0	0-0	2-1	2-0	1-0	0-2	11-7
Benes, Alan	0-0	0-0	0-0	0-1	0-0	0-0	1-1	1-0	0-0	0-0	0-0	0-0	0-0	0-0	0-0	0-0	2-2
Benes, Andy	0-1	0-1	0-1	3-1	1-0	0-0	0-2	1-0	0-2	0-0	0-0	1-0	1-0	3-0	0-0	2-1	12-9
Brunette, J.	0-0	0-0	0-0	0-0	0-0	0-0	0-0	0-0	0-0	0-0	0-0	0-0	0-0	0-0	0-0	0-0	0-0
Christiansen, J.	0-0	0-0	0-0	0-0	0-0	0-0	0-0	0-0	0-0	0-0	1-0	0-0	0-0	0-0	0-0	0-0	1-0
Hackman, L.	0-0	0-0	0-0	0-0	0-0	0-0	0-0	0-0	0-0	0-0	0-0	0-0	0-0	0-0	0-0	0-0	0-0
Hentgen, Pat	0-1	1-0	2-1	1-1	1-1	0-2	1-1	1-0	1-1	2-0	0-1	1-0	1-1	0-0	1-1	2-1	15-12
Holmes, D.	0-0	0-0	0-0	0-1	0-0	1-0	0-0	0-0	0-0	0-0	0-1	0-0	0-0	0-0	0-0	0-0	0-1
James, Mike	0-0	0-0	1-0	0-0	0-1	1-0	0-0	0-0	0-0	0-1	0-0	0-0	0-0	0-0	0-0	0-0	2-2
Kile, Darryl	1-0	1-1	3-0	2-0	0-1	1-0	0-1	0-2	2-1	2-0	1-1	1-0	1-1	3-0	0-0	2-1	20-9
Matthews, M.	0-0	0-0	0-0	0-0	0-0	0-0	0-0	0-0	0-0	0-0	0-0	0-0	0-0	0-0	0-0	0-0	0-0
Mohler, Mike	0-0	0-0	0-0	0-0	0-1	0-0	0-0	0-0	0-0	0-0	1-0	0-0	0-0	0-0	0-0	0-0	1-1
Morris, Matt	0-0	0-0	0-0	0-0	0-0	1-1	0-0	0-0	1-0	0-0	1-0	0-0	0-0	0-0	0-1	0-1	3-3
Orosco, Jesse	0-0	0-0	0-0	0-0	0-0	0-0	0-0	0-0	0-0	0-0	0-0	0-0	0-0	0-0	0-0	0-0	0-0
Radinsky, S.	0-0	0-0	0-0	0-0	0-0	0-0	0-0	0-0	1-0	0-0	0-0	0-0	0-0	0-0	0-0	0-0	0-0
Reames, Britt	0-0	0-0	1-0	0-0	0-0	0-0	0-0	0-0	0-0	1-0	0-0	0-1	0-0	0-0	0-0	0-0	2-1

Pitcher	Ari. W-L	Atl. W-L	Chi. W-L	Cin. W-L	Col. W-L	Fla. W-L	Hou. W-L	L.A. W-L	Mil. W-L	Mon. W-L	N.Y. W-L	Phi. W-L	Pit. W-L	S.D. W-L	S.F. W-L	A.L. W-L	Total W-L
Rodriguez, J.	0-0	0-0	0-0	0-0	0-0	0-0	0-0	0-0	0-0	0-0	0-0	0-0	0-0	0-0	0-0	0-0	0-0
Slocumb, H.	0-0	0-0	0-0	0-0	0-0	0-0	0-0	2-0	0-0	0-0	0-0	0-1	0-1	0-0	0-1	0-0	2-3
Stechschulte, G.	0-0	0-0	0-0	0-0	0-0	0-0	0-0	1-0	0-0	0-0	0-0	0-0	0-0	0-0	0-0	0-0	1-0
Stephenson, G.	2-1	2-0	2-0	0-2	0-0	1-0	1-0	0-0	0-0	0-1	0-1	2-0	3-0	1-0	1-2	1-2	16-9
Thompson, M.	0-0	0-0	0-0	0-0	0-0	0-0	1-0	0-0	0-0	0-0	0-1	0-0	0-0	0-0	0-0	0-0	1-1
Timlin, Mike	0-0	0-1	1-0	0-0	1-0	1-0	0-0	0-0	0-0	0-0	0-0	0-0	0-0	0-0	0-0	0-0	3-1
Veres, Dave	0-1	0-0	0-1	0-0	0-0	0-0	0-0	0-1	1-1	0-0	1-1	0-0	0-0	1-0	0-0	0-0	3-5
Wainhouse, D.	0-0	0-0	0-0	0-0	0-0	0-0	0-1	0-0	0-0	0-0	0-0	0-0	0-0	0-0	0-0	0-0	0-1
Totals	4-5	4-3	10-3	6-7	3-5	6-3	6-6	6-3	7-5	5-2	3-6	7-2	8-4	9-0	4-5	7-8	95-67

INTERLEAGUE: Benes 1-0, Stephenson 1-0, Kile 0-1 vs. White Sox; Kile 1-0, Stephenson 0-1, Morris 0-1 vs. Indians; Hentgen 1-0, Stephenson 0-1, Ankiel 0-1 vs. Tigers; Benes 1-0, Kile 1-0, Hentgen 0-1 vs. Royals; Hentgen 1-0, Ankiel 0-1, Benes 0-1 vs. Twins. Total: 7-8.

SAN DIEGO—76-86

Pitcher	Ari. W-L	Atl. W-L	Chi. W-L	Cin. W-L	Col. W-L	Fla. W-L	Hou. W-L	L.A. W-L	Mil. W-L	Mon. W-L	N.Y. W-L	Phi. W-L	Pit. W-L	S.F. W-L	StL. W-L	A.L. W-L	Total W-L
Almanzar, C.	0-0	0-0	1-0	0-0	0-1	0-0	0-0	0-0	1-0	0-0	0-0	1-0	0-2	1-1	0-0	0-1	4-5
Boehringer, B.	0-0	0-0	0-0	0-0	0-0	0-0	0-1	0-0	0-0	0-1	0-0	0-0	0-0	0-0	0-1	0-0	0-3
Carlyle, Buddy	0-0	0-0	0-0	0-0	0-0	0-0	0-0	0-0	0-0	0-0	0-0	0-0	0-0	0-0	0-0	0-0	0-0
Clement, Matt	0-2	0-0	1-0	1-1	1-2	1-1	1-0	2-2	0-0	0-1	2-1	2-0	1-2	0-1	0-1	1-3	13-17
Cunnane, Will	0-0	0-1	0-0	0-0	0-0	0-0	1-0	0-0	0-0	0-0	0-0	0-0	0-0	0-0	0-0	0-0	1-1
Davey, Tom	0-0	0-0	0-0	0-0	0-0	0-0	0-0	0-0	1-0	0-0	0-0	0-0	0-0	1-0	0-1	0-0	2-1
Eaton, Adam	0-0	0-0	1-0	0-0	2-1	1-0	0-0	1-0	1-0	0-0	1-0	0-0	0-1	0-1	0-1	0-1	7-4
Erdos, Todd	0-0	0-0	0-0	0-0	0-0	0-0	0-0	0-0	0-0	0-0	0-0	0-0	0-0	0-0	0-0	0-0	0-0
Guzman, D.	0-0	0-0	0-0	0-0	0-0	0-0	0-0	0-0	0-0	0-0	0-0	0-0	0-0	0-0	0-0	0-0	0-0
Hitchcock, S.	0-2	0-2	0-0	0-1	0-0	1-0	0-0	0-0	0-0	0-0	0-0	0-0	0-0	0-0	0-0	1-1	1-6
Hoffman, T.	0-0	0-0	0-1	1-0	1-1	0-0	0-0	0-1	0-0	0-0	1-1	0-0	0-1	0-0	0-0	1-1	4-7
Kolb, Brandon	0-1	0-0	0-0	0-0	0-0	0-0	0-0	0-0	0-0	0-0	0-0	0-0	0-0	0-0	0-0	0-0	0-1
Lopez, R.	0-1	0-0	0-0	0-0	0-0	0-0	0-0	0-0	0-0	0-0	0-0	0-0	0-0	0-0	0-1	0-1	0-3
Maurer, Dave	0-0	0-0	0-0	0-0	0-0	0-0	0-0	1-0	0-0	0-0	0-0	0-0	0-0	0-0	0-0	0-0	1-0
Meadows, B.	2-0	0-1	0-0	0-1	1-0	1-0	1-0	1-1	0-1	1-0	0-0	0-0	0-0	0-1	0-1	0-2	7-8
Montgomery, S.	0-0	0-0	0-0	0-0	0-0	0-0	0-1	0-0	0-0	0-0	0-0	0-0	0-0	0-0	0-0	0-0	0-2
Myers, R.	0-0	0-0	0-0	0-0	0-0	0-0	0-0	0-0	0-0	0-0	0-0	0-0	0-0	0-0	0-0	0-1	0-1
Palacios, V.	0-0	0-1	0-0	0-0	0-0	0-0	0-0	0-0	0-0	0-0	0-0	0-0	0-0	0-0	0-0	0-0	0-1
Reyes, Carlos	0-1	0-0	0-0	1-0	0-0	0-0	0-0	0-0	0-0	0-0	0-0	0-0	0-0	0-0	0-0	0-0	1-1
Serafini, Dan	0-0	0-0	0-0	0-0	0-0	0-0	0-0	0-0	0-0	0-0	0-0	0-0	0-0	0-0	0-0	0-0	0-0
Slocumb, H.	0-0	0-0	0-0	0-0	0-0	0-0	0-0	0-0	0-0	0-0	0-0	0-1	0-0	0-0	0-0	0-0	0-1
Spencer, Stan	0-1	0-0	0-0	0-0	1-0	0-0	0-0	0-0	0-0	0-0	0-0	0-0	0-0	0-1	1-0	2-2
Tollberg, Brian	1-0	0-0	0-1	0-0	0-1	0-0	0-0	1-0	0-0	0-0	0-0	0-1	1-0	0-1	0-0	4-5
Walker, Kevin	0-0	0-1	1-0	0-0	2-0	1-0	1-0	0-0	0-0	0-0	0-0	0-0	0-0	0-0	0-0	7-1
Wall, Donne	0-0	0-0	0-0	0-0	0-0	0-0	0-0	0-0	1-1	1-1	0-0	1-0	1-0	1-0	1-0	5-2
Whisenant, M.	1-0	0-0	0-0	0-1	0-0	0-0	1-0	0-0	0-0	0-0	0-0	0-0	0-0	0-0	0-0	2-2
Whiteside, M.	0-0	1-0	0-0	0-0	0-0	0-0	0-0	0-2	0-0	1-0	0-0	0-0	0-0	0-0	0-1	2-3
Williams, W.	0-1	0-1	0-1	0-0	1-0	0-1	2-0	0-2	2-0	0-0	1-0	0-0	0-0	1-2	0-0	10-8
Witasick, Jay	0-0	0-1	1-0	0-0	0-0	0-0	0-0	0-0	1-0	1-0	0-0	0-0	0-0	0-1	0-0	3-2
Totals	4-9	1-8	5-3	5-4	6-7	7-2	7-2	5-8	7-2	6-3	6-3	5-2	2-7	5-7	0-9	5-10	76-86

INTERLEAGUE: Almanzar 0-1, Lopez 0-1, Clement 0-1 vs. Athletics; Spencer 1-0, Hoffman 1-0, Williams 1-0, Meadows 0-2, Clement 0-1 vs. Mariners; Clement 1-0, Whiteside 0-1, Eaton 0-1 vs. Rangers; Wall 1-0, Hoffman 0-1. Total: 5-10.

SAN FRANCISCO—97-65

Pitcher	Ari. W-L	Atl. W-L	Chi. W-L	Cin. W-L	Col. W-L	Fla. W-L	Hou. W-L	L.A. W-L	Mil. W-L	Mon. W-L	N.Y. W-L	Phi. W-L	Pit. W-L	S.D. W-L	StL. W-L	A.L. W-L	Total W-L
del Toro, M.	1-0	0-0	0-0	0-0	0-0	0-0	0-0	0-0	0-0	1-0	0-0	0-0	0-0	0-0	0-0	0-0	2-0
Embree, Alan	0-1	0-0	0-0	0-0	0-0	0-0	0-0	0-0	0-0	0-0	0-0	0-0	1-0	1-2	1-0	0-2	3-5
Estes, Shawn	0-1	0-1	1-0	0-2	2-0	0-1	2-0	0-0	0-0	2-0	1-0	1-0	1-0	2-0	1-0	2-1	15-6
Fultz, Aaron	0-0	0-0	0-1	0-0	0-0	1-0	0-0	1-0	0-0	0-0	1-1	0-0	0-0	0-0	2-0	5-2
Gardner, Mark	0-1	1-0	2-0	0-0	1-1	2-0	0-0	0-1	0-1	1-0	0-1	0-0	1-0	2-0	0-1	0-0	11-7
Henry, Doug	1-0	0-0	0-0	0-0	0-0	0-0	0-0	0-0	1-0	0-0	0-0	1-0	0-1	0-0	0-0	0-0	3-1
Hernandez, L.	1-2	1-1	2-0	1-1	1-1	1-1	3-0	1-0	1-1	1-0	1-1	1-0	0-1	0-0	1-1	1-1	17-11
Johnstone, J.	0-0	0-0	0-0	0-0	0-2	1-1	0-0	0-0	0-0	1-1	0-0	0-0	0-0	0-0	0-0	0-0	3-4
Linebrink, S.	0-0	0-0	0-0	0-0	0-0	0-0	0-0	0-0	0-0	0-0	0-0	0-0	0-0	0-0	0-0	0-0	0-0
Nathan, Joe	1-0	0-0	0-0	1-0	2-2	0-0	1-0	0-0	0-0	0-0	0-0	0-0	0-0	0-0	0-1	5-2
Nen, Robb	0-0	0-0	0-0	1-0	1-0	0-0	1-1	1-0	0-1	0-0	0-0	0-0	0-0	0-0	0-1	4-3
Ortiz, Russ	2-1	1-2	0-1	1-0	0-0	1-0	0-3	2-0	0-1	1-0	2-0	2-0	0-1	0-2	1-1	14-12
Rodriguez, F.	0-0	0-0	0-0	0-0	0-0	0-0	0-1	1-0	0-0	2-1	0-0	0-0	1-0	0-0	4-2
Rueter, Kirk	1-0	0-2	0-2	2-0	0-0	0-0	0-0	2-1	1-0	0-1	0-1	1-0	2-1	1-0	1-1	11-9
Vogelsong, R.	0-0	0-0	0-0	0-0	0-0	0-0	0-0	0-0	0-0	0-0	0-0	0-0	0-0	0-0	0-0	0-0
Weber, Ben	0-0	0-0	0-0	0-0	0-0	0-0	0-1	0-0	0-0	0-0	0-0	0-0	0-0	0-0	0-0	0-1
Zerbe, Chad	0-0	0-0	0-0	0-0	0-0	0-0	0-0	0-0	0-0	0-0	0-0	0-0	0-0	0-0	0-0	0-0
Totals	7-6	3-6	5-4	6-3	7-6	6-3	8-1	5-7	6-3	6-3	5-3	7-2	6-2	7-5	5-4	8-7	97-65

INTERLEAGUE: Ortiz 1-1, Estes 1-0, Gardner 1-0, Rueter 0-1, Embree 0-1 vs. Athletics; Rueter 1-0, Estes 0-1, Hernandez 0-1 vs. Mariners; Estes 1-0, Hernandez 1-0, Fultz 1-0 vs. Rangers; Fultz 1-0, Nen 0-1, Embree 0-1 vs. Angels. Total: 8-7.

HOME RUNS BY PARKS

	At Ari.	At Atl.	At Chi.	At Cin.	At Col.	At Fla.	At Hou.	At L.A.	At Mil.	At Mon.	At N.Y.	At Phi.	At Pit.	At St.L.	At S.D.	At S.F.	At A.L. Parks	Totals 2000	1999	HR Allow.
Arizona	84	1	9	3	8	6	4	4	5	7	4	10	5	5	11	8	5	179	216	190
Atlanta	10	84	8	0	5	3	9	2	4	8	7	13	5	1	5	3	12	183	197	165
Chicago	4	3	84	8	11	3	14	3	5	8	*7	5	4	6	3	5	10	183	189	231
Cincinnati	4	3	9	98	13	3	10	8	7	4	3	2	8	9	9	4	6	200	209	190
Colorado	0	6	1	2	112	3	4	4	3	5	3	2	4	3	6	0	3	161	223	221
Florida	5	4	4	10	5	71	6	4	2	8	8	7	5	8	4	1	8	160	128	169

	At Ari.	At Atl.	At Chi.	At Cin.	At Col.	At Fla.	At Hou.	At L.A.	At Mil.	At Mon.	At N.Y.	At Phi.	At Pit.	At St.L.	At S.D.	At S.F.	At A.L. Parks	Totals 2000	1999	HR Allow.
Houston	1	1	15	11	12	4	135	9	9	7	3	7	5	12	6	2	10	249	168	234
Los Angeles	8	5	7	8	12	7	5	108	1	6	5	0	2	11	11	7	8	211	187	176
Milwaukee	10	4	7	14	5	7	6	4	78	4	5	3	5	9	5	0	11	177	165	174
Montreal	4	10	3	6	8	7	5	2	7	88	3	11	3	6	3	4	8	178	163	181
New York	2	5	*5	4	4	6	8	4	8	4	*93	8	10	10	5	3	15	198	181	164
Philadelphia	3	7	6	3	3	3	9	4	2	3	7	66	4	1	4	4	15	144	161	201
Pittsburgh	5	1	13	3	2	1	10	9	4	4	3	4	86	9	1	3	10	168	171	163
St. Louis	3	7	4	12	8	3	13	5	3	5	3	9	8	124	6	7	15	235	194	196
San Diego	9	9	3	10	9	6	2	6	2	5	2	6	5	2	72	3	6	157	153	191
San Francisco	13	6	2	4	17	8	14	7	6	7	0	1	4	7	4	110	16	226	188	151
A.L. clubs	8	10	8	10	11	11	12	6	9	13	9	4	9	6	7	7	....	140	155	....
2000 Totals	173	166	*188	206	245	152	266	193	151	190	*165	158	172	229	162	171	158	3005	....	2997
1999 Totals	185	161	222	213	303	123	118	194	187	152	161	185	171	187	†159	185	....	....	2893	....

*There were actually 187 home runs hit at Chicago and 162 hit at New York in 2000. The totals include two homers hit by the Cubs and one by the Mets when the Mets were the "home" team at Tokyo Stadium on March 29, and one homer hit by the Mets when the Cubs were the "home" team at Tokyo Stadium on March 30. †There were actually 158 home runs hit at San Diego in 1999. The total includes one home run hit by the Rockies when the Padres were the "home" team in a game against Colorado at Monterrey, Mexico.

AT ARIZONA (173):

Anaheim (5)—Anderson 2, Salmon 1, Gil 1, Glaus 1. **Arizona (84)**—Finley 17, Gonzalez 14, Bell 9, Colbrunn 6, Miller 6, Williams 5, Bautista 4, Womack 4, Durazo 3, Stinnett 2, Frias 2, Klassen 2, Cabrera 2, Harris 1, Gilkey 1, Daal 1, Mieske 1, Fox 1, Lee 1, Barajas 1, Conti 1. **Atlanta (10)**—Sanders 2, Jordan 2, A. Jones 2, Galarraga 1, Joyner 1, C. Jones 1, Furcal 1. **Chicago (4)**—Sosa 4. **Cincinnati (4)**—Boone 2, Bichette 1, Ochoa 1. **Florida (5)**—Wilson 2, Lowell 2, Lee 1. **Houston (1)**—Berkman 1. **Los Angeles (8)**—Hundley 2, Beltre 2, Sheffield 1, Hansen 1, Goodwin 1, Hollandsworth 1. **Milwaukee (10)**—Houston 3, Sexson 3, Loretta 2, Burnitz 1, Lopez 1. **Montreal (4)**—V. Guerrero 3, Stevens 1. **New York (2)**—Ventura 1, Bordick 1. **Philadelphia (3)**—Rolen 2, Relaford 1. **Pittsburgh (5)**—Giles 2, Vander Wal 1, Meares 1, Aven 1. **St. Louis (3)**—Dunston 1, McGwire 1, Perez 1. **San Diego (9)**—Sprague 3, Klesko 3, Boone 1, Owens 1, Nevin 1. **San Francisco (13)**—Bonds 3, Kent 2, Aurilia 2, Mueller 2, Benard 1, Crespo 1, Estalella 1, Murray 1, Minor 1. **Seattle (1)**—Oliver 1. **Texas (2)**—Clayton 1, Sheldon 1.

AT ATLANTA (166):

Arizona (1)—Colbrunn 1. **Atlanta (84)**—C. Jones 18, A. Jones 15, Galarraga 14, Lopez 12, Jordan 7, Bonilla 4, Sanders 4, Joyner 2, Veras 2, Bako 2, Surhoff 1, Hunter 1, Lockhart 1, Furcal 1. **Boston (1)**—Daubach 1. **Chicago (3)**—Hill 1, Nieves 1, Matthews Jr. 1. **Cincinnati (3)**—Young 1, Reese 1, LaRue 1. **Colorado (6)**—Helton 3, Shumpert 1, Goodwin 1, Hollandsworth 1. **Florida (4)**—Floyd 2, Wilson 1, Lowell 1. **Houston (1)**—Eusebio 1. **Los Angeles (5)**—Elster 1, Sheffield 1, Hundley 1, Karros 1, Green 1. **Milwaukee (4)**—Grissom 2, Burnitz 1, Houston 1. **Montreal (10)**—V. Guerrero 2, Vidro 2, Cabrera 2, Tracy 2, White 1, Seguignol 1. **New York A.L. (4)**—Brosius 1, Turner 1, Ledee 1, Bellinger 1. **New York N.L. (5)**—Bell 2, Zeile 1, Piazza 1, Alfonzo 1. **Philadelphia (7)**—Rolen 3, Gant 1, Lieberthal 1, Abreu 1, Brock 1. **Pittsburgh (1)**—A. Ramirez 1. **St. Louis (7)**—Clark 2, Lankford 2, Edmonds 2, Renteria 1. **San Diego (9)**—Nevin 3, Hernandez 1, Sprague 1, Martin 1, Boone 1, Mabry 1, Rivera 1. **San Francisco (6)**—Kent 3, Bonds 1, Crespo 1, Estalella 1. **Toronto (5)**—Delgado 2, Woodward 2, Mondesi 1.

AT CHICAGO (188):

Arizona (9)—Gonzalez 3, Bell 1, Finley 1, Gilkey 1, Colbrunn 1, Stinnett 1, Counsell 1. **Atlanta (8)**—Galarraga 4, C. Jones 3, Lopez 1. **Chicago (84)**—Sosa 22, Buford 9, Greene 7, Gutierrez 7, Andrews 7, Hill 6, Rodriguez 6, E. Young 5, Girardi 4, Grace 3, Matthews Jr. 2, Wood 1, Nieves 1, R. Brown 1, Zuleta 1, Patterson 1, Ojeda 1. **Chicago (6)**—Ordonez 2, Lee 2, Thomas 1, Perry 1. **Cincinnati (9)**—Young 2, Boone 2, LaRue 2, Griffey Jr. 1, Reese 1, Casey 1. **Colorado (1)**—T. Walker 1. **Detroit (2)**—Palmer 1, Higginson 1. **Florida (4)**—Bautista 1, Floyd 1, Millar 1, Gonzalez 1. **Houston (15)**—Hidalgo 6, Bogar 2, Ward 2, Berkman 2, Cedeno 1, Chavez 1, Lugo 1. **Los Angeles (7)**—Aven 2, Beltre 2, Hundley 1, Hansen 1, Green 1. **Milwaukee (7)**—Burnitz 5, Hernandez 1, Loretta 1. **Montreal (3)**—White 2, V. Guerrero 1. **New York (5)**—*Agbayani 3, Ventura 1, Piazza 1. **Philadelphia (6)**—Jordan 2, Gant 1, Arias 1, Glanville 1, Abreu 1. **Pittsburgh (13)**—Cordero 4, Sojo 3, Giles 2, Young 1, Meares 1, Kendall 1, A. Ramirez 1. **St. Louis (4)**—Dunston 1, Clark 1, Renteria 1, Polanco 1. **San Diego (3)**—Nevin 2, DeHaan 1. **San Francisco (2)**—Aurilia 1, Rios 1.

*Note: Agbayani hit one of his home runs at Tokyo Stadium.

AT CINCINNATI (206):

Arizona (3)—Finley 1, Durazo 1, Cabrera 1. **Chicago A.L. (4)**—Thomas 2, Valentin 1, Norton 1. **Chicago N.L. (8)**—Sosa 3, Grace 1, Hill 1, Buford 1, Andrews 1. **Cincinnati (98)**—Griffey Jr. 22, Bichette 11, Ochoa 9, Casey 9, Stynes 8, Santiago 7, Tucker 7, B. Larkin 6, Young 6, Boone 5, Reese 3, Morris 1, Harnisch 1, Castro 1, LaRue 1, M. Bell 1. **Cleveland (3)**—Vizquel 1, Lofton 1. **Colorado (2)**—Helton 2. **Florida (10)**—Floyd 2, Lee 2, Kotsay 2, Bautista 1, Fox 1, Wilson 1, Lowell 1. **Houston (11)**—Bagwell 3, Hidalgo 3, Lugo 2, Biggio 1, Alou 1, Berkman 1. **Los Angeles (8)**—Elster 2, Hundley 2, Sheffield 1, Karros 1, Green 1, Hollandsworth 1. **Milwaukee (14)**—Jenkins 4, Burnitz 3, Grissom 1, Sweeney 1, Houston 1, Belliard 1, Collier 1, Sexson 1, Barker 1. **Minnesota (2)**—Canizaro 1, Jones 1. **Montreal (6)**—V. Guerrero 3, O'Brien 1, White 1, Tracy 1. **New York (4)**—Zeile 1, Pratt 1, Piazza 1, M. Franco 1. **Philadelphia (3)**—Lieberthal 1, Rolen 1, Abreu 1. **Pittsburgh (3)**—Benjamin 1, Giles 1, Kendall 1. **St. Louis (12)**—Davis 3, Edmonds 2, Renteria 2, Dunston 1, McGwire 1, Lankford 1, Marrero 1, Drew 1. **San Diego (10)**—Boone 5, Rivera 1, Klesko 1, Owens 1, Nicholson 1. **San Francisco (4)**—Mirabelli 2, Bonds 1, Martinez 1.

AT COLORADO (245):

Arizona (8)—Bell 2, Colbrunn 2, Williams 1, Gonzalez 1, Bautista 1, Womack 1. **Atlanta (5)**—C. Jones 2, A. Jones 1, Jordan 1. **Chicago (11)**—Sosa 3, Greene 2, Reed 1, Hill 1, Girardi 1, Buford 1, Zuleta 1, Gload 1. **Cincinnati (13)**—Griffey Jr. 4, Reese 2, Casey 2, B. Larkin 1, Bichette 1, Morris 1, Young 1, Cromer 1. **Colorado (112)**—Helton 27, Hammonds 14, Lansing 9, Cirillo 9, L. Walker 7, Shumpert 7, Hollandsworth 7, Perez 7, T. Walker 5, Goodwin 4, Mayne 3, Bragg 3, Huskey 2, Petrick 2, Bohanon 1, Servais 1, White 1, Hunter 1, Yoshii 1, Carpenter 1. **Florida (5)**—Wilson 2, Rodriguez 1, Kotsay 1, Castro 1. **Houston (12)**—Berkman 3, Caminiti 2, Alou 2, Bagwell 1, Hidalgo 2, Eusebio 1. **Los Angeles (12)**—Sheffield 2, Cora 2, Beltre 2, Hundley 1, Hansen 1, Donnels 1, Karros 1, Green 1, Grudzielanek 1. **Milwaukee (8)**—Grissom 2, Lopez 1, Houston 1, Sexson 1, Jenkins 1. **Montreal (8)**—Widger 2, Stevens 1, White 1, Mordecai 1, Vidro 1, Coquillette 1, Bergeron 1. **New York (4)**—Zeile 1, Pratt 1, Alfonzo 1, Mora 1. **Oakland (6)**—Saenz 1, J. Giambi 1, Tejada 1, Grieve 1, J. Giambi 1, Long 1. **Philadelphia (3)**—Perez 1, Bennett 1, Rolen 1. **Pittsburgh (2)**—Cordero 1, Giles 1. **St. Louis (8)**—Edmonds 2, Polanco 2, Davis 1, Howard 1, Tatis 1, Marrero 1. **San Diego (9)**—Klesko 2, Davis 2, Magadan 1, Mabry 1, Nevin 1, Rivera 1, Gonzalez 1. **San Francisco (17)**—Kent 3, Rios 3, Bonds 3, Mueller 2, Estalella 2, Davis 1, Aurilia 1, Hernandez 1, Lowery 1, Nathan 1. **Texas (5)**—Rodriguez 2, Palmeiro 1, Martinez 1, Clayton 1.

AT FLORIDA (152):

Arizona (6)—Gonzalez 2, Williams 1, Finley 1, Colbrunn 1, Miller 1. **Atlanta (3)**—Sanders 1, Jordan 1, Lopez 1. **Boston (2)**—Everett 1, Garciaparra 1. **Chicago (3)**—Buford 1, B. Brown 1, Nieves 1. **Cincinnati (3)**—B. Larkin 1, Bichette 1, Ochoa 1. **Colorado (3)**—Lansing 2, Manto 1. **Florida (71)**—Floyd 13, Wilson 12, Lowell 11, Lee 9, Millar 6, Kotsay 5, Gonzalez 5, M. Smith 2, Brown 2, Rodriguez 1, Bautista 1, Fox 1, Castillo 1, Berg 1, Burnett 1. **Houston (4)**—Biggio 1, Alou 1, Bagwell 1, Berkman 1. **Los Angeles (7)**—Sheffield 2, Beltre 2, Karros 1, Green 1, Santangelo 1. **Milwaukee (7)**—Jenkins 2, Hayes 1, Grissom 1, Burnitz 1, Lopez 1, Houston 1. **Montreal (7)**—Blum 3, V. Guerrero 1, Seguignol 1, Tracy 1, de la Rosa 1. **New York (6)**—Bell 3, Zeile 1, Piazza 1, Alfonzo 1. **Philadelphia (3)**—Gant 1, Abreu 1, Burrell 1. **Pittsburgh (1)**—Osik 1. **St. Louis (3)**—Clark 1, Paquette 1, Renteria 1. **San Diego (6)**—Nevin 3, Klesko 2, Mabry 1. **San Francisco (8)**—Burks 3, Kent 2, Bonds 1, Davis 1, Aurilia 1. **Tampa Bay (5)**—McGriff 3, Vaughn 1, Williams 1. **Toronto (4)**—Mondesi 1, Delgado 1, Stewart 1, Cruz 1.

AT HOUSTON (266):

Arizona (4)—Miller 2, Gonzalez 1, Lee 1. **Atlanta (9)**—A. Jones 3, Lopez 2, Sanders 1, Jordan 1, C. Jones 1, Furcal 1. **Chicago A.L. (4)**—Thomas 1, Durham 1, Lee 1, Singleton 1. **Chicago N.L. (14)**—Rodriguez 3, Gutierrez 3, Sosa 2, White 2, E. Young 1, Greene 1, Buford 1, Andrews 1. **Cincinnati (10)**—Griffey Jr. 3, Boone 2, B. Larkin 1, Tucker 1, Graves 1, Young 1, Reese 1. **Colorado (4)**—Helton 3, Cirillo 1. **Florida (6)**—Lee 1, Clapinski 1, Millar 1, Wilson 1, Gonzalez 1, Lowell 1. **Houston (135)**—Bagwell 28, Alou 17, Hidalgo 16, Ward 13, Meluskey 11, Berkman 10, Caminiti 9, Truby 9, Lugo 6, Bogar 3, Cedeno 3, Biggio 2, Spiers 2, Eusebio 2, Barker 2, Mieske 1, Ginter 1. **Kansas City (6)**—Fabregas 1, Randa 1, Damon 1, Sweeney 1, Dye 1, Quinn 1. **Los Angeles (5)**—Sheffield 4, Karros 1. **Milwaukee (6)**—Jenkins 3, Burnitz 2, Belliard 1. **Minnesota (2)**—Canizaro 1, LeCroy 1. **Montreal (5)**—Stevens 1, Vidro 1, Seguignol 1, Blum 1, Tracy 1. **New York (8)**—Payton 2, Hamilton 1, Ventura 1, Bell 1, Piazza 1, Abbott 1, Agbayani 1. **Philadelphia (9)**—Abreu 3, Glanville 2, Gant 1, Relaford 1, Rolen 1, Burrell 1. **Pittsburgh (10)**—Giles 3, Vander Wal 2, Young 1, Meares 1, A. Brown 1, Nunez 1, A. Ramirez 1. **St. Louis (13)**—Edmonds 3, Renteria 3, Howard 2, McGwire 1, Lankford 1, Vina 1, Perez 1, Drew 1. **San Diego (2)**—Martin 1, Klesko 1. **San Francisco (14)**—Bonds 4, Snow 2, Benard 2, Burks 1, Kent 1, Mueller 1, Mirabelli 1, Estalella 1, Rios 1.

AT LOS ANGELES (193):

Anaheim (4)—Glaus 3, Erstad 1. **Arizona (4)**—Williams 1, Colbrunn 1, Miller 1, Lee 1. **Atlanta (2)**—Joyner 1, Veras 1. **Chicago (3)**—Reed 1, Sosa 1, Gutierrez 1. **Cincinnati (8)**—Taubensee 2, Tucker 2, B. Larkin 1, Griffey Jr. 1, Reese 1, Boone 1. **Colorado (4)**—Mayne 1, Huskey 1, Perez 1, Helton 1. **Florida (4)**—Lee 3, Lowell 1. **Houston (9)**—Caminiti 2, Bagwell 2, Biggio 1, Alou 1, Cedeno 1, Hidalgo 1, Berkman 1. **Los Angeles (108)**—Sheffield 23, Karros 16, Green 15, Hundley 10, Elster 7, Beltre 7, Hollandsworth 6, Kreuter 4, Hansen 4, Grudzielanek 4, Donnels 3, White 2, Dreifort 2, Cora 2, Leyritz 1, Park 1, Valdes 1. **Milwaukee (4)**—Jenkins 3, Blanco 1. **Montreal (2)**—Cabrera 1, Seguignol 1. **New York (8)**—Alfonzo 2, Harris 1, Bell 1, Pratt 1, Piazza 1, Abbott 1, Trammell 1. **Oakland (2)**—Saenz 1, Chavez 1. **Philadelphia (4)**—Ducey 1, Lieberthal 1, Relaford 1, Burrell 1. **Pittsburgh (9)**—Cordero 2, Meares 2, Giles 2, Vander Wal 1, Young 1, Kendall 1. **St. Louis (5)**—McGwire 2, Edmonds 2, Drew 1. **San Diego (6)**—Boone 1, Klesko 1, Nevin 1, Rivera 1, Relaford 1, Gonzalez 1. **San Francisco (7)**—Bonds 2, Snow 1, Aurilia 1, Crespo 1, Estalella 1, Rios 1.

AT MILWAUKEE (151):

Arizona (5)—Finley 2, Bell 1, Lee 1, Durazo 1. **Atlanta (4)**—Galarraga 1, Lopez 1, Lockhart 1, Veras 1. **Chicago (5)**—Rodriguez 2, Reed 1, R. Brown 1, Patterson 1. **Cincinnati (7)**—Castro 2, Casey 2, Tucker 1, Stynes 1, M. Bell 1. **Cleveland (6)**—Justice 3, Fryman 1, Sexson 1, Branyan 1. **Colorado (3)**—Hammonds 2, Helton 1. **Detroit (3)**—Polonia 1, Easley 1, Becker 1. **Florida (2)**—Bautista 1, Lee 1. **Houston (9)**—Hidalgo 3, Caminiti 1, Alou 1, Bagwell 1, Bogar 1, Ward 1, Meluskey 1. **Los Angeles (1)**—Beltre 1. **Milwaukee (78)**—Jenkins 15, Burnitz 12, Hernandez 8, Sexson 7, Houston 6, Grissom 4, Casanova 4, Belliard 4, Lopez 3, Loretta 3, Blanco 3, Hayes 2, L. Mouton 2, Berry 1, J. Mouton 1, D'Amico 1, Echevarria 1, Rigdon 1. **Montreal (7)**—Vidro 2, Stevens 1, White 1, Widger 1, V. Guerrero 1, Cabrera 1. **New York (4)**—Ventura 1, Piazza 1, Abbott 1, Agbayani 1. **Philadelphia (2)**—Hunter 1, Lieberthal 1. **Pittsburgh (4)**—Benjamin 1, Vander Wal 1, Young 1, Giles 1. **St. Louis (3)**—Dunston 1, Lankford 1, Matheny 1. **San Diego (2)**—Nevin 1, Gonzalez 1. **San Francisco (6)**—Bonds 3, Burks 1, Kent 1, Snow 1.

AT MONTREAL (190):

Arizona (7)—Finley 4, Gonzalez 1, Colbrunn 1, Womack 1. **Atlanta (8)**—A. Jones 3, Bonilla 1, Sanders 1, Lopez 1, C. Jones 1, Furcal 1. **Baltimore (4)**—Belle 2, Surhoff 1, C. Johnson 1. **Chicago (8)**—Rodriguez 3, Sosa 2, Reed 1, Tapani 1, Buford 1. **Cincinnati (4)**—Taubensee 2, Griffey Jr. 1, Young 1. **Colorado (5)**—Helton 2, L. Walker 1, Bohanon 1, Perez 1. **Florida (8)**—M. Smith 2, Wilson 2, Fox 1, Lee 1, Kotsay 1, Castro 1. **Houston (7)**—Caminiti 1, Spiers 1, Alou 1, Eusebio 1, Hidalgo 1, Ward 1, Meluskey 1. **Los Angeles (6)**—White 1, Sheffield 1, Hundley 1, Hansen 1, Karros 1, Beltre 1. **Milwaukee (4)**—Jenkins 3, Belliard 1. **Montreal (88)**—V. Guerrero 25, Stevens 14, Vidro 11, Cabrera 7, Widger 6, Tracy 6, Blum 5, White 3, Bergeron 3, Mordecai 2, W. Guerrero 2, Lira 1, Seguignol 1, Bradley 1, de la Rosa 1. **New York A.L. (4)**—Martinez 1, Williams 1, Posada 1, Ledee 1. **New York N.L. (8)**—Zeile 2, Ventura 2, Alfonzo 2, Piazza 1, Payton 1. **Philadelphia (3)**—Gant 1, Lieberthal 1, Rolen 1. **Pittsburgh (4)**—Vander Wal 3, Kendall 1. **St. Louis (5)**—Edmonds 2, Clark 1, Tatis 1, Drew 1. **San Diego (5)**—Klesko 2, Boone 1, Nevin 1, Rivera 1. **San Francisco (7)**—Bonds 2, Snow 2, Aurilia 1, Benard 1, Estalella 1. **Toronto (5)**—Mondesi 3, Fletcher 1, Cruz 1.

AT NEW YORK (165):

Arizona (4)—Finley 2, Colbrunn 1, Lee 1. **Atlanta (7)**—Galarraga 2, Lopez 2, Jordan 1, C. Jones 1, A. Jones 1. **Baltimore (4)**—Ripken Jr. 2, Surhoff 1, Bordick 1. **Chicago (7)**—*Grace 2, *Andrews 2, Sosa 1, Rodriguez 1, Buford 1. **Cincinnati (3)**—Griffey Jr. 1, Taubensee 1, Young 1. **Colorado (3)**—Perez 1, Helton 1, Carpenter 1. **Florida (3)**—Lee 2, Wilson 2, Lowell 1, Floyd 1, Millar 1. **Houston (3)**—Bagwell 1, Cedeno 1, Hidalgo 1. **Los Angeles (5)**—Karros 2, White 1, Sheffield 1, Grudzielanek 1. **Milwaukee (5)**—Hayes 2, J. Mouton 1, Sexson 1, Jenkins 1. **Montreal (3)**—Seguignol 2, Vidro 1. **New York A.L. (1)**—Martinez 1. **New York N.L. (93)**—*Piazza 17, Alfonzo 13, Ventura 12, Payton 9, Agbayani 9, Zeile 8, Bell 8, Mora 4, Bordick 3, Abbott 3, Pratt 2, Harris 1, Johnson 1, M. Franco 1, Trammell 1, McEwing 1. **Philadelphia (7)**—Burrell 3, Rolen 2, Gant 1, Hunter 1. **Pittsburgh (3)**—Vander Wal 1, Young 1, Giles 1. **St. Louis (3)**—Lankford 2, Edmonds 1. **San Diego (2)**—Sprague 1, Nevin 1. **Tampa Bay (4)**—McGriff 1, Yan 1, Trammell 1, F. Martinez 1.

*Note: Totals for Grace, Andrews and Piazza include one home run for each at Tokyo Stadium.

AT PHILADELPHIA (158):

Arizona (10)—Gonzalez 2, Stinnett 2, Bell 1, Williams 1, Stottlemyre 1, Finley 1, Lee 1, Durazo 1. **Atlanta (13)**—C. Jones 4, A. Jones 3, Jordan 2, Galarraga 1, Sanders 1, Veras 1, Sisco 1. **Baltimore (1)**—Clark 1. **Boston (3)**—Everett 2, Garciaparra 1. **Chicago (5)**—Grace 2, Sosa 2, Rodriguez 1. **Cincinnati (2)**—Taubensee 1, Casey 1. **Colorado (2)**—Petrick 1, Carpenter 1. **Florida (7)**—Wilson 3, Lee 2, Kotsay 1, Millar 1. **Houston (7)**—Alou 3, Bagwell 2, Hidalgo 1, Truby 1. **Milwaukee (3)**—Grissom 1, Burnitz 1, Casanova 1. **Montreal (11)**—V. Guerrero 3, Vidro 2, White 2, Mordecai 1, Lira 1, Cabrera 1, Blum 1, Bergeron 1. **New York (8)**—Zeile 2, Piazza 2, Payton 2, Alfonzo 1, Perez 1. **Philadelphia (66)**—Abreu 14, Rolen 12, Gant 9, Lieberthal 8, Burrell 7, Ducey 4, Hunter 3, Glanville 3, Jordan 2, Arias 1, Brogna 1, Lee 1, Anderson 1. **Pittsburgh (4)**—Osik 1, E. Brown 1, A. Brown 1, Hyzdu 1. **St. Louis (9)**—McGwire 4, Edmonds 2, A. Benes 1, Paquette 1, Renteria 1. **San Diego (6)**—Nevin 2, Boone 1, Vitiello 1, Rivera 1, Relaford 1. **San Francisco (1)**—Rios 1.

AT PITTSBURGH (172):

Arizona (5)—Gonzalez 2, Bell 1, Williams 1, Colbrunn 1. **Atlanta (5)**—A. Jones 3, Jordan 1, C. Jones 1. **Chicago (4)**—Sosa 1, B. Brown 1, Nieves 1, R. Brown 1. **Cincinnati (8)**—Griffey Jr. 2, Casey 2, Tucker 1, Castro 1, Ochoa 1, Young 1. **Colorado (4)**—Hammonds 1, Huskey 1, T. Walker 1, Helton 1. **Detroit (1)**—D. Cruz 1. **Florida (5)**—Lee 3, Floyd 1, Wilson 1. **Houston (5)**—Bagwell 1, Bogar 1, Hidalgo 1, Ward 1, Lugo 1. **Kansas City (6)**—Dye 3, Johnson 1, Zaun 1, Sweeney 1. **Los Angeles (2)**—Green 1, Beltre 1. **Milwaukee (5)**—Houston 2, Blanco 2, Hayes 1. **Minnesota (2)**—Koskie 2. **Montreal (3)**—Vidro 2, Stevens 1. **New York (10)**—Ventura 3, Piazza 3, Zeile 1, Bell 1, Nunnally 1, Alfonzo 1. **Philadelphia (4)**—Prince 2, Bennett 1, Abreu 1. **Pittsburgh (86)**—Giles 16, Vander Wal 13, Young 11, Cordero 8, Meares 7, Kendall 7, Aven 4, A. Ramirez 4, Morris 3, Sojo 2, E. Brown 2, A. Brown 2, Hermansen 2, Wehner 1, Osik 1, Wilson 1, A. Ramirez 1, Hernandez 1. **St. Louis (8)**—McGwire 2, Matheny 2, Dunston 1, Howard 1, Vina 1, Tatis 1. **San Diego (5)**—Klesko 2, Nevin 1, Rivera 1, Jackson 1. **San Francisco (4)**—Bonds 1, Kent 1, Davis 1, Mueller 1.

AT ST. LOUIS (229):

Arizona (5)—Gonzalez 2, Bautista 2, Cabrera 1. **Atlanta (1)**—Galarraga 1. **Chicago (6)**—Andrews 3, Sosa 1, Matthews Jr. 1, Ojeda 1. **Cincinnati (9)**—Tucker 2, Stynes 2, Casey 2, Ochoa 1, LaRue 1, Cromer 1. **Cleveland (5)**—Sexson 2, Justice 1, Thome 1, Lofton 1. **Colorado (3)**—L. Walker 1, Hammonds 1, Helton 1. **Florida (8)**—Millar 2, Floyd 1, M. Smith 1, Lee 1, Kotsay 1, Wilson 1, Lowell 1. **Houston (12)**—Hidalgo 6, Bagwell 3, Alou 1, Berkman 1, Truby 1. **Kansas City (1)**—Dye 1. **Los Angeles (11)**—Karros 3, Sheffield 2, Hundley 2, Green 1, Gilbert 1, LoDuca 1, Beltre 1. **Milwaukee (9)**—Burnitz 3, Hayes 1, Houston 1, Belliard 1, Blanco 1, Jenkins 1, Barker 1. **Montreal (6)**—V. Guerrero 2, Seguignol 1, Blum 1, Bradley 1. **New York (10)**—Zeile 3, Ventura 2, Pratt 1, Piazza 1, Alfonzo 1, Trammell 1, Payton 1. **Philadelphia (1)**—Glanville 1. **Pittsburgh (9)**—Giles 3, Vander Wal 1, Young 1, Kendall 1, Osik 1, Wilson 1, A. Ramirez 1. **St. Louis (124)**—Edmonds 22, McGwire 18, Lankford 18, Paquette 13, Tatis 11, Drew 11, Dunston 6, Clark 6, Renteria 4, Davis 2, Matheny 2, Marrero 2, Polanco 2, Ankiel 2, McDonald 2, Hernandez 1, Howard 1, Vina 1. **San Diego (2)**—Klesko 1, Gonzalez 1. **San Francisco (7)**—Snow 3, Burks 2, Kent 1, Mirabelli 1.

AT SAN DIEGO (162):

Anaheim (4)—Vaughn 1, Walbeck 1, Anderson 1, Erstad 1. **Arizona (11)**—Finley 4, Bell 2, Durazo 2, Womack 1, Stinnett 1, Lee 1. **Atlanta (5)**—Galarraga 2, Jordan 1, T. Hubbard 1, A. Jones 1. **Chicago (3)**—Grace 1, Girardi 1, Sosa 1. **Cincinnati (9)**—Bichette 2, Griffey Jr. 2, Reese 2, Stynes 1, Young 1, Casey 1. **Colorado (6)**—Hollandsworth 3, Mayne 1, Hammonds 1, Cirillo 1. **Florida (4)**—Floyd 1, Kotsay 1, Wilson 1, Nunez 1. **Houston (6)**—Bagwell 3, Biggio 1, Alou 1, Reynolds 1. **Los Angeles (11)**—Hundley 3, Kreuter 1, Sheffield 1, Karros 1, Green 1, Park 1, Dreifort 1, Grudzielanek 1, Beltre 1. **Milwaukee (5)**—Grissom 1, Loretta 1, Houston 1, Casanova 1, Sexson 1. **Montreal (3)**—Vidro 2, Stevens 1. **New York (5)**—Zeile 1, Pratt 1, Piazza 1, Alfonzo 1, Agbayani 1. **Philadelphia (4)**—Burrell 2, Hunter 1, Rolen 1. **Pittsburgh (1)**—Kendall 1. **St. Louis (6)**—McGwire 1, Clark 1, Edmonds 1, Matheny 1, Marrero 1, Drew 1. **San Diego (72)**—Nevin 13, Klesko 9, Martin 8, Boone 8, Rivera 8, Jackson 5, Sprague 4, Owens 4, Mabry 3, Gwynn 1, Magadan 1, Hernandez 1, Vitiello 1, G. Williams 1, Davis 1, Darr 1, Newhan 1, Gonzalez 1, DeHaan 1. **San Francisco (4)**—Burks 1, Kent 1, Benard 1, Estalella 1. **Seattle (3)**—Olerud 2, Cameron 1.

AT SAN FRANCISCO (171):

Arizona (8)—Williams 2, Gonzalez 2, Stinnett 2, Lee 1, Cabrera 1. **Atlanta (3)**—C. Jones 2, Lopez 1. **Chicago (5)**—Rodriguez 2, Sosa 1, Nieves 1, Zuleta 1. **Cincinnati (4)**—B. Larkin 1, Santiago 1, Griffey Jr. 1, Young 1. **Florida (1)**—Millar 1. **Houston (2)**—Biggio 1, Alou 1. **Los Angeles (7)**—Elster 3, Sheffield 2, Hundley 1, Green 1. **Montreal (4)**—White 1, Widger 1, Cabrera 1, Barrett 1. **New York (3)**—Zeile 1, Piazza 1, Nunnally 1. **Oakland (4)**—Fasano 1, Tejada 1, Chavez 1, Hernandez 1. **Philadelphia (4)**—Gant 2, Jordan 1, Burrell 1. **Pittsburgh (3)**—Meares 1, Wilson 1, A. Ramirez 1. **St. Louis (7)**—Renteria 2, McGwire 1, Lankford 1, Vina 1, Sutton 1, Drew 1. **San Diego (3)**—Klesko 1, W. Williams 1, Mabry 1. **San Francisco (110)**—Bonds 25, Burks 15, Kent 14, Aurilia 12, Snow 10, Benard 6, Estalella 6, Davis 5, Martinez 4, Mueller 3, Mirabelli 2, Rios 2, Minor 2, Estes 1, Crespo 1, Nathan 1, Murray 1. **Seattle (2)**—Henderson 1, A. Rodriguez 1. **Texas (1)**—Palmeiro 1.

HISTORY

All-time results

Award winners

Hall of Fame

Team by team

ALL-TIME RESULTS
AMERICAN LEAGUE CHAMPIONS

Year	Team	Manager	Year	Team	Manager
1901—Chicago		Clark Griffith	1952—New York		Casey Stengel
1902—Philadelphia		Connie Mack	1953—New York		Casey Stengel
1903—Boston		Jimmy Collins	1954—Cleveland		Al Lopez
1904—Boston		Jimmy Collins	1955—New York		Casey Stengel
1905—Philadelphia		Connie Mack	1956—New York		Casey Stengel
1906—Chicago		Fielder Jones	1957—New York		Casey Stengel
1907—Detroit		Hugh Jennings	1958—New York		Casey Stengel
1908—Detroit		Hugh Jennings	1959—Chicago		Al Lopez
1909—Detroit		Hugh Jennings	1960—New York		Casey Stengel
1910—Philadelphia		Connie Mack	1961—New York		Ralph Houk
1911—Philadelphia		Connie Mack	1962—New York		Ralph Houk
1912—Boston		Jake Stahl	1963—New York		Ralph Houk
1913—Philadelphia		Connie Mack	1964—New York		Yogi Berra
1914—Philadelphia		Connie Mack	1965—Minnesota		Sam Mele
1915—Boston		Bill Carrigan	1966—Baltimore		Hank Bauer
1916—Boston		Bill Carrigan	1967—Boston		Dick Williams
1917—Chicago		Pants Rowland	1968—Detroit		Mayo Smith
1918—Boston		Ed Barrow	1969—Baltimore (East Division)		Earl Weaver
1919—Chicago		Kid Gleason	1970—Baltimore (East Division)		Earl Weaver
1920—Cleveland		Tris Speaker	1971—Baltimore (East Division)		Earl Weaver
1921—New York		Miller Huggins	1972—Oakland (West Division)		Dick Williams
1922—New York		Miller Huggins	1973—Oakland (West Division)		Dick Williams
1923—New York		Miller Huggins	1974—Oakland (West Division)		Al Dark
1924—Washington		Bucky Harris	1975—Boston (East Division)		Darrell Johnson
1925—Washington		Bucky Harris	1976—New York (East Division)		Billy Martin
1926—New York		Miller Huggins	1977—New York (East Division)		Billy Martin
1927—New York		Miller Huggins	1978—New York (East Division)		Billy Martin, Bob Lemon
1928—New York		Miller Huggins	1979—Baltimore (East Division)		Earl Weaver
1929—Philadelphia		Connie Mack	1980—Kansas City (West Division)		Jim Frey
1930—Philadelphia		Connie Mack	1981—New York (East Division)		Gene Michael, Bob Lemon
1931—Philadelphia		Connie Mack	1982—Milwaukee (East Division)		Buck Rodgers, Harvey Kuenn
1932—New York		Joe McCarthy	1983—Baltimore (East Division)		Joe Altobelli
1933—Washington		Joe Cronin	1984—Detroit (East Division)		Sparky Anderson
1934—Detroit		Mickey Cochrane	1985—Kansas City (West Division)		Dick Howser
1935—Detroit		Mickey Cochrane	1986—Boston (East Division)		John McNamara
1936—New York		Joe McCarthy	1987—Minnesota (West Division)		Tom Kelly
1937—New York		Joe McCarthy	1988—Oakland (West Division)		Tony La Russa
1938—New York		Joe McCarthy	1989—Oakland (West Division)		Tony La Russa
1939—New York		Joe McCarthy	1990—Oakland (West Division)		Tony La Russa
1940—Detroit		Del Baker	1991—Minnesota (West Division)		Tom Kelly
1941—New York		Joe McCarthy	1992—Toronto (East Division)		Cito Gaston
1942—New York		Joe McCarthy	1993—Toronto (East Division)		Cito Gaston
1943—New York		Joe McCarthy	1994—None†		
1944—St. Louis		Luke Sewell	1995—Cleveland (Central Division)		Mike Hargrove
1945—Detroit		Steve O'Neill	1996—New York (East Division)		Joe Torre
1946—Boston		Joe Cronin	1997—Cleveland (Central Division)		Mike Hargrove
1947—New York		Bucky Harris	1998—New York (East Division)		Joe Torre
1948—Cleveland*		Lou Boudreau	1999—New York (East Division)		Joe Torre
1949—New York		Casey Stengel	2000—New York (East Division)		Joe Torre
1950—New York		Casey Stengel			
1951—New York		Casey Stengel			

*Defeated Boston in one-game playoff. †New York finished the strike-shortened season with the league's best record.

NATIONAL LEAGUE CHAMPIONS

Year	Team	Manager	Year	Team	Manager
1876—Chicago		Albert Spalding	1890—Brooklyn		William McGunnigle
1877—Boston		Harry Wright	1891—Boston		Frank Selee
1878—Boston		Harry Wright	1892—Boston		Frank Selee
1879—Providence		George Wright	1893—Boston		Frank Selee
1880—Chicago		Adrian Anson	1894—Baltimore		Edward Hanlon
1881—Chicago		Adrian Anson	1895—Baltimore		Edward Hanlon
1882—Chicago		Adrian Anson	1896—Baltimore		Edward Hanlon
1883—Boston		John Morrill	1897—Boston		Frank Selee
1884—Providence		Frank Bancroft	1898—Boston		Frank Selee
1885—Chicago		Adrian Anson	1899—Brooklyn		Edward Hanlon
1886—Chicago		Adrian Anson	1900—Brooklyn		Edward Hanlon
1887—Detroit		William Watkins	1901—Pittsburgh		Fred Clarke
1888—New York		James Mutrie	1902—Pittsburgh		Fred Clarke
1889—New York		James Mutrie	1903—Pittsburgh		Fred Clarke

Year	Team	Manager
1904	New York	John McGraw
1905	New York	John McGraw
1906	Chicago	Frank Chance
1907	Chicago	Frank Chance
1908	Chicago	Frank Chance
1909	Pittsburgh	Fred Clarke
1910	Chicago	Frank Chance
1911	New York	John McGraw
1912	New York	John McGraw
1913	New York	John McGraw
1914	Boston	George Stallings
1915	Philadelphia	Pat Moran
1916	Brooklyn	Wilbert Robinson
1917	New York	John McGraw
1918	Chicago	Fred Mitchell
1919	Cincinnati	Pat Moran
1920	Brooklyn	Wilbert Robinson
1921	New York	John McGraw
1922	New York	John McGraw
1923	New York	John McGraw
1924	New York	John McGraw
1925	Pittsburgh	Bill McKechnie
1926	St. Louis	Rogers Hornsby
1927	Pittsburgh	Donie Bush
1928	St. Louis	Bill McKechnie
1929	Chicago	Joe McCarthy
1930	St. Louis	Gabby Street
1931	St. Louis	Gabby Street
1932	Chicago	Charlie Grimm
1933	New York	Bill Terry
1934	St. Louis	Frank Frisch
1935	Chicago	Charlie Grimm
1936	New York	Bill Terry
1937	New York	Bill Terry
1938	Chicago	Gabby Hartnett
1939	Cincinnati	Bill McKechnie
1940	Cincinnati	Bill McKechnie
1941	Brooklyn	Leo Durocher
1942	St. Louis	Billy Southworth
1943	St. Louis	Billy Southworth
1944	St. Louis	Billy Southworth
1945	Chicago	Charlie Grimm
1946	St. Louis*	Eddie Dyer
1947	Brooklyn	Burt Shotton
1948	Boston	Billy Southworth
1949	Brooklyn	Burt Shotton
1950	Philadelphia	Eddie Sawyer
1951	New York†	Leo Durocher
1952	Brooklyn	Charlie Dressen
1953	Brooklyn	Charlie Dressen
1954	New York	Leo Durocher
1955	Brooklyn	Walter Alston
1956	Brooklyn	Walter Alston
1957	Milwaukee	Fred Haney
1958	Milwaukee	Fred Haney
1959	Los Angeles‡	Walter Alston
1960	Pittsburgh	Danny Murtaugh
1961	Cincinnati	Fred Hutchinson
1962	San Francisco§	Al Dark
1963	Los Angeles	Walter Alston
1964	St. Louis	Johnny Keane
1965	Los Angeles	Walter Alston
1966	Los Angeles	Walter Alston
1967	St. Louis	Red Schoendienst
1968	St. Louis	Red Schoendienst
1969	New York (East Division)	Gil Hodges
1970	Cincinnati (West Division)	Sparky Anderson
1971	Pittsburgh (East Division)	Danny Murtaugh
1972	Cincinnati (West Division)	Sparky Anderson
1973	New York (East Division)	Yogi Berra
1974	Los Angeles (West Division)	Walter Alston
1975	Cincinnati (West Division)	Sparky Anderson
1976	Cincinnati (West Division)	Sparky Anderson
1977	Los Angeles (West Division)	Tommy Lasorda
1978	Los Angeles (West Division)	Tommy Lasorda
1979	Pittsburgh (East Division)	Chuck Tanner
1980	Philadelphia (East Division)	Dallas Green
1981	Los Angeles (West Division)	Tommy Lasorda
1982	St. Louis (East Division)	Whitey Herzog
1983	Philadelphia (East Division)	Pat Corrales, Paul Owens
1984	San Diego (West Division)	Dick Williams
1985	St. Loius (East Division)	Whitey Herzog
1986	New York (East Division)	Dave Johnson
1987	St. Louis (East Division)	Whitey Herzog
1988	Los Angeles (West Division)	Tommy Lasorda
1989	San Francisco (West Division)	Roger Craig
1990	Cincinnati (West Division)	Lou Piniella
1991	Atlanta (West Division)	Bobby Cox
1992	Atlanta (West Division)	Bobby Cox
1993	Philadelphia (East Division)	Jim Fregosi
1994	None∞	
1995	Atlanta (East Division)	Bobby Cox
1996	Atlanta (East Division)	Bobby Cox
1997	Florida (East Division)	Jim Leyland
1998	San Diego (West Division)	Bruce Bochy
1999	Atlanta (East Division)	Bobby Cox
2000	New York (East Division)	Bobby Valentine

*Defeated Brooklyn, two games to none, in playoff for pennant.

†Defeated Brooklyn, two games to one, in playoff for pennant.

‡Defeated Milwaukee, two games to none, in playoff for pennant.

§Defeated Los Angeles, two games to one, in playoff for pennant.

∞Montreal finished the strike-shortened season with the league's best record.

WORLD SERIES

Year	Winner	Loser	Games
1903	Boston A.L.	Pittsburgh N.L.	5-3
1904	No Series		
1905	New York N.L.	Philadelphia A.L.	4-1
1906	Chicago A.L.	Chicago N.L.	4-2
1907	Chicago N.L.	Detroit A.L.	*4-0
1908	Chicago N.L.	Detroit A.L.	4-1
1909	Pittsburgh N.L.	Detroit A.L.	4-3
1910	Philadelphia A.L.	Chicago N.L.	4-1
1911	Philadelphia A.L.	New York N.L.	4-2
1912	Boston A.L.	New York N.L.	*4-3
1913	Philadelphia A.L.	New York N.L.	4-1
1914	Boston N.L.	Philadelphia A.L.	4-0
1915	Boston A.L.	Philadelphia N.L.	4-1
1916	Boston A.L.	Brooklyn N.L.	4-1
1917	Chicago A.L.	New York N.L.	4-2
1918	Boston A.L.	Chicago N.L.	4-2
1919	Cincinnati N.L.	Chicago A.L.	5-3
1920	Cleveland A.L.	Brooklyn N.L.	5-2
1921	New York N.L.	New York A.L.	5-3
1922	New York N.L.	New York A.L.	*4-0
1923	New York A.L.	New York N.L.	4-2
1924	Washington A.L.	New York N.L.	4-3
1925	Pittsburgh N.L.	Washington A.L.	4-3
1926	St. Louis N.L.	New York A.L.	4-3
1927	New York A.L.	Pittsburgh, N.L.	4-0
1928	New York A.L.	St. Louis N.L.	4-0
1929	Philadelphia A.L.	Chicago N.L.	4-1
1930	Philadelphia A.L.	St. Louis N.L.	4-2
1931	St. Louis N.L.	Philadelphia A.L.	4-3
1932	New York A.L.	Chicago N.L.	4-0
1933	New York N.L.	Washington A.L.	4-1
1934	St. Louis N.L.	Detroit A.L.	4-3
1935	Detroit A.L.	Chicago N.L.	4-2
1936	New York A.L.	New York N.L.	4-2

Year	Winner	Loser	Games
1937—New York A.L.	New York N.L.	4-1
1938—New York A.L.	Chicago N.L.	4-0
1939—New York A.L.	Cincinnati N.L.	4-0
1940—Cincinnati N.L.	Detroit A.L.	4-3
1941—New York A.L.	Brooklyn N.L.	4-1
1942—St. Louis N.L.	New York A.L.	4-1
1943—New York A.L.	St. Louis N.L.	4-1
1944—St. Louis N.L.	St. Louis A.L.	4-2
1945—Detroit A.L.	Chicago N.L.	4-3
1946—St. Louis N.L.	Boston A.L.	4-3
1947—New York A.L.	Brooklyn, N.L.	4-3
1948—Cleveland A.L.	Boston N.L.	4-2
1949—New York A.L.	Brooklyn N.L.	4-1
1950—New York A.L.	Philadelphia N.L.	4-0
1951—New York A.L.	New York N.L.	4-2
1952—New York A.L.	Brooklyn N.L.	4-3
1953—New York A.L.	Brooklyn N.L.	4-2
1954—New York N.L.	Cleveland A.L.	4-0
1955—Brooklyn N.L.	New York A.L.	4-3
1956—New York A.L.	Brooklyn N.L.	4-3
1957—Milwaukee N.L.	New York A.L.	4-3
1958—New York A.L.	Milwaukee N.L.	4-3
1959—Los Angeles N.L.	Chicago A.L.	4-2
1960—Pittsburgh N.L.	New York A.L.	4-3
1961—New York A.L.	Cincinnati N.L.	4-1
1962—New York A.L.	San Francisco N.L.	4-3
1963—Los Angeles N.L.	New York A.L.	4-0
1964—St. Louis N.L.	New York A.L.	4-3
1965—Los Angeles N.L.	Minnesota A.L.	4-3
1966—Baltimore A.L.	Los Angeles N.L.	4-0
1967—St. Louis N.L.	Boston A.L.	4-3
1968—Detroit A.L.	St. Louis N.L.	4-3
1969—New York N.L.	Baltimore A.L.	4-1

Year	Winner	Loser	Games
1970—Baltimore A.L.	Cincinnati N.L.	4-1
1971—Pittsburgh N.L.	Baltimore A.L.	4-3
1972—Oakland A.L.	Cincinnati N.L.	4-3
1973—Oakland A.L.	New York N.L.	4-3
1974—Oakland A.L.	Los Angeles N.L.	4-1
1975—Cincinnati N.L.	Boston A.L.	4-3
1976—Cincinnati N.L.	New York A.L.	4-0
1977—New York A.L.	Los Angeles N.L.	4-2
1978—New York A.L.	Los Angeles N.L.	4-2
1979—Pittsburgh N.L.	Baltimore A.L.	4-3
1980—Philadelphia N.L.	Kansas City A.L.	4-2
1981—Los Angeles N.L.	New York A.L.	4-2
1982—St. Louis N.L.	Milwaukee A.L.	4-3
1983—Baltimore A.L.	Philadelphia N.L.	4-1
1984—Detroit A.L.	San Diego N.L.	4-1
1985—Kansas City A.L.	St. Louis N.L.	4-3
1986—New York N.L.	Boston A.L.	4-3
1987—Minnesota A.L.	St. Louis N.L.	4-3
1988—Los Angeles N.L.	Oakland A.L.	4-1
1989—Oakland A.L.	San Francisco N.L.	4-0
1990—Cincinnati N.L.	Oakland A.L.	4-0
1991—Minnesota A.L.	Atlanta N.L.	4-3
1992—Toronto A.L.	Atlanta N.L.	4-2
1993—Toronto A.L.	Philadelphia N.L.	4-2
1994—No Series		
1995—Atlanta N.L.	Cleveland A.L.	4-2
1996—New York A.L.	Atlanta N.L.	4-2
1997—Florida N.L.	Cleveland A.L.	4-3
1998—New York A.L.	San Diego N.L.	4-0
1999—New York A.L.	Atlanta N.L.	4-0
2000—New York A.L.	New York N.L.	4-1

*Includes tie game.

DIVISION SERIES

AMERICAN LEAGUE

Year	Winner (Division)	Loser (Division)	Games
1981—New York (East)	Milwaukee (East)	3-2
Oakland (West)	Kansas City (West)	3-0
1995—Cleveland (Central)	Boston (East)	3-0
Seattle (West)	New York* (East)	3-2
1996—New York (East)	Texas (West)	3-1
Baltimore (East)*	Cleveland (Central)	3-1
1997—Baltimore (East)	Seattle (West)	3-1
Cleveland (Central)	New York (East)*	3-2
1998—New York (East)	Texas (West)	3-0
Cleveland (Central)	Boston (East)*	3-1
1999—New York (East)	Texas (West)	3-0
Boston (East)*	Cleveland (Central)	3-2
2000—New York (East)	Oakland (West)	3-2
Seattle (West)*	Chicago (Central)	3-0

NATIONAL LEAGUE

Year	Winner (Division)	Loser (Division)	Games
1981—Montreal (East)	Philadelphia (East)	3-2
Los Angeles (West)	Houston (West)	3-2
1995—Atlanta (East)	Colorado* (West)	3-1
Cincinnati (Central)	Los Angeles (West)	3-0
1996—Atlanta (East)	Los Angeles (West)*	3-0
St. Louis (Central)	San Diego (West)	3-0
1997—Atlanta (East)	Houston (Central)	3-0
Florida (East)*	San Francisco (West)	3-0
1998—Atlanta (East)	Chicago (Central)*	3-0
San Diego (West)	Houston (Central)	3-1
1999—Atlanta (East)	Houston (Central)	3-1
New York (East)*	Arizona (West)	3-1
2000—St. Louis (Central)	Atlanta (East)	3-0
New York (East)*	San Francisco (West)	3-1

*Wild-card team.

CHAMPIONSHIP SERIES

AMERICAN LEAGUE

Year	Winner (Division)	Loser (Division)	Games
1969—Baltimore (East)	Minnesota (West)	3-0
1970—Baltimore (East)	Minnesota (West)	3-0
1971—Baltimore (East)	Oakland (West)	3-0
1972—Oakland (West)	Detroit (East)	3-2
1973—Oakland (West)	Baltimore (East)	3-2
1974—Oakland (West)	Baltimore (East)	3-1
1975—Boston (East)	Oakland (West)	3-0
1976—New York (East)	Kansas City (West)	3-2
1977—New York (East)	Kansas City (West)	3-2
1978—New York (East)	Kansas City (West)	3-1
1979—Baltimore (East)	California (West)	3-1
1980—Kansas City (West)	New York (East)	3-0
1981—New York (East)	Oakland (West)	3-0

Year	Winner (Division)	Loser (Division)	Games
1982—Milwaukee (East)	California (West)	3-2
1983—Baltimore (East)	Chicago (West)	3-1
1984—Detroit (East)	Kansas City (West)	3-0
1985—Kansas City (West)	Toronto (East)	4-3
1986—Boston (East)	California (West)	4-3
1987—Minnesota (West)	Detroit (East)	4-1
1988—Oakland (West)	Boston (East)	4-0
1989—Oakland (West)	Toronto (East)	4-1
1990—Oakland (West)	Boston (East)	4-0
1991—Minnesota (West)	Toronto (East)	4-1
1992—Toronto (East)	Oakland (West)	4-2
1993—Toronto (East)	Chicago (West)	4-2
1994—No series		
1995—Cleveland (Central)	Seattle (West)	4-2
1996—New York (East)	Baltimore (East)*	4-1

Year	Winner (Division)	Loser (Division)	Games
1997—Cleveland (Central)	Baltimore (East)	4-2
1998—New York (East)	Cleveland (Central)	4-2
1999—New York (East)	Boston (East)*	4-1
2000—New York (East)	Seattle (West)	4-2

NATIONAL LEAGUE

Year	Winner (Division)	Loser (Division)	Games
1969—New York (East)	Atlanta (West)	3-0
1970—Cincinnati (West)	Pittsburgh (East)	3-0
1971—Pittsburgh (East)	San Francisco (West)	3-1
1972—Cincinnati (West)	Pittsburgh (East)	3-2
1973—New York (East)	Cincinnati (West)	3-2
1974—Los Angeles (West)	Pittsburgh (East)	3-1
1975—Cincinnati (West)	Pittsburgh (East)	3-0
1976—Cincinnati (West)	Philadelphia (East)	3-0
1977—Los Angeles (West)	Philadelphia (East)	3-1
1978—Los Angeles (West)	Philadelphia (East)	3-1
1979—Pittsburgh (East)	Cincinnati (West)	3-0
1980—Philadelphia (East)	Houston (West)	3-2
1981—Los Angeles (West)	Montreal (East)	3-2

Year	Winner (Division)	Loser (Division)	Games
1982—St. Louis (East)	Atlanta (West)	3-0
1983—Philadelphia (East)	Los Angeles (West)	3-1
1984—San Diego (West)	Chicago (East)	3-2
1985—St. Louis (East)	Los Angeles (West)	4-2
1986—New York (East)	Houston (West)	4-2
1987—St. Louis (East)	San Francisco (West)	4-3
1988—Los Angeles (West)	New York (East)	4-3
1989—San Francisco (West)	Chicago (East)	4-1
1990—Cincinnati (West)	Pittsburgh (East)	4-2
1991—Atlanta (West)	Pittsburgh (East)	4-3
1992—Atlanta (West)	Pittsburgh (East)	4-3
1993—Philadelphia (East)	Atlanta (West)	4-2
1994—No series
1995—Atlanta (East)	Cincinnati (Central)	4-0
1996—Atlanta (East)	St. Louis (Central)	4-3
1997—Florida (East)*	Atlanta (East)	4-2
1998—San Diego (West)	Atlanta (East)	4-2
1999—Atlanta (East)	New York (East)*	4-2
2000—New York (East)*	St. Louis (Central)	4-1

*Wild-card team.

ALL-STAR GAME

Date	Site	Score (Winner)	Winning pitcher (Losing pitcher)	Winning manager (Losing manager)	Att.
7-6-33	Comiskey Park Chicago	4-2 (A.L.)	Lefty Gomez, Yankees (Bill Hallahan, Cardinals)	Connie Mack, Athletics (John McGraw, Giants)	47,595
7-10-34	Polo Grounds New York	9-7 (A.L.)	Mel Harder, Indians (Van Mungo, Dodgers)	Joe Cronin, Senators (Bill Terry, Giants)	48,363
7-8-35	Municipal Stadium Cleveland	4-1 (A.L.)	Lefty Gomez, Yankees (Bill Walker, Cardinals)	Mickey Cochrane, Tigers (Frankie Frisch, Cardinals)	69,831
7-7-36	Braves Field Boston	4-3 (N.L.)	Dizzy Dean, Cardinals (Lefty Grove, Red Sox)	Charlie Grimm, Cubs (Joe McCarthy, Yankees)	25,556
7-7-37	Griffith Stadium Washington	8-3 (A.L.)	Lefty Gomez, Yankees (Dizzy Dean, Cardinals)	Joe McCarthy, Yankees (Bill Terry, Giants)	31,391
7-6-38	Crosley Field Cincinnati	4-1 (N.L.)	Johnny Vander Meer, Reds (Lefty Gomez, Yankees)	Bill Terry, Giants (Joe McCarthy, Yankees)	27,067
7-11-39	Yankee Stadium New York	3-1 (A.L.)	Tommy Bridges, Tigers (Bill Lee, Cubs)	Joe McCarthy, Yankees (Gabby Hartnett, Cubs)	62,892
7-9-40	Sportsman's Park St. Louis	4-0 (N.L.)	Paul Derringer, Reds (Red Ruffing, Yankees)	Bill McKechnie, Reds (Joe Cronin, Red Sox)	32,373
7-8-41	Briggs Stadium Detroit	7-5 (A.L.)	Ed Smith, White Sox (Claude Passeau, Cubs)	Del Baker, Tigers (Bill McKechnie, Reds)	54,674
7-6-42	Polo Grounds New York	3-1 (A.L.)	Spud Chandler, Yankees (Mort Cooper, Cardinals)	Joe McCarthy, Yankees (Leo Durocher, Dodgers)	34,178
7-13-43	Shibe Park Philadelphia	5-3 (A.L.)	Dutch Leonard, Senators (Mort Cooper, Cardinals)	Joe McCarthy, Yankees (Billy Southworth, Cardinals)	31,938
7-11-44	Forbes Field Pittsburgh	7-1 (N.L.)	Ken Raffensberger, Phillies (Tex Hughson, Red Sox)	Billy Southworth, Cardinals (Joe McCarthy, Yankees)	29,589
1945	No game played.				
7-9-46	Fenway Park Boston	12-0 (A.L.)	Bob Feller, Indians (Claude Passeau, Cubs)	Steve O'Neill, Tigers (Charlie Grimm, Cubs)	34,906
7-8-47	Wrigley Field Chicago	2-1 (A.L.)	Frank Shea, Yankees (Johnny Sain, Braves)	Joe Cronin, Red Sox (Eddie Dyer, Cardinals)	41,123
7-13-48	Sportsman's Park St. Louis	5-2 (A.L.)	Vic Raschi, Yankees (Johnny Schmitz, Cubs)	Bucky Harris, Yankees (Leo Durocher, Dodgers)	34,009
7-12-49	Ebbets Field Brooklyn	11-7 (A.L.)	Virgil Trucks, Tigers (Don Newcombe, Dodgers)	Lou Boudreau, Indians (Billy Southworth, Braves)	32,577
7-11-50	Comiskey Park Chicago	4-3* (N.L.)	Ewell Blackwell, Reds (Ted Gray, Tigers)	Burt Shotton, Dodgers (Casey Stengel, Yankees)	46,127
7-10-51	Briggs Stadium Detroit	8-3 (N.L.)	Sal Maglie, Giants (Ed Lopat, Yankees)	Eddie Sawyer, Phillies (Casey Stengel, Yankees)	52,075
7-8-52	Shibe Park Philadelphia	3-2† (N.L.)	Bob Rush, Cubs (Bob Lemon, Indians)	Leo Durocher, Giants (Casey Stengel, Yankees)	32,785
7-14-53	Crosley Field Cincinnati	5-1 (N.L.)	Warren Spahn, Braves (Allie Reynolds, Yankees)	Chuck Dressen, Dodgers (Casey Stengel, Yankees)	30,846
7-13-54	Municipal Stadium Cleveland	11-9 (A.L.)	Dean Stone, Senators (Gene Conley, Braves)	Casey Stengel, Yankees (Walter Alston, Dodgers)	68,751
7-12-55	Milwaukee Co. Stadium Milwaukee	6-5‡ (N.L.)	Gene Conley, Braves (Frank Sullivan, Red Sox)	Leo Durocher, Giants (Al Lopez, Indians)	45,643
7-10-56	Griffith Stadium Washington	7-3 (N.L.)	Bob Friend, Pirates (Billy Pierce, White Sox)	Walter Alston, Dodgers (Casey Stengel, Yankees)	28,843
7-9-57	Busch Stadium St. Louis	6-5 (A.L.)	Jim Bunning, Tigers (Curt Simmons, Phillies)	Casey Stengel, Yankees (Walter Alston, Dodgers)	30,693

Date	Site	Score (Winner)	Winning pitcher (Losing pitcher)	Winning manager (Losing manager)	Att.
7-8-58	Memorial Stadium Baltimore	4-3 (A.L.)	Early Wynn, White Sox (Bob Friend, Pirates)	Casey Stengel, Yankees (Fred Haney, Braves)	48,829
7-7-59	Forbes Field Pittsburgh	5-4 (N.L.)	Johnny Antonelli, Giants (Whitey Ford, Yankees)	Fred Haney, Braves (Casey Stengel, Yankees)	35,277
8-3-59	Memorial Coliseum Los Angeles	5-3 (A.L.)	Jerry Walker, Orioles (Don Drysdale, Dodgers)	Casey Stengel, Yankees (Fred Haney, Braves)	55,105
7-11-60	Municipal Stadium Kansas City	5-3 (N.L.)	Bob Friend, Pirates (Bill Monbouquette, Red Sox)	Walter Alston, Dodgers (Al Lopez, White Sox)	30,619
7-13-60	Yankee Stadium New York	6-0 (N.L.)	Vernon Law, Pirates (Whitey Ford, Yankees)	Walter Alston, Dodgers (Al Lopez, White Sox)	38,362
7-11-61	Candlestick Park San Francisco	5-4§ (N.L.)	Stu Miller, Giants (Hoyt Wilhelm, Orioles)	Danny Murtaugh, Pirates (Paul Richards, Orioles)	44,115
7-31-61	Fenway Park Boston	1-1 (tie)		Paul Richards, Orioles (A.L.) Danny Murtaugh, Pirates (N.L.)	31,851
7-10-62	District of Col. Stad. Washington	3-1 (N.L.)	Juan Marichal, Giants (Camilo Pascual, Twins)	Fred Hutchinson, Reds (Ralph Houk, Yankees)	45,480
7-30-62	Wrigley Field Chicago	9-4 (A.L.)	Ray Herbert, White Sox (Art Mahaffey, Phillies)	Ralph Houk, Yankees (Fred Hutchinson, Reds)	38,359
7-9-63	Municipal Stadium Cleveland	5-3 (N.L.)	Larry Jackson, Cubs (Jim Bunning, Tigers)	Alvin Dark, Giants (Ralph Houk, Yankees)	44,160
7-7-64	Shea Stadium New York	7-4 (N.L.)	Juan Marichal, Giants (Dick Radatz, Red Sox)	Walter Alston, Dodgers (Al Lopez, White Sox)	50,850
7-13-65	Metropolitan Stadium Bloomington, Minn.	6-5 (N.L.)	Sandy Koufax, Dodgers (Sam McDowell, Indians)	Gene Mauch, Phillies (Al Lopez, White Sox)	46,706
7-12-66	Busch Stadium St. Louis	2-1§ (N.L.)	Gaylord Perry, Giants (Pete Richert, Senators)	Walter Alston, Dodgers (Sam Mele, Twins)	49,936
7-11-67	Anaheim Stadium Anaheim, Calif.	2-1∞ (N.L.)	Don Drysdale, Dodgers (Jim Hunter, Athletics)	Walter Alston, Dodgers (Hank Bauer, Orioles)	46,309
7-9-68	Astrodome Houston	1-0 (N.L.)	Don Drysdale, Dodgers (Luis Tiant, Indians)	Red Schoendienst, Cardinals (Dick Williams, Red Sox)	48,321
7-23-69	R.F.K. Stadium Washington	9-3 (N.L.)	Steve Carlton, Cardinals (Mel Stottlemyre, Yankees)	Red Schoendienst, Cardinals (Mayo Smith, Tigers)	45,259
7-14-70	Riverfront Stadium Cincinnati	5-4‡ (N.L.)	Claude Osteen, Dodgers (Clyde Wright, Angels)	Gil Hodges, Mets (Earl Weaver, Orioles)	51,838
7-13-71	Tiger Stadium Detroit	6-4 (A.L.)	Vida Blue, Athletics (Dock Ellis, Pirates)	Earl Weaver, Orioles (Sparky Anderson, Reds)	53,559
7-25-72	Atlanta Stadium Atlanta	4-3§ (N.L.)	Tug McGraw, Mets (Dave McNally, Orioles)	Danny Murtaugh, Pirates (Earl Weaver, Orioles)	53,107
7-24-73	Royals Stadium Kansas City	7-1 (N.L.)	Rick Wise, Cardinals (Bert Blyleven, Twins)	Sparky Anderson, Reds (Dick Williams, Athletics)	40,849
7-23-74	Three Rivers Stadium Pittsburgh	7-2 (N.L.)	Ken Brett, Pirates (Luis Tiant, Red Sox)	Yogi Berra, Mets (Dick Williams, Athletics)	50,706
7-15-75	Milwaukee Co. Stadium Milwaukee	6-3 (N.L.)	Jon Matlack, Mets (Jim Hunter, Yankees)	Walter Alston, Dodgers (Alvin Dark, Athletics)	51,480
7-13-76	Veterans Stadium Philadelphia	7-1 (N.L)	Randy Jones, Padres (Mark Fidrych, Tigers)	Sparky Anderson, Reds (Darrell Johnson, Red Sox)	63,974
7-19-77	Yankee Stadium New York	7-5 (N.L.)	Don Sutton, Dodgers (Jim Palmer, Orioles)	Sparky Anderson, Reds (Billy Martin, Yankees)	56,683
7-11-78	San Diego Stadium San Diego	7-3 (N.L.)	Bruce Sutter, Cubs (Rich Gossage, Yankees)	Tommy Lasorda, Dodgers (Billy Martin, Yankees)	51,549
7-17-79	Kingdome Seattle	7-6 (N.L.)	Bruce Sutter, Cubs (Jim Kern, Rangers)	Tommy Lasorda, Dodgers (Bob Lemon, Yankees)	58,905
7-8-80	Dodger Stadium Los Angeles	4-2 (N.L.)	Jerry Reuss, Dodgers (Tommy John, Yankees)	Chuck Tanner, Pirates (Earl Weaver, Orioles)	56,088
8-9-81	Municipal Stadium Cleveland	5-4 (N.L.)	Vida Blue, Giants (Rollie Fingers, Brewers)	Dallas Green, Phillies (Jim Frey, Royals)	72,086
7-13-82	Olympic Stadium Montreal	4-1 (N.L.)	Steve Rogers, Expos (Dennis Eckersley, Red Sox)	Tommy Lasorda, Dodgers (Billy Martin, Athletics)	59,057
7-6-83	Comiskey Park Chicago	13-3 (A.L.)	Dave Stieb, Blue Jays (Mario Soto, Reds)	Harvey Kuenn, Brewers (Whitey Herzog, Cardinals)	43,801
7-10-84	Candlestick Park San Francisco	3-1 (N.L.)	Charlie Lea, Expos (Dave Stieb, Blue Jays)	Paul Owens, Phillies (Joe Altobelli, Orioles)	57,756
7-16-85	Metrodome Minneapolis	6-1 (N.L.)	LaMarr Hoyt, Padres (Jack Morris, Tigers)	Dick Williams, Padres (Sparky Anderson, Tigers)	54,960
7-15-86	Astrodome Houston	3-2 (A.L.)	Roger Clemens, Red Sox (Dwight Gooden, Mets)	Dick Howser, Royals (Whitey Herzog, Cardinals)	45,774
7-14-87	Oak.-Alameda Co. Col. Oakland	2-0▲ (N.L.)	Lee Smith, Cubs (Jay Howell, Athletics)	Dave Johnson, Mets (John McNamara, Red Sox)	49,671
7-12-88	Riverfront Stadium Cincinnati	2-1 (A.L.)	Frank Viola, Twins (Dwight Gooden, Mets)	Tom Kelly, Twins (Whitey Herzog, Cardinals)	55,837
7-11-89	Anaheim Stadium Anaheim, Calif.	5-3 (A.L.)	Nolan Ryan, Rangers (John Smoltz, Braves)	Tony La Russa, Athletics (Tommy Lasorda, Dodgers)	64,036
7-10-90	Wrigley Field Chicago	2-0 (A.L.)	Bret Saberhagen, Royals (Jeff Brantley, Giants)	Tony La Russa, Athletics (Roger Craig, Giants)	39,071

Date	Site	Score (Winner)	Winning pitcher (Losing pitcher)	Winning manager (Losing manager)	Att.
7-9-91	SkyDome Toronto	4-2 (A.L.)	Jimmy Key, Blue Jays (Dennis Martinez, Expos)	Tony La Russa, Athletics (Lou Piniella, Reds)	52,383
7-14-92	Jack Murphy Stadium San Diego	13-6 (A.L.)	Kevin Brown, Rangers (Tom Glavine, Braves)	Tom Kelly, Twins (Bobby Cox, Braves)	59,372
7-13-93	Oriole Park at Camden Yards, Baltimore	9-3 (A.L.)	Jack McDowell, White Sox (John Burkett, Giants)	Cito Gaston, Blue Jays (Bobby Cox, Braves)	48,147
7-12-94	Three Rivers Stadium Pittsburgh	8-7§ (N.L.)	Doug Jones, Phillies (Jason Bere, White Sox)	Jim Fregosi, Phillies (Cito Gaston, Blue Jays)	59,568
7-11-95	Ballpark in Arlington Arlington, Texas	3-2 (N.L.)	Heathcliff Slocumb, Phillies (Steve Ontiveros, A's)	Felipe Alou, Expos (Buck Showalter, Yankees)	50,920
7-9-96	Veterans Stadium Philadelphia	6-0 (N.L.)	John Smoltz, Braves (Charles Nagy, Indians)	Bobby Cox, Braves (Mike Hargrove, Indians)	62,670
7-8-97	Jacobs Field Cleveland	3-1 (A.L.)	Jose Rosado, Royals (Shawn Estes, Giants)	Joe Torre, Yankees (Bobby Cox, Braves)	44,916
7-7-98	Coors Field Colorado	13-8 (A.L.)	Bartolo Colon, Indians (Ugueth Urbina, Expos)	Mike Hargrove, Indians (Jim Leyland, Marlins)	51,267
7-13-99	Fenway Park Boston	4-1 (A.L.)	Pedro Martinez, Red Sox (Curt Schilling, Phillies)	Joe Torre, Yankees (Bruce Bochy, Padres)	34,187
7-11-00	Turner Field Atlanta	6-3 (A.L.)	James Baldwin, White Sox (Al Leiter, Mets)	Joe Torre, Yankees (Bobby Cox, Braves)	51,323

*14 innings. †5 innings (rain). ‡12 innings. §10 innings. ∞15 innings. ▲13 innings.

AWARD WINNERS

MOST VALUABLE PLAYER

AMERICAN LEAGUE

Year	Player	Team	Pos.	Points
1929—Al Simmons		Philadelphia	OF	40
1930—Joe Cronin		Washington	SS	52
1931—Lou Gehrig		New York	1B	40
1932—Jimmie Foxx		Philadelphia	1B	46
1933—Jimmie Foxx		Philadelphia	1B	49
1934—Lou Gehrig		New York	1B	51
1935—Hank Greenberg		Detroit	1B	64
1936—Lou Gehrig		New York	1B	55
1937—Charley Gehringer		Detroit	2B	78
1938—Jimmie Foxx		Boston	1B	304
1939—Joe DiMaggio		New York	OF	280
1940—Hank Greenberg		Detroit	OF	292
1941—Joe DiMaggio		New York	OF	291
1942—Joe Gordon		New York	2B	270
1943—Spud Chandler		New York	P	246
1944—Bobby Doerr		Boston	2B	
1945—Eddie Mayo		Detroit	2B	

NATIONAL LEAGUE

Year	Player	Team	Pos.	Points
1929—No selection				
1930—Bill Terry		New York	1B	47
1931—Chuck Klein		Philadelphia	OF	40
1932—Chuck Klein		Philadelphia	OF	46
1933—Carl Hubbell		New York	P	64
1934—Dizzy Dean		St. Louis	P	57
1935—Arky Vaughan		Pittsburgh	SS	42
1936—Carl Hubbell		New York	P	61
1937—Joe Medwick		St. Louis	OF	70
1938—Ernie Lombardi		Cincinnati	C	229
1939—Bucky Walters		Cincinnati	P	303
1940—Frank McCormick		Cincinnati	1B	274
1941—Dolf Camilli		Brooklyn	1B	300
1942—Mort Cooper		St. Louis	P	263
1943—Stan Musial		St. Louis	OF	267
1944—Marty Marion		St. Louis	SS	
1945—Tommy Holmes		Boston	OF	

PLAYER AND PITCHER OF THE YEAR

AMERICAN LEAGUE

Year	Player	Team	Pos.
1944—Bobby Doerr		Boston	2B
	Hal Newhouser	Detroit	P
1945—Eddie Mayo		Detroit	2B
	Hal Newhouser	Detroit	P
1946—No selections			
1947—No selections			
1948—Lou Boudreau		Cleveland	SS
	Bob Lemon	Cleveland	P
1949—Ted Williams		Boston	OF
	Ellis Kinder	Boston	P
1950—Phil Rizzuto		New York	SS
	Bob Lemon	Cleveland	P
1951—Ferris Fain		Philadelphia	1B
	Bob Feller	Cleveland	P
1952—Luke Easter		Cleveland	1B
	Bobby Shantz	Philadelphia	P
1953—Al Rosen		Cleveland	3B
	Bob Porterfield	Washington	P
1954—Bobby Avila		Cleveland	2B
	Bob Lemon	Cleveland	P
1955—Al Kaline		Detroit	OF
	Whitey Ford	New York	P
1956—Mickey Mantle		New York	OF
	Billy Pierce	Chicago	P
1957—Ted Williams		Boston	OF
	Billy Pierce	Chicago	P
1958—Jackie Jensen		Boston	OF
	Bob Turley	New York	P
1959—Nellie Fox		Chicago	2B
	Early Wynn	Chicago	P
1960—Roger Maris		New York	OF
	Chuck Estrada	Baltimore	P
1961—Roger Maris		New York	OF
	Whitey Ford	New York	P
1962—Mickey Mantle		New York	OF
	Dick Donovan	Cleveland	P
1963—Al Kaline		Detroit	OF
	Whitey Ford	New York	P
1964—Brooks Robinson		Baltimore	3B
	Dean Chance	Los Angeles	P
1965—Tony Oliva		Minnesota	OF
	Jim Grant	Minnesota	P
1966—Frank Robinson		Baltimore	OF
	Jim Kaat	Minnesota	P

NATIONAL LEAGUE

Year	Player	Team	Pos.
1944— Marty Marion		St. Louis	SS
	Bill Voiselle	New York	P
1945— Tommy Holmes		Boston	OF
	Hank Borowy	Chicago	P
1946— No selections			
1947— No selections			
1948— Stan Musial		St. Louis	OF-1B
	Johnny Sain	Boston	P
1949— Enos Slaughter		St. Louis	OF
	Howard Pollet	St. Louis	P
1950— Ralph Kiner		Pittsburgh	OF
	Jim Konstanty	Philadelphia	P
1951— Stan Musial		St. Louis	OF
	Preacher Roe	Brooklyn	P
1952— Hank Sauer		Chicago	OF
	Robin Roberts	Philadelphia	P
1953— Roy Campanella		Brooklyn	C
	Warren Spahn	Milwaukee	P
1954— Willie Mays		New York	OF
	Johnny Antonelli	New York	P
1955— Duke Snider		Brooklyn	OF
	Robin Roberts	Philadelphia	P
1956— Hank Aaron		Milwaukee	OF
	Don Newcombe	Brooklyn	P
1957— Stan Musial		St. Louis	1B
	Warren Spahn	Milwaukee	P
1958— Ernie Banks		Chicago	SS
	Warren Spahn	Milwaukee	P
1959— Ernie Banks		Chicago	SS
	Sam Jones	San Francisco	P
1960— Dick Groat		Pittsburgh	SS
	Vern Law	Pittsburgh	P
1961— Frank Robinson		Cincinnati	OF
	Warren Spahn	Milwaukee	P
1962— Maury Wills		Los Angeles	SS
	Don Drysdale	Los Angeles	P
1963— Hank Aaron		Milwaukee	OF
	Sandy Koufax	Los Angeles	P
1964— Ken Boyer		St. Louis	3B
	Sandy Koufax	Los Angeles	P
1965— Willie Mays		San Francisco	OF
	Sandy Koufax	Los Angeles	P
1966— Roberto Clemente		Pittsburgh	OF
	Sandy Koufax	Los Angeles	P

Year	Player	Team	Pos.	Year	Player	Team	Pos.
1967—	Carl Yastrzemski	Boston	OF	1967—	Orlando Cepeda	St. Louis	1B
	Jim Lonborg	Boston	P		Mike McCormick	San Francisco	P
1968—	Ken Harrelson	Boston	OF	1968—	Pete Rose	Cincinnati	OF
	Denny McLain	Detroit	P		Bob Gibson	St. Louis	P
1969—	Harmon Killebrew	Minnesota	1B-3B	1969—	Willie McCovey	San Francisco	1B
	Denny McLain	Detroit	P		Tom Seaver	New York	P
1970—	Harmon Killebrew	Minnesota	3B	1970—	Johnny Bench	Cincinnati	C
	Sam McDowell	Cleveland	P		Bob Gibson	St. Louis	P
1971—	Tony Oliva	Minnesota	OF	1971—	Joe Torre	St. Louis	3B
	Vida Blue	Oakland	P		Ferguson Jenkins	Chicago	P
1972—	Dick Allen	Chicago	1B	1972—	Billy Williams	Chicago	OF
	Wilbur Wood	Chicago	P		Steve Carlton	Philadelphia	P
1973—	Reggie Jackson	Oakland	OF	1973—	Bobby Bonds	San Francisco	OF
	Jim Palmer	Baltimore	P		Ron Bryant	San Francisco	P
1974—	Jeff Burroughs	Texas	OF	1974—	Lou Brock	St. Louis	OF
	Jim Hunter	Oakland	P		Mike Marshall	Los Angeles	P
1975—	Fred Lynn	Boston	OF	1975—	Joe Morgan	Cincinnati	2B
	Jim Palmer	Baltimore	P		Tom Seaver	New York	P
1976—	Thurman Munson	New York	C	1976—	George Foster	Cincinnati	OF
	Jim Palmer	Baltimore	P		Randy Jones	San Diego	P
1977—	Rod Carew	Minnesota	1B	1977—	George Foster	Cincinnati	OF
	Nolan Ryan	California	P		Steve Carlton	Philadelphia	P
1978—	Jim Rice	Boston	OF	1978—	Dave Parker	Pittsburgh	OF
	Ron Guidry	New York	P		Vida Blue	San Francisco	P
1979—	Don Baylor	California	OF	1979—	Keith Hernandez	St. Louis	1B
	Mike Flanagan	Baltimore	P		Joe Niekro	Houston	P
1980—	George Brett	Kansas City	3B	1980—	Mike Schmidt	Philadelphia	3B
	Steve Stone	Baltimore	P		Steve Carlton	Philadelphia	P
1981—	Tony Armas	Oakland	OF	1981—	Andre Dawson	Montreal	OF
	Jack Morris	Detroit	P		Fernando Valenzuela	Los Angeles	P
1982—	Robin Yount	Milwaukee	SS	1982—	Dale Murphy	Atlanta	OF
	Dave Stieb	Toronto	P		Steve Carlton	Philadelphia	P
1983—	Cal Ripken Jr.	Baltimore	SS	1983—	Dale Murphy	Atlanta	OF
	LaMarr Hoyt	Chicago	P		John Denny	Philadelphia	P
1984—	Don Mattingly	New York	1B	1984—	Ryne Sandberg	Chicago	2B
	Willie Hernandez	Detroit	P		Rick Sutcliffe	Chicago	P
1985—	Don Mattingly	New York	1B	1985—	Willie McGee	St. Louis	OF
	Bret Saberhagen	Kansas City	P		Dwight Gooden	New York	P
1986—	Don Mattingly	New York	1B	1986—	Mike Schmidt	Philadelphia	3B
	Roger Clemens	Boston	P		Mike Scott	Houston	P
1987—	George Bell	Toronto	OF	1987—	Andre Dawson	Chicago	OF
	Jimmy Key	Toronto	P		Rick Sutcliffe	Chicago	P
1988—	Jose Canseco	Oakland	OF	1988—	Andy Van Slyke	Pittsburgh	OF
	Frank Viola	Minnesota	P		Orel Hershiser	Los Angeles	P
1989—	Ruben Sierra	Texas	OF	1989—	Kevin Mitchell	San Francisco	OF
	Bret Saberhagen	Kansas City	P		Mark Davis	San Diego	P
1990—	Cecil Fielder	Detroit	1B	1990—	Barry Bonds	Pittsburgh	OF
	Bob Welch	Oakland	P		Doug Drabek	Pittsburgh	P
1991—	Cal Ripken Jr.	Baltimore	SS	1991—	Barry Bonds	Pittsburgh	OF
	Roger Clemens	Boston	P		Tom Glavine	Atlanta	P

PITCHER OF THE YEAR

AMERICAN LEAGUE

Year	Pitcher	Team
1992—	Dennis Eckersley	Oakland
1993—	Jack McDowell	Chicago
1994—	Jimmy Key	New York
1995—	Randy Johnson	Seattle
1996—	Pat Hentgen	Toronto
1997—	Roger Clemens	Toronto
1998—	Roger Clemens	Toronto
1999—	Pedro Martinez	Boston
2000—	Pedro Martinez	Boston

NATIONAL LEAGUE

Year	Pitcher	Team
1992—	Greg Maddux	Chicago
1993—	Greg Maddux	Atlanta
1994—	Greg Maddux	Atlanta
1995—	Greg Maddux	Atlanta
1996—	John Smoltz	Atlanta
1997—	Pedro Martinez	Montreal
1998—	Kevin Brown	San Diego
1999—	Mike Hampton	Houston
2000—	Tom Glavine	Atlanta

ROOKIE OF THE YEAR

1946—Combined selection—Del Ennis, Philadelphia N.L., OF
1947—Combined selection—Jackie Robinson, Brooklyn N.L., 1B
1948—Combined selection—Richie Ashburn, Philadelphia N.L., OF

AMERICAN LEAGUE

Year	Player	Team	Pos.
1949—	Roy Sievers	St. Louis	OF
1950—	Whitey Ford	New York	P

NATIONAL LEAGUE

Year	Player	Team	Pos.
1949—	Don Newcombe	Brooklyn	P
1950—	Combined A.L.-N.L. selection		

Year	Player	Team	Pos.	Year	Player	Team	Pos.
1951—Minnie Minoso	Chicago	OF		1951—Willie Mays	New York	OF	
1952—Clint Courtney	St. Louis	C		1952—Joe Black	Brooklyn	P	
1953—Harvey Kuenn	Detroit	SS		1953—Jim Gilliam	Brooklyn	2B	
1954—Bob Grim	New York	P		1954—Wally Moon	St. Louis	OF	
1955—Herb Score	Cleveland	P		1955—Bill Virdon	St. Louis	OF	
1956—Luis Aparicio	Chicago	SS		1956—Frank Robinson	Cincinnati	OF	
1957—Tony Kubek	New York	IF-OF		1957—Ed Bouchee	Philadelphia	1B	
(No pitcher named)				Jack Sanford	Philadelphia	P	
1958—Albie Pearson	Washington	OF		1958—Orlando Cepeda	San Francisco	1B	
Ryne Duren	New York	P		Carlton Willey	Milwaukee	P	
1959—Bob Allison	Washington	OF		1959—Willie McCovey	San Francisco	1B	
1960—Ron Hansen	Baltimore	SS		1960—Frank Howard	Los Angeles	OF	
1961—Dick Howser	Kansas City	SS		1961—Billy Williams	Chicago	OF	
Don Schwall	Boston	P		Ken Hunt	Cincinnati	P	
1962—Tom Tresh	New York	OF-SS		1962—Ken Hubbs	Chicago	2B	
1963—Pete Ward	Chicago	3B		1963—Pete Rose	Cincinnati	2B	
Gary Peters	Chicago	P		Ray Culp	Philadelphia	P	
1964—Tony Oliva	Minnesota	OF		1964—Dick Allen	Philadelphia	3B	
Wally Bunker	Baltimore	P		Billy McCool	Cincinnati	P	
1965—Curt Blefary	Baltimore	OF		1965—Joe Morgan	Houston	2B	
Marcelino Lopez	California	P		Frank Linzy	San Francisco	P	
1966—Tommie Agee	Chicago	OF		1966—Tommy Helms	Cincinnati	3B	
Jim Nash	Kansas City	P		Don Sutton	Los Angeles	P	
1967—Rod Carew	Minnesota	2B		1967—Lee May	Cincinnati	1B	
Tom Phoebus	Baltimore	P		Dick Hughes	St. Louis	P	
1968—Del Unser	Washington	OF		1968—Johnny Bench	Cincinnati	C	
Stan Bahnsen	New York	P		Jerry Koosman	New York	P	
1969—Carlos May	Chicago	OF		1969—Coco Laboy	Montreal	3B	
Mike Nagy	Boston	P		Tom Griffin	Houston	P	
1970—Roy Foster	Cleveland	OF		1970—Bernie Carbo	Cincinnati	OF	
Bert Blyleven	Minnesota	P		Carl Morton	Montreal	P	
1971—Chris Chambliss	Cleveland	1B		1971—Earl Williams	Atlanta	C	
Bill Parsons	Milwaukee	P		Reggie Cleveland	St. Louis	P	
1972—Carlton Fisk	Boston	C		1972—Dave Rader	San Francisco	C	
Dick Tidrow	Cleveland	P		Jon Matlack	New York	P	
1973—Al Bumbry	Baltimore	OF		1973—Gary Matthews	San Francisco	OF	
Steve Busby	Kansas City	P		Steve Rogers	Montreal	P	
1974—Mike Hargrove	Texas	1B		1974—Greg Gross	Houston	OF	
Frank Tanana	California	P		John D'Acquisto	San Francisco	P	
1975—Fred Lynn	Boston	OF		1975—Gary Carter	Montreal	OF-C	
Dennis Eckersley	Cleveland	P		John Montefusco	San Francisco	P	
1976—Butch Wynegar	Minnesota	C		1976—Larry Herndon	San Francisco	OF	
Mark Fidrych	Detroit	P		Butch Metzger	San Diego	P	
1977—Mitchell Page	Oakland	OF		1977—Andre Dawson	Montreal	OF	
Dave Rozema	Detroit	P		Bob Owchinko	San Diego	P	
1978—Paul Molitor	Milwaukee	2B		1978—Bob Horner	Atlanta	3B	
Rich Gale	Kansas City	P		Don Robinson	Pittsburgh	P	
1979—Pat Putnam	Texas	1B		1979—Jeff Leonard	Houston	OF	
Mark Clear	California	P		Rick Sutcliffe	Los Angeles	P	
1980—Joe Charboneau	Cleveland	OF		1980—Lonnie Smith	Philadelphia	OF	
Britt Burns	Chicago	P		Bill Gullickson	Montreal	P	
1981—Rich Gedman	Boston	C		1981—Tim Raines	Montreal	OF	
Dave Righetti	New York	P		Fernando Valenzuela	Los Angeles	P	
1982—Cal Ripken Jr.	Baltimore	SS-3B		1982—Johnny Ray	Pittsburgh	2B	
Ed Vande Berg	Seattle	P		Steve Bedrosian	Atlanta	P	
1983—Ron Kittle	Chicago	OF		1983—Darryl Strawberry	New York	OF	
Mike Boddicker	Baltimore	P		Craig McMurtry	Atlanta	P	
1984—Alvin Davis	Seattle	1B		1984—Juan Samuel	Philadelphia	2B	
Mark Langston	Seattle	P		Dwight Gooden	New York	P	
1985 Ozzie Guillen	Chicago	SS		1985—Vince Coleman	St. Louis	OF	
Teddy Higuera	Milwaukee	P		Tom Browning	Cincinnati	P	
1986—Jose Canseco	Oakland	OF		1986—Robby Thompson	San Francisco	2B	
Mark Eichhorn	Toronto	P		Todd Worrell	St. Louis	P	
1987—Mark McGwire	Oakland	1B		1987—Benito Santiago	San Diego	C	
Mike Henneman	Detroit	P		Mike Dunne	Pittsburgh	P	
1988—Walt Weiss	Oakland	SS		1988—Mark Grace	Chicago	1B	
Bryan Harvey	California	P		Tim Belcher	Los Angeles	P	
1989—Craig Worthington	Baltimore	3B		1989—Jerome Walton	Chicago	OF	
Tom Gordon	Kansas City	P		Andy Benes	San Diego	P	
1990—Sandy Alomar Jr.	Cleveland	C		1990—David Justice	Atlanta	OF	
Kevin Appier	Kansas City	P		Mike Harkey	Chicago	P	
1991—Chuck Knoblauch	Minnesota	2B		1991—Jeff Bagwell	Houston	1B	
Juan Guzman	Toronto	P		Al Osuna	Houston	P	
1992—Pat Listach	Milwaukee	SS		1992—Eric Karros	Los Angeles	1B	
Cal Eldred	Milwaukee	P		Tim Wakefield	Pittsburgh	P	
1993—Tim Salmon	California	OF		1993—Mike Piazza	Los Angeles	C	
Aaron Sele	Boston	P		Kirk Rueter	Montreal	P	

Year	Player	Team	Pos.
1994—	Bob Hamelin	Kansas City	DH
	Brian Anderson	California	P
1995—	Garret Anderson	California	OF
	Julian Tavarez	Cleveland	P
1996—	Derek Jeter	New York	SS
	James Baldwin	Chicago	P
1997—	Nomar Garciaparra	Boston	SS
	Jason Dickson	Anaheim	P
1998—	Ben Grieve	Oakland	OF
	Rolando Arrojo	Tampa Bay	P
1999—	Carlos Beltran	Kansas City	OF
	Tim Hudson	Oakland	P
2000—	Mark Quinn	Kansas City	OF-DH
	Kazuhiro Sasaki	Seattle	P

Year	Player	Team	Pos.
1994—	Raul Mondesi	Los Angeles	OF
	Steve Trachsel	Chicago	P
1995—	Chipper Jones	Atlanta	3B
	Hideo Nomo	Los Angeles	P
1996—	Jason Kendall	Pittsburgh	C
	Alan Benes	St. Louis	P
1997—	Scott Rolen	Philadelphia	3B
	Matt Morris	St. Louis	P
1998—	Todd Helton	Colorado	1B
	Kerry Wood	Chicago	P
1999—	Preston Wilson	Florida	OF
	Scott Williamson	Cincinnati	P
2000—	Rafael Furcal	Atlanta	2B-SS
	Rick Ankiel	St. Louis	P

FIREMAN OF THE YEAR

AMERICAN LEAGUE

Year	Pitcher	Team
1960—	Mike Fornieles	Boston
1961—	Luis Arroyo	New York
1962—	Dick Radatz	Boston
1963—	Stu Miller	Baltimore
1964—	Dick Radatz	Boston
1965—	Eddie Fisher	Chicago
1966—	Jack Aker	Kansas City
1967—	Minnie Rojas	California
1968—	Wilbur Wood	Chicago
1969—	Ron Perranoski	Minnesota
1970—	Ron Perranoski	Minnesota
1971—	Ken Sanders	Milwaukee
1972—	Sparky Lyle	New York
1973—	John Hiller	Detroit
1974—	Terry Forster	Chicago
1975—	Rich Gossage	Chicago
1976—	Bill Campbell	Minnesota
1977—	Bill Campbell	Boston
1978—	Rich Gossage	New York
1979—	Mike Marshall	Minnesota
	Jim Kern	Texas
1980—	Dan Quisenberry	Kansas City
1981—	Rollie Fingers	Milwaukee
1982—	Dan Quisenberry	Kansas City
1983—	Dan Quisenberry	Kansas City
1984—	Dan Quisenberry	Kansas City
1985—	Dan Quisenberry	Kansas City
1986—	Dave Righetti	New York
1987—	Dave Righetti	New York
	Jeff Reardon	Minnesota
1988—	Dennis Eckersley	Oakland
1989—	Jeff Russell	Texas
1990—	Bobby Thigpen	Chicago
1991—	Dennis Eckersley	Oakland
	Bryan Harvey	California
1992—	Dennis Eckersley	Oakland
1993—	Jeff Montgomery	Kansas City
1994—	Lee Smith	Baltimore
1995—	Jose Mesa	Cleveland
1996—	John Wetteland	New York
1997—	Mariano Rivera	New York
1998—	Tom Gordon	Boston
1999—	Mariano Rivera	New York
2000—	Todd Jones	Detroit

NATIONAL LEAGUE

Year	Pitcher	Team
1960—	Lindy McDaniel	St. Louis
1961—	Stu Miller	San Francisco
1962—	Roy Face	Pittsburgh
1963—	Lindy McDaniel	Chicago
1964—	Al McBean	Pittsburgh
1965—	Ted Abernathy	Chicago
1966—	Phil Regan	Los Angeles
1967—	Ted Abernathy	Cincinnati
1968—	Phil Regan	L.A.-Chicago
1969—	Wayne Granger	Cincinnati
1970—	Wayne Granger	Cincinnati
1971—	Dave Giusti	Pittsburgh
1972—	Clay Carroll	Cincinnati
1973—	Mike Marshall	Montreal
1974—	Mike Marshall	Los Angeles
1975—	Al Hrabosky	St. Louis
1976—	Rawly Eastwick	Cincinnati
1977—	Rollie Fingers	San Diego
1978—	Rollie Fingers	San Diego
1979—	Bruce Sutter	Chicago
1980—	Rollie Fingers	San Diego
	Tom Hume	Cincinnati
1981—	Bruce Sutter	St. Louis
1982—	Bruce Sutter	St. Louis
1983—	Al Holland	Philadelphia
	Lee Smith	Chicago
1984—	Bruce Sutter	St. Louis
1985—	Jeff Reardon	Montreal
1986—	Todd Worrell	St. Louis
1987—	Steve Bedrosian	Philadelphia
1988—	John Franco	Cincinnati
1989—	Mark Davis	San Diego
1990—	John Franco	New York
1991—	Lee Smith	St. Louis
1992—	Doug Jones	Houston
	Lee Smith	St. Louis
1993—	Randy Myers	Chicago
1994—	John Franco	New York
1995—	Randy Myers	Chicago
1996—	Trevor Hoffman	San Diego
1997—	Jeff Shaw	Cincinnati
1998—	Trevor Hoffman	San Diego
1999—	Ugueth Urbina	Montreal
2000—	Antonio Alfonseca	Florida

COMEBACK PLAYER OF THE YEAR

AMERICAN LEAGUE

Year	Pitcher	Team
1965—	Norm Cash	Detroit
1966—	Boog Powell	Baltimore
1967—	Dean Chance	Minnesota
1968—	Ken Harrelson	Boston

NATIONAL LEAGUE

Year	Pitcher	Team
1965—	Vernon Law	Pittsburgh
1966—	Phil Regan	Los Angeles
1967—	Mike McCormick	San Francisco
1968—	Alex Johnson	Cincinnati

Year	Pitcher	Team	Year	Pitcher	Team
1969—Tony Conigliaro	Boston		1969— Tommie Agee	New York
1970—Clyde Wright	California		1970— Jim Hickman	Chicago
1971—Norm Cash	Detroit		1971— Al Downing	Los Angeles
1972—Luis Tiant	Boston		1972— Bobby Tolan	Cincinnati
1973—John Hiller	Detroit		1973— Dave Johnson	Atlanta
1974—Ferguson Jenkins	Texas		1974— Jim Wynn	Los Angeles
1975—Boog Powell	Cleveland		1975— Randy Jones	San Diego
1976—Dock Ellis	New York		1976— Tommy John	Los Angeles
1977—Eric Soderholm	Chicago		1977— Willie McCovey	San Francisco
1978—Mike Caldwell	Milwaukee		1978— Willie Stargell	Pittsburgh
1979—Willie Horton	Seattle		1979— Lou Brock	St. Louis
1980—Matt Keough	Oakland		1980— Jerry Reuss	Los Angeles
1981—Richie Zisk	Seattle		1981— Bob Knepper	Houston
1982—Andre Thornton	Cleveland		1982— Joe Morgan	San Francisco
1983—Alan Trammell	Detroit		1983— John Denny	Philadelphia
1984—Dave Kingman	Oakland		1984— Joaquin Andujar	St. Louis
1985—Gorman Thomas	Seattle		1985— Rick Reuschel	Pittsburgh
1986—John Candelaria	California		1986— Ray Knight	New York
1987—Bret Saberhagen	Kansas City		1987— Rick Sutcliffe	Chicago
1988—Storm Davis	Oakland		1988— Tim Leary	Los Angeles
1989—Bert Blyleven	California		1989— Lonnie Smith	Atlanta
1990—Dave Winfield	California		1990— John Tudor	St. Louis
1991—Jose Guzman	Texas		1991— Terry Pendleton	Atlanta
1992—Rick Sutcliffe	Baltimore		1992— Gary Sheffield	San Diego
1993—Bo Jackson	Chicago		1993— Andres Galarraga	Colorado
1994—Jose Canseco	Texas		1994— Tim Wallach	Los Angeles
1995—Tim Wakefield	Boston		1995— Ron Gant	Cincinnati
1996—Kevin Elster	Texas		1996— Eric Davis	Cincinnati
1997—David Justice	Cleveland		1997— Darren Daulton	Phi.-Fla.
1998—Bret Saberhagen	Boston		1998— Greg Vaughn	San Diego
1999—John Jaha	Oakland		1999— Rickey Henderson	New York
2000—Frank Thomas	Chicago		2000— Andres Galarraga	Atlanta

MAJOR LEAGUE PLAYER OF THE YEAR

Year	Player	Team	Year	Player	Team	Year	Player	Team
1936—Carl Hubbell	New York N.L.		1958—Bob Turley	New York A.L.		1979—Willie Stargell	Pittsburgh N.L.
1937—Johnny Allen	Cleveland A.L.		1959—Early Wynn	Chicago A.L.		1980—George Brett	Kansas City A.L.
1938—Johnny Vander Meer	Cincinnati N.L.		1960—Bill Mazeroski	Pittsburgh N.L.		1981—Fernando Valenzuela	Los Angeles N.L.
1939—Joe DiMaggio	New York A.L.		1961—Roger Maris	New York A.L.		1982—Robin Yount	Milwaukee A.L.
1940—Bob Feller	Cleveland A.L.		1962—Maury Wills	Los Angeles N.L.		1983—Cal Ripken Jr.	Baltimore A.L.
1941—Ted Williams	Boston A.L.		Don Drysdale	Los Angeles N.L.		1984—Ryne Sandberg	Chicago N.L.
1942—Ted Williams	Boston A.L.		1963—Sandy Koufax	Los Angeles N.L.		1985—Don Mattingly	New York A.L.
1943—Spud Chandler	New York A.L.		1964—Ken Boyer	St. Louis N.L.		1986—Roger Clemens	Boston A.L.
1944—Marty Marion	St. Louis N.L.		1965—Sandy Koufax	Los Angeles N.L.		1987—George Bell	Toronto A.L.
1945—Hal Newhouser	Detroit A.L.		1966—Frank Robinson	Baltimore A.L.		1988—Orel Hershiser	Los Angeles N.L.
1946—Stan Musial	St. Louis N.L.		1967—Carl Yastrzemski	Boston A.L.		1989—Kevin Mitchell	San Francisco N.L.
1947—Ted Williams	Boston A.L.		1968—Denny McLain	Detroit A.L.		1990—Barry Bonds	Pittsburgh N.L.
1948—Lou Boudreau	Cleveland A.L.		1969—Willie McCovey	San Francisco N.L.		1991—Cal Ripken Jr.	Baltimore A.L.
1949—Ted Williams	Boston A.L.		1970—Johnny Bench	Cincinnati N.L.		1992—Gary Sheffield	San Diego N.L.
1950—Phil Rizzuto	New York A.L.		1971—Joe Torre	St. Louis N.L.		1993—Frank Thomas	Chicago A.L.
1951—Stan Musial	St. Louis N.L.		1972—Billy Williams	Chicago N.L.		1994—Jeff Bagwell	Houston N.L.
1952—Robin Roberts	Philadelphia N.L.		1973—Reggie Jackson	Oakland A.L.		1995—Albert Belle	Cleveland A.L.
1953—Al Rosen	Cleveland A.L.		1974—Lou Brock	St. Louis N.L.		1996—Alex Rodriguez	Seattle A.L.
1954—Willie Mays	New York N.L.		1975—Joe Morgan	Cincinnati N.L.		1997—Ken Griffey Jr.	Seattle A.L.
1955—Duke Snider	Brooklyn N.L.		1976—Joe Morgan	Cincinnati N.L.		1998—Sammy Sosa	Chicago N.L.
1956—Mickey Mantle	New York A.L.		1977—Rod Carew	Minnesota A.L.		1999—Rafael Palmeiro	Texas A.L.
1957—Ted Williams	Boston A.L.		1978—Ron Guidry	New York A.L.		2000—Carlos Delgado	Toronto A.L.

MAJOR LEAGUE MANAGER OF THE YEAR

Year	Manager	Team	Year	Manager	Team	Year	Manager	Team
1936—Joe McCarthy	New York A.L.		1949—Casey Stengel	New York A.L.		1962—Bill Rigney	Los Angeles A.L.
1937—Bill McKechnie	Boston N.L.		1950—Red Rolfe	Detroit A.L.		1963—Walter Alston	Los Angeles N.L.
1938—Joe McCarthy	New York A.L.		1951—Leo Durocher	New York N.L.		1964—Johnny Keane	St. Louis N.L.
1939—Leo Durocher	Brooklyn N.L.		1952—Eddie Stanky	St. Louis N.L.		1965—Sam Mele	Minnesota A.L.
1940—Bill McKechnie	Cincinnati N.L.		1953—Casey Stengel	New York A.L.		1966—Hank Bauer	Baltimore A.L.
1941—Billy Southworth	St. Louis N.L.		1954—Leo Durocher	New York N.L.		1967—Dick Williams	Boston A.L.
1942—Billy Southworth	St. Louis N.L.		1955—Walter Alston	Brooklyn N.L.		1968—Mayo Smith	Detroit A.L.
1943—Joe McCarthy	New York A.L.		1956—Birdie Tebbetts	Cincinnati N.L.		1969—Gil Hodges	New York N.L.
1944—Luke Sewell	St. Louis A.L.		1957—Fred Hutchinson	St. Louis N.L.		1970—Danny Murtaugh	Pittsburgh N.L.
1945—Ossie Bluege	Washington A.L.		1958—Casey Stengel	New York A.L.		1971—Charlie Fox	San Francisco N.L.
1946—Eddie Dyer	St. Louis N.L.		1959—Walter A.L.ston	Los Angeles N.L.		1972—Chuck Tanner	Chicago A.L.
1947—Bucky Harris	New York A.L.		1960—Danny Murtaugh	Pittsburgh N.L.		1973—Gene Mauch	Montreal N.L.
1948—Bill Meyer	Pittsburgh N.L.		1961—Ralph Houk	New York A.L.		1974—Bill Virdon	New York A.L.

Year	Manager	Team
1975—Darrell Johnson	Boston A.L.
1976—Danny Ozark	Philadelphia N.L.
1977—Earl Weaver	Baltimore A.L.
1978—George Bamberger	Milwaukee A.L.
1979—Earl Weaver	Baltimore A.L.
1980—Bill Virdon	Houston N.L.
1981—Billy Martin	Oakland A.L.
1982—Whitey Herzog	St. Louis N.L.
1983—Tony La Russa	Chicago A.L.
1984—Jim Frey	Chicago N.L.
1985—Bobby Cox	Toronto A.L.
1986—John McNamara	Boston A.L.
Hal Lanier	Houston N.L.
1987—Sparky Anderson	Detroit A.L.
Buck Rodgers	Montreal N.L.

Year	Manager	Team
1988—Tony La Russa	Oakland A.L.
Tom Lasorda	L.A. N.L. (tie)
Jim Leyland	Pit. N.L. (tie)
1989—Frank Robinson	Baltimore A.L.
Don Zimmer	Chicago N.L.
1990—Jeff Torborg	Chicago A.L.
Jim Leyland	Pittsburgh N.L.
1991—Tom Kelly	Minnesota A.L.
Bobby Cox	Atlanta N.L.
1992—Tony La Russa	Oakland A.L.
Jim Leyland	Pittsburgh N.L.
1993—Johnny Oates	Baltimore A.L.
Bobby Cox	Atlanta N.L.
1994—Buck Showalter	New York A.L.
Felipe Alou	Montreal N.L.

Year	Manager	Team
1995—Mike Hargrove	Cleveland A.L.
Don Baylor	Colorado N.L.
1996—Johnny Oates	Texas A.L.
Bruce Bochy	San Diego N.L.
1997—Dave Johnson	Baltimore A.L.
Dusty Baker	San Fran. N.L.
1998—Joe Torre	New York A.L.
Bruce Bochy	San Diego N.L.
1999—Jimy Williams	Boston A.L.
Bobby Cox	Atlanta N.L.
2000—Jerry Manuel	Chicago A.L.
Dusty Baker	San Fran. N.L.

MAJOR LEAGUE EXECUTIVE OF THE YEAR

Year	Executive	Team
1936—Branch Rickey	St. Louis N.L.
1937—Ed Barrow	New York A.L.
1938—Warren Giles	Cincinnati N.L.
1939—Larry MacPhail	Brooklyn N.L.
1940—Walter Briggs Sr.	Detroit A.L.
1941—Ed Barrow	New York A.L.
1942—Branch Rickey	St. Louis N.L.
1943—Clark Griffith	Washington A.L.
1944—Billy DeWitt	St. Louis A.L.
1945—Phil Wrigley	Chicago N.L.
1946—Tom Yawkey	Boston A.L.
1947—Branch Rickey	Brooklyn N.L.
1948—Bill Veeck	Cleveland A.L.
1949—Bob Carpenter	Philadelphia N.L.
1950—George Weiss	New York A.L.
1951—George Weiss	New York A.L.
1952—George Weiss	New York A.L.
1953—Lou Perini	Milwaukee N.L.
1954—Horace Stoneham	New York N.L.
1955—Walter O'Malley	Brooklyn N.L.
1956—Gabe Paul	Cincinnati N.L.
1957—Frank Lane	St. Louis N.L.

Year	Executive	Team
1958—Joe Brown	Pittsburgh N.L.
1959—Buzzie Bavasi	L.A. N.L.
1960—George Weiss	New York A.L.
1961—Dan Topping	New York A.L.
1962—Fred Haney	Los Angeles A.L.
1963—Bing Devine	St. Louis N.L.
1964—Bing Devine	St. Louis N.L.
1965—Cal Griffith	Minnesota A.L.
1966—Lee MacPhail	Commissioner's Office
1967—Dick O'Connell	Boston A.L.
1968—Jim Campbell	Detroit A.L.
1969—John Murphy	New York N.L.
1970—Harry Dalton	Baltimore A.L.
1971—Cedric Tallis	Kansas City A.L.
1972—Roland Hemond	Chicago A.L.
1973—Bob Howsam	Cincinnati N.L.
1974—Gabe Paul	New York A.L.
1975—Dick O'Connell	Boston A.L.
1976—Joe Burke	Kansas City A.L.
1977—Bill Veeck	Chicago A.L.
1978—Spec Richardson	San Francisco N.L.
1979—Hank Peters	Baltimore A.L.

Year	Executive	Team
1980—Tal Smith	Houston N.L.
1981—John McHale	Montreal N.L.
1982—Harry Dalton	Milwaukee A.L.
1983—Hank Peters	Baltimore A.L.
1984—Dallas Green	Chicago N.L.
1985—John Schuerholz	Kansas City A.L.
1986—Frank Cashen	New York N.L.
1987—Al Rosen	San Francisco N.L.
1988—Fred Claire	Los Angeles N.L.
1989—Roland Hemond	Baltimore A.L.
1990—Bob Quinn	Cincinnati N.L.
1991—Andy MacPhail	Minnesota A.L.
1992—Dan Duquette	Montreal N.L.
1993—Lee Thomas	Philadelphia N.L.
1994—John Hart	Cleveland A.L.
1995—John Hart	Cleveland A.L.
1996—Doug Melvin	Texas A.L.
1997—Cam Bonifay	Pittsburgh N.L.
1998—Gerry Hunsicker	Houston N.L.
1999—Billy Beane	Oakland A.L.
2000—Walt Jocketty	St. Louis N.L.

MAJOR LEAGUE ALL-STAR TEAMS

1925
1B— Jim Bottomley, St. Louis N.L.
2B— Rogers Hornsby, St. Louis N.L.
SS— Glenn Wright, Pittsburgh N.L.
3B— Pie Traynor, Pittsburgh N.L.
OF— Kiki Cuyler, Pittsburgh N.L.
OF— Max Carey, Pittsburgh N.L.
OF— Goose Goslin, Washington A.L.
C— Mickey Cochrane, Phil. A.L.
P— Walter Johnson, Washington A.L.
P— Ed Rommel, Philadelphia A.L.
P— Dazzy Vance, Brooklyn N.L.

1926
1B— George Burns, Cleveland A.L.
2B— Rogers Hornsby, St. Louis N.L.
SS— Joe Sewell, Cleveland A.L.
3B— Pie Traynor, Pittsburgh N.L.
OF— Goose Goslin, Washington A.L.
OF— John Mostil, Chicago A.L.
OF— Babe Ruth, New York A.L.
C— Bob O'Farrell, St. Louis N.L.
P— Herb Pennock, New York A.L.
P— George Uhle, Cleveland A.L.
P— Grover Alexander, St. Louis N.L.

1927
1B— Lou Gehrig, New York A.L.
2B— Rogers Hornsby, New York N.L.
SS— Travis Jackson, New York N.L.
3B— Pie Traynor, Pittsburgh N.L.
OF— Babe Ruth, New York A.L.

1928
1B— Lou Gehrig, New York A.L.
2B— Rogers Hornsby, Boston N.L.
SS— Travis Jackson, New York N.L.
3B— Fred Lindstrom, New York N.L.
OF— Babe Ruth, New York A.L.
OF— Heinie Manush, St. Louis A.L.
OF— Paul Waner, Pittsburgh N.L.
C— Mickey Cochrane, Phil. A.L.
P— Lefty Grove, Philadelphia A.L.
P— Waite Hoyt, New York A.L.

1929
1B— Jimmie Foxx, Philadelphia A.L.
2B— Rogers Hornsby, Chicago N.L.
SS— Travis Jackson, New York N.L.
3B— Pie Traynor, Pittsburgh, N.L.
OF— Al Simmons, Philadelphia A.L.
OF— Hack Wilson, Chicago N.L.
OF— Babe Ruth, New York A.L.
C— Mickey Cochrane, Phil. A.L.
P— Lefty Grove, Philadelphia A.L.
P— Burleigh Grimes, Pittsburgh N.L.

1930
1B— Bill Terry, New York N.L.
2B— Frank Frisch, St. Louis N.L.

OF— Al Simmons, Philadelphia A.L.
OF— Paul Waner, Pittsburgh N.L.
C— Gabby Hartnett, Chicago N.L.
P— Charley Root, Chicago N.L.
P— Ted Lyons, Chicago A.L.

SS— Joe Cronin, Washington A.L.
3B— Fred Lindstrom, New York N.L.
OF— Al Simmons, Philadelphia A.L.
OF— Hack Wilson, Chicago N.L.
OF— Babe Ruth, New York A.L.
C— Mickey Cochrane, Phil. A.L.
P— Lefty Grove, Philadelphia A.L.
P— Wes Ferrell, Cleveland A.L.

1931
1B— Lou Gehrig, New York A.L.
2B— Frank Frisch, St. Louis N.L.
SS— Joe Cronin, Washington A.L.
3B— Pie Traynor, Pittsburgh N.L.
OF— Al Simmons, Philadelphia A.L.
OF— Earl Averill, Cleveland A.L.
OF— Babe Ruth, New York A.L.
C— Mickey Cochrane, Phil. A.L.
P— Lefty Grove, Philadelphia A.L.
P— George Earnshaw, Phil. A.L.

1932
1B— Jimmie Foxx, Philadelphia A.L.
2B— Tony Lazzeri, New York A.L.
SS— Joe Cronin, Washington A.L.
3B— Pie Traynor, Pittsburgh N.L.
OF— Lefty O'Doul, Brooklyn N.L.
OF— Earl Averill, Cleveland A.L.
OF— Chuck Klein, Philadelphia N.L.
C— Bill Dickey, New York A.L.
P— Lefty Grove, Philadelphia A.L.
P— Lon Warneke, Chicago N.L.

1933

1B— Jimmie Foxx, Philadelphia A.L.
2B— Charley Gehringer, Detroit A.L.
SS— Joe Cronin, Washington A.L.
3B— Pie Traynor, Pittsburgh A.L.
OF— Al Simmons, Chicago A.L.
OF— Wally Berger, Boston N.L.
OF— Chuck Klein, Philadelphia N.L.
C— Bill Dickey, New York A.L.
P— Alvin Crowder, Washington A.L.
P— Carl Hubbell, New York N.L.

1934

1B— Lou Gehrig, New York A.L.
2B— Charley Gehringer, Detroit A.L.
SS— Joe Cronin, Washington A.L.
3B— Mike Higgins, Philadelphia A.L.
OF— Al Simmons, Chicago A.L.
OF— Earl Averill, Cleveland A.L.
OF— Mel Ott, New York N.L.
C— Mickey Cochrane, Detroit A.L.
P— Lefty Gomez, New York A.L.
P— Schoolboy Rowe, Detroit A.L.
P— Dizzy Dean, St. Louis N.L.

1935

1B— Hank Greenberg, Detroit A.L.
2B— Charley Gehringer, Detroit A.L.
SS— Arky Vaughan, Pittsburgh N.L.
3B— Pepper Martin, St. Louis N.L.
OF— Joe Medwick, St. Louis N.L.
OF— Doc Cramer, Philadelphia A.L.
OF— Mel Ott, New York N.L.
C— Mickey Cochrane, Detroit A.L.
P— Carl Hubbell, New York N.L.
P— Dizzy Dean, St. Louis N.L.

1936

1B— Lou Gehrig, New York A.L.
2B— Charley Gehringer, Detroit A.L.
SS— Luke Appling, Chicago A.L.
3B— Mike Higgins, Philadelphia A.L.
OF— Joe Medwick, St. Louis N.L.
OF— Earl Averill, Cleveland A.L.
OF— Mel Ott, New York N.L.
C— Bill Dickey, New York A.L.
P— Carl Hubbell, New York N.L.
P— Dizzy Dean, St. Louis N.L.

1937

1B— Lou Gehrig, New York A.L.
2B— Charley Gehringer, Detroit A.L.
SS— Dick Bartell, New York N.L.
3B— Red Rolfe, New York A.L.
OF— Joe Medwick, St. Louis N.L.
OF— Joe DiMaggio, New York A.L.
OF— Paul Waner, Pittsburgh N.L.
C— Gabby Hartnett, Chicago N.L.
P— Carl Hubbell, New York N.L.
P— Red Ruffing, New York A.L.

1938

1B— Jimmie Foxx, Boston A.L.
2B— Charley Gehringer, Detroit A.L.
SS— Joe Cronin, Boston A.L.
3B— Red Rolfe, New York A.L.
OF— Joe Medwick, St. Louis N.L.
OF— Joe DiMaggio, New York A.L.
OF— Mel Ott, New York N.L.
C— Bill Dickey, New York A.L.
P— Red Ruffing, New York A.L.
P— Lefty Gomez, New York A.L.
P— Johnny Vander Meer, Cin. N.L.

1939

1B— Jimmie Foxx, Boston A.L.
2B— Joe Gordon, New York A.L.
SS— Joe Cronin, Boston A.L.
3B— Red Rolfe, New York A.L.
OF— Joe Medwick, St. Louis N.L.
OF— Joe DiMaggio, New York A.L.

OF— Ted Williams, Boston A.L.
C— Bill Dickey, New York A.L.
P— Red Ruffing, New York A.L.
P— Bob Feller, Cleveland A.L.
P— Bucky Walters, Cincinnati N.L.

1940

1B— Frank McCormick, Cincinnati N.L.
2B— Joe Gordon, New York A.L.
SS— Luke Appling, Chicago A.L.
3B— Stan Hack, Chicago N.L.
OF— Hank Greenberg, Detroit A.L.
OF— Joe DiMaggio, New York A.L.
OF— Ted Williams, Boston A.L.
C— Harry Danning, New York N.L.
P— Bob Feller, Cleveland A.L.
P— Bucky Walters, Cincinnati N.L.
P— Paul Derringer, Cincinnati N.L.

1941

1B— Dolf Camilli, Brooklyn N.L.
2B— Joe Gordon, New York A.L.
SS— Cecil Travis, Washington A.L.
3B— Stan Hack, Chicago N.L.
OF— Ted Williams, Boston A.L.
OF— Joe DiMaggio, New York A.L.
OF— Pete Reiser, Brooklyn N.L.
C— Bill Dickey, New York A.L.
P— Bob Feller, Cleveland A.L.
P— Whitlow Wyatt, Brooklyn N.L.
P— Thornton Lee, Chicago A.L.

1942

1B— Johnny Mize, New York N.L.
2B— Joe Gordon, New York A.L.
SS— Johnny Pesky, Boston A.L.
3B— Stan Hack, Chicago N.L.
OF— Ted Williams, Boston A.L.
OF— Joe DiMaggio, New York A.L.
OF— Enos Slaughter, St. Louis N.L.
C— Mickey Owen, Brooklyn N.L.
P— Mort Cooper, St. Louis N.L.
P— Tiny Bonham, New York A.L.
P— Tex Hughson, Boston A.L.

1943

1B— Rudy York, Detroit A.L.
2B— Billy Herman, Brooklyn N.L.
SS— Luke Appling, Chicago A.L.
3B— Billy Johnson, New York A.L.
OF— Dick Wakefield, Detroit A.L.
OF— Stan Musial, St. Louis N.L.
OF— Bill Nicholson, Chicago N.L.
C— Walker Cooper, St. Louis N.L.
P— Spud Chandler, New York A.L.
P— Mort Cooper, St. Louis N.L.
P— Rip Sewell, Pittsburgh N.L.

1944

1B— Ray Sanders, St. Louis N.L.
2B— Bobby Doerr, Boston A.L.
SS— Marty Marion, St. Louis N.L.
3B— Bob Elliott, Pittsburgh N.L.
OF— Stan Musial, St. Louis N.L.
OF— Dick Wakefield, Detroit A.L.
OF— Dixie Walker, Brooklyn, N.L.
C— Walker Cooper, St. Louis N.L.
P— Hal Newhouser, Detroit A.L.
P— Mort Cooper, St. Louis N.L.
P— Dizzy Trout, Detroit A.L.

1945

1B— Phil Cavarretta, Chicago N.L.
2B— George Stirnweiss, N.Y. A.L.
SS— Marty Marion, St. Louis N.L.
3B— Whitey Kurowski, St. Louis N.L.
OF— Tommy Holmes, Boston N.L.
OF— Andy Pafko, Chicago N.L.
OF— Goody Rosen, Brooklyn N.L.
C— Paul Richards, Detroit A.L.
P— Hal Newhouser, Detroit A.L.

P— Boo Ferriss, Boston A.L.
P— Hank Borowy, Chicago N.L.

1946

1B— Stan Musial, St. Louis N.L.
2B— Bobby Doerr, Boston A.L.
SS— Johnny Pesky, Boston A.L.
3B— George Kell, Detroit A.L.
OF— Ted Williams, Boston A.L.
OF— Dom DiMaggio, Boston A.L.
OF— Enos Slaughter, St. Louis N.L.
C— Aaron Robinson, New York A.L.
P— Hal Newhouser, Detroit A.L.
P— Bob Feller, Cleveland A.L.
P— Boo Ferriss, Boston A.L.

1947

1B— Johnny Mize, New York N.L.
2B— Joe Gordon, Cleveland A.L.
SS— Lou Boudreau, Cleveland A.L.
3B— George Kell, Detroit A.L.
OF— Ted Williams, Boston A.L.
OF— Joe DiMaggio, New York A.L.
OF— Ralph Kiner, Pittsburgh N.L.
C— Walker Cooper, New York N.L.
P— Ewell Blackwell, Cincinnati N.L.
P— Bob Feller, Cleveland A.L.
P— Ralph Branca, Brooklyn N.L.

1948

1B— Johnny Mize, New York N.L.
2B— Joe Gordon, Cleveland A.L.
SS— Lou Boudreau, Cleveland A.L.
3B— Bob Elliott, Boston N.L.
OF— Ted Williams, Boston A.L.
OF— Joe DiMaggio, New York A.L.
OF— Stan Musial, St. Louis N.L.
C— Birdie Tebbetts, Boston A.L.
P— Johnny Sain, Boston N.L.
P— Bob Lemon, Cleveland A.L.
P— Harry Brecheen, St. Louis N.L.

1949

1B— Tommy Henrich, New York A.L.
2B— Jackie Robinson, Brooklyn N.L.
SS— Phil Rizzuto, New York A.L.
3B— George Kell, Detroit A.L.
OF— Ted Williams, Boston A.L.
OF— Stan Musial, St. Louis N.L.
OF— Ralph Kiner, Pittsburgh N.L.
C— Roy Campanella, Brooklyn N.L.
P— Mel Parnell, Boston A.L.
P— Ellis Kinder, Boston A.L.
P— Joe Page, New York A.L.

1950

1B— Walt Dropo, Boston A.L.
2B— Jackie Robinson, Brooklyn N.L.
SS— Phil Rizzuto, New York A.L.
3B— George Kell, Detroit A.L.
OF— Stan Musial, St. Louis N.L.
OF— Ralph Kiner, Pittsburgh N.L.
OF— Larry Doby, Cleveland A.L.
C— Yogi Berra, New York A.L.
P— Vic Raschi, New York A.L.
P— Bob Lemon, Cleveland A.L.
P— Jim Konstanty, Phil. N.L.

1951

1B— Ferris Fain, Philadelphia A.L.
2B— Jackie Robinson, Brooklyn N.L.
SS— Phil Rizzuto, New York A.L.
3B— George Kell, Detroit A.L.
OF— Stan Musial, St. Louis N.L.
OF— Ted Williams, Boston A.L.
OF— Ralph Kiner, Pittsburgh N.L.
C— Roy Campanella, Brooklyn N.L.
P— Sal Maglie, New York N.L.
P— Preacher Roe, Brooklyn N.L.
P— Allie Reynolds, New York A.L.

1952

1B— Ferris Fain, Philadelphia A.L.
2B— Jackie Robinson, Brooklyn N.L.
SS— Phil Rizzuto, New York A.L.
3B— George Kell, Boston A.L.
OF— Stan Musial, St. Louis N.L.
OF— Hank Sauer, Chicago N.L.
OF— Mickey Mantle, New York A.L.
C— Yogi Berra, New York A.L.
P— Robin Roberts, Philadelphia N.L.
P— Bobby Shantz, Philadelphia A.L.
P— Allie Reynolds, New York A.L.

1953

1B— Mickey Vernon, Washington A.L.
2B— Red Schoendienst, St. Louis N.L.
SS— Pee Wee Reese, Brooklyn N.L.
3B— Al Rosen, Cleveland A.L.
OF— Stan Musial, St. Louis N.L.
OF— Duke Snider, Brooklyn N.L.
OF— Carl Furillo, Brooklyn N.L.
C— Roy Campanella, Brooklyn N.L.
P— Robin Roberts, Philadelphia N.L.
P— Warren Spahn, Milwaukee N.L.
P— Bob Porterfield, Washington A.L.

1954

1B— Ted Kluszewski, Cincinnati N.L.
2B— Bobby Avila, Cleveland A.L.
SS— Alvin Dark, New York N.L.
3B— Al Rosen, Cleveland A.L.
OF— Willie Mays, New York N.L.
OF— Stan Musial, St. Louis N.L.
OF— Duke Snider, Brooklyn N.L.
C— Yogi Berra, New York A.L.
P— Bob Lemon, Cleveland A.L.
P— Johnny Antonelli, New York N.L.
P— Robin Roberts, Philadelphia N.L.

1955

1B— Ted Kluszewski, Cincinnati N.L.
2B— Nellie Fox, Chicago A.L.
SS— Ernie Banks, Chicago N.L.
3B— Ed Mathews, Milwaukee N.L.
OF— Duke Snider, Brooklyn N.L.
OF— Ted Williams, Boston A.L.
OF— Al Kaline, Detroit A.L.
C— Roy Campanella, Brooklyn N.L.
P— Robin Roberts, Philadelphia N.L.
P— Don Newcombe, Brooklyn N.L.
P— Whitey Ford, New York A.L.

1956

1B— Ted Kluszewski, Cincinnati N.L.
2B— Nellie Fox, Chicago A.L.
SS— Harvey Kuenn, Detroit A.L.
3B— Ken Boyer, St. Louis N.L.
OF— Mickey Mantle, New York A.L.
OF— Hank Aaron, Milwaukee N.L.
OF— Ted Williams, Boston A.L.
C— Yogi Berra, New York A.L.
P— Don Newcombe, Brooklyn N.L.
P— Whitey Ford, New York A.L.
P— Billy Pierce, Chicago A.L.

1957

1B— Stan Musial, St. Louis N.L.
2B— Red Schoendienst, N.Y.-Mil. N.L.
SS— Gil McDougald, New York A.L.
3B— Ed Mathews, Milwaukee N.L.
OF— Mickey Mantle, New York A.L.
OF— Ted Williams, Boston A.L.
OF— Willie Mays, New York N.L.
C— Yogi Berra, New York A.L.
P— Warren Spahn, Milwaukee N.L.
P— Billy Pierce, Chicago N.L.
P— Jim Bunning, Detroit A.L.

1958

1B— Stan Musial, St. Louis N.L.
2B— Nellie Fox, Chicago A.L.
SS— Ernie Banks, Chicago N.L.
3B— Frank Thomas, Pittsburgh N.L.
OF— Ted Williams, Boston A.L.
OF— Willie Mays, San Francisco N.L.
OF— Hank Aaron, Milwaukee N.L.
C— Del Crandall, Milwaukee N.L.
P— Bob Turley, New York A.L.
P— Warren Spahn, Milwaukee N.L.
P— Bob Friend, Pittsburgh N.L.

1959

1B— Orlando Cepeda, S.F. N.L.
2B— Nellie Fox, Chicago A.L.
SS— Ernie Banks, Chicago N.L.
3B— Ed Mathews, Milwaukee N.L.
OF— Minnie Minoso, Cleveland A.L.
OF— Willie Mays, San Francisco N.L.
OF— Hank Aaron, Milwaukee N.L.
C— Sherm Lollar, Chicago A.L.
P— Early Wynn, Chicago A.L.
P— Sam Jones, San Francisco N.L.
P— Johnny Antonelli, S.F. N.L.

1960

1B— Bill Skowron, New York A.L.
2B— Bill Mazeroski, Pittsburgh N.L.
SS— Ernie Banks, Chicago N.L.
3B— Ed Mathews, Milwaukee N.L.
OF— Minnie Minoso, Chicago A.L.
OF— Willie Mays, San Francisco N.L.
OF— Roger Maris, New York A.L.
C— Del Crandall, Milwaukee N.L.
P— Vernon Law, Pittsburgh N.L.
P— Warren Spahn, Milwaukee N.L.
P— Ernie Broglio, St. Louis N.L.

1961

AMERICAN LEAGUE

1B— Norm Cash, Detroit
2B— Bobby Richardson, New York
SS— Tony Kubek, New York
3B— Brooks Robinson, Baltimore
OF— Mickey Mantle, New York
OF— Roger Maris, New York
OF— Rocky Colavito, Detroit
C— Elston Howard, New York
P— Whitey Ford, New York
P— Frank Lary, Detroit

NATIONAL LEAGUE

1B— Orlando Cepeda, San Francisco
2B— Frank Bolling, Milwaukee
SS— Maury Wills, Los Angeles
3B— Ken Boyer, St. Louis
OF— Willie Mays, San Francisco
OF— Frank Robinson, Cincinnati
OF— Roberto Clemente, Pittsburgh
C— Smoky Burgess, Pittsburgh
P— Joey Jay, Cincinnati
P— Warren Spahn, Milwaukee

1962

AMERICAN LEAGUE

1B— Norm Siebern, Kansas City
2B— Bobby Richardson, New York
SS— Tom Tresh, New York
3B— Brooks Robinson, Baltimore
OF— Leon Wagner, Los Angeles
OF— Mickey Mantle, New York
OF— Al Kaline, Detroit
C— Earl Battey, Minnesota
P— Ralph Terry, New York
P— Dick Donovan, Cleveland

NATIONAL LEAGUE

1B— Orlando Cepeda, San Francisco
2B— Bill Mazeroski, Pittsburgh
SS— Maury Wills, Los Angeles
3B— Ken Boyer, St. Louis
OF— Tommy Davis, Los Angeles
OF— Willie Mays, San Francisco
OF— Frank Robinson, Cincinnati
C— Del Crandall, Milwaukee
P— Don Drysdale, Los Angeles
P— Bob Purkey, Cincinnati

1963

AMERICAN LEAGUE

1B— Joe Pepitone, New York
2B— Bobby Richardson, New York
SS— Luis Aparicio, Baltimore
3B— Frank Malzone, Boston
OF— Carl Yastrzemski, Boston
OF— Albie Pearson, Los Angeles
OF— Al Kaline, Detroit
C— Elston Howard, New York
P— Whitey Ford, New York
P— Gary Peters, Chicago

NATIONAL LEAGUE

1B— Bill White, St. Louis
2B— Jim Gilliam, Los Angeles
SS— Dick Groat, St. Louis
3B— Ken Boyer, St. Louis
OF— Tommy Davis, Los Angeles
OF— Willie Mays, San Francisco
OF— Hank Aaron, Milwaukee
C— John Edwards, Cincinnati
P— Sandy Koufax, Los Angeles
P— Juan Marichal, San Francisco

1964

AMERICAN LEAGUE

1B— Dick Stuart, Boston
2B— Bobby Richardson, New York
SS— Jim Fregosi, Los Angeles
3B— Brooks Robinson, Baltimore
OF— Harmon Killebrew, Minnesota
OF— Mickey Mantle, New York
OF— Tony Oliva, Minnesota
C— Elston Howard, New York
P— Dean Chance, Los Angeles
P— Gary Peters, Chicago

NATIONAL LEAGUE

1B— Bill White, St. Louis
2B— Ron Hunt, New York
SS— Dick Groat, St. Louis
3B— Ken Boyer, St. Louis
OF— Billy Williams, Chicago
OF— Willie Mays, San Francisco
OF— Roberto Clemente, Pittsburgh
C— Joe Torre, Milwaukee
P— Sandy Koufax, Los Angeles
P— Jim Bunning, Philadelphia

1965

AMERICAN LEAGUE

1B— Fred Whitfield, Cleveland
2B— Bobby Richardson, New York
SS— Zoilo Versalles, Minnesota
3B— Brooks Robinson, Baltimore
OF— Carl Yastrzemski, Boston
OF— Jimmie Hall, Minnesota
OF— Tony Oliva, Minnesota
C— Earl Battey, Minnesota
P— Jim Grant, Minnesota
P— Mel Stottlemyre, New York

NATIONAL LEAGUE

1B— Willie McCovey, San Francisco
2B— Pete Rose, Cincinnati
SS— Maury Wills, Los Angeles
3B— Deron Johnson, Cincinnati
OF— Willie Stargell, Pittsburgh
OF— Willie Mays, San Francisco
OF— Hank Aaron, Milwaukee
C— Joe Torre, Milwaukee
P— Sandy Koufax, Los Angeles
P— Juan Marichal, San Francisco

HISTORY *Award winners*

1966
AMERICAN LEAGUE
1B— Boog Powell, Baltimore
2B— Bobby Richardson, New York
SS— Luis Aparicio, Baltimore
3B— Brooks Robinson, Baltimore
OF— Frank Robinson, Baltimore
OF— Al Kaline, Detroit
OF— Tony Oliva, Minnesota
C— Paul Casanova, Washington
P— Jim Kaat, Minnesota
P— Earl Wilson, Detroit

NATIONAL LEAGUE
1B— Felipe Alou, Atlanta
2B— Pete Rose, Cincinnati
SS— Gene Alley, Pittsburgh
3B— Ron Santo, Chicago
OF— Willie Stargell, Pittsburgh
OF— Willie Mays, San Francisco
OF— Roberto Clemente, Pittsburgh
C— Joe Torre, Atlanta
P— Sandy Koufax, Los Angeles
P— Juan Marichal, San Francisco

1967
AMERICAN LEAGUE
1B— Harmon Killebrew, Minnesota
2B— Rod Carew, Minnesota
SS— Jim Fregosi, California
3B— Brooks Robinson, Baltimore
OF— Carl Yastrzemski, Boston
OF— Al Kaline, Detroit
OF— Frank Robinson, Baltimore
C— Bill Freehan, Detroit
P— Jim Lonborg, Boston
P— Earl Wilson, Detroit

NATIONAL LEAGUE
1B— Orlando Cepeda, St. Louis
2B— Bill Mazeroski, Pittsburgh
SS— Gene Alley, Pittsburgh
3B— Ron Santo, Chicago
OF— Hank Aaron, Atlanta
OF— Jim Wynn, Houston
OF— Roberto Clemente, Pittsburgh
C— Tim McCarver, St. Louis
P— Mike McCormick, San Francisco
P— Ferguson Jenkins, Chicago

1968
AMERICAN LEAGUE
1B— Boog Powell, Baltimore
2B— Rod Carew, Minnesota
SS— Luis Aparicio, Chicago
3B— Brooks Robinson, Baltimore
OF— Ken Harrelson, Boston
OF— Willie Horton, Detroit
OF— Frank Howard, Washington
C— Bill Freehan, Detroit
P— Dave McNally, Baltimore
P— Denny McLain, Detroit

NATIONAL LEAGUE
1B— Willie McCovey, San Francisco
2B— Tommy Helms, Cincinnati
SS— Don Kessinger, Chicago
3B— Ron Santo, Chicago
OF— Billy Williams, Chicago
OF— Curt Flood, St. Louis
OF— Pete Rose, Cincinnati
C— Johnny Bench, Cincinnati
P— Bob Gibson, St. Louis
P— Juan Marichal, San Francisco

1969
AMERICAN LEAGUE
1B— Boog Powell, Baltimore
2B— Rod Carew, Minnesota
SS— Rico Petrocelli, Boston
3B— Harmon Killebrew, Minnesota

OF— Frank Howard, Washington
OF— Paul Blair, Baltimore
OF— Reggie Jackson, Oakland
C— Bill Freehan, Detroit
RHP— Denny McLain, Detroit
LHP— Mike Cuellar, Baltimore

NATIONAL LEAGUE
1B— Willie McCovey, San Francisco
2B— Glenn Beckert, Chicago
SS— Don Kessinger, Chicago
3B— Ron Santo, Chicago
OF— Cleon Jones, New York
OF— Matty Alou, Pittsburgh
OF— Hank Aaron, Atlanta
C— Johnny Bench, Cincinnati
RHP— Tom Seaver, New York
LHP— Steve Carlton, St. Louis

1970
AMERICAN LEAGUE
1B— Boog Powell, Baltimore
2B— Dave Johnson, Baltimore
SS— Luis Aparicio, Chicago
3B— Harmon Killebrew, Minnesota
OF— Frank Howard, Washington
OF— Reggie Smith, Boston
OF— Tony Oliva, Minnesota
C— Ray Fosse, Cleveland
RHP— Jim Perry, Minnesota
LHP— Sam McDowell, Cleveland

NATIONAL LEAGUE
1B— Willie McCovey, San Francisco
2B— Glenn Beckert, Chicago
SS— Don Kessinger, Chicago
3B— Tony Perez, Cincinnati
OF— Billy Williams, Chicago
OF— Bobby Tolan, Cincinnati
OF— Hank Aaron, Atlanta
C— Johnny Bench, Cincinnati
RHP— Bob Gibson, St. Louis
LHP— Jim Merritt, Cincinnati

1971
AMERICAN LEAGUE
1B— Norm Cash, Detroit
2B— Cookie Rojas, Kansas City
SS— Leo Cardenas, Minnesota
3B— Brooks Robinson, Baltimore
OF— Merv Rettenmund, Baltimore
OF— Bobby Murcer, New York
OF— Tony Oliva, Minnesota
C— Bill Freehan, Detroit
RHP— Jim Palmer, Baltimore
LHP— Vida Blue, Oakland

NATIONAL LEAGUE
1B— Lee May, Cincinnati
2B— Glenn Beckett, Chicago
SS— Bud Harrelson, New York
3B— Joe Torre, St. Louis
OF— Willie Stargell, Pittsburgh
OF— Willie Davis, Los Angeles
OF— Hank Aaron, Atlanta
C— Manny Sanguillen, Pittsburgh
RHP— Ferguson Jenkins, Chicago
LHP— Steve Carlton, St. Louis

1972
AMERICAN LEAGUE
1B— Dick Allen, Chicago
2B— Rod Carew, Minnesota
SS— Luis Aparicio, Boston
3B— Brooks Robinson, Baltimore
OF— Joe Rudi, Oakland
OF— Bobby Murcer, New York
OF— Richie Scheinblum, Kansas City
C— Carlton Fisk, Boston
RHP— Gaylord Perry, Cleveland
LHP— Wilbur Wood, Chicago

NATIONAL LEAGUE
1B— Willie Stargell, Pittsburgh
2B— Joe Morgan, Cincinnati
SS— Chris Speier, San Francisco
3B— Ron Santo, Chicago
OF— Billy Williams, Chicago
OF— Cesar Cedeno, Houston
OF— Roberto Clemente, Pittsburgh
C— Johnny Bench, Cincinnati
RHP— Ferguson Jenkins, Chicago
LHP— Steve Carlton, Philadelphia

1973
AMERICAN LEAGUE
1B— John Mayberry, Kansas City
2B— Rod Carew, Minnesota
SS— Bert Campaneris, Oakland
3B— Sal Bando, Oakland
OF— Reggie Jackson, Oakland
OF— Amos Otis, Kansas City
OF— Bobby Murcer, New York
C— Thurman Munson, New York
RHP— Jim Palmer, Baltimore
LHP— Ken Holtzman, Oakland

NATIONAL LEAGUE
1B— Tony Perez, Cincinnati
2B— Dave Johnson, Atlanta
SS— Bill Russell, Los Angeles
3B— Darrell Evans, Atlanta
OF— Bobby Bonds, San Francisco
OF— Cesar Cedeno, Houston
OF— Pete Rose, Cincinnati
C— Johnny Bench, Cincinnati
RHP— Tom Seaver, New York
LHP— Ron Bryant, San Francisco

1974
AMERICAN LEAGUE
1B— Dick Allen, Chicago
2B— Rod Carew, Minnesota
SS— Bert Campaneris, Oakland
3B— Sal Bando, Oakland
OF— Joe Rudi, Oakland
OF— Paul Blair, Baltimore
OF— Jeff Burroughs, Texas
C— Thurman Munson, New York
DH— Tommy Davis, Baltimore
RHP— Jim Hunter, Oakland
LHP— Mike Cuellar, Baltimore

NATIONAL LEAGUE
1B— Steve Garvey, Los Angeles
2B— Joe Morgan, Cincinnati
SS— Dave Concepcion, Cincinnati
3B— Mike Schmidt, Philadelphia
OF— Lou Brock, St. Louis
OF— Jim Wynn, Los Angeles
OF— Richie Zisk, Pittsburgh
C— Johnny Bench, Cincinnati
RHP— Andy Messersmith, Los Angeles
LHP— Don Gullett, Cincinnati

1975
AMERICAN LEAGUE
1B— John Mayberry, Kansas City
2B— Rod Carew, Minnesota
SS— Toby Harrah, Texas
3B— Graig Nettles, New York
OF— Jim Rice, Boston
OF— Fred Lynn, Boston
OF— Reggie Jackson, Oakland
C— Thurman Munson, New York
DH— Willie Horton, Detroit
RHP— Jim Palmer, Baltimore
LHP— Jim Kaat, Chicago

NATIONAL LEAGUE
1B— Steve Garvey, Los Angeles
2B— Joe Morgan, Cincinnati
SS— Larry Bowa, Philadelphia

3B— Bill Madlock, Chicago
OF— Greg Luzinski, Philadelphia
OF— Al Oliver, Pittsburgh
OF— Dave Parker, Pittsburgh
C— Johnny Bench, Cincinnati
RHP— Tom Seaver, New York
LHP— Randy Jones, San Diego

1976
AMERICAN LEAGUE
1B— Chris Chambliss, New York
2B— Bobby Grich, Baltimore
3B— George Brett, Kansas City
SS— Mark Belanger, Baltimore
OF— Joe Rudi, Oakland
OF— Mickey Rivers, New York
OF— Reggie Jackson, Baltimore
C— Thurman Munson, New York
DH— Hal McRae, Kansas City
RHP— Jim Palmer, Baltimore
LHP— Frank Tanana, California

NATIONAL LEAGUE
1B— Willie Montanez, S.F.-Atl.
2B— Joe Morgan, Cincinnati
3B— Mike Schmidt, Philadelphia
SS— Dave Concepcion, Cincinnati
OF— George Foster, Cincinnati
OF— Cesar Cedeno, Houston
OF— Ken Griffey, Cincinnati
C— Bob Boone, Philadelphia
RHP— Don Sutton, Los Angeles
LHP— Randy Jones, San Diego

1977
AMERICAN LEAGUE
1B— Rod Carew, Minnesota
2B— Willie Randolph, New York
3B— Graig Nettles, New York
SS— Rick Burleson, Boston
OF— Jim Rice, Boston
OF— Larry Hisle, Minnesota
OF— Bobby Bonds, California
C— Carlton Fisk, Boston
DH— Hal McRae, Kansas City
RHP— Nolan Ryan, California
LHP— Frank Tanana, California

NATIONAL LEAGUE
1B— Steve Garvey, Los Angeles
2B— Joe Morgan, Cincinnati
3B— Mike Schmidt, Philadelphia
SS— Garry Templeton, St. Louis
OF— George Foster, Cincinnati
OF— Dave Parker, Pittsburgh
OF— Greg Luzinski, Philadelphia
C— Ted Simmons, St. Louis
RHP— Rick Reuschel, Chicago
LHP— Steve Carlton, Philadelphia

1978
AMERICAN LEAGUE
1B— Rod Carew, Minnesota
2B— Frank White, Kansas City
3B— Graig Nettles, New York
SS— Robin Yount, Milwaukee
OF— Jim Rice, Boston
OF— Larry Hisle, Milwaukee
OF— Fred Lynn, Boston
C— Jim Sundberg, Texas
DH— Rusty Staub, Detroit
RHP— Jim Palmer, Baltimore
LHP— Ron Guidry, New York

NATIONAL LEAGUE
1B— Steve Garvey, Los Angeles
2B— Dave Lopes, Los Angeles
3B— Pete Rose, Cincinnati
SS— Larry Bowa, Philadelphia
OF— George Foster, Cincinnati

OF— Dave Parker, Pittsburgh
OF— Jack Clark, San Francisco
C— Ted Simmons, St. Louis
RHP— Gaylord Perry, San Diego
LHP— Vida Blue, San Francisco

1979
AMERICAN LEAGUE
1B— Cecil Cooper, Milwaukee
2B— Bobby Grich, California
3B— George Brett, Kansas City
SS— Roy Smalley, Minnesota
OF— Jim Rice, Boston
OF— Fred Lynn, Boston
OF— Ken Singleton, Baltimore
C— Darrell Porter, Kansas City
DH— Don Baylor, California
RHP— Jim Kern, Texas
LHP— Mike Flanagan, Baltimore

NATIONAL LEAGUE
1B— Keith Hernandez, St. Louis
2B— Dave Lopes, Los Angeles
3B— Mike Schmidt, Philadelphia
SS— Garry Templeton, St. Louis
OF— Dave Kingman, Chicago
OF— Omar Moreno, Pittsburgh
OF— Dave Winfield, San Diego
C— Ted Simmons, St. Louis
RHP— Joe Niekro, Houston
LHP— Steve Carlton, Philadelphia

1980
AMERICAN LEAGUE
1B— Cecil Cooper, Milwaukee
2B— Willie Randolph, New York
3B— George Brett, Kansas City
SS— Robin Yount, Milwaukee
OF— Ben Oglivie, Milwaukee
OF— Al Bumbry, Baltimore
OF— Reggie Jackson, New York
DH— Reggie Jackson, New York
C— Rick Cerone, New York
RHP— Steve Stone, Baltimore
LHP— Tommy John, New York

NATIONAL LEAGUE
1B— Keith Hernandez, St. Louis
2B— Manny Trillo, Philadelphia
3B— Mike Schmidt, Philadelphia
SS— Garry Templeton, St. Louis
OF— Dusty Baker, Los Angeles
OF— Cesar Cedeno, Houston
OF— George Hendrick, St. Louis
C— Gary Carter, Montreal
RHP— Jim Bibby, Pittsburgh
LHP— Steve Carlton, Philadelphia

1981
AMERICAN LEAGUE
1B— Cecil Cooper, Milwaukee
2B— Bobby Grich, California
3B— Buddy Bell, Texas
SS— Rick Burleson, California
OF— Rickey Henderson, Oakland
OF— Dwayne Murphy, Oakland
OF— Tony Armas, Oakland
C— Jim Sundberg, Texas
DH— Richie Zisk, Seattle
RHP— Jack Morris, Detroit
LHP— Ron Guidry, New York

NATIONAL LEAGUE
1B— Pete Rose, Philadelphia
2B— Manny Trillo, Philadelphia
3B— Mike Schmidt, Philadelphia
SS— Dave Concepcion, Cincinnati
OF— George Foster, Cincinnati
OF— Andre Dawson, Montreal
OF— Pedro Guerrero, Los Angeles

C— Gary Carter, Montreal
RHP— Tom Seaver, Cincinnati
LHP— Fernando Valenzuela, Los Angeles

1982
AMERICAN LEAGUE
1B— Cecil Cooper, Milwaukee
2B— Damaso Garcia, Toronto
3B— Doug DeCinces, California
SS— Robin Yount, Milwaukee
OF— Dave Winfield, New York
OF— Gorman Thomas, Milwaukee
OF— Dwight Evans, Boston
C— Lance Parrish, Detroit
DH— Hal McRae, Kansas City
RHP— Dave Stieb, Toronto
LHP— Geoff Zahn, California

NATIONAL LEAGUE
1B— Al Oliver, Montreal
2B— Manny Trillo, Philadelphia
3B— Mike Schmidt, Philadelphia
SS— Ozzie Smith, St. Louis
OF— Lonnie Smith, St. Louis
OF— Dale Murphy, Atlanta
OF— Pedro Guerrero, Los Angeles
C— Gary Carter, Montreal
RHP— Steve Rogers, Montreal
LHP— Steve Carlton, Philadelphia

1983
AMERICAN LEAGUE
1B— Eddie Murray, Baltimore
2B— Lou Whitaker, Detroit
3B— Wade Boggs, Boston
SS— Cal Ripken, Baltimore
OF— Jim Rice, Boston
OF— Dave Winfield, New York
OF— Lloyd Moseby, Toronto
C— Carlton Fisk, Chicago
DH— Greg Luzinski, Chicago
RHP— LaMarr Hoyt, Chicago
LHP— Ron Guidry, New York

NATIONAL LEAGUE
1B— George Hendrick, St. Louis
2B— Glenn Hubbard, Atlanta
3B— Mike Schmidt, Philadelphia
SS— Dickie Thon, Houston
OF— Dale Murphy, Atlanta
OF— Andre Dawson, Montreal
OF— Tim Raines, Montreal
C— Tony Pena, Pittsburgh
RHP— John Denny, Philadelphia
LHP— Larry McWilliams, Pittsburgh

1984
AMERICAN LEAGUE
1B— Don Mattingly, New York
2B— Lou Whitaker, Detroit
3B— Buddy Bell, Texas
SS— Cal Ripken, Baltimore
OF— Tony Armas, Boston
OF— Dwight Evans, Boston
OF— Dave Winfield, New York
C— Lance Parrish, Detroit
DH— Dave Kingman, Oakland
RHP— Mike Boddicker, Baltimore
LHP— Willie Hernandez, Detroit

NATIONAL LEAGUE
1B— Keith Hernandez, New York
2B— Ryne Sandberg, Chicago
3B— Mike Schmidt, Philadelphia
SS— Ozzie Smith, St. Louis
OF— Dale Murphy, Atlanta
OF— Jose Cruz, Houston
OF— Tony Gwynn, San Diego
C— Gary Carter, Montreal
RHP— Rick Sutcliffe, Chicago
LHP— Mark Thurmond, San Diego

1985
AMERICAN LEAGUE
1B— Don Mattingly, New York
2B— Damaso Garcia, Toronto
3B— Wade Boggs, Boston
SS— Cal Ripken, Baltimore
OF— Rickey Henderson, New York
OF— Harold Baines, Chicago
OF— Phil Bradley, Seattle
C— Carlton Fisk, Chicago
DH— Don Baylor, New York
RHP— Bret Saberhagen, Kansas City
LHP— Ron Guidry, New York

NATIONAL LEAGUE
1B— Keith Hernandez, New York
2B— Tom Herr, St. Louis
3B— Tim Wallach, Montreal
SS— Ozzie Smith, St. Louis
OF— Dave Parker, Cincinnati
OF— Willie McGee, St. Louis
OF— Dale Murphy, Atlanta
C— Gary Carter, New York
RHP— Dwight Gooden, New York
LHP— John Tudor, St. Louis

1986
AMERICAN LEAGUE
1B— Don Mattingly, New York
2B— Tony Bernazard, Cleveland
3B— Wade Boggs, Boston
SS— Tony Fernandez, Toronto
OF— Jim Rice, Boston
OF— George Bell, Toronto
OF— Kirby Puckett, Minnesota
C— Rich Gedman, Boston
DH— Don Baylor, Boston
RHP— Roger Clemens, Boston
LHP— Teddy Higuera, Milwaukee

NATIONAL LEAGUE
1B— Keith Hernandez, New York
2B— Steve Sax, Los Angeles
3B— Mike Schmidt, Philadelphia
SS— Ozzie Smith, St. Louis
OF— Tim Raines, Montreal
OF— Tony Gwynn, San Diego
OF— Dave Parker, Cincinnati
C— Gary Carter, New York
RHP— Mike Scott, Houston
LHP— Fernando Valenzuela, Los Angeles

1987
AMERICAN LEAGUE
1B— Don Mattingly, New York
2B— Willie Randolph, New York
3B— Wade Boggs, Boston
SS— Alan Trammell, Detroit
OF— George Bell, Toronto
OF— Kirby Puckett, Minnesota
OF— Dwight Evans, Boston
C— Matt Nokes, Detroit
DH— Paul Molitor, Milwaukee
RHP— Roger Clemens, Boston
LHP— Jimmy Key, Toronto

NATIONAL LEAGUE
1B— Jack Clark, St. Louis
2B— Juan Samuel, Philadelphia
3B— Tim Wallach, Montreal
SS— Ozzie Smith, St. Louis
OF— Andre Dawson, Chicago
OF— Tony Gwynn, San Diego
OF— Eric Davis, Cincinnati
C— Benito Santiago, San Diego
RHP— Rick Sutcliffe, Chicago
LHP— Zane Smith, Atlanta

1988
AMERICAN LEAGUE
1B— George Brett, Kansas City
2B— Johnny Ray, California

3B— Wade Boggs, Boston
SS— Alan Trammell, Detroit
OF— Kirby Puckett, Minnesota
OF— Mike Greenwell, Boston
OF— Jose Canseco, Oakland
C— Ernie Whitt, Toronto
DH— Harold Baines, Chicago
RHP— Dave Stewart, Oakland
LHP— Frank Viola, Minnesota

NATIONAL LEAGUE
1B— Will Clark, San Francisco
2B— Ryne Sandberg, Chicago
3B— Bobby Bonilla, Pittsburgh
SS— Barry Larkin, Cincinnati
OF— Darryl Strawberry, New York
OF— Andy Van Slyke, Pittsburgh
OF— Kevin McReynolds, New York
C— Mike LaValliere, Pittsburgh
RHP— Orel Hershiser, Los Angeles
LHP— Danny Jackson, Cincinnati

1989
AMERICAN LEAGUE
1B— Fred McGriff, Toronto
2B— Julio Franco, Texas
3B— Carney Lansford, Oakland
SS— Cal Ripken, Baltimore
OF— Ruben Sierra, Texas
OF— Kirby Puckett, Minnesota
OF— Robin Yount, Milwaukee
C— Mickey Tettleton, Baltimore
DH— Harold Baines, Chi.-Tex.
RHP— Bret Saberhagen, Kansas City
LHP— Chuck Finley, California

NATIONAL LEAGUE
1B— Will Clark, San Francisco
2B— Ryne Sandberg, Chicago
3B— Howard Johnson, New York
SS— Shawon Dunston, Chicago
OF— Tony Gwynn, San Diego
OF— Kevin Mitchell, San Francisco
OF— Eric Davis, Cincinnati
C— Benito Santiago, San Diego
RHP— Mike Scott, Houston
LHP— Mark Davis, San Diego

1990
AMERICAN LEAGUE
1B— Cecil Fielder, Detroit
2B— Julio Franco, Texas
3B— Kelly Gruber, Toronto
SS— Alan Trammell, Detroit
OF— Rickey Henderson, Oakland
OF— Jose Canseco, Oakland
OF— Ellis Burks, Boston
C— Carlton Fisk, Chicago
DH— Dave Parker, Milwaukee
RHP— Bob Welch, Oakland
LHP— Chuck Finley, California

NATIONAL LEAGUE
1B— Eddie Murray, Los Angeles
2B— Ryne Sandberg, Chicago
3B— Matt Williams, San Francisco
SS— Barry Larkin, Cincinnati
OF— Barry Bonds, Pittsburgh
OF— Bobby Bonilla, Pittsburgh
OF— Darryl Strawberry, New York
C— Mike Scioscia, Los Angeles
RHP— Doug Drabek, Pittsburgh
LHP— Frank Viola, New York

1991
AMERICAN LEAGUE
1B— Cecil Fielder, Detroit
2B— Julio Franco, Texas
3B— Wade Boggs, Boston
SS— Cal Ripken, Baltimore
OF— Jose Canseco, Oakland
OF— Joe Carter, Toronto

OF— Ken Griffey Jr., Seattle
C— Mickey Tettleton, Detroit
RHP— Roger Clemens, Boston
LHP— Jim Abbott, California

NATIONAL LEAGUE
1B— Will Clark, San Francisco
2B— Ryne Sandberg, Chicago
3B— Terry Pendleton, Atlanta
SS— Barry Larkin, Cincinnati
OF— Barry Bonds, Pittsburgh
OF— Bobby Bonilla, Pittsburgh
OF— Ron Gant, Atlanta
C— Benito Santiago, San Diego
RHP— Jose Rijo, Cincinnati
LHP— Tom Glavine, Atlanta

1992
AMERICAN LEAGUE
1B— Mark McGwire, Oakland
2B— Roberto Alomar, Toronto
3B— Edgar Martinez, Seattle
SS— Travis Fryman, Detroit
OF— Joe Carter, Toronto
OF— Mike Devereaux, Baltimore
OF— Kirby Puckett, Minnesota
C— Mickey Tettleton, Detroit
RHP— Jack McDowell, Chicago
LHP— Dave Fleming, Seattle

NATIONAL LEAGUE
1B— Fred McGriff, San Diego
2B— Ryne Sandberg, Chicago
3B— Gary Sheffield, San Diego
SS— Barry Larkin, Cincinnati
OF— Barry Bonds, Pittsburgh
OF— Andy Van Slyke, Pittsburgh
OF— Larry Walker, Montreal
C— Darren Daulton, Philadelphia
RHP— Greg Maddux, Chicago
LHP— Tom Glavine, Atlanta

1993
AMERICAN LEAGUE
1B— Frank Thomas, Chicago
2B— Carlos Baerga, Cleveland
3B— Travis Fryman, Detroit
SS— Cal Ripken Jr., Baltimore
OF— Albert Belle, Cleveland
OF— Juan Gonzalez, Texas
OF— Ken Griffey Jr., Seattle
C— Mike Stanley, New York
DH— Paul Molitor, Toronto
RHP— Jack McDowell, Chicago
LHP— Jimmy Key, New York

NATIONAL LEAGUE
1B— Fred McGriff, S.D.-Atl.
2B— Robby Thompson, San Francisco
3B— Matt Williams, San Francisco
SS— Jay Bell, Pittsburgh
OF— Barry Bonds, San Francisco
OF— Lenny Dykstra, Philadelphia
OF— David Justice, Atlanta
C— Mike Piazza, Los Angeles
RHP— Greg Maddux, Atlanta
LHP— Steve Avery, Atlanta

1994
AMERICAN LEAGUE
1B— Frank Thomas, Chicago
2B— Chuck Knoblauch, Minnesota
3B— Wade Boggs, New York
SS— Cal Ripken Jr., Baltimore
OF— Albert Belle, Cleveland
OF— Ken Griffey Jr., Seattle
OF— Kirby Puckett, Minnesota
C— Ivan Rodriguez, Texas
DH— Paul Molitor, Toronto
RHP— David Cone, Kansas City
LHP— Jimmy Key, New York

NATIONAL LEAGUE
1B— Jeff Bagwell, Houston
2B— Craig Biggio, Houston
3B— Matt Williams, San Francisco
SS— Barry Larkin, Cincinnati
OF— Moises Alou, Montreal
OF— Barry Bonds, San Francisco
OF— Tony Gwynn, San Diego
C— Mike Piazza, Los Angeles
RHP— Greg Maddux, Atlanta
LHP— Danny Jackson, Philadelphia

1995
AMERICAN LEAGUE
1B— Mo Vaughn, Boston
2B— Carlos Baerga, Cleveland
3B— Jim Thome, Cleveland
SS— Cal Ripken Jr., Baltimore
OF— Albert Belle, Cleveland
OF— Tim Salmon, California
OF— Jim Edmonds, California
C— Ivan Rodriguez, Texas
DH— Edgar Martinez, Seattle
RHP— Mike Mussina, Baltimore
LHP— Randy Johnson, Seattle

NATIONAL LEAGUE
1B— Eric Karros, Los Angeles
2B— Craig Biggio, Houston
3B— Vinny Castilla, Colorado
SS— Barry Larkin, Cincinnati
OF— Reggie Sanders, Cincinnati
OF— Dante Bichette, Colorado
OF— Sammy Sosa, Chicago
C— Mike Piazza, Los Angeles
RHP— Greg Maddux, Atlanta
LHP— Pete Schourek, Cincinnati

1996
AMERICAN LEAGUE
1B— Mark McGwire, Oakland
2B— Roberto Alomar, Baltimore
3B— Jim Thome, Cleveland
SS— Alex Rodriguez, Seattle
OF— Albert Belle, Cleveland
OF— Juan Gonzalez, Texas
OF— Ken Griffey Jr., Seattle
C— Ivan Rodriguez, Texas
DH— Paul Molitor, Minnesota
RHP— Pat Hentgen, Toronto
LHP— Andy Pettitte, New York

NATIONAL LEAGUE
1B— Jeff Bagwell, Houston
2B— Eric Young, Colorado

3B— Ken Caminiti, San Diego
SS— Barry Larkin, Cincinnati
OF— Barry Bonds, San Francisco
OF— Ellis Burks, Colorado
OF— Gary Sheffield, Florida
C— Mike Piazza, Los Angeles
RHP— John Smoltz, Atlanta
LHP— Al Leiter, Florida

1997
AMERICAN LEAGUE
1B— Tino Martinez, New York
2B— Chuck Knoblauch, Minnesota
3B— Matt Williams, Cleveland
SS— Nomar Garciaparra, Boston
OF— Ken Griffey Jr., Seattle
OF— David Justice, Cleveland
OF— Tim Salmon, Anaheim
C— Ivan Rodriguez, Texas
DH— Edgar Martinez, Seattle
RHP— Roger Clemens, Toronto
LHP— Randy Johnson, Seattle

NATIONAL LEAGUE
1B— Jeff Bagwell, Houston
2B— Craig Biggio, Houston
3B— Vinny Castillo, Colorado
SS— Jeff Blauser, Atlanta
OF— Barry Bonds, San Francisco
OF— Tony Gwynn, San Diego
OF— Larry Walker, Colorado
C— Mike Piazza, Los Angeles
RHP— Pedro Martinez, Montreal
LHP— Denny Neagle, Atlanta

1998
AMERICAN LEAGUE
1B— Rafael Palmeiro, Baltimore
2B— Roberto Alomar, Baltimore
3B— Scott Brosius, New York
SS— Alex Rodriguez, Seattle
OF— Ken Griffey Jr., Seattle
OF— Juan Gonzalez, Texas
OF— Albert Belle, Chicago
C— Ivan Rodriguez, Texas
DH— Jose Canseco, Toronto
RHP— Pedro Martinez, Boston
LHP— David Wells, New York

NATIONAL LEAGUE
1B— Mark McGwire, St. Louis
2B— Craig Biggio, Houston
3B— Vinny Castillo, Colorado
SS— Barry Larkin, Cincinnati
OF— Sammy Sosa, Chicago

OF— Moises Alou, Houston
OF— Greg Vaughn, San Diego
C— Mike Piazza, L.A.-Fla.-N.Y.
RHP— Kevin Brown, San Diego
LHP— Tom Glavine, Atlanta

1999
AMERICAN LEAGUE
1B— Rafael Palmeiro, Texas
2B— Roberto Alomar, Cleveland
3B— Dean Palmer, Detroit
SS— Nomar Garciaparra, Boston
OF— Shawn Green, Toronto
OF— Ken Griffey Jr., Seattle
OF— Manny Ramirez, Cleveland
C— Ivan Rodriguez, Texas
RHP— Pedro Martinez, Boston
LHP— Jamie Moyer, Seattle

NATIONAL LEAGUE
1B— Jeff Bagwell, Houston
2B— Edgardo Alfonzo, New York
3B— Chipper Jones, Atlanta
SS— Barry Larkin, Cincinnati
OF— Sammy Sosa, Chicago
OF— Vladimir Guerrero, Montreal
OF— Larry Walker, Colorado
C— Mike Piazza, New York
RHP— Jose Lima, Houston
LHP— Mike Hampton, Houston

2000
AMERICAN LEAGUE
1B— Carlos Delgado, Toronto
2B— Roberto Alomar, Cleveland
3B— Travis Fryman, Cleveland
SS— Alex Rodriguez, Seattle
OF— Darin Erstad, Anaheim
OF— Magglio Ordonez, Chicago
OF— Bernie Williams, New York
C— Jorge Posada, New York
RHP— Pedro Martinez, Boston
LHP— David Wells, Toronto

NATIONAL LEAGUE
1B— Todd Helton, Colorado
2B— Jeff Kent, San Francisco
3B— Chipper Jones, Atlanta
SS— Edgar Renteria, St. Louis
OF— Barry Bonds, San Francisco
OF— Vladimir Guerrero, Montreal
OF— Sammy Sosa, Chicago
C— Mike Piazza, New York
RHP— Greg Maddux, Atlanta
LHP— Tom Glavine, Atlanta

MINOR LEAGUE PLAYER OF THE YEAR

Year	Player, Team, League
1936	John Vander Meer, Durham, Piedmont
1937	Charlie Keller, Newark, International
1938	Fred Hutchinson, Seattle, Pacific Coast
1939	Lou Novikoff, Tulsa, Texas; Los Angeles, Pacific Coast
1940	Phil Rizzuto, Kansas City, American Association
1941	John Lindell, Newark, International
1942	Dick Barrett, Seattle, Pacific Coast
1943	Chet Covington, Scranton, Eastern
1944	Rip Collins, Albany, Eastern
1945	Gil Coan, Chattanooga, Southern
1946	Sibby Sisti, Indianapolis, American Association
1947	Hank Sauer, Syracuse, International
1948	Gene Woodling, San Francisco, Pacific Coast
1949	Orie Arntzen, Albany, Eastern
1950	Frank Saucier, San Antonio, Texas
1951	Gene Conley, Hartford, Eastern
1952	Bill Skowron, Kansas City, American Association
1953	Gene Conley, Toledo, American Association
1954	Herb Score, Indianapolis, American Association
1955	John Murff, Dallas, Texas

Year	Player, Team, League
1956	Steve Bilko, Los Angeles, Pacific Coast
1957	Norm Siebern, Denver, American Association
1958	Jim O'Toole, Nashville, Southern
1959	Frank Howard, Victoria-Spokane
1960	Willie Davis, Spokane, Pacific Coast
1961	Howie Koplitz, Birmingham, Southern
1962	Bob Bailey, Columbus, International
1963	Don Buford, Indianapolis, International
1964	Mel Stottlemyre, Richmond, International
1965	Joe Foy, Toronto, International
1966	Mike Epstein, Rochester, International
1967	Johnny Bench, Buffalo, International
1968	Merv Rettenmund, Rochester, International
1969	Danny Walton, Oklahoma City, American Association
1970	Don Baylor, Rochester, International
1971	Bobby Grich, Rochester, International
1972	Tom Paciorek, Albuquerque, Pacific Coast
1973	Steve Ontiveros, Phoenix, Pacific Coast
1974	Jim Rice, Pawtucket, International
1975	Hector Cruz, Tulsa, American Association

Year	Player, Team, League
1976	Pat Putnam, Asheville, Western Carolina
1977	Ken Landreaux, S.L.C., Pacific Coast; El Paso, Texas
1978	Champ Summers, Indianapolis, American Association
1979	Mark Bomback, Vancouver, Pacific Coast
1980	Tim Raines, Denver, American Association
1981	Mike Marshall, Albuquerque, Pacific Coast
1982	Ron Kittle, Edmonton, Pacific Coast
1983	Kevin McReynolds, Las Vegas, Pacific Coast
1984	Alan Knicely, Wichita, American Association
1985	Jose Canseco, Hunt., Southern-Tac., Pacific Coast
1986	Tim Pyznarski, Las Vegas, Pacific Coast
1987	Randy Milligan, Tidewater, International
1988	Sandy Alomar Jr., Las Vegas, Pacific Coast Gary Sheffield, Denver, American Association (tie)

Year	Player, Team, League
1989	Sandy Alomar Jr., Las Vegas, Pacific Coast
1990	Jose Offerman, Albuquerque, Pacific Coast
1991	Pedro Martinez, Albuquerque, Pacific Coast
1992	Tim Salmon, Edmonton, Pacific Coast
1993	Cliff Floyd, Harrisburg, Eastern
1994	Derek Jeter, Tampa, Florida State; Albany, Eastern; Columbus, International
1995	Karim Garcia, Albuquerque, Pacific Coast
1996	Vladimir Guerrero, West Palm Beach, Florida State; Harrisburg, Eastern
1997	Ben Grieve, Huntsville, Southern; Edmonton, Pacific Coast
1998	Gabe Kapler, Jacksonville, Southern
1999	Rick Ankiel, Arkansas, Texas; Memphis, Pacific Coast
2000	Jon Rauch, Win.-Salem, Carolina; Birmingham, Southern

MINOR LEAGUE MANAGER OF THE YEAR

Year	Manager, Team, League
1936	Al Sothoron, Milwaukee, American Association
1937	Jake Flowers, Salisbury, Eastern Shore
1938	Paul Richards, Atlanta, Southern
1939	Bill Meyer, Kansas City, American Association
1940	Larry Gilbert, Nashville, Southern
1941	Burt Shotton, Columbus, American Association
1942	Eddie Dyer, Columbus, American Association
1943	Nick Cullop, Columbus, American Association
1944	Al Thomas, Baltimore, International
1945	Lefty O'Doul, San Francisco, Pacific Coast
1946	Clay Hopper, Montreal, International
1947	Nick Cullop, Milwaukee, American Association
1948	Casey Stengel, Oakland, Pacific Coast
1949	Fred Haney, Hollywood, Pacific Coast
1950	Rollie Hemsley, Columbus, American Association
1951	Charlie Grimm, Milwaukee, American Association
1952	Luke Appling, Memphis, Southern
1953	Bobby Bragan, Hollywood, Pacific Coast
1954	Kerby Farrell, Indianapolis, American Association
1955	Bill Rigney, Minneapolis, American Association
1956	Kerby Farrell, Indianapolis, American Association
1957	Ben Geraghty, Wichita, American Association
1958	Cal Ermer, Birmingham, Southern
1959	Pete Reiser, Victoria, Texas
1960	Mel McGaha, Toronto, International
1961	Kerby Farrell, Buffalo, International
1962	Ben Geraghty, Jacksonville, International
1963	Rollie Hemsley, Indianapolis, International
1964	Harry Walker, Jacksonville, International
1965	Grady Hatton, Oklahoma City, Pacific Coast
1966	Bob Lemon, Seattle, Pacific Coast
1967	Bob Skinner, San Diego, Pacific Coast
1968	Jack Tighe, Toledo, International

Year	Manager, Team, League
1969	Clyde McCullough, Tidewater, International
1970	Tom Lasorda, Spokane, Pacific Coast
1971	Del Rice, Salt Lake City, Pacific Coast
1972	Hank Bauer, Tidewater, International
1973	Joe Morgan, Charleston, International
1974	Joe Altobelli, Rochester, International
1975	Joe Frazier, Tidewater, International
1976	Vern Rapp, Denver, American Association
1977	Tommy Thompson, Arkan., Texas
1978	Les Moss, Evansville, American Association
1979	Vern Benson, Syracuse, International
1980	Hal Lanier, Springfield, American Association
1981	Del Crandall, Albuquerque, Pacific Coast
1982	George Scherger, Indianapolis, American Association
1983	Bill Dancy, Reading, Eastern
1984	Bob Rodgers, Indianapolis, American Association
1985	Jim Fregosi, Louisville, American Association
1986	Joe Sparks, Indianapolis, American Association
1987	Terry Collins, Albuquerque, Pacific Coast
1988	Joe Sparks, Indianapolis, American Association
1989	Bob Bailor, Syracuse, International
1990	Sal Rende, Omaha, American Association
1991	Chris Chambliss, Greenville, Southern
1992	Grady Little, Greenville, Southern
1993	Jim Tracy, Harrisburg, Eastern
1994	Mike Jirschele, Wilmington, Carolina
1995	Pete Mackanin, Ottawa, International
1996	John Mizerock, Wilmington, Carolina
1997	Marv Foley, Rochester, International
1998	Doug Davis, Columbia, South Atlantic
1999	DeMarlo Hale, Trenton, Eastern
2000	Joel Skinner, Buffalo, International

MINOR LEAGUE EXECUTIVE OF THE YEAR (HIGHER CLASSIFICATIONS, 1936-1992)

(Restricted to Class AAA starting in 1963)

Year	Executive, Team, League
1936	Earl Mann, Atlanta, Southern
1937	Robert LaMotte, Savannah, Sally
1938	Louis McKenna, St. Paul, American Association
1939	Bruce Dudley, Louisville, American Association
1940	Roy Hamey, Kansas City, American Association
1941	Emil Sick, Seattle, Pacific Coast
1942	Bill Veeck, Milwaukee, American Association
1943	Clarence Rowland, Los Angeles, Pacific Coast
1944	William Mulligan, Seattle, Pacific Coast
1945	Bruce Dudley, Louisville, American Association
1946	Earl Mann, Atlanta, Southern
1947	William Purnhage, Waterloo, I.I.I.
1948	Edward Glennon, Birmingham, Southern
1949	Ted Sullivan, Indianapolis, American Association
1950	Clearnce (Brick) Laws, Oakland, Pacific Coast
1951	Robert Howsam, Denver, West
1952	Jack Cooke, Toronto, International
1953	Richard Burnett, Dallas, Texas
1954	Edward Stumpf, Indianapolis, American Association

Year	Executive, Team, League
1955	Dewey Soriano, Seattle, Pacific Coast
1956	Robert Howsam, Denver American Association
1957	John Stiglmeier, Buffalo, International
1958	Edward Glennon, Birmingham, Southern
1959	Edward Leishman, Salt Lake City, Pacific Coast
1960	Ray Winder, Little Rock, Southern
1961	Elten Schiller, Omaha, American Association
1962	George Sisler Jr., Rochester, International
1963	Lewis Matlin, Hawaii, Pacific Coast
1964	Edward Leishman, San Diego, Pacific Coast
1965	Harold Cooper, Columbus, International
1966	John Quinn Jr., Hawaii, Pacific Coast
1967	Hillman Lyons, Richmond, International
1968	Gabe Paul Jr., Tulsa, Pacific Coast
1969	Bill Gardner, Louisville, International
1970	Dick King, Wichita, American Association
1971	Carl Steinfeldt Jr., Rochester, International
1972	Don Labbruzzo, Evansville, American Association
1973	Merle Miller, Tucson, Pacific Coast

Year	Executive, Team, League
1974—John Carbray, Sacramento, Pacific Coast
1975—Stan Naccarato, Tacoma, Pacific Coast
1976—Art Teece, Salt Lake City, Pacific Coast
1977—George Sisler Jr., Columbus, International
1978—Willie Sanchez, Albuquerque, Pacific Coast
1979—George Sisler Jr., Columbus, International
1980—Jim Burris, Denver, American Association
1981—Pat McKernan, Albuquerque, Pacific Coast
1982—A. Ray Smith, Louisville, American Association
1983—A. Ray Smith, Louisville, American Association

Year Executive, Team, League
1974—John Carbray, Sacramento, Pacific Coast
1975—Stan Naccarato, Tacoma, Pacific Coast
1976—Art Teece, Salt Lake City, Pacific Coast
1977—George Sisler Jr., Columbus, International
1978—Willie Sanchez, Albuquerque, Pacific Coast
1979—George Sisler Jr., Columbus, International
1980—Jim Burris, Denver, American Association
1981—Pat McKernan, Albuquerque, Pacific Coast
1982—A. Ray Smith, Louisville, American Association
1983—A. Ray Smith, Louisville, American Association

Year Executive, Team, League
1984—Mike Tamburro, Pawtucket, International
1985—Patty Cox Hampton, Oklahoma City, American Association
1986—Bob Goughan, Rochester, International
1987—Stu Kehoe, Vancouver, Pacific Coast
1988—Bob Rich, Buffalo, American Association
1989—Larry Schmittou, Nashville, American Association
1990—Greg Corns, Phoenix, Pacific Coast
1991—Tom Maloney, Denver, American Association
1992—Lou Schwechheimer, Pawtucket, International

MINOR LEAGUE EXECUTIVE OF THE YEAR (LOWER CLASSIFICATIONS, 1950-1990)

(Separate awards for Class AA and Class A started in 1963; for Short Class A in 1988)

Year Executive, Team, League
1950—H. Cooper, Hutchinson, Western Association
1951—O. W. (Bill) Hayes, Triple, B.S.
1952—Hillman Lyons, Danville, MOV
1953—Carl Roth, Peoria, I.I.I.
1954—James Meagham, Cedar Rapids, I.I.I.
1955—John Petrakis, Dubuque, MOV
1956—Marvin Milkes, Fresno, California
1957—Richard Wagner, Lincoln, West.
1958—Gerald Waring, Macon, Sally
1959—Clay Dennis, Des Moines, I.I.I.
1960—Hubert Kittle, Yakima, Northwest
1961—David Steele, Fresno, California
1962—John Quinn Jr., San Jose, California
1963—Hugh Finnerty, Tulsa, Texas
    Ben Jewell, M. Valley, Pioneer
1964—Glynn West, Birmingham, Southern
    James Bayens, Rock Hill, W. Carolina
1965—Dick Butler, Dallas-Ft. Worth, Texas
    Ken. Blackman, Quad Cities, Midwest
1966—Tom Fleming, Evansville, Southern
    Cappy Harada, Lodi, California
1967—Robert Quinn, Reading, Eastern
    Pat Williams, Spar'burg, W.C.
1968—Phil Howser, Charlotte, Southern
    Merle Miller, Burlington, Midwest
1969—Charlie Blaney, Albuquerque, Texas
    Bill Gorman, Visalia, California
1970—Carl Sawatski, Arkansas, Texas
    Bob Williams, Bakersfield, California
1971—Miles Wolff, Savannah, Dixie Association
    Ed Holtz, Appleton, Midwest
1972—John Begzos, S. Antonio, Texas
    Bob Piccinini, Modesto, California
1973—Dick Kravitz, Jacksonville, Southern
    Fritz Colschen, Clinton, Midwest
1974—Jim Paul, El Paso, Texas
    Bing Russell, Portland, Northwest

Year Executive, Team, League
1975—Jim Paul, El Paso, Texas
    Cordy Jensen, Eugene, Northwest
1976—Woodrow Reid, Chattanooga, Southern
    Don Buchheister, Cedar Rapids, Midwest
1977—Jim Paul, El Paso, Texas
    Harry Pells, Quad Cities, Midwest
1978—Larry Schmittou, Nashville, Southern
    Dave Hersh, Appleton, Midwest
1979—Bill Rigney Jr., Midland, Texas
    Tom Romenesko, Greensboro, W.C.
1980—Frances Crockett, Charlotte, Southern
    Tom Romenesko, Greensboro, W.C.
1981—Allie Prescott, Memphis, Southern
    Dan Overstreet, Hagerstown, Caro.
1982—Art Clarkson, Birmingham, Southern
    Bob Carruesco, Stockton, California
1983—Edward Kenney, New Britain, Eastern
    Terry Reynolds, Vero Beach, Florida State
1984—Bruce Baldwin, Greenville, Southern
    Dave Tarrolly, Beloit, Midwest
1985—Ben Bernard, Albany-Colonie, Eastern
    Pete Vonachen, Peoria, Midwest
1986—Bill Davidson, Midland, Texas
    Rob Dlugozima, Durham, Carolina
1987—Joe Preseren, Tulsa, Texas
    Skip Weisman, Greensboro, South Atlantic
1988—Bill Valentine, Arkansas, Texas
    Dennis Bastien, Charleston (W.Va.), South Atlantic
    Bob Beban, Eugene, Northwest
1989—Chuck Domino, Reading, Eastern
    John Baxter, South Bend, Midwest
    Bill Pereira, Boise, Northwest
1990—Joe Preseren, Tulsa, Texas
    Dan Chapman, Stockton, California
    Dave Baggott, Salt Lake City, Pioneer

MINOR LEAGUE EXECUTIVE OF THE YEAR

Year Executive, Team, League
1993—Todd Vander Woude, Harrisburg, Eastern (AA)
1994—Scott Lane, West Michigan, Midwest (A)
1995—Jack and Mary Cain, Portland, Northwest (A)
1996—Wayne Hodes, Trenton, Eastern (AA)

Year Executive, Team, League
1997—Andy Milovich, Erie, New York-Pennsylvania (A)
1998—Chuck Domino, Reading, Eastern (AA)
1999—Ben Mondor, Pawtucket, International (AAA)
2000—Art Savage, Sacramento, Pacific Coast (AAA)

RAWLINGS GOLD GLOVE TEAMS

1957
MAJORS
P— Bobby Shantz, New York A.L.
C— Sherm Lollar, Chicago A.L.
1B— Gil Hodges, Brooklyn N.L.
2B— Nellie Fox, Chicago A.L.
3B— Frank Malzone, Boston A.L.
SS— Roy McMillan, Cincinnati N.L.
OF— Minnie Minoso, Chicago A.L.
OF— Willie Mays, New York N.L.
OF— Al Kaline, Detroit A.L.

1958
AMERICAN LEAGUE
P— Bobby Shantz, New York
C— Sherm Lollar, Chicago
1B— Vic Power, Cleveland
2B— Frank Bolling, Detroit
3B— Frank Malzone, Boston
SS— Luis Aparicio, Chicago
OF— Norm Siebern, New York
OF— Jimmy Piersall, Boston
OF— Al Kaline, Detroit

NATIONAL LEAGUE
P— Harvey Haddix, Cincinnati
C— Del Crandall, Milwaukee
1B— Gil Hodges, Los Angeles
2B— Bill Mazeroski, Pittsburgh
3B— Ken Boyer, St. Louis
SS— Roy McMillan, Cincinnati
OF— Frank Robinson, Cincinnati
OF— Willie Mays, San Francisco
OF— Hank Aaron, Milwaukee

1959
AMERICAN LEAGUE
P— Bobby Shantz, New York
C— Sherm Lollar, Chicago
1B— Vic Power, Cleveland
2B— Nellie Fox, Chicago
3B— Frank Malzone, Boston
SS— Luis Aparicio, Chicago
OF— Minnie Minoso, Cleveland
OF— Al Kaline, Detroit
OF— Jackie Jensen, Boston

NATIONAL LEAGUE
P— Harvey Haddix, Pittsburgh
C— Del Crandall, Milwaukee
1B— Gil Hodges, Los Angeles
2B— Charley Neal, Los Angeles
3B— Ken Boyer, St. Louis
SS— Roy McMillan, Cincinnati
OF— Jackie Brandt, San Francisco
OF— Willie Mays, San Francisco
OF— Hank Aaron, Milwaukee

1960
AMERICAN LEAGUE
P— Bobby Shantz, New York
C— Earl Battey, Washington
1B— Vic Power, Cleveland
2B— Nellie Fox, Chicago
3B— Brooks Robinson, Baltimore
SS— Luis Aparicio, Chicago
OF— Minnie Minoso, Chicago
OF— Jim Landis, Chicago
OF— Roger Maris, New York

NATIONAL LEAGUE
P— Harvey Haddix, Pittsburgh
C— Del Crandall, Milwaukee
1B— Bill White, St. Louis
2B— Bill Mazeroski, Pittsburgh
3B— Ken Boyer, St. Louis
SS— Ernie Banks, Chicago
OF— Wally Moon, Los Angeles
OF— Willie Mays, San Francisco
OF— Hank Aaron, Milwaukee

1961
AMERICAN LEAGUE
P— Frank Lary, Detroit
C— Earl Battey, Minnesota
1B— Vic Power, Cleveland
2B— Bobby Richardson, New York
3B— Brooks Robinson, Baltimore
SS— Luis Aparicio, Chicago
OF— Al Kaline, Detroit
OF— Jimmy Piersall, Cleveland
OF— Jim Landis, Chicago

NATIONAL LEAGUE
P— Bobby Shantz, Pittsburgh
C— John Roseboro, Los Angeles
1B— Bill White, St. Louis
2B— Bill Mazeroski, Pittsburgh
3B— Ken Boyer, St. Louis
SS— Maury Wills, Los Angeles
OF— Willie Mays, San Francisco
OF— Roberto Clemente, Pittsburgh
OF— Vada Pinson, Cincinnati

1962
AMERICAN LEAGUE
P— Jim Kaat, Minnesota
C— Earl Battey, Minnesota
1B— Vic Power, Minnesota
2B— Bobby Richardson, New York
3B— Brooks Robinson, Baltimore
SS— Luis Aparicio, Chicago
OF— Jim Landis, Chicago

OF— Mickey Mantle, New York
OF— Al Kaline, Detroit

NATIONAL LEAGUE
P— Bobby Shantz, St. Louis
C— Del Crandall, Milwaukee
1B— Bill White, St. Louis
2B— Ken Hubbs, Chicago
3B— Jim Davenport, San Francisco
SS— Maury Wills, Los Angeles
OF— Willie Mays, San Francisco
OF— Roberto Clemente, Pittsburgh
OF— Bill Virdon, Pittsburgh

1963
AMERICAN LEAGUE
P— Jim Kaat, Minnesota
C— Elston Howard, New York
1B— Vic Power, Minnesota
2B— Bobby Richardson, New York
3B— Brooks Robinson, Baltimore
SS— Zoilo Versalles, Minnesota
OF— Al Kaline, Detroit
OF— Carl Yastrzemski, Boston
OF— Jim Landis, Chicago

NATIONAL LEAGUE
P— Bobby Shantz, St. Louis
C— Johnny Edwards, Cincinnati
1B— Bill White, St. Louis
2B— Bill Mazeroski, Pittsburgh
3B— Ken Boyer, St. Louis
SS— Bobby Wine, Philadelphia
OF— Willie Mays, San Francisco
OF— Roberto Clemente, Pittsburgh
OF— Curt Flood, St. Louis

1964
AMERICAN LEAGUE
P— Jim Kaat, Minnesota
C— Elston Howard, New York
1B— Vic Power, Los Angeles
2B— Bobby Richardson, New York
3B— Brooks Robinson, Baltimore
SS— Luis Aparicio, Baltimore
OF— Al Kaline, Detroit
OF— Jim Landis, Chicago
OF— Vic Davalillo, Cleveland

NATIONAL LEAGUE
P— Bobby Shantz, Philadelphia
C— Johnny Edwards, Cincinnati
1B— Bill White, St. Louis
2B— Bill Mazeroski, Pittsburgh
3B— Ron Santo, Chicago
SS— Ruben Amaro, Philadelphia
OF— Willie Mays, San Francisco
OF— Roberto Clemente, Pittsburgh
OF— Curt Flood, St. Louis

1965
AMERICAN LEAGUE
P— Jim Kaat, Minnesota
C— Bill Freehan, Detroit
1B— Joe Pepitone, New York
2B— Bobby Richardson, New York
3B— Brooks Robinson, Baltimore
SS— Zoilo Versalles, Minnesota
OF— Al Kaline, Detroit
OF— Tom Tresh, New York
OF— Carl Yastrzemski, Boston

NATIONAL LEAGUE
P— Bob Gibson, St. Louis
C— Joe Torre, Atlanta
1B— Bill White, St. Louis
2B— Bill Mazeroski, Pittsburgh
3B— Ron Santo, Chicago
SS— Leo Cardenas, Cincinnati

OF— Willie Mays, San Francisco
OF— Roberto Clemente, Pittsburgh
OF— Curt Flood, St. Louis

1966
AMERICAN LEAGUE
P— Jim Kaat, Minnesota
C— Bill Freehan, Detroit
1B— Joe Pepitone, New York
2B— Bobby Knoop, California
3B— Brooks Robinson, Baltimore
SS— Luis Aparicio, Baltimore
OF— Al Kaline, Detroit
OF— Tommie Agee, Chicago
OF— Tony Oliva, Minnesota

NATIONAL LEAGUE
P— Bob Gibson, St. Louis
C— John Roseboro, Los Angeles
1B— Bill White, Philadelphia
2B— Bill Mazeroski, Pittsburgh
3B— Ron Santo, Chicago
SS— Gene Alley, Pittsburgh
OF— Willie Mays, San Francisco
OF— Curt Flood, St. Louis
OF— Roberto Clemente, Pittsburgh

1967
AMERICAN LEAGUE
P— Jim Kaat, Minnesota
C— Bill Freehan, Detroit
1B— George Scott, Boston
2B— Bobby Knoop, California
3B— Brooks Robinson, Baltimore
SS— Jim Fregosi, California
OF— Carl Yastrzemski, Boston
OF— Paul Blair, Baltimore
OF— Al Kaline, Detroit

NATIONAL LEAGUE
P— Bob Gibson, St. Louis
C— Randy Hundley, Chicago
1B— Wes Parker, Los Angeles
2B— Bill Mazeroski, Pittsburgh
3B— Ron Santo, Chicago
SS— Gene Alley, Pittsburgh
OF— Roberto Clemente, Pittsburgh
OF— Curt Flood, St. Louis
OF— Willie Mays, San Francisco

1968
AMERICAN LEAGUE
P— Jim Kaat, Minnesota
C— Bill Freehan, Detroit
1B— George Scott, Boston
2B— Bobby Knoop, California
3B— Brooks Robinson, Baltimore
SS— Luis Aparicio, Chicago
OF— Mickey Stanley, Detroit
OF— Carl Yastrzemski, Boston
OF— Reggie Smith, Boston

NATIONAL LEAGUE
P— Bob Gibson, St. Louis
C— Johnny Bench, Cincinnati
1B— Wes Parker, Los Angeles
2B— Glenn Beckert, Chicago
3B— Ron Santo, Chicago
SS— Dal Maxvill, St. Louis
OF— Willie Mays, San Francisco
OF— Roberto Clemente, Pittsburgh
OF— Curt Flood, St. Louis

1969
AMERICAN LEAGUE
P— Jim Kaat, Minnesota
C— Bill Freehan, Detroit
1B— Joe Pepitone, New York
2B— Dave Johnson, Baltimore

3B— Brooks Robinson, Baltimore
SS— Mark Belanger, Baltimore
OF— Paul Blair, Baltimore
OF— Mickey Stanley, Detroit
OF— Carl Yastrzemski, Boston

NATIONAL LEAGUE
P— Bob Gibson, St. Louis
C— Johnny Bench, Cincinnati
1B— Wes Parker, Los Angeles
2B— Felix Millan, Atlanta
3B— Clete Boyer, Atlanta
SS— Don Kessinger, Chicago
OF— Roberto Clemente, Pittsburgh
OF— Curt Flood, St. Louis
OF— Pete Rose, Cincinnati

1970
AMERICAN LEAGUE
P— Jim Kaat, Minnesota
C— Ray Fosse, Cleveland
1B— Jim Spencer, California
2B— Dave Johnson, Baltimore
3B— Brooks Robinson, Baltimore
SS— Luis Aparicio, Chicago
OF— Mickey Stanley, Detroit
OF— Paul Blair, Baltimore
OF— Ken Berry, Chicago

NATIONAL LEAGUE
P— Bob Gibson, St. Louis
C— Johnny Bench, Cincinnati
1B— Wes Parker, Los Angeles
2B— Tommy Helms, Cincinnati
3B— Doug Rader, Houston
SS— Don Kessinger, Chicago
OF— Roberto Clemente, Pittsburgh
OF— Tommie Agee, New York
OF— Pete Rose, Cincinnati

1971
AMERICAN LEAGUE
P— Jim Kaat, Minnesota
C— Ray Fosse, Cleveland
1B— George Scott, Boston
2B— Dave Johnson, Baltimore
3B— Brooks Robinson, Baltimore
SS— Mark Belanger, Baltimore
OF— Paul Blair, Baltimore
OF— Amos Otis, Kansas City
OF— Carl Yastrzemski, Boston

NATIONAL LEAGUE
P— Bob Gibson, St. Louis
C— Johnny Bench, Cincinnati
1B— Wes Parker, Los Angeles
2B— Tommy Helms, Cincinnati
3B— Doug Rader, Houston
SS— Bud Harrelson, New York
OF— Roberto Clemente, Pittsburgh
OF— Bobby Bonds, San Francisco
OF— Willie Davis, Los Angeles

1972
AMERICAN LEAGUE
P— Jim Kaat, Minnesota
C— Carlton Fisk, Boston
1B— George Scott, Milwaukee
2B— Doug Griffin, Boston
3B— Brooks Robinson, Baltimore
SS— Ed Brinkman, Detroit
OF— Paul Blair, Baltimore
OF— Bobby Murcer, New York
OF— Ken Berry, California

NATIONAL LEAGUE
P— Bob Gibson, St. Louis
C— Johnny Bench, Cincinnati
1B— Wes Parker, Los Angeles
2B— Felix Millan, Atlanta

3B— Doug Rader, Houston
SS— Larry Bowa, Philadelphia
OF— Roberto Clemente, Pittsburgh
OF— Cesar Cedeno, Houston
OF— Willie Davis, Los Angeles

1973
AMERICAN LEAGUE
P— Jim Kaat, Chicago
C— Thurman Munson, New York
1B— George Scott, Milwaukee
2B— Bobby Grich, Baltimore
3B— Brooks Robinson, Baltimore
SS— Mark Belanger, Baltimore
OF— Paul Blair, Baltimore
OF— Amos Otis, Kansas City
OF— Mickey Stanley, Detroit

NATIONAL LEAGUE
P— Bob Gibson, St. Louis
C— Johnny Bench, Cincinnati
1B— Mike Jorgensen, Montreal
2B— Joe Morgan, Cincinnati
3B— Doug Rader, Houston
SS— Roger Metzger, Houston
OF— Bobby Bonds, San Francisco
OF— Cesar Cedeno, Houston
OF— Willie Davis, Los Angeles

1974
AMERICAN LEAGUE
P— Jim Kaat, Chicago
C— Thurman Munson, New York
1B— George Scott, Milwaukee
2B— Bobby Grich, Baltimore
3B— Brooks Robinson, Baltimore
SS— Mark Belanger, Baltimore
OF— Paul Blair, Baltimore
OF— Amos Otis, Kansas City
OF— Joe Rudi, Oakland

NATIONAL LEAGUE
P— Andy Messersmith, Los Angeles
C— Johnny Bench, Cincinnati
1B— Steve Garvey, Los Angeles
2B— Joe Morgan, Cincinnati
3B— Doug Rader, Houston
SS— Dave Concepcion, Cincinnati
OF— Cesar Cedeno, Houston
OF— Cesar Geronimo, Cincinnati
OF— Bobby Bonds, San Francisco

1975
AMERICAN LEAGUE
P— Jim Kaat, Chicago
C— Thurman Munson, New York
1B— George Scott, Milwaukee
2B— Bobby Grich, Baltimore
3B— Brooks Robinson, Baltimore
SS— Mark Belanger, Baltimore
OF— Paul Blair, Baltimore
OF— Joe Rudi, Oakland
OF— Fred Lynn, Boston

NATIONAL LEAGUE
P— Andy Messersmith, Los Angeles
C— Johnny Bench, Cincinnati
1B— Steve Garvey, Los Angeles
2B— Joe Morgan, Cincinnati
3B— Ken Reitz, St. Louis
SS— Dave Concepcion, Cincinnati
OF— Cesar Cedeno, Houston
OF— Cesar Geronimo, Cincinnati
OF— Garry Maddox, Philadelphia

1976
AMERICAN LEAGUE
P— Jim Palmer, Baltimore
C— Jim Sundberg, Texas

1B— George Scott, Milwaukee
2B— Bobby Grich, Baltimore
3B— Aurelio Rodriguez, Detroit
SS— Mark Belanger, Baltimore
OF— Joe Rudi, Oakland
OF— Dwight Evans, Boston
OF— Rick Manning, Cleveland

NATIONAL LEAGUE
P— Jim Kaat, Philadelphia
C— Johnny Bench, Cincinnati
1B— Steve Garvey, Los Angeles
2B— Joe Morgan, Cincinnati
3B— Mike Schmidt, Philadelphia
SS— Dave Concepcion, Cincinnati
OF— Cesar Cedeno, Houston
OF— Cesar Geronimo, Cincinnati
OF— Garry Maddox, Philadelphia

1977
AMERICAN LEAGUE
P— Jim Palmer, Baltimore
C— Jim Sundberg, Texas
1B— Jim Spencer, Chicago
2B— Frank White, Kansas City
3B— Graig Nettles, New York
SS— Mark Belanger, Baltimore
OF— Juan Beniquez, Texas
OF— Carl Yastrzemski, Boston
OF— Al Cowens, Kansas City

NATIONAL LEAGUE
P— Jim Kaat, Philadelphia
C— Johnny Bench, Cincinnati
1B— Steve Garvey, Los Angeles
2B— Joe Morgan, Cincinnati
3B— Mike Schmidt, Philadelphia
SS— Dave Concepcion, Cincinnati
OF— Cesar Geronimo, Cincinnati
OF— Garry Maddox, Philadelphia
OF— Dave Parker, Pittsburgh

1978
AMERICAN LEAGUE
P— Jim Palmer, Baltimore
C— Jim Sundberg, Texas
1B— Chris Chambliss, New York
2B— Frank White, Kansas City
3B— Graig Nettles, New York
SS— Mark Belanger, Baltimore
OF— Fred Lynn, Boston
OF— Dwight Evans, Boston
OF— Rick Miller, California

NATIONAL LEAGUE
P— Phil Niekro, Atlanta
C— Bob Boone, Philadelphia
1B— Keith Hernandez, St. Louis
2B— Dave Lopes, Los Angeles
3B— Mike Schmidt, Philadelphia
SS— Larry Bowa, Philadelphia
OF— Garry Maddox, Philadelphia
OF— Dave Parker, Pittsburgh
OF— Ellis Valentine, Montreal

1979
AMERICAN LEAGUE
P— Jim Palmer, Baltimore
C— Jim Sundberg, Texas
1B— Cecil Cooper, Milwaukee
2B— Frank White, Kansas City
3B— Buddy Bell, Texas
SS— Rick Burleson, Boston
OF— Dwight Evans, Boston
OF— Sixto Lezcano, Milwaukee
OF— Fred Lynn, Boston

NATIONAL LEAGUE
P— Phil Niekro, Atlanta
C— Bob Boone, Philadelphia

1B— Keith Hernandez, St. Louis
2B— Manny Trillo, Philadelphia
3B— Mike Schmidt, Philadelphia
SS— Dave Concepcion, Cincinnati
OF— Garry Maddox, Philadelphia
OF— Dave Parker, Pittsburgh
OF— Dave Winfield, San Diego

1980
AMERICAN LEAGUE
P— Mike Norris, Oakland
C— Jim Sundberg, Texas
1B— Cecil Cooper, Milwaukee
2B— Frank White, Kansas City
3B— Buddy Bell, Texas
SS— Alan Trammell, Detroit
OF— Fred Lynn, Boston
OF— Dwayne Murphy, Oakland
OF— Willie Wilson, Kansas City

NATIONAL LEAGUE
P— Phil Niekro, Atlanta
C— Gary Carter, Montreal
1B— Keith Hernandez, St. Louis
2B— Doug Flynn, New York
3B— Mike Schmidt, Philadelphia
SS— Ozzie Smith, San Diego
OF— Andre Dawson, Montreal
OF— Garry Maddox, Philadelphia
OF— Dave Winfield, San Diego

1981
AMERICAN LEAGUE
P— Mike Norris, Oakland
C— Jim Sundberg, Texas
1B— Mike Squires, Chicago
2B— Frank White, Kansas City
3B— Buddy Bell, Texas
SS— Alan Trammell, Detroit
OF— Dwayne Murphy, Oakland
OF— Dwight Evans, Boston
OF— Rickey Henderson, Oakland

NATIONAL LEAGUE
P— Steve Carlton, Philadelphia
C— Gary Carter, Montreal
1B— Keith Hernandez, St. Louis
2B— Manny Trillo, Philadelphia
3B— Mike Schmidt, Philadelphia
SS— Ozzie Smith, San Diego
OF— Andre Dawson, Montreal
OF— Garry Maddox, Philadelphia
OF— Dusty Baker, Los Angeles

1982
AMERICAN LEAGUE
P— Ron Guidry, New York
C— Bob Boone, California
1B— Eddie Murray, Baltimore
2B— Frank White, Kansas City
3B— Buddy Bell, Texas
SS— Robin Yount, Milwaukee
OF— Dwight Evans, Boston
OF— Dave Winfield, New York
OF— Dwayne Murphy, Oakland

NATIONAL LEAGUE
P— Phil Niekro, Atlanta
C— Gary Carter, Montreal
1B— Keith Hernandez, St. Louis
2B— Manny Trillo, Philadelphia
3B— Mike Schmidt, Philadelphia
SS— Ozzie Smith, St. Louis

OF— Andre Dawson, Montreal
OF— Dale Murphy, Atlanta
OF— Garry Maddox, Philadelphia

1983
AMERICAN LEAGUE
P— Ron Guidry, New York
C— Lance Parrish, Detroit
1B— Eddie Murray, Baltimore
2B— Lou Whitaker, Detroit
3B— Buddy Bell, Texas
SS— Alan Trammell, Detroit
OF— Dwight Evans, Boston
OF— Dave Winfield, New York
OF— Dwayne Murphy, Oakland

NATIONAL LEAGUE
P— Phil Niekro, Atlanta
C— Tony Pena, Pittsburgh
1B— Keith Hernandez, St.L.-N.Y.
2B— Ryne Sandberg, Chicago
3B— Mike Schmidt, Philadelphia
SS— Ozzie Smith, St. Louis
OF— Andre Dawson, Montreal
OF— Dale Murphy, Atlanta
OF— Willie McGee, St. Louis

1984
AMERICAN LEAGUE
P— Ron Guidry, New York
C— Lance Parrish, Detroit
1B— Eddie Murray, Baltimore
2B— Lou Whitaker, Detroit
3B— Buddy Bell, Texas
SS— Alan Trammell, Detroit
OF— Dwight Evans, Boston
OF— Dave Winfield, New York
OF— Dwayne Murphy, Oakland

NATIONAL LEAGUE
P— Joaquin Andujar, St. Louis
C— Tony Pena, Pittsburgh
1B— Keith Hernandez, New York
2B— Ryne Sandberg, Chicago
3B— Mike Schmidt, Philadelphia
SS— Ozzie Smith, St. Louis
OF— Dale Murphy, Atlanta
OF— Bob Dernier, Chicago
OF— Andre Dawson, Montreal

1985
AMERICAN LEAGUE
P— Ron Guidry, New York
C— Lance Parrish, Detroit
1B— Don Mattingly, New York
2B— Lou Whitaker, Detroit
3B— George Brett, Kansas City
SS— Alfredo Griffin, Oakland
OF— Gary Pettis, California
OF— Dave Winfield, New York
OF— Dwight Evans, Boston (tie)
      Dwayne Murphy, Oakland (tie)

NATIONAL LEAGUE
P— Rick Reuschel, Pittsburgh
C— Tony Pena, Pittsburgh
1B— Keith Hernandez, New York
2B— Ryne Sandberg, Chicago
3B— Tim Wallach, Montreal
SS— Ozzie Smith, St. Louis
OF— Willie McGee, St. Louis
OF— Dale Murphy, Atlanta
OF— Andre Dawson, Montreal

1986
AMERICAN LEAGUE
P— Ron Guidry, New York
C— Bob Boone, California

1B— Don Mattingly, New York
2B— Frank White, Kansas City
3B— Gary Gaetti, Minnesota
SS— Tony Fernandez, Toronto
OF— Gary Pettis, California
OF— Jesse Barfield, Toronto
OF— Kirby Puckett, Minnesota

NATIONAL LEAGUE
P— Fernando Valenzuela, Los Angeles
C— Jody Davis, Chicago
1B— Keith Hernandez, New York
2B— Ryne Sandberg, Chicago
3B— Mike Schmidt, Philadelphia
SS— Ozzie Smith, St. Louis
OF— Tony Gwynn, San Diego
OF— Dale Murphy, Atlanta
OF— Willie McGee, St. Louis

1987
AMERICAN LEAGUE
P— Mark Langston, Seattle
C— Bob Boone, California
1B— Don Mattingly, New York
2B— Frank White, Kansas City
3B— Gary Gaetti, Minnesota
SS— Tony Fernandez, Toronto
OF— Jesse Barfield, Toronto
OF— Kirby Puckett, Minnesota
OF— Dave Winfield, New York

NATIONAL LEAGUE
P— Rick Reuschel, Pit.-S.F.
C— Mike LaValliere, Pittsburgh
1B— Keith Hernandez, New York
2B— Ryne Sandberg, Chicago
3B— Terry Pendleton, St. Louis
SS— Ozzie Smith, St. Louis
OF— Eric Davis, Cincinnati
OF— Tony Gwynn, San Diego
OF— Andre Dawson, Chicago

1988
AMERICAN LEAGUE
P— Mark Langston, Seattle
C— Bob Boone, California
1B— Don Mattingly, New York
2B— Harold Reynolds, Seattle
3B— Gary Gaetti, Minnesota
SS— Tony Fernandez, Toronto
OF— Kirby Puckett, Minnesota
OF— Devon White, California
OF— Gary Pettis, Detroit

NATIONAL LEAGUE
P— Orel Hershiser, Los Angeles
C— Benito Santiago, San Diego
1B— Keith Hernandez, New York
2B— Ryne Sandberg, Chicago
3B— Tim Wallach, Montreal
SS— Ozzie Smith, St. Louis
OF— Andy Van Slyke, Pittsburgh
OF— Eric Davis, Cincinnati
OF— Andre Dawson, Chicago

1989
AMERICAN LEAGUE
P— Bret Saberhagen, Kansas City
C— Bob Boone, Kansas City
1B— Don Mattingly, New York
2B— Harold Reynolds, Seattle
3B— Gary Gaetti, Minnesota
SS— Tony Fernandez, Toronto
OF— Kirby Puckett, Minnesota
OF— Devon White, California
OF— Gary Pettis, Detroit

OF— Andre Dawson, Montreal
OF— Dale Murphy, Atlanta
OF— Garry Maddox, Philadelphia

NATIONAL LEAGUE
P— Ron Darling, New York
C— Benito Santiago, San Diego
1B— Andres Galarraga, Montreal
2B— Ryne Sandberg, Chicago
3B— Terry Pendleton, St. Louis
SS— Ozzie Smith, St. Louis
OF— Andy Van Slyke, Pittsburgh
OF— Tony Gwynn, San Diego
OF— Eric Davis, Cincinnati

1990
AMERICAN LEAGUE
P— Mike Boddicker, Boston
C— Sandy Alomar Jr., Cleveland
1B— Mark McGwire, Oakland
2B— Harold Reynolds, Seattle
3B— Kelly Gruber, Toronto
SS— Ozzie Guillen, Chicago
OF— Ken Griffey Jr., Seattle
OF— Ellis Burks, Boston
OF— Gary Pettis, Texas

NATIONAL LEAGUE
P— Greg Maddux, Chicago
C— Benito Santiago, San Diego
1B— Andres Galarraga, Montreal
2B— Ryne Sandberg, Chicago
3B— Tim Wallach, Montreal
SS— Ozzie Smith, St. Louis
OF— Barry Bonds, Pittsburgh
OF— Andy Van Slyke, Pittsburgh
OF— Tony Gwynn, San Diego

1991
AMERICAN LEAGUE
P— Mark Langston, California
C— Tony Pena, Boston
1B— Don Mattingly, New York
2B— Roberto Alomar, Toronto
3B— Robin Ventura, Chicago
SS— Cal Ripken, Baltimore
OF— Ken Griffey Jr., Seattle
OF— Kirby Puckett, Minnesota
OF— Devon White, Toronto

NATIONAL LEAGUE
P— Greg Maddux, Chicago
C— Tom Pagnozzi, St. Louis
1B— Will Clark, San Francisco
2B— Ryne Sandberg, Chicago
3B— Matt Williams, San Francisco
SS— Ozzie Smith, St. Louis
OF— Barry Bonds, Pittsburgh
OF— Andy Van Slyke, Pittsburgh
OF— Tony Gwynn, San Diego

1992
AMERICAN LEAGUE
P— Mark Langston, California
C— Ivan Rodriguez, Texas
1B— Don Mattingly, New York
2B— Roberto Alomar, Toronto
3B— Robin Ventura, Chicago
SS— Cal Ripken, Baltimore
OF— Ken Griffey Jr., Seattle
OF— Kirby Puckett, Minnesota
OF— Devon White, Toronto

NATIONAL LEAGUE
P— Greg Maddux, Chicago
C— Tom Pagnozzi, St. Louis
1B— Mark Grace, Chicago
2B— Jose Lind, Pittsburgh
3B— Terry Pendleton, Atlanta
SS— Ozzie Smith, St. Louis
OF— Barry Bonds, Pittsburgh

OF— Andy Van Slyke, Pittsburgh
OF— Larry Walker, Montreal

1993
AMERICAN LEAGUE
P— Mark Langston, California
C— Ivan Rodriguez, Texas
1B— Don Mattingly, New York
2B— Roberto Alomar, Toronto
3B— Robin Ventura, Chicago
SS— Omar Vizquel, Seattle
OF— Ken Griffey Jr., Seattle
OF— Kenny Lofton, Cleveland
OF— Devon White, Toronto

NATIONAL LEAGUE
P— Greg Maddux, Atlanta
C— Kirt Manwaring, San Francisco
1B— Mark Grace, Chicago
2B— Robby Thompson, San Fran.
3B— Matt Williams, San Francisco
SS— Jay Bell, Pittsburgh
OF— Barry Bonds, San Francisco
OF— Marquis Grissom, Montreal
OF— Larry Walker, Montreal

1994
AMERICAN LEAGUE
P— Mark Langston, California
C— Ivan Rodriguez, Texas
1B— Don Mattingly, New York
2B— Roberto Alomar, Toronto
3B— Wade Boggs, New York
SS— Omar Vizquel, Cleveland
OF— Ken Griffey Jr., Seattle
OF— Kenny Lofton, Cleveland
OF— Devon White, Toronto

NATIONAL LEAGUE
P— Greg Maddux, Atlanta
C— Tom Pagnozzi, St. Louis
1B— Jeff Bagwell, Houston
2B— Craig Biggio, Houston
3B— Matt Williams, San Francisco
SS— Barry Larkin, Cincinnati
OF— Barry Bonds, San Francisco
OF— Marquis Grissom, Montreal
OF— Darren Lewis, San Francisco

1995
AMERICAN LEAGUE
P— Mark Langston, California
C— Ivan Rodriguez, Texas
1B— J.T. Snow, California
2B— Roberto Alomar, Toronto
3B— Wade Boggs, New York
SS— Omar Vizquel, Cleveland
OF— Ken Griffey Jr., Seattle
OF— Kenny Lofton, Cleveland
OF— Devon White, Toronto

NATIONAL LEAGUE
P— Greg Maddux, Atlanta
C— Charles Johnson, Florida
1B— Mark Grace, Chicago
2B— Craig Biggio, Houston
3B— Ken Caminiti, San Diego
SS— Barry Larkin, Cincinnati
OF— Raul Mondesi, Los Angeles
OF— Marquis Grissom, Atlanta
OF— Steve Finley, San Diego

1996
AMERICAN LEAGUE
P— Mike Mussina, Baltimore
C— Ivan Rodriguez, Texas
1B— J.T. Snow, California

2B— Roberto Alomar, Baltimore
3B— Robin Ventura, Chicago
SS— Omar Vizquel, Cleveland
OF— Jay Buhner, Seattle
OF— Ken Griffey Jr., Seattle
OF— Kenny Lofton, Cleveland

NATIONAL LEAGUE
P— Greg Maddux, Atlanta
C— Charles Johnson, Florida
1B— Mark Grace, Chicago
2B— Craig Biggio, Houston
3B— Ken Caminiti, San Diego
SS— Barry Larkin, Cincinnati
OF— Barry Bonds, San Francisco
OF— Marquis Grissom, Atlanta
OF— Steve Finley, San Diego

1997
AMERICAN LEAGUE
P— Mike Mussina, Baltimore
C— Ivan Rodriguez, Texas
1B— Rafael Palmeiro, Baltimore
2B— Chuck Knoblauch, Minnesota
3B— Matt Williams, Cleveland
SS— Omar Vizquel, Cleveland
OF— Jim Edmonds, Anaheim
OF— Ken Griffey Jr., Seattle
OF— Bernie Williams, New York

NATIONAL LEAGUE
P— Greg Maddux, Atlanta
C— Charles Johnson, Florida
1B— J.T. Snow, San Francisco
2B— Craig Biggio, Houston
3B— Ken Caminiti, San Diego
SS— Rey Ordonez, New York
OF— Barry Bonds, San Francisco
OF— Raul Mondesi, Los Angeles
OF— Larry Walker, Colorado

1998
AMERICAN LEAGUE
P— Mike Mussina, Baltimore
C— Ivan Rodriguez, Texas
1B— Rafael Palmeiro, Baltimore
2B— Roberto Alomar, Baltimore
3B— Robin Ventura, White Sox
SS— Omar Vizquel, Cleveland
OF— Jim Edmonds, Anaheim
OF— Ken Griffey Jr., Seattle
OF— Bernie Williams, New York

NATIONAL LEAGUE
P— Greg Maddux, Atlanta
C— Charles Johnson, Fla.-L.A.
1B— J.T. Snow, San Francisco
2B— Bret Boone, Cincinnati
3B— Scott Rolen, Philadelphia
SS— Rey Ordonez, New York
OF— Barry Bonds, San Francisco
OF— Andruw Jones, Atlanta
OF— Larry Walker, Colorado

1999
AMERICAN LEAGUE
P— Mike Mussina, Baltimore
C— Ivan Rodriguez, Texas
1B— Rafael Palmeiro, Texas
2B— Roberto Alomar, Cleveland
3B— Scott Brosius, New York
SS— Omar Vizquel, Cleveland
OF— Shawn Green, Toronto
OF— Ken Griffey Jr., Seattle
OF— Bernie Williams, New York

HISTORY *Award winners*

NATIONAL LEAGUE
P— Greg Maddux, Atlanta
C— Mike Lieberthal, Philadelphia
1B— J.T. Snow, San Francisco
2B— Pokey Reese, Cincinnati
3B— Robin Ventura, New York
SS— Rey Ordonez, New York
OF— Steve Finley, Arizona
OF— Andruw Jones, Atlanta
OF— Larry Walker, Colorado

2000
AMERICAN LEAGUE
1B— John Olerud, Seattle
2B— Roberto Alomar, Cleveland
3B— Travis Fryman, Cleveland
SS— Omar Vizquel, Cleveland
OF— Jermaine Dye, Kansas City
OF— Darin Erstad, Anaheim
OF— Bernie Williams, New York
C— Ivan Rodriguez, Texas

NATIONAL LEAGUE
1B— J.T. Snow, San Francisco
2B— Pokey Reese, Cincinnati
3B— Scott Rolen, Philadelphia
SS— Neifi Perez, Colorado
OF— Jim Edmonds, St. Louis
OF— Steve Finley, Arizona
OF— Andruw Jones, Atlanta
C— Mike Matheny, St. Louis
P— Greg Maddux, Atlanta

HILLERICH & BRADSBY SILVER SLUGGER TEAMS

HISTORY Award winners

1980
AMERICAN LEAGUE
1B— Cecil Cooper, Milwaukee
2B— Willie Randolph, New York
3B— George Brett, Kansas City
SS— Robin Yount, Milwaukee
OF— Ben Oglivie, Milwaukee
OF— Al Oliver, Texas
OF— Willie Wilson, Kansas City
C— Lance Parrish, Detroit
DH— Reggie Jackson, New York

NATIONAL LEAGUE
1B— Keith Hernandez, St. Louis
2B— Manny Trillo, Philadelphia
3B— Mike Schmidt, Philadelphia
SS— Garry Templeton, St. Louis
OF— Dusty Baker, Los Angeles
OF— Andre Dawson, Montreal
OF— George Hendrick, St. Louis
C— Ted Simmons, St. Louis
P— Bob Forsch, St. Louis

1981
AMERICAN LEAGUE
1B— Cecil Cooper, Milwaukee
2B— Bobby Grich, California
3B— Carney Lansford, Boston
SS— Rick Burleson, California
OF— Rickey Henderson, Oakland
OF— Dwight Evans, Boston
OF— Dave Winfield, New York
C— Carlton Fisk, Chicago
DH— Al Oliver, Texas

NATIONAL LEAGUE
1B— Pete Rose, Philadelphia
2B— Manny Trillo, Philadelphia
3B— Mike Schmidt, Philadelphia
SS— Dave Concepcion, Cincinnati
OF— Andre Dawson, Montreal
OF— George Foster, Cincinnati
OF— Dusty Baker, Los Angeles
C— Gary Carter, Montreal
P— Fernando Valenzuela, Los Angeles

1982
AMERICAN LEAGUE
1B— Cecil Cooper, Milwaukee
2B— Damaso Garcia, Toronto
3B— Doug DeCinces, California
SS— Robin Yount, Milwaukee
OF— Dave Winfield, New York
OF— Willie Wilson, Kansas City
OF— Reggie Jackson, California
C— Lance Parrish, Detroit
DH— Hal McRae, Kansas City

NATIONAL LEAGUE
1B— Al Oliver, Montreal
2B— Joe Morgan, San Francisco
3B— Mike Schmidt, Philadelphia
SS— Dave Concepcion, Cincinnati
OF— Dale Murphy, Atlanta
OF— Pedro Guerrero, Los Angeles

OF— Leon Durham, Chicago
C— Gary Carter, Montreal
P— Don Robinson, Pittsburgh

1983
AMERICAN LEAGUE
1B— Eddie Murray, Baltimore
2B— Lou Whitaker, Detroit
3B— Wade Boggs, Boston
SS— Cal Ripken Jr., Baltimore
OF— Jim Rice, Boston
OF— Dave Winfield, New York
OF— Lloyd Moseby, Toronto
C— Lance Parrish, Detroit
DH— Don Baylor, New York

NATIONAL LEAGUE
1B— George Hendrick, St. Louis
2B— Johnny Ray, Pittsburgh
3B— Mike Schmidt, Philadelphia
SS— Dickie Thon, Houston
OF— Andre Dawson, Montreal
OF— Dale Murphy, Atlanta
OF— Jose Cruz, Houston
C— Terry Kennedy, San Diego
P— Fernando Valenzuela, Los Angeles

1984
AMERICAN LEAGUE
1B— Eddie Murray, Baltimore
2B— Lou Whitaker, Detroit
3B— Buddy Bell, Texas
SS— Cal Ripken Jr., Baltimore
OF— Tony Armas, Boston
OF— Jim Rice, Boston
OF— Dave Winfield, New York
C— Lance Parrish, Detroit
DH— Andre Thornton, Cleveland

NATIONAL LEAGUE
1B— Keith Hernandez, New York
2B— Ryne Sandberg, Chicago
3B— Mike Schmidt, Philadelphia
SS— Garry Templeton, San Diego
OF— Dale Murphy, Atlanta
OF— Jose Cruz, Houston
OF— Tony Gwynn, San Diego
C— Gary Carter, Montreal
P— Rick Rhoden, Pittsburgh

1985
AMERICAN LEAGUE
1B— Don Mattingly, New York
2B— Lou Whitaker, Detroit
3B— George Brett, Kansas City
SS— Cal Ripken Jr., Baltimore
OF— Rickey Henderson, New York
OF— Dave Winfield, New York
OF— George Bell, Toronto
C— Carlton Fisk, Chicago
DH— Don Baylor, New York

NATIONAL LEAGUE
1B— Jack Clark, St. Louis
2B— Ryne Sandberg, Chicago

3B— Tim Wallach, Montreal
SS— Hubie Brooks, Montreal
OF— Willie McGee, St. Louis
OF— Dale Murphy, Atlanta
OF— Dave Parker, Cincinnati
C— Gary Carter, New York
P— Rick Rhoden, Pittsburgh

1986
AMERICAN LEAGUE
1B— Don Mattingly, New York
2B— Frank White, Kansas City
3B— Wade Boggs, Boston
SS— Cal Ripken Jr., Baltimore
OF— George Bell, Toronto
OF— Kirby Puckett, Minnesota
OF— Jesse Barfield, Toronto
C— Lance Parrish, Detroit
DH— Don Baylor, Boston

NATIONAL LEAGUE
1B— Glenn Davis, Houston
2B— Steve Sax, Los Angeles
3B— Mike Schmidt, Philadelphia
SS— Hubie Brooks, Montreal
OF— Tony Gwynn, San Diego
OF— Tim Raines, Montreal
OF— Dave Parker, Cincinnati
C— Gary Carter, New York
P— Rick Rhoden, Pittsburgh

1987
AMERICAN LEAGUE
1B— Don Mattingly, New York
2B— Lou Whitaker, Detroit
3B— Wade Boggs, Boston
SS— Alan Trammell, Detroit
OF— George Bell, Toronto
OF— Dwight Evans, Boston
OF— Kirby Puckett, Minnesota
C— Matt Nokes, Detroit
DH— Paul Molitor, Milwaukee

NATIONAL LEAGUE
1B— Jack Clark, St. Louis
2B— Juan Samuel, Philadelphia
3B— Tim Wallach, Montreal
SS— Ozzie Smith, St. Louis
OF— Andre Dawson, Chicago
OF— Eric Davis, Cincinnati
OF— Tony Gwynn, San Diego
C— Benito Santiago, San Diego
P— Bob Forsch, St. Louis

1988
AMERICAN LEAGUE
1B— George Brett, Kansas City
2B— Julio Franco, Cleveland
3B— Wade Boggs, Boston
SS— Alan Trammell, Detroit
OF— Kirby Puckett, Minnesota
OF— Jose Canseco, Oakland
OF— Mike Greenwell, Boston
C— Carlton Fisk, Chicago
DH— Paul Molitor, Milwaukee

NATIONAL LEAGUE
1B— Andres Galarraga, Montreal
2B— Ryne Sandberg, Chicago
3B— Bobby Bonilla, Pittsburgh
SS— Barry Larkin, Cincinnati
OF— Darryl Strawberry, New York
OF— Andy Van Slyke, Pittsburgh
OF— Kirk Gibson, Los Angeles
C— Benito Santiago, San Diego
P— Tim Leary, Los Angeles

1989
AMERICAN LEAGUE
1B— Fred McGriff, Toronto
2B— Julio Franco, Texas
3B— Wade Boggs, Boston
SS— Cal Ripken Jr., Baltimore
OF— Kirby Puckett, Minnesota
OF— Ruben Sierra, Texas
OF— Robin Yount, Milwaukee
C— Mickey Tettleton, Baltimore
DH— Harold Baines, Chi.-Tex.

NATIONAL LEAGUE
1B— Will Clark, San Francisco
2B— Ryne Sandberg, Chicago
3B— Howard Johnson, New York
SS— Barry Larkin, Cincinnati
OF— Kevin Mitchell, San Francisco
OF— Tony Gwynn, San Diego
OF— Eric Davis, Cincinnati
C— Craig Biggio, Houston
P— Don Robinson, San Francisco

1990
AMERICAN LEAGUE
1B— Cecil Fielder, Detroit
2B— Julio Franco, Texas
3B— Kelly Gruber, Toronto
SS— Alan Trammell, Detroit
OF— Rickey Henderson, Oakland
OF— Jose Canseco, Oakland
OF— Ellis Burks, Boston
C— Lance Parrish, California
DH— Dave Parker, Milwaukee

NATIONAL LEAGUE
1B— Eddie Murray, Los Angeles
2B— Ryne Sandberg, Chicago
3B— Matt Williams, San Francisco
SS— Barry Larkin, Cincinnati
OF— Barry Bonds, Pittsburgh
OF— Bobby Bonilla, Pittsburgh
OF— Darryl Strawberry, New York
C— Benito Santiago, San Diego
P— Don Robinson, San Francisco

1991
AMERICAN LEAGUE
1B— Cecil Fielder, Detroit
2B— Julio Franco, Texas
3B— Wade Boggs, Boston
SS— Cal Ripken Jr., Baltimore
OF— Jose Canseco, Oakland
OF— Joe Carter, Toronto
OF— Ken Griffey Jr., Seattle
C— Mickey Tettleton, Detroit
DH— Frank Thomas, Chicago

NATIONAL LEAGUE
1B— Will Clark, San Francisco
2B— Ryne Sandberg, Chicago
3B— Howard Johnson, New York
SS— Barry Larkin, Cincinnati
OF— Barry Bonds, Pittsburgh
OF— Bobby Bonilla, Pittsburgh
OF— Ron Gant, Atlanta
C— Benito Santiago, San Diego
P— Tom Glavine, Atlanta

1992
AMERICAN LEAGUE
1B— Mark McGwire, Oakland
2B— Roberto Alomar, Toronto
3B— Edgar Martinez, Seattle
SS— Travis Fryman, Detroit
OF— Joe Carter, Toronto
OF— Juan Gonzalez, Texas
OF— Kirby Puckett, Minnesota
C— Mickey Tettleton, Detroit
DH— Dave Winfield, Toronto

NATIONAL LEAGUE
1B— Fred McGriff, San Diego
2B— Ryne Sandberg, Chicago
3B— Gary Sheffield, San Diego
SS— Barry Larkin, Cincinnati
OF— Barry Bonds, Pittsburgh
OF— Andy Van Slyke, Pittsburgh
OF— Larry Walker, Montreal
C— Darren Daulton, Philadelphia
P— Dwight Gooden, New York

1993
AMERICAN LEAGUE
1B— Frank Thomas, Chicago
2B— Carlos Baerga, Cleveland
3B— Wade Boggs, New York
SS— Cal Ripken Jr., Baltimore
OF— Albert Belle, Cleveland
OF— Juan Gonzalez, Texas
OF— Ken Griffey Jr., Seattle
C— Mike Stanley, New York
DH— Paul Molitor, Toronto

NATIONAL LEAGUE
1B— Fred McGriff, S.D.-Atl.
2B— Robby Thompson, San Fran.
3B— Matt Williams, San Francisco
SS— Jay Bell, Pittsburgh
OF— Barry Bonds, San Francisco
OF— Lenny Dykstra, Philadelphia
OF— David Justice, Atlanta
C— Mike Piazza, Los Angeles
P— Orel Hershiser, Los Angeles

1994
AMERICAN LEAGUE
1B— Frank Thomas, Chicago
2B— Carlos Baerga, Cleveland
3B— Wade Boggs, New York
SS— Cal Ripken Jr., Baltimore
OF— Albert Belle, Cleveland
OF— Ken Griffey Jr., Seattle
OF— Kirby Puckett, Minnesota
C— Ivan Rodriguez, Texas
DH— Julio Franco, Chicago

NATIONAL LEAGUE
1B— Jeff Bagwell, Houston
2B— Craig Biggio, Houston
3B— Matt Williams, San Francisco
SS— Wil Cordero, Montreal
OF— Moises Alou, Montreal
OF— Barry Bonds, San Francisco
OF— Tony Gwynn, San Diego
C— Mike Piazza, Los Angeles
P— Mark Portugal, San Francisco

1995
AMERICAN LEAGUE
1B— Mo Vaughn, Boston
2B— Chuck Knoblauch, Minnesota
3B— Gary Gaetti, Kansas City
SS— John Valentin, Boston
OF— Albert Belle, Cleveland
OF— Tim Salmon, California
OF— Manny Ramirez, Cleveland
C— Ivan Rodriguez, Texas
DH— Edgar Martinez, Seattle

NATIONAL LEAGUE
1B— Eric Karros, Los Angeles
2B— Craig Biggio, Houston
3B— Vinny Castilla, Colorado
SS— Barry Larkin, Cincinnati
OF— Dante Bichette, Colorado
OF— Tony Gwynn, San Diego
OF— Sammy Sosa, Chicago
C— Mike Piazza, Los Angeles
P— Tom Glavine, Atlanta

1996
AMERICAN LEAGUE
1B— Mark McGwire, Oakland
2B— Roberto Alomar, Baltimore
3B— Jim Thome, Cleveland
SS— Alex Rodriguez, Seattle
OF— Albert Belle, Cleveland
OF— Juan Gonzalez, Texas
OF— Ken Griffey Jr., Seattle
C— Ivan Rodriguez, Texas
DH— Paul Molitor, Minnesota

NATIONAL LEAGUE
1B— Andres Galarraga, Colorado
2B— Eric Young, Colorado
3B— Ken Caminiti, San Diego
SS— Barry Larkin, Cincinnati
OF— Barry Bonds, San Francisco
OF— Ellis Burks, Colorado
OF— Gary Sheffield, Florida
C— Mike Piazza, Los Angeles
P— Tom Glavine, Atlanta

1997
AMERICAN LEAGUE
1B— Tino Martinez, New York
2B— Chuck Knoblauch, Minnesota
3B— Matt Williams, Cleveland
SS— Nomar Garciaparra, Boston
OF— Juan Gonzalez, Texas
OF— Ken Griffey Jr., Seattle
OF— David Justice, Cleveland
C— Ivan Rodriguez, Texas
DH— Edgar Martinez, Seattle

NATIONAL LEAGUE
1B— Jeff Bagwell, Houston
2B— Craig Biggio, Houston
3B— Vinny Castilla, Colorado
SS— Jeff Blauser, Atlanta
OF— Barry Bonds, San Francisco
OF— Tony Gwynn, San Diego
OF— Larry Walker, Colorado
C— Mike Piazza, Los Angeles
P— John Smoltz, Atlanta

1998
AMERICAN LEAGUE
1B— Rafael Palmeiro, Baltimore
2B— Damion Easley, Detroit
3B— Dean Palmer, Kansas City
SS— Alex Rodriguez, Seattle
OF— Juan Gonzalez, Texas
OF— Ken Griffey Jr., Seattle
OF— Albert Belle, Chicago
C— Ivan Rodriguez, Texas
DH— Jose Canseco, Toronto

NATIONAL LEAGUE
1B— Mark McGwire, St. Louis
2B— Craig Biggio, Houston
3B— Vinny Castilla, Colorado
SS— Barry Larkin, Cincinnati
OF— Sammy Sosa, Chicago
OF— Moises Alou, Houston
OF— Greg Vaughn, San Diego
C— Mike Piazza, L.A.-Fla.-N.Y.
P— Tom Glavine, Atlanta

HISTORY *Award winners*

1999

AMERICAN LEAGUE
1B— Carlos Delgado, Toronto
2B— Roberto Alomar, Cleveland
3B— Dean Palmer, Detroit
SS— Alex Rodriguez, Seattle
OF— Shawn Green, Toronto
OF— Ken Griffey Jr., Seattle
OF— Manny Ramirez, Cleveland
C— Ivan Rodriguez, Texas
DH— Rafael Palmeiro, Texas

NATIONAL LEAGUE
1B— Jeff Bagwell, Houston
2B— Edgardo Alfonzo, New York
3B— Chipper Jones, Atlanta
SS— Barry Larkin, Cincinnati
OF— Sammy Sosa, Chicago
OF— Vladimir Guerrero, Montreal
OF— Larry Walker, Colorado
C— Mike Piazza, New York
P— Mike Hampton, Houston

2000

AMERICAN LEAGUE
1B— Carlos Delgado, Toronto
2B— Roberto Alomar, Cleveland
3B— Troy Glaus, Anaheim
SS— Alex Rodriguez, Seattle
OF— Darin Erstad, Anaheim
OF— Manny Ramirez, Cleveland
OF— Magglio Ordonez, Chicago
C— Jorge Posada, New York
DH— Frank Thomas, Chicago

NATIONAL LEAGUE
1B— Todd Helton, Colorado
2B— Jeff Kent, San Francisco
3B— Chipper Jones, Atlanta
SS— Edgar Renteria, St. Louis
OF— Sammy Sosa, Chicago
OF— Barry Bonds, San Francisco
OF— Vladimir Guerrero, Montreal
C— Mike Piazza, New York
P— Mike Hampton, New York

BASEBALL WRITERS' ASSOCIATION OF AMERICA
MOST VALUABLE PLAYER

AMERICAN LEAGUE

Year	Player	Team	Pos.	Points
1931	Lefty Grove	Philadelphia	P	78
1932	Jimmie Foxx	Philadelphia	1B	75
1933	Jimmie Foxx	Philadelphia	1B	74
1934	Mickey Cochrane	Detroit	C	67
1935	Hank Greenberg	Detroit	1B	*80
1936	Lou Gehrig	New York	1B	73
1937	Charley Gehringer	Detroit	2B	78
1938	Jimmie Foxx	Boston	1B	305
1939	Joe DiMaggio	New York	OF	280
1940	Hank Greenberg	Detroit	OF	292
1941	Joe DiMaggio	New York	OF	291
1942	Joe Gordon	New York	2B	270
1943	Spud Chandler	New York	P	246
1944	Hal Newhouser	Detroit	P	236
1945	Hal Newhouser	Detroit	P	236
1946	Ted Williams	Boston	OF	224
1947	Joe DiMaggio	New York	OF	202
1948	Lou Boudreau	Cleveland	SS	324
1949	Ted Williams	Boston	OF	272
1950	Phil Rizzuto	New York	SS	284
1951	Yogi Berra	New York	C	184
1952	Bobby Shantz	Philadelphia	P	280
1953	Al Rosen	Cleveland	3B	*336
1954	Yogi Berra	New York	C	230
1955	Yogi Berra	New York	C	218
1956	Mickey Mantle	New York	OF	*336
1957	Mickey Mantle	New York	OF	233
1958	Jackie Jensen	Boston	OF	233
1959	Nellie Fox	Chicago	2B	295
1960	Roger Maris	New York	OF	225
1961	Roger Maris	New York	OF	202
1962	Mickey Mantle	New York	OF	234
1963	Elston Howard	New York	C	248
1964	Brooks Robinson	Baltimore	3B	269
1965	Zoilo Versalles	Minnesota	SS	275
1966	Frank Robinson	Baltimore	OF	*280
1967	Carl Yastrzemski	Boston	OF	275
1968	Denny McLain	Detroit	P	*280
1969	Harmon Killebrew	Minnesota	1B-3B	294
1970	Boog Powell	Baltimore	1B	234
1971	Vida Blue	Oakland	P	268
1972	Dick Allen	Chicago	1B	321
1973	Reggie Jackson	Oakland	OF	*336
1974	Jeff Burroughs	Texas	OF	248
1975	Fred Lynn	Boston	OF	326
1976	Thurman Munson	New York	C	304
1977	Rod Carew	Minnesota	1B	273
1978	Jim Rice	Boston	OF	352
1979	Don Baylor	California	OF	347
1980	George Brett	Kansas City	3B	335
1981	Rollie Fingers	Milwaukee	P	319
1982	Robin Yount	Milwaukee	SS	385
1983	Cal Ripken Jr.	Baltimore	SS	322

NATIONAL LEAGUE

Year	Player	Team	Pos.	Points
1931	Frank Frisch	St. Louis	2B	65
1932	Chuck Klein	Philadelphia	OF	78
1933	Carl Hubbell	New York	P	77
1934	Dizzy Dean	St. Louis	P	78
1935	Gabby Hartnett	Chicago	C	75
1936	Carl Hubbell	New York	P	60
1937	Joe Medwick	St. Louis	OF	70
1938	Ernie Lombardi	Cincinnati	C	229
1939	Bucky Walters	Cincinnati	P	303
1940	Frank McCormick	Cincinnati	1B	274
1941	Dolf Camilli	Brooklyn	1B	300
1942	Mort Cooper	St. Louis	P	263
1943	Stan Musial	St. Louis	OF	267
1944	Marty Marion	St. Louis	SS	190
1945	Phil Cavarretta	Chicago	1B	279
1946	Stan Musial	St. Louis	1B	319
1947	Bob Elliott	Boston	3B	205
1948	Stan Musial	St. Louis	OF	303
1949	Jackie Robinson	Brooklyn	2B	264
1950	Jim Konstanty	Philadelphia	P	286
1951	Roy Campanella	Brooklyn	C	243
1952	Hank Sauer	Chicago	OF	226
1953	Roy Campanella	Brooklyn	C	297
1954	Willie Mays	New York	OF	283
1955	Roy Campanella	Brooklyn	C	226
1956	Don Newcombe	Brooklyn	P	223
1957	Hank Aaron	Milwaukee	OF	239
1958	Ernie Banks	Chicago	SS	283
1959	Ernie Banks	Chicago	SS	232 1/2
1960	Dick Groat	Pittsburgh	SS	276
1961	Frank Robinson	Cincinnati	OF	219
1962	Maury Wills	Los Angeles	SS	209
1963	Sandy Koufax	Los Angeles	P	237
1964	Ken Boyer	St. Louis	3B	243
1965	Willie Mays	San Francisco	OF	224
1966	Roberto Clemente	Pittsburgh	OF	218
1967	Orlando Cepeda	St. Louis	1B	*280
1968	Bob Gibson	St. Louis	P	242
1969	Willie McCovey	San Francisco	1B	265
1970	Johnny Bench	Cincinnati	C	326
1971	Joe Torre	St. Louis	3B	318
1972	Johnny Bench	Cincinnati	C	263
1973	Pete Rose	Cincinnati	OF	274
1974	Steve Garvey	Los Angeles	1B	270
1975	Joe Morgan	Cincinnati	2B	321 1/2
1976	Joe Morgan	Cincinnati	2B	311
1977	George Foster	Cincinnati	OF	291
1978	Dave Parker	Pittsburgh	OF	320
1979	Willie Stargell	Pittsburgh	1B	216
	Keith Hernandez	St. Louis	1B	216
1980	Mike Schmidt	Philadelphia	3B	*336
1981	Mike Schmidt	Philadelphia	3B	321
1982	Dale Murphy	Atlanta	OF	283
1983	Dale Murphy	Atlanta	OF	318

Year	Player	Team	Pos.	Points	Year	Player	Team	Pos.	Points
1984—Willie Hernandez	Detroit	P	306		1984—Ryne Sandberg	Chicago	2B	326
1985—Don Mattingly	New York	1B	367		1985—Willie McGee	St. Louis	OF	280
1986—Roger Clemens	Boston	P	339		1986—Mike Schmidt	Philadelphia	3B	287
1987—George Bell	Toronto	OF	332		1987—Andre Dawson	Chicago	OF	269
1988—Jose Canseco	Oakland	OF	*392		1988—Kirk Gibson	Los Angeles	OF	272
1989—Robin Yount	Milwaukee	OF	256		1989—Kevin Mitchell	San Francisco	OF	314
1990—Rickey Henderson	Oakland	OF	317		1990—Barry Bonds	Pittsburgh	OF	331
1991—Cal Ripken Jr.	Baltimore	SS	318		1991—Terry Pendleton	Atlanta	3B	274
1992—Dennis Eckersley	Oakland	P	306		1992—Barry Bonds	Pittsburgh	OF	304
1993—Frank Thomas	Chicago	1B	*392		1993—Barry Bonds	San Francisco	OF	372
1994—Frank Thomas	Chicago	1B	372		1994—Jeff Bagwell	Houston	1B	*392
1995—Mo Vaughn	Boston	1B	308		1995—Barry Larkin	Cincinnati	SS	281
1996—Juan Gonzalez	Texas	OF	290		1996—Ken Caminiti	San Diego	3B	*392
1997—Ken Griffey Jr.	Seattle	OF	*392		1997—Larry Walker	Colorado	OF	359
1998—Juan Gonzalez	Texas	OF	357		1998—Sammy Sosa	Chicago	OF	438
1999—Ivan Rodriguez	Texas	C	252		1999—Chipper Jones	Atlanta	3B	432
2000—Jason Giambi	Oakland	1B	317		2000　Jeff Kent	San Francisco	2B	392

*Unanimous selection.

CY YOUNG MEMORIAL AWARD

Year	Pitcher	Team	Votes	Year	Pitcher	Team	Votes
1956—Don Newcombe	Brooklyn	10		1982—A.L.—Pete Vuckovich	Milwaukee	87
1957—Warren Spahn	Milwaukee	15		N.L.—Steve Carlton	Philadelphia	112
1958—Bob Turley	New York A.L.	5		1983—A.L.—LaMarr Hoyt	Chicago	116
1959—Early Wynn	Chicago A.L.	13		N.L.—John Denny	Philadelphia	103
1960—Vernon Law	Pittsburgh	8		1984—A.L.—Willie Hernandez	Detroit	88
1961—Whitey Ford	New York A.L.	9		N.L.—Rick Sutcliffe	Chicago	*120
1962—Don Drysdale	Los Angeles N.L.	14		1985—A.L.—Bret Saberhagen	Kansas City	127
1963—Sandy Koufax	Los Angeles N.L.	*20		N.L.—Dwight Gooden	New York	*120
1964—Dean Chance	Los Angeles A.L.	17		1986—A.L.—Roger Clemens	Boston	*140
1965—Sandy Koufax	Los Angeles N.L.	*20		N.L.—Mike Scott	Houston	98
1966—Sandy Koufax	Los Angeles N.L.	*20		1987—A.L.—Roger Clemens	Boston	124
1967—A.L.—Jim Lonborg	Boston	18		N.L.—Steve Bedrosian	Philadelphia	57
N.L.—Mike McCormick	San Francisco	18		1988—A.L.—Frank Viola	Minnesota	138
1968—A.L.—Denny McLain	Detroit	*20		N.L.—Orel Hershiser	Los Angeles	*120
N.L.—Bob Gibson	St. Louis	*20		1989—A.L.—Bret Saberhagen	Kansas City	138
1969—A.L.—Denny McLain	Detroit	10		N.L.—Mark Davis	San Diego	107
Mike Cuellar	Baltimore	10		1990—A.L.—Bob Welch	Oakland	107
N.L.—Tom Seaver	New York	23		N.L.—Doug Drabek	Pittsburgh	118
1970—A.L.—Jim Perry	Minnesota	55		1991—A.L.—Roger Clemens	Boston	119
N.L.—Bob Gibson	St. Louis	118		N.L.—Tom Glavine	Atlanta	110
1971—A.L.—Vida Blue	Oakland	98		1992—A.L.—Dennis Eckersley	Oakland	107
N.L.—Fergie Jenkins	Chicago	97		N.L.—Greg Maddux	Chicago	112
1972—A.L.—Gaylord Perry	Cleveland	64		1993—A.L.—Jack McDowell	Chicago	124
N.L.—Steve Carlton	Philadelphia	*120		N.L.—Greg Maddux	Atlanta	119
1973—A.L.—Jim Palmer	Baltimore	88		1994—A.L.—David Cone	Kansas City	108
N.L.—Tom Seaver	New York	71		N.L.—Greg Maddux	Atlanta	*140
1974—A.L.—Jim Hunter	Oakland	90		1995—A.L.—Randy Johnson	Seattle	136
N.L.—Mike Marshall	Los Angeles	96		N.L.—Greg Maddux	Atlanta	*140
1975—A.L.—Jim Palmer	Baltimore	98		1996—A.L.—Pat Hentgen	Toronto	110
N.L.—Tom Seaver	New York	98		N.L.—John Smoltz	Atlanta	136
1976—A.L.—Jim Palmer	Baltimore	108		1997—A.L.—Roger Clemens	Toronto	134
N.L.—Randy Jones	San Diego	96		N.L.—Pedro Martinez	Montreal	134
1977—A.L.—Sparky Lyle	New York	56¹/₂		1998—A.L.—Roger Clemens	Toronto	*140
N.L.—Steve Carlton	Philadelphia	*104		N.L.—Tom Glavine	Atlanta	99
1978—A.L.—Ron Guidry	New York	*140		1999—A.L.—Pedro Martinez	Boston	*140
N.L.—Gaylord Perry	San Diego	116		N.L.—Randy Johnson	Arizona	134
1979—A.L.—Mike Flanagan	Baltimore	136		2000—A.L.—Pedro Martinez	Boston	*140
N.L.—Bruce Sutter	Chicago	72		N.L.—Randy Johnson	Arizona	133
1980—A.L.—Steve Stone	Baltimore	100		*Unanimous selection.		
N.L.—Steve Carlton	Philadelphia	118				
1981—A.L.—Rollie Fingers	Milwaukee	126				
N.L.—Fernando Valenzuela	Los Angeles	70				

ROOKIE OF THE YEAR

1947—Combined selection—Jackie Robinson, Brooklyn N.L., 1B
1948—Combined selection—Alvin Dark, Boston N.L., SS

AMERICAN LEAGUE

Year	Player	Team	Pos.	Votes
1949—Roy Sievers	St. Louis	OF	10
1950—Walt Dropo	Boston	1B	15
1951—Gil McDougald	New York	3B	13

NATIONAL LEAGUE

Year	Player	Team	Pos.	Votes
1949—Don Newcombe	Brooklyn	P	21
1950—Sam Jethroe	Boston	OF	11
1951—Willie Mays	New York	OF	18

Year	Player	Team	Pos.	Votes	Year	Player	Team	Pos.	Votes
1952	Harry Byrd	Philadelphia	P	9	1952	Joe Black	Brooklyn	P	19
1953	Harvey Kuenn	Detroit	SS	23	1953	Jim Gilliam	Brooklyn	2B	11
1954	Bob Grim	New York	P	15	1954	Wally Moon	St. Louis	OF	17
1955	Herb Score	Cleveland	P	18	1955	Bill Virdon	St. Louis	OF	15
1956	Luis Aparicio	Chicago	SS	22	1956	Frank Robinson	Cincinnati	OF	*24
1957	Tony Kubek	New York	IF-OF	23	1957	Jack Sanford	Philadelphia	P	16
1958	Albie Pearson	Washington	OF	14	1958	Orlando Cepeda	San Francisco	1B	*†21
1959	Bob Allison	Washington	OF	18	1959	Willie McCovey	San Francisco	1B	*24
1960	Ron Hansen	Baltimore	SS	22	1960	Frank Howard	Los Angeles	OF	12
1961	Don Schwall	Boston	P	7	1961	Billy Williams	Chicago	OF	10
1962	Tom Tresh	New York	OF-SS	13	1962	Ken Hubbs	Chicago	2B	19
1963	Gary Peters	Chicago	P	10	1963	Pete Rose	Cincinnati	2B	17
1964	Tony Oliva	Minnesota	OF	19	1964	Dick Allen	Philadelphia	3B	18
1965	Curt Blefary	Baltimore	OF	12	1965	Jim Lefebvre	Los Angeles	2B	13
1966	Tommie Agee	Chicago	OF	16	1966	Tommy Helms	Cincinnati	3B	12
1967	Rod Carew	Minnesota	2B	19	1967	Tom Seaver	New York	P	11
1968	Stan Bahnsen	New York	P	17	1968	Johnny Bench	Cincinnati	C	10½
1969	Lou Piniella	Kansas City	OF	9	1969	Ted Sizemore	Los Angeles	2B	14
1970	Thurman Munson	New York	C	23	1970	Carl Morton	Montreal	P	11
1971	Chris Chambliss	Cleveland	1B	11	1971	Earl Williams	Atlanta	C	18
1972	Carlton Fisk	Boston	C	*24	1972	Jon Matlack	New York	P	19
1973	Al Bumbry	Baltimore	OF	13½	1973	Gary Matthews	San Francisco	OF	11
1974	Mike Hargrove	Texas	1B	16½	1974	Bake McBride	St. Louis	OF	16
1975	Fred Lynn	Boston	OF	23	1975	John Montefusco	San Francisco	P	12
1976	Mark Fidrych	Detroit	P	22	1976	Butch Metzger	San Diego	P	11
						Pat Zachry	Cincinnati	P	11
1977	Eddie Murray	Baltimore	DH-1B	12½	1977	Andre Dawson	Montreal	OF	10
1978	Lou Whitaker	Detroit	2B	21	1978	Bob Horner	Atlanta	3B	12½
1979	John Castino	Minnesota	3B	7	1979	Rick Sutcliffe	Los Angeles	P	20
	Alfredo Griffin	Toronto	SS	7					
1980	Joe Charboneau	Cleveland	OF	103	1980	Steve Howe	Los Angeles	P	80
1981	Dave Righetti	New York	P	127	1981	Fernando Valenzuela	Los Angeles	P	107
1982	Cal Ripken	Baltimore	SS-3B	132	1982	Steve Sax	Los Angeles	2B	63
1983	Ron Kittle	Chicago	OF	104	1983	Darryl Strawberry	New York	OF	109
1984	Alvin Davis	Seattle	1B	134	1984	Dwight Gooden	New York	P	118
1985	Ozzie Guillen	Chicago	SS	101	1985	Vince Coleman	St. Louis	OF	*120
1986	Jose Canseco	Oakland	OF	110	1986	Todd Worrell	St. Louis	P	118
1987	Mark McGwire	Oakland	1B	*140	1987	Benito Santiago	San Diego	C	*120
1988	Walt Weiss	Oakland	SS	103	1988	Chris Sabo	Cincinnati	3B	79
1989	Gregg Olson	Baltimore	P	136	1989	Jerome Walton	Chicago	OF	116
1990	Sandy Alomar Jr.	Cleveland	C	*140	1990	Dave Justice	Atlanta	OF	118
1991	Chuck Knoblauch	Minnesota	2B	136	1991	Jeff Bagwell	Houston	1B	118
1992	Pat Listach	Milwaukee	SS	122	1992	Eric Karros	Los Angeles	1B	116
1993	Tim Salmon	California	OF	*140	1993	Mike Piazza	Los Angeles	C	*140
1994	Bob Hamelin	Kansas City	DH	134	1994	Raul Mondesi	Los Angeles	OF	*140
1995	Marty Cordova	Minnesota	3B	105	1995	Hideo Nomo	Los Angeles	P	118
1996	Derek Jeter	New York	SS	*140	1996	Todd Hollandsworth	Los Angeles	OF	105
1997	Nomar Garciaparra	Boston	SS	*140	1997	Scott Rolen	Philadelphia	3B	*140
1998	Ben Grieve	Oakland	OF	130	1998	Kerry Wood	Chicago	P	128
1999	Carlos Beltran	Kansas City	OF	133	1999	Scott Williamson	Cincinnati	P	118
2000	Kazuhiro Sasaki	Seattle	P	104	2000	Rafael Furcal	Atlanta	SS-2B	144

*Unanimous selection. †Three writers did not vote.

MANAGER OF THE YEAR

AMERICAN LEAGUE

NATIONAL LEAGUE

Year	Manager	Team	Points	Year	Manager	Team	Points
1983	Tony La Russa	Chicago	17	1983	Tommy Lasorda	Los Angeles	10
1984	Sparky Anderson	Detroit	96	1984	Jim Frey	Chicago	101
1985	Bobby Cox	Toronto	104	1985	Whitey Herzog	St. Louis	86
1986	John McNamara	Boston	95	1986	Hal Lanier	Houston	108
1987	Sparky Anderson	Detroit	90	1987	Buck Rodgers	Montreal	92
1988	Tony La Russa	Oakland	103	1988	Tommy Lasorda	Los Angeles	101
1989	Frank Robinson	Baltimore	125	1989	Don Zimmer	Chicago	118
1990	Jeff Torborg	Chicago	128	1990	Jim Leyland	Pittsburgh	99
1991	Tom Kelly	Minnesota	138	1991	Bobby Cox	Atlanta	96
1992	Tony La Russa	Oakland	132	1992	Jim Leyland	Pittsburgh	109
1993	Gene Lamont	Chicago	72	1993	Dusty Baker	San Francisco	105
1994	Buck Showalter	New York	132	1994	Felipe Alou	Montreal	138
1995	Lou Piniella	Seattle	86	1995	Don Baylor	Colorado	122
1996	Johnny Oates	Texas	89	1996	Bruce Bochy	San Diego	76
	Joe Torre	New York	89				
1997	Dave Johnson	Baltimore	88	1997	Dusty Baker	San Francisco	110
1998	Joe Torre	New York	128	1998	Larry Dierker	Houston	102
1999	Jimy Williams	Boston	115	1999	Jack McKeon	Cincinnati	115
2000	Jerry Manuel	Chicago	143	2000	Dusty Baker	San Francisco	154

EARLY MOST VALUABLE PLAYER AWARDS

CHALMERS AWARD

AMERICAN LEAGUE

Year	Player	Team	Pos.	Points
1911—Ty Cobb		Detroit	OF	64
1912—Tris Speaker		Boston	OF	59
1913—Walter Johnson		Washington	P	54
1914—Eddie Collins		Philadelphia	2B	63

NATIONAL LEAGUE

Year	Player	Team	Pos.	Points
1911—Frank Schulte		Chicago	OF	29
1912—Larry Doyle		New York	2B	48
1913—Jake Daubert		Brooklyn	1B	50
1914—Johnny Evers		Boston	2B	50

LEAGUE AWARDS

AMERICAN LEAGUE

Year	Player	Team	Pos.	Points
1922—George Sisler		St. Louis	1B	59
1923—Babe Ruth		New York	OF	64
1924—Walter Johnson		Washington	P	55
1925—Roger Peckinpaugh		Washington	SS	45
1926—George Burns		Cleveland	1B	63
1927—Lou Gehrig		New York	1B	56
1928—Mickey Cochrane		Philadelphia	C	53
1929—No selection				

NATIONAL LEAGUE

Year	Player	Team	Pos.	Points
1922—No selection				
1923—No selection				
1924—Dazzy Vance		Brooklyn	P	74
1925—Rogers Hornsby		St. Louis	2B	73
1926—Bob O'Farrell		St. Louis	C	79
1927—Paul Waner		Pittsburgh	OF	72
1928—Jim Bottomley		St. Louis	1B	76
1929—Rogers Hornsby		Chicago	2B	60

HISTORY *Award winners*

HALL OF FAME

Name	Des.*	Elec. year	Votes rec.†	Votes cast‡	% of vote	Teams as player
Aaron, Hank	P	1982	406	415	97.8	Milwaukee NL, Atlanta NL, Milwaukee AL
Alexander, Grover C.	P	1938	212	262	80.9	Philadelphia NL, Chicago NL, St. Louis NL
Alston, Walter	M	1983	CV	—	—	St. Louis NL
Anderson, Sparky	M	2000	CV	—	—	Philadelphia NL
Anson, Cap	P	1939	C1	—	—	Chicago NL
Aparicio, Luis	P	1984	341	403	84.6	Chicago AL, Baltimore AL, Boston AL
Appling, Luke	P	1964	189	225	84.0	Chicago AL
Ashburn, Richie	P	1995	CV	—	—	Philadelphia NL, Chicago NL, New York NL
Averill, Earl	P	1975	CV	—	—	Cleveland AL, Detroit AL, Boston AL
Baker, Home Run	P	1955	CV	—	—	Philadelphia AL, New York AL
Bancroft, Dave	P	1971	CV	—	—	Philadelphia NL, New York NL, Boston NL, Brooklyn NL
Banks, Ernie	P	1977	321	383	83.8	Chicago NL
Barlick, Al	U	1989	CV	—	—	
Barrow, Ed	E	1953	CV	—	—	
Beckley, Jake	P	1971	CV	—	—	Pittsburgh NL, Pittsburgh PL, New York NL, Cincinnati NL, St. Louis NL
Bell, Cool Papa	P	1974	SCNL	—	—	Negro Leagues
Bench, Johnny	P	1989	431	447	96.4	Cincinnati NL
Bender, Chief	P	1953	CV	—	—	Philadelphia AL, Philadelphia NL, Chicago AL
Berra, Yogi	P	1972	339	396	85.6	New York AL, New York NL
Bottomley, Jim	P	1974	CV	—	—	St. Louis NL, Cincinnati NL, St. Louis AL
Boudreau, Lou	P	1970	232	300	77.3	Cleveland AL, Boston AL
Bresnahan, Roger	P	1945	C2	—	—	Washington NL, Chicago NL, Baltimore AL, New York NL, St. Louis NL
Brett, George	P	1999	488	497	98.2	Kansas City AL
Brock, Lou	P	1985	315	395	79.7	Chicago NL, St. Louis NL
Brouthers, Dan	P	1945	C2	—	—	Troy NL, Buffalo NL, Detroit NL, Boston NL, Boston PL, Boston AA, Brooklyn NL, Baltimore NL, Louisville NL, Philadelphia NL, New York NL
Brown, Three Finger	P	1949	C2	—	—	St. Louis NL, Chicago NL, Cincinnati NL
Bulkeley, Morgan	E	1937	CC	—	—	
Bunning, Jim	P	1996	CV	—	—	Detroit AL, Philadelphia NL, Pittsburgh NL, Los Angeles AL
Burkett, Jesse	P	1946	C2	—	—	New York NL, Cleveland NL, St. Louis NL, St. Louis AL, Boston AL
Campanella, Roy	P	1969	270	340	79.4	Brooklyn NL
Carew, Rod	P	1991	401	443	90.5	Minnesota AL, California AL
Carey, Max	P	1961	CV	—	—	Pittsburgh NL, Brooklyn NL
Carlton, Steve	P	1994	436	455	95.8	St. Louis NL, Philadelphia NL, San Francisco NL, Chicago AL, Cleveland AL, Minnesota AL
Cartwright, Alexander	O	1938	CC	—	—	
Cepeda, Orlando	P	1999	CV	—	—	San Francisco NL, St. Louis NL, Atlanta NL, Oakland AL, Boston AL, Kansas City AL
Chadwick, Henry	O	1938	CC	—	—	
Chance, Frank	P	1946	C2	—	—	Chicago NL, New York AL
Chandler, Happy	E	1982	CV	—	—	
Charleston, Oscar	P	1976	SCNL	—	—	Negro Leagues
Chesbro, Jack	P	1946	C2	—	—	Pittsburgh NL, New York AL, Boston AL
Chylak, Nestor	U	1999	CV	—	—	
Clarke, Fred	P	1945	C2	—	—	Louisville NL, Pittsburgh NL
Clarkson, John	P	1963	CV	—	—	Worcester NL, Chicago NL, Boston NL, Cleveland NL
Clemente, Roberto	P	1973	393	424	92.7	Pittsburgh NL
Cobb, Ty	P	1936	222	226	98.2	Detroit AL, Philadelphia AL
Cochrane, Mickey	P	1947	128	161	79.5	Philadelphia AL, Detroit AL
Collins, Eddie	P	1939	213	274	77.7	Philadelphia AL, Chicago AL
Collins, Jimmy	P	1945	C2	—	—	Boston NL, Louisville NL, Boston AL, Philadelphia AL
Combs, Earle	P	1970	CV	—	—	New York AL
Comiskey, Charley	F/P	1939	C1	—	—	St. Louis AA, Chicago PL, Cincinnati NL
Conlan, Jocko	U	1974	CV	—	—	Chicago AL
Connolly, Tommy	U	1953	CV	—	—	
Connor, Roger	P	1976	CV	—	—	Troy NL, New York NL, New York PL, Philadelphia NL, St. Louis NL
Coveleski, Stan	P	1969	CV	—	—	Philadelphia AL, Cleveland AL, Washington AL, New York AL
Crawford, Sam	P	1957	CV	—	—	Cincinnati NL, Detroit AL
Cronin, Joe	P	1956	152	193	78.8	Pittsburgh NL, Washington AL, Boston AL
Cummings, Candy	P	1939	C1	—	—	Hartford NL, Cincinnati NL
Cuyler, Kiki	P	1968	CV	—	—	Pittsburgh NL, Chicago NL, Cincinnati NL, Brooklyn NL

HISTORY *Hall of Fame*

Name	Des.*	Elec. year	Votes rec.†	Votes cast‡	% of vote	Teams as player
Dandridge, Ray	P	1987	CV	—	—	Negro Leagues
Davis, George S.	P	1998	CV	—	—	Cleveland NL, New York NL, Chicago AL
Day, Leon	P	1995	CV	—	—	Negro Leagues
Dean, Dizzy	P	1953	209	264	79.2	St. Louis NL, Chicago NL, St. Louis AL
Delahanty, Ed	P	1945	C2	—	—	Philadelphia NL, Cleveland PL, Washington AL
Dickey, Bill	P	1954	202	252	80.2	New York AL
Dihigo, Martin	P	1977	SCNL	—	—	Negro Leagues
DiMaggio, Joe	P	1955	223	251	88.8	New York AL
Doby, Larry	P	1998	CV	—	—	Cleveland AL, Chicago AL, Detroit AL
Doerr, Bobby	P	1986	CV	—	—	Boston AL
Drysdale, Don	P	1984	316	403	78.4	Brooklyn NL, Los Angeles NL
Duffy, Hugh	P	1945	C2	—	—	Chicago NL, Chicago PL, Boston AA, Boston NL, Milwaukee AL, Philadelphia NL
Durocher, Leo	M	1994	CV	—	—	New York AL, Cincinnati NL, St. Louis NL, Brooklyn NL
Evans, Billy	U	1973	CV	—	—	
Evers, Johnny	P	1946	C2	—	—	Chicago NL, Boston NL, Philadelphia NL, Chicago AL
Ewing, Buck	P	1939	C1	—	—	Troy NL, New York NL, New York PL, Cleveland NL, Cincinnati NL
Faber, Red	P	1964	CV	—	—	Chicago AL
Feller, Bob	P	1962	150	160	93.8	Cleveland AL
Ferrell, Rick	P	1984	CV	—	—	St. Louis AL, Boston AL, Washington AL
Fingers, Rollie	P	1992	349	430	81.2	Oakland AL, San Diego NL, Milwaukee AL
Fisk, Carlton	P	2000	397	499	79.6	Boston AL, Chicago AL
Flick, Elmer	P	1963	CV	—	—	Philadelphia NL, Philadelphia AL, Cleveland AL
Ford, Whitey	P	1974	284	365	77.8	New York AL
Foster, Bill	P	1996	CV	—	—	Negro Leagues
Foster, Rube	P	1981	CV	—	—	Negro Leagues
Fox, Nellie	P	1997	CV	—	—	Philadelphia AL, Chicago AL, Houston NL
Foxx, Jimmie	P	1951	179	226	79.2	Philadelphia AL, Boston AL, Chicago NL, Philadelphia NL
Frick, Ford	E	1970	CV	—	—	
Frisch, Frank	P	1947	136	161	84.5	New York NL, St. Louis NL
Galvin, Pud	P	1965	CV	—	—	Buffalo NL, Pittsburgh AA, Pittsburgh NL, Pittsburgh PL, St. Louis NL
Gehrig, Lou	P	1939	SE	—	—	New York AL
Gehringer, Charley	P	1949	159	187	85.0	Detroit AL
Gibson, Bob	P	1981	337	401	84.0	St. Louis NL
Gibson, Josh	P	1972	SCNL	—	—	Negro Leagues
Giles, Warren	E	1979	CV	—	—	
Gomez, Lefty	P	1972	CV	—	—	New York AL, Washington AL
Goslin, Goose	P	1968	CV	—	—	Washington AL, St. Louis AL, Detroit AL
Greenberg, Hank	P	1956	164	193	85.0	Detroit AL, Pittsburgh NL
Griffith, Clark	M	1946	C2	—	—	St. Louis AA, Boston AA, Chicago NL, Chicago AL, New York AL, Cincinnati NL, Washington AL
Grimes, Burleigh	P	1964	CV	—	—	Pittsburgh NL, Brooklyn NL, New York NL, Boston NL, St. Louis NL, Chicago NL, New York AL
Grove, Lefty	P	1947	123	161	76.4	Philadelphia AL, Boston AL
Hafey, Chick	P	1971	CV	—	—	St. Louis NL, Cincinnati NL
Haines, Jesse	P	1970	CV	—	—	Cincinnati NL, St. Louis NL
Hamilton, Billy	P	1961	CV	—	—	Kansas City AA, Philadelphia NL, Boston NL
Hanlon, Ned	M	1996	CV	—	—	Cleveland NL, Detroit NL, Pittsburgh NL, Pittsburgh PL, Baltimore NL
Harridge, Will	E	1972	CV	—	—	
Harris, Bucky	M	1975	CV	—	—	Washington AL, Detroit AL
Hartnett, Gabby	P	1955	195	251	77.7	Chicago NL, New York NL
Heilmann, Harry	P	1952	203	234	86.8	Detroit AL, Cincinnati NL
Herman, Billy	P	1975	CV	—	—	Chicago NL, Brooklyn NL, Boston NL, Pittsburgh NL
Hooper, Harry	P	1971	CV	—	—	Boston AL, Chicago AL
Hornsby, Rogers	P	1942	182	233	78.1	St. Louis NL, New York NL, Boston NL, Chicago NL, St. Louis AL
Hoyt, Waite	P	1969	CV	—	—	New York NL, Boston AL, New York AL, Detroit AL, Philadelphia AL, Brooklyn NL, Pittsburgh NL
Hubbard, Cal	U	1976	CV	—	—	
Hubbell, Carl	P	1947	140	161	87.0	New York NL
Huggins, Miller	M	1964	CV	—	—	Cincinnati NL, St. Louis NL
Hulbert, William	F	1995	CV	—	—	
Hunter, Catfish	P	1987	315	413	76.3	Kansas City AL, Oakland AL, New York AL
Irvin, Monte	P	1973	SCNL	—	—	New York NL, Chicago NL, Negro Leagues
Jackson, Reggie	P	1993	396	423	93.6	Kansas City AL, Oakland AL, Baltimore AL, New York AL, California AL
Jackson, Travis	P	1982	CV	—	—	New York NL
Jenkins, Ferguson	P	1991	334	443	75.4	Philadelphia NL, Chicago NL, Texas AL, Boston AL
Jennings, Hugh	P	1945	C2	—	—	Louisville AA, Louisville NL, Baltimore NL, Brooklyn NL, Philadelphia NL, Detroit AL
Johnson, Ban	E	1937	CC	—	—	

Name	Des.*	Elec. year	Votes rec.†	Votes cast‡	% of vote	Teams as player
Johnson, Judy	P	1975	SCNL	—	—	Negro Leagues
Johnson, Walter	P	1936	189	226	83.6	Washington AL
Joss, Addie	P	1978	CV	—	—	Cleveland AL
Kaline, Al	P	1980	340	385	88.3	Detroit AL
Keefe, Tim	P	1964	CV	—	—	Troy NL, New York AA, New York NL, New York PL, Philadelphia NL
Keeler, Willie	P	1939	207	274	75.5	New York NL, Brooklyn, NL, Baltimore NL, New York AL
Kell, George	P	1983	CV	—	—	Philadelphia AL, Detroit AL, Boston AL, Chicago AL, Baltimore AL
Kelley, Joe	P	1971	CV	—	—	Boston NL, Pittsburgh NL, Baltimore NL, Brooklyn NL, Baltimore AL, Cincinnati NL
Kelly, George	P	1973	CV	—	—	New York NL, Pittsburgh NL, Cincinnati NL, Chicago NL, Brooklyn NL
Kelly, Mike	P	1945	C2	—	—	Cincinnati NL, Chicago NL, Boston NL, Boston PL, Cincinnati AA, Boston AA, New York NL
Killebrew, Harmon	P	1984	335	403	83.1	Washington AL, Minnesota AL, Kansas City AL
Kiner, Ralph	P	1975	273	362	75.4	Pittsburgh NL, Chicago NL, Cleveland AL
Klein, Chuck	P	1980	CV	—	—	Philadelphia NL, Chicago NL, Pittsburgh NL
Klem, Bill	U	1953	CV	—	—	
Koufax, Sandy	P	1972	344	396	86.9	Brooklyn NL, Los Angeles NL
Lajoie, Nap	P	1937	168	201	83.6	Philadelphia NL, Philadelphia AL, Cleveland AL
Landis, Kenesaw M.	E	1944	C2	—	—	
Lasorda, Tom	M	1997	CV	—	—	Brooklyn NL, Kansas City AL
Lazzeri, Tony	P	1991	CV	—	—	New York AL, Chicago NL, Brooklyn NL, New York NL
Lemon, Bob	P	1976	305	388	78.6	Cleveland AL
Leonard, Buck	P	1972	SCNL	—	—	Negro Leagues
Lindstrom, Fred	P	1976	CV	—	—	New York NL, Pittsburgh NL, Chicago NL, Brooklyn NL
Lloyd, John Henry	P	1977	SCNL	—	—	Negro Leagues
Lombardi, Ernie	P	1986	CV	—	—	Brooklyn NL, Cincinnati NL, Boston NL, New York NL
Lopez, Al	M	1977	CV	—	—	Brooklyn NL, Boston NL, Pittsburgh NL, Cleveland AL
Lyons, Ted	P	1955	217	251	86.5	Chicago AL
Mack, Connie	M	1937	CC	—	—	Washington NL, Buffalo PL, Pittsburgh NL
MacPhail, Larry	E	1978	CV	—	—	
MacPhail, Lee	E	1998	CV	—	—	
Mantle, Mickey	P	1974	322	365	88.2	New York AL
Manush, Heinie	P	1964	CV	—	—	Detroit AL, St. Louis AL, Washington AL, Boston AL, Brooklyn NL, Pittsburgh NL
Maranville, Rabbit	P	1954	209	252	82.9	Boston NL, Pittsburgh NL, Chicago NL, Brooklyn NL, St. Louis NL
Marichal, Juan	P	1983	313	374	83.7	San Francisco NL, Boston AL, Los Angeles NL
Marquard, Rube	P	1971	CV	—	—	New York NL, Brooklyn NL, Cincinnati NL, Boston NL
Mathews, Eddie	P	1978	301	379	79.4	Boston NL, Milwaukee NL, Atlanta NL, Houston NL, Detroit AL
Mathewson, Christy	P	1936	205	226	90.7	New York NL, Cincinnati NL
Mays, Willie	P	1979	409	432	94.7	New York (Giants)NL, San Francisco NL, New York (Mets)NL
McCarthy, Joe	M	1957	CV	—	—	
McCarthy, Tommy	P	1946	C2	—	—	Boston UA, Boston NL, Philadelphia NL, St. Louis AA, Brooklyn NL
McCovey, Willie	P	1986	346	425	81.4	San Francisco NL, San Diego NL, Oakland AL
McGinnity, Joe	P	1946	C2	—	—	Baltimore NL, Brooklyn NL, Baltimore AL, New York NL
McGowan, Bill	U	1992	CV	—	—	
McGraw, John	M	1937	CC	—	—	Baltimore AA, Baltimore NL, St. Louis NL, Baltimore AL, New York NL
McKechnie, Bill	M	1962	CV	—	—	Pittsburgh NL, Boston NL, New York AL, New York NL, Cincinnati
McPhee, Bid	P	2000	CV	—	—	Cincinnati AA, Cincinnati NL
Medwick, Joe	P	1968	240	283	84.8	St. Louis NL, Brooklyn NL, New York NL, Boston NL
Mize, Johnny	P	1981	CV	—	—	St. Louis NL, New York NL, New York AL
Morgan, Joe	P	1990	363	444	81.8	Houston NL, Cincinnati NL, San Francisco NL, Philadelphia NL, Oakland AL
Musial, Stan	P	1969	317	340	93.2	St. Louis NL
Newhouser, Hal	P	1992	CV	—	—	Detroit AL, Cleveland AL
Nichols, Kid	P	1949	C2	—	—	Boston NL, St. Louis NL, Philadelphia NL
Niekro, Phil	P	1997	380	473	80.3	Milwaukee NL, Atlanta NL, New York AL, Cleveland AL, Toronto AL
O'Rourke, Jim	P	1945	C2	—	—	Boston NL, Providence NL, Buffalo NL, New York NL, Washington NL, New York PL
Ott, Mel	P	1951	197	226	87.2	New York NL
Paige, Satchel	P	1971	SCNL	—	—	Cleveland AL, St. Louis AL, Kansas City AL, Negro Leagues
Palmer, Jim	P	1990	411	444	92.6	Baltimore AL
Pennock, Herb	P	1948	94	121	77.7	Philadelphia AL, Boston AL, New York AL

Name	Des.*	Elec. year	Votes rec.†	Votes cast‡	% of vote	Teams as player
Perez, Tony	P	2000	385	499	77.2	Cincinnati NL, Montreal NL, Boston AL, Philadelphia NL
Perry, Gaylord	P	1991	342	443	77.2	San Francisco NL, Cleveland AL, Texas AL, San Diego NL, New York AL, Atlanta NL, Seattle AL, Kansas City AL
Plank, Eddie	P	1946	C2	—	—	Philadelphia AL, St. Louis AL
Puckett, Kirby	P	2001	423	515	82.1	Minnesota AL
Radbourn, Hoss	P	1939	C1	—	—	Buffalo NL, Providence NL, Boston NL, Boston PL, Cincinnati NL
Reese, Pee Wee	P	1984	CV	—	—	Brooklyn NL, Los Angeles NL
Rice, Sam	P	1963	CV	—	—	Washington AL, Cleveland AL
Rickey, Branch	E	1967	CV	—	—	St. Louis AL, New York AL
Rixey, Eppa	P	1963	CV	—	—	Philadelphia NL, Cincinnati NL
Rizzuto, Phil	P	1994	CV	—	—	New York AL
Roberts, Robin	P	1976	337	388	86.9	Philadelphia NL, Baltimore AL, Houston NL, Chicago NL
Robinson, Brooks	P	1983	344	374	92.0	Baltimore AL
Robinson, Frank	P	1982	370	415	89.2	Cincinnati NL, Baltimore AL, Los Angeles NL, California AL, Cleveland AL
Robinson, Jackie	P	1962	124	160	77.5	Brooklyn NL
Robinson, Wilbert	M	1945	C2	—	—	Philadelphia AA, Baltimore AA, Baltimore NL, St. Louis NL, Baltimore AL
Rogan, Bullet Joe	P	1998	CV	—	—	
Roush, Edd	P	1962	CV	—	—	Chicago AL, New York NL, Cincinnati NL
Ruffing, Red	P	1967	266	306	86.9	Boston AL, New York AL, Chicago AL
Rusie, Amos	P	1977	CV	—	—	Indianapolis NL, New York NL, Cincinnati NL
Ruth, Babe	P	1936	215	226	95.1	Boston AL, New York AL, Boston NL
Ryan, Nolan	P	1999	491	497	98.8	New York NL, California AL, Houston NL, Texas AL
Schalk, Ray	P	1955	CV	—	—	Chicago AL, New York NL
Schmidt, Mike	P	1995	444	460	96.5	Philadelphia NL
Schoendienst, Red	P	1989	CV	—	—	St. Louis NL, New York (Giants) NL, Milwaukee NL
Seaver, Tom	P	1992	425	430	98.8	New York NL, Cincinnati NL, Chicago AL, Boston AL
Selee, Frank	M	1999	CV	—	—	
Sewell, Joe	P	1977	CV	—	—	Cleveland AL, New York AL
Simmons, Al	P	1953	199	264	75.4	Philadelphia AL, Chicago AL, Detroit AL, Washington AL, Boston NL, Cincinnati NL, Boston AL
Sisler, George	P	1939	235	274	85.8	St. Louis AL, Washington AL, Boston NL
Slaughter, Enos	P	1985	CV	—	—	St. Louis NL, New York AL, Kansas City AL, Milwaukee NL
Snider, Duke	P	1980	333	385	86.5	Brooklyn NL, Los Angeles NL, New York NL, San Francisco NL
Spahn, Warren	P	1973	316	380	83.2	Boston NL, Milwaukee NL, New York NL, San Francisco NL
Spalding, Al	P	1939	C1	—	—	Chicago NL
Speaker, Tris	P	1937	165	201	82.1	Boston AL, Cleveland AL, Washington AL, Philadelphia AL
Stargell, Willie	P	1988	352	427	82.4	Pittsburgh NL
Stearnes, Turkey	P	2000	CV	—	—	Negro Leagues
Stengel, Casey	M	1966	CV	—	—	Brooklyn NL, Pittsburgh NL, Philadelphia NL, New York NL, Boston NL
Sutton, Don	P	1998	386	473	81.6	Los Angeles NL, Houston NL, Milwaukee AL, Oakland AL, California AL
Terry, Bill	P	1954	195	252	77.4	New York NL
Thompson, Sam	P	1974	CV	—	—	Detroit NL, Philadelphia NL, Detroit AL
Tinker, Joe	P	1946	C2	—	—	Chicago NL, Cincinnati NL
Traynor, Pie	P	1948	93	121	76.9	Pittsburgh NL
Vance, Dazzy	P	1955	205	251	81.7	Pittsburgh NL, New York AL, Brooklyn NL, St. Louis NL, Cincinnati NL
Vaughan, Arky	P	1985	CV	—	—	Pittsburgh NL, Brooklyn NL
Veeck, Bill	E	1991	CV	—	—	
Waddell, Rube	P	1946	C2	—	—	Louisville NL, Pittsburgh NL, Chicago NL, Philadelphia AL, St. Louis AL
Wagner, Honus	P	1936	215	226	95.1	Louisville NL, Pittsburgh NL
Wallace, Bobby	P	1953	CV	—	—	Cleveland NL, St. Louis NL, St. Louis AL
Walsh, Ed	P	1946	C2	—	—	Chicago AL, Boston NL
Waner, Lloyd	P	1967	CV	—	—	Pittsburgh NL, Boston NL, Cincinnati NL, Philadelphia NL, Brooklyn NL
Waner, Paul	P	1952	195	234	83.3	Pittsburgh NL, Brooklyn NL, Boston NL, New York AL
Ward, John Montgomery	P	1964	CV	—	—	Providence NL, New York NL, Brooklyn PL, Brooklyn NL
Weaver, Earl	M	1996	CV	—	—	
Weiss, George	E	1971	CV	—	—	
Welch, Mickey	P	1973	CV	—	—	Troy NL, New York NL
Wells, Willie	P	1997	CV	—	—	

Name	Des.*	Elec. year	Votes rec.†	Votes cast‡	% of vote	Teams as player
Wheat, Zack	P	1959	CV	—	—	Brooklyn NL, Philadelphia AL
Wilhelm, Hoyt	P	1985	331	395	83.8	New York NL, St. Louis NL, Cleveland AL, Baltimore AL, Chicago AL California AL, Atlanta NL, Chicago NL, Los Angeles NL
Williams, Billy	P	1987	354	413	85.7	Chicago NL, Oakland AL
Williams, Smokey Joe	P	1999	CV	—	—	Negro Leagues
Williams, Ted	P	1966	282	302	93.4	Boston AL
Willis, Vic	P	1995	CV	—	—	Boston NL, Pittsburgh NL, St. Louis NL
Wilson, Hack	P	1979	CV	—	—	New York NL, Chicago NL, Brooklyn NL, Philadelphia NL
Winfield, Dave	P	2001	435	515	84.5	San Diego NL, New York AL, California AL, Toronto AL, Minnesota AL, Cleveland AL
Wright, George	M	1937	CC	—	—	Boston NL, Providence NL
Wright, Harry	M	1953	CV	—	—	Boston NL
Wynn, Early	P	1972	301	396	76.0	Washington AL, Cleveland AL, Chicago AL
Yastrzemski, Carl	P	1989	423	447	94.6	Boston AL
Yawkey, Tom	E	1980	CV	—	—	
Young, Cy	P	1937	153	201	76.1	Cleveland NL, St. Louis NL, Boston AL, Cleveland AL, Boston NL
Youngs, Ross	P	1972	CV	—	—	New York NL
Yount, Robin	P	1999	385	497	77.5	Milwaukee AL

*Designation for which he was honored. Abbreviations: E—executive; F—founder; M—manager; O—organizer; P—player; U—umpire.

†Where an abbreviation is listed rather than a vote total, the enshrinee was selected by one of the following groups: Centennial Commission (CC), committee of old-time players and writers (C1), committee on old-timers (C2), Committee on Veterans (CV), special election by Baseball Writers' Association of America (SE) or Special Committee on Negro Leagues (SCNL).

‡Votes cast by eligible members of the Baseball Writers' Association of America.

League abbreviations: AA—American Association; AL—American League; NL—National League; PL—Players League; UA—Union Association.

TEAM BY TEAM

AMERICAN LEAGUE

ANAHEIM ANGELS
YEARLY FINISHES

(Known as Los Angeles Angels through September 1, 1965 and California Angels through 1996)

Year	Position	W	L	Pct.	*GB	Manager	Attendance
1961	8th	70	91	.435	38.5	Bill Rigney	603,510
1962	3rd	86	76	.531	10.0	Bill Rigney	1,144,063
1963	9th	70	91	.435	34.0	Bill Rigney	821,015
1964	5th	82	80	.506	17.0	Bill Rigney	760,439
1965	7th	75	87	.463	27.0	Bill Rigney	566,727
1966	6th	80	82	.494	18.0	Bill Rigney	1,400,321
1967	5th	84	77	.522	7.5	Bill Rigney	1,317,713
1968	8th	67	95	.414	36.0	Bill Rigney	1,025,956

WEST DIVISION

Year	Position	W	L	Pct.	*GB	Manager	Attendance
1969	3rd	71	91	.438	26.0	Bill Rigney, Lefty Phillips	758,388
1970	3rd	86	76	.531	12.0	Lefty Phillips	1,077,741
1971	4th	76	86	.469	25.5	Lefty Phillips	926,373
1972	5th	75	80	.484	18.0	Del Rice	744,190
1973	4th	79	83	.488	15.0	Bobby Winkles	1,058,206
1974	6th	68	94	.420	22.0	Bobby Winkles, Dick Williams	917,269
1975	6th	72	89	.447	25.5	Dick Williams	1,058,163
1976	4th (tied)	76	86	.469	14.0	Dick Williams, Norm Sherry	1,006,774
1977	5th	74	88	.457	28.0	Norm Sherry, Dave Garcia	1,432,633
1978	2nd (tied)	87	75	.537	5.0	Dave Garcia, Jim Fregosi	1,755,386
1979	1st†	88	74	.543	+3.0	Jim Fregosi	2,523,575
1980	6th	65	95	.406	31.0	Jim Fregosi	2,297,327
1981	4th/7th	51	59	.464	‡	Jim Fregosi, Gene Mauch	1,441,545
1982	1st†	93	69	.574	+3.0	Gene Mauch	2,807,360
1983	5th (tied)	70	92	.432	29.0	John McNamara	2,555,016
1984	2nd (tied)	81	81	.500	3.0	John McNamara	2,402,997
1985	2nd	90	72	.556	1.0	Gene Mauch	2,567,427
1986	1st†	92	70	.568	+5.0	Gene Mauch	2,655,872
1987	6th (tied)	75	87	.463	10.0	Gene Mauch	2,696,299
1988	4th	75	87	.463	29.0	Cookie Rojas	2,340,925
1989	3rd	91	71	.562	8.0	Doug Rader	2,647,291
1990	4th	80	82	.494	23.0	Doug Rader	2,555,688
1991	7th	81	81	.500	14.0	Doug Rader, Buck Rodgers	2,416,236
1992	5th (tied)	72	90	.444	24.0	Buck Rodgers	2,065,444
1993	5th (tied)	71	91	.438	23.0	Buck Rodgers	2,057,460
1994	4th	47	68	.409	5.5	Buck Rodgers, Marcel Lachemann	1,512,622
1995	2nd§	78	67	.538	1.0	Marcel Lachemann	1,748,680
1996	4th	70	91	.435	19.5	Marcel Lachemann, John McNamara, Joe Maddon	1,820,521
1997	2nd	84	78	.519	6.0	Terry Collins	1,767,330
1998	2nd	85	77	.525	3.0	Terry Collins	2,519,210
1999	4th	70	92	.432	25.0	Terry Collins, Joe Maddon	2,253,123
2000	3rd	82	80	.506	9.5	Mike Scioscia	2,066,977

*Games behind winner. †Lost championship series. ‡First half 31-29; second 20-30. §Lost division playoff.

MANAGERIAL RECORDS

Terry Collins 220-237, Jim Fregosi 237-249, Dave Garcia 60-66, Marcel Lachemann 161-170, Joe Maddon 27-24, Gene Mauch 379-332, John McNamara 161-191, Lefty Phillips 222-225, Doug Rader 232-216, Del Rice 75-80, Bill Rigney 625-707, Buck Rodgers 179-223, Cookie Rojas 75-87, Mike Scioscia 82-80, Norm Sherry 76-71, Dick Williams 147-194, Bobby Winkles 109-127.

BALTIMORE ORIOLES
YEARLY FINISHES

(Known as Milwaukee Brewers in 1901 and St. Louis Browns through 1953)

Year	Position	W	L	Pct.	*GB	Manager	Attendance
1901	8th	48	89	.350	35.5	Hugh Duffy	139,034
1902	2nd	78	58	.574	5.0	Jimmy McAleer	272,283
1903	6th	65	74	.468	26.5	Jimmy McAleer	380,405
1904	6th	65	87	.428	29.0	Jimmy McAleer	318,108
1905	8th	54	99	.354	40.5	Jimmy McAleer	339,112

Year	Position	W	L	Pct.	*GB	Manager	Attendance
1906	5th	76	73	.510	16.0	Jimmy McAleer	389,157
1907	6th	69	83	.454	24.0	Jimmy McAleer	419,025
1908	4th	83	69	.546	6.5	Jimmy McAleer	618,947
1909	7th	61	89	.407	36.0	Jimmy McAleer	366,274
1910	8th	47	107	.305	57.0	John O'Connor	249,889
1911	8th	45	107	.296	56.5	Bobby Wallace	207,984
1912	7th	53	101	.344	53.0	Bobby Wallace, George Stovall	214,070
1913	8th	57	96	.373	39.0	George Stovall, Branch Rickey	250,330
1914	5th	71	82	.464	28.5	Branch Rickey	244,714
1915	6th	63	91	.409	39.5	Branch Rickey	150,358
1916	5th	79	75	.513	12.0	Fielder Jones	335,740
1917	7th	57	97	.370	43.0	Fielder Jones	210,486
1918	5th	58	64	.475	15.0	Fielder Jones, Jimmy Austin, Jimmy Burke	122,076
1919	5th	67	72	.482	20.5	Jimmy Burke	349,350
1920	4th	76	77	.497	21.5	Jimmy Burke	419,311
1921	3rd	81	73	.526	17.5	Lee Fohl	355,978
1922	2nd	93	61	.604	1.0	Lee Fohl	712,918
1923	5th	74	78	.487	24.0	Lee Fohl, Jimmy Austin	430,296
1924	4th	74	78	.487	17.0	George Sisler	533,349
1925	3rd	82	71	.536	15.0	George Sisler	462,898
1926	7th	62	92	.403	29.0	George Sisler	283,986
1927	7th	59	94	.336	50.5	Dan Howley	247,879
1928	3rd	82	72	.532	19.0	Dan Howley	339,497
1929	4th	79	73	.520	26.0	Dan Howley	280,697
1930	6th	64	90	.416	38.0	Bill Killefer	152,088
1931	5th	63	91	.409	45.0	Bill Killefer	179,126
1932	6th	63	91	.409	44.0	Bill Killefer	112,558
1933	8th	55	96	.364	43.5	Bill Killefer, Allen Sothoron, Rogers Hornsby	88,113
1934	6th	67	85	.441	33.0	Rogers Hornsby	115,305
1935	7th	65	87	.428	28.5	Rogers Hornsby	80,922
1936	7th	57	95	.375	44.5	Rogers Hornsby	93,267
1937	8th	46	108	.299	56.0	Rogers Hornsby, Jim Bottomley	123,121
1938	7th	55	97	.362	44.0	Gabby Street	130,417
1939	8th	43	111	.279	64.5	Fred Haney	109,159
1940	6th	67	87	.435	23.0	Fred Haney	239,591
1941	6th (tied)	70	84	.455	31.0	Fred Haney, Luke Sewell	176,240
1942	3rd	82	69	.543	19.5	Luke Sewell	255,617
1943	6th	72	80	.474	25.0	Luke Sewell	214,392
1944	1st	89	65	.578	+1.0	Luke Sewell	508,644
1945	3rd	81	70	.536	6.0	Luke Sewell	482,986
1946	7th	66	88	.429	38.0	Luke Sewell, Zack Taylor	526,435
1947	8th	59	95	.383	38.0	Muddy Ruel	320,474
1948	6th	59	94	.386	37.0	Zack Taylor	335,546
1949	7th	53	101	.344	44.0	Zack Taylor	270,936
1950	7th	58	96	.377	40.0	Zack Taylor	247,131
1951	8th	52	102	.338	46.0	Zack Taylor	293,790
1952	7th	64	90	.416	31.0	Rogers Hornsby, Marty Marion	518,796
1953	8th	54	100	.351	46.5	Marty Marion	297,238
1954	7th	54	100	.351	57.0	Jimmie Dykes	1,060,910
1955	7th	57	97	.370	39.0	Paul Richards	852,039
1956	6th	69	85	.448	28.0	Paul Richards	901,201
1957	5th	76	76	.500	21.0	Paul Richards	1,029,581
1958	6th	74	79	.484	17.5	Paul Richards	829,991
1959	6th	74	80	.481	20.0	Paul Richards	891,926
1960	2nd	89	65	.578	8.0	Paul Richards	1,187,849
1961	3rd	95	67	.586	14.0	Paul Richards, Luman Harris	951,089
1962	7th	77	85	.475	19.0	Billy Hitchcock	790,254
1963	4th	86	76	.531	18.5	Billy Hitchcock	774,343
1964	3rd	97	65	.599	2.0	Hank Bauer	1,116,215
1965	3rd	94	68	.580	8.0	Hank Bauer	781,649
1966	1st	97	63	.606	+9.0	Hank Bauer	1,203,366
1967	6th (tied)	76	85	.472	15.5	Hank Bauer	955,053
1968	2nd	91	71	.562	12.0	Hank Bauer, Earl Weaver	943,977

EAST DIVISION

Year	Position	W	L	Pct.	*GB	Manager	Attendance
1969	1st†	109	53	.673	+19.0	Earl Weaver	1,058,168
1970	1st†	108	54	.667	+15.0	Earl Weaver	1,057,069
1971	1st†	101	57	.639	+12.0	Earl Weaver	1,023,037
1972	3rd	80	74	.519	5.0	Earl Weaver	899,950
1973	1st‡	97	65	.599	+8.0	Earl Weaver	958,667
1974	1st‡	91	71	.562	+2.0	Earl Weaver	962,572
1975	2nd	90	69	.566	4.5	Earl Weaver	1,002,157
1976	2nd	88	74	.543	10.5	Earl Weaver	1,058,609
1977	2nd (tied)	97	64	.602	2.5	Earl Weaver	1,195,769

Year	Position	W	L	Pct.	*GB	Manager	Attendance
1978	4th	90	71	.559	9.0	Earl Weaver	1,051,724
1979	1st†	102	57	.642	+8.0	Earl Weaver	1,681,009
1980	2nd	100	62	.617	3.0	Earl Weaver	1,797,438
1981	2nd/4th	59	46	.562	§	Earl Weaver	1,024,652
1982	2nd	94	68	.580	1.0	Earl Weaver	1,613,031
1983	1st†	98	64	.605	+6.0	Joe Altobelli	2,042,071
1984	5th	85	77	.525	19.0	Joe Altobelli	2,045,784
1985	4th	83	78	.516	16.0	Joe Altobelli, Earl Weaver	2,132,387
1986	7th	73	89	.451	22.5	Earl Weaver	1,973,176
1987	6th	67	95	.414	31.0	Cal Ripken Sr.	1,835,692
1988	7th	54	107	.335	34.5	Cal Ripken Sr., Frank Robinson	1,660,738
1989	2nd	87	75	.537	2.0	Frank Robinson	2,535,208
1990	5th	76	85	.472	11.5	Frank Robinson	2,415,189
1991	6th	67	95	.414	24.0	Frank Robinson, Johnny Oates	2,552,753
1992	3rd	89	73	.549	7.0	Johnny Oates	3,567,819
1993	3rd (tied)	85	77	.525	10.0	Johnny Oates	3,644,965
1994	2nd	63	49	.563	6.5	Johnny Oates	2,535,359
1995	3rd	71	73	.493	15.0	Phil Regan	3,098,475
1996	2nd∞‡	88	74	.543	4.0	Dave Johnson	3,646,950
1997	1st∞‡	98	64	.605	+2.0	Dave Johnson	3,711,132
1998	4th	79	83	.488	35.0	Ray Miller	3,685,194
1999	4th	78	84	.481	20.0	Ray Miller	3,433,150
2000	4th	74	88	.457	13.5	Mike Hargrove	3,295,128

*Games behind winner. †Won championship series. ‡Lost championship series. §First half 31-23; second 28-23. ∞Won division series.

MANAGERIAL RECORDS

Joe Altobelli 212-167, Jimmy Austin 29-38, Hank Bauer 407-318, Jim Bottomley 21-56, Jimmy Burke 172-180, Hugh Duffy 48-89, Jimmie Dykes 54-100, Lee Fohl 226-183, Fred Haney 125-227, Mike Hargrove 74-88, Lum Harris 17-10, Billy Hitchcock 163-161, Rogers Hornsby 255-381, Dan Howley 220-239, Dave Johnson 186-138, Fielder Jones 158-196, Bill Killefer 224-329, Marty Marion 96-161, Jimmy McAleer 551-632, Ray Miller 157-167, Johnny Oates 291-270, Jack O'Connor 47-107, Phil Regan 71-73, Paul Richards 517-539, Branch Rickey 139-179, Cal Ripken Sr. 67-101, Frank Robinson 230-285, Luke Sewell 432-410, George Sisler 218-241, Al Sothoron 2-6, George Stovall 91-158, Gabby Street 55-97, Zack Taylor 235-410, Bobby Wallace 57-134, Earl Weaver 1,481-1,060.

BOSTON RED SOX
YEARLY FINISHES

Year	Position	W	L	Pct.	*GB	Manager	Attendance
1901	2nd	79	57	.581	4.0	Jimmy Collins	289,448
1902	3rd	77	60	.562	6.5	Jimmy Collins	348,567
1903	1st	91	47	.659	+14.5	Jimmy Collins	379,338
1904	1st	95	59	.617	+1.5	Jimmy Collins	623,295
1905	4th	78	74	.513	16.0	Jimmy Collins	468,828
1906	8th	49	105	.318	45.5	Jimmy Collins, Chick Stahl	410,209
1907	7th	59	90	.396	32.5	George Huff, Bob Unglaub, Deacon McGuire	436,777
1908	5th	75	79	.487	15.5	Deacon McGuire, Fred Lake	473,048
1909	3rd	88	63	.583	9.5	Fred Lake	668,965
1910	4th	81	72	.529	22.5	Patsy Donovan	584,619
1911	5th	78	75	.510	24.0	Patsy Donovan	503,961
1912	1st	105	47	.691	+14.0	Jake Stahl	597,096
1913	4th	79	71	.527	15.5	Jake Stahl, Bill Carrigan	437,194
1914	2nd	91	62	.595	8.5	Bill Carrigan	481,359
1915	1st	101	50	.669	+2.5	Bill Carrigan	539,885
1916	1st	91	63	.591	+2.0	Bill Carrigan	496,397
1917	2nd	90	62	.592	9.0	Jack Barry	387,856
1918	1st	75	51	.595	+2.5	Ed Barrow	249,513
1919	6th	66	71	.482	20.5	Ed Barrow	417,291
1920	5th	72	81	.471	25.5	Ed Barrow	402,445
1921	5th	75	79	.487	23.5	Hugh Duffy	279,273
1922	8th	61	93	.396	33.0	Hugh Duffy	259,184
1923	8th	61	91	.401	37.0	Frank Chance	229,668
1924	7th	67	87	.435	25.0	Lee Fohl	448,556
1925	8th	47	105	.309	49.5	Lee Fohl	267,782
1926	8th	46	107	.301	44.5	Lee Fohl	285,155
1927	8th	51	103	.331	59.0	Bill Carrigan	305,275
1928	8th	57	96	.373	43.5	Bill Carrigan	396,920
1929	8th	58	96	.377	48.0	Bill Carrigan	394,620
1930	8th	52	102	.338	50.0	Heinie Wagner	444,045
1931	6th	62	90	.408	45.0	Shano Collins	350,975
1932	8th	43	111	.279	64.0	Shano Collins, Marty McManus	182,150
1933	7th	63	86	.423	34.5	Marty McManus	268,715
1934	4th	76	76	.500	24.0	Bucky Harris	610,640
1935	4th	78	75	.510	16.0	Joseph Cronin	558,568
1936	6th	74	80	.481	28.5	Joe Cronin	626,895

Year	Position	W	L	Pct.	*GB	Manager	Attendance
1937	5th	80	72	.526	21.0	Joe Cronin	559,659
1938	2nd	88	61	.591	9.5	Joe Cronin	646,459
1939	2nd	89	62	.589	17.0	Joe Cronin	573,070
1940	4th (tied)	82	72	.532	8.0	Joe Cronin	716,234
1941	2nd	84	70	.545	17.0	Joe Cronin	718,497
1942	2nd	93	59	.612	9.0	Joe Cronin	730,340
1943	7th	68	84	.447	29.0	Joe Cronin	358,275
1944	4th	77	77	.500	12.0	Joe Cronin	506,975
1945	7th	71	83	.461	17.5	Joe Cronin	603,794
1946	1st	104	50	.675	+12.0	Joe Cronin	1,416,944
1947	3rd	83	71	.539	14.0	Joe Cronin	1,427,315
1948	2nd†	96	59	.619	1.0	Joe McCarthy	1,558,798
1949	2nd	96	58	.623	1.0	Joe McCarthy	1,596,650
1950	3rd	94	60	.610	4.0	Joe McCarthy, Steve O'Neill	1,344,080
1951	3rd	87	67	.565	11.0	Steve O'Neill	1,312,282
1952	6th	76	78	.494	19.0	Lou Boudreau	1,115,750
1953	4th	84	69	.549	16.0	Lou Boudreau	1,026,133
1954	4th	69	85	.448	42.0	Lou Boudreau	931,127
1955	4th	84	70	.545	12.0	Pinky Higgins	1,203,200
1956	4th	84	70	.545	13.0	Pinky Higgins	1,137,158
1957	3rd	82	72	.532	16.0	Pinky Higgins	1,181,087
1958	3rd	79	75	.513	13.0	Pinky Higgins	1,077,047
1959	5th	75	79	.487	19.0	Pinky Higgins, Billy Jurges	984,102
1960	7th	65	89	.422	32.0	Billy Jurges, Pinky Higgins	1,129,866
1961	6th	76	86	.469	33.0	Pinky Higgins	850,589
1962	8th	76	84	.475	19.0	Pinky Higgins	733,080
1963	7th	76	85	.472	28.0	Johnny Pesky	942,642
1964	8th	72	90	.444	27.0	Johnny Pesky, Billy Herman	883,276
1965	9th	62	100	.383	40.0	Billy Herman	652,201
1966	9th	72	90	.444	26.0	Billy Herman, Pete Runnels	811,172
1967	1st	92	70	.568	+1.0	Dick Williams	1,727,832
1968	4th	86	76	.531	17.0	Dick Williams	1,940,788

EAST DIVISION

Year	Position	W	L	Pct.	*GB	Manager	Attendance
1969	3rd	87	75	.537	22.0	Dick Williams, Eddie Popowski	1,833,246
1970	3rd	87	75	.537	21.0	Eddie Kasko	1,595,278
1971	3rd	85	77	.525	18.0	Eddie Kasko	1,678,732
1972	2nd	85	70	.548	0.5	Eddie Kasko	1,441,718
1973	2nd	89	73	.549	8.0	Eddie Kasko	1,481,002
1974	3rd	84	78	.519	7.0	Darrell Johnson	1,556,411
1975	1st‡	95	65	.594	+4.5	Darrell Johnson	1,748,587
1976	3rd	83	79	.512	15.5	Darrell Johnson, Don Zimmer	1,895,846
1977	2nd (tied)	97	64	.602	2.5	Don Zimmer	2,074,549
1978	2nd§	99	64	.607	1.0	Don Zimmer	2,320,643
1979	3rd	91	69	.569	11.5	Don Zimmer	2,353,114
1980	4th	83	77	.519	19.0	Don Zimmer, Johnny Pesky	1,956,092
1981	5th/2nd (tied)	59	49	.546	∞	Ralph Houk	1,060,379
1982	3rd	89	73	.549	6.0	Ralph Houk	1,950,124
1983	6th	78	84	.481	20.0	Ralph Houk	1,782,285
1984	4th	86	76	.531	18.0	Ralph Houk	1,661,618
1985	5th	81	81	.500	18.5	John McNamara	1,786,633
1986	1st‡	95	66	.590	+5.5	John McNamara	2,147,641
1987	5th	78	84	.481	20.0	John McNamara	2,231,551
1988	1st▲	89	73	.549	+1.0	John McNamara, Joe Morgan	2,464,851
1989	3rd	83	79	.512	6.0	Joe Morgan	2,510,012
1990	1st▲	88	74	.543	+2.0	Joe Morgan	2,528,986
1991	2nd (tied)	84	78	.519	7.0	Joe Morgan	2,562,435
1992	7th	73	89	.451	23.0	Butch Hobson	2,468,574
1993	5th	80	82	.494	15.0	Butch Hobson	2,422,021
1994	4th	54	61	.470	17.0	Butch Hobson	1,775,818
1995	1st◆	86	58	.597	+7.0	Kevin Kennedy	2,164,410
1996	3rd	85	77	.525	7.0	Kevin Kennedy	2,315,231
1997	4th	78	84	.481	20.0	Jimy Williams	2,226,136
1998	2nd◆	92	70	.568	22.0	Jimy Williams	2,343,947
1999	2nd■▲	94	68	.580	4.0	Jimy Williams	2,446,162
2000	2nd	85	77	.525	2.5	Jimy Williams	2,586,032

*Games behind winner. †Lost pennant playoff. ‡Won championship series. §Lost division playoff. ∞First half 30-26; second 29-23. ▲Lost championship series. ◆Lost division series. ■Won division series.

MANAGERIAL RECORDS

Ed Barrow 213-203, Jack Barry 90-62, Lou Boudreau 229-232, Bill Carrigan 489-500, Frank Chance 61-91, Jimmy Collins 455-376, Shano Collins 73-134, Joe Cronin 1,071-916, Patsy Donovan 159-147, Hugh Duffy 136-172, Lee Fohl 160-299, Bucky Harris 76-76, Billy Herman 128-182, Pinky Higgins 560-556, Butch Hobson 207-232, Ralph Houk 312-282, George Huff 2-6, Darrell Johnson 220-188, Billy Jurges 59-63, Eddie Kasko 346-295, Kevin Kennedy 171-135, Fred Lake 110-80, Joe McCarthy 223-145, Deacon McGuire

98-123, Marty McManus 95-153, John McNamara 297-273, Joe Morgan 301-262, Steve O'Neill 150-99, Johnny Pesky 147-179, Eddie Popowski 5-4, Pete Runnels 8-8, Chick Stahl 14-26, Jake Stahl 144-88, Bob Unglaub 9-20, Heinie Wagner 52-102, Dick Williams 260-217, Jimy Williams 349-299, Don Zimmer 411-304.

CHICAGO WHITE SOX
YEARLY FINISHES

Year	Position	W	L	Pct.	*GB	Manager	Attendance
1901	1st	83	53	.610	+4.0	Clark Griffith	354,350
1902	4th	74	60	.552	8.0	Clark Griffith	337,898
1903	7th	60	77	.438	30.5	Nixey Callahan	286,183
1904	3rd	89	65	.578	6.0	Nixey Callahan, Fielder Jones	557,123
1905	2nd	92	60	.605	2.0	Fielder Jones	687,419
1906	1st	93	58	.616	+3.0	Fielder Jones	585,202
1907	3rd	87	64	.576	5.5	Fielder Jones	666,307
1908	3rd	88	64	.579	1.5	Fielder Jones	636,096
1909	4th	78	74	.513	20.0	Billy Sullivan	478,400
1910	6th	68	85	.444	35.5	Hugh Duffy	552,084
1911	4th	77	74	.510	24.0	Hugh Duffy	583,208
1912	4th	78	76	.506	28.0	Nixey Callahan	602,241
1913	5th	78	74	.513	17.5	Nixey Callahan	644,501
1914	6th (tied)	70	84	.455	30.0	Nixey Callahan	469,290
1915	3rd	93	61	.604	9.5	Pants Rowland	539,461
1916	2nd	89	65	.578	2.0	Pants Rowland	679,923
1917	1st	100	54	.649	+9.0	Pants Rowland	684,521
1918	6th	57	67	.460	17.0	Pants Rowland	195,081
1919	1st	88	52	.629	+3.5	Kid Gleason	627,186
1920	2nd	96	58	.623	2.0	Kid Gleason	833,492
1921	7th	62	92	.403	36.5	Kid Gleason	543,650
1922	5th	77	77	.500	17.0	Kid Gleason	602,860
1923	7th	69	85	.448	30.0	Kid Gleason	573,778
1924	8th	66	87	.431	25.5	Johnny Evers	606,658
1925	5th	79	75	.513	18.5	Eddie Collins	832,231
1926	5th	81	72	.529	9.5	Eddie Collins	710,339
1927	5th	70	83	.458	29.5	Ray Schalk	614,423
1928	5th	72	82	.468	29.0	Ray Schalk, Lena Blackburne	494,152
1929	7th	59	93	.388	46.0	Lena Blackburne	426,795
1930	7th	62	92	.403	40.0	Donie Bush	406,123
1931	8th	56	97	.366	51.0	Donie Bush	403,550
1932	7th	49	102	.325	56.5	Lew Fonseca	233,198
1933	6th	67	83	.447	31.0	Lew Fonseca	397,789
1934	8th	53	99	.349	47.0	Lew Fonseca, Jimmie Dykes	236,559
1935	5th	74	78	.487	19.5	Jimmie Dykes	470,281
1936	3rd	81	70	.536	20.0	Jimmie Dykes	440,810
1937	3rd	86	68	.558	16.0	Jimmie Dykes	589,245
1938	6th	65	83	.439	32.0	Jimmie Dykes	338,278
1939	4th	85	69	.552	22.5	Jimmie Dykes	594,104
1940	4th (tied)	82	72	.532	8.0	Jimmie Dykes	660,336
1941	3rd	77	77	.500	24.0	Jimmie Dykes	677,077
1942	6th	66	82	.446	34.0	Jimmie Dykes	425,734
1943	4th	82	72	.532	16.0	Jimmie Dykes	508,962
1944	7th	71	83	.461	18.0	Jimmie Dykes	563,539
1945	6th	71	78	.477	15.0	Jimmie Dykes	657,981
1946	5th	74	80	.481	30.0	Jimmie Dykes, Ted Lyons	983,403
1947	6th	70	84	.455	27.0	Ted Lyons	876,948
1948	8th	51	101	.336	44.5	Ted Lyons	777,844
1949	6th	63	91	.409	34.0	Jack Onslow	937,151
1950	6th	60	94	.390	38.0	Jack Onslow, Red Corriden	781,330
1951	4th	81	73	.526	17.0	Paul Richards	1,328,234
1952	3rd	81	73	.526	14.0	Paul Richards	1,231,675
1953	3rd	89	65	.578	11.5	Paul Richards	1,191,353
1954	3rd	94	60	.610	17.0	Paul Richards, Marty Marion	1,231,629
1955	3rd	91	63	.591	5.0	Marty Marion	1,175,684
1956	3rd	85	69	.552	12.0	Marty Marion	1,000,090
1957	2nd	90	64	.584	8.0	Al Lopez	1,135,668
1958	2nd	82	72	.532	10.0	Al Lopez	797,451
1959	1st	94	60	.610	+5.0	Al Lopez	1,423,144
1960	3rd	87	67	.565	10.0	Al Lopez	1,644,460
1961	4th	86	76	.531	23.0	Al Lopez	1,146,019
1962	5th	85	77	.525	11.0	Al Lopez	1,131,562
1963	2nd	94	68	.580	10.5	Al Lopez	1,158,848
1964	2nd	98	64	.605	1.0	Al Lopez	1,250,053
1965	2nd	95	67	.586	7.0	Al Lopez	1,130,519
1966	4th	83	79	.512	15.0	Eddie Stanky	990,016
1967	4th	89	73	.549	3.0	Eddie Stanky	985,634
1968	8th (tied)	67	95	.414	36.0	Eddie Stanky, Al Lopez	803,775

WEST DIVISION

Year	Position	W	L	Pct.	*GB	Manager	Attendance
1969	5th	68	94	.420	29.0	Al Lopez, Don Gutteridge	589,546
1970	6th	56	106	.346	42.0	Don Gutteridge, Chuck Tanner	495,355
1971	3rd	79	83	.488	22.5	Chuck Tanner	833,891
1972	2nd	87	67	.565	5.5	Chuck Tanner	1,177,318
1973	5th	77	85	.475	17.0	Chuck Tanner	1,302,527
1974	4th	80	80	.500	9.0	Chuck Tanner	1,149,596
1975	5th	75	86	.466	22.5	Chuck Tanner	750,802
1976	6th	64	97	.398	25.5	Paul Richards	914,945
1977	3rd	90	72	.556	12.0	Bob Lemon	1,657,135
1978	5th	71	90	.441	20.5	Bob Lemon, Larry Doby	1,491,100
1979	5th	73	87	.456	14.0	Don Kessinger, Tony La Russa	1,280,702
1980	5th	70	90	.438	26.0	Tony La Russa	1,200,365
1981	3rd/6th	54	52	.509	†	Tony La Russa	946,651
1982	3rd	87	75	.537	6.0	Tony La Russa	1,567,787
1983	1st‡	99	63	.611	+20.0	Tony La Russa	2,132,821
1984	5th (tied)	74	88	.457	10.0	Tony La Russa	2,136,988
1985	3rd	85	77	.525	6.0	Tony La Russa	1,669,888
1986	5th	72	90	.444	20.0	Tony La Russa, Jim Fregosi	1,424,313
1987	5th	77	85	.475	8.0	Jim Fregosi	1,208,060
1988	5th	71	90	.441	32.5	Jim Fregosi	1,115,749
1989	7th	69	92	.429	29.5	Jeff Torborg	1,045,651
1990	2nd	94	68	.580	9.0	Jeff Torborg	2,002,357
1991	2nd	87	75	.537	8.0	Jeff Torborg	2,934,154
1992	3rd	86	76	.531	10.0	Gene Lamont	2,681,156
1993	1st‡	94	68	.580	+8.0	Gene Lamont	2,581,091

CENTRAL DIVISION

Year	Position	W	L	Pct.	*GB	Manager	Attendance
1994	1st	67	46	.593	+1.0	Gene Lamont	1,697,398
1995	3rd	68	76	.472	32.0	Gene Lamont, Terry Bevington	1,609,773
1996	2nd	85	77	.525	14.5	Terry Bevington	1,676,403
1997	2nd	80	81	.497	6.0	Terry Bevington	1,864,782
1998	2nd	80	82	.494	9.0	Jerry Manuel	1,391,146
1999	2nd	75	86	.466	21.5	Jerry Manuel	1,338,851
2000	1st§	95	67	.586	+5.0	Jerry Manuel	1,947,799

*Games behind winner. †First half 31-22; second 23-30. ‡Lost championship series. §Lost division series.

MANAGERIAL RECORDS

Terry Bevington 222-214, Lena Blackburne 99-133, Donie Bush 118-189, Nixey Callahan 309-329, Eddie Collins 160-147, Red Corriden 52-72, Larry Doby 37-50, Hugh Duffy 145-159, Jimmie Dykes 899-940, Johnny Evers 66-87, Lew Fonseca 120-196, Jim Fregosi 193-226, Kid Gleason 392-364, Clark Griffith 157-113, Don Gutteridge 109-172, Fielder Jones 426-293, Don Kessinger 46-60, Tony La Russa 522-510, Gene Lamont 258-210, Bob Lemon 124-112, Al Lopez 840-650, Ted Lyons 185-245, Jerry Manuel 250-235, Marty Marion 179-138, Jack Onslow 71-133, Paul Richards 406-362, Pants Rowland 339-247, Ray Schalk 102-125, Eddie Stanky 206-197, Billy Sullivan 78-74, Chuck Tanner 401-414, Jeff Torborg 250-235.

CLEVELAND INDIANS
YEARLY FINISHES

Year	Position	W	L	Pct.	*GB	Manager	Attendance
1901	7th	54	82	.397	29.0	James McAleer	131,380
1902	5th	69	67	.507	14.0	Bill Armour	275,395
1903	3rd	77	63	.550	15.0	Bill Armour	311,280
1904	4th	86	65	.570	7.5	Bill Armour	264,749
1905	5th	76	78	.494	19.0	Nap Lajoie	316,306
1906	3rd	89	64	.582	5.0	Nap Lajoie	325,733
1907	4th	85	67	.559	8.0	Nap Lajoie	382,046
1908	2nd	90	64	.584	0.5	Nap Lajoie	422,242
1909	6th	71	82	.464	27.5	Nap Lajoie, Deacon McGuire	354,627
1910	5th	71	81	.467	32.0	Deacon McGuire	293,456
1911	3rd	80	73	.523	22.0	Deacon McGuire, George Stovall	406,296
1912	5th	75	78	.490	30.5	Harry Davis, J.L. Birmingham	336,844
1913	3rd	86	66	.566	9.5	J.L. Birmingham	541,000
1914	8th	51	102	.333	48.5	J.L. Birmingham	185,997
1915	7th	57	95	.375	44.5	J.L. Birmingham, Lee Fohl	159,285
1916	6th	77	77	.500	14.0	Lee Fohl	492,106
1917	3rd	88	66	.571	12.0	Lee Fohl	477,298
1918	2nd	73	54	.575	2.5	Lee Fohl	295,515
1919	2nd	84	55	.604	3.5	Lee Fohl, Tris Speaker	538,135
1920	1st	98	56	.636	+2.0	Tris Speaker	912,832
1921	2nd	94	60	.610	4.5	Tris Speaker	748,705
1922	4th	78	76	.507	16.0	Tris Speaker	528,145

Year	Position	W	L	Pct.	*GB	Manager	Attendance
1923	3rd	82	71	.536	16.5	Tris Speaker	558,856
1924	6th	67	86	.438	24.5	Tris Speaker	481,905
1925	6th	70	84	.455	27.5	Tris Speaker	419,005
1926	2nd	88	66	.571	3.0	Tris Speaker	627,426
1927	6th	66	87	.431	43.5	Jack McAllister	373,138
1928	7th	62	92	.403	39.0	Roger Peckinpaugh	375,907
1929	3rd	81	71	.533	24.0	Roger Peckinpaugh	536,210
1930	4th	81	73	.536	21.0	Roger Peckinpaugh	528,657
1931	4th	78	76	.506	30.0	Roger Peckinpaugh	483,027
1932	4th	87	65	.572	19.0	Roger Peckinpaugh	468,953
1933	4th	75	76	.497	23.5	Roger Peckinpaugh, Walter Johnson	387,936
1934	3rd	85	69	.552	16.0	Walter Johnson	391,338
1935	3rd	82	71	.536	12.0	Walter Johnson, Steve O'Neill	397,615
1936	5th	80	74	.519	22.5	Steve O'Neill	500,391
1937	4th	83	71	.539	19.0	Steve O'Neill	564,849
1938	3rd	86	66	.566	13.0	Ossie Vitt	652,006
1939	3rd	87	67	.565	20.5	Ossie Vitt	563,926
1940	2nd	89	65	.578	1.0	Ossie Vitt	902,576
1941	4th (tied)	75	79	.487	26.0	Roger Peckinpaugh	745,948
1942	4th	75	79	.487	28.0	Lou Boudreau	459,447
1943	3rd	82	71	.536	15.5	Lou Boudreau	438,894
1944	5th (tied)	72	82	.468	17.0	Lou Boudreau	475,272
1945	5th	73	72	.503	11.0	Lou Boudreau	558,182
1946	6th	68	86	.442	36.0	Lou Boudreau	1,057,289
1947	4th	80	74	.519	17.0	Lou Boudreau	1,521,978
1948	1st†	97	58	.626	+1.0	Lou Boudreau	2,620,627
1949	3rd	89	65	.578	8.0	Lou Boudreau	2,233,771
1950	4th	92	62	.597	6.0	Lou Boudreau	1,727,464
1951	2nd	93	61	.604	5.0	Al Lopez	1,704,984
1952	2nd	93	61	.604	2.0	Al Lopez	1,444,607
1953	2nd	92	62	.597	8.5	Al Lopez	1,069,176
1954	1st	111	43	.721	+8.0	Al Lopez	1,335,472
1955	2nd	93	61	.604	3.0	Al Lopez	1,221,780
1956	2nd	88	66	.571	9.0	Al Lopez	865,467
1957	6th	76	77	.497	21.5	Kerby Farrell	722,256
1958	4th	77	76	.503	14.5	Bobby Bragan, Joe Gordon	663,805
1959	2nd	89	65	.578	5.0	Joe Gordon	1,497,976
1960	4th	76	78	.494	21.0	Joe Gordon, Jimmie Dykes	950,985
1961	5th	78	83	.484	30.5	Jimmie Dykes	725,547
1962	6th	80	82	.494	16.0	Mel McGaha	716,076
1963	5th (tied)	79	83	.488	25.5	Birdie Tebbetts	562,507
1964	6th (tied)	79	83	.488	20.0	Birdie Tebbetts	653,293
1965	5th	87	75	.537	15.0	Birdie Tebbetts	934,786
1966	5th	81	81	.500	17.0	Birdie Tebbetts, George Strickland	903,359
1967	8th	75	87	.463	17.0	Joe Adcock	662,980
1968	3rd	86	75	.534	16.5	Alvin Dark	857,994

EAST DIVISION

Year	Position	W	L	Pct.	*GB	Manager	Attendance
1969	6th	62	99	.385	46.5	Alvin Dark	619,970
1970	5th	76	86	.469	32.0	Alvin Dark	729,752
1971	6th	60	102	.370	43.0	Alvin Dark, John Lipon	591,361
1972	5th	72	84	.462	14.0	Ken Aspromonte	626,354
1973	6th	71	91	.438	26.0	Ken Aspromonte	615,107
1974	4th	77	85	.475	14.0	Ken Aspromonte	1,114,262
1975	4th	79	80	.497	15.5	Frank Robinson	977,039
1976	4th	81	78	.509	16.0	Frank Robinson	948,776
1977	5th	71	90	.441	28.5	Frank Robinson, Jeff Torborg	900,365
1978	6th	69	90	.434	29.0	Jeff Torborg	800,584
1979	6th	81	80	.503	22.0	Jeff Torborg, Dave Garcia	1,011,644
1980	6th	79	81	.494	23.0	Dave Garcia	1,033,827
1981	6th/5th	52	51	.504	‡	Dave Garcia	661,395
1982	6th (tied)	78	84	.481	17.0	Dave Garcia	1,044,021
1983	7th	70	92	.432	28.0	Mike Ferraro, Pat Corrales	768,941
1984	6th	75	87	.463	29.0	Pat Corrales	734,079
1985	7th	60	102	.370	39.5	Pat Corrales	655,181
1986	5th	84	78	.519	11.5	Pat Corrales	1,471,805
1987	7th	61	101	.377	37.0	Pat Corrales, Doc Edwards	1,077,898
1988	6th	78	84	.481	11.0	Doc Edwards	1,411,610
1989	6th	73	89	.451	16.0	Doc Edwards, John Hart	1,285,542
1990	4th	77	85	.475	11.0	John McNamara	1,225,240
1991	7th	57	105	.352	34.0	John McNamara, Mike Hargrove	1,051,863
1992	4th (tied)	76	86	.469	20.0	Mike Hargrove	1,224,274
1993	6th	76	86	.469	19.0	Mike Hargrove	2,177,908

CENTRAL DIVISION

Year	Position	W	L	Pct.	*GB	Manager	Attendance
1994	2nd.....................66		47	.584	1.0	Mike Hargrove	1,995,174
1995	1st§∞....................100		44	.694	+30.0	Mike Hargrove	2,842,745
1996	1st▲......................99		62	.615	+14.5	Mike Hargrove	3,318,174
1997	1st§∞....................86		75	.534	+6.0	Mike Hargrove	3,404,750
1998	1st§◆....................89		73	.549	+9.0	Mike Hargrove	3,467,299
1999	1st▲......................97		65	.599	+21.5	Mike Hargrove	3,468,456
2000	2nd.....................90		72	.556	5.0	Charlie Manuel	3,456,278

*Games behind winner. †Won pennant playoff. ‡First half 26-24; second 26-27. §Won division series. ∞Won championship series. ▲Lost division series. ◆Lost championship series.

MANAGERIAL RECORDS

Joe Adcock 75-87, Bill Armour 232-195, Ken Aspromonte 220-260, Joe Birmingham 170-191, Lou Boudreau 728-649, Bobby Bragan 31-36, Pat Corrales 280-355, Alvin Dark 266-321, Harry Davis 54-71, Jimmie Dykes 103-115, Doc Edwards 173-207, Kerby Farrell 76-77, Mike Ferraro 40-60, Lee Fohl 327-310, Dave Garcia 247-244, Joe Gordon 184-151, Mike Hargrove 721-591, John Hart 8-11, Walter Johnson 179-168, Nap Lajoie 377-309, Johnny Lipon 18-41, Al Lopez 570-354, Charlie Manuel 90-72, Jimmy McAleer 54-82, Jack McCallister 66-87, Mel McGaha 80-82, Deacon McGuire 91-117, John McNamara 102-137, Steve O'Neill 199-168, Roger Peckinpaugh 490-481, Frank Robinson 186-189, Tris Speaker 617-520, George Stovall 74-62, George Strickland 15-24, Birdie Tebbetts 269-298, Jeff Torborg 157-201, Oscar Vitt 262-198.

DETROIT TIGERS
YEARLY FINISHES

HISTORY Team by team

Year	Position	W	L	Pct.	*GB	Manager	Attendance
1901	3rd 74		61	.548	8.5	George Stallings	259,430
1902	7th 52		83	.385	30.5	Frank Dwyer	189,469
1903	5th 65		71	.478	25.0	Ed Barrow	224,523
1904	7th 62		90	.408	32.0	Ed Barrow, Bobby Lowe	177,796
1905	3rd 79		74	.516	15.5	Bill Armour	193,384
1906	6th 71		78	.477	21.0	Bill Armour	174,043
1907	1st..........................92		58	.613	+1.5	Hughey Jennings	297,079
1908	1st..........................90		63	.588	+ .5	Hughey Jennings	436,199
1909	1st..........................98		54	.645	+3.5	Hughey Jennings	490,490
1910	3rd 86		68	.558	18.0	Hughey Jennings	391,288
1911	2nd▲......................89		65	.578	13.5	Hughey Jennings	484,988
1912	6th 69		84	.451	36.5	Hughey Jennings	402,870
1913	6th 66		87	.431	30.0	Hughey Jennings	398,502
1914	4th 80		73	.523	19.5	Hughey Jennings	416,225
1915	2nd......................100		54	.649	2.5	Hughey Jennings	476,105
1916	3rd 87		67	.565	4.0	Hughey Jennings	616,772
1917	4th 78		75	.510	21.5	Hughey Jennings	457,289
1918	7th 55		71	.437	20.0	Hughey Jennings	203,719
1919	4th 80		60	.571	8.0	Hughey Jennings	643,805
1920	7th 61		93	.396	37.0	Hughey Jennings	579,650
1921	6th 71		82	.464	27.0	Ty Cobb	661,527
1922	3rd 79		75	.513	15.0	Ty Cobb	861,206
1923	2nd.........................83		71	.539	16.0	Ty Cobb	911,377
1924	3rd 86		68	.558	6.0	Ty Cobb	1,015,136
1925	4th 81		73	.526	16.5	Ty Cobb	820,766
1926	6th 79		75	.513	12.0	Ty Cobb	711,914
1927	4th 82		71	.536	27.5	George Moriarty	773,716
1928	6th 68		86	.442	33.0	George Moriarty	474,323
1929	6th 70		84	.455	36.0	Bucky Harris	869,318
1930	5th 75		79	.487	27.0	Bucky Harris	649,450
1931	7th 61		93	.396	47.0	Bucky Harris	434,056
1932	5th 76		75	.503	29.5	Bucky Harris	397,157
1933	5th 75		79	.487	25.0	Del Baker	320,972
1934	1st........................101		53	.656	+7.0	Mickey Cochrane	919,161
1935	1st..........................93		58	.616	+3.0	Mickey Cochrane	1,034,929
1936	2nd.........................83		71	.539	19.5	Mickey Cochrane	875,948
1937	2nd.........................89		65	.578	13.0	Mickey Cochrane	1,072,276
1938	4th 84		70	.545	16.0	Mickey Cochrane, Del Baker	799,557
1939	5th 81		73	.526	26.5	Del Baker	836,279
1940	1st..........................90		64	.584	+1.0	Del Baker	1,112,693
1941	4th (tied).................75		79	.487	26.0	Del Baker	684,915
1942	5th 73		81	.474	30.0	Del Baker	580,087
1943	5th 78		76	.506	20.0	Steve O'Neill	606,287
1944	2nd.........................88		66	.571	1.0	Steve O'Neill	923,176
1945	1st..........................88		65	.575	+1.5	Steve O'Neill	1,280,341
1946	2nd.........................92		62	.597	12.0	Steve O'Neill	1,722,590

Year	Position	W	L	Pct.	*GB	Manager	Attendance
1947	2nd	85	69	.552	12.0	Steve O'Neill	1,398,093
1948	5th	78	76	.506	18.5	Steve O'Neill	1,743,035
1949	4th	87	67	.565	10.0	Red Rolfe	1,821,204
1950	2nd	95	59	.617	3.0	Red Rolfe	1,951,474
1951	5th	73	81	.474	25.0	Red Rolfe	1,132,641
1952	8th	50	104	.325	45.0	Red Rolfe, Fred Hutchinson	1,026,846
1953	6th	60	94	.390	40.5	Fred Hutchinson	884,658
1954	5th	68	86	.442	43.0	Fred Hutchinson	1,079,847
1955	5th	79	75	.513	17.0	Bucky Harris	1,181,838
1956	5th	82	72	.532	15.0	Bucky Harris	1,051,182
1957	4th	78	76	.506	20.0	Jack Tighe	1,272,346
1958	5th	77	77	.500	15.0	Jack Tighe, Bill Norman	1,098,924
1959	4th	76	78	.494	18.0	Bill Norman, Jimmie Dykes	1,221,221
1960	6th	71	83	.461	26.0	Jimmie Dykes, Billy Hitchcock, Joe Gordon	1,167,669
1961	2nd	101	61	.623	8.0	Bob Scheffing	1,600,710
1962	4th	85	76	.528	10.5	Bob Scheffing	1,207,881
1963	5th (tied)	79	83	.488	25.5	Bob Scheffing, Charlie Dressen	821,952
1964	4th	85	77	.525	14.0	Charlie Dressen	816,139
1965	4th	89	73	.549	13.0	Charlie Dressen, Bob Swift	1,029,645
1966	3rd	88	74	.543	10.0	Charlie Dressen, Bob Swift, Frank Skaff	1,124,293
1967	2nd	91	71	.562	1.0	Mayo Smith	1,447,143
1968	1st	103	59	.636	+12.0	Mayo Smith	2,031,847

EAST DIVISION

Year	Position	W	L	Pct.	*GB	Manager	Attendance
1969	2nd	90	72	.556	19.0	Mayo Smith	1,577,481
1970	4th	79	83	.488	29.0	Mayo Smith	1,501,293
1971	2nd	91	71	.562	12.0	Billy Martin	1,591,073
1972	1st†	86	70	.551	+0.5	Billy Martin	1,892,386
1973	3rd	85	77	.525	12.0	Billy Martin, Joe Schultz	1,724,146
1974	6th	72	90	.444	19.0	Ralph Houk	1,243,080
1975	6th	57	102	.358	37.5	Ralph Houk	1,058,836
1976	5th	74	87	.460	24.0	Ralph Houk	1,467,020
1977	4th	74	88	.457	26.0	Ralph Houk	1,359,856
1978	5th	86	76	.531	13.5	Ralph Houk	1,714,893
1979	5th	85	76	.528	18.0	Les Moss, Dick Tracewski, Sparky Anderson	1,630,929
1980	5th	84	78	.519	19.0	Sparky Anderson	1,785,293
1981	4th/2nd (tied)	60	49	.550	‡	Sparky Anderson	1,149,144
1982	4th	83	79	.512	12.0	Sparky Anderson	1,636,058
1983	2nd	92	70	.568	6.0	Sparky Anderson	1,829,636
1984	1st§	104	58	.642	+15.0	Sparky Anderson	2,704,794
1985	3rd	84	77	.522	15.0	Sparky Anderson	2,286,609
1986	3rd	87	75	.537	8.5	Sparky Anderson	1,899,437
1987	1st†	98	64	.605	+2.0	Sparky Anderson	2,061,830
1988	2nd	88	74	.543	1.0	Sparky Anderson	2,081,162
1989	7th	59	103	.364	30.0	Sparky Anderson	1,543,656
1990	3rd	79	83	.488	9.0	Sparky Anderson	1,495,785
1991	2nd	84	78	.519	7.0	Sparky Anderson	1,641,661
1992	6th	75	87	.463	21.0	Sparky Anderson	1,423,963
1993	3rd (tied)	85	77	.525	10.0	Sparky Anderson	1,971,421
1994	5th	53	62	.461	18.0	Sparky Anderson	1,184,783
1995	4th	60	84	.417	26.0	Sparky Anderson	1,180,979
1996	5th	53	109	.327	39.0	Buddy Bell	1,168,610
1997	3rd	79	83	.488	19.0	Buddy Bell	1,365,157

CENTRAL DIVISION

Year	Position	W	L	Pct.	*GB	Manager	Attendance
1998	5th	65	97	.401	24.0	Buddy Bell, Larry Parrish	1,409,391
1999	3rd	69	92	.429	27.5	Larry Parrish	2,026,441
2000	3rd	79	83	.488	16.0	Phil Garner	2,533,752

*Games behind winner. †Lost championship series. ‡First half 31-26; second 29-23. §Won championship series.

MANAGERIAL RECORDS

Sparky Anderson 1,431-1,248, Bill Armour 150-152, Del Baker 392-336, Ed Barrow 97-117, Buddy Bell 184-277, Ty Cobb 479-444, Mickey Cochrane 379-278, Chuck Dressen 221-189, Frank Dwyer 52-83, Jimmie Dykes 118-115, Phil Garner 79-83, Joe Gordon 26-31, Bucky Harris 516-557, Ralph Houk 366-443, Fred Hutchinson 155-235, Hugh Jennings 1,131-972, Bobby Lowe 30-44, Billy Martin 248-204, George Moriarty 150-157, Les Moss 27-26, Bill Norman 58-64, Steve O'Neill 509-414, Larry Parrish 82-104, Red Rolfe 278-256, Bob Scheffing 210-173, Joe Schultz 14-14, Frank Skaff 40-39, Mayo Smith 363-285, George Stallings 74-61, Bob Swift 56-43, Jack Tighe 99-104.

YEARLY FINISHES

WEST DIVISION

Year	Position	W	L	Pct.	*GB	Manager	Attendance
1969	4th	69	93	.429	28	Joe Gordon	902,414
1970	4th (tied)	65	97	.401	33	Charlie Metro, Bob Lemon	693,047
1971	2nd	85	76	.528	16	Bob Lemon	910,784
1972	4th	76	78	.494	16.5	Bob Lemon	707,656
1973	2nd	88	74	.543	6	Jack McKeon	1,345,341
1974	5th	77	85	.475	13	Jack McKeon	1,173,292
1975	2nd	91	71	.562	7	Jack McKeon, Whitey Herzog	1,151,836
1976	1st†	90	72	.556	+2.5	Whitey Herzog	1,680,265
1977	1st†	102	60	.630	+8	Whitey Herzog	1,852,603
1978	1st†	92	70	.568	+5	Whitey Herzog	2,255,493
1979	2nd	85	77	.525	3	Whitey Herzog	2,261,845
1980	1st‡	97	65	.599	+14	Jim Frey	2,288,714
1981	5th/1st∞	50	53	.485	§	Jim Frey, Dick Howser	1,279,403
1982	2nd	90	72	.556	3	Dick Howser	2,284,464
1983	2nd	79	83	.488	20	Dick Howser	1,963,875
1984	1st†	84	78	.519	+3	Dick Howser	1,810,018
1985	1st‡	91	71	.562	+1	Dick Howser	2,162,717
1986	3rd (tied)	76	86	.469	16	Dick Howser, Mike Ferraro	2,320,794
1987	2nd	83	79	.512	2	Billy Gardner, John Wathan	2,392,471
1988	3rd	84	77	.522	19.5	John Wathan	2,350,181
1989	2nd	92	70	.568	7	John Wathan	2,477,700
1990	6th	75	86	.466	27.5	John Wathan	2,244,956
1991	6th	82	80	.506	13	John Wathan, Hal McRae	2,161,537
1992	5th (tied)	72	90	.444	24	Hal McRae	1,867,689
1993	3rd	84	78	.519	10	Hal McRae	1,934,578

CENTRAL DIVISION

Year	Position	W	L	Pct.	*GB	Manager	Attendance
1994	3rd	64	51	.557	4	Hal McRae	1,400,494
1995	2nd	70	74	.486	30	Bob Boone	1,233,530
1996	5th	75	86	.466	24	Bob Boone	1,435,997
1997	5th	67	94	.416	19	Bob Boone, Tony Muser	1,517,638
1998	3rd	72	89	.447	16.5	Tony Muser	1,494,875
1999	4th	64	97	.398	32.5	Tony Muser	1,506,068
2000	4th	77	85	.475	18.0	Tony Muser	1,677,915

*Games behind winner. †Lost championship series. ‡Won championship series. §First half 20-30; second 30-23. ∞Lost division series.

MANAGERIAL RECORDS

Bob Boone 181-206, Mike Ferraro 36-38, Jim Frey 127-105, Billy Gardner 62-64, Joe Gordon 69-93, Whitey Herzog 410-304, Dick Howser 404-365, Bob Lemon 207-218, Jack McKeon 215-205, Hal McRae 286-277, Charlie Metro 19-33, Tony Muser 244-319, John Wathan 288-270.

MINNESOTA TWINS

YEARLY FINISHES

(Known as original Washington Senators through 1960)

Year	Position	W	L	Pct.	*GB	Manager	Attendance
1901	6th	61	72	.459	20.5	Jimmy Manning	161,661
1902	6th	61	75	.449	22.0	Tom Loftus	188,158
1903	8th	43	94	.314	47.5	Tom Loftus	128,878
1904	8th	38	113	.251	55.5	Patsy Donovan	131,744
1905	7th	64	87	.421	29.5	Jake Stahl	252,027
1906	7th	55	95	.367	37.5	Jake Stahl	129,903
1907	8th	49	102	.325	43.5	Joe Cantillon	221,929
1908	7th	67	85	.441	22.5	Joe Cantillon	264,252
1909	8th	42	110	.276	56.0	Joe Cantillon	205,199
1910	7th	66	85	.437	36.5	Jimmy McAleer	254,591
1911	7th	64	90	.416	38.5	Jimmy McAleer	244,884
1912	2nd	91	61	.599	14.0	Clark Griffith	350,663
1913	2nd	90	64	.584	6.5	Clark Griffith	325,831
1914	3rd	81	73	.526	19.0	Clark Griffith	243,888
1915	4th	85	68	.556	17.0	Clark Griffith	167,332
1916	7th	76	77	.497	14.5	Clark Griffith	177,265
1917	5th	74	79	.484	25.5	Clark Griffith	89,682
1918	3rd	72	56	.563	4.0	Clark Griffith	182,122
1919	7th	56	84	.400	32.0	Clark Griffith	234,096

Year	Position	W	L	Pct.	*GB	Manager	Attendance
1920	6th	68	84	.447	29.0	Clark Griffith	359,260
1921	4th	80	73	.523	18.0	George McBride	456,069
1922	6th	69	85	.448	25.0	Clyde Milan	458,552
1923	4th	75	78	.490	23.5	Donie Bush	357,406
1924	1st	92	62	.597	+2.0	Bucky Harris	534,310
1925	1st	96	55	.636	+8.5	Bucky Harris	817,199
1926	4th	81	69	.540	8.0	Bucky Harris	551,580
1927	3rd	85	69	.552	25.0	Bucky Harris	528,976
1928	4th	75	79	.487	26.0	Bucky Harris	378,501
1929	5th	71	81	.467	34.0	Walter Johnson	355,506
1930	2nd	94	60	.610	8.0	Walter Johnson	614,474
1931	3rd	92	62	.597	16.0	Walter Johnson	492,657
1932	3rd	93	61	.604	14.0	Walter Johnson	371,396
1933	1st	99	53	.651	+7.0	Joe Cronin	437,533
1934	7th	66	86	.434	34.0	Joe Cronin	330,074
1935	6th	67	86	.438	27.0	Bucky Harris	255,011
1936	4th	82	71	.536	20.0	Bucky Harris	379,525
1937	6th	73	80	.477	28.5	Bucky Harris	397,799
1938	5th	75	76	.497	23.5	Bucky Harris	522,694
1939	6th	65	87	.428	41.5	Bucky Harris	339,257
1940	7th	64	90	.416	26.0	Bucky Harris	381,241
1941	6th (tied)	70	84	.455	31.0	Bucky Harris	415,663
1942	7th	62	89	.411	39.5	Bucky Harris	403,493
1943	2nd	84	69	.549	13.5	Ossie Bluege	574,694
1944	8th	64	90	.416	25.0	Ossie Bluege	525,235
1945	2nd	87	67	.565	1.5	Ossie Bluege	652,660
1946	4th	76	78	.494	28.0	Ossie Bluege	1,027,216
1947	7th	64	90	.416	33.0	Ossie Bluege	850,758
1948	7th	56	97	.366	40.0	Joe Kuhel	795,254
1949	8th	50	104	.325	47.0	Joe Kuhel	770,745
1950	5th	67	87	.435	31.0	Bucky Harris	699,697
1951	7th	62	92	.403	36.0	Bucky Harris	695,167
1952	5th	78	76	.506	17.0	Bucky Harris	699,457
1953	5th	76	76	.500	23.5	Bucky Harris	595,594
1954	6th	66	88	.429	45.0	Bucky Harris	503,542
1955	8th	53	101	.344	43.0	Chuck Dressen	425,238
1956	7th	59	95	.383	38.0	Chuck Dressen	431,647
1957	8th	55	99	.357	43.0	Chuck Dressen, Cookie Lavagetto	457,079
1958	8th	61	93	.396	31.0	Cookie Lavagetto	475,288
1959	8th	63	91	.409	31.0	Cookie Lavagetto	615,372
1960	5th	73	81	.474	24.0	Cookie Lavagetto	743,404
1961	7th	70	90	.438	38.0	Cookie Lavagetto, Sam Mele	1,256,723
1962	2nd	91	71	.562	5.0	Sam Mele	1,433,116
1963	3rd	91	70	.565	13.0	Sam Mele	1,406,652
1964	6th (tied)	79	83	.488	20.0	Sam Mele	1,207,514
1965	1st	102	60	.630	+7.0	Sam Mele	1,463,258
1966	2nd	89	73	.549	9.0	Sam Mele	1,259,374
1967	2nd (tied)	91	71	.562	1.0	Sam Mele, Cal Ermer	1,483,547
1968	7th	79	83	.488	24.0	Cal Ermer	1,143,257

WEST DIVISION

Year	Position	W	L	Pct.	*GB	Manager	Attendance
1969	1st†	97	65	.599	+9.0	Billy Martin	1,349,328
1970	1st†	98	64	.605	+9.0	Bill Rigney	1,261,887
1971	5th	74	86	.463	26.5	Bill Rigney	940,858
1972	3rd	77	77	.500	15.5	Bill Rigney, Frank Quilici	797,901
1973	3rd	81	81	.500	13.0	Frank Quilici	907,499
1974	3rd	82	80	.506	8.0	Frank Quilici	662,401
1975	4th	76	83	.478	20.5	Frank Quilici	737,156
1976	3rd	85	77	.525	5.0	Gene Mauch	715,394
1977	4th	84	77	.522	17.5	Gene Mauch	1,162,727
1978	4th	73	89	.451	19.0	Gene Mauch	787,878
1979	4th	82	80	.506	6.0	Gene Mauch	1,070,521
1980	3rd	77	84	.478	19.5	Gene Mauch, Johnny Goryl	769,206
1981	7th/4th	41	68	.376	‡	Johnny Goryl, Billy Gardner	469,090
1982	7th	60	102	.370	33.0	Billy Gardner	921,186
1983	5th (tied)	70	92	.432	29.0	Billy Gardner	858,939
1984	2nd (tied)	81	81	.500	3.0	Billy Gardner	1,598,422
1985	4th (tied)	77	85	.475	14.0	Billy Gardner, Ray Miller	1,651,814
1986	6th	71	91	.438	21.0	Ray Miller, Tom Kelly	1,255,453
1987	1st§	85	77	.525	+2.0	Tom Kelly	2,081,976
1988	2nd	91	71	.562	13.0	Tom Kelly	3,030,672
1989	5th	80	82	.494	19.0	Tom Kelly	2,277,438
1990	7th	74	88	.457	29.0	Tom Kelly	1,751,584

– 359 –

Year	Position	W	L	Pct.	*GB	Manager	Attendance
1991	1st§	95	67	.586	+8.0	Tom Kelly	2,293,842
1992	2nd	90	72	.556	6.0	Tom Kelly	2,482,428
1993	5th (tied)	71	91	.438	23.0	Tom Kelly	2,048,673

CENTRAL DIVISION

Year	Position	W	L	Pct.	*GB	Manager	Attendance
1994	4th	53	60	.469	14.0	Tom Kelly	1,398,565
1995	5th	56	88	.389	44.0	Tom Kelly	1,057,667
1996	4th	78	84	.481	21.5	Tom Kelly	1,437,352
1997	4th	68	94	.420	18.5	Tom Kelly	1,411,064
1998	4th	70	92	.432	19.0	Tom Kelly	1,165,980
1999	5th	63	97	.394	33.0	Tom Kelly	1,202,829
2000	5th	69	93	.426	26.0	Tom Kelly	1,059,715

*Games behind winner. †Lost championship series. ‡First half 17-39; second 24-29. §Won championship series.

MANAGERIAL RECORDS

Ossie Bluege 375-394, Donie Bush 75-78, Joe Cantillon 158-297, Joe Cronin 165-139, Patsy Donovan 38-113, Chuck Dressen 116-212, Cal Ermer 145-129, Billy Gardner 268-353, Johnny Goryl 34-38, Clark Griffith 693-646, Bucky Harris 1,336-1,416, Walter Johnson 350-264, Tom Kelly 1,055-1,167, Joe Kuhel 106-201, Cookie Lavagetto 271-384, Tom Loftus 104-169, Jimmy Manning 61-72, Billy Martin 97-65, Gene Mauch 378-394, Jimmy McAleer 130-175, George McBride 80-73, Sam Mele 524-436, Clyde Milan 69-85, Ray Miller 109-130, Frank Quilici 280-287, Bill Rigney 208-184, Jake Stahl 119-182.

NEW YORK YANKEES
YEARLY FINISHES

(Known as Baltimore Orioles through 1902)

Year	Position	W	L	Pct.	*GB	Manager	Attendance
1901	5th	68	65	.511	13.5	John McGraw	141,952
1902	8th	50	88	.362	34.0	John McGraw, Wilbert Robinson	174,606
1903	4th	72	62	.537	17.0	Clark Griffith	211,808
1904	2nd	92	59	.609	1.5	Clark Griffith	438,919
1905	6th	71	78	.477	21.5	Clark Griffith	309,100
1906	2nd	90	61	.596	3.0	Clark Griffith	434,709
1907	5th	70	78	.473	21.0	Clark Griffith	350,020
1908	8th	51	103	.331	39.5	Clark Griffith, Kid Elberfeld	305,500
1909	5th	74	77	.490	23.5	George Stallings	501,000
1910	2nd	88	63	.583	14.5	George Stallings, Hal Chase	355,857
1911	6th	76	76	.500	25.5	Hal Chase	302,444
1912	8th	50	102	.329	55.0	Harry Wolverton	242,194
1913	7th	57	94	.377	38.0	Frank Chance	357,551
1914	6th (tied)	70	84	.455	30.0	Frank Chance, Roger Peckinpaugh	359,477
1915	5th	69	83	.454	32.5	Bill Donovan	256,035
1916	4th	80	74	.519	11.0	Bill Donovan	469,211
1917	6th	71	82	.464	28.5	Bill Donovan	330,294
1918	4th	60	63	.488	13.5	Miller Huggins	282,047
1919	3rd	80	59	.576	7.5	Miller Huggins	619,164
1920	3rd	95	59	.617	3.0	Miller Huggins	1,289,422
1921	1st	98	55	.641	+4.5	Miller Huggins	1,230,696
1922	1st	94	60	.610	+1.0	Miller Huggins	1,026,134
1923	1st	98	54	.645	+16.0	Miller Huggins	1,007,066
1924	2nd	89	63	.586	2.0	Miller Huggins	1,053,533
1925	7th	69	85	.448	30.0	Miller Huggins	697,267
1926	1st	91	63	.591	+3.0	Miller Huggins	1,027,095
1927	1st	110	44	.714	+19.0	Miller Huggins	1,164,015
1928	1st	101	53	.656	+2.5	Miller Huggins	1,072,132
1929	2nd	88	66	.571	18.0	Miller Huggins, Art Fletcher	960,148
1930	3rd	86	68	.558	16.0	Bob Shawkey	1,169,230
1931	2nd	94	59	.614	13.5	Joe McCarthy	912,437
1932	1st	107	47	.695	+13.0	Joe McCarthy	962,320
1933	2nd	91	59	.607	7.0	Joe McCarthy	728,014
1934	2nd	94	60	.610	7.0	Joe McCarthy	854,682
1935	2nd	89	60	.597	3.0	Joe McCarthy	657,508
1936	1st	102	51	.667	+19.5	Joe McCarthy	976,913
1937	1st	102	52	.662	+13.0	Joe McCarthy	998,148
1938	1st	99	53	.651	+9.5	Joe McCarthy	970,916
1939	1st	106	45	.702	+17.0	Joe McCarthy	859,785
1940	3rd	88	66	.571	2.0	Joe McCarthy	988,975
1941	1st	101	53	.656	+17.0	Joe McCarthy	964,722
1942	1st	103	51	.669	+9.0	Joe McCarthy	988,251
1943	1st	98	56	.636	+13.5	Joe McCarthy	645,006

Year	Position	W	L	Pct.	*GB	Manager	Attendance
1944	3rd	83	71	.539	6.0	Joe McCarthy	822,864
1945	4th	81	71	.533	6.5	Joe McCarthy	881,846
1946	3rd	87	67	.565	17.0	Joe McCarthy, Bill Dickey, Johnny Neun	2,265,512
1947	1st	97	57	.630	+12.0	Bucky Harris	2,178,937
1948	3rd	94	60	.610	2.5	Bucky Harris	2,373,901
1949	1st	97	57	.630	+1.0	Casey Stengel	2,281,676
1950	1st	98	56	.636	+3.0	Casey Stengel	2,081,380
1951	1st	98	56	.636	+5.0	Casey Stengel	1,950,107
1952	1st	95	59	.617	+2.0	Casey Stengel	1,629,665
1953	1st	99	52	.656	+8.5	Casey Stengel	1,537,811
1954	2nd	103	51	.669	8.0	Casey Stengel	1,475,171
1955	1st	96	58	.623	+3.0	Casey Stengel	1,490,138
1956	1st	97	57	.630	+9.0	Casey Stengel	1,491,784
1957	1st	98	56	.636	+8.0	Casey Stengel	1,497,134
1958	1st	92	62	.597	+10.0	Casey Stengel	1,428,438
1959	3rd	79	75	.513	15.0	Casey Stengel	1,552,030
1960	1st	97	57	.630	+8.0	Casey Stengel	1,627,349
1961	1st	109	53	.673	+8.0	Ralph Houk	1,747,725
1962	1st	96	66	.593	+5.0	Ralph Houk	1,493,574
1963	1st	104	57	.646	+10.5	Ralph Houk	1,308,920
1964	1st	99	63	.611	+1.0	Yogi Berra	1,305,638
1965	6th	77	85	.475	25.0	Johnny Keane	1,213,552
1966	10th	70	89	.440	26.5	Johnny Keane, Ralph Houk	1,124,648
1967	9th	72	90	.444	20.0	Ralph Houk	1,259,514
1968	5th	83	79	.512	20.0	Ralph Houk	1,185,666

EAST DIVISION

Year	Position	W	L	Pct.	*GB	Manager	Attendance
1969	5th	80	81	.497	28.5	Ralph Houk	1,067,996
1970	2nd	93	69	.574	15.0	Ralph Houk	1,136,879
1971	4th	82	80	.506	21.0	Ralph Houk	1,070,771
1972	4th	79	76	.510	6.5	Ralph Houk	966,328
1973	4th	80	82	.494	17.0	Ralph Houk	1,262,103
1974	2nd	89	73	.549	2.0	Bill Virdon	1,273,075
1975	3rd	83	77	.519	12.0	Bill Virdon, Billy Martin	1,288,048
1976	1st†	97	62	.610	+10.5	Billy Martin	2,012,434
1977	1st†	100	62	.617	+2.5	Billy Martin	2,103,092
1978	1st‡†	100	63	.613	+1.0	Billy Martin, Bob Lemon	2,335,871
1979	4th	89	71	.556	13.5	Bob Lemon, Billy Martin	2,537,765
1980	1st§	103	59	.636	+3.0	Dick Howser	2,627,417
1981	1st/6th▲†	59	48	.551	∞	Gene Michael, Bob Lemon	1,614,533
1982	5th	79	83	.488	16.0	Bob Lemon, Gene Michael, Clyde King	2,041,219
1983	3rd	91	71	.562	7.0	Billy Martin	2,257,976
1984	3rd	87	75	.537	17.0	Yogi Berra	1,821,815
1985	2nd	97	64	.602	2.0	Yogi Berra, Billy Martin	2,214,587
1986	2nd	90	72	.556	5.5	Lou Piniella	2,268,030
1987	4th	89	73	.549	9.0	Lou Piniella	2,427,672
1988	5th	85	76	.528	3.5	Billy Martin, Lou Piniella	2,633,701
1989	5th	74	87	.460	14.5	Dallas Green, Bucky Dent	2,170,485
1990	7th	67	95	.414	21.0	Bucky Dent, Stump Merrill	2,006,436
1991	5th	71	91	.438	20.0	Stump Merrill	1,863,733
1992	4th (tied)	76	86	.469	20.0	Buck Showalter	1,748,733
1993	2nd	88	74	.543	7.0	Buck Showalter	2,416,965
1994	1st	70	43	.619	+6.5	Buck Showalter	1,675,556
1995	2nd◆	79	65	.549	7.0	Buck Showalter	1,705,263
1996	1st▲†	92	70	.568	+4.0	Joe Torre	2,250,877
1997	2nd◆	96	66	.593	2.0	Joe Torre	2,580,325
1998	1st▲†	114	48	.704	+22.0	Joe Torre	2,949,734
1999	1st▲†	98	64	.605	+4.0	Joe Torre	3,292,736
2000	1st▲†	87	74	.540	+2.5	Joe Torre	3,227,657

*Games behind winner. †Won championship series. ‡Won pennant playoff. §Lost championship series. ∞First half 34-22; second 25-26. ▲Won division series. ◆Lost division series.

MANAGERIAL RECORDS

Yogi Berra 192-148, Frank Chance 117-168, Hal Chase 86-80, Bucky Dent 36-53, Bill Dickey 57-48, Bill Donovan 220-239, Kid Elberfeld 27-71, Art Fletcher 6-5, Dallas Green 56-65, Clark Griffith 419-370, Bucky Harris 191-117, Ralph Houk 944-806, Dick Howser 103-59, Miller Huggins 1,067-719, Johnny Keane 81-101, Clyde King 29-33, Bob Lemon 99-73, Billy Martin 501-385, Joe McCarthy 1,460-867, John McGraw 94-96, Stump Merrill 120-155, Gene Michael 92-76, Johnny Neun 8-6, Roger Peckinpaugh 10-10, Lou Piniella 224-193, Wilbert Robinson 24-57, Bob Shawkey 86-68, Buck Showalter 311-268, George Stallings 152-136, Casey Stengel 1,149-696, Joe Torre 487-322, Bill Virdon 142-124, Harry Wolverton 50-102.

OAKLAND A'S
YEARLY FINISHES

(Known as Philadelphia A's through 1954 and Kansas City A's through 1967)

Year	Position	W	L	Pct.	*GB	Manager	Attendance
1901	4th	74	62	.544	9.0	Connie Mack	206,329
1902	1st	83	53	.610	+5.0	Connie Mack	442,473
1903	2nd	75	60	.556	14.5	Connie Mack	420,078
1904	5th	81	70	.536	12.5	Connie Mack	512,294
1905	1st	92	56	.622	+2.0	Connie Mack	554,576
1906	4th	78	67	.538	12.0	Connie Mack	489,129
1907	2nd	88	57	.607	1.5	Connie Mack	625,581
1908	6th	68	85	.444	22.0	Connie Mack	455,062
1909	2nd	95	58	.621	3.5	Connie Mack	674,915
1910	1st	102	48	.680	+14.5	Connie Mack	588,905
1911	1st	101	50	.669	+13.5	Connie Mack	605,749
1912	3rd	90	62	.592	15.0	Connie Mack	517,653
1913	1st	96	57	.627	+6.5	Connie Mack	571,896
1914	1st	99	53	.651	+8.5	Connie Mack	346,641
1915	8th	43	109	.283	58.5	Connie Mack	146,223
1916	8th	36	117	.235	54.5	Connie Mack	184,471
1917	8th	55	98	.359	44.5	Connie Mack	221,432
1918	8th	52	76	.406	24.0	Connie Mack	177,926
1919	8th	36	104	.257	52.0	Connie Mack	225,209
1920	8th	48	106	.312	50.0	Connie Mack	287,888
1921	8th	53	100	.346	45.0	Connie Mack	344,430
1922	7th	65	89	.422	29.0	Connie Mack	425,356
1923	6th	69	83	.454	29.0	Connie Mack	534,122
1924	5th	71	81	.467	20.0	Connie Mack	531,992
1925	2nd	88	64	.579	8.5	Connie Mack	869,703
1926	3rd	83	67	.553	6.0	Connie Mack	714,308
1927	2nd	91	63	.591	19.0	Connie Mack	605,529
1928	2nd	98	55	.641	2.5	Connie Mack	689,756
1929	1st	104	46	.693	+18.0	Connie Mack	839,176
1930	1st	102	52	.662	+8.0	Connie Mack	721,663
1931	1st	107	45	.704	+13.5	Connie Mack	627,464
1932	2nd	94	60	.610	13.0	Connie Mack	405,500
1933	3rd	79	72	.523	19.5	Connie Mack	297,138
1934	5th	68	82	.453	31.0	Connie Mack	305,847
1935	8th	58	91	.389	34.0	Connie Mack	233,173
1936	8th	53	100	.346	49.0	Connie Mack	285,173
1937	7th	54	97	.358	46.5	Connie Mack	430,733
1938	8th	53	99	.349	46.0	Connie Mack	385,357
1939	7th	55	97	.362	51.5	Connie Mack	395,022
1940	8th	54	100	.351	36.0	Connie Mack	432,145
1941	8th	64	90	.416	37.0	Connie Mack	528,894
1942	8th	55	99	.357	48.0	Connie Mack	423,487
1943	8th	49	105	.318	49.0	Connie Mack	376,735
1944	5th (tied)	72	82	.468	17.0	Connie Mack	505,322
1945	8th	52	98	.347	34.5	Connie Mack	462,631
1946	8th	49	105	.318	55.0	Connie Mack	621,793
1947	5th	78	76	.506	19.0	Connie Mack	911,566
1948	4th	84	70	.545	12.5	Connie Mack	945,076
1949	5th	81	73	.526	16.0	Connie Mack	816,514
1950	8th	52	102	.338	46.0	Connie Mack	309,805
1951	6th	70	84	.455	28.0	Jimmie Dykes	465,469
1952	4th	79	75	.513	16.0	Jimmie Dykes	627,100
1953	7th	59	95	.383	41.5	Jimmie Dykes	362,113
1954	8th	51	103	.331	60.0	Ed Joost	304,666
1955	6th	63	91	.409	33.0	Lou Boudreau	1,393,054
1956	8th	52	102	.338	45.0	Lou Boudreau	1,015,154
1957	7th	59	94	.386	38.5	Lou Boudreau, Harry Craft	901,067
1958	7th	73	81	.474	19.0	Harry Craft	925,090
1959	7th	66	88	.429	28.0	Harry Craft	963,683
1960	8th	58	96	.377	39.0	Bob Elliot	774,944
1961	9th (tied)	61	100	.379	47.5	Joe Gordon, Hank Bauer	683,817
1962	9th	72	90	.444	24.0	Hank Bauer	635,675
1963	8th	73	89	.451	31.5	Ed Lopat	762,364
1964	10th	57	105	.352	42.0	Ed Lopat, Mel McGaha	642,478
1965	10th	59	103	.364	43.0	Mel McGaha, Haywood Sullivan	528,344
1966	7th	74	86	.463	23.0	Alvin Dark	773,929
1967	10th	62	99	.385	29.5	Alvin Dark, Luke Appling	726,639
1968	6th	82	80	.506	21.0	Bob Kennedy	837,466

WEST DIVISION

Year	Position	W	L	Pct.	*GB	Manager	Attendance
1969	2nd	88	74	.543	9.0	Hank Bauer, John McNamara	778,232
1970	2nd	89	73	.549	9.0	John McNamara	778,355
1971	1st†	101	60	.627	+16.0	Dick Williams	914,993
1972	1st‡	93	62	.600	+5.5	Dick Williams	921,323
1973	1st‡	94	68	.580	+6.0	Dick Williams	1,000,763
1974	1st‡	90	72	.556	+5.0	Alvin Dark	845,693
1975	1st†	98	64	.605	+7.0	Alvin Dark	1,075,518
1976	2nd	87	74	.540	2.5	Chuck Tanner	780,593
1977	7th	63	98	.391	38.5	Jack McKeon, Bobby Winkles	495,599
1978	6th	69	93	.426	23.0	Bobby Winkles, Jack McKeon	526,999
1979	7th	54	108	.333	34.0	Jim Marshall	306,763
1980	2nd	83	79	.512	14.0	Billy Martin	842,259
1981	1st/2nd∞†	64	45	.587	§	Billy Martin	1,304,054
1982	5th	68	94	.420	25.0	Billy Martin	1,735,489
1983	4th	74	88	.457	25.0	Steve Boros	1,294,941
1984	4th	77	85	.475	7.0	Steve Boros, Jackie Moore	1,353,281
1985	4th (tied)	77	85	.475	14.0	Jackie Moore	1,334,599
1986	3rd (tied)	76	86	.469	16.0	Jackie Moore, Tony La Russa	1,314,646
1987	3rd	81	81	.500	4.0	Tony La Russa	1,678,921
1988	1st‡	104	58	.642	+13.0	Tony La Russa	2,287,335
1989	1st‡	99	63	.611	+7.0	Tony La Russa	2,667,225
1990	1st‡	103	59	.636	+9.0	Tony La Russa	2,900,217
1991	4th	84	78	.519	11.0	Tony La Russa	2,713,493
1992	1st†	96	66	.593	+6.0	Tony La Russa	2,494,160
1993	7th	68	94	.420	26.0	Tony La Russa	2,035,025
1994	2nd	51	63	.447	1.0	Tony La Russa	1,242,692
1995	4th	67	77	.465	11.5	Tony La Russa	1,174,310
1996	3rd	78	84	.481	12.0	Art Howe	1,148,380
1997	4th	65	97	.401	25.0	Art Howe	1,264,218
1998	4th	74	88	.457	14.0	Art Howe	1,232,339
1999	2nd	87	75	.537	8.0	Art Howe	1,434,610
2000	1st▲	91	70	.565	+0.5	Art Howe	1,728,888

*Games behind winner. †Lost championship series. ‡Won championship series. §First half 37-23; second 27-22. ∞Won division series. ▲Lost division series.

MANAGERIAL RECORDS

Luke Appling 10-30, Hank Bauer 187-226, Steve Boros 94-112, Lou Boudreau 151-260, Harry Craft 162-196, Alvin Dark 314-291, Jimmie Dykes 198-254, Bob Elliott 58-96, Joe Gordon 26-33, Art Howe 395-414, Eddie Joost 51-103, Bob Kennedy 82-80, Tony La Russa 695-614, Eddie Lopat 90-124, Connie Mack 3,582-3,814, Jim Marshall 54-108, Billy Martin 215-218, Mel McGaha 45-91, Jack McKeon 71-105, John McNamara 97-78, Jackie Moore 163-190, Haywood Sullivan 54-82, Chuck Tanner 87-74, Dick Williams 288-190, Bobby Winkles 61-86.

SEATTLE MARINERS
YEARLY FINISHES
WEST DIVISION

Year	Position	W	L	Pct.	*GB	Manager	Attendance
1977	6th	64	98	.395	38.0	Darrell Johnson	1,338,511
1978	7th	56	104	.350	35.0	Darrell Johnson	877,440
1979	6th	67	95	.414	21.0	Darrell Johnson	844,447
1980	7th	59	103	.364	38.0	Darrell Johnson, Maury Wills	836,204
1981	6th/5th	44	65	.404	†	Maury Wills, Rene Lachemann	636,276
1982	4th	76	86	.469	17.0	Rene Lachemann	1,070,404
1983	7th	60	102	.370	39.0	Rene Lachemann, Del Crandall	813,537
1984	5th (tied)	74	88	.457	10.0	Del Crandall, Chuck Cottier	870,372
1985	6th	74	88	.457	17.0	Chuck Cottier	1,128,696
1986	7th	67	95	.414	25.0	Chuck Cottier, Marty Martinez, Dick Williams	1,029,045
1987	4th	78	84	.481	7.0	Dick Williams	1,134,255
1988	7th	68	93	.422	35.5	Dick Williams, Jim Snyder	1,022,398
1989	6th	73	89	.451	26.0	Jim Lefebvre	1,298,443
1990	5th	77	85	.475	26.0	Jim Lefebvre	1,509,727
1991	5th	83	79	.512	12.0	Jim Lefebvre	2,147,905
1992	7th	64	98	.395	32.0	Bill Plummer	1,651,398
1993	4th	82	80	.506	12.0	Lou Piniella	2,051,853
1994	3rd	49	63	.438	2.0	Lou Piniella	1,104,206
1995	1st‡§∞	79	66	.545	+1.0	Lou Piniella	1,643,203
1996	2nd	85	76	.528	4.5	Lou Piniella	2,723,850
1997	1st▲	90	72	.556	+6.0	Lou Piniella	3,192,237
1998	3rd	76	85	.472	11.5	Lou Piniella	2,644,166
1999	3rd	79	83	.488	16.0	Lou Piniella	2,916,346
2000	2nd§∞	91	71	.562	0.5	Lou Piniella	3,148,317

*Games behind winner. †First half 21-36; second 23-29. ‡Won division playoff. §Won division series. ∞Lost championship series. ▲Lost division series.

MANAGERIAL RECORDS

Chuck Cottier 98-120, Del Crandall 93-141, Darrell Johnson 226-362, Rene Lachemann 140-180, Jim Lefebvre 233-253, Lou Piniella 631-596, Bill Plummer 64-98, Jimmy Snyder 45-60, Dick Williams 159-192, Maury Wills 26-56.

TAMPA BAY DEVIL RAYS
YEARLY FINISHES
EAST DIVISION

Year	Position	W	L	Pct.	*GB	Manager	Attendance
1998	5th	63	99	.389	51.0	Larry Rothschild	2,506,023
1999	5th	69	93	.426	29.0	Larry Rothschild	1,562,827
2000	5th	69	92	.429	18.0	Larry Rothschild	1,549,052

*Games behind winner.

MANAGERIAL RECORDS

Larry Rothschild 201-284.

TEXAS RANGERS
YEARLY FINISHES

(Known as second Washington Senators through 1971)

Year	Position	W	L	Pct.	*GB	Manager	Attendance
1961	9th (tied)	61	100	.379	47.5	Mickey Vernon	597,287
1962	10th	60	101	.373	35.5	Mickey Vernon	729,775
1963	10th	56	106	.346	48.5	Mickey Vernon, Gil Hodges	535,604
1964	9th	62	100	.383	37.0	Gil Hodges	600,106
1965	8th	70	92	.432	32.0	Gil Hodges	560,083
1966	8th	71	88	.447	25.5	Gil Hodges	576,260
1967	6th (tied)	76	85	.472	15.5	Gil Hodges	770,863
1968	10th	65	96	.404	37.5	Jim Lemon	546,661

EAST DIVISION

Year	Position	W	L	Pct.	*GB	Manager	Attendance
1969	4th	86	76	.531	23.0	Ted Williams	918,106
1970	6th	70	92	.432	38.0	Ted Williams	824,789
1971	5th	63	96	.396	38.5	Ted Williams	655,156

WEST DIVISION

Year	Position	W	L	Pct.	*GB	Manager	Attendance
1972	6th	54	100	.351	38.5	Ted Williams	662,974
1973	6th	57	105	.352	37.0	Whitey Herzog, Del Wilber, Billy Martin	686,085
1974	2nd	84	76	.525	5.0	Billy Martin	1,193,902
1975	3rd	79	83	.488	19.0	Billy Martin, Frank Lucchesi	1,127,924
1976	4th (tied)	76	86	.469	14.0	Frank Lucchesi	1,164,982
1977	2nd	94	68	.580	8.0	Frank Lucchesi, Eddie Stanky, Connie Ryan, Billy Hunter	1,250,722
1978	2nd (tied)	87	75	.537	5.0	Billy Hunter, Pat Corrales	1,447,963
1979	3rd	83	79	.512	5.0	Pat Corrales	1,519,671
1980	4th	76	85	.472	20.5	Pat Corrales	1,198,175
1981	2nd/3rd	57	48	.543	†	Don Zimmer	850,076
1982	6th	64	98	.395	29.0	Don Zimmer, Darrell Johnson	1,154,432
1983	3rd	77	85	.475	22.0	Doug Rader	1,363,469
1984	7th	69	92	.429	14.5	Doug Rader	1,102,471
1985	7th	62	99	.385	28.5	Doug Rader, Bobby Valentine	1,112,497
1986	2nd	87	75	.537	5.0	Bobby Valentine	1,692,002
1987	6th (tied)	75	87	.463	10.0	Bobby Valentine	1,763,053
1988	6th	70	91	.435	33.5	Bobby Valentine	1,581,901
1989	4th	83	79	.512	16.0	Bobby Valentine	2,043,993
1990	3rd	83	79	.512	20.0	Bobby Valentine	2,057,911
1991	3rd	85	77	.525	10.0	Bobby Valentine	2,297,720
1992	4th	77	85	.475	19.0	Bobby Valentine, Toby Harrah	2,198,231
1993	2nd	86	76	.531	8.0	Kevin Kennedy	2,244,616
1994	1st	52	62	.456	+1.0	Kevin Kennedy	2,503,198
1995	3rd	74	70	.514	4.5	Johnny Oates	1,985,910
1996	1st‡	90	72	.556	+4.5	Johnny Oates	2,889,020
1997	3rd	77	85	.475	13.0	Johnny Oates	2,945,228
1998	1st‡	88	74	.543	+3.0	Johnny Oates	2,927,409
1999	1st‡	95	67	.586	+8.0	Johnny Oates	2,771,469
2000	4th	71	91	.438	20.5	Johnny Oates	2,800,147

*Games behind winner. †First half 33-22; second 24-26. ‡Lost division series.

HISTORY Team by team

Pat Corrales 160-164, Toby Harrah 32-44, Whitey Herzog 47-91, Gil Hodges 321-444, Billy Hunter 146-108, Darrell Johnson 26-40, Kevin Kennedy 138-138, Jim Lemon 65-96, Frank Lucchesi 142-149, Billy Martin 137-141, Johnny Oates 495-459, Doug Rader 155-200, Connie Ryan 2-4, Eddie Stanky 1-0, Bobby Valentine 581-605, Mickey Vernon 135-227, Del Wilber 1-0, Ted Williams 273-364, Don Zimmer 95-106.

TORONTO BLUE JAYS
YEARLY FINISHES
EAST DIVISION

Year	Position	W	L	Pct.	*GB	Manager	Attendance
1977	7th	54	107	.335	45.5	Roy Hartsfield	1,701,052
1978	7th	59	102	.366	40.0	Roy Hartsfield	1,562,585
1979	7th	53	109	.327	50.5	Roy Hartsfield	1,431,651
1980	7th	67	95	.414	36.0	Bobby Mattick	1,400,327
1981	7th/7th	37	69	.349	†	Bobby Mattick	755,083
1982	6th (tied)	78	84	.481	17.0	Bobby Cox	1,275,978
1983	4th	89	73	.549	9.0	Bobby Cox	1,930,415
1984	2nd	89	73	.549	15.0	Bobby Cox	2,110,009
1985	1st‡	99	62	.615	+2.0	Bobby Cox	2,468,925
1986	4th	86	76	.531	9.5	Jimy Williams	2,455,477
1987	2nd	96	66	.593	2.0	Jimy Williams	2,778,429
1988	3rd (tied)	87	75	.537	2.0	Jimy Williams	2,595,175
1989	1st‡	89	73	.549	+2.0	Jimy Williams, Cito Gaston	3,375,883
1990	2nd	86	76	.531	2.0	Cito Gaston	3,885,284
1991	1st‡	91	71	.562	+7.0	Cito Gaston	4,001,527
1992	1st§	96	66	.593	+4.0	Cito Gaston	4,028,318
1993	1st§	95	67	.586	+7.0	Cito Gaston	4,057,947
1994	3rd	55	60	.478	16.0	Cito Gaston	2,907,933
1995	5th	56	88	.389	30.0	Cito Gaston	2,826,483
1996	4th	74	88	.457	18.0	Cito Gaston	2,559,573
1997	5th	76	86	.469	22.0	Cito Gaston, Mel Queen	2,589,297
1998	3rd	88	74	.543	26.0	Tim Johnson	2,454,183
1999	3rd	84	78	.519	14.0	Jim Fregosi	2,163,464
2000	3rd	83	79	.512	4.5	Jim Fregosi	1,819,886

*Games behind winner. †First half 16-42; second 21-27. ‡Lost championship series.§Won championship series.

Bobby Cox 355-292, Jim Fregosi 167-157, Cito Gaston 702-650, Roy Hartsfield 166-318, Tim Johnson 88-74, Bobby Mattick 104-164, Mel Queen 4-1, Jimy Williams 281-241.

NATIONAL LEAGUE
ARIZONA DIAMONDBACKS
YEARLY FINISHES
WEST DIVISION

Year	Position	W	L	Pct.	*GB	Manager	Attendance
1998	5th	65	97	.401	33.0	Buck Showalter	3,600,412
1999	1st†	100	62	.617	+14.0	Buck Showalter	3,019,654
2000	3rd	85	77	.525	12.0	Buck Showalter	2,942,516

*Games behind winner.

Buck Showalter 250-236.

ATLANTA BRAVES
YEARLY FINISHES

(Known as Boston Braves through 1952 and Milwaukee Braves through 1965)

Year	Position	W	L	Pct.	*GB	Manager	Attendance
1901	5th	69	69	.500	20.5	Frank Selee	146,502
1902	3rd	73	64	.533	29.0	Al Buckenberger	116,960
1903	6th	58	80	.420	32.0	Al Buckenberger	143,155
1904	7th	55	98	.359	51.0	Al Buckenberger	140,694
1905	7th	51	103	.331	54.5	Fred Tenney	150,003

HISTORY Team by team

Year	Position	W	L	Pct.	*GB	Manager	Attendance
1906	8th	49	102	.325	66.5	Fred Tenney	143,280
1907	7th	58	90	.392	47.0	Fred Tenney	203,221
1908	6th	63	91	.409	36.0	Joe Kelley	253,750
1909	8th	45	108	.294	65.5	Frank Bowerman, Harry Smith	195,188
1910	8th	53	100	.346	50.5	Fred Lake	149,027
1911	8th	44	107	.291	54.0	Fred Tenney	116,000
1912	8th	52	101	.340	52.0	Johnny Kling	121,000
1913	5th	69	82	.457	31.5	George Stallings	208,000
1914	1st	94	59	.614	+10.5	George Stallings	382,913
1915	2nd	83	69	.546	7.0	George Stallings	376,283
1916	3rd	89	63	.586	4.0	George Stallings	313,495
1917	6th	72	81	.471	25.5	George Stallings	174,253
1918	7th	53	71	.427	28.5	George Stallings	84,938
1919	6th	57	82	.410	38.5	George Stallings	167,401
1920	7th	62	90	.408	30.0	George Stallings	162,483
1921	4th	79	74	.516	15.0	Fred Mitchell	318,627
1922	8th	53	100	.346	39.5	Fred Mitchell	167,965
1923	7th	54	100	.351	41.5	Fred Mitchell	227,802
1924	8th	53	100	.346	40.0	Dave Bancroft	117,478
1925	5th	70	83	.458	25.0	Dave Bancroft	313,528
1926	7th	66	86	.434	22.0	Dave Bancroft	303,598
1927	7th	60	94	.390	34.0	Dave Bancroft	288,685
1928	7th	50	103	.327	44.5	Jack Slattery, Rogers Hornsby	227,001
1929	8th	56	98	.364	43.0	Emil Fuchs	372,351
1930	6th	70	84	.455	22.0	Bill McKechnie	464,835
1931	7th	64	90	.416	37.0	Bill McKechnie	515,005
1932	5th	77	77	.500	13.0	Bill McKechnie	507,606
1933	4th	83	71	.539	9.0	Bill McKechnie	517,803
1934	4th	78	73	.517	16.0	Bill McKechnie	303,205
1935	8th	38	115	.248	61.5	Bill McKechnie	232,754
1936	6th	71	83	.461	21.0	Bill McKechnie	340,585
1937	5th	79	73	.520	16.0	Bill McKechnie	385,339
1938	5th	77	75	.507	12.0	Casey Stengel	341,149
1939	7th	63	88	.417	32.5	Casey Stengel	285,994
1940	7th	65	87	.428	34.5	Casey Stengel	241,616
1941	7th	62	92	.403	38.0	Casey Stengel	263,680
1942	7th	59	89	.399	44.0	Casey Stengel	285,332
1943	6th	68	85	.444	36.5	Casey Stengel	271,289
1944	6th	65	89	.422	40.0	Bob Coleman	208,691
1945	6th	67	85	.441	30.0	Bob Coleman, Del Bissonette	374,178
1946	4th	81	72	.529	15.5	Billy Southworth	969,673
1947	3rd	86	68	.558	8.0	Billy Southworth	1,277,361
1948	1st	91	62	.595	+6.5	Billy Southworth	1,455,439
1949	4th	75	79	.487	22.0	Billy Southworth	1,081,795
1950	4th	83	71	.539	8.0	Billy Southworth	944,391
1951	4th	76	78	.494	20.5	Billy Southworth, Tommy Holmes	487,475
1952	7th	64	89	.418	32.0	Tommy Holmes, Charlie Grimm	281,278
1953	2nd	92	62	.597	13.0	Charlie Grimm	1,826,397
1954	3rd	89	65	.578	8.0	Charlie Grimm	2,131,388
1955	2nd	85	69	.552	13.5	Charlie Grimm	2,005,836
1956	2nd	92	62	.597	1.0	Charlie Grimm, Fred Haney	2,046,331
1957	1st	95	59	.617	+8.0	Fred Haney	2,215,404
1958	1st	92	62	.597	+8.0	Fred Haney	1,971,101
1959	2nd▲	86	70	.551	2.0	Fred Haney	1,749,112
1960	2nd	88	66	.571	7.0	Chuck Dressen	1,497,799
1961	4th	83	71	.539	10.0	Chuck Dressen, Birdie Tebbetts	1,101,441
1962	5th	86	76	.531	15.5	Birdie Tebbetts	766,921
1963	6th	84	78	.519	15.0	Bobby Bragan	773,018
1964	5th	88	74	.543	5.0	Bobby Bragan	910,911
1965	5th	86	76	.531	11.0	Bobby Bragan	555,584
1966	5th	85	77	.525	10.0	Bobby Bragan, Billy Hitchcock	1,539,801
1967	7th	77	85	.475	24.5	Billy Hitchcock, Ken Silvestri	1,389,222
1968	5th	81	81	.500	16.0	Lum Harris	1,126,540

WEST DIVISION

Year	Position	W	L	Pct.	*GB	Manager	Attendance
1969	1st†	93	69	.574	+3.0	Lum Harris	1,458,320
1970	5th	76	86	.469	26.0	Lum Harris	1,078,848
1971	3rd	82	80	.506	8.0	Lum Harris	1,006,320
1972	4th	70	84	.455	25.0	Lum Harris, Eddie Mathews	752,973
1973	5th	76	85	.472	22.5	Eddie Mathews	800,655
1974	3rd	88	74	.543	14.0	Eddie Mathews, Clyde King	981,085
1975	5th	67	94	.416	40.5	Clyde King, Connie Ryan	534,672
1976	6th	70	92	.432	32.0	Dave Bristol	818,179
1977	6th	61	101	.377	37.0	Dave Bristol, Ted Turner	872,464

Year	Position	W	L	Pct.	*GB	Manager	Attendance
1978	6th	69	93	.426	26.0	Bobby Cox	904,494
1979	6th	66	94	.413	23.5	Bobby Cox	769,465
1980	4th	81	80	.503	11.0	Bobby Cox	1,048,411
1981	4th/5th	50	56	.472	‡	Bobby Cox	535,418
1982	1st†	89	73	.549	+1.0	Joe Torre	1,801,985
1983	2nd	88	74	.543	3.0	Joe Torre	2,119,935
1984	2nd (tied)	80	82	.494	12.0	Joe Torre	1,724,892
1985	5th	66	96	.407	29.0	Eddie Haas, Bobby Wine	1,350,137
1986	6th	72	89	.447	23.5	Chuck Tanner	1,387,181
1987	5th	69	92	.429	20.5	Chuck Tanner	1,217,402
1988	6th	54	106	.338	39.5	Chuck Tanner, Russ Nixon	848,089
1989	6th	63	97	.394	28.0	Russ Nixon	984,930
1990	6th	65	97	.401	26.0	Russ Nixon, Bobby Cox	980,129
1991	1st§	94	68	.580	+1.0	Bobby Cox	2,140,217
1992	1st§	98	64	.605	+8.0	Bobby Cox	3,077,400
1993	1st†	104	58	.642	+1.0	Bobby Cox	3,884,725

EAST DIVISION

Year	Position	W	L	Pct.	*GB	Manager	Attendance
1994	2nd	68	46	.596	6.0	Bobby Cox	2,539,240
1995	1st∞§	90	54	.625	+21.0	Bobby Cox	2,561,831
1996	1st∞§	96	66	.593	+8.0	Bobby Cox	2,901,242
1997	1st∞†	101	61	.623	+9.0	Bobby Cox	3,464,488
1998	1st∞†	106	56	.654	+18.0	Bobby Cox	3,361,350
1999	1st∞§	103	59	.636	+6.5	Bobby Cox	3,284,897
2000	1st◆	95	67	.586	+1.0	Bobby Cox	3,234,301

*Games behind winner. †Lost championship series. ‡First half 25-29; second 25-27. §Won championship series. ∞Won division series. ▲Lost pennant playoff. ◆Lost division series.

MANAGERIAL RECORDS

Dave Bancroft 249-363, Del Bissonette 25-34, Frank Bowerman 23-55, Bobby Bragan 310-287, Dave Bristol 131-192, Al Buckenberger 186-242, Bob Coleman 107-140, Bobby Cox 1,261-979, Chuck Dressen 159-124, Emil Fuchs 56-98, Charlie Grimm 341-285, Eddie Haas 50-71, Fred Haney 341-231, Lum Harris 379-373, Billy Hitchcock 110-100, Tommy Holmes 61-69, Rogers Hornsby 39-83, Joe Kelley 63-91, Clyde King 96-101, Johnny Kling 52-101, Fred Lake 53-100, Eddie Mathews 149-161, Bill McKechnie 560-666, Fred Mitchell 186-274, Russ Nixon 130-216, Connie Ryan 9-18, Frank Selee 69-69, Ken Silvestri 0-3, Jack Slattery 11-20, Harry Smith 22-53, Billy Southworth 424-358, George Stallings 579-597, Casey Stengel 394-516, Chuck Tanner 153-208, Birdie Tebbetts 98-89, Fred Tenney 202-402, Joe Torre 257-229, Ted Turner 0-1, Bobby Wine 16-25.

CHICAGO CUBS
YEARLY FINISHES

Year	Position	W	L	Pct.	*GB	Manager	Attendance
1901	6th	53	86	.381	37.0	Tom Loftus	205,071
1902	5th	68	69	.496	34.0	Frank Selee	263,700
1903	3rd	82	56	.594	8.0	Frank Selee	386,205
1904	2nd	93	60	.608	13.0	Frank Selee	439,100
1905	3rd	92	61	.601	13.0	Frank Selee, Frank Chance	509,900
1906	1st	116	36	.763	+20.0	Frank Chance	654,300
1907	1st	107	45	.704	+17.0	Frank Chance	422,550
1908	1st	99	55	.643	+1.0	Frank Chance	665,325
1909	2nd	104	49	.680	6.5	Frank Chance	633,480
1910	1st	104	50	.675	+13.0	Frank Chance	526,152
1911	2nd	92	62	.597	7.5	Frank Chance	576,000
1912	3rd	91	59	.607	11.5	Frank Chance	514,000
1913	3rd	88	65	.575	13.5	Johnny Evers	419,000
1914	4th	78	76	.506	16.5	Hank O'Day	202,516
1915	4th	73	80	.477	17.5	Roger Bresnahan	217,058
1916	5th	67	86	.438	26.5	Joe Tinker	453,685
1917	5th	74	80	.481	24.0	Fred Mitchell	360,218
1918	1st	84	45	.651	+10.5	Fred Mitchell	337,256
1919	3rd	75	65	.536	21.0	Fred Mitchell	424,430
1950	5th (tied)	75	79	.487	18.0	Fred Mitchell	480,783
1921	7th	64	89	.418	30.0	Johnny Evers, Bill Killefer	410,107
1922	5th	80	74	.519	13.0	Bill Killefer	542,283
1923	4th	83	71	.539	12.5	Bill Killefer	703,705
1924	5th	81	72	.529	12.0	Bill Killefer	716,922
1925	8th	68	86	.442	27.5	Bill Killefer, Rabbit Maranville, George Gibson	622,610
1926	4th	82	72	.532	7.0	Joe McCarthy	885,063
1927	4th	85	68	.556	8.5	Joe McCarthy	1,159,168
1928	3rd	91	63	.591	4.0	Joe McCarthy	1,143,740
1929	1st	98	54	.645	+10.5	Joe McCarthy	1,485,166
1930	2nd	90	64	.584	2.0	Joe McCarthy, Rogers Hornsby	1,463,624
1931	3rd	84	70	.545	17.0	Rogers Hornsby	1,086,422

Year	Position	W	L	Pct.	*GB	Manager	Attendance
1932	1st	90	64	.584	+4.0	Rogers Hornsby, Charlie Grimm	974,688
1933	3rd	86	68	.558	6.0	Charlie Grimm	594,112
1934	3rd	86	65	.570	8.0	Charlie Grimm	707,525
1935	1st	100	54	.649	+4.0	Charlie Grimm	692,604
1936	2nd (tied)	87	67	.565	5.0	Charlie Grimm	699,370
1937	2nd	93	61	.604	3.0	Charlie Grimm	895,020
1938	1st	89	63	.586	+2.0	Charlie Grimm, Gabby Hartnett	951,640
1939	4th	84	70	.545	13.0	Gabby Hartnett	726,663
1940	5th	75	79	.487	25.5	Gabby Hartnett	534,878
1941	6th	70	84	.455	30.0	Jimmy Wilson	545,159
1942	6th	68	86	.442	38.0	Jimmy Wilson	590,872
1943	5th	74	79	.484	30.5	Jimmy Wilson	508,247
1944	4th	75	79	.487	30.0	Jimmy Wilson, Charlie Grimm	640,110
1945	1st	98	56	.636	+3.0	Charlie Grimm	1,036,386
1946	3rd	82	71	.536	14.5	Charlie Grimm	1,342,970
1947	6th	69	85	.448	25.0	Charlie Grimm	1,364,039
1948	8th	64	90	.416	27.5	Charlie Grimm	1,237,792
1949	8th	61	93	.396	36.0	Charlie Grimm, Frankie Frisch	1,143,139
1950	7th	64	89	.418	26.5	Frankie Frisch	1,165,944
1951	8th	62	92	.403	34.5	Frankie Frisch, Phil Cavarretta	894,415
1952	5th	77	77	.500	19.5	Phil Cavarretta	1,024,826
1953	7th	65	89	.422	40.0	Phil Cavarretta	763,658
1954	7th	64	90	.416	33.0	Stan Hack	748,183
1955	6th	72	81	.471	26.0	Stan Hack	875,800
1956	8th	60	94	.390	33.0	Stan Hack	720,118
1957	7th (tied)	62	92	.403	33.0	Bob Scheffing	670,629
1958	5th (tied)	72	82	.468	20.0	Bob Scheffing	979,904
1959	5th (tied)	74	80	.481	13.0	Bob Scheffing	858,255
1960	7th	60	94	.390	35.0	Charlie Grimm, Lou Boudreau	809,770
1961	7th	64	90	.416	29.0	Vedie Himsl, Harry Craft, Elvin Tappe, Lou Klein	673,057
1962	9th	59	103	.364	42.5	Charlie Metro, Elvin Tappe, Lou Klein	609,802
1963	7th	82	80	.506	17.0	Bob Kennedy	979,551
1964	8th	76	86	.469	17.0	Bob Kennedy	751,647
1965	8th	72	90	.444	25.0	Bob Kennedy, Lou Klein	641,361
1966	10th	59	103	.364	36.0	Leo Durocher	635,891
1967	3rd	87	74	.540	14.0	Leo Durocher	977,226
1968	3rd	84	78	.519	13.0	Leo Durocher	1,043,409

EAST DIVISION

Year	Position	W	L	Pct.	*GB	Manager	Attendance
1969	2nd	92	70	.568	8.0	Leo Durocher	1,674,993
1970	2nd	84	78	.519	5.0	Leo Durocher	1,642,705
1971	3rd (tied)	83	79	.512	14.0	Leo Durocher	1,653,007
1972	2nd	85	70	.548	11.0	Leo Durocher, Whitey Lockman	1,299,163
1973	5th	77	84	.478	5.0	Whitey Lockman	1,351,705
1974	6th	66	96	.407	22.0	Whitey Lockman, Jim Marshall	1,015,378
1975	5th (tied)	75	87	.463	17.5	Jim Marshall	1,034,819
1976	4th	75	87	.463	26.0	Jim Marshall	1,026,217
1977	4th	81	81	.500	20.0	Herman Franks	1,439,834
1978	3rd	79	83	.488	11.0	Herman Franks	1,525,311
1979	5th	80	82	.494	18.0	Herman Franks, Joe Amalfitano	1,648,587
1980	6th	64	98	.395	27.0	Preston Gomez, Joe Amalfitano	1,206,776
1981	6th/5th	38	65	.369	†	Joe Amalfitano	565,637
1982	5th	73	89	.451	19.0	Lee Elia	1,249,278
1983	5th	71	91	.438	19.0	Lee Elia, Charlie Fox	1,479,717
1984	1st‡	96	65	.596	+6.5	Jim Frey	2,104,219
1985	4th	77	84	.478	23.5	Jim Frey	2,161,534
1986	5th	70	90	.438	37.0	Jim Frey, John Vukovich, Gene Michael	1,859,102
1987	6th	76	85	.472	18.5	Gene Michael, Frank Lucchesi	2,035,130
1988	4th	77	85	.475	24.0	Don Zimmer	2,089,034
1989	1st‡	93	69	.574	+6.0	Don Zimmer	2,491,942
1990	4th	77	85	.475	18.0	Don Zimmer	2,243,791
1991	4th	77	83	.481	20.0	Don Zimmer, Joe Altobelli, Jim Essian	2,314,250
1992	4th	78	84	.481	18.0	Jim Lefebvre	2,126,720
1993	4th	84	78	.519	13.0	Jim Lefebvre	2,653,763

CENTRAL DIVISION

Year	Position	W	L	Pct.	*GB	Manager	Attendance
1994	5th	49	64	.434	16.5	Tom Trebelhorn	1,845,208
1995	3rd	73	71	.507	12.0	Jim Riggleman	1,918,265
1996	4th	76	86	.469	12.0	Jim Riggleman	2,219,110
1997	5th	68	94	.420	16.0	Jim Riggleman	2,190,308
1998	2nd§∞	90	73	.552	12.5	Jim Riggleman	2,623,000
1999	6th	67	95	.414	30.0	Jim Riggleman	2,813,854
2000	6th	65	97	.401	30.0	Don Baylor	2,789,511

*Games behind winner. †First half 15-37; second 23-28. ‡Lost championship series. §Won wild-card playoff. ∞Lost division series.

MANAGERIAL RECORDS

Joe Amalfitano 66-116, Don Baylor 65-97, Lou Boudreau 54-83, Roger Bresnahan 73-80, Phil Cavarretta 169-213, Frank Chance 753-379, Harry Craft 7-9, Leo Durocher 535-526, Lee Elia 127-158, Jim Essian 59-63, Johnny Evers 130-121, Charlie Fox 17-22, Herman Franks 238-241, Jim Frey 196-182, Frank Frisch 141-196, George Gibson 12-14, Preston Gomez 38-52, Charlie Grimm 946-784, Stan Hack 196-265, Gabby Hartnett 203-176, Vedie Himsl 10-21, Rogers Hornsby 141-114, Roy Johnson 0-1, Bob Kennedy 182-198, Bill Killefer 299-292, Lou Klein 65-83, Jim Lefebvre 162-162, Whitey Lockman 157-162, Tom Loftus 53-86, Frank Lucchesi 8-17, Rabbit Maranville 23-30, Jim Marshall 175-218, Joe McCarthy 442-321, Charlie Metro 43-69, Gene Michael 114-124, Fred Mitchell 308-269, Hank O'Day 78-76, Jim Riggleman 374-419, Bob Scheffing 208-254, Frank Selee 295-223, Elvin Tappe 46-69, Joe Tinker 67-86, Tom Trebelhorn 49-64, John Vukovich 1-1, Jimmy Wilson 213-258, Don Zimmer 265-259.

CINCINNATI REDS
YEARLY FINISHES

Year	Position	W	L	Pct.	*GB	Manager	Attendance
1901	8th	52	87	.374	38.0	Bid McPhee	205,728
1902	4th	70	70	.500	33.5	Bid McPhee, Frank Bancroft, Joe Kelley	217,300
1903	4th	74	65	.532	16.5	Joe Kelley	351,680
1904	3rd	88	65	.575	18.0	Joe Kelley	391,915
1905	5th	79	74	.516	26.0	Joe Kelley	313,927
1906	6th	64	87	.424	51.5	Ned Hanlon	330,056
1907	6th	66	87	.431	41.5	Ned Hanlon	317,500
1908	5th	73	81	.474	26.0	John Ganzel	399,200
1909	4th	77	76	.503	33.5	Clark Griffith	424,643
1910	5th	75	79	.487	29.0	Clark Griffith	380,622
1911	6th	70	83	.458	29.0	Clark Griffith	300,000
1912	4th	75	78	.490	29.0	Hank O'Day	344,000
1913	7th	64	89	.418	37.5	Joe Tinker	258,000
1914	8th	60	94	.390	34.5	Buck Herzog	100,791
1915	7th	71	83	.461	20.0	Buck Herzog	218,878
1916	7th (tied)	60	93	.392	33.5	Buck Herzog, Christy Mathewson	255,846
1917	4th	78	76	.506	20.0	Christy Mathewson	269,056
1918	3rd	68	60	.531	15.5	Christy Mathewson, Heinie Groh	163,009
1919	1st	96	44	.686	+9.0	Pat Moran	532,501
1920	3rd	82	71	.536	10.5	Pat Moran	568,107
1921	6th	70	83	.458	24.0	Pat Moran	311,227
1922	2nd	86	68	.558	7.0	Pat Moran	493,754
1923	2nd	91	63	.591	4.5	Pat Moran	575,063
1924	4th	83	70	.542	10.0	Jack Hendricks	437,707
1925	3rd	80	73	.523	15.0	Jack Hendricks	464,920
1926	2nd	87	67	.565	2.0	Jack Hendricks	672,987
1927	5th	75	78	.490	18.5	Jack Hendricks	442,164
1928	5th	78	74	.513	16.0	Jack Hendricks	490,490
1929	7th	66	88	.429	33.0	Jack Hendricks	295,040
1930	7th	59	95	.383	33.0	Dan Howley	386,727
1931	8th	58	96	.377	43.0	Dan Howley	263,316
1932	8th	60	94	.390	30.0	Dan Howley	356,950
1933	8th	58	94	.382	33.0	Donie Bush	218,281
1934	8th	52	99	.344	42.0	Bob O'Farrell, Chuck Dressen	206,773
1935	6th	68	85	.444	31.5	Chuck Dressen	448,247
1936	5th	74	80	.481	18.0	Chuck Dressen	466,245
1937	8th	56	98	.364	40.0	Chuck Dressen, Bobby Wallace	411,221
1938	4th	82	68	.547	6.0	Bill McKechnie	706,756
1939	1st	97	57	.630	+4.5	Bill McKechnie	981,443
1940	1st	100	53	.654	+12.0	Bill McKechnie	850,180
1941	3rd	88	66	.571	12.0	Bill McKechnie	643,513
1942	4th	76	76	.500	29.0	Bill McKechnie	427,031
1943	2nd	87	67	.565	18.0	Bill McKechnie	379,122
1944	3rd	89	65	.578	16.0	Bill McKechnie	409,567
1945	7th	61	93	.396	37.0	Bill McKechnie	290,070
1946	6th	67	87	.435	30.0	Bill McKechnie	715,751
1947	5th	73	81	.474	21.0	Johnny Neun	899,975
1948	7th	64	89	.418	27.0	Johnny Neun, Bucky Walters	823,386
1949	7th	62	92	.403	35.0	Bucky Walters	707,782
1950	6th	66	87	.431	24.5	Luke Sewell	538,794
1951	6th	68	86	.442	28.5	Luke Sewell	588,268
1952	6th	69	85	.448	27.5	Luke Sewell, Rogers Hornsby	604,197
1953	6th	68	86	.442	37.0	Rogers Hornsby, Buster Mills	548,086
1954	5th	74	80	.481	23.0	Birdie Tebbetts	704,167
1955	5th	75	79	.487	23.5	Birdie Tebbetts	693,662
1956	3rd	91	63	.591	2.0	Birdie Tebbetts	1,125,928
1957	4th	80	74	.519	15.0	Birdie Tebbetts	1,070,850
1958	4th	76	78	.494	16.0	Birdie Tebbetts, Jimmie Dykes	788,582
1959	5th (tied)	74	80	.481	13.0	Mayo Smith, Fred Hutchinson	801,289
1960	6th	67	87	.435	28.0	Fred Hutchinson	663,486

Year	Position	W	L	Pct.	*GB	Manager	Attendance
1961	1st	93	61	.604	+4.0	Fred Hutchinson	1,117,603
1962	3rd	98	64	.605	3.5	Fred Hutchinson	982,085
1963	5th	86	76	.531	13.0	Fred Hutchinson	858,805
1964	2nd (tied)	92	70	.549	1.0	Fred Hutchinson, Dick Sisler	862,466
1965	4th	89	73	.549	8.0	Dick Sisler	1,047,824
1966	7th	76	84	.475	18.0	Don Heffner, Dave Bristol	742,958
1967	4th	87	75	.537	14.5	Dave Bristol	958,300
1968	4th	83	79	.512	14.0	Dave Bristol	733,354

WEST DIVISION

Year	Position	W	L	Pct.	*GB	Manager	Attendance
1969	3rd	89	73	.549	4.0	Dave Bristol	987,991
1970	1st†	102	60	.630	+14.5	Sparky Anderson	1,803,568
1971	4th (tied)	79	83	.488	11.0	Sparky Anderson	1,501,122
1972	1st†	95	59	.617	+10.5	Sparky Anderson	1,611,459
1973	1st‡	99	63	.611	+3.5	Sparky Anderson	2,017,601
1974	2nd	98	64	.605	4.0	Sparky Anderson	2,164,307
1975	1st†	108	54	.667	+20.0	Sparky Anderson	2,315,603
1976	1st†	102	60	.630	+10.0	Sparky Anderson	2,629,708
1977	2nd	88	74	.543	10.0	Sparky Anderson	2,519,670
1978	2nd	92	69	.571	2.5	Sparky Anderson	2,532,497
1979	1st‡	90	71	.559	+1.5	John McNamara	2,356,933
1980	3rd	89	73	.549	3.5	John McNamara	2,022,450
1981	2nd/2nd	66	42	.611	§	John McNamara	1,093,730
1982	6th	61	101	.377	28.0	John McNamara, Russ Nixon	1,326,528
1983	6th	74	88	.457	17.0	Russ Nixon	1,190,419
1984	5th	70	92	.432	22.0	Vern Rapp, Pete Rose	1,275,887
1985	2nd	89	72	.553	5.5	Pete Rose	1,834,619
1986	2nd	86	76	.531	10.0	Pete Rose	1,692,432
1987	2nd	84	78	.519	6.0	Pete Rose	2,185,205
1988	2nd	87	74	.540	7.0	Pete Rose	2,072,528
1989	5th	75	87	.463	17.0	Pete Rose, Tommy Helms	1,979,320
1990	1st†	91	71	.562	+5.0	Lou Piniella	2,400,892
1991	5th	74	88	.457	20.0	Lou Piniella	2,372,377
1992	2nd	90	72	.556	8.0	Lou Piniella	2,315,946
1993	5th	73	89	.451	31.0	Tony Perez, Dave Johnson	2,453,232

CENTRAL DIVISION

Year	Position	W	L	Pct.	*GB	Manager	Attendance
1994	1st	66	48	.579	+0.5	Dave Johnson	1,897,681
1995	1st∞‡	85	59	.590	+9.0	Dave Johnson	1,837,649
1996	3rd	81	81	.500	7.0	Ray Knight	1,861,428
1997	3rd	76	86	.469	8.0	Ray Knight, Jack McKeon	1,785,788
1998	4th	77	85	.475	25.0	Jack McKeon	1,793,679
1999	2nd▲	96	67	.589	1.5	Jack McKeon	2,061,222
2000	2nd	85	77	.525	10.0	Jack McKeon	2,577,351

*Games behind winner. †Won championship series. ‡Lost championship series. §First half 35-21; second 31-21. ∞Won division series. ▲Lost wild-card playoff.

MANAGERIAL RECORDS

Sparky Anderson 863-586, Frank Bancroft 9-7, Dave Bristol 298-265, Donie Bush 58-94, Chuck Dressen 214-282, Jimmie Dykes 24-17, John Ganzel 73-81, Clark Griffith 222-238, Heinie Groh 7-3, Ned Hanlon 130-174, Don Heffner 37-46, Tommy Helms 14-21, Jack Hendricks 469-450, Buck Herzog 165-226, Rogers Hornsby 91-106, Dan Howley 177-285, Fred Hutchinson 443-372, Dave Johnson 204-172, Joe Kelley 275-230, Ray Knight 124-137, Christy Mathewson 164-176, Bill McKechnie 747-632, Jack McKeon 291-259, John McNamara 279-244, Bid McPhee 79-124, Buster Mills 4-4, Pat Moran 425-329, Johnny Neun 117-137, Russ Nixon 101-131, Hank O'Day 75-78, Bob O'Farrell 30-60, Tony Perez 20-24, Lou Piniella 255-231, Vern Rapp 51-70, Pete Rose 426-388, Luke Sewell 176-234, Dick Sisler 121-94, Mayo Smith 35-45, Birdie Tebbetts 372-357, Joe Tinker 64-89, Bobby Wallace 5-20, Bucky Walters 81-123.

COLORADO ROCKIES
YEARLY FINISHES
WEST DIVISION

Year	Position	W	L	Pct.	*GB	Manager	Attendance
1993	6th	67	95	.414	37.0	Don Baylor	4,483,350
1994	3rd	53	64	.453	6.5	Don Baylor	3,281,511
1995	2nd†	77	67	.535	1.0	Don Baylor	3,390,037
1996	3rd	83	79	.512	8.0	Don Baylor	3,891,014
1997	3rd	83	79	.512	7.0	Don Baylor	3,888,453
1998	4th	77	85	.475	21.0	Don Baylor	3,789,347
1999	5th	72	90	.444	28.0	Jim Leyland	3,481,065
2000	4th	82	80	.506	15.0	Buddy Bell	3,285,710

*Games behind winner. †Lost division series.

MANAGERIAL RECORDS

Don Baylor 440-469, Buddy Bell 82-80, Jim Leyland 72-90.

FLORIDA MARLINS
YEARLY FINISHES
EAST DIVISION

Year	Position	W	L	Pct.	*GB	Manager	Attendance
1993	6th	64	98	.395	33.0	Rene Lachemann	3,064,847
1994	5th	51	64	.443	23.5	Rene Lachemann	1,937,467
1995	4th	67	76	.469	22.5	Rene Lachemann	1,700,466
1996	3rd	80	82	.494	16.0	Rene Lachemann, John Boles	1,746,767
1997	2nd†‡	92	70	.568	9.0	Jim Leyland	2,364,387
1998	5th	54	108	.333	52.0	Jim Leyland	1,750,395
1999	5th	64	98	.395	39.0	John Boles	1,369,421
2000	3rd	79	82	.491	15.5	John Boles	1,218,326

*Games behind winner. †Won division series. ‡Won championship series.

MANAGERIAL RECORDS

John Boles 183-215, Rene Lachemann 222-285, Jim Leyland 146-178.

HOUSTON ASTROS
YEARLY FINISHES

(Known as Houston Colt .45s through 1964)

Year	Position	W	L	Pct.	*GB	Manager	Attendance
1962	8th	64	96	.400	36.5	Harry Craft	924,456
1963	9th	66	96	.407	33.0	Harry Craft	719,502
1964	9th	66	96	.407	27.0	Harry Craft, Luman Harris	725,773
1965	9th	65	97	.401	32.0	Luman Harris	2,151,470
1966	8th	72	90	.444	23.0	Grady Hatton	1,872,108
1967	9th	69	93	.426	32.5	Grady Hatton	1,348,303
1968	10th	72	90	.444	25.0	Grady Hatton, Harry Walker	1,312,887

WEST DIVISION

Year	Position	W	L	Pct.	*GB	Manager	Attendance
1969	5th	81	81	.500	12.0	Harry Walker	1,442,995
1970	4th	79	83	.488	23.0	Harry Walker	1,253,444
1971	4th (tied)	79	83	.488	11.0	Harry Walker	1,261,589
1972	2nd	84	69	.549	10.5	Harry Walker, Salty Parker, Leo Durocher	1,469,247
1973	4th	82	80	.506	17.0	Leo Durocher, Preston Gomez	1,394,004
1974	4th	81	81	.500	21.0	Preston Gomez	1,090,728
1975	6th	64	97	.398	43.5	Preston Gomez, Bill Virdon	858,002
1976	3rd	80	82	.494	22.0	Bill Virdon	886,146
1977	3rd	81	81	.500	17.0	Bill Virdon	1,109,560
1978	5th	74	88	.457	21.0	Bill Virdon	1,126,145
1979	2nd	89	73	.549	1.5	Bill Virdon	1,900,312
1980	1st†‡	93	70	.571	+1.0	Bill Virdon	2,278,217
1981	3rd/1st∞	61	49	.555	§	Bill Virdon	1,321,282
1982	5th	77	85	.475	12.0	Bill Virdon, Bob Lillis	1,558,555
1983	3rd	85	77	.525	6.0	Bob Lillis	1,351,962
1984	2nd (tied)	80	82	.494	12.0	Bob Lillis	1,229,862
1985	3rd (tied)	83	79	.512	12.0	Bob Lillis	1,184,314
1986	1st‡	96	66	.593	+10.0	Hal Lanier	1,734,276
1987	3rd	76	86	.469	14.0	Hal Lanier	1,909,902
1988	5th	82	80	.506	12.5	Hal Lanier	1,933,505
1989	3rd	86	76	.531	6.0	Art Howe	1,834,908
1990	4th (tied)	75	87	.463	16.0	Art Howe	1,310,927
1991	6th	65	97	.401	29.0	Art Howe	1,196,152
1992	4th	81	81	.500	17.0	Art Howe	1,211,412
1993	3rd	85	77	.525	19.0	Art Howe	2,084,546

CENTRAL DIVISION

Year	Position	W	L	Pct.	*GB	Manager	Attendance
1994	2nd	66	49	.574	0.5	Terry Collins	1,561,136
1995	2nd	76	68	.528	9.0	Terry Collins	1,363,801
1996	2nd	82	80	.506	6.0	Terry Collins	1,975,888
1997	1st∞	84	78	.519	+5.0	Larry Dierker	2,046,781
1998	1st∞	102	60	.630	+12.5	Larry Dierker	2,450,451
1999	1st∞	97	65	.599	+1.5	Larry Dierker	2,706,017
2000	4th	72	90	.444	23.0	Larry Dierker	3,056,139

*Games behind winner. †Won division playoff. ‡Lost championship series. §First half 28-29; second 33-20. ∞Lost division series.

MANAGERIAL RECORDS

Terry Collins 224-197, Harry Craft 191-280, Larry Dierker 355-293, Leo Durocher 98-95, Preston Gomez 128-161, Lum Harris 70-105, Grady Hatton 164-221, Art Howe 392-418, Hal Lanier 254-232, Bob Lillis 276-261, Bill Virdon 544-522, Harry Walker 355-353.

LOS ANGELES DODGERS
YEARLY FINISHES

(Known as Brooklyn Dodgers through 1957)

Year	Position	W	L	Pct.	*GB	Manager	Attendance
1901	3rd	79	57	.581	9.5	Ned Hanlon	189,200
1902	2nd	75	63	.543	27.5	Ned Hanlon	199,868
1903	5th	70	66	.515	19.0	Ned Hanlon	224,670
1904	6th	56	97	.366	50.0	Ned Hanlon	214,600
1905	8th	48	104	.316	56.5	Ned Hanlon	227,924
1906	5th	66	86	.434	50.0	Patsy Donovan	227,400
1907	5th	65	83	.439	40.0	Patsy Donovan	312,500
1908	7th	53	101	.344	46.0	Patsy Donovan	275,600
1909	6th	55	98	.359	55.5	Harry Lumley	321,300
1910	6th	64	90	.416	40.0	Bill Dahlen	279,321
1911	7th	64	86	.427	33.5	Bill Dahlen	269,000
1912	7th	58	95	.379	46.0	Bill Dahlen	243,000
1913	6th	65	84	.436	34.5	Bill Dahlen	347,000
1914	5th	75	79	.487	19.5	Wilbert Robinson	122,671
1915	3rd	80	72	.526	10.0	Wilbert Robinson	297,766
1916	1st	94	60	.610	+2.5	Wilbert Robinson	447,747
1917	7th	70	81	.464	26.5	Wilbert Robinson	221,619
1918	5th	57	69	.452	25.5	Wilbert Robinson	83,831
1919	5th	69	71	.493	27.0	Wilbert Robinson	360,721
1920	1st	93	61	.604	+7.0	Wilbert Robinson	808,722
1921	5th	77	75	.507	16.5	Wilbert Robinson	613,245
1922	6th	76	78	.494	17.0	Wilbert Robinson	498,856
1923	6th	76	78	.494	19.5	Wilbert Robinson	564,666
1924	2nd	92	62	.597	1.5	Wilbert Robinson	818,883
1925	6th (tied)	68	85	.444	27.0	Wilbert Robinson	659,435
1926	6th	71	82	.464	17.5	Wilbert Robinson	650,819
1927	6th	65	88	.425	28.5	Wilbert Robinson	637,230
1928	6th	77	76	.503	17.5	Wilbert Robinson	664,863
1929	6th	70	83	.458	28.5	Wilbert Robinson	731,886
1930	4th	86	68	.558	6.0	Wilbert Robinson	1,097,339
1931	4th	79	73	.520	21.0	Wilbert Robinson	753,133
1932	3rd	81	73	.526	9.0	Max Carey	681,827
1933	6th	65	88	.425	26.5	Max Carey	526,815
1934	6th	71	81	.467	23.5	Casey Stengel	434,188
1935	5th	70	83	.458	29.5	Casey Stengel	470,517
1936	7th	67	87	.435	25.0	Casey Stengel	489,618
1937	6th	62	91	.405	33.5	Burleigh Grimes	482,481
1938	7th	69	80	.463	18.5	Burleigh Grimes	663,087
1939	3rd	84	69	.549	12.5	Leo Durocher	955,668
1940	2nd	88	65	.575	12.0	Leo Durocher	975,978
1941	1st	100	54	.649	+2.5	Leo Durocher	1,214,910
1942	2nd	104	50	.675	2.0	Leo Durocher	1,037,765
1943	3rd	81	72	.529	23.5	Leo Durocher	661,739
1944	7th	63	91	.409	42.0	Leo Durocher	605,905
1945	3rd	87	67	.565	11.0	Leo Durocher	1,059,220
1946	2nd‡	96	60	.615	2.0	Leo Durocher	1,796,824
1947	1st	94	60	.610	+5.0	Clyde Sukeforth, Burt Shotton	1,807,526
1948	3rd	84	70	.545	7.5	Leo Durocher, Burt Shotton	1,398,967
1949	1st	97	57	.630	+1.0	Burt Shotton	1,633,747
1950	2nd	89	65	.578	2.0	Burt Shotton	1,185,896
1951	2nd‡	97	60	.618	1.0	Chuck Dressen	1,282,628
1952	1st	96	57	.627	+4.5	Chuck Dressen	1,088,704
1953	1st	105	49	.682	+13.0	Chuck Dressen	1,163,419
1954	2nd	92	62	.597	5.0	Walter Alston	1,020,531
1955	1st	98	55	.641	+13.5	Walter Alston	1,033,589
1956	1st	93	61	.604	+1.0	Walter Alston	1,213,562
1957	3rd	84	70	.545	11.0	Walter Alston	1,028,258
1958	7th	71	83	.461	21.0	Walter Alston	1,845,556
1959	1st†	88	68	.564	+2.0	Walter Alston	2,071,045
1960	4th	82	72	.532	13.0	Walter Alston	2,253,887
1961	2nd	89	65	.578	4.0	Walter Alston	1,804,250
1962	2nd‡	102	63	.618	1.0	Walter Alston	2,755,184
1963	1st	99	63	.611	+6.0	Walter Alston	2,538,602
1964	6th (tied)	80	82	.494	13.0	Walter Alston	2,228,751

Year	Position	W	L	Pct.	*GB	Manager	Attendance
1965	1st.................97	65	.599	+2.0		Walter Alston	2,553,577
1966	1st.................95	67	.586	+1.5		Walter Alston	2,617,029
1967	8th.................73	89	.451	28.5		Walter Alston	1,664,362
1968	7th 76	86	.469	21.0		Walter Alston	1,581,093

WEST DIVISION

Year	Position	W	L	Pct.	*GB	Manager	Attendance
1969	4th 85	77	.525	8.0		Walter Alston	1,784,527
1970	2nd.................87	74	.540	14.5		Walter Alston	1,697,142
1971	2nd.................89	73	.549	1.0		Walter Alston	2,064,594
1972	3rd.................85	70	.548	10.5		Walter Alston	1,860,858
1973	2nd.................95	66	.590	3.5		Walter Alston	2,136,192
1974	1st§.................102	60	.630	+4.0		Walter Alston	2,632,474
1975	2nd.................88	74	.543	20.0		Walter Alston	2,539,349
1976	2nd.................92	70	.568	10.0		Walter Alston, Tommy Lasorda.........................	2,386,301
1977	1st§.................98	64	.605	+10.0		Tommy Lasorda	2,955,087
1978	1st§.................95	67	.586	+2.5		Tommy Lasorda	3,347,845
1979	3rd 79	83	.488	11.5		Tommy Lasorda	2,860,954
1980	2nd∞.................92	71	.564	1.0		Tommy Lasorda	3,249,287
1981	1st/4th◆§ 63	47	.573	▲		Tommy Lasorda	2,381,292
1982	2nd.................88	74	.543	1.0		Tommy Lasorda	3,608,881
1983	1st■.................91	71	.652	+3.0		Tommy Lasorda	3,510,313
1984	4th 79	83	.488	13.0		Tommy Lasorda	3,134,824
1985	1st■.................95	67	.586	+5.5		Tommy Lasorda	3,264,593
1986	5th 73	89	.451	23.0		Tommy Lasorda	3,023,208
1987	4th 73	89	.451	17.0		Tommy Lasorda	2,797,409
1988	1st§.................94	67	.584	+7.0		Tommy Lasorda	2,980,262
1989	4th 77	83	.481	14.0		Tommy Lasorda	2,944,653
1990	2nd.................86	76	.531	5.0		Tommy Lasorda	3,002,396
1991	2nd.................93	69	.574	1.0		Tommy Lasorda	3,348,170
1992	6th 63	99	.389	35.0		Tommy Lasorda	2,473,266
1993	4th 81	81	.500	23.0		Tommy Lasorda	3,170,392
1994	1st 58	56	.509	+3.5		Tommy Lasorda	2,279,355
1995	1st▼.................78	66	.542	+1.0		Tommy Lasorda	2,766,251
1996	2nd▼.................90	72	.556	1.0		Tommy Lasorda, Bill Russell	3,188,454
1997	2nd.................88	74	.543	2.0		Bill Russell...	3,319,504
1998	3rd 83	79	.512	15.0		Bill Russell, Glenn Hoffman............................	3,089,201
1999	3rd 77	85	.475	23.0		Dave Johnson...	3,095,346
2000	2nd.................86	76	.531	11.0		Dave Johnson...	3,010,819

*Games behind winner. †Won pennant playoff. ‡Lost pennant playoff. §Won championship series. ∞Lost division playoff. ▲First half 36-21; second half 27-26. ◆Won division series. ■Lost championship series. ▼Lost division series.

MANAGERIAL RECORDS

Walter Alston 2,040-1,613, Max Carey 146-161, Bill Dahlen 251-355, Patsy Donovan 184-270, Chuck Dressen 298-166, Leo Durocher 738-565, Burleigh Grimes 131-171, Ned Hanlon 328-387, Glenn Hoffman 47-41, Dave Johnson 163-161, Tommy Lasorda 1,599-1,439, Harry Lumley 55-98, Wilbert Robinson 1,375-1,341, Bill Russell 173-149, Burt Shotton 326-215, Casey Stengel 208-251, Clyde Sukeforth 2-0.

MILWAUKEE BREWERS
YEARLY FINISHES

(Known as Seattle Pilots in 1969)

AMERICAN LEAGUE WEST DIVISION

Year	Position	W	L	Pct.	*GB	Manager	Attendance
1969	6th 64	98	.395	33		Joe Schultz	677,944
1970	4th 65	97	.401	33.0		Dave Bristol	933,690
1971	6th 69	92	.429	32.0		Dave Bristol	731,531

AMERICAN LEAGUE EAST DIVISION

Year	Position	W	L	Pct.	*GB	Manager	Attendance
1972	6th 65	91	.417	21.0		Dave Bristol, Del Crandall	600,440
1973	5th 74	88	.457	23.0		Del Crandall	1,092,158
1974	5th 76	86	.469	15.0		Del Crandall	955,741
1975	5th 68	94	.420	28.0		Del Crandall	1,213,357
1976	6th 66	95	.410	32.0		Alex Grammas	1,012,164
1977	6th 67	95	.414	33.0		Alex Grammas	1,114,938
1978	3rd 93	69	.574	6.5		George Bamberger..	1,601,406
1979	2nd..........................95	66	.590	8.0		George Bamberger..	1,918,343
1980	3rd 86	76	.531	17.0		George Bamberger, Buck Rodgers....................	1,857,408
1981	3rd/1st‡ 62	47	.569	†		Buck Rodgers	878,432

Year	Position	W	L	Pct.	*GB	Manager	Attendance
1982	1st§	95	67	.586	+1.0	Buck Rodgers, Harvey Kuenn	1,978,896
1983	5th	87	75	.537	11.0	Harvey Kuenn	2,397,131
1984	7th	67	94	.416	36.5	Rene Lachemann	1,608,509
1985	6th	71	90	.441	28.0	George Bamberger	1,360,265
1986	6th	77	84	.478	18.0	George Bamberger, Tom Trebelhorn	1,265,041
1987	3rd	91	71	.562	7.0	Tom Trebelhorn	1,909,244
1988	3rd (tied)	87	75	.537	2.0	Tom Trebelhorn	1,923,238
1989	4th	81	81	.500	8.0	Tom Trebelhorn	1,970,735
1990	6th	74	88	.457	14.0	Tom Trebelhorn	1,752,900
1991	4th	83	79	.512	8.0	Tom Trebelhorn	1,478,729
1992	2nd	92	70	.568	4.0	Phil Garner	1,857,314
1993	7th	69	93	.426	26.0	Phil Garner	1,688,080

AMERICAN LEAGUE CENTRAL DIVISION

Year	Position	W	L	Pct.	*GB	Manager	Attendance
1994	5th	53	62	.461	15.0	Phil Garner	1,268,399
1995	4th	65	79	.451	35.0	Phil Garner	1,087,560
1996	3rd	80	82	.494	19.5	Phil Garner	1,327,155
1997	3rd	78	83	.484	8.0	Phil Garner	1,444,027

NATIONAL LEAGUE CENTRAL DIVISION

Year	Position	W	L	Pct.	*GB	Manager	Attendance
1998	5th	74	88	.457	28.0	Phil Garner	1,811,548
1999	5th	74	87	.460	22.5	Phil Garner, Jim Lefebvre	1,701,796
2000	3rd	73	89	.451	22.0	Davey Lopes	1,573,621

*Games behind winner. †First half 31-25; second 31-22. ‡Lost division series. §Won championship series.

MANAGERIAL RECORDS

George Bamberger 377-351, Dave Bristol 144-209, Del Crandall 271-338, Phil Garner 563-617, Alex Grammas 133-190, Harvey Kuenn 160-118, Rene Lachemann 67-94, Jim Lefebvre 22-27, Davey Lopes 73-89, Buck Rodgers 124-102, Joe Schultz 64-98, Tom Trebelhorn 422-397.

MONTREAL EXPOS
YEARLY FINISHES
EAST DIVISION

Year	Position	W	L	Pct.	*GB	Manager	Attendance
1969	6th	52	110	.321	48.0	Gene Mauch	1,212,608
1970	6th	73	89	.451	16.0	Gene Mauch	1,424,683
1971	5th	71	90	.441	25.5	Gene Mauch	1,290,963
1972	5th	70	86	.449	26.5	Gene Mauch	1,142,145
1973	4th	79	83	.488	3.5	Gene Mauch	1,246,863
1974	4th	79	82	.491	8.5	Gene Mauch	1,019,134
1975	5th (tied)	75	87	.463	17.5	Gene Mauch	908,292
1976	6th	55	107	.340	46.0	Karl Kuehl, Charlie Fox	646,704
1977	5th	75	87	.463	26.0	Dick Williams	1,433,757
1978	4th	76	86	.469	14.0	Dick Williams	1,427,007
1979	2nd	95	65	.594	2.0	Dick Williams	2,102,173
1980	2nd	90	72	.556	1.0	Dick Williams	2,208,175
1981	3rd/1st‡§	60	48	.556	†	Dick Williams, Jim Fanning	1,534,564
1982	3rd	86	76	.531	6.0	Jim Fanning	2,318,292
1983	3rd§	82	80	.506	8.0	Bill Virdon	2,320,651
1984	5th	78	83	.484	18.0	Bill Virdon, Jim Fanning	1,606,531
1985	3rd	84	77	.522	16.5	Buck Rodgers	1,502,494
1986	4th	78	83	.484	29.5	Buck Rodgers	1,128,981
1987	3rd	91	71	.562	4.0	Buck Rodgers	1,850,324
1988	3rd	81	81	.500	20.0	Buck Rodgers	1,478,659
1989	4th	81	81	.500	12.0	Buck Rodgers	1,783,533
1990	3rd	85	77	.525	10.0	Buck Rodgers	1,373,087
1991	6th	71	90	.441	26.5	Buck Rodgers, Tom Runnells	934,742
1992	2nd	87	75	.537	9.0	Tom Runnells, Felipe Alou	1,669,077
1993	2nd	94	68	.580	3.0	Felipe Alou	1,641,437
1994	1st	74	40	.649	+6.0	Felipe Alou	1,276,250
1995	5th	66	78	.458	24.0	Felipe Alou	1,309,618
1996	2nd	88	74	.543	8.0	Felipe Alou	1,616,709
1997	4th	78	84	.481	23.0	Felipe Alou	1,497,609
1998	4th	65	97	.401	41.0	Felipe Alou	914,717
1999	4th	68	94	.420	35.0	Felipe Alou	773,277
2000	4th	67	95	.414	28.0	Felipe Alou	926,263

*Games behind winner. †First half 30-25; second 30-23. ‡Won division series. §Lost championship series.

MANAGERIAL RECORDS

Felipe Alou 670-685, Jim Fanning 116-103, Charlie Fox 12-22, Karl Kuehl 43-85, Gene Mauch 499-627, Buck Rodgers 520-499, Tom Runnells 68-81, Bill Virdon 146-147, Dick Williams 380-347.

NEW YORK METS
YEARLY FINISHES

Year	Position	W	L	Pct.	*GB	Manager	Attendance
1962	10th	40	120	.250	60.5	Casey Stengel	922,530
1963	10th	51	111	.315	48.0	Casey Stengel	1,080,108
1964	10th	53	109	.327	40.0	Casey Stengel	1,732,597
1965	10th	50	112	.309	47.0	Casey Stengel, Wes Westrum	1,768,389
1966	9th	66	95	.410	28.5	Wes Westrum	1,932,693
1967	10th	61	101	.377	40.5	Wes Westrum, Salty Parker	1,565,492
1968	9th	73	89	.451	24.0	Gil Hodges	1,781,657

EAST DIVISION

Year	Position	W	L	Pct.	*GB	Manager	Attendance
1969	1st†	100	62	.617	+8.0	Gil Hodges	2,175,373
1970	3rd	83	79	.512	6.0	Gil Hodges	2,697,479
1971	3rd (tied)	83	79	.512	14.0	Gil Hodges	2,266,680
1972	3rd	83	73	.532	13.5	Yogi Berra	2,134,185
1973	1st†	82	79	.509	+1.5	Yogi Berra	1,912,390
1974	5th	71	91	.438	17.0	Yogi Berra	1,722,209
1975	3rd (tied)	82	80	.506	10.5	Yogi Berra, Roy McMillan	1,730,566
1976	3rd	86	76	.531	15.0	Joe Frazier	1,468,754
1977	6th	64	98	.395	37.0	Joe Frazier, Joe Torre	1,066,825
1978	6th	66	96	.407	24.0	Joe Torre	1,007,328
1979	6th	63	99	.389	35.0	Joe Torre	788,905
1980	5th	67	95	.414	24.0	Joe Torre	1,192,073
1981	5th/4th	41	62	.398	‡	Joe Torre	704,244
1982	6th	65	97	.401	27.0	George Bamberger	1,323,036
1983	6th	68	94	.420	22.0	George Bamberger, Frank Howard	1,112,774
1984	2nd	90	72	.556	6.5	Dave Johnson	1,842,695
1985	2nd	98	64	.605	3.0	Dave Johnson	2,761,601
1986	1st†	108	54	.667	+21.5	Dave Johnson	2,767,601
1987	2nd	92	70	.568	3.0	Dave Johnson	3,034,129
1988	1st§	100	60	.625	+15.0	Dave Johnson	3,055,445
1989	2nd	87	75	.537	6.0	Dave Johnson	2,918,710
1990	2nd	91	71	.562	4.0	Dave Johnson, Bud Harrelson	2,732,745
1991	5th	77	84	.478	20.5	Bud Harrelson, Mike Cubbage	2,284,484
1992	5th	72	90	.444	24.0	Jeff Torborg	1,779,534
1993	7th	59	103	.364	38.0	Jeff Torborg, Dallas Green	1,873,183
1994	3rd	55	58	.487	18.5	Dallas Green	1,151,471
1995	2nd (tied)	69	75	.479	21.0	Dallas Green	1,273,183
1996	4th	71	91	.438	25.0	Dallas Green, Bobby Valentine	1,588,323
1997	3rd	88	74	.543	13.0	Bobby Valentine	1,766,174
1998	2nd	88	74	.543	18.0	Bobby Valentine	2,287,942
1999	2nd∞§	97	66	.595	6.5	Bobby Valentine	2,725,668
2000	2nd▲†	94	68	.580	1.0	Bobby Valentine	2,800,221

*Games behind winner. †Won championship series. ‡First half 17-34; second 24-28. §Lost championship series. ∞Won wild-card playoff. ▲Won division series.

MANAGERIAL RECORDS

George Bamberger 81-127, Yogi Berra 292-296, Mike Cubbage 3-4, Joe Frazier 101-106, Dallas Green 229-283, Bud Harrelson 145-129, Gil Hodges 339-309, Frank Howard 52-64, Davey Johnson 595-417, Roy McMillan 26-27, Salty Parker 4-7, Casey Stengel 175-404, Jeff Torborg 85-115, Joe Torre 286-420, Bobby Valentine 379-301, Wes Westrum 142-237.

PHILADELPHIA PHILLIES
YEARLY FINISHES

Year	Position	W	L	Pct.	*GB	Manager	Attendance
1901	2nd	83	57	.593	7.5	Bill Shettsline	234,937
1902	7th	56	81	.409	46.0	Bill Shettsline	112,066
1903	7th	49	86	.363	39.5	Chief Zimmer	151,729
1904	8th	52	100	.342	53.5	Hugh Duffy	140,771
1905	4th	83	69	.546	21.5	Hugh Duffy	317,932
1906	4th	71	82	.464	45.5	Hugh Duffy	294,680
1907	3rd	83	64	.565	21.5	Bill Murray	341,216
1908	4th	83	71	.539	16.0	Bill Murray	420,660
1909	5th	74	79	.484	36.5	Bill Murray	303,177

Year	Position	W	L	Pct.	*GB	Manager	Attendance
1910	4th	78	75	.510	25.5	Red Dooin	296,597
1911	4th	79	73	.520	19.5	Red Dooin	416,000
1912	5th	73	79	.480	30.5	Red Dooin	250,000
1913	2nd	88	63	.583	12.5	Red Dooin	470,000
1914	6th	74	80	.481	20.5	Red Dooin	138,474
1915	1st	90	62	.592	+7.0	Pat Moran	449,898
1916	2nd	91	62	.595	2.5	Pat Moran	515,365
1917	2nd	87	65	.572	10.0	Pat Moran	354,428
1918	6th	55	68	.447	26.0	Pat Moran	122,266
1919	8th	47	90	.343	47.5	Jack Coombs, Gavvy Cravath	240,424
1920	8th	62	91	.405	30.5	Gavvy Cravath	330,998
1921	8th	51	103	.331	43.5	Bill Donovan, Kaiser Wilhelm	273,961
1922	7th	57	96	.373	35.5	Kaiser Wilhelm	232,471
1923	8th	50	104	.325	45.5	Art Fletcher	228,168
1924	7th	55	96	.364	37.0	Art Fletcher	299,818
1925	6th (tied)	68	85	.444	27.0	Art Fletcher	304,905
1926	8th	58	93	.384	29.5	Art Fletcher	240,600
1927	8th	51	103	.331	43.0	Stuffy McInnis	305,420
1928	8th	43	109	.283	51.0	Burt Shotton	182,168
1929	5th	71	82	.464	27.5	Burt Shotton	281,200
1930	8th	52	102	.338	40.0	Burt Shotton	299,007
1931	6th	66	88	.429	35.0	Burt Shotton	284,849
1932	4th	78	76	.506	12.0	Burt Shotton	268,914
1933	7th	60	92	.395	31.0	Burt Shotton	156,421
1934	7th	56	93	.376	37.0	Jimmy Wilson	169,885
1935	7th	64	89	.418	35.5	Jimmy Wilson	205,470
1936	8th	54	100	.351	38.0	Jimmy Wilson	249,219
1937	7th	61	92	.399	34.5	Jimmy Wilson	212,790
1938	8th	45	105	.300	43.0	Jimmy Wilson, Hans Lobert	166,111
1939	8th	45	106	.298	50.5	Doc Prothro	277,973
1940	8th	50	103	.327	50.0	Doc Prothro	207,177
1941	8th	43	111	.279	57.0	Doc Prothro	231,401
1942	8th	42	109	.278	62.5	Hans Lobert	230,183
1943	7th	64	90	.416	41.0	Bucky Harris, Fred Fitzsimmons	466,975
1944	8th	61	92	.399	43.5	Fred Fitzsimmons	369,586
1945	8th	46	108	.299	52.0	Fred Fitzsimmons, Ben Chapman	285,057
1946	5th	69	85	.448	28.0	Ben Chapman	1,045,247
1947	7th (tied)	62	92	.403	32.0	Ben Chapman	907,332
1948	6th	66	88	.429	25.5	Ben Chapman, Dusty Cooke, Eddie Sawyer	767,429
1949	3rd	81	73	.526	16.0	Eddie Sawyer	819,698
1950	1st	91	63	.591	+2.0	Eddie Sawyer	1,217,035
1951	5th	73	81	.474	23.5	Eddie Sawyer	937,658
1952	4th	87	67	.565	9.5	Eddie Sawyer, Steve O'Neill	775,417
1953	3rd (tied)	83	71	.539	22.0	Steve O'Neill	853,644
1954	4th	75	79	.487	22.0	Steve O'Neill, Terry Moore	738,991
1955	4th	77	77	.500	21.5	Mayo Smith	922,886
1956	5th	71	83	.461	22.0	Mayo Smith	934,798
1957	5th	77	77	.500	19.0	Mayo Smith	1,146,230
1958	8th	69	85	.448	23.0	Mayo Smith, Eddie Sawyer	931,110
1959	8th	64	90	.416	23.0	Eddie Sawyer	802,815
1960	8th	59	95	.383	36.0	Eddie Sawyer, Andy Cohen, Gene Mauch	862,205
1961	8th	47	107	.305	46.0	Gene Mauch	590,039
1962	7th	81	80	.503	20.0	Gene Mauch	762,034
1963	4th	87	75	.537	12.0	Gene Mauch	907,141
1964	2nd (tied)	92	70	.568	1.0	Gene Mauch	1,425,891
1965	6th	85	76	.528	11.5	Gene Mauch	1,166,376
1966	4th	87	75	.537	8.0	Gene Mauch	1,108,201
1967	5th	82	80	.506	19.5	Gene Mauch	828,888
1968	7th (tied)	76	86	.469	21.0	Gene Mauch, George Myatt, Bob Skinner	664,546

EAST DIVISION

Year	Position	W	L	Pct.	*GB	Manager	Attendance
1969	5th	63	99	.389	37.0	Bob Skinner, George Myatt	519,414
1970	5th	73	88	.453	15.5	Frank Lucchesi	708,247
1971	6th	67	95	.414	30.0	Frank Lucchesi	1,511,223
1972	6th	59	97	.378	37.5	Frank Lucchesi, Paul Owens	1,343,329
1973	6th	71	91	.438	11.5	Danny Ozark	1,475,934
1974	3rd	80	82	.494	8.0	Danny Ozark	1,808,648
1975	2nd	86	76	.531	6.5	Danny Ozark	1,909,233
1976	1st†	101	61	.623	+9.0	Danny Ozark	2,480,150
1977	1st†	101	61	.623	+5.0	Danny Ozark	2,700,070
1978	1st†	90	72	.556	+1.5	Danny Ozark	2,583,389
1979	4th	84	78	.519	14.0	Danny Ozark, Dallas Green	2,775,011
1980	1st‡	91	71	.562	+1.0	Dallas Green	2,651,650

Year	Position	W	L	Pct.	*GB	Manager	Attendance
1981	1st/3rd∞	59	48	.551	§	Dallas Green	1,638,752
1982	2nd	89	73	.549	3.0	Pat Corrales	2,376,394
1983	1st‡	90	72	.556	+6.0	Pat Corrales, Paul Owens	2,128,339
1984	4th	81	81	.500	15.5	Paul Owens	2,062,693
1985	5th	75	87	.463	26.0	John Felske	1,830,350
1986	2nd	86	75	.534	21.5	John Felske	1,933,335
1987	4th (tied)	80	82	.494	15.0	John Felske, Lee Elia	2,100,110
1988	6th	65	96	.404	35.5	Lee Elia, John Vukovich	1,990,041
1989	6th	67	95	.414	26.0	Nick Leyva	1,861,985
1990	4th (tied)	77	85	.475	18.0	Nick Leyva	1,992,484
1991	3rd	78	84	.481	20.0	Nick Leyva, Jim Fregosi	2,050,012
1992	6th	70	92	.432	26.0	Jim Fregosi	1,927,448
1993	1st‡	97	65	.599	+3.0	Jim Fregosi	3,137,674
1994	4th	54	61	.470	20.5	Jim Fregosi	2,290,971
1995	2nd (tied)	69	75	.479	21.0	Jim Fregosi	2,043,598
1996	5th	67	95	.414	29.0	Jim Fregosi	1,801,677
1997	5th	68	94	.420	33.0	Terry Francona	1,490,638
1998	3rd	75	87	.463	31.0	Terry Francona	1,715,702
1999	3rd	77	85	.475	26.0	Terry Francona	1,825,337
2000	5th	65	97	.401	30.0	Terry Francona	1,612,769

*Games behind winner. †Lost championship series. ‡Won championship series. §First half 34-21; second 25-27. ∞Lost division series.

MANAGERIAL RECORDS

Ben Chapman 197-277, Andy Cohen 1-0, Dusty Cooke 6-6, Jack Coombs 18-44, Pat Corrales 132-115, Gavvy Cravath 91-137, Bill Donovan 31-71, Red Dooin 392-370, Hugh Duffy 206-251, Lee Elia 111-142, John Felske 190-194, Fred Fitzsimmons 102-179, Art Fletcher 231-378, Terry Francona 285-363, Jim Fregosi 431-463, Dallas Green 169-130, Bucky Harris 40-53, Nick Leyva 148-189, Hans Lobert 42-111, Frank Lucchesi 166-233, Gene Mauch 645-684, Stuffy McInnis 51-103, Terry Moore 35-42, Pat Moran 323-257, Bill Murray 240-214, George Myatt 21-35, Steve O'Neill 182-140, Paul Owens 161-158, Danny Ozark 594-510, Doc Prothro 138-320, Eddie Sawyer 390-424, Bill Shettsline 139-138, Burt Shotton 370-549, Bob Skinner 92-123, Mayo Smith 264-281, John Vukovich 5-4, Kaiser Wilhelm 77-128, Jimmy Wilson 280-477, Chief Zimmer 49-86.

PITTSBURGH PIRATES
YEARLY FINISHES

Year	Position	W	L	Pct.	*GB	Manager	Attendance
1901	1st	90	49	.647	+7.5	Fred Clarke	251,955
1902	1st	103	36	.741	+27.5	Fred Clarke	243,826
1903	1st	91	49	.650	+6.5	Fred Clarke	326,855
1904	4th	87	66	.569	19.0	Fred Clarke	340,615
1905	2nd	96	57	.627	9.0	Fred Clarke	369,124
1906	3rd	93	60	.608	23.5	Fred Clarke	394,877
1907	2nd	91	63	.591	17.0	Fred Clarke	319,506
1908	2nd	98	56	.636	1.0	Fred Clarke	382,444
1909	1st	110	42	.724	+6.5	Fred Clarke	534,950
1910	3rd	86	67	.562	17.5	Fred Clarke	436,586
1911	3rd	85	69	.552	14.5	Fred Clarke	432,000
1912	2nd	93	58	.616	10.0	Fred Clarke	384,000
1913	4th	78	71	.523	21.5	Fred Clarke	296,000
1914	7th	69	85	.448	25.5	Fred Clarke	139,620
1915	5th	73	81	.474	18.0	Fred Clarke	225,743
1916	6th	65	89	.422	29.0	Jimmy Callahan	289,132
1917	8th	51	103	.331	47.0	Jimmy Callahan, Honus Wagner, Hugo Bezdek	192,807
1918	4th	65	60	.520	17.0	Hugo Bezdek	213,610
1919	4th	71	68	.511	24.5	Hugo Bezdek	276,810
1920	4th	79	75	.513	14.0	George Gibson	429,037
1921	2nd	90	63	.588	4.0	George Gibson	701,567
1922	3rd (tied)	85	69	.552	8.0	George Gibson, Bill McKechnie	523,675
1923	3rd	87	67	.565	8.5	Bill McKechnie	611,082
1924	3rd	90	63	.588	3.0	Bill McKechnie	736,883
1925	1st	95	58	.621	+8.5	Bill McKechnie	804,354
1926	3rd	84	69	.549	4.5	Bill McKechnie	798,542
1927	1st	94	60	.610	+1.5	Donie Bush	869,720
1928	4th	85	67	.559	9.0	Donie Bush	495,070
1929	2nd	88	65	.575	10.5	Donie Bush, Jewel Ens	491,377
1930	5th	80	74	.519	12.0	Jewel Ens	357,795
1931	5th	75	79	.487	26.0	Jewel Ens	260,392
1932	2nd	86	68	.558	4.0	George Gibson	287,262
1933	2nd	87	67	.565	5.0	George Gibson	288,747
1934	5th	74	76	.493	19.5	George Gibson, Pie Traynor	322,622
1935	4th	86	67	.562	13.5	Pie Traynor	352,885
1936	4th	84	70	.545	8.0	Pie Traynor	372,524
1937	3rd	86	68	.558	10.0	Pie Traynor	459,679

Year	Position	W	L	Pct.	*GB	Manager	Attendance
1938	2nd	86	64	.573	2.0	Pie Traynor	641,033
1939	6th	68	85	.444	28.5	Pie Traynor	376,734
1940	4th	78	76	.506	22.5	Frankie Frisch	507,934
1941	4th	81	73	.526	19.0	Frankie Frisch	482,241
1942	5th	66	81	.449	36.5	Frankie Frisch	448,897
1943	4th	80	74	.519	25.0	Frankie Frisch	604,278
1944	2nd	90	63	.588	14.5	Frankie Frisch	498,740
1945	4th	82	72	.532	16.0	Frankie Frisch	604,694
1946	7th	63	91	.409	34.0	Frankie Frisch, Spud Davis	749,962
1947	7th (tied)	62	92	.403	32.0	Billy Herman, Bill Burwell	1,283,531
1948	4th	83	71	.539	8.5	Billy Meyer	1,517,021
1949	6th	71	83	.461	26.0	Billy Meyer	1,499,435
1950	8th	57	96	.373	33.5	Billy Meyer	1,166,267
1951	7th	64	90	.416	32.5	Billy Meyer	980,590
1952	8th	42	112	.273	54.5	Billy Meyer	686,673
1953	8th	50	104	.325	55.0	Fred Haney	572,757
1954	8th	53	101	.344	44.0	Fred Haney	475,494
1955	8th	60	94	.390	38.5	Fred Haney	469,397
1956	7th	66	88	.429	27.0	Bobby Bragan	949,878
1957	7th (tied)	62	92	.403	33.0	Bobby Bragan, Danny Murtaugh	850,732
1958	2nd	84	70	.545	8.0	Danny Murtaugh	1,311,988
1959	4th	78	76	.506	9.0	Danny Murtaugh	1,359,917
1960	1st	95	59	.617	+7.0	Danny Murtaugh	1,705,828
1961	6th	75	79	.487	18.0	Danny Murtaugh	1,199,128
1962	4th	93	68	.578	8.0	Danny Murtaugh	1,090,648
1963	8th	74	88	.457	25.0	Danny Murtaugh	783,648
1964	6th (tied)	80	82	.494	13.0	Danny Murtaugh	759,496
1965	3rd	90	72	.556	7.0	Harry Walker	909,279
1966	3rd	92	70	.568	3.0	Harry Walker	1,196,618
1967	6th	81	81	.500	20.5	Harry Walker, Danny Murtaugh	907,012
1968	6th	80	82	.494	17.0	Larry Shepard	693,485

EAST DIVISION

Year	Position	W	L	Pct.	*GB	Manager	Attendance
1969	3rd	88	74	.543	12.0	Larry Shepard, Alex Grammas	769,369
1970	1st†	89	73	.549	+5.0	Danny Murtaugh	1,341,947
1971	1st‡	97	65	.599	+7.0	Danny Murtaugh	1,501,132
1972	1st†	96	59	.619	+11.0	Bill Virdon	1,427,460
1973	3rd	80	82	.494	2.5	Bill Virdon, Danny Murtaugh	1,319,913
1974	1st†	88	74	.543	+1.5	Danny Murtaugh	1,110,552
1975	1st†	92	69	.571	+6.5	Danny Murtaugh	1,270,018
1976	2nd	92	70	.568	9.0	Danny Murtaugh	1,025,945
1977	2nd	96	66	.593	5.0	Chuck Tanner	1,237,349
1978	2nd	88	73	.547	1.5	Chuck Tanner	964,106
1979	1st‡	98	64	.605	+2.0	Chuck Tanner	1,435,454
1980	3rd	83	79	.512	8.0	Chuck Tanner	1,646,757
1981	4th/6th	46	56	.451	§.0	Chuck Tanner	541,789
1982	4th	84	78	.519	8.0	Chuck Tanner	1,024,106
1983	2nd	84	78	.519	6.0	Chuck Tanner	1,225,916
1984	6th	75	87	.463	21.5	Chuck Tanner	773,500
1985	6th	57	104	.354	43.5	Chuck Tanner	735,900
1986	6th	64	98	.395	44.0	Jim Leyland	1,000,917
1987	4th (tied)	80	82	.494	15.0	Jim Leyland	1,161,193
1988	2nd	85	75	.531	15.0	Jim Leyland	1,866,713
1989	5th	74	88	.457	19.0	Jim Leyland	1,374,141
1990	1st†	95	67	.586	+4.0	Jim Leyland	2,049,908
1991	1st†	98	64	.605	+14.0	Jim Leyland	2,065,302
1992	1st†	96	66	.593	+9.0	Jim Leyland	1,829,395
1993	5th	75	87	.463	22.0	Jim Leyland	1,650,593

CENTRAL DIVISION

Year	Position	W	L	Pct.	*GB	Manager	Attendance
1994	3rd (tied)	53	61	.465	13.0	Jim Leyland	1,222,520
1995	5th	58	86	.403	27.0	Jim Leyland	905,517
1996	5th	73	89	.451	15.0	Jim Leyland	1,332,150
1997	2nd	79	83	.488	5.0	Gene Lamont	1,657,022
1998	6th	69	93	.426	33.0	Gene Lamont	1,560,950
1999	3rd	78	83	.484	18.5	Gene Lamont	1,638,023
2000	5th	69	93	.426	26.0	Gene Lamont	1,748,908

*Games behind winner. †Lost championship series. ‡Won championship series. §First half 25-23; second half 21-33.

MANAGERIAL RECORDS

Hugo Bezdek 166-187, Bobby Bragan 102-155, Bill Burwell 1-0, Donie Bush 246-178, Jimmy Callahan 85-129, Fred Clarke 1,343-909, Spud Davis 1-2, Jewel Ens 176-167, Frank Frisch 539-528, George Gibson 401-330, Alex Grammas 4-1, Fred Haney 163-299, Billy

Herman 61-92, Gene Lamont 295-352, Jim Leyland 851-863, Bill McKechnie 409-293, Billy Meyer 317-452, Danny Murtaugh 1,115-950, Larry Shepard 164-155, Chuck Tanner 711-685, Pie Traynor 457-406, Bill Virdon 163-128, Honus Wagner 1-4, Harry Walker 224-184.

ST. LOUIS CARDINALS
YEARLY FINISHES

Year	Position	W	L	Pct.	*GB	Manager	Attendance
1901	4th	76	64	.543	14.5	Patsy Donovan	379,988
1902	6th	56	78	.418	44.5	Patsy Donovan	226,417
1903	8th	43	94	.314	46.5	Patsy Donovan	226,538
1904	5th	75	79	.487	31.5	Kid Nichols	386,750
1905	6th	58	96	.377	47.5	Kid Nichols, Jimmy Burke, Matt Robison	292,800
1906	7th	52	98	.347	63.0	John McCloskey	283,770
1907	8th	52	101	.340	55.5	John McCloskey	185,377
1908	8th	49	105	.318	50.0	John McCloskey	205,129
1909	7th	54	98	.355	56.0	Roger Bresnahan	299,982
1910	7th	63	90	.412	40.5	Roger Bresnahan	355,668
1911	5th	75	74	.503	22.0	Roger Bresnahan	447,768
1912	6th	63	90	.412	41.0	Roger Bresnahan	241,759
1913	8th	51	99	.340	49.0	Miller Huggins	203,531
1914	3rd	81	72	.529	13.0	Miller Huggins	256,099
1915	6th	72	81	.471	18.5	Miller Huggins	252,666
1916	7th (tied)	60	93	.392	33.5	Miller Huggins	224,308
1917	3rd	82	70	.539	15.0	Miller Huggins	288,491
1918	8th	51	78	.395	33.0	Jack Hendricks	110,599
1919	7th	54	83	.394	40.5	Branch Rickey	167,059
1920	5th (tied)	75	79	.487	18.0	Branch Rickey	326,836
1921	3rd	87	66	.569	7.0	Branch Rickey	384,773
1922	3rd (tied)	85	69	.552	8.0	Branch Rickey	536,998
1923	5th	79	74	.516	16.0	Branch Rickey	338,551
1924	6th	65	89	.422	28.5	Branch Rickey	272,885
1925	4th	77	76	.503	18.0	Branch Rickey, Rogers Hornsby	404,959
1926	1st	89	65	.578	+2.0	Rogers Hornsby	668,428
1927	2nd	92	61	.601	1.5	Bob O'Farrell	749,340
1928	1st	95	59	.617	+2.0	Bill McKechnie	761,574
1929	4th	78	74	.513	20.0	Bill McKechnie, Billy Southworth	399,887
1930	1st	92	62	.597	+2.0	Gabby Street	508,501
1931	1st	101	53	.656	+13.0	Gabby Street	608,535
1932	6th (tied)	72	82	.468	18.0	Gabby Street	279,219
1933	5th	82	71	.536	9.5	Gabby Street, Frankie Frisch	256,171
1934	1st	95	58	.621	+2.0	Frankie Frisch	325,056
1935	2nd	96	58	.623	4.0	Frankie Frisch	506,084
1936	2nd (tied)	87	67	.565	5.0	Frankie Frisch	448,078
1937	4th	81	73	.526	15.0	Frankie Frisch	430,811
1938	6th	71	80	.470	17.5	Frankie Frisch, Mike Gonzalez	291,418
1939	2nd	92	61	.601	4.5	Ray Blades	400,245
1940	3rd	84	69	.549	16.0	Ray Blades, Mike Gonzalez, Billy Southworth	324,078
1941	2nd	97	56	.634	2.5	Billy Southworth	633,645
1942	1st	106	48	.688	+2.0	Billy Southworth	553,552
1943	1st	105	49	.682	+18.0	Billy Southworth	517,135
1944	1st	105	49	.682	+14.5	Billy Southworth	461,968
1945	2nd	95	59	.617	3.0	Billy Southworth	594,630
1946	1st†	98	58	.628	+2.0	Eddie Dyer	1,061,807
1947	2nd	89	65	.578	5.0	Eddie Dyer	1,247,913
1948	2nd	85	69	.552	6.5	Eddie Dyer	1,111,440
1949	2nd	96	58	.623	1.0	Eddie Dyer	1,430,676
1950	5th	78	75	.510	12.5	Eddie Dyer	1,093,411
1951	3rd	81	73	.526	15.5	Marty Marion	1,013,429
1952	3rd	88	66	.571	8.5	Eddie Stanky	913,113
1953	3rd (tied)	83	71	.539	22.0	Eddie Stanky	880,242
1954	6th	72	82	.468	25.0	Eddie Stanky	1,039,698
1955	7th	68	86	.442	30.5	Eddie Stanky, Harry Walker	849,130
1956	4th	76	78	.494	17.0	Fred Hutchinson	1,029,773
1957	2nd	87	67	.565	8.0	Fred Hutchinson	1,183,575
1958	5th (tied)	72	82	.468	20.0	Fred Hutchinson, Stan Hack	1,063,730
1959	7th	71	83	.461	16.0	Solly Hemus	929,953
1960	3rd	86	68	.558	9.0	Solly Hemus	1,096,632
1961	5th	80	74	.519	13.0	Solly Hemus, Johnny Keane	855,305
1962	6th	84	78	.519	17.5	Johnny Keane	953,895
1963	2nd	93	69	.574	6.0	Johnny Keane	1,170,546
1964	1st	93	69	.574	+1.0	Johnny Keane	1,143,294
1965	7th	80	81	.497	16.5	Red Schoendienst	1,241,201
1966	6th	83	79	.512	12.0	Red Schoendienst	1,712,980
1967	1st	101	60	.627	+10.5	Red Schoendienst	2,090,145
1968	1st	97	65	.599	+9.0	Red Schoendienst	2,011,167

EAST DIVISION

Year	Position	W	L	Pct.	*GB	Manager	Attendance
1969	4th	87	75	.537	13.0	Red Schoendienst	1,682,783
1970	4th	76	86	.469	13.0	Red Schoendienst	1,629,736
1971	2nd	90	72	.556	7.0	Red Schoendienst	1,604,671
1972	4th	75	81	.481	21.5	Red Schoendienst	1,196,894
1973	2nd	81	81	.500	1.5	Red Schoendienst	1,574,046
1974	2nd	86	75	.534	1.5	Red Schoendienst	1,838,413
1975	3rd (tied)	82	80	.506	10.5	Red Schoendienst	1,695,270
1976	5th	72	90	.444	29.0	Red Schoendienst	1,207,079
1977	3rd	83	79	.512	18.0	Vern Rapp	1,659,287
1978	5th	69	93	.426	21.0	Vern Rapp, Jack Krol, Ken Boyer	1,278,215
1979	3rd	86	76	.531	12.0	Ken Boyer	1,627,256
1980	4th	74	88	.457	17.0	Ken Boyer, Jack Krol, Whitey Herzog, Red Schoendienst	1,385,147
1981	2nd/2nd	59	43	.578	‡	Whitey Herzog	1,010,247
1982	1st§	92	70	.568	+3.0	Whitey Herzog	2,111,906
1983	4th	79	83	.488	11.0	Whitey Herzog	2,317,914
1984	3rd	84	78	.519	12.5	Whitey Herzog	2,037,448
1985	1st§	101	61	.623	+3.0	Whitey Herzog	2,637,563
1986	3rd	79	82	.491	28.5	Whitey Herzog	2,471,974
1987	1st§	95	67	.586	+3.0	Whitey Herzog	3,072,122
1988	5th	76	86	.469	25.0	Whitey Herzog	2,892,799
1989	3rd	86	76	.531	7.0	Whitey Herzog	3,080,980
1990	6th	70	92	.432	25.0	Whitey Herzog, Red Schoendienst, Joe Torre	2,573,225
1991	2nd	84	78	.519	14.0	Joe Torre	2,448,699
1992	3rd	83	79	.512	13.0	Joe Torre	2,418,483
1993	3rd	87	75	.537	10.0	Joe Torre	2,844,328

CENTRAL DIVISION

Year	Position	W	L	Pct.	*GB	Manager	Attendance
1994	3rd (tied)	53	61	.465	13.0	Joe Torre	1,866,544
1995	4th	62	81	.434	22.5	Joe Torre, Mike Jorgensen	1,756,727
1996	1st∞▲	88	74	.543	+6.0	Tony La Russa	2,654,718
1997	4th	73	89	.451	11.0	Tony La Russa	2,634,014
1998	3rd	83	79	.512	19.0	Tony La Russa	3,194,092
1999	4th	75	86	.466	21.5	Tony La Russa	3,225,334
2000	1st∞▲	95	67	.586	+10.0	Tony La Russa	3,336,493

*Games behind winner. †Won pennant playoff. ‡First half 30-20; second 29-23. §Won championship series. ∞Won division series. ▲Lost championship series.

MANAGERIAL RECORDS

Ray Blades 106-85, Ken Boyer 166-190, Roger Bresnahan 255-352, Jimmy Burke 17-32, Patsy Donovan 175-236, Eddie Dyer 446-325, Frank Frisch 458-354, Mike Gonzalez 9-13, Stan Hack 3-7, Solly Hemus 190-192, Jack Hendricks 51-78, Whitey Herzog 835-739, Rogers Hornsby 153-116, Miller Huggins 346-415, Fred Hutchinson 232-220, Mike Jorgensen 42-54, Johnny Keane 317-249, Tony La Russa 414-395, Marty Marion 81-73, John McCloskey 153-304, Bill McKechnie 129-88, Kid Nichols 94-108, Bob O'Farrell 92-61, Vern Rapp 89-90, Branch Rickey 458-485, Stanley Robison 22-35, Red Schoendienst 1,028-944, Billy Southworth 620-346, Eddie Stanky 260-238, Gabby Street 312-242, Joe Torre 351-354, Harry Walker 51-67.

SAN DIEGO PADRES
YEARLY FINISHES
WEST DIVISION

Year	Position	W	L	Pct.	*GB	Manager	Attendance
1969	6th	52	110	.321	41.0	Preston Gomez	512,970
1970	6th	63	99	.389	39.0	Preston Gomez	643,679
1971	6th	61	100	.379	28.5	Preston Gomez	557,513
1972	6th	58	95	.379	36.5	Preston Gomez, Don Zimmer	644,273
1973	6th	60	102	.370	39.0	Don Zimmer	611,826
1974	6th	60	102	.370	42.0	John McNamara	1,075,399
1975	4th	71	91	.438	37.0	John McNamara	1,281,747
1976	5th	73	89	.451	29.0	John McNamara	1,458,478
1977	5th	69	93	.426	29.0	John McNamara, Bob Skinner, Alvin Dark	1,376,269
1978	4th	84	78	.519	11.0	Roger Craig	1,670,107
1979	5th	68	93	.422	22.0	Roger Craig	1,456,967
1980	6th	73	89	.451	19.5	Jerry Coleman	1,139,026
1981	6th/6th	41	69	.373	†	Frank Howard	519,161
1982	4th	81	81	.500	8.0	Dick Williams	1,607,516
1983	4th	81	81	.500	10.0	Dick Williams	1,539,815
1984	1st‡	92	70	.568	+12.0	Dick Williams	1,983,904
1985	3rd (tied)	83	79	.512	12.0	Dick Williams	2,210,352
1986	4th	74	88	.457	22.0	Steve Boros	1,805,716
1987	6th	65	97	.401	25.0	Larry Bowa	1,454,061
1988	3rd	83	78	.516	11.0	Larry Bowa, Jack McKeon	1,506,896

Year	Position	W	L	Pct.	*GB	Manager	Attendance
1989	2nd	89	73	.549	3.0	Jack McKeon	2,009,031
1990	4th (tied)	75	87	.463	16.0	Jack McKeon, Greg Riddoch	1,856,396
1991	3rd	84	78	.519	10.0	Greg Riddoch	1,804,289
1992	3rd	82	80	.506	16.0	Greg Riddoch, Jim Riggleman	1,722,102
1993	7th	61	101	.377	43.0	Jim Riggleman	1,375,432
1994	4th	47	70	.402	12.5	Jim Riggleman	953,857
1995	3rd	70	74	.486	8.0	Bruce Bochy	1,041,805
1996	1st§	91	71	.562	+1.0	Bruce Bochy	2,187,886
1997	4th	76	86	.469	14.0	Bruce Bochy	2,089,333
1998	1st∞	98	64	.605	+9.5	Bruce Bochy	2,555,901
1999	4th	74	88	.457	26.0	Bruce Bochy	2,523,538
2000	5th	76	86	.469	21.0	Bruce Bochy	2,423,149

*Games behind winner. †First half 23-33; second 18-36. ‡Won championship series. §Lost division series. ∞Won division series.

MANAGERIAL RECORDS

Bruce Bochy 485-469, Steve Boros 74-88, Larry Bowa 81-127, Jerry Coleman 73-89, Roger Craig 152-171, Alvin Dark 49-65, Preston Gomez 180-316, Frank Howard 41-69, Jack McKeon 193-164, John McNamara 224-310, Greg Riddoch 200-194, Jim Riggleman 112-179, Dick Williams 337-311, Don Zimmer 114-190.

SAN FRANCISCO GIANTS
YEARLY FINISHES

(Known as New York Giants through 1957)

Year	Position	W	L	Pct.	*GB	Manager	Attendance
1901	7th	52	85	.380	37.0	George Davis	297,650
1902	8th	48	88	.353	53.5	Horace Fogel, Heinie Smith, John McGraw	302,875
1903	2nd	84	55	.604	6.5	John McGraw	579,530
1904	1st	106	47	.693	+13.0	John McGraw	609,826
1905	1st	105	48	.686	+9.0	John McGraw	552,700
1906	2nd	96	56	.632	20.0	John McGraw	402,850
1907	4th	82	71	.536	25.5	John McGraw	538,350
1908	2nd (tied)	98	56	.636	1.0	John McGraw	910,000
1909	3rd	92	61	.601	18.5	John McGraw	783,700
1910	2nd	91	63	.591	13.0	John McGraw	511,785
1911	1st	99	54	.647	+7.5	John McGraw	675,000
1912	1st	103	48	.682	+10.0	John McGraw	638,000
1913	1st	101	51	.664	+12.5	John McGraw	630,000
1914	2nd	84	70	.545	10.5	John McGraw	364,313
1915	8th	69	83	.454	21.0	John McGraw	391,850
1916	4th	86	66	.566	7.0	John McGraw	552,056
1917	1st	98	56	.636	+10.0	John McGraw	500,264
1918	2nd	71	53	.573	10.5	John McGraw	256,618
1919	2nd	87	53	.621	9.0	John McGraw	708,857
1920	2nd	86	68	.558	7.0	John McGraw	929,609
1921	1st	94	59	.614	+4.0	John McGraw	773,477
1922	1st	93	61	.604	+7.0	John McGraw	945,809
1923	1st	95	58	.621	+4.5	John McGraw	820,780
1924	1st	93	60	.608	+1.5	John McGraw	844,068
1925	2nd	86	66	.566	8.5	John McGraw	778,993
1926	5th	74	77	.490	13.5	John McGraw	700,362
1927	3rd	92	62	.597	2.0	John McGraw	858,190
1928	2nd	93	61	.604	2.0	John McGraw	916,191
1929	3rd	84	67	.556	13.5	John McGraw	868,806
1930	3rd	87	67	.565	5.0	John McGraw	868,714
1931	2nd	87	65	.572	13.0	John McGraw	812,163
1932	6th (tied)	72	82	.468	18.0	John McGraw, Bill Terry	484,868
1933	1st	91	61	.599	+5.0	Bill Terry	604,471
1934	2nd	93	60	.608	2.0	Bill Terry	730,851
1935	3rd	91	62	.595	8.5	Bill Terry	748,748
1936	1st	92	62	.597	+5.0	Bill Terry	837,952
1937	1st	95	57	.625	+3.0	Bill Terry	926,887
1938	3rd	83	67	.553	5.0	Bill Terry	799,633
1939	5th	77	74	.510	18.5	Bill Terry	702,457
1940	6th	72	80	.474	27.5	Bill Terry	747,852
1941	5th	74	79	.484	25.5	Bill Terry	763,098
1942	3rd	85	67	.559	20.0	Mel Ott	779,621
1943	8th	55	98	.359	49.5	Mel Ott	466,095
1944	5th	67	87	.435	38.0	Mel Ott	674,083
1945	5th	78	74	.513	19.0	Mel Ott	1,016,468
1946	8th	61	93	.396	36.0	Mel Ott	1,219,873
1947	4th	81	73	.526	13.0	Mel Ott	1,600,793
1948	5th	78	76	.506	13.5	Mel Ott, Leo Durocher	1,459,269

Year	Position	W	L	Pct.	*GB	Manager	Attendance
1949	5th	73	81	.474	24.0	Leo Durocher	1,218,446
1950	3rd	86	68	.558	5.0	Leo Durocher	1,008,876
1951	1st (tied)†	98	59	.624	+1.0	Leo Durocher	1,059,539
1952	2nd	92	62	.597	4.5	Leo Durocher	984,940
1953	5th	70	84	.455	35.0	Leo Durocher	811,518
1954	1st	97	57	.630	+5.0	Leo Durocher	1,155,067
1955	3rd	80	74	.519	18.5	Leo Durocher	824,112
1956	6th	67	87	.435	26.0	Bill Rigney	629,179
1957	6th	69	85	.448	26.0	Bill Rigney	653,923
1958	3rd	80	74	.519	12.0	Bill Rigney	1,272,625
1959	3rd	83	71	.539	4.0	Bill Rigney	1,422,130
1960	5th	79	75	.513	16.0	Bill Rigney, Tom Sheehan	1,795,356
1961	3rd	85	69	.552	8.0	Alvin Dark	1,390,679
1962	1st†	103	62	.624	+1.0	Alvin Dark	1,592,594
1963	3rd	88	74	.543	11.0	Alvin Dark	1,571,306
1964	4th	90	72	.556	3.0	Alvin Dark	1,504,364
1965	2nd	95	67	.586	2.0	Herman Franks	1,546,075
1966	2nd	93	68	.578	1.5	Herman Franks	1,657,192
1967	2nd	91	71	.562	10.5	Herman Franks	1,242,480
1968	2nd	88	74	.543	9.0	Herman Franks	837,220

WEST DIVISION

Year	Position	W	L	Pct.	*GB	Manager	Attendance
1969	2nd	90	72	.556	3.0	Clyde King	873,603
1970	3rd	86	76	.531	16.0	Clyde King, Charlie Fox	740,720
1971	1st‡	90	72	.556	+1.0	Charlie Fox	1,106,043
1972	5th	69	86	.445	26.5	Charlie Fox	647,744
1973	3rd	88	74	.543	11.0	Charlie Fox	834,193
1974	5th	72	90	.444	30.0	Charlie Fox, Wes Westrum	519,987
1975	3rd	80	81	.497	27.5	Wes Westrum	522,919
1976	4th	74	88	.457	28.0	Bill Rigney	626,868
1977	4th	75	87	.463	23.0	Joe Altobelli	700,056
1978	3rd	89	73	.549	6.0	Joe Altobelli	1,740,477
1979	4th	71	91	.438	19.5	Joe Altobelli, Dave Bristol	1,456,402
1980	5th	75	86	.466	17.0	Dave Bristol	1,096,115
1981	5th/3rd	56	55	.505	§	Frank Robinson	632,274
1982	3rd	87	75	.537	2.0	Frank Robinson	1,200,948
1983	5th	79	83	.488	12.0	Frank Robinson	1,251,530
1984	6th	66	96	.407	26.0	Frank Robinson, Danny Ozark	1,001,545
1985	6th	62	100	.383	33.0	Jim Davenport, Roger Craig	818,697
1986	3rd	83	79	.512	13.0	Roger Craig	1,528,748
1987	1st‡	90	72	.556	+6.0	Roger Craig	1,917,168
1988	4th	83	79	.512	11.5	Roger Craig	1,785,297
1989	1st∞	92	70	.568	+3.0	Roger Craig	2,059,701
1990	3rd	85	77	.525	6.0	Roger Craig	1,975,528
1991	4th	75	87	.463	19.0	Roger Craig	1,737,478
1992	5th	72	90	.444	26.0	Roger Craig	1,561,987
1993	2nd	103	59	.636	1.0	Dusty Baker	2,606,354
1994	2nd	55	60	.478	3.5	Dusty Baker	1,704,608
1995	4th	67	77	.465	11.0	Dusty Baker	1,241,500
1996	4th	68	94	.420	23.0	Dusty Baker	1,413,922
1997	1st▲	90	72	.556	+2.0	Dusty Baker	1,690,869
1998	2nd◆	89	74	.546	9.5	Dusty Baker	1,925,634
1999	2nd	86	76	.531	14.0	Dusty Baker	2,078,399
2000	1st▲	97	65	.599	+11.0	Dusty Baker	3,315,330

*Games behind winner. †Won pennant playoff. ‡Lost championship series. §First half 27-32; second half 29-23. ∞Won championship series. ▲Lost division series. ◆Lost wild-card playoff.

MANAGERIAL RECORDS

Joe Altobelli 225-239, Dusty Baker 655-577, Dave Bristol 85-98, Roger Craig 586-566, Alvin Dark 366-277, Jim Davenport 56-88, George Davis 52-85, Leo Durocher 637-523, Horace Fogel 18-23, Charlie Fox 348-327, Herman Franks 367-280, Clyde King 109-95, John McGraw 2,604-1,801, Mel Ott 464-530, Danny Ozark 24-32, Bill Rigney 406-430, Frank Robinson 264-277, Tom Sheehan 46-50, Heinie Smith 5-27, Bill Terry 823-661, Wes Westrum 118-129.

MINOR LEAGUES

FARM SYSTEMS

ANAHEIM (6): AAA—Salt Lake. AA—Arkansas. A—Cedar Rapids, Rancho Cucamonga. Rookie—Mesa Angels, Provo.
BALTIMORE (6): AAA—Rochester. AA—Bowie. A—Delmarva, Frederick. Rookie—Bluefield, Gulf Coast Orioles.
BOSTON (6): AAA—Pawtucket. AA—Trenton. A—Augusta, Lowell, Sarasota. Rookie—Gulf Coast Red Sox.
CHICAGO (6): AAA—Charlotte. AA—Birmingham. A—Kannapolis, Winston-Salem. Rookie—Bristol, Tucson White Sox.
CLEVELAND (6): AAA—Buffalo. AA—Akron. A—Columbus (GA), Kinston, Mahoning Valley. Rookie—Burlington.
DETROIT (6): AAA—Toledo. AA—Erie. A—Lakeland, Oneonta, West Michigan. Rookie—Gulf Coast Tigers.
KANSAS CITY (6): AAA—Omaha. AA—Wichita. A—Burlington, Spokane, Wilmington. Rookie—Gulf Coast Royals.
MINNESOTA (6): AAA—Edmonton. AA—New Britain. A—Fort Myers, Quad City. Rookie—Elizabethton, Gulf Coast Twins.
NEW YORK (6): AAA—Columbus (OH). AA—Norwich. A—Greensboro, Staten Island, Tampa. Rookie—Gulf Coast Yankees.
OAKLAND (6): AAA—Sacramento. AA—Midland. A—Modesto, Vancouver, Visalia. Rookie—Scottsdale A's.
SEATTLE (6): AAA—Tacoma. AA—San Antonio. A—Everett, San Bernardino, Wisconsin. Rookie—Peoria Mariners.
TAMPA BAY (6): AAA—Durham. AA—Orlando. A—Bakersfield, Charleston (SC), Hudson Valley. Rookie—Princeton.
TEXAS (6): AAA—Oklahoma. AA—Tulsa. A—Charlotte, Savannah. Rookie—Gulf Coast Rangers, Pulaski.
TORONTO (6): AAA—Syracuse. AA—Tennessee. A—Auburn, Charleston (WV), Dunedin. Rookie—Medicine Hat.

ARIZONA (6): AAA—Tucson. AA—El Paso. A—Lancaster, South Bend, Yakima. Rookie—Missoula.
ATLANTA (7): AAA—Richmond. AA—Greenville. A—Jamestown, Macon, Myrtle Beach. Rookie—Danville, Gulf Coast Braves.
CHICAGO (6): AAA—Iowa. AA—West Tenn. A—Boise, Daytona, Lansing. Rookie—Mesa Cubs.
CINCINNATI (6): AAA—Louisville. AA—Chattanooga. A—Dayton, Mudville. Rookie—Billings, Gulf Coast Reds.
COLORADO (6): AAA—Colorado Springs. AA—Carolina. A—Asheville, Salem, Tri-City. Rookie—Casper.
FLORIDA (6): AAA—Calgary. AA—Portland (ME). A—Brevard County, Kane County, Utica. Rookie—Gulf Coast Marlins.
HOUSTON (6): AAA—New Orleans. AA—Round Rock. A—Lexington, Michigan, Pittsfield. Rookie—Martinsville.
LOS ANGELES (6): AAA—Las Vegas. AA—Jacksonville. A—Vero Beach, Wilmington. Rookie—Great Falls, Gulf Coast Dodgers.
MILWAUKEE (6): AAA—Indianapolis. AA—Huntsville. A—Beloit, High Desert. Rookie—Maryvale, Ogden.
MONTREAL (6): AAA—Ottawa. AA—Harrisburg. A—Clinton, Jupiter, Vermont. Rookie—Gulf Coast Expos.
NEW YORK (6): AAA—Norfolk. AA—Binghamton. A—Brooklyn, Capital City, St. Lucie. Rookie—Kingsport.
PHILADELPHIA (6): AAA—Scranton/Wilkes-Barre. AA—Reading. A—Batavia, Clearwater, Lakewood. Rookie—Gulf Coast Phillies.
PITTSBURGH (6): AAA—Nashville. AA—Altoona. A—Hickory, Lynchburg, Williamsport. Rookie—Gulf Coast Pirates.
ST. LOUIS (6): AAA—Memphis. AA—New Haven. A—New Jersey, Peoria (IL), Potomac. Rookie—Johnson City.
SAN DIEGO (6): AAA—Portland (OR). AA—Mobile. A—Eugene, Fort Wayne, Lake Elsinore. Rookie—Idaho Falls.
SAN FRANCISCO (6): AAA—Fresno. AA—Shreveport. A—Hagerstown, Salem-Keizer, San Jose. Rookie—Arizona Giants.

MINOR LEAGUES *Farm systems*

INTERNATIONAL LEAGUE

LEAGUE OFFICE

President
Randy Mobley

Address
55 S. High St., Suite 202
Dublin, OH 43017

Phone
614-791-9300

TEAMS

BUFFALO BISONS

General manager
Mike Buczkowski
Manager
Eric Wedge
Ballpark (capacity, surface)
Dunn Tire Park (21,050, grass)
Affiliation
Indians
Address
P.O. Box 450
Buffalo, NY 14205
Phone
716-846-2000

CHARLOTTE KNIGHTS

General manager
Tim Newman
Manager
Nick Leyva
Ballpark (capacity, surface)
Knights Stadium (10,005, grass)
Affiliation
White Sox
Address
2280 Deerfield Drive
Fort Mill, SC 29715
Phone
704-357-8071

COLUMBUS CLIPPERS

General manager
Ken Schnacke
Manager
Trey Hillman
Ballpark (capacity, surface)
Cooper Stadium (15,000, grass)
Affiliation
Yankees
Address
1155 W. Mound St.
Columbus, OH 43223
Phone
614-462-5250

DURHAM BULLS

General manager
George Habel
Manager
Bill Evers
Ballpark (capacity, surface)
Durham Bulls Athletic Park
(10,000, grass)
Affiliation
Devil Rays
Address
P.O. Box 507
Durham, NC 27702
Phone
919-687-6500

INDIANAPOLIS INDIANS

General manager
Cal Burleson
Manager
Wendell Kim
Ballpark (capacity, surface)
Victory Field (15,000, grass)
Affiliation
Brewers
Address
501 W. Maryland St.
Indianapolis, IN 46225
Phone
317-269-3542

LOUISVILLE RIVERBATS

President
Gary Ulmer
Manager
Dave Miley
Ballpark (capacity, surface)
Louisville Slugger Field (13,131, grass)
Affiliation
Reds
Address
P.O. Box 36407
Louisville, KY 40233
Phone
502-212-2287

NORFOLK TIDES

General manager
Dave Rosenfield
Manager
John Gibbons
Ballpark (capacity, surface)
Harbor Park (12,059, grass)
Affiliation
Mets
Address
150 Park Ave.
Norfolk, VA 23510
Phone
757-622-2222

OTTAWA LYNX

General manager
Kyle Bostwick
Manager
Stan Hough
Ballpark (capacity, surface)
JetForm Park (10,332, grass)
Affiliation
Expos
Address
300 Coventry Rd.
Ottawa, Ontario K1K 4P5
Phone
613-747-5969

PAWTUCKET RED SOX

General manager
Mike Tamburro
Manager
Gary Jones
Ballpark (capacity, surface)
McCoy Stadium (10,000, grass)
Affiliation
Red Sox
Address
P.O. Box 2365
Pawtucket, RI 02861
Phone
401-724-7303

RICHMOND BRAVES

General manager
Bruce Baldwin
Manager
Carlos Tosca
Ballpark (capacity, surface)
The Diamond (12,156, grass)
Affiliation
Braves
Address
P.O. Box 6667
Richmond, VA 23230
Phone
804-359-4444

ROCHESTER RED WINGS

General manager
Dan Mason
Manager
Andy Etchebarren
Ballpark (capacity, surface)
Frontier Field (22,844, grass)
Affiliation
Orioles
Address
1 Morrie Silver Way
Rochester, NY 14608
Phone
716-454-1001

SCRANTON/WILKES-BARRE RED BARONS

General manager
Rick Muntean
Manager
Marc Bombard
Ballpark (capacity, surface)
Lackawanna County Multi-Purpose
Stadium (10,982, artificial)
Affiliation
Phillies
Address
P.O. Box 3449
Scranton, PA 18505
Phone
570-969-2255

CLASS AAA *International League*

SYRACUSE SKY CHIEFS

General manager
John Simone
Manager
Omar Malave
Ballpark (capacity, surface)
P&C Stadium (11,100, artificial)
Affiliation
Blue Jays

Address
One Tex Simone
Syracuse, NY 13208
Phone
315-474-7833

TOLEDO MUD HENS

General manager
Joe Napoli
Manager
Bruce Fields

Ballpark (capacity, surface)
Ned Skeldon Stadium (10,025, grass)
Affiliation
Tigers
Address
2901 Key Street
Maumee, OH 43537
Phone
419-893-9483

2000 FINAL STANDINGS

NORTH DIVISION

Team	W	L	T	Pct.	GB
Buffalo (Indians)	86	59	0	.593	...
Scranton/Wilkes-Barre (Phillies)	85	60	0	.586	1.0
Pawtucket (Red Sox)	82	61	0	.573	3.0
Syracuse (Blue Jays)	74	66	0	.529	9.5
Rochester (Orioles)	65	79	0	.451	20.5
Ottawa (Expos)	53	88	0	.376	31.0

SOUTH DIVISION

Team	W	L	T	Pct.	GB
Durham (Devil Rays)	81	62	0	.566	...
Charlotte (White Sox)	78	65	0	.545	3.0
Norfolk (Mets)	65	79	0	.451	16.5
Richmond (Braves)	51	92	0	.357	30.0

WEST DIVISION

Team	W	L	T	Pct.	GB
Indianapolis (Brewers)	81	63	0	.563	...
Columbus (Yankees)	75	69	0	.521	6.0
Louisville (Reds)	71	73	0	.493	10.0
Toledo (Tigers)	55	86	0	.390	24.5

COMPOSITE

Team	Buf.	SWB.	Paw.	Dur.	Ind.	Char.	Syr.	Col.	Lou.	Roch.	Nor.	Tol.	Ott.	Rich.	W	L	T	Pct.	GB
Buffalo (Indians)	...	9	8	4	5	5	9	3	4	12	4	6	10	7	86	59	0	.593	...
Scranton/Wilkes-Barre (Phillies)	8	...	10	4	4	4	10	3	5	9	5	4	12	7	85	60	0	.586	1.0
Pawtucket (Red Sox)	8	6	...	7	5	6	8	3	5	11	4	4	9	6	82	61	0	.573	3.0
Durham (Devil Rays)	4	4	1	...	4	5	5	7	8	4	12	10	6	11	81	62	0	.566	4.0
Indianapolis (Brewers)	3	4	3	8	...	3	2	12	13	2	8	10	4	9	81	63	0	.563	4.5
Charlotte (White Sox)	3	4	2	10	9	...	6	3	6	2	10	6	6	11	78	65	0	.545	7.0
Syracuse (Blue Jays)	7	6	8	3	6	2	...	6	2	11	4	3	10	6	74	66	0	.529	9.5
Columbus (Yankees)	5	5	5	5	4	9	2	...	5	5	7	10	4	9	75	69	0	.521	10.5
Louisville (Reds)	4	3	3	4	3	6	6	11	...	4	5	11	3	8	71	73	0	.493	14.5
Rochester (Orioles)	4	7	5	4	6	6	5	3	4	...	5	3	10	3	65	79	0	.451	20.5
Norfolk (Mets)	4	3	4	4	4	6	4	5	7	3	...	7	4	10	65	79	0	.451	20.5
Toledo (Tigers)	2	4	4	2	6	6	3	6	5	5	5	...	5	2	55	86	0	.390	29.0
Ottawa (Expos)	6	4	7	2	4	2	4	4	5	6	4	2	...	3	53	88	0	.376	31.0
Richmond (Braves)	1	1	1	5	3	5	2	3	4	5	6	10	5	...	51	92	0	.357	34.0

Major league affiliations in parentheses.

PLAYOFFS: Indianapolis defeated Durham three games to two; Scranton/Wilkes-Barre defeated Buffalo three games to one; Indianapolis defeated Scranton/Wilkes-Barre three games to two to win league championship; Indianapolis defeated Memphis (Pacific Coast) three games to one in AAA World Series.

REGULAR-SEASON ATTENDANCE: Buffalo, 667,540; Charlotte, 338,928; Columbus, 458,806; Rochester, 459,494; Durham, 475,363; Indianapolis, 655,073; Louisville, 685,863; Norfolk, 479,741; Ottawa, 135,683; Pawtucket, 585,107; Richmond, 451,479; Scranton/Wilkes-Barre, 458,584; Syracuse, 402,450; Toledo, 298,564. Total—6,552,675. Playoffs (14 games)—49,298. Class AAA All-Star Game at Rochester, N.Y.—12,810.

MANAGERS: Buffalo, Joel Skinner; Charlotte, Nick Leyva; Columbus, Trey Hillman; Durham, Bill Evers; Indianapolis, Steve Smith; Louisville, Dave Miley; Norfolk, John Gibbons; Ottawa, Jeff Cox (Through July 20) and Rick Sweet (July 21 through end of season); Pawtucket, Gary Jones; Richmond, Randy Ingle; Rochester, Marv Foley; Scranton/Wilkes-Barre, Marc Bombard; Syracuse, Pat Kelly (Through May 16), Omar Malave (May 17 through May 22) and Mel Queen (May 23 through end of season); Toledo, Dave Anderson (Through June 23) and Glenn Ezell (June 24 through end of season).

ALL-STAR TEAM: 1B—Ryan Jackson, Durham; 2B—Marlon Anderson, Scranton/Wilkes-Barre; 3B—Aubrey Huff, Durham; SS—Chris Sexton, Louisville; C—Gary Bennett, Scranton/Wilkes-Barre; OF—Chad Mottola, Syracuse; OF—Billy McMillon, Toledo; OF—Ozzie Timmons, Durham; DH—Luis Lopez, Syracuse; Utility—Bill Selby, Buffalo; Starting pitcher—Jon Garland, Charlotte; Relief pitcher—Bob Scanlan, Indianapolis; Most Valuable Player—Jon Garland, Charlotte; Rookie of the Year—Aubrey Huff, Durham; Manager of the Year—Joel Skinner, Buffalo.

2000 BATTING
TEAM

Team	Avg.	G	TPA	AB	R	H	TB	2B	3B	HR	RBI	SH	SF	HP	BB	IBB	SO	SB	CS	GDP	LOB	ShO	Slg.	OBP
Durham	.284	143	5515	4888	746	1387	2151	281	27	143	703	41	44	48	494	23	894	167	63	113	1050	3	.440	.352
Scranton/W.-B.	.273	145	5556	4909	717	1341	2050	270	50	113	651	59	50	57	481	28	782	139	61	104	1024	6	.418	.342
Louisville	.273	144	5595	4951	748	1350	2182	305	28	157	701	39	48	55	502	27	854	86	45	126	1020	3	.441	.343
Rochester	.271	144	5450	4874	622	1319	1907	260	35	86	578	39	41	41	455	17	856	74	47	126	1050	8	.391	.335
Buffalo	.270	145	5423	4755	743	1284	2040	238	37	148	692	37	46	39	546	10	932	86	40	88	1015	4	.429	.347
Columbus	.270	144	5435	4784	729	1290	2108	272	39	156	686	30	38	42	541	21	913	132	60	113	979	7	.441	.347
Indianapolis	.267	144	5520	4860	704	1299	2023	299	37	117	657	40	48	41	531	32	905	121	42	111	1027	6	.416	.341
Norfolk	.265	145	5522	4841	654	1281	1871	254	24	96	603	50	42	60	529	26	873	152	93	105	1044	9	.386	.342
Syracuse	.264	140	5150	4659	632	1230	1999	250	36	149	609	29	36	42	384	15	798	136	63	89	904	11	.429	.323
Charlotte	.263	143	5352	4654	644	1224	1856	227	24	119	604	59	45	42	552	19	784	99	43	126	1036	11	.399	.343
Toledo	.260	141	5290	4712	657	1225	2028	259	20	168	617	19	42	38	479	18	867	33	35	124	980	8	.430	.330

Team	Avg.	G	TPA	AB	R	H	TB	2B	3B	HR	RBI	SH	SF	HP	BB	IBB	SO	SB	CS	GDP	LOB	ShO	Slg.	OBP
Richmond	.260	143	5382	4820	626	1253	1914	244	30	119	598	58	32	51	421	17	943	95	57	95	964	5	.397	.324
Ottawa	.258	141	5268	4602	599	1187	1745	260	29	80	542	49	43	55	519	25	870	73	45	112	1036	10	.379	.337
Pawtucket	.247	143	5417	4704	713	1163	1986	220	24	185	665	42	38	79	554	17	1028	67	31	97	979	5	.422	.334

INDIVIDUAL

TOP QUALIFIERS FOR BATTING CHAMPIONSHIP

Minimum 389 plate appearances. *Lefthanded batter. †Switch-hitter.

Player, Team	Avg.	G	TPA	AB	R	H	TB	2B	3B	HR	RBI	SH	SF	HP	BB	IBB	SO	SB	CS	GDP	Slg.	OBP
McMillon, Billy, Tol.*	.345	105	457	380	61	131	202	30	1	13	50	0	4	2	71	7	65	3	1	18	.532	.446
Lopez, Luis, Syr.	.328	130	549	491	64	161	211	27	1	7	79	0	8	2	48	1	33	3	1	10	.430	.384
Sexton, Chris, Lou.	.324	99	455	389	79	126	168	19	1	7	50	1	2	0	63	0	45	8	4	14	.432	.416
Robinson, Kerry, Col.*	.318	119	491	437	71	139	174	17	9	0	32	10	1	2	41	0	40	37	18	5	.398	.378
Huff, Aubrey, Dur.*	.316	108	464	408	73	129	231	36	3	20	76	2	1	2	51	4	72	2	3	15	.566	.394
Jackson, Ryan, Dur.*	.311	139	562	502	69	156	252	38	2	18	85	2	8	0	50	4	112	6	4	8	.502	.368
Mottola, Chad, Syr.	.309	134	552	505	85	156	286	25	3	33	102	0	5	5	37	2	99	30	15	11	.566	.359
Swann, Pedro, Rich.*	.305	125	504	442	70	135	188	22	2	9	57	2	1	5	54	6	68	6	5	10	.425	.386
Anderson, Marlon, S./W.B.*...	.305	103	448	397	57	121	179	18	8	8	53	2	5	5	39	12	43	24	10	2	.451	.370
Bradley, Milton, Ott.†	.304	88	391	342	58	104	144	20	1	6	29	1	2	1	45	3	56	10	15	5	.421	.385
Clark, Brady, Lou.	.304	132	577	487	90	148	249	41	6	16	79	0	9	9	72	0	51	12	8	14	.511	.397
Woods, Ken, S./W.B.	.303	133	565	512	89	155	201	28	6	2	35	8	1	5	39	0	47	20	7	7	.393	.357
Timmons, Ozzie, Dur.	.300	137	591	506	100	152	273	32	1	29	104	0	5	7	73	5	105	5	4	6	.540	.393
McGuire, Ryan, Nor.*	.298	122	487	392	63	117	172	23	1	10	62	1	6	1	87	5	84	6	3	3	.439	.422
Bartee, Kimera, Lou.	.298	119	514	453	69	135	186	19	4	8	48	8	3	2	48	0	64	28	11	7	.411	.366

DEPARTMENTAL LEADERS: G—Wakeland, 141; AB—Herrera, 552; R—Timmons, 100; H—J. Herrera, 163; TB—Mottola, 286; 2B—B. Clark, 41; 3B—Rollins, Kirby, 11; HR—Mottola, 33; RBI—Timmons, 104; SH—Li. Rodriguez, J. Garcia, 16; SF—B. Clark, Schneider, 9; HP—Eckstein, 20; BB—McGuire, 87; IBB—Anderson, 12; SO—Wakeland, 148; SB—Sanchez, 52; CS—Sanchez, 20; GIDP—Schall, 21; Slg.—Mottola, .566; OBP—McMillon, .446.

ALL PLAYERS

*Lefthanded batter. †Switch-hitter.

Player, Team	Avg.	G	TPA	AB	R	H	TB	2B	3B	HR	RBI	SH	SF	HP	BB	IBB	SO	SB	CS	GDP	Slg.	OBP
Abbott, Kurt, Nor.	.250	2	4	4	1	1	1	0	0	0	0	0	0	0	0	0	0	0	0	1	.250	.250
Abernathy, Brent, Syr.-Dur.	.290	119	505	449	61	130	176	27	2	5	50	6	8	5	37	1	43	23	15	7	.392	.345
Abreu, Winston, Rich.	.000	3	1	0	0	0	0	0	0	0	0	0	0	0	0	0	0	0	0	0	.000	.000
Alcantara, Israel, Paw.	.308	78	332	299	60	92	198	17	1	29	76	0	4	4	25	1	84	2	1	3	.662	.364
Alguacil, Jose, Char.*	.000	3	9	9	0	0	0	0	0	0	0	0	0	0	0	0	1	0	0	0	.000	.000
Allen, Dusty, Tol.	.222	25	96	90	9	20	31	5	0	2	12	0	0	1	5	0	27	0	2	2	.344	.271
Almonte, Wady, Roch.	.262	73	245	229	25	60	91	18	5	1	33	3	1	1	11	0	34	3	5	7	.397	.298
Alvarez, Clemente, S./W.B.	.000	5	12	11	0	0	0	0	0	0	0	0	0	0	0	0	2	0	0	1	.000	.083
Alvarez, Gabe, Tol.	.207	69	292	241	37	50	89	11	2	8	35	0	3	1	47	0	53	0	1	4	.369	.336
Amaral, Rich, Rich.	.136	7	26	22	3	3	4	1	0	0	0	0	0	0	4	0	6	0	0	1	.182	.269
Amezcua, Adan, Roch.	.235	38	148	132	9	31	41	5	1	1	14	1	1	0	14	0	25	0	0	7	.311	.306
Anderson, Marlon, S./W.B.*..	.305	103	448	397	57	121	179	18	8	8	53	2	5	5	39	12	43	24	10	2	.451	.370
Atchley, Justin, Lou.*	.143	33	23	21	1	3	4	1	0	0	2	2	0	0	0	0	5	0	0	0	.190	.143
Avery, Steve, Rich.*	.000	4	2	0	0	0	0	0	0	0	0	2	0	0	0	0	0	0	0	0	.000	.000
Azuaje, Jesus, Tol.	.217	61	265	235	32	51	72	9	0	4	13	1	2	4	23	0	17	3	2	9	.306	.295
Badeaux, Brooks, Dur.†	.327	33	108	98	11	32	36	2	1	0	3	1	0	0	9	0	21	1	0	1	.367	.383
Baez, Kevin, Nor.	.278	122	476	407	52	113	155	27	0	5	50	4	8	6	51	1	50	4	11	8	.381	.360
Banks, Willie, Nor.	.000	9	9	8	1	0	0	0	0	0	0	0	0	0	0	0	3	0	0	0	.000	.000
Barker, Kevin, Ind.*	.196	85	345	286	41	56	101	10	1	11	44	0	6	1	52	3	76	0	1	6	.353	.316
Barkett, Andy, Rich.*	.242	75	283	260	22	63	100	17	1	6	38	2	3	2	16	1	37	4	2	6	.385	.288
Baron, Jim, Nor.*	.000	2	2	1	0	0	0	0	0	0	0	0	0	0	1	0	0	0	0	0	.000	.000
Barrett, Michael, Ott.	.358	31	135	120	21	43	56	7	0	2	19	0	0	2	13	1	10	1	0	5	.467	.430
Barrios, Manny, S./W.B.	.000	47	2	2	0	0	0	0	0	0	0	1	0	0	0	0	0	0	0	0	.000	.000
Bartee, Kimera, Lou.	.298	119	514	453	69	135	186	19	4	8	48	8	3	2	48	0	64	28	11	7	.411	.366
Bates, Jason, Roch.†	.170	15	58	53	6	9	10	1	0	0	1	2	0	0	3	0	13	1	0	1	.189	.214
Battle, Howard, Lou.	.179	14	58	56	6	10	10	0	0	0	3	0	0	0	2	0	10	0	0	2	.179	.207
Belitz, Todd, Dur.*	.000	43	1	1	0	0	0	0	0	0	0	0	0	0	0	0	1	0	0	0	.000	.000
Bell, Mike, Lou.	.268	115	488	429	70	115	214	29	2	22	78	0	7	7	45	6	76	0	0	10	.499	.342
Bell, Rob, Lou.	.000	6	8	6	0	0	0	0	0	0	0	1	1	0	0	0	5	0	0	0	.000	.143
Bellinger, Clay, Col.	.321	8	30	28	3	9	11	2	0	0	2	0	0	0	2	0	5	1	0	1	.393	.367
Benitez, Yamil, Char.	.197	19	70	66	4	13	17	1	0	1	2	0	0	1	3	0	17	1	0	2	.258	.243
Bennett, Gary, S./W.B.	.306	92	369	317	47	97	157	24	0	12	52	3	2	7	40	1	44	1	0	9	.495	.393
Bennett, Shayne, Ott.	.000	22	10	9	0	0	0	0	0	0	0	1	0	0	0	0	5	0	0	0	.000	.000
Berry, Sean, Paw.-Buf.	.324	29	119	105	14	34	43	3	0	2	12	0	1	3	10	1	20	1	0	4	.410	.395
Besco, Derek, Tol.	.266	25	86	79	12	21	33	3	0	3	11	0	1	1	5	0	11	0	0	1	.418	.314
Bierek, Kurt, Ind.*	.265	128	493	430	61	114	197	22	2	19	72	1	3	2	57	5	77	1	0	9	.458	.352
Billingsley, Brent, Ott.*	.125	20	9	8	0	1	1	0	0	0	1	0	0	0	1	0	1	0	0	1	.125	.222
Blake, Casey, Lou.	.217	30	117	106	10	23	37	6	1	2	7	0	0	3	8	0	23	0	3	2	.349	.291
Blanco, Henry, Ind.	.333	1	4	3	1	1	2	1	0	0	0	0	0	0	1	0	0	0	0	1	.667	.500
Bolton, Rod, Ind.	.500	22	2	2	0	1	1	0	0	0	0	0	0	0	0	0	1	0	0	0	.500	.500
Borders, Pat, Dur.	.273	96	373	348	44	95	147	16	0	12	55	0	4	1	20	2	66	7	2	8	.422	.311
Bournigal, Rafael, Nor.	.307	19	81	75	7	23	27	4	0	0	4	1	0	0	5	2	2	1	1	3	.360	.350
Bowers, Shane, S./W.B.	.167	37	13	12	0	2	2	0	0	0	2	1	0	0	0	0	5	0	0	1	.167	.167
Bradley, Milton, Ott.†	.304	88	391	342	58	104	144	20	1	6	29	1	2	1	45	3	56	10	15	5	.421	.385
Branyan, Russell, Buf.*	.245	64	261	229	46	56	132	9	2	21	60	0	2	2	28	0	93	1	1	2	.576	.330
Brea, Lesli, Nor.	.000	1	2	2	0	0	0	0	0	0	0	0	0	0	0	0	1	0	0	0	.000	.000
Bridges, Kary, Ott.*	.338	61	245	210	35	71	95	12	3	2	27	5	2	1	27	0	7	10	3	9	.452	.413
Brinkley, Darryl, Roch.	.358	31	132	120	16	43	50	5	1	0	20	0	2	1	9	1	14	6	0	7	.417	.402
Brito, Tilson, Tol.	.265	15	56	49	4	13	17	2	1	0	7	0	1	1	5	0	12	1	0	3	.347	.339

– 387 –

Player, Team	Avg.	G	TPA	AB	R	H	TB	2B	3B	HR	RBI	SH	SF	HP	BB	IBB	SO	SB	CS	GDP	Slg.	OBP
Brown, Kevin, Syr.-Ind.	.307	74	277	261	31	80	126	20	1	8	35	0	1	1	14	1	70	0	0	8	.483	.343
Brown, Rich, Col.*	.216	10	38	37	1	8	10	2	0	0	2	0	0	1	1	0	7	0	0	1	.270	.237
Brownson, Mark, S./W.B.*	.462	33	18	13	0	6	7	1	0	0	0	5	0	0	0	1	0	0	0	0	.538	.462
Bruce, Mo, Nor.	.232	43	163	151	24	35	48	5	1	2	10	0	0	2	10	1	46	8	3	5	.318	.288
Brumfield, Jacob, Syr.-Char.	.220	62	244	223	30	49	76	16	1	3	20	0	1	1	19	0	31	5	1	7	.341	.283
Bruske, Jim, Ind.	.500	19	2	2	0	1	1	0	0	0	2	0	0	0	0	0	0	0	0	0	.500	.500
Buccheri, Jim, Dur.	.256	84	351	316	37	81	105	10	1	4	26	3	1	4	27	0	53	18	4	9	.332	.322
Buddie, Mike, Ind.	.500	30	2	2	0	1	1	0	0	0	0	0	0	0	0	0	0	0	0	0	.500	.500
Budzinski, Mark, Buf.*	.290	118	482	427	68	124	177	21	7	6	37	5	0	1	49	3	81	12	4	2	.415	.365
Burkhart, Morgan, Paw.†	.255	105	436	353	59	90	178	17	1	23	77	0	2	12	69	4	89	0	0	6	.504	.392
Burrell, Pat, S./W.B.	.294	40	176	143	31	42	71	15	1	4	25	0	1	0	32	0	36	1	1	1	.497	.420
Burton, Darren, S./W.B.†	.241	14	37	29	0	7	11	4	0	0	1	1	0	0	7	2	8	2	0	2	.379	.389
Byrd, Paul, S./W.B.	.333	3	3	3	0	1	1	0	0	0	0	0	0	0	0	0	0	0	0	1	.333	.333
Cabrera, Jolbert, Buf.	.338	20	82	74	18	25	42	6	1	3	11	1	1	1	5	0	8	2	1	0	.568	.383
Cabrera, Orlando, Ott.	.667	2	8	6	1	4	4	0	0	0	0	0	0	0	1	0	0	1	0	0	.667	.750
Calais, Ian, Ind.	.333	8	26	15	4	5	7	2	0	0	2	0	0	0	11	0	4	0	2	0	.467	.615
Camilli, Jason, Ott.	.156	21	81	77	7	12	18	4	1	0	11	0	1	0	3	0	21	0	0	1	.234	.185
Cardona, Javier, Tol.	.275	56	237	218	29	60	103	10	0	11	43	0	2	2	15	0	33	0	1	7	.472	.325
Carr, Dustin, Dur.	.219	111	428	365	38	80	107	14	2	3	36	7	3	3	49	0	61	9	2	9	.293	.314
Carroll, Jamey, Roch.	.278	91	392	349	53	97	124	17	2	2	23	6	2	2	33	1	32	6	3	9	.355	.342
Caruso, Mike, Char.*	.246	88	344	309	38	76	97	11	5	0	26	8	2	3	22	0	23	5	7	7	.314	.301
Carvajal, Jhonny, Ott.	.192	11	31	26	3	5	7	0	1	0	0	0	0	0	5	0	3	1	0	0	.269	.323
Casanova, Raul, Ind.†	.288	20	82	73	10	21	38	2	0	5	12	0	1	1	7	0	10	0	1	3	.521	.354
Casimiro, Carlos, Roch.	.222	24	85	81	9	18	34	4	0	4	10	0	0	0	4	0	16	0	0	1	.420	.259
Castilla, Vinny, Dur.	.375	2	8	8	1	3	7	1	0	1	3	0	0	0	0	0	1	0	0	0	.875	.375
Castro, Juan, Lou.	.317	19	74	60	9	19	32	5	1	2	10	1	1	0	12	3	12	0	1	3	.533	.425
Cedeno, Domingo, Nor.†	.200	3	7	5	1	1	2	1	0	0	2	0	2	0	0	0	1	0	0	0	.400	.143
Cepeda, Jose, Rich.	.200	4	16	15	2	3	3	0	0	0	0	0	0	0	1	0	2	0	0	0	.200	.250
Chamblee, Jim, Paw.	.258	127	468	407	72	105	190	26	4	17	56	2	2	7	50	1	129	8	3	4	.467	.348
Chapman, Jake, Ott.	1.000	7	1	1	1	1	1	0	0	0	1	0	0	0	0	0	0	0	0	0	1.000	1.000
Chen, Bruce, Rich.†	.000	1	3	3	0	0	0	0	0	0	0	0	0	0	0	0	0	0	0	0	.000	.000
Chevalier, Virgil, Paw.	.125	8	25	24	1	3	3	0	0	0	0	0	0	0	1	0	0	0	0	1	.125	.160
Christensen, McKay, Char.*	.264	90	382	337	49	89	124	13	2	6	29	7	5	1	32	1	51	28	6	2	.368	.325
Clark, Brady, Lou.	.304	132	577	487	90	148	249	41	6	16	79	0	9	9	72	0	51	12	8	14	.511	.390
Clark, Howie, Roch.*	.286	54	218	189	25	54	73	10	0	3	21	1	1	1	26	0	14	3	1	4	.386	.373
Clark, Tony, Tol.†	.091	6	23	22	1	2	6	1	0	1	2	0	0	0	1	0	1	0	0	0	.273	.130
Cline, Pat, Ind.	.216	11	39	37	3	8	13	2	0	1	6	0	0	0	2	0	5	0	0	3	.351	.256
Coffie, Ivanon, Roch.*	.218	21	83	78	4	17	21	2	1	0	10	1	1	1	2	0	21	0	0	1	.269	.244
Coggin, Dave, S./W.B.	.000	9	4	1	0	0	0	0	0	0	0	2	0	0	1	0	0	0	0	0	.000	.500
Coleman, Michael, Paw.	.258	18	70	66	11	17	42	5	1	6	15	0	1	0	3	0	23	3	0	0	.636	.286
Collier, Lou, Ind.	.250	17	51	56	7	14	20	4	1	0	12	1	2	1	11	0	9	2	2	1	.357	.371
Coolbaugh, Mike, Col.	.271	117	463	387	63	105	202	28	0	23	61	3	3	3	67	2	96	6	3	5	.522	.380
Coquillette, Trace, Ott.	.240	75	308	267	30	64	88	19	1	1	27	2	4	11	24	1	58	0	2	6	.330	.324
Corey, Mark, Nor.	.000	21	10	10	0	0	0	0	0	0	0	0	0	0	0	0	8	0	0	0	.000	.000
Coste, Chris, Buf.	.302	31	101	96	15	29	43	2	0	4	8	1	0	1	3	0	12	0	1	4	.448	.330
Cromer, Brandon, Ind.*	.211	23	78	71	7	15	25	3	2	1	6	0	0	0	7	2	14	1	0	3	.352	.282
Cromer, D.T., Lou.*	.270	106	456	415	58	112	186	26	3	14	67	0	7	1	33	1	84	6	4	11	.448	.320
Dalesandro, Mark, Syr.-Ind.	.184	38	109	98	11	18	25	1	0	2	8	3	1	4	3	0	11	0	0	5	.255	.236
D'Amico, Jeff, Ind.	.000	6	5	5	0	0	0	0	0	0	0	0	1	0	0	0	3	0	0	0	.000	.000
Davis, Kane, Ind.	.000	4	3	3	0	0	0	0	0	0	0	0	0	0	0	0	3	0	0	0	.000	.000
Davis, Lance, Lou.	.250	5	4	4	0	1	1	0	0	0	0	0	0	0	0	0	1	0	0	0	.250	.250
Davis, Tommy, Roch.	.287	122	514	456	65	131	203	27	0	15	64	0	6	7	45	2	93	2	1	17	.445	.356
De La Rosa, Tomas, Ott.	.203	103	390	340	27	69	84	10	1	1	36	12	5	2	31	0	43	10	3	9	.247	.270
De Leon, Jorge, Paw.	.125	5	16	16	0	2	3	1	0	0	0	0	0	0	0	0	4	0	0	1	.188	.125
De Los Santos, Eddy, Dur.	.251	78	300	271	27	68	83	4	1	3	32	5	1	2	21	0	50	3	2	9	.306	.308
Depastino, Joe, Roch.	.254	20	81	71	7	18	21	3	0	0	5	1	0	1	8	0	16	1	1	1	.296	.338
DeRosa, Mark, Rich.	.292	101	421	370	62	108	145	22	3	3	35	6	4	3	38	0	36	13	4	13	.392	.359
Dessens, Elmer, Lou.	.000	4	7	6	0	0	0	0	0	0	0	0	1	0	0	0	1	0	0	0	.000	.000
Diaz, Juan, Paw.	.279	13	51	43	11	12	33	0	0	7	17	0	2	0	6	0	9	1	0	2	.767	.353
Dishman, Richard, Rich.	.143	11	7	7	0	1	1	0	0	0	0	0	0	0	0	0	1	0	0	0	.143	.143
Dodd, Robert, Tol.*	.000	16	1	1	0	0	0	0	0	0	0	0	0	0	0	0	1	0	0	0	.000	.000
Doster, Dave, S./W.B.	.271	124	503	450	69	122	194	28	7	10	66	6	6	2	39	0	70	13	4	16	.431	.328
Dougherty, Tony, Ott.	.000	16	2	2	0	0	0	0	0	0	0	0	0	0	0	0	2	0	0	0	.000	.000
Dunn, Todd, Nor.	.215	62	187	172	20	37	68	10	0	7	19	0	0	3	12	0	67	4	2	3	.395	.278
Dykhoff, Radhames, Nor.*	.000	32	3	3	0	0	0	0	0	0	0	0	0	0	0	0	0	0	0	0	.000	.000
Easley, Damion, Tol.	.231	4	19	13	3	3	7	1	0	1	4	0	0	2	4	0	2	0	0	0	.538	.474
Ebert, Derrin, Rich.	.071	32	19	14	0	1	1	0	0	0	0	2	0	0	3	0	6	0	0	0	.071	.235
Eckstein, David, Paw.	.246	119	515	422	77	104	127	20	0	1	31	9	4	20	60	0	45	11	8	8	.301	.364
Eischen, Joey, Ott.*	.200	10	5	5	1	1	1	0	0	0	0	0	0	0	0	0	3	0	0	0	.200	.200
Encarnacion, Angelo, Paw.	.305	19	65	59	7	18	22	4	0	0	3	2	0	4	4	0	4	0	0	3	.373	.349
Estrada, Horacio, Ind.*	.176	25	21	17	4	3	3	0	0	0	1	1	0	0	3	0	3	1	0	1	.176	.300
Evans, Keith, Ott.	.000	15	4	3	1	0	0	0	0	0	0	0	0	0	0	0	1	0	0	0	.000	.250
Fernandez, Jose, Ind.	.286	133	530	468	70	134	212	37	4	11	68	1	6	4	49	0	93	10	3	11	.453	.357
Fernandez, Ozzie, Lou.	.000	10	9	7	0	0	0	0	0	0	0	0	1	0	1	0	4	0	0	0	.000	.125
Fick, Robert, Tol.*	.147	17	77	68	5	10	18	5	0	1	9	0	1	2	6	1	13	1	0	2	.265	.234
Figga, Mike, Paw.	.000	2	9	8	0	0	0	0	0	0	0	0	0	0	1	0	2	0	0	0	.000	.111
Figueroa, Nelson, S./W.B.†	.167	8	6	6	1	1	1	0	0	0	0	0	0	0	0	0	2	0	0	0	.167	.167
Flach, Jason, Rich.	.000	5	1	1	0	0	0	0	0	0	0	0	0	0	0	0	1	0	0	0	.000	.000
Fleming, Ryan, Syr.*	.182	3	11	11	1	2	2	0	0	0	1	0	0	0	0	0	1	0	0	0	.182	.182
Flury, Pat, Ott.	.000	40	3	3	0	0	0	0	0	0	0	0	0	0	0	0	1	0	0	0	.000	.000
Forbes, P.J., S./W.B.	.275	99	372	334	51	92	122	22	1	2	32	0	4	4	30	0	29	7	2	10	.365	.339
Fordham, Tom, Ind.*	.000	48	4	4	0	0	0	0	0	0	0	0	0	0	0	0	2	0	0	0	.000	.000
Fordyce, Brook, Char.	.239	17	76	67	9	16	27	5	0	2	12	0	1	0	8	0	13	0	1	2	.403	.316

Player, Team	Avg.	G	TPA	AB	R	H	TB	2B	3B	HR	RBI	SH	SF	HP	BB	IBB	SO	SB	CS	GDP	Slg.	OBP
Forster, Scott, Ott.	.000	23	2	2	0	0	0	0	0	0	0	0	0	0	0	0	1	0	0	0	.000	.000
Foster, Jim, Char.	.270	49	173	152	13	41	54	7	0	2	14	3	1	2	15	0	16	0	1	5	.355	.341
Francia, David, S./W.B.	.291	48	139	117	16	34	49	9	0	2	15	2	0	2	18	1	17	7	4	0	.419	.394
Franco, Matt, Nor.*	.137	14	54	51	3	7	8	1	0	0	1	0	0	0	3	0	10	0	0	2	.157	.185
Frank, Mike, Lou.-Col.*	.260	107	383	335	49	87	142	21	5	8	40	2	2	7	36	3	39	13	4	10	.424	.342
Fraraccio, Dan, Dur.	.174	15	55	46	6	8	8	0	0	0	4	3	0	1	5	0	6	1	1	2	.174	.269
Freel, Ryan, Syr.	.286	80	333	283	62	81	135	14	5	10	30	4	2	9	35	1	44	30	7	3	.477	.380
Garabito, Eddy, Roch.†	.086	9	37	35	3	3	4	1	0	0	0	0	0	0	2	0	10	1	0	2	.114	.135
Garcia, Carlos, Col.	.271	93	313	280	35	76	101	17	1	2	39	4	2	0	27	0	53	7	6	7	.361	.333
Garcia, Freddy, Paw.	.262	105	419	385	52	101	204	27	2	24	74	0	3	4	27	0	82	0	3	11	.530	.319
Garcia, Guillermo, Lou.	.272	102	360	327	38	89	159	24	2	14	55	1	5	2	25	1	54	2	2	9	.486	.323
Garcia, Jesse, Roch.	.242	106	420	372	44	90	109	12	2	1	23	16	1	4	27	0	60	9	4	8	.293	.300
Garcia, Karim, Tol.-Roch.*	.285	116	482	425	69	121	234	23	3	28	92	0	7	5	45	2	102	5	4	11	.551	.355
Garcia, Neil, Dur.†	.200	24	95	85	8	17	21	4	0	0	6	0	1	1	8	0	15	1	1	2	.247	.274
Gawer, Matt, Rich.*	.000	3	1	1	0	0	0	0	0	0	0	0	0	0	0	0	1	0	0	0	.000	.000
Gibralter, Steve, Char.	.253	65	258	237	33	60	106	9	2	11	37	1	2	1	17	3	54	7	0	8	.447	.304
Gillespie, Eric, Tol.*	.259	69	260	239	25	62	103	17	0	8	39	0	2	0	19	0	49	0	2	3	.431	.312
Gonzalez, Alex, Syr.	.000	1	5	5	0	0	0	0	0	0	0	0	0	0	0	0	2	0	0	0	.000	.000
Gonzalez, Gabe, Ott.	.000	14	4	4	0	0	0	0	0	0	0	0	0	0	0	0	1	0	0	0	.000	.000
Gonzalez, Lariel, Nor.	.000	52	1	0	0	0	0	0	0	0	0	0	0	0	1	0	0	0	0	0	.000	1.000
Gonzalez, Manny, Char.†	.250	2	4	4	0	1	1	0	0	0	0	0	0	0	0	0	0	0	1	0	.250	.250
Graffanino, Tony, Dur.	.286	10	42	35	9	10	19	3	0	2	6	0	0	0	7	0	8	2	0	0	.543	.405
Grahe, Joe, S./W.B.	.000	3	2	2	0	0	0	0	0	0	0	0	0	0	0	0	0	0	0	0	.000	.000
Granger, Jeff, Rich.	.000	10	1	1	0	0	0	0	0	0	0	0	0	0	0	0	1	0	0	0	.000	.000
Green, Chad, Ind.†	.203	43	137	123	18	25	46	8	2	3	10	2	1	1	10	0	36	6	2	2	.374	.267
Greene, Charlie, Syr.	.225	77	290	267	23	60	87	12	0	5	26	3	0	3	17	0	46	1	3	5	.326	.279
Greene, Rick, Lou.	.000	32	2	2	0	0	0	0	0	0	0	0	0	0	0	0	2	0	0	0	.000	.000
Greene, Todd, Syr.	.297	24	98	91	14	27	51	3	0	7	14	0	1	0	6	0	16	1	0	3	.560	.337
Gubanich, Creighton, Ind.	.284	109	422	380	48	108	190	34	0	16	71	2	3	2	35	6	95	0	1	11	.500	.345
Guerra, Mark, Nor.	.000	37	2	2	0	0	0	0	0	0	0	0	0	0	0	0	0	0	0	0	.000	.000
Guevara, Giomar, Tol.†	.282	109	439	383	61	108	156	23	2	7	33	5	3	4	44	0	65	4	5	10	.407	.359
Guillen, Jose, Dur.	.423	19	88	78	20	33	72	8	2	9	31	0	1	1	8	3	11	0	1	2	.923	.477
Hairston, Jerry, Roch.	.294	58	239	201	43	59	88	15	1	4	21	2	2	5	29	0	32	6	4	2	.438	.392
Hall, Toby, Dur.	.304	47	194	184	21	56	92	15	0	7	35	0	5	2	3	0	19	0	0	9	.500	.314
Hamilton, Darryl, Nor.*	.225	10	47	40	3	9	12	0	0	1	4	0	1	0	6	0	5	0	2	0	.300	.319
Hamilton, Joey, Syr.	.000	6	1	1	0	0	0	0	0	0	0	0	0	0	0	0	0	0	0	0	.000	.000
Hansen, Jed, Nor.-Lou.	.156	55	175	147	20	23	41	3	0	5	11	4	1	1	22	1	46	3	5	4	.279	.269
Harikkala, Tim, Ind.	.000	14	5	2	0	0	0	0	0	0	0	1	0	0	2	0	1	0	0	0	.000	.500
Harrison, Tommy, Rich.	.000	9	1	1	0	0	0	0	0	0	0	0	0	0	0	0	1	0	0	0	.000	.000
Hayes, Heath, Buf.	.128	11	43	39	4	5	9	1	0	1	5	0	2	0	2	0	16	1	0	1	.231	.163
Held, Dan, Nor.	.286	3	8	7	1	2	3	1	0	0	0	0	0	1	0	0	2	0	0	0	.429	.375
Helms, Wes, Rich.	.288	136	580	539	74	155	256	27	7	20	88	2	6	6	27	2	92	0	6	10	.475	.325
Hernandez, Jose, Ind.	.333	2	10	9	2	3	9	0	0	2	3	0	0	0	1	0	3	0	0	0	1.000	.400
Herrera, Jose, Roch.*	.295	132	599	552	79	163	224	35	7	4	54	3	3	4	37	1	73	12	8	11	.406	.342
Holbert, Aaron, Paw.	.252	80	314	294	38	74	100	13	2	3	23	1	0	4	15	0	54	8	6	4	.340	.297
Hollins, Damon, Ind.	.286	87	311	287	33	82	110	16	3	2	32	0	2	1	21	0	35	5	3	5	.383	.334
Hollins, Dave, Dur.-Roch.-Buf.†	.227	36	137	110	12	25	33	5	0	1	13	1	1	4	21	0	24	2	0	2	.300	.368
Holzemer, Mark, S./W.B.*	.000	24	4	3	0	0	0	0	0	0	0	1	0	0	0	0	1	0	0	0	.000	.000
Hoover, Paul, Dur.	.300	4	11	10	0	3	3	0	0	0	0	0	0	1	0	0	5	1	0	0	.300	.364
Horn, Jeff, Rich.	.188	13	37	32	2	6	12	3	0	1	5	1	0	1	3	0	11	0	0	0	.375	.278
Hubbard, Mike, Lou.-Rich.	.297	78	259	232	34	69	98	9	1	6	31	0	2	2	23	0	28	4	3	6	.422	.363
Hudson, Joe, Lou.	.000	29	2	2	0	0	0	0	0	0	0	0	0	0	0	0	2	0	0	0	.000	.000
Huff, Aubrey, Dur.*	.316	108	464	408	73	129	231	36	3	20	76	2	1	2	51	4	72	2	3	15	.566	.394
Hughes, Bobby, Buf.	.254	69	248	224	30	57	91	13	0	7	32	1	2	6	15	0	44	2	2	3	.406	.316
Hunter, Brian, Nor.	.125	2	9	8	2	1	4	0	0	1	1	0	0	0	1	0	1	1	0	1	.500	.222
Hunter, Scott, Ott.-Buf.	.190	8	26	21	2	4	6	2	0	0	3	1	1	1	2	0	6	1	0	0	.286	.280
Hyde, Brandon, Char.	.130	9	28	23	2	3	7	1	0	1	4	1	2	0	2	0	9	0	0	1	.304	.185
Iapoce, Anthony, Ind.†	.179	25	43	39	3	7	7	0	0	0	1	0	0	0	4	0	10	2	0	1	.179	.256
Inge, Brandon, Tol.†	.221	55	208	190	24	42	72	9	3	5	20	1	1	1	15	0	51	2	1	5	.379	.280
Inglin, Jeff, Char.	.301	45	162	146	19	44	69	8	1	5	31	1	1	2	12	0	17	3	0	7	.473	.360
Ingram, Garey, Char.	.238	103	374	311	44	74	125	17	2	10	36	5	4	9	45	1	53	5	2	9	.402	.347
Izturis, Cesar, Syr.†	.218	132	471	435	54	95	121	16	5	0	27	13	2	1	20	0	44	21	11	5	.278	.253
Jackson, Gavin, Paw.	.217	18	63	60	3	13	13	0	0	0	2	0	0	0	3	0	12	1	0	1	.217	.254
Jackson, Ryan, Dur.*	.311	139	562	502	69	156	252	38	2	18	85	2	8	0	50	4	112	6	4	8	.502	.368
Jacquez, Tom, S./W.B.*	.167	35	7	6	1	1	1	0	0	0	0	1	0	0	0	0	3	0	0	0	.167	.167
James, Kenny, Ott.†	.244	48	197	180	26	44	60	7	3	1	11	5	0	3	9	0	28	9	0	3	.333	.292
Jennings, Robin, Lou.*	.377	32	138	122	18	46	77	14	1	5	27	2	3	2	9	3	15	0	2	3	.631	.419
Jimenez, D'Angelo, Col.†	.233	21	81	73	11	17	25	3	1	1	5	0	0	1	7	1	12	2	0	2	.342	.309
Johnson, Barry, S./W.B.	.000	56	3	3	0	0	0	0	0	0	0	0	0	0	0	0	3	0	0	0	.000	.000
Johnson, Brian, Col.	.191	18	78	68	12	13	21	5	0	1	6	1	1	0	8	0	9	0	0	1	.309	.273
Johnson, Mark, Nor.*	.270	94	388	315	49	85	159	21	1	17	60	0	1	5	67	4	54	14	2	4	.505	.405
Johnson, Mike, Ott.*	.000	5	6	5	0	0	0	0	0	0	0	0	0	0	0	0	4	0	0	0	.000	.167
Jones, Bobby M., Nor.	.263	27	22	19	3	5	7	2	0	0	5	0	0	0	3	0	4	1	0	0	.368	.364
Jones, Chris, Ind.	.305	64	248	233	32	71	109	17	6	3	25	0	2	1	12	1	58	5	4	3	.468	.339
Jordan, Ricardo, Rich.*	.500	39	2	2	0	1	2	1	0	0	0	0	0	0	0	0	1	0	0	0	1.000	.500
Jose, Felix, Col.†	.310	59	235	210	31	65	119	17	2	11	38	0	1	1	23	1	60	4	3	7	.567	.379
Kieschnick, Brooks, Lou.*	.277	113	481	440	68	122	232	35	0	25	90	0	2	1	38	6	107	2	1	10	.527	.335
King, Cesar, S./W.B.	.233	43	142	129	13	30	43	7	0	2	19	1	2	2	8	0	25	0	0	4	.333	.284
King, Ray, Ind.*	.000	29	1	1	0	0	0	0	0	0	0	0	0	0	0	0	1	0	0	0	.000	.000
Kingsale, Eugene, Roch.†	.400	2	10	10	2	4	5	1	0	0	1	0	0	0	0	0	1	1	1	1	.500	.400
Kinkade, Mike, Roch.	.364	15	68	55	10	20	28	5	0	1	10	0	1	1	11	0	11	0	1	0	.509	.471
Kirby, Wayne, Roch.*	.284	129	557	507	76	144	208	24	11	6	60	1	2	1	46	5	61	10	4	12	.410	.344
Krause, Scott, Ind.	.269	67	230	208	29	56	92	15	0	7	33	1	1	5	15	1	57	1	0	2	.442	.332

Player, Team	Avg.	G	TPA	AB	R	H	TB	2B	3B	HR	RBI	SH	SF	HP	BB	IBB	SO	SB	CS	GDP	Slg.	OBP
Lamb, David, Nor.†	.225	109	419	356	45	80	111	23	1	2	35	9	6	8	40	3	49	8	3	9	.312	.312
Langaigne, Selwyn, Syr.*	.239	16	48	46	3	11	16	5	0	0	0	1	0	0	1	0	8	0	1	1	.348	.255
LaPlante, Mick, Rich.	.000	8	3	2	0	0	0	0	0	0	0	1	0	0	0	0	1	0	0	0	.000	.000
Larkin, Andy, Lou.	.000	27	2	0	0	0	0	0	0	0	0	1	0	0	1	0	0	0	0	0	.000	1.000
Larson, Brandon, Lou.	.286	17	67	63	11	18	33	7	1	2	4	0	0	0	4	0	16	0	0	1	.524	.328
LaRue, Jason, Lou.	.254	82	337	307	54	78	144	22	1	14	48	0	0	8	22	0	52	3	2	4	.469	.320
Leach, Jalal, S./W.B.*	.267	65	201	180	24	48	73	9	2	4	21	1	1	0	19	3	34	4	5	6	.406	.335
Lee, Derek, Ind.*	.000	3	1	1	0	0	0	0	0	0	0	0	0	0	0	0	0	0	0	0	.000	.000
Lee, Garrett, Rich.	.000	2	1	1	0	0	0	0	0	0	0	0	0	0	0	0	0	0	0	0	.000	.000
Lemonis, Chris, Tol.*	.215	84	307	288	30	62	98	21	3	3	23	1	0	1	17	2	53	1	1	10	.340	.261
Lennon, Pat, Ott.	.292	118	478	418	69	122	189	21	2	14	63	0	3	5	52	1	110	0	6	12	.452	.374
Leon, Donny, Col.†	.250	59	230	204	30	51	90	10	1	9	26	2	2	2	20	0	49	3	3	6	.441	.320
Levis, Jesse, Buf.*	.286	53	189	168	17	48	65	8	0	3	21	2	1	1	17	0	12	0	0	7	.387	.353
Levrault, Allen, Ind.	.077	21	15	13	0	1	1	0	0	0	0	2	0	0	0	0	7	0	0	0	.077	.077
Lewis, Richie, Nor.	.286	10	7	7	1	2	3	1	0	0	0	0	0	0	0	0	2	0	0	0	.429	.286
Liefer, Jeff, Char.*	.281	120	505	445	75	125	252	29	1	32	91	0	5	2	53	4	107	2	3	17	.566	.356
Ligtenberg, Kerry, Rich.	.000	5	1	1	0	0	0	0	0	0	0	0	0	0	0	0	1	0	0	0	.000	.000
Lindstrom, David, Tol.	.278	12	40	36	6	10	16	0	0	2	6	1	0	1	2	0	3	0	0	3	.444	.333
Lira, Felipe, Ott.	.000	4	4	3	0	0	0	0	0	0	0	0	0	0	1	0	2	0	0	0	.000	.250
Lombard, George, Rich.*	.276	112	493	424	72	117	186	25	7	10	48	5	3	6	55	3	130	32	9	3	.439	.365
Long, Ryan, Char.	.000	3	9	9	0	0	0	0	0	0	0	0	0	0	0	0	6	0	0	0	.000	.000
Lopez, Luis, Syr.	.328	130	549	499	64	161	211	27	1	7	79	0	8	2	48	1	33	3	1	10	.430	.384
Lopez, Mickey, Ind.†	.260	67	254	208	38	54	76	14	1	2	22	1	4	4	37	0	26	14	7	5	.365	.375
Loretta, Mark, Ind.	.240	10	29	25	6	6	7	1	0	0	5	0	1	0	2	0	4	0	0	1	.280	.310
Lotterhos, Chris, Lou.	.417	3	13	12	3	5	8	0	0	1	2	0	0	0	1	0	1	0	0	0	.667	.462
Loyd, Brian, Syr.	.135	22	57	52	2	7	10	0	0	1	4	0	1	1	3	0	9	0	2	2	.192	.193
Ludwick, Eric, Ind.	.300	14	12	10	2	3	6	0	0	1	2	1	0	0	1	0	1	0	0	0	.600	.364
Luebbers, Larry, Lou.	.556	19	11	9	1	5	6	1	0	0	3	1	0	0	1	0	1	0	0	0	.667	.600
Lydy, Scott, Char.	.272	116	448	368	66	100	165	15	4	14	45	0	3	8	69	3	70	15	2	9	.448	.395
Macias, Jose, Tol.†	.231	33	153	130	19	30	35	5	0	0	8	4	1	1	17	0	17	2	3	3	.269	.322
Magee, Wendell, Tol.	.571	2	8	7	1	4	5	1	0	0	1	0	0	0	1	0	1	0	1	0	.714	.625
Malave, Jaime, Ott.	.667	1	3	3	0	2	2	0	0	0	0	0	0	0	0	0	0	0	0	0	.667	.667
Malloy, Marty, Tol.	.235	30	124	115	16	27	47	8	0	4	16	1	1	0	7	0	18	0	0	0	.409	.276
Mann, Jim, Nor.	.400	49	5	5	0	2	2	0	0	0	0	0	0	0	0	0	3	0	0	0	.400	.400
Manto, Jeff, Buf.	.201	94	376	324	39	65	120	14	1	13	46	0	1	0	51	0	96	0	0	6	.370	.309
Marquez, Robert, Ott.	.000	53	4	3	0	0	0	0	0	0	0	0	0	0	1	0	2	0	0	0	.000	.250
Marquis, Jason, Rich.*	.000	6	3	3	0	0	0	0	0	0	0	0	0	0	0	0	0	0	0	0	.000	.000
Martin, Norberto, Ind.	.281	117	445	406	51	114	149	26	3	1	41	11	3	3	22	0	38	10	3	13	.367	.320
Martinez, Eddy, Roch.	.222	13	41	36	7	8	10	2	0	0	1	0	0	0	5	0	7	1	0	1	.278	.317
Martinez, Felix, Dur.†	.242	42	165	149	17	36	56	7	2	3	17	5	1	3	7	0	28	3	3	4	.376	.288
Martinez, Louis, Rich.	.169	28	77	71	3	12	17	3	1	0	2	3	1	0	2	1	12	2	0	0	.239	.189
Martinez, Pablo, Rich.†	.211	41	147	128	7	27	34	5	1	0	12	5	1	0	13	0	23	8	1	4	.266	.282
Matos, Francisco, Roch.	.279	91	352	333	37	93	121	19	3	1	24	4	1	1	13	1	34	7	3	15	.363	.307
Matos, Luis, Roch.	.171	11	40	35	2	6	7	1	0	0	0	1	0	1	3	0	8	2	0	0	.200	.256
Matos, Pascual, Rich.	.239	70	244	230	21	55	80	9	2	4	21	3	0	3	8	0	65	1	1	5	.348	.274
May, Derrick, Roch.*	.282	56	244	213	27	60	91	16	0	5	34	0	3	0	28	2	25	2	2	6	.427	.361
McClure, Brian, Tol.*	.313	16	57	48	7	15	19	2	1	0	3	0	0	0	9	0	8	1	0	0	.396	.421
McCracken, Quinton, Dur.†	.260	85	374	334	54	87	115	18	2	2	28	3	1	2	34	0	57	13	7	10	.344	.332
McDonald, Donzell, Col.†	.247	24	104	77	17	19	34	4	4	1	6	2	0	2	23	0	11	12	0	0	.442	.431
McDonald, John, Buf.	.269	75	321	286	37	77	101	17	2	1	36	7	6	1	21	1	29	4	3	7	.353	.315
McEwing, Joe, Nor.	.257	43	190	171	28	44	73	10	2	5	18	2	1	0	16	1	34	7	3	3	.427	.319
McGuire, Ryan, Nor.*	.298	122	487	392	63	117	172	23	1	10	62	1	6	1	87	5	84	6	3	3	.439	.422
McMillon, Billy, Tol.*	.345	105	457	380	61	131	202	30	1	13	50	0	4	2	71	7	65	3	1	18	.532	.446
Medina, Rafael, Syr.	.000	33	1	1	0	0	0	0	0	0	0	0	0	0	0	0	0	0	0	0	.000	.000
Mendez, Carlos, Tol.	.289	100	396	374	49	108	186	21	0	19	72	0	7	3	12	0	37	0	0	11	.497	.311
Mercado, Hector, Lou.*	.000	47	4	3	0	0	0	0	0	0	0	1	0	0	0	0	2	0	0	0	.000	.000
Merloni, Lou, Paw.	.410	11	42	39	6	16	21	2	0	1	5	0	0	0	3	0	3	0	1	2	.538	.452
Miller, David, Buf.*	.194	9	31	31	5	6	17	2	0	3	6	0	0	0	0	0	6	0	0	0	.548	.194
Minor, Ryan, Roch.	.295	68	285	241	33	71	124	9	1	14	48	0	7	5	32	2	57	1	4	4	.515	.379
Mitchell, Scott, Ott.	.313	29	20	16	4	5	8	3	0	0	1	0	0	0	4	0	3	0	0	0	.500	.450
Mix, Greg, Ind.	.000	38	4	3	0	0	0	0	0	0	0	1	0	0	0	0	1	0	0	2	.000	.000
Molina, Gabe, Rich.	.000	9	1	1	0	0	0	0	0	0	0	0	0	0	0	0	1	0	0	0	.000	.000
Monahan, Shane, Lou.*	.323	18	67	62	12	20	36	3	2	3	11	1	0	1	3	0	12	2	0	0	.581	.364
Moore, Brandon, Char.	.237	96	347	300	34	71	85	10	2	0	22	8	0	0	39	0	33	3	4	10	.283	.324
Moore, Mike, Rich.	.175	24	70	63	10	11	22	5	0	2	5	0	0	1	6	0	28	0	0	2	.349	.257
Moore, Trey, Ott.*	.182	12	14	11	1	2	2	0	0	0	0	3	0	0	0	0	3	0	0	0	.182	.182
Mora, Melvin, Nor.	.333	8	35	27	7	9	11	2	0	0	7	1	0	0	7	0	3	2	0	0	.407	.471
Morales, Willie, Roch.	.249	73	264	249	21	62	94	12	1	6	23	2	1	0	12	0	58	0	3	3	.378	.282
Morgan, Scott, Buf.	.364	11	42	33	5	12	15	3	0	0	4	0	1	1	7	0	7	1	0	1	.455	.476
Morris, Jeremy, Col.	.286	4	7	7	0	2	3	1	0	0	0	0	0	0	0	0	2	0	0	1	.429	.286
Mortimer, Mark, Rich.	.200	4	12	10	1	2	2	0	0	0	1	0	0	1	1	0	1	0	0	0	.200	.333
Mosquera, Julio, Col.	.238	35	117	101	17	24	37	6	2	1	14	1	1	6	8	0	20	6	0	3	.366	.328
Moss, Damian, Rich.	.278	30	22	18	3	5	7	2	0	0	2	1	0	0	3	0	0	0	0	0	.389	.381
Mota, Guillermo, Ott.	1.000	35	3	1	0	1	1	0	0	0	2	2	0	0	0	0	0	0	0	0	1.000	1.000
Mottola, Chad, Syr.	.309	134	552	505	85	156	286	25	3	33	102	0	5	5	37	2	99	30	15	11	.566	.359
Mouton, Lyle, Ind.	.305	52	230	197	33	60	119	23	0	12	51	0	6	4	23	2	41	4	1	7	.604	.378
Mulligan, Sean, Ott.	.220	15	52	50	3	11	15	4	0	0	3	0	1	1	0	0	7	0	0	2	.300	.231
Mummau, Rob, Syr.	.161	54	171	155	13	25	32	5	1	0	8	2	1	0	13	1	28	0	0	6	.206	.225
Munoz, Bobby, Lou.	.083	21	15	12	0	1	1	0	0	0	0	3	0	0	0	0	4	0	0	0	.083	.083
Myers, Rod, Char.*	.237	13	65	59	7	14	21	4	0	1	3	0	0	0	6	0	11	1	2	0	.356	.308
Nerei, Yuji, Ott.*	.247	55	193	162	18	40	58	10	1	2	16	0	3	1	27	3	35	0	0	5	.358	.352
Nevers, Tom, Lou.	.235	76	246	221	28	52	76	9	0	5	22	0	2	3	20	1	59	2	2	7	.344	.305
Newhan, David, S./W.B.*	.253	25	95	83	10	21	33	3	0	3	8	0	1	0	11	0	15	3	1	0	.398	.337

Player, Team	Avg.	G	TPA	AB	R	H	TB	2B	3B	HR	RBI	SH	SF	HP	BB	IBB	SO	SB	CS	GDP	Slg.	OBP
Norton, Greg, Char.†	.289	29	124	97	18	28	47	4	0	5	17	0	1	2	24	3	23	1	0	0	.485	.435
Nunnari, Talmadge, Ott.*	.281	44	161	135	17	38	52	12	1	0	12	0	1	2	23	1	31	0	1	1	.385	.391
Ochoa, Javier, Nor.	.000	1	1	1	0	0	0	0	0	0	0	0	0	0	0	0	0	0	0	0	.000	.000
Oquist, Mike, Tol.	.125	33	9	8	1	1	3	0	1	0	0	0	0	0	1	0	3	0	0	0	.375	.222
Orie, Kevin, Col.	.289	41	164	149	19	43	68	13	0	4	19	0	0	3	12	0	28	1	0	4	.456	.354
Osting, Jimmy, Rich.	.000	3	3	2	0	0	0	0	0	0	0	1	0	0	0	0	2	0	0	0	.000	.000
Otanez, Willis, Syr.	.171	22	83	76	6	13	22	3	0	2	14	0	1	0	6	0	15	0	0	4	.289	.229
Pacheco, Delvis, Rich.	.000	25	5	5	0	0	0	0	0	0	0	0	0	0	0	0	2	0	0	0	.000	.000
Patterson, Jarrod, Ott.*	.272	25	96	92	9	25	33	6	1	0	16	0	0	0	4	0	13	1	0	4	.359	.302
Patzke, Jeff, Buf.†	.248	69	250	210	35	52	76	14	2	2	18	3	2	1	34	0	57	4	1	4	.362	.352
Paul, Josh, Char.	.238	51	190	168	28	40	59	5	1	4	19	6	1	2	13	0	38	6	2	3	.351	.299
Pendergrass, Tyrone, Rich.†	.206	115	466	407	47	84	104	14	3	0	32	5	3	4	47	1	83	13	7	6	.256	.293
Peoples, Danny, Buf.	.260	124	491	420	68	109	195	19	2	21	74	0	4	4	63	1	122	2	4	8	.464	.358
Perez, Santiago, Ind.†	.275	106	457	408	74	112	167	26	7	5	34	3	1	1	44	3	96	31	8	2	.409	.346
Perez, Timoniel, Nor.*	.357	72	318	291	45	104	149	17	5	6	37	4	4	3	16	1	25	13	7	4	.512	.392
Perez, Tomas, S./W.B.†	.294	77	300	279	44	82	132	16	2	10	56	1	2	2	16	1	48	4	1	5	.473	.334
Perry, Chan, Buf.	.296	92	390	362	48	107	157	18	1	10	65	0	4	3	21	0	55	1	2	9	.434	.336
Petersen, Chris, Rich.	.226	79	275	252	12	57	67	10	0	0	21	6	1	2	14	0	42	2	4	4	.266	.271
Phillips, J.R., Char.*	.219	59	231	210	22	46	85	0	0	10	35	0	2	1	18	1	65	3	0	6	.405	.281
Pickering, Calvin, Roch.*	.218	60	237	197	20	43	71	10	0	6	30	0	2	1	36	2	70	2	2	4	.360	.339
Pickler, Jeff, Ind.*	.307	56	215	189	34	58	69	6	1	1	20	1	0	1	24	0	27	14	3	6	.365	.388
Polanco, Enohel, Buf.	.200	6	20	20	2	4	9	0	1	1	5	0	0	0	0	0	6	0	1	0	.450	.200
Politte, Cliff, S./W.B.	.063	22	19	16	3	1	2	1	0	0	0	2	0	0	1	0	3	0	0	0	.125	.118
Post, Dave, Ott.-Buf.	.257	120	451	378	46	97	141	22	5	4	43	4	1	7	61	2	46	8	3	10	.373	.369
Powell, Alonzo, Col.	.264	64	262	239	34	63	97	10	0	8	27	0	1	2	20	1	48	1	2	3	.406	.324
Powell, Corey, Paw.*	.111	3	9	9	0	1	1	0	0	0	1	0	0	0	0	0	5	0	0	0	.111	.111
Powell, Jeremy, Ott.	.133	26	18	15	1	2	3	1	0	0	3	0	0	0	0	0	4	0	0	0	.200	.133
Pratt, Scott, Buf.*	.083	4	13	12	0	1	1	0	0	0	1	0	1	0	0	0	4	0	0	1	.083	.077
Pride, Curtis, Nor.-Paw.*.	.303	63	243	185	53	56	106	12	4	10	35	5	2	2	49	1	38	15	3	3	.573	.450
Pritchett, Chris, S./W.B.*	.238	117	459	391	55	93	133	18	2	6	60	1	6	5	56	3	65	5	2	6	.340	.336
Probst, Alan, Nor.	.269	36	115	104	11	28	39	5	0	2	13	1	0	0	10	0	38	0	0	1	.375	.333
Pugh, Tim, Rich.	.100	18	10	10	0	1	1	0	0	0	1	0	0	0	0	0	3	0	0	0	.100	.100
Pulliam, Harvey, Rich.	.271	21	67	59	7	16	27	5	0	2	4	0	0	2	6	0	9	0	0	1	.458	.358
Pulsipher, Bill, Nor.*	.000	7	5	4	1	0	0	0	0	0	0	0	0	0	1	0	2	0	0	0	.000	.200
Ramirez, Hector, Ind.	.000	15	2	2	0	0	0	0	0	0	0	0	0	0	0	0	2	0	0	0	.000	.000
Ramirez, Manny, Buf.	.455	5	17	11	5	5	15	1	0	3	7	0	0	0	6	1	1	0	0	1	1.364	.647
Riedling, John, Lou.	.000	53	1	1	0	0	0	0	0	0	0	0	0	0	0	0	0	0	0	0	.000	.000
Rigby, Brad, Ott.	.231	24	13	13	2	3	3	0	0	0	1	0	0	0	0	0	3	0	0	1	.231	.231
Rivera, Luis, Rich.	.000	8	1	1	0	0	0	0	0	0	0	0	0	0	0	0	1	0	0	0	.000	.000
Rivera, Mike, Tol.	.231	4	13	13	0	3	6	3	0	0	1	0	0	0	0	0	2	0	0	0	.462	.231
Roberge, J.P., Col.	.117	29	84	77	7	9	15	3	0	1	6	1	0	1	5	0	10	0	0	1	.195	.181
Roberts, Dave, Buf.*	.292	120	532	462	93	135	196	16	3	13	55	7	2	2	59	2	68	39	11	3	.424	.373
Roberts, Grant, Nor.	.188	25	18	16	2	3	4	1	0	0	4	0	0	0	2	0	4	0	0	0	.250	.278
Roberts, Willis, Lou.	.056	25	19	18	1	1	1	0	0	0	0	1	0	0	0	0	9	0	0	0	.056	.056
Robinson, Kerry, Col.*	.318	119	491	437	71	139	174	17	9	0	32	10	1	2	41	0	40	37	18	5	.398	.378
Rodriguez, Liu, Char.†	.273	126	478	396	44	108	146	20	3	4	46	16	5	7	54	1	39	3	7	10	.369	.366
Rodriguez, Luis, Paw.	.193	28	87	83	7	16	23	4	0	1	3	1	0	0	3	0	30	1	1	1	.277	.221
Rodriguez, Rich, Paw.	.000	14	1	1	0	0	0	0	0	0	0	0	0	0	0	0	1	0	0	0	.000	.000
Rodriguez, Sammy, Nor.	.188	26	70	64	4	12	13	1	0	0	3	0	0	1	5	0	11	0	4	3	.203	.257
Rollins, Jimmy, S./W.B.†	.274	133	533	470	67	129	215	28	11	12	69	5	7	2	49	1	55	24	7	4	.457	.341
Romero, Mandy, Buf.†	.412	4	17	17	1	7	9	2	0	0	4	0	0	0	0	0	2	0	0	0	.529	.412
Roque, Rafael, Ind.*	.133	26	19	15	2	2	2	0	0	0	0	3	0	1	0	0	5	0	0	0	.133	.188
Rose, Ted, Lou.*	.333	24	5	3	0	1	1	0	0	0	1	1	1	0	0	0	0	0	0	0	.333	.250
Royster, Aaron, S./W.B.	.138	14	32	29	3	4	5	1	0	0	2	0	2	0	1	0	14	1	0	1	.172	.156
Ruebel, Matt, Ott.*	1.000	7	1	1	0	1	1	0	0	0	0	0	0	0	0	0	0	0	0	0	1.000	1.000
Rumfield, Toby, Rich.	.270	127	472	430	61	116	191	18	0	19	70	3	3	4	32	1	59	4	7	9	.444	.324
Runyan, Sean, Tol.*	.000	44	1	1	0	0	0	0	0	0	0	0	0	0	1	0	0	0	0	0	.000	1.000
Rust, Brian, Roch.	.140	14	48	43	2	6	9	3	0	0	5	0	1	1	3	0	17	0	0	2	.209	.208
Rutherford, Mark, S./W.B.	1.000	2	2	1	0	1	1	0	0	0	1	0	0	0	0	0	0	0	0	0	1.000	1.000
Sadler, Donnie, Paw.	.201	91	376	313	45	63	94	6	5	5	23	10	4	4	45	0	60	10	1	6	.300	.306
Sanchez, Alex, Dur.*	.291	107	486	446	76	130	160	18	3	2	33	3	2	5	30	1	66	52	20	6	.359	.342
Sandberg, Jared, Dur.*	.400	3	15	15	2	6	15	3	0	2	7	0	0	0	0	0	6	0	0	1	1.000	.400
Sanders, Deion, Lou.*	.200	25	121	105	13	21	33	1	1	3	7	1	1	0	14	0	9	10	4	2	.314	.292
Sandoval, Danny, Char.	.125	2	9	8	0	1	1	0	0	0	1	0	0	0	1	0	1	0	0	0	.125	.222
Sapp, Damian, Paw.	.250	5	14	12	3	3	6	0	0	1	1	0	0	0	1	0	5	0	0	0	.500	.357
Sasser, Rob, Tol.	.269	137	544	487	77	131	237	29	1	25	63	0	3	2	52	1	106	7	5	9	.487	.340
Saunders, Chris, Lou.	.174	26	76	69	6	12	15	1	1	0	2	1	1	2	3	0	12	0	0	2	.217	.227
Scanlan, Bob, Ind.	1.000	57	1	1	0	1	1	0	0	0	1	0	0	0	0	0	0	0	0	0	1.000	1.000
Schall, Gene, S./W.B.	.286	124	500	430	72	123	213	25	1	21	80	0	3	18	49	1	94	0	5	21	.495	.380
Schilling, Curt, S./W.B.	.000	1	1	1	0	0	0	0	0	0	0	0	0	0	0	0	0	0	0	0	.000	.000
Schmack, Brian, Char.	.000	51	1	1	0	0	0	0	0	0	0	0	0	0	0	0	1	0	0	0	.000	.000
Schneider, Brian, Ott.*	.248	67	265	238	22	59	99	22	3	4	31	2	9	0	16	1	42	1	0	5	.416	.285
Schrenk, Steve, S./W.B.	.000	26	1	1	0	0	0	0	0	0	0	0	0	0	0	0	1	0	0	0	.000	.000
Scott, Tim, Lou.	.000	16	1	1	0	0	0	0	0	0	0	0	0	0	0	0	1	0	0	0	.000	.000
Scutaro, Marcos, Buf.-Ind.	.283	128	523	438	72	124	175	21	6	6	57	7	7	9	62	0	55	10	6	9	.400	.378
Secoda, Jason, Char.	.000	34	1	1	0	0	0	0	0	0	0	0	0	1	0	0	0	0	0	0	.000	1.000
Seelbach, Chris, Rich.	.077	29	16	13	0	1	1	0	0	0	0	1	0	0	2	0	5	0	0	0	.077	.200
Seguignol, Fernando, Ott.†	.277	41	162	141	20	39	79	16	0	8	31	0	3	5	13	2	26	1	1	8	.560	.352
Seitzer, Brad, Char.	.293	80	318	283	42	77	130	20	0	11	42	5	4	0	46	1	47	0	1	12	.494	.393
Selby, Bill, Buf.*	.276	100	445	384	69	106	202	21	6	21	86	3	7	3	48	0	61	1	1	9	.526	.355
Sexton, Chris, Lou.	.324	99	455	389	79	126	168	19	1	7	50	1	2	0	63	0	45	8	4	14	.432	.416
Sheets, Andy, Paw.	.228	83	324	281	38	64	103	9	3	8	36	3	1	1	38	0	48	4	2	7	.367	.321
Sheets, Ben, Ind.	.000	14	5	5	0	0	0	0	0	0	0	0	0	0	0	0	2	0	0	0	.000	.000

Player, Team	Avg.	G	TPA	AB	R	H	TB	2B	3B	HR	RBI	SH	SF	HP	BB	IBB	SO	SB	CS	GDP	Slg.	OBP
Sheff, Chris, Nor.	.259	114	391	340	46	88	129	18	1	7	43	0	0	6	45	1	73	9	4	10	.379	.355
Short, Rick, Roch.	.243	13	43	37	3	9	13	1	0	1	3	0	0	2	4	0	4	0	0	0	.351	.349
Shumaker, Anthony, Nor.*	.143	22	14	14	0	2	2	0	0	0	1	0	0	0	0	0	5	0	0	0	.143	.143
Siddall, Joe, Paw.*	.234	23	86	77	7	18	31	4	0	3	14	0	1	0	8	0	16	0	0	3	.403	.302
Simon, Randall, Col.*	.266	94	406	364	52	97	176	20	4	17	74	0	7	0	35	5	42	6	5	17	.484	.325
Simons, Mitch, Nor.	.267	113	459	409	52	109	139	22	4	0	48	7	2	4	37	1	55	16	13	11	.340	.332
Sisco, Steve, Rich.	.295	75	303	275	46	81	133	16	0	12	35	3	2	2	21	2	46	3	2	4	.484	.347
Skrmetta, Matt, Ott.†	.000	32	2	2	0	0	0	0	0	0	0	0	0	0	0	0	1	0	0	0	.000	.000
Sledd, Aaron, Lou.*	.214	3	17	14	1	3	4	1	0	0	2	0	0	1	2	1	4	0	0	1	.286	.353
Small, Mark, Ott.	.000	12	3	3	0	0	0	0	0	0	0	0	0	0	0	0	2	0	0	0	.000	.000
Smith, Bobby, Dur.	.291	66	291	261	48	76	151	20	2	17	58	0	4	3	23	3	61	15	2	5	.579	.351
Smith, Dan, Rich.*	.000	53	2	2	0	0	0	0	0	0	0	0	0	0	0	0	0	0	0	0	.000	.000
Smith, Travis, Ind.	.000	3	2	1	0	0	0	0	0	0	0	1	0	0	0	0	0	0	0	0	.000	.000
Smothers, Stewart, Rich.	.056	5	19	18	3	1	1	0	0	0	0	0	0	0	1	0	9	0	0	0	.056	.105
Snusz, Chris, Ott.	.210	63	204	195	24	41	68	8	2	5	25	1	0	1	7	1	58	0	0	7	.349	.241
Snyder, John, Ind.	.000	1	2	2	0	0	0	0	0	0	0	0	0	0	0	0	0	0	0	0	.000	.000
Soderstrom, Steve, Lou.	.211	31	22	19	2	4	8	1	0	1	3	3	0	0	0	0	6	0	0	0	.421	.211
Sorensen, Zach, Buf.†	.263	12	42	38	5	10	13	1	1	0	2	0	1	0	3	0	9	1	0	2	.342	.310
Soriano, Alfonso, Col.	.290	111	495	459	90	133	213	32	6	12	66	2	6	3	25	1	85	14	7	8	.464	.327
Spehr, Tim, Paw.	.150	77	273	227	25	34	58	7	1	5	25	3	3	4	36	0	85	0	1	3	.256	.274
Springer, Dennis, Nor.	.059	25	22	17	0	1	1	0	0	0	2	3	1	0	1	0	5	0	0	1	.059	.105
Stankiewicz, Andy, Col.	.234	23	72	64	13	15	19	2	1	0	5	0	0	2	6	0	21	0	1	1	.297	.319
Staton, T.J., Ott.*	.240	47	170	146	14	35	49	5	0	3	16	0	0	1	23	3	35	2	2	2	.336	.347
Stefanski, Mike, Lou.	.229	32	103	96	12	22	35	7	0	2	10	0	0	3	4	1	17	0	0	3	.365	.282
Stenson, Dernell, Paw.*	.268	98	433	380	59	102	185	14	0	23	71	0	4	4	45	6	99	0	0	8	.487	.349
Stevens, Dave, Rich.	.200	51	5	5	0	1	1	0	0	0	0	0	0	0	0	0	2	0	0	0	.200	.200
Stevenson, Rod, Ott.	.000	10	2	2	0	0	0	0	0	0	0	0	0	0	0	0	0	0	0	1	.000	.000
Stewart, Scott, Nor.	.222	54	9	9	1	2	2	0	0	0	0	0	0	0	0	0	5	0	0	0	.222	.222
Stowers, Chris, Ott.*	.193	49	151	135	10	26	31	2	0	1	13	1	1	1	13	1	27	4	0	4	.230	.267
Stull, Everett, Ind.	.188	17	18	16	3	3	7	1	0	1	4	1	0	0	1	0	10	0	0	0	.438	.235
Swann, Pedro, Rich.*	.305	125	504	442	70	135	188	22	2	9	57	2	1	5	54	6	68	6	5	10	.425	.386
Sweeney, Mark, Ind.*	.509	18	65	55	13	28	42	8	0	2	14	0	0	0	10	0	8	0	0	3	.764	.585
Tamargo, John, Nor.†	.182	4	14	11	2	2	3	1	0	0	0	0	0	1	2	0	1	0	1	1	.273	.357
Taylor, Reggie, S./W.B.*	.275	98	454	422	60	116	187	10	8	15	43	5	4	2	21	3	87	23	12	4	.443	.310
Tebbs, Nate, Roch.†	.333	4	11	9	1	3	3	0	0	0	1	0	0	0	2	0	1	0	0	2	.333	.455
Tejero, Fausto, S./W.B.	.115	36	97	87	3	10	15	3	1	0	9	2	3	0	5	0	20	0	0	3	.172	.158
Telemaco, Amaury, S./W.B.	.000	21	14	10	0	0	0	0	0	0	0	4	0	0	0	0	4	0	0	0	.000	.000
Thomas, Evan, S./W.B.	.111	29	22	18	1	2	2	0	0	0	1	4	0	0	0	0	6	0	0	0	.111	.111
Thompson, Andy, Syr.	.246	121	491	426	59	105	202	27	2	22	65	0	6	9	50	1	95	9	2	4	.474	.334
Thompson, Ryan, Col.	.285	86	357	326	45	93	191	23	3	23	75	0	2	2	27	0	72	10	3	8	.586	.342
Thurman, Mike, Ott.	.000	4	2	1	0	0	0	0	0	0	0	0	0	0	1	0	1	0	0	0	.000	.500
Timmons, Ozzie, Dur.	.300	137	591	506	100	152	273	32	1	29	104	0	5	7	73	5	105	5	4	6	.540	.393
Toca, Jorge, Nor.	.272	120	477	453	58	123	187	25	3	11	70	0	3	4	17	3	72	9	8	18	.413	.302
Tomberlin, Andy, Buf.*	.333	11	40	30	4	10	16	2	2	0	6	0	0	2	8	1	6	0	0	0	.533	.500
Toth, Dave, Char.	.221	46	155	131	15	29	41	6	0	2	23	3	3	1	17	0	14	0	0	2	.313	.309
Tracy, Andy, Ott.*	.308	55	234	195	28	60	108	18	0	10	36	0	3	2	34	3	63	2	2	2	.554	.410
Turner, Chris, Col.	.273	14	47	44	6	12	21	3	0	2	3	0	0	0	3	0	11	0	0	2	.477	.319
Tyler, Brad, Ind.*	.248	113	445	371	59	92	138	16	3	8	49	1	5	1	67	9	63	13	3	4	.372	.360
Tyner, Jason, Nor.*	.321	84	369	327	54	105	114	5	2	0	28	8	2	2	30	1	32	33	14	3	.349	.380
Unroe, Tim, Rich.	.278	121	455	418	59	116	220	28	2	24	87	1	2	7	27	0	114	2	4	10	.526	.330
Valencia, Vic, Col.	.250	15	50	48	6	12	25	1	0	4	9	0	0	0	2	0	19	0	0	1	.521	.280
Valera, Yohanny, Ott.	.147	21	74	68	6	10	17	1	0	2	10	0	0	2	4	0	19	0	0	1	.250	.216
Velandia, Jorge, Nor.	.100	4	11	10	0	1	1	0	0	0	0	0	0	0	1	0	1	1	0	0	.100	.182
Veras, Wilton, Paw.	.211	60	234	218	18	46	64	9	0	3	25	1	1	2	12	1	18	0	1	6	.294	.258
Villafuerte, Brandon, Tol.	.000	46	1	0	0	0	0	0	0	0	0	0	0	0	1	0	0	0	0	0	.000	1.000
Villalobos, Carlos, Tol.	.125	18	59	48	2	6	8	0	1	0	4	2	0	0	9	0	12	0	0	1	.167	.263
Villegas, Ismael, Rich.	.333	41	3	3	0	1	1	0	0	0	0	0	0	0	0	0	0	0	0	0	.333	.333
Vinas, Julio, Paw.	.252	29	117	107	14	27	44	5	0	4	16	0	0	1	9	1	20	1	0	2	.411	.316
Wakeland, Chris, Tol.*	.270	141	561	492	65	133	246	25	2	28	76	0	5	4	60	6	148	4	5	8	.500	.351
Walker, Tyler, Nor.	.333	5	3	3	0	1	1	0	0	0	0	0	0	0	0	0	1	0	0	0	.333	.333
Watkins, Pat, Tol.	.250	77	330	304	50	76	112	12	0	8	36	3	2	2	19	0	28	2	4	13	.368	.297
Weber, Neil, Lou.*	1.000	2	1	1	0	1	1	0	0	0	0	0	0	0	0	0	0	0	0	0	1.000	1.000
Wells, Vernon, Syr.	.243	127	551	493	76	120	213	31	7	16	66	1	5	4	48	1	88	23	4	8	.432	.313
Wengert, Don, Rich.	.111	29	15	9	0	1	2	1	0	0	0	3	0	0	3	0	4	0	0	0	.222	.333
Wheeler, Dan, Dur.	.000	26	2	1	0	0	0	0	0	0	0	1	0	0	0	0	0	0	0	1	.000	.000
Whiten, Mark, Buf.†	.276	98	389	355	59	98	157	27	1	10	39	0	1	0	33	1	72	5	2	6	.442	.337
Wilcox, Luke, Col.*	.219	106	390	343	48	75	131	13	2	13	49	0	7	2	38	1	58	6	2	7	.382	.295
Wilkerson, Brad, Ott.*	.250	63	261	212	40	53	102	11	1	12	35	0	1	3	45	1	60	5	4	0	.481	.387
Williams, Jason, Lou.	.261	121	452	391	50	102	130	16	0	4	33	5	3	9	44	2	48	2	2	15	.332	.347
Wilson, Craig, Char.	.370	62	270	230	43	85	112	14	2	3	34	0	4	4	32	0	26	0	1	7	.487	.448
Wilson, Desi, Char.*	.269	124	496	439	58	118	152	23	1	3	55	0	2	4	51	2	79	17	4	11	.346	.349
Wilson, Paul, Nor.	.100	17	14	10	0	1	2	1	0	0	2	3	1	0	0	0	8	0	0	0	.200	.091
Wilson, Tom, Col.	.276	104	407	330	63	91	171	20	0	20	71	0	1	3	73	1	114	2	2	9	.518	.410
Wilson, Vance, Nor.	.260	111	440	400	47	104	177	23	1	16	62	1	3	12	24	1	65	11	6	12	.443	.319
Winchester, Scott, Lou.	.000	43	1	0	0	0	0	0	0	0	0	0	0	0	1	0	0	0	0	0	.000	1.000
Winkelsas, Joe, Rich.	.000	4	1	1	0	0	0	0	0	0	0	0	0	0	0	0	0	0	0	0	.000	.000
Winn, Randy, Dur.†	.330	79	358	303	67	100	155	24	5	7	40	3	1	3	48	1	53	18	5	5	.512	.425
Witt, Kevin, Syr.*	.247	135	539	489	58	121	233	24	5	26	72	1	0	4	45	6	132	1	1	9	.476	.316
Woods, Ken, S./W.B.	.303	133	565	512	89	155	201	28	6	2	35	8	1	5	39	0	47	20	7	7	.393	.357
Woodward, Chris, Syr.	.322	37	155	143	23	46	78	13	2	5	25	1	0	0	11	0	30	2	0	2	.545	.370
Wright, Jamey, Ind.	.000	1	2	1	0	0	0	0	0	0	0	1	0	0	0	0	1	0	0	0	.000	.000
Wright, Ron, Lou.	.200	18	68	60	10	12	23	5	0	2	13	0	0	0	8	0	18	0	0	1	.383	.294
Yarnall, Ed, Lou.*	.000	11	2	2	0	0	0	0	0	0	0	0	0	0	0	0	0	0	0	0	.000	.000
Zuber, Jon, Col.*	.293	87	355	294	36	86	104	15	0	1	39	3	2	4	52	7	28	9	2	8	.354	.403

GRAND SLAMS: M. Bell, Branyan, F. Garcia, Peoples, Unroe, Wakeland, T. Wilson, 2 each; Barker, Bartee, Bierek, Cardona, Coleman, Doster, Frank, Freel, Graffanino, Guillen, Helms, Hubbard, Inglin, Kieschnick, Larue, Minor, To. Perez, Perry, Phillips, Roberge, D. Roberts, Rollins, Rumfield, Schall, Schneider, Soriano, Stenson, Stull, A. Thompson, R. Thompson, Tyler, Veras, Watkins, Wilkerson, V. Wilson, R. Wright, 1 each.

AWARDED FIRST BASE ON CATCHER'S INTERFERENCE: Carr (Gubanich); Frank (Hubbard); Pickering (Dalesandro).

PLAYERS WITH TWO OR MORE TEAMS

Player, Team	Avg.	G	TPA	AB	R	H	TB	2B	3B	HR	RBI	SH	SF	HP	BB	IBB	SO	SB	CS	GDP	Slg.	OBP
Abernathy, Brent, Syr.	.296	92	391	358	47	106	143	21	2	4	35	3	1	26	1		32	14	13	7	.399	.343
Abernathy, Brent, Dur.	.264	27	114	91	14	24	33	6	0	1	15	3	5	4	11	0	11	9	2	0	.363	.351
Berry, Sean, Paw.	.368	16	65	57	12	21	30	3	0	2	4	0	0	2	6	1	17	0	0	1	.526	.446
Berry, Sean, Buf.	.271	13	54	48	2	13	13	0	0	0	8	0	1	1	4	0	3	1	0	3	.271	.333
Brown, Kevin, Syr.	.335	51	188	179	26	60	98	15	1	7	29	0	1	0	8	1	46	0	0	5	.547	.362
Brown, Kevin, Ind.	.244	23	89	82	5	20	28	5	0	1	6	0	0	1	6	0	24	0	0	3	.341	.303
Brumfield, Jacob, Syr.	.233	11	45	43	5	10	18	3	1	1	4	0	0	2	0		7	1	0	2	.419	.267
Brumfield, Jacob, Char.	.217	51	199	180	25	39	58	13	0	2	16	0	1	1	17	0	24	4	1	5	.322	.286
Dalesandro, Mark, Syr.	.333	1	3	3	1	1	4	0	0	1	1	0	0	0	0	0	1	0	0	0	1.333	.333
Dalesandro, Mark, Ind.	.179	37	106	95	10	17	21	1	0	1	7	3	1	4	3	0	10	0	0	5	.221	.233
Frank, Mike, Lou.*	.274	62	223	197	30	54	92	16	2	6	28	1	1	4	20	2	26	8	1	5	.467	.351
Frank, Mike, Col.*	.239	45	160	138	19	33	50	5	3	2	12	1	1	3	16	1	13	5	3	5	.362	.329
Garcia, Karim, Tol.*	.297	40	172	155	31	46	101	6	2	15	38	0	3	3	11	1	32	2	1	4	.652	.349
Garcia, Karim, Roch.*	.278	76	310	270	38	75	133	17	1	13	54	0	4	2	34	1	70	3	3	7	.493	.358
Hansen, Jed, Nor.	.146	39	119	96	13	14	28	2	0	4	9	3	1	1	18	1	31	2	4	2	.292	.284
Hansen, Jed, Lou.	.176	16	56	51	7	9	13	1	0	1	2	1	0	0	4	0	15	1	1	2	.255	.236
Hollins, Dave, Dur.†	.185	11	40	27	4	5	10	2	0	1	3	0	0	3	10	0	6	1	0	1	.370	.450
Hollins, Dave, Roch.†	.271	20	82	70	8	19	21	2	0	0	8	1	1	1	9	0	12	1	0	0	.300	.358
Hollins, Dave, Buf.†	.077	5	15	13	0	1	2	1	0	0	2	0	0	0	2	0	6	0	0	1	.154	.200
Hubbard, Mike, Lou.	.375	8	9	8	1	3	4	1	0	0	0	0	0	0	1	0	4	0	0	0	.500	.444
Hubbard, Mike, Rich.	.295	70	250	224	33	66	94	8	1	6	31	0	2	2	22	0	24	4	3	6	.420	.360
Hunter, Scott, Ott.	.200	7	24	20	2	4	6	2	0	0	3	1	1	1	1	0	5	1	0	0	.300	.261
Hunter, Scott, Buf.	.000	1	2	1	0	0	0	0	0	0	0	0	0	1	0		1	0	0	0	.000	.500
Post, Dave, Ott.	.254	115	430	362	45	92	136	22	5	4	43	4	1	7	56	2	44	8	3	10	.376	.364
Post, Dave, Buf.	.313	5	21	16	1	5	5	0	0	0	0	0	0	0	5	0	2	0	0	0	.313	.476
Pride, Curtis, Nor.*	.290	15	43	31	9	9	18	2	2	1	4	0	0	1	11	0	7	3	2	0	.581	.488
Pride, Curtis, Paw.*	.305	48	200	154	44	47	88	10	2	9	31	5	2	1	38	1	31	12	1	3	.571	.441
Scutaro, Marcos, Buf.	.275	124	509	425	67	117	162	20	5	5	54	7	7	9	61	0	53	9	6	8	.381	.373
Scutaro, Marcos, Ind.	.538	4	14	13	5	7	13	1	1	1	3	0	0	0	1	0	2	1	0	1	1.000	.571

2000 PITCHING

TEAM

Team	W	L	Pct.	ERA	G	CG	ShO	Sv.	IP	H	TBF	R	ER	HR	SH	SF	HB	BB	IBB	SO	WP	Bk.
Scranton/W.-B.	85	60	.586	3.63	145	14	10	34	1281.1	1184	5397	567	517	112	55	30	42	466	25	936	43	6
Syracuse	74	66	.529	3.89	140	16	9	35	1208.2	1137	5157	583	523	112	37	37	40	515	10	825	42	5
Charlotte	78	65	.545	3.96	143	5	8	42	1230.0	1233	5277	605	541	149	42	30	51	439	24	847	57	13
Indianapolis	81	63	.563	3.97	144	7	7	45	1270.0	1239	5511	644	560	132	58	43	54	530	23	879	73	5
Pawtucket	82	61	.573	4.13	143	11	9	35	1249.2	1206	5242	637	574	141	39	41	45	388	22	925	40	8
Rochester	65	79	.451	4.16	144	6	8	31	1253.2	1216	5397	675	580	141	36	41	58	483	11	944	53	12
Norfolk	65	79	.451	4.22	144	11	6	29	1270.0	1299	5534	697	596	113	42	40	55	508	44	895	75	9
Buffalo	86	59	.593	4.29	145	5	7	45	1235.0	1319	5404	654	589	125	40	41	46	456	21	838	55	6
Louisville	71	73	.493	4.31	145	5	7	36	1277.0	1321	5582	698	611	116	41	50	34	529	20	880	62	6
Columbus	75	69	.521	4.50	144	17	8	39	1245.0	1271	5485	700	623	132	43	52	40	531	26	970	69	22
Durham	81	62	.566	4.58	143	0	8	50	1251.0	1323	5516	719	636	144	32	25	55	534	23	871	62	6
Richmond	51	92	.357	5.08	143	3	2	23	1242.0	1390	5563	782	701	132	51	61	54	542	21	885	67	11
Toledo	55	86	.390	5.22	141	8	6	22	1203.0	1331	5402	808	698	155	32	56	45	552	13	869	59	6
Ottawa	53	88	.376	5.26	141	1	5	31	1195.2	1364	5411	795	699	132	43	46	71	515	12	789	60	12

INDIVIDUAL

TOP QUALIFIERS FOR EARNED-RUN AVERAGE TITLE

Minimum 115 innings. *Lefthanded pitcher.

Pitcher, Team	W	L	Pct.	ERA	G	GS	CG	ShO	GF	Sv.	IP	H	TBF	R	ER	HR	SH	SF	HB	BB	IBB	SO	WP	Bk.
Ohka, Tomo, Paw.	9	6	.600	2.96	19	19	3	2	0	0	130.2	111	513	52	43	15	2	7	3	23	1	78	2	0
Krivda, Rick, Roch.*	11	9	.550	3.12	26	26	0	0	0	0	152.2	142	645	75	53	15	3	8	3	61	0	99	5	0
Moss, Damian, Rich.*	9	6	.600	3.14	29	28	0	0	0	0	160.2	130	710	67	56	14	8	5	6	106	0	123	10	2
Taylor, Kerry, Syr.	9	8	.529	3.32	33	17	4	2	2	0	135.2	119	578	57	50	16	8	2	5	61	2	83	2	0
Estrada, Horacio, Ind.*	14	4	.778	3.33	25	25	3	2	0	0	159.1	149	663	63	59	14	7	2	7	45	0	103	9	0
Roberts, Grant, Nor.	7	8	.467	3.38	25	25	5	0	0	0	157.1	154	686	67	59	16	7	3	8	63	5	115	12	2
Towers, Josh, Roch.	8	6	.571	3.47	24	24	5	1	0	0	148.0	157	618	63	57	17	2	4	8	21	0	102	1	1
Thomas, Evan, S./W.B.	13	10	.565	3.53	29	27	3	2	1	0	171.0	163	720	70	67	17	4	0	6	50	1	127	7	0
Chantres, Carlos, Char.	10	4	.714	3.53	29	22	0	0	2	0	142.2	136	601	59	56	12	4	4	8	54	2	85	8	2
Telemaco, Amaury, S./W.B.	8	3	.727	3.87	21	21	0	0	0	0	123.1	115	514	60	53	15	4	4	0	42	0	88	5	0
Roque, Rafael, Ind.*	9	4	.692	4.15	21	21	1	1	0	0	132.1	127	576	66	61	18	7	2	6	63	1	111	2	0
Yarnall, Ed, Col.-Lou.*	5	5	.500	4.15	21	21	1	0	0	0	117.0	115	516	59	54	11	5	5	6	60	1	93	4	0
Lilly, Ted, Col.*	8	11	.421	4.19	22	22	3	1	0	0	137.1	157	610	77	64	14	6	5	4	48	0	127	5	4
Jones, Bobby M., Nor.*	10	8	.556	4.32	22	21	4	1	0	0	133.1	122	572	66	64	13	0	3	5	58	4	100	6	1
Springer, Dennis, Nor.	5	5	.500	4.38	25	17	1	1	1	0	117.0	120	501	65	57	15	3	4	6			35	7	1

DEPARTMENTAL LEADERS: W—Estrada, 14; L—Oquist, 15; Pct.—Garland, .818; G—Tessmer, 60; GS—Moss, 28; CG—Knight, 8; ShO—Ohka, K. Taylor, Estrada, Thomas, 2; GF—Tessmer, 53; Sv.—Scanlan, 35; IP—Knight, 184.2; H—Oquist, 214; TBF—Knight, 783; R—Wheeler, 109; ER—Powell, Daneker, 97; HR—Wheeler, 35; SH—Tessmer, Moss, K. Taylor, 8; SF—Dingman, Soderstrom, Krivda, Shumaker, 8; HB—Davenport, Marquez, 11; BB—Moss, 106; IBB—Tessmer, Guerra, 7; SO—Knight, 138; WP—Bradley, G. Roberts, Villafuerte, 12; BK—Several tied at 4.

CLASS AAA International League

ALL PITCHERS

*Lefthanded pitcher.

Pitcher, Team	W	L	Pct.	ERA	G	GS	CG	ShO	GF	Sv.	IP	H	TBF	R	ER	HR	SH	SF	HB	BB	IBB	SO	WP	Bk.
Abreu, Winston, Rich.	0	1	.000	7.00	3	0	0	0	0	0	9.0	7	42	8	7	2	1	1	1	10	0	5	0	0
Acevedo, Juan, Ind.	0	0	.000	0.00	2	2	0	0	0	0	4.0	3	15	0	0	0	0	0	0	0	0	4	1	0
Adams, Willie, Paw.	0	2	.000	5.47	22	0	0	0	15	4	26.1	38	124	18	16	4	2	0	1	7	2	21	0	0
Agosto, Stevenson, Dur.*	0	0	.000	0.00	1	0	0	0	0	0	4.0	0	12	0	0	0	0	0	0	1	0	4	0	0
Almonte, Wady, Roch.	0	0	.000	0.00	1	0	0	0	1	0	1.0	2	5	0	0	0	0	0	0	0	0	0	0	0
Andrews, Clayton, Syr.*	8	7	.533	4.82	19	18	0	0	0	0	102.2	114	449	56	55	8	2	3	2	42	0	59	1	2
Armas, Tony, Ott.	1	2	.333	3.79	4	4	0	0	0	0	19.0	22	83	11	8	3	0	0	2	4	0	12	0	0
Arteaga, J.D., Nor.*	1	0	1.000	1.59	1	1	0	0	0	0	5.2	4	23	1	1	0	0	0	0	2	0	1	0	0
Atchley, Justin, Lou.*	8	6	.571	5.89	30	19	0	0	5	0	122.1	168	547	83	80	19	2	5	3	26	1	69	8	0
Averette, Robert, Lou.	0	1	.000	8.38	2	2	0	0	0	0	9.2	9	49	10	9	1	1	1	0	10	0	4	0	0
Avery, Steve, Rich.*	1	3	.250	9.43	4	4	0	0	0	0	21.0	23	101	25	22	3	1	1	0	17	0	8	0	0
Aybar, Manny, Lou.	0	3	.000	13.50	3	2	0	0	0	0	6.2	10	39	10	10	0	0	0	0	10	0	1	1	1
Bacsik, Mike, Buf.*	0	3	.000	5.59	5	5	0	0	0	0	29.0	31	124	20	18	7	0	2	0	7	0	9	0	0
Bale, John, Syr.*	3	4	.429	3.19	21	12	0	0	0	0	79.0	68	338	35	28	4	1	3	2	41	0	70	4	0
Banks, Willie, Nor.	2	4	.333	5.08	9	9	0	0	0	0	51.1	56	224	32	29	5	0	2	5	25	2	20	5	1
Barcelo, Lorenzo, Char.	5	6	.455	4.26	17	17	0	0	0	0	99.1	114	433	53	47	20	1	4	4	17	1	62	3	2
Barkley, Brian, Paw.*	0	0	.000	4.50	2	0	0	0	1	0	4.0	3	15	2	2	0	0	1	0	1	0	1	0	0
Barnett, Marty, Dur.	3	3	.500	8.40	16	3	0	0	2	0	30.0	43	158	29	28	3	4	2	2	27	0	24	2	0
Baron, Jim, Nor.*	0	1	.000	14.73	2	2	0	0	0	0	7.1	26	50	15	12	1	0	0	1	4	1	3	1	0
Barrios, Manny, S./W.B.	6	5	.545	4.92	47	0	0	0	21	4	64.0	71	288	35	35	6	2	1	2	31	3	60	5	0
Beasley, Ray, Rich.*	0	2	.000	7.20	4	0	0	0	2	0	5.0	11	26	9	4	2	0	0	2	2	0	2	0	0
Beck, Rod, Paw.	1	0	1.000	0.00	3	0	0	0	0	0	6.0	4	22	0	0	0	0	0	0	0	0	5	0	0
Becks, Ryan, Ott.*	0	1	.000	9.75	3	1	0	0	0	0	12.0	21	64	16	13	5	0	0	0	7	0	4	1	0
Beirne, Kevin, Char.	2	3	.333	3.51	7	7	0	0	0	0	33.1	39	143	13	13	3	1	0	2	7	0	28	5	0
Belitz, Todd, Dur.*	1	1	.500	3.83	43	0	0	0	6	2	47.0	33	199	24	20	1	1	3	2	28	1	46	1	0
Bell, Jason, Syr.	3	4	.429	4.97	22	3	0	0	7	0	41.2	41	175	25	23	3	3	4	1	16	1	28	2	0
Bell, Rob, Lou.	4	0	1.000	3.73	6	6	0	0	0	0	41.0	35	170	18	17	6	0	1	3	13	0	47	1	0
Bennett, Joel, Paw.	1	1	.500	5.08	19	0	0	0	3	0	33.2	37	147	21	19	5	2	3	1	15	1	29	0	0
Bennett, Shayne, Ott.	3	5	.375	6.29	22	15	0	0	0	0	78.2	94	375	61	55	13	3	3	2	45	2	54	4	0
Bernero, Adam, Tol.	3	1	.750	2.47	7	7	1	1	0	0	47.1	34	182	16	13	5	0	3	0	10	0	37	1	0
Bertotti, Mike, Col.*	1	1	.500	4.50	7	3	0	0	2	0	24.0	23	104	16	12	2	0	0	0	8	0	23	2	0
Beverlin, Jason, Col.	0	3	.000	18.90	3	3	0	0	0	0	6.2	13	45	14	14	1	0	0	0	14	0	6	1	0
Billingsley, Brent, Ott.*	8	9	.471	5.66	20	20	0	0	0	0	103.1	118	464	73	65	14	4	2	3	46	0	76	7	0
Bogott, Kurt, Syr.*	1	0	1.000	4.01	20	0	0	0	6	1	24.2	25	109	12	11	4	2	1	4	12	1	17	2	0
Bolton, Rod, Ind.	2	6	.250	5.43	22	5	0	0	5	0	56.1	66	252	35	34	9	2	2	1	21	2	37	4	0
Borkowski, Dave, Tol.	3	1	.750	4.40	8	8	0	0	0	0	47.0	44	202	27	23	9	0	1	3	14	0	29	2	0
Bowers, Cedrick, Dur.*	3	1	.750	5.49	4	4	0	0	0	0	19.2	21	92	13	12	2	0	0	0	13	0	20	1	0
Bowers, Shane, S./W.B.	8	7	.533	4.65	36	17	3	0	4	1	137.1	129	567	73	71	19	3	1	2	37	1	99	4	1
Boyd, Jason, S./W.B.	1	0	1.000	1.72	11	2	0	0	1	0	15.2	8	66	3	3	1	0	0	0	14	0	10	1	0
Bradford, Chad, Char.	2	4	.333	1.51	55	0	0	0	25	10	53.2	38	212	18	9	2	5	2	3	12	1	42	1	0
Bradley, Ryan, Col.	5	1	.833	5.82	49	0	0	0	15	0	72.2	82	346	52	47	11	4	2	7	52	1	54	12	1
Brammer, J.D., Buf.	2	0	1.000	4.79	25	0	0	0	13	0	35.2	38	156	21	19	2	1	2	3	17	0	28	5	0
Brantley, Jeff, S./W.B.	0	0	.000	3.60	5	1	0	0	1	0	5.0	3	19	2	2	1	0	0	0	1	0	4	0	0
Brea, Lesli, Nor.-Roch.	1	2	.333	4.81	5	5	0	0	0	0	24.1	31	118	20	13	3	0	1	2	12	0	17	2	0
Brewer, Billy, Roch.*	0	2	.000	3.97	9	0	0	0	4	0	11.1	13	54	5	5	3	0	0	0	7	0	3	0	0
Brewington, Jamie, Buf.	1	0	1.000	3.04	17	0	0	0	6	0	23.2	19	99	8	8	3	0	1	0	12	0	25	1	0
Brower, Jim, Buf.	9	4	.692	3.11	16	15	1	0	0	0	101.1	99	425	41	35	7	4	3	3	24	1	68	2	0
Brown, Elliot, Dur.	0	1	.000	9.00	1	0	0	0	1	0	1.0	1	6	1	1	0	0	0	0	2	0	1	0	0
Brownson, Mark, S./W.B.	10	8	.556	4.55	31	20	4	0	4	0	132.2	134	556	70	67	15	4	6	6	36	1	104	2	3
Bruske, Jim, Ind.	2	4	.333	9.28	19	2	0	0	4	1	32.0	47	159	36	33	9	3	2	3	14	2	22	2	0
Buddie, Mike, Col.-Ind.	8	5	.615	4.28	36	6	0	0	7	2	88.1	74	390	50	42	12	3	4	5	49	2	55	6	0
Bullinger, Kirk, S./W.B.	0	1	.000	0.72	26	0	0	0	21	12	25.0	19	99	4	2	0	3	0	1	10	2	16	0	0
Busby, Mike, Ind.	2	1	.667	11.52	19	2	0	0	6	0	27.1	49	165	42	35	5	2	5	5	25	3	14	5	0
Byrd, Paul, S./W.B.	2	0	1.000	1.73	3	3	2	0	0	0	26.0	20	101	6	5	2	1	0	1	6	0	10	0	1
Cairncross, Cameron, Buf.*	0	1	.000	2.25	15	0	0	0	6	1	8.0	11	36	2	2	1	0	0	4	1	0	11	0	0
Callaway, Mickey, Dur.	11	6	.647	5.29	26	20	0	0	0	0	117.1	151	542	88	69	11	1	7	2	50	2	64	2	2
Cammack, Eric, Nor.	6	2	.750	1.70	47	0	0	0	27	9	63.2	38	259	14	12	2	3	0	2	31	3	67	2	1
Camp, Jared, Buf.	0	0	.000	2.25	3	0	0	0	2	0	4.0	5	20	2	1	0	1	0	1	2	0	1	0	0
Castillo, Carlos, Paw.	2	3	.400	4.66	16	4	0	0	4	0	48.1	42	195	26	25	9	3	1	2	8	1	27	0	1
Chantres, Carlos, Char.	10	4	.714	3.53	29	22	0	0	2	0	142.2	136	601	59	56	12	4	4	8	54	2	85	8	2
Chapman, Jake, Ott.*	1	0	1.000	2.08	7	1	0	0	0	0	8.2	9	40	2	2	0	0	0	0	5	0	8	0	0
Charlton, Norm, Lou.*	0	0	.000	0.00	4	0	0	0	2	0	2.2	0	10	0	0	0	0	0	0	2	0	5	1	0
Chen, Bruce, Rich.*	1	0	1.000	0.00	1	1	0	0	0	0	6.0	5	22	0	0	0	0	0	0	1	0	6	1	0
Cho, Jin Ho, Paw.	4	3	.571	4.65	13	9	1	0	2	0	71.2	77	298	37	37	9	3	2	0	13	3	37	0	0
Choate, Randy, Col.*	2	0	1.000	2.04	33	0	0	0	6	0	35.1	34	151	8	8	2	0	0	3	14	3	37	0	0
Clark, Howie, Roch.	0	0	.000	0.00	1	0	0	0	0	0	1.0	1	5	0	0	0	0	0	0	1	0	0	0	0
Clemons, Chris, Buf.	6	3	.667	4.42	12	12	0	0	0	0	59.0	68	264	34	29	8	4	3	6	24	1	39	4	0
Coggin, Dave, S./W.B.	3	2	.600	4.34	9	9	0	0	0	0	45.2	35	204	27	22	2	3	1	5	33	0	27	4	0
Colon, Bartolo, Buf.	1	0	1.000	1.80	1	1	0	0	0	0	5.0	6	21	1	1	0	0	0	0	0	0	4	0	0
Corbin, Archie, Char.	2	0	1.000	4.22	8	0	0	0	2	0	10.2	13	50	8	5	1	0	1	0	6	0	11	1	0
Corey, Mark, Nor.	3	7	.300	6.79	20	11	0	0	2	0	63.2	80	303	52	48	11	2	3	8	29	1	43	4	0
Cornett, Brad, Dur.	4	5	.444	4.26	19	12	0	0	3	0	88.2	100	383	46	42	7	1	2	2	24	1	72	1	1
Corsi, Jim, Roch.	0	0	.000	14.54	5	0	0	0	3	1	4.1	7	23	7	7	1	0	0	0	3	0	1	1	0
Crawford, Joe, Ind.*	0	0	.000	27.00	3	0	0	0	0	0	0.2	3	6	2	2	1	0	0	0	1	0	1	0	0
Crawford, Paxton, Paw.	7	4	.636	4.55	12	11	1	1	1	0	61.1	47	252	32	31	6	6	2	6	22	1	47	0	0
Creek, Doug, Dur.*	0	0	.000	1.96	10	1	0	0	2	0	18.1	10	80	5	4	1	0	0	0	14	0	22	4	0
Croushore, Rich, Paw.	0	1	.000	3.43	11	0	0	0	5	0	21.0	16	87	8	8	1	0	0	0	10	0	23	2	0
Cruz, Nelson, Tol.	2	4	.333	4.82	11	10	0	0	1	0	52.1	54	229	37	28	9	2	3	1	17	0	39	1	0
Cubillan, Darwin, Syr.	3	1	.750	0.55	24	0	0	0	14	8	32.2	14	123	2	2	0	1	0	1	13	1	41	1	0

Pitcher, Team	W	L	Pct.	ERA	G	GS	CG	ShO	GF	Sv.	IP	H	TBF	R	ER	HR	SH	SF	HB	BB	IBB	SO	WP	Bk.
Dale, Carl, Buf.	0	0	.000	5.79	7	0	0	0	5	0	14.0	17	68	9	9	1	0	0	0	9	0	6	1	0
D'Amico, Jeff, Ind.	1	1	.500	3.16	6	6	0	0	0	0	31.1	25	125	11	11	6	0	0	0	11	0	20	0	0
Daneker, Pat, Char.-Syr.	9	13	.409	5.54	29	27	0	0	0	0	157.2	186	691	108	97	28	2	4	5	51	1	73	5	4
Darwin, David, Tol.*	1	6	.143	5.85	24	5	0	0	8	0	64.2	70	292	44	42	11	1	3	2	41	0	47	3	0
Davenport, Joe, Char.	1	4	.200	4.58	59	0	0	0	33	9	70.2	74	314	41	36	6	7	4	11	27	2	42	7	1
Davis, Kane, Buf.-Ind.	3	1	.750	3.93	10	8	0	0	1	0	50.1	49	214	24	22	4	2	0	1	19	0	31	2	0
Davis, Lance, Lou.*	1	0	1.000	3.38	5	5	0	0	0	0	32.0	32	136	19	12	4	0	4	1	8	1	14	0	0
Dedrick, Jim, Buf.	0	2	.000	6.52	12	1	0	0	6	1	19.1	26	95	16	14	4	1	0	2	10	2	7	2	1
Delahoya, Javier, Roch.	7	6	.538	4.29	18	16	0	0	0	0	92.1	85	398	55	44	12	1	2	8	32	0	65	2	1
De Paula, Sean, Buf.	1	0	1.000	5.54	9	0	0	0	4	1	13.0	16	62	10	8	1	0	1	1	7	0	11	2	0
Dessens, Elmer, Lou.	2	0	1.000	3.18	4	4	0	0	0	0	22.2	24	98	10	8	1	1	1	0	7	0	14	1	0
Dewitt, Matt, Syr.	4	5	.444	4.87	31	7	0	0	23	15	64.2	78	296	42	35	6	2	5	2	25	0	41	0	0
Dingman, Craig, Col.	6	1	.857	3.05	47	2	0	0	10	1	73.2	60	304	31	25	5	3	8	0	20	2	65	1	1
Dishman, Richard, Rich.	2	5	.286	6.39	11	8	0	0	1	0	38.0	48	182	29	27	0	3	3	1	20	0	23	9	1
Dodd, Robert, S./W.B.*	0	2	.000	5.88	16	5	0	0	4	0	33.2	44	166	24	22	4	2	1	1	25	1	15	2	0
Donnelly, Brendan, Syr.	4	6	.400	5.48	37	0	0	0	7	0	42.2	47	203	34	26	5	4	1	1	27	2	34	1	0
Dougherty, Tony, Ott.	3	2	.600	7.18	16	1	0	0	5	0	26.1	37	130	23	21	2	0	3	1	11	0	10	1	1
Drew, Tim, Buf.	7	8	.467	5.87	16	16	2	0	0	0	95.0	122	432	69	62	12	3	6	1	31	0	53	5	1
Drews, Matt, Dur.	0	0	.000	54.00	1	1	0	0	0	0	0.2	0	8	4	4	0	0	0	2	4	0	1	3	0
Duvall, Mike, Dur.*	6	2	.750	4.59	30	8	0	0	1	0	80.1	85	363	47	41	8	1	3	3	44	0	49	7	0
Dykhoff, Radhames, Nor.*	2	3	.400	4.93	32	0	0	0	11	0	38.1	40	176	23	21	5	1	3	1	21	3	43	3	0
Ebert, Derrin, Rich.*	5	9	.357	4.78	32	23	0	0	2	0	150.2	192	670	94	80	21	4	7	4	44	0	91	4	0
Eichhorn, Mark, Syr.	1	0	1.000	1.10	17	0	0	0	4	0	16.1	5	57	2	2	2	0	0	0	2	0	17	0	0
Eiland, Dave, Dur.	2	1	.667	4.63	4	4	0	0	0	0	23.1	31	99	13	12	2	0	0	0	3	0	10	0	0
Einertson, Darrell, Col.	5	3	.625	3.24	26	0	0	0	10	1	33.1	31	154	19	12	4	1	2	1	18	3	20	5	1
Eischen, Joey, Buf.-Ott.*	0	4	.000	4.05	11	9	0	0	1	0	60.0	59	260	34	27	8	4	2	6	22	0	34	2	2
Eldred, Cal, Char.	0	1	.000	7.20	2	2	0	0	0	0	5.0	4	20	4	4	2	0	0	1	0	0	1	0	0
Ellis, Robert, Syr.	1	1	.500	4.50	16	0	0	0	10	2	18.0	17	85	10	9	2	3	0	2	15	1	18	3	1
Enders, Trevor, Dur.*	0	1	.000	2.70	15	0	0	0	5	0	26.2	22	104	8	8	3	1	0	1	6	0	16	2	0
Eshelman, Vaughn, Lou.*	0	1	.000	9.00	1	1	0	0	0	0	4.0	7	21	7	4	0	0	1	0	3	0	2	0	0
Estrada, Horacio, Ind.*	14	4	.778	3.33	25	25	3	2	0	0	159.1	149	663	63	59	14	7	2	7	45	0	103	9	0
Estrella, Leo, Syr.	5	4	.556	4.01	15	15	3	1	0	0	89.2	68	364	42	40	8	1	4	2	40	0	48	2	1
Evans, Bart, Tol.	5	4	.556	6.26	24	15	1	1	2	0	83.1	81	398	63	58	12	2	1	2	69	0	72	5	0
Evans, Keith, Ott.	2	4	.333	3.98	15	8	0	0	1	0	52.0	64	240	29	23	3	3	2	4	20	0	22	3	0
Eyre, Scott, Char.*	3	2	.600	3.00	47	0	0	0	26	12	48.0	33	191	18	16	1	6	0	0	20	3	46	2	0
Fernandez, Jared, Paw.	10	4	.714	3.02	31	9	2	0	17	4	113.1	103	464	51	38	10	4	4	5	36	0	65	11	1
Fernandez, Ozzie, Lou.	6	1	.857	4.13	10	10	0	0	0	0	56.2	57	243	27	26	3	3	3	0	19	0	44	2	0
Fesh, Sean, S./W.B.*	0	3	.000	3.27	37	0	0	0	10	2	55.0	46	245	22	20	0	6	0	4	38	5	44	2	0
Figueroa, Nelson, S./W.B.	4	3	.571	3.78	8	8	1	0	0	0	50.0	50	209	28	21	9	2	1	2	11	0	35	2	0
File, Bob, Syr.	2	0	1.000	0.93	20	0	0	0	11	8	19.1	14	69	2	2	1	0	0	1	2	0	10	0	0
Fiore, Tony, Dur.	8	5	.615	2.28	53	1	0	0	26	8	75.0	62	317	22	19	3	6	0	3	38	6	39	3	1
Flach, Jason, Rich.	2	0	1.000	5.12	5	1	1	0	1	0	19.1	29	90	11	11	1	0	2	2	5	0	8	1	0
Flores, Randy, Col.*	1	2	.333	7.33	4	4	0	0	0	0	23.1	43	117	21	19	3	0	0	0	7	0	16	1	1
Flury, Pat, Ott.	4	3	.571	1.42	40	0	0	0	25	5	57.0	40	232	10	9	0	2	2	3	26	1	46	2	1
Ford, Ben, Col.	3	0	1.000	3.07	20	2	0	0	5	0	44.0	37	194	15	15	3	0	1	4	24	0	41	8	0
Fordham, Tom, Ind.*	3	6	.333	3.55	48	3	0	0	11	0	66.0	48	295	29	26	2	2	2	0	49	0	64	6	0
Forster, Scott, Ott.*	1	0	1.000	2.32	23	0	0	0	9	2	31.0	24	135	11	8	0	1	1	1	22	1	22	5	0
Foster, Kevin, Paw.	2	4	.333	4.02	9	9	0	0	0	0	47.0	39	203	23	21	2	3	1	0	27	1	50	0	0
Frachiseur, Zach, Rich.	0	1	.000	14.40	1	1	0	0	0	0	5.0	12	27	8	8	1	0	1	0	1	0	0	0	0
Gardner, Lee, Dur.	1	0	1.000	3.38	21	0	0	0	9	5	18.2	12	75	7	7	1	1	0	0	9	1	8	1	0
Garland, Jon, Char.	9	2	.818	2.26	16	16	2	1	0	0	103.2	99	433	28	26	3	4	0	2	32	2	63	2	0
Gawer, Matt, Rich.*	0	0	.000	10.80	3	0	0	0	3	0	5.0	6	26	6	6	1	0	1	1	2	0	5	0	0
Glauber, Keith, Lou.	1	2	.333	1.52	18	0	0	0	10	4	29.2	26	116	5	5	1	1	1	0	6	1	15	1	0
Glover, Gary, Syr.	9	9	.500	5.02	27	27	1	0	0	0	166.2	181	731	104	93	21	2	4	2	62	0	119	5	0
Gomes, Wayne, S./W.B.	0	0	.000	2.25	3	0	0	0	1	0	4.0	3	16	1	1	0	0	0	0	1	0	1	0	0
Gonzalez, Gabe, Ott.	1	2	.333	6.84	14	0	0	0	5	1	25.0	34	130	21	19	3	0	2	1	20	0	11	2	0
Gonzalez, Lariel, Nor.	5	5	.500	4.19	52	0	0	0	19	5	66.2	68	304	33	31	4	3	6	4	38	3	61	8	0
Grace, Mike, Roch.	4	3	.571	4.01	34	3	0	0	5	1	76.1	66	317	36	34	5	3	0	8	16	1	43	1	0
Grahe, Joe, S./W.B.	1	0	1.000	4.50	3	3	0	0	0	0	16.0	19	67	8	8	0	0	1	0	3	0	5	0	0
Granger, Jeff, Rich.*	1	4	.200	10.27	10	3	0	0	3	0	23.2	45	127	33	27	2	2	2	3	11	1	11	1	0
Green, Tyler, Buf.	2	2	.500	8.38	11	4	0	0	3	0	29.0	42	144	28	27	2	0	2	1	20	2	11	3	0
Greene, Rick, Lou.	4	4	.500	2.82	32	0	0	0	26	7	38.1	31	162	21	12	2	2	1	1	19	2	13	0	0
Guerra, Mark, Nor.	1	4	.200	4.81	36	0	0	0	16	1	48.2	55	219	29	26	5	3	0	2	23	7	29	3	0
Gunderson, Eric, Syr.*	0	3	.000	2.67	33	0	0	0	10	2	27.0	26	117	12	8	2	2	1	1	11	0	17	4	1
Guzman, Juan, Dur.	0	2	.000	5.59	2	2	0	0	0	0	9.2	13	42	6	6	3	0	0	0	1	0	7	0	0
Haines, Talley, Dur.	0	1	.000	27.00	1	0	0	0	0	0	1.1	6	10	4	4	1	0	0	0	1	0	2	1	0
Halla, Ryan, Rich.	1	1	.500	4.32	18	0	0	0	10	1	16.2	19	80	11	8	1	0	0	0	12	3	19	2	0
Halladay, Roy, Syr.	2	3	.400	5.50	11	11	3	0	0	0	73.2	85	317	46	45	10	1	0	2	21	0	38	4	0
Hamilton, Jimmy, Roch.*	0	0	.000	0.00	2	0	0	0	2	0	1.0	0	4	0	0	0	0	0	0	1	0	1	0	0
Hamilton, Joey, Syr.	3	2	.600	3.66	6	6	1	0	0	0	39.1	41	167	18	16	1	1	4	4	12	0	17	0	0
Haney, Chris, Buf.*	8	3	.727	2.44	15	13	1	1	1	0	92.1	87	382	27	25	8	1	0	8	17	0	70	0	0
Harikkala, Tim, Ind.	4	2	.667	4.52	14	10	0	0	3	1	63.2	73	271	36	32	5	0	0	0	15	0	22	3	0
Harnisch, Pete, Lou.	0	0	.000	3.18	1	1	0	0	0	0	5.2	6	24	6	2	1	0	1	0	0	0	6	0	0
Harper, Travis, Dur.	7	4	.636	4.24	17	17	0	0	0	0	104.0	98	435	53	49	15	1	0	9	26	1	48	5	0
Harris, Reggie, Dur.-Rich.-Ind.	2	2	.500	6.75	38	0	0	0	18	0	49.1	66	238	41	37	12	2	2	3	24	2	34	3	0
Harrison, Tommy, Rich.	0	3	.000	7.97	9	1	0	0	0	0	20.1	27	101	20	18	5	2	1	1	12	0	11	0	0
Hasselhoff, Derek, Char.	7	4	.636	3.70	46	1	0	0	23	6	65.2	62	281	32	27	6	2	2	2	23	2	51	1	0
Hazlett, Andy, Paw.*	0	0	.000	24.00	3	0	0	0	0	0	3.0	11	20	8	8	1	0	1	0	0	0	4	0	0
Heams, Shane, Tol.	0	0	.000	11.17	6	0	0	0	2	0	9.2	13	52	12	12	3	0	2	1	12	0	7	3	0
Henriquez, Oscar, Nor.	0	1	.000	6.43	16	0	0	0	11	4	14.0	12	65	10	10	2	2	1	1	11	1	14	2	0
Hernandez, Adrian, Col.	2	1	.667	4.40	5	5	2	1	0	0	30.2	24	134	18	15	2	1	2	3	18	0	29	2	2
Hiljus, Erik, Tol.	5	3	.625	3.44	46	0	0	0	15	2	70.2	67	297	33	27	3	2	5	0	20	1	81	3	0

Pitcher, Team	W	L	Pct.	ERA	G	GS	CG	ShO	GF	Sv.	IP	H	TBF	R	ER	HR	SH	SF	HB	BB	IBB	SO	WP	Bk.
Hill, Ken, Char.	0	0	.000	4.50	1	1	0	0	0	0	4.0	6	18	2	2	0	0	0	0	0	0	7	0	0
Holzemer, Mark, S./W.B.*	3	2	.600	3.63	24	3	0	0	6	2	44.2	40	184	19	18	1	3	1	0	16	2	35	1	0
Hudson, Joe, Lou.	1	2	.333	4.88	29	0	0	0	19	6	31.1	34	152	20	17	2	1	0	2	21	2	21	1	0
Irabu, Hideki, Ott.	0	1	.000	3.18	1	1	0	0	0	0	5.2	5	23	2	2	1	0	0	0	2	0	6	0	0
Jackson, Ryan, Dur.*	0	0	.000	0.00	1	0	0	0	1	0	1.0	0	3	0	0	0	0	0	0	0	0	0	0	0
Jacquez, Tom, S./W.B.*	5	1	.833	1.98	35	1	0	0	8	1	54.2	53	229	15	12	3	2	4	3	20	1	34	1	0
Jimenez, Jason, Dur.*	1	1	.500	4.83	19	1	0	0	7	0	31.2	33	147	17	17	4	0	1	1	25	0	28	1	0
Johnson, Barry, S./W.B.	7	4	.636	2.67	56	1	0	0	22	3	81.0	66	339	25	24	6	3	2	4	30	4	57	1	0
Johnson, Craig, Tol.	0	0	.000	7.20	1	1	0	0	0	0	5.0	6	22	5	4	1	0	0	0	2	0	2	0	1
Johnson, Jason, Roch.	3	1	.750	1.47	8	8	1	1	0	0	55.0	32	216	12	9	2	2	2	3	21	0	56	2	0
Johnson, Mark, Tol.	2	11	.154	6.57	17	17	1	0	0	0	100.0	142	454	81	73	15	3	3	6	26	2	48	1	0
Johnson, Mike, Ott.	2	0	1.000	2.10	5	5	0	0	0	0	30.0	14	119	8	7	3	1	0	3	14	0	27	1	0
Jones, Bobby, Nor.	2	0	1.000	5.32	4	4	0	0	0	0	23.2	31	107	14	14	5	0	1	0	4	0	19	0	0
Jones, Bobby M., Nor.*	10	8	.556	4.32	22	21	4	1	0	0	133.1	122	572	66	64	13	0	3	5	58	4	100	6	1
Jordan, Ricardo, Ind.-Rich.*	3	2	.600	4.91	43	0	0	0	23	4	47.2	47	205	28	26	5	2	4	4	19	1	38	2	0
Keisler, Randy, Col.*	8	3	.727	3.02	17	17	1	1	0	0	113.1	104	479	44	38	9	3	4	4	42	1	86	5	3
Kida, Masao, Tol.	2	1	.667	2.16	21	0	0	0	20	7	25.0	21	96	6	6	3	1	1	0	4	1	26	1	0
Kim, Sun-Woo, Paw.*	11	7	.611	6.03	26	25	0	0	0	0	134.1	170	603	98	90	17	2	4	5	42	1	116	5	0
King, Ray, Ind.*	0	3	.000	3.51	29	0	0	0	6	1	25.2	26	113	15	10	1	3	1	1	12	0	20	3	0
Knight, Brandon, Col.	10	12	.455	4.44	28	28	8	1	0	0	184.2	172	783	105	91	21	5	7	3	61	3	138	10	3
Kohlmeier, Ryan, Roch.	1	4	.200	2.51	37	0	0	0	28	10	46.2	33	192	14	13	4	2	3	2	16	2	49	2	0
Krivda, Rick, Roch.*	11	9	.550	3.12	26	26	0	0	0	0	152.2	142	645	75	53	15	3	8	3	61	0	99	5	0
Lail, Denny, Col.	7	7	.500	4.64	27	22	0	0	3	0	147.1	149	625	83	76	23	2	4	1	52	1	114	4	4
LaPlante, Mick, Ott.-Rich.	0	3	.000	6.82	11	5	0	0	2	0	34.1	44	155	28	26	7	1	1	1	12	0	19	1	0
Larkin, Andy, Lou.	1	0	1.000	2.59	27	0	0	0	10	4	41.2	30	173	13	12	4	0	2	2	17	1	40	5	0
Lee, Derek, Ind.*	2	0	1.000	4.73	3	2	0	0	0	0	13.1	16	62	7	7	2	0	1	0	6	0	9	0	0
Lee, Garrett, Rich.	0	0	.000	2.57	2	1	0	0	0	0	7.0	6	30	2	2	0	0	0	3	3	0	3	0	0
Lee, Sang, Paw.*	5	2	.714	2.03	45	1	0	0	18	3	71.0	51	287	23	16	5	3	0	1	24	2	73	1	4
Leek, Randy, Tol.*	0	0	.000	9.64	1	1	0	0	0	0	4.2	6	22	5	5	1	0	0	0	3	0	1	0	0
Lemonis, Chris, Tol.	0	0	.000	0.00	1	0	0	0	1	0	1.0	0	4	0	0	0	0	0	0	1	0	0	0	0
Levrault, Allen, Ind.	6	8	.429	4.24	21	18	1	0	1	0	108.1	98	460	55	51	9	7	5	6	46	3	78	5	2
Lewis, Richie, Nor.-Buf.	4	4	.500	3.38	11	11	0	0	0	0	61.1	57	253	24	23	2	3	0	2	20	1	45	2	0
Lidle, Cory, Dur.	6	2	.750	2.52	9	9	0	0	0	0	50.0	52	205	15	14	3	1	0	1	8	0	44	1	0
Ligtenberg, Kerry, Rich.	0	0	.000	0.00	5	0	0	0	4	1	5.2	0	20	0	0	0	0	0	0	4	0	7	1	0
Lilly, Ted, Col.*	8	11	.421	4.19	22	22	3	1	0	0	137.1	157	610	77	64	14	6	5	4	48	0	127	5	4
Lira, Felipe, Ott.	0	3	.000	4.95	4	4	0	0	0	0	20.0	24	88	12	11	3	1	0	1	3	1	10	0	0
Lisio, Joe, Col.	0	0	.000	6.00	2	0	0	0	2	0	3.0	1	16	2	2	0	0	2	1	5	0	1	0	0
Looney, Brian, Buf.*	1	0	1.000	8.53	8	0	0	0	3	0	12.2	15	63	13	12	1	1	2	2	8	1	8	0	0
Lorraine, Andrew, Buf.*	8	3	.727	3.47	14	13	0	0	0	0	90.2	97	378	37	35	8	0	2	2	24	0	51	1	1
Lowe, Sean, Char.	0	0	.000	3.00	2	1	0	0	0	0	3.0	5	14	1	1	1	0	0	1	0	0	0	0	0
Ludwick, Eric, Ind.	6	3	.667	2.80	12	11	0	0	0	0	64.1	55	276	26	20	3	5	1	3	32	1	52	4	0
Luebbers, Larry, Lou.	7	6	.538	3.53	18	17	2	1	1	0	114.2	97	472	50	45	9	4	0	6	40	1	69	2	0
Lukasiewicz, Mark, Syr.*	2	1	.667	3.48	42	0	0	0	12	0	41.1	34	176	17	16	7	2	0	0	25	1	52	3	0
Maduro, Calvin, Roch.	1	0	1.000	0.00	4	1	0	0	0	0	4.0	1	16	1	0	1	0	0	0	4	0	6	0	0
Maeda, Kats, Col.	0	0	.000	9.00	1	0	0	0	0	0	2.0	3	9	2	2	2	0	1	0	0	0	1	0	0
Mairena, Ozwaldo, Col.*	1	1	.500	3.00	5	1	0	0	2	0	9.0	12	43	3	3	2	1	0	5	1	4	0	0	
Maloney, Sean, Roch.	2	5	.286	4.67	37	0	0	0	26	6	44.1	37	187	24	23	4	3	1	2	17	1	43	3	2
Mann, Jim, Nor.	3	4	.429	2.98	49	0	0	0	19	3	81.2	61	326	27	27	8	3	2	3	33	7	74	3	1
Marquez, Robert, Ott.	4	4	.500	5.06	53	0	0	0	15	3	96.0	116	435	61	54	7	5	5	11	34	1	63	6	0
Marquis, Jason, Rich.	0	3	.000	9.00	6	6	0	0	0	0	20.0	26	97	21	20	2	1	0	2	13	0	18	7	0
Martin, Tom, Buf.*	1	0	1.000	3.60	9	3	0	0	1	0	10.0	12	42	4	4	1	0	1	0	4	1	10	0	0
Martinez, Ramon, Paw.	1	0	1.000	2.31	2	2	0	0	0	0	11.2	8	46	4	3	1	0	1	0	4	0	10	0	0
Martinez, Willie, Buf.	8	5	.615	4.46	28	22	0	0	3	1	135.1	132	598	72	67	16	6	3	5	67	1	95	11	1
Matos, Francisco, Roch.	0	0	.000	108.00	1	0	0	0	1	0	0.1	5	6	4	4	0	0	0	0	1	0	0	1	0
McAvoy, Jeff, Ott.	1	0	1.000	0.00	6	0	0	0	2	0	7.2	3	26	0	0	0	1	0	2	0	4	0	0	
McDill, Allen, Tol.*	1	0	1.000	0.96	16	0	0	0	5	0	18.2	21	82	4	2	0	0	0	7	0	15	1	0	
McDougal, Mike, Roch.	1	2	.333	4.50	14	0	0	0	4	0	30.0	34	128	21	15	5	0	0	6	0	25	1	0	
McGlinchy, Kevin, Rich.	0	1	.000	3.60	9	0	0	0	3	1	10.0	9	42	4	4	0	0	0	3	2	9	0	0	
Medina, Rafael, Syr.	3	1	.750	2.80	33	2	0	0	16	1	54.2	37	235	18	17	0	0	2	3	35	1	33	4	0
Mendez, Carlos, Tol.	0	0	.000	0.00	1	0	0	0	1	0	1.0	1	4	0	0	0	0	0	0	0	0	0	0	0
Mercado, Hector, Lou.*	1	5	.167	3.04	47	5	0	0	10	2	77.0	69	339	26	26	2	6	2	48	2	67	6	0	
Michalak, Chris, Dur.*	0	0	.000	5.68	6	0	0	0	0	0	6.1	6	26	4	4	1	0	0	0	1	0	7	1	0
Mitchell, Scott, Ott.	6	5	.545	6.04	28	13	0	0	0	0	89.1	109	397	63	60	13	5	4	5	28	2	52	5	1
Mix, Greg, Ind.	3	2	.600	4.64	38	0	0	0	10	2	54.1	57	240	33	28	8	4	6	2	18	2	42	7	0
Mlicki, Dave, Tol.	0	1	.000	7.94	1	1	0	0	0	0	5.2	11	27	5	5	0	0	1	0	0	0	3	0	0
Mohler, Mike, Buf.*	0	0	.000	0.00	3	0	0	0	2	0	6.0	3	23	0	0	0	0	0	3	0	3	0	0	
Molina, Gabe, Roch.-Rich.	2	2	.500	4.58	27	4	0	0	17	8	37.1	37	161	21	19	5	2	2	0	13	0	35	2	2
Moore, Trey, Ott.*	3	2	.600	4.17	12	12	0	0	0	0	58.1	56	250	36	27	4	4	2	1	18	0	43	0	0
Morris, Jim, Dur.*	0	0	.000	9.00	1	0	0	0	0	0	1.0	1	6	1	1	0	0	0	0	2	0	1	0	0
Moss, Damian, Rich.*	9	6	.600	3.14	29	28	0	0	0	0	160.2	130	710	67	56	14	8	5	6	106	0	123	10	2
Mota, Guillermo, Ott.	4	5	.444	2.29	35	0	0	0	21	7	63.0	49	257	16	16	4	1	0	2	31	3	35	1	0
Munoz, Bobby, Lou.	6	8	.429	4.78	21	15	1	0	5	1	84.2	77	379	55	45	6	2	3	5	56	0	64	7	0
Munro, Peter, Syr.	4	3	.571	2.48	10	10	2	0	0	0	61.2	52	251	20	17	1	2	1	2	25	0	45	2	0
Myette, Aaron, Char.	5	5	.500	4.35	19	18	0	0	0	0	111.2	103	488	58	54	18	0	4	7	56	0	85	2	1
Nagy, Charles, Buf.	1	1	.500	4.30	3	3	0	0	0	0	14.2	12	63	7	7	2	0	1	2	4	0	5	0	0
Navarro, Jaime, Buf.	1	2	.333	4.44	12	2	0	0	4	0	26.1	36	121	16	13	1	0	0	0	12	1	13	0	0
Newman, Alan, Buf.*	7	4	.636	3.39	32	6	0	0	7	0	71.2	71	303	34	27	9	4	1	1	22	0	63	0	0
Nichting, Chris, Buf.	2	3	.400	4.23	47	3	0	0	36	26	66.0	65	275	31	31	6	2	3	1	16	1	60	0	1
Nussbeck, Mark, Roch.	1	2	.333	3.86	4	4	0	0	0	0	18.2	21	79	8	8	2	0	0	0	4	0	13	0	0
Ogea, Chad, Buf.	0	0	.000	40.50	1	1	0	0	0	0	1.1	8	13	6	6	2	0	0	0	1	0	0	0	0
Ohka, Tomo, Paw.	9	6	.600	2.96	19	19	3	2	0	0	130.2	111	513	52	43	15	2	7	3	23	1	78	2	0
Oquist, Mike, Tol.	7	15	.318	5.20	29	28	3	1	0	0	161.0	214	723	106	93	18	4	7	8	43	1	97	8	0

Pitcher, Team	W	L	Pct.	ERA	G	GS	CG	ShO	GF	Sv	IP	H	TBF	R	ER	HR	SH	SF	HB	BB	IBB	SO	WP	Bk.
Osting, Jimmy, Rich.*	0	2	.000	11.57	3	3	0	0	0	0	9.1	15	52	12	12	2	1	1	0	11	1	2	1	0
Pacheco, Delvis, Rich.	1	2	.333	4.76	25	0	0	0	6	0	58.2	61	238	32	31	6	3	4	2	18	2	44	2	0
Paronto, Chad, Roch.	1	1	.500	5.75	12	6	0	0	2	0	36.0	40	162	26	23	5	0	3	1	15	0	18	2	0
Parrish, John, Roch.*	6	7	.462	4.24	18	18	0	0	0	0	104.0	85	426	54	49	10	3	4	2	56	1	87	6	2
Pena, Jesus, Char.*	0	0	.000	3.12	21	0	0	0	9	4	17.1	10	69	6	6	1	0	0	0	10	0	19	1	1
Penney, Mike, Ind.	1	1	.500	3.44	17	0	0	0	10	1	18.1	16	80	9	7	2	2	0	0	10	1	13	1	0
Perez, Dario, Paw.	5	1	.833	3.27	14	0	0	0	6	0	33.0	28	135	14	12	2	0	2	1	23	3	27	1	0
Pettyjohn, Adam, Tol.*	0	4	.000	6.69	7	7	0	0	0	0	39.0	45	182	34	29	5	2	3	2	22	0	23	1	0
Phelps, Travis, Dur.	3	1	.750	4.85	6	6	0	0	0	0	29.2	29	131	17	16	6	2	0	0	16	0	21	0	0
Pichardo, Hipolito, Paw.	0	0	.000	0.00	3	0	0	0	3	0	4.2	2	16	0	0	0	0	0	0	0	0	4	0	0
Pina, Rafael, Roch.	0	6	.000	5.88	14	9	0	0	1	0	56.2	64	247	44	37	9	3	1	4	19	1	34	3	0
Pisciotta, Marc, Buf.	2	2	.500	5.60	19	0	0	0	7	0	27.1	31	135	23	17	2	1	3	0	22	1	22	6	1
Politte, Cliff, S./W.B.	8	4	.667	3.12	21	20	1	0	0	0	112.2	94	467	45	39	8	5	4	2	41	2	106	3	1
Poole, Jim, Buf.*	2	2	.500	6.00	18	0	0	0	2	1	12.0	16	60	10	8	2	1	2	0	6	0	8	1	0
Post, Dave, Ott.	0	0	.000	0.00	4	0	0	0	4	0	4.0	4	19	2	0	0	1	0	3	0	2	1	1
Powell, Jeremy, Ott.	5	13	.278	6.91	25	24	0	0	1	0	126.1	160	592	101	97	17	3	2	9	55	1	99	8	3
Pugh, Tim, Rich.	6	4	.600	5.18	18	16	0	0	0	0	88.2	117	407	55	51	10	1	2	7	26	1	69	3	0
Pujals, Denis, Dur.	4	2	.667	5.25	20	3	0	0	6	0	48.0	59	215	32	28	4	1	1	1	19	1	18	0	1
Pulsipher, Bill, Nor.*	2	3	.400	6.55	7	5	0	0	0	0	33.0	41	150	28	24	5	0	2	0	15	1	25	0	0
Ramirez, Hector, Ind.-Roch. ...	5	2	.714	5.79	41	0	0	0	14	1	65.1	79	291	45	42	13	3	1	1	24	2	46	8	4
Reed, Brandon, Tol.	7	6	.538	6.01	45	4	0	0	26	6	73.1	80	330	52	49	13	2	3	2	36	4	56	3	2
Rekar, Bryan, Dur.	3	0	1.000	2.05	4	4	0	0	0	0	22.0	16	85	5	5	1	1	3	4	0	18	1	0
Reyes, Al, Roch.	0	1	.000	7.71	9	0	0	0	8	2	11.2	13	57	11	10	2	0	0	9	1	17	2	0
Riedling, John, Lou.	6	3	.667	2.52	53	0	0	0	18	5	75.0	63	315	24	21	7	4	1	1	30	3	75	8	0
Rigby, Brad, Ott.	3	10	.231	6.67	24	14	0	0	2	0	83.2	117	396	77	62	8	2	5	9	26	0	51	4	2
Rigdon, Paul, Buf.	6	1	.857	3.30	12	12	1	0	0	0	71.0	72	291	27	26	4	2	1	1	18	0	41	1	0
Riley, Matt, Roch.*	0	2	.000	14.14	2	2	0	0	0	0	7.0	15	41	12	11	3	0	0	1	4	0	8	2	0
Rincon, Ricardo, Buf.*	0	0	.000	0.00	2	0	0	0	1	0	2.0	1	9	1	0	0	0	0	0	0	2	0	0
Riske, David, Buf.	0	0	.000	3.00	2	0	0	0	1	0	3.0	2	13	1	1	0	0	0	0	2	0	2	2	0
Rivera, Luis, Rich.-Roch.	0	3	.000	6.82	11	10	0	0	0	0	30.1	40	153	25	23	3	2	1	2	23	0	16	3	4
Robbins, Jake, Col.	0	0	.000	9.00	1	0	0	0	1	0	1.0	3	7	1	1	0	0	0	0	1	0	1	0	0
Roberts, Grant, Nor.	7	8	.467	3.38	25	25	5	0	0	0	157.1	154	686	67	59	6	5	3	8	63	5	115	12	2
Roberts, Mark, Char.	7	2	.778	2.10	14	10	1	0	1	0	64.1	58	262	16	15	7	1	3	3	20	1	38	2	1
Roberts, Willis, Lou.	7	8	.467	5.66	25	20	2	1	1	0	124.0	138	550	80	78	19	5	4	6	55	0	66	3	1
Rocker, John, Rich.*	0	0	.000	3.00	3	0	0	0	3	1	3.0	3	13	1	1	0	0	1	0	6	0	0
Rodriguez, Nerio, Paw.	0	1	.000	9.49	12	1	0	0	2	0	24.2	38	118	28	26	9	0	1	0	9	0	23	3	0
Rodriguez, Rich, Nor.*	0	1	.000	3.05	14	3	0	0	7	1	20.2	17	84	7	7	2	1	0	0	6	3	16	0	0
Rojas, Mel, Paw.	0	0	.000	3.00	1	0	0	0	2	0	3.0	1	13	1	1	0	0	0	3	1	2	0	0
Romano, Mike, Syr.	6	3	.667	3.25	10	10	2	1	0	0	63.2	53	259	23	23	7	0	1	2	26	0	34	1	0
Roque, Rafael, Ind.*	9	4	.692	4.15	25	20	1	1	0	0	132.1	127	576	66	61	18	7	2	6	63	1	111	2	0
Rose, Brian, Paw.	4	1	.800	3.19	5	5	1	0	0	0	31.0	28	134	13	11	2	0	2	1	13	0	20	0	0
Rose, Ted, Lou.	2	2	.500	4.97	23	0	0	0	6	2	38.0	36	158	23	21	5	1	2	1	13	0	33	1	0
Ruebel, Matt, Ott.*	0	2	.000	6.94	7	4	0	0	1	0	23.1	37	115	22	18	3	1	2	3	11	0	5	1	0
Runyan, Sean, Tol.*	1	2	.333	5.84	44	0	0	0	11	1	49.1	58	238	36	32	8	1	4	4	35	1	32	6	0
Rupe, Ryan, Dur.	0	1	.000	6.52	5	5	0	0	0	0	19.1	24	87	16	14	3	0	0	1	7	0	18	2	0
Rust, Brian, Roch.	0	0	.000	18.00	1	0	0	0	1	0	1.0	1	5	2	2	0	0	0	0	1	0	0	0	0
Rutherford, Mark, S./W.B.	1	1	.500	3.60	2	2	0	0	0	0	10.0	11	40	5	4	1	1	0	0	2	0	5	0	0
Ryan, B.J., Rich.*	0	1	.000	4.74	14	4	0	0	3	0	24.2	23	105	13	13	4	1	1	1	9	0	28	2	0
Ryan, Ken, Col.	0	0	.000	17.18	4	0	0	0	3	0	3.2	8	22	7	7	1	0	0	3	0	3	1	0
Ryan, Matt, Roch.	3	6	.333	3.57	46	0	0	0	14	2	63.0	55	289	34	25	5	7	2	6	43	1	35	5	0
Saberhagen, Bret, Paw.	0	0	.000	5.54	4	4	0	0	0	0	13.0	14	54	8	8	2	1	1	0	4	0	9	0	0
Salyers, Jeremy, Ott.	0	1	.000	9.00	1	1	0	0	0	0	5.0	5	24	5	5	0	1	0	5	0	1	1	0
Sanders, Frankie, Buf.	0	3	.000	8.31	5	3	0	0	0	0	17.1	26	86	16	16	3	0	0	2	8	0	7	0	0
Sanders, Scott, Buf.	3	1	.750	3.61	7	7	0	0	0	0	42.1	35	178	20	17	5	0	1	1	16	0	38	1	0
Santana, Julio, Paw.	5	3	.625	4.71	12	12	0	0	0	0	65.0	61	271	34	34	7	1	0	2	23	0	55	0	2
Santos, Victor, Tol.	0	1	.000	11.37	2	2	0	0	0	0	6.1	7	33	8	8	4	2	0	0	6	0	2	0	0
Scanlan, Bob, Ind.	2	2	.500	1.79	57	0	0	0	51	35	60.1	42	243	16	12	4	4	1	2	18	4	23	1	0
Schilling, Curt, S./W.B.	0	0	.000	3.60	1	1	0	0	0	0	5.0	9	25	2	2	0	0	0	1	0	7	0	0
Schmack, Brian, Char.	11	7	.611	2.78	51	0	0	0	13	1	90.2	82	379	32	28	10	4	1	1	29	5	84	4	0
Schourek, Pete, Paw.*	0	0	.000	0.00	1	1	0	0	0	0	3.0	1	11	0	0	0	0	0	0	1	0	3	0	0
Schrenk, Steve, S./W.B.	2	1	.667	1.31	26	0	0	0	15	3	34.1	18	126	5	5	2	2	1	2	5	2	27	0	0
Scott, Tim, Lou.	0	1	.000	2.77	16	0	0	0	2	0	26.0	26	113	13	8	1	2	0	1	9	0	25	0	0
Seberino, Ronni, Dur.*	1	0	1.000	2.12	12	0	0	0	4	1	17.0	6	74	9	4	3	1	0	1	14	0	14	4	0
Secoda, Jason, Char.	2	7	.222	6.01	32	11	0	0	4	0	100.1	122	461	76	67	20	4	1	3	49	3	75	8	1
Seelbach, Chris, Rich.	5	9	.357	4.78	29	22	1	1	2	2	118.2	118	520	71	63	12	2	4	5	55	1	96	8	1
Sekany, Jason, Paw.	3	3	.500	5.47	17	7	1	0	2	0	52.2	59	229	34	32	8	0	5	2	16	2	29	4	0
Sheets, Andy, Paw.	0	0	.000	0.00	2	0	0	0	2	0	2.0	1	7	0	0	0	0	0	0	0	0	1	0	0
Sheets, Ben, Ind.	3	5	.375	2.87	14	13	1	0	0	0	81.2	77	346	31	26	4	1	3	4	31	0	59	3	1
Shouse, Brian, Nor.-Roch.*	4	5	.444	3.39	47	0	0	0	14	2	61.0	69	260	25	23	6	0	2	2	16	1	53	2	0
Shumaker, A., S./W.B.-N.-Roch.*	7	8	.467	5.54	32	23	1	0	2	0	138.0	168	622	89	85	17	7	8	7	51	2	82	5	1
Sido, Wilson, Buf.	0	0	.000	4.50	1	0	0	0	1	0	2.0	2	9	1	1	1	0	0	2	0	0	0	0
Skrmetta, Matt, Ott.	0	3	.000	5.45	32	0	0	0	27	10	34.2	32	154	23	21	4	1	1	2	19	0	38	2	0
Small, Mark, Ott.	0	2	.000	6.00	12	0	0	0	4	0	21.0	24	94	16	14	2	0	1	0	10	0	21	0	0
Smart, J.D., Ott.	0	1	.000	10.80	4	0	0	0	0	0	6.2	15	34	8	8	2	0	0	1	0	3	0	0
Smith, Dan, Paw.	7	10	.412	4.84	24	21	2	1	1	0	124.2	134	546	72	67	15	2	3	9	41	1	70	7	0
Smith, Dan, Rich.*	8	6	.571	3.42	53	1	0	0	22	0	76.1	83	325	32	29	2	4	2	0	24	3	58	3	1
Smith, Travis, Ind.	1	1	.500	12.66	3	3	0	0	0	0	10.2	19	58	18	15	6	1	1	1	9	1	5	0	0
Snusz, Chris, Ott.	0	0	.000	0.00	2	0	0	0	2	0	1.1	2	5	0	0	0	0	0	0	0	0	0	0	0
Snyder, Bill, Tol.	0	0	.000	10.32	18	0	0	0	5	0	22.2	28	119	26	26	5	1	4	2	24	0	10	1	0
Snyder, John, Ind.	0	1	.000	2.57	1	1	0	0	0	0	7.0	6	26	2	2	1	1	0	0	0	0	5	0	0
Snyder, Matt, Roch.	1	0	1.000	5.09	10	1	0	0	2	1	23.0	23	97	13	13	7	6	1	8	0	18	0	0
Soderstrom, Steve, Lou.	9	11	.450	4.92	31	22	0	0	2	0	137.1	160	601	84	75	8	6	8	1	49	4	67	3	4

Pitcher, Team	W	L	Pct.	ERA	G	GS	CG	ShO	GF	Sv.	IP	H	TBF	R	ER	HR	SH	SF	HB	BB	IBB	SO	WP	Bk.
Sparks, Jeff, Dur.	0	1	.000	14.21	9	1	0	0	2	0	12.2	11	75	21	20	2	1	0	3	23	0	17	2	0
Sparks, Steve, Tol.	5	7	.417	3.77	16	14	1	0	0	0	90.2	86	397	53	38	8	4	4	4	41	0	44	0	1
Speier, Justin, Buf.	0	0	.000	4.15	13	0	0	0	13	9	13.0	13	55	6	6	0	1	0	0	3	0	12	0	0
Spencer, Sean, Ott.*	1	1	.500	9.90	10	0	0	0	5	1	10.0	15	52	12	11	2	0	1	1	6	0	8	0	0
Springer, Dennis, Nor.	5	5	.500	4.38	25	17	1	1	1	0	117.0	120	501	65	57	15	3	4	6	35	1	35	7	1
Spurgeon, Jay, Roch.	2	0	1.000	0.66	2	2	0	0	0	0	13.2	5	54	1	1	1	0	0	1	9	0	10	0	0
Stanifer, Rob, Paw.	3	4	.429	1.89	41	0	0	0	35	16	52.1	40	204	13	11	6	4	1	1	20	1	42	4	0
Stevens, Dave, Rich.	1	9	.100	5.00	51	0	0	0	32	7	72.0	73	318	44	40	10	1	6	2	31	3	50	7	1
Stevenson, Rod, Ott.	0	0	.000	15.23	10	0	0	0	2	0	13.0	31	76	25	22	6	0	2	1	7	0	8	3	1
Stewart, Scott, Nor.*	3	5	.375	3.50	53	1	0	0	18	5	72.0	80	313	32	28	3	5	2	3	18	2	57	8	0
Strickland, Scott, Ott.	0	0	.000	0.00	3	0	0	0	2	0	4.0	1	13	0	0	0	0	0	0	0	0	4	0	0
Stull, Everett, Ind.	7	5	.583	2.95	16	16	1	1	0	0	103.2	95	439	41	34	3	3	5	4	43	0	74	5	2
Tatis, Ramon, Col.*	0	1	.000	10.72	7	3	0	0	1	0	22.2	31	115	30	27	2	1	3	0	18	1	15	1	1
Taylor, Bill, Dur.	4	0	1.000	4.17	42	0	0	0	36	26	45.1	47	194	22	21	7	1	0	0	17	5	47	2	0
Taylor, Kerry, Syr.	9	8	.529	3.32	33	17	4	2	2	0	135.2	119	578	57	50	16	8	2	5	61	2	83	2	0
Tejero, Fausto, S./W.B.	0	0	.000	20.25	1	0	0	0	1	0	1.1	5	11	3	3	0	0	0	0	2	0	0	0	0
Telemaco, Amaury, S./W.B.	8	3	.727	3.87	21	21	0	0	0	0	123.1	115	514	60	53	15	4	4	0	42	0	88	5	0
Tessmer, Jay, Col.	4	8	.333	3.80	60	0	0	0	53	34	66.1	73	293	36	28	5	8	2	1	19	7	40	1	1
Thomas, Evan, S./W.B.	13	10	.565	3.53	29	27	3	2	1	0	171.0	163	720	70	67	17	4	0	6	50	1	127	7	0
Thurman, Mike, Ott.	0	3	.000	7.71	4	4	0	0	0	0	16.1	23	76	14	14	1	2	1	0	9	0	8	0	0
Tolar, Kevin, Tol.*	4	2	.667	3.30	33	0	0	0	12	2	46.1	37	203	23	17	4	0	3	0	26	1	42	4	0
Towers, Josh, Roch.	8	6	.571	3.47	24	24	5	1	0	0	148.0	157	618	63	57	17	2	4	8	21	0	102	1	1
Unroe, Tim, Rich.	0	0	.000	0.00	1	0	0	0	1	0	1.0	0	3	0	0	0	0	0	0	0	0	1	0	0
Valdes, Marc, Dur.	5	2	.714	4.15	9	9	0	0	0	0	47.2	52	204	25	22	2	1	0	4	17	1	25	0	1
Villafuerte, Brandon, Tol.	4	9	.308	6.67	46	6	0	0	21	4	87.2	112	417	70	65	7	2	3	1	49	1	85	12	1
Villegas, Ismael, Rich.	0	5	.000	4.81	41	0	0	0	13	3	63.2	66	286	38	34	7	5	6	2	31	1	51	1	0
Vosberg, Ed, S./W.B.*	0	0	.000	0.00	1	0	0	0	0	0	2.0	1	6	0	0	0	0	0	0	0	0	2	0	0
Wade, Terrell, Lou.*	0	2	.000	12.15	2	2	0	0	0	0	6.2	11	39	9	9	0	0	0	1	8	0	7	1	0
Walker, Tyler, Nor.	1	3	.250	2.39	5	5	0	0	0	0	26.1	29	111	7	7	0	0	0	9	0	17	1	0	
Walls, Doug, Tol.	3	7	.300	5.17	18	14	1	0	3	0	85.1	88	375	60	49	10	3	5	3	42	1	61	3	1
Ward, Bryan, S./W.B.*	3	2	.600	2.30	22	0	0	0	14	6	27.1	23	113	11	7	1	4	0	1	8	0	17	3	0
Wasdin, John, Paw.	1	0	1.000	2.25	5	3	0	0	2	1	16.0	7	57	4	4	0	0	1	2	0	11	0	0	
Watson, Allen, Col.*	0	1	.000	1.35	5	1	0	0	0	0	6.2	3	26	2	1	1	0	0	2	0	4	1	0	
Watson, Mark, Buf.*	1	2	.333	4.43	16	0	0	0	7	1	20.1	18	91	11	10	1	1	2	0	12	6	16	1	0
Weaver, Jeff, Tol.	0	1	.000	3.38	1	1	0	0	0	0	5.1	5	22	2	2	1	0	1	0	1	0	10	0	0
Weber, Neil, Lou.-Roch.*	0	4	.000	4.70	3	1	0	0	0	0	7.2	9	37	5	4	1	1	0	4	0	7	0	0	
Wells, Kip, Char.	5	3	.625	5.37	12	12	2	1	0	0	62.0	67	275	38	37	10	1	1	0	27	1	38	6	0
Wengert, Don, Rich.	4	7	.364	4.23	29	12	1	0	1	0	110.2	117	462	55	52	9	3	4	4	22	0	83	2	0
Westbrook, Jake, Col.	5	7	.417	4.65	16	15	2	0	0	0	89.0	94	393	53	46	3	4	1	4	38	0	61	2	0
Wheeler, Dan, Dur.	5	11	.313	5.63	26	26	0	0	0	0	150.1	183	668	109	94	35	2	6	7	42	1	91	4	0
White, Matt, Dur.	3	2	.600	2.83	6	6	0	0	0	0	35.0	36	153	14	11	1	0	3	16	1	28	3	0	
Williams, Brian, Buf.	4	3	.571	2.57	18	0	0	0	8	3	21.0	23	95	7	6	1	4	1	0	11	2	21	2	0
Williams, Matt, Col.*	4	2	.667	5.25	27	0	0	0	14	2	36.0	37	160	24	21	4	0	1	0	16	1	35	3	0
Wilson, Jeff, Roch.*	2	2	.500	3.86	11	3	0	0	1	0	35.0	26	157	16	15	1	0	3	2	29	0	25	1	1
Wilson, Paul, Nor.	5	5	.500	4.23	15	13	0	0	1	0	83.0	85	350	40	39	7	0	4	2	25	1	56	3	1
Winchester, Scott, Lou.	1	2	.333	4.08	43	0	0	0	16	3	57.1	67	249	29	26	4	3	0	3	15	2	33	3	0
Winkelsas, Joe, Rich.	0	1	.000	14.40	4	0	0	0	1	0	5.0	12	33	9	8	1	2	0	1	5	2	1	0	0
Wohlers, Mark, Lou.	1	2	.333	6.10	17	2	0	0	5	0	20.2	30	103	21	14	4	1	2	0	9	0	16	5	0
Wright, Jamey, Ind.	0	0	.000	1.80	1	1	0	0	0	0	5.0	8	25	5	1	0	0	0	3	0	7	0	0	
Wright, Jaret, Buf.	0	0	.000	0.00	1	1	0	0	0	0	2.0	0	6	0	0	0	0	0	1	0	1	0	0	
Yarnall, Ed, Col.-Lou.*	5	5	.500	4.15	21	21	1	0	0	0	117.0	115	516	59	54	11	5	5	6	60	1	93	4	0
Young, Tim, Paw.*	1	1	.500	2.40	32	0	0	0	11	6	41.1	35	171	13	11	5	1	0	3	12	1	43	0	0
Zambrano, Victor, Dur.	0	6	.000	5.03	53	0	0	0	27	8	62.2	72	290	38	35	9	4	0	4	29	2	55	6	0

COMBINATION SHUTOUTS: **Buffalo (6)**—Newman-Brewington, Lorraine-Brewington, Rigdon-Williams-Nichting, Lorraine-DePaula, Lorraine-Nichting, Brower-Cairncross-Williams-Nichting. **Charlotte (6)**—Beirne-Hasselhoff-Pena-Davenport, Garland-Chantres-Pena-Bradford-Davenport, Garland-Pena-Bradford-Davenport, Daneker-Davenport-Eyre, Garland-Schmack, Roberts-Schmack-Hasselhoff. **Columbus (4)**—Yarnall-Lail, Yarnall-Williams, Keisler-Tessmer, Lilly-Lisio. **Durham (8)**—Valdes-Zambrano-Taylor, Lidle-Belitz-Taylor, Wheeler-Creek, Harper-Zambrano, Cornett-Jimenez, Cornett-Fiore, White-Zambrano-Fiore, Phelps-Seberino-Zambrano. **Indianapolis (3)**—Acevedo-Ludwick-Fordham-Busby, Fordham-Mix-Buddie-Scanlan, Sheets-Mix-Scanlan-King. **Louisville (5)**—Soderstrom-Rose-Mercado, Mercado-Riedling-Winchester, Yarnall-Glauber-Greene, Yarnall-Winchester-Scott-Riedling-Hudson-Greene. **Norfolk (4)**—Wilson-Mann, Jones-Guerra-Mann-Cammack, Jones-Gonzalez-Cammack, Roberts-Cammack-Gonzalez-Stewart-Mann-Henriquez. **Ottawa (5)**—Billingsley-Mota-Skrmetta, Armas-Marquez-Skrmetta, Bennett-Forster, Billingsley-Skrmetta, Powell-Flury-Mota. **Pawtucket (5)**—Ohka-Lee, Smith-Fernandez, Crawford-Young, Rose-Lee-Rojas-Stanifer, Saberhagen-Perez-Young. **Richmond (1)**—Avery-Villegas-Stevens. **Rochester (6)**—Towers-Reyes, Delahoya-Brewer-Ryan-Kohlmeier, Delahoya-Molina-Shouse, Krivda-Ryan-Maloney, Spurgeon-Maloney-Corsi, Nussbeck-Shumaker-Maloney. **Scranton/Wilkes-Barre (7)**—Grahe-Fesh, Bowers-Holzemer-Johnson-Fesh-Ward, Brownson-Boyd-Johnson, Holzemer-Johnson-Schrenk, Telemaco-Dodd-Schrenk-Ward-Johnson-Bullinger, Coggin-Schrenk-Bullinger, Thomas-Barrios-Holzemer. **Syracuse (5)**—Medina-Dewitt, Andrews-Gunderson-Lukasiewicz, Estrella-Cubillan, Glover-Gunderson-Medina, Munro-Medina-File-Lukasiewicz. **Toledo (3)**—Sparks-McDill, Bernero-Villafuerte, Johnson-Runyan-Reed.

NO-HIT GAMES: Luebbers, Louisville, defeated Charlotte, 5-0, May 14; Ohka, Pawtucket, defeated Charlotte, 2-0, June 1; Estrella, Syracuse, defeated Indianapolis, 5-0, June 17; Crawford, Pawtucket, defeated Ottawa, 3-0, July 18.

PITCHERS WITH TWO OR MORE TEAMS

Pitcher, Team	W	L	Pct.	ERA	G	GS	CG	ShO	GF	Sv.	IP	H	TBF	R	ER	HR	SH	SF	HB	BB	IBB	SO	WP	Bk.
Brea, Lesli, Nor.	0	0	.000	5.40	2	1	0	0	0	0	5.0	4	23	2	0	0	1	0	4	0	4	0	0	
Brea, Lesli, Roch.	1	2	.333	6.05	4	4	0	0	0	0	19.1	27	95	18	13	3	0	1	8	0	13	2	0	
Buddie, Mike, Col.	1	3	.250	7.50	6	6	0	0	0	0	30.0	34	145	30	25	8	1	2	0	20	1	16	2	0
Buddie, Mike, Ind.	7	2	.778	2.62	30	0	0	0	7	2	58.1	40	245	20	17	4	2	2	5	29	1	39	4	0
Daneker, Pat, Char.	8	12	.400	5.75	27	25	0	0	0	0	144.0	168	633	102	92	26	2	3	4	49	3	69	4	4
Daneker, Pat, Syr.	1	1	.500	3.29	2	2	0	0	0	0	13.2	18	58	6	5	2	0	1	1	2	0	4	1	0
Davis, Kane, Buf.	2	0	1.000	4.20	6	4	0	0	1	0	30.0	30	131	16	14	2	2	0	1	12	0	19	2	0
Davis, Kane, Ind.	1	1	.500	3.54	4	4	0	0	0	0	20.1	19	83	8	8	2	0	1	0	7	0	12	0	0
Eischen, Joey, Buf.*	0	0	.000	40.50	1	0	0	0	1	0	0.2	4	6	3	3	0	0	0	0	0	0	0	0	0
Eischen, Joey, Ott.*	0	4	.000	3.64	10	9	0	0	1	0	59.1	55	254	31	24	8	4	2	6	22	0	34	2	2

Pitcher, Team	W	L	Pct.	ERA	G	GS	CG	ShO	GF	Sv.	IP	H	TBF	R	ER	HR	SH	SF	HB	BB	IBB	SO	WP	Bk.
Harris, Reggie, Dur.	0	0	.000	6.35	4	0	0	0	2	0	5.2	8	28	4	4	1	0	0	0	3	0	8	1	0
Harris, Reggie, Rich.	0	1	.000	12.15	5	0	0	0	1	0	6.2	14	39	9	9	3	1	0	1	4	0	4	0	0
Harris, Reggie, Ind.	2	1	.667	5.84	29	0	0	0	15	0	37.0	44	171	28	24	8	1	2	2	17	2	22	2	0
Jordan, Ricardo, Ind.*	0	0	.000	1.80	4	0	0	0	2	0	5.0	7	19	1	1	1	0	0	0	1	0	3	0	0
Jordan, Ricardo, Rich.*	3	2	.600	5.27	39	0	0	0	21	4	42.2	40	186	27	25	4	2	4	4	18	1	35	2	0
LaPlante, Mick, Ott.	0	0	.000	9.00	3	0	0	0	2	0	4.0	4	19	4	4	1	0	0	0	3	0	2	0	0
LaPlante, Mick, Rich.	0	3	.000	6.53	8	5	0	0	0	0	30.1	40	136	24	22	6	1	1	1	9	0	17	1	0
Lewis, Richie, Nor.	3	4	.429	3.21	9	9	0	0	0	0	53.1	49	221	20	19	0	3	0	2	17	1	40	2	0
Lewis, Richie, Buf.	1	0	1.000	4.50	2	2	0	0	0	0	8.0	8	32	4	4	2	0	0	0	3	0	5	0	0
Molina, Gabe, Roch.	1	2	.333	4.94	18	4	0	0	9	5	27.1	30	120	16	15	3	2	0	0	10	0	26	2	1
Molina, Gabe, Rich.	1	0	1.000	3.60	9	0	0	0	8	3	10.0	7	41	5	4	2	0	2	0	3	0	9	0	1
Ramirez, Hector, Ind.	3	0	1.000	3.04	15	0	0	0	6	0	23.2	24	98	9	8	5	1	0	1	5	0	18	5	0
Ramirez, Hector, Roch.	2	2	.500	7.34	26	0	0	0	8	1	41.2	55	193	36	34	8	2	1	0	19	2	28	3	4
Rivera, Luis, Rich.	0	2	.000	8.06	8	7	0	0	0	0	22.1	29	111	20	20	3	1	0	1	18	0	12	1	4
Rivera, Luis, Roch.	0	1	.000	3.38	3	3	0	0	0	0	8.0	11	42	5	3	0	1	1	5	0	4	2	0
Shouse, Brian, Nor.*	0	1	.000	13.50	4	0	0	0	0	0	3.1	6	16	5	5	2	0	0	2	0	1	0	0
Shouse, Brian, Roch.*	4	4	.500	2.81	43	0	0	0	14	2	57.2	63	244	20	18	4	0	2	2	14	1	52	2	0
Shumaker, Anthony, S./W.B.*..	1	0	1.000	9.00	1	1	0	0	0	0	4.0	6	20	4	4	0	0	2	0	3	0	1	0	0
Shumaker, Anthony, Nor.*	4	5	.444	4.99	21	17	1	0	1	0	101.0	121	451	58	56	12	6	5	6	35	2	55	5	1
Shumaker, Anthony, Roch.*	3	2	.600	6.82	10	5	0	0	1	0	33.0	41	151	27	25	5	1	1	1	13	0	26	0	0
Weber, Neil, Lou.*	0	0	.000	7.36	2	0	0	0	0	0	3.2	6	18	3	3	0	0	0	0	2	0	4	0	0
Weber, Neil, Roch.*	0	0	.000	2.25	1	1	0	0	0	0	4.0	3	19	2	1	0	0	0	1	2	0	3	0	0
Yarnall, Ed, Col.*	2	1	.667	4.56	10	10	1	0	0	0	49.1	43	210	27	25	4	3	4	4	26	1	34	2	0
Yarnall, Ed, Lou.*	3	4	.429	3.86	11	11	0	0	0	0	67.2	72	306	32	29	7	2	1	2	34	0	59	2	0

2000 FIELDING

TEAM

Team	Pct.	G	PO	A	E	TC	DP	TP	PB
Norfolk	.981	144	3810	1480	100	5390	131	0	19
Scranton/W.-B.	.981	145	3844	1557	103	5504	149	0	14
Syracuse	.979	140	3626	1428	108	5162	132	0	8
Charlotte	.979	143	3690	1493	111	5294	142	0	11
Pawtucket	.978	143	3749	1357	114	5220	113	0	17
Buffalo	.978	143	3705	1475	118	5298	132	0	12
Louisville	.977	144	3831	1624	126	5581	127	0	14
Durham	.976	143	3753	1499	130	5382	144	0	12
Indianapolis	.975	144	3810	1461	134	5405	118	0	6
Richmond	.975	143	3726	1459	133	5318	154	0	8
Ottawa	.973	141	3587	1479	140	5206	133	0	7
Toledo	.972	143	3609	1475	145	5229	152	0	22
Columbus	.970	144	3735	1387	157	5279	111	0	11
Rochester	.969	144	3761	1411	163	5335	118	0	17

INDIVIDUAL

FIRST BASEMEN

NOTE: All caps denotes fielding-percentage leader based on 72 games for catchers, 96 for all other non-pitchers and 115 innings for pitchers. *Throws lefthanded.

Player, Team	Pct.	G	PO	A	E	TC	DP
Alcantara, Israel, Paw.	.923	3	23	1	2	26	2
Allen, Dusty, Tol.	1.000	10	63	6	0	69	8
Alvarez, Gabe, Tol.	.972	32	253	26	8	287	31
Barker, Kevin, Ind.*	.995	74	605	57	3	665	58
Barkett, Andy, Rich.*	.990	51	382	26	4	412	41
Battle, Howard, Lou.	1.000	11	91	9	0	100	8
Bellinger, Clay, Col.	1.000	3	27	3	0	30	7
Bierek, Kurt, Ind.	.987	64	504	31	7	542	34
Borders, Pat, Dur.	1.000	3	26	6	0	32	4
Burkhart, Morgan, Paw.*	.992	61	482	46	4	532	49
Burrell, Pat, S./W.B.	.990	10	85	10	1	96	8
Carr, Dustin, Dur.	1.000	1	1	0	0	1	0
Clark, Howie, Roch.	1.000	2	16	2	0	18	2
Clark, Tony, Tol.	1.000	6	40	3	0	43	3
Coolbaugh, Mike, Col.	1.000	6	46	6	0	52	4
Coste, Chris, Buf.	1.000	1	8	0	0	8	1
Cromer, D.T., Lou.*	.984	55	436	49	8	493	37
Dalesandro, Mark, Ind.	1.000	4	14	3	0	17	1
Davis, Tommy, Roch.	.992	70	552	43	5	600	43
Diaz, Juan, Paw.	.980	10	94	4	2	100	7
Fernandez, Jose, Ind.	.897	4	25	1	3	29	2
Fick, Robert, Tol.	1.000	7	53	4	0	57	5
Foster, Jim, Char.	1.000	1	12	1	0	13	2
Franco, Matt, Nor.	1.000	1	6	1	0	7	1
Garcia, Guillermo, Lou.	.992	29	242	17	2	261	19
Gillespie, Eric, Tol.	.983	32	276	17	5	298	30
Graffanino, Tony, Dur.	1.000	1	1	0	0	1	1
Gubanich, Creighton, Ind.	.973	6	34	2	1	37	4

Player, Team	Pct.	G	PO	A	E	TC	DP
Hayes, Heath, Buf.	1.000	1	9	0	0	9	1
Held, Dan, Nor.	1.000	2	5	2	0	7	0
Hollins, Dave, Dur.	1.000	3	15	2	0	17	3
Horn, Jeff, Rich.	.923	2	11	1	1	13	1
Hubbard, Mike, Rich.	.957	3	17	5	1	23	1
Huff, Aubrey, Dur.	1.000	1	3	0	0	3	1
Hunter, Brian, Rich.*	1.000	2	16	1	0	17	0
Jackson, Ryan, Ind.*	.991	137	1195	96	12	1303	112
Johnson, Mark, Nor.*	.991	38	305	32	3	340	23
Kieschnick, Brooks, Lou.	.995	41	362	31	2	395	38
Kinkade, Mike, Roch.	.958	3	23	0	1	24	2
Langaigne, Selwyn, Syr.*	1.000	3	13	0	0	13	0
Lemonis, Chris, Tol.	1.000	14	107	5	0	112	11
Lennon, Pat, Ott.	.980	16	130	15	3	148	10
Liefer, Jeff, Char.	.988	62	544	50	7	601	50
Lindstrom, David, Tol.	1.000	1	9	1	0	10	0
Lopez, Luis, Syr.	1.000	31	270	13	0	283	33
Manto, Jeff, Buf.	.974	9	73	3	2	78	4
Matos, Francisco, Roch.	1.000	7	47	6	0	53	4
McGuire, Ryan, Nor.*	1.000	31	251	22	0	273	32
Mendez, Carlos, Tol.	.996	32	259	18	1	278	37
Merloni, Lou, Paw.	1.000	1	8	0	0	8	1
Minor, Ryan, Roch.	.967	7	55	3	2	60	1
Morales, Willie, Roch.	1.000	4	13	0	0	13	1
Mortimer, Mark, Rich.	1.000	1	2	0	0	2	0
Nerei, Yuji, Ott.*	1.000	9	78	6	0	84	5
Nevers, Tom, Lou.	1.000	2	1	0	0	1	0
Norton, Greg, Char.	1.000	4	28	0	0	28	6
Nunnari, Talmadge, Ott.*	.991	39	291	24	3	318	35
Otanez, Willis, Syr.	1.000	3	16	2	0	18	2
Peoples, Danny, Buf.	.993	112	945	60	7	1012	93
Perry, Chan, Buf.	.995	24	192	17	1	210	16
Phillips, J.R., Char.*	.993	48	402	33	3	438	36
Pickering, Calvin, Roch.*	.978	56	497	30	12	539	46
Post, Dave, Ott.	.987	8	69	7	1	77	5
PRITCHETT, Chris, S./W.B.	.996	101	904	50	4	958	92
Rumfield, Toby, Rich.	.986	63	406	30	6	442	53
Rust, Brian, Roch.	1.000	2	10	0	0	10	2
Sasser, Rob, Tol.	.987	17	132	21	2	155	19
Saunders, Chris, Lou.	.971	4	32	2	1	35	2
Schall, Gene, S./W.B.	.994	36	314	22	2	338	33
Schneider, Brian, Ott.	.981	7	47	5	1	53	5
Seguignol, Fernando, Ott.	.986	25	197	21	3	221	21
Seitzer, Brad, Char.	1.000	8	75	5	0	80	7
Sheets, Andy, Paw.	1.000	4	18	1	0	19	1
Short, Rick, Roch.	1.000	1	5	0	0	5	0
Simon, Randall, Col.*	.988	74	620	33	8	661	52
Sisco, Steve, Rich.	1.000	2	14	2	0	16	3
Snusz, Chris, Ott.	1.000	3	19	1	0	20	3
Stefanski, Mike, Lou.	1.000	1	12	3	0	15	1
Stenson, Dernell, Paw.*	.982	67	521	38	10	569	42
Swann, Pedro, Rich.	1.000	1	0	1	0	1	0
Sweeney, Mark, Ind.*	1.000	3	17	3	0	20	3
Timmons, Ozzie, Dur.	1.000	8	54	7	0	61	8

Player, Team	Pct.	G	PO	A	E	TC	DP
Toca, Jorge, Nor.	.987	80	638	45	9	692	57
Toth, Dave, Char.	1.000	3	23	1	0	24	1
Tracy, Andy, Ott.	.995	43	364	23	2	389	38
Turner, Chris, Col.	1.000	4	29	0	0	29	3
Unroe, Tim, Rich.	.991	40	299	33	3	335	35
Vinas, Julio, Paw.	1.000	2	9	0	0	9	1
Wilson, Desi, Char.*	.987	26	198	23	3	224	22
Wilson, Tom, Col.	1.000	5	34	2	0	36	2
Witt, Kevin, Syr.	.986	109	931	54	14	999	85
Wright, Ron, Lou.	.992	14	110	8	1	119	10
Zuber, Jon, Col.*	.990	58	427	63	5	495	34

SECOND BASEMEN

Player, Team	Pct.	G	PO	A	E	TC	DP
Abernathy, Brent, Syr.-Dur.	.973	114	199	313	14	526	74
Alguacil, Jose, Char.	1.000	1	4	0	0	4	0
Anderson, Marlon, S./W.B.	.969	99	167	269	14	450	62
Azuaje, Jesus, Tol.	.927	9	14	24	3	41	3
Badeaux, Brooks, Dur.	1.000	11	15	21	0	36	5
Baez, Kevin, Nor.	.992	25	55	75	1	131	17
Bates, Jason, Roch.	.937	13	25	34	4	63	10
Bridges, Kary, Ott.	.996	54	112	155	1	268	36
Brito, Tilson, Tol.	1.000	11	25	33	0	58	7
Cabrera, Jolbert, Buf.	1.000	2	5	6	0	11	2
Camilli, Jason, Ott.	1.000	12	31	28	0	59	7
Carr, Dustin, Dur.	.984	54	93	152	4	249	32
Carroll, Jamey, Ott.	.990	60	134	149	3	286	34
Caruso, Mike, Char.	.989	23	34	52	1	87	11
Casimiro, Carlos, Roch.	.981	14	22	30	1	53	6
Castro, Juan, Lou.	1.000	3	7	11	0	18	1
Cepeda, Jose, Rich.	.889	4	9	7	2	18	0
Clark, Howie, Roch.	.979	30	41	54	2	97	14
Collier, Lou, Ind.	.846	4	4	7	2	13	0
Coolbaugh, Mike, Col.	.983	28	44	75	2	121	12
Coquillette, Trace, Ott.	.969	17	28	34	2	64	10
Dalesandro, Mark, Ind.	1.000	1	1	1	0	2	0
De Leon, Jorge, Paw.	1.000	5	6	12	0	18	1
DeRosa, Mark, Rich.	.944	3	8	9	1	18	3
Doster, Dave, S./W.B.	.993	27	52	91	1	144	26
Easley, Damion, Tol.	1.000	3	5	9	0	14	4
ECKSTEIN, David, Paw.	.992	115	183	318	4	505	58
Fernandez, Jose, Ind.	1.000	1	1	3	0	4	1
Forbes, P.J., S./W.B.	.000	1	0	0	0	0	0
Fraraccio, Dan, Dur.	1.000	1	2	3	0	5	2
Freel, Ryan, Syr.	.965	24	42	69	4	115	16
Garcia, Carlos, Col.	.958	44	58	100	7	165	19
Garcia, Guillermo, Lou.	1.000	1	5	4	0	9	0
Garcia, Jesse, Roch.	.933	4	7	7	1	15	1
Gillespie, Eric, Tol.	.000	1	0	0	0	0	0
Graffanino, Tony, Dur.	1.000	3	5	8	0	13	5
Guevara, Giomar, Tol.	.988	35	75	95	2	172	24
Hairston, Jerry, Roch.	.967	52	128	135	9	272	43
Hansen, Jed, Nor.-Lou.	.987	35	66	83	2	151	14
Holbert, Aaron, Paw.	1.000	1	3	1	0	4	0
Ingram, Garey, Paw.	.909	3	5	5	1	11	0
Jackson, Gavin, Paw.	.941	3	6	10	1	17	2
Jimenez, D'Angelo, Col.	.943	14	28	22	3	53	4
Lamb, David, Nor.	1.000	10	15	22	0	37	3
Lemonis, Chris, Tol.	.967	45	85	147	8	240	45
Lopez, Mickey, Ind.	.955	44	86	105	9	200	27
Macias, Jose, Tol.	.846	4	3	8	2	13	4
Malloy, Marty, Tol.	1.000	27	51	78	0	129	19
Martin, Norberto, Ind.	.975	54	104	130	6	240	28
Martinez, Louis, Rich.	1.000	13	23	33	0	56	9
Martinez, Pablo, Rich.	.976	20	27	54	2	83	15
Matos, Francisco, Roch.	.985	36	50	79	2	131	7
McClure, Brian, Tol.	.981	12	19	34	1	54	6
McDonald, John, Buf.	1.000	3	5	10	0	15	1
McEwing, Joe, Nor.	.981	11	26	25	1	52	5
Merloni, Lou, Paw.	1.000	1	2	0	0	2	0
Moore, Brandon, Char.	.988	50	94	148	3	245	38
Mora, Melvin, Nor.	1.000	1	2	3	0	5	0
Mummau, Rob, Syr.	1.000	10	14	16	0	30	3
Nevers, Tom, Lou.	.962	9	21	30	2	53	8
Newhan, David, S./W.B.	.991	23	42	71	1	114	15
Patzke, Jeff, Buf.	1.000	7	16	19	0	35	5
Perez, Santiago, Paw.	1.000	4	3	6	0	9	2
Perez, Tomas, S./W.B.	1.000	1	4	2	0	6	2
Petersen, Chris, Rich.	.978	49	99	119	5	223	35
Pickler, Jeff, Ind.	.979	52	103	129	5	237	27
Post, Dave, Ott.-Buf.	.914	8	14	18	3	35	4

Player, Team	Pct.	G	PO	A	E	TC	DP
Pratt, Scott, Buf.	1.000	4	4	5	0	9	0
Roberge, J.P., Col.	.957	15	17	27	2	46	4
Rodriguez, Liu, Char.	.987	79	149	220	5	374	55
Rust, Brian, Roch.	1.000	1	1	4	0	5	1
Sadler, Donnie, Paw.	1.000	7	14	17	0	31	3
Sasser, Rob, Tol.	.000	1	0	0	0	0	0
Saunders, Chris, Lou.	1.000	2	7	3	0	10	1
Scutaro, Marcos, Buf.-Ind.	.982	111	250	291	10	551	85
Selby, Bill, Buf.	.964	21	31	50	3	84	8
Sexton, Chris, Lou.	.975	16	37	40	2	79	6
Sheets, Andy, Paw.	.979	11	25	22	1	48	5
Simons, Mitch, Syr.	.975	74	137	214	9	360	55
Sisco, Steve, Rich.	.980	61	128	163	6	297	48
Smith, Bobby, Dur.	.975	54	115	162	7	284	42
Soriano, Alfonso, Col.	.963	40	83	99	7	189	30
Stankiewicz, Andy, Col.	.955	18	22	41	3	66	6
Tamargo, John, Nor.	1.000	4	11	7	0	18	3
Unroe, Tim, Rich.	.955	8	8	13	1	22	2
Williams, Jason, Lou.	.980	113	213	363	12	588	69
Woodward, Chris, Syr.	.990	20	31	64	1	96	6

SECOND BASEMEN WITH TWO OR MORE TEAMS

Player, Team	Pct.	G	PO	A	E	TC	DP
Abernathy, Brent, Syr.	.973	90	146	258	11	415	59
Abernathy, Brent, Dur.	.973	24	53	55	3	111	15
Hansen, Jed, Nor.	.985	30	56	74	2	132	12
Hansen, Jed, Lou.	1.000	5	10	9	0	19	2
Post, Dave, Ott.	.950	4	9	10	1	20	5
Post, Dave, Buf.	.867	4	5	8	2	15	3
Scutaro, Marcos, Buf.	.981	109	244	283	10	537	82
Scutaro, Marcos, Ind.	1.000	2	6	8	0	14	3

THIRD BASEMEN

Player, Team	Pct.	G	PO	A	E	TC	DP
Alguacil, Jose, Char.	1.000	1	0	3	0	3	1
Alvarez, Gabe, Tol.	.783	11	9	9	5	23	3
Badeaux, Brooks, Dur.	.944	7	6	11	1	18	0
Baez, Kevin, Nor.	.917	34	20	68	8	96	4
Barrett, Michael, Ott.	.944	24	20	48	4	72	7
Battle, Howard, Lou.	1.000	2	1	1	0	2	0
Bell, Mike, Lou.	.928	111	68	228	23	319	19
Berry, Sean, Paw.-Buf.	.907	22	13	26	4	43	0
Blake, Casey, Syr.	.971	29	24	42	2	68	7
Branyan, Russell, Buf.	.930	35	36	70	8	114	4
Brito, Tilson, Tol.	.727	4	2	6	3	11	1
Bruce, Mo, Nor.	.937	39	23	81	7	111	11
Camilli, Jason, Ott.	.923	8	8	16	2	26	1
Carr, Dustin, Dur.	.943	35	25	58	5	88	8
Carroll, Jamey, Ott.	.893	25	9	58	8	75	4
Carvajal, Jhonny, Ott.	.667	3	0	2	1	3	0
Casimiro, Carlos, Roch.	.900	11	7	20	3	30	2
Castilla, Vinny, Dur.	1.000	2	0	2	0	2	0
Castro, Juan, Lou.	.800	2	1	3	1	5	0
Cedeno, Domingo, Nor.	.667	2	0	4	2	6	1
Clark, Howie, Roch.	.714	3	2	3	2	7	0
Coffie, Ivanon, Roch.	1.000	10	6	20	0	26	2
Collier, Lou, Ind.	.800	1	1	3	1	5	0
Coolbaugh, Mike, Col.	.881	13	10	27	5	42	3
Coquillette, Trace, Ott.	.850	18	5	29	6	40	3
Coste, Chris, Buf.	.900	4	5	4	1	10	1
Cromer, Brandon, Ind.	1.000	5	4	9	0	13	2
Dalesandro, Mark, Ind.	1.000	2	1	1	0	2	0
Davis, Tommy, Roch.	.909	7	4	6	1	11	1
DeRosa, Mark, Rich.	.875	3	2	5	1	8	0
Doster, Dave, S./W.B.	.958	72	53	150	9	212	18
FERNANDEZ, Jose, Ind.	.955	123	97	224	15	336	16
Forbes, P.J., S./W.B.	1.000	23	18	55	0	73	7
Franco, Matt, Nor.	.905	7	3	16	2	21	2
Fraraccio, Dan, Dur.	.900	3	3	6	1	10	2
Freel, Ryan, Syr.	.892	12	8	25	4	37	3
Garabito, Eddy, Roch.	1.000	3	1	5	0	6	1
Garcia, Carlos, Col.	.863	27	18	45	10	73	4
Garcia, Freddy, Paw.	.933	37	32	65	7	104	5
Garcia, Guillermo, Lou.	1.000	3	0	3	0	3	0
Garcia, Jesse, Roch.	.000	1	0	0	0	0	0
Gillespie, Eric, Tol.	.922	17	12	35	4	51	5
Graffanino, Tony, Dur.	1.000	1	0	4	0	4	1
Guevara, Giomar, Tol.	1.000	1	0	4	0	4	0
Hansen, Jed, Nor.	1.000	3	2	3	0	5	0
Held, Dan, Nor.	.000	1	0	0	1	1	0
Helms, Wes, Rich.	.933	130	96	222	23	341	28
Hernandez, Jose, Ind.	1.000	1	0	2	0	2	0

Player, Team	Pct.	G	PO	A	E	TC	DP
Holbert, Aaron, Paw.	.868	26	14	32	7	53	2
Hollins, Dave, Roch.-Buf.	.907	14	13	26	4	43	3
Hoover, Paul, Dur.	1.000	2	0	2	0	2	0
Huff, Aubrey, Dur.	.914	93	57	166	21	244	15
Jimenez, D'Angelo, Col.	1.000	3	3	3	0	6	0
Kinkade, Mike, Roch.	.667	2	2	4	3	9	1
Lamb, David, Nor.	.962	38	27	73	4	104	6
Larson, Brandon, Lou.	.929	16	6	46	4	56	4
Leon, Donny, Col.	.937	58	51	113	11	175	9
Liefer, Jeff, Char.	.976	13	11	29	1	41	3
Lopez, Luis, Syr.	.945	54	32	88	7	127	7
Lydy, Scott, Char.	1.000	2	1	0	0	1	0
Manto, Jeff, Buf.	.973	19	8	28	1	37	1
Martin, Norberto, Ind.	.907	18	24	25	5	54	4
Martinez, Louis, Rich.	1.000	2	0	3	0	3	0
Matos, Francisco, Roch.	.951	26	15	43	3	61	1
McEwing, Joe, Nor.	.941	11	10	22	2	34	4
Mendez, Carlos, Tol.	1.000	1	0	1	0	1	0
Merloni, Lou, Paw.	1.000	1	4	0	0	4	0
Minor, Ryan, Roch.	.910	61	42	109	15	166	8
Moore, Brandon, Char.	.977	43	30	56	2	88	4
Mummau, Rob, Syr.	.982	24	15	39	1	55	2
Nevers, Tom, Lou.	.900	8	5	4	1	10	0
Norton, Greg, Char.	.986	24	25	47	1	73	7
Orie, Kevin, Col.	.925	41	29	70	8	107	8
Otanez, Willis, Syr.	.958	18	11	35	2	48	4
Patterson, Jarrod, Ott.	.940	25	19	44	4	67	7
Patzke, Jeff, Buf.	.924	22	16	45	5	66	4
Perez, Tomas, S./W.B.	.947	56	48	112	9	169	6
Petersen, Chris, Rich.	1.000	2	0	4	0	4	1
Polanco, Enohel, Buf.	.750	4	3	9	4	16	1
Post, Dave, Ott.-Buf.	.967	34	22	67	3	92	6
Roberge, J.P., Col.	.875	7	3	4	1	8	0
Rust, Brian, Roch.	.875	10	2	19	3	24	1
Sandberg, Jared, Dur.	.933	3	1	13	1	15	1
Sasser, Rob, Tol.	.922	112	72	211	24	307	21
Saunders, Chris, Lou.	.941	9	4	12	1	17	0
Seitzer, Brad, Char.	.902	46	29	72	11	112	13
Selby, Bill, Buf.	.932	52	31	119	11	161	9
Sheets, Andy, Paw.	.978	21	14	31	1	46	1
Short, Rick, Roch.	.909	8	4	16	2	22	2
Simons, Mitch, Nor.	.966	20	15	42	2	59	4
Sisco, Steve, Rich.	.952	8	4	16	1	21	1
Smith, Bobby, Dur.	1.000	4	3	7	0	10	0
Stankiewicz, Andy, Col.	.833	2	1	4	1	6	0
Tracy, Andy, Ott.	.900	13	3	33	4	40	3
Tyler, Brad, Ind.	1.000	1	0	3	0	3	0
Unroe, Tim, Rich.	.944	7	9	8	1	18	2
Veras, Wilton, Paw.	.973	58	45	98	4	147	16
Wilson, Craig, Char.	.960	33	19	53	3	75	7
Woodward, Chris, Syr.	.964	12	5	22	1	28	0

THIRD BASEMEN WITH TWO OR MORE TEAMS

Player, Team	Pct.	G	PO	A	E	TC	DP
Berry, Sean, Paw.	.933	9	5	9	1	15	0
Berry, Sean, Buf.	.893	13	8	17	3	28	0
Hollins, Dave, Roch.	.935	10	11	18	2	31	2
Hollins, Dave, Buf.	.833	4	2	8	2	12	1
Post, Dave, Ott.	.965	32	21	62	3	86	6
Post, Dave, Buf.	1.000	2	1	5	0	6	0

SHORTSTOPS

Player, Team	Pct.	G	PO	A	E	TC	DP
Abbott, Kurt, Nor.	1.000	2	1	2	0	3	1
Alguacil, Jose, Char.	1.000	1	0	4	0	4	1
Azuaje, Jesus, Tol.	.979	52	75	161	5	241	38
Badeaux, Brooks, Dur.	.985	12	20	46	1	67	14
Baez, Kevin, Nor.	.968	61	92	147	8	247	24
Bates, Jason, Roch.	.727	2	3	5	3	11	0
Bellinger, Clay, Col.	.667	2	2	0	1	3	1
Blake, Casey, Syr.	.000	1	0	0	0	0	0
Bournigal, Rafael, Nor.	.985	19	24	41	1	66	6
Bruce, Mo, Nor.	1.000	1	0	2	0	2	0
Cabrera, Jolbert, Buf.	1.000	6	12	19	0	31	5
Cabrera, Orlando, Ott.	1.000	2	3	7	0	10	1
Calais, Ian, Rich.	.962	6	9	16	1	26	4
Carr, Dustin, Dur.	.950	4	7	12	1	20	4
Carroll, Jamey, Ott.	.941	7	13	19	2	34	4
Caruso, Mike, Char.	.952	66	96	204	15	315	42
Carvajal, Jhonny, Ott.	1.000	6	9	10	0	19	3
Castro, Juan, Lou.	.955	16	20	44	3	67	6
Coffie, Ivanon, Roch.	.927	12	13	25	3	41	4

Player, Team	Pct.	G	PO	A	E	TC	DP
Coolbaugh, Mike, Col.	.958	54	90	138	10	238	29
Cromer, Brandon, Ind.	.966	18	20	37	2	59	11
De La Rosa, Tomas, Ott.	.964	101	156	270	16	442	61
De Los Santos, Eddy, Dur.	.949	78	110	204	17	331	39
DeRosa, Mark, Rich.	.960	91	136	273	17	426	61
Eckstein, David, Paw.	1.000	1	0	6	0	6	2
Forbes, P.J., S./W.B.	1.000	1	3	3	0	6	2
Fraraccio, Dan, Dur.	1.000	1	0	2	0	2	0
Freel, Ryan, Syr.	1.000	1	3	2	0	5	0
Garcia, Carlos, Col.	.961	21	28	46	3	77	11
Garcia, Guillermo, Lou.	1.000	3	0	2	0	2	0
Garcia, Jesse, Roch.	.964	101	157	292	17	466	55
Gonzalez, Alex, Syr.	1.000	1	2	3	0	5	1
Graffanino, Tony, Dur.	1.000	5	7	15	0	22	4
Guevara, Giomar, Tol.	.953	73	108	219	16	343	63
Hairston, Jerry, Roch.	.917	8	8	14	2	24	4
Hansen, Jed, Nor.-Lou.	.936	7	11	18	2	31	6
Holbert, Aaron, Paw.	.961	47	73	100	7	180	27
IZTURIS, Cesar, Syr.	.981	131	231	395	12	638	87
Jackson, Gavin, Paw.	.952	15	27	33	3	63	10
Jimenez, D'Angelo, Col.	.917	3	2	9	1	12	0
Lamb, David, Nor.	.980	55	96	151	5	252	32
Lemonis, Chris, Tol.	1.000	1	1	0	0	1	0
Lopez, Mickey, Ind.	.930	14	16	37	4	57	9
Loretta, Mark, Ind.	1.000	7	4	14	0	18	4
Lotterhos, Chris, Lou.	.929	3	7	6	1	14	1
Macias, Jose, Tol.	.921	11	14	21	3	38	5
Malloy, Marty, Tol.	1.000	1	1	1	0	2	1
Martin, Norberto, Ind.	.905	15	23	34	6	63	5
Martinez, Eddy, Roch.	.936	13	15	29	3	47	6
Martinez, Felix, Dur.	.971	42	66	132	6	204	34
Martinez, Louis, Rich.	1.000	12	17	27	0	44	6
Martinez, Pablo, Rich.	.984	18	19	44	1	64	9
Matos, Francisco, Roch.	.920	13	15	31	4	50	5
McClure, Brian, Tol.	.905	3	7	12	2	21	4
McDonald, John, Buf.	.974	72	107	192	8	307	46
McEwing, Joe, Nor.	1.000	6	2	19	0	21	2
Merloni, Lou, Paw.	.840	7	9	12	4	25	2
Moore, Brandon, Char.	1.000	1	0	1	0	1	0
Mora, Melvin, Nor.	1.000	1	4	4	0	8	0
Mummau, Rob, Syr.	1.000	3	4	4	0	8	1
Nevers, Tom, Lou.	.973	41	60	120	5	185	19
Norton, Greg, Char.	1.000	3	2	7	0	9	0
Patzke, Jeff, Buf.	.974	39	61	124	5	190	25
Perez, Santiago, Ind.	.940	102	153	268	27	448	48
Perez, Tomas, S./W.B.	1.000	16	20	44	0	64	9
Petersen, Chris, Rich.	.975	27	51	66	3	120	22
Polanco, Enohel, Buf.	1.000	2	2	7	0	9	1
Post, Dave, Ott.	.948	33	49	98	8	155	17
Rodriguez, Liu, Dur.	.959	50	65	124	8	197	27
Rollins, Jimmy, S./W.B.	.958	132	183	411	26	620	82
Sadler, Donnie, Paw.	.970	34	76	86	5	167	28
Sandoval, Danny, Char.	.800	2	0	4	1	5	0
Sasser, Rob, Tol.	1.000	5	5	12	0	17	1
Scutaro, Marcos, Buf.-Ind.	.941	20	33	47	5	85	6
Sexton, Chris, Lou.	.981	81	141	263	8	412	55
Sheets, Andy, Paw.	.961	47	68	105	7	180	16
Sisco, Steve, Rich.	1.000	1	0	2	0	2	0
Smith, Bobby, Dur.	.895	5	2	15	2	19	2
Sorensen, Zach, Buf.	.972	12	28	42	2	72	8
Soriano, Alfonso, Col.	.944	71	92	146	14	252	23
Stankiewicz, Andy, Col.	1.000	1	1	1	0	2	1
Tebbs, Nate, Nor.	1.000	4	4	6	0	10	1
Velandia, Jorge, Nor.	1.000	4	7	10	0	17	4
Wilson, Craig, Char.	.954	31	29	75	5	109	17
Woodward, Chris, Syr.	1.000	6	12	24	0	36	9

SHORTSTOPS WITH TWO OR MORE TEAMS

Player, Team	Pct.	G	PO	A	E	TC	DP
Hansen, Jed, Nor.	1.000	1	0	1	0	1	0
Hansen, Jed, Lou.	.933	6	11	17	2	30	6
Scutaro, Marcos, Buf.	.936	19	30	43	5	78	6
Scutaro, Marcos, Ind.	1.000	1	3	4	0	7	0

OUTFIELDERS

Player, Team	Pct.	G	PO	A	E	TC	DP
Alcantara, Israel, Paw.	.945	46	98	6	6	110	0
Allen, Dusty, Tol.	1.000	16	21	0	0	21	0
Almonte, Wady, Roch.	.977	71	114	12	3	129	3
Amaral, Rich, Rich.	1.000	5	11	0	0	11	0
Barkett, Andy, Rich.*	1.000	23	35	3	0	38	1
Bartee, Kimera, Lou.	.993	113	263	3	2	268	1

Player, Team	Pct.	G	PO	A	E	TC	DP
Bellinger, Clay, Col.	1.000	3	8	0	0	8	0
Benitez, Yamil, Char.	1.000	17	40	3	0	43	0
Besco, Derek, Tol.	1.000	13	20	0	0	20	0
Bierek, Kurt, Ind.	.981	33	47	4	1	52	0
Bradley, Milton, Ott.	.987	87	216	7	3	226	2
Branyan, Russell, Buf.	.975	19	39	0	1	40	0
Brinkley, Darryl, Roch.	.979	28	45	2	1	48	0
Brown, Rich, Col.*	.923	7	12	0	1	13	0
Brumfield, Jacob, Syr.-Char.	.969	55	120	5	4	129	2
Buccheri, Jim, Dur.	.986	71	141	3	2	146	1
Budzinski, Mark, Buf.*	.991	118	216	8	2	226	4
Burkhart, Morgan, Paw.*	1.000	16	26	0	0	26	0
Burrell, Pat, S./W.B.	.982	30	50	6	1	57	2
Burton, Darren, S./W.B.	1.000	9	24	0	0	24	0
Cabrera, Jolbert, Char.	1.000	13	27	0	0	27	0
Carr, Dustin, Dur.	1.000	11	24	1	0	25	0
Carvajal, Jhonny, Ott.	1.000	1	2	0	0	2	0
Chamblee, Jim, Paw.	.987	121	225	9	3	237	2
Chevalier, Virgil, Paw.	1.000	7	25	0	0	25	0
Christensen, McKay, Char.*	.964	83	184	3	7	194	0
Clark, Brady, Lou.	.981	131	298	10	6	314	4
Clark, Howie, Roch.	.963	14	26	0	1	27	0
Coleman, Michael, Paw.	.964	18	26	1	1	28	0
Collier, Lou, Ind.	1.000	10	26	1	0	27	0
Coolbaugh, Mike, Col.	1.000	23	43	0	0	43	0
Coquillette, Trace, Ott.	.963	41	76	2	3	81	1
Coste, Chris, Buf.	1.000	1	3	0	0	3	0
Cromer, D.T., Lou.*	.926	17	25	0	2	27	0
Dalesandro, Mark, Ind.	1.000	4	7	0	0	7	0
Davis, Tommy, Roch.	1.000	11	24	0	0	24	0
Doster, Dave, S./W.B.	.931	18	24	3	2	29	2
Dunn, Todd, Nor.	.981	35	49	4	1	54	1
Fleming, Ryan, Syr.*	1.000	2	4	0	0	4	0
Forbes, P.J., S./W.B.	.991	66	105	2	1	108	1
Francia, David, S./W.B.*	.965	34	53	2	2	57	0
Franco, Matt, Nor.	1.000	2	2	0	0	2	0
Frank, Mike, Lou.-Col.*	1.000	101	196	8	0	204	1
Fraraccio, Dan, Dur.	.955	7	21	0	1	22	0
Freel, Ryan, Syr.	.981	23	48	3	1	52	1
Garcia, Freddy, Paw.	.833	15	14	1	3	18	0
Garcia, Karim, Tol.-Roch.*	.968	103	203	9	7	219	2
Gibralter, Steve, Tol.	.976	61	118	4	3	125	0
Gillespie, Eric, Tol.	1.000	6	15	1	0	16	0
Gonzalez, Manny, Char.	1.000	2	3	0	0	3	0
Green, Chad, Ind.	.967	42	86	2	3	91	1
Greene, Todd, Syr.	.947	11	18	0	1	19	0
Guillen, Jose, Dur.	.912	18	29	2	3	34	0
Hamilton, Darryl, Nor.	1.000	7	18	1	0	19	1
Hansen, Jed, Lou.	1.000	3	6	0	0	6	0
Herrera, Jose, Roch.*	.970	124	282	9	9	300	1
Hollins, Damon, Ind.*	1.000	82	202	8	0	210	1
Hoover, Paul, Dur.	.000	1	0	0	0	0	0
Hunter, Scott, Ott.-Buf.	1.000	8	13	1	0	14	0
Iapoce, Anthony, Ind.*	1.000	17	35	1	0	36	0
Inglin, Jeff, Char.	.985	39	60	5	1	66	0
Ingram, Garey, Paw.	.968	96	207	5	7	219	2
James, Kenny, Ott.	.978	47	130	5	3	138	0
Jennings, Robin, Lou.*	.946	31	48	5	3	56	0
Johnson, Mark, Nor.*	1.000	38	63	1	0	64	0
Jones, Chris, Ind.	.969	56	120	3	4	127	0
Jose, Felix, Col.	.970	16	30	2	1	33	2
Kieschnick, Brooks, Lou.	.966	49	82	4	3	89	1
Kingsale, Eugene, Roch.	1.000	2	11	1	0	12	0
Kirby, Wayne, Roch.	.966	103	222	7	8	237	1
Krause, Scott, Ind.	.990	57	96	3	1	100	1
Langaigne, Selwyn, Syr.*	1.000	12	24	0	0	24	0
Leach, Jalal, S./W.B.*	.988	52	83	2	1	86	0
Lennon, Pat, Ott.	.964	22	22	5	1	28	0
Liefer, Jeff, Char.	.963	17	25	1	1	27	0
Lombard, George, Rich.	.972	110	202	5	6	213	2
Long, Ryan, Char.	1.000	2	4	0	0	4	0
Lydy, Scott, Char.	.984	103	186	3	3	192	2
Macias, Jose, Tol.	.980	20	47	1	1	49	0
Magee, Wendell, Tol.	1.000	2	2	0	0	2	0
Martin, Norberto, Ind.	1.000	33	42	1	0	43	1
Matos, Luis, Roch.	1.000	11	26	0	0	26	0
May, Derrick, Roch.	.970	14	30	2	1	33	0
McClure, Brian, Tol.	1.000	1	2	0	0	2	0
McCracken, Quinton, Dur.	.977	83	161	8	4	173	2
McDonald, Donzell, Col.	1.000	24	51	2	0	53	1
McEwing, Joe, Nor.	.976	16	39	1	1	41	0
McGuire, Ryan, Nor.*	.993	83	143	4	1	148	1
McMillon, Billy, Tol.*	.973	100	208	7	6	221	1
Mendez, Carlos, Tol.	1.000	18	30	0	0	30	0
Miller, David, Buf.*	1.000	9	17	0	0	17	0
Monahan, Shane, Lou.	.968	15	29	1	1	31	0
Moore, Brandon, Char.	.000	1	0	0	0	0	0
Moore, Mike, Rich.	1.000	21	39	2	0	41	1
Mora, Melvin, Nor.	1.000	3	5	0	0	5	0
Morgan, Scott, Buf.	1.000	9	14	0	0	14	0
Morris, Jeremy, Col.	1.000	3	3	1	0	4	0
Mottola, Chad, Syr.	.964	126	259	8	10	277	2
Mouton, Lyle, Ind.	.991	50	107	2	1	110	0
Mummau, Rob, Syr.	1.000	3	6	0	0	6	0
Myers, Rod, Char.*	1.000	12	33	2	0	35	1
Nerei, Yuji, Ott.*	.971	45	66	2	2	70	1
Nevers, Tom, Lou.	1.000	2	3	0	0	3	0
Nunnari, Talmadge, Ott.*	1.000	5	8	0	0	8	0
Oquist, Mike, Tol.	.000	1	0	0	0	0	0
Paul, Josh, Char.	.000	1	0	0	0	0	0
Pendergrass, Tyrone, Rich.	.973	111	279	13	8	300	0
Perez, Timoniel, Nor.*	.976	70	198	7	5	210	3
Perry, Chan, Buf.	.979	52	94	0	2	96	0
Phillips, J.R., Char.*	1.000	1	2	0	0	2	0
Post, Dave, Ott.	1.000	29	50	1	0	51	0
Powell, Alonzo, Col.	.955	33	41	1	2	44	0
Powell, Corey, Nor.	1.000	2	11	0	0	11	0
Pride, Curtis, Nor.-Paw.	.983	53	115	0	2	117	0
Pulliam, Harvey, Rich.	.958	13	23	0	1	24	0
ROBERTS, Dave, Buf.*	.997	118	284	8	1	293	3
Robinson, Kerry, Col.*	.988	114	237	4	3	244	1
Royster, Aaron, S./W.B.	1.000	9	14	1	0	15	0
Rust, Brian, Roch.	1.000	1	2	0	0	2	0
Sadler, Donnie, Paw.	.984	50	121	5	2	128	1
Sanchez, Alex, Dur.*	.977	107	243	11	6	260	0
Sanders, Deion, Lou.*	.981	25	49	3	1	53	1
Sasser, Rob, Tol.	1.000	4	5	1	0	6	1
Schall, Gene, S./W.B.	1.000	14	22	1	0	23	0
Seguignol, Fernando, Ott.	.900	14	16	2	2	20	0
Selby, Bill, Buf.	.980	28	46	3	1	50	0
Sexton, Chris, Lou.	.000	2	0	0	0	0	0
Sheff, Chris, Nor.	1.000	92	181	8	0	189	2
Short, Rick, Roch.	1.000	2	2	1	0	3	0
Simon, Randall, Col.*	.889	3	7	1	1	9	0
Simons, Mitch, Nor.	.826	10	16	3	4	23	0
Sledd, Aaron, Lou.*	1.000	3	9	0	0	9	0
Smothers, Stewart, Rich.	1.000	5	14	2	0	16	0
Snusz, Chris, Ott.	.750	1	3	0	1	4	0
Staton, T.J., Ott.*	.958	42	69	0	3	72	0
Stenson, Dernell, Paw.*	.953	21	38	3	2	43	1
Stowers, Chris, Ott.*	1.000	43	63	4	0	67	0
Swann, Pedro, Rich.	.987	104	229	3	3	235	0
Sweeney, Mark, Ind.*	1.000	1	1	0	0	1	0
Taylor, Reggie, S./W.B.	.980	98	241	9	5	255	3
Thompson, Andy, Syr.	.969	113	205	17	7	229	0
Thompson, Ryan, Col.	.988	80	155	10	2	167	3
Timmons, Ozzie, Dur.	.972	64	102	4	3	109	1
Toca, Jorge, Nor.	.903	22	27	1	3	31	0
Tomberlin, Andy, Buf.*	1.000	5	5	0	0	5	0
Toth, Dave, Char.	.833	2	4	1	1	6	0
Turner, Chris, Col.	.875	5	7	0	1	8	0
Tyler, Brad, Ind.	.990	99	185	5	2	192	2
Tyner, Jason, Nor.*	.995	81	188	5	1	194	0
Unroe, Tim, Rich.	.983	60	110	7	2	119	1
Villalobos, Carlos, Tol.	.968	13	30	0	1	31	0
Vinas, Julio, Paw.	.961	24	46	3	2	51	1
Wakeland, Chris, Tol.*	.966	130	217	10	8	235	0
Watkins, Pat, Tol.	.994	75	161	9	1	171	0
Wells, Vernon, Syr.	.990	119	293	8	3	304	3
Whiten, Mark, Buf.	.955	78	139	9	7	155	0
Wilcox, Luke, Col.	.980	103	184	12	4	200	2
Wilkerson, Brad, Ott.*	.956	62	123	6	6	135	0
Wilson, Desi, Char.*	.981	61	101	5	2	108	1
Wilson, Tom, Col.	1.000	6	6	1	0	7	0
Winn, Randy, Dur.	.960	76	158	10	7	175	3
Witt, Kevin, Syr.	1.000	6	13	0	0	13	0
Woods, Ken, S./W.B.	.987	128	295	15	4	314	4
Zuber, Jon, Col.*	1.000	4	11	0	0	11	0

OUTFIELDERS WITH TWO OR MORE TEAMS

Player, Team	Pct.	G	PO	A	E	TC	DP
Brumfield, Jacob, Syr.	.966	10	27	1	1	29	0
Brumfield, Jacob, Char.	.970	45	93	4	3	100	2
Frank, Mike, Lou.*	1.000	57	106	4	0	110	1
Frank, Mike, Col.*	1.000	44	90	4	0	94	0

Player, Team	Pct.	G	PO	A	E	TC	DP
Garcia, Karim, Tol.*	.956	39	82	5	4	91	1
Garcia, Karim, Roch.*	.977	64	121	4	3	128	1
Hunter, Scott, Ott.	1.000	7	12	1	0	13	0
Hunter, Scott, Buf.	1.000	1	1	0	0	1	0
Pride, Curtis, Nor.	.929	8	13	0	1	14	0
Pride, Curtis, Paw.	.990	45	102	0	1	103	0

CATCHERS

Player, Team	Pct.	G	PO	A	E	TC	DP	PB
Alvarez, Clemente, S./W.B.	1.000	5	19	0	0	19	0	0
Amezcua, Adan, Roch.	.988	22	146	13	2	161	1	2
Barrett, Michael, Ott.	.947	5	17	1	1	19	0	0
Bellinger, Clay, Col.	1.000	1	1	0	0	1	0	0
BENNETT, Gary, S./W.B.	.996	82	483	34	.2	519	8	1
Borders, Pat, Dur.	.995	81	494	57	3	554	7	7
Brown, Kevin, Syr.-Ind.	.993	72	409	46	3	458	7	3
Cardona, Javier, Tol.	.986	51	317	25	5	347	3	9
Casanova, Raul, Ind.	.985	18	120	15	2	137	2	3
Cline, Pat, Ind.	.957	10	63	4	3	70	1	0
Coste, Chris, Buf.	.985	24	115	15	2	132	2	1
Dalesandro, Mark, Syr.-Ind.	.974	25	141	8	4	153	1	0
Davis, Tommy, Roch.	.983	33	214	15	4	233	3	2
Depastino, Joe, Roch.	.993	19	120	15	1	136	1	1
Encarnacion, Angelo, Paw.	.986	19	136	7	2	145	1	1
Figga, Mike, Paw.	1.000	2	14	1	0	15	0	1
Fordyce, Brook, Char.	1.000	13	76	3	0	79	0	2
Foster, Jim, Char.	.993	41	252	23	2	277	1	2
Garcia, Guillermo, Lou.	.994	51	306	27	2	335	2	3
Garcia, Neil, Dur.	.993	20	144	7	1	152	1	4
Greene, Charlie, Syr.	.983	77	468	41	9	518	3	5
Greene, Todd, Syr.	1.000	1	13	1	0	14	0	0
Gubanich, Creighton, Ind.	.985	78	466	52	8	526	8	3
Hall, Toby, Dur.	.993	44	249	22	2	273	1	1
Hayes, Heath, Buf.	.983	9	47	11	1	59	0	3
Hoover, Paul, Dur.	1.000	1	10	0	0	10	0	0
Horn, Jeff, Rich.	1.000	4	34	0	0	34	1	0
Hubbard, Mike, Lou.-Rich.	.989	57	346	15	4	365	2	2
Hughes, Bobby, Rich.	.988	66	390	37	5	432	7	6
Hyde, Brandon, Char.	.972	9	33	2	1	36	0	0
Inge, Brandon, Tol.	.991	49	308	37	3	348	2	4
Johnson, Brian, Col.	.993	18	139	8	1	148	1	2
King, Cesar, S./W.B.	.993	38	244	22	2	268	4	11
Kinkade, Mike, Roch.	1.000	6	45	7	0	52	3	2
LaRue, Jason, Lou.	.984	77	445	57	8	510	9	9
Levis, Jesse, Buf.	.997	51	286	20	1	307	2	2
Lindstrom, David, Tol.	1.000	10	64	6	0	70	2	2
Loyd, Brian, Syr.	.979	18	88	5	2	95	0	0
Matos, Pascual, Rich.	.974	62	336	44	10	390	5	4
Mendez, Carlos, Tol.	.980	32	190	11	4	205	0	6
Morales, Willie, Roch.	.990	67	450	32	5	487	5	10
Mortimer, Mark, Rich.	1.000	3	25	3	0	28	0	0
Mosquera, Julio, Col.	.988	34	213	24	3	240	1	3
Mulligan, Sean, Ind.	.949	12	49	7	3	59	1	0
Mummau, Rob, Syr.	1.000	4	2	0	0	2	0	0
Paul, Josh, Char.	.994	47	291	25	2	318	5	5
Probst, Alan, Nor.	1.000	34	195	18	0	213	4	1
Rivera, Mike, Tol.	.968	4	26	4	1	31	0	1
Rodriguez, Luis, Paw.	1.000	28	153	20	0	173	1	3
Rodriguez, Sammy, Nor.	.983	19	108	11	2	121	0	4
Romero, Mandy, Buf.	1.000	4	26	3	0	29	0	0
Rumfield, Toby, Rich.	.990	32	188	12	2	202	1	2
Sapp, Damian, Paw.	1.000	5	33	4	0	37	0	1
Schneider, Brian, Ott.	.982	60	344	47	7	398	7	4
Siddall, Joe, Paw.	.980	21	122	25	3	150	2	5
Sisco, Steve, Rich.	.000	1	0	0	0	0	0	1
Snusz, Chris, Ott.	.982	54	300	28	6	334	5	3
Spehr, Tim, Paw.	.991	77	506	51	5	562	3	6
Stefanski, Mike, Lou.	1.000	25	141	14	0	155	2	1
Tejero, Fausto, S./W.B.	.996	32	217	25	1	243	3	2
Toth, Dave, Char.	.992	40	221	26	2	249	3	2
Turner, Chris, Col.	1.000	4	22	3	0	25	0	0
Valencia, Vic, Col.	.965	15	100	10	4	114	2	2
Valera, Yohanny, Ott.	.969	21	113	11	4	128	0	0
Wilson, Tom, Col.	.986	81	525	31	8	564	2	4
Wilson, Vance, Nor.	.996	104	637	66	3	706	10	14

CATCHERS WITH TWO OR MORE TEAMS

Player, Team	Pct.	G	PO	A	E	TC	DP	PB
Brown, Kevin, Syr.	.990	49	280	32	3	315	5	3
Brown, Kevin, Ind.	1.000	23	129	14	0	143	2	0
Dalesandro, Mark, Syr.	.857	1	6	0	1	7	1	0
Dalesandro, Mark, Ind.	.979	24	135	8	3	146	0	0

Player, Team	Pct.	G	PO	A	E	TC	DP	PB
Hubbard, Mike, Lou.	1.000	5	14	0	0	14	0	1
Hubbard, Mike, Rich.	.989	52	332	15	4	351	2	1

PITCHERS

Player, Team	Pct.	G	PO	A	E	TC	DP
Abreu, Winston, Rich.	1.000	3	0	1	0	1	0
Acevedo, Juan, Ind.	.000	2	0	0	0	0	0
Adams, Willie, Paw.	1.000	22	0	2	0	2	0
Agosto, Stevenson, Dur.*	.000	1	0	0	0	0	0
Almonte, Wady, Roch.	.000	1	0	0	0	0	0
Andrews, Clayton, Syr.*	1.000	19	2	19	0	21	2
Armas, Tony, Ott.	1.000	4	0	6	0	6	0
Arteaga, J.D., Nor.*	1.000	1	1	1	0	2	0
Atchley, Justin, Lou.*	.947	30	7	11	1	19	1
Averette, Robert, Lou.	1.000	2	2	1	0	3	0
Avery, Steve, Rich.*	1.000	4	0	4	0	4	0
Aybar, Manny, Lou.	.000	3	0	0	0	0	0
Bacsik, Mike, Buf.*	1.000	5	2	2	0	4	0
Bale, John, Syr.*	.875	21	0	7	1	8	1
Banks, Willie, Nor.	.875	9	4	3	1	8	0
Barcelo, Lorenzo, Char.	1.000	17	5	10	0	15	0
Barkley, Brian, Paw.*	1.000	2	0	0	0	0	0
Barnett, Marty, Dur.	1.000	16	1	7	0	8	0
Baron, Jim, Nor.*	.000	2	0	0	0	0	0
Barrios, Manny, S./W.B.	1.000	47	3	7	0	10	0
Beasley, Ray, Rich.*	1.000	4	0	1	0	1	1
Beck, Rod, Paw.	.500	3	1	0	1	2	0
Becks, Ryan, Ott.*	1.000	3	1	2	0	3	0
Beirne, Kevin, Char.	1.000	7	3	6	0	9	0
Belitz, Todd, Dur.*	.846	43	4	7	2	13	2
Bell, Jason, Syr.	.900	22	1	8	1	10	2
Bell, Rob, Lou.	.857	6	4	2	1	7	0
Bennett, Joel, Paw.	1.000	19	2	5	0	7	1
Bennett, Shayne, Ott.	.882	22	2	13	2	17	0
Bernero, Adam, Tol.	1.000	7	7	4	0	11	1
Bertotti, Mike, Col.*	1.000	7	0	4	0	4	0
Beverlin, Jason, Col.	.000	3	0	0	0	0	0
Billingsley, Brent, Ott.*	.905	20	6	13	2	21	1
Bogott, Kurt, Syr.*	1.000	20	2	7	0	9	0
Bolton, Rod, Ind.	1.000	22	5	12	0	17	0
Borkowski, Dave, Tol.	.929	8	7	6	1	14	1
Bowers, Cedrick, Dur.*	1.000	4	0	2	0	2	0
Bowers, Shane, S./W.B.	.960	36	8	16	1	25	2
Boyd, Jason, S./W.B.	1.000	11	3	2	0	5	1
Bradford, Chad, Char.	1.000	55	8	16	0	24	1
Bradley, Ryan, Col.	.944	49	6	11	1	18	0
Brammer, J.D., Buf.	1.000	25	3	2	0	5	0
Brantley, Jeff, S./W.B.	.000	5	0	0	0	0	0
Brea, Lesli, Nor.-Roch.	.667	5	2	4	3	9	0
Brewer, Billy, Roch.*	1.000	9	2	2	0	4	0
Brewington, Jamie, Buf.	1.000	17	1	3	0	4	0
Brower, Jim, Buf.	.947	16	4	14	1	19	0
Brown, Elliot, Dur.	1.000	1	0	1	0	1	0
Brownson, Mark, S./W.B.	.913	31	6	15	2	23	1
Bruske, Jim, Ind.	1.000	19	1	3	0	4	0
Buddie, Mike, Col.-Ind.	.957	36	8	14	1	23	0
Bullinger, Kirk, S./W.B.	.833	26	1	4	1	6	2
Busby, Mike, Ind.	.667	19	2	2	2	6	0
Byrd, Paul, S./W.B.	.800	3	2	2	1	5	0
Cairncross, Cameron, Buf.*	1.000	15	0	3	0	3	1
Callaway, Mickey, Dur.	.947	26	18	18	2	38	3
Cammack, Eric, Nor.	.909	47	3	7	1	11	0
Camp, Jared, Dur.	1.000	3	1	2	0	3	0
Castillo, Carlos, Paw.	1.000	16	0	5	0	5	0
Chantres, Carlos, Char.	.939	29	14	17	2	33	0
Chapman, Jake, Ott.*	.000	3	0	0	0	0	0
Charlton, Norm, Lou.*	1.000	4	1	0	0	1	0
Chen, Bruce, Rich.*	1.000	1	2	1	0	3	1
Cho, Jin Ho, Paw.	1.000	13	4	9	0	13	2
Choate, Randy, Col.*	.875	33	3	4	1	8	0
Clark, Howie, Roch.	.000	1	0	0	0	0	0
Clemons, Chris, Buf.	.857	12	5	7	2	14	0
Coggin, Dave, S./W.B.	.778	9	2	5	2	9	0
Colon, Bartolo, Buf.	1.000	1	0	0	0	0	0
Corbin, Archie, Char.	1.000	8	0	2	0	2	0
Corey, Mark, Nor.	.867	20	2	11	2	15	1
Cornett, Brad, Dur.	1.000	19	11	11	0	22	0
Corsi, Jim, Roch.	1.000	5	0	1	0	1	0
Crawford, Joe, Ind.*	.000	3	0	0	0	0	0
Crawford, Paxton, Paw.	.923	12	4	8	1	13	0
Creek, Doug, Dur.*	.000	10	0	0	0	0	0
Croushore, Rich, Paw.	1.000	11	2	1	0	3	0
Cruz, Nelson, Tol.	.667	11	3	5	4	12	1

CLASS AAA International League

Player, Team	Pct.	G	PO	A	E	TC	DP
Cubillan, Darwin, Syr.	1.000	24	2	3	0	5	0
Dale, Carl, Buf.	.000	7	0	0	1	1	0
D'Amico, Jeff, Ind.	1.000	6	4	3	0	7	0
Daneker, Pat, Char.-Syr.	.964	29	11	16	1	28	2
Darwin, David, Tol.*	1.000	24	3	8	0	11	1
Davenport, Joe, Char.	.905	59	9	10	2	21	0
Davis, Kane, Buf.-Ind.	1.000	10	4	9	0	13	0
Davis, Lance, Lou.*	1.000	5	0	6	0	6	0
Dedrick, Jim, Buf.	.900	12	2	7	1	10	0
Delahoya, Javier, Roch.	.957	18	7	15	1	23	1
De Paula, Sean, Buf.	1.000	9	1	2	0	3	0
Dessens, Elmer, Lou.	.750	4	2	1	1	4	1
Dewitt, Matt, Syr.	.923	31	3	9	1	13	1
Dingman, Craig, Col.	.933	47	6	8	1	15	0
Dishman, Richard, Rich.	.909	11	4	6	1	11	0
Dodd, Robert, S./W.B.*	.857	16	1	5	1	7	0
Donnelly, Brendan, Syr.	.800	37	2	2	1	5	0
Dougherty, Tony, Ott.	1.000	16	2	3	0	5	0
Drew, Tim, Buf.	.944	16	5	12	1	18	1
Drews, Matt, Dur.	.000	1	0	0	0	0	0
Duvall, Mike, Dur.*	1.000	30	4	12	0	16	2
Dykhoff, Radhames, Nor.*	1.000	32	3	2	0	5	2
Ebert, Derrin, Rich.*	.903	32	9	19	3	31	2
Eichhorn, Mark, Syr.	1.000	17	0	5	0	5	0
Eiland, Dave, Dur.	1.000	4	2	3	0	5	0
Einertson, Darrell, Col.	.923	26	4	8	1	13	0
Eischen, Joey, Buf.-Ott.*	.846	11	2	9	2	13	0
Eldred, Cal, Char.	1.000	2	1	2	0	3	0
Ellis, Robert, Syr.	1.000	16	2	2	0	4	1
Enders, Trevor, Dur.*	1.000	15	2	5	0	7	0
Eshelman, Vaughn, Lou.*	1.000	1	0	1	0	1	0
ESTRADA, Horacio, Ind.*	1.000	25	14	28	0	42	0
Estrella, Leo, Syr.	.933	15	4	10	1	15	1
Evans, Bart, Tol.	.875	24	4	10	2	16	1
Evans, Keith, Ott.	.929	15	7	6	1	14	1
Eyre, Scott, Char.*	1.000	47	1	7	0	8	0
Fernandez, Jared, Paw.	.962	31	7	18	1	26	1
Fernandez, Ozzie, Lou.	1.000	10	3	11	0	14	0
Fesh, Sean, S./W.B.*	1.000	37	2	15	0	17	1
Figueroa, Nelson, S./W.B.	.857	8	3	3	1	7	1
File, Bob, Syr.	1.000	20	1	6	0	7	0
Fiore, Tony, Dur.	.957	53	13	9	1	23	0
Flach, Jason, Rich.	1.000	5	0	3	0	3	0
Flores, Randy, Col.*	.833	4	0	5	1	6	1
Flury, Pat, Ott.	.917	40	5	6	1	12	1
Ford, Ben, Col.	1.000	20	5	8	0	13	0
Fordham, Tom, Ind.*	.917	48	2	9	1	12	0
Forster, Scott, Ott.*	1.000	23	3	7	0	10	1
Foster, Kevin, Paw.	1.000	9	2	4	0	6	0
Frachiseur, Zach, Rich.	1.000	1	0	1	0	1	0
Gardner, Lee, Dur.	1.000	21	0	2	0	2	0
Garland, Jon, Char.	1.000	16	7	25	0	32	1
Gawer, Matt, Rich.*	1.000	3	1	1	0	2	0
Glauber, Keith, Lou.	1.000	18	0	2	0	2	0
Glover, Gary, Syr.	.897	27	11	15	3	29	1
Gomes, Wayne, S./W.B.	1.000	3	0	1	0	1	0
Gonzalez, Gabe, Ott.*	1.000	14	2	3	0	5	0
Gonzalez, Lariel, Nor.	1.000	52	8	6	0	14	1
Grace, Mike, Roch.	1.000	34	0	15	0	15	1
Grahe, Joe, S./W.B.	1.000	3	1	1	0	2	0
Granger, Jeff, Rich.*	1.000	10	0	4	0	4	0
Green, Tyler, Ind.	1.000	11	0	4	0	4	0
Greene, Rick, Lou.	1.000	32	3	7	0	10	1
Guerra, Mark, Nor.	1.000	36	8	8	0	16	3
Gunderson, Eric, Syr.*	1.000	33	1	9	0	10	2
Guzman, Juan, Dur.	1.000	2	0	1	0	1	0
Haines, Talley, Dur.	.000	1	0	0	0	0	0
Halla, Ryan, Rich.	1.000	18	1	0	0	1	0
Halladay, Roy, Tol.	1.000	11	9	10	0	19	1
Hamilton, Jimmy, Roch.*	1.000	2	0	1	0	1	0
Hamilton, Joey, Char.	1.000	6	4	4	0	8	0
Haney, Chris, Buf.*	.944	15	4	13	1	18	1
Harikkala, Tim, Ind.	.950	14	8	11	1	20	1
Harnisch, Pete, Lou.	1.000	1	1	0	0	1	0
Harper, Travis, Dur.	1.000	17	4	11	0	15	0
Harris, Reggie, Dur.-Rich.-Ind.	1.000	38	5	5	0	10	0
Harrison, Tommy, Rich.	1.000	9	1	1	0	2	0
Hasselhoff, Derek, Char.	.867	46	7	6	2	15	0
Hazlett, Andy, Paw.*	.000	3	0	0	0	0	0
Heams, Shane, Tol.	1.000	6	0	1	0	1	1
Henriquez, Oscar, Nor.	1.000	16	2	1	0	3	0
Hernandez, Adrian, Col.	.889	5	2	6	1	9	0
Hiljus, Erik, Tol.	.500	46	0	1	1	2	0
Hill, Ken, Char.	1.000	1	0	1	0	1	0
Holzemer, Mark, S./W.B.*	.900	24	2	7	1	10	0
Hudson, Joe, Lou.	.909	29	3	7	1	11	1
Irabu, Hideki, Ott.	.000	1	0	0	0	0	0
Jackson, Ryan, Dur.*	.000	1	0	0	0	0	0
Jacquez, Tom, S./W.B.*	1.000	35	3	6	0	9	1
Jimenez, Jason, Dur.*	1.000	19	0	3	0	3	1
Johnson, Barry, S./W.B.	.857	56	6	6	2	14	0
Johnson, Craig, Tol.	1.000	1	1	0	0	1	0
Johnson, Jason, Roch.	1.000	8	7	4	0	11	0
Johnson, Mark, Tol.	1.000	17	7	10	0	17	1
Johnson, Mike, Ott.	1.000	5	2	6	0	8	0
Jones, Bobby, Nor.	1.000	4	0	4	0	4	0
Jones, Bobby M., Nor.*	.944	22	7	10	1	18	2
Jordan, Ricardo, Ind.-Rich.*	1.000	43	6	4	0	10	0
Keisler, Randy, Col.*	.889	17	1	15	2	18	0
Kida, Masao, Tol.	1.000	21	3	4	0	7	0
Kim, Sun-Woo, Paw.	.963	26	9	17	1	27	2
King, Ray, Ind.*	.833	29	2	3	1	6	0
Knight, Brandon, Col.	.882	28	13	32	6	51	1
Kohlmeier, Ryan, Roch.	1.000	37	1	7	0	8	0
Krivda, Rick, Roch.*	.913	26	3	18	2	23	1
Lail, Denny, Col.	.943	27	13	20	2	35	1
Larkin, Andy, Col.	.714	27	1	4	2	7	0
LaPlante, Mick, Ott.-Rich.	1.000	11	1	3	0	4	0
Lee, Derek, Ind.*	1.000	3	1	0	0	1	0
Lee, Garrett, Rich.	1.000	2	0	1	0	1	0
Lee, Sang, Paw.*	1.000	45	3	9	0	12	0
Leek, Randy, Tol.*	1.000	1	0	1	0	1	0
Lemonis, Chris, Tol.	.000	1	0	0	0	0	0
Levrault, Allen, Ind.	.966	21	8	20	1	29	0
Lewis, Richie, Nor.-Buf.	1.000	11	9	13	0	22	0
Lidle, Cory, Dur.	.947	9	8	10	1	19	0
Ligtenberg, Kerry, Rich.	.000	5	0	0	0	0	0
Lilly, Ted, Col.*	.880	22	8	14	3	25	0
Lira, Felipe, Ott.	1.000	4	0	6	0	6	0
Lisio, Joe, Col.	1.000	2	0	1	0	1	0
Looney, Brian, Buf.*	1.000	8	0	1	0	1	0
Lorraine, Andrew, Buf.*	1.000	14	4	15	0	19	0
Lowe, Sean, Char.	1.000	2	0	1	0	1	0
Ludwick, Eric, Ind.	1.000	12	1	8	0	9	1
Luebbers, Larry, Lou.	.962	18	12	13	1	26	1
Lukasiewicz, Mark, Syr.*	.857	42	3	3	1	7	1
Maduro, Calvin, Roch.	1.000	4	0	1	0	1	0
Maeda, Kats, Col.	.000	1	0	0	0	0	0
Mairena, Ozwaldo, Col.*	1.000	5	1	1	0	2	0
Maloney, Sean, Roch.	.909	37	3	7	1	11	0
Mann, Jim, Nor.	1.000	49	5	6	0	11	1
Marquez, Robert, Ott.	.955	53	5	16	1	22	4
Marquis, Jason, Rich.	1.000	6	1	2	0	3	1
Martin, Tom, Buf.*	1.000	9	0	1	0	1	0
Martinez, Ramon, Paw.	1.000	2	2	0	0	2	0
Martinez, Willie, Buf.	1.000	28	7	13	0	20	2
Matos, Francisco, Roch.	.000	1	0	0	0	0	0
McAvoy, Jeff, Ott.	1.000	6	2	1	0	3	0
McDill, Allen, Tol.*	1.000	16	1	4	0	5	0
McDougal, Mike, Roch.	1.000	14	2	4	0	6	0
McGlinchy, Kevin, Rich.	1.000	9	0	1	0	1	0
Medina, Rafael, Syr.	.667	33	0	2	1	3	0
Mendez, Carlos, Tol.	.000	1	0	0	0	0	0
Mercado, Hector, Lou.*	.941	47	1	15	1	17	0
Michalak, Chris, Dur.*	1.000	6	0	1	0	1	0
Mitchell, Scott, Ott.	.882	28	7	8	2	17	1
Mix, Greg, Ind.	1.000	38	2	7	0	9	0
Milcki, Dave, Ind.	1.000	1	1	0	0	1	0
Mohler, Mike, Buf.*	1.000	3	2	2	0	4	0
Molina, Gabe, Roch.-Rich.	1.000	27	1	4	0	5	0
Moore, Trey, Ott.*	1.000	12	6	15	0	21	1
Morris, Jim, Dur.*	.000	1	0	0	0	0	0
Moss, Damian, Rich.*	.813	29	5	21	6	32	3
Mota, Guillermo, Ott.	1.000	35	7	20	0	27	1
Munoz, Bobby, Lou.	.793	21	6	17	6	29	3
Munro, Peter, Syr.	.933	10	7	7	1	15	3
Myette, Aaron, Char.	.889	19	5	11	2	18	1
Nagy, Charles, Buf.	1.000	3	1	2	0	3	0
Navarro, Jaime, Buf.	1.000	12	2	6	0	8	0
Newman, Alan, Buf.*	.692	32	1	8	4	13	0
Nichting, Chris, Buf.	.900	47	1	8	1	10	0
Nussbeck, Mark, Roch.	.000	4	0	0	0	0	0
Ogea, Chad, Buf.	1.000	1	0	1	0	1	0
Ohka, Tomo, Paw.	1.000	19	13	21	0	34	0
Oquist, Mike, Tol.	.911	29	17	24	4	45	4
Osting, Jimmy, Rich.*	1.000	3	0	1	0	1	0

Player, Team	Pct.	G	PO	A	E	TC	DP
Pacheco, Delvis, Rich.	1.000	25	1	3	0	4	0
Paronto, Chad, Roch.	1.000	12	2	2	0	4	0
Parrish, John, Roch.*	.886	18	3	28	4	35	2
Pena, Jesus, Char.*	1.000	21	3	1	0	4	0
Penney, Mike, Ind.	1.000	17	1	2	0	3	0
Perez, Dario, Paw.	.889	14	0	8	1	9	2
Pettyjohn, Adam, Tol.*	1.000	7	1	10	0	11	0
Phelps, Travis, Dur.	.900	6	1	8	1	10	0
Pichardo, Hipolito, Paw.	1.000	3	0	1	0	1	0
Pina, Rafael, Roch.	1.000	14	3	8	0	11	0
Pisciotta, Marc, Buf.	1.000	19	1	6	0	7	1
Politte, Cliff, S./W.B.	.962	21	10	15	1	26	3
Poole, Jim, Buf.*	1.000	10	0	3	0	3	0
Post, Dave, Ott.	1.000	4	1	0	0	1	0
Powell, Jeremy, Ott.	.962	25	12	13	1	26	0
Pugh, Tim, Rich.	1.000	18	10	13	0	23	2
Pujals, Denis, Dur.	.833	20	3	7	2	12	0
Pulsipher, Bill, Nor.*	.857	7	1	5	1	7	0
Ramirez, Hector, Ind.-Roch.	.875	41	4	3	1	8	1
Reed, Brandon, Tol.	1.000	45	5	2	0	7	1
Rekar, Bryan, Dur.	.875	4	4	3	1	8	0
Reyes, Al, Roch.	1.000	9	2	1	0	3	1
Riedling, John, Lou.	1.000	53	8	12	0	20	0
Rigby, Brad, Ott.	.765	24	6	7	4	17	1
Rigdon, Paul, Buf.	1.000	12	5	4	0	9	1
Riley, Matt, Roch.*	.000	2	0	0	1	1	0
Rincon, Ricardo, Buf.*	.500	2	0	1	1	2	0
Riske, David, Buf.	1.000	2	0	1	0	1	0
Rivera, Luis, Rich.-Roch.	1.000	11	3	9	0	12	2
Robbins, Jake, Col.	.000	1	0	0	0	0	0
Roberts, Grant, Nor.	.898	25	21	23	5	49	1
Roberts, Mark, Char.	1.000	14	7	4	0	11	0
Roberts, Willis, Lou.	.973	25	17	19	1	37	2
Rocker, John, Rich.*	.000	3	0	0	0	0	0
Rodriguez, Nerio, Paw.	1.000	12	3	5	0	8	0
Rodriguez, Rich, Nor.*	1.000	14	0	4	0	4	0
Rojas, Mel, Paw.	.000	3	0	0	0	0	0
Romano, Mike, Syr.	1.000	10	2	7	0	9	0
Roque, Rafael, Ind.*	.958	25	5	18	1	24	0
Rose, Brian, Paw.	1.000	5	3	2	0	5	1
Rose, Ted, Lou.	1.000	23	3	2	0	5	0
Ruebel, Matt, Ott.*	1.000	7	3	3	0	6	0
Runyan, Sean, Tol.*	1.000	44	1	1	0	2	0
Rupe, Ryan, Dur.	1.000	5	0	1	0	1	0
Rust, Brian, Roch.	.000	1	0	0	0	0	0
Rutherford, Mark, S./W.B.	1.000	2	0	2	0	2	2
Ryan, B.J., Roch.*	1.000	14	2	3	0	5	0
Ryan, Ken, Col.	1.000	4	0	2	0	2	0
Ryan, Matt, Roch.	.941	46	6	26	2	34	2
Saberhagen, Bret, Paw.	1.000	4	1	3	0	4	0
Salyers, Jeremy, Ott.	.000	1	0	0	0	0	0
Sanders, Frankie, Buf.	1.000	5	3	4	0	7	1
Sanders, Scott, Buf.	1.000	7	6	5	0	11	0
Santana, Julio, Paw.	.923	12	4	8	1	13	1
Santos, Victor, Tol.	.500	2	0	1	1	2	0
Scanlan, Bob, Ind.	.944	57	7	10	1	18	1
Schilling, Curt, S./W.B.	1.000	1	0	1	0	1	0
Schmack, Brian, Char.	.905	51	6	13	2	21	1
Schourek, Pete, Paw.*	1.000	1	0	1	0	1	0
Schrenk, Steve, S./W.B.	1.000	26	1	4	0	5	0
Scott, Tim, Lou.	1.000	16	0	1	0	1	0
Seberino, Ronni, Dur.*	.000	12	0	0	0	0	0
Secoda, Jason, Char.	.889	32	6	18	3	27	2
Seelbach, Chris, Rich.	1.000	29	9	17	0	26	2
Sekany, Jason, Paw.	1.000	17	5	5	0	10	0
Sheets, Andy, Paw.	.000	2	0	0	0	0	0
Sheets, Ben, Ind.	1.000	14	8	12	0	20	0
Shouse, Brian, Nor.-Roch.*	1.000	47	4	2	0	6	0
Shumaker, A., Roc.-S./W.B.-Nor.*	1.000	32	10	18	0	28	3
Sido, Wilson, Buf.	1.000	1	1	0	0	1	0
Skrmetta, Matt, Ott.	1.000	32	1	1	0	2	0
Small, Mark, Ott.	1.000	12	2	3	0	5	1
Smart, J.D., Ott.	.000	4	0	0	0	0	0
Smith, Dan, Rich.*	.905	53	3	16	2	21	0
Smith, Dan, Paw.	1.000	24	12	13	0	25	2
Smith, Travis, Ind.	1.000	3	1	5	0	6	0
Snusz, Chris, Ott.	1.000	2	0	1	0	1	0
Snyder, Bill, Tol.	1.000	18	2	3	0	5	1
Snyder, John, Ind.	1.000	1	0	4	0	4	0
Snyder, Matt, Roch.	1.000	10	1	3	0	4	0
Soderstrom, Steve, Lou.	.938	31	11	19	2	32	2
Sparks, Jeff, Dur.	1.000	9	0	1	0	1	0
Sparks, Steve, Tol.	.943	16	11	22	2	35	2
Speier, Justin, Buf.	1.000	13	1	2	0	3	0
Spencer, Sean, Ott.*	1.000	10	0	3	0	3	0
Springer, Dennis, Nor.	1.000	25	8	5	0	13	2
Spurgeon, Jay, Roch.	1.000	2	0	3	0	3	0
Stanifer, Rob, Paw.	1.000	41	2	11	0	13	1
Stevens, Dave, Rich.	.905	51	7	12	2	21	2
Stevenson, Rod, Ott.	.667	10	0	2	1	3	0
Stewart, Scott, Nor.*	1.000	53	2	11	0	13	0
Strickland, Scott, Ott.	.000	3	0	0	0	0	0
Stull, Everett, Ind.	1.000	16	6	17	0	23	1
Tatis, Ramon, Col.*	.889	7	4	4	1	9	0
Taylor, Bill, Dur.	.917	42	0	11	1	12	1
Taylor, Kerry, Syr.	1.000	33	5	21	0	26	0
Tejero, Fausto, S./W.B.	1.000	1	0	1	0	1	0
Telemaco, Amaury, S./W.B.	.955	21	10	11	1	22	0
Tessmer, Jay, Col.	.850	60	4	13	3	20	2
Thomas, Evan, S./W.B.	1.000	29	13	11	0	24	1
Thurman, Mike, Ott.	1.000	4	0	3	0	3	0
Tolar, Kevin, Tol.*	.875	33	2	5	1	8	0
Towers, Josh, Roch.	.886	24	11	20	4	35	2
Unroe, Tim, Rich.	.000	1	0	0	0	0	0
Valdes, Marc, Dur.	.857	9	2	4	1	7	1
Villafuerte, Brandon, Tol.	1.000	46	10	9	0	19	1
Villegas, Ismael, Rich.	.882	41	5	10	2	17	0
Vosberg, Ed, S./W.B.*	.000	1	0	0	0	0	0
Wade, Terrell, Lou.*	.000	2	0	0	1	1	0
Walker, Tyler, Nor.	1.000	5	0	2	0	2	0
Walls, Doug, Tol.	.875	18	2	5	1	8	0
Ward, Bryan, S./W.B.*	.800	22	0	4	1	5	0
Wasdin, John, Paw.	1.000	5	0	2	0	2	0
Watson, Allen, Col.*	1.000	5	0	3	0	3	0
Watson, Mark, Buf.*	.833	16	2	3	1	6	0
Weaver, Jeff, Tol.	1.000	1	1	1	0	2	0
Weber, Neil, Lou.-Roch.*	1.000	3	0	0	0	0	0
Wells, Kip, Char.	1.000	12	2	6	0	8	0
Wengert, Don, Rich.	1.000	29	10	8	0	18	1
Westbrook, Jake, Col.	.967	16	9	20	1	30	2
Wheeler, Dan, Nor.	1.000	26	12	20	0	32	2
White, Matt, Dur.	.500	6	0	1	1	2	0
Williams, Brian, Buf.	.875	18	3	4	1	8	0
Williams, Matt, Col.*	1.000	27	2	5	0	7	2
Wilson, Jeff, Roch.*	.000	11	0	0	0	0	0
Wilson, Paul, Nor.	1.000	15	4	9	0	13	2
Winchester, Scott, Lou.	1.000	43	8	9	0	17	0
Winkelsas, Joe, Rich.	.750	4	0	3	1	4	0
Wohlers, Mark, Lou.	.500	17	1	0	1	2	0
Wright, Jamey, Ind.	1.000	1	0	1	0	1	0
Wright, Jaret, Buf.	.000	1	0	0	0	0	0
Yarnall, Ed, Col.-Lou.*	1.000	21	3	15	0	18	0
Young, Tim, Paw.*	1.000	32	1	6	0	7	0
Zambrano, Victor, Dur.	.750	53	1	8	3	12	0

PITCHERS WITH TWO OR MORE TEAMS

Player, Team	Pct.	G	PO	A	E	TC	DP
Brea, Lesli, Nor.	1.000	1	0	2	0	2	0
Brea, Lesli, Roch.	.571	4	2	2	3	7	0
Buddie, Mike, Col.	1.000	6	4	5	0	9	0
Buddie, Mike, Ind.	.929	30	4	9	1	14	0
Daneker, Pat, Char.	.962	27	10	15	1	26	2
Daneker, Pat, Syr.	1.000	2	1	1	0	2	0
Davis, Kane, Buf.	1.000	1	1	6	0	7	0
Davis, Kane, Ind.	1.000	4	3	3	0	6	0
Eischen, Joey, Buf.*	.000	1	0	0	0	0	0
Eischen, Joey, Ott.*	.846	10	2	9	2	13	0
Harris, Reggie, Dur.	1.000	4	2	0	0	2	0
Harris, Reggie, Rich.	1.000	5	0	2	0	2	0
Harris, Reggie, Ind.	1.000	29	3	3	0	6	0
Jordan, Ricardo, Ind.*	1.000	4	1	0	0	1	0
Jordan, Ricardo, Rich.*	1.000	39	5	4	0	9	0
LaPlante, Mick, Ott.	.000	3	0	0	0	0	0
LaPlante, Mick, Rich.	1.000	8	1	3	0	4	0
Lewis, Richie, Nor.	1.000	9	9	12	0	21	0
Lewis, Richie, Buf.	1.000	2	0	1	0	1	0
Molina, Gabe, Roch.	1.000	18	1	3	0	4	0
Molina, Gabe, Rich.	1.000	9	0	1	0	1	0
Ramirez, Hector, Ind.	.667	15	1	1	1	3	0
Ramirez, Hector, Roch.	1.000	26	3	2	0	5	1
Rivera, Luis, Rich.	1.000	8	2	7	0	9	2
Rivera, Luis, Roch.	1.000	3	1	2	0	3	0
Shouse, Brian, Nor.*	.000	4	0	0	0	0	0
Shouse, Brian, Roch.*	1.000	43	4	2	0	6	0

CLASS AAA International League

Player, Team	Pct.	G	PO	A	E	TC	DP
Shumaker, Anthony, Roch.*	1.000	10	3	7	0	10	1
Shumaker, Anthony, S./W.B.*	1.000	1	0	1	0	1	0
Shumaker, Anthony, Nor.*	1.000	21	7	10	0	17	2
Weber, Neil, Lou.*	.000	2	0	0	0	0	0
Weber, Neil, Roch.*	.000	1	0	0	0	0	0

Player, Team	Pct.	G	PO	A	E	TC	DP
Yarnall, Ed, Col.*	1.000	10	0	7	0	7	0
Yarnall, Ed, Lou.*	1.000	11	3	8	0	11	0

The following players appeared only as designated hitter, pinch-hitter or pinch runner: Blanco, dh; Malave, dh; Ochoa, ph; M. Ramirez, dh.

LEAGUE CHAMPIONS

Year	Team	Pct.
1884—	Trenton	.520
1885—	Syracuse	.584
1886—	Utica	.646
1887—	Toronto	.644
1888—	Syracuse	.723
1889—	Detroit	.649
1890—	Detroit	.617
1891—	Buffalo (reg. season)	.727
	Buffalo (supplemental)	.680
1892—	Providence	.615
	Binghamton*	.667
1893—	Erie	.606
1894—	Providence	.696
1895—	Springfield	.687
1896—	Providence	.602
1897—	Syracuse	.632
1898—	Montreal	.586
1899—	Rochester	.624
1900—	Providence	.616
1901—	Rochester	.642
1902—	Toronto	.669
1903—	Jersey City	.742
1904—	Buffalo	.657
1905—	Providence	.638
1906—	Buffalo	.607
1907—	Toronto	.619
1908—	Baltimore	.593
1909—	Rochester	.596
1910—	Rochester	.601
1911—	Rochester	.645
1912—	Toronto	.595
1913—	Newark	.625
1914—	Providence	.617
1915—	Buffalo	.632
1916—	Buffalo	.586
1917—	Toronto	.604
1918—	Toronto	.693
1919—	Baltimore	.671
1920—	Baltimore	.719
1921—	Baltimore	.717
1922—	Baltimore	.689
1923—	Baltimore	.677
1924—	Baltimore	.709
1925—	Baltimore	.633
1926—	Toronto	.657
1927—	Buffalo	.667
1928—	Rochester	.549
1929—	Rochester	.613
1930—	Rochester	.629
1931—	Rochester	.601
1932—	Newark	.649
1933—	Newark	.622
	Buffalo (4th)†	.494
1934—	Newark	.608
	Toronto (3rd)†	.559
1935—	Montreal	.597
	Syracuse (2nd)†	.565
1936—	Buffalo‡	.610
1937—	Newark‡	.717
1938—	Newark‡	.684
1939—	Jersey City	.582
	Rochester (2nd)†	.556
1940—	Rochester	.611
	Newark (2nd)†	.594
1941—	Newark	.649
	Montreal (2nd)†	.584
1942—	Newark	.601
	Syracuse (3rd)†	.513
1943—	Toronto	.625
	Syracuse (3rd)†	.536
1944—	Baltimore‡	.553
1945—	Montreal	.621
	Newark (2nd)†	.582
1946—	Montreal‡	.649
1947—	Jersey City	.610
	Syracuse (3rd)†	.575
1948—	Montreal‡	.614
1949—	Buffalo	.584
	Montreal (3rd)†	.545
1950—	Rochester	.609
	Baltimore (3rd)†	.556
1951—	Montreal‡	.617
1952—	Montreal	.629
	Rochester (3rd)†	.619
1953—	Rochester	.630
	Montreal (2nd)†	.586
1954—	Toronto	.630
	Syracuse (4th)§	.510
1955—	Montreal	.617
	Rochester (4th)†	.497
1956—	Toronto	.566
	Rochester (2nd)†	.553
1957—	Toronto	.575
	Buffalo (2nd)†	.571
1958—	Montreal‡	.588
1959—	Buffalo	.582
	Havana (3rd)†	.523
1960—	Toronto‡	.649
	Buffalo (3rd)†	.559
1961—	Columbus	.597
	Buffalo (3rd)†	.559
1962—	Jacksonville	.610
	Atlanta (3rd)†	.539
1963—	Syracuse∞	.533
	Indianapolis‡	.562
1964—	Jacksonville	.589
	Rochester (4th)†	.532
1965—	Columbus	.582
	Toronto (3rd)†	.556
1966—	Rochester	.565
	Toronto (2nd-tied)†	.558
1967—	Richmond	.574
	Toledo (3rd)†	.525
1968—	Toledo	.565
	Jacksonville (4th)†	.514
1969—	Tidewater	.563
	Syracuse (3rd)†	.536
1970—	Syracuse‡	.600
1971—	Rochester‡	.614
1972—	Louisville	.563
	Tidewater (3rd)†	.545
1973—	Charleston	.586
	Pawtuckets†	.534
1974—	Memphis	.613
	Rochester ∞‡	.611
1975—	Tidewater‡	.610
1976—	Rochester	.638
	Syracuse (2nd)†	.590
1977—	Pawtucket	.571
	Charleston (2nd)‡	.557
1978—	Charleston	.607
	Richmond (4th)†	.511
1979—	Columbus‡	.612
1980—	Columbus‡	.593
1981—	Columbus‡	.633
1982—	Richmond	.590
	Tidewater (3rd)†	.540
1983—	Columbus	.593
	Tidewater (4th)†	.511
1984—	Columbus	.590
	Pawtucket (4th)†	.536
1985—	Syracuse	.564
	Tidewater (4th)†	.540
1986—	Richmond‡	.571
1987—	Tidewater	.579
	Columbus†	.550
1988—	Rochester◆	.546
	Tidewater	.546
1989—	Syracuse	.572
	Richmond◆	.555
1990—	Rochester◆	.614
	Columbus	.596
1991—	Columbus◆	.590
	Pawtucket	.552
1992—	Columbus◆	.660
	Scr. W.B.	.592
1993—	Charlotte◆	.610
	Rochester	.525
1994—	Richmond◆	.567
	Pawtucket	.549
1995—	Norfolk	.606
	Ottawa◆	.507
1996—	Columbus◆	.599
	Rochester	.511
1997—	Rochester◆	.589
	Columbus	.556
1998—	Buffalo■	.566
1999—	Columbus	.589
	Charlotte▲	.569
2000—	Buffalo	.593
	Indianapolis▲	.563

*Won split-season playoff. †Won four-team playoff. ‡Won championship and four-team playoff. §Defeated Havana in game to decide fourth place, then won four-team playoff. ∞League was divided into Northern, Southern divisions. ◆League divided into Eastern, Western divisions; won playoffs. ■League divided into Eastern, Northern and Southern divisions; won four-team playoff. ▲League divided into North, South and West divisions; won four-team playoff. (NOTE—Known as Eastern League in 1884, New York State League in 1885, International League in 1886-87, International Association in 1888, International League in 1889-90, Eastern Association in 1891 and Eastern League from 1892 until 1912.)

MEXICAN LEAGUE

Note: Final official Mexican League statistics were not available at publication time; therefore, following is an abbreviated set of final unofficial statistics.

2000 FINAL STANDINGS

FIRST HALF

NORTHERN ZONE

Team	W	L	T	Pct.	GB
Saltillo	39	22	1	.639	....
Torreon	30	32	0	.484	9.5
Monterrey	29	33	0	.468	10.5
Monclova	28	33	1	.459	11.0
Nuevo Laredo	28	33	0	.459	11.0
Reynosa	26	36	0	.419	13.5

CENTRAL ZONE

Team	W	L	T	Pct.	GB
Mexico City Reds	39	21	0	.650	....
Mexico City Tigers	36	23	1	.610	2.5
Oaxaca	30	28	1	.517	8.0
Cordoba	28	31	0	.475	10.5
Puebla	22	39	0	.361	17.5

SOUTHERN ZONE

Team	W	L	T	Pct.	GB
Yucatan	35	27	0	.565	....
Tabasco	34	28	0	.548	1.0
Veracruz	31	30	0	.508	3.5
Campeche	30	30	0	.500	4.0
Cancun	21	40	0	.344	13.5

SECOND HALF

NORTHERN ZONE

Team	W	L	T	Pct.	GB
Saltillo	38	20	0	.655	....
Monclova	30	30	0	.500	9.0
Monterrey	30	30	0	.500	9.0
Torreon	26	33	0	.441	12.5
Nuevo Laredo	26	33	0	.441	12.5
Reynosa	24	33	1	.421	13.5

CENTRAL ZONE

Team	W	L	T	Pct.	GB
Mexico City Tigers	38	21	1	.644	....
Mexico City Reds	31	26	0	.544	6.0
Oaxaca	29	29	1	.500	8.5
Puebla	28	29	1	.491	9.0
Cordoba	25	32	1	.439	12.0

SOUTHERN ZONE

Team	W	L	T	Pct.	GB
Yucatan	34	25	1	.576	....
Tabasco	32	27	0	.542	2.0
Veracruz	30	28	1	.517	3.5
Campeche	29	30	1	.492	5.0
Cancun	17	41	2	.293	16.5

COMPOSITE

NORTHERN ZONE

Team	W	L	T	Pct.	GB
Saltillo	77	42	1	.647	....
Monterrey	59	63	0	.484	19.5
Monclova	58	63	1	.479	20.0
Torreon	56	65	0	.463	22.0
Nuevo Laredo	54	66	0	.450	23.5
Reynosa	50	69	1	.420	27.0

CENTRAL ZONE

Team	W	L	T	Pct.	GB
Mexico City Tigers	74	44	2	.627	....
Mexico City Reds	70	47	0	.598	3.5
Oaxaca	59	57	2	.509	14.0
Cordoba	53	63	1	.457	20.0
Puebla	50	68	1	.424	24.0

SOUTHERN ZONE

Team	W	L	T	Pct.	GB
Yucatan	69	52	1	.570	....
Tabasco	66	55	0	.545	3.0
Veracruz	61	58	1	.513	7.0
Campeche	59	60	1	.496	9.0
Cancun	38	81	2	.319	30.0

PLAYOFFS—Monterrey defeated Saltillo, four games to one; Mexico City Reds defeated Veracruz, four games to two; Mexico City Tigers defeated Oaxaca, four games to two; Yucatan defeated Tabasco, four games to one, in the first round; Mexico City Tigers defeated Monterrey, two games to one; Yucatan defeated Mexico City Reds, two games to one, in the second round; Mexico City Tigers defeated Mexico City Reds, four games to one, in final series to capture league championship.

(Compiled by Ana Luisa Perea Talarico, League Statistician, Mexico, D.F.)

2000 BATTING

TEAM

Team	Avg.	AB	R	H	HR	BB	SO	SB	CS
Oaxaca	.324	4028	747	1306	146	493	539	50	42
Mexico City Reds	.320	4145	854	1328	212	515	707	50	24
Mexico City Tigers	.319	4173	845	1331	160	468	666	109	58
Saltillo	.312	4218	789	1318	177	590	764	99	49
Torreon	.312	4213	738	1314	139	527	701	45	25
Monterrey	.306	4218	688	1289	112	439	546	77	51
Nuevo Laredo	.293	4053	628	1187	139	470	614	38	53
Tabasco	.293	4119	583	1205	101	428	571	42	34
Cordoba	.291	3936	636	1146	116	408	660	100	58
Campeche	.287	3963	551	1138	63	415	565	72	46
Yucatan	.286	4073	612	1164	103	527	707	69	44
Monclova	.285	4113	684	1172	138	560	701	53	34
Veracruz	.284	4008	626	1139	118	502	591	99	47
Puebla	.282	3948	573	1115	103	401	728	27	26
Reynosa	.282	4082	620	1153	131	395	661	56	42
Cancun	.268	4134	556	1108	110	380	636	38	27

TOP QUALIFIERS FOR BATTING CHAMPIONSHIP

Minimum 329 plate appearances.

Player, Team	Avg.	G	TPA	AB	R	H	TB	2B	3B	HR	RBI	SH	SF	HP	BB	IBB	SO	SB	CS	GDP	Slg.	OBP
Newson, Warren, Tor.*	.386	112	509	417	104	161	306	26	1	39	121	1	0	1	90	3	91	3	2	8	.734	.496
Azocar, Oscar, Oax.*	.377	118	535	491	79	185	266	36	0	15	89	2	8	6	28	6	16	4	5	17	.542	.411
Gastelum, Sergio, Tig.	.377	111	510	438	108	165	248	18	13	13	77	8	2	16	46	1	40	31	11	8	.566	.452
Garcia, Cornelio, Tor.*	.371	94	447	372	75	138	167	24	1	1	35	7	1	1	66	4	52	8	4	5	.449	.466
Lopez, Fabian, Oax.*	.367	101	376	341	57	125	172	23	0	8	50	0	1	0	34	1	26	3	3	17	.504	.423
Rodarte, Raul, Lar.-Rey.	.364	107	447	393	81	143	247	28	2	24	98	2	6	3	43	1	64	15	3	15	.628	.425
De Los Santos, Luis, Sal.	.363	100	439	391	79	142	247	28	1	25	94	2	5	1	40	3	59	0	1	19	.632	.419
Alvarez, Hector, Oax.	.361	109	521	471	92	170	238	26	6	10	78	4	5	5	36	1	64	1	3	21	.505	.408
Munoz, Noe, Sal.	.360	106	479	394	86	142	207	30	1	11	64	4	2	2	77	5	48	0	2	15	.525	.465
Barron, Tony, Mont.	.356	118	513	432	82	154	244	34	1	18	93	0	4	4	73	6	78	8	1	17	.565	.450

DEPARTMENTAL LEADERS: G—L. Arredondo, Je. Gonzalez, Morejon, 121; AB—L. Arredondo, 513; R—Adriana, 113; H—Azocar, 185; TB—Newson, 306; 2B—Tellez, 37; 3B—S. Gastelum, 13; HR—Jimenez, 45; RBI—Yan, 129; SH—Guizar, En. Ramirez, 17; SF—Yan, 10; HP—Zambrano, 23; BB—Jimenez, 108; IBB—Jimenez, 23; SO—Chance, 115; SB—W. Romero, 45; CS—L. Arredondo, 22; GIDP—A. Cedeno, O. Romero, 30; Slg.—Newson, .734; OBP—Newson, .496.

ALL PLAYERS

Player, Team	Avg.	G	TPA	AB	R	H	TB	2B	3B	HR	RBI	SH	SF	HP	BB	IBB	SO	SB	CS	GDP	Slg.	OBP
Abrego, Jesus, Can.*	.258	81	276	240	30	62	77	6	0	3	26	5	3	3	25	2	36	2	2	8	.321	.332
Acosta, Francisco, Tab.	.357	9	21	14	3	5	8	0	0	1	2	2	0	0	5	0	3	0	3	0	.571	.526
Acuna, Jose Luis, Tor.†	.319	71	170	141	29	45	50	3	1	0	13	7	2	1	19	1	22	1	2	3	.355	.399
Adriana, Sharnol, Cor.-Cam.	.326	117	500	408	113	133	246	20	3	29	88	2	6	13	71	3	90	24	12	6	.603	.436
Aganza, Ruben, Monc.	.303	120	507	449	66	136	200	26	1	12	87	3	9	3	43	3	47	3	1	16	.445	.361
Aguilera, Antonio, Cor.*	.261	50	169	142	18	37	48	5	0	2	16	3	1	2	21	1	31	2	3	5	.338	.361
Aguilera, Armando, Sal.*	.204	49	105	93	14	19	26	1	0	2	11	3	0	1	8	0	19	1	1	1	.280	.275
Almeida, Shammar, Oax.*	.245	52	72	49	10	12	26	2	0	4	12	1	2	4	16	0	17	0	0	0	.531	.451
Alvarez, Hector, Oax.	.361	109	521	471	92	170	238	26	6	10	78	4	5	5	36	1	64	1	3	21	.505	.408
Alvarez, Jorge, Cor.	.292	48	210	195	27	57	88	13	0	6	40	0	3	0	12	1	37	1	0	4	.451	.329
Amescua, Alex, Mont.	.411	29	121	107	23	44	73	12	1	5	21	1	1	0	12	1	16	0	0	3	.682	.467
Arano, Eloy, Ver.†	.264	99	367	333	58	88	114	4	2	6	28	1	0	3	30	0	46	20	9	6	.342	.331
Arano, Marco, Tab.	.279	51	157	140	20	39	44	2	0	1	13	4	1	0	12	1	25	1	0	4	.314	.333
Arano, Wilfrido, Lar.*	.314	104	372	315	51	99	143	22	2	6	36	2	2	5	48	4	30	1	4	13	.454	.411
Arauz, Leobardo, Yuc.†	.211	98	257	223	24	47	66	8	1	3	20	2	3	1	28	1	51	0	0	3	.296	.298
Arias, Francisco, Oax.	.290	62	154	131	23	38	51	8	1	1	15	5	3	3	12	0	22	1	1	4	.389	.356
Armenta, Cristian, Lar.	.267	18	16	15	3	4	4	0	0	0	1	0	1	0	0	0	2	1	0	1	.267	.250
Armenta, Guillermo, Ver.†	.218	40	171	147	18	32	34	2	0	0	6	0	1	2	21	0	13	6	5	4	.231	.322
Arredondo, Hernando, Cam.	.285	99	369	344	43	98	140	21	3	5	47	7	1	1	16	2	62	3	3	9	.407	.318
Arredondo, Jesus, Pue.*	.296	111	484	402	74	119	154	17	6	2	33	4	1	11	66	4	51	3	2	4	.383	.408
Arredondo, Luis, Yuc.*	.339	121	568	513	94	174	232	21	8	7	43	3	1	5	46	4	68	43	22	9	.452	.388
Avila, Ruben, Tor.	.222	29	69	63	7	14	17	0	0	1	10	0	1	0	5	0	12	0	0	3	.270	.275
Azocar, Oscar, Oax.*	.377	118	535	491	79	185	266	36	0	15	89	2	8	6	28	6	16	4	5	17	.542	.411
Barajas, Edison, Cor.*	.209	59	151	139	7	29	39	7	0	1	13	1	0	5	6	1	32	0	0	4	.281	.247
Barrera, Nelson, Oax.	.286	93	375	346	55	99	184	16	0	23	71	0	4	4	21	2	74	2	1	11	.532	.331
Barron, Tony, Mont.	.356	118	513	432	82	154	244	34	1	18	93	0	4	4	73	6	78	8	1	17	.565	.450
Belk, Tim, Tab.	.321	36	148	134	15	43	63	5	0	5	30	2	4	2	6	1	17	0	0	5	.470	.349
Bell, Juan, Cor.-Cam.†	.271	96	425	351	65	95	149	17	2	11	57	2	8	7	57	3	49	8	5	10	.425	.376
Beltran, Gerardo, Tab.	.000	3	2	0	0	0	0	0	0	0	0	0	0	0	1	1	0	0	0	0	.000	.333
Beltran, Juan, Cam.	.205	33	48	44	10	9	11	2	0	0	3	0	0	0	4	0	13	2	2	0	.250	.271
Bojorquez, Victor, Mex.	.317	113	468	445	68	141	224	26	9	13	56	2	3	2	16	2	69	4	2	16	.503	.341
Bolado, Carlos, Ver.	.275	60	88	69	17	19	25	3	0	1	11	5	2	0	12	0	15	2	1	2	.362	.373
Brena, Jaime, Oax.	.222	4	9	9	0	2	2	0	0	0	0	0	0	0	0	0	1	0	1	0	.222	.222
Brewer, Rodney, Ver.	.283	119	513	410	75	116	211	23	0	24	86	0	6	9	88	4	72	2	1	13	.515	.415
Brooks, Jerry, Lar.-Yuc.	.158	11	43	38	5	6	9	0	0	1	5	0	0	0	5	0	6	0	1	1	.237	.256
Bruno, Julio, Tab.	.296	114	509	463	56	137	190	23	0	10	65	6	2	2	36	3	51	0	2	15	.410	.348
Bullett, Scott, Rey.	.333	119	515	471	94	157	293	23	4	35	100	1	5	9	29	8	78	24	9	7	.622	.379
Bustamante, Omar, Lar.	.211	53	116	109	10	23	37	2	0	4	12	1	0	2	4	0	22	0	1	2	.339	.252
Bustillos, Luis, Rey.	.193	84	277	243	32	47	70	6	1	5	29	9	2	3	20	0	48	1	0	9	.288	.261
Camacho, Reginaldo, Rey.	.239	43	98	92	5	22	29	4	0	1	8	2	0	1	3	0	23	0	0	3	.315	.271
Campusano, Silvestre, Can.	.256	33	146	129	18	33	49	5	1	3	11	1	1	1	14	0	21	1	1	0	.380	.331
Canales, Joel, Cam.	.000	2	4	3	0	0	0	0	0	0	0	0	0	0	1	0	1	0	0	0	.000	.250
Cancino, Jorge, Ver.*	.077	13	16	13	5	1	1	0	0	0	0	0	0	1	2	0	6	0	0	1	.077	.250
Canizalez, Juan, Mont.†	.344	116	494	436	74	150	217	19	3	14	71	0	5	4	49	5	52	1	3	24	.498	.411
Carbajal, Jovino, Tab.†	.230	14	65	61	6	14	18	4	0	0	5	0	0	0	4	1	11	4	0	2	.295	.277
Carrasco, Ernesto, Pue.†	.241	111	387	328	40	79	97	7	1	3	31	4	4	9	42	3	52	1	3	4	.296	.339
Carrillo, Matias, Tig.*	.331	113	504	438	98	145	252	26	3	25	110	0	1	4	61	10	44	5	4	8	.575	.417
Castaneda, Hector, Yuc.*	.285	108	451	372	52	106	157	20	2	9	63	2	3	4	70	4	80	4	2	17	.422	.401
Castaneda, Rafael, Yuc.	.270	112	489	411	63	111	148	16	0	7	44	11	3	3	61	2	40	7	2	19	.360	.364
Castellano, Pedro, Mex.	.331	115	532	450	108	149	269	26	2	30	111	0	9	5	68	5	78	2	0	25	.598	.425
Castro, Arnoldo, Can.	.296	118	527	473	64	140	179	22	1	5	49	13	2	0	39	1	31	2	2	16	.378	.348
Castro, Domingo, Monc.	.243	90	259	230	28	56	74	5	2	3	29	7	2	2	18	0	37	3	3	5	.322	.302
Castro, Guadulpo, Tab.	.000	6	15	13	0	0	0	0	0	0	0	0	0	0	2	0	6	0	0	2	.000	.133
Castro, Wilfredo, Oax.	.100	7	12	10	1	1	2	1	0	0	1	0	0	0	2	0	5	1	0	0	.200	.250
Cazarin, Manuel, Cam.	.296	113	415	371	41	110	154	20	0	8	55	10	5	7	22	1	26	1	2	15	.415	.343
Cedeno, Andujar, Can.	.318	119	526	485	79	154	255	26	0	25	88	1	4	5	31	4	55	2	0	30	.526	.362
Cedeno, Domingo, Cor.	.320	75	324	291	60	93	128	11	6	4	30	3	2	1	27	1	67	16	5	4	.440	.377
Cervantes, Ivan, Mex.	.186	34	65	59	7	11	15	1	0	1	4	1	0	1	4	0	6	0	0	1	.254	.250
Cervantes, Refugio, Lar.*	.286	56	68	56	4	16	30	5	0	3	22	0	2	1	9	3	6	0	0	4	.536	.382
Cervera, Francisco, Lar.	.240	98	399	338	51	81	146	20	0	15	50	0	1	12	48	3	71	3	7	15	.432	.353
Chance, Tony, Yuc.	.309	120	518	433	83	134	217	29	0	18	69	1	4	4	76	2	115	2	1	14	.501	.414
Charbonnet, Mark, Tor.-Pue.	.272	55	233	217	29	59	106	9	1	12	42	3	2	4	7	1	60	0	0	5	.488	.304
Chimelis, Joel, Lar.	.300	120	519	453	82	136	250	26	4	30	98	2	4	8	52	1	54	4	2	9	.552	.379

Player, Team	Avg.	G	TPA	AB	R	H	TB	2B	3B	HR	RBI	SH	SF	HP	BB	IBB	SO	SB	CS	GDP	Slg.	OBP
Cisneros, Ventura, Rey.	.283	32	68	60	8	17	27	4	0	2	8	0	0	1	7	1	14	0	0	3	.450	.368
Claudio, Patricio, Pue.	.200	6	6	5	1	1	1	0	0	0	0	1	0	0	0	0	1	0	0	0	.200	.200
Cobos, Rogelio, Cam.	.242	57	111	99	13	24	27	1	1	0	3	3	1	2	6	0	34	3	1	4	.273	.296
Colina, Roberto, Tig.-Pue.*	.323	113	491	427	74	138	209	21	1	16	86	2	6	8	48	4	22	3	2	13	.489	.397
Connell, Lino, Ver.†	.313	120	540	470	94	147	213	24	0	14	58	3	4	3	60	3	64	36	10	9	.453	.391
Cornelius, Brian, Lar.	.250	36	156	140	17	35	51	6	2	2	20	3	3	1	9	1	16	2	5	5	.364	.294
Cruz, Ivan, Mex.	.402	51	225	199	52	80	158	16	1	20	49	0	5	1	20	3	29	0	0	5	.794	.449
Cruz, Marco Ant., Tor.-Ver.	.289	48	110	97	7	28	40	7	1	1	19	0	4	1	8	1	17	0	1	3	.412	.336
DeLaCruz, Lorenzo, Pue.	.313	114	481	403	82	126	245	26	3	29	84	0	3	7	68	3	109	11	1	8	.608	.418
De Los Santos, Luis, Sal.	.363	100	439	391	79	142	247	28	1	25	94	2	5	1	40	3	59	0	1	19	.632	.419
Diaz, Alex, Tor.	.402	23	104	97	24	39	65	5	0	7	23	0	2	2	3	0	18	7	1	3	.670	.423
Diaz, Luis Fernando, Tor.-Tab.*	.271	70	241	199	34	54	97	8	1	11	35	2	3	1	36	5	33	1	1	7	.487	.381
Diaz, Pedro, Pue.	.289	80	297	273	38	79	115	14	2	6	36	4	0	4	16	0	48	1	2	6	.421	.338
Diaz, Remigio, Mont.	.283	115	449	410	71	116	159	22	3	5	51	10	6	2	21	0	34	25	8	15	.388	.317
Dilone, Juan, Tor.-Can.†	.270	57	248	200	37	54	85	6	2	7	33	5	2	5	36	4	52	2	0	1	.425	.391
Dominguez, David, Ver.	.280	90	340	296	38	83	113	12	0	6	37	5	2	1	36	4	49	0	2	13	.382	.358
Duran, Felipe, Monc.	.214	6	14	14	1	3	4	1	0	0	0	0	0	0	0	0	4	0	1	1	.286	.214
Escalante, Marcelo, Can.	.162	51	113	105	5	17	25	3	1	1	3	2	0	0	6	1	27	0	0	4	.238	.207
Espino, Daniel, Mont.	.301	56	180	163	23	49	52	3	0	0	11	3	0	3	11	0	15	2	3	5	.319	.356
Espino, Omar, Pue.	.230	29	78	61	6	14	18	2	1	0	6	3	1	1	12	0	20	0	0	2	.295	.360
Espinoza, Efren, Mex.	.263	22	41	38	6	10	11	1	0	0	4	0	1	1	1	0	9	2	0	2	.289	.293
Espinoza, Jose, Lar.*	.318	108	500	434	62	138	186	23	2	7	50	2	2	7	55	5	57	7	11	14	.429	.402
Espinoza, Ramon, Rey.	.304	110	491	450	82	137	231	22	3	22	79	3	4	9	25	3	60	12	7	15	.513	.350
Espinoza, Ramon, Tor.	.194	22	35	31	4	6	8	2	0	0	1	2	0	1	1	0	12	0	0	1	.258	.242
Esquer, Ramon, Mex.*	.295	110	507	431	81	127	174	20	3	7	57	7	6	1	62	2	53	4	1	13	.404	.380
Estrada, Hector, Yuc.	.276	114	453	402	48	111	181	11	1	19	83	4	4	4	39	2	58	0	0	17	.450	.343
Estrella, Isaac, Lar.	.200	50	31	25	15	5	5	0	0	0	1	1	0	1	4	0	12	1	0	3	.200	.333
Facundo, Armando, Tab.†	.231	31	44	39	6	9	9	0	0	0	1	1	0	1	3	0	7	1	0	0	.231	.302
Felix, Junior, Tor.-Yuc.†	.289	115	499	412	81	119	214	13	2	26	97	0	4	7	76	6	83	5	2	14	.519	.405
Felix, Lauro, Tab.	.300	47	184	150	32	45	66	10	1	3	13	6	0	4	24	0	24	8	4	2	.440	.410
Fentanes, Oscar, Tab.	.301	109	446	405	50	122	180	21	2	11	60	4	5	8	24	3	40	2	6	13	.444	.348
Fernandez, Daniel, Mex.*	.300	58	270	223	56	67	102	9	7	4	21	5	3	1	38	1	29	5	8	4	.457	.400
Figueroa, Jesus, Cor.	.333	3	3	3	0	1	1	0	0	0	0	0	0	0	0	0	0	0	0	1	.333	.333
Flores, Miguel, Mont.	.311	112	504	412	84	128	164	19	1	5	47	4	3	7	78	1	40	7	7	10	.398	.426
Fornes, Daniel, Rey.*	.270	114	450	392	50	106	156	11	0	13	58	4	6	4	44	2	44	0	6	10	.398	.345
Franco, Iker, Tig.	.255	19	55	51	4	13	25	6	0	2	9	2	0	1	1	0	15	1	0	2	.490	.283
Franco, Manuel, Can.	.176	18	37	34	2	6	10	1	0	1	8	0	1	0	2	0	12	0	0	0	.294	.216
Gainer, Jonathan, Tab.*	.317	113	485	407	80	129	245	21	1	31	81	1	3	1	73	10	79	2	3	16	.602	.419
Gainey, Ty, Yuc.*	.292	66	269	212	31	62	88	17	0	3	40	0	2	1	54	6	47	0	1	6	.415	.435
Garcia, Cornelio, Tor.*	.371	94	447	372	75	138	167	24	1	1	35	7	1	1	66	4	52	8	4	5	.449	.466
Garcia, Hector, Mont.	.303	111	442	403	62	122	161	17	2	6	49	10	6	6	17	1	31	15	8	12	.400	.336
Garcia, Heriberto, Oax.	.359	80	286	245	43	88	103	13	1	0	32	7	2	5	27	0	24	2	2	4	.420	.430
Garcia, Luis, Tig.	.354	120	526	477	89	169	266	27	2	22	81	0	8	2	39	5	91	33	9	15	.558	.399
Garcia, Omar, Ver.	.331	117	499	456	86	151	233	20	1	20	93	0	3	1	39	0	51	3	2	7	.511	.383
Garland, Tim, Cam.	.311	116	533	485	71	151	186	16	2	5	37	10	1	4	33	4	66	30	11	9	.384	.359
Garza, Gerardo, Lar.	.269	86	244	212	26	57	85	5	1	7	32	10	2	2	18	1	35	1	2	7	.401	.329
Garzon, Eliseo, Tor.	.239	91	345	289	40	69	86	11	0	2	25	10	2	2	42	1	39	0	4	10	.298	.337
Gastelum, Carlos, Pue.	.258	65	200	186	17	48	59	7	2	0	11	5	0	1	8	0	21	0	1	5	.317	.292
Gastelum, Sergio, Tig.	.377	111	510	438	108	165	248	18	13	13	77	8	2	16	46	1	40	31	11	8	.566	.452
Gavia, Jesus, Yuc.	.140	34	52	50	2	7	8	1	0	0	2	2	0	0	0	0	11	0	0	1	.160	.140
Gomez, Heber, Tab.	.307	119	523	463	67	142	210	25	2	13	56	7	3	8	42	3	36	5	6	10	.454	.372
Gonzalez, Fernando, Rey.	.173	40	93	81	6	14	19	5	0	0	9	1	1	2	8	0	12	0	0	4	.235	.261
Gonzalez, Jesus, Tor.	.338	121	559	465	100	157	253	19	1	25	99	2	3	5	84	7	76	2	3	19	.544	.442
Gonzalez, Jose, Mont.-Sal.	.215	22	100	79	16	17	25	5	0	1	9	0	1	2	18	1	14	4	3	4	.316	.370
Gonzalez, Rolando, Monc.	.281	54	111	96	14	27	34	4	0	1	15	2	2	2	9	0	16	1	0	3	.354	.349
Gonzalez, Roman, Cor.	.257	88	285	268	28	69	92	11	0	4	34	4	3	3	7	0	51	0	4	8	.343	.281
Gracia, Ernesto, Oax.	.235	11	19	17	4	4	9	0	1	1	1	0	0	0	2	0	7	1	1	1	.529	.316
Guerrero, Epy, Cam.*	.301	117	513	438	61	132	182	24	4	6	66	6	4	2	63	7	46	2	1	10	.416	.389
Guerrero, Sergio, Rey.	.335	117	545	471	72	158	197	23	2	4	39	13	4	12	45	1	37	5	10	13	.418	.404
Guiel, Aaron, Oax.*	.365	56	255	192	55	70	149	11	1	22	62	0	5	6	52	2	35	7	5	6	.776	.502
Guizar, Hector, Tor.	.291	114	477	436	56	127	178	18	0	11	67	17	4	4	16	0	45	7	1	18	.408	.320
Henry, Santiago, Cor.	.308	117	491	458	67	141	209	19	11	9	58	9	3	3	18	1	65	13	8	18	.456	.336
Hernandez, Esteban, Oax.	.000	3	5	4	0	0	0	0	0	0	0	0	0	0	1	0	2	0	0	0	.000	.200
Hernandez, Julio, Lar.	.280	120	485	397	71	111	146	21	4	2	29	10	3	14	61	1	56	4	5	16	.368	.392
Herrera, Christian, Ver.	.000	2	1	1	0	0	0	0	0	0	0	0	0	0	0	0	1	0	0	0	.000	.000
Hurtado, Hector, Monc.†	.240	48	129	121	17	29	50	3	0	6	19	0	0	3	5	0	35	0	0	2	.413	.287
Iglesias, Luis, Cam.-Ver.	.293	46	194	167	19	49	75	17	0	3	23	0	0	1	26	2	31	0	0	4	.449	.392
Iturbe, Pedro, Pue.*	.306	90	359	340	36	104	149	18	3	7	54	0	2	4	13	1	56	2	3	13	.438	.337
Jimenez, Eduardo, Sal.*	.317	117	529	416	108	132	285	18	0	45	107	0	1	4	108	23	106	0	1	12	.685	.461
Kapano, Randy, Lar.	.205	24	103	78	11	16	29	1	0	4	13	0	0	2	23	0	22	0	1	2	.372	.398
Lara, Idelfonso, Oax.	.000	3	6	5	1	0	0	0	0	0	0	0	0	0	1	0	1	0	0	0	.000	.167
Leal, Gerardo, Monc.	.350	10	20	20	3	7	11	1	0	1	1	0	0	0	0	0	5	0	0	0	.550	.350
Leal, Guadalupe, Can.-Monc.*	.239	67	184	176	21	42	70	8	1	6	25	1	1	0	6	0	38	1	0	3	.398	.262
Leyva, German, Ver.	.277	105	430	354	45	98	130	11	0	7	46	5	4	1	66	7	28	5	5	19	.367	.388
Leyva, Octavio, Ver.	.000	4	1	1	0	0	0	0	0	0	0	0	0	0	0	0	0	1	0	0	.000	.000
Lopez, Carlos, Pue.	.200	9	21	20	0	4	4	0	0	0	0	0	0	0	1	0	3	0	0	0	.200	.238
Lopez, Fabian, Oax.*	.367	101	376	341	57	125	172	23	0	8	50	0	1	0	34	1	26	3	3	17	.504	.423
Lopez, Fortunato, Tab.	.000	4	5	5	0	0	0	0	0	0	0	0	0	0	0	0	3	0	0	1	.000	.000
Lopez, Gonzalo, Yuc.	.279	41	91	86	14	24	28	4	0	0	11	2	0	1	2	0	13	0	0	2	.326	.303
Loredo, Jorge, Pue.	.152	20	41	33	4	5	7	2	0	0	2	1	0	1	6	0	7	0	0	1	.212	.300
Machiria, Pablo, Lar.-Mont.	.284	85	334	306	33	87	134	14	0	11	41	4	2	4	18	3	38	1	4	15	.438	.330
Machorro, Roberto, Oax.	.227	49	121	110	15	25	33	5	0	1	13	0	0	1	10	1	16	1	0	4	.300	.298
Macias, Roberto, Can.	.207	39	121	111	6	23	29	3	0	1	8	2	0	1	7	0	34	0	0	2	.261	.261
Maclin, Lonnie, Tab.*	.206	20	79	63	7	13	17	1	0	1	4	2	1	0	13	0	10	0	0	0	.270	.338
Maddox, Garry, Mont.*	.225	10	41	40	5	9	10	1	0	0	2	1	0	0	0	0	6	0	0	1	.250	.225
Magallanes, Ever, Mont.*	.292	118	521	462	67	135	187	23	1	9	60	3	4	6	46	2	53	2	3	15	.405	.361

Player, Team	Avg.	G	TPA	AB	R	H	TB	2B	3B	HR	RBI	SH	SF	HP	BB	IBB	SO	SB	CS	GDP	Slg.	OBP
Magallnes, Roberto, Tig.	.301	87	355	309	53	93	161	29	0	13	57	1	2	2	41	1	75	5	7	3	.521	.384
Marte, Julio, Tab.	.000	1	4	4	0	0	0	0	0	0	0	0	0	0	0	0	0	0	0	0	.000	.000
Martinez, Aguado, Tab.	.000	1	1	0	1	0	0	0	0	0	0	0	0	0	1	0	0	0	0	0	.000	1.000
Martinez, Enrique, Mont.	.301	64	156	143	19	43	61	7	1	3	23	2	2	1	8	0	28	2	4	4	.427	.338
Martinez, Grimaldo, Monc.	.237	103	416	359	52	85	106	12	0	3	23	6	1	7	43	1	24	2	1	12	.295	.329
Martinez, Luis, Sal.	.278	73	276	252	28	70	94	11	2	3	26	7	1	4	12	0	35	5	3	6	.373	.320
Martinez, Orlando, Tab.	.000	2	2	2	0	0	0	0	0	0	0	0	0	0	0	0	0	0	0	0	.000	.000
Martinez, Raul, Oax.-Mont.	.250	43	94	76	7	19	23	1	0	1	12	3	2	2	11	0	8	0	1	4	.303	.352
Martinez, Ray, Mex.	.309	118	513	414	98	128	263	20	2	37	113	1	5	7	86	2	110	9	1	12	.635	.432
Mashore, Damon, Tab.	.264	47	199	178	24	47	53	6	0	0	12	4	0	0	17	1	43	6	0	3	.298	.328
Mata, Noe, Ver.	.251	73	196	171	19	43	67	3	0	7	18	6	0	3	16	0	39	4	7	4	.392	.326
May, Derrick, Mont.*	.320	48	210	175	38	56	96	10	3	8	40	0	3	1	31	1	22	1	1	4	.549	.419
Medina, Ernesto, Mont.	.000	2	6	4	0	0	0	0	0	0	0	0	0	0	2	0	2	0	0	0	.000	.333
Medina, Jose Ramon, Sal.	.340	64	171	156	24	53	68	7	1	2	27	0	0	0	15	2	36	0	2	7	.436	.398
Mejia, Roberto, Oax.	.365	50	225	200	40	73	119	10	3	10	36	1	1	2	21	3	28	3	1	2	.595	.429
Mendez, Francisco, Mont.	.250	18	24	20	3	5	5	0	0	0	0	0	0	0	4	0	6	0	0	1	.250	.375
Mendez, Roberto, Oax.	.264	109	459	360	81	95	177	20	1	20	68	6	5	2	86	6	55	16	10	11	.492	.404
Mendoza, Omar, Ver.	.345	22	35	29	4	10	11	1	0	0	5	2	0	0	4	0	8	0	0	0	.379	.424
Mere, Pedro, Ver.	.288	112	458	389	71	112	181	21	0	16	66	8	3	10	48	1	55	5	2	18	.465	.378
Meulens, Hensley, Sal.	.317	88	413	347	72	110	200	14	2	24	73	4	2	6	54	2	105	4	1	5	.576	.416
Meza, Alfredo, Ver.†	.269	102	367	338	28	91	124	16	1	5	54	8	0	2	19	3	45	1	0	11	.367	.312
Meza, Gonzalo, Mex.*	.242	32	65	62	8	15	19	4	0	0	6	1	0	0	2	0	15	0	0	1	.306	.266
Michel, Keith, Tab.	.306	34	146	124	24	38	53	3	0	4	20	0	1	0	21	0	21	2	1	1	.427	.404
Miller, Orlando, Oax.	.125	3	10	8	1	1	4	0	0	1	1	0	0	0	2	0	1	0	0	0	.500	.300
Minjarez, Franco, Pue.*	.272	66	234	206	35	56	74	7	4	1	17	3	1	3	21	1	47	1	3	4	.359	.346
Montanez, Daniel, Ver.	.286	6	7	7	2	2	3	1	0	0	1	0	0	0	0	0	0	1	1	0	.429	.286
Montano, Angel, Cam.	.200	26	29	25	1	5	6	1	0	0	6	0	0	0	4	2	7	0	0	0	.240	.310
Moore, Mike, Tor.	.267	23	103	86	13	23	39	4	0	4	13	3	0	1	13	1	27	1	0	1	.453	.370
Morales, Juan, Oax.	.125	17	37	32	5	4	5	1	0	0	0	1	0	0	4	0	12	0	1	0	.156	.222
Morejon, Oswaldo, Yuc.*	.285	121	480	425	54	121	180	25	5	8	43	6	6	3	40	1	60	5	8	18	.424	.346
Moreno, Leonardo, Pue.*	.122	28	43	41	2	5	6	1	0	0	2	0	0	0	2	0	8	0	1	2	.146	.163
Munoz, Adan, Monc.*	.290	92	305	272	30	79	121	15	0	9	37	1	1	3	28	1	70	0	1	5	.445	.362
Munoz, Jose, Cor.	.210	18	73	62	6	13	14	1	0	0	8	0	1	0	10	0	8	0	1	3	.226	.315
Munoz, Jose De J., Sal.*	.261	111	534	425	87	111	183	19	7	13	59	2	4	5	98	2	84	26	16	7	.431	.402
Munoz, Noe, Sal.	.360	106	479	394	86	142	207	30	1	11	64	4	2	2	77	5	48	0	2	15	.525	.465
Nelson, Bryant, Mont.†	.348	59	250	227	51	79	157	18	0	20	72	0	1	0	22	2	23	8	6	7	.692	.404
Newson, Warren, Tor.*	.386	112	509	417	104	161	306	26	1	39	121	1	0	1	90	3	91	3	2	8	.734	.496
Nunez, Raymond, Pue.-Tig.	.343	61	270	245	49	84	144	5	2	17	64	1	1	4	19	0	48	1	1	10	.588	.398
Ochoa, Edgar, Mont.	.000	7	7	6	0	0	0	0	0	0	0	1	0	0	0	0	3	0	0	1	.000	.000
Ojeda, Miguel, Mex.	.318	92	378	330	59	105	213	25	4	25	73	2	2	1	43	1	47	1	1	14	.645	.396
Orantes, Ramon, Mont.	.312	86	287	263	38	82	118	6	0	10	35	5	0	6	13	0	43	0	2	10	.449	.358
Ortega, Antonio, Ver.	.147	29	39	34	1	5	6	1	0	0	3	2	0	0	3	0	11	0	0	1	.176	.216
Ortiz, Alejandro, Tab.	.297	112	486	411	61	122	164	18	0	8	63	7	8	3	57	1	47	1	0	11	.399	.380
Ortiz, Hector, Oax.	.000	1	5	4	1	0	0	0	0	0	0	0	0	0	1	0	2	0	0	0	.000	.200
Osuna, Hector, Can.	.173	40	86	75	6	13	16	3	0	0	3	1	0	2	8	0	20	0	0	2	.213	.271
Otero, Ricardo, Can.†	.287	111	515	464	75	133	178	16	4	7	41	5	0	4	42	4	40	17	8	5	.384	.351
Pacho, Carlos, Tab.	.137	32	55	51	4	7	7	0	0	0	1	0	0	1	3	0	17	0	1	3	.137	.200
Pacho, Juan Jose, Yuc.	.292	117	406	363	40	106	124	15	0	1	33	15	6	1	21	0	36	3	3	13	.342	.327
Paez, Hector, Can.*	.267	108	360	329	34	88	125	10	3	7	50	4	5	4	18	0	44	0	1	8	.380	.309
Paez, Raul, Cam.†	.290	82	274	241	28	70	101	19	0	4	35	0	2	1	30	2	38	0	1	6	.419	.369
Palafox, Sergio, Sal.	.273	13	13	11	1	3	4	1	0	0	0	0	0	1	1	0	2	1	0	2	.364	.385
Parra, Franklin, Cam.†	.290	93	388	348	59	101	151	19	5	7	47	4	4	0	32	10	64	12	4	17	.434	.346
Patron, Damian, Oax.	.240	51	86	75	15	18	22	4	0	0	6	5	1	0	5	0	13	1	1	1	.293	.284
Payro, Edison, Cam.*	.274	81	218	179	26	49	57	6	1	0	10	6	0	0	33	0	25	2	4	5	.318	.387
Pearson, Eddie, Tig.†	.320	29	137	125	23	40	68	4	0	8	34	0	3	0	9	1	13	0	0	5	.544	.358
Peguero, Julio, Tab.*	.310	54	256	226	37	70	98	16	0	4	33	4	1	2	23	0	35	5	3	1	.434	.377
Pemberton, Rudy, Mex.	.333	117	523	454	99	151	253	26	2	24	92	0	6	16	47	3	50	7	5	20	.557	.409
Perez, Alfredo, Cam.†	.283	33	68	60	7	17	18	1	0	0	7	1	1	0	6	0	14	1	1	4	.300	.343
Perez, F., Mont.	.000	1	2	2	0	0	0	0	0	0	0	0	0	0	0	0	2	0	0	0	.000	.000
Perez, Francisco, Rey.*	.266	86	228	207	26	55	83	9	2	5	26	2	0	2	17	2	50	2	1	4	.401	.327
Perez, L. Antonio, Monc.	.143	6	7	7	1	1	1	0	0	0	0	0	0	0	0	0	2	0	0	0	.143	.143
Pinto, Placido, Cor.	.158	42	108	101	8	16	26	4	0	2	10	1	1	1	4	0	35	1	0	5	.257	.196
Poe, Charles, Tab.	.282	10	44	39	3	11	14	0	0	1	4	1	0	0	4	0	4	0	1	2	.359	.349
Powell, Corey, Mex.-Oax.	.334	90	393	356	72	119	209	13	1	25	89	0	3	3	31	1	101	3	0	10	.587	.389
Pozo, Arquimedes, Tig.	.256	47	210	168	28	43	83	11	1	9	37	1	5	0	36	2	20	2	1	3	.494	.378
Presichi, Cristian, Sal.	.208	13	26	24	5	5	6	1	0	0	2	0	0	0	2	0	8	0	0	1	.250	.269
Prieto, Chris, Mex.	.378	24	125	98	29	37	53	4	3	2	13	0	1	1	25	0	10	12	3	3	.541	.504
Quinonez, Ruben, Monc.	.000	2	1	1	0	0	0	0	0	0	0	0	0	0	0	0	0	0	0	0	.000	.000
Quintero, Alan, Mex.	.211	54	99	90	14	19	24	1	2	0	5	2	1	0	6	0	10	0	1	2	.267	.258
Quintero, Edgar, Mont.-Pue.	.266	101	374	331	48	88	154	11	2	17	56	2	2	2	37	2	108	4	3	7	.465	.341
Quintero, Guillermo, Cor.	.287	55	104	87	14	25	29	4	0	0	8	3	0	1	13	0	14	2	0	2	.333	.386
Ramirez, Efren, Cor.	.241	99	354	303	37	73	104	10	0	7	33	8	4	5	34	0	53	2	3	11	.343	.324
Ramirez, Enrique, Pue.	.287	86	342	303	39	87	100	11	1	0	26	17	1	2	19	1	29	0	1	12	.330	.332
Ramirez, Jaime, Can.	.122	24	51	41	2	5	6	1	0	0	4	1	0	1	8	0	7	0	1	0	.146	.280
Ramirez, Jesus, Oax.	.332	95	349	298	58	99	140	18	4	5	41	9	3	5	34	0	29	2	4	5	.470	.406
Resendez, Carlos, Monc.	.202	50	104	89	14	18	30	3	0	3	11	0	1	4	10	1	26	0	1	2	.337	.308
Rincon, Isaias, Mex.	.214	18	29	28	6	6	7	1	0	0	0	1	0	0	0	0	8	1	0	2	.250	.214
Rivera, Jesus, Tab.*	.267	55	132	120	13	32	34	2	0	0	12	7	0	0	5	1	13	0	2	6	.283	.296
Roberson, Kevin, Mont.-Lar.†	.292	59	240	216	38	63	116	6	1	15	33	0	0	2	22	2	59	1	0	7	.537	.363
Robles, Javier, Tig.	.328	97	380	338	62	111	158	17	3	8	55	3	2	2	35	4	39	6	3	6	.467	.393
Robles, Juan Jose, Rey.	.262	85	266	233	34	61	82	10	1	3	29	3	2	7	21	0	47	0	1	8	.352	.338
Robles, Oscar, Mex.-Oax.*	.348	85	387	310	63	108	136	14	1	4	45	4	4	0	69	0	35	3	3	10	.439	.462
Robles, Trinidad, Tig.	.300	73	244	203	47	61	88	10	1	5	27	2	1	6	32	0	48	10	1	7	.433	.409
Rodarte, Raul, Lar.-Rey.	.364	107	447	393	81	143	247	28	2	24	98	2	6	3	43	1	64	15	3	15	.628	.425
Rodriguez, Armando, Tig.	.278	73	276	234	49	65	98	8	2	7	31	2	1	3	36	1	49	7	9	7	.419	.380
Rodriguez, Boi, Monc.*	.293	111	495	393	84	115	226	18	0	31	87	0	7	5	90	3	102	12	4	7	.575	.424

Player, Team	Avg.	G	TPA	AB	R	H	TB	2B	3B	HR	RBI	SH	SF	HP	BB	IBB	SO	SB	CS	GDP	Slg.	OBP
Rodriguez, Carlos, Rey.	.274	49	220	175	25	48	59	7	2	0	6	9	1	5	30	0	18	5	3	8	.337	.393
Rodriguez, Fernando, Cam.	.337	108	442	386	56	130	190	21	0	13	82	2	8	8	38	3	34	2	5	12	.492	.400
Rodriguez, Jose, Monc.	.500	4	16	4	6	2	2	0	0	0	0	0	0	0	12	1	0	0	0	1	.500	.875
Rojas, Homar, Oax.	.297	81	315	279	49	83	154	20	0	17	57	4	3	4	25	3	31	1	0	6	.552	.360
Romero, Marco, Sal.	.317	109	445	398	65	126	220	25	0	23	80	2	1	4	40	5	81	8	0	10	.553	.384
Romero, Oscar, Monc.	.282	118	503	436	75	123	183	31	1	9	54	5	0	4	58	2	55	4	7	30	.420	.371
Romero, Wilfredo, Sal.	.335	118	566	489	102	164	263	28	4	21	82	12	5	5	55	0	88	45	12	14	.538	.404
Royster, Aaron, Ver.	.277	26	116	101	14	28	40	3	0	3	9	0	0	0	15	0	33	5	2	4	.396	.371
Rubio, Sergio, Yuc.	.188	38	17	16	11	3	3	0	0	0	0	0	0	0	1	0	3	0	0	0	.188	.235
Ruiz, Juan, Cor.	.268	78	299	272	35	73	110	12	2	7	37	3	3	0	21	1	30	1	1	4	.404	.318
Saenz, Ricardo, Monc.	.314	115	481	417	80	131	242	21	3	28	94	0	2	3	59	2	99	3	1	9	.580	.401
Salas, Heriberto, Cam.	.238	86	313	265	35	63	85	16	0	2	24	9	5	10	24	1	37	0	0	5	.321	.319
Salomon, Abraham, Can.	.222	14	23	18	3	4	5	1	0	0	0	1	0	2	2	0	4	0	0	0	.278	.364
Sanchez, Gerardo, Lar.	.284	73	252	208	25	59	87	13	0	5	29	3	2	4	35	1	29	2	1	10	.418	.394
Sanchez, Orlando, Mont.	.156	52	66	64	3	10	10	0	0	0	1	0	0	0	2	0	14	0	0	0	.156	.182
Sanchez, Raul, Can.	.262	110	439	397	50	104	144	12	2	8	40	4	5	4	29	2	89	9	7	9	.363	.315
Sanchez, Roque, Cam.	.259	49	150	135	11	35	42	7	0	0	11	4	2	1	8	1	15	1	0	5	.311	.301
Sanders, Tracy, Yuc.*	.200	13	58	45	10	9	15	3	0	1	6	0	0	1	12	0	17	1	0	0	.333	.379
Sandoval, Jose, Mex.	.333	112	469	400	75	133	242	29	1	26	105	2	5	3	59	3	80	0	0	17	.605	.418
Sandoval, Octavio, Tig.	.322	85	225	202	41	65	103	14	3	6	37	2	1	2	18	0	33	4	4	5	.510	.381
Santana, Mario, Mont.†	.293	94	309	270	29	79	108	7	5	4	32	10	1	4	24	0	33	5	3	9	.400	.358
Santos, Andres, Lar.	.308	68	143	130	13	40	63	6	1	5	17	1	1	3	8	0	26	0	0	2	.485	.359
Sauceda, Victor, Can.†	.254	114	444	393	53	100	123	15	1	2	28	9	4	1	37	2	56	4	3	10	.313	.317
Saucedo, Roberto, Mont.-Rey.	.214	42	96	84	9	18	32	2	0	4	11	0	1	0	11	1	13	0	0	3	.381	.302
Sherman, Darrell, Monc.*	.342	119	563	462	98	158	213	25	3	8	53	4	4	6	87	6	35	19	5	6	.461	.449
Sierra, Ruben, Can.*	.355	16	73	62	8	22	35	2	1	3	12	0	1	0	10	1	10	0	1	2	.565	.438
Sievers, Carlos, Yuc.*	.328	56	133	122	16	40	63	9	1	4	26	0	1	1	9	0	27	0	2	5	.516	.376
Simmons, Nelson, Rey.†	.216	10	45	37	2	8	12	1	0	1	6	0	1	0	7	0	7	0	0	1	.324	.333
Soriano, Ricardo, Cor.*	.341	73	277	246	37	84	105	10	1	3	35	3	2	3	23	1	22	5	4	5	.427	.401
Sotmayor, Gilberto, Monc.	.274	50	78	73	11	20	23	3	0	0	4	1	0	0	4	0	8	0	0	1	.315	.312
Soto, Saul, Mex.	.360	19	58	50	13	18	22	4	0	0	4	1	0	0	7	1	11	1	1	1	.440	.439
Suarez, Luis, Tig.*	.344	102	355	317	66	109	190	23	5	16	73	3	4	5	26	2	47	1	2	8	.599	.398
Tatum, Jim, Mex.	.302	10	48	43	3	13	18	0	1	1	4	0	1	1	3	0	9	1	1	2	.419	.354
Tavarez, Jesus, Ver.†	.291	52	233	213	32	62	92	13	1	5	17	1	0	1	18	2	20	8	0	3	.432	.349
Tellez, Alonso, Rey.	.282	120	500	444	54	125	206	37	1	14	67	1	0	4	51	6	82	0	0	9	.464	.361
Tinsley, Lee, Monc.-Tab.†	.259	51	218	193	28	50	82	6	1	8	38	1	3	2	19	3	45	3	2	6	.425	.327
Tiquet, Lazaro, Tab.	.125	26	38	32	1	4	4	0	0	0	4	0	0	2	4	0	7	0	0	1	.125	.263
Torres, Sebastian, Oax.	.167	10	7	6	3	1	1	0	0	0	0	0	0	1	0	0	1	0	0	0	.167	.286
Tovar, Jose DeJesus, Rey.†	.150	46	66	60	9	9	12	3	0	0	4	1	0	1	4	0	7	1	1	3	.200	.215
Trapaga, Julio, Tig.	.330	49	105	94	21	31	49	11	2	1	16	2	3	1	5	0	24	1	1	1	.521	.359
Tredaway, Chad, Rey.†	.196	45	183	163	18	32	45	7	0	2	12	0	0	3	17	0	22	0	1	3	.276	.284
Valdez, Emmanuel, Tig.	.183	49	131	109	20	20	34	5	0	3	12	3	1	2	16	0	48	2	0	1	.312	.297
Valdez, Francisco, Tab.	.326	113	420	374	46	122	158	21	0	5	44	9	3	7	27	1	30	4	1	15	.422	.380
Valdez, Jesus, Cam.	.385	11	15	13	2	5	5	0	0	0	0	0	0	0	2	0	1	0	0	0	.385	.467
Valdez, Ramon, Cor.	.302	108	499	398	76	120	134	9	1	1	19	11	2	11	77	0	42	28	19	6	.337	.426
Valencia, Carlos, Lar.	.400	5	5	5	0	2	2	0	0	0	0	0	0	0	0	0	1	0	1	0	.400	.400
Valencia, Carlos, Cor.	.256	53	151	133	13	34	42	5	0	1	16	2	1	3	12	0	15	0	0	5	.316	.329
Valenzuela, Irving, Monc.†	.233	84	202	176	16	41	55	7	2	1	19	7	1	3	15	0	31	2	6	3	.313	.303
Valenzula, Armando, Sal.	.292	43	122	113	14	33	47	9	1	1	16	1	2	0	6	0	16	0	3	3	.416	.322
Valle, Cosme, Mex.	.321	32	89	81	13	26	35	3	0	2	15	2	1	1	4	0	18	0	0	3	.432	.356
Valle, Jorge Luis, Tor.	.307	76	298	264	33	81	111	16	1	4	43	2	3	5	24	1	44	0	2	12	.420	.372
Valle, Jose Luis, Yuc.	.147	31	34	34	2	5	8	1	1	0	4	0	0	0	0	0	9	0	0	2	.235	.147
Valle, Roberto, Tor.	.174	31	52	46	9	8	12	1	0	1	6	1	0	1	4	0	14	0	0	0	.261	.255
Valverde, Raul, Tor.	.250	8	18	16	1	4	6	0	1	0	2	0	0	0	2	0	4	1	1	0	.375	.333
Vazquez, Felipe, Lar.	.290	23	69	62	7	18	28	4	0	2	13	2	0	0	5	0	8	1	3	3	.452	.343
Vazquez, Gregorio, Tab.	.306	55	119	111	16	34	37	3	0	0	7	2	0	1	5	0	16	1	0	5	.333	.342
Vazquez, Jorge, Monc.-Pue. .	.248	63	153	133	14	33	43	5	1	1	14	1	1	2	16	1	48	1	2	4	.323	.336
Vazquez, Jose, Tig.	.242	41	71	66	9	16	24	2	0	2	9	0	0	2	3	0	20	0	0	2	.364	.296
Vega, Edgar, Pue.	.245	77	232	212	26	52	68	10	0	2	17	6	2	1	11	1	46	0	2	5	.321	.283
Velazquez, G'mo, Mont.-Rey.* ..	.260	77	321	273	47	71	120	13	0	12	43	0	2	2	44	3	67	0	1	7	.440	.364
Velez, Manuel, Lar.	.347	114	490	435	77	151	217	30	0	12	60	10	3	2	40	1	50	1	5	18	.499	.402
Verdugo, Vicente, Sal.	.320	120	464	409	54	131	157	20	0	2	52	16	2	4	33	1	30	4	4	19	.384	.375
Villarreal, Alex, Lar.	.167	14	19	18	3	3	5	0	1	0	2	0	1	0	0	0	4	0	0	1	.278	.158
Villarreal, Salvador, Rey.	.125	51	37	32	7	4	4	0	0	0	0	2	0	1	2	0	17	0	0	0	.125	.200
Villegas, Fernando, Sal.	.156	31	58	45	8	7	8	1	0	0	4	3	0	1	9	1	6	0	1	1	.178	.309
Villegas, Fernando, Tor.	.301	39	165	133	16	40	57	5	3	2	23	3	1	4	24	1	16	1	0	5	.429	.420
Vizcarra, Roberto, Tig.	.294	120	558	479	99	141	221	32	0	16	76	7	5	15	52	1	37	1	5	10	.461	.377
Walton, Jerome, Cam.	.282	39	151	124	21	35	55	6	1	4	20	1	1	1	24	3	16	4	3	7	.444	.400
Williams, Eddie, Monc.	.288	61	261	205	44	59	101	12	0	10	56	0	2	1	53	1	31	0	1	12	.493	.433
Yan, Julian, Cor.	.332	117	506	434	86	144	281	23	0	38	129	0	10	5	57	4	77	6	1	11	.647	.407
Yuriar, Jesus, Can.	.233	83	245	219	17	51	65	6	1	2	28	4	1	0	21	1	36	0	1	5	.297	.299
Zambrano, Roberto, Can.	.305	110	478	383	84	117	253	17	1	39	100	0	2	23	70	5	70	0	0	13	.661	.439
Zamudio, Rafael, Pue.	.278	25	92	79	12	22	31	4	1	1	6	1	1	1	10	2	24	0	0	3	.392	.363
Zazueta, Juan, Tor.†	.310	109	450	403	73	125	176	20	2	9	47	16	4	6	21	1	40	5	3	11	.437	.350
Zazueta, Mauricio, Tor.	.301	117	508	439	63	132	185	22	2	9	55	10	7	4	48	9	85	5	1	14	.421	.369

PLAYERS WITH TWO OR MORE TEAMS

Player, Team	Avg.	G	TPA	AB	R	H	TB	2B	3B	HR	RBI	SH	SF	HP	BB	IBB	SO	SB	CS	GDP	Slg.	OBP
Adriana, Sharnol, Cor.	.352	88	382	310	95	109	213	17	3	27	77	1	6	12	53	2	64	20	8	5	.687	.457
Adriana, Sharnol, Cam.	.245	29	118	98	18	24	33	3	0	2	11	1	0	1	18	1	26	4	4	1	.337	.368
Bell, Juan, Cor.†	.298	24	110	94	22	28	46	2	2	4	20	0	2	1	13	0	17	3	1	2	.489	.382
Bell, Juan, Cam.†	.261	72	315	257	43	67	103	15	0	7	37	2	6	6	44	3	32	5	4	8	.401	.374
Brooks, Jerry, Lar.	.188	6	19	16	3	3	3	0	0	0	1	0	0	0	3	0	2	0	0	1	.188	.316
Brooks, Jerry, Yuc.	.136	5	24	22	2	3	6	0	0	1	4	0	0	0	2	0	4	0	1	0	.273	.208
Charbonnet, Mark, Tor.	.264	30	132	125	17	33	55	4	0	6	21	2	0	1	4	1	31	0	0	2	.440	.292

Player, Team	Avg.	G	TPA	AB	R	H	TB	2B	3B	HR	RBI	SH	SF	HP	BB	IBB	SO	SB	CS	GDP	Slg.	OBP
Charbonnet, Mark, Pue.	.283	25	101	92	12	26	51	5	1	6	21	1	2	3	3	0	29	0	0	3	.554	.320
Colina, Roberto, Tig.*	.289	11	53	45	9	13	14	1	0	0	8	1	2	1	4	0	2	0	0	0	.311	.346
Colina, Roberto, Pue.*	.327	102	438	382	65	125	195	20	1	16	78	1	4	7	44	4	20	3	2	13	.510	.403
Cruz, Marco Antonio, Tor.	.333	27	51	45	4	15	20	3	1	0	8	0	3	1	2	0	5	0	1	1	.444	.353
Cruz, Marco Antonio, Ver.	.250	21	59	52	3	13	20	4	0	1	11	0	1	0	6	1	12	0	0	2	.385	.322
Diaz, Luis Fernando, Tor.*	.257	45	161	136	23	35	63	2	1	8	27	1	3	1	20	1	20	1	0	6	.463	.350
Diaz, Luis Fernando, Tab.*	.302	25	80	63	11	19	34	6	0	3	8	1	0	0	16	4	13	0	1	1	.540	.443
Dilone, Juan, Tor.†	.312	39	175	141	31	44	70	6	1	6	30	0	2	3	29	3	33	2	0	0	.496	.434
Dilone, Juan, Can.†	.169	18	73	59	6	10	15	0	1	1	3	5	0	2	7	1	19	0	0	1	.254	.279
Felix, Junior, Tor.†	.265	17	79	68	16	18	32	2	0	4	15	0	1	0	10	0	15	1	0	2	.471	.354
Felix, Junior, Yuc.†	.294	98	420	344	65	101	182	11	2	22	82	0	3	7	66	6	68	4	2	12	.529	.414
Gonzalez, Jose, Mont.	.077	5	21	13	1	1	1	0	0	0	2	0	1	0	7	0	2	0	2	1	.077	.381
Gonzalez, Jose, Sal.	.242	17	79	66	15	16	24	5	0	1	7	0	0	2	11	1	12	4	1	3	.364	.367
Iglesias, Luis, Cam.	.271	14	56	48	5	13	18	5	0	0	6	0	0	1	7	0	9	0	0	1	.375	.375
Iglesias, Luis, Ver.	.303	32	138	119	14	36	57	12	0	3	17	0	0	0	19	2	22	0	0	3	.479	.399
Leal, Guadalupe, Can.*	.206	35	112	107	12	22	35	5	1	2	10	0	1	0	4	0	23	1	0	2	.327	.232
Leal, Guadalupe, Monc.*	.290	32	72	69	9	20	35	3	0	4	15	1	0	0	2	0	15	0	0	1	.507	.310
Machiria, Pablo, Lar.	.292	77	317	291	33	85	131	13	0	11	39	4	2	3	17	3	34	0	4	13	.450	.335
Machiria, Pablo, Mont.	.133	8	17	15	0	2	3	1	0	0	2	0	0	1	1	0	4	1	0	2	.200	.235
Martinez, Raul, Oax.	.273	27	70	55	5	15	16	1	0	0	9	2	2	2	9	0	5	0	1	3	.291	.382
Martinez, Raul, Mont.	.190	16	24	21	2	4	7	0	0	1	3	1	0	0	2	0	3	0	0	1	.333	.261
Nunez, Raymond, Pue.	.321	41	179	165	30	53	98	2	2	13	41	1	1	1	11	0	27	1	0	9	.594	.365
Nunez, Raymond, Tig.	.388	20	91	80	19	31	46	3	0	4	23	0	0	3	8	0	21	0	1	1	.575	.462
Powell, Corey, Mex.	.368	62	274	247	57	91	161	8	1	20	71	0	3	1	23	1	64	1	0	4	.652	.420
Powell, Corey, Oax.	.257	28	119	109	15	28	48	5	0	5	18	0	0	2	8	0	37	2	0	6	.440	.319
Quintero, Edgar, Mont.	.000	4	3	3	1	0	0	0	0	0	0	0	0	0	0	0	1	0	0	0	.000	.000
Quintero, Edgar, Pue.	.268	97	371	328	47	88	154	11	2	17	56	2	2	2	37	2	107	4	3	7	.470	.344
Roberson, Kevin, Mont.†	.178	13	50	45	3	8	12	1	0	1	6	0	0	2	3	1	13	0	0	2	.267	.260
Roberson, Kevin, Lar.†	.322	46	190	171	35	55	104	5	1	14	27	0	0	0	19	1	46	1	0	5	.608	.389
Robles, Oscar, Mex.*	.000	1	2	1	0	0	0	0	0	0	0	0	1	0	1	0	0	0	0	0	.000	1.000
Robles, Oscar, Oax.*	.348	84	385	310	62	108	136	14	1	4	45	3	4	0	68	0	35	3	3	10	.439	.461
Rodarte, Raul, Lar.	.328	55	227	201	33	66	115	8	1	13	48	1	3	1	21	1	37	9	1	7	.572	.389
Rodarte, Raul, Rey.	.401	52	220	192	48	77	132	20	1	11	50	1	3	2	22	0	27	6	2	8	.688	.461
Saucedo, Roberto, Mont.	.000	18	29	24	0	0	0	0	0	0	1	0	1	0	4	0	7	0	0	0	.000	.138
Saucedo, Roberto, Rey.	.300	24	67	60	9	18	32	2	0	4	10	0	0	0	7	1	6	0	0	3	.533	.373
Tinsley, Lee, Monc.†	.292	43	192	168	28	49	81	6	1	8	38	0	3	2	19	3	33	3	2	5	.482	.365
Tinsley, Lee, Tab.†	.040	8	26	25	0	1	1	0	0	0	0	0	1	0	0	0	12	0	0	1	.040	.040
Vazquez, Jorge, Monc.	.234	31	52	47	7	11	18	4	0	1	6	0	0	0	5	0	25	1	0	1	.383	.308
Vazquez, Jorge, Pue.	.256	32	101	86	7	22	25	1	1	0	8	1	1	2	11	1	23	0	2	3	.291	.350
Velazquez, Guillermo, Mont.* ..	.242	20	75	66	10	16	27	2	0	3	8	0	0	1	8	0	17	0	0	3	.409	.333
Velazquez, Guillermo, Rey.* ...	.266	57	246	207	37	55	93	11	0	9	35	0	2	1	36	3	50	1	0	4	.449	.374

2000 PITCHING

TEAM

Team	W	L	Pct.	ERA	CG	H	Sv.	HR	BB	SO	Team	W	L	Pct.	ERA	CG	H	Sv.	HR	BB	SO
Tabasco	66	55	.545	4.31	13	1156	30	96	353	519	Cancun	38	81	.319	5.46	6	1227	17	147	508	567
Yucatan	69	52	.570	4.45	10	1172	39	117	399	796	M.C. Reds	70	47	.598	5.47	10	1321	28	129	409	626
Saltillo	77	42	.647	4.67	2	1242	32	108	477	708	Puebla	50	68	.424	5.48	15	1126	26	118	525	599
Campeche	59	60	.496	4.70	12	1149	24	92	447	645	Cordoba	53	63	.457	5.54	7	1188	24	144	500	565
Veracruz	61	58	.513	4.71	17	1160	30	121	411	678	Nuevo Laredo ..	54	66	.450	5.60	8	1274	28	156	441	680
Monterrey	59	63	.484	4.85	4	1166	16	130	497	725	Monclova	58	63	.479	5.92	8	1290	26	153	540	683
Reynosa	50	69	.420	5.13	8	1206	21	124	495	612	Torreon	56	65	.463	5.95	10	1304	19	153	504	673
M.C. Tigers	74	44	.627	5.32	1	1200	48	124	496	686	Oaxaca	59	57	.509	6.28	13	1232	26	156	516	595

INDIVIDUAL

TOP QUALIFIERS FOR EARNED-RUN AVERAGE TITLE

Minimum 98 innings.

Pitcher, Team	W	L	Pct.	ERA	G	GS	CG	ShO	GF	Sv.	IP	H	TBF	R	ER	HR	SH	SF	HB	BB	IBB	SO	WP	Bk.
Morales, Luis, Ver.	10	7	.588	2.04	34	14	1	0	11	5	119.0	100	466	37	27	14	4	4	2	26	2	82	1	0
Flynt, Will, Sal.	13	4	.765	2.68	26	25	1	0	0	0	174.1	175	745	71	52	14	4	5	67	0	157	5	0	
Campos, Francisco, Cam.	11	4	.733	3.10	28	26	8	3	2	1	189.0	159	759	73	65	14	9	2	4	57	3	172	6	0
Aguirre, Gaudencio, Tab.	10	6	.625	3.34	39	16	5	0	17	8	143.0	134	650	59	53	4	8	6	9	32	2	66	6	1
Mora, Eleazar, Ver.	10	8	.556	3.39	23	23	3	2	0	0	148.2	159	621	67	56	9	5	5	3	37	3	98	3	1
Alvarez, Juan, Tab.	6	8	.429	3.54	24	24	3	1	0	0	152.1	157	654	70	60	14	7	2	6	57	3	71	3	3
Manzanillo, Ravelo, Yuc.	10	6	.625	3.55	23	23	5	0	0	0	157.1	140	688	65	62	14	9	3	5	91	1	183	7	2
Magee, Danny, Monc.	9	3	.750	3.60	16	16	2	1	0	0	100.0	91	445	44	40	6	1	2	5	68	0	104	4	0
Rivera, Oscar, Ver.	8	5	.615	3.86	22	21	4	1	1	0	137.2	141	615	71	59	11	7	2	7	67	3	92	12	0
Pimentel, Roberto, Tab.	6	9	.400	3.87	26	25	2	1	1	0	151.1	146	646	72	65	12	18	4	2	60	4	88	1	0

DEPARTMENTAL LEADERS: W—Flynt, E. Lopez, A. Moreno, J. Nunez, E. Valdez, 13; L—J.M. Martinez, Pulido, Qintanilla, 13; Pct.—Flynt, .765; G—Ayala, J. Garcia, Rubio, Wishnevski, 55; GS—J. Nunez, 29; CG—Campos, 8; ShO—Campos, 3; GF—Ayala, Wishnevski, 52; Sv.—S. Hernandez, 36; IP—J. Nunez, 214.2; H—J. Nunez, 234; TBF—J. Nunez, 905; R—J. Nunez, 110; ER—Carasco, 107; HR—Carasco, E. Lopez, 26; SH—Pimentel, 18; SF—J. Nunez, J. Rios, 9; HB—A. Acosta, Vazquez, 13; BB—Manzanillo, 91; IBB—Almeida, 10; SO—Manzanillo, 183; WP—Barron, 16; BK—Tijerina, 4.

ALL PITCHERS

Pitcher, Team	W	L	Pct.	ERA	G	GS	CG	ShO	Rel.	Sv.	IP	H	TBF	R	ER	HR	SH	SF	HB	BB	IBB	SO	WP	Bk.
Acosta, Aaron, Cor.	10	10	.500	5.54	24	23	2	0	0	0	125.0	148	574	86	77	22	6	2	13	60	2	84	5	0
Acosta, Jaciel, Monc.	1	1	.500	5.32	38	0	0	0	6	1	44.0	44	197	31	26	7	1	1	2	26	2	30	0	0
Aguilar, Hugo, Monc.	0	0	.000	16.20	8	0	0	0	3	0	5.0	16	36	11	9	3	2	1	2	3	0	2	0	0
Aguilar, Jose , Pue.	5	5	.500	5.45	45	1	0	0	2	1	38.0	46	174	26	23	3	2	3	0	19	1	20	2	1

Pitcher, Team	W	L	Pct.	ERA	G	GS	CG	ShO	Rel.	Sv.	IP	H	TBF	R	ER	HR	SH	SF	HB	BB	IBB	SO	WP	Bk.
Aguilar, Mario, Cam.	0	0	.000	11.25	3	0	0	0	1	0	4.0	7	23	6	5	0	0	0	0	4	0	3	1	0
Aguilera, Adrian, Yuc.	0	0	.000	27.00	1	0	0	0	1	0	1.0	5	9	3	3	0	0	0	0	1	0	1	0	0
Aguirre, Gaudencio, Tab.	10	6	.625	3.34	39	16	5	0	17	8	143.0	134	650	59	53	4	8	6	9	32	2	66	6	1
Aleman, Paulo, Cor.	1	4	.200	6.55	13	9	0	0	0	0	44.0	59	207	34	32	5	3	3	4	23	0	12	1	0
Almeida, Rowsell, Lar.	5	1	.833	2.79	43	0	0	0	19	2	48.1	31	201	19	15	4	3	2	1	33	10	42	6	0
Alvarez, Antonio, Monc.	6	0	.375	6.55	30	23	3	2	1	0	115.1	147	551	95	84	16	5	5	4	70	5	44	3	3
Alvarez, Juan, Tab.	6	8	.429	3.54	24	24	3	1	0	0	152.1	157	654	70	60	14	7	2	6	57	3	71	3	3
Alvarez, Juan Azael, Monc.	3	2	.600	4.42	23	8	0	0	4	0	53.0	56	253	26	26	5	0	2	7	40	1	52	4	1
Alvarez, Octavio, Mex.	11	5	.688	4.64	26	26	2	0	0	0	172.2	228	734	100	89	18	9	2	6	45	0	93	6	0
Alvarez, Victor, Mex.*	0	2	.000	6.33	7	6	0	0	0	0	21.1	30	105	15	15	3	0	1	3	14	0	14	0	0
Angulo, Victor, Pue.	2	2	.500	5.34	28	4	0	0	6	0	62.1	70	277	38	37	8	0	0	2	42	0	36	1	0
Arias, Joel, Mont.	0	1	.000	4.42	13	0	0	0	6	1	18.1	21	89	14	9	3	2	0	0	14	1	11	1	0
Armenta, Alejandro, Tig.	7	0	1.000	5.26	37	16	0	0	7	1	104.1	121	467	65	61	13	3	3	4	52	0	75	5	0
Arteaga, Ivan, Oax.	1	2	.333	15.00	4	2	0	0	1	0	9.0	14	48	15	15	1	1	0	1	8	0	8	3	0
Atondo, Sergio, Yuc.	0	0	.000	3.86	16	0	0	0	6	0	16.1	11	71	9	7	1	1	0	0	11	1	21	3	0
Avila, Mauricio, Can.	0	1	.000	11.57	5	0	0	0	2	0	4.2	5	26	7	6	2	2	0	1	6	1	2	0	0
Ayala, Luis, Sal.	5	3	.625	2.76	55	0	0	0	52	25	65.1	69	269	22	20	4	4	0	3	13	1	38	1	0
Babineaux, Darrin, Lar.	5	2	.714	3.77	10	9	1	0	1	0	57.1	49	234	25	24	7	0	0	6	24	0	33	1	0
Baez, Sixto, Oax.	6	8	.429	4.69	50	0	0	0	42	23	55.2	81	269	31	29	5	2	1	3	22	4	32	1	0
Baez, Victor, Cor.	0	1	.000	6.75	22	0	0	0	6	0	30.2	36	145	26	23	3	2	2	3	24	1	12	0	0
Baker, Scott, Oax.	0	1	.000	8.44	2	2	0	0	0	0	10.2	17	50	11	10	3	0	0	0	6	0	1	0	0
Barradas, Roberto, Mex.	0	3	.000	7.86	13	5	0	0	4	0	26.1	41	127	23	23	4	2	1	2	10	0	7	3	0
Barron, Abelino, Sal.	2	1	.667	4.43	30	2	0	0	0	0	69.0	77	331	37	34	8	3	1	8	39	0	49	16	1
Bautista, Jose, Mont.	9	8	.529	5.52	26	22	0	0	2	0	122.1	161	375	84	75	20	7	1	7	40	1	69	3	1
Beckett, Robbie, Pue.*	0	1	.000	15.43	7	1	0	0	2	0	7.0	6	43	14	12	0	1	0	1	15	0	10	2	0
Beltran, Alonso, Tig.	5	5	.500	5.93	16	7	0	0	1	0	60.2	61	272	43	40	11	1	2	6	35	1	34	5	1
Bernal, Manuel, Mex.	10	3	.769	5.33	27	22	2	2	1	0	145.1	189	644	90	86	16	5	1	4	46	1	61	4	0
Berumen, Andres, Rey.	1	3	.250	8.22	5	5	0	0	0	0	15.1	19	72	14	14	3	2	1	2	8	0	6	3	0
Blancas, Rigoberto, Tab.	1	3	.250	6.27	23	0	0	0	4	0	18.2	22	86	14	13	3	1	0	0	7	2	9	0	0
Borowski, Joe, Mont.	4	2	.667	3.19	12	5	0	0	5	1	42.1	31	173	15	15	5	3	1	1	18	1	44	3	0
Bravo, Armando, Oax.	1	0	1.000	1.42	5	0	0	0	2	0	6.1	3	25	1	1	1	0	0	1	2	0	6	0	0
Briones, Jose Luis, Tor.	0	1	.000	8.10	13	2	0	0	3	0	20.0	35	108	20	18	3	1	1	1	13	0	11	0	1
Brito, Mario, Tor.	1	1	.500	5.14	21	0	0	0	18	7	28.0	26	120	16	16	5	2	0	3	13	1	27	1	0
Burgos, Enrique, Monc.-Cam.*	6	7	.462	3.88	17	17	1	0	0	0	92.2	85	413	48	40	4	6	1	3	60	3	79	6	0
Cabrales, Gabriel, Pue.	5	9	.357	5.53	34	21	3	0	2	0	128.2	156	573	84	79	15	11	4	5	53	7	54	2	0
Camara, Pedro, Cam.	1	0	1.000	7.15	9	3	0	0	4	0	11.1	13	58	9	9	5	0	1	0	10	1	5	0	0
Campillo, Jorge, Tig.	9	7	.563	6.84	25	17	1	0	4	0	98.2	128	456	79	75	22	3	2	0	42	2	58	7	1
Campos, Francisco, Cam.	11	4	.733	3.10	28	26	8	3	2	1	189.0	159	759	73	65	14	9	2	4	57	3	172	6	0
Cantu, Jacobo, Tor.	0	1	.000	7.04	12	0	0	0	4	0	15.1	25	76	13	12	3	0	0	2	10	0	6	1	0
Carasco, Alejandro, Oax.-Ver.	9	11	.450	6.42	29	23	5	0	3	1	150.0	181	644	108	107	26	6	7	8	61	2	64	3	0
Cardenas, Faustino, Can.	0	0	.000	7.36	7	0	0	0	2	0	11.0	17	54	9	9	0	1	1	3	4	0	4	0	1
Carranza, Javier, Lar.-Cam.-Tor.*	0	2	.000	8.13	31	2	0	0	5	0	31.0	45	160	29	28	7	3	4	1	26	2	13	2	0
Caruso, Eugene, Lar.	3	4	.429	6.59	10	10	0	0	0	0	56.0	78	240	43	41	8	5	0	1	34	0	23	5	0
Castaneda, Aurelio, Pue.	2	11	.154	6.75	25	15	0	0	4	1	89.1	132	426	75	67	17	5	3	3	34	1	37	4	0
Castillo, Daniel, Tab.	1	1	.500	6.14	6	0	0	0	3	1	7.1	10	31	5	5	0	1	0	0	3	0	6	2	0
Castro, Carlos, Tor.	0	0	.000	3.86	3	0	0	0	2	0	4.2	4	22	2	2	1	0	0	1	3	0	5	1	0
Cazares, Rosario, Sal.	0	0	.000	4.00	31	0	0	0	7	0	45.0	54	190	28	20	6	3	5	1	15	2	42	1	0
Cazarez, Tomas, Monc.	3	5	.375	5.96	13	9	0	0	2	0	48.1	70	233	37	32	5	0	0	1	25	3	27	1	0
Cazas, Tor.	0	0	.000	36.00	1	0	0	0	1	0	1.0	3	7	4	4	1	0	0	0	1	0	0	0	0
Cecena, Jose, Monc.	5	6	.455	6.31	36	10	0	0	3	0	87.0	100	379	62	61	11	4	6	1	43	2	81	5	0
Cera, Aquiles, Cor.	3	4	.429	3.70	28	2	0	0	22	4	41.1	27	184	19	17	5	2	0	3	32	3	37	4	0
Chapa, Javier, Cam.-Tor.	4	1	.800	6.95	30	5	0	0	8	1	66.0	94	315	54	51	9	4	3	2	31	0	21	6	0
Chavez, Anthony, Pue.	3	1	.750	2.10	20	0	0	0	18	9	25.2	18	106	7	6	1	2	3	1	15	3	22	1	0
Chavez, Carlos, Lar.	2	0	1.000	2.57	5	0	0	0	2	0	7.0	8	31	2	2	1	0	0	0	3	0	6	2	0
Chazaro, Jose, Lar.	0	0	.000	81.00	1	0	0	0	0	0	0.1	2	4	3	3	1	0	0	0	1	0	0	0	0
Conde, Argenis, Tor.-Rey.	7	11	.389	4.41	27	18	2	0	4	0	126.2	152	562	78	62	17	7	5	5	42	0	89	6	0
Correa, Ramser, Mont.	1	3	.250	9.35	5	5	0	0	0	0	17.1	26	87	22	18	3	0	1	0	12	0	8	1	0
Cortes, Jonathan, Cor.	0	0	.000	0.00	1	0	0	0	0	0	2.2	2	12	0	0	0	0	0	1	1	0	4	0	0
Cortez, Martin, Cor.	0	0	.000	0.00	1	0	0	0	1	0	1.0	0	5	0	0	0	0	0	0	2	0	1	0	0
Couoh, Enrique, Yuc.	4	3	.571	3.39	32	9	1	1	9	0	95.2	92	393	39	36	14	6	1	1	18	2	68	5	0
Crawford, Joseph, Sal.*	2	1	.667	6.86	4	4	0	0	0	0	21.0	26	97	17	16	1	1	0	2	9	0	10	1	0
Cruz, Javier, Mex.	7	3	.700	5.83	53	0	0	0	18	3	58.2	64	266	41	38	8	4	4	3	27	2	60	2	1
Cruz, Luis Manuel, Pue.	3	2	.600	4.14	22	4	0	0	6	0	37.0	55	177	23	17	3	1	2	2	16	1	14	6	0
Cuervo, Bernardo, Yuc.	9	7	.563	4.83	20	19	1	0	0	0	119.1	156	491	70	64	9	7	3	4	35	1	46	3	0
Darley, Ned, Sal.	3	1	.750	5.21	30	2	0	0	7	0	38.0	51	190	22	22	2	4	2	0	32	0	24	5	0
De La Rosa, Jorge, Mont.	3	2	.600	6.28	37	0	0	0	5	1	38.2	38	184	27	27	2	2	0	2	32	1	50	6	1
DeLaFuente, Julian, Mex.-Rey.	0	0	.000	8.71	9	0	0	0	3	0	10.1	19	53	10	10	1	0	0	0	5	0	7	4	0
Diaz, Alejandro, Can.	0	0	.000	10.80	2	0	0	0	0	0	1.2	2	9	2	2	0	0	2	0	2	1	0	0	0
Diaz, Marco Antonio, Sal.	7	1	.875	3.95	37	5	0	0	6	0	66.0	61	281	29	29	6	5	2	3	23	0	58	3	0
Dominguez, Carlos, Rey.	0	2	.000	7.50	9	0	0	0	2	0	6.0	10	36	5	5	1	0	3	1	5	0	6	0	0
Drumheller, Al, Pue.	1	0	1.000	7.17	5	5	1	1	0	0	21.1	24	101	18	17	2	0	0	0	17	2	16	1	0
Duarte, Miguel, Sal.	6	1	.857	4.13	45	0	0	0	11	2	61.0	65	269	29	28	2	5	1	1	29	2	66	6	0
Dunbar, Matt, Oax.	4	3	.571	3.81	9	8	3	0	0	0	56.2	57	239	27	24	8	2	1	1	18	1	50	2	1
Ellis, Robert, Mont.	8	5	.615	3.51	15	14	3	0	0	0	92.1	78	379	39	36	8	5	1	2	32	0	70	6	1
Elvira, Abraham, Cor.	1	1	.500	8.36	15	0	0	0	2	0	14.0	26	79	17	13	2	0	0	1	15	2	8	1	0
Enriquez, Martin, Rey.	2	1	.667	3.95	17	1	0	0	1	0	27.1	30	126	16	12	2	2	1	2	14	0	12	1	0
Esparza, Emerson, Monc.	4	4	.500	7.73	23	15	0	0	2	0	80.1	120	383	69	69	20	4	0	4	29	2	43	6	1
Espejo, Humberto, Can.	3	4	.429	5.70	43	0	0	0	12	0	53.2	60	243	38	34	7	3	2	1	33	1	25	5	1
Espinoza, Mario, Can.	0	1	.000	8.44	4	1	0	0	1	0	5.1	6	32	5	5	2	0	0	2	8	0	1	0	0
Esquer, Mercedes, Rey.	11	3	.786	4.21	23	21	1	0	0	0	130.1	149	562	65	61	16	6	3	5	32	0	73	1	0
Federico, Gustavo, Mont.	4	2	.667	4.81	31	5	0	0	11	0	76.2	82	333	45	41	10	2	5	5	34	2	31	3	0
Ferrer, Jesus, Can.	2	1	.667	2.76	7	4	0	0	1	0	32.2	24	144	11	10	3	2	2	0	22	0	18	2	0
Flores, Ignacio, Tor.	4	6	.400	5.11	35	15	0	0	10	1	98.2	114	454	63	56	11	5	6	7	47	2	81	4	1
Flores, Jordan, Sal.	3	3	.500	6.51	12	11	0	0	0	0	56.2	71	276	49	41	8	3	3	6	41	1	23	4	0
Flores, Jorge, Tab.-Tor.*	2	6	.250	5.37	43	4	0	0	8	2	52.0	66	243	37	31	7	4	0	0	26	7	18	2	1
Flores, Pedro, Yuc.*	1	0	1.000	6.23	8	1	0	0	3	0	17.1	24	83	13	12	7	0	0	1	10	0	9	0	0

Pitcher, Team	W	L	Pct.	ERA	G	GS	CG	ShO	Rel.	Sv.	IP	H	TBF	R	ER	HR	SH	SF	HB	BB	IBB	SO	WP	Bk.
Flynt, Will, Sal.	13	4	.765	2.68	26	25	1	0	0	0	174.1	175	745	71	52	11	5	4	5	67	0	157	5	0
Fontes, Agustin, Can.-Tab.	1	2	.333	5.11	20	8	0	0	7	1	56.1	75	230	41	32	11	1	2	1	18	0	25	3	1
Fregoso, Raul, Cam.	3	3	.500	5.10	31	8	0	0	6	1	67.0	79	324	39	38	9	3	3	2	50	1	30	4	1
Galvez, Randy, Mex.	4	4	.500	6.65	12	12	1	0	0	0	66.1	88	295	51	49	7	3	0	1	24	1	39	1	0
Galvez, Rosario, Pue.-Rey.*	1	3	.250	6.75	32	0	0	0	7	0	25.1	35	134	21	19	0	2	1	0	25	2	18	2	0
Garcia, Adolfo, Cam.	3	3	.500	4.33	36	0	0	0	7	0	70.2	81	308	39	34	3	6	1	5	21	2	19	2	2
Garcia, Alfredo, Mex.	1	2	.333	3.94	6	5	0	0	0	0	16.0	17	65	8	7	2	0	1	0	3	0	10	1	0
Garcia, Gerardo, Tig.	2	2	.500	4.75	15	1	0	0	5	0	30.1	27	128	16	16	0	0	0	0	18	1	16	8	0
Garcia, Jose, Tig.	6	4	.600	2.97	55	0	0	0	14	5	69.2	88	299	26	23	6	3	2	1	19	7	43	4	1
Garcia, Jose Luis, Pue.	7	5	.583	3.19	15	12	4	0	1	0	87.1	69	351	32	31	7	4	1	0	30	0	69	3	1
Garcia, Manuel, Can.	0	0	.000	5.40	4	0	0	0	1	0	3.1	6	17	6	2	0	0	0	0	1	0	1	3	1
Garcia, Ramon, Tab.	1	2	.333	8.00	10	4	1	1	3	0	27.0	34	127	26	24	3	1	0	0	12	0	21	3	0
Garibay, Roberto, Rey.	5	11	.313	6.57	25	24	2	0	0	0	124.2	166	579	102	91	16	1	5	6	49	3	49	5	0
Garibay, Salvador, Lar.	0	3	.000	7.18	37	4	0	0	6	1	62.2	85	291	52	50	9	3	3	1	25	1	28	6	1
Gomez, Alejandro, Cor.	0	0	.000	6.58	31	3	0	0	8	0	53.1	75	239	42	39	10	2	3	4	27	2	31	3	0
Gomez, Gustavo, Rey.	0	0	.000	7.99	17	0	0	0	2	0	23.2	39	124	25	21	5	0	1	3	13	0	12	5	0
Gomez, Martin, Cor.	5	9	.357	5.38	40	7	0	0	13	3	72.0	87	328	53	43	10	6	4	4	36	4	29	2	0
Gonzalez, Arnulfo, Can.	0	0	.000	13.50	1	1	0	0	0	0	2.2	4	13	4	4	3	0	0	0	1	0	1	1	0
Gonzalez, Arturo, Mont.	7	5	.583	4.01	16	16	1	1	0	0	94.1	101	402	43	42	11	6	2	4	27	1	40	1	0
Gonzalez, Erubiel, Ver.	0	0	.000	30.38	5	0	0	0	1	0	2.2	7	23	9	9	1	1	0	3	4	0	3	1	0
Gonzalez, Victor, Monc.	1	1	.500	11.01	28	0	0	0	4	0	34.1	56	179	45	42	14	3	2	3	22	5	14	1	0
Grajales, Norberto, Tor.	2	4	.333	5.35	9	6	1	0	1	0	33.2	42	149	25	20	7	1	2	4	7	1	16	0	0
Graterol, Beiker, Tig.	5	3	.625	7.13	26	7	0	0	5	2	70.2	88	334	59	56	10	5	7	1	40	2	38	1	1
Guerra, Pascual, Tab.	0	0	.000	5.87	9	0	0	0	1	0	15.1	23	72	12	10	1	0	1	0	8	1	3	1	0
Gutierrez, Cosme, Oax.	1	1	.500	6.19	21	0	0	0	8	0	16.0	23	73	11	11	5	0	0	0	6	0	9	0	0
Gutierrez, J., Tor.	0	0	.000	0.00	1	0	0	0	1	1	3.0	0	9	0	0	0	0	0	0	1	0	0	0	0
Gutierrez, Marco, Mex.	0	1	.000	7.65	6	2	0	0	0	0	20.0	34	98	18	17	4	1	1	0	14	1	10	0	0
Gutierrez, Pablo, Cor.	2	2	.500	5.40	22	0	0	0	8	1	33.1	42	148	23	20	3	5	2	3	6	4	14	1	0
Guzman, Ricardo, Monc.	0	0	.000	5.52	9	0	0	0	2	0	14.2	21	70	12	9	3	0	1	0	6	1	6	0	0
Hartmann, Pete, Lar.*	3	5	.375	5.93	15	10	0	0	1	1	57.2	65	264	38	38	8	2	1	4	38	0	52	5	0
Henriquez, Oscar, Mex.	7	2	.778	3.86	36	0	0	0	9	0	46.2	38	202	26	20	4	1	3	6	23	1	65	2	0
Henry, Santiago, Cor.	0	0	.000	0.00	1	0	0	0	1	0	1.0	0	4	0	0	0	0	0	1	1	0	1	0	0
Henthorne, Kevin, Pue.-Tig.	11	4	.733	4.34	21	19	4	0	0	0	124.1	128	495	67	60	18	4	4	1	31	1	69	0	0
Heredia, Hector, Yuc.	4	4	.500	4.20	29	2	0	0	20	3	40.2	50	180	20	19	3	7	2	0	8	3	19	1	0
Heredia, Julian, Rey.-Tor.	6	7	.462	3.76	45	2	0	0	37	12	81.1	75	343	42	34	7	7	1	4	28	2	69	3	0
Heredia, Maximo, Mont.	3	4	.429	7.29	13	11	0	0	0	0	54.1	69	264	47	44	9	5	2	1	35	0	35	5	0
Hernandez, Martin, Sal.	10	8	.556	6.20	22	20	1	0	1	0	101.2	121	429	75	70	16	2	1	0	47	1	36	4	0
Hernandez, Santos, Tig.	4	4	.500	2.80	49	0	0	0	45	36	54.2	59	243	20	17	4	2	0	6	19	2	54	3	0
Herrera, Calixto, Ver.	2	1	.667	4.97	29	0	0	0	10	4	38.0	42	164	25	21	6	0	3	2	16	0	16	1	0
Herrera, Enrique, Tab.	5	3	.625	5.50	47	0	0	0	15	7	37.2	45	167	24	23	6	2	0	1	20	4	27	1	0
Hidalgo, Romeo, Rey.	0	0	.000	4.67	15	0	0	0	3	0	17.1	12	76	12	9	1	0	1	1	16	1	6	2	0
Huerta, Francisco, Ver.	0	0	.000	10.80	8	0	0	0	4	0	10.0	15	55	12	12	2	0	2	2	9	0	4	0	0
Huerta, Luis, Lar.	3	4	.429	7.01	14	12	0	0	0	0	60.1	86	277	47	47	13	2	1	6	21	1	37	1	0
Hurtado, Edwin, Oax.	7	7	.500	6.56	25	23	2	0	2	0	133.0	168	619	106	97	24	5	2	7	72	2	84	11	0
Ishee, Gabe, Can.	0	1	.000	13.50	2	2	0	0	0	0	7.1	14	41	11	11	1	0	1	0	7	0	4	2	0
Izabal, Luis, Pue.	0	0	.000	6.10	9	0	0	0	6	0	10.1	13	53	7	7	2	0	0	1	9	0	7	0	0
Janzen, Marty, Cam.	3	0	1.000	1.05	7	3	1	1	3	0	25.2	22	103	4	3	0	0	0	1	7	1	25	2	0
Jimenez, German, Mont.	0	1	.000	3.41	20	2	0	0	2	0	31.2	35	138	15	12	3	4	2	0	19	1	19	1	0
Jimenez, Isaac, Mont.	3	2	.600	4.88	19	4	0	0	3	0	31.1	40	139	18	17	5	1	1	2	8	0	23	1	0
Jimenez, Jose, Oax.	3	4	.429	7.09	14	12	2	0	1	0	53.1	62	255	48	42	7	3	1	3	43	0	34	2	1
Jimenez, Julio, Sal.-Tor.*	1	1	.500	4.89	26	2	0	0	6	0	35.0	28	160	22	19	3	0	1	3	23	1	22	7	1
Jones, Calvin, Tab.	2	1	.667	1.23	17	0	0	0	17	11	22.0	11	82	3	3	1	0	1	0	7	1	18	0	0
Kamar, Emil, Monc.-Tor.	2	7	.222	10.46	21	18	0	0	1	0	68.0	109	357	82	79	12	3	7	9	48	1	46	7	0
Landeros, Lorenzo, Oax.	3	4	.429	8.22	24	11	0	0	4	0	65.2	95	315	63	60	16	1	3	2	30	1	35	4	0
Lara, Jorge, Sal.	4	8	.333	8.69	24	15	0	0	1	0	76.2	118	381	84	74	16	4	4	8	36	0	33	0	2
Larranaga, Miguel, Tab.	0	0	.000	13.50	2	0	0	0	0	0	2.2	4	14	4	4	1	0	0	0	3	0	0	0	0
Leal, Gerardo, Monc.-Can.	1	2	.333	5.98	14	5	0	0	2	0	40.2	54	192	31	27	6	4	2	1	18	0	15	1	1
Leon, Cupertino, Oax.	6	3	.667	4.39	25	15	2	0	5	0	104.2	115	466	57	51	11	2	2	4	52	2	46	3	1
Leon, Juan Antonio, Tor.	1	3	.250	9.73	20	7	0	0	2	0	45.1	71	230	50	49	10	1	3	6	25	1	30	9	1
Leyva, Edgar, Cor.	7	5	.583	5.12	19	18	2	0	1	1	110.2	120	463	66	63	16	7	3	6	38	1	82	5	0
Lezama, Rafael, Tab.*	2	0	1.000	6.50	18	0	0	0	3	0	18.0	21	90	13	13	1	0	2	1	12	0	9	1	0
Linares, Yfrain, Pue.	0	0	.000	37.80	4	0	0	0	2	0	1.2	6	16	8	7	1	0	0	0	5	1	2	0	0
Loaiza, Sabino, Cam.	2	11	.154	6.65	28	9	0	0	6	0	69.0	96	321	56	51	8	2	4	4	23	2	29	1	0
Lomeli, Israel, Oax.	3	0	1.000	9.23	20	1	0	0	4	0	26.1	30	139	31	27	3	2	2	6	23	0	19	2	0
Lopez, Emigdio, Tor.	13	8	.619	4.86	26	25	1	0	1	0	157.1	175	662	89	85	26	6	6	11	52	2	80	1	0
Lopez, Gilberto, Ver.	2	2	.500	7.53	35	2	0	0	7	2	34.2	53	162	30	29	5	5	1	4	23	0	14	1	1
Lopez, J. Dionisio, Pue.	0	2	.000	7.82	26	1	0	0	5	0	35.2	36	182	35	31	2	3	0	3	41	1	25	7	0
Lopez, Jesus Nain, Oax.-Ver.*	1	0	1.000	9.53	39	0	0	0	5	1	28.1	42	144	33	30	9	5	1	0	14	1	22	0	0
Lopez, Jose Juan, Sal.	8	2	.800	3.51	50	0	0	0	21	5	56.1	67	246	29	22	5	6	2	3	15	2	34	0	0
Lopez, Miguel Angel, Tig.	1	0	1.000	4.97	18	0	0	0	5	1	29.0	30	117	17	16	5	2	0	4	20	3	18	4	0
Lopez, Roberto, Mex.	1	1	.500	9.14	16	1	0	0	5	0	21.2	38	108	22	22	9	0	3	0	12	0	14	0	0
Loya, Rigoberto, Mont.	0	3	.000	5.88	18	9	0	0	3	0	52.0	78	255	39	34	5	4	3	3	26	0	26	5	0
Lozano, Ivan, Tab.	0	0	.000	81.00	1	0	0	0	0	0	0.1	5	8	3	3	1	0	0	0	1	0	0	0	0
Luevano, Juan, Ver.-Oax.	3	3	.500	5.18	44	3	0	0	17	4	57.1	87	272	36	33	9	5	2	5	18	5	27	0	0
Lugo, Aaron, Mont.	0	0	.000	8.31	3	0	0	0	0	0	4.1	6	23	4	4	1	0	1	0	4	0	2	0	0
Macias, Luis, Monc.	0	0	.000	7.03	17	0	0	0	8	0	24.1	30	115	20	19	4	0	5	2	11	0	11	3	0
Madero, Francisco, Mex.-Can.	4	6	.400	5.10	24	16	0	0	2	0	97.0	115	441	58	55	9	9	3	3	51	4	67	5	1
Magee, Danny, Monc.	9	3	.750	3.60	16	16	2	1	0	0	100.0	91	445	44	40	6	1	2	5	68	0	104	4	0
Manrique, Alberto, Rey.	3	7	.300	5.43	31	12	0	0	6	0	106.0	133	489	76	64	20	7	5	3	42	2	73	4	0
Manzanillo, Ravelo, Yuc.	10	6	.625	3.55	23	23	5	0	0	0	157.1	140	688	65	62	14	9	3	5	91	1	183	7	2
Manzano, Rafael, Can.	0	0	.000	5.40	4	0	0	0	2	0	3.1	1	16	2	2	1	0	0	1	4	0	3	0	0
Marquez, Isidro, Cam.	3	9	.250	3.62	51	0	0	0	47	22	59.2	70	263	29	24	4	4	2	4	18	4	53	3	0
Martinez, Cesar, Tor.-Sal.*	6	7	.462	8.14	29	19	0	0	0	0	87.1	116	450	90	79	12	0	1	10	79	0	62	6	0
Martinez, Jesus, Ver.*	2	2	.500	8.16	10	7	0	0	1	0	28.2	49	148	34	26	3	1	3	0	18	1	14	1	0
Martinez, Jose, Tab.-Mont.	3	13	.188	5.05	20	20	0	0	0	0	114.0	125	483	71	64	15	12	3	2	30	5	65	3	1
Martinez, Juan J., Mex.	0	2	.000	12.10	11	2	0	0	1	0	19.1	30	106	27	26	3	1	2	2	21	0	9	1	0

Pitcher, Team	W	L	Pct.	ERA	G	GS	CG	ShO	Rel.	Sv.	IP	H	TBF	R	ER	HR	SH	SF	HB	BB	IBB	SO	WP	Bk.
Martinez, Pedro, Oax.	11	8	.579	4.28	23	23	3	2	0	0	143.0	149	618	82	68	16	6	2	1	55	0	89	0	1
Martinez, Uriel, Cam.	0	0	.000	7.71	5	0	0	0	1	0	4.2	7	25	5	4	0	0	0	1	3	0	3	1	0
Mascorro, David, Mex.	0	0	.000	3.86	11	0	0	0	2	0	11.2	10	53	5	5	1	0	1	1	10	1	1	0	0
Medina, Alonso, Mont.	0	0	.000	7.04	7	0	0	0	6	0	7.2	12	36	6	6	0	1	0	0	3	0	8	1	0
Medina, Osvaldo, Pue.	2	1	.667	6.05	20	2	0	0	8	0	38.2	46	177	26	26	5	4	0	2	20	2	23	5	0
Melendez, Nestor, Rey.	5	8	.385	4.10	46	10	0	0	22	5	107.2	94	477	59	49	11	8	2	1	78	7	76	13	1
Mendoza, Marco, Rey.	0	0	.000	3.60	5	0	0	0	2	0	5.0	5	23	3	2	0	0	1	1	3	0	5	1	0
Mere, Fernando, Can.	4	5	.444	6.00	39	4	0	0	18	1	69.0	77	318	48	46	15	3	3	4	35	2	38	4	0
Meza, Leobardo, Ver.	11	8	.579	4.36	24	24	3	2	0	0	152.2	159	666	80	74	7	11	5	8	59	2	114	0	0
Minor, Blas, Tor.	3	2	.600	6.75	17	5	1	0	4	2	46.2	57	216	35	35	8	1	1	5	23	2	35	3	0
Miranda, Julio, Pue.	0	4	.000	5.80	43	0	0	0	16	5	45.0	56	202	29	29	7	2	4	2	19	8	33	2	0
Molina, Primitivo, Mont.-Lar.	1	2	.333	7.08	11	1	0	0	1	0	20.1	28	93	16	16	7	0	1	1	6	0	6	1	0
Montano, Ignacio, Cor.	1	3	.250	6.33	53	2	0	0	10	4	42.2	42	206	32	30	7	2	1	5	40	6	29	5	0
Montmayor, Humberto, Mont.	3	2	.600	5.05	42	7	0	0	7	0	76.2	90	352	46	43	8	4	6	7	38	1	60	3	1
Mora, Eleazar, Ver.	10	8	.556	3.39	23	23	3	2	0	0	148.2	159	621	67	56	9	5	5	3	37	3	98	3	1
Morales, Fernando, Cam.	0	0	.000	3.18	2	1	0	0	1	0	5.2	7	26	2	2	0	1	0	1	5	0	2	0	0
Morales, Luis, Ver.	10	7	.588	2.04	34	14	1	0	11	1	119.0	100	466	37	27	14	4	4	2	26	2	82	1	0
Moreno, Angel, Mex.	13	8	.619	5.41	24	24	5	1	0	0	158.0	214	712	100	95	21	7	6	5	46	1	79	7	0
Moreno, Claudio, Mex.	10	4	.714	4.59	43	7	0	0	5	0	96.0	122	444	61	49	9	6	2	4	40	5	52	6	0
Moreno, Edgar, Oax.	0	0	.000	6.97	7	0	0	0	2	0	10.1	12	51	9	8	1	0	1	1	8	0	5	0	0
Moreno, Leobardo, Sal.*	2	3	.400	5.51	9	9	0	0	0	0	47.1	62	213	29	29	2	2	3	1	22	0	23	2	0
Munoz, Leonardo, Mont.-Lar.*	2	5	.286	6.52	31	5	0	0	7	0	48.1	60	229	40	35	10	4	2	0	35	1	25	5	1
Munoz, Miguel, Cor.-Tab.	6	7	.462	5.01	22	22	1	0	0	0	120.1	150	529	76	67	20	6	3	3	25	6	60	1	1
Murillo, Felipe, Monc.	2	2	.500	6.34	45	0	0	0	12	0	61.0	70	275	44	43	9	8	4	3	28	6	31	1	0
Navarro, Hector, Sal.	0	0	.000	4.58	12	0	0	0	5	0	19.2	25	88	12	10	1	0	1	2	5	0	12	1	0
Navarro, Joel, Mex.	0	0	.000	5.91	7	0	0	0	2	0	10.2	18	52	7	7	2	0	1	0	3	0	9	1	0
Navarro, Jose Felix, Tig.	5	8	.385	6.05	23	19	0	0	2	0	108.2	131	496	81	73	16	9	3	8	40	4	72	5	0
Navarro, Luis, Yuc.	3	1	.750	2.73	5	5	0	0	0	0	26.1	30	108	10	8	2	0	0	1	4	0	10	0	0
Neri, Braulio, Sal.	0	0	.000	2.45	14	0	0	0	2	0	7.1	8	31	2	2	1	0	0	0	2	0	6	1	1
Neri, Eduardo, Ver.-Oak.*	1	4	.200	4.53	52	1	0	0	5	1	47.2	54	209	27	24	5	2	3	3	14	3	34	1	0
Nieblas, Mauro, Mont.	0	1	.000	10.38	3	1	0	0	1	0	4.1	4	23	5	5	0	0	0	2	6	1	3	0	0
Nieblas, Omar, Tab.	0	1	.000	9.35	19	0	0	0	4	0	17.1	19	85	19	18	1	0	1	0	17	0	9	6	0
Nunez, Jose, Lar.	13	10	.565	3.98	31	29	6	0	0	0	214.2	234	905	110	95	25	12	9	3	45	7	147	5	0
Nunez, Jose Javier, Tor.	0	0	.000	5.14	3	0	0	0	0	0	7.0	14	40	5	4	3	0	0	2	2	0	4	0	0
Nunez, Juan Jose, Oax.	4	3	.571	5.52	27	6	1	0	7	0	60.1	65	266	42	37	7	2	2	4	32	0	32	1	0
Ochoa, Jesus, Oax.	0	0	.000	4.22	8	0	0	0	5	1	10.2	10	45	5	5	0	1	2	1	7	0	2	1	0
Olague, Jesus, Pue.	5	6	.455	6.19	28	12	1	0	1	0	75.2	87	333	54	52	13	4	1	1	34	2	59	5	1
Orea, Flavio, Cor.	0	0	.000	9.00	1	0	0	0	0	0	1.0	2	6	1	1	0	0	0	0	0	0	0	1	0
Orozco, Jaime, Tor.	0	0	.000	9.00	7	1	0	0	2	1	8.0	18	44	8	8	2	0	1	0	3	0	5	0	0
Ortega, Pablo, Tig.	11	3	.786	4.34	24	23	0	0	0	0	122.1	139	535	61	59	7	2	6	8	68	1	91	7	0
Ortega, Raul, Yuc.-Cor.	0	1	.000	5.73	19	0	0	0	3	0	11.0	10	47	7	7	1	1	2	0	7	0	3	1	0
Ortega, Roberto, Pue.*	0	0	.000	5.74	6	4	0	0	1	0	15.2	19	82	12	10	0	0	0	0	18	1	15	0	0
Ortega, Wilbert, Yuc.	1	1	.500	4.39	48	0	0	0	3	0	26.2	33	118	15	13	3	2	0	0	15	2	26	4	2
Osuna, Adrian, Oax.	0	0	.000	14.73	9	0	0	0	3	0	7.1	10	45	12	12	1	0	0	2	12	0	4	0	0
Osuna, Ricardo, Lar.	0	3	.000	6.48	15	11	0	0	2	0	58.1	85	275	51	42	10	3	1	2	22	0	39	7	0
Ozuna, Gabriel, Yuc.	5	1	.833	2.54	8	8	0	0	0	0	49.2	43	194	15	14	4	0	1	0	6	0	41	2	0
Pacheco, Alex, Pue.	2	1	.667	1.80	19	0	0	0	18	10	20.0	16	81	5	4	1	1	2	0	10	1	12	2	0
Palafox, Juan, Monc.	12	9	.571	4.70	24	24	3	1	0	0	159.0	191	714	96	83	20	13	6	12	51	9	82	3	2
Palomares, Manuel, Pue.	0	0	.000	6.08	15	0	0	0	4	0	23.2	30	119	19	16	2	2	1	0	16	0	16	4	0
Parra, Julio, Lar.	4	7	.364	4.64	50	0	0	0	47	21	52.1	59	220	31	27	7	1	3	2	17	3	53	3	0
Pena, Joel, Ver.	2	1	.667	4.96	30	1	0	0	9	2	45.1	49	204	29	25	10	1	1	1	27	1	33	2	0
Perez, Edgar, Cor.	7	6	.538	5.48	30	14	2	1	2	0	108.1	141	508	71	66	16	4	8	7	50	3	56	6	0
Perez, Leonardo, Cor.	6	5	.545	5.45	21	21	0	0	0	0	105.2	138	493	80	64	10	4	3	6	45	2	43	7	0
Perez, Oliver, Yuc.*	3	2	.600	4.36	11	6	0	0	1	1	43.1	39	182	24	21	3	4	2	0	17	1	37	1	1
Pesqueira, Omar, Yuc.	4	1	.800	5.43	34	5	0	0	4	0	59.2	78	270	46	36	8	1	0	0	26	1	19	5	0
Picota, Lenin, Tor.	2	0	1.000	6.28	11	0	0	0	6	1	14.1	16	72	11	10	1	2	1	0	13	0	10	0	0
Pimentel, Roberto, Tab.	6	9	.400	3.87	26	25	2	1	1	0	151.1	146	646	72	65	12	18	4	2	60	4	88	1	0
Pulido, Raymundo, Can.	7	13	.350	4.29	32	15	2	1	5	1	115.1	116	499	62	55	14	11	3	7	51	5	63	6	2
Purata, Julio, Rey.	2	4	.333	6.31	13	11	1	0	0	0	51.1	54	246	38	36	9	3	2	3	45	1	28	2	0
Qintanilla, Enrique, Lar.	9	13	.409	6.03	51	10	1	0	10	0	115.0	156	543	87	77	16	4	4	12	39	4	73	12	2
Quinones, Enrique, Rey.	6	12	.333	4.29	28	18	2	1	9	2	130.0	151	530	69	62	15	9	1	5	33	1	73	3	0
Quiroz, Aaron, Sal.	7	4	.636	3.91	18	18	0	0	0	0	89.2	114	244	50	39	12	4	2	2	30	0	57	4	0
Ramirez, Jose, Monc.	0	0	.000	4.29	17	0	0	0	7	0	21.0	21	90	11	10	0	0	2	1	17	2	9	3	0
Ramon, Jose Andres, Tab.	8	4	.667	4.19	43	0	0	0	13	0	58.0	72	247	28	27	5	3	3	2	18	5	43	2	1
Raygoza, Martin, Tor.	1	0	1.000	4.50	6	1	0	0	1	0	8.0	13	41	6	4	0	0	0	1	4	1	1	0	0
Retes, Lorenzo, Oax.*	2	1	.667	10.55	15	1	0	0	2	0	21.1	27	117	26	25	3	4	2	2	29	4	22	3	0
Retes, Luis, Ver.	0	0	.000	15.58	4	0	0	0	1	0	8.2	19	54	15	15	2	0	0	3	6	0	7	1	0
Reyes, Nathanael, Mex.	5	3	.625	6.61	48	6	0	0	6	0	66.2	102	321	59	49	14	5	0	2	34	2	35	6	1
Reyes, Pablo, Pue.*	0	3	.000	4.86	3	3	0	0	0	0	16.2	21	81	15	9	2	0	1	0	10	0	10	1	0
Ricken, Ray, Pue.	2	3	.400	3.68	5	5	2	0	0	0	36.2	31	157	21	15	1	1	3	1	20	1	19	5	0
Rios, Alejandro, Tor.	2	1	.667	5.44	29	0	0	0	3	0	46.1	61	217	35	28	7	3	0	2	21	1	35	3	0
Rios, Daniel, Tor.	6	3	.667	3.21	12	7	5	0	5	0	61.2	60	261	22	22	4	1	1	5	30	0	28	4	0
Rios, Jesus, Tor.	6	2	.333	6.60	33	20	2	1	2	2	132.1	160	605	104	97	17	3	9	8	58	1	89	7	2
Rivas, Jesus, Tig.	0	1	.000	8.10	29	0	0	0	8	0	20.0	22	101	19	18	3	1	1	2	20	2	6	3	1
Rivera, Francisco, Tor.	2	0	1.000	7.43	20	1	0	0	7	0	36.1	60	182	34	30	4	0	0	5	17	0	15	3	0
Rivera, Oscar, Ver.	8	5	.615	3.86	22	21	4	1	1	0	137.2	141	615	71	59	11	7	2	7	67	3	92	12	0
Rivera, Paul, Can.	2	4	.333	6.25	47	0	0	0	9	2	59.0	68	267	48	41	10	4	2	3	28	1	26	4	1
Rivera, Roberto, Mont.-Sal.*	4	7	.364	4.31	30	9	0	0	17	6	64.2	64	291	33	31	5	6	3	4	38	3	34	3	1
Rodriguez, Enoc, Can.-Lar.*	0	0	.000	9.82	9	2	0	0	4	0	14.2	22	78	18	16	5	0	1	3	12	0	3	0	0
Rodriguez, Hugo, Can.	0	0	.000	0.00	2	0	0	0	2	0	1.1	1	5	0	0	0	0	0	0	1	0	1	0	0
Rodriguez, Jesus, Monc.	0	0	.000	8.44	7	0	0	0	1	0	5.1	10	30	5	5	1	0	0	1	5	1	3	2	1
Rodriguez, Manuel, Cor.	3	3	.500	4.93	44	2	0	0	13	4	73.0	69	329	45	40	9	1	4	3	45	3	45	4	0
Rodriguez, Rosario, Sal.*	0	0	.000	4.85	21	0	0	0	1	0	13.0	13	50	9	7	2	0	0	2	6	0	4	2	0
Rodriguez, Salvador, Yuc.	2	2	.500	5.74	5	5	1	0	0	0	31.1	42	144	21	20	5	1	1	1	8	0	28	0	0
Rojo, Oscar, Rey.	0	1	.000	19.80	7	0	0	0	4	0	5.0	14	34	11	11	0	1	0	0	6	1	3	0	0
Romero, Alejandro, Yuc.	8	7	.533	4.55	22	21	2	1	0	0	118.2	151	539	77	60	11	4	3	6	40	3	88	6	1

Pitcher, Team	W	L	Pct.	ERA	G	GS	CG	ShO	Rel.	Sv.	IP	H	TBF	R	ER	HR	SH	SF	HB	BB	IBB	SO	WP	Bk.
Romero, Cesar, Lar.	1	0	1.000	5.40	24	0	0	0	13	1	38.1	43	170	26	23	8	1	1	4	20	2	26	2	0
Romero, Juan Jose, Cor.	3	4	.429	5.77	37	0	0	0	20	7	43.2	49	202	32	28	7	5	0	3	27	6	23	4	0
Romo, Eduardo, Lar.	0	0	.000	6.75	2	1	0	0	1	0	4.0	5	19	3	3	0	1	0	0	3	0	0	0	0
Roque, Jorge, Tor.	0	1	.000	4.66	25	0	0	0	6	0	36.2	42	162	21	19	4	3	1	2	11	0	21	1	0
Rosenkranz, Terry, Cam.*	1	1	.500	5.92	20	0	0	0	4	0	24.1	22	105	16	16	3	2	1	0	14	0	24	1	0
Rosenkranz, Terry, Oax.	0	1	.000	7.36	11	0	0	0	2	1	14.2	16	69	13	12	2	3	0	0	9	0	15	0	0
Rubio, Miguel, Mont.	8	2	.800	1.73	55	0	0	0	32	7	83.1	57	333	16	16	3	4	2	2	36	6	82	3	0
Ruiz, Cecilio, Tab.*	7	4	.636	3.32	20	18	0	0	2	1	89.1	112	387	43	33	7	3	4	3	10	1	29	0	0
Ruiz, Juan Manuel, Cor.	0	0	.000	9.00	2	0	0	0	1	0	3.0	1	16	3	3	0	0	1	2	4	0	0	0	0
Sanchez, Alejandro, Can.	1	0	1.000	8.20	18	0	0	0	4	0	26.1	40	127	25	24	4	3	1	0	14	1	13	2	1
Sanchez, Efrain, Cam.	6	4	.600	5.44	29	15	1	1	3	0	99.1	116	439	64	60	11	3	1	3	42	1	36	1	0
Sanchez, Hector, Pue.	1	2	.333	4.40	6	6	0	0	0	0	28.2	29	126	17	14	3	0	1	0	14	0	15	0	0
Sanchez, Sergio, Tab.	0	0	.000	16.88	3	0	0	0	2	0	2.2	8	16	5	5	0	0	0	0	2	0	2	0	0
Sandoval, Guillermo, Can.-Pue.	2	9	.182	6.43	24	15	1	0	0	0	78.1	92	380	64	56	12	2	3	4	61	2	53	9	0
Sandoval, Ricardo, Tor.	0	0	.000	14.54	7	0	0	0	0	0	4.1	11	25	8	7	2	1	2	0	1	0	2	0	0
Serrano, Jorge, Lar.	0	1	.000	7.47	15	2	0	0	2	0	31.1	43	152	28	26	6	1	1	0	21	0	15	3	0
Seung, Choi, Can.	1	2	.333	6.63	3	3	1	0	0	0	19.0	28	85	16	14	4	0	1	1	3	0	6	1	0
Sierra, Abel, Tab.	3	2	.600	5.73	26	2	0	0	8	0	63.0	87	293	47	41	14	4	1	2	30	2	23	7	0
Sinohui, David, Cam.	3	4	.429	6.12	19	2	0	0	3	0	32.1	42	147	22	22	5	1	2	2	8	2	18	3	0
Solarte, Jose, Monc.	7	6	.538	3.27	49	0	0	0	45	23	63.1	60	262	24	23	7	7	5	4	20	8	46	2	0
Solis, Ricardo, Lar.	0	4	.000	8.48	40	5	0	0	4	2	40.1	74	206	44	38	5	3	2	1	16	3	14	2	0
Sombra, Francisco, Cam.	2	2	.500	2.11	29	0	0	0	4	0	21.1	22	90	9	5	0	1	3	1	9	0	8	2	0
Soto, Cruz Ant., Can.-Mont.	1	8	.111	7.90	21	0	0	0	3	0	49.0	59	239	47	43	9	2	2	3	43	1	34	3	0
Soto, Daniel, Oax.-Ver.	1	3	.250	9.56	24	1	0	0	5	0	32.0	52	174	38	34	11	3	1	3	22	2	16	2	0
Sulu, Mario, Cam.	0	1	.000	5.68	15	0	0	0	6	0	19.0	28	94	19	12	2	1	3	2	9	2	12	0	0
Tejeda, Felix, Pue.-Can.*	2	6	.250	7.79	26	9	0	0	3	0	52.0	80	245	47	45	9	3	0	4	17	2	18	1	0
Tijerina, Carlos, Rey.	1	1	.500	5.63	28	0	0	0	11	0	40.0	45	195	28	25	2	3	6	4	32	4	21	11	4
Trujillo, Jorge, Ver.	0	2	.000	8.10	16	0	0	0	3	0	30.0	36	140	30	27	8	0	4	0	17	2	18	1	0
Turner, Matt, Can.-Monc.	3	1	.750	3.88	39	0	0	0	28	10	60.1	56	249	29	26	6	7	1	1	27	4	45	5	0
Uribe, Juan Carlos, Oax.	2	3	.400	5.87	32	3	0	0	4	1	46.0	57	196	32	30	6	2	1	3	14	0	28	1	0
Uzcanga, Alejandro, Ver.-Tor.*	1	1	.500	3.09	24	2	0	0	8	0	32.0	28	115	14	11	1	2	2	1	20	1	28	4	3
Valdez, Armando, Mont.	2	1	.667	4.66	28	0	0	0	6	2	46.1	55	207	26	24	6	2	2	3	16	4	43	3	0
Valdez, Carlos, Yuc.	0	0	.000	13.50	3	0	0	0	2	0	6.0	14	32	9	9	3	0	0	2	0	4	0	0
Valdez, Efrain, Tig.	13	6	.684	5.86	25	25	0	0	0	0	138.1	162	615	99	90	11	3	3	5	59	1	87	10	1
Valdez, Rodolfo, Can.	1	4	.200	4.61	32	1	0	0	18	3	54.2	62	238	30	28	9	2	5	4	13	0	32	2	0
Valenzuela, Jesus, Oax.	0	0	.000	43.20	3	0	0	0	1	0	1.2	7	16	8	8	2	0	1	0	4	0	1	0	0
Valenzuela, Jose, Tig.	1	0	1.000	5.59	28	0	0	0	5	1	38.2	44	187	24	24	4	2	2	4	27	3	28	2	0
Valenzuela, Juan, Mont.	0	0	.000	9.00	1	0	0	0	1	0	1.0	0	4	1	1	0	0	0	0	1	0	1	0	0
Valenzuela, Saul, Cam.-Mont.	2	5	.286	8.92	13	10	0	0	1	0	35.1	54	183	39	35	8	2	0	8	21	2	9	3	0
Valera, Julio, Ver.	2	8	.200	4.74	38	10	1	0	25	14	100.2	115	438	58	53	16	5	3	3	26	2	83	2	0
Valerio, Julio, Monc.	1	6	.333	6.10	46	2	0	0	9	1	48.2	68	225	40	33	10	0	1	1	14	2	29	2	0
Vargas, Joel, Tab.	7	1	.875	2.44	17	11	2	1	3	0	84.2	77	335	23	23	4	2	3	2	19	1	34	1	0
Vazquez, Adrian, Cam.	9	6	.600	4.46	26	25	1	0	1	0	143.1	153	642	78	71	14	11	3	13	57	0	94	9	0
Vega, Obed, Can.	5	10	.333	4.38	26	26	2	1	0	0	148.0	177	644	84	72	16	5	4	2	50	1	81	4	0
Velaquez, Alonso, Yuc.	3	0	1.000	4.60	6	5	0	0	0	0	31.1	28	136	16	16	4	3	0	0	16	0	19	1	0
Verdugo, Jose, Lar.	4	4	.500	5.38	23	11	0	0	1	0	88.2	102	397	57	53	12	4	2	10	45	1	76	6	0
Verdugo, Orlando, Yuc.	1	9	.100	8.66	27	10	0	0	2	0	70.2	97	345	71	68	14	4	2	5	39	0	46	11	1
Verdugo, Osvaldo, Yuc.	6	4	.600	4.58	42	2	0	0	10	2	57.0	54	247	30	29	2	0	1	1	28	1	42	2	0
Verdugo, Roberto, Mont.	0	0	.000	0.00	2	0	0	0	2	0	2.0	1	8	0	0	0	0	0	0	1	0	1	0	0
Vilavicncio, Ismael, Tig.	0	0	.000	1.62	13	0	0	0	9	1	16.2	15	70	3	3	3	1	0	0	9	1	11	1	0
Villalobos, Noe, Can.	1	8	.111	6.28	30	13	0	0	2	0	96.0	122	457	78	67	11	6	4	11	47	2	65	5	1
Villaluna, Juan, Mont.	0	0	.000	0.00	3	0	0	0	1	0	3.1	0	13	0	0	0	0	0	3	0	5	0	0
Villareal, Tony, Yuc.	0	2	.000	3.79	19	1	0	0	6	0	38.0	39	158	18	16	7	2	2	1	4	1	24	4	0
Villarreal, Carlos, Tor.	0	0	.000	7.94	13	0	0	0	2	0	5.2	7	31	6	5	1	0	3	0	8	1	4	0	0
Villegas, Jose, Tor.	3	3	.500	7.56	19	0	0	0	7	1	25.0	34	117	23	21	8	2	1	3	8	1	10	3	0
Vizcarra, Enrique, Sal.	0	0	.000	13.50	2	0	0	0	1	0	2.0	4	13	3	3	0	0	0	0	3	0	4	0	0
Wallace, Kent, Yuc.	5	1	.833	1.74	49	0	0	0	43	33	51.2	38	196	10	10	3	2	3	0	11	0	64	3	0
Wishnevski, Rob, Mex.	1	4	.200	2.49	55	0	0	0	52	25	61.1	45	261	21	17	2	5	2	7	33	7	61	9	0
Yepiz, Heriberto, Yuc.	0	0	.000	0.00	2	0	0	0	2	0	2.0	1	12	2	0	0	0	1	0	4	0	1	0	0
Young, Ray, Cam.	2	4	.333	5.53	8	8	0	0	0	0	40.2	40	159	27	25	2	3	1	4	36	0	35	4	0
Zambrano, Baudel, Rey.	0	1	.000	6.14	5	0	0	0	0	0	7.1	5	34	5	5	0	1	0	0	8	0	4	1	0
Zamudio, Jeovanni, Rey.	3	0	1.000	5.64	43	0	0	0	18	4	52.2	57	244	37	33	4	2	3	3	30	2	32	3	0
Zavala, Marco, Tig.	3	1	.750	4.74	51	0	0	0	8	1	38.0	39	169	21	20	4	3	2	1	20	4	31	3	0

PITCHERS WITH TWO OR MORE TEAMS

Pitcher, Team	W	L	Pct.	ERA	G	GS	CG	ShO	Rel.	Sv.	IP	H	TBF	R	ER	HR	SH	SF	HB	BB	IBB	SO	WP	Bk.
Burgos, Enrique, Monc.*	1	2	.333	5.24	4	4	0	0	0	0	22.1	21	109	18	13	1	1	0	1	21	3	21	0	0
Burgos, Enrique, Cam.*	5	5	.500	3.45	13	13	1	0	0	0	70.1	64	304	30	27	3	5	1	2	39	0	58	6	0
Carasco, Alejandro, Oax.	3	5	.375	8.66	13	10	0	0	1	0	62.1	93	276	61	60	14	3	4	2	29	1	24	2	0
Carasco, Alejandro, Ver.	6	6	.500	4.83	16	13	5	0	2	0	87.2	88	368	47	47	12	3	3	6	32	1	40	1	0
Carranza, Javier, Lar.*	0	2	.000	9.82	14	2	0	0	2	0	14.2	21	80	17	16	6	1	2	1	18	1	6	2	0
Carranza, Javier, Cam.*.	0	0	.000	6.14	13	0	0	0	3	0	14.2	21	71	10	10	1	2	1	0	7	1	6	0	0
Carranza, Javier, Tor.*	0	0	.000	10.80	4	0	0	0	0	0	1.2	3	9	2	2	0	0	1	0	1	0	0	0	0
Chapa, Javier, Cam.	3	0	1.000	8.02	23	2	0	0	7	0	42.2	71	214	41	38	6	4	3	2	19	0	9	6	0
Chapa, Javier, Tor.	1	1	.500	5.01	7	3	0	0	1	1	23.1	23	101	13	13	3	0	0	0	12	0	12	0	0
Conde, Argenis, Tor.	1	3	.250	5.21	11	2	0	0	4	0	19.0	27	89	18	11	3	0	0	1	7	0	20	2	0
Conde, Argenis, Rey.	6	8	.429	4.26	16	16	2	0	0	0	107.2	125	473	60	51	14	7	5	4	35	0	69	4	0
DeLaFuente, Julian, Mex.	0	0	.000	4.91	3	0	0	0	3	0	3.2	3	15	2	2	0	0	0	1	0	0	3	0	0
DeLaFuente, Julian, Rey.	0	0	.000	10.80	4	0	0	0	1	0	6.2	16	38	8	8	1	0	0	0	4	0	4	4	0
Flores, Jorge, Tab.	2	2	.500	4.91	29	2	0	0	3	2	36.2	40	160	21	20	5	2	0	0	15	4	9	0	1
Flores, Jorge, Tor.	0	0	.000	6.46	14	2	0	0	6	0	15.1	26	83	16	11	2	2	0	0	11	3	9	2	0
Fontes, Agustin, Can.	0	1	.000	4.15	8	5	0	0	3	1	34.2	43	127	22	16	8	0	2	0	12	0	15	2	1
Fontes, Agustin, Tor.	1	1	.500	6.65	12	3	0	0	0	2	21.2	32	103	19	16	3	1	0	1	6	0	10	1	0
Galvez, Rosario, Pue.*	0	1	.000	23.14	1	0	0	0	1	0	2.1	7	17	6	6	0	0	0	0	0	0	0	0	0
Galvez, Rosario, Rey.*	1	2	.333	5.09	28	0	0	0	6	0	23.0	28	117	15	13	0	2	1	0	22	2	14	2	0

Pitcher, Team	W	L	Pct.	ERA	G	GS	CG	ShO	Rel.	Sv.	IP	H	TBF	R	ER	HR	SH	SF	HB	BB	IBB	SO	WP	Bk.
Henthorne, Kevin, Pue.	9	4	.692	3.94	14	14	4	0	0	0	89.0	82	339	43	39	12	2	3	1	23	0	45	0	0
Henthorne, Kevin, Tig.	2	0	1.000	5.35	7	5	0	0	0	0	35.1	46	156	24	21	6	2	1	0	8	1	24	0	0
Heredia, Julian, Rey.	4	5	.444	3.88	30	2	0	0	24	10	58.0	54	248	32	25	4	6	1	4	20	1	46	2	0
Heredia, Julian, Tor.	2	2	.500	3.47	15	0	0	0	13	2	23.1	21	95	10	9	3	1	0	0	8	1	23	1	0
Jimenez, Julio, Sal.*	1	0	1.000	9.35	10	0	0	0	3	0	8.2	13	47	10	9	2	0	0	1	5	0	7	2	0
Jimenez, Julio, Tor.*	0	1	.000	3.42	16	2	0	0	3	0	26.1	15	113	12	10	1	0	1	2	18	1	15	5	1
Kamar, Emil, Monc.	0	5	.000	11.16	14	11	0	0	1	0	40.1	67	215	50	50	8	3	4	5	31	1	27	5	0
Kamar, Emil, Tor.	2	2	.500	9.43	7	7	0	0	0	0	27.2	42	142	32	29	4	0	3	4	17	0	19	2	0
Leal, Gerardo, Monc.	0	0	.000	22.09	2	0	0	0	1	0	3.2	14	28	11	9	2	0	1	0	2	0	4	0	0
Leal, Gerardo, Can.	1	2	.333	4.38	12	5	0	0	1	0	37.0	40	164	20	18	4	4	1	1	16	0	11	1	1
Lopez, Jesus Nain, Oax.*	1	0	1.000	13.50	18	0	0	0	1	0	12.2	26	70	21	19	8	1	0	0	4	0	8	0	0
Lopez, Jesus Nain, Ver.*	0	0	.000	6.32	21	0	0	0	4	1	15.2	16	74	12	11	1	4	1	0	10	1	14	0	0
Luevano, Juan, Ver.	3	1	.750	5.16	18	3	0	0	11	4	29.2	49	145	18	17	5	0	0	3	9	2	15	0	0
Luevano, Juan, Oax.	0	2	.000	5.20	26	0	0	0	6	0	27.2	38	127	18	16	4	5	2	2	9	3	12	0	0
Madero, Francisco, Mex.	0	0	.000	18.00	6	0	0	0	2	0	4.0	10	23	8	8	2	0	0	0	3	0	4	0	0
Madero, Francisco, Can.	4	6	.400	4.55	18	16	0	0	0	0	93.0	105	418	50	47	7	9	3	3	48	4	63	5	1
Martinez, Cesar, Tor.*	4	6	.400	8.41	17	14	0	0	0	0	61.0	85	314	66	57	9	0	1	5	50	0	41	2	0
Martinez, Cesar, Sal.*	2	1	.667	7.52	12	5	0	0	0	0	26.1	31	136	24	22	3	0	0	5	29	0	21	4	0
Martinez, Jose, Tab.	2	6	.250	5.64	11	11	0	0	0	0	59.0	68	253	41	37	8	5	3	1	13	1	33	2	0
Martinez, Jose, Mont.	1	7	.125	4.42	9	9	0	0	0	0	55.0	57	230	30	27	7	7	0	1	17	4	32	1	1
Molina, Primitivo, Mont.	0	2	.000	9.58	5	1	0	0	0	0	10.1	15	49	11	11	4	0	1	1	4	0	3	1	0
Molina, Primitivo, Lar.	1	0	1.000	4.50	6	0	0	0	1	0	10.0	13	44	5	5	3	0	0	0	2	0	3	0	0
Munoz, Leonardo, Mont.*	1	2	.333	5.86	25	1	0	0	7	0	27.2	30	130	21	18	5	3	0	0	23	1	19	4	1
Munoz, Leonardo, Lar.*	1	3	.250	7.40	6	4	0	0	0	0	20.2	30	99	19	17	5	1	2	0	12	0	6	1	0
Munoz, Miguel, Cor.	4	6	.400	5.55	17	17	1	0	0	0	97.1	121	430	69	60	18	4	3	2	22	5	51	0	1
Munoz, Miguel, Tab.	2	1	.667	2.74	5	5	0	0	0	0	23.0	29	99	7	7	2	2	0	1	3	1	9	1	0
Neri, Eduardo, Ver.*	0	3	.000	5.01	26	0	0	0	4	1	23.1	23	100	15	13	2	1	3	1	7	2	15	0	0
Neri, Eduardo, Oax.*	1	1	.500	4.07	26	1	0	0	1	0	24.1	31	109	12	11	3	1	0	2	7	1	19	1	0
Ortega, Raul, Yuc.	0	1	.000	7.20	13	0	0	0	0	0	5.0	7	25	4	4	0	1	2	0	5	0	0	0	0
Ortega, Raul, Cor.	0	0	.000	4.50	6	0	0	0	3	0	6.0	3	22	3	3	1	0	0	0	2	0	3	1	0
Rivera, Roberto, Mont.*	2	6	.250	5.40	26	5	0	0	17	6	46.2	47	212	29	28	5	5	1	4	29	3	30	3	1
Rivera, Roberto, Sal.*	2	1	.667	1.50	4	4	0	0	0	0	18.0	17	79	4	3	0	1	2	0	9	0	4	0	0
Rodriguez, Enoc, Can.*	0	0	.000	7.71	8	2	0	0	4	0	14.0	17	70	14	12	3	0	0	3	11	0	2	0	0
Rodriguez, Enoc, Lar.*	0	0	.000	54.00	1	0	0	0	0	0	0.2	5	8	4	4	2	0	1	0	1	0	1	0	0
Sandoval, Guillermo, Can.	2	4	.333	4.75	6	6	1	0	0	0	30.1	32	146	24	16	5	0	1	2	23	0	21	3	0
Sandoval, Guillermo, Pue.	0	5	.000	7.50	18	9	0	0	0	0	48.0	60	234	40	40	7	2	2	2	38	2	32	6	0
Soto, Cruz Antonio, Can.	1	8	.111	8.18	16	8	0	0	1	0	44.0	52	210	43	40	8	1	2	3	36	1	29	1	0
Soto, Cruz Antonio, Mont.	0	0	.000	5.40	5	0	0	0	2	0	5.0	7	29	4	3	1	1	0	0	7	0	5	2	0
Soto, Daniel, Oax.	0	0	.000	9.37	11	0	0	0	1	0	16.1	26	91	19	17	5	1	0	1	15	2	10	1	0
Soto, Daniel, Ver.	1	3	.250	9.77	13	1	0	0	4	0	15.2	26	83	19	17	6	2	1	2	7	0	6	1	0
Tejeda, Felix, Pue.*	1	0	1.000	9.00	11	0	0	0	1	0	9.0	11	40	9	9	4	0	0	2	4	0	4	0	0
Tejeda, Felix, Can.*	1	6	.143	7.53	15	9	0	0	2	0	43.0	69	205	38	36	5	3	0	2	13	2	14	1	0
Turner, Matt, Can.	2	0	1.000	4.46	28	0	0	0	25	9	38.1	39	162	22	19	5	6	0	1	19	3	28	3	0
Turner, Matt, Monc.	1	1	.500	2.86	11	0	0	0	3	1	22.0	17	87	7	7	1	1	1	0	8	1	17	2	0
Uzcanga, Alejandro, Ver.*	1	1	.500	5.14	12	1	0	0	6	0	14.0	14	43	8	8	1	1	1	1	11	0	10	3	2
Uzcanga, Alejandro, Tor.*	0	0	.000	1.50	12	1	0	0	2	0	18.0	14	72	6	3	0	1	1	0	9	1	18	1	1
Valenzuela, Saul, Cam.	2	3	.400	9.98	6	5	0	0	0	0	15.1	29	83	19	17	2	1	0	3	9	2	4	1	0
Valenzuela, Saul, Mont.	0	2	.000	8.10	7	5	0	0	1	0	20.0	25	100	20	18	6	1	0	5	12	0	5	2	0

2000 FIELDING

TEAM

Team	Pct.	G	PO	A	E	TC	DP	TP	PB
Monterrey	.984	122	3196	1364	73	4633	124	0	5
Yucatan	.981	122	3195	1209	84	4488	123	0	13
M.C. Tigers	.980	120	3108	1366	91	4565	149	0	6
M.C. Reds	.980	118	3079	1432	94	4605	167	0	8
Veracruz	.977	120	3128	1321	105	4554	123	0	6
Tabasco	.977	121	3153	1417	109	4679	136	0	6
Puebla	.976	119	2980	1354	108	4442	138	0	10
Monclova	.976	122	3159	1210	109	4478	126	0	7
Cordoba	.975	118	3029	1270	111	4410	121	0	9
Saltillo	.975	120	3189	1338	117	4644	158	0	3
Nuevo Laredo	.974	120	3116	1316	117	4549	151	0	11
Campeche	.974	120	3090	1348	119	4557	139	0	8
Oaxaca	.974	118	2988	1294	115	4397	128	0	6
Cancun	.973	121	3146	1311	122	4579	146	0	5
Torreon	.973	121	3165	1313	123	4601	142	0	4
Reynosa	.973	120	3135	1251	123	4509	129	0	7

INDIVIDUAL

Player, Team	—Games played at positions— 1B	2B	3B	SS	OF	C	Err.
Abrego, Jesus, Can.	0	0	0	1	45	10	3
Acosta, Francisco, Tab.	0	7	0	0	0	0	2
Acuna, Jose Luis, Tor.	0	0	0	0	62	1	0
Adriana, Sharnol, Cor.-Cam.	0	6	67	0	0	0	10
Aganza, Ruben, Monc.	108	0	8	0	0	0	9
Aguilera, Antonio, Cor.	0	0	0	0	41	1	1
Aguilera, Armando, Sal.	18	0	2	0	2	24	6
Almeida, Shammar, Oax.	8	0	0	1	1	1	1
Alvarez, Hector, Oax.	0	0	0	0	108	0	7
Alvarez, Jorge, Cor.	0	0	0	0	46	0	3
Amescua, Alex, Mont.	0	0	0	0	0	29	0
Arano, Eloy, Ver.	0	0	0	0	88	0	3
Arano, Marco, Tab.	11	16	19	2	0	0	8
Arano, Wilfrido, Lar.	0	0	0	0	92	0	5
Arauz, Leobardo, Yuc.	0	0	0	0	85	0	2
Arias, Francisco, Sal.	0	19	6	34	0	0	7
Armenta, Cristian, Lar.	0	0	0	0	14	0	0
Armenta, Guillermo, Ver.	0	23	1	5	0	1	5
Arredondo, Hernando, Cam.	0	0	27	0	71	0	8
Arredondo, Jesus, Pue.	0	106	0	2	1	0	13
Arredondo, Luis, Yuc.	0	0	0	0	120	0	1
Avila, Ruben, Tor.	0	0	0	0	0	23	2
Azocar, Oscar, Oax.	113	0	0	0	1	0	20
Barajas, Edison, Cor.	5	1	0	0	2	0	0
Barrera, Nelson, Oax.	1	0	0	0	0	0	0
Barron, Tony, Mont.	95	1	1	0	13	0	2
Belk, Tim, Tab.	3	0	0	0	35	0	4
Bell, Juan, Cor.-Cam.	1	93	0	0	0	0	21
Beltran, Gerardo, Tab.	0	0	0	0	0	0	0
Beltran, Juan, Cam.	0	1	0	17	0	0	6
Bojorquez, Victor, Mex.	0	0	0	0	111	0	3
Bolado, Carlos, Ver.	0	0	0	0	43	0	2
Brena, Jaime, Oax.	0	1	0	2	0	0	1
Brewer, Rodney, Ver.	111	0	0	0	0	0	8
Brooks, Jerry, Lar.-Yuc.	0	0	0	0	0	0	0
Bruno, Julio, Tab.	1	9	104	0	0	0	23
Bullett, Scott, Rey.	0	0	0	0	118	0	8
Bustamante, Omar, Lar.	0	0	0	0	0	52	5
Bustillos, Luis, Rey.	0	0	4	75	0	0	24
Camacho, Reginaldo, Rey.	3	0	30	1	0	0	6
Campusano, Silvestre, Can.	0	0	0	0	25	0	3

CLASS AAA Mexican League

—Games played at positions—

Player, Team	1B	2B	3B	SS	OF	C	Err.
Canales, Joel, Cam.	0	0	0	0	1	0	0
Cancino, Jorge, Ver.	0	3	2	3	0	0	0
Canizalez, Juan, Mont.	0	0	0	0	115	0	7
Carbajal, Jovino, Tab.	0	0	0	0	14	0	1
Carrasco, Ernesto, Pue.	0	0	88	1	0	0	13
Carrillo, Matias, Tig.	0	0	0	0	104	0	2
Castaneda, Hector, Yuc.	104	0	0	0	0	0	4
Castaneda, Rafael, Yuc.	2	0	110	1	0	0	20
Castellano, Pedro, Mex.	93	0	22	0	0	0	8
Castro, Arnoldo, Can.	0	117	0	0	0	0	16
Castro, Domingo, Monc.	0	0	1	87	0	0	20
Castro, Guadulpo, Tab.	0	0	0	0	5	0	0
Castro, Wilfredo, Oax.	0	1	0	1	4	0	0
Cazarin, Manuel, Cam.	0	0	0	0	0	112	9
Cedeno, Andujar, Cam.	0	0	114	10	0	0	18
Cedeno, Domingo, Cor.	0	72	0	4	0	0	10
Cervantes, Ivan, Mex.	0	14	15	4	3	0	4
Cervantes, Refugio, Sal.	6	2	0	1	0	1	0
Cervera, Francisco, Lar.	1	0	96	1	0	0	15
Chance, Tony, Yuc.	0	0	0	0	119	0	5
Charbonnet, Mark, Tor.-Pue.	0	0	0	0	41	0	0
Chimelis, Joel, Lar.	109	12	0	0	0	0	6
Cisneros, Ventura, Rey.	0	0	0	0	15	0	0
Claudio, Patricio, Pue.	0	0	0	1	0	0	0
Cobos, Rogelio, Cam.	17	0	0	0	6	33	2
Colina, Roberto, Tig.-Pue.	83	0	0	0	5	0	10
Connell, Lino, Ver.	0	1	2	112	6	0	37
Cornelius, Brian, Lar.	0	0	0	0	36	0	2
Cruz, Ivan, Mex.	5	0	0	0	39	0	0
Cruz, Marco Antonio, Tor.-Ver.	1	0	0	0	0	44	3
De Los Santos, Luis, Sal.	16	0	93	0	0	0	20
DeLaCruz, Lorenzo, Pue.	0	0	0	0	101	0	2
Diaz, Alex, Tor.	0	0	0	0	22	0	1
Diaz, Luis Fernando, Tor.-Tab.	1	0	0	0	50	0	1
Diaz, Pedro, Pue.	15	1	27	1	0	0	4
Diaz, Remigio, Mont.	0	0	0	114	0	0	10
Dilone, Juan, Tor.-Can.	8	0	0	0	45	0	2
Dominguez, David, Ver.	0	0	0	0	49	0	0
Duran, Felipe, Monc.	0	0	0	5	0	0	0
Escalante, Marcelo, Can.	4	0	1	0	18	1	0
Espino, Daniel, Mont.	13	0	0	0	9	0	2
Espino, Omar, Pue.	0	0	0	0	17	0	2
Espinoza, Efren, Mex.	0	8	0	11	1	0	4
Espinoza, Jose, Lar.	0	0	0	0	106	0	8
Espinoza, Ramon, Rey.	0	0	0	0	109	0	3
Espinoza, Ramon, Tor.	0	0	0	0	0	21	1
Esquer, Ramon, Mex.	0	109	0	0	0	0	10
Estrada, Hector, Yuc.	0	0	0	0	0	11	4
Estrella, Isaac, Lar.	1	5	0	1	13	1	0
Facundo, Armando, Tab.	0	27	0	0	0	0	2
Felix, Junior, Tor.-Yuc.	0	0	0	0	76	0	5
Felix, Lauro, Tab.	0	45	0	3	0	1	7
Fentanes, Oscar, Tab.	0	0	0	0	106	0	3
Fernandez, Daniel, Mex.	0	0	0	0	56	0	3
Figueroa, Jesus, Cor.	0	0	0	0	0	3	0
Flores, Miguel, Mont.	0	110	0	0	0	0	8
Fornes, Daniel, Rey.	54	0	1	0	59	0	8
Franco, Iker, Tig.	0	0	0	0	0	19	2
Franco, Manuel, Can.	0	0	8	0	0	0	0
Gainer, Jonathan, Tab.	111	0	0	0	0	0	8
Gainey, Ty, Yuc.	0	0	0	0	0	0	0
Garcia, Cornelio, Tor.	2	0	0	0	34	0	3
Garcia, Hector, Mont.	0	0	0	1	107	0	6
Garcia, Heriberto, Oax.	0	4	0	78	0	0	11
Garcia, Luis, Tig.	0	0	0	0	118	0	4
Garcia, Omar, Ver.	1	0	0	0	66	0	0
Garland, Tim, Cam.	0	0	0	0	115	0	3
Garza, Gerardo, Lar.	0	0	0	0	84	8	
Garzon, Eliseo, Tor.	0	0	0	0	88	3	
Gastelum, Carlos, Pue.	0	0	0	0	65	6	
Gastelum, Sergio, Tig.	0	102	1	0	9	0	10
Gavia, Jesus, Yuc.	2	0	0	0	30	0	0
Gomez, Heber, Tab.	0	0	0	117	0	0	20
Gonzalez, Fernando, Rey.	0	0	0	0	0	0	3
Gonzalez, Jesus, Tor.	118	0	0	0	0	2	9
Gonzalez, Jose, Mont.-Sal.	0	0	0	0	22	0	1
Gonzalez, Rolando, Monc.	2	18	13	2	0	0	7
Gonzalez, Roman, Cor.	0	3	1	0	77	1	8
Gracia, Ernesto, Oax.	0	1	5	0	0	0	1
Guerrero, Epy, Cam.	25	46	2	0	30	0	14
Guerrero, Sergio, Rey.	0	68	13	38	0	0	18
Guiel, Aaron, Oax.	0	0	0	0	44	0	4
Guizar, Hector, Tor.	0	2	0	112	0	0	37
Henry, Santiago, Cor.	0	0	2	114	0	0	29
Hernandez, Esteban, Oax.	0	0	0	0	0	3	0
Hernandez, Julio, Lar.	0	0	1	118	0	0	20
Herrera, Christian, Ver.	0	1	0	0	0	0	0
Hurtado, Hector, Monc.	0	0	0	0	0	39	3
Iglesias, Luis, Cam.-Ver.	10	0	16	0	17	0	6
Iturbe, Pedro, Pue.	2	0	1	0	82	0	4
Jimenez, Eduardo, Sal.	0	0	0	0	0	0	0
Kapano, Randy, Lar.	0	0	0	0	5	0	0
Lara, Idelfonso, Oax.	0	0	3	0	0	0	1
Leal, Gerardo, Monc.	1	0	0	0	2	0	0
Leal, Guadalupe, Can.-Monc.	12	2	0	0	20	0	1
Leyva, German, Ver.	2	0	103	0	0	0	14
Leyva, Octavio, Ver.	0	0	0	0	0	0	0
Lopez, Carlos, Pue.	0	3	0	4	0	0	2
Lopez, Fabian, Oax.	0	25	60	10	13	0	16
Lopez, Fortunato, Tab.	0	0	0	0	0	3	0
Lopez, Gonzalo, Yuc.	0	3	20	7	1	0	3
Loredo, Jorge, Pue.	0	4	10	3	0	0	1
Machiria, Pablo, Lar.-Mont.	1	0	0	0	16	0	2
Machorro, Roberto, Oax.	0	0	0	1	5	37	1
Macias, Roberto, Can.	26	0	3	0	0	0	3
Maclin, Lonnie, Tab.	0	0	0	0	19	0	0
Maddox, Garry, Mont.	0	0	0	0	10	0	0
Magallanes, Ever, Mont.	1	11	107	4	0	0	9
Magallanes, Roberto, Tig.	0	0	85	0	0	0	12
Marte, Julio, Tab.	0	0	0	1	0	0	0
Martinez, Aguado, Tab.	0	0	0	0	0	0	0
Martinez, Enrique, Mont.	1	0	0	0	39	0	1
Martinez, Grimaldo, Monc.	0	102	0	0	0	0	8
Martinez, Luis, Sal.	0	0	0	0	73	0	13
Martinez, Orlando, Tab.	0	0	0	0	0	2	0
Martinez, Raul, Oax.-Mont.	0	0	0	0	0	42	1
Martinez, Ray, Mex.	21	0	97	0	0	0	17
Mashore, Damon, Tab.	0	0	0	0	46	0	0
Mata, Noe, Ver.	0	1	0	0	64	0	1
May, Derrick, Mont.	0	0	0	0	45	0	1
Medina, Ernesto, Mont.	0	0	0	0	2	0	0
Medina, Jose Ramon, Sal.	0	0	0	1	46	1	5
Mejia, Roberto, Oax.	0	49	0	0	0	0	7
Mendez, Francisco, Mont.	8	0	0	0	0	0	1
Mendez, Roberto, Oax.	1	0	0	0	96	2	8
Mendoza, Omar, Ver.	0	7	8	2	0	0	6
Mere, Pedro, Ver.	0	95	11	0	0	0	10
Meulens, Hensley, Sal.	4	0	20	3	76	0	4
Meza, Alfredo, Ver.	0	0	0	0	0	101	5
Meza, Gonzalo, Mex.	0	0	0	0	19	0	0
Michel, Keith, Tab.	1	0	0	0	32	0	3
Miller, Orlando, Oax.	0	2	0	1	0	0	0
Minjarez, Franco, Pue.	0	18	4	37	0	0	13
Montanez, Daniel, Ver.	0	1	0	3	0	0	0
Montano, Angel, Cam.	0	0	0	0	1	8	0
Moore, Mike, Tor.	0	0	0	0	23	0	0
Morales, Juan, Oax.	0	1	2	12	0	0	7
Morejon, Oswaldo, Yuc.	0	120	0	0	0	0	14
Moreno, Leonardo, Pue.	0	0	0	0	15	0	0
Munoz, Adan, Monc.	0	0	0	0	0	82	8
Munoz, Jose, Cor.	0	1	0	0	2	0	0
Munoz, Jose De J., Sal.	2	0	0	0	109	0	4
Munoz, Noe, Sal.	0	0	0	1	1	103	7
Nelson, Bryant, Mont.	0	0	13	0	43	0	4
Newson, Warren, Tor.	0	0	0	0	84	0	5
Nunez, Raymond, Pue.-Tig.	26	0	2	0	0	0	2
Ochoa, Edgar, Mont.	0	0	0	0	0	7	0
Ojeda, Miguel, Mex.	5	0	0	0	0	90	10
Orantes, Ramon, Mont.	7	1	12	1	0	0	2
Ortega, Antonio, Ver.	0	0	0	0	0	26	0
Ortiz, Alejandro, Tab.	0	0	1	0	0	0	0
Ortiz, Hector, Oax.	0	0	0	0	1	0	0
Osuna, Hector, Can.	0	0	0	0	0	40	6
Otero, Ricardo, Can.	0	0	0	0	110	0	4
Pacho, Carlos, Tab.	0	0	0	0	0	28	2
Pacho, Juan Jose, Yuc.	0	5	0	116	0	0	11
Paez, Hector, Can.	1	0	0	0	0	98	16
Paez, Raul, Cam.	74	0	0	0	0	0	3
Palafox, Sergio, Sal.	0	12	0	1	0	0	1
Parra, Franklin, Cam.	0	0	24	27	47	0	14
Patron, Damian, Oax.	0	4	2	39	0	0	3
Payro, Edison, Cam.	3	0	0	0	67	0	2
Pearson, Eddie, Tig.	8	0	0	0	0	0	0
Peguero, Julio, Tab.	2	1	0	0	53	0	4
Pemberton, Rudy, Mex.	0	1	0	0	20	0	0
Perez, Alfredo, Cam.	0	14	7	4	1	0	4
Perez, F., Mont.	0	0	0	0	0	0	0
Perez, Francisco, Rey.	8	0	0	0	57	0	6
Perez, L. Antonio, Monc.	1	1	0	1	0	0	0
Pinto, Placido, Cor.	0	0	0	0	0	39	2

Player, Team	1B	2B	3B	SS	OF	C	Err.
Poe, Charles, Tab.	0	0	0	0	10	0	0
Powell, Corey, Mex.-Oax.	0	0	0	0	79	0	6
Pozo, Arquimedes, Tig.	0	0	0	0	9	0	1
Presichi, Cristian, Sal.	1	1	8	0	1	0	3
Prieto, Chris, Mex.	0	1	0	0	24	0	0
Quinonez, Ruben, Monc.	0	0	0	0	0	1	0
Quintero, Alan, Mex.	0	0	0	0	50	0	2
Quintero, Edgar, Mont.-Pue.	0	0	0	0	94	0	3
Quintero, Guillermo, Cor.	0	25	7	5	1	0	3
Ramirez, Efren, Cor.	0	0	0	0	0	96	4
Ramirez, Enrique, Pue.	0	0	0	86	0	0	12
Ramirez, Jaime, Cam.	0	7	4	9	0	0	2
Ramirez, Jesus, Oax.	0	24	0	1	67	0	6
Resendez, Carlos, Monc.	0	0	0	1	5	33	1
Rincon, Isaias, Mex.	0	0	0	0	18	0	0
Rivera, Jesus, Tab.	1	48	1	1	0	0	9
Roberson, Kevin, Mont.-Lar.	0	0	0	0	52	0	1
Robles, Javier, Tig.	0	1	0	94	0	0	13
Robles, Juan Jose, Rey.	0	0	0	0	0	0	3
Robles, Oscar, Mex.-Oax.	0	25	56	13	0	0	10
Robles, Trinidad, Tig.	0	3	31	31	2	0	6
Rodarte, Raul, Lar.-Rey.	11	0	55	1	44	0	21
Rodriguez, Armando, Tig.	0	0	0	0	1	72	8
Rodriguez, Boi, Monc.	11	0	0	0	64	0	6
Rodriguez, Carlos, Rey.	0	48	0	0	0	0	3
Rodriguez, Fernando, Cam.	0	0	0	0	35	0	1
Rodriguez, Jose, Monc.	1	0	1	0	2	0	1
Rojas, Homar, Oax.	0	0	0	0	0	80	6
Romero, Marco, Sal.	108	0	0	0	1	0	13
Romero, Oscar, Monc.	0	0	113	9	0	0	21
Romero, Wilfredo, Sal.	0	1	1	0	117	0	5
Royster, Aaron, Ver.	0	0	0	0	26	0	0
Rubio, Sergio, Yuc.	0	0	0	1	16	0	1
Ruiz, Juan, Cor.	0	0	65	0	0	0	11
Saenz, Ricardo, Monc.	0	0	0	0	109	0	2
Salas, Heriberto, Cam.	0	0	1	82	0	0	19
Salomon, Abraham, Can.	0	0	0	0	9	0	0
Sanchez, Gerardo, Lar.	2	0	0	0	36	0	4
Sanchez, Orlando, Mont.	0	15	1	32	0	0	6
Sanchez, Raul, Can.	0	0	0	2	106	0	6
Sanchez, Roque, Cam.	6	0	28	0	0	0	5
Sanders, Tracy, Yuc.	0	0	0	0	0	0	0
Sandoval, Jose, Mex.	0	0	0	111	0	0	15
Sandoval, Octavio, Tig.	0	0	0	0	79	0	5
Santana, Mario, Mont.	0	0	0	0	0	86	10
Santos, Andres, Lar.	10	0	19	1	3	0	5
Sauceda, Victor, Can.	0	1	0	111	0	0	25
Saucedo, Roberto, Mont.-Rey.	2	0	0	0	1	0	2
Sherman, Darrell, Monc.	0	0	0	0	118	0	5
Sierra, Ruben, Can.	0	0	0	0	7	0	1
Sievers, Carlos, Yuc.	22	0	0	1	0	0	2
Simmons, Nelson, Rey.	0	0	0	0	10	0	0
Soriano, Ricardo, Cor.	0	0	0	0	67	0	4
Sotmayor, Gilberto, Monc.	0	1	0	0	32	1	1
Soto, Saul, Mex.	1	0	0	0	0	18	1
Suarez, Luis, Tig.	2	0	0	0	83	0	4
Tatum, Jim, Mex.	0	0	0	0	9	0	0
Tavarez, Jesus, Ver.	0	0	0	0	51	0	1
Tellez, Alonso, Rey.	0	0	0	1	0	0	0
Tinsley, Lee, Monc.-Tab.	0	0	0	0	45	0	2
Tiquet, Lazaro, Tab.	0	0	0	0	3	0	0
Torres, Sebastian, Oax.	0	1	5	1	0	0	0
Tovar, Jose DeJesus, Rey.	0	9	0	20	1	0	6
Trapaga, Julio, Tig.	2	34	0	5	0	0	3
Tredaway, Chad, Rey.	0	0	42	1	0	0	9
Valdez, Emmanuel, Tig.	3	0	0	0	0	0	0
Valdez, Francisco, Tab.	0	0	0	0	1	108	7
Valdez, Jesus, Cam.	7	0	0	0	3	0	0
Valdez, Ramon, Cor.	0	0	0	0	107	0	6
Valencia, Carlos, Lar.	0	0	0	0	1	0	0
Valencia, Carlos, Cor.	0	0	0	0	35	0	0
Valenzuela, Irving, Monc.	0	24	0	61	1	0	6
Valenzula, Armando, Sal.	0	13	0	26	1	0	4
Valle, Cosme, Mex.	4	0	0	0	5	23	1
Valle, Jorge Luis, Tor.	0	0	71	0	0	1	8
Valle, Jose Luis, Yuc.	0	0	1	29	0	0	1
Valle, Roberto, Tor.	1	4	8	10	5	0	4
Valverde, Raul, Tor.	0	0	0	0	5	0	0
Vazquez, Felipe, Lar.	0	0	0	0	0	23	3
Vazquez, Gregorio, Tab.	0	0	0	0	38	0	0
Vazquez, Jorge, Monc.-Pue.	1	1	0	2	32	2	1
Vazquez, Jose, Tig.	6	0	11	0	0	4	5
Vega, Edgar, Pue.	0	0	0	0	0	75	6
Velazquez, Guillermo, Mont.-Rey.	70	0	0	0	0	0	5
Velez, Manuel, Lar.	0	113	0	0	0	0	11
Verdugo, Vicente, Sal.	0	114	0	0	0	0	12
Villarreal, Alex, Lar.	0	0	9	0	0	0	0
Villarreal, Salvador, Rey.	0	0	0	0	40	0	3
Villegas, Fernando, Sal.	1	0	0	0	22	0	1
Villegas, Fernando, Tor.	0	0	0	0	34	0	4
Vizcarra, Roberto, Tig.	98	8	0	0	0	0	7
Walton, Jerome, Cam.	15	0	0	0	15	0	3
Williams, Eddie, Monc.	1	0	0	0	0	0	0
Yan, Julian, Cor.	115	0	0	0	0	0	12
Yuriar, Jesus, Can.	14	1	0	0	50	1	3
Zambrano, Roberto, Can.	70	0	0	0	0	0	5
Zamudio, Rafael, Pue.	6	0	0	0	12	0	2
Zazueta, Juan, Tor.	0	8	53	13	34	0	12
Zazueta, Mauricio, Tor.	0	115	1	0	1	0	10

FIELDERS WITH TWO OR MORE TEAMS

Player, Team	1B	2B	3B	SS	OF	C	Err.
Adriana, Sharnol, Cor.	0	6	38	0	0	0	8
Adriana, Sharnol, Cam.	0	0	29	0	0	0	2
Bell, Juan, Cor.	0	23	0	0	0	0	6
Bell, Juan, Cam.	1	70	0	0	0	0	15
Brooks, Jerry, Lar.	0	0	0	0	0	0	0
Brooks, Jerry, Yuc.	0	0	0	0	0	0	0
Charbonnet, Mark, Tor.	0	0	0	0	20	0	0
Charbonnet, Mark, Pue.	0	0	0	0	21	0	0
Colina, Roberto, Tig.	11	0	0	0	0	0	0
Colina, Roberto, Pue.	72	0	0	0	0	0	10
Cruz, Marco Antonio, Tor.	0	0	0	0	0	26	2
Cruz, Marco Antonio, Ver.	1	0	0	0	0	18	1
Diaz, Luis Fernando, Tor.	1	0	0	0	35	0	1
Diaz, Luis Fernando, Tab.	0	0	0	0	15	0	0
Dilone, Juan, Tor.	0	0	0	0	35	0	2
Dilone, Juan, Can.	8	0	0	0	10	0	0
Felix, Junior, Tor.	0	0	0	0	10	0	3
Felix, Junior, Can.	0	0	0	0	66	0	2
Gonzalez, Jose, Mont.	0	0	0	0	5	0	0
Gonzalez, Jose, Sal.	0	0	0	0	17	0	1
Iglesias, Luis, Cam.	0	0	14	0	1	0	2
Iglesias, Luis, Ver.	10	0	2	16	0	0	4
Leal, Guadalupe, Can.	8	0	0	0	8	0	1
Leal, Guadalupe, Monc.	4	2	0	0	12	0	0
Machiria, Pablo, Lar.	1	0	0	0	13	0	2
Machiria, Pablo, Mont.	0	0	0	0	3	0	0
Martinez, Raul, Oax.	0	0	0	0	0	26	1
Martinez, Raul, Mont.	0	0	0	0	0	16	0
Nunez, Raymond, Pue.	24	0	2	0	0	0	2
Nunez, Raymond, Tig.	2	0	0	0	0	0	0
Powell, Corey, Mex.	0	0	0	0	51	0	6
Powell, Corey, Oax.	0	0	0	0	28	0	0
Quintero, Edgar, Mont.	0	0	0	0	1	0	0
Quintero, Edgar, Pue.	0	0	0	0	93	0	3
Roberson, Kevin, Mont.	0	0	0	0	8	0	0
Roberson, Kevin, Lar.	0	0	0	0	44	0	1
Robles, Oscar, Mex.	0	1	0	0	0	0	0
Robles, Oscar, Oax.	0	24	56	13	0	0	10
Rodarte, Raul, Lar.	7	0	9	0	41	0	8
Rodarte, Raul, Rey.	4	0	46	1	3	0	13
Saucedo, Roberto, Mont.	0	0	0	0	0	12	0
Saucedo, Roberto, Rey.	2	0	0	0	1	0	2
Tinsley, Lee, Monc.	0	0	0	0	38	0	1
Tinsley, Lee, Tab.	0	0	0	0	7	0	1
Vazquez, Jorge, Monc.	0	1	0	1	11	0	0
Vazquez, Jorge, Pue.	1	0	0	1	21	2	1
Velazquez, Guillermo, Mont.	14	0	0	0	0	0	0
Velazquez, Guillermo, Rey.	56	0	0	0	0	0	5

Year	Team	Pct.	Year	Team	Pct.	Year	Team	Pct.
1955—	Mexico City Tigers*	.539	1975—	Tampico∞	.541	1989—	Nuevo Laredo◆	.621
1956—	Mexico City Reds	.692		Cordoba	.649		Yucatan	.539
1957—	Yucatan	.567	1976—	Mexico City Reds∞	.543	1990—	Nuevo Laredo	.618
	Mex. C. Reds (2nd)†	.550		Union Laguna	.547		Leon◆	.565
1958—	Nuevo Laredo	.625	1977—	Mexico City Reds	.623	1991—	Monterrey◆	.683
1959—	Poza Rica	.575		Nuevo Laredo∞	.507		Mexico City Reds	.627
	Mex. C. Reds (3rd)†	.507	1978—	Aguascalientes∞	.589	1992—	Mexico City Tigers◆	.594
1960—	Mexico City Tigers	.538		Union Laguna	.523		Nuevo Laredo	.538
1961—	Veracruz	.575	1979—	Saltillo	.704	1993—	Nuevo Laredo	.589
1962—	Monterrey	.592		Puebla∞	.628		Tabasco◆	.528
1963—	Puebla	.606	1980—	No champion▲		1994—	Mexico City Red Devils◆	.646
1964—	Mexico City Reds	.586	1981—	Mexico City Reds	.615		Monterrey Sultans	.608
1965—	Mexico City Tigers	.590		Reynosa	.492	1995—	Mexico City Red Devils	.708
1966—	Mexico City Tigers‡	.614	1982—	Ciudad Juarez∞	.570		Monterrey Sultans◆	.570
	Mexico City Reds	.571		Mexico City Tigers	.508	1996—	Monterrey Sultans	.713
1967—	Jalisco	.607	1983—	Campeche◆	.614		Mexico City Reds◆	.619
1968—	Mexico City Reds	.586		Ciudad Juarez	.535	1997—	Mexico City Red Devils	.686
1969—	Reynosa	.591	1984—	Yucatan◆	.560		Mexico City Tigers■	.658
1970—	Aguila§	.580		Ciudad Juarez	.509	1998—	Monterrey	.672
	Mexico City Reds	.607	1985—	Mexico City Reds◆	.606		Oaxaca■	.576
1971—	Jalisco§	.558		Nuevo Laredo	.5275	1999—	Mexico City Tigers	.664
	Saltillo	.593	1986—	Puebla◆	.682		Mexico City Reds■	.632
1972—	Saltillo	.636		Monclova	.598	2000—	Saltillo	.647
	Cordoba§	.541	1987—	Mexico City Reds◆	.605		Mexico City Tigers■	.627
1973—	Saltillo	.656		Monterrey	.536			
	Mexico City Reds∞	.590	1988—	Mexico City Reds◆	.646			
1974—	Jalisco	.627		Nuevo Laredo	.602			
	Mexico City Reds∞	.551						

*Defeated Nuevo Laredo, two games to none, in playoff for pennant. †Won four-team playoff. ‡Won split-season playoff. §League divided into Northern, Southern divisions; won two-team playoff. ∞League divided into Northern, Southern zones; sub-divided into Eastern, Western divisions, won eight-team playoff. ▲ A players strike on July 1 forced the cancellation of the regular season and playoff schedule. ◆ League divided into Northern, Southern zones; four clubs from each zone qualified for postseason play. Won final series for league championship. ■ League divided into Northern, Central and Southern zones; played split season, with top eight teams qualifying for playoffs. Won final series for league championship.

PACIFIC COAST LEAGUE

LEAGUE OFFICE

President
Branch Rickey

Address
1631 Mesa Ave.
Colorado Springs, CO 80906-2917

Phone
719-636-3399

TEAMS

CALGARY CANNONS

V.p, baseball operations/g.m.
John Traub
Manager
Chris Chambliss
Ballpark (capacity, surface)
Burn Stadium (8,000, grass)
Affiliation
Marlins
Address
2255 Crowchild Trail N.W.
Calgary, Alberta T2M 4S7
Phone
403-284-1111

COLORADO SPRINGS SKY SOX

General manager/president
Robert Goughan
Manager
Chris Cron
Ballpark (capacity, surface)
Sky Sox Stadium (9,000, grass)
Affiliation
Rockies
Address
4385 Tutt Blvd.
Colorado Springs, CO 80922
Phone
719-597-1449

EDMONTON TRAPPERS

General manager
Mel Kowalchuk
Manager
John Russell
Ballpark (capacity, surface)
Telus Field (10,000; artificial infield,
grass outfield)
Affiliation
Twins
Address
10233 96th Ave.
Edmonton, Alberta T5K 0A5
Phone
780-414-4450

FRESNO GRIZZLIES

General manager
Joe Hart
Manager
Shane Turner
Ballpark (capacity, surface)
Beinden Field (6,500, grass)
Affiliation
Giants
Address
700 Van Ness Avenue
Fresno, CA 93721

Phone
559-442-1994

IOWA CUBS

General manager
Sam Bernabe
Manager
Bruce Kimm
Ballpark (capacity, surface)
Sec Taylor Stadium (10,500, grass)
Affiliation
Cubs
Address
350 SW First Street
Des Moines, IA 50309
Phone
515-243-6111

LAS VEGAS STARS

General manager
Don Logan
Manager
Rick Sofield
Ballpark (capacity, surface)
Cashman Field (9,370, grass)
Affiliation
Dodgers
Address
850 Las Vegas Blvd. N
Las Vegas, NV 89101
Phone
702-386-7200

MEMPHIS REDBIRDS

President/general manager
Allie Prescott
Manager
Gaylen Pitts
Ballpark (capacity, surface)
Autozone Park (14,200; grass)
Affiliation
Cardinals
Address
200 Union Avenue
Memphis, TN 38103
Phone
901-721-6050

NASHVILLE SOUNDS

General manager
Tom Moncrief
Manager
Marty Brown
Ballpark (capacity, surface)
Greer Stadium (11,500, grass)
Affiliation
Pirates
Address
534 Chestnut Street
Nashville, TN 37203

Phone
615-242-4371

NEW ORLEANS ZEPHYRS

General manager
Dan Hanrahan
Manager
Tony Pena
Ballpark (capacity, surface)
Zephyr Field (11,000, grass)
Affiliation
Astros
Address
6000 Airline Highway
Metairie, LA 70003
Phone
504-734-5155

OKLAHOMA REDHAWKS

President/general manager
Tim O'Toole
Manager
DeMarlo Hale
Ballpark (capacity, surface)
Southwestern Bell Bricktown Ball Park
(13,066, grass)
Affiliation
Rangers
Address
2 South Mickey Mantle Drive
Oklahoma City, OK 73104
Phone
405-218-1000

OMAHA GOLDEN SPIKES

Vice president/general manager
Bill Gorman
Manager
John Mizerock
Ballpark (capacity, surface)
Omaha's Rosenblatt Stadium (23,000,
grass)
Affiliation
Royals
Address
1202 Bert Murphy Drive
Omaha, NE 68107
Phone
402-734-2550

PORTLAND BEAVERS

General manager
Mike Higgins
Manager
Rick Sweet
Ballpark (capacity, surface)
PGE Park (20,000, artificial)
Affiliation
Padres
Address
920 SW Sixth Avenue, Mezzanine Level
Portland Ore. 97204

Phone
503-553-5400

SACRAMENTO RIVER CATS

General Manager
Gary Arthur
Manager
Bob Geren
Ballpark (capacity, surface)
Raley Field (10,500, grass)
Affiliation
Athletics
Address
400 Ballpark Drive
West Sacramento, CA 95691
Phone
916-376-4700

SALT LAKE BUZZ

General manager
Dorsena Picknell

Manager
Garry Templeton
Ballpark (capacity, surface)
Franklin-Covey Field (15,500, grass)
Affiliation
Angels
Address
P.O. Box 4108
Salt Lake City, UT 84110
Phone
801-485-3800

TACOMA RAINIERS

General manager
Dave Lewis
Manager
Dan Rohn
Ballpark (capacity, surface)
Cheney Stadium (10,106, grass)
Affiliation
Mariners

Address
P.O. Box 11087
Tacoma, WA 98411
Phone
253-752-7707

TUCSON SIDEWINDERS

Vice president of baseball operations
Mike Feder
Manager
Tom Spencer
Ballpark (capacity, surface)
Tucson Electric Park (11,000, grass)
Affiliation
Diamondbacks
Address
P.O. Box 27045
Tucson, AZ 85716
Phone
520-434-1021

2000 FINAL STANDINGS

EAST DIVISION

Team	W	L	T	Pct.	GB
Memphis (Cardinals)	83	61	0	.576	...
Oklahoma (Rangers)	69	74	0	.483	13.5
New Orleans (Astros)	68	74	0	.479	14.0
Nashville (Pirates)	63	79	0	.444	19.0

CENTRAL DIVISION

Team	W	L	T	Pct.	GB
Albuquerque (Dodgers)	86	58	0	.597	...
Colorado Springs (Rockies)	74	68	0	.521	11.0
Omaha (Royals)	64	79	0	.448	21.5
Iowa (Cubs)	57	87	0	.396	29.0

NORTH DIVISION

Team	W	L	T	Pct.	GB
Salt Lake (Twins)	90	53	0	.629	...
Tacoma (Mariners)	76	67	0	.531	14.0
Edmonton (Angels)	63	78	0	.447	26.0
Calgary (Marlins)	60	82	0	.423	29.5

SOUTH DIVISION

Team	W	L	T	Pct.	GB
Sacramento (Athletics)	90	54	0	.625	...
Las Vegas (Padres)	73	70	0	.510	16.5
Tucson (Diamondbacks)	68	73	0	.482	20.5
Fresno (Giants)	57	84	0	.404	31.5

COMPOSITE

Team	S.L.	Sac.	Alb.	Mem.	Tac.	C.S.	L.V.	Okla.	Tuc.	N.O.	Oma.	Edm.	Nash.	Cal.	Fres.	iowa	W	L	T	Pct.	GB
Salt Lake (Twins)	...	8	1	1	10	2	14	4	10	2	2	8	4	11	10	3	90	53	0	.629	...
Sacramento (Athletics)	8	...	3	1	9	3	12	2	7	2	3	9	3	11	13	4	90	54	0	.625	0.5
Albuquerque (Dodgers)	3	1	...	10	3	9	1	8	2	11	10	3	10	3	3	9	86	58	0	.597	4.5
Memphis (Cardinals)	3	3	6	...	3	8	2	11	3	8	9	3	8	3	3	10	83	61	0	.576	7.5
Tacoma (Mariners)	6	7	1	1	...	4	8	1	11	2	2	11	3	6	9	4	76	67	0	.531	14.0
Colo. Springs (Rockies)	2	1	8	8	0	...	2	7	1	14	8	3	8	2	2	8	74	68	0	.521	15.5
Las Vegas (Padres)	2	4	3	2	9	2	...	3	12	2	3	8	3	10	8	2	73	70	0	.510	17.0
Oklahoma (Rangers)	0	2	8	6	3	9	1	...	1	8	9	2	8	0	4	8	69	74	0	.483	21.0
Tucson (Diamondbacks)	6	9	2	2	5	2	4	2	...	2	2	11	2	9	9	1	68	73	0	.482	21.0
New Orleans (Astros)	2	2	4	8	2	3	2	7	2	...	9	3	9	2	3	10	68	74	0	.479	21.5
Omaha (Royals)	2	1	6	6	1	8	1	7	2	7	...	1	8	3	1	10	64	79	0	.448	26.0
Edmonton (Angels)	7	7	1	1	5	1	8	2	4	1	3	...	3	9	8	3	63	78	0	.447	26.0
Nashville (Pirates)	0	1	6	7	1	8	1	7	2	5	9	1	...	1	2	12	63	79	0	.444	26.5
Calgary (Marlins)	5	5	1	1	10	1	6	4	8	2	1	5	3	...	8	0	60	82	0	.423	29.5
Fresno (Giants)	6	3	1	1	6	1	6	1	6	1	3	9	2	8	...	3	57	84	0	.404	32.0
Iowa (Cubs)	1	0	7	6	0	7	2	8	2	7	6	1	5	4	1	...	57	87	0	.396	33.5

Major league affiliations in parentheses.

PLAYOFFS: Memphis defeated Albuquerque three games to two; Salt Lake defeated Sacramento three games to two; Memphis defeated Salt Lake three games to one to win league championship; Memphis was defeated by Indianapolis (International) three games to one in AAA World Series.

REGULAR-SEASON ATTENDANCE: Albuquerque, 338,103; Calgary, 270,682; Colorado Springs, 255,301; Edmonton, 359,697; Fresno, 309,147; Iowa, 483,176; Las Vegas, 322,354; Memphis, 859,851; Nashville, 271,857; New Orleans, 443,526; Oklahoma, 416,196; Omaha, 413,713; Sacramento, 861,808; Salt Lake, 511,423; Tacoma, 265,702; Tucson, 270,832. Total—6,653,368. Playoffs (14 games)—108,046; Class AAA All-Star Game at Rochester, N.Y.—12,810.

MANAGERS: Albuquerque, Tom Gamboa; Calgary, Lynn Jones; Colorado Springs, Chris Cron; Edmonton, Garry Templeton; Fresno, Shane Turner; Iowa, Dave Trembley; Las Vegas, Duane Espy (Through May 29) and Tony Franklin, (May 30 through end of season); Memphis, Gaylen Pitts; Nashville, Trent Jewett (Through June 5) and Richie Hebner (June 6 through end of season); New Orleans, Tony Pena; Oklahoma, Demarlo Hale; Omaha, John Mizerock; Sacramento, Bob Geren; Salt Lake, Phil Roof; Tacoma, Dave Myers; Tucson, Tom Spencer.

ALL-STAR TEAM: 1B—Phil Hiatt, Colorado Springs; 2B—Hiram Bocachica, Albuquerque; 3B—Pedro Feliz, Fresno; SS—Jose Ortiz, Sacramento; OF—John Barnes, Salt Lake; OF—Brian Buchanan, Salt Lake; OF—Ernie Young; Memphis; C—Craig Wilson, Nashville; DH—Doug Mientkiewicz, Salt Lake; RHP—Ryan Franklin, Tacoma; LHP—Ryan Anderson, Tacoma; Relief pitcher—Todd Williams, Tacoma; Most Valuable Player—Jose Ortiz, Sacramento; Rookie of the Year—Nate Rolison, Calgary; Manager of the Year—Phil Roof, Salt Lake.

TEAM

Team	Avg.	G	TPA	AB	R	H	TB	2B	3B	HR	RBI	SH	SF	HP	BB	IBB	SO	SB	CS	GDP	LOB	ShO	Slg.	OBP
Salt Lake	.312	143	5779	5064	1016	1580	2577	358	42	185	970	34	70	49	562	13	865	85	36	131	1020	2	.509	.381
Albuquerque	.300	144	5748	5020	943	1506	2414	310	44	170	855	61	34	45	588	21	945	156	103	106	1033	2	.481	.376
Colo. Springs	.295	142	5547	4812	823	1419	2219	286	53	136	764	67	57	38	573	27	959	149	63	110	1038	4	.461	.370
Tucson	.289	141	5397	4843	752	1399	2076	300	46	95	696	56	49	49	400	22	735	69	44	125	978	6	.429	.346
Calgary	.285	142	5447	4873	768	1390	2245	297	30	166	710	49	42	47	436	16	1012	117	62	103	972	4	.461	.347
Sacramento	.285	144	5778	4956	864	1410	2204	274	32	152	796	28	49	54	691	28	968	161	67	114	1141	4	.445	.375
Las Vegas	.282	143	5626	4831	830	1364	2159	333	36	130	769	49	52	45	649	15	998	95	43	107	1114	4	.447	.369
Tacoma	.278	143	5496	4835	696	1342	2046	283	35	117	638	45	48	58	510	20	865	120	56	107	1083	3	.423	.350
Oklahoma	.270	143	5463	4775	735	1289	1990	249	40	124	671	32	42	44	570	18	909	73	52	131	1038	5	.417	.350
Omaha	.267	143	5333	4741	658	1266	1954	238	27	132	600	36	43	67	446	14	754	135	70	119	963	8	.412	.336
Iowa	.264	144	5416	4794	715	1267	2067	277	20	161	681	50	40	63	469	23	921	114	62	104	933	9	.431	.335
Edmonton	.264	141	5292	4689	695	1239	1989	260	50	130	645	30	39	53	481	20	916	104	65	100	933	5	.424	.337
Memphis	.264	144	5721	4994	771	1318	2097	266	33	149	716	45	40	62	580	25	1001	106	49	111	1073	4	.420	.345
Fresno	.262	141	5388	4793	692	1255	2027	228	29	162	641	44	33	34	484	16	947	100	59	120	951	11	.423	.332
Nashville	.258	142	5424	4821	681	1246	1967	251	28	138	639	38	37	70	458	9	1008	129	58	99	961	15	.408	.329
New Orleans	.258	142	5425	4775	633	1233	1760	210	37	81	574	47	45	57	501	28	949	116	63	131	981	10	.369	.333

INDIVIDUAL

TOP QUALIFIERS FOR BATTING CHAMPIONSHIP

Minimum 389 plate appearances. *Lefthanded batter. †Switch-hitter.

Player, Team	Avg.	G	TPA	AB	R	H	TB	2B	3B	HR	RBI	SH	SF	HP	BB	IBB	SO	SB	CS	GDP	Slg.	OBP
Barnes, John, S.L.	.365	119	513	441	107	161	249	37	6	13	87	1	7	7	57	0	48	7	6	10	.565	.439
Mendoza, Carlos, C.S.*	.354	107	431	359	79	127	171	16	14	0	42	8	1	3	60	2	50	26	13	5	.476	.449
Ortiz, Jose, Sac.	.351	131	571	518	107	182	298	34	5	24	108	0	2	4	47	0	64	22	9	21	.575	.408
Darr, Mike, L.V.*	.344	91	421	366	79	126	186	23	5	9	65	0	9	2	44	0	55	13	6	7	.508	.409
Valdez, Mario, S.L.-Sac.*	.344	105	458	378	87	130	219	27	1	20	96	1	7	5	66	4	59	1	1	13	.579	.441
Mientkiewicz, Doug, S.L.*	.334	130	560	485	96	162	254	32	3	18	96	3	8	3	61	2	68	9	5	17	.524	.406
Valdes, Pedro, Okla.*	.332	92	405	352	64	117	199	30	2	16	78	0	5	3	45	4	41	2	0	7	.565	.407
Rolison, Nate, Cal.*	.330	123	518	443	88	146	258	37	3	23	88	0	2	3	70	5	117	3	1	7	.582	.423
Donnels, Chris, Alb.*	.328	105	402	332	79	109	219	27	1	27	84	0	2	2	66	2	52	6	1	9	.660	.440
Sell, Chip, Tuc.*	.326	112	448	405	65	132	181	23	7	4	54	5	2	8	28	2	71	8	6	1	.447	.379
Sierra, Ruben, Okla.†	.326	112	498	439	70	143	229	26	3	18	82	0	4	0	55	6	63	5	2	24	.522	.398
Bocachica, Hiram, Alb.	.322	124	548	482	99	155	270	38	4	23	84	9	2	15	40	0	100	10	14	7	.560	.390
Ramirez, Omar, N.O.	.320	133	553	469	73	150	184	24	2	2	53	5	4	6	69	1	36	19	13	23	.392	.411
Roskos, John, L.V.*	.318	99	436	377	75	120	203	29	0	18	74	0	4	2	53	1	67	2	5	14	.538	.401
Gulan, Mike, Cal.	.317	119	463	426	66	135	230	40	2	17	74	0	2	8	27	1	94	5	1	12	.540	.367

DEPARTMENTAL LEADERS: G—LaRocca, 137; AB—J. Ortiz, 518; R—Bellhorn, 111; H—J. Ortiz, 182; TB—Hiatt, 303; 2B—LaRocca, 42; 3B—Mendoza, 14; HR—Hiatt, 36; RBI—Hiatt, 109; SH—several tied, 9 each; SF—Barajas, Buchanan, 11 each; HP—C. Wilson, 25; BB—Bellhorn, 94; IBB—Vaz, 10; SO—Hiatt, 149; SB—Porter, 39; CS—Byas, Redman, 18; GIDP—R. Sierra, 24; Slg.—Donnels, .660; OBP—Mendoza, .449.

ALL PLAYERS

*Lefthanded batter. †Switch-hitter.

Player, Team	Avg.	G	TPA	AB	R	H	TB	2B	3B	HR	RBI	SH	SF	HP	BB	IBB	SO	SB	CS	GDP	Slg.	OBP
Abbott, Chuck, Edm.	.200	5	15	15	0	3	4	1	0	0	4	0	0	0	0	0	5	0	0	0	.267	.200
Ah Yat, Paul, Nash.	.150	19	24	20	0	3	3	0	0	0	0	3	0	0	1	0	13	0	0	0	.150	.190
Akers, Chad, Tac.	.272	103	426	389	56	106	165	31	5	6	34	4	3	6	24	0	41	13	5	7	.424	.322
Alcala, Juan, Tac.	.300	3	11	10	1	3	4	1	0	0	1	0	0	0	0	0	2	0	0	0	.400	.300
Alexander, Chad, Tac.	.270	120	488	440	58	119	186	27	2	12	55	1	6	2	39	1	70	6	3	14	.423	.329
Allen, Chad, S.L.	.311	96	424	389	71	121	179	21	5	9	67	2	1	1	31	1	72	10	2	13	.460	.363
Allen, Dusty, L.V.	.311	67	283	222	52	69	133	14	4	14	55	0	3	0	58	0	50	3	0	6	.599	.449
Alston, Garvin, Alb.	.000	10	3	2	0	0	0	0	0	0	0	0	0	1	0	0	1	0	0	0	.000	.000
Alvarado, Damien, Tac.*	.000	1	1	1	0	0	0	0	0	0	0	0	0	0	1	0	0	0	0	0	.000	1.000
Alvarez, Gabe, L.V.	.305	43	181	141	33	43	81	11	0	9	26	1	2	4	33	0	44	2	0	3	.574	.444
Ambrose, John, Mem.	.000	13	1	1	0	0	0	0	0	0	0	0	0	0	0	0	0	0	0	1	.000	.000
Ametller, Jesus, Mem.*	.214	10	29	28	2	6	8	2	0	0	2	0	1	0	0	0	3	0	1	0	.286	.207
Anderson, Jimmy, Nash.*	.500	2	2	2	1	1	1	0	0	0	0	0	0	0	0	0	0	0	0	0	.500	.500
Andra, Jeff, Fres.*	.200	7	5	5	0	1	1	0	0	0	0	0	0	0	0	0	2	0	0	0	.200	.200
Andrews, Jeff, Tuc.	.000	16	3	2	1	0	0	0	0	0	0	0	0	0	0	0	0	0	0	0	.000	.000
Andrews, Shane, Iowa	.184	15	46	38	5	7	16	3	0	2	7	0	1	0	7	1	10	0	0	2	.421	.304
Andujar, Luis, Nash.	.000	25	2	2	0	0	0	0	0	0	0	0	0	0	0	0	2	0	0	0	.000	.000
Ardoin, Danny, Sac.-S.L.	.276	70	293	243	43	67	103	16	1	6	34	3	2	8	37	3	76	6	0	5	.424	.386
Arnold, Jamie, Alb.-Iowa	.286	23	31	28	5	8	9	1	0	0	3	3	0	0	0	0	5	0	0	0	.321	.286
Arroyo, Bronson, Nash.	.296	15	30	27	3	8	9	1	0	0	3	0	0	0	0	0	6	0	0	0	.333	.296
Arroyo, Luis, Cal.*	1.000	7	1	1	0	1	1	0	0	0	0	0	0	0	0	0	0	0	0	0	1.000	1.000
Ashby, Chris, Alb.	.297	134	524	465	98	138	199	34	3	7	59	1	1	2	55	1	74	16	11	10	.428	.373
Aven, Bruce, Nash.-Alb.	.286	12	49	42	8	12	14	2	0	0	6	0	0	0	7	1	9	0	0	1	.333	.388
Bailey, Cory, Nash.	.000	55	3	3	0	0	0	0	0	0	0	0	0	0	0	0	2	0	0	0	.000	.000
Ball, Jeff, Fres.	.242	72	244	223	32	54	79	8	1	5	11	1	0	5	15	1	45	1	1	8	.354	.305
Baptist, Travis, Nash.*	.150	34	27	20	3	3	3	0	0	0	3	0	0	4	0	0	10	0	0	0	.150	.292
Barajas, Rod, Tuc.	.226	110	446	416	43	94	158	25	0	13	75	0	11	5	14	0	65	4	3	13	.380	.253
Bard, Josh, C.S.†	.235	4	17	17	0	4	4	0	0	0	1	0	0	0	0	0	2	0	0	0	.235	.235
Barker, Glen, N.O.†	.271	26	118	107	15	29	40	5	0	2	10	0	0	0	10	1	12	11	3	3	.374	.333
Barkett, Andy, Okla.*	.178	13	47	45	4	8	10	2	0	0	1	0	0	0	2	0	6	0	0	0	.222	.213
Barnes, Brian, Cal.*	.000	26	5	5	0	0	0	0	0	0	0	0	0	0	0	0	5	0	0	0	.000	.000

CLASS AAA Pacific Coast League

Player, Team	Avg.	G	TPA	AB	R	H	TB	2B	3B	HR	RBI	SH	SF	HP	BB	IBB	SO	SB	CS	GDP	Slg.	OBP
Barnes, John, S.L.	.365	119	513	441	107	161	249	37	6	13	87	1	7	7	57	0	48	7	6	10	.565	.439
Barnes, Larry, Edm.*	.257	103	448	397	56	102	167	22	11	7	54	0	3	0	48	5	81	3	6	4	.421	.335
Baughman, Justin, Edm.	.234	80	350	303	44	71	85	7	2	1	35	4	6	7	30	1	41	28	5	6	.281	.312
Bautista, Juan, Okla.-N.O.	.214	40	110	103	12	22	27	5	0	0	6	2	0	2	3	0	24	4	3	4	.262	.250
Bellhorn, Mark, Sac.†	.266	117	545	436	111	116	227	17	11	24	73	6	4	5	94	3	121	20	5	5	.521	.399
Beltran, Carlos, Oma.*	.333	5	22	18	4	6	13	1	0	2	2	0	0	1	3	0	3	1	0	0	.722	.455
Beltran, Rigo, C.S.*	.290	29	38	31	5	9	11	2	0	0	2	3	0	0	4	0	3	1	0	0	.355	.371
Beltre, Esteban, Tuc.	.314	129	485	452	52	142	182	23	4	3	60	3	2	0	28	0	71	6	9	12	.403	.353
Benes, Alan, Mem.	.300	10	13	10	1	3	4	1	0	0	1	2	0	0	1	0	2	0	0	0	.400	.364
Benz, Jake, Cal.*	.000	15	2	1	0	0	0	0	0	0	0	1	0	0	0	0	1	0	0	0	.000	.000
Berblinger, Jeff, Oma.	.667	1	4	3	1	2	4	2	0	0	0	0	0	1	0	0	0	0	0	0	1.333	.750
Bergman, Sean, Cal.	.200	13	9	5	1	1	4	0	0	1	1	4	0	0	0	0	2	0	0	0	.800	.200
Berkman, Lance, N.O.†	.330	31	144	112	18	37	63	4	2	6	27	0	0	1	31	2	20	4	4	7	.563	.479
Berry, Mike, Alb.	.000	1	2	2	0	0	0	0	0	0	0	0	0	0	0	0	1	0	0	0	.000	.000
Betts, Todd, Cal.*	.000	1	1	1	0	0	0	0	0	0	0	0	0	0	0	0	0	0	0	0	.000	.000
Betzsold, James, N.O.	.283	93	348	314	47	89	132	17	1	8	49	0	1	4	29	1	101	16	7	8	.420	.351
Bevins, Andy, Mem.	.182	5	23	22	1	4	6	2	0	0	3	0	0	1	0	0	3	0	0	1	.273	.217
Bierbrodt, Nick, Tuc.*	.000	5	3	2	0	0	0	0	0	0	0	0	0	0	1	0	0	0	0	0	.000	.333
Bieser, Steve, Mem.*	.256	94	309	262	41	67	84	11	3	0	14	4	1	7	35	2	29	10	3	2	.321	.357
Blake, Casey, S.L.	.317	80	342	293	59	93	155	22	2	12	52	2	2	6	39	0	59	7	2	4	.529	.406
Bloomquist, Willie, Tac.	.225	51	205	191	17	43	53	5	1	1	23	4	3	0	7	0	28	5	0	3	.277	.249
Blosser, Greg, Fres.*	.159	18	52	44	4	7	10	3	0	0	8	0	1	0	7	1	9	2	0	1	.227	.269
Bocachica, Hiram, Alb.	.322	124	548	482	99	155	270	38	4	23	84	9	2	15	40	0	100	10	14	7	.560	.390
Boskie, Shawn, Tac.	.000	6	3	3	0	0	0	0	0	0	0	0	0	0	0	0	2	0	0	0	.000	.000
Bost, Heath, C.S.	.000	7	4	3	1	0	0	0	0	0	0	0	0	0	1	0	2	0	0	0	.000	.250
Bourgeois, Steve, C.S.	.182	9	12	11	1	2	2	0	0	0	0	1	0	0	0	0	2	0	0	0	.182	.182
Bowie, Micah, Iowa*	.222	9	10	9	1	2	2	0	0	0	0	1	0	0	0	0	3	0	0	0	.222	.222
Branson, Jeff, Alb.*	.289	108	365	332	45	96	138	23	2	5	41	2	4	0	27	3	71	6	4	3	.416	.339
Brede, Brent, Nash.*	.249	101	310	269	38	67	85	15	0	1	23	2	2	1	35	0	51	2	1	8	.316	.336
Brinkley, Darryl, Nash.	.301	38	128	113	19	34	47	5	1	2	16	0	1	1	13	1	27	3	3	2	.416	.375
Brito, Juan, Oma.	.286	17	53	49	8	14	18	1	0	1	2	1	0	0	3	0	10	1	1	0	.367	.327
Brock, Tarrik, Iowa*	.263	104	435	388	60	102	167	19	5	12	47	2	1	1	43	2	109	15	7	5	.430	.337
Brohawn, Troy, Tuc.*	.000	11	1	1	0	0	0	0	0	0	0	0	0	0	0	0	1	0	0	0	.000	.000
Brown, Adrian, Nash.†	.231	8	29	26	3	6	7	1	0	0	2	0	0	1	2	0	4	3	0	0	.269	.310
Brown, Dee, Oma.*	.269	125	522	479	76	129	235	25	6	23	70	0	3	3	37	5	112	20	3	14	.491	.324
Brown, Emil, Nash.	.312	70	284	237	44	74	111	20	1	5	25	0	1	6	40	1	44	26	4	8	.468	.423
Brown, Roosevelt, Iowa*	.309	100	409	363	67	112	180	32	0	12	55	0	2	7	37	3	60	10	3	7	.496	.381
Brown, Vick, C.S.-Tuc.	.228	80	208	180	30	41	57	9	2	1	14	2	0	1	25	2	35	8	3	6	.317	.325
Brumbaugh, Cliff, Okla.	.278	127	547	454	81	126	192	28	4	10	56	4	3	1	85	1	72	9	12	13	.423	.390
Brunette, Justin, Mem.*	.000	30	2	1	0	0	0	0	0	0	0	0	0	0	1	0	1	0	0	0	.000	.500
Buchanan, Brian, S.L.	.297	95	419	364	82	108	211	20	1	27	103	0	11	3	41	1	75	5	1	16	.580	.363
Bullett, Scott, C.S.*	.475	11	42	40	6	19	22	3	0	0	8	0	0	0	2	0	5	2	3	1	.550	.500
Burke, Jamie, Edm.	.240	75	291	263	25	63	75	12	0	0	17	2	2	5	19	2	42	1	1	5	.285	.301
Burns, Kevin, N.O.*	.214	4	15	14	3	3	6	1	1	0	1	0	0	0	1	0	2	0	0	0	.429	.267
Bush, Darren, L.V.*	.500	1	4	4	0	2	3	1	0	0	1	0	0	0	0	0	0	0	0	0	.750	.500
Butler, Brent, C.S.	.292	122	502	438	73	128	189	35	1	8	54	7	9	4	44	1	46	1	3	15	.432	.356
Butler, Rich, Tac.-Okla.*	.199	44	188	171	15	34	56	8	1	4	14	2	2	0	13	1	34	2	1	4	.327	.253
Byas, Mike, Fres.*	.264	135	602	516	84	136	154	10	1	2	34	5	2	1	78	0	89	36	18	5	.298	.360
Byrnes, Eric, Sac.	.333	67	279	243	55	81	133	23	1	9	47	1	2	2	31	0	30	12	5	3	.547	.410
Cabrera, Alex, Tuc.	.282	21	85	78	18	22	41	5	1	4	12	0	0	2	5	0	19	0	1	1	.526	.341
Campusano, Carlos, Fres.	.000	2	3	3	0	0	0	0	0	0	0	0	0	0	0	0	1	0	0	0	.000	.000
Candaele, Casey, Cal.†	.214	22	98	84	11	18	26	4	2	0	11	0	2	1	11	0	5	4	1	3	.310	.306
Canizaro, Jay, S.L.	.356	27	123	101	21	36	67	9	2	6	32	0	1	4	17	2	17	4	1	2	.663	.439
Carlson, Dan, Tuc.	.200	5	6	5	0	1	1	0	0	0	1	1	0	0	0	0	1	0	0	0	.200	.200
Carlyle, Buddy, L.V.*	.087	29	30	23	2	2	3	1	0	0	0	6	0	0	1	0	8	0	0	1	.130	.125
Carpenter, Bubba, C.S.*	.223	53	192	157	23	35	58	7	2	4	19	1	1	0	33	3	37	3	2	2	.369	.356
Carr, Jeremy, Oma.	.242	53	216	190	20	46	60	9	1	1	15	4	0	5	17	0	33	18	9	4	.316	.321
Carrara, Giovanni, C.S.	.167	18	27	24	2	4	4	0	0	0	1	3	0	0	0	0	3	0	0	1	.167	.167
Carvajal, Jhonny, Tuc.	.296	56	201	179	28	53	65	8	2	0	14	4	0	2	16	1	37	4	4	5	.363	.360
Castillo, Carlos, Cal.	.100	13	14	10	0	1	1	0	0	0	0	2	0	0	2	0	3	0	0	1	.100	.250
Castillo, Luis, Cal.†	.308	4	17	13	4	4	7	1	1	0	0	0	0	0	4	0	2	1	0	0	.538	.471
Castro, Nelson, Fres.†	.254	67	261	244	27	62	88	7	2	5	20	1	1	0	14	0	51	10	4	7	.361	.293
Castro, Ramon, Cal.	.335	67	234	218	44	73	137	22	0	14	45	0	0	0	16	0	36	0	0	5	.628	.380
Catalanotto, Frank, Okla.*	.273	3	12	11	2	3	3	0	0	0	1	0	0	1	0	0	4	0	0	0	.273	.333
Cather, Mike, Cal.	.000	43	3	3	0	0	0	0	0	0	0	0	0	0	0	0	1	0	0	0	.000	.000
Cedeno, Roger, N.O.†	.350	6	23	20	2	7	9	0	1	0	3	0	1	0	2	0	5	1	1	0	.450	.391
Cey, Dan, S.L.	.185	8	27	27	1	5	6	1	0	0	4	0	0	0	0	0	5	2	0	1	.222	.185
Charles, Frank, N.O.	.261	84	313	284	29	74	105	10	3	5	37	2	3	3	21	1	62	1	3	9	.370	.315
Chavez, Raul, N.O.	.244	99	349	303	31	74	93	13	0	2	36	4	4	4	34	5	44	3	0	12	.307	.325
Checo, Robinson, Alb.	.095	16	24	21	2	2	2	0	0	0	2	3	0	0	0	0	7	0	0	0	.095	.095
Chiaramonte, Giuseppe, Fres.	.255	122	498	443	70	113	227	30	6	24	79	1	3	3	47	1	81	2	1	7	.512	.329
Chouinard, Bobby, C.S.	.000	9	2	1	0	0	0	0	0	0	0	0	0	0	1	0	1	0	0	0	.000	.500
Clapinski, Chris, Cal.†	.280	62	252	214	41	60	94	10	3	6	24	1	2	2	33	0	36	3	3	4	.439	.378
Clapp, Stubby, Mem.*	.273	129	600	505	89	138	185	28	8	1	52	6	4	5	80	0	88	10	5	7	.366	.375
Clemente, Edgard, Edm.	.241	22	98	87	14	21	33	4	1	2	10	0	0	2	9	0	23	0	2	2	.379	.327
Cleto, Ambioris, Nash.	.143	4	16	14	0	2	2	0	0	0	0	1	0	1	0	0	5	0	0	0	.143	.250
Cline, Pat, Iowa	.333	3	3	3	0	1	1	0	0	0	0	0	0	0	0	0	2	0	0	0	.333	.333
Cole, Victor, Mem.*	.000	5	6	5	0	0	0	0	0	0	0	0	0	0	1	0	4	0	0	0	.000	.167
Connelly, Steve, Fres.	.333	43	4	3	1	1	1	0	0	0	1	0	0	0	0	0	0	0	0	0	.333	.500
Conti, Jason, Tuc.*	.305	92	418	383	75	117	180	20	5	11	57	2	5	5	23	1	57	11	3	8	.470	.349
Cookson, Brent, Alb.	.313	34	138	115	30	36	74	5	0	11	38	0	1	0	22	2	22	4	2	4	.643	.420
Cora, Alex, Alb.*	.373	30	122	110	18	41	55	8	3	0	20	2	1	2	7	0	10	5	3	1	.500	.417
Cornelius, Reid, Cal.	.154	8	13	13	0	2	3	1	0	0	3	0	0	0	0	0	6	0	0	0	.231	.154

Player, Team	Avg.	G	TPA	AB	R	H	TB	2B	3B	HR	RBI	SH	SF	HP	BB	IBB	SO	SB	CS	GDP	Slg.	OBP
Corsi, Jim, Tuc.	.000	32	1	1	0	0	0	0	0	0	0	0	0	0	0	0	1	0	0	0	.000	.000
Cotton, John, C.S.*	.328	103	347	314	58	103	182	21	5	16	62	0	2	1	30	3	97	13	0	6	.580	.386
Counsell, Craig, Tuc.*	.348	50	224	198	45	69	98	14	3	3	27	1	2	1	22	3	20	4	1	1	.495	.413
Cox, Darron, C.S.	.320	78	284	244	37	78	101	14	0	3	46	2	7	4	27	2	34	3	3	10	.414	.387
Crabtree, Robbie, Fres.	.125	63	10	8	2	1	1	0	0	0	0	0	0	0	2	0	5	0	0	0	.125	.300
Creek, Ryan, Cal.	.000	3	1	1	0	0	0	0	0	0	0	0	0	0	0	0	1	0	0	0	.000	.000
Cromer, Tripp, N.O.	.214	66	244	224	21	48	73	7	3	4	24	1	2	0	17	1	47	1	0	4	.326	.267
Croushore, Rich, C.S.	.000	33	3	2	1	0	0	0	0	0	0	0	0	0	1	0	2	0	0	0	.000	.333
Cruz, Ivan, Nash.*	.314	36	138	121	15	38	70	11	0	7	28	0	1	1	15	0	26	0	0	3	.579	.391
Cumberland, Chris, Fres.	.250	9	4	4	0	1	1	0	0	0	0	0	0	0	0	0	1	0	0	0	.250	.250
Cunnane, Will, L.V.	.250	20	25	16	5	4	4	0	0	0	2	5	1	1	2	0	2	0	0	0	.250	.350
Curl, John, L.V.*	.291	111	331	292	43	85	133	25	4	5	53	0	4	0	35	1	80	2	1	4	.455	.363
Dace, Derek, Tuc.*	.000	31	5	4	0	0	0	0	0	0	0	1	0	0	0	0	1	0	0	0	.000	.000
Dalesandro, Mark, Iowa	.388	15	50	49	5	19	24	3	1	0	8	0	0	0	1	0	4	0	0	2	.490	.400
Darr, Mike, L.V.*	.344	91	421	366	79	126	186	23	5	9	65	0	9	2	44	0	55	13	6	7	.508	.409
Davis, Ben, L.V.†	.262	59	261	221	38	58	97	16	1	7	40	1	0	1	38	3	43	5	2	5	.439	.373
Davis, Clint, Tuc.	.286	49	7	7	0	2	2	0	0	0	0	0	0	0	0	0	1	0	0	0	.286	.286
Davis, Jason, Fres.*	.000	46	9	8	0	0	0	0	0	0	0	0	0	0	1	0	3	0	0	0	.000	.111
Decker, Steve, Edm.-Sac.	.284	110	486	405	51	115	176	23	1	12	78	0	5	2	74	5	62	1	2	13	.435	.393
DeHaan, Kory, L.V.*	.293	10	46	41	7	12	16	4	0	0	3	1	1	1	2	0	11	3	0	1	.390	.333
De Jean, Mike, C.S.	.000	12	1	1	0	0	0	0	0	0	0	0	0	0	0	0	1	0	0	0	.000	.000
Dellucci, David, Tuc.*	.230	33	137	122	16	28	49	6	3	3	17	1	1	0	13	0	15	4	0	0	.402	.301
Del Toro, Miguel, Fres.	.067	21	16	15	0	1	1	0	0	0	1	0	0	0	1	0	10	0	1	0	.067	.125
Demetral, Chris, Okla.*	.239	106	423	355	55	85	128	9	5	8	47	9	3	1	55	2	53	2	3	5	.361	.341
Deschaine, James, Iowa	.250	4	10	8	3	2	8	0	0	2	5	0	0	0	2	0	1	0	0	0	1.000	.400
DeSilva, John, Cal.	.111	29	27	18	2	2	3	1	0	0	3	8	0	0	1	0	5	0	0	1	.167	.158
Diaz, Edwin, Okla.	.227	55	217	198	27	45	73	10	0	6	28	3	4	1	11	0	43	1	0	2	.369	.266
Dillon, Joe, Oma.	.282	45	168	149	19	42	60	11	2	1	11	0	0	2	17	0	26	1	0	6	.403	.363
Diorio, Mike, Nash.	.000	6	4	3	0	0	0	0	0	0	0	1	0	0	0	0	2	0	0	0	.000	.000
Donnelly, Brendan, Iowa	.000	9	4	3	0	0	0	0	0	0	0	1	0	0	0	0	2	0	0	0	.000	.000
Donnels, Chris, Alb.*	.328	105	402	332	79	109	219	27	1	27	84	0	2	2	66	2	52	6	1	9	.660	.440
Dougherty, Jim, Mem.	.000	60	4	4	0	0	0	0	0	0	0	0	0	0	0	0	2	0	0	1	.000	.000
Dransfeldt, Kelly, Okla.	.247	117	487	441	60	109	161	22	3	8	42	1	3	4	38	0	123	10	5	7	.365	.311
Driskill, Travis, N.O.	.000	28	41	36	1	0	0	0	0	0	0	2	0	0	3	0	18	0	0	2	.000	.077
Drumright, Mike, Cal.*	.125	34	26	24	0	3	3	0	0	0	1	2	0	0	0	0	8	0	0	1	.125	.125
Duncan, Geoff, Cal.	.000	24	1	1	0	0	0	0	0	0	0	0	0	0	0	0	0	0	0	0	.000	.000
Dunwoody, Todd, Oma.*	.323	9	38	31	5	10	14	1	0	1	5	1	1	1	4	0	8	1	2	1	.452	.405
Duplissea, William, Alb.	.263	9	20	19	3	5	10	2	0	1	4	0	0	1	0	0	8	0	0	0	.526	.300
Durazo, Erubiel, Tuc.*	.419	13	49	43	9	18	33	6	0	3	10	0	0	0	6	0	7	0	0	0	.767	.490
Durocher, Jayson, L.V.	.000	31	1	1	0	0	0	0	0	0	0	0	0	0	0	0	1	0	0	0	.000	.000
Durrington, Trent, Edm.	.219	28	126	105	19	23	38	4	1	3	14	3	1	1	16	0	25	8	6	3	.362	.325
Echevarria, Angel, C.S.	.335	74	319	284	46	95	143	23	2	7	50	0	4	5	26	4	44	1	1	5	.504	.395
Eckelman, Alex, Mem.	.375	6	16	16	2	6	6	0	0	0	1	0	0	0	0	0	1	0	0	0	.375	.375
Eckstein, David, Edm.	.346	15	66	52	17	18	35	8	0	3	8	0	0	5	9	0	1	5	3	0	.673	.485
Elarton, Scott, N.O.	.000	2	3	3	0	0	0	0	0	0	0	0	0	0	0	0	1	0	0	0	.000	.000
Encarnacion, Angelo, Iowa	.250	10	25	24	2	6	7	1	0	0	1	0	0	0	1	0	3	0	0	0	.292	.280
Encarnacion, Mario, Sac.	.269	81	346	301	51	81	142	16	3	13	61	1	5	3	36	2	95	15	7	8	.472	.348
Escandon, Emiliano, Oma.†	.228	103	367	302	35	69	102	12	0	7	32	7	6	2	50	0	58	4	0	6	.338	.336
Espada, Josue, Sac.	.234	40	176	145	21	34	41	7	0	0	10	3	0	1	27	0	23	7	2	5	.283	.358
Estrella, Luis, Fres.	.111	16	10	9	1	1	1	0	0	0	1	0	0	0	1	0	1	1	0	0	.111	.200
Evans, Dave, Tuc.	.000	41	9	8	0	0	0	0	0	0	0	0	0	0	1	0	4	0	0	0	.000	.111
Everett, Adam, N.O.	.245	126	547	453	82	111	155	25	2	5	37	4	4	11	75	0	100	13	4	6	.342	.363
Eversgerd, Bryan, Mem.	.400	48	5	5	1	2	2	0	0	0	0	0	0	0	0	0	0	0	0	1	.400	.400
Fabregas, Jorge, Oma.*	.248	37	142	129	8	32	42	5	1	1	18	0	1	0	12	1	9	1	1	5	.326	.310
Faggett, Ethan, L.V.*	.277	34	155	137	21	38	67	7	2	6	15	0	0	2	16	0	31	7	3	4	.489	.361
Fajardo, Alejandro, Fres.	.250	4	13	12	1	3	5	0	1	0	1	1	0	0	0	0	3	0	0	0	.417	.250
Falteisek, Steve, Cal.	.000	5	1	0	0	0	0	0	0	0	0	1	0	0	0	0	0	0	0	0	.000	.000
Febles, Carlos, Oma.	.214	11	50	42	6	9	16	4	0	1	5	0	0	1	7	0	10	3	3	2	.381	.340
Feliz, Pedro, Fres.	.298	128	542	503	85	150	287	34	2	33	105	2	5	2	30	4	94	1	1	18	.571	.337
Ferguson, Jeff, S.L.	.243	78	274	235	46	57	81	14	2	2	31	4	2	4	29	0	51	4	0	5	.345	.333
Figga, Mike, Alb.	.371	15	38	35	10	13	17	4	0	0	8	0	1	0	2	0	12	0	0	2	.486	.395
Figueroa, Eduardo, Tac.	.077	4	13	13	0	1	1	0	0	0	1	0	0	0	0	0	2	0	0	0	.077	.077
Figueroa, Luis, Nash.†	.250	23	65	64	6	16	26	1	0	3	8	0	0	0	1	0	8	2	1	2	.406	.262
Figueroa, Nelson, Tuc.†	.125	17	23	16	2	2	2	0	0	0	1	5	0	0	2	0	2	0	0	0	.125	.222
Flores, Ignacio, Alb.	.000	2	2	2	0	0	0	0	0	0	0	0	0	0	0	0	0	0	0	0	.000	.000
Flores, Jose, Tac.	.284	91	390	328	53	93	124	14	4	3	30	1	3	5	53	0	44	19	7	6	.378	.388
Florez, Tim, Iowa	.262	14	46	42	4	11	15	4	0	0	3	0	1	0	3	0	10	0	0	0	.357	.304
Flury, Pat, Cal.	.500	12	3	2	2	1	1	0	0	0	0	0	0	0	1	0	0	0	0	0	.500	.667
Ford, Ben, Iowa	.000	8	8	4	0	0	0	0	0	0	0	3	0	0	1	0	2	0	0	0	.000	.200
Fox, Andy, Tuc.*	.231	3	13	13	1	3	5	0	1	0	3	0	0	0	0	0	1	0	1	1	.385	.231
Franklin, Wayne, N.O.*	.000	48	3	2	1	0	0	0	0	0	0	0	0	0	1	0	1	0	0	0	.000	.333
Fraraccio, Dan, L.V.	.190	20	71	63	6	12	18	3	0	1	12	0	1	2	5	0	19	2	0	0	.286	.268
Funaro, Joe, Cal.	.282	49	174	142	22	40	43	1	1	0	11	3	1	5	23	3	13	0	2	3	.303	.398
Gagne, Eric, Alb.	.200	9	16	15	0	3	4	1	0	0	4	1	0	0	0	0	2	0	0	0	.267	.200
Gallagher, Shawn, Okla.	.237	64	249	219	27	52	85	9	3	6	30	1	5	1	23	1	43	1	4	6	.388	.306
Gann, Jamie, Tuc.	.250	65	219	208	35	52	83	12	2	5	33	1	3	4	3	0	44	3	1	6	.399	.271
Garcia , Osmani, Okla.	.270	43	161	148	17	40	53	7	0	2	20	1	1	1	10	0	14	1	2	2	.358	.319
Garcia, Amaury, Cal.	.292	120	534	479	83	140	211	26	3	13	47	7	3	4	41	0	79	35	15	15	.441	.351
Garcia, Luis, Mem.	.290	112	410	386	53	112	168	17	3	11	44	4	2	5	13	0	65	5	5	11	.435	.320
Garcia, Mike, Nash.	.000	24	1	1	0	0	0	0	0	0	0	0	0	0	0	0	1	0	0	0	.000	.000
Garrett, Hal, Alb.	.000	27	2	1	0	0	0	0	0	0	0	1	0	0	0	0	1	0	0	0	.000	.000
Giambi, Jeremy, Sac.*	.355	8	39	31	8	11	19	2	0	2	8	0	0	0	8	0	7	1	1	1	.613	.487
Gibbs, Kevin, Alb.†	.000	2	6	6	0	0	0	0	0	0	0	0	0	0	0	0	2	0	0	0	.000	.000

Player, Team	Avg.	G	TPA	AB	R	H	TB	2B	3B	HR	RBI	SH	SF	HP	BB	IBB	SO	SB	CS	GDP	Slg.	OBP
Gibson, Derrick, Cal.	.279	100	370	340	43	95	141	12	2	10	43	1	2	9	18	2	84	13	7	5	.415	.331
Gil, Geronimo, Alb.	.380	15	57	50	9	19	30	5	0	2	22	0	2	0	5	0	8	0	1	1	.600	.421
Gilbert, Shawn, Alb.	.333	86	363	297	67	99	168	19	4	14	49	0	1	5	60	1	69	11	10	3	.566	.452
Gipson, Charles, Tac.	.248	67	256	214	27	53	74	6	6	1	22	4	3	3	31	1	38	16	7	7	.346	.347
Glendenning, Mike, Fres.	.194	40	155	139	17	27	52	7	0	6	18	0	2	1	13	0	41	0	1	1	.374	.265
Gload, Ross, Iowa*	.404	28	115	104	24	42	98	10	2	14	39	0	1	1	9	1	13	1	1	2	.942	.452
Goldberg, Lonnie, C.S.	.320	7	29	25	5	8	13	2	0	1	6	0	1	0	2	0	5	0	0	0	.520	.357
Gonzalez, Enrique, Tuc.	.000	1	2	2	0	0	0	0	0	0	0	0	0	0	0	0	0	0	0	1	.000	.000
Gonzalez, Raul, Oma.	.266	69	265	241	35	64	91	13	1	4	33	0	1	2	21	1	20	5	5	6	.378	.328
Graves, Bryan, Edm.	.238	25	79	63	8	15	18	3	0	0	13	0	3	0	13	0	18	0	1	2	.286	.354
Green, Jason, N.O.	.000	10	1	1	0	0	0	0	0	0	0	0	0	0	0	0	1	0	0	0	.000	.000
Green, Scarborough, Okla.†	.313	27	125	99	20	31	40	6	0	1	10	3	0	1	22	0	24	14	2	0	.404	.443
Greene, Willie, Iowa*	.294	6	21	17	4	5	10	2	0	1	4	0	1	0	3	0	5	1	0	0	.588	.381
Grijak, Kevin, Alb.*	.285	112	376	337	61	96	173	20	3	17	79	0	5	3	31	5	55	10	9	8	.513	.346
Grilli, Jason, Cal.	.125	8	11	8	3	1	1	0	0	0	0	0	0	0	1	0	3	0	0	0	.125	.222
Gross, Kip, N.O.	.135	25	41	37	3	5	6	1	0	0	3	2	0	0	2	0	11	0	0	0	.162	.179
Guerra, Mark, N.O.	.077	10	15	13	0	1	1	0	0	0	1	1	0	0	1	0	3	0	0	0	.077	.143
Guiel, Aaron, Oma.*	.287	73	301	258	47	74	132	15	2	13	40	0	0	8	35	0	54	6	0	3	.512	.389
Guillen, Carlos, Tac.†	.299	24	102	87	19	26	38	4	1	2	11	1	1	1	12	0	17	4	1	3	.437	.386
Gulan, Mike, Cal.	.317	119	463	426	66	135	230	40	2	17	74	0	2	8	27	1	94	5	1	12	.540	.367
Guzman, Domingo, L.V.	.000	43	2	2	0	0	0	0	0	0	0	0	0	0	0	0	1	0	0	0	.000	.000
Guzman, Edwards, Fres.*	.280	115	450	421	52	118	162	24	1	6	52	4	3	5	17	0	43	1	5	17	.385	.314
Guzman, Geraldo, Tuc.	.091	6	15	11	1	1	1	0	0	0	0	2	1	0	2	0	5	0	0	0	.091	.231
Haas, Chris, Mem.*	.214	23	65	56	7	12	16	1	0	1	9	0	0	0	9	0	11	0	0	2	.286	.343
Hacker, Steve, S.L.	.208	17	51	48	3	10	11	1	0	0	2	0	0	0	3	0	12	0	0	1	.229	.255
Hackman, Luther, Mem.	.200	22	27	20	4	4	6	2	0	0	1	3	0	0	4	0	9	0	0	0	.300	.333
Hansen, Jed, L.V.	.208	14	30	24	3	5	12	1	0	2	5	1	0	0	5	0	11	1	0	2	.500	.345
Hardtke, Jason, C.S.†	.200	5	22	20	3	4	4	0	0	0	1	0	0	0	2	1	3	0	0	1	.200	.273
Harper, Brian, Tac.	.000	1	4	4	0	0	0	0	0	0	0	0	0	0	0	0	1	0	0	1	.000	.000
Hart, Jason, Sac.	.278	5	21	18	4	5	9	1	0	1	4	0	0	0	3	0	7	0	0	0	.500	.381
Hatcher, Chris, Iowa-Edm.	.295	116	453	403	65	119	245	23	5	31	95	0	3	13	34	2	88	5	4	7	.608	.366
Hayes, Heath, Alb.	.111	6	19	18	0	2	2	0	0	0	3	0	0	0	1	0	5	0	1	0	.111	.158
Heathcott, Mike, Iowa	.167	38	6	6	1	1	2	1	0	0	2	0	0	0	0	0	3	0	0	1	.333	.167
Heiserman, Rick, Mem.	.000	55	3	3	0	0	0	0	0	0	0	0	0	0	0	0	2	0	0	0	.000	.000
Hemphill, Bret, Edm.†	.279	41	168	147	22	41	71	10	1	6	21	0	0	0	21	0	28	0	0	2	.483	.369
Henderson, Ryan, Cal.	.000	11	3	3	0	0	0	0	0	0	1	0	0	0	0	0	2	0	0	0	.000	.000
Henderson, Scott, Cal.	.000	8	1	1	0	0	0	0	0	0	0	0	0	0	0	0	0	0	0	0	.000	.000
Hermansen, Chad, Nash.	.224	78	329	294	47	66	113	12	1	11	38	0	1	9	25	0	89	16	4	2	.384	.304
Hernandez, Alex, Nash.*	.275	76	288	276	29	76	121	17	2	8	37	0	0	1	11	1	60	6	3	6	.438	.304
Hernandez, Carlos, Tac.	.238	62	232	210	21	50	62	10	1	0	15	4	0	3	15	0	38	9	0	8	.295	.298
Herndon, Junior, L.V.	.136	26	30	22	1	3	3	0	0	0	1	3	6	0	2	0	13	0	0	1	.136	.208
Hiatt, Phil, C.S.	.310	136	584	507	106	157	303	36	1	36	109	0	9	5	63	1	149	14	2	9	.598	.385
Hinch, A.J., Sac.	.266	109	476	417	65	111	156	23	2	6	47	2	5	7	45	2	67	5	5	8	.374	.344
Hinchliffe, Brett, Iowa	.200	7	11	10	1	2	2	0	0	0	1	0	0	0	1	0	5	0	0	1	.200	.273
Holbert, Aaron, Cal.	.279	29	115	104	18	29	48	5	1	4	18	0	0	1	10	0	12	3	4	2	.462	.348
Holbert, Ray, Oma.	.254	94	376	338	41	86	106	12	1	2	40	1	2	0	35	0	49	14	9	10	.314	.323
Holmes, Darren, Mem.-Tuc.	.000	12	2	2	0	0	0	0	0	0	0	0	0	0	0	0	0	0	0	0	.000	.000
Hopper, Shane, L.V.	.381	5	21	21	3	8	11	3	0	0	5	0	0	0	0	0	5	0	0	0	.524	.381
Hosey, Dwayne, Edm.†	.233	46	175	150	25	35	62	5	2	6	19	2	2	1	20	2	25	7	1	2	.413	.324
House, Craig, C.S.	.000	8	1	1	0	0	0	0	0	0	0	0	0	0	0	0	0	0	0	0	.000	.000
Howard, Thomas, Mem.†	.265	17	43	34	7	9	11	2	0	0	5	0	0	2	7	1	6	0	1	2	.324	.419
Huckaby, Ken, Tuc.	.276	76	258	243	31	67	92	11	1	4	33	0	3	2	10	2	30	2	2	10	.379	.306
Huisman, Rick, N.O.	.000	48	1	1	0	0	0	0	0	0	0	0	0	0	0	0	0	0	0	1	.000	.000
Hundley, Todd, Alb.†	.556	3	10	9	2	5	8	0	0	1	5	0	0	0	1	0	0	0	0	0	.889	.600
Hunter, Torii, S.L.	.368	55	227	209	58	77	152	17	2	18	61	1	3	3	11	0	28	11	3	4	.727	.403
Huskey, Butch, S.L.	.333	2	10	9	2	3	9	0	0	2	5	0	0	1	0	0	2	0	0	0	1.000	.400
Hutchins, Norm, C.S.†	.227	15	49	44	8	10	18	1	2	1	4	1	1	1	2	0	15	2	1	1	.409	.271
Hutchinson, Chad, Mem.	.000	5	2	2	0	0	0	0	0	0	0	0	0	0	0	0	2	0	0	0	.000	.000
Hutton, Mark, N.O.	.000	46	2	1	1	0	0	0	0	0	0	0	0	0	1	0	1	0	0	0	.000	.500
Ibanez, Raul, Tac.*	.250	10	41	40	3	10	14	4	0	0	6	0	0	0	1	0	3	0	0	1	.350	.268
Iglesias, Mario, Iowa†	.250	10	4	4	1	1	1	0	0	0	0	0	0	0	0	0	0	0	0	0	.250	.250
Jaha, John, Sac.	.444	3	13	9	0	4	5	1	0	0	2	0	0	0	4	2	2	0	0	0	.556	.615
Janzen, Marty, Tuc.	.125	10	8	8	1	1	2	1	0	0	0	0	0	0	0	0	3	0	0	0	.250	.125
Jarvis, Kevin, C.S.†	.000	7	8	5	0	0	0	0	0	0	0	2	0	0	1	0	1	0	0	0	.000	.167
Jennings, Doug, Oma.*	.323	33	139	124	23	40	72	12	1	6	18	0	0	2	13	0	21	2	3	2	.581	.396
Jennings, Robin, S.L.*	.310	91	395	345	70	107	185	33	6	11	61	4	8	3	35	1	45	4	2	4	.536	.371
Jensen, Marcus, S.L.†	.291	15	70	55	10	16	23	4	0	1	12	1	1	2	11	0	10	0	2	3	.418	.420
Jensen, Ryan, Fres.	.263	27	26	19	4	5	9	1	0	1	5	3	1	0	3	0	4	0	0	0	.474	.343
Jester, Joe, Fres.	.200	4	17	15	1	3	4	1	0	0	0	0	0	0	2	0	4	0	0	1	.267	.294
Johns, Keith, Iowa	.244	115	393	353	50	86	116	24	0	2	26	1	3	2	33	1	75	3	4	3	.329	.309
Johnson, Brian, Mem.	.250	15	54	48	6	12	24	6	0	2	7	0	0	2	4	0	10	0	0	2	.500	.308
Johnson, Keith, Edm.	.307	109	460	423	63	130	204	31	2	13	64	6	5	7	19	0	71	7	8	14	.482	.344
Jones, Chris, L.V.	.269	13	30	26	6	7	12	2	0	1	6	0	2	0	2	0	9	1	0	0	.462	.300
Judd, Mike, Alb.	.227	25	28	22	1	5	7	2	0	0	0	4	0	0	3	0	7	0	0	1	.318	.346
Kapler, Gabe, Okla.	.333	3	12	9	3	3	3	0	0	0	0	0	0	0	3	0	2	0	0	0	.333	.500
Karchner, Matt, Iowa	.000	20	10	10	0	0	0	0	0	0	0	0	0	0	0	0	5	0	0	0	.000	.000
Karl, Scott, C.S.*	.500	3	3	2	0	1	1	0	0	0	0	1	0	0	0	0	0	0	0	0	.500	.667
Karnuth, Jason, Mem.	.364	17	26	22	4	8	13	2	0	1	4	2	0	0	2	0	6	0	0	0	.591	.417
Kaufman, Brad, N.O.	.000	40	4	4	0	0	0	0	0	0	0	0	0	0	0	0	2	0	0	0	.000	.000
Keith, Rusty, Sac.	.500	4	18	16	5	8	18	4	0	2	6	0	0	0	2	0	2	0	0	1	1.125	.556
Kielty, Bobby, S.L.†	.242	9	40	33	8	8	12	4	0	0	2	0	0	0	7	0	10	0	0	0	.364	.375
King, Brett, Iowa-Edm.	.171	29	80	70	5	12	21	3	0	2	5	3	1	0	6	1	24	0	2	1	.300	.247
King, Cesar, Okla.	.143	13	47	42	3	6	10	2	1	0	7	0	0	1	4	0	10	0	1	1	.238	.234

Player, Team	Avg.	G	TPA	AB	R	H	TB	2B	3B	HR	RBI	SH	SF	HP	BB	IBB	SO	SB	CS	GDP	Slg.	OBP
Klassen, Danny, Tuc.	.320	28	119	97	25	31	48	7	2	2	14	2	0	1	19	1	23	1	2	2	.495	.436
Knoll, Brian, Fres.	.200	10	12	10	0	2	2	0	0	0	0	2	0	0	0	0	3	1	0	0	.200	.200
Knorr, Randy, Nash.-Okla.	.240	83	321	292	39	70	110	17	1	7	45	0	1	0	28	0	61	0	1	13	.377	.305
Knott, Eric, Tuc.*	.000	11	5	4	0	0	0	0	0	0	0	1	0	0	0	0	1	0	0	0	.000	.000
Kolb, Brandon, L.V.	.000	47	3	2	0	0	0	0	0	0	0	1	0	0	0	0	0	0	0	0	.000	.000
Kubenka, Jeff, Tuc.	.000	4	1	0	0	0	0	0	0	0	0	1	0	0	0	0	0	0	0	0	.000	.000
Laker, Tim, Nash.	.247	121	484	421	70	104	197	28	4	19	75	0	8	1	54	1	73	5	0	9	.468	.329
Lamb, Mike, Okla.*	.255	14	60	55	8	14	27	5	1	2	5	0	0	0	5	0	6	2	1	5	.491	.317
Lampkin, Tom, Tac.*	.250	3	11	8	1	2	3	1	0	0	0	0	0	0	3	0	2	0	0	0	.375	.455
LaRocca, Greg, L.V.	.295	137	553	482	90	142	225	42	7	9	80	1	2	12	54	1	62	13	4	9	.467	.378
Latham, Chris, C.S.†	.245	126	421	339	76	83	132	16	6	7	49	3	6	2	71	3	105	29	7	8	.389	.373
Lawrence, Brian, L.V.	.100	12	10	10	1	1	2	1	0	0	2	0	0	0	0	0	0	0	0	1	.200	.100
Leach, Jalal, Fres.*	.379	51	216	198	34	75	137	16	5	12	45	0	0	0	18	1	28	8	3	2	.692	.431
LeCroy, Matthew, S.L.	.308	16	69	65	15	20	40	5	0	5	15	0	0	0	4	0	11	0	0	4	.615	.348
Ledesma, Aaron, C.S.	.344	59	247	224	31	77	88	9	1	0	37	2	3	1	17	1	30	10	1	6	.393	.388
Lee, David, C.S.	.000	47	2	2	0	0	0	0	0	0	0	0	0	0	0	0	1	0	0	0	.000	.000
Lee, Travis, Tuc.*	.367	7	31	30	4	11	15	4	0	0	3	0	0	0	1	0	6	1	0	1	.500	.387
Leon, Danny, Nash.	.000	3	2	2	0	0	0	0	0	0	0	0	0	0	0	0	0	0	0	0	.000	.000
Lesher, Brian, Tac.	.288	132	567	489	77	141	255	33	3	25	92	2	4	2	70	5	104	4	4	10	.521	.377
Linebrink, Scott, Fres.	.000	28	7	4	0	0	0	0	0	0	0	2	0	0	1	0	2	0	0	0	.000	.200
Liniak, Cole, Iowa	.236	123	461	411	63	97	180	24	1	19	58	4	4	3	39	0	77	5	3	16	.438	.304
Linton, Doug, C.S.*	.114	28	41	35	3	4	5	1	0	0	4	4	1	0	1	0	8	0	0	0	.143	.135
Little, Mark, Mem.	.283	107	489	424	70	120	208	29	7	15	64	1	2	11	51	1	98	22	11	2	.491	.373
Livingstone, Scott, Okla.*	.304	25	102	92	16	28	36	5	0	1	9	0	0	0	10	1	12	0	0	7	.391	.373
Lockwood, Mike, Sac.*	.254	36	149	126	14	32	38	3	0	1	13	2	3	1	17	1	14	0	2	1	.302	.340
LoDuca, Paul, Alb.	.351	78	319	279	47	98	143	27	3	4	54	2	2	2	33	0	14	8	5	13	.513	.421
Loewer, Carlton, L.V.†	.000	1	1	1	0	0	0	0	0	0	0	0	0	0	0	0	0	0	0	0	.000	.000
Long, Terrence, Sac.*	.400	15	67	60	11	24	39	6	0	3	15	1	1	0	4	0	4	0	3	2	.650	.431
Looney, Brian, Cal.*	.000	3	1	1	0	0	0	0	0	0	0	0	0	0	0	0	1	0	0	0	.000	.000
Lopez, Mendy, Cal.	.324	56	240	225	34	73	116	20	1	7	29	2	0	0	13	0	38	1	1	2	.516	.361
Lopez, Pedro, N.O.	.222	8	10	9	2	2	2	0	0	0	1	0	0	1	0	0	0	0	0	0	.222	.300
Lopez, Rodrigo, L.V.	.000	20	16	16	0	0	0	0	0	0	0	0	0	0	0	0	10	0	0	0	.000	.000
Lowery, Terrell, Fres.	.199	84	343	301	48	60	119	9	1	16	44	1	2	3	36	0	88	6	1	12	.395	.289
Lucca, Lou, Mem.	.284	122	508	462	70	131	208	31	2	14	70	2	3	9	32	3	61	7	4	10	.450	.340
Lugo, Julio, N.O.	.327	24	114	101	22	33	48	4	1	3	12	2	0	0	11	0	20	12	7	2	.475	.393
Luuloa, Keith, Edm.-Iowa	.252	80	325	286	43	72	121	18	2	9	48	1	4	2	32	1	31	3	4	12	.423	.327
Lynch, Jim, Fres.	.500	2	2	2	0	1	1	0	0	0	0	0	0	0	0	0	0	0	0	0	.500	.500
Mabry, John, Tac.*	.214	4	14	14	1	3	4	1	0	0	1	0	0	0	0	0	4	0	0	0	.286	.214
Machado, Robert, Tac.	.300	92	369	330	41	99	146	20	0	9	58	5	3	3	28	1	43	1	5	10	.442	.357
Magdaleno, Ricky, Tac.	.130	18	66	54	7	7	11	1	0	1	5	1	0	0	11	0	14	0	0	1	.204	.277
Mahoney, Mike, Iowa	.304	63	207	181	29	55	87	14	0	6	28	1	3	6	16	0	28	2	1	2	.481	.374
Mairena, Ozwaldo, Iowa*	.000	11	2	2	0	0	0	0	0	0	0	0	0	0	0	0	0	0	0	0	.000	.000
Manning, David, Iowa	.000	19	14	10	0	0	0	0	0	0	0	2	0	0	2	0	7	0	1	0	.000	.167
Manzanillo, Josias, Nash.	.000	15	3	3	0	0	0	0	0	0	0	0	0	0	0	0	2	0	0	0	.000	.000
Marcinczyk, T.R., Sac.	.231	11	44	39	4	9	13	1	0	1	3	0	0	1	4	0	7	0	0	1	.333	.318
Marrero, Eli, Mem.	.067	6	15	15	1	1	1	0	0	0	0	0	0	0	0	0	0	0	0	1	.067	.067
Martinez, Gabby, Iowa	.169	25	68	65	6	11	15	1	0	1	5	1	0	1	1	0	9	2	1	1	.231	.194
Martinez, Manny, Cal.	.266	124	424	380	57	101	149	19	1	9	54	3	9	1	31	0	58	20	6	4	.392	.316
Martinez, Pablo, Mem.†	.219	52	168	151	16	33	41	5	0	1	15	4	2	1	10	0	42	6	2	8	.272	.268
Martinez, Sandy, Cal.*	.300	86	299	277	45	83	148	20	0	15	48	0	4	2	16	1	57	2	1	5	.534	.338
Martins, Eric, Sac.	.253	76	301	261	35	66	84	10	1	2	21	2	1	0	37	0	32	1	5	11	.322	.344
Marval, Raul, Fres.	.208	50	175	159	15	33	44	5	0	2	12	6	0	0	10	0	23	4	5	4	.277	.254
Masaoka, Onan, Alb.	.250	18	5	4	1	1	4	0	0	1	1	1	0	0	0	0	1	0	0	1	1.000	.250
Mashore, Damon, Tuc.	.182	23	81	66	10	12	16	2	1	0	3	0	0	1	14	0	11	2	1	3	.242	.333
Matthews, Gary, Iowa†	.242	60	230	211	29	51	83	11	3	5	22	0	1	0	18	3	41	6	1	4	.393	.300
Matthews, Mike, Mem.*	.273	10	11	11	0	3	5	2	0	0	2	0	0	0	0	0	4	0	0	0	.455	.273
Mattson, Rob, Nash.*	.150	18	26	20	2	3	3	0	0	0	0	6	0	0	0	0	9	0	0	0	.150	.150
Maurer, Dave, L.V.	1.000	35	1	1	1	1	1	0	0	0	0	0	0	0	0	0	0	0	0	0	1.000	1.000
McCarthy, Greg, Cal.*	1.000	40	1	1	0	1	1	0	0	0	1	0	0	0	0	0	0	0	0	0	1.000	1.000
McClain, Scott, C.S.	.276	123	512	438	76	121	227	25	3	25	87	0	6	6	62	2	89	8	9	11	.518	.369
McClendon, Travis, Tac.	.000	1	1	1	0	0	0	0	0	0	0	0	0	0	0	0	0	0	0	0	.000	.000
McConnell, Sam, Nash.*	.125	8	9	8	0	1	1	0	0	0	0	0	0	0	1	0	2	0	0	3	.125	.222
McDonald, Jason, Okla.†	.238	32	124	105	13	25	39	6	1	2	12	2	1	2	14	0	29	2	4	1	.371	.336
McDonald, Keith, Mem.	.263	83	308	266	34	70	100	15	0	5	30	5	6	3	28	1	59	0	2	8	.376	.333
McKay, Cody, Sac.*	.224	16	64	58	8	13	20	4	0	1	7	0	0	1	5	1	14	0	0	1	.345	.297
McKnight, Tony, N.O.*	.192	21	27	26	1	5	5	0	0	0	3	1	0	0	0	0	6	0	0	0	.192	.192
McMullen, Mike, Fres.	.000	36	1	1	0	0	0	0	0	0	0	0	0	0	0	0	0	0	0	0	.000	.000
McNally, Sean, Cal.	.262	112	427	374	58	98	164	22	4	12	41	3	3	5	42	0	104	2	4	12	.439	.342
McNichol, Brian, Iowa*	.238	43	28	21	5	5	6	1	0	0	3	3	0	1	3	0	4	0	0	2	.286	.360
Meacham, Rusty, N.O.	.000	33	6	6	0	0	0	0	0	0	0	0	0	0	0	0	3	0	0	0	.000	.000
Medrano, Tony, Oma.	.266	128	532	485	65	129	178	23	1	8	55	7	4	3	33	0	45	18	8	14	.367	.314
Melconian, Alex, Cal.	.286	10	24	21	5	6	8	2	0	0	2	1	0	0	2	0	7	1	0	0	.381	.348
Melhuse, Adam, Alb.-C.S.†	.306	78	293	248	44	76	104	14	1	4	37	2	0	0	43	0	56	6	5	6	.419	.409
Melo, Juan, Fres.†	.295	123	460	417	58	123	197	26	6	12	50	4	1	3	35	3	89	13	13	8	.472	.353
Mendoza, Carlos, C.S.*	.354	107	431	359	79	127	171	16	14	0	42	8	1	3	60	2	50	26	13	5	.476	.449
Menechino, Frankie, Sac.	.316	9	43	38	8	12	20	2	0	2	2	0	0	0	5	0	4	1	0	0	.526	.395
Menhart, Paul, C.S.	.500	14	2	2	0	1	1	0	0	0	0	0	0	0	0	0	1	0	0	0	.500	.500
Merced, Orlando, N.O.*	.269	17	69	67	8	18	25	4	0	1	14	0	0	0	2	0	4	0	1	2	.373	.290
Mercedes, Henry, Mem.	.333	5	15	12	4	4	9	0	1	1	3	1	0	0	2	0	6	0	0	0	.750	.429
Metcalfe, Mike, Alb.†	.302	35	165	149	22	45	57	6	3	0	21	2	2	2	10	0	16	9	11	2	.383	.350
Meyers, Chad, Iowa	.269	80	355	301	54	81	97	10	0	2	26	4	2	5	43	0	41	34	15	5	.322	.368
Meyers, Mike, Iowa	.067	13	16	15	0	1	1	0	0	0	0	1	0	0	0	0	4	0	0	0	.067	.067
Michalak, Chris, Alb.*	.282	24	46	39	7	11	14	3	0	0	4	4	0	0	3	0	13	0	0	1	.359	.333

Player, Team	Avg.	G	TPA	AB	R	H	TB	2B	3B	HR	RBI	SH	SF	HP	BB	IBB	SO	SB	CS	GDP	Slg.	OBP
Mientkiewicz, Doug, S.L.*	.334	130	560	485	96	162	254	32	3	18	96	3	8	3	61	2	68	9	5	17	.524	.406
Mieske, Matt, Tuc.	.240	6	26	25	2	6	11	2	0	1	3	0	1	0	0	0	7	0	0	1	.440	.231
Miller, Orlando, Alb.	.280	7	28	25	2	7	12	2	0	1	4	0	0	0	3	1	3	0	1	1	.480	.357
Miller, Ryan, N.O.	.251	111	335	299	31	75	104	18	1	3	35	3	5	10	18	1	58	1	5	7	.348	.310
Miller, Trever, Alb.	.154	12	17	13	1	2	2	0	0	0	2	1	0	0	3	0	4	0	0	0	.154	.313
Miller, Wade, N.O.	.000	16	20	14	1	0	0	0	0	0	1	3	0	0	3	0	4	0	0	0	.000	.176
Milliard, Ralph, L.V.	.280	108	448	371	61	104	151	26	3	5	40	7	2	5	63	2	63	18	9	7	.407	.390
Minor, Damon, Fres.*	.290	133	579	482	84	140	259	27	1	30	106	0	9	1	87	4	97	0	0	11	.537	.394
Mitchell, Mike, Tuc.*	.308	84	326	279	50	86	127	25	2	4	40	3	2	2	40	2	41	2	2	7	.455	.396
Moeller, Chad, S.L.	.287	47	178	167	30	48	78	13	1	5	20	1	1	0	9	1	45	0	1	6	.467	.322
Molina, Izzy, Oma.	.235	90	332	311	39	73	114	9	1	10	36	0	5	2	14	0	55	5	4	6	.367	.268
Molina, Jose, Iowa	.234	76	275	248	22	58	70	9	0	1	17	1	3	0	23	1	61	1	4	6	.282	.296
Monahan, Shane, Tac.-L.V.-C.S.*	.264	48	159	144	14	38	58	7	2	3	24	3	1	1	10	0	29	2	4	1	.403	.314
Montgomery, Ray, Nash.	.259	71	254	228	36	59	92	10	1	7	29	0	0	7	19	1	38	3	5	8	.404	.335
Montilla, Samuel, Tuc.	.500	2	2	2	0	1	1	0	0	0	1	0	0	0	0	0	0	0	0	0	.500	.500
Montoya, Saul, Tuc.	.000	3	1	1	0	0	0	0	0	0	0	0	0	0	0	0	0	0	0	0	.000	.000
Moody, Eric, Cal.	.667	35	3	3	1	2	2	0	0	0	0	0	0	0	0	0	0	0	0	0	.667	.667
Moraga, David, C.S.*	.000	6	5	2	1	0	0	0	0	0	0	2	0	0	1	0	1	0	0	0	.000	.333
Morales, Steve, Cal.†	.000	3	3	3	0	0	0	0	0	0	0	0	0	0	0	0	0	0	0	1	.000	.000
Morgan, Scott, Edm.	.247	90	357	320	53	79	135	25	2	9	54	0	2	3	32	1	74	8	3	5	.422	.319
Moriarty, Mike, S.L.	.249	127	471	390	73	97	167	23	4	13	55	9	4	5	63	0	58	1	2	9	.428	.357
Morris, Matt, Mem.	.000	3	3	2	0	0	0	0	0	0	0	1	0	0	0	0	0	0	0	0	.000	.000
Mota, Tony, Alb.†	.269	102	402	372	57	100	137	11	4	6	47	0	2	0	28	2	61	8	6	9	.368	.318
Munoz, Juan, Mem.*	.215	32	82	79	6	17	24	7	0	0	7	0	1	0	2	0	10	2	1	2	.304	.323
Murphy, Mike, Tac.	.283	97	397	360	54	102	146	18	4	6	38	1	1	3	32	0	86	10	3	4	.406	.346
Murphy, Nate, Edm.*	.257	119	453	393	60	101	154	17	6	8	38	3	2	2	52	3	91	6	4	11	.392	.345
Murray, Heath, Alb.*	.171	29	42	35	4	6	6	0	0	0	4	4	0	0	3	0	9	0	0	1	.171	.237
Nathan, Joe, Fres.	1.000	3	3	1	1	1	1	0	0	0	0	1	0	0	1	0	0	0	0	0	1.000	1.000
Navarro, Jaime, C.S.	.000	5	10	8	0	0	0	0	0	0	0	2	0	0	0	0	3	0	0	0	.000	.000
Neill, Mike, Tac.*	.310	112	488	397	69	123	196	38	1	11	63	6	4	6	75	6	105	9	4	10	.494	.423
Nelson, Bry, Tuc.†	.310	69	279	261	34	81	117	21	0	5	31	0	2	0	16	0	20	4	2	8	.448	.348
Newhan, David, L.V.*	.254	66	284	244	41	62	86	5	2	5	35	2	1	0	37	1	61	9	3	4	.352	.351
Newman, Eric, Iowa	.083	30	16	12	1	1	1	0	0	0	0	3	0	0	1	0	2	0	0	0	.083	.154
Newstrom, Doug, Tuc.*	.294	57	164	143	16	42	52	7	0	1	20	2	3	0	16	1	25	2	1	5	.364	.358
Nicholson, Kevin, L.V.†	.279	91	370	326	48	91	141	26	3	6	44	1	5	3	35	0	62	4	4	5	.433	.350
Niebla, Ruben, Alb.*	.000	24	2	2	0	0	0	0	0	0	0	0	0	0	0	0	1	0	0	0	.000	.000
Nieves, Jose, Iowa	.281	7	34	32	7	9	18	4	1	1	7	0	0	0	2	0	5	1	0	0	.563	.324
Nieves, Wilbert, L.V.	.000	1	1	1	0	0	0	0	0	0	0	0	0	0	0	0	0	0	0	0	.000	.000
Norman, Les, Oma.	.258	109	456	411	53	106	169	22	4	11	63	2	6	7	30	4	62	7	4	5	.411	.315
Norris, Ben, Tuc.*	.000	12	18	14	0	0	0	0	0	0	0	3	0	0	1	0	6	0	0	0	.000	.067
Norton, Chris, Sac.	.244	13	55	45	7	11	17	0	0	2	9	0	1	1	8	0	10	0	0	2	.378	.364
Norton, Phillip, Iowa	.135	28	46	37	3	5	5	0	0	0	2	9	0	0	0	0	15	0	0	0	.135	.135
Nunez, Abraham, Nash.†	.276	90	394	351	49	97	119	11	1	3	29	4	2	1	36	0	46	20	5	7	.339	.344
Nunez, Argelis, Tuc.	.333	4	4	3	0	1	1	0	0	0	2	0	1	0	0	0	2	0	0	0	.333	.250
Nunez, Jorge, Alb.	.000	1	3	3	0	0	0	0	0	0	0	0	0	0	0	0	0	0	0	0	.000	.000
Nunez, Vladimir, Cal.	.300	15	12	10	2	3	5	2	0	0	0	0	2	0	0	0	2	0	0	0	.500	.300
Nussbeck, Mark, Mem.*	.120	21	27	25	2	3	4	1	0	0	1	1	0	0	1	0	6	0	0	1	.160	.154
O'Connor, Brian, Nash.*	.100	5	10	10	0	1	2	1	0	0	0	0	0	0	0	0	3	0	0	0	.200	.100
Ojeda, Augie, Iowa†	.280	113	443	396	56	111	162	23	2	8	43	3	4	7	33	1	27	16	6	10	.409	.343
Oliver, Joe, Tac.	.197	18	68	61	2	12	14	2	0	0	8	0	1	1	5	0	12	0	0	3	.230	.265
Ontiveros, Steve, C.S.	.500	8	13	6	3	3	3	0	0	0	1	4	0	1	2	0	0	0	0	0	.500	.667
Orie, Kevin, Oma.	.280	54	210	175	30	49	79	11	2	5	23	0	2	5	28	0	24	3	3	8	.451	.390
Ortiz, Hector, Oma.	.322	68	254	227	30	73	103	12	0	6	24	3	1	1	22	2	18	4	3	8	.454	.382
Ortiz, Jose, Sac.	.351	131	571	518	107	182	298	34	5	24	108	0	2	4	47	0	64	22	9	21	.575	.408
Ortiz, Luis, Tuc.	.302	92	337	308	50	93	155	26	3	10	65	3	6	4	16	0	17	0	0	17	.503	.338
Osteen, Gavin, Nash.	.000	14	2	1	0	0	0	0	0	0	0	0	0	0	0	0	0	0	0	0	.000	.000
Padilla, Vicente, Tuc.	.500	12	2	2	1	1	1	0	0	0	0	0	0	0	0	0	1	0	0	0	.500	.500
Palacios, Vicente, L.V.-Iowa	.083	44	16	12	2	1	1	0	0	0	0	1	0	1	2	0	4	0	0	2	.083	.267
Parra, Jose, Nash.	.063	23	21	16	2	1	1	0	0	0	1	2	0	0	3	0	7	0	0	0	.063	.211
Patrick, Bronswell, Cal.	.182	27	25	22	2	4	7	0	0	1	2	3	0	0	0	0	4	0	0	0	.318	.182
Patterson, Jarrod, Nash.*	.278	70	217	198	25	55	80	10	0	5	30	2	2	2	13	0	40	0	2	2	.404	.326
Patterson, John, Tuc.	1.000	3	2	1	1	1	1	0	0	0	0	0	0	0	1	0	0	0	0	0	1.000	1.000
Pavlas, Dave, Nash.†	.000	45	5	3	0	0	0	0	0	0	0	2	0	0	0	0	3	0	0	0	.000	.000
Pelaez, Alex, L.V.	.250	34	119	108	13	27	33	3	0	1	15	5	1	1	4	1	20	0	0	2	.306	.283
Pellow, Kit, Oma.	.249	117	481	421	61	105	194	17	3	22	75	1	5	16	38	1	89	6	4	5	.461	.331
Pena, Angel, Alb.	.308	87	346	315	52	97	166	12	3	17	61	1	2	0	28	0	75	3	1	4	.527	.362
Perez, Eduardo, Mem.	.289	77	324	277	57	80	155	12	3	19	66	0	3	1	43	1	48	10	3	9	.560	.383
Peters, Chris, Nash.*	.000	11	15	14	0	0	0	0	0	0	0	1	0	0	0	0	8	0	0	0	.000	.000
Petersen, Chris, Iowa	.056	9	20	18	1	1	2	1	0	0	0	0	0	0	2	0	5	0	0	1	.111	.150
Petrick, Ben, C.S.	.315	63	282	248	38	78	133	22	3	9	47	0	2	0	32	1	40	7	2	2	.536	.390
Phillips, J.R., N.O.*	.268	73	304	269	35	72	122	8	0	14	52	0	3	4	28	4	77	1	0	4	.454	.342
Phillips, Jason, Nash.	.000	6	3	3	0	0	0	0	0	0	0	0	0	0	0	0	2	0	0	0	.000	.000
Piatt, Adam, Sac.	.283	65	287	254	36	72	111	15	0	8	42	0	3	4	26	1	57	3	2	3	.437	.355
Pierre, Juan, C.S.*	.471	4	17	17	3	8	10	0	1	0	1	0	0	0	0	0	1	1	0	0	.588	.471
Pierzynski, A.J., S.L.*	.335	41	166	155	22	52	80	14	1	4	25	2	3	1	5	1	22	1	1	3	.516	.354
Plantenberg, Erik, N.O.†	.000	24	1	1	0	0	0	0	0	0	0	0	0	0	0	0	0	0	0	0	.000	.000
Polanco, Enohel, Cal.	.100	9	22	20	1	2	2	0	0	0	1	0	1	0	1	0	7	1	0	0	.100	.136
Porter, Bo, Sac.	.272	129	585	481	94	131	200	21	3	14	64	4	6	5	88	1	117	39	10	9	.416	.386
Porzio, Mike, C.S.*	.125	6	10	8	1	1	1	0	0	0	0	1	0	0	1	0	5	0	0	1	.125	.222
Powell, Alonzo, C.S.	.259	21	68	58	9	15	25	7	0	1	4	0	0	0	10	0	12	0	0	1	.431	.368
Powell, Brian, N.O.	.188	19	21	16	1	3	3	0	0	0	1	4	0	0	1	0	7	0	0	1	.188	.235
Powell, Dante, Alb.	.221	65	208	181	36	40	67	7	1	6	21	2	1	3	21	0	51	13	4	4	.370	.311
Pride, Curtis, Alb.*	.293	38	156	133	30	39	70	7	3	6	17	2	1	0	20	3	37	7	5	2	.526	.383
Prieto, Alejandro, Oma.	.263	118	429	384	54	101	141	19	0	7	37	8	2	6	26	0	40	14	6	12	.367	.318

Player, Team	Avg.	G	TPA	AB	R	H	TB	2B	3B	HR	RBI	SH	SF	HP	BB	IBB	SO	SB	CS	GDP	Slg.	OBP
Prieto, Chris, Alb.*	.278	85	306	248	53	69	112	13	3	8	31	3	1	4	50	1	42	25	5	3	.452	.406
Pujols, Albert, Mem.	.214	3	15	14	1	3	4	1	0	0	2	0	0	0	1	0	2	1	0	0	.286	.267
Pulsipher, Bill, Tuc.*	.250	13	11	8	1	2	3	1	0	0	2	2	0	0	1	0	1	0	0	0	.375	.333
Quevedo, Ruben, Iowa	.143	13	17	14	1	2	2	0	0	0	0	0	0	0	1	0	8	0	0	1	.143	.200
Quinn, Mark, Oma.	.377	13	62	61	8	23	37	5	0	3	13	0	1	0	0	0	8	0	1	5	.607	.371
Radmanovich, Ryan, L.V.*	.273	120	464	399	74	109	179	31	3	11	59	0	5	0	60	3	84	4	3	9	.449	.364
Rain, Steve, Iowa	.000	28	1	1	0	0	0	0	0	0	0	0	0	0	0	0	0	0	0	0	.000	.000
Raleigh, Matt, Cal.	.333	4	8	6	1	2	3	1	0	0	1	0	0	0	2	0	2	0	0	0	.500	.500
Ramirez, Aramis, Nash.	.353	44	182	167	28	59	87	12	2	4	26	0	0	4	11	0	26	2	1	5	.521	.407
Ramirez, Julio, Cal.	.266	94	380	350	45	93	138	18	3	7	52	2	4	3	21	1	86	20	14	5	.394	.310
Ramirez, Omar, N.O.	.320	133	553	469	73	150	184	24	2	2	53	5	4	6	69	1	36	19	13	23	.392	.411
Randolph, Steve, Tuc.*	.250	5	4	4	1	1	1	0	0	0	1	0	0	0	0	0	2	0	0	0	.250	.250
Rath, Fred, Mem.-Nash.	.143	37	31	28	3	4	5	1	0	0	1	2	0	0	1	0	9	0	0	0	.179	.172
Raven, Luis, Cal.	.274	115	463	420	68	115	214	23	2	24	81	0	6	3	34	2	98	3	1	10	.510	.328
Reames, Britt, Mem.	.235	14	20	17	2	4	7	0	0	1	1	3	0	0	0	0	1	0	0	0	.412	.235
Redman, Tike, Nash.*	.261	121	547	506	62	132	190	24	11	4	51	2	4	3	32	0	73	24	18	4	.375	.306
Revenig, Todd, Tuc.	.000	17	2	2	0	0	0	0	0	0	0	0	0	0	0	0	1	0	0	0	.000	.000
Reyes, Al, Alb.	.500	30	4	2	0	1	1	0	0	0	1	1	0	0	1	0	0	0	0	0	.500	.667
Reyes, Carlos, L.V.†	.000	16	1	1	0	0	0	0	0	0	0	0	0	0	0	0	1	0	0	0	.000	.000
Richard, Chris, Mem.*	.277	95	432	375	64	104	176	24	0	16	75	0	3	4	50	4	70	9	3	5	.469	.366
Richardson, Brian, S.L.-N.O.	.257	119	442	404	53	104	141	16	6	3	52	3	5	4	26	0	97	3	0	11	.349	.305
Ricketts, Chad, Alb.	.250	54	4	4	0	1	1	0	0	0	0	0	0	0	0	0	1	0	0	1	.250	.250
Riggs, Adam, Alb.	.313	124	394	348	71	109	177	24	4	12	57	6	3	2	35	0	67	11	7	11	.509	.376
Riley, Mike, Fres.*	.083	14	13	12	2	1	1	0	0	0	1	0	0	0	3	0	7	0	0	0	.083	.267
Rivas, Luis, S.L.	.318	41	173	157	33	50	75	14	1	3	25	0	1	2	13	0	21	7	4	3	.478	.371
Rivera, Ruben, L.V.	.200	2	10	10	1	2	2	0	0	0	1	0	0	0	0	0	3	0	0	0	.200	.200
Roberge, J.P., Oma.	.391	6	24	23	5	9	16	4	0	1	1	0	0	0	1	0	3	0	0	0	.696	.417
Roberson, Kevin, S.L.†	.250	36	137	120	22	30	57	7	1	6	26	0	3	2	12	0	38	0	0	3	.475	.321
Robertson, Jeriome, N.O.*	.182	9	13	11	0	2	2	0	0	0	2	2	0	0	0	0	1	0	0	0	.182	.182
Robertson, Mike, N.O.*	.242	121	455	401	57	97	157	23	5	9	49	1	2	6	45	8	56	1	3	13	.392	.326
Rodriguez, Jose, Mem.*	.000	40	2	2	0	0	0	0	0	0	0	0	0	0	0	0	1	0	0	0	.000	.000
Rolison, Nate, Cal.*	.330	123	518	443	88	146	258	37	3	23	88	0	2	3	70	5	117	3	1	7	.582	.423
Root, Derek, L.V.*	.250	9	4	4	2	1	2	1	0	0	1	0	0	0	0	0	0	0	0	0	.500	.250
Rosario, Omar, Sac.*	.296	8	30	27	4	8	9	1	0	0	1	0	0	1	2	0	5	0	0	0	.333	.367
Roskos, John, L.V.	.318	99	436	377	75	120	203	29	0	18	74	0	4	2	53	1	67	2	5	14	.538	.401
Ruffin, Johnny, Tuc.	.000	45	4	4	0	0	0	0	0	0	0	0	0	0	0	0	1	0	0	0	.000	.000
Ryan, Jason, S.L.†	1.000	18	1	1	1	1	2	1	0	0	0	0	0	0	0	0	0	0	0	0	2.000	1.000
Ryan, Mike, S.L.*	.222	3	12	9	1	2	2	0	0	0	2	0	0	0	3	0	2	0	0	1	.222	.417
Ryan, Rob, Tuc.*	.307	92	390	332	56	102	147	19	1	8	55	0	2	11	45	5	35	1	1	9	.443	.405
Sabel, Erik, Tuc.	.083	29	16	12	0	1	1	0	0	0	0	2	0	0	2	0	5	0	0	0	.083	.214
Saenz, Olmedo, Sac.	.500	1	4	4	1	2	2	0	0	0	1	0	0	0	0	0	0	0	0	0	.500	.500
Sagmoen, Marc, N.O.*	.268	122	463	414	65	111	176	15	7	12	43	4	4	1	40	1	82	20	5	3	.425	.331
Saipe, Mike, C.S.	.273	15	12	11	3	3	5	2	0	0	4	0	1	0	0	0	3	0	0	0	.455	.250
Salazar, Oscar, Sac.	.154	4	14	13	0	2	3	1	0	0	1	0	0	0	1	0	1	1	0	2	.231	.214
Sanchez, Victor, N.O.-Tuc.	.105	15	21	19	1	2	3	1	0	0	1	0	1	0	1	0	10	1	0	2	.158	.143
Sanders, Anthony, Tac.	.306	114	479	428	72	131	218	21	3	20	80	2	9	6	33	2	109	9	8	9	.509	.357
Sanders, Scott, Cal.	.000	6	8	7	0	0	0	0	0	0	0	0	0	0	0	0	1	0	0	0	.000	.000
Sanders, Tracy, Nash.*	.143	4	7	7	0	1	1	0	0	0	1	0	0	0	0	0	4	0	0	1	.143	.143
Santos, Sneideer, Tuc.*	.000	1	1	1	0	0	0	0	0	0	0	0	0	0	0	0	0	0	0	1	.000	.000
Saylor, Jamie, N.O.*	.233	25	71	60	3	14	19	5	0	0	7	1	1	1	8	0	17	1	2	2	.317	.329
Scheschuk, John, L.V.*	.429	2	8	7	2	3	4	1	0	0	1	0	0	0	1	0	1	0	0	0	.571	.500
Scott, Darryl, Tuc.	.000	14	4	3	0	0	0	0	0	0	1	0	1	0	0	0	3	0	0	0	.000	.000
Sears, Todd, S.L.*	.364	3	12	11	2	4	8	1	0	1	4	0	0	0	1	0	2	0	0	1	.727	.417
Secrist, Reed, Okla.*	.240	31	119	104	13	25	41	2	1	4	14	1	0	1	13	0	24	0	0	1	.394	.331
Sell, Chip, Tuc.*	.326	112	448	405	65	132	181	23	7	4	54	5	2	8	28	2	71	8	6	1	.447	.379
Serafini, Dan, L.V.-Nash.†	.053	33	19	19	0	1	2	1	0	0	3	0	0	0	0	0	11	0	0	0	.105	.053
Sergio, Tom, Okla.*	.271	18	63	59	13	16	27	5	3	0	4	0	0	0	4	0	11	1	0	1	.458	.317
Serrano, Wascar, L.V.	.250	4	4	4	1	1	1	0	0	0	0	0	0	0	0	0	0	0	0	0	.250	.250
Servais, Scott, C.S.	.292	20	71	65	7	19	32	2	1	3	12	1	0	1	4	0	8	0	1	1	.492	.343
Shave, Jon, Okla.	.290	131	573	510	85	148	209	21	5	10	54	3	3	17	40	3	65	12	5	16	.410	.360
Sierra, Ruben, Okla.†	.326	112	498	439	70	143	229	26	3	18	82	0	4	0	55	6	63	5	2	24	.522	.398
Simon, Randall, Cal.*	.294	22	69	68	5	20	26	3	0	1	11	0	1	0	0	0	3	0	0	1	.382	.290
Small, Aaron, C.S.	.308	36	30	26	4	8	12	1	0	1	4	4	0	0	0	0	6	0	0	1	.462	.308
Smith, Bud, Mem.*	.188	9	21	16	1	3	3	0	0	0	2	2	0	0	3	0	5	0	0	0	.188	.316
Smith, Cam, Alb.	.250	39	6	4	1	1	1	0	0	0	1	2	0	0	0	0	0	0	0	0	.250	.250
Smith, Jeff, S.L.*	.286	25	87	84	10	24	34	4	0	2	9	0	0	1	2	1	20	1	0	1	.405	.310
Snopek, Chris, Tac.	.300	104	448	393	76	118	185	24	2	13	48	2	5	4	44	2	40	12	6	5	.471	.372
Soliz, Steve, L.V.	.218	34	138	119	16	26	34	8	0	0	8	1	1	2	14	1	22	0	0	3	.286	.309
Sollecito, Gabe, Okla.†	.000	8	1	1	0	0	0	0	0	0	0	0	0	0	0	0	0	0	0	0	.000	.000
Sorrento, Paul, Sac.*	.273	40	175	139	25	38	67	9	1	6	32	0	3	0	33	0	34	1	0	2	.482	.406
Sosa, Juan, C.S.	.274	118	494	449	67	123	193	25	9	9	69	9	2	3	31	1	54	23	10	16	.430	.324
Spencer, Stan, L.V.	.286	7	11	7	1	2	3	1	0	0	0	4	0	0	0	0	1	0	0	1	.429	.286
Spivey, Junior, Tuc.	.282	28	130	117	21	33	58	8	4	3	16	1	1	0	11	0	17	3	1	4	.496	.341
Stahoviak, Scott, Iowa*	.278	15	48	36	3	10	17	4	0	1	13	0	1	0	11	2	2	1	0	1	.472	.438
Stechschulte, Gene, Mem.	1.000	41	1	1	1	1	2	1	0	0	0	0	0	0	0	0	0	0	0	0	2.000	1.000
Steenstra, Kennie, Mem.-Tuc.	.174	34	28	23	4	4	8	1	0	1	1	5	0	0	0	0	10	0	0	0	.348	.174
Stone, Ricky, Alb.	.067	48	18	15	1	1	1	0	0	0	2	2	0	0	1	0	7	0	0	0	.067	.125
Stoner, Mike, Edm.-Iowa	.287	111	449	414	64	119	185	17	2	15	61	0	3	10	22	1	48	1	2	11	.447	.336
Stovall, DaRond, Edm.†	.262	79	290	252	35	66	114	7	7	9	32	2	0	1	35	0	76	10	4	4	.452	.354
Strittmatter, Mark, C.S.-L.V.	.254	28	77	67	4	17	19	2	0	0	7	1	1	2	6	0	20	0	0	0	.284	.329
Strong, Joe, Cal.†	.667	29	4	3	0	2	2	0	0	0	0	0	0	0	1	0	1	0	0	0	.667	.750
Sullivan, Brendan, L.V.	.250	45	5	4	1	1	1	0	0	0	0	0	0	0	1	0	1	0	0	0	.250	.400
Summers, John, Fres.†	.308	6	13	13	0	4	4	0	0	0	1	0	0	0	0	0	4	0	0	1	.308	.308

Player, Team	Avg.	G	TPA	AB	R	H	TB	2B	3B	HR	RBI	SH	SF	HP	BB	IBB	SO	SB	CS	GDP	Slg.	OBP
Sutton, Larry, Mem.*	.256	95	422	347	61	89	150	21	2	12	70	0	5	3	67	5	56	4	1	12	.432	.377
Tabaka, Jeff, C.S.	.000	22	2	2	0	0	0	0	0	0	0	0	0	0	0	0	1	0	0	0	.000	.000
Tatis, Fernando, Mem.	.000	3	10	9	0	0	0	0	0	0	0	0	0	0	1	0	3	0	0	0	.000	.100
Tatum, Jim, Fres.	.190	30	114	100	10	19	33	5	0	3	12	0	1	1	12	0	17	1	0	2	.330	.281
Tebbs, Nate, L.V.†	.256	38	145	133	18	34	44	4	0	2	21	1	4	0	7	0	24	4	0	4	.331	.285
t'Hoen, E.J., Edm.	.208	39	130	120	13	25	40	6	0	3	10	1	0	1	8	0	36	1	1	1	.333	.264
Thompson, Mark, Mem.	.286	7	7	7	0	2	2	0	0	0	0	0	0	0	0	0	2	0	0	0	.286	.286
Thrower, Jake, L.V.†	.313	4	18	16	4	5	5	0	0	0	2	0	0	0	2	0	2	0	0	0	.313	.389
Thurston, Jerrey, N.O.	.167	13	30	30	3	5	7	2	0	0	0	0	0	0	0	0	10	0	0	1	.233	.167
Tolentino, Juan, Edm.	.245	122	479	432	58	106	175	30	3	11	58	3	4	3	37	0	106	16	14	6	.405	.307
Tollberg, Brian, L.V.	.158	13	23	19	3	3	3	0	0	0	2	3	0	0	1	0	2	0	0	1	.158	.200
Tomlinson, Goef, Oma.*	.286	29	121	98	12	28	35	3	2	0	9	1	4	1	17	0	11	5	5	2	.357	.383
Tonis, Michael, Oma.	.500	2	8	8	1	4	4	0	0	0	3	0	0	0	0	0	3	0	0	0	.500	.500
Torres, Gabby, S.L.	.000	1	1	1	0	0	0	0	0	0	0	0	0	0	0	0	0	0	0	0	.000	.000
Tremie, Chris, Cal.	.267	46	136	120	16	32	47	7	1	2	17	1	0	0	15	1	24	0	1	4	.392	.348
Truby, Chris, N.O.	.284	64	292	268	31	76	99	11	3	2	30	0	7	0	17	2	32	6	2	7	.369	.318
Tuttle, Dave, Tuc.	.000	20	11	9	0	0	0	0	0	0	0	2	0	0	0	0	1	0	0	0	.000	.000
Tyler, Josh, Fres.	.274	78	243	212	24	58	70	10	1	0	11	1	1	5	24	0	29	12	4	11	.330	.360
Valdes, Pedro, Okla.*	.332	92	405	352	64	117	199	30	2	16	78	0	5	3	45	4	41	2	0	7	.565	.409
Valdez, Mario, S.L.-Sac.*	.344	105	458	378	87	130	219	27	1	20	96	1	7	5	66	4	59	1	1	13	.579	.441
Valentin, Javier, S.L.†	.357	39	151	140	25	50	91	16	2	7	35	0	1	1	9	0	27	1	0	1	.650	.397
Van Poppel, Todd, Iowa	.167	10	7	6	0	1	1	0	0	0	0	1	0	0	0	0	4	0	0	0	.167	.167
Vaz, Roberto, Sac.*	.289	114	482	426	56	123	181	22	3	10	72	1	4	2	49	10	72	20	6	9	.425	.362
Velandia, Jorge, Sac.	.278	83	345	302	56	84	133	20	1	9	57	2	2	5	34	0	52	4	3	8	.440	.359
Velarde, Randy, Sac.	.455	3	16	11	3	5	5	0	0	0	2	0	0	1	4	0	2	2	0	0	.455	.625
Verdugo, Jason, Fres.	.000	11	1	1	0	0	0	0	0	0	0	0	0	0	0	0	0	0	0	0	.000	.000
Verplancke, Jeff, Fres.	.000	1	2	1	0	0	0	0	0	0	0	0	0	1	0	0	0	0	0	0	.000	.000
Vieira, Scott, Iowa	.000	2	3	3	0	0	0	0	0	0	0	0	0	0	0	0	2	0	0	1	.000	.000
Villano, Mike, Nash.	.133	46	15	15	1	2	2	0	0	0	0	0	0	0	0	0	3	0	0	0	.133	.133
Vililo, Miguel, Tac.†	.125	4	16	16	2	2	6	1	0	1	1	0	0	0	0	0	3	0	0	1	.375	.125
Vitiello, Joe, L.V.	.350	77	304	274	43	96	160	31	0	11	46	0	1	2	27	0	59	2	0	11	.584	.411
Voigt, Jack, Okla.	.176	13	41	34	9	6	6	0	0	0	4	0	2	0	5	0	8	0	0	2	.176	.268
Vosberg, Ed, C.S.*	.167	29	6	6	1	1	1	0	0	0	0	0	0	0	0	0	0	0	0	0	.167	.167
Wainhouse, David, Mem.*	.000	20	8	7	0	0	0	0	0	0	0	0	1	0	0	0	5	0	0	1	.000	.125
Walker, Pete, C.S.	.000	58	3	2	0	0	0	0	0	0	0	1	0	0	0	0	1	0	0	0	.000	.000
Walker, Todd, S.L.*	.325	63	287	249	51	81	103	14	1	2	37	3	3	0	32	0	32	8	3	6	.414	.398
Ward, Turner, Tuc.†	.378	32	99	82	24	31	55	10	1	4	16	0	0	0	17	2	7	0	1	3	.671	.485
Waszgis, B.J., Okla.	.263	77	319	259	45	68	124	11	3	13	62	0	1	4	55	0	68	2	2	8	.479	.398
Wathan, Dusty, Tac.	.325	64	235	203	25	66	87	12	0	3	29	4	1	12	15	1	28	0	2	4	.429	.403
Watkins, Scott, C.S.*	.364	44	13	11	0	4	5	1	0	0	1	2	0	0	0	0	3	0	0	0	.455	.364
Weber, Ben, Fres.	.000	38	6	6	0	0	0	0	0	0	0	0	0	0	0	0	4	0	0	0	.000	.000
Wehner, John, Nash.	.255	121	489	427	57	109	180	23	0	16	63	0	2	4	56	1	65	14	5	11	.422	.346
Weibl, Clint, Mem.	.179	19	34	28	3	5	6	1	0	0	1	2	0	0	4	0	11	0	0	0	.214	.333
Whisenant, Matt, L.V.	.000	33	3	3	0	0	0	0	0	0	0	0	0	0	0	0	2	0	0	0	.000	.000
White, Walt, Tuc.	.273	23	62	55	4	15	22	4	0	1	10	2	0	0	5	1	10	1	0	1	.400	.333
Whitmore, Darrell, Mem.*	.281	89	272	256	36	72	120	14	2	10	34	0	2	1	13	0	64	4	2	3	.469	.316
Wilkins, Marc, Nash.	.000	17	7	7	0	0	0	0	0	0	0	0	0	0	0	0	2	0	0	0	.000	.000
Wilkins, Rick, Mem.*	.230	63	218	187	23	43	63	6	1	4	25	1	1	2	27	1	57	0	1	1	.337	.332
Williams, George, L.V.†	.239	63	218	176	27	42	78	8	2	8	35	0	3	3	36	1	44	0	1	3	.443	.372
Williams, Jeff, Alb.	.200	12	18	15	2	3	3	0	0	0	1	1	0	1	1	0	4	0	0	0	.200	.294
Williams, Keith, Fres.	.217	60	211	184	29	40	62	5	1	5	23	0	1	4	22	1	52	1	1	7	.337	.313
Williams, Woody, L.V.	.000	1	3	1	0	0	0	0	0	0	0	0	1	0	1	0	0	0	0	0	.000	.500
Wilson, Craig, Nash.	.283	124	472	396	83	112	239	24	2	33	86	0	7	25	44	2	121	1	2	7	.604	.383
Wilson, Dan, Tac.	.250	4	4	4	0	1	2	1	0	0	0	0	0	0	0	0	1	0	0	0	.500	.250
Wilson, Enrique, Nash.†	.286	2	7	7	0	2	2	0	0	0	1	0	0	0	0	0	1	0	0	2	.286	.286
Wojciechowski, Steve, Fre.-Cal.*	.125	33	8	8	0	1	1	0	0	0	0	0	0	0	0	0	3	0	0	0	.125	.125
Wolff, Bryan, N.O.	.143	11	18	14	1	2	2	0	0	0	0	1	0	0	3	0	6	0	0	0	.143	.294
Wood, Jason, Nash.	.237	88	351	316	40	75	114	18	0	7	45	2	4	1	28	0	84	2	2	7	.361	.298
Wood, Kerry, Iowa	.333	1	3	3	0	1	1	0	0	0	0	0	0	0	0	0	1	0	0	0	.333	.333
Woolf, Jason, Mem.†	.243	32	114	103	21	25	32	5	1	0	6	0	0	2	19	0	23	5	3	1	.311	.371
Wooten, Shawn, Edm.	.353	66	274	252	43	89	149	21	3	11	42	0	1	3	18	0	38	0	0	4	.591	.401
Worrell, Tim, Iowa	.000	6	2	1	0	0	0	0	0	0	0	0	0	0	1	0	0	0	0	0	.000	.500
Young, Danny, Iowa	.000	27	3	2	1	0	0	0	0	0	1	0	0	0	1	0	1	0	0	0	.000	.333
Young, Ernie, Mem.	.263	124	527	453	76	119	240	16	0	35	98	0	4	4	66	6	117	11	1	17	.530	.359
Young, Travis, Fres.	.156	13	37	32	2	5	5	0	0	0	2	0	0	0	3	0	8	0	0	1	.156	.229
Zambrano, Carlos, Iowa*	.200	34	6	5	1	1	4	0	0	1	1	0	0	0	0	0	3	0	0	0	.800	.200
Zancanaro, Dave, Iowa*	.125	29	31	24	1	3	3	0	0	0	2	5	1	0	1	0	5	1	0	0	.125	.154
Zaun, Greg, Oma.†	.280	9	29	25	7	7	10	3	0	0	3	0	0	0	4	1	3	1	1	1	.400	.379
Zeber, Ryan, Edm.	.250	2	4	4	1	1	1	0	0	0	0	0	0	0	0	0	1	0	0	0	.250	.250
Zerbe, Chad, Fres.*	.529	17	20	17	4	9	9	0	0	0	3	0	0	0	0	0	5	0	0	0	.529	.529
Zinter, Alan, Iowa-Tuc.†	.245	101	321	269	36	66	134	17	3	15	40	0	3	2	47	3	86	0	0	4	.498	.358
Zosky, Eddie, Nash.-N.O.	.232	64	180	164	17	38	53	5	2	2	19	2	2	1	10	0	32	0	2	4	.323	.281
Zuleta, Julio, Iowa	.311	107	436	392	76	122	227	25	1	26	94	0	4	9	31	2	77	5	4	14	.579	.372
Zywica, Mike, Okla.	.262	126	478	420	57	110	170	25	4	9	58	3	4	5	46	0	123	8	7	6	.405	.339

GRAND SLAMS: R. Castro, Feliz, Hatcher, Hunter, Sorrento, 3 each; D. Allen, Bellhorn, Gload, Liniak, Lowery, Minor, Pellow, Perez, Pierzynski, E. Young; 2 each; Blake, Branson, Brede, Brock, Byas, Canizaro, Carr, Chiaramonte, Cruz, Decker, Donnels, Durrington, Grijak, Hiatt, T. Hundley, K. Johnson, Leach, Lesher, Lucca, McClain, Newhan, J. Ortiz, Petrick, Piatt, Radmanovich, Raven, Richard, Roskos, Sierra, Sosa, Stahoviak, Sutton, Tolentino, Valdes, Valdez, Vaz, T. Walker, Waszgis, J. Wood, Zuleta, 1 each.

AWARDED FIRST BASE ON CATCHER'S INTERFERENCE: Prieto 3 (McDonald, Secrist, Wilson); LaRocca 2 (Guzman, McDonald); Barker (McDonald); Brede (King); Castro (Huckaby); Chiaramonte (Huckaby); Goldberg (Dalesandro); Gipson (Barajas); Johns (Waszgis); LoDuca (Chiaramonte); Long (Chiaramonte); Murphy (Barajas); Porter (Torres); A. Sanders (Petrick); S. Sanders (Williams); Soliz (Ardoin); Valdez (Machado).

PLAYERS WITH TWO OR MORE TEAMS

Player, Team	Avg.	G	TPA	AB	R	H	TB	2B	3B	HR	RBI	SH	SF	HP	BB	IBB	SO	SB	CS	GDP	Slg.	OBP
Ardoin, Danny, Sac.	.278	67	281	234	42	65	101	16	1	6	34	3	2	8	34	3	72	6	0	5	.432	.385
Ardoin, Danny, S.L.	.222	3	12	9	1	2	2	0	0	0	0	0	0	0	3	0	4	0	0	0	.222	.417
Arnold, Jamie, Alb.	.227	20	25	22	4	5	5	0	0	0	2	3	0	0	0	0	5	0	0	0	.227	.227
Arnold, Jamie, Iowa	.500	3	6	6	1	3	4	1	0	0	1	0	0	0	0	0	0	0	0	0	.667	.500
Aven, Bruce, Nash.	.300	3	11	10	1	3	4	1	0	0	3	0	0	0	1	1	3	0	0	0	.400	.364
Aven, Bruce, Alb.	.281	9	38	32	7	9	10	1	0	0	3	0	0	0	6	0	6	0	0	1	.313	.395
Bautista, Juan, Okla.	.240	7	26	25	3	6	7	1	0	0	1	1	0	0	0	0	6	1	1	2	.280	.240
Bautista, Juan, N.O.	.205	33	84	78	9	16	20	4	0	0	5	1	0	2	3	0	18	3	2	2	.256	.253
Brown, Vick, C.S.	.205	47	92	78	14	16	22	6	0	0	7	1	0	0	13	2	20	2	0	3	.282	.319
Brown, Vick, Tuc.	.245	33	116	102	16	25	35	3	2	1	7	1	0	1	12	0	15	6	3	3	.343	.330
Butler, Rich, Tac.*	.185	32	136	124	11	23	38	7	1	2	9	2	0	0	10	1	26	2	0	1	.306	.246
Butler, Rich, Okla.*	.234	12	52	47	4	11	18	1	0	2	5	0	2	0	3	0	8	0	1	3	.383	.269
Decker, Steve, Edm.	.302	48	205	162	29	49	86	11	1	8	35	0	1	2	40	4	22	0	0	5	.531	.444
Decker, Steve, Sac.	.272	62	281	243	22	66	90	12	0	4	43	0	4	0	34	1	40	1	2	8	.370	.356
Hatcher, Chris, Iowa	.278	86	326	288	46	80	169	15	1	24	71	0	2	10	26	1	64	4	4	4	.587	.356
Hatcher, Chris, Edm.	.339	30	127	115	19	39	76	8	4	7	24	0	1	3	8	1	24	1	0	3	.661	.394
Holmes, Darren, Mem.	.000	9	1	1	0	0	0	0	0	0	0	0	0	0	0	0	0	0	0	0	.000	.000
Holmes, Darren, Tuc.	.000	3	1	1	0	0	0	0	0	0	0	0	0	0	0	0	0	0	0	0	.000	.000
King, Brett, Iowa	.171	18	40	35	1	6	9	3	0	0	0	0	0	0	5	1	8	0	2	0	.257	.275
King, Brett, Edm.	.171	11	40	35	4	6	12	0	0	2	5	3	0	1	1	0	16	0	0	1	.343	.216
Knorr, Randy, Nash.	.150	13	46	40	3	6	10	1	0	1	4	0	0	0	6	0	11	0	1	1	.250	.261
Knorr, Randy, Okla.	.254	70	275	252	36	64	100	16	1	6	41	0	1	0	22	0	50	0	0	12	.397	.313
Luuloa, Keith, Edm.	.244	76	307	270	39	66	111	17	2	8	44	1	4	2	30	1	30	2	4	11	.411	.320
Luuloa, Keith, Iowa	.375	4	18	16	4	6	10	1	0	1	4	0	0	0	2	0	1	1	0	1	.625	.444
Melhuse, Adam, Alb.†	.343	36	132	108	21	37	49	9	0	1	19	2	0	0	22	0	21	4	2	2	.454	.454
Melhuse, Adam, C.S.†	.279	42	161	140	23	39	55	5	1	3	18	0	0	0	21	0	35	2	3	4	.393	.373
Monahan, Shane, Tac.*	.296	8	30	27	3	8	14	1	1	1	8	0	1	1	1	0	4	1	1	0	.519	.333
Monahan, Shane, L.V.*	.179	13	45	39	5	7	9	2	0	0	5	1	0	0	5	0	6	0	2	0	.231	.273
Monahan, Shane, C.S.*	.295	27	84	78	6	23	35	4	1	2	11	2	0	0	4	0	19	1	1	1	.449	.329
Palacios, Vicente, L.V.	.000	38	7	4	2	0	0	0	0	0	0	0	0	1	2	0	2	0	0	0	.000	.429
Palacios, Vicente, Iowa	.125	6	9	8	0	1	1	0	0	0	0	1	0	0	0	0	2	0	0	2	.125	.125
Rath, Fred, Mem.	.200	18	16	15	3	3	4	1	0	0	1	0	0	0	1	0	5	0	0	0	.267	.250
Rath, Fred, Nash.	.077	7	15	13	0	1	1	0	0	0	0	2	0	0	0	0	4	0	0	0	.077	.077
Richardson, Brian, S.L.	.252	42	163	155	20	39	48	7	1	0	17	0	1	1	6	0	35	2	0	3	.310	.282
Richardson, Brian, N.O.	.261	77	279	249	33	65	93	9	5	3	35	3	4	3	20	0	62	1	0	8	.373	.319
Sanchez, Victor, N.O.	.000	9	11	11	0	0	0	0	0	0	0	0	0	0	0	0	5	0	0	2	.000	.000
Sanchez, Victor, Tuc.	.250	6	10	8	1	2	3	1	0	0	1	0	1	0	1	0	3	0	0	1	.375	.300
Serafini, Dan, L.V.†	.100	26	10	10	0	1	2	1	0	0	3	0	0	0	0	0	6	0	0	0	.200	.100
Serafini, Dan, Nash.†	.000	7	9	9	0	0	0	0	0	0	0	0	0	0	0	0	5	0	0	0	.000	.000
Steenstra, Kennie, Mem.	.000	10	3	2	1	0	0	0	0	0	0	0	1	0	0	0	2	0	0	0	.000	.000
Steenstra, Kennie, Tuc.	.190	24	25	21	3	4	8	1	0	1	1	4	0	0	0	0	8	0	0	0	.381	.190
Stoner, Mike, Edm.	.274	85	351	329	48	90	144	11	2	13	44	0	2	4	16	0	42	1	2	9	.438	.313
Stoner, Mike, Iowa	.341	26	98	85	16	29	41	6	0	2	17	0	1	6	6	1	6	0	0	2	.482	.418
Strittmatter, Mark, C.S.	.296	13	33	27	3	8	8	0	0	0	3	1	1	1	3	0	9	0	0	0	.296	.375
Strittmatter, Mark, L.V.	.225	15	44	40	1	9	11	2	0	0	4	0	0	1	3	0	11	0	0	0	.275	.295
Valdez, Mario, S.L.*	.366	88	385	317	76	116	196	24	1	18	85	1	6	3	57	3	46	1	1	10	.618	.460
Valdez, Mario, Sac.*	.230	17	73	61	11	14	23	3	0	2	11	0	1	2	9	1	13	0	0	3	.377	.342
Wojciechowski, Steve, Fres.*.	.000	13	6	6	0	0	0	0	0	0	0	0	0	0	0	0	2	0	0	0	.000	.000
Wojciechowski, Steve, Cal.* ..	.500	20	2	2	0	1	1	0	0	0	0	0	0	0	0	0	1	0	0	0	.500	.500
Zinter, Alan, Iowa†	.227	90	277	233	27	53	111	12	2	14	35	0	3	2	39	2	78	0	0	3	.476	.339
Zinter, Alan, Tuc.†	.361	11	44	36	9	13	23	5	1	1	5	0	0	0	8	1	8	0	0	1	.639	.477
Zosky, Eddie, Nash.	.221	53	142	131	14	29	44	5	2	2	16	2	2	1	6	0	24	0	1	2	.336	.257
Zosky, Eddie, N.O.	.273	11	38	33	3	9	9	0	0	0	3	0	0	1	4	0	8	0	1	2	.273	.368

2000 PITCHING
TEAM

Team	W	L	Pct.	ERA	G	CG	ShO	Sv.	IP	H	TBF	R	ER	HR	SH	SF	HB	BB	IBB	SO	WP	Bk.
Memphis	83	61	.576	3.97	144	5	12	45	1301.2	1275	5561	659	574	118	63	40	48	513	19	906	39	7
New Orleans	68	74	.479	4.13	142	6	8	29	1266.0	1260	5448	688	581	118	54	37	55	462	32	934	43	5
Sacramento	90	54	.625	4.16	144	1	6	42	1273.0	1291	5462	681	588	133	37	41	36	452	17	940	59	8
Tacoma	76	67	.531	4.19	143	11	12	42	1244.1	1243	5370	676	579	120	35	31	45	503	25	999	51	12
Albuquerque	86	58	.597	4.48	144	7	8	36	1273.1	1368	5664	754	634	115	52	46	72	614	12	950	75	9
Las Vegas	73	70	.510	4.74	143	6	7	32	1231.1	1359	5501	754	648	142	37	44	59	479	21	1034	47	5
Oklahoma	69	74	.483	4.79	143	14	8	30	1227.2	1310	5438	756	653	113	30	60	43	591	22	912	66	11
Tucson	68	73	.482	4.80	141	3	4	34	1219.1	1369	5448	746	650	137	50	48	36	519	26	876	44	9
Nashville	63	79	.444	4.80	142	4	8	34	1252.2	1279	5513	758	668	140	61	39	64	577	32	854	91	7
Salt Lake	90	53	.629	4.95	143	6	4	43	1266.0	1449	5625	795	697	151	30	41	45	465	18	936	67	12
Omaha	64	79	.448	5.03	143	3	3	35	1230.1	1352	5406	771	687	184	26	45	58	487	22	875	64	9
Edmonton	63	78	.447	5.12	141	8	4	35	1214.0	1316	5442	774	691	124	23	52	49	549	6	828	74	7
Colo. Springs	68	73	.521	5.28	142	9	7	32	1229.1	1363	5493	811	721	144	52	47	62	482	10	928	73	9
Iowa	57	87	.396	5.36	144	4	4	29	1242.1	1358	5628	836	740	155	51	48	51	624	32	980	74	10
Fresno	57	84	.404	5.56	141	1	1	31	1239.0	1413	5600	887	765	179	54	44	59	505	7	920	64	9
Calgary	60	82	.423	5.99	142	6	0	30	1228.1	1518	5701	926	818	155	56	57	53	576	14	880	76	7

CLASS AAA Pacific Coast League

TOP QUALIFIERS FOR EARNED-RUN AVERAGE TITLE

Minimum 114 innings.*Lefthanded pitcher.

Pitcher, Team	W	L	Pct.	ERA	G	GS	CG	ShO	GF	Sv.	IP	H	TBF	R	ER	HR	SH	SF	HB	BB	IBB	SO	WP	Bk.
Weibl, Clint, Mem.	9	4	.692	2.83	19	18	2	2	0	0	120.2	98	481	45	38	11	1	2	6	37	0	92	1	1
Wise, Matt, Edm.	9	6	.600	3.69	19	19	2	1	0	0	124.1	122	510	54	51	10	2	7	2	26	0	82	0	1
Crabtree, Robbie, Fres.	5	6	.455	3.81	63	0	0	0	21	8	127.2	126	544	67	54	8	7	4	7	31	5	116	2	0
Ahearne, Pat, Tac.	13	8	.619	3.86	29	26	1	0	0	0	168.0	190	725	92	72	11	5	2	1	53	5	92	5	1
Franklin, Ryan, Tac.	11	5	.688	3.90	31	22	4	0	2	0	164.0	147	665	85	71	28	3	3	12	35	1	142	2	0
Gross, Kip, N.O.	8	7	.533	3.94	25	25	4	0	0	0	157.2	156	664	80	69	20	10	6	4	44	1	94	3	0
Nussbeck, Mark, Mem.	9	4	.692	3.96	21	21	1	1	0	0	125.0	127	536	69	55	11	4	1	2	44	0	76	3	2
Steenstra, Kennie, Mem.-Tuc.	9	5	.643	3.98	34	20	1	0	5	2	156.0	187	689	79	69	16	10	4	6	53	0	75	0	0
Driskill, Travis, N.O.	12	11	.522	4.01	28	28	2	1	0	0	179.1	201	774	101	80	15	5	3	7	45	0	113	6	0
Sikorski, Brian, Okla.	10	9	.526	4.04	24	23	5	2	1	1	140.1	131	591	73	63	9	2	8	3	60	1	99	3	5
Michalak, Chris, Alb.*	11	3	.786	4.26	23	21	1	0	0	0	133.0	166	587	72	63	18	6	4	4	55	0	83	4	3
Carlyle, Buddy, L.V.	8	6	.571	4.29	27	27	1	0	0	0	151.0	165	656	93	72	25	5	1	2	44	0	127	3	0
Austin, Jeff, Oma.	7	9	.438	4.48	23	19	1	1	1	0	126.2	150	551	85	63	16	3	7	4	35	1	57	8	1
Dickey, R.A., Okla.	8	9	.471	4.49	30	23	2	0	2	1	158.1	167	680	83	79	13	4	9	7	65	1	85	5	2
Judd, Mike, Alb.	7	6	.538	4.51	24	23	1	0	1	0	141.2	153	628	86	71	12	7	4	12	62	0	92	9	1

DEPARTMENTAL LEADERS: W—Ahearne, 13; L—Norton, Shields, Linton, 13 each; Pct.—Ryan, .818; G—Gandarillas, Crabtree, 63 each; GS—Linton, Driskill, 28 each; CG—Linton, 6; ShO—Linton, 3; GF—T. Williams, 46; Sv.—T. Williams, 32; IP—Driskill, 179.1; H—Perkins, 207; TBF—Driskill, 774; R—Perkins, 131; ER—Perkins, 115; HR—R. Franklin, 28; SH—Linton, 3; SF—Linton, 10; HB—Shields, 14; BB—Norton, 104; IBB—Bailey, 10; SO—Shields, 156; WP—Parra, 14; BK—Sikorski, 5.

ALL PITCHERS

*Lefthanded pitcher.

Pitcher, Team	W	L	Pct.	ERA	G	GS	CG	ShO	GF	Sv.	IP	H	TBF	R	ER	HR	SH	SF	HB	BB	IBB	SO	WP	Bk.
Adkins, Jon, Sac.	0	1	.000	9.00	1	1	0	0	0	0	4.0	6	19	4	4	2	0	0	0	1	0	2	0	0
Ahearne, Pat, Tac.	13	8	.619	3.86	29	26	1	0	0	0	168.0	190	725	92	72	11	5	2	1	53	5	92	5	1
Ah Yat, Paul, Nash.*	3	9	.250	4.07	19	18	0	0	0	1	110.2	110	468	55	50	14	1	5	3	36	0	60	6	0
Akers, Chad, Tac.	0	0	.000	0.00	1	0	0	0	0	0	0.0	0	1	0	0	0	0	0	0	1	0	0	0	0
Alexander, Chad, Tac.	0	1	.000	6.75	1	0	0	0	0	0	1.1	1	8	1	1	0	0	0	0	4	0	0	0	0
Almanzar, Carlos, L.V.	0	0	.000	4.50	4	0	0	0	0	0	6.0	9	28	4	3	1	0	0	0	0	0	7	0	0
Almonte, Hector, Cal.	0	4	.000	11.17	18	0	0	0	13	3	19.1	36	98	24	24	7	1	0	0	9	0	16	2	1
Alston, Garvin, Alb.	2	0	1.000	3.96	10	0	0	0	2	0	25.0	23	107	12	11	2	0	3	2	12	0	19	3	0
Alvarez, Juan, Edm.*	3	1	.750	2.82	44	0	0	0	15	0	38.1	30	158	12	12	3	3	0	1	19	1	27	2	0
Ambrose, John, Mem.	1	1	.500	5.49	13	0	0	0	3	1	19.2	24	97	12	12	1	0	3	0	20	0	8	4	0
Anderson, Jimmy, Nash.*	0	0	.000	4.15	2	2	0	0	0	0	13.0	18	55	6	6	0	0	1	4	0	7	1	0	0
Anderson, Ryan, Tac.*	5	8	.385	3.98	20	20	1	1	0	0	104.0	83	439	51	46	8	0	1	3	55	0	146	7	3
Andra, Jeff, Fres.*	0	3	.000	8.73	7	7	0	0	0	0	33.0	49	171	35	32	9	1	1	1	24	0	16	1	0
Andrews, Jeff, Tuc.	1	2	.333	6.63	16	5	0	0	2	0	38.0	47	182	31	28	2	2	4	1	26	1	21	3	1
Andujar, Luis, L.V.-Nash.	3	5	.375	5.70	35	0	0	0	15	3	53.2	64	252	38	34	11	3	2	2	22	2	37	2	0
Arnold, Jamie, Alb.-Iowa	6	8	.429	4.99	23	16	0	0	1	0	110.0	116	498	72	61	7	4	1	8	64	0	57	4	0
Arroyo, Bronson, Nash.	8	2	.800	3.65	13	13	1	0	0	0	88.2	82	363	43	36	7	6	2	3	25	3	52	5	1
Arroyo, Luis, Cal.*	1	1	.500	5.74	7	0	0	0	2	0	15.2	16	71	10	11	3	1	2	0	8	0	9	0	1
Atchison, Scott, Tac.	1	1	.500	3.81	5	5	0	0	0	0	26.0	22	103	11	11	3	0	0	0	6	0	18	0	0
Austin, Jeff, Oma.	7	9	.438	4.48	23	19	1	1	1	0	126.2	150	551	85	63	16	3	7	4	35	1	57	8	1
Ayala, Bobby, Iowa-Alb.	3	2	.600	4.83	34	0	0	0	23	6	41.0	41	180	23	22	3	1	2	2	18	1	48	3	0
Ayers, Mike, Nash.*	0	0	.000	5.74	11	0	0	0	6	1	15.2	22	74	11	10	5	0	0	6	0	11	1	0
Bailey, Cory, Nash.	2	4	.333	3.47	55	0	0	0	41	12	72.2	76	318	32	28	2	4	5	1	35	10	62	8	1
Baker, Jason, Oma.	1	3	.250	6.25	7	6	0	0	1	0	36.0	40	161	28	25	9	0	2	2	14	0	18	4	0
Baptist, Travis, Nash.*	4	10	.286	5.62	34	16	3	0	6	0	133.0	146	578	85	83	17	8	4	7	51	3	93	11	2
Barker, Richie, Iowa	0	1	.000	7.62	10	0	0	0	2	1	13.0	20	70	12	11	0	0	0	1	9	0	10	3	1
Barnes, Brian, Cal.*	1	3	.250	7.85	26	3	0	0	5	1	36.2	54	182	32	32	3	1	5	3	24	1	15	3	0
Barnes, John, S.L.	0	0	.000	18.00	1	0	0	0	1	0	1.0	8	8	2	2	0	0	0	1	4	0	1	0	0
Batista, Miguel, Oma.	2	2	.500	6.04	18	1	0	0	12	3	28.1	35	127	20	19	6	1	1	2	7	0	27	2	0
Beaumont, Matt, Edm.*	0	0	.000	12.27	2	1	0	0	1	0	7.1	11	40	10	10	1	0	0	1	9	0	4	1	0
Belcher, Tim, Edm.	1	1	.500	3.86	3	3	0	0	0	0	14.0	12	60	7	6	2	0	1	7	0	6	0	0
Belitz, Todd, Sac.*	0	1	.000	4.38	12	0	0	0	1	1	12.1	12	52	6	6	2	0	0	2	5	0	10	2	0
Beltran, Rigo, C.S.*	6	10	.375	5.90	25	21	1	1	1	0	125.0	132	563	85	82	15	5	3	7	63	0	95	8	2
Benes, Alan, Mem.	1	2	.333	5.95	9	8	0	0	2	0	39.1	45	179	31	26	7	2	2	1	21	0	26	3	0
Benz, Jake, Cal.*	0	0	.000	5.33	15	0	0	0	4	0	25.1	21	116	16	15	2	0	1	1	20	1	24	0	0
Bergman, Sean, Cal.	4	3	.571	5.73	13	13	0	0	0	0	81.2	107	363	55	52	8	1	3	1	23	1	48	6	0
Bierbrodt, Nick, Tuc.*	2	1	.667	4.82	4	3	0	0	0	0	18.2	13	77	10	10	3	0	0	2	14	0	11	0	0
Bieser, Steve, Mem.	0	0	.000	0.00	1	0	0	0	0	0	0.0	0	2	1	1	0	0	0	0	2	0	0	0	0
Bluma, Jaime, Oma.	5	3	.625	5.00	30	2	0	0	13	1	54.0	58	236	34	30	8	1	3	4	19	2	30	3	0
Bochtler, Doug, Oma.	2	1	.667	4.02	27	0	0	0	13	2	40.1	37	179	19	18	4	1	2	0	28	6	28	3	0
Boskie, Shawn, Edm.-Tuc.	5	6	.455	4.63	20	7	0	0	3	0	72.0	88	327	48	37	8	2	6	5	22	0	38	6	0
Bost, Heath, C.S.	0	0	.000	4.91	7	0	0	0	1	0	11.0	8	46	8	6	1	0	1	0	4	0	7	0	0
Bourgeois, Steve, C.S.	2	3	.400	5.11	9	6	0	0	1	0	44.0	40	194	30	25	6	1	0	2	21	0	39	5	0
Bowie, Micah, Iowa*	1	7	.125	7.94	9	9	0	0	0	0	45.1	59	220	44	40	9	3	1	1	31	3	35	2	0
Brohawn, Troy, Tuc.*	0	0	.000	3.78	11	1	0	0	0	0	16.2	18	71	7	7	5	1	2	1	5	0	16	0	1
Brunette, Justin, Mem.*	1	2	.333	6.15	30	0	0	0	7	0	33.2	42	159	27	23	4	3	2	1	14	2	27	1	0
Brunson, Will, Sac.*	3	0	1.000	3.65	18	0	0	0	5	0	24.2	26	111	12	10	0	2	0	1	11	1	22	0	0
Burnett, A.J., Cal.	0	0	.000	0.00	1	1	0	0	0	0	5.0	0	18	0	0	0	0	0	0	3	0	6	2	0
Burrows, Terry, Sac.*	0	1	.000	1.38	2	2	1	0	0	0	13.0	8	51	2	2	1	0	1	1	4	1	7	0	0
Busby, Mike, S.L.	0	0	.000	6.75	7	0	0	0	1	0	9.1	16	52	7	7	2	0	0	0	9	0	8	2	0
Byrdak, Tim, Oma.*	6	2	.750	4.44	34	1	0	0	17	4	52.2	59	244	27	26	5	4	1	4	29	3	47	3	2
Cabrera, Jose, N.O.	0	1	.000	2.93	12	0	0	0	8	4	15.1	15	67	6	5	0	1	1	0	5	0	12	0	0

Pitcher, Team	W	L	Pct.	ERA	G	GS	CG	ShO	GF	Sv.	IP	H	TBF	R	ER	HR	SH	SF	HB	BB	IBB	SO	WP	Bk.
Callier, Jeremy, Edm.	2	2	.500	5.64	9	2	0	0	3	0	22.1	29	104	14	14	0	2	1	1	7	1	16	0	0
Camp, Jared, Oma.	1	2	.333	13.50	13	0	0	0	2	0	12.2	19	71	24	19	4	0	0	2	13	0	13	1	0
Carlson, Dan, Tuc.	0	1	.000	1.64	4	3	0	0	1	0	22.0	25	96	9	4	1	1	2	0	7	0	12	1	0
Carlyle, Buddy, L.V.	8	6	.571	4.29	27	27	1	0	0	0	151.0	165	656	93	72	25	5	1	2	44	0	127	3	0
Carmona, Rafael, Tac.	0	1	.000	20.25	3	0	0	0	1	0	4.0	12	26	9	9	3	0	0	0	2	0	1	1	1
Carrara, Giovanni, C.S.	7	2	.778	3.26	18	15	0	0	1	0	96.2	89	403	39	35	8	3	1	5	30	1	89	4	0
Carter, Lance, Oma.	2	8	.200	4.95	34	6	0	0	13	5	76.1	88	321	46	42	13	2	2	1	18	1	51	0	1
Castillo, Carlos, Cal.	1	7	.125	7.15	13	10	0	0	1	1	61.2	94	291	59	49	6	3	3	6	16	0	37	3	2
Cather, Mike, Cal.	4	5	.444	3.98	43	0	0	0	28	8	63.1	66	280	34	28	6	4	3	3	27	2	62	0	0
Checo, Robinson, Alb.	8	3	.727	3.63	16	15	1	0	0	0	86.2	78	358	36	35	11	2	1	3	33	0	85	2	1
Chouinard, Bobby, C.S.	0	0	.000	3.63	9	0	0	0	1	1	17.1	18	73	10	7	3	0	0	3	0	0	12	1	0
Clontz, Brad, Nash.	0	0	.000	0.00	4	0	0	0	2	1	4.2	1	17	0	0	0	0	0	0	2	0	5	0	0
Cloude, Ken, Tac.	5	5	.500	5.14	14	14	1	0	0	0	75.1	88	345	56	43	10	2	1	4	36	0	62	2	2
Cole, Victor, Mem.	1	0	1.000	2.89	5	3	0	0	1	0	18.2	13	74	6	6	0	0	1	8	1	16	0	1	0
Connelly, Steve, Fres.	8	6	.571	4.37	43	0	0	0	36	9	59.2	63	254	33	29	9	3	1	2	20	0	44	1	0
Cooper, Brian, Edm.	3	7	.300	7.23	11	11	1	1	0	0	61.0	87	288	51	49	12	1	3	3	18	0	37	3	0
Corbin, Archie, Oma.	1	5	.167	8.10	32	0	0	0	15	6	43.1	56	221	44	39	5	3	2	3	40	1	29	9	0
Cordero, Francisco, Okla.	0	0	.000	4.15	3	0	0	0	3	1	4.1	7	23	3	2	0	0	0	0	3	0	5	1	0
Corey, Bryan, Sac.	8	3	.727	4.24	47	6	0	0	16	4	85.0	88	362	43	40	11	4	3	3	29	2	55	2	1
Cornelius, Reid, Cal.	2	2	.500	4.57	8	8	0	0	0	0	43.1	45	190	23	22	5	2	1	1	18	0	22	1	0
Corsi, Jim, Tuc.	4	3	.571	5.20	32	2	0	0	9	2	36.1	35	156	23	21	4	1	1	0	21	0	33	1	2
Cox, Ryan, Fres.	0	0	.000	18.00	1	0	0	0	1	0	1.0	3	6	2	2	0	0	0	0	0	0	1	1	0
Crabtree, Robbie, Fres.	5	6	.455	3.81	63	0	0	0	21	8	127.2	126	544	67	54	8	7	4	7	31	5	116	2	0
Crafton, John, Oma.	0	0	.000	6.75	2	0	0	0	1	0	2.2	4	12	2	2	0	0	0	1	0	0	0	0	0
Creek, Ryan, Cal.-Tuc.	0	1	.000	16.88	7	0	0	0	2	0	10.2	20	64	20	20	1	0	4	0	12	1	7	0	0
Cressend, Jack, S.L.	4	4	.500	3.44	54	1	0	0	20	8	86.1	87	380	40	33	3	4	3	1	39	4	87	6	0
Croushore, Rich, C.S.	2	4	.333	7.36	33	2	0	0	12	0	36.2	40	178	31	30	4	2	4	2	32	1	30	6	0
Cubillan, Darwin, Okla.	0	0	.000	1.08	8	0	0	0	6	2	16.2	9	61	2	2	0	0	0	4	0	12	0	0
Cumberland, Chris, Fres.*	0	3	.000	9.93	9	4	0	0	0	0	29.0	40	137	32	32	12	1	2	1	15	0	10	1	0
Cunnane, Will, L.V.	7	4	.636	3.98	17	17	1	1	0	0	97.1	96	407	46	43	7	1	3	3	26	0	97	1	0
Curl, John, L.V.	0	1	.000	13.50	1	0	0	0	1	0	0.2	2	5	1	1	0	0	1	0	1	0	0	0	0
Dace, Derek, Tuc.*	2	0	1.000	4.11	31	1	0	0	11	1	35.0	37	155	17	16	2	2	0	0	15	1	21	1	0
D'Amico, Jeff, Oma.	3	3	.500	3.83	16	16	1	0	0	0	91.2	87	386	39	39	16	1	0	7	26	1	66	6	2
Davey, Tom, Tac.-L.V.	9	8	.529	4.53	41	12	0	0	8	2	109.1	131	498	72	55	10	0	2	3	44	0	94	4	0
Davis, Clint, Tuc.	1	3	.250	4.10	49	2	0	0	19	3	74.2	80	336	43	34	3	4	3	2	30	5	56	2	1
Davis, Doug, Okla.*	8	3	.727	2.84	12	12	2	0	0	0	69.2	62	290	32	22	8	2	2	3	41	1	53	4	0
Davis, Jason, Fres.*	5	4	.444	6.26	46	0	0	0	16	0	77.2	104	372	60	54	10	2	1	3	36	0	39	9	1
De Jean, Mike, C.S.	1	1	.500	2.51	12	0	0	0	9	5	14.1	15	59	4	4	0	0	0	4	0	12	1	0
Del Toro, Miguel, Fres.	6	6	.500	6.01	21	20	0	0	0	0	112.1	117	502	82	75	17	6	3	7	42	0	98	4	1
DeLucia, Rich, Sac.*	1	3	.750	3.96	10	10	0	0	0	0	50.0	50	212	27	22	7	0	1	0	18	0	34	3	0
Demouy, Chris, Edm.*	0	0	.000	3.00	1	0	0	0	1	0	3.0	1	11	1	1	0	0	0	1	0	0	0	0	0
DeSilva, John, Cal.	10	9	.526	4.68	29	19	3	0	5	2	140.1	150	613	78	73	21	6	8	5	43	2	94	3	2
Dickey, R.A., Okla.	8	9	.471	4.49	30	23	2	0	2	1	158.1	167	680	83	79	13	4	9	7	65	1	85	5	2
Dickson, Jason, Edm.	0	2	.000	10.13	2	2	0	0	0	0	8.0	13	38	9	9	1	0	0	4	4	0	4	1	0
Diorio, Mike, Nash.	0	0	.000	3.86	6	3	0	0	1	0	16.1	11	76	7	7	2	0	1	17	1	12	1	0
DiPoto, Jerry, C.S.	1	0	1.000	2.00	9	0	0	0	2	1	9.0	6	35	2	2	1	0	0	3	1	12	0	0
Donnelly, Brendan, Iowa	0	3	.000	7.56	9	0	0	0	3	1	16.2	25	83	19	14	3	0	1	2	6	1	14	2	0
Dougherty, Jim, Mem.	3	7	.300	3.32	60	0	0	0	24	6	81.1	76	342	33	30	5	6	4	5	29	5	82	3	2
Driskill, Travis, N.O.	12	11	.522	4.01	28	28	2	1	0	0	179.1	201	774	101	80	15	5	3	7	45	0	113	6	0
Drumright, Mike, Cal.	9	8	.529	6.24	34	22	1	0	3	0	131.1	164	641	105	91	10	3	5	4	101	0	87	12	1
Duarte, Renney, Edm.	0	0	.000	9.00	1	0	0	0	1	0	2.0	3	10	2	2	1	0	0	0	1	0	1	0	0
Duncan, Geoff, Oma.	2	0	1.000	8.56	24	0	0	0	13	1	27.1	35	132	26	26	7	2	1	1	15	2	30	5	0
Durbin, Chad, Oma.	4	4	.500	4.46	12	12	0	0	0	0	72.2	75	303	37	36	10	0	1	1	22	0	53	0	0
Durocher, Jayson, L.V.	3	5	.375	4.95	31	0	0	0	18	7	40.0	44	187	25	22	2	2	2	3	25	3	38	6	0
Elarton, Scott, N.O.	1	0	1.000	0.75	2	2	0	0	0	0	12.0	3	42	1	1	0	0	1	4	0	12	0	0
Estes, Shawn, Fres.*	0	1	.000	9.00	1	1	0	0	0	0	3.0	5	19	3	3	2	0	0	2	2	0	2	0	0
Estrella, Luis, Fres.	1	5	.167	7.42	16	7	0	0	0	0	57.0	75	267	52	47	9	1	1	2	31	0	32	4	0
Etherton, Seth, Edm.	3	2	.600	4.01	9	9	0	0	0	0	58.1	60	248	30	26	6	0	1	1	19	0	50	3	0
Evans, Dave, Tuc.	6	4	.600	4.94	41	3	0	0	15	2	74.2	82	343	47	41	11	4	2	4	41	2	60	8	0
Eversgerd, Bryan, Mem.*	4	4	.500	3.50	48	0	0	0	8	0	72.0	67	299	32	28	9	1	4	1	20	0	52	0	0
Falteisek, Steve, Cal.	0	1	.000	19.96	5	1	0	0	0	0	7.2	23	53	18	17	2	0	1	5	0	5	1	0
Farnsworth, Kyle, Iowa	0	2	.000	3.20	22	0	0	0	22	9	25.1	24	115	10	9	1	0	1	0	18	2	22	4	1
Feliciano, Pedro, Alb.*	0	0	.000	18.00	1	0	0	0	1	0	1.0	3	9	3	2	2	0	0	0	1	0	2	0	0
Fesh, Sean, C.S.*	0	0	.000	8.59	8	0	0	0	1	0	7.1	11	39	7	7	0	0	1	5	0	4	0	0
Figueroa, Nelson, Tuc.	9	4	.692	4.31	17	16	1	0	0	0	112.0	101	455	41	35	9	2	2	0	28	2	78	8	0
Flores, Ignacio, Alb.	0	0	.000	7.56	2	2	0	0	0	0	8.1	10	43	9	7	1	0	0	0	9	0	5	0	0
Flury, Pat, Cal.	1	0	1.000	7.91	12	0	0	0	4	1	19.1	28	100	18	17	5	2	0	1	14	0	15	6	0
Ford, Ben, Iowa	1	3	.250	6.63	8	8	0	0	0	0	36.2	36	178	30	27	4	2	4	3	31	0	30	2	0
Franklin, Ryan, Tac.	11	5	.688	3.90	31	22	4	0	2	0	164.0	147	665	85	71	28	3	3	12	35	1	142	2	0
Franklin, Wayne, N.O.*	3	3	.500	3.63	48	0	0	0	15	4	44.2	51	208	29	18	4	3	1	2	19	3	37	1	0
Freehill, Mike, Okla.	2	2	.500	5.63	16	0	0	0	7	0	24.0	32	122	16	15	3	0	2	20	1	17	2	0
Fuller, Jody, Tuc.	1	0	1.000	3.60	1	0	0	0	0	0	5.0	3	18	2	2	1	0	0	0	4	0	0	0
Fussell, Chris, Oma.	1	1	.500	4.98	6	6	0	0	0	0	21.2	22	99	13	12	5	1	0	3	12	0	12	0	0
Fyhrie, Mike, Edm.	2	1	.667	2.30	9	0	0	0	3	1	15.2	6	63	4	4	1	0	0	0	12	0	9	1	0
Gagne, Eric, Alb.	5	1	.833	3.88	9	9	0	0	0	0	55.2	56	233	30	24	8	2	0	15	0	59	1	0
Gajkowski, Steve, Sac.	3	3	.500	4.09	36	0	0	0	14	5	61.2	73	260	32	28	8	2	1	1	11	0	41	1	0
Gandarillas, Gus, S.L.	9	4	.692	4.94	63	1	0	0	26	7	89.2	105	399	50	49	9	4	7	2	33	4	75	6	0
Garcia, Freddy, Sac.	1	0	1.000	2.57	1	1	0	0	0	0	7.0	5	26	2	2	2	0	0	0	2	0	11	0	0
Garcia, Mike, Nash.	2	2	.500	3.55	24	0	0	0	3	0	33.0	31	137	17	13	5	1	2	8	0	31	0	0
Garibay, Daniel, Iowa*	0	0	.000	2.08	1	1	0	0	0	0	4.1	3	20	1	1	0	0	0	5	1	2	0	0
Garrett, Hal, Alb.	3	4	.429	5.40	27	2	0	0	8	1	40.0	42	182	27	24	4	1	0	2	23	0	29	5	0
Garza, Chris, S.L.*	1	1	.500	6.10	19	0	0	0	11	0	20.2	28	101	19	14	1	2	1	0	13	1	19	2	0
George, Chris, Oma.*	3	2	.600	4.84	8	8	0	0	0	0	44.2	47	194	29	24	8	0	1	1	20	0	27	1	1

– 433 –

Pitcher, Team	W	L	Pct.	ERA	G	GS	CG	ShO	GF	Sv.	IP	H	TBF	R	ER	HR	SH	SF	HB	BB	IBB	SO	WP	Bk.
Gilbert, Shawn, Alb.	0	0	.000	0.00	1	0	0	0	1	1	1.0	0	3	0	0	0	0	0	0	0	0	2	0	0
Gilfillan, Jason, Oma.	0	0	.000	0.00	1	0	0	0	1	0	1.0	0	4	0	0	0	0	0	0	1	0	2	0	0
Glynn, Ryan, Okla.	4	2	.667	3.55	15	14	2	2	0	0	83.2	72	347	36	33	5	0	3	3	33	1	66	7	1
Gonzalez, Enrique, Tuc.	1	0	1.000	0.00	1	0	0	0	0	0	4.0	1	12	0	0	0	0	0	0	1	0	1	0	0
Granger, Jeff, Alb.*	0	1	.000	63.00	2	0	0	0	0	0	1.0	7	11	7	7	0	0	0	0	1	0	1	0	0
Green, Jason, N.O.	2	1	.667	2.08	10	0	0	0	7	1	13.0	10	55	3	3	0	1	0	2	4	2	12	0	0
Green, Steve, Edm.	0	4	.000	7.29	8	8	0	0	0	0	42.0	55	208	35	34	4	1	0	2	27	1	24	1	2
Greene, Rick, S.L.	2	2	.500	5.81	22	0	0	0	9	3	26.1	30	125	21	17	2	1	0	3	19	3	15	1	1
Grilli, Jason, Cal.	1	4	.200	7.19	8	8	0	0	0	0	41.1	58	204	37	33	4	3	3	2	23	0	21	6	0
Gross, Kip, N.O.	8	7	.533	3.94	25	25	2	0	0	0	157.2	156	664	80	69	20	10	6	4	44	1	94	3	0
Gryboski, Kevin, Tac.	2	2	.500	4.83	31	0	0	0	18	2	41.0	45	181	23	22	3	2	0	0	23	4	35	7	0
Guerra, Mark, N.O.	1	4	.200	6.00	9	8	0	0	1	0	45.0	58	199	32	30	3	2	1	4	5	1	25	0	0
Gunderson, Eric, Fres.*	2	1	.667	5.01	13	0	0	0	7	2	23.1	34	109	18	13	2	1	0	1	7	1	14	0	0
Guzman, Domingo, L.V.	3	5	.375	5.97	43	3	0	0	10	1	63.1	56	282	47	42	10	3	6	8	35	3	54	6	2
Guzman, Geraldo, Tuc.	4	1	.800	1.42	6	6	1	1	0	0	38.0	23	148	7	6	3	0	0	3	10	1	44	0	0
Hackman, Luther, Mem.	8	9	.471	4.74	21	21	0	0	0	0	119.2	134	522	71	63	11	5	3	5	36	1	66	1	0
Harville, Chad, Sac.	5	3	.625	4.50	53	0	0	0	29	9	64.0	53	280	35	32	8	2	1	3	35	0	77	8	0
Haynes, Heath, N.O.	0	0	.000	23.63	2	0	0	0	1	0	2.2	6	17	7	7	1	0	0	1	3	2	3	0	0
Heathcott, Mike, Iowa-Edm.	6	4	.600	5.32	41	3	0	0	20	2	88.0	107	397	58	52	8	1	6	4	39	1	41	9	0
Heaverlo, Jeff, Tac.	0	1	.000	4.85	2	2	0	0	0	0	13.0	14	54	7	7	2	0	1	0	6	0	4	1	0
Heflin, Bronson, Nash.	0	0	.000	0.00	4	0	0	0	2	0	4.2	1	15	0	0	0	0	0	0	0	0	3	0	0
Heiserman, Rick, Mem.	6	3	.667	4.09	55	1	0	0	22	6	77.0	85	340	36	35	10	6	3	2	29	3	55	6	0
Henderson, Rod, Tac.	2	1	.667	6.06	4	4	0	0	0	0	16.1	19	77	11	11	1	0	0	1	14	0	12	0	0
Henderson, Ryan, Cal.	0	0	.000	8.34	11	0	0	0	1	0	22.2	33	119	27	21	5	0	1	2	18	0	21	2	0
Henderson, Scott, Cal.	0	1	.000	5.06	8	0	0	0	2	0	10.2	10	51	10	6	1	0	1	1	6	0	12	4	0
Hernandez, Fernando, N.O.	3	3	.500	3.26	36	1	0	0	13	3	60.2	41	257	28	22	5	2	0	3	33	4	88	4	0
Herndon, Junior, L.V.	10	11	.476	5.13	26	26	3	0	0	0	135.0	151	610	90	77	13	5	2	4	65	2	75	5	0
Hiatt, Phil, C.S.	0	0	.000	0.00	1	0	0	0	1	0	1.0	0	4	0	0	0	0	0	0	1	0	1	0	0
Hill, Ken, Edm.	0	0	.000	6.52	2	2	0	0	0	0	9.2	14	47	8	7	4	1	0	0	8	0	5	0	0
Hinchliffe, Brett, Edm.-Iowa	4	3	.571	3.47	34	7	1	1	10	2	96.0	95	405	39	37	10	2	2	3	32	1	52	8	1
Hoane, Wes, Tac.	0	0	.000	18.00	1	0	0	0	1	0	1.0	3	7	2	2	0	0	0	0	1	0	2	0	0
Hodges, Kevin, Tac.	4	3	.571	2.76	30	11	2	1	6	3	98.0	87	393	32	30	3	3	3	8	21	1	73	1	0
Holmes, Darren, Mem.-Tuc.	1	1	.500	2.37	12	0	0	0	6	1	19.0	14	74	5	5	0	2	0	0	7	1	10	1	0
Holtz, Mike, Edm.*	0	1	.000	10.80	6	0	0	0	1	0	5.0	5	22	6	6	1	0	0	1	1	0	1	0	0
Hooten, Dave, S.L.	1	2	.333	3.90	13	0	0	0	4	1	27.2	26	112	14	12	7	0	0	0	10	0	15	0	0
House, Craig, C.S.	0	0	.000	3.24	8	0	0	0	8	4	8.1	6	32	4	3	0	0	1	1	2	0	8	1	0
Huisman, Rick, N.O.	3	5	.375	3.48	48	0	0	0	27	10	54.1	36	217	26	21	5	1	2	0	20	1	64	5	0
Hundley, Jeff, Edm.*	0	2	.000	11.57	2	1	0	0	0	0	9.1	14	47	12	12	0	0	3	2	4	0	2	2	0
Hutchinson, Chad, Mem.	0	1	.000	25.92	5	4	0	0	0	0	8.1	10	63	24	24	1	2	3	3	27	0	9	3	0
Hutton, Mark, N.O.	4	2	.667	3.60	46	0	0	0	19	3	60.0	58	259	27	24	8	2	3	3	24	0	27	1	0
Iglesias, Mario, Iowa	1	1	.500	11.07	8	2	0	0	3	0	20.1	31	105	30	25	5	0	1	0	11	2	15	4	0
James, Mike, Mem.	2	1	.667	0.93	8	0	0	0	1	1	9.2	6	39	3	1	1	0	0	1	4	0	8	1	0
Janzen, Marty, Tuc.	1	0	1.000	5.61	10	3	0	0	2	1	25.2	30	123	16	16	9	1	0	3	14	1	15	0	0
Jarvis, Kevin, C.S.	3	2	.600	0.69	7	7	0	0	0	0	39.0	18	145	6	3	1	1	1	0	13	0	18	3	0
Jennings, Robin, S.L.*	0	0	.000	9.00	1	0	0	0	1	0	1.0	3	7	1	1	0	0	1	0	1	0	1	0	0
Jensen, Ryan, Fres.	5	8	.385	5.79	26	26	1	0	0	0	135.1	167	628	106	87	18	4	9	4	63	0	114	3	1
Johnson, Jon, Okla.	4	7	.364	5.08	36	2	0	0	18	5	56.2	55	243	38	32	8	1	2	0	26	2	63	3	1
Johnstone, John, Fres.	0	0	.000	0.00	1	1	0	0	0	0	2.0	0	7	0	0	0	0	0	0	1	0	1	0	0
Jones, Greg, Edm.	2	2	.500	7.65	25	0	0	0	13	1	42.1	57	217	42	36	5	1	3	4	33	1	21	6	0
Jones, Marcus, Sac.	6	4	.600	4.35	17	17	0	0	0	0	101.1	108	434	57	49	7	3	5	2	36	0	51	3	1
Judd, Mike, Alb.	7	6	.538	4.51	24	23	1	0	1	0	141.2	153	628	86	71	12	7	4	12	62	0	92	9	1
Karchner, Matt, Iowa	2	1	.667	4.01	20	1	0	0	5	2	42.2	46	184	23	19	2	3	3	2	12	1	35	2	0
Karl, Scott, C.S.*	0	3	.000	5.66	3	2	0	0	1	0	20.2	21	88	17	13	2	1	0	0	4	1	16	0	0
Karnuth, Jason, Mem.	5	4	.556	4.04	16	13	0	0	1	0	78.0	89	341	47	35	7	4	2	5	27	0	28	3	0
Kaufman, Brad, N.O.	1	6	.143	5.70	40	1	0	0	16	2	60.0	74	297	51	38	5	3	5	4	44	3	53	5	0
Keagle, Greg, Edm.	0	0	.000	15.00	1	0	0	0	0	0	3.0	5	16	5	5	1	0	0	0	2	0	2	1	0
Kelley, Rich, Edm.*	0	1	.000	6.64	7	2	0	0	3	0	20.1	29	100	17	15	4	0	1	1	10	0	12	0	1
Kim, Byung-Hyun, Tuc.	0	0	.000	0.00	2	2	0	0	0	0	8.1	1	29	0	0	0	0	0	1	4	0	13	0	0
King, Ray, Iowa*	1	0	1.000	0.00	1	0	0	0	1	0	1.1	1	5	0	0	0	0	0	0	0	0	1	0	0
Kinney, Matt, S.L.	5	2	.714	4.25	9	9	0	0	0	0	55.0	42	228	26	26	5	1	1	1	26	0	59	2	1
Knoll, Brian, Fres.	3	4	.429	6.24	10	10	0	0	0	0	62.0	76	277	46	43	13	5	4	5	19	0	36	1	0
Knott, Eric, Tuc.*	3	2	.600	6.35	11	7	0	0	1	0	39.2	59	180	30	28	6	2	3	1	8	0	21	0	0
Kolb, Brandon, L.V.	3	3	.500	4.47	47	0	0	0	35	16	56.1	53	250	35	28	2	0	1	5	21	0	59	2	0
Kolb, Dan, Okla.	4	1	.800	0.98	13	0	0	0	13	4	18.1	11	74	6	2	0	2	1	0	8	1	18	1	0
Kroon, Marc, Alb.	0	1	.000	7.36	4	1	0	0	2	1	3.2	6	23	4	3	0	0	0	0	7	0	1	0	0
Kubenka, Jeff, Tuc.-Sac.*	2	3	.400	6.55	21	5	0	0	7	1	57.2	67	265	48	42	9	2	2	3	29	1	39	3	0
Kubinski, Tim, Sac.*	6	5	.545	5.99	41	1	0	0	14	1	67.2	84	309	52	45	10	3	3	0	22	3	51	4	1
Lankford, Frank, Sac.	1	5	.167	3.76	29	7	0	0	4	0	67.0	68	284	32	28	4	1	2	3	25	1	33	3	1
Lawrence, Brian, L.V.	4	0	1.000	1.93	8	8	0	0	0	0	46.2	48	193	13	10	6	0	0	4	7	0	46	0	0
Laxton, Brett, Oma.	5	9	.357	5.32	21	21	0	0	0	0	108.1	118	492	69	64	4	3	5	7	61	0	88	7	0
Lee, Corey, Okla.*	2	12	.143	8.76	26	21	0	0	0	0	112.0	163	569	128	109	15	3	3	2	87	1	84	3	2
Lee, David, C.S.	2	3	.400	5.96	47	0	0	0	39	12	48.1	50	223	38	32	9	2	2	2	28	1	44	1	1
Lee, Jonathan, Tuc.	1	0	1.000	0.00	1	0	0	0	0	0	2.2	1	11	0	0	0	0	0	2	0	0	1	0	0
Lehr, Charles, Sac.	0	0	.000	11.25	1	1	0	0	0	0	4.0	7	21	5	5	1	0	0	0	3	0	3	0	0
Leon, Danny, Nash.	1	2	.333	4.02	3	3	0	0	0	0	15.2	11	69	8	7	1	0	2	1	12	1	9	0	0
Lincoln, Mike, S.L.	4	1	.800	3.87	12	12	2	1	0	0	74.1	72	306	35	32	4	0	2	2	16	1	37	3	0
Linebrink, Scott, Fres.-N.O.	3	4	.429	4.56	39	7	0	0	18	5	77.0	69	321	46	39	10	0	3	1	19	0	71	6	1
Linton, Doug, C.S.	10	13	.435	5.38	28	28	6	3	0	0	174.0	189	753	109	104	15	11	10	12	42	2	136	7	2
Loewer, Carlton, L.V.	0	0	.000	0.00	1	1	0	0	0	0	4.2	3	17	0	0	0	0	0	0	0	0	4	0	0
Loiselle, Rich, Nash.	0	0	.000	0.00	4	0	0	0	1	0	4.2	2	20	0	0	0	1	1	0	2	0	3	0	0
Looney, Brian, Cal.*	0	2	.000	7.00	3	2	0	0	1	0	9.0	11	39	7	7	1	1	1	0	2	0	6	0	0
Lopez, Johan, Okla.	6	2	.750	4.15	29	0	0	0	16	5	56.1	44	230	28	26	6	0	3	2	20	2	42	3	0
Lopez, Rodrigo, L.V.	8	7	.533	4.69	20	20	1	0	0	0	109.1	123	483	66	57	9	3	7	2	45	1	100	0	0

Pitcher, Team	W	L	Pct.	ERA	G	GS	CG	ShO	GF	Sv.	IP	H	TBF	R	ER	HR	SH	SF	HB	BB	IBB	SO	WP	Bk.
Lynch, Jim, Fres.	1	0	1.000	6.30	2	2	0	0	0	0	10.0	9	46	7	7	2	0	0	1	7	0	6	1	0
Magnante, Mike, Sac.*	0	0	.000	4.05	5	2	0	0	0	0	6.2	6	27	3	3	2	0	0	1	1	0	4	0	0
Mahaffey, Alan, S.L.*	7	3	.700	5.29	34	15	0	0	5	2	102.0	118	449	62	60	16	2	4	3	40	0	74	2	3
Mahay, Ron, Cal.*	0	1	.000	4.85	8	0	0	0	3	0	13.0	7	50	7	7	1	2	1	0	7	1	15	1	0
Mahoney, Mike, Iowa	0	0	.000	45.00	1	0	0	0	1	0	1.0	4	9	5	5	1	0	0	1	1	0	0	0	0
Mairena, Ozwaldo, Iowa*	1	0	1.000	4.91	11	0	0	0	3	0	14.2	13	62	9	8	1	1	0	0	2	0	4	3	0
Manning, David, Iowa	2	5	.286	6.35	19	11	0	0	2	0	66.2	82	304	52	47	11	2	1	3	25	1	40	3	0
Mantei, Matt, Tuc.	0	0	.000	2.45	4	2	0	0	0	0	3.2	1	14	1	1	0	0	1	0	3	0	2	0	0
Manwiller, Tim, Sac.	1	2	.333	6.49	5	5	0	0	0	0	26.1	34	124	23	19	6	1	2	0	12	0	22	0	1
Manzanillo, Josias, Nash.	0	2	.000	2.70	15	0	0	0	6	3	23.1	19	93	8	7	0	0	1	2	6	1	23	1	0
Martinez, Jose, Okla.	2	5	.286	7.30	11	10	0	0	0	0	53.0	77	248	49	43	10	2	2	4	14	0	23	6	0
Masaoka, Onan, Alb.*	3	1	.750	3.86	18	5	0	0	4	0	37.1	31	172	17	16	1	1	1	0	36	1	22	2	0
Mathews, T.J., Sac.	0	0	.000	0.00	3	1	0	0	1	0	3.2	2	15	1	0	0	0	0	1	1	0	5	2	0
Mathews, Terry, Okla.	0	1	.000	6.35	7	0	0	0	3	1	11.1	13	53	10	8	1	1	1	0	5	1	10	2	0
Matthews, Mike, Mem.*	3	1	.750	3.12	9	9	0	0	0	0	52.0	33	216	19	18	4	2	0	1	32	1	50	3	0
Mattson, Rob, Nash.	6	8	.429	5.60	17	17	0	0	0	0	98.0	103	437	67	61	13	7	1	9	48	0	66	4	1
Maurer, Dave, L.V.*	4	1	.800	3.25	35	0	0	0	10	0	44.1	47	193	19	16	5	0	0	0	15	1	44	1	0
Mays, Joe, S.L.	2	0	1.000	1.72	3	3	0	0	0	0	15.2	16	64	4	3	0	1	0	1	2	0	18	2	0
McCarthy, Greg, Cal.*	4	3	.571	7.28	40	0	0	0	10	1	38.1	43	198	38	31	3	8	1	8	30	0	30	1	0
McConnell, Sam, Nash.*	1	4	.200	6.43	8	8	0	0	0	0	49.0	58	216	36	35	8	1	2	4	16	0	22	1	0
McDill, Allen, Mem.*	0	2	.000	4.38	23	0	0	0	5	0	24.2	24	114	13	12	1	1	0	0	17	0	28	1	0
McKnight, Tony, N.O.	4	8	.333	4.56	19	19	0	0	0	0	118.1	129	511	66	60	10	7	3	5	36	3	63	2	2
McMullen, Mike, Fres.	4	2	.667	4.83	36	0	0	0	12	1	50.1	37	246	35	27	2	3	5	12	52	1	41	12	1
McNichol, Brian, Iowa*	3	8	.273	5.87	43	13	0	0	14	1	115.0	131	519	81	75	20	2	6	4	52	1	105	2	1
Meacham, Rusty, N.O.	4	3	.571	2.20	33	4	0	0	8	0	57.1	43	227	16	14	5	4	1	3	14	1	56	2	0
Meche, Gil, Tac.	1	1	.500	3.86	3	3	0	0	0	0	14.0	10	61	7	6	1	0	1	0	10	0	15	0	0
Menhart, Paul, C.S.	2	1	.667	5.75	14	0	0	0	4	1	20.1	29	104	19	13	3	1	0	1	12	0	20	3	0
Meyer, Jake, Tac.	0	1	.000	3.55	8	0	0	0	4	0	12.2	9	52	5	5	2	1	0	0	5	1	14	3	0
Meyers, Mike, Iowa	2	6	.250	7.28	13	12	0	0	0	0	59.1	74	278	51	48	9	2	5	6	30	2	44	2	1
Miadich, Bart, Edm.	2	1	.667	4.57	10	0	0	0	3	1	21.2	25	101	14	11	3	1	0	0	9	0	20	2	0
Michalak, Chris, Alb.*	11	3	.786	4.26	23	21	1	0	0	0	133.0	166	587	72	63	18	6	4	4	55	0	83	4	3
Middlebrook, Jason, L.V.	0	1	.000	216.00	1	1	0	0	0	0	0.1	8	9	8	8	1	0	1	0	0	0	0	0	0
Miller, Ernie, Edm.*	0	0	.000	2.70	1	1	0	0	0	0	3.1	1	12	1	1	0	0	0	0	1	0	0	0	0
Miller, Justin, Sac.	4	1	.800	2.47	9	9	0	0	0	0	54.2	42	217	18	15	3	0	1	3	13	0	34	2	0
Miller, Matt, Okla.	3	3	.500	3.58	39	0	0	0	25	4	60.1	61	276	29	24	6	4	4	3	34	4	69	4	0
Miller, Trever, Alb.*	4	2	.667	3.41	12	9	1	1	0	0	58.0	60	248	29	22	5	2	1	1	20	0	39	2	0
Miller, Wade, N.O.	4	5	.444	3.67	16	15	0	0	0	0	105.1	95	437	46	43	6	7	1	3	38	1	81	0	1
Mintz, Steve, Edm.	4	4	.500	7.56	32	2	0	0	19	2	41.2	60	210	42	35	4	4	3	0	28	1	24	3	0
Mitchell, Dean, Okla.	3	4	.429	5.95	45	0	0	0	18	3	59.0	69	272	43	39	5	2	4	2	32	3	39	6	0
Mohler, Mike, Sac.*	2	0	1.000	6.50	18	0	0	0	6	1	18.0	22	91	13	13	6	1	0	0	16	1	14	1	0
Montane, Ivan, Tac.	0	2	.000	5.92	16	0	0	0	5	0	24.1	29	124	18	16	2	0	2	3	23	0	24	1	0
Montgomery, Matt, Alb.	1	0	1.000	7.20	7	0	0	0	1	0	10.0	15	51	8	8	3	0	0	0	7	0	6	2	0
Montgomery, Steve, L.V.	0	1	.000	27.00	1	1	0	0	0	0	0.2	2	4	2	2	0	0	0	0	0	0	1	0	0
Montoya, Saul, Tuc.	0	0	.000	2.45	3	1	0	0	0	0	7.1	6	29	2	2	1	0	0	0	2	0	8	0	0
Moody, Eric, L.V.-Cal.	1	4	.200	6.09	39	2	0	0	12	2	57.2	87	260	41	39	13	1	0	1	8	1	30	0	0
Moraga, David, C.S.*	4	1	.800	7.76	6	6	2	0	0	0	31.1	50	147	27	27	6	1	0	1	7	0	6	0	0
Morgan, Russ, Tac.*	0	0	.000	33.75	1	0	0	0	0	0	1.1	3	8	5	5	1	0	0	0	2	0	1	1	1
Morris, Matt, Mem.	1	2	.333	7.98	3	3	0	0	0	0	14.2	20	67	13	13	2	1	2	1	6	1	8	0	0
Morse, Paul, Edm.	6	5	.545	4.76	13	11	0	0	0	0	73.2	73	334	47	39	9	0	6	1	44	0	31	7	0
Mota, Danny, S.L.	0	0	.000	1.59	4	0	0	0	1	0	5.2	5	23	1	1	0	1	0	0	1	0	5	0	0
Mounce, Tony, Okla.*	1	4	.200	5.66	32	4	0	0	6	1	62.0	74	287	49	39	4	2	6	1	30	1	48	4	0
Mulder, Mark, Sac.*	1	1	.500	5.40	2	2	0	0	0	0	8.1	15	44	11	5	1	0	0	0	4	0	6	1	0
Mullen, Scott, Oma.*	2	1	.667	3.05	16	0	0	0	5	0	20.2	15	85	10	7	1	1	2	1	8	0	21	0	0
Munro, Peter, Okla.	1	2	.333	4.65	5	5	1	1	0	0	31.0	27	136	17	16	3	0	1	3	14	0	15	1	0
Murray, Dan, Oma.	10	9	.526	5.57	27	22	1	1	3	1	140.2	148	618	99	87	22	2	9	7	60	3	102	9	1
Murray, Heath, Alb.*	7	10	.412	4.73	29	24	3	1	0	0	156.0	184	703	96	82	8	4	7	8	66	5	110	7	1
Nathan, Joe, Fres.	0	2	.000	4.40	3	3	0	0	0	0	14.1	15	64	8	7	4	1	0	0	7	0	9	1	0
Naulty, Dan, Oma.	0	0	.000	48.60	4	0	0	0	0	0	1.2	5	19	9	9	1	0	0	1	8	0	0	1	0
Navarro, Jaime, C.S.	3	2	.600	5.30	5	5	0	0	0	0	35.2	48	160	26	21	8	4	0	0	6	0	20	2	0
Newman, Eric, Iowa	3	5	.375	5.47	30	8	0	0	10	0	79.0	74	350	54	48	12	6	3	1	52	4	68	5	0
Newstrom, Doug, Tuc.	0	0	.000	9.00	1	0	0	0	1	0	1.0	2	5	1	1	0	0	0	0	0	0	1	0	0
Niebla, Ruben, Alb.*	0	2	.000	6.89	24	0	0	0	11	1	32.2	42	151	25	25	3	2	2	3	15	0	25	1	3
Niedermaier, Brad, C.S.	0	0	.000	6.23	7	0	0	0	6	0	8.2	15	43	6	6	1	0	0	0	5	0	6	2	0
Nina, Elvin, Edm.	0	0	.000	2.89	3	2	0	0	0	0	9.1	11	44	6	3	0	0	1	0	6	0	3	0	1
Norris, Ben, Tuc.*	2	6	.250	7.97	12	10	0	0	0	0	55.1	88	275	56	49	7	5	2	2	29	1	28	2	1
Norton, Phillip, Iowa*	8	13	.381	4.96	28	26	2	1	0	0	159.2	166	733	100	88	16	9	6	2	104	4	126	8	2
Nunez, Maximo, Alb.	0	0	.000	4.50	1	0	0	0	0	0	2.0	1	12	1	1	0	0	1	1	5	0	0	1	0
Nunez, Vladimir, Cal.	6	7	.462	4.12	15	15	1	0	0	0	89.2	92	385	43	41	9	3	4	2	38	1	95	6	0
Nussbeck, Mark, Mem.	9	4	.692	3.96	21	21	1	1	0	0	125.0	127	536	69	55	11	4	1	2	44	0	76	3	2
O'Connor, Brian, Nash.*	2	2	.500	6.84	5	5	0	0	0	0	26.1	30	121	23	20	2	1	2	1	14	0	19	5	0
Olivares, Omar, Sac.	0	0	.000	0.00	1	1	0	0	0	0	6.0	3	21	1	0	0	0	0	0	2	0	3	0	0
Oliver, Darren, Okla.*	2	1	.667	1.97	7	7	1	1	0	0	32.0	22	128	11	7	2	0	1	1	14	0	28	0	0
Olson, Gregg, Alb.	0	0	.000	4.50	4	0	0	0	0	0	4.0	3	16	2	2	0	0	0	0	2	0	2	1	0
Ontiveros, Steve, C.S.	4	1	.800	2.91	8	8	0	0	0	0	43.1	36	177	15	14	6	1	0	3	10	1	33	2	0
Orosco, Jesse, Mem.*	0	1	.000	9.00	2	1	0	0	0	0	1.0	1	4	1	1	0	0	0	0	0	0	0	0	0
Ortiz, Ramon, Edm.	6	6	.500	4.55	15	15	1	0	0	0	89.0	74	381	49	45	7	1	7	4	37	0	76	7	1
Osteen, Gavin, Nash.*	4	1	.800	5.56	14	0	0	0	7	0	11.1	11	50	8	7	2	0	0	1	4	0	7	1	0
Osuna, Antonio, Alb.	0	0	.000	0.00	3	1	0	0	0	0	5.2	2	27	2	0	0	0	0	1	5	0	7	0	0
Padilla, Vicente, Tuc.	0	1	.000	4.42	12	3	0	0	4	1	18.1	22	82	9	9	2	2	0	0	8	0	22	2	0
Palacios, Vicente, L.V.-Iowa	6	3	.667	4.31	42	5	1	0	23	7	77.1	80	332	40	37	8	2	4	4	23	3	63	0	1
Parra, Jose, Nash.	6	5	.545	5.22	23	21	0	0	1	1	101.2	106	466	66	59	7	5	2	7	65	0	68	14	0
Patrick, Bronswell, Cal.	5	12	.294	7.08	27	23	0	0	1	0	128.1	174	595	114	101	18	8	4	3	42	0	72	1	0
Patterson, John, Tuc.	0	2	.000	7.80	3	2	0	0	0	0	15.0	21	76	14	13	1	1	1	0	9	0	10	2	0

Pitcher, Team	W	L	Pct.	ERA	G	GS	CG	ShO	GF	Sv.	IP	H	TBF	R	ER	HR	SH	SF	HB	BB	IBB	SO	WP	Bk.
Pavlas, Dave, Nash.	4	2	.667	3.39	45	0	0	0	17	5	71.2	71	311	36	27	8	7	3	4	23	3	61	2	0
Penny, Brad, Cal.	2	0	1.000	1.80	3	3	0	0	0	0	15.0	8	65	8	3	1	0	1	3	10	1	16	0	0
Perez, Eduardo, Mem.	1	0	1.000	0.00	1	0	0	0	1	0	2.0	2	9	0	0	0	1	0	0	3	0	1	0	0
Perkins, Dan, S.L.	9	10	.474	7.34	33	22	0	0	3	1	141.0	207	667	131	115	26	1	7	5	51	0	97	6	3
Peters, Chris, Nash.*	2	4	.333	5.47	11	11	0	0	0	0	52.2	71	252	38	32	6	3	1	0	26	1	32	6	0
Petersen, Chris, Iowa	0	0	.000	18.00	1	0	0	0	1	0	1.0	1	6	2	2	1	0	0	1	0	0	0	0	0
Phillips, Jason, Nash.	2	4	.333	4.70	6	6	0	0	0	0	30.2	30	138	20	16	4	2	0	3	18	0	18	0	0
Pineiro, Joel, Tac.	7	1	.875	2.80	10	9	2	2	0	0	61.0	53	256	20	19	3	2	1	3	22	1	41	2	0
Plantenberg, Erik, N.L.-Cal.*	2	0	1.000	6.41	30	0	0	0	7	1	26.2	23	122	20	19	5	0	2	0	25	1	18	4	0
Porzio, Mike, C.S.*	0	3	.000	10.04	6	6	0	0	0	0	26.0	39	133	30	29	7	3	2	0	20	0	26	0	1
Pote, Lou, Edm.	2	1	.667	3.52	24	0	0	0	22	12	30.2	27	133	14	12	2	1	1	0	14	0	28	3	0
Powell, Brian, N.O.	9	4	.692	4.95	18	18	1	0	0	0	103.2	103	442	63	57	9	1	4	5	41	1	57	3	1
Powell, Jay, N.O.	0	0	.000	4.50	2	1	0	0	0	0	2.0	2	9	1	1	0	0	0	0	2	0	2	0	0
Prieto, Ariel, Sac.	8	4	.667	3.27	20	18	0	0	1	0	113.0	110	469	51	41	9	1	3	1	31	1	79	4	1
Pulsipher, Bill, Tuc.*	3	8	.273	4.95	13	13	0	0	0	0	70.2	73	309	39	31	7	1	1	1	37	0	51	1	2
Quevedo, Ruben, Iowa	7	2	.778	4.22	13	13	0	0	0	0	74.2	68	322	37	35	7	4	3	1	30	1	77	1	1
Radlosky, Rob, S.L.	0	0	.000	4.26	5	2	0	0	0	0	19.0	18	81	10	9	3	0	0	2	7	0	19	1	1
Rain, Steve, Iowa	0	2	.000	3.45	28	0	0	0	21	6	31.1	31	132	14	12	4	2	1	0	6	1	34	2	0
Rakers, Jason, Oma.	3	2	.600	5.52	32	6	0	0	9	2	75.0	83	319	49	46	14	0	2	1	17	2	68	2	1
Ramirez, Hector, N.O.	0	0	.000	1.80	5	0	0	0	4	0	5.0	6	22	1	1	1	0	0	1	1	0	4	0	0
Ramsay, Robert, Tac.*	0	1	.000	4.50	3	3	0	0	0	0	16.0	16	68	8	8	1	0	0	0	6	0	6	0	0
Randall, Scott, S.L.-Okla.	7	6	.538	5.45	30	24	0	0	2	0	150.1	201	683	101	91	17	4	7	5	55	1	89	7	0
Randolph, Steve, Tuc.*	0	0	.000	8.78	5	3	0	0	1	0	13.1	11	69	13	13	3	1	1	0	19	0	6	0	0
Rath, Fred, S.L.-Mem.-Nash.	7	8	.467	4.57	37	16	0	0	3	0	124.1	135	547	83	66	18	6	2	5	52	1	62	5	0
Rath, Gary, Tuc.*	0	0	.000	10.61	11	1	0	0	5	0	9.1	16	52	12	11	2	1	1	0	10	2	8	1	0
Ratliff, Jon, Sac.	8	4	.667	3.44	20	18	0	0	1	1	107.1	102	442	48	41	12	2	3	4	31	2	72	7	1
Ray, Ken, Fres.	0	0	.000	7.45	7	0	0	0	1	0	9.2	13	49	10	8	4	1	1	0	8	0	8	2	0
Reames, Britt, Mem.	6	2	.750	2.28	13	13	2	1	0	0	75.0	55	289	20	19	2	3	4	2	20	0	77	1	0
Revenig, Todd, Tuc.	2	1	.667	2.73	17	0	0	0	9	2	26.1	29	110	8	8	1	1	0	0	4	0	28	1	0
Reyes, Al, Alb.	3	2	.600	3.72	30	0	0	0	22	8	38.2	33	173	20	16	5	3	2	1	21	0	39	4	0
Reyes, Carlos, L.V.	0	2	.000	2.86	16	0	0	0	5	1	28.1	28	125	13	9	5	2	1	0	9	1	24	1	0
Ricketts, Chad, Alb.	6	2	.750	3.46	54	0	0	0	27	7	67.2	59	294	35	26	7	5	2	5	36	2	75	3	0
Riley, Mike, Fres.*	6	8	.429	5.91	24	24	0	0	0	0	128.0	141	578	92	84	21	5	3	4	54	0	114	6	0
Rivette, Scott, Tac.	0	0	.000	8.10	3	0	0	0	1	0	3.1	5	17	3	3	0	0	0	3	0	4	2	0
Rizzo, Todd, S.L.*	6	4	.600	3.39	61	0	0	0	14	1	71.2	76	315	31	27	1	3	1	0	27	1	43	4	0
Robertson, Jeriome, N.O.*	1	7	.125	7.07	9	9	0	0	0	0	49.2	64	228	42	39	10	2	2	3	23	1	27	1	0
Rodriguez, Frank, Tac.	2	1	.667	4.84	9	6	0	0	1	0	35.1	30	148	20	19	1	0	1	4	11	0	26	0	0
Rodriguez, Jose, Mem.*	4	2	.667	3.80	40	0	0	0	17	3	47.1	48	200	21	20	4	5	1	0	19	1	37	0	1
Romano, Mike, S.L.	7	6	.538	6.14	16	16	1	0	0	0	95.1	122	435	71	65	11	3	2	8	30	0	54	6	1
Romero, J.C., S.L.*	4	2	.667	3.44	17	11	1	0	4	4	65.1	60	278	40	25	6	1	2	4	25	0	38	3	0
Root, Derek, L.V.*	0	1	.000	9.00	9	2	0	0	2	0	14.0	18	71	15	14	1	0	1	1	10	1	7	2	0
Rosengren, John, Nash.*	0	1	.000	6.75	4	0	0	0	0	0	2.2	0	14	2	2	0	0	0	1	4	0	4	1	0
Ruffin, Johnny, Tuc.	5	3	.625	2.98	45	0	0	0	36	20	57.1	48	245	21	19	4	1	0	0	25	1	66	2	0
Ryan, Jason, S.L.	9	2	.818	4.38	17	17	2	1	0	0	96.2	94	419	52	47	16	1	2	6	31	0	66	6	0
Sabel, Erik, Tuc.	4	11	.267	7.23	29	15	0	0	5	1	98.1	149	473	90	79	16	4	8	5	31	4	61	4	0
Saipe, Mike, C.S.-L.V.-Edm.	4	6	.400	9.41	21	13	0	0	2	1	80.1	133	399	93	84	24	3	6	4	32	0	55	1	0
Sak, Jim, Nash.	0	0	.000	51.30	6	0	0	0	3	0	3.1	6	35	19	19	2	1	0	2	18	0	4	4	0
Sampson, Benj, S.L.*	5	3	.625	8.19	18	13	0	0	0	0	70.1	114	342	67	64	15	2	3	3	22	3	47	4	1
Sanders, Scott, Edm.-Cal.-Sac.	6	8	.429	6.51	22	15	1	0	1	0	103.2	133	470	76	75	14	4	5	1	40	0	86	5	0
Santiago, Jose, Oma.	0	1	.000	3.18	11	0	0	0	7	4	17.0	19	71	7	6	2	0	0	0	3	1	14	1	0
Sauerbeck, Scott, Nash.*	0	0	.000	0.00	2	0	0	0	0	0	2.0	1	6	0	0	0	0	0	0	0	0	0	0	0
Sauveur, Rich, Sac.*	5	2	.714	4.57	25	11	0	0	2	1	82.2	88	357	48	42	7	0	3	4	25	1	59	0	0
Scheffer, Aaron, Tac.	1	6	.143	5.06	21	0	0	0	6	1	32.0	26	141	22	18	5	6	5	1	15	1	21	2	0
Schoeneweis, Scott, Edm.*	0	0	.000	0.00	1	1	0	0	0	0	7.0	2	25	1	0	0	0	0	1	0	0	6	0	0
Scott, Darryl, C.S.-Tuc.	2	2	.500	9.89	16	0	0	0	6	0	23.2	36	117	30	26	6	0	0	0	12	1	23	3	0
Serafini, Dan, L.V.-Nash.*	6	7	.462	4.87	33	11	0	0	0	0	98.0	113	448	61	53	10	5	5	7	41	2	67	4	0
Sergio, Tom, Okla.	0	0	.000	0.00	1	0	0	0	0	0	0.2	0	5	0	0	0	0	0	0	3	1	0	0	0
Serrano, Wascar, L.V.	0	1	.000	14.18	4	4	0	0	0	0	13.1	24	75	23	21	5	0	0	2	10	0	19	4	1
Service, Scott, Sac.	6	2	.750	1.30	33	0	0	0	31	13	41.2	27	166	8	6	1	1	0	0	11	4	50	5	1
Shields, Scot, Edm.	7	13	.350	5.41	27	27	4	1	0	0	163.0	158	734	114	98	16	1	6	14	82	0	156	7	0
Sikorski, Brian, Okla.	10	9	.526	4.04	24	23	5	2	1	1	140.1	131	591	73	63	9	2	8	3	60	1	99	3	5
Sinclair, Steve, Tac.*	4	3	.571	4.50	45	0	0	0	8	3	58.0	68	265	36	29	6	3	2	1	27	5	45	3	1
Skrmetta, Matt, Nash.	1	0	1.000	3.24	7	0	0	0	6	2	8.1	6	34	4	3	2	0	0	0	2	0	13	1	0
Slusarski, Joe, N.O.	2	1	.667	2.25	13	0	0	0	6	0	20.0	14	84	9	5	2	0	0	1	7	5	21	0	0
Small, Aaron, C.S.	11	6	.647	5.61	36	18	0	0	2	0	131.2	152	596	87	82	14	1	6	13	43	0	85	3	0
Smith, Bud, Mem.*	5	1	.833	2.15	9	8	0	0	0	0	54.1	40	213	24	13	4	2	1	1	15	0	34	0	0
Smith, Cam, Alb.	7	3	.700	4.28	39	0	0	0	12	5	61.0	61	297	43	29	3	5	6	12	48	0	56	5	0
Smith, Chuck, Okla.	5	3	.625	3.78	11	11	1	0	0	0	66.2	73	300	31	28	3	2	2	2	38	1	73	5	0
Snow, Bert, Sac.	0	0	.000	4.50	3	0	0	0	2	0	2.0	1	10	1	1	0	0	0	0	3	0	3	0	0
Sodowsky, Clint, Okla.	2	1	.667	2.91	13	0	0	0	7	2	21.2	23	88	7	7	2	0	0	2	4	0	13	3	0
Sollecito, Gabe, Okla.	0	0	.000	7.71	7	0	0	0	1	0	9.1	12	46	8	8	2	0	1	0	6	0	10	0	0
Spencer, Sean, Tac.*	3	2	.600	3.38	42	0	0	0	20	0	45.1	35	208	21	17	3	5	2	1	37	3	46	3	2
Spencer, Stan, L.V.	4	0	1.000	1.72	6	6	0	0	0	0	36.2	29	146	9	7	2	1	3	1	7	0	40	3	1
Spoljaric, Paul, Oma.*	2	2	.333	2.82	43	0	0	0	25	7	51.0	44	210	17	16	5	1	4	0	19	0	56	4	0
Stechschultc, Gene, Mem.	4	1	.800	2.45	41	0	0	0	38	26	47.2	38	195	13	13	4	5	0	1	18	4	37	1	0
Steenstra, Kennie, Mem.-Tuc.	9	5	.643	3.98	34	20	1	0	5	2	156.0	187	689	79	69	16	10	4	6	53	0	75	0	0
Stein, Blake, Oma.	2	0	1.000	0.73	2	2	0	0	0	0	12.1	9	49	1	1	1	0	0	2	0	14	0	0
Stentz, Brent, S.L.	4	2	.667	1.93	42	0	0	0	35	6	46.2	31	183	14	10	6	1	0	1	13	1	47	1	1
Stone, Ricky, Alb.	9	5	.643	4.94	48	7	0	0	22	5	120.1	146	535	79	66	9	7	6	7	42	3	75	10	0
Stoops, Jim, C.S.	0	0	.000	2.45	3	0	0	0	0	0	3.2	6	23	2	1	0	0	0	0	6	0	4	2	0
Strong, Joe, Cal.	2	1	.667	4.03	29	1	0	0	21	9	44.2	44	198	21	20	1	1	2	4	20	1	33	7	0
Suarez, Felipe, Edm.	0	0	.000	18.00	1	0	0	0	0	0	1.0	2	5	2	2	0	0	0	0	0	0	0	1	0
Sullivan, Brendan, L.V.	2	5	.286	6.21	45	5	0	0	10	0	82.2	101	390	60	57	9	8	1	6	47	1	52	2	0

– 436 –

Pitcher, Team	W	L	Pct.	ERA	G	GS	CG	ShO	GF	Sv.	IP	H	TBF	R	ER	HR	SH	SF	HB	BB	IBB	SO	WP	Bk.
Sweeney, Brian, Tac.	0	1	.000	6.00	2	1	0	0	0	0	6.0	9	26	4	4	2	0	0	0	1	0	1	1	0
Tabaka, Jeff, C.S.*	0	2	.000	7.66	22	0	0	0	8	0	22.1	30	109	19	19	3	2	3	1	9	0	26	4	0
Tebbs, Nate, L.V.	0	0	.000	10.13	3	0	0	0	3	0	2.2	2	11	3	3	2	0	0	0	1	0	1	0	0
Thompson, Justin, Okla.*	0	0	.000	11.12	1	1	0	0	0	0	5.2	10	30	8	7	0	0	1	0	4	0	4	1	0
Thompson, Mark, Mem.	2	0	1.000	2.03	6	5	0	0	0	0	31.0	31	126	9	7	1	2	0	2	5	0	15	0	0
Tollberg, Brian, L.V.	6	0	1.000	2.83	13	13	0	0	0	0	76.1	72	311	28	24	5	1	2	2	11	0	60	0	0
Tomko, Brett, Tac.	1	0	1.000	2.84	2	2	0	0	0	0	12.2	13	53	4	4	1	0	0	0	5	1	8	0	0
Torres, Melqui, Tac.	1	0	1.000	5.06	1	1	0	0	0	0	5.1	7	22	3	3	0	0	0	0	1	0	2	2	0
Tremie, Chris, Cal.	0	0	.000	0.00	2	0	0	0	2	0	1.1	1	6	0	0	0	0	0	0	1	0	0	0	0
Tuttle, Dave, Tuc.	3	4	.429	4.80	20	13	0	0	1	0	80.2	85	355	52	43	7	1	5	3	36	1	62	2	1
Tyler, Josh, Fres.	0	0	.000	9.00	2	0	0	0	2	0	3.0	6	17	3	3	0	0	0	0	1	0	0	1	0
Ulloa, Enmanuel, Tac.	0	1	.000	5.40	1	1	0	0	0	0	5.0	2	21	3	3	0	0	0	0	4	0	4	0	0
Van Poppel, Todd, Iowa	3	4	.429	3.10	10	6	0	0	2	0	40.2	37	172	18	14	2	1	0	5	10	0	52	6	0
Verdugo, Jason, Fres.	0	5	.000	8.60	11	7	0	0	0	0	30.1	44	144	32	29	10	1	0	0	11	0	20	1	1
Verplancke, Jeff, Fres.	0	0	.000	1.80	1	0	0	0	0	0	5.0	3	20	1	1	0	0	0	0	2	0	6	0	0
Villano, Mike, Nash.	5	3	.625	6.42	45	1	0	0	11	2	75.2	77	338	64	54	13	3	2	3	43	3	56	6	2
Villarreal, Oscar, Tuc.	1	0	1.000	2.08	2	0	0	0	0	0	4.1	6	19	1	1	0	0	0	0	2	0	4	0	0
Vizcaino, Luis, Sac.	6	2	.750	5.03	33	2	0	0	12	5	48.1	48	204	27	27	4	5	3	1	21	0	41	1	0
Vosberg, Ed, C.S.*	1	2	.333	6.86	29	3	0	0	4	2	42.0	59	204	41	32	4	3	2	1	20	0	37	4	1
Wainhouse, David, Mem.	4	4	.500	6.28	20	6	0	0	2	0	43.0	55	199	32	30	8	1	2	3	20	0	20	1	0
Walker, Jamie, Oma.*	3	10	.231	5.22	24	15	0	0	3	0	101.2	138	446	65	59	25	2	1	7	25	1	52	0	0
Walker, Pete, C.S.	7	3	.700	3.07	58	0	0	0	22	5	73.1	64	315	29	25	3	4	1	3	30	1	61	6	0
Wall, Donne, L.V.	0	0	.000	0.00	2	0	0	0	0	0	2.0	3	10	0	0	0	0	0	0	2	0	1	1	0
Wallace, Jeff, Nash.*	0	0	.000	0.64	13	0	0	0	6	1	14.0	11	56	1	1	1	0	1	1	6	1	12	2	0
Ward, Bryan, Edm.*	0	0	.000	4.26	6	0	0	0	2	1	6.1	12	30	4	3	0	0	0	0	1	1	3	0	0
Ward, Jeremy, Tuc.	0	1	.000	5.40	5	0	0	0	2	0	3.1	3	17	2	2	0	0	0	1	5	0	1	0	0
Washburn, Jarrod, Edm.*	3	0	1.000	3.52	5	5	0	0	0	0	30.2	35	131	13	12	2	0	1	0	13	0	20	3	0
Watkins, Scott, C.S.*	3	1	.750	4.33	43	7	0	0	7	1	81.0	93	364	51	39	6	3	4	3	43	1	42	6	2
Watson, Mark, Tac.*	2	1	.667	3.96	16	0	0	0	4	0	25.0	30	111	16	11	3	0	3	0	6	0	17	0	1
Weaver, Eric, Edm.	1	2	.333	4.14	34	0	0	0	28	13	37.0	37	164	20	17	5	1	1	2	13	0	36	3	0
Weber, Ben, Fres.	4	8	.333	2.42	38	3	0	0	26	7	78.0	72	328	31	21	7	7	4	3	20	0	66	6	2
Wehner, John, Nash.	0	0	.000	16.20	2	0	0	0	2	0	1.2	6	12	3	3	0	0	0	1	1	0	1	0	0
Weibl, Clint, Mem.	9	4	.692	2.83	19	18	2	2	0	0	120.2	98	481	45	38	11	1	2	6	37	0	92	1	1
Whisenant, Matt, L.V.*	0	3	.000	5.31	33	0	0	0	8	0	39.0	49	190	26	23	3	0	0	3	26	2	24	4	0
Whiteside, Matt, L.V.	2	5	.286	5.28	23	1	0	0	5	0	30.2	34	144	21	18	6	2	2	3	15	2	31	1	1
Wilkins, Marc, Nash.	2	3	.400	4.97	17	4	0	0	7	3	38.0	34	172	23	21	4	3	0	4	24	1	33	7	0
Williams, Jeff, Alb.*	4	3	.571	4.26	12	12	0	0	0	0	63.1	64	266	33	30	6	2	1	2	28	0	38	7	0
Williams, Shad, Edm.	1	5	.167	5.50	22	5	0	0	5	1	54.0	67	247	41	33	5	1	1	2	23	0	34	1	0
Williams, Todd, Tac.	2	3	.400	2.98	50	0	0	0	46	32	51.1	51	213	20	17	2	3	2	0	18	1	26	0	0
Williams, Woody, L.V.	0	0	.000	1.50	1	1	0	0	0	0	6.0	7	24	2	1	1	0	0	0	0	0	5	0	0
Wise, Matt, Edm.	9	6	.600	3.69	19	19	2	1	0	0	124.1	122	510	54	51	10	2	7	2	26	0	82	0	1
Wojciechowski, Steve, Fres.-Cal.*	2	6	.250	6.21	33	14	0	0	7	1	91.1	130	432	74	63	15	3	3	0	39	1	64	5	0
Wolff, Bryan, N.O.-S.L.	6	4	.600	5.23	20	18	1	1	1	0	113.2	116	495	71	66	14	4	4	4	45	0	89	8	1
Wood, Kerry, Iowa	0	0	.000	2.57	1	1	0	0	0	0	7.0	4	27	2	2	1	0	0	0	4	0	7	1	0
Worrell, Tim, Iowa	2	0	1.000	5.06	6	0	0	0	0	0	10.2	9	44	6	6	3	0	0	1	5	1	7	2	0
Young, Danny, Iowa*	2	1	.667	5.59	27	0	0	0	10	1	37.0	36	169	27	23	3	3	1	2	22	1	30	3	0
Zambrano, Carlos, Iowa	2	5	.286	3.97	34	0	0	0	17	6	56.2	54	259	30	25	3	5	4	2	40	2	46	3	0
Zancanaro, Dave, Iowa*	4	10	.286	5.23	25	20	0	0	2	0	115.1	131	517	80	67	19	3	0	6	54	2	67	5	2
Zerbe, Chad, Fres.*	7	3	.700	4.32	17	11	0	0	1	0	81.1	94	347	46	39	5	3	2	5	17	0	41	1	1
Zimmerman, Jordan, Tac.*	0	1	.000	6.65	15	0	0	0	2	0	23.0	27	108	20	17	3	0	0	0	11	1	23	1	0
Zito, Barry, Sac.*	8	5	.615	3.19	18	18	0	0	0	0	101.2	88	437	44	36	4	5	3	2	45	0	91	5	0
Zosky, Eddie, Nash.	0	0	.000	9.00	1	0	0	0	1	0	1.0	1	7	1	1	0	0	0	1	2	0	1	0	0

COMBINATION SHUTOUTS: **Albuquerque (6)**—Osuna-Arnold, Arnold-Garrett-Niebla, Judd-Garrett-Ricketts, Checo-Stone, Gagne-Ayala. **Calgary (0)**—None. **Colorado Springs (3)**—Small-Croushore-Tabaka, Small-Chouinard-Tabaka, Small-Menhart. **Edmonton (1)**—Wise-Hinchliffe. **Fresno (1)**—Riley-Connelly. **Iowa (2)**—Van Poppel-Ayala-Rain, Van Poppel-Heathcott. **Las Vegas (6)**—Tollberg-Serafini-Whiteside-Kolb, Herndon-Serafini-Whiteside, Carlyle-Serafini-Guzman, Tollberg-Maurer-Guzman-Whisenant-Palacios, Sullivan-Guzman-Maurer-Kolb, Herndon-Whiteside-Durocher. **Memphis (8)**—Matthews-Stechschulte, Steenstra-Heiserman, Nussbeck-Stechschulte-Dougherty-Rath, Thompson-Stechschulte, Weibl-Heiserman, Weibl-Stechschulte, Reames-Rodriguez-Heiserman, Smith-Brunette-Bougherty. **Nashville (8)**—Diorio-Garcia-Manzanillo, Phillips-Garcia-Bailey, Phillips-Wilkins, Peters-Andujar-Wilkins, Serafini-Andujar, Serafini-Villano, Rath-Wallace-Bailey, Parra-Ayers-Heflin. **New Orleans (6)**—Miller-Hutton, Powell-Kaufman-Huisman, Powell-Miller-Franklin-Huisman, Gross-Huisman-Hutton, Guerra-Hutton-Kaufman, McKnight-Linebrink. **Oklahoma (2)**—Davis-Mathews, Davis-Sollecito. **Omaha (1)**—Durbin-Corbin-Byrdak. **Salt Lake (2)**—Randall-Rath-Gandarillas, Ryan-Rizzo-Mota-Garza. **Sacramento (6)**—Sauver-Kubinski-Service, Zito-Kubinski-Service, Prieto-Service, Zito-Corey-Harville, Zito-Corey-Kubinski-Gajkowski, Corey-Vizcaino-Harville. **Tacoma (8)**—Anderson-Hodges-Williams, Davey-Williams, Ahearne-Montane-Spencer-Williams, Anderson-Montane-Spencer-Hodges, Ahearne-Watson, Henderson-Rodriguez-Heiserman, Franklin-Williams, Hodges-Rodriguez. **Tucson (3)**—Randolph-Evans-Padilla, Figueroa-Ruffin, Tuttle-Ruffin.

NO-HIT GAMES: None.

PITCHERS WITH TWO OR MORE TEAMS

Pitcher, Team	W	L	Pct.	ERA	G	GS	CG	ShO	GF	Sv.	IP	H	TBF	R	ER	HR	SH	SF	HB	BB	IBB	SO	WP	Bk.
Andujar, Luis, L.V.	2	1	.667	6.46	10	0	0	0	4	0	15.1	18	73	13	11	6	0	2	2	4	0	8	1	0
Andujar, Luis, Nash.	1	4	.200	5.40	25	0	0	0	11	3	38.1	46	179	25	23	5	3	0	0	18	2	29	1	0
Arnold, Jamie, Alb.	4	7	.364	5.07	20	13	0	0	1	0	92.1	94	415	62	52	5	3	1	6	54	0	47	3	0
Arnold, Jamie, Iowa	2	1	.667	4.58	3	3	0	0	0	0	17.2	22	83	10	9	2	1	0	2	10	0	10	1	0
Ayala, Bobby, Iowa	1	2	.333	4.61	10	0	0	0	1	0	13.2	12	60	7	7	1	0	0	0	7	0	17	0	0
Ayala, Bobby, Alb.	2	0	1.000	4.94	24	0	0	0	22	9	27.1	29	120	16	15	2	1	2	2	11	1	31	3	0
Boskie, Shawn, Edm.	3	2	.600	4.28	14	2	0	0	2	0	40.0	51	180	22	19	4	0	2	2	16	0	22	5	0
Boskie, Shawn, Tuc.	2	4	.333	5.06	6	5	0	0	1	0	32.0	37	147	26	18	4	2	4	3	6	0	16	1	0
Creek, Ryan, Cal.	0	0	.000	19.64	3	0	0	0	2	0	3.2	8	25	8	8	0	0	3	0	6	0	3	0	0
Creek, Ryan, Tuc.	0	1	.000	15.43	4	0	0	0	0	0	7.0	12	39	12	12	1	0	1	0	6	1	4	0	0
Davey, Tom, Tac.	8	6	.571	4.61	28	12	0	0	6	2	93.2	104	418	59	48	10	0	1	3	37	0	77	4	0
Davey, Tom, L.V.	1	2	.333	4.02	13	0	0	0	2	0	15.2	27	80	13	7	0	0	1	0	7	0	17	0	0
Heathcott, Mike, Iowa	5	3	.625	5.62	38	1	0	0	20	2	73.2	93	336	52	46	8	0	6	2	32	1	37	8	0
Heathcott, Mike, Edm.	1	1	.500	3.77	3	2	0	0	0	0	14.1	14	61	6	6	0	1	0	2	7	0	4	1	0
Hinchliffe, Brett, Edm.	2	3	.400	3.80	27	3	0	0	10	2	64.0	63	272	29	27	6	1	2	2	24	0	30	8	1

Pitcher, Team	W	L	Pct.	ERA	G	GS	CG	ShO	GF	Sv.	IP	H	TBF	R	ER	HR	SH	SF	HB	BB	IBB	SO	WP	Bk.
Hinchliffe, Brett, Iowa	2	0	1.000	2.81	7	4	1	1	0	0	32.0	32	133	10	10	4	1	0	1	8	1	22	0	0
Holmes, Darren, Mem.	0	0	.000	2.45	9	0	0	0	3	0	14.2	10	54	4	4	0	2	0	0	3	0	8	1	0
Holmes, Darren, Tuc.	1	1	.500	2.08	3	0	0	0	3	1	4.1	4	20	1	1	0	0	0	0	4	1	2	0	0
Kubenka, Jeff, Tuc.*	0	2	.000	6.75	4	0	0	0	1	0	9.1	10	42	7	7	1	0	0	1	6	1	6	0	0
Kubenka, Jeff, Sac.*	2	1	.667	6.52	17	5	0	0	6	1	48.1	57	223	41	35	8	2	2	2	23	0	33	3	0
Linebrink, Scott, Fres.	1	4	.200	5.23	28	7	0	0	14	4	62.0	54	255	42	36	10	0	2	1	12	0	49	3	1
Linebrink, Scott, N.O.	2	0	1.000	1.80	11	0	0	0	4	1	15.0	15	66	4	3	0	0	1	0	7	0	22	3	0
Moody, Eric, L.V.	0	1	.000	4.91	4	1	0	0	0	0	7.1	12	34	4	4	1	0	0	0	0	0	4	0	0
Moody, Eric, Cal.	1	3	.250	6.26	35	1	0	0	12	2	50.1	75	226	37	35	12	1	0	1	8	1	26	0	0
Palacios, Vicente, L.V.	4	1	.800	3.42	36	0	0	0	23	7	47.1	41	199	20	18	5	1	3	2	17	2	40	0	0
Palacios, Vicente, Iowa	2	2	.500	5.70	6	5	1	0	0	0	30.0	39	133	20	19	3	1	1	2	6	1	23	0	1
Plantenberg, Erik, N.O.*	2	0	1.000	3.91	24	0	0	0	7	1	23.0	17	98	11	10	3	0	2	0	17	1	15	3	0
Plantenberg, Erik, Cal.*	0	0	.000	22.09	6	0	0	0	0	0	3.2	6	24	9	9	2	0	0	0	8	0	3	1	0
Randall, Scott, S.L.	5	3	.625	5.47	14	14	0	0	0	0	75.2	105	344	52	46	9	1	1	1	22	0	54	5	0
Randall, Scott, Okla.	2	3	.400	5.42	16	10	0	0	0	2	74.2	96	339	49	45	8	3	6	4	33	1	35	2	0
Rath, Fred, S.L.	2	1	.667	3.00	12	0	0	0	1	0	18.0	21	80	12	6	1	0	0	1	5	0	14	1	0
Rath, Fred, Mem.	2	3	.400	5.14	18	9	0	0	2	0	63.0	72	274	40	36	9	4	1	2	24	0	33	2	0
Rath, Fred, Nash.	3	4	.429	4.98	7	7	0	0	0	0	43.1	42	193	31	24	8	2	1	2	23	1	15	2	0
Saipe, Mike, C.S.	4	5	.444	9.61	15	8	0	0	1	0	54.1	94	270	67	58	18	3	5	4	16	0	37	1	0
Saipe, Mike, L.V.	0	0	.000	13.50	2	2	0	0	0	0	7.1	13	39	11	11	4	0	0	0	6	0	4	0	0
Saipe, Mike, Edm.	0	1	.000	7.23	4	3	0	0	0	1	18.2	26	90	15	15	2	0	1	0	10	0	14	0	0
Sanders, Scott, Edm.	0	2	.000	5.56	6	2	0	0	1	0	22.2	25	101	15	14	3	0	0	0	12	0	18	2	0
Sanders, Scott, Cal.	2	3	.400	7.18	6	6	1	0	0	0	31.1	45	149	25	25	2	2	1	0	15	0	30	1	0
Sanders, Scott, Sac.	4	3	.571	6.52	10	7	0	0	0	0	49.2	63	220	36	36	9	2	4	1	13	0	38	2	0
Scott, Darryl, C.S.	1	0	1.000	6.00	2	0	0	0	1	0	3.0	5	13	2	2	0	0	0	0	0	0	2	1	0
Scott, Darryl, Tuc.	1	2	.333	10.45	14	0	0	0	5	0	20.2	31	104	28	24	6	0	0	0	12	1	21	2	0
Serafini, Dan, L.V.*	2	4	.333	6.88	26	4	0	0	1	0	51.0	74	255	44	39	6	3	4	6	23	1	45	4	0
Serafini, Dan, Nash.*	4	3	.571	2.68	7	7	0	0	0	0	47.0	39	193	17	14	4	2	1	1	18	1	22	0	0
Steenstra, Kennie, Mem.	1	0	1.000	3.86	10	1	0	0	3	2	25.2	28	115	11	11	1	0	0	2	12	0	13	0	0
Steenstra, Kennie, Tuc.	8	5	.615	4.01	24	19	1	0	2	0	130.1	159	574	68	58	15	10	4	4	41	0	62	0	0
Wojciechowski, Steve, Fres.*	0	4	.000	6.75	13	8	0	0	4	0	44.0	66	213	38	33	5	2	1	0	23	0	37	3	0
Wojciechowski, Steve, Cal.*	2	2	.500	5.70	20	6	0	0	3	1	47.1	64	219	36	30	10	1	2	0	16	1	27	2	0
Wolff, Bryan, N.O.	2	3	.400	4.94	11	11	1	1	0	0	62.0	63	268	38	34	6	3	1	3	26	0	46	4	1
Wolff, Bryan, S.L.	4	1	.800	5.57	9	7	0	0	1	0	51.2	53	227	33	32	8	1	3	1	19	0	43	4	0

2000 FIELDING

TEAM

Team	Pct.	G	PO	A	E	TC	DP	TP	PB
Edmonton	.976	141	3642	1400	124	5166	121	0	19
Omaha	.976	143	3691	1453	128	5272	133	0	7
Memphis	.975	144	3905	1608	140	5653	160	0	11
Salt Lake	.975	143	3798	1555	136	5489	148	0	13
Calgary	.975	143	3685	1446	133	5264	137	1	11
Nashville	.974	142	3758	1595	141	5494	141	1	26
Sacramento	.974	144	3819	1500	142	5461	150	0	24
Tacoma	.974	143	3733	1444	139	5316	136	0	18
Las Vegas	.974	143	3694	1379	138	5211	117	0	15
New Orleans	.973	142	3798	1528	146	5472	136	0	13
Albuquerque	.973	144	3820	1654	153	5627	177	0	21
Colo. Springs	.972	143	3688	1462	148	5298	124	0	21
Oklahoma	.970	143	3683	1474	158	5315	146	0	21
Iowa	.970	144	3727	1466	161	5354	137	0	19
Fresno	.970	141	3717	1491	162	5370	129	1	24
Tucson	.969	141	3658	1456	164	5278	132	0	5

INDIVIDUAL

FIRST BASEMEN

NOTE: All caps denotes fielding-percentage leader based on 72 games for catchers, 95 for all other non-pitchers and 115 innings for pitchers. *Throws lefthanded.

Player, Team	Pct.	G	PO	A	E	TC	DP
Allen, Dusty, L.V.	1.000	3	11	0	0	11	2
Alvarez, Gabe, L.V.	.985	34	248	19	4	271	24
Ardoin, Danny, Sac.	1.000	13	94	5	0	99	8
Ashby, Chris, Alb.	.969	21	87	6	3	96	16
Ball, Jeff, Fres.	1.000	7	47	3	0	50	2
Barajas, Rod, Tuc.	.972	14	93	10	3	106	9
Barkett, Andy, Okla.*	.989	12	85	7	1	93	6
Barnes, Larry, Edm.*	.996	94	772	50	3	825	70
Bellhorn, Mark, Sac.	.972	4	34	1	1	36	2
Berkman, Lance, N.O.*	.984	9	55	5	1	61	6
Betzold, James, N.O.	1.000	1	10	0	0	10	0
Bevins, Andy, Mem.	1.000	1	5	0	0	5	0
Blake, Casey, S.L.	1.000	1	2	0	0	2	0
Branson, Jeff, Alb.	1.000	1	3	0	0	3	0
Brede, Brent, Nash.*	1.000	17	101	8	0	109	13
Brumbaugh, Cliff, Okla.	.992	47	342	35	3	380	36
Buchanan, Brian, S.L.	.981	8	45	6	1	52	6
Burns, Kevin, N.O.*	.950	2	18	1	1	20	3
Cabrera, Alex, Tuc.	1.000	10	73	2	0	75	6
Charles, Frank, N.O.	.976	18	115	7	3	125	9
Cotton, John, C.S.	1.000	2	4	0	0	4	0
Cromer, Tripp, N.O.	1.000	2	12	0	0	12	3
Cruz, Ivan, Nash.*	.992	28	232	25	2	259	26
Curl, John, L.V.	1.000	15	80	7	0	87	9
Dalesandro, Mark, Iowa	1.000	1	2	0	0	2	0
Decker, Steve, Edm.-Sac.	.989	38	356	14	4	374	45
Donnels, Chris, Alb.	.992	67	491	38	4	533	51
Durazo, Erubiel, Tuc.*	.957	11	61	5	3	69	6
Echevarria, Angel, C.S.	.974	15	103	9	3	115	8
Fabregas, Jorge, Oma.	1.000	6	34	5	0	39	3
Figga, Mike, Alb.	1.000	1	4	0	0	4	0
Fraraccio, Dan, L.V.	1.000	2	19	1	0	20	3
Gallagher, Shawn, Okla.	.978	30	208	14	5	227	21
Giambi, Jeremy, Sac.*	1.000	2	13	0	0	13	0
Gilbert, Shawn, Alb.	.000	1	0	0	0	0	0
Greene, Willie, Iowa	1.000	2	8	0	0	8	0
Grijak, Kevin, Iowa	.996	60	427	30	2	459	62
Guzman, Edwards, Fres.	1.000	6	37	3	0	40	2
Haas, Chris, Mem.	.977	10	81	4	2	87	11
Hacker, Steve, S.L.	.979	4	44	3	1	48	5
Hart, Jason, Sac.	1.000	4	33	2	0	35	2
Hatcher, Chris, Iowa-Edm.	.981	20	133	20	3	156	12
Hernandez, Alex, Nash.*	.990	49	388	25	4	417	47
Hiatt, Phil, C.S.	.991	118	1015	66	10	1091	87
Hinch, A.J., Sac.	1.000	1	6	0	0	6	0
Huckaby, Ken, Tuc.	1.000	1	1	0	0	1	0
Jennings, Doug, Oma.*	1.000	1	2	2	0	4	0
Jennings, Robin, S.L.*	1.000	10	58	8	0	66	7
Johns, Keith, Iowa	.875	1	6	1	1	8	1
Johnson, Keith, Edm.	1.000	4	29	1	0	30	3
Knorr, Randy, Okla.	1.000	1	2	0	0	2	1
Laker, Tim, Nash.	.996	31	249	24	1	274	20
LeCroy, Matthew, S.L.	1.000	1	12	0	0	12	1
Ledesma, Aaron, C.S.	1.000	4	27	3	0	30	4
Lee, Travis, Tuc.*	1.000	5	37	3	0	40	6
Lesher, Brian, Tac.*	.995	130	1018	85	6	1109	108
Livingstone, Scott, Okla.	1.000	7	51	5	0	56	7
LoDuca, Paul, Alb.	.974	8	37	1	1	39	3
Lucca, Lou, Mem.	1.000	3	7	0	0	7	0
Mabry, John, Tac.	1.000	1	2	1	0	3	1

Player, Team	Pct.	G	PO	A	E	TC	DP
Mahoney, Mike, Iowa	1.000	4	3	0	0	3	0
Marcinczyk, T.R., Sac.	.969	11	80	14	3	97	9
McKay, Cody, Sac.	1.000	5	43	3	0	46	5
McNally, Sean, Cal.	.974	4	34	4	1	39	3
Medrano, Tony, Oma.	.987	20	137	17	2	156	16
Melhuse, Adam, Alb.-C.S.	.993	17	139	11	1	151	17
Merced, Orlando, N.O.	1.000	1	11	0	0	11	0
Mientkiewicz, Doug, S.L.	.994	95	755	67	5	827	81
Minor, Damon, Fres.*	.991	131	1134	60	11	1205	115
Mitchell, Mike, Tuc.	.992	70	565	37	5	607	50
Molina, Jose, Iowa	.000	1	0	0	0	0	0
Monahan, Shane, C.S.	1.000	3	21	3	0	24	1
Morgan, Scott, Edm.	1.000	1	5	1	0	6	1
Munoz, Juan, Mem.*	1.000	4	22	0	0	22	2
Murphy, Mike, Tac.	1.000	3	26	1	0	27	3
Nelson, Bry, Tuc.	1.000	1	2	0	0	2	1
Newstrom, Doug, Tuc.	1.000	11	48	4	0	52	7
Norman, Les, Oma.	1.000	1	11	0	0	11	1
Norton, Chris, Sac.	.982	12	102	7	2	111	10
Ortiz, Luis, Tuc.	.996	29	226	15	1	242	23
Patterson, Jarrod, Nash.	.933	1	14	0	1	15	1
Pelaez, Alex, L.V.	1.000	8	62	2	0	64	7
Pellow, Kit, Oma.	.992	116	938	80	8	1026	96
Pena, Angel, Alb.	.985	18	119	10	2	131	14
Perez, Eduardo, Mem.	.994	36	301	18	2	321	31
Phillips, J.R., N.O.*	.995	23	189	12	1	202	13
Piatt, Adam, Sac.	.992	14	116	10	1	127	12
Powell, Alonzo, C.S.	1.000	3	12	0	0	12	1
Raleigh, Matt, Cal.	1.000	1	8	1	0	9	1
Raven, Luis, Cal.	1.000	14	108	3	0	111	7
Richard, Chris, Mem.*	1.000	13	99	6	0	105	6
Richardson, Brian, S.L.	1.000	2	18	2	0	20	3
Roberge, J.P., Oma.	1.000	5	46	3	0	49	3
ROBERTSON, Mike, N.O.*	.995	105	895	42	5	942	94
Rolison, Nate, Cal.	.988	113	945	76	12	1033	106
Roskos, John, L.V.	.995	34	190	10	1	201	14
Sanchez, Victor, N.O.-Tuc.	.923	3	12	0	1	13	0
Sanders, Tracy, Nash.	1.000	2	9	0	0	9	0
Scheschuk, John, L.V.*	1.000	2	24	1	0	25	3
Sears, Todd, S.L.	1.000	3	32	1	0	33	3
Secrist, Reed, Okla.	1.000	7	59	5	0	64	8
Shave, Jon, Iowa	.990	36	286	20	3	309	37
Simon, Randall, Cal.*	.966	14	104	9	4	117	11
Smith, Jeff, S.L.	1.000	2	6	0	0	6	0
Snopek, Chris, Tac.	1.000	11	72	5	0	77	9
Sorrento, Paul, Sac.	1.000	33	298	19	0	317	34
Stahoviak, Scott, Iowa	1.000	3	18	0	0	18	0
Stoner, Mike, Edm.-Iowa	.991	37	303	23	3	329	28
Summers, John, Fres.	1.000	2	18	2	0	20	3
Sutton, Larry, Mem.*	.991	86	771	84	8	863	88
Tyler, Josh, Fres.	.909	3	8	2	1	11	1
Valdez, Mario, S.L.-Sac.	.990	54	467	37	5	509	45
Vaz, Roberto, Sac.*	.000	1	0	0	0	0	0
Vitiello, Joe, L.V.	.991	63	492	46	5	543	47
Voigt, Jack, Okla.	.987	7	70	4	1	75	8
Waszgis, B.J., Okla.	.982	8	51	5	1	57	2
Wathan, Dusty, Tac.	1.000	5	33	2	0	35	2
Wehner, John, Nash.	1.000	10	29	1	0	30	5
Wilkins, Rick, Mem.	1.000	1	4	0	0	4	0
Williams, George, L.V.	.950	4	16	3	1	20	0
Wilson, Craig, Nash.	.989	30	240	22	3	265	21
Wood, Jason, Nash.	1.000	2	8	0	0	8	0
Wooten, Shawn, Edm.	1.000	7	67	2	0	69	5
Zinter, Alan, Iowa-Tuc.	.988	47	319	21	4	344	35
Zuleta, Julio, Iowa	.983	86	648	48	12	708	75

TRIPLE PLAY: Minor.

FIRST BASEMEN WITH TWO OR MORE TEAMS

Player, Team	Pct.	G	PO	A	E	TC	DP
Decker, Steve, Edm.	.935	5	43	0	3	46	4
Decker, Steve, Sac.	.997	33	313	14	1	328	41
Hatcher, Chris, Iowa	1.000	14	85	11	0	96	9
Hatcher, Chris, Edm.	.950	6	48	9	3	60	3
Melhuse, Adam, Alb.	1.000	11	89	7	0	96	11
Melhuse, Adam, C.S.	.982	6	50	4	1	55	6
Sanchez, Victor, N.O.	.889	2	8	0	1	9	0
Sanchez, Victor, Tuc.	1.000	1	4	0	0	4	0
Stoner, Mike, Edm.	.991	26	213	18	2	233	18
Stoner, Mike, Iowa	.990	11	90	5	1	96	10
Valdez, Mario, S.L.	.987	39	345	31	5	381	31
Valdez, Mario, Sac.	1.000	15	122	6	0	128	14
Zinter, Alan, Iowa	.986	39	261	19	4	284	31
Zinter, Alan, Tuc.	1.000	8	58	2	0	60	4

SECOND BASEMEN

Player, Team	Pct.	G	PO	A	E	TC	DP
Abbott, Chuck, Edm.	1.000	1	2	3	0	5	0
Akers, Chad, Tac.	.982	24	51	59	2	112	14
Ametller, Jesus, Mem.	1.000	5	9	7	0	16	0
Ball, Jeff, Fres.	.000	1	0	0	0	0	0
Baughman, Justin, Edm.	.929	4	7	6	1	14	1
Bautista, Juan, N.O.	.909	6	8	12	2	22	4
Bellhorn, Mark, Sac.	.981	12	18	34	1	53	5
Beltre, Esteban, Tuc.	.965	32	74	92	6	172	32
Berblinger, Jeff, Oma.	1.000	1	3	1	0	4	0
Bieser, Steve, Mem.	1.000	2	8	6	0	14	1
Bloomquist, Willie, Tac.	.987	50	105	123	3	231	36
Bocachica, Hiram, Alb.	.963	118	273	326	23	622	99
Brown, Vick, C.S.-Tuc.	.977	53	88	122	5	215	24
Burke, Jamie, Edm.	1.000	1	1	1	0	2	0
Butler, Brent, C.S.	.970	100	174	243	13	430	51
Candaele, Casey, Cal.	1.000	8	12	23	0	35	10
Canizaro, Jay, S.L.	.965	22	36	75	4	115	21
Carvajal, Jhonny, Tuc.	.941	25	58	53	7	118	19
Castillo, Luis, Cal.	.944	4	7	10	1	18	3
Catalanotto, Frank, Okla.	1.000	1	0	1	0	1	0
Cey, Dan, S.L.	.941	4	7	9	1	17	3
Clapinski, Chris, Cal.	.965	16	23	32	2	57	7
Clapp, Stubby, Mem.	.977	127	284	341	15	640	89
Cleto, Ambioris, Nash.	.885	4	9	14	3	26	2
Cotton, John, C.S.	1.000	12	19	14	0	33	5
Counsell, Craig, Tuc.	1.000	22	43	45	0	88	8
Cromer, Tripp, N.O.	.972	39	89	85	5	179	26
Demetral, Chris, Okla.	.984	78	153	213	6	372	57
Diaz, Edwin, Okla.	.969	25	41	54	3	98	13
Donnels, Chris, Alb.	1.000	1	0	1	0	1	0
Durrington, Trent, Edm.	.985	26	55	79	2	136	19
Eckelman, Alex, Mem.	1.000	1	2	2	0	4	0
Eckstein, David, Edm.	1.000	15	27	28	0	55	4
Escandon, Emiliano, Oma.	.982	60	112	159	5	276	35
Espada, Josue, Sac.	.953	37	73	89	8	170	15
Febles, Carlos, Oma.	.983	10	27	31	1	59	14
Ferguson, Jeff, S.L.	.973	27	46	62	3	111	15
Figueroa, Luis, Nash.	1.000	6	10	3	0	13	3
Flores, Jose, Tac.	.938	7	11	19	2	32	5
Florez, Tim, Iowa	.981	12	24	27	1	52	6
Fox, Andy, Tuc.	.833	1	4	1	1	6	0
Funaro, Joe, Cal.	.965	11	20	35	2	57	10
Garcia, Amaury, Cal.	.962	92	195	262	18	475	58
Garcia, Luis, Mem.	.778	4	9	5	4	18	1
Gilbert, Shawn, Alb.	.864	7	7	12	3	22	3
Gipson, Charles, Tac.	1.000	1	1	3	0	4	0
Goldberg, Lonnie, C.S.	.938	7	9	21	2	32	5
Guzman, Edwards, Fres.	.957	33	72	82	7	161	22
Hansen, Jed, L.V.	1.000	6	6	9	0	15	2
Hardtke, Jason, C.S.	1.000	5	4	8	0	12	2
Hernandez, Carlos, Tac.	.979	45	90	98	4	192	30
Holbert, Aaron, Cal.	.975	8	18	21	1	40	2
Holbert, Ray, Oma.	.922	17	27	44	6	77	11
Jester, Joe, Fres.	.900	4	6	12	2	20	4
Johns, Keith, Iowa	.978	73	139	176	7	322	46
Johnson, Keith, Edm.	.978	63	111	161	6	278	39
King, Brett, Iowa-Edm.	.970	16	25	40	2	67	10
Klassen, Danny, Tuc.	1.000	2	3	1	0	4	0
Lagana, Shawn, Tuc.	.000	1	0	0	0	0	0
LaRocca, Greg, L.V.	.968	23	44	48	3	95	14
Ledesma, Aaron, C.S.	.981	16	19	32	1	52	6
Liniak, Cole, Iowa	1.000	1	1	1	0	2	0
LoDuca, Paul, Alb.	.875	1	4	3	1	8	2
Lopez, Mendy, Cal.	.985	14	34	31	1	66	8
Lucca, Lou, Mem.	1.000	2	5	6	0	11	2
Lugo, Julio, N.O.	.971	17	47	55	3	105	18
Luuloa, Keith, Edm.-Iowa	.947	20	45	45	5	95	8
Mahoney, Mike, Iowa	.000	1	0	0	0	1	0
Martinez, Gabby, Iowa	1.000	2	3	2	0	5	0
Martinez, Pablo, Mem.	1.000	5	6	20	0	26	5
Martins, Eric, Sac.	.970	25	48	80	4	132	20
Marval, Raul, Fres.	.959	38	70	117	8	195	27
Medrano, Tony, Oma.	.971	22	43	56	3	102	15
Melo, Juan, Fres.	.992	47	116	119	2	237	32
Metcalfe, Mike, Alb.	.889	2	2	6	1	9	1
Meyers, Chad, Iowa	.947	64	145	141	16	302	42
Mientkiewicz, Doug, S.L.	1.000	4	7	12	0	19	5
Miller, Ryan, N.O.	.960	77	134	176	13	323	38
Milliard, Ralph, L.V.	.958	46	84	121	9	214	26
Nelson, Bry, Tuc.	1.000	1	1	2	0	3	0
Newhan, David, L.V.	.974	58	118	140	7	265	35

CLASS AAA Pacific Coast League

Player, Team	Pct.	G	PO	A	E	TC	DP
Newstrom, Doug, Tuc.	.895	6	8	9	2	19	0
Nicholson, Kevin, L.V.	1.000	2	2	2	0	4	0
Nieves, Jose, Iowa.	1.000	1	2	3	0	5	2
Nunez, Abraham, Nash.	1.000	10	18	27	0	45	6
Ojeda, Augie, Iowa.	1.000	2	5	0	0	5	0
Ortiz, Jose, Sac.	.959	75	165	209	16	390	64
Pelaez, Alex, L.V.	1.000	1	1	0	0	1	0
Petersen, Chris, Iowa	.000	1	0	0	0	0	0
Prieto, Alejandro, Oma.	.985	47	83	116	3	202	25
Richardson, Brian, S.L.-N.O.	1.000	2	2	0	0	2	0
Riggs, Adam, Alb.	.984	33	55	68	2	125	19
Rivas, Luis, S.L.	.994	36	63	93	1	157	25
Saylor, Jamie, N.O.	.967	17	27	32	2	61	7
Shave, Jon, Okla.	.979	42	72	119	4	195	24
Snopek, Chris, Tac.	.988	24	40	45	1	86	12
Spivey, Junior, Tuc.	.966	21	54	59	4	117	16
Tebbs, Nate, L.V.	.962	21	45	55	4	104	13
t'Hoen, E.J., Edm.	.960	7	8	16	1	25	2
Thrower, Jake, L.V.	1.000	4	5	14	0	19	4
Tyler, Josh, Fres.	.958	20	31	38	3	72	8
Velarde, Randy, Sac.	1.000	3	6	11	0	17	5
Walker, Todd, S.L.	.964	59	114	180	11	305	46
WEHNER, John, Nash.	.984	98	218	260	8	486	69
White, Walt, Tuc.	1.000	20	42	35	0	77	7
Wilson, Enrique, Nash.	1.000	2	3	2	0	5	1
Wood, Jason, Nash.	1.000	18	43	35	0	78	12
Young, Travis, Fres.	.966	10	23	33	2	58	8
Zosky, Eddie, Nash.-N.O.	.991	28	47	66	1	114	15

TRIPLE PLAYS: A. Garcia, Marval.

SECOND BASEMEN WITH TWO OR MORE TEAMS

Player, Team	Pct.	G	PO	A	E	TC	DP
Brown, Vick, C.S.	.975	23	30	49	2	81	7
Brown, Vick, Tuc.	.978	30	58	73	3	134	17
King, Brett, Iowa	.947	7	8	10	1	19	5
King, Brett, Edm.	.979	9	17	30	1	48	5
Luuloa, Keith, Edm.	.947	19	44	45	5	94	8
Luuloa, Keith, Iowa	1.000	1	1	0	0	1	0
Richardson, Brian, S.L.	1.000	1	2	0	0	2	0
Richardson, Brian, N.O.	.000	1	0	0	0	0	0
Zosky, Eddie, Nash.	.989	23	37	54	1	92	12
Zosky, Eddie, N.O.	1.000	5	10	12	0	22	3

THIRD BASEMEN

Player, Team	Pct.	G	PO	A	E	TC	DP
Abbott, Chuck, Edm.	.800	1	2	2	1	5	1
Akers, Chad, Tac.	.947	71	57	140	11	208	19
Andrews, Shane, Iowa	1.000	12	2	20	0	22	4
Ardoin, Danny, Sac.	.750	2	1	2	1	4	0
Ball, Jeff, Fres.	.800	5	2	6	2	10	0
Barajas, Rod, Tuc.	1.000	2	2	1	0	3	0
Bautista, Juan, Okla.-N.O.	.903	13	4	24	3	31	1
Bellhorn, Mark, Sac.	.948	94	52	169	12	233	20
Beltre, Esteban, Tuc.	.885	26	12	34	6	52	3
Berry, Mike, Alb.	.000	1	0	0	0	0	0
Bieser, Steve, Mem.	1.000	3	1	5	0	6	0
Blake, Casey, S.L.	.927	71	36	128	13	177	12
Branson, Jeff, Alb.	.974	74	43	142	5	190	13
Brumbaugh, Cliff, Okla.	.955	17	11	31	2	44	2
Burke, Jamie, Edm.	.970	56	33	129	5	167	8
Cabrera, Alex, Tuc.	1.000	1	0	1	0	1	0
Campusano, Carlos, Fres.	1.000	2	1	0	0	1	0
Canizaro, Jay, S.L.	.000	1	0	0	0	0	0
Carvajal, Jhonny, Tuc.	1.000	6	2	14	0	16	1
Cey, Dan, S.L.	.000	1	0	0	0	0	0
Charles, Frank, N.O.	.792	10	4	15	5	24	3
Clapinski, Chris, Cal.	1.000	5	0	4	0	4	0
Clapp, Stubby, Mem.	.000	1	0	0	0	0	0
Cotton, John, C.S.	1.000	2	0	3	0	3	0
Counsell, Craig, Tuc.	.962	22	11	39	2	52	4
Cromer, Tripp, N.O.	.933	11	3	25	2	30	7
Dalesandro, Mark, Iowa	.000	1	0	0	0	0	0
Decker, Steve, Edm.-Sac.	.879	15	4	25	4	33	0
Demetral, Chris, Oma.	.907	17	10	29	4	43	1
Diaz, Edwin, Okla.	.907	23	10	39	5	54	4
Dillon, Joe, Oma.	.959	39	22	71	4	97	11
Donnels, Chris, Alb.	.923	30	20	40	5	65	8
Eckelman, Alex, Mem.	1.000	2	1	3	0	4	0
Escandon, Emiliano, Oma.	.000	3	0	0	0	0	0
Feliz, Pedro, Fres.	.939	121	83	287	24	394	31
Ferguson, Jeff, S.L.	.943	14	10	23	2	35	2
Figueroa, Luis, Nash.	.000	1	0	0	0	0	0

Player, Team	Pct.	G	PO	A	E	TC	DP
Flores, Jose, Tac.	.932	24	17	38	4	59	4
Fox, Andy, Tuc.	1.000	1	0	2	0	2	0
Fraraccio, Dan, L.V.	.920	10	7	16	2	25	1
Garcia , Osmani, Okla.	.952	42	30	89	6	125	7
Garcia, Luis, Mem.	.846	9	5	6	2	13	2
Gil, Geronimo, Alb.	.667	1	1	1	1	3	1
Gipson, Charles, Tac.	.963	16	6	46	2	54	6
Greene, Willie, Iowa.	.875	4	5	2	1	8	0
Guillen, Carlos, Tac.	.930	13	17	23	3	43	1
Gulan, Mike, Cal.	.953	53	36	87	6	129	7
Guzman, Edwards, Fres.	.938	14	7	38	3	48	1
Haas, Chris, Mem.	1.000	2	1	2	0	3	1
Hardtke, Jason, C.S.	1.000	1	0	1	0	1	0
Hernandez, Carlos, Tac.	.800	2	1	3	1	5	1
Hiatt, Phil, C.S.	.958	7	7	16	1	24	0
Holbert, Ray, Oma.	.882	13	8	22	4	34	4
Huckaby, Ken, Tuc.	.933	5	3	11	1	15	0
Huskey, Butch, S.L.	1.000	2	1	3	0	4	0
Johns, Keith, Iowa	.949	20	7	30	2	39	4
Johnson, Keith, Edm.	.918	21	17	28	4	49	3
King, Brett, Edm.	.833	1	3	2	1	6	2
Klassen, Danny, Tuc.	.750	1	0	3	1	4	0
Laker, Tim, Nash.	1.000	4	2	5	0	7	0
Lamb, Mike, Okla.	.806	12	12	17	7	36	1
LaRocca, Greg, L.V.	.928	109	83	199	22	304	17
Ledesma, Aaron, C.S.	.923	20	21	39	5	65	5
Liniak, Cole, Iowa	.926	116	91	196	23	310	21
Livingstone, Scott, Okla.	1.000	4	2	6	0	8	1
LoDuca, Paul, Alb.	.875	5	3	4	1	8	1
Lopez, Mendy, Cal.	.800	1	3	1	1	5	0
LUCCA, Lou, Mem.	.954	117	82	248	16	346	32
Luuloa, Keith, Edm.	.966	27	21	65	3	89	2
Mabry, John, Tac.	.500	1	0	1	1	2	0
Magdaleno, Ricky, Tac.	.909	7	6	14	2	22	1
Martinez, Gabby, Iowa	.000	1	0	0	0	0	0
Martinez, Pablo, Mem.	1.000	1	1	1	0	2	0
Martins, Eric, Sac.	.893	27	10	65	9	84	8
McClain, Scott, C.S.	.948	120	80	227	17	324	19
McNally, Sean, Cal.	.958	93	54	151	9	214	12
Medrano, Tony, Oma.	.967	22	19	40	2	61	3
Melhuse, Adam, Alb.	.000	1	0	0	0	0	0
Menechino, Frankie, Sac.	1.000	2	2	7	0	9	1
Merced, Orlando, N.O.	.944	4	2	15	1	18	0
Meyers, Chad, Iowa	.750	2	1	2	1	4	1
Mientkiewicz, Doug, S.L.	.951	36	22	75	5	102	10
Miller, Orlando, Alb.	1.000	1	0	1	0	1	1
Miller, Ryan, N.O.	1.000	1	0	1	0	1	0
Milliard, Ralph, L.V.	.963	13	10	16	1	27	0
Monahan, Shane, Tac.	.000	1	0	0	0	0	0
Nelson, Bry, Tuc.	.911	51	34	78	11	123	8
Newstrom, Doug, Tuc.	.870	21	9	38	7	54	3
Nieves, Jose, Iowa.	.889	5	0	8	1	9	1
Orie, Kevin, Oma.	.951	54	48	88	7	143	11
Ortiz, Jose, Sac.	1.000	1	0	2	0	2	0
Ortiz, Luis, Tuc.	.879	32	16	42	8	66	6
Patterson, Jarrod, Nash.	.942	56	26	105	8	139	8
Pelaez, Alex, L.V.	1.000	23	14	31	0	45	2
Pena, Angel, Alb.	.000	1	0	0	0	0	0
Perez, Eduardo, Mem.	.912	21	11	51	6	68	5
Petersen, Chris, Iowa	1.000	1	0	1	0	1	0
Piatt, Adam, Sac.	.879	21	14	37	7	58	4
Prieto, Alejandro, Oma.	.945	21	10	42	3	55	4
Pujols, Albert, Mem.	1.000	2	2	1	0	3	0
Ramirez, Aramis, Nash.	.930	42	34	85	9	128	4
Richardson, Brian, S.L.-N.O.	.930	87	49	164	16	229	14
Riggs, Adam, Alb.	.907	76	34	131	17	182	13
Roskos, John, L.V.	.000	2	0	0	0	0	0
Shave, Jon, Okla.	.949	26	10	46	3	59	5
Snopek, Chris, Tac.	.870	16	18	29	7	54	6
Spivey, Junior, Tuc.	1.000	1	0	2	0	2	0
Stahoviak, Scott, Iowa	1.000	3	2	2	0	4	0
Tatis, Fernando, Mem.	1.000	3	3	2	0	5	0
Tebbs, Nate, L.V.	1.000	2	0	9	0	9	1
t'Hoen, E.J., Edm.	.940	16	10	37	3	50	5
Thrower, Jake, L.V.	1.000	1	1	3	0	4	0
Tremie, Chris, Cal.	1.000	3	2	5	0	7	0
Truby, Chris, N.O.	.943	62	46	151	12	209	20
Tyler, Josh, Fres.	1.000	4	2	10	0	12	1
Valdez, Mario, S.L.	1.000	4	2	3	0	5	0
Villilo, Miguel, Tac.	.714	2	2	3	2	7	0
Wathan, Dusty, Tac.	.000	3	0	0	0	0	0
Wehner, John, Nash.	.933	20	14	42	4	60	4
White, Walt, Tuc.	1.000	2	0	2	0	2	0

Player, Team	Pct.	G	PO	A	E	TC	DP
Williams, George, L.V.	.000	1	0	0	0	0	0
Wood, Jason, Nash.	.957	36	22	88	5	115	8
Wooten, Shawn, Edm.	.957	12	5	17	1	23	1
Zeber, Ryan, Edm.	.500	1	1	0	1	2	0
Zinter, Alan, Iowa	1.000	3	0	2	0	2	0
Zosky, Eddie, N.O.	.000	3	0	0	0	0	0
Zuleta, Julio, Iowa	.800	1	2	2	1	5	0

TRIPLE PLAYS: Feliz, Gulan, Wood.

THIRD BASEMEN WITH TWO OR MORE TEAMS

Player, Team	Pct.	G	PO	A	E	TC	DP
Bautista, Juan, Okla.	.909	5	0	10	1	11	0
Bautista, Juan, N.O.	.900	8	4	14	2	20	1
Decker, Steve, Edm.	.903	13	4	24	3	31	0
Decker, Steve, Sac.	.500	2	0	1	1	2	0
Richardson, Brian, S.L.	.908	30	10	59	7	76	5
Richardson, Brian, N.O.	.941	57	39	105	9	153	9

SHORTSTOPS

Player, Team	Pct.	G	PO	A	E	TC	DP
Abbott, Chuck, Edm.	1.000	2	0	1	0	1	0
Baughman, Justin, Edm.	.956	74	110	216	15	341	38
Bautista, Juan, Okla.-N.O.	.867	11	11	28	6	45	4
Bellhorn, Mark, Sac.	.950	7	7	12	1	20	2
Beltre, Esteban, Tuc.	.924	75	99	217	26	342	28
Blake, Casey, S.L.	.971	9	11	22	1	34	4
Branson, Jeff, Alb.	.977	31	40	85	3	128	21
Butler, Brent, C.S.	.975	25	48	68	3	119	18
Canizaro, Jay, S.L.	.870	5	6	14	3	23	4
Carvajal, Jhonny, Tuc.	.939	30	33	74	7	114	12
Castro, Nelson, Fres.	.924	66	78	201	23	302	38
Cey, Dan, L.V.	.750	1	2	1	1	4	1
Clapinski, Chris, Cal.	.974	36	52	99	4	155	24
Cora, Alex, Alb.	.959	30	74	90	7	171	28
Counsell, Craig, Tuc.	.973	17	23	49	2	74	12
Cromer, Tripp, N.O.	1.000	8	8	21	0	29	5
Demetral, Chris, Okla.	1.000	2	5	8	0	13	2
Deschaine, James, Iowa	.833	4	1	4	1	6	0
Diaz, Edwin, Okla.	.969	6	15	16	1	32	6
Dransfeldt, Kelly, Okla.	.962	114	208	345	22	575	86
Durrington, Trent, Edm.	1.000	2	4	6	0	10	3
Eckelman, Alex, Mem.	1.000	1	3	1	0	4	0
Everett, Adam, N.O.	.959	124	172	410	25	607	69
Feliz, Pedro, Fres.	1.000	1	1	1	0	2	0
Ferguson, Jeff, S.L.	.724	13	4	17	8	29	4
Figueroa, Luis, Nash.	.891	12	13	28	5	46	7
Flores, Jose, Tac.	.928	59	78	142	17	237	25
Florez, Tim, Iowa	1.000	2	1	0	0	1	0
Fox, Andy, Tuc.	1.000	1	1	3	0	4	1
Funaro, Joe, Cal.	.973	34	60	85	4	149	19
Garcia, Luis, Mem.	.944	94	158	277	26	461	68
Gilbert, Shawn, Alb.	.950	63	97	206	16	319	42
Gipson, Charles, Tac.	.925	14	23	26	4	53	6
Guillen, Carlos, Tac.	.921	7	10	25	3	38	6
Gulan, Mike, Cal.	.923	12	16	32	4	52	8
Hardtke, Jason, C.S.	.750	1	1	2	1	4	1
Hernandez, Carlos, Tac.	.901	15	29	35	7	71	8
Holbert, Aaron, Cal.	.980	21	25	73	2	100	18
Holbert, Ray, Oma.	.955	59	73	161	11	245	31
Johns, Keith, Iowa	.956	15	19	46	3	68	9
Johnson, Keith, Iowa	.952	22	26	53	4	83	11
King, Brett, Iowa-Edm.	.964	10	9	18	1	28	3
Klassen, Danny, Tuc.	.950	25	39	93	7	139	26
LaRocca, Greg, L.V.	1.000	5	13	4	0	17	0
Ledesma, Aaron, C.S.	.977	10	19	24	1	44	10
Lopez, Mendy, Cal.	.948	37	60	123	10	193	22
Lucca, Lou, Mem.	1.000	1	2	3	0	5	2
Lugo, Julio, N.O.	.833	1	1	4	1	6	0
Luuloa, Keith, Edm.	.948	27	41	86	7	134	20
Magdaleno, Ricky, Tac.	.938	11	20	25	3	48	7
Martinez, Gabby, Iowa	.962	20	25	50	3	78	16
Martinez, Pablo, Mem.	.968	33	53	97	5	155	18
Marval, Raul, Fres.	.969	8	9	22	1	32	7
McNally, Sean, Cal.	1.000	3	2	6	0	8	2
Medrano, Tony, Oma.	.974	36	58	94	4	156	17
Melo, Juan, Fres.	.961	74	101	196	12	309	34
Menechino, Frankie, Sac.	1.000	6	11	23	0	34	6
Metcalfe, Mike, Alb.	.964	29	38	94	5	137	20
Meyers, Chad, Iowa	.000	1	0	0	1	1	0
Miller, Orlando, Alb.	.867	6	8	18	4	30	3
Miller, Ryan, N.O.	1.000	1	0	1	0	1	0
Milliard, Ralph, L.V.	.950	52	77	133	11	221	27
Moriarty, Mike, S.L.	.968	126	219	394	20	633	84
Nicholson, Kevin, L.V.	.945	90	114	230	20	364	51
Nieves, Jose, Iowa	1.000	2	1	4	0	5	1
Nunez, Abraham, Nash.	.966	80	119	251	13	383	58
Nunez, Jorge, Alb.	.000	1	0	0	0	0	0
OJEDA, Augie, Iowa	.976	110	156	294	11	461	57
Ortiz, Jose, Sac.	.932	48	82	136	16	234	23
Petersen, Chris, Iowa	.963	6	10	16	1	27	5
Polanco, Enohel, Cal.	.926	8	9	16	2	27	2
Prieto, Alejandro, Oma.	.962	54	73	156	9	238	30
Rivas, Luis, S.L.	.955	4	7	14	1	22	4
Salazar, Oscar, Sac.	1.000	4	5	8	0	13	1
Saylor, Jamie, N.O.	.750	1	1	2	1	4	1
Shave, Jon, Okla.	.961	20	30	44	3	77	9
Snopek, Chris, Tac.	.942	48	81	131	13	225	31
Sosa, Juan, C.S.	.955	116	171	333	24	528	54
Spivey, Junior, Tuc.	.917	6	9	13	2	24	1
Tebbs, Nate, L.V.	1.000	3	1	6	0	7	1
t'Hoen, E.J., Edm.	.957	16	20	47	3	70	4
Velandia, Jorge, Sac.	.973	82	127	262	11	400	64
White, Walt, Tuc.	1.000	1	3	5	0	8	1
Wilson, Enrique, Nash.	.750	1	1	2	1	4	0
Wood, Jason, Nash.	.982	33	53	107	3	163	24
Woolf, Jason, Nash.	.933	26	42	69	8	119	10
Zosky, Eddie, Nash.-N.O.	.952	32	47	73	6	126	16

TRIPLE PLAY: A. Nunez.

SHORTSTOPS WITH TWO OR MORE TEAMS

Player, Team	Pct.	G	PO	A	E	TC	DP
Bautista, Juan, Okla.	.800	2	4	8	3	15	1
Bautista, Juan, N.O.	.900	9	7	20	3	30	3
King, Brett, Iowa	.958	9	9	14	1	24	3
King, Brett, Edm.	1.000	1	0	4	0	4	0
Zosky, Eddie, Nash.	.952	27	36	64	5	105	15
Zosky, Eddie, N.O.	.952	5	11	9	1	21	1

OUTFIELDERS

Player, Team	Pct.	G	PO	A	E	TC	DP
Akers, Chad, Tac.	1.000	5	5	0	0	5	0
Alcala, Juan, Tac.	.000	2	0	0	1	1	0
Alexander, Chad, Tac.	.981	105	195	11	4	210	2
Allen, Chad, S.L.	.993	86	146	2	1	149	0
Allen, Dusty, L.V.	.964	65	102	4	4	110	0
Alvarez, Gabe, L.V.	.909	7	10	0	1	11	0
Ashby, Chris, Alb.	.969	121	173	13	6	192	3
Aven, Bruce, Nash.-Alb.	1.000	12	17	1	0	18	0
Ball, Jeff, Fres.	.861	31	29	2	5	36	0
Barker, Glen, N.O.	.970	25	63	2	2	67	0
Barnes, John, S.L.	.977	111	244	8	6	258	3
Barnes, Larry, Edm.*	1.000	6	7	1	0	8	0
Bautista, Juan, N.O.	1.000	5	2	0	0	2	0
Beltran, Carlos, Oma.	1.000	2	6	0	0	6	0
Berkman, Lance, N.O.*	.980	27	48	2	1	51	0
Betzsold, James, N.O.	.968	76	144	9	5	158	0
Bevins, Andy, Mem.	1.000	4	8	0	0	8	0
Bieser, Steve, Mem.	.985	59	127	6	2	135	4
Blosser, Greg, Fres.*	1.000	6	5	0	0	5	0
Brede, Brent, Nash.*	.992	68	116	4	1	121	2
Brinkley, Darryl, Nash.	1.000	26	41	0	0	41	0
Brock, Tarrik, Iowa*	.989	103	262	7	3	272	1
Brown, Adrian, Nash.	1.000	8	11	1	0	12	0
Brown, Dee, Oma.	.966	115	193	6	7	206	2
Brown, Emil, Nash.	.978	68	127	9	3	139	0
Brown, Roosevelt, Iowa	.943	89	159	6	10	175	0
Brown, Vick, C.S.-Tuc.	1.000	5	8	0	0	8	0
Brumbaugh, Cliff, Okla.	1.000	69	154	10	0	164	2
Buchanan, Brian, S.L.	.980	77	139	5	3	147	2
Bullett, Scott, C.S.*	1.000	10	12	0	0	12	0
Butler, Rich, Tac.-Okla.	.969	28	60	2	2	64	0
Byas, Mike, Fres.	.973	132	351	11	10	372	3
Byrnes, Eric, Sac.	.980	51	94	3	2	99	0
Cabrera, Alex, Tuc.	1.000	4	5	0	0	5	0
Candaele, Casey, Cal.	1.000	14	12	1	0	13	0
Carpenter, Bubba, C.S.*	.972	49	103	2	3	108	0
Carr, Jeremy, Oma.	.981	50	94	8	2	104	0
Catalanotto, Frank, Okla.	.000	1	0	0	0	0	0
Cedeno, Roger, N.O.	1.000	5	6	0	0	6	0
Clapinski, Chris, Cal.	1.000	5	9	0	0	9	0
Clemente, Edgard, Edm.	.982	20	54	1	1	56	0
Conti, Jason, Tuc.	.950	90	186	6	10	202	1
Cookson, Brent, Alb.	.977	31	40	2	1	43	0
Cotton, John, C.S.	.918	61	74	4	7	85	2

Player, Team	Pct.	G	PO	A	E	TC	DP
Curl, John, L.V.	.987	59	77	0	1	78	0
Darr, Mike, L.V.	.977	89	205	6	5	216	2
DeHaan, Kory, L.V.	1.000	10	37	0	0	37	0
Dellucci, David, Tuc.*	.966	27	55	1	2	58	0
Demetral, Chris, Okla.	.000	2	0	0	0	0	0
Dougherty, Jim, Mem.	.000	1	0	0	0	0	0
Dunwoody, Todd, Oma.*	1.000	8	11	0	0	11	0
Echevarria, Angel, C.S.	.990	52	93	4	1	98	1
Eckelman, Alex, Mem.	.000	2	0	0	0	0	0
Encarnacion, Mario, Sac.	.972	74	165	10	5	180	3
Faggett, Ethan, L.V.*	1.000	34	70	1	0	71	0
Fajardo, Alejandro, Fres.	1.000	3	10	1	0	11	1
Ferguson, Jeff, S.L.	1.000	11	14	0	0	14	0
Figga, Mike, Alb.	1.000	2	3	0	0	3	0
Figueroa, Eduardo, Tac.	1.000	4	5	2	0	7	0
Fraraccio, Dan, L.V.	1.000	6	6	0	0	6	0
Funaro, Joe, Cal.	1.000	3	6	0	0	6	0
Gallagher, Shawn, Okla.	1.000	4	9	0	0	9	0
Gann, Jamie, Tuc.	1.000	60	128	11	0	139	2
Garcia, Amaury, Cal.	.960	27	46	2	2	50	0
Giambi, Jeremy, Sac.*	.917	6	10	1	1	12	1
Gibbs, Kevin, Alb.	1.000	2	4	0	0	4	0
Gibson, Derrick, Cal.	.980	94	187	6	4	197	0
Gil, Geronimo, Alb.	1.000	4	6	0	0	6	0
Gilbert, Shawn, Alb.	.923	19	31	5	3	39	2
Gipson, Charles, Tac.	1.000	40	89	5	0	94	1
Glendenning, Mike, Fres.	.959	34	66	4	3	73	0
Gload, Ross, Iowa*	.917	28	42	2	4	48	0
Gonzalez, Raul, Iowa	.974	66	110	4	3	117	1
Green, Scarborough, Okla.	.985	27	62	3	1	66	2
Grijak, Kevin, Alb.	1.000	37	47	2	0	49	0
Guiel, Aaron, Oma.	.977	70	152	18	4	174	7
Gulan, Mike, Cal.	.974	48	73	3	2	78	0
Guzman, Domingo, L.V.	.000	1	0	0	0	0	0
Guzman, Edwards, Fres.	.840	12	18	3	4	25	2
Haas, Chris, Mem.	.000	1	0	0	0	0	0
Hatcher, Chris, Iowa-Edm.	.970	53	62	2	2	66	0
Hayes, Heath, Alb.	1.000	3	5	0	0	5	0
Hermansen, Chad, Nash.	.975	74	156	2	4	162	0
Hernandez, Alex, Nash.*	1.000	26	48	1	0	49	0
Hiatt, Phil, C.S.	.833	9	9	1	2	12	0
Hopper, Shane, L.V.	.875	4	6	1	1	8	0
Hosey, Dwayne, Edm.	.979	21	46	0	1	47	0
Howard, Thomas, Mem.	.905	13	19	0	2	21	0
Huckaby, Ken, Tuc.	1.000	2	1	0	0	1	0
Hunter, Torii, S.L.	.973	52	105	5	3	113	1
Hutchins, Norm, C.S.*	.955	12	21	0	1	22	0
Ibanez, Raul, Tac.	1.000	5	9	0	0	9	0
Jennings, Doug, Oma.*	.978	25	43	2	1	46	0
Jennings, Robin, S.L.*	.962	67	100	2	4	106	0
Johns, Keith, Iowa	1.000	6	8	0	0	8	0
Jones, Chris, L.V.	1.000	6	7	1	0	8	0
Kapler, Gabe, Okla.	1.000	2	1	1	0	2	0
Keith, Rusty, Sac.	1.000	2	1	0	0	1	0
Kielty, Bobby, S.L.	.957	9	22	0	1	23	0
King, Brett, Iowa	.000	1	0	0	0	0	0
LaRocca, Greg, L.V.	1.000	2	1	0	0	1	0
Latham, Chris, C.S.	.971	117	228	6	7	241	2
Leach, Jalal, Fres.*	.976	44	80	2	2	84	0
Ledesma, Aaron, C.S.	1.000	11	16	0	0	16	0
Lee, Travis, Tuc.*	1.000	3	7	0	0	7	0
Lesher, Brian, Tac.*	1.000	2	1	0	0	1	0
Little, Mark, Mem.	.974	104	253	13	7	273	3
Lockwood, Mike, Sac.*	1.000	32	51	3	0	54	1
LoDuca, Paul, Alb.	1.000	9	12	2	0	14	1
Long, Terrence, Sac.*	.903	15	28	0	3	31	0
Lowery, Terrell, Fres.	.974	76	146	2	4	152	0
Lugo, Julio, N.O.	1.000	6	10	0	0	10	0
Luuloa, Keith, Edm.-Iowa	1.000	8	11	0	0	11	0
Martinez, Manny, Cal.	.976	116	231	10	6	247	2
Martinez, Pablo, Mem.	1.000	4	9	0	0	9	0
Martins, Eric, Sac.	1.000	15	21	1	0	22	0
Mashore, Damon, Tuc.	.978	19	43	1	1	45	0
Matthews, Gary, Iowa	.970	58	125	5	4	134	2
McDonald, Jason, Okla.	.974	30	71	5	2	78	2
Medrano, Tony, Oma.	.989	35	82	4	1	87	0
Melconian, Alex, Cal.	1.000	5	7	1	0	8	0
Melhuse, Adam, Alb.-C.S.	1.000	27	43	2	0	45	0
Mendoza, Carlos, C.S.*	.976	99	159	5	4	168	1
Merced, Orlando, N.O.	1.000	12	24	1	0	25	1
Metcalfe, Mike, Alb.	.929	6	13	0	1	14	0
Meyers, Chad, Iowa	.962	18	25	0	1	26	0
Mientkiewicz, Doug, S.L.	1.000	2	2	0	0	2	0
Mieske, Matt, Tuc.	1.000	6	10	0	0	10	0
Monahan, Shane, Tac.-L.V.-C.S.	.964	35	77	4	3	84	1
Montgomery, Ray, Nash.	.972	64	105	1	3	109	0
Morgan, Scott, Edm.	.984	85	173	6	3	182	1
Mota, Tony, Alb.	.982	94	155	6	3	164	0
Munoz, Juan, Mem.*	.967	19	27	2	1	30	0
Murphy, Mike, Tac.	.967	80	173	2	6	181	0
Murphy, Nate, Edm.*	.980	114	276	16	6	298	8
Neill, Mike, Tac.*	.993	77	128	8	1	137	2
Nelson, Bry, Tuc.	.889	14	24	0	3	27	0
Newhan, David, L.V.	1.000	9	14	0	0	14	0
Newstrom, Doug, Tuc.	1.000	12	15	0	0	15	0
Norman, Les, Oma.	.979	95	220	9	5	234	0
Nunez, Argelis, Tuc.	1.000	4	0	1	0	1	0
Perez, Eduardo, Mem.	1.000	10	17	0	0	17	0
Phillips, J.R., N.O.*	.968	46	59	2	2	63	0
Piatt, Adam, Sac.	.970	22	30	2	1	33	0
Pierre, Juan, C.S.*	1.000	4	11	0	0	11	0
Porter, Bo, Sac.	.990	123	299	6	3	308	1
Powell, Alonzo, C.S.	.917	9	11	0	1	12	0
Powell, Dante, Alb.	.967	56	84	3	3	90	0
Pride, Curtis, Alb.	.959	34	68	2	3	73	0
Prieto, Alejandro, Oma.	1.000	1	3	0	0	3	0
Prieto, Chris, Alb.*	.982	75	157	10	3	170	4
Pujols, Albert, Mem.	1.000	2	5	1	0	6	1
Quinn, Mark, Iowa	1.000	11	23	1	0	24	0
RADMANOVICH, Ryan, L.V.	.994	108	168	3	1	172	0
Ramirez, Julio, Cal.	.954	90	220	9	11	240	3
Ramirez, Omar, N.O.	.979	125	277	5	6	288	2
Raven, Luis, Cal.	.938	67	88	3	6	97	0
Redman, Tike, Nash.*	.981	120	251	5	5	261	0
Richard, Chris, Mem.*	.989	84	175	9	2	186	2
Richardson, Brian, S.L.-N.O.	.975	29	37	2	1	40	0
Riggs, Adam, Alb.	1.000	4	5	0	0	5	0
Rivera, Ruben, L.V.	1.000	2	1	0	0	1	0
Roberson, Kevin, S.L.	.980	28	48	2	1	51	0
Robertson, Mike, N.O.*	1.000	7	5	0	0	5	0
Rosario, Omar, Sac.*	.952	8	18	2	1	21	0
Roskos, John, L.V.	.958	51	66	2	3	71	0
Ryan, Mike, S.L.	1.000	3	5	1	0	6	0
Ryan, Rob, Tuc.*	.994	87	156	7	1	164	2
Sagmoen, Marc, N.O.*	.991	112	204	12	2	218	2
Sanchez, Victor, Tuc.	.000	1	0	0	0	0	0
Sanders, Anthony, Tac.	.984	101	177	11	3	191	1
Saylor, Jamie, N.O.	.500	3	1	0	1	2	0
Secrist, Reed, Okla.	.895	12	17	0	2	19	0
Sell, Chip, Tuc.	.986	102	210	7	3	220	0
Sergio, Tom, Okla.	1.000	15	29	1	0	30	0
Shave, Jon, Okla.	1.000	1	1	0	0	1	0
Sierra, Ruben, Okla.	.962	81	141	9	6	156	3
Sosa, Juan, C.S.	.875	3	6	1	1	8	0
Stahoviak, Scott, Iowa	1.000	8	13	1	0	14	0
Stoner, Mike, Iowa	1.000	11	23	0	0	23	0
Stovall, DaRond, Edm.*	.983	62	112	6	2	120	2
Tatum, Jim, Fres.	1.000	24	44	1	0	45	0
Tebbs, Nate, L.V.	1.000	5	4	1	0	5	0
Tolentino, Juan, Edm.	.971	120	301	3	9	313	1
Tomlinson, Goef, Oma.*	.965	28	81	2	3	86	1
Tyler, Josh, Fres.	.941	31	45	3	3	51	0
Valdes, Pedro, Okla.*	.987	71	153	4	2	159	1
Valdez, Mario, S.L.	1.000	9	6	0	0	6	0
Vaz, Roberto, Sac.*	.985	93	188	10	3	201	0
Vieira, Scott, Iowa	1.000	1	1	0	0	1	0
Voigt, Jack, Okla.	1.000	2	3	0	0	3	0
Ward, Turner, Tuc.	1.000	21	30	1	0	31	0
Wehner, John, Nash.	1.000	2	3	0	0	3	0
Whitmore, Darrell, Mem.	.988	53	82	2	1	85	0
Williams, Keith, Fres.	.954	49	80	3	4	87	0
Woolf, Jason, Mem.	1.000	3	2	0	0	2	0
Young, Ernie, Mem.	.990	112	184	13	2	199	3
Zinter, Alan, Iowa-Tuc.	.857	11	12	0	2	14	0
Zuleta, Julio, Iowa	1.000	21	30	1	0	31	0
Zywica, Mike, Okla.	.958	123	217	11	10	238	1

TRIPLE PLAY: M. Martinez.

OUTFIELDERS WITH TWO OR MORE TEAMS

Player, Team	Pct.	G	PO	A	E	TC	DP
Aven, Bruce, Nash.	1.000	3	6	0	0	6	0
Aven, Bruce, Alb.	1.000	9	11	1	0	12	0
Brown, Vick, C.S.	.000	2	0	0	0	0	0
Brown, Vick, Tuc.	1.000	3	8	0	0	8	0
Butler, Rich, Tac.	.969	19	30	1	1	32	0
Butler, Rich, Okla.	.969	9	30	1	1	32	0

Player, Team	Pct.	G	PO	A	E	TC	DP
Hatcher, Chris, Iowa	.964	48	52	2	2	56	0
Hatcher, Chris, Edm.	1.000	5	10	0	0	10	0
Luuloa, Keith, Edm.	1.000	5	6	0	0	6	0
Luuloa, Keith, Iowa	1.000	3	5	0	0	5	0
Melhuse, Adam, Alb.	1.000	1	1	0	0	1	0
Melhuse, Adam, C.S.	1.000	26	42	2	0	44	0
Monahan, Shane, Tac.	1.000	4	10	1	0	11	0
Monahan, Shane, L.V.	.958	11	23	0	1	24	0
Monahan, Shane, C.S.	.959	20	44	3	2	49	1
Richardson, Brian, S.L.	1.000	12	17	1	0	18	0
Richardson, Brian, N.O.	.955	17	20	1	1	22	0
Zinter, Alan, Iowa	.800	6	8	0	2	10	0
Zinter, Alan, Tuc.	1.000	5	4	0	0	4	0

CATCHERS

Player, Team	Pct.	G	PO	A	E	TC	DP	PB
Ardoin, Danny, Sac.-S.L.	.978	44	298	19	7	324	3	12
Barajas, Rod, Tuc.	.982	89	528	69	11	608	8	5
Bard, Josh, C.S.	.923	2	11	1	1	13	0	0
Bieser, Steve, Mem.	1.000	4	18	0	0	18	0	1
Brito, Juan, Oma.	1.000	9	54	5	0	59	0	2
Burke, Jamie, Edm.	.992	19	117	13	1	131	0	3
Castro, Ramon, Cal.	.990	59	360	32	4	396	3	5
Charles, Frank, N.O.	.987	53	336	35	5	376	3	6
Chavez, Raul, N.O.	.987	92	571	52	8	631	3	7
Chiaramonte, Giuseppe, Fres.	.990	111	726	44	8	778	6	12
Cline, Pat, Iowa	1.000	1	1	1	0	2	0	0
Cotton, John, C.S.	1.000	1	4	0	0	4	0	0
Cox, Darron, C.S.	.993	58	366	39	3	408	2	5
Dalesandro, Mark, Iowa	.965	13	77	6	3	86	1	2
Davis, Ben, L.V.	.986	59	441	37	7	485	5	5
Decker, Steve, Edm.-Sac.	.990	26	174	15	2	191	5	3
Donnels, Chris, Alb.	1.000	1	2	0	0	2	0	0
Duplissea, William, Alb.	1.000	9	32	3	0	35	1	0
Encarnacion, Angelo, Iowa	.985	10	61	3	1	65	0	1
Fabregas, Jorge, Oma.	.982	22	149	15	3	167	0	1
Figga, Mike, Alb.	1.000	11	48	2	0	50	1	0
Gil, Geronimo, Alb.	.969	11	55	8	2	65	0	2
Graves, Bryan, Edm.	1.000	25	153	5	0	158	2	3
Grijak, Kevin, Alb.	1.000	1	1	0	0	1	0	0
Guzman, Edwards, Fres.	.981	30	184	18	4	206	1	11
Harper, Brian, Tac.	1.000	1	8	0	0	8	0	0
Hayes, Heath, Alb.	1.000	1	6	0	0	6	0	1
Hemphill, Bret, Edm.	.986	37	205	12	3	220	3	3
HINCH, A.J., Sac.	.994	87	580	47	4	631	4	10
Huckaby, Ken, Tuc.	.983	61	377	40	7	424	3	0
Hundley, Todd, Alb.	1.000	3	15	0	0	15	0	0
Jensen, Marcus, S.L.	.974	12	71	4	2	77	0	1
Johnson, Brian, Mem.	.976	13	78	5	2	85	2	3
King, Cesar, Oma.	.958	13	105	10	5	120	0	0
Knorr, Randy, Nash.-Okla.	.986	76	435	43	7	485	9	6
Laker, Tim, Nash.	.976	67	409	46	11	466	2	8
Lampkin, Tom, Tac.	1.000	2	12	2	0	14	0	1
LeCroy, Matthew, S.L.	1.000	10	64	3	0	67	1	2
LoDuca, Paul, Alb.	.983	49	308	38	6	352	3	7
Lopez, Pedro, N.O.	1.000	2	8	1	0	9	0	0
Machado, Robert, Tac.	.980	75	491	57	11	559	7	7
Mahoney, Mike, Iowa	.991	54	298	37	3	338	4	6
Marrero, Eli, Mem.	1.000	6	16	1	0	17	0	0
Martinez, Sandy, Cal.	.990	67	373	38	4	415	3	4
McDonald, Keith, Mem.	.987	76	466	51	7	524	7	3
McKay, Cody, Sac.	.980	8	44	4	1	49	1	1
Melconian, Alex, Cal.	1.000	2	6	1	0	7	0	0
Melhuse, Adam, Alb.-C.S.	.994	29	148	20	1	169	2	8
Mercedes, Henry, Mem.	1.000	4	25	5	0	30	1	0
Moeller, Chad, S.L.	.993	46	256	25	2	283	2	3
Molina, Izzy, Oma.	.980	59	365	26	8	399	7	5
Molina, Jose, Iowa	.981	73	505	67	11	583	6	6
Monahan, Shane, C.S.	1.000	1	4	0	0	4	0	0
Montilla, Samuel, Tuc.	1.000	1	1	0	0	1	0	0
Morales, Steve, Cal.	1.000	3	5	0	0	5	0	0
Norton, Chris, Sac.	1.000	1	1	0	0	1	0	0
Oliver, Joe, Tac.	.992	16	118	12	1	131	3	3
Ortiz, Hector, Oma.	.982	53	291	28	6	325	5	0
Patterson, Jarrod, Nash.	.000	1	0	0	0	0	0	0
Pena, Angel, Alb.	.989	64	412	50	5	467	10	5
Petrick, Ben, C.S.	.986	58	375	39	6	420	4	14
Pierzynski, A.J., S.L.	.990	38	263	20	3	286	1	3
Roskos, John, L.V.	1.000	2	12	2	0	14	0	0
Secrist, Reed, Okla.	.960	9	44	4	2	50	2	2
Servais, Scott, C.S.	.989	14	80	8	1	89	2	0
Smith, Jeff, S.L.	.983	18	106	13	2	121	1	2
Soliz, Steve, L.V.	.991	29	210	12	2	224	0	5

Player, Team	Pct.	G	PO	A	E	TC	DP	PB
Strittmatter, Mark, C.S.-L.V.	.988	24	158	10	2	170	3	2
Tatum, Jim, Fres.	1.000	1	5	2	0	7	0	0
Thurston, Jerrey, N.O.	.980	9	47	1	1	49	0	0
Tonis, Michael, Oma.	1.000	2	15	0	0	15	0	0
Torres, Gabby, S.L.	.000	1	0	1	0	1	0	0
Tremie, Chris, Cal.	.994	33	162	13	1	176	0	2
Tyler, Josh, Fres.	1.000	8	29	1	0	30	0	1
Valentin, Javier, S.L.	.994	24	155	11	1	167	2	1
Waszgis, B.J., Okla.	.979	62	432	42	10	484	6	16
Wathan, Dusty, Tac.	.995	57	396	43	2	441	3	7
Wilkins, Rick, Mem.	.990	57	340	42	4	386	5	4
Williams, George, L.V.	.972	45	290	23	9	322	4	5
Wilson, Craig, Nash.	.978	71	398	37	10	445	2	15
Wooten, Shawn, Edm.	.980	49	269	32	6	307	3	9
Zaun, Greg, Oma.	1.000	7	44	3	0	47	1	0
Zeber, Ryan, Edm.	1.000	1	3	1	0	4	0	0
Zinter, Alan, Iowa	.986	19	70	3	1	74	1	4

TRIPLE PLAYS: Martinez, Wilson.

CATCHERS WITH TWO OR MORE TEAMS

Player, Team	Pct.	G	PO	A	E	TC	DP	PB
Ardoin, Danny, Sac.	.977	41	276	17	7	300	3	11
Ardoin, Danny, S.L.	1.000	3	22	2	0	24	0	1
Decker, Steve, Edm.	.991	15	97	8	1	106	4	1
Decker, Steve, Sac.	.988	11	77	7	1	85	1	2
Knorr, Randy, Nash.	.963	12	69	9	3	81	1	3
Knorr, Randy, Okla.	.990	64	366	34	4	404	8	3
Melhuse, Adam, Alb.	1.000	17	95	16	0	111	1	6
Melhuse, Adam, C.S.	.983	12	53	4	1	58	1	2
Strittmatter, Mark, C.S.	.984	12	59	4	1	64	2	0
Strittmatter, Mark, L.V.	.991	12	99	6	1	106	1	2

PITCHERS

Player, Team	Pct.	G	PO	A	E	TC	DP
Adkins, Jon, Sac.	1.000	1	0	1	0	1	0
Ahearne, Pat, Tac.	.973	29	4	32	1	37	0
Ah Yat, Paul, Nash.*	.923	19	8	16	2	26	1
Akers, Chad, Tac.	.000	1	0	0	0	0	0
Alexander, Chad, Tac.	1.000	1	0	2	0	2	0
Almanzar, Carlos, L.V.	.000	4	0	0	0	0	0
Almonte, Hector, Cal.	.857	18	2	4	1	7	1
Alston, Garvin, Alb.	1.000	10	0	2	0	2	1
Alvarez, Juan, Edm.*	1.000	44	3	11	0	14	1
Ambrose, John, Mem.	1.000	13	1	2	0	3	0
Anderson, Jimmy, Nash.*	1.000	2	0	1	0	1	0
Anderson, Ryan, Tac.*	1.000	20	0	6	0	6	0
Andra, Jeff, Fres.*	1.000	7	1	4	0	5	0
Andrews, Jeff, Tuc.	.750	16	1	2	1	4	0
Andujar, Luis, L.V.-Nash.	1.000	35	5	12	0	17	0
Arnold, Jamie, Alb.-Iowa	.905	23	5	14	2	21	1
Arroyo, Bronson, Nash.	.875	13	10	18	4	32	2
Arroyo, Luis, Cal.*	1.000	7	3	2	0	5	1
Atchison, Scott, Tac.	1.000	5	2	2	0	4	0
Austin, Jeff, Oma.	.781	23	9	16	7	32	1
Ayala, Bobby, Iowa-Alb.	1.000	34	4	5	0	9	0
Ayers, Mike, Nash.*	1.000	11	0	3	0	3	0
Bailey, Cory, Nash.	.900	55	9	9	2	20	4
Baker, Jason, Oma.	.889	7	5	3	1	9	0
Baptist, Travis, Nash.*	1.000	34	11	29	0	40	3
Barker, Richie, Iowa	1.000	10	0	1	0	1	0
Barnes, Brian, Cal.*	1.000	26	6	0	0	6	1
Barnes, John, S.L.	.000	1	0	0	0	0	0
Batista, Miguel, Oma.	1.000	18	1	1	0	2	0
Beaumont, Matt, Edm.*	1.000	2	0	2	0	2	1
Belcher, Tim, Edm.	1.000	3	1	0	0	1	0
Belitz, Todd, Sac.*	1.000	12	1	0	0	1	0
Beltran, Rigo, C.S.*	1.000	25	7	27	0	34	1
Benes, Alan, Mem.	1.000	9	2	5	0	7	0
Benz, Jake, Cal.*	1.000	15	2	0	0	2	0
Bergman, Sean, Cal.	1.000	13	6	6	0	12	1
Bierbrodt, Nick, Tuc.*	1.000	4	1	3	0	4	0
Bieser, Steve, Mem.	.000	1	0	0	0	0	0
Bluma, Jaime, Oma.	1.000	30	3	6	0	9	0
Bochtler, Doug, Oma.	1.000	27	2	5	0	7	0
Boskie, Shawn, Edm.-Tuc.	.950	20	2	17	1	20	0
Bost, Heath, C.S.	1.000	7	0	2	0	2	0
Bourgeois, Steve, C.S.	.600	9	1	2	2	5	0
Bowie, Micah, Iowa*	1.000	9	1	4	0	5	0
Brohawn, Troy, Tuc.*	1.000	11	0	3	0	3	0
Brunette, Justin, Mem.*	.800	30	0	4	1	5	1
Brunson, Will, Sac.*	1.000	18	0	4	0	4	1
Burnett, A.J., Cal.	.000	1	0	0	0	0	0
Burrows, Terry, Sac.*	1.000	2	0	3	0	3	0

Player, Team	Pct.	G	PO	A	E	TC	DP
Busby, Mike, S.L.	1.000	7	0	1	0	1	0
Byrdak, Tim, Oma.*	1.000	34	1	5	0	6	0
Cabrera, Jose, N.O.	1.000	12	0	3	0	3	0
Callier, Jeremy, Edm.	1.000	9	2	5	0	7	1
Camp, Jared, Oma.	1.000	13	2	3	0	5	0
Carlson, Dan, Tuc.	.000	4	0	0	0	0	0
Carlyle, Buddy, L.V.	.962	27	7	18	1	26	1
Carmona, Rafael, Tac.	.000	3	0	0	0	0	0
Carrara, Giovanni, C.S.	.957	18	9	13	1	23	0
Carter, Lance, Oma.	1.000	34	7	10	0	17	1
Castillo, Carlos, Cal.	.778	13	0	7	2	9	0
Cather, Mike, Cal.	1.000	43	4	7	0	11	0
Checo, Robinson, Alb.	.933	16	4	10	1	15	1
Chouinard, Bobby, C.S.	.750	9	1	2	1	4	0
Clontz, Brad, Nash.	.000	4	0	0	0	0	0
Cloude, Ken, Tac.	.889	14	4	12	2	18	0
Cole, Victor, Mem.	1.000	5	2	3	0	5	0
Connelly, Steve, Fres.	1.000	43	2	10	0	12	0
Cooper, Brian, Edm.	.857	11	2	4	1	7	0
Corbin, Archie, Oma.	1.000	32	5	8	0	13	0
Cordero, Francisco, Okla.	1.000	3	0	0	0	0	0
Corey, Bryan, Sac.	1.000	47	3	6	0	9	1
Cornelius, Reid, Cal.	1.000	8	1	10	0	11	0
Corsi, Jim, Tuc.	1.000	32	0	7	0	7	0
Cox, Ryan, Fres.	.000	1	0	0	0	0	0
Crabtree, Robbie, Fres.	1.000	63	10	18	0	28	0
Crafton, Kevin, Mem.	.000	2	0	0	0	0	0
Creek, Ryan, Cal.-Tuc.	1.000	7	1	0	0	1	0
Cressend, Jack, S.L.	1.000	54	10	4	0	14	0
Croushore, Rich, C.S.	1.000	33	3	4	0	7	1
Cubillan, Darwin, Okla.	1.000	8	3	2	0	5	0
Cumberland, Chris, Fres.*	1.000	9	0	4	0	4	1
Cunnane, Will, L.V.	1.000	17	4	15	0	19	0
Curl, John, L.V.	.000	1	0	0	0	0	0
Dace, Derek, Tuc.*	1.000	31	3	3	0	6	0
D'Amico, Jeff, Oma.	.947	16	6	12	1	19	0
Davey, Tom, Tac.-L.V.	.952	41	13	7	1	21	0
Davis, Clint, Tuc.	.929	49	2	11	1	14	1
Davis, Doug, Okla.*	.909	12	1	19	2	22	0
Davis, Jason, Fres.*	1.000	46	4	10	0	14	0
De Jean, Mike, C.S.	1.000	12	1	1	0	2	0
Del Toro, Miguel, Fres.	.950	21	7	12	1	20	0
DeLucia, Rich, Sac.*	1.000	10	2	3	0	5	0
Demouy, Chris, Edm.*	1.000	1	1	0	0	1	0
DeSilva, John, Cal.	.950	29	8	11	1	20	0
Dickey, R.A., Okla.	.882	30	10	20	4	34	1
Dickson, Jason, Edm.	1.000	2	1	0	0	1	0
Diorio, Mike, Nash.	1.000	6	0	1	0	1	1
DiPoto, Jerry, C.S.	1.000	9	1	0	0	1	0
Donnelly, Brendan, Iowa	1.000	9	2	1	0	3	1
Dougherty, Jim, Mem.	.960	60	6	18	1	25	3
Driskill, Travis, N.O.	.957	28	5	17	1	23	2
Drumright, Mike, Cal.	.952	34	3	17	1	21	1
Duarte, Renney, Edm.	1.000	1	2	0	0	2	0
Duncan, Geoff, Cal.	1.000	24	1	4	0	5	0
Durbin, Chad, Oma.	1.000	12	5	9	0	14	1
Durocher, Jayson, L.V.	1.000	31	5	2	0	7	0
Elarton, Scott, N.O.	1.000	2	1	2	0	3	0
Estes, Shawn, Fres.*	.000	1	0	0	1	1	0
Etherton, Seth, Edm.	1.000	9	4	3	0	7	0
Evans, Dave, Tuc.	1.000	41	1	11	0	12	0
Eversgerd, Bryan, Mem.*	.957	48	5	17	1	23	1
Falteisek, Steve, Cal.	1.000	5	0	3	0	3	0
Farnsworth, Kyle, Iowa	.833	22	0	5	1	6	1
Feliciano, Pedro, Alb.*	.000	1	0	0	0	0	0
Fesh, Sean, C.S.*	1.000	8	1	2	0	3	0
Figueroa, Nelson, Tuc.	.941	17	13	19	2	34	0
Flores, Ignacio, Alb.	1.000	2	2	2	0	4	0
Flury, Pat, Cal.	1.000	12	1	2	0	3	0
Ford, Ben, Iowa	1.000	8	2	5	0	7	1
Franklin, Ryan, Tac.	.964	31	9	18	1	28	0
Franklin, Wayne, N.O.*	1.000	48	2	5	0	7	0
Freehill, Mike, Okla.	1.000	16	2	1	0	3	0
Fuller, Jody, Tuc.	.000	1	0	0	0	0	0
Fussell, Chris, Oma.	1.000	6	3	1	0	4	0
Fyhrie, Mike, Edm.	1.000	9	1	3	0	4	0
Gagne, Eric, Alb.	.750	9	0	3	1	4	0
Gajkowski, Steve, Sac.	.889	36	3	5	1	9	2
Gandarillas, Gus, S.L.	.947	63	7	11	1	19	2
Garcia, Freddy, Tac.	1.000	1	0	1	0	1	0
Garcia, Mike, Nash.	.833	24	3	2	1	6	1
Garibay, Daniel, Iowa*	1.000	1	0	3	0	3	0

Player, Team	Pct.	G	PO	A	E	TC	DP
Garrett, Hal, Alb.	.750	27	1	5	2	8	0
Garza, Chris, S.L.*	1.000	19	1	2	0	3	0
George, Chris, Oma.*	1.000	8	1	6	0	7	0
Gilbert, Shawn, Alb.	.000	1	0	0	0	0	0
Gilfillan, Jason, Oma.	.000	1	0	0	0	0	0
Glynn, Ryan, Okla.	.933	15	7	7	1	15	0
Gonzalez, Enrique, Tuc.	1.000	1	0	1	0	1	0
Granger, Jeff, Alb.*	1.000	2	0	0	0	0	0
Green, Jason, N.O.	1.000	10	3	0	0	3	0
Green, Steve, Edm.	.889	8	0	8	1	9	0
Greene, Rick, S.L.	1.000	22	2	3	0	5	0
Grilli, Jason, Cal.	.923	8	3	9	1	13	1
Gross, Kip, N.O.	.975	25	5	34	1	40	2
Gryboski, Kevin, Tac.	1.000	31	2	5	0	7	0
Guerra, Mark, N.O.	1.000	9	3	6	0	9	0
Gunderson, Eric, Fres.*	.750	13	1	2	1	4	1
Guzman, Domingo, L.V.	.929	43	5	8	1	14	1
Guzman, Geraldo, Tuc.	1.000	6	2	4	0	6	0
Hackman, Luther, Mem.	.889	21	3	13	2	18	1
Harville, Chad, Sac.	.875	53	6	8	2	16	0
Haynes, Heath, N.O.	.000	2	0	0	0	0	0
Heathcott, Mike, Iowa-Edm.	.939	41	10	21	2	33	0
Heaverlo, Jeff, Tac.	1.000	2	0	1	0	1	0
Heflin, Bronson, Nash.	1.000	4	1	1	0	2	0
Heiserman, Rick, Mem.	1.000	55	4	11	0	15	1
Henderson, Rod, Tac.	1.000	4	0	2	0	2	0
Henderson, Ryan, Cal.	1.000	11	2	0	0	2	0
Henderson, Scott, Cal.	.000	8	0	0	0	0	0
Hernandez, Fernando, N.O.	.750	36	1	5	2	8	1
Herndon, Junior, L.V.	.923	26	12	24	3	39	3
Hiatt, Phil, C.S.	.000	1	0	0	0	0	0
Hill, Ken, Edm.	.000	2	0	0	0	0	0
Hinchliffe, Brett, Edm.-Iowa	.941	34	6	10	1	17	1
Hoane, Wes, Tac.	.000	1	0	0	0	0	0
Hodges, Kevin, Tac.	1.000	30	11	15	0	26	2
Holmes, Darren, Mem.-Tuc.	1.000	12	0	1	0	1	0
Holtz, Mike, Edm.*	.000	6	0	0	0	0	0
Hooten, Dave, S.L.	.889	13	2	6	1	9	0
House, Craig, C.S.	1.000	8	2	0	0	2	0
Huisman, Rick, N.O.	1.000	48	2	6	0	8	0
Hundley, Jeff, Edm.*	.750	2	1	2	1	4	0
Hutchinson, Chad, Mem.	.000	5	0	0	0	0	0
Hutton, Mark, N.O.	1.000	46	4	9	0	13	2
Iglesias, Mario, Iowa	1.000	8	1	0	0	1	0
James, Mike, Mem.	1.000	8	2	0	0	2	0
Janzen, Marty, Tuc.	.667	10	1	1	1	3	0
Jarvis, Kevin, C.S.	1.000	7	4	3	0	7	1
Jennings, Robin, S.L.*	.000	1	0	0	0	0	0
Jensen, Ryan, Fres.	1.000	26	4	13	0	17	0
Johnson, Jon, Okla.	.857	36	4	8	2	14	0
Johnstone, John, Fres.	.000	1	0	0	0	0	0
Jones, Greg, Edm.	1.000	25	5	2	0	7	0
Jones, Marcus, Sac.	.857	17	3	3	1	7	0
Judd, Mike, Alb.	.958	25	9	14	1	24	3
Karchner, Matt, Iowa	1.000	20	5	6	0	11	0
Karl, Scott, C.S.*	.833	3	2	3	1	6	0
Karnuth, Jason, Mem.	.852	16	8	15	4	27	3
Kaufman, Brad, N.O.	.778	40	2	5	2	9	0
Keagle, Greg, Edm.	.000	1	0	0	0	0	0
Kelley, Rich, Edm.*	1.000	7	2	3	0	5	0
Kim, Byung-Hyun, Tuc.	1.000	2	1	0	0	1	1
King, Ray, Iowa*	.500	1	0	1	1	2	0
Kinney, Matt, S.L.	1.000	9	2	4	0	6	0
Knoll, Brian, Fres.	1.000	10	1	6	0	7	1
Knott, Eric, Tuc.*	1.000	11	1	3	0	4	0
Kolb, Brandon, L.V.	.714	47	1	4	2	7	0
Kolb, Dan, Okla.	1.000	13	2	5	0	7	1
Kroon, Marc, Alb.	.000	4	0	0	0	0	0
Kubenka, Jeff, Tuc.-Sac.*	1.000	21	0	5	0	5	0
Kubinski, Tim, Sac.*	.941	41	5	11	1	17	0
Lankford, Frank, Sac.	1.000	29	5	14	0	19	2
Lawrence, Brian, L.V.	1.000	8	1	12	0	13	0
Laxton, Brett, Oma.	.935	21	11	18	2	31	0
Lee, Corey, Okla.*	.864	26	5	14	3	22	2
Lee, David, C.S.	.917	47	5	6	1	12	0
Lee, Jonathan, Tuc.	1.000	1	1	0	0	1	0
Lehr, Charles, Sac.	.000	1	0	0	0	0	0
Leon, Danny, Nash.	1.000	3	1	4	0	5	0
Lincoln, Mike, S.L.	1.000	12	11	9	0	20	0
Linebrink, Scott, Fres.-N.O.	1.000	39	1	2	0	3	0
Linton, Doug, C.S.	.897	28	10	25	4	39	0
Loewer, Carlton, L.V.	1.000	1	2	1	0	3	0
Loiselle, Rich, Nash.	1.000	4	0	1	0	1	0

Player, Team	Pct.	G	PO	A	E	TC	DP
Looney, Brian, Cal.*	1.000	3	1	2	0	3	0
Lopez, Johan, Okla.	1.000	29	2	5	0	7	1
Lopez, Rodrigo, L.V.	1.000	20	5	9	0	14	0
Lynch, Jim, Fres.	.000	2	0	0	0	0	0
Magnante, Mike, Sac.*	.500	5	0	1	1	2	0
Mahaffey, Alan, S.L.*	.882	34	2	13	2	17	1
Mahay, Ron, Cal.*	.000	8	0	0	0	0	0
Mahoney, Mike, Iowa	.000	1	0	0	0	0	0
Mairena, Ozwaldo, Iowa*	1.000	11	1	3	0	4	0
Manning, David, Iowa	1.000	19	5	12	0	17	1
Mantei, Matt, Tuc.	.000	4	0	0	0	0	0
Manwiller, Tim, Sac.	1.000	5	0	2	0	2	0
Manzanillo, Josias, Nash.	1.000	15	2	1	0	3	0
Martinez, Jose, Okla.	1.000	11	4	10	0	14	1
Masaoka, Onan, Alb.*	1.000	18	2	1	0	3	0
Mathews, T.J., Sac.	1.000	3	0	4	0	4	0
Mathews, Terry, Okla.	.800	7	2	2	1	5	0
Matthews, Mike, Mem.*	.923	9	1	11	1	13	1
Mattson, Rob, Nash.	.914	17	6	26	3	35	0
Maurer, Dave, L.V.*	1.000	35	4	7	0	11	0
Mays, Joe, S.L.	1.000	3	0	1	0	1	0
McCarthy, Greg, Cal.*	.875	40	2	5	1	8	0
McConnell, Sam, Nash.*	1.000	8	3	12	0	15	1
McDill, Allen, Mem.*	1.000	23	1	4	0	5	0
McKnight, Tony, N.O.	.913	19	5	16	2	23	1
McMullen, Mike, Fres.	.850	36	3	14	3	20	3
McNichol, Brian, Iowa*	.923	43	3	9	1	13	1
Meacham, Rusty, N.O.	1.000	33	2	14	0	16	0
Meche, Gil, Tac.	.500	3	1	0	1	2	0
Menhart, Paul, C.S.	1.000	14	1	2	0	3	0
Meyer, Jake, Tac.	1.000	8	0	2	0	2	0
Meyers, Mike, Iowa	1.000	13	5	8	0	13	0
Miadich, Bart, Edm.	1.000	10	0	1	0	1	0
MICHALAK, Chris, Alb.*	1.000	23	9	39	0	48	3
Middlebrook, Jason, L.V.	.000	1	0	0	0	0	0
Miller, Ernie, Edm.*	1.000	1	0	1	0	1	0
Miller, Justin, Sac.	.889	9	2	6	1	9	1
Miller, Matt, Okla.	.889	39	2	6	1	9	0
Miller, Trever, Alb.*	1.000	12	7	9	0	16	0
Miller, Wade, N.O.	.968	16	7	23	1	31	0
Mintz, Steve, Edm.	.750	32	0	3	1	4	0
Mitchell, Dean, Okla.	.810	45	5	12	4	21	4
Mohler, Mike, Sac.*	.750	18	0	3	1	4	0
Montane, Ivan, Tac.	1.000	16	0	6	0	6	3
Montgomery, Matt, Alb.	1.000	7	1	2	0	3	0
Montgomery, Steve, L.V.	.000	1	0	0	0	0	0
Montoya, Saul, Tuc.	.000	3	0	0	0	0	0
Moody, Eric, L.V.-Cal.	1.000	39	4	7	0	11	1
Moraga, David, C.S.*	1.000	6	3	4	0	7	0
Morgan, Russ, Tac.*	.000	1	0	0	0	0	0
Morris, Matt, Mem.	1.000	3	0	3	0	3	1
Morse, Paul, Edm.	.944	13	3	14	1	18	1
Mota, Danny, S.L.	1.000	4	1	1	0	2	0
Mounce, Tony, Okla.*	.846	32	2	9	2	13	0
Mulder, Mark, Sac.*	1.000	2	0	2	0	2	0
Mullen, Scott, Oma.*	.750	16	2	1	1	4	1
Munro, Peter, Okla.	1.000	5	4	7	0	11	0
Murray, Dan, Oma.	.871	27	17	10	4	31	1
Murray, Heath, Alb.*	.969	29	4	27	1	32	1
Nathan, Joe, Fres.	1.000	3	0	1	0	1	0
Naulty, Dan, Oma.	1.000	4	1	0	0	1	0
Navarro, Jaime, C.S.	1.000	5	1	7	0	8	0
Newman, Eric, Iowa	.917	30	4	7	1	12	0
Newstrom, Doug, Tuc.	.000	1	0	0	0	0	0
Niebla, Ruben, Alb.*	1.000	24	4	6	0	10	1
Niedermaier, Brad, C.S.	1.000	7	1	2	0	3	1
Nina, Elvin, Edm.	.500	3	0	1	1	2	1
Norris, Ben, Tuc.*	1.000	12	3	8	0	11	0
Norton, Phillip, Iowa*	.846	28	3	30	6	39	2
Nunez, Maximo, Alb.	.000	1	0	0	0	0	0
Nunez, Vladimir, Cal.	.933	15	3	11	1	15	1
Nussbeck, Mark, Mem.	.958	21	7	16	1	24	3
O'Connor, Brian, Nash.*	1.000	5	2	5	0	7	0
Olivares, Omar, Sac.	1.000	1	1	0	0	1	0
Oliver, Darren, Okla.*	1.000	7	0	5	0	5	0
Olson, Gregg, Alb.	.000	4	0	0	0	0	0
Ontiveros, Steve, C.S.	1.000	8	4	8	0	12	1
Orosco, Jesse, Mem.*	.000	2	0	0	0	0	0
Ortiz, Ramon, Edm.	.842	15	7	9	3	19	0
Osteen, Gavin, Nash.*	1.000	14	1	1	0	2	0
Osuna, Antonio, Alb.	.000	3	0	0	0	0	0
Padilla, Vicente, Tuc.	1.000	12	1	4	0	5	0
Palacios, Vicente, L.V.-Iowa	1.000	42	5	8	0	13	1
Parra, Jose, Nash.	.923	23	7	5	1	13	1
Patrick, Bronswell, Cal.	1.000	27	14	20	0	34	2
Patterson, John, Tuc.	1.000	3	0	2	0	2	0
Pavlas, Dave, Nash.	.769	45	1	9	3	13	0
Penny, Brad, Cal.	1.000	3	1	0	0	1	0
Perez, Eduardo, Mem.	1.000	1	0	1	0	1	0
Perkins, Dan, S.L.	.962	33	14	11	1	26	2
Peters, Chris, Nash.*	1.000	11	4	6	0	10	0
Petersen, Chris, Iowa	1.000	1	0	1	0	1	0
Phillips, Jason, Nash.	1.000	6	4	1	0	5	0
Pineiro, Joel, Tac.	1.000	10	2	8	0	10	2
Plantenberg, Erik, N.O.-Cal.*	.833	30	1	4	1	6	0
Porzio, Mike, C.S.*	1.000	6	0	5	0	5	0
Pote, Lou, Edm.	1.000	24	0	5	0	5	0
Powell, Brian, N.O.	.923	18	2	10	1	13	1
Powell, Jay, N.O.	1.000	2	0	1	0	1	0
Prieto, Ariel, Sac.	.906	20	9	20	3	32	5
Pulsipher, Bill, Tuc.*	.818	13	2	7	2	11	0
Quevedo, Ruben, Iowa	.917	13	3	8	1	12	1
Radlosky, Rob, S.L.	1.000	5	0	2	0	2	0
Rain, Steve, Iowa.	.667	28	1	1	1	3	0
Rakers, Jason, Oma.	1.000	32	2	3	0	5	0
Ramirez, Hector, N.O.	.000	5	0	0	0	0	0
Ramsay, Robert, Tac.*	1.000	3	0	1	0	1	0
Randall, Scott, S.L.-Okla.	.950	30	15	23	2	40	1
Randolph, Steve, Tuc.*	1.000	5	0	2	0	2	0
Rath, Fred, S.L.-Mem.-Nash.	.857	37	11	13	4	28	3
Rath, Gary, Tuc.*	1.000	11	0	1	0	1	0
Ratliff, Jon, Sac.	.889	20	5	11	2	18	0
Ray, Ken, Fres.	1.000	7	0	1	0	1	0
Reames, Britt, Mem.	.955	13	9	12	1	22	2
Revenig, Todd, Tuc.	.750	17	1	2	1	4	0
Reyes, Al, Alb.	1.000	30	3	3	0	6	0
Reyes, Carlos, L.V.	1.000	16	1	4	0	5	0
Ricketts, Chad, Alb.	1.000	54	3	3	0	6	0
Riley, Mike, Fres.*	.941	24	3	13	1	17	0
Rivette, Scott, Tac.	1.000	3	0	1	0	1	1
Rizzo, Todd, S.L.*	.923	61	0	12	1	13	1
Robertson, Jeriome, N.O.*	1.000	9	0	8	0	8	0
Rodriguez, Frank, Tac.	1.000	9	6	3	0	9	1
Rodriguez, Jose, Mem.*	1.000	40	1	8	0	9	1
Romano, Mike, S.L.	1.000	16	9	17	0	26	3
Romero, J.C., S.L.*	.958	17	8	15	1	24	0
Root, Derek, L.V.*	1.000	9	0	2	0	2	0
Rosengren, John, Nash.*	.000	4	0	0	0	0	0
Ruffin, Johnny, Tuc.	1.000	45	6	2	0	8	0
Ryan, Jason, S.L.	.929	17	6	7	1	14	1
Sabel, Erik, Tuc.	.947	29	10	8	1	19	1
Saipe, Mike, C.S.-L.V.-Edm.	.813	21	4	9	3	16	1
Sak, Jim, Nash.	.000	6	0	0	0	0	0
Sampson, Benj, S.L.*	.929	18	4	9	1	14	0
Sanders, Scott, Edm.-Cal.-Sac.	1.000	22	6	9	0	15	0
Santiago, Jose, Oma.	1.000	11	2	1	0	3	0
Sauerbeck, Scott, Nash.*	.000	2	0	0	0	0	0
Sauveur, Rich, Sac.*	.941	25	4	12	1	17	1
Scheffer, Aaron, Tac.	.917	21	4	7	1	12	0
Schoeneweis, Scott, Edm.*	1.000	1	0	1	0	1	0
Scott, Darryl, C.S.-Tuc.	.750	16	1	2	1	4	0
Serafini, Dan, L.V.-Nash.*	.923	33	5	19	2	26	0
Sergio, Tom, Okla.	.000	1	0	0	0	0	0
Serrano, Wascar, L.V.	1.000	4	0	2	0	2	0
Service, Scott, Sac.	1.000	33	3	2	0	5	0
Shields, Scot, Edm.	.917	27	7	15	2	24	0
Sikorski, Brian, Okla.	.862	24	11	14	4	29	0
Sinclair, Steve, Tac.*	.955	45	8	13	1	22	1
Skrmetta, Matt, Nash.	1.000	7	0	1	0	1	0
Slusarski, Joe, N.O.	1.000	13	1	1	0	2	0
Small, Aaron, C.S.	1.000	36	10	10	0	20	1
Smith, Bud, Mem.*	1.000	9	3	12	0	15	0
Smith, Cam, Alb.	1.000	39	5	6	0	11	0
Smith, Chuck, Okla.	.813	11	4	9	3	16	1
Snow, Bert, Sac.	.000	3	0	0	0	0	0
Sodowsky, Clint, Okla.	1.000	13	0	1	0	1	0
Sollecito, Gabe, Okla.	1.000	7	2	2	0	4	0
Spencer, Sean, Tac.*	.875	42	2	5	1	8	0
Spencer, Stan, L.V.	.875	6	2	5	1	8	0
Spoljaric, Paul, Oma.*	1.000	43	3	6	0	9	0
Stechschulte, Gene, Mem.	1.000	41	4	6	0	10	0
Steenstra, Kennie, Mem.-Tuc.	1.000	34	5	20	0	25	3
Stein, Blake, Oma.	1.000	2	1	0	0	1	0
Stentz, Brent, S.L.	.667	42	2	2	2	6	0
Stone, Ricky, Alb.	.900	48	10	17	3	30	3
Stoops, Jim, C.S.	.000	3	0	0	0	0	0

CLASS AAA Pacific Coast League

Player, Team	Pct.	G	PO	A	E	TC	DP
Strong, Joe, Cal.	1.000	29	1	7	0	8	0
Suarez, Felipe, Edm.	.000	1	0	0	0	0	0
Sullivan, Brendan, L.V.	.913	45	6	15	2	23	1
Sweeney, Brian, Tac.	.000	2	0	0	0	0	0
Tabaka, Jeff, C.S.*	1.000	22	0	4	0	4	0
Tebbs, Nate, L.V.	.000	3	0	0	0	0	0
Thompson, Justin, Okla.*	1.000	1	0	1	0	1	0
Thompson, Mark, Mem.	.800	6	1	3	1	5	0
Tollberg, Brian, L.V.	1.000	13	4	7	0	11	0
Tomko, Brett, Tac.	1.000	2	1	0	0	1	0
Torres, Melqui, Tac.	1.000	1	0	1	0	1	0
Tremie, Chris, Cal.	.000	2	0	0	0	0	0
Tuttle, Dave, Tuc.	1.000	20	4	14	0	18	0
Tyler, Josh, Fres.	.000	2	0	0	0	0	0
Ulloa, Enmanuel, Tac.	.000	1	0	0	0	0	0
Van Poppel, Todd, Iowa	1.000	10	1	4	0	5	0
Verdugo, Jason, Fres.	1.000	11	1	3	0	4	0
Verplancke, Jeff, Fres.	.000	1	0	0	0	0	0
Villano, Mike, Nash.	.857	45	8	16	4	28	2
Villarreal, Oscar, Tac.	.000	2	0	0	0	0	0
Vizcaino, Luis, Sac.	1.000	33	3	7	0	10	1
Vosberg, Ed, C.S.*	.783	29	1	17	5	23	1
Wainhouse, David, Mem.	.889	20	3	5	1	9	1
Walker, Jamie, Oma.*	1.000	24	2	14	0	16	1
Walker, Pete, C.S.	1.000	58	1	9	0	10	0
Wall, Donne, L.V.	1.000	2	0	0	0	0	0
Wallace, Jeff, Nash.*	1.000	13	0	3	0	3	0
Ward, Bryan, Edm.*	.000	6	0	0	0	0	0
Ward, Jeremy, Tuc.	1.000	5	1	0	0	1	0
Washburn, Jarrod, Edm.*	1.000	5	1	2	0	3	1
Watkins, Scott, C.S.*	.667	43	2	6	4	12	0
Watson, Mark, Tac.*	1.000	16	3	4	0	7	1
Weaver, Eric, Edm.	1.000	34	5	7	0	12	1
Weber, Ben, Fres.	1.000	38	4	11	0	15	0
Wehner, John, Nash.	.000	2	0	0	0	0	0
Weibl, Clint, Mem.	.952	19	7	13	1	21	0
Whisenant, Matt, L.V.*	1.000	33	4	4	0	8	0
Whiteside, Matt, L.V.	1.000	23	3	3	0	6	0
Wilkins, Marc, Nash.	.778	17	1	6	2	9	1
Williams, Jeff, Alb.*	1.000	12	6	10	0	16	0
Williams, Shad, Edm.	1.000	22	3	1	0	4	0
Williams, Todd, Tac.	.917	50	1	10	1	12	0
Williams, Woody, L.V.	.000	1	0	0	0	0	0
Wise, Matt, Edm.	.923	19	6	6	1	13	1
Wojciechowski, Steve, Fres.-Cal.*	.933	33	2	12	1	15	1
Wolff, Bryan, N.O.-S.L.	.800	20	4	8	3	15	0
Wood, Kerry, Iowa	1.000	1	0	4	0	4	0
Worrell, Tim, Iowa	1.000	6	2	0	0	2	0
Young, Danny, Iowa*	.875	27	0	7	1	8	1
Zambrano, Carlos, Iowa	.913	34	9	12	2	23	2
Zancanaro, Dave, Iowa*	.923	25	7	17	2	26	2
Zerbe, Chad, Fres.*	.800	17	3	13	4	20	0
Zimmerman, Jordan, Tac.*	.667	15	1	3	2	6	0
Zito, Barry, Sac.*	.960	18	4	20	1	25	3
Zosky, Eddie, Nash.	.000	1	0	0	0	0	0

PITCHERS WITH TWO OR MORE TEAMS

Player, Team	Pct.	G	PO	A	E	TC	DP
Andujar, Luis, L.V.	1.000	10	3	1	0	4	0
Andujar, Luis, Nash.	1.000	25	2	11	0	13	0
Arnold, Jamie, Alb.	.857	20	4	8	2	14	1
Arnold, Jamie, Iowa	1.000	3	1	6	0	7	0
Ayala, Bobby, Iowa	1.000	10	3	1	0	4	0
Ayala, Bobby, Alb.	1.000	24	1	4	0	5	0
Boskie, Shawn, Edm.	1.000	14	1	10	0	11	0
Boskie, Shawn, Tuc.	.889	6	1	7	1	9	0
Creek, Ryan, Cal.	1.000	3	1	0	0	1	0
Creek, Ryan, Tuc.	.000	4	0	0	0	0	0
Davey, Tom, Tac.	1.000	28	11	7	0	18	0
Davey, Tom, L.V.	.667	13	2	0	1	3	0
Heathcott, Mike, Iowa	.931	38	8	19	2	29	0
Heathcott, Mike, Edm.	1.000	3	2	2	0	4	0
Hinchliffe, Brett, Edm.	.909	27	4	6	1	11	1
Hinchliffe, Brett, Iowa	1.000	7	2	4	0	6	0
Holmes, Darren, Mem.	.000	9	0	0	0	0	0
Holmes, Darren, Tuc.	1.000	3	0	1	0	1	0
Kubenka, Jeff, Tuc.*	.000	4	0	0	0	0	0
Kubenka, Jeff, Sac.*	1.000	17	0	5	0	5	0
Linebrink, Scott, Fres.	1.000	28	1	2	0	3	0
Linebrink, Scott, N.O.	.000	11	0	0	0	0	0
Moody, Eric, L.V.	1.000	4	0	1	0	1	0
Moody, Eric, Cal.	1.000	35	4	6	0	10	1
Palacios, Vicente, L.V.	1.000	36	3	3	0	6	0
Palacios, Vicente, Iowa	1.000	6	2	5	0	7	1
Plantenberg, Erik, N.O.*	.833	24	1	4	1	6	0
Plantenberg, Erik, Cal.*	.000	6	0	0	0	0	0
Randall, Scott, S.L.	1.000	14	6	13	0	19	0
Randall, Scott, Okla.	.905	16	9	10	2	21	1
Rath, Fred, S.L.	.750	12	1	2	1	4	1
Rath, Fred, Mem.	.923	18	5	7	1	13	1
Rath, Fred, Nash.	.818	7	5	4	2	11	1
Saipe, Mike, C.S.	.786	15	2	9	3	14	1
Saipe, Mike, L.V.	.000	2	0	0	0	0	0
Saipe, Mike, Edm.	1.000	4	2	0	0	2	0
Sanders, Scott, Edm.	1.000	6	1	2	0	3	0
Sanders, Scott, Cal.	1.000	6	3	1	0	4	0
Sanders, Scott, Sac.	1.000	10	2	6	0	8	0
Scott, Darryl, C.S.	1.000	2	0	1	0	1	0
Scott, Darryl, Tuc.	.667	14	1	1	1	3	0
Serafini, Dan, L.V.*	.923	26	4	8	1	13	0
Serafini, Dan, Nash.*	.923	7	1	11	1	13	0
Steenstra, Kennie, Mem.	1.000	10	1	4	0	5	2
Steenstra, Kennie, Tuc.	1.000	24	4	16	0	20	1
Wojciechowski, Steve, Fres.*	1.000	13	1	8	0	9	0
Wojciechowski, Steve, Cal.*	.833	20	1	4	1	6	1
Wolff, Bryan, N.O.	.714	11	1	4	2	7	0
Wolff, Bryan, S.L.	.875	9	3	4	1	8	0

The following players appeared only as designated hitter, pinch-hitter or pinch runner: Alvarado, ph; Betts, ph; Bush, dh; Jaha, dh; McClendon, ph; W. Nieves, ph; Saenz, dh; Santos, ph; D. Wilson, dh.

LEAGUE CHAMPIONS

Year	Team	Pct.
1903—	Los Angeles	.630
1904—	Tacoma	.589
	Tacoma§	.571
	Los Angeles§	.571
1905—	Tacoma	.583
	Los Angeles*	.604
1906—	Portland	.657
1907—	Los Angeles	.608
1908—	Los Angeles	.585
1909—	San Francisco	.623
1910—	Portland	.567
1911—	Portland	.589
1912—	Oakland	.591
1913—	Portland	.559
1914—	Portland	.574
1915—	San Francisco	.570
1916—	Los Angeles	.601
1917—	San Francisco	.561
1918—	Vernon	.569
	Los Angeles (2nd)◆	.548
1919—	Vernon	.613
1920—	Vernon	.556
1921—	Los Angeles	.574

Year	Team	Pct.
1922—	San Francisco	.638
1923—	San Francisco	.617
1924—	Seattle	.545
1925—	San Francisco	.643
1926—	Los Angeles	.599
1927—	Oakland	.615
1928—	San Francisco*	.630
	Sacramento∞	.626
	San Francisco∞	.626
1929—	Mission	.643
	Hollywood*	.592
1930—	Los Angeles	.576
	Hollywood*	.650
1931—	Hollywood	.626
	San Francisco*	.608
1932—	Portland	.587
1933—	Los Angeles	.610
1934—	Los Angeles▼	.786
	Los Angeles▼	.689
1935—	Los Angeles	.648
	San Francisco*	.608
1936—	Portland‡	.549
1937—	Sacramento	.573

Year	Team	Pct.
	San Diego (3rd)†	.545
1938—	Los Angeles	.590
	Sacramento (3rd)†	.537
1939—	Seattle	.589
	Sacramento (4th)†	.500
1940—	Seattle‡	.629
1941—	Seattle‡	.598
1942—	Sacramento	.590
	Seattle (3rd)†	.539
1943—	Los Angeles	.710
	S. Francisco (2nd)†	.574
1944—	Los Angeles	.586
	S. Francisco (3rd)†	.509
1945—	Portland	.622
	S. Francisco (4th)†	.525
1946—	San Francisco‡	.628
1947—	Los Angeles▲	.567
1948—	Oakland‡	.606
1949—	Hollywood‡	.583
1950—	Oakland	.590
1951—	Seattle‡	.593
1952—	Hollywood	.606
1953—	Hollywood	.589

Year	Team	Pct.	Year	Team	Pct.	Year	Team	Pct.
1954—	San Diego■	.604		Eugene	.534		Las Vegas*	.563
1955—	Seattle	.552	1973—	Tucson	.583	1987—	Calgary	.596
1956—	Los Angeles	.637		Spokane•	.563		Albuquerque*	.542
1957—	San Francisco	.601	1974—	Spokane•	.549	1988—	Vancouver	.599
1958—	Phoenix	.578		Albuquerque	.535		Las Vegas*	.529
1959—	Salt Lake City	.552	1975—	Salt Lake City	.556	1989—	Albuquerque	.563
1960—	Spokane	.601		Hawaii•	.611		Vancouver*	.514
1961—	Tacoma	.630	1976—	Salt Lake City	.625	1990—	Albuquerque*	.641
1962—	San Diego	.604		Hawaii•	.531		Edmonton	.553
1963—	Spokane	.620	1977—	Phoenix•	.579	1991—	Albuquerque	.580
	Oklahoma City•	.632		Hawaii	.541		Tucson*	.564
1964—	Arkansas	.609	1978—	Tacoma††	.584	1992—	Colorado Springs*	.596
	San Diego•	.576		Albuquerque††	.557		Portland	.576
1965—	Oklahoma City	.628	1979—	Albuquerque	.581	1993—	Portland	.608
	Portland	.547		Salt Lake City‡‡	.541		Tucson*	.580
1966—	Seattle•	.561	1980—	Albuquerque	.578	1994—	Albuquerque*	.597
	Tulsa	.578		Hawaii	.539		Vancouver	.542
1967—	San Diego•	.574	1981—	Albuquerque*	.712	1995—	Salt Lake	.549
	Spokane	.541		Tacoma	.561		Colorado Springs*	.538
1968—	Tulsa•	.642	1982—	Albuquerque*	.594	1996—	Edmonton*	.592
	Spokane	.586		Spokane	.545		Phoenix	.479
1969—	Tacoma•	.589	1983—	Albuquerque	.594	1997—	Phoenix	.615
	Eugene	.603		Portland*	.528		Edmonton*	.556
1970—	Spokane•	.644	1984—	Hawaii	.621	1998—	Iowa	.590
	Hawaii	.671		Edmonton*	.486		New Orleans†	.535
1971—	Salt Lake City	.534	1985—	Vancouver*	.522	1999—	Vancouver‡	.592
	Tacoma	.545		Phoenix	.563	2000—	Salt Lake	.629
1972—	Albuquerque	.622	1986—	Vancouver	.616		Memphis‡	.576

*Won split-season playoff. †Won four-team playoff. ‡Won pennant and four-team playoff. §Tied for second-half title with Tacoma winning playoff. ∞Tied for second-half title, with Sacramento winning playoff. ▲Ended regular season in tie with San Francisco and won one-game playoff for pennant, then won four-club playoff. ◆Won playoff from first-place Vernon and awarded championship. ■Defeated Hollywood in one-game playoff for pennant. ▼Won both halves, no playoff. •League was divided into Northern, Southern divisions in 1963, 1969-70-71, and Eastern, Western divisions in 1964 through 1968 and 1972 through 1977, won two-team playoff. ††League divided into Eastern and Western divisions, Tacoma and Albuquerque declared co-champions following cancellation of four-team playoff due to continuing rain and wet grounds. ‡‡Won second-half title and defeated Hawaii in four-team playoff.

CLASS AAA Pacific Coast League

EASTERN LEAGUE

LEAGUE OFFICE

President
Bill Troubh

Address
P.O. Box 9711
Portland, ME 04104

Phone
207-761-2700

TEAMS

AKRON AEROS

General manager/vice president
Jeff Auman
Manager
Willie Upshaw
Ballpark (capacity, surface)
Canal Park (9,097, grass)
Affiliation
Indians
Address
300 S. Main St.
Akron, OH 44308
Phone
330-253-5151

ALTOONA CURVE

General manager
Jeff Parker
Manager
Dale Sveum
Ballpark (capacity, surface)
Blair County Ballpark (6,120, grass)
Affiliation
Pirates
Address
P.O. Box 1029
Altoona, PA 16603
Phone
814-943-5400

BINGHAMTON METS

General manager
Bill Terlecky
Manager
Howie Freiling
Ballpark (capacity, surface)
Binghamton Municipal Stadium (6,012, grass)
Affiliation
Mets
Address
211 Henry Street
Binghamton, NY 13901
Phone
607-723-6387

BOWIE BAYSOX

General manager
Jon Danos
Manager
Dave Machemer
Ballpark (capacity, surface)
Prince George's Stadium (10,000, grass)
Affiliation
Orioles
Address
4101 NE Crain Highway
Bowie, MD 20716
Phone
301-805-6000

ERIE SEAWOLVES

General manager
John Frey
Manager
To be announced
Ballpark (capacity, surface)
Jerry Uht Park (6,000, grass)
Affiliation
Tigers
Address
110 E. 10th Street
Erie, PA 16501
Phone
814-456-1300

HARRISBURG SENATORS

General manager
Todd Vander Woude
Manager
Luis Dorante
Ballpark (capacity, surface)
RiverSide Stadium (6,300, grass)
Affiliation
Expos
Address
RiverSide Stadium/City Island
Harrisburg, PA 17101
Phone
717-231-4444

NEW BRITAIN ROCK CATS

General manager
Bill Dowling
Manager
Stan Cliburn
Ballpark (capacity, surface)
New Britain Stadium (6,146, grass)
Affiliation
Twins
Address
South Main Street
New Britain, CT 06051
Phone
860-224-8383

NEW HAVEN RAVENS

General manager
Bob Flannery
Manager
Dan Sheaffer
Ballpark (capacity, surface)
Yale Field (6,200, grass)
Affiliation
Cardinals
Address
252 Derby Ave.
West Haven, CT 06516
Phone
203-782-1666

NORWICH NAVIGATORS

General manager
Brian Mahoney
Manager
Dan Radison
Ballpark (capacity, surface)
Thomas J. Dodd Memorial Stadium (6,000, grass)
Affiliation
Yankees
Address
14 Stott Ave.
Norwich, CT 06360
Phone
860-887-7962

PORTLAND SEA DOGS

General manager
Charles Eshbach
Manager
Rick Renteria
Ballpark (capacity, surface)
Hadlock Field (6,850, grass)
Affiliation
Marlins
Address
271 Park Avenue
Portland, ME 04102
Phone
207-874-9300

READING PHILLIES

General manager
Chuck Domino
Manager
Gary Varsho
Ballpark (capacity, surface)
GPU Stadium (8,500, grass)
Affiliation
Phillies
Address
Route 61 South/1900 Centre Ave.
Reading, PA 19605
Phone
610-375-8469

TRENTON THUNDER

General manager
Rick Brenner
Manager
Billy Gardner Jr.
Ballpark (capacity, surface)
Samuel J. Plumeri, Sr. Field at Mercer County Waterfront Park (6,300, grass)
Affiliation
Red Sox
Address
One Thunder Road
Trenton, NJ 08611
Phone
609-394-3300

CLASS AA *Eastern League*

NORTH DIVISION

Team	W	L	T	Pct.	GB
Binghamton (Mets)	82	58	0	.586	...
New Haven (Mariners)	82	60	0	.577	1.0
Norwich (Yankees)	76	66	0	.535	7.0
Portland (Marlins)	71	70	0	.504	11.5
Trenton (Red Sox)	67	75	0	.472	16.0
New Britain (Twins)	51	91	0	.359	32.0

SOUTH DIVISION

Team	W	L	T	Pct.	GB
Reading (Phillies)	85	57	0	.599	...
Harrisburg (Expos)	76	67	0	.531	9.5
Akron (Indians)	75	68	0	.524	10.5
Altoona (Pirates)	74	68	0	.521	11.0
Bowie (Orioles)	65	77	0	.458	20.0
Erie (Angels)	47	94	0	.333	37.5

COMPOSITE

Team	Read.	Bing.	N.H.	Nor.	Har.	Akr.	Alt.	Por.	Tren.	Bow.	N.B.	Erie	W	L	T	Pct.	GB
Reading (Phillies)	...	3	4	3	11	11	11	5	6	16	1	14	85	57	0	.599	...
Binghamton (Mets)	4	...	11	9	4	5	5	12	11	2	15	4	82	58	0	.586	2.0
New Haven (Mariners)	3	9	...	12	1	3	5	10	14	5	14	6	82	60	0	.577	3.0
Norwich (Yankees)	4	11	8	...	5	5	2	7	10	5	14	5	76	66	0	.535	9.0
Harrisburg (Expos)	9	3	6	2	...	10	8	5	5	11	5	12	76	67	0	.531	9.5
Akron (Indians)	9	2	4	2	11	...	11	6	5	11	3	11	75	68	0	.524	10.5
Altoona (Pirates)	9	2	2	5	12	9	...	6	2	10	4	13	74	68	0	.521	11.0
Portland (Marlins)	2	7	10	13	2	1	1	...	10	3	16	6	71	70	0	.504	13.5
Trenton (Red Sox)	1	9	6	10	2	2	5	10	...	4	12	6	67	75	0	.472	18.0
Bowie (Orioles)	4	5	2	2	9	9	10	4	3	...	4	13	65	77	0	.458	20.0
New Britain (Twins)	6	5	6	6	2	4	3	4	8	3	...	4	51	91	0	.359	34.0
Erie (Angels)	6	2	1	2	8	5	9	7	1	7	3	...	47	94	0	.333	37.5

Major league affiliations in parentheses.

PLAYOFFS: New Haven defeated Binghamton three games to one; Reading defeated Harrisburg three games to none; New Haven defeated Reading three games to one to win league championship.

REGULAR-SEASON ATTENDANCE: Akron, 481,060; Altoona, 333,968; Binghamton, 184,695; Bowie, 400,338; Erie, 206,208; Harrisburg, 250,384; New Britain, 220,127; New Haven, 185,086; Norwich, 226,551; Portland, 370,702; Reading, 452,343; Trenton, 408,262. Total—3,719,724. Class AA All-Star Game at Bowie, Md.—14,077.

MANAGERS: Akron, Eric Wedge; Altoona, Marty Brown; Binghamton, Doug Davis; Bowie, Andy Etchebarren; Erie, Don Wakamatsu; Harrisburg, Doug Sisson; New Britain, John Russell; New Haven, Dan Rohn; Norwich, Dan Radison; Portland, Rick Renteria; Reading, Gary Varsho; Trenton, Billy Gardner Jr.

ALL-STAR TEAM—1B—Shea Hillenbrand, Trenton; 2B—Pablo Osuna, Portland; 3B—Scott Seabol, Norwich; SS—Ramon Vazquez, New Haven; OF—Adam Hyzdu, Altoona; OF—Eric Valent, Reading; OF—Alex Escobar, Binghamton; C—Mike Kinkade, Binghamton; DH—Juan Thomas, New Haven; Utility—Rick Short, Bowie; RHP—Greg Wooten, New Haven; Donnie Bridges, Harrisburg; LHP—Sam McConnell, Altoona; Wilson Guzman, Altoona; Relief pitcher—Jerrod Riggan, Binghamton; Player of the Year—Adam Hyzdu, Altoona; Pitcher of the Year—Greg Wooten, New Haven; Rookie of the Year—Alex Escobar, Binghamton; Manager of the Year—Gary Varsho, Reading.

2000 BATTING

TEAM

Team	Avg.	G	TPA	AB	R	H	TB	2B	3B	HR	RBI	SH	SF	HP	BB	IBB	SO	SB	CS	GDP	LOB	ShO	Slg.	OBP
Trenton	.272	142	5370	4832	691	1314	1954	258	29	108	648	17	40	60	421	6	947	83	66	110	958	9	.404	.335
Portland	.269	141	5391	4674	736	1257	1858	232	42	95	677	45	48	69	555	17	957	145	78	77	1034	8	.398	.352
New Haven	.267	142	5447	4778	668	1274	1892	253	40	95	607	41	39	63	526	17	858	91	42	111	1079	5	.396	.345
Bowie	.265	142	5375	4733	664	1255	1826	246	32	87	603	41	48	66	487	11	818	117	58	111	1044	12	.386	.339
Binghamton	.265	140	5030	4498	650	1191	1808	239	30	106	592	45	34	64	389	15	1021	133	73	93	861	9	.402	.330
Reading	.265	142	5522	4797	730	1269	2003	262	29	138	680	68	52	75	530	12	763	98	51	92	1037	10	.418	.344
Altoona	.264	142	5437	4764	682	1257	1888	230	31	113	621	55	43	48	527	23	941	75	48	93	1038	7	.396	.340
New Britain	.264	142	5329	4721	631	1244	1845	251	49	84	589	28	33	63	484	16	883	67	38	136	1021	9	.391	.338
Akron	.259	143	5436	4804	656	1243	1874	237	41	104	609	38	41	50	503	15	948	110	56	83	1046	9	.390	.333
Norwich	.256	142	5383	4743	653	1213	1876	260	32	113	617	38	30	42	530	23	1019	106	61	102	1018	11	.396	.334
Harrisburg	.251	143	5322	4638	644	1166	1677	217	54	62	570	60	41	69	514	14	916	197	80	84	1002	8	.362	.332
Erie	.248	141	5185	4582	581	1136	1687	206	39	89	531	45	38	76	444	7	1006	125	66	79	945	12	.368	.322

INDIVIDUAL

TOP QUALIFIERS FOR BATTING CHAMPIONSHIP

Minimum 383 plate appearances. *Lefthanded batter. †Switch-hitter.

Player, Team	Avg.	G	TPA	AB	R	H	TB	2B	3B	HR	RBI	SH	SF	HP	BB	IBB	SO	SB	CS	GDP	Slg.	OBP
Kinkade, Mike, Bing.-Bow.	.358	98	396	344	70	123	193	25	3	13	72	0	3	11	38	5	46	18	7	8	.561	.434
Short, Rick, Bow.	.331	116	507	447	63	148	216	39	1	9	82	0	8	8	44	2	54	3	3	14	.483	.394
Hillenbrand, Shea, Tren.	.323	135	558	529	77	171	245	35	3	11	79	0	2	8	19	0	39	3	3	15	.463	.355
Betts, Todd, Port.*	.321	119	498	421	74	135	192	26	2	9	71	0	5	8	64	3	57	4	3	6	.456	.416
Held, Dan, Bing.	.312	114	429	381	66	119	177	23	1	11	69	0	3	17	28	3	71	4	3	9	.465	.382
Chevalier, Virgil, Tren.	.309	89	390	346	58	107	155	25	1	7	67	0	8	2	34	1	35	3	2	11	.448	.367
Ozuna, Pablo, Port.	.308	118	521	464	74	143	201	25	6	7	59	5	5	7	40	0	55	35	24	9	.433	.368
Ottavinia, Paul, Nor.*	.302	127	548	477	80	144	211	27	8	8	58	0	5	10	56	7	50	15	5	10	.442	.383
Erickson, Matt, Port.*	.301	100	407	335	56	101	138	23	4	2	41	1	3	9	59	3	62	8	3	9	.412	.416
Mackowiak, Rob, Alt.*	.297	134	568	526	82	156	236	33	4	13	87	4	7	9	22	0	96	18	5	8	.449	.332
Seabol, Scott, Nor.	.296	132	542	493	82	146	255	45	2	20	78	1	2	4	42	1	108	2	4	11	.517	.355
Edwards, Mike, Akr.	.295	136	560	481	72	142	204	25	2	11	63	3	5	5	68	2	86	7	3	9	.424	.386
Michaels, Jason, Read.	.295	113	478	437	71	129	197	30	4	10	74	3	7	3	28	1	87	7	4	9	.451	.337
McNamara, Rusty, Read.	.294	125	534	466	79	137	215	24	6	14	76	1	6	18	43	1	41	3	3	10	.461	.371
Clark, Jermaine, N.H.*	.293	133	569	447	80	131	178	23	9	2	44	18	3	14	87	3	69	38	8	7	.398	.421

DEPARTMENTAL LEADERS: G—Hyzdu, 142; AB—Mateo, 530; R—Hyzdu, Crespo, 96 each; H—Hillenbrand, 171; TB—Hyzdu, 285; 2B—Seabol, 45; 3B—McKinley, 14; HR—Hyzdu, 31; RBI—Hyzdu, 106; SH—J. Clark, 18; SF—Gibralter, Guiel, 9 each; HP—Blakely, 20; BB—Kielty, 98; IBB—Hyzdu, Ottavinia, 7 each; SO—Blakely, 136; SB—Mateo, 48; CS—Ozuna, 24; GIDP—Gibralter, 18; Slg.—Kinkade, .561; OBP—Kinkade, .434.

ALL PLAYERS

*Lefthanded batter. †Switch-hitter.

Player, Team	Avg.	G	TPA	AB	R	H	TB	2B	3B	HR	RBI	SH	SF	HP	BB	IBB	SO	SB	CS	GDP	Slg.	OBP
Abbott, Chuck, Erie	.248	97	365	330	39	82	117	14	3	5	39	7	2	4	22	0	96	3	3	11	.355	.302
Ackerman, Scott, Har.	.000	1	3	3	0	0	0	0	0	0	0	0	0	0	0	0	0	0	0	0	.000	.000
Agamennone, Brandon, Har.	.000	30	15	13	1	0	0	0	0	0	0	1	0	0	1	0	4	0	0	0	.000	.071
Alcala, Juan, N.H.	.222	2	9	9	1	2	2	0	0	0	0	0	0	0	0	0	2	1	0	0	.222	.222
Almanzar, Rich, Nor.	.219	58	218	183	18	40	48	8	0	0	9	5	0	4	26	1	14	9	6	6	.262	.329
Almonte, Erick, Nor.	.271	131	506	454	56	123	194	18	4	15	77	12	2	3	35	0	129	12	2	3	.427	.326
Alvarado, Carlos, Alt.	.000	16	3	2	0	0	0	0	0	0	0	1	0	0	0	0	2	0	0	0	.000	.000
Alvarez, Clemente, Read.	.222	9	25	18	2	4	5	1	0	0	5	2	2	0	3	0	3	0	0	1	.278	.304
Alvarez, Rafael, N.B.*	.259	97	316	274	35	71	111	15	2	7	46	0	2	4	35	2	65	3	1	8	.405	.349
Amezcua, Adan, Bow.	.314	17	54	51	4	16	23	4	0	1	6	0	0	0	3	0	9	1	0	0	.451	.352
Aracena, Juan, Bing.	.000	7	1	0	0	0	0	0	0	0	0	0	0	0	1	0	0	0	0	0	.000	1.000
Arroyo, Luis, Port.*	.000	31	1	1	0	0	0	0	0	0	0	0	0	0	0	0	1	0	0	0	.000	.000
Arteaga, J.D., Bing.*	.000	34	11	11	0	0	0	0	0	0	0	0	0	0	0	0	6	0	0	0	.000	.000
Ayers, Mike, Alt.*	.000	38	1	1	0	0	0	0	0	0	0	0	0	0	0	0	0	0	0	0	.000	.000
Barthol, Blake, N.H.	.298	74	280	248	43	74	106	9	1	7	30	2	2	2	26	1	44	1	1	13	.427	.367
Bass, Jayson, Alt.†	.244	19	51	45	7	11	13	0	1	0	5	0	1	0	5	0	8	3	0	1	.289	.314
Baughman, Justin, Erie	.286	31	136	126	15	36	45	2	2	1	6	1	0	1	8	0	20	11	2	1	.357	.333
Beimel, Joe, Alt.*	.250	10	10	8	3	2	3	1	0	0	0	1	0	0	1	0	4	0	0	0	.375	.333
Benefield, Brian, Akr.	.000	1	3	2	0	0	0	0	0	0	0	0	0	0	1	0	2	0	0	0	.000	.333
Benz, Jake, Port.*	.000	14	2	2	0	0	0	0	0	0	0	0	0	0	0	0	0	0	0	0	.000	.000
Betts, Todd, Port.*	.321	119	498	421	74	135	192	26	2	9	71	0	5	8	64	3	57	4	3	6	.456	.416
Bigbie, Larry, Bow.*	.241	31	124	112	11	27	33	6	0	0	5	1	0	0	11	0	28	3	0	3	.295	.309
Blakely, Darren, Erie†	.237	122	497	439	72	104	186	20	7	16	54	6	2	20	30	1	136	13	5	11	.424	.314
Bolivar, Papo, N.B.	.278	117	442	406	46	113	152	19	7	2	42	3	4	5	24	0	69	14	8	14	.374	.323
Brea, Lesli, Bing.	.000	19	13	12	0	0	0	0	0	0	1	1	0	0	0	0	9	0	0	0	.000	.000
Brester, Jason, Read.*	.267	25	17	15	3	4	7	0	0	1	1	0	0	0	2	0	2	0	0	0	.467	.353
Bridges, Donnie, Har.	.261	24	24	23	2	6	11	2	0	1	5	1	0	0	0	0	2	1	0	1	.478	.261
Brittan, Corey, Bing.	.000	55	4	3	0	0	0	0	0	0	0	1	0	0	0	0	0	0	0	0	.000	.000
Brown, Adrian, Alt.†	.000	2	8	5	1	0	0	0	0	0	0	0	0	0	3	0	1	0	0	0	.000	.375
Brown, Rich, Nor.*	.238	82	346	319	52	76	109	15	3	4	30	1	0	1	25	0	34	15	7	6	.342	.296
Bruce, Mo, Bing.	.274	81	345	314	50	86	114	16	3	2	23	2	1	1	27	0	55	21	10	8	.363	.332
Budzinski, Mark, Akr.*	.239	18	79	71	7	17	22	2	0	1	5	1	0	1	6	1	20	3	2	0	.310	.308
Bump, Nate, Port.	.154	26	18	13	1	2	3	1	0	0	0	4	0	0	1	0	3	0	0	0	.231	.214
Burnham, Gary, Read.*	.268	111	411	355	53	95	162	28	0	13	61	0	2	14	40	2	47	0	1	10	.456	.363
Burton, Darren, Alt.†	.328	63	263	229	44	75	102	8	2	5	33	3	3	5	23	0	42	3	0	3	.445	.396
Butler, Rich, N.H.*	.243	26	115	103	16	25	45	3	1	5	23	0	2	2	8	0	22	1	0	3	.437	.304
Calabrese, Anthony, Nor.	.000	1	1	1	0	0	0	0	0	0	0	0	0	0	0	0	1	0	0	0	.000	.000
Camilli, Jason, Har.	.213	65	273	240	27	51	76	10	3	3	19	4	2	3	24	1	51	3	6	2	.317	.290
Candelaria, Ben, Port.*	.258	20	77	66	8	17	26	3	0	2	15	1	2	1	7	1	16	0	0	1	.394	.329
Capista, Aaron, Tren.†	.237	126	479	434	52	103	135	20	3	2	36	2	2	4	37	0	68	9	4	6	.311	.322
Cappuccio, Carmine, Read.*	.230	60	202	187	23	43	80	5	1	10	36	1	3	1	10	0	22	0	1	7	.428	.269
Carrasco, Dan, Alt.	.000	9	2	2	0	0	0	0	0	0	0	0	0	0	0	0	1	0	0	0	.000	.000
Carroll, Jamey, Har.	.290	45	183	169	23	49	60	5	3	0	18	1	1	0	12	0	13	8	2	5	.355	.335
Carvajal, Jhony, Har.	.247	24	82	73	8	18	28	7	0	1	11	0	1	1	7	0	12	2	1	3	.384	.317
Casimiro, Carlos, Bow.	.262	87	319	290	44	76	110	12	2	6	32	3	1	1	23	0	66	2	4	5	.379	.317
Cedeno, Blas, Read.	.000	36	4	2	0	0	0	0	0	0	0	1	0	0	1	0	1	0	0	0	.000	.333
Cerros, Juan, Bing.	.000	50	3	2	1	0	0	0	0	0	0	1	0	0	0	0	1	0	0	0	.000	.000
Chapman, Jake, Har.	.000	49	1	1	0	0	0	0	0	0	0	0	0	0	0	0	0	0	0	0	.000	.000
Chevalier, Virgil, Tren.	.309	89	390	346	58	107	155	25	1	7	67	0	8	2	34	1	35	3	2	11	.448	.367
Clark, Chris, Port.	.200	32	7	5	0	1	1	0	0	0	0	2	0	0	0	0	1	0	0	0	.200	.200
Clark, Howie, Bow.*	.340	13	58	53	11	18	27	6	0	1	9	0	1	1	3	0	6	0	0	1	.509	.379
Clark, Jermaine, N.H.*	.293	133	569	447	80	131	178	23	9	2	44	18	3	14	87	3	69	38	8	7	.398	.421
Coffie, Ivanon, Bow.*	.267	87	384	341	49	91	145	21	3	9	44	0	3	4	36	3	53	1	4	6	.425	.341
Coggin, Dave, Read.	.000	7	5	5	0	0	0	0	0	0	0	0	0	0	0	0	0	0	0	0	.000	.000
Cole, Brian, Bing.	.278	46	196	176	31	49	74	9	2	4	25	3	3	1	13	0	28	15	4	2	.420	.326
Comer, Scott, Port.*	.286	25	9	7	0	2	2	0	0	0	1	2	0	0	0	0	1	0	0	0	.286	.286
Connors, Greg, N.H.	.279	123	513	452	64	126	188	29	3	9	58	2	5	7	47	0	83	0	1	7	.416	.352
Corey, Mark, Bing.	.000	14	1	0	0	0	0	0	0	0	0	1	0	0	0	0	0	0	0	0	.000	.000
Coste, Chris, Akr.	.333	65	260	240	32	80	114	20	4	2	31	0	1	4	15	2	33	1	2	7	.475	.381
Cota, Humberto, Alt.	.261	112	459	429	49	112	158	20	1	8	44	1	5	3	21	1	80	6	4	8	.368	.297
Cota, Marino, Bing.	.000	22	1	1	0	0	0	0	0	0	0	0	0	0	0	0	1	0	0	0	.000	.000
Cotton, Joe, Read.	.000	33	3	3	0	0	0	0	0	0	0	0	0	0	0	0	0	0	0	0	.000	.000
Crespo, Cesar, Port.†	.257	134	574	482	96	124	184	21	6	9	60	8	5	2	77	3	118	41	15	8	.382	.359
Crumpton, Chuck, Har.	.167	31	8	6	0	1	1	0	0	0	1	0	0	0	1	0	3	0	0	0	.167	.286
Cuddyer, Mike, N.B.	.263	138	565	490	72	129	193	30	8	6	61	6	2	12	55	2	93	5	4	16	.394	.351
Curtis, Matt, Akr.†	.000	1	4	4	0	0	0	0	0	0	0	0	0	0	0	0	0	0	0	0	.000	.000
Daniels, John, Read.†	.000	41	10	9	0	0	0	0	0	0	0	0	0	1	0	0	3	0	0	1	.000	.100
Davidson, Cleatus, N.B.†	.229	119	487	445	42	102	129	13	7	0	31	10	1	3	28	0	93	15	7	6	.290	.279
De Leon, Jorge, Tren.	.307	88	370	339	47	104	128	16	1	2	38	2	0	5	24	1	51	1	8	8	.378	.361
Dennis, Les, Tren.	.200	20	67	60	8	12	15	0	0	1	3	0	0	0	7	0	15	0	1	0	.250	.284
Dent, Darrell, Bow.*	.260	115	429	362	52	94	107	11	1	0	25	7	2	2	56	0	63	20	11	4	.296	.360
Depastino, Joe, Bow.	.215	19	71	65	11	14	26	6	0	2	9	0	0	0	6	0	13	0	0	4	.400	.282
Depippo, Jeff, Akr.	.227	57	200	172	20	39	56	6	1	3	19	7	2	6	13	0	60	2	1	2	.326	.301
Derosso, Tony, Tren.	.281	120	501	449	77	126	222	28	4	20	85	0	2	5	45	1	91	0	1	14	.494	.351
Diaz, Juan, Tren.	.313	50	210	198	36	62	129	14	1	17	53	0	2	0	10	0	56	0	0	6	.652	.343
Diaz, Maikell, Bow.	.133	5	16	15	1	2	2	0	0	0	1	0	0	0	0	0	6	0	0	0	.133	.133

Player, Team	Avg.	G	TPA	AB	R	H	TB	2B	3B	HR	RBI	SH	SF	HP	BB	IBB	SO	SB	CS	GDP	Slg.	OBP
Dina, Allen, Bing.	.258	121	464	419	58	108	159	22	4	7	46	9	3	11	22	0	78	21	10	7	.379	.310
Dominique, Andy, Read	.239	104	378	327	46	78	144	27	0	13	50	3	4	8	35	0	56	0	1	9	.440	.324
Dougherty, Jeb, Erie	.240	76	318	267	33	64	82	9	3	1	32	6	7	2	36	0	42	20	7	2	.307	.327
Duckworth, Brandon, Read.†	.263	30	22	19	2	5	6	1	0	0	4	1	0	0	2	0	5	0	0	0	.316	.333
Duff, Matt, Alt.	.400	48	5	5	0	2	2	0	0	0	0	0	0	0	0	0	1	0	0	0	.400	.400
Dykhoff, Radhames, Bing.*	1.000	17	2	1	0	1	1	0	0	0	0	1	0	0	0	0	0	0	0	0	1.000	1.000
Edwards, Mike, Akr.	.295	136	560	481	72	142	204	25	2	11	63	3	3	5	68	2	86	7	3	9	.424	.386
Epperson, Chad, Bow.*	.214	10	45	42	6	9	15	3	0	1	5	0	0	0	3	0	9	1	0	1	.357	.267
Erickson, Corey, Akr.	.214	7	30	28	4	6	17	2	0	3	9	0	0	0	2	0	11	0	0	0	.607	.267
Erickson, Matt, Port.*	.301	100	407	335	56	101	138	23	4	2	41	1	3	9	59	3	62	8	3	9	.412	.416
Escobar, Alex, Bing.	.288	122	506	437	79	126	213	25	7	16	67	0	5	7	57	5	114	24	5	8	.487	.375
Espinal, Juan, Tren.	.296	15	62	54	13	16	31	4	1	3	9	0	2	0	6	0	13	0	0	0	.574	.355
Estrada, Johnny, Read.†	.295	95	372	356	42	105	159	18	0	12	42	2	0	4	10	2	20	1	0	8	.447	.322
Evans, Lee, Alt.†	.237	32	137	118	18	28	37	4	1	1	8	4	0	1	14	2	28	1	1	3	.314	.323
Fernandez, Alex, N.H.*	.254	101	365	350	32	89	125	22	1	4	40	1	2	1	11	1	51	10	4	9	.357	.277
Figga, Mike, Tren.	.185	8	29	27	1	5	8	0	0	1	2	0	0	0	2	0	8	0	0	0	.296	.241
Figueroa, Luis, N.H.	.272	117	467	427	49	116	145	24	1	1	37	2	2	2	34	1	39	0	1	14	.340	.327
Figueroa, Luis, Alt.†	.284	94	392	342	45	97	118	10	4	1	28	10	1	2	37	1	32	14	5	8	.345	.356
Fischer, Mark, Tren.	.204	34	125	108	15	22	33	6	1	1	15	0	4	1	12	0	39	1	1	1	.306	.280
Fitzgerald, Jason, Akr.*	.279	56	236	208	27	58	86	8	4	4	30	1	2	1	23	1	38	7	6	0	.413	.350
Flores, Jose, N.H.	.184	12	48	38	5	7	10	3	0	0	1	1	0	2	7	0	5	0	0	0	.263	.340
Foster, Quincy, Port.*	.310	65	283	248	60	77	98	7	4	2	21	3	2	7	23	0	42	25	8	2	.395	.382
France, Aaron, Alt.*	.100	23	11	10	1	1	1	0	0	0	0	0	0	0	1	0	6	0	0	0	.100	.182
Francia, David, Read.*	.290	56	241	210	36	61	84	8	3	3	26	8	2	10	11	0	29	16	7	2	.400	.352
Fuentes, Javier, Tren.	.167	2	7	6	0	1	1	0	0	0	0	0	0	0	1	0	0	0	1	0	.167	.286
Funaro, Joe, Port.	.250	26	93	68	7	17	19	2	0	0	5	2	1	5	17	0	12	1	0	3	.279	.429
Furniss, Eddy, Alt.*	.239	121	425	348	50	83	134	16	1	11	52	1	5	3	68	3	82	4	4	4	.385	.363
Gainey, Bryon, Bing.*	.203	106	370	345	36	70	121	18	0	11	49	1	1	0	23	3	132	1	2	9	.351	.252
Gallagher, Shawn, Har.	.191	21	80	68	7	13	16	3	0	0	5	0	1	4	7	0	14	3	1	3	.235	.300
Garabito, Eddy, Bow.†	.251	116	529	482	72	121	166	21	3	6	52	8	7	5	27	1	55	22	9	7	.344	.294
Geary, Geoff, Read.	.118	22	19	17	1	2	2	0	0	0	0	0	0	0	2	0	10	0	0	0	.118	.211
Gibralter, David, Bow.	.284	134	575	497	70	141	220	20	1	19	87	2	9	12	39	0	81	3	1	18	.443	.345
Gload, Ross, Port.*	.284	100	439	401	60	114	198	28	4	16	65	3	4	2	29	3	53	4	1	4	.494	.333
Goetz, Geoff, Port.*	.000	17	1	1	0	0	0	0	0	0	0	0	0	0	0	0	0	0	0	0	.000	.000
Gonzalez, Dicky, Bing.	.143	26	16	14	0	2	2	0	0	0	2	1	0	0	1	0	4	0	0	0	.143	.200
Gonzalez, Gabe, Har.*	.333	44	3	3	1	1	1	0	0	0	0	0	0	0	0	0	0	0	0	0	.333	.333
Gonzalez, Jimmy, Bing.	.278	73	261	234	32	65	104	13	1	8	30	0	1	5	21	0	52	1	2	3	.444	.349
Gordon, Keith, N.H.	.247	23	81	77	4	19	29	4	0	2	9	0	0	1	3	0	24	0	0	2	.377	.284
Grabow, John, Alt.*	.111	24	20	18	1	2	2	0	0	0	1	2	0	0	0	0	7	0	0	0	.111	.111
Graham, Jess, Tren.*	.238	75	285	256	28	61	93	11	3	5	33	2	2	5	20	2	61	0	3	8	.363	.304
Graves, Bryan, Erie	.216	34	121	97	12	21	29	5	0	1	14	0	2	1	21	0	23	0	1	5	.299	.355
Guiel, Jeff, Erie*	.254	118	481	410	55	104	183	25	3	16	59	1	9	10	49	3	97	2	4	8	.446	.341
Gunderson, Shane, N.B.	.280	19	54	50	9	14	21	4	0	1	3	0	0	2	2	0	8	0	0	0	.420	.333
Guy, Brad, Alt.	.000	55	3	3	0	0	0	0	0	0	0	0	0	0	0	0	1	0	0	0	.000	.000
Guzman, Wilson, Alt.*	.000	18	18	12	2	0	0	0	0	0	0	5	0	0	1	0	6	0	0	0	.000	.077
Haad, Yamid, Alt.	.197	59	203	183	24	36	55	7	0	4	13	1	1	0	18	0	44	1	1	4	.301	.267
Hafer, Jeff, Bing.	.000	29	1	1	0	0	0	0	0	0	0	0	0	0	0	0	1	0	0	0	.000	.000
Hagins, Steve, Erie	.186	12	44	43	2	8	15	4	0	1	7	0	0	0	1	0	12	0	1	0	.349	.205
Hall, Noah, Har.	.259	45	189	147	25	38	59	8	2	3	24	2	2	3	35	2	19	8	5	3	.401	.406
Hamilton, Jon, Akr.*	.249	137	562	493	57	123	178	28	3	7	56	0	4	3	62	2	117	12	6	8	.361	.335
Hardge, Mike, Nor.	.241	24	92	83	9	20	29	7	1	0	6	0	0	0	9	0	26	2	3	1	.349	.315
Harper, Brandon, Port.	.208	37	138	125	15	26	44	3	0	5	17	0	0	1	12	0	23	0	0	4	.352	.283
Harris, Brian, Read.†	.268	110	407	351	46	94	152	22	3	10	41	10	4	4	38	0	48	12	5	7	.433	.343
Haverbusch, Kevin, Alt.	.279	43	153	140	23	39	59	3	1	5	21	0	0	2	11	0	15	2	2	5	.421	.340
Haynes, Nathan, Erie*	.254	118	509	457	56	116	158	16	4	6	43	8	2	9	33	0	107	37	20	3	.346	.315
Hebson, Bryan, Har.	.087	29	29	23	1	2	3	1	0	0	1	6	0	0	0	0	10	0	0	2	.130	.087
Held, Dan, Bing.	.312	114	429	381	66	119	177	23	1	11	69	0	3	17	28	3	71	4	3	9	.465	.382
Hemphill, Bret, Erie†	.232	59	235	207	31	48	72	6	3	4	24	3	2	1	22	0	41	0	1	4	.348	.306
Henderson, Scott, Port.	.333	39	3	3	1	1	2	1	0	0	1	0	0	0	0	0	1	0	0	0	.667	.333
Henson, Drew, Nor.	.287	59	245	223	39	64	98	9	2	7	39	0	1	1	20	1	75	0	5	6	.439	.347
Hernandez, Alex, Alt.*	.337	50	214	199	28	67	97	16	1	4	34	1	1	0	13	2	42	1	2	4	.487	.376
Hernandez, Michel, Nor.	.212	21	73	66	7	14	16	2	0	0	4	2	1	0	4	0	13	1	0	1	.242	.254
Hillenbrand, Shea, Tren.	.323	135	558	529	77	171	245	35	3	11	79	0	2	8	19	0	39	3	3	15	.463	.355
Hodges, Scott, Har.*	.176	6	21	17	2	3	6	0	0	1	5	0	2	0	2	2	4	1	0	0	.353	.238
Honeycutt, Heath, Port.	.182	50	189	170	19	31	43	4	1	2	15	0	3	4	12	0	58	3	0	3	.253	.249
Hood, Jay, Erie	.213	71	259	240	25	51	79	16	0	4	29	1	0	2	16	0	50	3	0	6	.329	.267
Horne, Tyrone, Nor.*	.253	31	114	99	11	25	35	4	0	2	9	0	0	0	15	1	26	1	1	3	.354	.351
Horner, Jim, N.H.	.241	65	272	245	36	59	101	11	2	9	33	0	2	5	20	1	42	4	1	7	.412	.309
Huff, B.J., Bing.	.212	73	233	208	18	44	66	8	1	4	24	1	1	1	22	0	79	1	2	3	.317	.289
Huisman, Jason, Erie	.274	120	494	441	52	121	161	23	4	3	42	3	1	9	40	1	75	14	4	9	.365	.346
Huls, Steve, N.B.	.205	102	288	249	24	51	59	4	2	0	15	3	1	3	32	0	51	4	2	2	.237	.302
Hunter, Scott, Akr.	.228	94	377	347	35	79	116	16	3	5	33	3	5	8	14	0	61	11	6	5	.334	.270
Hyzdu, Adam, Alt.	.290	142	619	514	96	149	285	39	2	31	106	0	3	8	94	7	102	3	7	6	.554	.405
Jackson, Gavin, Bing.	.224	33	124	98	13	22	24	0	1	0	9	1	2	1	22	0	21	1	2	4	.245	.366
Jacquez, Tom, Read.*	.000	13	3	3	0	0	0	0	0	0	0	0	0	0	0	0	2	0	0	0	.000	.000
James, Kenny, Har.†	.240	91	373	321	47	77	103	12	4	2	32	4	2	4	42	0	54	31	5	7	.321	.333
Johnson, Gary, Erie†	.287	71	297	258	44	74	122	10	4	10	56	0	1	3	35	0	63	4	4	4	.473	.377
Johnson, Rontrez, Tren.	.269	134	592	524	83	141	184	21	2	6	53	3	4	6	55	1	73	30	19	12	.351	.343
Jones, Jaime, Port.*	.227	50	203	185	25	42	70	6	2	6	30	0	2	3	13	0	47	0	4	2	.378	.286
Jones, Ryan, Akr.	.258	56	239	209	30	54	98	13	2	9	38	0	5	4	21	1	40	0	1	7	.469	.331
Kershner, Jason, Read.*	.182	28	25	22	2	4	4	0	0	0	0	1	0	0	2	0	7	0	0	1	.182	.250
Kielty, Bobby, N.B.†	.262	129	558	451	79	118	196	30	3	14	65	0	4	5	98	4	109	6	4	16	.435	.396
Kiil, Skip, Read	.203	58	231	182	24	37	65	10	0	6	19	4	2	3	40	0	60	5	3	2	.357	.352

Player, Team	Avg.	G	TPA	AB	R	H	TB	2B	3B	HR	RBI	SH	SF	HP	BB	IBB	SO	SB	CS	GDP	Slg.	OBP
Kilburg, Joe, Akr.*	.000	1	2	2	0	0	0	0	0	0	0	0	0	0	0	0	1	0	0	0	.000	.000
King, Brett, Erie	.192	9	28	26	0	5	6	1	0	0	3	0	0	1	1	0	11	0	1	0	.231	.250
Kingman, Brendan, N.H.	.282	11	41	39	3	11	14	3	0	0	5	0	0	2	0	0	4	0	0	2	.359	.317
Kingsale, Eugene, Bow.†	.364	3	14	11	5	4	9	2	0	1	5	0	0	0	3	0	1	0	1	0	.818	.500
Kinkade, Mike, Bing.-Bow.	.358	98	396	344	70	123	193	25	3	13	72	0	3	11	38	5	46	18	7	8	.561	.434
Knotts, Gary, Port.	.111	27	9	9	1	1	1	0	0	0	0	0	0	0	0	0	4	0	0	1	.111	.111
Knupfer, Jason, Read.	.269	84	332	279	53	75	103	14	1	4	24	11	3	0	39	1	46	6	6	4	.369	.355
Lankford, Derrick, Alt.*	.293	96	365	314	41	92	142	16	2	10	40	0	3	0	47	3	60	4	1	7	.452	.382
Lara, Giovanny, Har.	.000	33	3	3	0	0	0	0	0	0	0	0	0	0	0	0	3	0	0	0	.000	.000
Leach, Nick, Nor.*	.277	113	416	354	44	98	144	23	1	7	49	2	1	3	56	3	79	5	3	6	.407	.379
LeBron, Juan, Bing.	.227	72	259	238	26	54	89	17	0	6	25	0	2	3	16	0	82	2	4	3	.374	.282
LeCroy, Matthew, N.B.	.282	54	230	195	33	55	99	12	1	10	38	0	0	6	29	3	34	0	0	8	.508	.391
Leese, Brandon, Port.	.263	27	23	19	4	5	6	1	0	0	4	1	0	0	3	0	2	0	0	0	.316	.364
Leon, Carlos, Tren.†	.204	15	57	49	4	10	14	4	0	0	4	2	0	1	5	0	13	1	2	1	.286	.291
Leon, Jose, Bow.	.250	18	74	68	7	17	21	1	0	1	6	0	0	2	4	0	13	5	2	2	.309	.311
Lewis, Marc, Tren.	.280	63	220	207	26	58	93	14	3	5	30	1	1	1	10	0	44	4	2	3	.449	.315
Lidle, Kevin, Erie†	.220	29	94	82	11	18	20	2	0	0	3	0	0	2	10	2	14	1	2	0	.244	.319
Lomasney, Steve, Tren.	.245	66	272	233	30	57	99	16	1	8	27	1	2	12	24	0	81	4	6	8	.425	.343
Long, Garrett, Alt.	.230	42	142	122	18	28	48	8	0	4	18	0	1	2	17	0	33	0	1	6	.393	.331
Lopez-Cao, Mike, Bow.*	.224	17	54	49	7	11	14	3	0	0	4	0	0	1	4	0	7	0	0	1	.286	.296
Lorenzana, Luis, Alt.	.157	24	57	51	7	8	10	2	0	0	2	2	0	0	4	0	15	0	0	0	.196	.218
Lunar, Fernando, Bow.	.288	22	89	80	12	23	32	7	1	0	8	0	0	3	6	0	8	0	0	4	.400	.360
Machado, Anderson, Read.†	.364	3	11	11	2	4	8	1	0	1	2	0	0	0	0	0	4	0	0	0	.727	.364
Mackowiak, Rob, Alt.*	.297	134	568	526	82	156	236	33	4	13	87	4	7	9	22	0	96	18	5	8	.449	.332
Maddox, Garry, Tren.*	.275	100	406	363	58	100	131	13	3	4	40	2	2	2	36	0	87	7	5	2	.361	.342
Malave, Jaime, Har.	.255	77	215	192	26	49	101	13	0	13	36	0	3	3	17	1	63	0	0	4	.526	.321
Maloney, Sean, Bow.	1.000	6	1	1	0	1	1	0	0	0	0	0	0	0	0	0	0	0	0	0	1.000	1.000
Maness, Dwight, N.H.	.229	114	453	407	54	93	159	20	5	12	52	3	6	8	29	1	98	9	5	3	.391	.289
Maness, Nick, Bing.	.000	2	3	2	0	0	0	0	0	0	0	1	0	0	0	0	1	0	0	0	.000	.000
Manning, Nate, N.B.	.275	18	57	51	8	14	19	5	0	0	6	0	0	1	5	0	11	0	0	1	.373	.351
Manon, Julio, Har.	.000	14	2	2	0	0	0	0	0	0	0	0	0	0	0	0	0	0	0	1	.000	.000
Manzueta, Roberto, Alt.*	.000	8	4	4	0	0	0	0	0	0	0	0	0	0	0	0	2	0	0	0	.000	.000
Marcinczyk, T.R., N.B.	.225	60	220	191	21	43	73	9	0	7	23	0	0	2	27	1	53	1	2	6	.382	.327
Martin, Jeff, Alt.	1.000	17	1	1	1	1	1	0	0	0	0	0	0	0	0	0	0	0	0	0	1.000	1.000
Martinez, Eddy, Bow.	.252	41	153	127	17	32	41	2	2	1	20	3	1	5	17	1	21	0	0	2	.323	.360
Martinez, Gabby, Bing.	.248	48	182	165	22	41	57	4	3	2	12	6	0	0	11	0	22	8	8	3	.345	.295
Martinez, Jesus, Bing.*	.000	6	2	2	0	0	0	0	0	0	0	0	0	0	0	0	2	0	0	0	.000	.000
Mateo, Henry, Har.†	.287	140	600	530	91	152	214	25	11	5	63	4	2	6	58	0	97	48	16	4	.404	.362
Matos, Luis, Bow.	.271	50	207	181	26	49	72	7	5	2	33	1	3	5	17	0	23	14	8	3	.398	.345
Mattes, Troy, Har.	.400	29	22	20	5	8	14	1	1	1	2	1	0	0	1	0	8	1	0	0	.700	.429
Mattson, Rob, Alt.*	.000	7	8	7	0	0	0	0	0	0	0	1	0	0	0	0	3	0	0	0	.000	.000
Matz, Brian, Har.*	.200	41	5	5	1	1	1	0	0	0	0	0	0	0	0	0	2	0	0	0	.200	.200
McClendon, Travis, N.H.	.154	3	13	13	1	2	2	0	0	0	0	0	0	0	0	0	1	0	0	0	.154	.154
McConnell, Sam, Alt.*	.125	20	11	8	0	1	1	0	0	0	1	2	0	0	1	0	4	0	0	0	.125	.222
McCurtain, Paul, Port.	.400	41	6	5	0	2	2	0	0	0	0	0	0	0	1	0	2	0	0	0	.400	.500
McDonald, Darnell, Bow.	.242	116	502	459	59	111	152	13	5	6	43	6	4	4	29	0	87	11	4	7	.331	.290
McDonald, Donzell, Nor.†	.241	44	205	170	23	41	58	7	2	2	10	0	0	3	35	1	36	13	7	1	.341	.371
McKinley, Dan, Har.*	.280	131	562	517	66	145	205	20	14	4	57	8	3	9	25	1	75	23	7	3	.397	.323
McNamara, Rusty, Read.	.294	125	534	466	79	137	215	24	6	14	76	1	6	18	43	1	41	3	3	10	.461	.371
Medrano, Ryan, N.H.	.241	77	262	216	25	52	67	9	0	2	26	2	3	2	39	0	45	2	1	8	.310	.358
Melconian, Alex, Port.	.178	61	163	146	15	26	45	7	0	4	30	1	1	6	9	0	58	0	1	2	.308	.253
Melian, Jackson, Nor.	.252	81	316	290	34	73	116	8	4	9	38	2	3	3	18	1	69	17	1	6	.400	.299
Michaels, Jason, Read.	.295	113	478	437	71	129	197	30	4	10	74	3	7	3	28	1	87	7	4	9	.451	.337
Miller, David, Akr.*	.242	56	229	198	28	48	84	16	1	6	31	1	1	0	29	0	26	6	1	5	.424	.338
Mills, Ryan, N.B.	.000	8	1	1	0	0	0	0	0	0	0	0	0	0	0	0	0	0	0	0	.000	.000
Mirizzi, Marc, Nor.†	.239	93	363	318	40	76	110	16	0	6	29	2	1	2	40	2	73	5	4	13	.346	.327
Moraga, David, Har.*	.000	12	7	7	0	0	0	0	0	0	0	0	0	0	0	0	2	0	0	0	.000	.000
Moreno, Juan, Bing.	.200	32	101	90	6	18	22	4	0	0	8	3	1	0	7	0	18	3	2	1	.244	.255
Morris, Jeremy, Nor.	.227	17	50	44	7	10	16	3	0	1	5	0	0	0	6	1	12	1	0	1	.364	.320
Moskau, Ryan, Port.	.000	16	7	5	1	0	0	0	0	0	0	1	0	1	0	0	2	0	0	0	.000	.167
Mosquera, Julio, Nor.	.230	29	86	74	9	17	24	3	2	0	3	2	1	1	8	0	12	2	2	2	.324	.310
Munoz, Billy, Akr.*	.274	74	316	281	41	77	142	15	4	14	48	1	1	4	29	2	66	1	0	3	.505	.349
Myers, Adrian, N.H.	.284	92	396	334	60	95	126	19	3	2	34	0	1	2	59	1	69	8	10	5	.377	.394
Ndungidi, Ntema, Bow.*	.235	41	165	136	17	32	47	6	0	3	14	0	0	3	25	0	33	2	2	5	.346	.366
Nerei, Yuji, Har.	.250	12	33	24	5	6	7	1	0	0	1	0	0	2	7	0	7	1	1	0	.292	.455
Niles, Drew, Port.†	.242	39	135	124	14	30	35	3	1	0	10	1	0	1	9	0	21	2	0	3	.282	.299
Norton, Chris, Port.	.277	61	243	206	39	57	95	8	0	10	43	0	4	2	31	0	55	1	0	5	.461	.370
Nunez, Abraham, Port.†	.276	74	268	221	39	61	102	17	3	6	42	0	3	0	44	1	64	8	6	3	.462	.392
Nunnari, Talmadge, Har.*	.268	92	374	317	46	85	120	16	2	5	54	0	5	2	48	1	66	10	6	6	.379	.363
O'Brien, Charlie, Har.	.222	5	20	18	3	4	9	2	0	1	5	0	0	0	2	0	5	0	0	0	.500	.300
Ochoa, Pablo, Bing.	.100	26	22	20	1	2	2	0	0	0	2	2	0	0	0	0	6	0	0	0	.100	.100
O'Connor, Brian, Alt.*	.214	22	19	14	1	3	4	1	0	0	5	3	1	0	1	0	4	0	0	0	.286	.250
Oliver, Brian, Erie	.203	17	69	59	3	12	12	0	0	0	3	2	0	4	4	0	9	2	1	0	.203	.299
Olsen, Kevin, Port.	.000	9	7	7	0	0	0	0	0	0	0	0	0	0	0	0	4	0	0	0	.000	.000
Ortiz, Nick, Nor.	.162	11	45	37	4	6	6	0	0	0	0	0	0	1	7	0	8	0	0	2	.162	.311
Osilka, Garret, Har.	.163	20	49	43	3	7	9	0	1	0	6	2	1	1	2	0	16	2	0	1	.209	.213
Osting, Jimmy, Read.	.143	10	8	7	0	1	1	0	0	0	0	0	0	0	1	0	3	0	0	0	.143	.250
Ottavinia, Paul, Nor.*	.302	127	548	477	80	144	211	27	8	8	58	0	5	10	56	7	50	15	5	10	.442	.383
Ozuna, Pablo, Port.	.308	118	521	464	74	143	201	25	6	7	59	5	5	7	40	0	55	35	24	9	.433	.368
Pachot, John, Port.	.291	97	356	323	35	94	122	19	0	3	57	5	4	2	22	0	41	0	4	6	.378	.336
Padua, Geraldo, Alt.	.000	9	2	2	0	0	0	0	0	0	0	0	0	0	0	0	1	0	0	0	.000	.000
Patterson, Jarrod, Alt.*	.139	11	41	36	1	5	6	1	0	0	4	0	1	1	3	0	11	0	0	1	.167	.220
Patzke, Jeff, Akr.†	.316	7	30	19	8	6	6	0	0	0	2	0	0	0	11	0	5	1	1	0	.316	.567

Player, Team	Avg.	G	TPA	AB	R	H	TB	2B	3B	HR	RBI	SH	SF	HP	BB	IBB	SO	SB	CS	GDP	Slg.	OBP
Paz, Rich, Bow.	.285	40	171	137	18	39	57	9	3	1	17	4	1	2	27	0	28	3	2	0	.416	.407
Perez, Josue, Read.†	.240	32	107	96	10	23	33	5	1	1	8	1	1	0	9	0	19	2	5	1	.344	.302
Person, Robert, Read.	.500	1	3	2	0	1	1	0	0	0	2	0	0	0	1	0	1	0	0	0	.500	.667
Peterman, Tommy, N.B.*	.272	118	434	394	54	107	154	18	1	9	43	1	2	3	34	2	54	2	1	13	.391	.333
Phillips, Andy, Nor.	.250	7	32	28	5	7	11	2	1	0	3	1	0	0	3	0	11	1	0	1	.393	.323
Phillips, Jason, Bing.	.388	27	108	98	16	38	42	4	0	0	13	0	1	2	7	0	9	0	0	3	.429	.435
Phoenix, Wynter, Port.*	.257	121	457	385	69	99	164	23	6	10	62	2	2	7	61	3	95	10	7	6	.426	.367
Pickford, Kevin, Alt.*	.286	10	8	7	0	2	2	0	0	0	0	0	0	0	1	0	1	0	0	0	.286	.375
Pierzynski, A.J., N.B.*	.298	62	249	228	36	68	101	17	2	4	34	0	4	9	8	0	22	0	0	13	.443	.341
Pinto, Rene, Nor.	.234	28	86	77	10	18	32	2	0	4	13	2	2	2	3	0	24	0	1	1	.416	.274
Pointer, Corey, Alt.	.154	19	50	39	6	6	9	1	1	0	4	1	3	0	7	0	18	0	0	1	.231	.265
Polanco, Enohel, Port.-Akr.	.107	8	31	28	2	3	5	0	1	0	1	0	0	2	1	0	9	1	1	0	.179	.194
Pratt, Scott, Akr.*	.236	129	550	500	67	118	169	18	6	7	51	7	3	1	39	1	98	22	12	7	.338	.291
Punto, Nick, Read.†	.254	121	547	456	77	116	154	15	4	5	47	14	6	2	69	0	71	33	10	5	.338	.351
Raleigh, Matt, Port.	.200	18	58	50	8	10	17	1	0	2	6	0	0	1	7	0	24	0	0	0	.340	.310
Ramirez, Manny, Akr.	.500	1	4	2	1	1	4	0	0	1	2	0	0	0	2	0	1	0	0	0	2.000	.750
Ramos, Kelly, Tren.†	.200	8	28	25	2	5	6	1	0	0	0	1	0	0	2	0	8	0	0	0	.240	.259
Reding, Josh, Har.	.219	137	538	457	58	100	127	11	5	2	48	9	4	10	58	0	110	25	6	10	.278	.318
Reese, Nate, Port.	.250	3	9	8	0	2	2	0	0	0	3	1	0	0	0	0	3	0	0	0	.250	.250
Rickon, Jim, Akr.	.500	3	4	4	1	2	3	1	0	0	0	0	0	0	0	0	0	0	0	0	.750	.500
Riggan, Jerrod, Bing.	.000	52	1	1	0	0	0	0	0	0	0	0	0	0	0	0	0	0	0	0	.000	.000
Rigsby, Randy, Port.*	.222	4	11	9	1	2	2	0	0	0	1	2	0	0	0	0	3	0	0	0	.222	.222
Rivas, Luis, N.B.	.250	82	373	328	56	82	126	23	6	3	40	1	3	4	36	0	41	11	4	3	.384	.329
Rivera, Juan, Nor.	.226	17	68	62	9	14	25	5	0	2	12	0	0	0	6	0	15	0	0	2	.403	.294
Rivera, Roberto, Bow.†	.224	80	309	272	31	61	92	13	3	4	34	1	4	1	31	1	62	10	2	10	.338	.302
Roach, Jason, Bing.	1.000	1	2	2	2	2	3	1	0	0	0	0	0	0	0	0	0	0	0	0	1.500	1.000
Rodgers, Bobby, Port.	.667	48	3	3	0	2	2	0	0	0	0	0	0	0	0	0	1	0	0	0	.667	.667
Rodriguez, John, Nor.*	.196	17	65	56	4	11	18	4	0	1	10	0	0	1	8	0	22	0	0	1	.321	.308
Rodriguez, Juan, Erie†	.244	68	261	238	24	58	73	10	1	1	14	2	0	1	20	0	66	0	1	1	.307	.305
Rodriguez, Luis, Tren.	.280	27	102	93	14	26	45	1	0	6	14	0	1	1	7	0	23	2	0	6	.484	.333
Rodriguez, Nerio, Tren.	.500	20	4	4	0	2	3	1	0	0	0	0	0	0	0	0	1	0	0	0	.750	.500
Rodriguez, Sammy, Bing.	.250	2	8	8	1	2	4	2	0	0	3	0	0	0	0	0	1	0	0	0	.500	.250
Rodriguez, Victor, Akr.	.242	35	145	132	20	32	45	7	0	2	14	1	1	2	9	0	14	1	2	2	.341	.299
Rogers, Ed, Bow.	.286	13	53	49	4	14	20	3	0	1	8	0	1	0	3	0	15	1	1	0	.408	.321
Romero, Mandy, Akr.†	.311	79	330	280	55	87	146	19	2	12	46	1	4	2	43	3	34	1	1	6	.521	.401
Rose, Pete, Read.*	.247	109	418	356	56	88	136	22	1	8	56	1	3	2	56	4	47	8	2	6	.382	.350
Rosengren, John, Alt.*	.000	22	1	1	0	0	0	0	0	0	0	0	0	0	0	0	1	0	0	0	.000	.000
Royster, Aaron, Read.	.353	27	118	102	19	36	59	8	0	5	15	0	1	1	14	0	27	3	0	2	.578	.432
Rust, Brian, Bow.	.330	30	119	103	16	34	63	14	0	5	24	0	2	1	13	1	21	5	2	2	.612	.403
Rutherford, Mark, Read.	.214	30	17	14	1	3	4	1	0	0	0	2	0	0	1	0	4	0	0	0	.286	.267
Ryan, Mike, N.B.*	.277	122	526	481	64	133	205	23	8	11	69	3	6	2	34	1	79	4	3	13	.426	.323
Salyers, Jeremy, Har.	.000	20	2	1	0	0	0	0	0	0	0	1	0	0	0	0	1	0	0	0	.000	.000
Sanchez, Yuri, Akr.*	.111	4	9	9	1	1	1	0	0	0	0	0	0	0	0	0	3	0	0	0	.111	.111
Sanders, Tracy, Alt.*	.184	26	89	76	11	14	30	4	0	4	12	0	0	1	12	1	29	0	0	0	.395	.303
Sandusky, Scott, Har.	.126	47	137	127	11	16	19	3	0	0	11	1	1	1	7	0	33	3	1	2	.150	.176
Santana, Osmany, Akr.*	.283	51	208	191	16	54	63	6	0	1	23	5	0	1	11	0	23	14	1	3	.330	.325
Santos, Angel, Tren.†	.258	80	314	275	32	71	101	17	2	3	32	1	4	2	32	0	60	18	8	7	.367	.335
Sapp, Damian, Tren.	.216	69	260	222	27	48	76	10	0	6	26	0	1	5	32	0	76	0	0	2	.342	.327
Schaeffer, Jon, N.B.	.143	8	25	21	0	3	4	1	0	0	2	0	2	0	2	0	2	0	0	0	.190	.200
Scharrer, Jim, Erie	.172	11	31	29	1	5	5	0	0	0	1	0	0	0	2	0	12	1	0	0	.172	.226
Scott, Darryl, Read.	.000	19	2	2	0	0	0	0	0	0	0	0	0	0	0	0	1	0	0	0	.000	.000
Seabol, Scott, Nor.	.296	132	542	493	82	146	255	45	2	20	78	1	2	4	42	1	108	2	4	11	.517	.355
Sears, Todd, N.B.*	.314	40	159	140	15	44	63	8	1	3	15	0	0	1	18	1	40	1	0	5	.450	.396
Serrano, Jim, Har.	.000	55	2	1	0	0	0	0	0	0	0	0	0	0	1	0	0	0	0	0	.000	.500
Sherlock, Brian, Har.	.240	44	146	129	14	31	39	5	0	1	8	0	0	2	15	1	28	0	2	4	.302	.329
Short, Rick, Bow.	.331	116	507	447	63	148	216	39	1	9	82	0	8	8	44	2	54	3	3	14	.483	.394
Shrum, Allen, N.B.	.220	41	137	127	13	28	39	5	0	2	20	0	1	0	9	0	32	0	0	8	.307	.270
Skrehot, Shaun, Alt.	.228	57	178	158	14	36	42	4	1	0	9	1	0	3	16	0	32	7	2	4	.266	.311
Smith, Brian, Alt.	.000	22	1	1	0	0	0	0	0	0	0	0	0	0	0	0	0	0	0	0	.000	.000
Smith, Casey, Akr.	.174	6	25	23	3	4	8	2	1	0	4	1	0	0	1	0	3	0	0	0	.348	.208
Smith, Jeff, N.B.*	.386	37	147	140	23	54	84	13	1	5	30	0	0	0	7	0	17	1	1	2	.600	.415
Smith, Rod, Nor.†	.171	18	43	35	5	6	9	3	0	0	1	0	0	0	8	0	9	1	2	0	.257	.326
Sneed, John, Read.*	.000	6	5	4	0	0	0	0	0	0	0	0	0	0	1	0	3	0	0	0	.000	.200
Snow, Casey, Akr.†	.200	5	17	15	3	3	6	0	0	1	2	0	0	0	2	0	3	0	0	1	.400	.294
Sorensen, Zach, Akr.†	.259	96	433	382	62	99	142	17	4	6	38	4	3	2	42	0	62	16	6	8	.372	.333
Soriano, Jose, Tren.	.194	12	33	31	3	6	7	1	0	0	2	0	1	0	1	0	5	0	0	0	.226	.212
Sparks, Steve, Alt.	.250	24	21	20	3	5	7	2	0	0	2	0	0	1	0	0	6	0	0	0	.350	.286
Stevens, Kris, Read.	.500	7	8	6	1	3	3	0	0	0	1	1	0	0	1	0	1	0	0	0	.500	.571
Stevens, Tony, N.B.†	.261	11	50	46	1	12	14	2	0	0	4	1	1	1	1	0	9	0	1	2	.304	.286
Stevenson, Rod, Har.	.000	41	1	1	0	0	0	0	0	0	0	0	0	0	0	0	0	0	0	0	.000	.000
Strange, Pat, Bing.	.000	10	5	5	0	0	0	0	0	0	0	0	0	0	0	0	3	0	0	0	.000	.000
Sulentor, Joe, N.B.†	.231	4	13	13	0	3	3	0	0	0	2	0	0	0	0	0	1	0	0	0	.231	.231
Tamargo, John, Bing.†	.258	96	344	291	47	75	98	18	1	1	29	8	0	2	43	0	47	5	6	10	.337	.357
Thames, Marcus, Nor.	.241	131	537	474	72	114	193	30	2	15	79	0	8	4	50	1	89	1	5	13	.407	.313
t'Hoen, E.J., Erie	.217	62	230	198	24	43	74	13	0	6	26	2	3	3	24	0	54	6	1	4	.374	.307
Thomas, Juan, N.H.	.275	127	551	495	66	136	251	28	3	27	100	0	3	9	44	2	128	5	0	16	.507	.343
Toca, Jorge, Bing.	.091	3	11	11	1	1	2	1	0	0	0	0	0	0	0	0	0	0	0	0	.182	.091
Tucker, T.J., Har.	.286	8	9	7	0	2	2	0	0	0	0	2	0	0	0	0	1	0	0	0	.286	.286
Urquhart, Derick, Erie*	.238	57	227	189	30	45	69	8	2	4	21	2	2	0	34	0	23	4	4	2	.365	.351
Valencia, Vic, Nor.	.199	84	305	256	23	51	87	12	0	8	36	6	1	2	40	2	74	1	1	5	.340	.311
Valent, Eric, Read.*	.258	128	550	469	81	121	219	22	5	22	90	0	6	5	70	1	89	2	3	7	.467	.356
Valera, Yohanny, Har.	.235	92	321	281	28	66	89	8	3	3	34	5	2	9	24	1	56	1	3	4	.317	.313
Vargas, Claudio, Port.	.000	3	1	1	0	0	0	0	0	0	0	0	0	0	0	0	1	0	0	0	.000	.000

Player, Team	Avg.	G	TPA	AB	R	H	TB	2B	3B	HR	RBI	SH	SF	HP	BB	IBB	SO	SB	CS	GDP	Slg.	OBP
Vazquez, Ramon, N.H.*	.286	124	471	405	58	116	173	25	4	8	59	8	4	2	52	4	76	1	6	6	.427	.367
Vinas, Julio, Akr.	.254	20	78	63	12	16	24	3	1	1	8	0	1	3	11	0	10	0	0	2	.381	.385
Walker, Tyler, Bing.	.000	22	9	8	0	0	0	0	0	0	0	0	0	0	0	0	3	0	0	1	.000	.000
Walther, Chris, Erie	.255	71	273	251	20	64	79	10	1	1	19	1	1	1	19	0	25	0	3	5	.315	.309
Ware, Jeremy, Har.	.278	123	488	442	62	123	180	23	2	10	63	0	5	2	39	2	87	12	11	10	.407	.336
Washington, Rico, Alt.*	.258	135	576	503	74	130	190	22	7	8	59	9	4	5	55	1	74	4	9	11	.378	.335
Wathan, Derek, Port.†	.220	41	157	141	13	31	38	3	2	0	17	0	2	1	13	0	20	3	1	1	.270	.287
Weber, Jake, N.H.*	.256	129	541	473	71	121	171	21	7	5	56	2	4	2	60	2	56	11	4	9	.362	.340
Werth, Jayson, Bow.	.228	85	339	276	47	63	98	16	2	5	26	4	1	4	54	1	50	9	3	10	.355	.361
Whitaker, Chad, Akr.*	.234	104	413	367	44	86	124	11	3	7	50	1	4	1	40	0	96	3	4	5	.338	.308
Whitlock, Brian, Akr.	.147	33	78	68	9	10	15	2	0	1	6	1	1	0	8	0	33	1	1	3	.221	.234
Wigginton, Ty, Bing.	.285	122	487	453	64	129	222	27	3	20	77	1	7	2	24	0	107	5	5	4	.490	.319
Wilcox, Luke, Nor.*	.271	18	82	70	10	19	32	7	0	2	18	0	2	0	10	1	10	2	2	1	.457	.354
Wilkerson, Brad, Har.*	.336	66	279	229	53	77	135	36	2	6	44	1	3	4	42	1	38	8	4	4	.590	.442
Williams, Keith, Alt.	.256	36	138	121	14	31	45	5	0	3	17	0	1	0	16	1	29	3	1	6	.372	.341
Wilson, Jack, Alt.	.252	33	159	139	17	35	49	7	2	1	16	2	2	2	14	1	17	1	3	3	.353	.325
Wimberly, Larry, Alt.*	.000	10	2	1	0	0	0	0	0	0	0	0	0	0	1	0	1	0	0	0	.000	.500
Wooten, Shawn, Erie............	.293	51	214	191	32	56	99	12	2	9	35	0	4	2	17	0	30	4	1	3	.518	.350
Zamora, Junior, Erie.............	.162	40	141	130	14	21	36	3	0	4	11	0	0	2	9	0	29	3	1	4	.277	.242
Zamora, Pete, Read.*	.000	43	10	9	0	0	0	0	0	0	0	1	0	0	0	0	4	0	0	1	.000	.000
Zeber, Ryan, Erie	.250	1	4	4	0	1	1	0	0	0	0	0	0	0	0	0	0	0	0	0	.250	.250
Zech, Scott, Har.	.197	87	225	178	28	35	42	5	1	0	18	6	1	3	37	1	31	6	3	5	.236	.342

GRAND SLAMS: Mackowiak, J. Thomas, 3 each; E. Almonte, Kielty, 2 each; Cappuccio, Chevalier, Coffie, Cole, DeLeon, J. Diaz, Gibralter, Guiel, Jo. Hamilton, Horner, Hyzdu, James, R. Jones, Kiil, Kinkade, Knupfer, LeCroy, L. Matos, McKinley, Miller, Nunnari, V. Rodriguez, Rose, Ryan, T. Sanders, Santana, Shrum, Sorensen, Thames, Vinas, Ware, J. Zamora, 1 each.

AWARDED FIRST BASE ON CATCHER'S INTERFERENCE: Gibralter 16 (H. Cota 2, Kinkade 2, Lidle 2, Ackerman, Coste, Dominique, LeCroy, Lomasney, Malave, Pachot, Romero, Snow, Valera); Guiel 2 (H. Cota, Sapp); Nunnari 2 (LeCroy 2); R. Alvarez (Melconian); Casimiro (Estrada); Dominique (Valencia); J. Fitzgerald (LeCroy); Lankford (Werth); Maddox (H. Cota); Ndungidi (LeCroy); Rivas (Kinkade); Thames (H. Cota).

PLAYERS WITH TWO OR MORE TEAMS

Player, Team	Avg.	G	TPA	AB	R	H	TB	2B	3B	HR	RBI	SH	SF	HP	BB	IBB	SO	SB	CS	GDP	Slg.	OBP
Kinkade, Mike, Bing.	.366	90	364	317	66	116	176	24	3	10	67	0	3	9	35	4	39	18	7	6	.555	.440
Kinkade, Mike, Bow.	.259	8	32	27	4	7	17	1	0	3	5	0	0	2	3	1	7	0	0	2	.630	.375
Polanco, Enohel, Port.	.133	4	15	15	1	2	4	0	1	0	1	0	0	0	0	0	7	0	1	0	.267	.133
Polanco, Enohel, Akr.	.077	4	16	13	1	1	1	0	0	0	0	0	0	2	1	0	2	1	0	0	.077	.250

2000 PITCHING
TEAM

Team	W	L	Pct.	ERA	G	CG	ShO	Sv.	IP	H	TBF	R	ER	HR	SH	SF	HB	BB	IBB	SO	WP	Bk.
New Haven.......	82	60	.577	3.50	142	10	18	43	1243.1	1172	5224	529	483	76	34	34	73	402	14	1043	70	10
Norwich	76	66	.535	3.65	142	14	11	35	1241.2	1182	5420	632	504	78	41	39	66	570	26	976	71	21
Reading...........	85	57	.599	3.79	142	4	10	53	1269.1	1211	5409	596	535	115	54	28	56	451	16	987	44	9
Binghamton......	82	58	.586	3.95	140	6	12	49	1184.0	1140	5125	609	519	86	40	42	58	487	5	957	57	10
Akron	75	68	.524	4.03	143	4	5	32	1246.0	1187	5404	639	558	90	55	42	83	497	16	928	73	4
Harrisburg.......	76	67	.531	4.05	143	14	11	30	1229.0	1230	5317	647	553	115	45	45	61	457	11	775	47	4
Altoona...........	74	68	.521	4.06	142	16	8	32	1244.0	1223	5493	696	561	97	65	45	43	61	565	20	856	65	11
Bowie	65	77	.458	4.29	142	10	9	34	1222.2	1233	5352	676	583	121	42	45	47	504	26	916	45	2
Trenton...........	67	75	.472	4.37	142	8	8	29	1237.0	1312	5385	698	600	83	39	45	48	420	16	981	54	9
Portland	71	70	.504	4.53	141	14	8	34	1206.2	1282	5342	714	608	130	54	35	61	496	11	864	52	5
Erie.................	47	94	.333	4.90	141	10	5	22	1198.2	1296	5360	757	652	125	36	49	71	557	6	797	58	11
New Britain	51	91	.359	5.02	142	5	4	21	1206.2	1351	5425	793	673	108	36	41	60	504	9	997	76	4

INDIVIDUAL

TOP QUALIFIERS FOR EARNED-RUN AVERAGE TITLE

Minimum 114 innings.*Lefthanded pitcher.

Pitcher, Team	W	L	Pct.	ERA	G	GS	CG	ShO	GF	Sv.	IP	H	TBF	R	ER	HR	SH	SF	HB	BB	IBB	SO	WP	Bk.
Wooten, Greg, N.H.	17	3	.850	2.31	26	26	6	4	0	0	179.1	166	702	50	46	9	2	3	7	15	1	115	5	0
Bridges, Donnie, Har.	11	7	.611	2.39	19	19	6	4	0	0	128.0	104	528	39	34	5	3	4	8	49	0	84	7	0
Walker, Tyler, Bing.	7	6	.538	2.75	22	22	0	0	0	0	121.0	82	495	43	37	3	2	2	55	1	111	9	1
Beverlin, Jason, Nor.	8	9	.471	2.82	24	24	1	0	0	0	143.2	110	618	61	45	7	3	4	10	87	2	100	6	0
Flores, Randy, Nor.*	10	9	.526	2.94	31	20	3	0	3	1	141.0	138	601	64	46	8	4	2	5	58	1	97	8	1
Guzman, Wilson, Alt.*..........	10	4	.714	3.02	18	18	3	1	0	0	119.1	99	492	49	40	6	8	3	2	45	1	77	1	3
Parker, Christian, Nor.	14	6	.700	3.13	28	28	4	0	0	0	204.0	196	860	86	71	8	11	6	9	58	5	147	8	5
Duckworth, Brandon, Read. ...	13	7	.650	3.16	27	27	1	0	0	0	165.0	145	688	70	58	17	5	2	7	52	0	178	6	3
Duchscherer, Justin, Tren.	7	9	.438	3.39	24	24	2	2	0	0	143.1	134	593	59	54	7	3	6	6	35	1	126	6	1
Leese, Brandon, Port.	12	9	.571	3.47	27	25	6	1	1	1	173.2	179	728	82	67	18	8	5	7	47	1	96	6	1
Kershner, Jason, Read.*	9	2	.818	3.63	27	19	0	0	3	1	119.0	125	501	49	48	15	6	1	5	25	0	80	3	0
O'Connor, Brian, Alt.*	7	4	.750	3.76	22	22	4	0	0	0	129.1	120	562	69	54	4	4	2	7	61	0	76	12	0
Beaumont, Matt, Erie*..........	5	10	.333	3.80	30	21	0	0	3	0	118.1	95	539	62	50	11	4	1	17	92	0	84	4	1
Gonzalez, Dicky, Bing.	13	5	.722	3.84	26	25	2	1	0	0	147.2	130	609	75	63	14	4	2	11	36	0	138	6	0
Rogers, Brian, Nor.	11	6	.647	3.94	27	27	1	0	0	0	164.1	155	717	90	72	10	5	7	10	70	0	132	14	2

DEPARTMENTAL LEADERS: W—Wooten, 17; L—Lohse, 18; Pct.—Wooten, .850; G—Jean, 62; GS—Hebson, 29; CG—Bridges, Leese, Wooten, 6 each; ShO—Bridges, Wooten, 4 each; GF—Rodgers, Jean, 46 each; Sv.—Riggan, Jean, 28 each; IP—Parker, 204; H—Lohse, Parker, 196 each; TBF—Parker, 860; R—Lohse, 123; ER—Lohse, 112; HR—Comer, 28; SH—Parker, 11; SF—Ochoa, 9; HB—Beaumont, 92; BB—Beaumont, 92; IBB—Duff, 9; SO—Duckworth, 178; WP—Fuentes, B. Rogers, 14 each; BK—Parker, Walling, 5 each.

ALL PITCHERS

*Lefthanded pitcher.

Pitcher, Team	W	L	Pct.	ERA	G	GS	CG	ShO	GF	Sv.	IP	H	TBF	R	ER	HR	SH	SF	HB	BB	IBB	SO	WP	Bk.
Adkins, Tim, Nor.*	1	0	1.000	3.86	9	0	0	0	1	0	7.0	9	33	3	3	0	1	0	0	3	0	8	0	0
Agamennone, Brandon, Har.	8	7	.533	4.13	30	15	0	0	8	4	96.0	102	411	58	44	10	4	8	3	26	2	55	6	0
Almonte, Hector, Port.	0	1	.000	3.60	4	0	0	0	4	3	5.0	5	25	2	2	1	0	0	0	4	0	6	0	0
Alvarado, Carlos, Alt.	3	0	1.000	4.11	16	1	0	0	4	1	30.2	31	140	16	14	2	2	2	1	18	1	27	2	0
Anderson, Jimmy, Alt.	1	0	1.000	0.00	1	1	1	0	0	0	9.0	7	34	1	0	0	0	0	0	1	0	6	0	0
Aracena, Juan, Bow.-Bing.	3	4	.429	7.91	40	2	0	0	23	9	46.2	63	232	44	41	9	0	1	0	34	5	33	1	0
Arroyo, Luis, Port.*	3	2	.600	3.79	31	0	0	0	14	0	57.0	50	249	26	24	2	6	0	2	33	1	47	1	1
Arteaga, J.D., Bing.*	10	7	.588	3.45	34	14	2	1	2	1	112.1	125	490	60	43	6	7	5	6	25	0	76	1	0
Ayala, Julio, N.H.*	7	1	.875	2.70	11	11	1	0	0	0	63.1	55	259	21	19	4	2	3	0	23	0	41	3	0
Ayers, Mike, Alt.*	3	2	.600	3.24	38	0	0	0	12	1	58.1	47	250	30	21	2	5	1	1	29	2	49	4	0
Bacsik, Mike, Akr.*	7	1	.875	2.78	11	11	1	1	0	0	71.1	61	287	23	22	3	4	1	3	15	0	44	3	0
Baez, Danny, Akr.	4	9	.308	3.68	18	18	0	0	0	0	102.2	98	426	46	42	6	5	6	5	32	0	77	7	0
Barkley, Brian, Tren.*	5	5	.500	5.19	17	12	2	0	0	0	69.1	85	313	44	40	1	3	4	4	29	0	65	1	1
Barnett, Marty, Nor.	0	0	.000	6.43	6	0	0	0	4	0	7.0	8	32	6	5	1	0	0	0	3	1	6	1	0
Baron, Jim, Bing.*	1	0	1.000	3.38	13	0	0	0	3	0	21.1	23	88	8	8	2	1	0	0	3	0	21	0	1
Bauer, Rick, Bow.	6	8	.429	5.30	26	23	1	0	1	1	129.0	154	583	89	76	16	3	3	12	39	1	87	4	0
Beaumont, Matt, Erie*	5	10	.333	3.80	30	21	0	0	3	0	118.1	95	539	62	50	11	4	1	17	92	0	84	4	1
Beimel, Joe, Alt.*	1	6	.143	4.16	10	10	1	0	0	0	62.2	72	279	38	29	8	0	2	6	21	0	28	1	3
Belcher, Tim, Erie	1	0	1.000	0.00	1	1	0	0	0	0	7.0	4	26	0	0	0	0	0	0	0	0	6	0	0
Bell, Mike, Bow.*	0	1	.000	9.72	6	1	0	0	3	1	8.1	12	41	9	9	3	1	0	1	2	0	4	0	0
Bennett, Joel, Tren.	4	3	.571	4.48	23	6	1	0	10	2	64.1	60	272	35	32	4	4	1	1	32	0	54	3	0
Benz, Jake, Port.*	1	1	.500	4.42	14	0	0	0	4	0	18.1	21	85	11	9	1	1	2	0	10	1	11	1	0
Beverlin, Jason, Nor.	8	9	.471	2.82	24	24	1	0	0	0	143.2	110	618	61	45	7	3	4	10	87	2	100	6	0
Borland, Toby, Erie	3	1	.250	4.50	9	1	0	0	5	1	12.0	12	57	8	6	0	1	1	7	0	12	4	0
Boskie, Shawn, Erie.	0	2	.000	6.43	6	6	0	0	0	0	28.0	38	133	22	20	3	3	3	2	10	0	21	1	0
Brammer, J.D., Akr.	2	1	.667	1.16	16	0	0	0	6	1	23.1	12	88	4	3	1	0	1	0	6	0	20	3	0
Brea, Lesli, Bing.-Bow.	6	9	.400	4.25	21	20	0	0	0	0	106.0	97	477	59	50	11	3	6	7	70	0	89	8	2
Brester, Jason, Read.*	11	6	.647	4.27	25	19	0	0	2	0	116.0	107	539	65	55	7	7	6	12	89	2	74	7	3
Bridges, Donnie, Har.	11	7	.611	2.39	19	19	6	4	0	0	128.0	104	528	39	34	5	3	4	8	49	0	84	7	0
Brittan, Corey, Bing.	7	1	.875	2.39	55	0	0	0	27	12	74.1	67	305	28	19	1	2	1	2	28	1	48	2	1
Brooks, Jacob, Erie	2	1	.667	4.07	5	5	0	0	0	0	24.1	25	110	13	11	2	0	1	0	10	0	11	2	1
Brown, Alvin, Erie	0	0	.000	9.82	7	0	0	0	3	0	7.1	12	44	9	8	0	0	1	9	0	3	2	0
Brown, Jamie, Akr.	7	6	.538	4.38	17	17	1	0	0	0	96.2	95	416	49	47	12	4	1	6	26	0	57	1	0
Brummett, Sean, Erie*	0	7	.000	5.33	9	9	1	0	0	0	49.0	63	225	33	29	6	1	2	1	25	0	30	0	0
Bullinger, Kirk, Read.	0	0	.000	0.00	2	1	0	0	0	0	3.0	3	12	0	0	0	0	1	1	0	1	0	0
Bump, Nate, Port.	8	9	.471	4.57	26	26	3	1	0	0	149.2	169	663	85	76	16	5	4	15	49	1	98	5	0
Burton, Darren, Alt.	0	0	.000	0.00	1	0	0	0	1	0	1.0	0	3	0	0	0	0	0	0	0	0	1	0	0
Cairncross, Cameron, Akr.*	1	0	1.000	1.52	28	0	0	0	15	4	29.2	22	114	5	5	2	1	1	3	6	2	23	1	0
Callier, Jeremy, Erie	2	3	.400	4.03	41	0	0	0	28	11	58.0	52	238	30	26	5	0	2	2	24	1	44	2	0
Camp, Jared, Akr.	0	0	.000	9.35	9	0	0	0	1	0	17.1	28	88	21	18	6	0	1	1	7	0	13	2	0
Carnes, Matt, N.B.	1	8	.111	5.18	14	14	0	0	0	0	88.2	99	392	59	51	7	1	6	4	37	1	63	4	0
Carrasco, Dan, Alt.	1	1	.500	8.36	9	0	0	0	3	0	14.0	16	68	14	13	0	0	1	13	0	10	1	0
Cedeno, Blas, Read.	3	1	.750	4.77	36	0	0	0	20	7	54.2	47	228	31	29	4	0	3	4	24	1	34	3	0
Cerros, Juan, Bing.	10	4	.714	3.50	50	2	0	0	23	3	74.2	71	327	33	29	8	0	3	4	30	1	52	6	0
Chapman, Jake, Har.*	4	5	.444	3.80	49	0	0	0	11	1	66.1	73	295	34	28	4	3	2	1	26	1	53	1	0
Cho, Jin Ho, Tren.	3	5	.375	5.83	10	10	0	0	0	0	58.2	76	260	45	38	8	2	3	8	30	0	32	0	0
Clark, Chris, Port.	7	3	.700	3.84	32	8	0	0	2	0	86.2	83	381	42	37	5	3	3	2	48	0	54	6	0
Clemons, Chris, Akr.	1	3	.250	5.96	10	9	0	0	0	0	48.1	63	229	37	32	5	3	5	8	15	0	26	1	0
Clontz, Brad, Alt.	0	0	.000	1.93	4	0	0	0	4	0	4.2	4	19	2	1	0	1	1	1	2	0	4	0	0
Coggin, Dave, Read.	2	3	.400	4.93	7	7	0	0	0	0	42.0	49	181	24	23	5	2	0	1	13	0	30	2	0
Comer, Scott, Port.*	4	10	.286	6.42	25	15	1	1	0	0	130.1	180	598	113	93	28	3	5	2	32	1	60	2	0
Corey, Mark, Bing.	0	0	.000	1.05	14	2	0	0	2	0	25.2	15	101	5	3	0	1	1	0	11	0	19	2	0
Corona, Ronnie, N.B.	0	0	.000	6.35	3	0	0	0	1	0	5.2	6	28	4	4	0	0	0	2	0	9	1	0
Cota, Marino, Bing.	6	3	.667	3.89	22	12	1	1	2	0	74.0	74	326	37	32	9	3	1	7	27	1	57	2	2
Cotton, Joe, Read.	4	1	.800	2.00	33	2	0	0	18	6	72.0	48	273	17	16	5	0	2	1	19	1	51	0	0
Crawford, Paxton, Tren.	2	3	.400	3.10	9	9	0	0	0	0	52.1	50	211	20	18	3	1	0	0	6	0	54	2	0
Crumpton, Chuck, Har.	3	2	.600	4.29	31	11	0	0	7	1	77.2	90	340	43	37	7	0	1	5	23	0	34	7	0
Cummings, Ryan, Erie	4	9	.308	6.23	26	16	0	0	5	0	99.2	122	465	80	69	14	0	2	10	45	1	53	6	2
Dagley, Corey, Read.	0	1	.000	34.71	1	1	0	0	0	0	2.1	9	18	9	9	0	0	0	0	1	0	0	0	0
Dale, Carl, Akr.-Tren.	0	0	.000	7.71	10	0	0	0	2	0	14.0	17	72	12	12	1	1	1	1	13	0	12	1	0
Daniels, John, Read.	7	5	.583	3.63	41	0	0	0	22	10	84.1	78	346	35	34	10	3	0	2	23	1	75	2	0
Darrell, Tommy, Tren.	0	0	.000	0.00	2	0	0	0	1	0	2.0	2	8	0	0	0	0	0	1	0	1	1	0
Davis, Kane, Akr.	0	1	.000	2.70	5	5	0	0	0	0	20.0	17	78	7	6	2	0	0	0	5	0	13	3	0
Day, Zach, Akr.	4	2	.667	3.52	8	8	0	0	0	0	46.0	38	192	20	18	1	4	0	3	21	0	43	4	0
Dedrick, Jim, Akr.-Tren.	4	3	.571	3.05	18	3	0	0	4	0	44.1	45	186	17	15	1	1	3	0	17	0	27	1	3
De La Cruz, Fernando, Tren.	3	5	.375	6.37	41	0	0	0	15	2	65.0	80	310	49	46	4	3	5	4	37	2	42	10	1
Delgado, Ernie, Akr.	4	4	.429	4.67	34	0	0	0	22	6	44.1	43	210	26	23	5	0	1	0	40	1	31	6	0
Della Ratta, Pete, Bing.	1	2	.333	6.75	13	0	0	0	5	0	17.1	18	79	16	13	3	1	0	0	8	0	8	1	0
Demouy, Chris, Erie*	0	1	.000	5.09	9	0	0	0	4	0	17.2	22	83	12	10	2	1	2	0	7	1	11	0	0
De Paula, Sean, Akr.	0	0	.000	1.80	4	0	0	0	1	0	5.0	1	18	1	1	0	0	1	0	2	0	4	0	0
DePriest, Derrick, Har.	0	0	.000	6.00	7	0	0	0	2	0	9.0	8	42	6	6	1	0	0	0	6	0	3	0	0
Deschenes, Marc, Akr.	2	4	.333	3.98	41	0	0	0	31	2	54.1	43	238	27	24	3	2	4	3	31	3	64	4	0
Douglass, Sean, Bow.	9	8	.529	4.03	27	27	1	0	0	0	160.2	155	687	79	72	17	3	2	5	55	1	118	5	0
Drew, Tim, Akr.	3	2	.600	2.42	9	9	0	0	0	0	52.0	41	210	19	14	1	3	2	1	15	0	22	3	1
Duarte, Renney, Erie.	0	1	.000	6.11	10	0	0	0	3	1	22.1	25	106	20	16	3	2	1	2	9	0	12	1	0
Duchscherer, Justin, Tren.	7	9	.438	3.39	24	24	2	2	0	0	143.1	134	593	59	54	7	3	5	6	35	1	126	6	1
Duckworth, Brandon, Read.	13	7	.650	3.16	27	27	1	0	0	0	165.0	145	688	70	58	17	5	2	7	52	0	178	6	3
Duff, Matt, Alt.	0	4	.000	3.93	47	0	0	0	22	6	55.0	50	253	31	24	1	4	2	1	36	9	61	2	1
Duncan, Geoff, Port.	0	0	.000	0.00	2	0	0	0	1	0	1.1	1	6	0	0	0	0	0	0	1	0	1	0	0

Pitcher, Team	W	L	Pct.	ERA	G	GS	CG	ShO	GF	Sv.	IP	H	TBF	R	ER	HR	SH	SF	HB	BB	IBB	SO	WP	Bk.
Dykhoff, Radhames, Bing.*	3	0	1.000	2.10	17	1	0	0	2	1	25.2	16	104	7	6	2	0	0	1	8	0	30	0	1
Eibey, Scott, Bow.*	4	4	.500	5.05	37	0	0	0	15	0	57.0	59	256	34	32	8	4	4	2	25	4	32	0	0
Ellison, Jason, Nor.	1	1	.500	8.68	10	0	0	0	8	4	9.1	18	48	11	9	1	2	0	0	2	1	5	0	1
Erickson, Scott, Bow.	0	0	.000	0.00	1	1	0	0	0	0	7.0	4	25	0	0	0	0	0	0	0	0	5	1	0
Escalante, Jaime, Erie.	0	1	.000	15.00	3	1	0	0	0	0	3.0	4	19	6	5	0	1	1	0	6	0	2	0	0
Farnsworth, Jeff, N.H.	9	3	.750	3.46	39	8	0	0	6	2	101.1	91	414	40	39	6	2	2	9	25	1	70	3	1
Figueroa, Juan, Bow.	2	2	.500	5.54	7	7	0	0	0	0	39.0	46	183	24	24	3	2	2	21	2	42	3	0
Fish, Steve, Erie	2	5	.286	6.68	24	7	0	0	2	0	62.0	76	287	47	46	7	0	2	6	29	1	44	3	0
Fisher, Peter, N.B.	2	5	.286	6.68	15	12	0	0	2	0	60.2	89	286	55	45	4	1	3	5	14	0	36	2	1
Fitzgerald, Brian, N.H.*	6	4	.600	3.53	44	2	0	0	18	4	79.0	84	331	33	31	7	1	1	3	19	0	62	1	1
Flores, Randy, Nor.*	10	9	.526	2.94	31	20	3	0	3	1	141.0	138	601	64	46	8	4	2	5	58	1	97	8	1
Florie, Bryce, Tren.	0	0	.000	0.00	3	1	0	0	0	0	5.0	2	20	0	0	0	0	0	0	2	0	11	0	0
Foote, Joe, N.B.	0	1	.000	12.60	1	1	0	0	0	0	5.0	7	26	7	7	2	0	0	1	4	0	3	0	0
Foster, Kevin, Tren.	4	3	.571	4.19	11	11	1	0	0	0	62.1	49	261	30	29	0	0	1	2	30	0	52	1	0
France, Aaron, Alt.	5	2	.714	3.44	22	12	0	0	0	0	81.0	83	355	41	31	4	0	5	1	27	1	57	6	0
Fuentes, Brian, N.H.*	7	12	.368	4.51	26	26	1	0	0	0	139.2	127	610	80	70	7	4	7	13	70	0	152	14	0
Garrett, Josh, Tren.	1	3	.250	8.92	13	5	0	0	0	0	37.1	69	198	48	37	3	2	4	2	16	1	22	2	1
Garza, Chris, N.B.*	2	4	.333	3.50	39	0	0	0	10	0	43.2	34	195	21	17	1	2	2	2	26	2	52	1	0
Geary, Geoff, Read.	7	6	.538	4.11	22	22	1	0	0	0	129.1	141	553	66	59	15	2	4	7	22	0	112	1	2
Goetz, Geoff, Port.*	1	2	.333	5.96	17	0	0	0	7	1	22.2	27	105	15	15	3	4	0	1	11	0	21	1	0
Gonzalez, Dicky, Bing.	13	5	.722	3.84	26	25	2	1	0	0	147.2	130	609	75	63	14	4	2	11	36	0	138	6	0
Gonzalez, Gabe, Har.*	2	0	1.000	3.83	44	0	0	0	8	0	44.2	46	188	24	19	4	2	3	0	12	1	25	0	1
Grabow, John, Alt.*	8	7	.533	4.33	24	24	1	0	0	0	145.1	145	637	81	70	10	1	6	5	65	0	109	8	1
Graman, Alex, Nor.*	0	1	.000	11.81	1	1	0	0	0	0	5.1	6	25	7	7	3	0	0	1	4	0	3	0	0
Green, Steve, Erie	7	4	.636	3.40	13	13	0	0	0	0	79.1	71	330	34	30	7	2	0	3	34	0	66	1	0
Gryboski, Kevin, N.H.	1	1	.500	2.50	16	0	0	0	14	9	18.0	15	78	5	5	0	1	0	1	8	1	20	4	0
Guy, Brad, Alt.	4	6	.400	3.53	54	1	0	0	27	7	81.2	82	354	35	32	3	2	1	1	25	1	37	6	0
Guzman, Juan, Bow.	5	9	.357	4.64	18	18	1	0	0	0	97.0	114	449	59	50	5	4	2	3	46	3	57	2	2
Guzman, Wilson, Alt.*	10	4	.714	3.02	18	18	3	1	0	0	119.1	99	492	49	40	6	8	3	2	45	1	77	1	3
Hafer, Jeff, Bing.	1	3	.250	7.90	29	0	0	0	17	2	49.0	64	236	46	43	6	1	2	8	20	0	29	4	1
Hamilton, Jimmy, Bow.*	5	4	.556	3.75	51	0	0	0	14	4	57.2	53	252	26	24	6	1	4	1	29	1	49	3	0
Harris, Jeff, N.B.	2	0	1.000	4.82	24	0	0	0	12	0	28.0	35	129	17	15	5	2	2	3	10	0	28	2	0
Hazlett, Andy, Tren.*	6	6	.500	3.31	42	4	0	0	18	6	92.1	85	389	43	34	9	5	1	5	23	4	84	1	0
Hebson, Bryan, Har.	7	15	.318	4.57	29	29	3	1	0	0	171.1	175	753	102	87	23	7	2	14	66	2	90	3	0
Henderson, Rod, Bing.	1	0	1.000	4.38	9	0	0	0	7	0	12.1	7	50	6	6	0	0	1	0	5	0	10	1	0
Henderson, Ryan, Port.	2	3	.400	5.19	10	1	0	0	4	0	17.1	22	89	16	10	1	1	1	3	12	1	19	3	0
Henderson, Scott, Port.	7	2	.778	3.13	39	0	0	0	20	4	63.1	47	266	23	22	5	1	1	1	25	0	73	6	1
Heredia, Maximo, Bow.	0	2	.000	2.30	9	0	0	0	0	0	15.2	19	72	6	4	2	1	0	0	6	0	12	1	0
Hernandez, Adrian, Nor.	5	1	.833	4.04	6	6	1	0	0	0	35.2	34	159	17	16	1	0	1	3	18	0	44	2	2
Herrera, Alex, Akr.*	0	0	.000	0.00	2	0	0	0	1	0	1.1	2	6	1	0	0	0	0	0	1	0	1	0	0
Hill, Terrance, Tren.*	2	3	.400	4.38	18	0	0	0	9	1	24.2	25	112	15	12	1	1	0	3	13	3	28	2	0
Holzemer, Mark, Read.*	0	0	.000	0.00	3	1	0	0	0	0	2.2	0	10	0	0	0	0	0	0	2	0	1	0	0
Hooten, Dave, N.B.	4	3	.571	5.28	37	2	0	0	8	1	61.1	59	264	38	36	6	1	4	4	26	1	64	1	0
Howard, Tom, N.B.*	0	1	.000	3.65	13	2	0	0	4	0	24.2	32	114	12	10	1	0	0	1	13	0	8	1	0
Huls, Steve, N.B.	0	0	.000	0.00	1	0	0	0	1	0	1.0	1	5	0	0	0	0	0	0	1	0	1	0	0
Hundley, Jeff, Erie*	0	8	.000	9.20	10	9	0	0	0	0	45.0	74	230	51	46	10	1	2	2	27	0	21	2	0
Iglesias, Mario, Bow.	3	3	.500	3.53	37	0	0	0	14	2	58.2	63	258	29	23	6	5	6	4	22	3	49	4	0
Jacquez, Tom, Read.*	0	0	.000	2.96	13	0	0	0	8	3	27.1	26	115	11	9	2	2	0	0	9	0	21	1	0
Jean, Domingo, Nor.	9	4	.692	3.13	62	0	0	0	46	28	86.1	63	357	30	30	8	4	1	5	39	5	73	12	3
Jensen, Justin, Tren.*	1	1	.500	7.53	10	0	0	0	7	0	14.1	13	64	12	12	3	1	1	1	8	0	6	2	0
Jodie, Brett, Nor.	2	1	.667	3.15	3	3	1	1	0	0	20.0	16	77	8	7	3	0	1	0	5	0	9	0	0
Jones, Greg, Erie	0	2	.000	5.40	11	0	0	0	8	2	15.0	19	66	9	9	1	0	0	0	4	0	7	0	0
Kaye, Justin, N.H.	2	5	.286	2.67	50	0	0	0	23	8	84.1	80	368	32	25	3	3	3	5	36	4	109	4	3
Keisler, Randy, Nor.*	6	2	.750	2.60	11	11	1	0	0	0	72.2	63	313	29	21	4	0	1	1	34	1	70	4	1
Kelley, Rich, Erie*	5	6	.455	4.44	44	4	1	0	18	2	97.1	120	428	58	48	12	3	8	3	32	1	72	3	3
Kershner, Jason, Read.*	9	2	.818	3.63	27	19	0	0	3	1	119.0	125	501	49	48	15	6	1	5	25	0	80	3	0
Kinney, Matt, N.B.	6	1	.857	2.71	15	15	0	0	0	0	86.1	74	358	31	26	7	2	0	1	35	0	93	4	0
Knotts, Gary, Port.	9	8	.529	4.66	27	27	2	0	0	0	156.1	161	687	102	81	15	3	5	7	63	1	113	8	0
Lackey, John, Erie	6	1	.857	3.30	8	8	2	0	0	0	57.1	58	234	23	21	6	1	0	1	9	0	43	0	0
Lakman, Jason, Bow.	1	3	.250	5.64	17	0	0	0	5	0	22.1	18	102	17	14	5	5	0	0	15	2	24	3	0
Lampley, Dan, Tren.	1	1	.500	8.59	3	0	0	0	0	0	7.1	12	38	10	7	0	1	0	0	2	0	12	1	0
Lankford, Derrick, Alt.	0	0	.000	0.00	2	0	0	0	2	0	4.0	2	16	0	0	0	0	0	0	4	0	2	0	0
Lara, Giovanny, Har.	3	2	.600	2.83	33	0	0	0	19	5	41.1	40	182	15	13	2	3	2	2	22	1	34	3	0
Lara, Nelson, Port.	1	1	.500	8.22	21	0	0	0	8	1	30.2	35	165	31	28	5	1	1	7	32	0	38	3	2
Leese, Brandon, Port.	12	9	.571	3.47	27	25	6	1	1	1	173.2	179	728	82	67	18	8	5	7	47	1	96	6	1
Levine, Alan, Erie	0	0	.000	0.00	1	1	0	0	0	0	2.0	3	9	2	0	0	0	0	0	0	0	0	0	0
Lewis, Marc, Tren.	0	0	.000	9.00	1	0	0	0	1	0	1.0	1	7	1	1	0	0	0	0	3	0	2	0	0
Lidle, Kevin, Erie	0	0	.000	0.00	1	0	0	0	0	0	1.0	1	5	0	0	0	0	0	0	1	0	0	0	0
Lisio, Joe, Nor.	1	3	.250	4.97	42	0	0	0	14	2	50.2	55	240	30	28	4	2	3	2	33	4	42	0	0
Lohse, Kyle, N.B.	3	18	.143	6.04	28	28	0	0	0	0	167.0	196	744	123	112	23	5	6	3	55	0	124	6	0
Loiselle, Rich, Alt.	0	1	.000	5.27	13	0	0	0	6	2	13.2	17	65	9	8	1	1	0	0	6	1	18	1	0
Lontayo, Alejandro, Erie*	1	1	.500	5.21	34	2	0	0	11	2	57.0	55	249	39	33	7	3	6	3	27	1	37	2	1
Lubozynski, Matt, Erie*	1	8	.111	4.45	23	11	2	0	5	0	83.0	88	356	47	41	9	3	0	26	0	66	6	2
Lyons, Curt, Akr.	2	1	.667	5.40	3	3	0	0	0	0	15.0	15	68	9	9	1	0	0	2	8	0	20	1	0
Maeda, Kats, Nor.	2	3	.400	4.80	39	2	0	0	19	0	50.2	44	235	31	27	1	2	3	44	1	54	7	0
Mairena, Ozwaldo, Nor.*	0	4	.000	2.78	35	0	0	0	5	0	32.1	29	137	16	10	0	1	2	1	11	3	30	0	0
Malko, Bryan, N.B.	3	2	.600	3.25	18	3	0	0	5	1	36.0	34	151	14	13	5	0	1	1	14	0	28	5	0
Maloney, Sean, Bow.	0	0	.000	1.42	6	0	0	0	5	1	6.1	3	23	1	1	0	0	0	1	0	9	0	0
Maness, Nick, Bing.	1	0	1.000	1.93	2	1	0	0	0	0	9.1	8	38	2	2	1	0	0	4	0	3	0	1
Manon, Julio, Har.	2	1	.667	5.17	14	4	0	0	4	1	31.1	32	136	19	18	7	1	2	2	8	0	25	1	0
Manzueta, Roberto, Alt.	0	1	.000	5.06	8	2	0	0	0	0	21.1	26	104	16	12	0	0	0	13	0	14	2	0
Marshall, Lee, N.B.	5	4	.556	4.02	59	0	0	0	43	8	69.1	82	308	35	31	8	2	2	2	27	2	52	5	0

Pitcher, Team	W	L	Pct.	ERA	G	GS	CG	ShO	GF	Sv.	IP	H	TBF	R	ER	HR	SH	SF	HB	BB	IBB	SO	WP	Bk.
Marte, Damaso, N.H.*	0	0	.000	1.59	4	0	0	0	2	0	5.2	6	23	1	1	1	0	0	2	0	4	0	1
Martin, Jeff, Alt.	0	2	.000	4.64	17	0	0	0	9	0	21.1	28	109	16	11	2	0	3	6	15	0	16	1	0
Martinez, Jesus, Akr.-Bing.*	1	2	.333	4.15	13	4	0	0	1	0	34.2	37	158	19	16	3	0	2	3	22	0	21	3	1
Matos, Josue, N.H.	4	5	.444	3.63	14	14	1	0	0	0	84.1	77	349	36	34	11	2	2	6	23	0	60	1	1
Mattes, Troy, Har.	11	9	.550	4.18	28	28	4	0	0	0	174.1	170	729	91	81	20	5	3	4	56	1	109	6	0
Mattson, Rob, Alt.	1	1	.500	6.32	7	6	0	0	0	0	37.0	48	179	33	26	4	2	2	5	16	1	19	0	0
Matz, Brian, Har.*	7	6	.538	4.60	41	13	0	0	15	2	94.0	95	409	62	48	10	3	4	4	34	0	57	2	1
McConnell, Sam, Alt.*	9	2	.818	1.61	20	13	3	1	0	0	106.0	83	422	24	19	3	2	2	2	26	0	61	1	1
McCrary, Scott, Bing.	0	0	.000	8.18	5	0	0	0	1	1	11.0	15	53	10	10	1	0	2	0	8	0	11	1	0
McCurtain, Paul, Port.	6	1	.857	4.11	41	2	0	0	16	2	85.1	98	382	46	39	9	4	3	5	34	2	56	1	0
McLeary, Marty, Tren.	2	9	.182	4.56	43	8	0	0	22	5	96.2	114	449	66	49	5	2	6	2	53	3	53	8	1
McNatt, Josh, Bow.*	0	0	.000	0.00	1	0	0	0	1	0	0.1	0	1	0	0	0	0	0	0	0	0	0	0	0
Meyer, Jake, N.H.	1	0	1.000	2.29	15	0	0	0	10	2	19.2	17	81	5	5	0	0	0	1	8	0	20	4	0
Miadich, Bart, Erie	3	1	.750	3.35	28	0	0	0	17	2	40.1	27	171	16	15	2	1	2	4	21	0	38	4	0
Mills, Ryan, N.B.*	0	7	.000	9.28	8	8	0	0	0	0	32.0	47	185	49	33	6	1	2	6	34	0	21	3	0
Mirizzi, Marc, N.H.	0	0	.000	27.00	1	0	0	0	1	0	1.0	5	8	4	3	1	0	0	0	0	0	1	0	0
Montane, Ivan, N.H.	2	5	.286	7.45	26	0	0	0	15	0	38.2	50	189	36	32	3	1	0	4	22	1	39	6	1
Moraga, David, Har.*	7	3	.700	3.41	12	12	1	0	0	0	71.1	67	299	28	27	2	2	1	1	24	1	39	0	2
Moreno, Julio, Bow.	1	1	.500	5.52	13	0	0	0	4	0	31.0	43	144	21	19	6	0	2	1	10	1	14	3	0
Morse, Paul, Erie	3	8	.273	4.37	14	14	2	1	0	0	80.1	80	368	48	39	4	5	4	7	58	0	46	11	0
Moskau, Ryan, Port.*	3	8	.273	5.53	16	16	2	0	0	0	84.2	96	377	58	52	9	8	2	3	38	0	53	3	0
Mota, Danny, N.B.	3	1	.750	2.86	24	0	0	0	16	4	28.1	19	110	13	9	1	0	1	8	1	40	0	0	
Nagy, Charles, Akr.	1	0	1.000	1.00	2	2	0	0	0	0	9.0	4	33	1	1	0	0	0	2	0	10	1	0	
Nickle, Doug, Read.	8	3	.727	2.44	49	0	0	0	36	16	77.1	55	311	25	21	4	4	1	3	22	2	58	4	0
Nina, Elvin, Erie	2	4	.333	4.24	12	10	2	0	0	0	57.1	51	243	31	27	3	4	1	3	24	0	30	2	0
Norton, Jason, Tren.	1	0	1.000	0.00	1	1	0	0	0	0	7.0	3	26	0	0	0	0	0	3	0	10	1	0	
Ochoa, Pablo, Bing.	9	12	.429	5.22	26	26	1	1	0	0	146.2	171	659	94	85	10	6	9	4	75	0	106	8	1
O'Connor, Brian, Alt.*	12	4	.750	3.76	22	22	4	0	0	0	129.1	120	562	69	54	4	4	2	7	61	0	76	12	0
Ogea, Chad, Alt.	2	1	.667	4.62	4	4	0	0	0	0	25.1	26	111	17	13	4	1	2	3	5	0	16	0	0
Ojala, Kirt, Tren.*	0	0	.000	2.45	7	0	0	0	4	1	11.0	7	43	3	3	2	0	1	0	3	0	6	0	0
Olore, Kevin, N.H.	0	0	.000	8.31	3	0	0	0	2	0	4.1	7	21	5	4	1	0	0	2	0	2	0	0	
Olsen, Kevin, Port.	3	4	.429	4.83	9	9	0	0	0	0	54.0	54	234	30	29	8	1	0	2	21	0	47	3	0
Osteen, Gavin, Alt.*	0	0	.000	0.00	1	0	0	0	0	0	1.2	1	9	0	0	0	0	0	0	2	0	2	0	0
Osting, Jimmy, Read.*	4	2	.667	2.38	10	9	1	1	0	0	56.2	53	245	17	15	1	6	2	4	26	2	31	2	0
Padilla, Juan, N.B.	0	1	.000	3.74	23	0	0	0	6	0	33.2	35	144	15	14	1	1	0	2	11	0	24	0	0
Padilla, Roy, Akr.*	0	1	.000	4.24	16	0	0	0	7	0	23.1	20	117	16	11	0	0	1	3	25	0	18	3	0
Padua, Geraldo, Alt.	1	6	.143	6.97	9	9	0	0	0	0	41.1	59	202	42	32	3	3	1	2	20	0	31	3	0
Parker, Christian, Nor.	14	6	.700	3.13	28	28	4	0	0	0	204.0	196	860	86	71	8	11	6	9	58	5	147	8	5
Paronto, Chad, Bow.	4	2	.667	2.87	8	8	1	0	0	0	47.0	29	183	19	15	2	1	2	2	16	0	31	0	0
Parrish, John, Bow.*	2	0	1.000	1.69	3	3	0	0	0	0	16.0	12	64	3	3	0	0	1	0	7	0	16	0	0
Perez, Dario, Tren.	4	3	.571	3.74	29	6	0	0	10	1	74.2	82	330	42	31	9	0	1	3	16	1	67	2	2
Person, Robert, Read.	1	0	1.000	5.79	1	0	0	0	0	0	4.2	3	20	3	3	1	0	0	0	3	0	7	0	0
Pickford, Kevin, Alt.*	0	5	.000	9.97	10	4	0	0	1	0	21.2	38	115	29	24	2	3	3	2	14	0	9	1	1
Pineiro, Joel, N.H.	2	1	.667	4.13	9	9	0	0	0	0	52.1	42	207	25	24	6	0	1	1	12	0	43	0	0
Pipes, Joey, Erie	0	2	.000	11.37	2	2	0	0	0	0	6.1	10	36	10	8	1	1	0	0	6	0	3	0	0
Pugmire, Rob, Akr.	1	1	.500	5.51	4	4	0	0	0	0	16.1	22	77	11	10	0	0	3	6	14	1	6	0	0
Pumphrey, Ken, N.B.	0	9	.000	7.11	12	12	1	0	0	0	63.1	68	289	54	50	7	1	1	8	31	0	39	3	0
Quezada, Ed, Har.	0	0	.000	8.44	4	0	0	0	0	0	5.1	10	31	5	5	1	0	1	0	5	0	0	0	0
Radlosky, Rob, N.B.-Tren.	2	4	.333	5.19	14	14	1	0	0	0	67.2	81	302	43	39	5	2	4	8	12	0	56	0	0
Rakers, Aaron, Bow.	3	2	.600	2.79	24	0	0	0	18	8	29.0	20	118	11	9	5	1	3	1	10	0	21	0	0
Rangel, Julio, Nor.	0	3	.000	5.45	17	2	0	0	7	0	38.0	48	177	28	23	2	1	2	2	20	0	24	2	1
Rath, Gary, Tren.*	0	1	.000	7.36	9	0	0	0	1	0	11.0	13	53	11	9	1	0	1	1	6	0	9	1	0
Rayborn, Kenny, N.H.	4	3	.571	4.86	13	7	0	0	3	0	46.1	54	207	25	25	1	2	1	5	19	0	26	1	0
Reinike, Chris, Akr.	0	0	.000	4.50	1	0	0	0	0	0	2.0	1	8	1	1	0	0	0	0	2	0	3	0	0
Reitsma, Chris, Tren.	7	2	.778	2.58	14	14	1	0	0	0	90.2	78	361	28	26	7	1	1	2	21	1	58	1	0
Reyes, Carlos, Read.	0	0	.000	0.00	2	0	0	0	0	0	3.0	1	9	0	0	0	0	0	0	0	0	4	0	0
Riggan, Jerrod, Bing.	2	0	1.000	1.11	52	0	0	0	41	28	65.0	43	252	9	8	2	3	2	2	18	0	79	1	0
Riley, Matt, Bow.*	5	7	.417	6.08	19	14	2	0	2	1	74.0	74	333	56	50	9	0	0	2	49	0	66	7	0
Rincon, Juan, N.B.	3	9	.250	4.65	15	15	2	0	0	0	89.0	96	399	55	46	9	0	0	1	39	0	79	9	1
Riske, David, Akr.	0	0	.000	0.00	3	1	0	0	1	1	4.0	2	16	1	0	0	0	0	1	0	0	4	0	0
Rivera, Saul, N.H.	1	0	1.000	3.89	22	0	0	0	7	0	37.0	28	163	16	16	0	2	1	2	22	0	47	8	0
Rivette, Scott, N.H.	0	0	.000	13.50	2	0	0	0	1	0	2.0	6	12	3	3	0	0	1	0	1	0	0	0	0
Roa, Joe, Akr.	6	5	.545	3.41	19	14	1	0	2	0	103.0	91	439	48	39	7	5	2	7	38	0	59	3	0
Roach, Jason, Bing.	0	0	.000	3.60	1	0	0	0	0	0	5.0	7	24	3	2	0	1	0	0	3	0	3	0	0
Robbins, Jake, Nor.	3	5	.375	2.78	48	4	0	0	13	0	71.1	68	326	45	22	4	2	3	6	40	1	53	5	0
Rodgers, Bobby, Port.	3	5	.375	3.25	48	0	0	0	46	22	55.1	38	234	23	20	3	4	1	2	31	2	58	3	0
Rodriguez, Nerio, Tren.	7	7	.500	4.77	19	19	1	0	0	0	109.1	115	466	64	58	9	4	5	3	34	0	93	3	0
Rogers, Brian, Nor.	11	6	.647	3.94	27	27	1	0	0	0	164.1	155	717	90	72	10	5	7	10	70	0	132	14	2
Root, Derek, Bing.*	0	1	.000	7.82	9	0	0	0	1	0	12.2	13	61	13	11	0	2	0	1	11	1	7	0	0
Rosengren, John, Alt.*	2	1	.667	7.17	22	0	0	0	10	3	21.1	17	100	17	17	1	2	0	1	21	1	24	1	1
Rosenkranz, Terry, Bow.*	1	0	1.000	5.63	10	0	0	0	1	0	16.0	16	70	13	10	3	1	0	0	8	2	16	1	0
Rutherford, Mark, Read.	7	9	.438	4.34	29	14	0	0	6	3	114.0	121	493	65	55	13	8	5	3	34	3	62	1	1
Sabathia, C.C., Akr.*	3	7	.300	3.59	17	17	0	0	0	0	90.1	75	394	41	36	6	2	1	7	48	0	90	2	1
Saberhagen, Bret, Tren.	0	0	.000	6.00	1	1	0	0	0	0	3.0	1	13	2	2	1	0	0	3	1	0	3	0	0
Sak, Jim, Alt.	0	1	.000	10.80	7	0	0	0	3	0	5.0	2	32	9	6	1	0	0	2	13	0	5	2	0
Salkeld, Roger, Akr.	0	0	.000	0.00	3	0	0	0	1	0	4.0	2	16	0	0	0	1	0	0	4	0	4	0	0
Salter, Cody, Erie	0	2	.000	5.90	18	0	0	0	4	0	29.0	40	131	20	19	4	0	1	1	6	0	10	0	0
Salyers, Jeremy, Har.	1	3	.250	5.94	20	4	0	0	3	0	33.1	44	166	27	22	3	2	1	4	19	0	20	3	0
Sanders, Frankie, Akr.	5	5	.500	5.19	19	9	0	0	3	1	69.1	77	312	47	40	9	5	3	6	29	2	50	2	0
Scheffer, Aaron, N.H.*	2	2	.500	3.49	29	0	0	0	22	14	38.2	33	173	15	15	4	3	4	19	5	53	5	0	
Scott, Darryl, Read.	1	0	1.000	2.83	19	0	0	0	10	1	28.2	20	113	9	9	2	1	1	0	10	1	31	6	0
Serrano, Jim, Har.	4	5	.444	4.20	55	0	0	0	34	16	75.0	64	335	39	35	6	6	5	7	43	2	80	6	0

Pitcher, Team	W	L	Pct.	ERA	G	GS	CG	ShO	GF	Sv.	IP	H	TBF	R	ER	HR	SH	SF	HB	BB	IBB	SO	WP	Bk.
Sherlock, Brian, Har.	0	0	.000	0.00	1	0	0	0	1	0	1.0	0	3	0	0	0	0	0	0	1	0	1	0	0
Shuey, Paul, Akr.	0	0	.000	4.50	2	1	0	0	0	0	2.0	1	8	1	1	0	0	0	1	0	1	0	0	0
Sido, Wilson, Akr.	1	0	1.000	1.29	1	1	1	0	0	0	7.0	4	25	2	1	0	0	0	2	0	0	6	0	0
Smith, Brian, Alt.	3	4	.429	0.99	22	0	0	0	19	12	27.1	14	106	6	3	0	2	1	1	8	2	23	0	0
Smith, Roy, Akr.	5	1	.833	1.96	28	0	0	0	15	6	55.0	36	217	14	12	0	4	0	1	22	2	50	6	0
Sneed, John, Read.	1	3	.250	8.77	6	6	0	0	0	0	25.2	31	126	28	25	5	4	2	2	19	0	24	0	0
Snyder, Matt, Bow.	2	7	.222	3.90	23	12	0	0	3	1	90.0	84	385	50	39	9	4	6	5	38	1	77	1	0
Sodowsky, Clint, Akr.	2	1	.667	5.36	23	0	0	0	9	3	45.1	59	211	35	27	3	4	4	2	12	2	39	2	0
Sparks, Steve, Alt.	6	7	.462	4.77	23	17	3	2	3	0	109.1	103	484	66	58	6	3	4	11	54	0	66	8	0
Spiegel, Mike, Akr.*	1	3	.250	7.12	9	7	0	0	1	0	36.2	48	182	32	29	6	0	3	2	24	1	18	2	0
Spiers, Corey, N.B.*	4	5	.444	6.24	17	9	0	0	1	0	62.0	94	294	53	43	6	3	2	2	18	0	28	4	0
Spurgeon, Jay, Bow.	3	1	.750	1.62	6	6	2	1	0	0	39.0	32	152	10	7	3	0	1	2	7	0	27	0	0
Stanford, Jason, Akr.*	1	0	1.000	1.59	1	1	0	0	0	0	5.2	5	23	1	1	0	0	0	1	1	0	5	0	0
Stark, Dennis, N.H.	4	3	.571	2.19	8	8	1	0	0	0	49.1	31	194	13	12	1	2	1	3	17	0	42	2	0
Stentz, Brent, N.B.	1	2	.333	4.32	24	0	0	0	18	7	25.0	32	110	14	12	2	0	1	0	5	0	27	2	0
Stevens, Kris, Read.*	5	2	.714	4.69	7	7	0	0	0	0	40.1	44	173	22	21	3	1	0	0	12	0	20	1	0
Stevenson, Rod, Har.	4	1	.800	3.86	41	0	0	0	14	0	53.2	63	238	26	23	3	2	3	3	15	0	38	0	0
Strange, Pat, Bing.	4	3	.571	4.55	10	10	0	0	0	0	55.1	62	252	30	28	2	3	2	1	30	0	36	3	0
Sturdy, Tim, N.B.	0	1	.000	5.14	1	1	0	0	0	0	7.0	7	31	5	4	0	1	0	1	1	0	5	0	0
Suarez, Felipe, Erie	2	0	1.000	4.86	20	0	0	0	10	1	37.0	46	161	22	20	5	1	5	1	7	0	23	2	1
Sweeney, Brian, N.H.	4	3	.571	3.40	19	7	0	0	5	1	47.2	49	207	20	18	3	1	2	2	19	0	27	5	0
Taglienti, Jeff, Tren.	3	1	.750	3.71	38	0	0	0	31	10	51.0	59	216	26	21	3	3	0	0	7	0	33	2	0
Thomas, Brad, N.B.*	6	6	.500	4.06	14	13	1	1	0	0	75.1	80	346	47	34	3	3	4	4	46	1	66	9	2
Thurman, Mike, Har.	0	0	.000	4.15	1	0	0	0	0	0	4.1	4	19	2	2	0	0	1	0	3	0	1	0	0
Tucker, T.J., Har.	2	1	.667	3.60	8	8	0	0	0	0	45.0	33	182	19	18	7	2	1	3	17	0	24	1	0
Turman, Jason, N.H.	3	4	.429	4.38	39	7	0	0	11	3	100.2	102	429	53	49	7	3	2	4	34	1	94	8	0
Vael, Rob, Har.	0	0	.000	12.00	6	0	0	0	3	0	6.0	10	31	8	8	0	0	2	2	0	3	1	0
Vargas, Claudio, Port.	1	1	.500	3.60	3	2	0	0	0	0	15.0	16	68	9	6	1	1	2	1	6	0	13	0	0
Vargas, Martin, Akr.	10	8	.556	5.42	53	0	0	0	26	7	81.1	96	374	52	49	4	6	3	6	30	3	58	10	0
Veras, Dario, Akr.	0	0	.000	15.43	4	0	0	0	1	1	4.2	7	23	8	8	1	0	0	1	1	0	6	0	0
Walker, Tyler, Bing.	7	6	.538	2.75	22	22	0	0	0	0	121.0	82	495	43	37	3	2	4	2	55	1	111	9	1
Walling, Dave, Nor.	3	9	.250	5.27	14	14	2	0	0	0	85.1	101	378	54	50	10	3	3	6	26	0	70	2	5
Weber, Ben, Erie	0	1	.000	16.20	2	0	0	0	0	0	1.2	3	11	5	3	1	0	0	0	2	0	2	0	0
Weber, Neil, Bow.*	0	2	.000	4.71	43	0	0	0	20	3	57.1	68	267	38	30	2	4	2	1	25	0	51	3	0
Weidert, Chris, Bow.	0	0	.000	2.08	2	0	0	0	0	0	4.1	3	17	1	1	0	0	0	1	0	5	0	0
Westfall, Allan, N.H.	7	5	.583	2.64	18	17	0	0	0	0	88.2	80	370	31	26	2	3	2	5	28	0	64	4	2
Whiteley, Shad, Nor.	0	0	.000	7.07	8	0	0	0	6	0	14.0	14	71	11	11	2	0	0	2	15	1	6	0	0
Whitlock, Brian, Akr.	0	0	.000	0.00	1	0	0	0	1	0	0.2	0	2	0	0	0	0	1	0	0	0	0	0
Wilson, Jeff, Bow.*	6	7	.462	3.32	19	18	2	0	0	0	111.0	101	464	51	41	6	2	3	3	38	0	79	3	0
Wimberly, Larry, Alt.*	4	1	.800	6.86	10	2	0	0	4	0	21.0	29	104	22	16	4	0	1	2	11	0	25	2	0
Wood, Stanton, Nor.	0	0	.000	4.50	1	0	0	0	1	0	2.0	2	8	1	1	0	0	0	0	1	0	1	0	0
Wooten, Greg, N.H.	17	3	.850	2.31	26	26	6	4	0	0	179.1	166	702	50	46	9	2	3	7	15	1	115	5	0
Wright, Jaret, Akr.	0	0	.000	3.38	2	2	0	0	0	0	8.0	4	33	3	3	0	0	0	3	0	5	1	1
Yeskie, Nate, N.B.	4	1	.800	5.80	21	1	0	0	3	0	45.0	62	214	35	29	4	1	0	2	20	1	34	6	0
Zamora, Pete, Read.*	2	3	.400	4.09	43	7	1	1	13	6	101.1	105	455	50	46	6	3	1	7	45	3	94	5	0

COMBINATION SHUTOUTS: **Akron (4)**—Brown-Vargas, Sabathia-Delgado, Bacsik-Cairncross, Roa-Delgado. **Altoona (4)**—Padua-Martin, France-Duff, Grabow-Ayers-Smith, Grabow-Smith. **Binghamton (8)**—Gonzalez-Corey-Cerros-Della Ratta, Brea-Riggan-Brittan, Walker-Cerros, Walker-Maness-Hafer, Brea-Brittan, Strange-Arteaga-Brittan, Cerros-Brittan-Dykhoff-Riggan, Arteage-Cota. **Bowie (8)**—Parrish-Heredia-Aracena, Bauer-Hamilton-Aracena, Wilson-Aracena, Douglass-Hamilton, Guzman-Aracena-Weber, Douglass-Hamilton-Weber, Bauer-Snyder, Riley-Weber. **Erie (4)**—Green-Fish-Cummings, Morse-Callier, Kelley-Borland-Suarez-Miadich, Belcher-Suarez. **Harrisburg (6)**—Matz-Chapman-Stevenson-Serrano, Mattes-Gonzalez, Tucker-Chapman-Serrano, Bridges-Agamennone, Matz-Serrano, Hebson-Stevenson. **New Britain (3)**—Kinney-Hooten, Hooten-Rivera-Padilla-Mota, Howard-Marshall-Harris. **New Haven (15)**—Stark-Turman-Gryboski, Fuentes-Farnsworth-Meyer, Westfall-Farnsworth, Fuentes-Kaye, Westfall-Fitzgerald-Turman-Kaye, Wooten-Kaye, Rayborn-Montane-Kaye, Ayala-Farnsworth-Scheffer, Wooten-Scheffer, Wooten-Fitzgerald-Scheffer, Farnsworth-Kaye, Westfall-Fitzgerald-Kaye-Scheffer, Sweeney-Montane-Fitzgerald, Westfall-Turman, Westfall-Turman. **Norwich (10)**—Keisler-Ellison, Beverlin-Robbins-Maeda-Jean, Flores-Maeda-Jean, Flores-Robbins-Lisio-Whiteley, Rogers-Flores, Parker-Jean, Parker-Jean, Beverlin-Robbins-Jean, Flores-Jean, Parker-Robbins-Maeda. **Portland (4)**—Leese-Rodgers, Clark-Henderson-Rodgers, Olsen-Clark, Leese-Henderson-Almonte. **Reading (8)**—Geary-Zamora-Nickle, Geary-Cotton, Duckworth-Cedeno, Kershner-Nickle, Geary-Cedeno, Brester-Daniels, Brester-Cotton, Kershner-Nickle. **Trenton (6)**—Foster-Hazlett-Taglienti, Florie-McLeary, Reitsma-Florie-Taglienti, Duchscherer-McLeary, Foster-Hazlett-Bennett, Duchscherer-Bennett.

NO-HIT GAMES: None.

PITCHERS WITH TWO OR MORE TEAMS

Pitcher, Team	W	L	Pct.	ERA	G	GS	CG	ShO	GF	Sv.	IP	H	TBF	R	ER	HR	SH	SF	HB	BB	IBB	SO	WP	Bk.
Aracena, Juan, Bow.	3	2	.600	5.94	33	0	0	0	22	8	36.1	39	168	24	24	4	0	1	0	25	5	22	1	0
Aracena, Juan, Bing.	0	2	.000	14.81	7	2	0	0	1	1	10.1	24	64	20	17	5	0	0	9	0	11	0	0
Brea, Lesli, Bing.	5	8	.385	4.24	19	18	0	0	0	0	93.1	85	422	53	44	10	3	5	7	61	0	86	8	2
Brea, Lesli, Bow.	1	1	.500	4.26	2	2	0	0	0	0	12.2	12	55	6	6	1	0	1	0	9	0	3	0	0
Dale, Carl, Akr.	0	0	.000	9.00	4	0	0	0	1	0	6.0	10	31	6	6	0	0	0	1	3	0	7	0	0
Dale, Carl, Tren.	0	0	.000	6.75	6	0	0	0	1	0	8.0	7	41	6	6	1	1	1	0	10	0	5	1	0
Dedrick, Jim, Akr.	1	0	1.000	0.00	3	0	0	0	3	0	5.0	1	17	0	0	0	0	0	0	2	0	2	0	1
Dedrick, Jim, Tren.	3	3	.500	3.43	15	3	0	0	4	0	39.1	44	169	17	15	1	1	3	0	15	0	25	1	2
Martinez, Jesus, Akr.*	0	1	.000	3.68	7	0	0	0	1	0	14.2	17	68	8	6	2	0	0	1	10	0	5	1	0
Martinez, Jesus, Bing.*	1	1	.500	4.50	6	4	0	0	0	0	20.0	20	90	11	10	1	0	2	2	12	0	16	2	1
Radlosky, Rob, N.B.	1	2	.333	5.12	6	6	1	0	0	0	31.2	35	140	21	18	4	1	3	5	6	0	26	0	0
Radlosky, Rob, Tren.	1	2	.333	5.25	6	6	0	0	0	0	36.0	46	162	22	21	1	1	1	3	6	0	30	0	0

TEAM

Team	Pct.	G	PO	A	E	TC	DP	TP	PB
New Haven	.977	142	3730	1394	121	5245	126	0	11
Akron	.977	143	3738	1545	127	5410	111	0	18
Reading	.976	142	3808	1559	131	5498	108	0	18
Harrisburg	.973	143	3687	1431	144	5262	118	0	25
Trenton	.972	142	3711	1360	148	5219	112	0	26
Bowie	.971	142	3668	1348	149	5165	98	1	8
New Britain	.970	142	3620	1438	158	5216	150	0	22
Binghamton	.970	140	3552	1380	155	5087	122	0	10
Portland	.969	141	3620	1390	160	5170	131	0	21
Altoona	.969	142	3732	1552	170	5454	122	0	33
Erie	.968	141	3596	1535	171	5302	138	0	25
Norwich	.965	142	3725	1451	187	5363	120	1	26

INDIVIDUAL

FIRST BASEMEN

NOTE: All caps denotes fielding-percentage leader based on 71 games for catchers, 95 for all other non-pitchers and 114 innings for pitchers. *Throws lefthanded.

Player, Team	Pct.	G	PO	A	E	TC	DP
Barthol, Blake, N.H.	1.000	1	5	0	0	5	0
Betts, Todd, Port.	.985	57	453	20	7	480	49
Bruce, Mo, Bing.	.000	1	0	0	0	0	0
Burnham, Gary, Read.*	.993	73	606	58	5	669	53
Camilli, Jason, Har.	.972	5	32	3	1	36	0
Cappuccio, Carmine, Read.	.975	14	109	8	3	120	10
Carvajal, Jhonny, Har.	1.000	3	15	0	0	15	1
Chevalier, Virgil, Tren.	1.000	8	56	2	0	58	5
Clark, Howie, Bow.	1.000	1	1	0	0	1	0
CONNORS, Greg, N.H.	.996	112	872	59	4	935	83
Coste, Chris, Akr.	.995	21	177	13	1	191	14
Cota, Humberto, Alt.	1.000	1	1	0	0	1	0
Depastino, Joe, Bow.	1.000	3	11	3	0	14	1
Derosso, Tony, Tren.	.992	37	234	22	2	258	29
Diaz, Juan, Tren.	.973	37	275	17	8	300	15
Dominique, Andy, Read.	1.000	39	242	19	0	261	17
Epperson, Chad, Bow.	1.000	2	12	0	0	12	1
Evans, Lee, Alt.	.984	19	177	10	3	190	11
Francia, David, Read.*	1.000	1	1	0	0	1	1
Furniss, Eddy, Alt.*	.987	77	685	57	10	752	62
Gainey, Bryon, Bing.	.982	86	638	57	13	708	53
Gallagher, Shawn, Har.	.993	17	140	9	1	150	13
Gibralter, David, Bow.	.989	125	978	79	12	1069	74
Gload, Ross, Port.*	.990	48	381	24	4	409	37
Gonzalez, Jimmy, Bing.	1.000	1	1	0	0	1	0
Guiel, Jeff, Erie	.978	24	203	17	5	225	15
Gunderson, Shane, N.B.	1.000	1	11	0	0	11	1
Haad, Yamid, Har.	1.000	3	25	1	0	26	3
Hagins, Steve, Erie	.947	2	16	2	1	19	2
Held, Dan, Bing.	.986	65	441	49	7	497	45
Hemphill, Bret, Erie	.923	1	11	1	1	13	0
Hernandez, Alex, Alt.*	.985	8	61	5	1	67	6
Hillenbrand, Shea, Tren.	.993	65	562	39	4	605	49
Huisman, Jason, Erie	1.000	45	407	43	0	450	50
Huls, Steve, N.B.	.980	6	43	5	1	49	3
Hyzdu, Adam, Alt.	1.000	1	1	0	0	1	0
Jones, Ryan, Akr.	.969	7	61	2	2	65	4
Kingman, Brendan, N.H.	.956	10	81	5	4	90	5
Knupfer, Jason, Read.	.996	28	224	21	1	246	17
Lankford, Derrick, Alt.	.966	14	105	10	4	119	9
Leach, Nick, Nor.	.989	86	679	47	8	734	65
Long, Garrett, Alt.	.989	10	88	4	1	93	13
Lopez-Cao, Mike, Bow.	1.000	1	2	1	0	3	0
Malave, Jaime, Har.	1.000	6	21	4	0	25	1
Manning, Nate, N.B.	1.000	13	95	2	0	97	9
Marcinczyk, T.R., N.B.	.981	15	93	8	2	103	15
Miller, David, Akr.*	.992	43	342	35	3	380	27
Mirizzi, Marc, Nor.	1.000	5	33	2	0	35	2
Morris, Jeremy, Nor.	1.000	3	4	1	0	5	0
Mosquera, Julio, Nor.	1.000	1	4	0	0	4	1
Munoz, Billy, Akr.*	.993	71	632	50	5	687	54
Nerei, Yuji, Har.*	1.000	1	1	0	0	1	1
Norton, Chris, Port.	.992	29	230	14	2	246	22
Nunnari, Talmadge, Har.*	.992	87	709	64	6	779	61

Player, Team	Pct.	G	PO	A	E	TC	DP
Osilka, Garret, Har.	.950	3	18	1	1	20	1
Ottavinia, Paul, Nor.*	.997	43	317	29	1	347	27
Pachot, John, Port.	1.000	3	15	1	0	16	2
Peterman, Tommy, N.B.*	.983	83	610	71	12	693	67
Raleigh, Matt, Port.	.989	10	84	4	1	89	6
Rivera, Roberto, Bow.	1.000	1	1	0	0	1	0
Rodriguez, John, Nor.*	.969	9	59	3	2	64	5
Rodriguez, Juan, Erie*	.973	55	472	33	14	519	44
Rose, Pete, Read.	.976	10	75	5	2	82	4
Rust, Brian, Bow.	1.000	3	14	1	0	15	1
Sanders, Tracy, Alt.	.994	17	147	10	1	158	9
Sapp, Damian, Tren.	1.000	2	9	0	0	9	1
Schaeffer, Jon, N.B.	1.000	4	22	1	0	23	4
Scharrer, Jim, Erie	1.000	6	32	3	0	35	3
Seabol, Scott, Nor.	.991	14	97	11	1	109	13
Sears, Todd, N.B.	.993	35	275	18	2	295	35
Sherlock, Brian, Har.	.947	9	35	1	2	38	3
Short, Rick, Bow.	.982	15	104	5	2	111	8
Smith, Jeff, N.B.	1.000	1	2	0	0	2	1
Thomas, Juan, N.H.	.991	27	224	8	2	234	24
Toca, Jorge, Bing.	1.000	2	13	3	0	16	1
Valencia, Vic, Nor.	1.000	1	1	0	0	1	0
Valera, Yohanny, Har.	1.000	1	2	0	0	2	0
Vinas, Julio, Akr.	1.000	5	35	5	0	40	2
Walther, Chris, Erie	.984	15	120	7	2	129	9
Wilkerson, Brad, Har.*	1.000	6	51	5	0	56	5
Zech, Scott, Har.	.994	22	149	18	1	168	15

TRIPLE PLAYS: Leach, Short.

SECOND BASEMEN

Player, Team	Pct.	G	PO	A	E	TC	DP
Abbott, Chuck, Erie	.974	83	160	218	10	388	57
Almanzar, Rich, Nor.	.980	54	109	136	5	250	32
Baughman, Justin, Erie	.978	18	37	53	2	92	11
Calabrese, Anthony, Nor.	1.000	1	0	1	0	1	0
Camilli, Jason, Har.	1.000	2	4	8	0	12	0
Carroll, Jamey, Har.	.971	6	12	21	1	34	4
CLARK, Jermaine, N.H.	.977	132	232	329	13	574	86
Crespo, Cesar, Port.	.938	18	34	42	5	81	9
Davidson, Cleatus, N.B.	.895	8	24	27	6	57	9
De Leon, Jorge, Tren.	.990	42	80	120	2	202	27
Dennis, Les, Tren.	1.000	5	8	8	0	16	4
Erickson, Corey, Akr.	.957	7	16	29	2	47	8
Erickson, Matt, Port.	1.000	12	22	21	0	43	8
Fuentes, Javier, Tren.	1.000	1	1	2	0	3	0
Funaro, Joe, Port.	.923	5	6	6	1	13	0
Garabito, Eddy, Bow.	.959	102	225	242	20	487	52
Hardge, Mike, Nor.	.972	22	39	64	3	106	14
Harris, Brian, Read.	.976	87	169	272	11	452	49
Huisman, Jason, Erie	.988	33	79	85	2	166	19
Huls, Steve, N.B.	.967	51	80	123	7	210	34
Jackson, Gavin, Bing.	.973	18	31	41	2	74	5
Kilburg, Joe, Akr.	.800	1	4	0	1	5	0
King, Brett, Erie	1.000	4	5	14	0	19	3
Knupfer, Jason, Read.	.971	42	57	110	5	172	16
Leon, Carlos, Tren.	.974	15	35	40	2	77	12
Lorenzana, Luis, Alt.	.929	7	7	19	2	28	4
Mackowiak, Rob, Alt.	.977	71	138	201	8	347	39
Martinez, Eddy, Bow.	1.000	4	8	8	0	16	2
Mateo, Henry, Har.	.962	132	233	374	24	631	69
McNamara, Rusty, Read.	.906	27	39	67	11	117	7
Medrano, Ryan, N.H.	.926	19	25	38	5	68	8
Mirizzi, Marc, Nor.	.962	56	92	162	10	264	29
Niles, Drew, Port.	1.000	1	2	2	0	4	0
Oliver, Brian, Erie	.969	7	12	19	1	32	3
Ortiz, Nick, Nor.	1.000	11	27	36	0	63	10
Osilka, Garret, Har.	.800	2	2	2	1	5	1
Ozuna, Pablo, Port.	.956	116	242	302	25	569	79
Patzke, Jeff, Akr.	1.000	2	5	6	0	11	0
Paz, Rich, Bow.	1.000	19	32	46	0	78	4
Pratt, Scott, Akr.	.964	127	235	354	22	611	68
Rivas, Luis, N.B.	.972	75	133	210	10	353	53
Rust, Brian, Bow.	1.000	1	1	1	0	2	0
Ryan, Mike, N.B.	.920	19	27	42	6	75	15
Sanchez, Yuri, Akr.	.929	3	7	6	1	14	0
Santos, Angel, Tren.	.968	80	144	224	12	380	44
Seabol, Scott, Nor.	.750	2	1	2	1	4	1

Player, Team	Pct.	G	PO	A	E	TC	DP
Short, Rick, Bow.	1.000	23	33	51	0	84	9
Skrehot, Shaun, Alt.	.975	13	16	23	1	40	6
Smith, Rod, Nor.	.886	12	16	23	5	44	1
Tamargo, John, Bing.	.981	60	108	148	5	261	35
t'Hoen, E.J., Erie	.833	1	0	5	1	6	1
Washington, Rico, Alt.	.954	61	128	162	14	304	46
Whitlock, Brian, Akr.	.938	4	10	20	2	32	3
Wigginton, Ty, Bing.	.958	68	112	161	12	285	29
Zech, Scott, Har.	1.000	5	9	5	0	14	2

THIRD BASEMEN

Player, Team	Pct.	G	PO	A	E	TC	DP
Abbott, Chuck, Erie	.000	1	0	0	0	0	0
Betts, Todd, Port.	.923	53	46	97	12	155	5
Bruce, Mo, Bing.	.880	27	15	51	9	75	5
Camilli, Jason, Har.	.902	54	28	73	11	112	5
Carroll, Jamey, Har.	.957	33	24	64	4	92	10
Carvajal, Jhonny, Har.	.976	15	14	26	1	41	2
Casimiro, Carlos, Bow.	.883	84	68	158	30	256	12
Coffie, Ivanon, Bow.	.917	4	2	9	1	12	0
Coste, Chris, Akr.	.923	6	1	11	1	13	0
Cuddyer, Mike, N.B.	.903	138	84	231	34	349	22
De Leon, Jorge, Tren.	.927	33	22	67	7	96	5
Dennis, Les, Tren.	.765	6	1	12	4	17	1
Derosso, Tony, Tren.	.905	69	43	110	16	169	13
Dominique, Andy, Read.	.000	2	0	0	0	0	0
Duff, Matt, Alt.	.000	1	0	0	0	0	0
Edwards, Mike, Akr.	.943	131	98	234	20	352	16
Erickson, Matt, Port.	.974	42	19	93	3	115	8
Espinal, Juan, Tren.	.917	6	8	14	2	24	1
FIGUEROA, Luis, N.H.	.954	115	94	216	15	325	27
Funaro, Joe, Port.	1.000	4	3	6	0	9	1
Gallagher, Shawn, Har.	.000	1	0	0	0	0	0
Guiel, Jeff, Erie	.822	14	10	27	8	45	3
Haverbusch, Kevin, Alt.	.809	34	17	59	18	94	6
Held, Dan, Bing.	.947	17	10	26	2	38	4
Henson, Drew, Nor.	.917	48	33	67	9	109	7
Hillenbrand, Shea, Tren.	.889	35	32	56	11	99	9
Hodges, Scott, Har.	1.000	6	3	3	0	6	0
Honeycutt, Heath, Port.	.927	49	38	102	11	151	18
Huisman, Jason, Erie	.869	41	28	65	14	107	6
Huls, Steve, N.B.	1.000	6	4	9	0	13	1
King, Brett, Erie	.750	3	1	5	2	8	1
Kinkade, Mike, Bing.-Bow.	.912	17	10	21	3	34	3
Knupfer, Jason, Read.	.971	16	6	28	1	35	2
Leach, Nick, Nor.	1.000	1	1	1	0	2	0
Leon, Jose, Bow.	.955	18	13	29	2	44	2
Lorenzana, Luis, Alt.	1.000	7	0	10	0	10	2
Mackowiak, Rob, Alt.	.906	23	12	46	6	64	5
Malave, Jaime, Har.	1.000	1	0	1	0	1	0
Martinez, Eddy, Bow.	1.000	2	0	4	0	4	1
McNamara, Rusty, Read.	.945	52	34	87	7	128	11
Medrano, Ryan, N.H.	.921	32	26	56	7	89	5
Mirizzi, Marc, Nor.	.931	11	11	16	2	29	1
Ortiz, Nick, Nor.	1.000	1	1	1	0	2	0
Osilka, Garret, Har.	1.000	2	1	5	0	6	0
Patterson, Jarrod, Alt.	.778	11	6	22	8	36	2
Patzke, Jeff, Akr.	.857	2	2	4	1	7	0
Paz, Rich, Bow.	.967	10	13	16	1	30	1
Phillips, Andy, Nor.	.913	7	3	18	2	23	0
Rose, Pete, Read.	.932	85	76	143	16	235	10
Rust, Brian, Bow.	.750	7	1	5	2	8	1
Seabol, Scott, Nor.	.905	81	49	132	19	200	12
Sherlock, Brian, Har.	.955	28	20	44	3	67	7
Short, Rick, Bow.	.918	26	14	42	5	61	5
Skrehot, Shaun, Alt.	.857	3	1	5	1	7	0
t'Hoen, E.J., Erie	.976	31	23	58	2	83	4
Walther, Chris, Erie	.940	53	43	114	10	167	15
Washington, Rico, Alt.	.937	73	57	150	14	221	13
Wathan, Derek, Port.	.000	1	0	0	0	0	0
Whitlock, Brian, Akr.	.917	5	3	8	1	12	1
Wigginton, Ty, Bing.	.909	53	27	83	11	121	10
Wooten, Shawn, Erie	1.000	6	2	12	0	14	0
Zamora, Junior, Bing.	.919	36	32	70	9	111	7
Zech, Scott, Har.	.902	27	15	31	5	51	2

TRIPLE PLAY: Mirizzi.

THIRD BASEMEN WITH TWO OR MORE TEAMS

Player, Team	Pct.	G	PO	A	E	TC	DP
Kinkade, Mike, Bing.	.909	16	9	21	3	33	3
Kinkade, Mike, Bow.	1.000	1	1	0	0	1	0

SHORTSTOPS

Player, Team	Pct.	G	PO	A	E	TC	DP
Abbott, Chuck, Erie	.970	15	21	43	2	66	10
Almonte, Erick, Nor.	.943	129	235	308	33	576	65
Baughman, Justin, Erie	.967	13	20	39	2	61	6
Bruce, Mo, Bing.	.918	53	78	113	17	208	35
Camilli, Jason, Har.	.925	12	13	24	3	40	3
Capista, Aaron, Tren.	.955	125	181	287	22	490	58
Carroll, Jamey, Har.	.957	8	8	14	1	23	3
Carvajal, Jhonny, Har.	1.000	1	1	2	0	3	1
Coffie, Ivanon, Bow.	.941	75	96	190	18	304	30
Crespo, Cesar, Port.	.750	3	0	3	1	4	0
Davidson, Cleatus, N.B.	.940	109	167	288	29	484	70
De Leon, Jorge, Tren.	.959	14	20	27	2	49	6
Dennis, Les, Tren.	.939	8	12	19	2	33	4
Diaz, Maikell, Bow.	.857	5	4	8	2	14	1
Erickson, Matt, Port.	.969	51	78	138	7	223	32
Figueroa, Luis, Alt.	.948	93	166	307	26	499	57
Flores, Jose, N.H.	.960	12	12	36	2	50	5
Fuentes, Javier, Tren.	1.000	1	1	5	0	6	1
Funaro, Joe, Port.	.943	16	22	28	3	53	7
Garabito, Eddy, Bow.	.862	9	6	19	4	29	1
Guy, Brad, Alt.	1.000	1	1	0	0	1	0
Harris, Brian, Read.	.943	23	34	65	6	105	8
Hood, Jay, Erie	.968	71	106	225	11	342	55
Huisman, Jason, Erie	1.000	1	0	3	0	3	0
Huls, Steve, N.B.	.951	26	46	70	6	122	23
Jackson, Gavin, Bing.	1.000	16	14	39	0	53	6
King, Brett, Erie	1.000	2	2	3	0	5	0
Knupfer, Jason, Read.	1.000	3	0	1	0	1	0
Lorenzana, Luis, Alt.	.958	7	14	9	1	24	2
Machado, Anderson, Read.	.929	3	2	11	1	14	1
Mackowiak, Rob, Alt.	.750	2	1	5	2	8	2
Martinez, Eddy, Bow.	.967	35	55	91	5	151	15
Martinez, Gabby, Bing.	.961	47	66	130	8	204	18
Medrano, Ryan, N.H.	.794	13	11	16	7	34	4
Mirizzi, Marc, Nor.	.959	21	27	43	3	73	14
Niles, Drew, Port.	.937	34	48	85	9	142	14
Oliver, Brian, Erie	.923	10	21	27	4	52	10
Osilka, Garret, Har.	.667	1	0	2	1	3	0
Patzke, Jeff, Akr.	1.000	2	7	10	0	17	3
Paz, Rich, Bow.	.972	9	17	18	1	36	4
Polanco, Enohel, Port.-Akr.	.879	8	11	18	4	33	2
Pratt, Scott, Akr.	.889	1	3	5	1	9	0
PUNTO, Nick, Read.	.963	120	186	331	20	537	57
Reding, Josh, Har.	.960	136	250	332	24	606	64
Rivas, Luis, N.B.	.960	8	8	16	1	25	8
Rodriguez, Victor, Akr.	1.000	35	41	82	0	123	10
Rogers, Ed, Bow.	1.000	13	22	20	0	42	5
Sanchez, Yuri, Alt.	.000	1	0	0	0	0	0
Skrehot, Shaun, Alt.	.980	13	15	35	1	51	4
Sorensen, Zach, Akr.	.961	96	161	288	18	467	58
Stevens, Tony, N.B.	1.000	7	13	22	0	35	8
Tamargo, John, Bing.	.981	29	38	66	2	106	9
t'Hoen, E.J., Erie	.926	34	38	88	10	136	13
Vazquez, Ramon, N.H.	.961	123	194	350	22	566	75
Wathan, Derek, Port.	.933	41	62	120	13	195	24
Whitlock, Brian, Akr.	1.000	9	13	19	0	32	3
Wilson, Jack, Alt.	.966	33	47	93	5	145	16
Zamora, Junior, Bing.	.923	3	4	8	1	13	1
Zech, Scott, Har.	.857	3	2	4	1	7	1

TRIPLE PLAY: Coffie.

SHORTSTOPS WITH TWO OR MORE TEAMS

Player, Team	Pct.	G	PO	A	E	TC	DP
Polanco, Enohel, Port.	.818	4	5	4	2	11	0
Polanco, Enohel, Akr.	.909	4	6	14	2	22	2

OUTFIELDERS

Player, Team	Pct.	G	PO	A	E	TC	DP
Alvarez, Rafael, N.B.*	.979	73	131	7	3	141	1
Bass, Jayson, Alt.	1.000	15	29	0	0	29	0
Bigbie, Larry, Bow.*	1.000	31	63	2	0	65	0
Blakely, Darren, Erie	.974	111	213	9	6	228	2
Bolivar, Papo, N.B.	.972	112	201	5	6	212	2
Brown, Adrian, Alt.	1.000	2	3	1	0	4	0
Brown, Rich, Nor.*	.944	76	115	2	7	124	0
Bruce, Mo, Bing.	.000	1	0	0	0	0	0
Budzinski, Mark, Akr.*	1.000	18	38	1	0	39	0
Burton, Darren, Alt.	1.000	60	145	4	0	149	0
Butler, Rich, N.H.	.972	21	33	2	1	36	0
Camilli, Jason, Har.	1.000	2	1	0	0	1	0
Candelaria, Ben, Port.	.931	19	26	1	2	29	0

Player, Team	Pct.	G	PO	A	E	TC	DP
Cappuccio, Carmine, Read.	1.000	27	37	3	0	40	0
Chevalier, Virgil, Tren.	.981	78	148	7	3	158	2
Clark, Howie, Bow.	1.000	5	5	0	0	5	0
Cole, Brian, Bing.	.944	43	81	3	5	89	1
Connors, Greg, N.H.	.750	1	3	0	1	4	0
Crespo, Cesar, Port.	.967	114	254	6	9	269	0
DENT, Darrell, Bow.*	1.000	111	255	9	0	264	2
Dina, Allen, Bing.	.972	113	199	6	6	211	1
Dougherty, Jeb, Erie	.972	57	97	7	3	107	2
Escobar, Alex, Bing.	.983	119	276	10	5	291	3
Fernandez, Alex, N.H.*	.974	87	142	10	4	156	2
Fischer, Mark, Tren.	.891	28	40	1	5	46	0
Fitzgerald, Jason, Akr.*	.991	50	102	5	1	108	3
Foster, Quincy, Port.	.977	64	160	8	4	172	0
Francia, David, Read.*	1.000	55	101	5	0	106	1
Funaro, Joe, Port.	1.000	4	1	0	0	1	0
Gallagher, Shawn, Har.	.000	1	0	0	0	0	0
Gload, Ross, Port.*	.967	54	81	6	3	90	0
Gordon, Keith, N.H.	.970	19	31	1	1	33	0
Graham, Jess, Tren.*	.972	72	133	6	4	143	0
Guiel, Jeff, Erie	1.000	35	70	2	0	72	0
Gunderson, Shane, N.B.	1.000	7	8	0	0	8	0
Haad, Yamid, Alt.	1.000	1	1	0	0	1	0
Hall, Noah, Har.	.969	42	90	4	3	97	1
Hamilton, Jon, Akr.*	.973	129	242	7	7	256	1
Hardge, Mike, Nor.	.000	1	0	0	0	0	0
Haverbusch, Kevin, Alt.	.000	1	0	0	0	0	0
Haynes, Nathan, Erie*	.965	115	244	7	9	260	0
Hernandez, Alex, Alt.*	.988	43	79	2	1	82	0
Horne, Tyrone, Nor.	.000	1	0	0	0	0	0
Huff, B.J., Bing.	.969	53	89	4	3	96	2
Huisman, Jason, Erie	.000	1	0	0	0	0	0
Huls, Steve, N.B.	1.000	7	12	1	0	13	0
Hunter, Scott, Akr.	.953	85	136	7	7	150	2
Hyzdu, Adam, Alt.	.996	137	268	9	1	278	2
James, Kenny, Har.	.992	89	251	4	2	257	2
Johnson, Gary, Erie*	.980	68	94	2	2	98	0
Johnson, Rontrez, Tren.	.979	133	370	6	8	384	1
Jones, Jaime, Port.*	.976	46	79	4	2	85	0
Kielty, Bobby, N.B.	.988	127	243	6	3	252	2
Kiil, Skip, Read.	.946	54	83	5	5	93	0
Kingsale, Eugene, Bow.	1.000	2	3	0	0	3	0
Kinkade, Mike, Bing.	.952	11	15	5	1	21	1
Lankford, Derrick, Alt.	.972	65	99	5	3	107	0
LeBron, Juan, Bing.	.979	67	131	11	3	145	7
Lewis, Marc, Tren.	.966	37	54	2	2	58	0
Long, Garrett, Alt.	1.000	26	39	2	0	41	0
Mackowiak, Rob, Alt.	.984	39	57	3	1	61	1
Maddox, Garry, Tren.	.972	91	169	2	5	176	0
Maness, Dwight, N.H.	.982	108	215	7	4	226	0
Marcinczyk, T.R., N.B.	1.000	1	1	0	0	1	0
Matos, Luis, Bow.	.984	48	117	4	2	123	1
McDonald, Darnell, Bow.	.960	104	206	9	9	224	0
McDonald, Donzell, Nor.	.980	43	96	1	2	99	0
McKinley, Dan, Har.	.986	124	279	7	4	290	1
McNamara, Rusty, Read.	.976	25	39	1	1	41	0
Medrano, Ryan, N.H.	1.000	4	3	0	0	3	0
Melconian, Alex, Port.	.962	23	45	5	2	52	2
Melian, Jackson, Nor.	.954	78	181	4	9	194	2
Michaels, Jason, Read.	.977	111	244	8	6	258	1
Miller, David, Akr.*	1.000	13	31	2	0	33	0
Moreno, Juan, Bing.	.914	23	30	2	3	35	1
Morris, Jeremy, Nor.	1.000	7	11	1	0	12	0
Myers, Adrian, N.H.	.995	84	191	2	1	194	0
Ndungidi, Ntema, Bow.	.985	40	65	1	1	67	0
Niles, Drew, Port.	.000	1	0	0	0	0	0
Norton, Chris, Port.	1.000	2	1	0	0	1	0
Nunez, Abraham, Port.	1.000	5	5	0	0	5	0
Nunnari, Talmadge, Har.*	1.000	3	9	0	0	9	0
Osilka, Garret, Har.	1.000	1	1	1	0	2	0
Ottavinia, Paul, Nor.*	.975	82	152	2	4	158	0
Perez, Josue, Read.	.984	31	61	1	1	63	0
Peterman, Tommy, N.B.*	.846	11	10	1	2	13	1
Phoenix, Wynter, Port.*	.983	108	224	12	4	240	2
Pointer, Corey, Alt.	.967	14	28	1	1	30	0
Rigsby, Randy, Port.*	1.000	3	2	0	0	2	0
Rivera, Juan, Nor.	.955	15	20	1	1	22	0
Rivera, Roberto, Bow.	.973	66	138	6	4	148	0
Rodriguez, Juan, Erie*	1.000	6	6	0	0	6	0
Rose, Pete, Read.	1.000	3	6	1	0	7	0
Royster, Aaron, Read.	1.000	25	33	2	0	35	0
Rust, Brian, Bow.	1.000	15	31	0	0	31	0
Ryan, Mike, N.B.	.984	109	175	7	3	185	0
Sanders, Tracy, Alt.	1.000	8	7	0	0	7	0

Player, Team	Pct.	G	PO	A	E	TC	DP
Santana, Osmany, Akr.*	1.000	46	89	2	0	91	1
Seabol, Scott, Nor.	.947	15	17	1	1	19	0
Short, Rick, Bow.	1.000	15	28	1	0	29	1
Skrehot, Shaun, Alt.	.964	22	26	1	1	28	1
Soriano, Jose, Tren.	.944	9	15	2	1	18	1
Stevens, Tony, N.B.	1.000	4	9	0	0	9	0
Thames, Marcus, Nor.	.959	111	197	11	9	217	0
Urquhart, Derick, Erie*	.984	46	119	3	2	124	1
Valent, Eric, Read.*	.984	122	233	16	4	253	3
Ware, Jeremy, Har.	.984	115	235	13	4	252	5
Weber, Jake, N.H.	.986	122	200	4	3	207	0
Werth, Jayson, Bow.	.000	1	0	0	0	0	0
Whitaker, Chad, Akr.	.983	93	171	3	3	177	2
Whitlock, Brian, Akr.	1.000	3	4	0	0	4	0
Wilcox, Luke, Nor.	1.000	16	32	2	0	34	0
Wilkerson, Brad, Har.*	.976	57	117	3	3	123	1
Williams, Keith, Alt.	.985	30	64	3	1	68	2
Zech, Scott, Har.	1.000	7	9	0	0	9	0

CATCHERS

Player, Team	Pct.	G	PO	A	E	TC	DP	PB
Ackerman, Scott, Har.	.750	1	2	1	1	4	0	1
Alcala, Juan, N.H.	1.000	2	13	1	0	14	0	1
Alvarez, Clemente, Read.	1.000	9	40	4	0	44	0	1
Amezcua, Adan, Bow.	1.000	10	65	9	0	74	2	0
Barthol, Blake, N.H.	.995	67	530	40	3	573	0	3
Chevalier, Virgil, Tren.	1.000	4	18	1	0	19	0	0
Connors, Greg, N.H.	1.000	10	71	10	0	81	1	3
Coste, Chris, Akr.	.974	5	37	1	1	39	0	1
Cota, Humberto, Alt.	.973	90	571	51	17	639	6	15
Depastino, Joe, Bow.	1.000	11	63	4	0	67	1	0
Depippo, Jeff, Akr.	.981	56	368	39	8	415	6	10
Dominique, Andy, Read.	.990	60	370	33	4	407	2	12
Epperson, Chad, Bow.	.984	7	50	10	1	61	1	0
Estrada, Johnny, Read.	.990	86	603	64	7	674	5	5
Evans, Lee, Alt.	.976	13	70	10	2	82	0	5
Figga, Mike, Tren.	.971	7	32	2	1	35	0	2
Gonzalez, Jimmy, Bing.	.989	55	317	29	4	350	5	1
Graves, Bryan, Erie	.981	25	144	10	3	157	0	1
Haad, Yamid, Alt.	.990	41	257	30	3	290	2	13
Harper, Brandon, Port.	.985	35	235	20	4	259	1	4
Hemphill, Bret, Erie	.991	53	302	34	3	339	4	9
Hernandez, Michel, Nor.	.975	21	134	24	4	162	1	5
Horner, Jim, N.H.	.986	62	440	48	7	495	6	4
Kinkade, Mike, Bing.-Bow.	.991	68	520	57	5	582	8	10
LeCroy, Matthew, N.B.	.970	42	297	31	10	338	6	12
Lidle, Kevin, Erie	.960	28	126	17	6	149	2	7
Lomasney, Steve, Tren.	.987	60	418	36	6	459	2	9
Lopez-Cao, Mike, Bow.	1.000	13	66	7	0	73	1	0
Lunar, Fernando, Bow.	.989	21	165	22	2	189	3	2
Malave, Jaime, Har.	.969	38	135	21	5	161	5	9
McClendon, Travis, N.H.	1.000	3	23	1	0	24	0	0
Melconian, Alex, Port.	.986	31	128	10	2	140	2	5
Mosquera, Julio, Nor.	.988	25	146	12	2	160	0	5
O'Brien, Charlie, Har.	1.000	3	8	0	0	8	0	0
Pachot, John, Port.	.990	87	519	70	6	595	8	11
Phillips, Jason, Bing.	.983	25	164	14	3	181	3	0
Pierzynski, A.J., N.B.	.982	50	304	31	6	341	2	4
Pinto, Rene, Nor.	.984	28	160	26	3	189	2	6
Ramos, Kelly, Tren.	1.000	8	54	10	0	64	1	2
Reese, Nate, Port.	1.000	3	18	1	0	19	0	1
Rickon, Jim, Akr.	1.000	3	4	1	0	5	0	0
Rodriguez, Luis, Tren.	1.000	17	114	13	0	127	2	2
Rodriguez, Nerio, Tren.	1.000	1	7	4	0	11	0	0
Rodriguez, Sammy, Bing.	1.000	2	10	0	0	10	0	0
ROMERO, Mandy, Akr.	.996	74	484	46	2	532	2	4
Sandusky, Scott, Har.	.992	44	206	28	2	236	3	6
Sapp, Damian, Tren.	.987	50	344	42	5	391	4	11
Shrum, Allen, N.B.	1.000	38	232	18	0	250	1	4
Smith, Casey, Akr.	1.000	6	32	4	0	36	1	0
Smith, Jeff, N.B.	.985	14	123	8	2	133	0	2
Snow, Casey, Akr.	.969	5	29	2	1	32	0	3
Sulentor, Joe, N.B.	.971	4	32	1	1	34	1	0
Tamargo, John, Bing.	.000	2	0	0	0	0	0	0
Valencia, Vic, Nor.	.978	82	546	64	14	624	3	10
Valera, Yohanny, Har.	.986	88	441	59	7	507	8	9
Werth, Jayson, Bow.	.988	82	502	51	7	560	5	5
Wooten, Shawn, Erie	.968	38	230	45	9	284	4	8

CATCHERS WITH TWO OR MORE TEAMS

Player, Team	Pct.	G	PO	A	E	TC	DP	PB
Kinkade, Mike, Bing.	.991	64	492	54	5	551	8	9
Kinkade, Mike, Bow.	1.000	4	28	3	0	31	0	1

PITCHERS

Player, Team	Pct.	G	PO	A	E	TC	DP
Adkins, Tim, Nor.*	1.000	9	1	1	0	2	0
Agamennone, Brandon, Har.	1.000	30	8	7	0	15	1
Almonte, Hector, Port.	.000	4	0	0	0	0	0
Alvarado, Carlos, Alt.	1.000	16	2	2	0	4	0
Anderson, Jimmy, Alt.	1.000	1	0	5	0	5	0
Aracena, Juan, Bow.-Bing.	1.000	40	1	4	0	5	1
Arroyo, Luis, Port.*	1.000	31	3	7	0	10	1
Arteaga, J.D., Bing.*	.921	34	7	28	3	38	2
Ayala, Julio, N.H.*	.917	11	3	8	1	12	0
Ayers, Mike, Alt.*	.750	38	3	6	3	12	0
Bacsik, Mike, Akr.*	1.000	11	5	13	0	18	0
Baez, Danny, Akr.	1.000	18	11	15	0	26	2
Barkley, Brian, Tren.*	1.000	17	7	8	0	15	0
Barnett, Marty, Nor.	.000	6	0	0	1	1	0
Baron, Jim, Bing.*	1.000	13	0	7	0	7	0
Bauer, Rick, Bow.	.943	26	12	21	2	35	2
Beaumont, Matt, Erie*	.840	30	6	15	4	25	0
Beimel, Joe, Alt.*	1.000	10	2	13	0	15	1
Belcher, Tim, Erie*	1.000	1	1	0	0	1	0
Bell, Mike, Bow.*	1.000	6	0	1	0	1	0
Bennett, Joel, Tren.	1.000	23	1	10	0	11	0
Benz, Jake, Port.*	.800	14	0	4	1	5	0
Beverlin, Jason, Nor.	1.000	24	5	19	0	24	2
Borland, Toby, Erie.	1.000	9	1	2	0	3	0
Boskie, Shawn, Erie.	.889	6	3	5	1	9	0
Brammer, J.D., Akr.	1.000	16	1	1	0	2	0
Brea, Lesli, Bing.-Bow.	.913	21	8	13	2	23	2
Brester, Jason, Read.*	.963	25	11	15	1	27	4
Bridges, Donnie, Har.	.926	19	12	13	2	27	1
Brittan, Corey, Bing.	.967	55	4	25	1	30	1
Brooks, Jacob, Erie	1.000	5	2	1	0	3	0
Brown, Alvin, Erie	1.000	7	4	0	0	4	0
Brown, Jamie, Akr.	.967	17	14	15	1	30	0
Brummett, Sean, Erie*	.909	9	2	8	1	11	1
Bullinger, Kirk, Read.	1.000	2	0	2	0	2	1
Bump, Nate, Port.	.947	26	14	22	2	38	3
Burton, Darren, Alt.	.000	1	0	0	0	0	0
Cairncross, Cameron, Akr.*	1.000	28	5	11	0	16	0
Callier, Jeremy, Erie	.778	41	1	6	2	9	2
Camp, Jared, Akr.	1.000	9	0	4	0	4	0
Carnes, Matt, N.B.	.957	14	10	12	1	23	3
Carrasco, Dan, Alt.	.000	9	0	0	0	0	0
Cedeno, Blas, Read.	.826	36	6	13	4	23	0
Cerros, Juan, Bing.	.923	50	3	9	1	13	0
Chapman, Jake, Har.*	.941	49	6	10	1	17	1
Cho, Jin Ho, Tren.	.600	10	2	1	2	5	0
Clark, Chris, Port.	.917	32	3	8	1	12	1
Clemons, Chris, Akr.	1.000	10	5	10	0	15	0
Clontz, Brad, Alt.	1.000	4	0	1	0	1	0
Coggin, Dave, Read.	.941	7	10	6	1	17	1
Comer, Scott, Port.*	1.000	25	3	13	0	16	0
Corey, Mark, Bing.	.875	14	4	3	1	8	0
Corona, Ronnie, N.B.	1.000	3	1	0	0	1	0
Cota, Marino, Bing.	.941	22	8	8	1	17	0
Cotton, Joe, Read.	1.000	34	4	9	0	13	1
Crawford, Paxton, Tren.	.938	9	3	12	1	16	0
Crumpton, Chuck, Har.	.950	31	8	11	1	20	1
Cummings, Ryan, Erie	.846	26	9	13	4	26	1
Dagley, Corey, Read.	.000	1	0	0	0	0	0
Dale, Carl, Akr.-Tren.	1.000	10	2	3	0	5	1
Daniels, John, Read.	.950	41	6	13	1	20	2
Darrell, Tommy, Tren.	.000	2	0	0	0	0	0
Davis, Kane, Akr.	1.000	5	2	4	0	6	0
Day, Zach, Akr.	.938	8	4	11	1	16	1
Dedrick, Jim, Akr.-Tren.	.909	18	2	8	1	11	1
De La Cruz, Fernando, Tren.	.909	41	5	5	1	11	1
Delgado, Ernie, Alt.	.875	34	2	5	1	8	1
Della Ratta, Pete, Bing.	1.000	13	2	2	0	4	0
Demouy, Chris, Erie*	1.000	9	0	1	0	1	0
De Paula, Sean, Akr.	1.000	4	0	1	0	1	0
DePriest, Derrick, Har.	.667	7	0	2	1	3	0
Deschenes, Marc, Akr.	.857	41	2	4	1	7	0
Douglass, Sean, Bow.	.977	27	22	21	1	44	2
Drew, Tim, Akr.	1.000	9	7	11	0	18	0
Duarte, Renney, Erie	1.000	11	1	4	0	5	0
Duchscherer, Justin, Tren.	.939	24	8	23	2	33	0
Duckworth, Brandon, Read.	.905	27	5	14	2	21	0
Duff, Matt, Alt.	1.000	47	8	6	0	14	1
Duncan, Geoff, Port.	.000	2	0	0	0	0	0
Dykhoff, Radhames, Bing.*	1.000	17	2	2	0	4	0
Eibey, Scott, Bow.*	.909	37	5	5	1	11	0
Ellison, Jason, Nor.	1.000	10	1	4	0	5	0
Erickson, Scott, Bow.	1.000	1	0	3	0	3	0
Escalante, Jaime, Erie	1.000	3	0	1	0	1	0
Farnsworth, Jeff, N.H.	.789	39	2	13	4	19	0
Figueroa, Juan, Bow.	1.000	7	1	3	0	4	0
Fish, Steve, Erie	.895	24	2	15	2	19	0
Fisher, Peter, N.B.	.929	15	4	9	1	14	2
Fitzgerald, Brian, N.H.*	1.000	44	5	13	0	18	0
Flores, Randy, Nor.*	.958	31	11	35	2	48	2
Florie, Bryce, Tren.	.000	3	0	0	0	0	0
Foote, Joe, N.B.	1.000	1	0	2	0	2	0
Foster, Kevin, Tren.	1.000	11	2	5	0	7	0
France, Aaron, Alt.	1.000	22	1	9	0	10	0
Fuentes, Brian, N.H.*	.870	26	4	16	3	23	0
Garrett, Josh, Tren.	1.000	13	5	9	0	14	0
Garza, Chris, N.B.*	.889	39	4	4	1	9	0
Geary, Geoff, Read.	.875	22	5	9	2	16	0
Goetz, Geoff, Port.*	1.000	17	2	7	0	9	0
Gonzalez, Dicky, Bing.	.918	26	24	21	4	49	0
Gonzalez, Gabe, Har.*	1.000	44	4	10	0	14	0
Grabow, John, Alt.*	.880	24	7	15	3	25	0
Graman, Alex, Nor.*	.000	1	0	0	0	0	0
Green, Steve, Erie	.852	13	3	20	4	27	2
Gryboski, Kevin, N.H.	1.000	16	1	3	0	4	0
Guy, Brad, Alt.	.952	54	9	11	1	21	0
Guzman, Juan, Bow.	1.000	18	6	13	0	19	1
Guzman, Wilson, Alt.*	.971	18	6	27	1	34	0
Hafer, Jeff, Bing.	1.000	29	6	7	0	13	1
Hamilton, Jimmy, Bow.*	1.000	51	2	5	0	7	0
Harris, Jeff, N.B.	1.000	24	4	4	0	8	0
Hazlett, Andy, Tren.*	1.000	42	9	11	0	20	0
Hebson, Bryan, Har.	.806	29	11	18	7	36	2
Henderson, Rod, Bing.	1.000	9	2	0	0	2	0
Henderson, Ryan, Port.	.875	10	1	6	1	8	0
Henderson, Scott, Port.	.667	39	0	2	1	3	0
Heredia, Maximo, Bow.	1.000	9	3	5	0	8	0
Hernandez, Adrian, Nor.	1.000	6	2	5	0	7	0
Herrera, Alex, Akr.*	.000	2	0	0	0	0	0
Hill, Terrance, Tren.*	1.000	18	0	1	0	1	0
Holzemer, Mark, Read.*	.000	3	0	0	0	0	0
Hooten, Dave, N.B.	.875	37	2	12	2	16	1
Howard, Tom, N.B.*	1.000	13	0	2	0	2	0
Huls, Steve, N.B.*	.000	1	0	0	0	0	0
Hundley, Jeff, Erie*	.857	10	5	7	2	14	0
Iglesias, Mario, Bow.	1.000	37	2	12	0	14	0
Jacquez, Tom, Read.*	1.000	13	0	7	0	7	1
Jean, Domingo, Nor.	1.000	62	6	11	0	17	1
Jensen, Justin, Tren.*	.800	10	1	3	1	5	0
Jodie, Brett, Nor.	.800	3	0	4	1	5	0
Jones, Greg, Erie	1.000	11	1	2	0	3	0
Kaye, Justin, N.H.	.857	50	4	8	2	14	0
Keisler, Randy, Nor.*	.727	11	4	4	3	11	0
Kelley, Rich, Erie*	1.000	44	2	22	0	24	1
Kershner, Jason, Read.*	1.000	27	5	24	0	29	2
Kinney, Matt, N.B.	1.000	15	10	4	0	14	0
Knotts, Gary, Port.	.950	27	5	14	1	20	1
Lackey, John, Erie	.900	8	2	7	1	10	3
Lakman, Jason, Bow.	.500	17	1	1	2	4	0
Lampley, Dan, Tren.	1.000	3	0	2	0	2	1
Lankford, Derrick, Alt.	1.000	2	0	3	0	3	1
Lara, Giovanny, Har.	1.000	33	2	5	0	7	0
Lara, Nelson, Port.	1.000	21	1	1	0	2	0
Leese, Brandon, Port.	.933	27	7	21	2	30	2
Levine, Alan, Erie	.500	1	1	0	1	2	0
Lewis, Marc, Tren.	.000	1	0	0	0	0	0
Lidle, Kevin, Erie	.000	1	0	0	0	0	0
Lisio, Joe, Nor.	.833	42	6	4	2	12	0
LOHSE, Kyle, N.B.	1.000	28	20	25	0	45	2
Loiselle, Rich, Alt.	1.000	13	0	1	0	1	0
Lontayo, Alejandro, Erie*	1.000	34	3	12	0	15	0
Lubozynski, Matt, Erie*	1.000	23	2	16	0	18	0
Lyons, Curt, Akr.	1.000	3	1	2	0	3	0
Maeda, Kats, Nor.	.833	39	2	8	2	12	0
Mairena, Ozwaldo, Nor.*	.875	35	1	6	1	8	0
Malko, Bryan, N.B.	1.000	18	2	3	0	5	0
Maloney, Sean, Bow.	1.000	6	1	0	0	1	0
Maness, Nick, Bing.	1.000	2	1	2	0	3	0
Manon, Julio, Har.	1.000	14	1	1	0	2	0
Manzueta, Roberto, Alt.	1.000	8	2	1	0	3	0
Marshall, Lee, N.B.	1.000	59	6	9	0	15	2
Marte, Damaso, N.H.*	1.000	4	0	1	0	1	0
Martin, Jeff, Alt.	1.000	17	0	1	0	1	0
Martinez, Jesus, Akr.-Bing.*	.889	13	3	5	1	9	0

Player, Team	Pct.	G	PO	A	E	TC	DP
Matos, Josue, N.H.	1.000	14	3	6	0	9	0
Mattes, Troy, Har.	.975	28	11	28	1	40	3
Mattson, Rob, Alt.	1.000	7	2	7	0	9	1
Matz, Brian, Har.*	1.000	41	8	18	0	26	1
McConnell, Sam, Alt.*	1.000	20	6	13	0	19	1
McCrary, Scott, Bing.	1.000	5	2	3	0	5	1
McCurtain, Paul, Port.	.833	41	2	8	2	12	0
McLeary, Marty, Tren.	.933	43	6	22	2	30	1
McNatt, Josh, Bow.*	.000	1	0	0	0	0	0
Meyer, Jake, N.H.	1.000	15	0	1	0	1	0
Miadich, Bart, Erie	1.000	28	3	2	0	5	0
Mills, Ryan, N.B.*	1.000	8	1	3	0	4	0
Mirizzi, Marc, Nor.	.000	1	0	0	0	0	0
Montane, Ivan, N.H.	1.000	26	3	5	0	8	1
Moraga, David, Har.*	.923	12	4	8	1	13	0
Moreno, Julio, Bow.	1.000	13	1	1	0	2	0
Morse, Paul, Erie	1.000	14	8	16	0	24	0
Moskau, Ryan, Port.*	.900	16	7	11	2	20	1
Mota, Danny, N.B.	1.000	24	0	3	0	3	0
Nagy, Charles, Akr.	1.000	2	1	0	0	1	0
Nickle, Doug, Read.	1.000	49	5	25	0	30	0
Nina, Elvin, Erie	.875	12	8	6	2	16	1
Norton, Jason, Tren.	.000	1	0	0	0	0	0
Ochoa, Pablo, Bing.	.976	26	23	18	1	42	2
O'Connor, Brian, Alt.*	1.000	22	8	28	0	36	1
Ogea, Chad, Akr.	1.000	4	0	7	0	7	1
Ojala, Kirt, Tren.*	1.000	7	2	2	0	4	0
Olore, Kevin, N.H.	.000	3	0	0	0	0	0
Olsen, Kevin, Port.	.727	9	4	4	3	11	1
Osteen, Gavin, Alt.*	.000	1	0	0	0	0	0
Osting, Jimmy, Read.*	1.000	10	4	11	0	15	1
Padilla, Juan, N.B.	1.000	23	2	6	0	8	0
Padilla, Roy, Akr.*	.909	16	4	6	1	11	0
Padua, Geraldo, Alt.	1.000	9	2	3	0	5	2
Parker, Christian, Nor.	.944	28	17	51	4	72	4
Paronto, Chad, Bow.	1.000	8	6	5	0	11	2
Parrish, John, Bow.*	.667	3	0	4	2	6	0
Perez, Dario, Tren.	1.000	29	1	10	0	11	1
Person, Robert, Read.	.000	1	0	0	0	0	0
Pickford, Kevin, Alt.*	.833	10	0	5	1	6	0
Pineiro, Joel, N.H.	1.000	9	1	6	0	7	0
Pipes, Joey, Erie	1.000	2	0	1	0	1	0
Pugmire, Rob, Akr.	1.000	4	1	3	0	4	0
Pumphrey, Ken, N.B.	1.000	12	6	14	0	20	1
Quezada, Ed, Har.	1.000	4	1	1	0	2	0
Radlosky, Rob, N.B.-Tren.	1.000	14	5	5	0	10	0
Rakers, Aaron, Bow.	1.000	24	2	3	0	5	0
Rangel, Julio, Nor.	.850	17	8	9	3	20	1
Rath, Gary, Tren.*	1.000	9	0	2	0	2	0
Rayborn, Kenny, N.H.	1.000	13	2	8	0	10	1
Reinike, Chris, Akr.	.000	1	0	0	0	0	0
Reitsma, Chris, Tren.	1.000	14	10	9	0	19	1
Reyes, Carlos, Read.	.000	2	0	0	0	0	0
Riggan, Jerrod, Bing.	.900	52	3	6	1	10	0
Riley, Matt, Bow.*	.750	19	1	11	4	16	0
Rincon, Juan, N.B.	1.000	15	9	7	0	16	2
Riske, David, Akr.	1.000	3	1	0	0	1	0
Rivera, Saul, N.H.	1.000	22	2	6	0	8	0
Rivette, Scott, N.H.	1.000	2	0	1	0	1	1
Roa, Joe, Akr.	1.000	19	8	18	0	26	3
Roach, Jason, Bing.	.000	1	0	0	0	0	0
Robbins, Jake, Nor.	.650	48	5	8	7	20	2
Rodgers, Bobby, Port.	1.000	48	0	7	0	7	1
Rodriguez, Nerio, Tren.	.833	19	3	7	2	12	0
Rogers, Brian, Nor.	1.000	27	5	19	0	24	1
Root, Derek, Bing.*	1.000	9	1	1	0	2	0
Rosengren, John, Alt.*	1.000	22	4	2	0	6	0
Rosenkranz, Terry, Bow.*	.000	10	0	1	1	1	0
Rutherford, Mark, Read.	.964	29	11	16	1	28	1
Sabathia, C.C., Akr.*	.958	17	2	21	1	24	0
Saberhagen, Bret, Tren.	.000	1	0	0	0	0	0

Player, Team	Pct.	G	PO	A	E	TC	DP
Sak, Jim, Alt.	1.000	7	0	1	0	1	0
Salkeld, Roger, Akr.	.000	3	0	0	0	0	0
Salter, Cody, Erie	1.000	18	4	4	0	8	0
Salyers, Jeremy, Har.	.700	20	2	5	3	10	0
Sanders, Frankie, Akr.	1.000	19	5	10	0	15	0
Scheffer, Aaron, N.H.	1.000	29	2	5	0	7	0
Scott, Darryl, Read.	1.000	19	3	6	0	9	0
Serrano, Jim, Har.	.786	55	5	6	3	14	0
Sherlock, Brian, Har.	.000	1	0	0	0	0	0
Shuey, Paul, Akr.	1.000	2	1	0	0	1	0
Sido, Wilson, Akr.	1.000	1	0	2	0	2	0
Smith, Brian, Alt.	.750	22	0	3	1	4	0
Smith, Roy, Akr.	.913	28	7	14	2	23	1
Sneed, John, Read.	1.000	6	2	5	0	7	0
Snyder, Matt, Bow.	.900	23	3	15	2	20	1
Sodowsky, Clint, Akr.	1.000	23	6	9	0	15	0
Sparks, Steve, Alt.	.970	23	11	21	1	33	2
Spiegel, Mike, Akr.*	.750	9	2	4	2	8	0
Spiers, Corey, N.B.*	1.000	17	9	12	0	21	2
Spurgeon, Jay, Bow.	.933	6	7	7	1	15	3
Stanford, Jason, Akr.*	1.000	1	1	0	0	1	0
Stark, Dennis, N.H.	1.000	8	5	12	0	17	4
Stentz, Brent, N.B.	1.000	24	3	5	0	8	0
Stevens, Kris, Read.*	.867	7	8	5	2	15	1
Stevenson, Rod, Har.	1.000	41	4	4	0	8	1
Strange, Pat, Bing.	.944	10	4	13	1	18	0
Sturdy, Tim, N.B.	1.000	1	2	2	0	4	0
Suarez, Felipe, Erie	1.000	20	7	3	0	10	1
Sweeney, Brian, N.H.	.900	19	2	7	1	10	0
Taglienti, Jeff, Tren.	1.000	38	0	3	0	3	0
Thomas, Brad, N.B.*	1.000	14	0	25	0	25	0
Thurman, Mike, Har.	.000	1	0	0	0	0	0
Tucker, T.J., Har.	1.000	8	3	2	0	5	0
Turman, Jason, N.H.	1.000	39	2	10	0	12	1
Vael, Rob, Har.	.667	6	1	1	1	3	0
Vargas, Claudio, Port.	.000	3	0	0	0	0	0
Vargas, Martin, Akr.	.912	53	10	21	3	34	1
Veras, Dario, Akr.	1.000	4	1	0	0	1	0
Walker, Tyler, Bing.	1.000	22	9	10	0	19	0
Walling, Dave, Nor.	.929	14	4	9	1	14	0
Weber, Ben, Erie	1.000	2	1	1	0	2	0
Weber, Neil, Bow.*	.889	43	3	5	1	9	0
Weidert, Chris, Bow.	.000	2	0	0	0	0	0
Westfall, Allan, N.H.	.895	18	10	7	2	19	1
Whiteley, Shad, Nor.	1.000	8	2	0	0	2	0
Whitlock, Brian, Akr.	.000	1	0	0	0	0	0
Wilson, Jeff, Bow.*	.950	19	2	17	1	20	0
Wimberly, Larry, Alt.*	.750	10	0	3	1	4	0
Wood, Stanton, Nor.	.000	1	0	0	0	0	0
Wooten, Greg, N.H.	.946	26	10	25	2	37	1
Wright, Jaret, Akr.	1.000	2	0	1	0	1	0
Yeskie, Nate, N.B.	.929	21	6	7	1	14	1
Zamora, Pete, Read.*	1.000	43	13	10	0	23	1

TRIPLE PLAY: Iglesias.

PITCHERS WITH TWO OR MORE TEAMS

Player, Team	Pct.	G	PO	A	E	TC	DP
Aracena, Juan, Bow.	1.000	33	1	4	0	5	1
Aracena, Juan, Bing.	.000	7	0	0	0	0	0
Brea, Lesli, Bing.	.889	19	5	11	2	18	2
Brea, Lesli, Bow.	1.000	2	3	2	0	5	0
Dale, Carl, Akr.	1.000	4	1	1	0	2	0
Dale, Carl, Tren.	1.000	6	1	2	0	3	1
Dedrick, Jim, Akr.	1.000	3	0	1	0	1	0
Dedrick, Jim, Tren.	.900	15	2	7	1	10	1
Martinez, Jesus, Akr.*	.875	7	2	5	1	8	0
Martinez, Jesus, Bing.*	1.000	6	1	0	0	1	0
Radlosky, Rob, N.B.	1.000	6	2	3	0	5	0
Radlosky, Rob, Tren.	1.000	8	3	2	0	5	0

The following players appeared only as designated hitter, pinch-hitter or pinch runner: Benefield, dh; Curtis, dh; Ramirez, dh; Zeber, dh.

LEAGUE CHAMPIONS

Year	Team	Pct.	Year	Team	Pct.	Year	Team	Pct.
1923—	Williamsport	.661	1929—	Binghamton	.597	1935—	Scranton	.657
1924—	Williamsport	.654	1930—	Wilkes-Barre	.572		Binghamton*	.580
1925—	York§	.583	1931—	Harrisburg	.597	1936—	Scranton*	.609
	Williamsport§	.583	1932—	Wilkes-Barre	.561		Elmira	.629
1926—	Scranton	.627	1933—	Binghamton	.690	1937—	Elmira†	.622
1927—	Harrisburg	.630	1934—	Binghamton	.694	1938—	Binghamton	.622
1928—	Harrisburg	.603		Williamsport*	.603		Elmira (3rd)‡	.522

CLASS AA Eastern League

Year	Team	Pct.	Year	Team	Pct.	Year	Team	Pct.
1939—	Scranton†	.571	1961—	Springfield	.612	1983—	Lynn	.554
1940—	Scranton	.568	1962—	Williamsport	.593		New Britain‡	.518
	Binghamton (2nd)‡	.554		Elmira (2nd)‡	.514	1984—	Waterbury	.543
1941—	Wilkes-Barre	.630	1963—	Charleston	.593		Vermont‡	.536
	Elmira (3rd)‡	.514	1964—	Elmira	.586	1985—	Albany	.540
1942—	Albany	.600	1965—	Pittsfield	.607		Vermont‡	.514
	Scranton (2nd)‡	.593	1966—	Elmira	.633	1986—	Reading	.566
1943—	Scranton	.630	1967—	Binghamton♦	.586		Vermont‡	.554
	Elmira (2nd)‡	.568		Elmira	.532	1987—	Pittsfield	.630
1944—	Hartford	.723	1968—	Pittsfield	.604		Harrisburg‡	.550
	Binghamton (4th)‡	.474		Reading (2nd)‡	.579	1988—	Glens Falls	.584
1945—	Utica	.615	1969—	York	.640		Albany‡	.522
	Albany (3rd)‡	.564	1970—	Waterbury■	.560	1989—	Albany‡	.657
1946—	Scranton†	.691		Reading■	.553		Harrisburg	.522
1947—	Utica†	.652	1971—	Three Rivers	.569	1990—	Albany	.568
1948—	Scranton†	.636		Elmira▼	.561		London‡	.547
1949—	Albany	.664	1972—	West Haven▼	.600	1991—	Harrisburg	.621
	Binghamton (4th)‡	.500		Three Rivers	.559		Albany‡	.543
1950—	Wilkes-Barre‡	.652	1973—	Reading▼	.551	1992—	Canton/Akron	.580
1951—	Wilkes-Barre‡	.612		Pittsfield	.551		Binghamton‡	.572
	Scranton (2nd)†	.562	1974—	Thetford Miners (2nd)•	.536	1993—	Harrisburg‡	.681
1952—	Albany	.603		Pittsfield (2nd)	.496		Canton/Akron	.543
	Binghamton (2nd)‡	.562	1975—	Reading	.613	1994—	Harrisburg	.633
1953—	Reading	.682		Bristol*	.587		Binghamton‡	.582
	Binghamton (2nd)‡	.636	1976—	Three Rivers	.601	1995—	New Haven	.556
1954—	Wilkes-Barre	.576		West Haven††	.576		Reading‡	.514
	Albany (3rd)‡	.540	1977—	West Haven‡‡	.623	1996—	Portland	.589
1955—	Reading	.613		Three Rivers	.551		Harrisburg‡	.521
	Allentown (2nd)‡	.565	1978—	Reading	.642	1997—	Harrisburg‡	.606
1956—	Schenectady†	.609		Bristol*	.580		Portland	.556
1957—	Binghamton	.607	1979—	West Haven§§	.597	1998—	New Britain	.585
	Reading (3rd)‡	.529	1980—	Holyoke*	.561		Harrisburg‡	.514
1958—	Lancaster∞	.568		Waterbury	.540	1999—	Trenton	.648
	Binghamton (6th)‡	.493	1981—	Glens Falls	.615		Harrisburg‡	.535
1959—	Springfield†	.607		Bristol*	.577	2000—	Reading	.599
1960—	Williamsport▲	.551	1982—	West Haven*	.614		New Haven‡	.577
	Springfield (3rd)▲	.496		Lynn	.590			

*Won split-season playoff. †Won championship and four-team playoff. ‡Won four-team playoff. §Tied for pennant, York winning playoff. ∞League was divided into Northern, Southern divisions and played a split season; Lancaster was overall season leader. ▲Playoff finals canceled after one game because of rain with Williamsport and Springfield declared playoff co-champions. ♦League was divided into Eastern, Western divisions; Binghamton won playoff. ■Tied for pennant, Waterbury winning playoff. ▼League was divided into American, National divisions; won playoff. •League was divided into American and National divisions; won four-team playoff. ††League was divided into Northern, Southern divisions, won playoff. ‡‡League was divided into New England and Canadian-American divisions; won playoff. §§Won both halves of split season (no playoffs). (NOTE—Known as New York-Pennsylvania League prior to 1938.)

SOUTHERN LEAGUE

LEAGUE OFFICE

President/secretary-treasurer
Don Mincher

Address
1 Depot St., Suite 300
Marietta, GA 30060

Phone
770-428-4749

TEAMS

BIRMINGHAM BARONS
General manager
Tony Ensor
Manager
Nick Capra
Ballpark (capacity, surface)
Hoover Metropolitan Stadium
(10,800, grass)
Affiliation
White Sox
Address
P.O. Box 360007
Birmingham, AL 35236
Phone
205-988-3200

CAROLINA MUDCATS
General manager
Joe Kremer
Manager
Ron Gideon
Ballpark (capacity, surface)
Five County Stadium (6,500, grass)
Affiliation
Rockies
Address
P.O. Drawer 1218
Zebulon, NC 27597
Phone
919-269-2287

CHATTANOOGA LOOKOUTS
President
J. Frank Burke
General manager
Rich Mozingo
Manager
Philip Wellman
Ballpark (capacity, surface)
BellSouth Park (6,100, grass)
Affiliation
Reds
Address
201 Power Alley
Chattanooga, TN 37402
Phone
423-267-2208

GREENVILLE BRAVES
General manager
Steve DeSalvo
Manager
Paul Runge
Ballpark (capacity, surface)
Greenville Municipal Stadium (7,027, grass)
Affiliation
Braves
Address
P.O. Box 16683
Greenville, SC 29606
Phone
864-299-3456

HUNTSVILLE STARS
President/general manager
Bryan Dingo
Manager
Ed Romero
Ballpark (capacity, surface)
Joe W. Davis Stadium (10,400, grass)
Affiliation
Brewers
Address
3125 Leeman Ferry Road
Huntsville, AL 35801
Phone
256-882-2562

JACKSONVILLE SUNS
Vice president/general manager
Peter Bragan Jr.
Manager
John Shoemaker
Ballpark (capacity, surface)
Wolfson Park (8,200, grass)
Affiliation
Dodgers
Address
P.O. Box 4756
Jacksonville, FL 32201
Phone
904-358-2846

MOBILE BAYBEARS
Vice president/general manager
Bill Shanahan
Manager
Tracy Woodson
Ballpark (capacity, surface)
Hank Aaron Stadium (6,000, grass)
Affiliation
Padres
Address
755 Bolling Brothers Blvd.
Mobile, AL 36606
Phone
334-479-2327

ORLANDO RAYS
General manager
Mitch Lukevics
Manager
Mike Ramsey
Ballpark (capacity, surface)
Disney's Wide World of Sports
Complex (9,500, grass)
Affiliation
Devil Rays
Address
P.O. Box 10000
Lake Buena Vista, FL 32830
Phone
407-939-4263

TENNESSEE SMOKIES
General manager
Dan Rajkowski
Manager
Rocket Wheeler
Ballpark (capacity, surface)
Smokies Park (6,000, grass)
Affiliation
Blue Jays
Address
3540 Line Drive
Kodak, TN 37764
Phone
865-637-9494

WEST TENN DIAMOND JAXX
General manager
David Hersh
Manager
Dave Bialas
Ballpark (capacity, surface)
Pringles Park (6,000, grass)
Affiliation
Cubs
Address
4 Fun Place
Jackson, TN 38305
Phone
901-664-2020

CLASS AA Southern League

2000 FINAL STANDINGS
FIRST HALF

EAST DIVISION

Team	W	L	T	Pct.	GB
Orlando (Devil Rays)	36	34	0	.514	...
Greenville (Braves)	36	34	0	.514	...
Carolina (Rockies)	34	36	0	.486	2.0
Tennessee (Blue Jays)	33	37	0	.471	3.0
Jacksonville (Tigers)	29	41	0	.414	7.0

WEST DIVISION

Team	W	L	T	Pct.	GB
Birmingham (White Sox)	43	27	0	.614	...
Chattanooga (Reds)	40	30	0	.571	3.0
West Tenn (Cubs)	35	35	0	.500	8.0
Mobile (Padres)	33	37	0	.471	10.0
Huntsville (Brewers)	31	39	0	.443	12.0

SECOND HALF

EAST DIVISION

Team	W	L	T	Pct.	GB
Jacksonville (Tigers)	40	30	0	.571	...
Tennessee (Blue Jays)	38	32	0	.543	2.0
Greenville (Braves)	32	37	0	.464	7.5
Orlando (Devil Rays)	29	37	0	.439	9.0
Carolina (Rockies)	30	39	0	.435	9.5

WEST DIVISION

Team	W	L	T	Pct.	GB
West Tenn (Cubs)	45	23	0	.662	...
Birmingham (White Sox)	34	36	0	.486	12.0
Mobile (Padres)	33	36	0	.478	12.5
Huntsville (Brewers)	33	36	0	.478	12.5
Chattanooga (Reds)	30	38	0	.441	15.0

COMPOSITE

Team	W.T.	Birm.	Chat.	Tenn.	Jax.	Gre.	Orl.	Mob.	Hunt.	Car.	W	L	T	Pct.	GB
West Tenn (Cubs)	...	16	10	6	3	7	4	11	18	5	80	58	0	.580	...
Birmingham (White Sox)	12	...	16	6	6	5	4	12	13	3	77	63	0	.550	4.0
Chattanooga (Reds)	10	4	...	6	5	4	3	16	15	7	70	68	0	.507	10.0
Tennessee (Blue Jays)	2	2	10	...	11	16	10	6	4	10	71	69	0	.507	10.0
Jacksonville (Tigers)	5	2	7	9	...	10	15	3	1	17	69	71	0	.493	12.0
Greenville (Braves)	1	3	4	8	14	...	14	5	7	12	68	71	0	.489	12.5
Orlando (Devil Rays)	3	4	3	10	13	13	...	3	2	14	65	71	0	.478	14.0
Mobile (Padres)	12	16	8	2	5	3	5	...	11	4	66	73	0	.475	14.5
Huntsville (Brewers)	10	11	9	4	7	1	6	13	...	3	64	75	0	.460	16.5
Carolina (Rockies)	3	5	1	18	7	12	10	4	4	...	64	75	0	.460	16.5

Carolina's home games played in Zebulon, N.C.; Tennessee's home games played in Knoxville, Tenn.; West Tenn's home games played in Jackson, Tenn.

Major league affiliations in parentheses.

PLAYOFFS: West Tenn defeated Birmingham three games to two; Jacksonville defeated Greenville three games to two; West Tenn defeated Jacksonville three games to two to win league championship.

REGULAR-SEASON ATTENDANCE: Birmingham, 321,307; Carolina, 252,713; Chattanooga, 290,165; Greenville, 217,558; Huntsville, 238,930; Jacksonville, 221,221; Mobile, 261,496; Orlando, 61,960; Tennessee, 256,141; West Tenn, 303,355. Total—2,424,846. Playoffs (15 games)—33,066. Class AA All-Star Game at Bowie, Md.—14,077.

MANAGERS: Birmingham, Nick Capra; Carolina, Ron Gideon; Chattanooga, Mike Rojas; Greenville, Paul Runge; Huntsville, Carlos Lezcano; Jacksonville, Gene Roof; Mobile, Mike Basso; Orlando, Mike Ramsey; Tennessee, Rocket Wheeler; West Tenn, Dave Bialas.

ALL-STAR TEAM: 1B—Jay Gibbons, Tennessee; 2B—Marcus Giles, Greenville; 3B—Joe Crede, Birmingham; SS—Elvis Pena, Carolina; OF—Corey Patterson, West Tenn; OF—Juan Pierre, Carolina; OF—Aaron Rowand, Birmingham; OF—Robert Perez, Tennessee; C—Brandon Inge, Jacksonville; DH—Alejandro Freire, Jacksonville; Utility—Paul Hoover, Orlando; RHP—Pasqual Coco, Tennessee; LHP—Mark Buehrle, Birmingham; Relief pitcher—Bob File, Tennessee; Most Valuable Player—Joe Crede, Birmingham; Most Outstanding Pitcher—Mark Buehrle; Best Hustler—Juan Pierre, Carolina; Manager of the Year—Dave Bialas, West Tenn.

2000 BATTING
TEAM

Team	Avg.	G	TPA	AB	R	H	TB	2B	3B	HR	RBI	SH	SF	HP	BB	IBB	SO	SB	CS	GDP	LOB	ShO	Slg.	OBP
Tennessee	.265	140	5346	4686	640	1241	1862	242	29	107	584	50	46	70	494	23	880	105	72	102	1018	11	.397	.341
Chattanooga	.255	138	5236	4592	646	1171	1819	229	37	115	587	44	36	75	489	16	994	160	110	81	925	10	.396	.334
Carolina	.255	139	5196	4508	570	1149	1630	215	28	70	510	67	37	72	512	27	907	208	85	95	1017	9	.362	.338
Birmingham	.252	140	5306	4639	629	1168	1724	224	25	94	585	40	39	66	522	20	935	121	62	94	987	7	.372	.333
Mobile	.252	139	5341	4707	591	1185	1767	242	23	98	553	44	42	56	492	19	912	71	54	102	1025	14	.375	.327
Orlando	.251	140	5077	4467	512	1121	1573	194	30	66	450	44	40	65	461	11	869	83	81	88	1005	12	.352	.327
Huntsville	.246	139	5304	4561	603	1122	1638	222	21	84	547	61	40	77	565	19	1018	133	79	84	1023	9	.359	.336
West Tenn	.245	138	5222	4595	609	1125	1728	209	41	104	549	39	36	66	486	23	1125	147	78	88	939	8	.376	.324
Jacksonville	.244	140	5306	4628	594	1131	1715	240	25	98	546	39	40	81	518	11	1031	140	47	94	1037	15	.371	.328
Greenville	.232	139	5143	4538	565	1054	1662	225	16	117	508	36	35	55	479	19	1048	126	49	100	926	8	.366	.311

INDIVIDUAL
TOP QUALIFIERS FOR BATTING CHAMPIONSHIP

Minimum 378 plate appearances. *Lefthanded batter. †Switch-hitter.

Player, Team	Avg.	G	TPA	AB	R	H	TB	2B	3B	HR	RBI	SH	SF	HP	BB	IBB	SO	SB	CS	GDP	Slg.	OBP
Pierre, Juan, Car.*	.326	107	489	439	63	143	167	16	4	0	32	8	4	5	33	0	26	46	12	4	.380	.376
Gibbons, Jay, Tenn.*	.321	132	552	474	85	152	249	38	1	19	75	0	7	10	61	5	67	3	1	10	.525	.404
Crede, Joe, Birm.	.306	138	610	533	84	163	261	35	0	21	94	1	5	15	56	10	111	3	4	18	.490	.384
Sears, Todd, Car.*	.301	86	378	299	54	90	147	21	0	12	72	0	5	2	72	11	76	12	3	7	.492	.434
Pena, Elvis, Car.†	.300	126	561	477	92	143	182	16	7	3	37	4	1	10	69	2	76	48	13	11	.382	.399
Burroughs, Sean, Mob.*	.291	108	461	392	46	114	157	29	4	2	42	4	3	2	58	6	45	6	8	10	.401	.383
Giles, Marcus, Gre.	.290	132	533	458	73	133	216	28	2	17	62	0	1	2	72	6	71	25	5	11	.472	.388
Rexrode, Jackie, Birm.*	.288	90	412	337	60	97	113	10	3	0	14	3	2	2	68	1	39	19	11	3	.335	.408

Player, Team	Avg.	G	TPA	AB	R	H	TB	2B	3B	HR	RBI	SH	SF	HP	BB	IBB	SO	SB	CS	GDP	Slg.	OBP
Perez, Robert, Tenn...............	.287	136	584	547	66	157	249	33	1	19	92	2	3	6	26	3	82	8	7	12	.455	.325
Gerut, Jody, Car.*	.285	109	448	362	48	103	150	32	3	3	57	1	7	2	76	2	54	18	11	9	.414	.405
Amrhein, Mike, W.T.	.284	104	406	352	45	100	145	18	0	9	49	2	2	14	35	2	40	0	3	10	.412	.370
Leday, A.J., Mob.	.283	117	451	407	45	115	175	20	2	12	70	0	4	14	26	1	84	4	2	9	.430	.344
Santana, Pedro, Jack.............	.281	112	497	448	61	126	172	20	4	6	53	4	4	3	38	1	83	40	8	2	.384	.339
Klimek, Josh, Hun.*	.280	108	418	378	53	106	170	22	0	14	62	0	6	5	29	0	71	3	4	4	.450	.335
Peeples, Mike, Tenn.	.280	123	541	475	70	133	221	26	4	18	73	4	7	46	1	71	11	8	14	.465	.350

DEPARTMENTAL LEADERS: G—Rowand, 139; AB—R. Perez, 547; R—E. Pena, 92; H—Crede, 163; TB—Crede, 261; 2B—Briggs, 39; 3B—Hinske, 9; HR—Freire, 25; RBI—Rowand, 98; SH—Prieto, 14; SF—Tucci, Pomierski, 8 each; HP—C. Miller, 30; BB—Prieto, 86; IBB—Sears, 11; SO—Hessman, 178; SB—E. Pena, 48; CS—Kelly, 21; GIDP—Crede, 18; Slg.—Gibbons, .525; OBP—Sears, .434.

ALL PLAYERS

*Lefthanded batter. †Switch-hitter.

Player, Team	Avg.	G	TPA	AB	R	H	TB	2B	3B	HR	RBI	SH	SF	HP	BB	IBB	SO	SB	CS	GDP	Slg.	OBP
Abreu, Dennis, W.T.	.241	52	181	166	24	40	56	8	1	2	13	3	0	3	9	0	36	7	5	4	.337	.292
Airoso, Kurt, Jack.	.239	98	387	326	43	78	106	14	1	4	41	2	3	5	49	0	69	6	1	7	.325	.345
Alguacil, Jose, Birm.*	.053	9	22	19	1	1	1	0	0	0	0	0	0	0	3	0	3	2	0	1	.053	.182
Amrhein, Mike, W.T.	.284	104	406	352	45	100	145	18	0	9	49	2	2	14	35	2	40	0	3	10	.412	.370
Andreopoulos, Alex, Hun.*	.200	5	12	10	1	2	3	1	0	0	2	0	1	0	1	0	2	0	0	0	.300	.250
Aragon, Angel, Mob.	.111	54	9	9	0	1	1	0	0	0	0	0	0	0	0	0	5	0	0	0	.111	.111
Averette, Robert, Chat.-Car. ...	.171	24	41	35	1	6	6	0	0	0	4	0	0	2	0	14	2	0	1	.171	.216
Avery, Steve, Gre.*	.250	6	4	4	0	1	1	0	0	0	0	0	0	0	0	0	0	0	0	0	.250	.250
Backe, Brandon, Orl.	.250	4	10	8	1	2	2	0	0	0	0	0	0	0	2	0	1	0	2	0	.250	.400
Badeaux, Brooks, Orl.†	.262	73	305	260	37	68	91	8	6	1	27	5	1	5	34	1	29	2	2	5	.350	.357
Bair, Rod, Car.	.169	27	107	89	13	15	24	6	0	1	6	0	1	5	12	1	16	1	2	2	.270	.299
Balfe, Ryan, Mob.†	.262	130	521	462	61	121	186	21	4	12	66	0	4	9	46	2	120	3	3	12	.403	.338
Barnes, Brian, Gre.*	.500	24	2	2	0	1	1	0	0	0	0	0	0	0	0	0	1	0	0	0	.500	.500
Bass, Jayson, Gre.†	.138	31	76	65	9	9	14	0	1	1	4	0	1	2	8	1	18	5	2	0	.215	.250
Bass, Jayson, W.T.*	.317	50	173	145	27	46	65	7	0	4	17	0	2	4	22	1	20	4	5	4	.448	.416
Battersby, Eric, Birm.	.238	127	474	411	59	98	148	20	3	8	43	1	4	3	55	1	84	6	8	8	.360	.330
Beck, Greg, Hun.	.333	48	7	6	0	2	2	0	0	0	1	0	0	0	0	0	2	0	0	0	.333	.333
Becker, Brian, Orl.	.278	132	551	503	45	140	198	27	2	9	58	0	3	5	40	1	88	1	3	11	.394	.336
Beinbrink, Andy, Orl.	.455	3	12	11	2	5	8	0	0	1	3	0	0	0	1	0	1	0	0	1	.727	.500
Besco, Derek, Jack.	.200	32	118	105	10	21	38	5	0	4	10	2	0	1	10	0	14	3	0	2	.362	.276
Booker, Chris, W.T.	.000	12	1	1	0	0	0	0	0	0	0	0	0	0	0	0	1	0	0	0	.000	.000
Borchard, Joe, Birm.†	.227	6	26	22	3	5	7	0	1	0	3	0	1	0	3	0	8	0	0	1	.318	.308
Bost, Heath, Car.	.500	6	2	2	1	1	1	0	0	0	0	0	0	0	0	0	0	0	0	0	.500	.500
Bowers, Brent, Chat.*	.095	6	26	21	5	2	5	0	0	1	5	0	0	0	5	0	4	0	1	0	.238	.269
Bowie, Micah, W.T.*	.000	18	28	21	0	0	0	0	0	0	1	5	0	0	2	0	9	0	0	0	.000	.087
Bravo, Danny, Birm.†	.232	96	390	340	48	79	100	12	0	3	29	2	3	2	42	0	56	11	9	5	.294	.318
Briggs, Stoney, Jack.	.254	134	568	496	65	126	220	39	2	17	65	2	4	6	60	1	145	17	6	14	.444	.339
Broussard, Benjamin, Chat.* ..	.255	87	366	286	64	73	131	8	4	14	51	0	2	6	72	3	78	15	2	6	.458	.413
Brown, Jason, Orl.	.261	69	256	230	21	60	98	12	1	8	29	1	4	7	14	0	53	1	0	8	.426	.318
Brumfield, Jacob, Birm.	.186	18	69	59	6	11	13	2	0	0	2	1	0	0	9	0	8	3	2	0	.220	.294
Burkhart, Lance, Hun.	.194	51	179	155	17	30	56	6	1	6	19	4	0	1	19	3	43	0	0	2	.361	.286
Burress, Andy, Chat.	.250	123	462	400	54	100	147	15	7	6	41	5	3	3	51	0	78	15	14	7	.368	.337
Burroughs, Sean, Mob.*	.291	108	461	392	46	114	157	29	4	2	42	4	4	3	58	6	45	6	8	10	.401	.383
Butler, Garrett, Orl.†	.239	38	128	117	14	28	36	5	0	1	7	0	0	4	7	0	17	3	4	5	.308	.305
Bynum, Mike, Mob.*	.000	6	5	5	0	0	0	0	0	0	0	0	0	0	0	0	1	0	0	0	.000	.000
Caceres, Wilmy, Chat.†	.268	130	585	534	69	143	180	23	4	2	33	5	5	4	37	3	71	36	19	10	.337	.317
Calais, Ian, Gre.	.161	14	39	31	5	5	5	0	0	0	1	0	1	0	7	0	11	0	1	0	.161	.316
Camp, Shawn, Mob.	.125	45	10	8	2	1	1	0	0	0	0	0	0	1	1	0	0	0	0	0	.125	.300
Cancel, Robinson, Hun.	.268	22	83	71	11	19	25	3	0	1	12	0	1	0	11	0	16	5	1	2	.352	.361
Cannon, Jon, W.T.	.667	32	4	3	0	2	2	0	0	0	1	1	0	0	0	0	0	0	0	0	.667	.667
Carr, Dustin, Orl.	.273	2	11	11	1	3	3	0	0	0	1	0	0	0	0	0	2	0	0	0	.273	.273
Cepeda, Jose, Gre.	.284	30	74	67	4	19	21	0	1	0	3	0	1	0	6	0	10	0	0	2	.313	.338
Ceriani, Matt, Hun.	.000	8	20	16	1	0	0	0	0	0	0	1	2	1	0	1	4	0	0	0	.000	.056
Chacon, Shawn, Car.	.217	28	27	23	4	5	9	1	0	1	2	2	0	0	2	0	5	0	0	0	.391	.280
Chiaffredo, Paul, Tenn.	.111	18	69	63	6	7	8	1	0	0	2	0	0	1	5	0	16	0	1	0	.127	.188
Choi, Hee, W.T.*	.303	36	148	122	25	37	76	9	0	10	25	0	1	0	25	0	38	3	1	5	.623	.419
Christensen, Ben, W.T.	.182	7	14	11	2	2	2	0	0	0	0	2	0	0	1	0	5	0	0	0	.182	.250
Cleveland, Russell, Jack.........	.000	1	1	1	0	0	0	0	0	0	0	0	0	0	0	0	1	0	0	0	.000	.000
Cline, Pat, Hun.	.118	19	60	51	2	6	10	4	0	0	4	0	1	2	6	0	11	0	0	1	.196	.233
Colina, Javier, Car.	.217	130	490	429	34	93	113	12	1	2	35	10	4	3	44	2	81	5	2	8	.263	.292
Collier, Lou, Hun.	.267	50	206	172	29	46	60	4	2	2	29	0	3	1	30	1	44	7	3	5	.349	.374
Condrey, Clay, Mob.	.000	35	4	3	0	0	0	0	0	0	0	0	0	0	0	0	2	0	0	0	.000	.000
Connacher, Kevin, Birm.	.200	4	16	15	3	3	3	0	0	0	2	0	0	1	0	0	6	1	0	1	.200	.250
Corey, Michael, Gre.	.000	52	7	7	0	0	0	0	0	0	0	0	0	0	0	0	3	0	0	0	.000	.000
Crede, Joe, Birm.	.306	138	610	533	84	163	261	35	0	21	94	1	5	15	56	10	111	3	4	18	.490	.384
Cripps, Bobby, Chat.*	.238	8	21	21	2	5	7	2	0	0	6	0	0	0	0	0	5	0	0	1	.333	.238
Cromer, Brandon, Hun.*	.206	22	83	68	11	14	25	5	0	2	8	1	0	1	13	0	17	2	1	0	.368	.341
Crowell, Jim, Chat.	.250	23	4	4	0	1	1	0	0	0	0	0	0	0	0	0	3	0	0	0	.250	.250
Cumberland, Chris, Gre..........	.000	12	2	1	0	0	0	0	0	0	0	0	0	0	0	0	1	0	0	0	.000	.000
Da Luz, Craig, Jack.	.222	4	11	9	2	2	7	0	1	1	2	0	0	0	2	0	1	0	0	0	.778	.364
Daniels, David, Mob.	.000	9	2	1	0	0	0	0	0	0	0	0	0	0	1	0	0	0	0	0	.000	.000
Darula, Bobby, Hun.*	.239	35	135	117	17	28	38	7	0	1	10	0	1	3	14	0	17	3	1	1	.325	.333
Davis, Lance, Chat.	.200	25	31	25	1	5	5	0	0	0	3	0	0	3	0	6	0	0	0	.200	.286
Dawkins, Travis, Chat.	.231	90	415	368	54	85	135	20	6	6	31	2	2	3	40	0	71	22	10	3	.367	.310
DeCinces, Tim, Mob.*	.271	72	256	207	34	56	98	9	0	11	44	0	7	0	42	1	28	1	0	4	.473	.383
Dellaero, Jason, Birm.	.185	122	473	438	36	81	122	18	1	7	42	7	2	6	20	0	142	9	6	7	.279	.230
De Los Santos, Eddy, Orl.	.234	48	180	171	11	40	48	6	1	0	8	1	1	2	5	0	26	2	3	2	.281	.263
Dent, Doug, Mob...................	.077	18	16	13	1	1	1	0	0	0	0	3	0	0	0	0	5	0	0	0	.077	.077

Player, Team	Avg.	G	TPA	AB	R	H	TB	2B	3B	HR	RBI	SH	SF	HP	BB	IBB	SO	SB	CS	GDP	Slg.	OBP
Dewey, Jason, Car.	.226	96	366	318	29	72	123	24	0	9	44	6	2	6	34	1	101	1	3	9	.387	.311
DeWitt, Scott, Car.	.333	34	4	3	0	1	1	0	0	0	0	1	0	0	0	0	0	0	0	0	.333	.333
Diaz, Alejandro, Chat.	.267	122	515	491	69	131	205	19	8	13	66	0	5	4	14	1	77	18	20	5	.418	.290
Difelice, Mark, Car.	.056	23	20	18	2	1	2	1	0	0	1	0	0	0	2	0	11	0	0	0	.111	.150
Dishman, Glenn, Hun.	.143	42	9	7	1	1	1	0	0	0	0	0	2	0	0	0	1	0	0	0	.143	.143
Dixon, Tim, Hun.*	.000	35	4	3	0	0	0	0	0	0	0	0	0	0	1	0	2	0	0	0	.000	.250
Donaldson, Bo, Chat.	.000	57	2	2	0	0	0	0	0	0	0	0	0	0	0	0	1	0	0	0	.000	.000
Dorame, Randey, Car.*	1.000	2	1	1	0	1	1	0	0	0	0	0	0	0	0	0	0	0	0	0	1.000	1.000
Doughty, Brian, Mob.	.182	32	36	33	2	6	8	2	0	0	2	2	0	0	1	0	7	0	0	0	.242	.206
Duncan, Courtney, W.T.*	.000	61	2	2	0	0	0	0	0	0	0	0	0	0	0	0	2	0	0	0	.000	.000
Eaton, Adam, Mob.	.286	10	15	14	0	4	4	0	0	0	1	0	0	0	1	0	7	0	0	0	.286	.333
Eberwein, Kevin, Mob.	.263	100	423	372	57	98	172	16	2	18	71	0	4	2	45	3	77	2	2	8	.462	.343
Emiliano, Jamie, Car.	.500	47	3	2	0	1	1	0	0	0	0	1	0	0	0	0	1	0	0	0	.500	.500
Ernster, Mark, Hun.	.244	57	245	205	27	50	74	9	0	5	26	3	1	1	35	2	46	10	6	6	.361	.355
Faggett, Ethan, Mob.*	.241	97	421	370	55	89	123	20	4	2	23	2	1	6	42	0	84	12	15	9	.332	.327
Fernandez, Ozzie, Chat.	.000	1	2	0	0	0	0	0	0	0	0	0	2	0	0	0	0	0	0	0	.000	.000
Flach, Jason, Gre.	.091	28	11	11	0	1	1	0	0	0	0	0	0	0	0	0	3	0	0	0	.091	.091
Fleming, Ryan, Tenn.*	.171	37	129	105	16	18	28	4	0	2	9	3	0	1	20	0	17	2	1	1	.267	.310
Flener, Huck, Mob.†	.000	15	3	2	0	0	0	0	0	0	0	1	0	0	0	0	1	0	0	0	.000	.000
Florez, Tim, Chat.	.163	42	110	98	11	16	27	3	1	2	6	2	0	2	8	0	24	1	6	1	.276	.241
Font, Franklin, W.T.	.261	104	365	329	39	86	101	9	3	0	26	4	1	5	26	1	44	9	4	6	.307	.324
Foster, Jim, Birm.	.257	10	36	35	1	9	10	1	0	0	3	0	0	0	1	0	3	0	0	0	.286	.286
Frachiseur, Zach, Gre.	.250	43	8	8	1	2	2	0	0	0	0	0	0	0	0	0	2	0	0	0	.250	.250
Frank, Mike, Chat.*	.267	8	31	30	6	8	13	1	2	0	5	0	0	0	1	0	1	0	0	1	.433	.290
Fraraccio, Dan, Orl.	.107	9	29	28	2	3	6	0	0	1	1	0	0	0	1	0	5	0	0	1	.214	.138
Freel, Ryan, Tenn.	.295	12	55	44	11	13	18	3	1	0	8	0	2	1	8	0	6	2	3	3	.409	.400
Freire, Alejandro, Jack.	.274	135	562	471	73	129	220	16	0	25	77	0	6	16	69	1	111	2	4	13	.467	.381
Furcal, Rafael, Gre.†	.200	3	11	10	1	2	5	0	0	1	3	0	0	0	1	0	0	0	0	0	.500	.273
Garcia, Jose, Hun.	.379	20	30	29	4	11	15	4	0	0	4	0	0	0	1	0	9	1	0	0	.517	.400
Garcia, Neil, Orl.†	.202	34	116	99	11	20	30	3	2	1	6	0	1	0	16	1	27	0	0	1	.303	.310
Gazarek, Marty, Gre.	.287	61	230	202	27	58	89	10	0	7	28	0	2	8	18	0	32	5	3	4	.441	.365
Gerut, Jody, Car.*	.285	109	448	362	48	103	150	32	3	3	57	1	7	2	76	2	54	18	11	9	.414	.405
Gibbons, Jay, Tenn.*	.321	132	552	474	85	152	249	38	1	19	75	0	7	10	61	5	67	3	1	10	.525	.404
Gibbs, Kevin, Car.†	1.000	1	1	1	0	1	1	0	0	0	0	0	0	0	0	0	0	0	0	0	1.000	1.000
Gil, David, Chat.	.000	6	3	2	1	0	0	0	0	0	0	0	0	0	1	0	1	0	0	0	.000	.333
Giles, Marcus, Gre.	.290	132	533	458	73	133	216	28	2	17	62	0	1	2	72	6	71	25	5	11	.472	.388
Giles, Tim, Tenn.*	.264	115	456	397	43	105	162	18	0	13	56	0	5	1	53	6	98	1	6	11	.408	.349
Giron, Isabel, Mob.	.429	70	7	7	1	3	6	0	0	1	3	0	0	0	0	0	2	0	0	1	.857	.429
Gissell, Chris, W.T.	.190	16	24	21	0	4	5	1	0	0	3	3	0	0	0	0	9	0	0	0	.238	.190
Glauber, Keith, Chat.	.000	32	1	1	0	0	0	0	0	0	0	0	0	0	0	0	0	0	0	0	.000	.000
Glavine, Mike, Gre.*	.234	128	471	423	37	99	158	26	0	11	81	0	7	5	36	3	83	1	1	8	.374	.297
Gooch, Arnie, Chat.	.143	21	25	21	2	3	3	0	0	0	3	2	0	0	2	0	9	0	0	1	.143	.217
Goodell, Steve, Car.	.258	76	288	229	39	59	107	13	1	11	42	0	1	10	48	2	48	2	1	7	.467	.406
Granger, Jeff, Gre.	.000	16	2	1	1	0	0	0	0	0	0	0	0	0	1	0	0	0	0	0	.000	.500
Green, Chad, Hun.†	.233	85	351	317	44	74	109	22	2	3	27	1	3	1	29	1	85	19	6	2	.344	.297
Greene, Ryan, Gre.	.000	24	1	1	0	0	0	0	0	0	0	0	0	0	0	0	0	0	0	0	.000	.000
Guiliano, Matt, Hun.	.182	20	55	44	3	8	8	0	0	0	3	0	1	2	8	1	14	1	0	1	.182	.327
Gulin, Lindsay, W.T.*	.000	9	12	9	1	0	0	0	0	0	0	1	0	0	2	0	7	0	0	0	.000	.182
Guttormson, Rick, Mob.	.250	20	14	12	1	3	3	0	0	0	1	2	0	0	0	0	5	0	0	0	.250	.250
Guzman, Domingo, Mob.	.333	14	3	3	1	1	4	0	0	1	3	0	0	0	0	0	2	0	0	0	1.333	.333
Hall, Toby, Orl.	.343	68	294	271	37	93	134	14	0	9	50	0	5	1	17	2	24	3	2	6	.494	.378
Harikkala, Tim, Hun.	.000	22	8	7	0	0	0	0	0	0	0	0	0	0	1	0	4	0	0	0	.000	.125
Haring, Brett, Chat.	.235	23	23	17	1	4	4	0	0	0	1	5	0	0	1	0	5	0	0	1	.235	.278
Harrison, Adonis, Orl.*	.213	25	90	80	10	17	20	3	0	0	5	2	0	0	8	1	11	5	3	3	.250	.281
Hart, Len, Mob.*	.200	32	5	5	1	1	1	0	0	0	0	0	0	0	0	0	0	0	0	0	.200	.200
Hawkins, Al, Hun.	.313	18	16	16	0	5	6	1	0	0	4	0	0	0	0	0	1	0	0	1	.375	.313
Heintz, Chris, Birm.	.268	73	267	239	27	64	87	15	1	2	34	1	6	0	21	0	33	4	1	2	.364	.320
Henson, Drew, Chat.	.172	16	68	64	7	11	22	8	0	1	9	0	0	0	4	0	25	2	0	2	.344	.221
Hessman, Mike, Greenv.	.183	127	484	437	52	80	162	23	1	19	50	0	2	8	37	0	178	3	1	9	.371	.258
Hinske, Eric, W.T.*	.259	131	520	436	76	113	212	21	9	20	73	0	3	3	78	3	133	14	5	7	.486	.374
Hite, Kevin, Mob.	.000	27	5	3	0	0	0	0	0	0	0	2	0	0	0	0	2	0	0	0	.000	.000
Hoover, Paul, Orl.	.250	106	446	360	54	90	127	20	4	3	44	1	5	13	67	2	66	9	8	5	.353	.382
House, Craig, Car.	.000	18	1	1	0	0	0	0	0	0	0	0	0	0	0	0	0	0	0	0	.000	.000
Hudson, Orlando, Tenn.†	.239	39	154	134	17	32	48	4	3	2	15	1	2	2	15	1	18	3	2	3	.358	.320
Huff, Jake, Mob.	.250	4	8	8	0	2	2	0	0	0	0	0	0	0	0	0	0	0	0	0	.250	.250
Huntsman, Marcel, Mob.	.000	59	5	4	0	0	0	0	0	0	0	0	0	0	1	0	3	0	0	0	.000	.000
Hutchins, Norm, Car.†	.242	77	314	281	31	68	101	13	4	4	29	3	2	6	21	0	69	19	6	4	.359	.306
Iapoce, Anthony, Hun.	.223	72	279	247	24	55	62	7	0	0	20	3	3	3	23	1	57	16	4	4	.251	.293
Iglesias, Mike, Hun.	.333	13	4	3	1	1	1	0	0	0	0	0	0	0	1	0	0	0	0	0	.333	.500
Inge, Brandon, Jack.†	.258	78	330	298	39	77	122	25	1	6	53	1	5	0	26	1	73	10	3	10	.409	.313
Inglin, Jeff, Birm.	.291	65	288	244	43	71	104	12	3	5	40	2	4	4	34	0	43	5	2	7	.426	.381
Jacobs, Ryan, Hun.	.000	18	4	3	0	0	0	0	0	0	0	0	1	0	0	0	1	0	0	0	.000	.000
Jacobsen, Bucky, Hun.	.276	81	327	268	44	74	142	14	0	18	50	0	4	4	51	2	69	4	2	8	.530	.394
Jennings, Jason, Car.*	.143	6	8	7	0	1	1	0	0	0	1	0	0	0	1	0	0	0	0	0	.143	.143
Johnson, Adam, Birm.*	.232	105	426	379	42	88	146	21	2	11	60	0	3	2	42	2	74	3	5	10	.385	.310
Johnson, James, Hun.†	.083	16	15	12	1	1	1	0	0	0	0	0	2	0	1	0	6	0	0	0	.083	.154
Johnston, Doug, Hun.-W.T.	.241	32	30	29	1	7	7	0	0	0	4	0	0	0	1	0	7	0	0	1	.241	.267
Kalinowski, Josh, Car.*	.000	6	5	5	0	0	0	0	0	0	0	0	0	0	0	0	4	0	0	0	.000	.000
Keck, Brian, Car.	.261	63	233	203	22	53	74	10	1	3	28	6	3	3	18	1	44	9	5	6	.365	.326
Kelly, Kenny, Orl.	.252	124	560	489	73	123	165	17	8	3	29	4	2	6	59	1	119	31	21	9	.337	.338
Kent, Robbie, Mob.	.082	29	71	61	6	5	6	1	0	0	4	0	1	2	7	0	10	0	0	3	.098	.197
King, Brad, Chat.	.250	41	132	108	18	27	38	5	0	2	11	0	3	2	18	1	26	3	3	2	.352	.364
King, Brett, W.T.	.143	48	158	126	12	18	32	4	2	2	14	1	0	3	28	1	41	3	2	2	.254	.312

Player, Team	Avg.	G	TPA	AB	R	H	TB	2B	3B	HR	RBI	SH	SF	HP	BB	IBB	SO	SB	CS	GDP	Slg.	OBP
Kirby, Scott, Hun.	.218	118	425	344	54	75	124	11	1	12	45	2	1	12	66	2	112	7	5	4	.360	.362
Klimek, Josh, Hun.*	.280	108	418	378	53	106	170	22	0	14	62	0	6	5	29	0	71	3	4	4	.450	.335
Kominek, Toby, Hun.	.260	130	510	427	56	111	171	18	6	10	68	2	5	14	62	0	104	16	7	8	.400	.368
Krause, Scott, Hun.	.321	11	28	28	2	9	12	3	0	0	5	0	0	0	0	0	8	0	0	1	.429	.321
Kremblas, Mike, Tenn.	.275	30	95	69	16	19	26	4	0	1	6	5	2	10	9	0	14	1	1	2	.377	.422
Lackey, Steve, Gre.	.233	129	543	489	61	114	132	9	0	3	33	10	2	3	39	0	95	24	8	15	.270	.293
Langaigne, Selwyn, Tenn.*	.244	76	238	213	26	52	58	4	1	0	22	2	1	1	21	1	43	1	5	7	.272	.314
Larkin, Stephen, Chat.*	.220	64	165	150	15	33	47	5	3	1	17	0	0	1	14	1	30	4	5	0	.313	.291
Larson, Brandon, Chat.	.272	111	469	427	61	116	202	26	0	20	64	0	3	8	31	5	122	15	5	8	.473	.330
Lawrence, Brian, Mob.	.241	21	31	29	1	7	9	2	0	0	1	1	1	0	0	0	6	0	0	0	.310	.233
Lawrence, Joe, Tenn.	.263	39	168	133	22	35	44	9	0	0	9	1	1	3	30	0	27	7	1	2	.331	.407
Leday, A.J., Mob.	.283	117	451	407	45	115	175	20	2	12	70	0	4	14	26	1	84	4	2	9	.430	.344
Lee, Derek, Hun.*	.115	28	33	26	4	3	4	1	0	0	1	3	0	0	4	0	7	0	0	0	.154	.233
LeRoy, John, Chat.	.000	6	2	2	0	0	0	0	0	0	0	0	0	0	0	0	0	0	0	0	.000	.000
Lewis, Derrick, Gre.	.000	27	26	21	1	0	0	0	0	0	1	0	1	0	4	0	9	0	0	1	.000	.154
Lindsey, Rodney, Jack.	.224	114	452	393	57	88	107	11	4	0	20	10	1	10	38	0	100	46	14	4	.272	.308
Lindstrom, David, Jack.	.234	68	248	222	26	52	84	11	0	7	36	0	3	4	19	0	17	1	0	6	.378	.302
Long, Ryan, Birm.	.241	89	350	315	37	76	120	14	0	10	39	2	0	10	23	0	86	1	0	9	.381	.313
Lopez, Felipe, Tenn.†	.257	127	506	463	52	119	172	18	4	9	41	8	3	1	31	0	110	12	11	6	.371	.303
Lopez, Mickey, Hun.†	.335	53	249	212	42	71	113	22	4	4	26	6	1	0	30	0	32	16	7	5	.533	.416
Lopez, Rafael, W.T.	.260	69	245	227	19	59	76	12	1	1	26	2	1	1	14	1	33	0	1	13	.335	.305
Loyd, Brian, Tenn.	.299	58	227	194	21	58	73	10	1	1	23	0	2	2	29	1	22	7	3	6	.376	.392
Lunar, Fernando, Gre.	.167	31	110	102	6	17	20	3	0	0	4	0	0	0	8	0	15	0	0	2	.196	.227
Lutz, Manuel, Jack.*	.333	1	3	3	1	1	2	1	0	0	3	0	0	0	0	0	0	0	0	0	.667	.333
Mackiewitz, Richard, Car.*	.267	10	34	30	2	8	9	1	0	0	1	0	0	1	3	0	5	0	0	1	.300	.353
MacRae, Scott, Chat.	.000	55	3	1	0	0	0	0	0	0	0	2	0	0	0	0	1	0	0	0	.000	.000
Magdaleno, Ricky, Mob.	.201	57	178	144	14	29	44	7	1	2	12	3	0	0	31	0	23	1	1	3	.306	.343
Mahoney, Mike, W.T.	.303	24	86	76	12	23	30	7	0	0	7	0	1	2	7	0	16	0	0	0	.395	.372
Manias, Jim, Chat.*	.333	15	9	6	1	2	2	0	0	0	1	1	0	0	2	0	0	0	0	0	.333	.500
Manning, Nate, W.T.	.200	2	5	5	1	1	1	0	0	0	0	0	0	0	0	0	1	0	0	0	.200	.200
Marquis, Jason, Gre.*	.182	11	12	11	0	2	3	1	0	0	0	0	0	0	1	0	4	0	0	0	.273	.250
Martin, Chandler, Car.	.000	4	4	3	0	0	0	0	0	0	0	0	0	0	1	0	1	0	0	0	.000	.250
Martinez, Belvani, Car.	.249	115	428	406	50	101	136	18	4	3	36	6	0	5	11	2	63	25	10	11	.335	.277
Martinez, Gabby, W.T.†	.214	13	47	42	5	9	16	1	0	2	5	2	0	0	3	1	6	5	2	1	.381	.267
Mashore, Justin, Car.	.233	17	49	43	4	10	16	1	1	1	4	0	0	2	4	1	8	2	1	2	.372	.327
Matcuk, Steve, Car.	.000	5	2	2	0	0	0	0	0	0	0	0	0	0	0	0	0	0	0	0	.000	.000
Mathis, Jared, Hun.	.259	101	386	351	49	91	122	23	1	2	21	9	1	13	12	1	49	5	9	6	.348	.308
Matos, Julius, Mob.	.264	135	586	546	61	144	189	30	0	5	35	7	0	2	31	0	57	11	9	13	.346	.306
Matos, Pascual, Gre.	.167	24	91	84	7	14	21	7	0	0	5	0	1	1	5	0	26	1	0	5	.250	.220
McClendon, Matt, Gre.	.133	22	19	15	2	2	2	0	0	0	0	3	0	0	1	0	6	0	0	0	.133	.188
McClure, Brian, Jack.*	.285	81	288	246	33	70	90	17	0	1	18	1	1	0	40	0	46	2	1	4	.366	.383
McKeel, Walt, Car.	.225	72	270	227	29	51	90	15	0	8	26	2	2	8	31	0	45	3	3	7	.396	.336
Meadows, Tydus, W.T.	.261	80	280	249	33	65	102	14	4	5	32	2	5	4	20	0	72	4	2	2	.410	.320
Meggers, Mike, Car.	.178	47	173	157	12	28	56	7	0	7	19	1	1	1	13	1	51	0	0	2	.357	.244
Melian, Jackson, Chat.	.167	2	6	6	0	1	1	0	0	0	0	0	0	0	0	0	0	0	0	0	.167	.167
Meran, Jorge, Jack.	.154	4	14	13	2	2	2	0	0	0	0	0	0	1	0	0	1	0	0	0	.154	.214
Merrell, Phil, Chat.	.333	7	7	6	0	2	2	0	0	0	0	1	0	0	0	0	3	0	0	0	.333	.333
Meyers, Mike, W.T.	.154	9	14	13	0	2	2	0	0	0	1	1	0	0	0	0	5	0	0	0	.154	.154
Middlebrook, Jason, Mob.	.040	24	31	25	2	1	1	0	0	0	0	2	0	0	4	0	8	0	0	1	.040	.172
Miller, Corky, Chat.	.233	103	390	317	40	74	119	18	0	9	44	1	1	30	41	1	51	5	8	12	.375	.373
Miller, David, Gre.*	.239	31	100	92	8	22	33	8	0	1	11	0	0	0	8	0	18	3	0	2	.359	.300
Mitchell, Derek, Jack.	.197	116	392	330	38	65	82	14	0	1	27	7	1	0	54	0	76	3	3	4	.248	.309
Monahan, Shane, Chat.*	.250	25	89	80	10	20	40	8	0	4	16	0	1	1	7	0	18	3	0	1	.500	.315
Moon, Brian, Hun.†	.183	106	374	312	34	57	75	13	1	1	33	3	4	10	45	5	49	2	4	9	.240	.302
Moore, Mike, Hun.-Gre.	.206	55	194	180	17	37	73	5	2	9	22	0	0	3	11	0	87	1	1	3	.406	.263
Moraga, David, Car.*	.000	8	7	7	0	0	0	0	0	0	0	0	0	0	0	0	2	0	0	0	.000	.000
Morris, Bobby, Chat.*	.273	87	283	245	34	67	98	14	1	5	35	1	3	2	32	0	42	6	2	9	.400	.358
Mortimer, Mark, Gre.	.178	41	132	118	14	21	36	3	0	4	12	1	0	1	12	0	15	0	0	2	.305	.260
Munson, Eric, Jack.*	.252	98	428	365	52	92	166	21	4	15	68	0	6	18	39	5	96	5	2	8	.455	.348
Nation, Joey, W.T.*	.075	27	42	40	1	3	3	0	0	0	1	0	0	0	2	0	11	0	0	1	.075	.119
Neuberger, Scott, Orl.	.218	118	469	418	36	91	132	15	1	8	40	8	2	10	31	0	75	4	5	8	.316	.286
Neugebauer, Nickolas, Hun.	.222	10	10	9	0	2	2	0	0	0	0	1	0	0	0	0	2	0	0	0	.222	.222
Nieves, Jose, W.T.	.571	2	7	7	2	4	10	0	0	2	2	0	0	0	0	0	0	0	0	0	1.429	.571
Nieves, Wilbert, Mob.	.266	68	234	214	18	57	73	4	0	4	30	2	1	1	16	4	22	1	1	9	.341	.319
Norris, Dax, Gre.	.252	132	548	484	56	122	188	27	0	13	72	0	5	8	50	5	74	1	1	12	.388	.329
Ochoa, Alex, Chat.	.188	4	19	16	3	3	8	2	0	1	2	0	0	1	2	0	1	1	0	2	.500	.316
Ohman, Will, W.T.*	.333	59	4	3	0	1	1	0	0	0	0	0	0	0	1	0	2	0	0	0	.333	.500
Osting, Jimmy, Gre.	.100	11	11	10	0	1	1	0	0	0	0	0	0	0	1	0	5	0	0	0	.100	.182
Otanez, Willis, Tenn.	.320	27	115	103	13	33	53	5	0	5	19	0	1	1	10	1	16	0	0	2	.515	.383
Pacheco, Delvis, Gre.	.250	11	4	4	1	1	2	1	0	0	0	0	0	0	0	0	0	0	0	0	.500	.250
Patterson, Corey, W.T.*	.261	118	507	444	73	116	218	26	5	22	82	0	7	10	45	5	115	27	14	7	.491	.338
Peeples, Mike, Tenn.	.280	123	541	475	70	133	221	26	4	18	73	9	4	7	46	1	71	11	8	14	.465	.350
Pelaez, Alex, Mob.	.267	28	101	90	8	24	33	3	0	2	11	0	1	0	10	0	15	0	0	5	.367	.337
Pena, Elvis, Car.†	.300	126	561	477	92	143	182	16	7	3	37	4	1	10	69	2	76	48	13	11	.382	.399
Perez, Nestor, Orl.	.204	75	269	240	15	49	53	4	0	0	14	13	0	2	14	0	40	0	3	5	.221	.254
Perez, Robert, Tenn.	.287	136	584	547	66	157	249	33	1	19	92	2	3	6	26	3	82	8	7	12	.455	.325
Pernell, Brandon, W.T.	.199	61	221	196	20	39	63	14	2	2	26	0	4	3	18	2	67	7	1	1	.321	.271
Peterson, Kyle, Hun.	.000	1	2	1	0	0	0	0	0	0	0	1	0	0	0	0	1	0	0	0	.000	.000
Phelps, Josh, Tenn.	.228	56	209	184	23	42	80	9	1	9	28	1	2	7	15	0	66	1	0	6	.435	.308
Pickler, Jeff, Hun.*	.303	71	291	254	34	77	88	11	0	0	26	4	2	1	30	0	28	15	12	7	.346	.376
Pierce, Tony, Gre.	.000	1	1	1	0	0	0	0	0	0	0	0	0	0	0	0	1	0	0	0	.000	.000
Pierre, Juan, Car.*	.326	107	489	439	63	143	167	16	4	0	32	8	4	5	33	0	26	46	12	4	.380	.376
Piersoll, Chris, W.T.	.000	47	2	1	0	0	0	0	0	0	0	0	0	0	1	0	0	0	0	0	.000	.500

Player, Team	Avg.	G	TPA	AB	R	H	TB	2B	3B	HR	RBI	SH	SF	HP	BB	IBB	SO	SB	CS	GDP	Slg.	OBP
Pigott, Anthony, Orl..............	.240	43	134	125	13	30	35	5	0	0	9	3	0	0	6	0	29	2	3	4	.280	.275
Poe, Ryan, Hun...................	.333	9	3	3	0	1	1	0	0	0	2	0	0	0	0	0	1	0	0	0	.333	.333
Pomierski, Joe, Orl.*	.235	131	542	459	60	108	187	25	3	16	65	1	8	4	70	2	137	0	3	6	.407	.336
Porzio, Mike, Car.*	.000	20	16	15	0	0	0	0	0	0	0	0	0	1	0	0	8	0	0	0	.000	.063
Powers, John, Mob.*	.262	93	364	305	61	80	114	23	1	3	22	1	2	6	50	0	56	6	3	2	.374	.375
Price, Ryan, Car.	.077	20	16	13	0	1	1	0	0	0	0	3	0	0	0	0	10	0	0	0	.077	.077
Priest, Eddie, Chat.	.056	28	45	36	3	2	2	0	0	0	2	3	0	0	6	0	21	0	0	0	.056	.190
Prieto, Rick, Birm.†	.255	118	537	432	65	110	134	15	3	1	40	14	3	2	86	1	59	30	5	7	.310	.379
Ramirez, Dan, Car.	.257	110	414	382	40	98	116	8	2	2	39	11	4	3	14	1	89	17	13	4	.304	.285
Randolph, Jaisen, W.T.†	.243	126	554	490	76	119	147	15	5	1	31	3	3	2	56	2	96	46	20	3	.300	.321
Reinoso, Nataniel, Gre.*	.175	24	84	80	6	14	20	3	0	1	7	1	1	0	2	0	16	0	2	3	.250	.193
Reith, Brian, Chat.	.000	5	4	4	0	0	0	0	0	0	0	0	0	0	0	0	1	0	0	0	.000	.000
Rexrode, Jackie, Birm.*	.288	90	412	337	60	97	113	10	3	0	14	3	2	2	68	1	39	19	11	3	.335	.408
Rios, Brian, Jack.	.260	95	359	315	42	82	126	23	3	5	36	3	4	8	29	0	59	1	1	3	.400	.334
Rivera, Mike, Jack.	.193	39	158	150	10	29	45	8	1	2	9	0	1	0	7	0	30	0	0	4	.300	.228
Roberts, Willis, Chat.	.500	5	12	10	3	5	5	0	0	0	0	1	0	0	1	0	4	0	0	0	.500	.545
Rolls, Damian, Orl................	.255	14	60	51	6	13	18	5	0	0	3	0	1	1	7	0	6	1	1	0	.353	.350
Rosario, Mel, Birm.†	.260	83	319	289	34	75	122	23	3	6	42	2	2	5	21	1	63	2	2	3	.422	.319
Rose, Ted, Chat.*	.333	31	6	6	1	2	3	1	0	0	1	0	0	0	0	0	2	0	0	1	.500	.333
Ross, Jason, Gre.	.251	73	276	251	32	63	115	16	0	12	26	0	0	3	22	3	91	13	5	7	.458	.319
Rowand, Aaron, Birm............	.258	139	592	532	80	137	233	26	5	20	98	4	4	14	38	4	117	22	7	12	.438	.321
Runion, Tony, Mob...............	.167	19	7	6	1	1	1	0	0	0	0	1	0	0	0	0	2	0	0	0	.167	.167
Sachs, Brent, W.T...............	.125	11	18	16	2	2	3	1	0	0	1	0	1	0	1	0	3	1	0	0	.188	.167
Saipe, Mike, Car.	.000	4	2	2	0	0	0	0	0	0	0	0	0	0	0	0	0	0	0	0	.000	.000
Salzano, Jerry, Gre.	.157	24	95	83	7	13	23	4	0	2	11	0	1	3	8	0	17	5	0	0	.277	.253
Sanchez, Alex, Orl.*	.291	20	89	86	12	25	29	2	1	0	4	1	0	1	1	0	13	2	6	1	.337	.307
Sanchez, Wellington, Hun.	.258	85	285	244	26	63	79	9	2	1	28	5	0	2	34	0	47	1	6	5	.324	.354
Sandberg, Jared, Orl.	.258	67	282	244	30	63	95	15	1	5	35	0	3	2	33	0	55	5	3	6	.389	.348
Santana, Pedro, Jack.	.281	112	497	448	61	126	172	20	4	6	53	4	4	3	38	1	83	40	8	2	.384	.339
Saunders, Chris, Chat.	.350	61	234	200	30	70	114	15	1	9	37	0	2	3	28	1	53	1	6	2	.570	.433
Schifano, Tony, Tenn.	.233	87	311	275	24	64	78	11	0	1	24	8	2	7	19	2	53	6	4	4	.284	.297
Schmidt, Bryan, Mob.	.207	13	32	29	1	6	7	1	0	0	3	1	0	1	1	0	5	0	1	3	.241	.258
Sears, Todd, Car.*	.301	86	378	299	54	90	147	21	0	12	72	0	5	2	72	11	76	12	3	7	.492	.434
Seifert, Ryan, Car.	.000	32	5	5	0	0	0	0	0	0	0	0	0	0	0	0	3	0	0	0	.000	.000
Sekany, Jason, Chat.	.000	10	9	4	0	0	0	0	0	0	0	1	0	0	4	0	3	0	0	0	.000	.500
Serrano, Wascar, Mob.	.261	20	26	23	1	6	6	0	0	0	2	2	1	0	0	0	5	0	0	1	.261	.250
Sexton, Jeff, Car.	.000	17	8	7	0	0	0	0	0	0	0	0	0	0	0	0	3	0	0	0	.000	.000
Sheets, Ben, Hun.	.143	13	15	14	2	2	2	0	0	0	0	0	0	0	1	0	2	0	0	0	.143	.200
Simmons, Jerry, Gre.	.444	3	10	9	0	4	5	1	0	0	1	0	0	0	1	0	2	1	1	0	.556	.500
Smith, Demond, Gre.†	.274	117	512	431	78	118	204	33	7	13	48	5	3	6	67	0	93	30	14	5	.473	.377
Smith, Jason, W.T.*	.237	119	508	481	55	114	186	22	7	12	61	2	1	2	22	3	130	16	10	7	.387	.273
Smith, Rod, Orl.†	.243	60	244	206	21	50	58	8	0	0	12	4	4	2	28	0	45	12	9	1	.282	.333
Smith, Travis, Hun.	.286	31	46	42	4	12	12	0	0	0	3	3	0	0	1	0	9	0	0	1	.286	.302
Smothers, Stewart, Gre..........	.222	57	192	158	28	35	57	6	2	4	11	2	1	0	31	1	51	7	0	7	.361	.347
Snellgrove, Clay, Mob.	.200	12	39	35	1	7	9	2	0	0	3	0	0	2	2	0	3	0	1	0	.257	.282
Sobkowiak, Scott, Gre.	.000	4	5	2	0	0	0	0	0	0	0	3	0	0	0	0	2	0	0	0	.000	.000
Soliz, Steve, Mob.	.204	44	158	137	14	28	39	5	0	2	10	3	0	0	17	0	30	0	1	4	.285	.292
Sollmann, Scott, Tenn.*	.236	114	455	385	66	91	117	16	5	0	27	6	3	8	53	1	58	19	10	6	.304	.339
Speed, Dorian, Tenn.	.074	8	27	27	2	2	2	0	0	0	0	0	0	0	0	0	11	2	1	0	.074	.074
Stewart, Paul, Hun.	.143	10	8	7	0	1	1	0	0	0	0	0	1	0	0	0	4	0	0	0	.143	.143
Stoops, Jim, Car..................	.000	33	2	2	0	0	0	0	0	0	0	0	0	0	0	0	1	0	0	0	.000	.000
Strange, Doug, Gre.†	.207	18	66	58	4	12	15	3	0	0	5	0	1	2	5	0	12	0	1	0	.259	.284
Tebbs, Nate, Mob.†	.287	37	147	136	16	39	58	6	2	3	10	2	1	1	7	1	29	3	3	1	.426	.324
Terhune, Mike, Gre.†	.226	82	218	186	31	42	57	10	1	1	15	8	5	1	17	0	32	1	4	5	.306	.287
Teut, Nate, W.T.	.043	27	25	23	0	1	1	0	0	0	1	2	0	0	0	0	11	0	0	0	.043	.043
Thrower, Jake, Mob.†	.278	31	134	115	16	32	41	6	0	1	11	2	2	1	14	1	22	3	0	1	.357	.356
Torres, Andres, Jack.†	.148	14	59	54	3	8	8	0	0	0	0	0	0	1	5	0	14	2	0	1	.148	.220
Tucci, Pete, Mob.	.216	133	528	476	63	103	195	35	3	17	73	0	8	5	39	0	147	18	4	4	.410	.278
Ust, Brant, Jack..................	.217	111	433	383	37	83	118	15	4	4	28	7	1	9	33	2	95	2	4	12	.308	.293
Vidal, Gilbert, Gre.	.071	9	16	14	1	1	1	0	0	0	0	0	0	0	2	0	5	0	0	0	.071	.188
Vieira, Scott, W.T.	.220	97	377	322	44	71	112	16	2	7	34	0	3	8	44	1	112	1	3	8	.348	.326
Wade, Terrell, Chat.*	.200	28	6	5	0	1	1	0	0	0	0	1	0	0	0	0	2	0	0	0	.200	.200
Walker, Ron, W.T.	.231	68	198	173	14	40	53	4	0	3	13	0	1	2	22	0	52	0	0	5	.306	.323
Watkins, Pat, Chat.	.292	33	132	120	16	35	42	4	0	1	16	1	2	0	9	0	21	4	2	3	.350	.336
Welsh, Eric, Chat.*	.281	53	191	171	23	48	75	12	0	5	29	1	2	2	15	0	44	5	5	2	.439	.342
Whitehead, Braxton, Chat.	.368	5	21	19	5	7	12	2	0	1	5	0	0	0	2	0	6	0	0	0	.632	.429
Wise, Dewayne, Tenn.*	.250	15	63	56	10	14	29	5	2	2	8	0	0	0	7	0	13	3	2	2	.518	.333
Wright, Ron, Chat.	.266	79	278	237	36	63	117	18	0	12	50	0	2	2	37	0	70	2	2	3	.494	.367
Yankosky, L.J., Gre.	.235	27	23	17	1	4	4	0	0	0	1	1	0	0	5	0	1	0	0	0	.235	.409
Yennaco, Jay, W.T.	.000	60	2	2	0	0	0	0	0	0	0	0	0	0	0	0	0	0	0	0	.000	.000
Yoder, Jeff, W.T.*	.333	8	4	3	0	1	1	0	0	0	0	1	0	0	0	0	1	0	0	1	.333	.333
Young, Mike, Tenn.	.275	91	392	345	51	95	147	24	5	6	47	4	6	1	36	1	72	16	5	5	.426	.340
Zambrano, Carlos, W.T.*	.000	9	14	11	0	0	0	0	0	0	0	2	0	0	1	0	6	0	0	0	.000	.083

GRAND SLAMS: Broussard, Burkhart, Dewey, Goodell, Inge, Keck, Kirby, Leday, Long, B. Martinez, Monahan, Munson, Rowand, Sandberg, J. Smith, 1 each.

AWARDED FIRST BASE ON CATCHER'S INTERFERENCE: Airoso 2 (Loyd, J. Phelps); Amrhein (Rivera); Bravo (Kremblas); Diaz (Kremblas); Hutchins (Hoover); Norris (C. Miller); Patterson (M. Rosario); Saunders (C. Miller); Soliz (Brad King); Terhune (Moon).

PLAYERS WITH TWO OR MORE TEAMS

Player, Team	Avg.	G	TPA	AB	R	H	TB	2B	3B	HR	RBI	SH	SF	HP	BB	IBB	SO	SB	CS	GDP	Slg.	OBP
Averette, Robert, Chat...........	.194	19	36	31	1	6	6	0	0	0	0	4	0	0	1	0	13	2	0	1	.194	.219
Averette, Robert, Car............	.000	5	5	4	0	0	0	0	0	0	0	0	0	0	1	0	1	0	0	0	.000	.200
Johnston, Doug, Hun.............	.000	2	2	2	0	0	0	0	0	0	0	0	0	0	0	0	1	0	0	0	.000	.000

Player, Team	Avg.	G	TPA	AB	R	H	TB	2B	3B	HR	RBI	SH	SF	HP	BB	IBB	SO	SB	CS	GDP	Slg.	OBP
Johnston, Doug, W.T...........	.259	30	28	27	1	7	7	0	0	0	4	0	0	0	1	0	6	0	0	1	.259	.286
Moore, Mike, Hun..............	.184	26	82	76	5	14	24	2	1	2	8	0	0	1	5	0	37	0	1	1	.316	.244
Moore, Mike, Gre.	.221	29	112	104	12	23	49	3	1	7	14	0	0	2	6	0	50	1	0	2	.471	.277

2000 PITCHING

TEAM

Team	W	L	Pct.	ERA	G	CG	ShO	Sv.	IP	H	TBF	R	ER	HR	SH	SF	HB	BB	IBB	SO	WP	Bk.
West Tenn	80	58	.580	3.08	138	7	15	43	1238.0	1013	5232	493	423	84	58	38	54	546	18	1105	56	5
Birmingham	77	63	.550	3.15	140	7	13	36	1235.2	1142	5169	547	433	77	35	32	68	432	22	954	69	4
Orlando	65	71	.478	3.44	136	8	10	37	1182.0	1021	5031	549	452	87	37	37	4	478	11	905	64	7
Chattanooga	70	68	.507	3.70	138	11	7	37	1227.1	1187	5329	617	504	84	66	34	65	553	47	987	80	8
Greenville	68	71	.489	3.76	139	4	11	38	1217.1	1184	5256	581	509	92	48	50	41	518	21	961	62	3
Carolina............	64	75	.460	3.86	139	12	6	32	1199.1	1162	5219	605	515	87	45	37	66	500	11	992	89	1
Mobile	66	73	.475	3.95	139	3	10	35	1238.0	1170	5318	635	544	115	53	30	69	481	12	971	60	7
Tennessee	71	69	.507	3.98	140	7	8	34	1227.2	1169	5376	651	543	100	45	46	94	524	15	961	74	9
Huntsville	64	75	.460	4.04	139	2	13	41	1221.2	1224	5305	647	549	115	42	40	63	487	15	952	76	5
Jacksonville	69	71	.493	4.18	140	6	10	33	1222.0	1195	5253	634	567	112	35	47	59	499	16	931	70	5

INDIVIDUAL

TOP QUALIFIERS FOR EARNED-RUN AVERAGE TITLE

Minimum 112 innings.*Lefthanded pitcher.

Pitcher, Team	W	L	Pct.	ERA	G	GS	CG	ShO	GF	Sv.	IP	H	TBF	R	ER	HR	SH	SF	HB	BB	IBB	SO	WP	Bk.
Davis, Lance, Chat.*	7	5	.583	2.18	25	16	1	1	3	0	115.2	96	484	41	28	4	6	2	2	52	3	98	9	1
Ginter, Matt, Birm.	11	8	.579	2.25	27	26	0	0	0	0	179.2	153	741	72	45	6	5	5	13	60	2	126	12	0
Buehrle, Mark, Birm.*	8	4	.667	2.28	16	16	1	1	0	0	118.2	95	458	37	30	8	1	1	10	17	0	68	1	0
Lawrence, Brian, Mob.	7	6	.538	2.42	21	21	0	0	0	0	126.2	99	496	40	34	6	1	0	10	28	0	119	1	0
Lee, Derek, Hun.*	11	3	.786	2.54	28	20	1	1	2	0	131.1	121	544	48	37	6	2	5	6	41	0	87	6	2
Fogg, Josh, Birm.	11	7	.611	2.57	27	27	2	0	0	0	192.1	190	787	68	55	7	5	4	6	44	2	136	9	1
Averette, Robert, Chat.-Car. ...	13	9	.591	2.58	24	24	5	2	0	0	167.1	151	686	63	48	9	3	1	5	38	3	116	9	1
Priest, Eddie, Chat.*	11	7	.611	2.80	27	27	3	1	0	0	180.0	182	770	78	56	5	10	5	8	59	1	149	11	0
Serrano, Wascar, Mob.	9	4	.692	2.80	20	20	1	0	1	0	112.1	93	471	42	35	11	6	1	4	42	0	112	9	0
Teut, Nate, W.T.*	11	6	.647	3.06	27	21	1	1	2	0	138.1	133	583	53	47	13	4	2	10	44	0	106	4	0
Biddle, Rocky, Birm.	11	6	.647	3.08	23	23	2	2	0	0	146.1	138	619	63	50	10	2	3	8	54	0	118	4	0
Chacon, Shawn, Car.	10	10	.500	3.16	27	27	4	3	0	0	173.2	151	739	71	61	10	4	2	9	85	1	172	16	0
Miller, Matt, Jack.*	9	6	.615	3.18	20	20	1	0	0	0	121.2	126	513	50	43	10	4	3	5	32	1	99	4	0
Lewis, Derrick, Gre.	7	9	.438	3.30	27	27	1	1	0	0	163.2	146	706	70	60	5	4	4	6	83	2	143	10	0
Nation, Joey, W.T.*	11	10	.524	3.31	27	27	1	1	0	0	166.0	137	695	72	61	17	6	6	6	65	2	165	9	0

DEPARTMENTAL LEADERS: W—Averette, 13; L—Maroth, 14; Pct.—Lee, .786; G—Giron, 69; GS—several tied, 27 each; CG—Averette, 5; ShO—Chacon, 3; GF—Keller, 58; Sv.—Keller, 26; IP—Fogg, 192.1; H—Fogg, 190; TBF—Fogg, 787; R—McClellan, 100; ER—McClellan, 90; HR—Phelps, Nation, 17 each; SH—Priest, Johnston, 10 each; SF—Maroth, 9; HB—Coco, 17; BB—Chacon, 85; IBB—MacRae, 9; SO—Chacon, 172; WP—Price, 25; BK—several tied, 3 each.

ALL PITCHERS

*Lefthanded pitcher.

Pitcher, Team	W	L	Pct.	ERA	G	GS	CG	ShO	GF	Sv.	IP	H	TBF	R	ER	HR	SH	SF	HB	BB	IBB	SO	WP	Bk.
Abreu, Winston, Gre.	0	1	.000	2.25	1	1	0	0	0	0	4.0	4	17	1	1	0	0	0	0	3	0	5	0	0
Agosto, Stevenson, Orl.*	2	2	.500	2.47	28	3	0	0	5	1	51.0	37	210	18	14	4	1	1	2	24	1	38	2	0
Almonte, Edwin, Birm.	1	3	.250	4.54	7	6	0	0	0	0	39.2	45	159	22	20	5	0	1	1	9	0	21	2	0
Aragon, Angel, Mob.	3	6	.333	5.17	54	2	0	0	20	5	76.2	84	338	46	44	9	5	1	1	30	3	61	8	0
Averette, Robert, Chat.-Car.	13	9	.591	2.58	24	24	5	2	0	0	167.1	151	686	63	48	9	3	1	5	38	3	116	9	1
Avery, Steve, Gre.*	0	5	.000	8.69	6	6	0	0	0	0	29.0	43	147	32	28	6	1	5	0	22	1	17	2	0
Barnes, Brian, Gre.*	2	2	.500	1.38	24	0	0	0	18	11	39.0	37	165	7	6	1	7	3	1	9	1	45	1	0
Beasley, Ray, Gre.*	3	4	.429	3.05	48	0	0	0	16	3	59.0	54	255	25	20	2	5	1	1	25	3	64	4	0
Beck, Greg, Hun.	3	6	.333	4.95	48	1	0	0	14	2	83.2	97	367	51	46	8	2	4	4	26	5	60	2	0
Becker, Tom, Jack.	0	4	.000	6.63	37	0	0	0	16	0	58.1	65	261	47	43	5	0	2	6	24	2	47	6	0
Bell, Jason, Tenn.	4	3	.571	3.53	12	2	0	0	3	0	35.2	30	151	19	14	2	6	4	2	10	1	32	0	0
Bernero, Adam, Jack.	2	5	.286	2.79	10	10	0	0	0	0	61.1	54	260	26	19	6	2	3	3	24	0	46	5	0
Biddle, Rocky, Birm.	11	6	.647	3.08	23	23	2	2	0	0	146.1	138	619	63	50	10	2	3	8	54	0	118	4	0
Booker, Chris, W.T.	1	0	1.000	3.68	12	0	0	0	3	0	14.2	10	65	8	6	1	0	0	12	0	21	0	0
Bost, Heath, Car.	1	0	1.000	1.00	6	0	0	0	1	0	9.0	6	33	2	1	1	0	0	2	0	10	0	0
Bowers, Cedrick, Orl.*	5	8	.385	2.74	20	19	1	0	0	0	106.2	85	443	45	33	8	4	2	3	44	0	92	3	1
Bowie, Micah, W.T.*	7	6	.538	3.45	18	18	1	1	0	0	117.1	91	481	47	45	6	7	1	3	48	1	106	1	0
Bowles, Brian, Tenn.	4	4	.500	2.98	49	0	0	0	12	6	81.2	64	343	31	27	1	2	3	8	36	1	72	11	0
Brantley, Brian, Car.	0	0	.000	13.50	1	0	0	0	0	0	4.0	7	23	6	6	0	0	0	0	4	0	4	1	0
Brown, Elliot, Orl.	3	4	.429	4.77	45	0	0	0	7	1	71.2	75	321	44	38	5	2	3	8	24	3	39	5	0
Brown, Tighe, Chat.	0	0	.000	0.00	2	0	0	0	1	0	5.2	3	22	0	0	0	0	1	2	0	4	0	0
Buehrle, Mark, Birm.*	8	4	.667	2.28	16	16	1	1	0	0	118.2	95	458	37	30	8	1	1	10	17	0	68	1	0
Burress, Andy, Chat.	1	0	1.000	27.00	1	0	0	0	0	0	1.1	1	11	4	4	0	0	0	1	5	0	2	0	0
Bynum, Mike, Mob.*	3	1	.750	2.91	6	6	0	0	0	0	34.0	31	144	12	11	2	1	2	2	16	0	27	1	1
Camp, Shawn, Mob.	3	3	.500	2.43	45	0	0	0	11	4	59.1	47	252	23	16	4	2	2	1	30	2	53	4	0
Cannon, Jon, W.T.*	1	2	.333	3.06	32	1	0	0	9	1	53.0	35	225	19	18	4	4	2	3	31	1	44	1	0
Carrasco, Troy, Orl.*	0	0	.000	9.35	8	0	0	0	4	0	8.2	15	46	9	9	1	0	0	1	6	0	5	0	0
Cassidy, Scott, Tenn.	2	2	.500	5.91	8	7	0	0	0	0	42.2	48	190	30	28	7	1	4	4	15	0	39	3	0
Chacin, Gustavo, Tenn.*	0	2	.000	12.60	2	2	0	0	0	0	5.0	10	31	7	7	1	0	1	0	6	0	5	0	1
Chacon, Shawn, Car.	10	10	.500	3.16	27	27	4	3	0	0	173.2	151	739	71	61	10	4	2	9	85	1	172	16	0
Christensen, Ben, W.T.	3	1	.750	2.76	7	7	0	0	0	0	42.1	36	177	18	13	2	2	3	1	15	0	42	1	0
Christman, Tim, Car.*	0	0	.000	2.53	8	0	0	0	3	0	10.2	6	48	3	3	0	0	0	2	7	0	13	0	0
Coco, Pasqual, Tenn.	12	7	.632	3.76	27	26	2	0	0	0	167.2	154	723	83	70	16	1	4	17	68	0	142	6	3

CLASS AA Southern League

Pitcher, Team	W	L	Pct.	ERA	G	GS	CG	ShO	GF	Sv.	IP	H	TBF	R	ER	HR	SH	SF	HB	BB	IBB	SO	WP	Bk.
Colome, Jesus, Orl.	1	2	.333	6.75	3	3	0	0	0	0	14.2	18	72	12	11	2	1	0	2	7	0	9	0	0
Condrey, Clay, Mob.	2	2	.500	5.36	35	0	0	0	19	6	43.2	41	195	27	26	4	3	2	5	20	0	25	1	0
Corey, Michael, Gre.	7	6	.538	4.50	52	0	0	0	20	2	66.0	67	294	35	33	6	4	3	2	29	3	66	1	1
Cornejo, Nate, Jack.	5	7	.417	4.61	16	16	0	0	0	0	91.2	91	389	52	47	6	3	3	4	43	1	60	1	1
Crowell, Jim, Chat.*	0	0	.000	5.90	23	0	0	0	5	0	29.0	35	148	23	19	3	1	0	3	22	2	20	0	0
Cumberland, Chris, Gre.*	2	1	.667	4.57	12	2	0	0	3	0	21.2	19	97	12	11	1	1	0	1	10	1	10	0	0
Daniels, David, Mob.	0	1	.000	3.97	9	0	0	0	0	0	11.1	10	50	7	5	0	0	0	0	5	0	11	0	0
Davis, Lance, Chat.*	7	5	.583	2.18	25	16	1	1	3	0	115.2	96	484	41	28	4	6	2	2	52	3	98	9	1
Dean, Aaron, Tenn.	0	1	.000	1.50	1	1	1	0	0	0	6.0	5	28	1	1	1	0	0	1	5	0	4	2	0
De La Cruz, Francisco, Orl.	0	0	.000	7.00	7	0	0	0	3	0	9.0	12	44	9	7	2	0	0	0	3	0	6	1	0
Dent, Doug, Mob.	4	9	.308	5.88	18	16	0	0	0	0	82.2	97	392	65	54	8	3	5	11	44	0	47	10	1
DeWitt, Scott, Car.*	5	2	.714	3.16	34	0	0	0	12	1	51.1	44	224	22	18	5	2	2	7	19	1	36	4	0
Difelice, Mark, Car.	7	5	.583	3.59	23	22	2	0	0	0	133.0	152	556	58	53	15	2	3	0	19	0	98	2	0
Dishman, Glenn, Hun.*	1	2	.333	5.04	42	1	0	0	5	0	64.1	67	295	39	36	12	4	1	6	35	3	59	8	1
Dixon, Tim, Hun.*	2	4	.333	5.62	35	0	0	0	10	0	41.2	41	189	31	26	6	2	5	6	17	1	38	7	0
Donaldson, Bo, Chat.	1	4	.200	3.65	57	0	0	0	46	24	61.2	50	284	31	25	7	4	1	4	48	6	78	6	2
Dorame, Randey, Car.*	0	2	.000	5.06	2	2	0	0	0	0	10.2	7	46	6	6	3	0	0	2	4	0	9	0	0
Doughty, Brian, Mob.	9	10	.474	4.16	31	22	1	1	2	0	134.0	154	577	83	62	13	4	2	6	26	0	67	1	1
Duncan, Courtney, W.T.	5	4	.556	3.07	61	0	0	0	41	25	73.1	57	307	32	25	2	4	3	0	33	2	72	3	0
Durocher, Jayson, Mob.	1	1	.500	2.08	27	0	0	0	23	14	30.1	26	132	7	7	4	2	1	3	12	1	43	3	0
Eaton, Adam, Mob.	4	1	.800	2.68	10	10	1	1	0	0	57.0	47	238	20	17	3	1	3	1	18	0	58	4	1
Eiland, Dave, Orl.	1	0	1.000	1.59	2	2	0	0	0	0	11.1	7	42	3	2	0	2	0	1	1	0	8	0	0
Emiliano, Jamie, Car.	3	4	.429	2.64	47	0	0	0	11	2	58.0	52	250	27	17	1	4	1	4	23	3	37	3	0
Enders, Trevor, Orl.*	6	3	.667	3.22	29	5	0	0	8	0	67.0	63	264	26	24	7	0	1	1	11	0	41	3	3
Espina, Rendy, Tenn.*	6	1	.857	2.11	53	0	0	0	19	3	59.2	49	264	22	14	1	2	2	5	35	1	41	2	1
Estrella, Leo, Tenn.	5	5	.500	3.67	13	13	3	2	0	0	76.0	68	324	36	31	6	4	3	10	30	1	63	2	0
Fernandez, Ozzie, Chat.	0	0	.000	12.71	1	1	0	0	0	0	5.2	11	30	9	8	2	2	0	0	3	1	1	0	0
Figueroa, Juan, Birm.	2	3	.400	3.40	10	9	0	0	0	0	55.2	57	241	25	21	4	1	3	6	24	0	42	3	1
File, Bob, Tenn.	4	3	.571	3.12	36	0	0	0	32	20	34.2	29	153	20	12	1	2	1	2	13	0	40	0	1
Fisher, Louis, W.T.	1	0	1.000	6.75	4	0	0	0	1	0	6.2	7	31	6	5	2	0	1	0	5	0	5	0	0
Flach, Jason, Gre.	4	6	.400	4.33	28	13	0	0	3	0	95.2	95	399	47	46	12	6	3	3	30	2	64	4	0
Fleck, Will, Gre.	0	0	.000	27.00	2	0	0	0	1	0	2.0	6	15	6	6	1	0	0	3	1	0	2	0	0
Flener, Huck, Mob.*	0	0	.000	3.21	15	0	0	0	1	0	14.0	12	59	5	5	2	0	0	0	4	0	10	1	0
Fogg, Josh, Birm.	11	7	.611	2.57	27	27	2	0	0	0	192.1	190	787	68	55	7	5	4	6	44	2	136	9	1
Frachiseur, Zach, Gre.	2	7	.222	4.78	42	5	0	0	14	2	86.2	92	379	54	46	8	0	8	4	29	1	58	4	0
Freeman, Kai, Birm.	3	2	.600	3.93	30	2	0	0	8	0	52.2	57	238	32	23	5	3	4	1	22	1	31	4	0
Garcia, Jose, Hun.	4	8	.333	3.76	19	18	0	0	0	0	103.0	107	463	52	43	8	3	4	5	54	0	78	6	0
Gardner, Lee, Orl.	3	2	.600	3.40	36	0	0	0	24	12	45.0	34	186	19	17	0	4	3	2	14	1	48	6	0
Garland, Jon, Birm.	0	0	.000	0.00	1	1	0	0	0	0	6.0	4	22	0	0	0	1	0	0	1	0	10	0	0
Gil, David, Chat.	2	0	1.000	2.16	6	3	0	0	1	1	25.0	15	105	7	6	1	0	0	8	13	0	25	3	0
Giles, Tim, Tenn.	0	0	.000	27.00	1	0	0	0	1	0	1.0	3	8	4	3	0	0	0	2	0	0	0	0	0
Ginter, Matt, Birm.	11	8	.579	2.25	27	26	0	0	0	0	179.2	153	741	72	45	6	5	1	3	60	2	126	12	0
Giron, Isabel, Mob.	5	5	.500	5.58	69	0	0	0	21	5	79.0	71	339	52	49	9	5	1	7	32	2	77	4	1
Gissell, Chris, W.T.	7	5	.583	3.10	16	16	0	0	0	0	93.0	80	395	39	32	6	3	2	6	41	1	65	2	0
Glauber, Keith, Chat.	4	0	1.000	3.51	32	0	0	0	9	2	41.0	42	176	19	16	2	5	2	4	12	3	27	2	1
Gooch, Arnie, Chat.	9	7	.563	4.11	21	21	1	0	0	0	135.2	133	583	78	62	13	4	1	8	55	4	80	16	0
Granger, Jeff, Gre.*	3	2	.600	3.50	16	2	1	0	6	1	36.0	38	150	17	14	0	2	1	0	12	2	12	0	0
Greene, Ryan, Gre.	1	0	1.000	2.78	24	0	0	0	9	0	32.1	29	140	10	10	3	1	2	0	18	0	25	3	0
Guerrier, Matt, Birm.	3	1	.750	2.70	23	0	0	0	19	7	23.1	17	95	9	7	1	0	0	1	12	1	19	3	0
Gulin, Lindsay, W.T.*	5	2	.714	4.99	9	9	1	1	0	0	52.1	49	237	33	29	4	1	3	4	30	0	54	4	2
Guttormson, Rick, Mob.	4	4	.500	3.98	17	15	0	0	0	0	81.1	88	361	44	36	9	4	2	5	35	0	36	1	2
Guzman, Domingo, Mob.	0	0	.000	2.08	14	1	0	0	4	0	17.1	13	76	8	4	2	1	1	2	11	0	14	4	0
Guzman, Juan, Orl.	0	1	.000	8.44	1	1	0	0	0	0	5.1	6	26	6	5	1	0	1	0	3	0	5	0	0
Haines, Talley, Hun.	3	3	.500	1.49	33	0	0	0	21	3	54.1	36	222	18	9	2	6	2	1	21	5	47	3	0
Harikkala, Tim, Hun.	5	3	.625	2.98	22	4	0	0	5	0	48.1	54	205	20	16	1	3	1	8	0	0	34	0	0
Haring, Brett, Chat.*	6	7	.462	5.15	23	17	0	0	1	0	106.2	133	491	73	61	5	7	5	7	53	2	69	4	0
Harper, Travis, Orl.	3	1	.750	2.63	9	9	0	0	0	0	51.1	49	215	19	15	1	2	3	7	11	0	33	2	1
Hart, Len, Mob.*	1	1	.500	3.92	32	0	0	0	14	1	39.0	37	168	17	17	2	1	0	1	20	1	29	3	0
Hawkins, Al, Hun.	7	7	.500	3.71	18	18	0	0	0	0	97.0	88	414	49	40	12	7	2	3	43	0	66	7	0
Heams, Shane, Jack.	6	2	.750	2.59	39	0	0	0	19	5	55.2	35	238	17	16	4	3	1	2	34	2	67	2	0
Hendrickson, Mark, Tenn.*	3	1	.750	3.63	6	6	0	0	0	0	39.2	32	161	17	16	5	1	0	0	12	0	29	4	0
Hite, Kevin, Mob.	0	1	.000	3.86	27	0	0	0	7	1	37.1	38	162	19	16	6	2	2	1	14	2	33	0	0
House, Craig, Car.	0	2	.000	3.80	18	0	0	0	14	9	21.1	14	96	11	9	1	0	1	5	15	0	28	6	0
Huggins, David, Tenn.	1	1	.500	8.38	6	0	0	0	2	1	9.2	10	47	10	9	0	1	0	4	5	0	10	1	0
Huntsman, Scott, Hun.	4	4	.500	4.65	59	1	0	0	26	6	71.2	81	315	45	37	6	1	3	6	19	2	43	4	0
Iapoce, Anthony, Hun.*	0	0	.000	0.00	1	0	0	0	1	0	0.2	1	3	0	0	0	0	0	0	1	0	1	0	0
Iglesias, Mike, Hun.	0	2	.000	6.75	13	1	0	0	7	0	32.0	37	141	24	24	5	1	2	0	8	1	21	0	0
Izquierdo, Hansel, Birm.	1	2	.333	7.50	8	1	0	0	5	0	12.0	12	53	11	10	2	1	1	0	5	1	5	1	0
Jacobs, Ryan, Hun.*	1	2	.333	4.34	18	0	0	0	5	0	29.0	32	134	18	14	5	1	1	0	16	0	23	2	0
James, Delvin, Orl.	1	3	.250	2.92	6	6	1	0	0	0	37.0	31	153	15	12	3	0	3	0	7	0	26	1	0
Jennings, Jason, Car.	1	3	.250	3.44	6	6	0	0	0	0	36.2	32	149	19	14	4	1	0	0	11	0	33	1	0
Jimenez, Jason, Orl.*	5	1	.833	1.94	30	1	0	0	8	6	46.1	29	185	13	10	4	2	1	2	12	0	53	3	0
Johnson, James, Hun.*	4	3	.571	4.63	16	10	0	0	1	0	68.0	74	299	42	35	9	2	1	0	22	0	74	11	0
Johnston, Doug, Hun.-W.T.	4	5	.444	4.39	32	18	0	0	3	1	123.0	116	534	63	60	8	10	3	6	57	3	87	10	0
Kalinowski, Josh, Car.*	1	3	.250	6.23	6	6	0	0	0	0	26.0	30	119	22	18	0	1	1	1	12	0	27	2	1
Keller, Kris, Jack.	2	3	.400	2.91	62	0	0	0	58	26	68.0	58	299	24	22	0	1	5	0	44	3	60	9	0
King, Brad, Chat.	0	0	.000	0.00	1	0	0	0	1	0	0.2	0	3	0	0	0	0	0	0	1	0	0	0	0
Kingrey, Jarrod, Tenn.	2	0	1.000	2.12	16	0	0	0	15	7	17.0	11	76	6	4	2	1	1	0	15	2	16	1	0
Kirsten, Rick, Jack.	1	1	.500	5.79	4	1	0	0	2	0	9.1	9	37	6	6	4	0	1	1	3	0	5	0	0
Krawczyk, Jack, Hun.	0	0	.000	4.50	1	0	0	0	1	0	4.0	4	16	2	2	1	0	0	0	1	0	2	0	0
Kusiewicz, Mike, Tenn.*	7	9	.438	3.63	27	26	1	0	1	0	156.0	149	684	83	63	14	8	4	9	59	1	115	10	0
Lakman, Jason, Birm.	2	2	.500	4.14	27	2	0	0	12	1	45.2	49	210	25	21	2	0	2	3	30	0	44	7	0
LaPlante, Mick, Gre.	1	0	1.000	1.29	1	1	0	0	0	0	7.0	4	28	1	1	0	0	1	0	2	0	6	0	1

Pitcher, Team	W	L	Pct.	ERA	G	GS	CG	ShO	GF	Sv.	IP	H	TBF	R	ER	HR	SH	SF	HB	BB	IBB	SO	WP	Bk.
Lawrence, Brian, Mob.	7	6	.538	2.42	21	21	0	0	0	0	126.2	99	496	40	34	6	1	0	10	28	0	119	1	0
Lawrence, Clint, Tenn.*	3	3	.500	5.30	34	1	0	0	18	0	54.1	63	268	33	32	7	3	2	1	43	2	31	6	0
Lee, Derek, Hun.*	11	3	.786	2.54	28	20	1	1	2	0	131.1	121	544	48	37	6	2	5	6	41	0	87	6	2
Leek, Randy, Jack.*	2	2	.500	7.84	7	6	0	0	0	0	31.0	43	146	29	27	6	1	1	2	8	0	21	0	0
LeRoy, John, Chat.	1	0	1.000	5.73	6	0	0	0	2	0	11.0	9	48	7	7	3	0	1	0	6	0	9	1	0
Lewis, Derrick, Gre.	7	9	.438	3.30	27	27	1	1	0	0	163.2	146	706	70	60	5	4	4	6	83	2	143	10	0
Lira, Jim, Orl.	0	0	.000	12.00	2	0	0	0	0	0	3.0	4	17	4	4	1	0	0	0	3	0	4	0	0
Loux, Shane, Jack.	12	9	.571	3.82	26	26	2	0	0	0	157.2	150	670	78	67	12	3	7	14	55	0	130	7	0
Lowe, Benny, Jack.*	0	0	.000	8.10	17	0	0	0	4	0	23.1	28	117	21	21	3	2	0	1	17	1	25	5	0
Lukasiewicz, Mark, Tenn.*	0	0	.000	5.79	3	0	0	0	1	0	4.2	4	22	3	3	1	0	0	0	4	0	6	0	0
MacRae, Scott, Chat.	4	1	.800	3.59	55	0	0	0	17	1	77.2	75	339	32	31	4	8	1	5	40	9	61	4	0
Mairena, Ozwaldo, W.T.*	0	1	.000	0.00	2	0	0	0	1	0	2.0	3	10	1	0	0	1	0	1	1	1	0	0	0
Manias, Jim, Chat.*	1	4	.200	4.14	15	5	1	0	3	0	45.2	41	200	23	21	6	2	1	0	23	6	45	3	0
Maroth, Mike, Jack.*	9	14	.391	3.94	27	26	2	1	0	0	164.1	176	689	79	72	14	9	9	3	58	0	85	6	1
Marquis, Jason, Gre.	4	2	.667	3.57	11	11	0	0	0	0	68.0	68	287	35	27	10	1	2	1	23	0	49	2	1
Martin, Chandler, Car.	0	3	.000	3.91	4	4	1	0	0	0	23.0	27	105	10	10	1	1	1	1	11	0	10	1	0
Matcuk, Steve, Car.	1	0	1.000	7.00	5	1	0	0	1	0	18.0	25	90	14	14	1	0	4	4	10	0	6	2	0
Mathis, Jared, Hun.	0	0	.000	0.00	1	1	0	0	0	0	0.1	1	2	0	0	0	0	0	0	0	0	1	0	0
Maurer, Dave, Mob.*	1	2	.333	2.70	24	0	0	0	8	0	26.2	15	98	8	8	2	3	0	1	3	1	28	1	0
McBride, Chris, Tenn.	2	2	.500	2.39	22	4	0	0	9	1	60.1	51	240	18	16	5	2	2	4	9	0	37	5	0
McClellan, Matt, Tenn.	6	12	.333	4.80	28	27	0	0	0	0	168.2	174	743	100	90	16	2	4	11	69	1	140	11	3
McClendon, Matt, Gre.	7	6	.538	3.78	22	21	1	1	1	0	131.0	124	561	59	55	6	4	8	5	54	0	90	12	0
McClure, Brian, Jack.	0	0	.000	0.00	1	0	0	0	1	0	0.2	1	3	0	0	0	0	0	0	0	0	0	0	0
McGlinchy, Kevin, Gre.	0	0	.000	0.00	4	0	0	0	0	0	4.0	2	15	1	0	0	0	1	0	0	0	7	1	0
Merrell, Phil, Chat.	1	4	.200	6.40	7	7	0	0	0	0	32.1	34	150	26	23	3	3	2	3	24	0	25	3	0
Meyers, Mike, W.T.	5	2	.714	2.44	9	9	3	1	0	0	59.0	41	242	18	16	4	5	2	4	26	0	51	2	0
Middlebrook, Jason, Mob.	5	13	.278	6.15	24	24	0	0	0	0	120.0	133	533	89	82	15	5	4	4	52	0	75	3	0
Milburn, Adam, Gre.*	1	1	.500	6.55	12	0	0	0	1	0	11.0	13	49	8	8	2	1	1	1	5	1	5	0	0
Miller, Matt, Jack.*	8	5	.615	3.18	20	20	1	0	0	0	121.2	126	513	50	43	10	4	3	5	32	1	99	4	0
Mobley, Kevin, Jack.	6	0	1.000	2.70	43	5	1	1	8	0	90.0	62	368	31	27	5	0	4	3	42	2	72	7	0
Moraga, David, Car.*	3	3	.500	1.06	8	8	3	0	0	0	59.1	52	243	18	7	3	3	1	3	11	0	53	2	0
Myette, Aaron, Birm.	2	0	1.000	3.52	3	3	0	0	0	0	15.1	11	68	7	6	1	0	0	2	8	0	21	1	0
Nation, Joey, W.T.*	11	10	.524	3.31	27	27	1	1	0	0	166.0	137	695	72	61	17	6	6	6	65	2	165	9	0
Neugebauer, Nickolas, Hun.	1	3	.250	3.73	10	10	0	0	0	0	50.2	35	229	28	21	2	0	0	3	47	0	57	1	0
Ohman, Will, W.T.*	6	4	.600	1.89	59	0	0	0	23	3	71.1	53	312	20	15	3	3	5	3	36	5	85	8	0
Osting, Jimmy, Gre.*	2	6	.250	2.65	11	11	0	0	0	0	71.1	67	302	30	21	6	2	1	0	29	1	52	1	0
Pacheco, Delvis, Gre.	6	2	.750	3.07	11	10	0	0	0	0	58.2	55	245	22	20	9	0	0	1	23	0	51	2	0
Pearsall, J.J., Chat.*	4	1	.800	6.87	22	0	0	0	10	1	18.1	18	88	16	14	5	1	1	1	15	2	23	1	1
Pena, Jesus, Birm.*	1	2	.333	3.38	23	0	0	0	20	10	21.1	19	89	9	8	2	1	0	2	6	2	25	0	1
Penney, Mike, Hun.	0	1	.000	2.66	20	0	0	0	11	7	20.1	19	83	7	6	0	0	0	1	6	0	22	4	0
Peterson, Kyle, Hun.	0	1	.000	7.71	1	1	0	0	0	0	4.2	6	25	7	4	1	1	0	0	4	0	1	1	0
Pettyjohn, Adam, Jack.*	2	2	.500	3.40	8	8	0	0	0	0	50.1	43	203	20	19	4	1	0	4	12	0	45	2	0
Phelps, Tommy, Jack.*	6	6	.500	4.94	38	11	0	0	7	0	102.0	111	435	59	56	17	1	0	7	26	2	62	1	0
Phelps, Travis, Orl.	7	8	.467	3.00	21	21	2	0	0	0	108.0	85	448	44	36	5	1	1	13	46	0	106	5	0
Pierce, Tony, Gre.	0	0	.000	0.00	1	0	0	0	0	0	2.0	0	8	0	0	0	0	0	0	1	0	2	0	0
Piersoll, Chris, W.T.	3	3	.500	2.08	47	0	0	0	16	2	60.2	51	258	17	14	4	4	1	2	28	1	54	5	3
Plunk, Eric, W.T.	2	0	1.000	2.00	7	0	0	0	2	1	9.0	5	41	3	2	1	0	0	1	6	0	9	0	0
Poe, Ryan, Hun.	1	3	.250	3.38	9	0	0	0	8	3	21.1	18	94	8	8	1	2	1	2	9	2	20	1	0
Porzio, Mike, Car.*	7	4	.636	3.41	20	18	1	1	2	0	121.1	111	502	53	46	11	5	4	5	31	0	90	5	0
Price, Ryan, Car.	6	7	.462	6.17	20	18	0	0	1	0	86.0	86	415	69	59	5	3	3	8	76	2	67	25	0
Priest, Eddie, Chat.*	11	7	.611	2.80	27	27	3	1	0	0	180.0	182	770	78	56	5	10	5	8	59	1	149	11	0
Pujals, Denis, Orl.	1	2	.333	2.37	6	2	0	0	0	0	19.0	14	75	6	5	1	0	1	2	4	0	7	1	0
Purvis, Rob, Birm.	0	1	.000	4.50	1	1	0	0	0	0	4.0	6	24	8	2	1	0	1	0	3	0	3	0	0
Ramirez, Jose, Jack.*	2	2	.500	5.76	19	0	0	0	3	0	25.0	33	117	18	16	4	1	4	1	10	0	11	7	1
Rauch, Jon, Birm.	5	1	.833	2.25	8	8	2	2	0	0	56.0	36	220	18	14	4	1	0	2	16	0	63	2	0
Reith, Brian, Chat.	1	3	.250	3.90	5	5	0	0	0	0	30.0	31	128	14	13	3	2	2	1	11	0	29	2	0
Reyes, Eddy, Orl.	2	5	.286	3.94	50	0	0	0	35	14	59.1	52	280	32	26	5	1	1	11	48	0	44	3	0
Roberts, Mark, Birm.	6	3	.667	3.75	17	8	0	0	7	3	60.0	65	256	27	25	4	1	1	1	17	1	46	1	0
Roberts, Willis, Chat.	4	0	1.000	3.06	5	5	0	0	0	0	32.1	33	137	12	11	0	3	1	2	13	1	28	0	0
Root, Derek, Mob.*	4	0	1.000	3.63	15	2	0	0	3	2	22.1	15	96	9	9	1	0	0	0	18	0	13	0	0
Rosario, Juan, Orl.	1	3	.250	3.83	28	0	0	0	12	6	44.2	43	202	26	19	4	3	1	10	18	0	21	4	1
Rose, Ted, Chat.	4	2	.667	1.10	31	0	0	0	17	8	41.0	24	154	8	5	1	1	3	0	9	2	51	1	2
Rossiter, Mike, Hun.	0	5	.000	6.15	48	0	0	0	38	22	45.1	47	217	32	31	7	2	2	9	31	1	41	2	0
Runion, Tony, Mob.	1	1	.500	1.61	19	0	0	0	1	0	28.0	15	120	8	5	1	4	0	5	18	0	27	1	0
Runyan, Sean, Jack.*	0	0	.000	21.60	3	0	0	0	1	0	1.2	4	11	4	4	0	0	0	0	2	0	1	0	0
Saipe, Mike, Car.	1	3	.250	5.47	4	4	1	0	0	0	26.1	29	118	17	16	2	3	0	1	12	1	13	1	0
Schmidt, Bryan, Mob.	0	1	.000	27.00	1	0	0	0	1	0	1.0	3	7	3	3	1	0	0	0	2	0	0	0	0
Seanez, Rudy, Gre.	0	0	.000	0.00	2	1	0	0	0	0	2.0	2	8	0	0	0	0	0	0	0	0	3	0	0
Seay, Bobby, Orl.*	8	7	.533	3.88	24	24	0	0	0	0	132.1	132	568	64	57	13	4	5	8	53	1	106	4	0
Seberino, Ronni, Orl.*	0	0	.000	2.08	4	0	0	0	1	0	8.2	6	36	2	2	0	2	2	0	6	0	6	3	0
Seifert, Ryan, Car.	3	6	.333	4.05	32	9	0	0	8	0	97.2	97	422	49	44	6	1	6	4	37	1	95	3	0
Sekany, Jason, Chat.	1	6	.143	7.06	10	9	0	0	1	0	43.1	49	200	36	34	8	3	1	1	28	1	28	5	0
Serrano, Wascar, Mob.	9	4	.692	2.80	20	20	1	0	0	0	112.1	93	471	42	35	11	6	1	4	42	0	112	9	0
Sexton, Jeff, Car.	5	4	.556	5.08	17	9	0	0	5	1	67.1	78	306	41	38	3	4	1	2	31	0	58	4	0
Sheets, Ben, Hun.	5	3	.625	1.88	13	13	0	0	0	0	72.0	55	288	17	15	4	1	4	2	25	0	60	2	0
Shumate, Jacob, Gre.	2	1	.667	4.14	47	0	0	0	39	18	45.2	32	208	23	21	3	1	0	2	41	0	41	10	0
Smith, Dan, Gre.*	0	0	.000	5.40	2	0	0	0	1	0	1.2	2	10	1	1	0	1	0	0	3	0	1	0	0
Smith, Travis, Hun.	12	7	.632	3.73	27	24	1	1	1	0	154.1	141	631	77	64	13	4	2	5	37	0	113	3	1
Sneed, John, Tenn.	5	9	.357	4.54	21	21	0	0	0	0	121.0	124	548	81	61	9	4	7	10	56	0	100	5	0
Snyder, Bill, Jack.	1	2	.333	3.60	29	0	0	0	13	2	40.0	33	177	16	16	4	2	2	2	23	2	38	1	1
Snyder, John, Hun.	1	1	.500	2.19	2	2	0	0	0	0	12.1	6	46	3	3	1	1	0	1	5	0	6	0	0
Sobkowiak, Scott, Gre.	2	1	.667	4.63	4	4	0	0	0	0	23.1	26	107	16	12	2	0	2	2	15	0	27	0	0
Sparks, Jeff, Orl.	0	2	.000	6.75	3	3	0	0	0	0	10.2	9	55	13	8	2	1	0	0	11	0	8	4	0

Pitcher, Team	W	L	Pct.	ERA	G	GS	CG	ShO	GF	Sv.	IP	H	TBF	R	ER	HR	SH	SF	HB	BB	IBB	SO	WP	Bk.
Spille, Ryan, Tenn.*	1	1	.500	4.18	4	4	0	0	0	0	23.2	23	99	11	11	1	2	2	0	10	0	8	0	0
Standridge, Jason, Orl.	6	8	.429	3.62	17	17	2	0	0	0	97.0	85	416	46	39	4	2	1	1	43	0	55	4	0
Stewart, Paul, Hun.	1	7	.125	6.13	10	10	0	0	0	0	47.0	75	224	36	32	5	2	0	2	22	0	30	5	1
Stoops, Jim, Car.	5	3	.625	2.75	33	0	0	0	15	2	52.1	37	222	20	16	3	4	4	5	33	2	47	4	0
Tabaka, Jeff, Car.*	0	0	.000	1.93	9	0	0	0	4	0	9.1	7	36	2	2	0	1	0	0	1	0	7	1	0
Taglienti, Jeff, Car.	1	1	.500	1.46	10	0	0	0	9	0	12.1	9	51	4	2	1	1	0	0	3	0	7	0	0
Teut, Nate, W.T.*	11	6	.647	3.06	27	21	1	1	2	0	138.1	133	583	53	47	13	4	2	10	44	0	106	4	0
Thompson, Travis, Car.	3	7	.300	6.33	50	0	0	0	41	17	58.1	70	278	44	41	8	3	2	7	30	0	43	4	0
Thompson, Travis, Chat.	1	1	.500	4.63	2	2	0	0	0	0	11.2	12	51	6	6	0	0	0	1	8	0	6	0	0
Tokarse, Brian, Birm.	6	3	.667	5.62	34	0	0	0	15	1	41.2	40	188	26	26	5	5	1	3	28	3	52	7	1
Tolar, Kevin, Jack.*	2	0	1.000	0.52	9	0	0	0	2	0	17.1	7	66	3	1	0	0	0	0	8	0	19	1	0
Vavrek, Mike, Car.*	0	0	.000	16.88	2	0	0	0	2	0	2.2	8	17	5	5	1	0	1	0	3	0	0	0	0
Villegas, Ismael, Gre.	2	1	.667	4.50	8	0	0	0	3	1	16.0	20	75	12	8	2	2	1	0	7	1	16	1	0
Vining, Ken, Birm.*	1	5	.167	4.08	43	0	0	0	13	1	46.1	36	188	26	21	2	1	1	3	18	4	41	4	0
Wade, Terrell, Chat.*	0	5	.000	4.08	28	1	0	0	10	0	39.2	34	172	23	18	3	2	1	4	23	1	42	2	0
Walker, Kevin, Mob.*	0	1	.000	2.25	4	0	0	0	1	0	4.0	1	14	1	1	1	0	0	0	1	0	6	0	0
Walls, Doug, Jack.	3	7	.300	7.69	11	11	0	0	0	0	52.2	66	254	54	45	8	2	2	1	34	0	38	6	1
Weimer, Matt, Tenn.	4	3	.571	4.60	49	0	0	0	20	2	62.2	68	273	36	32	6	2	3	4	22	5	31	5	0
Weymouth, Marty, Birm.	0	5	.000	3.65	37	0	0	0	23	13	44.1	47	194	26	18	3	6	3	3	15	3	33	2	0
White, Matt, Orl.	7	6	.538	3.75	20	20	2	0	0	0	120.0	94	505	56	50	10	2	5	15	58	0	98	7	1
Whitley, Curtis, Birm.*	1	1	.500	5.74	29	1	0	0	11	0	31.1	37	144	21	20	2	1	1	2	19	2	19	3	0
Wright, Danny, Birm.	2	4	.333	2.49	7	7	0	0	0	0	43.1	28	175	15	12	3	0	0	1	24	0	31	3	0
Wright, Jamey, Hun.	2	0	1.000	0.00	2	2	0	0	0	0	12.1	7	46	0	0	0	0	0	1	5	0	10	1	0
Yankosky, L.J., Gre.	10	8	.556	3.45	26	24	1	1	0	0	140.2	139	589	57	54	7	5	3	11	42	1	100	4	0
Yennaco, Jay, W.T.	5	4	.556	2.67	60	0	0	0	30	10	70.2	53	292	25	21	5	2	4	1	31	1	79	3	0
Yoder, Jeff, W.T.	0	3	.000	4.31	8	5	0	0	1	0	31.1	27	141	16	15	2	2	1	1	22	0	22	2	0
Zambrano, Carlos, W.T.	3	1	.750	1.34	9	9	0	0	0	0	60.1	39	241	14	9	2	1	0	3	21	0	43	4	0

COMBINATION SHUTOUTS: **Birmingham (8)**—Fogg-Izquierdo, Biddle-Freeman, Ginter-Weymouth-Tokarse, Fugueroa-Vining-Guerrier, Rauch-Guerrier-Pena, Almonte-Guerrier, Wright-Weymouth-Pena, Fogg-Pena. **Carolina (2)**—Sexton-DeWitt-Thompson, Price-Stoops-Seifert. **Chattanooga (3)**—Davis-Glauber-MacRae-Donaldson, Priest-Glauber, Gooch-MacRae-Wade-Donaldson. **Greenville (8)**—Seanez-Yankosky-Beasley, Lewis-Shumate, Yankosky-Greene-Flach-Beasley-Shumate, Marquis-Franchiseur-Shumate, Lewis-Greene-Beasley, McClendon-Beasley-Villegas, Yankosky-Cumberland-Barnes, Lewis-Barnes. **Huntsville (11)**—Stewart-Huntsman-Dixon, Sheets-Dishman-Iglesias, Lee-Huntsman-Rossiter, Wright-Huntsman-Rossiter, Wright-Lee-Harikkala, Sheets-Rossiter, Smith-Harikkala-Huntsman, Hawkins-Beck, Smith-Rossiter-Jacobs-Huntsman, Garcia-Jacobs-Beck-Huntsman, Neugebauer-Poe. **Jacksonville (8)**—Loux-Heams, Loux-Heams-Keller, Miller-Mobley-Keller, Pettyjohn-Mobley, Maroth-Snyder, Cornejo-Snyder, Leek-Snyder-Keller, Leek-Snyder-Keller. **Mobile (8)**—Root-Daniels-Camp-Giron, Serrano-Hite-Aragon-Giron, Serrano-Camp-Giron, Doughty-Camp-Maurer-Durocher, Lawrence-Camp-Hart, Doughty-Hart-Condrey, Bynum-Giron-Hart-Condrey, Serrano-Runion-Camp. **Orlando (10)**—Phelps-Rosario-Enders-Gardner, Harper-Jimenez-Reyes, White-Enders-Reyes, Bowers-Haines-Agosto, Standridge-Agosto-Brown, White-Reyes, Bowers-Haines, Seay-Reyes-Agosto, Seay-Haines, Standridge-Jimenez. **Tennessee (6)**—Estrella-Lawrence-Bowles-Espina-File, Kusiewicz-Bowles-Files, McClellan-Lawrence-Weimer, Coco-File, Sneed-Weimer, Hendrickson-Espina. **West Tenn (10)**—Zambrano-Ohman-Piersoll, Teut-Ohman, Zambrano-Ohman, Christensen-Plunk-Cannon, Gissell-Piersoll, Bowie-Yennaco-Ohman-Piersoll-Johnston-Duncan, Nation-Piersoll-Ohman-Duncan, Bowie-Yennaco, Teut-Ohman-Duncan, Bowie-Duncan.

NO-HIT GAMES: Estrella, Tennessee defeated Orlando, 3-0, May 27; Mobley, Jacksonville defeated Tennessee, 1-0, August 3.

PITCHERS WITH TWO OR MORE TEAMS

Pitcher, Team	W	L	Pct.	ERA	G	GS	CG	ShO	GF	Sv.	IP	H	TBF	R	ER	HR	SH	SF	HB	BB	IBB	SO	WP	Bk.
Averette, Robert, Chat.	12	6	.667	2.44	19	19	5	2	0	0	136.1	126	555	51	37	6	2	1	4	28	3	87	7	1
Averette, Robert, Car.	1	3	.250	3.19	5	5	0	0	0	0	31.0	25	131	12	11	3	1	0	1	10	0	29	2	0
Johnston, Doug, Hun.	0	1	.000	14.21	2	2	0	0	0	0	6.1	10	35	11	10	2	1	1	0	6	0	5	3	0
Johnston, Doug, W.T.	4	4	.500	3.86	30	16	0	0	3	1	116.2	106	499	52	50	6	9	2	6	51	3	82	7	0

2000 FIELDING

TEAM

Team	Pct.	G	PO	A	E	TC	DP	TP	PB
Mobile	.975	139	3714	1413	132	5259	93	0	16
Greenville	.974	139	3652	1442	134	5228	113	0	9
Jacksonville	.974	140	3666	1530	138	5334	127	0	18
Orlando	.974	138	3546	1375	133	5054	114	0	18
Birmingham	.973	140	3707	1463	145	5315	122	0	17
West Tenn	.971	138	3714	1287	148	5149	95	0	17
Huntsville	.970	139	3665	1507	160	5332	126	0	20
Chattanooga	.969	138	3682	1635	170	5487	138	0	23
Carolina	.968	139	3598	1308	161	5067	103	0	23
Tennessee	.965	140	3683	1462	188	5333	120	1	15

INDIVIDUAL

FIRST BASEMEN

NOTE: All caps denotes fielding-percentage leader based on 70 games for catchers, 93 for all other non-pitchers and 112 innings for pitchers. *Throws lefthanded.

Player, Team	Pct.	G	PO	A	E	TC	DP
Amrhein, Mike, W.T.	.996	35	253	25	1	279	16
Balfe, Ryan, Mob.	1.000	7	66	2	0	68	7
Battersby, Eric, Birm.*	.992	124	1066	76	9	1151	94
Becker, Brian, Orl.	.987	129	1063	87	15	1165	100
Bravo, Danny, Birm.	1.000	2	13	2	0	15	1
Broussard, Benjamin, Chat.*	.971	15	126	10	4	140	16
Brown, Jason, Orl.	1.000	1	10	0	0	10	1
Burkhart, Lance, Hun.	.994	21	160	11	1	172	14

Player, Team	Pct.	G	PO	A	E	TC	DP
Cancel, Robinson, Hun.	.500	1	2	0	2	4	0
Chiaffredo, Paul, Tenn.	1.000	2	11	0	0	11	1
Choi, Hee, W.T.*	.997	35	285	14	1	300	23
DeCinces, Tim, Mob.	1.000	4	46	2	0	48	3
Eberwein, Kevin, Mob.	.992	97	769	50	7	826	50
Freire, Alejandro, Jack.	.989	61	486	42	6	534	47
Garcia, Neil, Orl.	1.000	2	8	1	0	9	1
Gibbons, Jay, Tenn.*	.991	101	818	36	8	862	78
Giles, Tim, Tenn.	.981	43	322	35	7	364	26
GLAVINE, Mike, Gre.*	.995	108	849	71	5	925	73
Goodell, Steve, Car.	.987	20	142	8	2	152	14
Heintz, Chris, Birm.	.967	10	75	14	3	92	9
Hinske, Eric, W.T.	1.000	6	17	5	0	22	1
Hoover, Paul, Orl.	1.000	7	45	5	0	50	4
Jacobsen, Bucky, Hun.	.989	77	659	34	8	701	62
Johnson, Adam, Birm.*	1.000	9	68	2	0	70	9
Keck, Brian, Orl.	1.000	16	125	7	0	132	10
Kent, Robbie, Mob.	.989	9	88	6	1	95	8
Kominek, Toby, Hun.	.985	47	375	28	6	409	34
Kremblas, Chris, Tenn.	1.000	1	1	0	0	1	0
Langaigne, Selwyn, Tenn.*	.933	4	13	1	1	15	2
Larkin, Stephen, Chat.*	1.000	1	6	0	0	6	0
Lindstrom, David, Jack.	1.000	1	4	1	0	5	1
Loyd, Brian, Tenn.	1.000	1	1	0	0	1	0
Lutz, Manuel, Jack.	1.000	1	5	0	0	5	0
Mackiewitz, Richard, Car.*	.968	9	54	7	2	63	5
Magdaleno, Ricky, Mob.	.984	21	173	16	3	192	14
Manning, Nate, W.T.	.917	1	11	0	1	12	1
Mathis, Jared, Hun.	1.000	1	2	0	0	2	0
McClure, Brian, Jack.	.974	6	32	5	1	38	7

CLASS AA Southern League

Player, Team	Pct.	G	PO	A	E	TC	DP
McKeel, Walt, Car.	1.000	4	35	1	0	36	2
Meggers, Mike, Car.	1.000	14	110	7	0	117	8
Miller, David, Gre.*	1.000	5	15	3	0	18	0
Moon, Brian, Hun.	1.000	1	6	0	0	6	1
Mortimer, Mark, Gre.	1.000	6	11	1	0	12	1
Munson, Eric, Jack.	.989	74	640	51	8	699	61
Nieves, Wilbert, Mob.	1.000	4	34	2	0	36	2
Norris, Dax, Gre.	.996	30	210	15	1	226	19
Otanez, Willis, Tenn.	1.000	6	40	5	0	45	1
Pelaez, Alex, Mob.	1.000	2	6	0	0	6	0
Pomierski, Joe, Orl.	1.000	1	0	1	0	1	0
Rios, Brian, Jack.	1.000	10	34	2	0	36	2
Rosario, Mel, Birm.	1.000	1	7	0	0	7	1
Saunders, Chris, Chat.	1.000	33	319	16	0	335	28
Schifano, Tony, Tenn.	1.000	1	2	0	0	2	0
Schmidt, Bryan, Mob.	1.000	1	5	0	0	5	1
Sears, Todd, Car.	.982	80	634	30	12	676	54
Strange, Doug, Gre.	1.000	5	39	4	0	43	2
Terhune, Mike, Gre.	.933	9	12	2	1	15	1
Tucci, Pete, Mob.	1.000	1	2	0	0	2	1
Vieira, Scott, W.T.	.984	47	344	27	6	377	29
Walker, Ron, W.T.	.993	20	137	13	1	151	11
Welsh, Eric, Chat.*	.990	39	354	24	4	382	29
Wright, Ron, Chat.	.989	56	483	34	6	523	52

TRIPLE PLAY: Gibbons.

SECOND BASEMEN

Player, Team	Pct.	G	PO	A	E	TC	DP
Abreu, Dennis, W.T.	.969	41	66	91	5	162	15
Alguacil, Jose, Birm.	1.000	4	6	8	0	14	3
Badeaux, Brooks, Orl.	.982	67	166	164	6	336	43
Bravo, Danny, Birm.	.963	46	90	118	8	216	23
Caceres, Wilmy, Chat.	.961	56	119	180	12	311	44
Carr, Dustin, Orl.	.875	2	1	6	1	8	2
Cepeda, Jose, Gre.	1.000	4	6	15	0	21	2
Colina, Javier, Car.	.857	4	2	4	1	7	0
Collier, Lou, Hun.	.875	1	4	3	1	8	1
Connacher, Kevin, Birm.	1.000	4	10	7	0	17	2
Da Luz, Craig, Jack.	1.000	2	6	10	0	16	4
Dawkins, Travis, Chat.	.980	39	88	113	4	205	30
Ernster, Mark, Hun.	1.000	1	0	1	0	1	0
Florez, Tim, Chat.	.980	15	21	28	1	50	5
Font, Franklin, W.T.	.972	74	162	154	9	325	34
Freel, Ryan, Tenn.	1.000	2	3	7	0	10	1
GILES, Marcus, Gre.	.973	125	304	333	18	655	70
Goodell, Steve, Car.	.986	18	36	37	1	74	11
Guiliano, Matt, Hun.	.000	2	0	0	0	0	0
Harrison, Adonis, Orl.	.917	5	13	9	2	24	3
Hoover, Paul, Orl.	.909	2	4	6	1	11	1
Keck, Brian, Car.	1.000	12	13	19	0	32	5
King, Brett, W.T.	.969	24	46	49	3	98	7
Kremblas, Mike, Tenn.	1.000	1	3	3	0	6	0
Lackey, Steve, Gre.	1.000	5	9	10	0	19	3
Lindstrom, David, Jack.	1.000	2	5	4	0	9	2
Lopez, Mickey, Hun.	.975	53	100	137	6	243	35
Magdaleno, Ricky, Mob.	.938	12	32	28	4	64	5
Martinez, Belvani, Car.	.960	106	198	258	19	475	53
Martinez, Gabby, W.T.	.942	11	20	29	3	52	4
Mathis, Jared, Hun.	.963	23	45	58	4	107	11
Matos, Julius, Mob.	.913	5	8	13	2	23	2
McClure, Brian, Jack.	.950	10	21	17	2	40	5
Morris, Bobby, Chat.	.924	40	72	87	13	172	13
Nieves, Wilbert, Mob.	1.000	2	0	3	0	3	0
Peeples, Mike, Tenn.	.973	31	83	59	4	146	19
Pelaez, Alex, Mob.	.941	3	7	9	1	17	2
Pena, Elvis, Car.	1.000	11	21	20	0	41	2
Pickler, Jeff, Hun.	.961	67	134	188	13	335	42
Powers, John, Mob.	.961	57	120	151	11	282	27
Rexrode, Jackie, Birm.	.950	90	147	267	22	436	50
Rios, Brian, Jack.	.968	21	38	52	3	93	12
Sachs, Brent, W.T.	1.000	3	1	4	0	5	0
Santana, Pedro, Jack.	.965	112	230	292	19	541	64
Schifano, Tony, Tenn.	.978	21	38	50	2	90	13
Schmidt, Bryan, Mob.	.875	4	3	4	1	8	1
Smith, Rod, Orl.	.968	60	125	147	9	281	32
Snellgrove, Clay, Mob.	.930	9	20	20	3	43	2
Tebbs, Nate, Mob.	.991	28	53	61	1	115	10
Terhune, Mike, Gre.	1.000	16	21	30	0	51	1
Thrower, Jake, Mob.	.977	24	54	74	3	131	16
Young, Mike, Tenn.	.967	90	185	248	15	448	56

TRIPLE PLAY: Young.

THIRD BASEMEN

Player, Team	Pct.	G	PO	A	E	TC	DP
Abreu, Dennis, W.T.	1.000	1	0	1	0	1	0
Badeaux, Brooks, Orl.	1.000	5	3	11	0	14	0
Balfe, Ryan, Mob.	.000	2	0	0	0	0	0
Beinbrink, Andy, Orl.	1.000	3	1	8	0	9	1
Bravo, Danny, Birm.	.900	6	6	3	1	10	2
BURROUGHS, Sean, Mob.	.947	108	98	188	16	302	11
Colina, Javier, Car.	.908	121	77	210	29	316	24
Collier, Lou, Hun.	.933	34	18	66	6	90	1
Crede, Joe, Birm.	.942	135	91	218	19	328	20
Cromer, Brandon, Hun.	.960	18	10	38	2	50	3
Eberwein, Kevin, Mob.	1.000	2	1	0	0	1	0
Ernster, Mark, Hun.	.500	1	0	1	1	2	0
Florez, Tim, Chat.	.913	6	6	15	2	23	4
Font, Franklin, W.T.	.778	14	8	13	6	27	2
Fraraccio, Dan, Orl.	.955	7	5	16	1	22	2
Garcia, Neil, Orl.	1.000	1	1	2	0	3	1
Goodell, Steve, Car.	.789	8	6	9	4	19	1
Harrison, Adonis, Orl.	.853	11	12	17	5	34	1
Henson, Drew, Chat.	.933	16	13	29	3	45	3
Hessman, Mike, Gre.	.926	123	67	219	23	309	17
Hinske, Eric, W.T.	.906	115	80	189	28	297	15
Hoover, Paul, Orl.	.926	41	33	79	9	121	8
Hudson, Orlando, Tenn.	.921	39	32	96	11	139	11
Keck, Brian, Car.	.975	16	11	28	1	40	4
King, Brett, W.T.	1.000	7	4	2	0	6	0
Kirby, Scott, Hun.	.869	21	13	40	8	61	2
Klimek, Josh, Hun.	.922	48	31	75	9	115	8
Kremblas, Mike, Tenn.	.800	2	3	5	2	10	0
Larson, Brandon, Chat.	.917	108	54	212	24	290	12
Lindstrom, David, Jack.	1.000	5	0	2	0	2	0
Lopez, Mickey, Hun.	.000	1	0	0	0	0	0
Magdaleno, Ricky, Mob.	.667	1	1	3	2	6	0
Mashore, Justin, Car.	.875	6	1	6	1	8	1
Mathis, Jared, Hun.	.975	29	20	59	2	81	8
McClure, Brian, Jack.	1.000	2	0	1	0	1	0
Morris, Bobby, Chat.	.800	5	2	6	2	10	0
Nieves, Jose, W.T.	1.000	1	2	0	0	2	0
Otanez, Willis, Tenn.	.963	22	24	53	3	80	5
Peeples, Mike, Tenn.	.828	41	22	60	17	99	1
Pelaez, Alex, Mob.	.959	21	17	53	3	73	2
Rios, Brian, Jack.	.952	30	22	58	4	84	4
Rolls, Damian, Orl.	.906	8	7	22	3	32	0
Sachs, Brent, W.T.	.500	4	0	1	1	2	0
Sanchez, Wellington, Hun.	1.000	2	0	1	0	1	0
Sandberg, Jared, Orl.	.946	60	45	131	10	186	9
Saunders, Chris, Chat.	.900	7	2	7	1	10	0
Schifano, Tony, Tenn.	.993	41	37	102	1	140	14
Schmidt, Bryan, Mob.	.889	3	2	6	1	9	0
Snellgrove, Clay, Mob.	.667	1	1	1	1	3	0
Strange, Doug, Gre.	1.000	1	0	1	0	1	0
Tebbs, Nate, Mob.	.909	6	5	5	1	11	1
Terhune, Mike, Gre.	.971	22	8	26	1	35	2
Ust, Brant, Jack.	.941	111	73	232	19	324	16
Walker, Ron, W.T.	.917	14	1	21	2	24	0
Watkins, Pat, Chat.	1.000	1	0	1	0	1	0

TRIPLE PLAY: Schifano.

SHORTSTOPS

Player, Team	Pct.	G	PO	A	E	TC	DP
Abreu, Dennis, W.T.	1.000	5	9	14	0	23	5
Alguacil, Jose, Birm.	1.000	2	2	5	0	7	0
Backe, Brandon, Orl.	.000	1	0	0	0	0	0
Bravo, Danny, Birm.	.970	19	37	59	3	99	13
Caceres, Wilmy, Chat.	.965	79	137	274	15	426	50
Calais, Ian, Gre.	1.000	11	12	27	0	39	3
Collier, Lou, Hun.	.000	1	0	0	0	0	0
Cromer, Brandon, Hun.	1.000	3	3	3	0	6	1
Da Luz, Craig, Jack.	.000	1	0	0	0	0	0
Dawkins, Travis, Chat.	.948	56	97	177	15	289	42
Dellaero, Jason, Birm.	.956	122	201	347	25	573	64
De Los Santos, Eddy, Orl.	.942	48	70	142	13	225	24
Ernster, Mark, Hun.	.947	51	65	132	11	208	27
Florez, Tim, Chat.	1.000	9	8	22	0	30	8
Font, Franklin, W.T.	1.000	1	2	3	0	5	1
Fraraccio, Dan, Orl.	.667	1	1	1	1	3	1
Furcal, Rafael, Gre.	.889	3	0	8	1	9	1
Goodell, Steve, Car.	1.000	5	10	7	0	17	1
Guiliano, Matt, Hun.	.897	15	17	44	7	68	5
Harrison, Adonis, Orl.	1.000	5	12	16	0	28	4
Hoover, Paul, Orl.	.932	9	15	26	3	44	7

Player, Team	Pct.	G	PO	A	E	TC	DP
Keck, Brian, Car.	1.000	19	20	36	0	56	1
King, Brett, W.T.	.958	16	27	41	3	71	3
Lackey, Steve, Gre.	.940	125	165	348	33	546	63
Lopez, Felipe, Tenn.	.923	127	177	351	44	572	64
Magdaleno, Ricky, Mob.	.920	8	11	12	2	25	3
Martinez, Belvani, Car.	.882	7	7	8	2	17	1
Martinez, Gabby, W.T.	1.000	2	0	4	0	4	0
Mathis, Jared, Hun.	.979	14	19	28	1	48	5
Matos, Julius, Mob.	.955	128	202	372	27	601	62
McClure, Brian, Jack.	1.000	1	1	0	0	1	0
MITCHELL, Derek, Jack.	.964	115	176	335	19	530	70
Morris, Bobby, Chat.	1.000	1	2	4	0	6	1
Nieves, Jose, W.T.	1.000	1	2	1	0	3	0
Pena, Elvis, Car.	.936	115	184	301	33	518	55
Perez, Nestor, Orl.	.975	75	75	197	7	279	37
Rios, Brian, Jack.	.944	36	56	97	9	162	25
Sachs, Brent, W.T.	1.000	1	1	4	0	5	1
Sanchez, Wellington, Hun.	.937	68	91	205	20	316	44
Schifano, Tony, Tenn.	.925	18	23	51	6	80	11
Smith, Jason, W.T.	.927	117	190	281	37	508	51
Tebbs, Nate, Mob.	1.000	3	2	2	0	4	0
Terhune, Mike, Gre.	1.000	11	17	26	0	43	8
Thrower, Jake, Mob.	1.000	5	7	13	0	20	1
Ust, Brant, Jack.	1.000	5	1	2	0	3	0
Young, Mike, Tenn.	.800	2	2	2	1	5	2

OUTFIELDERS

Player, Team	Pct.	G	PO	A	E	TC	DP
Airoso, Kurt, Jack.	.974	87	148	2	4	154	0
Backe, Brandon, Orl.	1.000	3	6	1	0	7	0
Bair, Rod, Car.	.976	25	38	2	1	41	0
Balfe, Ryan, Mob.	.973	108	166	12	5	183	1
Bass, Jayson, W.T.*	.981	27	48	3	1	52	0
Bass, Jayson, Gre.	.900	21	33	3	4	40	0
Battersby, Eric, Birm.*	1.000	4	5	2	0	7	0
Besco, Derek, Jack.	1.000	27	37	1	0	38	0
Borchard, Joe, Birm.	.875	6	6	1	1	8	0
Bowers, Brent, Chat.	1.000	5	11	0	0	11	0
Bravo, Danny, Birm.	.971	22	32	1	1	34	0
Briggs, Stoney, Jack.	.972	132	231	11	7	249	2
Broussard, Benjamin, Chat.*	.939	70	88	5	6	99	0
Brumfield, Jacob, Birm.	1.000	18	41	1	0	42	1
Burkhart, Lance, Hun.	.000	1	0	0	0	0	0
Burress, Andy, Chat.	.972	119	159	17	5	181	3
Butler, Garrett, Orl.	.986	36	67	1	1	69	1
Calais, Ian, Gre.	1.000	2	3	0	0	3	0
Cepeda, Jose, Gre.	1.000	7	11	0	0	11	0
Cline, Pat, Hun.	.000	1	0	0	0	0	0
Collier, Lou, Hun.	.929	9	13	0	1	14	0
Cripps, Bobby, Chat.	1.000	6	7	0	0	7	0
Da Luz, Craig, Jack.	1.000	1	3	0	0	3	0
Darula, Bobby, Hun.	.958	29	46	0	2	48	0
Diaz, Alejandro, Chat.	.983	122	273	17	5	295	2
Durocher, Jayson, Mob.	.000	1	0	0	0	0	0
Faggett, Ethan, Mob.*	.983	93	173	1	3	177	0
Fleming, Ryan, Tenn.*	.986	36	71	2	1	74	0
Font, Franklin, W.T.	1.000	5	8	0	0	8	0
Frank, Mike, Chat.*	1.000	7	9	0	0	9	0
Freel, Ryan, Tenn.	1.000	11	22	0	0	22	0
Freire, Alejandro, Jack.	1.000	7	6	0	0	6	0
Garcia, Jose, Hun.	.000	1	0	0	0	0	0
Gazarek, Marty, Gre.	.983	56	109	6	2	117	3
Gerut, Jody, Car.*	.977	90	158	10	4	172	0
Gibbons, Jay, Tenn.*	1.000	12	13	1	0	14	1
Gibbs, Kevin, Car.	1.000	1	1	0	0	1	0
Glavine, Mike, Gre.*	1.000	15	14	0	0	14	0
Green, Chad, Hun.	.982	83	204	9	4	217	6
Guttormson, Rick, Mob.	1.000	1	1	0	0	1	0
Hinske, Eric, W.T.*	1.000	6	15	0	0	15	0
Hoover, Paul, Orl.	.957	27	40	5	2	47	1
Hutchins, Norm, Car.*	.960	72	138	7	6	151	1
Iapoce, Anthony, Hun.*	1.000	64	142	2	0	144	0
Inge, Brandon, Jack.	1.000	1	1	0	0	1	0
Inglin, Jeff, Birm.	.964	16	25	2	1	28	0
Johnson, Adam, Birm.*	.952	35	59	1	3	63	0
Keck, Brian, Car.	.000	1	0	0	0	0	0
Kelly, Kenny, Orl.	.974	124	286	9	8	303	4
Kirby, Scott, Hun.	.961	82	141	7	6	154	1
Klimek, Josh, Hun.	.980	49	94	2	2	98	0
Kominek, Toby, Hun.	.968	75	118	4	4	126	0
Krause, Scott, Hun.	1.000	3	6	0	0	6	0
Kremblas, Mike, Tenn.	.714	3	5	0	2	7	0

Player, Team	Pct.	G	PO	A	E	TC	DP
Langaigne, Selwyn, Tenn.*	.985	69	129	4	2	135	1
Larkin, Stephen, Chat.*	.934	36	56	1	4	61	0
LEDAY, A.J., Mob.	.994	109	168	9	1	178	1
Lindsey, Rodney, Jack.	.973	114	273	12	8	293	1
Lindstrom, David, Jack.	1.000	12	10	1	0	11	0
Long, Ryan, Birm.	.977	70	122	5	3	130	2
Lopez, Rafael, W.T.	.000	1	0	0	0	0	0
Magdaleno, Ricky, Mob.	1.000	4	3	1	0	4	0
Mashore, Justin, Car.	.957	9	20	2	1	23	1
Mathis, Jared, Hun.	1.000	35	73	3	0	76	2
McClure, Brian, Jack.	.986	50	67	4	1	72	0
Meadows, Tydus, W.T.	.961	68	117	5	5	127	2
Meggers, Mike, Car.	.958	23	21	2	1	24	0
Melian, Jackson, Chat.	.667	2	2	0	1	3	0
Miller, David, Gre.*	1.000	20	35	3	0	38	0
Monahan, Shane, Chat.	1.000	21	27	1	0	28	0
Moore, Mike, Hun.-Gre.	.944	42	66	2	4	72	0
Mortimer, Mark, Gre.	.000	1	0	0	0	0	0
Neuberger, Scott, Orl.	.988	117	239	16	3	258	3
Ochoa, Alex, Chat.	1.000	4	7	0	0	7	0
Patterson, Corey, W.T.	.990	118	296	7	3	306	2
Peeples, Mike, Tenn.	.986	52	68	5	1	74	1
Perez, Robert, Tenn.	.983	134	222	13	4	239	2
Pernell, Brandon, W.T.	.972	57	100	5	3	108	1
Pierre, Juan, Car.*	.992	103	261	2	2	265	0
Pigott, Anthony, Orl.	.970	41	60	4	2	66	1
Pomierski, Joe, Orl.	1.000	55	79	0	0	79	0
Priest, Eddie, Chat.*	.000	1	0	0	0	0	0
Prieto, Rick, Birm.	.980	118	238	7	5	250	0
Ramirez, Dan, Car.	.973	102	200	19	6	225	3
Randolph, Jaisen, W.T.	.971	123	222	11	7	240	2
Reinoso, Nataniel, Gre.*	.971	23	32	2	1	35	0
Ross, Jason, Gre.	.952	69	156	4	8	168	0
Rowand, Aaron, Birm.	.975	138	299	18	8	325	4
Sachs, Brent, W.T.	.000	1	0	0	0	0	0
Salzano, Jerry, Gre.	.957	24	44	1	2	47	0
Sanchez, Alex, Orl.*	.972	20	34	1	1	36	0
Schifano, Tony, Tenn.	1.000	10	16	2	0	18	0
Schmidt, Bryan, Mob.	.000	1	0	0	1	1	0
Simmons, Jerry, Gre.	1.000	1	2	0	0	2	0
Smith, Demond, Gre.	.975	115	194	5	5	204	1
Smothers, Stewart, Gre.	.971	56	128	4	4	136	1
Sollmann, Scott, Tenn.*	.967	108	200	4	7	211	1
Speed, Dorian, Tenn.	1.000	7	7	0	0	7	0
Strange, Doug, Gre.	.000	1	0	0	0	0	0
Terhune, Mike, Gre.	.971	26	32	2	1	35	0
Torres, Andres, Jack.	.971	14	32	1	1	34	0
Tucci, Pete, Mob.	.987	128	288	5	4	297	0
Vieira, Scott, W.T.	.979	30	44	2	1	47	0
Watkins, Pat, Chat.	.981	32	50	1	1	52	0
Welsh, Eric, Chat.*	1.000	7	8	1	0	9	0
Wise, Dewayne, Tenn.*	.882	15	29	1	4	34	0

OUTFIELDERS WITH TWO OR MORE TEAMS

Player, Team	Pct.	G	PO	A	E	TC	DP
Moore, Mike, Hun.	.958	16	23	0	1	24	0
Moore, Mike, Gre.	.938	26	43	2	3	48	0

CATCHERS

Player, Team	Pct.	G	PO	A	E	TC	DP	PB
Amrhein, Mike, W.T.	.990	58	461	30	5	496	4	7
Andreopoulos, Alex, Hun.	1.000	3	10	5	0	15	0	0
Brown, Jason, Orl.	.989	40	245	14	3	262	4	4
Burkhart, Lance, Hun.	.979	24	168	15	4	187	1	5
Burress, Andy, Chat.	.000	1	0	0	0	0	0	0
Cancel, Robinson, Hun.	1.000	8	33	5	0	38	1	2
Ceriani, Matt, Hun.	1.000	4	20	4	0	24	0	0
Chiaffredo, Paul, Tenn.	.991	15	96	13	1	110	0	1
Cleveland, Russell, Jack.	1.000	1	1	0	0	1	0	1
Cline, Pat, Hun.	.961	7	46	3	2	51	0	2
Cripps, Bobby, Chat.	1.000	1	7	0	0	7	0	1
DeCinces, Tim, Mob.	.986	47	311	32	5	348	0	4
Dewey, Jason, Car.	.984	83	622	38	11	671	3	18
Foster, Jim, Birm.	.978	9	82	5	2	89	0	2
Garcia, Jesse, Orl.	.968	23	135	17	5	157	1	3
Hall, Toby, Orl.	.984	55	395	33	7	435	2	8
Heintz, Chris, Birm.	.987	56	361	28	5	394	0	6
Hoover, Paul, Orl.	.984	23	165	20	3	188	0	3
Huff, Jake, Mob.	.900	2	9	0	1	10	0	1
INGE, Brandon, Jack.	.990	71	437	73	5	515	6	10
Jones, Jay, Car.	1.000	1	2	0	0	2	0	0
King, Brad, Chat.	.977	39	231	24	6	261	2	9

Player, Team	Pct.	G	PO	A	E	TC	DP	PB
Kremblas, Mike, Tenn.	.987	20	134	18	2	154	2	3
Lawrence, Joe, Tenn.	.978	29	207	19	5	231	3	4
Lindstrom, David, Jack.	.986	36	263	26	4	293	2	2
Lopez, Rafael, W.T.	.987	63	486	52	7	545	4	5
Loyd, Brian, Tenn.	.981	38	284	23	6	313	0	1
Lunar, Fernando, Gre.	.989	30	228	37	3	268	2	0
Magdaleno, Ricky, Mob.	1.000	1	8	1	0	9	0	1
Mahoney, Mike, W.T.	.995	23	177	30	1	208	0	5
Mathis, Jared, Hun.	1.000	5	21	1	0	22	0	0
Matos, Pascual, Gre.	.988	23	152	19	2	173	4	2
McKeel, Walt, Car.	.987	57	391	56	6	453	5	4
Meran, Jorge, Jack.	1.000	4	24	3	0	27	0	2
Miller, Corky, Chat.	.981	103	732	103	16	851	8	11
Moon, Brian, Hun.	.990	100	665	120	8	793	10	11
Mortimer, Mark, Gre.	.990	28	193	15	2	210	1	3
Nieves, Wilbert, Mob.	.991	55	380	44	4	428	1	4
Norris, Dax, Gre.	.996	64	416	51	2	469	5	4
Phelps, Josh, Tenn.	.983	39	274	15	5	294	1	6
Rivera, Mike, Jack.	.969	31	231	17	8	256	1	3
Rosario, Mel, Birm.	.986	78	540	81	9	630	10	9
Soliz, Steve, Mob.	.994	43	297	38	2	337	4	7
Vidal, Gilbert, Car.	.500	1	1	0	1	2	0	0
Whitehead, Braxton, Chat.	1.000	5	37	4	0	41	0	2

PITCHERS

Player, Team	Pct.	G	PO	A	E	TC	DP
Abreu, Winston, Gre.	1.000	1	1	0	0	1	0
Agosto, Stevenson, Orl.*	1.000	28	4	9	0	13	2
Almonte, Edwin, Birm.	1.000	7	4	5	0	9	0
Aragon, Angel, Mob.	1.000	54	2	16	0	18	0
Averette, Robert, Chat.-Car.	.959	24	12	35	2	49	2
Avery, Steve, Gre.*	.875	6	4	3	1	8	2
Barnes, Brian, Gre.*	.867	24	4	9	2	15	0
Beasley, Ray, Gre.*	.909	48	2	8	1	11	0
Beck, Greg, Hun.	.867	48	4	9	2	15	1
Becker, Tom, Jack.	.909	37	5	5	1	11	0
Bell, Jason, Tenn.	1.000	12	1	5	0	6	0
Bernero, Adam, Jack.	1.000	10	2	9	0	11	0
Biddle, Rocky, Birm.	.923	23	9	15	2	26	3
Booker, Chris, W.T.	1.000	12	1	2	0	3	0
Bost, Heath, Car.	1.000	6	3	2	0	5	1
Bowers, Cedrick, Orl.*	1.000	20	4	13	0	17	0
Bowie, Micah, W.T.*	1.000	18	7	13	0	20	0
Bowles, Brian, Tenn.	.895	49	3	14	2	19	0
Brantley, Brian, Car.	.000	1	0	0	0	0	0
Brown, Elliot, Orl.	1.000	45	7	10	0	17	0
Brown, Tighe, Chat.	.000	2	0	0	0	0	0
Buehrle, Mark, Birm.*	.956	16	5	38	2	45	3
Burress, Andy, Chat.	.000	1	0	0	0	0	0
Bynum, Mike, Mob.*	.900	6	1	8	1	10	0
Camp, Shawn, Mob.	1.000	45	5	12	0	17	1
Cannon, Jon, W.T.*	.889	32	7	9	2	18	2
Carrasco, Troy, Orl.*	.000	8	0	0	0	0	0
Cassidy, Scott, Tenn.	.909	8	2	8	1	11	1
Chacin, Gustavo, Tenn.*	.000	2	0	0	0	0	0
Chacon, Shawn, Car.	.889	27	9	23	4	36	2
Christensen, Ben, W.T.	1.000	7	2	4	0	6	0
Christman, Tim, Car.*	1.000	8	3	0	0	3	0
Coco, Pasqual, Tenn.	.840	27	7	14	4	25	0
Colome, Jesus, Orl.	1.000	3	2	4	0	6	0
Condrey, Clay, Mob.	.909	35	5	5	1	11	1
Corey, Michael, Gre.	1.000	52	8	7	0	15	0
CORNEJO, Nate, Jack.	1.000	16	9	20	0	29	4
Crowell, Jim, Chat.*	.833	23	2	3	1	6	1
Cumberland, Chris, Gre.*	1.000	12	1	1	0	2	0
Daniels, David, Mob.	1.000	9	1	1	0	2	0
Davis, Lance, Chat.*	.848	25	6	22	5	33	0
Dean, Aaron, Tenn.	1.000	1	0	1	0	1	0
De La Cruz, Francisco, Orl.	.000	7	0	0	0	0	0
Dent, Doug, Mob.	.889	18	5	19	3	27	2
DeWitt, Scott, Car.*	.923	34	3	9	1	13	0
Difelice, Mark, Car.	.933	23	13	15	2	30	0
Dishman, Glenn, Hun.*	1.000	42	3	3	0	6	0
Dixon, Tim, Hun.*	.571	35	1	3	3	7	0
Donaldson, Bo, Chat.	1.000	57	1	5	0	6	1
Dorame, Randey, Car.*	.000	2	0	0	0	0	0
Doughty, Brian, Mob.	.905	31	6	13	2	21	1
Duncan, Courtney, W.T.	.909	61	6	14	2	22	0
Durocher, Jayson, Mob.	.000	27	1	6	0	7	0
Eaton, Adam, Mob.	1.000	10	3	7	0	10	1
Eiland, Dave, Orl.	1.000	2	1	1	0	2	0
Emiliano, Jamie, Car.	.944	47	2	15	1	18	1
Enders, Trevor, Orl.*	1.000	29	2	12	0	14	0
Espina, Rendy, Tenn.*	1.000	53	3	13	0	16	1
Estrella, Leo, Tenn.	.950	13	8	11	1	20	1
Fernandez, Ozzie, Chat.	1.000	1	0	6	0	6	0
Figueroa, Juan, Birm.	.625	10	1	4	3	8	0
File, Bob, Tenn.	.929	36	6	7	1	14	1
Fisher, Louis, W.T.	1.000	4	0	2	0	2	0
Flach, Jason, Gre.	1.000	28	9	17	0	26	2
Fleck, Will, Gre.	.000	2	0	0	0	0	0
Flener, Huck, Mob.*	1.000	15	0	1	0	1	0
Fogg, Josh, Birm.	.980	27	14	36	1	51	3
Frachiseur, Zach, Gre.	1.000	42	3	2	0	5	1
Freeman, Kai, Birm.	1.000	30	2	7	0	9	0
Garcia, Jose, Hun.	.842	19	4	12	3	19	0
Gardner, Lee, Orl.	.947	36	7	11	1	19	1
Garland, Jon, Birm.	1.000	1	1	0	0	1	0
Gil, David, Chat.	1.000	6	2	1	0	3	1
Giles, Tim, Tenn.	1.000	1	0	1	0	1	0
Ginter, Matt, Birm.	.907	27	19	30	5	54	2
Giron, Isabel, Mob.	.909	69	4	6	1	11	1
Gissell, Chris, W.T.	1.000	16	7	9	0	16	1
Glauber, Keith, Chat.	1.000	32	3	9	0	12	1
Gooch, Arnie, Chat.	.950	21	13	25	2	40	3
Granger, Jeff, Gre.*	1.000	16	2	5	0	7	1
Greene, Ryan, Gre.	1.000	24	1	5	0	6	1
Guerrier, Matt, Birm.	1.000	23	2	5	0	7	0
Gulin, Lindsay, W.T.*	1.000	9	1	6	0	7	0
Guttormson, Rick, Mob.	.955	17	10	11	1	22	3
Guzman, Domingo, Mob.	1.000	14	0	3	0	3	0
Guzman, Juan, Orl.	1.000	1	0	1	0	1	0
Haines, Talley, Orl.	1.000	33	5	9	0	14	1
Harikkala, Tim, Hun.	.889	22	1	7	1	9	0
Haring, Brett, Chat.*	.944	23	5	29	2	36	2
Harper, Travis, Orl.	1.000	9	0	5	0	5	0
Hart, Len, Mob.*	1.000	32	3	5	0	8	0
Hawkins, Al, Hun.	.920	18	3	20	2	25	1
Heams, Shane, Jack.	1.000	39	5	1	0	6	0
Hendrickson, Mark, Tenn.*	1.000	6	1	6	0	7	0
Hite, Kevin, Mob.	1.000	27	1	6	0	7	0
House, Craig, Car.	.500	18	0	1	1	2	0
Huggins, David, Tenn.	1.000	6	1	2	0	3	1
Huntsman, Scott, Hun.	.900	59	2	16	2	20	3
Iapoce, Anthony, Hun.*	.000	1	0	0	0	0	0
Iglesias, Mike, Hun.	1.000	13	3	5	0	8	1
Izquierdo, Hansel, Birm.	.000	8	0	0	0	0	0
Jacobs, Ryan, Hun.*	1.000	18	1	4	0	5	0
James, Delvin, Orl.	1.000	6	2	3	0	5	0
Jennings, Jason, Car.	.875	6	2	5	1	8	1
Jimenez, Jason, Orl.*	1.000	30	1	4	0	5	0
Johnson, James, Hun.*	1.000	16	7	10	0	17	0
Johnston, Doug, Hun.-W.T.	.917	32	13	9	2	24	1
Kalinowski, Josh, Car.*	1.000	6	1	6	0	7	0
Keller, Kris, Jack.	1.000	62	1	2	0	3	0
King, Brad, Chat.	1.000	1	0	0	0	0	0
Kingrey, Jarrod, Tenn.	1.000	16	1	2	0	3	0
Kirsten, Rick, Jack.	1.000	4	0	1	0	1	0
Krawczyk, Jack, Hun.	.000	2	0	0	0	0	0
Kusiewicz, Mike, Tenn.*	.789	27	5	25	8	38	2
Lakman, Jason, Birm.	.600	27	2	1	2	5	0
Lawrence, Brian, Mob.	.944	21	6	11	1	18	1
Lawrence, Clint, Tenn.*	.778	34	3	4	2	9	0
LaPlante, Mick, Gre.	1.000	1	1	1	0	2	0
Lee, Derek, Hun.*	.977	28	11	31	1	43	3
Leek, Randy, Jack.*	.875	7	2	5	1	8	0
Lewis, Derrick, Gre.	.935	27	10	19	2	31	0
LeRoy, John, Chat.	1.000	6	2	1	0	3	0
Lira, Jim, Orl.	.000	2	0	0	0	0	0
Loux, Shane, Jack.	.964	26	6	21	1	28	2
Lowe, Benny, Jack.	.750	17	0	3	1	4	0
Lukasiewicz, Mark, Tenn.*	.000	3	0	0	0	0	0
MacRae, Scott, Chat.	.944	55	2	15	1	18	2
Mairena, Ozwaldo, W.T.*	.000	2	0	0	0	0	0
Manias, Jim, Chat.*	1.000	15	2	3	0	5	0
Maroth, Mike, Jack.*	.982	27	10	45	1	56	4
Marquis, Jason, Gre.	1.000	11	3	15	0	18	1
Martin, Chandler, Car.	1.000	4	1	2	0	3	0
Matcuk, Steve, Car.	1.000	5	0	3	0	3	0
Mathis, Jared, Hun.	.000	1	0	0	0	0	0
Maurer, Dave, Mob.*	1.000	24	2	6	0	8	0
McBride, Chris, Tenn.	1.000	22	2	9	0	11	0
McClellan, Matt, Tenn.	.932	28	12	29	3	44	1
McClendon, Matt, Gre.	.875	22	6	8	2	16	1

CLASS AA Southern League

Player, Team	Pct.	G	PO	A	E	TC	DP
McClure, Brian, Jack.	.000	1	0	0	0	0	0
McGlinchy, Kevin, Gre.	.000	4	0	0	1	1	0
Merrell, Phil, Chat.	.778	7	0	7	2	9	1
Meyers, Mike, W.T.	.933	9	6	8	1	15	0
Middlebrook, Jason, Mob.	1.000	24	9	13	0	22	0
Milburn, Adam, Gre.*	1.000	12	1	4	0	5	1
Miller, Matt, Jack.*	.957	20	6	16	1	23	2
Mobley, Kevin, Jack.	.846	43	4	7	2	13	0
Moraga, David, Car.*	1.000	8	0	10	0	10	0
Myette, Aaron, Birm.	1.000	3	1	1	0	2	0
Nation, Joey, W.T.*	1.000	27	0	22	0	22	1
Neugebauer, Nickolas, Hun.	1.000	10	3	2	0	5	0
Ohman, Will, W.T.*	.889	59	3	5	1	9	1
Osting, Jimmy, Gre.*	1.000	11	8	11	0	19	1
Pacheco, Delvis, Gre.	1.000	11	4	4	0	8	0
Pearsall, J.J., Chat.*	1.000	22	1	5	0	6	1
Pena, Jesus, Birm.*	1.000	23	1	1	0	2	0
Penney, Mike, Hun.	1.000	20	0	3	0	3	0
Peterson, Kyle, Hun.	1.000	1	1	0	0	1	0
Pettyjohn, Adam, Jack.*	1.000	8	2	4	0	6	0
Phelps, Tommy, Jack.*	.964	38	6	21	1	28	1
Phelps, Travis, Orl.	.964	21	10	17	1	28	0
Pierce, Tony, Gre.	.000	1	0	0	0	0	0
Piersoll, Chris, W.T.	1.000	47	2	19	0	21	0
Plunk, Eric, W.T.	.000	7	0	0	1	1	0
Poe, Ryan, Hun.	1.000	9	1	3	0	4	0
Porzio, Mike, Car.*	.958	20	4	19	1	24	1
Price, Ryan, Car.	.917	20	2	9	1	12	0
Priest, Eddie, Chat.*	.977	27	11	31	1	43	0
Pujals, Denis, Orl.	1.000	6	2	4	0	6	1
Purvis, Rob, Birm.	.000	1	0	0	0	0	0
Ramirez, Jose, Jack.*	.875	19	1	6	1	8	0
Rauch, Jon, Birm.	.889	8	2	6	1	9	2
Reith, Brian, Chat.	1.000	5	0	4	0	4	1
Reyes, Eddy, Orl.	.778	50	2	5	2	9	0
Roberts, Mark, Birm.	1.000	17	2	7	0	9	0
Roberts, Willis, Chat.	1.000	5	3	4	0	7	0
Root, Derek, Mob.*	1.000	15	1	2	0	3	0
Rosario, Juan, Orl.	.882	28	7	8	2	17	0
Rose, Ted, Chat.	.833	31	2	3	1	6	0
Rossiter, Mike, Hun.	1.000	48	1	9	0	10	0
Runion, Tony, Mob.	.875	19	3	4	1	8	0
Runyan, Sean, Jack.*	.000	3	0	0	0	0	0
Saipe, Mike, Car.	.857	4	0	6	1	7	0
Schmidt, Bryan, Mob.	1.000	1	0	1	0	1	1
Seanez, Rudy, Gre.	1.000	2	1	0	0	1	0
Seay, Bobby, Orl.*	.950	24	4	15	1	20	0
Seberino, Ronni, Orl.*	1.000	4	1	0	0	1	0

Player, Team	Pct.	G	PO	A	E	TC	DP
Seifert, Ryan, Car.	1.000	32	7	9	0	16	0
Sekany, Jason, Chat.	.667	10	1	5	3	9	0
Serrano, Wascar, Mob.	.839	20	8	18	5	31	0
Sexton, Jeff, Car.	1.000	17	4	7	0	11	0
Sheets, Ben, Hun.	.900	13	4	5	1	10	0
Shumate, Jacob, Gre.	1.000	47	0	1	0	1	0
Smith, Dan, Gre.*	.000	2	0	0	0	0	0
Smith, Travis, Hun.	.971	27	15	18	1	34	1
Sneed, John, Tenn.	.857	21	10	14	4	28	0
Snyder, Bill, Jack.	1.000	29	4	3	0	7	0
Snyder, John, Hun.	1.000	2	1	2	0	3	0
Sobkowiak, Scott, Gre.	1.000	4	1	0	0	1	0
Sparks, Jeff, Orl.	.857	3	1	5	1	7	1
Spille, Ryan, Tenn.*	1.000	4	0	3	0	3	0
Standridge, Jason, Orl.	.900	17	6	12	2	20	0
Stewart, Paul, Hun.	.875	10	1	6	1	8	1
Stoops, Jim, Car.	.889	33	1	7	1	9	1
Tabaka, Jeff, Car.*	1.000	9	0	2	0	2	0
Taglienti, Jeff, Car.	1.000	10	0	3	0	3	0
TEUT, Nate, W.T.*	1.000	27	7	22	0	29	4
Thompson, Travis, Chat.	1.000	2	1	5	0	6	1
Thompson, Travis, Car.	.923	50	2	10	1	13	0
Tokarse, Brian, Birm.	1.000	34	1	1	0	2	0
Tolar, Kevin, Jack.*	1.000	9	5	3	0	8	1
Vavrek, Mike, Car.*	.000	1	0	0	0	0	0
Villegas, Ismael, Gre.	1.000	8	2	1	0	3	0
Vining, Ken, Birm.*	1.000	43	4	9	0	13	2
Wade, Terrell, Chat.*	1.000	28	2	8	0	10	0
Walker, Kevin, Mob.*	1.000	4	1	0	0	1	0
Walls, Doug, Jack.	1.000	11	4	4	0	8	0
Weimer, Matt, Tenn.	1.000	49	2	9	0	11	2
Weymouth, Marty, Birm.	.909	37	1	9	1	11	0
White, Matt, Orl.	.923	20	12	12	2	26	3
Whitley, Curtis, Birm.*	1.000	29	3	0	0	3	1
Wright, Danny, Birm.	1.000	7	4	10	0	14	2
Wright, Jamey, Hun.	1.000	2	1	5	0	6	1
Yankosky, L.J., Gre.	.927	26	10	28	3	41	2
Yennaco, Jay, W.T.	1.000	60	2	8	0	10	2
Yoder, Jeff, W.T.	1.000	8	2	1	0	3	0
Zambrano, Carlos, W.T.	1.000	9	6	5	0	11	0

PITCHERS WITH TWO OR MORE TEAMS

Player, Team	Pct.	G	PO	A	E	TC	DP
Averette, Robert, Chat.	.953	19	10	31	2	43	2
Averette, Robert, Car.	1.000	5	2	4	0	6	0
Johnston, Doug, Hun.	.667	2	0	2	1	3	0
Johnston, Doug, W.T.	.952	30	13	7	1	21	1

LEAGUE CHAMPIONS

Year	Team	Pct.
1904—	Macon	.598
1905—	Macon	.625
1906—	Savannah	.637
1907—	Charleston	.620
1908—	Jackonsville	.694
1909—	Chattanooga*	.738
	Augusta	.702
1910—	Columbus	.588
1911—	Columbus*	.681
	Columbia	.710
1912—	Jacksonville*	.679
	Columbus	.632
1913—	Savannah	.754
	Savannah	.593
1914—	Savannah*	.667
	Albany	.650
1915—	Macon	.588
	Columbus*	.686
1916—	Augusta*	.617
	Columbia	.631
1917—	Charleston	.741
	Columbia*	.667
1918—	Did not operate.	
1919—	Columbia	.585
1920—	Columbia	.633
1921—	Columbia	.642
1922—	Charleston	.625
1923—	Charlotte*	.653
	Macon	.580
1924—	Augusta	.612
1925—	Spartanburg	.620

Year	Team	Pct.
1926—	Greenville	.662
1927—	Greenville	.622
1928—	Asheville	.664
1929—	Asheville	.605
	Knoxville*	.634
1930—	Greenville*	.620
	Macon	.643
1931-35—	Did not operate.	
1936—	Jacksonville	.652
	Columbus*	.650
1937—	Columbus	.572
	Savannah (3rd)†	.565
1938—	Savannah	.574
	Macon (2nd)†	.570
1939—	Columbus	.601
	Augusta (2nd)†	.597
1940—	Savannah	.627
	Columbus (2nd)†	.583
1941—	Macon	.643
	Columbia (2nd)†	.636
1942—	Charleston	.620
	Macon (2nd)†	.585
1943-45—	Did not operate.	
1946—	Columbus	.568
	Augusta (4th)†	.547
1947—	Columbus	.575
	Savannah (2nd)†	.563
1948—	Charleston	.572
	Greenville (3rd)†	.549
1949—	Macon‡	.623
1950—	Macon‡	.588

Year	Team	Pct.
1951—	Montgomery	.607
1952—	Columbia	.649
	Montgomery (3rd)†	.558
1953—	Jacksonville	.679
	Savannah (2nd)†	.571
1954—	Jacksonville	.593
	Savannah (2nd)†	.571
1955—	Columbia	.636
	Augusta (3rd)†	.543
1956—	Jacksonville‡	.621
1957—	Augusta	.636
	Charlotte (2nd)†	.562
1958—	Augusta	.550
	Macon (3rd)†	.500
1959—	Knoxville	.557
	Gastonia (4th)†	.504
1960—	Columbia	.597
	Savannah (3rd)†	.561
1961—	Asheville	.635
1962—	Savannah	.662
	Macon (3rd)†	.576
1963—	Augusta*	.661
	Lynchburg	.662
1964—	Lynchburg	.579
1965—	Columbus	.572
1966—	Mobile	.629
1967—	Birmingham	.604
1968—	Asheville	.614
1969—	Charlotte	.579
1970—	Columbus	.569

Year	Team	Pct.
1971—	Did not operate as league—clubs were members of Dixie Association.	
1972—	Asheville	.583
	Montgomery§	.561
1973—	Montgomery§	.580
	Jacksonville	.559
1974—	Jacksonville	.565
	Knoxville§	.533
1975—	Orlando	.587
	Montgomery§	.545
1976—	Montgomery∞	.591
	Orlando	.540
1977—	Montgomery∞	.628
	Jacksonville	.522
1978—	Knoxville∞	.611
	Savannah	.500
1979—	Columbus	.587
	Nashville∞	.576
1980—	Memphis	.576
	Charlotte∞	.500

Year	Team	Pct.
1981—	Nashville	.566
	Orlando∞	.556
1982—	Jacksonville	.576
	Nashville∞	.535
1983—	Birmingham∞	.628
	Jacksonville	.531
1984—	Charlotte∞	.510
	Knoxville	.483
1985—	Charlotte	.545
	Huntsville∞	.542
1986—	Huntsville	.553
	Columbus∞	.500
1987—	Charlotte	.586
	Birmingham∞	.476
1988—	Greenville	.604
	Chattanooga∞	.566
1989—	Birmingham∞	.615
	Greenville	.504
1990—	Orlando	.590
	Memphis∞	.507

Year	Team	Pct.
1991—	Greenville	.611
	Orlando∞	.535
1992—	Greenville∞	.699
	Chattanooga	.629
1993—	Birmingham∞	.549
	Knoxville	.500
1994—	Huntsville∞	.587
	Carolina	.529
1995—	Carolina∞	.618
	Chattanooga	.580
1996—	Chattanooga	.579
	Jacksonville∞	.543
1997—	Huntsville	.554
	Greenville∞	.529
1998—	Mobile∞	.614
	Jacksonville	.614
1999—	West Tenn.	.596
	Orlando∞	.507
2000—	West Tenn∞	.580
	Jacksonville	.493

*Won split season playoff. †Won four-club playoff. ‡Won championship and four-club playoff. §League was divided into Eastern and Western divisions; won play-off. ∞League was divided into Eastern and Western divisions and played split season; won playoff.

CLASS AA Southern League

TEXAS LEAGUE

LEAGUE OFFICE

President/treasurer
Tom Kayser

Address
2442 Facet Oak
San Antonio, TX 78232

Phone
210-545-5297

TEAMS

ARKANSAS TRAVELERS

Vice president/general manager
Bill Valentine
Manager
Mike Brumley
Ballpark (capacity, surface)
Ray Winder Field (6,083, grass)
Affiliation
Angels
Address
P.O. Box 55066
Little Rock, AR 72215
Phone
501-664-1555

EL PASO DIABLOS

President
Rick Parr
Manager
Al Pedrique
Ballpark (capacity, surface)
Cohen Stadium (9,765, grass)
Affiliation
Diamondbacks
Address
9700 Gateway Blvd. N.
El Paso, TX 79924
Phone
915-755-2000

MIDLAND ROCKHOUNDS

General manager
Monty Hoppel
Manager
Tony DeFrancesco
Ballpark (capacity, surface)
Christensen Stadium (5,000, grass)
Affiliation
Athletics
Address
P.O. Box 51187
Midland, TX 79710

Phone
915-683-4251

ROUND ROCK EXPRESS

General manager
Jay Miller
Manager
Jackie Moore
Ballpark (capacity, surface)
To be announced (7,500, grass)
Affiliation
Astros
Address
P.O. Box 5309
Round Rock, TX 78683
Phone
512-255-2255

SAN ANTONIO MISSIONS

President
Burl Yarbrough
Manager
Dave Brundage
Ballpark (capacity, surface)
Nelson Wolff Stadium (6,300, grass)
Affiliation
Mariners
Address
5757 Highway 90 West
San Antonio, TX 78227
Phone
210-675-7275

SHREVEPORT CAPTAINS

General manager
Daniel Robinson
Manager
Bill Russell
Ballpark (capacity, surface)
Fair Grounds Field (6,200, grass)
Affiliation
Giants

Address
P.O. Box 3448
Shreveport, LA 71133
Phone
318-636-5555

TULSA DRILLERS

Executive v.p./general manager
Chuck Lamson
Manager
Paul Carey
Ballpark (capacity, surface)
Drillers Stadium (10,842, grass)
Affiliation
Rangers
Address
4802 E. 15th
Tulsa, OK 74112
Phone
918-744-5998

WICHITA WRANGLERS

General manager
Steve Shaad
Manager
Keith Bodie
Ballpark (capacity, surface)
Lawrence-Dumont Stadium (6,111, artificial infield, grass outfield)
Affiliation
Royals
Address
P.O. Box 1420
Wichita, KS 67201
Phone
316-267-3372

2000 FINAL STANDINGS

FIRST HALF

EAST DIVISION

Team	W	L	T	Pct.	GB
Shreveport (Giants)	37	32	0	.536	...
Wichita (Royals)	34	33	0	.507	2.0
Arkansas (Cardinals)	33	36	0	.478	4.0
Tulsa (Rangers)	27	43	0	.386	10.5

WEST DIVISION

Team	W	L	T	Pct.	GB
Round Rock (Astros)	43	27	0	.614	...
San Antonio (Dodgers)	41	29	0	.586	2.0
Midland (Athletics)	32	37	0	.464	10.5
El Paso (Diamondbacks)	30	40	0	.429	13.0

SECOND HALF

EAST DIVISION

Team	W	L	T	Pct.	GB
Wichita (Royals)	42	28	0	.600	...
Tulsa (Rangers)	37	33	0	.529	5.0
Arkansas (Cardinals)	35	35	0	.500	7.0
Shreveport (Giants)	21	49	0	.300	21.0

WEST DIVISION

Team	W	L	T	Pct.	GB
El Paso (Diamondbacks)	44	26	0	.629	...
Round Rock (Astros)	40	30	0	.571	4.0
Midland (Athletics)	38	32	0	.543	6.0
San Antonio (Dodgers)	23	47	0	.329	21.0

CLASS AA *Texas League*

COMPOSITE

Team	R.R.	Wich.	E.P.	Mid.	Ark.	Tul.	S.A.	Shre.	W	L	T	Pct.	GB
Round Rock (Astros)	...	10	12	14	11	9	16	11	83	57	0	.593	...
Wichita (Royals)	6	...	7	9	14	16	9	15	76	61	0	.555	5.5
El Paso (Diamondbacks)	16	9	...	13	7	10	12	7	74	66	0	.529	9.0
Midland (Athletics)	10	6	11	...	7	10	16	10	70	69	0	.504	12.5
Arkansas (Cardinals)	5	11	9	9	...	10	9	15	68	71	0	.489	14.5
Tulsa (Rangers)	7	8	6	6	16	...	8	13	64	76	0	.457	19.0
San Antonio (Dodgers)	8	7	12	12	7	8	...	10	64	76	0	.457	19.0
Shreveport (Giants)	5	10	9	6	9	13	6	...	58	81	0	.417	24.5

Arkansas' home games played in Little Rock, Ark.

Major league affiliations in parentheses.

PLAYOFFS: Wichita defeated Shreveport three games to one; Round Rock defeated El Paso three games to two; Round Rock defeated Wichita four games to one to win league championship.

REGULAR-SEASON ATTENDANCE: Arkansas, 197,125; El Paso, 289,856; Midland, 170,545; Round Rock, 660,110; San Antonio, 325,137; Shreveport, 125,575; Tulsa, 334,207; Wichita, 165,352; Total—2,267,907. Playoffs (14 games)—50,127. Class AA All-Star Game at Bowie, Md.—14,077.

MANAGERS: Arkansas, Chris Maloney; El Paso, Bobby Dickerson; Midland, Tony DeFrancesco; Round Rock, Jackie Moore; San Antonio, Rick Burleson; Shreveport, Bill Hayes; Tulsa, Bobby Jones (Through May 8), Moe Hill (May 9 through May 17), James Byrd (May 18 through end of season); Wichita, Keith Bodie.

ALL-STAR TEAM: 1B—Jason Hart, Midland; 2B—Keith Ginter, Round Rock; 3B—Morgan Ensberg, Round Rock; SS—Alex Cintron, El Paso; OF—Andy Bevins, Arkansas; OF—Eric Cole, Round Rock; OF—Jack Cust, El Paso; OF—Bill Ortega, Arkansas; C—Cody McKay, Midland; DH—Alex Cabrera, El Paso; Utility—Joe Caruso, Wichita; RHP—Kurt Ainsworth, Shreveport; Roy Oswalt, Round Rock; Bret Prinz, El Paso; Luke Prokopec, San Antonio; LHP—Bud Smith, Arkansas; Most Valuable Player—Keith Ginter, Round Rock; Pitcher of the Year—Bud Smith, Arkansas; Manager of the Year—Jackie Moore, Round Rock.

2000 BATTING
TEAM

Team	Avg.	G	TPA	AB	R	H	TB	2B	3B	HR	RBI	SH	SF	HP	BB	IBB	SO	SB	CS	GDP	LOB	ShO	Slg.	OBP
Round Rock	.281	140	5471	4781	745	1343	2104	274	23	147	706	44	38	85	523	30	1079	127	81	102	1033	3	.440	.359
Midland	.280	139	5591	4835	788	1353	2098	301	27	130	738	27	58	72	599	21	937	86	61	124	1078	8	.434	.364
Wichita	.280	137	5360	4635	725	1297	1867	218	29	98	656	50	48	83	544	26	793	187	87	105	1041	7	.403	.362
Arkansas	.279	139	5268	4692	696	1309	2053	243	45	137	644	44	33	65	434	27	916	73	61	112	987	6	.438	.346
Tulsa	.276	141	5652	4830	806	1335	2099	284	36	136	731	54	59	48	661	34	967	162	71	98	1162	6	.435	.365
El Paso	.271	141	5471	4801	759	1302	1999	251	52	114	690	46	39	42	543	32	1065	142	75	115	984	7	.416	.348
San Antonio	.249	140	5295	4638	612	1156	1705	203	35	92	558	69	34	45	509	25	964	157	72	110	964	11	.368	.327
Shreveport	.248	139	5172	4591	572	1139	1681	221	21	93	534	52	37	56	436	21	957	80	52	113	941	12	.366	.319

INDIVIDUAL

TOP QUALIFIERS FOR BATTING CHAMPIONSHIP

Minimum 378 plate appearances. *Lefthanded batter. †Switch-hitter.

Player, Team	Avg.	G	TPA	AB	R	H	TB	2B	3B	HR	RBI	SH	SF	HP	BB	IBB	SO	SB	CS	GDP	Slg.	OBP
Ginter, Keith, R.R.	.333	125	569	462	108	154	268	30	3	26	92	0	1	24	82	3	127	24	11	9	.580	.457
Hart, Jason, Mid.	.326	135	626	546	98	178	318	44	3	30	121	0	7	6	67	5	112	4	0	18	.582	.401
Hallmark, Pat, Wich.	.326	132	562	479	80	156	218	26	3	10	79	5	6	20	52	6	74	41	14	10	.455	.409
Lane, Ryan, Tul.	.322	117	502	425	75	137	218	29	2	16	79	0	5	3	69	4	94	15	7	5	.513	.416
Bevins, Andy, Ark.	.321	125	478	430	84	138	248	27	4	25	88	0	3	11	34	0	87	0	4	11	.577	.383
McKay, Cody, Mid.*	.319	115	514	427	70	136	190	35	2	5	89	0	10	10	67	6	54	1	5	15	.445	.414
Caruso, Joe, Wich.	.313	108	460	400	69	125	192	26	1	13	66	5	5	16	34	3	45	10	5	4	.480	.385
McNeal, Aaron, Ark.†	.310	97	390	361	40	112	169	20	2	11	69	1	3	1	24	3	91	0	4	11	.468	.352
Cintron, Alex, E.P.†	.301	125	573	522	83	157	211	30	6	4	59	13	7	2	29	0	56	9	9	22	.404	.336
Ensberg, Morgan, R.R.	.300	137	592	483	95	145	263	34	0	28	90	3	6	8	92	3	107	9	12	15	.545	.416
Salazar, Oscar, Mid.	.300	111	473	427	70	128	196	27	1	13	57	2	3	2	39	0	71	4	4	9	.459	.359
Pena, Carlos, Tul.*	.299	138	648	529	117	158	282	36	2	28	105	1	8	9	101	10	108	12	0	7	.533	.414
Wilson, Jack, Ark.	.294	88	391	343	65	101	155	20	8	6	34	5	2	5	36	0	59	2	3	5	.452	.368
Ortiz, Nick, Wich.	.294	111	445	381	59	112	165	19	2	10	62	9	2	1	52	1	66	14	6	13	.433	.378
Maier, T.J., Ark.	.294	110	422	364	59	107	147	16	3	6	42	1	2	6	49	1	42	13	7	7	.404	.385

DEPARTMENTAL LEADERS: G—Pena, 138; AB—Hart, 546; R—Pena, 117; H—Hart, 178; TB—Hart, 318; 2B—Cole, 46; 3B—Saturria, Saylor, 10 each; HR—Cabrera, 35; RBI—Hart, 121; SH—Romano, 16; SF—McKay, 10; HP—Ginter, 24; BB—Cust, 117; IBB—Cust, 12; SO—Cust, 150; SB—Curry, 52; CS—Moreta, 20; GIDP—Cintron, 22; Slg.—Hart, .582; OBP—Ginter, .457.

ALL PLAYERS

*Lefthanded batter. †Switch-hitter.

Player, Team	Avg.	G	TPA	AB	R	H	TB	2B	3B	HR	RBI	SH	SF	HP	BB	IBB	SO	SB	CS	GDP	Slg.	OBP
Ainsworth, Kurt, Shre.	.188	28	35	32	4	6	7	1	0	0	2	1	0	0	2	0	6	0	0	0	.219	.235
Allen, Jeff, Shre.	.237	128	485	447	40	106	154	23	2	7	52	3	5	4	26	0	97	8	10	9	.345	.282
Allen, Luke, S.A.*	.265	90	385	339	55	90	136	15	5	7	60	0	5	1	40	3	71	14	5	10	.401	.340
Alvarez, Victor, S.A.*	.375	9	9	8	0	3	3	0	0	0	1	0	0	0	0	0	2	0	0	1	.375	.375
Amado, Jose, Wich.	.292	88	368	318	41	93	125	17	0	5	56	0	4	7	39	1	26	6	2	9	.393	.378
Ambrose, John, Ark.	.000	45	2	2	0	0	0	0	0	0	0	1	0	0	0	0	1	0	0	0	.000	.000
Ametller, Jesus, Ark.*	.250	5	16	16	1	4	5	1	0	0	2	0	0	0	0	0	1	0	0	2	.313	.250
Andra, Jeff, Shre.*	.143	17	17	14	3	2	2	0	0	0	2	0	0	0	3	0	5	0	0	0	.143	.294
Andrews, Jeff, E.P.	.200	22	16	15	2	3	4	1	0	0	2	1	0	0	0	0	2	0	0	0	.267	.200
Avrard, Corey, Ark.	.000	57	3	2	1	0	0	0	0	0	0	0	0	0	1	0	1	0	0	0	.000	.333
Bates, Fletcher, E.P.†	.276	109	395	355	52	98	162	24	5	10	62	1	3	1	35	1	73	13	9	4	.456	.340
Bautista, Juan, Tul.	.250	50	188	172	24	43	70	10	1	5	25	1	1	1	13	0	29	8	6	5	.407	.305
Benes, Adam, Ark.*	.200	26	13	10	0	2	2	0	0	0	6	0	0	0	7	0	7	0	0	0	.200	.333
Benham, David, Ark.	.228	18	64	57	9	13	20	5	1	0	6	0	0	0	7	1	10	0	3	0	.351	.313

Player, Team	Avg.	G	TPA	AB	R	H	TB	2B	3B	HR	RBI	SH	SF	HP	BB	IBB	SO	SB	CS	GDP	Slg.	OBP
Benham, Jason, Ark.*	.545	5	12	11	3	6	8	2	0	0	1	0	0	0	1	0	0	0	0	0	.727	.583
Berger, Brandon, Wich.	.163	27	97	86	9	14	25	2	0	3	8	1	1	2	7	0	27	6	1	2	.291	.240
Berrios, Harry, Tul.	.324	24	107	102	20	33	56	6	1	5	18	1	1	0	3	0	12	5	1	3	.549	.340
Berry, Mike, S.A.	.366	30	126	112	13	41	59	7	1	3	20	0	0	0	14	0	17	2	3	4	.527	.437
Bevel, Bobby, S.A.*	.250	47	8	8	1	2	2	0	0	0	0	0	0	0	0	0	2	0	0	0	.250	.250
Bevins, Andy, Ark.	.321	125	478	430	84	138	248	27	4	25	88	0	3	11	34	0	87	0	4	11	.577	.383
Bierbrodt, Nick, E.P.*	.200	7	11	5	0	1	1	0	0	0	1	4	0	0	2	0	3	1	0	0	.200	.429
Bowles, Justin, Mid.*	.271	124	492	443	76	120	204	24	6	16	65	1	6	2	40	0	111	6	6	11	.460	.330
Braswell, Bryan, R.R.*	.111	19	12	9	1	1	1	0	0	0	1	0	0	2	0	0	4	0	0	0	.111	.273
Brito, Juan, Wich.	.257	34	119	105	9	27	29	2	0	0	10	0	2	1	11	2	15	2	1	4	.276	.328
Brown, Vick, E.P.	.250	18	64	56	14	14	17	3	0	0	4	0	0	0	8	0	8	2	0	0	.304	.344
Brumbaugh, Cliff, Tul.	.222	7	36	27	5	6	13	1	0	2	3	0	0	0	9	0	10	1	0	2	.481	.417
Buckley, Brandon, R.R.	.400	1	5	5	1	2	3	1	0	0	1	0	0	0	0	0	0	0	0	0	.600	.400
Burns, Kevin, R.R.*	.318	87	289	255	48	81	126	17	2	8	46	0	3	3	28	5	58	1	2	5	.494	.388
Burnside, Adrian, S.A.	.278	17	20	18	1	5	8	0	0	1	6	1	0	0	1	0	5	0	0	1	.444	.316
Byrnes, Eric, Mid.	.301	67	311	259	49	78	122	25	2	5	37	2	6	1	43	0	38	21	11	5	.471	.395
Cabrera, Alex, E.P.	.382	53	239	212	56	81	209	19	2	35	82	0	0	2	25	6	52	3	2	9	.986	.452
Campusano, Carlos, Shre.	.200	11	25	25	5	5	6	1	0	0	1	0	0	0	0	0	9	0	0	0	.240	.200
Carter, Charley, R.R.	.267	24	97	90	12	24	40	7	0	3	21	0	1	0	6	0	15	0	0	2	.444	.309
Caruso, Joe, Wich.	.313	108	460	400	69	125	192	26	1	13	66	5	5	16	34	3	45	10	5	4	.480	.385
Cervantes, Chris, E.P.*	.176	17	19	17	3	3	3	0	0	0	1	0	0	0	2	0	10	1	0	0	.176	.263
Cesar, Dionys, Mid.†	.277	111	478	433	62	120	157	21	2	4	37	4	3	0	38	0	65	13	10	7	.363	.333
Chen, Chin-Feng, S.A.	.277	133	584	516	66	143	194	27	3	6	67	1	3	3	61	3	131	23	15	7	.376	.355
Cintron, Alex, E.P.†	.301	125	573	522	83	157	211	30	6	4	59	13	7	2	29	0	56	9	9	22	.404	.336
Clark, Doug, Shre.*	.272	131	548	492	68	134	198	20	7	10	75	1	7	5	43	5	102	12	4	13	.402	.333
Clark, Kevin, E.P.	.179	27	86	78	7	14	21	4	0	1	10	0	2	2	4	0	29	0	0	0	.269	.233
Clemons, Chris, E.P.	.000	2	2	1	0	0	0	0	0	0	0	1	1	0	0	0	0	0	0	0	.000	.000
Cole, Eric, R.R.	.291	132	601	543	90	158	270	46	0	22	94	0	6	9	43	3	98	21	10	12	.497	.349
Coogan, Patrick, Ark.	.143	27	29	21	1	3	4	1	0	0	1	5	0	0	3	0	10	0	0	0	.190	.250
Corps, Edwin, Shre.	.133	36	17	15	0	2	2	0	0	0	0	2	0	0	0	0	5	0	0	0	.133	.133
Cox, Ryan, Shre.	.000	7	8	6	0	0	0	0	0	0	0	1	0	0	1	0	2	0	0	0	.000	.143
Crafton, Kevin, Ark.	.667	57	5	3	0	2	2	0	0	0	2	0	0	0	2	0	1	0	0	0	.667	.800
Creek, Ryan, E.P.	.000	2	1	1	0	0	0	0	0	0	0	0	0	0	0	0	1	0	0	0	.000	.000
Cresse, Brad, E.P.	.262	15	52	42	9	11	15	1	0	1	10	0	1	3	6	0	12	0	0	1	.357	.385
Curry, Mike, Wich.*	.289	123	566	461	104	133	175	18	6	4	52	4	2	5	94	2	99	52	16	4	.380	.413
Curtis, Chris, E.P.	.167	5	8	6	2	1	1	0	0	0	0	2	0	0	0	0	3	1	0	0	.167	.167
Cust, Jack, E.P.*	.293	129	568	447	100	131	235	32	6	20	75	0	2	2	117	12	150	12	9	10	.526	.440
Dace, Derek, E.P.*	1.000	28	1	1	0	1	1	0	0	0	0	0	0	0	0	0	0	0	0	0	1.000	1.000
Daeley, Scott, Shre.	.000	3	2	2	1	0	0	0	0	0	0	0	0	0	0	0	1	0	0	0	.000	.000
Dallimore, Brian, R.R.-E.P.	.275	112	407	367	51	101	135	17	1	5	56	3	5	6	26	3	58	17	3	13	.368	.329
Davis, Allen, S.A.*	.214	29	35	28	1	6	7	1	0	0	2	3	0	0	4	0	12	0	0	3	.250	.313
Davis, Clint, E.P.	.000	11	1	1	0	0	0	0	0	0	0	0	0	0	0	0	0	0	0	0	.000	.000
Davis, Glenn, S.A.†	.207	113	441	377	54	78	134	17	6	9	40	2	1	3	58	2	113	2	0	11	.355	.317
Depastino, Joe, Wich.	.444	5	18	18	3	8	16	0	1	2	4	0	0	0	0	0	2	0	1	0	.889	.444
Dillon, Joe, Wich.	.318	62	273	220	35	70	120	16	2	10	43	2	5	7	39	1	38	0	0	6	.545	.428
Dodson, Jeremy, Wich.*	.238	128	514	450	69	107	185	16	4	18	57	5	0	7	52	2	111	17	8	7	.411	.326
Dorame, Randey, S.A.*	.130	9	23	23	2	3	3	0	0	0	1	0	0	0	0	0	9	0	0	1	.130	.130
Eckelman, Alex, Ark.	.311	85	322	280	42	87	121	16	3	4	33	7	3	8	24	1	27	4	1	6	.432	.378
Edsell, Geoff, S.A.	.214	25	15	14	1	3	3	0	0	0	1	1	0	0	0	0	2	0	0	1	.214	.214
Elarton, Scott, R.R.	.000	1	2	1	0	0	0	0	0	0	0	1	0	0	0	0	1	0	0	0	.000	.000
Ellis, Mark, Wich.	.318	7	27	22	4	7	8	1	0	0	4	0	0	0	5	0	5	1	0	0	.364	.444
Ensberg, Morgan, R.R.	.300	137	592	483	95	145	263	34	0	28	90	3	6	8	92	3	107	9	12	15	.545	.416
Espada, Josue, Mid.	.265	23	112	98	17	26	33	7	0	0	7	0	0	2	12	0	12	2	2	4	.337	.357
Estrella, Luis, Shre.	.500	21	4	4	0	2	3	1	0	0	0	0	0	0	0	0	0	0	0	0	.750	.500
Faircloth, Chad, Shre.*	.231	23	56	52	3	12	12	0	0	0	4	1	0	1	2	0	10	0	2	1	.231	.273
Farley, Cordell, Ark.	.229	96	280	249	37	57	87	7	1	7	24	5	1	3	22	0	76	17	8	1	.349	.298
Febles, Carlos, Wich.	.133	4	19	15	2	2	2	0	0	0	1	0	1	1	2	0	4	2	0	0	.133	.263
Figga, Mike, S.A.	.236	43	161	148	16	35	64	5	0	8	21	0	0	1	12	0	37	0	0	5	.432	.298
Flaherty, Tim, Shre.	.205	92	309	264	29	54	91	13	0	8	34	3	2	9	31	3	97	8	2	5	.345	.307
Flores, Ignacio, S.A.	.000	3	1	1	0	0	0	0	0	0	0	0	0	0	0	0	0	0	0	1	.000	.000
Flores, Javier, Mid.	.242	12	39	33	3	8	12	4	0	0	4	1	0	0	5	0	5	0	0	0	.364	.342
Fox, Andy, E.P.*	.400	4	17	15	3	6	8	2	0	0	4	0	0	0	2	1	1	1	0	0	.533	.471
Franks, Lance, Ark.	.375	44	18	16	2	6	6	0	0	0	1	0	0	0	1	0	5	0	0	0	.375	.412
Fuentes, Javier, E.P.	.286	5	9	7	1	2	2	0	0	0	0	0	0	0	2	0	1	0	0	0	.286	.444
Fuller, Jody, E.P.	.000	8	2	2	0	0	0	0	0	0	0	0	0	0	0	0	1	0	0	0	.000	.000
Gallagher, Shawn, Tul.	.283	29	128	113	22	32	55	8	0	5	24	0	2	1	12	0	30	0	0	3	.487	.352
Galvez, Randy, S.A.	.200	12	6	5	0	1	1	0	0	0	1	0	0	0	0	0	2	0	0	0	.200	.200
Gann, Jamie, E.P.	.203	42	161	153	19	31	48	5	0	4	10	0	0	2	6	0	35	4	2	4	.314	.242
Garcia, Apostol, S.A.	.000	18	4	3	0	0	0	0	0	0	0	0	0	0	1	0	1	0	0	0	.000	.250
Garrett, Hal, S.A.	.250	21	10	8	0	2	2	0	0	0	1	0	0	1	0	0	2	0	0	0	.250	.333
Garrick, Matt, Ark.	.234	101	365	325	33	76	105	17	0	4	35	1	1	2	36	3	71	1	2	12	.323	.313
German, Esteban, Mid.	.213	24	97	75	13	16	20	1	0	1	6	2	0	2	18	0	21	5	3	1	.267	.379
Gibbs, Kevin, S.A.†	.190	11	50	42	5	8	10	0	1	0	4	0	1	1	6	0	9	1	0	0	.238	.300
Gil, Geronimo, S.A.	.284	100	397	352	42	100	154	19	1	11	58	1	5	6	33	3	65	3	2	8	.438	.351
Ginter, Keith, R.R.	.333	125	569	462	108	154	268	30	3	26	92	0	1	24	82	3	127	24	11	9	.580	.457
Glendenning, Mike, Shre.	.261	85	334	291	50	76	138	14	0	16	54	0	2	5	36	4	87	1	1	5	.474	.350
Glick, Dave, R.R.*	.000	33	1	1	0	0	0	0	0	0	0	0	0	0	0	0	0	0	0	1	.000	.000
Gomez, Ramon, E.P.	.284	74	295	264	42	75	105	8	8	2	37	1	2	2	26	0	50	18	2	2	.398	.350
Gooding, Jason, Wich.	.000	29	1	1	0	0	0	0	0	0	0	0	0	0	0	0	0	0	0	0	.000	.000
Goodrich, Randy, Shre.	.000	51	3	3	0	0	0	0	0	0	0	0	0	0	0	0	3	0	0	0	.000	.000
Goodwin, Curtis, Wich.*	.263	11	44	38	8	10	11	1	0	0	2	0	0	0	6	0	5	2	1	1	.289	.364
Gorr, Robb, S.A.	.261	87	315	280	32	73	111	14	0	8	41	6	3	5	21	1	54	3	3	8	.396	.320
Grabowski, Jason, Tul.*	.274	135	592	493	93	135	235	33	5	19	90	0	7	4	88	1	106	8	7	12	.477	.383

Player, Team	Avg.	G	TPA	AB	R	H	TB	2B	3B	HR	RBI	SH	SF	HP	BB	IBB	SO	SB	CS	GDP	Slg.	OBP
Green, Jason, R.R.	.000	31	2	1	0	0	0	0	0	0	0	1	0	0	0	0	0	0	0	0	.000	.000
Greer, Rusty, Tul.*	.143	2	8	7	0	1	1	0	0	0	1	0	0	0	1	0	3	0	0	0	.143	.250
Guzman, Geraldo, E.P.	.083	17	13	12	1	1	1	0	0	0	0	0	0	0	0	0	8	0	0	0	.083	.154
Haas, Chris, Ark.*	.271	82	339	291	52	79	148	14	2	17	59	1	3	4	40	2	84	0	1	11	.509	.364
Hallmark, Pat, Wich.	.326	132	562	479	80	156	218	26	3	10	79	5	6	20	52	6	74	41	14	10	.455	.409
Hammock, Rob, E.P.	.250	45	154	140	22	35	45	5	1	1	15	0	2	1	11	1	25	1	2	1	.321	.305
Harkrider, Kip, S.A.*	.231	97	316	286	29	66	89	9	1	4	35	9	1	2	18	1	39	1	0	10	.311	.280
Hart, Jason, Mid.	.326	135	626	546	98	178	318	44	3	30	121	0	7	6	67	5	112	4	0	18	.582	.401
Hayes, Heath, S.A.	.400	3	7	5	1	2	3	1	0	0	2	0	1	0	1	1	1	0	0	0	.600	.429
Herbert, Russ, R.R.	.167	38	8	6	0	1	1	0	0	0	0	2	0	0	0	0	5	0	0	0	.167	.167
Hernandez, Fernando, R.R.	.000	15	1	1	0	0	0	0	0	0	0	0	0	0	0	0	0	0	0	0	.000	.000
Hillman, Eric, R.R.*	.500	1	3	2	1	1	1	0	0	0	0	0	1	0	0	0	0	0	0	0	.500	.500
Horgan, Joe, Shre.*	1.000	1	2	2	0	2	2	0	0	0	0	0	0	0	0	0	0	0	0	0	1.000	1.000
Huff, Larry, Wich.	.300	83	354	290	48	87	112	14	1	3	43	7	3	3	51	0	48	13	8	9	.386	.406
Huffman, Royce, R.R.	.353	4	18	17	2	6	7	1	0	0	2	0	0	1	0	0	2	1	1	1	.412	.389
Husted, Brent, S.A.	.333	52	9	6	0	2	2	0	0	0	2	2	0	0	1	0	2	0	0	0	.333	.429
Hutchinson, Chad, Ark.	.143	11	8	7	0	1	1	0	0	0	0	0	0	0	1	0	5	0	0	0	.143	.250
Hutton, Mark, R.R.	1.000	3	1	1	0	1	1	0	0	0	0	0	0	0	0	0	0	0	0	0	1.000	1.000
Ireland, Eric, R.R.	.182	29	45	33	5	6	11	2	0	1	4	7	0	0	5	0	7	0	0	1	.333	.289
Jerue, Tristan, Ark.	.000	4	4	4	0	0	0	0	0	0	0	0	0	0	0	0	1	0	0	0	.000	.000
Jones, Jeremy, Tul.	.289	30	115	97	18	28	42	6	1	2	13	3	2	0	13	0	19	0	2	2	.433	.366
Joseph, Kevin, Shre.	.083	27	15	12	2	1	1	0	0	0	0	1	0	0	2	0	2	0	0	0	.083	.214
Kapler, Gabe, Tul.	.583	3	13	12	3	7	10	0	0	1	4	0	0	0	1	0	2	0	0	0	.833	.615
Karnuth, Jason, Ark.	.500	8	3	2	0	1	2	1	0	0	2	1	0	0	0	0	0	0	0	0	1.000	.500
Keith, Rusty, Mid.	.197	18	71	61	8	12	17	2	0	1	6	0	0	1	9	0	11	0	0	2	.279	.310
Kellner, Ryan, S.A.	.091	15	48	44	4	4	4	0	0	0	1	0	0	0	4	0	14	0	0	1	.091	.167
Kessel, Kyle, R.R.	.313	15	22	16	1	5	6	1	0	0	1	3	0	0	3	0	7	0	0	0	.375	.421
Knoll, Brian, Shre.	.000	22	12	7	3	0	0	0	0	0	0	0	2	0	3	0	1	0	0	0	.000	.300
Koplove, Mike, E.P.	.250	35	4	4	1	1	1	0	0	0	1	0	0	0	0	0	1	0	0	0	.250	.250
Lambert, Jeremy, Ark.	.333	39	3	3	0	1	1	0	0	0	2	0	0	0	0	0	2	0	0	0	.333	.333
Landry, Jacques, Mid.	.255	127	532	470	83	120	212	32	3	18	80	0	5	10	47	2	143	9	5	5	.451	.333
Lane, Ryan, Tul.	.322	117	502	425	75	137	218	29	2	16	79	0	5	3	69	4	94	15	7	5	.513	.416
Lanfranco, Otoniel, Ark.	.286	33	18	14	0	4	5	1	0	0	4	3	0	0	1	0	1	0	0	0	.357	.333
Lee, Travis, E.P.*	.200	3	12	10	0	2	2	0	0	0	0	0	0	0	2	0	1	0	0	1	.200	.333
Leon, Jose, Ark.	.269	90	320	297	41	80	144	16	3	14	41	2	0	5	16	0	66	2	1	7	.485	.318
Lockwood, Mike, Mid.*	.309	56	267	236	45	73	103	16	1	4	31	2	2	6	21	0	33	1	1	4	.436	.377
Logan, Kyle, R.R.*	.219	109	388	343	44	75	110	17	0	6	31	1	5	4	35	2	63	13	5	4	.321	.295
Luderer, Brian, Mid.	.315	33	126	108	18	34	52	6	0	4	16	0	3	0	15	0	11	0	1	4	.481	.389
Macrory, Bob, Ark.	.211	9	41	38	3	8	8	0	0	0	2	0	0	0	3	0	5	1	0	1	.211	.268
Magruder, Chris, Shre.†	.282	134	580	496	85	140	191	33	3	4	39	6	3	8	67	2	75	18	10	11	.385	.375
Maier, T.J., Ark.	.294	110	422	364	59	107	147	16	3	6	42	1	2	6	49	1	42	13	7	7	.404	.385
Maldonado, Carlos, R.R.	.270	116	474	423	46	114	157	24	2	5	52	5	6	5	35	3	71	5	4	15	.371	.328
Martine, Chris, Ark.	.063	5	16	16	1	1	1	0	0	0	0	0	0	0	0	0	6	0	0	0	.063	.063
Martines, Jason, E.P.*	.000	55	9	9	0	0	0	0	0	0	0	1	0	0	0	0	8	0	0	0	.000	.000
Martinez, Greg, Mid.†	.272	28	95	81	13	22	25	1	1	0	7	2	0	0	12	0	14	10	1	2	.309	.366
Marval, Raul, Shre.	.213	53	166	150	9	32	40	0	1	2	15	4	1	2	9	0	14	1	1	9	.267	.265
Matranga, David, R.R.	.233	120	441	373	50	87	125	14	3	6	44	2	1	17	48	0	99	5	5	1	.335	.343
Mayo, Blake, E.P.	.188	38	22	16	2	3	4	1	0	0	1	2	0	0	4	0	9	0	0	0	.250	.350
McAffee, Josh, Tul.	.250	4	10	8	1	2	4	2	0	0	0	1	0	0	1	0	3	0	1	0	.500	.333
McCutcheon, Mike, E.P.*	.000	30	2	2	0	0	0	0	0	0	0	0	0	0	0	0	2	0	0	0	.000	.000
McGowan, Sean, Shre.	.348	18	70	69	5	24	28	4	0	0	12	0	0	0	1	0	8	0	0	2	.406	.357
McKay, Cody, Mid.*	.319	115	514	427	70	136	190	35	2	5	89	0	10	10	67	6	54	1	5	15	.445	.414
McKnight, Tony, R.R.*	.000	6	2	1	0	0	0	0	0	0	0	1	0	0	0	0	0	0	0	0	.000	.000
McNeal, Aaron, S.A.	.310	97	390	361	40	112	169	20	2	11	69	1	3	1	24	3	91	0	4	11	.468	.352
Medrano, Steve, Wich.†	.224	16	53	49	5	11	11	0	0	0	4	1	1	0	2	0	9	0	2	1	.224	.250
Meier, Dan, E.P.*	.194	25	66	62	8	12	21	1	1	2	7	0	1	0	3	0	25	0	1	3	.339	.227
Melhuse, Adam, S.A.†	.397	16	73	58	17	23	36	7	0	2	9	1	1	2	11	1	9	3	0	2	.621	.500
Meliah, Dave, Tul.*	.250	10	38	36	2	9	14	1	2	0	5	0	1	0	1	1	7	0	0	0	.389	.263
Mensik, Todd, Mid.*	.263	124	498	414	56	109	206	24	2	23	84	2	5	5	72	6	114	0	0	11	.498	.375
Messman, Joe, Shre.	.000	38	3	2	0	0	0	0	0	0	0	0	0	0	1	0	0	0	0	0	.000	.333
Messner, Jake, Shre.*	.345	22	67	58	7	20	35	6	0	3	9	0	0	0	9	0	14	2	1	2	.603	.433
Metcalfe, Mike, S.A.†	.245	52	232	196	42	48	65	5	3	2	25	4	1	1	30	1	18	34	9	0	.332	.346
Metzler, Rod, Wich.†	.266	111	400	361	50	96	132	15	3	5	44	5	1	5	28	4	74	7	8	4	.366	.327
Miller, Benji, Shre.	.000	58	6	3	1	0	0	0	0	0	0	1	0	0	2	0	1	0	0	0	.000	.400
Miller, Orlando, S.A.	.283	14	57	53	6	15	28	4	0	3	8	0	0	4	0	0	12	0	0	2	.528	.333
Mitchell, Mike, Ark.*	.304	13	50	46	3	14	19	5	0	0	4	0	0	0	4	0	8	0	1	1	.413	.360
Monroe, Craig, Tul.	.282	120	539	464	89	131	235	34	5	20	89	1	8	2	64	4	91	12	13	12	.506	.366
Montas, Ricardo, Wich.	.216	11	37	37	5	8	10	2	0	0	3	0	0	0	0	0	5	0	0	1	.270	.216
Montgomery, Matt, S.A.	.000	41	13	11	0	0	0	0	0	0	0	2	0	0	0	0	5	0	0	0	.000	.000
Moreta, Ramon, S.A.	.239	126	519	468	61	112	165	16	2	11	31	7	2	5	37	1	86	26	20	8	.353	.301
Morillo, Cesar, E.P.-R.R.†	.288	99	334	302	43	87	112	16	0	3	38	0	2	5	25	4	62	9	7	5	.371	.350
Morris, Matt, Ark.	.000	2	1	1	0	0	0	0	0	0	0	0	0	0	0	0	1	0	0	0	.000	.000
Munoz, Juan, Ark.*	.344	68	266	247	41	85	116	14	1	5	31	1	1	1	16	0	16	5	2	7	.470	.385
Murray, Glenn, Ark.	.243	10	42	37	9	9	21	1	1	3	5	0	0	2	3	0	8	0	0	1	.568	.333
Navarro, Jason, Ark.*	.000	33	1	1	0	0	0	0	0	0	0	0	0	0	0	0	0	0	0	0	.000	.000
Navarro, Scott, R.R.*	.000	22	3	1	0	0	0	0	0	0	0	2	0	0	0	0	1	0	0	0	.000	.000
Newstrom, Doug, E.P.*	.211	40	119	109	9	23	32	9	0	0	6	0	1	0	9	0	24	4	1	3	.294	.269
Niebla, Ruben, S.A.*	.000	10	2	1	0	0	0	0	0	0	0	0	0	0	1	0	1	0	0	0	.000	.500
Norris, Ben, E.P.*	.000	7	6	6	0	0	0	0	0	0	0	0	0	0	0	0	3	0	0	0	.000	.000
Norton, Chris, Mid.	.217	20	83	69	10	15	23	6	1	0	11	0	1	1	12	1	17	0	0	3	.333	.337
Nunez, Maximo, S.A.	.333	38	9	9	2	3	6	0	0	1	4	0	0	0	0	0	3	0	0	0	.667	.333
Olivo, Miguel, Mid.	.237	19	65	59	8	14	19	2	0	1	9	1	0	0	5	0	15	0	0	3	.322	.297
Oropesa, Eddie, Shre.*	.000	59	3	3	0	0	0	0	0	0	0	0	0	0	0	0	2	0	0	1	.000	.000

– 483 –

CLASS AA Texas League

Player, Team	Avg.	G	TPA	AB	R	H	TB	2B	3B	HR	RBI	SH	SF	HP	BB	IBB	SO	SB	CS	GDP	Slg.	OBP
Ortega, Bill, Ark.	.325	86	368	332	51	108	172	18	5	12	62	0	4	4	28	4	42	1	5	10	.518	.380
Ortiz, Nick, Wich.	.294	111	445	381	59	112	165	19	2	10	62	9	2	1	52	1	66	14	6	13	.433	.378
Oswalt, Roy, R.R.	.138	19	33	29	2	4	5	1	0	0	0	1	0	0	3	0	5	0	0	1	.172	.219
Otero, William, Shre.	.207	46	174	145	14	30	43	7	0	2	20	4	2	3	20	2	30	0	2	2	.297	.312
Overbay, Lyle, E.P.*	.352	62	276	244	43	86	130	16	2	8	49	0	2	2	28	0	39	3	2	6	.533	.420
Owens, Ryan, E.P.	.216	60	232	208	30	45	75	7	4	5	24	1	0	2	21	1	60	5	4	3	.361	.294
Pachot, John, E.P.	.143	5	14	14	1	2	3	1	0	0	1	0	0	0	0	0	1	0	0	1	.214	.143
Pearce, Josh, Ark.	.083	17	27	24	0	2	2	0	0	0	2	3	0	0	0	0	15	0	0	2	.083	.083
Pearson, Eddie, Ark.†	.300	74	282	257	28	77	122	15	0	10	38	0	2	1	22	6	34	0	0	12	.475	.355
Pecci, Jay, Mid.†	.246	102	422	353	52	87	114	15	3	2	36	4	5	15	44	1	50	5	7	13	.323	.350
Pena, Carlos, Tul.*	.299	138	648	529	117	158	282	36	2	28	105	1	8	9	101	10	108	12	0	7	.533	.414
Perez, Jhonny, R.R.	.297	79	300	273	44	81	113	9	1	7	31	5	0	1	17	0	40	14	4	6	.414	.340
Persails, Mark, R.R.	.333	50	6	3	1	1	1	0	0	0	0	2	0	0	1	0	1	0	0	0	.333	.500
Phillips, Paul, Wich.	.292	82	318	291	49	85	118	11	5	4	30	1	4	1	21	1	22	4	5	11	.405	.338
Pina, Rafael, E.P.	.000	13	19	18	1	0	0	0	0	0	0	0	0	0	1	0	7	0	0	1	.000	.053
Piniella, Juan, Tul.	.246	126	531	447	68	110	144	17	1	5	40	12	1	4	67	0	105	24	8	5	.322	.349
Podsednik, Scott, Tul.*	.249	49	203	169	20	42	59	7	2	2	13	1	2	1	30	1	33	19	4	4	.349	.361
Porter, Colin, R.R.*	.274	124	498	435	76	119	196	25	5	14	57	0	1	6	56	4	130	17	9	6	.451	.363
Powell, Dante, S.A.	.266	17	76	64	12	17	24	4	0	1	6	0	0	0	12	0	16	10	3	2	.375	.382
Powell, Jay, R.R.	.000	1	1	1	0	0	0	0	0	0	0	0	0	0	0	0	1	0	0	0	.000	.000
Priess, Matt, Shre.	.245	52	159	143	16	35	56	6	0	5	18	1	0	0	15	0	26	1	1	5	.392	.316
Prinz, Bret, E.P.	.500	53	2	2	0	1	1	0	0	0	0	0	0	0	0	0	0	0	0	0	.500	.500
Prokopec, Luke, S.A.*	.258	23	36	31	3	8	14	3	0	1	2	3	0	0	2	0	8	1	0	1	.452	.303
Ramirez, Erasmo, Shre.*	.000	39	6	4	0	0	0	0	0	0	0	1	0	0	1	0	1	0	0	0	.000	.200
Ransom, Cody, Shre.	.200	130	505	459	58	92	138	21	2	7	47	3	3	0	40	1	141	9	3	9	.301	.263
Reames, Britt, Ark.	.400	8	6	5	1	2	4	0	1	0	2	0	1	0	0	0	1	0	0	0	.800	.333
Redding, Tim, R.R.	.000	5	1	1	0	0	0	0	0	0	0	0	0	0	0	0	1	0	0	0	.000	.000
Regalado, Maximo, S.A.	.000	26	1	1	0	0	0	0	0	0	0	0	0	0	0	0	0	0	0	0	.000	.000
Revenig, Todd, E.P.	.214	12	17	14	0	3	3	0	0	0	0	3	0	0	0	0	8	0	0	0	.214	.214
Riggs, Eric, S.A.†	.223	117	494	421	56	94	142	19	4	7	39	15	2	2	54	2	85	18	6	8	.337	.313
Roberge, J.P., Wich.	.242	36	135	124	20	30	39	6	0	1	13	0	0	1	10	1	17	1	1	3	.315	.304
Robertson, Jeriome, R.R.*	.211	12	20	19	0	4	4	0	0	0	0	0	0	0	1	0	8	0	0	0	.211	.250
Rodriguez, Wilfredo, R.R.*	.267	11	15	15	2	4	6	0	1	0	1	0	0	0	0	0	4	0	0	2	.400	.267
Romano, Jason, Tul.	.271	131	620	535	87	145	208	35	2	8	70	16	7	6	56	0	84	25	10	13	.389	.343
Ronan, Marc, Ark.*	.207	40	128	116	8	24	28	4	0	0	9	1	1	1	9	1	22	0	0	2	.241	.268
Rose, Mike, E.P.†	.284	117	426	352	58	100	154	22	1	10	62	1	4	1	68	2	70	8	11	16	.438	.398
Ross, David, S.A.	.209	24	79	67	11	14	27	2	1	3	12	1	1	1	9	1	17	1	0	0	.403	.308
Rupp, Brian, Ark.	.000	1	1	1	0	0	0	0	0	0	0	0	0	0	0	0	0	0	0	0	.000	.000
Saitta, Rich, S.A.	.251	106	391	351	48	88	119	14	4	3	36	3	4	7	26	2	65	9	2	10	.339	.312
Salazar, Oscar, Mid.	.300	111	473	427	70	128	196	27	1	13	57	2	3	2	39	0	71	4	4	9	.459	.359
Samboy, Nelson, R.R.	.277	13	51	47	11	13	19	3	0	1	3	0	1	0	3	0	9	2	3	1	.404	.314
Sanchez, Martin, E.P.	.263	28	19	19	0	5	5	0	0	0	2	0	0	0	0	0	12	0	0	0	.263	.263
Sanchez, Victor, E.P.	.281	31	104	96	12	27	34	2	1	1	17	0	0	2	6	1	21	2	2	5	.354	.337
Saturria, Luis, Ark.	.274	129	537	478	78	131	236	25	10	20	76	2	6	6	45	5	124	18	11	7	.494	.340
Saylor, Jamie, E.P.*	.213	90	340	286	50	61	96	12	10	1	28	2	2	6	44	2	71	14	2	3	.336	.328
Schaeffer, Jon, Mid.	.216	14	44	37	5	8	13	2	0	1	8	0	2	0	5	0	6	0	0	1	.351	.295
Scott, Brian, E.P.	.133	16	15	15	1	2	2	0	0	0	1	0	0	0	0	0	9	1	0	0	.133	.133
Secoda, Joe, Ark.	.200	17	34	30	4	6	7	1	0	0	2	0	2	2	0	0	11	0	0	2	.233	.235
Secrist, Reed, Tul.*	.323	42	151	133	19	43	64	10	1	3	20	0	1	4	13	2	28	3	0	0	.481	.397
Sedlacek, Shawn, Wich.	.000	35	3	3	0	0	0	0	0	0	0	0	0	0	0	0	1	0	0	0	.000	.000
Sergio, Tom, Tul.*	.255	37	167	141	20	36	47	8	0	1	19	1	1	3	21	0	14	7	0	1	.333	.361
Sessions, Doug, R.R.	.000	56	4	2	0	0	0	0	0	0	1	1	0	0	1	0	1	0	0	0	.000	.333
Shearn, Tom, R.R.	.207	25	33	29	2	6	9	3	0	0	0	3	0	0	1	0	9	0	0	0	.310	.233
Sheredy, Kevin, Ark.	.000	21	1	1	0	0	0	0	0	0	0	0	0	0	0	0	1	0	0	0	.000	.000
Simon, Ben, S.A.	.214	29	18	14	2	3	3	0	0	0	0	2	0	0	2	0	8	0	0	0	.214	.313
Smith, Bud, Ark.*	.261	18	28	23	4	6	10	1	0	1	6	0	1	0	4	0	1	0	0	0	.435	.357
Smith, Cam, S.A.	.000	7	2	2	0	0	0	0	0	0	0	0	0	0	0	0	2	0	0	0	.000	.000
Solano, Danny, Tul.	.251	109	417	359	36	90	130	13	3	7	33	10	2	6	40	0	66	10	6	11	.362	.334
Spivey, Junior, E.P.	.421	6	20	19	5	8	16	5	0	1	2	1	0	0	0	0	5	0	0	1	.842	.421
Stephenson, Brian, S.A.	.000	4	2	2	0	0	0	0	0	0	0	0	0	0	0	0	0	0	0	0	.000	.000
Summers, John, Shre.†	.258	54	162	151	15	39	52	8	1	1	10	1	1	2	7	0	31	0	1	2	.344	.298
Sykes, Jamie, E.P.	.201	48	176	154	16	31	49	5	2	3	21	0	3	0	19	1	45	6	3	1	.318	.284
Taveras, Luis, Tul.	.232	82	329	285	44	66	101	14	3	5	37	2	6	2	34	0	73	3	2	8	.354	.312
Tebbs, Nate, Ark.†	.250	29	125	116	13	29	36	7	0	0	14	1	0	0	8	0	20	2	4	2	.310	.298
Theodorou, Nick, S.A.†	.241	113	321	266	29	64	87	14	3	1	25	2	3	1	49	3	39	3	3	9	.327	.357
Thomas, Gary, Mid.	.247	74	227	190	28	47	57	7	0	1	26	4	0	9	24	0	30	5	5	6	.300	.359
Thompson, Mark, Ark.	.000	1	1	1	0	0	0	0	0	0	0	0	0	0	0	0	0	0	0	0	.000	.000
Thorn, Todd, E.P.*	.125	23	9	8	0	1	1	0	0	0	1	1	0	0	0	0	3	0	0	0	.125	.125
Thurston, Jerrey, R.R.	.247	24	80	77	4	19	26	2	1	1	7	1	0	1	1	0	19	0	1	2	.338	.266
Torcato, Tony, Shre.*	.500	2	8	8	1	4	4	0	0	0	2	0	0	0	0	0	1	0	0	0	.500	.500
Torrealba, Yorvit, Shre.	.286	108	450	398	50	114	149	21	1	4	32	10	2	6	34	2	55	2	3	17	.374	.350
Tsoukalas, John, Shre.*	.217	31	66	60	8	13	19	3	0	1	11	0	1	1	4	0	11	0	0	0	.317	.273
Tuttle, Dave, E.P.	.250	21	4	4	0	1	1	0	0	0	1	0	0	0	0	0	3	0	0	0	.250	.250
Ullery, Dave, Wich.*	.287	62	227	202	22	58	82	9	0	5	42	2	7	1	15	1	47	1	2	6	.406	.329
Urquiola, Carlos, E.P.*	.302	68	254	225	33	68	78	8	1	0	18	5	1	3	20	1	17	13	8	2	.347	.365
Vasquez, Geraldo, Ark.	.000	3	3	3	0	0	0	0	0	0	0	0	0	0	0	0	2	0	0	0	.000	.000
Velarde, Randy, Mid.	.125	5	20	16	4	2	5	0	0	1	1	0	0	0	4	0	4	0	0	0	.313	.300
Vogelsong, Ryan, Shre.	.074	27	31	27	0	2	2	0	0	0	0	1	0	0	3	0	5	0	0	0	.074	.167
Wade, Travis, R.R.	.000	23	2	2	0	0	0	0	0	0	0	0	0	0	0	0	1	0	0	0	.000	.000
Weibl, Clint, Ark.	.000	10	9	7	0	0	0	0	0	0	0	2	0	0	0	0	2	0	0	1	.000	.000
Wesson, Barry, R.R.	.236	39	122	110	12	26	37	1	2	2	15	0	2	0	10	0	32	6	2	2	.336	.295
White, Walt, E.P.	.285	53	181	158	20	45	59	9	1	1	19	4	1	3	15	1	37	3	2	3	.373	.356
Williams, Matt, E.P.	.462	5	15	13	3	6	8	2	0	0	1	0	0	0	2	0	1	0	0	0	.615	.533

Player, Team	Avg.	G	TPA	AB	R	H	TB	2B	3B	HR	RBI	SH	SF	HP	BB	IBB	SO	SB	CS	GDP	Slg.	OBP
Willis, Dave, Wich.	.219	87	338	302	37	66	108	17	2	7	37	3	4	5	24	1	55	8	7	10	.358	.284
Wilson, Jack, Ark.	.294	88	391	343	65	101	155	20	8	6	34	5	2	5	36	0	59	2	3	5	.452	.368
Woolf, Jason, Ark.†	.236	45	186	165	22	39	60	8	2	3	13	1	0	4	16	3	40	7	8	2	.364	.319
Wright, Corey, Tul.*	.188	17	76	69	6	13	13	0	0	0	3	1	0	1	5	0	20	1	1	1	.188	.253
Young, Mike, Tul.	.319	43	212	188	30	60	86	13	5	1	32	3	4	0	17	1	28	9	3	4	.457	.368
Young, Travis, Shre.	.249	97	373	334	41	83	123	14	4	6	31	2	4	7	25	0	65	14	7	8	.368	.311
Zamarripa, Mark, E.P.	.250	12	4	4	0	1	1	0	0	0	0	0	0	0	0	0	1	0	0	0	.250	.250
Zerbe, Chad, Shre.*	.500	9	6	6	0	3	4	1	0	0	2	0	0	0	0	0	1	0	0	0	.667	.500
Zuniga, Tony, Shre.	.260	125	466	407	54	106	181	24	0	17	62	3	4	3	49	2	50	3	4	12	.445	.341
Zywica, Mike, Tul.	.421	5	22	19	7	8	12	1	0	1	8	0	0	1	2	0	2	0	0	0	.632	.500

GRAND SLAMS: Pena 3; Bates, Bowles, Cole, 2 each; Bautista, Bevins, Caruso, Cust, Garrick, Ginter, Glendenning, Grabowski, Hart, Lane, Matranga, McNeal, Monroe, Ortega, Ortiz, Otero, Ransom, Ross, 1 each.

AWARDED FIRST BASE ON CATCHER'S INTERFERENCE: Perez 4 (Brito, Garrick, J. Jones, Newstrom), Pecci (Rose), T. Young (Garrick).

PLAYERS WITH TWO OR MORE TEAMS

Player, Team	Avg.	G	TPA	AB	R	H	TB	2B	3B	HR	RBI	SH	SF	HP	BB	IBB	SO	SB	CS	GDP	Slg.	OBP
Dallimore, Brian, R.R.	.182	5	12	11	1	2	6	1	0	1	3	0	0	0	1	0	3	0	0	0	.545	.250
Dallimore, Brian, E.P.	.278	107	395	356	50	99	129	16	1	4	53	3	5	6	25	3	55	17	3	13	.362	.332
Morillo, Cesar, E.P.†	.190	10	21	21	0	4	5	1	0	0	1	0	0	0	0	0	6	0	0	0	.238	.190
Morillo, Cesar, R.R.†	.295	88	313	281	43	83	107	15	0	3	37	0	2	5	25	4	56	9	7	5	.381	.361

2000 PITCHING

TEAM

Team	W	L	Pct.	ERA	G	CG	ShO	Sv.	IP	H	TBF	R	ER	HR	SH	SF	HB	BB	IBB	SO	WP	Bk.
Shreveport	58	81	.417	3.94	139	3	8	27	1212.2	1264	5279	631	531	110	61	49	41	466	44	931	41	12
Round Rock	83	57	.593	4.11	140	5	11	38	1245.1	1224	5414	671	569	130	55	40	48	546	19	1003	56	4
Wichita	76	61	.555	4.22	137	3	4	40	1204.2	1229	5237	661	565	134	35	30	64	505	32	905	66	11
San Antonio	64	76	.457	4.39	140	4	9	29	1231.1	1264	5431	707	601	108	62	48	81	552	21	1007	52	5
El Paso	74	66	.529	4.54	141	1	3	42	1242.2	1371	5525	740	627	100	50	37	83	498	16	1018	67	7
Midland	70	69	.504	4.60	139	1	7	40	1243.2	1307	5566	766	636	110	36	40	61	531	28	981	76	5
Arkansas	68	71	.489	4.72	139	6	9	40	1196.1	1240	5283	723	627	131	52	47	56	538	35	904	62	7
Tulsa	64	76	.457	4.86	141	1	9	33	1238.0	1335	5610	804	668	124	35	55	62	613	11	928	91	3

INDIVIDUAL

TOP QUALIFIERS FOR EARNED-RUN AVERAGE TITLE

Minimum 112 innings.*Lefthanded pitcher.

Pitcher, Team	W	L	Pct.	ERA	G	GS	CG	ShO	GF	Sv.	IP	H	TBF	R	ER	HR	SH	SF	HB	BB	IBB	SO	WP	Bk.
Oswalt, Roy, R.R.	11	4	.733	1.94	19	18	2	2	0	0	129.2	106	521	37	28	5	4	2	3	22	1	141	4	1
Prokopec, Luke, S.A.	7	3	.700	2.45	22	22	1	0	0	0	128.2	118	524	40	35	8	4	3	7	23	1	124	0	0
Lundberg, Spike, Tul.	14	7	.667	3.05	40	13	0	0	16	4	150.2	148	637	61	51	9	5	5	8	54	4	102	5	1
Corps, Edwin, Shre.	5	6	.455	3.12	36	14	1	0	7	0	112.1	120	480	47	39	10	5	2	0	34	3	63	3	0
Ainsworth, Kurt, Shre.	10	9	.526	3.30	28	28	0	0	0	0	158.0	138	667	67	58	12	4	5	3	63	3	130	7	1
Ireland, Eric, R.R.	11	9	.550	3.41	29	29	2	2	0	0	179.2	171	754	84	68	14	7	4	5	64	0	123	12	0
Calero, Enrique, Wich.	10	7	.588	3.63	28	25	0	0	0	0	153.2	141	648	74	62	16	7	3	10	66	2	130	7	1
Sedlacek, Shawn, Wich.	15	6	.714	3.66	35	16	1	0	11	3	140.1	153	612	69	57	6	5	2	12	43	4	81	8	2
Mayo, Blake, E.P.	8	3	.727	4.09	38	17	0	0	1	0	136.1	157	617	73	62	5	8	4	8	57	1	120	11	0
Vogelsong, Ryan, Shre.	6	10	.375	4.23	27	27	1	0	0	0	155.1	153	682	82	73	15	5	7	13	69	2	147	5	4
Manwiller, Tim, Mid.	4	5	.444	4.41	25	19	0	0	1	0	114.1	122	495	65	56	16	5	3	7	36	0	80	3	0
Davis, Allen, S.A.*	10	8	.556	4.53	29	26	3	1	0	0	163.0	187	706	91	82	18	6	6	6	51	0	123	1	0
Wagner, Denny, Mid.	7	9	.438	4.55	29	29	1	0	0	0	180.0	209	793	100	91	13	4	4	10	63	2	109	11	0
Cook, Derrick, Tul.	5	8	.385	4.59	21	20	0	0	0	0	113.2	111	498	71	58	12	0	3	8	54	1	72	8	0
Shearn, Tom, R.R.	9	6	.600	4.69	25	23	0	0	0	0	136.1	134	602	79	71	14	4	5	8	67	1	102	7	0

DEPARTMENTAL LEADERS: W—Sedlacek, 15; L—Gregg, 14; Pct.—R. Smith, .923; G—Snow, Oropesa, 59 each; GS—Ireland, Wagner, 29 each; CG—R. Smith, A. Davis, 3 each; ShO—R. Smith, 3; GF—Snow, 53; Sv.—Snow, 27; IP—Wagner, 180; H—Wagner, 209; TBF—Wagner, 793; R—Gregg, 120; ER—Gregg, 100; HR—Guerrero, 25; SH—Mayo, Bevel, Montgomery, 8 each; SF—Poeck, 9; HB—Vogelsong, 13; BB—Elder, 88; IBB—Lamber, 10; SO—Vogelsong, 147; WP—Scott, 15; BK—Vogelsong, 4.

ALL PITCHERS

*Lefthanded pitcher.

Pitcher, Team	W	L	Pct.	ERA	G	GS	CG	ShO	GF	Sv.	IP	H	TBF	R	ER	HR	SH	SF	HB	BB	IBB	SO	WP	Bk.
Ainsworth, Kurt, Shre.	10	9	.526	3.30	28	28	0	0	0	0	158.0	138	667	67	58	12	4	5	3	63	3	130	7	1
Alston, Garvin, Wich.	3	2	.600	6.46	18	0	0	0	10	0	30.2	30	137	23	22	5	1	0	5	9	3	24	3	0
Alvarez, Victor, S.A.*	0	3	.000	3.91	11	8	0	0	0	0	48.1	44	218	27	21	3	5	3	7	30	1	43	0	0
Ambrose, John, Ark.	3	4	.429	4.22	45	0	0	0	28	15	49.0	48	226	31	23	3	2	1	3	32	3	49	8	0
Anderson, Jason, Mid.*	4	0	.000	4.83	28	0	0	0	9	1	41.0	47	192	36	22	3	1	4	1	20	3	17	3	0
Andra, Jeff, Shre.*	6	6	.500	3.84	17	17	0	0	0	0	91.1	106	403	51	39	6	7	5	1	35	2	64	1	0
Andrews, Jeff, E.P.	3	4	.429	7.57	21	8	0	0	4	0	60.2	88	292	54	51	12	2	4	3	30	0	35	3	1
Austin, Jeff, Wich.	2	2	.500	2.93	6	6	1	0	0	0	43.0	33	168	16	14	3	0	2	5	4	0	31	2	0
Avrard, Corey, Ark.	0	6	.000	5.45	57	0	0	0	33	14	71.0	64	323	46	43	10	5	6	1	53	4	57	10	0
Baez, Benito, Mid.*	5	4	.556	4.89	37	0	0	0	9	0	53.1	61	246	35	29	4	1	1	1	27	3	50	4	0
Baker, Jason, Wich.	4	5	.444	6.26	17	12	0	0	1	0	69.0	87	323	50	48	8	1	2	6	35	0	49	6	0
Benes, Adam, Ark.	2	5	.286	4.32	26	10	0	0	4	0	83.1	93	355	43	40	8	5	5	1	20	5	55	3	0
Benoit, Joaquin, Tul.	4	4	.500	3.83	16	16	0	0	0	0	82.1	73	346	40	35	6	0	4	4	30	0	72	6	0
Bevel, Bobby, S.A.*	5	4	.556	5.63	47	1	0	0	19	2	78.1	86	365	52	49	8	8	0	6	44	5	75	7	0
Bierbrodt, Nick, E.P.*	1	3	.250	7.13	7	7	0	0	0	0	35.1	37	166	30	28	1	2	1	3	24	0	36	5	0
Bluma, Jaime, Wich.	0	0	.000	18.00	2	0	0	0	2	0	2.0	3	12	4	4	0	0	0	0	3	0	2	0	0

Pitcher, Team	W	L	Pct.	ERA	G	GS	CG	ShO	GF	Sv.	IP	H	TBF	R	ER	HR	SH	SF	HB	BB	IBB	SO	WP	Bk.
Braswell, Bryan, R.R.*	5	4	.556	5.05	19	10	1	0	1	0	71.1	78	309	48	40	13	4	2	0	22	1	38	2	1
Brink, Jim, Mid.	0	0	.000	7.71	6	0	0	0	3	0	9.1	13	44	8	8	2	0	1	0	5	1	5	1	0
Brunette, Justin, Ark.*	0	0	.000	3.00	3	0	0	0	1	0	3.0	5	13	4	1	1	0	0	0	0	0	1	0	0
Burnside, Adrian, S.A.*	6	5	.545	2.90	17	17	0	0	0	0	93.0	73	400	40	30	6	7	4	7	55	3	82	3	0
Byrdak, Tim, Wich.*	0	0	.000	5.40	4	0	0	0	1	0	6.2	9	29	4	4	1	0	0	0	3	0	1	0	0
Calero, Enrique, Wich.	10	7	.588	3.63	28	25	0	0	0	0	153.2	141	648	74	62	16	7	3	10	66	2	130	7	1
Camp, Jared, Tul.	0	0	.000	0.00	7	0	0	0	3	1	10.0	10	48	6	0	1	1	0	1	7	0	4	2	0
Cervantes, Chris, E.P.*	7	5	.583	4.36	16	15	0	0	0	0	95.0	108	411	50	46	13	5	1	7	21	0	72	3	2
Clemons, Chris, E.P.	2	2	.000	15.26	2	2	0	0	0	0	7.2	19	40	13	13	0	0	0	3	6	0	5	0	0
Cogan, Tony, Wich.*	1	1	.500	11.57	2	0	0	0	1	0	2.1	6	15	4	3	0	1	0	0	2	1	1	0	0
Colome, Jesus, Mid.	9	4	.692	3.59	20	20	0	0	0	0	110.1	99	478	62	44	10	4	4	5	50	0	95	6	1
Coogan, Patrick, Ark.	9	13	.409	5.10	27	26	1	0	1	0	150.0	164	661	96	85	21	6	6	9	62	0	79	7	1
Cook, Derrick, Tul.	5	8	.385	4.59	21	20	0	0	0	0	113.2	111	498	71	58	12	0	3	8	54	1	72	8	0
Corps, Edwin, Shre.	5	6	.455	3.12	36	14	1	0	7	0	112.1	120	480	47	39	10	5	2	0	34	3	63	3	0
Cox, Ryan, Shre.	2	2	.500	8.10	7	7	0	0	0	0	33.1	53	158	35	30	5	0	1	3	5	0	24	0	0
Crafton, Kevin, Ark.	9	5	.643	2.55	57	0	0	0	28	4	70.2	69	302	24	20	5	4	4	2	28	4	48	1	0
Creek, Ryan, E.P.	0	0	.000	0.00	2	1	0	0	0	0	5.0	2	19	0	0	0	0	0	1	2	0	5	0	0
Crowell, Jim, Ark.*	1	1	.500	5.40	12	0	0	0	6	1	15.0	16	68	10	9	1	1	0	1	8	1	10	0	0
Curtis, Chris, E.P.	0	4	.000	7.20	5	5	0	0	0	0	25.0	40	120	22	20	5	1	0	1	9	0	20	1	0
Dace, Derek, E.P.*	2	2	.500	3.51	28	0	0	0	12	0	33.1	28	139	15	13	1	3	1	1	19	3	25	1	0
Davis, Adam, S.A.*	10	8	.556	4.53	29	26	3	1	0	0	163.0	187	706	91	82	18	6	6	6	51	0	123	1	0
Davis, Clint, E.P.	0	1	.000	0.87	11	0	0	0	7	1	10.1	6	43	2	1	0	1	0	6	6	0	16	0	0
Dorame, Randey, S.A.*	3	4	.429	3.86	9	9	0	0	0	0	58.1	53	238	29	25	5	3	3	1	18	0	28	2	1
Dubose, Eric, Mid.*	5	1	.833	4.13	18	0	0	0	1	0	28.1	25	131	16	13	1	0	3	18	2	0	20	2	0
Duncan, Sean, Tul.*	3	5	.375	4.63	46	0	0	0	23	2	79.2	69	368	56	41	10	3	2	3	60	2	57	8	0
Eckelman, Alex, Ark.	0	0	.000	0.00	2	0	0	0	2	0	1.0	1	4	0	0	0	1	0	0	0	0	1	0	0
Edsell, Geoff, S.A.	5	5	.500	4.45	25	10	0	0	4	1	83.0	84	365	50	41	9	1	1	5	33	2	74	3	0
Elarton, Scott, R.R.	1	0	1.000	2.84	1	1	0	0	0	0	6.1	7	26	2	2	1	1	0	0	0	0	7	0	0
Elder, David, Tul.	7	6	.538	4.94	33	21	0	0	8	3	116.2	121	554	80	64	9	4	4	4	88	0	104	11	0
Estrella, Luis, Shre.	1	4	.200	2.75	21	6	0	0	7	1	59.0	51	237	24	18	2	6	1	1	22	3	31	5	0
Everly, Bill, S.A.	2	0	1.000	6.14	11	0	0	0	7	2	14.2	16	68	12	10	0	1	1	1	7	1	4	0	0
Feliciano, Pedro, S.A.*	0	0	.000	1.93	9	0	0	0	3	2	9.1	7	37	2	2	0	1	0	1	4	1	11	0	2
Flores, Ignacio, S.A.	0	0	.000	2.57	3	0	0	0	1	1	7.0	5	30	2	2	0	1	0	6	0	7	2	0	0
Franks, Lance, Ark.	6	4	.600	5.16	43	7	0	0	5	0	89.0	90	396	59	51	16	5	3	44	4	56	3	1	0
Freehill, Mike, Tul.	0	3	.000	5.56	26	0	0	0	14	1	45.1	52	215	30	28	5	3	2	7	26	1	31	7	0
Fuller, Jody, E.P.	0	0	.000	4.84	8	1	0	0	3	0	22.1	24	89	12	12	1	0	3	1	5	0	10	1	0
Gajkowski, Steve, Mid.	1	1	.500	4.50	10	0	0	0	7	1	16.0	13	68	11	8	2	0	2	0	6	1	18	0	0
Galvez, Randy, S.A.	4	4	.500	5.12	12	12	0	0	0	0	63.1	74	281	40	36	5	1	1	4	30	0	35	3	0
Garcia, Apostol, S.A.	1	3	.250	7.34	18	4	0	0	6	0	34.1	49	171	39	28	4	3	3	3	23	1	22	4	0
Garrett, Hal, S.A.	1	6	.143	6.27	21	5	0	0	6	0	47.1	57	236	39	33	3	2	1	5	40	1	32	5	1
George, Chris, Wich.*	8	5	.615	3.14	18	18	0	0	0	0	97.1	92	429	41	34	5	3	6	6	51	1	80	2	2
Glick, Dave, R.R.*	2	2	.500	5.45	32	0	0	0	18	0	33.0	40	163	23	20	2	3	0	4	27	0	21	2	0
Gooding, Jason, Wich.*	6	3	.667	4.00	29	6	0	0	7	2	81.0	97	348	47	36	12	3	0	1	26	2	46	2	0
Goodrich, Randy, Shre.	4	5	.444	3.72	51	1	0	0	25	12	75.0	90	331	36	31	10	7	1	0	17	4	48	2	1
Green, Jason, R.R.	8	2	.800	1.98	31	0	0	0	29	15	41.0	38	169	10	9	0	0	0	11	3	54	1	0	0
Gregg, Kevin, Mid.	5	14	.263	6.40	28	27	0	0	0	0	140.2	171	655	120	100	18	5	6	8	73	0	97	6	0
Guerrero, Junior, Wich.	4	10	.286	4.13	28	24	0	0	2	0	131.0	153	603	93	83	25	1	6	3	69	2	79	8	3
Guzman, Geraldo, E.P.	3	3	.500	3.75	17	7	0	0	5	3	50.1	47	220	23	21	2	3	3	22	2	53	3	0	0
Guzman, Leiby, Tul.	7	9	.438	5.70	24	20	0	0	2	0	115.1	143	544	86	73	15	1	4	8	58	1	84	4	0
Herbert, Russ, R.R.	4	2	.667	4.23	38	3	0	0	6	2	87.1	84	374	45	41	10	2	4	4	48	0	83	4	0
Hernandez, Fernando, R.R.	4	1	.800	3.30	15	0	0	0	6	2	30.0	19	123	12	11	1	2	2	1	15	2	43	3	0
Hillman, Eric, R.R.*	1	0	1.000	0.00	1	1	0	0	0	0	5.0	3	20	0	0	0	0	0	0	2	0	4	0	0
Horgan, Joe, Shre.*	0	0	.000	3.38	1	0	0	0	1	0	5.1	2	20	2	2	0	0	0	0	2	1	3	0	0
Huff, Larry, Wich.	0	0	.000	0.00	1	0	0	0	1	0	1.0	0	4	0	0	0	0	0	0	1	0	0	0	0
Husted, Brent, S.A.	4	9	.308	4.09	52	0	0	0	26	3	70.1	64	300	37	32	7	5	3	4	22	2	48	0	0
Hutchinson, Chad, Ark.	2	3	.400	3.38	11	11	1	1	0	0	48.0	40	206	21	18	1	0	1	2	27	0	54	2	0
Hutton, Mark, R.R.	0	0	.000	7.71	3	0	0	0	1	0	4.2	6	24	4	4	1	0	1	1	3	0	4	0	0
Ireland, Eric, R.R.	11	9	.550	3.41	29	29	2	2	0	0	179.2	171	754	84	68	14	7	4	5	64	0	123	12	0
Jacob, Russell, E.P.	1	0	1.000	1.86	7	1	0	0	1	0	9.2	10	40	2	2	0	1	0	0	3	0	4	0	0
Jerue, Tristan, Ark.	0	0	.000	8.44	4	4	0	0	0	0	10.2	14	60	13	10	2	6	1	1	16	0	5	1	0
Jones, Marcus, Mid.	2	0	1.000	2.74	5	5	0	0	0	0	23.0	24	92	8	7	0	2	1	0	1	0	12	0	1
Joseph, Kevin, Shre.	3	11	.214	5.17	27	16	0	0	8	1	102.2	116	454	60	59	8	5	7	5	48	1	71	4	0
Karnuth, Jason, Ark.	2	3	.400	3.75	8	8	1	0	0	0	50.1	59	220	30	21	3	1	2	1	14	0	31	5	1
Kaufman, Brad, R.R.	0	3	.000	4.09	6	0	0	0	1	0	11.0	13	49	7	5	3	1	0	1	5	0	7	0	0
Kessel, Kyle, R.R.*	6	5	.545	4.88	14	13	0	0	0	0	72.0	68	320	45	39	12	4	1	4	48	1	43	0	0
Kimball, Andrew, Mid.	3	4	.429	7.42	29	0	0	0	11	2	47.1	60	223	42	39	9	1	1	6	20	0	38	2	0
Knoll, Brian, Shre.	7	5	.583	3.39	21	10	1	0	5	3	79.2	80	346	34	30	8	4	7	4	26	2	62	0	0
Koplove, Mike, R.R.	4	3	.571	3.88	35	0	0	0	16	6	46.1	38	197	28	20	2	0	2	7	19	1	47	1	1
Lamber, Justin, Wich.*	5	3	.625	6.55	43	0	0	0	19	2	68.2	85	327	54	50	8	5	2	2	58	10	43	6	1
Lambert, Jeremy, Ark.	0	2	.000	3.83	39	0	0	0	5	3	47.0	41	207	27	20	1	2	1	1	28	7	63	0	0
Lane, Ryan, Tul.	0	0	.000	0.00	1	0	0	0	1	0	1.0	1	4	0	0	0	0	0	0	0	0	3	0	0
Lanfranco, Otoniel, Ark.	9	6	.600	5.04	33	18	0	0	4	0	119.2	123	527	75	67	17	3	5	6	52	0	70	3	1
Lundberg, Spike, Tul.	14	7	.667	3.05	40	13	0	0	16	4	150.2	148	637	61	51	9	5	5	8	54	4	102	5	1
MacDougal, Mike, Wich.	0	1	.000	7.71	2	2	0	0	0	0	11.2	16	54	10	10	0	0	1	1	7	0	9	1	0
Malerich, Will, Shre.*	0	1	.000	17.36	4	0	0	0	3	0	4.2	12	30	9	9	2	0	0	1	3	0	4	0	0
Manwiller, Tim, Mid.	4	5	.444	4.41	25	19	0	0	1	0	114.1	122	495	65	56	16	3	3	7	36	0	80	3	0
Martines, Jason, E.P.	9	1	.900	2.81	55	0	0	0	20	2	86.1	72	356	32	27	3	2	6	4	27	3	77	0	0
Martinez, Jose, Tul.	5	6	.455	3.14	18	13	1	1	1	0	103.1	97	431	44	36	7	6	2	0	21	0	79	10	0
Marval, Raul, Shre.	0	0	.000	0.00	1	0	0	0	0	0	1.0	0	3	0	0	0	0	0	0	0	0	0	0	0
Maurer, Mike, Mid.	0	0	.000	6.28	12	0	0	0	4	2	14.1	16	70	11	10	1	0	0	12	1	17	1	0	0
Mayo, Blake, E.P.	8	3	.727	4.09	38	17	0	0	1	0	136.1	157	617	73	62	5	8	4	8	57	1	120	11	0
McCutcheon, Mike, E.P.*	4	1	.800	3.98	30	0	0	0	13	0	40.2	40	173	21	18	2	1	0	2	13	0	32	6	0
McKnight, Tony, R.R.	0	2	.000	4.78	6	6	0	0	0	0	32.0	39	141	19	17	4	0	1	1	10	1	24	1	0

Pitcher, Team	W	L	Pct.	ERA	G	GS	CG	ShO	GF	Sv.	IP	H	TBF	R	ER	HR	SH	SF	HB	BB	IBB	SO	WP	Bk.
Messman, Joe, Shre.	5	2	.714	3.41	38	0	0	0	11	1	60.2	51	248	27	23	7	2	4	0	23	2	46	8	1
Miller, Benji, Shre.	4	9	.308	3.35	58	0	0	0	29	4	86.0	81	372	44	32	10	6	2	2	37	7	71	3	3
Miller, Greg, R.R.*	0	0	.000	0.00	2	0	0	0	0	0	2.1	0	8	0	0	0	0	0	1	0	2	0	0
Miller, Justin, Mid.	5	4	.556	4.55	18	18	0	0	0	0	87.0	74	371	49	44	8	2	0	6	41	1	82	9	1
Miller, Matt, Tul.	0	0	.000	14.73	3	0	0	0	0	0	3.2	7	22	7	6	0	0	1	0	4	0	4	1	0
Montgomery, Matt, S.A.	5	5	.500	3.94	41	4	0	0	19	5	89.0	98	402	55	39	5	8	5	5	37	0	82	5	0
Moreno, Juan, Tul.*	0	0	.000	5.40	5	0	0	0	3	1	6.2	6	30	4	4	0	0	1	0	5	0	12	1	0
Morris, Matt, Ark.	0	0	.000	6.43	2	2	0	0	0	0	7.0	8	31	5	5	0	0	0	0	4	0	7	0	0
Morrison, Robbie, Wich.	3	3	.500	3.38	34	1	0	0	18	5	61.1	58	263	30	23	6	2	0	0	29	3	49	5	0
Mullen, Scott, Wich.*	3	2	.600	3.19	33	1	0	0	16	7	73.1	65	299	27	26	5	3	1	1	26	1	61	3	0
Munoz, Juan, Ark.*	0	0	.000	9.00	1	0	0	0	1	0	1.0	1	4	1	1	1	0	0	0	0	0	2	0	0
Navarro, Jason, Ark.*	2	2	.500	5.71	33	0	0	0	8	2	34.2	36	154	25	22	2	1	3	5	18	2	35	2	0
Navarro, Scott, R.R.*	4	4	.500	5.29	22	7	0	0	5	0	64.2	76	293	49	38	9	2	1	2	23	0	30	0	1
Newstrom, Doug, E.P.	0	0	.000	0.00	1	0	0	0	1	0	0.2	1	3	0	0	0	0	0	0	0	0	0	0	0
Niebla, Ruben, S.A.*	1	0	1.000	2.40	10	0	0	0	5	0	15.0	13	59	5	4	2	0	0	0	4	0	10	0	0
Niles, Randy, Mid.	5	0	1.000	5.31	38	1	0	0	11	1	76.1	87	346	52	45	6	0	3	5	35	1	45	7	0
Noriega, Ray, Mid.*	3	0	1.000	3.71	21	0	0	0	7	1	26.2	21	113	13	11	1	1	2	2	11	0	17	0	1
Norris, Ben, E.P.*	4	1	.800	2.20	7	7	1	0	0	0	45.0	41	192	14	11	1	2	0	3	18	1	24	1	0
Nunez, Maximo, S.A.	2	6	.250	6.65	38	2	0	0	10	1	65.0	79	319	57	48	8	2	5	8	43	1	59	7	0
Oliver, Darren, Tul.*	0	1	.000	11.57	1	1	0	0	0	0	4.2	10	27	7	6	0	0	1	0	2	0	5	1	0
Oropesa, Eddie, Shre.*	4	4	.333	3.07	59	2	0	0	23	4	76.1	70	341	38	26	6	3	1	3	40	6	76	3	2
Oswalt, Roy, R.R.	11	4	.733	1.94	19	18	2	2	0	0	129.2	106	521	37	28	5	4	2	3	22	1	141	4	1
Ozias, Todd, Shre.	0	0	.000	9.00	1	0	0	0	0	0	2.0	5	12	2	2	1	0	0	0	1	0	1	0	0
Pamus, Javier, Wich.	0	0	.000	1.80	3	0	0	0	1	0	5.0	5	19	1	1	0	0	0	1	0	1	0	0
Pearce, Josh, Ark.	5	6	.455	5.46	17	17	0	0	0	0	97.1	117	441	68	59	13	6	2	6	35	2	63	5	1
Pearsall, J.J., Tul.*	4	0	1.000	3.32	28	0	0	0	10	3	43.1	40	197	22	16	3	4	0	6	20	1	37	1	0
Persails, Mark, R.R.	3	2	.600	6.32	50	2	0	0	16	3	78.1	101	375	64	55	10	7	3	4	41	4	63	8	0
Pina, Rafael, E.P.	3	3	.500	3.93	12	11	0	0	0	0	71.0	82	318	40	31	6	3	1	4	21	0	65	3	1
Poeck, Chad, Tul.	2	3	.400	4.22	46	1	0	0	29	10	79.0	87	349	46	37	6	3	9	3	34	0	65	4	0
Poland, Trey, Tul.*	6	8	.429	6.66	30	14	0	0	4	0	98.2	115	449	85	73	12	1	7	2	46	0	67	9	0
Powell, Jay, R.R.	0	0	.000	0.00	1	1	0	0	0	0	2.0	0	6	0	0	0	0	0	0	1	0	1	0	0
Pratt, Andy, Tul.*	1	6	.143	7.22	11	11	0	0	0	0	52.1	66	255	48	42	7	0	2	2	33	0	42	5	1
Prinz, Bret, E.P.	9	1	.900	3.56	53	0	0	0	42	26	60.2	71	265	24	24	6	1	1	5	16	3	69	3	0
Prokopec, Luke, S.A.	7	3	.700	2.45	22	22	1	0	0	0	128.2	118	524	40	35	8	4	3	7	23	1	124	0	1
Ramirez, Erasmo, Shre.*	0	5	.000	6.44	39	2	0	0	13	1	58.2	80	269	45	42	7	6	4	3	21	5	46	0	0
Ramos, Mario, Mid.*	2	0	1.000	1.32	4	4	0	0	0	0	27.1	24	107	6	4	0	1	1	0	6	0	19	0	0
Reames, Britt, Ark.	2	3	.400	6.13	8	8	0	0	0	0	39.2	46	178	28	27	4	0	0	2	18	0	39	1	0
Redding, Tim, R.R.	2	0	1.000	3.46	5	5	0	0	0	0	26.0	14	111	12	10	4	2	2	1	22	0	22	4	0
Regalado, Maximo, S.A.	1	2	.333	3.09	26	0	0	0	22	9	23.1	22	103	8	8	1	0	0	0	15	0	27	2	0
Revenig, Todd, E.P.	2	4	.333	6.27	12	11	0	0	0	0	60.1	90	276	50	42	7	3	3	6	14	0	50	0	1
Robertson, Jeriome, R.R.*	2	2	.500	4.13	11	10	0	0	1	0	61.0	62	265	36	28	8	3	1	2	18	1	30	4	1
Rodriguez, Jose, Ark.*	1	0	1.000	2.45	10	0	0	0	2	1	11.0	7	47	3	3	0	2	0	0	4	2	8	0	0
Rodriguez, Wilfredo, R.R.*	2	4	.333	5.77	11	11	0	0	0	0	57.2	54	275	42	37	10	4	6	1	52	0	55	2	0
Sanchez, Martin, E.P.	7	6	.538	4.96	28	19	0	0	3	1	110.2	112	484	70	61	15	0	6	3	42	0	88	4	1
Scott, Brian, E.P.	3	8	.273	6.71	16	14	0	0	1	0	61.2	73	303	55	46	6	4	0	6	46	0	43	15	0
Sedlacek, Shawn, Wich.	15	6	.714	3.66	35	16	1	0	11	3	140.1	153	612	69	57	10	5	2	12	43	4	81	8	2
Sessions, Doug, R.R.	6	4	.600	3.39	56	0	0	0	34	10	82.1	78	351	35	31	7	5	2	1	37	4	80	1	0
Shearn, Tom, R.R.	9	6	.600	4.69	25	23	0	0	0	0	136.1	134	602	79	71	14	4	5	8	67	1	102	7	0
Sheredy, Kevin, Ark.	0	2	.000	14.18	21	0	0	0	4	0	26.2	42	154	45	42	7	1	1	6	29	0	12	5	2
Simon, Ben, S.A.	8	8	.500	4.49	29	16	0	0	5	2	108.1	102	460	58	54	15	5	2	8	44	2	91	4	1
Smith, Bud, Ark.*	12	1	.923	2.32	18	18	3	3	0	0	108.0	93	439	32	28	5	2	3	4	27	1	102	5	0
Smith, Cam, S.A.	0	0	.000	7.63	7	1	0	0	3	1	15.1	13	74	13	13	0	0	2	2	15	0	16	3	0
Snow, Bert, Mid.	1	7	.125	3.59	59	0	0	0	53	27	67.2	58	297	33	27	6	4	4	2	36	6	98	12	0
Sodowsky, Clint, Tul.	0	0	.000	4.82	6	0	0	0	3	0	9.1	6	41	6	5	0	1	0	0	6	0	8	0	1
Sonnier, Shawn, Wich.	0	3	.000	2.25	48	0	0	0	42	21	64.0	41	260	22	16	6	0	0	3	26	3	90	4	0
Stechschulte, Gene, Ark.	0	0	.000	0.00	2	0	0	0	1	0	2.0	0	8	0	0	0	0	0	1	0	0	3	0	0
Stein, Blake, Wich.	1	0	1.000	6.23	2	2	0	0	0	0	8.2	10	37	6	6	2	0	0	1	0	12	1	0
Stephenson, Brian, S.A.	1	0	1.000	4.96	4	3	0	0	1	0	16.1	19	73	11	9	1	0	4	0	8	0	14	1	0
Theodorou, Nick, Ark.	0	0	.000	0.00	1	0	0	0	0	0	0.0	1	2	0	0	0	0	0	1	0	0	0	0	0
Thompson, Eric, Mid.	6	6	.500	3.91	18	15	0	0	1	1	101.1	107	425	52	44	5	2	1	0	23	0	79	0	1
Thompson, Justin, Tul.*	1	0	1.000	4.76	1	1	0	0	0	0	5.2	8	25	3	3	1	0	0	1	0	4	0	0
Thompson, Mark, Ark.	0	0	.000	4.91	1	1	0	0	0	0	3.2	6	16	2	2	0	0	0	0	0	0	3	0	0
Thorn, Todd, E.P.*	3	8	.273	5.03	23	10	0	0	4	2	87.2	113	410	63	49	4	6	3	10	32	1	65	5	0
Thurman, Corey, Wich.	4	5	.444	4.83	9	9	0	0	0	0	50.1	46	222	34	27	10	2	1	3	24	0	47	4	1
Trejo, Francisco, E.P.*	0	0	.000	1.80	2	1	0	0	0	0	5.0	2	21	2	1	1	0	0	0	5	0	4	0	0
Tuttle, Dave, E.P.	0	0	.000	2.48	21	0	0	0	5	1	36.1	30	152	15	10	1	0	0	0	19	0	31	0	0
Vasquez, Leo, Mid.*	6	5	.545	2.72	36	1	0	0	13	4	53.0	48	239	21	16	3	1	0	5	33	4	59	7	0
Verdugo, Jason, Shre.	0	1	.000	3.18	5	0	0	0	3	0	5.2	8	28	6	2	0	1	0	2	4	0	4	0	0
Vogelsong, Ryan, Shre.	10	6	.375	4.23	27	27	1	0	0	0	155.1	153	682	82	73	15	5	7	13	69	2	147	5	4
Wade, Travis, R.R.	2	1	.667	4.26	23	0	0	0	17	6	31.2	33	135	18	15	2	0	3	5	7	0	26	1	0
Wagner, Denny, Mid.	7	9	.438	4.55	29	29	1	0	0	0	180.0	209	793	106	91	13	4	4	10	63	2	109	11	0
Webb, Alan, Tul.*	4	0	.000	11.72	10	6	0	0	3	0	25.1	35	131	33	33	9	2	1	1	24	0	17	4	0
Weibl, Clint, Ark.	3	3	.500	4.74	10	9	0	0	0	0	57.0	57	243	35	30	10	0	2	1	19	0	51	1	0
Wells, Matt, Shre.	1	0	1.000	7.71	4	0	0	0	0	0	7.0	11	42	11	6	0	0	1	9	3	6	0	0
Willis, Dave, Wich.	0	0	.000	0.00	1	0	0	0	0	0	1.0	0	3	0	0	0	0	0	0	0	0	0	0	0
Wilson, Kris, Wich.	7	3	.700	3.51	21	15	1	0	1	0	102.2	99	425	52	40	12	1	4	6	21	0	69	4	1
Woodman, Hank, Tul.	5	6	.455	5.72	42	4	0	0	20	8	91.1	130	439	69	58	12	3	6	5	40	1	60	4	0
Yates, Tyler, Mid.	1	1	.500	6.53	8	7	0	0	0	0	26.1	28	121	20	18	2	2	0	15	3	24	2	0
Zamarripa, Mark, E.P.	1	3	.250	4.35	12	4	0	0	2	0	39.1	40	179	30	19	6	2	1	5	25	1	22	1	1
Zerbe, Chad, Shre.*	2	1	.667	2.33	9	0	0	0	5	0	38.2	37	156	11	10	1	1	1	1	9	0	34	0	0

COMBINATION SHUTOUTS: **Arkansas (5)**—Lanfranco-Rodriguez-Avrard, Franks-Crafton-Avrard, Coogan-Lambert-Crafton-Ambrose, Lanfranco-Lambert-Crafton-Ambrose, Hutchinson-Franks-Navarro. **El Paso (3)**—Guzman-Sanchez, Mayo-Koplove-Prinz, Cervantes-Koplove-McCutcheon-Fuller. **Midland (7)**—Wagner-Baez-

Maurer, Manwiller-Gajkowski, Miller-Niles-Brink, Wagner-Maurer, Manwiller-Thompson, Manwiller-Baez-Niles-Snow, Thompson-Vasquez. **Round Rock (7)**—Braswell-Hutton-Green, Shearn-Persails, Navarro-Hernandez, Shearn-Sessions, Oswalt-Sessions, Shearn-Wade-Persails, Ireland-Wade. **San Antonio (8)**—Simon-Garcia-Husted, Galvez-Smith, Simon-Husted, Prokopec-Husted, Prokopec-Edsell-Husted, Prokopec-Edsell, Prokopec-Edsell-Husted-Regalado, Simon-Feliciano-Regalado. **Shreveport (8)**—Zerbe-Knoll, Ainsworth-Oropesa-Miller, Andra-Messman-Knoll, Ainsworth-Oropesa, Zerbe-Corps-Ramirez, Joseph-Knoll, Corps-Miller-Oropesa, Ainsworth-Miller. **Tulsa (7)**—Cook-Moreno, Elder-Duncan-Poeck, Benoit-Poland-Duncan, Elder-Pearsall-Poeck, Lundberg-Camp-Poeck, Cook-Pearsall, Lundberg-Duncan. **Wichita (4)**—George-Mullen, George-Gooding-Lamber-Soonier, Morrison-Sonnier, Baker-Gooding-Sonnier.

NO-HIT GAMES: R. Smith, Arkansas defeated Midland, 5-0, May 6; R. Smith, Arkansas defeated San Antonio, 1-0, June 11.

2000 FIELDING

TEAM

Team	Pct.	G	PO	A	E	TC	DP	TP	PB
Wichita	.975	137	3614	1474	132	5220	145	0	19
Shreveport	.973	139	3638	1525	142	5305	115	0	17
Round Rock	.973	140	3736	1535	149	5420	110	0	17
San Antonio	.970	140	3694	1472	159	5325	144	0	17
Arkansas	.969	139	3589	1336	155	5080	134	0	18
Midland	.968	139	3731	1565	176	5472	135	0	29
El Paso	.966	141	3728	1601	190	5519	147	0	14
Tulsa	.964	141	3714	1469	192	5375	121	0	19

INDIVIDUAL

FIRST BASEMEN

NOTE: All caps denotes fielding-percentage leader based on 70 games for catchers, 93 for all other non-pitchers and 112 innings for pitchers. *Throws lefthanded.

Player, Team	Pct.	G	PO	A	E	TC	DP
Allen, Luke, S.A.	1.000	2	10	0	0	10	1
Amado, Jose, Wich.	.988	55	455	36	6	497	52
Bevins, Andy, Ark.	.919	8	56	1	5	62	5
Burns, Kevin, R.R.*	.989	36	255	16	3	274	24
Cabrera, Alex, E.P.	.992	52	478	39	4	521	50
Carter, Charley, R.R.	.983	21	211	14	4	229	19
Clark, Kevin, E.P.	1.000	9	62	4	0	66	6
Davis, Glenn, S.A.*	.989	72	578	55	7	640	66
Figga, Mike, S.A.	1.000	4	32	2	0	34	5
Flaherty, Tim, Shre.	.992	80	591	62	5	658	46
Fuentes, Javier, E.P.	1.000	1	8	0	0	8	1
Gallagher, Shawn, Tul.	1.000	1	6	0	0	6	0
Gil, Geronimo, S.A.	1.000	3	6	0	0	6	1
Glendenning, Mike, Shre.	.994	20	156	9	1	166	11
Gorr, Robb, S.A.	.981	63	477	50	10	537	52
Haas, Chris, Ark.	.982	19	105	4	2	111	10
Hallmark, Pat, Wich.	.988	11	71	8	1	80	4
Harkrider, Kip, S.A.	.000	1	0	0	0	0	0
HART, Jason, Mid.	.991	126	1184	66	11	1261	117
Lane, Ryan, Tul.	1.000	5	36	2	0	38	3
Lee, Travis, E.P.*	1.000	2	13	1	0	14	0
Leon, Jose, Ark.	.993	22	138	3	1	142	20
Marval, Raul, Shre.	1.000	2	2	0	0	2	0
McGowan, Sean, Shre.	1.000	17	151	9	0	160	13
McKay, Cody, Mid.	1.000	2	1	0	0	1	0
McNeal, Aaron, R.R.	.989	91	733	61	9	803	61
Meier, Dan, E.P.*	1.000	16	127	10	0	137	13
Melhuse, Adam, S.A.	1.000	1	7	0	0	7	0
Mensik, Todd, Mid.*	1.000	15	123	12	0	135	8
Miller, Orlando, S.A.	.929	2	11	2	1	14	4
Mitchell, Mike, Ark.	.958	11	77	14	4	95	8
Morillo, Cesar, R.R.	1.000	1	4	0	0	4	0
Munoz, Juan, Ark.*	.982	46	310	15	6	331	36
Newstrom, Doug, E.P.	1.000	3	21	1	0	22	3
Overbay, Lyle, E.P.*	.979	61	536	37	12	585	60
Pearson, Eddie, Ark.	.987	45	343	24	5	372	42
Pena, Carlos, Tul.*	.982	136	1101	79	22	1202	109
Priess, Matt, Shre.	1.000	1	6	1	0	7	0
Roberge, J.P., Wich.	1.000	1	7	1	0	8	1
Ronan, Marc, Ark.	.950	5	37	1	2	40	3
Sanchez, Victor, E.P.	1.000	2	15	3	0	18	0
Saylor, Jamie, E.P.	1.000	1	7	1	0	8	3
Summers, John, Shre.	.991	25	202	19	2	223	23
Theodorou, Nick, S.A.	1.000	1	2	3	0	5	0
Tsoukalas, John, Shre.*	.986	12	68	4	1	73	9
Ullery, Dave, Wich.	1.000	1	3	0	0	3	0
Wesson, Barry, R.R.	1.000	1	1	0	0	1	0
Willis, Dave, Wich.	.990	82	692	35	7	734	70
Young, Travis, Shre.	1.000	1	1	0	0	1	0

SECOND BASEMEN

Player, Team	Pct.	G	PO	A	E	TC	DP
Ametller, Jesus, Ark.	1.000	4	4	6	0	10	1
Bautista, Juan, Tul.	1.000	3	8	3	0	11	0
Benham, Jason, Ark.	1.000	2	2	3	0	5	1
Brown, Vick, E.P.	.959	15	29	42	3	74	10
Campusano, Carlos, Shre.	.933	3	4	10	1	15	2
Caruso, Joe, Wich.	.953	14	23	38	3	64	10
Cesar, Dionys, Mid.	.979	15	45	49	2	96	16
Dallimore, Brian, E.P.	.967	38	74	100	6	180	28
Eckelman, Alex, Ark.	.958	35	65	73	6	144	12
Ellis, Mark, Wich.	1.000	7	15	15	0	30	7
Espada, Josue, Mid.	.983	12	25	32	1	58	6
Febles, Carlos, Wich.	1.000	4	5	13	0	18	2
German, Esteban, Mid.	.951	21	33	64	5	102	8
Ginter, Keith, R.R.	.972	122	255	338	17	610	73
Harkrider, Kip, S.A.	.963	5	15	11	1	27	9
Huff, Larry, Wich.	.969	7	13	18	1	32	4
Huffman, Royce, R.R.	1.000	3	5	7	0	12	2
Macrory, Bob, Ark.	.980	9	31	17	1	49	5
Maier, T.J., Ark.	.970	91	215	232	14	461	73
Marval, Raul, Shre.	.940	11	23	24	3	50	9
Meliah, Dave, Tul.	.941	3	4	12	1	17	1
Metcalfe, Mike, S.A.	.986	43	98	120	3	221	35
Metzler, Rod, Wich.	.967	109	209	263	16	488	71
Miller, Orlando, S.A.	1.000	2	4	5	0	9	2
Montas, Ricardo, Wich.	1.000	3	2	6	0	8	2
Morillo, Cesar, E.P.-R.R.	.977	20	31	53	2	86	13
Otero, William, Shre.	.948	43	84	118	11	213	27
Pecci, Jay, Mid.	.979	94	187	318	11	516	65
Perez, Jhonny, R.R.	1.000	3	2	3	0	5	0
Riggs, Eric, S.A.	.981	36	60	93	3	156	15
Roberge, J.P., Wich.	.857	6	5	7	2	14	2
Romano, Jason, Tul.	.963	125	292	336	24	652	77
Saitta, Rich, S.A.	.947	59	118	151	15	284	31
Saylor, Jamie, E.P.	.977	49	78	130	5	213	36
Solano, Danny, Tul.	.928	14	32	32	5	69	7
Spivey, Junior, E.P.	1.000	5	12	11	0	23	2
Tebbs, Nate, Ark.	.947	3	8	10	1	19	5
Theodorou, Nick, S.A.	.842	3	13	3	3	19	4
Velarde, Randy, Mid.	.941	4	7	9	1	17	2
White, Walt, E.P.	.982	44	97	116	4	217	35
YOUNG, Travis, Shre.	.988	93	165	247	5	417	39
Zuniga, Tony, Shre.	.947	3	8	10	1	19	5

SECOND BASEMEN WITH TWO OR MORE TEAMS

Player, Team	Pct.	G	PO	A	E	TC	DP
Morillo, Cesar, E.P.	.917	3	2	9	1	12	2
Morillo, Cesar, R.R.	.986	17	29	44	1	74	11

THIRD BASEMEN

Player, Team	Pct.	G	PO	A	E	TC	DP
Allen, Luke, S.A.	.890	86	53	166	27	246	13
Amado, Jose, Wich.	.923	10	7	17	2	26	3
Bautista, Juan, Tul.	1.000	2	2	3	0	5	0
Berry, Mike, S.A.	.931	26	24	43	5	72	6
Brumbaugh, Cliff, Tul.	.857	2	0	6	1	7	1
Campusano, Carlos, Shre.	.000	3	0	0	0	0	0
Caruso, Joe, Wich.	.889	23	14	42	7	63	3
Cesar, Dionys, Mid.	1.000	7	2	10	0	12	0
Dallimore, Brian, E.P.	.907	54	32	105	14	151	10
Dillon, Joe, Wich.	.950	56	34	119	8	161	7
Eckelman, Alex, Ark.	.915	27	19	35	5	59	3
ENSBERG, Morgan, R.R.	.942	136	84	307	24	415	22
Flaherty, Tim, Shre.	1.000	1	1	2	0	3	0
Fox, Andy, E.P.	.500	2	0	2	2	4	0
Garrick, Matt, Ark.	.000	1	0	0	0	0	0
Gil, Geronimo, S.A.	.667	2	1	1	1	3	0
Grabowski, Jason, Tul.	.898	130	84	270	40	394	22
Haas, Chris, Ark.	.936	66	39	122	11	172	13
Hammock, Rob, E.P.	.857	3	1	5	1	7	0
Harkrider, Kip, S.A.	.981	24	9	43	1	53	3

Player, Team	Pct.	G	PO	A	E	TC	DP
Huff, Larry, Wich.	.935	54	49	94	10	153	10
Huffman, Royce, R.R.	1.000	1	0	2	0	2	0
Landry, Jacques, Mid.	.910	122	72	262	33	367	23
Lane, Ryan, Tul.	1.000	4	2	7	0	9	1
Leon, Jose, Ark.	.901	46	32	86	13	131	8
Marval, Raul, Shre.	.926	28	11	52	5	68	5
McKay, Cody, Mid.	.840	10	4	17	4	25	2
Melhuse, Adam, S.A.	.000	1	0	0	1	1	0
Meliah, Dave, Tul.	1.000	2	3	3	0	6	1
Montas, Ricardo, Wich.	1.000	3	3	6	0	9	0
Morillo, Cesar, E.P.-R.R.	1.000	4	4	8	0	12	1
Newstrom, Doug, E.P.	.902	20	8	38	5	51	6
Owens, Ryan, E.P.	.908	58	39	100	14	153	7
Roberge, J.P., Wich.	.773	6	5	12	5	22	2
Rupp, Brian, Ark.	1.000	1	1	1	0	2	1
Salazar, Oscar, Mid.	.778	6	2	5	2	9	0
Sanchez, Victor, E.P.	.875	5	1	6	1	8	0
Saylor, Jamie, E.P.	.909	15	6	24	3	33	3
Solano, Danny, Tul.	.700	3	1	6	3	10	0
Theodorou, Nick, S.A.	.714	11	4	6	4	14	1
Torcato, Tony, Shre.	1.000	2	0	1	0	1	0
Tsoukalas, John, Shre.*	1.000	2	1	2	0	3	0
White, Walt, E.P.	1.000	1	1	0	0	1	0
Williams, Matt, E.P.	1.000	4	2	4	0	6	1
Woolf, Jason, Ark.	.923	9	5	7	1	13	1
Young, Travis, Shre.	1.000	2	1	0	0	1	0
Zuniga, Tony, Shre.	.930	116	68	226	22	316	20

THIRD BASEMEN WITH TWO OR MORE TEAMS

Player, Team	Pct.	G	PO	A	E	TC	DP
Morillo, Cesar, E.P.	1.000	1	1	3	0	4	1
Morillo, Cesar, R.R.	1.000	3	3	5	0	8	0

SHORTSTOPS

Player, Team	Pct.	G	PO	A	E	TC	DP
Bautista, Juan, Tul.	.933	20	33	65	7	105	15
Campusano, Carlos, Shre.	1.000	2	1	3	0	4	0
Caruso, Joe, Wich.	1.000	2	3	9	0	12	5
Cesar, Dionys, Mid.	.938	33	62	90	10	162	18
Cintron, Alex, E.P.	.950	124	219	387	32	638	78
Dallimore, Brian, R.R.-E.P.	.750	5	1	11	4	16	1
Espada, Josue, Mid.	.951	10	15	24	2	41	5
Fox, Andy, E.P.	1.000	1	1	1	0	2	0
Harkrider, Kip, S.A.	.966	49	77	124	7	208	30
Huff, Larry, Wich.	.966	19	14	43	2	59	5
Maier, T.J., Ark.	.962	9	8	17	1	26	4
Marval, Raul, Shre.	.921	12	11	24	3	38	4
Matranga, David, R.R.	.951	115	163	360	27	550	61
Medrano, Steve, Wich.	1.000	15	15	33	0	48	9
Metcalfe, Mike, S.A.	1.000	1	3	2	0	5	1
Miller, Orlando, S.A.	.909	9	14	26	4	44	4
Montas, Ricardo, Wich.	1.000	3	0	12	0	12	0
Morillo, Cesar, R.R.	.957	37	38	72	5	115	15
ORTIZ, Nick, Wich.	.980	108	198	347	11	556	84
Pecci, Jay, Mid.	.971	7	14	19	1	34	4
Perez, Jhonny, R.R.	.889	3	4	4	1	9	2
Ransom, Cody, Shre.	.958	128	210	366	25	601	69
Riggs, Eric, S.A.	.966	81	123	244	13	380	62
Saitta, Rich, S.A.	1.000	8	7	15	0	22	1
Salazar, Oscar, Mid.	.935	96	166	297	32	495	66
Saylor, Jamie, E.P.	.914	14	21	43	6	70	9
Solano, Danny, Tul.	.959	83	137	236	16	389	41
Tebbs, Nate, Ark.	.962	24	37	64	4	105	16
Theodorou, Nick, S.A.	1.000	1	0	3	0	3	0
White, Walt, E.P.	1.000	4	1	7	0	8	1
Wilson, Jack, Ark.	.971	88	140	262	12	414	58
Woolf, Jason, Ark.	.960	23	29	67	4	100	16
Young, Mike, Tul.	.965	41	67	125	7	199	23
Young, Travis, Shre.	1.000	2	3	6	0	9	1

SHORTSTOPS WITH TWO OR MORE TEAMS

Player, Team	Pct.	G	PO	A	E	TC	DP
Dallimore, Brian, R.R.	.667	3	0	4	2	6	0
Dallimore, Brian, E.P.	.800	2	1	7	2	10	1

OUTFIELDERS

Player, Team	Pct.	G	PO	A	E	TC	DP
Allen, Jeff, Shre.	.983	122	228	9	4	241	2
Bates, Fletcher, E.P.	.950	95	147	5	8	160	1
Bautista, Juan, Tul.	1.000	8	12	1	0	13	0
Berger, Brandon, Wich.	1.000	19	21	3	0	24	1
Berrios, Harry, Tul.	.932	19	41	0	3	44	0
Bevel, Bobby, S.A.*	.000	1	0	0	0	0	0
Bevins, Andy, Ark.	.972	84	134	7	4	145	1
Bowles, Justin, Mid.*	.956	117	186	9	9	204	0
Brumbaugh, Cliff, Tul.	1.000	4	6	1	0	7	0
Byrnes, Eric, Mid.	.983	66	114	5	2	121	0
Cabrera, Alex, E.P.	1.000	1	2	0	0	2	0
Caruso, Joe, Wich.	.974	67	109	5	3	117	1
Cesar, Dionys, Mid.	.916	61	92	6	9	107	0
Chen, Chin-Feng, S.A.	.988	127	239	11	3	253	2
Clark, Doug, Shre.	.965	122	213	9	8	230	0
Clark, Kevin, E.P.	.000	2	0	0	0	0	0
Cole, Eric, R.R.	.963	128	227	7	9	243	0
Curry, Mike, Wich.	.981	121	256	7	5	268	2
Cust, Jack, E.P.	.944	127	176	10	11	197	0
Daeley, Scott, Shre.	1.000	1	1	0	0	1	0
Dallimore, Brian, E.P.	1.000	1	3	0	0	3	0
Davis, Glenn, S.A.*	.982	31	51	5	1	57	0
Dodson, Jeremy, Wich.	.962	127	214	13	9	236	2
Eckelman, Alex, Ark.	.950	16	19	0	1	20	0
Faircloth, Chad, Shre.	.947	16	18	0	1	19	0
Farley, Cordell, Ark.	.988	76	152	7	2	161	2
Figga, Mike, S.A.	1.000	2	3	0	0	3	0
Flaherty, Tim, Shre.	1.000	2	1	0	0	1	0
Fox, Andy, E.P.	1.000	1	1	0	0	1	0
Fuentes, Javier, E.P.	.000	1	0	0	0	0	0
Gallagher, Shawn, Tul.	1.000	5	7	0	0	7	0
Gann, Jamie, E.P.	.961	37	68	6	3	77	2
Garrick, Matt, Ark.	.000	1	0	0	0	0	0
Gibbs, Kevin, S.A.	1.000	11	22	0	0	22	0
Gil, Geronimo, S.A.	1.000	16	19	0	0	19	0
Glendenning, Mike, Shre.	.848	27	37	2	7	46	0
Gomez, Ramon, E.P.	.961	70	142	7	6	155	1
Goodwin, Curtis, Wich.*	1.000	9	13	0	0	13	0
Greer, Rusty, Tul.*	1.000	1	2	1	0	3	0
Hallmark, Pat, Wich.	.975	89	146	12	4	162	2
Hammock, Rob, E.P.	.833	3	5	0	1	6	0
Huff, Larry, Wich.	1.000	2	2	0	0	2	0
Huffman, Royce, R.R.	.000	1	0	0	0	0	0
Kapler, Gabe, Tul.	1.000	3	6	0	0	6	0
Keith, Rusty, Mid.	1.000	18	19	0	0	19	0
Lane, Ryan, Tul.	.959	54	112	6	5	123	2
Lee, Travis, E.P.*	1.000	1	2	0	0	2	0
Leon, Jose, Ark.	1.000	4	9	1	0	10	0
Lockwood, Mike, Mid.*	.971	55	93	6	3	102	1
Logan, Kyle, R.R.	.963	95	165	15	7	187	0
Magruder, Chris, Shre.	.983	132	277	6	5	288	0
Martinez, Greg, Mid.	1.000	27	37	2	0	39	0
Melhuse, Adam, S.A.	1.000	4	2	0	0	2	0
Meliah, Dave, Tul.	.000	1	0	0	0	0	0
Mensik, Todd, Mid.*	.949	38	36	1	2	39	1
Messner, Jake, Shre.*	.968	18	29	1	1	31	0
Metcalfe, Mike, S.A.	1.000	9	16	0	0	16	0
Metzler, Rod, Wich.	.000	1	0	0	0	0	0
Monroe, Craig, Tul.	.948	119	199	18	12	229	3
Moreta, Ramon, S.A.	.971	121	257	10	8	275	1
Morillo, Cesar, R.R.	.917	6	9	2	1	12	0
Munoz, Juan, Ark.*	.969	22	30	1	1	32	0
Murray, Glenn, Ark.	1.000	8	12	0	0	12	0
Newstrom, Doug, E.P.	1.000	5	6	1	0	7	0
Ortega, Bill, Ark.	.955	84	163	8	8	179	0
Ortiz, Nick, Wich.	.000	1	0	0	0	0	0
Perez, Jhonny, R.R.	.951	61	92	6	5	103	1
Phillips, Paul, Wich.	.000	1	0	0	0	0	0
Piniella, Juan, Tul.	.982	124	269	7	5	281	1
Podsednik, Scott, Tul.*	.968	42	90	1	3	94	0
Porter, Colin, R.R.*	.985	121	254	9	4	267	0
Powell, Dante, S.A.	.979	16	44	2	1	47	0
Roberge, J.P., Wich.	.000	1	0	0	0	0	0
Rose, Mike, E.P.	.750	3	3	0	1	4	0
Saitta, Rich, S.A.	.980	32	45	3	1	49	0
Salazar, Oscar, Mid.	1.000	9	14	1	0	15	0
Samboy, Nelson, R.R.	1.000	7	15	0	0	15	0
Sanchez, Victor, E.P.	.857	6	6	0	1	7	0
SATURRIA, Luis, Ark.	.991	127	338	9	3	350	1
Saylor, Jamie, E.P.	.947	9	17	1	1	19	1
Secoda, Joe, Ark.	.933	9	14	0	1	15	0
Sergio, Tom, Tul.	1.000	35	80	2	0	82	1
Sykes, Jamie, E.P.	.976	40	72	8	2	82	2
Tebbs, Nate, Ark.	1.000	2	7	0	0	7	0
Theodorou, Nick, S.A.	.971	87	132	3	4	139	1
Thomas, Gary, Mid.	.970	73	124	5	4	133	1
Ullery, Dave, Wich.	.000	1	0	0	0	0	0
Urquiola, Carlos, E.P.	.957	44	66	1	3	70	0

CLASS AA Texas League

Player, Team	Pct.	G	PO	A	E	TC	DP
Wesson, Barry, R.R.	1.000	34	45	2	0	47	1
Woolf, Jason, Ark.	.926	12	24	1	2	27	0
Wright, Corey, Tul.*	.959	17	46	1	2	49	0
Zywica, Mike, Tul.	.917	5	9	2	1	12	1

CATCHERS

Player, Team	Pct.	G	PO	A	E	TC	DP	PB
Benham, David, Ark.	.989	16	87	5	1	93	1	2
Brito, Juan, Wich.	.990	33	182	16	2	200	1	2
Buckley, Brandon, R.R.	1.000	1	9	0	0	9	0	0
Clark, Kevin, E.P.	1.000	11	62	6	0	68	2	2
Cresse, Brad, E.P.	1.000	14	64	18	0	82	1	0
Depastino, Joe, R.R.	1.000	4	27	6	0	33	0	0
Figga, Mike, S.A.	.967	23	132	14	5	151	0	2
Flores, Javier, Mid.	1.000	12	61	5	0	66	0	2
Garrick, Matt, Ark.	.981	98	636	69	14	719	4	8
Gil, Geronimo, S.A.	.989	80	555	59	7	621	10	8
Hallmark, Pat, Wich.	1.000	1	1	0	0	1	0	0
Hammock, Rob, E.P.	1.000	29	178	15	0	193	0	3
Hayes, Heath, S.A.	1.000	2	12	2	0	14	0	0
Jones, Jeremy, Tul.	.978	30	200	19	5	224	2	1
Kellner, Ryan, S.A.	.992	15	104	13	1	118	0	2
Luderer, Brian, Mid.	.966	21	125	16	5	146	2	3
Maldonado, Carlos, R.R.	.988	116	882	80	12	974	4	14
Martine, Chris, Ark.	1.000	5	26	0	0	26	0	0
McAffee, Josh, Tul.	1.000	3	15	3	0	18	0	0
McKay, Cody, Mid.	.985	84	626	53	10	689	1	16
Melhuse, Adam, S.A.	.984	8	56	7	1	64	2	2
Newstrom, Doug, E.P.	.950	3	18	1	1	20	0	0
Norton, Chris, Mid.	1.000	7	48	7	0	55	0	2
Olivo, Miguel, Mid.	.980	14	95	5	2	102	0	4
Pachot, John, E.P.	1.000	5	34	2	0	36	2	0
Phillips, Paul, Wich.	.983	72	463	50	9	522	6	9
Priess, Matt, Shre.	.993	43	253	27	2	282	3	5
Ronan, Marc, Ark.	.995	34	189	26	1	216	4	5
Rose, Mike, E.P.	.981	96	681	90	15	786	7	9
Ross, David, S.A.	.994	22	165	11	1	177	3	3
Schaeffer, Jon, Mid.	1.000	10	59	7	0	66	0	2
Secrist, Reed, Tul.	.987	35	208	17	3	228	1	2
Taveras, Luis, Tul.	.982	81	531	65	11	607	7	16
Theodorou, Nick, S.A.	1.000	3	10	1	0	11	0	0
Thurston, Jerrey, R.R.	.993	22	132	13	1	146	1	3
TORREALBA, Yorvit, Shre.	.990	106	719	86	8	813	7	12
Ullery, Dave, Wich.	.997	42	293	26	1	320	5	8

PITCHERS

Player, Team	Pct.	G	PO	A	E	TC	DP
Ainsworth, Kurt, Shre.	.971	28	12	21	1	34	1
Alston, Garvin, Wich.	1.000	18	2	2	0	4	1
Alvarez, Victor, S.A.*	.941	11	3	13	1	17	0
Ambrose, John, Ark.	.833	45	3	7	2	12	1
Anderson, Jason, Mid.*	1.000	28	0	14	0	14	2
Andra, Jeff, Shre.*	.947	17	5	13	1	19	0
Andrews, Jeff, E.P.	.952	21	6	14	1	21	1
Austin, Jeff, Wich.	.875	6	4	3	1	8	0
Avrard, Corey, Ark.	1.000	57	5	4	0	9	1
Baez, Benito, Mid.*	1.000	37	4	13	0	17	2
Baker, Jason, Wich.	1.000	17	5	7	0	12	1
Benes, Adam, Ark.	.909	26	4	6	1	11	1
Benoit, Joaquin, Tul.	.933	16	6	8	1	15	1
Bevel, Bobby, S.A.*	.875	47	6	15	3	24	2
Bierbrodt, Nick, E.P.*	.875	7	1	6	1	8	0
Bluma, Jaime, Wich.	1.000	2	1	0	0	1	0
Braswell, Bryan, R.R.*	.944	19	7	10	1	18	0
Brink, Jim, Mid.	1.000	6	1	2	0	3	0
Brunette, Justin, Ark.*	.000	3	0	0	0	0	0
Burnside, Adrian, S.A.*	.864	17	5	14	3	22	0
Byrdak, Tim, Wich.*	1.000	4	1	2	0	3	0
Calero, Enrique, Wich.	.976	28	9	31	1	41	2
Camp, Jared, Tul.	1.000	7	3	5	0	8	0
Cervantes, Chris, E.P.*	.923	16	6	18	2	26	0
Clemons, Chris, E.P.	1.000	2	2	0	0	2	0
Cogan, Tony, Wich.*	1.000	2	0	1	0	1	0
Colome, Jesus, Mid.	.909	20	2	18	2	22	2
Coogan, Patrick, Ark.	.833	27	5	15	4	24	1
Cook, Derrick, Tul.	.952	21	6	14	1	21	1
Corps, Edwin, Shre.	.963	36	7	19	1	27	0
Cox, Ryan, Shre.	1.000	7	1	4	0	5	0
Crafton, Kevin, Ark.	1.000	57	3	8	0	11	0
Creek, Ryan, E.P.	1.000	2	1	0	0	1	0
Crowell, Jim, Ark.*	1.000	12	0	1	0	1	0
Curtis, Chris, E.P.	1.000	5	1	3	0	4	0
Dace, Derek, E.P.*	1.000	28	1	5	0	6	0
Davis, Allen, S.A.*	.909	29	3	17	2	22	2
Davis, Clint, E.P.	1.000	11	0	1	0	1	0
Dorame, Randey, S.A.*	1.000	9	3	12	0	15	2
Dubose, Eric, Mid.*	1.000	18	3	3	0	6	1
Duncan, Sean, Tul.*	.905	46	9	10	2	21	0
Eckelman, Alex, Ark.	.000	2	0	0	0	0	0
Edsell, Geoff, S.A.	.833	25	7	8	3	18	1
Elarton, Scott, R.R.	.000	1	0	0	0	0	0
Elder, David, Tul.	.864	33	5	14	3	22	1
Estrella, Luis, Shre.	.885	21	6	17	3	26	2
Everly, Bill, S.A.	.750	11	0	3	1	4	0
Feliciano, Pedro, S.A.*	1.000	9	1	1	0	2	0
Flores, Ignacio, S.A.	1.000	3	0	1	0	1	0
Franks, Lance, Ark.	.960	43	3	21	1	25	2
Freehill, Mike, Tul.	1.000	26	1	4	0	5	0
Fuller, Jody, E.P.	1.000	8	2	3	0	5	1
Gajkowski, Steve, Mid.	1.000	10	1	2	0	3	0
Galvez, Randy, S.A.	1.000	12	7	6	0	13	3
Garcia, Apostol, S.A.	.889	18	2	6	1	9	0
Garrett, Hal, S.A.	1.000	21	5	4	0	9	0
George, Chris, Wich.*	.826	18	7	12	4	23	0
Glick, Dave, R.R.*	1.000	33	4	6	0	10	0
GOODING, Jason, Wich.*	1.000	29	7	18	0	25	2
Goodrich, Randy, Shre.	.960	51	11	13	1	25	5
Green, Jason, R.R.	1.000	31	3	5	0	8	0
Gregg, Kevin, Mid.	.900	28	10	17	3	30	2
Guerrero, Junior, Wich.	.905	28	6	13	2	21	0
Guzman, Geraldo, E.P.	1.000	17	3	6	0	9	0
Guzman, Leiby, Tul.	.882	24	3	12	2	17	0
Herbert, Russ, R.R.	.909	38	6	14	2	22	1
Hernandez, Fernando, R.R.	1.000	15	2	3	0	5	0
Hillman, Eric, R.R.*	1.000	1	1	1	0	2	0
Horgan, Joe, Shre.*	1.000	1	0	1	0	1	0
Huff, Larry, Wich.	.000	1	0	0	0	0	0
Husted, Brent, S.A.	.950	52	9	10	1	20	3
Hutchinson, Chad, Ark.	1.000	11	5	2	0	7	0
Hutton, Mark, R.R.	1.000	3	1	0	0	1	0
Ireland, Eric, R.R.	.977	29	21	22	1	44	2
Jacob, Russell, E.P.	1.000	7	0	1	0	1	0
Jerue, Tristan, Ark.	.857	4	1	5	1	7	0
Jones, Marcus, Mid.	.875	5	3	4	1	8	0
Joseph, Kevin, Shre.	.833	27	7	13	4	24	0
Karnuth, Jason, Ark.	.818	8	2	7	2	11	0
Kaufman, Brad, R.R.	.500	6	0	1	1	2	0
Kessel, Kyle, R.R.*	.957	14	11	11	1	23	0
Kimball, Andrew, Mid.	.889	29	1	7	1	9	0
Knoll, Brian, Shre.	1.000	21	10	12	0	22	2
Koplove, Mike, E.P.	1.000	35	3	9	0	12	2
Lamber, Justin, Wich.*	.842	43	1	15	3	19	2
Lambert, Jeremy, Ark.	.500	39	0	1	1	2	0
Lane, Ryan, Tul.	.000	1	0	0	0	0	0
Lanfranco, Otoniel, Ark.	.857	33	3	15	3	21	0
Lundberg, Spike, Tul.	.925	40	14	23	3	40	0
MacDougal, Mike, Wich.	1.000	2	0	2	0	2	0
Malerich, Will, Shre.*	1.000	4	0	1	0	1	0
Manwiller, Tim, Mid.	.857	25	3	9	2	14	0
Martines, Jason, E.P.	.957	55	4	18	1	23	3
Martinez, Jose, Tul.	1.000	18	5	12	0	17	0
Marval, Raul, Shre.	.000	1	0	0	0	0	0
Maurer, Mike, Mid.	1.000	12	2	4	0	6	1
Mayo, Blake, E.P.	.857	38	12	30	7	49	3
McCutcheon, Mike, E.P.*	1.000	30	3	8	0	11	0
McKnight, Tony, R.R.	1.000	6	6	1	0	7	0
Messman, Joe, Shre.	1.000	38	6	7	0	13	1
Miller, Benji, Shre.	.963	58	8	18	1	27	2
Miller, Greg, R.R.*	.000	2	0	0	0	0	0
Miller, Justin, Mid.	.938	18	4	11	1	16	0
Miller, Matt, Tul.	.000	3	0	0	0	0	0
Montgomery, Matt, S.A.	1.000	41	2	9	0	11	0
Moreno, Juan, Tul.*	.000	5	0	0	0	0	0
Morris, Matt, Ark.	.000	2	0	0	0	0	0
Morrison, Robbie, Wich.	.700	34	1	6	3	10	2
Mullen, Scott, Wich.*	1.000	33	4	10	0	14	1
Munoz, Juan, Ark.*	.000	1	0	0	0	0	0
Navarro, Jason, Ark.*	1.000	33	2	4	0	6	0
Navarro, Scott, R.R.*	1.000	22	0	10	0	10	0
Newstrom, Doug, E.P.	.000	1	0	0	0	0	0
Niebla, Ruben, S.A.*	1.000	10	2	3	0	5	1
Niles, Randy, Mid.	1.000	38	0	8	0	8	0
Noriega, Ray, Mid.*	1.000	21	2	6	0	8	0
Norris, Ben, E.P.*	.750	7	2	4	2	8	0
Nunez, Maximo, S.A.	.867	38	7	6	2	15	1

Player, Team	Pct.	G	PO	A	E	TC	DP
Oliver, Darren, Tul.*	.000	1	0	0	0	0	0
Oropesa, Eddie, Shre.*	.852	59	7	16	4	27	0
Oswalt, Roy, R.R.	.917	19	3	19	2	24	1
Ozias, Todd, Shre.	.000	1	0	0	0	0	0
Pamus, Javier, Wich.	.000	3	0	0	0	0	0
Pearce, Josh, Ark.	.923	17	5	7	1	13	0
Pearsall, J.J., Tul.*	1.000	28	1	6	0	7	0
Persails, Mark, R.R.	.867	50	3	10	2	15	1
Pina, Rafael, E.P.	.917	12	6	5	1	12	1
Poeck, Chad, Tul.	.933	46	8	6	1	15	0
Poland, Trey, Tul.*	.917	30	5	6	1	12	0
Powell, Jay, R.R.	1.000	1	0	1	0	1	1
Pratt, Andy, Tul.*	.857	11	1	5	1	7	0
Prinz, Bret, E.P.	1.000	53	1	7	0	8	0
Prokopec, Luke, S.A.	.926	22	5	20	2	27	1
Ramirez, Erasmo, Shre.*	.950	39	6	13	1	20	1
Ramos, Mario, Mid.*	1.000	4	2	7	0	9	1
Reames, Britt, Ark.	.875	8	2	5	1	8	0
Redding, Tim, R.R.	.833	5	0	5	1	6	0
Regalado, Maximo, S.A.	1.000	26	1	0	0	1	0
Revenig, Todd, E.P.	1.000	12	6	3	0	9	0
Robertson, Jeriome, R.R.*	.895	11	6	11	2	19	0
Rodriguez, Jose, Ark.*	.750	10	0	3	1	4	0
Rodriguez, Wilfredo, R.R.*	.571	11	0	4	3	7	0
Sanchez, Martin, E.P.	.960	28	8	16	1	25	1
Scott, Brian, E.P.	.900	16	3	6	1	10	0
Sedlacek, Shawn, Wich.	.962	35	8	17	1	26	2
Sessions, Doug, R.R.	1.000	56	3	9	0	12	0
Shearn, Tom, R.R.	.960	25	13	11	1	25	1
Sheredy, Kevin, Ark.	.833	21	1	4	1	6	0
Simon, Ben, S.A.	.960	29	11	13	1	25	3
Smith, Bud, Ark.*	1.000	18	4	15	0	19	2

Player, Team	Pct.	G	PO	A	E	TC	DP
Smith, Cam, S.A.	1.000	7	1	1	0	2	1
Snow, Bert, Mid.	.800	59	1	3	1	5	0
Sodowsky, Clint, Tul.	1.000	6	0	1	0	1	0
Sonnier, Shawn, Wich.	.833	48	2	3	1	6	1
Stechschulte, Gene, Ark.	.000	2	0	0	0	0	0
Stein, Blake, Wich.	1.000	2	1	1	0	2	0
Stephenson, Brian, S.A.	1.000	4	4	1	0	5	0
Theodorou, Nick, S.A.	.000	1	0	0	0	0	0
Thompson, Eric, Mid.	.882	18	8	7	2	17	0
Thompson, Justin, Tul.*	1.000	1	0	2	0	2	0
Thompson, Mark, Ark.	.000	1	0	0	0	0	0
Thorn, Todd, E.P.*	.957	23	4	18	1	23	0
Thurman, Corey, Wich.	1.000	9	2	9	0	11	0
Trejo, Francisco, E.P.*	.000	2	0	0	1	1	0
Tuttle, Dave, E.P.	1.000	21	5	6	0	11	0
Vasquez, Leo, Mid.*	1.000	36	2	4	0	6	1
Verdugo, Jason, Shre.	1.000	5	1	3	0	4	1
Vogelsong, Ryan, Shre.	.889	27	7	17	3	27	1
Wade, Travis, R.R.	1.000	23	2	4	0	6	1
Wagner, Denny, Mid.	.941	29	11	21	2	34	0
Webb, Alan, Tul.*	1.000	10	0	2	0	2	0
Weibl, Clint, Ark.	1.000	10	0	8	0	8	1
Wells, Matt, Shre.	.500	4	1	0	1	2	0
Willis, Dave, Wich.	1.000	1	0	1	0	1	0
Wilson, Kris, Wich.	.929	21	12	14	2	28	1
Woodman, Hank, Tul.	.941	42	6	10	1	17	2
Yates, Tyler, Mid.	1.000	22	0	3	0	3	0
Zamarripa, Mark, E.P.	.750	12	2	7	3	12	0
Zerbe, Chad, Shre.*	1.000	9	2	5	0	7	0

The following player appeared only as a designated hitter, pinch-hitter or pinch runner; G. Vasquez, ph.

LEAGUE CHAMPIONS

Year	Team	Pct.
1888—	Dallas	.671
1889—	Houston	.551
1890—	Galveston	.705
1892—	Dallas	.741
	Houston	.613
1895—	Dallas	.754
	Fort Worth*	.750
1896—	Fort Worth	.757
	Houston*	.679
	Galveston	.548
1897—	San Antonio†	.657
	Galveston†	.717
1898—League disbanded.		
1899—	Galveston	.632
	Galveston	.762
1900-01—Did not operate.		
1902—	Corsicana	.866
	Corsicana	.682
1903—	Paris-Waco	.615
	Dallas*	.648
1904—	Corsicana*	.615
	Fort Worth	.800
1905—	Fort Worth	.545
1906—	Fort Worth	.677
	Cleburne∞	.609
1907—	Austin	.629
1908—	San Antonio	.664
1909—	Houston	.601
1910—	Dallas†	.586
	Houston†	.586
1911—	Austin	.575
1912—	Houston	.626
1913—	Houston	.620
1914—	Houston†	.671
	Waco†	.671
1915—	Waco	.592
1916—	Waco	.587
1917—	Dallas	.600
1918—	Dallas	.584
1919—	Shreveport*	.677
	Fort Worth	.651
1920—	Fort Worth	.703
	Fort Worth	.750
1921—	Fort Worth	.691
	Fort Worth	.662
1922—	Fort Worth	.694

Year	Team	Pct.
	Fort Worth	.711
1923—	Fort Worth	.632
1924—	Fort Worth	.689
	Fort Worth	.763
1925—	Fort Worth	.711
	Fort Worth▲	.653
1926—	Dallas	.574
1927—	Wichita Falls	.654
1928—	Houston*	.679
	Wichita Falls	.731
1929—	Dallas*	.588
	Wichita Falls	.620
1930—	Wichita Falls	.697
	Fort Worth*	.632
1931—	Houston◆	.625
	Houston	.734
1932—	Beaumont*	.640
	Dallas	.727
1933—	Houston	.623
	San Antonio (4th)§	.523
1934—	Galveston‡	.579
1935—	Oklahoma City‡	.590
1936—	Dallas	.604
	Tulsa (3rd)§	.519
1937—	Oklahoma City	.635
	Fort Worth (3rd)§	.535
1938—	Beaumont	.635
1939—	Houston	.606
	Fort Worth (4th)§	.540
1940—	Houston‡	.652
1941—	Houston	.673
	Dallas (4th)§	.519
1942—	Beaumont	.605
	Shreveport (2nd)§	.576
1943-44-45—Did not operate.		
1946—	Fort Worth	.656
	Dallas (2nd)§	.591
1947—	Houston‡	.623
1948—	Fort Worth‡	.601
1949—	Fort Worth	.649
	Tulsa (2nd)§	.584
1950—	Beaumont	.595
	San Antonio (4th)§	.513
1951—	Houston‡	.619
1952—	Dallas	.571
	Shreveport (3rd)§	.522

Year	Team	Pct.
1953—	Dallas‡	.571
1954—	Shreveport	.559
	Houston (2nd)§	.553
1955—	Dallas	.581
	Shreveport (3rd)§	.540
1956—	Houston‡	.623
1957—	Dallas	.662
	Houston (2nd)§	.630
1958—	Fort Worth	.582
	Cor. Christi (3rd)§	.507
1959—	Victoria	.589
	Austin (2nd)§	.548
1960—	Rio Grande Valley	.590
	Tulsa (3rd)§	.528
1961—	Amarillo	.643
	San Antonio (3rd)§	.532
1962—	El Paso	.571
	Tulsa (2nd)§	.550
1963—	San Antonio	.564
	Tulsa (3rd)§	.529
1964—	San Antonio‡	.607
1965—	Tulsa	.574
	Albuquerque■	.550
1966—	Arkansas	.579
1967—	Albuquerque	.557
1968—	Arkansas	.586
	El Paso■	.562
1969—	Amarillo	.593
	Memphis■	.504
1970—	Albuquerque◆	.615
	Memphis	.507
1971— Did not operate as league—clubs were members of Dixie Association.		
1972—	Alexandria	.600
	El Paso■	.557
1973—	San Antonio	.590
	Memphis■	.558
1974—	Victoria■	.581
	El Paso	.555
1975—	Lafayette▼	.558
	Midland▼	.604
1976—	Amarillo■	.600
	Shreveport	.515
1977—	El Paso	.600
	Arkansas•	.485
1978—	El Paso•	.593

Year	Team	Pct.	Year	Team	Pct.	Year	Team	Pct.
	Jackson	.567	1986—	El Paso•	.630		Jackson•	.541
1979—	Arkansas•	.571		Jackson	.533	1994—	El Paso•	.647
	Midland	.563	1987—	Wichita•	.515		Jackson	.548
1980—	Arkansas•	.596		Jackson	.515	1995—	Shreveport•	.652
	San Antonio	.544	1988—	El Paso	.552		Midland	.485
1981—	San Antonio	.571		Tulsa•	.522	1996—	Jackson•	.547
	Jackson•	.507	1989—	Arkansas•	.585		Wichita	.500
1982—	El Paso	.559		Wichita	.537	1997—	San Antonio•	.604
	Tulsa•	.515	1990—	San Antonio	.582		Shreveport	.551
1983—	Jackson	.507		Shreveport•	.489	1998—	Arkansas	.571
	Beaumont•	.500	1991—	Shreveport•	.632		Tulsa•	.557
1984—	Beaumont	.654		El Paso	.596	1999—	Wichita•	.593
	Jackson•	.610	1992—	Shreveport	.566	2000—	Round Rock*	.593
1985—	El Paso	.632		Wichita•	.515			
	Jackson•	.537	1993—	El Paso	.563			

*Won split-season playoff. †Won playoff for title. ‡Finished first and won four-club playoff. §Won four-club playoff. ∞Title to Cleburne by default. ▲Tied with Dallas in second half and won playoff for championship. ◆Tied with Beaumont at end of first half and won title in best-of-five series played as part of second-half schedule. ■League divided into Eastern, Western divisions; won two-team playoff. ▼League divided into Eastern, Western divisions; declared co-champions when playoffs were not completed. •League divided into Eastern and Western divisions and played split-season; won playoffs. NOTE—Championship awarded to winner of four-team play-off, 1933-51; first-place team and playoff winner co-champions, 1952-64.

CALIFORNIA LEAGUE

LEAGUE OFFICE

President
Joe Gagliardi
Address
2380 S. Bascom Ave., Suite 200
Campbell, CA 95008
Phone
408-369-8038

Teams (affiliation)
Bakersfield Blaze (Devil Rays)
High Desert Mavericks (Brewers)
Lake Elsinore Storm (Padres)
Lancaster Jethawks (Diamondbacks)
Modesto A's (A's)
Rancho Cucamonga Quakes (Angels)

San Bernardino Stampede (Mariners)
San Jose Giants (Giants)
Mudville Nine (Reds)
Visalia Oaks (A's)

2000 FINAL STANDINGS

FIRST HALF

NORTHERN DIVISION

Team	W	L	T	Pct.	GB
Modesto (Athletics)	39	31	0	.557	...
Visalia (Athletics)	38	32	0	.543	1.0
Bakersfield (Giants)	37	33	0	.529	2.0
Mudville (Brewers)	33	37	0	.471	6.0
San Jose (Giants)	29	41	0	.414	10.0

SOUTHERN DIVISION

Team	W	L	T	Pct.	GB
Lancaster (Mariners)	40	30	0	.571	...
San Bernardino (Dodgers)	38	32	0	.543	2.0
Rancho Cucamonga (Padres)	37	33	0	.529	3.0
Lake Elsinore (Angels)	36	34	0	.514	4.0
High Desert (Diamondbacks)	23	47	0	.329	17.0

SECOND HALF

NORTHERN DIVISION

Team	W	L	T	Pct.	GB
Bakersfield (Giants)	43	27	0	.614	...
Visalia (Athletics)	40	30	0	.571	3.0
Modesto (Athletics)	37	33	0	.529	6.0
Mudville (Brewers)	35	35	0	.500	8.0
San Jose (Giants)	24	46	0	.343	19.0

SOUTHERN DIVISION

Team	W	L	T	Pct.	GB
Lancaster (Mariners)	49	21	0	.700	...
San Bernardino (Dodgers)	39	31	0	.557	10.0
Lake Elsinore (Angels)	34	36	0	.486	15.0
High Desert (Diamondbacks)	25	45	0	.357	24.0
Rancho Cucamonga (Padres)	24	46	0	.343	25.0

COMPOSITE

Team	Lan.	Bak.	Vis.	S.B.	Mod.	L.E.	Mud.	R.C.	S.J.	H.D.	W	L	T	Pct.	GB
Lancaster (Mariners)	...	5	5	13	7	14	9	14	8	14	89	51	0	.636	...
Bakersfield (Giants)	7	...	13	5	10	5	11	7	14	8	80	60	0	.571	9.0
Visalia (Athletics)	7	8	...	7	11	8	9	7	11	10	78	62	0	.557	11.0
San Bernardino (Dodgers)	7	7	5	...	6	11	6	14	7	14	77	63	0	.550	12.0
Modesto (Athletics)	5	9	10	6	...	5	14	5	11	11	76	64	0	.543	13.0
Lake Elsinore (Angels)	6	7	4	9	6	...	5	12	11	10	70	70	0	.500	19.0
Mudville (Brewers)	3	9	11	6	6	7	...	5	12	9	68	72	0	.486	21.0
Rancho Cucamonga (Padres)	6	5	5	6	7	8	7	...	6	11	61	79	0	.436	28.0
San Jose (Giants)	4	6	7	5	10	2	8	6	...	5	53	87	0	.379	36.0
High Desert (Diamondbacks)	6	4	2	6	1	10	3	9	7	...	48	92	0	.343	41.0

Major league affiliations in parentheses.

High Desert plays home games in Adelanto, Calif.; Mudville plays home games in Stockton, Calif.

PLAYOFFS: San Bernardino defeated Lake Elsinore two games to none; Visalia defeated Bakersfield two games to one; San Bernardino defeated Lancaster three games to two; Visalia defeated Modesto three games to two; San Bernardino defeated Visalia three games to none to win league championship.

REGULAR-SEASON ATTENDANCE: Bakersfield, 96,538; High Desert, 137,464; Lake Elsinore, 238,201; Lancaster, 191,319; Modesto, 144,049; Mudville, 66,420; Rancho Cucamonga, 312,333; San Bernardino, 165,113; San Jose, 136,472; Visalia, 61,879. Total—1,549,788. Playoffs (18 games)—23,951. California-Carolina League All-Star Game at Kinston, N.C. 4,669.

MANAGERS: Bakersfield, Lenn Sakata; High Desert, Scott Coolbaugh; Lake Elsinore, Mario Mendoza; Lancaster, Mark Parent; Modesto, Greg Sparks; Mudville, Barry Moss (Through May 24), Lonnie Keeter (May 25 through June 12), Frank Kremblas (June 14 through end of season); Rancho Cucamonga, Tom Levasseur; San Bernardino, Dino Ebel; San Jose, Keith Comstock; Visalia, Juan Navarrete.

ALL-STAR TEAM: 1B—Sean McGowan, San Jose; 2B—Willie Bloomquist, Lancaster; 3B—Bo Robinson, Lancaster; SS—Joe Thurston, San Bernardino; OF—Ryan Ludwick, Modesto; OF—Juan Silvestre, Lancaster; OF—Terrmel Sledge, Lancaster; C—Guillermo Rodriguez, Bakersfield; RHP—Carlos Garcia, San Bernardino; Jack Krawczyk, Mudville; LHP—Mike Bynum, Rancho Cucamonga; Mario Ramos, Modesto; Most Valuable Player—Juan Silvestre, Lancaster; Pitcher of the Year—Carlos Garcia, San Bernardino; Rookie of the Year—Willie Bloomquist, Lancaster; Manager of the Year—Mark Parent, Lancaster.

2000 BATTING

TEAM

Team	Avg.	G	TPA	AB	R	H	TB	2B	3B	HR	RBI	SH	SF	HP	BB	IBB	SO	SB	CS	GDP	LOB	ShO	Slg.	OBP
Lancaster	.288	140	5700	4882	933	1405	2125	257	53	119	860	30	46	87	655	15	1031	178	119	99	1056	3	.435	.379
High Desert	.271	140	5423	4851	738	1313	2003	254	50	112	657	23	40	46	463	6	1100	128	92	82	966	8	.413	.337
Lake Elsinore	.270	140	5528	4808	770	1296	1890	245	53	81	688	54	57	58	551	14	962	244	106	84	1011	3	.393	.348
R. Cucamonga	.268	140	5428	4825	703	1294	1915	255	45	92	636	24	48	59	472	20	1012	164	83	138	960	9	.397	.338
Bakersfield	.265	140	5512	4702	807	1246	1904	238	36	116	703	50	58	80	622	14	1144	254	87	77	1017	5	.405	.357
San Bern.	.265	140	5418	4731	713	1252	1851	228	52	89	628	64	48	67	508	16	1006	207	121	74	975	7	.391	.341
Visalia	.257	140	5460	4634	754	1191	1819	217	42	109	658	39	52	77	658	22	1061	273	103	91	1020	2	.393	.355
Modesto	.257	140	5621	4721	767	1211	1788	247	33	88	685	45	45	69	741	9	1212	156	69	114	1162	7	.379	.362
San Jose	.255	140	5485	4744	656	1208	1646	201	30	59	597	53	43	76	569	14	982	196	89	93	1073	9	.347	.341
Mudville	.244	140	5241	4606	604	1122	1658	218	27	88	516	33	42	73	487	13	1049	167	94	87	930	8	.360	.323

TOP QUALIFIERS FOR BATTING CHAMPIONSHIP

Minimum 378 plate appearances. *Lefthanded batter. †Switch-hitter.

Player, Team	Avg.	G	TPA	AB	R	H	TB	2B	3B	HR	RBI	SH	SF	HP	BB	IBB	SO	SB	CS	GDP	Slg.	OBP
Sledge, Terrmel, Lan.*	.339	103	479	384	90	130	199	22	7	11	75	1	5	17	72	3	49	35	11	4	.518	.458
McGowan, Sean, S.J.	.327	114	508	456	58	149	221	32	2	12	106	0	3	6	43	1	71	4	3	12	.485	.390
Torcato, Tony, S.J.*	.324	119	544	490	77	159	221	37	2	7	88	0	7	6	41	8	62	19	4	2	.451	.379
Pujols, Rafael, Vis.	.322	117	481	422	61	136	183	16	2	9	74	0	8	1	50	5	57	11	6	8	.434	.389
Quinlan, Robb, L.E.	.317	127	563	482	79	153	213	35	5	5	85	2	9	2	67	1	82	6	4	7	.442	.396
Keith, Rusty, Mod.	.316	104	481	389	84	123	171	22	1	8	61	4	3	3	82	1	72	10	3	11	.440	.436
Valderrama, Carlos, Bak.	.315	121	491	435	78	137	207	21	5	13	81	5	8	4	39	1	96	54	11	4	.476	.370
Robinson, Bo, Lan.	.313	136	595	515	93	161	224	33	0	10	97	1	9	5	65	2	69	2	5	23	.435	.389
Gordon, Brian, H.D.*	.311	127	532	476	98	148	236	26	13	10	66	0	6	2	47	1	107	19	14	8	.496	.371
Powers, Jeff, H.D.*	.309	112	455	408	55	126	158	20	3	2	52	5	4	4	34	0	29	3	6	2	.387	.364
Silvestre, Juan, Lan.	.304	127	580	506	104	154	265	15	3	30	137	0	7	7	60	1	126	9	6	5	.524	.381
Thurston, Joe, S.B.*	.303	138	641	551	97	167	226	31	8	4	70	9	8	17	56	1	61	43	25	8	.410	.380
Hopper, Shane, R.C.	.302	108	485	447	77	135	210	28	7	11	58	1	3	5	28	1	110	15	11	15	.470	.348
Mott, Bill, L.E.*	.301	115	488	396	83	119	190	20	9	11	82	1	5	10	76	5	78	29	8	5	.480	.421
Luther, Ryan, Bak.	.300	110	483	414	78	124	174	25	2	7	48	5	6	10	48	1	94	14	8	6	.420	.381

DEPARTMENTAL LEADERS: G—Owens, Thruston, 138 each; AB—Owens, 570; R—Kuzmic, 106; H—Thurston, 167; TB—Silvestre, 265; 2B—Koonce, 40; 3B—Guzman, 16; HR—Silvestre, 30; RBI—Silvestre, 137; SH—Wenner, 18; SF—Guzman, 11; HP—Basabe, 23; BB—Koonce, 107; IBB—Torcato, 8; SO—Owens, 183; SB—German, 78; CS—Thurston, 25; GIDP—Berroa, 25; Slg.—A. Perez, .527; OBP—Sledge, .458.

ALL PLAYERS

*Lefthanded batter. †Switch-hitter.

Player, Team	Avg.	G	TPA	AB	R	H	TB	2B	3B	HR	RBI	SH	SF	HP	BB	IBB	SO	SB	CS	GDP	Slg.	OBP
Abate, Mike, Lan.	.232	24	81	69	14	16	25	3	0	2	12	0	0	3	9	0	21	5	2	2	.362	.346
Adams, John, R.C.	.230	110	417	395	47	91	146	12	2	13	57	0	2	3	17	2	103	14	5	23	.370	.266
Alexander, Kevin, S.J.	.167	2	7	6	0	1	1	0	0	0	0	0	0	0	1	0	1	0	1	1	.167	.286
Alfano, Jeff, Mud.	.232	22	75	69	9	16	25	4	1	1	10	0	1	0	5	0	18	1	0	3	.362	.293
Amezaga, Alfredo, L.E.†	.279	108	497	420	90	117	150	13	4	4	44	5	5	4	63	0	70	73	21	4	.357	.374
Ardoin, Danny, Mod.	.300	4	11	10	1	3	4	1	0	0	2	0	0	1	0	0	4	0	0	0	.400	.364
Asche, Kirk, Vis.	.247	118	494	421	65	104	196	30	4	18	63	1	2	4	66	3	128	17	8	4	.466	.353
Barski, Chris, L.E.*	.152	19	73	66	6	10	14	4	0	0	4	1	0	0	6	0	18	0	1	2	.212	.222
Basabe, Jesus, Mod.	.258	125	538	445	64	115	192	35	3	12	85	3	6	23	61	0	142	9	10	9	.431	.372
Bazzani, Matt, Bak.	.130	13	27	23	2	3	4	1	0	0	4	0	2	0	2	0	9	0	0	1	.174	.185
Beatriz, Ramy, Mud.*	.250	7	24	20	1	5	5	0	0	0	2	0	0	0	4	0	3	2	0	0	.250	.375
Belliard, Francisco, H.D.†	.226	111	404	368	46	83	114	14	4	3	39	2	3	7	24	0	96	7	9	7	.310	.284
Benjamin, Al, R.C.	.279	137	587	552	71	154	227	30	4	9	81	1	5	5	24	1	89	16	16	14	.411	.312
Berroa, Angel, Vis.	.277	129	474	429	61	119	186	25	6	10	63	2	3	10	30	1	70	11	9	10	.434	.337
Berroa, Cristian, R.C.†	.270	130	542	488	76	132	171	19	4	4	50	4	5	17	28	0	62	30	16	25	.350	.329
Bloomquist, Willie, Lan.	.379	64	295	256	63	97	134	19	6	2	51	1	1	0	37	2	27	22	12	3	.523	.456
Brito, Obispo, Mud.	.214	55	210	201	23	43	67	10	1	4	28	0	0	3	5	1	42	4	3	3	.333	.244
Brooks, Jeff, H.D.	.245	127	542	506	62	124	188	29	4	9	78	0	4	7	25	0	117	8	4	11	.372	.288
Bubela, Jaime, Lan.*	.138	9	36	29	6	4	5	1	0	0	2	1	0	1	5	0	12	4	0	1	.172	.286
Bush, Darren, R.C.*	.276	108	402	340	50	94	137	23	1	6	60	3	3	2	54	2	57	1	3	11	.403	.376
Caiazzo, Nick, Mud.	.253	101	411	356	43	90	124	16	0	6	48	0	7	7	41	2	73	5	5	2	.348	.336
Campbell, Sean, R.C.*	.209	50	182	163	19	34	52	8	2	2	22	0	4	2	13	2	46	3	2	2	.319	.269
Campusano, Carlos, S.J.-Bak.	.253	69	276	249	33	63	84	10	4	1	26	8	1	7	11	0	47	13	3	5	.337	.302
Casper, Brett, Bak.	.243	128	551	436	85	106	184	27	3	15	70	2	3	13	97	1	146	22	4	8	.422	.393
Castro, Nelson, Bak.†	.284	53	248	218	38	62	97	14	3	5	41	4	6	0	20	0	40	27	8	5	.445	.336
Cepeda, Ali, S.J.	.118	19	43	34	4	4	4	0	0	0	3	0	0	0	9	0	14	1	0	0	.118	.302
Ceriani, Matt, Mud.	.260	48	170	150	14	39	55	8	1	2	16	5	0	0	15	0	22	2	3	4	.367	.327
Cesar, Dionys, Vis.†	.227	5	24	22	3	5	13	2	0	2	6	0	1	0	1	0	4	0	0	2	.591	.250
Chirinos, Germain, Mod.	.224	21	80	67	11	15	25	1	3	1	8	1	2	0	10	0	21	4	0	2	.373	.316
Christensen, Mike, L.E.	.270	129	563	523	66	141	217	30	2	14	95	2	5	3	26	1	101	3	3	14	.415	.305
Clements, Jason, Mod.†	.250	24	100	84	13	21	30	2	2	1	11	1	1	2	12	0	19	3	2	1	.357	.354
Clifton, Rodney, Mod.	.143	12	32	28	4	4	6	2	0	0	2	0	0	0	4	0	11	2	0	0	.214	.250
Collins, Mike, S.B.	.292	103	401	342	50	100	112	12	0	0	36	6	8	1	44	0	45	11	6	6	.327	.367
Cook, Joshua, S.J.	.240	15	58	50	9	12	18	0	0	2	2	0	0	1	7	0	13	0	1	0	.360	.345
Cordido, Julio, Bak.	.252	130	524	460	70	116	169	17	3	10	64	5	6	7	46	0	99	13	12	3	.367	.326
Cosme, Caonabo, Mod.	.241	133	621	546	73	132	175	33	2	2	53	12	3	2	56	0	163	44	15	9	.319	.312
Cresse, Brad, H.D.	.324	48	199	173	35	56	114	7	0	17	56	0	2	7	17	1	50	0	0	3	.659	.402
Cridland, Mark, Mud.*	.260	131	565	503	78	131	231	25	6	21	66	1	3	9	49	4	101	20	9	11	.459	.335
Crosby, Bubba, S.B.*	.250	3	12	12	2	3	3	0	0	0	2	0	0	0	0	0	4	1	0	1	.250	.250
Cruz, Israel, Lan.	.000	1	4	4	0	0	0	0	0	0	1	0	0	0	0	0	1	0	0	0	.000	.000
Daeley, Scott, S.J.	.263	106	498	418	83	110	137	20	2	1	44	6	2	8	64	0	71	33	12	7	.328	.370
Davis, Monty, Vis.	.478	11	34	23	7	11	13	2	0	0	5	1	0	2	8	1	1	1	2	0	.565	.636
Davis, Ryan, S.J.*	.400	2	6	5	0	2	2	0	0	0	1	0	0	0	1	0	0	0	0	0	.400	.500
Deardorff, Jeff, Vis.	.245	111	460	421	48	103	167	20	7	10	54	0	6	1	32	2	120	7	10	9	.397	.296
DeHaan, Kory, R.C.*	.214	4	15	14	2	3	7	1	0	1	1	0	0	0	1	0	4	0	0	0	.500	.267
De La Cruz, Jose, Mod.	.177	59	198	164	17	29	39	7	0	1	20	1	2	1	30	0	47	1	5	5	.238	.305
Delgado, Ariel, L.E.*	.248	48	168	153	17	38	52	8	0	2	16	0	1	4	10	0	22	0	4	3	.340	.310
De Los Santos, Nelson, Mud.†.	.255	14	54	51	5	13	23	2	1	2	8	0	0	0	3	0	8	0	1	2	.451	.296
Diaz, Angel, Lan.	.353	45	159	133	24	47	69	11	1	3	18	1	2	4	19	0	29	7	3	4	.519	.443
Dougherty, Jeb, L.E.	.288	18	76	59	12	17	19	2	0	0	5	3	1	1	12	0	12	7	3	0	.322	.411
Dunaway, Jason, R.C.	.244	55	182	156	25	38	43	3	1	0	10	3	2	1	17	0	39	9	5	5	.276	.330
Duplissea, William, S.B.	.222	7	11	9	1	2	2	0	0	0	1	0	0	0	2	0	6	0	0	0	.222	.364
Encarnacion, Bienvenido, L.E.	.226	76	287	266	24	60	69	9	0	0	33	7	0	3	11	0	40	5	4	6	.259	.264
Encarnacion, Mario, Mod.	.200	5	16	15	1	3	3	0	0	0	1	0	0	1	0	0	2	1	0	0	.200	.250

Player, Team	Avg.	G	TPA	AB	R	H	TB	2B	3B	HR	RBI	SH	SF	HP	BB	IBB	SO	SB	CS	GDP	Slg.	OBP
Enochs, Chris, Vis.	.000	19	1	0	1	0	0	0	0	0	0	0	0	0	1	0	0	0	0	0	.000	1.000
Ernster, Mark, Mud.	.230	61	224	204	30	47	67	9	1	3	22	3	1	3	13	0	40	4	2	8	.328	.285
Faircloth, Chad, S.J.*	.213	31	86	80	12	17	25	2	0	2	8	1	0	2	3	0	22	2	1	1	.313	.259
Fajardo, Alejandro, S.J.	.281	93	396	331	47	93	108	9	3	0	39	4	4	3	54	0	67	23	6	8	.326	.383
Feliciano, Jesus, S.B.*	.289	114	449	405	56	117	136	13	3	0	43	8	3	1	32	0	41	31	11	8	.336	.340
Figueroa, Eduardo, Mud.*	.256	85	346	289	42	74	100	8	0	6	36	0	3	9	45	1	75	0	3	5	.346	.370
Flaherty, Tim, Bak.	.258	18	79	62	17	16	33	2	0	5	15	0	2	1	14	0	20	2	0	2	.532	.392
Flores, Javier, Vis.	.257	77	299	257	35	66	89	9	1	4	41	1	4	4	33	1	34	2	3	5	.346	.346
Forbes, Matt, Mod.	.247	52	204	178	23	44	52	6	1	0	17	4	1	1	20	0	52	9	3	2	.292	.325
Ford, Will, Mud.*	.289	13	49	45	7	13	20	1	0	2	8	0	0	1	3	1	13	2	0	1	.444	.347
Fox, Jason, Mud.†	.249	130	563	493	58	123	150	17	2	2	43	10	5	3	52	1	92	53	17	4	.304	.322
Freeman, Corey, Lan.	.214	27	123	112	19	24	32	6	1	0	7	0	1	2	8	0	23	5	6	2	.286	.265
French, Ron, R.C.	.125	12	20	16	1	2	2	0	0	0	1	0	1	2	1	0	5	0	0	1	.125	.250
Fulse, Sheldon, Lan.†	.274	17	73	62	11	17	27	4	3	0	7	2	0	1	8	0	18	0	1	0	.435	.366
Gandolfo, Rob, Lan.*	.212	55	209	184	28	39	48	4	1	1	12	0	2	7	16	0	20	4	7	4	.261	.297
Gastelum, Carlos, L.E.	.209	27	87	67	11	14	18	4	0	0	8	5	0	4	11	0	17	3	4	2	.269	.354
German, Esteban, Vis.	.264	109	500	428	82	113	153	14	10	2	35	4	2	5	61	0	86	78	8	4	.357	.361
Gibbs, Kevin, S.B.†	.358	13	65	53	13	19	29	3	2	1	13	0	1	0	11	0	9	5	3	0	.547	.462
Glassey, Josh, S.B.-H.D.*	.225	43	159	129	18	29	43	14	0	0	10	0	1	0	29	1	36	0	1	2	.333	.371
Goldfield, Josh, H.D.*	.235	29	87	85	9	20	29	6	0	1	10	0	1	0	1	0	17	2	2	2	.341	.241
Gomez, Ramon, H.D.	.308	41	143	130	21	40	57	3	4	2	9	1	0	1	11	0	30	10	4	1	.438	.366
Gonzalez, Jimmy, S.B.	.284	125	556	510	71	145	192	19	5	6	66	9	4	5	28	0	54	30	21	9	.376	.325
Gonzalez, Jose, Bak.	.000	4	4	4	0	0	0	0	0	0	0	0	0	0	0	0	3	0	0	0	.000	.000
Gordon, Brian, H.D.*	.311	127	532	476	98	148	236	26	13	12	66	0	6	2	47	1	107	19	14	8	.496	.371
Greene, Clay, S.J.	.252	103	386	326	49	82	105	15	1	2	35	8	4	3	45	0	63	38	15	4	.322	.344
Gregg, Mitch, Mod.*	.217	52	209	175	22	38	50	6	0	2	22	1	0	3	30	0	50	2	0	1	.286	.341
Gustafson, Troy, S.J.	.200	3	6	5	0	1	1	1	0	0	1	0	0	0	1	0	0	0	0	0	.200	.333
Guzman, Elpidio, L.E.*	.282	135	612	532	96	150	229	20	16	9	72	5	11	3	61	2	116	53	14	6	.430	.353
Hall, Justin, Mod.	.255	90	409	341	59	87	119	17	3	3	38	2	4	6	56	0	65	12	3	7	.349	.366
Hammock, Rob, H.D.	.353	40	167	136	25	48	74	15	1	3	23	0	3	1	27	1	24	3	3	5	.544	.455
Hammond, Derry, Mud.	.167	66	237	210	23	35	56	6	0	5	23	1	5	6	15	0	87	2	2	3	.267	.237
Hargrove, Harvey, Lan.	.258	120	484	399	60	103	138	22	2	3	58	1	3	10	69	0	76	10	14	10	.346	.378
Harris, Cedrick, H.D.	.264	34	144	129	27	34	48	6	4	0	14	1	1	1	12	0	29	10	4	1	.372	.329
Haynes, Larry, Lan.	.222	7	28	27	3	6	8	2	0	0	0	0	1	0	0	0	9	2	0	0	.296	.222
Hernandez, John, S.B.	.249	80	307	273	30	68	91	17	0	2	20	7	1	12	14	1	53	6	2	5	.333	.313
Hill, Jason, L.E.	.249	70	267	233	23	58	82	12	0	4	33	4	2	4	23	1	44	0	1	5	.352	.324
Hochgesang, Joshua, Vis.	.246	126	551	443	78	109	198	23	3	20	80	2	9	7	90	4	135	20	9	11	.447	.375
Hood, Jay, L.E.	.184	26	111	103	9	19	22	3	0	0	9	1	1	2	4	0	25	1	2	1	.214	.227
Hopper, Shane, R.C.	.302	108	485	447	77	135	210	28	7	11	58	1	3	5	28	1	110	15	11	5	.470	.348
Howe, Matt, Vis.	.255	104	426	364	60	93	151	17	1	13	55	3	7	7	45	1	77	10	5	8	.415	.343
Ingram, Darron, S.B.	.265	100	435	396	58	105	178	16	6	15	71	0	2	0	37	1	136	5	5	10	.449	.326
Jaha, John, Mod.	.000	1	4	2	1	0	0	0	0	0	0	0	0	0	2	1	1	0	0	0	.000	.500
Jaramillo, Frank, Mud.	.239	84	312	276	34	66	98	13	2	5	27	5	1	5	24	0	63	12	7	4	.355	.310
Jaramillo, Milko, S.B.†	.190	34	122	105	11	20	22	0	1	0	6	6	1	2	8	0	24	4	1	2	.210	.259
Jaroncyk, Ryan, S.B.†	.105	11	43	38	4	4	5	1	0	0	1	3	0	0	2	0	11	1	0	1	.132	.150
Jester, Joe, S.J.	.263	114	524	429	94	113	158	13	4	8	46	3	6	17	69	0	75	24	8	7	.368	.382
Johnson, Gary, L.E.*	.338	70	316	266	56	90	153	20	2	13	62	0	5	4	41	1	59	13	6	6	.575	.427
Kasper, Todd, H.D.*	.234	45	160	137	16	32	41	6	0	1	19	1	2	1	19	1	26	2	4	3	.299	.327
Keating, Matthew, S.J.*	.318	10	23	22	1	7	8	1	0	0	0	0	0	0	1	0	2	0	1	0	.364	.348
Keith, Rusty, Mod.	.316	104	481	389	84	123	171	22	1	8	61	4	3	3	82	1	72	10	3	11	.440	.436
Keller, G.W., Vis.	.234	28	90	77	15	18	27	3	3	0	9	2	1	1	9	0	15	3	2	2	.351	.318
Kenney, Jeff, Mud.	.266	56	230	188	27	50	63	13	0	0	16	3	1	4	34	0	34	5	7	3	.335	.388
Knight, Marcus, L.E.†	.234	55	220	192	26	45	71	10	2	4	20	4	2	2	20	1	39	4	4	4	.370	.310
Koonce, Graham, R.C.*	.295	137	595	475	92	140	240	40	3	18	93	0	4	4	107	7	105	0	0	4	.505	.425
Kuzmic, Craig, Lan.†	.297	136	609	522	106	155	259	27	10	19	104	0	6	10	71	3	124	5	8	10	.496	.388
Laird, Gerald, Vis.	.243	33	120	103	14	25	28	3	0	0	13	0	2	1	14	0	27	7	2	3	.272	.333
Lockwood, Mike, Mod.*	.314	47	219	159	42	50	80	12	0	6	35	3	7	4	46	6	25	9	1	3	.503	.463
Loggins, Joshua, R.C.	.300	78	333	293	52	88	127	13	4	6	43	0	4	6	30	2	84	9	4	5	.433	.372
Lopez, Norberto, L.E.	.038	30	90	79	2	3	4	1	0	0	2	2	0	0	9	0	29	0	0	3	.051	.136
Luderer, Brian, Mod.	.301	40	164	136	22	41	55	2	0	4	23	2	1	3	22	0	22	1	1	4	.404	.407
Ludwick, Ryan, Mod.	.264	129	578	493	86	130	249	26	3	29	102	1	7	9	68	0	128	10	6	6	.505	.359
Luster, Jeremy, Bak.†	.282	137	612	517	86	146	233	35	5	14	99	0	8	10	77	6	104	17	2	11	.451	.381
Luther, Ryan, Bak.	.300	110	483	414	78	124	174	25	2	7	48	5	6	10	48	1	94	14	8	6	.420	.381
Macalutas, Jon, Mud.	.251	137	604	483	79	121	184	31	1	10	48	0	6	11	104	1	68	38	16	8	.381	.391
Marcinczyk, T.R., Mod.	.325	10	44	40	9	13	21	5	0	1	11	0	0	1	3	0	6	1	0	1	.525	.386
Martinez, Greg, Mod.†	.364	3	14	11	1	4	4	0	0	0	0	1	0	0	2	0	0	1	1	0	.364	.500
Martinez, Guillermo, Lan.†.	.219	30	108	96	11	21	34	7	3	0	13	2	1	0	9	0	25	1	2	2	.354	.283
Martinez, Hipolito, Vis.	.203	113	456	400	51	81	146	16	5	13	48	2	2	6	46	1	135	8	6	11	.365	.293
Matthews, Lamont, S.B.*	.245	131	575	473	79	116	234	28	9	24	90	1	6	6	88	2	170	12	13	5	.495	.366
May, Freddy, S.B.-Lan.*	.296	86	345	287	57	85	111	12	4	2	39	1	2	3	52	3	47	9	9	9	.387	.407
Maynard, Scott, Lan.	.260	94	387	342	43	89	125	15	0	7	59	1	3	2	39	0	96	4	2	7	.365	.337
McAffee, Josh, H.D.	.167	5	13	12	0	2	4	2	0	0	4	0	0	0	1	0	2	0	0	0	.333	.231
McClendon, Travis, Lan.	.250	43	163	136	17	34	39	5	0	0	20	3	2	4	18	0	23	7	3	3	.287	.350
McDowell, Arturo, Bak.*	.214	122	549	453	77	97	139	13	4	7	53	7	6	6	77	1	129	38	13	5	.307	.332
McGowan, Sean, H.D.	.327	114	508	456	58	149	221	32	2	12	106	0	3	6	43	1	71	4	3	12	.485	.390
Meier, Dan, H.D.*	.267	11	38	30	6	8	15	1	0	2	4	0	1	0	7	0	8	0	0	1	.500	.395
Mejia, Max, S.B.	.233	82	346	305	43	71	106	13	2	6	30	2	3	7	29	2	76	19	12	3	.348	.311
Mendoza, Carlos, S.J.†	.256	112	464	394	52	101	140	16	4	5	45	9	3	9	49	0	82	25	13	11	.355	.349
Messner, Jake, Bak.*	.315	98	348	311	56	98	168	18	2	16	59	0	2	3	32	2	67	7	5	3	.540	.382
Moore, Kevin, Mud.†	.213	20	71	61	10	13	18	2	0	1	8	0	1	0	9	0	19	0	0	1	.295	.310
Mota, Pedro, S.J.*	.227	49	182	154	17	35	52	6	4	1	18	3	1	1	23	2	33	7	3	2	.338	.330
Mott, Bill, L.E.*	.301	115	488	396	83	119	190	20	9	11	82	1	5	10	76	5	78	29	8	5	.480	.421
Neal, Steve, H.D.*	.296	111	455	395	59	117	195	27	3	15	70	0	1	3	56	1	92	11	4	8	.494	.387

Player, Team	Avg.	G	TPA	AB	R	H	TB	2B	3B	HR	RBI	SH	SF	HP	BB	IBB	SO	SB	CS	GDP	Slg.	OBP
Nieckula, Aaron, Vis.-Mod.	.262	87	327	260	51	68	84	10	2	0	34	0	2	14	51	1	66	17	7	4	.323	.407
Niemet, Robert, S.J.	.091	7	11	11	0	1	1	0	0	0	0	0	0	0	0	0	4	0	0	0	.091	.091
Nieves, Wilbert, R.C.	.257	31	119	101	16	26	31	5	0	0	9	2	1	0	15	0	17	2	0	3	.307	.350
Oglesby, Travis, H.D.	.245	88	303	265	40	65	122	16	1	13	45	0	0	1	37	1	100	0	0	8	.460	.340
Olivo, Miguel, Mod.	.282	58	247	227	40	64	100	11	5	5	35	0	2	2	16	0	53	5	2	8	.441	.332
Otero, William, S.J.	.211	59	237	209	22	44	63	8	1	3	22	3	3	1	21	0	53	6	2	7	.301	.282
Owens, Jeremy, R.C.	.256	138	650	570	99	146	243	29	10	16	63	8	4	5	63	1	183	54	12	5	.426	.333
Paciorek, Pete, S.B.*	.279	134	588	499	80	139	222	29	9	12	83	1	5	7	76	6	106	10	10	6	.445	.378
Patten, Chris, Mud.	.260	118	491	443	60	115	167	28	3	6	49	5	3	9	31	0	111	10	7	15	.377	.319
Pecci, Jay, Vis.†	.373	26	120	102	21	38	56	9	0	3	23	0	1	2	15	2	12	6	4	3	.549	.458
Pelaez, Alex, R.C.	.281	62	262	235	29	66	92	20	0	2	28	0	4	0	23	0	27	2	2	11	.391	.340
Perez, Antonio, Lan.	.276	98	474	395	90	109	208	36	6	17	63	9	4	8	58	1	99	28	16	3	.527	.376
Pernalete, Marco, Bak.†	.256	91	368	301	53	77	110	16	1	5	27	6	1	3	57	2	88	15	3	5	.365	.378
Pini, Ryan, S.J.*	.212	123	479	416	47	88	123	13	2	6	47	3	4	3	52	1	124	6	7	10	.296	.301
Powers, Jeff, H.D.*	.309	112	455	408	55	126	158	20	3	2	52	5	4	4	34	0	29	3	6	2	.387	.364
Pujols, Rafael, Vis.	.322	117	481	422	61	136	183	16	2	9	74	0	8	1	50	5	57	11	6	8	.434	.389
Quinlan, Robb, L.E.	.317	127	563	482	79	153	213	35	5	5	85	2	9	2	67	1	82	6	4	7	.442	.396
Quintana, Wilfredo, Lan.	.369	33	115	103	25	38	70	7	2	7	24	2	0	1	9	0	17	3	4	1	.680	.425
Ramirez, Domingo, S.J.	.000	5	10	9	0	0	0	0	0	0	0	0	0	0	1	0	3	0	0	1	.000	.100
Reyes, Christian, Mod.†	.222	68	256	225	26	50	63	7	3	0	19	2	1	1	27	0	62	4	3	15	.280	.307
Reynoso, Ismael, S.J.	.174	51	163	144	16	25	32	2	1	1	5	2	0	5	12	0	22	1	4	3	.222	.261
Risinger, Ben, R.C.	.260	15	58	50	5	13	23	4	0	2	9	0	1	1	6	0	13	0	0	3	.460	.345
Robinson, Bo, Lan.	.313	136	595	515	93	161	224	33	0	10	97	1	9	5	65	2	69	2	5	23	.435	.389
Rodriguez, Guillermo, Bak.	.240	118	487	437	63	105	164	27	1	10	58	4	3	13	30	0	101	20	8	11	.375	.306
Rodriguez, Juan, L.E.†	.283	30	107	92	14	26	37	6	1	1	14	4	1	0	10	0	11	0	3	0	.402	.350
Rosario, Carlos, Mod.†	.236	86	345	284	45	67	92	11	4	2	38	4	0	2	54	0	93	20	7	4	.324	.362
Rosario, Omar, Vis.*	.252	102	414	333	56	84	116	16	2	4	39	2	2	4	73	2	76	24	14	5	.348	.391
Ross, David, S.B.	.257	51	213	191	27	49	83	11	1	7	21	3	1	1	17	1	43	3	2	3	.435	.319
Rowan, Chris, Mud.	.175	39	147	143	13	25	38	5	1	2	4	0	0	1	3	0	55	0	2	3	.266	.197
Ruiz, Ramon, S.B.	.224	39	144	125	21	28	46	8	2	2	23	4	2	1	12	0	28	6	3	3	.368	.293
Sanchez, Yuri, H.D.*	.217	42	157	138	18	30	53	5	0	6	16	4	1	0	14	0	42	1	3	2	.384	.288
Sandoval, Jhensy, H.D.	.236	42	158	148	17	35	63	13	0	5	19	0	1	1	8	0	45	2	5	1	.426	.278
Santangelo, F.P., S.B.†	.474	7	21	19	2	9	13	2	1	0	1	0	0	0	2	0	1	0	0	0	.684	.524
Santos, Luis, H.D.	.228	49	164	145	12	33	43	5	1	1	15	2	3	0	14	0	15	1	3	6	.297	.290
Schaeffer, Jon, Mod.	.262	52	224	191	33	50	76	10	2	4	32	1	2	2	28	0	34	2	3	7	.398	.359
Scharrer, Jim, L.E.	.233	24	100	90	10	21	24	3	0	0	10	0	1	0	9	0	31	1	0	2	.267	.300
Schill, Vaughn, Lan.	.250	6	21	16	4	4	4	0	0	0	2	0	0	0	5	0	5	2	1	0	.250	.429
Schmidt, Bryan, R.C.	.143	32	106	98	4	14	16	2	0	0	3	0	0	0	8	0	19	0	0	6	.163	.208
Schneidmiller, Gary, Mod.	.223	77	306	242	36	54	68	11	0	1	21	1	1	1	61	0	62	4	3	10	.281	.380
Serrano, Sammy, S.J.	.182	38	145	132	12	24	37	3	2	2	17	0	1	0	12	0	30	4	1	5	.280	.248
Silvestre, Juan, Lan.	.304	127	580	506	104	154	265	15	3	30	137	0	7	7	60	1	126	9	4	5	.524	.381
Sledge, Terrmel, Lan.*	.339	103	479	384	90	130	199	22	7	11	75	1	5	17	72	3	49	35	11	4	.518	.458
Snellgrove, Clay, R.C.	.276	104	432	388	33	107	132	18	2	1	44	1	5	3	35	2	36	9	7	7	.340	.336
Sosa, Nicolas, Mod.	.279	61	261	219	38	61	99	18	1	6	44	2	2	0	38	0	64	0	0	6	.452	.382
Soto, Jorge, Vis.	.168	44	145	119	17	20	42	4	0	6	22	1	0	4	21	0	58	4	1	6	.353	.313
Specht, Brian, L.E.†	.269	89	395	334	70	90	128	22	5	2	35	3	3	3	52	2	80	25	12	6	.383	.370
Sprague, Ed, R.C.	.286	2	8	7	1	2	5	0	0	1	2	0	0	0	1	0	0	0	0	0	.714	.375
Stone, Jon, R.C.†	.243	12	39	37	4	9	11	0	1	0	2	1	0	0	1	0	13	0	0	0	.297	.263
Stuart, Rich, L.E.	.246	83	324	293	52	72	118	11	4	9	39	3	3	4	21	0	56	14	9	5	.403	.302
Summers, John, S.J.†	.281	66	280	249	24	70	87	12	1	1	32	0	3	5	23	2	44	2	7	6	.349	.350
Sykes, Jamie, H.D.	.287	83	351	303	64	87	162	15	6	16	57	0	2	1	45	0	80	11	6	3	.535	.379
Terrero, Luis, H.D.	.190	19	83	79	10	15	20	3	1	0	1	0	1	0	3	0	16	5	5	2	.253	.229
Thurston, Joe, S.B.*	.303	138	641	551	97	167	226	31	8	4	70	9	8	17	56	1	61	43	25	8	.410	.380
Tommasini, Kevin, Bak.	.256	98	355	297	59	76	118	12	3	8	47	1	3	5	51	0	81	11	7	8	.397	.367
Torcato, Tony, S.J.*	.324	119	544	490	77	159	221	37	2	7	88	0	7	6	41	8	62	19	4	2	.451	.379
Turco, Anthony, S.J.*	.167	28	80	72	3	12	14	2	0	0	5	0	2	0	6	0	24	0	0	1	.194	.225
Turco, Paul, Bak.†	.239	33	114	88	12	21	21	0	0	0	11	4	1	0	21	0	20	1	3	0	.239	.382
Urquiola, Carlos, H.D.*	.364	40	185	165	34	60	70	6	2	0	12	1	1	3	15	0	16	24	5	1	.424	.424
Valderrama, Carlos, Bak.	.315	121	491	435	78	137	207	21	5	13	81	5	8	4	39	1	96	54	11	4	.476	.370
Valdez, Mario, Vis.*	.500	1	3	2	0	1	1	0	0	0	0	0	0	0	1	0	1	0	0	0	.500	.667
Vasquez, Sandy, S.B.	.215	93	367	331	55	71	123	6	3	10	43	5	2	5	24	0	115	11	8	0	.372	.276
Vizcaino, Maximo, H.D.	.225	48	163	160	11	36	49	6	2	1	10	1	0	0	2	0	33	1	2	3	.306	.235
Wenner, Michael, Vis.	.237	122	562	477	82	113	152	20	5	3	53	18	6	6	55	0	91	57	18	6	.319	.320
White, Devon, S.B.†	.400	2	7	5	2	2	3	1	0	0	1	0	0	1	1	0	0	0	0	0	.600	.571
Williams, Jason, H.D.	.222	7	32	27	4	6	7	1	0	0	1	0	0	1	4	0	4	1	0	1	.259	.344
Williams, Matt, H.D.	.375	2	8	8	1	3	6	0	0	1	1	0	0	0	0	0	1	0	0	0	.750	.375
Williams, P.J., Lan.	.291	51	207	175	37	51	64	3	5	0	27	3	0	1	28	0	38	20	9	4	.366	.392
Williams, Peanut, Lan.	.253	76	323	292	53	74	113	15	0	8	55	1	1	5	24	0	109	3	2	6	.387	.320
Williford, Dan, H.D.*	.191	31	98	94	15	18	23	5	0	0	5	0	0	2	2	0	31	0	1	0	.245	.224
Woodward, Steve, H.D.†	.260	69	303	265	45	69	87	10	1	2	25	5	4	2	27	0	74	7	7	3	.328	.329
Wright, Mike, S.J.	.191	97	346	299	29	57	87	10	1	6	33	10	0	6	31	0	102	1	0	6	.291	.280
Zeber, Ryan, L.E.	.207	10	31	29	0	6	11	1	2	0	2	1	0	1	0	0	3	0	0	0	.379	.233

GRAND SLAMS: Brito, Casper, McGowan, Sosa, Soto, Sykes, 2 each; Asche, Castro, Cordido, Cresse, Ji. Gonzalez, Hargrove, Hopper, Ingram, Knight, Koonce, Kuzmic, Loggins, Ludwick, Luster, Luther, Matthews, C. Mendoza, Owens, Pujols, C. Rosario, Silvestre, Stuart, Tommasini, Valderrama, Vasquez, 1 each.

AWARDED FIRST BASE ON CATCHER'S INTERFERENCE: Koonce 5 (McClendon 2, Ardoin, Angel Diaz, Laird); Christensen 4 (Hernandez 2, Hammock, Loggins); Hargrove 2 (Caiazzo, Pujols); Brito (Wright); Gordon (Loggins); J. Hill (Pujols); Hopper (Zeber); F. Jaramillo (Niemet); Matthews (Laird); Pini (Brito); Quinlan (Wright).

PLAYERS WITH TWO OR MORE TEAMS

Player, Team	Avg.	G	TPA	AB	R	H	TB	2B	3B	HR	RBI	SH	SF	HP	BB	IBB	SO	SB	CS	GDP	Slg.	OBP
Campusano, Carlos, S.J.	.333	1	4	3	0	1	1	0	0	0	1	0	0	0	0	0	0	0	0	0	.333	.333
Campusano, Carlos, Bak.	.252	68	272	246	33	62	83	10	4	1	26	7	1	7	11	0	47	13	3	5	.337	.302
Glassey, Josh, S.B.*	.183	20	79	60	10	11	18	7	0	0	4	0	0	1	18	1	20	0	0	2	.300	.380

Player, Team	Avg.	G	TPA	AB	R	H	TB	2B	3B	HR	RBI	SH	SF	HP	BB	IBB	SO	SB	CS	GDP	Slg.	OBP
Glassey, Josh, H.D.*	.261	23	80	69	8	18	25	7	0	0	6	0	0	0	11	0	16	0	1	0	.362	.363
May, Freddy, S.B.*	.207	10	37	29	1	6	7	1	0	0	3	0	1	0	7	0	3	2	1	0	.241	.351
May, Freddy, Lan.*	.306	76	308	258	56	79	104	11	4	2	36	1	1	3	45	3	44	7	8	9	.403	.414
Nieckula, Aaron, Vis.	.259	72	266	212	45	55	69	8	0	2	29	0	2	13	39	1	54	14	6	3	.325	.402
Nieckula, Aaron, Mod.	.271	15	61	48	6	13	15	2	0	0	5	0	0	1	12	0	12	3	1	1	.313	.426

2000 PITCHING

TEAM

Team	W	L	Pct.	ERA	G	CG	ShO	Sv.	IP	H	TBF	R	ER	HR	SH	SF	HB	BB	IBB	SO	WP	Bk.
San Bernardino .	77	63	.550	3.73	140	3	5	37	1253.0	1220	5388	604	519	79	43	36	81	519	14	1002	73	12
Mudville	68	72	.486	3.85	140	1	9	31	1235.1	1106	5354	638	529	83	35	43	73	605	8	1213	87	15
Modesto	76	64	.543	3.90	140	2	7	46	1240.1	1213	5354	668	538	71	49	54	53	493	39	1083	94	15
Bakersfield	80	60	.571	4.14	140	1	7	46	1237.1	1305	5457	680	569	89	45	39	72	524	7	980	77	17
Lake Elsinore	70	70	.500	4.18	140	6	7	29	1251.2	1266	5515	748	581	85	42	56	59	542	22	955	104	19
Lancaster	89	51	.636	4.20	140	1	5	39	1254.2	1320	5500	721	585	115	26	46	71	449	17	1064	73	14
Visalia	78	62	.557	4.35	140	2	10	46	1235.2	1254	5414	726	597	107	41	37	55	507	16	1143	66	15
R. Cucamonga ..	61	79	.436	4.85	140	0	5	33	1249.2	1153	5635	808	673	93	50	53	71	774	6	1245	142	27
San Jose	53	87	.379	5.03	140	2	4	28	1237.1	1321	5593	855	691	103	50	61	81	612	9	926	115	15
High Desert	48	92	.343	6.13	140	1	2	23	1215.1	1380	5626	987	828	128	34	54	76	701	5	948	100	21

INDIVIDUAL

TOP QUALIFIERS FOR EARNED-RUN AVERAGE TITLE

Minimum 112 innings.*Lefthanded pitcher.

Pitcher, Team	W	L	Pct.	ERA	G	GS	CG	ShO	GF	Sv.	IP	H	TBF	R	ER	HR	SH	SF	HB	BB	IBB	SO	WP	Bk.
Garcia, Carlos, S.B.	14	7	.667	2.57	27	27	2	1	0	0	182.0	162	737	61	52	5	5	4	14	49	0	106	2	3
Surkont, Keith, Vis.	8	7	.533	2.72	27	22	0	0	1	1	125.2	104	535	60	38	6	4	3	11	54	0	122	5	4
Bermudez, Manny, Bak.	9	7	.563	2.84	59	0	0	0	25	7	120.1	107	487	41	38	3	9	2	9	27	3	66	4	0
Ramos, Mario, Mod.*	12	5	.706	2.90	26	24	1	1	1	0	152.0	131	624	63	49	6	9	3	3	50	4	134	3	1
Williams, Jerome, S.J.	7	6	.538	2.94	23	19	0	0	2	0	125.2	89	512	53	41	6	5	6	10	48	3	115	9	2
Bynum, Mike, R.C.*	9	6	.600	3.00	21	21	0	0	0	0	126.0	101	517	55	42	4	3	5	8	51	0	129	7	1
Chiasson, Scott, Vis.	11	4	.733	3.06	31	23	0	0	4	2	156.0	146	666	66	53	17	3	2	6	57	2	150	8	1
Lehr, Charles, Mod.	13	6	.684	3.19	29	25	0	0	1	0	175.0	161	709	71	62	10	8	4	5	46	1	138	15	5
Junge, Eric, S.B.	8	1	.889	3.36	29	24	0	0	2	1	158.0	159	666	69	59	8	3	5	9	53	0	116	8	2
Childers, Jason, Mud.	12	10	.545	3.49	28	28	0	0	0	0	157.1	140	646	71	61	12	3	3	0	54	0	177	6	0
Watkins, Steve, R.C.	7	6	.538	3.70	27	27	0	0	0	0	151.0	118	652	75	62	10	8	6	1	90	0	163	10	2
Devey, Phil, S.B.*	6	11	.353	3.76	29	24	1	0	1	0	172.1	179	737	86	72	13	5	7	13	54	1	112	3	1
Pena, Juan, Mod.*	6	9	.400	3.86	29	27	0	0	0	0	154.0	132	659	85	66	7	5	4	1	75	2	177	16	3
Cozier, Vance, Bak.	10	8	.556	3.89	28	28	0	0	0	0	150.1	164	665	82	65	6	6	7	4	61	0	106	6	2
Seabury, Jaron, Mud.	10	7	.588	4.07	33	21	1	0	0	0	150.1	135	650	83	68	6	5	6	19	72	0	97	14	4

DEPARTMENTAL LEADERS: W—Heaverlo, Horgan, C. Garcia, 14 each; L—Cunningham, Verplancke, 14 each; Pct.—Caraccioli, .769; G—Forbes, 74; GS—Cozier, Mears, Childers, 28 each; CG—Lackey, Emanuel, C. Garcia, 2 each; ShO—Lackey, Nix, Ramos, C. Garcia, 1 each; GF—Bullard, 52; Sv.—Bullard, 30; IP—C. Garcia, 182; H—Horgan, 190; TBF—Horgan, 739; R—Mendoza, 140; ER—Mendoza, 110; HR—Calzada, 25; SH—Flores, 10; HB—Seabury, 19; BB—Howard, 111; IBB—Brink, 5; SO—Pena, Childers, 177 each; WP—Cunningham, 21; BK—Forbes, Lehr, 5 each.

ALL PITCHERS

*Lefthanded pitcher.

Pitcher, Team	W	L	Pct.	ERA	G	GS	CG	ShO	GF	Sv.	IP	H	TBF	R	ER	HR	SH	SF	HB	BB	IBB	SO	WP	Bk.
Adkins, Jon, Mod.	5	2	.714	1.81	9	7	1	0	0	0	49.2	41	203	17	10	1	1	2	1	17	0	38	2	0
Aguilera, Adrian, S.B.*	0	1	.000	10.03	9	0	0	0	6	1	11.2	10	56	13	13	1	2	0	3	9	1	4	2	0
Allen, Rodney, Mud.	0	2	.000	4.94	16	3	0	0	2	0	31.0	40	151	25	17	2	0	2	4	14	0	34	2	2
Anderson, Jason, Vis.*	3	3	.500	6.98	19	0	0	0	6	2	29.2	36	137	26	23	3	2	1	2	12	0	19	0	0
Atchison, Scott, Lan.	5	5	.500	3.69	18	18	1	0	0	0	97.2	117	436	58	40	10	2	4	4	21	0	77	2	0
Avery, Paul, H.D.*	0	0	.000	18.00	3	0	0	0	1	0	3.0	8	20	6	6	1	0	1	0	4	0	2	1	0
Ayala, Julio, Lan.*	4	1	.800	5.13	14	3	0	0	1	0	26.1	34	124	19	15	4	0	0	4	5	0	20	2	0
Balbuena, Caleb, Lan.	3	1	.750	4.54	21	3	0	0	11	3	39.2	47	185	29	20	3	2	1	3	18	2	24	2	0
Barber, Scott, H.D.	0	2	.000	6.89	4	4	0	0	0	0	15.2	18	69	15	12	0	0	2	1	5	0	12	0	1
Bausher, Andy, R.C.*	1	0	1.000	3.18	5	0	0	0	2	0	5.2	6	28	4	2	0	2	0	0	4	1	3	0	0
Bazzani, Matt, Bak.	0	0	.000	0.00	1	0	0	0	1	0	1.1	2	6	0	0	0	0	0	0	0	0	0	0	0
Bazzell, Shane, Mod.	3	4	.429	5.75	32	5	0	0	10	1	72.0	91	331	57	46	6	1	4	1	30	4	71	7	1
Beckman, Jacob, Mod.	1	0	1.000	4.50	11	0	0	0	5	0	14.0	16	69	8	7	0	0	2	1	15	2	4	0	2
Belcher, Tim, L.E.	1	0	1.000	3.21	3	3	0	0	0	0	14.0	6	50	5	5	1	1	1	1	2	0	16	0	0
Bell, Casey, L.E.	0	1	.000	12.27	3	0	0	0	1	0	3.2	5	21	8	5	0	1	2	0	4	0	2	1	0
Belson, Gregory, H.D.	2	0	1.000	2.49	22	0	0	0	21	8	25.1	19	107	8	7	3	1	0	0	13	0	23	2	0
Bergman, Dusty, L.E.*	0	1	.000	2.25	1	1	0	0	0	0	4.0	3	18	4	1	0	0	0	1	0	3	0	0
Bermudez, Manny, Bak.	9	7	.563	2.84	59	0	0	0	25	7	120.1	107	487	41	38	3	9	2	9	27	3	66	4	0
Berry, Jon, S.B.	7	4	.636	5.14	40	0	0	0	24	5	68.2	57	310	33	24	3	6	2	5	47	2	68	6	0
Berryman, Chad, L.E.	0	4	.000	7.05	25	0	0	0	8	2	37.0	46	169	32	29	4	2	1	1	13	1	22	7	0
Blood, Darin, Bak.-S.J.	0	1	.000	18.00	5	2	0	0	2	0	4.0	6	32	8	8	0	0	0	1	14	0	1	2	0
Boehringer, Brian, R.C.	0	2	.000	5.40	4	2	0	0	0	0	5.0	8	24	3	3	0	0	0	2	1	0	5	0	0
Bonilla, Ben, H.D.*	0	0	.000	9.00	1	0	0	0	1	0	1.0	1	5	1	1	0	0	1	0	0	0	0	0	0
Bridenbaugh, Christian, S.B.* .	2	0	1.000	7.97	11	0	0	0	3	1	20.1	29	103	20	18	6	1	1	1	10	0	18	5	0
Bridges, Dou, L.E.*	6	10	.375	5.72	31	22	1	0	3	0	140.0	166	626	103	89	15	7	9	3	62	0	85	10	2
Brink, Jim, Mod.	3	2	.600	3.42	42	0	0	0	33	19	47.1	49	209	21	18	2	3	2	2	17	5	41	3	0
Brooks, Jacob, L.E.	7	3	.700	4.25	28	7	0	0	7	0	78.1	82	354	52	37	5	3	3	5	33	2	80	8	4
Brous, David, S.J.*	1	3	.250	4.59	9	7	0	0	1	0	33.1	26	143	17	17	1	1	0	0	20	0	25	2	1
Bullard, Jason, Bak.	4	4	.500	4.02	58	0	0	0	52	30	65.0	69	287	33	29	6	3	2	4	26	1	65	5	0
Bynum, Mike, R.C.*	9	6	.600	3.00	21	21	0	0	0	0	126.0	101	517	55	42	4	3	5	8	51	0	129	7	1

CLASS A California League

Pitcher, Team	W	L	Pct.	ERA	G	GS	CG	ShO	GF	Sv.	IP	H	TBF	R	ER	HR	SH	SF	HB	BB	IBB	SO	WP	Bk.
Calzada, Javier, Vis.	7	8	.467	4.68	31	24	1	0	2	2	150.0	149	643	83	78	25	4	2	6	55	1	127	4	0
Camp, Shawn, R.C.	1	0	1.000	1.45	14	0	0	0	13	6	18.2	10	72	3	3	0	0	0	2	5	0	18	2	0
Caraccioli, Lance, S.B.*	10	3	.769	3.92	34	9	0	0	12	4	105.2	105	476	56	46	8	3	3	6	68	1	95	4	2
Ceriani, Matt, Mud.	0	0	.000	9.00	1	0	0	0	1	0	1.0	1	5	1	1	1	0	0	1	0	0	0	0	0
Chavez, Carlos, Vis.	5	2	.714	2.73	34	0	0	0	11	5	56.0	51	235	21	17	4	4	1	2	14	2	66	5	0
Chiasson, Scott, Vis.	11	4	.733	3.06	31	23	0	0	4	2	156.0	146	666	66	53	17	3	2	6	57	2	150	8	1
Childers, Jason, Mud.	12	10	.545	3.49	28	28	0	0	0	0	157.1	140	646	71	61	12	3	3	0	54	0	177	6	0
Childers, Matt, Mud.	3	9	.250	4.75	15	15	0	0	0	0	85.1	103	388	59	45	10	2	2	3	32	0	43	3	2
Clark, Jeffrey, S.J.	0	0	.000	2.25	2	0	0	0	0	0	4.0	2	14	1	1	0	0	0	0	0	0	8	1	0
Condrey, Clay, R.C.	1	1	.500	3.48	18	0	0	0	9	4	20.2	18	85	9	8	1	1	0	2	7	0	21	2	1
Connolly, Keith, S.J.	3	6	.333	4.17	54	0	0	0	22	1	77.2	66	336	45	36	12	4	8	3	33	1	71	9	0
Cooper, Brian, L.E.	0	0	.000	0.00	1	1	0	0	0	0	7.0	4	27	1	0	0	0	0	1	2	0	3	2	0
Correa, Elvis, S.B.	3	9	.250	3.06	41	0	0	0	34	14	67.2	74	285	25	23	5	9	2	2	16	3	58	6	0
Coscia, Tony, Bak.	7	8	.467	4.14	21	21	0	0	0	0	119.2	115	503	63	55	1	2	11	31	0	124	7	4
Cox, Ryan, S.J.	5	8	.385	4.61	19	19	0	0	0	0	107.1	122	463	67	55	12	3	7	5	28	0	54	5	0
Cozier, Vance, Bak.	10	8	.556	3.89	28	28	0	0	0	0	150.1	164	665	82	65	6	6	7	4	61	0	106	6	2
Cramblitt, Joey, H.D.	4	1	.800	6.21	22	0	0	0	7	0	42.0	62	194	35	29	8	2	0	2	14	0	28	0	1
Crawford, Wesley, L.E.*	7	8	.467	4.38	27	22	1	0	0	0	141.2	145	625	84	69	9	6	5	12	66	1	102	10	4
Cunningham, Jeremy, S.J.	5	14	.263	5.94	34	19	0	0	6	0	133.1	169	625	105	88	8	9	4	9	61	0	90	21	4
Davis, Monty, Vis.	0	0	.000	0.00	1	0	0	0	1	0	1.2	1	7	0	0	0	0	0	0	1	0	1	0	0
De Hart, Blair, R.C.	0	7	.000	7.31	9	9	0	0	0	0	48.0	55	217	45	39	5	1	3	4	18	0	36	2	1
De La Cruz, Jose, Mod.	0	1	.000	27.00	1	0	0	0	1	0	0.1	2	5	1	1	0	1	0	1	1	0	0	0	0
Demouy, Chris, L.E.*	7	2	.778	2.28	40	1	0	0	17	2	59.1	62	264	21	15	0	1	2	3	26	0	44	3	0
Dent, Doug, R.C.	2	1	.667	2.43	10	7	0	0	1	0	40.2	34	176	17	11	2	1	1	3	19	0	31	4	0
Devey, Phil, S.B.*	6	11	.353	3.76	29	24	1	0	1	0	172.1	179	737	86	72	13	5	7	13	54	1	112	3	1
Diaz, Alex, Vis.	0	0	.000	18.41	7	0	0	0	3	0	7.1	18	41	15	15	2	0	0	0	5	0	3	2	0
Diaz, Antonio, R.C.	2	4	.333	7.68	24	0	0	0	5	0	38.2	58	190	40	33	5	5	4	1	17	1	18	7	3
Dotel, Melido, S.B.	1	1	.500	3.72	8	0	0	0	0	0	9.2	7	50	6	4	0	0	0	4	12	0	11	2	0
Duarte, Renney, L.E.	2	2	.500	4.65	17	0	0	0	3	0	31.0	33	141	22	16	3	1	3	1	13	2	24	0	0
Dubose, Eric, Vis.*	0	1	.000	1.69	5	0	0	0	2	1	10.2	8	46	2	2	0	0	1	5	1	0	12	1	0
Emanuel, Brandon, L.E.	4	10	.286	6.27	19	17	2	0	1	0	103.1	136	489	89	72	14	2	5	7	43	2	54	12	1
Encarnacion, Bienvenido, L.E.	0	0	.000	9.00	1	0	0	0	1	0	1.0	3	7	1	1	0	0	0	0	1	0	0	0	0
Enochs, Chris, Vis.	2	5	.286	4.64	18	18	0	0	0	0	97.0	116	429	61	50	6	5	5	0	38	0	75	6	1
Escalante, Jaime, L.E.	1	1	.500	2.08	6	0	0	0	4	1	8.2	6	37	2	2	1	0	0	0	4	0	18	0	0
Estes, Shawn, S.J.*	1	0	1.000	0.00	1	1	0	0	0	0	7.0	2	23	0	0	0	0	0	1	0	0	11	1	0
Fahrner, Evan, H.D.	1	12	.077	5.34	45	5	0	0	15	1	87.2	102	411	79	52	10	4	3	4	43	1	92	12	3
Faircloth, Chad, S.J.	0	0	.000	0.00	1	0	0	0	1	0	1.0	0	3	0	0	0	0	0	0	0	0	0	0	0
Featherstone, Deron, S.J.	0	0	.000	5.40	1	0	0	0	1	0	3.1	7	19	3	2	0	1	0	0	2	0	0	0	0
Fikac, Jeremy, R.C.	5	3	.625	1.80	61	0	0	0	43	20	75.0	46	298	19	15	2	4	1	4	24	0	101	6	0
Fischer, Mike, S.B.	2	2	.500	3.97	11	10	0	0	0	0	45.1	53	198	24	20	4	0	1	2	17	0	33	3	0
Fleming, John, H.D.	2	3	.400	6.12	13	7	0	0	2	0	42.2	53	202	36	29	3	1	2	1	26	0	39	0	0
Flores, Benito, S.J.*	2	9	.182	4.64	48	2	0	0	17	0	108.2	131	504	74	56	9	10	4	4	55	3	62	3	0
Forbes, Derek, H.D.	0	0	.000	8.26	20	2	0	0	4	0	40.1	37	186	40	37	9	1	3	0	31	1	38	2	0
Forbes, Keith, R.C.	5	6	.455	4.04	74	0	0	0	24	1	98.0	79	437	59	44	10	7	5	3	59	0	99	10	5
Foster, Kris, S.B.	0	0	.000	0.77	10	1	0	0	5	2	11.2	7	42	2	1	0	0	0	1	1	0	19	0	0
Galva, Claudio, Vis.*	7	4	.636	3.61	48	7	0	0	30	15	97.1	103	421	54	39	9	1	3	1	29	0	98	3	1
Garcia, Apostol, S.B.	1	2	.333	4.05	4	4	0	0	0	0	20.0	24	86	10	9	1	0	1	0	6	0	17	4	0
Garcia, Carlos, S.B.	14	7	.667	2.57	27	27	2	1	0	0	182.0	162	737	61	52	5	5	4	14	49	0	106	2	3
German, Franklyn, Mod.	5	5	.500	5.50	17	14	0	0	2	0	72.0	88	333	55	44	4	0	3	6	37	0	52	7	2
Gonzalez, Cristian, Mod.	0	0	.000	8.64	4	0	0	0	0	0	8.1	16	45	9	8	1	0	1	5	0	4	2	0
Greene, Clay, S.J.	0	0	.000	0.00	1	0	0	0	1	0	1.0	0	5	0	0	0	0	0	0	2	0	1	0	0
Grezlovski, Ben, L.E.	2	4	.333	5.23	43	0	0	0	33	13	53.1	48	241	33	31	2	3	1	2	30	4	51	5	0
Harris, Toby, H.D.	2	2	.500	11.07	14	0	0	0	2	0	20.1	34	108	28	25	3	0	1	15	1	19	0	3
Hart, Len, R.C.*	0	0	.000	1.72	13	0	0	0	2	0	15.2	13	61	4	3	0	3	0	0	4	1	12	1	0
Haworth, Brent, L.E.	3	2	.600	4.01	17	0	0	0	4	0	33.2	42	142	18	15	5	1	0	0	6	0	13	0	1
Heaverlo, Jeff, Lan.	14	6	.700	4.22	27	27	0	0	0	0	155.2	170	685	84	73	18	4	5	6	52	0	159	9	2
Hensley, Matthew, L.E.	0	0	.000	0.00	1	0	0	0	0	0	1.0	1	4	0	0	0	0	0	0	0	0	2	0	0
Hershiser, Orel, S.B.	1	0	1.000	3.06	3	3	0	0	0	0	17.2	18	73	7	6	1	0	1	1	5	0	8	1	0
Hill, Ken, L.E.	0	0	.000	0.00	1	1	0	0	0	0	4.0	5	18	2	0	0	0	0	1	3	0	3	0	0
Holmes, Mike, Mod.	4	0	1.000	4.50	21	2	0	0	6	1	54.0	60	237	32	27	4	2	5	1	14	1	40	2	0
Horgan, Joe, S.J.*	14	10	.583	4.60	27	27	1	0	0	0	166.1	190	739	104	85	15	5	6	14	66	0	92	14	0
Howard, Ben, R.C.	5	11	.313	6.37	32	19	0	0	4	0	107.1	88	506	87	76	8	2	2	111	1	150	14	1
Hundley, Jeff, L.E.*	5	5	.500	2.78	18	15	0	0	1	0	97.0	85	403	48	30	3	5	2	2	36	1	69	6	0
Hunter, Johnny, S.J.	5	5	.500	4.67	47	8	0	0	7	0	106.0	92	469	68	55	7	3	6	2	65	0	87	14	4
Jacobs, Dwayne, S.B.	3	2	.600	4.03	21	0	0	0	11	4	29.0	23	135	14	13	2	1	0	1	30	0	41	5	0
Jacobs, Greg, L.E.*	2	1	.667	6.80	32	0	0	0	11	0	41.0	39	205	37	31	2	0	3	5	43	2	37	9	1
Jacobs, Ryan, Mud.*	2	3	.400	7.50	26	1	0	0	4	0	36.0	41	175	35	30	4	2	1	1	29	0	31	6	0
Jensen, Jared, Vis.	1	3	.250	4.92	30	6	0	0	3	0	75.0	94	345	56	41	7	2	1	6	28	1	60	4	2
Jensen, Jason, H.D.*	6	12	.333	5.66	28	26	0	0	0	0	154.1	181	697	115	97	13	2	5	5	82	0	103	13	1
Johnson, Eric, S.J.-Bak.	0	0	.000	8.12	18	4	0	0	4	0	41.0	56	209	43	37	5	2	3	2	35	0	20	5	1
Johnson, James, Mud.*	3	5	.375	3.07	11	11	0	0	0	0	58.2	45	241	25	20	1	1	2	0	20	0	66	4	0
Johnstone, John, S.J.	0	0	.000	9.00	2	2	0	0	0	0	2.0	4	10	2	2	0	0	0	0	0	0	3	0	0
Jones, Chris, S.J.*	3	6	.333	10.71	36	7	0	0	7	0	61.1	74	341	89	73	8	0	8	6	85	0	50	20	0
Jones, Fontella, Mud.	1	1	.500	4.99	25	0	0	0	12	3	30.2	30	141	19	17	5	1	1	1	24	0	35	3	1
Jones, Greg, L.E.	0	0	.000	4.08	16	0	0	0	12	3	17.2	19	81	9	8	2	1	1	10	3	12	3	0
Jones, Marcus, Vis.	0	1	.000	6.55	3	2	0	0	1	0	11.0	15	49	8	8	1	0	1	3	0	11	0	0
Junge, Eric, S.B.	8	1	.889	3.36	29	24	0	0	2	1	158.0	159	666	69	59	8	3	5	9	53	0	116	8	2
Karl, Scott, L.E.*	1	0	1.000	0.00	1	0	0	0	0	0	7.0	5	27	0	0	0	1	0	1	0	5	0	0
Kees, Justin, H.D.	4	5	.571	7.63	32	0	0	0	0	0	59.0	75	285	54	50	6	2	5	6	38	0	34	9	2
Kimball, Andrew, Mod.	1	6	.143	2.76	16	0	0	0	0	0	32.2	31	140	22	10	1	0	2	1	13	3	29	5	0
Koplove, Mike, H.D.	2	0	1.000	1.42	20	0	0	0	19	8	25.1	14	100	4	4	0	3	0	1	10	0	31	2	0
Krawczyk, Jack, Mud.	7	1	.875	1.47	49	0	0	0	42	15	86.0	62	321	14	14	2	5	1	1	9	1	80	1	0
Kuo, Hong-chih, S.B.*	0	0	.000	0.00	1	1	0	0	0	0	3.0	0	10	0	0	0	1	0	0	0	7	0	1
Lackey, John, L.E.	6	6	.500	3.40	15	15	2	1	0	0	100.2	94	433	56	38	9	0	5	9	42	0	74	12	3

Pitcher, Team	W	L	Pct.	ERA	G	GS	CG	ShO	GF	Sv.	IP	H	TBF	R	ER	HR	SH	SF	HB	BB	IBB	SO	WP	Bk.
Lankford, Frank, Mod.	0	0	.000	0.00	1	1	0	0	0	0	2.0	0	6	0	0	0	0	0	0	0	0	2	0	0
Lee, Fletcher, Bak.	0	1	.000	3.07	9	0	0	0	6	1	14.2	19	73	6	5	0	0	0	4	9	1	13	0	0
Lehr, Charles, Mod.	13	6	.684	3.19	29	25	0	0	1	0	175.0	161	709	71	62	10	8	4	5	46	1	138	15	5
Leyva, Julian, Mod.	4	4	.500	4.38	42	0	0	0	27	5	74.0	64	312	41	36	5	7	6	2	27	4	56	2	0
Lineweaver, Aaron, H.D.	0	0	.000	0.00	1	0	0	0	0	0	2.0	3	9	0	0	0	0	0	0	0	0	2	0	0
Loewer, Carlton, R.C.	0	0	.000	2.57	1	1	0	0	0	0	7.0	7	27	3	2	2	0	0	0	0	0	4	0	0
Longo, Neil, Lan.	2	1	.667	7.28	34	0	0	0	6	1	50.2	76	249	49	41	11	0	0	3	22	0	34	12	0
Lontayo, Alejandro, L.E.*	2	0	1.000	3.32	6	3	0	0	1	1	21.2	21	95	14	8	0	1	1	0	12	0	19	0	0
Looper, Aaron, Lan.	5	3	.625	5.70	51	0	0	0	8	0	72.2	105	357	62	46	7	3	5	8	22	1	47	8	1
Lopez, Javier, H.D.*	4	8	.333	5.22	30	21	0	0	4	2	136.1	152	602	87	79	14	4	7	6	57	0	98	8	2
Luque, Roger, R.C.*	3	3	.500	5.98	29	2	0	0	8	1	43.2	55	213	35	29	1	3	1	5	27	0	34	13	0
Lynch, Jim, Bak.	6	4	.600	2.87	18	18	0	0	0	0	100.1	74	422	36	32	3	1	4	1	56	0	109	8	1
Malerich, Will, Bak.*	2	1	.667	3.97	36	1	0	0	8	0	56.2	64	258	33	25	4	2	1	4	31	0	49	2	1
Mallette, Brian, Mud.	4	4	.500	3.30	50	0	0	0	15	2	71.0	52	316	35	26	6	1	3	5	52	1	94	11	0
Malloy, Bill, Bak.	3	3	.500	4.84	10	10	0	0	0	0	44.2	52	205	27	24	4	0	2	3	26	0	27	5	0
Martin, Scott, S.B.	6	5	.545	3.32	33	12	0	0	7	1	111.0	97	451	45	41	7	0	4	6	28	1	90	5	1
Matos, Josue, Lan.	3	3	.500	2.64	14	14	0	0	0	0	88.2	78	358	29	26	8	2	0	3	22	1	93	3	4
Maurer, Mike, Vis.	2	1	.667	3.48	14	0	0	0	4	0	20.2	15	84	9	8	2	3	0	0	8	1	21	1	1
Mazur, Bryan, Mod.*	5	3	.625	3.64	36	2	0	0	19	7	76.2	81	333	34	31	3	3	2	3	23	3	68	9	0
McAdoo, Duncan, R.C.	1	4	.200	7.76	6	6	0	0	0	0	26.2	41	133	25	23	3	0	2	1	17	1	21	2	3
McCall, Travis, Vis.*	2	5	.286	5.30	43	0	0	0	28	7	52.2	58	244	36	31	7	3	4	3	23	2	40	1	1
McDaniel, Denny, Lan.*	5	0	1.000	4.06	43	0	0	0	14	1	44.1	42	208	29	20	2	0	6	5	25	2	37	5	0
Mears, Chris, Lan.	11	8	.579	4.76	28	28	0	0	0	0	151.1	178	670	92	80	13	4	8	10	54	0	89	6	1
Mendoza, Hatuey, H.D.	8	12	.400	6.57	29	27	0	0	0	0	150.2	170	710	140	110	17	1	4	12	98	0	107	19	0
Mendoza, Mario, L.E.	1	1	.500	3.51	12	8	0	0	0	0	51.1	51	222	27	20	4	2	2	1	19	1	35	1	0
Mercker, Kent, L.E.*	0	0	.000	0.00	1	1	0	0	0	0	4.0	0	12	0	0	0	0	0	0	0	0	3	0	0
Meyer, Dave, S.B.	0	1	.000	4.09	8	0	0	0	8	1	11.0	13	46	5	5	0	0	1	0	1	0	5	0	1
Mieses, Jose, Mud.	4	1	.800	2.65	6	6	0	0	0	0	34.0	25	144	11	10	1	1	1	2	18	0	40	3	1
Miller, Corey, Vis.	6	4	.600	3.44	47	0	0	0	23	7	55.0	56	242	27	21	2	4	2	3	25	4	59	2	1
Miller, Jim, Mud.	0	4	.000	6.65	12	2	0	0	5	0	21.2	33	116	21	16	4	1	3	4	15	1	22	5	2
Miller, Tom, Bak.*	4	2	.667	4.47	32	16	0	0	2	0	108.2	126	494	71	54	10	2	3	2	53	0	92	17	4
Montero, Agustin, S.B.	0	2	.000	9.72	7	0	0	0	3	0	8.1	13	52	14	9	0	0	1	2	12	0	10	2	0
Montgomery, Steve, R.C.	0	1	.000	7.50	6	0	0	0	0	0	6.0	8	29	7	5	0	1	1	0	2	0	8	1	0
Moore, Darin, Mod.	0	2	.000	22.09	3	1	0	0	0	0	3.2	5	30	12	9	1	0	0	6	6	0	5	2	0
Morrison, Cody, Lan.	8	7	.533	4.28	52	0	0	0	21	3	82.0	78	342	42	39	5	2	1	6	29	3	60	5	2
Myers, Aaron, Mud.	2	3	.400	3.57	50	0	0	0	19	2	88.1	64	374	36	35	9	2	3	6	44	0	104	3	0
Myers, Rodney, R.C.	0	0	.000	0.00	3	2	0	0	0	0	4.0	2	14	0	0	0	1	0	0	0	0	4	0	0
Nall, T. J., S.B.	1	1	.500	4.38	3	3	0	0	0	0	12.1	10	50	6	6	2	0	0	2	2	0	11	0	0
Nathan, Joe, S.J.-Bak.	1	1	.500	4.35	2	2	0	0	0	0	10.1	6	44	5	5	1	0	1	1	8	0	8	2	0
Neugebauer, Nickolas, Mud.	4	4	.500	4.19	18	18	0	0	0	0	77.1	43	349	40	36	0	0	2	4	87	0	117	10	1
Nix, Wayne, Vis.	9	5	.643	5.30	30	24	1	1	2	1	139.1	125	615	99	82	7	3	4	7	76	2	146	19	1
Noriega, Ray, Mod.*	0	3	.000	1.03	24	0	0	0	18	12	26.1	22	114	8	3	0	2	1	0	15	2	20	5	0
Obando, Omar, Lan.	0	1	.000	4.43	21	0	0	0	9	3	20.1	11	92	10	10	1	0	1	3	17	1	10	0	0
O'Brien, Matt, Mod.*	2	0	1.000	1.50	4	3	0	0	0	0	18.0	10	70	6	3	1	1	0	0	7	0	24	0	0
Olivares, Omar, Mod.	0	0	.000	1.50	2	2	0	0	0	0	6.0	3	21	1	1	1	0	0	0	1	0	3	0	0
Olson, Gregg, S.B.	0	0	.000	4.05	6	4	0	0	0	0	6.2	8	31	4	3	0	0	0	0	4	0	8	2	0
Ortiz, Omar, R.C.	3	9	.250	6.36	21	21	0	0	0	0	99.0	111	485	82	70	12	4	6	9	81	0	97	11	3
Ortiz, Ramon, L.E.	1	0	1.000	3.00	1	1	0	0	0	0	6.0	8	26	2	2	0	0	0	0	2	0	7	0	0
Osuna, Antonio, S.B.	0	2	.000	4.91	3	3	0	0	0	0	7.1	4	28	4	4	2	0	0	1	3	0	11	0	0
Ozias, Todd, S.J.	2	1	.667	3.46	47	0	0	0	44	21	52.0	49	227	28	20	4	2	3	1	17	0	61	7	0
Parker, Brandon, Lan.	4	2	.667	3.71	52	0	0	0	45	22	53.1	49	235	25	22	3	3	2	4	28	2	74	5	0
Parrish, Wade, S.B.*	2	3	.400	3.18	29	0	0	0	12	2	51.0	39	221	22	18	3	1	0	0	32	3	56	3	0
Pavon, Julio, Bak.	3	0	1.000	3.46	7	0	0	0	0	0	13.0	15	58	11	5	2	1	0	0	5	0	15	1	0
Pena, Juan, Mod.*	6	9	.400	3.86	29	27	0	0	0	0	154.0	132	659	85	66	7	5	4	1	75	2	177	16	3
Penney, Mike, Mud.	2	4	.333	3.24	13	13	0	0	0	0	66.2	63	287	31	24	3	2	4	6	28	0	45	6	0
Percival, Troy, L.E.	0	0	.000	4.50	2	2	0	0	0	0	2.0	1	8	1	1	0	0	0	0	1	0	1	0	0
Perez, Beltran, H.D.	0	1	.000	3.60	2	2	0	0	0	0	10.0	8	43	4	4	3	0	0	0	5	0	11	0	1
Petkovsek, Mark, L.E.	0	0	.000	3.38	2	0	0	0	0	0	2.2	3	13	1	1	0	0	0	0	3	0	3	0	0
Poe, Ryan, Mud.	7	5	.583	1.96	33	7	0	0	21	9	82.2	56	323	19	18	5	1	3	3	21	1	98	2	1
Polanco, Elvis, Mud.	4	3	.571	4.21	35	0	0	0	14	0	57.2	52	260	37	27	3	5	3	6	36	3	49	4	0
Prata, Danny, S.J.-Bak.*	2	2	.500	6.00	23	10	0	0	2	0	69.0	74	322	55	46	8	2	3	6	47	0	42	1	0
Rajotte, Jason, S.J.*	1	4	.200	4.43	44	1	0	0	26	5	61.0	70	276	42	30	3	2	3	3	23	0	41	4	0
Ramos, Mario, Mod.*	12	5	.706	2.90	26	24	1	1	1	0	152.0	131	624	63	49	6	9	3	3	50	4	134	3	1
Rayborn, Kenny, Lan.	5	1	.833	2.91	21	1	0	0	3	0	55.2	47	228	24	18	2	0	4	1	19	3	43	4	0
Roberts, Rick, S.B.*	8	5	.615	5.05	29	15	0	0	5	1	108.2	112	480	66	61	7	3	3	5	53	1	88	8	2
Rodriguez, Francisco, L.E.	4	4	.500	2.81	13	12	0	0	0	0	64.0	43	265	29	20	2	2	2	1	32	0	79	12	1
Rooney, Mike, H.D.	2	8	.200	7.55	17	15	1	0	0	0	70.1	85	326	64	59	13	1	5	7	37	0	29	3	1
Rosario, Carlos, Mod.	0	0	.000	10.80	1	0	0	0	1	0	1.2	3	10	2	2	0	0	0	1	1	0	2	2	0
Ross, Lew, H.D.*	2	2	.500	4.29	23	0	0	0	9	1	35.2	39	160	22	17	2	0	4	3	17	1	49	2	0
Royer, Jason, H.D.	0	1	.000	12.79	8	0	0	0	2	0	12.2	21	74	20	18	1	0	3	1	14	0	7	0	0
Sanchez, Cade, Vis.	4	0	1.000	4.76	14	0	0	0	2	0	11.1	14	57	9	6	0	0	2	1	9	0	8	1	1
Schoeneweis, Scott, L.E.*	0	0	.000	1.93	1	1	0	0	0	0	4.2	3	19	1	1	0	0	0	1	3	0	3	0	0
Schultz, Jeff, Vis.	7	6	.538	5.83	35	7	0	0	11	2	83.1	96	390	63	54	4	2	6	4	47	0	64	4	1
Schultz, Michael, H.D.	1	2	.333	3.63	7	7	0	0	0	0	22.1	15	90	9	9	2	0	1	0	11	0	16	1	0
Scott, Brian, H.D.	2	4	.333	7.12	14	5	0	0	2	0	43.0	46	202	38	34	6	2	0	7	31	0	20	5	1
Seabury, Jaron, Mud.	10	7	.588	4.07	33	21	1	0	0	0	150.1	135	650	83	68	6	5	6	19	72	0	97	14	4
Seaver, Mark, Mod.	8	10	.444	5.44	29	27	0	0	0	0	144.0	157	657	100	87	16	5	13	16	70	3	114	4	1
Shabansky, Rob, H.D.*	0	2	.000	13.24	6	3	0	0	0	0	17.0	35	98	28	25	1	0	2	1	14	0	9	3	0
Shiell, Jason, R.C.	7	5	.583	5.33	16	14	0	0	0	0	81.0	73	356	54	48	9	0	3	6	41	0	80	10	2
Shiyuk, Todd, R.C.*	1	0	1.000	4.75	29	0	0	0	9	0	30.1	32	142	19	16	1	0	0	2	19	0	35	6	1
Simonson, Chris, Mud.	1	2	.333	8.03	14	5	0	0	1	0	40.1	65	204	44	36	3	2	3	5	19	1	20	1	0
Simpson, Allan, Lan.	3	2	.600	2.08	46	0	0	0	20	6	52.0	34	217	17	12	1	0	2	2	27	1	67	2	0
Smith, Justin, Lan.*	0	1	.000	3.38	1	1	0	0	0	0	2.2	1	11	2	1	0	0	0	0	2	0	4	0	0
Snellgrove, Clay, R.C.	0	1	.000	3.38	1	0	0	0	1	0	2.2	2	11	1	1	1	1	0	0	1	0	1	0	0

Pitcher, Team	W	L	Pct.	ERA	G	GS	CG	ShO	GF	Sv.	IP	H	TBF	R	ER	HR	SH	SF	HB	BB	IBB	SO	WP	Bk.
Stabile, Paul, H.D.*	0	0	.000	3.80	21	0	0	0	9	1	21.1	17	106	10	9	0	0	0	1	24	0	26	4	0
Stewart, Paul, Mud.	2	4	.333	4.40	17	10	0	0	3	0	59.1	56	263	32	29	6	1	0	2	31	0	61	3	1
Suarez, Felipe, L.E.	5	5	.500	2.20	31	0	0	0	17	5	57.1	51	248	24	14	3	2	5	1	18	3	40	1	1
Surkont, Keith, Vis.	8	7	.533	2.72	27	22	0	0	1	1	125.2	104	535	60	38	6	4	3	11	54	0	122	5	4
Taschner, Jack, S.J.*	2	2	.500	4.10	10	2	0	0	1	1	26.1	23	119	17	12	0	0	1	4	17	0	22	3	3
Temple, Jason, R.C.	3	3	.500	8.01	57	0	0	0	11	1	82.0	78	433	81	73	8	0	6	13	105	1	72	18	0
Thames, Charles, L.E.	0	0	.000	8.68	6	0	0	0	5	2	9.1	15	46	11	9	2	0	1	0	1	0	6	0	0
Thompson, Eric, Vis.	4	3	.571	4.98	13	7	0	0	4	1	56.0	49	228	31	31	5	0	0	2	18	0	61	0	0
Thorn, Todd, H.D.*	0	5	.000	7.23	8	8	0	0	0	0	42.1	64	199	39	34	5	1	0	3	15	0	24	2	1
Torres, Melqui, Lan.	8	4	.667	4.38	18	18	0	0	0	0	102.2	119	448	60	50	7	3	3	4	29	0	79	4	2
Tucker, Ben, S.B.	5	2	.714	5.30	12	12	0	0	0	0	56.0	73	257	37	33	4	1	4	8	22	0	41	3	0
Turuda, Miyoki, S.B.	2	1	.667	7.71	6	0	0	0	3	0	14.0	17	65	12	12	1	4	0	2	7	1	10	2	0
Ulloa, Enmanuel, Lan.	9	5	.643	4.34	27	27	0	0	0	0	155.2	134	642	90	75	20	1	4	4	55	1	145	4	2
Uzzell, Todd, S.J.	0	0	.000	6.75	2	0	0	0	1	0	2.2	4	14	2	2	0	0	0	1	2	0	3	1	0
Valenti, Jon, Bak.	13	5	.722	3.86	58	0	0	0	30	7	95.2	87	417	49	41	9	2	2	6	42	0	89	6	0
Vardijan, Dan, H.D.	1	0	1.000	7.65	16	0	0	0	7	0	20.0	16	99	22	17	0	1	0	5	23	1	12	3	0
Vent, Kevin, Bak.	4	7	.364	5.16	26	21	0	0	2	0	83.2	115	397	65	48	6	4	2	1	44	0	65	6	4
Verplancke, Jeff, S.J.	6	14	.300	5.86	26	25	1	0	0	0	139.2	159	642	111	91	12	5	6	11	67	1	129	7	4
Villarreal, Oscar, H.D.	0	3	.000	3.65	9	4	0	0	0	0	24.2	24	117	20	10	4	4	1	3	14	0	18	2	0
Volkman, Keith, R.C.*	0	1	.000	15.00	6	0	0	0	0	0	6.0	15	42	13	10	2	0	1	6	6	0	6	1	0
Walk, Mitch, S.J.*	0	1	.000	3.00	1	1	0	0	0	0	6.0	7	25	2	2	0	0	0	1	6	0	6	0	0
Washburn, Jarrod, L.E.*	0	0	.000	6.00	1	1	0	0	0	0	3.0	3	14	2	2	0	0	0	2	0	0	7	0	1
Watkins, Steve, R.C.	7	6	.538	3.70	27	27	0	0	0	0	151.0	118	652	75	62	10	8	6	1	90	0	163	10	2
Wells, Matt, S.J.	1	0	1.000	4.32	16	0	0	0	2	0	25.0	24	116	15	12	1	0	1	9	19	1	25	1	0
Wells, Zach, Bak.	0	2	.000	4.75	40	0	0	0	7	0	72.0	74	305	41	38	2	6	4	5	23	1	42	3	0
Williams, Jerome, S.J.	7	6	.538	2.94	23	19	0	0	2	0	125.2	89	512	53	41	6	5	6	10	48	3	115	9	2
Williams, Woody, R.C.	0	0	.000	0.00	1	1	0	0	0	0	5.0	3	18	0	0	0	0	0	0	0	0	10	1	0
Williamson, Charles, H.D.	1	0	1.000	6.88	19	0	0	0	6	0	17.0	16	80	13	13	1	1	0	1	14	0	28	1	1
Wilson, Philip, L.E.	3	0	1.000	1.96	6	6	0	0	0	0	41.1	32	165	9	9	1	0	2	10	9	0	33	2	0
Wood, Brandon, H.D.	3	6	.333	5.92	35	0	0	0	18	2	51.2	52	242	43	34	3	2	3	4	32	0	48	5	1
Yates, Tyler, Mod.	4	2	.667	2.86	30	0	0	0	5	1	56.2	50	237	23	18	2	1	1	1	23	4	61	8	0
Zamarripa, Mark, H.D.	1	1	.500	2.91	5	4	0	0	1	0	21.2	13	85	7	7	0	1	2	1	·13	0	23	1	2
Zimmerman, Jordan, Lan.*	0	0	.000	0.00	3	0	0	0	1	0	3.1	0	13	0	0	0	0	0	1	2	0	2	0	0
Zirelli, Mike, Bak.	8	4	.667	4.08	40	3	1	0	5	1	103.2	110	453	52	47	13	7	1	7	28	1	61	1	1

COMBINATION SHUTOUTS: **Bakersfield (7)**—Cozier-Valenti, Lynch-Valenti-Wells-Bullard, Cozier-Bermudez, Lynch-Valenti, Lynch-Bullard, Cozier-Bullard, Zirelli-Malerich-Bermudez-Bullard. **High Desert (2)**—Zamarripa-Wood, Jensen-Williamson-Ross. **Lake Elsinore (6)**—Brooks-Berryman, Crawford-Jacobs, Mendoza-Haworth-Duarte-Grezlovski, Wilson-Grezlovski, Percival-Karl-Haworth, Rodriguez-Thames. **Lancaster (5)**—Matos-Ayala-Morrison-Parker, Ulloa-Ayala-Parker, Ulloa-Simpson-Parker, Mears-Morrison-Simpson-Parker, Atchison-Looper-Parker. **Modesto (6)**—Ramos-Yates-Noriega-Brink, Bazeell-Leyva, Ramos-Brink, Seaver-Kimball-Brink, Lehr-Kimball, Adkins-Kimball-Leyva. **Mudville (9)**—Johnson-Poe-Mallette, Penney-Seabury-Poe, Johnson-Mallette, Neugbauer-Krawczyk-Poe, Childers-Krawczyk, Childers-Allen-Mallette, Poe-Jones, Childers-Mallette-Krawczyk, Childers-Allen-Jones. **Rancho Cucamonga (5)**—Bynum-Myers-Temple, Howard-Condrey-Fikac-Camp, Bynum-Hart-Fikac, Watkins-Hart-Hunter, Bynum-Fikac. **San Bernardino (4)**—Roberts-Devey-Parrish, Garcia-Correa, Garcia-Caraccioli, Roberts-Martin-Meyer. **San Jose (4)**—Estes-Wells-Ozias, Verplancke-Connolly, Williams-Prata-Ozias, Flores-Connolly-Ozias. **Visalia (9)**—Thompson-Chiasson, Surkont-Schultz-Diaz, Surkont-Calzada, Surkont-Calzada, Chiasson-Chavez-Schultz, Calzada-Schultz-McCall, Surkont-Chavez-Jensen, Chiasson-Jensen-Galva-McCall, Chiasson-McCall.

NO-HIT GAMES: None.

PITCHERS WITH TWO OR MORE TEAMS

Pitcher, Team	W	L	Pct.	ERA	G	GS	CG	ShO	GF	Sv.	IP	H	TBF	R	ER	HR	SH	SF	HB	BB	IBB	SO	WP	Bk.
Blood, Darin, Bak.	0	1	.000	15.00	4	2	0	0	1	0	3.0	4	23	5	5	0	0	0	1	10	0	0	1	0
Blood, Darin, S.J.	0	0	.000	27.00	1	0	0	0	1	0	1.0	2	9	3	3	0	0	0	4	0	1	1	0
Johnson, Eric, S.J.	0	0	.000	8.78	13	5	0	0	4	0	26.2	37	136	31	26	4	2	1	2	20	0	15	4	1
Johnson, Eric, Bak.	0	0	.000	6.91	5	4	0	0	0	0	14.1	19	73	12	11	1	0	2	0	15	0	5	1	0
Nathan, Joe, S.J.	0	1	.000	3.60	1	1	0	0	0	0	5.0	4	19	2	2	1	0	0	1	0	2	4	0	0
Nathan, Joe, Bak.	0	0	1.000	5.06	1	1	0	0	0	0	5.1	2	25	3	3	0	0	0	1	7	0	6	1	0
Prata, Danny, S.J.*	1	1	.500	5.25	20	7	0	0	2	0	60.0	60	273	42	35	7	2	2	5	39	0	37	1	0
Prata, Danny, Bak.*	1	1	.500	11.00	3	3	0	0	0	0	9.0	14	49	13	11	1	0	1	1	8	0	5	0	0

2000 FIELDING

TEAM

Team	Pct.	G	PO	A	E	TC	DP	TP	PB
San Bernardino	.972	140	3759	1668	159	5586	121	0	23
Bakersfield	.971	140	3712	1498	154	5364	97	0	31
Lancaster	.970	140	3764	1401	162	5327	92	0	23
R. Cucamonga	.967	140	3749	1402	176	5327	97	1	27
Mudville	.965	140	3706	1450	189	5345	107	0	21
Modesto	.964	140	3721	1516	195	5432	97	2	29
San Jose	.959	140	3712	1514	221	5447	153	0	24
Visalia	.959	140	3707	1501	224	5432	107	0	25
Lake Elsinore	.958	140	3755	1642	239	5636	134	1	44
High Desert	.955	140	3646	1617	247	5510	150	0	17

INDIVIDUAL

FIRST BASEMEN

NOTE: All caps denotes fielding-percentage leader based on 70 games for catchers, 93 for all other non-pitchers and 112 innings for pitchers. *Throws lefthanded.

Player, Team	Pct.	G	PO	A	E	TC	DP
Brooks, Jeff, H.D.	.974	19	173	16	5	194	19
Caiazzo, Nick, Mud.	.991	36	299	18	3	320	26
Cesar, Dionys, Vis.	1.000	2	14	0	0	14	0
Cosme, Caonabo, Mod.	.000	1	0	0	0	0	0
Davis, Monty, Vis.	1.000	3	11	0	0	11	1
Deardorff, Jeff, Mud.	.980	31	224	18	5	247	19
De La Cruz, Jose, Mod.	.992	17	113	9	1	123	9
Delgado, Ariel, L.E.*	.971	10	92	9	3	104	13
Diaz, Angel, L.E.	.000	1	0	0	0	0	0
Encarnacion, Bienvenido, L.E.	.000	1	0	0	1	1	0
Figueroa, Eduardo, Mud.*	.992	70	575	37	5	617	47
Flaherty, Tim, Bak.	.900	3	23	4	3	30	2
Flores, Javier, Vis.	.987	9	73	5	1	79	5
Glassey, Josh, H.D.	1.000	1	5	0	0	5	0
Gregg, Mitch, Mod.	.991	47	402	27	4	433	22
Hammock, Rob, H.D.	.957	3	19	3	1	23	2
Hopper, Shane, R.C.	1.000	8	40	2	0	42	2
Howe, Matt, Vis.	.985	54	457	17	7	481	35
Keating, Matthew, S.J.	1.000	5	19	4	0	23	3
Koonce, Graham, R.C.*	.984	135	1068	74	18	1160	78
Kuzmic, Craig, Lan.	.987	80	660	43	9	712	45
Loggins, Joshua, R.C.	1.000	1	5	0	0	5	0
Luster, Jeremy, Bak.	.984	134	1171	78	20	1269	81
Macalutas, Jon, Mud.	.987	8	75	1	1	77	4
Marcinczyk, T.R., Mod.	.965	7	54	1	2	57	6
Maynard, Scott, Lan.	1.000	1	5	2	0	7	0
McGowan, Sean, S.J.	.979	101	904	45	20	969	97

Player, Team	Pct.	G	PO	A	E	TC	DP
Meier, Dan, H.D.*	1.000	1	10	0	0	10	2
Neal, Steve, H.D.*	.984	102	828	75	15	918	83
Nieckula, Aaron, Vis.	1.000	1	1	0	0	1	0
Oglesby, Travis, H.D.	.988	20	153	15	2	170	20
PACIOREK, Pete, S.B.*	.992	117	1097	89	10	1196	85
Pelaez, Alex, R.C.	1.000	1	4	0	0	4	0
Pernalete, Marco, Bak.	1.000	6	28	3	0	31	1
Pini, Ryan, S.J.*	.989	23	161	15	2	178	15
Pujols, Rafael, Vis.	.981	44	343	18	7	368	25
Quinlan, Robb, L.E.	.987	113	1048	76	15	1139	100
Reyes, Christian, Mod.	.875	3	14	0	2	16	0
Robinson, Bo, Lan.	1.000	2	3	2	0	5	1
Rodriguez, Juan, L.E.*	.978	10	84	6	2	92	6
Rosario, Omar, Vis.*	1.000	3	16	4	0	20	1
Schaeffer, Jon, Mod.	.981	31	247	14	5	266	15
Scharrer, Jim, L.E.	.989	11	91	3	1	95	6
Schmidt, Bryan, R.C.	.875	2	12	2	2	16	2
Snellgrove, Clay, R.C.	1.000	1	1	0	0	1	0
Sosa, Nicolas, Mod.	.975	45	377	18	10	405	32
Soto, Jorge, Vis.	.990	40	270	18	3	291	22
Summers, John, S.J.	.984	14	122	5	2	129	17
Valdez, Mario, Vis.	1.000	1	5	1	0	6	0
Vasquez, Sandy, S.B.	.987	23	209	14	3	226	18
Williams, Peanut, Lan.	.978	62	514	31	12	557	41
Williford, Dan, H.D.*	1.000	8	42	5	0	47	5

TRIPLE PLAYS: Gregg, Koonce.

SECOND BASEMEN

Player, Team	Pct.	G	PO	A	E	TC	DP
Amezaga, Alfredo, L.E.	.961	94	196	274	19	489	66
Belliard, Francisco, H.D.	.959	79	152	227	16	395	62
Bloomquist, Willie, Lan.	.961	53	97	147	10	254	21
Campusano, Carlos, S.J.-Bak.	1.000	3	9	8	0	17	2
Cesar, Dionys, Vis.	1.000	1	1	3	0	4	0
Clements, Jason, Mod.	.926	7	10	15	2	27	3
Collins, Mike, S.B.	.985	69	130	194	5	329	44
Cruz, Israel, Lan.	1.000	1	1	1	0	2	0
Davis, Monty, Vis.	1.000	5	7	7	0	14	1
Dunaway, Jason, R.C.	.942	27	36	61	6	103	6
Encarnacion, Bienvenido, L.E.	.974	31	80	67	4	151	23
Flores, Javier, Vis.	1.000	5	5	11	0	16	1
Gandolfo, Rob, Lan.	.979	42	80	104	4	188	18
Gastelum, Carlos, L.E.	.974	20	50	64	3	117	19
German, Esteban, Vis.	.959	109	221	271	21	513	51
Goldfield, Josh, H.D.	.600	1	1	2	2	5	0
Gonzalez, Jimmy, S.B.	.971	38	74	93	5	172	15
Hall, Jason, Mod.	.971	78	155	212	11	378	33
Hargrove, Harvey, Lan.	1.000	2	3	5	0	8	1
Jaramillo, Frank, Mud.	.948	14	22	33	3	58	7
Jaramillo, Milko, S.B.	.923	11	21	27	4	52	3
Jester, Joe, S.J.	.971	107	244	287	16	547	86
Keller, G.W., Vis.	.976	8	16	24	1	41	3
Kenney, Jeff, Mud.	.914	8	17	15	3	35	3
Kuzmic, Craig, Lan.	.985	25	53	75	2	130	13
Loggins, Joshua, R.C.	.875	2	2	5	1	8	0
Luther, Ryan, Bak.	.954	86	139	212	17	368	33
Martinez, Guillermo, Lan.	.950	29	61	71	7	139	9
Mendoza, Carlos, S.J.	.969	6	19	12	1	32	4
Otero, William, S.J.	.936	27	57	75	9	141	17
Patten, Chris, Mud.	.982	114	201	278	9	488	53
Pecci, Jay, Vis.	1.000	23	41	64	0	105	7
Pelaez, Alex, R.C.	.935	9	8	21	2	31	4
Pernalete, Marco, Bak.	.994	43	70	108	1	179	22
Powers, Jeff, H.D.	.975	53	106	129	6	241	37
Reynoso, Ismael, S.J.	1.000	4	2	6	0	8	0
Risinger, Ben, R.C.	.971	7	17	16	1	34	6
Rosario, Carlos, Mod.	.954	63	131	162	14	307	22
Rowan, Chris, Mud.	.927	6	15	23	3	41	4
Santangelo, F.P., S.B.	1.000	2	6	1	0	7	0
Santos, Luis, H.D.	1.000	22	45	46	0	91	15
Schill, Vaughn, Lan.	1.000	1	2	1	0	3	0
Schmidt, Bryan, R.C.	1.000	12	17	28	0	45	5
Schneidmiller, Gary, Mod.	1.000	1	0	1	0	1	0
SNELLGROVE, Clay, R.C.	.993	95	192	228	3	423	42
Sprague, Ed, R.C.	1.000	2	0	6	0	6	0
Thurston, Joe, S.B.	.978	28	64	72	3	139	19
Turco, Paul, Bak.	.973	21	25	48	2	75	7

SECOND BASEMEN WITH TWO OR MORE TEAMS

Player, Team	Pct.	G	PO	A	E	TC	DP
Campusano, Carlos, S.J.	1.000	1	3	3	0	6	2
Campusano, Carlos, Bak.	1.000	2	6	5	0	11	0

TRIPLE PLAYS: Amezaga, Dunaway, Hall.

THIRD BASEMEN

Player, Team	Pct.	G	PO	A	E	TC	DP
Belliard, Francisco, H.D.	.908	31	29	79	11	119	6
Brooks, Jeff, H.D.	.839	91	57	182	46	285	20
Caiazzo, Nick, Mud.	.800	7	3	13	4	20	0
Campusano, Carlos, Bak.	.973	12	12	24	1	37	0
Christensen, Mike, L.E.	.904	129	77	272	37	386	23
Clements, Jason, Mod.	.929	6	5	8	1	14	1
Collins, Mike, S.B.	.939	26	10	67	5	82	5
Cook, Joshua, S.J.	.880	15	14	30	6	50	4
CORDIDO, Julio, Bak.	.950	130	110	286	21	417	23
Cosme, Caonabo, Mod.	1.000	8	6	20	0	26	2
Deardorff, Jeff, Mud.	.901	72	47	154	22	223	15
De La Cruz, Jose, Mod.	.000	1	0	0	0	0	0
Dunaway, Jason, R.C.	.963	13	7	19	1	27	3
Encarnacion, Bienvenido, L.E.	.919	13	4	30	3	37	5
Gonzalez, Jimmy, S.B.	.934	90	68	201	19	288	17
Hochgesang, Joshua, Vis.	.920	116	72	240	27	339	17
Hopper, Shane, R.C.	.874	62	45	87	19	151	11
Howe, Matt, Vis.	.951	27	20	57	4	81	5
Jaramillo, Frank, Mud.	.878	17	21	22	6	49	0
Kenney, Jeff, Mud.	.851	45	37	83	21	141	5
Kuzmic, Craig, Lan.	.867	9	3	10	2	15	1
Luther, Ryan, Bak.	.000	1	0	0	0	0	0
Martinez, Guillermo, Lan.	1.000	2	2	2	0	4	0
Moore, Kevin, Mud.	1.000	1	2	2	0	4	1
Otero, William, S.J.	.806	11	7	22	7	36	3
Patten, Chris, Mud.	1.000	2	1	2	0	3	0
Pelaez, Alex, R.C.	.950	53	28	87	6	121	6
Powers, Jeff, H.D.	.933	27	19	51	5	75	11
Reyes, Christian, Mod.	.906	64	31	142	18	191	10
Reynoso, Ismael, S.J.	1.000	3	0	6	0	6	0
Risinger, Ben, R.C.	1.000	4	0	10	0	10	0
Robinson, Bo, Lan.	.946	134	87	231	18	336	8
Rosario, Carlos, Mod.	1.000	1	0	2	0	2	0
Ruiz, Ramon, S.B.	.902	33	19	64	9	92	5
Santos, Luis, H.D.	.750	2	1	2	1	4	0
Schill, Vaughn, Lan.	.833	3	1	4	1	6	0
Schmidt, Bryan, R.C.	.900	15	9	27	4	40	2
Schneidmiller, Gary, Mod.	.901	69	52	112	18	182	9
Snellgrove, Clay, R.C.	1.000	2	0	1	0	1	0
Summers, John, S.J.	.778	8	5	16	6	27	1
Torcato, Tony, S.J.	.882	105	77	222	40	339	24
Turco, Anthony, S.J.	.000	1	0	0	0	0	0
Williams, Matt, H.D.	1.000	1	1	1	0	2	0

TRIPLE PLAYS: Christensen, Schneidmiller.

SHORTSTOPS

Player, Team	Pct.	G	PO	A	E	TC	DP
Alexander, Kevin, S.J.	1.000	1	1	0	0	1	0
Amezaga, Alfredo, L.E.	.959	14	22	49	3	74	12
Berroa, Angel, Vis.	.909	128	195	344	54	593	63
Berroa, Cristian, R.C.	.936	129	195	328	36	559	49
Bloomquist, Willie, Lan.	.962	11	21	29	2	52	5
Campusano, Carlos, Bak.	.955	53	74	140	10	224	27
Castro, Nelson, Bak.	.953	53	97	145	12	254	21
Cesar, Dionys, Vis.	1.000	1	1	5	0	6	1
Clements, Jason, Mod.	1.000	2	4	5	0	9	2
Collins, Mike, S.B.	.932	12	18	23	3	44	4
COSME, Caonabo, Mod.	.960	123	176	349	22	547	53
Cruz, Israel, Lan.	.800	1	2	2	1	5	1
Dunaway, Jason, R.C.	.946	12	12	23	2	37	6
Encarnacion, Bienvenido, L.E.	.938	9	14	31	3	48	4
Ernster, Mark, Mud.	.925	61	82	151	19	252	29
Flores, Javier, Vis.	.894	15	16	43	7	66	6
Freeman, Corey, Lan.	.945	25	36	67	6	109	8
Gandolfo, Rob, Lan.	.960	13	24	24	2	50	5
Gastelum, Carlos, L.E.	.750	5	5	10	5	20	0
German, Esteban, Vis.	.733	2	7	4	4	15	1
Hood, Jay, L.E.	.949	26	37	112	8	157	16
Jaramillo, Frank, Mud.	.952	53	67	149	11	227	28
Jaramillo, Milko, S.B.	.932	22	31	79	8	118	11
Kenney, Jeff, Mud.	1.000	1	1	1	0	2	1
Mendoza, Carlos, S.J.	.954	104	155	339	24	518	72
Otero, William, S.J.	.857	1	4	2	1	7	2
Patten, Chris, Mud.	.500	1	1	0	1	2	0
Pecci, Jay, Vis.	.923	5	4	8	1	13	0
Perez, Antonio, Lan.	.939	96	144	271	27	442	53
Pernalete, Marco, Bak.	.914	39	60	79	13	152	12
Powers, Jeff, H.D.	.957	38	46	89	6	141	21
Reynoso, Ismael, S.J.	.927	41	51	114	13	178	20
Rosario, Carlos, Mod.	.893	18	30	37	8	75	6
Rowan, Chris, Mud.	.897	27	38	75	13	126	14

CLASS A *California League*

Player, Team	Pct.	G	PO	A	E	TC	DP
Sanchez, Yuri, H.D.	.937	41	66	112	12	190	18
Santos, Luis, H.D.	.916	23	33	65	9	107	22
Schill, Vaughn, Lan.	.889	1	2	6	1	9	1
Snellgrove, Clay, R.C.	.933	7	9	19	2	30	6
Specht, Brian, L.E.	.928	89	153	285	34	472	50
Thurston, Joe, S.B.	.947	110	185	374	31	590	68
Turco, Paul, Bak.	1.000	1	1	0	0	1	0
Vizcaino, Maximo, H.D.	.926	48	87	125	17	229	32
Williams, Jason, H.D.	.974	7	10	28	1	39	4

TRIPLE PLAYS: C. Berroa, Clements.

OUTFIELDERS

Player, Team	Pct.	G	PO	A	E	TC	DP
Abate, Mike, Lan.	.857	16	17	1	3	21	0
Adams, John, R.C.	.967	103	168	7	6	181	1
Asche, Kirk, Vis.	.947	110	154	8	9	171	1
Basabe, Jesus, Mod.	.930	91	139	7	11	157	1
Beatriz, Ramy, Mud.*	1.000	6	4	0	0	4	0
Benjamin, Al, R.C.	.954	133	178	7	9	194	0
Bubela, Jaime, Lan.	1.000	9	10	0	0	10	0
Bush, Darren, R.C.	.000	3	0	0	0	0	0
Caiazzo, Nick, Mud.	1.000	3	4	0	0	4	0
Casper, Brett, Bak.	.977	123	241	18	6	265	6
Cepeda, Al, S.J.	.947	13	17	1	1	19	0
Cesar, Dionys, Vis.	.000	1	0	0	0	0	0
Chirinos, Germain, Mod.	1.000	19	36	0	0	36	0
Clements, Jason, Mod.	1.000	6	6	1	0	7	0
Clifton, Rodney, Mod.	1.000	9	11	1	0	12	1
Collins, Mike, S.B.	.000	1	0	0	0	0	0
Cridland, Mark, Mud.	.980	104	181	12	4	197	2
Daeley, Scott, S.J.	.975	106	258	10	7	275	3
Davis, Ryan, S.J.*	1.000	2	3	0	0	3	0
Delgado, Ariel, L.E.*	.920	28	45	1	4	50	0
DeHaan, Kory, R.C.	1.000	4	4	0	0	4	0
Dougherty, Jeb, L.E.	1.000	16	22	2	0	24	0
Encarnacion, Bienvenido, L.E.	.882	21	29	1	4	34	0
Encarnacion, Mario, Mod.	1.000	5	11	2	0	13	1
Faircloth, Chad, S.J.	.978	26	44	1	1	46	0
Fajardo, Alejandro, S.J.	.984	79	175	7	3	185	2
FELICIANO, Jesus, S.B.*	.996	113	233	8	1	242	2
Forbes, Matt, Mod.	.944	50	82	3	5	90	0
Ford, Will, Mud.*	.900	12	18	0	2	20	0
Fox, Jason, Mud.	.979	129	227	7	5	239	0
Fulse, Sheldon, Lan.	.957	17	22	0	1	23	0
Gibbs, Kevin, S.B.	1.000	6	10	0	0	10	0
Gomez, Ramon, H.D.	.939	37	62	0	4	66	0
Gordon, Brian, H.D.	.948	122	175	7	10	192	2
Greene, Clay, S.J.	.952	85	138	0	7	145	0
Gustafson, Troy, S.J.	1.000	2	2	1	0	3	0
Guzman, Elpidio, L.E.*	.957	133	297	15	14	326	0
Hammond, Derry, Mud.	.971	57	99	0	3	102	0
Hargrove, Harvey, Lan.	.992	112	229	6	2	237	1
Harris, Cedrick, H.D.	.986	32	67	3	1	71	0
Haynes, Larry, Lan.	1.000	4	4	0	0	4	0
Hopper, Shane, R.C.	.969	20	29	2	1	32	0
Ingram, Darron, S.B.	.977	40	42	1	1	44	0
Jaroncyk, Ryan, S.B.	.917	4	11	0	1	12	0
Johnson, Gary, L.E.*	.948	69	107	3	6	116	1
Keith, Rusty, Mod.	.976	86	116	4	3	123	0
Keller, G.W., Vis.	1.000	21	26	0	0	26	0
Kenney, Jeff, Mod.	1.000	1	1	0	0	1	0
Knight, Marcus, L.E.	.953	52	116	7	6	129	0
Kuzmic, Craig, Lan.	1.000	2	2	0	0	2	0
Lockwood, Mike, Mod.*	.958	44	63	5	3	71	1
Loggins, Joshua, R.C.	.917	31	51	4	5	60	0
Ludwick, Ryan, Mod.*	.983	118	281	9	5	295	3
Luther, Ryan, Bak.	1.000	2	3	0	0	3	0
Macalutas, Jon, Mud.	.952	113	150	7	8	165	1
Martinez, Greg, Mod.	1.000	2	4	0	0	4	0
Martinez, Hipolito, Vis.	.974	97	139	12	4	155	4
Matthews, Lamont, S.B.*	.956	128	238	23	12	273	4
May, Freddy, S.B.-Lan.*	.921	27	33	2	3	38	0
McClendon, Travis, Lan.	.000	1	0	0	0	0	0
McDowell, Arturo, Bak.*	.990	120	281	11	3	295	2
Mejia, Max, S.B.	.924	73	92	5	8	105	2
Messner, Jake, Bak.*	.950	15	15	4	1	20	0
Moore, Kevin, Mud.	1.000	7	7	1	0	8	0
Mota, Pedro, S.J.*	.903	41	56	0	6	62	0
Mott, Bill, L.E.	1.000	9	5	0	0	5	0
Owens, Jeremy, R.C.	.986	138	344	16	5	365	5
Pini, Ryan, S.J.*	.973	94	173	10	5	188	1
Powers, Jeff, H.D.	1.000	1	3	0	0	3	0
Quinlan, Robb, L.E.	.957	16	20	2	1	23	1
Quintana, Wilfredo, Lan.	.939	26	43	3	3	49	1
Risinger, Ben, R.C.	1.000	1	1	0	0	1	0
Rodriguez, Juan, L.E.*	1.000	17	35	2	0	37	1
Rosario, Omar, Vis.*	.953	89	135	7	7	149	2
Sandoval, Jhensy, H.D.	.949	40	50	6	3	59	2
Santangelo, F.P., S.B.	1.000	4	4	0	0	4	0
Santos, Luis, H.D.	1.000	3	5	0	0	5	0
Silvestre, Juan, Lan.	.957	114	168	10	8	186	1
Sledge, Terrmel, Lan.*	.981	72	147	5	3	155	0
Stuart, Rich, L.E.	.956	75	124	6	6	136	3
Sykes, Jamie, H.D.	.957	77	148	6	7	161	2
Terrero, Luis, H.D.	.941	19	46	2	3	51	0
Tommasini, Kevin, Bak.	.981	60	93	9	2	104	1
Urquiola, Carlos, H.D.	.959	27	45	2	2	49	1
Valderrama, Carlos, Bak.	.972	117	199	8	6	213	0
Vasquez, Sandy, S.B.	.917	54	62	4	6	72	1
Wenner, Michael, Vis.	.966	122	244	9	9	262	2
White, Devon, S.B.	1.000	2	3	0	0	3	0
Williams, P.J., Lan.	.977	49	126	1	3	130	0
Williford, Dan, H.D.*	.900	13	18	0	2	20	0
Woodward, Steve, H.D.*	.974	68	108	3	3	114	0

TRIPLE PLAY: Knight.

OUTFIELDERS WITH TWO OR MORE TEAMS

Player, Team	Pct.	G	PO	A	E	TC	DP
May, Freddy, S.B.*	.667	7	3	1	2	6	0
May, Freddy, Lan.*	.969	20	30	1	1	32	0

CATCHERS

Player, Team	Pct.	G	PO	A	E	TC	DP	PB
Alfano, Jeff, Mud.	.992	17	111	11	1	123	0	4
Ardoin, Danny, Mod.	.960	4	23	1	1	25	1	0
Barski, Chris, L.E.	.984	17	111	10	2	123	0	2
Bazzani, Matt, Bak.	1.000	4	4	0	0	4	0	0
Brito, Obispo, Mud.	.971	46	364	70	13	447	1	6
Bush, Darren, R.C.	.982	30	184	30	4	218	2	10
Caiazzo, Nick, Mud.	.986	22	193	19	3	215	1	6
Campbell, Sean, R.C.	.985	44	351	38	6	395	3	6
Ceriani, Matt, Mud.	.986	47	427	60	7	494	6	2
Cresse, Brad, H.D.	.955	39	232	44	13	289	5	2
Davis, Monty, Vis.	.000	1	0	0	0	0	0	0
De La Cruz, Jose, Mod.	.988	40	281	40	4	325	2	15
De Los Santos, Nelson, Mud.	1.000	14	110	16	0	126	1	3
Diaz, Angel, L.E.	.981	38	209	50	5	264	4	12
Duplissea, William, S.B.	1.000	5	13	1	0	14	0	0
Encarnacion, Bienvenido, L.E.	.000	1	0	0	1	1	0	1
Flores, Javier, Vis.	.979	48	369	57	9	435	3	9
French, Ron, R.C.	1.000	10	28	4	0	32	1	1
Glassey, Josh, S.B.-H.D.	.980	37	220	27	5	252	3	4
Goldfield, Josh, H.D.	.986	20	120	25	2	147	1	3
Gonzalez, Jose, Bak.	1.000	4	9	2	0	11	0	0
Hammock, Rob, H.D.	.963	35	228	30	10	268	0	4
HERNANDEZ, John, S.B.	.990	79	587	81	7	675	1	16
Hill, Jason, L.E.	.982	62	379	66	8	453	2	19
Kasper, Todd, H.D.	.958	30	203	26	10	239	0	3
Kuzmic, Craig, Lan.	.987	11	68	7	1	76	0	3
Laird, Gerald, Vis.	.969	27	220	31	8	259	1	10
Loggins, Joshua, R.C.	.976	38	319	46	9	374	2	2
Lopez, Norberto, L.E.	.968	30	164	17	6	187	2	10
Luderer, Brian, Mod.	.979	33	205	25	5	235	1	3
Luther, Ryan, Bak.	1.000	27	159	22	0	181	1	8
Maynard, Scott, Lan.	.988	93	700	73	9	782	2	15
McAfee, Josh, H.D.	.905	3	16	3	2	21	0	0
McClendon, Travis, Lan.	.986	41	317	40	5	362	1	5
Nieckula, Aaron, Vis.-Mod.	.980	78	603	81	14	698	7	4
Niemet, Robert, S.J.	.882	3	15	0	2	17	0	1
Nieves, Wilbert, R.C.	.984	29	261	45	5	311	6	3
Oglesby, Travis, H.D.	.983	11	56	1	1	58	0	2
Olivo, Miguel, Mod.	.959	50	375	64	19	458	5	11
Pujols, Rafael, Vis.	.971	9	64	3	2	69	1	2
Ramirez, Domingo, S.J.	1.000	4	16	2	0	18	0	1
Risinger, Ben, R.C.	1.000	2	4	0	0	4	0	0
Rodriguez, Guillermo, Bak.	.984	118	823	112	15	950	8	23
Ross, David, S.B.	.992	42	314	53	3	370	4	6
Schaeffer, Jon, Mod.	.991	14	106	10	1	117	0	0
Serrano, Sammy, S.J.	.964	31	221	22	9	252	3	7
Stone, Jon, R.C.	.971	8	58	10	2	70	1	5
Turco, Anthony, S.J.	.989	27	164	17	2	183	1	1
Wright, Mike, S.J.	.985	96	538	72	9	619	7	14
Zeber, Ryan, L.E.	.942	12	60	5	4	69	0	0

TRIPLE PLAY: Olivo.

CATCHERS WITH TWO OR MORE TEAMS

Player, Team	Pct.	G	PO	A	E	TC	DP	PB
Glassey, Josh, S.B.	.986	19	125	17	2	144	2	1
Glassey, Josh, H.D.	.972	18	95	10	3	108	1	3
Nieckula, Aaron, Vis.	.981	65	497	70	11	578	6	4
Nieckula, Aaron, Mod.	.975	13	106	11	3	120	1	0

PITCHERS

Player, Team	Pct.	G	PO	A	E	TC	DP
Adkins, Jon, Mod.	1.000	9	4	6	0	10	1
Aguilera, Adrian, S.B.*	1.000	9	2	6	0	8	1
Allen, Rodney, Mud.	1.000	16	1	3	0	4	0
Anderson, Jason, Vis.*	1.000	19	4	5	0	9	0
Atchison, Scott, Lan.	1.000	18	12	10	0	22	3
Avery, Paul, H.D.*	.000	3	0	0	0	0	0
Ayala, Julio, Lan.*	1.000	14	3	2	0	5	0
Balbuena, Caleb, Lan.	1.000	21	3	1	0	4	0
Barber, Scott, H.D.	1.000	4	2	1	0	3	0
Bausher, Andy, R.C.*	1.000	5	0	1	0	1	0
Bazzani, Matt, Bak.	1.000	1	0	1	0	1	0
Bazzell, Shane, Mud.	1.000	32	2	8	0	10	0
Beckman, Jacob, Mod.	1.000	11	0	5	0	5	2
Belcher, Tim, L.E.	1.000	3	1	0	0	1	0
Bell, Casey, L.E.	1.000	3	1	0	0	1	0
Belson, Gregory, H.D.	1.000	22	1	3	0	4	0
Bergman, Dusty, L.E.*	1.000	1	0	2	0	2	0
Bermudez, Manny, Bak.	.885	59	9	14	3	26	2
Berry, Jon, L.E.	1.000	40	6	8	0	14	1
Berryman, Chad, L.E.	1.000	25	2	3	0	5	0
Blood, Darin, Bak.-S.J.	.885	5	0	0	0	0	0
Boehringer, Brian, R.C.	1.000	4	0	1	0	1	0
Bonilla, Ben, H.D.*	.000	1	0	0	0	0	0
Bridenbaugh, Christian, S.B.*	1.000	11	1	3	0	4	0
Bridges, Dou, L.E.*	.962	31	8	17	1	26	2
Brink, Jim, Mod.	1.000	42	7	4	0	11	0
Brooks, Jacob, L.E.	.769	28	3	7	3	13	0
Brous, David, S.J.*	1.000	9	1	5	0	6	0
Bullard, Jason, Bak.	.882	58	7	8	2	17	0
Bynum, Mike, R.C.*	.971	21	4	29	1	34	1
Calzada, Javier, Vis.	.900	31	3	24	3	30	0
Camp, Shawn, R.C.	1.000	14	2	0	0	2	0
Caraccioli, Lance, S.B.*	.941	34	10	22	2	34	1
Ceriani, Matt, Mud.	.000	1	0	0	0	0	0
Chavez, Carlos, Vis.	.889	34	1	7	1	9	0
Chiasson, Scott, Vis.	.939	31	11	20	2	33	2
Childers, Jason, Mud.	.969	28	10	21	1	32	2
Childers, Matt, Mud.	1.000	15	3	10	0	13	0
Clark, Jeffrey, S.J.	.000	2	0	0	0	0	0
Condrey, Clay, R.C.	.857	18	2	4	1	7	0
Connolly, Keith, S.J.	.727	54	3	5	3	11	0
Cooper, Brian, L.E.	.000	1	0	1	0	1	0
Correa, Elvis, S.B.	.933	41	4	10	1	15	1
Coscia, Tony, Bak.	1.000	21	5	14	0	19	2
Cox, Ryan, S.J.	1.000	19	3	11	0	14	1
Cozier, Vance, Bak.	.778	28	6	15	6	27	1
Cramblitt, Joey, H.D.	1.000	22	3	5	0	8	0
Crawford, Wesley, L.E.*	.925	27	10	27	3	40	1
Cunningham, Jeremy, S.J.	.963	34	6	20	1	27	2
Davis, Monty, Vis.	.000	1	0	0	0	0	0
De Hart, Blair, R.C.	.917	9	5	6	1	12	0
De La Cruz, Jose, Mod.	.000	1	0	0	0	0	0
Demouy, Chris, L.E.*	1.000	40	1	10	0	11	1
Dent, Doug, R.C.	.875	10	3	4	1	8	0
Devey, Phil, S.B.*	.929	29	3	23	2	28	1
Diaz, Alex, Vis.	1.000	7	0	2	0	2	1
Diaz, Antonio, R.C.	.909	24	2	8	1	11	0
Dotel, Melido, S.B.	1.000	8	2	1	0	3	0
Duarte, Renney, L.E.	.800	17	0	4	1	5	0
Dubose, Eric, Vis.*	1.000	5	0	1	0	1	0
Emanuel, Brandon, L.E.	.893	19	8	17	3	28	2
Encarnacion, Bienvenido, L.E.	.000	1	0	0	0	0	0
Enochs, Chris, Vis.	.889	18	3	5	1	9	1
Escalante, Jaime, L.E.	1.000	6	0	1	0	1	0
Estes, Shawn, S.J.*	.000	1	0	0	0	0	0
Fahrner, Evan, H.D.	.933	45	5	9	1	15	0
Faircloth, Chad, S.J.	.000	1	0	0	0	0	0
Featherstone, Deron, S.J.	.000	1	0	0	0	0	0
Fikac, Jeremy, R.C.	1.000	61	3	11	0	14	1
Fischer, Mike, S.B.	1.000	11	2	3	0	5	0
Fleming, John, H.D.	.889	13	5	3	1	9	0
Flores, Benito, S.J.*	.964	48	5	22	1	28	2
Forbes, Derek, H.D.	1.000	20	1	8	0	9	0
Forbes, Keith, R.C.	.765	74	2	11	4	17	1
Foster, Kris, S.B.	1.000	10	2	0	0	2	0
Galva, Claudio, Vis.*	.852	48	6	17	4	27	0
Garcia, Apostol, S.B.	1.000	4	0	1	0	1	0
Garcia, Carlos, S.B.	.983	27	20	38	1	59	2
German, Franklyn, Mod.	.867	17	4	9	2	15	0
Gonzalez, Cristian, Mod.	1.000	4	0	1	0	1	0
Greene, Clay, S.J.	.000	1	0	0	0	0	0
Grezlovski, Ben, L.E.	.667	43	4	2	3	9	0
Harris, Toby, H.D.	1.000	14	2	3	0	5	0
Hart, Len, R.C.*	1.000	13	1	4	0	5	1
Haworth, Brent, L.E.	.778	17	2	5	2	9	1
Heaverlo, Jeff, Lan.	.852	27	9	14	4	27	1
Hensley, Matthew, L.E.	.000	1	0	0	0	0	0
Hershiser, Orel, S.B.	1.000	3	4	3	0	7	0
Hill, Ken, L.E.	1.000	1	0	1	0	1	0
Holmes, Mike, Mod.	.900	21	5	4	1	10	0
HORGAN, Joe, S.J.*	1.000	27	10	26	0	36	4
Howard, Ben, R.C.	.800	32	4	4	2	10	0
Hundley, Jeff, L.E.*	.917	18	8	14	2	24	1
Hunter, Johnny, R.C.	.944	47	5	12	1	18	0
Jacobs, Dwayne, S.B.	1.000	21	3	7	0	10	1
Jacobs, Greg, L.E.*	.833	32	1	4	1	6	0
Jacobs, Ryan, Mud.*	1.000	26	1	7	0	8	0
Jensen, Jared, Vis.	.846	30	3	8	2	13	1
Jensen, Jason, H.D.*	.972	28	6	29	1	36	1
Johnson, Eric, S.J.-Bak.	1.000	18	3	8	0	11	1
Johnson, James, Mud.*	.800	11	5	7	3	15	0
Johnstone, John, S.J.	.000	2	0	0	0	0	0
Jones, Chris, S.J.*	.700	36	3	4	3	10	0
Jones, Fontella, Mud.	1.000	25	2	5	0	7	1
Jones, Greg, L.E.	1.000	16	2	3	0	5	0
Jones, Marcus, Vis.	.333	3	0	1	2	3	0
Junge, Eric, S.B.	.960	29	10	14	1	25	1
Karl, Scott, L.E.*	1.000	1	1	0	0	1	0
Kees, Justin, H.D.	.947	32	6	12	1	19	1
Kimball, Andrew, Mod.	1.000	16	1	5	0	6	0
Koplove, Mike, H.D.	1.000	20	2	5	0	7	0
Krawczyk, Jack, Mud.	1.000	49	7	18	0	25	2
Kuo, Hong-chih, S.B.*	1.000	1	0	1	0	1	0
Lackey, John, L.E.	.952	15	11	9	1	21	1
Lankford, Frank, Mod.	1.000	1	0	0	0	0	0
Lee, Fletcher, Bak.	1.000	9	2	1	0	3	0
Lehr, Charles, Mod.	.911	29	16	35	5	56	3
Leyva, Julian, Mod.	.895	42	3	14	2	19	0
Lineweaver, Aaron, H.D.	.000	1	0	0	0	0	0
Loewer, Carlton, R.C.	1.000	1	1	0	0	1	0
Longo, Neil, Lan.	1.000	34	3	2	0	5	0
Lontayo, Alejandro, L.E.*	.727	6	3	5	3	11	0
Looper, Aaron, Lan.	.857	51	1	11	2	14	0
Lopez, Javier, H.D.*	1.000	30	6	26	0	32	0
Luque, Roger, R.C.*	1.000	29	1	9	0	10	0
Lynch, Jim, Bak.	.826	18	9	10	4	23	0
Malerich, Will, Bak.*	.952	36	2	18	1	21	0
Mallette, Brian, Mud.	.800	50	4	4	2	10	0
Malloy, Bill, Bak.	1.000	10	3	8	0	11	0
Martin, Scott, S.B.	1.000	33	11	5	0	16	0
Matos, Josue, Lan.	1.000	14	1	7	0	8	1
Maurer, Mike, Vis.	.900	14	2	7	1	10	0
Mazur, Bryan, Mod.*	1.000	3	1	18	0	19	1
McAdoo, Duncan, R.C.	.625	6	3	2	3	8	0
McCall, Travis, Vis.*	.923	43	2	10	1	13	2
McDaniel, Denny, Lan.*	.800	43	4	4	2	10	0
Mears, Chris, Lan.	.931	28	9	18	2	29	0
Mendoza, Hatuey, H.D.	.905	29	18	20	4	42	3
Mendoza, Mario, L.E.	.933	12	3	11	1	15	0
Mercker, Kent, L.E.*	1.000	1	0	1	0	1	0
Meyer, Dave, S.B.	.500	8	0	1	1	2	0
Mieses, Jose, Mud.	.818	6	3	6	2	11	0
Miller, Corey, Vis.	.917	47	2	9	1	12	1
Miller, Jim, Mud.	1.000	12	1	2	0	3	0
Miller, Tom, Bak.*	1.000	32	3	12	0	15	0
Montero, Agustin, S.B.	.000	7	0	0	0	0	0
Montgomery, Steve, R.C.	1.000	6	1	0	0	1	0
Moore, Darin, Mod.	.500	3	0	1	1	2	0
Morrison, Cody, Lan.	.875	52	4	10	2	16	3
Myers, Aaron, Mud.	1.000	50	7	13	0	20	1
Myers, Rodney, R.C.	1.000	3	0	2	0	2	0
Nall, T. J., S.B.	1.000	3	1	3	0	4	1
Nathan, Joe, S.J.-Bak.	1.000	2	0	1	0	1	0
Neugebauer, Nickolas, Mud.	.889	18	3	5	1	9	0
Nix, Wayne, Vis.	.929	30	6	7	1	14	0
Noriega, Ray, Mod.*	.833	24	2	3	1	6	1
Obando, Omar, Lan.	1.000	21	0	1	0	1	0

CLASS A *California League*

Player, Team	Pct.	G	PO	A	E	TC	DP
O'Brien, Matt, Mod.*	1.000	4	0	3	0	3	0
Olivares, Omar, Mod.	1.000	2	0	1	0	1	0
Olson, Gregg, S.B.	.000	6	0	0	0	0	0
Ortiz, Omar, R.C.	.917	21	2	9	1	12	1
Ortiz, Ramon, L.E.	.000	1	0	0	0	0	0
Osuna, Antonio, S.B.	1.000	3	1	3	0	4	0
Ozias, Todd, S.J.	.833	47	0	5	1	6	0
Parker, Brandon, Lan.	.889	52	2	6	1	9	0
Parrish, Wade, S.B.*	1.000	29	2	3	0	5	0
Pavon, Julio, Bak.	1.000	7	0	2	0	2	0
Pena, Juan, Mod.*	.931	29	3	24	2	29	1
Penney, Mike, Mud.	1.000	13	8	13	0	21	2
Percival, Troy, L.E.	.000	2	0	0	0	0	0
Perez, Beltran, H.D.	.500	2	1	0	1	2	0
Petkovsek, Mark, L.E.	.000	2	0	0	0	0	0
Poe, Ryan, Mud.	1.000	33	5	5	0	10	0
Polanco, Elvis, Mud.	.867	35	4	9	2	15	1
Prata, Danny, S.J.-Bak.*	.778	23	0	14	4	18	0
Rajotte, Jason, S.J.*	.867	44	2	11	2	15	1
Ramos, Mario, Mod.*	.953	26	7	34	2	43	2
Rayborn, Kenny, Lan.	1.000	21	2	8	0	10	0
Roberts, Rick, S.B.*	.889	29	6	18	3	27	1
Rodriguez, Francisco, L.E.	.846	13	2	9	2	13	0
Rooney, Mike, H.D.	1.000	17	4	13	0	17	0
Rosario, Carlos, Mod.	.000	1	0	0	0	0	0
Ross, Lew, H.D.*	1.000	23	1	5	0	6	0
Royer, Jason, H.D.	1.000	8	0	5	0	5	0
Sanchez, Cade, Vis.	1.000	14	1	0	0	1	0
Schoeneweis, Scott, L.E.*	1.000	1	0	1	0	1	1
Schultz, Jeff, Vis.	.789	35	5	10	4	19	1
Schultz, Michael, H.D.	.857	7	3	3	1	7	0
Scott, Brian, H.D.	1.000	14	7	5	0	12	2
Seabury, Jaron, Mud.	.952	33	12	28	2	42	1
Seaver, Mark, Mod.	.966	29	8	20	1	29	0
Shabansky, Rob, H.D.*	.600	6	1	2	2	5	0
Shiell, Jason, R.C.	.895	16	4	13	2	19	0
Shiyuk, Todd, R.C.*	1.000	29	0	1	0	1	0
Simonson, Chris, Mud.	.938	14	2	13	1	16	1
Simpson, Allan, Lan.	.818	46	2	7	2	11	1
Smith, Justin, Lan.*	.000	1	0	0	0	0	0
Snellgrove, Clay, R.C.	1.000	1	1	0	0	1	0
Stabile, Paul, H.D.*	1.000	21	1	1	0	2	0
Stewart, Paul, Mud.	1.000	17	4	3	0	7	0
Suarez, Felipe, L.E.	.769	31	1	9	3	13	0

Player, Team	Pct.	G	PO	A	E	TC	DP
Surkont, Keith, Vis.	.853	27	9	20	5	34	2
Taschner, Jack, S.J.*	.500	10	0	2	2	4	1
Temple, Jason, R.C.	.933	57	7	7	1	15	3
Thames, Charles, L.E.	1.000	6	2	2	0	4	0
Thompson, Eric, Vis.	1.000	13	5	7	0	12	1
Thorn, Todd, H.D.*	.909	8	4	6	1	11	0
Torres, Melqui, Lan.	.913	18	8	13	2	23	1
Tucker, Ben, Bak.	1.000	12	4	10	0	14	1
Turuda, Miyoki, S.B.	1.000	6	0	3	0	3	0
Ulloa, Enmanuel, Lan.	.931	27	16	11	2	29	1
Uzzell, Todd, S.J.	.000	2	0	0	0	0	0
Valenti, Jon, Bak.	.923	58	5	19	2	26	0
Vardijan, Dan, H.D.	1.000	16	1	9	0	10	2
Vent, Kevin, Bak.	1.000	26	6	14	0	20	1
Verplancke, Jeff, S.J.	.808	26	5	16	5	26	1
Villarreal, Oscar, H.D.	.875	9	1	6	1	8	0
Volkman, Keith, R.C.*	.000	6	0	0	0	0	0
Walk, Mitch, S.J.*	1.000	1	2	2	0	4	0
Washburn, Jarrod, L.E.*	.000	1	0	0	0	0	0
Watkins, Steve, R.C.	.909	27	9	11	2	22	0
Wells, Matt, S.J.	1.000	16	1	2	0	3	0
Wells, Zach, Bak.	.917	40	4	7	1	12	1
Williams, Jerome, S.J.	.964	23	6	21	1	28	1
Williams, Woody, R.C.	.000	1	0	0	0	0	0
Williamson, Charles, H.D.	1.000	19	1	2	0	3	0
Wilson, Philip, L.E.	.889	6	5	3	1	9	0
Wood, Brandon, H.D.	.846	35	2	9	2	13	1
Yates, Tyler, Mod.	1.000	30	6	4	0	10	0
Zamarripa, Mark, H.D.	1.000	5	2	7	0	9	0
Zimmerman, Jordan, Lan.*	1.000	3	1	1	0	2	0
Zirelli, Mike, Bak.	.955	40	1	20	1	22	0

PITCHERS WITH TWO OR MORE TEAMS

Player, Team	Pct.	G	PO	A	E	TC	DP
Blood, Darin, Bak.	.000	4	0	0	0	0	0
Blood, Darin, S.J.	.000	1	0	0	0	0	0
Johnson, Eric, S.J.	1.000	13	0	5	0	5	1
Johnson, Eric, Bak.	1.000	5	3	3	0	6	0
Nathan, Joe, S.J.	.000	1	0	0	0	0	0
Nathan, Joe, Bak.	1.000	1	0	1	0	1	0
Prata, Danny, S.J.*	.786	20	0	11	3	14	0
Prata, Danny, Bak.*	.750	3	0	3	1	4	0

The following players appeared only as designated hitter, pinch-hitter or pinch runner: Crosby, dh; Jaha, dh.

LEAGUE CHAMPIONS

Year	Team	Pct.
1914—	Fresno	.571
1915—	Modesto	.857
1916-40—	Did not operate.	
1941—	Fresno	.643
	Santa Barbara (2nd)*	.597
1942—	Santa Barbara†	.642
1943-44-45—	Did not operate.	
1946—	Stockton‡	.600
1947—	Stockton‡	.679
1948—	Fresno	.607
	Santa Barbara (3rd)*	.529
1949—	Bakersfield	.612
	San Jose (4th)*	.543
1950—	Ventura	.607
	Modesto (2nd)*	.586
1951—	Santa Barbara‡	.599
1952—	Fresno‡	.629
1953—	San Jose‡	.664
1954—	Modesto‡	.623
1955—	Stockton	.733
	Fresno§	.718
1956—	Fresno§	.650
1957—	Visalia∞	.622
	Salinas (4th)*	.504
1958—	Fresno*	.639
	Bakersfield	.672
1959—	Bakersfield	.592
	Modesto§	.643
1960—	Reno	.614
	Reno	.657
1961—	Reno	.743
	Reno	.643

Year	Team	Pct.
1962—	San Jose§	.686
	Reno	.587
1963—	Modesto	.589
	Stockton§	.687
1964—	Fresno	.638
	Fresno	.600
1965—	San Jose	.586
	Stockton§	.614
1966—	Modesto	.577
	Modesto	.671
1967—	San Jose§	.676
	Modesto	.586
1968—	San Jose	.629
	Fresno§	.623
1969—	Stockton§	.600
	Visalia	.614
1970—	Bakersfield	.667
	Bakersfield	.671
1971—	Visalia§	.583
	Fresno	.500
1972—	Modesto§	.547
	Bakersfield	.629
1973—	Lodi§	.657
	Bakersfield	.571
1974—	Fresno§	.607
	San Jose	.579
1975—	Reno	.614
	Reno	.614
1976—	Salinas	.650
	Reno§	.547
1977—	Salinas	.564
	Lodi§	.579

Year	Team	Pct.
1978—	Visalia§	.698
	Lodi	.607
1979—	San Jose§	.636
	Reno	.525
1980—	Stockton§	.638
	Visalia	.507
1981—	Visalia	.621
	Lodi§	.521
1982—	Modesto§	.671
	Visalia	.586
1983—	Visalia	.621
	Redwood§	.529
1984—	Modesto§	.597
	Bakersfield	.486
1985—	Fresno§	.575
	Stockton	.566
1986—	Palm Springs	.613
	Stockton§	.585
1987—	Fresno§	.559
	Reno	.535
1988—	Stockton	.657
	Riverside§	.599
1989—	Stockton	.627
	Bakersfield§	.577
1990—	Visalia	.638
	Stockton§	.582
1991—	San Jose	.676
	High Desert§	.537
1992—	Stockton§	.610
	Visalia	.551
1993—	High Desert§	.620
	Modesto	.529

CLASS A *California League*

Year	Team	Pct.	Year	Team	Pct.	Year	Team	Pct.
1994—	Modesto	.706		Lake Elsinore‡	.550	1999—	Modesto	.629
	Rancho Cucamonga§	.566	1997—	High Desert▲	.593		San Bernardino▲	.567
1995—	San Bernardino§	.612		San Bernardino	.486	2000—	Lancaster	.636
	San Jose	.550	1998—	San Jose▲	.593		San Bernardino▲	.550
1996—	San Jose	.636		Rancho Cucamonga	.550			

*Won four-club playoff. †League disbanded June 28. ‡Won championship and four-club playoff. §Won split-season playoff. ∞Won both halves of split season. ▲Played split season and won six-club playoff.

CAROLINA LEAGUE

LEAGUE OFFICE

President/treasurer
John Hopkins
Address
P.O. Box 9503
Greensboro, NC 27429
Phone
336-691-9030

Teams (affiliation)
Frederick Keys (Orioles)
Kinston Indians (Indians)
Lynchburg Hillcats (Pirates)
Myrtle Beach Pelicans (Braves)
Potomac Cannons (Cardinals)
Salem Avalanche (Rockies)

Wilmington Blue Rocks (Royals)
Winston-Salem Warthogs (White Sox)

2000 FINAL STANDINGS

FIRST HALF

NORTHERN DIVISION

Team	W	L	T	Pct.	GB
Frederick (Orioles)	38	32	0	.543	...
Potomac (Cardinals)	35	35	0	.500	3.0
Wilmington (Royals)	29	41	0	.414	9.0
Lynchburg (Pirates)	27	43	0	.386	11.0

SOUTHERN DIVISION

Team	W	L	T	Pct.	GB
Myrtle Beach (Braves)	42	28	0	.600	...
Salem (Rockies)	38	32	0	.543	4.0
Kinston (Indians)	36	34	0	.514	6.0
Winston-Salem (White Sox)	35	35	0	.500	7.0

SECOND HALF

NORTHERN DIVISION

Team	W	L	T	Pct.	GB
Lynchburg (Pirates)	39	29	0	.574	...
Wilmington (Royals)	34	35	0	.493	5.5
Frederick (Orioles)	28	39	0	.418	10.5
Potomac (Cardinals)	27	41	0	.397	12.0

SOUTHERN DIVISION

Team	W	L	T	Pct.	GB
Myrtle Beach (Braves)	46	24	0	.657	...
Salem (Rockies)	35	35	0	.500	11.0
Winston-Salem (White Sox)	33	36	0	.478	12.5
Kinston (Indians)	32	35	0	.478	12.5

COMPOSITE

Team	M.B.	Sal.	Kin.	W.S.	Fred.	Lyn.	Wil.	Poto.	W	L	T	Pct.	GB
Myrtle Beach (Braves)	...	11	12	15	15	11	12	12	88	52	0	.629	...
Salem (Rockies)	9	...	10	8	12	12	10	12	73	67	0	.521	15.0
Kinston (Indians)	8	10	...	9	6	10	12	13	68	69	0	.496	18.5
Winston-Salem (White Sox)	5	12	10	...	10	11	10	10	68	71	0	.489	19.5
Frederick (Orioles)	5	8	13	10	...	10	13	7	66	71	0	.482	20.5
Lynchburg (Pirates)	9	8	10	9	8	...	9	13	66	72	0	.478	21.0
Wilmington (Royals)	8	10	8	10	7	11	...	9	63	76	0	.453	24.5
Potomac (Cardinals)	8	8	6	10	13	7	10	...	62	76	0	.449	25.0

Major league affiliations in parentheses.

PLAYOFFS: Lynchburg defeated Frederick two games to none; Myrtle Beach defeated Lynchburg three games to none to win championship.

REGULAR-SEASON ATTENDANCE: Frederick, 310,753; Kinston, 112,084; Lynchburg, 109,599; Myrtle Beach, 234,019; Potomac, 167,988; Salem, 200,863; Wilmington, 324,019; Winston-Salem, 151,930. Total—1,611,255. Playoffs (5 games)—10,100. Carolina-California League All-Star Game at Kinston, N.C.—4,699.

MANAGERS: Frederick, Dave Machemer; Kinston, Brad Komminsk; Lynchburg, Tracy Woodson; Myrtle Beach, Brian Snitker; Potomac, Joe Cunningham; Salem, Alan Cockrell; Wilmington, Jeff Garber; Winston-Salem, Brian Dayett.

ALL-STAR TEAM: 1B—A.J. Zapp, Myrtle Beach; 2B—Chone Figgins, Salem; 3B—Corey Erickson, Kinston; SS—Mark Ellis, Wilmington; Utility IF—Victor Rodriguez, Kinston; OF—Kevin Burford, Salem; OF—Esix Snead, Potomac; OF—Mario Valenzuela, Winston-Salem; C—Lee Evans, Lynchburg; DH—Troy Farnsworth, Potomac; Utility OF—J.J. Davis, Lynchburg; Starting Pitcher—Christian Parra, Myrtle Beach; Relief pitcher—Jason Marr, Potomac; Most Valuable Player—Troy Farnsworth, Potomac; Pitcher of the Year—Christian Parra, Myrtle Beach; Manager of the Year—Brian Snitker, Myrtle Beach.

2000 BATTING

TEAM

Team	Avg.	G	TPA	AB	R	H	TB	2B	3B	HR	RBI	SH	SF	HP	BB	IBB	SO	SB	CS	GDP	LOB	ShO	Slg.	OBP
Salem	.268	140	5162	4625	654	1239	1854	273	45	84	595	25	44	63	405	4	866	140	66	95	914	7	.401	.332
Kinston	.260	137	5208	4572	618	1189	1758	258	31	83	562	47	36	65	488	11	973	177	71	96	1005	13	.385	.338
Frederick	.257	137	5242	4472	658	1151	1632	220	24	71	582	60	49	64	597	19	974	202	82	111	1015	8	.365	.350
Wilmington	.252	139	5204	4551	584	1145	1560	199	30	52	519	60	37	81	475	9	981	127	51	105	1024	11	.343	.331
Lynchburg	.250	138	5078	4416	594	1105	1663	213	30	95	540	46	43	64	509	9	1128	145	51	102	950	10	.377	.333
Win.-Salem	.245	139	5192	4497	630	1104	1725	267	33	96	568	45	44	62	544	12	978	118	54	97	968	8	.384	.332
Potomac	.242	138	5141	4517	597	1092	1622	241	29	77	531	54	32	91	447	6	1019	181	82	94	924	11	.359	.320
Myrtle Beach	.237	140	5073	4502	567	1069	1632	225	31	92	503	32	29	79	431	8	1166	104	57	64	939	12	.363	.313

INDIVIDUAL

TOP QUALIFIERS FOR BATTING CHAMPIONSHIP

Minimum 378 plate appearances. *Lefthanded batter. †Switch-hitter.

Player, Team	Avg.	G	TPA	AB	R	H	TB	2B	3B	HR	RBI	SH	SF	HP	BB	IBB	SO	SB	CS	GDP	Slg.	OBP
Rodriguez, Victor, Kin.	.327	96	432	382	59	125	172	31	2	4	42	7	1	5	37	1	48	24	9	7	.450	.393
Ellis, Mark, Wil.	.302	132	576	484	83	146	199	27	4	6	62	4	3	7	78	0	72	25	7	11	.411	.404

Player, Team	Avg.	G	TPA	AB	R	H	TB	2B	3B	HR	RBI	SH	SF	HP	BB	IBB	SO	SB	CS	GDP	Slg.	OBP
Burford, Kevin, Sal.*	.292	127	537	465	73	136	232	40	4	16	80	0	4	10	58	2	79	11	4	6	.499	.380
Connacher, Kevin, W.S.	.286	97	428	360	70	103	163	24	3	10	43	2	2	5	59	2	100	24	8	4	.453	.392
Berger, Brandon, Wil.	.285	102	443	379	63	108	179	18	4	15	71	4	3	17	40	2	71	12	4	8	.472	.376
Ndungidi, Ntema, Fred.*	.284	90	384	313	53	89	143	16	4	10	59	3	5	3	60	2	83	16	5	4	.457	.399
Lindsey, John, Sal.	.280	104	398	343	43	96	148	23	1	9	56	0	3	15	37	0	76	5	3	6	.431	.372
Figgins, Chone, Sal.†	.278	134	601	522	92	145	208	26	14	3	48	6	5	1	67	0	107	37	19	7	.398	.358
McNaughton, Troy, Pot.*	.275	125	506	458	63	126	195	26	2	13	70	2	3	2	41	2	124	16	9	8	.426	.335
Wilson, Travis, M.B.	.275	125	516	484	62	133	212	33	5	12	63	3	4	9	16	0	111	7	8	9	.438	.308
Holliday, Matt, Sal.	.274	123	510	460	64	126	179	28	2	7	72	0	5	2	43	1	74	11	5	12	.389	.335
Bowers, Jason, Pot.	.272	91	399	342	53	93	124	16	6	1	35	3	0	6	48	0	72	10	5	5	.363	.371
Segura, Rolando, Lyn.	.270	108	416	378	42	102	150	19	1	9	47	2	3	8	25	0	105	0	1	9	.397	.326
Erickson, Corey, Kin.	.268	120	489	422	66	113	206	27	0	22	72	0	5	11	51	3	109	9	2	3	.488	.358
Hankins, Ryan, W.S.	.268	96	391	321	43	86	136	27	1	7	52	3	8	2	57	1	64	6	4	4	.424	.374
Zapp, A.J., M.B.*	.268	107	452	385	59	103	157	28	1	8	49	0	0	10	57	3	106	3	2	4	.408	.376

DEPARTMENTAL LEADERS: G—Valenzuela, 138; AB—Valenzuela, 524; R—Figgins, 92; H—Ellis, 146; TB—Valenzuela, 235; 2B—Burford, 40; 3B—Figgins, 14; HR—Farnsworth, 23; RBI—Farnsworth, 113; SH—L. Gonzalez, 12; SF—Farnsworth, 11; HP—Berger, 17; BB—Merriman, 94; IBB—Shackelford, 4; SO—Davis, 171; SB—Snead, 109; CS—Snead, 35; GIDP—Figueroa, 15; Slg.—Burford, .499; OBP—Ellis, .404.

ALL PLAYERS

*Lefthanded batter. †Switch-hitter.

Player, Team	Avg.	G	TPA	AB	R	H	TB	2B	3B	HR	RBI	SH	SF	HP	BB	IBB	SO	SB	CS	GDP	Slg.	OBP
Acevas, Jon, W.S.	.212	76	287	259	41	55	85	17	2	3	17	1	2	5	20	2	65	3	1	9	.328	.280
Aldridge, Cory, M.B.*	.249	109	444	401	51	100	173	18	5	15	64	0	9	1	33	2	118	10	5	0	.431	.302
Alguacil, Jose, W.S.*	.268	40	153	138	18	37	50	9	2	0	18	5	1	2	7	0	19	10	3	3	.362	.311
Alley, Charles, Fred.†	.245	35	120	98	15	24	33	3	0	2	12	2	1	1	18	0	20	0	0	4	.337	.364
Alviso, Jerome, Sal.†	.271	95	358	321	39	87	107	11	3	1	44	7	7	6	17	0	46	11	9	8	.333	.313
Bard, Josh, Sal.†	.285	93	345	309	40	88	111	17	0	2	25	1	2	1	32	1	33	3	1	6	.359	.352
Barns, B.J., Lyn.*	.244	120	458	398	46	97	143	20	1	8	48	2	5	9	44	2	95	8	5	8	.359	.329
Beltran, Carlos, Wil.†	.308	3	13	13	2	4	12	0	1	2	6	0	0	0	0	0	5	0	0	0	.923	.308
Benefield, Brian, Kin.	.284	66	276	236	45	67	104	19	6	2	19	2	2	1	35	0	55	10	3	9	.441	.376
Benham, David, Pot.	.188	28	102	85	12	16	25	4	1	1	7	2	1	8	6	0	20	0	0	5	.294	.300
Benham, Jason, Fred.*	.197	28	72	66	7	13	16	1	1	0	9	0	0	0	6	0	17	1	0	5	.242	.264
Berger, Brandon, Wil.	.285	102	443	379	63	108	179	18	4	15	71	4	3	17	40	2	71	12	4	8	.472	.376
Berger, Matt, W.S.	.228	128	519	430	65	98	176	32	2	14	65	1	6	5	77	0	106	3	4	10	.409	.347
Bigbie, Larry, Fred.*	.294	55	229	201	33	59	76	11	0	2	28	1	4	0	23	2	34	7	3	3	.378	.360
Borchard, Joe, W.S.†	.288	14	61	52	7	15	24	3	0	2	7	0	1	2	6	0	9	0	0	0	.462	.377
Bost, Tom, Kin.*	.226	10	34	31	3	7	10	1	1	0	1	1	0	1	1	0	8	0	1	1	.323	.273
Bowers, Jason, Pot.	.272	91	399	342	53	93	124	16	6	1	35	3	0	6	48	0	72	10	5	5	.363	.371
Brignac, Junior, M.B.	.211	128	536	475	58	100	144	17	3	7	42	9	1	8	43	1	145	27	8	5	.303	.287
Brito, Juan, Wil.	.222	22	63	54	4	12	16	4	0	0	9	0	1	0	8	0	7	1	0	2	.296	.317
Bronowicz, Scott, M.B.*	.222	11	38	36	5	8	8	0	0	0	2	0	0	1	1	0	8	0	0	0	.222	.263
Burford, Kevin, Sal.*	.292	127	537	465	73	136	232	40	4	16	80	0	4	10	58	2	79	11	4	6	.499	.380
Calais, Ian, M.B.	.077	5	15	13	3	1	1	0	0	0	1	0	0	1	1	0	4	1	1	0	.077	.200
Calderon, Henry, Wil.	.263	122	460	419	52	110	141	11	4	4	45	10	4	8	19	0	76	14	6	14	.337	.304
Cameron, Troy, M.B.†	.212	123	470	401	53	85	159	23	3	15	51	0	2	8	59	0	131	0	2	6	.397	.323
Caradonna, Brett, W.S.*	.208	103	398	365	39	76	106	20	2	2	32	1	0	2	29	2	70	3	1	11	.290	.270
Castro, Alfredo, M.B.†	.252	108	445	385	52	97	138	20	3	5	44	3	1	12	44	0	76	13	5	4	.358	.346
Cleto, Ambioris, Lyn.	.500	4	7	6	2	3	6	1	1	0	0	0	0	1	0	0	1	0	0	0	1.000	.571
Connacher, Kevin, W.S.	.286	97	428	360	70	103	163	24	3	10	43	2	2	5	59	2	100	24	8	4	.453	.392
Copeland, Brandon, Pot.	.179	42	138	112	13	20	35	3	3	2	15	2	1	5	18	0	39	2	4	2	.313	.316
Curtis, Matt, Kin.†	.309	82	292	256	37	79	128	19	0	10	48	0	3	0	33	3	46	4	2	5	.500	.384
Daedelow, Craig, Fred.	.200	62	179	145	24	29	35	6	0	0	9	4	2	2	26	0	26	4	1	3	.241	.326
Dalton, David, M.B.	.244	82	326	275	36	67	99	12	1	6	21	3	0	10	38	0	77	9	5	3	.360	.356
Darr, Ryan, Pot.	.243	88	332	280	43	68	91	17	0	2	26	3	2	4	43	0	90	7	1	4	.325	.350
Davis, J.J., Lyn.	.243	130	545	485	77	118	216	36	1	20	80	0	4	4	52	2	171	9	4	11	.445	.319
Deck, Billy, Pot.*	.221	99	350	290	36	64	95	13	0	6	30	3	3	12	42	0	79	3	3	6	.328	.340
Diaz, Maikell, Fred.	.258	74	282	240	31	62	73	7	2	0	22	7	1	3	31	1	58	9	7	9	.304	.349
Diaz, Miguel, Pot.	.250	105	338	312	35	78	105	23	2	0	32	4	3	5	14	0	47	5	3	8	.337	.290
Dunn, Casey, Wil.	.283	62	228	205	18	58	72	11	0	1	28	3	3	5	12	0	35	1	0	9	.351	.333
Dyt, Darren, Pot.*	.183	24	74	71	5	13	18	3	1	0	3	0	0	0	3	0	27	1	0	2	.254	.216
Ellis, Mark, Wil.	.302	132	576	484	83	146	199	27	4	6	62	4	3	7	78	0	72	25	7	11	.411	.404
Erickson, Corey, Kin.	.268	120	489	422	66	113	206	27	0	22	72	0	5	11	51	3	109	9	2	3	.488	.358
Esquerra, Marques, Kin.†	.247	29	86	77	6	19	20	1	0	0	9	2	0	1	6	1	12	0	1	1	.260	.310
Evans, Lee, Lyn.†	.259	90	354	305	45	79	127	15	3	9	37	2	2	2	43	0	88	16	1	6	.416	.352
Ewing, Byron, Kin.	.166	98	367	314	38	52	74	11	1	3	22	2	0	7	44	0	102	16	5	7	.236	.282
Farnsworth, Troy, Pot.	.240	137	578	512	67	123	222	24	3	23	113	0	11	11	44	1	133	7	2	7	.434	.308
Fennell, Jason, W.S.†	.180	17	64	50	7	9	11	2	0	0	4	4	0	0	10	0	12	1	2	1	.220	.317
Figgins, Chone, Sal.†	.278	134	601	522	92	145	208	26	14	3	48	6	5	1	67	0	107	37	19	7	.398	.358
Figueroa, Franky, Fred.	.255	126	526	490	58	125	199	23	0	17	87	1	7	6	22	3	109	1	3	15	.406	.291
Fitzgerald, Jason, Kin.*	.252	82	355	318	42	80	114	16	3	4	44	1	4	2	29	2	55	21	4	3	.358	.314
Freeman, Choo, Sal.	.266	127	476	429	73	114	161	18	7	5	54	1	5	4	37	0	104	16	8	7	.375	.326
Gallaher, T.T., Kin.	.215	20	76	65	7	14	20	4	1	0	11	2	1	1	7	0	12	1	2	2	.308	.297
Garcia, Tony, W.S.	.277	77	277	238	33	66	91	14	1	3	32	4	1	14	20	0	55	5	1	7	.382	.366
Gettis, Byron, Wil.	.155	30	115	97	13	15	17	2	0	0	10	2	1	2	13	0	33	2	1	1	.175	.265
Gomez, Alexis, Wil.*	.254	121	516	461	63	117	141	13	4	1	33	7	1	2	45	1	121	21	10	8	.306	.322
Gonzalez, Luis, Kin.	.246	79	325	284	32	70	87	11	0	2	33	12	2	6	21	0	54	6	6	6	.306	.310
Goodwin, David, Wil.	.248	89	350	311	29	77	107	21	0	3	38	2	3	8	26	1	83	1	0	9	.344	.319
Green, Nick, M.B.	.242	27	105	91	13	22	31	6	0	1	6	1	0	3	10	0	23	3	2	0	.341	.337
Griswold, Matt, Fred.*	.191	24	75	68	5	13	18	3	1	0	6	0	1	0	6	0	15	2	2	2	.265	.253
Gutierrez, Vic, Lyn.	.242	107	386	339	42	82	102	9	4	1	29	6	0	1	40	0	53	15	8	7	.301	.324
Haad, Yamid, Lyn.	.253	25	103	91	14	23	40	8	0	3	9	0	1	0	11	0	16	2	0	4	.440	.330
Hage, Tom, Fred.*	.227	25	109	97	10	22	32	8	1	0	15	0	1	0	11	0	17	1	0	4	.330	.303
Hairston, Jerry, Fred.	.375	2	9	8	1	3	5	2	0	0	1	0	0	0	1	0	0	0	0	0	.625	.444

Player, Team	Avg.	G	TPA	AB	R	H	TB	2B	3B	HR	RBI	SH	SF	HP	BB	IBB	SO	SB	CS	GDP	Slg.	OBP
Hammond, Joey, Fred.	.257	126	511	432	47	111	137	22	2	0	39	4	5	5	65	1	88	5	8	7	.317	.357
Hankins, Ryan, W.S.	.268	96	391	321	43	86	136	27	1	7	52	3	8	2	57	1	64	6	4	4	.424	.374
Hart, Bo, Pot.	.256	75	314	273	42	70	103	25	4	0	20	4	1	13	23	0	42	9	6	2	.377	.342
Hart, Corey, Wil.†	.218	88	316	243	45	53	66	6	2	1	22	6	1	2	64	0	62	6	6	7	.272	.384
Harvey, Ken, Wil.	.335	46	185	164	20	55	77	10	0	4	25	0	0	7	14	0	29	0	2	4	.470	.411
Hemme, Justin, Sal.*	.221	76	274	249	27	55	90	17	0	6	30	1	1	3	20	0	59	0	0	8	.361	.286
Hernandez, Javier, Kin.†	.167	3	13	12	1	2	3	1	0	0	2	0	0	0	1	0	5	1	0	0	.250	.231
Hernandez, Jesus, Kin.*	.279	62	259	222	30	62	96	12	5	4	30	1	2	1	33	0	57	11	7	1	.432	.372
Hernandez, Jose, Lyn.	.333	4	10	9	1	3	4	1	0	0	1	0	1	0	0	0	4	0	0	0	.444	.300
Hill, Jeremy, Wil.	.197	99	345	299	33	59	84	12	2	3	26	6	3	3	33	1	84	1	2	6	.281	.281
Hobbs, Jay, Lyn.*	.229	98	348	297	38	68	118	22	2	8	52	2	3	2	44	1	102	2	2	10	.397	.329
Holliday, Matt, Sal.	.274	123	510	460	64	126	179	28	2	7	72	0	5	2	43	1	74	11	5	12	.389	.335
Hummel, Timothy, W.S.	.327	27	113	98	15	32	42	7	0	1	9	0	0	2	13	1	12	1	1	4	.429	.416
Hyde, Brandon, W.S.	.184	47	164	136	15	25	34	6	0	1	15	0	3	4	21	0	42	1	2	8	.250	.305
Johnson, Eric, Kin.	.207	55	253	213	23	44	58	4	2	2	21	6	2	5	27	0	47	15	5	1	.272	.308
Johnson, Erik, Sal.	.242	83	271	252	32	61	99	17	3	5	26	1	3	4	11	0	38	3	2	5	.393	.281
Jones, Jay, Sal.*	.286	36	138	126	15	36	54	10	1	2	24	1	2	0	9	0	13	1	0	3	.429	.328
Kidwell, Tommy, Pot.	.077	9	13	13	0	1	1	0	0	0	0	0	0	0	0	0	3	0	0	0	.077	.077
Kilburg, Joe, Kin.*	.209	25	103	86	12	18	24	4	1	0	7	0	1	5	11	0	23	2	3	4	.279	.330
Kim, Dave, Pot.	.241	42	168	141	15	34	59	10	0	5	18	1	0	5	21	0	31	1	1	4	.418	.359
Kingsale, Eugene, Fred.†	.440	6	26	25	8	11	17	3	0	1	3	0	0	0	1	0	6	2	1	0	.680	.462
Landaeta, Luis, Sal.*	.253	89	306	288	34	73	111	11	0	9	33	3	3	2	9	0	51	10	5	8	.385	.278
Landreth, Jason, Lyn.	.193	22	69	57	5	11	15	1	0	1	6	0	1	2	9	0	23	1	0	1	.263	.319
Langerhans, Ryan, M.B.*	.212	116	437	392	55	83	129	14	7	6	37	4	0	9	32	1	104	25	11	3	.329	.286
Lehr, Ryan, M.B.	.198	64	232	207	15	41	57	8	1	2	22	2	1	1	21	0	43	1	1	5	.275	.274
Leon, Alfredo, Fred.	.239	35	127	117	8	28	34	3	0	1	10	0	1	1	8	0	24	0	1	3	.291	.291
Lindsey, John, Sal.	.280	104	398	343	43	96	148	23	1	9	56	0	3	15	37	0	76	5	3	6	.431	.372
Long, Ryan, W.S.	.282	19	84	71	15	20	53	1	1	10	18	0	2	2	9	1	17	0	1	0	.746	.369
Lopez-Cao, Mike, Fred.*	.197	49	139	117	15	23	52	8	0	7	24	1	2	5	14	0	23	0	1	5	.444	.304
Lorenzana, Luis, Lyn.	.229	58	202	170	22	39	53	3	4	1	9	9	1	2	20	0	35	3	3	2	.312	.316
Macrory, Bob, Pot.	.241	49	190	170	23	41	50	7	1	0	14	4	2	2	12	0	26	3	4	10	.294	.296
Malave, Dennis, Kin.*	.348	19	53	46	8	16	27	4	2	1	11	1	0	0	6	0	8	4	0	0	.587	.423
Manuel, Marcellous, W.S.*	.228	75	269	246	18	56	68	10	1	0	26	3	2	1	17	0	31	0	1	4	.276	.278
Martin, Justin, Lyn.†	.262	98	426	355	52	93	104	9	1	0	26	4	1	8	58	0	70	37	10	6	.293	.377
Martinez, Eddy, Fred.	.303	40	183	152	23	46	58	10	1	0	15	5	0	2	24	0	34	7	6	6	.382	.404
Martinez, Octavio, Fred.	.375	2	9	8	0	3	3	0	0	0	1	0	0	1	0	0	0	0	0	0	.375	.444
Martinez, Victor, Kin.†	.217	26	99	83	9	18	25	7	0	0	8	3	1	1	11	0	5	1	1	3	.301	.313
Maxwell, Keith, Lyn.	.214	11	32	28	1	6	6	0	0	0	2	0	0	2	2	0	11	0	0	2	.214	.313
McDonald, John, Kin.	.333	1	3	3	0	1	1	0	0	0	0	0	0	0	0	0	0	0	0	0	.333	.333
McGee, Tom, Fred.	.222	85	289	252	29	56	76	12	1	2	27	6	2	4	25	0	74	5	1	9	.302	.300
McKinley, Dan, Kin.*	.323	18	66	62	8	20	25	5	0	0	7	1	0	1	2	0	11	4	1	1	.403	.354
McNaughton, Troy, Pot.*	.275	125	506	458	63	126	195	26	2	13	70	2	3	2	41	2	124	16	9	8	.426	.335
Medrano, Steve, Wil.†	.154	3	14	13	1	2	2	0	0	0	0	1	0	0	0	0	0	0	0	0	.154	.154
Meier, Dan, Lyn.*	.307	57	239	202	45	62	120	12	2	14	43	0	1	7	29	1	46	2	2	5	.594	.410
Merriman, Terrell, W.S.*	.232	134	546	439	64	102	178	22	9	12	67	1	5	7	94	1	109	28	7	6	.405	.372
Minges, Tyler, Kin.	.223	110	446	404	46	90	133	17	4	6	51	2	5	3	32	0	78	12	9	12	.329	.282
Minor, Ryan, Fred.	.333	2	9	9	3	3	3	0	0	0	0	0	0	0	0	0	4	0	0	0	.333	.333
Montas, Ricardo, Wil.	.277	93	367	314	43	87	104	17	0	0	36	2	4	5	42	0	49	6	1	9	.331	.367
Mortimer, Mark, M.B.	.267	41	160	135	17	36	45	4	1	1	14	1	0	2	22	0	26	0	1	5	.333	.377
Munoz, Billy, Kin.*	.315	63	240	213	28	67	115	13	1	11	39	0	3	3	21	0	46	0	1	5	.540	.379
Myers, Rod, W.S.*	.254	17	71	59	11	15	15	0	0	0	3	1	0	3	8	0	10	3	1	0	.254	.371
Ndungidi, Ntema, Fred.*	.284	90	384	313	53	89	143	16	4	10	59	3	5	3	60	2	83	16	5	4	.457	.399
Nelson, Eric, Wil.†	.211	106	421	370	44	78	102	13	4	1	28	7	4	6	34	0	94	10	4	2	.276	.285
Nunez, Jose, Pot.	.252	87	259	242	25	61	85	18	0	2	24	2	0	4	11	0	36	4	2	5	.351	.296
Nykoluk, Kevin, Pot.	.209	61	208	177	16	37	51	5	0	3	14	7	0	3	21	0	30	0	0	3	.288	.303
Olmeda, Jose, W.S.†	.205	45	177	166	14	34	61	14	2	3	20	3	2	1	5	1	45	4	3	4	.367	.230
Pagan, Carlos, Wil.	.250	3	5	4	1	1	3	0	1	0	1	0	0	1	0	0	1	0	0	0	.750	.400
Paz, Rich, Fred.	.306	79	354	268	53	82	107	13	0	4	45	6	6	3	71	0	47	15	8	5	.399	.448
Pichardo, Henry, Kin.	.188	16	51	48	7	9	14	2	0	1	6	0	0	0	3	0	11	4	2	1	.292	.235
Polanco, Enohel, Kin.	.000	3	11	11	1	0	0	0	0	0	0	0	0	0	0	0	5	0	0	1	.000	.000
Pond, Simon, Kin.*	.321	64	264	237	40	76	112	18	0	6	37	0	2	3	22	1	49	14	3	9	.473	.385
Pride, Joshua, Sal.	.227	10	28	22	3	5	7	2	0	0	2	0	1	2	3	0	8	0	0	1	.318	.357
Prieto, Jon, Lyn.†	.237	112	463	392	61	93	120	12	6	1	31	9	2	2	58	0	88	23	5	10	.306	.337
Puffinbarger, Rusty, Kin.	.121	13	40	33	4	4	4	0	0	0	1	0	0	1	6	0	9	0	0	1	.121	.275
Pugh, Josh, M.B.	.174	38	126	115	11	20	32	6	0	2	10	0	0	1	10	0	30	0	1	2	.278	.246
Pujols, Albert, Pot.	.284	21	89	81	11	23	39	8	1	2	10	1	0	0	7	0	8	1	1	3	.481	.341
Raines, Tim, Fred.†	.236	127	551	457	89	108	141	21	3	2	36	11	3	13	67	0	106	81	19	8	.309	.348
Reed, Keith, Fred.	.235	65	272	243	33	57	93	10	1	8	31	0	3	4	21	2	58	9	1	4	.383	.303
Reese, Nate, M.B.	.111	6	20	18	1	2	3	1	0	0	1	0	0	0	2	0	2	0	0	0	.167	.200
Reinoso, Nataniel, M.B.*	.229	85	314	297	27	68	99	17	1	4	37	2	5	1	9	1	66	0	3	6	.333	.259
Rickon, Jim, Kin.	.385	8	29	26	6	10	16	3	0	1	2	0	0	2	1	0	6	0	0	1	.615	.448
Rivera, Carlos, Lyn.*	.270	64	250	233	20	63	95	17	0	5	47	0	9	2	6	1	34	0	1	7	.408	.284
Rivera, Roberto, Fred.†	.250	36	134	116	14	29	43	5	3	1	18	1	2	2	12	3	30	4	0	0	.371	.326
Roberts, Brian, Fred.†	.301	48	198	163	27	49	61	6	3	0	16	7	0	1	27	1	24	13	10	4	.374	.403
Rodriguez, Victor, Kin.	.327	96	432	382	59	125	172	31	2	4	42	7	1	5	37	1	48	24	9	7	.450	.393
Ruiz, Willy, Wil.	.167	8	16	12	1	2	3	1	0	0	1	0	0	0	4	0	3	2	0	1	.250	.375
Rust, Brian, Fred.	.290	70	305	252	53	73	133	22	1	12	46	0	1	7	45	1	50	15	4	5	.528	.410
Salargo, Steve, Fred.	.196	20	55	51	3	10	12	2	0	0	5	0	0	1	3	0	12	0	0	3	.235	.255
Sanders, Tracy, Lyn.*	.278	43	172	144	25	40	79	9	0	10	26	0	2	3	23	1	47	1	0	1	.549	.384
Sandoval, Danny, W.S.	.266	52	225	199	29	53	74	11	2	2	17	7	0	1	18	1	21	11	7	7	.372	.330
Santana, Osmany, Kin.*	.326	44	208	190	27	62	78	12	2	0	14	2	1	0	15	0	27	13	4	2	.411	.374
Schneider, Matt, Lyn.*	.200	6	22	20	0	4	4	0	0	0	0	0	0	0	2	0	7	0	0	0	.200	.273
Seal, Scott, Sal.*	.267	103	377	344	55	92	147	31	3	6	35	0	1	9	23	0	75	10	5	6	.427	.329
Segura, Rolando, Lyn.	.270	108	416	378	42	102	150	19	1	9	47	2	3	8	25	0	105	0	1	9	.397	.326

Player, Team	Avg.	G	TPA	AB	R	H	TB	2B	3B	HR	RBI	SH	SF	HP	BB	IBB	SO	SB	CS	GDP	Slg.	OBP
Shackelford, Brian, Wil.*	.234	113	464	423	44	99	157	23	1	11	63	2	4	5	30	4	83	4	1	10	.371	.290
Sickles, Jeremy, Lyn.	.200	40	128	115	8	23	29	6	0	0	16	2	4	3	4	0	26	1	0	4	.252	.238
Simmons, Jerry, M.B.	.176	12	36	34	3	6	7	1	0	0	1	0	0	0	2	0	8	0	1	0	.206	.222
Skrehot, Shaun, Lyn.	.233	42	145	129	9	30	37	3	2	0	7	4	2	1	9	0	22	5	3	2	.287	.284
Smith, Casey, Kin.	.226	69	266	230	27	52	75	14	0	3	21	2	1	5	28	0	60	3	0	10	.326	.322
Smith, Sam, Sal.	.100	3	11	10	0	1	1	0	0	0	1	0	0	0	1	0	3	0	0	1	.100	.182
Smothers, Stewart, M.B.	.292	11	25	24	3	7	11	1	0	1	3	0	0	1	0	0	9	0	0	0	.458	.320
Snead, Esix, Pot.†	.235	132	582	493	82	116	139	14	3	1	34	9	1	7	72	1	98	109	35	7	.282	.340
Suarez, Luis, W.S.	.246	102	374	346	39	85	123	17	3	5	38	8	3	2	15	0	81	4	4	7	.355	.279
Taveras, Jose, Wil.	.217	99	308	286	25	62	78	10	3	0	15	4	2	3	13	0	73	21	7	4	.273	.257
Thames, Damon, Pot.	.260	30	108	104	12	27	50	5	0	6	16	2	0	1	0	0	18	1	0	3	.481	.274
Torrealba, Steve, M.B.	.269	99	376	334	43	90	127	16	0	7	35	4	6	1	31	0	79	5	1	12	.380	.328
Uribe, Juan, Sal.	.256	134	533	485	64	124	199	22	7	13	65	4	2	4	38	0	100	22	5	11	.410	.314
Valenzuela, Mario, W.S.	.261	138	592	524	87	137	235	31	2	21	85	1	6	2	59	0	110	11	3	8	.448	.335
Weichard, Paul, Lyn.†	.251	80	303	263	39	66	95	10	2	5	26	4	1	5	30	1	84	20	6	9	.361	.338
Weidert, Chris, Fred.	.000	24	1	1	0	0	0	0	0	0	0	0	0	0	0	0	0	0	0	0	.000	.000
Werth, Jayson, Fred.	.277	24	96	83	16	23	32	3	0	2	18	1	2	0	10	1	15	5	1	3	.386	.347
Whitlock, Brian, Kin.	.176	24	73	68	5	12	17	2	0	1	4	0	0	0	5	0	25	2	0	0	.250	.233
William, Jovany, Pot.	.217	87	339	314	37	68	114	20	1	8	43	4	3	3	15	2	86	0	3	9	.363	.257
Wilson, Jack, Pot.	.277	13	54	47	7	13	21	0	1	2	7	1	1	0	5	0	10	2	3	1	.447	.340
Wilson, Travis, M.B.	.275	125	516	484	62	133	212	33	5	12	63	3	4	9	16	0	111	7	8	9	.438	.308
Zapp, A.J., M.B.*	.268	107	452	385	59	103	157	28	1	8	49	0	0	10	57	3	106	3	2	4	.408	.376

GRAND SLAMS: Farnsworth, 2; Alley, B. Berger, M. Berger, Castro, Davis, F. Figueroa, Holliday, Langerhans, Minges, Pichardo, T. Sanders, Snead, Uribe, Zapp, 1 each.

AWARDED FIRST BASE ON CATCHER'S INTERFERENCE: Caradonna (Leon), Fitzgerald (Erik Johnson), Hill (William), Landaeta (Hill), Reed (Garcia), R. Rivera (William).

2000 PITCHING

TEAM

Team	W	L	Pct.	ERA	G	CG	ShO	Sv.	IP	H	TBF	R	ER	HR	SH	SF	HB	BB	IBB	SO	WP	Bk.
Myrtle Beach	88	52	.629	2.51	140	8	27	43	1205.2	908	4831	395	336	68	38	33	38	382	11	1089	63	12
Salem	73	67	.521	3.82	140	9	7	37	1203.0	1100	5276	615	510	56	61	42	80	562	2	1088	92	17
Wilmington	63	76	.453	3.89	139	4	12	27	1189.0	1128	5146	627	514	62	56	35	80	521	13	951	94	21
Kinston	68	69	.496	4.00	137	7	8	25	1194.1	1127	5173	624	531	94	45	38	83	516	13	1105	58	9
Winston-Salem	68	71	.489	4.12	139	9	7	34	1200.1	1184	5303	673	549	72	46	36	87	523	7	1032	123	10
Frederick	66	71	.482	4.13	137	6	1	27	1187.0	1225	5530	658	545	105	36	44	73	441	9	1004	64	8
Potomac	62	76	.449	4.17	138	2	9	40	1205.2	1200	5230	642	558	95	37	46	75	491	11	896	72	6
Lynchburg	66	72	.478	4.28	138	3	9	36	1170.0	1222	5145	668	557	98	50	40	53	460	12	920	66	3

INDIVIDUAL

TOP QUALIFIERS FOR EARNED-RUN AVERAGE TITLE

Minimum 112 innings. *Lefthanded pitcher.

Pitcher, Team	W	L	Pct.	ERA	G	GS	CG	ShO	GF	Sv.	IP	H	TBF	R	ER	HR	SH	SF	HB	BB	IBB	SO	WP	Bk.
Thurman, Corey, Wil.	10	5	.667	2.26	19	19	1	0	0	0	115.2	97	468	33	29	6	1	5	4	46	0	96	7	0
Parra, Christian, M.B.	17	4	.810	2.28	26	25	2	2	1	0	157.2	98	608	46	40	6	2	5	3	56	0	163	8	2
Kent, Nathan, M.B.	10	6	.625	2.55	24	20	1	0	0	0	137.2	97	537	50	39	3	4	3	4	30	0	89	3	1
Stephens, John, Fred.	7	6	.538	3.05	20	20	0	0	0	0	118.0	119	497	45	40	5	3	4	8	22	1	121	6	0
Ramirez, Horacio, M.B.*	15	8	.652	3.22	27	26	3	2	0	0	148.1	136	609	57	53	14	1	1	2	42	0	125	6	4
Walrond, Les, Pot.*	10	5	.667	3.34	27	27	0	0	0	0	151.0	134	632	66	56	9	1	3	7	54	0	153	12	1
Beimel, Joe, Lyn.*	10	6	.625	3.36	18	18	2	1	0	0	120.2	111	515	49	45	6	7	6	8	44	1	82	2	0
Purvis, Rob, W.S.	11	10	.524	3.38	27	27	2	0	0	0	167.2	139	727	81	63	6	2	2	11	87	0	114	22	0
Mendoza, Geronimo, W.S.	11	6	.647	3.41	31	19	4	3	4	0	145.0	146	635	65	55	7	5	3	4	65	0	117	13	0
Achilles, Matt, Fred.	8	11	.421	3.42	26	26	0	0	0	0	150.0	166	667	75	57	13	2	5	12	65	0	137	7	0
Jennings, Jason, Sal.	7	10	.412	3.47	22	22	3	1	0	0	150.1	136	632	66	58	6	3	5	2	42	0	133	8	1
Crowder, Chuck, Sal.*	14	9	.609	3.52	28	28	0	0	0	0	168.2	124	710	78	66	6	10	9	10	86	0	154	8	6
Sanches, Brian, Wil.	6	12	.333	3.53	28	27	2	1	0	0	158.0	132	665	77	62	9	5	7	15	69	0	122	11	3
Cameron, Ryan, Sal.	13	7	.650	3.59	26	26	1	0	0	0	160.1	152	715	81	64	9	7	5	9	78	0	168	12	2
Sido, Wilson, Kin.	11	6	.647	3.70	29	19	1	1	3	0	126.1	131	550	58	52	9	8	1	7	51	2	105	4	0

DEPARTMENTAL LEADERS: W—Parra, 17; L—Affeldt, 15; Pct.—Wimberly, .857; G—Sanders, Chrysler, 51 each; GS—Crowder, 28; CG—Mendoza, 4; ShO—Mendoza, 3; GF—Marr, 46; Sv.—Marr, 30; IP—Crowder, 168.2; H—Bechler, 179; TBF—Purvis, 727; R—Bechler, 98; ER—Bechler, 87; HR—Bechler, 19; SH—Crowder, 10; SF—Crowder, 9; HB—Sanches, 15; BB—Purvis, 87; IBB—Foster, 4; SO—Cameron, 168; WP—Purvis, 22; BK—Crowder, 6.

ALL PITCHERS

*Lefthanded pitcher.

Pitcher, Team	W	L	Pct.	ERA	G	GS	CG	ShO	GF	Sv.	IP	H	TBF	R	ER	HR	SH	SF	HB	BB	IBB	SO	WP	Bk.
Achilles, Matt, Fred.	8	11	.421	3.42	26	26	0	0	0	0	150.0	166	667	75	57	13	2	5	12	65	0	137	7	0
Affeldt, Jeremy, Wil.*	5	15	.250	4.09	27	26	0	0	0	0	147.1	158	656	87	67	7	8	5	10	59	0	92	17	1
Almonte, Edwin, W.S.	3	1	.750	3.16	33	7	0	0	10	2	77.0	66	320	32	27	2	3	1	5	20	0	73	4	1
Alvarado, Carlos, Lyn.	0	5	.000	4.20	15	7	0	0	2	0	49.1	50	216	30	23	2	2	2	1	25	0	37	5	0
Alviso, Jerome, Sal.	0	0	.000	0.00	1	0	0	0	1	0	1.0	1	4	0	0	0	0	0	0	1	0	0	0	0
Ammons, Cary, Wil.*	3	4	.429	3.26	17	9	1	0	4	2	80.0	79	338	34	29	4	4	3	4	30	0	85	7	0
Aracena, Juan, Fred.	1	1	.500	5.59	11	0	0	0	11	2	9.2	9	44	9	6	3	0	0	0	5	0	12	2	0
Arroyo, Bronson, Lyn.	0	0	.000	3.86	1	1	0	0	0	0	7.0	8	32	3	3	0	0	0	0	2	0	3	0	0
Avery, Steve, M.B.*	3	3	.500	1.53	7	7	1	0	0	0	47.0	40	195	11	8	2	2	1	0	25	0	32	1	0
Babula, Shaun, Fred.*	3	2	.600	3.30	37	0	0	0	17	2	46.1	40	206	25	17	4	3	2	3	25	2	47	1	0
Bacsik, Mike, Kin.*	5	6	.333	4.57	11	11	0	0	0	0	65.0	72	269	36	33	4	1	2	2	8	0	56	0	0
Baerlocher, Ryan, Wil.	5	1	.833	2.98	8	8	0	0	0	0	51.1	35	206	18	17	3	1	1	2	17	0	54	0	1
Baez, Danny, Kin.	2	2	.500	4.71	9	9	0	0	0	0	49.2	45	221	29	26	5	3	1	6	20	0	56	4	1

Pitcher, Team	W	L	Pct.	ERA	G	GS	CG	ShO	GF	Sv.	IP	H	TBF	R	ER	HR	SH	SF	HB	BB	IBB	SO	WP	Bk.
Bajenaru, Jeffrey, W.S.	2	0	1.000	4.38	10	0	0	0	7	2	12.1	7	52	6	6	1	0	3	2	5	0	15	4	0
Bauer, Rick, Fred.	0	1	.000	5.21	3	3	0	0	0	0	19.0	20	79	13	11	1	0	1	0	6	0	15	2	0
Bausher, Andy, Lyn.*	1	5	.167	5.97	30	5	0	0	10	0	66.1	77	299	48	44	8	4	2	6	27	0	44	1	1
Bechler, Steven, Fred.	8	12	.400	4.83	27	27	2	0	0	0	162.0	179	712	98	87	19	3	1	6	57	1	137	6	0
Beimel, Joe, Lyn.*	10	6	.625	3.36	18	18	2	1	0	0	120.2	111	515	49	45	6	7	6	8	44	1	82	2	0
Belisle, Matt, M.B.	3	4	.429	3.43	12	12	0	0	0	0	78.2	72	314	32	30	5	3	5	2	11	0	71	9	1
Bello, Jilberto, Fred.	0	0	.000	7.88	4	0	0	0	1	0	8.0	17	47	10	7	0	1	0	2	5	0	3	0	0
Bohannan, Kyle, W.S.	0	1	.000	3.18	4	0	0	0	3	2	5.2	5	22	2	2	0	1	1	0	0	0	5	0	0
Bong, Jung, M.B.*	3	1	.750	2.18	7	6	0	0	0	0	41.1	33	163	14	10	1	1	0	5	7	0	37	4	0
Bost, Heath, Sal.	2	1	.667	6.14	7	1	0	0	2	0	14.2	24	69	10	10	2	0	0	1	0	14	1	0
Brantley, Brian, Sal.	3	3	.500	2.59	41	0	0	0	19	4	59.0	38	264	22	17	1	7	3	9	40	0	75	5	0
Bravo, Franklin, Lyn.	2	9	.182	6.30	20	12	0	0	2	0	75.2	91	355	60	53	7	2	5	6	34	1	55	6	0
Brown, Derek, Fred.	2	5	.286	4.01	41	0	0	0	31	8	51.2	52	221	25	23	4	1	3	2	13	0	39	4	0
Brueggemann, Dean, Sal.*	3	1	.750	4.13	44	0	0	0	21	1	52.1	51	228	31	24	1	4	4	3	16	0	41	4	0
Buirley, Matt, Lyn.	0	1	.000	5.51	11	0	0	0	3	0	16.1	17	85	14	10	2	1	0	2	17	0	18	6	0
Bukvich, Ryan, Wil.	0	1	.000	18.00	2	0	0	0	0	0	2.0	3	15	4	4	0	1	0	1	5	2	3	1	0
Burch, Matt, Wil.	5	9	.357	5.38	32	17	0	0	2	0	113.2	125	517	82	68	11	8	1	12	59	2	71	5	2
Burger, Rob, Sal.	0	1	.000	5.79	8	0	0	0	4	0	14.0	9	68	10	9	0	1	0	4	15	0	15	3	1
Cameron, Ryan, Sal.	13	7	.650	3.59	26	26	1	0	0	0	160.1	152	715	81	64	9	7	5	9	78	0	168	12	2
Caple, Chance, Pot.	7	9	.438	4.39	22	22	0	0	0	0	125.0	128	529	68	61	11	4	4	6	34	0	97	5	3
Carr, Tim, Wil.	1	2	.333	3.84	45	0	0	0	27	0	58.2	74	275	35	25	2	3	2	5	27	3	39	2	1
Carrasco, Dan, Lyn.	1	0	1.000	3.48	8	0	0	0	6	2	10.1	8	45	5	4	1	1	0	0	8	0	10	1	0
Carter, Justin, Sal.*	5	8	.385	4.13	17	17	1	0	0	0	106.2	113	480	61	49	4	9	4	9	58	0	75	6	0
Chavez, Christopher, M.B.	3	5	.375	2.39	35	0	0	0	14	2	52.2	40	224	20	14	5	3	4	3	24	2	56	2	0
Christenson, Ryan, Pot.	6	6	.500	5.36	22	13	0	0	1	0	84.0	90	362	54	50	4	2	4	4	27	0	61	3	1
Chrysler, Clint, Lyn.*	5	1	.833	2.57	51	0	0	0	32	14	63.0	48	260	20	18	1	0	1	0	22	2	63	4	0
Cogan, Tony, Wil.*	2	4	.333	4.35	16	3	0	0	6	1	39.1	39	168	22	19	1	1	1	0	18	0	31	3	4
Colmenares, Luis, Sal.	0	1	.000	3.29	9	0	0	0	6	0	13.2	15	58	6	5	0	1	0	2	2	0	13	1	3
Colon, Jose, Kin.	2	1	.667	8.15	17	0	0	0	13	2	17.2	29	92	19	16	3	1	1	2	8	2	16	0	0
Cook, Aaron, Sal.	1	6	.143	5.44	7	7	1	0	0	0	43.0	52	196	33	26	4	1	1	7	12	0	37	3	0
Cook, B.R., Pot.	0	4	.000	5.53	8	8	0	0	0	0	42.1	48	193	31	26	3	3	3	2	27	0	23	3	0
Correa, Cristobal, Pot.	6	6	.500	3.24	18	18	0	0	0	0	100.0	82	419	41	36	9	1	3	5	49	0	76	6	0
Cowie, Steve, Kin.	2	5	.286	4.52	12	12	1	0	0	0	69.2	82	313	45	35	7	1	4	6	24	1	48	3	0
Crowder, Chuck, Sal.*	14	9	.609	3.52	28	28	0	0	0	0	168.2	124	710	78	66	6	10	9	10	86	0	154	8	6
Crudale, Mike, Pot.	2	4	.333	4.56	21	0	0	0	9	2	25.2	31	120	17	13	3	2	2	1	11	1	28	0	0
Curtis, Dan, M.B.	3	2	.600	2.68	8	8	1	0	0	0	50.1	48	213	18	15	5	4	2	3	15	1	34	0	2
Daniels, David, Pot.	2	2	.500	1.28	31	0	0	0	3	0	42.1	27	158	8	6	1	0	1	3	8	0	36	3	0
De Leon, Jose, Sal.*	0	3	.000	10.20	11	0	0	0	5	0	15.0	28	86	21	17	4	3	0	0	9	0	6	1	0
Delgado, Ernie, Kin.	1	0	1.000	1.59	9	0	0	0	2	0	17.0	11	71	3	3	0	0	1	0	10	0	22	2	0
Drese, Ryan, Kin.	0	1	.000	3.86	1	1	0	0	0	0	2.1	2	9	1	1	0	1	0	0	1	0	4	1	0
Eibey, Scott, Fred.*	1	1	.500	4.05	4	0	0	0	3	0	6.2	9	30	4	3	1	0	0	0	5	0	5	1	0
Erickson, Scott, Fred.	0	0	.000	2.70	1	1	0	0	0	0	6.2	3	24	2	2	0	0	0	1	0	5	0	0
Felix, Miguel, W.S.-Fred.	0	0	.000	9.06	35	0	0	0	14	0	46.2	57	232	49	47	5	1	2	12	32	0	37	9	0
Figueroa, Juan, W.S.	4	4	.500	4.67	9	7	1	0	2	0	52.0	58	224	30	27	3	3	1	3	8	0	65	3	0
Fiora, Chris, Pot.	0	0	.000	27.00	1	0	0	0	0	0	0.1	0	3	1	1	0	0	0	1	1	0	1	0	0
Fischer, Eric, W.S.*	4	9	.308	7.23	25	12	0	0	0	0	69.2	91	338	66	56	8	4	0	1	36	1	49	7	1
Fleck, Will, Fred.	0	0	.000	9.00	1	0	0	0	1	0	2.0	1	8	2	2	1	0	0	0	1	0	2	0	0
Forystek, Brian, Fred.*	1	0	1.000	1.35	3	0	0	0	0	0	6.2	5	28	1	1	0	0	0	0	1	0	7	1	0
Foster, John, M.B.*	2	1	.667	1.85	38	0	0	0	17	3	48.2	48	204	13	10	2	4	2	2	14	4	46	4	0
Gandy, Josh, Kin.*	1	0	1.000	4.91	9	0	0	0	4	0	18.1	22	85	11	10	3	0	2	1	9	0	18	1	0
Garcia, Tony, W.S.	0	1	.000	9.00	1	0	0	0	1	0	1.0	3	5	1	1	0	0	0	0	0	0	0	0	0
Gargano, Mike, Pot.	1	3	.250	5.09	38	3	0	0	9	0	63.2	71	294	37	36	6	5	1	7	38	3	23	6	0
Garza, Alberto, Kin.	4	10	.286	5.63	22	15	0	0	3	0	78.1	61	372	58	49	8	3	3	11	81	0	85	8	0
Gilfillan, Jason, Wil.	3	1	.750	1.76	12	0	0	0	3	1	15.1	13	74	6	3	0	0	0	1	13	1	20	2	0
Gonzalez, Mike, Lyn.*	4	3	.571	4.66	12	10	0	0	1	0	56.0	57	256	34	29	6	5	2	3	34	0	53	1	0
Gorman, Pat, Fred.	0	0	.000	1.29	7	0	0	0	7	5	7.0	6	31	1	1	0	0	0	4	0	7	0	0
Graham, Brian, W.S.	0	0	.000	3.18	1	1	0	0	0	0	5.2	7	27	5	2	0	1	0	0	0	0	1	1	0
Gray, Michael, M.B.*	2	3	.400	3.76	30	0	0	0	17	1	52.2	50	212	24	22	7	2	2	0	10	1	53	0	0
Green, Tyler, Kin.	0	1	.000	3.60	1	1	0	0	0	0	5.0	7	23	4	2	0	0	1	1	0	1	1	0
Greene, Ryan, M.B.	2	2	.500	4.50	14	0	0	0	8	1	22.0	16	94	16	11	3	1	0	1	10	0	23	2	0
Griffin, Kirk, Pot.	2	6	.250	3.65	50	0	0	0	24	2	61.2	64	269	35	25	4	2	6	6	18	3	34	4	0
Gross, Rafael, Kin.	2	2	.500	3.59	29	0	0	0	17	5	52.2	50	225	24	21	7	0	0	1	19	1	42	3	1
Guerrier, Matt, W.S.	0	3	.000	1.30	30	0	0	0	28	19	34.2	25	147	13	5	0	2	1	3	12	0	35	2	0
Guzman, Juan, Fred.	3	0	1.000	1.53	3	3	0	0	0	0	17.2	11	68	3	3	0	0	0	4	0	20	2	0
Guzman, Wilson, Lyn.*	4	3	.571	2.88	10	10	0	0	0	0	59.1	65	259	28	19	5	2	0	1	19	0	58	1	0
Halpin, Jeremy, Fred.	2	2	.500	7.20	25	0	0	0	13	0	40.0	52	192	37	32	6	3	1	2	17	0	13	4	0
Haynie, Jason, Lyn.*	6	12	.333	5.52	23	21	0	0	1	1	109.1	133	487	76	67	17	4	4	4	43	1	76	5	0
Herrera, Alex, Kin.*	0	1	.000	2.32	17	0	0	0	6	1	31.0	28	138	11	8	1	0	1	1	19	0	40	3	1
House, Craig, Sal.	2	0	1.000	2.25	13	0	0	0	12	8	16.0	7	69	4	4	0	1	0	1	10	0	24	7	0
Hudson, Luke, Sal.	5	8	.385	3.27	19	19	2	2	0	0	110.0	101	462	47	40	9	3	4	10	34	0	80	5	1
Izquierdo, Hansel, Kin.	1	3	.250	4.79	10	5	0	0	2	1	41.1	39	178	29	22	4	2	2	5	13	0	34	1	0
Jennings, Jason, Sal.	7	10	.412	3.47	22	22	3	1	0	0	150.1	136	632	66	58	6	3	5	2	42	0	133	8	1
Jerue, Tristan, Pot.	1	1	.500	5.40	10	0	0	0	0	0	10.0	12	49	7	6	1	1	0	1	8	0	12	3	0
Johnston, Clint, Lyn.*	1	2	.333	5.35	10	6	0	0	2	0	37.0	48	167	28	22	3	3	3	0	15	0	23	3	1
Jones, Sean, Fred.	0	0	.000	0.00	1	0	0	0	0	0	2.0	2	10	2	0	0	0	0	1	0	3	0	0
Kane, Kyle, W.S.	1	2	.333	5.86	32	0	0	0	7	0	50.2	57	243	39	33	3	2	1	6	31	3	47	1	0
Kearney, Ryan, Kin.	5	4	.556	4.22	32	0	0	0	20	1	53.1	54	231	25	25	7	4	1	2	18	1	59	1	0
Kent, Nathan, M.B.	10	6	.625	2.55	24	20	1	0	0	0	137.2	97	537	50	39	3	4	3	4	30	0	89	3	1
King, Jim, Wil.*	2	2	.500	3.29	46	0	0	0	23	6	52.0	48	207	19	19	2	3	2	2	11	0	45	4	0
Koeth, Mark, Kin.	0	0	.000	9.00	1	0	0	0	1	0	3.0	5	17	4	3	0	1	0	0	1	0	1	0	0
Kurtz-Nicholl, Jesse, Wil.*	0	1	.000	5.00	8	0	0	0	3	0	9.0	10	47	9	5	1	5	0	0	8	1	12	0	1
Lamattina, Ryan, Sal.*	0	0	.000	4.24	27	0	0	0	8	2	34.0	42	174	19	16	2	0	2	29	0	41	4	1
Lambert, Jeremy, Pot.	0	0	.000	4.40	16	3	0	0	2	0	28.2	30	121	17	14	1	1	1	1	7	0	28	1	0
Landreth, Jason, Lyn.	0	0	.000	9.00	2	0	0	0	1	0	2.0	5	12	2	2	0	0	0	0	1	0	0	0	0

Pitcher, Team	W	L	Pct.	ERA	G	GS	CG	ShO	GF	Sv.	IP	H	TBF	R	ER	HR	SH	SF	HB	BB	IBB	SO	WP	Bk.
Langen, Brian, Pot.*	1	0	1.000	1.90	31	0	0	0	6	0	42.2	34	181	14	9	2	3	1	5	21	0	28	2	0
Ledden, Ryan, Lyn.	3	0	1.000	3.15	15	0	0	0	5	0	20.0	14	92	12	7	0	2	2	0	16	1	14	3	1
Lee, Garrett, M.B.	7	3	.700	2.03	29	6	0	0	5	1	79.2	61	322	19	18	2	3	1	7	21	0	60	2	1
Lopez, Jose, Lyn.	4	1	.800	3.11	6	6	1	1	0	0	37.2	29	161	14	13	2	0	1	1	19	2	38	0	0
Lorenzana, Luis, Lyn.	0	0	.000	18.00	1	0	0	0	1	0	1.0	3	6	2	2	0	0	0	0	1	0	1	0	0
MacDougal, Mike, Wil.	9	7	.563	3.92	26	25	0	0	1	1	144.2	115	620	79	63	5	5	1	14	76	0	129	21	4
Maduro, Calvin, Fred.	0	0	.000	0.00	1	1	0	0	0	0	2.0	1	7	0	0	0	0	0	0	0	0	6	0	0
Majewski, Gary, W.S.	2	4	.333	5.11	6	6	0	0	0	0	37.0	32	163	21	21	1	2	2	8	17	0	24	2	0
Maleski, Eric, Kin.	0	0	.000	7.88	5	0	0	0	3	0	8.0	9	37	7	7	0	0	1	0	6	1	3	0	0
Manzueta, Roberto, Lyn.	0	4	.000	4.85	23	2	0	0	9	0	42.2	49	194	28	23	3	2	1	1	13	0	38	6	0
Marini, Anthony, Kin.*	0	1	.000	3.86	1	0	0	0	0	0	2.1	1	9	2	1	0	1	0	0	0	0	2	0	0
Marr, Jason, Pot.	2	4	.333	3.56	48	0	0	0	46	30	55.2	52	235	24	22	5	2	2	3	17	0	45	0	1
Martin, Chandler, Sal.	5	1	.833	3.55	7	7	1	0	0	0	45.2	41	184	18	18	1	2	1	1	12	0	25	1	0
Martin, Jeff, Lyn.	2	2	.500	4.60	28	1	0	0	8	0	43.0	36	183	27	22	5	1	0	2	20	1	33	4	0
Martin, Justin, Lyn.	0	1	.000	27.00	1	0	0	0	1	0	0.1	2	5	1	1	0	0	0	1	1	0	0	0	0
Martinez, Jesus, Kin.*	0	0	.000	0.00	2	0	0	0	2	0	4.0	3	17	0	0	0	0	0	0	3	0	3	0	0
Matcuk, Steve, Sal.	4	3	.571	6.68	22	7	0	0	9	5	60.2	72	287	48	45	5	3	1	5	33	0	42	4	0
Mays, Jarrod, Kin.	2	0	1.000	2.14	14	0	0	0	11	7	21.0	17	90	8	5	1	1	1	1	10	3	19	0	0
McClendon, Matt, M.B.	3	1	.750	1.59	6	6	0	0	0	0	39.2	24	147	7	7	1	1	0	0	8	0	43	1	0
McDade, Neal, Lyn.	1	2	.333	4.66	7	7	0	0	0	0	29.0	35	131	18	15	2	1	3	1	11	1	24	0	0
Mejia, Francisco, Fred.*	0	0	.000	4.50	4	1	0	0	1	0	10.0	9	43	5	5	1	0	1	0	6	0	7	0	0
Mendoza, Geronimo, W.S.	11	6	.647	3.41	31	19	4	3	4	0	145.0	146	635	65	55	7	5	3	4	65	0	117	13	0
Mills, Alan, Fred.	0	0	.000	4.50	1	1	0	0	0	0	2.0	2	8	1	1	0	0	0	0	0	0	1	0	0
Montgomery, Greg, W.S.	0	0	.000	3.00	2	0	0	0	0	0	3.0	0	11	1	1	0	0	0	0	2	0	5	2	0
Moreno, Julio, Fred.	0	0	.000	4.50	2	0	0	0	0	0	4.0	2	15	2	2	2	0	0	1	0	1	0	0	0
Navarro, Jason, Pot.*	1	2	.333	3.25	23	0	0	0	8	0	27.2	22	114	11	10	3	1	2	4	10	2	24	0	0
Negrette, Richard, Fred.	0	1	.000	0.00	4	0	0	0	1	0	5.2	3	28	5	0	0	1	1	0	4	0	5	0	1
Nunez, Jose, Pot.	0	0	.000	6.75	1	0	0	0	1	0	1.1	1	6	1	1	1	0	0	1	0	1	0	0	0
Ormond, Rodney, Fred.	2	5	.286	3.63	39	0	0	0	12	6	67.0	66	294	38	27	3	5	2	3	25	0	59	4	0
Osting, Jimmy, M.B.*	2	2	.500	3.13	4	4	0	0	0	0	23.0	25	94	8	8	0	0	1	0	5	0	17	0	0
Padilla, Roy, Kin.*	1	1	.500	4.94	14	0	0	0	4	0	23.2	14	110	21	13	0	0	1	4	21	0	32	4	0
Padua, Geraldo, Lyn.	4	9	.308	4.21	17	14	0	0	2	0	92.0	102	396	57	43	11	5	2	1	22	0	57	7	0
Pamus, Javier, Wil.	2	3	.400	5.82	32	0	0	0	9	0	43.1	56	207	35	28	0	2	2	2	18	3	19	4	0
Paradis, Mike, Fred.	2	5	.286	4.17	8	8	1	0	0	0	45.1	55	212	24	21	1	0	2	4	24	0	32	2	0
Parra, Christian, M.B.	17	4	.810	2.28	26	25	2	2	1	0	157.2	98	608	46	40	6	2	5	3	56	0	163	8	2
Pavlovich, Tony, Lyn.	2	1	.667	3.60	36	0	0	0	27	14	40.0	38	171	18	16	0	1	0	3	13	1	33	1	0
Pearce, Josh, Pot.	5	3	.625	3.45	10	10	1	0	0	0	62.2	70	259	25	24	5	0	1	1	10	0	42	0	0
Pederson, Justin, Wil.	8	6	.571	4.74	47	0	0	0	27	9	68.1	64	304	42	36	4	4	1	5	34	0	66	4	2
Pickford, Kevin, Lyn.*	1	2	.333	6.16	10	6	0	0	1	0	30.2	42	153	30	21	3	1	2	8	14	0	13	1	0
Pierce, Tony, M.B.	2	5	.286	4.11	18	14	0	0	1	0	72.1	64	316	35	33	8	1	1	3	44	0	63	5	1
Prather, Scott, Pot.*	5	3	.625	5.00	42	7	0	0	7	2	75.2	61	339	50	42	6	3	6	1	56	0	70	5	0
Price, Ryan, Sal.	1	3	.250	6.00	6	6	0	0	0	0	30.0	27	159	26	20	1	2	1	5	37	0	32	13	0
Purvis, Rob, W.S.	11	10	.524	3.38	27	27	2	0	0	0	167.2	139	727	81	63	6	2	2	11	87	0	114	22	0
Rakers, Aaron, Fred.	1	1	.500	1.55	26	0	0	0	19	8	40.2	23	157	8	7	2	0	2	2	12	1	57	1	0
Ramirez, Horacio, M.B.*	15	8	.652	3.22	27	26	3	2	0	0	148.1	136	609	57	53	14	1	1	2	42	0	125	6	4
Rauch, Jon, W.S.	11	3	.786	2.86	18	18	1	0	0	0	110.0	102	456	49	35	10	4	3	5	33	0	124	4	1
Reinike, Chris, Kin.	0	1	.000	2.18	11	0	0	0	3	0	20.2	13	83	7	5	0	1	1	2	8	0	25	2	0
Roberts, Mike, Kin.	0	0	.000	3.30	31	0	0	0	18	5	43.2	39	185	17	16	3	5	2	3	18	1	30	1	1
Sabathia, C.C., Kin.*	3	2	.600	3.54	10	10	2	2	0	0	56.0	48	232	23	22	4	0	1	2	24	0	69	2	1
Salargo, Steve, Fred.	0	0	.000	0.00	1	0	0	0	1	0	1.0	0	3	0	0	0	0	0	0	0	0	0	0	0
Sanches, Brian, Wil.	6	12	.333	3.53	28	27	2	1	0	0	158.0	132	665	77	62	9	5	7	15	69	0	122	11	3
Sanders, David, W.S.*	3	2	.600	5.21	51	0	0	0	20	6	48.1	39	228	35	28	4	2	2	4	39	1	50	12	1
Sequea, Jacobo, Fred.	9	11	.450	5.09	23	22	2	1	0	0	123.2	121	544	80	70	11	6	6	8	58	0	94	4	5
Sheredy, Kevin, Pot.	2	5	.286	5.13	30	1	0	0	15	4	40.1	46	193	25	23	2	1	2	5	26	1	24	2	0
Sido, Wilson, Kin.	11	6	.647	3.70	29	19	1	1	3	0	126.1	131	550	58	52	9	8	1	7	51	2	105	4	0
Sims, Ken, Fred.	5	3	.625	3.89	29	9	0	0	5	0	81.0	98	361	44	35	10	3	3	9	27	1	44	6	1
Sirianni, Jay, Kin.*	0	2	.000	4.58	7	2	0	0	3	0	17.2	18	81	14	9	1	1	0	0	11	1	6	1	0
Smith, Roy, Kin.*	2	2	.500	2.80	21	0	0	0	9	2	45.0	35	183	15	14	0	0	1	3	21	1	45	3	0
Snyder, Kyle, Wil.	0	0	.000	0.00	1	1	0	0	0	0	0.0	0	1	1	0	0	0	0	0	1	0	0	0	0
Spiegel, Mike, Kin.*	3	2	.600	3.67	5	5	0	0	0	0	27.0	23	117	12	11	4	1	1	3	11	0	23	3	1
Spooneybarger, Tim, M.B.	3	0	1.000	0.91	19	6	0	0	5	0	49.2	18	187	7	5	0	4	0	1	19	0	57	6	0
Spurgeon, Jay, Fred.	8	2	.800	4.12	16	15	1	0	0	0	91.2	75	379	47	42	8	3	7	3	31	0	92	8	0
Spurling, Chris, Lyn.	1	0	1.000	0.98	9	0	0	0	6	5	18.1	8	66	2	2	1	0	1	0	3	0	17	0	0
Stabile, Paul, Lyn.*	0	0	.000	9.82	10	0	0	0	5	0	14.2	21	75	19	16	1	1	1	1	8	0	11	1	0
Stanford, Jason, Kin.*	4	3	.571	2.57	11	11	1	0	0	0	70.0	68	294	22	20	2	1	2	2	17	0	58	0	0
Stein, Blake, Wil.	0	0	.000	6.75	2	2	0	0	0	0	5.1	6	24	4	4	1	0	0	0	2	0	12	1	0
Stein, Ethan, Wil.	2	3	.400	4.35	26	2	0	0	12	2	41.1	35	169	23	20	3	2	2	0	10	0	25	4	1
Sternle, Steve, Pot.	9	10	.474	4.80	26	26	1	0	0	0	150.0	169	668	89	80	15	2	4	12	59	1	84	16	0
Stephens, John, Fred.	7	6	.538	3.05	20	20	0	0	0	0	118.0	119	497	45	40	5	3	4	8	22	1	121	6	0
Sullivan, Ted, Kin.	0	0	.000	0.00	4	0	0	0	4	3	3.1	0	12	1	0	0	0	0	0	3	0	3	0	2
Sylvester, Billy, M.B.	3	0	1.000	0.79	32	0	0	0	27	16	45.2	16	172	8	4	2	1	1	3	15	1	48	2	0
Thompson, Doug, Sal.	5	3	.625	3.05	46	0	0	0	13	1	62.0	43	267	29	21	2	3	1	5	35	1	80	3	2
Thurman, Corey, Wil.	10	5	.667	2.26	19	19	1	0	0	0	115.2	97	468	33	29	6	1	5	4	46	0	96	7	0
Vargas, Jose, Kin.	3	4	.429	4.27	27	9	0	0	7	0	78.0	69	326	43	37	4	4	2	5	29	0	76	3	1
Veras, Dario, Kin.	3	0	1.000	3.41	17	0	0	0	10	3	34.1	27	134	13	13	5	2	0	5	4	0	29	0	0
Voyles, Brad, M.B.	5	2	.714	1.11	39	0	0	0	36	19	56.2	21	212	8	7	1	1	3	0	25	2	70	8	0
Walrond, Les, Pot.*	10	5	.667	3.34	27	27	0	0	0	0	151.0	134	632	66	56	9	7	3	5	54	0	153	12	1
Weidert, Chris, Fred.-Kin.	4	2	.667	4.85	28	1	0	0	6	0	55.2	66	251	39	30	9	2	4	2	18	3	38	4	1
West, Brian, W.S.	0	1	.000	11.37	2	2	0	0	0	0	6.1	10	37	12	8	2	0	0	0	6	1	3	1	1
Whatley, Brannon, W.S.*	1	5	.167	4.14	26	1	0	0	16	2	41.1	49	187	21	19	7	1	1	3	20	0	31	3	1
White, Matt, Kin.*	11	9	.550	4.07	28	26	2	0	1	0	143.2	136	616	76	65	14	7	7	10	63	0	115	7	1
Whitecotton, Billy, Fred.	0	0	.000	0.00	1	0	0	0	0	0	2.2	2	10	0	0	0	0	0	1	0	0	2	0	0
Whitlock, Brian, Kin.	1	0	1.000	9.00	1	0	0	0	1	0	1.0	2	7	1	1	0	0	0	0	3	0	0	0	0
Williams, Dave, Lyn.*	1	0	1.000	6.55	2	2	0	0	0	0	11.0	18	51	8	8	2	1	0	0	3	0	8	2	0

Pitcher, Team	W	L	Pct.	ERA	G	GS	CG	ShO	GF	Sv.	IP	H	TBF	R	ER	HR	SH	SF	HB	BB	IBB	SO	WP	Bk.
Williams, Larry, Lyn.	1	1	.500	3.80	14	0	0	0	4	0	21.1	25	103	12	9	1	0	1	0	10	0	21	3	0
Williams, Mike, W.S.	3	4	.429	3.73	46	1	0	0	22	1	70.0	62	315	39	29	4	5	4	13	37	1	79	14	0
Wimberly, Larry, Lyn.*	12	2	.857	1.88	24	10	0	0	6	0	96.0	82	370	23	20	9	4	1	3	16	0	90	3	0
Wright, Danny, W.S.	9	8	.529	3.74	21	21	1	0	0	0	132.1	135	577	64	55	4	4	5	10	50	0	106	18	2
Wrigley, Jase, Sal.	3	2	.600	2.66	47	0	0	0	36	16	61.0	52	250	26	18	3	5	2	1	22	1	38	4	0
Wylie, Mitch, W.S.	3	7	.300	4.34	17	17	0	0	0	0	95.1	112	422	59	46	8	4	4	3	34	0	57	1	2

COMBINATION SHUTOUTS: **Frederick (0)**—None. **Kinston (5)**—Bacsik-Maleski, White-Delgado-Mays, Sido-Kearney-Smith-Mays, Baez-Smith, Stanford-Garza-Vargas. **Lynchburg (6)**—Alvarado-Wimberly-Pavlovich, Guzman-Buirley-Chrystler-Pavlovich, Wimberly-Martin-Manzueta, Wimberly-Ledden-Carrasco, Lopez-Martin-Pickford, Gonzalez-Ledden-Chrystler. **Myrtle Beach (23)**—Lee-Sylvester-Voyles, McClendon-Gray, Ramirez-Chavez-Voyles, McClendon-Sylvester-Foster, Spooneybarger-Lee-Foster, McClendon-Sylvester, Kent-Voyles, Avery-Foster-Voyles, Ramirez-Voyles, Ramirez-Sylvester, Kent-Foster, Avery-Sylvester, Parra-Voyles, Parra-Sylvester, Ramirez-Gray-Sylvester, Pierce-Lee-Voyles, Spooneybarger-Parra, Parra-Gray, Ramirez-Foster, Parra-Spooneybarger, Bong-Greene-Voyles, Belisle-Lee-Voyles, Lee-Foster-Spooneybarger. **Potomac (9)**—Correa-Prather-Marr, Walrond-Navarro, Correa-Prather-Griffin-Christenson, Pearce-Prather-Navarro, Pearce-Griffin-Navarro, Caple-Griffin-Marr, Walrond-Lambert-Marr, Walrond-Daniels-Sheredy, Stemle-Marr. **Salem (4)**—Carter-Thompson-Lamattina, Crowder-Lamattina, Jennings-Matchuk, Cameron-Wrigley. **Wilmington (11)**—Sanches-Carr, Burch-King-Roberts, Thurman-Roberts, Stein-Burch, Sanches-Affeldt-Pederson, Stein-King-Pederson-Carr, Thurman-King, Thurman-Pederson, MacDougal-Carr, Thurman-Pederson-King, MacDougal-Burch-Gilfillan. **Winston-Salem (4)**—Fischer-Figueroa, Purvis-Almonte-Guerrier, Purvis-Felix, Purvis-Sanders.

NO-HIT GAME: Sanches, Wilmington defeated Lynchburg, 5-0, May 2.

PITCHERS WITH TWO OR MORE TEAMS

Pitcher, Team	W	L	Pct.	ERA	G	GS	CG	ShO	GF	Sv.	IP	H	TBF	R	ER	HR	SH	SF	HB	BB	IBB	SO	WP	Bk.
Felix, Miguel, W.S.	0	0	.000	7.64	27	0	0	0	10	0	35.1	39	167	32	30	2	1	2	6	21	0	32	9	0
Felix, Miguel, Fred.	0	0	.000	13.50	8	0	0	0	4	0	11.1	18	65	17	17	3	0	0	6	11	0	5	0	0
Weidert, Chris, Fred.	3	2	.600	5.29	24	0	0	0	5	0	47.2	60	220	37	28	8	2	3	2	16	3	28	3	1
Weidert, Chris, Kin.	1	0	1.000	2.25	4	1	0	0	1	0	8.0	6	31	2	2	1	0	1	0	2	0	10	1	0

2000 FIELDING

TEAM

Team	Pct.	G	PO	A	E	TC	DP	TP	PB
Potomac	.973	138	3617	1511	145	5273	139	1	14
Myrtle Beach	.970	137	3617	1387	154	5158	114	1	13
Wilmington	.969	139	3567	1544	165	5276	125	0	26
Frederick	.969	137	3561	1260	156	4977	106	0	21
Kinston	.968	137	3583	1290	159	5032	122	0	18
Winston-Salem	.966	139	3601	1489	178	5268	117	0	29
Salem	.965	140	3609	1527	188	5324	103	1	23
Lynchburg	.963	138	3510	1442	192	5144	128	0	21

INDIVIDUAL

FIRST BASEMEN

NOTE: All caps denotes fielding-percentage leader based on 70 games for catchers, 93 for all other non-pitchers and 112 innings for pitchers. *Throws lefthanded.

Player, Team	Pct.	G	PO	A	E	TC	DP
Alviso, Jerome, Sal.	.990	33	274	20	3	297	23
Berger, Matt, W.S.	.986	117	1006	62	15	1083	92
Burford, Kevin, Sal.*	.951	16	145	10	8	163	13
Castro, Alfredo, M.B.	.800	1	3	1	1	5	2
Curtis, Matt, Kin.	.986	17	138	5	2	145	14
Daedelow, Craig, Fred.	1.000	8	23	1	0	24	3
Darr, Ryan, Pot.	1.000	1	1	0	0	1	0
Deck, Billy, Pot.*	.991	89	694	45	7	746	77
Dyt, Darren, Pot.	1.000	1	6	0	0	6	0
Esquerra, Marques, Kin.	1.000	4	15	2	0	17	2
Evans, Lee, Lyn.	.952	3	16	4	1	21	2
Ewing, Byron, Kin.	.976	68	480	41	13	534	47
Farnsworth, Troy, Pot.	.990	64	537	40	6	583	54
Figueroa, Franky, Fred.	.985	106	805	67	13	885	68
Goodwin, David, Wil.	.995	21	190	14	1	205	20
Hage, Tom, Fred.	1.000	6	46	3	0	49	4
Harvey, Ken, Wil.	.983	18	162	8	3	173	9
Hemme, Justin, Sal.*	.987	59	493	24	7	524	35
Hobbs, Jay, Lyn.*	.983	21	163	11	3	177	19
Hyde, Brandon, W.S.	.987	25	204	16	3	223	16
Johnson, Erik, Sal.	.971	5	29	4	1	34	2
Jones, Jay, Sal.	1.000	2	18	2	0	20	0
Kilburg, Joe, Kin.	1.000	3	17	0	0	17	2
Landreth, Jason, Lyn.	1.000	10	74	2	0	76	2
Lehr, Adam, M.B.	.987	35	272	29	4	305	30
Leon, Alfredo, Fred.	.966	8	54	2	2	58	6
Lindsey, John, Sal.	.990	34	289	12	3	304	16
Long, Ryan, W.S.	1.000	1	7	1	0	8	0
Lorenzana, Luis, Lyn.	1.000	1	0	1	0	1	0
Maxwell, Keith, Lyn.	1.000	2	21	1	0	22	0
Meier, Dan, Lyn.*	.990	34	275	20	3	298	28
Montas, Ricardo, Wil.	.994	86	707	65	5	777	59
Mortimer, Mark, M.B.	1.000	9	85	6	0	91	6
Munoz, Billy, Kin.*	.990	48	361	26	4	391	33
Nunez, Jose, Pot.	1.000	1	2	1	0	3	1

Player, Team	Pct.	G	PO	A	E	TC	DP
Nykoluk, Kevin, Pot.	1.000	2	1	0	0	1	0
Pond, Simon, Kin.	1.000	5	36	2	0	38	2
Rivera, Carlos, Lyn.*	.998	60	487	29	1	517	51
Rust, Brian, Fred.	.968	18	137	12	5	154	12
Sanders, Tracy, Lyn.	1.000	18	139	7	0	146	12
Shackelford, Brian, Wil.*	.983	24	159	12	3	174	22
Sickles, Jeremy, Lyn.	.929	1	12	1	1	14	0
Smith, Sam, Sal.	1.000	2	16	1	0	17	2
ZAPP, A.J., M.B.	.987	96	784	51	11	846	68

TRIPLE PLAYS: Burford, Farnsworth, Zapp.

SECOND BASEMEN

Player, Team	Pct.	G	PO	A	E	TC	DP
Alguacil, Jose, W.S.	.961	18	33	40	3	76	9
Alviso, Jerome, Sal.	1.000	7	11	15	0	26	3
Benefield, Brian, Kin.	.965	24	36	73	4	113	17
Benham, Jason, Fred.	.867	8	4	9	2	15	0
Bowers, Jason, Pot.	.983	12	22	35	1	58	9
Castro, Alfredo, M.B.	.976	11	21	20	1	42	3
Connacher, Kevin, W.S.	.980	90	166	267	9	442	54
Daedelow, Craig, Fred.	1.000	21	51	39	0	90	13
Dalton, David, M.B.	.917	5	4	7	1	12	2
Diaz, Maikell, Fred.	.974	39	69	83	4	156	16
Ellis, Mark, Wil.	1.000	3	5	6	0	11	1
Erickson, Corey, Kin.	.947	53	98	115	12	225	27
Figgins, Chone, Sal.	.955	134	226	373	28	627	60
Gonzalez, Luis, Kin.	.980	51	82	119	4	205	28
Green, Nick, M.B.	.943	9	14	19	2	35	5
Hairston, Jerry, Fred.	1.000	2	2	7	0	9	0
Hammond, Joey, Fred.	1.000	3	3	4	0	7	1
Hart, Bo, Pot.	.954	72	115	156	13	284	36
Hart, Corey, Wil.	.959	38	64	99	7	170	21
Hernandez, Javier, Kin.	1.000	3	5	8	0	13	0
Kidwell, Tommy, Pot.	.800	4	2	6	2	10	1
Kilburg, Joe, Kin.	1.000	2	4	7	0	11	2
Lopez-Cao, Mike, Fred.	.000	1	0	0	0	0	0
Lorenzana, Luis, Lyn.	.939	8	17	14	2	33	5
Macrory, Bob, Pot.	.980	49	87	157	5	249	41
Martin, Justin, Lyn.	.970	17	23	42	2	67	5
Montas, Ricardo, Wil.	1.000	2	0	2	0	2	0
Nelson, Eric, Wil.	.948	100	194	280	26	500	68
Nunez, Jose, Pot.	.980	9	19	30	1	50	11
Olmeda, Jose, W.S.	.962	12	20	30	2	52	10
Paz, Rich, Fred.	.968	74	117	184	10	311	33
Pichardo, Henry, Kin.	.950	8	13	6	1	20	5
Prieto, Jon, Lyn.	.963	106	222	278	19	519	77
Rodriguez, Victor, Kin.	.947	6	9	9	1	19	1
Ruiz, Willy, Wil.	.964	5	7	20	1	28	5
Rust, Brian, Fred.	1.000	4	4	5	0	9	2
Sandoval, Danny, W.S.	.949	24	43	68	6	117	11
Skrehot, Shaun, Lyn.	.976	10	16	24	1	41	4
Whitlock, Brian, Kin.	1.000	1	1	0	0	1	0
WILSON, Travis, M.B.	.967	119	214	287	17	518	61

TRIPLE PLAYS: Bowers, Wilson.

THIRD BASEMEN

Player, Team	Pct.	G	PO	A	E	TC	DP
Acevas, Jon, W.S.	.667	1	1	1	1	3	0
Alguacil, Jose, W.S.	.933	7	6	8	1	15	2
Alviso, Jerome, Sal.	.938	29	26	64	6	96	6
Benefield, Brian, Kin.	.892	15	12	21	4	37	2
Benham, Jason, Fred.	.884	16	13	25	5	43	1
Berger, Matt, W.S.	.933	5	3	11	1	15	1
Bowers, Jason, Pot.	.000	1	0	0	0	0	0
CALDERON, Henry, Wil.	.947	120	73	215	16	304	27
Cameron, Troy, M.B.	.920	123	85	224	27	336	15
Curtis, Matt, Kin.	.865	13	12	20	5	37	0
Daedelow, Craig, Fred.	1.000	5	2	3	0	5	0
Dalton, David, M.B.	.937	18	11	48	4	63	7
Darr, Ryan, Pot.	.937	37	38	80	8	126	12
Diaz, Maikell, Fred.	1.000	3	3	2	0	5	0
Erickson, Corey, Kin.	.949	68	45	124	9	178	14
Esquerra, Marques, Kin.	.864	12	4	15	3	22	4
Farnsworth, Troy, Pot.	.917	46	26	95	11	132	11
Griswold, Matt, Fred.	1.000	1	0	1	0	1	0
Hammond, Joey, Fred.	.939	91	68	149	14	231	12
Hankins, Ryan, W.S.	.905	78	49	123	18	190	18
Hart, Corey, Wil.	.953	21	6	35	2	43	2
Holliday, Matt, Sal.	.893	112	55	213	32	300	13
Hummel, Timothy, W.S.	.900	25	21	51	8	80	1
Johnson, Erik, Sal.	.000	1	0	0	0	0	0
Kidwell, Tommy, Pot.	.800	3	0	4	1	5	1
Leon, Alfredo, Fred.	1.000	5	6	5	0	11	0
Lorenzana, Luis, Lyn.	.897	28	7	45	6	58	1
Martin, Justin, Lyn.	.886	14	8	23	4	35	6
McGee, Tom, Fred.	.000	4	0	0	1	1	0
Minor, Ryan, Fred.	1.000	2	1	1	0	2	0
Montas, Ricardo, Wil.	1.000	3	1	7	0	8	1
Nunez, Jose, Pot.	.948	56	33	77	6	116	8
Olmeda, Jose, W.S.	.760	12	5	14	6	25	0
Paz, Rich, Fred.	1.000	1	0	1	0	1	0
Polanco, Enohel, Kin.	1.000	3	0	4	0	4	1
Pond, Simon, Kin.	.903	35	28	56	9	93	3
Pujols, Albert, Pot.	.957	21	12	54	3	69	4
Rust, Brian, Fred.	.891	20	9	40	6	55	1
Sandoval, Danny, W.S.	.960	16	5	43	2	50	3
Segura, Rolando, Lyn.	.835	90	41	151	38	230	21
Skrehot, Shaun, Lyn.	.951	20	13	26	2	41	3
Smith, Sam, Sal.	.750	1	0	3	1	4	0
Whitlock, Brian, Kin.	1.000	3	5	5	0	10	1

TRIPLE PLAY: Darr.

SHORTSTOPS

Player, Team	Pct.	G	PO	A	E	TC	DP
Alguacil, Jose, W.S.	.873	11	12	36	7	55	7
Alviso, Jerome, Sal.	.977	9	17	26	1	44	6
Benham, Jason, Fred.	1.000	1	0	2	0	2	0
Bowers, Jason, Pot.	.969	79	123	252	12	387	53
Calais, Ian, M.B.	.938	5	5	10	1	16	5
Castro, Alfredo, M.B.	.967	91	125	254	13	392	49
Cleto, Ambioris, Lyn.	1.000	2	2	7	0	9	0
Daedelow, Craig, Fred.	1.000	2	0	2	0	2	0
Dalton, David, M.B.	.934	33	45	97	10	152	16
Diaz, Maikell, Fred.	.954	32	41	84	6	131	22
Ellis, Mark, Wil.	.953	128	219	415	31	665	78
Erickson, Corey, Kin.	1.000	1	0	1	0	1	0
Esquerra, Marques, Kin.	.000	1	0	0	0	0	0
Gonzalez, Luis, Kin.	.922	28	36	59	8	103	13
Green, Nick, M.B.	.851	16	19	21	7	47	7
Gutierrez, Vic, Lyn.	.949	106	134	328	25	487	47
Hammond, Joey, Fred.	.950	24	41	54	5	100	10
Hart, Corey, Wil.	.897	10	17	18	4	39	4
Hummel, Timothy, W.S.	1.000	2	3	8	0	11	0
Lorenzana, Luis, Lyn.	.964	22	37	69	4	110	21
Martinez, Eddy, Fred.	.938	40	46	89	9	144	15
McDonald, John, Kin.	1.000	1	1	3	0	4	0
Medrano, Steve, Wil.	.909	3	7	13	2	22	2
Nunez, Jose, Pot.	.936	23	21	67	6	94	10
Olmeda, Jose, W.S.	.896	20	23	63	10	96	10
Pichardo, Henry, Kin.	.905	8	7	12	2	21	1
Roberts, Brian, Fred.	.952	42	60	97	8	165	24
Rodriguez, Victor, Kin.	.965	89	133	200	12	345	53
Sandoval, Danny, W.S.	.973	8	9	27	1	37	6
Skrehot, Shaun, Lyn.	.908	14	24	47	7	76	7
Suarez, Luis, W.S.	.947	99	170	296	26	492	56
Thames, Damon, Pot.	.931	29	50	84	10	144	23
URIBE Juan, Sal.	.961	133	213	428	26	667	65
Whitlock, Brian, Kin.	.918	16	16	29	4	49	6
Wilson, Jack, Pot.	.967	13	20	39	2	61	8

TRIPLE PLAYS: Green, Uribe.

OUTFIELDERS

Player, Team	Pct.	G	PO	A	E	TC	DP
Aldridge, Cory, M.B.	.977	109	165	2	4	171	0
Alguacil, Jose, W.S.	1.000	1	2	0	0	2	0
Alviso, Jerome, Sal.	.931	18	25	2	2	29	1
Barns, B.J., Lyn.*	.979	118	225	7	5	237	0
Beltran, Carlos, Wil.	1.000	1	2	0	0	2	0
Benefield, Brian, Kin.	.926	19	24	1	2	27	0
Berger, Brandon, Wil.	.983	100	169	7	3	179	0
Bigbie, Larry, Fred.*	.975	55	111	5	3	119	1
Borchard, Joe, W.S.	1.000	13	17	4	0	21	0
Bost, Tom, Kin.	.818	7	9	0	2	11	0
BRIGNAC, Junior, M.B.	.993	128	283	15	2	300	6
Burford, Kevin, Sal.*	.973	74	68	4	2	74	0
Caradonna, Brett, W.S.	.977	58	84	1	2	87	0
Copeland, Brandon, Pot.	.955	28	40	2	2	44	0
Curtis, Matt, Kin.	.941	11	15	1	1	17	0
Daedelow, Craig, Fred.	1.000	17	36	0	0	36	0
Dalton, David, M.B.	1.000	11	22	0	0	22	0
Darr, Ryan, Pot.	1.000	7	11	0	0	11	0
Davis, J.J., Lyn.	.925	122	214	7	18	239	4
Deck, Billy, Pot.*	1.000	11	22	0	0	22	0
Diaz, Miguel, Pot.	.986	101	197	10	3	210	1
Dyt, Darren, Pot.	1.000	7	4	0	0	4	0
Esquerra, Marques, Kin.	.000	1	0	0	1	1	0
Fennell, Jason, W.S.	1.000	2	3	0	0	3	0
Fitzgerald, Jason, Kin.*	.986	71	134	8	2	144	0
Freeman, Choo, Sal.	.965	127	213	9	8	230	3
Gallaher, T.T., Kin.	.976	20	40	0	1	41	0
Garcia, Tony, W.S.	1.000	1	2	1	0	3	0
Gettis, Byron, Wil.	.976	30	40	1	1	42	1
Gomez, Alexis, Wil.*	.950	119	261	3	14	278	2
Griswold, Matt, Fred.	.976	22	40	0	1	41	0
Hart, Bo, Pot.	1.000	3	3	0	0	3	0
Hart, Corey, Wil.	.941	12	14	2	1	17	0
Hernandez, Jesus, Kin.*	.933	53	101	11	8	120	4
Hobbs, Jay, Lyn.*	.966	48	53	4	2	59	0
Johnson, Eric, Kin.	.986	53	133	7	2	142	1
Johnson, Erik, Sal.	.887	44	42	5	6	53	1
Kilburg, Joe, Kin.	1.000	14	28	1	0	29	1
Kim, Dave, Pot.	.982	38	54	1	1	56	0
Kingsale, Eugene, Fred.	1.000	5	12	0	0	12	0
Landaeta, Luis, Sal.*	.935	85	135	10	10	155	0
Landreth, Jason, Lyn.	1.000	5	6	1	0	7	1
Langerhans, Ryan, M.B.*	.961	91	142	4	6	152	0
Lehr, Ryan, M.B.	1.000	3	7	0	0	7	0
Long, Ryan, W.S.	.964	16	25	2	1	28	0
Macrory, Bob, Pot.	.000	1	0	0	0	0	0
Malave, Dennis, Kin.*	1.000	13	19	1	0	20	0
Manuel, Marcellous, W.S.*	.984	49	62	1	1	64	0
Martin, Justin, Lyn.	.978	60	127	5	3	135	0
Maxwell, Keith, Lyn.	1.000	4	8	0	0	8	0
McGee, Tom, Fred.	1.000	2	2	0	0	2	0
McKinley, Dan, Kin.	1.000	13	22	0	0	22	0
McNaughton, Troy, Pot.*	.975	118	185	14	5	204	0
Meier, Dan, Lyn.*	1.000	3	2	0	0	2	0
Merriman, Terrell, W.S.*	.978	131	256	9	6	271	1
Minges, Tyler, Lyn.	.968	103	171	13	6	190	3
Myers, Rod, W.S.*	.900	15	18	0	2	20	0
Ndungidi, Ntema, Fred.	.960	88	139	6	6	151	1
Pond, Simon, Kin.	1.000	1	1	0	0	1	0
Raines, Tim, Fred.	.972	124	302	8	9	319	2
Reed, Keith, Fred.	.953	65	116	6	6	128	0
Reinoso, Nataniel, M.B.*	.971	70	131	3	4	138	0
Rickon, Jim, Kin.	.750	1	3	0	1	4	0
Rivera, Roberto, Fred.	.952	33	60	0	3	63	0
Rust, Brian, Fred.	1.000	10	12	0	0	12	0
Salargo, Steve, Fred.	.964	14	27	0	1	28	0
Santana, Osmany, Kin.*	.988	35	80	0	1	81	0
Seal, Scott, Sal.*	.974	99	140	11	4	155	1
Shackelford, Brian, Wil.*	.977	83	120	8	3	131	1
Simmons, Jerry, M.B.	1.000	7	9	1	0	10	1
Smothers, Stewart, M.B.	1.000	8	16	0	0	16	0
Snead, Esix, Pot.	.979	132	313	10	7	330	4
Taveras, Jose, Wil.	.968	94	144	9	5	158	0
Valenzuela, Mario, W.S.	.977	138	242	15	6	263	2
Weichard, Paul, Lyn.*	.947	70	154	7	9	170	4
Whitlock, Brian, Kin.	1.000	2	3	0	0	3	0
William, Jovany, Pot.	.000	1	0	0	0	0	0
Wilson, Travis, M.B.	.000	1	0	0	0	0	0

TRIPLE PLAY: Landaeta.

CATCHERS

Player, Team	Pct.	G	PO	A	E	TC	DP	PB
Acevas, Jon, W.S.	.984	67	489	56	9	554	4	18
Alley, Charles, Fred.	.995	30	189	25	1	215	0	6

CLASS A Carolina League

Player, Team	Pct.	G	PO	A	E	TC	DP	PB
Bard, Josh, Sal.	.987	92	702	77	10	789	5	12
Benham, David, Pot.	.986	28	186	24	3	213	3	5
Brito, Juan, Wil.	.972	22	117	20	4	141	1	3
Bronowicz, Scott, M.B.	.927	8	50	1	4	55	0	5
Curtis, Matt, Kin.	.984	28	219	20	4	243	3	5
Dunn, Casey, Wil.	.978	35	204	14	5	223	0	5
EVANS, Lee, Lyn.	.990	76	518	57	6	581	6	9
Garcia, Tony, W.S.	.976	71	513	59	14	586	1	7
Haad, Yamid, Lyn.	.972	25	159	13	5	177	3	5
Hernandez, Jose, Lyn.	1.000	4	14	3	0	17	0	0
Hill, Jeremy, Wil.	.980	98	611	86	14	711	7	17
Hyde, Brandon, W.S.	.968	5	30	0	1	31	0	4
Johnson, Erik, Sal.	.982	22	152	13	3	168	0	8
Jones, Jay, Sal.	.976	23	189	16	5	210	3	1
Leon, Alfredo, Fred.	.952	12	73	6	4	83	0	3
Lopez-Cao, Mike, Fred.	.976	26	140	20	4	164	0	0
Martinez, Octavio, Fred.	1.000	1	5	1	0	6	0	0
Martinez, Victor, Kin.	.980	25	232	16	5	253	2	3
McGee, Tom, Fred.	.982	71	489	65	10	564	8	11
Mortimer, Mark, M.B.	.990	14	95	5	1	101	1	2
Nykoluk, Kevin, Pot.	.975	52	321	29	9	359	0	2
Pagan, Carlos, Wil.	1.000	3	10	1	0	11	0	1
Pride, Joshua, Sal.	1.000	10	59	8	0	67	0	2
Puffinbarger, Rusty, Kin.	.976	13	79	4	2	85	1	1
Pugh, Josh, M.B.	.982	32	193	20	4	217	2	3
Reese, Nate, M.B.	1.000	3	19	4	0	23	1	0
Rickon, Jim, Kin.	1.000	7	56	6	0	62	0	0
Sickles, Jeremy, Lyn.	.985	39	236	21	4	261	2	7
Smith, Casey, Kin.	.990	67	541	69	6	616	12	9
Torrealba, Steve, M.B.	.988	90	723	82	10	815	1	8
Werth, Jayson, Fred.	.985	16	116	12	2	130	2	1
Whitlock, Brian, Kin.	1.000	1	9	0	0	9	0	0
William, Jovany, Pot.	.983	66	404	49	8	461	3	7

PITCHERS

Player, Team	Pct.	G	PO	A	E	TC	DP
Achilles, Matt, Fred.	1.000	26	5	16	0	21	0
Affeldt, Jeremy, Wil.*	.970	27	5	27	1	33	3
Almonte, Edwin, W.S.	.944	33	4	13	1	18	1
Alvarado, Carlos, Lyn.	1.000	15	3	4	0	7	1
Alviso, Jerome, Sal.	.000	1	0	0	0	0	0
Ammons, Cary, Wil.*	.938	17	2	13	1	16	1
Aracena, Juan, Fred.	1.000	11	1	0	0	1	0
Arroyo, Bronson, Lyn.	1.000	1	1	4	0	5	0
Avery, Steve, M.B.*	1.000	7	5	10	0	15	3
Babula, Shaun, Fred.*	.875	37	3	4	1	8	0
Bacsik, Mike, Kin.*	.941	11	5	11	1	17	1
Baerlocher, Ryan, Wil.	.875	8	3	4	1	8	0
Baez, Danny, Kin.	1.000	9	4	11	0	15	0
Bajenaru, Jeffrey, W.S.	1.000	10	1	0	0	1	0
Bauer, Rick, Fred.	1.000	3	6	3	0	9	2
Bausher, Andy, Lyn.*	1.000	30	1	5	0	6	0
Bechler, Steven, Fred.	.963	27	5	21	1	27	2
Beimel, Joe, Lyn.*	.885	18	6	17	3	26	0
Belisle, Matt, M.B.	.952	12	9	11	1	21	0
Bello, Jilberto, Fred.	.667	4	1	1	1	3	0
Bohannan, Kyle, W.S.	1.000	4	0	1	0	1	0
Bong, Jung, M.B.*	.917	7	4	7	1	12	1
Bost, Heath, Sal.	1.000	7	1	1	0	2	0
Brantley, Brian, Sal.	1.000	41	3	8	0	11	0
Bravo, Franklin, Lyn.	1.000	20	6	15	0	21	0
Brown, Derek, Fred.	.833	41	5	5	2	12	0
Brueggemann, Dean, Sal.*	.938	44	6	9	1	16	0
Buirley, Matt, Lyn.	.800	11	2	2	1	5	0
Bukvich, Ryan, Wil.	1.000	3	0	2	0	2	0
Burch, Matt, Wil.	.872	32	12	22	5	39	2
Burger, Rob, Sal.	1.000	8	0	2	0	2	0
Cameron, Ryan, Sal.	.969	26	9	22	1	32	1
Caple, Chance, Pot.	.952	22	3	17	1	21	1
Carr, Tim, Wil.	1.000	45	5	3	0	8	1
Carrasco, Dan, Lyn.	1.000	8	1	1	0	2	0
Carter, Justin, Sal.*	.903	17	5	23	3	31	2
Chavez, Christopher, M.B.	.909	35	0	10	1	11	1
Christenson, Ryan, Pot.	.864	22	6	13	3	22	0
Chrysler, Clint, Lyn.*	.889	51	2	6	1	9	0
Cogan, Tony, Wil.*	1.000	16	1	3	0	4	0
Colmenares, Luis, Sal.	.000	9	0	0	0	0	0
Colon, Jose, Kin.	1.000	17	4	1	0	5	0
Cook, Aaron, Sal.	1.000	7	1	8	0	9	1
Cook, B.R., Fred.	1.000	8	2	5	0	7	0
Correa, Cristobal, Pot.	1.000	18	6	6	0	12	0
Cowie, Steve, Kin.	1.000	12	5	10	0	15	0
Crowder, Chuck, Sal.*	.872	28	13	21	5	39	1

Player, Team	Pct.	G	PO	A	E	TC	DP
Crudale, Mike, Pot.	1.000	21	2	2	0	4	0
Curtis, Dan, M.B.	.750	8	6	3	3	12	0
Daniels, David, Pot.	1.000	31	2	2	0	4	0
De Leon, Jose, Pot.	1.000	11	0	3	0	3	0
Delgado, Ernie, Kin.	1.000	9	2	3	0	5	0
Drese, Ryan, Kin.	.000	1	0	0	0	0	0
Eibey, Scott, Fred.*	.000	4	0	0	0	0	0
Erickson, Scott, Fred.	1.000	1	1	1	0	2	0
Felix, Miguel, W.S.-Fred.	1.000	35	5	2	0	7	0
Figueroa, Juan, W.S.	1.000	9	1	5	0	6	0
Fiora, Chris, Pot.	.000	1	0	0	0	0	0
Fischer, Eric, W.S.*	.938	25	2	13	1	16	0
Fleck, Will, M.B.	.000	1	0	0	0	0	0
Forystek, Brian, Fred.*	.000	3	0	0	0	0	0
Foster, John, M.B.*	.917	38	1	10	1	12	1
Gandy, Josh, Kin.*	1.000	9	0	2	0	2	0
Garcia, Tony, W.S.	.000	1	0	0	0	0	0
Gargano, Mike, Pot.	1.000	38	6	10	0	16	2
Garza, Alberto, Kin.	.813	22	5	8	3	16	2
Gilfillan, Jason, Wil.	1.000	12	1	0	0	1	1
Gonzalez, Mike, Lyn.*	.947	12	1	17	1	19	0
Gorman, Pat, Fred.	1.000	7	1	2	0	3	0
Graham, Brian, W.S.	.800	1	1	3	1	5	0
Gray, Michael, M.B.*	.923	30	2	10	1	13	1
Green, Tyler, Wil.	1.000	1	0	1	0	1	0
Greene, Ryan, M.B.	.833	14	1	4	1	6	0
Griffin, Kirk, Pot.	1.000	50	4	9	0	13	2
Gross, Rafael, Kin.	1.000	29	1	7	0	8	1
Guerrier, Matt, W.S.	1.000	30	3	5	0	8	0
Guzman, Juan, Fred.	1.000	3	1	0	0	1	0
Guzman, Wilson, Lyn.*	1.000	10	1	16	0	17	0
Halpin, Jeremy, Fred.	.857	25	5	7	2	14	0
Haynie, Jason, Lyn.*	.929	23	2	24	2	28	2
Herrera, Alex, Kin.*	1.000	17	1	4	0	5	0
House, Craig, Sal.	1.000	13	4	2	0	6	0
Hudson, Luke, Sal.	.864	19	4	15	3	22	0
Izquierdo, Hansel, Kin.	1.000	10	2	4	0	6	0
Jennings, Jason, Sal.	.909	22	9	21	3	33	1
Jerue, Tristan, Pot.	.000	10	0	0	0	0	0
Johnston, Clint, Lyn.*	1.000	10	3	8	0	11	0
Jones, Sean, Fred.	.000	1	0	0	0	0	0
Kane, Kyle, W.S.	.909	32	4	6	1	11	0
Kearney, Ryan, Kin.	1.000	32	1	9	0	10	0
Kent, Nathan, M.B.	.944	24	4	13	1	18	0
King, Jim, Wil.*	1.000	46	5	16	0	21	0
Koeth, Mark, Kin.	1.000	1	1	1	0	2	0
Kurtz-Nicholl, Jesse, Wil.*	1.000	8	0	2	0	2	0
Lamattina, Ryan, Sal.*	1.000	27	3	3	0	6	0
Lambert, Jeremy, Pot.	1.000	16	0	3	0	3	0
Landreth, Jason, Lyn.	.000	2	0	0	0	0	0
Langen, Brian, Pot.*	1.000	31	3	14	0	17	0
Ledden, Ryan, Lyn.	.750	15	3	3	2	8	0
Lee, Garrett, M.B.	1.000	29	4	11	0	15	2
Lopez, Jose, Lyn.	1.000	6	3	4	0	7	0
Lorenzana, Luis, Lyn.	.000	1	0	0	0	0	0
MacDOUGAL, Mike, Wil.	1.000	26	12	27	0	39	0
Maduro, Calvin, Fred.	1.000	1	0	0	0	0	0
Majewski, Gary, W.S.	1.000	6	2	6	0	8	0
Maleski, Eric, Kin.	.667	5	0	2	1	3	0
Manzueta, Roberto, Lyn.	.600	23	0	3	2	5	0
Marini, Anthony, Kin.*	.667	1	0	2	1	3	0
Marr, Jason, Pot.	1.000	48	8	6	0	14	3
Martin, Chandler, Sal.	1.000	7	5	10	0	15	0
Martin, Jeff, Lyn.	.750	28	3	3	2	8	0
Martin, Justin, Lyn.	1.000	1	1	0	0	1	0
Martinez, Jesus, Kin.*	.000	2	0	0	0	0	0
Matcuk, Steve, Sal.	.833	22	1	9	2	12	0
Mays, Jarrod, Kin.	1.000	14	1	0	0	1	0
McClendon, Matt, M.B.	1.000	6	2	4	0	6	1
McDade, Neal, Lyn.	.714	7	1	4	2	7	0
Mejia, Francisco, Fred.	.667	4	1	1	1	3	0
Mendoza, Geronimo, W.S.	.909	31	14	16	3	33	1
Mills, Alan, Fred.	.000	1	0	0	0	0	0
Montgomery, Greg, W.S.	.000	2	0	0	0	0	0
Moreno, Julio, Fred.	.000	2	0	0	0	0	0
Navarro, Jason, Pot.*	1.000	23	1	7	0	8	0
Negrette, Richard, Fred.	.500	4	0	1	1	2	0
Nunez, Jose, Pot.	1.000	1	0	0	0	0	0
Ormond, Rodney, Fred.	.885	39	11	12	3	26	0
Osting, Jimmy, M.B.*	1.000	4	2	3	0	5	0
Padilla, Roy, Kin.*	.857	14	4	2	1	7	0
Padua, Geraldo, Lyn.	.955	17	9	12	1	22	1
Pamus, Javier, Wil.	.875	32	2	12	2	16	0

Player, Team	Pct.	G	PO	A	E	TC	DP
Paradis, Mike, Fred.	1.000	8	6	7	0	13	2
Parra, Christian, M.B.	.923	26	13	23	3	39	3
Pavlovich, Tony, Lyn.	1.000	36	3	11	0	14	1
Pearce, Josh, Pot.	1.000	10	3	4	0	7	0
Pederson, Justin, Wil.	.933	47	1	13	1	15	1
Pickford, Kevin, Lyn.*	1.000	10	2	5	0	7	1
Pierce, Tony, M.B.	.867	18	5	8	2	15	1
Prather, Scott, Pot.*	.833	42	2	8	2	12	0
Price, Ryan, Sal.	.333	6	0	1	2	3	0
Purvis, Rob, W.S.	.958	27	16	30	2	48	3
Rakers, Aaron, Fred.	1.000	26	1	2	0	3	0
Ramirez, Horacio, M.B.*	1.000	27	4	26	0	30	2
Rauch, Jon, W.S.	1.000	18	2	11	0	13	0
Reinike, Chris, Kin.	.750	11	1	2	1	4	0
Roberts, Mike, Wil.	1.000	31	4	6	0	10	0
Sabathia, C.C., Kin.*	1.000	10	1	9	0	10	2
Salargo, Steve, Fred.	.000	1	0	0	0	0	0
Sanches, Brian, Wil.	.957	28	3	19	1	23	0
Sanders, David, W.S.*	.833	51	0	5	1	6	1
Sequea, Jacobo, Fred.	.966	23	10	18	1	29	0
Sheredy, Kevin, Pot.	.857	30	5	7	2	14	2
Sido, Wilson, Kin.	.943	29	11	22	2	35	0
Sims, Ken, Fred.	.952	29	9	11	1	21	1
Sirianni, Jay, Kin.*	1.000	7	4	4	0	8	0
Smith, Roy, Kin.	.923	21	2	10	1	13	0
Snyder, Kyle, Wil.	.000	1	0	0	0	0	0
Spiegel, Mike, Kin.*	1.000	5	1	3	0	4	0
Spooneybarger, Tim, M.B.	.824	19	5	9	3	17	0
Spurgeon, Jay, Fred.	.917	16	6	5	1	12	1
Spurling, Chris, Lyn.	1.000	9	4	4	0	8	1
Stabile, Paul, Lyn.*	1.000	10	0	1	0	1	0
Stanford, Jason, Kin.*	.917	11	3	8	1	12	1
Stein, Blake, Wil.	.000	2	0	0	0	0	0

Player, Team	Pct.	G	PO	A	E	TC	DP
Stein, Ethan, Wil.	1.000	26	0	2	0	2	0
Stemle, Steve, Pot.	.958	26	6	17	1	24	2
Stephens, John, Fred.	1.000	20	4	11	0	15	0
Sullivan, Ted, Kin.	.000	4	0	0	0	0	0
Sylvester, Billy, M.B.	.818	32	5	4	2	11	0
Thompson, Doug, Sal.	.909	46	2	8	1	11	0
Thurman, Corey, Wil.	.913	19	8	13	2	23	2
Vargas, Jose, Kin.	1.000	27	5	13	0	18	1
Veras, Dario, Kin.	.500	17	1	1	2	4	0
Voyles, Brad, M.B.	1.000	39	3	10	0	13	3
Walrond, Les, Pot.*	.867	27	9	17	4	30	1
Weidert, Chris, Fred.-Kin.	.909	28	4	6	1	11	1
West, Brian, W.S.	.000	2	0	0	1	1	0
Whatley, Brannon, W.S.	1.000	26	3	9	0	12	2
White, Matt, Kin.*	.862	28	5	20	4	29	0
Whitecotton, Billy, Fred.	1.000	1	0	1	0	1	0
Whitlock, Brian, Kin.	.000	1	0	0	0	0	0
Williams, Dave, Lyn.*	1.000	2	0	3	0	3	1
Williams, Larry, Lyn.	.500	14	0	1	1	2	0
Williams, Mike, W.S.	.889	46	3	13	2	18	2
Wimberly, Larry, Lyn.*	.875	24	1	20	3	24	1
Wright, Danny, W.S.	.962	21	7	18	1	26	0
Wrigley, Jase, Sal.	.952	47	6	14	1	21	0
Wylie, Mitch, W.S.	.893	17	5	20	3	28	2

PITCHERS WITH TWO OR MORE TEAMS

Player, Team	Pct.	G	PO	A	E	TC	DP
Felix, Miguel, W.S.	1.000	27	4	2	0	6	0
Felix, Miguel, Fred.	1.000	8	1	0	0	1	0
Weidert, Chris, Fred.	.909	24	4	6	1	11	1
Weidert, Chris, Kin.	.000	4	0	0	0	0	0

The following player appeared only as designated hitter, pinch-hitter or pinch runner: Schneider, dh.

LEAGUE CHAMPIONS

Year	Team	Pct.
1945—	Danville	.681
1946—	Greensboro	.599
	Raleigh (2nd)†	.563
1947—	Burlington	.613
	Raleigh (3rd)†	.574
1948—	Raleigh	.592
	Martinsville (2nd)†	.570
1949—	Danville	.601
	Burlington (4th)†	.500
1950—	Winston-Salem*	.693
1951—	Durham	.600
	Winston-Salem (2nd)†	.583
1952—	Raleigh	.581
	Reidsville (4th)†	.536
1953—	Raleigh	.593
	Danville (2nd)†	.572
1954—	Fayetteville*	.628
1955—	HP-Thomasville	.580
	Danville (2nd)†	.533
1956—	HP-Thomasville	.591
	Fayetteville (4th)§	.523
1957—	Durham	.632
	HP-Thomasville	.622
1958—	Danville	.576
	Burlington (4th)†	.511
1959—	Raleigh	.600
	Wilson (2nd)†	.550
1960—	Greensboro‡	.636
	Burlington	.586
1961—	Wilson	.594
1962—	Durham	.636
	Wilson	.600
	Kinston (2nd)†	.593
1963—	Kinston§	.538
	Greensboro§	.590
	Wilson (2nd)†	.535
1964—	Kinston§	.572
	Winston-Salem§†	.590

Year	Team	Pct.
1965—	Peninsula§	.597
	Durham§	.580
	Tidewater†	.528
1966—	Kinston§	.547
	Winston-Salem§	.586
	Rocky Mount†	.533
1967—	Durham∞(West.)	.536
	Raleigh (East.)	.542
1968—	Salem (West.)	.607
	Ral-Dur (East.)	.597
	HP-Thom.▲(W.)	.493
1969—	Rocky M (East.)	.569
	Salem (West.)	.542
	Ral-Dur◆(East.)	.560
1970—	Winston-Salem‡	.586
	Burlington	.597
1971—	Peninsula‡	.647
	Kinston	.623
1972—	Salem‡	.657
	Burlington	.632
1973—	Lynchburg	.588
	Winston-Salem‡	.557
1974—	Salem	.671
	Salem	.582
1975—	Rocky Mount	.667
	Rocky Mount	.614
1976—	Winston-Salem	.618
	Winston-Salem	.551
1977—	Lynchburg	.591
	Peninsula‡	.556
1978—	Peninsula	.696
	Lynchburg‡	.614
1979—	Winston-Salem■	.607
1980—	Peninsula‡	.714
	Durham	.600
1981—	Peninsula	.522
	Hagerstown‡	.507
1982—	Alexandria‡	.597

Year	Team	Pct.
	Durham	.588
1983—	Lynchburg‡	.691
	Winston-Salem	.529
1984—	Lynchburg‡	.645
	Durham	.486
1985—	Lynchburg	.679
	Winston-Salem‡	.417
1986—	Hagerstown	.655
	Winston-Salem‡	.594
1987—	Salem‡	.576
	Kinston	.536
1988—	Kinston§	.629
	Lynchburg	.486
1989—	Durham	.609
	Prince William‡	.522
1990—	Kinston	.652
	Frederick‡	.544
1991—	Kinston‡	.645
	Lynchburg	.482
1992—	Lynchburg	.570
	Peninsula‡	.536
1993—	Wilmington	.532
	Winston-Salem‡	.514
1994—	Wilmington‡	.681
	Winston-Salem	.555
1995—	Wilmington	.601
	Kinston‡	.591
1996—	Wilmington▼	.571
	Kinston	.551
1997—	Kinston	.621
	Lynchburg†	.586
1998—	Wilmington▼	.614
	Winston-Salem	.568
1999—	Kinston	.577
	Myrtle Beach•	.568
	Wilmington•	.568
2000—	Myrtle Beach▼	.629

*Won championship and four-club playoff. †Won four-club playoff. ‡Won split-season playoff. §League was divided into Eastern, Western divisions. ∞Won eight-club, two-division playoff. ▲Won eight-club, two-division playoff against Raleigh-Durham. ◆Won eight-club, two-division playoff against Burlington. ■Won both halves of split season (no playoffs). ▼League divided into Northern and Southern divisions and played a split-season, won playoffs. •Declared co-champions after final series cancelled due to hurricane.

CLASS A Carolina League

FLORIDA STATE LEAGUE

LEAGUE OFFICE

President
Chuck Murphy

Address
P.O. Box 349
Daytona Beach, FL 32115

Phone
904-252-7479

Teams (affiliation)
Brevard County Manatees (Marlins)
Charlotte Rangers (Rangers)
Clearwater Phillies (Phillies)
Daytona Cubs (Cubs)
Dunedin Blue Jays (Blue Jays)
Fort Myers Miracle (Twins)
Jupiter Hammerheads (Expos)
Lakeland Tigers (Tigers)
St. Lucie Mets (Mets)
Sarasota Red Sox (Red Sox)
Tampa Yankees (Yankees)
Vero Beach Dodgers (Dodgers)

2000 FINAL STANDINGS

FIRST HALF

EAST DIVISION

Team	W	L	T	Pct.	GB
St. Lucie (Mets)	47	22	0	.681	...
Brevard County (Marlins)	39	31	0	.557	8.5
Kissimmee (Astros)	38	32	0	.543	9.5
Vero Beach (Dodgers)	36	34	0	.514	11.5
Daytona (Cubs)	32	38	0	.457	15.5
Jupiter (Expos)	27	43	0	.386	20.5

WEST DIVISION

Team	W	L	T	Pct.	GB
Dunedin (Blue Jays)	40	29	0	.580	...
Fort Myers (Twins)	38	32	0	.543	2.5
Tampa (Yankees)	37	33	0	.529	3.5
Clearwater (Phillies)	37	33	0	.529	3.5
Charlotte (Rangers)	36	34	0	.514	4.5
Sarasota (Red Sox)	29	41	0	.414	11.5
Lakeland (Tigers)	28	43	0	.394	13.0
St. Petersburg (Devil Rays)	25	46	0	.352	16.0

SECOND HALF

EAST DIVISION

Team	W	L	T	Pct.	GB
Daytona (Cubs)	44	25	0	.638	...
Kissimmee (Astros)	35	34	0	.507	9.0
St. Lucie (Mets)	34	36	0	.486	10.5
Jupiter (Expos)	34	36	0	.486	10.5
Vero Beach (Dodgers)	30	37	0	.448	13.0
Brevard County (Marlins)	27	43	0	.386	17.5

WEST DIVISION

Team	W	L	T	Pct.	GB
Fort Myers (Twins)	45	25	0	.643	...
Dunedin (Blue Jays)	44	25	0	.638	0.5
Charlotte (Rangers)	42	27	0	.609	2.5
St. Petersburg (Devil Rays)	33	35	0	.485	11.0
Tampa (Yankees)	33	37	0	.471	12.0
Sarasota (Red Sox)	31	38	0	.449	13.5
Clearwater (Phillies)	27	38	0	.415	15.5
Lakeland (Tigers)	24	45	0	.348	20.5

COMPOSITE

Team	Dun.	F.M.	St.L.	Char.	Day.	Kis.	Tam.	V.B.	Cle.	B.C.	Jup.	Sar.	St.P.	Lak.	W	L	T	Pct.	GB
Dunedin (Blue Jays)	...	8	4	6	6	4	8	4	10	4	5	8	7	10	84	54	0	.609	...
Fort Myers (Twins)	4	...	6	9	4	6	7	4	5	8	5	9	11	5	83	57	0	.593	2.0
St. Lucie (Mets)	3	2	...	6	8	7	5	12	7	7	11	3	6	4	81	58	0	.583	3.5
Charlotte (Rangers)	6	7	2	...	4	5	5	6	6	5	5	10	8	9	78	61	0	.561	6.5
Daytona (Cubs)	2	4	8	4	...	9	5	8	1	10	7	5	6	7	76	63	0	.547	8.5
Kissimmee (Astros)	4	2	7	3	7	...	5	8	7	8	8	4	4	6	73	66	0	.525	11.5
Tampa (Yankees)	6	5	3	7	3	3	...	3	7	3	4	8	8	10	70	70	0	.500	15.0
Vero Beach (Dodgers)	4	4	4	1	6	6	5	...	2	9	10	6	4	5	66	71	0	.482	17.5
Clearwater (Phillies)	5	7	1	6	6	1	7	4	...	4	3	6	6	8	64	71	0	.474	18.5
Brevard County (Marlins)	4	0	7	3	6	8	5	7	4	...	10	4	4	4	66	74	0	.471	19.0
Jupiter (Expos)	3	3	5	2	3	7	8	4	6	5	...	4	2	7	61	79	0	.436	24.0
Sarasota (Red Sox)	4	3	5	6	3	3	4	2	6	4	4	...	9	7	60	79	0	.432	24.5
St. Petersburg (Devil Rays)	5	5	2	4	2	4	4	5	4	6	7	4	...	6	58	81	0	.417	26.5
Lakeland (Tigers)	4	7	4	3	1	2	6	3	6	4	1	5	6	...	52	88	0	.371	33.0

Brevard County played home games in Melbourne, Fla.; Charlotte played home games in Port Charlotte, Fla.

Major league affiliations in parentheses.

PLAYOFFS: Daytona defeated St. Lucie two games to none; Dunedin defeated Fort Myers two games to none; Daytona defeated Dunedin three games to none to win league championship.

REGULAR-SEASON ATTENDANCE: Brevard County, 130,950; Charlotte, 36,917; Clearwater, 83,895; Daytona, 70,042; Dunedin, 35,184; Fort Myers, 116,041; Jupiter, 98,781; Kissimmee, 29,650; Lakeland, 23,937; St. Lucie, 61,481; St. Petersburg, 61,962; Sarasota, 47,491; Tampa, 97,839; Vero Beach, 59,550. Total—953,720. Playoffs (7 games)—5,284. All-Star Game at Jupiter, Fla.—5,342.

MANAGERS: Brevard County, Dave Huppert; Charlotte, James Byrd (Through May 14), Bob Miscik (May 15 through end of season); Clearwater, Ken Oberkfell; Daytona, Richie Zisk; Dunedin, Marty Pevey; Fort Myers, Jose Marzan; Jupiter, Luis Dorante; Kissimmee, Manny Acta; Lakeland, Skeeter Barnes; St. Lucie, Dave Engle; St. Petersburg, Julio Garcia; Sarasota, Ron Johnson; Tampa, Tom Nieto; Vero Beach, John Shoemaker.

ALL-STAR TEAM: 1B—Travis Hafner, Charlotte; 2B—Ruben Salazar, Fort Myers; 3B—Scott Hodges, Jupiter; SS—Anderson Machado, Clearwater; Utility IF—Royce Huffman, Kissimmee; OF—Kevin Mench, Charlotte; Andres Torres, Lakeland; Brian Cole, St. Lucie; Utility OF—Matt Cepicky, Jupiter; C—Joe Lawrence, Dunedin; Brandon Marsters, Fort Myers; DH—Earl Snyder, St. Lucie; RHP—Aaron Harang, Charlotte; Brett Jodie, Tampa; Tim Redding, Kissimmee; LHP—Lindsay Gulin, Daytona; Relief pitcher—Jarrod Kingrey, Dunedin; Most Valuable Player—Kevin Mench, Charlotte; Most Valuable Pitcher—Tim Redding, Kissimmee; Manager—Marty Pevey, Dunedin; Coach—Dave Engle, St. Lucie; Richie Zisk, Daytona.

2000 BATTING
TEAM

Team	Avg.	G	TPA	AB	R	H	TB	2B	3B	HR	RBI	SH	SF	HP	BB	IBB	SO	SB	CS	GDP	LOB	ShO	Slg.	OBP
Dunedin	.279	138	5323	4642	760	1294	2023	298	28	125	703	32	49	71	529	19	1026	127	57	104	993	4	.436	.358
Charlotte	.279	139	5434	4707	748	1311	1941	252	57	88	663	40	37	88	562	19	863	119	70	94	1086	5	.412	.364
Vero Beach	.270	137	5157	4590	661	1238	1695	194	40	61	574	30	51	69	417	13	819	177	71	110	953	6	.369	.336
St. Lucie	.265	139	5327	4691	702	1245	1833	235	22	103	641	41	48	72	475	31	965	189	85	96	982	7	.391	.339
Fort Myers	.265	140	5236	4685	641	1243	1748	254	31	63	577	33	34	54	430	14	831	86	43	125	972	8	.373	.332
Jupiter	.263	140	5387	4705	669	1237	1705	205	40	61	595	53	52	60	517	25	870	190	96	93	1000	8	.362	.340
Daytona	.263	139	5315	4693	696	1233	1887	247	43	107	622	38	53	71	460	17	905	145	86	73	947	7	.402	.334
Clearwater	.257	135	5044	4444	562	1141	1583	237	41	41	500	38	44	73	445	16	912	149	76	91	972	9	.356	.331
Lakeland	.255	140	5146	4607	589	1176	1707	214	46	75	518	37	30	46	426	18	1120	173	82	92	923	8	.371	.323
St. Petersburg	.255	139	5036	4555	549	1162	1635	236	33	57	483	44	37	54	346	19	860	75	54	106	927	8	.359	.313
Kissimmee	.253	139	5116	4532	627	1147	1727	253	33	87	563	27	47	57	453	11	917	131	63	111	906	13	.381	.326
Sarasota	.251	139	5111	4537	596	1137	1623	206	35	70	513	31	43	67	436	18	935	125	91	95	895	13	.358	.323
Tampa	.244	140	5080	4493	551	1095	1666	229	21	100	505	16	43	58	470	19	940	72	60	95	951	10	.371	.320
Brev. County	.242	140	5325	4630	581	1121	1565	202	31	60	515	37	42	64	552	25	914	128	56	102	1057	12	.338	.328

INDIVIDUAL

TOP QUALIFIERS FOR BATTING CHAMPIONSHIP

Minimum 378 plate appearances. *Lefthanded batter. †Switch-hitter.

Player, Team	Avg.	G	TPA	AB	R	H	TB	2B	3B	HR	RBI	SH	SF	HP	BB	IBB	SO	SB	CS	GDP	Slg.	OBP
Hafner, Travis, Char.*	.346	122	528	436	90	151	253	34	1	22	109	0	7	18	67	2	86	0	4	9	.580	.447
Gallo, Ismael, V.B.*	.340	113	466	424	55	144	182	32	3	0	68	3	5	3	31	0	25	6	2	10	.429	.384
Mench, Kevin, Char.	.334	132	583	491	118	164	302	39	9	27	121	0	7	7	78	3	72	19	7	9	.615	.427
Bledsoe, Hunter, V.B.	.320	116	496	447	61	143	193	25	2	7	75	0	7	6	36	2	49	17	4	14	.432	.373
Cole, Brian, St.L.	.312	91	413	375	73	117	198	26	5	15	61	0	8	1	29	3	51	54	11	7	.528	.356
Salazar, Ruben, F.M.	.311	124	541	499	80	155	213	25	0	11	64	0	3	2	37	1	81	3	5	18	.427	.359
Marsters, Brandon, F.M.	.310	118	447	407	46	126	180	25	4	7	77	2	3	4	31	6	61	2	1	9	.442	.362
Hodges, Scott, Jup.*	.306	111	487	422	75	129	205	32	1	14	83	2	11	3	49	6	66	8	2	8	.486	.373
Lawrence, Joe, Dun.	.301	101	452	375	69	113	186	32	1	13	67	0	3	5	69	6	74	21	7	9	.496	.414
Piedra, Jorge, V.B.-Day.*	.301	126	553	499	83	150	207	22	7	7	69	5	9	5	35	1	72	29	9	6	.415	.347
Cepicky, Matt, Jup.*	.299	131	569	536	61	160	221	32	7	5	88	1	5	2	24	4	64	32	13	9	.412	.328
Smith, Nestor, F.M.†	.298	106	405	359	53	107	139	21	4	1	41	2	5	5	34	0	72	6	3	6	.387	.362
Chavez, Endy, St.L.*	.298	111	490	433	84	129	156	20	2	1	43	7	3	0	47	4	48	38	16	3	.360	.364
Burns, Pat, St.L.†	.298	109	444	386	53	115	152	21	2	4	61	0	4	5	49	5	109	3	1	8	.394	.381
Huffman, Royce, Kis.	.298	129	547	450	82	134	189	32	4	5	55	1	6	6	84	2	49	31	4	12	.420	.410

DEPARTMENTAL LEADERS: G—Aguila, 136; AB—Cepicky, 536; R—Mench, 118; H—Mench, 164; TB—Mench, 302; 2B—Mench, 39; 3B—Andres Torres, 11; HR—Stratton, 29; RBI—Mench, 121; SH—Machado, 18; SF—Hodges, 11; HP—Auterson, 22; BB—Huffman, 84; IBB—several tied, 6 each; SO—Stratton, 180; SB—Andres Torres, 65; CS—Nunez, 22; GIDP—M. Diaz, 21; Slg.—Mench, .615; OBP—Hafner, .447.

ALL PLAYERS

*Lefthanded batter. †Switch-hitter.

Player, Team	Avg.	G	TPA	AB	R	H	TB	2B	3B	HR	RBI	SH	SF	HP	BB	IBB	SO	SB	CS	GDP	Slg.	OBP
Aaron, Oginga, St.P.	.000	1	1	1	0	0	0	0	0	0	0	0	0	0	0	0	0	0	0	0	.000	.000
Abreu, Dave, St.L.†	.333	8	35	30	3	10	10	0	0	0	3	1	0	0	4	1	6	3	2	0	.333	.412
Abreu, Dennis, Day.	.322	39	127	118	18	38	48	4	0	2	10	2	0	3	4	1	24	8	5	4	.407	.360
Ackerman, Scott, Jup.	.280	48	201	182	14	51	62	5	0	2	25	2	1	1	15	2	22	1	0	8	.341	.337
Aguila, Chris, B.C.	.241	136	563	518	68	125	185	27	3	9	56	3	3	1	37	1	105	8	8	11	.357	.292
Ahumada, Alejandro, Sar.	.265	125	485	457	55	121	163	18	3	6	47	1	3	8	16	0	80	9	7	8	.357	.300
Alfaro, Jason, Kis.	.250	117	496	460	58	115	158	20	1	7	41	5	5	1	25	1	63	2	6	15	.343	.287
Alvarez, Clemente, Cle.	.268	12	44	41	1	11	11	0	0	0	1	0	0	1	2	1	7	0	0	1	.268	.318
Anderson, Dennis, B.C.†	.196	23	70	56	6	11	13	2	0	0	3	1	0	4	9	0	16	0	1	0	.232	.348
Auterson, Jeff, V.B.	.238	108	405	344	61	82	129	16	2	9	45	2	2	22	34	0	109	17	4	7	.375	.343
Autry, Brian, Jup.	.167	23	79	72	5	12	17	2	0	1	7	0	1	3	3	0	27	0	0	1	.236	.228
Backe, Brandon, St.P.	.247	112	426	376	38	93	133	25	6	1	34	4	5	10	31	2	99	3	6	8	.354	.318
Bailey, Jeff, B.C.	.247	125	520	458	56	113	180	19	3	14	66	1	4	7	50	2	116	3	3	9	.393	.328
Baker, Derek, Char.*	.294	127	526	449	50	132	199	28	3	11	81	0	1	9	67	3	67	1	2	8	.443	.395
Ballard, Ryan, St.P.	.154	14	45	39	2	6	8	2	0	0	1	1	0	0	5	0	18	0	0	1	.205	.250
Barningham, Steve, Char.*	.274	102	410	351	68	96	136	15	8	3	30	6	2	10	41	3	52	16	7	8	.387	.364
Barr, Clint, Tam.	.150	13	22	20	0	3	4	1	0	0	1	0	0	0	2	0	8	0	0	0	.200	.227
Basak, Chris, St.L.	.412	4	21	17	2	7	8	1	0	0	3	0	0	0	4	0	2	3	1	1	.471	.524
Batson, Tom, Cle.	.245	40	166	147	16	36	48	9	0	1	16	0	1	2	16	1	28	0	2	4	.327	.325
Beinbrink, Andy, St.P.	.297	130	535	475	70	141	190	28	0	7	58	2	6	8	43	3	70	3	4	10	.400	.361
Bell, Ricky, V.B.	.254	127	528	481	59	122	155	18	0	5	45	1	6	3	37	2	75	7	3	13	.322	.307
Bennett, Ryan, St.L.	.277	53	191	166	20	46	55	7	1	0	15	3	0	1	20	0	35	0	1	4	.331	.358
Berg, Dave, B.C.	.273	3	13	11	2	3	3	0	0	0	2	0	0	1	0	0	3	0	1	1	.273	.385
Bernhardt, Jossephang, Dun.	.250	3	5	4	0	1	2	1	0	0	3	0	0	1	1	0	1	0	0	0	.500	.400
Berry, Sean, Sar.	.250	1	4	4	0	1	1	0	0	0	0	0	0	0	0	0	2	0	0	1	.250	.250
Besco, Derek, Lake.	.280	20	87	82	15	23	33	4	0	2	12	0	0	1	4	0	15	1	0	1	.402	.322
Bledsoe, Hunter, V.B.	.320	116	496	447	61	143	193	25	2	7	75	0	7	6	36	2	49	17	4	14	.432	.373
Bly, Derrick, Day.	.245	83	323	294	30	72	110	10	5	6	31	5	2	4	17	0	75	2	4	3	.374	.293
Boone, Matt, Lake.	.249	119	478	441	47	110	155	21	3	6	48	1	0	1	35	2	112	5	6	12	.351	.306
Borjas, Henry, Sar.†	.000	1	3	3	0	0	0	0	0	0	0	0	0	0	0	0	0	0	0	0	.000	.000
Borrego, Ramon, F.M.†	.223	79	302	265	29	59	67	6	1	0	20	3	1	5	28	0	37	8	2	6	.253	.308
Boyer, Bret, Jup.	.391	8	25	23	1	9	12	1	1	0	5	0	1	0	1	0	1	0	2	1	.522	.400
Brogna, Rico, Cle.*	.219	7	33	32	2	7	8	1	0	0	2	0	0	0	1	1	4	0	0	0	.250	.242
Brosius, Scott, Tam.	.250	2	5	4	0	1	1	0	0	0	0	0	0	1	0	0	1	0	0	0	.250	.400

Player, Team	Avg.	G	TPA	AB	R	H	TB	2B	3B	HR	RBI	SH	SF	HP	BB	IBB	SO	SB	CS	GDP	Slg.	OBP
Brown, Billy, Tam.	.247	109	409	361	41	89	119	20	2	2	26	2	1	10	35	0	90	12	8	5	.330	.329
Brown, Tonayne, Sar.	.272	127	562	507	83	138	170	16	5	2	40	11	2	9	33	1	79	33	13	3	.335	.327
Bryan, Jason, Char.	.000	2	4	3	0	0	0	0	0	0	0	0	0	0	1	0	2	0	0	0	.000	.250
Bryant, Matt, Cle.	.258	67	261	221	27	57	69	8	2	0	30	1	2	3	34	0	31	2	2	10	.312	.362
Buckley, Brandon, Kis.	.264	45	144	129	19	34	45	3	1	2	16	2	0	2	11	0	27	0	1	3	.349	.331
Bundy, Ryan, Dun.	.000	2	5	5	1	0	0	0	0	0	0	0	0	0	0	0	2	0	0	0	.000	.000
Burns, Pat, St.L.†	.298	109	444	386	53	115	152	21	2	4	61	0	4	5	49	5	109	3	1	8	.394	.381
Bush, Brian, Cle.	.223	65	233	215	27	48	60	7	1	1	21	0	1	7	10	0	62	7	2	2	.279	.279
Calloway, Ron, Jup.*	.277	135	596	530	78	147	201	24	6	6	65	1	6	4	55	3	89	34	14	13	.379	.346
Camilo, Juan, Lake.*	.247	114	426	373	49	92	145	13	2	12	45	2	3	2	46	5	142	4	9	4	.389	.330
Cantu, Jorge, St.P.	.292	36	137	130	18	38	50	5	2	1	14	3	0	1	3	0	13	4	2	3	.385	.313
Carreno, Jose, Jup.	.256	38	140	125	6	32	35	3	0	0	3	3	0	2	10	0	18	0	1	2	.280	.321
Carter, Charley, Kis.	.276	106	428	398	51	110	172	32	0	10	66	0	8	1	21	0	64	2	1	16	.432	.308
Casillas, Uriel, Cle.	.307	48	178	140	17	43	55	7	1	1	14	2	1	3	32	0	17	0	3	3	.393	.443
Castillo, Carlos, St.L.†	.286	3	9	7	1	2	3	1	0	0	0	1	0	0	1	0	1	1	0	1	.429	.375
Cepicky, Matt, Jup.*	.299	131	569	536	61	160	221	32	7	5	88	1	5	2	24	4	64	32	13	9	.412	.328
Chapman, Scott, Kis.	.255	107	432	373	51	95	147	26	1	8	59	0	6	3	50	1	85	0	1	9	.394	.343
Chavez, Endy, St.L.*	.298	111	490	433	84	129	156	20	2	1	43	7	3	0	47	4	48	38	16	3	.360	.364
Chiaffredo, Paul, Dun.	.289	11	44	38	7	11	18	1	0	2	6	0	0	1	5	0	9	0	0	0	.474	.386
Choi, Hee, Day.*	.296	96	394	345	60	102	184	25	6	15	70	0	5	6	37	5	78	4	1	7	.533	.369
Clapinski, Chris, B.C.†	.353	4	17	17	4	6	9	0	0	1	1	0	0	0	0	0	2	0	0	0	.529	.353
Clarke, Jason, Day.†	.167	13	44	42	8	7	12	2	0	1	4	0	0	0	2	0	8	2	0	0	.286	.205
Cleveland, Russell, Lake.	.182	10	36	33	4	6	6	0	0	0	2	1	1	0	1	0	9	0	1	0	.182	.200
Close, James, B.C.	.200	2	5	5	0	1	1	0	0	0	0	0	0	0	0	0	1	0	0	0	.200	.200
Cole, Brian, St.L.	.312	91	413	375	73	117	198	26	5	15	61	0	8	1	29	3	51	54	11	7	.528	.356
Cooper, Sam, Day.†	.222	10	29	27	4	6	9	1	1	0	4	1	1	0	0	0	4	0	0	0	.333	.214
Copeland, Brandon, St.L.	.245	35	118	102	18	25	35	4	0	2	13	1	1	3	11	1	17	4	4	2	.343	.333
Crosby, Bubba, V.B.*	.266	73	316	274	50	73	126	13	8	8	51	3	1	7	31	3	41	27	10	9	.460	.355
Curry, Chris, Day.	.153	20	65	59	5	9	9	0	0	0	3	1	0	1	4	0	17	0	0	4	.153	.219
Curtice, John, Sar.*	.000	26	1	1	0	0	0	0	0	0	0	0	0	0	0	0	0	0	0	0	.000	.000
Daigle, Leo, Lake.	.236	113	439	398	26	94	139	20	2	7	52	1	8	5	27	2	108	1	2	12	.349	.288
Da Luz, Craig, Lake.	.243	102	407	382	40	93	135	25	4	3	46	1	4	3	17	0	72	3	8	13	.353	.278
De Aza, Modesto, Kis.	.000	4	1	1	0	0	0	0	0	0	0	0	0	0	0	0	1	0	0	0	.000	.000
De Leon, Jorge, Sar.	.275	10	44	40	5	11	17	4	1	0	3	0	0	0	4	0	7	1	0	1	.425	.341
Dennis, Les, Sar.	.378	23	98	82	11	31	39	5	0	1	12	0	1	3	12	0	17	0	1	1	.476	.469
Diaz , Jorge, Char.	.274	51	213	179	27	49	59	2	4	0	13	1	2	4	27	0	26	4	5	1	.330	.377
Diaz, Juan, Sar.	.275	14	57	51	7	14	30	2	1	4	12	0	1	1	4	0	15	0	0	1	.588	.333
Diaz, Matt, St.P.	.270	106	420	392	37	106	151	21	3	6	53	1	5	11	11	0	54	2	3	21	.385	.305
Dorman, John, St.L.	.188	35	114	96	13	18	24	1	1	1	4	1	0	3	13	0	25	5	1	3	.250	.304
Duncan, Carlos, Cle.	.264	107	431	390	49	103	158	25	3	8	47	3	3	9	26	0	113	13	9	3	.405	.322
Duplissea, William, V.B.	.143	3	9	7	1	1	2	1	0	0	0	0	0	0	2	0	1	0	0	0	.286	.333
Dusan, Joe, Dun.*	.198	77	228	197	30	39	61	7	0	5	19	2	4	1	24	0	55	1	1	6	.310	.283
Dwyer, Mike, Sar.*	.209	110	411	383	36	80	126	20	4	6	43	1	2	0	25	3	103	2	5	8	.329	.256
Elwood, Brad, Tam.	.189	42	133	122	9	23	25	2	0	0	9	0	1	0	10	0	31	0	0	6	.205	.248
Escalona, Felix, Kis.	.252	42	163	143	19	36	43	5	1	0	8	3	1	6	9	0	21	5	3	3	.301	.321
Espinal, Juan, Sar.	.270	93	397	330	51	89	150	17	1	14	66	0	6	6	55	3	81	3	7	8	.455	.373
Fischer, Mark, Sar.	.300	51	204	180	31	54	96	15	0	9	30	0	2	1	21	1	45	5	2	1	.533	.373
Fleming, Ryan, Dun.*	.304	90	349	309	42	94	126	18	1	4	32	6	5	1	28	1	38	6	8	1	.408	.359
Francia, Juan, Lake.†	.225	11	49	40	3	9	11	2	0	0	2	0	0	2	7	0	9	5	2	0	.275	.340
Franco, Iker, St.P.	.000	1	4	4	0	0	0	0	0	0	0	0	0	0	0	0	2	0	0	0	.000	.000
Franco, Raul, B.C.	.238	85	347	315	25	75	90	13	1	0	29	3	3	4	22	0	29	10	7	4	.286	.294
Freel, Ryan, Dun.	.500	4	18	18	7	9	19	1	0	3	6	0	0	0	0	0	1	0	0	0	1.056	.500
Freeman, Terrence, Lake.†	.263	50	197	167	32	44	53	3	3	0	12	3	0	7	20	0	26	12	5	1	.317	.366
Frese, Nate, Day.	.296	117	507	425	70	126	181	24	5	7	52	8	4	6	64	0	84	10	6	9	.426	.393
Fuentes, Javier, Sar.	.300	4	13	10	2	3	4	1	0	0	3	1	0	0	1	0	1	0	0	0	.400	.364
Fukuhara, Pete, Day.	.229	96	365	323	43	74	105	25	0	2	18	3	3	5	31	1	54	2	9	8	.325	.304
Gallo, Ismael, V.B.*	.340	113	466	424	55	144	182	32	3	0	68	3	5	3	31	0	25	6	2	10	.429	.384
Garcia , Osmani, Char.	.335	44	182	170	26	57	89	12	1	6	34	4	2	1	5	0	14	1	2	3	.524	.354
Garcia, Douglas, Char.*	.257	56	149	140	16	36	48	7	1	1	17	1	0	0	8	0	28	3	3	1	.343	.297
Garcia, Gabe, Kis.	.000	40	1	1	0	0	0	0	0	0	0	0	0	0	0	0	0	0	0	0	.000	.000
Gibbs, Kevin, V.B.†	.500	3	10	8	3	4	7	0	0	1	3	0	0	0	2	0	0	2	1	0	.875	.600
Giron, Alejandro, Cle.	.291	115	481	433	59	126	183	31	7	4	47	3	6	6	33	2	100	16	7	9	.423	.345
Goelz, Jim, V.B.	.244	75	277	242	36	59	70	7	2	0	19	4	4	2	25	1	45	2	4	6	.289	.315
Goetz, Geoff, B.C.*	.000	27	1	0	0	0	0	0	0	0	0	0	0	0	0	0	0	0	0	0	.000	.000
Goldbach, Jeff, Day.	.200	119	469	420	49	84	131	15	1	10	60	0	7	8	31	1	76	6	5	1	.312	.264
Gomez, Rich, Lake.	.277	128	522	455	78	126	190	20	10	8	57	6	3	8	50	1	102	48	8	4	.418	.357
Gonzalez, Alex, B.C.	.118	4	18	17	1	2	2	0	0	0	2	0	0	0	1	0	3	1	0	0	.118	.167
Goodson, Steve, St.P.*	.217	105	398	351	30	76	89	5	4	0	23	5	1	0	41	5	85	5	1	10	.254	.298
Graham, Jess, Sar.*	.167	13	50	42	4	7	11	1	0	1	2	0	1	1	6	0	7	2	1	2	.262	.280
Greene, Claude, Tam.†	.212	78	236	212	22	45	72	7	1	6	19	0	1	9	14	3	53	1	6	4	.340	.288
Greene, Todd, Dun.	.200	5	23	20	2	4	8	1	0	1	4	0	0	1	2	1	4	0	0	0	.400	.304
Guerrero, Pedro, Char.	.189	85	326	275	40	52	66	6	4	0	21	8	1	6	36	0	65	7	5	7	.240	.296
Gutierrez, Ricky, Day.	.400	4	12	10	0	4	5	1	0	0	1	0	0	0	2	0	2	1	0	1	.500	.500
Haas, Danny, Sar.*	.254	118	438	398	44	101	127	12	1	4	39	1	2	7	30	2	63	5	8	5	.319	.316
Hadden, Randy, V.B.	.000	36	1	0	0	0	0	0	0	0	0	0	0	0	0	0	0	0	0	0	.000	.000
Hafner, Travis, Char.*	.346	122	528	436	90	151	253	34	1	22	109	0	7	18	67	2	86	0	4	9	.580	.447
Hall, Noah, Jup.	.287	90	378	310	64	89	110	8	2	3	40	1	2	8	57	1	36	26	11	3	.355	.408
Halloran, Matt, Char.	.143	5	18	14	1	2	4	2	0	0	5	0	1	1	1	0	4	0	0	2	.286	.235
Haltiwanger, Garrick, Dun.	.291	100	396	354	57	103	166	27	3	10	56	0	1	3	37	1	67	18	4	10	.469	.362
Hamilton, Darryl, St.L.*	.333	1	4	3	0	1	1	0	0	0	0	0	0	0	0	0	0	0	0	0	.333	.500
Hargreaves, Brad, Day.	.223	46	115	103	18	23	28	5	0	0	6	2	0	0	8	0	14	0	1	2	.272	.292
Hawthorne, Kyle, F.M.	.234	67	264	235	42	55	81	16	2	2	18	3	0	5	21	0	52	4	2	5	.345	.310
Henson, Drew, Tam.	.333	5	22	21	4	7	12	2	0	1	1	0	0	0	1	0	7	0	1	0	.571	.364
Hernandez, Michel, Tam.	.221	75	270	231	17	51	66	12	0	1	28	4	3	3	29	0	23	3	4	4	.286	.312

Player, Team	Avg.	G	TPA	AB	R	H	TB	2B	3B	HR	RBI	SH	SF	HP	BB	IBB	SO	SB	CS	GDP	Slg.	OBP
Hernandez, Victor, Sar.	.232	30	107	99	12	23	32	4	1	1	7	1	1	0	6	0	30	3	4	2	.323	.274
Herrick, Jason, V.B.*	.211	28	120	109	12	23	39	4	3	2	18	2	1	0	8	1	27	3	2	2	.358	.263
Hill, Bobby, St.L.*	.248	92	320	290	41	72	91	11	1	2	25	11	4	2	12	0	63	11	9	4	.314	.279
Hill, Willy, B.C.*	.315	42	167	143	18	45	56	5	3	0	15	4	1	1	18	0	11	9	4	4	.392	.393
Hlousek, Rob, Lake.	.125	3	9	8	0	1	1	0	0	0	0	1	0	0	0	0	2	0	0	0	.125	.125
Hodge, Kevin, F.M.	.278	130	522	450	60	125	190	29	3	10	56	5	4	5	54	2	91	6	3	12	.422	.359
Hodges, Scott, Jup.*	.306	111	487	422	75	129	205	32	1	14	83	2	11	3	49	6	66	8	2	8	.486	.373
Honeycutt, Heath, B.C.	.259	16	61	54	8	14	19	2	0	1	3	0	0	1	6	1	13	1	0	3	.352	.344
Hudson, Orlando, Dun.†	.285	96	402	358	54	102	143	16	2	7	48	4	1	2	37	1	42	9	5	15	.399	.354
Huffman, Royce, Kis.	.298	129	547	450	82	134	189	32	4	5	55	1	6	6	84	2	49	31	4	12	.420	.410
Illig, Brett, V.B.	.218	74	269	234	34	51	74	9	1	4	26	1	4	4	26	2	73	1	1	6	.316	.302
Infante, Omar, Lake.	.274	79	289	259	35	71	88	11	0	2	24	5	4	1	20	0	29	11	5	4	.340	.324
Jackson, Brandon, Dun.	.313	6	21	16	6	5	7	2	0	0	2	0	1	1	3	0	0	2	0	0	.438	.429
Jaile, Chris, Char.	.250	4	12	8	1	2	2	0	0	0	1	0	0	0	4	0	2	0	0	0	.250	.500
Jaroncyk, Ryan, V.B.†	.333	1	3	3	1	1	1	0	0	0	0	0	0	0	0	0	1	0	1	0	.333	.333
Jeter, Derek, Tam.	.667	1	3	3	2	2	3	1	0	0	0	0	0	0	0	0	0	0	0	0	1.000	.667
Jimenez, D'Angelo, Tam.†	.195	12	50	41	8	8	14	1	1	1	2	0	1	0	8	1	7	0	0	1	.341	.320
Joffrion, Jack, St.P.	.216	67	239	218	14	47	69	13	0	3	22	3	2	4	12	0	64	4	6	3	.317	.267
Johnson, Gary, Day.	.289	124	514	436	75	126	202	21	5	15	65	1	7	15	55	2	74	25	7	11	.463	.382
Johnson, Jason, Cle.	.275	95	387	335	56	92	125	18	3	3	34	4	6	10	32	1	60	22	7	6	.373	.350
Johnson, Reed, Dun.	.316	36	162	133	26	42	67	9	2	4	28	1	3	11	14	0	27	3	2	1	.504	.416
Jones, Aaron, Tam.*	.230	113	425	365	41	84	130	19	0	9	37	2	3	1	54	4	86	3	4	10	.356	.329
Jones, Jeremy, Char.	.290	50	177	155	17	45	66	11	2	2	24	0	1	4	17	1	24	1	1	4	.426	.373
Jordan, Kevin, Kis.	.252	38	144	127	22	32	56	6	3	4	19	0	1	5	11	0	23	2	5	7	.441	.333
Joyce, Jesse, Kis.	.214	56	172	154	17	33	52	14	1	1	16	2	4	0	12	0	25	7	0	3	.338	.265
Kawabata, Kenichiro, Sar.†	.223	44	110	94	11	21	29	2	0	2	6	2	0	2	12	0	30	2	1	1	.309	.324
Kellner, Ryan, V.B.	.262	62	247	221	23	58	80	13	0	3	24	1	4	3	18	1	44	0	4	7	.362	.321
Kelly, Heath, B.C.	.230	50	165	152	17	35	58	8	0	5	25	2	0	2	9	1	54	2	1	3	.382	.282
Kelton, Dave, Day.	.268	132	569	523	75	140	238	30	7	18	84	1	5	2	38	4	120	7	8	9	.455	.317
Kerrigan, Joe, Sar.*	.205	83	320	264	28	54	68	14	0	0	21	1	3	1	51	2	48	4	8	6	.258	.332
Kidd, Scott, Tam.	.282	88	327	301	38	85	130	16	1	9	41	0	2	5	19	0	63	1	2	8	.432	.333
Kiil, Skip, Cle.	.270	40	177	148	25	40	65	13	0	4	25	1	1	4	23	0	46	7	2	1	.439	.381
Knoblauch, Chuck, Tam.	.000	1	2	1	0	0	0	0	0	0	0	0	0	1	0	0	1	0	0	0	.000	.500
Koerner, Mike, V.B.*	.262	21	72	65	7	17	22	2	0	1	5	0	0	2	5	0	13	0	1	2	.338	.333
Kremblas, Mike, Dun.	.281	25	87	64	15	18	22	2	1	0	10	0	1	6	16	0	7	1	0	1	.344	.460
Kropf, Andrew, Lake.	.253	29	94	87	7	22	31	3	0	2	8	0	1	0	6	0	29	0	0	2	.356	.298
LaForest, Pete, St.P.*	.270	129	542	474	85	128	212	28	7	14	70	1	5	6	56	4	108	2	4	4	.447	.351
Langaigne, Selwyn, Dun.*	.600	5	11	10	2	6	7	1	0	0	1	0	0	0	1	1	2	0	0	0	.700	.636
Lawrence, Joe, Dun.	.301	101	452	375	69	113	186	32	1	13	67	0	3	5	69	6	74	21	7	9	.496	.414
Leatherman, Dan, F.M.*	.204	93	295	265	34	54	86	15	1	5	31	6	4	2	18	0	40	2	4	6	.325	.256
LeBron, Juan, St.L.	.200	24	98	90	6	18	26	2	0	2	8	0	1	1	6	0	25	0	0	3	.289	.255
Lentz, Ryan, Jup.*	.368	7	26	19	3	7	11	2	1	0	3	0	0	0	7	2	7	0	0	0	.579	.538
Leon, Carlos, Sar.†	.308	88	352	302	61	93	118	14	4	1	31	4	3	6	37	2	24	12	10	14	.391	.391
Leon, Donny, Tam.	.215	23	87	79	5	17	26	6	0	1	14	0	1	1	6	2	23	0	0	1	.329	.276
Logan, Exavier, Lake.	.333	11	45	42	4	14	15	1	0	0	3	1	0	0	2	0	13	2	1	0	.357	.364
Logan, Kyle, Kis.*	.275	17	68	51	8	14	19	1	2	0	4	0	2	2	13	2	6	7	0	0	.373	.426
Logan, Matt, Dun.*	.279	124	424	373	58	104	159	26	1	9	55	2	6	7	36	0	93	4	1	13	.426	.348
Lopez, Luis, Kis.	.204	74	247	226	33	46	79	10	4	5	25	2	1	3	15	0	67	7	6	3	.350	.261
Lorenzo, Juan, F.M.	.283	119	468	431	57	122	158	25	1	3	44	7	4	6	20	0	33	8	3	10	.367	.321
Lucca, Tony, B.C.*	.237	102	395	329	38	78	105	14	2	3	31	2	2	4	58	6	54	0	0	10	.319	.356
Lugo, Felix, Jup.†	.143	2	7	7	2	1	1	0	0	0	0	0	0	0	0	0	3	0	1	0	.143	.143
Lutz, Manuel, Lake.*	.259	59	219	205	19	53	81	16	0	4	34	0	0	3	11	2	58	1	5	3	.395	.306
Machado, Albenis, Jup.†	.245	128	539	428	79	105	126	10	4	1	39	18	9	5	79	2	67	16	11	6	.294	.363
Machado, Anderson, Cle.†	.245	117	478	417	55	102	138	19	7	1	35	5	2	0	54	0	103	32	18	7	.331	.330
Malloy, Marty, Lake.	.231	7	28	26	4	6	10	1	0	1	4	0	0	1	1	0	1	1	0	0	.385	.286
Mann, Derek, St.P.*	.246	65	228	195	25	48	67	7	3	2	14	8	2	2	21	0	28	5	3	3	.344	.323
Manning, Nate, F.M.	.216	66	265	245	28	53	74	13	1	2	23	0	0	3	17	1	52	0	0	9	.302	.275
Marcinczyk, T.R., F.M.	.188	4	18	16	1	3	3	0	0	0	1	0	1	1	0	0	3	0	0	2	.188	.222
Marciniak, Dave, F.M.	.333	4	15	15	2	5	5	0	0	0	3	0	0	0	0	0	4	0	1	0	.333	.333
Marsters, Brandon, F.M.	.310	118	447	407	46	126	180	25	4	7	77	2	3	4	31	6	61	2	1	9	.442	.362
Martin, Tyler, Char.†	.167	6	24	18	2	3	3	0	0	0	1	2	0	0	4	0	2	0	0	1	.167	.318
Martinez, Ramon, Char.	.289	42	161	152	12	44	56	7	1	1	20	3	1	0	5	0	28	8	3	2	.368	.310
McAffee, Josh, Kis.	.155	26	94	84	10	13	23	1	0	3	15	0	0	5	5	0	33	1	0	2	.274	.245
McCrary, Scott, St.L.	.000	23	1	1	0	0	0	0	0	0	0	0	0	0	0	0	0	0	0	0	.000	.000
McCrotty, Will, V.B.	.215	76	293	256	19	55	74	10	0	3	34	0	3	3	31	0	53	0	2	6	.289	.304
McDonald, Jason, Char.†	.333	5	19	15	4	5	7	2	0	0	1	0	0	0	4	0	5	1	0	0	.467	.474
McMillan, Andrew, Jup.	.136	8	25	22	2	3	3	0	0	0	1	1	0	0	2	0	4	1	0	0	.136	.208
McMillin, Brian, F.M.	.224	86	345	312	42	70	98	15	2	3	28	2	1	1	29	1	67	17	5	4	.314	.292
Meadows, Randy, Jup.	.232	47	151	142	16	33	40	5	1	0	9	3	0	1	4	0	27	2	1	3	.282	.259
Meadows, Tydus, Day.	.311	46	191	167	30	52	85	11	2	6	24	1	2	4	17	0	36	11	4	1	.509	.384
Medrano, Jesus, B.C.	.219	117	532	466	56	102	135	18	3	3	46	3	10	5	48	2	98	32	8	9	.290	.293
Mejias, Erick, Char.†	.000	3	12	12	1	0	0	0	0	0	1	0	0	0	0	0	3	1	0	0	.000	.000
Melconian, Alex, B.C.	.167	3	9	6	2	1	4	0	0	1	5	0	1	0	2	0	0	1	0	0	.667	.333
Meliah, Dave, Char.*	.290	104	434	407	65	118	174	24	7	6	50	3	5	3	16	2	53	2	2	7	.428	.318
Mench, Kevin, Char.	.334	132	583	491	118	164	302	39	9	27	121	0	7	7	78	3	72	19	7	9	.615	.427
Mendoza, Angel, Sar.	.264	76	302	280	35	74	114	19	6	3	23	0	2	1	19	2	62	19	6	10	.407	.311
Meran, Jorge, Lake.	.268	63	234	224	22	60	97	10	3	7	19	0	0	0	10	0	45	2	3	2	.433	.299
Merhoff, Aaron, Cle.	.231	8	31	26	3	6	8	0	1	0	3	0	0	3	2	0	8	1	0	0	.308	.355
Miles, Aaron, Kis.†	.292	75	326	295	40	86	114	20	1	2	36	2	1	0	28	0	29	11	6	7	.386	.352
Minus, Steve, Sar.	.190	46	165	147	14	28	38	5	1	1	17	2	1	1	14	0	51	0	2	1	.259	.264
Mohr, Dustan, F.M.	.265	101	418	370	58	98	154	19	2	11	75	1	4	8	35	1	65	7	4	11	.416	.338
Moreno, Juan, St.L.	.280	68	279	243	42	68	87	7	3	2	31	5	3	1	27	0	38	37	8	1	.358	.350
Murch, Jeremy, St.P.*	.230	26	106	100	11	23	37	8	0	2	9	0	0	0	6	0	25	4	0	1	.370	.274
Myers, Tootie, Jup.	.243	110	504	449	70	109	164	16	9	7	43	9	2	3	41	1	111	26	16	3	.365	.309

Player, Team	Avg.	G	TPA	AB	R	H	TB	2B	3B	HR	RBI	SH	SF	HP	BB	IBB	SO	SB	CS	GDP	Slg.	OBP
Nelson, Reggie, Lake.	.220	52	184	159	17	35	44	5	2	0	14	1	1	4	19	0	29	6	8	2	.277	.317
Newton, Kimani, V.B.	.212	34	124	104	17	22	30	3	1	1	16	0	1	1	18	0	31	3	3	3	.288	.331
Nieves, Jose, Day.	.167	2	7	6	2	1	1	0	0	0	0	0	0	0	1	0	0	0	0	0	.167	.286
Niles, Drew, B.C.†	.234	32	111	94	9	22	26	2	1	0	5	3	1	0	13	0	22	2	1	3	.277	.324
Nina, Amuarys, Char.	.257	102	418	354	52	91	122	10	9	1	39	5	1	10	48	1	86	11	7	11	.345	.361
Norton, Chris, B.C.	.429	2	7	7	1	3	4	1	0	0	1	0	0	0	0	0	2	0	0	0	.571	.429
Nunez, Abraham, B.C.†	.194	31	133	103	17	20	27	4	0	1	9	0	0	2	28	1	34	11	3	3	.262	.376
Nunez, Jorge, V.B.	.288	128	582	534	86	154	199	17	8	4	39	5	2	2	38	0	104	54	22	5	.373	.337
Nunez, Sergio, Cle.	.225	105	433	378	44	85	109	18	3	0	39	8	6	1	40	0	46	23	3	16	.288	.296
Nye, Rodney, St.L.	.272	132	536	464	70	126	174	28	1	6	62	0	4	10	58	4	74	8	8	15	.375	.362
Olivares, Teuris, Tam.	.252	121	515	468	56	118	167	22	3	7	47	3	5	0	39	0	70	20	11	10	.357	.307
Osilka, Garret, Jup.	.226	57	220	186	21	42	53	8	0	1	23	4	0	10	20	0	41	8	5	7	.285	.333
Pascucci, Val, Jup.	.284	113	487	405	70	115	191	30	2	14	66	0	5	11	66	0	98	14	6	9	.472	.394
Pearson, Shawn, Dun.	.600	4	11	10	3	6	7	1	0	0	3	0	0	1	0	0	1	0	0	0	.700	.636
Peguero, Miguel, Lake.	.182	4	11	11	0	2	3	1	0	0	1	0	0	0	0	0	4	0	0	0	.273	.182
Pena, Rodolfo, Sar.	.194	78	245	217	18	42	51	9	0	0	18	4	1	8	15	0	40	3	2	5	.235	.270
Perez, Franklin, Lake.	.000	10	1	1	0	0	0	0	0	0	0	0	0	0	0	0	0	0	0	0	.000	.000
Perez, Jersen, Dun.	.271	126	546	509	69	138	211	35	7	8	64	8	5	4	20	0	106	8	4	11	.415	.301
Perez, Jhonny, Kis.	.353	13	59	51	6	18	19	1	0	0	4	1	0	0	5	0	8	5	2	1	.373	.411
Perez, Josue, Cle.†	.297	70	319	279	41	83	117	9	8	3	32	3	3	6	28	2	48	18	14	2	.419	.370
Perez, Nestor, St.P.	.249	47	208	193	16	48	56	8	0	0	13	6	0	0	9	0	21	3	2	4	.290	.282
Perez, Timoniel, St.L.	.355	8	37	31	3	11	18	4	0	1	8	2	1	1	2	0	1	3	3	0	.581	.400
Pernell, Brandon, Day.	.257	59	235	210	34	54	87	6	3	7	35	1	6	2	16	0	44	20	5	5	.414	.308
Peters, Tony, Dun.	.268	127	541	455	97	122	201	30	2	15	61	4	3	7	71	1	164	23	8	9	.442	.373
Pfister, Billy, Lake.	.375	4	10	8	0	3	3	0	0	0	0	0	0	0	2	0	1	0	0	0	.375	.500
Phelps, Josh, Dun.	.319	30	127	113	26	36	79	7	0	12	34	0	1	1	12	0	34	0	0	2	.699	.386
Phillips, Andy, Tam.	.287	127	534	478	66	137	213	33	2	13	58	0	8	2	46	0	98	2	0	9	.446	.346
Phillips, Jason, St.L.	.276	80	330	297	53	82	121	21	0	6	41	1	1	8	23	2	19	1	1	12	.407	.343
Piedra, Jorge, V.B.-Day.*	.301	126	553	499	83	150	207	22	7	7	69	5	9	5	35	1	72	29	9	6	.415	.347
Pigott, Anthony, St.P.	.267	62	251	243	36	65	85	12	1	2	17	1	0	1	6	0	50	11	5	2	.350	.288
Pimentel, Franklin, Lake.†	.243	46	173	152	18	37	46	7	1	0	12	1	1	1	18	0	39	1	1	2	.303	.326
Pinto, Rene, Tam.	.137	24	79	73	4	10	20	4	0	2	7	0	0	2	4	0	24	0	0	2	.274	.203
Pittman, Tom, Jup.	.243	58	248	226	24	55	70	8	2	1	31	0	5	1	16	1	60	6	5	8	.310	.290
Pohle, Ike, Tam.	.000	1	2	2	0	0	0	0	0	0	0	0	0	0	0	0	1	0	0	0	.000	.000
Pond, Simon, Jup.*	.206	19	73	63	7	13	23	1	0	3	8	0	0	1	9	0	13	1	0	0	.365	.315
Preston, Brian, Jup.	.208	18	58	53	7	11	16	2	0	1	6	0	1	0	4	0	6	0	1	1	.302	.259
Quatraro, Matt, St.P.*	.204	15	51	49	6	10	16	1	1	1	3	0	0	0	2	0	14	0	0	4	.327	.235
Ralph, Brian, Day.-V.B.*	.260	110	436	366	71	95	122	13	4	2	37	5	3	4	58	1	38	31	11	1	.333	.363
Reese, Nate, B.C.	.207	9	31	29	3	6	8	2	0	0	2	0	0	0	2	0	6	0	0	0	.276	.258
Restovich, Mike, F.M.	.263	135	543	475	73	125	194	27	9	8	64	0	3	4	61	1	100	19	7	11	.408	.350
Reyes, Ivan, Tam.	.000	1	3	3	0	0	0	0	0	0	0	0	0	0	0	0	2	0	0	0	.000	.000
Rhodes, Dusty, Tam.*	.192	65	179	146	21	28	45	6	4	1	11	1	1	2	29	1	40	2	6	2	.308	.331
Riepe, Andy, Sar.	.204	41	118	103	11	21	26	2	0	1	9	0	0	2	13	0	21	2	4	2	.252	.305
Rigsby, Randy, B.C.*	.271	71	275	247	40	67	105	16	5	4	29	1	3	1	23	0	41	15	1	3	.425	.332
Rivera, Juan, Tam.	.276	115	453	409	62	113	183	26	1	14	69	0	5	6	33	1	56	11	7	9	.447	.336
Rivera, Mike, Lake.	.292	64	262	243	30	71	131	19	4	11	53	0	2	1	16	3	45	2	0	6	.539	.336
Robertson, Mike, Sar.	.164	17	67	55	7	9	15	1	1	1	5	1	1	2	8	0	10	2	1	2	.273	.288
Rodriguez, John, Tam.*	.268	105	412	362	59	97	163	14	2	16	44	1	0	8	40	5	81	3	2	6	.450	.354
Rodriguez, Luis, Sar.	.237	53	212	190	26	45	72	10	4	3	34	0	2	3	17	2	36	10	4	6	.379	.307
Rodriguez, Mike, Dun.	.274	73	261	223	34	61	77	11	1	1	23	2	4	4	28	2	44	1	3	6	.345	.359
Rodriguez, Ronny, Sar.	.000	1	3	3	0	0	0	0	0	0	0	0	0	0	0	0	2	0	0	0	.000	.000
Rodriguez, Sammy, St.L.	.264	17	66	53	11	14	19	2	0	1	5	0	1	4	8	1	9	0	0	2	.358	.394
Rolls, Damian, St.P.	.188	5	20	16	2	3	5	2	0	0	1	0	1	1	2	0	3	1	0	0	.313	.316
Romano, Jimmie, Char.	.326	45	147	129	15	42	52	5	1	1	12	1	1	1	15	0	24	4	3	2	.403	.397
Roneberg, Brett, B.C.*	.261	125	532	445	51	116	144	18	2	2	45	4	4	1	77	5	60	4	2	13	.324	.368
Rosamond, Mike, Kis.	.206	129	516	446	60	92	168	14	7	16	60	2	6	2	60	3	151	17	13	6	.377	.300
Rowe, Casey, Lake.	.000	11	2	1	0	0	0	0	0	0	0	1	0	0	0	0	1	0	0	0	.000	.000
Ryan, Kelvin, St.P.	.179	34	300	279	26	50	74	11	2	3	27	2	1	4	13	0	56	5	5	8	.265	.229
Sachs, Brent, Day.	.302	82	335	298	44	90	120	19	1	3	42	3	3	5	26	1	56	14	10	5	.403	.364
Salazar, Jeremy, Cle.	.250	45	180	164	18	41	57	11	1	1	25	1	1	1	13	0	37	0	0	6	.348	.307
Salazar, Ruben, F.M.	.311	124	541	499	80	155	213	25	0	11	64	0	3	2	37	1	81	3	5	18	.427	.359
Sandusky, Scott, Jup.	.257	43	155	140	18	36	48	4	1	2	25	4	2	1	8	0	29	0	1	7	.343	.298
Santana, Pedro, Tam.	.225	20	77	71	8	16	22	3	0	1	13	0	1	0	5	1	22	2	1	0	.310	.273
Santoro, Pat, Sar.	.226	17	60	53	3	12	17	3	1	0	5	0	2	0	5	0	9	0	1	0	.321	.283
Santos, Jose, B.C.	.216	129	518	444	55	96	137	16	2	7	54	0	5	14	55	2	125	7	2	14	.309	.319
Sapp, Damian, Sar.	.333	11	46	39	9	13	26	4	0	3	14	0	0	1	6	0	14	0	0	0	.667	.435
Scanlon, Matt, F.M.*	.278	5	21	18	2	5	6	1	0	0	0	0	0	0	3	0	3	1	0	2	.333	.381
Schaeffer, Jon, F.M.	.276	20	93	76	12	21	26	5	0	0	7	0	0	1	16	0	17	2	2	1	.342	.409
Schrager, Tony, Day.	.230	116	444	378	48	87	139	19	3	9	49	3	4	7	56	0	83	7	3	2	.368	.333
Schreimann, Eric, Cle.	.235	40	172	153	19	36	50	8	0	2	21	0	1	6	11	0	29	0	1	5	.327	.310
Seale, Marvin, St.L.†	.353	5	20	17	5	6	10	1	0	1	2	1	0	0	2	0	6	0	1	1	.588	.421
Shipp, Brian, St.L.	.197	42	160	147	17	29	47	4	1	4	25	1	2	4	6	0	42	8	0	0	.320	.245
Shrum, Allen, F.M.	.274	25	82	73	12	20	24	4	0	0	10	0	0	1	8	0	17	0	0	2	.329	.354
Smith, Nestor, F.M.†	.298	106	405	359	53	107	139	21	4	1	41	2	5	5	34	0	72	6	3	6	.387	.362
Smith, Rod, St.P.†	.289	36	164	142	27	41	62	14	2	1	10	1	0	0	21	0	37	18	5	2	.437	.380
Snyder, Earl, St.L.	.282	134	587	514	84	145	256	36	0	25	93	0	8	8	57	6	127	4	4	8	.498	.358
Solano, Fausto, Dun.	.241	50	182	158	20	38	54	8	1	2	22	0	3	3	19	2	27	6	2	4	.342	.330
Soules, Ryan, Tam.*	.247	106	398	336	50	83	143	25	1	11	42	0	4	2	56	1	89	1	0	7	.426	.354
Spear, Russell, Lake.	.000	14	1	1	0	0	0	0	0	0	0	0	0	0	0	0	0	0	0	0	.000	.000
Steele, Alex, Lake.	.217	89	326	286	43	62	96	16	0	6	31	0	1	2	37	0	121	2	1	8	.336	.310
Stewart, Shannon, Dun.	1.000	1	5	3	2	3	4	1	0	0	1	0	0	0	2	1	0	0	1	0	1.333	1.000
Strange, Mike, Dun.	.250	16	47	36	6	9	11	2	0	0	2	0	0	0	11	0	14	0	2	0	.306	.426
Stratton, Rob, St.L.	.228	108	452	381	61	87	200	18	4	29	87	1	2	8	60	3	180	3	5	3	.525	.344
Sulentor, Joe, F.M.	.242	46	143	128	5	31	38	5	1	0	12	2	0	0	12	1	31	1	1	8	.297	.307

Player, Team	Avg.	G	TPA	AB	R	H	TB	2B	3B	HR	RBI	SH	SF	HP	BB	IBB	SO	SB	CS	GDP	Slg.	OBP
Suriel, Miguel, St.P..............	.246	94	368	325	44	80	106	14	0	4	32	5	5	2	31	0	54	3	5	3	.326	.311
Taylor, Seth, Tam...............	.206	110	401	354	37	73	100	9	3	4	32	2	5	5	35	0	53	10	8	11	.282	.283
Terrell, Jeff, Cle.†................	.265	87	363	317	27	84	119	17	3	4	54	3	7	3	33	3	52	7	5	5	.375	.333
Thomas, J.J., Kis...............	.274	112	434	380	58	104	190	27	1	19	58	1	3	12	38	0	139	2	5	6	.500	.356
Thomas, Mark, Jup.*..........	.240	76	260	225	35	54	63	7	1	0	17	4	1	3	27	1	58	11	3	5	.280	.328
Thompson, Andy, St.L.*	.148	38	124	108	5	16	20	4	0	0	8	1	2	3	10	1	18	0	0	3	.185	.236
Thompson, Tyler, Dun.........	.280	103	403	350	51	98	161	26	2	11	57	2	2	4	45	1	93	20	5	5	.460	.367
Tolli, Barry, Lake...............	.100	14	44	40	4	4	7	1	1	0	1	0	0	1	3	0	11	1	1	1	.175	.182
Torres, Andres, Lake.†........	.296	108	477	398	82	118	160	11	11	3	33	10	0	5	63	2	82	65	16	10	.402	.399
Torres, Frederick, Char.........	.236	80	302	275	34	65	92	18	0	3	20	2	2	4	19	0	65	1	1	6	.335	.293
Torres, Gabby, F.M.............	.196	20	54	46	5	9	12	3	0	0	3	0	1	1	6	0	5	0	0	3	.261	.296
Treanor, Matt, B.C.............	.246	109	419	350	51	86	112	17	0	3	37	4	3	14	48	0	65	3	3	6	.320	.357
Turnquist, Tyler, Kis.	.240	74	273	246	25	59	76	15	1	0	29	2	0	3	22	1	34	0	1	8	.309	.310
Valdez, Jerry, Cle...............	.225	59	241	218	24	49	74	14	1	3	21	0	0	4	19	1	41	1	1	4	.339	.299
Van Horn, Ryan, Day.........	.154	15	16	13	1	2	2	0	0	0	1	1	0	1	1	0	2	0	1	0	.154	.267
Van Iten, Robert, Cle.*	.236	108	438	390	52	92	129	22	0	5	33	4	3	4	36	4	80	0	0	7	.331	.305
Vasquez, Alejandro, Kis.*.....	.201	61	226	209	17	42	51	5	2	0	17	0	2	4	11	1	26	8	4	8	.244	.252
Velazquez, Gil, St.L...........	.230	125	481	440	37	101	122	16	1	1	43	4	3	9	25	0	69	3	9	15	.277	.283
Velazquez, Jose, St.P.*	.296	135	551	513	60	152	216	30	2	10	79	0	5	4	29	5	48	2	2	16	.421	.336
Vento, Mike, Tam.............	.167	10	37	30	1	5	8	0	0	1	4	1	1	1	4	0	12	1	0	0	.267	.278
Villalobos, Carlos, Lake.......	.235	25	97	85	10	20	27	4	0	1	7	0	1	0	11	1	15	0	0	3	.318	.320
Volquez, Bolivar, St.P.	.152	12	37	33	2	5	7	2	0	0	4	0	0	0	4	0	9	0	1	3	.212	.243
Wakakuwa, Kenn, St.P.........	.286	2	7	7	0	2	2	0	0	0	0	0	0	0	0	0	2	0	0	0	.286	.286
Waldron, Jeff, Sar.*	.158	19	45	38	4	6	7	1	0	0	4	0	1	0	6	0	9	0	0	3	.184	.267
Walker, Ron, Day..................	.288	30	129	111	19	32	51	7	0	4	23	0	1	1	16	1	17	0	4	1	.459	.380
Warriax, Brandon, Char.........	.207	84	326	304	33	63	90	13	1	4	39	1	1	0	20	0	74	8	7	7	.296	.253
Wathan, Derek, B.C.†..........	.258	91	418	364	53	94	142	18	6	6	49	5	2	2	45	4	54	19	11	6	.390	.341
Watson, Matt, Jup.*	.175	40	156	137	10	24	33	5	2	0	8	0	0	1	18	2	23	4	3	6	.241	.276
Weekly, Chris, Dun.*............	.250	34	139	120	23	30	52	7	0	5	22	1	1	3	14	0	30	0	2	0	.433	.341
Wesson, Barry, Kis.............	.273	81	348	308	50	84	126	21	3	5	35	4	1	2	33	0	66	24	5	2	.409	.346
Wiese, Brian, Sar..................	.279	50	193	165	28	46	76	7	1	7	22	1	3	4	20	0	49	8	4	4	.461	.365
Williams, Glenn, Dun.	.261	107	436	391	53	102	175	26	4	13	77	0	6	6	33	1	91	4	2	11	.448	.323
Wren, Cliff, V.B..................	.247	98	382	356	45	88	123	11	3	6	40	3	3	4	16	0	55	4	0	13	.346	.285
Wright, Corey, Char.*..........	.254	99	464	370	76	94	121	17	5	0	24	3	2	10	79	4	81	31	11	6	.327	.397
Zech, Scott, Jup.................	.000	2	5	3	1	0	0	0	0	0	0	0	0	0	2	0	0	0	0	0	.000	.400

GRAND SLAMS: Choi, Snyder, 2 each; Carter, Chiaffredo, Duncan, Fischer, Hodges, Jordan, Manning, Melconian, Mench, Minus, Mohr, Moraga, A Nunez, J. Nunez, Nye, Peters, A. Phillips, J. Rivera, J. Rodriguez, Sachs, Sandusky, Sapp, Schrager, Shipp, Stratton, Warriax, Wesson, 1 each.

AWARDED FIRST BASE ON CATCHER'S INTERFERENCE: Hodge 4 (Lawrence 2, McCrotty 2); Goldbach 3 (Carreno, LaForest, Suriel); Goldbach 2 (Goldbach 2); Aguila (Pena); Auterson (G. Torres); Beinbrink (M. Rivera); Bennett (Treanor); Bly (Suriel); Cepicky (Pena); Choi (Suriel); Dorman (Pena); Escalona (LaForest); Fuentes (Kellner); Halloran (Kremblas); Haltiwanger (LaForest); B. Hill (Chapman); R. Meadows (A. Thompson); J. Nunez (Bennett); J. Rodriguez (LaForest); Roneberg (Chapman); Ryan (Kellner); Schreimann (LaForest); Sulentor (LaForest); An. Torres (Suriel); Van Iten (Sapp).

PLAYERS WITH TWO OR MORE TEAMS

Player, Team	Avg.	G	TPA	AB	R	H	TB	2B	3B	HR	RBI	SH	SF	HP	BB	IBB	SO	SB	CS	GDP	Slg.	OBP
Piedra, Jorge, V.B.*	.283	92	404	360	59	102	143	11	6	6	52	3	7	5	29	1	57	21	5	6	.397	.339
Piedra, Jorge, Day.*............	.345	34	149	139	24	48	64	11	1	1	17	2	2	0	6	0	15	8	4	0	.460	.367
Ralph, Brian, Day.*	.228	77	281	246	39	56	76	11	3	1	23	3	2	2	28	1	22	18	9	0	.309	.309
Ralph, Brian, V.B.*	.325	33	155	120	32	39	46	2	1	1	14	2	1	2	30	0	16	13	2	1	.383	.464

2000 PITCHING

TEAM

Team	W	L	Pct.	ERA	G	CG	ShO	Sv.	IP	H	TBF	R	ER	HR	SH	SF	HB	BB	IBB	SO	WP	Bk.
Fort Myers........	83	57	.593	3.21	140	5	11	43	1221.0	1118	5177	536	436	59	30	32	63	462	27	1037	84	7
Tampa	70	70	.500	3.41	140	11	14	37	1193.2	1121	5065	548	452	43	36	30	42	441	28	1023	61	10
St. Lucie...........	81	58	.583	3.57	139	4	14	37	1226.0	1198	5275	613	486	74	37	45	73	475	16	921	60	18
Dunedin............	84	54	.609	3.59	138	3	10	47	1205.2	1089	5192	595	481	87	31	44	62	573	26	887	92	10
Daytona...........	76	63	.547	3.73	139	6	7	37	1233.0	1172	5332	615	511	84	46	33	46	532	24	1045	90	15
Clearwater........	64	71	.474	3.75	135	9	6	36	1167.2	1227	5062	594	486	61	33	33	49	428	8	750	55	12
Brevard County .	66	74	.471	3.81	140	4	11	34	1227.1	1174	5263	645	519	91	39	38	78	455	22	972	51	10
Kissimmee	73	66	.525	3.84	139	6	9	36	1195.2	1200	5161	605	510	71	35	33	59	415	21	1026	62	10
Charlotte..........	78	61	.561	4.01	139	11	7	36	1210.0	1212	5198	639	539	80	39	40	75	430	9	946	77	11
Lakeland...........	52	88	.371	4.16	140	8	3	31	1194.2	1180	5308	708	552	87	23	63	74	581	16	847	85	11
St. Petersburg	58	81	.417	4.23	139	10	10	24	1176.0	1182	5122	676	553	69	28	51	64	446	12	840	86	7
Sarasota...........	60	79	.432	4.38	139	6	7	27	1198.0	1296	5277	684	570	85	48	47	77	390	30	977	46	7
Jupiter..............	61	79	.436	4.38	140	4	5	27	1227.0	1305	5358	722	597	82	43	55	69	403	14	784	44	3
Vero Beach.......	66	71	.482	4.73	137	6	4	39	1182.0	1306	5282	752	621	125	29	63	73	487	11	822	69	11

INDIVIDUAL

TOP QUALIFIERS FOR EARNED-RUN AVERAGE TITLE

Minimum 112 innings. *Lefthanded pitcher.

Pitcher, Team	W	L	Pct.	ERA	G	GS	CG	ShO	GF	Sv.	IP	H	TBF	R	ER	HR	SH	SF	HB	BB	IBB	SO	WP	Bk.
Reith, Brian, Tam.	9	4	.692	2.18	18	18	1	1	0	0	119.2	101	487	39	29	4	2	3	5	33	0	100	6	1
Jodie, Brett, Tam.	11	4	.733	2.57	25	18	3	1	2	0	143.2	134	582	53	41	5	3	3	29	5	122	5	1
Redding, Tim, Kis.	12	5	.706	2.68	24	24	0	0	0	0	154.2	125	649	62	46	5	4	6	9	57	1	170	13	0
Walker, Adam, Cle.*.............	9	8	.529	3.08	18	17	1	0	0	0	114.0	116	486	50	39	6	3	6	4	39	1	87	7	1
Maness, Nick, St.L.	11	7	.611	3.22	26	25	0	0	1	0	145.1	116	602	58	52	14	5	4	5	68	1	124	3	5
Smyth, Steve, Day.*	8	8	.500	3.25	24	23	1	0	0	0	138.1	134	589	62	50	9	0	2	5	57	0	100	9	1

Pitcher, Team	W	L	Pct.	ERA	G	GS	CG	ShO	GF	Sv.	IP	H	TBF	R	ER	HR	SH	SF	HB	BB	IBB	SO	WP	Bk.
Vargas, Claudio, B.C.	10	5	.667	3.28	24	23	0	0	0	0	145.1	126	596	64	53	10	4	2	7	44	3	143	3	0
Harang, Aaron, Char.	13	5	.722	3.32	28	27	3	2	0	0	157.0	128	642	68	58	10	1	3	7	50	0	136	5	1
Lampley, Dan, Sar.	6	7	.462	3.35	27	16	2	0	5	2	121.0	133	527	59	45	8	2	4	6	36	2	107	7	0
Cook, Andy, St.L.	10	4	.714	3.36	28	16	1	1	7	4	126.0	123	537	51	47	7	3	4	11	37	1	94	7	0
Leek, Randy, Lake.*	3	6	.333	3.41	20	20	2	0	0	0	126.2	122	520	60	48	9	1	6	5	25	1	97	3	0
Anderson, Wes, B.C.	6	9	.400	3.42	22	21	0	0	0	0	115.2	108	517	55	44	5	2	4	4	66	1	91	5	1
Fossum, Casey, Sar.*	9	10	.474	3.44	27	27	3	3	0	0	149.1	147	623	71	57	7	2	6	7	36	0	143	3	0
Fleming, Emar, Char.	6	6	.500	3.49	42	8	1	1	18	4	118.2	121	509	53	46	8	5	6	6	39	1	93	4	1
Flohr, Adam, St.P.*	6	11	.353	3.53	27	27	2	1	0	0	173.1	173	729	88	68	7	5	2	9	51	0	134	10	0

DEPARTMENTAL LEADERS: W—Harang, 13; L—C. Silva, 13; Pct.—Strange, .909; G—Waligora, 55; GS—Graman, Saenz, Wuertz, 28 each; CG—C. Silva, 4; ShO—Fossum, 3; GF—Belovsky, 43; Sv.—Kingrey, Bell, 23 each; IP—C. Silva, 176.1; H—C. Silva, 229; TBF—Silva, 778; R—Williams, 110; ER—Williams, 92; HR—M. Castillo, 18; SH—Sams, 9; SF—Saenz, 10; HB—Kalita, 16; BB—Saenz, 83; IBB—Krug, 9; SO—Redding, 170; WP—Casey, 21; BK—Palma, Kegley, Maness, 5 each.

ALL PITCHERS

*Lefthanded pitcher.

Pitcher, Team	W	L	Pct.	ERA	G	GS	CG	ShO	GF	Sv.	IP	H	TBF	R	ER	HR	SH	SF	HB	BB	IBB	SO	WP	Bk.
Agosto, Stevenson, St.P.*	0	1	.000	5.40	13	0	0	0	1	0	16.2	22	90	17	10	0	0	2	1	16	0	18	2	0
Akin, Aaron, B.C.	3	8	.273	4.26	17	16	0	0	0	0	82.1	91	368	56	39	5	2	1	6	33	0	51	4	0
Albin, Scott, Jup.	4	3	.571	2.96	49	0	0	0	25	2	67.0	66	290	31	22	2	7	3	2	23	3	51	1	0
Almonte, Hector, B.C.	1	1	.500	2.35	8	2	0	0	3	0	15.1	11	61	6	4	2	1	0	2	5	0	16	1	0
Alvarez, Victor, V.B.*	1	1	.500	5.16	4	4	0	0	0	0	22.2	17	94	14	13	6	0	0	0	11	0	20	1	0
Alvarez, Wilson, St.P.*	0	0	.000	0.00	1	1	0	0	0	0	4.0	0	12	0	0	0	0	0	0	0	0	2	0	0
Anderson, Wes, B.C.	6	9	.400	3.42	22	21	0	0	0	0	115.2	108	517	55	44	5	2	4	4	66	1	91	5	1
Arias, Pablo, Lake.	2	1	.667	5.86	5	5	0	0	0	0	27.2	26	120	21	18	2	0	5	3	13	0	21	1	1
Armas, Tony, Jup.	0	0	.000	0.00	1	1	0	0	0	0	4.2	4	18	0	0	0	0	0	0	8	0	9	0	0
Armstrong, Jack, B.C.	1	1	.500	6.35	4	4	0	0	0	0	17.0	15	70	14	12	3	1	0	3	6	0	13	0	0
Ascencio, Miguel, Cle.	2	1	.667	2.73	5	5	0	0	0	0	33.0	22	132	10	10	2	0	0	0	17	0	24	1	1
Avery, Paul, V.B.*	2	5	.286	7.11	22	10	0	0	8	0	63.1	92	313	67	50	9	0	5	2	31	1	34	7	1
Baisley, Brad, Cle.	3	9	.250	3.74	16	15	2	0	1	1	89.0	95	391	47	37	9	0	2	3	34	0	60	4	0
Baker, Chris, Dun.	9	5	.643	3.20	41	6	0	0	10	5	104.0	91	440	50	37	11	2	1	5	29	2	85	9	1
Balfour, Grant, F.M.	8	5	.615	4.25	35	10	0	0	13	6	89.0	91	392	46	42	8	3	1	8	34	2	90	10	1
Batchelor, Rich, Tam.	0	2	.000	5.87	8	0	0	0	8	2	7.2	10	40	6	5	0	1	0	0	6	3	7	1	0
Becker, Tom, Lake.	1	0	1.000	1.50	2	0	0	0	1	1	6.0	3	22	1	1	0	1	0	0	2	0	7	1	0
Becks, Ryan, Jup.*	5	10	.333	5.06	30	17	0	0	5	0	110.1	139	507	74	62	4	3	6	11	42	0	45	2	0
Bell, Heath, St.L.	5	1	.833	2.55	48	0	0	0	37	23	60.0	43	241	19	17	4	2	2	2	21	2	75	1	0
Belovsky, Josh, Sar.	3	8	.273	4.12	51	0	0	0	43	14	63.1	83	305	36	29	5	5	1	2	31	6	72	5	1
Bess, Steve, Lake.	1	3	.250	5.50	26	0	0	0	11	5	36.0	40	178	26	22	2	2	2	1	27	2	23	6	0
Blevins, Jeremy, Tam.	3	7	.300	4.44	42	12	0	0	26	20	95.1	96	417	50	47	5	2	3	2	49	2	104	6	1
Bohannon, Gary, St.L.	6	4	.600	2.58	39	3	0	0	14	2	90.2	81	375	38	26	5	3	3	7	24	2	63	0	0
Bond, Aaron, Char.	0	0	.000	6.14	3	1	0	0	0	0	7.1	13	38	6	5	0	0	0	0	5	0	4	1	0
Booker, Chris, Day.	0	2	.000	2.28	31	0	0	0	24	10	27.2	25	122	12	7	0	2	0	1	14	1	34	2	0
Borkowski, Dave, Lake.	0	1	.000	8.59	2	2	0	0	0	0	7.1	11	35	7	7	1	0	0	0	4	0	5	0	0
Boyd, Jason, Cle.	1	0	1.000	2.38	6	3	0	0	1	0	11.1	11	50	4	3	0	0	0	2	4	0	12	0	1
Brantley, Jeff, Cle.	2	0	1.000	3.00	5	1	0	0	0	0	6.0	5	24	2	2	0	0	0	0	3	0	5	1	0
Bridges, Donnie, Jup.	5	5	.500	3.19	11	11	0	0	0	0	73.1	58	296	29	26	0	1	4	1	20	0	66	2	0
Bruback, Matt, Day.	5	5	.500	4.85	18	18	0	0	0	0	89.0	101	404	57	48	6	5	4	6	50	1	69	12	0
Buller, Sean, Lake.*	5	2	.714	1.99	29	1	0	0	13	1	49.2	45	212	19	11	3	0	1	0	18	1	29	3	0
Burke, Erick, Lake.*	0	1	.000	5.09	12	0	0	0	3	0	17.2	20	91	17	10	2	0	2	4	15	1	13	3	0
Burnett, A.J., B.C.	0	0	.000	3.68	2	2	0	0	0	0	7.1	4	31	3	3	0	0	0	0	6	0	6	0	2
Campos, David, B.C.*	0	0	.000	4.50	2	0	0	0	1	0	6.0	7	29	3	3	0	0	1	1	4	0	4	2	0
Cannon, Jon, Day.*	0	0	.000	0.00	7	1	0	0	3	1	16.1	7	62	0	0	0	0	0	0	7	0	11	1	0
Carnes, Matt, F.M.	0	2	.000	2.65	19	9	0	0	1	0	54.1	54	228	20	16	1	1	3	1	19	3	48	4	0
Casey, Joe, Dun.	10	8	.556	4.21	27	27	0	0	0	0	158.1	151	677	88	74	7	1	5	14	74	2	96	21	1
Cassidy, Scott, Dun.	9	3	.750	1.33	14	13	1	0	1	0	88.0	53	342	15	13	4	3	2	3	34	2	89	4	0
Castellanos, Hugo, Dun.	0	0	.000	4.50	4	0	0	0	4	1	8.0	5	37	4	4	1	1	1	0	10	1	5	0	0
Castelli, Rob, Jup.	0	0	.000	13.50	11	0	0	0	5	0	11.1	15	66	19	17	2	0	0	3	15	0	8	6	0
Castillo, Jose, Lake.	0	0	.000	0.00	1	0	0	0	0	0	1.0	1	5	0	0	0	0	0	0	1	1	1	0	0
Castillo, Marcos, V.B.	7	9	.438	3.89	25	22	2	2	2	0	141.0	150	614	77	61	18	3	6	12	34	1	91	10	0
Castro, Eleuterio, Sar.	0	1	.000	8.76	7	0	0	0	3	0	12.1	18	65	17	12	3	1	0	1	8	1	9	0	0
Chacin, Gustavo, Dun.*	9	5	.643	4.02	25	21	0	0	1	0	127.2	138	584	69	57	14	1	2	3	64	0	77	9	0
Chiavacci, Ron, Dun.	11	11	.500	3.65	28	26	1	0	2	0	158.0	145	674	80	64	12	4	7	7	59	0	131	7	0
Cho, Jin Ho, Sar.	1	1	.500	2.40	3	3	0	0	0	0	15.0	13	60	5	4	1	0	0	0	0	0	15	0	0
Christensen, Ben, Day.	4	2	.667	2.10	10	10	1	0	0	0	64.1	43	253	18	15	6	0	0	3	15	0	63	2	0
Cisar, Mark, Sar.	0	0	.000	2.76	10	0	0	0	4	0	16.1	15	70	8	5	1	0	0	1	4	1	14	0	0
Clackum, Scott, B.C.	6	3	.667	2.59	33	0	0	0	12	1	59.0	53	234	20	17	2	6	1	1	12	2	39	1	0
Claussen, Brandon, Tam.*	2	5	.286	3.10	9	9	1	0	2	0	52.1	49	220	24	18	1	1	0	2	17	0	44	2	1
Coggin, Dave, Cle.	2	2	.500	2.67	6	5	0	0	0	0	33.2	25	131	11	10	1	1	1	0	13	0	26	0	0
Collins, Pat, Jup.	0	1	.000	6.55	2	2	0	0	0	0	11.0	10	47	9	8	1	0	1	0	6	0	3	0	0
Colyer, Steve, V.B.*	5	7	.417	5.76	26	18	1	0	2	0	95.1	97	442	74	61	9	2	7	7	68	0	80	6	0
Comer, Scott, B.C.*	0	1	.000	5.06	3	3	0	0	0	0	16.0	24	73	13	9	2	1	1	1	14	0	10	0	0
Cook, Andy, St.L.	10	4	.714	3.36	28	16	1	1	7	4	126.0	123	537	51	47	7	3	4	11	37	1	94	2	1
Cornejo, Jesse, St.P.*	0	2	.000	4.60	10	0	0	0	4	0	15.2	13	67	8	8	1	3	2	0	12	2	14	0	0
Cornejo, Nate, Lake.	5	5	.500	3.04	12	12	1	0	0	0	77.0	67	322	37	26	5	0	1	4	31	0	60	2	1
Cosgrove, Mike, Kis.	1	1	.500	5.06	8	0	0	0	4	0	10.2	13	49	9	6	3	0	0	1	3	0	4	1	0
Cotton, Joe, Cle.	0	1	.000	3.94	9	0	0	0	4	0	16.0	16	65	7	7	1	1	0	2	0	0	14	0	0
Crumpton, Chuck, Jup.	0	0	.000	5.89	16	0	0	0	13	7	18.1	20	82	13	12	1	0	2	0	6	1	12	0	0
Cruz, Juan, Day.	3	0	1.000	3.25	8	7	1	0	0	0	44.1	30	182	22	16	5	0	0	3	18	0	54	4	0
Cuello, Manolin, Lake.	0	1	.000	6.00	2	1	0	0	0	0	6.0	6	31	7	4	0	1	0	0	8	0	1	0	0
Curtice, John, Sar.*	4	10	.286	6.49	25	23	0	0	1	0	112.1	114	526	87	81	5	6	8	12	68	0	83	7	1
Dagley, Corey, Cle.	0	1	.000	8.10	3	3	0	0	0	0	13.1	17	62	13	12	1	1	1	1	8	0	8	0	0
Dant, Larry, Day.	0	0	.000	13.06	8	0	0	0	2	0	10.1	18	56	15	15	0	0	2	1	8	1	3	0	0
Darrell, Tommy, Sar.	4	4	.500	4.10	44	3	0	0	21	5	96.2	98	422	53	44	8	3	4	9	34	6	71	2	0

Pitcher, Team	W	L	Pct.	ERA	G	GS	CG	ShO	GF	Sv.	IP	H	TBF	R	ER	HR	SH	SF	HB	BB	IBB	SO	WP	Bk.
Day, Zach, Tam.	2	4	.333	4.19	7	7	0	0	0	0	34.1	33	150	22	16	2	0	0	1	15	1	36	1	0
Dean, Aaron, Dun.	1	0	1.000	6.46	3	3	0	0	0	0	15.1	22	77	15	11	1	0	1	1	7	0	13	3	0
Della Ratta, Pete, St.L.	0	0	.000	0.00	2	0	0	0	0	0	1.1	2	7	0	0	0	0	0	0	0	0	2	0	0
DePriest, Derrick, Jup.	1	0	1.000	2.25	4	0	0	0	4	3	4.0	3	14	1	1	0	0	0	0	0	0	4	1	0
Detillion, Jamie, Lake.*	0	0	.000	10.80	4	0	0	0	2	0	5.0	7	23	6	6	2	0	0	0	2	0	2	1	0
Dimma, Doug, Dun.*	6	3	.667	3.84	43	0	0	0	17	1	79.2	74	361	46	34	6	1	3	9	48	4	42	7	0
Dobis, Jason, F.M.	3	4	.429	3.24	37	3	1	0	13	4	77.2	74	321	34	28	2	3	3	1	29	1	39	6	0
Dorame, Randey, V.B.*	7	1	.875	2.21	9	9	2	0	0	0	57.0	50	226	15	14	3	3	2	2	13	0	49	2	0
Dorman, John, St.L.	0	0	.000	45.00	1	0	0	0	1	0	1.0	3	8	5	5	1	0	0	1	1	0	0	0	0
Dunn, Keith, Tam.	4	4	.500	2.31	24	1	0	0	9	0	58.1	45	240	16	15	2	1	0	1	26	2	31	0	2
Duprey, Pete, Day.*	0	0	.000	0.00	1	0	0	0	0	0	1.2	2	8	0	0	0	0	0	0	1	0	1	0	0
Eichhorn, Mark, Dun.	0	0	.000	0.00	5	0	0	0	4	0	5.1	3	20	0	0	0	1	0	0	0	0	8	1	0
Everly, Bill, V.B.	1	5	.167	3.36	39	0	0	0	29	12	61.2	57	260	23	23	2	2	4	8	24	2	20	2	0
Eversgerd, Randy, Sar.	2	0	1.000	2.49	8	2	0	0	2	1	21.2	23	91	7	6	1	0	3	0	4	0	19	0	0
Farizo, Brad, B.C.	1	2	.333	6.58	7	2	0	0	1	1	26.0	35	121	24	19	2	0	0	2	8	1	10	2	1
Feliciano, Pedro, V.B.*	4	5	.444	3.82	25	2	0	0	7	0	61.1	76	289	31	26	4	4	4	5	24	1	48	3	0
Figueroa, Carlos, Char.*	6	3	.667	5.74	33	1	0	0	7	1	58.0	53	270	41	37	0	2	1	5	44	1	51	6	1
Fisher, Peter, F.M.	8	3	.727	3.15	14	14	2	0	0	0	88.2	75	370	34	31	9	3	0	7	37	0	67	2	0
Fleming, Emar, Char.	6	6	.500	3.49	42	8	1	1	18	4	118.2	121	509	53	46	8	5	6	6	39	1	93	4	1
Flohr, Adam, St.P.*	6	11	.353	3.53	27	27	2	1	0	0	173.1	173	729	88	68	7	5	2	9	51	0	134	10	0
Florie, Bryce, Sar.	0	0	.000	0.00	1	1	0	0	0	0	3.0	3	13	1	0	0	0	0	0	1	0	2	0	0
Fossum, Casey, Sar.*	9	10	.474	3.44	27	27	3	3	0	0	149.1	147	623	71	57	7	2	6	7	36	0	143	3	0
Frederick, Kevin, F.M.	2	1	.667	2.70	19	0	0	0	7	3	30.0	20	123	11	9	0	1	1	1	14	1	37	4	2
Frey, Chris, Char.	5	2	.714	2.63	30	0	0	0	21	7	51.1	43	218	21	15	2	1	1	2	14	0	40	2	0
Gagliano, Steve, Day.	1	1	.500	2.77	16	3	0	0	3	3	39.0	29	161	14	12	4	1	0	4	10	0	40	7	1
Garcia, Gabe, Kis.	2	3	.400	5.59	40	4	0	0	12	1	77.1	90	358	54	48	6	8	2	10	34	1	62	4	0
Garcia, Rosman, Tam.	0	2	.000	5.50	4	3	0	0	1	1	18.0	18	77	13	11	1	0	3	2	4	0	6	0	1
Garibaldi, Cecilio, St.P.	5	7	.417	3.68	25	17	2	0	2	0	110.0	101	465	59	45	9	1	7	10	36	2	73	6	0
Garrett, Josh, Sar.	2	6	.250	6.83	16	8	0	0	1	0	54.0	68	248	46	41	9	4	1	8	9	2	36	1	1
Geigel, Rolando, B.C.	2	0	1.000	3.60	5	0	0	0	1	0	10.0	9	43	5	4	1	1	0	0	4	1	5	2	0
German, Yon, St.L.*	4	4	.500	2.67	14	12	0	0	0	0	70.2	76	297	33	21	5	2	1	1	14	0	33	1	0
Giese, Daniel, Sar.	1	0	1.000	3.14	8	0	0	0	2	0	14.1	19	64	8	5	2	0	1	0	2	0	13	0	0
Glick, Dave, Kis.*	0	0	.000	4.50	3	0	0	0	2	0	4.0	4	17	2	2	0	0	0	0	1	0	4	1	0
Goetz, Geoff, B.C.*	6	2	.750	1.75	27	0	0	0	15	5	67.0	43	270	19	13	1	3	1	0	36	1	61	6	0
Grace, Bryan, Tam.	0	1	.000	9.00	5	0	0	0	2	0	6.0	10	32	6	6	0	0	0	0	6	0	1	1	0
Graman, Alex, Tam.*	8	9	.471	3.65	28	28	3	1	0	0	143.0	120	598	64	58	6	5	2	3	58	1	111	9	1
Gulin, Lindsay, Day.*	11	2	.846	2.46	19	17	0	0	1	0	109.2	93	447	34	30	8	5	1	3	43	0	97	5	3
Guzman, Ambiorix, Char.	1	4	.200	4.13	31	2	0	0	16	3	56.2	65	234	29	26	5	1	2	2	6	2	35	1	0
Guzman, Juan, St.P.	1	0	1.000	0.00	1	1	0	0	0	0	5.0	4	21	0	0	0	0	0	0	2	0	6	0	0
Hadden, Randy, V.B.	9	3	.750	4.42	36	5	0	0	11	1	95.2	113	426	52	47	12	3	6	6	29	2	52	4	2
Hafer, Jeff, St.L.	1	1	.500	3.86	11	0	0	0	9	1	16.1	14	69	8	7	0	1	0	1	4	0	12	0	0
Haines, Talley, St.P.	2	1	.667	2.78	16	0	0	0	10	3	22.2	22	94	10	7	1	0	0	0	2	1	22	0	0
Hamann, Robert, Dun.	2	1	.667	1.50	16	0	0	0	13	5	24.0	16	91	5	4	2	1	1	0	7	3	14	2	1
Hamulack, Tim, Kis.*	3	1	.750	4.98	41	0	0	0	20	1	56.0	67	251	37	31	3	2	1	1	21	1	54	0	0
Hancock, Josh, Sar.	5	10	.333	4.45	26	24	1	0	0	0	143.2	164	628	89	71	9	5	6	6	37	0	95	8	2
Harang, Aaron, Char.	13	5	.722	3.32	28	27	3	2	0	0	157.0	128	642	68	58	10	1	3	7	50	0	136	5	1
Harber, Ryan, B.C.*	5	4	.556	4.82	22	11	1	0	5	0	89.2	95	389	53	48	8	2	3	0	34	0	54	4	0
Hargreaves, Brad, Day.	0	0	.000	13.50	2	0	0	0	1	0	2.0	3	10	3	3	1	0	0	0	1	0	0	0	0
Harrell, Tim, V.B.	7	7	.500	5.00	30	18	1	1	5	2	117.0	121	508	77	65	9	1	7	3	44	1	89	8	1
Heath, Woody, Dun.	0	2	.000	6.30	8	1	0	0	3	1	20.0	27	97	17	14	1	0	2	1	16	0	11	4	0
Hendrickson, Mark, Dun.*	2	2	.500	5.61	12	12	1	0	0	0	51.1	63	235	34	32	7	1	5	0	29	0	38	1	0
Hernandez, Adrian, Tam.	1	0	1.000	1.35	1	1	0	0	0	0	6.2	3	24	1	1	0	0	0	0	1	0	13	1	0
Hernandez, Orlando, Tam.	0	0	.000	0.00	1	0	0	0	0	0	4.0	1	14	0	0	0	0	0	0	1	0	5	0	0
Hiles, Cary, Cle.	8	3	.727	3.16	46	0	0	0	41	20	62.2	76	280	27	22	0	5	1	3	22	2	41	3	1
Hill, Terrance, Sar.*	4	0	1.000	2.98	34	0	0	0	13	2	60.1	50	246	20	20	3	2	2	5	18	3	54	1	0
Hoard, Brent, F.M.*	5	9	.357	4.30	19	18	0	0	1	0	92.0	98	412	57	44	6	3	2	3	44	2	55	8	0
Howard, Tom, F.M.*	2	2	.500	4.12	27	2	0	0	3	2	59.0	65	268	32	27	2	1	3	2	21	0	52	3	0
Hubbel, Travis, Dun.	0	0	.000	3.38	3	0	0	0	1	0	5.1	4	20	2	2	2	1	0	0	2	0	3	1	0
Hughes, Travis, Char.	9	9	.500	4.42	39	14	1	0	19	9	126.1	122	553	76	62	9	6	1	12	54	3	96	11	0
Irabu, Hideki, Jup.	1	0	1.000	1.04	2	2	0	0	0	0	8.2	7	34	1	1	1	0	0	0	1	0	9	0	0
James, Delvin, St.P.	7	9	.438	4.26	22	22	3	1	0	0	137.1	142	576	74	65	10	2	2	7	27	2	74	5	0
Jensen, Justin, Sar.*	1	1	.500	6.75	12	1	0	0	5	1	16.0	24	79	12	12	2	1	1	0	5	0	15	0	0
Jodie, Brett, Tam.	11	4	.733	2.57	25	18	3	1	2	0	143.2	134	582	53	41	4	5	3	3	29	5	122	5	1
Johnson, Adam, F.M.	5	4	.556	2.47	13	12	1	1	0	0	69.1	45	267	21	19	2	0	2	3	20	1	92	2	1
Johnson, Craig, Lake.	3	6	.333	4.19	19	14	1	1	2	0	86.0	85	357	51	40	9	0	3	5	16	0	60	4	1
Johnston, Dave, B.C.	0	2	.000	7.30	5	1	0	0	3	0	12.1	18	62	13	10	3	2	0	3	6	1	7	1	0
Julio, Jorge, Jup.	2	10	.167	5.90	21	15	0	0	3	1	79.1	93	363	60	52	4	1	5	4	35	0	67	1	3
Kalita, Tim, Lake.*	7	12	.368	4.57	27	25	1	0	0	0	149.2	146	672	93	76	7	3	4	16	73	0	107	11	0
Kegley, Charles, Dun.	3	9	.250	3.88	23	23	0	0	0	0	111.1	96	490	60	48	6	4	4	8	74	1	66	11	5
Kershner, Jason, Cle.*	1	0	1.000	0.64	2	2	0	0	0	0	14.0	7	52	1	1	1	0	0	0	5	0	15	0	0
Kessel, Kyle, Kis.*	4	5	.444	3.36	12	12	0	0	0	0	75.0	74	315	37	28	3	3	0	2	24	1	56	1	0
Kingrey, Jarrod, Dun.	4	2	.667	2.97	37	0	0	0	34	23	39.1	33	177	20	13	2	2	2	3	23	1	35	5	1
Kirsten, Rick, Lake.	5	4	.556	3.30	14	13	2	0	0	0	87.1	80	364	42	32	8	4	4	11	23	0	45	3	1
Klepacki, Ed, Jup.	2	2	.500	4.53	11	11	0	0	0	0	55.2	75	253	37	28	1	2	4	0	14	0	28	1	0
Kofler, Ed, St.P.	9	10	.474	5.28	28	26	1	0	1	0	148.1	180	658	98	87	11	3	9	8	46	0	98	11	2
Kosderka, Matt, Char.	1	3	.250	5.12	12	5	0	0	1	0	38.2	49	170	28	22	3	1	0	3	10	0	27	0	0
Koutrouba, Tom, Lake.*	2	7	.222	3.20	40	1	0	0	20	3	70.1	67	299	31	25	4	1	2	2	22	2	49	4	0
Krug, Dustin, Day.	5	7	.417	3.52	52	1	0	0	16	0	79.1	82	353	39	31	6	1	3	4	37	9	64	7	1
Kubes, Greg, Cle.*	5	9	.357	4.56	24	24	0	0	0	0	136.1	158	612	81	69	6	5	5	5	64	1	70	4	0
LaChapelle, Yan, Dun.	5	1	.833	2.60	18	7	0	0	3	0	55.1	42	234	22	16	4	2	2	2	27	1	49	2	0
Lajara, Eudy, B.C.*	0	2	.000	8.10	6	0	0	0	2	0	10.0	12	48	11	9	2	0	0	0	8	0	6	0	0
Lampley, Dan, Sar.	6	7	.462	3.35	27	16	2	0	5	2	121.0	133	527	59	45	8	2	4	6	36	2	107	7	0
Lara, Nelson, B.C.	0	0	.000	9.28	7	0	0	0	1	0	10.2	12	57	11	11	0	1	1	4	10	0	6	2	0

Pitcher, Team	W	L	Pct.	ERA	G	GS	CG	ShO	GF	Sv.	IP	H	TBF	R	ER	HR	SH	SF	HB	BB	IBB	SO	WP	Bk.
Leek, Randy, Lake.*	3	6	.333	3.41	20	20	2	0	0	0	126.2	122	520	60	48	9	1	6	5	25	1	97	3	0
Levan, Matt, B.C.*	0	1	.000	8.31	4	0	0	0	3	2	8.2	10	40	8	8	1	0	0	0	5	0	12	0	0
Lewis, Colby, Char.	11	10	.524	4.07	28	27	3	1	0	0	163.2	169	692	83	74	11	4	7	10	45	0	153	11	2
Lewis, Craig, Tam.	0	0	.000	13.50	1	0	0	0	0	0	2.0	3	10	3	3	0	0	1	0	1	0	1	0	0
Lidge, Brad, Kis.	2	1	.667	2.81	8	8	0	0	0	0	41.2	28	164	14	13	3	1	0	1	15	0	46	1	2
Lilly, Ted, Tam.*	0	0	.000	1.35	1	1	0	0	0	0	6.2	5	28	3	1	0	0	1	0	1	0	6	1	0
Lira, Jim, St.P.	2	4	.333	2.24	42	0	0	0	22	2	52.1	47	214	15	13	2	1	2	1	15	0	39	2	0
Lockwood, Luke, Jup.*	0	1	.000	10.93	3	3	0	0	0	0	14.0	24	65	17	17	3	0	0	1	5	0	2	0	0
Lohrman, Dave, St.L.	1	6	.143	4.86	43	0	0	0	19	3	63.0	75	310	40	34	1	2	3	5	42	2	70	12	0
Lombardi, Justin, B.C.*	0	2	.000	15.00	3	1	0	0	0	0	6.0	13	37	12	10	2	0	1	1	6	0	1	0	1
Lopez, Gustavo, B.C.	0	0	.000	0.00	2	0	0	0	2	0	4.0	1	14	2	0	1	0	0	0	0	0	5	0	0
Loux, Shane, Lake.	0	1	.000	1.80	1	1	0	0	0	0	5.0	2	19	1	1	0	1	0	0	3	0	6	0	0
Lowe, Benny, Lake.*	0	2	.000	2.37	20	0	0	0	19	11	19.0	11	78	6	5	1	1	0	0	10	0	17	0	0
Lutz, Manuel, Lake.	0	0	.000	18.00	1	0	0	0	1	0	1.0	3	6	2	2	0	0	1	0	0	0	0	0	0
Lyons, Jon, Sar.	4	3	.571	4.92	33	0	0	0	11	0	53.0	64	232	31	29	5	3	3	19	3	30	2	0
Maldonado, Esteban, Kis.	3	12	.200	5.33	36	14	0	0	11	2	106.1	123	487	76	63	9	2	2	5	46	3	70	16	1
Malko, Bryan, F.M.	2	1	.667	2.67	19	0	0	0	13	2	27.0	16	106	10	8	0	0	1	1	12	1	26	0	0
Maness, Nick, St.L.	11	7	.611	3.22	26	25	0	0	1	0	145.1	116	602	58	52	14	5	4	5	68	1	124	3	5
Mangum, Mark, Jup.	6	8	.429	4.11	20	19	1	0	1	0	114.0	109	487	62	52	11	4	5	12	30	0	55	4	0
Marin, Willy, V.B.	0	0	.000	27.00	1	0	0	0	0	0	1.0	5	10	6	3	0	0	0	0	1	0	1	0	0
Marrero, Darwin, Jup.	0	1	.000	13.50	1	0	0	0	0	0	1.1	4	10	5	2	1	0	0	0	2	0	2	0	0
Marriott, Mike, B.C.	0	0	.000	7.71	2	1	0	0	0	0	2.1	4	14	3	2	0	1	1	0	3	0	0	0	0
Mastrolonardo, Dave, Char.	1	0	1.000	5.11	8	0	0	0	1	0	12.1	16	65	8	7	1	0	1	1	12	0	11	0	0
McClaskey, Tim, B.C.	7	4	.636	2.25	46	0	0	0	38	13	84.0	72	333	26	21	6	2	2	5	18	4	97	2	1
McCrary, Scott, St.L.	2	3	.400	4.05	23	0	0	0	10	2	40.0	39	172	20	18	3	3	1	0	12	1	34	1	0
McCurtain, Paul, B.C.	0	0	.000	3.00	3	0	0	0	0	0	6.0	6	24	2	2	0	0	0	0	2	1	8	1	0
McDonald, Jonathan, F.M.	3	3	.500	3.99	10	10	0	0	0	0	49.2	42	207	24	22	1	1	1	6	16	0	33	3	1
McGowan, Brian, St.P.	0	2	.000	5.56	11	3	0	0	1	0	22.2	23	106	19	14	0	0	1	1	17	1	13	8	1
Meadows, Randy, Jup.	0	0	.000	0.00	1	0	0	0	1	0	1.0	1	4	0	0	0	0	0	0	0	0	1	0	0
Medina, Carlos, St.L.*	1	2	.333	3.38	11	1	0	0	2	0	21.1	22	87	10	8	0	1	1	9	0	16	0	2
Melendez, Dave, Lake.	0	4	.000	9.13	7	4	0	0	1	0	22.2	37	125	30	23	2	0	3	3	17	0	13	2	0
Mendoza, Ramiro, Tam.	0	2	.000	7.20	2	2	0	0	0	0	5.0	9	22	4	4	0	0	0	0	0	0	7	0	0
Meyer, Dave, V.B.	1	0	1.000	1.00	11	0	0	0	7	0	18.0	12	69	2	2	1	2	0	1	5	0	12	0	0
Miceli, Danny, B.C.	1	0	1.000	3.00	5	4	0	0	0	0	6.0	3	21	2	2	1	0	0	0	0	0	7	0	0
Miller, Greg, Kis.*	10	8	.556	3.70	24	24	1	0	0	0	146.0	131	604	63	60	13	4	5	2	46	1	109	5	2
Montero, Agustin, V.B.	0	0	.000	6.00	3	0	0	0	1	0	3.0	2	17	2	2	0	0	0	0	6	0	4	2	0
Montero, Francisco, Cle.	2	1	.667	4.38	26	2	0	0	17	1	61.2	72	267	32	30	4	1	1	1	15	1	39	2	3
Moore, Chris, B.C.	0	1	1.000	12.71	4	0	0	0	1	1	5.2	7	31	9	8	1	1	1	1	6	1	2	3	0
Moreno, Juan, Char.*	0	0	.000	0.00	1	1	0	0	0	0	2.0	0	7	0	0	0	0	0	1	0	0	1	0	0
Moskau, Ryan, B.C.*	2	5	.286	6.49	10	9	1	0	0	0	52.2	74	245	40	38	6	0	2	2	15	0	43	1	0
Mota, Danny, F.M.	2	2	.500	2.05	29	1	0	0	13	4	48.1	38	209	20	11	0	1	3	1	23	5	52	5	0
Munro, Peter, Dun.	0	1	.000	5.56	3	3	0	0	0	0	11.1	11	47	7	7	0	0	0	4	0	12	1	0
Murphy, Matt, Day.*	0	7	.000	4.65	47	2	0	0	19	5	60.0	65	279	38	31	2	4	3	0	41	5	46	3	0
Nakamura, Mike, F.M.	1	0	1.000	1.52	32	0	0	0	19	12	41.1	33	162	9	7	0	2	1	2	11	1	46	2	0
Nannini, Mike, Kis.	7	3	.700	3.33	12	12	2	1	0	0	78.1	83	329	34	29	3	0	0	14	0	56	0	0
Navarro, Scott, Kis.*	2	2	.500	3.24	4	3	1	0	1	0	25.0	23	106	12	9	1	0	2	1	6	0	20	1	0
Neal, Blaine, B.C.	2	2	.500	2.15	41	0	0	0	34	11	54.1	40	231	27	13	1	1	2	4	24	3	65	1	0
Niedermaier, Brad, Tam.	1	0	1.000	5.14	5	0	0	0	0	0	7.0	11	36	5	4	1	1	1	2	1	5	0	0
Noel, Todd, Tam.	0	0	.000	10.80	4	4	0	0	0	0	10.0	18	55	13	12	2	0	0	0	8	0	11	3	0
Norton, Jason, Sar.	7	7	.500	3.86	40	5	0	0	12	1	91.0	102	405	53	39	6	4	2	3	29	3	89	4	2
Noyce, Dave, B.C.-Day.*	7	5	.583	3.67	21	20	1	1	0	0	105.1	100	469	59	43	12	3	4	12	44	0	69	4	1
Nunez, Franklin, Cle.	10	4	.714	3.62	23	14	1	0	6	2	112.0	112	492	54	45	4	1	3	7	57	0	81	9	1
Olsen, Kevin, B.C.	4	8	.333	2.86	18	18	1	0	0	0	110.0	93	436	40	35	2	2	4	6	25	2	77	4	0
Ortega, Carlos, V.B.*	4	2	.667	4.55	14	10	0	0	2	0	61.1	70	279	39	31	9	0	4	4	29	0	53	1	2
Oswalt, Roy, Kis.	4	3	.571	2.98	8	8	0	0	0	0	45.1	52	191	15	15	1	1	1	1	11	0	47	0	1
Pageler, Mick, B.C.	0	1	.000	6.43	4	0	0	0	2	0	7.0	10	33	5	5	0	1	0	1	3	0	4	0	0
Painter, Lance, Dun.*	0	0	.000	0.00	1	1	0	0	0	0	1.0	0	3	0	0	0	0	0	0	0	0	1	0	0
Palki, Jeromy, F.M.	6	3	.667	3.21	42	0	0	0	16	3	73.0	72	314	32	26	6	0	2	3	30	1	75	4	0
Palma, Rick, Day.*	4	8	.333	4.70	20	19	0	0	1	1	99.2	109	446	61	52	9	5	5	0	44	0	72	9	5
Partenheimer, Brian, B.C.*	2	5	.286	3.77	34	3	0	0	12	0	86.0	79	376	44	36	12	2	6	12	26	1	49	2	2
Penny, Brad, B.C.	0	1	1.000	1.13	2	2	0	0	0	0	8.0	5	33	2	1	0	0	0	4	0	11	0	1
Perez, Franklin, Lake.	2	3	.400	3.78	10	8	0	0	0	0	50.0	54	231	34	21	4	0	6	1	34	1	25	2	0
Perez, Julio, Jup.	0	1	.000	3.38	7	0	0	0	4	1	13.1	13	58	6	5	0	0	1	2	5	1	7	0	0
Person, Robert, Cle.	0	0	.000	6.75	1	0	0	0	0	0	2.2	3	12	2	2	0	0	0	1	0	2	0	0
Pichardo, Hipolito, Sar.	1	1	.500	1.38	7	2	0	0	2	0	13.0	9	51	3	2	1	0	0	2	0	12	0	0
Pineda, Isauro, Sar.	1	1	.500	3.57	7	6	0	0	0	0	22.2	25	105	12	9	3	0	1	0	14	0	17	2	0
Pineda, Luis, Lake.	1	3	.250	3.38	18	0	0	0	13	4	26.2	23	122	13	10	3	2	1	1	19	0	42	4	1
Place, Eric, Dun.*	5	2	.714	4.24	24	1	0	0	11	0	46.2	47	220	27	22	3	5	5	2	33	3	32	1	0
Pool, Matt, V.B.	2	1	.667	3.57	8	2	0	0	3	0	22.2	28	98	9	9	2	0	1	7	0	12	1	0
Porter, Scott, Dun.	1	2	.333	2.67	24	0	0	0	12	4	33.2	20	135	14	10	2	1	0	3	15	3	41	2	0
Pratt, Andy, Char.*	7	4	.636	2.72	16	16	2	1	0	0	92.2	68	365	37	28	8	1	2	1	26	0	95	1	2
Proctor, Scott, V.B.	3	7	.300	5.16	35	5	0	0	15	1	89.0	93	413	65	51	13	2	4	6	54	1	70	6	1
Prokop, Mike, St.L.	3	2	.600	4.03	38	0	0	0	21	1	51.1	63	236	31	23	3	1	3	24	5	33	2	0
Pruett, Jason, St.P.*	2	1	.667	0.84	18	0	0	0	8	2	10.2	11	45	2	1	0	3	0	3	0	7	1	0
Puffer, Brandon, Kis.	2	3	.400	1.27	18	0	0	0	18	9	21.1	18	95	6	3	0	0	1	11	4	26	3	0
Pumphrey, Ken, F.M.	4	4	.500	4.02	14	13	1	0	0	0	83.1	68	343	32	28	7	1	6	35	0	58	3	0
Quarnstrom, Rob, Char.*	2	0	1.000	3.10	10	0	0	0	4	1	20.1	30	96	12	7	0	1	2	4	0	11	1	0
Queen, Mike, St.L.*	3	5	.375	3.41	33	1	0	0	11	1	68.2	74	304	39	26	6	4	4	3	24	1	34	5	3
Quezada, Ed, Jup.	2	2	.500	3.91	17	0	0	0	5	1	25.1	24	110	17	11	4	1	3	8	1	7	2	0
Ramos, Fernando, Cle.	0	1	.000	4.33	27	1	0	0	15	1	54.0	53	240	31	26	6	0	2	7	0	37	2	1
Rangel, Julio, Tam.	7	1	.875	2.84	12	10	0	0	1	0	63.1	59	266	24	20	1	2	0	3	26	0	67	1	1
Redding, Tim, Kis.	12	5	.706	2.68	24	24	0	0	0	0	154.2	125	649	62	46	5	4	6	9	57	1	170	13	0
Regalado, Maximo, V.B.	0	0	.000	0.88	30	0	0	0	29	21	30.2	15	114	4	3	0	0	1	8	1	45	2	0

Pitcher, Team	W	L	Pct.	ERA	G	GS	CG	ShO	GF	Sv.	IP	H	TBF	R	ER	HR	SH	SF	HB	BB	IBB	SO	WP	Bk.
Regilio, Nick, Char.	4	3	.571	4.52	20	20	0	0	0	0	85.2	94	369	54	43	8	3	1	7	29	0	63	10	2
Reith, Brian, Tam.	9	4	.692	2.18	18	18	1	1	0	0	119.2	101	487	39	29	4	2	3	5	33	0	100	6	1
Reitsma, Chris, Sar.	3	4	.429	3.66	11	11	0	0	0	0	64.0	57	267	29	26	3	4	1	5	17	0	47	0	0
Rincon, Juan, F.M.	5	3	.625	2.12	13	13	0	0	0	0	76.1	67	309	26	18	3	1	0	4	23	2	55	10	0
Rivera, Saul, F.M.	8	1	.889	3.58	29	0	0	0	22	5	37.2	34	166	15	15	0	2	0	0	19	3	45	6	1
Roach, Jason, St.L.	5	3	.625	2.59	9	9	0	0	0	0	48.2	42	191	15	14	2	1	2	0	12	0	22	1	0
Robertson, Jeriome, Kis.*	2	1	.667	4.66	5	5	1	1	0	0	29.0	28	121	19	15	1	1	0	2	5	0	13	0	1
Robinson, Jeremy, St.P.*	3	3	.500	4.37	37	0	0	0	16	0	57.2	60	265	38	28	1	3	5	4	28	0	28	3	0
Rodney, Thomas, Lake.	0	0	.000	1.59	1	1	0	0	0	0	5.2	4	23	1	1	0	0	0	0	4	0	3	2	2
Rodriguez, Wilfredo, Kis.*	3	5	.375	4.75	9	9	1	0	0	0	53.0	43	234	29	28	5	1	4	6	30	0	52	4	1
Rojas, Mel, Sar.	0	1	.000	7.71	5	4	0	0	0	0	7.0	10	30	6	6	1	0	0	0	2	0	5	1	0
Roller, Adam, Tam.	1	4	.200	4.21	19	0	0	0	14	1	25.2	29	118	17	12	1	1	3	3	9	0	26	5	0
Romero, J.C., F.M.*	0	0	.000	1.93	2	0	0	0	0	0	4.2	4	20	1	1	0	0	0	1	1	0	3	0	0
Root, Derek, St.L.*	0	0	.000	3.68	5	0	0	0	2	0	7.1	10	33	3	3	0	0	0	1	2	0	9	1	0
Rosado, Juan, Lake.*	2	2	.500	4.73	21	0	0	0	12	0	26.2	26	129	16	14	0	1	2	2	23	1	17	3	1
Rowe, Casey, Lake.	1	7	.125	5.75	11	11	0	0	0	0	51.2	57	250	46	33	7	1	6	1	37	0	37	5	0
Ruebel, Matt, Jup.*	0	0	.000	0.90	4	0	0	0	1	0	10.0	7	34	1	1	0	1	0	0	0	0	10	1	0
Ruhl, Nathan, St.P.	4	6	.400	5.82	40	5	1	0	22	7	72.2	82	346	58	47	5	1	5	3	41	1	53	9	1
Saberhagen, Bret, Sar.	0	1	.000	27.00	1	1	0	0	0	0	1.0	5	8	3	3	0	0	0	0	0	0	2	0	0
Sachs, Brent, Day.	0	0	.000	0.00	1	0	0	0	0	0	1.0	0	3	0	0	0	0	0	0	0	0	1	0	0
Saenz, Jason, St.L.*	6	9	.400	4.40	28	28	0	0	0	0	153.1	165	684	98	75	7	4	10	8	83	0	107	14	4
Salyers, Jeremy, Jup.	3	4	.429	5.49	14	6	0	0	3	0	41.0	55	201	35	25	0	2	3	1	23	0	22	1	0
Sams, Aaron, Day.*	2	4	.333	5.46	35	2	0	0	13	1	57.2	69	284	49	35	3	9	3	3	40	4	56	8	1
Santos, Alex, St.P.	3	9	.250	4.69	17	16	0	0	0	0	88.1	86	387	54	46	6	0	2	6	34	0	69	5	3
Santos, Victor, Lake.	1	0	1.000	0.00	1	1	0	0	0	0	5.0	5	20	0	0	0	0	0	1	0	0	4	0	0
Saunders, Tony, St.P.*	0	0	.000	3.86	2	2	0	0	0	0	7.0	7	30	4	3	1	0	1	0	3	0	3	1	0
Schilling, Curt, Cle.*	1	0	1.000	1.31	4	4	0	0	0	0	20.2	10	76	3	3	0	0	0	1	2	0	23	1	0
Schoening, Brent, F.M.	6	4	.600	3.21	12	12	0	0	0	0	70.0	61	295	27	25	3	2	4	4	27	2	57	4	0
Schourek, Pete, Sar.*	0	0	.000	2.08	1	1	0	0	0	0	4.1	2	15	1	1	0	0	0	0	0	0	5	0	0
Scott, Darryl, Cle.	0	1	.000	1.29	4	0	0	0	3	0	7.0	4	29	1	1	0	0	0	1	4	1	5	3	0
Scuglik, Mike, Char.*	0	0	.000	0.00	1	0	0	0	1	0	0.2	2	4	0	0	0	0	0	0	0	0	0	0	0
Seale, Dustin, Jup.*	0	0	.000	2.28	23	0	0	0	12	0	27.2	23	118	11	7	3	0	2	3	14	0	14	0	0
Seberino, Ronni, St.P.*	6	0	1.000	2.75	33	1	0	0	13	4	39.1	30	166	17	12	0	0	4	0	20	1	33	2	0
Serrano, Willy, Lake.	3	3	.500	3.10	26	0	0	0	11	2	40.2	31	190	22	14	4	3	3	1	38	4	27	5	1
Severino, Jose, Lake.	3	3	.500	4.06	7	5	1	0	0	0	31.0	28	134	19	14	3	1	0	4	14	0	19	2	1
Sheldon, Kyle, Jup.	5	0	1.000	4.44	40	1	0	0	13	2	77.0	87	337	48	38	8	2	4	4	15	1	46	2	0
Sierra, Jr., Auvin, Lake.*	0	0	.000	0.00	2	0	0	0	1	0	4.0	2	16	0	0	0	0	0	0	3	0	5	0	0
Silva, Carlos, Cle.	8	13	.381	3.57	26	24	4	0	0	0	176.1	229	778	99	70	7	6	5	11	26	1	82	4	2
Silva, Doug, Char.	5	5	.500	4.54	45	0	0	0	28	10	67.1	74	299	37	34	7	4	3	1	24	1	55	5	0
Simon, Ben, V.B.	1	0	1.000	3.80	4	4	0	0	0	0	23.2	23	97	12	10	4	1	1	3	5	0	16	0	1
Sismondo, Bobby, Cle.*	5	7	.417	4.00	32	6	0	0	11	1	87.2	85	375	49	39	7	2	2	3	35	0	62	5	1
Smith, Clint, Lake.	4	11	.267	5.76	37	13	0	0	14	0	104.2	131	486	76	67	9	1	4	6	50	2	76	10	1
Smith, Taylor, Dun.	0	1	.000	3.52	13	0	0	0	5	0	23.0	21	101	19	9	1	1	1	0	10	1	20	2	0
Smuin, Shane, B.C.	0	0	.000	0.00	1	0	0	0	0	0	3.0	3	13	0	0	0	0	0	0	6	0	0	0	0
Smyth, Steve, Day.*	8	8	.500	3.25	24	23	1	0	0	0	138.1	134	589	62	50	9	2	5	5	57	0	100	9	1
Sparks, Jeff, St.P.	1	4	.200	3.21	13	1	0	0	6	3	28.0	9	121	13	10	0	2	1	7	26	0	33	3	0
Spear, Russell, Lake.	1	0	1.000	1.66	13	2	0	0	6	0	34.2	24	156	11	10	0	2	2	2	35	0	21	6	0
Spille, Ryan, Dun.*	10	6	.625	4.27	20	19	1	0	0	0	109.2	107	451	55	52	9	2	4	5	35	1	82	4	0
Spurling, Chris, Tam.	4	6	.400	3.79	34	0	0	0	15	1	57.0	50	239	27	24	1	2	3	1	22	5	55	3	0
Stafford, Mike, Tam.*	4	0	1.000	3.88	44	0	0	0	12	2	46.1	51	197	21	20	3	3	1	1	8	0	38	2	0
Standridge, Jason, St.P.	2	4	.333	3.38	10	10	1	0	0	0	56.0	45	243	28	21	4	0	1	1	31	0	41	6	0
Stewart, John, Char.*	1	1	.500	6.93	11	1	0	0	4	1	24.2	35	114	23	19	3	1	4	5	9	0	8	2	0
Strange, Pat, St.L.	10	1	.909	3.58	19	13	2	0	1	0	88.0	78	374	48	35	4	2	5	9	32	0	77	9	1
Surridge, Lance, Sar.	2	3	.400	4.85	20	1	0	0	11	1	42.2	50	197	27	23	2	6	3	7	16	3	22	3	0
Tetz, Kris, Jup.	1	3	.250	3.91	25	0	0	0	18	9	25.1	30	124	13	11	0	4	0	1	18	3	19	1	0
Thomas, Brad, F.M.*	6	2	.750	1.66	12	12	0	0	0	0	65.0	62	279	33	12	3	1	0	3	16	0	57	3	0
Thomas, Joe, F.M.*	7	2	.778	4.48	22	11	0	0	5	1	66.1	77	294	35	33	9	4	1	5	16	1	34	2	1
Thompson, Justin, Char.*	0	0	.000	2.08	1	1	0	0	0	0	4.1	3	17	1	1	0	0	0	0	3	0	2	0	0
Thurman, Mike, Jup.	1	1	.500	2.08	3	3	0	0	0	0	13.0	14	50	3	3	1	0	0	0	6	0	8	0	0
Torres, Alex, Lake.*	0	0	.000	0.00	1	0	0	0	1	0	0.2	0	4	0	0	0	0	0	0	2	0	0	0	0
Torres, Leo, Day.*	4	5	.444	3.43	46	0	0	0	18	5	76.0	72	316	35	29	1	3	3	2	24	1	64	2	1
Tranchina, Scott, Day.	2	0	1.000	1.77	15	0	0	0	13	5	20.1	14	86	5	4	0	0	0	2	9	0	21	3	0
Tremblay, Max, Kis.*	0	0	.000	4.22	13	0	0	0	1	0	21.1	20	95	13	10	1	0	1	1	11	0	23	2	0
Ugas, Juan, V.B.	2	2	.500	6.32	7	0	0	0	3	1	15.2	21	69	13	11	3	0	1	0	2	0	14	0	0
Urdaneta, Lino, V.B.	5	4	.556	5.42	27	5	0	0	7	1	78.0	103	351	60	47	7	2	5	3	24	1	40	6	0
Vael, Rob, Jup.	2	1	.667	4.84	26	0	0	0	8	1	44.2	51	195	27	24	3	2	1	6	11	1	25	7	0
Valdes, Ismael, Day.	1	0	1.000	1.80	1	1	0	0	0	0	5.0	3	20	2	1	0	0	0	0	3	0	5	0	0
Valera, Nelson, St.P.	0	0	.000	9.00	1	0	0	0	1	0	1.0	2	6	1	1	0	0	0	1	0	1	2	0
Vargas, Claudio, B.C.	10	5	.667	3.28	24	23	0	0	0	0	145.1	126	596	64	53	10	4	2	7	44	3	143	3	0
Vega, Rene, St.L.*	11	6	.647	4.40	27	26	1	0	0	0	147.1	150	648	88	72	12	3	4	14	62	1	97	8	2
Victoria, Lester, F.M.*	0	2	.000	7.36	17	0	0	0	9	1	18.1	22	92	17	15	3	0	1	1	15	1	16	3	0
Vigeland, Will, Char.	1	2	.333	6.00	23	0	0	0	8	0	39.0	44	176	26	26	2	4	3	3	16	1	26	3	0
Villalon, Julio, St.P.	0	2	.000	8.33	6	6	0	0	0	0	31.1	48	153	30	29	2	1	3	11	0	20	2	0
Wade, Travis, Kis.	4	1	.800	0.74	38	0	0	0	33	18	48.2	36	187	9	4	2	1	0	1	10	2	51	1	1
Waldron, Brad, Jup.	3	5	.375	4.90	44	0	0	0	12	0	79.0	89	338	47	43	8	4	3	2	19	3	50	1	0
Waligora, Tom, Day.	10	4	.714	5.26	55	0	0	0	18	5	78.2	78	345	51	46	8	5	3	6	29	1	61	7	0
Walker, Adam, Cle.*	9	8	.529	3.08	18	17	1	0	0	0	114.0	116	486	50	39	6	3	6	4	39	1	87	7	1
Wallace, Chris, Tam.	2	4	.333	4.50	39	0	0	0	22	7	48.0	55	217	28	24	3	3	0	1	24	4	32	4	0
Walling, Dave, Tam.	7	2	.778	1.99	9	9	2	0	0	0	58.2	48	237	17	13	1	1	2	4	12	0	45	2	0
Wambach, Trevor, Jup.	7	7	.500	3.85	19	18	2	0	1	0	112.1	113	471	54	48	10	4	0	6	21	0	62	3	0
Watson, Allen, Tam.*	0	0	.000	0.00	1	1	0	0	0	0	2.0	0	6	0	0	0	0	0	0	1	0	1	0	0
Wayne, Justin, Jup.	0	3	.000	5.81	5	5	0	0	0	0	26.1	26	112	22	17	2	1	1	0	11	0	24	1	0
Webb, Alan, Char.*	5	4	.556	3.24	16	15	1	1	0	0	83.1	83	360	36	30	3	4	3	9	39	0	40	14	2

Pitcher, Team	W	L	Pct.	ERA	G	GS	CG	ShO	GF	Sv.	IP	H	TBF	R	ER	HR	SH	SF	HB	BB	IBB	SO	WP	Bk.
Webb, John, Day.	1	1	.500	4.76	4	2	0	0	1	1	17.0	17	71	11	9	1	0	0	0	3	0	18	2	0
Weber, Brett, Tam.	0	1	.000	5.87	14	0	0	0	5	2	15.1	15	64	10	10	0	0	1	0	6	2	19	1	0
Wedel, Jeremy, Cle.	5	4	.556	2.13	39	0	0	0	23	9	71.2	43	283	19	17	1	7	2	3	30	1	45	4	0
Westmoreland, Ken, Cle.	0	6	.000	8.26	12	8	1	0	4	1	44.2	68	225	51	41	5	0	2	4	20	0	12	5	0
Whiteley, Shad, Tam.	2	0	1.000	2.05	33	1	0	0	11	5	57.0	42	245	21	13	1	4	1	3	30	2	62	3	0
Whitesides, Johnny, Kis.	2	3	.400	5.18	21	3	0	0	7	1	41.2	43	181	25	24	4	1	1	4	13	1	27	4	1
Whitney, Jacob, Kis.*	9	7	.563	4.24	40	11	0	0	6	3	104.0	135	464	55	49	7	2	6	1	29	5	93	4	1
Wiggins, Scott, Tam.*	2	8	.200	4.11	28	15	1	1	1	0	100.2	106	444	61	46	4	2	3	5	46	0	68	4	1
Wilkerson, Byron, Kis.	1	2	.333	4.31	30	2	0	0	18	0	56.1	64	264	34	27	1	1	2	10	28	1	43	1	0
Williams, Adam, V.B.*	5	12	.294	6.68	27	23	0	0	0	0	124.0	161	593	110	92	14	4	7	9	68	0	72	8	3
Wilson, Paul, St.L.	2	0	1.000	1.40	5	5	0	0	0	0	25.2	22	100	9	4	0	0	1	1	4	0	19	0	0
Wood, Kerry, Day.	2	0	1.000	1.50	2	2	0	0	0	0	12.0	3	42	2	2	0	0	0	0	5	0	17	0	1
Woodards, Orlando, Dun.	8	1	.889	2.27	41	1	0	0	16	7	87.1	65	353	26	22	4	1	3	3	32	1	69	2	0
Wright, Barrett, St.P.	0	0	.000	6.75	3	0	0	0	2	0	4.0	5	19	3	3	0	0	0	1	2	0	3	0	0
Wright, Chris, St.P.	5	5	.500	4.38	46	1	0	0	20	3	72.0	70	306	40	35	7	3	2	2	24	2	56	8	0
Wuertz, Mike, Day.	12	7	.632	3.78	28	28	3	2	0	0	171.1	166	732	79	72	15	6	4	3	64	1	142	7	1
Yount, Andy, Lake.	0	0	.000	8.03	8	0	0	0	1	0	12.1	16	68	13	11	0	4	2	4	15	0	14	1	0

COMBINATION SHUTOUTS: **Brevard County (10)**—Olsen-Goetz, Anderson-Clackum-Neal, Vargas-Goetz, Anderson-Levan, Noyce-Farizo, Vargas-McClaskey, Vargas-Goetz, Olsen-Neal, Akin-Neal, Vargas-Almonte. **Charlotte (1)**—Webb-Silva. **Clearwater (6)**—Baisley-Boyd, Coggin-Wedel, Ascencio-Wedel, Nunez-Wedel-Hiles, Boyd-Walker-Hiles, Silva-Nunez. **Dunedin (10)**—Cassidy-Porter-Kingrey, Cassidy-Baker-Porter, Kegley-Woodards-Porter-Kingrey, Cassidy-Porter-Kingrey, Cassidy-Woodards, Kegley-Chacin-Dimma-Baker-Kingrey, Chacin-LaChapelle, Casey-Hamann, Casey-Dimma, LaChapelle-Chacin-Castellanos. **Fort Myers (10)**—Rincon-Carnes-Palki-Malko, Thomas-Rivera-Howard, Hoard-Palki-Mota, Thomas-Rivera, Fisher-Nakamura, Schoening-Nakamura, Johnson-Palki-Nakamura, Fisher-Balfour, Johnson-Balfour, Johnson-Balfour. **Jupiter (5)**—Chiavacci-Albin-Crumpton, Bridges-Seale, Mangum-Vael-Albin, Mangum-Tetz, Wamback-Albin-DePriest. **Kissimmee (7)**—Kessel-Wade, Redding-Hamulack-Wade, Miller-Maldonado-Wade, Kessel-Wade, Redding-Wade, Whitney-Navarro, Garcia-Whitesides-Tremblay-Puffer. **Lakeland (2)**—Kalita-Smith-Buller-Serrano-Rosado, Santo-Bess-Lowe. **St. Lucie (13)**—Saenz-Cook, German-Hafer, German-Bell, Maness-McCrary-Prokop, Vega-Bell, Strange-Prokop-Bell, Saenz-Bell, Cook-McCrary, Maness-Prokop-Lohrman, Roach-Bohannon, Maness-McCrary-Prokop, Vega-Bell, Queen-German-Bohannon. **St. Petersburg (8)**—Standridge-Lira-Garibaldi, James-Seberino-Haines, Santos-Wright, Kofler-Sparks, Garibaldi-Robinson, Garibaldi-Cornejo-Wright, Sparks-Ruhl, Garibaldi-Lira-Pruett. **Sarasota (4)**—Cho-Darrell-Surridge-Lyons, Reitsma-Norton-Belovsky, Norton-Darrell, Curtice-Hill. **Tampa (9)**—Graman-Whiteley-Wallace, Walling-Wallace, Jodie-Stafford-Wallace, Walling-Spurling-Blevins, Graman-Dunn-Roller, Rangel-Blevins, Watson-Rangel, Rangel-Stafford-Blevins, Whiteley-Stafford-Wallace. **Vero Beach (1)**—Williams-Proctor-Hadden.

NO-HIT GAME: Fossum, Sarasota defeated Clearwater, 2-0, August 7.

PITCHERS WITH TWO OR MORE TEAMS

Pitcher, Team	W	L	Pct.	ERA	G	GS	CG	ShO	GF	Sv.	IP	H	TBF	R	ER	HR	SH	SF	HB	BB	IBB	SO	WP	Bk.
Noyce, Dave, B.C.*	6	5	.545	3.87	18	17	1	1	0	0	93.0	91	413	53	40	12	3	4	12	35	0	63	4	1
Noyce, Dave, Day.*	1	0	1.000	2.19	3	3	0	0	0	0	12.1	9	56	6	3	0	0	0	0	9	0	6	0	0

2000 FIELDING

TEAM

Team	Pct.	G	PO	A	E	TC	DP	TP	PB
Tampa	.973	140	3581	1455	139	5175	99	0	25
Brevard County	.972	140	3682	1451	150	5283	116	0	23
Dunedin	.971	138	3617	1539	155	5311	139	0	52
Kissimmee	.970	139	3587	1281	150	5018	106	0	21
Charlotte	.970	139	3630	1397	158	5185	113	0	40
Daytona	.969	139	3699	1466	165	5330	122	0	26
St. Petersburg	.969	139	3528	1481	161	5170	106	0	59
Fort Myers	.968	140	3663	1495	173	5331	119	0	18
St. Lucie	.966	139	3678	1698	187	5563	144	0	17
Jupiter	.966	140	3681	1500	181	5362	122	0	34
Clearwater	.964	135	3503	1550	186	5239	149	0	23
Sarasota	.962	139	3594	1361	198	5153	107	0	27
Vero Beach	.960	137	3546	1509	208	5263	144	0	19
Lakeland	.960	140	3584	1472	211	5267	130	0	30

INDIVIDUAL

FIRST BASEMEN

NOTE: All caps denotes fielding-percentage leader based on 70 games for catchers, 93 for all other non-pitchers and 112 innings for pitchers. *Throws lefthanded.

Player, Team	Pct.	G	PO	A	E	TC	DP
Autry, Brian, Jup.	1.000	17	119	12	0	131	13
Bailey, Jeff, B.C.	.988	40	320	18	4	342	24
Baker, Derek, Char.	.995	78	587	33	3	623	47
Ballard, Ryan, St.P.	1.000	2	4	1	0	5	0
Bernhardt, Jossephang, Dun.	.000	1	0	0	0	0	0
Bledsoe, Hunter, V.B.	.977	23	239	13	6	258	23
Bly, Derrick, Day.	.983	30	212	15	4	231	26
Brogna, Rico, Cle.*	1.000	7	72	6	0	78	7
Burns, Pat, St.L.*	.985	21	187	14	3	204	18
CARTER, Charley, Kis.	.996	93	693	38	3	734	62
Casillas, Uriel, Cle.	.951	7	71	7	4	82	11
Choi, Hee, Day.*	.995	85	722	52	4	778	64
Daigle, Leo, Lake.	.987	107	920	60	13	993	88
Da Luz, Craig, Lake.	.976	20	149	16	4	169	14
Diaz, Juan, Sar.	.992	14	112	8	1	121	8
Dorman, John, St.L.	1.000	1	3	0	0	3	0
Dusan, Joe, Dun.*	1.000	28	190	18	0	208	19
Dwyer, Mike, Sar.*	.989	100	748	55	9	812	61
Espinal, Juan, Sar.	.990	12	97	6	1	104	9
Goelz, Jim, V.B.	1.000	1	1	0	0	1	0
Greene, Claude, Tam.	.990	15	94	3	1	98	5
Hafner, Travis, Char.	.985	59	494	32	8	534	49
Hawthorne, Kyle, F.M.	.987	18	139	11	2	152	11
Hodges, Scott, Jup.	1.000	1	2	1	0	3	0
Illig, Brett, V.B.	.988	39	315	27	4	346	31
Jaile, Chris, Char.	1.000	2	13	1	0	14	2
Joffrion, Jack, St.P.	1.000	5	29	2	0	31	0
Jones, Aaron, Tam.*	.988	88	767	36	10	813	53
Jones, Jeremy, Char.	.000	1	0	0	0	0	0
Kelly, Heath, B.C.	1.000	1	7	1	0	8	1
Kerrigan, Joe, Sar.	.955	6	35	7	2	44	5
Kidd, Scott, Tam.	1.000	4	24	2	0	26	1
Leatherman, Dan, F.M.*	.992	80	558	33	5	596	47
Logan, Matt, Dun.	.992	117	970	81	9	1060	104
Lucca, Tony, B.C.*	.991	88	720	63	7	790	71
Lugo, Felix, Jup.	1.000	1	4	0	0	4	1
Lutz, Manuel, Lake.	.962	9	69	6	3	78	7
Manning, Nate, F.M.	.984	29	231	18	4	253	22
Marcinczyk, T.R., F.M.	1.000	2	13	2	0	15	1
Marciniak, Dave, F.M.	1.000	4	34	5	0	39	3
Meadows, Randy, Jup.	1.000	7	35	2	0	37	5
Meliah, Dave, Char.	.971	5	33	1	1	35	3
Minus, Steve, Sar.	.991	14	98	9	1	108	11
Norton, Chris, B.C.	.875	1	6	1	1	8	1
Osilka, Garret, Jup.	1.000	3	21	2	0	23	1
Pascucci, Val, Jup.	.974	10	72	4	2	78	5
Peters, Tony, Dun.	1.000	1	0	1	0	1	0
Pittman, Tom, Jup.	.972	47	429	24	13	466	36
Pond, Simon, Jup.	1.000	10	84	10	0	94	9
Rigsby, Randy, B.C.*	.978	5	42	3	1	46	5
Rivera, Juan, Tam.	.909	1	8	2	1	11	1
Rivera, Mike, Lake.	.980	5	46	3	1	50	4
Rodriguez, Mike, Dun.	.987	14	74	4	1	79	5
Romano, Jimmie, Char.	.926	3	22	3	2	27	1
Roneberg, Brett, B.C.*	1.000	9	92	7	0	99	4
Sachs, Brent, Day.	.914	4	30	2	3	35	2
Salazar, Ruben, F.M.	.933	1	14	0	1	15	1

CLASS A Florida State League

Player, Team	Pct.	G	PO	A	E	TC	DP
Sandusky, Scott, Jup.	1.000	1	1	0	0	1	0
Sapp, Damian, Sar.	.933	2	14	0	1	15	2
Schaeffer, Jon, F.M.	.992	15	115	13	1	129	12
Snyder, Earl, St.L.	.988	121	1146	82	15	1243	117
Solano, Fausto, Dun.	.875	2	7	0	1	8	2
Soules, Ryan, Tam.	.995	43	358	16	2	376	29
Strange, Mike, Dun.	.000	1	0	0	0	0	0
Sulentor, Joe, F.M.	.993	15	128	8	1	137	6
Suriel, Miguel, St.P.	.943	3	32	1	2	35	0
Terrell, Jeff, Cle.	.991	19	199	14	2	215	16
Thomas, J.J., Kis.	.980	49	372	28	8	408	31
Thomas, Mark, Jup.*	.986	59	453	28	7	488	41
Torres, Gabby, F.M.	1.000	1	2	0	0	2	0
Treanor, Matt, B.C.	1.000	1	1	2	0	3	1
Turnquist, Tyler, Kis.	1.000	2	8	0	0	8	2
Van Iten, Robert, Cle.	.988	104	882	57	11	950	103
Vasquez, Alejandro, Kis.*	.000	1	0	0	0	0	0
Velazquez, Jose, St.P.*	.992	132	1128	85	10	1223	94
Walker, Ron, Day.	.992	28	232	16	2	250	15
Wren, Cliff, V.B.	.988	77	649	66	9	724	75

Player, Team	Pct.	G	PO	A	E	TC	DP
Osilka, Garret, Jup.	.960	22	45	51	4	100	16
Perez, Jersen, Dun.	.000	1	0	0	0	0	0
Perez, Jhonny, Kis.	1.000	7	14	19	0	33	2
Pfister, Billy, Lake.	1.000	3	7	5	0	12	2
Pimentel, Franklin, Lake.	.931	17	35	32	5	72	12
Rodriguez, Mike, Dun.	1.000	4	4	10	0	14	1
Sachs, Brent, Day.	.971	11	11	23	1	35	2
Salazar, Ruben, F.M.	.956	100	197	281	22	500	59
Santoro, Pat, Sar.	.948	17	30	43	4	77	7
Schrager, Tony, Day.	.972	112	211	270	14	495	70
Shipp, Brian, St.L.	.976	32	75	88	4	167	30
Smith, Rod, St.P.	.983	36	68	104	3	175	24
Solano, Fausto, Dun.	.955	11	20	22	2	44	4
Strange, Mike, Dun.	1.000	6	10	14	0	24	4
Taylor, Seth, Tam.	.981	90	157	212	7	376	37
Terrell, Jeff, Cle.	.970	15	17	48	2	67	10
Velazquez, Gil, St.L.	.974	8	15	22	1	38	5
Villalobos, Carlos, Lake.	1.000	1	0	1	0	1	0
Volquez, Bolivar, St.P.	.966	8	15	13	1	29	2
Weekly, Chris, Dun.	1.000	4	6	10	0	16	1
Williams, Glenn, Dun.	.975	99	207	291	13	511	82

SECOND BASEMEN

Player, Team	Pct.	G	PO	A	E	TC	DP
Aaron, Oginga, St.P.	.000	1	0	0	0	0	0
Abreu, Dave, St.L.	.907	8	15	24	4	43	5
Abreu, Dennis, Day.	.943	19	40	42	5	87	9
Alfaro, Jason, Kis.	1.000	1	1	2	0	3	1
Backe, Brandon, St.P.	1.000	1	2	2	0	4	2
Berg, Dave, B.C.	1.000	1	3	3	0	6	0
Bernhardt, Jossephang, Dun.	1.000	1	1	1	0	2	0
Borrego, Ramon, F.M.	.967	30	45	74	4	123	19
Boyer, Bret, Jup.	.926	6	13	12	2	27	4
Bush, Brian, Cle.	1.000	1	2	0	0	2	0
Casillas, Uriel, Cle.	.946	17	32	56	5	93	15
Castillo, Carlos, St.L.	1.000	2	9	6	0	15	1
Clapinski, Chris, B.C.	1.000	1	6	1	0	7	1
Clarke, Jason, Day.	1.000	3	9	13	0	22	2
Cooper, Sam, Day.	.944	3	5	12	1	18	1
Da Luz, Craig, Lake.	.967	27	50	66	4	120	17
De Leon, Jorge, Sar.	.917	2	6	5	1	12	4
Dennis, Les, Sar.	.935	7	9	20	2	31	5
Diaz , Jorge, Char.	.978	50	106	120	5	231	30
Dorman, John, St.L.	.951	20	41	56	5	102	14
Escalona, Felix, Kis.	.976	12	20	21	1	42	2
Francia, Juan, Lake.	.944	11	27	24	3	54	8
Franco, Raul, B.C.	.970	18	33	32	2	67	7
Freeman, Terrence, Lake.	.953	45	95	127	11	233	42
Fuentes, Javier, Sar.	1.000	2	5	4	0	9	1
GALLO, Ismael, V.B.	.976	107	214	283	12	509	74
Goelz, Jim, V.B.	.970	34	69	94	5	168	25
Guerrero, Pedro, Char.	.938	60	119	140	17	276	34
Hargreaves, Brad, Day.	1.000	1	1	5	0	6	1
Hawthorne, Kyle, F.M.	.983	12	25	33	1	59	6
Hernandez, Victor, Sar.	.895	6	13	4	2	19	0
Hill, Bobby, St.L.	.973	76	161	233	11	405	52
Hlousek, Rob, Lake.	.923	3	6	6	1	13	1
Hodge, Kevin, F.M.	1.000	2	3	3	0	6	0
Hudson, Orlando, Dun.	.972	17	46	24	2	72	8
Huffman, Royce, Kis.	.970	50	91	106	6	203	23
Illig, Brett, V.B.	1.000	1	1	1	0	2	0
Jackson, Brandon, Dun.	.958	5	6	17	1	24	1
Jimenez, D'Angelo, Tam.	1.000	5	10	6	0	16	4
Joffrion, Jack, St.P.	.948	35	65	98	9	172	16
Kelly, Heath, B.C.	1.000	6	11	16	0	27	2
Kerrigan, Joe, Sar.	.924	24	22	51	6	79	5
Kidd, Scott, Tam.	.981	45	88	120	4	212	23
Knoblauch, Chuck, Tam.	1.000	1	0	1	0	1	0
Leon, Carlos, Sar.	.973	87	192	212	11	415	50
Lutz, Manuel, Lake.	.000	2	0	0	0	0	0
Machado, Albenis, Jup.	.000	1	0	0	0	0	0
Malloy, Marty, Lake.	.920	7	6	17	2	25	2
Mann, Derek, St.P.	.967	62	122	140	9	271	34
Marciniak, Dave, F.M.	1.000	1	0	3	0	3	0
Meadows, Randy, Jup.	.947	24	53	54	6	113	11
Medrano, Jesus, B.C.	.945	114	222	273	29	524	63
Mejias, Erick, Char.	.900	2	3	6	1	10	1
Meliah, Dave, Char.	.969	31	52	74	4	130	12
Miles, Aaron, Kis.	.950	71	140	186	17	343	40
Myers, Tootie, Jup.	.953	96	226	259	24	509	55
Nelson, Reggie, Lake.	.988	34	65	100	2	167	17
Niles, Drew, B.C.	1.000	5	13	13	0	26	3
Nunez, Sergio, Cle.	.972	105	234	326	16	576	84
Olivares, Teuris, Tam.	.952	5	9	11	1	21	3

THIRD BASEMEN

Player, Team	Pct.	G	PO	A	E	TC	DP
Ahumada, Alejandro, Sar.	.000	1	0	0	0	0	0
Alfaro, Jason, Kis.	1.000	2	0	3	0	3	0
Backe, Brandon, St.P.	.800	1	0	4	1	5	1
Baker, Derek, Char.	.818	5	5	13	4	22	1
Batson, Tom, Cle.	.896	36	31	81	13	125	8
BEINBRINK, Andy, St.P.	.935	125	83	290	26	399	35
Bell, Ricky, V.B.	.891	125	90	293	47	430	22
Berg, Dave, B.C.	1.000	1	0	2	0	2	0
Bly, Derrick, Day.	.893	24	7	43	6	56	1
Boone, Matt, Lake.	.861	101	64	196	42	302	26
Borjas, Henry, Sar.	1.000	1	0	1	0	1	0
Borrego, Ramon, F.M.	.923	17	10	26	3	39	2
Brosius, Scott, Tam.	1.000	2	2	2	0	4	0
Bryant, Matt, Cle.	.917	59	48	140	17	205	19
Casillas, Uriel, Cle.	.947	7	7	11	1	19	1
Clapinski, Chris, B.C.	1.000	1	1	2	0	3	0
Clarke, Jason, Day.	.824	6	2	12	3	17	0
Da Luz, Craig, Lake.	.952	24	20	60	4	84	7
De Leon, Jorge, Sar.	.900	3	3	6	1	10	0
Dennis, Les, Sar.	.933	13	11	31	3	45	4
Escalona, Felix, Kis.	1.000	7	4	22	0	26	2
Espinal, Juan, Sar.	.862	55	53	103	25	181	5
Franco, Raul, B.C.	.885	28	14	63	10	87	4
Garcia , Osmani, Char.	.939	41	21	87	7	115	4
Garcia, Douglas, Char.*	1.000	1	0	4	0	4	1
Guerrero, Pedro, Char.	.964	8	11	16	1	28	3
Hafner, Travis, Char.	.902	18	20	26	5	51	3
Haltiwanger, Garrick, Dun.*	.000	1	0	0	0	0	0
Hawthorne, Kyle, F.M.	.873	21	11	44	8	63	4
Henson, Drew, Tam.	1.000	5	1	4	0	5	0
Hernandez, Victor, Sar.	.822	19	14	46	13	73	6
Hill, Bobby, St.L.	.850	11	9	25	6	40	4
Hodge, Kevin, F.M.	.921	101	52	217	23	292	23
Hodges, Scott, Jup.	.932	105	80	247	24	351	18
Honeycutt, Heath, B.C.	1.000	11	9	28	0	37	1
Hudson, Orlando, Dun.	.931	82	48	183	17	248	17
Huffman, Royce, Kis.	.919	64	42	128	15	185	7
Illig, Brett, V.B.	.800	15	12	24	9	45	4
Joffrion, Jack, St.P.	.786	5	3	8	3	14	1
Kelly, Heath, B.C.	.892	24	15	43	7	65	1
Kelton, Dave, Day.	.896	97	49	176	26	251	10
Kerrigan, Joe, Sar.	.855	22	14	33	8	55	2
Kidd, Scott, Tam.	.906	9	5	24	3	32	0
Logan, Matt, Dun.	.917	6	5	6	1	12	0
Lugo, Felix, Jup.	.000	1	0	0	0	0	0
Lutz, Manuel, Lake.	.929	6	2	11	1	14	2
Manning, Nate, F.M.	.905	7	6	13	2	21	1
Martin, Tyler, Char.	1.000	5	2	10	0	12	1
Martinez, Ramon, Char.	1.000	1	0	1	0	1	0
Meadows, Randy, Jup.	1.000	6	3	8	0	11	0
Mejias, Erick, Char.	1.000	1	2	0	0	3	1
Meliah, Dave, Char.	.924	64	35	123	13	171	8
Minus, Steve, Sar.	.967	26	17	70	3	90	11
Nieves, Jose, Day.	1.000	1	2	1	0	3	0
Niles, Drew, B.C.	1.000	2	5	3	0	8	0
Nye, Rodney, St.L.	.926	132	61	327	31	419	18
Osilka, Garret, Jup.	.862	27	12	63	12	87	7
Phillips, Andy, Tam.	.912	125	61	251	30	342	20
Pond, Simon, Jup.	.941	7	3	13	1	17	0

Player, Team	Pct.	G	PO	A	E	TC	DP
Rodriguez, Mike, Dun.	.910	26	22	59	8	89	6
Rolls, Damian, St.P.	1.000	4	2	9	0	11	0
Sachs, Brent, Day.	1.000	16	5	33	0	38	0
Santos, Jose, B.C.	.909	77	50	160	21	231	7
Scanlon, Matt, F.M.	.833	5	3	7	2	12	1
Schaeffer, Jon, F.M.	.000	1	0	0	0	0	0
Solano, Fausto, Dun.	1.000	1	0	2	0	2	0
Strange, Mike, Dun.	.800	8	1	3	1	5	0
Suriel, Miguel, St.P.	.667	5	3	3	3	9	0
Taylor, Seth, Tam.	.333	1	0	1	2	3	1
Terrell, Jeff, Cle.	.810	33	28	40	16	84	6
Turnquist, Tyler, Kis.	.902	68	50	116	18	184	7
Villalobos, Carlos, Lake.	.816	12	12	19	7	38	1
Weekly, Chris, Dun.	.930	27	18	48	5	71	7
Wren, Cliff, V.B.	1.000	1	0	1	0	1	0
Zech, Scott, Jup.	1.000	2	1	5	0	6	0

SHORTSTOPS

Player, Team	Pct.	G	PO	A	E	TC	DP
Abreu, Dennis, Day.	.935	9	13	16	2	31	2
Ahumada, Alejandro, Sar.	.917	124	192	318	46	556	58
Alfaro, Jason, Kis.	.945	113	159	324	28	511	67
Backe, Brandon, St.P.	.960	37	64	102	7	173	23
Basak, Chris, St.L.	.952	4	10	10	1	21	1
Bell, Ricky, V.B.	.000	1	0	0	0	0	0
Berg, Dave, B.C.	1.000	1	3	2	0	5	1
Bernhardt, Jossephang, Dun.	1.000	1	0	5	0	5	0
Boone, Matt, Lake.	.500	2	0	1	1	2	0
Borrego, Ramon, F.M.	.925	26	22	52	6	80	5
Bryant, Matt, Cle.	.857	4	9	15	4	28	5
Cantu, Jorge, St.P.	.944	34	46	88	8	142	11
Casillas, Uriel, Cle.	.944	14	21	46	4	71	14
Clapinski, Chris, B.C.	1.000	1	0	3	0	3	1
Clarke, Jason, Day.	.800	4	5	7	3	15	2
Cooper, Sam, Day.	.875	5	6	15	3	24	1
Da Luz, Craig, Lake.	.900	9	10	35	5	50	6
De Leon, Jorge, Sar.	.750	1	2	1	1	4	0
Dennis, Les, Sar.	.750	2	0	3	1	4	0
Diaz , Jorge, Char.	.000	1	0	0	0	0	0
Dorman, John, St.L.	.833	1	5	25	6	36	4
Escalona, Felix, Kis.	.932	25	29	53	6	88	10
Espinal, Juan, Sar.	1.000	1	2	5	0	7	1
Franco, Raul, B.C.	.972	24	42	63	3	108	11
FRESE, Nate, Day.	.975	113	139	364	13	516	74
Fuentes, Javier, Sar.	1.000	1	0	1	0	1	0
Garcia , Osmani, Char.	1.000	1	1	9	0	10	2
Goelz, Jim, V.B.	.986	14	25	43	1	69	13
Gonzalez, Alex, B.C.	1.000	4	8	11	0	19	3
Guerrero, Pedro, Char.	.929	9	10	16	2	28	3
Gutierrez, Ricky, Day.	.727	4	2	6	3	11	2
Halloran, Matt, Char.	1.000	5	5	13	0	18	3
Hawthorne, Kyle, F.M.	.925	13	17	32	4	53	2
Hill, Bobby, St.L.	.000	1	0	0	0	0	0
Hodge, Kevin, F.M.	1.000	1	3	2	0	5	2
Hudson, Orlando, Dun.	1.000	1	0	4	0	4	0
Infante, Omar, Lake.	.951	79	121	244	19	384	48
Jeter, Derek, Tam.	1.000	1	1	3	0	4	0
Jimenez, D'Angelo, Tam.	.825	6	9	24	7	40	5
Joffrion, Jack, St.P.	.931	21	25	69	7	101	7
Kelly, Heath, B.C.	1.000	2	1	0	0	1	0
Kerrigan, Joe, Sar.	.915	10	18	25	4	47	5
Leon, Carlos, Sar.	.000	1	0	0	0	0	0
Logan, Exavier, Lake.	.860	11	16	27	7	50	2
Lorenzo, Juan, F.M.	.946	113	149	321	27	497	63
Machado, Albenis, Jup.	.966	128	187	384	20	591	67
Machado, Anderson, Char.	.934	117	210	394	43	647	79
Martinez, Ramon, Cle.	.947	41	72	125	11	208	18
Meadows, Randy, Jup.	.865	12	12	20	5	37	7
Meran, Jorge, Lake.	1.000	1	0	2	0	2	0
Nelson, Reggie, Lake.	.972	16	20	49	2	71	11
Nieves, Jose, Day.	1.000	1	0	3	0	3	0
Niles, Drew, V.B.	.940	25	23	71	6	100	11
Nunez, Jorge, V.B.	.912	127	212	386	58	656	84
Olivares, Teuris, Tam.	.968	117	148	370	17	535	48
Osilka, Garret, Jup.	.862	5	7	18	4	29	2
Peguero, Miguel, Lake.	.938	4	6	9	1	16	0
Perez, Jersen, Dun.	.946	123	192	388	33	613	84
Perez, Jhonny, Kis.	1.000	3	5	6	0	11	2
Perez, Nestor, St.P.	.973	47	52	163	6	221	22
Pfister, Billy, Lake.	.800	1	1	3	1	5	0
Pimentel, Franklin, Lake.	.898	26	42	72	13	127	11
Reyes, Ivan, Tam.	.714	1	1	4	2	7	0
Rodriguez, Ronny, Sar.	1.000	1	0	3	0	3	1
Sachs, Brent, Day.	.954	16	22	40	3	65	12

Player, Team	Pct.	G	PO	A	E	TC	DP
Shipp, Brian, St.L.	.889	12	17	39	7	63	11
Solano, Fausto, Dun.	.833	7	5	20	5	30	2
Strange, Mike, Dun.	.857	3	5	7	2	14	2
Taylor, Seth, Tam.	.897	16	18	43	7	68	10
Velazquez, Gil, St.L.	.948	117	175	407	32	614	85
Volquez, Bolivar, St.P.	1.000	3	4	8	0	12	0
Warriax, Brandon, Char.	.959	84	107	241	15	363	45
Wathan, Derek, B.C.	.976	90	133	280	10	423	48
Williams, Glenn, Dun.	.905	7	18	20	4	42	3

OUTFIELDERS

Player, Team	Pct.	G	PO	A	E	TC	DP
Abreu, Dennis, Day.	1.000	5	6	0	0	6	0
Aguila, Chris, B.C.	.985	136	327	6	5	338	2
Anderson, Dennis, B.C.	.000	2	0	0	0	0	0
Auterson, Jeff, V.B.	.968	107	203	8	7	218	3
Backe, Brandon, St.P.	.975	74	148	9	4	161	3
Barningham, Steve, Char.	.971	85	163	6	5	174	1
Besco, Derek, Lake.	1.000	12	25	1	0	26	0
Bly, Derrick, Day.	1.000	11	12	0	0	12	0
Brown, Billy, Tam.	.962	106	196	4	8	208	1
Brown, Tonayne, Sar.*	.993	126	296	5	2	303	2
Bryan, Jason, Day.	.000	1	0	0	0	0	0
Bryant, Matt, Cle.	1.000	1	1	1	0	2	0
Burns, Pat, St.L.*	.914	25	30	2	3	35	0
Bush, Brian, Cle.	.985	61	127	6	2	135	3
Calloway, Ron, Jup.*	.994	117	323	8	2	333	0
Camilo, Juan, Lake.	.973	105	202	12	6	220	2
Cepicky, Matt, Jup.	.983	106	220	7	4	231	0
Chavez, Endy, St.L.*	.980	106	228	15	5	248	0
Clapinski, Chris, B.C.	.000	1	0	0	0	0	0
Close, James, B.C.	1.000	2	1	0	0	1	0
Cole, Brian, St.L.	.988	86	158	11	2	171	1
Copeland, Brandon, St.L.	.949	33	37	0	2	39	0
Crosby, Bubba, V.B.*	.969	72	115	8	4	127	0
Da Luz, Craig, Lake.	1.000	17	22	1	0	23	0
Diaz, Matt, St.P.	.957	104	217	8	10	235	0
Dorman, John, St.L.	1.000	1	1	0	0	1	0
Duncan, Carlos, Cle.	.932	82	127	10	10	147	0
Dusan, Joe, Char.*	1.000	8	5	0	0	5	0
Dwyer, Mike, Sar.*	.500	3	1	0	1	2	0
Fischer, Mark, Sar.	.979	24	46	0	1	47	0
Fleming, Ryan, Dun.*	1.000	85	175	1	0	176	0
Franco, Raul, B.C.	1.000	14	22	1	0	23	1
Freel, Ryan, Dun.	1.000	4	3	0	0	3	0
Fukuhara, Pete, Day.	.981	91	153	5	3	161	0
Garcia, Douglas, Char.*	.977	26	42	1	1	44	0
Gibbs, Kevin, V.B.	1.000	1	2	0	0	2	0
Giron, Alejandro, Cle.	.982	78	156	6	3	165	1
Goelz, Jim, V.B.	.939	27	44	2	3	49	0
Gomez, Rich, Lake.	.959	117	226	9	10	245	2
Goodson, Brian, St.P.	.977	92	159	11	4	174	1
Graham, Jess, Sar.*	1.000	13	18	3	0	21	0
Greene, Claude, Tam.	.974	50	75	0	2	77	0
Greene, Todd, Dun.	1.000	2	4	0	0	4	0
Haas, Danny, Sar.	.968	79	112	8	4	124	0
Hall, Noah, Jup.	.982	77	157	6	3	166	3
Haltiwanger, Garrick, Dun.*	.970	89	152	9	5	166	0
Hawthorne, Kyle, F.M.	1.000	2	5	0	0	5	0
Hernandez, Victor, Sar.	1.000	3	6	0	0	6	0
Herrick, Jason, V.B.*	1.000	28	53	2	0	55	0
Hill, Bobby, St.L.	.000	1	0	0	0	0	0
Hill, Willy, B.C.*	1.000	42	72	4	0	76	0
Hodge, Kevin, F.M.	.979	31	38	8	1	47	1
Huffman, Royce, Kis.	1.000	8	16	0	0	16	0
Jaroncyk, Ryan, V.B.	1.000	1	4	0	0	4	0
Johnson, Gary, Day.	.993	123	265	4	2	271	1
Johnson, Jason, Cle.	.977	81	166	7	4	177	3
Johnson, Reed, Dun.	.975	36	72	5	2	79	2
Jones, Aaron, Tam.*	.000	1	0	0	0	0	0
Jordan, Kevin, Kis.	1.000	25	30	0	0	30	0
Joyce, James, Kis.	.978	54	87	3	2	92	0
Kawabata, Kenichiro, Sar.*	.976	43	78	5	2	85	2
Kelly, Heath, B.C.	.950	14	19	0	1	20	0
Kerrigan, Joe, Sar.	1.000	2	2	3	0	5	2
Kill, Skip, Cle.	1.000	40	81	4	0	85	1
Koerner, Mike, V.B.*	.977	18	38	4	1	43	0
Langaigne, Selwyn, Dun.*	1.000	4	5	0	0	5	0
Leatherman, Dan, F.M.*	.923	8	12	0	1	13	0
LeBron, Juan, St.L.	.895	14	17	0	2	19	0
Logan, Kyle, Kis.	.923	16	22	2	2	26	0
Lopez, Luis, Kis.	.927	64	99	2	8	109	1
Lutz, Manuel, Lake.	.909	16	18	2	2	22	0
Manning, Nate, F.M.	.971	27	32	2	1	35	0

Player, Team	Pct.	G	PO	A	E	TC	DP
Marcinczyk, T.R., F.M.	.000	1	0	0	0	0	0
Marsters, Brandon, F.M.	.000	1	0	0	0	0	0
McDonald, Jason, Char.	1.000	3	4	0	0	4	0
McMillin, Brian, F.M.	.963	62	103	2	4	109	1
Meadows, Randy, Jup.	1.000	1	1	0	0	1	0
Meadows, Tydus, Day.	.940	44	73	5	5	83	0
Melconian, Alex, B.C.	1.000	2	1	1	0	2	0
Meliah, Dave, Char.	1.000	5	7	1	0	8	0
MENCH, Kevin, Char.	.996	124	228	12	1	241	2
Mendoza, Angel, Sar.	.959	73	132	9	6	147	2
Merhoff, Aaron, Cle.	1.000	2	5	0	0	5	0
Minus, Steve, Sar.	1.000	2	2	0	0	2	0
Mohr, Dustan, F.M.	.978	89	170	6	4	180	1
Moreno, Juan, St.L.	.991	64	110	6	1	117	1
Murch, Jeremy, St.P.*	.935	23	26	3	2	31	0
Myers, Tootie, Jup.	.000	1	0	0	0	0	0
Newton, Kimani, V.B.	1.000	33	64	1	0	65	0
Niles, Drew, B.C.	.000	1	0	0	0	0	0
Nina, Amuarys, Char.	.985	96	192	4	3	199	1
Pascucci, Val, Jup.	.975	94	189	7	5	201	1
Pearson, Shawn, Dun.	1.000	3	2	0	0	2	0
Perez, Jhonny, Kis.	.500	3	1	0	1	2	0
Perez, Josue, Cle.	.993	67	143	7	1	151	0
Perez, Timoniel, St.L.*	1.000	8	11	2	0	13	0
Pernell, Brandon, Day.	.973	57	105	3	3	111	0
Peters, Tony, Dun.	.995	109	193	12	1	206	1
Piedra, Jorge, V.B.-Day.*	.981	125	296	12	6	314	5
Pigott, Anthony, St.P.	.994	62	154	4	1	159	0
Preston, Brian, Jup.	1.000	1	1	0	0	1	0
Ralph, Brian, Day.-V.B.*	.975	106	219	11	6	236	1
Restovich, Mike, F.M.	.975	127	229	6	6	241	2
Rhodes, Dusty, Tam.	.989	50	82	5	1	88	0
Riepe, Andy, Sar.	1.000	6	6	1	0	7	0
Rigsby, Randy, B.C.*	.967	59	88	1	3	92	0
Rivera, Juan, Tam.	.982	115	198	15	4	217	3
Robertson, Mike, Sar.	1.000	16	30	2	0	32	0
Rodriguez, John, Tam.*	.986	101	139	4	2	145	1
Rodriguez, Luis, Sar.	.824	6	14	0	3	17	0
Rodriguez, Mike, Dun.	1.000	10	16	1	0	17	0
Roneberg, Brett, B.C.*	.975	117	223	12	6	241	3
Rosamond, Mike, Kis.	.979	127	318	14	7	339	2
Ryan, Kelvin, St.P.	.958	64	134	4	6	144	0
Sachs, Brent, Day.	1.000	8	12	0	0	12	0
Santana, Pedro, Tam.	.973	20	34	2	1	37	0
Santos, Jose, B.C.	.944	44	65	2	4	71	0
Sapp, Damian, Sar.	.500	1	1	0	1	2	0
Schaeffer, Jon, F.M.	1.000	1	3	0	0	3	0
Seale, Marvin, St.L.	1.000	5	8	0	0	8	0
Smith, Nestor, F.M.	.966	92	165	3	6	174	1
Solano, Fausto, Dun.	.714	6	4	1	2	7	0
Soules, Ryan, Tam.	1.000	1	1	0	0	1	0
Steele, Alex, Lake.	.989	49	91	1	1	93	0
Stewart, Shannon, Dun.	.000	1	0	0	0	0	0
Stratton, Rob, St.L.	.944	94	158	12	10	180	5
Suriel, Miguel, St.P.	1.000	11	15	2	0	17	0
Thomas, J.J., Kis.	1.000	5	12	1	0	13	1
Thomas, Mark, Jup.*	.967	16	29	0	1	30	0
Thompson, Tyler, Dun.	.988	80	162	7	2	171	0
Timaure, Jesus, B.C.	.000	1	0	0	0	0	0
Tolli, Barry, Lake.	.889	11	7	1	1	9	0
Torres, Andres, Lake.	.979	104	267	18	6	291	4
Turnquist, Tyler, Kis.	1.000	2	1	0	0	1	0
Vasquez, Alejandro, Kis.*	.983	56	114	5	2	121	1
Vento, Mike, Tam.	1.000	4	9	0	0	9	0
Villalobos, Carlos, Lake.	1.000	2	2	0	0	2	0
Watson, Matt, Jup.	.951	18	39	0	2	41	0
Weekly, Chris, Dun.	1.000	1	3	0	0	3	0
Wesson, Barry, Kis.	.988	81	154	4	2	163	0
Wiese, Brian, Sar.	.971	47	67	1	2	70	0
Williams, Glenn, Dun.	.000	1	0	0	0	0	0
Wren, Cliff, V.B.	1.000	8	6	0	0	6	0
Wright, Corey, Char.*	.974	98	259	8	7	274	2

Player, Team	Pct.	G	PO	A	E	TC	DP	PB
Anderson, Dennis, B.C.	.983	20	111	7	2	120	1	3
Bailey, Jeff, B.C.	.991	14	104	6	1	111	1	1
Ballard, Ryan, St.P.	.955	4	21	0	1	22	0	1
Barr, Clint, Tam.	1.000	13	56	6	0	62	0	3
Bennett, Ryan, St.L.	.996	32	205	21	1	227	1	4
Buckley, Brandon, Kis.	.993	45	284	19	2	305	0	5
Carreno, Jose, Jup.	.974	38	206	19	6	231	5	7
Casillas, Uriel, Cle.	1.000	1	1	0	0	1	0	0
CHAPMAN, Scott, Kis.	.994	84	646	42	4	692	5	13
Chiaffredo, Paul, Dun.	.973	9	65	7	2	74	2	2
Cleveland, Russell, Lake.	1.000	9	49	5	0	54	0	2
Curry, Chris, Day.	.989	15	77	12	1	90	0	2
Duplissea, William, V.B.	.941	3	14	2	1	17	0	1
Elwood, Brad, Tam.	.979	42	279	40	7	326	2	14
Franco, Iker, St.P.	.875	1	7	0	1	8	0	1
Goldbach, Jeff, Day.	.973	102	738	70	22	830	9	16
Hargreaves, Brad, Day.	.995	41	199	17	1	217	2	5
Hernandez, Michel, Tam.	.988	75	504	59	7	570	2	5
Jaile, Chris, Char.	1.000	2	6	1	0	7	0	0
Jones, Jeremy, Char.	.985	43	290	36	5	331	4	11
Kellner, Ryan, V.B.	.966	61	360	37	14	411	4	6
Kremblas, Mike, Dun.	.972	18	95	10	3	108	0	3
Kropf, Andrew, Lake.	.992	20	120	7	1	128	1	5
LaForest, Pete, St.P.	.974	61	334	38	10	382	0	37
Lawrence, Joe, Dun.	.978	68	438	48	11	497	3	28
Lentz, Ryan, Jup.	1.000	1	1	0	0	1	0	1
Marsters, Brandon, F.M.	.991	113	812	95	8	915	10	9
McAffee, Josh, Kis.	.985	20	116	13	2	131	1	3
McCrotty, Will, V.B.	.980	76	465	68	11	544	4	12
McMillan, Andrew, Jup.	1.000	8	22	8	0	30	1	2
Meadows, Randy, Jup.	.000	1	0	0	0	0	0	1
Meran, Jorge, Lake.	.992	59	334	51	3	388	5	19
Norton, Chris, B.C.	1.000	1	4	0	0	4	0	2
Pena, Rodolfo, Sar.	.990	75	514	54	6	574	2	10
Peters, Tony, Dun.	.990	14	84	11	1	96	1	9
Phelps, Josh, Dun.	.992	18	98	19	1	118	0	7
Phillips, Jason, St.L.	.989	74	478	52	6	536	4	5
Pinto, Rene, Tam.	.990	24	191	12	2	205	1	3
Pohle, Ike, Tam.	1.000	1	1	0	0	1	0	0
Preston, Brian, Jup.	.951	14	64	13	4	81	1	4
Quatraro, Matt, St.P.	.971	12	58	8	2	68	0	5
Reese, Nate, B.C.	1.000	7	27	2	0	29	2	0
Riepe, Andy, Sar.	.991	21	92	13	1	106	1	2
Rivera, Mike, Lake.	.988	56	374	43	5	422	3	4
Rodriguez, Luis, Sar.	.991	44	296	38	3	337	1	10
Rodriguez, Mike, Dun.	.967	17	108	9	4	121	0	3
Rodriguez, Sammy, St.L.	.988	14	76	7	1	84	0	3
Romano, Jimmie, Char.	.957	37	176	24	9	209	1	11
Salazar, Jeremy, Cle.	.985	44	291	35	5	331	1	3
Sandusky, Scott, Jup.	.974	42	260	37	8	305	2	10
Sapp, Damian, Sar.	.963	6	47	5	2	54	1	4
Schaeffer, Jon, F.M.	1.000	3	23	2	0	25	1	1
Schrager, Tony, Day.	1.000	1	5	0	0	5	1	0
Schreimann, Eric, Cle.	.972	40	185	27	6	218	4	9
Shrum, Allen, F.M.	.966	17	73	11	3	87	0	3
Sulentor, Joe, F.M.	.987	16	69	7	1	77	0	4
Suriel, Miguel, St.P.	.967	65	431	40	16	487	3	15
Thompson, Andy, St.L.	.995	28	172	26	1	199	1	5
Torres, Frederick, Char.	.982	72	496	57	10	563	4	18
Torres, Gabby, F.M.	.977	15	74	12	2	88	0	1
Treanor, Matt, B.C.	.986	106	763	73	12	848	4	17
Valdez, Jerry, Cle.	.993	45	245	37	2	284	0	11
Van Horn, Ryan, Day.	.964	13	23	4	1	28	0	3
Waldron, Jeff, Sar.	.970	16	58	7	2	67	0	1
Wren, Cliff, V.B.	1.000	1	1	0	0	1	0	0

OUTFIELDERS WITH TWO OR MORE TEAMS

Player, Team	Pct.	G	PO	A	E	TC	DP
Piedra, Jorge, V.B.*	.974	91	215	7	6	228	1
Piedra, Jorge, Day.*	1.000	34	81	5	0	86	4
Ralph, Brian, Day.*	.963	73	151	7	6	164	0
Ralph, Brian, V.B.*	1.000	33	68	4	0	72	1

CATCHERS

Player, Team	Pct.	G	PO	A	E	TC	DP	PB
Ackerman, Scott, Jup.	.969	45	255	24	9	288	2	9
Alvarez, Clemente, Cle.	1.000	8	55	9	0	64	0	0

PITCHERS

Player, Team	Pct.	G	PO	A	E	TC	DP
Agosto, Stevenson, St.P.*	1.000	13	1	6	0	7	0
Akin, Aaron, B.C.	.941	17	3	13	1	17	3
Albin, Scott, Jup.	.846	49	2	9	2	13	0
Almonte, Hector, B.C.	1.000	8	1	2	0	3	0
Alvarez, Victor, V.B.*	1.000	4	1	6	0	7	0
Alvarez, Wilson, St.P.*	1.000	1	0	1	0	1	0
Anderson, Wes, B.C.	.909	22	5	15	2	22	0
Arias, Pablo, Lake.	1.000	5	1	2	0	3	0
Armas, Tony, Jup.	.000	1	0	0	0	0	0
Armstrong, Jack, B.C.	1.000	4	1	1	0	2	0
Ascencio, Miguel, Cle.	1.000	5	3	5	0	8	1
Avery, Paul, V.B.*	.900	22	4	5	1	10	0
Baisley, Brad, Cle.	.923	16	2	10	1	13	1
Baker, Chris, Dun.	.955	41	13	8	1	22	0
Balfour, Grant, F.M.	.889	35	5	11	2	18	0
Batchelor, Rich, Tam.	1.000	8	0	2	0	2	0

Player, Team	Pct.	G	PO	A	E	TC	DP
Becker, Tom, Lake.	1.000	2	1	1	0	2	0
Becks, Ryan, Jup.*	.955	30	5	16	1	22	1
Bell, Heath, St.L.	1.000	48	1	6	0	7	0
Belovsky, Josh, Sar.	.857	51	1	11	2	14	0
Bess, Steve, Lake.	.800	26	0	4	1	5	0
Blevins, Jeremy, Tam.	.950	42	5	14	1	20	1
Bohannon, Gary, St.L.	.895	39	5	12	2	19	0
Bond, Aaron, Char.	1.000	3	1	0	0	1	0
Booker, Chris, Day.*	.600	31	1	2	2	5	0
Borkowski, Dave, Lake.	.833	2	1	4	1	6	0
Boyd, Jason, Cle.	.000	6	0	0	0	0	0
Brantley, Jeff, Cle.	.000	5	0	0	0	0	0
Bridges, Donnie, Jup.	1.000	11	2	9	0	11	0
Bruback, Matt, Day.	.867	18	4	9	2	15	0
Buller, Sean, Lake.*	.889	29	1	7	1	9	0
Burke, Erick, Lake.*	1.000	12	0	1	0	1	0
Burnett, A.J., B.C.	.000	2	0	0	0	0	0
Campos, David, B.C.*	1.000	2	0	1	0	1	0
Cannon, Jon, Day.*	1.000	7	1	2	0	3	0
Carnes, Matt, F.M.	1.000	19	3	6	0	9	0
Casey, Joe, Dun.	.923	27	11	25	3	39	2
Cassidy, Scott, Dun.	.917	14	2	9	1	12	1
Castellanos, Hugo, Dun.	.800	4	3	1	1	5	0
Castelli, Rob, Jup.	.667	11	1	1	1	3	0
Castillo, Jose, Lake.	.000	1	0	0	0	0	0
Castillo, Marcos, V.B.	.971	25	12	21	1	34	1
Castro, Eleuterio, Sar.	1.000	7	0	1	0	1	0
Chacin, Gustavo, Dun.*	.920	25	6	17	2	25	0
Chiavacci, Ron, Jup.	.941	28	4	12	1	17	0
Cho, Jin Ho, Sar.	.000	3	0	0	2	2	0
Christensen, Ben, Day.	.917	10	4	7	1	12	0
Cisar, Mark, Sar.	1.000	10	4	3	0	7	1
Clackum, Scott, B.C.	.947	33	4	14	1	19	1
Claussen, Brandon, Tam.*	1.000	9	4	8	0	12	0
Coggin, Dave, Cle.	.750	6	1	2	1	4	0
Collins, Pat, Jup.	1.000	2	1	3	0	4	0
Colyer, Steve, V.B.*	.857	26	2	10	2	14	0
Comer, Scott, B.C.*	1.000	3	0	2	0	2	0
Cook, Andy, St.L.	1.000	28	11	18	0	29	0
Cornejo, Jesse, St.P.*	1.000	10	0	4	0	4	0
Cornejo, Nate, Lake.	.917	12	1	10	1	12	0
Cosgrove, Mike, Kis.	1.000	8	1	2	0	3	0
Cotton, Joe, Cle.	1.000	9	0	1	0	1	0
Crumpton, Chuck, Jup.	1.000	16	1	0	0	1	0
Cruz, Juan, Day.	1.000	8	5	2	0	7	0
Cuello, Manolin, Lake.	1.000	2	0	1	0	1	0
Curtice, John, Sar.*	1.000	25	3	9	0	12	0
Dagley, Corey, Cle.	1.000	3	1	3	0	4	0
Dant, Larry, Day.	1.000	8	1	2	0	3	0
Darrell, Tommy, Sar.	.963	44	7	19	1	27	1
Day, Zach, Tam.	1.000	7	0	4	0	4	0
Dean, Aaron, Dun.	1.000	3	0	1	0	1	0
Della Ratta, Pete, St.L.	.000	2	0	0	0	0	0
DePriest, Derrick, Jup.	1.000	4	0	1	0	1	0
Detillion, Jamie, Lake.*	1.000	4	2	1	0	3	0
Dimma, Doug, Dun.*	.941	43	5	11	1	17	1
Dobis, Jason, F.M.	1.000	37	8	18	0	26	2
Dorame, Randey, V.B.*	1.000	9	2	13	0	15	0
Dorman, John, St.L.	1.000	1	1	0	0	1	0
Dunn, Keith, Tam.	.923	24	3	9	1	13	1
Duprey, Pete, Day.*	.000	1	0	0	0	0	0
Eichhorn, Mark, Dun.	1.000	5	0	1	0	1	0
Everly, Bill, V.B.	1.000	39	6	10	0	16	1
Eversgerd, Randy, Sar.	1.000	8	1	2	0	3	0
Farizo, Brad, B.C.	1.000	7	2	2	0	4	1
Feliciano, Pedro, V.B.*	.900	25	4	5	1	10	0
Figueroa, Carlos, Char.*	1.000	33	2	8	0	10	1
Fisher, Peter, F.M.	.938	14	6	9	1	16	0
Fleming, Emar, Char.	.958	42	3	20	1	24	0
FLOHR, Adam, St.P.*	1.000	27	8	30	0	38	0
Florie, Bryce, Sar.	.000	1	0	0	0	0	0
Fossum, Casey, Sar.*	.846	27	6	16	4	26	0
Frederick, Kevin, F.M.	.000	19	0	0	1	1	0
Frey, Chris, Char.	1.000	30	1	3	0	4	1
Gagliano, Steve, Day.	.750	16	1	5	2	8	0
Garcia, Gabe, Kis.	1.000	40	5	14	0	19	3
Garcia, Rosman, St.P.	1.000	4	2	6	0	8	0
Garibaldi, Cecilio, St.P.	.929	25	6	7	1	14	2
Garrett, Josh, Sar.	1.000	16	5	5	0	10	0
Geigel, Rolando, B.C.	.500	5	0	1	1	2	0
German, Yon, St.L.*	.955	14	4	17	1	22	0
Giese, Daniel, Sar.	1.000	8	1	1	0	2	0
Glick, Dave, Kis.*	1.000	3	0	2	0	2	0
Goetz, Geoff, B.C.*	1.000	27	8	15	0	23	1
Grace, Bryan, Tam.	1.000	5	0	1	0	1	1
Graman, Alex, Tam.*	.970	28	8	24	1	33	0
Gulin, Lindsay, Day.*	.914	19	7	25	3	35	3
Guzman, Ambiorix, Char.	1.000	31	5	7	0	12	1
Guzman, Juan, St.P.	.000	1	0	0	0	0	0
Hadden, Randy, V.B.	.941	36	6	10	1	17	0
Hafer, Jeff, St.L.	1.000	11	2	2	0	4	0
Haines, Talley, St.P.	1.000	16	1	5	0	6	0
Hamann, Robert, Dun.	1.000	16	1	4	0	5	1
Hamulack, Tim, Kis.*	.600	41	1	2	2	5	0
Hancock, Josh, Sar.	.964	26	11	16	1	28	0
Harang, Aaron, Char.	.933	28	2	12	1	15	0
Harber, Ryan, B.C.*	.905	22	8	11	2	21	2
Hargreaves, Brad, Day.	.000	2	0	0	0	0	0
Harrell, Tim, V.B.	1.000	30	11	8	0	19	0
Heath, Woody, Dun.	1.000	8	1	0	0	1	0
Hendrickson, Mark, Dun.*	1.000	12	2	7	0	9	1
Hernandez, Adrian, Tam.	.000	1	0	0	0	0	0
Hernandez, Orlando, Tam.	.000	1	0	0	0	0	0
Hiles, Cary, Cle.	1.000	46	1	16	0	17	1
Hill, Terrance, Sar.*	1.000	34	2	5	0	7	0
Hoard, Brent, F.M.*	.750	19	5	10	5	20	0
Howard, Tom, F.M.*	1.000	27	4	7	0	11	0
Hubbel, Travis, Dun.	1.000	3	1	3	0	4	1
Hughes, Travis, Char.	.758	39	7	18	8	33	0
Irabu, Hideki, Jup.	.000	2	0	0	0	0	0
James, Delvin, St.P.	.964	22	8	19	1	28	1
Jensen, Justin, Sar.*	1.000	12	0	1	0	1	0
Jodie, Brett, Tam.	1.000	25	5	24	0	29	0
Johnson, Adam, F.M.	.917	13	3	8	1	12	1
Johnson, Craig, Lake.	.909	19	3	7	1	11	0
Johnston, Dave, B.C.	1.000	5	0	4	0	4	0
Julio, Jorge, Jup.	1.000	21	8	6	0	14	0
Kalita, Tim, Lake.*	.909	27	7	13	2	22	0
Kegley, Charles, Dun.	.958	23	5	18	1	24	0
Kershner, Jason, Cle.*	1.000	2	0	2	0	2	0
Kessel, Kyle, Tam.*	1.000	12	3	7	0	10	0
Kingrey, Jarrod, Dun.	1.000	37	5	5	0	10	1
Kirsten, Rick, Lake.	.944	14	4	13	1	18	0
Klepacki, Ed, Jup.	.923	11	4	8	1	13	2
Kofler, Ed, St.P.	.963	28	10	16	1	27	1
Kosderka, Matt, Char.	.778	12	2	5	2	9	0
Koutrouba, Tom, Lake.*	.938	40	3	12	1	16	0
Krug, Dustin, Day.	.889	52	6	10	2	18	0
Kubes, Greg, Cle.*	.833	24	5	20	5	30	1
LaChapelle, Yan, Dun.	1.000	18	0	1	0	1	0
Lajara, Eudy, B.C.*	.000	6	0	0	0	0	0
Lampley, Dan, Sar.	.938	27	9	6	1	16	0
Lara, Nelson, B.C.	1.000	7	1	0	0	1	0
Leek, Randy, Lake.*	.964	20	8	19	1	28	1
Levan, Matt, B.C.*	.000	4	0	0	0	0	0
Lewis, Colby, Tam.	1.000	28	11	13	0	24	0
Lewis, Craig, Tam.	.000	1	0	0	0	0	0
Lidge, Brad, Kis.	1.000	8	3	7	0	10	0
Lilly, Ted, Tam.*	1.000	1	0	2	0	2	0
Lira, Jim, St.P.	1.000	42	2	8	0	10	0
Lockwood, Luke, Jup.*	1.000	3	0	3	0	3	0
Lohrman, Dave, St.L.	.857	43	1	11	2	14	1
Lombardi, Justin, B.C.*	.000	3	0	0	0	0	0
Lopez, Gustavo, B.C.	.000	2	0	0	0	0	0
Loux, Shane, Lake.	1.000	1	0	1	0	1	0
Lowe, Benny, Lake.*	.857	20	4	2	1	7	0
Lutz, Manuel, Lake.	.000	1	0	0	0	0	0
Lyons, Jon, Sar.	1.000	33	3	11	0	14	1
Maldonado, Esteban, Kis.	.913	36	10	11	2	23	1
Malko, Bryan, F.M.	.667	19	3	3	3	9	0
Maness, Nick, St.L.	.917	26	10	23	3	36	1
Mangum, Mark, Jup.	.909	20	4	16	2	22	0
Marin, Willy, V.B.	.000	1	0	0	0	0	0
Marrero, Darwin, Jup.	1.000	1	0	0	0	0	0
Marriott, Mike, B.C.	.000	2	0	0	0	0	0
Mastrolonardo, Dave, Char.	1.000	8	1	0	0	1	0
McClaskey, Tim, B.C.	.889	46	5	11	2	18	2
McCrary, Scott, St.L.	1.000	23	1	8	0	9	0
McCurtain, Paul, B.C.	.000	3	0	0	0	0	0
McDonald, Jonathan, F.M.	.923	10	6	6	1	13	0
McGowan, Brian, St.P.	1.000	11	1	2	0	3	0
Meadows, Randy, Jup.	.000	4	0	0	0	0	0
Medina, Carlos, St.L.*	1.000	11	0	2	0	2	1
Melendez, Dave, Lake.	1.000	7	1	4	0	5	0
Mendoza, Ramiro, Tam.	1.000	1	0	1	0	1	0
Meyer, Dave, V.B.	1.000	11	0	3	0	3	0
Miceli, Danny, B.C.	1.000	5	0	1	0	1	0
Miller, Greg, Kis.*	1.000	24	4	19	0	23	0

Player, Team	Pct.	G	PO	A	E	TC	DP
Montero, Agustin, V.B.	.000	3	0	0	0	0	0
Montero, Francisco, Cle.	1.000	26	3	7	0	10	0
Moore, Chris, B.C.	.667	4	1	1	1	3	0
Moreno, Juan, Char.*	.000	1	0	0	0	0	0
Moskau, Ryan, B.C.*	1.000	10	5	11	0	16	1
Mota, Danny, F.M.	1.000	29	3	3	0	6	0
Munro, Peter, Dun.	.800	3	1	3	1	5	1
Murphy, Matt, Day.*	1.000	47	0	19	0	19	3
Nakamura, Mike, F.M.	1.000	32	3	2	0	5	0
Nannini, Mike, Kis.	.889	12	3	5	1	9	0
Navarro, Scott, Kis.*	.667	4	0	4	2	6	0
Neal, Blaine, B.C.	1.000	41	5	3	0	8	0
Niedermaier, Brad, Tam.	1.000	5	0	2	0	2	0
Noel, Todd, Tam.	1.000	4	0	1	0	1	0
Norton, Jason, Sar.	1.000	40	4	12	0	16	1
Noyce, Dave, B.C.-Day.*	.875	21	4	10	2	16	0
Nunez, Franklin, Cle.	.929	23	6	7	1	14	2
Olsen, Kevin, B.C.	.960	18	9	15	1	25	0
Ortega, Carlos, V.B.*	.917	14	0	11	1	12	1
Oswalt, Roy, Kis.	1.000	8	1	6	0	7	1
Pageler, Mick, B.C.	1.000	4	1	1	0	2	0
Painter, Lance, Dun.*	.000	1	0	0	0	0	0
Palki, Jeromy, F.M.	.833	42	1	4	1	6	1
Palma, Rick, Day.*	.850	20	3	14	3	20	1
Partenheimer, Brian, B.C.*	.958	34	8	15	1	24	0
Penny, Brad, B.C.	1.000	2	1	1	0	2	0
Perez, Franklin, Lake.	.700	10	2	5	3	10	2
Perez, Julio, Jup.	1.000	7	0	3	0	3	1
Person, Robert, Cle.	.000	1	0	0	0	0	0
Pichardo, Hipolito, Sar.	.750	7	2	1	1	4	0
Pineda, Isauro, Sar.	.667	7	1	1	1	3	0
Pineda, Luis, Lake.	.500	18	0	1	1	2	0
Place, Eric, Dun.*	.833	24	3	7	2	12	0
Pool, Matt, V.B.	1.000	8	1	3	0	4	0
Porter, Scott, Dun.	.800	24	1	3	1	5	1
Pratt, Andy, Char.*	.944	16	1	16	1	18	0
Proctor, Scott, V.B.	.900	35	4	5	1	10	0
Prokop, Mike, St.L.	1.000	38	3	6	0	9	1
Pruett, Jason, St.P.*	1.000	8	3	1	0	4	0
Puffer, Brandon, Kis.	1.000	18	2	0	0	2	0
Pumphrey, Ken, F.M.	.900	14	6	3	1	10	1
Quarnstrom, Rob, Char.*	.875	10	0	7	1	8	0
Queen, Mike, St.L.*	1.000	33	3	11	0	14	1
Quezada, Ed, Jup.	1.000	17	1	6	0	7	0
Ramos, Fernando, Cle.	1.000	27	1	4	0	5	1
Rangel, Julio, Tam.	.917	12	6	5	1	12	1
Redding, Tim, Kis.	.778	24	6	15	6	27	0
Regalado, Maximo, V.B.	1.000	30	0	1	0	1	0
Regilio, Nick, Char.	.875	20	5	9	2	16	0
Reith, Brian, Tam.	.957	18	6	16	1	23	1
Reitsma, Chris, Sar.	.933	11	5	9	1	15	2
Rincon, Juan, F.M.	1.000	13	6	13	0	19	1
Rivera, Saul, F.M.	.917	29	4	7	1	12	0
Roach, Jason, St.L.	.929	9	2	11	1	14	2
Robertson, Jeriome, Kis.*	.900	5	4	5	1	10	1
Robinson, Jeremy, St.P.*	.813	37	4	9	3	16	1
Rodney, Thomas, Lake.	1.000	1	1	0	0	1	0
Rodriguez, Wilfredo, Kis.*	.833	9	1	4	1	6	0
Rojas, Mel, Sar.	.000	5	0	0	0	0	0
Roller, Adam, Tam.	.500	19	0	2	2	4	0
Romero, J.C., F.M.*	1.000	2	2	0	0	2	0
Root, Derek, St.L.*	1.000	5	0	1	0	1	0
Rosado, Juan, Lake.*	.500	21	0	2	2	4	0
Rowe, Casey, Lake.	.778	11	4	3	2	9	0
Ruebel, Matt, Jup.*	1.000	4	1	3	0	4	2
Ruhl, Nathan, St.P.	.917	40	8	3	1	12	0
Saberhagen, Bret, Sar.	.000	1	0	0	0	0	0
Sachs, Brent, Day.	.000	1	0	0	0	0	0
Saenz, Jason, St.L.*	.677	28	5	16	10	31	1
Salyers, Jeremy, Jup.	1.000	14	4	4	0	8	0
Sams, Aaron, Day.*	.947	35	7	11	1	19	0
Santos, Alex, St.P.	1.000	17	6	15	0	21	3
Santos, Victor, Lake.	1.000	1	1	0	0	1	0
Saunders, Tony, St.P.*	1.000	2	0	2	0	2	0
Schilling, Curt, Cle.	1.000	4	1	1	0	2	0
Schoening, Brent, F.M.	1.000	12	2	7	0	9	0
Schourek, Pete, Sar.*	1.000	1	0	2	0	2	0
Scott, Darryl, Cle.	1.000	4	1	0	0	1	0
Scuglik, Mike, Char.*	.000	1	0	0	0	0	0
Seale, Dustin, Jup.*	1.000	23	2	6	0	8	1
Seberino, Ronni, St.P.*	.909	33	2	8	1	11	0
Serrano, Willy, Lake.	1.000	26	1	3	0	4	1
Severino, Jose, Lake.	1.000	7	2	5	0	7	0
Sheldon, Kyle, Jup.	.846	40	2	9	2	13	0
Sierra, Jr., Auvin, Lake.*	1.000	2	0	1	0	1	0
Silva, Carlos, Cle.	.929	26	14	25	3	42	2
Silva, Doug, Char.	.917	45	2	9	1	12	0
Simon, Ben, V.B.	.833	4	2	3	1	6	0
Sismondo, Bobby, Cle.*	.905	32	2	17	2	21	1
Smith, Clint, Lake.	.929	37	8	5	1	14	1
Smith, Taylor, Dun.	1.000	13	5	0	0	5	0
Smuin, Shane, B.C.	.000	1	0	0	0	0	0
Smyth, Steve, Day.*	.889	24	2	14	2	18	1
Sparks, Jeff, St.P.	1.000	13	2	2	0	4	0
Spear, Russell, Lake.	.800	13	2	2	1	5	1
Spille, Ryan, Dun.*	1.000	20	5	23	0	28	1
Spurling, Chris, Tam.	.833	34	1	4	1	6	1
Stafford, Mike, Tam.*	1.000	44	6	11	0	17	0
Standridge, Jason, St.P.	1.000	10	10	9	0	19	1
Stewart, John, Char.*	1.000	11	1	2	0	3	2
Strange, Pat, St.L.	.857	19	3	15	3	21	2
Surridge, Lance, Sar.	.833	20	4	6	2	12	1
Tetz, Kris, Jup.	.750	25	0	3	1	4	1
Thomas, Brad, F.M.*	.875	12	4	10	2	16	0
Thomas, Joe, F.M.*	.941	22	1	15	1	17	0
Thompson, Justin, Char.*	1.000	1	0	2	0	2	0
Thurman, Mike, Jup.	1.000	3	0	3	0	3	0
Torres, Alex, Lake.*	.000	1	0	0	0	0	0
Torres, Leo, Day.*	.864	46	7	12	3	22	2
Tranchina, Scott, Day.	1.000	15	0	2	0	2	0
Tremblay, Max, Kis.*	1.000	13	2	0	0	2	0
Ugas, Juan, V.B.	1.000	7	1	1	0	2	0
Urdaneta, Lino, V.B.	1.000	27	5	5	0	10	1
Vael, Rob, Jup.	1.000	26	0	8	0	8	0
Valdes, Ismael, Day.	1.000	1	0	1	0	1	0
Valera, Nelson, St.P.	.000	1	0	0	0	0	0
Vargas, Claudio, B.C.	.963	24	4	22	1	27	2
Vega, Rene, St.L.*	.882	27	6	24	4	34	2
Victoria, Lester, F.M.*	1.000	17	3	1	0	4	0
Vigeland, Will, Char.	1.000	23	3	7	0	10	0
Villalon, Julio, St.P.	.875	6	1	6	1	8	0
Wade, Travis, Kis.	1.000	38	3	3	0	6	0
Waldron, Brad, Jup.	.833	44	1	9	2	12	0
Waligora, Tom, Day.	.905	55	8	11	2	21	1
Walker, Adam, Cle.*	.944	18	6	11	1	18	1
Wallace, Chris, Tam.	1.000	39	1	9	0	10	0
Walling, Dave, Tam.	1.000	9	1	3	0	4	0
Wamback, Trevor, Jup.	1.000	19	7	15	0	22	0
Watson, Allen, Tam.*	1.000	1	0	1	0	1	1
Wayne, Justin, Jup.	1.000	5	2	1	0	3	0
Webb, Alan, Char.*	.933	16	1	13	1	15	0
Webb, John, Day.	.667	4	0	2	1	3	0
Weber, Brett, Tam.	1.000	14	0	1	0	1	0
Wedel, Jeremy, Cle.	.964	39	8	19	1	28	2
Westmoreland, Ken, Cle.	1.000	12	2	10	0	12	2
Whiteley, Shad, Tam.	.875	33	2	5	1	8	0
Whitesides, Johnny, Kis.	.833	21	2	3	1	6	0
Whitney, Jacob, Kis.*	1.000	40	2	12	0	14	2
Wiggins, Scott, Tam.*	.920	28	5	18	2	25	0
Wilkerson, Byron, Kis.	1.000	30	3	3	0	6	1
Williams, Adam, V.B.*	.955	27	6	15	1	22	1
Wilson, Paul, St.L.	.833	5	2	3	1	6	1
Wood, Kerry, Day.	1.000	2	1	1	0	2	1
Woodards, Orlando, Dun.	.917	41	8	14	2	24	0
Wright, Barrett, St.P.	.000	3	0	0	0	0	0
Wright, Chris, St.P.	1.000	46	4	11	0	15	0
Wuertz, Mike, Day.	.970	28	15	17	1	33	1
Yount, Andy, Lake.	.250	8	0	1	3	4	0

PITCHERS WITH TWO OR MORE TEAMS

Player, Team	Pct.	G	PO	A	E	TC	DP
Noyce, Dave, B.C.*	.867	18	3	10	2	15	0
Noyce, Dave, B.C.*	1.000	3	1	0	0	1	0

The following players appeared only as designated hitter, pinch-hitter or pinch runner: Berry, dh; Bundy, dh-pr; De Aza, pr-dh; Hamilton, dh; Leon, dh-ph; Nunez, dh; Wakakuwa, dh.

CLASS A *Florida State League*

Year	Team	Pct.
1919—	Sanford*	.605
	Orlando*	.703
1920—	Tampa	.654
	Tampa	.722
1921—	Orlando	.635
1922—	St. Petersburg	.503
	St. Petersburg	.618
1923—	Orlando	.667
	Orlando	.678
1924—	Lakeland	.695
	Lakeland	.683
1925—	St. Petersburg	.667
	Tampa†	.696
1926—	Sanford	.647
	Sanford	.623
1927—	Orlando†	.600
	Miami	.661
1928-35—	Did not operate.	
1936—	Gainesville	.542
	St. Augustine (4th)†	.492
1937—	Gainesville§	.616
1938—	Leesburg	.626
	Gainesville (2nd)‡	.615
1939—	Sanford§	.787
1940—	Daytona Beach	.619
	Orlando (4th)‡	.507
1941—	St. Augustine	.659
	Leesburg (4th)‡	.488
1942-45—	Did not operate.	
1946—	Orlando§	.681
1947—	St. Augustine	.625
	Gainesville (2nd)‡	.584
1948—	Orlando	.643
	Daytona Beach (2nd)‡	.616
1949—	Gainesville	.635
	St. Augustine (3rd)‡	.556
1950—	Orlando	.629
	DeLand (3rd)‡	.590
1951—	DeLand§	.643
1952—	DeLand∞	.704
	Palatka (3rd)‡	.569
1953—	Daytona Beach†	.657
	DeLand	.703
1954—	Jacksonville Beach	.629
	Lakeland†	.594
1955—	Orlando	.671
	Orlando	.643
1956—	Cocoa	.614
	Cocoa	.671
1957—	Palatka	.629
	Tampa†	.681
1958—	St. Petersburg	.732
	St. Petersburg	.681
1959—	Tampa	.591
	St. Petersburg†	.612
1960—	Lakeland	.731
	Palatka†	.614
1961—	Tampa†	.710
	Sarasota	.696
1962—	Sarasota	.689
	Fort Lauderdale†	.623
1963—	Sarasota	.645
	Sarasota	.667
1964—	Fort Lauderdale†	.629
	St. Petersburg	.594
1965—	Fort Lauderdale	.627
	Fort Lauderdale	.634
1966—	Leesburg†	.781
	St. Petersburg	.700
1967—	St. Petersburg▲	.691
	Orlando	.638
1968—	Miami	.613
	Orlando◆	.579
1969—	Miami■	.606
	Orlando	.606
1970—	Miami▼	.662
	St. Petersburg	.600
1971—	Miami▼	.667
	Daytona Beach	.586
1972—	Miami•	.562
	Daytona Beach	.606
1973—	St. Petersburg††	.575
	West Palm Beach	.580
1974—	West Palm Beach††	.598
	Fort Lauderdale	.626
1975—	St. Petersburg††	.652
	Miami	.581
1976—	Tampa	.559
	Lakeland††	.536
1977—	Lakeland††	.616
	West Palm Beach	.583
1978—	Lakeland	.565
	Miami§	.539
1979—	Fort Lauderdale	.643
	Winter Haven‡‡	.577
1980—	Daytona Beach	.628
	Fort Lauderdale††	.606
1981—	Fort Myers	.554
	Daytona Beach§§	.504
1982—	Fort Lauderdale§§	.621
	Tampa	.546
1983—	Daytona Beach	.634
	Vero Beach§§	.515
1984—	Tampa	.532
	Fort Lauderdale§§	.521
1985—	Fort Myers∞∞∞	.590
	Fort Lauderdale	.550
1986—	St. Petersburg∞∞∞	.647
	West Palm Beach	.593
1987—	Fort Lauderdale∞∞∞	.616
	Osceola	.576
1988—	Osceola	.606
	St. Lucie▲▲	.532
1989—	Port Charlotte▲▲	.540
	St. Lucie	.540
1990—	West Palm Beach	.697
	Vero Beach▲▲	.585
1991—	Clearwater	.623
	West Palm Beach▲▲	.550
1992—	Sarasota	.639
	Lakeland◆◆	.530
1993—	St. Lucie	.600
	Clearwater§§	.556
1994—	Tampa§§	.606
	Brevard County	.561
1995—	Daytona§§	.644
	Fort Myers	.577
1996—	Tampa	.627
	St. Lucie§§	.534
1997—	St. Petersburg■ ■	.591
	Vero Beach	.511
1998—	Charlotte	.594
	St. Lucie■ ■	.515
1999—	Dunedin	.628
	Kissimmee■ ■	.578
2000—	Dunedin	.609
	Daytona■ ■	.547

*Split-season playoff abandoned after each team won three games. †Won split-season playoff. ‡Won four-club playoff. §Won championship and four-club playoff. ∞Won both halves of split season. ▲League divided into Eastern and Western divisions with split season. St. Petersburg and Orlando won both halves of split season; St. Petersburg won playoff. ◆League divided into Eastern and Western divisions. Miami won regular-season pennant on basis of highest won-lost percentage. Orlando won four-club playoff involving first two teams in each division. ■ League divided into Southern and Central divisions. Miami won playoff between division leaders. (NOTE—Pennant awarded to playoff winner in 1936.) ▼League divided into Eastern and Western divisions. Miami won regular-season pennant on basis of highest won-loss percentage, and also won four-club playoff involving first two teams in each division. •League divided into Eastern and Western divisions. Won four-club playoff involving first two teams in each division. ††League divided into Northern and Southern divisions. Won four-club playoff involving first two teams in each division. ‡‡League divided into Northern and Southern divisions. Same two clubs won both halves; won playoffs. §§Won split-season playoff. ∞∞∞League divided into Western, Central and Southern divisions. Won four-club playoff. ▲▲League divided into Eastern, Western and Central divisions; played split-season. Won six-club playoff. ◆◆League divided into Eastern, Western and Central divisions; played split-season. Won eight-club playoff. ■ ■ League divided into East and West divisions and played split season; won four-club playoff.

MIDWEST LEAGUE

LEAGUE OFFICE

President
George H. Spelius

Address
P.O. Box 936
Beloit, WI 53512

Phone
608-364-1188

Teams (affiliation)
Beloit Snappers (Brewers)
Burlington Bees (Royals)
Cedar Rapids Kernels (Angels)
Clinton Lumber Kings (Expos)
Dayton Dragons (Reds)
Fort Wayne Wizards (Padres)
Kane County Cougars (Marlins)

Lansing Lugnuts (Cubs)
Michigan Battle Cats (Astros)
Peoria Chiefs (Cardinals)
Quad City River Bandits (Twins)
South Bend Silver Hawks
  (Diamondbacks)
West Michigan Whitecaps (Tigers)
Wisconsin Timber Rattlers (Mariners)

2000 FINAL STANDINGS

FIRST HALF

EASTERN DIVISION

Team	W	L	T	Pct.	GB
West Michigan (Tigers)	44	26	0	.629	...
Fort Wayne (Padres)	36	31	0	.537	6.5
Lansing (Cubs)	36	32	0	.529	7.0
Michigan (Astros)	34	34	0	.500	9.0
Dayton (Reds)	31	36	0	.463	11.5
South Bend (Diamondbacks)	28	40	0	.412	15.0

WESTERN DIVISION

Team	W	L	T	Pct.	GB
Beloit (Brewers)	41	26	0	.612	...
Wisconsin (Mariners)	38	30	0	.559	3.5
Quad City (Twins)	37	32	0	.536	5.0
Kane County (Marlins)	36	33	0	.522	6.0
Clinton (Reds)	33	37	0	.471	9.5
Peoria (Cardinals)	30	39	0	.435	12.0
Burlington (White Sox)	29	40	0	.420	13.0
Cedar Rapids (Angels)	26	43	0	.377	16.0

SECOND HALF

EASTERN DIVISION

Team	W	L	T	Pct.	GB
Michigan (Astros)	48	22	0	.686	...
West Michigan (Tigers)	44	26	0	.629	4.0
Dayton (Reds)	39	31	0	.557	9.0
Fort Wayne (Padres)	36	34	0	.514	12.0
Lansing (Cubs)	34	36	0	.486	14.0
South Bend (Diamondbacks)	32	38	0	.457	16.0

WESTERN DIVISION

Team	W	L	T	Pct.	GB
Wisconsin (Mariners)	40	30	0	.571	...
Kane County (Marlins)	38	32	0	.543	2.0
Clinton (Reds)	38	32	0	.543	2.0
Peoria (Cardinals)	33	35	0	.485	6.0
Beloit (Brewers)	30	38	0	.441	9.0
Quad City (Twins)	27	43	0	.386	13.0
Cedar Rapids (Angels)	27	43	0	.386	13.0
Burlington (White Sox)	22	48	0	.314	18.0

COMPOSITE

Team	W.M.	Mich.	Wis.	K.C.	Bel.	F.W.	Day.	Lan.	Clin.	Q.C.	Peo.	S.B.	C.R.	Burl.	W	L	T	Pct.	GB
West Michigan (Tigers)	...	7	7	7	7	8	5	11	6	6	2	8	6	8	88	52	0	.629	...
Michigan (Astros)	9	...	4	4	2	8	8	6	6	5	7	11	5	7	82	56	0	.594	5.0
Wisconsin (Mariners)	4	4	...	9	6	3	5	2	6	8	7	6	9	9	78	60	0	.565	9.0
Kane County (Marlins)	1	4	7	...	6	5	4	5	9	9	4	6	6	8	74	65	0	.532	13.5
Beloit (Brewers)	1	6	5	10	...	5	3	3	3	5	9	4	11	6	71	64	0	.526	14.5
Fort Wayne (Padres)	8	6	5	3	3	...	7	10	3	3	7	8	6	3	72	65	0	.526	14.5
Dayton (Reds)	4	8	3	4	4	9	...	8	6	4	2	5	6	7	70	67	0	.511	16.5
Lansing (Cubs)	5	6	5	3	5	6	8	...	4	5	3	10	4	6	70	68	0	.507	17.0
Clinton (Reds)	2	2	3	7	5	5	5	4	...	6	7	5	10	10	71	69	0	.507	17.0
Quad City (Twins)	2	3	4	7	6	5	4	3	6	...	7	3	7	7	64	74	0	.460	23.5
Peoria (Cardinals)	6	1	9	3	5	1	6	5	5	9	...	5	3	5	63	74	0	.460	23.5
South Bend (Diamondbacks)	8	5	2	2	4	4	5	6	3	5	7	...	3	6	60	78	0	.435	27.0
Cedar Rapids (Angels)	2	3	3	2	5	2	2	3	6	5	9	5	...	6	53	86	0	.381	34.5
Burlington (White Sox)	0	1	3	4	6	4	5	2	6	5	3	2	10	...	51	88	0	.367	36.5

Quad City's home games played in Davenport, Iowa; Kane County's home games played in Geneva, Ill.; Michgan's home games played in Battle Creek, Mich.; West Michigan's home games played in Comstock Park, Mich.

Major league affiliations in parentheses.

PLAYOFFS: Michigan defeated Fort Wayne two games to one; Dayton defeated West Michigan two games to one; Beloit defeated Clinton two games to one; Wisconsin defeated Kane County two games to one; Michigan defeated Dayton two games to none; Beloit defeated Wisconsin two games to one; Michigan defeated Beloit three games to none to win league championship.

REGULAR-SEASON ATTENDANCE: Beloit, 69,199; Burlington, 56,539; Cedar Rapids, 129,652; Clinton, 69,242; Dayton, 581,853; Fort Wayne, 252,605; Kane County, 470,906; Lansing, 416,332; Michigan, 86,297; Peoria, 150,439; Quad City, 138,394; South Bend, 194,652; West Michigan, 436,751; Wisconsin, 215,612. Total—3,268,473. Playoffs (20 games)—40,936. All-Star Game at Kane County, Ill.—8,162.

MANAGERS: Beloit, Don Money; Burlington, Jerry Terrell; Cedar Rapids, Mitch Seoane (Through May 4), Tyrone Boykin (May 5 through end of season); Clinton, Jay Sorg; Dayton, Freddie Benavides; Fort Wayne, Craig Colbert; Kane County, Russ Morman; Lansing, Steve McFarland; Michigan, Al Pedrique; Peoria, Tom Lawless; Quad City, Stan Cliburn; South Bend, Dave Jorn; West Michigan, Bruce Fields; Wisconsin, Gary Thurman.

ALL-STAR TEAM: 1B—Shawn McCorkle, Wisconsin; 2B—Mark Burnett, Clinton; 3B—Albert Pujols, Peoria; SS—Ramon Santiago, West Michigan; OF—Austin Kearns, Dayton; Jason Lane, Michigan; Corey Richardson, West Michigan; Chris Snelling, Wisconsin; C—Braxton Whitehead, Dayton; DH—Billy Martin, South Bend; RHP—Calvin Chipperfield, West Michigan; LHP—Andy Van Hekken, West Michigan; RHR—John Trujillo, Fort Wayne; LHR—Cliff Bartosh, Fort Wayne; Most Valuable Player—Albert Pujols, Peoria; Prospects of the Year—Austin Kearns, Dayton; Albert Pujols, Peoria; Manager of the Year—Bruce Fields, West Michigan.

TEAM

Team	Avg.	G	TPA	AB	R	H	TB	2B	3B	HR	RBI	SH	SF	HP	BB	IBB	SO	SB	CS	GDP	LOB	ShO	Slg.	OBP
Michigan	.269	138	5424	4624	747	1245	1812	255	36	80	659	42	60	71	627	20	959	189	78	99	1088	3	.392	.361
Dayton	.263	137	5303	4567	730	1201	1844	271	15	114	658	33	37	73	593	22	969	116	54	120	1003	5	.404	.354
Lansing	.262	138	5225	4616	642	1209	1801	230	25	104	596	30	42	81	456	20	863	156	70	95	985	9	.390	.336
Clinton	.254	140	5281	4650	655	1182	1755	238	19	99	591	34	42	71	484	20	1078	149	66	90	958	11	.377	.331
South Bend	.253	138	5250	4520	654	1142	1702	220	44	84	574	47	36	65	582	21	928	192	73	81	1027	9	.377	.344
W. Michigan	.253	140	5308	4592	685	1160	1574	179	32	57	584	46	41	84	545	14	1073	175	50	98	1019	9	.343	.340
Beloit	.253	135	5022	4395	594	1110	1615	230	31	71	527	87	38	77	425	17	943	126	57	92	923	8	.367	.327
Fort Wayne	.249	137	5105	4477	598	1113	1631	252	25	72	528	23	33	64	508	20	992	112	51	112	977	10	.364	.332
Wisconsin	.248	138	5272	4538	689	1126	1674	222	28	90	602	48	51	81	554	17	1087	164	85	76	984	11	.369	.337
Burlington	.247	139	5050	4501	542	1112	1498	191	30	45	462	43	33	46	427	10	873	215	93	97	899	11	.333	.317
Peoria	.242	137	5113	4524	590	1095	1662	240	36	85	507	57	29	56	447	18	1078	144	70	83	937	9	.367	.316
Kane County	.241	139	5130	4446	586	1070	1604	208	37	84	521	29	37	80	538	25	1033	120	62	98	989	12	.361	.331
Quad City	.238	139	5219	4535	581	1081	1512	183	22	68	517	56	42	97	489	16	858	77	51	101	1020	8	.333	.323
Cedar Rapids	.234	139	5222	4530	588	1060	1494	186	22	68	516	49	39	62	542	20	996	160	77	93	974	9	.330	.322

INDIVIDUAL

TOP QUALIFIERS FOR BATTING CHAMPIONSHIP

Minimum 378 plate appearances. *Lefthanded batter. †Switch-hitter.

Player, Team	Avg.	G	TPA	AB	R	H	TB	2B	3B	HR	RBI	SH	SF	HP	BB	IBB	SO	SB	CS	GDP	Slg.	OBP
Gripp, Ryan, Lan.	.333	135	574	498	87	166	262	36	0	20	92	0	3	5	68	2	86	4	0	13	.526	.416
Pujols, Albert, Peo.	.324	109	440	395	62	128	223	32	6	17	84	0	2	5	38	7	37	2	4	10	.565	.389
Nicholson, Derek, Mich.*	.311	116	486	408	62	127	181	25	4	7	69	0	8	5	65	2	54	9	7	6	.444	.405
Stegall, Randy, Day.	.309	123	535	466	84	144	208	43	3	5	60	1	1	14	53	3	81	5	5	13	.446	.395
Medina, Luis, Lan.	.307	126	511	476	53	146	178	19	2	3	44	4	3	5	23	2	34	5	4	22	.374	.343
Kearns, Austin, Day.	.306	136	590	484	110	148	270	37	2	27	104	0	9	7	90	5	93	18	5	14	.558	.415
Beattie, Andy, Day.-Clin.†	.301	121	520	455	80	137	195	32	4	6	59	9	5	1	49	5	72	19	10	7	.429	.367
Burnett, Mark, Clin.*	.301	131	580	489	92	147	207	33	3	7	65	2	4	4	81	2	73	24	13	5	.423	.401
Lane, Jason, Mich.	.299	133	594	511	98	153	260	38	0	23	104	0	13	8	62	7	91	20	7	9	.509	.375
Deschaine, James, Lan.	.293	130	561	478	81	140	229	33	4	16	73	2	6	6	69	2	91	19	9	13	.479	.385
Devore, Doug, S.B.*	.292	127	508	452	64	132	212	27	4	15	60	2	4	2	47	5	101	9	6	9	.469	.358
Zoccolillo, Peter, Lan.*	.291	109	416	358	58	104	154	22	2	8	56	0	4	8	46	5	47	5	2	4	.430	.380
McCorkle, Shawn, Wis.*	.289	129	531	432	77	125	213	29	4	17	73	2	4	6	87	4	112	4	6	7	.493	.412
Schmitt, Brian, Mich.*	.289	123	506	447	61	129	184	24	2	9	71	6	4	5	44	1	94	13	2	9	.412	.356
Ward, Brian, Ft.W.	.286	106	446	377	58	108	153	24	3	5	36	3	4	5	56	3	60	4	4	12	.406	.382
Spoerl, Josh, Clin.	.286	110	441	405	46	116	172	20	3	10	57	5	7	5	24	0	106	15	6	6	.425	.323

DEPARTMENTAL LEADERS: G—Kearns, 136; AB—Kata, 521; R—Kearns, 110; H—Gripp, 166; TB—Kearns, 270; 2B—Stegall, 43; 3B—Topolski, 12; HR—Kearns, 27; RBI—Kearns, Lane, 104 each; SH—L. Rodriguez, 19; SF—Lane, 13; HP—Johnstone, 20; BB—Topolski, 105; IBB—Sandberg, 8; SO—Peters, 198; SB—Durham, 58; CS—Topolski, 22; GIDP—Medina, 22; Slg.—Pujols, .565; OBP—Dunn, .428.

ALL PLAYERS

*Lefthanded batter. †Switch-hitter.

Player, Team	Avg.	G	TPA	AB	R	H	TB	2B	3B	HR	RBI	SH	SF	HP	BB	IBB	SO	SB	CS	GDP	Slg.	OBP
Abate, Mike, Wis.	.286	24	100	91	9	26	30	4	0	0	8	2	2	0	5	0	22	1	2	3	.330	.316
Acevedo, Luis, Day.-Clin.	.205	26	83	73	6	15	17	2	0	0	4	0	1	2	7	0	21	2	1	1	.233	.289
Ahlers, Steve, C.R.	.204	15	66	54	3	11	14	3	0	0	3	2	1	0	9	0	12	2	3	2	.259	.313
Alcala, Juan, Wis.	.275	23	76	69	9	19	28	6	0	1	14	0	2	1	4	0	16	1	0	2	.406	.316
Alfieri, Frank, Bel.	.171	21	77	70	8	12	18	1	1	1	5	0	1	2	4	1	17	0	1	3	.257	.234
Alfonzo, Eliezer, Peo.-Bel.	.285	109	424	396	50	113	169	26	0	10	48	1	4	9	14	0	93	4	2	12	.427	.322
Alvarado, Damien, Wis.*	.213	23	82	61	7	13	19	3	0	1	7	2	0	2	17	0	10	0	0	0	.311	.400
Alvarez, Jimmy, Q.C.†	.224	43	158	134	14	30	53	7	2	4	21	3	0	2	19	1	38	3	1	0	.396	.329
Amador, Gerardo, W.M.	.239	96	378	331	38	79	105	11	0	5	45	1	3	5	38	2	69	2	2	5	.317	.324
Ambres, Chip, K.C.	.231	84	380	320	46	74	117	16	3	7	28	3	2	3	52	0	72	26	8	3	.366	.334
Anderson, Dennis, K.C.	.222	29	98	81	7	18	23	3	1	0	9	0	2	6	9	0	17	0	0	2	.284	.337
Anthony, Jacob, W.M.*	.233	111	404	377	36	88	108	14	0	2	48	4	2	15	32	0	105	5	4	10	.286	.317
Araujo, Danilo, Peo.	.224	62	206	183	22	41	51	6	2	0	9	3	1	3	16	0	36	5	3	4	.279	.296
Arroyo, Abner, Ft.W.*	.221	36	143	131	14	29	42	7	0	2	11	1	1	0	10	0	28	4	3	3	.321	.275
Aspito, Jason, Burl.	.248	61	226	206	17	51	72	10	1	3	27	1	2	3	14	0	48	3	4	5	.350	.302
Baderdeen, Kevin, Day.	.258	47	177	159	26	41	64	11	0	4	20	4	1	1	12	0	50	0	0	4	.403	.312
Bailey, Travis, Peo.	.246	118	487	418	64	103	161	21	5	9	58	3	4	4	58	4	154	10	7	4	.385	.341
Barski, Chris, C.R.*	.244	36	142	123	13	30	38	5	0	1	9	0	0	0	19	0	32	0	1	4	.309	.345
Bass, Kevin, Lan.†	.201	108	403	358	41	72	130	17	1	13	47	2	1	3	39	4	120	1	3	8	.363	.284
Beattie, Andy, Day.-Clin.†‡	.301	121	520	455	80	137	195	32	4	6	59	9	5	1	49	5	72	19	10	7	.429	.367
Betancourt, Tony, Q.C.†	.056	14	20	18	1	1	3	0	1	0	3	0	1	0	1	0	8	0	0	0	.167	.100
Bikowski, Scott, C.R.*	.246	117	497	422	53	104	148	14	3	8	55	4	3	7	61	2	79	6	9	6	.351	.349
Bitter, Jarrod, Ft.W.	.230	33	132	113	10	26	42	10	0	2	17	0	3	6	10	0	27	1	1	2	.372	.318
Bookout, Casey, Day.*	.272	83	338	298	37	81	129	19	1	9	55	0	2	5	33	3	57	0	0	8	.433	.352
Bordenick, Ryan, Bel.	.217	87	356	300	30	65	106	18	1	7	39	7	2	5	42	1	82	4	1	7	.353	.321
Buck, John, Mich.	.282	109	455	390	57	110	173	33	0	10	71	0	5	5	55	6	81	2	4	8	.444	.374
Burkhart, Lance, Bel.	.282	58	245	202	42	57	126	18	0	17	64	0	5	4	34	4	42	0	2	5	.624	.388
Burnett, Mark, Clin.*	.301	131	580	489	92	147	207	33	3	7	65	2	4	4	81	2	73	24	13	5	.423	.401
Burns, Kevan, S.B.*	.267	110	455	401	62	107	147	15	8	4	53	2	6	1	45	2	65	26	6	8	.367	.338
Callahan, Dave, K.C.*	.264	131	528	455	55	120	174	29	2	7	60	1	3	5	64	4	110	17	5	14	.382	.359
Campana, Wandel, Clin.	.155	39	113	103	8	16	21	2	0	1	9	5	1	2	2	0	18	5	5	1	.204	.185
Candela, Frank, Bel.	.274	67	274	241	43	66	75	7	1	0	19	8	1	7	17	0	28	28	7	6	.311	.338
Carvajal, Ramon, Peo.†	.235	92	410	361	55	85	127	20	8	2	23	13	2	3	31	0	79	20	6	3	.352	.300

Player, Team	Avg.	G	TPA	AB	R	H	TB	2B	3B	HR	RBI	SH	SF	HP	BB	IBB	SO	SB	CS	GDP	Slg.	OBP
Castillo, Ruben, Wis.	.214	123	459	416	57	89	117	14	4	2	46	8	4	2	29	0	101	21	6	3	.281	.266
Christianson, Ryan, Wis.	.249	119	482	418	60	104	163	20	0	13	59	0	10	4	50	1	98	1	6	10	.390	.328
Clark, Greg, Peo.	.213	35	128	108	8	23	32	0	0	3	11	1	0	0	19	0	25	1	0	0	.296	.331
Cline, Pat, Day.	.286	32	139	112	15	32	56	9	0	5	16	0	1	3	23	2	18	0	0	5	.500	.417
Close, James, K.C.	.476	7	23	21	4	10	14	0	2	0	5	0	1	0	1	0	5	1	0	1	.667	.478
Closser, J.D., S.B.†	.224	101	396	331	54	74	119	19	1	8	37	1	1	3	60	4	61	6	2	7	.360	.347
Cochrane, Mark, Burl.	.188	6	19	16	2	3	5	2	0	0	0	0	0	0	3	0	7	0	0	1	.313	.316
Cook, Jon, Ft.W.	.217	24	83	69	6	15	17	2	0	0	5	3	0	1	10	0	21	12	3	0	.246	.325
Cosentino, Tony, Ft.W.	.261	80	315	276	25	72	102	19	1	3	38	0	2	5	32	0	50	1	0	13	.370	.346
Cripps, Bobby, Clin.*	.229	83	326	301	31	69	120	9	0	14	47	0	6	1	18	3	62	2	0	5	.399	.270
Crisp, Covelli, Peo.†	.276	27	118	98	14	27	36	9	0	0	7	4	0	0	16	0	15	7	3	1	.367	.377
Curry, Chris, Lan.	.206	48	145	131	17	27	50	3	1	6	23	0	1	1	12	0	41	0	0	0	.382	.276
Curry, Jesse, Ft.W.*	.189	23	87	74	14	14	30	7	0	3	15	0	1	1	11	0	20	3	0	1	.405	.299
Curtis, Bill, C.R.†	.071	9	21	14	1	1	1	0	0	0	1	0	0	1	6	1	2	0	0	0	.071	.381
Darula, Bobby, Bel.*	.384	71	293	237	56	91	124	18	3	3	43	0	3	9	44	2	25	16	2	2	.523	.491
Day, Nick, Ft.W.	.227	29	106	97	12	22	38	7	0	3	11	0	2	1	6	0	22	0	0	5	.392	.274
De Aza, Modesto, Mich.	.221	25	83	77	8	17	25	2	3	0	6	1	1	2	2	0	24	11	1	1	.325	.256
Dehner, Matt, Clin.	.234	109	367	325	48	76	105	18	1	3	26	4	2	13	23	0	80	15	8	11	.323	.309
De La Cruz, Eric, Bel.	.274	68	214	190	25	52	68	10	0	2	17	6	1	3	14	0	26	2	5	6	.358	.332
Dellucci, David, S.B.*	.200	2	8	5	3	1	2	1	0	0	1	0	1	0	2	0	0	0	1	0	.400	.375
Demarco, Matt, K.C.*	.228	29	102	92	12	21	34	8	1	1	16	0	0	1	9	0	15	1	0	2	.370	.304
Deschaine, James, Lan.	.293	130	561	478	81	140	229	33	4	16	73	2	6	6	69	2	91	19	9	13	.479	.385
Devore, Doug, S.B.*	.292	127	508	452	64	132	212	27	4	15	60	2	4	2	47	5	101	9	6	9	.469	.358
Domero, William, W.M.	.333	8	36	33	5	11	17	3	0	1	9	0	0	0	3	0	10	2	0	1	.515	.389
Dominguez, Luis, Mich.	.206	84	304	247	44	51	63	5	2	1	26	1	5	3	48	1	48	8	2	12	.255	.337
Donovan, Todd, Ft.W.	.284	53	235	204	39	58	78	12	4	0	23	0	2	4	25	0	45	18	9	1	.382	.370
Doudt, Anthony, C.R.	.260	34	119	104	8	27	35	2	0	2	11	0	1	3	11	0	32	0	1	2	.337	.345
Drobiak, Jayson, W.M.*	.224	94	354	313	38	70	102	17	0	5	43	0	4	2	35	2	88	5	1	2	.326	.302
Duncan, Chris, Peo.*	.256	122	494	450	52	115	173	34	0	8	57	1	1	6	36	1	111	1	2	11	.384	.318
Dunn, Adam, Day.*	.281	122	538	420	101	118	197	29	1	16	79	0	6	12	100	4	101	24	5	10	.469	.428
Duran, Francisco, C.R.	.225	115	466	405	58	91	113	17	1	1	39	7	5	4	45	1	97	12	10	7	.279	.305
Durango, Ariel, Wis.†	.262	117	495	447	80	117	158	19	2	6	59	7	3	9	29	1	110	49	17	5	.353	.318
Durham, Chad, Burl.	.275	132	575	517	80	142	172	15	6	1	33	4	6	2	46	2	85	58	18	5	.333	.333
Dzurilla, Mike, Lan.	.243	67	296	263	32	64	88	10	1	4	33	1	5	2	25	1	33	6	4	3	.335	.308
Edwards, Dytarious, Clin.*	.182	12	24	22	4	4	4	0	0	0	0	0	0	0	2	0	4	1	1	1	.182	.250
Edwards, John, Q.C.	.241	92	347	323	46	78	118	15	2	7	32	1	2	3	18	1	90	8	4	9	.365	.286
Egly, John, S.B.†	.226	9	36	31	0	7	8	1	0	0	5	0	0	0	5	0	11	0	1	1	.258	.333
Escalona, Felix, Mich.	.259	64	282	251	42	65	99	14	1	6	35	3	2	4	22	1	49	7	0	4	.394	.326
Escobar, Gustavo, Peo.	.180	43	149	128	12	23	30	3	2	0	10	4	2	0	15	1	29	3	3	4	.234	.262
Estrella, Gorky, Wis.	.199	104	422	342	52	68	114	14	1	10	48	3	4	9	64	2	109	4	6	6	.333	.337
Faison, Vince, Ft.W.*	.219	117	492	457	65	100	160	20	2	12	39	2	2	5	26	0	159	21	4	5	.350	.267
Fatheree, Danny, Mich.	.265	46	154	132	18	35	48	4	0	3	17	1	1	1	19	0	18	1	1	5	.364	.359
Fennell, Jason, Burl.†	.237	79	291	249	26	59	86	13	1	4	36	3	2	5	32	0	42	3	2	3	.345	.333
Fernandez, Medardo, K.C.†	.171	25	84	70	8	12	15	3	0	0	6	1	1	2	10	0	15	3	3	2	.214	.289
Ferrand, Francisco, K.C.*	.251	77	296	267	38	67	122	7	6	12	42	2	2	1	24	1	45	1	4	1	.457	.313
Figueroa, Eduardo, Bel.*	.185	21	78	65	6	12	20	2	0	2	4	0	0	0	13	0	29	1	1	1	.308	.321
Flores, Ralphs, Burl.	.245	84	334	298	33	73	96	13	2	2	34	3	1	3	29	2	33	14	7	6	.322	.317
Ford, Will, Bel.*	.208	62	230	202	30	42	64	12	2	2	17	3	0	1	24	0	59	1	1	3	.317	.295
Foreman, Julius, S.B.*	.288	50	169	139	22	40	46	0	3	0	10	0	0	0	30	0	29	14	6	1	.331	.414
Frank, Nick, Bel.	.234	79	298	244	30	57	71	9	1	1	22	7	0	7	40	1	48	3	1	1	.291	.357
Frick, Matt, K.C.	.263	100	376	327	48	86	132	12	2	10	59	0	4	8	37	2	67	4	4	12	.404	.348
Fuentes, Javier, S.B.	.288	80	327	278	38	80	100	9	1	3	33	6	4	7	32	0	24	7	2	6	.360	.371
Fulse, Sheldon, Wis.†	.255	64	265	216	45	55	69	8	0	2	22	3	3	5	38	2	58	30	7	1	.319	.374
Garbe, B.J., Q.C.	.233	133	557	476	62	111	144	12	3	5	51	5	3	10	63	2	91	14	7	10	.303	.333
Garcia, Cip, S.B.	.045	11	24	22	1	1	2	1	0	0	3	1	0	1	0	0	7	0	0	1	.091	.087
Garcia, Hector, Bel.	.250	111	463	436	43	109	165	18	4	10	61	3	2	7	15	1	81	2	2	21	.378	.285
Garrett, Shawn, Ft.W.†	.272	123	500	438	59	119	183	28	3	10	55	1	7	3	47	2	79	6	5	8	.418	.341
Garza, Rolando, Burl.	.242	92	317	277	30	67	85	14	2	0	24	4	1	2	33	0	63	5	7	4	.307	.326
Gauch, Barry, Burl.	.164	24	72	67	4	11	15	4	0	0	7	1	1	0	3	0	14	1	1	1	.224	.197
German, Franklin, Lan.	.279	100	336	308	42	86	119	14	2	5	32	2	1	4	21	1	86	37	10	5	.386	.332
Gillikin, Joe, Burl.	.225	36	130	111	14	25	47	7	0	5	13	1	1	3	14	0	33	0	1	0	.423	.326
Goodman, Scott, K.C.*	.234	129	513	423	68	99	178	27	2	16	54	0	2	15	73	5	110	1	4	5	.421	.365
Gosewisch, Ian, C.R.	.203	59	197	177	20	36	49	10	0	1	14	4	0	2	14	0	38	2	0	7	.277	.269
Graham, Justin, S.B.	.132	24	67	53	4	7	10	3	0	0	7	1	2	1	10	0	21	2	0	0	.189	.273
Green, Andy, S.B.	.000	3	11	9	1	0	0	0	0	0	0	0	0	0	2	0	1	0	0	0	.000	.182
Gregorio, Tom, C.R.	.245	106	426	379	46	93	128	17	0	6	41	3	2	7	35	4	79	2	1	13	.338	.319
Gripp, Ryan, Lan.	.333	135	574	498	87	166	262	36	0	20	92	0	3	5	68	2	86	4	0	13	.526	.416
Gsell, Tony, Lan.	.193	92	344	296	43	57	109	15	2	11	37	3	2	15	27	0	95	3	3	2	.368	.291
Guerrero, Cris, Bel.	.164	15	58	55	5	9	19	4	0	2	8	0	1	1	1	0	18	1	0	2	.345	.190
Gulledge, Kelley, Q.C.	.153	39	147	124	8	19	23	4	0	0	12	1	0	6	16	0	37	0	3	1	.185	.281
Gundrum, Kris, Wis.*	.250	75	287	256	40	64	87	14	0	3	28	4	2	3	22	1	60	13	2	2	.340	.314
Gutierrez, Said, Ft.W.	.189	19	39	37	5	7	11	1	0	1	4	0	0	0	2	0	6	2	0	2	.297	.231
Hall, Victor, S.B.*	.232	41	180	164	19	38	58	4	5	2	16	1	0	2	13	0	41	12	5	1	.354	.296
Hall, Will, Bel.	.262	130	506	470	57	123	174	30	6	3	41	12	5	1	18	0	127	10	11	12	.370	.287
Hawes, Bobby, Day.	.257	39	148	136	23	35	44	4	1	1	7	2	0	1	9	0	24	7	2	5	.324	.308
Haynes, Larry, Wis.	.208	17	58	53	6	11	14	1	1	0	2	0	1	0	4	0	17	5	0	1	.264	.276
Helquist, Jon, Mich.	.238	96	377	320	59	76	114	19	2	5	42	1	4	4	48	0	101	4	6	4	.356	.340
Hernandez, Johnny, Peo.†	.222	109	432	379	47	84	119	13	2	6	33	6	3	3	41	2	85	27	12	7	.314	.300
Hernandez, Orlando, Wis.	.245	91	351	331	31	81	93	7	1	1	34	2	0	3	15	2	55	5	11	7	.281	.284
Hill, Mike, Mich.	.313	56	217	198	38	62	106	18	4	6	35	0	4	4	11	0	43	6	1	6	.535	.355
Hills, Chris, C.R.	.221	61	269	231	36	51	67	6	5	0	17	2	0	8	28	0	54	10	8	3	.290	.326
Hlousek, Rob, W.M.	.247	30	107	89	15	22	31	2	2	1	9	3	0	1	14	0	14	1	1	3	.348	.356
Hooper, Kevin, K.C.	.249	123	546	457	73	114	160	25	6	3	38	9	1	6	73	2	83	17	2	6	.350	.359
Huff, Jake, Ft.W.	.240	61	228	200	15	48	65	11	0	2	22	0	1	2	25	0	62	1	0	6	.325	.329

Player, Team	Avg.	G	TPA	AB	R	H	TB	2B	3B	HR	RBI	SH	SF	HP	BB	IBB	SO	SB	CS	GDP	Slg.	OBP
Hummel, Timothy, Burl.	.326	39	168	144	22	47	61	9	1	1	21	0	2	1	21	0	20	8	3	2	.424	.411
Hurtado, Omar, Clin.	.278	125	520	460	58	128	184	31	2	7	65	2	7	4	47	2	129	19	10	15	.400	.346
Huth, Jason, Day.	.181	49	157	127	16	23	29	6	0	0	12	2	1	0	27	0	31	4	3	0	.228	.323
Infante, Omar, W.M.	.229	12	55	48	7	11	11	0	0	0	5	0	0	2	5	0	7	1	0	2	.229	.327
Jenkins, Neil, W.M.	.253	112	456	411	56	104	169	16	5	13	65	2	4	1	38	1	151	0	1	7	.411	.315
Jimenez, Carlos, W.M.	.227	102	379	335	47	76	111	18	7	1	33	4	3	2	35	0	107	13	6	6	.331	.301
Johnson, Ben, Peo.-Ft.W.	.230	122	512	439	69	101	183	28	3	16	59	2	3	8	60	1	103	17	9	13	.417	.331
Johnson, Gabe, Peo.	.157	58	219	197	20	31	51	8	0	4	22	4	1	4	13	1	91	1	2	5	.259	.223
Johnstone, Benjamin, Lan.	.250	128	574	512	82	128	157	15	4	2	43	10	3	20	29	1	62	54	21	2	.307	.314
Jones, Brian, Day.*	.230	41	131	122	14	28	51	8	0	5	25	1	1	3	4	0	43	0	0	4	.418	.269
Jordan, Yustin, Q.C.	.234	87	276	231	35	54	84	9	0	7	28	1	3	3	38	0	67	6	4	2	.364	.345
Kalczynski, Joe, S.B.	.157	50	140	115	12	18	21	3	0	0	8	3	0	5	17	0	23	1	2	0	.183	.292
Kata, Matt, S.B.†	.255	133	587	521	82	133	191	22	9	6	59	3	5	6	52	2	58	38	12	10	.367	.327
Kearns, Austin, Day.	.306	136	590	484	110	148	270	37	2	27	104	0	9	7	90	5	93	18	5	14	.558	.415
Kelley, Casey, C.R.*	.254	82	318	256	39	65	122	13	1	14	43	3	3	0	56	1	97	4	3	2	.477	.384
Kelly, Chris, Peo.	.063	8	19	16	0	1	1	0	0	0	1	1	0	1	1	0	9	0	0	1	.063	.167
Kilburg, Joe, Day.-Clin.*	.252	32	144	115	23	29	33	2	1	0	7	1	0	6	22	0	19	11	2	3	.287	.399
Kison, Robbie, Clin.-Day.	.217	77	256	207	29	45	50	3	1	0	21	1	1	4	43	0	42	12	5	3	.242	.361
Knox, Ryan, Bel.	.272	125	534	460	72	125	162	19	6	2	41	16	7	17	34	3	61	42	10	5	.352	.340
Kopitzke, Casey, Lan.	.224	68	228	201	18	45	58	10	0	1	22	3	3	3	18	0	28	1	1	8	.289	.293
Lane, Jason, Mich.	.299	133	594	511	98	153	260	38	0	23	104	0	13	8	62	7	91	20	7	9	.509	.375
Lara, David, W.M.	.239	105	414	372	64	89	129	14	1	8	52	0	2	5	35	1	81	11	1	7	.347	.312
Layton, Blane, Day.*	.229	86	326	279	48	64	101	17	1	6	27	3	0	1	43	0	70	15	9	3	.362	.334
Lemon, Tim, Peo.	.225	127	497	466	64	105	170	25	5	10	52	8	1	5	17	0	105	25	10	6	.365	.260
Leone, Justin, Wis.	.267	115	469	374	77	100	192	32	3	18	63	2	3	11	79	1	107	9	2	3	.513	.407
Lindsey, Cordell, C.R.	.213	105	440	409	42	87	129	22	1	6	56	3	4	4	20	0	65	16	9	9	.315	.254
Lotterhos, Chris, S.B.	.111	3	10	9	0	1	2	1	0	0	0	1	0	0	0	0	3	0	0	0	.222	.111
Lundquist, Ryan, Clin.	.251	120	496	438	61	110	183	24	2	15	61	3	2	10	43	1	106	10	1	7	.418	.331
Lutz, Manuel, W.M.*	.318	12	51	44	8	14	19	2	0	1	7	0	0	1	6	2	9	0	0	2	.432	.412
Markray, Thad, Clin.	.118	14	39	34	1	4	4	0	0	0	4	1	1	0	3	0	9	0	0	3	.118	.184
Martin, Billy, S.B.	.280	123	512	415	78	116	225	26	4	25	90	0	3	11	83	6	130	7	1	6	.542	.410
Massey, John, S.B.	.267	41	163	146	9	39	49	10	0	0	13	0	1	4	12	0	30	3	1	5	.336	.337
Matan, Jim, Day.	.204	72	255	225	22	46	65	7	0	4	30	0	1	1	28	0	59	0	0	8	.289	.294
Mauck, Matt, Lan.*	.152	31	112	99	6	15	27	4	1	2	13	0	2	0	11	0	43	2	0	2	.273	.232
Maule, Jason, Mich.*	.282	68	295	241	46	68	79	11	0	0	26	2	2	2	48	0	47	26	6	9	.328	.403
Maya, Johan, Mich.†	.206	55	192	155	19	32	41	4	1	1	19	6	1	7	23	0	30	2	1	7	.265	.333
McCorkle, Shawn, Wis.*	.289	129	531	432	77	125	213	29	4	17	73	2	4	6	87	4	112	4	6	7	.493	.412
McKinney, Antonio, W.M.	.278	88	351	316	48	88	125	12	2	7	44	1	1	7	26	1	70	23	2	8	.396	.346
Medina, Luis, Lan.	.307	126	511	476	53	146	178	19	2	3	44	4	3	5	23	2	34	5	4	22	.374	.343
Mendez, Donaldo, Mich.	.270	101	425	370	65	100	123	17	0	2	51	6	2	14	33	1	68	39	10	3	.332	.351
Montanez, Luis, Lan.	.138	8	32	29	2	4	5	1	0	0	0	0	0	0	3	0	6	0	1	0	.172	.219
Moore, Jason, Ft.W.†	.233	123	492	438	62	102	133	18	2	3	42	3	1	3	47	2	86	10	7	10	.304	.311
Morales, Steve, K.C.†	.219	42	131	114	9	25	40	3	0	4	19	2	1	3	11	0	24	0	0	2	.351	.302
Morrow, Alvin, Bel.	.260	64	247	204	32	53	99	17	1	9	27	0	1	4	37	2	77	0	3	4	.485	.382
Mounts, J.R., Burl.	.171	50	190	164	19	28	41	3	2	2	13	1	1	1	23	0	67	13	2	1	.250	.275
Munoz, Arnaldo, Burl.*	.000	23	1	1	0	0	0	0	0	0	0	0	0	0	0	0	0	0	0	0	.000	.000
Myers, Corey, S.B.	.125	19	73	64	5	8	10	2	0	0	4	1	1	0	7	0	23	1	1	3	.156	.208
Nelson, Reggie, W.M.	.272	56	236	202	35	55	60	5	0	0	15	4	3	1	26	0	26	19	3	2	.297	.353
Nicholson, Derek, Mich.*	.311	116	486	408	62	127	181	25	4	7	69	0	8	5	65	2	54	9	7	6	.444	.405
Nicholson, Tommy, Burl.*	.260	66	283	250	33	65	79	10	2	0	24	3	2	5	22	1	33	10	2	10	.316	.330
Niles, Drew, K.C.†	.175	14	47	40	4	7	11	0	2	0	5	1	2	0	4	0	9	1	1	1	.275	.239
Noboa, Joel, S.B.	.225	19	72	71	5	16	16	0	0	0	1	0	0	1	0	0	30	3	1	0	.225	.236
Nunez, Argelis, S.B.	.130	24	85	77	4	10	19	0	3	1	9	4	0	0	4	0	26	0	2	2	.247	.173
Oborn, Spencer, Burl.	.250	127	513	448	56	112	162	23	3	7	52	3	5	3	54	1	94	28	6	1	.362	.331
O'Connor, Brian, Mich.	.169	32	112	89	7	15	19	1	0	1	11	2	1	2	18	0	34	1	1	3	.213	.318
O'Keefe, Mike, C.R.*	.218	118	453	377	56	82	136	14	2	12	45	2	4	9	60	2	72	6	5	5	.361	.336
Olmedo, Ranier, Day.	.255	111	418	369	50	94	127	19	1	4	41	14	4	1	30	1	70	17	11	11	.344	.309
Olson, Tim, S.B.	.218	68	285	261	37	57	81	14	2	2	26	0	1	8	15	0	49	15	3	5	.310	.281
Orgill, Pete, C.R.*	.224	25	86	76	5	17	22	5	0	0	8	2	1	1	6	1	18	0	1	2	.289	.286
Ortiz, Matt, Peo.	.174	9	25	23	2	4	7	0	0	1	3	0	0	0	2	0	6	0	0	1	.304	.240
Ortiz, Miguel, C.R.*	.264	86	359	330	42	87	124	17	1	6	50	4	6	7	12	2	51	25	7	14	.376	.299
Overbay, Lyle, S.B.*	.332	71	290	259	47	86	129	19	3	6	47	0	2	2	27	0	36	9	2	2	.498	.397
Owens, Ryan, S.B.	.248	71	322	270	52	67	114	20	0	9	43	1	0	4	47	1	76	15	4	6	.422	.368
Padgett, Matt, K.C.*	.233	125	506	446	60	104	166	22	2	12	60	0	3	4	53	5	139	5	3	13	.372	.318
Palmieri, Jon, C.R.	.235	28	101	85	10	20	24	2	1	0	4	0	0	2	14	0	10	1	0	1	.282	.356
Parker, Chris, W.M.	.333	6	23	18	2	6	8	2	0	0	2	0	0	1	4	0	1	0	0	1	.444	.478
Parnell, Sean, Wis.	.226	95	362	318	40	72	103	16	0	5	35	7	4	6	27	0	82	5	9	7	.324	.296
Paulino, Dave, K.C.*	.100	15	28	20	2	2	2	0	0	0	1	0	0	0	8	0	5	2	2	1	.100	.357
Perkins, Kevin, K.C.	.282	91	301	255	34	72	96	12	0	4	27	2	2	10	32	4	49	9	5	8	.376	.381
Peters, Samone, Clin.	.204	125	496	456	51	93	178	22	0	21	64	0	1	7	32	1	198	0	0	6	.390	.266
Pogue, Jamie, Peo.	.167	22	83	66	8	11	17	1	1	1	6	2	0	3	12	0	20	0	1	2	.258	.321
Pujols, Albert, Peo.	.324	109	440	395	62	128	223	32	6	17	84	0	2	5	38	7	37	2	4	10	.565	.389
Quintero, Humberto, Burl.	.238	75	272	248	23	59	75	12	2	0	24	4	2	3	15	1	31	10	6	8	.302	.287
Ramirez, Oscar, Wis.	.234	70	260	209	34	49	71	13	3	1	24	3	1	7	40	0	34	7	5	3	.340	.374
Ramsey, Brad, Lan.	.083	4	16	12	0	1	1	0	0	0	0	1	0	0	3	0	5	0	0	0	.083	.267
Reyes, Eduardo, Bel.	.208	54	196	173	25	36	48	5	2	1	15	6	0	3	14	0	39	4	3	1	.277	.279
Richardson, Corey, W.M.	.264	126	564	454	80	120	139	12	2	1	50	6	2	8	94	1	124	41	10	1	.306	.398
Rios, Fernando, Clin.-Day.	.266	92	387	350	49	93	121	23	1	1	46	2	2	2	31	1	43	4	4	14	.346	.327
Risinger, Ben, Ft.W.	.176	50	182	159	10	28	32	4	0	0	8	3	0	5	15	0	31	0	1	3	.201	.268
Rivera, Francisco, Clin.*	.231	67	233	195	28	45	58	4	0	3	22	2	2	2	32	1	38	0	0	6	.297	.342
Robles, Kevin, Wis.	.220	62	237	223	16	49	67	11	2	1	21	2	0	5	7	0	59	1	2	13	.300	.260
Rodriguez, Luis, Q.C.†	.225	106	408	342	35	77	92	11	2	0	28	19	2	5	40	1	29	4	5	10	.269	.314
Rodriguez, Serafin, Clin.-Day.	.271	95	402	369	42	100	125	14	1	3	36	2	3	2	26	1	49	14	5	7	.339	.320
Rogowski, Casey, Burl.*	.231	122	467	412	62	95	134	19	1	6	41	3	1	4	47	2	89	11	3	10	.325	.315

Player, Team	Avg.	G	TPA	AB	R	H	TB	2B	3B	HR	RBI	SH	SF	HP	BB	IBB	SO	SB	CS	GDP	Slg.	OBP
Rosa, Wally, Burl.	.211	27	102	95	7	20	24	4	0	0	9	0	1	2	4	0	25	1	0	3	.253	.255
Ross, Cody, W.M.	.267	122	507	434	71	116	172	17	9	7	68	2	7	9	55	0	83	11	3	14	.396	.356
Rowden, Monte, Lan.	.000	6	5	3	0	0	0	0	0	0	0	0	0	1	1	0	1	0	0	0	.000	.400
Ryan, Jeff, Lan.	.243	56	206	169	29	41	63	9	2	3	20	2	2	5	28	0	25	11	6	2	.373	.363
Saba, Cesar, Ft.W.†	.177	35	134	124	5	22	28	6	0	0	14	2	0	0	8	0	23	2	0	3	.226	.227
Sachs, Brent, Lan.	.267	15	67	60	10	16	20	4	0	0	7	0	1	0	6	0	10	6	2	2	.333	.328
St. Pierre, Maxim, W.M.	.249	73	281	229	41	57	75	10	1	2	28	2	3	5	42	1	37	2	2	10	.328	.373
Salinas, Trey, Day.	.189	14	43	37	4	7	8	1	0	0	4	0	0	0	6	1	10	0	0	2	.216	.302
Sandberg, Eric, Q.C.*	.257	128	532	424	72	109	165	11	0	15	59	0	5	8	95	8	71	0	0	11	.389	.398
Sandoval, Danny, Burl.	.323	75	298	269	34	87	102	9	3	0	34	8	1	2	18	1	22	37	18	6	.379	.369
Sandoval, Jhensy, S.B.	.258	18	72	62	8	16	26	4	0	2	14	1	3	1	5	0	16	3	2	1	.419	.310
Santamarina, Juan, Burl.*	.192	17	56	52	5	10	15	3	1	0	2	0	0	0	4	0	11	1	0	2	.288	.250
Santiago, Daniel, Day.†	.095	9	23	21	1	2	2	0	0	0	0	1	0	1	0	0	7	0	0	1	.095	.136
Santiago, Ramon, W.M.†	.272	98	446	379	69	103	123	15	1	1	42	15	6	12	34	1	60	39	12	11	.325	.346
Santora, Jack, S.B.†	.247	102	399	316	38	78	103	16	3	1	28	18	2	4	59	1	61	20	13	6	.326	.370
Santos, Luis, S.B.	.208	22	59	48	8	10	12	2	0	0	7	1	0	0	10	0	6	1	0	1	.250	.345
Scales, Bobby, Ft.W.†	.283	81	314	269	42	76	99	14	3	1	27	3	0	3	39	5	52	14	7	9	.368	.379
Scanlon, Matt, Q.C.*	.257	120	504	439	59	113	173	29	5	7	58	1	6	19	39	1	61	5	4	12	.394	.340
Scarborough, Steve, Bel.	.241	127	530	452	51	109	143	24	2	2	64	13	7	3	55	2	80	8	2	4	.316	.323
Schader, Troy, Ft.W.	.305	77	316	279	51	85	151	23	2	13	53	0	2	6	29	1	71	5	1	7	.541	.380
Scheschuk, John, Ft.W.*	.280	131	553	461	72	129	178	25	0	8	85	0	5	6	80	5	51	6	1	13	.386	.389
Schmitt, Brian, Mich.*	.289	123	506	447	61	129	184	24	2	9	71	6	4	5	44	1	94	13	2	9	.412	.356
Schnall, Kevin, Day.	.250	2	5	4	1	1	1	0	0	0	0	0	0	0	1	0	2	0	0	0	.250	.400
Schumacher, Shawn, Peo.*	.283	13	48	46	5	13	18	5	0	0	5	0	0	0	2	0	6	0	0	0	.391	.313
Secoda, Joe, Peo.	.281	36	104	89	9	25	28	1	1	0	11	1	0	0	14	0	29	2	3	0	.315	.379
Seever, Brian, C.R.	.258	109	459	380	74	98	137	14	5	5	48	4	5	5	65	4	90	57	11	6	.361	.369
Selander, Craig, Q.C.*	.237	45	145	131	19	31	50	7	3	2	17	0	1	0	13	1	23	1	1	2	.382	.303
Senjem, Guye, Clin.*	.444	3	9	9	2	4	10	3	0	1	2	0	0	0	0	0	3	0	0	0	1.111	.444
Shaffer, Josh, C.R.*	.239	116	436	394	43	94	111	10	2	1	36	7	4	1	30	0	73	3	2	4	.282	.291
Simpson, Andre, Burl.	.000	47	1	1	0	0	0	0	0	0	0	0	0	0	0	0	0	0	0	0	.000	.000
Sledge, Terrmel, Wis.*	.217	7	27	23	5	5	11	2	2	0	3	0	0	1	3	0	3	1	0	1	.478	.333
Snelling, Chris, Wis.*	.305	72	309	259	44	79	125	9	5	9	56	1	9	6	34	3	34	7	4	2	.483	.386
Solorzano, Lenin, Burl.	.200	70	230	210	14	42	46	2	1	0	13	3	2	4	11	0	50	6	4	14	.219	.251
Soriano, Carlos, Bel.	.094	9	34	32	3	3	6	1	1	0	4	0	0	0	2	0	12	0	1	1	.188	.147
Southward, Deshawn, Q.C.	.178	62	144	118	19	21	22	1	0	0	12	1	3	2	20	0	34	4	4	3	.186	.301
Spadt, Eric, Clin.	.321	13	37	28	5	9	16	1	0	2	7	1	0	1	7	0	12	0	0	0	.571	.472
Sparks, Eddie, Day.-Clin.	.100	8	13	10	1	1	1	0	0	0	1	0	0	0	3	0	3	0	0	0	.100	.308
Spoerl, Josh, Clin.	.286	110	441	405	46	116	172	20	3	10	57	0	5	7	24	0	106	15	6	6	.425	.333
Sprowl, Jon-Mark, Lan.*	.000	2	7	4	3	0	0	0	0	0	0	0	0	0	3	0	2	0	0	0	.000	.429
Stegall, Randy, Day.	.309	123	535	466	84	144	208	43	3	5	60	1	1	14	53	3	81	5	5	13	.446	.395
Stevens, Tony, Q.C.†	.233	116	503	443	53	103	122	15	2	0	30	13	4	9	34	0	61	14	11	4	.275	.298
Stone, Jon, Ft.W.†	.194	12	39	31	7	6	6	0	0	0	2	0	0	2	6	0	9	1	0	2	.194	.359
Suarez, Marc, Clin.	.000	1	2	2	0	0	0	0	0	0	0	0	0	0	0	0	0	0	0	0	.000	.000
Tamburrino, Brett, Q.C.†	.172	8	34	29	2	5	5	0	0	0	1	1	0	2	2	0	7	1	0	1	.172	.273
Teilon, Nilson, Burl.	.249	126	506	466	61	116	181	19	2	14	55	1	2	3	34	0	106	6	9	15	.388	.303
Thames, Damon, Peo.	.232	82	306	280	23	65	89	11	2	3	29	3	4	2	17	1	59	9	3	4	.318	.277
Tiffee, Terry, Q.C.†	.254	129	527	493	59	125	171	25	0	7	60	0	5	0	29	0	73	2	0	14	.347	.292
Toomey, Chris, Clin.	.186	23	79	70	6	13	13	0	0	0	6	0	0	3	6	1	16	1	0	1	.186	.278
Topolski, Jon, Mich.*	.257	133	598	475	84	122	175	20	12	3	40	12	2	4	105	1	124	24	22	7	.368	.394
Torres, Gabby, Q.C.	.272	71	298	268	36	73	105	14	0	6	33	3	1	7	19	0	39	1	1	8	.392	.336
Trout, Casey, Bel.	.246	17	65	57	8	14	19	5	0	0	5	3	0	0	5	0	9	1	0	2	.333	.306
Truitt, Steve, Bel.	.182	19	73	66	6	12	20	2	0	2	4	3	0	0	4	0	20	1	1	0	.303	.229
Ugueto, Luis, K.C.†	.234	114	437	393	43	92	112	13	2	1	32	7	4	5	28	0	83	12	14	10	.285	.291
Vandemore, Tony, Ft.W.*	.241	10	34	29	1	7	11	2	1	0	3	0	0	1	4	0	12	0	0	0	.379	.353
Van Horn, Ryan, Lan.	.200	11	25	20	1	4	5	1	0	0	2	0	0	0	5	1	3	0	1	0	.250	.360
Van Rossum, Chris, Clin.*	.255	59	238	216	28	55	80	6	2	5	34	0	1	6	15	0	52	11	3	3	.370	.319
Vargas, Inakel, W.M.	.246	66	240	207	25	51	70	9	2	2	19	2	1	7	23	2	31	0	2	6	.338	.340
Vasquez, Alejandro, Mich.*	.240	38	160	150	17	36	49	10	0	1	17	0	3	1	6	0	16	6	4	4	.327	.269
Venales, Luis, K.C.	.231	6	15	13	1	3	3	0	0	0	2	0	0	0	2	0	4	0	0	0	.231	.333
Villarreal, Oscar, S.B.*	.000	13	1	1	0	0	0	0	0	0	0	0	0	0	0	0	0	0	0	0	.000	.000
Villero, Armando, Bel.*	.222	6	18	18	0	4	4	0	0	0	0	0	0	0	0	0	5	0	1	0	.222	.222
Vincent, Matt, Peo.*	.000	58	1	0	1	0	0	0	0	0	0	0	0	0	1	0	0	0	0	0	.000	1.000
Voshell, Key, Peo.	.300	12	45	40	5	12	16	1	0	1	5	1	0	1	3	0	6	1	0	1	.400	.364
Wagner, Mike, Ft.W.	.181	35	120	105	15	19	32	6	2	1	5	0	0	2	13	1	53	1	2	2	.305	.283
Wallis, Jacob, Clin.	.000	8	16	14	0	0	0	0	0	0	0	0	0	0	2	1	7	0	0	0	.000	.125
Ward, Brian, Ft.W.	.286	106	446	377	58	108	153	24	3	5	36	3	4	5	56	3	60	4	4	12	.406	.382
Warner, Bryan, Lan.*	.273	99	368	341	37	93	146	17	3	10	52	0	5	3	19	1	45	2	3	9	.428	.313
Washington, Kelley, K.C.	.205	107	401	365	45	75	100	14	4	1	30	1	4	5	25	1	113	20	9	6	.274	.263
Weber, Jon, Clin.*	.221	108	382	321	60	71	107	14	2	6	34	4	2	5	50	1	50	8	6	5	.333	.333
Welch, Edward, C.R.*	.176	32	112	102	9	18	18	0	0	0	1	1	0	0	9	1	32	9	3	2	.176	.243
Welsh, Eric, Day.*	.282	41	163	142	29	40	90	11	0	13	35	0	1	3	17	1	35	0	0	2	.634	.368
West, Kevin, Q.C.	.239	112	419	368	42	88	124	14	2	6	54	0	5	12	34	0	85	10	4	8	.337	.320
White, Greg, C.R.	.226	65	256	212	30	48	78	15	0	5	35	1	0	1	42	1	63	5	3	4	.368	.357
Whitehead, Braxton, Day.	.307	83	323	287	37	88	131	23	1	6	48	0	5	5	26	2	56	1	0	10	.456	.368
Williams, Charles, Peo.†	.236	82	321	276	31	65	85	12	1	2	14	1	3	5	36	1	63	11	5	5	.308	.331
Williamson, Chris, Day.*	.177	21	73	62	8	11	22	2	0	3	9	0	0	4	7	0	28	1	0	0	.355	.301
Wilson, Josh, K.C.	.269	13	57	52	2	14	22	3	1	1	6	0	1	1	3	0	14	0	0	2	.423	.316
Woody, Dominic, K.C.	.234	64	262	235	27	55	83	11	1	5	22	0	2	5	20	1	54	0	0	4	.353	.305
Wrenn, Michael, Q.C.	.247	52	200	174	19	43	58	9	0	2	18	7	1	9	9	1	44	4	2	6	.333	.316
Wright, Gavin, Mich.	.288	43	184	163	22	47	73	10	5	2	19	1	2	0	18	0	37	10	3	2	.448	.355
Zoccolillo, Peter, Lan.*	.291	109	416	358	58	104	154	22	2	8	56	0	4	8	46	5	47	5	2	4	.430	.380

GRAND SLAMS: Helquist, Hurtado, Snelling, Welsh, 2 each; Alvarado, Beattie, Cripps, A. Dunn, Estrella, Ferrand, Frick, H. Garcia, Gregorio, Gripp, Gsell, B. Johnson, Johnstone, Jordan, Lane, Lundquist, Matan, McKinney, D. Nicholson, Padgett, Schader, Scheschuk, G. Torres, Woody, 1 each.

CLASS A Midwest League

AWARDED FIRST BASE ON CATCHER'S INTERFERENCE: Garrett 4 (Rosa 2, Doudt, F. Rivera); Beattie (Bordenick); Devore (Vargas); Gsell (Alfonzo); Morrow (Christianson); O'Keefe (Bordenick); Scheschuk (Mauck); Ward (Christianson); Washington (G. Torres).

PLAYERS WITH TWO OR MORE TEAMS

Player, Team	Avg.	G	TPA	AB	R	H	TB	2B	3B	HR	RBI	SH	SF	HP	BB	IBB	SO	SB	CS	GDP	Slg.	OBP
Acevedo, Luis, Day..	.233	20	67	60	4	14	16	2	0	0	3	0	0	1	6	0	15	1	1	1	.267	.313
Acevedo, Luis, Clin.	.077	6	16	13	2	1	1	0	0	0	1	0	1	1	1	0	6	1	0	0	.077	.188
Alfonzo, Eliezer, Peo.	.309	49	190	175	28	54	85	16	0	5	21	1	2	6	6	0	35	2	0	6	.486	.349
Alfonzo, Eliezer, Bel.	.267	60	234	221	22	59	84	10	0	5	27	0	2	3	8	0	58	2	2	6	.380	.299
Beattie, Andy, Day.†	.228	20	64	57	15	13	21	2	0	2	7	2	0	0	5	0	14	1	3	2	.368	.290
Beattie, Andy, Clin.†	.312	101	456	398	65	124	174	30	4	4	52	7	5	1	44	5	58	18	7	5	.437	.377
Johnson, Ben, Peo.	.242	93	391	330	58	80	143	22	1	13	46	0	3	5	53	0	78	17	6	8	.433	.353
Johnson, Ben, Ft.W.	.193	29	121	109	11	21	40	6	2	3	13	2	0	3	7	1	25	0	3	5	.367	.261
Kilburg, Joe, Day.*	.188	20	93	80	14	15	17	0	1	0	4	1	0	4	8	0	13	5	2	2	.213	.293
Kilburg, Joe, Clin.*	.400	12	51	35	9	14	16	2	0	0	3	0	0	2	14	0	6	6	0	1	.457	.588
Kison, Robbie, Clin.	.207	34	107	92	15	19	20	1	0	0	6	0	0	1	14	0	17	6	3	1	.217	.318
Kison, Robbie, Day.	.226	43	149	115	14	26	30	2	1	0	15	1	1	3	29	0	25	6	2	2	.261	.392
Rios, Fernando, Clin.	.333	30	138	123	22	41	53	12	0	0	20	2	1	1	11	1	16	2	1	6	.431	.390
Rios, Fernando, Day.	.229	62	249	227	27	52	68	11	1	1	26	0	1	1	20	0	27	2	3	8	.300	.293
Rodriguez, Serafin, Clin.	.232	27	112	99	13	23	29	6	0	0	6	1	1	0	11	1	11	5	2	2	.293	.306
Rodriguez, Serafin, Day.	.285	68	290	270	29	77	96	8	1	3	30	1	2	2	15	0	38	9	3	5	.356	.325
Sparks, Eddie, Day.	.125	6	9	8	1	1	1	0	0	0	1	0	0	0	1	0	2	0	0	0	.125	.222
Sparks, Eddie, Clin.	.000	2	4	2	0	0	0	0	0	0	0	0	0	0	2	0	1	0	0	0	.000	.500

2000 PITCHING

TEAM

Team	W	L	Pct.	ERA	G	CG	ShO	Sv.	IP	H	TBF	R	ER	HR	SH	SF	HB	BB	IBB	SO	WP	Bk.
West Michigan..	88	52	.629	2.98	140	9	19	40	1218.2	1023	5205	502	404	69	41	31	70	536	8	975	50	5
Wisconsin	78	60	.565	3.42	138	8	9	37	1204.0	1087	5138	587	457	74	43	33	93	487	21	1019	63	10
Fort Wayne	72	65	.526	3.58	137	1	10	49	1186.2	1011	5083	584	472	78	35	42	76	538	16	1140	80	14
Quad City	64	75	.460	3.67	139	9	8	35	1200.2	1155	5220	620	490	84	42	34	72	509	43	1015	92	12
Kane County	74	65	.532	3.70	139	6	10	38	1188.2	1184	5055	571	489	83	53	32	60	353	5	942	78	4
Beloit	71	64	.526	3.71	135	4	10	48	1171.0	1085	4990	586	483	98	30	32	70	409	13	966	75	9
Peoria	63	74	.460	3.76	137	2	12	34	1191.0	1139	5215	665	497	62	57	37	61	484	37	880	89	9
Michigan	82	56	.594	3.76	138	12	9	41	1206.2	1064	5211	607	504	85	40	44	77	568	20	992	91	6
Clinton	71	69	.507	3.84	140	13	9	34	1223.0	1128	5269	641	522	70	48	44	36	566	29	1122	117	4
South Bend	60	78	.435	4.06	138	6	4	27	1183.2	1149	5205	659	534	65	43	45	76	542	23	930	82	13
Lansing	70	68	.507	4.09	138	8	8	35	1193.2	1204	5320	678	542	80	48	53	93	561	8	932	101	9
Burlington	51	88	.367	4.29	139	4	8	27	1189.2	1140	5321	718	567	82	58	48	86	650	24	997	86	14
Cedar Rapids	53	86	.381	4.46	139	15	5	26	1201.0	1278	5341	747	595	98	51	44	58	495	8	837	101	9
Dayton	70	67	.511	4.46	137	13	3	31	1199.1	1259	5364	716	595	93	35	41	80	519	5	983	100	9

INDIVIDUAL

TOP QUALIFIERS FOR EARNED-RUN AVERAGE TITLE

Minimum 112 innings. *Lefthanded pitcher.

Pitcher, Team	W	L	Pct.	ERA	G	GS	CG	ShO	GF	Sv.	IP	H	TBF	R	ER	HR	SH	SF	HB	BB	IBB	SO	WP	Bk.
Chipperfield, Calvin, W.M.	12	3	.800	2.13	24	22	3	3	0	0	143.2	95	588	45	34	12	3	1	9	65	0	151	3	0
Vanhekken, Andrew, W.M.*	16	6	.727	2.45	26	25	3	1	1	1	158.0	139	648	48	43	3	3	2	7	30	0	126	3	0
Webb, John, Lan.	7	6	.538	2.47	21	21	1	1	0	0	134.2	125	559	53	37	4	3	6	8	40	0	108	9	1
Mieses, Jose, Bel.	13	6	.684	2.53	21	21	2	2	0	0	135.0	107	530	43	38	8	5	1	3	37	1	132	6	1
Thompson, Travis, Clin.-Day.	16	5	.762	2.54	25	23	5	2	0	0	177.0	154	727	60	50	9	5	1	5	52	0	157	6	1
Moser, Todd, K.C.*	9	5	.643	2.83	21	21	3	0	0	0	136.2	136	566	54	43	6	5	3	9	26	0	101	7	0
Soriano, Rafael, Wis.	8	4	.667	2.87	21	21	1	0	0	0	122.1	97	500	41	39	3	2	5	12	50	0	90	5	2
Peavy, Jacob, Ft.W.	13	8	.619	2.90	26	25	0	0	0	0	133.2	107	565	61	43	6	4	3	9	53	0	164	8	2
Sturdy, Tim, Q.C.	9	7	.563	2.96	23	21	2	1	0	0	133.2	121	552	61	44	6	1	1	8	39	3	73	11	2
Majewski, Gary, Burl.	6	7	.462	3.07	22	22	3	3	0	0	134.2	83	546	53	46	8	3	6	12	68	0	137	2	0
Roberts, Nick, Mich.	13	6	.684	3.10	22	20	2	1	1	0	139.1	121	587	58	48	10	1	5	5	61	1	107	5	1
Fuller, Jody, S.B.	9	6	.600	3.13	20	20	1	0	0	0	123.2	116	516	58	43	8	4	6	6	37	3	76	9	0
Putz, Joseph, Wis.	12	6	.667	3.15	26	25	3	2	0	0	142.2	130	611	71	50	4	6	7	9	63	2	105	8	0
Manias, Jim, Day.*	6	6	.500	3.22	17	16	6	1	0	0	120.1	112	496	53	43	11	0	4	2	25	0	109	5	0
Wilson, Philip, C.R.	8	5	.615	3.41	21	21	1	0	0	0	129.1	114	544	61	49	9	4	4	7	49	0	82	9	1

DEPARTMENTAL LEADERS: W—Vanhekken, T. Thompson, 16 each; L—Howington, Bergman, 15 each; Pct.—Childers, Chipperfield, .800 each; G—Trujillo, 63; GS—Ulacia, Sauer, Sanchez, 28 each; CG—Manias, Bergman, 6 each; ShO—Majewski, Chipperfield, 3 each; GF—Watson, Trujillo, 59 each; Sv.—Trujillo, 42; IP—T. Thompson, 177; H—Sauer, 177; TBF—Stanford, 736; R—Ulacia, 109; ER—Howington, 83; HR—Sauer, 21; SH—Darnell, 10; SF—Howington, Cordova, 8 each; HB—Conroy, 19; BB—Stanford, 92; IBB—Centro, 9; SO—Peavy, Darnell, 164 each; WP—Dunn, 20; BK—Munoz, 5.

ALL PITCHERS

*Lefthanded pitcher.

Pitcher, Team	W	L	Pct.	ERA	G	GS	CG	ShO	GF	Sv.	IP	H	TBF	R	ER	HR	SH	SF	HB	BB	IBB	SO	WP	Bk.
Acevedo, Jose, Day.	11	5	.688	3.89	25	23	0	0	2	0	141.0	135	610	74	61	16	1	4	6	53	0	123	6	0
Acosta, Jhon, Lan.	0	0	.000	5.40	5	0	0	0	0	0	10.0	6	45	7	6	2	0	1	0	10	0	9	0	0
Altman, Gene, Day.-Bel.	6	0	1.000	2.65	42	0	0	0	30	17	54.1	49	246	21	16	1	1	0	7	31	0	52	2	0
Anderson, Craig, Wis.*	11	8	.579	3.71	26	26	1	0	0	0	157.2	161	659	81	65	14	4	5	6	40	1	131	2	3
Anderson, Travis, Mich.	8	10	.444	5.10	27	27	1	0	0	0	143.0	142	646	99	81	14	4	5	9	73	1	106	18	0
Arias, Pablo, W.M.	6	3	.667	2.46	15	13	0	0	0	0	84.0	61	336	26	23	8	1	3	4	30	1	54	2	0
Artieta, Corey, Bel.*	7	3	.700	3.49	32	5	0	0	8	0	90.1	94	404	48	35	7	1	5	2	38	4	63	5	0
Baek, Cha, Wis.	8	5	.615	3.95	24	24	0	0	0	0	127.2	137	547	71	56	13	6	2	5	36	0	99	6	0

Pitcher, Team	W	L	Pct.	ERA	G	GS	CG	ShO	GF	Sv.	IP	H	TBF	R	ER	HR	SH	SF	HB	BB	IBB	SO	WP	Bk.
Bailey, David, Lan.	1	3	.250	2.53	45	0	0	0	27	14	57.0	45	240	16	16	3	4	4	3	25	1	48	0	0
Bailey, Travis, Peo.	0	0	.000	0.00	1	0	0	0	1	0	1.0	1	4	0	0	0	0	0	0	0	0	0	0	0
Balbuena, Caleb, Wis.	5	3	.625	3.34	12	11	1	0	1	1	62.0	51	269	28	23	1	2	1	10	37	0	46	1	1
Barnett, Aaron, W.M.*	2	2	.500	4.16	46	0	0	0	13	4	62.2	68	295	39	29	1	3	5	3	40	2	33	3	0
Barreto, Joel, Q.C.	2	1	.667	4.50	14	0	0	0	6	0	24.0	21	109	12	12	1	1	0	1	19	3	26	5	0
Bartosh, Cliff, Ft.W.*	8	4	.667	3.04	50	4	0	0	18	1	77.0	50	335	40	26	6	2	3	5	44	3	94	8	2
Baxter, Gerik, Ft.W.	5	6	.455	3.40	20	19	0	0	0	0	100.2	81	418	46	38	5	1	6	6	44	0	103	7	0
Beckett, Josh, K.C.	2	3	.400	2.12	13	12	0	0	0	0	59.1	45	232	18	14	4	5	0	2	15	0	61	1	1
Belicic, Adam, C.R.*	1	0	1.000	7.20	6	0	0	0	2	0	10.0	17	50	8	8	2	0	0	0	7	0	5	1	0
Bell, Casey, Ft.W.	1	0	1.000	2.08	3	0	0	0	0	0	4.1	3	20	2	1	0	0	0	0	6	0	2	1	0
Beltran, Francis, Lan.	1	1	.500	9.68	16	0	0	0	11	0	17.2	24	97	22	19	0	0	3	4	19	0	16	4	0
Bergman, Dusty, C.R.*	4	15	.211	3.90	28	25	6	1	0	0	163.2	174	727	102	71	12	9	2	5	60	0	108	10	0
Berryman, Chad, C.R.	2	2	.500	6.26	11	10	1	1	1	0	54.2	70	259	45	38	7	6	0	4	27	0	34	5	0
Birdsong, Tim, Day.	6	6	.500	5.19	20	13	2	0	1	0	78.0	100	359	56	45	5	2	2	3	24	0	61	3	1
Blackwell, Scott, Q.C.	3	3	.500	4.40	11	8	0	0	2	0	47.0	40	199	24	23	3	1	3	5	23	3	27	5	2
Blake, Peter, Q.C.*	2	2	.500	4.50	18	0	0	0	6	0	26.0	30	122	18	13	2	1	2	0	18	3	18	5	0
Bludau, Frank, Day.	1	0	1.000	0.00	2	0	0	0	1	0	4.2	2	14	0	0	0	0	0	0	0	0	1	0	0
Bonilla, Ben, S.B.*	1	4	.200	5.96	11	9	0	0	0	0	45.1	65	210	39	30	3	1	5	2	16	0	23	4	2
Bonilla, Vincent, Q.C.	2	8	.200	4.50	15	10	1	0	2	0	62.0	70	277	39	31	3	6	3	3	25	1	50	7	0
Borne, Matt, Burl.	1	6	.143	5.40	25	5	0	0	10	0	56.2	78	279	46	34	9	4	4	6	30	3	41	5	1
Bowe, Brandon, K.C.	7	3	.700	3.73	61	0	0	0	25	6	79.2	73	345	36	33	4	2	4	5	32	0	89	5	0
Bradley, David, Clin.	3	6	.333	3.26	41	4	0	0	13	4	88.1	61	353	37	32	3	2	2	4	41	3	84	7	0
Brewer, Clint, Day.	1	4	.200	7.05	16	1	0	0	4	0	37.0	53	172	36	29	5	1	2	3	8	0	26	3	2
Brown, Paul, Day.*	1	0	1.000	5.35	14	1	0	0	2	0	33.2	42	148	23	20	2	2	2	4	8	0	11	2	2
Brown, Tighe, Day.	2	2	.500	7.85	21	2	0	0	4	0	39.0	55	189	39	34	4	2	3	3	20	0	25	4	0
Bruback, Matt, Lan.	4	2	.667	2.93	9	9	2	0	0	0	55.1	49	237	23	18	2	1	0	4	19	0	36	3	1
Brummett, Sean, C.R.*	7	4	.636	1.00	32	5	1	0	17	5	72.1	58	290	16	8	0	5	0	3	23	3	53	4	1
Buirley, Matt, Day.	1	1	.500	6.30	16	0	0	0	10	1	20.0	17	100	14	14	2	0	3	5	20	0	20	8	0
Bukowski, Stanislaw, C.R.	0	5	.000	11.44	5	5	0	0	0	0	19.2	26	105	29	25	2	1	3	4	17	0	15	2	0
Burke, Erick, W.M.*	1	1	.500	7.03	21	0	0	0	16	0	32.0	45	165	27	25	4	2	0	0	28	1	32	2	0
Burns, Casey, Ft.W.	1	1	.500	10.03	5	3	0	0	0	0	11.2	13	57	13	13	0	0	0	3	9	0	12	2	3
Burton, Timothy, Wis.	2	0	1.000	2.96	17	0	0	0	8	1	24.1	26	109	11	8	0	1	2	1	13	0	15	1	0
Byron, Terence, K.C.	1	2	.333	4.18	6	4	0	0	0	0	23.2	18	102	16	11	1	0	1	0	15	0	13	1	0
Calvo, Jose, Mich.	2	1	.667	7.36	4	3	0	0	0	0	14.2	15	70	13	12	2	0	3	0	11	0	15	1	0
Capuano, Chris, S.B.*	10	4	.714	2.21	18	18	0	0	0	0	101.2	68	408	35	25	2	4	1	5	45	0	105	2	2
Cassel, Jack, Ft.W.	2	2	.500	4.71	22	0	0	0	6	0	36.1	42	160	24	19	2	0	2	2	12	0	25	4	0
Cento, Tony, Q.C.*	6	7	.462	1.97	52	1	0	0	14	5	82.1	56	335	31	18	3	4	3	2	34	9	72	1	2
Cepeda, Wellington, S.B.	2	3	.400	5.90	26	2	0	0	7	0	50.1	59	231	39	33	4	0	4		26	1	32	5	0
Cervantes, Chris, S.B.*	4		.556	3.03	11	11	0	0	0	0	59.1	62	247	29	20	3	0	3	2	11	0	54	2	0
Chapman, Dennis, Ft.W.	0	0	.000	14.21	5	0	0	0	0	0	6.1	9	40	10	10	0	1	2	1	11	1	5	3	0
Childers, Matt, Bel.	8	2	.800	2.71	12	12	1	1	0	0	73.0	64	300	33	22	4	0	1		17	0	47	2	1
Chipperfield, Calvin, W.M.	12	3	.800	2.13	24	22	3	3	0	0	143.2	95	588	45	34	12	3	1	9	65	0	151	3	0
Conroy, Ken, Lan.	11	6	.647	4.33	27	25	1	0	1	0	137.1	151	635	90	66	7	6	5	19	78	0	108	17	0
Cook, B.R., Peo.	5	7	.417	3.69	18	18	0	0	0	0	97.2	90	438	66	40	7	3	1	3	52	2	83	7	1
Cordero, Frangil, Lan.*	2	3	.400	6.14	23	4	0	0	9	7	36.2	39	174	27	25	2	2	2	1	28	1	28	2	1
Cordero, Victor, Bel.	1	1	.500	4.20	15	0	0	0	4	1	30.0	26	137	16	14	5	0	1	4	18	0	31	7	0
Cordova, Jorge, K.C.-Clin.	9	9	.500	4.01	30	23	1	0	2	1	143.2	142	611	67	64	10	5	8	4	49	1	144	17	1
Corona, Ronnie, Q.C.	2	1	.667	2.66	18	0	0	0	14	8	23.2	17	99	8	7	1	1	1	3	8	2	36	2	1
Crudale, Mike, Peo.	6	1	.857	2.31	38	0	0	0	14	5	50.2	40	209	17	13	2	5	0	3	16	3	45	4	0
Cruz, Juan, Lan.	5	5	.500	3.28	17	17	2	1	0	0	96.0	75	423	50	35	6	1	0	13	60	0	106	8	1
Cueto, Jose, Lan.	0	4	.000	5.74	16	1	0	0	6	0	26.2	26	132	19	17	1	3	2	0	25	1	35	9	1
Cummings, Jeremy, Peo.	1	1	.500	6.35	3	3	0	0	0	0	11.1	15	51	9	8	3	0	0	0	3	0	8	1	0
Curreri, Joe, Burl.	4	4	.500	3.69	41	0	0	0	29	12	53.2	46	237	24	22	5	2	4	3	35	5	56	3	1
Curtis, Bill, C.R.	0	0	.000	21.60	2	0	0	0	1	1	1.2	3	10	4	4	1	0	0	0	2	0	1	0	0
Cyr, Eric, Ft.W.*	2	2	.500	4.68	9	6	0	0	0	0	32.2	28	140	18	17	2	0	1	4	15	0	31	1	0
Dant, Larry, Lan.	1	0	1.000	6.53	6	3	0	0	1	0	20.2	27	92	17	15	5	1	0	6	6	0	8	0	0
Darnell, Paul, Clin.*	9	10	.474	3.51	26	25	3	1	0	0	161.2	131	679	81	63	11	10	4	7	67	1	164	12	1
De Hart, Chris, Ft.W.	5	4	.556	4.05	20	10	0	0	1	1	73.1	85	314	38	33	7	1	2	5	14	1	64	2	0
Dehart, Casey, Day.*	6	3	.667	4.26	50	0	0	0	20	2	63.1	67	291	39	30	3	4	3	0	38	0	52	9	0
Delgado, Danny, Wis.	5	2	.714	3.18	37	3	1	0	15	4	79.1	67	324	31	28	8	4	1	4	26	0	71	0	1
Devine, Travis, Wis.	4	7	.364	4.45	23	16	1	0	4	0	99.0	102	423	57	49	8	5	1	4	35	0	61	10	0
Diaz, Antonio, Ft.W.	1	0	1.000	1.00	6	0	0	0	1	0	9.0	5	33	1	1	1	1	0	1	4	2	2	1	0
Dunn, Scott, Clin.	11	3	.786	3.96	26	26	2	1	0	0	147.2	123	638	78	65	9	2	3	4	89	1	159	20	0
Duprey, Pete, Wis.-Lan.*	2	1	.667	3.06	31	0	0	0	13	2	50.0	54	222	26	17	3	1	3	2	17	3	43	3	0
Ebanks, Palmer, C.R.	1	4	.200	4.59	21	2	0	0	8	0	49.0	55	224	36	25	4	2	2	2	16	1	27	4	0
Eckenstahler, Eric, W.M.*	0	2	.000	5.79	10	3	0	0	4	1	18.2	21	89	15	12	4	1	1	1	10	0	22	0	1
Eppeneder, James, Lan.*	7	1	.875	3.10	44	1	0	0	14	3	81.1	66	336	33	28	9	3	4	2	33	3	59	5	1
Escalante, Jaime, C.R.	0	1	.000	2.43	25	0	0	0	16	7	40.2	24	171	14	11	1	1	2	3	23	2	41	2	0
Escamilla, Paco, Clin.	0	0	.000	1.80	2	1	0	0	1	1	10.0	9	43	3	2	0	0	0	0	5	0	10	1	0
Eshelman, Vaughn, Day.*	2	2	.500	6.43	2	2	0	0	0	0	7.0	8	32	5	5	0	0	0	1	4	0	4	1	0
Eyre, Willie, Q.C.	5	7	.417	4.61	26	18	1	1	3	0	99.2	104	457	64	51	9	2	3	5	56	0	81	9	0
Fahs, Paul, Peo.	0	1	.000	4.67	30	2	0	0	7	0	52.0	54	234	30	27	1	4	4	1	29	1	22	6	1
Farizo, Brad, K.C.	3	4	.429	3.65	10	8	0	0	1	0	49.1	50	209	23	20	3	3	0	1	10	0	37	4	1
Fitzgerald, Ryan, Mich.	3	2	.600	3.75	28	0	0	0	11	1	50.1	44	217	24	21	6	1	0	3	21	1	43	4	0
Foote, Joe, Q.C.	9	8	.529	3.88	28	25	4	1	0	0	146.0	152	634	86	63	13	7	1	7	43	2	128	9	0
Frank, Nick, Bel.	0	0	.000	0.00	1	0	0	0	1	0	2.0	3	9	0	0	0	0	0	0	0	0	2	0	0
Franke, Aaron, C.R.	0	6	.000	7.75	8	8	0	0	0	0	40.2	60	206	46	35	4	2	4	1	30	0	37	3	1
Frasor, Jason, W.M.	5	3	.625	3.88	14	14	0	0	0	0	71.1	55	300	32	26	2	0	2	4	29	0	65	5	1
Frederick, Kevin, Q.C.	5	0	1.000	2.35	27	0	0	0	11	4	46.0	34	193	17	12	1	3	1	4	23	4	51	4	0
Fuller, Jody, S.B.	9	6	.600	3.13	20	20	1	0	0	0	123.2	116	516	58	43	8	4	6	6	37	3	76	9	0
Gagliano, Steve, Lan.	2	0	1.000	4.22	12	2	0	0	3	0	32.0	34	145	18	15	0	0	1	1	13	0	13	1	0
Gallo, Mike, Mich.*	8	3	.727	4.86	24	13	0	0	3	0	90.2	104	406	58	49	6	5	3		27	1	56	4	1
Gangemi, Joe, Bel.*	1	1	.500	7.20	11	4	0	0	4	0	25.0	34	115	20	20	2	1	0	3	8	0	19	4	1
Garza, Rolando, Burl.	1	0	1.000	6.75	4	0	0	0	1	0	4.0	6	21	3	3	0	0	1		2	0	5	2	0

CLASS A Midwest League

Pitcher, Team	W	L	Pct.	ERA	G	GS	CG	ShO	GF	Sv.	IP	H	TBF	R	ER	HR	SH	SF	HB	BB	IBB	SO	WP	Bk.
George, Chris, Mich.	3	2	.600	1.38	48	0	0	0	43	24	58.2	34	221	12	9	3	1	4	1	21	3	54	3	0
Gil, David, Day.	1	1	.500	2.70	4	4	0	0	0	0	26.2	20	109	13	8	1	2	0	1	11	0	15	1	0
Giuliano, Joe, Day.	0	3	.000	5.45	22	1	0	0	15	4	38.0	48	179	31	23	4	1	2	3	13	0	30	2	2
Gold, J.M., Bel.	3	1	.750	2.91	7	7	0	0	0	0	34.0	27	143	13	11	0	2	0	1	16	0	33	1	0
Gomer, Jeramy, Lan.*	6	8	.429	4.60	24	24	1	0	0	0	135.0	141	607	84	69	15	6	6	11	55	0	98	12	1
Gomez, Odalis, C.R.	1	0	1.000	8.82	7	0	0	0	0	0	16.1	27	92	20	16	2	0	3	1	19	0	13	10	1
Gonzalez, Jeremi, Lan.	0	0	.000	0.00	1	1	0	0	0	0	0.2	0	2	0	0	0	0	0	0	0	0	2	0	0
Gordon, Kevin, K.C.	2	1	.667	3.96	23	0	0	0	6	1	36.1	31	161	17	16	3	1	2	2	19	0	43	6	1
Gosewisch, Ian, C.R.	1	0	1.000	3.00	2	0	0	0	2	0	3.0	4	16	1	1	0	0	0	1	2	1	1	0	0
Grater, Kevin, Bel.	2	1	.667	2.98	17	7	0	0	4	2	60.1	51	251	23	20	8	1	1	3	18	0	52	2	0
Gray, Brett, Day.	5	3	.625	3.02	13	4	1	0	4	0	47.2	37	193	19	16	6	3	1	3	13	2	43	1	0
Grezlovski, Ben, C.R.	0	1	.000	3.72	11	0	0	0	10	6	9.2	9	45	6	4	0	0	0	0	6	1	12	0	0
Grippo, Mike, Peo.*	0	0	.000	2.70	5	0	0	0	2	0	6.2	2	28	4	2	0	1	0	0	6	0	8	0	0
Gruban, Jarret, C.R.	0	1	.000	3.00	1	1	0	0	0	0	6.0	4	25	2	2	0	0	1	0	5	0	0	0	0
Grunwald, Erik, Wis.	2	1	.667	2.04	37	0	0	0	19	3	66.1	53	276	24	15	3	3	2	3	18	2	59	5	0
Handy, Russell, Ft.W.	0	0	.000	45.00	2	0	0	0	1	0	1.0	1	10	6	5	0	0	1	0	5	0	0	1	0
Hannah, Shawn, W.M.	1	0	1.000	0.00	2	0	0	0	1	1	8.0	3	27	0	0	0	0	0	1	0	0	5	0	0
Haring, Brett, Day.*	1	2	.333	2.88	5	5	0	0	0	0	34.1	36	147	14	11	1	2	0	2	8	0	15	0	0
Harris, J.T., C.R.	3	5	.375	4.66	28	6	0	0	11	1	63.2	75	283	41	33	6	3	1	1	20	0	43	4	0
Harris, Julian, C.R.*	2	7	.222	4.30	31	9	0	0	13	2	90.0	93	416	61	43	8	3	6	8	48	0	56	13	0
Harris, Toby, Bel.	1	2	.333	6.50	11	0	0	0	3	0	18.0	22	92	18	13	4	1	0	4	9	0	9	2	1
Hayden, Terry, Day.*	0	1	.000	5.60	15	3	0	0	5	2	35.1	44	157	23	22	5	2	1	4	7	0	19	3	0
Hebert, Cedric, Day.	0	0	.000	3.38	2	0	0	0	2	0	2.2	2	16	2	1	0	0	1	1	4	0	2	0	0
Henriquez, Hector, K.C.*	5	5	.500	5.68	50	3	0	0	22	1	71.1	82	328	52	45	7	2	3	36	1	67	8	0
Hensley, Matthew, C.R.	2	2	.500	4.15	5	5	1	0	0	0	30.1	33	129	16	14	1	0	2	2	10	0	26	1	2
Hernandez, Carlos, Mich.*	6	6	.500	3.82	22	22	2	1	0	0	110.2	92	490	57	47	8	5	3	11	63	0	115	10	1
Hickman, Ben, K.C.	1	0	1.000	1.56	8	2	0	0	5	0	17.1	15	74	4	3	0	1	0	1	5	0	13	0	0
Hoard, Brent, Q.C.*	0	3	.000	5.40	6	6	1	0	0	0	28.1	34	130	22	17	5	0	0	0	11	0	14	2	0
Hoerman, Jared, Wis.	0	4	.000	4.70	22	0	0	0	7	1	38.1	35	177	25	20	4	2	2	7	22	4	44	8	1
Horney, Micke, Clin.	0	3	.000	4.56	15	0	0	0	6	0	25.2	30	121	17	13	2	3	2	3	8	2	23	4	0
Howington, Ty, Day.*	5	15	.250	5.27	27	26	0	0	0	0	141.2	150	656	91	83	7	3	8	13	86	1	119	19	1
Huggins, David, Day.	2	5	.286	3.72	38	0	0	0	28	16	38.2	24	186	21	16	1	3	2	7	39	1	46	10	0
Hunter, Johnny, Ft.W.	1	1	.500	5.14	4	0	0	0	2	0	7.0	7	32	5	4	1	1	0	0	4	0	10	1	0
Hussman, Darrell, Clin.	2	3	.400	5.14	9	8	0	0	0	0	42.0	46	181	26	24	1	1	0	3	14	0	33	7	0
Jackson, Stosh, Lan.*	5	6	.455	5.49	42	4	0	0	23	2	83.2	93	381	58	51	5	3	5	9	40	0	54	9	0
Jamison, Ryan, Mich.	8	3	.727	2.10	41	7	0	0	15	7	98.2	66	402	32	23	3	4	3	10	38	3	95	8	1
Janke, Cheyenne, Peo.	10	10	.500	4.04	28	27	0	0	0	0	167.0	169	734	97	75	8	7	4	10	53	3	90	11	0
Johnston, Rikki, W.M.*	1	0	1.000	1.50	1	1	0	0	0	0	6.0	8	30	4	1	0	1	0	4	0	4	1	0
Jolliffe, Brian, Ft.W.*	5	5	.500	4.35	48	0	0	0	11	0	70.1	64	325	44	34	6	2	3	7	49	4	47	5	1
Jones, Fontella, Bel.	0	3	.000	2.59	25	0	0	0	23	18	24.1	21	97	10	7	2	1	2	1	5	0	23	2	1
Jones, Travis, Ft.W.*	0	2	.000	3.38	8	0	0	0	1	0	10.2	13	50	4	4	2	0	0	1	7	1	10	0	0
Kata, Matt, S.B.	0	1	.000	27.00	1	0	0	0	1	0	0.1	0	3	1	1	0	0	0	1	0	0	0	0	0
Kees, Justin, S.B.	1	1	.500	4.91	17	2	0	0	6	0	33.0	29	145	18	18	4	4	1	1	20	1	24	2	0
Key, Chris, K.C.*	0	2	.000	3.71	5	2	0	0	1	0	17.0	21	76	11	7	0	0	2	1	1	0	18	2	0
Kirsten, Rick, W.M.	4	1	.800	1.83	6	6	0	0	0	0	39.1	36	163	10	8	1	1	0	3	8	0	25	2	0
Kohl, Doug, S.B.-Peo.	2	4	.333	3.55	36	0	0	0	13	1	58.1	49	239	26	23	6	3	2	3	15	0	48	2	1
Koronka, John, Clin.*	4	13	.235	4.33	20	18	4	0	0	0	104.0	123	452	65	50	7	2	3	0	38	2	74	4	0
Koziara, Matt, Clin.	3	3	.500	3.38	38	0	0	0	17	2	72.0	80	314	34	27	2	5	2	0	31	3	42	9	0
Lackey, John, C.R.	3	2	.600	2.08	5	5	0	0	0	0	30.1	20	115	7	7	1	0	0	2	5	0	21	4	0
Lacorte, Vince, C.R.	5	7	.417	6.46	17	9	0	0	4	0	69.2	94	323	59	50	13	2	4	2	21	0	54	3	0
Landkamer, Michael, Day.	0	0	.000	24.00	3	0	0	0	1	0	3.0	13	25	11	8	1	0	0	1	1	0	2	0	0
Law, Keith, W.M.	4	4	.500	4.83	33	1	0	0	13	0	50.1	43	237	33	27	3	3	2	5	34	1	46	1	0
Layfield, Scotty, Peo.	2	4	.333	5.13	53	0	0	0	29	15	54.1	65	277	46	31	4	2	4	2	40	5	50	6	0
Leclair, Aric, S.B.*	1	1	.500	5.12	23	0	0	0	9	0	38.2	41	188	29	22	3	1	3	4	30	4	38	5	0
Lee, Jonathan, S.B.	0	0	.000	6.43	7	0	0	0	4	2	7.0	9	35	5	5	1	2	0	1	4	0	4	2	0
Leuenberger, Jeffrey, W.M.	3	1	.750	2.73	12	9	0	0	1	0	59.1	54	255	24	18	0	2	2	2	27	0	33	4	0
Lewis, Peyton, Lan.	2	4	.333	2.63	15	0	0	0	5	2	24.0	21	104	11	7	2	2	0	1	14	1	23	2	0
Lima, Lescano, Mich.	3	2	.600	3.34	18	0	0	0	7	1	29.2	26	127	14	11	2	3	0	1	14	0	31	1	0
Lincoln, Jeff, Q.C.	0	0	.000	4.24	17	0	0	0	9	0	23.1	25	114	16	11	2	0	1	1	19	1	27	4	1
Lopez, Aquilino, Wis.	6	1	.857	1.85	39	5	1	1	29	17	68.0	47	268	16	14	1	0	1	4	20	4	67	3	0
Lopez, Gustavo, K.C.	5	4	.556	4.33	29	15	0	0	1	1	97.2	99	416	51	47	4	5	4	2	28	1	73	8	1
Lopez, Juan, Burl.*	2	7	.222	4.53	28	1	0	0	11	0	47.2	32	220	29	24	2	6	3	4	48	3	43	4	1
Loudon, Gary, S.B.	0	0	.000	3.48	7	0	0	0	2	0	10.1	3	45	5	4	0	0	0	0	11	0	8	1	0
Love, Brandon, Day.	2	1	.667	3.63	7	7	0	0	0	0	34.2	33	159	18	14	1	1	0	4	19	0	32	4	0
Lowe, Matt, Bel.	1	1	.500	5.45	24	0	0	0	8	2	33.0	48	147	24	20	2	3	1	0	8	0	15	1	0
Luque, Roger, Ft.W.*	4	3	.571	4.24	14	12	0	0	0	0	63.2	66	283	37	30	3	1	2	6	20	0	56	1	0
Madritsch, Robert, Day.*	0	0	.000	0.90	2	2	0	0	0	0	10.0	8	44	1	1	0	0	1	0	7	1	17	1	0
Majewski, Gary, Burl.	6	7	.462	3.07	22	22	3	3	0	0	134.2	83	546	53	46	8	3	6	12	68	0	137	2	0
Malone, Corwin, Burl.*	2	3	.400	4.90	38	1	0	0	16	0	71.2	67	345	52	39	4	4	4	2	60	4	82	17	2
Manias, Jim, Day.*	6	6	.500	3.22	17	16	6	1	0	0	120.1	112	496	53	43	11	0	4	2	25	0	109	5	0
Martinez, Dan, Burl.*	0	0	.000	6.75	8	0	0	0	5	0	9.1	12	49	7	7	0	0	0	1	9	0	6	1	0
Martinez, Javier, Day.	4	1	.800	6.35	16	1	0	0	7	1	17.0	20	82	13	12	3	0	0	1	10	1	24	1	0
Martinez, Luis, Bel.*	5	7	.417	3.79	28	13	0	0	7	0	92.2	71	412	49	39	8	0	6	5	61	1	77	7	1
Martinez, Renan, C.R.*	1	1	.500	4.02	7	5	0	0	2	0	31.1	37	141	15	14	4	0	1	2	12	0	18	2	0
Marx, Tommy, W.M.*	7	6	.538	2.74	18	18	1	1	0	0	98.2	74	416	35	30	6	4	1	51	0	83	4	1
Mateo, Julio, Wis.	4	8	.333	4.19	36	1	0	0	15	4	68.2	63	295	38	32	12	4	1	6	23	1	73	9	0
Mathews, Dan, Bel.	4	4	.500	2.10	45	0	0	0	25	8	68.2	54	278	20	16	0	3	0	4	17	2	58	7	0
Matzenbacher, Brian, S.B.	5	6	.455	3.02	51	0	0	0	22	5	65.2	56	282	25	22	3	2	1	3	31	2	61	4	0
Maysonet, Roberto, Bel.	0	0	.000	15.00	1	1	0	0	0	0	3.0	5	18	5	5	0	0	0	1	4	0	5	0	0
McClain, Kevin, C.R.	4	3	.571	3.13	30	0	0	0	19	3	46.0	36	187	21	16	5	0	3	2	15	0	47	4	0
McCutcheon, Mike, S.B.*	2	6	.250	3.90	10	10	1	0	0	0	57.2	62	251	34	25	1	3	1	4	20	1	37	3	0
McWhirter, Kris, Burl.	3	9	.250	3.75	28	17	2	0	4	0	122.1	118	532	67	51	11	7	4	7	46	1	103	6	1
Meche, Gil, Wis.	0	0	.000	0.00	1	1	0	0	0	0	5.0	1	17	0	0	0	0	0	0	2	0	6	0	0
Medina, Franklin, S.B.	0	1	.000	10.80	2	1	0	0	0	0	3.1	4	21	5	4	1	0	0	0	7	0	1	0	0

– 540 –

Pitcher, Team	W	L	Pct.	ERA	G	GS	CG	ShO	GF	Sv.	IP	H	TBF	R	ER	HR	SH	SF	HB	BB	IBB	SO	WP	Bk.
Mendoza, Mario, C.R.	6	6	.500	4.30	14	14	4	0	0	0	98.1	101	414	54	47	10	5	1	4	19	0	67	5	1
Merrell, Phil, Day.	0	1	.000	7.02	13	1	0	0	3	1	16.2	19	89	17	13	2	1	0	5	20	0	14	7	0
Mieses, Jose, Bel.	13	6	.684	2.53	21	21	2	2	0	0	135.0	107	530	43	38	8	5	1	3	37	1	132	6	1
Miller, Colby, Q.C.	0	1	.000	6.75	2	2	0	0	0	0	6.2	10	39	6	5	0	2	0	1	7	0	6	2	0
Miller, Ernie, C.R.*	2	5	.286	4.67	15	5	1	0	5	1	54.0	63	240	33	28	4	4	1	1	19	0	26	3	0
Mills, Ryan, Q.C.*	3	6	.333	3.53	20	20	0	0	0	0	119.2	101	518	54	47	5	7	3	15	64	0	110	9	0
Minaya, Pedro, Day.	0	1	.000	11.17	16	0	0	0	12	4	19.1	30	103	27	24	4	0	1	2	19	0	15	4	0
Mlicki, Dave, W.M.	1	0	1.000	0.00	1	1	0	0	0	0	6.0	1	21	0	0	0	0	0	0	1	0	6	0	0
Moehler, Brian, W.M.	0	1	.000	4.26	1	1	0	0	0	0	6.1	5	24	3	3	1	0	0	1	0	0	4	0	0
Montero, Oscar, Lan.	4	1	.800	0.37	17	0	0	0	15	6	24.1	18	103	6	1	0	2	0	1	12	1	27	0	0
Montoya, Saul, S.B.	0	0	.000	2.57	2	1	0	0	0	0	7.0	4	28	2	2	0	0	0	5	0	3	0	0
Moore, Bryan, K.C.	5	2	.714	3.10	58	0	0	0	54	27	69.2	78	291	28	24	3	7	2	3	12	1	58	4	0
Moore, Greg, C.R.	0	2	.000	5.48	15	0	0	0	2	0	21.1	24	93	15	13	2	4	2	0	10	0	10	2	1
Morse, Bryan, K.C.*	3	4	.429	2.70	16	0	0	0	2	0	36.2	30	152	13	11	0	2	0	5	13	0	30	3	0
Moser, Todd, K.C.*	9	5	.643	2.83	21	21	3	0	0	0	136.2	136	566	54	43	6	5	3	9	26	0	101	7	0
Mosher, Andy, Bel.	1	1	.500	6.39	17	0	0	0	6	0	25.1	28	116	22	18	1	1	6	4	12	0	18	3	0
Mottl, Ryan, Clin.	1	3	.250	7.45	9	4	0	0	1	0	29.0	41	141	27	24	4	1	2	2	8	1	28	0	0
Mozingo, Dan, Burl.*	0	0	.000	19.16	10	0	0	0	3	0	10.1	17	68	24	22	2	0	0	6	16	0	9	0	0
Munoz, Arnaldo, Burl.*	2	3	.400	6.81	22	0	0	0	8	0	38.1	45	185	34	29	2	1	0	6	25	0	44	7	5
Nanninga, Matthew, Clin.	0	0	.000	27.00	1	0	0	0	0	0	1.2	6	13	5	5	0	0	0	0	2	0	1	0	0
Nannini, Mike, Mich.	7	4	.636	3.55	15	15	3	0	0	0	101.1	85	411	45	40	4	1	3	2	33	0	86	1	0
Neu, Mike, Clin.	7	7	.500	3.13	58	0	0	0	54	24	69.0	47	306	27	24	5	4	3	1	52	8	95	10	0
Neubauer, Marc, K.C.*	6	2	.750	3.86	17	3	0	0	1	0	35.0	40	146	16	15	4	2	2	1	11	0	14	4	0
Odom, Lance, Q.C.	0	0	.000	8.22	6	0	0	0	3	0	7.2	14	43	10	7	0	0	0	5	0	6	0	2
Olean, Chris, Bel.	2	3	.400	3.54	12	5	1	0	1	0	40.2	28	155	16	16	3	1	0	1	4	0	27	3	0
Olore, Kevin, Wis.	1	3	.250	7.20	12	0	0	0	4	0	20.0	25	101	16	16	1	1	1	4	14	1	17	1	0
Orosco, Jesse, Peo.*	0	0	.000	0.00	2	2	0	0	0	0	1.2	0	6	0	0	0	0	0	0	1	0	1	0	0
Ortiz, Miguel, C.R.	0	0	.000	0.00	1	0	0	0	1	0	0.2	2	5	1	0	0	0	0	0	1	0	1	0	1
Ortiz, Omar, Ft.W.	2	1	.667	4.55	6	6	0	0	0	0	29.2	28	134	21	15	7	0	1	1	18	1	27	2	0
Ovalles, Juan, S.B.	1	4	.200	6.45	8	8	0	0	0	0	37.2	51	181	32	27	4	1	5	3	16	0	24	5	1
Padilla, Juan, Q.C.	2	2	.500	1.91	32	0	0	0	27	16	33.0	24	133	7	7	0	3	0	1	9	2	40	1	0
Parker, Matt, Peo.-Bel.	6	4	.600	3.21	40	12	0	0	18	3	109.1	96	456	52	39	10	4	3	3	32	2	74	10	0
Peavy, Jacob, Ft.W.	13	8	.619	2.90	26	25	0	0	0	0	133.2	107	565	61	43	6	4	3	9	53	0	164	8	2
Peck, Brandon, Peo.*	2	2	.500	4.82	29	1	0	0	5	0	46.2	58	222	33	25	4	2	0	1	23	3	24	4	1
Peguero, Darwin, Mich.*	3	4	.429	3.13	39	3	0	0	14	0	77.2	67	331	33	27	4	2	6	4	36	4	62	8	0
Pember, Dave, Bel.	2	10	.167	4.68	17	16	0	0	0	0	98.0	118	434	56	51	9	3	4	8	25	2	70	5	2
Perkins, Kevin, K.C.	0	0	.000	0.00	2	0	0	0	0	0	1.1	2	7	0	0	0	0	0	0	1	0	0	0	0
Perkins, Mike, Peo.	2	3	.400	4.56	8	6	0	0	0	0	23.2	31	116	23	12	1	0	2	0	14	0	28	4	0
Peterson, Kyle, Bel.	1	1	.500	1.80	3	3	0	0	0	0	15.0	10	58	4	3	2	0	1	4	0	17	0	0
Pike, Tom, Clin.	3	1	.750	3.52	31	0	0	0	14	1	46.0	55	216	26	18	0	2	3	2	24	1	41	4	1
Pineda, Jairo, W.M.	5	2	.714	3.04	42	1	0	0	9	1	68.0	53	288	29	23	6	3	2	12	25	0	37	1	0
Prater, Andy, Ft.W.	0	1	.000	4.20	26	3	0	0	6	0	45.0	38	204	23	21	4	1	3	2	28	0	44	1	0
Pridie, Jon, Q.C.	7	7	.500	3.43	45	8	0	0	9	2	97.0	89	421	47	37	5	1	3	6	42	4	91	5	0
Prinz, Bret, S.B.	1	0	1.000	0.00	6	0	0	0	5	1	7.1	2	26	2	0	0	0	0	1	9	0	10	1	0
Putz, Joseph, Wis.	12	6	.667	3.15	26	25	3	2	0	0	142.2	130	611	71	50	4	6	7	9	63	2	105	8	0
Ramirez, Santiago, Mich.	3	3	.500	6.07	23	0	0	0	12	5	29.2	27	146	28	20	6	1	0	3	32	1	22	3	1
Ramos, Juan, Wis.	6	3	.667	2.78	36	0	0	0	15	3	58.1	39	252	25	18	3	4	1	13	30	2	51	2	0
Randazzo, Jeffrey, Q.C.*	1	1	.500	3.97	2	2	0	0	0	0	11.1	10	49	5	5	3	0	0	0	8	0	12	0	0
Reith, Brian, Day.	2	1	.667	2.88	5	5	0	0	0	0	34.1	33	139	12	11	2	0	0	0	8	0	30	2	0
Risinger, Ben, Ft.W.	0	0	.000	0.00	1	0	0	0	1	1	1.0	1	5	0	0	0	0	0	1	0	0	0	0
Rivera, Homero, W.M.*	3	4	.429	3.42	36	0	0	0	10	2	47.1	45	202	23	18	4	2	2	3	15	1	40	1	0
Rivera, Samuel, W.M.	1	2	.333	4.29	18	0	0	0	3	0	21.0	18	112	14	10	0	1	1	2	29	0	18	5	1
Roberts, Nick, Mich.	13	6	.684	3.10	22	20	2	1	1	0	139.1	121	587	53	48	10	1	5	5	61	1	107	5	1
Robertson, Nathan, K.C.*	0	2	.000	5.09	6	6	0	0	0	0	17.2	24	81	13	10	0	0	1	6	0	15	0	0
Robinson, Dustin, Clin.	7	4	.636	3.94	40	4	0	0	12	1	89.0	81	374	49	39	3	4	2	30	4	61	5	0
Robinson, Jeff, Bel.	5	8	.385	4.68	17	16	0	0	0	0	82.2	63	357	50	43	10	6	1	7	43	1	88	8	1
Rodney, Fernando, W.M.	6	4	.600	2.94	22	10	0	0	1	0	82.2	74	353	34	27	2	5	0	2	35	0	56	3	0
Rohling, Stuart, Burl.	2	4	.333	2.85	26	2	0	0	7	0	60.0	42	269	25	19	3	2	2	2	51	1	58	4	1
Rojas, Chris, Ft.W.	5	4	.556	2.72	15	15	0	0	0	0	79.1	64	339	26	24	4	3	2	3	38	0	69	3	4
Rowe, Casey, W.M.	8	5	.615	3.06	15	15	2	1	0	0	97.0	85	400	40	33	11	1	3	4	27	1	67	5	0
Salmon, Brad, Clin.	7	5	.583	4.29	22	22	1	0	0	0	123.2	134	538	71	59	4	3	4	2	46	0	119	11	1
Sams, Aaron, Lan.*	0	4	.000	5.97	6	4	0	0	1	0	28.2	38	128	22	19	1	2	4	1	11	0	20	2	0
Sanchez, Duaner, S.B.	8	9	.471	3.65	28	28	4	0	0	0	165.1	152	700	80	67	6	5	5	11	54	1	121	6	2
Sansom, Trevor, Peo.	2	8	.200	2.84	49	5	0	0	13	3	87.1	81	378	42	28	2	4	2	6	33	4	45	4	0
Sauer, Marc, K.C.	8	10	.444	4.23	28	28	2	0	0	0	164.0	177	696	92	77	21	9	3	8	29	1	95	4	0
Sawyer, Steve, K.C.	1	0	1.000	0.00	3	0	0	0	0	0	4.0	14	0	0	0	0	0	0	3	0	6	0	0
Schultz, Bryan, Peo.	1	1	.500	1.15	12	0	0	0	9	0	15.2	9	63	2	2	1	0	0	0	9	0	10	0	0
Schurman, Ryan, Clin.	1	2	.333	4.74	22	0	0	0	9	1	38.0	29	174	22	20	2	3	2	3	30	3	21	7	0
Secoda, Joe, Peo.	0	0	.000	36.00	1	0	0	0	1	0	1.0	2	7	4	4	2	0	0	0	2	0	1	0	0
Sergent, Joe, K.C.*	8	3	.727	2.67	46	10	0	0	4	1	101.0	97	417	34	30	7	1	2	2	20	0	70	5	0
Shaffar, Ben, Lan.	6	9	.400	4.94	19	18	1	0	0	0	102.0	127	469	70	56	7	6	2	10	30	1	72	11	0
Shiyuk, Todd, Ft.W.*	0	2	.000	2.13	32	0	0	0	9	4	38.0	31	166	14	9	4	3	1	2	17	1	40	5	0
Shrout, Kevin, Bel.	1	0	1.000	0.00	4	2	0	0	0	0	14.0	8	54	2	0	0	0	0	4	0	10	1	0
Sikaras, Pete, S.B.	0	3	.000	6.14	20	0	0	0	2	1	29.1	33	146	25	20	1	1	2	2	22	0	17	0	0
Simonson, Chris, Bel.	4	4	.500	4.55	14	9	0	0	4	0	61.1	61	258	37	31	5	0	0	7	14	0	47	1	0
Simpson, Andre, Burl.	5	6	.455	3.01	45	1	0	0	34	15	80.2	68	339	34	27	5	5	5	4	32	2	68	5	1
Smuin, Shane, K.C.	1	0	1.000	0.00	4	0	0	0	2	0	5.1	3	23	3	0	0	0	0	0	4	0	4	0	0
Soriano, Rafael, Wis.	8	4	.667	2.87	21	21	1	0	0	0	125.0	93	500	41	39	3	2	5	12	50	0	90	5	2
Sprague, Kevin, Peo.*	8	9	.471	4.03	24	24	0	0	0	0	120.2	117	520	60	54	5	3	4	6	53	1	117	15	1
Stanford, Derek, Mich.	11	6	.647	3.99	28	25	3	1	0	0	169.0	141	736	85	75	11	8	2	18	92	3	133	15	0
Stanton, Timothy, S.B.*	5	5	.500	3.88	51	0	0	0	21	2	65.0	61	291	33	28	5	5	2	6	33	4	55	4	1
Steele, Matt, S.B.	0	0	.000	10.80	6	0	0	0	2	0	8.1	12	49	11	10	0	0	2	9	0	4	2	0
Stegall, Randy, Day.	0	0	.000	0.00	1	0	0	0	1	0	0.0	0	1	1	0	0	0	0	1	0	0	0	0
Stewart, Josh, Burl.*	9	9	.500	4.57	25	25	1	1	0	0	138.0	157	617	84	70	14	5	3	10	58	2	82	9	0

CLASS A Midwest League

Pitcher, Team	W	L	Pct.	ERA	G	GS	CG	ShO	GF	Sv.	IP	H	TBF	R	ER	HR	SH	SF	HB	BB	IBB	SO	WP	Bk.
Stewart, Steve, Bel.*	1	3	.250	6.83	21	1	0	0	5	0	29.0	38	135	23	22	7	0	2	0	10	1	27	1	0
Stiehl, Robert, Mich.	0	0	.000	9.00	1	0	0	0	1	0	1.0	1	5	1	1	0	0	0	0	1	0	1	1	0
Stocks, Nick, Peo.	10	10	.500	3.78	25	24	1	0	0	0	150.0	133	643	88	63	4	4	4	15	52	5	118	8	2
Stockstill, Jason, C.R.*	0	2	.000	7.36	10	1	0	0	5	0	22.0	29	104	18	18	0	0	1	0	9	0	22	4	0
Stokes, Shaun, Peo.	2	2	.500	3.55	8	8	0	0	0	0	45.2	47	192	22	18	5	5	0	2	12	2	36	3	0
Stumm, Jason, Burl.	2	7	.222	4.61	13	13	2	0	0	0	66.1	66	289	46	34	6	4	1	2	30	2	62	3	1
Sturdy, Tim, Q.C.	9	7	.563	2.96	23	21	2	1	0	0	133.2	121	552	61	44	6	1	1	8	39	3	73	11	2
Szuminski, Jason, Lan.	3	1	.750	3.38	4	4	0	0	0	0	21.1	19	89	8	8	0	0	1	1	10	0	7	1	1
Takach, Ryan, S.B.*	1	1	.667	4.24	12	0	0	0	6	0	17.0	16	82	13	8	1	1	1	1	14	1	12	1	1
Tankersley, Dennis, Ft.W.	5	2	.714	2.85	12	12	0	0	0	0	66.1	48	265	25	21	5	2	2	2	25	0	87	2	0
Tejeda, Franklin, Peo.	6	6	.500	3.47	19	17	1	1	1	0	106.1	100	453	57	41	4	3	6	5	31	3	64	4	1
Thomas, Don, Mich.*	4	1	.800	3.03	43	1	0	0	14	2	62.1	65	279	28	21	3	4	1	5	34	2	44	6	1
Thomas, Gaige, K.C.	0	0	.000	16.39	10	0	0	0	5	0	9.1	10	57	17	17	0	0	0	1	21	0	5	5	0
Thompson, Mike, Ft.W.	1	3	.250	5.13	6	6	0	0	0	0	26.1	28	122	19	15	1	2	3	5	15	0	17	3	0
Thompson, Travis, Clin.-Day.	5	6	.762	2.54	25	23	5	2	0	0	177.0	154	727	60	50	9	5	1	5	52	0	157	6	1
Thornton, Matt, Wis.*	6	9	.400	4.01	26	17	0	0	3	0	103.1	94	465	59	46	2	3	0	6	72	1	88	12	2
Timmerman, Heath, C.R.	0	0	.000	5.06	13	3	0	0	5	0	26.2	26	127	16	15	0	0	1	0	20	0	17	6	0
Torres, Melqui, Wis.	2	3	.400	4.01	9	4	0	0	1	0	33.2	35	154	33	15	3	0	2	2	13	1	28	0	0
Trejo, Francisco, S.B.*	1	2	.333	2.96	5	4	0	0	0	0	27.1	24	114	14	9	3	1	1	2	11	1	16	1	0
Trujillo, John, Ft.W.	3	4	.429	1.33	63	0	0	0	59	42	74.2	39	286	16	11	3	3	0	5	25	1	85	4	2
Ulacia, Dennis, Burl.*	4	14	.222	4.73	28	28	1	0	0	0	148.1	157	671	109	78	8	8	6	11	67	0	111	7	0
Valdez, Jose, Clin.	5	3	.625	2.72	14	14	2	1	0	0	86.0	63	357	39	26	7	5	4	3	40	1	76	5	1
Valera, Greg, S.B.	5	7	.417	4.46	29	18	0	0	5	0	119.0	119	525	67	59	9	4	2	6	56	0	93	9	2
Valverde, Jose, S.B.	0	5	.000	5.40	31	0	0	0	21	14	31.2	31	152	20	19	1	2	0	3	25	0	39	8	0
Vanhekken, Andrew, W.M.*	16	6	.727	2.45	26	25	3	1	1	1	158.0	139	648	48	43	3	3	2	7	37	0	126	3	0
Vasquez, Luis, Mich.*	0	1	.000	14.54	2	2	0	0	0	0	4.1	9	24	8	7	1	0	0	2	2	0	5	1	0
Villanueva, Bill, K.C.	1	6	.143	3.67	13	10	0	0	0	0	61.1	59	267	32	25	7	4	3	9	25	0	36	2	0
Villarreal, Oscar, S.B.	1	3	.250	4.41	13	5	0	0	5	0	32.2	37	155	19	16	0	0	0	3	17	3	30	2	1
Vincent, Matt, Peo.*	3	4	.429	3.92	58	0	0	0	19	1	66.2	65	303	36	29	5	8	4	5	30	3	65	6	2
Warner, Bryan, Lan.*	0	0	.000	3.24	5	0	0	0	5	0	8.1	5	37	4	3	1	0	0	2	4	0	8	1	0
Watson, Gregory, W.M.	2	2	.500	2.16	62	0	0	0	59	30	58.1	40	256	21	14	1	5	1	8	38	1	68	5	1
Webb, Brandon, S.B.	0	0	.000	3.24	12	0	0	0	7	2	16.2	10	69	7	6	0	0	0	2	9	0	18	1	0
Webb, John, Lan.	7	6	.538	2.47	21	21	1	1	0	0	134.2	125	559	53	37	4	3	6	8	40	0	108	9	1
Weis, Brad, Q.C.*	1	2	.333	2.55	40	0	0	0	22	0	60.0	55	255	20	17	9	0	3	6	22	5	56	4	1
West, Brian, Burl.	8	9	.471	3.78	24	24	0	0	0	0	147.2	146	654	81	62	3	7	6	9	73	1	90	11	0
White, Bill, S.B.*	0	0	.000	3.38	1	1	0	0	0	0	2.2	3	14	1	1	0	0	0	3	0	5	1	0
Whitesides, Johnny, Mich.	0	2	.000	4.56	13	0	0	0	5	1	25.2	25	113	17	13	2	0	3	0	9	0	17	2	0
Wiggins, Dan, Lan.	1	3	.250	6.75	24	0	0	0	7	1	34.2	50	171	31	26	7	3	4	1	20	0	32	2	1
Wiles, Chad, Wis.	0	0	.000	0.00	2	0	0	0	2	1	2.0	0	6	0	0	0	0	0	0	0	0	1	0	0
Wilson, Philip, C.R.	8	5	.615	3.41	21	21	1	0	0	0	129.1	114	544	61	49	9	4	4	7	49	0	82	9	1
Wohlers, Mark, Day.	0	0	.000	3.00	3	3	0	0	0	0	3.0	1	11	1	1	1	0	0	0	1	0	7	0	0
Wolfe, Brian, Q.C.	5	9	.357	4.74	31	18	0	0	2	0	123.1	148	541	73	65	13	2	6	4	34	1	91	7	1
Yates, Chad, Peo.	0	1	.000	1.72	17	0	0	0	17	6	15.2	7	60	5	3	0	1	1	6	1	13	1	0
Young, Douglas, Ft.W.	5	2	.714	2.91	62	0	0	0	12	0	89.2	58	357	34	29	1	2	4	1	40	1	85	5	0

COMBINATION SHUTOUTS: **Beloit (7)**—Mieses-Mathews-Mosher, Childers-Jones, Grater-Jones, Martinez-Cordero-Altman, Parker-Mathews, Simonson-Cordero-Mathews, Parker-Mathews. **Burlington (4)**—West-Simpson, Majewski-Simpson-Curreri, Simpson-Malone-Curreri, Majewski-Simpson. **Cedar Rapids (3)**—Martinez-Harris, Brummett-Escalante, Hensley-McClain. **Clinton (5)**—Darnell-Neu, Thompson-Robinson, Dunn-Schurman-Neu, Cordova-Bradley-Neu, Cordova-Mottl-Pike. **Dayton (1)**—Acevedo-DeHart. **Fort Wayne (10)**—Ortiz-Prater-Bartosh-Hunter, Baxter-Trujillo, Baxter-Shiyuk-Trujillo, Peavy-Young, Peavy-Prater-Jolliffe, Rojas-Trujillo, Tankersley-Young-Trujillo, Rojas-Young-Bartosh, Peavy-Jolliffe-Cassel-Trujillo, Tankersley-Young-Bartosh-Trujillo. **Kane County (10)**—Henriquez-Gordon-Bowe, Villanueva-Moore, Cordova-Gordon, Farizo-Bowe-Henriquez-Moore, Lopez-Morse-Bowe-Moore, Moser-Henriquez, Lopez-Neubauer-Bowe, Sauer-Moore, Sergeant-Moore, Lopez-Gordon. **Lansing (6)**—Webb-Cordero, Webb-Bailey-Montero, Cruz-Eppeneder, Cordero-Jackson, Szuminski-Lewis, Gomer-Jackson. **Michigan (5)**—Stanford-George-Ramirez, Roberts-Whitesides-Peguero, Hernandez-Peguero-Jamison, Anderson-Jamison-George, Jamison-George. **Peoria (11)**—Janke-Yates, Cook-Crudale-Yates, Sprague-Sansom-Layfield-Vincent, Stocks-Crudale-Fahs, Sprague-Sansom, Cook-Sansom, Stocks-Vincent-Layfield, Stocks-Sansom-Layfield, Sprague-Sansom-Layfield-Kohl-Peck, Stocks-Fahs-Kohl, Janke-Kohl. **Quad City (5)**—Wolfe-Frederick-Cento, Pridie-Frederick-Cento-Padilla, Sturdy-Pride, Mills-Barreto, Blackwell-Wolfe-Cento. **South Bend (4)**—Villarreal-Stanton-Valverde, Valera-Matzenbacher-Kohl, Valera-Matzenbacher-Valverde, Capuano-Matzenbacher-Stanton. **West Michigan (13)**—Marx-Burke, Marx-Barnett-Rivera, Marx-Watson, Van Hekken-Watson, Marx-Rodney-Watson, Van Hekken-Pineda-Watson, Van Hekken-Rodney-Watson, Rodney-Barnett-Eckenstahler-Burke, Frasor-Rivera-Watson, Arias-Barnett-Pineda, Frasor-Rivera-Eckstahler, Arias-Eckstahler, Mlicki-Van Hekken. **Wisconsin (6)**—Baek-Torres, Delgado-Ramos-Lopez, Baek-Mateo-Lopez, Thornton-Burton-Lopez, Putz-Ramos-Lopez, Meche-Delgado-Ramos.

NO-HIT GAMES: Putz, Wisconsin defeated Kane County, 6-1, April 29; Sturdy, Quad City defeated Cedar Rapids, 1-0, May 19; Hernandez, Michigan, defeated West Michigan, 2-0, May 28; Marx, West Michigan defeated Kane County, 8-0, June 10; Chipperfield, West Michigan defeated Kane County, 2-0, June 13; Dunn, Clinton defeated Lansing, 7-0, August 3.

PITCHERS WITH TWO OR MORE TEAMS

Pitcher, Team	W	L	Pct.	ERA	G	GS	CG	ShO	GF	Sv.	IP	H	TBF	R	ER	HR	SH	SF	HB	BB	IBB	SO	WP	Bk.
Altman, Gene, Day.	2	0	1.000	3.78	9	0	0	0	3	0	16.2	17	83	10	7	0	1	0	1	13	0	16	0	0
Altman, Gene, Bel.	4	0	1.000	2.15	33	0	0	0	27	17	37.2	32	163	11	9	1	0	6	18	0	42	2	0
Cordova, Jorge, K.C.	6	7	.462	3.88	22	15	1	0	2	1	95.0	94	395	41	41	9	4	2	4	21	1	94	9	0
Cordova, Jorge, Clin.	3	2	.600	4.25	8	8	0	0	0	0	48.2	48	216	26	23	1	1	6	0	28	0	50	8	1
Duprey, Pete, Wis.*	0	0	.000	4.44	19	0	0	0	11	2	24.1	26	108	17	12	2	1	0	1	8	2	28	0	0
Duprey, Pete, Lan.*	2	1	.667	1.75	12	0	0	0	2	0	25.2	28	114	9	5	1	0	3	1	9	1	15	3	0
Kohl, Doug, S.B.	1	2	.333	4.43	11	0	0	0	7	0	20.1	20	91	11	10	2	1	2	2	8	0	20	2	1
Kohl, Doug, Peo.	1	2	.333	3.08	25	0	0	0	6	1	38.0	29	148	15	13	4	2	0	1	7	0	28	0	0
Parker, Matt, Peo.	2	2	.500	2.59	26	0	0	0	17	3	31.1	24	129	9	9	0	3	1	0	13	1	20	5	0
Parker, Matt, Bel.	2	4	.667	3.46	14	12	0	0	1	0	78.0	72	327	43	30	10	1	2	3	19	1	54	5	0
Thompson, Travis, Clin.	5	1	.833	1.77	6	6	1	1	0	0	40.2	21	153	8	8	0	0	0	0	13	0	42	2	0
Thompson, Travis, Day.	11	4	.733	2.77	19	17	4	1	0	0	136.1	133	574	52	42	6	4	1	5	39	0	115	4	1

TEAM

Team	Pct.	G	PO	A	E	TC	DP	TP	PB
Kane County	.970	139	3566	1485	156	5207	120	0	22
Fort Wayne	.967	137	3560	1362	166	5088	101	0	24
Beloit	.965	135	3513	1484	179	5176	106	0	20
West Michigan	.965	140	3656	1440	183	5279	109	0	31
Wisconsin	.965	138	3612	1454	185	5251	140	0	26
Michigan	.964	138	3620	1455	187	5262	133	0	23
Lansing	.964	138	3581	1455	186	5222	127	1	50
South Bend	.963	138	3551	1548	198	5297	103	1	47
Burlington	.962	139	3569	1395	197	5161	122	0	37
Dayton	.962	137	3598	1401	199	5198	133	0	15
Quad City	.961	139	3602	1614	213	5429	144	0	32
Clinton	.961	140	3669	1446	210	5325	120	0	24
Peoria	.959	137	3573	1605	222	5400	109	0	31
Cedar Rapids	.957	139	3603	1628	236	5467	117	0	23

INDIVIDUAL

FIRST BASEMEN

NOTE: All caps denotes fielding-percentage leader based on 70 games for catchers, 93 for all other non-pitchers and 112 innings for pitchers. *Throws lefthanded.

Player, Team	Pct.	G	PO	A	E	TC	DP
Amador, Gerardo, W.M.	1.000	1	6	0	0	6	0
Anthony, Jacob, W.M.*	.985	110	937	61	15	1013	76
Bailey, Travis, Peo.	.981	56	495	30	10	535	39
Beattie, Andy, Day.	1.000	1	0	0	0	1	1
Bookout, Casey, Day.	.992	59	459	22	4	485	55
Bordenick, Ryan, Bel.	1.000	3	35	2	0	37	1
Callahan, Dave, K.C.*	.987	128	1135	81	16	1232	98
Cline, Pat, Day.	.000	1	0	0	0	0	0
Closser, J.D., S.B.	.952	3	18	2	1	21	2
Curtis, Bill, C.R.	1.000	2	11	1	0	12	1
Darula, Bobby, Bel.	1.000	1	15	1	0	16	1
Dehner, Matt, Clin.	.972	18	95	8	3	106	11
Demarco, Matt, K.C.	.960	3	23	1	1	25	0
Domero, William, W.M.	.977	4	37	5	1	43	5
Dominguez, Luis, Mich.	.990	23	193	14	2	209	17
Drobiak, Jayson, W.M.	.993	19	126	9	1	136	10
Duncan, Chris, Peo.	.962	85	848	44	35	927	58
Egly, John, S.B.	.941	9	74	6	5	85	4
Estrella, Gorky, Wis.	1.000	4	26	2	0	28	2
Fennell, Jason, Burl.	1.000	6	43	1	0	44	5
Figueroa, Eduardo, Bel.*	.993	17	146	6	1	153	9
Frick, Matt, K.C.	.989	10	83	8	1	92	9
Fuentes, Javier, S.B.	.981	7	49	3	1	53	6
Garcia, Hector, Bel.	.983	98	887	65	16	968	72
Garrett, Shawn, Ft.W.	.972	8	64	5	2	71	6
Garza, Rolando, Burl.	.991	15	108	6	1	115	6
Gripp, Ryan, Lan.	1.000	1	1	0	0	1	0
Jordan, Yustin, Q.C.	.957	8	39	5	2	46	2
Kelley, Casey, C.R.	.987	75	693	74	10	777	56
Kelly, Chris, Peo.	1.000	3	11	0	0	11	0
Lane, Jason, Mich.*	.995	26	201	12	1	214	22
Lutz, Manuel, W.M.	.968	11	85	6	3	94	6
Markray, Thad, Clin.	1.000	1	3	0	0	3	1
Martin, Billy, S.B.	.991	58	517	40	5	562	30
Massey, John, S.B.	1.000	1	5	0	0	5	0
Matan, Jim, Day.	.995	40	360	8	2	370	38
McCORKLE, Shawn, Wis.	.994	124	1023	58	7	1088	111
Medina, Luis, Lan.	.985	122	998	88	16	1102	102
Morrow, Alvin, Bel.	.969	18	146	10	5	161	15
Oborn, Spencer, Burl.	.833	1	3	2	1	6	0
Ortiz, Matt, Peo.	1.000	1	3	0	0	3	0
Ortiz, Miguel, C.R.	.978	13	131	4	3	138	13
Overbay, Lyle, S.B.*	.983	65	587	45	11	643	46
Owens, Ryan, S.B.	1.000	3	13	3	0	16	2
Palmieri, Jon, C.R.	.985	15	121	10	2	133	9
Peters, Samone, Clin.	.980	122	1021	61	22	1104	92
Robles, Kevin, Wis.	.987	17	146	4	2	152	11
Rogowski, Casey, Burl.*	.986	122	982	54	15	1051	95
Sandberg, Eric, Q.C.*	.985	127	1186	103	19	1308	123
Santamarina, Juan, Burl.	1.000	1	4	1	0	5	2
Scheschuk, John, Ft.W.*	.988	131	1017	80	13	1110	82
Schmitt, Brian, Mich.*	.983	96	812	63	15	890	82
Selander, Craig, Q.C.	1.000	5	37	1	0	38	1
Solorzano, Lenin, Burl.	.800	3	4	0	1	5	0
Spoerl, Josh, Clin.	.937	11	85	4	6	95	8
Stegall, Randy, Day.	.981	11	100	5	2	107	6
Tiffee, Terry, Q.C.	.964	4	25	2	1	28	1
Welsh, Eric, Day.*	.985	16	123	9	2	134	8
White, Greg, C.R.	.992	46	374	22	3	399	31
Whitehead, Braxton, Day.	.957	3	22	0	1	23	2
Williamson, Chris, Day.*	.972	15	98	6	3	107	11
Wrenn, Michael, Q.C.	.667	2	2	0	1	3	1
Zoccolillo, Peter, Lan.	.987	21	129	18	2	149	10

TRIPLE PLAY: Egly.

SECOND BASEMEN

Player, Team	Pct.	G	PO	A	E	TC	DP
Acevedo, Luis, Day.	.976	20	40	43	2	85	13
Ahlers, Steve, C.R.	.896	15	19	41	7	67	8
Alvarez, Jimmy, Q.C.	.939	34	57	98	10	165	24
Araujo, Danilo, Peo.	.935	58	95	163	18	276	30
Beattie, Andy, Day.-Clin.	.966	13	21	35	2	58	5
Burnett, Mark, Clin.	.944	120	204	332	32	568	65
Campana, Wandel, Clin.	.974	11	14	23	1	38	6
Carvajal, Ramon, Peo.	.956	39	74	120	9	203	22
Demarco, Matt, K.C.	1.000	4	14	10	0	24	5
Dominguez, Luis, Mich.	.667	2	2	4	3	9	1
Drobiak, Jayson, W.M.	.950	11	9	29	2	40	4
Duran, Francisco, C.R.	.955	85	163	244	19	426	50
Durango, Ariel, Wis.	.963	103	179	287	18	484	70
Dzurilla, Mike, Lan.	.982	66	140	186	6	332	50
Edwards, Dytarious, Clin.	.857	4	7	5	2	14	3
Escalona, Felix, Mich.	.952	53	90	149	12	251	37
Escobar, Gustavo, Peo.	.977	35	56	112	4	172	15
Flores, Ralphs, Burl.	.923	8	7	17	2	26	6
Frank, Nick, Bel.	1.000	14	25	49	0	74	9
Fuentes, Javier, S.B.	.983	27	51	65	2	118	13
German, Franklin, Lan.	.942	23	61	52	7	120	11
Gosewisch, Ian, C.R.	.963	16	30	49	3	82	5
Green, Andy, S.B.	1.000	3	5	2	0	7	0
Gsell, Tony, Lan.	.969	34	77	77	5	159	20
Hawes, Bobby, Day.	.000	1	0	0	0	0	0
Hlousek, Rob, W.M.	.977	30	59	67	3	129	14
HOOPER, Kevin, K.C.	.978	121	234	339	13	586	78
Huth, Jason, Day.	.969	31	56	71	4	131	20
Jimenez, Carlos, W.M.	.953	63	105	160	13	278	34
Kata, Matt, S.B.	.965	9	24	31	2	57	5
Kilburg, Joe, Day.-Clin.	.962	21	41	59	4	104	10
Kison, Richie, Clin.-Day.	.977	40	62	111	4	177	25
Leone, Justin, Wis.	.875	2	4	3	1	8	0
Lotterhos, Chris, S.B.	1.000	2	1	2	0	3	0
Maule, Jason, Mich.	.959	64	125	157	12	294	41
Maya, Johan, Mich.	.957	30	50	62	5	117	20
Moore, Jason, Ft.W.	.926	8	7	18	2	27	2
Nelson, Reggie, W.M.	.971	44	87	150	7	244	27
Nicholson, Derek, Mich.	1.000	1	1	4	0	5	1
Nicholson, Tommy, Burl.	.973	65	116	175	8	299	36
Olmedo, Ranier, Day.	.959	15	37	57	4	98	13
Ortiz, Miguel, C.R.	.927	25	47	67	9	123	14
Owens, Ryan, S.B.	.972	16	30	40	2	72	3
Paulino, Dave, K.C.	.970	10	8	24	1	33	0
Perkins, Kevin, K.C.	1.000	5	7	7	0	14	1
Ramirez, Oscar, Wis.	.945	44	65	108	10	183	23
Risinger, Ben, Ft.W.	.977	28	54	73	3	130	18
Rodriguez, Luis, Q.C.	.970	85	126	258	12	396	51
Ryan, Jeff, Lan.	.915	8	21	22	4	47	5
Sachs, Brent, Lan.	.985	14	31	35	1	67	11
Sandoval, Danny, Burl.	.909	3	5	5	1	11	2
Santiago, Daniel, Day.	1.000	2	2	2	0	4	1
Santora, Jack, S.B.	.969	83	152	226	12	390	41
Santos, Luis, Q.C.	.966	11	15	13	1	29	3
Scales, Bobby, Ft.W.	.949	59	119	159	15	293	27
Scanlon, Matt, Q.C.	.912	22	32	51	8	91	14
Scarborough, Steve, Bel.	.976	122	214	352	14	580	62
Secoda, Joe, Peo.	.000	1	0	0	0	0	0
Shaffer, Josh, C.R.	.895	5	6	11	2	19	2
Solorzano, Lenin, Burl.	.833	6	7	8	3	18	1
Spadt, Eric, Clin.	1.000	2	2	1	0	3	1
Stegall, Randy, Day.	.906	21	46	41	9	96	9
Tamburrino, Brett, Q.C.	.900	8	8	19	3	30	6
Teilon, Nilson, Burl.	.936	62	116	147	18	281	33
Voshell, Key, Peo.	.962	12	17	34	2	53	5
Ward, Brian, Ft.W.	.947	44	81	98	10	189	17
Wilson, Josh, K.C.	.920	4	12	11	2	25	5

TRIPLE PLAYS: Gsell, Kata.

CLASS A Midwest League

SECOND BASEMEN WITH TWO OR MORE TEAMS

Player, Team	Pct.	G	PO	A	E	TC	DP
Beattie, Andy, Day.	.951	9	16	23	2	41	1
Beattie, Andy, Clin.	1.000	4	5	12	0	17	4
Kilburg, Joe, Day.	.959	19	38	56	4	98	10
Kilburg, Joe, Clin.	1.000	2	3	3	0	6	0
Kison, Robbie, Clin.	.941	4	7	9	1	17	3
Kison, Robbie, Day.	.981	36	55	102	3	160	22

THIRD BASEMEN

Player, Team	Pct.	G	PO	A	E	TC	DP
Alfieri, Frank, Bel.	.939	13	7	24	2	33	1
Alvarado, Damien, Wis.	.833	2	2	3	1	6	0
Araujo, Danilo, Peo.	.000	1	0	0	0	0	0
Aspito, Jason, Burl.	.944	36	29	56	5	90	5
Baderdeen, Kevin, Day.	.906	44	27	88	12	127	7
Bailey, Travis, Peo.	.837	12	12	29	8	49	5
Beattie, Andy, Clin.	.950	11	5	14	1	20	0
Dehner, Matt, Clin.	.924	91	60	147	17	224	17
Demarco, Matt, K.C.	.839	13	4	22	5	31	2
Domero, William, W.M.	1.000	4	2	4	0	6	0
Dominguez, Luis, Mich.	.908	57	32	96	13	141	7
Drobiak, Jayson, W.M.	.872	43	31	51	12	94	4
Escobar, Gustavo, Peo.	1.000	5	1	2	0	3	0
Estrella, Gorky, Wis.	.913	66	43	103	14	160	10
Fennell, Jason, Burl.	1.000	1	1	0	0	1	0
Flores, Ralphs, Burl.	.891	45	34	56	11	101	5
Frank, Nick, Bel.	.906	62	26	137	17	180	11
Fuentes, Javier, S.B.	.930	46	27	93	9	129	8
Garrett, Shawn, Ft.W.	.914	14	14	18	3	35	4
Garza, Rolando, Burl.	.895	9	6	11	2	19	0
German, Franklin, Lan.	.933	4	4	10	1	15	0
Gosewisch, Ian, C.R.	.813	8	5	8	3	16	1
Gripp, Ryan, Lan.	.924	124	69	248	26	343	25
Gsell, Tony, Lan.	.857	10	1	17	3	21	2
Helquist, Jon, Mich.	.899	62	37	114	17	168	11
Huth, Jason, Day.	.879	13	4	25	4	33	2
Jenkins, Neil, W.M.	.842	99	68	177	46	291	13
Johnson, Gabe, Peo.	.894	21	14	45	7	66	6
Jordan, Yustin, Q.C.	.778	13	8	13	6	27	2
Kelly, Chris, Peo.	1.000	1	0	1	0	1	0
Kilburg, Joe, Clin.	.864	9	8	11	3	22	0
Kison, Robbie, Day.	.000	1	0	0	0	0	0
Leone, Justin, Wis.	.894	74	46	132	21	199	16
Lindsey, Cordell, C.R.	.916	104	65	251	29	345	16
Lundquist, Ryan, Clin.	.000	1	0	0	0	0	0
Markray, Thad, Clin.	.958	13	8	15	1	24	1
Martin, Billy, S.B.	1.000	2	0	1	0	1	0
Matan, Jim, Day.	.000	1	0	0	0	0	0
Maya, Johan, Mich.	.842	8	1	15	3	19	3
Medina, Luis, Lan.	.714	4	2	3	2	7	0
Moore, Jason, Ft.W.	.898	15	11	33	5	49	5
Myers, Corey, S.B.	.797	19	14	41	14	69	2
Nelson, Reggie, W.M.	1.000	2	1	4	0	5	0
Nicholson, Derek, Mich.	.836	22	12	34	9	55	4
Niles, Drew, K.C.	.667	1	0	2	1	3	0
Olson, Tim, S.B.	.907	20	12	37	5	54	2
Ortiz, Miguel, C.R.	.941	31	21	59	5	85	5
Owens, Ryan, S.B.	.899	50	29	104	15	148	7
Perkins, Kevin, K.C.	.901	29	13	51	7	71	6
PUJOLS, Albert, Peo.	.948	104	92	254	19	365	21
Ramirez, Oscar, Wis.	.829	11	8	21	6	35	2
Reyes, Eduardo, Bel.	.868	52	25	106	20	151	2
Risinger, Ben, Ft.W.	.974	15	10	27	1	38	2
Rodriguez, Luis, Q.C.	.900	7	2	7	1	10	0
Ryan, Jeff, Lan.	1.000	1	1	1	0	2	0
Sachs, Brent, Lan.	1.000	1	0	3	0	3	0
Sandoval, Danny, Burl.	1.000	1	3	2	0	5	0
Santamarina, Juan, Burl.	.808	9	6	15	5	26	0
Santos, Luis, S.B.	.952	7	4	16	1	21	0
Scanlon, Matt, Q.C.	.881	55	28	113	19	160	9
Schader, Troy, Ft.W.	.901	73	54	147	22	223	11
Shaffer, Josh, C.R.	1.000	1	1	1	0	2	0
Solorzano, Lenin, Burl.	.926	53	30	82	9	121	9
Spadt, Eric, Clin.	.853	10	4	25	5	34	3
Spoerl, Josh, Clin.	.727	23	7	25	12	44	0
Stegall, Randy, Day.	.903	89	64	150	23	237	20
Tiffee, Terry, Q.C.	.860	69	47	138	30	215	16
Trout, Casey, Bel.	.906	12	11	18	3	32	4
Ward, Brian, Ft.W.	.899	24	16	46	7	69	1
Washington, Kelley, K.C.	.921	102	67	167	20	254	13
White, Greg, C.R.	.000	1	0	0	0	0	0
Whitehead, Braxton, Day.	.000	1	0	0	0	0	0

Player, Team	Pct.	G	PO	A	E	TC	DP
Wilson, Josh, K.C.	.875	2	1	6	1	8	0
Wrenn, Michael, Q.C.	1.000	6	2	7	0	9	1

TRIPLE PLAY: Olson.

SHORTSTOPS

Player, Team	Pct.	G	PO	A	E	TC	DP
Acevedo, Luis, Day.-Clin.	.966	7	13	15	1	29	3
Alvarez, Jimmy, Q.C.	.882	9	12	18	4	34	6
Baderdeen, Kevin, Day.	1.000	1	1	0	0	1	0
Beattie, Andy, Clin.	.922	89	132	234	31	397	43
Campana, Wandel, Clin.	.925	24	42	44	7	93	10
Carvajal, Ramon, Peo.	.937	53	81	187	18	286	24
Castillo, Ruben, Wis.	.947	120	234	322	31	587	74
Dehner, Matt, Clin.	1.000	1	1	1	0	2	0
Demarco, Matt, K.C.	.960	6	9	15	1	25	3
Deschaine, James, Lan.	.950	107	169	305	25	499	63
Dominguez, Luis, Mich.	.500	1	0	1	1	2	0
Duran, Francisco, C.R.	.923	32	61	71	11	143	15
Durango, Ariel, Wis.	.927	10	17	21	3	41	5
Edwards, Dytarious, Clin.	.857	3	2	4	1	7	1
Escalona, Felix, Mich.	.960	14	18	30	2	50	6
Escobar, Gustavo, Peo.	1.000	4	3	9	0	12	3
Estrella, Gorky, Wis.	.800	1	1	3	1	5	1
Flores, Ralphs, Burl.	.917	27	43	89	12	144	22
German, Franklin, Lan.	.861	20	27	35	10	72	7
Gsell, Tony, Lan.	.927	11	17	34	4	55	7
Hall, Will, Bel.	.939	130	214	397	40	651	79
Hawes, Bobby, Day.	.892	37	44	105	18	167	12
Helquist, Jon, Mich.	.935	14	16	27	3	46	5
Hummel, Timothy, Burl.	.964	39	46	87	5	138	15
Infante, Omar, W.M.	.983	12	28	31	1	60	11
Jimenez, Carlos, W.M.	.947	43	69	129	11	209	21
Jordan, Yustin, Q.C.	.913	7	6	15	2	23	2
Kata, Matt, S.B.	.933	122	164	355	37	556	56
Kilburg, Joe, Clin.	1.000	1	1	1	0	2	1
Kison, Robbie, Clin.-Day.	.959	36	48	93	6	147	22
Leone, Justin, Wis.	.949	21	32	42	4	78	11
Maya, Johan, Mich.	1.000	16	31	37	0	68	8
Mendez, Donaldo, Mich.	.957	100	166	326	22	514	59
Montanez, Luis, Lan.	.929	4	6	20	2	28	6
Moore, Jason, Ft.W.	.946	96	135	232	21	388	47
Nelson, Reggie, W.M.	.935	10	13	30	3	46	1
Nicholson, Derek, Mich.	1.000	1	1	2	0	3	0
Niles, Drew, K.C.	.981	13	16	36	1	53	5
Olmedo, Ranier, Day.	.943	95	137	274	25	436	63
Ortiz, Miguel, C.R.	.750	1	2	1	1	4	0
Owens, Ryan, S.B.	1.000	2	3	8	0	11	1
Perkins, Kevin, K.C.	.938	6	8	7	1	16	1
Reyes, Eduardo, Bel.	.000	2	0	0	0	0	0
Risinger, Ben, Ft.W.	.962	6	12	13	1	26	3
Rodriguez, Luis, Q.C.	.986	16	24	45	1	70	14
Saba, Cesar, Ft.W.	.916	35	42	89	12	143	14
Sandoval, Danny, Burl.	.927	68	97	195	23	315	36
Santiago, Ramon, W.M.	.976	81	110	220	8	338	45
Santora, Jack, S.B.	.971	16	22	45	2	69	7
Santos, Luis, S.B.	.846	5	2	9	2	13	2
Scarborough, Steve, Bel.	.962	5	8	17	1	26	6
Schader, Troy, Ft.W.	1.000	2	4	6	0	10	0
Shaffer, Josh, C.R.	.932	109	141	338	35	514	58
Solorzano, Lenin, Burl.	1.000	8	14	29	0	43	8
Stegall, Randy, Day.	.733	4	5	6	4	15	2
STEVENS, Tony, Q.C.	.958	116	202	342	24	568	80
Thames, Damon, Peo.	.928	82	92	232	25	349	34
Ugueto, Luis, K.C.	.941	113	179	343	33	555	70
Wilson, Josh, K.C.	.950	5	7	12	1	20	2

TRIPLE PLAY: Deschaine.

SHORTSTOPS WITH TWO OR MORE TEAMS

Player, Team	Pct.	G	PO	A	E	TC	DP
Acevedo, Luis, Day.	1.000	2	1	1	0	2	0
Acevedo, Luis, Clin.	.963	5	12	14	1	27	3
Kison, Robbie, Clin.	.967	28	41	78	4	123	18
Kison, Robbie, Day.	.917	7	15	2	2	24	4

OUTFIELDERS

Player, Team	Pct.	G	PO	A	E	TC	DP
Abate, Mike, Wis.	1.000	22	20	2	0	22	0
Alfieri, Frank, Bel.	.857	5	6	0	1	7	0
Amador, Gerardo, W.M.	.982	74	111	1	2	114	0
Ambres, Chip, K.C.	.989	81	180	5	2	187	1
Arroyo, Abner, Ft.W.*	.974	31	36	1	1	38	0
Aspito, Jason, Burl.	.938	19	30	0	2	32	0

Player, Team	Pct.	G	PO	A	E	TC	DP
Bailey, Travis, Peo.	.000	1	0	0	0	0	0
Bass, Kevin, Lan.	.963	91	148	7	6	161	1
Beattie, Andy, Day.-Clin.	1.000	8	6	2	0	8	1
Bikowski, Scott, C.R.*	.968	113	203	9	7	219	1
Burns, Kevan, S.B.*	.980	95	141	4	3	148	1
Callahan, Dave, K.C.*	.000	1	0	0	0	0	0
Candela, Frank, Bel.	.963	65	125	5	5	135	0
Close, James, K.C.	1.000	6	8	0	0	8	0
Cook, Jon, Ft.W.	1.000	24	36	1	0	37	0
Cripps, Bobby, Clin.	.000	2	0	0	0	0	0
Crisp, Covelli, Peo.	1.000	22	42	0	0	42	0
Curry, Jesse, Ft.W.*	1.000	15	16	1	0	17	0
Curtis, Bill, C.R.	1.000	3	4	0	0	4	0
Darula, Bobby, Bel.	1.000	28	39	2	0	41	0
Day, Nick, Ft.W.	.950	26	37	1	2	40	0
De Aza, Modesto, Mich.	.971	12	31	3	1	35	2
Dehner, Matt, Clin.	1.000	2	1	1	0	2	0
De La Cruz, Eric, Bel.	.976	67	117	6	3	126	1
Dellucci, David, S.B.*	1.000	1	1	0	0	1	0
Deschaine, James, Lan.	1.000	9	11	1	0	12	0
Devore, Doug, S.B.*	.941	118	178	14	12	204	4
Dominguez, Luis, Mich.	.000	1	0	0	0	0	0
Donovan, Todd, Ft.W.	.991	53	101	4	1	106	0
Dunn, Adam, Day.	.958	122	197	10	9	216	1
Durham, Chad, Burl.	.958	130	261	14	12	287	0
Edwards, John, Q.C.	.961	70	83	15	4	102	2
Faison, Vince, Ft.W.	.953	117	188	13	10	211	1
Fennell, Jason, Burl.	1.000	10	9	0	0	9	0
Fernandez, Medardo, K.C.	.976	25	38	2	1	41	0
Ferrand, Francisco, K.C.*	.952	66	133	5	7	145	4
Ford, Will, Bel.*	.968	55	85	6	3	94	0
Foreman, Julius, S.B.	.979	46	94	0	2	96	0
Fulse, Sheldon, Wis.	.978	62	128	5	3	136	1
Garbe, B.J., Q.C.	.948	133	234	5	13	252	1
Garcia, Hector, Bel.	.810	11	14	3	4	21	0
Garrett, Shawn, Ft.W.	1.000	77	125	4	0	129	1
Garza, Rolando, Burl.	.973	56	102	8	3	113	0
German, Franklin, Lan.	.967	50	80	8	3	91	0
Gillikin, Joe, Burl.	.000	1	0	0	0	0	0
Goodman, Scott, K.C.*	.964	106	156	6	6	168	0
Gosewisch, Ian, C.R.	.955	20	21	0	1	22	0
Graham, Justin, S.B.	.966	21	28	0	1	29	0
Guerrero, Cris, Bel.	.960	15	24	0	1	25	0
Gundrum, Kris, Wis.*	.959	71	107	11	5	123	1
Hall, Victor, S.B.*	.922	40	70	1	6	77	0
Haynes, Larry, Wis.	.909	16	17	3	2	22	0
Hernandez, Johnny, Peo.*	.951	103	189	7	10	206	2
Hernandez, Orlando, Wis.	.994	90	160	4	1	165	2
Hill, Mike, Mich.	.988	42	77	4	1	82	1
Hills, Chris, C.R.	.941	54	125	2	8	135	0
Huff, Jake, Ft.W.	.750	2	2	1	1	4	0
Hurtado, Omar, Clin.	.974	124	207	15	6	228	5
Huth, Jason, Day.	1.000	1	1	0	0	1	0
Johnson, Ben, Peo.-Ft.W.	.972	119	196	14	6	216	5
Johnstone, Benjamin, Lan.	.969	127	277	4	9	290	1
Jordan, Yustin, Q.C.	.921	48	52	6	5	63	1
Kata, Matt, S.B.	1.000	1	1	0	0	1	0
Kearns, Austin, Day.	.955	133	231	23	12	266	5
Kilburg, Joe, Day.	1.000	2	2	0	0	2	0
Knox, Ryan, Bel.	.983	125	220	9	4	233	1
Lane, Jason, Mich.*	.973	91	137	6	4	147	0
Lara, David, W.M.	.921	34	57	1	5	63	1
Layton, Blane, Day.*	.972	70	133	7	4	144	1
Lemon, Tim, Peo.	.970	124	215	13	7	235	0
Leone, Justin, Wis.	1.000	4	10	1	0	11	0
Lundquist, Ryan, Clin.	.982	78	104	7	2	113	1
Matan, Jim, Day.	1.000	2	1	0	0	1	0
McKinney, Antonio, W.M.	.969	80	120	7	4	131	1
Morrow, Alvin, Bel.	.936	32	42	2	3	47	1
Mounts, J.R., Burl.	.956	49	84	2	4	90	1
Munoz, Arnaldo, Burl.*	1.000	1	1	0	0	1	0
Nicholson, Derek, Mich.	.973	68	100	8	3	111	2
Noboa, Joel, S.B.	.958	19	22	1	1	24	0
Nunez, Argelis, S.B.	.947	23	34	2	2	38	0
O'Keefe, Mike, C.R.*	.954	114	179	9	9	197	2
Oborn, Spencer, Burl.	.981	124	239	13	5	257	4
Olson, Tim, S.B.	.966	50	104	8	4	116	1
Ortiz, Matt, Peo.	.800	3	4	0	1	5	0
Ortiz, Miguel, C.R.	1.000	9	12	1	0	13	0
Padgett, Matt, K.C.*	.979	114	187	4	4	195	0
Parnell, Sean, Wis.	.971	94	128	4	4	136	0
Perkins, Kevin, K.C.	1.000	35	44	2	0	46	0
RICHARDSON, Corey, W.M.	.989	122	265	13	3	281	4
Rios, Fernando, Clin.-Day.	.986	87	205	5	3	213	2
Rodriguez, Serafin, Clin.-Day.	.977	64	123	2	3	128	0
Ross, Cody, W.M.*	.978	120	251	10	6	267	3
Ryan, Jeff, Lan.	.962	43	70	5	3	78	2
Sandoval, Jhensy, S.B.	1.000	18	30	2	0	32	1
Scales, Bobby, Ft.W.	.929	16	11	2	1	14	0
Schmitt, Brian, Mich.*	1.000	12	22	0	0	22	0
Secoda, Joe, Peo.	.933	17	26	2	2	30	0
Seever, Brian, C.R.	.941	84	151	8	10	169	0
Selander, Craig, Q.C.	.952	18	20	0	1	21	0
Simpson, Andre, Bel.	.000	2	0	0	0	0	0
Sledge, Terrmel, Wis.*	1.000	2	3	1	0	4	0
Snelling, Chris, Wis.*	.983	71	116	3	2	121	1
Soriano, Carlos, Bel.	1.000	8	9	0	0	9	0
Southward, Deshawn, Q.C.	.946	51	50	3	3	56	1
Stegall, Randy, Day.	.000	1	0	0	0	0	0
Teilon, Nilson, Burl.	.913	41	59	4	6	69	1
Toomey, Chris, Clin.	.846	10	9	2	2	13	0
Topolski, Jon, Mich.	.965	130	235	14	9	258	1
Truitt, Steve, Bel.	1.000	19	25	1	0	26	0
Vandemore, Tony, Ft.W.	1.000	10	22	0	0	22	0
Van Rossum, Chris, Clin.*	.968	59	116	4	4	124	1
Vasquez, Alejandro, Mich.*	.957	28	44	1	2	47	0
Villero, Armando, Bel.	1.000	6	8	0	0	8	0
Wagner, Mike, Ft.W.	.963	31	51	1	2	54	0
Warner, Bryan, Lan.*	.962	35	50	1	2	53	1
Weber, Jon, Clin.*	.960	98	174	17	8	199	1
Welch, Edward, C.R.	.954	32	60	2	3	65	1
Welsh, Eric, Day.*	1.000	1	2	0	0	2	0
West, Kevin, Q.C.	.980	110	187	8	4	199	4
White, Greg, C.R.	1.000	6	5	1	0	6	0
Williams, Charles, Peo.	.983	61	109	6	2	117	3
Williamson, Chris, Day.*	1.000	4	3	0	0	3	0
Wrenn, Michael, Q.C.	1.000	16	32	1	0	33	0
Wright, Gavin, Mich.	.978	41	86	1	2	89	0
Zoccolillo, Peter, Lan.	.967	83	143	3	5	151	0

OUTFIELDERS WITH TWO OR MORE TEAMS

Player, Team	Pct.	G	PO	A	E	TC	DP
Beattie, Andy, Day.	1.000	5	5	1	0	6	0
Beattie, Andy, Clin.	1.000	3	1	1	0	2	1
Johnson, Ben, Peo.	.962	90	140	11	6	157	4
Johnson, Ben, Ft.W.	1.000	29	56	3	0	59	1
Rios, Fernando, Clin.	1.000	30	56	2	0	58	1
Rios, Fernando, Day.	.981	57	149	3	3	155	1
Rodriguez, Serafin, Clin.	.943	27	50	0	3	53	0
Rodriguez, Serafin, Day.	1.000	37	73	2	0	75	0

CATCHERS

Player, Team	Pct.	G	PO	A	E	TC	DP	PB
Alcala, Juan, Wis.	.989	14	77	11	1	89	0	5
Alfonzo, Eliezer, Peo.-Bel.	.983	78	515	57	10	582	3	12
Alvarado, Damien, Wis.	.961	9	67	7	3	77	0	3
Anderson, Dennis, K.C.	1.000	22	131	15	0	146	0	0
Barski, Chris, C.R.	.952	16	110	8	6	124	0	3
Betancourt, Tony, Q.C.	1.000	9	24	2	0	26	0	1
Bitter, Jarrod, Ft.W.	1.000	22	170	19	0	189	0	2
Bordenick, Ryan, Bel.	.990	54	436	49	5	490	2	5
Buck, John, Mich.	.982	100	748	81	15	844	11	14
Burkhart, Lance, Bel.	.985	44	283	45	5	333	0	10
Christianson, Ryan, Wis.	.981	94	709	81	15	805	5	12
Clark, Greg, Peo.	.995	34	190	28	1	219	0	7
Cline, Pat, Day.	1.000	24	149	8	0	157	0	4
Closser, J.D., S.B.	.980	74	484	51	11	546	7	25
Cosentino, Tony, Ft.W.	.991	59	504	39	5	548	2	15
Cripps, Bobby, Clin.	.985	67	512	76	9	597	3	15
Curry, Chris, Lan.	.986	48	247	32	4	283	1	17
Doudt, Anthony, C.R.	.989	25	158	18	2	178	1	0
Edwards, John, Q.C.	.969	15	81	14	3	98	0	4
Fatheree, Danny, Mich.	.982	18	104	5	2	111	0	3
Fennell, Jason, Burl.	.979	10	84	9	2	95	1	3
Frank, Nick, Bel.	1.000	1	3	0	0	3	0	0
Frick, Matt, K.C.	.995	65	373	52	2	427	4	7
Garcia, Cip, S.B.	1.000	9	39	4	0	43	0	1
Gauch, Barry, Burl.	.969	20	121	6	4	131	1	3
Gillikin, Joe, Burl.	.982	20	149	12	3	164	3	13
Gosewisch, Ian, C.R.	1.000	1	2	0	0	2	0	0
Gregorio, Tom, C.R.	.979	102	587	104	15	706	8	20
Gulledge, Kelley, Q.C.	.990	39	279	25	3	307	2	9
Gutierrez, Said, Ft.W.	.979	11	86	8	2	96	0	3
Huff, Jake, Ft.W.	.983	39	310	38	6	354	2	2
Johnson, Gabe, Peo.	.974	33	196	25	6	227	2	10
Jones, Brian, Day.	.986	31	190	19	3	212	2	6

Player, Team	Pct.	G	PO	A	E	TC	DP	PB
Kalczynski, Joe, S.B.	.996	36	214	29	1	244	2	9
Kopitzke, Casey, Lan.	.990	68	457	61	5	523	3	21
Lundquist, Ryan, Clin.	1.000	14	70	10	0	80	1	2
Massey, John, S.B.	.996	32	210	23	1	234	2	12
Mauck, Matt, Lan.	.967	28	179	24	7	210	1	12
Morales, Steve, K.C.	.977	31	193	18	5	216	1	2
O'Connor, Brian, Mich.	.974	30	173	18	5	196	0	6
Ortiz, Matt, Peo.	1.000	4	29	3	0	32	0	2
Parker, Chris, W.M.	.917	6	39	5	4	48	0	0
Pogue, Jamie, Peo.	.987	21	134	13	2	149	0	3
Quintero, Humberto, Burl.	.986	71	501	74	8	583	6	6
Ramsey, Brad, Lan.	1.000	2	11	0	0	11	0	0
Risinger, Ben, Ft.W.	1.000	1	2	0	0	2	0	0
Rivera, Francisco, Clin.	.979	65	471	44	11	526	5	7
Robles, Kevin, Wis.	.986	30	190	22	3	215	1	6
Rosa, Wally, Burl.	.975	27	174	23	5	202	2	12
Rowden, Monte, Lan.	1.000	5	16	0	0	16	0	0
ST. PIERRE, Maxim, W.M.	.990	73	518	52	6	576	2	18
Salinas, Trey, Day.	.955	14	57	7	3	67	2	0
Santiago, Daniel, Day.	.977	7	39	3	1	43	2	0
Schnall, Kevin, Day.	1.000	2	8	2	0	10	0	0
Schumacher, Shawn, Peo.	.975	11	65	14	2	81	0	2
Senjem, Guye, Clin.	1.000	3	20	0	0	20	0	0
Sparks, Eddie, Day.-Clin.	.944	6	14	3	1	18	0	0
Stegall, Randy, Day.	1.000	1	3	0	0	3	0	0
Stone, Jon, Ft.W.	.979	11	81	12	2	95	0	2
Suarez, Marc, Clin.	1.000	1	3	1	0	4	0	0
Torres, Gabby, Q.C.	.975	64	467	69	14	550	5	11
Van Horn, Ryan, Lan.	.964	9	46	8	2	56	0	0
Vargas, Inakel, W.M.	.990	66	439	49	5	493	3	13
Venales, Luis, K.C.	.971	6	30	3	1	34	0	2
Wallis, Jacob, Clin.	1.000	8	30	4	0	34	0	0
Whitehead, Braxton, Day.	.987	75	553	50	8	611	0	5
Woody, Dominic, K.C.	.996	32	212	26	1	239	3	11
Wrenn, Michael, Q.C.	.995	25	169	27	1	197	1	7

TRIPLE PLAY: Kopitzke.

CATCHERS WITH TWO OR MORE TEAMS

Player, Team	Pct.	G	PO	A	E	TC	DP	PB
Alfonzo, Eliezer, Peo.	.987	40	268	29	4	301	3	7
Alfonzo, Eliezer, Bel.	.979	38	247	28	6	281	0	5
Sparks, Eddie, Day.	.917	4	11	0	1	12	0	0
Sparks, Eddie, Clin.	1.000	2	3	3	0	6	0	0

PITCHERS

Player, Team	Pct.	G	PO	A	E	TC	DP
Acevedo, Jose, Day.	.840	25	6	15	4	25	3
Acosta, Jhon, Lan.	1.000	5	1	0	0	1	0
Altman, Gene, Day.-Bel.	.800	42	3	1	1	5	0
Anderson, Craig, Wis.*	1.000	26	2	21	0	23	2
Anderson, Travis, Mich.	.941	27	12	20	2	34	3
Arias, Pablo, W.M.	1.000	15	3	9	0	12	0
Artieta, Corey, Bel.*	.917	32	2	9	1	12	0
Baek, Cha, Wis.	.889	24	9	23	4	36	2
Bailey, David, Lan.	.900	45	3	6	1	10	0
Bailey, Travis, Peo.	.000	1	0	0	0	0	0
Balbuena, Caleb, Wis.	.800	12	1	11	3	15	1
Barnett, Aaron, W.M.*	.923	46	3	9	1	13	1
Barreto, Joel, Q.C.	1.000	14	4	4	0	8	1
Bartosh, Cliff, Ft.W.*	1.000	50	2	9	0	11	2
Baxter, Gerik, Ft.W.	.857	20	3	9	2	14	2
Beckett, Josh, K.C.	1.000	13	2	10	0	12	0
Belicic, Adam, C.R.*	1.000	6	1	1	0	2	1
Bell, Casey, Ft.W.	.000	3	0	0	0	0	0
Beltran, Francis, Lan.	1.000	16	0	1	0	1	0
Bergman, Dusty, C.R.*	.870	28	11	29	6	46	3
Berryman, Chad, C.R.	.857	11	2	4	1	7	0
Birdsong, Tim, Day.	.857	20	2	10	2	14	0
Blackwell, Scott, Q.C.	.889	11	0	8	1	9	1
Blake, Peter, Q.C.*	1.000	18	2	5	0	7	0
Bludau, Frank, Day.	1.000	2	1	0	0	1	0
Bonilla, Ben, S.B.*	1.000	11	0	9	0	9	0
Bonilla, Vincent, Q.C.	.850	15	6	11	3	20	0
Borne, Matt, Burl.	.818	25	4	5	2	11	1
Bowe, Brandon, K.C.	.955	61	6	15	1	22	1
Bradley, David, Clin.	.938	41	8	7	1	16	1
Brewer, Clint, Day.	.571	16	2	2	3	7	0
Brown, Paul, Day.*	1.000	14	0	9	0	9	0
Brown, Tighe, Day.	1.000	21	1	3	0	4	0
Bruback, Matt, Lan.	.933	9	4	10	1	15	0
Brummett, Sean, C.R.*	1.000	32	3	12	0	15	0
Buirley, Matt, Day.	.000	16	0	0	0	0	0
Bukowski, Stanislaw, C.R.	.750	5	0	3	1	4	1

Player, Team	Pct.	G	PO	A	E	TC	DP
Burke, Erick, W.M.*	.500	21	0	2	2	4	0
Burns, Casey, Ft.W.	1.000	5	1	3	0	4	0
Burton, Timothy, Wis.	1.000	17	1	2	0	3	0
Byron, Terence, K.C.	.875	6	1	6	1	8	0
Calvo, Jose, Mich.	1.000	4	2	0	0	2	0
Capuano, Chris, S.B.*	.902	18	7	30	4	41	0
Cassel, Jack, Ft.W.	.917	22	5	6	1	12	1
Cento, Tony, Q.C.*	1.000	52	5	16	0	21	2
Cepeda, Wellington, S.B.	1.000	26	1	8	0	9	2
Cervantes, Chris, S.B.*	1.000	11	5	11	0	16	0
Chapman, Dennis, Ft.W.	1.000	5	1	2	0	3	0
Childers, Matt, Bel.	.900	12	3	15	2	20	3
Chipperfield, Calvin, W.M.	.852	24	7	16	4	27	1
Conroy, Ken, Lan.	.914	27	12	20	3	35	2
Cook, B.R., Peo.	.946	18	10	25	2	37	0
Cordero, Frangil, Lan.*	1.000	23	1	8	0	9	0
Cordero, Victor, Bel.	1.000	15	0	3	0	3	2
Cordova, Jorge, K.C.-Clin.	.944	30	3	14	1	18	0
Corona, Ronnie, Q.C.	1.000	18	0	3	0	3	0
Crudale, Mike, Peo.	.941	38	5	11	1	17	1
Cruz, Juan, Lan.	.900	17	7	11	2	20	0
Cueto, Jose, Lan.	.667	17	2	2	2	6	0
Cummings, Jeremy, Peo.	.750	3	0	3	1	4	0
Curreri, Joe, Burl.	1.000	41	2	11	0	13	2
Curtis, Bill, C.R.	.000	2	0	0	0	0	0
Cyr, Eric, Ft.W.*	.778	9	1	6	2	9	1
Dant, Larry, Lan.	1.000	6	2	2	0	4	0
Darnell, Paul, Clin.*	.880	26	4	18	3	25	0
De Hart, Blair, Ft.W.	.933	20	5	9	1	15	0
Dehart, Casey, Day.*	.867	50	2	11	2	15	2
Delgado, Danny, Wis.	.923	37	6	6	1	13	0
Devine, Travis, Ft.W.	1.000	23	5	9	0	14	0
Diaz, Antonio, Ft.W.	1.000	6	0	1	0	1	0
DUNN, Scott, Clin.	1.000	26	12	27	0	39	3
Duprey, Pete, Wis.-Lan.*	1.000	31	2	5	0	7	0
Ebanks, Palmer, C.R.	.889	21	9	23	4	36	2
Eckenstahler, Eric, W.M.*	1.000	10	2	2	0	4	0
Eppeneder, James, Lan.*	.867	44	5	8	2	15	1
Escalante, Jaime, C.R.	.750	25	1	5	2	8	0
Escamilla, Paco, Clin.	1.000	2	1	0	0	1	0
Eshelman, Vaughn, Day.*	.000	2	0	0	0	0	0
Eyre, Willie, Q.C.	.947	26	7	11	1	19	0
Fahs, Paul, Peo.	1.000	30	2	6	0	8	0
Farizo, Brad, K.C.	.824	10	7	7	3	17	1
Fitzgerald, Ryan, Mich.	.800	28	1	3	1	5	0
Foote, Joe, Q.C.	.912	25	8	23	3	34	2
Frank, Nick, Bel.	.000	1	0	0	0	0	0
Franke, Aaron, C.R.	.778	8	5	2	2	9	0
Frasor, Jason, W.M.	.933	14	12	16	2	30	1
Frederick, Kevin, Q.C.	1.000	27	3	9	0	12	1
Fuller, Jody, S.B.	.838	20	10	21	6	37	2
Gagliano, Steve, Lan.	1.000	12	2	5	0	7	1
Gallo, Mike, Mich.*	1.000	24	8	19	0	27	0
Gangemi, Joe, Bel.*	.750	11	2	1	1	4	0
Garza, Rolando, Burl.	.000	4	0	0	0	0	0
George, Chris, Mich.	1.000	48	2	8	0	10	0
Gil, David, Day.	1.000	4	1	2	0	3	0
Giuliano, Joe, Day.	1.000	22	1	6	0	7	1
Gold, J.M., Bel.	.889	7	2	6	1	9	0
Gomer, Jeramy, Lan.*	.967	24	9	20	1	30	0
Gomez, Odalis, C.R.	1.000	7	1	7	0	8	1
Gonzalez, Jeremi, Lan.	1.000	1	0	0	0	0	0
Gordon, Kevin, K.C.	1.000	23	2	5	0	7	0
Gosewisch, Ian, C.R.	.000	2	0	0	0	0	0
Grater, Kevin, Bel.	1.000	17	4	7	0	11	1
Gray, Brett, Day.	.900	13	1	8	1	10	0
Grezlovski, Ben, C.R.	.000	11	0	0	0	0	0
Grippo, Mike, Peo.*	1.000	5	0	0	0	0	0
Gruban, Jarret, C.R.	1.000	1	1	0	0	1	0
Grunwald, Erik, Wis.	.909	37	0	10	1	11	0
Handy, Russell, Ft.W.	1.000	2	2	0	0	2	0
Hannah, Shawn, W.M.	1.000	2	1	3	0	4	0
Haring, Brett, Day.*	1.000	5	2	5	0	7	1
Harris, J.T., C.R.	.895	28	9	8	2	19	0
Harris, Julian, C.R.*	.850	31	4	13	3	20	0
Harris, Toby, Bel.	.833	11	0	5	1	6	0
Hayden, Terry, Day.*	.909	15	2	8	1	11	1
Hebert, Cedric, Day.	.000	2	0	0	0	0	0
Henriquez, Hector, K.C.*	.733	50	0	11	4	15	0
Hensley, Matthew, C.R.	.857	5	2	4	1	7	0
Hernandez, Carlos, Mich.*	.875	22	0	14	2	16	0
Hickman, Ben, K.C.	1.000	8	0	5	0	5	0
Hoard, Brent, Q.C.*	1.000	6	1	1	0	2	0

Player, Team	Pct.	G	PO	A	E	TC	DP
Hoerman, Jared, Wis.	.778	22	0	7	2	9	0
Horney, Micke, Clin.	1.000	15	2	3	0	5	0
Howington, Ty, Day.*	.917	27	3	19	2	24	1
Huggins, David, Day.	.667	38	1	5	3	9	0
Hunter, Johnny, Ft.W.	1.000	4	1	2	0	3	0
Hussman, Darrell, Clin.	1.000	9	2	8	0	10	1
Jackson, Stosh, Lan.*	.833	42	6	9	3	18	1
Jamison, Ryan, Mich.	.833	41	9	16	5	30	1
Janke, Cheyenne, Peo.	.977	28	13	29	1	43	1
Johnston, Rikki, W.M.*	1.000	1	1	1	0	2	0
Jolliffe, Brian, Ft.W.*	.960	48	7	17	1	25	1
Jones, Fontella, Bel.	1.000	25	1	2	0	3	0
Jones, Travis, Ft.W.*	1.000	8	1	1	0	2	1
Kata, Matt, S.B.	1.000	1	0	1	0	1	0
Kees, Justin, S.B.	1.000	17	3	8	0	11	0
Key, Chris, K.C.*	.750	5	0	6	2	8	1
Kirsten, Rick, W.M.	.875	6	1	6	1	8	0
Kohl, Doug, S.B.-Peo.	1.000	36	3	4	0	7	0
Koronka, John, Clin.*	.971	20	6	28	1	35	0
Koziara, Matt, Clin.	.955	38	5	16	1	22	2
Lackey, John, C.R.	1.000	5	2	8	0	10	1
Lacorte, Vince, C.R.	.952	17	10	10	1	21	0
Landkamer, Michael, Day.	.000	3	0	0	0	0	0
Law, Keith, W.M.	.813	33	7	6	3	16	1
Layfield, Scotty, Peo.	.833	53	4	6	2	12	1
Leclair, Aric, S.B.*	.727	23	2	6	3	11	1
Lee, Jonathan, S.B.	.500	7	1	0	1	2	0
Leuenberger, Jeffrey, W.M.	1.000	12	2	5	0	7	0
Lewis, Peyton, Lan.	.833	15	2	3	1	6	1
Lima, Lescano, Mich.	.667	18	2	0	1	3	0
Lincoln, Jeff, Q.C.	.750	17	0	3	1	4	0
Lopez, Aquilino, Wis.	.950	39	9	10	1	20	2
Lopez, Gustavo, K.C.	.955	29	3	18	1	22	0
Lopez, Juan, Burl.*	.800	28	1	7	2	10	0
Loudon, Gary, S.B.	1.000	7	2	3	0	5	0
Love, Brandon, Day.	.917	7	5	6	1	12	1
Lowe, Matt, Bel.	1.000	24	2	2	0	4	0
Luque, Roger, Ft.W.*	1.000	14	3	14	0	17	0
Madritsch, Robert, Day.*	1.000	2	0	1	0	1	0
Majewski, Gary, Burl.	1.000	22	5	19	0	24	0
Malone, Corwin, Burl.*	.714	38	0	10	4	14	0
Manias, Jim, Day.*	.833	17	4	11	3	18	1
Martinez, Dan, Burl.*	1.000	8	0	1	0	1	1
Martinez, Javier, Day.	1.000	16	2	1	0	3	0
Martinez, Luis, Bel.*	.615	28	1	7	5	13	0
Martinez, Renan, C.R.	.750	7	1	2	1	4	0
Marx, Tommy, W.M.*	1.000	18	8	12	0	20	1
Mateo, Julio, Wis.	.769	36	0	10	3	13	1
Mathews, Dan, Bel.	.960	45	4	20	1	25	0
Matzenbacher, Brian, S.B.	.933	51	4	10	1	15	1
Maysonet, Roberto, Bel.	1.000	1	1	0	0	1	0
McClain, Kevin, C.R.	.714	30	2	3	2	7	0
McCutcheon, Mike, S.B.*	.923	10	4	20	2	26	0
McWhirter, Kris, Burl.	.917	28	3	19	2	24	0
Meche, Gil, Wis.	1.000	1	1	1	0	2	1
Medina, Franklin, S.B.	.000	2	0	0	0	0	0
Mendoza, Mario, C.R.	.940	14	13	34	3	50	2
Merrell, Phil, Day.	1.000	13	0	3	0	3	1
Mieses, Jose, Bel.	.972	21	14	21	1	36	1
Miller, Colby, Q.C.	1.000	2	1	0	0	1	0
Miller, Ernie, C.R.*	.917	15	3	8	1	12	0
Mills, Ryan, Q.C.*	.857	20	7	17	4	28	2
Minaya, Pedro, Day.	1.000	16	2	3	0	5	0
Mlicki, Dave, W.M.	.000	1	0	0	0	0	0
Moehler, Brian, W.M.	1.000	1	0	3	0	3	0
Montero, Oscar, Lan.	.750	17	2	1	1	4	0
Montoya, Saul, S.B.	.667	2	0	2	1	3	0
Moore, Bryan, K.C.	1.000	58	6	12	0	18	1
Moore, Greg, C.R.	1.000	15	0	6	0	6	1
Morse, Bryan, K.C.*	.929	16	1	12	1	14	0
Moser, Todd, K.C.*	.944	21	8	26	2	36	3
Mosher, Andy, Bel.	.667	17	0	4	2	6	0
Mottl, Ryan, Clin.	.667	9	2	0	1	3	0
Mozingo, Dan, Burl.*	.000	10	0	0	0	0	0
Munoz, Arnaldo, Burl.*	1.000	22	0	9	0	9	0
Nanninga, Matthew, Clin.	.000	1	0	0	0	0	0
Nannini, Mike, Mich.	.941	15	7	9	1	17	0
Neu, Mike, Clin.	.833	58	7	8	3	18	0
Neubauer, Marc, K.C.*	.900	17	1	8	1	10	0
Odom, Lance, Q.C.	.000	6	0	0	0	0	0
Olean, Chris, Bel.	1.000	12	5	2	0	7	0
Olore, Kevin, Wis.	.714	12	2	3	2	7	0
Orosco, Jesse, Peo.*	.000	2	0	0	0	0	0
Ortiz, Miguel, C.R.	.000	1	0	0	0	0	0
Ortiz, Omar, Ft.W.	1.000	6	4	2	0	6	0
Ovalles, Juan, S.B.	1.000	8	2	5	0	7	0
Padilla, Juan, Q.C.	1.000	32	6	7	0	13	0
Parker, Matt, Peo.-Bel.	.826	40	9	10	4	23	0
Peavy, Jacob, Ft.W.	.880	26	11	11	3	25	0
Peck, Brandon, Peo.*	.917	29	1	10	1	12	0
Peguero, Darwin, Mich.*	.833	39	3	12	3	18	0
Pember, Dave, Bel.	1.000	17	9	4	0	13	0
Perkins, Kevin, K.C.	1.000	2	1	0	0	1	0
Perkins, Mike, Peo.	.750	8	1	2	1	4	1
Peterson, Kyle, Bel.	1.000	3	1	2	0	3	1
Pike, Tom, Clin.	1.000	31	3	7	0	10	3
Pineda, Jairo, W.M.	.842	42	4	12	3	19	0
Prater, Andy, Ft.W.	1.000	26	0	7	0	7	0
Pridie, Jon, Q.C.	1.000	45	8	11	0	19	0
Prinz, Bret, S.B.	.667	6	1	1	1	3	0
Putz, Joseph, Wis.	.917	26	7	26	3	36	1
Ramirez, Santiago, Mich.	1.000	23	2	7	0	9	1
Ramos, Juan, Wis.	.800	36	2	10	3	15	0
Randazzo, Jeffrey, Q.C.*	1.000	2	1	2	0	3	0
Reith, Brian, Day.	1.000	5	0	2	0	2	0
Risinger, Ben, Ft.W.	1.000	1	0	2	0	2	0
Rivera, Homero, W.M.*	1.000	36	4	9	0	13	0
Rivera, Samuel, W.M.	.625	18	0	5	3	8	0
Roberts, Nick, Mich.	1.000	22	9	19	0	28	1
Robertson, Nathan, K.C.*	1.000	6	1	4	0	5	0
Robinson, Dustin, Clin.	1.000	40	5	19	0	24	0
Robinson, Jeff, Bel.	.929	17	5	8	1	14	0
Rodney, Fernando, W.M.	1.000	22	3	12	0	15	3
Rohling, Stuart, Burl.	.923	26	4	8	1	13	1
Rojas, Chris, Ft.W.	.889	15	7	17	3	27	1
Rowe, Casey, W.M.	.952	15	8	12	1	21	2
Salmon, Brad, Clin.	.957	22	3	19	1	23	1
Sams, Aaron, Lan.*	1.000	6	4	7	0	11	1
Sanchez, Duaner, S.B.	.953	28	13	28	2	43	1
Sansom, Trevor, Peo.	.955	44	9	12	1	22	0
Sauer, Marc, W.M.	.897	28	8	18	3	29	0
Sawyer, Steve, K.C.	1.000	3	0	1	0	1	0
Schultz, Bryan, Peo.	1.000	12	1	3	0	4	1
Schurman, Ryan, Clin.	1.000	22	1	8	0	9	0
Secoda, Joe, Peo.	.000	1	0	0	0	0	0
Sergent, Joe, K.C.*	1.000	46	4	11	0	15	0
Shaffar, Ben, Lan.	.929	19	9	17	2	28	1
Shiyuk, Todd, Ft.W.*	1.000	32	5	4	0	9	0
Shrout, Kevin, Bel.	1.000	4	3	1	0	4	0
Sikaras, Pete, S.B.	.769	20	2	8	3	13	0
Simonson, Chris, Bel.	1.000	14	2	14	0	16	1
Simpson, Andre, Burl.	1.000	45	2	13	0	15	1
Smuin, Shane, K.C.	.000	4	0	0	0	0	0
Soriano, Rafael, Wis.	.947	21	5	13	1	19	2
Sprague, Kevin, Peo.*	.900	24	6	12	2	20	0
Stanford, Derek, Mich.	.919	28	6	28	3	37	1
Stanton, Timothy, S.B.*	.941	51	5	11	1	17	1
Steele, Matt, S.B.	1.000	6	1	1	0	2	0
Stegall, Randy, Day.	.000	1	0	0	0	0	0
Stewart, Josh, Burl.*	.933	25	6	22	2	30	2
Stewart, Steve, Bel.*	1.000	21	3	6	0	9	0
Stiehl, Robert, Mich.	.000	1	0	0	0	0	0
Stocks, Nick, Peo.	.816	25	6	25	7	38	2
Stockstill, Jason, C.R.*	1.000	10	1	3	0	4	1
Stokes, Shaun, Peo.	1.000	8	2	4	0	6	0
Stumm, Jason, Burl.	.941	13	4	12	1	17	2
Sturdy, Tim, Q.C.	.961	23	9	40	2	51	4
Szuminski, Jason, Lan.	1.000	4	1	0	0	1	0
Takach, Ryan, S.B.*	1.000	12	1	2	0	3	1
Tankersley, Dennis, Ft.W.	1.000	12	3	4	0	7	0
Tejeda, Franklin, Peo.	.871	19	6	21	4	31	1
Thomas, Don, Mich.*	.850	43	7	10	3	20	0
Thomas, Gaige, K.C.	.800	10	1	3	1	5	0
Thompson, Mike, Ft.W.	.857	6	2	4	1	7	0
Thompson, Travis, Clin.-Day.	.939	25	11	35	3	49	2
Thornton, Matt, Wis.*	1.000	26	6	29	0	35	2
Timmerman, Heath, C.R.	1.000	13	2	3	0	5	1
Torres, Melqui, Wis.	.700	9	3	4	3	10	0
Trejo, Francisco, S.B.*	1.000	5	3	11	0	14	0
Trujillo, John, Ft.W.	.943	63	8	25	2	35	1
Ulacia, Dennis, Burl.*	.868	28	4	29	5	38	2
Valdez, Jose, Clin.	.833	14	8	7	3	18	0
Valera, Greg, S.B.	.931	29	8	19	2	29	1
Valverde, Jose, S.B.	1.000	31	5	2	0	7	0
Vanhekken, Andrew, W.M.*	.926	26	9	16	2	27	1
Vasquez, Luis, Mich.*	.500	2	1	0	1	2	0

Player, Team	Pct.	G	PO	A	E	TC	DP
Villanueva, Bill, K.C.	.923	13	7	17	2	26	2
Villarreal, Oscar, S.B.	1.000	13	2	3	0	5	0
Vincent, Matt, Peo.*	1.000	58	0	14	0	14	0
Warner, Bryan, Lan.*	.000	5	0	0	0	0	0
Watson, Gregory, W.M.	1.000	62	8	13	0	21	1
Webb, Brandon, S.B.	.000	12	0	0	0	0	0
Webb, John, Lan.	.848	21	13	15	5	33	2
Weis, Brad, Q.C.*	.900	40	4	14	2	20	2
West, Brian, Burl.	.956	24	16	27	2	45	4
White, Bill, S.B.*	.000	1	0	0	0	0	0
Whitesides, Johnny, Mich.	.857	13	4	2	1	7	0
Wiggins, Dan, Lan.	.750	24	5	1	2	8	0
Wiles, Chad, Wis.	.000	2	0	0	0	0	0
Wilson, Philip, C.R.	.927	21	12	26	3	41	1
Wohlers, Mark, Day.	.000	3	0	0	0	0	0
Wolfe, Brian, Q.C.	.933	31	9	19	2	30	0
Yates, Chad, Peo.	1.000	17	1	2	0	3	0
Young, Douglas, Ft.W.	1.000	62	9	6	0	15	1

PITCHERS WITH TWO OR MORE TEAMS

Player, Team	Pct.	G	PO	A	E	TC	DP
Altman, Gene, Day.	1.000	9	2	1	0	3	0
Altman, Gene, Bel.	.500	33	1	0	1	2	0
Cordova, Jorge, K.C.	1.000	22	2	10	0	12	0
Cordova, Jorge, Clin.	.833	8	1	4	1	6	0
Duprey, Pete, Wis.*	1.000	19	0	4	0	4	0
Duprey, Pete, Lan.*	1.000	12	2	1	0	3	0
Kohl, Doug, S.B.	1.000	11	1	2	0	3	0
Kohl, Doug, Peo.	1.000	25	2	2	0	4	0
Parker, Matt, Peo.	.889	26	3	5	1	9	0
Parker, Matt, Bel.	.786	14	6	5	3	14	0
Thompson, Travis, Clin.	1.000	6	3	9	0	12	1
Thompson, Travis, Day.	.919	19	8	26	3	37	1

The following player appeared only as designated hitter, pinch-hitter or pinch runner: Cochrane, dh; Orgill, dh-ph; Sprowl, dh.

LEAGUE CHAMPIONS

Year	Team	Pct.	Year	Team	Pct.	Year	Team	Pct.
1947—	Belleville	.667		Cedar Rapids	.762	1984—	Appleton•	.640
	Belleville	.672	1967—	Wisconsin Rapids	.685		Springfield	.504
1948—	West Frankfort*	.708		Appleton◆	.587	1985—	Kenosha▼	.568
1949—	Centralia	.627	1968—	Decatur	.656		Peoria	.536
	Paducah (4th)†	.454		Quad Cities◆	.648	1986—	Springfield	.621
1950—	Centralia‡	.675	1969—	Appleton	.648		Waterloo▼	.557
1951—	Paris§	.700		Appleton	.690	1987—	Springfield	.671
	Danville (4th)†	.432	1970—	Quincy◆	.691		Kenosha▼	.586
1952—	Danville∞	.685		Quad Cities	.581	1988—	Cedar Rapids■	.621
	Decatur (3rd)†	.584	1971—	Appleton	.642		Kenosha	.579
1953—	Decatur*	.576		Quad Cities■	.548	1989—	South Bend■	.644
1954—	Decatur	.587	1972—	Appleton	.598		Springfield	.541
	Danville (2nd)‡	.528		Danville■	.584	1990—	Cedar Rapids	.657
1955—	Dubuque*	.587	1973—	Wisconsin Rapids■	.562		Quad City■	.579
1956—	Paris▲	.656		Danville	.537	1991—	Clinton■	.583
	Dubuque	.603	1974—	Appleton	.593		Madison	.558
1957—	Decatur▲	.683		Danville■	.517	1992—	Quad City	.664
	Clinton	.623	1975—	Waterloo■	.727		Cedar Rapids■	.594
1958—	Michigan City	.623		Quad Cities	.624	1993—	Clinton	.597
	Waterloo◆	.613	1976—	Waterloo■	.600		South Bend■	.566
1959—	Waterloo	.613		Cedar Rapids	.595	1994—	Rockford	.640
	Waterloo	.613	1977—	Waterloo	.580		Cedar Rapids■	.554
1960—	Waterloo	.629		Burlington■	.511	1995—	Beloit††	.633
	Waterloo	.677	1978—	Appleton■	.708		Michigan	.543
1961—	Waterloo	.613		Burlington	.500	1996—	Wisconsin	.570
	Quincy◆	.594	1979—	Waterloo	.600		West Michigan††	.558
1962—	Dubuque◆	.667		Quad Cities■	.579	1997—	Kane County	.507
	Waterloo	.625	1980—	Waterloo■	.610		Lansing**	.504
1963—	Clinton	.710		Quad Cities	.532	1998—	West Michigan††	.593
	Clinton	.629	1981—	Wausau■	.636	1999—	Kane County	.569
1964—	Clinton	.667		Quad Cities	.570		Burlington**	.511
	Fox Cities◆	.667	1982—	Madison	.626	2000—	West Michigan	.629
1965—	Burlington	.667		Appleton▼	.579		Michigan‡‡	.594
	Burlington	.677	1983—	Appleton•	.635			
1966—	Fox Cities◆	.689		Springfield	.576			

*Won championship and four-club playoff. †Won four-club playoff. ‡Playoff finals canceled because of bad weather. §Won both halves of split season. ∞Won first half of split season and tied Paris for second-half title. ▲Won first-half title and four-team playoff. ◆Won split season playoff. ■League divided into Northern and Southern divisions and played split season. Playoff winner. ▼League divided into Northern, Central and Southern divisions. Playoff winner. •League divided into Northern, Central and Southern divisions; regular season and playoff winner. ††League divided into Eastern, Central and Western divisions; regular season and playoff winner. **League divided into Eastern, Central and Western divisions, playoff winner. ‡‡League divided into Eastern and Western divisions and played split season. Playoff winner. (NOTE— Known as Illinois State League in 1947-48 and Mississippi-Ohio Valley League from 1949 through 1955.)

CLASS A *Midwest League*

NEW YORK-PENN LEAGUE

LEAGUE OFFICE

President
Bob Julian

Address
1629 Oneida St.
Utica, NY 13501

Phone
315-733-8036

Teams (affiliation)
Auburn Doubledays (Blue Jays)
Batavia Muck Dogs (Phillies)
Brooklyn Cyclones (Mets)
Hudson Valley Renegades (Devil Rays)
Jamestown Jammers (Braves)
Lowell Spinners (Red Sox)
Mahoning Valley Scrappers (Indians)

New Jersey Cardinals (Cardinals)
Oneonta Tigers (Tigers)
Pittsfield Astros (Astros)
Staten Island Yankees (Yankees)
Utica Blue Sox (Marlins)
Vermont Expos (Expos)
Williamsport Crosscutters (Pirates)

2000 FINAL STANDINGS

McNAMARA DIVISION

Team	W	L	T	Pct.	GB
Mahoning Valley (Indians)	43	33	0	.566	...
Batavia (Phillies)	42	34	0	.553	1.0
Jamestown (Braves)	38	38	0	.500	5.0
Utica (Marlins)	42	33	0	.560	...
Oneonta (Tigers)	41	34	0	.547	1.0
Auburn (Astros)	39	37	0	.513	4.0
Williamsport (Pirates)	32	44	0	.421	11.0

STEDLER DIVISION

Team	W	L	T	Pct.	GB
Staten Island (Yankees)	39	34	0	.527	2.5
Queens (Blue Jays)	34	42	0	.447	9.0
Vermont (Expos)	33	43	0	.434	9.5
Lowell (Red Sox)	34	42	0	.447	8.5
Pittsfield (Mets)	41	35	0	.539	1.5
New Jersey (Cardinals)	30	46	0	.395	12.5
Hudson Valley (Devil Rays)	42	34	0	.553	0.5

COMPOSITE

Team	M.V.	S.I.	Que.	Ver.	Low.	Bat.	Pit.	Jam.	Uti.	One.	Aub.	N.J.	Wpt.	H.V.	W	L	T	Pct.	GB
Mahoning Valley (Indians)	...	1	2	1	1	5	3	6	6	6	5	3	7	2	48	28	0	.632	...
Staten Island (Yankees)	3	...	4	4	4	2	3	3	3	2	3	6	1	8	46	28	0	.622	1.0
Queens (Blue Jays)	2	4	...	5	4	2	5	3	2	3	3	6	2	5	46	29	0	.613	1.5
Vermont (Expos)	3	3	3	...	7	3	7	2	1	1	3	4	1	7	45	30	0	.600	2.5
Lowell (Red Sox)	3	4	4	1	...	2	3	2	2	4	4	2	7	4	41	34	0	.547	6.5
Batavia (Phillies)	3	2	2	1	2	...	2	5	5	5	3	6	1	5	2	39	37	0	.513	9.0
Pittsfield (Mets)	1	5	3	1	5	2	...	2	1	2	1	7	4	4	38	37	0	.507	9.5
Jamestown (Braves)	2	1	1	2	1	3	2	...	4	4	5	3	5	4	37	38	0	.493	10.5
Utica (Marlins)	2	1	2	3	2	3	2	4	...	4	4	1	4	3	35	40	0	.467	12.5
Oneonta (Tigers)	2	2	1	3	1	5	2	4	4	...	4	3	3	1	35	41	0	.461	13.0
Auburn (Astros)	3	1	1	1	0	2	3	3	4	4	...	1	5	4	32	42	0	.432	15.0
New Jersey (Cardinals)	1	2	2	4	4	3	1	1	3	1	3	...	2	4	31	45	0	.408	17.0
Williamsport (Pirates)	1	2	2	3	2	3	0	3	4	5	1	2	...	1	29	44	0	.397	17.5
Hudson Valley (Devil Rays)	2	0	2	1	1	2	4	0	1	3	0	4	3	...	23	52	0	.307	24.5

Major league affiliations in parentheses.

PLAYOFFS: Staten Island defeated Queens two games to one; Mahoning Valley defeated Batavia two games to none; Staten Island defeated Mahoning Valley two games to one to win league championship.

REGULAR-SEASON ATTENDANCE: Auburn, 53,075; Batavia, 38,663; Hudson Valley, 155,621; Jamestown, 60,883; Lowell, 180,000; Mahoning Valley, 206,287; New Jersey, 128,252; Oneonta, 50,608; Pittsfield, 63,679; Queens, 38,662; Staten Island, 102,697; Utica, 54,029; Vermont, 122,863; Williamsport, 67,220. Total—1,322,739. Playoffs (8 games)—13,255.

MANAGERS: Auburn, Lyle Yates; Batavia, Frank Klebe; Hudson Valley, Dave Silvestri; Jamestown, Jim Saul; Lowell, Arnie Beyeler; Mahoning Valley, Ted Kubiak; New Jersey, Jeff Shireman; Oneonta, Gary Green; Pittsfield, Tony Tijerina; Queens, Eddie Rodriguez; Staten Island, Joe Arnold; Utica, Joe Deeble; Vermont, Tim Leiper; Williamsport, Curtis Wilkerson.

ALL-STAR TEAM: 1B—Dario Delgado, Batavia; 2B—Dominic Rich, Queens; 3B—Elvis Corporan, Staten Island; SS—Josh Wilson, Utica; Res. INF—Chris Basak, Pittsfield; OF—Ryan Church, Mahoning Valley; Nathan Janowicz, Mahoning Valley; Mitch Jones, Staten Island; Ron Acuna, Pittsfield; C—Ryan Doumit, Williamsport; Bryce Terveen, Jamestown; DH—John Wilson, Pittsfield; RHP—Landon Jacobsen, Williamsport; Doug Waechter, Hudson Valley; LHP—Mauricio Lara, Lowell; Andy Beal, Staten Island; Most Valuable Player—Ryan Church, Mahoning Valley.

2000 BATTING

TEAM

Team	Avg.	G	TPA	AB	R	H	TB	2B	3B	HR	RBI	SH	SF	HP	BB	IBB	SO	SB	CS	GDP	LOB	ShO	Slg.	OBP
Jamestown	.271	75	2896	2588	383	702	1043	136	32	47	342	9	33	30	236	9	561	56	29	49	565	2	.403	.335
Staten Island	.264	74	2893	2506	375	662	960	140	19	40	325	22	24	50	291	5	560	61	29	48	577	5	.383	.349
Oneonta	.261	76	2908	2494	355	652	871	88	34	21	309	17	22	49	326	7	609	88	47	53	592	3	.349	.355
Utica	.253	75	2870	2509	361	635	908	132	18	35	311	12	18	40	291	7	589	86	54	45	558	3	.362	.338
Vermont	.253	75	2960	2554	407	645	842	101	21	18	302	16	25	56	309	8	546	184	59	39	554	3	.330	.343
Queens	.251	75	2940	2538	364	637	868	106	25	25	321	19	24	31	328	6	530	88	40	52	582	5	.342	.341
Pittsfield	.250	75	2767	2409	336	602	808	112	26	14	267	37	22	51	248	9	535	155	50	49	490	5	.335	.330
Mahoning Val.	.249	76	3020	2539	432	633	946	112	42	39	359	31	20	83	347	8	578	92	44	49	554	1	.373	.356
Batavia	.248	76	2919	2557	354	634	875	107	19	32	312	18	30	36	278	5	537	128	26	45	574	1	.342	.327
Auburn	.239	74	2696	2440	305	584	826	113	24	27	260	12	15	37	192	5	553	96	47	38	437	7	.339	.303
Hudson Val.	.239	75	2718	2412	298	576	768	100	13	22	251	21	27	24	234	3	647	91	56	49	442	7	.318	.309
Lowell	.234	75	2801	2458	292	575	772	93	16	24	242	24	19	28	272	5	579	68	36	26	526	3	.314	.315
Williamsport	.232	73	2743	2435	280	566	777	90	20	27	240	18	19	45	226	4	547	75	28	51	526	7	.319	.307
New Jersey	.213	76	2793	2432	264	517	679	90	15	14	216	27	22	32	280	5	585	156	55	48	513	6	.279	.300

TOP QUALIFIERS FOR BATTING CHAMPIONSHIP

Minimum 205 plate appearances. *Lefthanded batter. †Switch-hitter.

Player, Team	Avg.	G	TPA	AB	R	H	TB	2B	3B	HR	RBI	SH	SF	HP	BB	IBB	SO	SB	CS	GDP	Slg.	OBP
Basak, Chris, Pit.	.349	63	281	249	46	87	113	18	4	0	15	3	0	3	26	2	36	32	12	1	.454	.417
Wilson, Josh, Uti.	.344	66	295	259	43	89	123	13	6	3	43	1	1	5	29	3	47	9	8	6	.475	.418
Janowicz, Nathan, M.V.*	.340	71	305	265	40	90	123	14	5	3	43	5	3	1	31	1	34	10	12	5	.464	.407
Betemit, Wilson, Jam.†	.331	69	308	269	54	89	123	15	2	5	37	3	5	1	30	2	37	3	4	4	.457	.393
Terveen, Bryce, Jam.*	.327	55	224	196	30	64	86	11	1	3	41	1	2	2	23	3	38	0	1	3	.439	.399
Wilson, John, Pit.	.324	69	289	247	36	80	98	16	1	0	48	0	5	12	24	0	30	18	3	4	.397	.403
Forbes, Michael, Jam.*	.321	61	241	196	29	63	97	13	3	5	43	2	4	3	36	1	43	2	0	5	.495	.427
Harris, Corey, Pit.	.320	61	238	194	38	62	97	17	3	4	30	1	5	4	34	0	28	23	4	3	.500	.422
Barnette, Jason, Bat.*	.315	62	240	213	31	67	81	5	3	1	25	3	0	3	21	0	55	28	3	3	.380	.384
Doumit, Ryan, Wil.†	.313	66	280	246	25	77	108	15	5	2	40	0	7	4	23	1	33	2	2	7	.439	.371
Navarrete, Raymond, Wil.	.310	66	278	248	19	77	101	13	1	3	36	1	5	3	20	2	27	1	1	4	.407	.362
Magness, Pat, Uti.*	.309	50	208	175	31	54	87	18	0	5	40	0	1	2	30	2	34	2	0	2	.497	.413
Donato, Gregorio, Jam.	.308	67	284	266	56	82	128	12	5	8	40	1	4	0	13	0	56	12	3	5	.481	.336
Acuna, Ron, Pit.	.307	72	306	287	52	88	105	11	0	2	35	4	2	3	10	0	55	31	10	3	.366	.334
Thomas, Charles, Jam.	.303	68	285	264	39	80	119	20	8	1	25	0	1	1	19	0	58	10	2	7	.451	.351
Ravelo, Manuel, Wil.	.303	52	231	195	38	59	77	4	7	0	17	5	0	5	26	0	30	28	9	2	.395	.398

DEPARTMENTAL LEADERS: G—M. Jones, 74; AB—Acuna, 287; R—Donato, 56; H—Janowicz, 90; TB—M. Jones, 143; 2B—M. Jones, 28; 3B—C. Thomas, Downing, Malave, 8 each; HR—M. Jones, 11; RBI—Church, 65; SH—Volquez, 9; SF—Volquez, Doumit, 7 each; HP—Becker, 20; BB—Hensley, 60; IBB—several tied, 3 each; SO—Harper, 89; SB—Hensley, 43; CS—Janowicz, Morris, Basak, 12 each; GIDP—Salas, 11; Slg.—M. Jones, Church, .504 each; OBP—Hensley, .430.

ALL PLAYERS

*Lefthanded batter. †Switch-hitter.

Player, Team	Avg.	G	TPA	AB	R	H	TB	2B	3B	HR	RBI	SH	SF	HP	BB	IBB	SO	SB	CS	GDP	Slg.	OBP
Abreu, Nielsen, Bat.	.125	6	8	8	2	1	1	0	0	0	1	0	0	0	0	0	1	0	0	0	.125	.125
Acevedo, Carlos, Bat.	.257	63	254	230	28	59	69	5	1	1	22	2	1	3	18	1	47	13	3	1	.300	.317
Acuna, Ron, Pit.	.307	72	306	287	52	88	105	11	0	2	35	4	2	3	10	1	55	31	10	3	.366	.334
Alvarado, Oscar, Aub.	.105	8	19	19	0	2	2	0	0	0	1	0	0	0	0	0	5	0	0	0	.105	.105
Avila, Rob, Bat.	.237	44	159	139	14	33	49	7	0	3	21	1	3	5	10	0	23	2	0	2	.353	.306
Barnette, Jason, Bat.*	.315	62	240	213	31	67	81	5	3	1	25	3	0	3	21	0	55	28	3	3	.380	.384
Barnowski, Bryan, Low.	.188	5	17	16	1	3	4	1	0	0	1	0	0	0	1	0	4	0	0	0	.250	.235
Basak, Chris, Pit.	.349	63	281	249	46	87	113	18	4	0	15	3	0	3	26	2	36	32	12	1	.454	.417
Bastardo, Angel, M.V.	.176	51	199	182	20	32	51	11	1	2	25	3	0	4	10	0	47	2	1	6	.280	.235
Bay, Jason, Ver.	.304	35	148	135	17	41	52	5	0	2	12	0	1	1	11	0	25	17	4	2	.385	.358
Becker, Jeff, M.V.	.216	71	324	264	52	57	98	12	4	7	30	2	2	20	36	1	56	1	1	5	.371	.351
Bernhardt, Jossephang, Que.	.136	17	63	59	1	8	10	2	0	0	3	0	0	4	0	0	10	0	0	5	.169	.190
Betemit, Wilson, Jam.†	.331	69	308	269	54	89	123	15	2	5	37	3	5	1	30	2	37	3	4	4	.457	.393
Blanco, Tony, Low.	.143	9	31	28	1	4	5	1	0	0	0	0	0	1	2	0	12	1	0	0	.179	.226
Blum, Gregory, Ver.	.240	42	175	146	22	35	48	7	0	2	17	1	1	10	17	1	34	9	3	1	.329	.356
Bonner, Adam, H.V.	.236	59	235	191	27	45	65	11	0	3	23	1	4	5	34	0	56	12	4	1	.340	.359
Borjas, Henry, Low.†	.246	35	134	122	10	30	33	3	0	0	10	3	0	0	9	0	17	2	2	2	.270	.298
Bozanich, Sam, S.I.	.264	71	301	239	40	63	85	11	1	3	25	4	3	5	50	0	30	15	4	8	.356	.397
Brandes, Landon, N.J.	.234	52	205	184	11	43	55	12	0	0	14	4	3	6	8	0	53	11	2	3	.299	.284
Brisson, Dustin, Low.*	.244	65	275	238	25	58	87	7	2	6	39	0	5	3	29	0	63	1	2	0	.366	.324
Brosseau, Richard, Que.*	.164	15	60	55	9	9	15	0	3	0	2	1	0	0	4	0	15	2	0	0	.273	.220
Buttler, Victor, Wil.*	.298	36	150	131	22	39	49	3	2	1	17	1	0	3	15	0	13	9	0	1	.374	.383
Cabrera, Miguel, Uti.	.250	8	34	32	3	8	10	2	0	0	6	0	0	0	2	0	6	0	0	0	.313	.294
Calabrese, Anthony, S.I.	.311	43	91	74	16	23	26	1	1	0	8	1	1	0	15	0	12	2	1	5	.351	.422
Campos, Julio, Bat.	.250	3	12	12	1	3	3	0	0	0	0	0	0	0	0	0	5	1	0	1	.250	.250
Candelaria, Tito, S.I.*	.000	4	3	3	0	0	0	0	0	0	0	0	0	0	0	0	1	0	0	0	.000	.000
Candelario, Luis, H.V.	.206	68	270	248	29	51	69	7	1	3	17	0	0	2	20	0	85	4	3	4	.278	.270
Caraway, Brandon, Bat.†	.218	53	231	206	24	45	53	6	1	0	19	1	4	1	19	0	40	16	5	2	.257	.283
Carrillo, Robert, Aub.	.149	42	145	141	9	21	29	5	0	1	8	0	1	2	1	0	47	1	0	4	.206	.166
Castaneda, Jose, Pit.	.202	24	91	84	6	17	18	1	0	0	9	1	0	1	5	0	9	2	0	5	.214	.256
Castillo, Carlos, Pit.†	.269	15	58	52	6	14	16	2	0	0	2	1	1	1	3	0	11	5	0	0	.308	.316
Caudill, Clarke, Low.	.202	30	103	89	8	18	20	2	0	0	6	0	0	2	12	0	26	0	2	1	.225	.311
Centeno, Irwin, H.V.	.250	65	281	232	37	58	70	12	0	0	18	5	2	5	36	0	50	26	8	5	.302	.360
Chapman, Travis, Bat.	.316	49	197	174	23	55	72	10	2	1	28	2	2	7	12	0	24	0	1	1	.414	.379
Chaves, Brandon, Wil.†	.154	55	201	169	14	26	30	4	0	0	11	3	2	9	18	0	37	0	7	1	.178	.264
Chourio, Jorjanis, Wil.	.238	11	42	42	4	10	13	3	0	0	2	0	0	0	0	0	15	1	0	0	.310	.238
Church, Ryan, M.V.*	.298	73	321	292	51	81	137	16	5	10	65	0	3	8	38	3	49	11	4	4	.504	.396
Ciarrachi, Kevin, Wil.	.197	22	77	71	4	14	15	1	0	0	1	0	0	6	0	0	13	0	1	3	.211	.260
Clark, Chivas, Que.*	.220	15	61	41	9	9	12	1	1	0	5	2	1	0	17	0	9	2	1	0	.293	.441
Clark, Jeremy, Low.	.138	18	66	58	4	8	14	3	0	1	3	1	0	0	7	0	27	0	0	3	.241	.231
Cleto, Ambioris, Wil.	.103	24	87	78	4	8	9	1	0	0	5	0	0	0	9	0	16	5	0	3	.115	.195
Cleveland, Russell, One.	.233	46	184	163	20	38	45	5	1	0	15	1	0	1	19	0	35	2	3	4	.276	.317
Close, James, Uti.	.257	46	203	175	34	45	71	9	1	5	20	0	2	3	23	0	54	15	5	3	.406	.350
Corporan, Elvis, S.I.†	.260	73	313	281	37	73	115	14	2	8	36	1	5	3	23	2	61	7	2	8	.409	.317
Cortes, Jorge, Wil.*	.202	51	197	173	18	35	58	11	0	4	22	0	2	2	20	1	48	0	2	5	.335	.289
Cosby, Rob, Que.†	.270	42	178	163	15	44	52	8	0	0	22	0	1	0	14	1	22	4	2	3	.319	.326
Cotten, Jeremy, Wil.	.000	2	6	5	0	0	0	0	0	0	0	0	0	0	1	0	2	0	0	0	.000	.167
Coyne, Anthony, Pit.	.208	21	77	72	5	15	18	3	0	0	4	1	0	2	2	0	21	2	4	1	.250	.250
Crisp, Covelli, N.J.†	.239	36	151	134	18	32	37	5	0	0	14	5	0	1	11	0	22	25	3	1	.276	.301
Crocker, Nickolas, Jam.*	.125	2	9	8	2	1	1	0	0	0	0	0	0	0	0	0	4	0	0	0	.125	.222
Crozier, Eric, M.V.*	.212	52	211	179	31	38	59	9	0	4	24	1	0		30	0	61	4	2	3	.330	.324
De Aza, Modesto, Aub.	.278	16	66	54	11	15	18	1	1	0	3	1	0	5	6	0	14	15	4	0	.333	.400
DeGroote, Casey, S.I.*	.159	34	74	69	4	11	15	1	0	1	4	1	1	0	3	0	36	0	0	0	.217	.192

Player, Team	Avg.	G	TPA	AB	R	H	TB	2B	3B	HR	RBI	SH	SF	HP	BB	IBB	SO	SB	CS	GDP	Slg.	OBP
Delgado, Dario, Bat.	.241	63	254	216	37	52	85	8	2	7	40	0	5	4	29	0	44	0	0	6	.394	.335
De Renne, Keoni, Jam.†	.303	20	80	66	19	20	29	6	0	1	9	0	1	2	11	0	5	6	1	3	.439	.413
Docen, Jose, Ver.†	.293	59	270	229	44	67	87	16	2	0	30	2	1	4	34	0	33	27	7	6	.380	.392
Donato, Gregorio, Jam.	.308	67	284	266	56	82	128	12	5	8	40	1	4	0	13	0	56	12	3	5	.481	.336
Douglas, Harley, Pit.*	.163	20	54	43	3	7	8	1	0	0	2	2	1	3	5	1	13	2	2	0	.186	.288
Doumit, Ryan, Wil.†	.313	66	280	246	25	77	108	15	5	2	40	0	7	4	23	1	33	2	2	7	.439	.371
Downing, Phillip, Ver.*	.243	61	272	218	38	53	81	9	8	1	24	0	2	4	48	1	62	15	3	2	.372	.386
Duarte, Justin, Bat.	.205	24	83	73	9	15	23	2	0	2	12	0	0	1	9	0	17	0	0	1	.315	.301
Duncan, Jeffrey, Pit.*	.242	53	228	186	39	45	64	3	5	2	13	4	0	4	34	0	46	20	3	1	.344	.371
Easterday, Matt, Uti.	.255	60	255	220	36	56	81	14	1	3	26	1	6	6	22	0	45	8	4	6	.368	.331
Ellis, Ryan, Ver.	.198	34	117	101	14	20	24	4	0	0	8	1	2	6	7	0	25	5	1	1	.238	.284
Encarnacion, Arismendy, Uti..	.212	60	206	193	21	41	49	4	2	0	15	1	2	2	8	0	38	15	6	2	.254	.249
Escobar, Gustavo, N.J.	.162	12	41	37	6	6	8	0	1	0	3	1	0	0	3	0	7	3	2	2	.216	.225
Espino, Jose, N.J.	.188	58	204	181	13	34	45	4	0	1	15	4	5	6	8	2	56	5	10	4	.249	.240
Esposito, Brian, Low.	.240	42	169	154	15	37	57	9	1	3	20	1	2	1	11	0	31	0	1	2	.370	.292
Fagan, Shawn, Que.	.289	25	106	90	17	26	40	6	1	2	13	0	1	3	12	1	22	0	1	3	.444	.387
Fera, Aaron, Que.	.167	10	39	36	3	6	13	1	0	2	7	0	2	0	1	0	9	0	0	0	.361	.179
Fernandez, Alejandro, S.I.	.333	4	8	6	1	2	2	0	0	0	0	1	0	0	1	0	2	0	0	0	.333	.429
Fernandez, Medardo, Uti.†	.246	47	186	167	22	41	50	3	3	0	9	2	0	4	13	0	28	11	7	1	.299	.315
Filson, Gregory, Low.*	.249	54	217	185	20	46	57	6	1	1	25	1	1	1	29	1	48	2	2	1	.308	.352
Finnerty, Francis, M.V.†	.300	1	11	10	2	3	6	0	0	1	3	0	1	0	0	0	1	0	1	0	.600	.273
Firlit, Dan, N.J.	.191	54	190	173	14	33	42	4	1	1	12	1	2	3	11	0	57	10	4	2	.243	.249
Flanagan, Kevin, S.I.	.000	5	3	3	0	0	0	0	0	0	0	0	0	0	0	0	2	0	0	0	.000	.000
Flannigan, Timothy, Pit.	.201	58	235	199	20	40	53	7	3	0	22	2	2	1	31	1	60	2	1	2	.266	.309
Floyd, Mike, N.J.	.145	45	162	145	16	21	31	6	2	0	9	2	0	1	14	0	61	5	3	0	.214	.225
Forbes, Michael, Jam.*	.321	61	241	196	29	63	97	13	3	5	43	2	4	3	36	1	43	2	0	5	.495	.427
Fowler, David, S.I.	.254	49	161	138	25	35	47	6	0	2	15	4	2	5	12	0	51	6	5	0	.341	.331
Franco, Iker, H.V.	.260	22	81	73	11	19	30	5	0	2	15	0	1	2	5	0	18	1	1	1	.411	.321
Frazier, Charles, Uti.	.115	7	29	26	3	3	3	0	0	0	2	0	0	0	3	0	11	2	0	0	.115	.207
Friar, Roddy, N.J.	.165	30	100	91	6	15	19	1	0	1	8	0	0	0	9	0	33	1	1	1	.209	.240
Galante, Matt, N.J.	.224	54	197	165	12	37	41	4	0	0	14	3	1	2	26	0	24	4	0	3	.248	.335
Gall, John, N.J.	.239	71	290	259	28	62	78	10	0	2	27	0	4	1	25	0	37	16	5	7	.301	.304
Garcia, Juan-Carlos, Uti.†	.192	17	66	52	6	10	12	2	0	0	6	0	2	0	12	0	28	1	1	1	.231	.333
Garcia, Kevys, Aub.	.242	53	176	161	11	39	47	6	3	0	15	3	0	2	10	1	42	9	5	4	.292	.295
Gates, Jeff, S.I.	.313	47	139	112	15	35	43	8	0	0	12	3	0	7	17	0	23	5	4	3	.384	.434
Gentry, Garett, Aub.*	.286	62	259	231	38	66	99	15	3	4	34	0	1	1	26	0	27	5	0	3	.429	.359
Gerber, Joseph, One.*	.228	56	231	189	27	43	63	9	1	3	23	1	1	4	36	2	43	0	1	6	.333	.361
Gingrich, Troy, Ver.*	.292	16	76	65	12	19	27	3	1	1	5	0	1	1	9	0	16	5	2	4	.415	.382
Gonzalez, Adrian, Uti.*	.310	8	36	29	7	9	12	3	0	0	3	0	0	0	7	0	6	0	0	0	.414	.444
Gonzalez, Edgar, H.V.	.221	41	158	145	17	32	44	4	4	0	8	1	0	0	12	0	32	5	1	3	.303	.280
Goodeill, Harold, H.V.	.190	11	27	21	2	4	7	0	0	1	4	0	0	1	5	0	5	0	0	2	.333	.370
Gotauco, David, Jam.	.271	21	69	59	5	16	28	6	0	2	9	0	1	3	6	0	9	1	0	1	.475	.362
Green, Kevin, Jam.	.125	17	62	56	5	7	11	1	0	1	7	0	0	1	5	0	25	0	0	2	.196	.210
Guerrero, Julio, Low.	.240	43	160	146	21	35	42	3	2	0	13	1	0	1	12	0	26	17	4	5	.288	.302
Haase, Jeff, M.V.	.250	69	299	244	46	61	95	12	5	4	45	2	3	10	40	1	72	14	2	6	.389	.374
Hambrick, Marcus, Jam.*	.267	60	214	195	17	52	80	9	5	3	25	1	4	1	13	0	44	5	5	1	.410	.310
Harper, Shaun, Jam.	.226	72	275	257	33	58	95	12	5	5	24	1	3	1	13	1	89	5	4	2	.370	.263
Harris, Corey, Pit.	.320	61	238	194	38	62	97	17	3	4	30	1	5	4	34	0	28	23	4	3	.500	.422
Hattig, John, Low.†	.289	61	264	242	30	70	80	8	1	0	28	1	1	0	20	1	43	1	1	1	.331	.342
Haynes, Dee, N.J.	.255	64	263	243	31	62	109	18	4	7	37	0	3	1	16	0	53	4	1	4	.449	.300
Hensley, Anthony, Bat.†	.277	68	302	235	48	65	86	9	3	2	28	2	1	4	60	1	52	43	9	2	.366	.430
Hernandez, Jose, Wil.	.118	5	18	17	2	2	5	0	0	1	2	1	0	0	0	0	3	0	0	1	.294	.118
Herrera, Franklyn, N.J.	.280	21	55	50	6	14	16	2	0	0	1	0	0	0	5	1	12	2	0	2	.320	.345
Hicks, Scott, Uti.*	.202	58	203	178	17	36	46	5	1	1	18	1	1	2	21	0	43	4	8	1	.258	.292
Hill, John, H.V.	.212	56	223	189	24	40	57	6	4	1	27	1	3	2	28	0	64	13	5	3	.302	.315
Holland, Tapley, One.	.178	46	164	135	20	24	31	4	0	1	11	1	1	4	23	1	39	2	4	6	.230	.313
Hooper, Clay, S.I.	.246	64	260	228	33	56	71	15	0	0	15	3	3	1	25	0	28	6	3	2	.311	.319
Hudnall, Joshua, Wil.	.197	38	131	117	13	23	26	1	1	0	6	1	0	1	12	0	48	5	1	2	.222	.277
Hunter, David, Pit.*	.138	29	98	94	6	13	15	2	0	0	4	1	1	0	2	0	26	1	1	0	.160	.155
Inglett, Joe, M.V.*	.287	56	238	202	37	58	84	12	4	2	37	0	0	5	31	1	30	4	5	1	.416	.395
Jacobs, John, H.V.	.222	40	137	126	13	28	41	7	0	2	11	0	1	0	9	0	46	7	8	1	.325	.272
Janowicz, Nathan, M.V.*	.340	71	305	265	40	90	123	14	5	3	43	5	3	1	31	1	34	10	12	5	.464	.407
Jimenez, Richard, Que.†	.219	9	36	32	5	7	8	1	0	0	3	0	0	1	3	0	9	0	0	0	.250	.306
Johnson, Forrest, One.	.264	34	131	110	20	29	43	4	2	2	17	0	2	6	13	0	20	3	2	6	.391	.366
Johnson, Patrick, Low.*	.200	26	84	70	8	14	25	5	0	2	4	0	0	0	14	2	20	0	2	2	.357	.312
Jones, Mitch, S.I.	.268	74	324	284	46	76	143	28	3	11	54	0	2	3	35	0	66	8	2	1	.504	.352
Katz, Damon, M.V.	.250	24	89	76	11	19	28	3	3	0	7	3	1	6	3	0	17	1	1	1	.368	.326
Kaup, Nathan, H.V.	.331	55	144	136	21	45	60	9	0	2	22	0	2	1	5	0	25	3	2	4	.441	.354
Kavourias, Jim, Uti.	.320	15	60	50	7	16	26	4	0	2	7	0	0	0	10	0	6	1	0	0	.520	.433
Keene, Kurt, Que.	.261	11	52	46	10	12	13	1	0	0	5	0	0	0	6	0	10	4	1	3	.283	.346
Kerner, Craig, Ver.*	.269	33	131	108	24	29	34	1	2	0	11	3	0	5	15	0	25	12	4	0	.315	.383
Kinchen, Jason, S.I.*	.281	66	264	231	39	65	113	16	1	10	50	0	3	8	22	1	47	0	1	2	.489	.360
Langill, Eric, Ver.	.136	14	54	44	3	6	7	1	0	0	7	0	2	1	7	0	14	0	0	0	.159	.259
Langlois, Jean-Sebastien, Jam.	.073	13	49	41	4	3	3	0	0	0	3	0	1	3	4	0	12	1	1	0	.073	.204
Leaumont, Jeff, S.I.*	.267	25	101	86	10	23	27	2	1	0	9	0	1	3	11	0	17	0	0	4	.314	.366
Lee, Eric, Aub.	.181	59	222	199	27	36	55	6	2	3	15	0	1	4	18	0	48	8	7	2	.276	.261
Leer, David, One.	.313	29	126	115	20	36	44	8	0	0	6	0	2	5	7	0	35	10	5	0	.383	.373
Lichay, Donald, Pit.	.194	35	112	93	15	18	26	3	1	1	8	3	0	3	13	0	32	6	2	1	.280	.312
Lockhart, Paul, Aub.	.255	67	251	231	20	59	83	15	3	1	29	0	2	2	16	1	44	4	6	4	.359	.307
Lopez, Aristides, Aub.	.201	41	144	134	19	27	40	8	1	1	16	1	0	1	8	0	27	9	4	2	.299	.252
Lopez, Guillermo, Low.	.143	8	32	28	3	4	5	1	0	0	1	0	0	0	4	0	13	1	0	0	.179	.250
Lopez, Raul, Jam.*	.221	72	298	267	32	59	93	15	2	5	41	0	2	3	26	2	52	0	0	9	.348	.295
Lotterhos, Chris, M.V.	.188	5	20	16	2	3	4	1	0	0	1	0	0	1	3	0	6	0	0	0	.250	.350

CLASS A New York-Pennsylvania League

Player, Team	Avg.	G	TPA	AB	R	H	TB	2B	3B	HR	RBI	SH	SF	HP	BB	IBB	SO	SB	CS	GDP	Slg.	OBP
Louwsma, Chris, Uti.	.238	71	290	265	28	63	82	13	0	2	34	1	0	1	23	1	55	3	4	10	.309	.301
Lowe, Steve, M.V.	.243	41	172	140	27	34	48	1	2	3	14	1	0	10	21	0	31	1	0	3	.343	.380
Lucas, William, Aub.	.303	29	94	89	11	27	30	3	0	0	10	1	1	0	3	0	19	3	2	1	.337	.323
Lugo, Felix, Ver.†	.250	39	156	140	22	35	57	13	0	3	19	0	1	6	7	0	47	11	4	2	.407	.312
Luna, Hector, M.V.	.316	5	21	19	2	6	8	2	0	0	4	1	0	0	1	0	3	0	0	0	.421	.350
Lutz, David, Ver.*	.220	35	145	118	18	26	27	1	0	0	13	0	2	0	25	1	25	9	1	0	.229	.352
Luuloa, Miles, One.†	.207	53	209	169	28	35	42	5	1	0	15	4	2	4	30	0	58	3	4	8	.249	.337
Lydic, Joe, Aub.	.273	67	278	260	37	71	111	16	3	6	30	0	2	5	11	2	60	1	2	2	.427	.313
Magness, Pat, Uti.*	.309	50	208	175	31	54	87	18	0	5	40	0	1	2	30	2	34	2	0	2	.497	.413
Malave, Dennis, M.V.*	.298	42	208	178	39	53	79	4	8	2	26	4	1	2	23	1	30	15	5	3	.444	.382
Malpica, Martin, Que.	.278	55	226	216	30	60	80	14	0	2	34	1	0	2	7	0	35	0	3	5	.370	.307
Marconi, Alex, H.V.	.291	24	94	86	11	25	33	1	2	1	10	0	1	0	7	1	15	2	2	3	.384	.340
Marsh, Jason, H.V.	.253	53	207	194	20	49	59	7	0	1	19	1	3	4	5	0	41	3	6	1	.304	.282
Martinez, Casey, Que.	.136	7	25	22	2	3	3	0	0	0	0	1	0	1	1	0	7	0	0	0	.136	.208
McDonald, John, M.V.	.118	5	19	17	0	2	3	1	0	0	1	0	0	0	2	0	3	0	0	0	.176	.211
McGrath, Ryan, Aub.	.274	37	125	106	13	29	34	5	0	0	4	1	1	5	12	0	21	6	2	2	.321	.371
McIntyre, Robert, Pit.	.176	5	21	17	1	3	3	0	0	0	1	1	0	0	3	0	5	0	0	0	.176	.300
McKee, Mickey, Aub.	.291	51	176	165	20	48	65	11	3	0	18	2	4	0	5	0	32	6	4	1	.394	.305
McMillan, Andrew, Ver.	.143	23	88	77	6	11	12	1	0	0	4	0	0	3	8	0	22	1	0	1	.156	.250
Melo, Hanlet, Jam.	.217	8	24	23	1	5	6	1	0	0	1	0	0	0	1	0	6	0	0	2	.261	.250
Merrill, Jr., Ronald, One.†	.311	33	150	135	21	42	54	5	2	1	21	0	2	12	1	23	6	3	1	.400	.376
Meseberg, Michael, H.V.*	.128	29	105	94	9	12	13	1	0	0	6	1	0	0	10	0	31	2	0	0	.138	.212
Miller, Eric, Ver.	.300	47	178	160	25	48	61	9	2	0	18	0	0	3	15	3	18	6	2	6	.381	.371
Moccia, Mark, One.	.232	51	225	203	23	47	65	6	6	0	20	2	3	3	14	0	40	6	4	1	.320	.287
Money, Freddie, Low.	.197	55	228	203	28	40	58	4	4	2	16	1	2	3	19	0	40	10	5	1	.286	.273
Mooney, Daniel, Low.	.182	34	122	110	10	20	33	4	0	3	13	1	3	3	5	0	31	2	0	1	.300	.231
Morris, Ken, N.J.†	.170	63	240	182	34	31	35	2	1	0	15	4	1	3	50	1	48	42	12	1	.192	.356
Moylan, Dan, N.J.*	.274	56	216	168	20	46	52	6	0	0	14	0	2	4	42	0	28	8	8	6	.310	.426
Muthig, Dean, Bat.	.225	36	128	120	13	27	46	2	1	5	15	0	2	0	6	0	33	2	0	3	.383	.258
Navarrete, Raymond, Wil.	.310	66	278	248	19	77	101	13	1	3	36	1	5	3	20	2	27	1	1	4	.407	.362
Neill, John, One.	.274	64	289	230	41	63	95	7	5	5	39	0	4	10	45	1	74	16	8	3	.413	.408
Nettles, Tim, S.I.	.245	36	59	53	9	13	16	1	1	0	5	0	0	2	4	0	12	3	3	2	.302	.322
Nicolas, Jose, Wil.	.225	55	225	204	25	46	73	9	0	6	16	0	0	1	19	0	67	3	0	4	.358	.295
Nieves, Raul, Low.	.248	56	229	202	23	50	59	7	1	0	13	4	1	0	22	1	33	5	2	2	.292	.320
O'Brien, Kevin, H.V.*	.213	22	82	75	9	16	21	2	0	1	7	1	0	0	6	1	23	0	1	1	.280	.272
O'Brien, Mike, One.*	.266	68	276	241	34	64	94	9	3	5	45	0	3	2	30	2	63	10	2	4	.390	.348
Ochoa, Javier, Pit.	.059	5	18	17	0	1	1	0	0	0	0	0	0	1	0	0	2	0	0	1	.059	.111
O'Neill, Daniel, Bat.	.198	29	106	91	10	18	26	2	0	2	7	0	0	0	15	0	24	0	0	2	.286	.311
Orr, Peterson, Jam.*	.242	69	299	265	40	64	80	8	1	2	15	0	4	6	24	0	51	9	5	4	.302	.314
Ortiz, Matt, N.J.	.184	28	92	87	6	16	27	3	1	2	8	0	0	0	5	0	16	0	0	2	.310	.228
Osborn, Jason, Pit.	.174	7	24	23	0	4	4	0	0	0	3	0	0	0	1	0	7	0	1	1	.174	.208
Osborne, Mark, M.V.*	.150	6	25	20	1	3	5	0	1	0	1	0	0	1	4	0	6	0	0	0	.250	.320
O'Sullivan, Patrick, Pit.	.250	1	4	4	0	1	1	0	0	0	0	0	0	0	0	0	2	0	0	0	.250	.250
Pagan, Jon, Wil.	.205	54	207	185	19	38	64	11	0	5	14	0	0	3	19	0	75	0	1	6	.346	.290
Parker, Chris, One.	.259	34	134	108	13	28	32	4	0	0	11	3	1	2	20	0	22	2	0	1	.296	.382
Parrish, Dave, S.I.	.240	63	251	221	29	53	87	20	1	4	29	1	0	4	25	0	54	0	0	4	.394	.328
Paulino, Dave, Uti.*	.500	2	4	4	1	2	4	0	1	0	0	0	0	0	0	0	0	2	0	0	1.000	.500
Pearson, Shawn, Que.	.351	20	94	74	18	26	27	1	0	0	3	0	2	0	18	0	8	7	4	1	.365	.468
Peguero, Miguel, One.	.319	22	81	72	7	23	23	0	0	0	9	3	0	0	6	0	21	1	2	1	.319	.372
Pelfrey, Brice, Wil.	.228	49	179	162	27	37	42	5	0	0	10	1	2	2	12	0	27	6	1	3	.259	.287
Pena, Wily, S.I.	.301	20	79	73	7	22	27	1	2	0	10	0	0	4	2	0	23	2	0	1	.370	.354
Perich, Josh, Pit.	.145	21	78	69	6	10	15	1	2	0	4	1	0	0	8	0	24	1	2	1	.217	.234
Peterson, Brian, M.V.	.222	24	92	72	9	16	20	2	1	0	6	3	1	4	12	0	20	2	0	2	.278	.340
Pfister, Billy, One.	.259	26	96	81	9	21	30	1	4	0	6	0	0	0	15	0	24	6	1	1	.370	.375
Pichardo, Henry, M.V.	.100	3	11	10	2	1	1	0	0	0	0	0	0	0	1	0	3	1	0	1	.100	.182
Pietro, Jim, M.V.	.193	35	147	119	19	23	25	2	0	0	5	4	1	4	19	0	32	4	2	3	.210	.322
Pogue, Jamie, N.J.	.233	28	116	90	12	21	27	6	0	0	9	0	1	1	24	1	18	1	0	4	.300	.397
Pohle, Ike, S.I.	.190	14	23	21	0	4	6	2	0	0	3	0	0	1	1	0	7	0	0	0	.286	.261
Pollaro, Dallas, N.J.	.145	20	62	55	5	8	8	0	0	0	3	1	0	3	3	0	10	3	0	2	.145	.230
Postell, Matthew, Uti.*	.301	46	171	156	24	47	66	10	3	1	15	1	0	2	12	0	29	2	1	3	.423	.359
Pugh, Dwayne, Que.	.000	8	17	16	2	0	0	0	0	0	0	0	0	0	1	0	5	1	0	0	.000	.059
Quattlebaum, Hugh, One.	.301	49	215	186	27	56	73	5	6	0	26	0	2	3	24	0	28	4	2	4	.392	.386
Quiroz, Guillermo, Que.	.224	55	228	196	27	44	68	9	0	5	29	0	1	4	27	0	48	1	2	4	.347	.329
Ravelo, Manuel, Wil.	.303	52	231	195	38	59	77	4	7	0	17	5	0	5	26	0	30	28	9	2	.395	.398
Rich, Dominic, Que.	.263	67	286	236	37	62	81	11	4	0	25	4	3	5	38	0	33	10	4	8	.343	.372
Richardson, Juan, Bat.	.154	10	42	39	0	6	8	2	0	0	2	0	0	0	3	0	15	0	0	2	.205	.214
Rickon, Jim, M.V.	.300	3	12	10	0	3	3	0	0	0	3	0	0	0	2	0	2	0	0	0	.300	.417
Ridley, Jeremy, Que.†	.000	1	2	2	0	0	0	0	0	0	0	0	0	0	0	0	0	0	0	0	.000	.000
Riek, Cliff, Wil.	.140	29	98	86	9	12	21	3	0	2	12	0	0	6	5	0	25	0	0	0	.244	.237
Riera, Zack, Wil.†	.133	15	52	45	4	6	7	1	0	0	2	0	0	3	4	0	11	1	0	3	.156	.250
Rikert, Wade, Que.*	.250	36	129	108	19	27	32	5	0	0	14	1	1	1	18	0	22	8	3	1	.296	.359
Rincon, Carlos, Aub.	.130	11	25	23	3	3	4	1	0	0	4	0	0	0	2	0	7	2	0	0	.174	.200
Rios, Alexis, Que.	.267	50	224	206	22	55	71	9	2	1	25	1	2	4	11	2	22	5	5	5	.345	.314
Rodriguez, Ronny, Low.	.105	13	46	38	7	4	5	1	0	0	2	0	2	4	0	18	1	2	0	.132	.227
Rodriguez, Wilson, M.V.	.000	3	10	9	3	0	0	0	0	0	1	0	0	0	1	0	2	0	0	0	.000	.100
Rojas, Alex, Bat.†	.168	46	149	137	27	23	29	4	1	0	13	3	3	1	5	0	31	12	2	4	.212	.199
Rombley, Danny, Ver.	.234	49	216	192	32	45	52	3	2	0	28	1	3	4	16	0	51	14	8	2	.271	.302
Rooi, Vince, Ver.	.231	65	283	234	36	54	83	9	1	6	43	0	4	4	40	2	60	9	2	3	.355	.348
Ryan, Jeff, M.V.	.125	2	8	8	0	1	1	0	0	0	0	0	0	0	0	0	3	0	1	0	.125	.125
Salas, Juan, H.V.	.284	38	145	134	22	38	53	7	1	2	14	1	0	1	9	0	31	3	5	11	.396	.333
Sanchez, Frederick, Low.	.288	34	146	132	24	38	58	13	2	1	14	2	0	3	9	0	16	2	4	1	.439	.347
Santana, Pedro, S.I.	.301	19	84	73	17	22	29	4	0	1	13	0	2	1	8	1	16	0	0	3	.397	.369
Santos, Juan, Que.†	.241	9	36	29	2	7	9	2	0	0	3	1	0	2	4	0	6	0	0	0	.310	.371

Player, Team	Avg.	G	TPA	AB	R	H	TB	2B	3B	HR	RBI	SH	SF	HP	BB	IBB	SO	SB	CS	GDP	Slg.	OBP
Schell, Barry, Uti.*	.227	44	147	128	20	29	52	5	0	6	21	0	0	1	18	0	52	0	1	4	.406	.327
Schuda, Justin, H.V.*	.268	65	262	231	25	62	89	16	1	3	27	0	3	0	28	1	70	2	1	2	.385	.344
Scott, Charles, M.V.	.250	1	5	4	0	1	1	0	0	0	0	0	0	0	1	0	1	0	0	1	.250	.400
Seiber, Antron, Low.	.190	6	21	21	2	4	6	0	1	0	2	0	0	0	0	0	5	1	0	0	.286	.190
Self, Todd, Aub.*	.194	52	195	160	13	31	39	3	1	1	19	2	1	4	28	0	42	10	4	1	.244	.326
Sellier, Brian, Que.*	.258	66	259	209	34	54	82	5	4	5	33	1	6	2	41	0	51	11	2	6	.392	.376
Serrano, Raymond, Jam.	.321	21	82	78	9	25	44	4	0	5	14	0	1	1	2	0	9	1	0	0	.564	.341
Sherrill, J.J., M.V.†	.280	24	112	93	16	26	37	6	1	1	5	2	0	3	14	0	25	9	8	2	.398	.391
Sherrod, Justin, Low.	.225	59	235	204	31	46	73	10	1	5	20	1	2	3	25	0	74	2	0	4	.358	.316
Skeens, Jeremy, Ver.	.100	7	22	20	2	2	3	1	0	0	0	1	0	0	1	0	8	0	0	0	.150	.143
Small, Chris, Que.	.133	4	16	15	2	2	3	1	0	0	1	0	0	0	1	0	5	0	0	0	.200	.188
Smith, Ryan, Pit.	.195	16	51	41	5	8	13	3	1	0	3	0	0	0	10	0	13	0	1	0	.317	.353
Smith, Will, Low.	.267	51	222	172	21	46	51	5	0	0	14	5	2	5	38	0	32	20	7	0	.297	.410
Snyder, Mike, Que.*	.278	57	251	227	28	63	92	11	3	4	34	0	1	1	22	1	49	4	3	2	.405	.343
Soto, Tony, Aub.	.221	67	265	235	40	52	93	6	4	9	32	0	1	5	24	0	66	10	2	5	.396	.306
Stevens, Jeff, Uti.	.200	39	122	110	11	22	30	8	0	0	9	0	1	3	8	0	29	2	2	3	.273	.270
Sullivan, Kevin, Bat.	.176	12	44	34	4	6	7	1	0	0	1	2	0	0	8	0	10	1	0	0	.206	.333
Sutter, Tony, S.I.†	.236	38	88	72	14	17	20	3	0	0	9	0	0	0	16	1	15	2	1	1	.278	.375
Tablado, Raul, Que.	.212	52	234	198	27	42	63	8	2	3	29	1	3	1	31	0	76	1	1	6	.318	.318
Terveen, Bryce, Jam.*	.327	55	224	196	30	64	86	11	1	3	41	1	2	2	23	3	38	0	1	3	.439	.399
Thomas, Charles, Jam.	.303	68	285	264	39	80	119	20	8	1	25	0	1	1	19	0	58	10	2	7	.451	.351
Thompson, Eric, M.V.*	.000	1	4	3	0	0	0	0	0	0	0	0	0	1	0	0	1	2	0	0	.000	.250
Thompson, Richard, Que.*	.262	68	309	252	42	66	88	9	5	1	27	5	0	6	45	1	57	28	8	0	.349	.386
Timaure, Jesus, Uti.	.300	4	13	10	1	3	5	2	0	0	1	0	0	0	3	0	2	0	0	1	.500	.462
Tolli, Barry, One.	.269	64	264	242	29	65	88	8	3	3	33	2	2	2	16	0	65	9	5	3	.364	.317
Tood, Jeremy, Pit.*	.248	63	247	214	31	53	92	14	5	5	47	2	3	6	22	3	52	6	3	3	.430	.331
Tosca, Daniel, Bat.*	.260	42	171	150	15	39	56	13	2	0	16	1	3	2	15	0	34	1	0	2	.373	.329
Umbria, Jose, Que.	.500	3	10	10	3	5	6	1	0	0	4	0	0	0	0	0	0	0	0	0	.600	.500
Underdown, Preston, Bat.	.196	17	64	56	6	11	13	2	0	0	4	0	0	2	6	0	13	2	0	1	.232	.297
Utley, Chase, Bat.*	.307	40	175	153	21	47	68	13	1	2	22	0	2	2	18	1	23	5	3	3	.444	.383
Valdez, Darlin, Ver.	.171	12	48	41	7	7	16	1	1	2	3	0	0	0	7	0	11	2	0	2	.390	.292
Valdez, Wilson, Ver.	.266	65	272	248	32	66	79	8	1	1	30	3	3	1	17	0	32	16	9	3	.319	.312
Vasquez, Geraldo, N.J.	.191	57	210	188	26	36	49	3	5	0	13	2	0	0	20	0	50	15	4	4	.261	.269
Veleber, Troy, Wil.†	.237	44	193	169	28	40	52	1	4	1	15	5	0	2	16	0	31	14	3	5	.308	.310
Villar, Jose, Jam.	.171	23	93	82	7	14	20	3	0	1	8	0	0	2	9	0	23	1	3	1	.244	.269
Volquez, Bolivar, H.V.	.217	68	248	217	16	47	51	4	0	0	22	9	7	1	14	0	51	7	9	7	.235	.259
Vriesenga, Matt, N.J.	.000	22	0	0	0	0	0	0	0	0	0	0	0	0	0	0	0	1	0	0	.000	.000
Wakakuwa, Kenn, H.V.	.250	7	21	20	5	5	6	1	0	0	1	0	0	0	1	0	4	1	0	0	.300	.286
Walker, Matt, One.	.330	31	134	115	16	38	49	8	0	1	12	0	1	2	16	0	19	8	1	4	.426	.418
Watson, Brandon, Ver.*	.291	69	312	278	53	81	92	9	1	0	30	4	2	3	25	0	38	26	9	4	.331	.354
Whiteman, Thomas, Aub.	.250	70	256	232	33	58	77	10	3	1	22	1	0	1	22	1	52	7	5	7	.332	.318
Willingham, Josh, Uti.	.263	65	256	205	37	54	88	16	0	6	29	1	2	9	39	1	55	9	5	2	.429	.400
Wilson, John, Pit.	.324	69	289	247	36	80	98	16	1	0	48	0	5	12	24	0	30	18	3	4	.397	.403
Wilson, Josh, Uti.	.344	66	295	259	43	89	123	13	6	3	43	1	1	5	29	3	47	9	8	6	.475	.418
Winrow, Gary, S.I.*	.289	63	267	239	33	69	88	7	6	0	28	3	1	3	21	0	57	5	3	4	.368	.352
Womack, Robert, M.V.*	.174	31	111	86	16	15	19	2	1	0	10	0	2	3	20	0	24	9	1	1	.221	.342
Woodcock, Lance, M.V.	.171	10	46	41	6	7	11	2	1	0	3	0	1	0	4	0	19	2	0	0	.268	.239
Wright, Daron, Bat.*	.150	7	23	20	0	3	3	0	0	0	1	0	0	1	2	0	6	2	0	0	.150	.261
Yancy, Michael, Pit.	.115	18	67	61	3	7	8	1	0	0	4	2	0	1	3	1	19	1	1	1	.131	.169
Young, Walter, Wil.*	.185	24	95	92	5	17	27	4	0	2	12	0	1	1	0	0	26	0	0	1	.293	.200
Youngbauer, Scott, Bat.†	.235	66	278	251	41	59	97	16	2	6	35	1	4	0	22	0	40	0	0	9	.386	.292
Zapey, Winton, Uti.	.093	28	87	75	9	7	11	1	0	1	7	3	0	0	8	0	21	0	2	0	.147	.181
Zaragoza, Joel, Pit.†	.178	54	191	163	18	29	40	9	1	0	13	8	2	6	12	1	44	3	0	2	.245	.257

GRAND SLAMS: M. Jones, 2 each; Church, Donato, Kinchen, Merrill, Riek, Rooi, W. Young, 1 each.

AWARDED FIRST BASE ON CATCHER'S INTERFERENCE: Lugo 2 (Alvarado, Castaneda); Avila (Lucas); Centeno (Quiroz); Gall (Bastardo); Jacobs (Mooney); Merrill (Osborn); Navarette (Alvarado); Nicolas (Gentry); Riek (Bastardo); Rooi (Franco); R. Thompson (John Wilson); Veleber (Alvarado); John Wilson (Cleveland); Zapey (Pogue).

2000 PITCHING
TEAM

Team	W	L	Pct.	ERA	G	CG	ShO	Sv.	IP	H	TBF	R	ER	HR	SH	SF	HB	BB	IBB	SO	WP	Bk.
Staten Island	46	28	.622	2.85	74	3	5	22	654.1	542	2688	258	207	19	20	9	31	217	3	602	56	12
Lowell	41	34	.547	3.07	75	3	7	26	664.2	600	2763	290	227	10	33	22	25	213	3	590	44	8
Queens	46	29	.613	3.15	75	1	4	19	671.1	568	2853	304	235	23	21	31	40	295	5	663	62	5
Vermont	45	30	.600	3.17	75	1	7	20	676.2	572	2879	325	238	31	14	26	40	299	0	548	42	7
Auburn	32	42	.432	3.49	74	0	2	18	645.1	569	2813	330	250	28	23	20	64	279	7	562	58	8
Pittsfield	38	37	.507	3.50	75	2	4	19	647.2	580	2805	324	252	19	15	17	50	300	5	620	47	11
Mahoning Val.	48	28	.632	3.71	76	0	5	14	676.1	646	2892	328	279	33	14	26	35	257	3	537	52	10
Jamestown	37	38	.493	3.77	75	0	4	20	648.2	646	2854	367	272	40	16	19	29	275	5	543	34	9
Batavia	39	37	.513	3.89	76	8	5	20	667.0	633	2891	356	288	29	25	18	52	263	22	500	53	11
Williamsport	29	44	.397	3.93	73	2	3	12	639.2	637	2858	369	279	33	19	33	52	311	1	549	33	15
Utica	35	40	.467	4.00	75	0	3	16	650.1	636	2860	365	289	43	25	21	32	287	5	552	69	11
Oneonta	35	41	.461	4.06	76	3	1	13	649.2	644	2873	365	293	25	19	25	39	264	7	545	58	12
Hudson Valley	23	52	.307	4.18	75	3	3	11	647.1	659	2909	411	301	26	21	27	47	282	16	567	64	10
New Jersey	31	45	.408	4.45	76	0	3	21	665.1	688	3001	414	329	26	18	26	56	316	2	578	79	1

TOP QUALIFIERS FOR EARNED-RUN AVERAGE TITLE

Minimum 61 innings. *Lefthanded pitcher.

Pitcher, Team	W	L	Pct.	ERA	G	GS	CG	ShO	GF	Sv.	IP	H	TBF	R	ER	HR	SH	SF	HB	BB	IBB	SO	WP	Bk.
Young, Simon, M.V.*	7	2	.778	1.75	14	13	0	0	0	0	77.0	62	295	20	15	1	1	1	4	21	0	56	3	1
Elmore, Christopher, Low.*	3	3	.500	1.89	15	10	1	1	3	2	71.1	55	279	20	15	0	1	1	6	14	0	46	3	2
Campos, Juan, Aub.	3	1	.750	1.92	29	0	0	0	13	7	61.0	44	248	21	13	1	3	3	4	19	0	59	5	1
Lara, Mauricio, Low.*	4	3	.571	2.12	15	14	1	0	0	0	85.0	70	330	22	20	0	2	0	3	21	0	83	2	2
Beal, Andy, S.I.*	9	3	.750	2.34	14	14	1	1	0	0	92.1	72	361	27	24	6	3	0	2	17	0	87	8	1
Waechter, Doug, H.V.	4	4	.500	2.35	14	14	2	2	0	0	72.2	53	302	23	19	2	2	1	4	37	0	58	7	3
Smith, Matt, S.I.*	5	4	.556	2.38	14	14	0	0	0	0	75.2	74	308	32	20	1	3	0	2	20	0	59	4	0
Cox, Michael, Pit.*	2	3	.400	2.48	14	12	1	0	0	0	61.2	43	261	23	17	3	0	2	5	30	0	81	6	0
Wang, Chien-ming, S.I.	4	4	.500	2.48	14	14	2	1	0	0	87.0	77	358	34	24	2	3	1	2	21	1	75	7	1
Fontana, Tony, Low.	5	4	.556	2.49	14	11	1	1	1	1	72.1	61	294	29	20	1	3	2	5	17	0	46	6	1
Song, Seung, Low.	5	2	.714	2.60	13	13	0	0	0	0	72.2	63	293	26	21	1	0	2	0	20	0	93	6	1
Bullock, Trevor, Bat.*	6	3	.667	2.61	15	7	1	0	4	1	62.0	57	264	23	18	2	0	0	3	17	3	54	1	0
Mendez, David, Jam.*	4	4	.556	2.87	15	15	0	0	0	0	84.2	75	360	33	27	7	0	1	6	31	0	84	3	0
Dequin, Benjamin, Ver.*	6	3	.667	2.89	16	16	0	0	0	0	74.2	60	328	33	24	2	0	3	4	50	0	79	6	0
Girdley, Josh, Ver.*	5	0	1.000	2.95	14	14	0	0	0	0	79.1	60	321	32	26	4	1	5	5	28	0	70	5	0

DEPARTMENTAL LEADERS: W—Beal, 9; L—Axelson, 9; Pct.—Hannah, .857; G—Samora, Cook, 32 each; GS—several tied, 15 each; CG—Waechter, Wang, Dagley, 2 each; ShO—Waechter, 2; GF—Jackson, 29; Sv.—Samora, 17; IP—Dagley, 102.2; H—Montana, 12; TBF—Dagley, 428; R—Cromer, 57; ER—Johnston, 44; HR—Flannery, 8; SH—several tied, 5 each; SF—several tied, 6 each; HB—Montana, 12; BB—Dequin, 50; IBB—Dagley, 5; SO—Song, 93; WP—Cali, Thomas, 11 each; BK—Roman, Anderson, 4 each.

ALL PITCHERS

*Lefthanded pitcher.

Pitcher, Team	W	L	Pct.	ERA	G	GS	CG	ShO	GF	Sv.	IP	H	TBF	R	ER	HR	SH	SF	HB	BB	IBB	SO	WP	Bk.
Adams, Brian, Low.*	3	4	.429	4.44	12	10	0	0	0	0	52.2	61	225	30	26	2	2	4	0	13	0	38	1	0
Adams, Daniel, Bat.	2	0	1.000	2.17	23	0	0	0	13	5	29.0	27	124	8	7	0	4	3	4	13	4	30	3	1
Albertus, Roberto, Jam.*	2	0	1.000	1.54	4	1	0	0	1	0	11.2	7	47	3	2	0	1	0	0	4	0	13	0	0
Alcala, Jason, Wil.	2	4	.333	3.25	17	8	1	0	6	1	63.2	67	270	26	23	3	1	5	0	22	1	49	2	3
Alston, Travis, Bat.	3	2	.600	2.68	20	5	1	1	13	6	47.0	43	218	19	14	0	5	0	3	28	2	40	3	0
Anderson, Jason, S.I.*	6	5	.545	4.03	15	15	0	0	0	0	80.1	84	342	41	36	1	2	2	5	25	0	73	5	4
Ascencio, Miguel, Bat.	2	2	.500	4.99	7	7	1	0	0	0	39.2	32	165	23	22	3	1	1	3	17	0	28	2	0
Axelson, Josh, N.J.	3	9	.250	5.13	15	14	0	0	0	0	73.2	79	330	53	42	2	2	3	4	34	0	63	9	0
Baker, Ryan, Jam.	4	2	.667	3.41	21	2	0	0	12	3	34.1	33	141	14	13	2	1	0	0	13	0	36	1	1
Baum, David, Wil.*	1	1	.500	5.84	14	0	0	0	5	0	24.2	36	121	19	16	1	0	2	2	12	0	25	1	0
Bautista, Denny, Uti.	0	0	.000	3.60	1	1	0	0	0	0	5.0	4	21	3	2	0	0	1	2	0	0	5	0	0
Bazan, Juan, Wil.	0	0	.000	1.46	3	1	0	0	0	0	12.1	6	45	2	2	1	0	0	1	1	0	10	0	0
Beal, Andy, S.I.*	9	3	.750	2.34	14	14	1	1	0	0	92.1	72	361	27	24	6	3	0	2	17	0	87	8	1
Bean, Colter, S.I.	0	0	.000	4.50	3	0	0	0	2	0	2.0	3	14	3	1	0	0	3	1	2	0	1	0	1
Benedetti, John, H.V.	4	3	.571	4.14	26	0	0	0	17	3	41.1	44	178	26	19	3	2	0	0	17	4	37	0	0
Bennett, Jamie, Bat.*	4	1	.800	3.73	25	0	0	0	12	1	31.1	23	133	18	13	2	1	1	1	13	1	37	3	1
Bennett, Steven, Pit.	4	4	.500	2.82	13	13	0	0	0	0	54.1	42	222	25	17	1	0	2	8	17	0	50	3	3
Bentley, Brian, Low.	4	1	.800	1.88	21	0	0	0	12	3	38.1	28	147	8	8	3	0	1	7	0	48	2	0
Bolson, Michael, Ver.	3	3	.500	5.76	21	0	0	0	6	1	29.2	30	137	25	19	1	1	2	2	19	0	18	2	1
Borrell, Danny, S.I.*	4	2	.667	3.20	10	10	0	0	0	0	56.1	39	224	21	20	2	1	1	2	19	0	44	1	0
Bottenfield, Jason, Low.	0	0	.000	0.00	1	0	0	0	0	0	2.1	0	8	0	0	0	0	0	1	0	0	0	0	0
Brito, Eude, Bat.*	1	1	.500	5.40	4	3	0	0	1	0	18.1	16	75	14	11	0	0	1	3	0	11	5	0	
Brookman, Ryan, Bat.	0	2	.000	4.09	9	1	0	0	6	2	22.0	27	101	11	10	2	0	1	3	8	1	17	0	0
Bullock, Trevor, Bat.*	6	3	.667	2.61	15	7	1	0	4	1	62.0	57	264	23	18	2	0	0	3	17	3	54	1	0
Bumatay, Mike, Wil.*	1	0	1.000	2.84	7	0	0	0	6	2	12.2	10	53	4	4	1	0	0	0	7	0	17	2	1
Button, Sammy, M.V.*	2	2	.500	4.20	11	6	0	0	0	0	40.2	44	178	24	19	4	1	3	0	15	0	42	2	1
Bye, Christopher, Ver.	3	3	.500	2.25	22	0	0	0	10	2	36.0	27	159	15	9	1	0	0	2	20	0	39	3	0
Cabell, Shannon, Wil.*	2	1	.667	4.88	16	0	0	0	7	0	31.1	32	140	20	17	2	0	3	2	12	0	33	0	1
Cali, Carmen, N.J.*	2	7	.222	4.89	14	14	0	0	0	0	70.0	68	301	45	38	3	2	3	5	30	0	55	11	0
Calvo, Jose, Aub.	1	1	.500	4.50	5	5	0	0	0	0	22.0	26	99	12	11	1	1	1	2	6	0	17	2	0
Campbell, Jarrett, H.V.	0	2	.000	3.82	21	0	0	0	7	0	37.2	41	172	25	16	2	3	1	2	20	1	42	4	1
Campos, David, Uti.*	0	2	.000	3.58	15	5	0	0	4	2	37.2	33	160	19	15	4	1	1	2	16	0	42	3	0
Campos, Juan, Aub.	3	1	.750	1.92	29	0	0	0	13	7	61.0	44	248	21	13	1	3	3	4	19	0	59	5	1
Canale, Tom, M.V.	0	1	.000	3.63	11	0	0	0	2	0	22.1	24	105	9	9	1	0	0	3	5	0	19	0	1
Carbajal, Alex, H.V.*	1	1	.500	2.25	21	0	0	0	7	0	28.0	26	123	13	7	1	1	2	1	9	1	32	3	3
Cardwell, Brian, Que.	2	4	.333	4.71	12	11	1	0	1	0	42.0	49	213	32	26	6	2	3	6	19	0	61	4	0
Carter, Ryan, Bat.*	5	6	.455	4.00	13	13	1	0	0	0	72.0	63	304	36	32	2	2	0	2	33	1	67	8	0
Castillo, Ramon, Uti.	4	4	.500	4.75	13	13	0	0	0	0	66.1	80	307	44	35	2	1	6	6	31	0	47	3	2
Cerda, Jaime, Pit.*	4	1	.800	0.57	20	1	0	0	6	5	47.0	33	176	6	3	0	0	6	1	5	2	51	2	0
Chisnall, Wesley, Ver.	5	5	.500	4.31	13	13	1	0	0	0	71.0	76	296	44	34	4	1	4	2	13	0	29	1	0
Christ, John, M.V.	4	2	.667	3.12	18	0	0	0	10	1	26.0	20	112	10	9	0	0	0	1	12	1	27	3	0
Clark, Chris, Jam.	0	3	.000	5.52	15	1	0	0	3	1	29.1	38	135	20	18	2	0	0	11	0	27	0	1	
Clark, Jeremy, Low.	0	0	.000	0.00	1	0	0	0	1	0	2.0	1	7	0	0	0	0	1	0	2	0	0	
Classen, Ender, Wil.	2	4	.333	4.15	12	12	0	0	0	0	60.2	60	278	39	28	4	0	6	5	37	0	41	3	0
Clifton, Derek, Jam.	3	2	.600	0.95	14	0	0	0	6	0	19.0	10	85	7	2	0	1	3	0	10	0	24	0	0
Cole, Joseph, Pit.	4	2	.667	4.56	10	10	0	0	0	0	49.1	41	221	28	25	0	2	0	9	32	0	50	0	2
Collazo, Rafael, Ver.*	0	0	.000	4.50	3	0	0	0	2	1	4.0	5	17	2	2	0	0	1	0	0	2	0	0	
Colvard, Ron, M.V.	2	0	1.000	1.50	3	0	0	0	1	0	6.0	4	26	1	1	0	0	0	2	2	0	6	0	0
Cook, Jeremy, N.J.	2	1	.667	2.37	32	0	0	0	0	0	49.1	51	211	21	13	3	1	0	2	17	0	34	1	0
Correa, Dominic, Jam.	0	0	.000	1.35	15	0	0	0	1	0	20.0	10	78	3	3	0	2	0	3	9	0	21	3	0
Coughenour, Jory, Aub.	4	7	.364	5.06	15	15	0	0	0	0	74.2	90	339	53	42	7	2	1	8	25	0	34	8	1
Coward, Timothy, H.V.	2	3	.400	3.42	6	6	1	0	0	0	33.2	34	153	22	16	1	0	4	2	14	0	31	5	0
Cox, Michael, Pit.*	2	3	.400	2.48	14	12	1	0	0	0	61.2	43	261	23	17	3	0	2	5	30	0	81	6	0

Pitcher, Team	W	L	Pct.	ERA	G	GS	CG	ShO	GF	Sv.	IP	H	TBF	R	ER	HR	SH	SF	HB	BB	IBB	SO	WP	Bk.
Crawford, Chris, H.V.	0	0	.000	0.00	2	0	0	0	1	0	2.0	2	9	0	0	0	0	0	0	1	0	2	0	0
Crist, Ryan, One.	0	0	.000	3.18	3	0	0	0	1	0	5.2	3	23	2	2	0	0	1	0	4	0	3	0	0
Cromer, Nathan, H.V.*	2	7	.222	5.97	13	13	0	0	0	0	60.1	63	280	57	40	3	1	3	4	29	0	45	6	0
Cummings, Frank, Jam.	0	3	.000	3.94	22	0	0	0	12	2	32.0	36	146	25	14	6	2	1	1	14	0	27	0	0
Curtin, Brian, M.V.	1	2	.333	5.29	4	3	0	0	0	0	17.0	16	69	10	10	1	0	0	4	0	4	0	9	2	0
Curtiss, Tom, Jam.*	1	1	.500	1.23	24	0	0	0	16	9	29.1	17	127	6	4	0	1	0	1	15	0	41	5	0
Dagley, Corey, Bat.	4	4	.500	3.59	15	15	2	1	0	0	102.2	83	428	53	41	4	4	2	11	28	5	45	3	1
DeLaCruz, Juan, Wil.	2	2	.500	6.14	13	0	0	0	10	1	22.0	24	102	18	15	4	1	1	1	10	0	24	2	0
Dequin, Benjamin, Ver.*	6	3	.667	2.89	16	14	0	0	0	0	74.2	60	328	33	24	2	0	3	4	50	0	79	6	0
Detwiler, James, Que.*	3	1	.750	2.83	20	0	0	0	8	1	35.0	25	146	12	11	0	2	0	2	19	1	38	3	1
Donaghey, Steve, M.V.	3	1	.750	2.17	21	0	0	0	6	1	49.2	43	202	14	12	1	1	3	3	9	1	21	1	1
Donovan, Kevin, Bat.*	0	1	.000	10.97	7	0	0	0	2	0	10.2	17	57	15	13	2	0	2	1	6	0	13	1	0
Dorman, Rich, H.V.	2	6	.250	3.47	14	14	0	0	0	0	70.0	71	331	47	27	0	2	4	4	40	2	46	9	1
Dougherty, Kevin, Pit.*	0	0	.000	6.75	2	0	0	0	0	0	2.2	5	13	3	2	1	0	0	0	1	0	1	0	0
Earl, Ryan, One.*	2	7	.222	5.49	12	12	0	0	0	0	57.1	61	264	45	35	5	1	1	5	23	0	53	9	0
Eckenstahler, Eric, One.*	0	3	.000	1.64	8	0	0	0	4	0	11.0	7	46	3	2	0	0	1	2	3	0	13	1	0
Elliott, Chad, Pit.	1	4	.200	4.89	11	8	0	0	1	0	49.2	58	227	33	27	3	2	1	2	22	1	54	3	0
Ellis, Ryan, Ver.	0	1	.000	45.00	1	0	0	0	1	0	1.0	1	9	5	5	1	0	0	2	3	0	1	0	0
Elmore, Christopher, Low.*	3	3	.500	1.89	15	10	1	1	3	2	71.1	55	279	20	15	0	1	1	6	14	0	46	3	2
Encarnacion, Orlando, Pit.	4	0	1.000	0.34	8	2	0	0	1	1	26.2	17	100	2	1	0	1	0	1	6	0	18	1	0
Esquivia, Manuel, Uti.	1	0	1.000	2.45	2	2	0	0	0	0	11.0	9	46	3	3	0	0	1	0	4	0	14	2	0
Estel, Justin, Ver.	0	0	.000	1.80	3	0	0	0	1	0	5.0	3	21	1	1	0	0	1	3	0	3	0	1
Evans, Kyle, M.V.	5	2	.714	3.14	12	11	0	0	1	0	63.0	56	259	29	22	4	0	4	1	22	0	53	3	1
Everett, Matt, M.V.	1	0	1.000	0.00	1	0	0	0	1	0	1.0	1	5	0	0	0	0	0	1	0	1	0	1
Evert, Brett, Jam.	8	3	.727	3.38	15	15	0	0	0	0	77.1	92	344	52	29	6	0	1	5	19	0	64	2	0
Ewin, Ryan, Jam.	0	1	.000	5.73	2	2	0	0	0	0	11.0	10	48	8	7	0	1	1	0	4	0	10	1	0
Faigin, Jason, S.I.	2	2	.500	4.06	22	0	0	0	6	1	31.0	25	137	19	14	0	2	0	2	18	0	27	5	2
Ferrari, Anthony, Ver.*	2	2	.500	1.71	25	0	0	0	21	5	47.1	31	190	14	9	2	3	0	5	15	0	37	2	1
Field, Luke, M.V.	2	3	.400	4.89	22	1	0	0	6	0	49.2	56	221	36	27	3	0	3	3	21	0	31	4	2
Fiora, Chris, N.J.	2	0	1.000	7.22	27	0	0	0	7	1	28.2	33	159	31	23	0	0	5	35	0	30	9	0
Fitch, Steve, M.V.	5	1	.833	4.28	12	10	0	0	0	0	61.0	68	255	30	29	3	4	1	0	12	0	38	1	0
Flannery, Michael, Uti.	2	7	.222	4.89	13	13	0	0	0	0	70.0	71	304	51	38	8	0	4	3	20	0	44	5	1
Fontana, Tony, Low.	5	4	.556	2.49	14	11	1	1	1	1	72.1	61	294	29	20	1	3	2	5	17	0	46	6	1
Fortin, Michael, Wil.	0	2	.000	4.76	16	0	0	0	7	0	28.1	36	137	20	15	2	1	2	3	16	0	12	2	0
Franco, Jose, S.I.	0	0	.000	0.00	5	0	0	0	2	1	5.2	3	24	0	0	0	0	0	4	1	7	0	0
Frias, Juan, H.V.	0	4	.000	6.38	23	0	0	0	9	0	36.2	44	178	32	26	4	2	3	5	19	2	33	4	0
Fugarino, Steve, M.V.	1	0	.000	5.29	14	0	0	0	8	1	17.0	16	78	10	10	3	0	0	3	9	0	14	3	0
Garris, Antonio, Ver.	3	1	.750	1.82	24	0	0	0	18	10	34.2	17	144	9	7	1	1	1	0	25	0	44	2	0
Gerk, Jordan, One.*	1	2	.333	3.38	11	7	0	0	0	0	42.2	42	179	20	16	1	1	3	0	11	0	31	0	1
Giese, Daniel, Low.	0	0	.000	0.92	15	0	0	0	13	9	19.2	12	75	3	2	1	1	0	0	1	0	20	1	0
Girdley, Josh, Ver.*	5	0	1.000	2.95	14	14	0	0	0	0	79.1	60	321	32	26	4	1	6	5	28	0	70	5	0
Gomez, Ricardo, S.I.	3	1	.750	1.76	20	0	0	0	7	1	41.0	25	165	8	8	1	2	1	2	21	0	40	7	1
Grippo, Mike, N.J.*	1	2	.000	4.88	22	0	0	0	9	1	24.0	21	118	16	13	0	1	0	6	18	0	36	9	0
Hamilton, Ryan, Aub.	0	3	.000	5.76	5	5	0	0	0	0	25.0	28	112	17	16	1	3	1	2	9	0	15	3	0
Hannah, Shawn, One.	6	1	.857	1.31	16	1	1	0	5	0	41.1	31	157	8	6	0	1	1	0	7	1	25	3	0
Hawk, David, Wil.*	1	7	.125	6.75	12	9	0	0	0	0	40.0	47	199	37	30	0	0	1	9	33	0	30	4	1
Hazelton, Justin, M.V.	0	0	.000	21.60	4	0	0	0	4	0	5.0	11	37	12	12	2	0	0	0	11	0	5	6	0
Hee, Aaron, Pit.*	2	1	.667	4.04	18	0	0	0	2	0	35.2	32	169	21	16	0	0	3	2	35	1	39	6	0
Henderson, Kenneth, Wil.*	2	5	.286	4.19	15	6	0	0	0	0	53.2	58	241	34	25	4	0	3	1	25	0	35	0	3
Hernandez, Buddy, Jam.	1	1	.500	1.57	12	0	0	0	4	3	23.0	17	90	5	4	0	0	1	0	7	0	35	0	1
Hernandez, John-eric, One.	0	1	.000	21.60	2	0	0	0	0	0	1.2	3	14	4	4	0	1	0	0	5	0	1	0	0
Hicks, Ralph, Aub.*	1	3	.250	4.33	26	0	0	0	8	1	35.1	19	159	19	17	0	1	3	7	26	1	48	7	1
Higgins, Joshua, Wil.	3	1	.750	1.04	23	0	0	0	18	8	34.2	25	137	7	4	1	4	0	2	8	0	40	2	1
Hodges, Trey, Jam.	0	2	.000	5.95	13	2	0	0	2	0	19.2	22	93	14	13	3	1	0	1	12	0	13	1	2
Hopper, Joshua, Pit.*	1	0	1.000	4.11	15	0	0	0	8	0	30.2	27	131	17	14	2	1	1	2	19	0	24	3	0
Houston, Ryan, Que.	1	2	.333	2.83	12	0	0	0	2	0	28.2	23	118	11	9	1	1	0	3	8	0	29	1	0
Huesgen, Daniel, Que.	2	1	.667	2.42	16	0	0	0	2	1	26.0	27	115	9	7	2	3	1	0	10	0	17	1	0
Jackson, Brian, M.V.	2	2	.500	3.24	30	0	0	0	29	11	33.1	34	151	18	12	1	0	1	3	10	0	32	3	0
Jacobsen, Landon, Wil.	3	2	.600	1.41	9	9	0	0	0	0	57.1	38	228	15	9	1	1	2	6	17	0	57	1	0
Johnson, Derrick, Aub.*	0	0	.000	2.14	21	0	0	0	7	1	42.0	32	179	13	10	1	0	2	5	24	0	44	3	1
Johnson, Jeremy, One.	0	1	.000	2.89	2	2	0	0	0	0	9.1	8	39	5	3	0	0	0	4	0	5	2	0
Johnston, Rikki, One.*	6	4	.600	4.07	15	15	1	0	0	0	97.1	98	417	47	44	3	1	5	6	33	0	58	7	0
Jones, Rob, Uti.*	1	0	1.000	2.89	14	0	0	0	5	0	18.2	18	84	10	6	0	1	1	1	10	0	17	2	0
Journell, Jimmy, N.J.*	1	0	1.000	1.97	13	1	0	0	3	0	32.0	12	136	12	7	0	0	2	24	0	39	8	0
Kelley, Chris, M.V.	3	2	.600	3.99	11	1	0	0	2	0	29.1	25	127	15	13	1	2	3	2	15	0	33	5	1
Kelly, Dan, Jam.*	1	1	.500	1.80	2	0	0	0	2	0	5.0	4	19	1	1	0	0	0	0	1	0	3	1	0
Key, Chris, Uti.*	3	2	.600	0.79	19	0	0	0	16	7	34.1	19	124	3	3	1	3	0	5	1	0	42	3	0
Kleine, Victor, M.V.*	0	0	.000	4.50	3	1	0	0	0	0	4.0	2	18	2	2	0	0	0	3	4	0	2	1	0
Kozlowski, Kristopher, Que.*	4	1	.800	3.52	21	0	0	0	3	0	44.2	38	194	21	14	2	1	1	0	20	0	58	3	2
Kozol, Anthony, Low.	1	3	.250	2.79	16	1	0	0	14	6	29.0	32	129	15	9	1	2	1	4	7	2	30	2	0
Krysa, Jonathan, Aub.	3	4	.429	2.92	21	2	0	0	7	1	37.0	27	162	21	12	1	1	1	2	21	0	28	6	1
Lara, Mauricio, Low.*	3	4	.571	2.12	15	14	1	0	0	0	85.0	70	330	22	20	0	2	0	3	21	0	83	2	0
Lavigne, Tim, Pit.	2	1	.667	2.70	15	0	0	0	12	6	16.2	11	66	5	5	1	1	0	2	7	0	15	2	0
Law, Keith, One.	2	2	.500	3.94	11	0	0	0	7	0	16.0	19	75	12	7	2	0	0	2	5	2	15	1	0
Lawson, Jarrod, Bat.	1	1	.500	9.58	4	4	0	0	0	0	10.1	8	52	11	11	0	0	0	2	15	0	2	2	0
Lelless, Alexander, Jam.	0	1	.000	4.15	19	0	0	0	8	1	39.0	37	179	24	18	1	1	3	1	30	1	23	7	0
Leuenberger, Jeffrey, One.	0	0	.000	0.00	2	0	0	0	0	0	2.0	2	11	0	0	0	0	1	2	0	2	0	0
Levesque, Benjamin, Wil.	3	4	.429	5.52	17	0	0	0	6	0	29.1	31	156	30	18	1	1	2	4	33	0	23	3	0
Lewis, Jeremy, One.*	1	0	1.000	0.00	2	1	0	0	1	0	7.0	6	29	1	0	0	0	0	3	0	6	0	0
Lima, Lescano, Aub.	0	0	.000	0.00	5	0	0	0	1	0	14.1	5	53	0	0	0	2	0	1	2	0	16	1	0
Litman, Johri, M.V.	0	0	.000	2.70	3	0	0	0	1	0	6.2	5	28	2	2	0	0	0	3	0	5	0	0
Lockwood, Luke, Ver.*	1	0	1.000	2.25	2	2	0	0	0	0	12.0	12	45	3	3	1	1	0	1	0	8	1	0
Lopez, Rafael, Pit.	3	1	.750	3.27	4	4	1	1	0	0	22.0	22	91	10	8	0	2	0	4	0	23	0	0

Pitcher, Team	W	L	Pct.	ERA	G	GS	CG	ShO	GF	Sv.	IP	H	TBF	R	ER	HR	SH	SF	HB	BB	IBB	SO	WP	Bk.
Lyon, Brandon, Que.	5	3	.625	2.39	15	13	0	0	0	0	60.1	43	230	20	16	1	2	2	2	6	0	55	1	1
Malaska, Mark, H.V.*	0	2	.000	4.91	10	5	0	0	0	0	40.1	44	176	27	22	1	0	1	14	2	36	8	0
Malpica, Martin, Que.	0	0	.000	0.00	1	0	0	0	1	0	0.2	0	2	0	0	0	0	0	0	0	0	1	0	0
Marini, Anthony, M.V.*	1	0	1.000	1.80	1	0	0	0	0	0	5.0	3	19	1	1	0	0	0	0	0	0	1	1	0
Markwell, Diegomar, Que.*	4	3	.571	3.05	14	13	0	0	1	0	73.2	59	306	29	25	2	1	4	3	31	0	66	2	0
Martinez, David, S.I.*	2	2	.500	2.51	6	4	0	0	1	0	32.1	20	129	12	9	2	0	4	11	0	33	2	0
Martinez, Mark, Low.*	2	0	1.000	3.56	17	1	0	0	2	0	43.0	28	193	25	17	0	4	4	1	42	1	29	10	0
Martinez, Oscar, S.I.	2	0	1.000	0.36	26	0	0	0	22	13	25.0	11	88	2	1	0	0	1	0	6	0	40	5	0
Martunas, Matthew, H.V.*	1	0	1.000	9.00	3	0	0	0	2	0	5.0	8	26	7	5	0	1	1	1	2	1	3	0	0
Massingale, Matt, Uti.	3	0	1.000	0.50	6	6	0	0	0	0	35.2	23	133	4	2	1	0	0	9	9	0	31	2	0
Matheny, Brandon, M.V.*	6	3	.667	3.29	15	15	0	0	0	0	76.2	70	317	30	28	3	1	3	3	32	0	69	6	0
Mattioni, Nick, Pit.	1	1	.500	4.45	16	0	0	0	6	0	28.1	23	119	16	14	2	1	1	1	11	2	28	4	0
McCasland, Ralph, Ver.*	0	2	.000	1.37	11	0	0	0	6	1	26.1	19	107	11	4	1	1	1	1	8	0	23	3	0
McClung, Michael, H.V.	2	2	.500	1.85	8	8	0	0	0	0	43.2	37	186	18	9	0	1	2	3	17	0	38	6	1
McCormick, Terry, H.V.*	2	4	.333	4.61	12	0	0	0	7	3	27.1	23	112	15	14	2	1	1	5	3	0	26	4	0
McFarland, Stuart, Que.*	2	1	.667	2.08	19	0	0	0	10	2	26.0	12	115	9	6	0	2	2	8	22	1	21	1	0
McGinnis, Johnny, Jam.	0	1	.000	6.00	11	0	0	0	2	0	15.0	11	76	14	10	0	2	0	5	16	0	13	3	0
McKay, John, Uti.	2	0	1.000	1.91	17	4	0	0	5	1	37.2	35	156	11	8	3	1	0	8	0	42	2	1
McKey, Dustin, H.V.	1	3	.250	5.14	11	0	0	0	9	1	14.0	18	65	11	8	0	1	3	4	1	7	1	1
McNutt, Michael, Uti.	2	6	.250	5.08	15	10	0	0	2	0	62.0	68	273	39	35	4	1	0	5	18	1	38	5	2
Medlock, Chet, H.V.	2	4	.333	7.00	7	7	0	0	0	0	27.0	35	131	24	21	2	0	0	4	13	0	22	2	0
Meldahl, Todd, Bat.*	3	3	.500	3.33	18	5	1	0	4	0	48.2	52	205	24	18	2	2	1	3	13	1	46	3	0
Mendez, David, Jam.*	5	4	.556	2.87	15	15	0	0	0	0	84.2	75	360	33	27	7	0	1	6	31	0	84	3	0
Meyer, Mike, N.J.	1	1	.500	6.29	27	0	0	0	5	0	34.1	48	166	29	24	3	2	3	2	15	0	24	7	0
Meza, Nathan, N.J.	3	7	.300	5.76	12	11	0	0	0	0	54.2	67	254	38	35	2	3	3	2	22	1	37	2	1
Miller, Matt, Jam.*	0	2	.000	5.29	18	0	0	0	6	1	32.1	36	151	23	19	1	0	1	1	16	1	33	0	0
Mitchel, Yaqui, H.V.	0	0	.000	5.25	19	0	0	0	11	3	24.0	30	122	14	14	1	1	1	3	18	2	27	1	0
Montalbano, Greg, Low.*	0	1	.000	1.74	2	2	0	0	0	0	10.1	4	39	3	2	0	1	0	4	0	15	0	0
Montilla, Felix, Wil.	3	5	.375	3.69	15	15	1	1	0	0	83.0	81	375	49	34	2	2	4	12	43	0	82	5	2
Morse, Bryan, Uti.*	1	0	1.000	0.00	2	0	0	0	1	0	2.2	1	10	0	0	0	0	0	1	0	2	0	0
Mowday, Chris, Que.	5	2	.714	3.39	15	13	0	0	2	0	71.2	61	310	32	27	1	0	3	4	41	0	65	8	0
Muldoon, Tommy, One.	1	1	.500	4.26	12	0	0	0	5	0	19.0	14	89	13	9	0	3	0	2	17	0	19	1	0
Nelson, Joe, Jam.	0	0	.000	2.25	3	0	0	0	1	0	4.0	3	16	3	1	0	0	0	1	0	7	0	0
Norderum, Jason, Ver.*	5	3	.625	3.77	15	15	0	0	0	0	76.1	66	343	44	32	3	0	2	7	47	0	40	7	0
Nunez, Maximo, Low.	3	2	.600	5.67	16	0	0	0	6	1	33.1	39	150	24	21	1	4	0	1	11	0	39	4	0
Nunley, Derrek, Que.	2	0	1.000	5.12	11	1	0	0	2	0	19.1	23	88	12	11	1	0	2	0	8	0	20	0	0
O'Brien, Mike, One.*	0	0	.000	27.00	1	0	0	0	1	0	0.1	1	3	1	1	0	0	0	0	1	0	0	0	0
Orloski, Joe, Que.	4	0	1.000	1.38	22	0	0	0	8	3	52.0	32	206	13	8	2	2	1	2	16	1	66	2	0
Parker, Daniel, Aub.	4	3	.571	4.32	19	10	0	0	7	1	58.1	59	257	31	28	3	0	2	6	21	1	50	3	0
Patterson, Quenten, Pit.	3	4	.429	5.83	8	6	0	0	0	0	29.1	41	143	28	19	0	1	2	5	16	0	9	2	0
Payne, Jerrod, Que.	0	0	.000	9.00	2	0	0	0	1	0	2.0	3	8	2	2	1	0	0	0	0	0	1	1	0
Pepen, Robert, Pit.	0	1	.000	3.12	7	0	0	0	4	0	8.2	7	40	4	3	0	0	0	5	8	0	8	0	0
Perez, Elvis, Jam.	7	5	.583	4.17	15	15	0	0	0	0	77.2	79	331	40	36	5	3	3	2	29	0	56	3	1
Perez, George, Que.	5	1	.833	0.78	29	0	0	0	25	12	34.2	21	138	3	3	1	2	2	3	15	2	35	3	0
Perez, Keino, M.V.	0	0	.000	0.00	1	0	0	0	0	0	2.0	4	11	2	0	0	1	0	0	0	0	2	0	0
Perio, Ian, Low.*	5	2	.714	3.78	13	2	0	0	8	1	33.1	33	146	20	14	2	5	2	1	11	0	31	2	0
Perkins, Mike, N.J.	5	6	.455	4.27	15	15	0	0	0	0	84.1	85	376	47	40	4	1	4	7	41	0	77	3	0
Pett, Jose, M.V.	0	0	.000	0.00	1	0	0	0	0	0	1.0	0	3	0	0	0	0	0	0	0	0	2	0	0
Pitney, James, One.	4	1	.800	3.71	17	1	0	0	7	0	34.0	28	149	15	14	1	0	2	3	15	1	42	3	1
Pollaro, Dallas, N.J.	0	0	.000	0.00	1	0	0	0	1	0	1.0	0	3	0	0	0	0	0	0	0	0	1	0	0
Polo, Bienvenido, N.J.	3	0	1.000	7.24	25	0	0	0	6	1	32.1	45	174	36	26	1	2	3	6	26	0	32	7	0
Ponce Deleon, Damon, N.J.	0	0	.000	6.00	2	0	0	0	1	0	3.0	6	15	3	2	0	0	1	0	0	0	1	0	0
Postell, Matthew, Uti.	0	0	.000	2.25	2	0	0	0	0	0	4.0	2	14	1	1	1	0	1	0	1	0	3	1	0
Pugmire, Rob, M.V.	0	1	.000	4.26	5	5	0	0	0	0	12.2	16	62	10	6	0	1	0	8	0	10	1	0
Ramirez, Santiago, Aub.	3	6	.333	4.25	20	9	0	0	9	2	53.0	36	228	34	25	3	0	2	4	39	1	57	9	1
Rayborn, Kris, N.J.*	0	1	.000	5.02	11	0	0	0	4	0	14.1	19	71	12	8	0	0	2	8	0	12	2	0
Renwick, Tyler, Que.	2	2	.500	2.55	7	7	0	0	0	0	35.1	26	156	19	10	1	0	1	23	0	31	5	0
Reynolds, Josh, Pit.	1	1	.500	4.39	7	6	0	0	0	0	26.2	35	119	13	13	1	0	3	11	0	23	0	0
Riethmaier, Matthew, Bat.	4	4	.500	4.26	14	9	1	0	1	0	69.2	67	303	43	33	3	3	2	8	28	1	47	8	2
Rivera, Samuel, One.	0	0	.000	8.03	9	0	0	0	1	0	12.1	9	65	11	11	0	0	3	2	15	0	14	3	0
Roach, Jason, Pit.	1	1	.500	2.36	5	5	0	0	0	0	26.2	18	108	11	7	0	0	2	7	0	26	0	1
Roberts, Marquis, H.V.*	0	2	.000	3.79	17	0	0	0	2	1	38.0	33	162	20	16	1	0	4	14	0	39	2	0
Rodney, Thomas, One.	2	4	.333	4.60	9	9	1	0	0	0	45.0	52	204	30	23	2	2	0	26	0	37	6	1
Rodriguez, Alejandro, Bat.	2	2	.500	5.12	6	4	0	0	0	0	31.2	37	146	24	18	4	1	1	3	11	0	14	4	3
Rogers, Lionel, Pit.	1	3	.250	2.05	23	0	0	0	15	5	30.2	17	132	11	7	0	2	0	2	20	0	31	5	0
Roman, Orlando, Pit.	3	5	.375	6.15	11	8	0	0	0	0	33.2	40	159	29	23	1	2	2	2	18	0	27	4	4
Roque, Darryl, Ver.	0	0	.000	2.45	5	0	0	0	0	0	7.1	9	29	3	2	1	0	1	0	1	0	4	1	0
Rosario, Rodrigo, Aub.	5	6	.455	3.45	14	14	0	0	0	0	75.2	67	330	36	29	3	2	1	6	32	1	67	2	0
Rose, Michael, Ver.	0	0	.000	0.00	2	0	0	0	1	1	3.0	2	13	0	0	0	0	0	0	2	0	3	0	0
Russo, Dennis, Jam.	4	4	.500	4.93	11	10	0	0	0	0	49.1	56	218	38	27	4	1	6	2	19	0	17	5	0
Russo, Scott, Ver.*	2	1	.667	1.78	14	0	0	0	4	0	25.1	25	103	10	5	1	1	0	6	0	21	0	1
Saberhagen, Bret, Low.	0	0	.000	0.00	1	1	0	0	0	0	3.0	1	10	0	0	0	0	0	0	0	3	0	0
Sadler, Carl, M.V.*	0	0	.000	3.00	5	0	0	0	1	0	6.0	5	25	2	2	0	1	0	0	3	0	3	0	0
Sadowski, Chad, Bat.	1	1	.500	3.29	20	1	0	0	6	2	38.1	42	168	21	14	2	0	2	1	13	0	31	3	0
St. Amand, Reuben, Que.	2	4	.333	5.87	17	5	0	0	3	0	46.0	65	219	42	30	1	1	5	2	22	0	28	8	0
Saladin, Miguel, Aub.	2	3	.400	0.68	27	0	0	0	16	4	40.0	32	182	19	3	0	4	0	6	20	3	42	4	0
Salazar, Luis, Uti.	2	4	.333	2.43	19	1	0	0	9	2	37.0	23	165	13	10	0	5	2	1	24	0	38	4	1
Samora, Santo, N.J.	2	3	.400	3.93	32	0	0	0	27	17	36.2	37	157	17	16	2	2	0	4	9	0	20	6	0
Santos, Bernaldo, Aub.	0	0	.000	3.51	15	0	0	0	6	0	25.2	31	121	13	10	1	1	1	3	11	0	10	2	1
Sawyer, Steve, Uti.	4	1	.800	2.00	15	0	0	0	5	2	27.0	14	110	8	6	0	1	1	2	12	0	22	5	0
Schilling, Tim, Uti.*	1	1	.500	5.61	10	3	0	0	1	0	25.2	31	121	19	16	3	4	0	2	18	0	22	2	0
Schiml, Anthony, Low.*	1	1	.500	1.80	2	2	0	0	0	0	5.0	6	22	1	1	0	0	0	4	0	2	0	1
Schmitt, Eric, S.I.	2	1	.667	2.10	15	0	0	0	9	1	30.0	21	121	9	7	0	0	1	8	0	35	0	1

Pitcher, Team	W	L	Pct.	ERA	G	GS	CG	ShO	GF	Sv.	IP	H	TBF	R	ER	HR	SH	SF	HB	BB	IBB	SO	WP	Bk.
Schultz, Bryan, N.J.	0	0	.000	0.00	4	0	0	0	2	0	6.0	4	25	0	0	0	0	1	2	0	8	0	0
Searles, Jonathan, Wil.	0	5	.000	4.11	6	6	0	0	0	0	35.0	44	156	20	16	1	4	2	1	8	0	21	2	1
Severino, Jose, One.	1	2	.333	6.00	3	3	0	0	0	0	18.0	23	79	14	12	0	1	1	2	0	0	13	2	2
Shelley, Jason, Wil.	2	1	.667	3.13	7	6	0	0	0	0	31.2	25	135	14	11	3	2	2	3	17	0	34	1	1
Sierra, Jr., Auvin, One.*	0	0	.000	0.00	4	0	0	0	3	0	7.0	4	26	0	0	0	0	1	0	1	0	11	0	0
Silverio, Carlos, Bat.	0	0	.000	2.25	1	1	0	0	0	0	4.0	3	15	1	1	0	0	0	0	2	0	1	1	0
Sloan, Brandon, Uti.	4	4	.500	4.79	14	14	0	0	0	0	73.1	89	328	49	39	5	0	2	1	24	0	50	7	2
Smalley, Mike, Jam.*	0	0	.000	0.90	3	2	0	0	0	0	10.0	6	38	1	1	0	0	2	0	8	1	8	1	0
Smith, Matt, S.I.*	5	4	.556	2.38	14	14	0	0	0	0	75.2	74	308	32	20	1	3	0	2	20	0	59	4	0
Smith, Matthew, Pit.	0	2	.000	4.61	20	0	0	0	13	0	27.1	35	138	21	14	0	0	0	2	19	0	23	2	0
Smith, Michael, Que.	2	2	.500	2.29	14	12	0	0	0	0	51.0	41	205	18	13	1	1	2	2	17	0	55	9	1
Smuin, Shane, Uti.	2	5	.286	6.87	26	0	0	0	13	1	38.0	50	190	43	29	6	2	2	5	23	2	34	6	0
Solano, Alex, Low.	0	0	.000	0.00	1	0	0	0	1	1	1.0	0	3	0	0	0	0	0	0	0	0	2	0	0
Sollenberger, Matt, Pit.*	1	2	.333	3.83	20	0	0	0	5	2	40.0	33	170	18	17	3	0	1	2	14	0	39	4	1
Song, Seung, Low.	5	2	.714	2.60	13	13	0	0	0	0	72.2	63	293	26	21	1	0	2	0	20	0	93	6	1
Sosebee, Chad, Low.	1	2	.333	5.30	12	0	0	0	7	2	18.2	27	95	15	11	1	0	1	1	11	0	19	1	0
Southard, Lee, Que.	0	1	1.000	12.00	5	0	0	0	1	0	6.0	7	37	10	8	0	0	1	0	12	0	7	5	0
Stanton, Jeff, S.I.	1	2	.333	3.38	11	0	0	0	6	0	18.2	16	78	8	7	1	1	1	2	3	0	17	1	0
Stasio, Doug, Bat.	1	4	.200	3.64	18	1	0	0	7	3	29.2	36	133	12	12	1	2	2	3	15	3	17	3	3
Staveland, Toby, Jam.	2	2	.500	5.20	11	10	0	0	0	0	45.0	57	210	36	26	3	1	1	1	21	0	24	1	1
Steele, Michael, One.	2	1	.667	2.70	22	0	0	0	20	9	26.2	21	117	11	8	0	1	0	3	11	1	41	4	0
Stevens, Jeff, Uti.	0	0	.000	0.00	2	0	0	0	2	0	2.0	0	7	0	0	0	0	0	0	1	0	1	0	0
Stiehl, Robert, Aub.	1	0	1.000	0.93	5	0	0	0	1	1	9.2	4	37	1	1	0	0	0	0	4	0	19	1	1
Stokes, Shaun, N.J.	0	0	.000	0.53	4	4	0	0	0	0	17.0	10	60	1	1	0	0	0	0	1	0	23	0	0
Story, Aaron, Wil.*	2	0	1.000	5.59	10	1	0	0	6	0	19.1	17	85	15	12	2	2	0	0	10	0	16	3	1
Sullivan, Ted, M.V.	0	0	1.000	0.00	2	0	0	0	2	0	2.0	1	7	0	0	0	1	0	0	2	0	1	0	0
Sunderman, Nick, M.V.*	4	4	.500	6.94	18	4	0	0	4	0	46.2	50	220	39	36	5	2	2	2	33	1	37	6	1
Swindell, Jeremy, One.*	1	3	.250	4.02	18	0	0	0	6	1	31.1	29	136	20	14	3	1	1	1	16	0	28	1	1
Tallet, Brian, M.V.*	1	0	1.000	1.15	6	6	0	0	0	0	15.2	10	62	2	2	0	0	1	3	0	0	20	0	0
Taylor, John, Que.	0	1	.000	9.35	10	0	0	0	3	0	8.2	13	47	10	9	0	1	2	2	6	0	9	4	0
Tekavec, Nate, One.	4	4	.500	4.60	11	11	0	0	0	0	60.2	75	270	38	31	6	1	4	1	9	1	44	4	1
Thomas, Gaige, Uti.	3	0	1.000	5.35	21	0	0	0	5	1	38.2	40	186	23	23	3	1	0	1	35	0	37	11	0
Torres, Luis, Ver.	7	5	.583	3.43	15	15	0	0	0	0	86.2	82	372	45	33	6	2	3	3	34	0	56	6	1
Urbina, Ulmer, One.	2	1	.667	3.77	25	0	0	0	6	0	43.0	30	186	20	18	2	2	1	5	22	0	57	2	2
Valle, Yoiset, S.I.*	0	0	.000	15.19	3	1	0	0	1	1	5.1	13	33	10	9	1	0	0	1	2	0	4	1	0
Vandermeer, Scott, H.V.	2	6	.250	5.33	15	15	0	0	0	0	72.2	88	334	54	43	5	2	4	5	24	0	65	4	0
Van Vessen, Joshua, One.*	0	0	.000	2.92	15	0	0	0	9	2	24.2	25	114	13	8	1	1	3	0	10	1	19	1	3
Villanueva, Bill, Uti.	4	3	.250	7.15	14	3	0	0	0	0	22.2	20	116	22	18	3	3	0	2	23	1	20	6	2
Villegas, Felix, Low.	4	6	.400	5.02	16	10	0	0	3	0	71.2	79	318	49	40	0	5	4	2	28	0	42	4	1
Vriesenga, Matt, N.J.	2	3	.400	2.77	22	4	0	0	3	0	48.2	48	202	22	15	3	2	3	1	12	1	39	1	0
Waechter, Doug, H.V.	4	4	.500	2.35	14	14	2	2	0	0	72.2	53	302	23	19	2	2	1	4	37	0	58	7	3
Wang, Chien-ming, S.I.	4	4	.500	2.48	14	14	2	1	0	0	87.0	77	358	34	24	2	3	1	2	21	1	75	7	1
Washburn, Ben, Ver.	1	0	1.000	3.50	9	2	0	0	0	0	18.0	22	76	11	7	0	0	2	1	2	0	16	1	0
Wheatland, Matthew, One.	1	2	.333	5.55	5	5	0	0	0	0	24.1	30	107	18	15	1	1	1	2	4	0	25	2	2
Williams, Blake, N.J.	3	1	.750	1.59	6	6	0	0	0	0	28.1	20	112	7	5	1	0	1	3	9	0	25	1	0
Willis, Jason, S.I.	4	0	1.000	4.50	13	2	0	0	1	1	32.0	29	141	18	16	0	1	1	1	20	0	25	4	0
Wombacher, Mike, S.I.*	1	2	.667	5.03	21	0	0	0	9	1	19.2	20	87	11	11	2	0	1	2	10	0	15	3	1
Woodyard, Mark, One.	1	5	.167	4.59	11	9	0	0	1	0	51.0	48	243	32	26	0	1	0	6	39	0	38	8	0
Yee, Damon, Aub.	5	5	.500	4.40	14	14	0	0	0	0	71.2	69	307	40	35	6	3	2	8	20	0	56	3	1
Young, Simon, M.V.*	7	2	.778	1.75	14	13	0	0	0	0	77.0	62	295	20	15	1	1	4	21	0	56	3	1
Zapey, Winton, Uti.	0	0	.000	0.00	1	0	0	0	0	0	1.0	1	5	0	0	0	0	0	1	0	1	0	0

COMBINATION SHUTOUTS: **Auburn (2)**—Yee-Lima-Saladin, Yee-Johnson. **Batavia (2)**—Carter-Stasio, Bullock-Bennett-Meldahl. **Hudson Valley (1)**—Waechter-Mitchel. **Jamestown (4)**—Evert-McGinnis-Curtis-Baker, Russo-Clark, Evert-McGinnis-Cummings, Mendez-Hernandez. **Lowell (5)**—Lara-Martinez-Perio, Lara-Elmore, Saberhagen-Adams-Giese, Elmore-Kozol, Song-Perio-Bentley. **Mahoning Valley (5)**—Young-Donaghey-Jackson, Matheny-Pett-Sadler-Jackson, Field-Sunderman-Fugarino-Christ, Pugmire-Fitch-Jackson, Young-Donaghey. **New Jersey (3)**—Cali-Fiora, Stokes-Cook-Samora, Perkins-Fiora-Grippo. **Oneonta (1)**—Earl-Swindall-Law-Steele. **Pittsfield (2)**—Cox-Cerda, Reynolds-Patterson-Smith. **Queens (4)**—Markwell-Mowday, Markwell-Orloski-McFarland, Mowday-Taylor, Markwell-Orloski. **Staten Island (3)**—Wang-Faigin, Anderson-Faigin-Wombacher, Anderson-Schmitt-Correa. **Utica (3)**—Massingale-Thomas-Key, Castillo-Salazar, Massingale-Campos. **Vermont (7)**—Torres-Estel-Rose, Girdley-Estel-Bye, Chisnall-Washburn-Urbina-Ferrari, Norderum-Washburn-Garris, Chisnall-Bolson-Garris, Torres-Russo, Girdley-Bolson-Garris. **Williamsport (2)**—Shelley-Henderson-Alcala, Montilla-Story.

NO-HIT GAME: Waechter, Hudson Valley defeated Pittsfield, 2-0, August 10.

2000 FIELDING

TEAM

Team	Pct.	G	PO	A	E	TC	DP	TP	PB
Mahoning Valley	.967	76	2029	800	97	2926	65	0	21
Staten Island	.965	74	1963	848	102	2913	62	0	10
Batavia	.964	76	2001	856	106	2963	73	0	6
Utica	.963	75	1951	741	103	2795	57	0	26
Queens	.963	75	2014	761	107	2882	56	0	12
Lowell	.963	75	1994	829	109	2932	60	0	13
Pittsfield	.963	75	1943	769	105	2817	74	0	21
Jamestown	.956	75	1946	785	125	2856	73	0	17
Vermont	.956	75	2030	798	131	2959	71	0	14
Oneonta	.955	76	1949	754	126	2829	63	0	11
New Jersey	.952	76	1996	798	142	2936	70	0	17
Williamsport	.951	73	1919	752	137	2808	62	0	14
Auburn	.951	74	1936	818	143	2897	66	0	13
Hudson Valley	.950	75	1942	809	146	2897	55	0	21

INDIVIDUAL

FIRST BASEMEN

NOTE: All caps denotes fielding-percentage leader based on 38 games for catchers, 51 for all other non-pitchers and 61 innings for pitchers. *Throws lefthanded.

Player, Team	Pct.	G	PO	A	E	TC	DP
Avila, Rob, Bat.	.000	1	0	0	0	0	0
Bastardo, Angel, M.V.	.958	2	23	0	1	24	2
Bernhardt, Jossephang, Que.	.956	6	39	4	2	45	2
Brandes, Landon, N.J.	.875	2	7	0	1	8	1
BRISSON, Dustin, Low.	.991	56	518	38	5	561	40
Calabrese, Anthony, S.I.	1.000	4	12	1	0	13	2
Carrillo, Robert, Aub.	.995	23	182	7	1	190	18
Cotten, Jeremy, Wil.	1.000	2	13	1	0	14	0
Crocker, Nickolas, Jam.*	1.000	1	11	0	0	11	1
Crozier, Eric, M.V.*	.978	16	130	2	3	135	11

Player, Team	Pct.	G	PO	A	E	TC	DP
Delgado, Dario, Bat.	.989	61	569	47	7	623	49
Duarte, Justin, Bat.	1.000	6	36	5	0	41	4
Ellis, Ryan, Ver.	1.000	7	48	3	0	51	5
Espino, Jose, N.J.	1.000	4	29	3	0	32	5
Finnerty, Francis, M.V.	1.000	1	11	1	0	12	0
Flannigan, Timothy, Pit.	.833	1	5	0	1	6	0
Forbes, Michael, Jam.	1.000	3	10	0	0	10	1
Franco, Iker, H.V.	1.000	1	10	1	0	11	0
Gall, John, N.J.	.987	58	510	35	7	552	42
Gerber, Joseph, One.*	.987	40	363	27	5	395	29
Gonzalez, Adrian, Uti.*	.976	8	75	5	2	82	5
Haase, Jeff, M.V.	.987	54	485	30	7	522	41
Hattig, John, Low.	.988	18	161	7	2	170	12
Hicks, Scott, Uti.	.986	19	134	8	2	144	18
Hunter, David, Pit.*	.987	19	137	15	2	154	21
Inglett, Joe, H.V.	.000	1	0	0	0	0	0
Jones, Mitch, S.I.	1.000	3	11	1	0	12	0
Kaup, Nathan, H.V.	1.000	28	236	22	0	258	19
Kavourias, Jim, Uti.	1.000	3	27	4	0	31	3
Keene, Kurt, Que.	1.000	2	17	2	0	19	1
Kinchen, Jason, S.I.	.993	42	380	17	3	400	25
Leaumont, Jeff, S.I.*	.995	24	207	11	1	219	16
Lopez, Raul, Jam.	.986	72	578	36	9	623	63
Louwsma, Chris, Uti.	1.000	3	30	2	0	32	0
Lugo, Felix, Ver.	.974	9	69	5	2	76	4
Lutz, David, Ver.	.974	34	274	25	8	307	26
Lydic, Joe, Aub.	1.000	4	43	0	0	43	5
Magness, Pat, Uti.	.984	36	293	24	5	322	21
Malpica, Martin, Que.	.984	13	114	8	2	124	13
Marconi, Alex, H.V.	1.000	2	18	3	0	21	4
Marsh, Jason, H.V.	1.000	8	88	6	0	94	3
McGrath, Ryan, Aub.	1.000	1	4	1	0	5	1
McKee, Mickey, Aub.	.994	38	304	27	2	333	22
Miller, Eric, Ver.	.994	23	161	13	1	175	19
Moylan, Dan, N.J.	1.000	3	13	1	0	14	2
Muthig, Dean, Bat.	.975	13	110	6	3	119	15
O'Brien, Kevin, H.V.*	.982	17	152	10	3	165	10
O'Brien, Mike, One.*	.975	36	289	19	8	316	23
Ortiz, Matt, N.J.	.947	4	35	1	2	38	4
Osborne, Mark, M.V.	.981	5	50	2	1	53	3
Pagan, Jon, Wil.	.987	36	288	21	4	313	25
Peterson, Brian, N.J.	1.000	1	4	0	0	4	0
Pogue, Jamie, N.J.	.986	10	67	6	1	74	5
Postell, Matthew, Uti.	1.000	10	51	10	0	61	2
Riek, Cliff, Wil.	1.000	22	135	13	0	148	15
Rooi, Vince, Ver.	.988	11	78	6	1	85	10
Schell, Barry, Uti.*	1.000	2	11	0	0	11	0
Schuda, Justin, H.V.	.979	20	183	7	4	194	14
Sherrod, Justin, Low.	1.000	1	4	1	0	5	0
Snyder, Mike, Que.	.987	54	422	35	6	463	37
Soto, Tony, Aub.	.973	17	133	11	4	148	13
Sutter, Tony, S.I.	.984	13	115	5	2	122	10
Terveen, Bryce, Jam.	.939	4	26	5	2	33	2
Tood, Jeremy, Pit.	.986	59	457	38	7	502	39
Willingham, Josh, Uti.	.000	1	0	0	0	0	0
Young, Walter, Wil.	.955	18	133	14	7	154	16
Zapey, Winton, Uti.	.000	1	2	0	0	2	0

SECOND BASEMEN

Player, Team	Pct.	G	PO	A	E	TC	DP
Abreu, Nielsen, Bat.	.857	1	1	5	1	7	1
Basak, Chris, Pit.	1.000	1	3	3	0	6	1
Borjas, Henry, Low.	.956	30	49	81	6	136	19
Bozanich, Sam, S.I.	.956	71	97	165	12	274	42
Cabrera, Miguel, Uti.	1.000	1	2	5	0	7	2
Calabrese, Anthony, S.I.	1.000	1	1	4	0	5	1
Castillo, Carlos, Pit.	.981	11	24	29	1	54	10
Centeno, Irwin, H.V.	.965	65	91	183	10	284	31
Cleto, Ambioris, Wil.	.957	13	34	32	3	69	9
Close, James, Uti.	.833	2	2	3	1	6	0
Coyne, Anthony, Pit.	.950	21	42	53	5	100	13
Crisp, Covelli, N.J.	.952	4	7	13	1	21	5
De Renne, Keoni, Jam.	1.000	10	12	34	0	46	5
Docen, Jose, Ver.	.950	58	118	130	13	261	34
Donato, Gregorio, Jam.	.967	30	60	86	5	151	25
Easterday, Matt, Uti.	.968	55	102	141	8	251	28
Ellis, Ryan, Ver.	.944	19	39	45	5	89	12
Escobar, Gustavo, N.J.	.800	2	3	5	2	10	1
Filson, Gregory, Low.	.974	16	27	48	2	77	9
GALANTE, Matt, N.J.	.972	54	85	123	6	214	32
Garcia, Juan-Carlos, Uti.	.926	7	14	11	2	27	2
Garcia, Kevys, Aub.	.899	38	74	105	20	199	26
Gonzalez, Edgar, H.V.	1.000	1	1	1	0	2	1

Player, Team	Pct.	G	PO	A	E	TC	DP
Hattig, John, Low.	.000	1	0	0	1	1	0
Herrera, Franklyn, N.J.	1.000	1	0	1	0	1	0
Hudnall, Joshua, Wil.	.941	11	22	26	3	51	7
Inglett, Joe, H.V.	.963	44	80	102	7	189	22
Jacobs, John, H.V.	.966	14	22	35	2	59	6
Jimenez, Richard, Que.	1.000	4	6	9	0	15	2
Katz, Damon, M.V.	1.000	1	1	6	0	7	0
Keene, Kurt, Que.	1.000	5	9	13	0	22	2
Lichay, Donald, Pit.	1.000	1	0	3	0	3	0
Lotterhos, Chris, M.V.	1.000	1	3	4	0	7	1
Lowe, Steve, M.V.	.933	4	7	7	1	15	1
Luuloa, Miles, One.	.939	53	89	141	15	245	28
McGrath, Ryan, Aub.	1.000	1	1	1	0	2	0
McIntyre, Robert, Pit.	.917	4	5	6	1	12	1
McKee, Mickey, Aub.	.976	11	22	19	1	42	5
Moccia, Mark, One.	.968	19	32	58	3	93	7
Navarrete, Raymond, Wil.	1.000	2	2	6	0	8	0
Nieves, John, Low.	.963	18	32	45	3	80	9
Orr, Peterson, Jam.	.949	38	61	108	9	178	29
Paulino, Dave, Uti.	.889	1	4	4	1	9	1
Pelfrey, Brice, Wil.	.958	49	80	104	8	192	22
Pfister, Billy, One.	.750	5	6	6	4	16	0
Pietro, Jim, M.V.	.964	28	48	58	4	110	13
Pollaro, Dallas, N.J.	.948	16	13	42	3	58	6
Rich, Dominic, Que.	.955	67	116	141	12	269	27
Rodriguez, Ronny, Low.	.939	13	25	37	4	66	6
Rojas, Alex, Bat.	.926	22	44	44	7	95	7
Ryan, Jeff, M.V.	1.000	2	3	6	0	9	2
Soto, Tony, Aub.	.905	32	64	79	15	158	16
Sutter, Tony, S.I.	.968	15	8	22	1	31	1
Underdown, Preston, Bat.	.980	17	33	64	2	99	19
Utley, Chase, Bat.	.983	34	75	101	3	179	21
Vasquez, Geraldo, N.J.	1.000	6	4	13	0	17	2
Willingham, Josh, Uti.	1.000	11	24	20	0	44	8
Wright, Daron, Bat.	.923	5	10	14	2	26	6
Zaragoza, Joel, Pit.	.967	42	66	79	5	150	21

THIRD BASEMEN

Player, Team	Pct.	G	PO	A	E	TC	DP
Avila, Rob, Bat.	.844	8	6	21	5	32	3
BECKER, Jeff, M.V.	.936	71	62	159	15	236	15
Bernhardt, Jossephang, Que.	.923	4	4	8	1	13	2
Blanco, Tony, Low.	.818	9	8	10	4	22	2
Brandes, Landon, N.J.	.812	42	22	99	28	149	6
Cabrera, Miguel, Uti.	1.000	1	1	0	0	1	0
Calabrese, Anthony, S.I.	1.000	1	1	1	0	2	0
Chapman, Travis, Bat.	.938	46	32	103	9	144	8
Corporan, Elvis, S.I.	.936	73	42	162	14	218	7
Cosby, Rob, Que.	.920	31	21	59	7	87	3
DeGroote, Casey, S.I.	.900	11	2	7	1	10	0
De Renne, Keoni, Jam.	1.000	4	2	15	0	17	2
Donato, Gregorio, Jam.	.750	2	1	2	1	4	0
Ellis, Ryan, Ver.	1.000	2	0	2	0	2	0
Escobar, Gustavo, N.J.	1.000	1	1	1	0	2	0
Fagan, Shawn, Que.	.871	23	18	36	8	62	5
Filson, Gregory, Low.	.838	27	14	43	11	68	3
Flannigan, Timothy, Pit.	.858	52	35	86	20	141	5
Forbes, Michael, Jam.	.899	46	36	88	14	138	11
Gall, John, N.J.	.912	12	8	23	3	34	3
Garcia, Juan-Carlos, Uti.	.933	4	3	11	1	15	2
Garcia, Kevys, Aub.	.933	7	3	11	1	15	2
Gonzalez, Edgar, H.V.	.840	34	24	60	16	100	3
Haase, Jeff, M.V.	.923	3	0	12	1	13	0
Hattig, John, Low.	.849	36	25	65	16	106	6
Hudnall, Joshua, Wil.	.800	10	11	13	6	30	2
Jacobs, John, H.V.	.667	4	3	3	3	9	0
Katz, Damon, M.V.	1.000	2	2	2	0	4	0
Kaup, Nathan, H.V.	.833	3	1	4	1	6	0
Lichay, Donald, Pit.	.913	26	11	52	6	69	3
Louwsma, Chris, Uti.	.899	68	52	135	21	208	12
Lugo, Felix, Ver.	.840	24	9	54	12	75	3
Lydic, Joe, Aub.	.917	60	46	120	15	181	8
Malpica, Martin, Que.	.950	20	14	43	3	60	2
McGrath, Ryan, Aub.	.000	1	0	0	1	1	0
Miller, Eric, Ver.	.923	9	9	15	2	26	2
Moccia, Mark, One.	.833	20	18	27	9	54	5
Muthig, Dean, Bat.	1.000	7	2	14	0	16	1
Navarrete, Raymond, Wil.	.909	59	55	94	15	164	11
Orr, Peterson, Jam.	.886	25	18	52	9	79	6
Pfister, Billy, One.	.929	9	5	8	1	14	1
Pichardo, Henry, N.J.	.667	1	1	1	1	3	0
Pollaro, Dallas, N.J.	1.000	1	0	2	0	2	0
Quattlebaum, Hugh, One.	.942	49	34	96	8	138	6

Player, Team	Pct.	G	PO	A	E	TC	DP
Richardson, Juan, Bat.	.935	10	6	23	2	31	1
Riek, Cliff, Wil.	.826	5	6	13	4	23	0
Rojas, Alex, Bat.	.880	10	5	17	3	25	2
Rooi, Vince, Ver.	.846	45	35	86	22	143	5
Salas, Juan, H.V.	.903	38	30	72	11	113	4
Sherrod, Justin, Low.	.833	6	4	11	3	18	0
Soto, Tony, Aub.	.920	10	3	20	2	25	0
Vasquez, Geraldo, N.J.	.882	24	15	30	6	51	3
Willingham, Josh, Uti.	.857	2	2	4	1	7	0

SHORTSTOPS

Player, Team	Pct.	G	PO	A	E	TC	DP
Abreu, Nielsen, Bat.	.857	4	3	3	1	7	1
BASAK, Chris, Pit.	.965	58	93	155	9	257	37
Bernhardt, Jossephang, Que.	.857	1	3	3	1	7	0
Betemit, Wilson, Jam.	.910	68	111	183	29	323	40
Borjas, Henry, Low.	.786	4	11	11	6	28	1
Brosseau, Richard, Que.	.931	14	27	40	5	72	4
Cabrera, Miguel, Uti.	.879	5	7	22	4	33	1
Calabrese, Anthony, S.I.	.938	22	20	41	4	65	7
Campos, Julio, Bat.	.933	3	5	9	1	15	5
Castillo, Carlos, Pit.	1.000	5	6	11	0	17	1
Chaves, Brandon, Wil.	.958	54	79	169	11	259	32
Cleto, Ambioris, Wil.	.933	11	18	24	3	45	2
De Renne, Keoni, Jam.	1.000	3	2	11	0	13	3
Easterday, Matt, Uti.	.857	2	3	3	1	7	0
Escobar, Gustavo, N.J.	.963	7	9	17	1	27	4
Firlit, Dan, N.J.	.940	52	94	141	15	250	32
Garcia, Juan-Carlos, Uti.	1.000	5	7	12	0	19	3
Garcia, Kevys, Aub.	.950	7	5	14	1	20	5
Gonzalez, Edgar, H.V.	.929	4	6	7	1	14	1
Hooper, Clay, S.I.	.944	64	112	172	17	301	38
Hudnall, Joshua, Wil.	.903	13	26	30	6	62	7
Jacobs, John, H.V.	.818	5	8	10	4	22	3
Jimenez, Richard, Que.	.885	5	12	11	3	26	2
Katz, Damon, M.V.	.988	18	24	57	1	82	13
Keene, Kurt, Que.	.600	3	1	5	4	10	0
Lotterhos, Chris, M.V.	1.000	4	7	9	0	16	2
Lowe, Steve, M.V.	.933	37	52	129	13	194	17
Luna, Hector, M.V.	.875	5	5	9	2	16	1
McDonald, John, M.V.	1.000	4	2	16	0	18	4
McIntyre, Robert, Pit.	1.000	1	6	0	0	6	1
Merrill, Jr., Ronald, One.	.936	33	45	86	9	140	21
Miller, Eric, Ver.	.909	14	24	36	6	66	5
Moccia, Mark, One.	.907	11	20	29	5	54	6
Nieves, Raul, Low.	.973	38	69	111	5	185	20
Orr, Peterson, Jam.	1.000	5	2	15	0	17	5
Peguero, Miguel, One.	.914	22	30	66	9	105	14
Pfister, Billy, One.	.846	11	19	25	8	52	5
Rojas, Alex, Bat.	.929	9	10	29	3	42	7
Sanchez, Frederick, Low.	.974	34	56	93	4	153	20
Soto, Tony, Aub.	.864	6	10	9	3	22	2
Sutter, Tony, S.I.	1.000	4	2	4	0	6	1
Tablado, Raul, Que.	.919	52	70	147	19	236	28
Valdez, Wilson, Ver.	.944	64	136	198	20	354	51
Vasquez, Geraldo, N.J.	.905	23	37	58	10	105	11
Volquez, Bolivar, H.V.	.914	68	107	202	29	338	36
Whiteman, Thomas, Aub.	.915	69	93	199	27	319	38
Willingham, Josh, Uti.	.923	2	7	5	1	13	2
Wilson, Josh, Uti.	.929	62	79	157	18	254	28
Woodcock, Lance, M.V.	.895	10	12	22	4	38	7
Youngbauer, Scott, Bat.	.920	66	80	186	23	289	33
Zaragoza, Joel, Pit.	.966	14	22	35	2	59	13

OUTFIELDERS

Player, Team	Pct.	G	PO	A	E	TC	DP
Acevedo, Carlos, Bat.	.944	60	99	2	6	107	0
Acuna, Ron, Pit.	.976	68	106	14	3	123	5
Barnette, Jason, Bat.*	.963	49	74	3	3	80	0
Bay, Jason, Ver.	1.000	14	20	3	0	23	1
Bonner, Adam, H.V.*	.956	56	84	2	4	90	0
Buttler, Victor, Wil.*	.967	36	57	1	2	60	0
Calabrese, Anthony, S.I.	1.000	2	1	0	0	1	0
Candelario, Luis, H.V.	.891	64	116	7	15	138	1
Caraway, Brandon, Bat.	.969	52	121	2	4	127	2
Caudill, Clarke, Low.	1.000	25	37	1	0	38	0
Chourio, Jorjanis, Wil.	1.000	10	13	1	0	14	0
Church, Ryan, M.V.*	.973	67	102	8	3	113	3
Clark, Chivas, Que.*	1.000	11	19	1	0	20	0
Clark, Jeremy, Low.	.000	1	0	0	0	0	0
Close, James, Uti.	.975	44	72	5	2	79	1
Cortes, Jorge, Wil.*	.931	47	85	9	7	101	1

Player, Team	Pct.	G	PO	A	E	TC	DP
Crisp, Covelli, N.J.	.980	30	47	3	1	51	0
Crozier, Eric, M.V.*	1.000	25	51	1	0	52	0
De Aza, Modesto, Aub.	1.000	16	25	3	0	28	0
De Renne, Keoni, Jam.	.000	1	0	0	0	0	0
Donato, Gregorio, Jam.	.000	1	0	0	0	0	0
Douglas, Harley, Pit.*	.895	18	16	1	2	19	0
DOWNING, Phillip, Ver.*	.992	56	117	4	1	122	0
Duncan, Jeffrey, Pit.*	.990	51	96	6	1	103	1
Encarnacion, Arismendy, Uti.	.967	58	115	4	4	123	1
Espino, Jose, N.J.	.956	52	93	16	5	114	5
Fera, Aaron, Que.	1.000	9	13	2	0	15	0
Fernandez, Medardo, Uti.	.971	38	67	1	2	70	0
Filson, Gregory, Low.	1.000	2	6	0	0	6	0
Floyd, Mike, N.J.	.933	42	50	6	4	60	2
Fowler, David, S.I.	.940	49	62	1	4	67	0
Frazier, Charles, Uti.	1.000	7	10	0	0	10	0
Gerber, Joseph, One.*	1.000	6	13	0	0	13	0
Gingrich, Troy, Ver.*	.967	15	28	1	1	30	0
Gonzalez, Edgar, H.V.	1.000	3	1	1	0	2	0
Goodeill, Harold, H.V.	.909	11	10	0	1	11	0
Guerrero, Julio, Low.	.958	40	64	5	3	72	2
Hambrick, Marcus, Jam.*	.979	54	93	2	2	97	1
Harper, Shaun, Jam.	.954	72	117	7	6	130	0
Harris, Corey, Pit.	.980	56	94	2	2	98	0
Haynes, Dee, N.J.	.941	63	109	3	7	119	1
Hensley, Anthony, Bat.	.936	59	82	6	6	94	1
Hicks, Scott, Uti.	.967	38	57	2	2	61	2
Hill, John, H.V.	.983	56	112	4	2	118	1
Holland, Tapley, One.	.979	42	88	6	2	96	0
Hudnall, Joshua, Wil.	1.000	2	1	1	0	2	0
Hunter, David, Pit.*	.000	1	0	0	0	0	0
Inglett, Joe, M.V.	.929	6	13	0	1	14	0
Jacobs, John, H.V.	.929	20	13	0	1	14	0
Janowicz, Nathan, M.V.*	.968	68	142	7	5	154	0
Johnson, Forrest, One.	.750	5	3	0	1	4	0
Johnson, Patrick, Low.*	.850	17	15	2	3	20	0
Jones, Mitch, S.I.	.980	74	92	5	2	99	1
Katz, Damon, M.V.	1.000	2	3	0	0	3	0
Kaup, Nathan, H.V.	1.000	2	1	0	0	1	0
Kavourias, Jim, Uti.	1.000	10	6	1	0	7	0
Kerner, Craig, Ver.	.951	23	36	3	2	41	0
Langlois, Jean-Sebastien, Jam.	1.000	14	23	1	0	24	0
Lee, Eric, Aub.	.976	55	80	3	2	85	0
Leer, David, One.	.960	28	47	1	2	50	0
Lichay, Donald, Pit.	1.000	3	3	1	0	4	0
Lockhart, Paul, Aub.	.978	60	81	8	2	91	2
Lopez, Aristides, Aub.	.939	38	61	1	4	66	1
Malave, Dennis, M.V.*	.981	41	99	2	2	103	0
Marsh, Jason, H.V.	.000	1	0	0	0	0	0
McGrath, Jason, S.I.	.750	5	3	0	1	4	0
McKee, Mickey, Aub.	.833	3	5	0	1	6	0
Melo, Hanlet, Jam.	1.000	8	13	0	0	13	0
Meseberg, Michael, H.V.	.971	28	32	1	1	34	0
Miller, Eric, Ver.	1.000	1	1	0	0	1	0
Money, Freddie, Low.	.977	53	122	4	3	129	3
Mooney, Daniel, Low.	1.000	1	1	0	0	1	0
Morris, Ken, N.J.	.991	54	112	2	1	115	1
Neill, John, One.	.961	61	121	3	5	129	0
Nettles, Tim, S.I.	.967	26	26	3	1	30	0
Nicolas, Jose, Wil.	.905	42	63	4	7	74	0
O'Brien, Mike, One.*	1.000	2	3	0	0	3	0
O'Neill, Daniel, Bat.*	1.000	16	22	1	0	23	1
Ortiz, Matt, N.J.	1.000	1	1	0	0	1	0
Pearson, Shawn, Que.	.978	20	41	3	1	45	0
Pena, Wily, S.I.	1.000	20	37	0	0	37	0
Perich, Josh, Pit.	.870	20	19	1	3	23	1
Pugh, Dwayne, Que.	.923	6	12	0	1	13	0
Ravelo, Manuel, Wil.	.901	51	107	2	12	121	0
Rikert, Wade, Que.*	1.000	18	28	2	0	30	0
Rincon, Carlos, Aub.	.833	9	9	1	2	12	0
Rios, Alexis, Que.	.957	41	65	2	3	70	0
Rodriguez, Wilson, M.V.	1.000	3	3	1	0	4	1
Rombley, Danny, Ver.	.957	49	102	8	5	115	0
Santana, Pedro, S.I.	1.000	17	26	1	0	27	0
Schell, Barry, Uti.*	.961	26	48	1	2	51	0
Seiber, Antron, Low.	.909	6	8	2	1	11	0
Self, Todd, Aub.	.930	50	79	1	6	86	0
Sellier, Brian, Que.	.990	63	99	2	1	102	2
Sherrill, J.J., M.V.	1.000	3	3	0	0	3	0
Sherrod, Justin, Low.	.919	40	53	4	5	62	0
Skeens, Jeremy, Ver.	1.000	6	9	0	0	9	0
Smith, Will, Low.	1.000	44	77	2	0	79	0
Soto, Tony, Aub.	1.000	3	4	1	0	5	0

Player, Team	Pct.	G	PO	A	E	TC	DP
Stevens, Jeff, Uti.	1.000	1	1	0	0	1	0
Sutter, Tony, S.I.	.000	1	0	0	0	0	0
Thomas, Charles, Jam.	.974	67	143	5	4	152	2
Thompson, Eric, M.V.*	1.000	1	3	0	0	3	0
Thompson, Richard, Que.	.942	67	124	7	8	139	1
Timaure, Jesus, Uti.	1.000	4	4	0	0	4	0
Tolli, Barry, One.	.974	64	109	4	3	116	2
Veleber, Troy, Wil.	.951	38	73	5	4	82	1
Villar, Jose, Jam.	.955	22	41	1	2	44	0
Walker, Matt, One.	.952	28	39	1	2	42	1
Watson, Brandon, Ver.	.948	68	121	7	7	135	1
Willingham, Josh, Uti.	1.000	24	46	2	0	48	0
Winrow, Gary, S.I.*	.934	62	97	2	7	106	0
Womack, Robert, M.V.*	1.000	21	33	3	0	36	0
Yancy, Michael, Pit.	.900	18	27	0	3	30	0

CATCHERS

Player, Team	Pct.	G	PO	A	E	TC	DP	PB
Alvarado, Oscar, Aub.	.941	6	40	8	3	51	1	2
Avila, Rob, Bat.	.986	30	180	26	3	209	1	4
Bastardo, Angel, M.V.	.977	47	303	33	8	344	1	10
Blum, Gregory, Ver.	.988	39	291	27	4	322	1	8
Candelaria, Tito, S.I.	1.000	4	5	1	0	6	0	0
Castaneda, Jose, Pit.	.981	15	136	15	3	154	3	5
Ciarrachi, Kevin, Wil.	.964	18	122	12	5	139	2	3
Clark, Jeremy, Low.	1.000	6	45	3	0	48	1	1
Cleveland, Russell, One.	.962	34	209	16	9	234	1	3
Doumit, Ryan, Wil.	.985	46	346	36	6	388	3	10
Duarte, Justin, Bat.	.986	11	62	9	1	72	0	0
Esposito, Brian, Low.	.975	36	271	35	8	314	0	8
Fernandez, Alejandro, S.I.	1.000	4	17	5	0	22	0	1
Flanagan, Kevin, S.I.	1.000	5	9	0	0	9	0	0
Franco, Iker, H.V.	.956	10	80	7	4	91	1	0
Friar, Roddy, N.J.	.976	22	140	24	4	168	2	7
Gates, Jeff, S.I.	.975	25	134	23	4	161	1	3
Gentry, Garett, Aub.	.982	34	234	32	5	271	1	6
Gotauco, David, Jam.	.963	16	94	9	4	107	1	2
Green, Kevin, Jam.	.951	15	110	6	6	122	1	6
Haase, Jeff, M.V.	.951	11	66	12	4	82	2	8
Hernandez, Jose, Wil.	1.000	5	41	5	0	46	1	1
Herrera, Franklyn, N.J.	.800	5	4	0	1	5	0	1
Johnson, Forrest, One.	.936	13	89	14	7	110	1	2
Langill, Eric, Ver.	.984	11	57	3	1	61	0	0
Lopez, Guillermo, Low.	.979	4	43	3	1	47	0	0
Lucas, William, Aub.	.991	18	103	10	1	114	0	1
Marconi, Alex, H.V.	.985	22	178	24	3	205	1	12
Marsh, Jason, H.V.	.969	41	278	32	10	320	0	7
Martinez, Casey, Que.	1.000	7	60	7	0	67	0	1
McGrath, Ryan, Aub.	.977	26	190	18	5	213	1	4
McKee, Mickey, Aub.	.500	1	2	0	2	4	0	0
McMillan, Andrew, Ver.	.955	19	128	20	7	155	2	3
Mooney, Daniel, Low.	.985	32	226	33	4	263	2	4
Moylan, Dan, N.J.	.978	48	357	44	9	410	2	5
Ochoa, Javier, Pit.	.963	5	45	7	2	54	0	1
Ortiz, Matt, N.J.	1.000	3	15	0	0	15	0	3
Osborn, Jason, Pit.	.966	7	48	9	2	59	0	0
Parker, Chris, One.	.989	34	236	23	3	262	2	6
Parrish, Dave, S.I.	.979	54	399	70	10	479	5	4
Peterson, Brian, M.V.	.994	21	141	26	1	168	1	3
Pogue, Jamie, N.J.	.962	10	69	6	3	78	0	0
Pohle, Ike, S.I.	1.000	8	15	0	0	15	0	2
Pollaro, Dallas, N.J.	.750	1	3	0	1	4	0	1
Postell, Matthew, Uti.	.987	34	199	21	3	223	0	15
Quiroz, Guillermo, Que.	.987	55	487	61	7	555	3	7
Rickon, Jim, M.V.	1.000	3	19	4	0	23	1	0
Riera, Zack, Wil.	1.000	8	58	4	0	62	0	0
Santos, Juan, Que.	1.000	9	86	8	0	94	0	3
Schuda, Justin, H.V.	1.000	1	1	0	0	1	0	0
Scott, Charles, M.V.	.923	1	12	0	1	13	1	0
Serrano, Raymond, Jam.	.983	19	154	22	3	179	2	1
Small, Chris, Que.	.976	4	34	6	1	41	0	1
Smith, Ryan, Pit.	.955	14	102	3	5	110	2	3
Stevens, Jeff, Uti.	.990	23	177	19	2	198	2	7
Sullivan, Kevin, Bat.	1.000	8	46	6	0	52	0	1
Terveen, Bryce, Jam.	.974	29	199	25	6	230	1	8
Tosca, Daniel, Bat.	.992	35	234	22	2	258	2	1
Umbria, Jose, Que.	1.000	1	9	1	0	10	0	0
Valdez, Darlin, Ver.	1.000	10	77	13	0	90	1	3
Wakakuwa, Kenn, H.V.	1.000	2	22	1	0	23	0	2
WILSON, John, Pit.	.988	39	302	31	4	337	5	12
Zapey, Winton, Uti.	.975	25	173	23	5	201	2	4

PITCHERS

Player, Team	Pct.	G	PO	A	E	TC	DP
Adams, Brian, Low.*	1.000	12	0	9	0	9	0
Adams, Daniel, Bat.	.857	23	0	6	1	7	0
Albertus, Roberto, Jam.*	1.000	4	0	2	0	2	0
Alcala, Jason, Wil.	.947	17	8	10	1	19	1
Alston, Travis, Bat.	.900	20	3	6	1	10	0
Anderson, Jason, S.I.*	.880	15	4	18	3	25	1
Ascencio, Miguel, Jam.	1.000	7	3	1	0	4	0
Axelson, Josh, N.J.	.929	15	6	7	1	14	0
Baker, Ryan, Jam.	.750	21	0	3	1	4	0
Baum, David, Wil.*	1.000	14	3	5	0	8	1
Bautista, Denny, Uti.	1.000	1	1	0	0	1	0
Bazan, Juan, Wil.	1.000	3	1	0	0	1	0
Beal, Andy, S.I.*	1.000	14	8	11	0	19	0
Bean, Colter, S.I.	.000	3	0	0	0	0	0
Benedetti, John, H.V.	.875	26	1	6	1	8	0
Bennett, Jamie, Bat.*	.750	25	3	3	2	8	0
Bennett, Steven, Pit.	.909	13	2	8	1	11	0
Bentley, Brian, Low.	.667	21	0	2	1	3	0
Bolson, Michael, Ver.	.714	21	2	3	2	7	0
Borrell, Danny, S.I.*	1.000	10	1	16	0	17	0
Bottenfield, Jason, Low.	.000	1	0	0	0	0	0
Brito, Eude, Bat.*	1.000	4	4	2	0	6	0
Brookman, Ryan, Bat.	1.000	9	2	2	0	4	0
Bullock, Trevor, Bat.*	.969	15	12	19	1	32	0
Bumatay, Mike, Wil.*	1.000	7	0	1	0	1	0
Button, Sammy, M.V.*	.800	11	0	4	1	5	0
Bye, Christopher, Ver.	1.000	22	3	2	0	5	0
Cabell, Shannon, Wil.*	.857	16	3	3	1	7	0
Cali, Carmen, N.J.*	.714	14	2	8	4	14	0
Calvo, Jose, Aub.	1.000	5	0	5	0	5	0
Campbell, Jarrett, H.V.	1.000	21	3	4	0	7	0
Campos, David, Uti.*	1.000	15	1	5	0	6	1
Campos, Juan, Aub.	.889	29	2	14	2	18	0
Canale, Tom, M.V.	.750	11	1	2	1	4	0
Carbajal, Alex, H.V.*	1.000	21	2	6	0	8	1
Cardwell, Brian, Que.	.875	12	2	5	1	8	1
Carter, Ryan, Bat.*	1.000	13	3	6	0	9	0
Castillo, Ramon, Uti.	.846	13	6	5	2	13	1
Cerda, Jaime, Pit.*	.909	20	1	9	1	11	0
Chisnall, Wesley, Ver.	.938	13	6	9	1	16	1
Christ, John, M.V.	1.000	18	0	3	0	3	0
Clark, Chris, Jam.	.889	15	0	8	1	9	1
Clark, Jeremy, Low.	.000	1	0	0	0	0	0
Classen, Ender, Wil.	.778	12	1	13	4	18	2
Clifton, Derek, Jam.	.667	14	2	6	4	12	1
Cole, Joseph, Pit.	.857	10	4	14	3	21	1
Collazo, Rafael, One.*	.000	3	0	0	0	0	0
Colvard, Ron, M.V.	.000	3	0	0	0	0	0
Cook, Jeremy, N.J.	.846	32	1	10	2	13	1
Correa, Dominic, S.I.	1.000	15	1	5	0	6	0
Coughenour, Jory, Aub.	.947	15	5	13	1	19	1
Coward, Timothy, H.V.	1.000	6	5	5	0	10	0
Cox, Michael, Pit.*	.857	14	2	4	1	7	0
Crawford, Chris, H.V.	.000	2	0	0	0	0	0
Crist, Ryan, One.	.000	3	0	0	0	0	0
Cromer, Nathan, H.V.*	.647	13	1	10	6	17	0
Cummings, Frank, Jam.	.750	22	0	3	1	4	0
Curtin, Brian, M.V.	1.000	4	1	0	0	1	0
Curtiss, Tom, Jam.*	.750	24	1	2	1	4	0
Dagley, Corey, Bat.	.929	15	4	22	2	28	1
Dequin, Benjamin, Ver.*	.857	16	1	11	2	14	1
DeLaCruz, Juan, Wil.	.857	13	1	5	1	7	0
Detwiler, James, Que.*	1.000	20	1	7	0	8	0
Donaghey, Steve, M.V.	.889	21	4	4	1	9	0
Donovan, Kevin, Bat.*	1.000	7	1	0	0	1	0
Dorman, Rich, H.V.	.850	14	5	12	3	20	1
Dougherty, Kevin, Pit.*	.000	2	0	0	0	0	0
Earl, Ryan, One.	.800	12	0	4	1	5	0
Eckenstahler, Eric, One.*	1.000	8	0	1	0	1	0
Elliott, Chad, Pit.	1.000	11	2	10	0	12	0
Ellis, Ryan, Ver.	.000	1	0	0	0	0	0
ELMORE, Christopher, Low.*	1.000	15	5	25	0	30	2
Encarnacion, Orlando, Pit.	1.000	8	2	6	0	8	1
Esquivia, Manuel, Uti.	.000	2	0	0	1	1	0
Estel, Justin, Ver.	1.000	3	1	0	0	1	0
Evans, Kyle, M.V.	.917	12	4	7	1	12	1
Everett, Matt, M.V.	1.000	1	0	0	0	0	0
Evert, Brett, Jam.	1.000	15	3	9	0	12	0
Ewin, Ryan, Jam.	1.000	2	1	1	0	2	0
Faigin, Jason, S.I.	.750	22	4	5	3	12	0
Ferrari, Anthony, Ver.*	1.000	25	2	10	0	12	0
Field, Luke, M.V.	.800	22	1	7	2	10	0

Player, Team	Pct.	G	PO	A	E	TC	DP
Fiora, Chris, N.J.	.750	27	1	2	1	4	0
Fitch, Steve, M.V.	1.000	12	1	6	0	7	3
Flannery, Michael, Uti.	1.000	13	6	7	0	13	0
Fontana, Tony, Low.	1.000	14	3	15	0	18	1
Fortin, Michael, Wil.	.900	16	0	9	1	10	2
Franco, Jose, S.I.	.500	5	0	1	1	2	0
Frias, Juan, H.V.	.571	23	3	1	3	7	0
Fugarino, Steve, M.V.	1.000	14	1	1	0	2	0
Garris, Antonio, Ver.	1.000	24	2	2	0	4	0
Gerk, Jordan, One.*	.667	11	2	2	2	6	1
Giese, Daniel, Low.	1.000	15	1	3	0	4	0
Girdley, Josh, Ver.*	.955	14	7	14	1	22	0
Gomez, Ricardo, S.I.	1.000	20	4	6	0	10	2
Grippo, Mike, N.J.*	1.000	22	2	3	0	5	0
Hamilton, Ryan, Aub.	1.000	5	3	2	0	5	0
Hannah, Shawn, One.	1.000	16	4	7	0	11	0
Hawk, David, Wil.*	.867	12	2	11	2	15	0
Hazelton, Justin, M.V.	.667	4	1	1	1	3	0
Hee, Aaron, Pit.*	.857	18	1	5	1	7	1
Henderson, Kenneth, Wil.*	.875	15	7	7	2	16	0
Hernandez, Buddy, Jam.	1.000	12	0	2	0	2	0
Hernandez, John-eric, One.	1.000	2	0	1	0	1	0
Hicks, Ralph, Aub.*	.833	26	0	5	1	6	1
Higgins, Joshua, Wil.	1.000	23	3	8	0	11	0
Hodges, Trey, Jam.	1.000	13	1	4	0	5	0
Hopper, Joshua, Pit.*	.909	15	3	7	1	11	0
Houston, Ryan, Que.	1.000	12	0	4	0	4	0
Huesgen, Daniel, Que.	1.000	16	3	9	0	12	0
Jackson, Brian, M.V.	1.000	30	2	2	0	4	0
Jacobsen, Landon, Wil.	.913	9	9	12	2	23	1
Johnson, Derrick, Aub.*	.875	21	0	7	1	8	0
Johnson, Jeremy, One.	1.000	2	3	0	0	3	2
Johnston, Rikki, One.*	.964	15	5	22	1	28	2
Jones, Rob, Uti.*	1.000	14	0	3	0	3	0
Journell, Jimmy, N.J.	.833	13	2	8	2	12	0
Kelley, Chris, M.V.	.750	11	2	1	1	4	0
Kelly, Dan, Jam.*	1.000	2	1	1	0	2	0
Key, Chris, Uti.*	1.000	19	3	7	0	10	0
Kleine, Victor, M.V.*	.000	3	0	0	0	0	0
Kozlowski, Kristopher, Que.*	.750	21	2	4	2	8	0
Kozol, Anthony, Low.	.917	16	3	8	1	12	1
Krysa, Jonathan, Aub.	.933	21	2	12	1	15	0
Lara, Mauricio, Low.*	1.000	15	3	20	0	23	2
Lavigne, Tim, Pit.	1.000	15	3	4	0	7	1
Law, Keith, One.	1.000	11	1	2	0	3	0
Lawson, Jarrod, Bat.	1.000	4	1	2	0	3	0
Lelless, Alexander, Jam.	.600	19	1	2	2	5	1
Leuenberger, Jeffrey, One.	1.000	2	0	1	0	1	0
Levesque, Benjamin, Wil.	.667	17	4	4	4	12	1
Lewis, Jeremy, One.*	1.000	2	0	3	0	3	0
Lima, Lescano, Aub.	1.000	5	1	4	0	5	0
Litman, Johri, M.V.	.000	3	0	0	0	0	0
Lockwood, Luke, Ver.*	1.000	2	2	7	0	9	0
Lopez, Rafael, Pit.	.600	4	1	2	2	5	0
Lyon, Brandon, Que.	.941	15	8	8	1	17	1
Malaska, Mark, H.V.*	1.000	10	2	8	0	10	1
Malpica, Martin, Que.	.000	1	0	0	0	0	0
Marini, Anthony, M.V.*	1.000	1	1	0	0	1	0
Markwell, Diegomar, Que.*	.900	14	3	6	1	10	1
Martinez, David, S.I.*	.909	6	2	8	1	11	0
Martinez, Mark, Low.*	.700	17	0	7	3	10	0
Martinez, Oscar, S.I.	.750	26	0	3	1	4	0
Martunas, Matthew, H.V.*	1.000	3	1	2	0	3	0
Massingale, Matt, Uti.	.800	6	4	4	2	10	0
Matheny, Brandon, M.V.*	1.000	15	0	10	0	10	2
Mattioni, Nick, Pit.	.778	16	2	5	2	9	0
McCasland, Ralph, Ver.*	1.000	11	2	5	0	7	0
McClung, Michael, H.V.	.667	8	1	3	2	6	0
McCormick, Terry, H.V.*	.833	12	2	8	2	12	0
McFarland, Stuart, Que.*	.750	19	1	2	1	4	0
McGinnis, Johnny, Jam.	1.000	11	1	0	0	1	0
McKay, John, Uti.	1.000	17	1	5	0	6	0
McKey, Dustin, H.V.	1.000	11	0	7	0	7	0
McNutt, Michael, Uti.	.923	15	4	8	1	13	0
Medlock, Chet, N.J.	.857	7	4	2	1	7	0
Meldahl, Todd, Bat.*	.900	18	3	6	1	10	0
Mendez, David, Jam.*	.875	15	4	10	2	16	0
Meyer, Mike, N.J.	1.000	27	1	1	0	2	0
Meza, Nathan, N.J.	.857	12	0	6	1	7	0
Miller, Matt, Jam.*	1.000	18	1	5	0	6	0
Mitchel, Yaqui, H.V.	1.000	19	1	1	0	2	0
Montalbano, Greg, Low.*	1.000	2	1	1	0	2	0
Montilla, Felix, Wil.	.789	15	4	11	4	19	1
Morse, Bryan, Uti.*	.000	2	0	0	0	0	0
Mowday, Chris, Que.	1.000	15	5	8	0	13	1
Muldoon, Tommy, One.	1.000	12	3	1	0	4	0
Nelson, Joe, Jam.	.500	3	1	1	2	4	0
Norderum, Jason, Ver.*	.875	15	3	11	2	16	1
Nunez, Maximo, Low.	1.000	16	1	6	0	7	0
Nunley, Derrek, Que.	1.000	11	1	2	0	3	0
O'Brien, Mike, One.*	.000	1	0	0	0	0	0
Orloski, Joe, Que.	.889	22	2	14	2	18	1
Parker, Daniel, Aub.	.917	19	4	7	1	12	0
Patterson, Quenten, Pit.	.889	8	4	4	1	9	1
Payne, Jerrod, Que.	1.000	2	1	0	0	1	0
Pepen, Robert, Pit.	1.000	7	1	0	0	1	0
Perez, Elvis, Jam.	1.000	15	7	5	0	12	0
Perez, George, Que.	1.000	29	2	6	0	8	1
Perez, Keino, M.V.	.000	1	0	0	0	0	0
Perio, Ian, Low.*	1.000	13	2	6	0	8	0
Perkins, Mike, N.J.	.786	15	3	8	3	14	1
Pett, Jose, M.V.	1.000	1	0	0	0	0	0
Pitney, James, One.	1.000	17	1	5	0	6	0
Pollaro, Dallas, N.J.	.000	1	0	0	0	0	0
Polo, Bienvenido, N.J.	1.000	25	3	2	0	5	1
Ponce Deleon, Damon, N.J.	1.000	2	0	1	0	1	0
Postell, Matthew, Uti.	.000	2	0	0	0	0	0
Pugmire, Rob, M.V.	.000	5	0	0	0	0	0
Ramirez, Santiago, Aub.	.950	20	4	15	1	20	3
Rayborn, Kris, N.J.*	.400	11	1	1	3	5	0
Renwick, Tyler, Que.	1.000	7	5	3	0	8	0
Reynolds, Josh, Pit.	1.000	7	1	6	0	7	1
Riethmaier, Matthew, Bat.	1.000	14	6	7	0	13	1
Rivera, Samuel, One.	1.000	9	1	4	0	5	0
Roach, Jason, Pit.	1.000	5	2	2	0	4	0
Roberts, Marquis, H.V.*	.889	17	1	7	1	9	1
Rodney, Thomas, One.	.778	9	2	5	2	9	2
Rodriguez, Alejandro, Bat.	.750	6	2	1	1	4	0
Rogers, Lionel, Pit.	.923	23	5	7	1	13	0
Roman, Orlando, Pit.	.923	11	4	8	1	13	0
Roque, Darryl, Ver.	1.000	5	3	2	0	5	1
Rosario, Rodrigo, Aub.	.727	14	3	5	3	11	0
Rose, Michael, Ver.	.000	2	0	0	0	0	0
Russo, Dennis, Jam.	1.000	11	2	3	0	5	0
Russo, Scott, Ver.	1.000	14	0	1	0	1	0
Saberhagen, Bret, Low.	.000	1	0	0	0	0	0
Sadler, Carl, M.V.*	.667	5	1	1	1	3	0
Sadowski, Chad, Bat.	1.000	20	4	2	0	6	1
St. Amand, Reuben, Que.	.400	17	1	1	3	5	0
Saladin, Miguel, Aub.	.727	27	3	5	3	11	1
Salazar, Luis, Uti.	1.000	19	3	4	0	7	1
Samora, Santo, N.J.	.929	32	5	8	1	14	0
Santos, Bernaldo, Aub.	1.000	15	1	2	0	3	0
Sawyer, Steve, Uti.	1.000	15	1	2	0	3	0
Schilling, Tim, Uti.*	1.000	10	1	4	0	5	0
Schiml, Anthony, Low.*	1.000	2	0	1	0	1	0
Schmitt, Eric, S.I.	.714	15	1	4	2	7	0
Schultz, Bryan, N.J.	1.000	4	0	1	0	1	0
Searles, Jonathan, Wil.	1.000	6	3	8	0	11	0
Severino, Jose, One.	1.000	3	1	3	0	4	1
Shelley, Jason, Wil.	.750	7	0	3	1	4	1
Sierra, Jr., Auvin, One.*	1.000	4	0	1	0	1	0
Silverio, Carlos, Bat.	.000	1	0	0	0	0	0
Sloan, Brandon, Uti.	.944	14	6	11	1	18	1
Smalley, Mike, Jam.*	.000	3	0	0	0	0	0
Smith, Matt, S.I.*	.882	14	1	14	2	17	1
Smith, Matthew, Pit.	.667	20	0	2	1	3	0
Smith, Michael, Que.	.947	14	4	14	1	19	1
Smuin, Shane, Uti.	.750	26	4	2	2	8	0
Solano, Alex, Low.	.000	1	0	0	0	0	0
Sollenberger, Matt, Pit.*	1.000	20	3	5	0	8	0
Song, Seung, Low.	.923	13	0	12	1	13	0
Sosebee, Chad, Low.	1.000	12	2	5	0	7	1
Southard, Lee, Que.	1.000	5	3	1	0	4	1
Stanton, Jeff, S.I.	.667	11	1	1	1	3	0
Stasio, Doug, Bat.	1.000	18	3	3	0	6	1
Staveland, Toby, Jam.	1.000	11	3	5	0	8	0
Steele, Michael, One.	1.000	22	2	6	0	8	0
Stevens, Jeff, Uti.	.000	2	0	0	0	0	0
Stiehl, Robert, Aub.	1.000	5	1	0	0	1	0
Stokes, Shaun, N.J.	1.000	4	1	0	0	1	0
Story, Aaron, Wil.*	.800	10	2	2	1	5	0
Sullivan, Ted, M.V.	.000	2	0	0	0	0	0
Sunderman, Nick, M.V.*	.909	18	3	7	1	11	1
Swindell, Jeremy, One.*	.857	18	2	4	1	7	0
Tallet, Brian, M.V.*	.667	6	0	2	1	3	0

CLASS A New York-Pennsylvania League

Player, Team	Pct.	G	PO	A	E	TC	DP
Taylor, John, Que.	1.000	10	0	1	0	1	0
Tekavec, Nate, One.	.955	11	8	13	1	22	1
Thomas, Gaige, Uti.	.778	21	3	4	2	9	0
Torres, Luis, Ver.	.941	15	6	10	1	17	1
Urbina, Ulmer, Ver.	.750	25	2	4	2	8	0
Valle, Yoiset, S.I.*	.600	3	0	3	2	5	0
Vandermeer, Scott, H.V.	1.000	15	4	14	0	18	1
Van Vessen, Joshua, One.*	1.000	15	1	3	0	4	0
Villanueva, Bill, Uti.	.714	14	0	5	2	7	0
Villegas, Felix, Low.	.842	16	2	14	3	19	0
Vriesenga, Matt, N.J.	.909	22	3	7	1	11	1
Waechter, Doug, H.V.	.800	14	2	10	3	15	0

Player, Team	Pct.	G	PO	A	E	TC	DP
Wang, Chien-ming, S.I.	.905	14	2	17	2	21	0
Washburn, Ben, Ver.	1.000	9	1	0	0	1	0
Wheatland, Matthew, One.	1.000	5	2	2	0	4	0
Williams, Blake, N.J.	1.000	6	2	5	0	7	0
Willis, Jason, S.I.	.875	13	2	5	1	8	1
Wombacher, Mike, S.I.*	1.000	21	2	7	0	9	0
Woodyard, Mark, One.	1.000	11	4	8	0	12	0
Yee, Damon, Aub.	.895	14	4	13	2	19	0
Young, Simon, M.V.*	1.000	14	1	11	0	12	0
Zapey, Winton, Uti.	.000	1	0	0	0	0	0

The following players appeared only as designated hitter, pinch-hitter or pinch runner: Barnowski, dh; O'Sullivan, dh; Ridley, dh-ph.

LEAGUE CHAMPIONS

Year	Team	Pct.	Year	Team	Pct.	Year	Team	Pct.
1939—	Olean*	.631		Auburn (3rd)†	.521	1984—	Newark	.622
1940—	Olean*	.625	1963—	Auburn	.585		Little Falls▲	.587
1941—	Jamestown	.618		Batavia (3rd)†	.485	1985—	Oneonta*	.705
	Bradford (2nd)†	.549	1964—	Auburn§	.622		Auburn	.603
1942—	Jamestown*	.672	1965—	Binghamton	.677	1986—	Oneonta	.766
1943—	Lockport	.591		Binghamton	.607		St. Catharines◆	.632
	Wellsville (3rd)†	.532	1966—	Auburn∞	.620	1987—	Geneva▲	.632
1944—	Lockport	.608		Binghamton	.646		Watertown	.579
	Jamestown (2nd)†	.565	1967—	Auburn	.667	1988—	Oneonta▲	.632
1945—	Batavia*	.677	1968—	Auburn	.645		Jamestown	.618
1946—	Jamestown‡	.672		Oneonta (2nd)*	.558	1989—	Pittsfield	.697
	Batavia‡	.672	1969—	Oneonta	.662		Jamestown▲	.579
1947—	Jamestown*	.690	1970—	Auburn	.623	1990—	Oneonta■	.667
1948—	Lockport*	.603	1971—	Oneonta	.662		Geneva	.662
1949—	Bradford*	.635	1972—	Niagara Falls	.686	1991—	Pittsfield	.662
1950—	Hornell	.653	1973—	Auburn	.667		Jamestown■	.654
	Olean (2nd)†	.568	1974—	Oneonta	.768	1992—	Hamilton	.737
1951—	Olean	.622	1975—	Newark	.688		Geneva▼	.547
	Hornell (3rd)†	.568		Newark	.714	1993—	Niagara Falls▼	.603
1952—	Hamilton	.659	1976—	Elmira	.727		Pittsfield	.533
	Jamestown (2nd)†	.643		Elmira	.703	1994—	Auburn	.592
1953—	Jamestown*	.704	1977—	Oneonta▲	.671		New Jersey▼	.573
1954—	Corning*	.621		Batavia	.600	1995—	Vermont	.645
1955—	Hamilton*	.656	1978—	Oneonta	.729		Watertown▼	.630
1956—	Wellsville*	.617		Geneva◆	.718	1996—	Vermont▼	.649
1957—	Wellsville	.632	1979—	Geneva	.725		St. Catharines	.579
	Erie (2nd)†	.598		Oneonta◆	.618	1997—	Batavia	.635
1958—	Wellsville	.556	1980—	Oneonta▲	.662		Pittsfield▼	.568
	Geneva (2nd)†	.548		Geneva	.649	1998—	Hudson Valley	.658
1959—	Wellsville†	.635	1981—	Oneonta▲	.658		Oneonta††	.592
1960—	Erie	.643		Jamestown	.649		Auburn††	.573
	Wellsville (2nd)†	.535	1982—	Oneonta	.566	1999—	Mahoning Valley	.566
1961—	Geneva	.616		Niagara Falls▲	.553		Hudson Valley‡‡	.553
	Olean (4th)†	.512	1983—	Utica▲	.649	2000—	Mahoning Valley	.632
1962—	Jamestown	.580		Newark	.649		Staten Island§§	.622

*Won championship and four-club playoff. †Won four-club playoff. ‡Jamestown and Batavia declared co-champions; Batavia defeated Jamestown in final of four-club playoff. §Won championship and two-club playoff. ∞Won split-season playoff. ▲League divided into Eastern and Western divisions; won playoff. League divided into Wrigley and Yawkey divisions; won playoff. ■League divided into Eastern, Western and Stedler divisions; won playoff. ▼League divided into McNamara, Pinckney and Stedler divisions; won playoff. ††Named co-champions due to final series being rained out. ‡‡League divided into McNamara and Pinckney divisions; won playoff. §§League divided into McNamara and Stedler divisions; won playoff. (NOTE—Known as Pennsylvania-Ontario-New York League from 1939 through 1956.)

NORTHWEST LEAGUE

LEAGUE OFFICE

President/treasurer
Bob Richmond
Address
P.O. Box 1645
Boise, ID 83701
Phone
208-429-1511

Teams (affiliation)
Boise Hawks (Cubs)
Eugene Emeralds (Padres)
Everett AquaSox (Mariners)
Salem-Keizer Volcanoes (Giants)

Spokane Indians (Royals)
Tri-Cities Dust Devils (Rockies)
Vancouver Canadians (A's)
Yakima Bears (Diamondbacks)

2000 FINAL STANDINGS

NORTH DIVISION

Team	W	L	T	Pct.	GB
Yakima (Dodgers)	41	35	0	.539	...
Boise (Angels)	41	35	0	.539	...
Spokane (Royals)	38	38	0	.500	3.0
Everett (Mariners)	37	39	0	.487	4.0

SOUTH DIVISION

Team	W	L	T	Pct.	GB
Eugene (Cubs)	40	36	0	.526	...
Vancouver (Athletics)	39	37	0	.513	1.0
Salem-Keizer (Giants)	36	40	0	.474	4.0
Portland (Rockies)	32	44	0	.421	8.0

COMPOSITE

Team	Yak.	Boi.	Eug.	Van.	Spo.	Ever.	S.K.	Port.	W	L	T	Pct.	GB
Yakima (Dodgers)	...	7	5	5	4	8	7	5	41	35	0	.539	...
Boise (Angels)	5	...	7	4	6	8	6	5	41	35	0	.539	...
Eugene (Cubs)	5	3	...	6	6	4	6	10	40	36	0	.526	1.0
Vancouver (Athletics)	5	6	6	...	3	6	6	7	39	37	0	.513	2.0
Spokane (Royals)	8	6	4	7	...	4	4	5	38	38	0	.500	3.0
Everett (Mariners)	4	4	6	4	8	...	7	4	37	39	0	.487	4.0
Salem-Keizer (Giants)	3	4	6	6	6	3	...	8	36	40	0	.474	5.0
Portland (Rockies)	5	5	2	5	5	6	4	...	32	44	0	.421	9.0

Major league affiliations in parentheses.

PLAYOFFS: Yakima defeated Eugene three games to two to win league championship.

REGULAR-SEASON ATTENDANCE: Boise, 133,715; Eugene, 139,790; Everett, 114,024; Portland, 161,446; Salem-Keizer, 125,409; Spokane, 188,774; Vancouver, 109,576; Yakima, 68,905. Total—1,041,639. Playoffs (5 games)—11,493.

MANAGERS: Boise, Tom Kotchman; Eugene, Danny Sheaffer; Everett, Terry Pollreisz; Portland, Billy White; Salem-Keizer, Fred Stanley; Spokane, Tom Poquette; Vancouver, Dave Joppie; Yakima, Butch Hughes.

ALL-STAR TEAM: 1B—Garrett Atkins, Portland; 2B—Blake Blasi, Eugene; 3B—Lance Niekro, Salem-Keizer; SS—Freddie Bynum, Vancouver; OF—Jamal Strong, Everett; Nicolas Alvarez, Yakima; Brad Hawpe, Portland; C—Ryan Jorgensen, Eugene; Trey Lunsford, Salem-Keizer; DH—Brad Downing, Boise; RHP—Wilton Chavez, Eugene; LHP—Mark Freed, Eugene; RHRP—Charlie Thames, Boise; LHRP—Adrian Aguilera, Yakima; Most Valuable Player—Jamal Strong, Everett; Garrett Atkins, Portland; Manager of the Year—Fred Stanley, Boise.

2000 BATTING

TEAM

Team	Avg.	G	TPA	AB	R	H	TB	2B	3B	HR	RBI	SH	SF	HP	BB	IBB	SO	SB	CS	GDP	LOB	ShO	Slg.	OBP
Boise	.257	76	3110	2665	440	686	1019	146	14	53	382	22	16	59	348	7	687	102	29	58	621	5	.382	.354
Yakima	.255	76	2896	2535	326	646	899	121	15	34	294	47	19	45	250	14	583	109	56	52	536	6	.355	.330
Spokane	.253	76	3008	2559	389	647	893	117	12	35	341	36	23	50	340	8	629	80	30	52	590	3	.349	.349
Salem-Keizer	.251	76	3024	2653	361	667	916	127	22	26	313	31	21	40	279	7	584	52	25	46	614	6	.345	.329
Everett	.244	76	3003	2610	376	637	916	111	15	46	327	23	17	36	317	18	685	141	60	38	547	3	.351	.332
Eugene	.244	76	2965	2574	340	627	941	129	22	47	306	20	26	49	296	7	615	120	48	43	567	6	.366	.330
Portland	.239	76	2870	2531	317	606	863	120	22	31	280	16	23	36	264	8	664	69	41	44	571	8	.341	.317
Vancouver	.238	76	2941	2511	344	597	806	124	11	21	303	25	21	48	336	12	649	47	28	44	592	4	.321	.336

INDIVIDUAL

TOP QUALIFIERS FOR BATTING CHAMPIONSHIP

Minimum 205 plate appearances. *Lefthanded batter. †Switch-hitter.

Player, Team	Avg.	G	TPA	AB	R	H	TB	2B	3B	HR	RBI	SH	SF	HP	BB	IBB	SO	SB	CS	GDP	Slg.	OBP
Niekro, Lance, S.K.	.362	49	213	196	27	71	108	14	4	5	44	0	2	4	11	2	25	2	0	6	.551	.404
Downing, Brad, Boi.*	.337	75	333	285	52	96	134	17	0	7	46	0	2	5	41	4	57	1	1	3	.470	.426
Strong, Jamal, Ever.	.314	75	358	296	63	93	109	7	3	1	28	5	1	4	52	1	29	60	14	0	.368	.422
Cowan, Justin, Spo.	.312	48	216	189	24	59	80	12	0	3	31	2	5	2	18	0	32	3	2	4	.423	.369
Martinez, Abel, Spo.	.308	62	269	247	30	76	89	4	3	1	31	0	1	1	17	0	29	5	5	5	.360	.353
Roper, Zachary, Boi.	.308	54	230	195	36	60	88	16	0	4	34	0	0	2	31	0	44	4	1	7	.451	.408
Atkins, Garrett, Port.	.303	69	299	251	34	76	109	12	0	7	47	0	1	2	45	1	48	2	0	3	.434	.411
Thomas, Charles, Yak.	.301	64	275	249	31	75	97	12	2	2	28	1	2	4	19	3	59	16	4	5	.390	.358
Ellison, Jason, S.K.	.300	74	341	300	67	90	109	15	2	0	28	4	1	7	29	1	45	13	7	1	.363	.374
Alvarez, Nicholas, Yak.	.300	61	254	217	39	65	113	14	2	10	36	5	3	5	24	0	31	20	5	4	.521	.378
Barbier, Blair, Eug.	.295	67	278	234	28	69	96	13	1	4	34	0	7	8	29	2	37	4	1	1	.410	.381
Hawpe, Bradley, Port.*	.288	62	254	205	38	59	103	19	2	7	29	0	7	2	40	2	51	2	0	1	.502	.398
Melebeck, Aaron, Spo.	.283	47	207	166	23	47	56	6	0	1	23	5	4	6	26	1	31	8	3	4	.337	.391

CLASS A *Northwest League*

Player, Team	Avg.	G	TPA	AB	R	H	TB	2B	3B	HR	RBI	SH	SF	HP	BB	IBB	SO	SB	CS	GDP	Slg.	OBP
Bone, Blake, Ever.*	.282	68	293	241	50	68	112	16	2	8	43	1	2	2	47	5	55	7	6	3	.465	.401
Wilfong, Nick, S.K.*	.282	65	263	227	35	64	103	14	5	5	31	1	1	4	30	2	83	6	2	3	.454	.374
Barmes, Clint, Port.	.282	45	205	181	37	51	71	6	4	2	16	0	1	5	18	0	28	12	9	1	.392	.361

DEPARTMENTAL LEADERS: G—Downing, Strong, Cunningham, Schied, 75 each; AB—Ellison, 300; R—Ellison, 67; H—Downing, 96; TB—Downing, 134; 2B—Cordova, 20; 3B—N. Jackson, 7; HR—C. Santos, 14; RBI—Wagner, 53; SH—Gann, 15; SF—Barbier, Hawpe, 7 each; HP—Hattenburg, Spokane; BB—Cunningham, Raburn, 54 each; IBB—Bowser, 6; SO—C. Santos, 103; SB—Strong, 60; CS—Strong, 14; GIDP—Wagner, 13; Slg.—Niekro, .551; OBP—Downing, .426.

ALL PLAYERS

*Lefthanded batter. †Switch-hitter.

Player, Team	Avg.	G	TPA	AB	R	H	TB	2B	3B	HR	RBI	SH	SF	HP	BB	IBB	SO	SB	CS	GDP	Slg.	OBP
Alexander, Kevin, S.K.	.182	24	85	66	6	12	13	1	0	0	4	1	0	1	17	0	9	0	2	1	.197	.357
Alvarez, Henrry, Spo.	.183	21	67	60	10	11	14	3	0	0	4	1	0	3	3	0	29	0	1	0	.233	.258
Alvarez, Nicholas, Yak.	.300	61	254	217	39	65	113	14	2	10	36	5	3	5	24	0	31	20	5	4	.521	.378
Aracena, Sandy, Yak.	.217	27	101	92	7	20	25	5	0	0	12	2	1	0	6	0	20	6	1	5	.272	.263
Atkins, Garrett, Port.	.303	69	299	251	34	76	109	12	0	7	47	0	1	2	45	1	48	2	0	3	.434	.411
Barbier, Blair, Eug.	.295	67	278	234	28	69	96	13	1	4	34	0	7	8	29	2	37	4	1	1	.410	.381
Barmes, Clint, Port.	.282	45	205	181	37	51	71	6	4	2	16	0	1	5	18	0	28	12	9	1	.392	.361
Bauer, Gregory, Van.*	.000	21	1	1	0	0	0	0	0	0	0	0	0	0	0	0	1	0	0	0	.000	.000
Bell, Derek, S.K.†	.245	66	251	204	30	50	77	12	3	3	37	0	6	4	37	0	39	4	1	2	.377	.363
Bernard, Dagoberto, Port.	.201	54	191	179	16	36	49	11	1	0	10	5	1	3	3	0	42	5	4	2	.274	.226
Betts, Dewayne, Van.	.063	6	19	16	2	1	1	0	0	0	1	0	0	0	3	0	10	1	0	0	.063	.211
Blasi, Blake, Eug.†	.236	72	333	276	52	65	88	12	1	3	28	6	1	6	44	0	50	27	7	2	.319	.352
Blocker, Kevin, Port.	.247	20	92	85	11	21	26	3	1	0	14	0	0	1	6	0	12	5	1	1	.306	.304
Bone, Blake, Ever.*	.282	68	293	241	50	68	112	16	2	8	43	1	2	2	47	5	55	7	6	3	.465	.401
Bowser, Matt, Van.*	.228	68	274	237	29	54	81	11	2	4	39	0	1	4	32	6	61	1	1	7	.342	.328
Bubela, Jaime, Ever.*	.230	30	131	113	11	26	36	1	3	1	13	1	0	3	14	1	25	13	3	0	.319	.331
Bynum, Freddie, Van.*	.256	72	320	281	52	72	87	10	1	1	26	3	0	5	31	0	58	22	12	3	.310	.341
Cappola, Anthony, Boi.	.212	16	37	33	4	7	9	2	0	0	4	1	0	0	3	0	7	0	0	0	.273	.278
Carroll, Mark, Ever.	.219	40	156	128	14	28	40	6	0	2	14	0	1	2	24	2	38	0	1	1	.313	.348
Carter, Bryan, S.K.*	.265	63	251	226	24	60	81	8	2	3	28	2	0	3	20	0	37	13	3	3	.358	.333
Cash, Condor, Eug.	.236	55	199	178	21	42	65	10	2	3	17	2	2	4	13	0	41	7	3	4	.365	.299
Cerda, Jose, S.K.	.232	17	62	56	8	13	19	3	0	1	5	0	0	0	6	0	15	1	0	0	.339	.306
Chirinos, Germain, Van.	.175	21	73	63	7	11	15	2	1	0	3	0	0	3	7	0	22	0	0	1	.238	.288
Cirone, Joseph, Van.	.212	57	215	189	25	40	63	14	0	3	18	2	0	6	18	1	72	2	1	6	.333	.300
Clements, Jason, Van.†	.239	23	76	67	8	16	20	1	0	1	4	2	0	0	7	0	23	2	4	1	.299	.311
Conway, Dan, Port.	.158	45	162	139	13	22	27	5	0	0	12	2	2	2	15	1	40	1	1	5	.194	.247
Cook, Joshua, S.K.	.192	34	138	130	14	25	32	7	0	0	14	1	0	1	6	0	19	0	2	3	.246	.234
Cooper, Sam, Eug.†	.148	14	35	27	4	4	4	0	0	0	1	1	0	2	5	0	2	0	0	0	.148	.324
Cordova, Ben, Spo.*	.236	67	286	242	43	57	94	20	1	5	34	1	2	0	41	3	54	6	2	6	.388	.344
Coulie, Jason, Boi.	.264	62	271	242	34	64	114	16	2	10	39	2	1	5	21	0	66	8	6	5	.471	.335
Covington, Kevin, Yak.	.248	48	157	141	17	35	55	12	1	2	13	3	0	0	10	0	29	2	1	0	.390	.298
Cowan, Justin, Spo.	.312	48	216	189	24	59	80	12	0	3	31	2	5	2	18	0	32	3	2	4	.423	.369
Craig, Beau, Van.†	.247	24	84	77	6	19	27	8	0	0	11	1	1	0	5	0	19	0	0	2	.351	.289
Crespo, Manny, Ever.	.259	46	187	162	28	42	57	6	0	3	25	1	1	4	19	1	53	2	2	4	.352	.349
Cunningham, Marco, Spo.	.277	75	356	282	58	78	108	16	4	2	42	9	1	10	54	1	51	31	7	4	.383	.409
Dacey, Ryan, Van.	.323	59	196	155	27	50	64	11	0	1	16	5	1	8	27	0	32	3	3	2	.413	.445
Daubert, Jake, Ever.*	.237	49	203	177	21	42	55	10	0	1	33	1	1	0	24	1	39	4	3	4	.311	.327
Declet, Miguel, Van.	.225	55	200	178	20	40	52	9	0	1	19	2	3	2	14	0	60	3	0	1	.292	.284
D'Jesus, Francisco, S.K.	.333	3	3	3	0	1	2	1	0	0	1	0	0	0	0	0	1	0	0	0	.667	.333
Delgado, Chris, Port.	.385	3	14	13	2	5	5	0	0	0	2	0	0	1	0	0	2	0	0	0	.385	.429
Devine, Rich, Spo.*	.281	24	70	57	15	16	17	1	0	0	8	0	0	2	11	0	11	12	2	0	.298	.414
Downing, Brad, Boi.*	.337	75	333	285	52	96	134	17	0	7	46	0	2	5	41	4	57	1	1	3	.470	.426
Duncheon, Ryan, Boi.*	.217	19	26	23	2	5	8	3	0	0	3	0	0	0	3	0	9	0	0	0	.348	.308
Duverge, Alcides, Boi.	.250	4	4	4	1	1	1	0	0	0	1	0	0	0	0	0	2	0	0	0	.250	.250
Ellison, Jason, S.K.	.300	74	341	300	67	90	109	15	2	0	28	4	1	7	29	1	45	13	7	1	.363	.374
Felix, Hersy, Spo.	.137	50	147	131	17	18	30	6	0	2	10	1	0	4	11	0	39	0	0	5	.229	.226
Felker, Jeffrey, Eug.*	.182	27	68	66	3	12	19	7	0	0	5	0	0	1	1	0	14	0	1	3	.288	.206
Fenster, Darren, Spo.	.236	60	222	182	30	43	53	5	1	1	23	4	3	1	32	0	34	4	2	3	.291	.352
Figueroa, Carlos, Port.*	.250	28	121	108	11	27	35	5	0	1	6	0	1	0	12	1	14	3	2	0	.324	.322
Freeman, Corey, Ever.	.218	65	249	216	32	47	63	12	2	0	11	6	3	0	24	0	64	12	6	3	.292	.292
Gann, Bryan, S.K.	.273	66	294	256	33	70	79	9	0	0	15	15	1	3	19	0	40	5	3	2	.309	.330
Gastelum, Carlos, Boi.	.199	66	236	206	23	41	46	5	0	0	14	9	0	7	14	0	36	13	4	4	.223	.273
Gemoll, Justin, Spo.	.314	9	42	35	8	11	16	2	0	1	5	0	0	3	4	0	10	0	0	1	.457	.429
Goelz, Jim, Yak.	.222	4	12	9	1	2	2	0	0	0	0	0	0	0	0	0	0	0	0	0	.222	.417
Graham, Peter, Eug.	.278	46	131	108	20	30	44	9	1	1	7	2	3	4	14	1	32	7	4	2	.407	.372
Guzman, Javier, Eug.†	.269	33	117	108	16	29	39	8	1	0	13	0	1	1	5	0	45	2	0	1	.361	.304
Guzman, Juan, Spo.†	.197	34	85	71	8	14	22	1	2	1	9	3	0	1	10	0	22	0	3	0	.310	.305
Halgren, Chris, Van.	.227	43	126	88	10	20	21	1	0	0	11	1	3	2	32	2	26	0	0	3	.239	.432
Hattenburg, Ray, Spo.†	.233	64	244	202	28	47	55	5	0	1	26	0	3	12	27	0	55	2	2	7	.272	.352
Hawpe, Bradley, Port.*	.288	62	254	205	38	59	103	19	2	7	29	0	7	2	40	2	51	2	0	1	.502	.398
Henderson, Bradley, Van.	.255	64	258	212	26	54	67	10	0	1	33	7	4	2	33	1	41	2	0	4	.316	.355
Hertel, Brian, Ever.	.236	63	240	199	29	47	74	12	3	3	22	2	2	5	32	1	54	4	4	0	.372	.353
Herzog, Jason, Spo.	.262	29	93	84	12	22	28	3	0	1	8	2	0	1	6	0	29	1	0	3	.333	.319
Higgins, Brett, Ever.*	.210	52	196	181	19	38	58	5	0	5	23	0	1	1	13	1	47	3	2	5	.320	.265
Hill, Koyie, Yak.†	.259	64	283	251	26	65	86	13	1	2	29	5	2	0	25	2	47	0	7	7	.343	.324
Hoffpauir, Josh, Van.*	.280	7	27	25	1	7	11	2	1	0	5	0	0	1	1	0	0	0	1	0	.440	.333
Holt, Daylan, Van.	.271	32	132	118	17	32	44	6	0	2	17	0	2	2	10	0	26	1	0	3	.373	.333
Jackson, Brandon, Boi.	.125	8	8	8	0	1	1	0	0	0	0	0	0	0	0	0	3	0	0	0	.125	.125
Jackson, Nicolas, Eug.*	.255	74	318	294	39	75	119	12	7	6	47	0	1	0	22	2	64	25	3	6	.405	.308
Jackson, Steve, Van.	.125	12	40	32	1	4	6	2	0	0	3	0	0	0	8	1	12	4	0	0	.188	.300
Jaramillo, Milko, Yak.†	.216	10	44	37	3	8	9	1	0	0	1	2	0	1	4	1	12	4	0	0	.243	.319
Jorgensen, Ryan, Eug.	.300	41	152	130	17	39	56	10	2	1	23	2	2	1	17	0	27	2	4	1	.431	.380
Kay, Kevin, Boi.*	.240	28	63	50	9	12	17	3	1	0	8	0	0	3	10	0	12	5	0	2	.340	.397

Player, Team	Avg.	G	TPA	AB	R	H	TB	2B	3B	HR	RBI	SH	SF	HP	BB	IBB	SO	SB	CS	GDP	Slg.	OBP
Keating, Matthew, S.K.*	.228	34	122	114	12	26	32	6	0	0	16	0	2	1	5	0	13	0	0	6	.281	.262
Keller, G.W., Van.	.249	62	249	217	32	54	71	8	3	1	33	3	2	7	20	0	41	5	2	4	.327	.329
Kent, Mat, Ever.*	.212	34	103	99	7	21	31	7	0	1	7	1	0	0	3	0	39	0	0	0	.313	.235
Keppinger, William, Spo.*	.276	51	173	152	22	42	59	11	0	2	21	0	2	1	18	0	32	4	2	1	.388	.353
King, Brennan, Yak.	.239	61	274	238	27	57	72	10	1	1	30	1	1	5	29	3	49	14	5	7	.303	.333
Knight, Marcus, Boi.†	.667	1	4	3	2	2	8	0	0	2	4	0	0	0	1	0	0	1	0	0	2.667	.750
Kweon, Yoon-Min, Eug.	.255	44	172	145	15	37	63	9	1	5	18	0	0	5	22	0	29	5	3	5	.434	.372
Langs, Ronte, Yak.	.224	55	203	170	26	38	45	5	1	0	17	4	1	4	24	2	45	11	6	4	.265	.332
Liriano, Pedro, Ever.	.200	4	19	15	2	3	3	0	0	0	2	0	0	0	4	0	4	4	0	1	.200	.368
Lopez, Chuck, Ever.*	.264	34	139	121	18	32	47	6	0	3	21	0	1	4	13	2	22	2	0	1	.388	.353
Lunsford, James, S.K.	.270	59	254	215	23	58	76	9	0	3	30	0	1	8	30	2	40	1	0	6	.353	.378
Madera, Sandy, Van.	.263	16	66	57	7	15	17	2	0	0	2	0	0	1	8	0	7	0	0	3	.298	.364
Maldonado, Edwin, S.K.	.188	57	213	191	23	36	48	9	0	1	16	5	3	1	13	0	46	0	3	4	.251	.240
Mallory, Michael, Eug.	.210	70	288	262	39	55	91	12	3	6	30	0	2	8	16	0	98	9	3	4	.347	.274
Martinez, Abel, Spo.	.308	62	269	247	30	76	89	4	3	1	31	0	1	1	17	0	29	5	5	5	.360	.353
Martinez, Candido, Yak.	.270	39	149	137	20	37	57	7	2	3	14	0	2	1	9	0	53	6	4	3	.416	.315
Martinez, Dionnar, Eug.†	.215	53	191	172	23	37	41	4	0	0	16	2	0	3	14	0	34	8	2	5	.238	.286
Martinez, Guillermo, Ever.†	.217	46	189	175	23	38	43	5	0	0	13	3	0	1	10	1	36	10	4	5	.246	.263
McDougall, Marshall, Van.	.275	27	121	102	17	28	36	4	2	0	11	0	1	0	18	0	19	5	3	1	.353	.380
Melebeck, Aaron, Spo.	.283	47	207	166	23	47	56	6	0	1	23	5	4	6	26	1	31	8	3	4	.337	.391
Michaelis, Derek, Yak.*	.199	60	231	211	23	42	65	6	1	5	28	1	1	0	18	0	77	1	2	2	.308	.261
Morency, Vernand, Port.	.228	48	203	180	17	41	57	6	2	2	18	0	1	4	18	1	57	6	6	6	.317	.310
Morrissey, Adam, Eug.	.275	73	321	269	32	74	115	16	2	7	36	3	4	3	42	1	50	12	11	2	.428	.374
Mounts, J.R., Boi.	.247	55	215	190	31	47	74	9	3	4	28	3	1	3	18	0	69	6	1	4	.389	.321
Mulqueen, Dave, Port.†	.150	13	42	40	5	6	9	1	1	0	4	0	0	0	2	0	20	1	0	1	.225	.190
Murphy, Tommy, Boi.	.225	55	235	213	38	48	74	18	1	2	25	1	1	5	15	0	52	14	7	1	.347	.291
Niekro, Lance, S.K.	.362	49	213	196	27	71	108	14	4	5	44	0	2	4	11	2	25	2	0	6	.551	.404
Ortega, Sixto, Port.	.250	6	20	20	1	5	7	2	0	0	2	0	0	0	0	0	6	0	0	0	.350	.250
Paredes, Reny, Eug.	.146	21	49	48	2	7	14	2	1	1	5	0	0	0	1	0	21	0	0	2	.292	.163
Paulino, Miguel, Eug.†	.167	18	56	48	7	8	8	0	0	0	4	0	0	1	7	1	16	7	1	0	.167	.286
Peck, Bryan, Port.	.224	54	216	196	21	44	64	9	1	3	16	1	2	4	13	1	35	0	3	3	.327	.284
Pekar, Jason, S.K.	.169	24	74	65	10	11	15	4	0	0	7	0	3	0	6	0	20	1	0	2	.231	.230
Pena, Pelagio, Ever.	.181	47	159	144	11	26	37	5	0	2	8	0	0	3	12	0	56	4	1	4	.257	.258
Pena, Wilton, Van.	.187	46	143	123	16	23	34	5	0	2	13	1	0	3	14	0	44	0	0	2	.276	.286
Pina, Enmanuel, Eug.	.000	1	1	1	0	0	0	0	0	0	0	0	0	0	0	0	1	0	0	0	.000	.000
Pride, Joshua, Port.	.123	16	61	57	4	7	9	0	1	0	4	0	0	2	2	0	15	1	0	3	.158	.180
Quintana, Wilfredo, Ever.	.305	22	92	82	16	25	49	3	0	7	26	0	1	0	9	1	24	2	1	1	.598	.370
Raburn, Johnny, Boi.†	.254	72	343	280	49	71	91	12	4	0	34	4	3	2	54	0	72	28	3	2	.325	.375
Repko, Jason, Yak.	.294	8	18	17	3	5	7	2	0	0	1	0	0	1	0	0	7	0	0	0	.412	.333
Reyes, Christian, Van.†	.322	25	100	87	12	28	40	9	0	1	14	0	1	0	12	0	20	0	2	0	.460	.410
Reynoso, Ismael, S.K.	.150	18	63	60	4	9	13	4	0	0	5	2	0	0	1	0	12	0	0	3	.217	.164
Richardson, Miguel, Ever.	.215	56	199	181	19	39	69	7	1	7	25	1	2	3	12	1	77	5	7	5	.381	.273
Riley, Brett, Boi.	.000	1	1	1	0	0	0	0	0	0	0	0	0	0	0	0	1	0	0	0	.000	.000
Rock, Jamie, Port.	.254	57	230	209	33	53	72	14	1	1	22	0	1	4	16	0	53	7	2	6	.344	.317
Rogers, Brandon, Boi.	.247	31	99	89	9	22	27	2	0	1	11	0	0	3	7	0	24	0	0	4	.303	.323
Roper, Zachary, Boi.	.308	54	230	195	36	60	88	16	0	4	34	0	0	2	31	0	44	4	1	7	.451	.408
Rosario, Vicente, Ever.	.269	21	88	78	11	21	29	3	1	1	12	1	1	4	4	0	23	9	6	1	.372	.333
Santos, Chad, Spo.*	.251	73	308	267	40	67	127	18	0	14	47	3	0	2	36	3	103	1	0	2	.476	.344
Santos, Deivis, S.K.*	.000	2	7	7	0	0	0	0	0	0	0	0	0	0	0	0	4	0	0	0	.000	.000
Sarna, Kenny, Spo.	.250	1	4	4	0	1	1	0	0	0	0	0	0	0	0	0	2	0	0	0	.250	.250
Schied, Jeremy, Van.*	.233	75	297	236	37	55	77	16	0	2	28	0	4	9	48	0	51	2	1	1	.326	.377
Schmidt, J.P., Van.*	.235	48	120	102	19	24	36	4	1	2	12	3	0	0	15	1	35	1	1	2	.353	.333
Shabala, Adam, S.K.	.216	59	209	176	27	38	62	6	3	4	19	0	1	2	30	0	60	2	1	4	.352	.335
Sing, Brandon, Eug.	.229	61	258	218	29	50	90	11	1	9	28	1	2	2	35	0	75	4	5	6	.413	.339
Smiley, Jermaine, Spo.*	.222	51	184	153	19	34	39	3	1	0	17	4	1	1	25	0	56	2	0	5	.255	.333
Socarras, Antonio, Boi.*	.255	55	192	161	26	41	65	9	0	5	28	0	3	4	24	1	47	0	4	3	.404	.359
Sosa, Jorge, Port.†	.230	62	241	200	24	46	75	7	5	4	26	0	1	3	37	0	102	4	6	3	.375	.357
Soto, Jorge, Van.	.000	2	4	4	0	0	0	0	0	0	0	0	0	0	0	0	2	0	0	0	.000	.000
Soto, Saul, Yak.	.255	55	222	192	26	49	79	12	0	6	26	2	0	9	19	1	46	1	3	5	.411	.350
Sprowl, Jon-Mark, Eug.*	.235	40	115	98	9	23	28	2	0	1	7	1	2	0	14	0	24	3	0	0	.286	.325
Storey, Eric, Port.	.100	6	24	20	3	2	5	0	0	1	3	1	0	0	3	0	7	0	0	1	.250	.217
Strankland, Elliott, S.K.	.167	3	6	6	2	1	3	0	1	0	0	0	0	0	0	0	2	0	0	0	.500	.167
Strong, Jamal, Ever.	.314	75	358	296	63	93	109	7	3	1	28	5	1	4	52	1	29	60	14	3	.368	.422
Tejada, Michael, Port.†	.230	41	144	126	16	29	39	2	1	2	19	1	2	0	15	1	42	3	0	1	.310	.308
Templeton, Garry, Boi.	.160	20	29	25	2	4	5	1	0	0	1	0	0	3	0	11	1	1	0	.200	.276
Testa, Chris, Port.*	.211	5	19	19	1	4	5	1	0	0	2	0	0	0	0	0	9	1	1	0	.263	.211
Thomas, Charles, Yak.	.301	64	275	249	31	75	97	12	2	2	28	1	2	4	19	3	59	16	4	5	.390	.358
Trumble, Dan, S.K.	.167	15	55	48	1	8	11	1	1	0	3	0	1	1	6	0	24	1	0	0	.229	.273
Turco, Anthony, S.K.*	.500	3	12	12	3	6	7	1	0	0	3	0	0	0	0	0	2	0	0	0	.583	.500
Van Buizen, Rodney, Yak.	.220	48	196	173	17	38	46	4	2	0	21	4	3	3	13	1	27	4	6	5	.266	.281
Ventura, Juan, Port.	.221	56	219	195	24	43	57	9	1	1	15	6	2	2	14	0	36	14	6	6	.292	.277
Victorino, Shane, Van.	.246	61	273	236	32	58	75	7	2	2	20	12	2	3	20	1	44	21	9	3	.318	.310
Wagner, Jeffrey, Boi.	.253	72	309	253	50	64	117	17	0	12	53	0	5	6	45	2	62	3	0	13	.462	.372
Walker, Mark, S.K.	.189	35	108	95	12	18	26	3	1	1	7	0	0	0	13	0	52	3	1	0	.274	.287
Walter, Scott, Spo.	.114	13	38	35	2	4	5	1	0	0	2	1	1	0	1	0	10	1	0	1	.143	.135
Warner, J.R., Boi.*	.278	74	312	266	54	74	109	14	3	5	33	0	0	4	42	0	68	6	1	7	.410	.385
Welch, Edward, Boi.*	.215	31	106	93	15	20	20	0	0	0	11	1	0	1	11	0	27	9	0	2	.215	.305
Wilfong, Nick, S.K.*	.282	65	263	227	35	64	103	14	5	5	31	1	1	4	30	2	83	6	2	3	.454	.374
Wilson, Dan, Ever.	.500	1	3	2	2	1	4	0	0	1	1	0	0	0	1	0	0	0	0	0	2.000	.667
Withey, Ryan, Boi.	.133	16	59	45	3	6	11	2	0	1	5	1	0	8	5	0	18	3	0	1	.244	.328
Wright, Nate, Van.	.222	4	10	9	1	2	2	0	0	0	2	0	0	0	1	0	4	0	0	0	.222	.300

GRAND SLAMS: Quintana 2; N. Alvarez, Cash, Henderson, N. Jackson, Mounts, Socarras, Sosa, C. Thomas, Wagner, 1 each.

AWARDED FIRST BASE ON CATCHER'S INTERFERENCE: Covington 3 (H. Alvarez 2, M. Kent), A. Martinez 3 (M. Kent, Lunsford, S. Soto), Conway 2 (Hill 2), Ja. Guzman 2 (Hill, S. Soto), W. Pena 2 (Aracena, Lunsford), Roper 2 (P. Pena, S. Sosa), Carroll (W. Pena), Declet (S. Soto).

TEAM

Team	W	L	Pct.	ERA	G	CG	ShO	Sv.	IP	H	TBF	R	ER	HR	SH	SF	HB	BB	IBB	SO	WP	Bk.
Vancouver	39	37	.513	3.24	76	0	7	22	671.1	585	2877	322	242	23	31	14	40	260	13	603	67	9
Eugene	40	36	.526	3.38	76	1	8	24	688.2	583	2904	314	259	30	26	18	32	264	14	707	37	8
Yakima	41	35	.539	3.54	76	0	6	20	681.1	628	2882	322	268	41	25	13	32	215	9	687	41	8
Spokane	38	38	.500	3.78	76	0	3	19	677.0	642	2961	347	284	29	28	19	41	315	8	596	62	13
Portland	32	44	.421	3.81	76	0	7	12	657.0	621	2927	362	278	35	24	21	47	314	13	541	40	12
Everett	37	39	.487	4.03	76	0	4	14	691.2	669	3095	399	310	50	32	26	57	329	7	716	80	5
Salem-Keizer	36	40	.474	4.21	76	0	4	21	681.1	669	3100	386	319	49	34	26	56	401	2	631	74	10
Boise	41	35	.539	4.73	76	0	2	23	685.2	716	3087	441	360	36	20	29	58	332	15	615	48	8

INDIVIDUAL

TOP QUALIFIERS FOR EARNED-RUN AVERAGE TITLE

Minimum 61 innings. *Lefthanded pitcher.

Pitcher, Team	W	L	Pct.	ERA	G	GS	CG	ShO	GF	Sv.	IP	H	TBF	R	ER	HR	SH	SF	HB	BB	IBB	SO	WP	Bk.
Farmer, Jason, S.K.	3	3	.500	1.62	16	9	0	0	0	0	66.2	58	287	19	12	2	4	2	7	31	0	47	1	1
Chavez, Wilton, Eug.	7	1	.875	1.69	15	15	0	0	0	0	90.1	69	371	28	17	0	4	1	10	25	0	103	4	3
Johnson, Everrett, Ever.	5	4	.556	2.07	17	8	0	0	2	0	69.2	51	286	26	16	1	3	3	2	21	0	88	5	1
Totten, Heath, Yak.	8	2	.800	2.30	13	13	0	0	0	0	74.1	55	292	24	19	4	0	2	2	15	0	67	3	0
Krawiec, Aaron, Eug.*	6	4	.600	2.54	14	14	0	0	0	0	78.0	59	323	28	22	4	4	1	4	26	0	99	1	2
Van Buren, Jermaine, Port.	4	5	.444	2.61	13	13	0	0	0	0	69.0	54	291	27	20	1	4	2	3	30	0	41	3	2
Buglovsky, Christopher, Port.	5	5	.500	2.63	14	12	0	0	0	0	65.0	50	273	30	19	5	0	2	3	32	1	50	4	2
Landestoy, Gilbert, Boi.	4	2	.667	2.81	28	0	0	0	8	0	64.0	47	263	27	20	0	1	4	7	21	1	54	2	0
DeJesus, Tony, Ever.*	4	6	.400	2.91	15	12	0	0	1	0	65.0	60	277	28	21	5	2	3	0	28	0	72	3	0
Crowell, Kyle, Van.	4	4	.500	2.91	17	9	0	0	4	2	65.0	63	274	28	21	0	4	0	4	12	0	64	5	3
Wolensky, David, Boi.	8	3	.727	3.07	15	15	0	0	0	0	76.1	60	317	29	26	1	0	1	2	35	1	88	3	0
Langone, Steve, Yak.	4	4	.500	3.08	15	12	0	0	1	1	84.2	76	353	30	29	6	4	2	3	5	0	79	1	0
Roney, Matt, Port.	7	5	.583	3.14	15	15	0	0	0	0	80.1	75	360	35	28	6	1	1	7	44	0	85	8	2
Kennedy, Casey, Yak.	6	4	.600	3.24	13	13	0	0	0	0	72.1	73	303	33	26	3	2	0	2	10	0	69	2	1
Ferguson, Ian, Spo.	5	6	.455	3.28	15	15	0	0	0	0	71.1	76	312	38	26	6	5	2	4	16	0	66	9	1

DEPARTMENTAL LEADERS: W—Freed, 9; L—Hampson, 8; Pct.—Chavez, .875; G—Butler, 30; GS—several tied, 15 each; CG—Freed, 1; ShO—None; GF—Butler, 25; Sv.—Anderson, 12; IP—Chavez, 90.1; H—Faust, 102; TBF—Chavez, 371; R—Taylor, 54; ER—Taylor, 52; HR—Pace, 10; SH—Minaya, 7; SF—Faas, 5; HB—O'Neal, D. Moore, 11 each; BB—Farley, 56; IBB—Stokley, Fries, Bauer, 4 each; SO—Chavez, 103; WP—D. Moore, 12; BK—A. Thomas, Metzger, 5 each.

ALL PITCHERS

*Lefthanded pitcher.

Pitcher, Team	W	L	Pct.	ERA	G	GS	CG	ShO	GF	Sv.	IP	H	TBF	R	ER	HR	SH	SF	HB	BB	IBB	SO	WP	Bk.
Abell, Joe, Port.	1	1	.500	3.13	24	0	0	0	12	3	31.2	19	128	11	11	2	0	3	2	12	1	28	0	0
Aguilera, Adrian, Yak.*	0	3	.000	3.93	17	0	0	0	12	5	36.2	36	164	21	16	1	5	0	1	14	0	36	2	1
Albright, Eric, Eug.	1	5	.167	3.59	27	0	0	0	19	6	42.2	45	179	19	17	4	0	2	0	8	2	36	2	0
Alvarez, Larry, Eug.	1	1	.500	3.86	18	0	0	0	7	0	32.2	33	149	21	14	0	3	0	2	12	0	34	2	0
Anderson, Luke, S.K.	4	0	1.000	1.45	25	0	0	0	19	12	31.0	19	124	5	5	1	2	1	1	10	0	55	3	0
Ashlock, Chad, S.K.	0	0	.000	2.25	2	2	0	0	0	0	4.0	5	21	2	1	0	0	0	4	2	1	0		
Baker, Joseph, Spo.	4	4	.500	5.43	14	14	0	0	0	0	63.0	77	291	48	38	5	3	0	4	25	0	31	3	0
Baranowski, Brannon, Spo.	2	0	1.000	2.45	19	0	0	0	3	2	36.2	20	154	14	10	1	1	1	1	24	1	44	5	1
Barker, Richie, Eug.	0	1	.000	3.27	10	0	0	0	9	4	11.0	6	43	5	4	2	0	0	1	4	0	11	0	0
Bauer, Gregory, Yak.	2	1	.667	3.48	21	0	0	0	16	9	33.2	26	148	17	13	2	1	1	2	19	4	50	5	2
Beckman, Jacob, Van.	3	2	.600	0.92	12	0	0	0	8	1	19.2	13	81	3	2	0	2	0	1	9	2	11	0	0
Beltran, Francis, Eug.	2	2	.500	2.68	25	0	0	0	13	8	43.2	28	180	16	13	1	1	1	1	20	2	52	6	0
Berney, Scott, Port.	0	0	.000	8.72	15	0	0	0	6	0	21.2	29	102	22	21	1	0	0	1	12	0	14	0	2
Bonser, Boof, S.K.	1	4	.200	6.00	10	0	0	0	0	0	33.0	21	145	23	22	2	1	2	1	29	0	41	4	0
Bridenbaugh, Christian, Yak.*	2	3	.400	4.06	7	6	0	0	0	0	37.2	48	161	19	17	2	0	0	0	10	0	24	1	0
Brooks, Conor, Van.	2	2	.500	3.47	18	8	0	0	3	0	62.1	60	260	31	24	3	1	1	1	18	2	56	4	1
Buglovsky, Christopher, Port.	5	5	.500	2.63	14	12	0	0	0	0	65.0	50	273	30	19	5	0	2	3	32	1	50	4	2
Bukowski, Stanislaw, Boi.	0	0	.000	7.36	5	0	0	0	0	0	3.2	5	19	3	3	1	0	0	1	2	0	3	3	0
Bukvich, Ryan, Spo.	2	0	1.000	0.64	10	0	0	0	8	2	14.0	5	56	1	1	0	1	0	1	9	0	15	1	0
Bullinger, Frederick, Spo.	2	1	.667	3.63	16	0	0	0	4	1	22.1	23	105	9	9	2	0	0	1	15	0	38	1	0
Burton, Timothy, Ever.	0	0	.000	3.00	3	0	0	0	0	0	3.0	4	12	2	1	1	0	0	0	0	0	3	0	0
Butler, John, Ever.	5	2	.714	1.42	30	0	0	0	25	10	38.0	22	159	12	6	0	4	3	4	18	3	39	1	1
Chavez, Wilton, Eug.	7	1	.875	1.69	15	15	0	0	0	0	90.1	69	371	28	17	0	4	1	10	25	0	103	4	3
Cordero, Frangil, Eug.*	1	1	.500	2.96	6	5	0	0	0	0	24.1	23	106	10	8	3	0	0	0	15	0	19	3	1
Crowell, Kyle, Van.	4	4	.500	2.91	17	9	0	0	4	2	65.0	63	274	28	21	0	4	0	4	12	0	64	5	3
Cueto, Jose, Eug.	2	5	.286	5.24	13	7	0	0	1	1	44.2	43	200	27	26	1	0	1	4	24	0	51	5	1
DeJesus, Tony, Ever.*	4	6	.400	2.91	15	12	0	0	1	0	65.0	60	277	28	21	5	2	3	0	28	0	72	3	0
Diaz, Alex, Van.	0	0	.000	0.00	2	0	0	0	1	0	3.2	5	17	1	0	0	0	1	0	2	1	4	0	0
Diaz, Felix, S.K.	0	1	.000	8.10	3	0	0	0	2	0	3.1	6	19	6	3	2	2	0	1	1	0	2	0	0
Dohmann, Christopher, Port.	2	1	.667	0.78	5	4	0	0	0	0	23.0	14	85	3	2	0	0	0	1	5	0	23	0	0
Drain, Bradley, Ever.	2	0	1.000	2.37	14	0	0	0	6	1	19.0	17	79	8	5	1	0	1	1	4	0	17	2	0
Duverge, Alcides, Boi.	0	0	.000	40.50	2	0	0	0	0	0	1.1	4	13	6	6	0	0	1	1	4	0	0	2	0
Ericks, Dave, Eug.	2	1	.667	9.82	10	0	0	0	4	0	14.2	17	74	18	16	2	1	1	1	13	1	11	3	0
Faas, Matthew, S.K.	3	1	.750	2.83	24	0	0	0	9	0	35.0	33	160	14	11	3	3	5	5	21	0	18	6	0
Farley, Joseph, S.K.*	4	4	.500	4.38	16	14	0	0	0	0	76.0	80	345	42	37	9	1	8	6	56	0	87	3	2
Farmer, Jason, S.K.	3	3	.500	1.62	16	9	0	0	0	0	66.2	58	287	19	12	2	4	2	7	31	0	47	1	1
Faust, Matthew, S.K.	6	4	.600	3.84	15	11	0	0	1	0	84.1	102	363	44	36	9	2	0	2	24	0	56	5	1
Featherstone, Deron, S.K.	0	2	.000	9.33	12	3	0	0	2	0	18.1	25	111	23	19	3	1	0	3	34	0	15	9	0
Ferguson, Ian, Spo.	5	6	.455	3.28	15	15	0	0	0	0	71.1	76	312	38	26	6	5	2	4	16	0	66	9	1

Pitcher, Team	W	L	Pct.	ERA	G	GS	CG	ShO	GF	Sv.	IP	H	TBF	R	ER	HR	SH	SF	HB	BB	IBB	SO	WP	Bk.
Fingers, Jason, Spo.	1	2	.333	3.68	18	0	0	0	12	2	29.1	35	134	18	12	1	0	0	0	11	0	24	4	0
Fischer, Steve, Van.	3	2	.600	2.93	18	2	0	0	3	1	46.0	35	186	19	15	1	1	2	1	12	1	42	1	0
Flading, Cameron, Boi.	0	0	.000	9.00	3	0	0	0	2	0	4.0	7	19	4	4	0	0	1	0	1	0	5	0	0
Flores, Ron, Van.*	1	1	.500	5.11	13	0	0	0	1	0	12.1	16	60	10	7	2	0	1	1	4	0	10	1	0
Franke, Aaron, Boi.	3	1	.750	5.34	6	6	0	0	0	0	28.2	24	129	19	17	2	0	3	2	23	1	19	4	0
Freed, Mark, Eug.*	9	2	.818	3.58	15	13	1	0	1	0	88.0	77	351	36	35	3	3	1	1	30	1	66	1	0
Fries, Scott, Eug.*	2	1	.667	2.54	26	0	0	0	10	3	46.0	35	189	17	13	1	1	2	1	16	4	51	1	0
Garcia, Freddy, Ever.	0	0	.000	4.50	2	2	0	0	0	0	10.0	11	44	5	5	1	0	0	0	2	0	15	2	1
Garner, Brandon, Port.	0	1	.000	5.91	18	0	0	0	2	0	32.0	33	141	22	21	3	1	0	1	10	0	23	2	1
German, Franklyn, Van.	1	0	1.000	1.77	9	2	0	0	2	0	20.1	13	86	4	4	0	0	0	1	10	0	20	4	0
Gilmore, Travis, Boi.*	0	0	.000	0.00	3	0	0	0	3	0	2.2	2	11	0	0	0	0	0	2	0	0	4	0	0
Gilpatrick, Tyler, Van.	2	2	.500	8.86	15	2	0	0	5	0	21.1	34	109	24	21	0	0	0	0	17	0	17	1	0
Glidewell, Clifton, Yak.*	0	1	.000	10.54	10	0	0	0	5	0	13.2	24	70	18	16	4	1	1	0	6	0	12	2	0
Gomez, Diogenes, Port.	2	2	.500	1.82	25	0	0	0	23	6	24.2	22	104	7	5	1	1	0	0	8	2	17	1	0
Goure, Sam, Port.*	1	1	.500	6.21	22	3	0	0	5	0	29.0	33	147	24	20	1	1	2	5	24	1	23	3	0
Graham, Elgin, S.K.	1	1	.500	6.17	19	2	0	0	6	0	35.0	37	165	24	24	1	1	2	2	25	0	24	3	0
Green, Sean, Port.	1	4	.200	8.48	22	0	0	0	4	0	28.2	45	155	32	27	2	1	2	5	19	2	17	5	0
Gross, Kyle, S.K.	1	2	.333	7.62	8	2	0	0	0	0	13.0	15	75	14	11	1	2	2	5	18	0	9	1	0
Gruban, Jarret, Boi.	2	2	.333	5.19	6	6	0	0	0	0	26.0	28	120	20	15	3	1	2	3	17	0	18	3	0
Gwyn, Marcus, Van.	2	1	.667	2.86	12	2	0	0	5	1	28.1	29	124	16	9	0	2	0	4	2	0	31	3	1
Haase, Frank, Port.*	0	0	.000	14.40	5	0	0	0	0	0	5.0	9	33	8	8	0	0	1	3	6	1	4	0	0
Hampson, Justin, Port.*	1	8	.111	3.54	14	13	0	0	0	0	68.2	74	309	43	27	5	3	2	4	27	0	44	1	0
Hannaman, Ryan, S.K.*	0	0	.000	0.00	1	0	0	0	1	0	1.0	1	5	0	0	0	0	0	1	0	0	1	0	0
Harrelson, Ralph, S.K.	1	4	.200	12.18	6	4	0	0	0	0	17.0	27	95	23	23	4	0	0	9	9	0	11	6	0
Haworth, Brent, S.K.	0	0	.000	4.76	5	0	0	0	3	2	11.1	17	60	7	6	1	0	0	2	7	0	6	0	0
Head, Daniel, Ever.	0	0	.000	4.50	10	0	0	0	3	0	16.0	21	78	10	8	1	1	1	2	7	0	17	0	0
Henderson, Bradley, Van.	0	0	.000	0.00	1	0	0	0	1	0	3.0	1	11	0	0	0	0	0	1	0	0	1	0	0
Herrera, Jose, Ever.	1	4	.200	3.84	14	10	0	0	1	0	61.0	63	276	37	26	3	2	4	7	29	0	31	5	1
Hertel, Brian, Ever.	0	0	.000	0.00	2	0	0	0	2	0	1.0	1	4	0	0	0	0	0	0	0	0	0	0	0
Hughes, Nial, Yak.*	3	1	.750	2.85	16	5	0	0	4	1	47.1	35	211	20	15	3	3	2	4	30	2	61	5	1
Huie, Bryan, Ever.*	2	1	.667	7.63	10	0	0	0	2	0	15.1	9	75	13	13	0	1	1	2	17	0	15	8	0
Huisman, Justin, Port.	3	6	.333	1.85	16	3	0	0	6	1	43.2	31	180	16	9	1	2	2	1	17	1	32	0	0
Johnson, Eric, S.K.	2	2	.500	3.18	8	8	0	0	0	0	39.2	30	172	19	14	0	1	3	1	24	0	24	4	0
Johnson, Everett, Ever.	5	4	.556	2.07	17	8	0	0	2	0	69.2	51	286	26	16	1	3	3	2	21	0	88	5	1
Kennedy, Casey, Yak.	6	4	.600	3.24	13	13	0	0	0	0	72.1	73	303	33	26	3	2	0	2	10	0	69	2	1
Kent, Steven, Ever.*	4	1	.800	2.56	24	3	0	0	6	0	52.2	38	219	16	15	5	2	0	2	23	1	61	5	0
Keppinger, William, Spo.*	0	0	.000	0.00	1	0	0	0	1	0	0.2	0	1	0	0	0	0	0	0	0	0	0	0	0
Krawiec, Aaron, Eug.*	6	4	.600	2.54	14	14	0	0	0	0	78.0	59	323	28	22	4	4	1	4	26	0	99	1	2
Landesto, Gilbert, Boi.	4	2	.667	2.81	28	0	0	0	8	0	64.0	47	263	27	20	0	1	4	7	21	1	54	2	0
Langone, Steve, Yak.	4	4	.500	3.08	15	12	0	0	1	1	84.2	76	335	30	29	6	4	2	3	5	0	79	1	0
Lee, Tymber, Boi.	1	2	.333	5.28	22	0	0	0	10	1	29.0	34	143	28	17	0	1	2	4	21	2	19	5	0
Leicester, Jon, Lineman, Eug.	1	5	.167	5.44	17	7	0	0	1	0	49.2	47	224	36	30	4	6	4	2	22	1	31	2	0
Little, Roger, Port.	1	1	.500	8.62	13	0	0	0	2	0	15.2	31	95	23	15	3	2	1	4	13	2	6	4	0
Lorenzo, Javier, Port.	1	1	.500	3.04	18	0	0	0	10	1	26.2	16	112	10	9	0	0	2	0	13	0	35	1	1
Mangrum, Micah, Spo.	0	3	.000	2.75	20	0	0	0	6	0	39.1	35	160	14	12	2	0	0	2	10	1	39	2	0
Marin, Willy, Yak.	4	1	.800	5.46	19	0	0	0	10	1	31.1	42	144	23	19	4	0	1	2	11	0	23	2	0
Markert, Jackson, S.K.	3	1	.750	2.27	21	0	0	0	13	6	35.2	28	152	9	9	0	1	0	2	15	0	38	4	0
Martin, Chandler, Port.	3	0	1.000	1.32	3	3	0	0	0	0	16.0	15	67	5	5	0	0	0	2	1	0	14	0	0
Martinez, Carlos, Spo.*	1	1	.500	6.17	21	0	0	0	6	0	35.0	36	159	24	24	3	1	3	4	22	0	26	2	2
McClellan, Zachary, Spo.	2	3	.400	3.58	13	13	0	0	0	0	55.1	52	244	24	22	1	2	2	4	29	0	46	3	1
McGerry, Kevin, Van.	2	2	.500	5.91	13	5	0	0	1	0	35.0	29	155	27	23	2	1	2	3	24	0	37	8	1
Meche, Gil, Ever.	0	1	.000	9.00	1	1	0	0	0	0	1.0	3	5	1	1	0	0	0	0	0	0	0	0	0
Metzger, Jon, Spo.*	2	6	.250	3.92	13	12	0	0	0	0	62.0	46	259	32	27	0	2	2	3	34	0	64	5	5
Milo, Anthony, Boi.*	4	0	1.000	2.53	9	4	0	0	0	0	32.0	26	130	9	9	2	0	0	2	11	0	51	0	0
Minaya, Edwin, Van.	4	6	.400	4.22	19	14	0	0	0	0	74.2	71	328	46	35	5	7	2	3	28	0	55	7	0
Montero, Agustin, Yak.	1	0	1.000	6.08	7	0	0	0	3	0	13.1	12	64	9	9	0	1	0	5	7	1	21	3	0
Moore, Darin, Van.	2	7	.222	4.78	18	14	0	0	0	0	69.2	68	312	45	37	2	6	1	11	37	1	61	12	0
Moore, Greg, Boi.	3	0	.000	7.45	13	0	0	0	6	1	29.0	48	146	29	24	1	1	3	3	6	1	19	1	0
Nance, Shane, Yak.*	2	4	.333	2.48	12	9	0	0	0	0	58.0	41	228	19	16	1	2	0	2	22	0	66	2	0
Natale, Michael, Spo.	2	1	.667	1.32	23	0	0	0	18	8	41.0	30	162	7	6	0	3	1	1	13	0	43	4	0
Negron, Alex, Van.-Eug.	0	2	.000	4.30	12	0	0	0	4	0	14.2	15	68	11	7	2	1	1	2	7	1	18	1	0
Newell, Mark, Spo.*	3	3	.500	2.25	19	1	0	0	7	2	40.0	32	165	14	10	0	4	1	3	12	3	35	5	1
O'Brien, Matt, Van.*	3	3	.500	2.55	13	8	0	0	1	0	49.1	46	209	21	14	5	3	0	2	19	0	38	1	1
Olore, Kevin, Ever.	1	3	.250	2.95	26	0	0	0	7	2	55.0	50	246	28	18	5	2	1	3	28	2	64	5	0
Olson, Jason, Yak.	0	1	.000	4.34	18	0	0	0	8	1	37.1	37	170	22	18	4	2	1	2	18	1	43	3	2
O'Neal, Brandon, Boi.	1	5	.167	5.60	13	10	0	0	1	0	53.0	66	248	45	33	3	2	1	11	22	1	45	0	0
Pace, Adam, Boi.*	0	5	.000	7.10	16	9	0	0	3	2	52.0	67	238	44	41	10	4	2	3	20	0	39	2	1
Padgett, Daniel, S.K.*	2	1	.667	5.23	20	0	0	0	11	1	20.2	17	88	12	12	2	2	0	0	9	0	37	3	1
Pavon, Julio, S.K.	5	1	.833	5.63	14	2	0	0	3	1	48.0	62	221	33	30	5	3	1	2	16	1	50	3	1
Peralta, Joel, Boi.	0	0	.000	6.48	4	0	0	0	1	0	8.1	12	41	6	6	0	0	1	1	5	0	9	0	0
Ramsay, Robert, Ever.*	0	0	.000	0.00	1	1	0	0	0	0	2.0	2	8	0	0	0	0	0	0	2	0	4	0	0
Rigueiro, Rafael, S.K.	0	0	.000	4.65	28	0	0	0	4	0	40.2	38	188	24	21	1	2	1	2	31	1	52	9	1
Rijo, Fernando, Yak.	0	0	.000	3.18	3	0	0	0	2	1	5.2	5	26	3	2	0	0	0	1	0	0	5	0	0
Rincones, Rafael, Spo.	2	1	.667	2.89	18	0	0	0	11	3	28.0	26	126	11	9	2	0	1	1	17	3	37	1	1
Rodarmel, Rich, Van.	1	0	1.000	1.17	18	0	0	0	15	10	23.0	15	90	3	3	0	0	1	1	8	0	33	4	0
Rojas, Jose, Yak.	4	4	.500	3.25	19	0	0	0	2	1	52.2	45	222	26	19	3	2	1	5	19	0	47	8	1
Roney, Matt, Port.	7	5	.583	3.14	15	15	0	0	0	0	80.1	75	360	35	28	6	1	1	7	44	0	85	8	2
Russo, Mike, Ever.	0	0	.000	5.40	6	0	0	0	2	0	8.1	8	44	5	5	1	0	1	1	10	0	7	2	0
Sachse, Matt, Ever.*	2	3	.400	6.30	24	0	0	0	5	0	40.0	60	204	43	28	5	6	0	3	20	1	47	6	0
Sanchez, Cade, Van.	0	2	.000	2.20	16	0	0	0	14	6	16.1	10	73	5	4	0	1	0	1	13	2	13	3	1
Scarcella, Christopher, Van.	3	1	.750	1.64	21	0	0	0	4	0	22.0	20	103	10	4	0	0	1	0	16	0	15	6	0
Schneider, Scott, Boi.	5	2	.714	2.61	26	0	0	0	9	5	51.2	44	228	25	15	2	3	0	4	28	2	44	8	0
Seaman, John, Eug.	1	0	1.000	1.86	11	0	0	0	3	1	19.1	16	86	7	4	0	1	0	0	8	1	22	2	0

Pitcher, Team	W	L	Pct.	ERA	G	GS	CG	ShO	GF	Sv.	IP	H	TBF	R	ER	HR	SH	SF	HB	BB	IBB	SO	WP	Bk.
Smith, Joseph, S.K.	0	0	.000	0.00	3	0	0	0	0	0	5.0	3	20	0	0	0	0	0	4	0	5	0	0
Smith, Justin, Ever.*	1	0	1.000	0.75	6	0	0	0	1	0	12.0	8	47	1	1	1	1	0	1	0	11	0	0
Snider, John, Van.	1	0	1.000	3.86	7	0	0	0	2	0	9.1	11	39	4	4	1	0	0	1	2	1	7	1	0
Sprowl, Jon-Mark, Eug.	0	0	.000	0.00	1	0	0	0	1	0	2.0	1	6	0	0	0	0	0	0	0	1	0	0
Stiles, Brad, Spo.*	8	3	.727	3.78	15	15	0	0	0	0	78.2	76	344	42	33	3	4	3	7	39	0	44	6	0
Stokley, William, Boi.	5	1	.833	6.80	25	0	0	0	5	0	41.0	52	199	37	31	4	0	0	5	20	4	33	4	0
Swanson, Erick, Ever.*	3	2	.600	3.46	18	0	0	0	8	1	26.0	18	117	19	10	1	3	0	2	23	0	24	3	0
Taylor, Aaron, Ever.	1	4	.200	7.43	15	14	0	0	1	0	63.0	76	298	54	52	5	0	2	9	37	0	57	10	1
Thames, Charles, Boi.	1	1	.500	0.35	17	0	0	0	17	11	26.0	18	102	2	1	0	2	0	1	5	1	30	1	0
Thomas, Adam, Boi.	2	4	.333	7.23	8	8	0	0	0	0	37.1	47	170	37	30	3	2	2	2	13	0	28	1	5
Thomas, Jebson, Spo.	1	0	1.000	5.57	14	1	0	0	1	0	21.0	20	99	16	13	0	0	1	2	19	0	20	9	1
Thomson, John, Port.	0	0	.000	2.25	1	0	0	0	0	0	4.0	4	17	1	1	0	0	0	1	0	3	0	0
Torres, Joseph, Boi.*	4	1	.800	2.54	11	10	0	0	0	0	46.0	27	186	17	13	0	1	2	1	23	0	52	4	1
Totten, Heath, Yak.	8	2	.800	2.30	13	13	0	0	0	0	74.1	55	292	24	19	4	0	2	2	15	0	67	3	0
Tranchina, Scott, Eug.	1	2	.333	1.59	10	0	0	0	4	1	17.0	12	69	5	3	0	0	2	1	4	0	24	1	0
Treadway, Brion, S.K.	2	3	.400	2.31	8	8	0	0	0	0	35.0	35	157	19	9	2	1	2	4	17	0	29	0	2
Turner, Kyle, Spo.*	1	3	.250	5.56	5	5	0	0	0	0	22.2	29	103	16	14	1	0	1	1	11	0	16	1	0
Ugas, Juan, Yak.	1	3	.250	3.67	20	0	0	0	13	0	34.1	30	142	17	14	2	1	1	0	9	0	27	2	0
Uzzell, Todd, S.K.	1	5	.167	4.62	16	2	0	0	5	1	39.0	44	187	31	20	2	5	3	2	22	0	28	9	1
Van Buren, Jermaine, Port.	4	5	.444	2.61	13	13	0	0	0	0	69.0	54	291	27	20	1	4	2	3	30	0	41	3	2
Vance, Cory, Port.*	0	2	.000	1.11	7	3	0	0	1	0	24.1	11	93	5	3	1	3	0	2	8	0	26	1	0
Van Dusen, Derrick, Ever.	1	1	.500	3.60	4	2	0	0	0	0	15.0	17	72	13	6	1	0	1	3	5	0	24	5	0
Villacis, Eduardo, Port.	0	0	.000	0.00	5	0	0	0	2	1	4.1	4	20	1	0	0	0	0	3	1	4	0	0
Walton, Sam, Ever.*	2	0	1.000	1.44	7	6	0	0	0	0	31.1	27	133	6	5	1	1	1	0	10	0	39	4	0
Ward, Jeremy, Boi.*	2	2	.500	6.14	16	7	0	0	1	0	48.1	67	231	35	33	3	1	4	2	27	1	30	4	1
Wawrzyniak, Alan, Boi.	0	1	.000	7.45	10	0	0	0	5	0	9.2	9	53	8	8	0	1	0	1	17	0	15	1	0
Wayne, Hawkeye, Ever.	0	2	.000	12.66	12	4	0	0	1	0	21.1	29	125	31	30	3	2	1	9	29	0	22	11	0
Webb, Nicholas, Port.*	0	1	.000	5.56	16	6	0	0	3	0	43.2	52	215	37	27	3	3	3	1	29	1	52	7	2
Wellemeyer, Todd, Eug.	4	4	.500	3.67	15	15	0	0	0	0	76.0	62	315	35	31	3	1	1	4	33	2	85	3	1
Wells, Roy, Ever.	3	5	.375	5.18	14	13	0	0	0	0	66.0	74	287	41	38	9	2	2	7	17	0	59	3	0
Wilkerson, George, Spo.	0	1	.000	9.72	12	0	0	0	5	0	16.2	24	87	19	18	2	0	2	2	9	0	8	1	0
Withelder, Gregory, Yak.*	4	3	.571	3.72	10	9	0	0	0	0	48.1	43	202	21	20	2	1	1	2	19	1	57	0	0
Withers, Darvin, Van.	2	1	.667	1.74	13	6	0	0	1	1	41.1	27	166	10	8	0	1	2	1	16	2	33	3	0
Wolensky, David, Boi.	8	3	.727	3.07	15	15	0	0	0	0	76.1	60	317	29	26	1	0	1	2	35	1	88	3	0
Wright, Shayne, Boi.	0	0	.000	4.15	1	1	0	0	0	0	4.1	5	21	4	2	0	1	0	0	2	0	4	0	0
Ziegler, Mike, Van.	3	0	1.000	1.27	12	4	0	0	3	0	42.2	27	167	10	6	2	2	0	1	8	0	48	3	1

COMBINATION SHUTOUTS: **Boise (2)**—Torres-Schneider, Wolensky-Landestoy-Schneider. **Eugene (8)**—Krawiec-Beltran-Fries, Freed-Cueto, Chavez-Trachina-Albright, Krawiec-Trachina, Chavez-Albright, Freed-Beltran, Chavez-Negron-Seaman-Albright, Wellemeyer-Negron-Fries-Beltran. **Everett (4)**—Walton-Johnson-Butler, Herrera-Kent-Butler, Kent-Drain-Butler, DeJesus-Olore-Butler. **Portland (7)**—Martin-Buglovsky-Gomez, Dohmann-Goure-Little-Huisman, Van Buren-Huisman-Abell-Gomez, Roney-Lorenzo-Abell, Buglovsky-Lorenzo-Berney, Buglovsky-Goure-Lorenzo, Roney-Lorenzo. **Salem-Keizer (4)**—Farley-Farmer-Anderson-Markert, Faust-Uzzell, Ashlock-Faust, Farmer-Markert. **Spokane (3)**—Ferguson-Baranowski-Mangrum, Stiles-Rincones-Natale, Stiles-Bullinger. **Vancouver (7)**—Minaya-Brooks-Beckman-Sanchez, O'Brien-Gilpatrick-Withers, O'Brien-Fischer, Minaya-Gwyn-Ziegler-German, Brooks-Moore-Flores-Rodarmel, Brooks-Beckman, Crowell-German-Beckman. **Yakima (6)**—Kennedy-Hughes-Bauer, Langone-Bauer, Withelder-Aguilera, Kennedy-Montero, Withelder-Aguilera, Langone-Rojas.

NO-HIT GAMES: None.

PITCHERS WITH TWO OR MORE TEAMS

Pitcher, Team	W	L	Pct.	ERA	G	GS	CG	ShO	GF	Sv.	IP	H	TBF	R	ER	HR	SH	SF	HB	BB	IBB	SO	WP	Bk.
Negron, Alex, Van.	0	1	.000	1.50	4	0	0	0	2	0	6.0	5	29	5	1	0	0	0	2	3	1	7	0	0
Negron, Alex, Eug.	0	1	.000	6.23	8	0	0	0	2	0	8.2	10	39	6	6	2	1	1	0	4	0	11	1	0

2000 FIELDING

TEAM

Team	Pct.	G	PO	A	E	TC	DP	TP	PB
Yakima	.967	76	2044	812	96	2952	59	0	15
Salem-Keizer	.965	76	2044	806	102	2952	70	0	25
Everett	.964	76	2075	827	109	3011	60	0	20
Spokane	.963	76	2031	847	110	2988	61	0	11
Eugene	.960	76	2066	839	121	3026	56	0	12
Vancouver	.957	76	2014	875	130	3019	57	0	14
Boise	.954	76	2057	848	141	3046	80	0	13
Portland	.953	76	1971	803	137	2911	57	0	25

INDIVIDUAL

FIRST BASEMEN

NOTE: All caps denotes fielding-percentage leader based on 38 games for catchers, 51 for all other non-pitchers and 61 innings for pitchers. *Throws lefthanded.

Player, Team	Pct.	G	PO	A	E	TC	DP
Atkins, Garrett, Port.	.988	35	316	17	4	337	29
Barbier, Blair, Eug.	.986	59	536	36	8	580	38
Bell, Derek, S.K.	.982	45	356	21	7	384	33
Bernard, Dagoberto, Port.	1.000	1	3	1	0	4	0
Bowser, Matt, Van.*	1.000	3	30	3	0	33	1
Conway, Dan, Port.	1.000	1	4	1	0	5	0
Cook, Joshua, S.K.	.950	3	16	3	1	20	1
Dacey, Ryan, Yak.	1.000	1	2	0	0	2	1

Player, Team	Pct.	G	PO	A	E	TC	DP
Delgado, Chris, Port.	.974	3	36	1	1	38	3
Duncheon, Ryan, Boi.	.956	12	41	2	2	45	6
Felker, Jeffrey, Eug.	.971	16	92	9	3	104	8
Hattenburg, Ray, Spo.	.980	6	47	1	1	49	5
Hawpe, Bradley, Port.*	.980	25	227	19	5	251	12
Henderson, Bradley, Van.	1.000	3	15	3	0	18	0
HERTEL, Brian, Ever.	.988	58	455	22	6	483	34
Higgins, Brett, Ever.	.973	31	207	13	6	226	18
Jackson, Steve, Van.	1.000	4	27	1	0	28	0
Keating, Matthew, S.K.	.991	25	206	12	2	220	17
Kent, Mat, Ever.	1.000	2	10	0	0	10	1
Keppinger, William, Spo.*	.962	9	42	8	2	52	3
Michaelis, Derek, Yak.*	.983	58	470	38	9	517	37
Mulqueen, Dave, Port.	1.000	13	82	8	0	90	7
Rock, Jamie, Port.	1.000	2	14	0	0	14	1
Roper, Zachary, Boi.	1.000	11	71	4	0	75	8
Santos, Chad, Spo.*	.980	67	595	55	13	663	50
Santos, Deivis, S.K.*	1.000	2	14	2	0	16	2
Schied, Jeremy, Van.*	.987	73	632	53	9	694	49
Sing, Brandon, Eug.	1.000	1	3	1	0	4	0
Soto, Jorge, Van.	1.000	1	5	0	0	5	0
Soto, Saul, Yak.	.969	8	54	9	2	65	6
Sprowl, Jon-Mark, Eug.	.987	10	68	6	1	75	6
Trumble, Dan, S.K.	.974	8	74	1	2	77	3
Van Buizen, Rodney, Yak.	1.000	14	107	9	0	116	7
Wagner, Jeffrey, Boi.	.976	67	517	43	14	574	50

SECOND BASEMEN

Player, Team	Pct.	G	PO	A	E	TC	DP
Alexander, Kevin, S.K.	.967	7	15	14	1	30	7
Bernard, Dagoberto, Port.	.938	5	4	11	1	16	1
Blasi, Blake, Eug.	.969	65	120	195	10	325	38
Blocker, Kevin, Port.	.978	7	12	32	1	45	5
Bone, Blake, Ever.	.973	18	30	41	2	73	12
Cappola, Anthony, Boi.	1.000	2	1	2	0	3	1
Clements, Jason, Van.	1.000	3	2	8	0	10	1
Cook, Joshua, S.K.	.875	1	4	3	1	8	1
Crespo, Manny, Ever.	.967	28	53	66	4	123	8
Declet, Miguel, Van.	1.000	1	0	1	0	1	0
Fenster, Darren, Spo.	.966	36	61	82	5	148	15
Figueroa, Carlos, Port.	.927	27	42	72	9	123	9
Gann, Bryan, S.K.	.961	66	126	167	12	305	37
GASTELUM, Carlos, Boi.	.988	66	154	172	4	330	48
Guzman, Juan, Spo.	1.000	25	37	36	0	73	7
Hattenburg, Ray, Spo.	.941	4	8	8	1	17	1
Henderson, Bradley, Van.	.973	46	84	129	6	219	23
Herzog, Jason, Spo.	.946	9	20	15	2	37	4
Hill, Koyie, Yak.	1.000	1	1	1	0	2	1
Hoffpauir, Josh, Van.	.778	5	11	10	6	27	2
Liriano, Pedro, Ever.	.909	4	10	10	2	22	2
Martinez, Abel, Spo.	.937	19	37	37	5	79	5
Martinez, Guillermo, Ever.	.976	30	38	84	3	125	13
McDougall, Marshall, Van.	.958	24	56	81	6	143	12
Morrissey, Adam, Eug.	.968	12	19	42	2	63	4
Paulino, Miguel, Eug.	.000	1	0	0	0	0	0
Raburn, Johnny, Boi.	.980	24	46	51	2	99	12
Reynoso, Ismael, S.K.	1.000	5	10	11	0	21	4
Schmidt, J.P., Van.	1.000	1	0	1	0	1	0
Strankman, Elliott, S.K.	.833	2	1	4	1	6	0
Templeton, Garry, Boi.	.000	1	0	0	0	0	0
Van Buizen, Rodney, Yak.	.963	18	35	44	3	82	12
Ventura, Juan, Port.	.963	38	68	112	7	187	20
Victorino, Shane, Yak.	.964	60	125	172	11	308	30

THIRD BASEMEN

Player, Team	Pct.	G	PO	A	E	TC	DP
Atkins, Garrett, Port.	.913	13	4	17	2	23	2
Barbier, Blair, Eug.	.000	1	0	0	0	0	0
Bell, Derek, S.K.	.893	13	5	20	3	28	2
Bernard, Dagoberto, Port.	1.000	1	1	1	0	2	0
Blocker, Kevin, Port.	.825	12	9	24	7	40	6
Bone, Blake, Ever.	.869	34	19	54	11	84	4
Cappola, Anthony, Boi.	.792	12	1	18	5	24	1
Cook, Joshua, S.K.	.925	28	29	69	8	106	7
Cowan, Justin, Spo.	1.000	2	1	1	0	2	0
Daubert, Jake, Ever.	.937	42	34	99	9	142	13
Declet, Miguel, Van.	.839	45	24	80	20	124	8
Gemoll, Justin, Spo.	.909	8	5	15	2	22	1
Guzman, Juan, Spo.	1.000	2	0	2	0	2	0
Hattenburg, Ray, Spo.	.875	27	21	42	9	72	3
Herzog, Jason, Spo.	.727	7	1	7	3	11	0
Hill, Koyie, Yak.	.898	15	6	38	5	49	5
Hoffpauir, Josh, Van.	1.000	1	2	3	0	5	0
Kay, Kevin, Boi.	.778	4	3	4	2	9	1
KING, Brennan, Yak.	.951	54	26	128	8	162	12
Martinez, Abel, Spo.	.929	43	30	88	9	127	8
Martinez, Guillermo, Ever.	1.000	3	1	9	0	10	0
McDougall, Marshall, Van.	.909	3	4	6	1	11	0
Morrissey, Adam, Eug.	.902	47	16	85	11	112	7
Murphy, Tommy, Boi.	.933	7	1	13	1	15	2
Niekro, Lance, S.K.	.939	35	23	54	5	82	7
Peck, Bryan, Port.	.833	44	24	61	17	102	2
Raburn, Johnny, Boi.	.896	30	11	49	7	67	5
Reyes, Christian, Van.	.914	21	10	43	5	58	5
Reynoso, Ismael, S.K.	.944	5	4	13	1	18	0
Roper, Zachary, Boi.	.826	43	31	59	19	109	6
Schmidt, J.P., Van.	.905	16	13	25	4	42	0
Sing, Brandon, Eug.	.866	30	16	42	9	67	2
Sprowl, Jon-Mark, Eug.	.000	1	0	0	2	2	0
Storey, Eric, Port.	.857	6	2	10	2	14	0
Templeton, Garry, Boi.	.538	7	6	1	6	13	1
Van Buizen, Rodney, Yak.	.857	8	6	24	5	35	3

SHORTSTOPS

Player, Team	Pct.	G	PO	A	E	TC	DP
Alexander, Kevin, S.K.	.912	18	18	34	5	57	3
Barmes, Clint, Port.	.925	33	52	96	12	160	20
Bernard, Dagoberto, Port.	.911	42	74	120	19	213	21
Blocker, Kevin, Port.	1.000	1	0	3	0	3	0
Bynum, Freddie, Van.	.917	68	114	205	29	348	35
Cooper, Sam, Eug.	.943	11	6	27	2	35	5
DACEY, Ryan, Yak.	.937	54	39	109	10	158	14
Fenster, Darren, Spo.	.940	23	37	57	6	100	8
Freeman, Corey, Ever.	.934	65	93	189	20	302	33
Gemoll, Justin, Spo.	.833	1	1	4	1	6	0
Goelz, Jim, Yak.	1.000	4	5	5	0	10	2
Guzman, Juan, Spo.	.882	6	7	8	2	17	1
Herzog, Jason, Spo.	.923	10	6	18	2	26	3
Jaramillo, Milko, Yak.	.850	10	9	25	6	40	2
King, Brennan, Yak.	1.000	1	1	0	0	1	0
Maldonado, Anthony, S.K.	.933	56	74	163	17	254	31
Martinez, Dionnar, Eug.	.892	53	64	150	26	240	25
Martinez, Guillermo, Ever.	.919	14	20	48	6	74	7
Melebeck, Aaron, Spo.	.967	47	71	166	8	245	28
Morrissey, Adam, Eug.	.840	7	10	11	4	25	2
Murphy, Tommy, Boi.	.920	48	69	137	18	224	30
Paulino, Miguel, Eug.	.923	12	9	27	3	39	4
Raburn, Johnny, Boi.	.913	33	55	102	15	172	28
Repko, Jason, Yak.	.813	8	2	11	3	16	4
Reynoso, Ismael, S.K.	1.000	8	9	20	0	29	2
Schmidt, J.P., Van.	.860	13	12	31	7	50	5
Van Buizen, Rodney, Yak.	1.000	8	13	16	0	29	4
Victorino, Shane, Yak.	.000	1	0	0	0	0	0
Wright, Nate, Yak.	1.000	3	2	7	0	9	1

OUTFIELDERS

Player, Team	Pct.	G	PO	A	E	TC	DP
Alvarez, Nicholas, Yak.	.943	56	76	6	5	87	0
Barmes, Clint, Port.	1.000	9	23	0	0	23	0
Betts, Dewayne, Van.	1.000	6	7	0	0	7	0
Bowser, Matt, Van.*	.966	58	83	2	3	88	0
Bubela, Jaime, Ever.	.940	30	43	4	3	50	0
Carter, Bryan, S.K.*	1.000	48	61	4	0	65	1
Cash, Condor, Eug.	.937	50	58	1	4	63	0
Chirinos, Germain, Van.	.933	21	27	1	2	30	0
Cirone, Joseph, Van.	.970	50	63	2	2	67	0
Clements, Jason, Van.	.941	13	15	1	1	17	0
Cordova, Ben, Spo.*	.926	59	106	7	9	122	1
Coulie, Jason, Boi.	.948	61	119	9	7	135	1
Covington, Kevin, Yak.	.973	43	71	2	2	75	1
Cowan, Justin, Spo.	.923	24	21	3	2	26	0
Crespo, Manny, Ever.	1.000	7	5	0	0	5	0
Cunningham, Marco, Spo.	.979	71	135	4	3	142	2
Declet, Miguel, Van.	1.000	2	1	0	0	1	0
Devine, Rich, Spo.	.917	12	11	0	1	12	0
Ellison, Jason, S.K.	.976	70	155	7	4	166	2
Felker, Jeffrey, Eug.	.000	3	0	0	0	0	0
Graham, Peter, Eug.	.925	38	36	1	3	40	0
Guzman, Javier, Port.	.982	27	53	2	1	56	0
Hattenburg, Ray, Spo.	1.000	4	4	0	0	4	0
Hawpe, Bradley, Port.*	1.000	26	33	3	0	36	0
Hertel, Brian, Ever.	.857	5	6	0	1	7	0
Holt, Daylan, Van.	1.000	30	40	0	0	40	0
Jackson, Brandon, Boi.*	1.000	5	2	0	0	2	0
Jackson, Nicolas, Eug.	.962	73	120	6	5	131	3
Kay, Kevin, Boi.	.000	1	0	0	0	0	0
Keller, G.W., Van.	.990	61	90	6	1	97	1
Keppinger, William, Spo.*	.960	31	45	3	2	50	0
Knight, Marcus, Boi.	1.000	1	4	0	0	4	0
Langs, Ronte, Van.	.969	55	94	1	3	98	0
Lopez, Chuck, Ever.*	.938	29	29	1	2	32	1
Mallory, Michael, Eug.	.944	69	129	5	8	142	2
Martinez, Abel, Spo.	.000	1	0	0	0	0	0
Martinez, Candido, Yak.	.942	28	48	1	3	52	0
Morency, Vernand, Port.	.976	48	121	2	3	126	0
Mounts, J.R., Boi.	.974	54	110	4	3	117	3
Paredes, Reny, Eug.	1.000	20	15	2	0	17	0
Peck, Bryan, Port.	1.000	6	3	0	0	3	0
Pekar, Jason, S.K.	.944	9	15	2	1	18	0
Pena, Pelagio, Ever.	1.000	6	6	2	0	8	0
Pride, Joshua, Port.	1.000	3	3	0	0	3	0
Quintana, Wilfredo, Ever.	.897	21	21	5	3	29	0
Raburn, Johnny, Boi.	.000	1	0	0	0	0	0
Richardson, Miguel, Ever.	.958	50	65	4	3	72	1
Rock, Jamie, Port.	.967	50	81	8	3	92	0
Roper, Zachary, Boi.	1.000	4	9	0	0	9	0
Rosario, Vicente, Ever.	.931	21	27	0	2	29	0
Schmidt, J.P., Van.	1.000	6	2	0	0	2	0
Shabala, Adam, S.K.	.971	41	63	3	2	68	1
Smiley, Jermaine, Spo.*	.984	45	56	5	1	62	0
Sosa, Jorge, Port.	.903	44	61	4	7	72	1

Player, Team	Pct.	G	PO	A	E	TC	DP
Strong, Jamal, Ever.	.988	74	159	3	2	164	1
Templeton, Garry, Boi.	1.000	4	1	0	0	1	0
Testa, Chris, Port.*	1.000	5	10	0	0	10	0
THOMAS, Charles, Yak.	1.000	55	102	3	0	105	2
Trumble, Dan, S.K.	.000	3	0	0	0	0	0
Ventura, Juan, Port.	.935	17	28	1	2	31	0
Walker, Mark, S.K.	.962	28	24	1	1	26	0
Warner, J.R., Boi.*	.964	74	69	12	3	84	1
Welch, Edward, Boi.	1.000	30	47	1	0	48	0
Wilfong, Nick, S.K.	1.000	52	58	7	0	65	0
Withey, Ryan, Boi.	.821	15	21	2	5	28	0

CATCHERS

Player, Team	Pct.	G	PO	A	E	TC	DP	PB
Alvarez, Henrry, Spo.	.968	16	84	8	3	95	1	2
Aracena, Sandy, Yak.	.991	26	211	19	2	232	3	8
Carroll, Mark, Ever.	.984	39	330	40	6	376	2	6
Cerda, Jose, S.K.	.979	15	129	12	3	144	1	4
Conway, Dan, Port.	.973	44	298	32	9	339	0	15
Cowan, Justin, Spo.	.993	22	132	15	1	148	0	1
Craig, Beau, Van.	.961	19	110	12	5	127	0	2
D'Jesus, Francisco, S.K.	1.000	1	10	1	0	11	1	1
Duncheon, Ryan, Boi.	1.000	1	1	0	0	1	0	0
Duverge, Alcides, Boi.	1.000	1	1	1	0	2	0	0
Felix, Hersy, Spo.	.988	50	298	42	4	344	0	5
Halgren, Chris, Van.	.985	24	119	11	2	132	3	13
Hill, Koyie, Yak.	.964	11	79	2	3	84	0	2
Jorgensen, Ryan, Eug.	.986	38	336	29	5	370	2	6
Kay, Kevin, Boi.	.970	15	64	1	2	67	0	0
Kent, Mat, Ever.	.977	21	160	10	4	174	0	5
KWEON, Yoon-Min, Eug.	1.000	41	374	35	0	409	2	4
Lunsford, James, S.K.	.987	59	490	58	7	555	9	17
Madera, Sandy, Van.	.979	12	84	9	2	95	1	2
Mounts, J.R., Boi.	1.000	1	3	0	0	3	0	1
Ortega, Sixto, Port.	1.000	6	34	5	0	39	0	1
Peck, Bryan, Port.	1.000	1	1	0	0	1	0	0
Pena, Pelagio, Ever.	.971	29	215	20	7	242	1	9
Pena, Wilton, Van.	.988	43	282	40	4	326	3	9
Pina, Enmanuel, Eug.	1.000	1	0	2	0	2	0	1
Pride, Joshua, Port.	1.000	8	54	11	0	65	1	0
Rogers, Brandon, Boi.	.986	31	192	27	3	222	1	6
Socarras, Antonio, Boi.	.988	51	367	35	5	407	2	7
Soto, Saul, Yak.	.989	46	417	24	5	446	2	5
Sprowl, Jon-Mark, Eug.	1.000	3	4	0	0	4	0	1
Tejada, Michael, Port.	.949	25	152	15	9	176	0	9
Turco, Anthony, S.K.	1.000	3	20	5	0	25	0	3
Walter, Scott, Spo.	1.000	12	67	9	0	76	0	3
Wilson, Dan, Ever.	1.000	1	3	1	0	4	0	0

PITCHERS

Player, Team	Pct.	G	PO	A	E	TC	DP
Abell, Joe, Port.	1.000	24	2	2	0	4	0
Aguilera, Adrian, Yak.*	.929	17	3	10	1	14	2
Albright, Eric, Eug.	1.000	27	2	10	0	12	1
Alvarez, Larry, Eug.	.750	18	3	6	3	12	0
Anderson, Luke, S.K.	1.000	25	5	4	0	9	0
Ashlock, Chad, S.K.	1.000	2	0	2	0	2	0
Baker, Joseph, Spo.	.900	14	8	10	2	20	2
Baranowski, Brannon, Spo.	.857	19	2	4	1	7	0
Barker, Richie, Eug.	1.000	10	0	4	0	4	0
Bauer, Gregory, Yak.	.889	21	4	4	1	9	0
Beckman, Jacob, Van.	1.000	12	2	5	0	7	0
Beltran, Francis, Eug.	.857	25	2	4	1	7	0
Berney, Scott, Port.	1.000	15	2	5	0	7	0
Bonser, Boof, S.K.	1.000	10	3	2	0	5	0
Bridenbaugh, Christian, Yak.*	1.000	7	0	11	0	11	0
Brooks, Conor, Van.	1.000	18	3	13	0	16	0
Buglovsky, Christopher, Port.	1.000	14	5	7	0	12	1
Bukowski, Stanislaw, Boi.	.000	5	0	0	0	0	0
Bukvich, Ryan, Spo.	1.000	10	1	4	0	5	0
Bullinger, Frederick, Spo.	.000	16	0	0	0	0	0
Burton, Timothy, Ever.	.000	3	0	0	0	0	0
Butler, John, Ever.	.875	30	1	6	1	8	0
Chavez, Wilton, Eug.	.818	15	6	12	4	22	1
Cordero, Frangil, Eug.*	.714	6	0	5	2	7	0
Crowell, Kyle, Van.	.889	17	7	9	2	18	1
Cueto, Jose, Eug.	.889	13	4	4	1	9	0
DeJesus, Tony, Ever.*	.944	15	3	14	1	18	0
Diaz, Alex, Van.	.000	2	0	0	1	1	0
Diaz, Felix, S.K.	1.000	3	2	0	0	2	0
Dohmann, Christopher, Port.	.700	5	2	5	3	10	0
Drain, Bradley, Ever.	.500	14	0	1	1	2	0

Player, Team	Pct.	G	PO	A	E	TC	DP
Duverge, Alcides, Boi.	.000	2	0	0	0	0	0
Ericks, Dave, Eug.	1.000	10	0	4	0	4	0
Faas, Matthew, S.K.	.889	24	1	7	1	9	1
Farley, Joseph, S.K.*	.900	16	2	7	1	10	1
Farmer, Jason, S.K.	.818	16	3	6	2	11	0
Faust, Wesley, S.K.	.957	15	6	16	1	23	0
Featherstone, Deron, S.K.	.333	12	0	1	2	3	0
Ferguson, Ian, Spo.	1.000	15	6	10	0	16	1
Fingers, Jason, Spo.	1.000	18	2	9	0	11	0
Fischer, Steve, Van.	1.000	18	2	8	0	10	1
Flading, Cameron, Boi.	.000	3	0	0	0	0	0
Flores, Ron, Van.*	1.000	13	1	2	0	3	0
Franke, Aaron, Boi.	.800	6	1	3	1	5	0
Freed, Mark, Eug.*	.966	15	4	24	1	29	2
Fries, Scott, Eug.*	1.000	26	2	13	0	15	2
Garcia, Freddy, Ever.	1.000	2	0	5	0	5	0
Garner, Brandon, Port.	1.000	18	2	5	0	7	0
German, Franklyn, Van.	1.000	9	1	2	0	3	0
Gilmore, Travis, Boi.*	.000	3	0	0	0	0	0
Gilpatrick, Tyler, Van.	1.000	15	4	4	0	8	0
Glidewell, Clifton, Yak.*	1.000	10	0	1	0	1	0
Gomez, Diogenes, Port.	1.000	25	1	5	0	6	0
Goure, Sam, Port.*	1.000	22	3	3	0	6	0
Graham, Elgin, S.K.	1.000	19	2	5	0	7	0
Green, Sean, Port.	.714	22	0	5	2	7	0
Gross, Kyle, S.K.	.833	8	2	3	1	6	0
Gruban, Jarret, Boi.	1.000	6	1	2	0	3	1
Gwyn, Marcus, Van.	.917	12	2	9	1	12	0
Haase, Frank, Port.*	1.000	5	0	1	0	1	0
Hampson, Justin, Port.*	.875	14	6	15	3	24	2
Hannaman, Ryan, S.K.*	.000	1	0	0	0	0	0
Harrelson, Ralph, S.K.	1.000	6	0	5	0	5	0
Haworth, Brent, Boi.	1.000	5	2	2	0	4	0
Head, Daniel, Ever.	.500	10	1	0	1	2	0
Henderson, Bradley, Van.	1.000	1	0	3	0	3	0
Herrera, Jose, Ever.	.917	14	4	7	1	12	0
Hertel, Brian, Ever.	1.000	2	1	0	0	1	0
Hughes, Nial, Yak.*	.875	16	2	5	1	8	0
Huie, Bryan, Ever.*	1.000	10	1	3	0	4	0
Huisman, Justin, Port.	.933	16	4	10	1	15	0
Johnson, Eric, S.K.	.444	8	1	3	5	9	0
Johnson, Everett, Ever.	1.000	17	3	14	0	17	2
Kennedy, Casey, Yak.	.870	13	4	16	3	23	0
Kent, Steven, Ever.*	1.000	24	4	7	0	11	1
Keppinger, William, Spo.*	1.000	1	0	1	0	1	1
KRAWIEC, Aaron, Eug.*	1.000	14	3	17	0	20	0
Landestoy, Gilbert, Boi.	1.000	28	7	11	0	18	0
Langone, Steve, Yak.	.962	15	9	16	1	26	0
Lee, Tymber, Boi.	1.000	22	0	3	0	3	0
Leicester, Jonathan, Eug.	.929	17	2	11	1	14	0
Little, Roger, Port.	1.000	13	1	3	0	4	1
Lorenzo, Javier, Port.	.800	18	0	4	1	5	0
Mangrum, Micah, Spo.	.857	20	2	4	1	7	0
Marin, Willy, Yak.	.900	19	3	6	1	10	0
Markert, Jackson, S.K.	1.000	21	1	4	0	5	0
Martin, Chandler, Port.	.667	3	0	2	1	3	0
Martinez, Carlos, Spo.*	.833	21	1	9	2	12	2
McClellan, Zachary, Spo.	.938	13	5	10	1	16	2
McGerry, Kevin, Van.	1.000	13	2	4	0	6	0
Meche, Gil, Ever.	1.000	1	0	1	0	1	0
Metzger, Jon, Spo.*	.909	13	5	5	1	11	0
Milo, Anthony, Boi.*	.917	9	3	8	1	12	0
Minaya, Edwin, Van.	.810	19	7	10	4	21	0
Montero, Agustin, Yak.	1.000	7	0	1	0	1	0
Moore, Darin, Van.	.852	18	9	14	4	27	0
Moore, Greg, Boi.	1.000	13	2	4	0	6	1
Nance, Shane, Yak.*	1.000	12	6	8	0	14	0
Natale, Michael, Spo.	1.000	23	1	3	0	4	0
Negron, Alex, Van.-Eug.	1.000	12	0	3	0	3	0
Newell, Mark, Spo.*	1.000	19	5	6	0	11	1
O'Brien, Matt, Van.*	1.000	13	3	7	0	10	0
Olore, Kevin, Ever.	1.000	26	1	5	0	6	1
Olson, Jason, Yak.	.667	18	1	3	2	6	0
O'Neal, Brandon, Boi.	.778	13	4	10	4	18	0
Pace, Adam, Boi.*	.900	16	0	9	1	10	0
Padgett, Daniel, S.K.*	.600	20	0	3	2	5	0
Pavon, Julio, S.K.	.938	14	1	14	1	16	0
Peralta, Joel, Boi.	1.000	4	1	0	0	1	0
Ramsay, Robert, Ever.*	.000	1	0	0	0	0	0
Riguero, Rafael, S.K.	1.000	28	1	4	0	5	0
Rijo, Fernando, Yak.	.500	3	0	1	1	2	0
Rincones, Rafael, Spo.	.500	18	0	1	1	2	0
Rodarmel, Rich, Van.	1.000	18	2	0	0	2	0

Player, Team	Pct.	G	PO	A	E	TC	DP
Rojas, Jose, Yak.	1.000	13	3	14	0	17	1
Roney, Matt, Port.	.947	15	6	12	1	19	1
Russo, Mike, Ever.	1.000	6	0	1	0	1	0
Sachse, Matt, Ever.*	1.000	24	2	8	0	10	0
Sanchez, Cade, Van.	.750	16	1	2	1	4	0
Scarcella, Christopher, Van.	.750	21	2	1	1	4	0
Schneider, Scott, Boi.	.786	26	3	8	3	14	0
Seaman, John, Eug.	.833	11	1	4	1	6	1
Smith, Joseph, S.K.	1.000	3	1	0	0	1	0
Smith, Justin, Ever.*	1.000	6	0	1	0	1	0
Snider, John, Van.	1.000	7	0	1	0	1	0
Sprowl, Jon-Mark, Eug.	.000	1	0	0	0	0	0
Stiles, Brad, Spo.*	.870	15	3	17	3	23	2
Stokley, William, Boi.	.857	25	4	8	2	14	1
Swanson, Erick, Ever.*	1.000	18	0	1	0	1	0
Taylor, Aaron, Ever.	1.000	15	6	10	0	16	2
Thames, Charles, Boi.	1.000	17	2	4	0	6	0
Thomas, Adam, Boi.	.667	8	0	4	2	6	0
Thomas, Jebson, Spo.	1.000	14	1	2	0	3	0
Thomson, John, Port.	.000	1	0	0	0	0	0
Torres, Joseph, Boi.*	1.000	11	2	4	0	6	1
Totten, Heath, Yak.	1.000	13	3	9	0	12	0
Tranchina, Scott, Eug.	.800	10	2	2	1	5	0
Treadway, Brion, S.K.	.800	8	1	3	1	5	0
Turner, Kyle, Spo.*	1.000	5	2	5	0	7	0
Ugas, Juan, Yak.	1.000	20	4	5	0	9	0

Player, Team	Pct.	G	PO	A	E	TC	DP
Uzzell, Todd, S.K.	.900	16	3	6	1	10	0
Van Buren, Jermaine, Port.	.905	13	5	14	2	21	1
Van Dusen, Derrick, Ever.	.500	4	1	0	1	2	0
Vance, Cory, Port.*	1.000	7	2	5	0	7	0
Villacis, Eduardo, Port.	1.000	5	0	2	0	2	0
Walton, Sam, Ever.*	1.000	7	1	4	0	5	0
Ward, Jeremy, Boi.*	.900	16	2	7	1	10	0
Wawrzyniak, Alan, Boi.	.000	10	0	0	0	0	0
Wayne, Hawkeye, Ever.	.889	12	2	6	1	9	0
Webb, Nicholas, Port.*	.833	16	1	9	2	12	1
Wellemeyer, Todd, Eug.	1.000	15	4	5	0	9	1
Wells, Roy, Ever.	1.000	14	5	8	0	13	1
Wilkerson, George, Spo.	.667	12	1	1	1	3	0
Withelder, Gregory, Yak.*	1.000	10	1	8	0	9	0
Withers, Darvin, Van.	.800	13	0	4	1	5	0
Wolensky, David, Boi.	.850	15	6	11	3	20	1
Wright, Shayne, Boi.	1.000	1	0	1	0	1	0
Ziegler, Mike, Van.	1.000	12	2	9	0	11	0

PITCHERS WITH TWO OR MORE TEAMS

Player, Team	Pct.	G	PO	A	E	TC	DP
Negron, Alex, Van.	1.000	4	0	1	0	1	0
Negron, Alex, Eug.	1.000	8	0	2	0	2	0

The following players appeared only as designated hitter, pinch-hitter or pinch runner: Downing, dh-ph; Riley, ph; Sarna, dh.

LEAGUE CHAMPIONS

Year	Team	Pct.
1901—	Portland	.675
1902—	Butte	.608
1903—	Butte	.578
1904—	Boise	.625
1905—	Vancouver	.586
	Everett*	.667
1906—	Tacoma	.600
1907—	Aberdeen	.625
1908—	Vancouver	.578
1909—	Seattle	.653
1910—	Spokane	.596
1911—	Vancouver	.628
1912—	Seattle	.600
1913—	Vancouver	.600
1914—	Vancouver	.632
1915—	Seattle	.564
1916—	Spokane	.622
1917—	Great Falls	.592
1918—	Seattle	.588
1919—	Seattle	.590
1920—	Victoria	.600
1921—	Yakima	.710
	Yakima	.660
1922—	Calgary‡	.600
1923-36—Did not operate.		
1937—	Wenatchee	.603
	Tacoma*	.627
1938—	Yakima	.583
	Bellingham (2nd)†	.511
1939—	Wenatchee	.601
	Tacoma (2nd)†	.533
1940—	Spokane	.587
	Tacoma (4th)†	.500
1941—	Spokane	.669
1942—	Vancouver	.594
1943-45—Did not operate.		
1946—	Wenatchee	.622
1947—	Vancouver	.566
1948—	Spokane	.614
1949—	Yakima	.660
	Vancouver (2nd)†	.615
1950—	Yakima	.613
1951—	Spokane	.655
1952—	Victoria	.631
1953—	Salem	.635
	Spokane*	.590

Year	Team	Pct.
1954—	Vancouver*	.636
	Lewiston	.629
1955—	Salem	.646
	Eugene*	.639
1956—	Yakima	.691
	Yakima	.619
1957—	Eugene	.576
	Wenatchee*	.647
1958—	Lewiston	.621
	Yakima*	.594
1959—	Salem	.623
	Yakima*	.563
1960—	Yakima	.638
	Yakima	.562
1961—	Lewiston*	.621
	Yakima	.600
1962—	Wenatchee*	.574
	Tri-City	.580
1963—	Lewiston	.594
	Yakima*	.613
1964—	Eugene	.636
	Yakima*	.611
1965—	Lewiston	.667
	Tri-City*	.681
1966—	Tri-City	.679
1967—	Medford	.607
1968—	Tri-City	.600
1969—	Rogue Valley	.633
1970—	Lewiston§	.538
	Coos Bay-No. Bend	.563
1971—	Tri-City§	.625
	Bend	.538
1972—	Lewiston§	.675
	Walla Walla	.513
1973—	Walla Walla∞	.638
	Portland	.563
1974—	Bellingham	.619
	Eugene▲	.571
1975—	Portland	.545
	Eugene◆	.684
1976—	Portland	.556
	Walla Walla◆	.639
1977—	Bellingham■	.618
	Portland	.667
1978—	Grays Harbor▼	.671
	Eugene	.514

Year	Team	Pct.
1979—	Central Oregon◆	.606
	Walla Walla	.571
1980—	Bellingham•	.643
	Eugene•	.529
1981—	Medford◆	.600
	Bellingham	.557
1982—	Medford	.757
	Salem◆	.486
1983—	Medford††	.735
	Bellingham	.588
1984—	Tri-Cities††	.622
	Medford	.608
1985—	Everett††	.541
	Eugene	.541
1986—	Bellingham††	.608
	Eugene	.608
1987—	Spokane▲	.711
	Everett	.653
1988—	Southern Oregon	.605
	Spokane◆	.553
1989—	Southern Oregon	.600
	Spokane◆	.547
1990—	Boise	.697
	Spokane◆	.645
1991—	Boise◆	.658
	Yakima	.579
1992—	Bellingham◆	.566
	Bend	.566
1993—	Bellingham	.579
	Boise◆	.539
1994—	Yakima	.645
	Boise◆	.579
1995—	Boise◆	.640
	Bellingham	.566
1996—	Eugene	.645
	Yakima§	.526
1997—	Boise	.671
	Portland◆	.579
1998—	Spokane	.618
	Boise	.618
	Salem-Keizer◆	.566
1999—	Spokane◆	.579
2000—	Yakima◆	.539
	Boise	.539

*Won split-season playoff. †Won four-club playoff. ‡League disbanded June 18. §League divided into Northern and Southern divisions, declared champion under league rules. ∞League divided into Eastern and Western divisions, declared champion under league rules. ▲League divided into Eastern and Western divisions; won two-team playoff. ◆League divided into North and South divisions; won two-team playoff. ■League divided into Affiliate and Independent divisions; won two-team playoff. ▼Declared league champion after winning one-game playoff. Balance of playoff canceled due to rain and wet grounds. •Declared co-champion after winning one game. Balance of playoff canceled due to rain and wet grounds. ††League divided into Washington and Oregon divisions; won two-team playoff. (NOTE—Known as Pacific Northwest League 1901-02, Pacific National League 1903-04, Northwestern League 1905-18, Pacific Coast International League 1919-22 and Western International League 1937-54.)

CLASS A Northwest League

SOUTH ATLANTIC LEAGUE

LEAGUE OFFICE

President/secretary-treasurer
John Moss
Address
P.O. Box 38
Kings Mountain, NC 28086
Phone
704-739-3466

Teams (affiliation)
Asheville Tourists (Rockies)
Augusta Greenjackets (Red Sox)
Capital City Bombers (Mets)
Charleston (S.C.) Riverdogs (Devil Rays)
Charleston (W.Va.) Alley Cats (Blue Jays)
Columbus Redstixx (Indians)
Delmarva Shorebirds (Orioles)
Greensboro Bats (Yankees)

Hagerstown Suns (Giants)
Hickory Crawdads (Pirates)
Kannapolis Intimidators (White Sox)
Lakewood BlueClaws (Phillies)
Lexington Legends (Astros)
Macon Braves (Braves)
Savannah Sand Gnats (Rangers)
Wilmington (N.C.) Waves (Dodgers)

2000 FINAL STANDINGS

FIRST HALF

NORTHERN DIVISION

Team	W	L	T	Pct.	GB
Piedmont (Phillies)	47	24	0	.662	...
Delmarva (Orioles)	38	32	0	.543	8.5
Cape Fear (Expos)	38	33	0	.535	9.0
Hickory (Pirates)	36	35	0	.507	11.0
Hagerstown (Blue Jays)	34	36	0	.486	12.5
Greensboro (Yankees)	34	37	0	.479	13.0
Charleston, W.Va. (Royals)	24	47	0	.338	23.0

SOUTHERN DIVISION

Team	W	L	T	Pct.	GB
Columbus (Indians)	42	29	0	.592	...
Augusta (Red Sox)	38	33	0	.535	4.0
Charleston, S.C. (Devil Rays)	35	35	0	.500	6.5
Asheville (Rockies)	34	35	0	.493	7.0
Macon (Braves)	35	36	0	.493	7.0
Savannah (Rangers)	33	38	0	.465	9.0
Columbia (Mets)	26	44	0	.371	15.5

SECOND HALF

NORTHERN DIVISION

Team	W	L	T	Pct.	GB
Piedmont (Phillies)	43	23	0	.652	...
Hickory (Pirates)	39	31	0	.557	6.0
Delmarva (Orioles)	36	30	0	.545	7.0
Charleston, W.Va. (Royals)	29	33	0	.468	12.0
Hagerstown (Blue Jays)	29	38	0	.433	14.5
Cape Fear (Expos)	26	41	0	.388	17.5
Greensboro (Yankees)	22	44	0	.333	21.0

SOUTHERN DIVISION

Team	W	L	T	Pct.	GB
Augusta (Red Sox)	45	25	0	.643	...
Savannah (Rangers)	41	27	0	.603	3.0
Charleston, S.C. (Devil Rays)	38	31	0	.551	6.5
Macon (Braves)	34	34	0	.500	10.0
Asheville (Rockies)	32	34	0	.485	11.0
Columbia (Mets)	30	37	0	.448	13.5
Columbus (Indians)	25	41	0	.379	18.0

COMPOSITE

Team	Pied.	Aug.	Del.	Sav.	Hick.	CSC	Mac.	C'bus	Ash.	C.F.	Hag.	Gbr.	C'bia	CWV	W	L	T	Pct.	GB
Piedmont (Phillies)	...	6	6	7	12	8	4	3	6	7	8	10	5	8	90	47	0	.657	...
Augusta (Red Sox)	5	...	8	6	3	6	6	11	8	5	6	4	9	6	83	58	0	.589	9.0
Delmarva (Orioles)	8	0	...	2	8	2	6	4	4	9	10	7	4	10	74	62	0	.544	15.5
Savannah (Rangers)	1	10	6	...	2	7	4	10	7	6	4	5	7	5	74	65	0	.532	17.0
Hickory (Pirates)	4	5	4	6	...	4	6	4	4	6	7	12	6	7	75	66	0	.532	17.0
Charleston, S.C. (Devil Rays)	0	6	5	8	4	...	10	9	7	2	5	4	10	3	73	66	0	.525	18.0
Macon (Braves)	4	5	2	11	2	5	...	8	8	4	3	4	8	5	69	70	0	.496	22.0
Columbus (Indians)	5	5	4	5	4	7	7	...	5	4	1	7	6	7	67	70	0	.489	23.0
Asheville (Rockies)	2	4	4	4	7	5	8	3	...	3	6	2	11	7	66	69	0	.489	23.0
Cape Fear (Expos)	2	3	6	2	6	5	4	4	5	...	6	8	5	8	64	74	0	.464	26.5
Hagerstown (Blue Jays)	4	2	4	4	5	3	4	6	1	10	...	8	4	8	63	74	0	.460	27.0
Greensboro (Yankees)	5	4	5	3	3	3	4	1	6	8	8	...	3	3	56	81	0	.409	34.0
Columbia (Mets)	3	6	4	4	2	6	4	6	7	3	3	5	...	3	56	81	0	.409	34.0
Charleston, W.Va. (Royals)	4	2	4	3	8	5	3	1	1	7	7	5	3	...	53	80	0	.398	35.0

FORFEIT: Columbus forfeited to Hagerstown, July 9 (Hagerstown won 9-0).

Major league affiliations in parentheses.

PLAYOFFS: Columbus defeated Augusta two games to one; Delmarva defeated Piedmont two games to one; Delmarva defeated Columbus three games to none to win league championship.

REGULAR-SEASON ATTENDANCE: Asheville, 162,395; Augusta, 136,060; Cape Fear, 33,510; Charleston, S.C., 240,069; Charleston, W.Va., 91,434; Columbia, 108,852; Columbus, 113,856; Delmarva, 264,924; Greensboro, 131,925; Hagerstown, 102,443; Hickory, 183,922; Macon, 127,470; Piedmont, 119,234; Savannah, 135,351. Total—1,951,445. Playoffs (9 games)—12,752. All-Star Game at Charleston, S.C.—5,565.

MANAGERS: Asheville, Joe Mikulik; Augusta, Mike Boulanger; Cape Fear, Bill Masse; Charleston, S.C., Charlie Montoyo; Charleston, W.Va., Joe Szekely; Columbia, John Stephenson; Columbus, Ricky Gutierrez; Delmarva, Joe Ferguson; Greensboro, Stan Hough; Hagerstown, Rolando Pino; Hickory, Jay Loviglio; Macon, Jeff Treadway; Piedmont, Greg Legg; Savannah, Paul Carey.

ALL-STAR TEAM: 1B—Nate Espy, Piedmont; 2B—Torre Tyson, Greensboro; 3B—Nate Grindell, Columbus; SS—Brandon Jackson, Hagerstown; Utility INF—Napolean Calzado, Delmarva; OF—Josh Hamilton, Charleston, S.C.; Marlon Byrd, Piedmont; Lew Ford, Augusta; Utility OF—Jay Sitzman, Piedmont; Casey Crawford, Charleston, S.C.; C—J.R. House, Hickory; RHP—Chin-Hui Tsao, Asheville; LHP—Dave Williams, Hickory; Manager—Greg Legg, Piedmont; Coach—Jerry Martin, Piedmont; Most Valuable Player—Josh Hamilton, Charleston, S.C.; J.R. House, Asheville; Most Outstanding Major League Prospect—Josh Hamilton, Charleston, S.C.

TEAM

Team	Avg.	G	TPA	AB	R	H	TB	2B	3B	HR	RBI	SH	SF	HP	BB	IBB	SO	SB	CS	GDP	LOB	ShO	Slg.	OBP
Hickory	.275	141	5532	4935	762	1359	2068	255	32	130	689	27	37	77	456	15	1261	178	77	86	981	4	.419	.344
Piedmont	.270	137	5214	4600	709	1244	1829	233	38	92	626	38	45	76	455	11	1020	209	59	90	984	6	.398	.343
Charleston, S.C.	.262	139	5309	4820	670	1265	1844	266	32	83	590	29	43	91	326	12	1079	145	42	79	958	3	.383	.319
Augusta	.258	141	5329	4675	692	1206	1817	248	39	95	609	35	32	93	494	16	1131	158	64	105	989	5	.389	.339
Delmarva	.256	136	5271	4557	700	1166	1607	201	42	52	590	55	37	71	551	12	908	188	66	83	1018	8	.353	.343
Columbus	.254	137	5205	4569	651	1159	1665	198	37	78	562	24	46	69	497	7	1106	237	55	85	958	3	.364	.333
Savannah	.253	139	5154	4518	585	1144	1638	209	36	71	512	51	47	71	467	11	923	202	78	87	957	11	.363	.330
Cape Fear	.253	138	5131	4583	633	1158	1603	209	37	54	567	22	36	61	429	11	931	239	70	87	892	7	.350	.323
Greensboro	.250	137	5228	4605	630	1153	1690	213	27	90	566	29	32	79	483	8	1234	112	65	74	1019	14	.367	.330
Macon	.250	139	5284	4675	626	1168	1760	234	23	104	574	27	30	79	473	9	1024	128	67	89	1004	8	.376	.327
Columbia	.247	137	5107	4511	533	1113	1534	225	26	48	458	36	33	83	444	11	1039	185	80	71	993	9	.340	.323
Hagerstown	.245	137	5116	4444	621	1088	1555	204	31	67	543	30	31	86	525	5	1056	152	65	76	986	7	.350	.334
Asheville	.244	135	5005	4444	560	1085	1684	229	14	114	503	18	26	82	435	8	1228	173	105	82	883	6	.379	.321
Charleston, W.V.	.236	133	4901	4274	505	1010	1401	179	37	46	449	42	33	72	480	6	966	114	56	106	936	12	.328	.321

INDIVIDUAL

TOP QUALIFIERS FOR BATTING CHAMPIONSHIP

Minimum 383 plate appearances. *Lefthanded batter. †Switch-hitter.

Player, Team	Avg.	G	TPA	AB	R	H	TB	2B	3B	HR	RBI	SH	SF	HP	BB	IBB	SO	SB	CS	GDP	Slg.	OBP
House, J.R., Hick.	.348	110	478	420	78	146	246	29	1	23	90	0	6	6	46	2	91	1	2	7	.586	.414
Sitzman, Jim, Pied.*	.316	107	478	418	95	132	183	17	8	6	55	2	5	15	38	3	88	53	12	3	.438	.389
Ford, Lew, Aug.	.315	126	583	514	122	162	246	35	11	9	74	3	2	12	52	3	83	52	4	12	.479	.390
Jackson, Brandon, Hag.	.312	110	456	391	71	122	170	17	8	5	52	1	8	13	43	0	83	5	6	6	.435	.391
Espy, Nate, Pied.	.312	130	561	452	88	141	240	32	2	21	87	0	4	4	101	7	105	7	0	12	.531	.439
Byrd, Marlon, Pied.	.309	133	582	515	104	159	265	29	13	17	93	1	5	10	51	0	110	41	5	7	.515	.379
Cadiente, Brett, Sav.*	.309	129	566	499	83	154	205	15	9	6	50	7	8	1	51	1	112	31	15	6	.411	.369
Rodriguez, Carlos, Aug.	.306	116	504	470	62	144	236	28	5	18	94	0	5	12	17	2	108	24	12	9	.502	.343
Padilla, Jorge, Pied.	.305	108	445	413	62	126	199	24	8	11	67	0	4	2	26	0	89	8	4	10	.482	.346
Pressley, Josh, C.S.C.*	.303	130	544	488	61	148	210	44	0	6	61	0	3	4	49	2	61	2	1	17	.430	.369
Ross, Donovan, C.W.Va.*	.303	105	429	360	54	109	178	20	5	13	61	5	1	7	56	1	72	1	4	13	.494	.406
Hamilton, Josh, C.S.C.*	.302	96	423	391	62	118	186	23	3	13	61	0	3	2	27	3	71	14	6	5	.476	.348
Crawford, Carl, C.S.C.*	.301	135	611	564	99	170	231	21	11	6	57	9	1	3	32	1	102	55	9	1	.410	.342
Blalock, Hank, Sav.*	.299	139	590	512	66	153	219	32	2	10	77	0	11	5	62	3	53	31	8	14	.428	.373
Castillo, Jose, Hick.	.299	125	577	529	95	158	254	32	8	16	72	7	2	10	29	0	107	16	12	10	.480	.346

DEPARTMENTAL LEADERS: G—Blalock, 139; AB—Ruan, 574; R—Ford, 122; H—Crawford, 170; TB—M. Byrd, 265; 2B—Pressley, 44; 3B—M. Byrd, 13; HR—House, 23; RBI—Grindell, 98; SH—Cates, 12; SF—Blalock, 11; HP—Grummitt, 22; BB—Espy, 101; IBB—Espy, 7; SO—Brown, 182; SB—Requena, 87; CS—Alvarez, 21; GIDP—Pressley, 17; Slg.—House, .586; OBP—Espy, .439.

ALL PLAYERS

*Lefthanded batter. †Switch-hitter.

Player, Team	Avg.	G	TPA	AB	R	H	TB	2B	3B	HR	RBI	SH	SF	HP	BB	IBB	SO	SB	CS	GDP	Slg.	OBP
Abreu, Dave, C'bia†	.288	78	323	285	40	82	105	14	3	1	35	8	0	4	26	1	51	29	12	6	.368	.356
Acevedo, Carlos, Pied.	.226	37	121	106	10	24	29	3	1	0	8	2	1	0	12	0	23	5	2	3	.274	.303
Acevedo, Inocencio, Sav.	.226	57	199	177	25	40	51	6	1	1	13	6	2	5	9	0	37	17	7	2	.288	.280
Ackerman, Scott, C.F.	.281	54	223	210	27	59	91	8	0	8	41	0	1	0	12	0	35	1	2	11	.433	.318
Acuna, Ron, C'bia	.179	13	40	39	1	7	9	2	0	0	0	0	0	0	1	0	17	3	1	0	.231	.200
Alamo, Efrain, C.S.C.	.147	10	36	34	2	5	9	1	0	1	6	0	1	1	0	0	15	0	0	0	.265	.167
Alley, Charles, Del.	.273	15	61	44	10	12	14	2	0	0	0	0	0	2	15	1	5	1	0	1	.318	.475
Alvarez, Henrry, C.W.Va.	.200	10	32	30	2	6	11	2	0	1	2	0	0	0	2	0	9	0	0	1	.367	.250
Alvarez, Jimmy, Hag.†	.232	50	183	155	19	36	52	5	1	3	15	1	0	2	25	0	44	12	5	0	.335	.346
Alvarez, Tony, Hick.	.285	118	504	442	75	126	204	25	4	15	77	0	8	15	39	2	93	52	21	8	.462	.357
Anderson, Jon, Aug.†	.240	87	350	287	40	69	78	9	0	0	35	11	4	2	46	0	39	12	11	11	.272	.345
Angell, Rick, Sav.	.239	123	467	418	46	100	142	11	8	5	44	10	3	7	29	0	79	28	8	5	.340	.298
Autry, Brian, C.F.	.259	25	88	81	7	21	37	5	1	3	13	0	1	2	4	1	21	1	0	4	.457	.307
Baker, Jacob, C.W.Va.	.203	88	335	295	26	60	87	12	3	3	26	0	3	0	37	0	99	3	2	10	.295	.290
Barnes, Clint, Ash.	.173	19	95	81	11	14	18	4	0	0	4	2	1	1	10	0	13	4	1	3	.222	.269
Batista, Angel, C.S.C.*	.212	44	152	137	28	29	46	7	2	2	8	3	0	0	12	0	37	8	2	0	.336	.275
Batista, Carlos, C'bus	.223	54	225	202	20	45	63	9	0	3	17	0	1	4	18	0	52	2	2	2	.312	.298
Batson, Tom, Pied.	.288	52	215	191	26	55	81	15	1	3	35	1	3	2	18	0	27	7	4	6	.424	.350
Bernhardt, Jossephang, Hag.	.125	2	8	8	1	1	2	1	0	0	0	0	0	0	0	0	3	0	0	0	.250	.125
Beverly, Shomari, Pied.	.217	80	335	309	30	67	89	14	1	2	20	2	3	0	21	0	108	19	9	1	.288	.264
Blalock, Hank, Sav.*	.299	139	590	512	66	153	219	32	2	10	77	0	11	5	62	3	53	31	8	14	.428	.373
Bonifay, Josh, Hick.	.281	106	433	377	62	106	169	17	2	14	62	2	3	3	48	3	104	11	5	6	.448	.364
Boscan, Jean, Mac.	.205	93	352	302	31	62	101	12	0	9	35	2	1	5	42	1	74	1	1	6	.334	.311
Bost, Tom, C'bus*	.288	54	225	208	30	60	108	14	5	8	42	0	2	3	11	1	36	18	1	4	.519	.330
Boyer, Bret, C.F.	.220	55	206	191	25	42	52	5	1	1	13	2	1	1	11	0	38	15	4	2	.272	.265
Brazeal, Spencer, Gre.	.200	14	48	35	8	7	10	3	0	0	4	0	0	4	9	0	10	0	0	1	.286	.417
Brazell, Craig, C'bia*	.241	112	439	406	35	98	150	28	0	8	57	1	8	9	15	1	82	3	3	6	.369	.279
Brazoban, Yhency, Gre.	.188	12	52	48	6	9	12	3	0	0	8	0	1	0	3	0	15	1	0	0	.250	.231
Brett, Jason, C'bus	.274	80	229	190	31	52	64	7	1	1	20	4	2	4	29	1	52	14	7	3	.337	.378
Brewer, Jace, C.S.C.	.219	37	147	137	10	30	41	7	2	0	15	0	3	1	6	0	28	3	0	1	.299	.252
Bronowicz, Scott, Mac.*	.250	11	35	32	3	8	10	0	1	0	2	1	0	0	2	0	7	0	0	1	.313	.294
Brown, Andy, Gre.*	.257	122	507	463	56	119	209	31	1	19	63	0	0	8	35	2	182	4	5	3	.451	.320
Bubela, Brent, Sav.*	.173	28	86	75	8	13	22	4	1	1	4	0	1	3	7	0	22	1	2	2	.293	.267

Player, Team	Avg.	G	TPA	AB	R	H	TB	2B	3B	HR	RBI	SH	SF	HP	BB	IBB	SO	SB	CS	GDP	Slg.	OBP
Bultmann, Kurt, Hick.	.207	47	166	145	20	30	40	7	0	1	9	1	0	2	18	0	25	2	1	6	.276	.303
Bundy, Ryan, Hag.	.230	25	99	87	10	20	32	6	0	2	13	1	0	0	11	0	31	2	2	1	.368	.316
Byrd, Marlon, Pied.	.309	133	582	515	104	159	265	29	13	17	93	1	5	10	51	0	110	41	5	7	.515	.379
Cabrera, Ray, Del.	.279	122	467	437	51	122	156	17	4	3	56	1	4	13	12	0	66	10	4	15	.357	.315
Cadiente, Brett, Sav.*	.309	129	566	499	83	154	205	15	9	6	50	7	8	1	51	1	112	31	15	6	.411	.369
Calzado, Napolean, Del.	.278	131	557	503	81	140	193	20	6	7	83	4	8	11	31	0	68	29	11	11	.384	.329
Cantu, Jorge, C.S.C.	.301	46	202	186	25	56	79	13	2	2	24	2	1	3	10	1	39	3	3	3	.425	.345
Carreno, Jose, C.F.	.328	18	72	58	3	19	21	2	0	0	8	0	3	1	10	0	4	0	0	1	.362	.417
Carter, Shannon, Hag.*	.273	123	500	443	74	121	150	15	7	0	39	1	0	11	45	0	129	33	6	5	.339	.355
Cash, Kevin, Hag.	.245	59	221	196	28	48	90	10	1	10	27	1	1	1	22	1	54	5	3	7	.459	.323
Castaneda, Cesar, Sav.	.194	40	106	98	6	19	30	5	0	2	12	0	0	3	5	1	34	0	0	2	.306	.255
Castaneda, Jose, C'bia	.116	14	50	43	5	5	5	0	0	0	0	0	0	0	7	0	8	0	0	2	.116	.240
Castillo, Carlos, C'bia†	.217	31	113	106	7	23	27	4	0	0	6	2	0	1	4	0	26	2	2	0	.255	.252
Castillo, Jose, Hick.	.299	125	577	529	95	158	254	32	8	16	72	7	2	10	29	0	107	16	12	10	.480	.346
Castillo, Victor, Gre.	.223	82	332	282	37	63	70	7	0	0	28	4	2	5	39	0	73	8	4	4	.248	.326
Castro, Martires, C.F.	.254	131	499	456	58	116	152	18	3	4	69	2	7	3	31	2	104	17	13	11	.333	.302
Castro, Vince, Hick.	.262	16	48	42	3	11	11	0	0	0	4	1	1	2	2	0	13	2	1	0	.262	.319
Catalanotte, Greg, Ash.†	.264	122	520	454	59	120	214	30	2	20	75	0	2	3	61	4	149	2	5	10	.471	.354
Cates, Gary, Del.	.251	107	347	311	40	78	103	18	2	1	30	12	2	4	18	0	48	11	8	3	.331	.299
Centeno, Irwin, C.S.C.	.268	30	131	112	17	30	37	5	1	0	13	1	2	4	12	0	20	7	2	2	.330	.354
Cervenak, Mike, Gre.	.329	38	170	155	19	51	74	4	5	3	20	3	1	4	7	0	21	3	3	1	.477	.371
Chiaffredo, Paul, Hag.	.356	13	57	45	9	16	25	6	0	1	5	0	0	3	9	0	6	0	0	0	.556	.491
Chwan, Brian, C.S.C.*	.288	19	58	52	7	15	17	2	0	0	7	0	1	2	3	0	12	0	0	1	.327	.345
Clark, Chivas, Hag.*	.159	37	131	113	15	18	24	6	0	0	10	2	0	1	15	1	27	1	2	0	.212	.254
Clay, Mike, C.W.Va.	.237	71	259	228	17	54	73	8	1	3	18	1	4	8	18	0	33	1	1	5	.320	.310
Cleto, Ambioris, Hick.	.250	5	17	12	4	3	3	0	0	0	0	0	1	0	2	2	5	1	1	0	.250	.438
Collazo, Julio, Pied.	.208	89	345	293	40	61	72	6	1	1	21	6	6	5	35	0	76	11	5	5	.246	.298
Contreras, Erick, Mac.†	.256	18	51	39	9	10	12	2	0	0	2	0	1	1	11	0	9	1	1	1	.308	.431
Cordova, Ben, C.W.Va.*	.198	26	101	86	11	17	23	4	1	0	7	2	0	0	13	0	24	1	0	2	.267	.303
Corporan, Elvis, Gre.†	.247	63	284	255	37	63	87	10	1	4	31	1	0	0	28	0	66	10	2	7	.341	.322
Cosby, Rob, Hag.	.237	77	309	291	31	69	90	9	0	4	29	0	2	0	16	0	37	2	3	7	.309	.275
Cotten, Jeremy, Hick.	.286	59	234	210	39	60	107	18	1	9	32	0	0	3	20	0	55	0	2	1	.510	.354
Crawford, Carl, C.S.C.*	.301	135	611	564	99	170	231	21	11	6	57	9	1	3	32	1	102	55	9	1	.410	.342
Crocker, Nickolas, Mac.*	.231	58	242	221	24	51	87	12	0	8	38	1	3	3	14	0	61	7	4	1	.394	.282
Cruz, Edgar, C'bus.	.181	90	358	320	44	58	106	13	1	11	38	3	6	8	21	1	81	0	0	8	.331	.245
Cruz, Enrique, C'bia	.185	49	185	157	19	29	44	12	0	1	12	1	1	1	25	1	44	1	3	1	.280	.299
De Caster, Yurendell, C.S.C.	.240	69	270	242	34	58	100	21	0	7	28	2	4	6	16	0	89	4	1	2	.413	.299
Dees, Charlie, Del.	.150	13	22	20	3	3	7	0	2	0	1	0	1	0	1	0	12	0	0	1	.350	.182
Deitrick, Jeremy, Pied.	.283	54	173	159	21	45	62	8	0	3	18	1	2	1	10	0	34	2	1	5	.390	.326
De La Cruz, Ruddi, C'bia	.207	55	179	164	20	34	50	6	2	2	12	3	0	2	10	0	43	15	1	2	.305	.261
Delgado, Chris, Ash.	.136	18	67	59	4	8	12	1	0	1	3	0	1	0	7	0	25	1	1	2	.203	.224
De Los Santos, Hector, Aug.	.188	7	17	16	1	3	3	0	0	0	2	0	1	0	0	0	3	1	0	0	.188	.176
Dennis, Les, Aug.	.247	23	99	81	10	20	30	7	0	1	13	4	0	3	11	1	23	2	0	3	.370	.358
De Renne, Keoni, Mac.	.262	38	160	145	13	38	52	9	1	1	11	0	2	2	11	0	20	3	3	1	.359	.319
Deschenes, Pat, C'bia*	.259	125	508	441	53	114	159	27	3	4	57	1	4	9	53	2	90	4	1	7	.361	.347
Docen, Jose, C.F.†	.276	34	139	116	19	32	35	3	0	0	15	5	1	3	14	0	18	6	5	4	.302	.366
Duck, Kevin, Ash.*	.168	39	140	125	7	21	26	5	0	0	5	1	0	2	12	0	39	1	1	5	.208	.252
Elder, Rick, Del.*	.083	14	58	48	4	4	8	1	0	1	6	0	1	0	9	0	18	0	2	0	.167	.224
Elwood, Brad, Gre.	.308	11	46	39	9	12	14	0	1	0	2	0	0	0	7	0	4	0	1	2	.359	.413
Elzy, Steve, C'bia	.225	57	201	182	22	41	56	9	0	2	12	0	1	1	17	0	28	2	0	5	.308	.294
Espinoza, Andres, C.F.	.182	38	117	99	13	18	25	1	0	2	11	2	0	0	16	0	28	6	1	3	.253	.296
Espy, Nate, Pied.	.312	130	561	452	88	141	240	32	2	21	87	0	4	4	101	7	105	7	0	12	.531	.439
Esquerra, Marques, C'bus†	.284	48	179	162	22	46	60	6	1	2	16	3	0	3	11	0	18	6	3	5	.370	.341
Ewan, Bry, Mac.	.173	29	93	81	9	14	21	1	0	2	14	1	0	1	10	0	32	0	0	2	.259	.272
Fagan, Shawn, Hag.	.279	45	191	172	20	48	64	8	1	2	23	0	0	1	18	0	28	5	1	2	.372	.351
Fera, Aaron, Hag.	.241	50	194	166	22	40	63	11	0	4	32	0	2	6	20	0	53	5	0	1	.380	.340
Fiore, Curt, Mac.	.283	108	423	360	64	102	145	17	1	8	47	2	2	14	42	0	56	8	1	11	.403	.378
Ford, Lew, Aug.	.315	126	583	514	122	162	246	35	11	9	74	3	2	12	52	3	83	52	4	12	.479	.390
Fowler, David, Gre.	.188	26	102	96	12	18	40	5	1	5	11	0	0	1	5	0	43	0	0	0	.417	.235
Freitas, Jeremy, C.W.Va.*	.241	59	226	187	27	45	91	9	5	9	31	1	3	1	34	0	47	1	0	4	.487	.356
Fuentes, Omar, Gre.	.248	69	277	250	30	62	93	16	0	5	39	1	3	6	17	0	49	2	0	2	.372	.308
Gallaher, T.T., C'bia	.260	72	257	215	36	56	75	6	2	3	21	5	2	1	34	0	39	18	5	5	.349	.361
Gambino, Michael, Aug.	.286	20	71	63	8	18	20	2	0	0	2	2	0	1	5	0	8	2	1	4	.317	.348
Garcia, Luis, Aug.	.260	128	547	493	72	128	225	27	5	20	77	0	2	1	51	0	112	8	1	8	.456	.329
Garcia, Oscar, C'bus	.254	41	165	138	22	35	45	5	1	1	14	0	2	4	21	0	30	9	2	4	.326	.364
Gay, Curt, C'bus*	.169	97	370	337	30	57	94	14	1	7	37	1	1	1	30	0	128	2	0	4	.279	.238
Gettis, Byron, C.W.Va.	.215	94	392	344	43	74	113	18	3	5	50	2	4	11	31	0	95	11	7	5	.328	.297
Gingrich, Troy, C.F.	.250	44	180	144	21	36	46	8	1	0	12	1	0	4	31	1	32	13	3	1	.319	.397
Gomez, Rafael, C'bia	.000	10	1	1	0	0	0	0	0	0	0	0	0	0	0	0	0	0	0	0	.000	.000
Gonzalez, Julian, C.W.Va.	.211	16	61	57	6	12	17	2	0	1	5	1	0	2	1	0	18	1	0	1	.298	.250
Gordon, Alexis, Del.*	.000	1	2	2	0	0	0	0	0	0	0	0	0	0	0	0	2	0	0	0	.000	.000
Goudie, Jaime, Hag.	.243	116	468	412	53	100	143	19	3	6	51	8	3	9	36	0	68	26	10	6	.347	.315
Gredvig, Doug, Del.	.220	56	222	186	28	41	71	12	0	6	24	0	0	1	35	0	48	3	5	2	.382	.347
Green, Nick, Mac.	.245	91	374	339	47	83	143	19	4	11	43	1	6	5	22	0	75	10	4	4	.422	.296
Griffin, Justin, C'bus	.154	8	14	13	0	2	4	0	1	0	1	1	0	0	0	0	5	0	0	0	.308	.154
Grindell, Nate, C'bus	.286	132	571	500	80	143	239	36	3	18	98	0	7	9	55	3	74	17	2	8	.478	.363
Grummitt, Dan, C.S.C.	.260	111	475	412	70	107	190	22	2	19	73	0	5	22	36	1	117	6	2	7	.461	.347
Gutierrez, Derrick, Del.	.250	4	9	8	1	2	2	0	0	0	0	1	0	0	0	0	3	0	0	0	.250	.333
Guyton, Eric, C'bia	.279	94	377	323	44	90	131	12	4	7	55	2	2	11	39	0	70	1	2	4	.406	.373
Guzman, Juan, C.W.Va.†	.175	19	74	63	5	11	15	2	1	0	2	0	0	1	10	0	24	2	3	0	.238	.297
Halloran, Matt, Sav.	.171	35	93	82	5	14	17	3	0	0	5	0	2	1	8	0	15	2	1	1	.207	.247
Hamilton, Josh, C.S.C.*	.302	96	423	391	62	118	186	23	3	13	61	0	3	2	27	3	71	14	6	5	.476	.348

Player, Team	Avg.	G	TPA	AB	R	H	TB	2B	3B	HR	RBI	SH	SF	HP	BB	IBB	SO	SB	CS	GDP	Slg.	OBP
Hannahan, Buzz, Pied.	.275	76	289	240	47	66	82	13	0	1	24	6	2	5	36	0	37	25	1	1	.342	.378
Harris, Willie, Del.*	.274	133	583	474	106	130	195	27	10	6	60	7	4	9	89	4	89	38	15	3	.411	.396
Harts, Jeremy, Hick.†	.242	124	510	459	75	111	165	14	2	12	62	7	3	9	32	0	147	25	7	11	.359	.302
Headley, Justin, Aug.*	.210	20	73	62	9	13	24	2	0	3	3	0	0	3	8	0	10	1	0	5	.387	.329
Heard, Scott, Sav.*	.250	2	8	8	0	2	2	0	0	0	0	0	0	0	0	0	3	0	0	1	.250	.250
Hernandez, Javier, C'bus†	.271	13	52	48	7	13	16	3	0	0	8	0	1	0	3	0	18	3	0	2	.333	.308
Hernandez, Jose, Hick	.143	9	29	28	1	4	4	0	0	0	1	0	0	1	0	0	8	0	0	0	.143	.172
Hine, Steve, Sav.*	.272	95	331	279	50	76	96	15	1	1	27	6	1	2	43	1	39	13	5	3	.344	.372
Hitchcox, Brian, Pied.*	.268	112	453	407	48	109	141	19	2	3	42	2	3	16	25	1	35	10	8	5	.346	.333
Holliday, Josh, Hag.†	.220	74	284	218	46	48	81	13	1	6	29	3	4	7	52	1	64	2	0	2	.372	.381
Hopper, Norris, C.W.Va.	.280	116	514	454	70	127	159	20	6	0	29	4	1	4	51	0	55	24	10	10	.350	.357
House, J.R., Hick.	.348	110	478	420	78	146	246	29	1	23	90	0	6	6	46	2	91	1	2	7	.586	.414
Humrich, Chris, C.F.	.000	39	2	1	0	0	0	0	0	0	0	0	0	0	1	0	1	0	0	0	.000	.500
Ide, Antoine, Del.	.254	26	75	67	13	17	21	2	1	0	9	0	0	0	8	0	12	6	0	1	.313	.333
Isenia, Chairon, C.S.C.	.269	102	413	383	37	103	142	21	0	6	59	2	5	6	17	2	54	5	3	9	.371	.307
Isturiz, Maicer, C'bus†	.276	10	32	29	4	8	9	1	0	0	1	0	0	0	3	0	3	0	0	1	.310	.344
Jackson, Brandon, Hag.	.312	110	456	391	71	122	170	17	8	5	52	1	8	13	43	0	83	5	6	6	.435	.391
Jacobs, John, C.S.C.	.197	20	65	61	5	12	18	4	1	0	7	0	0	1	3	0	19	6	0	1	.295	.246
Jacobs, Mike, C'bia*	.214	18	62	56	1	12	17	5	0	0	8	0	0	0	6	1	19	1	1	2	.304	.290
Jacobson, Russ, Pied.	.247	102	391	348	43	86	160	17	0	19	71	2	1	11	29	0	105	0	1	8	.460	.324
Jarvais, Kregg, Aug.	.184	26	91	76	10	14	22	3	1	1	14	0	1	1	13	0	30	1	0	0	.289	.308
Jenkins, Brian, C'bia	.267	60	236	217	25	58	83	12	2	3	23	0	2	3	14	2	41	5	2	1	.382	.318
Johannes, Todd, C.F.	.196	37	119	102	8	20	22	2	0	0	10	2	1	5	9	0	20	0	1	1	.216	.291
Johnson, Brian, C.W.Va.	.219	61	227	201	15	44	57	13	0	0	21	3	5	10	8	0	39	1	1	5	.284	.277
Johnson, Eric, C'bus	.309	67	310	262	63	81	108	11	2	4	45	1	3	7	37	1	49	41	7	1	.412	.405
Johnson, Reed, Hag.	.290	95	405	324	66	94	152	24	5	8	70	2	3	14	62	1	49	14	2	9	.469	.422
Jones, Damien, Mac.*	.268	126	570	503	82	135	164	18	4	1	33	3	0	1	63	0	98	44	19	7	.326	.351
Jones, Jason, Sav.†	.268	132	542	466	59	125	198	34	6	9	61	1	5	4	65	1	97	9	5	15	.425	.359
Kasper, Todd, C.F.*	.172	19	64	58	1	10	13	3	0	0	5	0	0	0	6	0	15	2	0	2	.224	.250
Kawabata, Kenichiro, Aug.†	.125	12	38	32	5	4	5	1	0	0	2	0	0	0	6	0	14	0	0	1	.156	.263
Keene, Kurt, Hag.	.261	55	211	199	16	52	66	11	0	1	25	0	1	3	8	0	33	4	6	3	.332	.299
Kelly, Shane, C.S.C.	.115	8	30	26	2	3	3	0	0	0	2	0	2	0	2	0	11	1	0	1	.115	.167
Kerrigan, Joe, Aug.*	.294	27	120	102	18	30	39	3	3	0	10	1	1	0	16	0	21	1	0	2	.382	.387
Kessick, Jon, Del.	.187	103	351	294	40	55	67	7	1	1	21	5	2	2	48	0	107	5	1	3	.228	.303
Landreth, Jason, Hick.	.304	72	314	260	43	79	115	16	4	4	41	0	2	3	49	3	50	21	9	6	.442	.417
Lane, Rich, C.F.*	.310	74	306	277	46	86	117	15	2	4	47	0	2	2	25	0	46	3	0	8	.422	.369
Langston, James, Hick.†	.292	113	472	435	62	127	180	23	3	8	77	3	4	2	27	2	99	3	1	8	.414	.333
Larned, Drew, Aug.	.225	59	220	178	29	40	49	9	0	0	16	1	3	2	36	0	50	3	2	2	.275	.356
Leal, Jaeme, Mac.	.258	107	436	387	44	100	170	20	1	16	65	0	4	10	35	0	133	0	0	5	.439	.333
Leaumont, Jeff, Gre.*	.282	88	369	323	45	91	142	18	3	9	59	0	2	5	39	1	83	2	1	5	.440	.366
Lebron, Francisco, C'bia	.186	14	54	43	4	8	15	4	0	1	5	1	0	1	9	0	13	0	1	1	.349	.340
Lee, Monte, Sav.	.200	44	141	110	17	22	27	2	0	1	8	3	2	8	18	0	32	10	3	1	.245	.348
Lehr, Ryan, Mac.	.326	46	195	184	25	60	83	15	1	2	36	0	0	2	9	1	22	2	2	6	.451	.364
Leon, Alfredo, Del.	.000	8	11	11	0	0	0	0	0	0	0	0	0	0	0	0	3	0	0	1	.000	.000
Lincoln, Justin, Ash.	.235	126	495	451	58	106	179	22	0	17	60	0	3	5	35	1	161	18	10	7	.397	.296
Lopez, Youanny, Aug	.152	10	35	33	3	5	9	1	0	1	2	0	0	0	2	0	17	0	0	1	.273	.200
Lora, Thomas, C.W.Va.†	.203	105	395	359	39	73	88	13	1	0	18	5	1	4	26	0	86	30	12	7	.245	.264
Lowe, Steve, C'bus	.267	46	163	135	16	36	49	4	3	1	19	1	3	10	14	0	43	3	1	0	.363	.370
Lugo, Felix, C.F.†	.186	16	62	59	7	11	19	2	0	2	7	1	0	0	2	0	20	3	1	1	.322	.213
Lutz, David, C.F.*	.216	11	42	37	5	8	8	0	0	0	5	0	0	0	5	0	15	0	0	0	.216	.310
Maduro, Jorge, C.S.C.	.000	1	2	2	0	0	0	0	0	0	0	0	0	0	0	0	1	0	0	0	.000	.000
Manning, Pat, Mac.	.202	124	515	435	48	88	136	27	0	7	49	4	5	6	63	2	82	9	2	9	.313	.308
Martin, Brian, C.S.C.	.197	87	324	279	36	55	86	14	4	3	27	0	2	11	32	1	104	3	0	7	.308	.302
Martinez, Edgar, Aug.	.100	16	54	50	4	5	9	1	0	1	4	0	0	1	3	0	13	0	0	2	.180	.167
Martinez, Louis, Mac.	.219	33	129	114	16	25	28	3	0	0	4	2	0	2	11	0	10	4	1	2	.246	.299
Martinez, Ramon, Sav.†	.311	39	175	164	19	51	63	9	0	1	17	6	0	3	2	0	29	6	5	3	.384	.331
Martinez, Victor, C'bus†	.371	21	84	70	11	26	43	9	1	2	12	0	2	1	11	0	6	0	0	1	.614	.452
Massiatte, Daniel, C.S.C.	.308	9	33	26	5	8	9	1	0	0	4	0	0	1	6	0	6	3	0	1	.346	.455
Matos, Angel, Sav.	.247	31	77	73	9	18	37	1	0	6	16	0	1	0	3	0	25	0	0	1	.507	.273
Matthews, Michael, C.W.Va.†	.000	1	4	4	0	0	0	0	0	0	0	0	0	0	0	0	1	0	0	0	.000	.000
McAuley, Jim, C.W.Va.	.244	53	190	160	21	39	49	5	1	1	23	3	1	3	23	0	44	4	1	7	.306	.348
McKinley, Josh, C.F.†	.256	129	545	480	73	123	178	34	3	5	64	1	6	4	54	3	100	46	14	10	.371	.333
McMillan, Andrew, C.F.	.106	29	103	94	6	10	10	0	0	0	4	0	0	4	5	0	19	0	0	1	.106	.184
McQueen, Eric, Ash.	.201	61	228	209	22	42	72	12	0	6	27	1	1	5	12	0	76	5	0	3	.344	.260
Medrano, Steve, C.W.Va.†	.215	44	193	163	30	35	38	3	0	0	9	4	1	1	24	0	28	5	1	6	.233	.317
Melucci, Lou, C.F.	.232	68	223	198	27	46	65	9	2	2	18	0	1	4	20	0	58	8	0	1	.328	.314
Mento, Al, C'bia	.134	48	180	149	10	20	31	8	0	1	16	2	5	3	21	0	40	12	6	2	.208	.247
Mercado, Wilkins, C.W.Va.	.276	42	163	145	12	40	58	8	2	2	22	1	0	2	15	0	45	0	0	1	.400	.352
Merhoff, Aaron, Pied.	.179	38	127	112	11	20	25	2	0	1	11	2	1	1	11	0	37	4	1	3	.223	.256
Minus, Steve, Aug.	.285	71	287	256	36	73	103	14	2	4	32	0	4	0	27	0	61	2	1	5	.402	.348
Mitchell, Todd, Gre.	.232	53	182	155	19	36	55	8	1	3	14	0	2	3	22	0	34	1	2	1	.355	.335
Moore, Chris, Ash.*	.267	77	336	292	43	78	126	12	0	12	43	0	3	2	39	2	58	13	8	1	.432	.354
Moore, Frank, C.S.C.*	.263	96	400	372	53	98	135	18	2	5	41	3	4	5	16	1	78	12	5	3	.363	.300
Moraga, Omar, C'bus*	.297	114	478	424	53	126	164	18	4	4	59	1	5	3	45	1	71	10	4	7	.387	.365
Morban, Jose, Sav.	.220	80	323	273	44	60	88	8	4	4	28	5	0	4	41	0	79	27	13	6	.322	.330
Moreno, Jorge, C'bus	.303	55	238	211	37	64	104	15	2	7	32	1	5	2	19	0	57	10	2	2	.493	.359
Morrow, Alvin, Hag.	.210	32	121	105	15	22	37	3	0	4	8	0	0	2	14	0	42	2	0	3	.352	.314
Moyer, Kyle, C'bus*	.249	52	199	177	13	44	57	4	0	3	24	0	2	1	19	0	67	0	0	6	.322	.322
Mulvehill, Chase, C'bia	.231	47	182	160	21	37	52	5	2	2	11	0	1	3	18	0	55	4	7	1	.325	.319
Murch, Jeremy, C.S.C.*	.273	56	205	187	30	51	89	15	1	7	27	1	0	1	14	0	56	3	2	5	.476	.327
Muth, Edmund, Ash.*	.237	50	206	173	15	41	55	11	0	1	13	1	1	7	24	0	57	8	5	2	.318	.351
Nerei, Yuji, C.F.*	.294	14	45	34	8	10	25	4	1	3	8	0	0	2	9	0	8	0	0	0	.735	.467

Player, Team	Avg.	G	TPA	AB	R	H	TB	2B	3B	HR	RBI	SH	SF	HP	BB	IBB	SO	SB	CS	GDP	Slg.	OBP
Nettles, Jeff, Gre.	.258	84	316	283	34	73	111	14	0	8	45	2	3	6	22	0	43	2	3	8	.392	.322
Neubart, Adam, C.W.Va.	.273	34	148	128	24	35	43	4	2	0	13	1	1	4	14	0	29	9	4	2	.336	.361
Norrell, Troy, Gre.	.148	52	186	162	13	24	36	6	0	2	15	3	2	2	17	0	76	0	1	4	.222	.235
Nowlin, Cody, Sav.*	.244	136	556	501	66	122	200	27	3	15	68	2	3	6	44	1	104	3	0	7	.399	.310
Ochoa, Javier, C'bia	.278	35	132	126	13	35	50	9	0	2	13	0	0	2	4	0	21	0	2	1	.397	.311
Olson, Eric, Gre.	.143	20	77	63	3	9	15	3	0	1	6	2	0	5	7	0	29	0	1	2	.238	.280
O'Neill, Daniel, Pied.	.243	12	47	37	6	9	12	3	0	0	1	1	0	0	9	0	11	0	0	0	.324	.391
Oropeza, Asdrubal, Mac.	.222	115	456	397	54	88	150	25	2	11	44	3	2	7	47	1	92	6	6	5	.378	.313
Padilla, Jorge, Pied.	.305	108	445	413	62	126	199	24	8	11	67	0	4	2	26	0	89	8	4	10	.482	.346
Palmieri, Jon, C.F.	.268	49	217	183	28	49	68	12	2	1	21	0	1	5	28	0	22	8	2	1	.372	.378
Pascucci, Val, C.F.	.319	20	86	69	17	22	35	4	0	3	10	0	1	0	16	0	15	5	0	2	.507	.442
Paulino, Ron, Hick.	.289	88	333	301	38	87	125	16	2	6	39	0	1	4	27	0	71	3	2	9	.415	.354
Pearson, Shawn, Hag.	.141	33	109	92	9	13	15	0	1	0	5	1	0	1	15	1	20	4	2	3	.163	.269
Pena, Jose, Aug.	.214	32	130	117	12	25	40	7	1	2	11	0	0	5	8	0	29	4	5	1	.342	.292
Pena, Wily, Gre.	.205	67	276	249	41	51	90	7	1	10	28	0	4	5	18	1	91	6	5	9	.361	.268
Peralta, John, C'bus	.241	106	413	349	52	84	108	13	1	3	34	1	2	2	59	0	102	7	6	13	.309	.352
Perea, Jean, Sav.†	.208	42	139	130	13	27	41	2	0	4	15	0	1	3	5	0	25	2	0	3	.315	.252
Perez, Deivi, Hick.	.179	82	250	224	32	40	58	11	2	1	12	1	2	2	21	0	76	4	2	4	.259	.253
Perich, Josh, C'bia	.158	6	21	19	0	3	3	0	0	0	0	0	0	0	2	0	8	0	0	0	.158	.238
Phillips, Brandon, C.F.	.242	126	536	484	74	117	183	17	8	11	72	0	5	9	38	3	97	23	8	11	.378	.306
Phillips, Dan, Ash.	.273	123	501	473	71	129	204	32	2	13	45	2	0	8	18	0	130	39	17	9	.431	.311
Poe, Adam, Sav.	.251	114	448	383	37	96	128	20	0	4	39	3	4	12	46	3	81	20	4	10	.334	.346
Pohle, Ike, Gre.	.083	4	15	12	1	1	1	0	0	0	1	0	0	0	3	0	4	0	0	0	.083	.267
Pressley, Josh, C.S.C.*	.303	130	544	488	61	148	210	44	0	6	61	0	3	4	49	2	61	2	1	17	.430	.369
Preston, Brian, C.F.	.155	18	65	58	7	9	16	4	0	1	6	0	0	0	7	0	13	1	0	0	.276	.246
Puffinbarger, Rusty, C'bus	.123	19	66	57	8	7	11	0	2	0	6	2	0	2	5	0	20	2	0	4	.193	.219
Pugh, Dwayne, Hag.	.133	6	21	15	2	2	2	0	0	0	0	0	0	1	5	0	0	2	0	0	.133	.381
Pugh, Josh, Mac.	.280	37	149	125	20	35	48	2	1	3	19	1	1	3	19	1	30	1	0	3	.384	.385
Quiroz, Guillermo, Hag.	.162	43	159	136	14	22	29	4	0	1	12	3	0	4	16	0	44	0	1	3	.213	.269
Rachels, Wesley, Del.	.260	122	485	373	58	97	113	14	1	0	46	7	4	5	96	0	58	7	0	13	.303	.414
Ramirez, Charlie, C.W.Va.	.222	16	54	54	3	12	15	1	1	0	5	0	0	0	0	0	8	0	0	2	.278	.222
Ramos, Kelly, Aug.†	.250	73	291	260	27	65	105	17	1	7	37	1	0	6	24	1	54	1	2	9	.404	.328
Raymundo, Gregg, C.W.Va.	.276	85	313	268	29	74	96	11	1	3	35	1	2	8	34	1	61	0	1	9	.358	.372
Redman, Prentice, C'bia	.260	131	556	497	60	129	159	19	1	3	46	1	2	3	52	1	90	26	10	5	.320	.332
Reed, Keith, Del.	.290	70	303	269	43	78	129	16	1	11	59	1	3	5	25	5	56	20	4	3	.480	.358
Requena, Alex, C'bus†	.259	126	560	482	90	125	146	6	6	1	24	4	2	6	66	0	137	87	20	1	.303	.354
Reyes, Ambiorix, Pied.	.255	64	218	204	28	52	60	8	0	0	27	8	2	0	4	0	31	8	2	9	.294	.267
Rhodes, Dusty, Gre.*	.236	14	64	55	8	13	21	3	1	1	5	0	0	1	8	0	13	0	1	1	.382	.344
Richardson, Juan, Pied.	.242	43	168	149	19	36	53	11	0	2	15	0	0	2	17	0	43	0	1	5	.356	.327
Rickon, Jim, C'bus	.200	17	45	40	3	8	12	2	1	0	1	0	0	0	5	0	17	0	0	1	.300	.289
Riepe, Andy, Aug.	.175	11	44	40	5	7	8	1	0	0	4	1	0	0	3	0	8	0	0	2	.200	.233
Riggins, Auntwan, Hag.†	.221	67	213	195	25	43	48	5	0	0	9	4	0	2	12	0	56	16	4	4	.246	.273
Rinne, Jim, Ash.	.278	112	466	385	66	107	169	21	1	13	48	1	3	5	72	1	96	15	12	8	.439	.396
Riordan, Matt, Del.	.283	109	446	389	54	110	148	22	2	4	51	1	1	8	47	2	74	11	4	5	.380	.371
Rios, Alexis, Hag.	.230	22	78	74	5	17	22	3	1	0	5	0	1	1	2	0	14	2	3	0	.297	.256
Rivas, Justo, Mac.	.288	129	554	504	67	145	203	30	2	8	65	4	3	10	33	2	103	7	8	11	.403	.342
Rodriguez, Carlos, Aug.	.306	116	504	470	62	144	236	28	5	18	94	0	5	12	17	2	108	24	12	9	.502	.343
Rodriguez, Jeff, Mac.	.154	15	43	39	3	6	6	0	0	0	0	1	0	0	3	0	9	1	0	0	.154	.214
Rodriguez, Ronny, Aug.	.105	6	24	19	5	2	3	1	0	0	1	0	0	1	4	0	10	0	0	1	.158	.292
Rogers, Ed, Del.	.274	80	367	332	46	91	130	14	5	5	42	10	3	0	22	0	63	27	6	3	.392	.317
Rojas, Alex, Pied.†	.170	33	110	100	16	17	21	2	1	0	11	1	0	1	8	0	26	7	2	3	.210	.239
Rombley, Danny, C.F.	.258	24	93	89	8	23	28	1	2	0	10	1	0	1	2	0	30	2	1	1	.315	.283
Roper, Douglas, Hag.†	.171	25	88	76	16	13	15	2	0	0	9	0	0	0	12	0	31	3	0	1	.197	.284
Rosario, Melvin, Ash.*	.192	78	249	219	26	42	46	2	1	0	10	2	2	3	23	0	57	8	9	5	.210	.275
Ross, Donovan, C.W.Va.*	.303	105	429	360	54	109	178	20	5	13	61	5	1	7	56	1	72	1	4	13	.494	.406
Ruan, Wilken, C.F.	.287	134	611	574	95	165	214	29	10	0	51	2	3	8	24	1	75	64	10	4	.373	.323
Ruiz, Willy, C.W.Va.	.243	77	309	272	32	66	74	4	2	0	24	4	3	2	28	0	35	18	8	10	.272	.315
Ryan, Jeff, C'bus	.400	3	6	5	0	2	2	0	0	0	1	0	0	0	1	0	1	0	0	0	.400	.500
Saba, Cesar, Aug.†	.266	47	210	192	26	51	73	10	3	2	30	1	4	1	12	0	33	2	5	4	.380	.306
Salargo, Steve, Del.	.239	71	243	205	42	49	71	11	1	3	28	1	0	4	33	0	53	5	0	5	.346	.355
Salas, Juan, C.S.C.	.241	60	234	220	25	53	67	11	0	1	26	0	3	7	3	0	50	6	3	4	.305	.270
Sanchez, Frederick, Aug.	.303	30	125	109	17	33	40	7	0	0	15	4	0	1	11	0	19	4	0	1	.367	.372
Sanchez, Tino, Ash.†	.251	58	211	187	15	47	56	4	1	1	16	0	1	2	21	0	27	7	1	2	.299	.332
Santana, Emmanuel, C.W.Va.*	.140	38	152	129	13	18	24	3	0	1	13	1	0	3	19	0	30	1	0	1	.186	.265
Santana, Pedro, Gre.	.239	83	330	309	29	74	98	10	1	4	26	1	3	3	14	0	89	17	9	3	.317	.277
Santini, Travis, C'bus	.178	52	196	185	10	33	42	9	0	0	12	0	0	2	9	0	52	2	0	6	.227	.224
Santoro, Pat, Aug.	.265	30	128	113	13	30	47	6	1	3	15	0	1	4	10	1	27	4	2	2	.416	.344
Santos, Chad, C.W.Va.*	.209	59	217	187	16	39	64	9	2	4	18	2	1	0	27	3	62	0	1	4	.342	.307
Santos, Juan, Hag.†	.146	14	49	41	4	6	13	1	0	2	5	1	1	1	5	0	20	1	1	1	.317	.250
Saucke, Casey, Del.	.267	9	16	15	1	4	5	1	0	0	1	0	0	0	1	0	6	0	0	0	.333	.313
Schneider, Matt, Hick.*	.262	80	331	305	35	80	101	18	0	1	25	0	1	5	20	0	93	6	2	5	.331	.317
Schreimann, Eric, Pied.	.245	29	117	110	7	27	39	6	0	2	16	0	2	1	4	0	31	1	1	3	.355	.274
Schrock, Chris, C.S.C.	.259	71	234	216	28	56	71	9	0	2	19	3	1	4	10	0	39	0	1	2	.329	.303
Seale, Marvin, C'bia†	.291	120	526	453	76	132	185	23	6	6	37	6	1	13	53	1	125	52	14	7	.408	.381
Seestedt, Mike, Del.	.222	59	177	158	19	35	50	6	0	3	19	2	0	1	16	0	29	2	0	8	.316	.297
Sherlock, Brian, C.F.	.285	42	163	130	25	37	49	9	0	1	15	0	0	0	33	0	27	10	3	2	.377	.429
Shipp, Brian, C'bia	.181	49	173	155	14	28	39	5	0	2	6	1	1	6	10	0	57	7	2	5	.252	.256
Simmons, Jerry, Mac.	.298	77	275	252	31	75	122	15	4	8	41	0	0	3	20	1	42	16	9	7	.484	.356
Sitzman, Jim, Pied.*	.316	107	478	418	95	132	183	17	8	6	55	2	5	15	38	3	88	53	12	3	.438	.389
Smith, Brett, C.S.C.†	.272	34	123	103	14	28	40	3	0	3	10	2	0	2	16	0	25	2	2	3	.388	.380
Smith, Ryan, C'bia	.197	26	96	71	12	14	20	2	2	0	3	2	0	4	19	0	18	1	0	4	.282	.394
Smith, Sam, Ash.	.206	94	358	321	31	66	97	14	4	3	22	1	0	14	22	0	100	6	4	7	.302	.286

Player, Team	Avg.	G	TPA	AB	R	H	TB	2B	3B	HR	RBI	SH	SF	HP	BB	IBB	SO	SB	CS	GDP	Slg.	OBP
Snyder, Mike, Hag.*	.182	54	199	165	26	30	43	8	1	1	13	0	0	1	32	0	48	4	1	2	.261	.318
Sosa, Jovanny, Hick.	.248	117	482	431	48	107	179	16	1	18	65	0	4	7	40	2	135	3	3	5	.415	.320
Sullivan, Kevin, Pied.	.324	11	39	37	8	12	16	4	0	0	4	1	0	0	0	0	4	1	0	1	.432	.316
Terni, Chaz, Aug.	.210	91	350	309	39	65	94	14	3	3	24	4	2	10	25	0	91	11	8	7	.304	.289
Ticehurst, Brad, Gre.*	.246	22	81	69	10	17	23	4	1	0	10	1	1	0	10	0	26	1	2	0	.333	.338
Tonis, Michael, C.W.Va.	.200	28	113	100	10	20	28	8	0	0	17	1	2	1	9	1	22	1	0	1	.280	.268
Torres, Jason, Sav.*	.193	94	308	270	32	52	72	15	1	1	28	2	3	4	29	0	57	2	2	5	.267	.278
Tucker, Mamon, Del.	.238	117	469	411	60	98	124	11	6	1	54	4	4	6	44	0	88	13	6	5	.302	.318
Tyson, Torre, Gre.†	.291	124	566	475	87	138	168	15	3	3	41	7	1	5	76	2	70	33	14	3	.354	.393
Umbria, Jose, Hag.	.209	27	103	91	3	19	21	2	0	0	8	1	2	1	8	0	19	0	2	2	.231	.275
Valdez, Angel, Gre.	.309	66	249	230	46	71	105	15	5	3	29	2	3	1	13	1	58	3	2	3	.457	.344
Valdez, Castulo, C.S.C.	.175	60	136	126	13	22	28	4	1	0	11	1	2	5	2	0	33	0	0	3	.222	.215
Valdez, Wilson, C.F.	.245	15	53	49	6	12	14	2	0	0	3	2	0	0	2	0	9	3	0	0	.286	.275
Vento, Mike, Gre.	.261	84	381	318	49	83	120	15	2	6	52	2	3	11	47	0	66	13	8	11	.377	.372
Villar, Jose, Mac.	.199	61	238	216	36	43	79	7	1	9	26	1	1	4	16	0	69	8	6	7	.366	.266
Vilorio, Miguel, Ash.	.278	92	394	363	47	101	131	15	3	3	29	7	2	3	19	0	52	25	17	4	.361	.318
Volquez, Bolivar, C.S.C.	.133	17	62	60	6	8	8	0	0	0	4	0	0	2	0	0	12	2	0	1	.133	.161
Wakakuwa, Kenn, C.S.C.	.500	1	4	4	1	2	2	0	0	0	0	0	0	0	0	0	0	0	0	0	.500	.500
Waldron, Jeff, Aug.*	.288	16	60	52	6	15	16	1	0	0	1	0	0	0	8	0	9	0	1	1	.308	.383
Warren, Chris, Aug.	.258	135	554	484	72	125	200	26	2	15	61	1	2	19	48	2	152	19	8	11	.413	.347
Warren, Chris, Ash.†	.231	77	287	255	23	59	95	15	0	7	30	0	1	2	29	0	79	12	7	7	.373	.314
Washington, Dion, Gre.	.244	83	321	279	31	68	96	16	0	4	29	0	1	4	37	1	89	6	1	4	.344	.340
Weekly, Chris, Hag.*	.291	66	260	234	21	68	106	15	1	7	49	0	3	1	22	0	53	2	5	8	.453	.350
Weston, Aron, Hick.*	.267	82	356	315	52	84	107	13	2	2	21	4	0	1	36	1	89	28	6	0	.340	.344
Williams, Brady, Aug.†	.225	83	324	267	41	60	93	16	1	5	30	1	0	8	48	0	107	4	1	1	.348	.359
Williams, Clyde, C.F.*	.226	72	272	252	19	57	80	12	1	3	29	1	2	3	14	0	61	2	2	5	.317	.273
Winchester, Jeff, Ash.	.262	110	453	397	62	104	184	29	0	17	73	0	5	20	31	0	109	9	7	7	.463	.342
Wright, Brad, C'bia*	.276	65	234	217	19	60	78	12	0	2	23	1	3	0	10	0	37	3	2	6	.359	.313
Yancy, Michael, C'bia	.182	3	11	11	1	2	2	0	0	0	1	0	0	0	0	0	4	0	1	0	.182	.182

GRAND SLAMS: Jacobson 3; J. Castillo, C. Warren (Aug.), 2 each; T. Alvarez, Batson, Cash, Catalanotte, Crawford, L. Ford, Gettis, Grummitt, Holliday, House, Isenia, Leal, Moraga, Reed, Ca. Rodriguez, E. Santana, P. Santana, M. Seale, Weekly, Winchester, 1 each.

AWARDED FIRST BASE ON CATCHER'S INTERFERENCE: Fiore 3 (Larned 2, Winchester); Crawford 2 (House, Larned); P. Manning 2 (Ed. Cruz, Perea); Murch 2 (Bronowicz, Larned); Tyson 2 (Ewan, Seestedt); Bost (Perea); Brown (K. Sullivan); Cotten (Larned); Green (Larned); J. Jones (Boscan); Langston (Perea); Lincoln (Ochoa); Redman (Ramos); Salas (E. Martinez); Snyder (Larned).

2000 PITCHING

TEAM

Team	W	L	Pct.	ERA	G	CG	ShO	Sv.	IP	H	TBF	R	ER	HR	SH	SF	HB	BB	IBB	SO	WP	Bk.
Piedmont	90	47	.657	2.91	137	10	13	39	1195.2	1030	5026	492	386	62	34	39	84	455	8	1031	63	5
Augusta	83	58	.589	3.45	141	2	10	47	1229.0	1155	5280	607	471	77	39	38	70	461	5	1125	82	2
Savannah	74	65	.532	3.52	139	7	12	32	1207.2	1033	5147	551	472	83	23	34	72	507	5	1061	83	7
Macon	69	70	.496	3.52	139	6	9	29	1219.2	1112	5188	613	477	91	33	42	62	442	8	1072	61	9
Hickory	75	66	.532	3.74	141	12	6	34	1266.2	1270	5554	709	527	96	43	41	90	447	10	1148	62	7
Charleston, S.C.	73	66	.525	3.75	139	9	7	37	1236.1	1237	5368	648	515	84	36	33	64	427	16	1149	110	7
Charleston, W.V.	53	80	.398	3.81	133	5	9	20	1139.2	1134	4949	628	482	72	26	31	57	434	2	895	64	11
Asheville	66	69	.489	3.82	135	6	9	38	1187.1	1171	5113	605	504	86	28	31	93	413	6	1196	57	4
Delmarva	74	62	.544	3.87	136	3	5	27	1189.1	1190	5134	603	512	64	28	24	58	426	15	1100	75	11
Hagerstown	63	74	.460	4.05	137	5	3	34	1167.2	1184	5087	681	525	85	33	39	90	460	13	896	99	6
Columbus	67	70	.489	4.06	137	2	5	40	1196.1	1223	5255	647	540	79	47	47	82	485	16	1049	71	3
Cape Fear	64	74	.464	4.25	138	3	3	33	1195.0	1229	5291	714	564	80	33	41	86	506	8	953	94	9
Greensboro	56	81	.409	4.28	137	7	2	27	1180.2	1222	5222	697	561	87	36	26	77	509	15	1025	113	8
Columbia	56	81	.409	4.29	137	1	6	39	1179.2	1128	5193	682	562	78	24	42	5	543	15	1206	140	4

INDIVIDUAL

TOP QUALIFIERS FOR EARNED-RUN AVERAGE TITLE

Minimum 114 innings. *Lefthanded pitcher.

Pitcher, Team	W	L	Pct.	ERA	G	GS	CG	ShO	GF	Sv.	IP	H	TBF	R	ER	HR	SH	SF	HB	BB	IBB	SO	WP	Bk.
Cedeno, Jovanny, Sav.	11	4	.733	2.42	24	22	0	0	0	0	130.1	95	530	40	35	1	1	3	7	53	0	153	5	0
Madson, Ryan, Pied.	14	5	.737	2.59	21	21	2	1	0	0	135.2	113	564	50	39	5	3	0	13	45	0	123	5	1
Tsao, Chin-hui, Ash.	11	8	.579	2.73	24	24	0	0	0	0	145.0	119	591	54	44	8	3	2	5	40	0	187	6	1
Magrane, Jim, C.S.C.	12	5	.706	2.76	27	27	1	1	0	0	173.0	158	710	64	53	9	3	0	4	43	0	162	14	1
Butler, Matt, Mac.	13	7	.650	2.94	26	26	2	2	0	0	156.1	132	662	75	51	13	1	10	2	66	0	122	5	1
Williams, Dave, Hick.*	11	9	.550	2.96	24	24	1	1	0	0	170.0	145	687	66	56	14	11	2	9	39	2	193	4	0
Cook, Aaron, Ash.	10	7	.588	2.96	21	21	4	2	0	0	142.2	130	579	54	47	10	1	0	16	23	0	118	5	0
Reid, Justin, Hick.	9	8	.529	3.02	27	22	5	0	4	3	170.0	146	694	82	57	12	3	4	3	30	0	176	5	0
Denney, Kyle, C'bus.	8	6	.571	3.05	28	24	0	0	1	0	138.2	135	584	55	47	12	4	1	4	46	0	131	5	0
Baker, Brad, Aug.	12	7	.632	3.07	27	27	0	0	0	0	137.2	125	591	58	47	3	3	6	15	55	0	126	10	0
Myers, Brett, Pied.	13	7	.650	3.18	27	27	2	1	0	0	175.1	165	738	78	62	7	1	4	9	69	0	140	8	0
Moreno, Edwin, Sav.	9	8	.529	3.25	23	22	1	0	0	0	133.0	127	562	58	48	9	1	2	7	46	0	89	6	0
Riccobono, Rick, Aug.	10	7	.588	3.27	25	24	0	0	0	0	124.0	116	548	69	45	11	3	4	11	49	0	72	5	0
Kennedy, Joe, C.S.C.*	11	6	.647	3.30	22	22	3	2	0	0	136.1	122	546	59	50	6	2	6	4	29	1	142	9	2
Glaser, Eric, Aug.	9	6	.600	3.33	32	16	1	1	8	1	124.1	103	493	53	46	14	0	4	3	34	1	120	4	0

DEPARTMENTAL LEADERS: W—Madson, Brooks, 14 each; L—Knowles, Kibler, Douglass, 14 each; Pct.—Backsmeyer, .900; G—Leach, 60; GS—Dittfurth, 29; CG—Reid, 5; ShO—several tied, 2 each; GF—Leach, 58; Sv.—Leach, 40; IP—Brooks, 177.2; H—Bennett, 189; TBF—Bennett, 761; R—Bennett, 116; ER—Bennett, 84; HR—Sandoval, 20; SH—Williams, 11; SF—Butler, 10; HB—Collins, 24; BB—Dittfurth, 99; IBB—Fry, 5; SO—Williams, 193; WP—Dunning, 31; BK—Andrade, 4.

ALL PITCHERS

*Lefthanded pitcher.

Pitcher, Team	W	L	Pct.	ERA	G	GS	CG	ShO	GF	Sv.	IP	H	TBF	R	ER	HR	SH	SF	HB	BB	IBB	SO	WP	Bk.
Abreu, Winston, Mac.	2	1	.667	1.88	11	1	0	0	8	3	28.2	11	103	6	6	2	0	0	6	0	0	48	1	0
Alston, Travis, Pied.	0	1	.000	4.85	5	2	0	0	2	0	13.0	13	62	9	7	2	0	0	0	10	0	8	2	0
Andersen, Derek, C.S.C.*	1	1	.500	4.12	15	0	0	0	9	0	19.2	25	86	11	9	3	1	0	2	0	0	22	1	0
Andrade, Jancy, Del.	7	7	.500	5.37	29	19	0	0	0	0	114.0	121	499	76	68	7	2	3	3	43	1	99	3	4
Angell, Rick, Sav.	0	0	.000	0.00	1	0	0	0	1	0	1.0	0	3	0	0	0	0	0	0	0	0	0	0	0
Aramboles, Ricardo, Gre.	5	13	.278	4.31	25	25	2	0	0	0	137.2	150	603	81	66	12	3	1	5	47	0	150	9	0
Arthurs, Shane, C.F.	4	3	.571	4.22	14	14	0	0	0	0	70.1	88	321	40	33	5	1	2	6	26	0	40	6	0
Avery, Steve, Mac.*	0	1	.000	1.50	2	2	0	0	0	0	6.0	6	25	5	1	2	0	0	0	1	0	7	0	0
Babula, Shaun, Del.*	1	0	1.000	0.64	9	0	0	0	4	0	14.0	13	60	2	1	0	1	0	2	4	0	11	0	0
Backsmeyer, Justin, Sav.	9	1	.900	4.13	40	0	0	0	21	0	72.0	60	314	37	33	7	1	2	6	35	1	54	2	1
Baerlocher, Ryan, C.W.Va.	5	6	.455	2.14	19	19	0	0	0	0	113.2	88	457	43	27	6	0	0	3	33	0	139	5	0
Bailie, Matt, Pied.	7	0	1.000	1.39	44	0	0	0	17	6	71.1	50	285	15	11	2	4	6	2	24	0	82	1	0
Baker, Brad, Aug.	12	7	.632	3.07	27	27	0	0	0	0	137.2	125	591	58	47	3	3	6	15	55	0	126	10	0
Baranowski, Brannon, C.W.Va.	1	1	.500	5.09	10	0	0	0	4	0	17.2	22	87	14	10	4	0	1	0	13	0	19	0	0
Barr, Adam, C'bus.*	3	5	.375	5.80	13	13	0	0	0	0	59.0	77	288	46	38	2	2	4	3	48	0	41	4	0
Bass, Brian, C.W.Va.	0	0	.000	6.75	1	1	0	0	0	0	4.0	6	18	3	3	0	0	0	0	0	0	1	0	0
Batista, Carlos, C'bus	0	0	.000	0.00	1	0	0	0	1	0	0.2	0	3	0	0	0	0	0	1	0	0	1	0	0
Bauer, Pete, Hag.	1	5	.167	5.06	9	9	0	0	0	0	32.0	37	141	27	18	2	2	3	8	0	0	22	4	0
Bazan, Juan, Hick.	3	4	.429	1.74	15	0	0	0	12	1	20.2	15	94	8	4	1	4	1	0	14	0	15	0	0
Bean, Colter, Gre.	1	0	1.000	4.91	18	0	0	0	9	0	25.2	21	110	16	14	1	0	0	1	11	0	35	4	0
Bedard, Erik, Del.*	9	4	.692	3.57	29	22	1	1	2	2	111.0	98	466	48	44	2	1	0	10	35	0	131	14	0
Belisle, Matt, Mac.	9	5	.643	2.37	15	15	1	0	0	0	102.1	79	392	37	27	7	2	3	4	18	0	97	7	0
Bello, Jilberto, Del.	2	2	.500	3.08	34	0	0	0	11	0	64.1	58	266	27	22	3	1	0	2	18	1	33	7	1
Bennett, Jeff, Hick.	10	13	.435	4.40	27	27	1	0	0	0	171.2	189	761	116	84	14	5	7	16	47	1	126	11	2
Bluma, Marc, Hag.	2	2	.500	4.28	48	0	0	0	19	1	67.1	75	306	48	32	3	3	4	5	27	3	52	1	0
Bong, Jung, Mac.*	7	7	.500	4.23	20	19	0	0	0	0	112.2	119	500	65	53	4	5	3	14	45	0	90	10	2
Bottenfield, Jason, Aug.	1	2	.333	7.18	14	0	0	0	4	0	26.1	44	132	28	21	3	2	1	3	6	0	21	2	0
Bradley, Bobby, Hick.	8	2	.800	2.29	14	14	3	0	0	0	82.2	62	336	31	21	3	1	4	4	21	0	118	2	0
Brito, Juan, C.F.*	2	0	1.000	4.32	14	0	0	0	11	1	25.0	20	111	15	12	2	0	2	4	7	0	15	4	0
Brookman, Ryan, Pied.	2	0	1.000	2.60	8	1	0	0	4	1	17.1	12	65	5	5	2	0	2	0	2	0	7	2	0
Brooks, Frank, Pied.*	14	8	.636	3.44	29	27	3	2	1	0	177.2	152	734	78	68	17	7	8	14	60	0	138	8	1
Buchanan, Brian, Gre.*	0	0	.000	3.63	19	0	0	0	6	1	22.1	22	99	9	9	1	0	1	0	15	0	19	3	0
Bukvich, Ryan, C.W.Va.	0	0	.000	1.88	11	0	0	0	9	4	14.1	6	57	3	3	0	2	0	1	7	0	17	1	0
Bullock, Jeremiah, Sav.*	1	3	.250	7.04	4	4	0	0	0	0	15.1	22	80	18	12	3	2	1	1	6	0	11	2	0
Bumatay, Mike, Hick.*	3	0	1.000	1.78	16	0	0	0	13	6	25.1	20	108	7	5	1	2	0	2	12	0	32	1	1
Burger, Rob, Ash.	0	0	.000	2.84	3	0	0	0	2	0	6.1	4	27	3	2	0	0	1	1	2	0	4	0	0
Butler, Matt, Mac.	13	7	.650	2.94	26	26	2	2	0	0	156.1	132	662	75	51	13	1	10	2	66	0	122	5	1
Button, Sammy, C'bus*	0	3	.000	35.31	3	3	0	0	0	0	4.1	9	36	17	17	4	0	1	1	13	0	4	0	0
Byrd, Mike, C'bus	0	2	.000	24.00	2	0	0	0	0	0	3.0	7	20	10	8	2	0	0	0	3	0	0	0	0
Cardwell, Brian, Hag.	0	5	.000	9.09	11	6	0	0	2	0	31.2	41	154	38	32	7	0	1	1	21	0	29	2	1
Carrasco, Dan, Hick.	5	4	.556	1.34	27	0	0	0	25	6	40.1	35	176	10	6	0	1	0	7	20	1	40	2	0
Casadiego, Gerardo, C.F.	5	7	.417	4.40	30	1	0	0	10	1	61.1	58	271	33	30	7	2	2	5	26	2	50	4	0
Castellanos, Hugo, Hag.	0	3	.000	1.64	29	0	0	0	19	7	38.1	16	155	11	7	1	2	0	5	18	1	30	5	0
Castro, Eleuterio, Aug.	3	1	.750	3.22	30	0	0	0	13	1	58.2	57	251	33	21	2	1	1	3	19	0	41	6	0
Cavazos, Andy, Sav.	2	5	.286	4.70	20	15	0	0	1	1	82.1	67	364	49	43	13	2	1	3	55	0	71	10	0
Cedeno, Jovanny, Sav.	11	4	.733	2.42	24	22	0	0	0	0	130.1	95	530	40	35	1	1	3	7	53	0	153	5	0
Cercy, Rick, Ash.	4	1	.800	1.18	44	0	0	0	18	6	61.0	38	236	10	8	3	0	0	4	21	0	78	1	0
Charron, Eric, C.F.	5	10	.333	4.60	26	15	0	0	2	0	94.0	113	418	57	48	4	0	4	7	29	1	71	7	1
Chenard, Ken, C'bia	4	5	.444	2.86	21	21	0	0	0	0	94.1	75	396	39	30	2	1	1	4	48	0	112	9	0
Claussen, Brandon, Gre.*	8	5	.615	4.05	17	17	1	0	0	0	97.2	91	416	49	44	9	4	4	1	44	0	98	3	0
Coa, Jesus, C.W.Va.	4	9	.308	4.63	21	12	0	0	3	1	81.2	98	390	65	42	9	2	0	3	41	0	34	3	2
Cogan, Tony, C.W.Va.*	6	2	.750	1.83	13	13	0	0	0	0	78.2	65	303	19	16	3	1	1	5	14	0	51	5	1
Cole, Joseph, C'bia	1	3	.250	6.53	4	4	0	0	0	0	20.2	25	99	19	15	3	0	0	1	16	0	16	2	0
Collins, Pat, C.F.	7	12	.368	3.82	24	23	1	0	0	0	143.2	140	636	81	61	10	4	1	24	75	1	96	11	1
Colmenares, Luis, Ash.	0	0	.000	2.57	6	0	0	0	4	0	7.0	5	31	2	2	1	0	0	1	5	0	8	0	0
Colon, Jose, C'bus	1	1	.500	1.67	28	0	0	0	27	19	32.1	23	133	8	6	1	0	0	1	8	0	31	0	0
Cook, Aaron, Ash.	10	7	.588	4.25	21	21	4	2	0	0	142.2	130	579	54	47	10	1	0	16	23	0	118	5	0
Corcoran, Tim, C'bia	3	5	.375	4.05	31	0	0	0	13	1	53.1	46	230	28	24	7	0	4	27	2	58	11	0
Cornejo, Jesse, C.S.C.*	4	1	.800	3.08	30	1	0	0	12	1	52.2	50	230	22	18	4	6	2	0	21	3	48	3	1
Correa, Dominic, Gre.	1	0	1.000	0.00	5	0	0	0	3	0	7.1	2	28	0	0	0	1	0	2	2	0	7	0	1
Cowie, Steve, C'bus	1	1	.875	3.39	14	14	0	0	0	0	85.0	77	346	35	32	12	1	2	2	21	0	64	1	0
Crowther, Jackson, C.F.	1	2	.333	5.87	18	1	0	0	5	0	30.2	32	146	22	20	2	0	4	0	20	0	23	6	0
Cullen, Ryan, Sav.*	6	6	.500	3.04	48	0	0	0	36	9	94.2	79	389	33	32	3	5	2	1	35	2	103	3	1
Curtis, Dan, Mac.	5	0	1.000	1.97	7	6	2	1	0	0	45.2	35	171	10	10	4	0	1	0	7	0	45	0	0
Curtiss, Tom, Mac.*	0	1	.000	6.75	10	0	0	0	4	0	17.1	17	86	16	13	0	1	1	1	17	0	14	0	0
Day, Zach, Gre.	9	3	.750	1.90	13	13	1	1	0	0	85.1	72	343	29	18	6	0	0	1	31	0	101	11	1
Dean, Aaron, Hag.	8	3	.727	3.28	19	19	0	0	0	0	112.2	99	472	55	41	8	2	6	6	38	0	89	4	0
DeLaCruz, Andres, Gre.	0	1	.000	7.33	26	0	0	0	15	1	27.0	31	145	28	22	3	0	2	6	30	0	16	3	0
Denney, Kyle, C'bus.	8	6	.571	3.05	28	24	0	0	1	0	138.2	135	584	55	47	12	4	1	4	46	0	131	5	0
De Paula, Julio, Ash.	8	13	.381	4.70	28	27	1	1	0	0	155.0	151	663	90	81	16	2	5	13	62	0	187	7	2
DePriest, Derrick, C.F.	0	2	.000	1.45	21	0	0	0	17	8	31.0	21	119	8	5	1	1	0	1	6	0	28	0	1
Dickinson, Rodney, Aug.	1	1	.500	1.00	13	0	0	0	3	1	27.0	20	103	4	3	2	1	1	4	1	0	31	1	0
Dittfurth, Ryan, Sav.	8	13	.381	4.25	29	29	2	1	0	0	158.2	127	699	83	75	8	2	5	17	99	1	158	16	3
Dobson, Scott, C.F.	0	0	.000	11.12	14	0	0	0	3	0	17.0	27	98	26	21	4	0	1	4	17	0	13	7	0
Dohmann, Christopher, Ash.	1	5	.167	6.46	7	7	0	0	0	0	32.2	43	149	24	22	3	0	3	3	8	0	36	3	1
Dorn, Grant, C.F.	3	6	.333	5.22	17	17	1	0	0	0	91.1	106	404	60	53	6	1	7	1	36	1	55	4	0
Douglass, Ryan, C.W.Va.	6	14	.300	4.02	27	27	2	0	0	0	159.0	174	668	88	71	9	3	1	6	34	0	105	6	1
Dukeman, Greg, Hick.	6	4	.455	4.57	25	19	0	0	2	0	132.0	151	606	91	67	13	3	14	46	0	82	16	1
Dunn, Keith, Gre.	1	5	.167	4.40	8	8	0	0	0	0	45.0	54	201	29	22	7	2	1	2	13	0	38	1	1
Dunning, Justin, C'bia	5	11	.313	6.08	28	26	0	0	1	0	120.0	114	545	91	81	8	1	5	17	71	0	128	31	0
Encarnacion, Orlando, C'bia	1	2	.333	6.37	19	0	0	0	10	0	41.0	43	181	31	29	5	1	4	3	14	1	36	5	1

Pitcher, Team	W	L	Pct.	ERA	G	GS	CG	ShO	GF	Sv.	IP	H	TBF	R	ER	HR	SH	SF	HB	BB	IBB	SO	WP	Bk.
Ennis, John, Mac.	7	4	.636	2.55	18	16	0	0	0	0	98.2	77	403	37	28	5	2	1	6	25	0	105	3	0
Esslinger, Cam, Ash.	4	2	.667	3.06	47	2	0	0	39	24	64.2	55	271	23	22	2	2	2	3	23	1	84	4	0
Evert, Brett, Mac.	1	4	.200	4.64	7	7	0	0	0	0	42.2	53	190	27	22	7	0	0	3	9	0	29	7	1
Field, Nathan, C.W.Va.	1	2	.333	2.23	17	0	0	0	4	0	36.1	28	152	10	9	2	4	1	2	15	0	31	3	1
Fiore, Curt, Mac.	0	0	.000	0.00	1	0	0	0	0	0	0.0	0	1	0	0	0	0	0	0	1	1	0	0	0
Fleming, Travis, Del.	7	2	.778	3.88	53	0	0	0	32	11	72.0	74	308	32	31	7	0	0	2	21	3	85	2	0
Ford, Matt, Hag.*	5	3	.625	3.87	18	14	1	0	0	0	83.2	81	353	42	36	5	0	4	3	36	0	86	5	0
Franco, Jose, Gre.	3	3	.500	3.07	39	0	0	0	36	17	44.0	34	185	17	15	2	3	0	1	20	2	47	3	0
Franco, Martire, Pied.	8	6	.571	4.13	24	23	2	2	0	0	126.1	146	573	70	58	7	3	4	6	57	0	89	10	2
Frendling, Neal, C.S.C.	8	8	.500	3.38	27	27	4	0	0	0	157.0	137	654	73	59	13	3	6	10	46	0	174	13	1
Frias, Juan, C.S.C.	2	0	1.000	5.06	7	0	0	0	1	0	10.2	13	46	6	6	1	0	0	4	0	0	9	1	0
Fry, Justin, Pied.	4	4	.500	2.51	44	0	0	0	32	13	57.1	40	241	19	16	2	2	2	5	23	5	77	2	0
Gamble, Jerome, Aug.	5	3	.625	2.52	15	15	0	0	0	0	78.2	69	335	26	22	1	0	3	5	32	0	71	9	0
Garcia, Raul, C.W.Va.	0	5	.000	4.69	40	0	0	0	15	0	55.2	63	253	35	29	5	2	2	5	28	0	57	4	0
Garcia, Reynaldo, Sav.	6	7	.462	2.69	49	2	1	0	35	14	97.0	87	410	37	29	6	2	4	5	33	1	82	8	0
Garcia, Rosman, Gre.	6	6	.500	4.57	23	15	1	0	1	0	104.1	115	454	67	53	12	3	1	4	35	0	73	5	1
Garcia, Sonny, Del.	6	7	.462	3.74	26	21	1	0	0	0	110.2	106	478	55	46	12	2	2	5	38	1	123	2	1
Garris, Antonio, C.F.	0	0	.000	9.00	1	0	0	0	1	0	2.0	2	9	2	2	1	0	0	0	1	0	2	0	0
Gawer, Matt, Mac.*	5	1	.833	2.98	30	0	0	0	14	1	51.1	36	211	20	17	2	4	1	2	20	1	59	2	0
Gehrke, Jay, C.W.Va.	1	4	.200	3.75	43	0	0	0	28	4	60.0	50	276	36	25	3	3	4	2	42	1	38	4	1
Gilfillan, Jason, C.W.Va.	1	2	.333	4.20	30	0	0	0	19	7	45.0	45	202	24	21	3	0	3	4	21	0	44	4	0
Glaser, Eric, Aug.	9	6	.600	3.33	32	16	1	1	8	1	124.1	103	493	53	46	14	0	4	3	34	1	120	4	0
Gobble, Jimmy, C.W.Va.*	12	10	.545	3.66	25	25	3	2	0	0	145.0	144	604	75	59	10	1	2	4	34	0	115	1	1
Gomez, Rafael, C'bia	1	2	.333	6.64	10	0	0	0	7	1	20.1	25	90	16	15	4	0	0	1	6	0	18	0	0
Good, Eric, C.F.*	1	2	.333	2.75	8	8	0	0	0	0	36.0	31	157	15	11	1	0	3	5	12	0	32	3	1
Gorman, Pat, C'bia-Del.	2	2	.500	1.80	32	0	0	0	29	16	40.0	25	174	10	8	1	1	1	2	29	2	59	9	0
Gracesqui, Franklyn, Hag.*	0	1	.000	4.91	3	1	0	0	1	0	7.1	4	33	4	4	1	0	0	1	9	0	6	0	0
Graham, Frank, C'bia	10	12	.455	4.33	27	25	1	0	0	0	143.1	152	636	80	69	7	3	5	23	52	0	109	11	0
Griffiths, Jeremy, C'bia	7	12	.368	4.34	26	26	0	0	0	0	128.2	120	548	78	62	12	1	4	8	39	0	138	8	0
Gross, Rafael, C'bus	1	0	1.000	2.50	8	0	0	0	7	1	18.0	11	66	5	5	3	0	0	0	3	0	23	0	0
Halvorson, Greg, C'bia	3	8	.273	5.73	29	14	0	0	7	1	108.1	132	502	82	69	9	2	3	10	49	0	90	17	0
Hamann, Robert, Hag.	8	4	.667	2.95	34	1	0	0	19	6	58.0	48	244	25	19	4	3	2	5	21	4	34	9	0
Harris, Silas, C.F.*	1	2	.333	4.38	14	0	0	0	9	1	24.2	23	114	23	12	2	0	0	0	17	1	17	7	0
Harvey, Ian, Aug.	2	1	.667	2.63	9	0	0	0	5	0	13.2	12	57	5	4	2	1	0	0	4	1	17	1	0
Hawkins, Chad, Sav.	0	0	.000	0.93	5	1	0	0	1	0	9.2	7	43	1	1	1	1	0	0	5	0	11	0	0
Heimbach, Andy, C.S.C.	1	1	.500	5.85	6	4	0	0	0	0	20.0	25	94	14	13	2	1	0	4	8	1	13	5	0
Hendricks, John, C'bia*	0	1	.000	8.76	7	0	0	0	3	0	12.1	15	63	18	12	3	0	1	4	6	0	12	0	0
Hernandez, Jose, Hick.	0	1	.000	0.00	1	0	0	0	0	0	1.1	0	1	1	0	0	0	0	1	0	0	0	0	0
Herrera, Alex, C'bus*	4	3	.571	3.43	20	0	0	0	2	0	42.0	41	186	25	16	1	3	3	3	21	1	41	2	1
Hertzel, Pat, C.S.C.	6	2	.250	5.33	14	14	0	0	0	0	79.1	105	352	57	47	12	2	1	5	19	0	53	4	0
Hopper, Joshua, C'bia*	1	4	.200	6.88	23	0	0	0	9	1	34.0	35	160	30	26	2	2	2	4	26	3	34	4	0
Houston, Ryan, Hag.	5	1	.833	2.21	6	6	0	0	0	0	36.2	17	136	9	9	2	0	1	0	13	0	27	1	0
Hubbel, Travis, Hag.	8	6	.571	3.89	19	19	0	0	0	0	113.1	103	478	62	49	7	3	3	10	55	0	75	13	0
Humrich, Chris, C.F.	4	1	.800	5.43	38	0	0	0	16	2	66.1	72	305	45	40	9	2	3	5	28	0	51	9	0
Hurley, Derek, Hick.*	2	1	.667	5.82	18	0	0	0	12	1	38.2	58	194	33	25	6	2	1	1	14	2	25	2	0
Igualada, Eric, Gre.	0	2	.000	8.56	9	0	0	0	3	0	13.2	17	66	13	13	1	3	0	0	10	2	9	2	0
Jackson, Jeremy, C'bia*	0	0	.000	0.00	2	0	0	0	1	0	3.0	4	13	0	0	0	0	0	1	0	1	2	1	0
Jacobsen, Landon, Hick.	3	0	1.000	3.64	5	4	0	0	0	0	29.2	40	141	16	12	0	0	3	4	13	0	25	1	0
Jarvais, Kregg, Aug.	0	0	.000	0.00	1	0	0	0	1	0	0.1	1	1	0	0	0	0	0	0	0	0	0	0	0
Jauregui, Miguel, C'bus	3	3	.500	4.20	29	1	0	0	8	2	64.1	59	287	34	30	1	1	2	11	30	1	64	3	0
Johnston, Mike, Hick.*	4	2	.667	6.22	26	0	0	0	7	2	50.2	66	245	42	35	2	2	5	30	0	52	0	2	
Jones, Sean, Del.	8	4	.667	4.33	39	3	0	0	9	0	68.2	72	303	38	33	2	2	4	8	23	1	65	3	0
Joseph, Jake, C'bia	4	3	.571	2.85	15	15	0	0	0	0	85.1	81	365	45	27	2	3	0	7	29	0	59	6	0
Kaanoi, Jason, C.W.Va.	0	1	.000	4.29	4	4	0	0	0	0	21.0	23	93	13	10	0	0	1	0	11	0	9	1	0
Kearney, Ryan, C'bus	0	0	.000	0.00	2	0	0	0	2	0	2.0	0	6	0	0	0	0	0	0	0	0	2	0	0
Keelin, Chris, Pied.	3	2	.600	3.25	45	1	0	0	21	1	61.0	36	255	26	22	4	5	0	6	37	0	82	5	1
Kelley, Chris, C'bus	1	1	.500	3.60	8	0	0	0	5	3	20.0	15	85	9	8	0	0	2	4	7	0	28	4	0
Kelly, Dan, Mac.*	1	0	1.000	2.37	12	0	0	0	6	0	19.0	17	78	5	5	2	1	1	0	3	0	18	0	0
Kennedy, Joe, C.S.C.*	11	6	.647	3.30	22	22	3	2	0	0	136.1	122	546	59	50	6	2	6	4	29	1	142	9	2
Kent, Nathan, Mac.	1	1	.500	4.66	5	1	0	0	4	0	9.2	9	42	5	5	0	1	3	0	5	1	7	0	0
Kibler, Ryan, Ash.	10	14	.417	4.41	26	26	0	0	0	0	155.0	173	711	107	76	9	3	1	14	67	0	110	7	0
Kidd, Jake, Ash.	1	1	.500	4.70	20	0	0	0	11	0	30.2	43	140	16	16	0	1	1	3	9	0	25	3	0
Klepacki, Ed, C.F.	7	4	.636	3.01	14	14	0	0	0	0	83.2	85	343	39	28	2	3	0	2	17	0	64	4	0
Knowles, Mike, Gre.	4	14	.222	5.83	24	22	0	0	0	0	114.1	150	544	98	74	7	4	5	12	53	1	66	15	0
Koeth, Mark, C'bus	2	1	.667	6.34	20	0	0	0	14	4	32.2	45	152	25	23	3	0	5	1	13	0	31	1	0
Kosderka, Matt, Sav.	5	4	.556	2.57	20	12	0	0	6	2	87.2	65	356	36	25	7	1	3	27	0	70	5	0	
Kozlowski, Ben, Mac.*	3	8	.273	4.21	15	14	0	0	0	0	77.0	76	353	53	36	6	2	4	6	39	0	67	4	2
Kremer, John, Gre.	1	6	.143	5.30	38	1	0	0	15	0	73.0	79	335	52	43	5	6	2	6	38	4	82	11	0
Kurtz-Nicholl, Jesse, C.W.Va.*	3	1	.750	2.56	29	0	0	0	14	1	38.2	29	161	13	11	2	2	2	17	0	31	3	0	
Labitzke, Jesse, Ash.*	1	0	1.000	4.96	36	0	0	0	9	0	52.2	64	248	32	29	3	3	2	0	36	0	38	2	0
Landreth, Jason, Hick.	0	0	.000	36.00	1	0	0	0	1	0	1.0	3	8	4	4	0	0	0	2	0	1	1	0	
Lara, Mauricio, Aug.*	1	0	1.000	1.41	16	0	0	0	4	0	32.0	25	133	11	5	2	0	1	2	13	0	33	5	0
Leach, Bryan, Aug.	3	3	.500	1.62	60	0	0	0	58	40	72.1	45	289	23	13	4	6	1	2	20	1	87	5	0
Ledden, Ryan, Hick.	1	2	.333	3.35	30	0	0	0	24	7	45.2	39	204	25	17	2	0	2	5	25	0	37	1	0
Ledezma, Wil, Aug.*	2	4	.333	5.13	14	14	0	0	0	0	52.2	51	240	33	30	3	1	1	2	36	0	60	5	0
Lee, Clifton, C.F.*	1	4	.200	5.24	11	11	0	0	0	0	44.2	50	217	39	26	1	1	1	36	0	63	3	2	
Lewis, Peyton, Hag.	0	3	.000	5.20	23	0	0	0	17	6	27.2	34	129	17	16	2	1	1	1	12	0	25	2	0
Lockwood, Luke, C.F.*	2	4	.333	4.50	9	9	0	0	0	0	48.0	49	209	32	24	3	2	1	5	20	1	33	2	0
Lopez, Jose, Hick.	3	4	.429	2.35	29	7	2	1	10	1	76.2	54	315	27	20	3	2	3	1	35	3	73	6	1
Lorenzo, Javier, Ash.	0	0	.000	14.63	6	0	0	0	1	1	8.0	12	52	15	13	1	1	1	3	11	0	9	2	0
Lowe, Matt, C'bia	0	1	.000	18.00	2	0	0	0	0	0	2.0	5	13	4	4	0	0	0	2	0	1	0	0	
Madson, Ryan, Pied.	14	5	.737	2.59	21	21	2	1	0	0	135.2	113	564	50	39	5	3	0	13	45	0	123	5	1
Magrane, Jim, C.S.C.	12	5	.706	2.76	27	27	1	1	0	0	173.0	158	710	64	53	9	3	0	4	43	0	162	14	1
Malaska, Mark, C.S.C.*	0	0	.000	9.00	2	0	0	0	2	0	2.0	3	8	2	2	1	0	0	0	0	0	3	0	0

Pitcher, Team	W	L	Pct.	ERA	G	GS	CG	ShO	GF	Sv.	IP	H	TBF	R	ER	HR	SH	SF	HB	BB	IBB	SO	WP	Bk.
Manning, Mike, C'bus	0	0	.000	12.46	5	0	0	0	3	2	4.1	4	25	7	6	0	1	2	1	6	0	2	0	0
Marietta, Ron, C'bus*	0	1	.000	0.00	1	0	0	0	1	0	0.0	1	3	1	0	0	0	1	1	1	0	1	0	0
Marini, Anthony, C'bus*	4	2	.667	3.18	11	10	0	0	1	0	62.1	63	267	24	22	2	3	3	4	26	1	44	0	0
Markwell, Diegomar, Hag.*	0	1	.000	9.00	2	0	0	0	0	0	2.0	3	15	2	2	0	1	0	0	5	0	2	0	0
Marsonek, Sam, Gre.	6	7	.462	4.25	18	18	1	0	0	0	114.1	114	510	64	54	8	1	3	23	51	0	78	15	2
Martinez, Anastacio, Aug.	9	6	.600	4.64	23	23	0	0	0	0	120.1	130	526	69	62	8	4	4	2	50	0	107	12	1
Martinez, David, Gre.*	2	5	.286	2.92	8	8	1	0	0	0	49.1	33	207	24	16	0	0	0	4	27	0	44	5	1
Matsko, Rick, C'bus	3	2	.600	2.29	26	0	0	0	10	3	55.0	37	222	16	14	1	3	1	4	21	1	68	2	0
McAvoy, Jeff, C.F.	1	2	.333	4.42	22	0	0	0	8	2	38.2	46	170	20	19	2	3	3	1	9	0	25	3	0
McClung, Michael, C.S.C.	2	1	.667	3.19	6	6	0	0	0	0	31.0	30	145	14	11	0	1	0	3	19	0	26	8	0
McCormick, Terry, C.S.C.*	0	0	.000	3.86	5	0	0	0	1	0	7.0	11	38	7	3	0	0	0	0	5	0	7	1	0
McGill, Frank, Sav.	3	6	.333	5.69	26	12	1	1	6	1	93.1	107	419	65	59	11	1	4	4	32	0	66	2	0
McNatt, Josh, Del.*	0	1	.000	8.10	7	0	0	0	1	0	10.0	15	49	9	9	1	1	0	0	7	1	2	1	0
Mikels, Jason, Mac.	1	5	.167	5.99	31	6	0	0	10	1	70.2	87	329	56	47	14	2	2	2	27	0	59	4	1
Minix, Travis, C.S.C.	4	2	.667	3.33	48	1	0	0	16	2	78.1	85	346	36	29	5	1	0	2	27	1	73	1	0
Miyamoto, Eij, C.F.	0	2	.000	3.78	3	3	0	0	0	0	16.2	15	74	8	7	1	0	0	2	9	0	20	1	0
Montero, Jose, Sav.	5	2	.714	2.92	34	0	0	0	13	3	61.2	44	274	26	20	1	2	2	9	36	0	62	8	2
Monzon, Yoel, Ash.	4	1	.800	3.23	39	0	0	0	10	2	64.0	48	271	28	23	9	0	2	9	20	0	83	2	0
Moore, Chris, Ash.	0	0	.000	13.50	1	0	0	0	1	0	0.2	2	4	1	1	0	0	1	0	0	0	0	0	0
Moreno, Edwin, Sav.	9	8	.529	3.25	23	22	1	0	0	0	133.0	127	562	58	48	9	1	2	7	46	0	89	6	0
Myers, Brett, Pied.	13	7	.650	3.18	27	27	2	1	0	0	175.1	165	738	78	62	7	1	4	9	69	0	140	8	0
Neil, Dan, C'bus*	6	4	.600	3.80	33	0	0	0	10	2	73.1	74	313	39	31	1	5	2	8	24	2	57	2	0
Nunez, Jose, C'bia*	3	4	.429	3.02	34	5	0	0	16	8	95.1	82	396	36	32	6	2	7	10	23	0	112	4	2
Obermueller, Wes, C.W.Va.	3	0	1.000	1.14	8	7	0	0	0	0	31.2	19	117	6	4	0	0	3	5	0	29	1	0
Oliver, Scott, Gre.	4	7	.364	5.03	29	7	0	0	8	1	96.2	108	441	61	54	7	2	1	5	45	0	71	8	1
Ortiz, Jose, C.S.C.	4	5	.444	3.84	46	0	0	0	27	9	58.2	49	267	35	25	4	5	3	2	38	4	51	9	0
Outlaw, Mark, Pied.*	5	2	.714	0.94	48	0	0	0	25	11	48.0	28	197	15	5	1	1	3	2	18	2	61	2	0
Pacheco, Enemencio, Ash.	8	10	.444	3.69	21	21	0	0	0	0	117.0	129	508	67	48	9	3	4	10	35	0	79	8	0
Paradis, Mike, Del.	6	5	.545	3.99	18	18	0	0	0	0	97.0	95	438	53	43	5	1	2	7	49	0	81	10	2
Pautz, Brad, Pied.	3	2	.600	2.33	13	11	1	0	0	0	65.2	53	272	20	17	2	0	5	4	24	0	33	3	0
Payne, Jerrod, Hag.	0	2	.000	3.71	19	0	0	0	17	8	17.0	15	70	9	7	0	2	0	6	6	0	6	2	0
Peguero, Radhame, C.S.C.	0	2	.000	5.06	4	4	0	0	0	0	16.0	16	80	17	9	2	0	3	15	0	13	2	0
Pena, Alex, Hick.	0	0	.000	5.00	3	2	0	0	0	0	9.0	8	39	5	5	0	0	1	7	0	3	0	0
Perez, Frank, Pied.	5	5	.500	3.04	36	9	0	0	12	2	97.2	85	410	47	33	3	2	4	9	39	1	64	7	0
Perez, Julio, Del.	6	2	.750	3.19	41	0	0	0	27	11	67.2	59	284	26	24	3	2	1	3	26	1	79	3	0
Perez, Randy, Del.*	10	9	.526	3.56	25	25	1	1	0	0	154.0	147	630	70	61	4	4	2	1	33	2	123	4	0
Pichardo, Carlos, C.W.Va.	5	6	.455	3.96	34	9	0	0	11	2	91.0	98	403	52	40	4	2	5	4	35	1	59	5	3
Pierce, Tony, Mac.	0	1	.000	7.20	1	1	0	0	0	0	5.0	7	22	4	4	2	0	0	0	4	0	4	0	0
Place, Eric, Hag.*	0	1	.000	5.40	4	0	0	0	3	0	5.0	6	21	3	3	0	0	1	0	0	6	0	0
Plank, Terry, Del.	3	7	.300	3.63	48	0	0	0	25	5	74.1	74	329	36	30	2	4	2	5	32	2	73	5	0
Polk, Scott, C'bia	7	2	.778	2.48	40	0	0	0	16	5	69.0	49	295	28	19	4	3	4	2	40	3	95	9	0
Powalski, Rich, Mac.*	2	5	.286	3.53	43	0	0	0	26	8	58.2	57	258	31	23	3	2	1	6	23	3	58	3	1
Pruett, Jason, C.S.C.*	6	4	.600	2.49	49	0	0	0	25	13	68.2	55	290	30	19	4	6	4	1	20	0	73	2	0
Pruitt, Jason, Del.*	0	0	.000	16.20	2	0	0	0	1	0	1.2	5	12	5	3	0	0	0	1	2	0	2	0	0
Puffer, Brandon, Ash.	0	0	.000	8.16	14	0	0	0	9	5	14.1	19	75	16	13	3	2	0	3	11	3	15	3	0
Reames, Jay, Sav.	0	0	.000	0.00	3	0	0	0	2	0	2.2	0	13	0	0	0	0	1	5	0	1	0	0
Reece, Dana, Hag.*	0	0	.000	7.33	34	1	0	0	11	0	43.0	65	226	47	35	5	1	1	2	31	0	37	11	1
Reid, Justin, Hick.	9	8	.529	3.04	27	22	5	0	4	3	170.0	146	694	82	57	12	3	4	3	30	0	176	5	0
Reimers, Cameron, Hag.	7	11	.389	3.73	26	26	2	0	0	0	154.1	158	671	79	64	10	5	4	21	45	0	112	14	2
Reinike, Chris, C'bus	0	0	.000	1.50	7	0	0	0	1	0	12.0	6	49	2	2	0	0	2	4	0	19	2	0
Renwick, Tyler, Hag.	3	2	.600	5.40	7	7	0	0	0	0	35.0	44	170	28	21	2	2	1	5	21	0	17	11	0
Riccobono, Rick, Aug.	10	7	.588	3.27	25	24	0	0	0	0	124.0	116	548	69	45	11	3	4	11	49	0	72	5	0
Richardson, Kasey, Ash.*	0	1	.000	5.11	9	0	0	0	4	0	12.1	16	56	10	7	3	0	1	0	5	0	9	1	0
Rincones, Rafael, C.W.Va.	0	0	.000	9.00	6	0	0	0	6	0	27.0	42	134	31	27	6	1	0	1	14	0	24	2	0
Rleal, Sendy, Del.	0	1	.000	10.80	1	1	0	0	0	0	3.1	3	18	5	4	0	0	1	3	0	4	0	0
Rodriguez, Alfredo, Sav.	1	0	1.000	6.52	6	0	0	0	2	0	9.2	10	43	7	7	2	0	0	2	3	0	6	1	0
Rodriguez, Cristobal, C.F.	5	6	.455	5.31	14	14	1	0	0	0	76.1	77	344	53	45	9	5	3	4	35	0	70	7	3
Rodriguez, Eddy, Del.	0	0	.000	1.80	4	0	0	0	1	0	5.0	5	21	1	1	0	0	0	2	0	3	0	0
Rodriguez, Jose, C.S.C.	1	3	.250	5.40	16	3	0	0	3	0	38.1	49	186	31	23	2	1	2	5	17	1	29	7	0
Rogers, Devin, C'bus	4	5	.444	4.52	20	20	0	0	0	0	89.2	78	409	59	45	6	5	2	7	66	0	83	8	0
Roller, Adam, Gre.	0	1	.000	1.31	13	0	0	0	5	1	20.2	15	87	6	3	1	1	1	1	5	1	22	6	0
Roque, Darryl, C.F.	1	1	.500	2.51	9	1	0	0	3	1	28.2	32	127	14	8	1	2	1	2	6	0	23	1	0
Rose, Michael, C.F.	0	0	.000	9.00	1	0	0	0	0	0	1.0	1	4	1	1	0	1	0	0	0	0	1	0	0
Rosengren, Phil, C'bus	3	5	.375	4.57	23	17	1	0	2	0	102.1	121	445	56	52	11	1	2	8	19	0	71	11	1
Rupp, Mike, Aug.	6	4	.600	3.78	30	0	0	0	5	0	64.1	65	282	30	27	4	2	3	3	29	0	44	1	0
Russ, Christopher, Sav.	3	1	.750	2.43	7	7	0	0	0	0	40.2	38	172	14	11	2	0	1	14	0	34	8	0
Sadler, Carl, C'bus*	1	3	.250	6.61	10	0	0	0	3	0	16.1	20	73	13	12	0	0	0	7	0	21	5	0
Sandoval, Marcos, Hag.	8	13	.381	4.56	28	25	2	1	0	0	163.2	188	721	105	83	20	3	3	15	49	3	100	3	2
Santos, Josh, C'bus*	3	8	.273	4.04	28	0	0	0	17	0	49.0	54	227	27	22	4	5	2	5	19	3	53	2	1
Saunders, Tony, C.S.C.*	0	0	.000	1.80	2	2	0	0	0	0	5.0	2	20	1	1	0	1	0	2	0	3	0	0
Schrock, Chris, C.S.C.	0	1	.000	0.00	1	0	0	0	1	0	0.0	1	1	1	1	0	0	0	0	0	0	0	0	0
Schwager, Matt, Del.	6	5	.545	3.29	47	0	0	0	23	5	76.2	78	324	35	28	6	5	4	4	21	3	66	4	1
Seale, Dustin, C.F.*	2	1	.667	1.64	5	0	0	0	5	0	11.0	8	48	3	2	0	1	1	1	7	0	13	0	0
Seestedt, Mike, Del.	0	0	.000	0.00	2	0	0	0	2	0	2.0	2	9	0	0	0	0	0	0	0	0	0	0	0
Serrano, Elio, Pied.	4	2	.667	2.27	38	0	0	0	13	5	67.1	67	287	26	17	5	4	1	10	15	0	56	3	0
Shelley, Jason, Hick.	0	0	.000	9.00	3	0	0	0	2	1	6.0	8	29	8	6	3	1	0	0	2	0	6	1	0
Simpson, Cory, Mac.	0	1	.000	2.55	7	3	1	0	3	0	17.2	16	83	10	5	1	1	0	1	10	0	16	1	0
Sirianni, Jay, C'bus*	1	3	.250	3.29	13	3	0	0	6	0	38.1	41	171	15	14	2	3	1	1	15	4	28	3	0
Smalley, Mike, Mac.*	4	4	.500	4.21	12	12	0	0	0	0	68.1	72	291	37	32	5	2	2	2	29	0	45	3	0
Smith, Hans, C.F.*	1	2	.333	1.74	17	0	0	0	11	7	31.0	33	132	8	6	0	2	0	6	2	23	2	0
Solano, Alex, Aug.	3	7	.300	5.46	33	1	0	0	19	0	56.0	65	259	45	34	8	5	2	5	22	1	38	6	0
Sollenberger, Matt, C'bia*	0	0	.000	6.35	4	0	0	0	3	0	5.2	7	29	5	4	0	1	1	4	1	0	8	2	0
Spencer, Corey, Aug.*	8	2	.800	2.61	53	0	0	0	11	2	96.2	90	423	46	28	4	3	4	5	34	0	119	4	0
Sperring, Jayme, Del.	0	0	.000	4.15	13	0	0	0	6	0	21.2	19	92	12	10	1	0	0	2	9	0	28	2	0

Pitcher, Team	W	L	Pct.	ERA	G	GS	CG	ShO	GF	Sv.	IP	H	TBF	R	ER	HR	SH	SF	HB	BB	IBB	SO	WP	Bk.
Spiers, Corey, Sav.*	4	3	.571	2.33	12	9	2	0	0	0	65.2	51	255	19	17	3	2	3	2	10	0	54	3	0
Stabile, Paul, Hick.*	0	0	.000	4.22	7	0	0	0	2	0	10.2	11	53	10	5	1	0	0	0	9	0	18	0	0
Stahl, Rich, Del.*	5	6	.455	3.34	20	20	0	0	0	0	89.0	97	399	47	33	3	2	0	0	51	0	83	9	1
Stamler, Keith, Sav.	0	1	.000	3.00	1	1	0	0	0	0	6.0	5	23	2	2	1	0	0	1	0	3	0	0
Stanford, Jason, C'bus*	7	4	.636	2.73	14	14	0	0	0	0	79.0	82	335	32	24	3	1	3	2	20	0	72	3	0
Stanton, Jeff, Gre.	1	0	1.000	0.82	4	0	0	0	2	1	11.0	11	47	1	1	1	1	0	0	3	2	4	1	0
Stepka, Tom, Ash.	0	5	.000	6.88	16	7	1	0	2	0	52.1	82	246	43	40	4	4	4	1	12	0	34	2	0
Stevens, Josh, Hag.	4	4	.500	2.99	47	3	0	0	15	5	84.1	97	363	42	28	4	3	2	3	19	1	95	9	0
Stiles, Brad, C.W.Va.*	1	5	.167	6.45	6	4	0	0	0	0	22.1	25	103	19	16	3	1	3	3	12	0	11	3	0
Stine, Justin, Hag.*	3	4	.429	3.13	41	0	0	0	9	1	54.2	53	229	28	19	2	2	1	0	26	1	46	3	0
Stodolka, Michael, C.W.Va.*	0	0	.000	7.71	1	1	0	0	0	0	4.2	3	21	4	4	0	0	0	0	4	0	0	0	0
Stokes, Brian, C.S.C.	5	6	.455	2.56	46	0	0	0	16	5	70.1	45	293	24	20	1	2	1	4	34	2	66	10	0
Sullivan, Ted, C'bus	1	0	1.000	5.87	10	0	0	0	10	3	15.1	24	77	16	10	1	2	4	1	4	1	5	1	0
Surridge, Lance, Aug.	3	1	.750	3.45	23	4	0	0	6	2	60.0	56	254	24	23	1	6	2	4	19	0	57	5	0
Tankersley, Dennis, Aug.	5	3	.625	4.06	15	15	1	1	0	0	75.1	73	326	41	34	4	0	4	32	0	74	1	1	
Taylor, Brien, C'bus*	0	0	.000	27.00	5	0	0	0	2	0	2.2	5	25	11	8	1	0	0	2	9	0	2	7	0
Terni, Chaz, Aug.	0	0	.000	45.00	1	0	0	0	1	0	1.0	5	11	8	5	2	0	0	2	0	0	0	0	0
Tetz, Kris, C.F.	1	0	1.000	5.64	19	0	0	0	16	6	22.1	15	96	19	14	2	1	0	0	18	0	19	1	0
Theodile, Simieon, Del.	3	1	.750	3.52	36	1	0	0	15	3	69.0	75	297	34	27	4	2	3	3	17	0	58	6	1
Toriz, Steve, C.F.	2	1	.667	6.75	10	0	0	0	2	0	14.2	19	78	19	11	1	0	0	2	14	0	16	1	0
Torres, Luis, Hick.	5	7	.417	4.49	23	21	0	0	1	0	110.1	121	511	73	55	10	3	5	12	60	0	68	4	0
Troilo, Joseph, Aug.	0	0	.000	1.17	2	1	0	0	1	0	7.2	4	26	1	1	1	0	0	0	1	0	8	0	0
Truitt, Derrick, Mac.	1	2	.333	1.97	40	0	0	0	11	2	73.0	55	306	29	16	3	2	4	8	27	1	43	4	0
Tsao, Chin-hui, Ash.	11	8	.579	2.73	24	24	0	0	0	0	145.0	119	591	54	44	8	3	2	5	40	0	187	6	1
Turner, Kyle, C.W.Va.*	2	3	.400	5.63	8	5	0	0	1	0	32.0	42	155	25	20	1	0	3	2	14	0	29	3	0
Valera, Nelson, C.S.C.	0	2	.000	7.50	18	0	0	0	8	0	30.0	46	150	29	25	4	0	3	1	13	1	22	4	0
Valle, Yoiset, Gre.*	1	0	1.000	3.04	6	3	0	0	2	0	23.2	23	98	10	8	0	1	2	0	8	0	16	5	0
Veras, Enger, C.S.C.	8	8	.500	4.81	20	20	1	0	0	0	106.2	125	493	74	57	7	2	1	11	41	0	102	11	1
Veronie, Shanin, Mac.	4	4	.500	2.71	43	0	0	0	34	13	66.1	48	269	22	20	4	3	1	4	26	2	69	2	0
Villalon, Julio, C.S.C.	1	0	1.000	6.38	4	3	0	0	0	0	18.1	18	78	14	13	2	0	0	3	6	0	25	0	0
Viole, Paul, C'bia	1	0	1.000	5.75	18	0	0	0	3	0	20.1	18	100	13	13	0	0	1	1	9	0	26	2	1
Wade, Matt, C'bus	2	4	.333	6.69	10	10	0	0	0	0	40.1	61	195	33	30	0	3	4	3	16	0	24	1	0
Walker, Adam, Pied.*	6	1	.857	2.05	8	8	0	0	0	0	48.1	37	196	11	11	1	1	0	2	14	0	50	3	0
Wallace, Shane, C'bus*	2	2	.500	2.82	13	8	1	0	2	1	54.1	53	227	27	17	6	4	1	3	14	1	40	2	0
Warren, Chris, Ash.	0	0	1.000	0.00	1	0	0	0	1	0	2.0	1	8	0	0	0	0	0	0	1	0	1	0	0
Washburn, Ben, C.F.	3	0	1.000	1.30	7	7	0	0	0	0	48.1	30	188	14	7	1	2	0	1	9	0	34	0	0
Watkins, David, Mac.	0	2	.000	7.16	4	4	0	0	0	0	16.1	24	76	17	13	4	0	2	1	5	0	8	1	1
Weaver, Joe, Sav.	1	1	.500	4.47	22	3	0	0	8	1	46.1	42	198	26	23	5	0	2	3	12	0	33	4	0
Weber, Brett, Gre.	0	0	.000	2.60	16	0	0	0	10	2	17.1	14	71	5	5	0	0	1	0	6	0	18	1	0
Weslowski, Robert, C'bia	3	4	.429	2.48	39	1	0	0	18	7	83.1	75	362	28	23	2	3	4	4	43	3	98	9	0
Westmoreland, Ken, Pied.	2	2	.500	4.28	7	7	0	0	0	0	33.2	33	147	23	16	2	1	0	2	18	0	21	2	0
Whitecotton, Billy, Del.	1	1	.500	5.72	6	6	0	0	0	0	28.1	32	125	18	18	4	0	2	17	0	25	3	0	
Williams, Dave, Hick.*	11	9	.550	2.96	24	24	1	1	0	0	170.0	145	687	66	56	14	11	2	9	39	2	193	4	0
Willoughby, Justin, Mac.*	3	6	.333	5.07	38	6	0	0	13	1	76.1	79	337	46	43	2	3	3	0	35	0	64	3	0
Witte, Lou, Gre.	3	3	.500	4.83	31	0	0	0	15	3	50.1	66	232	38	27	4	1	2	0	15	3	31	2	0
Wright, Barrett, C.S.C.	0	2	.000	5.81	5	5	0	0	0	0	26.1	34	123	19	17	1	0	2	1	12	0	10	3	1
Wright, Brad, C'bia*	0	0	.000	4.50	2	0	0	0	2	0	2.0	1	7	1	1	1	0	0	0	0	0	1	0	0
Wright, Shane, Hick.	3	3	.500	5.00	32	1	0	0	14	4	75.2	99	352	54	42	7	3	4	6	20	1	58	5	0
Yen, Buddy, C.W.Va.	1	1	.500	5.09	29	0	0	0	16	0	35.1	35	179	30	20	1	5	1	5	29	0	38	6	0
Young, Colin, Ash.*	3	1	.750	1.41	36	0	0	0	18	2	64.0	37	247	10	10	2	3	1	4	22	2	91	1	0
Zurita, Thomas, C.W.Va.	1	2	.333	5.76	14	0	0	0	4	1	25.0	29	116	20	16	0	1	3	2	11	0	14	4	1

COMBINATION SHUTOUTS: **Asheville (6)**—Chin-hui-Cercy-Esslinger, Pacheco-Young-Esslinger, Tsao-Monzon-Esslinger, Pacheco-Esslinger, De Paula-Monzon-Esslinger, Dohmann-Cercy. **Augusta (8)**—Baker-Leach, Ledezma-Surridge-Castro, Gamble-Harvey-Leach, Matinez-Solano, Gamble-Dickinson-Harvey-Leach, Martinez-Leach, Glaser-Surridge-Harvey, Glaser-Leach. **Cape Fear (3)**—Klepacki-Perez, Klepacki-Casadiego-Tetz, Dorn-Perez. **Charleston, S.C. (4)**—Kennedy-Rodriguez-Pruett-Ortiz, Frendling-Pruett, Frendling-Smith-Ortiz, Veras-Smith. **Charleston, W.Va. (7)**—Obermueller-Garcia, Obermueller-Coa, Douglass-Gehrke, Baerlocher-Gehrke-Gilfillan, Obermueller-Pichardo-Gehrke, Gobble-Coa, Pichardo-Kurtz-Nicholl. **Columbia (6)**—Dunning-Lowe-Nunez-Weslowski, Chenard-Polk, Graham-Polk, Joseph-Polk, Graham-Halvorson-Polk, Graham-Corcoran. **Columbus (5)**—Rogers-Jauregui-Manning, Stanford-Neil-Colon, Rogers-Neil-Colon, Rosengren-Matsko, Marini-Kelley. **Delmarva (3)**—Bedard-Fleming-Babula-Schwager, Stahl-Fleming, Perez-Fleming. **Greensboro (1)**—Day-Franco. **Hagerstown (2)**—Hubbel-Hamann, Houston-Stevens. **Hickory (4)**—Williams-Carrasco, Bradley-Carrasco, Williams-Ledden, Bradley-Bumatay-Wright-Pena. **Macon (6)**—Butler-Gawer-Curtiss, Kozlowski-Gawer-Veronie-Powalski, Ennis-Powalski, Butler-Gawer-Powalski, Ennis-Powalski, Butler-Kelly-Veronie. **Piedmont (7)**—Myers-Perez, Walker-Bailie, Myers-Bailie, Madson-Bailie, Brooks-Bailie, Pautz-Keelin-Outlaw-Fry, Pautz-Bailie-Keelin-Outlaw. **Savannah (10)**—Kosderka-Cavazos, Dittfurth-Garcia, Moreno-Weaver, Dittfurth-Backsmeyer, Kosderka-Garcia, Dittfurth-Montero, Garcia-Montero, Cedeno-Cullen, Spiers-Backsmeyer-Montero-Reames, Spiers-Backsmeyer-McGill.

NO-HIT GAMES: De Paula, Asheville defeated Cape Fear, 1-0, June 26; Glaser, Augusta defeated Hagerstown, 3-0, August 18.

PITCHERS WITH TWO OR MORE TEAMS

Pitcher, Team	W	L	Pct.	ERA	G	GS	CG	ShO	GF	Sv.	IP	H	TBF	R	ER	HR	SH	SF	HB	BB	IBB	SO	WP	Bk.
Gorman, Pat, C'bia	2	2	.500	1.93	30	0	0	0	27	15	37.1	24	163	10	8	1	1	1	1	28	2	54	9	0
Gorman, Pat, Del.	0	0	.000	0.00	2	0	0	0	2	1	2.2	1	11	0	0	0	0	1	1	0	5	0	0	

2000 FIELDING

TEAM

Team	Pct.	G	PO	A	E	TC	DP	TP	PB
Savannah	.969	139	3623	1382	158	5163	106	0	22
Delmarva	.969	136	3568	1429	159	5156	64	0	29
Piedmont	.969	137	3587	1394	159	5140	108	0	27
Augusta	.966	141	3687	1341	175	5203	83	0	30
Asheville	.965	135	3562	1426	183	5171	129	0	21
Macon	.963	139	3659	1468	195	5322	102	0	16
Charleston, S.C.	.963	139	3709	1537	202	5448	121	0	27
Charleston, W.V.	.963	133	3419	1453	188	5060	111	0	26
Columbia	.963	137	3539	1409	191	5139	111	0	38
Greensboro	.963	137	3542	1544	197	5283	104	0	35
Columbus	.963	137	3589	1444	195	5228	107	0	31
Cape Fear	.962	138	3585	1441	199	5225	97	0	51
Hagerstown	.960	137	3503	1468	206	5177	150	0	31
Hickory	.952	141	3800	1542	272	5614	96	0	24

INDIVIDUAL

FIRST BASEMEN

NOTE: All caps denotes fielding-percentage leader based on 71 games for catchers, 95 for all other non-pitchers and 114 innings for pitchers. *Throws lefthanded.

Player, Team	Pct.	G	PO	A	E	TC	DP
Alvarez, Tony, Hick.	.938	7	70	6	5	81	7
Angell, Rick, Sav.	1.000	4	35	3	0	38	3
Autry, Brian, C.F.	.987	8	75	3	1	79	4
Baker, Jacob, C.W.Va.	.989	21	169	17	2	188	13
Batista, Carlos, C'bus	.985	49	428	19	7	454	31
Bost, Tom, C'bus	1.000	1	6	1	0	7	1
Brazell, Craig, C'bia	.973	86	615	44	18	677	56
Bubela, Brent, Sav.	.973	21	176	6	5	187	14
Calzado, Napolean, Del.	1.000	6	9	1	0	10	0
Castaneda, Cesar, Sav.	1.000	28	169	6	0	175	10
Chiaffredo, Paul, Hag.	1.000	5	23	5	0	28	2
Chwan, Brian, C.S.C.	1.000	2	2	0	0	2	1
Clay, Mike, C.W.Va.	.972	17	126	11	4	141	10
Cotten, Jeremy, Hick.	.989	52	416	21	5	442	30
Crocker, Nickolas, Mac.*	.000	1	0	0	0	0	0
Delgado, Chris, Ash.	.986	17	136	4	2	142	17
Deschenes, Pat, C'bia	1.000	9	29	0	0	29	4
Duck, Kevin, Ash.*	.994	39	318	19	2	339	33
Elder, Rick, Del.*	.980	10	96	2	2	100	4
Espy, Nate, Pied.	.993	128	1069	67	8	1144	93
Esquerra, Marques, C'bus	.991	13	101	5	1	107	9
Fiore, Curt, Mac.	.991	65	498	39	5	542	33
Garcia, Luis, Aug.	.985	115	941	52	15	1008	65
Gay, Curt, C'bus*	.983	54	438	28	8	474	39
Gredvig, Doug, Del.	.979	12	89	4	2	95	7
Grindell, Nate, C'bus	.952	3	17	3	1	21	2
Grummitt, Dan, C.S.C.	.995	58	513	32	3	548	40
Guyton, Eric, C'bia	.991	28	202	8	2	212	24
Halloran, Matt, Sav.	1.000	1	6	0	0	6	1
Hitchcox, Brian, Pied.	.943	5	30	3	2	35	3
Holliday, Josh, Hag.	.985	30	243	28	4	275	36
House, J.R., Hick.	.980	5	48	2	1	51	5
Isenia, Chairon, C.S.C.	1.000	3	12	0	0	12	3
Jacobs, John, C.S.C.	1.000	2	9	0	0	9	1
Jenkins, Brian, C'bia	1.000	2	6	0	0	6	1
Johannes, Todd, C.F.	1.000	1	1	1	0	2	0
Jones, Jason, Sav.	.990	98	840	42	9	891	68
Keene, Kurt, Hag.	.983	42	374	21	7	402	47
Landreth, Jason, Hick.	.986	18	133	9	2	144	8
Lane, Rich, C.F.*	.989	62	536	21	6	563	43
Leal, Jaeme, Mac.	.984	57	467	33	8	508	37
Leaumont, Jeff, Gre.*	.990	79	693	31	7	731	58
Lebron, Francisco, C'bia	.965	10	78	4	3	85	5
Lehr, Ryan, Mac.	.982	27	207	12	4	223	20
Leon, Alfredo, Del.	.909	6	20	0	2	22	0
Lutz, David, C.F.	.987	9	67	8	1	76	6
McQueen, Eric, Ash.	1.000	7	47	1	0	48	3
Melucci, Lou, C.F.	1.000	3	17	4	0	21	1
Merhoff, Aaron, Pied.	.977	8	42	0	1	43	3
Moore, Chris, Ash.	1.000	3	23	3	0	26	2
Moyer, Kyle, C'bus*	.988	19	158	11	2	171	15
Nettles, Jeff, Gre.	1.000	1	6	0	0	6	0
Olson, Eric, Gre.	1.000	4	44	2	0	46	2
Palmieri, Jon, C.F.	.991	27	218	15	2	235	13
Paulino, Ron, Hick.	1.000	1	4	0	0	4	0
Pressley, Josh, C.S.C.	.992	82	726	47	6	779	63
RACHELS, Wesley, Del.	.996	113	893	57	4	954	46
Ramos, Kelly, Aug.	.967	5	28	1	1	30	2
Raymundo, Gregg, C.W.Va.	.963	5	48	4	2	54	6
Rickon, Jim, C'bus	1.000	2	5	1	0	6	0
Rinne, Jim, Ash.	.667	1	2	0	1	3	0
Sanchez, Tino, Ash.	.989	40	336	17	4	357	24
Santana, Emmanuel, C.W.Va.	.990	36	294	17	3	314	27
Santos, Chad, C.W.Va.*	.988	59	530	32	7	569	43
Santos, Juan, Hag.	.981	6	48	3	1	52	6
Schneider, Matt, Hick.	.980	66	551	26	12	589	40
Schrock, Chris, C.S.C.	1.000	2	3	0	0	3	0
Seestedt, Mike, Del.	1.000	14	51	2	0	53	2
Sherlock, Brian, C.F.	.941	3	15	1	1	17	1
Smith, Sam, Ash.	.987	34	289	19	4	312	29
Snyder, Mike, Hag.	.975	53	408	28	11	447	31
Umbria, Jose, Hag.	.936	7	70	3	5	78	8
Washington, Dion, Gre.	.982	56	526	19	10	555	39
Williams, Brady, Aug.	.989	21	164	22	2	188	10
Williams, Clyde, C.F.*	.976	28	228	19	6	253	20
Wright, Brad, C'bia*	.979	23	173	12	4	189	15

SECOND BASEMEN

Player, Team	Pct.	G	PO	A	E	TC	DP
Abreu, Dave, C'bia	.940	64	106	161	17	284	39
Acevedo, Inocencio, Sav.	.965	47	64	102	6	172	15
Alvarez, Jimmy, Hag.	.975	24	46	71	3	120	15
Anderson, Jon, Aug.	.964	25	46	61	4	111	11
Angell, Rick, Sav.	.885	9	11	12	3	26	3
Barmes, Clint, Ash.	.959	14	16	31	2	49	5
Bonifay, Josh, Hick.	.956	98	181	278	21	480	47
Boyer, Bret, C.F.	.968	47	73	80	5	158	18
Brett, Jason, C'bia	.958	43	75	108	8	191	24
Brewer, Jace, C.S.C.	1.000	1	1	2	0	3	0
Bultmann, Kurt, Hick.	.958	36	67	94	7	168	17
Cantu, Jorge, C.S.C.	1.000	1	2	3	0	5	1
Castillo, Carlos, C'bia	.948	15	26	29	3	58	8
Cates, Gary, Del.	.983	31	47	72	2	121	10
Centeno, Irwin, C.S.C.	.932	29	73	91	12	176	27
De La Cruz, Ruddi, C'bia	.965	24	51	60	4	115	7
De Los Santos, Hector, Aug.	1.000	3	7	8	0	15	1
Dennis, Les, Aug.	1.000	9	20	25	0	45	9
De Renne, Keoni, Mac.	1.000	5	4	9	0	13	0
Docen, Jose, C.F.	.962	31	54	96	6	156	13
Elzy, Steve, C'bia	1.000	1	0	2	0	2	0
Gambino, Michael, Aug.	.971	17	31	37	2	70	7
Garcia, Oscar, C'bus	.968	12	28	33	2	63	12
Goudie, Jaime, Hag.	.969	99	203	233	14	450	67
Green, Nick, Mac.	1.000	2	3	5	0	8	1
Halloran, Matt, Sav.	.982	16	23	31	1	55	8
Hannahan, Buzz, Pied.	.943	25	51	65	7	123	13
Harris, Willie, Del.	.972	111	216	298	15	529	37
Hine, Steve, Sav.	.969	86	146	234	12	392	44
Hitchcox, Brian, Pied.	.979	80	148	221	8	377	56
Hopper, Norris, C.W.Va.	.923	29	53	55	9	117	12
Isenia, Chairon, C.S.C.	.750	1	0	3	1	4	0
Jackson, Brandon, Hag.	.938	3	7	8	1	16	2
Jacobs, John, C.S.C.	.917	7	9	24	3	36	5
Kerrigan, Joe, Aug.	.990	22	33	68	1	102	14
Leal, Jaeme, Mac.	.000	1	0	0	0	0	0
Lora, Thomas, C.W.Va.	.964	76	163	189	13	365	47
Lowe, Steve, C'bus	.960	18	35	37	3	75	8
Manning, Pat, Mac.	.973	119	218	326	15	559	73
Martinez, Louis, Mac.	.981	14	23	29	1	53	5
McKinley, Josh, C.F.	.934	18	32	39	5	76	9
Melucci, Lou, C.F.	.938	25	42	64	7	113	15
Mitchell, Todd, Gre.	.967	21	35	54	3	92	9
Moore, Chris, Ash.	.963	17	32	45	3	80	7
Moore, Frank, C.S.C.	.950	95	167	268	23	458	43
MORAGA, Omar, C'bus	.975	111	196	263	12	471	63
Perez, Deivi, Hick.	.918	18	19	37	5	61	10
Phillips, Brandon, C.F.	.857	2	3	3	1	7	2
Rachels, Wesley, Del.	1.000	10	9	7	0	16	0
Reyes, Ambiorix, Pied.	.939	9	20	26	3	49	5
Rodriguez, Ronny, Aug.	.923	4	9	3	1	13	0
Rogers, Ed, Del.	1.000	1	1	0	0	1	0
Rojas, Alex, Pied.	.952	27	48	70	6	124	10
Ruiz, Willy, C.W.Va.	.955	30	56	91	7	154	15
Santoro, Pat, Aug.	.945	28	52	68	7	127	11
Saucke, Casey, Del.	1.000	2	1	3	0	4	1
Schrock, Chris, C.S.C.	.909	6	4	6	1	11	1
Seale, Marvin, C'bia	.000	1	0	0	0	0	0
Sherlock, Brian, C.F.	.952	9	20	20	2	42	4
Smith, Brett, C.S.C.	1.000	3	1	4	0	5	1
Smith, Sam, Ash.	1.000	1	2	0	0	2	0
Terni, Chaz, Aug.	.981	37	71	84	3	158	13
Tyson, Torre, Gre.	.963	119	231	348	22	601	67
Valdez, Wilson, C.F.	.952	10	16	24	2	42	4
Vilorio, Miguel, Ash.	.964	89	156	241	15	412	58
Wakakuwa, Kenn, C.S.C.	.750	1	0	3	1	4	0
Warren, Chris, Ash.	.954	19	42	61	5	108	14
Weekly, Chris, Hag.	.959	15	32	38	3	73	10
Williams, Brady, Aug.	1.000	1	2	2	0	4	0

THIRD BASEMEN

Player, Team	Pct.	G	PO	A	E	TC	DP
Abreu, Dave, C'bia	.500	2	0	2	2	4	0
Baker, Jacob, C.W.Va.	.970	13	3	29	1	33	2
Barmes, Clint, Ash.	1.000	2	3	6	0	9	0
Batson, Tom, Pied.	.877	48	44	84	18	146	8
Bernhardt, Jossephang, Hag.	.600	1	0	3	2	5	0
BLALOCK, Hank, Sav.	.942	139	72	253	20	345	22
Boyer, Bret, C.F.	1.000	1	0	1	0	1	0
Brett, Jason, C'bia	.933	17	9	19	2	30	2
Bultmann, Kurt, Hick.	1.000	4	2	5	0	7	0

Player, Team	Pct.	G	PO	A	E	TC	DP
Calzado, Napolean, Del.	.916	131	95	242	31	368	10
Castaneda, Cesar, Sav.	1.000	6	4	7	0	11	0
Cates, Gary, Del.	.963	19	6	20	1	27	1
Centeno, Irwin, C.S.C.	1.000	1	0	1	0	1	1
Cervenak, Mike, Gre.	.971	34	23	77	3	103	2
Clay, Mike, C.W.Va.	.935	41	36	108	10	154	7
Corporan, Elvis, Gre.	.915	61	59	123	17	199	13
Cosby, Rob, Hag.	.898	70	45	149	22	216	10
Cruz, Enrique, C'bia	.800	7	3	1	1	5	0
De Caster, Yurendell, C.S.C.	.916	68	51	124	16	191	5
De La Cruz, Ruddi, C'bia	.000	1	0	0	0	0	0
Dennis, Les, Aug.	.929	11	7	19	2	28	1
Deschenes, Pat, C'bia	.936	121	79	229	21	329	13
Esquerra, Marques, C'bus	.903	10	11	17	3	31	0
Fagan, Shawn, Hag.	.889	43	36	100	17	153	11
Fiore, Curt, Mac.	.804	18	11	30	10	51	1
Garcia, Oscar, C'bus	1.000	13	7	30	0	37	0
Grindell, Nate, C'bus	.890	114	84	222	38	344	21
Guyton, Eric, C'bia	.952	9	6	14	1	21	2
Halloran, Matt, Sav.	1.000	1	1	1	0	2	0
Hannahan, Buzz, Pied.	.902	34	18	56	8	82	3
Hine, Steve, Sav.	.000	1	0	0	0	0	0
Hitchcox, Brian, Pied.	.952	17	6	14	1	21	0
Holliday, Josh, Hag.	1.000	3	1	4	0	5	0
Humrich, Chris, C.F.	1.000	1	0	1	0	1	0
Isenia, Chairon, C.S.C.	.500	3	1	3	4	8	0
Jackson, Brandon, Hag.	.842	8	7	9	3	19	0
Jacobs, John, C.S.C.	1.000	1	1	0	0	1	0
Kessick, Jon, Del.	.000	1	0	0	0	0	0
Langston, James, Hick.	.878	106	66	207	38	311	10
Lowe, Steve, C'bus	.000	1	0	0	0	0	0
Lugo, Felix, C.F.	.907	15	17	22	4	43	2
Manning, Pat, Mac.	.889	2	1	7	1	9	0
Martinez, Louis, Mac.	1.000	7	3	21	0	24	3
McKinley, Josh, C.F.	.866	96	90	176	41	307	14
Melucci, Lou, C.F.	.943	21	18	48	4	70	3
Mercado, Wilkins, C.W.Va.	.943	42	26	90	7	123	6
Minus, Steve, Aug.	.915	65	31	119	14	164	7
Mitchell, Todd, Gre.	1.000	1	1	3	0	4	0
Moore, Chris, Ash.	.955	36	20	65	4	89	2
Nettles, Jeff, Gre.	.905	33	21	74	10	105	5
Olson, Eric, Gre.	.739	8	5	12	6	23	1
Oropeza, Asdrubal, Mac.	.900	113	64	251	35	350	12
Palmieri, Jon, C.F.	1.000	1	0	3	0	3	0
Paulino, Ron, Hick.	.000	1	0	0	0	0	0
Peralta, John, C'bus	.833	1	1	4	1	6	1
Perez, Deivi, Hick.	.930	38	19	74	7	100	2
Pressley, Josh, C.S.C.	1.000	1	2	1	0	3	0
Raymundo, Gregg, C.W.Va.	.896	12	6	37	5	48	5
Reyes, Ambiorix, Pied.	.800	3	2	2	1	5	0
Richardson, Juan, Pied.	.887	40	20	66	11	97	5
Rickon, Jim, C'bus	.000	1	0	0	0	0	0
Ross, Donovan, C.W.Va.	.897	29	24	63	10	97	3
Ruiz, Willy, C.W.Va.	.500	1	0	1	1	2	0
Salas, Juan, C.S.C.	.898	55	46	86	15	147	7
Sanchez, Tino, Ash.	.000	1	0	0	0	0	0
Saucke, Casey, Del.	1.000	4	1	1	0	2	0
Schrock, Chris, C.S.C.	.971	14	12	22	1	35	0
Seestedt, Mike, Del.	1.000	1	0	1	0	1	0
Sherlock, Brian, C.F.	1.000	9	8	17	0	25	3
Smith, Brett, C.S.C.	1.000	2	1	3	0	4	0
Smith, Sam, Ash.	.882	51	32	80	15	127	13
Terni, Chaz, Aug.	.890	38	28	77	13	118	4
Warren, Chris, Ash.	.887	48	33	93	16	142	8
Weekly, Chris, Hag.	.844	15	9	29	7	45	5
Williams, Brady, Aug.	.917	30	16	50	6	72	1

SHORTSTOPS

Player, Team	Pct.	G	PO	A	E	TC	DP
Acevedo, Inocencio, Sav.	.973	11	11	25	1	37	2
Alvarez, Jimmy, Hag.	.871	23	36	65	15	116	20
Anderson, Jon, Aug.	.956	62	78	161	11	250	19
Barmes, Clint, Ash.	1.000	4	8	16	0	24	1
Bernhardt, Jossephang, Hag.	1.000	1	1	6	0	7	0
Boyer, Bret, C.F.	1.000	5	4	9	0	13	2
Brett, Jason, C'bia	.944	11	13	21	2	36	5
Brewer, Jace, C.S.C.	.933	29	37	89	9	135	18
Cantu, Jorge, C.S.C.	.927	45	66	149	17	232	33
Castillo, Carlos, C'bia	.926	16	32	43	6	81	8
Castillo, Jose, Hick.	.908	123	198	392	60	650	62
Castillo, Victor, Gre.	.926	81	112	251	29	392	40
Cates, Gary, Del.	.936	57	67	122	13	202	19
Clay, Mike, C.W.Va.	.956	11	19	24	2	45	6

Player, Team	Pct.	G	PO	A	E	TC	DP
Cleto, Ambioris, Hick.	.842	4	6	10	3	19	2
Collazo, Julio, Pied.	.952	86	128	247	19	394	48
Contreras, Erick, Mac.	.932	14	20	35	4	59	5
Cruz, Enrique, C'bia	.909	45	69	111	18	198	11
De La Cruz, Ruddi, C'bia	.920	32	26	77	9	112	17
Dennis, Les, Aug.	1.000	3	5	8	0	13	2
De Renne, Keoni, Mac.	.959	34	51	90	6	147	20
Esquerra, Marques, C'bus	.800	1	1	3	1	5	0
Garcia, Oscar, C'bus	.872	8	12	22	5	39	4
Green, Nick, Mac.	.909	83	128	242	37	407	45
Griffin, Justin, C'bus	1.000	2	0	4	0	4	0
Gutierrez, Derrick, Del.	.867	4	4	9	2	15	0
Guzman, Juan, C.W.Va.	.927	19	29	60	7	96	17
Halloran, Matt, Sav.	.896	15	11	32	5	48	5
Hannahan, Buzz, Pied.	.875	9	6	15	3	24	4
Harris, Willie, Del.	.818	7	7	11	4	22	1
Hine, Steve, Sav.	1.000	7	8	16	0	24	3
Isturiz, Maicer, C'bus	.846	5	3	8	2	13	0
Jackson, Brandon, Hag.	.957	92	151	273	19	443	58
Keene, Kurt, Hag.	.962	6	6	19	1	26	6
Leal, Jaeme, Mac.	.000	1	0	0	0	0	0
Lincoln, Justin, Ash.	.933	126	180	359	39	578	81
Lora, Thomas, C.W.Va.	.919	27	44	92	12	148	14
Lowe, Steve, C'bus	.894	23	28	56	10	94	6
Martinez, Louis, Mac.	.942	12	14	35	3	52	5
Martinez, Ramon, Sav.	.917	39	48	118	15	181	16
Medrano, Steve, C.W.Va.	.974	43	65	119	5	189	22
Melucci, Lou, C.F.	.897	10	6	29	4	39	4
Mitchell, Todd, Gre.	.946	31	35	87	7	129	18
Moore, Chris, Ash.	.880	6	6	16	3	25	2
Morban, Jose, Sav.	.934	78	114	228	24	366	42
Nettles, Jeff, Gre.	.916	33	43	88	12	143	13
Oropeza, Asdrubal, Mac.	.833	1	2	3	1	6	1
PERALTA, John, C'bus	.949	105	151	319	25	495	56
Perez, Deivi, Hick.	.932	20	35	47	6	88	5
Phillips, Brandon, C.F.	.941	121	207	356	35	598	57
Reyes, Ambiorix, Pied.	.961	51	53	142	8	203	24
Rogers, Ed, Del.	.947	80	117	222	19	358	27
Roper, Douglas, Hag.	.934	22	35	50	6	91	11
Ruiz, Willy, C.W.Va.	.940	34	56	115	11	182	17
Saba, Cesar, Aug.	.915	41	57	104	15	176	20
Salas, Juan, C.S.C.	.950	5	9	10	1	20	1
Sanchez, Frederick, Aug.	.976	30	49	75	3	127	16
Saucke, Casey, Del.	.000	2	0	0	0	0	0
Schrock, Chris, C.S.C.	.922	41	58	107	14	179	18
Shipp, Brian, C'bia	.936	49	68	150	15	233	28
Smith, Brett, C.S.C.	.923	7	5	19	2	26	4
Terni, Chaz, Aug.	.931	8	14	13	2	29	2
Valdez, Wilson, C.F.	.857	5	6	12	3	21	3
Volquez, Bolivar, C.S.C.	.970	17	28	68	3	99	14
Warren, Chris, Ash.	.727	3	4	4	3	11	1

OUTFIELDERS

Player, Team	Pct.	G	PO	A	E	TC	DP
Abreu, Dave, C'bia	.000	1	0	0	0	0	0
Acevedo, Carlos, Pied.	.975	24	39	0	1	40	0
Acuna, Ron, C.W.Va.	1.000	10	14	0	0	14	0
Alamo, Efrain, C.S.C.	1.000	8	9	0	0	9	0
Alvarez, Tony, Hick.	.956	101	184	13	9	206	3
Anderson, Jon, Aug.	1.000	1	1	0	0	1	0
Angell, Rick, Sav.	.970	103	183	10	6	199	2
Baker, Jacob, C.W.Va.	.976	55	78	2	2	82	1
Barmes, Clint, Ash.	1.000	1	3	1	0	4	1
Batista, Angel, C.S.C.*	1.000	38	73	4	0	77	3
Batista, Carlos, C'bus	1.000	1	2	0	0	2	0
Beverly, Shomari, Pied.	.984	76	178	7	3	188	1
Bonifay, Josh, Hick.	1.000	7	9	0	0	9	0
Bost, Tom, C'bus	.988	50	79	4	1	84	0
Brazell, Craig, C'bia	.000	1	0	0	0	0	0
Brazoban, Yhency, Gre.	1.000	11	7	0	0	7	0
Brown, Andy, Gre.*	.970	114	177	14	6	197	3
Bultmann, Kurt, Hick.	1.000	4	3	0	0	3	0
Bundy, Ryan, Hag.	.944	16	16	1	1	18	0
Byrd, Marlon, Pied.	.980	103	192	9	4	205	0
Cabrera, Ray, Del.	.961	101	160	13	7	180	0
Cadiente, Brett, Sav.*	.977	122	253	1	6	260	0
Carter, Shannon, Hag.*	.941	114	207	15	14	236	4
Castaneda, Cesar, Sav.	.000	2	0	0	0	0	0
Castillo, Carlos, C'bia.	.000	1	0	0	0	0	0
Castro, Martires, C.F.	.965	123	235	13	9	257	1
Castro, Vince, Hick.	1.000	14	24	0	0	24	0
Catalanotte, Greg, Ash.	.946	116	144	15	9	168	1
Cates, Gary, Del.	1.000	3	2	0	0	2	0

Player, Team	Pct.	G	PO	A	E	TC	DP
Clark, Chivas, Hag.*	1.000	30	38	1	0	39	0
Cordova, Ben, C.W.Va.*	.977	26	43	0	1	44	0
Crawford, Carl, C.S.C.*	.968	131	232	7	8	247	3
Crocker, Nickolas, Mac.*	.951	58	90	7	5	102	1
Dees, Charlie, Del.	1.000	4	2	0	0	2	0
De Los Santos, Hector, Aug.	.667	3	2	0	1	3	0
Elzy, Steve, C'bia	.000	1	0	0	0	0	0
Espinoza, Andres, C.F.	1.000	33	63	1	0	64	0
Esquerra, Marques, C'bus	.857	7	6	0	1	7	0
Fera, Aaron, Hag.	.982	36	50	4	1	55	1
Fiore, Curt, Mac.	1.000	2	1	0	0	1	0
Ford, Lew, Aug.	.994	124	309	12	2	323	0
Fowler, David, Gre.	.945	26	51	1	3	55	0
Freitas, Jeremy, C.W.Va.	.968	34	26	4	1	31	2
Gallaher, T.T., C'bus	.977	67	119	8	3	130	1
Garcia, Oscar, C'bus	1.000	2	7	0	0	7	0
Gettis, Byron, C.W.Va.	.979	94	169	17	4	190	0
Gingrich, Troy, C.F.*	.944	42	64	3	4	71	1
Gonzalez, Julian, C.W.Va.	.885	16	23	0	3	26	0
Gordon, Alexis, Del.*	.750	1	3	0	1	4	0
Griffin, Justin, C'bus	1.000	3	4	0	0	4	0
Halloran, Matt, Sav.	.000	1	0	0	0	0	0
Hamilton, Josh, C.S.C.*	.976	81	159	7	4	170	0
Harris, Willie, Del.	1.000	20	37	4	0	41	0
Harts, Jeremy, Hick.*	.948	116	209	9	12	230	2
Headley, Justin, Aug.*	.900	15	17	1	2	20	0
Hernandez, Javier, C'bus	.968	13	27	3	1	31	0
Hine, Steve, Sav.	.000	1	0	0	0	0	0
Holliday, Josh, Hag.	1.000	8	7	1	0	8	0
Hopper, Norris, C.W.Va.	.976	87	198	2	5	205	1
Ide, Antoine, Del.	.967	21	26	3	1	30	0
Jacobs, John, C.S.C.	.875	8	7	0	1	8	0
Jenkins, Brian, C'bia	.988	56	71	8	1	80	2
Johnson, Brian, C.W.Va.	1.000	1	1	0	0	1	0
Johnson, Eric, C'bus	.988	64	149	12	2	163	1
JOHNSON, Reed, Hag.	.995	95	183	12	1	196	3
Jones, Damien, Mac.*	.960	123	233	8	10	251	2
Jones, Jason, Sav.	1.000	3	4	0	0	4	0
Kawabata, Kenichiro, Aug.*	.900	12	18	0	2	20	0
Keene, Kurt, Hag.	1.000	5	8	0	0	8	0
Kelly, Dan, Mac.*	.000	1	0	0	0	0	0
Kelly, Shane, C.S.C.	.889	8	8	0	1	9	0
Landreth, Jason, Hick.	.938	32	43	2	3	48	0
Lane, Rich, C.F.*	1.000	1	2	0	0	2	0
Lee, Monte, Sav.*	.983	40	53	4	1	58	1
Lehr, Ryan, Mac.	1.000	9	13	2	0	15	0
Lopez, Youanny, Aug.	.909	10	19	1	2	22	0
Martin, Brian, C.S.C.	.952	82	114	4	6	124	1
Matos, Angel, Sav.	.000	1	0	0	0	0	0
McKinley, Josh, C.F.	1.000	3	5	0	0	5	0
Mento, Al, C'bia	.983	47	53	5	1	59	2
Merhoff, Aaron, Pied.	1.000	22	35	1	0	36	0
Moore, Frank, C.S.C.	1.000	1	0	1	0	1	0
Moreno, Jorge, C'bus	.962	53	70	5	3	78	1
Morrow, Alvin, Hag.	.977	29	42	0	1	43	0
Mulvehill, Chase, C'bia	.917	34	30	3	3	36	0
Murch, Jeremy, C.S.C.*	1.000	53	63	1	0	64	0
Muth, Edmund, Ash.*	.968	50	90	1	3	94	0
Nerei, Yuji, C.F.*	.923	9	11	1	1	13	0
Nettles, Jeff, Gre.	.833	5	5	0	1	6	0
Neubart, Adam, C.W.Va.	.947	34	66	6	4	76	3
Nowlin, Cody, Sav.	.968	105	171	8	6	185	4
O'Neill, Daniel, Pied.*	1.000	10	17	1	0	18	0
Padilla, Jorge, Pied.	.976	94	199	8	5	212	0
Pascucci, Val, C.F.	.975	19	37	2	1	40	0
Pearson, Shawn, Hag.	1.000	33	41	4	0	45	2
Pena, Jose, Aug.	.968	30	60	1	2	63	0
Pena, Wily, Gre.	.964	57	102	6	4	112	0
Perich, Josh, C'bia	1.000	4	6	0	0	6	0
Phillips, Dan, Ash.	.957	117	141	13	7	161	1
Poe, Adam, Sav.	.931	57	92	3	7	102	1
Pugh, Dwayne, Hag.	1.000	2	4	0	0	4	0
Ramirez, Charlie, C.W.Va.	.900	16	27	0	3	30	0
Raymundo, Gregg, C.W.Va.	1.000	1	1	0	0	1	0
Redman, Prentice, C'bia	.963	128	165	15	7	187	1
Reed, Keith, Del.	.962	65	119	8	5	132	0
Requena, Alex, C'bus	.977	120	247	9	6	262	2
Rhodes, Dusty, Gre.	1.000	8	12	2	0	14	0
Riepe, Andy, Aug.	1.000	3	6	0	0	6	0
Riggins, Auntwan, Hag.	.985	64	132	3	2	137	0
Rinne, Jim, Ash.	.986	53	69	4	1	74	0
Riordan, Matt, Del.	.974	99	174	10	5	189	1
Rivas, Justo, Mac.	.971	119	224	9	7	240	2

Player, Team	Pct.	G	PO	A	E	TC	DP
Rodriguez, Carlos, Aug.	.923	109	162	5	14	181	0
Rombley, Danny, C.F.	.923	23	35	1	3	39	0
Rosario, Melvin, Ash.*	.947	76	151	9	9	169	2
Ross, Donovan, C.W.Va.	.934	36	52	5	4	61	2
Ruan, Wilken, C.F.	.990	131	292	18	3	313	1
Ruiz, Willy, C.W.Va.	1.000	7	12	0	0	12	0
Ryan, Jeff, C'bia	1.000	3	5	0	0	5	0
Salargo, Steve, Del.	.982	45	53	2	1	56	0
Sanchez, Tino, Ash.	1.000	4	2	0	0	2	0
Santana, Pedro, Gre.	.962	75	93	7	4	104	0
Santini, Travis, C'bus	.891	48	46	3	6	55	1
Saucke, Casey, Del.	1.000	1	1	0	0	1	0
Schneider, Matt, Hick.	.818	6	9	0	2	11	0
Schrock, Chris, C.S.C.	1.000	4	2	0	0	2	0
Seale, Marvin, C'bia	.963	112	199	8	8	215	2
Sherlock, Brian, C.F.	1.000	8	13	1	0	14	0
Simmons, Jerry, Mac.	.970	63	93	3	3	99	0
Sitzman, Jim, Pied.*	.950	92	164	6	9	179	0
Smith, Brett, C.S.C.	.900	22	26	1	3	30	0
Sosa, Jovanny, Hick.	.931	92	152	10	12	174	2
Ticehurst, Brad, Gre.	.929	11	12	1	1	14	0
Tucker, Mamon, Del.	.958	85	107	7	5	119	2
Valdez, Angel, Gre.	.960	52	91	5	4	100	1
Vento, Mike, Gre.	.956	58	101	7	5	113	1
Villar, Jose, Mac.	.986	60	137	3	2	142	1
Warren, Chris, Aug.	.981	123	188	17	4	209	1
Warren, Chris, Ash.	1.000	2	5	1	0	6	1
Weekly, Chris, Hag.	.889	8	8	0	1	9	0
Weston, Aron, Hick.*	.966	74	138	5	5	148	1
Williams, Clyde, C.F.*	.940	32	45	2	3	50	0
Wright, Brad, C'bia*	1.000	37	43	1	0	44	0
Yancy, Michael, C'bia	1.000	2	6	0	0	6	0

CATCHERS

Player, Team	Pct.	G	PO	A	E	TC	DP	PB
Ackerman, Scott, C.F.	.982	48	334	57	7	398	2	14
Alley, Charles, Del.	.988	11	78	6	1	85	0	5
Alvarez, Henrry, C.W.Va.	1.000	9	51	8	0	59	1	3
BOSCAN, Jean, Mac.	.995	88	681	67	4	752	3	8
Brazeal, Spencer, Gre.	.971	14	90	12	3	105	0	3
Bronowicz, Scott, Mac.	.955	10	62	2	3	67	0	0
Bundy, Ryan, Hag.	.939	7	41	5	3	49	3	1
Carreno, Jose, C.F.	.986	10	60	10	1	71	0	7
Cash, Kevin, Hag.	.974	50	318	60	10	388	9	4
Castaneda, Jose, C'bia	.984	13	112	10	2	124	0	2
Chiaffredo, Paul, Hag.	.979	8	38	9	1	48	0	3
Chwan, Brian, C.S.C.	1.000	13	85	15	0	100	0	3
Cruz, Edgar, C'bus	.981	90	703	81	15	799	6	24
Cruz, Enrique, C'bia	1.000	1	13	1	0	14	0	0
Deitrick, Jeremy, Pied.	.983	50	309	40	6	355	2	11
Elwood, Brad, Gre.	.972	11	90	15	3	108	0	5
Elzy, Steve, C'bia	.992	55	463	54	4	521	2	14
Ewan, Bry, Mac.	.973	23	136	8	4	148	0	4
Fuentes, Omar, Gre.	.990	66	510	77	6	593	3	12
Heard, Scott, Sav.	1.000	1	5	0	0	5	0	0
Hernandez, Jose, Hick.	.976	8	37	4	1	42	0	1
Holliday, Josh, Hag.	.974	16	104	10	3	117	0	4
House, J.R., Hick.	.991	77	686	58	7	751	2	14
Isenia, Chairon, C.S.C.	.983	89	709	81	14	804	4	14
Jacobs, Mike, C'bia	.989	18	163	17	2	182	0	7
Jacobson, Russ, Pied.	.993	79	544	65	4	613	1	5
Jarvais, Kregg, Aug.	.991	16	103	8	1	112	0	5
Johannes, Todd, C.F.	.985	32	183	15	3	201	0	6
Johnson, Brian, C.W.Va.	.978	60	476	46	12	534	2	7
Kasper, Todd, C.F.	.965	16	122	16	5	143	0	3
Kessick, Jon, Del.	.985	99	733	79	12	824	0	17
Larned, Drew, Aug.	.963	55	418	27	17	462	0	17
Leon, Alfredo, Del.	1.000	1	3	0	0	3	0	1
Maduro, Jorge, C.S.C.	1.000	1	4	0	0	4	0	0
Martinez, Edgar, Aug.	.972	16	127	14	4	145	2	0
Martinez, Victor, C'bus	.988	20	154	14	2	170	1	1
Massiatte, Daniel, C.S.C.	.985	8	60	7	1	68	0	1
Matos, Angel, Sav.	.982	28	149	13	3	165	0	7
McAuley, Jim, C.W.Va.	.968	43	217	25	8	250	0	14
McMillan, Andrew, C.F.	.987	29	191	34	3	228	1	13
McQueen, Eric, Ash.	.997	39	329	40	1	370	5	6
Norrell, Troy, Gre.	.980	48	297	42	7	346	2	10
Ochoa, Javier, C.W.Va.	.980	34	280	19	6	305	1	12
Paulino, Ron, Hick.	.982	64	436	60	9	505	2	9
Perea, Jean, Sav.	.982	41	306	20	6	332	3	5
Pohle, Ike, Gre.	.962	4	22	3	1	26	0	5
Preston, Brian, C.F.	.968	12	79	12	3	94	1	8
Puffinbarger, Rusty, C'bus	.980	19	130	18	3	151	1	4

Player, Team	Pct.	G	PO	A	E	TC	DP	PB
Pugh, Josh, Mac.	.985	17	118	10	2	130	1	4
Quiroz, Guillermo, Hag.	.994	41	276	35	2	313	2	13
Ramos, Kelly, Aug.	.983	53	465	48	9	522	0	5
Rickon, Jim, C'bus	.988	12	70	12	1	83	0	2
Riepe, Andy, Aug.	1.000	1	7	1	0	8	0	0
Rodriguez, Jeff, Mac.	.980	15	92	4	2	98	0	0
Sanchez, Tino, Ash.	1.000	11	97	6	0	103	0	1
Santos, Juan, Hag.	1.000	3	16	2	0	18	0	0
Schreimann, Eric, Pied.	.982	14	98	14	2	114	0	0
Seestedt, Mike, Del.	.987	45	279	28	4	311	0	6
Smith, Ryan, C'bia	.995	24	193	14	1	208	2	3
Sullivan, Kevin, Pied.	.987	10	73	4	1	78	0	1
Tonis, Michael, C.W.Va.	.973	26	166	17	5	188	4	2
Torres, Jason, Sav.	.993	93	619	49	5	673	4	10
Umbria, Jose, Hag.	.993	19	126	14	1	141	1	1
Valdez, Castulo, C.S.C.	.980	55	255	32	6	293	1	9
Waldron, Jeff, Aug.	1.000	4	32	4	0	36	0	3
Washington, Dion, Gre.	1.000	1	1	0	0	1	0	0
Winchester, Jeff, Ash.	.982	89	777	72	16	865	10	14

PITCHERS

Player, Team	Pct.	G	PO	A	E	TC	DP
Abreu, Winston, Mac.	1.000	11	4	1	0	5	0
Alston, Travis, Pied.	1.000	5	2	0	0	2	0
Andersen, Derek, C.S.C.*	1.000	15	1	1	0	2	1
Andrade, Jancy, Del.	1.000	29	11	7	0	18	0
Angell, Rick, Sav.	.000	1	0	0	0	0	0
Aramboles, Ricardo, Gre.	.800	25	4	12	4	20	0
Arthurs, Shane, C.F.	.882	14	3	12	2	17	0
Avery, Steve, Mac.*	1.000	2	0	3	0	3	0
Babula, Shaun, Del.*	1.000	9	1	8	0	9	0
Backsmeyer, Justin, Sav.	1.000	40	2	6	0	8	1
Baerlocher, Ryan, C.W.Va.	.958	19	4	19	1	24	0
Bailie, Matt, Pied.	1.000	44	4	12	0	16	2
Baker, Brad, Aug.	.875	27	9	12	3	24	1
Baranowski, Brannon, C.W.Va.	.000	10	0	0	0	0	0
Barr, Adam, C'bus*	1.000	13	1	9	0	10	0
Bass, Brian, C.W.Va.	1.000	1	0	1	0	1	0
Batista, Carlos, C'bus	.000	1	0	0	0	0	0
Bauer, Pete, Hag.	1.000	9	2	4	0	6	0
Bazan, Juan, Hick.	.800	15	1	3	1	5	0
Bean, Colter, Gre.	1.000	18	1	4	0	5	0
Bedard, Erik, Del.*	.958	29	4	19	1	24	1
Belisle, Matt, Mac.	.813	15	6	7	3	16	0
Bello, Jilberto, Del.	1.000	34	5	6	0	11	0
Bennett, Jeff, Hick.	.833	27	15	25	8	48	0
Bluma, Marc, Hag.	.750	48	3	3	2	8	0
Bong, Jung, Mac.*	.979	20	5	42	1	48	0
Bottenfield, Jason, Aug.	1.000	14	1	2	0	3	0
Bradley, Bobby, Hick.	.769	14	0	10	3	13	0
Brito, Juan, C.F.*	.900	14	3	6	1	10	1
Brookman, Ryan, Pied.	1.000	8	2	1	0	3	0
Brooks, Frank, Pied.*	.960	29	3	21	1	25	1
Buchanan, Brian, Gre.*	1.000	19	1	1	0	2	0
Bukvich, Ryan, C.W.Va.	.857	11	0	6	1	7	1
Bullock, Jeremiah, Sav.*	.600	4	1	2	2	5	0
Bumatay, Mike, Hick.*	1.000	16	1	4	0	5	0
Burger, Rob, Ash.	1.000	3	1	1	0	2	0
Butler, Matt, Mac.	.800	26	4	12	4	20	1
Button, Sammy, C'bus*	1.000	3	0	2	0	2	0
Byrd, Mike, C'bus	.000	2	0	0	0	0	0
Cardwell, Brian, Hag.	.800	11	1	3	1	5	1
Carrasco, Dan, Hick.	.889	27	1	7	1	9	0
Casadiego, Gerardo, C.F.	1.000	30	1	11	0	12	0
Castellanos, Hugo, Hag.	1.000	29	5	11	0	16	1
Castro, Eleuterio, Aug.	.889	30	1	7	1	9	0
Cavazos, Andy, Sav.	.800	20	3	9	3	15	0
Cedeno, Jovanny, Sav.	.958	24	10	13	1	24	1
Cercy, Rick, Ash.	.952	44	9	11	1	21	3
Charron, Eric, C.F.	.923	24	4	8	1	13	1
Chenard, Ken, C'bia	1.000	21	5	8	0	13	0
Claussen, Brandon, Gre.*	1.000	17	1	22	0	23	1
Coa, Jesus, C.W.Va.	.933	21	5	9	1	15	0
Cogan, Tony, C.W.Va.*	.920	13	7	16	2	25	2
Cole, Joseph, C'bia	.800	4	0	4	1	5	0
Collins, Pat, C.F.	.909	24	7	33	4	44	2
Colmenares, Luis, Ash.	.000	6	0	0	0	0	0
Colon, Jose, C'bus	.846	28	2	9	2	13	0
Cook, Aaron, Ash.	.911	21	13	28	4	45	1
Corcoran, Tim, C'bia	1.000	31	2	10	0	12	1
Cornejo, Jesse, C.S.C.*	1.000	30	2	13	0	15	0
Correa, Dominic, Gre.	.750	5	1	2	1	4	0
Cowie, Steve, C'bus	1.000	14	6	12	0	18	0

Player, Team	Pct.	G	PO	A	E	TC	DP
Crowther, Jackson, C.F.	.875	18	2	5	1	8	0
Cullen, Ryan, Sav.*	1.000	48	1	19	0	20	3
Curtis, Dan, Mac.	1.000	7	3	6	0	9	0
Curtiss, Tom, Mac.*	1.000	10	1	2	0	3	0
Day, Zach, Gre.	1.000	13	2	6	0	8	2
Dean, Aaron, Hag.	.700	19	2	5	3	10	0
DeLaCruz, Andres, Gre.	.667	26	1	1	1	3	1
Denney, Kyle, C'bus	.920	28	3	20	2	25	0
De Paula, Julio, Ash.	.900	28	6	12	2	20	0
DePriest, Derrick, C.F.	1.000	21	5	7	0	12	0
Dickinson, Rodney, Aug.	1.000	13	2	3	0	5	0
Dittfurth, Ryan, Sav.	.889	29	7	25	4	36	0
Dobson, Scott, C.F.	.833	14	3	2	1	6	0
Dohmann, Christopher, Ash.	1.000	7	0	4	0	4	0
Dorn, Grant, C.F.	.944	17	7	10	1	18	2
Douglass, Ryan, C.W.Va.	.957	27	16	29	2	47	0
Dukeman, Greg, Hick.	.964	25	3	24	1	28	0
Dunn, Keith, Gre.	.933	8	1	13	1	15	0
Dunning, Justin, C'bia	.708	28	9	8	7	24	1
Encarnacion, Orlando, C'bia	1.000	19	5	5	0	10	1
Ennis, John, Mac.	1.000	18	7	14	0	21	0
Esslinger, Cam, Ash.	1.000	47	2	9	0	11	0
Evert, Brett, Mac.	1.000	7	2	2	0	4	0
Field, Nathan, C.W.Va.	1.000	17	3	4	0	7	0
Fiore, Curt, Mac.	.000	1	0	0	0	0	0
Fleming, Travis, Del.	1.000	53	2	8	0	10	0
Ford, Matt, Hag.*	1.000	18	3	5	0	8	0
Franco, Jose, Gre.	1.000	39	0	8	0	8	0
Franco, Martire, Pied.	.889	24	6	18	3	27	1
Frendling, Neal, C.S.C.	.864	27	5	14	3	22	0
Frias, Juan, C.S.C.	.500	7	1	0	1	2	0
Fry, Justin, Pied.	1.000	44	1	5	0	6	0
Gamble, Jerome, Aug.	1.000	15	6	7	0	13	2
Garcia, Raul, C.W.Va.	1.000	40	2	12	0	14	0
Garcia, Reynaldo, Sav.	.882	49	3	12	2	17	0
Garcia, Rosman, Gre.	.815	23	5	17	5	27	0
Garcia, Sonny, Del.	.923	26	5	19	2	26	0
Garris, Antonio, C.F.	.000	1	0	0	0	0	0
Gawer, Matt, Mac.*	.692	30	2	7	4	13	1
Gehrke, Jay, C.W.Va.	.813	43	5	8	3	16	0
Gilfillan, Jason, C.W.Va.	1.000	30	2	5	0	7	0
Glaser, Eric, Aug.	.941	32	8	8	1	17	0
Gobble, Jimmy, C.W.Va.*	.900	25	2	16	2	20	0
Gomez, Rafael, C'bia	1.000	10	0	2	0	2	0
Good, Eric, C.F.*	1.000	8	0	7	0	7	0
Gorman, Pat, C'bia-Del.	1.000	32	2	3	0	5	0
Gracesqui, Franklyn, Hag.*	1.000	3	0	2	0	2	0
Graham, Frank, C'bia	.949	27	8	29	2	39	3
Griffiths, Jeremy, C'bia	.905	26	5	14	2	21	0
Gross, Rafael, C'bus	1.000	8	0	1	0	1	0
Halvorson, Greg, C'bia	1.000	29	5	11	0	16	1
Hamann, Robert, Hag.	1.000	34	9	11	0	20	0
Harris, Silas, C.F.*	.500	14	0	1	1	2	0
Harvey, Ian, Aug.	1.000	9	0	3	0	3	0
Hawkins, Chad, Sav.	1.000	5	1	1	0	2	0
Heimbach, Andy, C.S.C.	.800	6	1	3	1	5	0
Hendricks, John, C'bia*	1.000	7	3	1	0	4	0
Hernandez, Jose, Hick.	.000	1	0	0	0	0	0
Herrera, Alex, C'bus*	.938	20	1	14	1	16	0
Hertzel, Pat, C.S.C.	.909	14	6	14	2	22	1
Hopper, Joshua, C'bia*	.875	23	2	5	1	8	0
Houston, Ryan, Hag.	.889	6	3	5	1	9	0
Hubbel, Travis, Hag.	.813	19	10	16	6	32	6
Humrich, Chris, C.F.	.933	38	2	12	1	15	0
Hurley, Derek, Hick.*	.727	18	2	6	3	11	0
Igualada, Eric, Gre.	1.000	9	2	4	0	6	0
Jackson, Jeremy, C'bia*	1.000	2	1	2	0	3	0
Jacobsen, Landon, Hick.	1.000	5	2	0	0	2	0
Jarvais, Kregg, Aug.	.000	1	0	0	0	0	0
Jauregui, Miguel, C'bus	.917	29	3	8	1	12	0
Johnston, Mike, Hick.*	.833	26	2	8	2	12	0
Jones, Sean, Del.	.933	39	4	10	1	15	0
Joseph, Jake, C'bia	.889	15	1	15	2	18	1
Kaanoi, Jason, C.W.Va.	.750	4	1	2	1	4	2
Kearney, Ryan, C'bus.	1.000	2	1	0	0	1	0
Keelin, Chris, Pied.	.833	45	5	5	2	12	0
Kelley, Chris, C'bus	1.000	8	3	3	0	6	0
Kelly, Dan, Mac.*	1.000	12	2	6	0	8	0
Kennedy, Joe, C.S.C.*	.940	22	8	39	3	50	3
Kent, Nathan, Mac.	1.000	5	0	1	0	1	0
Kibler, Ryan, Ash.	.837	26	10	26	7	43	3
Kidd, Jake, Ash.	1.000	20	1	6	0	7	1
Klepacki, Ed, C.F.	1.000	14	6	14	0	20	0

CLASS A South Atlantic League

Player, Team	Pct.	G	PO	A	E	TC	DP
Knowles, Mike, Gre.	.923	24	7	17	2	26	0
Koeth, Mark, C'bus	1.000	20	5	2	0	7	0
Kosderka, Matt, Sav.	.944	20	3	14	1	18	0
Kozlowski, Ben, Mac.*	.769	15	1	9	3	13	0
Kremer, John, Gre.	.938	38	2	13	1	16	0
Kurtz-Nicholl, Jesse, C.W.Va.*	.938	29	5	10	1	16	0
Labitzke, Jesse, Ash.*	1.000	36	2	7	0	9	0
Landreth, Jason, Hick.	.000	1	0	0	0	0	0
Lara, Mauricio, Aug.*	.917	16	2	9	1	12	3
Leach, Bryan, Aug.	1.000	60	4	8	0	12	0
Ledden, Ryan, Hick.	.889	30	4	4	1	9	0
Ledezma, Wil, Aug.*	.833	14	5	5	2	12	0
Lee, Clifton, C.F.*	.900	11	2	7	1	10	0
Lewis, Peyton, Hag.	1.000	23	3	1	0	4	0
Lockwood, Luke, C.F.*	1.000	9	3	12	0	15	1
Lopez, Jose, Hick.	.909	29	1	9	1	11	0
Lorenzo, Javier, Ash.	1.000	6	0	2	0	2	0
Lowe, Matt, C'bia	.000	2	0	0	0	0	0
Madson, Ryan, Pied.	.958	21	9	14	1	24	1
Magrane, Jim, C.S.C.	.947	27	9	27	2	38	6
Malaska, Mark, C.S.C.*	.000	2	0	0	0	0	0
Manning, Mike, C'bus	1.000	5	1	0	0	1	0
Marietta, Ron, C'bus*	.000	1	0	0	0	0	0
Marini, Anthony, C'bus*	.929	11	1	12	1	14	0
Markwell, Diegomar, Hag.*	.000	2	0	0	0	0	0
Marsonek, Sam, Gre.	.861	18	7	24	5	36	1
Martinez, Anastacio, Aug.	1.000	23	9	11	0	20	1
Martinez, David, Gre.*	.917	8	2	9	1	12	0
Matsko, Rick, C'bus	.909	26	2	8	1	11	1
McAvoy, Jeff, C.F.	1.000	22	1	4	0	5	1
McClung, Michael, C.S.C.	1.000	6	4	4	0	8	1
McCormick, Terry, C.S.C.*	1.000	5	0	2	0	2	0
McGill, Frank, Sav.	1.000	26	4	8	0	12	0
McNatt, Josh, Del.*	.800	7	1	3	1	5	0
Mikels, Jason, Mac.	.875	31	4	3	1	8	0
Minix, Travis, C.S.C.	1.000	48	2	8	0	10	1
Miyamoto, Eij, C.F.	.000	3	0	0	0	0	0
Montero, Jose, Sav.	.727	34	2	6	3	11	0
Monzon, Yoel, Ash.	1.000	39	4	7	0	11	0
Moore, Chris, Ash.	.000	1	0	0	0	0	0
MORENO, Edwin, Sav.	1.000	23	6	18	0	24	1
Myers, Brett, Pied.	.921	27	9	26	3	38	0
Neil, Dan, C'bus*	.870	33	5	15	3	23	1
Nunez, Jose, C'bia*	.895	34	1	16	2	19	0
Obermueller, Wes, C.W.Va.	1.000	8	3	4	0	7	1
Oliver, Scott, Gre.	.952	29	6	14	1	21	2
Ortiz, Jose, C.S.C.	.786	46	3	8	3	14	0
Outlaw, Mark, Pied.*	.900	48	0	9	1	10	1
Pacheco, Enemencio, Ash.	.900	21	10	17	3	30	2
Paradis, Mike, Del.	.923	18	12	24	3	39	1
Pautz, Brad, Pied.	.929	13	4	9	1	14	0
Payne, Jerrod, Hag.	1.000	19	1	4	0	5	1
Peguero, Radhame, C.S.C.	1.000	4	0	3	0	3	0
Pena, Alex, Hick.	1.000	3	1	0	0	1	0
Perez, Frank, Pied.	.885	36	6	17	3	26	1
Perez, Julio, C.F.	1.000	41	5	9	0	14	0
Perez, Randy, Del.*	.917	25	6	27	3	36	3
Pichardo, Carlos, C.W.Va.	1.000	34	7	11	0	18	0
Pierce, Tony, Mac.	.000	1	0	0	0	0	0
Place, Eric, Hag.*	1.000	4	0	0	0	0	0
Plank, Terry, Del.	1.000	48	0	12	0	12	1
Polk, Scott, C'bia	.875	40	3	11	2	16	1
Powalski, Rich, Mac.*	1.000	43	3	11	0	14	1
Pruett, Jason, C.S.C.*	.906	49	3	26	3	32	4
Pruitt, Jason, Del.*	.000	2	0	0	0	0	0
Puffer, Brandon, Ash.	1.000	14	1	4	0	5	1
Reames, Jay, Sav.	.000	3	0	0	0	0	0
Reece, Dana, Hag.*	.500	34	0	2	2	4	0
Reid, Justin, Hick.	.897	27	9	17	3	29	0
Reimers, Cameron, Hag.	.905	26	9	29	4	42	2
Reinike, Chris, C'bus	.667	7	2	0	1	3	0
Renwick, Tyler, Hag.	1.000	7	2	3	0	5	0
Riccobono, Rick, Aug.	.895	25	3	14	2	19	1
Richardson, Kasey, Ash.*	1.000	9	2	3	0	5	0
Rincones, Rafael, C.W.Va.	1.000	6	1	2	0	3	1
Rleal, Sendy, Del.	.000	1	0	0	0	0	0
Rodriguez, Alfredo, Sav.	1.000	6	0	1	0	1	0
Rodriguez, Cristobal, C.F.	.833	14	5	10	3	18	1
Rodriguez, Eddy, Del.	1.000	4	0	1	0	1	0
Rodriguez, Jose, C.S.C.	.818	16	3	6	2	11	0
Rogers, Devin, C'bus	.850	20	3	14	3	20	0
Roller, Adam, Gre.	1.000	13	0	1	0	1	0
Roque, Darryl, C.F.	1.000	9	0	3	0	3	0
Rose, Michael, C.F.	.000	1	0	0	0	0	0
Rosengren, Phil, C'bus	.833	23	10	15	5	30	1
Rupp, Mike, Aug.	.941	30	5	11	1	17	0
Russ, Christopher, Sav.*	1.000	7	1	6	0	7	0
Sadler, Carl, C'bus*	.800	10	0	4	1	5	0
Sandoval, Marcos, Hag.	.917	28	5	17	2	24	3
Santos, Josh, C'bus*	.750	28	2	4	2	8	0
Saunders, Tony, C.S.C.*	1.000	2	0	1	0	1	0
Schrock, Chris, C.S.C.	.000	1	0	0	0	0	0
Schwager, Matt, Del.	.933	47	0	14	1	15	1
Seale, Dustin, C.F.*	1.000	6	0	2	0	2	0
Seestedt, Mike, Del.	.000	2	0	0	0	0	0
Serrano, Elio, Pied.	1.000	38	1	9	0	10	1
Shelley, Jason, Hick.	.000	3	0	0	1	1	0
Simpson, Cory, Mac.	.714	7	4	1	2	7	0
Sirianni, Jay, C'bus*	.750	13	0	6	2	8	0
Smalley, Mike, Mac.*	.955	12	5	16	1	22	0
Smith, Hans, C.S.C.*	.833	17	2	3	1	6	1
Solano, Alex, Aug.	.933	33	2	12	1	15	0
Sollenberger, Matt, C'bia*	1.000	4	0	1	0	1	0
Spencer, Corey, Aug.*	1.000	53	1	10	0	11	0
Sperring, Jayme, Del.	1.000	13	0	2	0	2	0
Spiers, Corey, Sav.*	1.000	12	5	9	0	14	0
Stabile, Paul, Hick.*	1.000	7	0	3	0	3	0
Stahl, Rich, Del.*	.895	20	6	28	4	38	1
Stamler, Keith, Sav.	1.000	1	0	3	0	3	0
Stanford, Jason, C'bus*	.882	14	3	12	2	17	0
Stanton, Jeff, Gre.	1.000	4	0	2	0	2	0
Stepka, Tom, Ash.	.917	16	0	11	1	12	0
Stevens, Josh, Hag.	.895	47	6	11	2	19	3
Stiles, Brad, C.W.Va.*	1.000	6	1	4	0	5	0
Stine, Justin, Hag.*	.947	41	3	15	1	19	0
Stodolka, Michael, C.W.Va.*	1.000	1	0	1	0	1	0
Stokes, Brian, C.S.C.	1.000	46	6	12	0	18	1
Sullivan, Ted, C'bus	1.000	10	2	5	0	7	0
Surridge, Lance, Aug.	.938	23	3	12	1	16	0
Tankersley, Dennis, Aug.	1.000	15	3	11	0	14	0
Taylor, Brien, C'bus*	.000	5	0	0	0	0	0
Terni, Chaz, Aug.	.000	1	0	0	0	0	0
Tetz, Kris, C.F.	1.000	19	0	2	0	2	0
Theodile, Simieon, Del.	1.000	36	5	5	0	10	0
Toriz, Steve, C.F.	.000	10	0	0	0	0	0
Torres, Luis, Hick.	.706	23	2	10	5	17	0
Troilo, Joseph, Aug.	.000	2	0	0	0	0	0
Truitt, Derrick, Mac.	.955	40	5	16	1	22	1
Tsao, Chin-hui, Ash.	.968	24	6	24	1	31	1
Turner, Kyle, C.W.Va.*	.667	8	2	4	3	9	0
Valera, Nelson, C.S.C.	.750	18	1	5	2	8	0
Valle, Yoiset, Gre.*	.833	6	2	3	1	6	2
Veras, Enger, C.S.C.	.958	20	4	19	1	24	2
Veronie, Shanin, Mac.	.889	43	3	5	1	9	0
Villalon, Julio, C.S.C.	1.000	4	1	1	0	2	0
Viole, Paul, C'bia	.857	18	4	2	1	7	0
Wade, Matt, C'bus	1.000	10	3	2	0	5	0
Walker, Adam, Pied.*	.667	8	0	6	3	9	0
Wallace, Shane, C'bus*	.842	13	2	14	3	19	0
Warren, Chris, Ash.	1.000	1	0	1	0	1	0
Washburn, Ben, C.F.	1.000	7	2	6	0	8	0
Watkins, David, Mac.	1.000	4	0	1	0	1	0
Weaver, Joe, Sav.	.857	22	0	6	1	7	0
Weber, Brett, Gre.	1.000	16	0	5	0	5	1
Weslowski, Robert, C'bia	1.000	39	6	11	0	17	2
Westmoreland, Ken, Pied.	.846	7	2	9	2	13	0
Whitecotton, Billy, Del.	.333	6	0	2	4	6	0
Williams, Dave, Hick.*	.857	24	4	32	6	42	1
Willoughby, Justin, Mac.*	.895	38	4	13	2	19	0
Witte, Lou, Gre.	1.000	31	2	5	0	7	0
Wright, Barrett, C.S.C.	.714	5	2	3	2	7	0
Wright, Brad, C'bia*	1.000	2	0	1	0	1	0
Wright, Shane, Hick.	.818	32	7	11	4	22	1
Yen, Buddy, C.W.Va.	.667	29	0	2	1	3	0
Young, Colin, Ash.*	1.000	36	2	11	0	13	1
Zurita, Thomas, C.W.Va.	1.000	14	0	2	0	2	0

PITCHERS WITH TWO OR MORE TEAMS

Player, Team	Pct.	G	PO	A	E	TC	DP
Gorman, Pat, C'bia	1.000	30	2	3	0	5	0
Gorman, Pat, Del.	.000	2	0	0	0	0	0

The following player appeared only as designated hitter, pinch-hitter or pinch runner: Matthews, dh; Rios, dh.

LEAGUE CHAMPIONS

Year	Team	Pct.	Year	Team	Pct.	Year	Team	Pct.
1948—	Lincolnton*	.627		Greenville	.619	1986—	Columbia‡	.682
1949—	Newton-Conover	.667	1971—	Greenwood	.631		Asheville	.643
	Rutherford Co. (2nd)†	.627		Greenwood	.759	1987—	Asheville	.655
1950—	Newton-Conover	.627	1972—	Spartanburg‡	.788		Myrtle Beach‡	.597
	Lenoir (2nd)†	.626		Greenville	.652	1988—	Charleston (S.C.)	.616
1951—	Morganton	.645	1973—	Spartanburg‡	.646		Spartanburg‡	.500
	Shelby (2nd)†	.604		Gastonia	.619	1989—	Gastonia	.657
1952—	Lincolnton	.649	1974—	Gastonia	.606		Augusta‡	.535
	Shelby (2nd)†	.645		Gastonia	.672	1990—	Columbia	.580
1953-59—League inactive.			1975—	Spartanburg	.543		Charleston (W.Va.)‡	.538
1960—	Lexington	.707		Spartanburg	.614	1991—	Charleston (W.Va.)	.648
	Salisbury (2nd)†	.650	1976—	Asheville	.544		Columbia‡	.614
1961—	Salisbury	.627		Greenwood‡	.600	1992—	Columbia	.572
	Shelby (4th)†	.481	1977—	Greenwood	.557		Myrtle Beach‡	.522
1962—	Statesville	.563		Gastonia‡	.590	1993—	Savannah‡	.662
	Statesville	.700	1978—	Greenwood	.614		Greensboro	.603
1963—	Greenville†	.576		Greenwood	.565	1994—	Columbus	.630
	Salisbury	.631	1979—	Greenwood‡	.565		Savannah‡	.599
1964—	Rock Hill	.672		Spartanburg	.525	1995—	Piedmont	.586
	Salisbury‡	.631	1980—	Greensboro	.590		Augusta‡	.551
1965—	Salisbury	.641		Charleston	.561	1996—	Delmarva	.585
	Rock Hill‡	.603	1981—	Greensboro‡	.695		Savannah†	.511
1966—	Spartanburg	.682		Greenwood	.549	1997—	Delmarva§	.543
	Spartanburg	.767	1982—	Greensboro‡	.681		Greensboro	.536
1967—	Spartanburg	.730		Florence	.546	1998—	Columbia§	.638
	Spartanburg	.567	1983—	Columbia	.620		Hagerstown	.574
1968—	Spartanburg	.597		Gastonia‡	.587	1999—	Hagerstown	.600
	Greenwood‡	.597	1984—	Charleston	.549		Augusta§	.496
1969—	Greenwood‡	.587		Asheville‡	.510	2000—	Piedmont	.657
	Shelby	.565	1985—	Florence‡	.599		Delmarva∞	.544
1970—	Greenville	.576		Greensboro	.540			

*Won championship and four-club playoff. †Won four-club playoff. ‡Won split-season playoff. §Won split season, eight-club playoff. ∞Won split season, four-club playoff. (NOTE—Known as Western Carolina League from 1948 through 1962 and known as Western Carolinas League through 1979.)

APPALACHIAN LEAGUE

LEAGUE OFFICE

President
Lee Landers

Address
283 Deerchase Circle
Statesville, NC 28625

Phone
704-873-5300

Teams (affiliation)
Bluefield Orioles (Orioles)
Bristol White Sox (White Sox)
Burlington Indians (Indians)
Danville Braves (Braves)
Elizabethton Twins (Twins)
Johnson City Cardinals (Cardinals)

Kingsport Mets (Mets)
Martinsville Astros (Astros)
Princeton Devil Rays (Devil Rays)
Pulaski Rangers (Rangers)

2000 FINAL STANDINGS

NORTH DIVISION

Team	W	L	T	Pct.	GB
Danville (Braves)	37	29	0	.561	...
Princeton (Devil Rays)	34	34	0	.500	4.0
Bluefield (Orioles)	31	32	0	.492	4.5
Martinsville (Astros)	30	36	0	.455	7.0
Burlington (Indians)	21	46	0	.313	16.5

SOUTH DIVISION

Team	W	L	T	Pct.	GB
Elizabethton (Twins)	46	18	0	.719	...
Pulaski (Rangers)	40	28	0	.588	8.0
Kingsport (Mets)	35	32	0	.522	12.5
Bristol (White Sox)	34	33	0	.507	13.5
Johnson City (Cardinals)	24	44	0	.353	24.0

COMPOSITE

Team	Eliz.	Pul.	Dan.	King.	Bris.	Prin.	Blu.	Mar.	J.C.	Burl.	W	L	T	Pct.	GB
Elizabethton (Twins)	...	3	5	7	8	3	1	5	10	4	46	18	0	.719	...
Pulaski (Rangers)	3	...	2	3	5	4	7	6	4	6	40	28	0	.588	8.0
Danville (Braves)	1	4	...	3	4	6	4	5	4	6	37	29	0	.561	10.0
Kingsport (Mets)	3	3	3	...	7	2	4	4	5	4	35	32	0	.522	12.5
Bristol (White Sox)	2	1	2	4	...	5	4	3	8	5	34	33	0	.507	13.5
Princeton (Devil Rays)	3	6	2	4	1	...	3	3	3	9	34	34	0	.500	14.0
Bluefield (Orioles)	1	3	5	2	2	7	...	5	3	3	31	32	0	.492	14.5
Martinsville (Astros)	1	4	4	2	3	3	3	...	5	5	30	36	0	.455	17.0
Johnson City (Cardinals)	2	2	2	5	2	3	3	1	...	4	24	44	0	.353	24.0
Burlington (Indians)	2	2	4	2	1	1	3	4	2	...	21	46	0	.313	26.5

Major league affiliations in parentheses.

PLAYOFFS: Elizabethton defeated Danville two games to none to win league championship.

REGULAR-SEASON ATTENDANCE: Bluefield, 28,579; Bristol, 18,671; Burlington, 43,014; Danville, 25,721; Elizabethton, 15,692; Johnson City, 23,324; Kingsport, 27,174; Martinsville, 40,533; Princeton, 33,215; Pulaski, 20,508. Total—276,431. Playoffs (2 games)—950.

MANAGERS: Bluefield, Duffy Dyer; Bristol, R.J. Reynolds; Burlington, David Turgeon; Danville, J.J. Cannon; Elizabethton, Jeff Carter; Johnson City, Luis Melendez; Kingsport, Edgar Alfonzo; Martinsville, Brad Wellman; Princeton, Edwin Rodriguez; Pulaski, Bruce Crabbe.

ALL-STAR TEAM: 1B—Ramon German, Martinsville; 2B—Alejandro Machado, Danville; 3B—Kelly Eddleman, Princeton; SS—Luis Maza, Elizabethton; Utility INF—Dan Dement, Princeton; OF—Anthony Acevedo, Martinsville; Charlie Dees, Bluefield-Pulaski; Alex Gordon, Bluefield; Utility OF—Rafael Boitel, Elizabethton; C—Octavio Martinez, Bluefield; DH—Ryan Hamill, Johnson City; Angel Matos, Pulaski; RHP—Chad Bowen, Kingsport; Domingo Valdez, Pulaski; LHP—Luke Martin, Elizabethton; Relief pitcher—Robert Pepen, Kingsport; Player of the Year—Octavio Martinez, Bluefield; Pitcher of the Year—Chad Bowen, Kingsport; Domingo Valdez, Pulaski; Manager of the Year—Jeff Carter, Elizabethton.

2000 BATTING

TEAM

Team	Avg.	G	TPA	AB	R	H	TB	2B	3B	HR	RBI	SH	SF	HP	BB	IBB	SO	SB	CS	GDP	LOB	ShO	Slg.	OBP
Bristol	.267	67	2492	2212	319	591	824	101	27	26	278	30	20	38	192	4	417	93	33	39	478	1	.373	.333
Danville	.267	66	2544	2234	341	596	862	108	22	38	290	16	23	36	235	4	509	55	42	46	456	1	.386	.343
Bluefield	.263	63	2396	2068	344	544	829	100	19	49	284	11	20	32	265	2	554	61	16	49	476	1	.401	.353
Kingsport	.263	67	2509	2159	334	567	870	114	21	49	290	36	19	41	254	4	540	145	72	33	439	3	.403	.349
Princeton	.259	68	2454	2196	292	569	797	108	21	26	245	15	19	33	191	1	555	53	35	52	440	3	.363	.325
Elizabethton	.257	64	2475	2137	378	549	825	106	16	46	332	22	17	45	254	4	461	75	28	28	457	3	.386	.346
Pulaski	.254	68	2630	2204	412	560	876	107	19	57	346	24	20	42	340	3	568	112	33	34	509	3	.397	.361
Martinsville	.252	66	2426	2131	317	538	819	125	24	36	265	5	15	50	225	1	471	114	43	36	423	3	.384	.336
Johnson City	.249	68	2530	2221	335	553	809	98	13	44	272	19	16	49	225	6	537	95	46	46	431	4	.364	.329
Burlington	.241	67	2476	2195	282	529	724	88	10	29	248	10	14	37	220	1	513	102	37	44	455	4	.330	.319

INDIVIDUAL

TOP QUALIFIERS FOR BATTING CHAMPIONSHIP

Minimum 184 plate appearances. *Lefthanded batter. †Switch-hitter.

Player, Team	Avg.	G	TPA	AB	R	H	TB	2B	3B	HR	RBI	SH	SF	HP	BB	IBB	SO	SB	CS	GDP	Slg.	OBP
Martinez, Octavio, Blue.	.387	49	212	181	45	70	107	14	1	7	46	1	3	8	19	0	21	0	1	4	.591	.460
Machado, Aleyandro, Dan.	.341	61	281	217	45	74	84	6	2	0	16	2	3	6	53	0	29	30	12	3	.387	.477
German, Ramon, Mar.†	.320	59	250	225	42	72	119	24	1	7	44	0	1	1	23	0	64	16	8	1	.529	.384
La Roche, Adam, Dan.*	.308	56	232	201	38	62	102	13	3	7	45	1	4	2	24	2	46	4	1	2	.507	.381
Devanez, Noel, King.	.305	58	219	197	33	60	105	14	2	9	35	3	0	5	14	0	46	8	8	3	.533	.366
Coleman, Alph, Dan.	.302	47	188	179	25	54	84	10	7	2	22	2	2	1	4	0	19	12	3	7	.469	.361
Matos, Angel, Pul.	.302	54	239	199	41	60	105	14	2	9	56	1	1	1	37	0	59	10	3	0	.528	.412
Dement, Dan, Prin.	.301	60	242	206	48	62	100	9	4	7	39	1	1	3	31	0	48	7	1	5	.485	.398

Player, Team	Avg.	G	TPA	AB	R	H	TB	2B	3B	HR	RBI	SH	SF	HP	BB	IBB	SO	SB	CS	GDP	Slg.	OBP
Dees, Charlie, Blue.-Pul.	.298	53	222	191	40	57	114	10	4	13	48	1	3	2	25	0	66	9	1	2	.597	.380
Reyes, Guillermo, Bris.†	.296	66	288	257	45	76	99	10	2	3	31	4	2	2	22	0	24	21	10	3	.385	.353
Maza, Luis, Eliz.	.295	56	249	210	40	62	108	16	3	8	35	7	1	12	19	1	41	12	4	1	.514	.384
Acevedo, Anthony, Mar.*	.295	56	238	200	33	59	100	20	3	5	43	0	4	3	31	0	41	7	3	4	.500	.391
McIntyre, Robert, King.	.294	53	222	197	33	58	86	13	3	3	29	1	2	8	14	0	60	13	13	2	.437	.362
Eddlemon, Kelly, Prin.	.293	65	267	239	44	70	121	21	0	10	42	0	5	4	19	0	47	7	3	2	.506	.348
Littleton, Brandon, Blue.†	.292	55	248	209	39	61	88	11	5	2	25	1	0	3	35	0	42	12	2	3	.421	.401

DEPARTMENTAL LEADERS: G—G. Reyes, Evans, 66 each; AB—G. Reyes, 257; R—Sowers, Dement, Evans, 48 each; H—G. Reyes, 76; TB—Gordon, 122; 2B—German, 24; 3B—Coleman, 7; HR—Gordon, Dees, 13 each; RBI—Matos, 56; SH—Maza, 7; SF—Eddlemon, Martin, Wilken, 5 each; HP—Maza, 12; BB—Machado, 53; IBB—several tied, 2 each; SO—Gordon, 105; SB—Taveras, 36; CS—McIntyre, 13; GIDP—N. Nelson, 9; Slg.—Dees, .597; OBP—Machado, .477.

ALL PLAYERS

*Lefthanded batter. †Switch-hitter.

Player, Team	Avg.	G	TPA	AB	R	H	TB	2B	3B	HR	RBI	SH	SF	HP	BB	IBB	SO	SB	CS	GDP	Slg.	OBP
Aaron, Oginga, Prin.	.236	42	162	144	23	34	38	2	1	0	6	2	0	3	13	0	33	5	5	2	.264	.313
Acevedo, Anthony, Mar.*	.295	56	238	200	33	59	100	20	3	5	43	0	4	3	31	0	41	7	3	4	.500	.391
Acosta, Emilio, J.C.	.244	36	136	119	22	29	35	6	0	0	13	1	2	1	13	0	19	6	2	4	.294	.319
Albertson, Justin, J.C.	.223	33	112	94	22	21	33	4	1	2	13	1	1	1	15	0	37	13	0	3	.351	.333
Alvarado, Oscar, Mar.	.169	25	78	71	6	12	18	1	1	1	2	0	0	2	5	0	19	3	1	2	.254	.244
Andrianoff, Jonathan, Mar.	.147	33	109	95	6	14	19	5	0	0	5	1	2	4	7	0	43	2	2	1	.200	.231
Angel, Anthony, Mar.	.234	46	171	154	21	36	57	9	3	2	20	0	1	2	14	0	28	7	2	3	.370	.304
Ayala, Abraham, Mar.	.292	38	144	130	19	38	47	6	0	1	11	1	0	3	10	0	8	4	3	4	.362	.357
Baetzel, Mike, Bris.†	.167	15	14	12	7	2	2	0	0	0	3	0	1	0	1	0	5	0	1	0	.167	.214
Baez, Manuel, Pul.	.267	56	229	180	35	48	60	8	2	0	22	3	1	2	43	0	37	13	6	3	.333	.412
Baldelli, Rocco, Prin.	.216	60	251	232	33	50	72	9	2	3	25	2	0	5	12	0	56	11	3	3	.310	.269
Baldiris, Aaron, King.	.219	32	117	105	14	23	34	3	1	2	20	0	4	1	7	0	20	2	1	4	.324	.265
Batista, Carlos, Burl.	.236	32	119	110	8	26	35	4	1	1	14	1	0	1	7	0	33	1	4	2	.318	.288
Bell, Josh, King.	.210	27	78	62	9	13	18	5	0	0	5	4	0	3	9	0	27	0	2	0	.290	.338
Boitel, Rafael, Eliz.†	.263	55	252	224	43	59	76	7	2	2	27	2	0	1	25	1	47	16	6	1	.339	.340
Bowen, Rob, Eliz.†	.288	21	84	73	17	21	36	3	0	4	19	0	0	0	11	0	11	8	0	0	.493	.381
Boyd, Shaun, J.C.	.263	43	166	152	15	40	55	9	0	2	15	1	1	2	10	1	22	6	5	1	.362	.315
Bruntlett, Eric, Mar.	.273	50	214	172	40	47	69	11	4	1	21	1	0	11	30	0	22	14	1	2	.401	.413
Burrows, Angelo, Dan.*	.275	44	187	171	28	47	57	6	2	0	20	2	1	2	11	1	20	8	3	3	.333	.324
Caperton, Freddy, Pul.	.292	9	28	24	7	7	13	4	1	0	4	0	0	2	2	0	7	0	0	1	.542	.393
Cardona, Raynier, King.†	.250	5	18	12	1	3	3	0	0	0	2	0	0	1	5	0	5	1	0	1	.250	.500
Castellanos, Jose, Dan.	.212	31	99	85	12	18	29	3	1	2	8	1	2	2	9	0	26	8	3	2	.341	.296
Cedano, Francisco, J.C.	.185	12	27	27	3	5	6	1	0	0	1	0	0	0	0	0	13	1	0	0	.222	.185
Centeno, Edwin, Blue.†	.226	37	120	93	26	21	28	2	1	1	12	1	0	5	21	0	36	10	0	1	.301	.395
Clark, Tommy, Dan.	.220	36	138	123	21	27	51	12	0	4	20	2	0	2	11	0	39	3	1	0	.415	.294
Cochrane, Mark, Bris.	.236	28	99	89	9	21	25	1	0	1	11	0	1	1	8	0	16	0	1	2	.281	.303
Coleman, Alph, Dan.	.302	47	188	179	25	54	84	10	7	2	22	2	2	1	4	0	19	12	3	7	.469	.317
Colmenter, Jesus, Burl.†	.270	42	165	152	20	41	55	8	0	2	23	3	0	1	8	0	21	3	1	4	.362	.311
Compton, Jack, Mar.	.118	6	20	17	2	2	3	1	0	0	1	0	0	1	2	0	4	2	0	0	.176	.250
Contreras, Erick, Dan.†	.405	13	42	37	10	15	18	3	0	0	5	1	0	0	4	0	4	3	3	0	.486	.463
Coyne, Anthony, King.	.225	13	46	40	6	9	15	3	0	1	3	1	0	1	4	0	10	2	1	0	.375	.311
Cruz, Enrique, King.	.251	63	258	223	35	56	97	14	0	9	39	4	2	3	26	1	56	19	7	3	.435	.335
Decola, Daniel, Eliz.	.338	35	154	136	27	46	67	10	1	3	28	1	1	9	7	0	24	0	0	6	.493	.405
Dees, Charlie, Blue.-Pul.	.298	53	222	191	40	57	114	10	4	13	48	1	3	2	25	0	66	9	1	2	.597	.380
De Los Santos, Santo, J.C.* ..	.326	15	47	43	6	14	18	4	0	0	9	1	0	0	3	0	10	4	2	0	.419	.370
Del Rosario, Emmanuel, Blue.†	.249	54	221	185	23	46	54	6	1	0	15	4	2	3	27	1	23	11	1	8	.292	.350
Dement, Dan, Prin.	.301	60	242	206	48	62	100	9	4	7	39	1	1	3	31	0	48	7	1	5	.485	.398
De Paula, Luis, Prin.	.293	30	126	116	9	34	42	8	0	0	10	1	2	0	7	1	26	1	3	5	.362	.328
Devanez, Noel, King.	.305	58	219	197	33	60	105	14	2	9	35	3	0	5	14	0	46	8	8	3	.533	.366
Diaz, Aneuris, J.C.	.268	53	195	179	27	48	76	11	1	5	25	2	1	3	10	1	65	4	4	3	.425	.316
Dillard, Thomas, Eliz.	.214	31	101	84	18	18	19	1	0	0	5	2	0	3	12	0	16	7	1	1	.226	.333
Dion, Nathanael, Prin.	.174	50	173	155	18	27	36	4	1	1	6	0	2	2	14	0	51	1	1	3	.232	.249
Dogero, Matt, J.C.	.215	22	78	65	7	14	25	2	0	3	7	0	0	4	9	0	22	0	1	0	.385	.346
Dorner, Dwight, Prin.*	.281	35	112	89	12	25	30	3	1	0	14	2	1	2	18	0	18	2	3	7	.337	.409
Dougherty, Andy, Burl.	.077	6	16	13	0	1	1	0	0	0	1	0	0	0	2	0	3	0	0	0	.077	.200
Douglas, Harley, King.*	.277	16	53	47	6	13	17	2	1	0	4	2	1	0	3	0	11	6	1	0	.362	.314
Eddlemon, Kelly, Prin.	.293	65	267	239	44	70	121	21	0	10	42	0	5	4	19	0	47	7	3	2	.506	.348
Eldridge, Rashad, Burl.†	.173	48	188	173	11	30	38	5	0	1	12	0	0	3	12	0	42	1	3	6	.220	.239
Ernst, Michael, Burl.†	.188	6	18	16	2	3	7	1	0	1	3	0	0	0	2	0	4	0	0	0	.438	.278
Esprit, Jermaine, Burl.†	.188	28	95	85	13	16	16	0	0	0	3	0	0	2	8	0	31	11	2	0	.188	.274
Estevez, Jose, King.	.250	2	6	4	0	1	1	0	0	0	0	0	0	0	2	0	2	0	1	0	.250	.500
Evans, Robert, Pul.*	.264	66	311	254	48	67	82	8	2	1	29	2	2	1	52	1	29	23	7	1	.323	.388
Fatur, Brian, J.C.	.233	60	257	223	38	52	72	2	0	6	30	3	3	11	16	0	37	10	9	5	.323	.312
Finnerty, Francis, Burl.†	.286	55	228	213	23	61	92	8	1	7	35	0	2	3	10	0	31	2	0	4	.432	.325
Flores, Ralphs, Bris.	.272	39	161	147	18	40	57	7	5	0	24	1	0	1	12	0	9	6	1	4	.388	.331
Folsom, Kenneth, Burl.	.227	51	189	176	11	40	60	8	0	4	16	0	0	3	10	0	62	3	0	3	.341	.280
Franco, Esterlin, Eliz.	.253	43	166	154	17	39	55	9	2	1	14	0	0	2	10	0	22	8	5	5	.357	.307
Gajewski, Matt, Pul.†	.246	38	154	118	26	29	44	6	0	3	18	0	1	4	31	0	24	8	0	5	.373	.416
Garcia, Nicolas, Blue.	.283	41	166	159	21	45	58	7	0	2	13	1	0	1	5	0	31	6	2	5	.365	.309
German, Amado, Prin.†	.268	48	171	149	20	40	55	9	0	2	9	2	1	1	18	0	38	8	9	1	.369	.349
German, Ramon, Mar.†	.320	59	250	225	42	72	119	24	1	7	44	0	1	1	23	0	64	16	8	1	.529	.384
Gomez, Jose, J.C.	.235	53	193	162	25	38	50	7	1	1	17	2	0	4	25	2	46	6	4	6	.309	.351
Gonzalez, Edgar, Prin.	.270	20	78	63	6	17	26	3	0	2	8	1	0	1	13	0	14	4	1	2	.413	.403
Gonzalez, Reggie, Eliz.	.286	52	203	189	28	54	88	11	1	7	39	2	2	0	10	0	26	8	1	1	.466	.318
Goodeill, Harold, Prin.	.444	3	12	9	1	4	7	0	0	1	3	0	0	2	1	0	3	0	0	0	.778	.583
Gordon, Alexis, Blue.*	.269	60	257	223	36	60	122	17	3	13	48	0	4	1	29	0	105	3	0	1	.547	.350
Guilliams, Earl, Dan.	.333	2	3	3	1	1	1	0	0	0	1	0	0	0	0	0	0	0	0	0	.333	.333
Hamill, Ryan, J.C.	.263	59	250	213	35	56	103	11	0	12	46	1	4	4	28	0	42	7	4	6	.484	.353
Hamilton, Mark, Mar.*	.269	56	225	201	27	54	74	11	0	3	23	0	2	3	19	0	48	11	3	1	.368	.338

Player, Team	Avg.	G	TPA	AB	R	H	TB	2B	3B	HR	RBI	SH	SF	HP	BB	IBB	SO	SB	CS	GDP	Slg.	OBP
Harriman, Preston, J.C.	.217	50	157	129	23	28	39	7	2	0	9	1	0	4	23	0	33	6	2	3	.302	.353
Hartley, Will, Burl.†	.327	16	58	52	11	17	19	2	0	0	3	0	0	1	5	0	10	1	0	0	.365	.397
Hernandez, Javier, Burl.†	.242	38	137	124	14	30	47	6	1	3	14	3	1	1	8	0	30	4	3	1	.379	.291
Hilario, Enderson, Bris.	.226	23	65	62	2	14	15	1	0	0	4	0	0	1	2	0	9	0	0	3	.242	.262
Hileman, Jutt, J.C.	.250	5	14	12	4	3	8	0	1	1	4	0	0	0	2	0	4	2	1	0	.667	.357
Holt, Todd, Bris.	.224	38	107	98	11	22	37	5	2	2	10	2	1	3	3	0	32	3	0	1	.378	.267
Jacobs, Mike, King.*	.270	59	241	204	28	55	99	15	4	7	40	1	2	1	33	1	62	6	3	3	.485	.371
Johnson, Kareem, Eliz.	.167	4	12	12	0	2	2	0	0	0	0	0	0	0	0	0	2	1	0	0	.167	.167
Jones, Garrett, Dan.*	.174	40	153	138	12	24	35	7	2	0	16	0	2	0	13	0	55	0	3	2	.254	.242
King, Jason, Dan.	.279	35	139	122	14	34	50	4	0	4	14	1	1	0	15	0	19	2	1	3	.410	.355
Krga, Mike, Prin.	.273	35	141	132	14	36	45	4	1	1	11	1	0	0	8	0	29	1	0	2	.341	.314
Lackaff, John, Bris.	.286	59	244	217	30	62	86	9	3	3	34	2	2	9	14	1	36	9	4	7	.396	.351
Lama, Jesus, Prin.	.245	54	208	184	23	45	60	10	1	1	19	0	4	1	19	0	59	4	2	7	.326	.313
Lantigua, Denys, Burl.	.206	38	130	107	18	22	31	6	0	1	13	0	1	5	17	0	14	4	0	6	.290	.338
La Roche, Adam, Dan.*	.308	56	232	201	38	62	102	13	3	7	45	1	4	2	24	2	46	4	1	2	.507	.387
Lawson, Forrest, King.	.271	60	238	203	27	55	77	12	2	2	22	3	0	4	28	0	43	12	7	4	.379	.370
Leon, Alfredo, Blue.	.231	7	30	26	5	6	9	1	1	0	0	0	0	1	3	0	1	0	0	1	.346	.333
Littleton, Brandon, Blue.†	.292	55	248	209	39	61	88	11	5	2	25	1	0	3	35	0	42	12	2	3	.421	.401
Lopez, Aristides, Mar.	.344	11	36	32	4	11	16	3	1	0	4	0	0	1	3	0	3	5	2	0	.500	.417
Lowe, Ernesto, Bris.	.254	44	146	130	21	33	41	3	1	1	7	2	1	3	10	0	20	5	3	3	.315	.319
Lucas, William, Mar.	.083	3	12	12	0	1	1	0	0	0	0	0	0	0	0	0	5	0	0	0	.083	.083
Lugo, Roberto, King.*	.182	14	33	22	2	4	10	1	1	1	4	1	0	0	10	0	6	1	2	0	.455	.438
Luna, Hector, Burl.	.204	55	232	201	25	41	49	5	0	1	15	0	1	3	27	0	35	19	4	4	.244	.306
Lydon, Wayne, King.*	.203	55	204	172	34	35	50	4	1	3	20	4	3	1	24	0	47	35	6	2	.291	.300
Lynn, Brody, Burl.†	.100	9	31	30	3	3	4	1	0	0	0	0	0	1	0	0	13	0	0	0	.133	.129
Machado, Aleyandro, Dan.	.341	61	281	217	45	74	84	6	2	0	16	2	3	6	53	0	29	30	12	3	.387	.477
Mack, Antonio, Blue.	.172	41	105	93	12	16	25	3	0	2	8	2	0	0	10	0	41	5	1	3	.269	.252
Maduro, Jorge, Prin.	.252	40	129	119	7	30	37	7	0	0	15	2	1	2	5	0	30	1	1	5	.311	.291
Marconi, Alex, Prin.	.338	19	70	65	8	22	32	10	0	0	9	1	0	0	4	0	10	0	0	5	.492	.377
Martin, Kyle, Blue.	.155	23	79	71	5	11	14	1	1	0	8	0	0	2	6	0	29	0	1	4	.197	.241
Martin, Tyler, Pul.†	.283	53	230	191	43	54	80	13	2	3	30	5	5	1	28	0	42	14	2	5	.419	.369
Martinez, Octavio, Blue.	.387	49	212	181	45	70	107	14	1	7	46	1	3	8	19	0	21	0	1	4	.591	.460
Matos, Angel, Pul.	.302	54	239	199	41	60	105	14	2	9	56	1	1	1	37	0	59	10	3	0	.528	.412
Matos, Watson, Eliz.	.307	31	105	88	18	27	43	5	1	3	14	1	1	0	15	0	30	1	4	1	.489	.404
Maza, Luis, Eliz.	.295	56	249	210	40	62	108	16	3	8	35	7	1	12	19	1	41	12	4	1	.514	.384
McCall, Gerard, Bris.	.287	47	185	164	20	47	71	10	1	4	23	4	2	1	14	0	28	1	1	2	.433	.343
McIntyre, Robert, King.	.294	53	222	197	33	58	86	13	3	3	29	1	2	8	14	0	60	13	13	2	.437	.362
Mejias, Aureliano, J.C.†	.148	11	29	27	3	4	5	1	0	0	2	0	0	2	0	0	10	0	1	0	.185	.207
Mejias, Erick, Pul.†	.214	45	174	154	24	33	39	4	1	0	14	0	1	3	16	0	46	7	4	1	.253	.299
Monegan, Anthony, Bris.*	.208	45	144	120	12	25	29	4	0	0	11	3	2	2	17	1	43	6	2	0	.242	.312
Mongeluzzo, Anthony, Pul.	.218	38	154	142	18	31	56	7	0	6	24	2	1	3	6	0	42	1	1	2	.394	.263
Montgomery, Billy, Pul.†	.220	49	200	164	25	36	42	3	0	1	9	4	0	6	26	0	44	7	3	1	.256	.347
Moose, Robert, Dan.	.286	3	8	7	1	2	2	0	0	0	1	0	0	0	1	0	3	0	0	0	.286	.375
Morban, Jose, Pul.	.225	30	136	120	21	27	43	3	2	3	17	3	1	0	12	2	35	6	3	0	.358	.294
Morneau, Justin, Eliz.*	.217	6	24	23	4	5	8	0	0	1	3	0	0	0	1	0	6	0	0	0	.348	.250
Nelson, Nathan, Mar.	.266	42	173	158	19	42	63	9	0	4	24	2	2	5	6	0	22	10	5	9	.399	.310
Nelson, Timothy, Blue.	.000	1	4	4	1	0	0	0	0	0	0	0	0	0	0	0	0	0	0	0	.000	.000
Nunez, Felix, Prin.	.285	56	210	200	20	57	73	8	4	0	23	0	0	4	6	0	58	1	2	3	.365	.319
O'Brien, Kevin, Prin.*	.103	11	43	39	2	4	4	0	0	0	4	0	2	1	1	0	17	0	0	0	.103	.140
Ortiz, Daniel, Prin.	.218	15	59	55	4	12	19	1	0	2	2	0	0	2	2	0	18	0	1	0	.345	.271
Osborn, Jason, King.	.143	11	38	35	1	5	7	2	0	0	2	0	1	1	1	0	6	0	0	1	.200	.184
Pack, Branden, Pul.†	.234	57	235	205	28	48	84	10	1	8	32	0	1	2	27	0	68	2	1	7	.410	.328
Pagan, Angel, Pul.	.361	19	78	72	13	26	33	5	1	0	8	0	0	0	6	0	8	6	1	1	.458	.410
Parrott, Tom, Dan.	.181	22	81	72	13	13	22	4	1	1	5	0	1		8	0	21	2	2	2	.306	.272
Pena, Amaury, Bris.	.280	37	140	125	20	35	53	7	1	3	14	2	0	2	11	0	33	4	0	3	.424	.348
Pena, Tony, Dan.	.214	55	224	215	22	46	57	5	0	2	20	2	2	0	5	0	53	6	2	8	.265	.230
Perez, Felipe, Blue.	.212	38	147	137	13	29	43	3	1	3	13	0	1	4	5	0	49	1	1	1	.314	.259
Perez, Jay, Mar.†	.237	50	204	173	25	41	63	6	2	4	23	0	0	9	22	1	39	7	1	3	.364	.353
Perez, Juan, J.C.	.247	23	98	85	13	21	31	3	2	1	4	1	0	3	9	0	17	6	1	1	.365	.340
Perich, Josh, King.	.238	24	88	80	12	19	29	1	0	3	11	0	0	0	8	0	24	2	4	4	.363	.307
Peterson, Brian, Burl.	.371	10	38	35	5	13	15	2	0	0	5	0	0	0	3	0	8	0	0	0	.429	.421
Pichardo, Henry, Burl.	.322	49	175	146	34	47	67	12	1	2	21	1	2	3	23	0	25	8	5	5	.459	.420
Pinales, Franklin, Eliz.	.212	40	138	113	13	24	32	8	0	0	12	0	3	2	20	0	26	10	5	2	.283	.333
Ponce Deleon, Damon, J.C.	1.000	20	1	1	0	1	1	0	0	0	1	0	0	0	0	0	0	0	0	0	1.000	1.000
Quickstad, Barry, Eliz.*	.236	52	211	178	28	42	73	11	4	4	33	5	0	1	27	1	48	6	1	1	.410	.340
Rabe, Joshua, Eliz.	.221	44	183	154	33	34	48	5	0	3	11	0	4	0	25	0	34	2	0	6	.312	.344
Raffo, John, King.	.272	52	193	158	28	43	74	10	0	7	20	3	1	1	30	2	30	4	0	2	.468	.389
Rasmussen, Wes, Dan.	.172	19	71	64	8	11	13	2	0	0	3	1	0	0	6	0	27	3	0	0	.203	.243
Reyes, Guillermo, Bris.†	.296	66	288	257	45	76	99	10	2	3	31	4	2		22	0	24	21	10	3	.385	.353
Reyes, Jose, King.†	.250	49	159	132	22	33	42	3	3	0	8	3	1	3	20	0	37	10	4	1	.318	.359
Reyes, Julio, Bris.*	.281	41	158	146	20	41	64	12	4	1	18	3	2	0	7	0	35	2	2	1	.438	.310
Ridley, Shayne, Blue.†	.260	41	171	150	22	39	49	7	0	1	16	1	1	1	18	0	32	3	1	3	.327	.341
Rincon, Carlos, Mar.	.140	15	47	43	8	6	12	0	0	2	4	0	0	1	3	0	17	1	1	0	.279	.213
Rodgers, Albert, J.C.†	.218	62	247	220	25	48	80	12	1	6	20	2	2	8	15	1	68	4	5	3	.364	.290
Rodriguez, Ricardo, Dan.	.172	11	33	29	4	5	6	1	0	0	1	0	1	0	2	0	8	0	0	0	.207	.250
Royer, Lissandro, King.	.268	25	69	56	14	15	20	0	1	2	4	0	3		6	0	9	5	5	0	.357	.369
Salas, Jose, Dan.†	.301	41	174	156	17	47	62	6	0	3	23	0	1	7	10	1	31	2	1	4	.397	.368
Salvesen, Matthew, Bris.*	.244	39	130	123	11	30	45	8	2	1	20	0	0	2	5	0	32	0	0	2	.366	.285
Sandoval, Michael, Eliz.	.268	42	181	149	27	40	60	10	2	2	30	0	4	4	24	0	22	4	0	1	.403	.346
Santana, Mayobanex, Bris.	.184	34	120	98	12	18	29	4	2	1	8	2	0	1	19	0	26	2	3	3	.296	.322
Santana, Sandy, J.C.	.258	35	140	124	21	32	50	7	1	3	17	1	1	3	11	0	27	9	1	2	.403	.331
Santor, John, J.C.	.174	14	48	46	3	8	11	3	0	0	4	0	0	2	6	0	13	1	0	0	.239	.208
Schmitt, Billy, J.C.	.321	46	178	165	21	53	70	5	3	2	21	1	1	1	10	0	23	3	1	6	.424	.362
Serrano, Raymond, Dan.	.328	21	76	67	16	22	38	4	0	4	16	0	1	1	7	0	11	2	0	0	.567	.395

Player, Team	Avg.	G	TPA	AB	R	H	TB	2B	3B	HR	RBI	SH	SF	HP	BB	IBB	SO	SB	CS	GDP	Slg.	OBP
Shier, Peter, Blue...............	.198	30	119	101	13	20	31	3	1	2	10	0	1	1	16	0	32	5	1	3	.307	.311
Smith, Bradley, Pul.............	.156	35	114	90	13	14	21	2	1	1	7	3	2	6	13	0	33	1	1	2	.233	.297
Smith, Corey, Burl.............	.256	57	239	207	21	53	77	8	2	4	39	0	4	1	27	0	50	8	1	4	.372	.339
Sosa, Francisco, King.	.321	32	86	78	12	25	29	2	1	0	10	2	2	2	12	0	12	12	4	1	.372	.345
Sowers, Douglas, Blue.*........	.281	59	262	221	48	62	113	14	2	11	41	0	3	1	37	1	59	4	2	2	.511	.382
Stanley, Derek, Bris.	.255	65	291	251	47	64	78	9	1	1	33	5	3	7	24	0	39	25	4	3	.311	.333
Stanley, Henry, Mar.*	.248	46	194	165	34	41	73	8	6	4	20	0	2	1	25	0	37	10	4	1	.442	.347
Stokes, Gregory, Eliz............	.197	30	86	76	10	15	17	2	0	0	4	0	1	1	8	0	29	1	2	1	.224	.279
Suraci, Scott, Eliz.*	.223	40	151	130	22	29	47	6	0	4	26	0	2	5	14	1	36	1	2	1	.362	.318
Swedlow, Sean, Burl.*	.226	36	140	115	13	26	31	5	0	0	7	0	0	2	23	0	41	1	2	4	.270	.364
Tapia, Roman, Bris.	.286	13	34	28	8	8	9	1	0	0	0	0	0	0	6	1	7	1	0	0	.321	.412
Taveras, Willy, Burl...........	.263	50	223	190	46	50	63	4	3	1	16	1	3	6	23	0	44	36	9	0	.332	.356
Thompson, Alva, Dan............	.319	39	168	144	27	46	75	7	2	6	26	0	4	6	14	0	31	5	2	6	.521	.393
Torres, Digno, Eliz.*	.250	51	207	184	35	46	72	9	1	5	31	0	0	1	22	0	32	2	1	3	.391	.333
Villegas, Ernest, Pul.	.279	47	211	179	43	50	95	16	1	9	37	0	1	9	22	0	40	11	1	4	.531	.384
Watkins, Thomas, Eliz...........	.221	37	133	113	15	25	29	2	1	0	15	2	2	2	14	0	23	4	1	1	.257	.313
Wendt, Justin, King...........	.364	9	34	33	4	12	20	5	0	1	5	0	0	1	0	0	4	0	1	0	.606	.382
Whitesides, Jake, Mar.*	.178	37	146	129	14	23	30	2	1	1	6	0	1	1	15	0	49	7	2	0	.233	.267
Wigginton, Derek, Bris.*	.366	47	168	145	26	53	84	10	3	5	27	0	3	3	17	1	23	8	1	2	.579	.435
Wilken, Kristopher, Blue.†	.274	58	248	208	35	57	86	10	2	5	28	0	5	1	34	0	49	1	3	5	.413	.371
Wilson, Brandon, King...........	.160	8	27	25	0	4	4	0	0	0	1	0	0	1	1	0	13	0	1	1	.160	.222
Wilson, Heath, Burl...........	.219	12	35	32	4	7	15	3	1	1	7	0	0	1	2	0	10	0	0	0	.469	.286
Womack, Robert, Burl.*.........	.111	5	21	18	0	2	2	0	0	0	3	0	0	0	3	0	6	0	0	1	.111	.238
Woodrow, Justin, J.C.*	.281	40	158	135	22	38	41	3	0	0	14	1	0	0	22	1	29	7	3	3	.304	.382
Zumwalt, Sean, Dan.............	.235	59	247	204	27	48	76	15	2	3	28	0	0	5	38	0	67	5	5	4	.373	.368

PLAYERS WITH TWO OR MORE TEAMS

Player, Team	Avg.	G	TPA	AB	R	H	TB	2B	3B	HR	RBI	SH	SF	HP	BB	IBB	SO	SB	CS	GDP	Slg.	OBP
Dees, Charlie, Blue...............	.143	2	7	7	0	1	2	1	0	0	1	0	0	0	0	0	4	0	0	0	.286	.143
Dees, Charlie, Pul...............	.304	51	215	184	40	56	112	9	4	13	47	1	3	2	25	0	62	9	1	2	.609	.388

GRAND SLAMS: Boitel, R. Bowen, Castellanos, Cruz, DeCola, Quickstad, G. Reyes, M. Santana, D. Stanley, 1 each.

AWARDED FIRST BASE ON CATCHER'S INTERFERENCE: Colmenter (Alvarado), Fatur (Sosa), G. Reyes (A. Matos), D. Stanley (Salas), H. Stanley (Acosta).

2000 PITCHING

TEAM

Team	W	L	Pct.	ERA	G	CG	ShO	Sv.	IP	H	TBF	R	ER	HR	SH	SF	HB	BB	IBB	SO	WP	Bk.
Pulaski	40	28	.588	3.29	68	3	2	14	574.2	503	2451	276	210	20	16	19	43	223	4	582	50	8
Kingsport	35	32	.522	3.65	67	2	1	17	581.1	567	2537	305	236	32	23	8	42	207	5	480	56	8
Danville	37	29	.561	3.80	66	3	2	22	589.2	577	2545	294	249	33	24	18	29	226	1	531	46	8
Elizabethton	46	18	.719	3.80	64	4	7	16	558.1	481	2365	279	236	42	17	13	33	248	2	536	64	8
Princeton	34	34	.500	4.00	68	1	3	21	571.1	588	2553	327	254	39	18	19	38	256	1	534	74	4
Bristol	34	33	.507	4.02	67	3	1	19	564.2	535	2428	311	252	41	23	22	36	221	8	537	63	5
Martinsville	30	36	.455	4.36	66	1	3	13	559.2	524	2468	358	271	46	15	15	51	271	5	504	58	8
Burlington	21	46	.313	4.66	67	0	3	10	568.0	584	2569	416	294	48	23	31	46	258	0	503	88	12
Johnson City	24	44	.353	4.96	68	1	2	11	580.1	625	2635	409	320	46	15	18	29	263	3	489	57	6
Bluefield	31	32	.492	5.32	63	1	2	12	524.2	612	2385	379	310	53	14	20	56	228	0	428	45	11

INDIVIDUAL

TOP QUALIFIERS FOR EARNED-RUN AVERAGE TITLE

Minimum 54 innings.*Lefthanded pitcher.

Pitcher, Team	W	L	Pct.	ERA	G	GS	CG	ShO	GF	Sv.	IP	H	TBF	R	ER	HR	SH	SF	HB	BB	IBB	SO	WP	Bk.
Valdez, Domingo, Pul.	6	2	.750	1.63	11	11	0	0	0	0	60.2	45	250	23	11	1	0	0	5	25	0	71	5	2
Ridgway, Jeff, Prin.*	3	4	.429	2.47	12	12	0	0	0	0	54.2	47	237	24	15	2	0	2	1	30	0	60	6	0
Martin, Lucas, Eliz.*	7	0	1.000	2.48	15	8	0	0	1	1	61.2	58	237	20	17	3	0	0	8	50	0	53	0	1
Urena, Sixto, Pul.	6	2	.750	2.83	11	11	1	0	0	0	60.1	53	255	24	19	0	0	0	5	25	0	47	3	1
Bowen, Chad, King.	7	2	.778	3.00	11	11	0	0	0	0	63.0	59	274	22	21	4	2	0	4	23	0	41	2	0
Lopez, Rafael, King.	3	3	.500	3.04	9	9	1	0	0	0	56.1	50	226	20	19	1	0	1	5	9	0	43	4	0
Caraballo, Angel, Bris.	7	4	.636	3.14	13	13	0	0	0	0	77.1	67	319	39	27	8	3	2	2	27	0	61	6	0
Narveson, Chris, J.C.*.........	2	4	.333	3.27	12	12	0	0	0	0	55.0	57	247	33	20	7	1	1	3	25	0	63	3	0
Trevino, Chris, Dan.*	1	4	.200	3.36	12	12	1	0	0	0	56.1	56	242	28	21	7	2	1	1	23	0	51	5	0
Rleal, Sendy, Blue.	6	2	.750	3.39	13	13	0	1	0	0	61.0	61	265	26	23	5	1	3	8	25	0	55	3	1
Stamler, Keith, Pul.	5	4	.556	3.55	14	9	1	0	2	0	66.0	59	276	32	26	2	5	0	7	15	1	59	2	0
Watkins, David, Dan.	3	3	.500	3.67	10	9	0	0	0	0	61.1	58	258	28	25	2	1	2	5	16	0	56	5	0
Ferrand, Dario, Bris.	5	5	.500	3.73	13	12	2	0	0	0	82.0	92	352	39	34	6	2	2	4	20	0	73	9	2
Graham, Brian, Bris.	5	4	.556	3.84	12	12	0	0	0	0	65.2	63	274	35	28	3	3	1	2	19	0	52	2	1
Waters, Chris, Dan.	5	3	.625	3.91	13	13	1	0	0	0	69.0	64	286	33	30	4	2	2	2	29	0	73	6	0

DEPARTMENTAL LEADERS: W—Martin, Bowen, Caraballo, 7 each; L—Lantigua, Burns, F. Cabrera, 7 each; Pct.—Martin, 1.000; G—Grassing, 27; GS—several tied, 13 each; CG—Richardson, Romero, Ferrand, 2 each; ShO—Romero, 1; GF—Ramirez, 21; Sv.—Jones, 9; IP—Ferrand, 82; H—Ferrand, 92; TBF—Ferrand, 352; R—Burns, 52; ER—Bethancour, Romero, 38 each; HR—Burns, 12; SH—Romero, Stamler, 5 each; SF—Anderson, Gilbert, Lantigua, 5 each; HB—Mead, 12; BB—Moseley, 43; IBB—several tied, 2 each; SO—Gilbert, 82; WP—Shaw, 15; BK—Bent, 4.

ALL PITCHERS

*Lefthanded pitcher.

Pitcher, Team	W	L	Pct.	ERA	G	GS	CG	ShO	GF	Sv.	IP	H	TBF	R	ER	HR	SH	SF	HB	BB	IBB	SO	WP	Bk.
Abbott, Jim, Eliz.	0	0	.000	2.19	2	2	0	0	0	0	12.1	9	47	4	3	1	0	0	0	1	0	19	2	0
Abrams, Grant, Dan.	2	5	.286	4.76	18	0	0	0	10	0	28.1	33	128	19	15	0	1	0	1	10	0	30	1	0

Pitcher, Team	W	L	Pct.	ERA	G	GS	CG	ShO	GF	Sv.	IP	H	TBF	R	ER	HR	SH	SF	HB	BB	IBB	SO	WP	Bk.
Advincola, Jose, Blue.*	1	0	1.000	7.71	17	0	0	0	1	0	30.1	43	155	26	26	6	0	1	6	21	0	22	11	1
Albers, Mike, Burl.*	0	2	.000	8.31	6	0	0	0	2	0	8.2	11	42	9	8	0	1	2	2	5	0	7	1	1
Albertson, Justin, J.C.	0	0	.000	40.50	1	0	0	0	0	0	0.2	1	8	3	3	0	0	0	0	5	0	2	3	0
Alvarez, Oscar, Burl.*	2	3	.400	4.54	16	1	0	0	2	0	37.2	32	166	29	19	2	1	3	1	19	0	39	3	0
Anderson, Julius, Prin.	4	4	.500	4.91	11	8	1	0	0	0	47.2	61	223	36	26	4	0	5	3	18	0	26	3	0
Bajenaru, Jeffrey, Bris.	1	1	.500	3.77	12	0	0	0	11	5	14.1	10	61	6	6	2	0	0	0	5	0	31	2	0
Barreto, Joel, Eliz.	1	3	.250	4.31	22	0	0	0	15	3	31.1	30	140	18	15	2	2	0	1	18	1	36	9	0
Barrett, Jimmy, Mar.	6	2	.750	4.73	13	13	0	0	0	0	66.2	60	294	37	35	4	0	1	10	32	0	72	4	1
Batista, Carlos, Burl.	0	0	.000	0.00	1	0	0	0	1	0	1.0	0	5	0	0	0	0	1	2	0	0	0	0	0
Batista, Roberto, J.C.	1	3	.250	3.11	7	7	0	0	0	0	37.2	42	167	23	13	2	0	2	1	13	0	12	3	0
Beltre, Sandy, Bris.	2	1	.667	3.68	4	4	0	0	0	0	22.0	19	90	13	9	3	1	1	6	0	0	15	3	0
Bent, Andy, Dan.	5	2	.714	2.66	16	5	0	0	6	1	47.1	42	197	18	14	1	3	1	4	11	1	55	1	4
Berube, Martin, Blue.	1	1	.500	4.60	5	5	0	0	0	0	29.1	34	121	15	15	4	2	0	1	4	0	22	0	1
Bethancourt, Euclides, Prin.	1	5	.167	7.33	13	11	0	0	0	0	46.2	60	232	48	38	7	2	1	8	23	0	31	7	1
Blackwell, Scott, Eliz.	1	1	.500	3.24	4	4	0	0	0	0	16.2	14	66	7	6	1	0	0	1	5	1	18	2	0
Bohannan, Kyle, Bris.	4	2	.667	1.09	15	0	0	0	11	4	24.2	16	99	5	3	0	2	3	3	10	2	29	1	0
Bouie, Aaron, Blue.	1	4	.200	4.42	10	7	0	0	0	0	36.2	38	163	24	18	1	0	2	3	18	0	29	6	2
Bowen, Chad, King.	7	2	.778	3.00	11	11	0	0	0	0	63.0	59	274	22	21	4	2	0	4	23	0	41	2	0
Burgess, Richie, J.C.	1	4	.200	7.06	9	9	0	0	0	0	43.1	59	203	37	34	5	3	3	4	16	0	26	2	0
Burns, Mike, Mar.	2	7	.222	4.52	12	12	0	0	0	0	65.2	75	286	52	33	12	4	2	4	9	0	51	2	1
Bustillos, Oscar, Prin.	0	1	.000	1.59	13	0	0	0	8	2	17.0	9	65	4	3	0	0	0	1	5	0	25	2	0
Byard, David, King.	2	1	.667	4.05	17	0	0	0	12	4	20.0	20	94	10	9	1	1	1	1	12	2	19	2	0
Cabrera, Fernando, Burl.	3	7	.300	4.61	13	13	0	0	0	0	68.1	64	282	42	35	4	2	4	2	20	0	50	14	0
Cabrera, Walin, Burl.	0	1	.000	10.38	10	0	0	0	3	0	13.0	20	73	20	15	1	0	2	1	10	0	10	3	1
Cabrera, Yunior, King.*	4	1	.800	2.76	13	7	0	0	1	0	45.2	44	201	23	14	1	3	0	1	21	1	44	3	2
Caraballo, Angel, Bris.	7	4	.636	3.14	13	13	0	0	0	0	77.1	67	319	39	27	8	3	2	2	27	0	61	6	0
Cetani, Bryan, Dan.*	3	1	.750	4.15	16	1	0	0	4	0	30.1	37	145	18	14	0	0	3	2	17	0	17	3	0
Christ, John, Blue.	0	0	.000	0.00	2	0	0	0	2	1	2.0	2	13	2	0	0	0	0	1	2	0	3	1	1
Cislak, Chad, Burl.	0	0	.000	4.76	6	0	0	0	2	0	11.1	10	53	11	6	0	3	1	0	8	0	9	6	0
Colton, Kyle, Dan.	1	0	.000	6.65	8	6	0	0	1	0	23.0	19	111	19	17	0	2	2	3	20	0	13	2	1
Colvard, Ron, Burl.	3	2	.600	2.56	19	0	0	0	9	1	38.2	41	168	24	11	2	0	4	0	12	0	38	6	1
Corn, Terry, Eliz.	2	0	1.000	3.99	19	0	0	0	8	3	29.1	17	123	15	13	3	1	2	5	18	0	31	6	0
Corona, Ronnie, Eliz.	0	0	.000	3.52	3	1	0	0	1	0	7.2	8	35	4	3	0	1	1	2	0	0	8	0	0
Coward, Timothy, Prin.	2	1	.667	2.08	6	6	0	0	0	0	30.1	27	130	13	7	1	1	1	1	16	0	41	4	0
Cox, Adam, Burl.*	2	4	.333	4.82	12	12	0	0	0	0	46.2	42	201	31	25	5	2	0	6	27	0	50	9	1
Cromer, Jason, Prin.*	3	4	.429	3.95	13	13	0	0	0	0	70.2	88	304	36	31	5	4	1	3	15	0	50	4	0
Davis, Jason, Burl.	4	4	.500	4.40	10	10	0	0	0	0	45.0	48	201	27	22	5	3	3	5	16	0	35	5	1
Deaton, Kevin, King.	0	1	.000	3.15	12	0	0	0	4	2	20.0	15	84	7	7	1	0	1	4	0	19	1	0
DeJesus, Rigoberto, J.C.	1	1	.500	4.80	12	0	0	0	4	0	15.0	16	73	16	8	3	0	0	11	0	13	4	0
De La Cruz, Carlos, Burl.	1	1	.500	6.98	19	0	0	0	13	3	29.2	34	143	30	23	5	1	2	5	15	0	28	5	1
D'Frank, Carlos, Burl.	2	2	.500	4.71	6	3	0	0	1	0	21.0	20	97	16	11	1	2	2	3	9	0	19	1	0
Dischiavo, John, Prin.	0	2	.000	5.40	11	8	0	0	0	0	35.0	39	160	22	21	3	1	0	6	7	0	27	6	0
Doyne, Michael, Mar.	3	6	.333	5.45	12	8	0	0	0	0	39.2	25	177	27	24	1	0	1	1	35	0	54	8	0
Echols, Justin, Pul.	0	4	.000	4.41	9	5	0	0	3	0	32.2	34	146	21	16	2	1	1	1	15	0	39	6	2
Esdaile, Ferrin, Burl.	1	4	.200	5.46	17	0	0	0	7	0	28.0	30	145	24	17	3	2	2	3	24	0	28	8	0
Farren, Dave, Blue.	2	4	.333	8.03	15	5	0	0	4	0	37.0	59	189	45	33	3	2	2	4	17	0	27	4	0
Fereira, Ramon, Mar.	2	3	.400	7.71	16	2	0	0	6	0	35.0	43	165	36	30	3	0	0	3	16	1	31	3	0
Ferrand, Dario, Bris.	5	5	.500	3.73	13	12	2	0	0	0	82.0	92	352	39	34	6	2	2	4	20	0	73	9	2
Flanagan, Ryan, Eliz.	0	0	.000	7.84	18	0	0	0	7	0	20.2	18	105	21	18	3	1	0	3	23	0	21	5	0
Ford, Jr, Thomas, Blue.*	1	0	1.000	3.93	19	0	0	0	6	3	36.2	27	146	19	16	2	1	0	2	15	0	41	1	2
Fortunato, Bartolome, Prin.	3	4	.429	4.63	17	5	0	0	2	1	46.2	56	223	31	24	4	2	1	4	19	0	51	8	0
Gilbert, Richard, Pul.*	3	4	.429	4.83	12	12	1	0	0	0	69.0	63	300	45	37	5	2	5	4	32	0	82	6	1
Gomez, Benito, Prin.*	4	1	.800	3.89	25	0	0	0	10	0	39.1	35	179	19	17	5	2	2	4	24	0	46	4	0
Gomez, Mariano, Burl.*	0	5	.000	4.31	13	11	0	0	0	0	54.1	77	247	44	26	7	1	3	1	16	0	30	5	3
Gomez, Rafael, King.	1	1	.500	3.96	5	5	0	0	0	0	25.0	26	110	12	11	2	0	0	1	9	0	20	2	1
Graham, Brian, Bris.	5	4	.556	3.84	12	12	0	0	0	0	65.2	63	274	35	28	3	3	1	2	19	0	52	2	1
Granadillo, Adel, Burl.	0	0	.000	1.08	3	3	0	0	0	0	8.1	3	34	1	1	0	0	0	5	4	0	9	1	1
Grassing, Bryan, J.C.	1	3	.250	5.90	27	0	0	0	7	0	39.2	53	184	32	26	3	1	1	2	9	0	36	6	0
Graves, Donovan, J.C.	3	4	.429	4.50	13	12	0	0	0	0	56.0	58	251	42	28	2	0	3	1	33	0	48	3	0
Guerrero, Neftali, King.	0	1	.000	4.70	15	0	0	0	7	0	23.0	31	109	16	12	0	1	1	0	8	0	19	3	0
Hamilton, Ryan, Mar.	3	3	.500	3.40	8	8	1	0	0	0	50.1	45	205	23	19	2	2	3	3	9	0	31	4	0
Harriman, Preston, J.C.	0	0	.000	0.00	2	0	0	0	1	0	1.2	3	8	0	0	0	0	0	0	1	0	0	1	0
Hollifield, Alec, Bris.	0	4	.000	9.82	5	5	0	0	0	0	22.0	32	105	25	24	0	0	1	11	0	20	1	0
Holubec, Kenneth, Eliz.*	4	1	.800	3.03	9	6	0	0	0	0	32.2	22	129	11	11	1	1	1	2	12	0	43	2	0
Hopper, Kevin, Dan.	2	0	1.000	3.52	16	0	0	0	7	3	30.2	27	128	13	12	2	1	0	1	7	0	26	4	0
Hughes, Rocky, Bris.*	1	1	.500	3.78	16	3	0	0	4	1	33.1	23	144	18	14	2	2	0	1	20	1	40	3	1
Hunt, Jordan, Mar.	1	2	.333	6.20	14	7	0	0	2	1	45.0	56	211	39	31	5	0	1	2	22	0	42	7	0
Johnson, Kareem, Eliz.	0	0	.000	0.00	1	0	0	0	1	0	1.0	0	4	0	0	0	0	0	1	0	1	0	0
Johnson, Kelly, J.C.	2	6	.250	7.96	22	0	0	0	12	1	26.0	24	128	25	23	3	2	1	3	23	1	21	9	0
Jones, Quentin, Dan.	4	2	.667	3.67	21	0	0	0	18	9	27.0	27	116	13	11	1	2	1	1	5	0	32	2	1
Kemp, Bo, Eliz.	1	0	1.000	2.18	17	0	0	0	16	7	20.2	12	81	6	5	2	1	0	1	6	0	28	0	0
Keppel, Bob, King.	1	2	.333	6.83	8	6	0	0	0	0	29.0	31	136	22	22	1	0	4	13	0	29	6	0
Knapp, Ben, Blue.	1	3	.250	5.83	7	6	0	0	0	0	29.1	37	135	24	19	4	1	1	2	11	0	26	2	2
Lama, Jesus, Prin.	0	0	.000	0.00	1	0	0	0	0	0	0.1	0	2	0	0	0	0	0	1	0	1	0	0
Lantigua, Delvis, Bris.	2	7	.222	5.31	12	12	1	0	0	0	59.1	63	273	42	35	4	3	5	10	30	2	59	6	0
La Rosa, Dancy, Eliz.	6	5	.545	4.55	16	8	0	0	2	1	55.1	71	258	37	28	2	3	3	2	23	0	33	9	1
Larson, Ryan, Burl.	2	0	1.000	2.54	19	0	0	0	10	2	46.0	32	189	17	13	5	2	2	17	0	56	9	0
Lazo, Rafael, King.	0	2	.000	2.92	15	0	0	0	4	1	24.2	17	107	9	8	3	3	0	3	11	1	30	2	0
Lee, Adam, J.C.	0	0	.000	3.56	19	0	0	0	4	0	30.1	26	127	14	12	2	1	2	1	13	0	20	6	0
Lindsey, David, J.C.	2	3	.400	6.08	19	0	0	0	9	2	40.0	46	190	32	27	3	0	2	2	22	0	25	1	2
Lockhart, John, J.C.	0	1	.000	5.09	19	0	0	0	9	2	23.0	26	107	19	13	0	1	0	2	7	0	22	1	0
Lopez, Albie, Prin.	0	0	.000	0.00	1	0	0	0	0	0	0.2	0	2	0	0	0	0	0	0	0	0	1	0	0
Lopez, Miguel, Prin.	4	3	.571	3.03	21	0	0	0	13	4	32.2	28	139	14	11	0	2	1	0	19	0	40	1	0
Lopez, Rafael, King.	3	3	.500	3.04	9	9	1	0	0	0	56.1	50	226	20	19	1	0	1	5	9	0	43	4	0

Pitcher, Team	W	L	Pct.	ERA	G	GS	CG	ShO	GF	Sv.	IP	H	TBF	R	ER	HR	SH	SF	HB	BB	IBB	SO	WP	Bk.
Mack, Antonio, Blue.	0	0	.000	0.00	2	0	0	0	2	0	0.2	0	3	0	0	0	0	0	0	1	0	1	0	0
Mansfield, Monte, Mar.	2	1	.667	2.22	18	0	0	0	15	3	24.1	16	100	7	6	2	2	1	2	14	2	32	6	0
Marchetti, Daniel, Blue.	3	2	.600	5.76	22	0	0	0	9	0	29.2	42	137	29	19	4	0	1	3	8	0	31	4	0
Martin, Lucas, Eliz.*	7	0	1.000	2.48	15	8	0	0	1	1	61.2	58	237	20	17	3	0	0	0	8	0	53	0	1
Martinez, Dan, Bris.*	0	0	.000	6.23	12	0	0	0	3	0	17.1	21	86	17	12	3	2	1	4	7	2	12	4	0
Martinez, Eduardo, Mar.*	1	1	.500	3.08	17	0	0	0	6	0	38.0	41	171	27	13	3	2	0	3	16	0	30	4	0
Martinez, Miguel, J.C.	2	5	.286	5.31	13	13	1	0	0	0	62.2	75	280	44	37	4	2	1	1	16	0	43	0	1
McKey, Dustin, Prin.	3	1	.750	0.79	17	0	0	0	8	4	22.2	12	84	3	2	0	2	1	1	6	1	11	1	1
Mead, David, Pul.	6	2	.750	4.62	12	12	0	0	0	0	62.1	57	274	35	32	2	1	4	12	24	0	66	5	1
Medlock, Chet, J.C.	2	0	1.000	1.99	5	4	0	0	0	0	22.2	12	89	7	5	2	0	0	1	11	0	17	1	1
Mejia, Francisco, Blue.*	2	1	.667	6.23	4	4	0	0	0	0	17.1	18	78	17	12	3	0	0	3	10	0	11	0	0
Miller, Jason, Eliz.*	2	1	.667	4.50	9	5	0	0	0	0	26.0	23	104	16	13	7	0	1	1	5	0	22	0	1
Morban, Domingo, King.*	1	0	1.000	4.82	11	0	0	0	3	0	18.2	24	93	18	10	3	1	0	4	9	0	16	5	2
Moseley, Marcus, Eliz.	2	1	.667	8.15	18	5	0	0	3	0	38.2	41	197	42	35	3	1	1	4	43	0	38	8	0
Mozingo, Dan, Bris.*	0	0	.000	3.00	9	0	0	0	6	1	15.0	13	63	5	5	1	1	1	0	6	0	16	4	0
Murray, Brad, Bris.*	2	1	.667	4.26	16	4	0	0	5	1	50.2	49	215	28	24	1	2	1	5	16	0	37	4	1
Musser, Neal, King.*	3	2	.600	2.10	7	7	0	0	0	0	34.1	33	138	10	8	1	0	0	1	6	0	21	3	0
Narveson, Chris, J.C.*	2	4	.333	3.27	12	12	0	0	0	0	55.0	57	247	33	20	7	1	1	3	25	0	63	3	0
Nichols, Brian, King.	2	5	.286	6.14	12	8	0	0	2	0	48.1	61	230	42	33	3	1	1	6	25	0	40	7	1
Novoa, Niquel, Prin.*	0	0	.000	16.88	3	0	0	0	2	0	2.2	7	16	5	5	1	0	0	0	2	0	2	0	0
Olivo, Carlos, J.C.	1	4	.200	5.18	24	0	0	0	7	0	40.0	41	182	26	23	5	3	0	4	20	1	40	3	0
Osberg, Tanner, King.	1	2	.333	2.11	12	0	0	0	5	1	21.1	18	89	10	5	2	2	1	1	6	1	22	1	1
Ough, Wayne, King.	3	2	.600	3.56	9	3	1	0	2	1	30.1	24	124	13	12	2	0	2	14	0	22	3	1	
Peeples, Ross, King.*	1	2	.333	2.61	15	2	0	0	5	0	31.0	25	128	15	9	1	1	1	0	10	0	29	1	0
Pena, Francisco, Mar.	3	2	.600	2.40	13	1	0	0	5	2	30.0	18	130	14	8	3	1	1	3	22	0	36	6	0
Pepen, Robert, King.	1	1	.500	1.20	13	0	0	0	11	7	15.0	13	63	3	2	1	2	1	0	4	0	18	1	0
Perez, Keino, Burl.	1	4	.200	3.41	21	0	0	0	14	3	34.1	34	161	23	13	5	2	2	3	14	0	27	1	0
Persby, Andrew, Eliz.	6	1	.857	1.07	20	2	0	0	4	1	42.0	21	158	5	5	0	0	1	0	24	0	45	5	2
Petulla, Craig, Mar.	0	1	.000	4.66	13	0	0	0	5	2	19.1	18	88	11	10	1	0	2	5	9	1	11	1	0
Phillips, James, Blue.	2	3	.400	10.80	22	0	0	0	8	0	28.1	49	154	38	34	6	3	2	3	22	0	17	1	0
Pichardo, Henry, Burl.	0	0	.000	0.00	1	0	0	0	1	0	0.2	0	2	0	0	0	0	0	0	0	0	0	0	0
Ponce Deleon, Damon, J.C.	2	0	1.000	2.70	20	0	0	0	17	8	23.1	13	94	7	7	1	0	1	0	8	0	26	4	1
Portobanco, Luz, King.	3	3	.500	4.89	16	9	0	0	2	0	57.0	62	257	43	31	3	4	1	8	18	0	38	7	0
Ramirez, Enrique, Blue.	1	3	.250	4.57	25	0	0	0	21	8	21.2	23	104	15	11	0	2	0	1	17	0	18	4	1
Reese, Josh, J.C.	1	4	.200	8.53	12	3	0	0	2	0	19.0	28	100	21	18	1	0	0	2	12	0	31	6	0
Renteria, Juan, Prin.	1	0	1.000	3.47	24	1	0	0	17	6	36.1	38	162	20	14	2	0	0	1	20	0	50	8	1
Reynolds, Jacob, Burl.	0	2	.000	6.30	10	2	0	0	0	0	30.0	34	146	28	21	1	1	1	1	24	0	25	6	1
Richardson, Jason, Eliz.	5	1	.833	1.71	10	9	2	0	0	0	47.1	29	194	11	9	2	1	0	8	16	0	51	5	0
Ridgway, Jeff, Prin.*	3	4	.429	2.47	12	12	0	0	0	0	54.2	47	237	24	15	2	0	2	1	30	0	60	6	0
Riviere, Rhett, Pul.	6	0	1.000	2.59	15	3	0	0	11	1	48.2	44	209	20	14	2	1	3	2	18	0	29	6	1
Rleal, Sendy, Blue.	2	2	.750	3.39	13	12	0	0	1	0	61.0	61	265	26	23	5	1	3	8	25	0	55	3	1
Rodriguez, Jose, Dan.	3	1	.750	3.96	12	12	1	0	0	0	61.1	59	280	33	27	6	1	2	4	40	0	31	7	1
Rodriguez, Luis, Pul.	2	1	.667	1.11	10	0	0	0	7	3	24.1	17	100	6	3	1	0	1	1	11	1	40	1	0
Rogers, Bradley, Blue.	2	1	.667	4.42	4	3	0	0	0	0	18.1	21	80	10	9	1	1	0	2	4	0	15	0	0
Romero, Josmir, Eliz.	5	2	.714	4.48	13	13	2	1	0	0	76.1	80	319	42	38	9	5	3	2	18	0	52	3	2
Rondon, Gabriel, King.	2	1	.667	1.45	14	0	0	0	7	1	18.2	14	77	10	3	2	1	0	0	5	0	10	3	0
Rowland, Carl, J.C.	2	2	.500	5.97	15	2	0	0	3	0	31.2	38	144	24	21	3	1	1	1	11	1	25	1	1
Runser, Greg, Pul.	3	3	.500	1.12	21	0	0	0	16	6	48.1	35	196	18	6	2	1	2	0	14	1	47	6	0
Russ, Christopher, Pul.*	2	0	1.000	0.83	6	2	0	0	1	0	21.2	14	85	4	2	0	2	0	1	4	0	26	2	0
Rust, Evan, Prin.	2	5	.714	2.89	26	0	0	0	5	1	43.2	37	184	17	14	3	1	3	3	13	0	34	3	0
Ryan, Jeremy, Mar.	0	4	.000	4.91	7	7	0	0	0	0	25.2	26	116	20	14	2	2	0	2	15	0	25	1	0
Santillan, Manuel, Mar.	1	0	1.000	4.76	19	0	0	0	13	1	22.2	21	110	18	12	1	0	0	3	24	0	20	3	2
Santos, Bernaldo, Mar.	0	0	.000	9.64	3	0	0	0	1	0	4.2	6	22	5	5	0	0	0	0	2	0	5	2	1
Sclafani, Anthony, Dan.	1	0	1.000	3.62	19	0	0	0	12	8	27.1	27	124	13	11	1	1	1	2	18	0	25	3	0
Scuglik, Mike, Pul.*	0	2	.000	5.16	18	0	0	0	12	1	29.2	26	135	19	17	1	2	0	2	22	1	27	5	0
Shaw, Elliott, Prin.	0	1	.000	4.62	18	4	0	0	4	0	37.0	38	181	28	19	2	0	1	2	34	0	29	15	1
Smart, Richard, Eliz.	3	2	.600	4.48	15	1	0	0	1	0	34.1	26	151	20	17	3	1	0	3	24	0	36	8	1
Smith, Hans, Prin.*	1	1	.500	8.59	7	0	0	0	6	3	7.1	6	30	7	7	0	1	0	0	4	0	9	2	0
Smith, Toebius, Dan.	2	1	.667	4.39	19	0	0	0	4	1	41.0	37	167	21	20	4	3	1	0	9	0	35	5	1
Sperring, Jayme, Blue.	1	0	1.000	0.00	4	0	0	0	2	1	4.0	2	16	1	0	0	0	0	0	2	0	5	1	0
Stamler, Keith, Pul.	5	4	.556	3.55	14	9	1	0	2	0	66.0	59	276	32	26	2	5	0	7	15	1	59	2	0
Staveland, Toby, Dan.	2	0	1.000	1.20	5	1	0	0	0	0	15.0	10	58	2	2	1	1	0	0	5	0	12	0	0
Stewart, John, Pul.*	0	4	.000	4.40	21	2	0	0	13	3	45.0	45	196	24	22	2	0	3	2	17	0	42	2	0
Sullivan, Thomas, Eliz.*	1	0	1.000	0.00	4	0	0	0	4	0	4.1	2	17	0	0	0	0	0	1	0	1	0	0	0
Sweeney, James, Bris.*	3	1	.750	1.60	17	2	0	0	1	0	39.1	31	156	10	7	1	0	2	0	16	0	36	3	0
Tate, Matthew, Blue.	1	3	.250	7.86	7	5	0	0	1	0	26.1	40	127	26	23	3	2	3	5	8	0	16	2	0
Tavarez, David, Blue.	2	2	.600	6.03	7	7	0	0	0	0	34.1	47	166	30	23	8	0	3	14	0	23	2	0	
Teekel, Josh, J.C.	1	0	1.000	1.42	4	3	0	0	0	0	12.2	7	53	4	2	0	0	0	1	8	0	18	1	0
Thompson, Derek, Burl.*	0	4	.000	5.82	12	12	0	0	0	0	43.1	50	201	38	28	2	0	2	2	14	0	40	4	0
Tillery, Josh, Dan.	2	1	.667	3.83	17	1	0	0	1	0	42.1	53	190	23	18	1	3	2	2	14	0	36	1	0
Tomaszewski, Eliot, Blue.	1	1	.500	5.24	21	1	0	0	6	0	34.1	36	158	22	20	1	0	7	15	0	36	4	0	
Tremont, Harold, Pul.	1	0	1.000	7.50	2	1	0	0	0	0	6.0	11	29	5	5	0	0	1	1	0	0	7	1	0
Trevino, Chris, Dan.*	1	4	.200	3.36	12	12	1	0	0	0	56.1	56	242	28	21	7	2	1	1	23	0	51	5	0
Urena, Sixto, Pul.	6	2	.750	2.83	11	11	0	0	0	0	60.1	53	255	24	19	0	0	5	25	0	47	3	1	
Valdez, Domingo, Pul.	6	2	.750	1.63	11	11	0	0	0	0	60.2	45	250	23	11	1	0	5	25	0	71	5	2	
Valentine, Joseph, Bris.	1	2	.667	2.88	19	0	0	0	16	7	25.0	14	104	10	8	1	2	2	12	1	30	9	0	
Valles, Rolando, Mar.*	5	2	.714	3.43	19	0	0	0	11	3	39.1	34	165	17	15	4	1	2	4	20	0	32	2	2
Wainwright, Adam, Dan.	2	2	.500	3.68	6	6	0	0	0	0	29.1	28	115	13	12	3	1	0	1	2	0	39	1	0
Waters, Chris, Dan.	5	3	.625	3.91	13	13	1	0	0	0	69.0	64	286	33	30	4	2	2	29	0	73	6	0	
Watkins, David, Dan.	3	3	.500	3.67	10	9	0	0	0	0	61.1	58	258	28	25	2	1	2	5	16	0	56	5	0
Whitecotton, Billy, Blue.	2	2	.500	1.64	8	8	1	0	0	0	49.1	35	188	12	9	2	1	0	3	16	0	33	0	1
Williams, Ruddy, Mar.	2	4	.333	2.70	12	8	0	0	1	1	53.1	40	228	25	16	3	1	2	6	26	1	26	5	1
Young, Curtis, Bris.	0	1	.000	8.64	15	0	0	0	7	0	16.2	22	87	19	16	0	0	1	1	16	0	26	6	0

COMBINATION SHUTOUTS: **Bluefield (2)**—Whitecotton-Marchetti, Mejia-Phillips-Sperring. **Bristol (1)**—Sweeney-Young-Bohannan. **Burlington (3)**—Davis-De La Cruz, Thompson-Alvarez, Cox-Perez-Colvard. **Danville (2)**—Waters-Smith-Jones, Bent-Smith. **Elizabethton (6)**—Moesley-Persby-Sullivan-Corn, Blackwell-Martin-Corn, Richardson-Smart-Martin-Barreto-Kemp, Persby-Kemp, Martin-Persby-Kemp, Romero-Barreto. **Johnson City (2)**—Graves-Lockhart, Narveson-Lee-Grassing-Ponce Deleon. **Kingsport (1)**—Bowen-Byard-Lazo-Rondon-Pepen. **Martinsville (3)**—Barrett-Valles, Barrett-Hunt-Santillan, Barrett-Pena. **Princeton (3)**—Ridgway-Rust-Renteria, Cromer-Lopez-Renteria-McKey, Ridgway-Lopez. **Pulaski (2)**—Russ-Runser, Valdez-Runser.

NO-HIT GAMES: None.

2000 FIELDING

TEAM

Team	Pct.	G	PO	A	E	TC	DP	TP	PB
Bristol	.966	67	1694	723	85	2502	49	0	26
Elizabethton	.966	64	1675	647	82	2404	43	0	10
Danville	.962	66	1769	722	98	2589	49	0	22
Pulaski	.958	68	1724	669	105	2498	43	0	18
Kingsport	.955	67	1744	753	118	2615	57	0	23
Princeton	.953	68	1714	710	119	2543	50	0	22
Martinsville	.952	66	1679	696	121	2496	64	0	25
Bluefield	.951	63	1574	701	116	2391	49	0	19
Johnson City	.947	68	1741	735	139	2615	47	0	25
Burlington	.933	67	1704	704	173	2581	47	0	27

INDIVIDUAL

FIRST BASEMEN

NOTE: All caps denotes fielding-percentage leader based on 34 games for catchers, 45 for all other non-pitchers and 54 innings for pitchers. *Throws lefthanded.

Player, Team	Pct.	G	PO	A	E	TC	DP
Acosta, Emilio, J.C.	.969	6	28	3	1	32	1
Ayala, Abraham, Mar.	.982	7	49	5	1	55	3
Baetzel, Mike, Bris.	1.000	1	5	0	0	5	0
Baldiris, Aaron, King.	.981	18	142	10	3	155	16
Batista, Carlos, Burl.	.951	25	239	15	13	267	20
Cardona, Raynier, King.	.000	1	0	0	0	0	0
Dees, Charlie, Pul.	.981	12	92	9	2	103	5
Dement, Dan, Prin.	1.000	2	1	0	0	1	1
Dorner, Dwight, Prin.	1.000	7	45	4	0	49	4
Finnerty, Francis, Burl.	.979	22	175	15	4	194	13
Gajewski, Matt, Pul.	.991	12	97	8	1	106	9
German, Ramon, Mar.	.992	40	351	21	3	375	38
Hamill, Ryan, J.C.	.940	8	61	2	4	67	4
Hamilton, Mark, Mar.*	.970	20	145	15	5	165	17
Jones, Garrett, Dan.*	.989	31	257	9	3	269	17
Krga, Mike, Prin.	1.000	1	4	0	0	4	0
La Roche, Adam, Dan.*	.994	37	325	12	2	339	31
Lugo, Roberto, King.*	.985	7	61	5	1	67	1
Maduro, Jorge, Prin.	1.000	1	11	0	0	11	0
Marconi, Alex, Prin.	1.000	1	6	0	0	6	1
Matos, Watson, Eliz.	.987	27	208	13	3	224	13
Moose, Robert, Dan.	1.000	2	4	0	0	4	0
Nelson, Timothy, Blue.	1.000	1	6	0	0	6	0
Nunez, Felix, Prin.	.979	54	426	31	10	467	36
O'Brien, Kevin, Prin.*	1.000	6	54	1	0	55	1
Ortiz, Daniel, Prin.	.974	4	36	2	1	39	2
Perez, Felipe, Blue.	1.000	12	82	6	0	88	11
Raffo, John, King.	.983	42	378	25	7	410	34
Rodgers, Albert, J.C.	.978	43	411	24	10	445	27
Salvesen, Matthew, Bris.	.979	34	271	11	6	288	17
Santana, Mayobanex, Bris.	.990	33	271	25	3	299	21
Santor, John, J.C.	.969	13	118	5	4	127	12
Schmitt, Billy, J.C.	1.000	2	10	1	0	11	0
Sowers, Douglas, Blue.	.982	54	463	29	9	501	29
Swedlow, Sean, Burl.	.955	22	158	13	8	179	9
Tapia, Roman, Bris.	.978	7	42	2	1	45	5
Torres, Digno, Eliz.*	.983	42	325	31	6	362	20
VILLEGAS, Ernest, Pul.	.984	45	346	25	6	377	24
Wendt, Justin, King.	1.000	5	53	1	0	54	3

SECOND BASEMEN

Player, Team	Pct.	G	PO	A	E	TC	DP
Aaron, Oginga, Prin.	.956	25	38	70	5	113	13
Andrianoff, Jonathan, Mar.	.939	7	10	21	2	33	4
Angel, Anthony, Mar.	.977	38	67	103	4	174	23
Baetzel, Mike, Bris.	1.000	3	6	8	0	14	2
Bell, Josh, King.	.914	18	16	37	5	58	3
Colmenter, Jesus, Burl.	.926	27	47	53	8	108	14
Contreras, Erick, Dan.	1.000	1	4	2	0	6	1
Coyne, Anthony, King.	.955	7	11	10	1	22	3
Cruz, Enrique, King.	.000	1	0	0	0	0	0
DEL ROSARIO, Emmanuel, Blue.	.982	54	82	134	4	220	24

Player, Team	Pct.	G	PO	A	E	TC	DP
Dement, Dan, Prin.	.932	16	29	40	5	74	10
Eddlemon, Kelly, Prin.	.000	1	0	0	0	0	0
Fatur, Brian, J.C.	1.000	2	3	3	0	6	0
Flores, Ralphs, Bris.	1.000	1	0	2	0	2	0
Franco, Esterlin, Mar.	.925	23	37	49	7	93	18
Garcia, Nicolas, Blue.	.909	2	2	8	1	11	0
German, Amado, Prin.	.830	12	21	18	8	47	4
Gonzalez, Edgar, Prin.	1.000	1	1	0	0	1	0
Gonzalez, Reggie, Eliz.	.977	50	70	102	4	176	22
Harriman, Preston, J.C.	.938	37	62	90	10	162	13
King, Jason, Dan.	1.000	2	3	4	0	7	0
Krga, Mike, Prin.	.989	21	37	51	1	89	9
Lackaff, John, Bris.	.667	2	2	0	1	3	0
Lantigua, Denys, Burl.	1.000	6	12	19	0	31	3
Machado, Aleyandro, Dan.	.973	59	127	159	8	294	30
Martin, Tyler, Pul.	.977	38	70	99	4	173	20
McIntyre, Robert, King.	.960	41	73	97	7	177	22
Mejias, Erick, Pul.	1.000	25	42	60	0	102	8
Parrott, Tom, Dan.	1.000	1	4	2	0	6	0
Pena, Amaury, Bris.	.980	21	37	61	2	100	12
Pena, Tony, Dan.	.000	1	0	0	0	0	0
Pichardo, Henry, Burl.	.955	39	69	80	7	156	15
Rasmussen, Wes, Dan.	1.000	5	1	7	0	8	0
Reyes, Guillermo, Bris.	.960	46	82	110	8	200	21
Reyes, Jose, King.	1.000	2	0	1	0	1	0
Ridley, Shayne, Blue.	.870	4	7	13	3	23	3
Rodgers, Albert, J.C.	.800	2	2	2	1	5	0
Royer, Lissandro, King.	.982	14	26	30	1	57	9
Santana, Sandy, J.C.	.955	34	61	108	8	177	20
Shier, Peter, Blue.	.952	5	9	11	1	21	1
Smith, Bradley, Pul.	.931	8	11	16	2	29	1
Stanley, Henry, Mar.*	1.000	1	2	2	0	4	1
Stokes, Gregory, Eliz.	.667	3	1	1	1	3	0
Watkins, Thomas, Eliz.	.969	17	32	31	2	65	5

THIRD BASEMEN

Player, Team	Pct.	G	PO	A	E	TC	DP
Andrianoff, Jonathan, Mar.	.727	3	4	4	3	11	1
Angel, Anthony, Mar.	.667	1	1	1	1	3	0
Baldelli, Rocco, Prin.	.000	1	0	0	0	0	0
Baldiris, Aaron, King.	.932	12	13	28	3	44	1
Bell, Josh, King.	.778	2	4	5	2	9	1
Colmenter, Jesus, Burl.	.667	1	2	0	1	3	0
Coyne, Anthony, King.	.842	7	5	11	3	19	0
Cruz, Enrique, King.	.910	46	24	108	13	145	9
Dement, Dan, Prin.	.818	6	4	5	2	11	0
Diaz, Aneuris, J.C.	.916	43	40	91	12	143	8
Dorner, Dwight, Prin.	.000	1	0	0	0	0	0
Eddlemon, Kelly, Prin.	.918	64	43	126	15	184	8
Finnerty, Francis, Burl.	.800	14	4	16	5	25	0
Flores, Ralphs, Bris.	1.000	1	0	2	0	2	0
Franco, Esterlin, Mar.	.731	10	5	14	7	26	0
Gajewski, Matt, Pul.	.945	19	17	35	3	55	1
Garcia, Nicolas, Blue.	.800	4	0	4	1	5	0
German, Amado, Prin.	.000	1	0	0	0	0	0
German, Ramon, Mar.	.854	14	10	31	7	48	0
King, Jason, Dan.	.879	31	20	67	12	99	4
LACKAFF, John, Bris.	.945	56	31	123	9	163	7
Lantigua, Denys, Burl.	.000	1	0	0	0	0	0
Leon, Alfredo, Blue.	.923	7	8	16	2	26	2
Martin, Tyler, Pul.	.958	12	4	19	1	24	0
Mongeluzzo, Anthony, Pul.	.831	31	16	48	13	77	6
Nelson, Nathan, Mar.	.892	41	28	79	13	120	6
Parrott, Tom, Dan.	.860	21	17	32	8	57	2
Pena, Amaury, Bris.	.905	6	4	15	2	21	2
Pichardo, Henry, Burl.	.917	2	4	7	1	12	0
Rasmussen, Wes, Dan.	.925	14	8	29	3	40	2
Reyes, Jose, King.	.933	7	2	12	1	15	0
Ridley, Shayne, Blue.	.867	18	6	33	6	45	3
Rodgers, Albert, J.C.	.000	1	0	0	0	0	0
Rodriguez , Ricardo, Dan.	.857	4	2	4	1	7	0
Royer, Lissandro, King.	1.000	2	0	5	0	5	0
Sandoval, Michael, Eliz.	.913	39	24	71	9	104	6

Player, Team	Pct.	G	PO	A	E	TC	DP
Santana, Mayobanex, Bris.	.000	1	0	0	0	0	0
Schmitt, Billy, J.C.	.876	29	18	60	11	89	4
Shier, Peter, Blue.	.000	1	0	0	0	0	0
Smith, Bradley, Pul.	.875	12	4	17	3	24	0
Smith, Corey, Burl.	.828	52	46	108	32	186	11
Sosa, Francisco, King.	.667	2	0	2	1	3	1
Sowers, Douglas, Blue.	.917	6	4	7	1	12	0
Stokes, Gregory, Eliz.	.806	21	9	16	6	31	0
Tapia, Roman, Bris.	.909	6	3	7	1	11	1
Thompson, Alva, Dan.	.750	1	1	2	1	4	0
Watkins, Thomas, Eliz.	.917	9	9	13	2	24	0
Wilken, Kristopher, Blue.	.948	32	23	68	5	96	5

SHORTSTOPS

Player, Team	Pct.	G	PO	A	E	TC	DP
Andrianoff, Jonathan, Mar.	.871	19	36	52	13	101	17
BRUNTLETT, Eric, Mar.	.948	47	70	132	11	213	30
Colmenter, Jesus, Burl.	.837	13	12	24	7	43	2
Contreras, Erick, Dan.	.857	8	4	14	3	21	4
Cruz, Enrique, King.	.918	20	29	60	8	97	11
De Los Santos, Santo, J.C.	.909	15	22	48	7	77	7
Dement, Dan, Prin.	.917	28	31	68	9	108	10
De Paula, Luis, Prin.	.913	30	47	90	13	150	17
Eddlemon, Kelly, Prin.	.000	1	0	0	1	1	0
Fatur, Brian, J.C.	.905	46	65	125	20	210	16
Flores, Ralphs, Bris.	.949	36	48	83	7	138	15
Franco, Esterlin, Mar.	1.000	1	2	3	0	5	2
Garcia, Nicolas, Blue.	.939	36	63	107	11	181	23
Gonzalez, Edgar, Prin.	.933	14	22	34	4	60	8
Harriman, Preston, J.C.	.862	9	7	18	4	29	3
Hileman, Jutt, J.C.	.850	5	7	10	3	20	0
King, Jason, Dan.	.800	1	2	2	1	5	0
Lackaff, John, Bris.	1.000	1	2	3	0	5	1
Luna, Hector, Burl.	.900	55	74	161	26	261	31
Machado, Aleyandro, Dan.	1.000	1	1	0	0	1	0
Martin, Tyler, Pul.	1.000	2	1	6	0	7	0
Maza, Luis, Eliz.	.932	56	94	154	18	266	27
McIntyre, Robert, King.	.912	16	24	28	5	57	5
Mejias, Erick, Pul.	.902	21	25	49	8	82	9
Morban, Jose, Pul.	.937	30	49	84	9	142	14
Pena, Amaury, Bris.	.917	12	13	20	3	36	4
Pena, Tony, Dan.	.930	54	70	184	19	273	31
Rasmussen, Wes, Dan.	.000	1	0	0	0	0	0
Reyes, Guillermo, Bris.	.950	21	29	67	5	101	10
Reyes, Jose, King.	.942	40	50	113	10	173	20
Ridley, Shayne, Blue.	.824	5	8	6	3	17	2
Rodriguez, Ricardo, Dan.	.955	7	10	11	1	22	2
Royer, Lissandro, King.	1.000	3	4	3	0	7	1
Shier, Peter, Blue.	.910	25	40	71	11	122	10
Smith, Bradley, Pul.	.893	16	12	38	6	56	9
Watkins, Thomas, Eliz.	.958	13	18	28	2	48	5

OUTFIELDERS

Player, Team	Pct.	G	PO	A	E	TC	DP
Acevedo, Anthony, Mar.*	.964	54	75	5	3	83	0
Albertson, Justin, J.C.	.914	32	31	1	3	35	0
Baez, Manuel, Pul.	.937	55	86	3	6	95	0
Baldelli, Rocco, Prin.	.966	60	109	6	4	119	1
Boitel, Rafael, Eliz.*	.964	55	100	8	4	112	2
Boyd, Shaun, J.C.	.961	42	72	1	3	76	1
Bruntlett, Eric, Mar.	.500	2	1	0	1	2	0
Burrows, Angelo, Dan.	.980	44	97	2	2	101	0
Castellanos, Jose, Dan.	.951	22	37	2	2	41	0
Centeno, Edwin, Blue.	.948	36	49	6	3	58	2
Clark, Tommy, Dan.	.948	36	55	0	3	58	0
COLEMAN, Alph, Dan.	1.000	47	85	7	0	92	0
Compton, Jack, Mar.	1.000	6	9	1	0	10	0
Dees, Charlie, Blue.-Pul.	.935	36	65	7	5	77	2
Dement, Dan, Prin.	.000	1	0	0	0	0	0
Devanez, Noel, King.	.981	57	97	7	2	106	2
Dion, Nathanael, Prin.	.959	50	69	2	3	74	1
Dorner, Dwight, Prin.	.667	4	4	0	2	6	0
Douglas, Harley, King.*	.923	15	11	1	1	13	0
Eddlemon, Kelly, Prin.	.000	1	0	0	0	0	0
Eldridge, Rashad, Burl.	.961	47	73	1	3	77	0
Esprit, Jermaine, Burl.	.788	28	39	2	11	52	0
Estevez, Jose, King.	.000	1	0	0	0	0	0
Evans, Robert, Pul.*	.967	66	114	4	4	122	0
Fatur, Brian, J.C.	1.000	14	17	0	0	17	0
Folsom, Kenneth, Burl.	.944	49	67	1	4	72	0
Franco, Esterlin, Mar.	1.000	5	8	0	0	8	0
Gajewski, Matt, Pul.	1.000	1	3	1	0	4	0
German, Amado, Prin.	.932	35	53	2	4	59	0

Player, Team	Pct.	G	PO	A	E	TC	DP
Gomez, Jose, J.C.	.932	53	64	5	5	74	0
Gonzalez, Edgar, Prin.	1.000	8	4	1	0	5	0
Goodeill, Harold, Prin.	.909	3	10	0	1	11	0
Gordon, Alexis, Blue.*	.892	59	75	8	10	93	1
Hamilton, Mark, Mar.*	.963	33	52	0	2	54	0
Hernandez, Javier, Burl.	.953	31	39	2	2	43	0
Holt, Todd, Bris.	.957	38	44	1	2	47	1
Johnson, Kareem, Eliz.	1.000	2	3	0	0	3	0
Lama, Jesus, Prin.	.899	54	56	6	7	69	2
Lantigua, Denys, Burl.	1.000	3	4	0	0	4	0
Lawson, Forrest, King.	.927	55	70	6	6	82	1
Littleton, Brandon, Blue.*	.979	55	89	5	2	96	0
Lopez, Aristides, Mar.	.955	11	20	1	1	22	0
Lowe, Ernesto, Bris.	.967	40	53	6	2	61	0
Lydon, Wayne, King.	.949	52	105	7	6	118	1
Mack, Antonio, Blue.	.946	36	69	1	4	74	0
Mejias, Aureliano, J.C.	1.000	9	11	1	0	12	0
Monegan, Anthony, Bris.	.982	41	53	1	1	55	0
Montgomery, Billy, Pul.	.950	49	54	3	3	60	0
Pagan, Angel, King.	.923	12	22	2	2	26	0
Perez, Felipe, Blue.	.950	17	18	1	1	20	0
Perez, Juan, J.C.	1.000	22	39	1	0	40	0
Perich, Josh, King.	.857	21	18	0	3	21	0
Pinales, Franklin, Eliz.	.949	40	67	8	4	79	2
Quickstad, Barry, Eliz.	.945	45	48	4	3	55	1
Rabe, Joshua, Eliz.	.977	31	38	4	1	43	2
Reyes, Jose, King.	.000	1	0	0	0	0	0
Reyes, Julio, Bris.	1.000	29	37	3	0	40	0
Rincon, Carlos, Mar.	.935	14	26	3	2	31	0
Rodgers, Albert, J.C.	.870	16	19	1	3	23	0
Royer, Lissandro, King.	1.000	2	2	0	0	2	0
Santor, John, J.C.	1.000	1	1	0	0	1	0
Stanley, Derek, Bris.	.982	64	105	5	2	112	2
Stanley, Henry, Mar.*	.963	45	76	1	3	80	0
Suraci, Scott, Eliz.	.955	27	41	1	2	44	0
Taveras, Willy, Burl.	.961	50	117	6	5	128	0
Torres, Digno, Eliz.*	1.000	4	13	0	0	13	0
Whitesides, Jake, Mar.	.952	35	58	2	3	63	0
Wigginton, Derek, Bris.*	1.000	10	5	0	0	5	0
Womack, Robert, Burl.*	1.000	5	9	1	0	10	0
Woodrow, Justin, J.C.	.960	34	46	2	2	50	0
Zumwalt, Sean, Dan.	.934	59	89	10	7	106	1

OUTFIELDERS WITH TWO OR MORE TEAMS

Player, Team	Pct.	G	PO	A	E	TC	DP
Dees, Charlie, Blue.	.833	2	4	1	1	6	0
Dees, Charlie, Pul.	.944	34	61	6	4	71	2

CATCHERS

Player, Team	Pct.	G	PO	A	E	TC	DP	PB
Acosta, Emilio, J.C.	.988	31	224	27	3	254	1	14
Alvarado, Oscar, Mar.	.961	20	127	20	6	153	1	4
Ayala, Abraham, Mar.	.971	17	115	20	4	139	1	4
Bowen, Rob, Eliz.	.983	19	147	29	3	179	0	3
Caperton, Freddy, Pul.	1.000	6	33	4	0	37	0	0
Cardona, Raynier, King.	.917	2	9	2	1	12	0	1
Cedano, Francisco, J.C.	.966	11	50	6	2	58	0	2
Cochrane, Mark, Bris.	.984	15	117	9	2	128	2	4
Decola, Daniel, Eliz.	.978	15	120	11	3	134	1	1
Dillard, Thomas, Eliz.	.985	30	230	30	4	264	4	6
Dogero, Matt, J.C.	1.000	8	52	2	0	54	0	5
Dorner, Dwight, Prin.	.980	22	177	17	4	198	2	4
Dougherty, Andy, Burl.	.944	5	29	5	2	36	0	1
Eddlemon, Kelly, Prin.	1.000	1	2	0	0	2	0	0
Ernst, Michael, Burl.	.957	6	42	3	2	47	0	2
Gajewski, Matt, Pul.	1.000	1	11	1	0	12	0	0
Guilliams, Earl, Dan.	1.000	2	4	0	0	4	0	0
Hamill, Ryan, J.C.	.974	26	162	24	5	191	0	4
Hartley, Will, Burl.	1.000	10	44	7	0	51	0	5
Hilario, Enderson, Bris.	.988	22	142	27	2	171	1	5
Jacobs, Mike, King.	.973	38	255	31	8	294	3	16
Lantigua, Denys, Burl.	.985	28	158	42	3	203	0	6
Lucas, William, Mar.	1.000	2	21	3	0	24	0	1
Lynn, Brody, Burl.	.975	9	65	13	2	80	0	5
Maduro, Jorge, Prin.	.971	37	231	33	8	272	0	15
Marconi, Alex, Prin.	.979	17	122	16	3	141	0	3
Martin, Kyle, Blue.	.977	10	72	12	2	86	0	4
Martinez, Octavio, Blue.	.969	37	232	53	9	294	1	8
Matos, Angel, Pul.	.967	19	126	19	5	150	0	11
McCall, Gerard, Bris.	.971	36	260	41	9	310	0	17
Morneau, Justin, Eliz.	1.000	5	34	6	0	40	0	0
Osborn, Jason, King.	.954	9	57	5	3	65	0	4
PACK, Branden, Pul.	.978	45	407	45	10	462	1	7

SUMMER CLASS A Appalachian League

Player, Team	Pct.	G	PO	A	E	TC	DP	PB
Perez, Jay, Mar.	.985	32	245	23	4	272	2	16
Peterson, Brian, Burl.	.943	10	69	13	5	87	0	3
Salas, Jose, Dan.	.975	41	334	53	10	397	1	18
Serrano, Raymond, Dan.	.980	20	133	15	3	151	0	3
Sosa, Francisco, King.	.975	21	134	19	4	157	2	2
Thompson, Alva, Dan.	1.000	8	57	6	0	63	0	1
Wilken, Kristopher, Blue.	.980	18	127	19	3	149	1	7
Wilson, Brandon, King.	.952	4	20	0	1	21	0	0
Wilson, Heath, Burl.	.988	12	72	9	1	82	0	5

PITCHERS

Player, Team	Pct.	G	PO	A	E	TC	DP
Abbott, Jim, Eliz.	.000	2	0	0	1	1	0
Abrams, Grant, Dan.	1.000	18	0	5	0	5	0
Advincola, Jose, Blue.*	1.000	17	2	4	0	6	0
Albers, Mike, Burl.*	.857	6	0	6	1	7	0
Albertson, Justin, J.C.	.000	1	0	0	0	0	0
Alvarez, Oscar, Burl.*	.917	16	5	6	1	12	0
Anderson, Julius, Prin.	.600	11	1	2	2	5	0
Bajenaru, Jeffrey, Bris.	1.000	12	0	1	0	1	0
Barreto, Joel, Eliz.	.800	22	4	0	1	5	0
Barrett, Jimmy, Mar.	1.000	13	3	6	0	9	1
Batista, Carlos, Burl.	.000	1	0	0	0	0	0
Batista, Roberto, J.C.	.833	7	0	5	1	6	0
Beltre, Sandy, Bris.	1.000	4	2	2	0	4	0
Bent, Andy, Dan.	.857	16	2	10	2	14	1
Berube, Martin, Blue.	1.000	5	2	2	0	4	0
Bethancour, Euclides, Prin.	1.000	13	1	5	0	6	1
Blackwell, Scott, Eliz.	.667	4	1	1	1	3	0
Bohannan, Kyle, Bris.	.833	15	0	5	1	6	0
Bouie, Aaron, Blue.	.667	10	2	6	4	12	0
Bowen, Chad, King.	.824	11	1	13	3	17	0
Burgess, Richie, J.C.	.800	9	7	5	3	15	1
Burns, Mike, Mar.	1.000	12	5	14	0	19	0
Bustillos, Oscar, Prin.	1.000	13	1	0	0	1	0
Byard, David, King.	.857	17	1	5	1	7	1
Cabrera, Fernando, Burl.	.952	13	4	16	1	21	1
Cabrera, Walin, Burl.	.000	10	0	0	0	0	0
Cabrera, Yunior, King.*	.833	13	0	5	1	6	0
Caraballo, Angel, Bris.	.870	13	9	11	3	23	0
Cetani, Bryan, Dan.*	.750	16	0	3	1	4	0
Christ, John, Burl.	.000	2	0	0	0	0	0
Cislak, Chad, Burl.	1.000	6	2	3	0	5	0
Colton, Kyle, Dan.	.667	8	0	4	2	6	0
Colvard, Ron, Burl.	.875	19	3	4	1	8	0
Corn, Terry, Eliz.	1.000	19	1	3	0	4	1
Corona, Ronnie, Eliz.	1.000	3	0	1	0	1	0
Coward, Timothy, Prin.	1.000	6	2	4	0	6	0
Cox, Adam, Burl.*	1.000	12	1	11	0	12	0
Cromer, Jason, Prin.*	.933	13	1	13	1	15	1
Davis, Jason, Burl.	.889	10	5	11	2	18	1
Deaton, Kevin, King.	1.000	12	2	1	0	3	0
DeJesus, Rigoberto, J.C.	.750	12	2	1	1	4	0
De La Cruz, Carlos, Burl.	1.000	19	1	2	0	3	0
D'Frank, Carlos, Burl.	.500	6	0	2	2	4	0
Dischiavo, John, Prin.	1.000	11	3	5	0	8	0
Doyne, Michael, Mar.	.500	12	0	4	4	8	1
Echols, Justin, Pul.	.667	9	0	4	2	6	1
Esdaile, Kremlin, Burl.	.667	17	1	3	2	6	0
Farren, Dave, Blue.	.400	15	2	0	3	5	0
Fereira, Ramon, Mar.	1.000	16	2	3	0	5	0
Ferrand, Dario, Bris.	1.000	13	1	13	0	14	0
Flanagan, Ryan, Eliz.	1.000	18	1	2	0	3	0
Ford, Jr, Thomas, Blue.*	.900	19	5	4	1	10	0
Fortunato, Bartolome, Prin.	1.000	17	3	8	0	11	0
Gilbert, Richard, Pul.*	.833	12	8	7	3	18	1
Gomez, Benito, Prin.*	.889	25	1	7	1	9	0
Gomez, Mariano, Burl.*	.692	13	2	7	4	13	0
Gomez, Rafael, King.	.900	5	1	8	1	10	0
Graham, Brian, Bris.	.833	12	3	12	3	18	0
Granadillo, Adel, Burl.	1.000	3	1	2	0	3	0
Grassing, Bryan, J.C.	1.000	27	4	3	0	7	1
Graves, Donovan, J.C.	.917	13	4	7	1	12	1
Guerrero, Neftali, King.	.667	15	0	2	1	3	0
Hamilton, Ryan, Mar.	1.000	8	4	9	0	13	0
Harriman, Preston, J.C.	1.000	2	1	0	0	1	0
Hollifield, Alec, Bris.	.833	5	0	5	1	6	0
Holubec, Kenneth, Eliz.*	1.000	9	2	4	0	6	0
Hopper, Kevin, Dan.	1.000	16	0	8	0	8	0
Hughes, Rocky, Bris.*	.909	16	2	8	1	11	0
Hunt, Jordan, Mar.	.833	14	1	4	1	6	2
Johnson, Kareem, Eliz.	.000	1	0	0	0	0	0
Johnson, Kelly, J.C.	1.000	22	3	4	0	7	0
Jones, Quentin, Dan.	.857	21	2	4	1	7	1
Kemp, Bo, Eliz.	1.000	17	0	3	0	3	0
Keppel, Bob, King.	1.000	8	2	0	0	2	0
Knapp, Ben, Blue.	.857	7	2	4	1	7	0
Lama, Jesus, Prin.	.000	1	0	0	0	0	0
Lantigua, Delvis, Bris.	.700	12	0	7	3	10	1
La Rosa, Dancy, Eliz.	1.000	16	4	3	0	7	1
Larson, Ryan, Burl.	.909	19	3	7	1	11	0
Lazo, Rafael, King.	1.000	15	2	0	0	2	0
Lee, Adam, J.C.	.714	19	0	5	2	7	1
Lindsey, David, J.C.	1.000	19	3	0	0	3	0
Lockhart, John, J.C.	1.000	19	3	3	0	6	0
Lopez, Albie, Prin.	.000	1	0	0	0	0	0
Lopez, Miguel, Prin.	.833	21	1	4	1	6	1
Lopez, Rafael, King.	1.000	9	5	14	0	19	3
Mack, Antonio, Blue.	1.000	2	0	1	0	1	0
Mansfield, Monte, Mar.	1.000	18	1	6	0	7	1
Marchetti, Daniel, Blue.	1.000	22	4	13	0	17	0
Martin, Lucas, Eliz.*	1.000	15	3	12	0	15	2
Martinez, Dan, Bris.*	.750	12	1	2	1	4	0
Martinez, Eduardo, Mar.*	.813	17	1	12	3	16	0
Martinez, Miguel, J.C.	.929	13	3	10	1	14	1
McKey, Dustin, Prin.	1.000	17	1	6	0	7	0
Mead, David, Mar.	.900	12	6	3	1	10	0
Medlock, Chet, J.C.	.889	5	1	7	1	9	0
Mejia, Francisco, Blue.*	.833	4	0	5	1	6	0
Miller, Jason, Eliz.*	1.000	9	2	8	0	10	0
Morban, Domingo, King.*	.000	11	0	0	0	0	0
Moseley, Marcus, Eliz.	1.000	18	3	7	0	10	0
Mozingo, Dan, Bris.*	1.000	9	1	5	0	6	0
Murray, Brad, Bris.*	.842	16	6	10	3	19	1
Musser, Neal, King.*	.857	7	1	5	1	7	0
Narveson, Chris, J.C.*	.909	12	3	7	1	11	1
Nichols, Brian, King.	.857	12	5	7	2	14	1
Novoa, Niquel, Prin.*	.000	3	0	0	0	0	0
Olivo, Carlos, J.C.	.625	24	1	4	3	8	0
Osberg, Tanner, King.	1.000	12	1	3	0	4	0
Ough, Wayne, King.	1.000	9	4	1	0	5	1
Peeples, Ross, King.*	1.000	15	1	5	0	6	0
Pena, Francisco, Mar.	.667	13	1	3	2	6	0
Pepen, Robert, King.	1.000	13	1	2	0	3	1
Perez, Keino, Burl.	1.000	21	2	1	0	3	0
Persby, Andrew, Eliz.	.929	20	4	9	1	14	0
Petulla, Craig, Mar.	.833	13	4	1	1	6	0
Phillips, James, Blue.	.857	22	5	1	1	7	0
Pichardo, Henry, Burl.	.000	1	0	0	0	0	0
Ponce Deleon, Damon, J.C.	.667	20	1	3	2	6	0
Portobanco, Luz, King.	1.000	16	3	7	0	10	0
Ramirez, Enrique, Blue.	.750	25	4	2	2	8	0
Reese, Josh, J.C.	.000	12	0	0	1	1	0
Renteria, Juan, Prin.	.889	24	2	6	1	9	0
Reynolds, Jacob, Burl.	.727	10	2	6	3	11	0
Richardson, Jason, Eliz.	.889	10	4	4	1	9	0
Ridgway, Jeff, Prin.*	.857	12	2	10	2	14	1
Riviere, Rhett, Pul.	1.000	15	3	4	0	7	0
Rleal, Sendy, Blue.	.842	13	5	11	3	19	0
Rodriguez, Jose, Dan.	1.000	12	4	8	0	12	1
Rodriguez, Luis, Pul.	.800	10	0	4	1	5	0
Rogers, Bradley, Blue.	.500	4	0	2	2	4	0
ROMERO, Josmir, Eliz.	1.000	13	12	19	0	31	0
Rondon, Gabriel, King.	1.000	14	1	4	0	5	0
Rowland, Carl, J.C.	.909	15	2	8	1	11	1
Runser, Greg, Pul.	.800	21	3	5	2	10	0
Russ, Christopher, Pul.*	1.000	6	0	4	0	4	0
Rust, Evan, Prin.	1.000	26	1	11	0	12	0
Ryan, Jeremy, Mar.	.833	7	0	5	1	6	2
Santillan, Manuel, Mar.	.750	19	1	2	1	4	1
Santos, Bernaldo, Mar.	1.000	3	1	0	0	1	0
Sclafani, Anthony, Dan.	1.000	19	0	3	0	3	1
Scuglik, Mike, Pul.*	.909	18	5	5	1	11	0
Shaw, Elliott, Prin.	.800	18	1	3	1	5	1
Smart, Richard, Eliz.	1.000	15	2	9	0	11	0
Smith, Hans, Prin.*	1.000	7	0	3	0	3	0
Smith, Toebius, Dan.	.778	19	1	6	2	9	0
Sperring, Jayme, Pul.	.000	4	0	0	0	0	0
Stamler, Keith, Pul.	.870	14	9	11	3	23	1
Staveland, Toby, Dan.	1.000	5	1	2	0	3	0
Stewart, John, Pul.*	1.000	21	1	5	0	6	1
Sullivan, Thomas, Eliz.*	1.000	4	1	1	0	2	0
Sweeney, James, Bris.*	1.000	17	4	8	0	12	0
Tate, Matthew, Blue.	.889	7	1	7	1	9	0
Tavarez, David, Blue.	.857	7	1	5	1	7	0
Teekel, Josh, J.C.	1.000	4	0	2	0	2	0

Player, Team	Pct.	G	PO	A	E	TC	DP
Thompson, Derek, Burl.*	.571	12	3	1	3	7	0
Tillery, Josh, Dan.	1.000	17	0	6	0	6	0
Tomaszewski, Eliot, Blue.	.833	21	0	5	1	6	0
Tremont, Harold, Pul.	1.000	2	2	0	0	2	0
Trevino, Chris, Dan.*	1.000	12	2	6	0	8	0
Urena, Sixto, Pul.	.944	11	4	13	1	18	2
Valdez, Domingo, Pul.	.875	11	2	5	1	8	0
Valentine, Joseph, Bris.	.750	19	1	2	1	4	0

Player, Team	Pct.	G	PO	A	E	TC	DP
Valles, Rolando, Mar.*	.846	19	2	9	2	13	1
Wainwright, Adam, Dan.	.750	6	1	2	1	4	0
Waters, Chris, Dan.	1.000	13	5	13	0	18	0
Watkins, David, Dan.	1.000	10	0	7	0	7	1
Whitecotton, Billy, Blue.	.846	8	1	10	2	13	1
Williams, Ruddy, Mar.	1.000	12	3	7	0	10	0
Young, Curtis, Bris.	1.000	15	2	0	0	2	0

LEAGUE CHAMPIONS

Year	Team	Pct.
1921—	Greenville	.608
	Johnson City*	.627
1922—	Bristol	.557
1923—	Knoxville	.635
1924—	Knoxville*	.642
	Bristol	.607
1925—	Greenville	.667
1926-36—Did not operate.		
1937—	Elizabethton	.559
	Pennington Gap*	.580
1938—	Elizabethton	.664
	Greenville (3rd)†	.571
1939—	Elizabethton‡	.597
1940—	Johnson City§	.726
	Elizabethton	.750
1941—	Johnson City	.614
	Elizabethton*	.661
1942—	Bristol	.667
	Bristol∞	.660
1943—	Bristol	.755
	Bristol▲	.617
1944—	Kingsport‡	.575
1945—	Kingsport‡	.670
1946—	New River‡	.675
1947—	Pulaski	.648
	New River (3rd)†	.516
1948—	Pulaski‡	.680
1949—	Bluefield‡	.721
1950—	Bluefield	.600
	Bluefield♦	.745
1951—	Kingsport‡	.659
1952—	Johnson City	.595
	Welch (3rd)†	.509
1953—	Welch*	.705
	Johnson City	.672
1954—	Bluefield‡	.619

Year	Team	Pct.
1955—	Salem■	.689
1956—	Did not operate.	
1957—	Bluefield	.701
1958—	Johnson City	.662
1959—	Morristown	.603
1960—	Wytheville	.614
1961—	Middlesboro	.591
1962—	Bluefield	.671
1963—	Bluefield	.652
1964—	Johnson City	.662
1965—	Salem	.614
1966—	Marion	.623
1967—	Bluefield	.627
1968—	Marion	.583
1969—	Pulaski▼	.576
	Johnson City	.544
1970—	Bluefield	.638
1971—	Bluefield▼	.609
	Kingsport	.559
1972—	Bristol▼	.588
	Covington	.586
1973—	Kingsport	.757
1974—	Bristol▼	.754
	Bluefield	.536
1975—	Marion	.515
	Johnson City▼	.603
1976—	Johnson City▼	.714
	Bluefield	.600
1977—	Kingsport	.623
1978—	Elizabethton	.594
1979—	Paintsville	.800
1980—	Paintsville	.657
1981—	Paintsville	.657
1982—	Bluefield▼	.681
	Johnson City	.478

Year	Team	Pct.
1983—	Paintsville	.653
1984—	Elizabethton•	.580
	Pulaski	.536
1985—	Bristol††	.638
1986—	Johnson City	.667
	Pulaski•	.621
1987—	Burlington•	.729
	Johnson City	.609
1988—	Kingsport•	.644
	Burlington	.529
1989—	Elizabethton•	.691
	Pulaski	.618
1990—	Elizabethton	.761
1991—	Pulaski•	.662
	Burlington	.597
1992—	Elizabethton	.742
	Bluefield•	.597
1993—	Burlington•	.647
	Elizabethton	.552
1994—	Princeton•	.621
	Johnson City	.618
1995—	Bluefield	.754
	Kingsport•	.727
1996—	Kingsport	.716
	Bluefield▼	.618
1997—	Pulaski	.632
	Bluefield•	.580
1998—	Bristol•	.636
	Princeton	.559
1999—	Pulaski	.696
	Martinsville•	.586
2000—	Elizabethton•	.719

*Won split-season playoff. †Won four-team playoff. ‡Won championship and four-team playoff. §Johnson City, first-half winner, won playoff involving six clubs. ∞Won both halves and defeated second-place Elizabethton in playoff. ▲Won both halves, but Erwin won four-team playoff. ♦Won both halves, but Bristol won two-club playoff. ■Salem and Johnson City declared playoff co-champions when weather forced cancellation of final series. ▼League was divided into Northern, Southern divisions; declared league champion based on highest won-lost percentage. •League was divided into North and South divisions; won playoff. ††Bristol declared league champion based on regular-season record.

ARIZONA LEAGUE

LEAGUE OFFICE

President/treasurer
Bob Richmond
Address
P.O. Box 1645
Boise, ID 83701
Phone
208-429-1511

Teams*
Angels
Athletics
Brewers
Cubs
Giants

Mariners
White Sox

*Teams play their games in Mesa, Peoria, Phoenix, Tucson and other Arizona sites to be announced.

2000 FINAL STANDINGS
COMPOSITE

Team	Mar.	Roc.	Cubs	Ath.	Dia.	Mex.	Gia.	W.S.	Pad.	W	L	T	Pct.	GB
Mariners	...	1	8	5	1	1	10	1	12	39	16	0	.709	...
Rockies	1	...	1	0	10	11	1	10	1	35	19	0	.648	3.5
Cubs	4	1	...	8	2	1	7	2	7	32	24	0	.571	7.5
Athletics	6	1	4	...	0	1	8	0	9	29	25	0	.537	9.5
Diamondbacks	1	5	0	1	...	7	0	11	2	27	27	0	.500	11.5
Mexico	0	5	1	1	8	...	1	6	1	23	32	0	.418	16.0
Giants	3	0	5	4	1	1	...	2	6	22	32	0	.407	16.5
White Sox	1	5	0	1	5	10	0	...	0	22	33	0	.400	17.0
Padres	0	1	5	5	0	0	5	1	...	17	38	0	.309	22.0

NOTE: Certain portions of the August 18th game between the Rockies and Mexico, the August 20th game between the Diamondbacks and Mexico, the August 22nd game between the White Sox and Mexico and the August 27th game between the Diamondbacks and Mexico were unattainable. Due to these unavoidable circumstances, individual Mexico player statistics do not match Mexico team statistics.

Club names are major league affiliations.

Games played in Mesa, Peoria, Phoenix and Tucson.

PLAYOFFS: Mariners defeated Rockies one game to none to win league championship.

REGULAR-SEASON ATTENDANCE: No total official attendance figures reported.

MANAGERS: Athletics, John Kuehl; Cubs, Carmelo Martinez; Diamondbacks, Joe Almaraz; Giants, Lemmie Miller; Mariners, Omar Munoz; Mexico, Jose Ortiz; Padres, Howard Bushong; Rockies, P.J. Carey; White Sox, Jerry Hairston.

ALL-STAR TEAM: 1B—David Mulqueen, Rockies; 2B—Pedro Liriano, Mariners; 3B—Christian Presichi, Mexico; Miguel Villilo, Mariners; SS—Luis Montanez, Cubs; OF—Daniel Trumble, Giants; Syketo Anderson, Cubs; Antoine Cameron, Cubs; C—Alvin Colina, Rockies; DH—Josh Hoffpauir, Athletics; Jose Vasquez, Rockies; RHP—Jorge Buret, Rockies; LHP—Derrick Van Dusen, Mariners; RHRP—Chad Wiles, Mariners; LHRP—Edgar Huerta, Mexico; Most Valuable Player—Luis Montanez, Cubs; Manager of the Year—P.J. Carey, Rockies.

2000 BATTING
TEAM

Team	Avg.	G	TPA	AB	R	H	TB	2B	3B	HR	RBI	SH	SF	HP	BB	IBB	SO	SB	CS	GDP	LOB	ShO	Slg.	OBP
Mariners	.316	55	2293	2009	408	634	870	117	16	29	341	14	32	43	195	6	330	60	25	27	469	2	.433	.383
Rockies	.309	54	2224	1917	417	592	893	102	50	33	356	5	19	48	235	0	446	91	33	24	440	1	.466	.394
White Sox	.298	55	2247	1919	381	571	776	124	27	9	314	7	26	28	267	4	389	143	53	33	432	3	.404	.387
Cubs	.296	56	2235	1969	371	582	849	104	44	25	328	20	25	32	189	7	411	61	36	32	387	2	.431	.363
Athletics	.287	54	2272	1915	403	550	798	106	32	26	326	15	17	27	298	4	421	87	27	39	459	1	.417	.388
Diamondbacks	.268	54	2126	1846	314	494	698	92	29	18	257	17	19	27	217	1	443	58	38	22	392	2	.378	.350
Giants	.264	54	2021	1751	273	463	604	64	19	13	203	29	22	32	187	3	355	117	63	36	342	1	.345	.342
Mexico	.262	55	2156	1835	305	480	654	90	21	14	223	9	27	33	252	1	323	44	19	41	439	2	.356	.356
Padres	.241	55	2098	1840	252	443	584	78	15	11	206	16	17	52	173	6	403	71	27	37	382	2	.317	.321

INDIVIDUAL

TOP QUALIFIERS FOR BATTING CHAMPIONSHIP

Minimum 151 plate appearances. *Lefthanded batter. †Switch-hitter.

Player, Team	Avg.	G	TPA	AB	R	H	TB	2B	3B	HR	RBI	SH	SF	HP	BB	IBB	SO	SB	CS	GDP	Slg.	OBP
Liriano, Pedro, Mar.	.400	43	197	170	46	68	90	15	2	1	30	0	4	2	21	0	11	18	5	1	.529	.462
Anderson, Syketo, Cubs*	.387	40	165	150	44	58	77	8	4	1	21	3	0	4	8	1	14	12	7	1	.513	.432
Hoffpauir, Josh, Ath.*	.384	45	204	172	51	66	95	13	2	4	31	0	2	4	26	1	9	15	4	0	.552	.471
Bojorquez, Jose, Mex.	.382	46	193	173	33	66	93	13	4	2	32	0	4	4	12	0	20	5	5	2	.538	.425
Trumble, Dan, Gia.	.366	42	185	161	40	59	106	15	4	8	36	0	3	6	15	0	53	9	3	3	.658	.432
Villilo, Miguel, Mar.†	.347	44	192	167	30	58	87	14	3	3	37	0	1	1	23	1	37	2	0	2	.521	.427
Testa, Chris, Rock.*	.345	44	197	177	43	61	83	10	3	2	30	0	2	2	16	0	24	8	4	0	.469	.401
Olkowski, Kevin, Mar.*	.344	41	171	154	32	53	67	12	1	0	21	0	2	2	13	0	27	3	3	0	.435	.398
Montanez, Luis, Cubs	.344	50	229	192	50	66	102	16	7	2	37	3	1	8	25	1	42	11	6	5	.531	.438
Romero, Flavio, Mex.	.343	51	235	178	40	61	77	8	4	0	26	0	3	1	52	0	27	8	7	2	.433	.487
Rosario, Vicente, Mar.	.343	34	162	143	33	49	65	2	4	2	16	1	4	2	12	0	27	10	2	1	.455	.391
Santos, Sneidder, Dia.*	.342	43	167	152	28	52	76	6	6	2	23	0	2	3	10	0	32	4	3	3	.500	.392
Ivy, Bjorn, W.S.	.341	36	165	129	35	44	52	4	2	0	13	0	2	0	34	0	24	34	11	0	.403	.473
Sadler, Raymond, Cubs	.339	42	185	165	32	56	74	5	5	1	27	0	3	1	16	1	27	4	3	1	.448	.395
Storey, Eric, Rock.	.328	47	222	180	40	59	107	13	4	9	40	0	3	3	36	0	56	10	3	2	.594	.441

ALL PLAYERS

*Lefthanded batter. †Switch-hitter.

Player, Team	Avg.	G	TPA	AB	R	H	TB	2B	3B	HR	RBI	SH	SF	HP	BB	IBB	SO	SB	CS	GDP	Slg.	OBP
Abate, Mike, Mar.	.167	7	34	24	3	4	7	0	0	1	3	0	0	1	9	0	11	0	0	1	.292	.412
Alexander, Kevin, Gia.	.419	14	54	43	8	18	22	1	0	1	8	2	0	0	9	0	5	4	1	3	.512	.519
Allegra, Matthew, Ath.	.270	42	175	141	26	38	51	7	3	0	13	3	3	3	25	0	44	15	2	1	.362	.384
Alvarado, Damien, Mar.*	.111	7	25	18	2	2	2	0	0	0	2	1	0	1	5	0	4	0	0	0	.111	.333
Amador, Christopher, W.S. ...	.302	53	250	212	48	64	80	10	3	0	31	1	0	6	30	0	46	40	13	6	.377	.403
Anderson, Syketo, Cubs*	.387	40	165	150	44	58	77	8	4	1	21	3	0	4	8	1	14	12	7	1	.513	.432
Avila, Carlos, Mex.	.227	50	226	207	40	47	57	8	1	0	25	1	3	2	13	0	26	7	3	4	.275	.276
Baez, Carlos, Mex.	.255	50	208	153	26	39	55	10	3	0	20	0	5	12	38	0	28	1	1	8	.359	.428
Banks, Gary, Cubs................	.273	31	122	110	19	30	40	3	2	1	11	3	0	3	6	0	35	3	2	1	.364	.328
Barrera, Reinaldo, Dia.†	.326	37	152	138	30	45	62	5	6	0	27	1	2	3	8	0	16	5	2	0	.449	.371
Biercan,, Mex.	.500	1	2	2	0	1	2	1	0	0	1	0	0	0	0	0	0	0	0	1	1.000	.500
Bingler, Travis, W.S.	1.000	19	1	1	0	1	1	0	0	0	1	0	0	0	0	0	0	0	0	0	1.000	1.000
Bird, T.J., Rock.*	.287	45	199	171	38	49	81	8	6	4	38	1	1	5	21	0	27	3	2	4	.474	.379
Bojorquez, Jose, Mex.	.382	46	193	173	33	66	93	13	4	2	32	0	4	4	12	0	20	5	5	2	.538	.425
Borchard, Joe, W.S.†	.414	7	33	29	3	12	16	4	0	0	8	0	0	0	4	0	4	0	0	0	.552	.485
Brack, Josh, Ath...................	.297	47	222	165	44	49	74	12	5	1	29	0	1	4	52	0	48	6	2	2	.448	.473
Brown, Larry, Mar.*	.331	35	144	121	24	40	52	6	0	2	15	0	1	8	14	0	30	1	2	2	.430	.431
Bullard, Kevin, Dia...............	.286	3	9	7	2	2	3	1	0	0	2	0	0	0	2	0	2	0	0	0	.429	.444
Cabrera, Alex, Dia.	.200	2	5	5	0	1	1	0	0	0	0	0	0	0	0	0	1	0	0	0	.200	.200
Cabrera, Leonel, Gia.	.295	39	123	112	14	33	43	6	2	0	9	3	3	0	5	0	17	6	3	1	.384	.317
Cadena, Alejandro, Mar.	.301	35	148	123	27	37	61	9	0	5	34	1	3	6	15	1	12	0	2	2	.496	.395
Cameron, Antoine, Cubs*	.326	53	216	190	34	62	109	20	3	7	48	0	7	0	19	1	39	1	2	2	.574	.375
Canales, Joel, Mex.	.151	27	106	86	8	13	19	3	0	1	12	1	3	1	15	0	12	0	0	2	.221	.276
Cano, Octavio, Mex.	.176	9	37	34	2	6	8	2	0	0	3	1	0	0	2	0	6	0	0	1	.235	.222
Carrera, Franklin, Pad.	.227	20	47	44	4	10	14	2	1	0	4	1	0	0	2	0	15	0	0	1	.318	.261
Castro, Juan, Cubs	.107	22	64	56	11	6	12	1	1	1	5	3	0	2	3	0	19	1	0	0	.214	.180
Castro, Julio, W.S.	.286	47	198	161	34	46	61	9	3	0	36	1	6	5	25	1	35	20	2	1	.379	.386
Cavin, Jonathan, W.S.*	.288	48	196	156	36	45	60	9	3	0	26	0	0	2	38	3	25	7	3	1	.385	.434
Cerda, Jose, Gia.	.348	8	26	23	3	8	10	2	0	0	6	0	0	1	2	0	3	1	2	0	.435	.423
Chavez, Angel, Gia.	.276	7	31	29	2	8	13	0	1	1	7	1	0	0	1	0	5	1	1	2	.448	.300
Chiarini, Mario, Mar.	.313	24	79	67	15	21	24	3	0	0	8	1	3	5	3	0	16	2	0	0	.358	.372
Chilsom, Marques, Dia..........	.176	53	229	199	25	35	49	12	1	0	19	2	2	3	23	0	63	5	6	4	.246	.269
Chilsom, Tawan, Dia.............	.128	27	49	39	2	5	5	0	0	0	2	1	1	0	8	0	13	5	1	0	.128	.271
Ciraco, Darren, W.S.	.324	33	113	105	21	34	47	7	0	2	18	0	0	0	8	0	25	1	2	2	.448	.372
Coats, Buck, Cubs*	.296	30	114	98	20	29	41	6	3	0	14	0	0	4	12	2	24	7	1	1	.418	.395
Colina, Alvin, Rock.	.352	35	139	122	25	43	64	7	1	4	28	0	2	6	9	0	26	2	3	2	.525	.417
Collins, Kevin, Cubs*	.244	36	145	127	18	31	50	5	1	4	18	1	1	2	14	0	35	0	2	3	.394	.326
Conyer, Darryl, Dia.*	.318	7	24	22	3	7	10	1	1	0	2	1	0	0	1	0	8	1	0	0	.455	.348
Corporan, Roberto, Dia.†	.198	38	130	91	21	18	29	4	2	1	16	2	2	2	33	0	35	5	6	1	.319	.414
Cruz, Israel, Mar.................	.318	47	186	176	33	56	70	9	1	1	34	2	2	0	6	0	18	6	3	3	.398	.337
Daniels, Claiborne, Pad.	.117	33	84	77	10	9	14	3	1	0	8	1	2	2	2	0	36	3	0	1	.182	.157
Davis, Ryan, Gia..................	.266	50	197	154	24	41	48	5	1	0	24	2	6	3	32	0	35	8	4	3	.312	.390
Dean, Mike, Gia.	.298	46	161	131	19	39	48	5	2	0	21	2	4	2	22	0	40	8	10	4	.366	.396
Delanuez, Orlando, Dia.†	.254	47	150	130	19	33	36	3	0	0	8	3	1	1	15	0	24	10	4	1	.277	.333
Delgado, Jorge, Dia.............	.310	8	34	29	7	9	13	2	1	0	6	0	0	0	5	0	4	0	1	0	.448	.412
Dellucci, David, Dia.*	.333	2	6	6	0	2	3	1	0	0	2	0	0	0	0	0	1	0	0	0	.500	.333
D'Jesus, Francisco, Gia........	.238	50	173	164	11	39	46	3	2	0	19	2	2	1	4	0	19	3	3	6	.280	.257
Durazo, Erubiel, Dia.*	.600	2	6	5	2	3	6	0	0	1	2	0	0	1	0	0	0	0	0	1	1.200	.667
Elguezabal, Octavio, Mex.* ...	.000	6	11	10	1	0	0	0	0	0	0	0	0	1	0	0	3	0	0	0	.000	.091
Ellis, Alvyn, Ath.	.296	48	200	169	31	50	74	10	1	4	28	2	0	3	26	1	46	1	2	4	.438	.399
Encarnacion, Julio, W.S.	.304	48	176	168	24	51	73	16	3	0	25	0	1	1	6	0	46	4	5	2	.435	.330
Esqueda, Jonathan, Mex.	.247	31	116	97	17	24	29	5	0	0	12	1	2	4	12	0	19	2	1	0	.299	.348
Essery, Frederick, Rock........	.333	19	45	39	9	13	16	3	0	0	9	1	0	1	4	0	3	0	0	1	.410	.409
Essian, James, Cubs†	.000	1	1	1	0	0	0	0	0	0	0	0	0	0	0	0	1	0	0	0	.000	.000
Esterlin, Ivan, Cubs*	.224	33	112	98	19	22	30	6	1	0	14	1	3	0	10	0	37	1	4	4	.306	.288
Falcon, Omar, Pad................	.275	40	147	120	23	33	58	9	2	4	25	0	1	4	22	0	43	1	1	2	.483	.401
Figueroa, Carlos, Rock.*	.341	24	107	88	21	30	42	4	4	0	12	1	1	1	16	0	12	4	1	0	.477	.443
Figueroa, Eduardo, Mar.	.302	48	212	179	47	54	89	8	3	7	33	3	3	6	21	1	37	7	1	1	.497	.388
Floyd, Daniel, Mar................	.321	43	209	190	32	61	83	14	1	2	34	2	4	2	11	1	18	3	1	3	.437	.357
Frazier, Carlos, Gia.	.134	40	90	82	5	11	13	0	1	0	4	2	1	0	5	0	22	5	6	0	.159	.182
Gann, Jamie, Dia..................	.474	6	20	19	5	9	12	3	0	0	7	0	0	1	0	0	1	2	0	0	.632	.500
Garcia, Isaac, Ath.	.318	52	252	223	52	71	103	13	5	3	28	2	2	2	23	1	29	18	5	1	.462	.384
Garrido, Tomas, Gia.	.234	51	213	188	32	44	49	5	0	0	11	7	0	5	13	0	29	13	4	3	.261	.301
Gearlds, Aaron, Rock.	.327	41	192	168	36	55	67	5	2	1	20	1	1	3	19	0	28	16	5	2	.399	.403
Giorgis, David, Pad.†	.267	53	221	206	26	55	72	9	1	2	28	0	3	2	10	1	38	3	2	4	.350	.303
Golden, Bryan, Cubs	.267	16	52	45	6	12	17	3	1	0	7	1	0	1	5	1	15	0	0	1	.378	.353
Goldfield, Josh, Dia.*	.235	5	19	17	3	4	7	0	0	1	2	0	0	0	2	0	2	0	0	1	.412	.316
Gomez, Andre, Pad.	.222	28	85	63	13	14	15	1	0	0	5	0	2	7	13	0	4	6	1	2	.238	.400
Gomez, Francis, Ath.	.355	17	73	62	17	22	36	3	1	3	28	0	0	0	11	0	10	8	1	1	.581	.452
Gonzalez, Carlos, Mar.	.326	16	52	46	10	15	21	3	0	1	7	0	1	0	5	0	7	3	0	1	.457	.385
Gonzalez, Jose, Gia.	.000	2	3	3	0	0	0	0	0	0	0	0	0	0	0	0	2	0	0	0	.000	.000
Gustafson, Troy, Gia............	.267	49	198	172	26	46	52	6	0	0	12	1	0	5	20	2	20	21	4	2	.302	.360
Hoffpauir, Josh, Ath.*	.384	45	204	172	51	66	95	13	2	4	31	0	2	4	26	1	9	15	4	0	.552	.471
Infantes, Juan, Pad.	.260	35	117	96	20	25	27	2	0	0	11	2	0	7	12	0	14	10	0	0	.281	.383
Ivy, Bjorn, W.S.	.341	36	165	129	35	44	52	4	2	0	13	0	2	0	34	0	24	34	11	0	.403	.473
Jackson, Steve, Ath.	.350	25	104	80	13	28	42	9	1	1	26	0	2	2	20	0	22	0	1	1	.525	.481
Johnson, Jonathan, Cubs	.316	44	192	177	27	56	82	9	4	3	43	0	3	0	12	0	19	3	2	6	.463	.354

SUMMER CLASS A *Arizona League*

Player, Team	Avg.	G	TPA	AB	R	H	TB	2B	3B	HR	RBI	SH	SF	HP	BB	IBB	SO	SB	CS	GDP	Slg.	OBP
Jones, Jared, Mar.	.111	6	21	18	2	2	2	0	0	0	2	0	0	0	3	0	7	1	0	0	.111	.238
Jung, Young-jin, Pad.	.183	37	127	120	10	22	25	3	0	0	3	1	0	2	4	0	28	0	1	4	.208	.222
Klatt, Joel, Pad.	.209	51	194	177	12	37	56	12	2	1	15	2	0	5	10	0	29	1	1	5	.316	.271
Koreger, Joshua, Dia.*	.297	54	245	222	40	66	93	9	3	4	28	0	1	1	21	1	41	5	4	3	.419	.359
Laird, Gerald, Ath.	.300	14	58	50	10	15	19	2	1	0	9	0	1	1	6	0	7	2	0	3	.380	.379
Liriano, Pedro, Mar.	.400	43	197	170	46	68	90	15	2	1	30	0	4	2	21	0	11	18	5	1	.529	.462
Lopez, Oliver, Pad.	.195	20	48	41	6	8	9	1	0	0	3	2	0	0	5	0	14	0	1	0	.220	.283
Madera, Sandy, Ath.	.279	28	121	104	19	29	47	6	3	2	24	0	0	0	17	1	10	4	2	8	.452	.380
Mapes, Jake, Gia.	.152	22	37	33	5	5	5	0	0	0	2	0	0	0	4	0	10	0	1	2	.152	.243
Martinez, Greg, Ath.†	.227	6	27	22	4	5	5	0	0	0	2	0	0	1	4	0	5	2	0	1	.227	.370
Martinez, Orlando, Mex.	.242	40	147	132	19	32	43	6	1	1	10	1	2	0	12	0	28	0	0	2	.326	.301
Materano, Oscar, Rock.	.243	31	130	115	19	28	37	3	3	0	13	0	0	5	10	0	25	5	3	2	.322	.331
Matos, Cesar, Ath.	.253	23	84	79	10	20	32	6	0	2	14	0	0	1	4	0	26	2	1	5	.405	.298
McKnight, Lukas, Cubs*	.290	35	126	107	16	31	39	3	1	1	15	1	0	3	15	0	18	2	2	3	.364	.392
Mejia, Anderson, Cubs	.342	29	86	76	13	26	32	4	1	0	15	0	2	1	7	0	11	4	3	0	.421	.395
Melton, John, Dia.	.339	22	68	59	12	20	29	7	1	0	9	0	1	3	5	0	24	0	1	1	.492	.412
Mendoza, Carlos, Gia.†	.300	6	22	20	1	6	10	2	1	0	0	0	0	0	2	1	2	1	0	1	.500	.364
Molina, Gustavo, W.S.	.243	31	134	115	15	28	41	10	0	1	22	1	3	2	13	0	13	3	1	0	.357	.323
Montanez, Luis, Cubs	.344	50	229	192	50	66	102	16	7	2	37	3	1	8	25	1	42	11	6	5	.531	.438
Montero, Esteban, Rock.	.314	49	209	175	41	55	75	12	4	0	28	0	2	3	29	0	49	9	3	1	.429	.416
Montilla, Samuel, Dia.	.272	45	136	125	23	34	51	8	0	3	18	0	1	1	9	0	23	6	1	2	.408	.324
Mora, Ruben, Pad.†	.181	33	87	72	14	13	14	1	0	0	4	1	0	5	9	0	25	4	2	1	.194	.314
Morse, Michael, W.S.†	.256	45	201	180	32	46	60	6	1	2	24	0	5	1	15	0	29	5	2	6	.333	.308
Mulqueen, Dave, Rock.†	.306	46	211	180	43	55	103	14	8	6	48	0	2	10	19	0	43	7	2	2	.572	.398
Nacar, Yimmy, Gia.	.000	12	1	1	0	0	0	0	0	0	0	0	0	0	0	0	1	0	0	0	.000	.000
Nulton, Kevin, Pad.	.316	52	206	187	29	59	71	7	1	1	23	2	4	4	9	0	25	17	4	4	.380	.353
Nunez, Argelis, Dia.	.342	23	81	73	15	25	42	6	1	3	15	1	0	2	5	0	20	2	2	0	.575	.400
O'Donnell, Ryan, Pad.	.312	37	158	141	24	44	62	9	3	1	25	1	2	3	11	1	17	7	3	3	.440	.369
Oliveros, Luis, Mar.	.356	28	92	87	15	31	36	5	0	0	19	1	1	2	1	0	7	3	3	3	.414	.374
Olkowski, Kevin, Mar.*	.344	41	171	154	32	53	67	12	1	0	21	0	2	2	13	0	27	3	3	0	.435	.398
Olson, David, Pad.	.147	19	42	34	3	5	5	0	0	0	1	0	0	0	8	0	22	2	0	0	.147	.310
Ortega, Sixto, Rock.	.321	24	89	81	16	26	32	2	2	0	13	1	0	0	7	0	18	3	1	2	.395	.375
Ortiz, Jorge, Ath.	.211	31	105	90	16	19	25	4	1	0	9	1	0	1	13	0	36	0	1	3	.278	.317
Ortiz, Luis, Dia.	1.000	1	4	3	3	3	4	1	0	0	2	0	0	0	1	0	0	0	0	0	1.333	1.000
Paulino, Miguel, Cubs†	.200	10	26	20	5	4	4	0	0	0	1	0	0	0	6	0	5	3	1	0	.200	.385
Pena, Amaury, W.S.	.319	17	86	69	21	22	42	7	5	1	16	0	3	3	11	0	9	8	2	1	.609	.419
Perez-Bermudez, Jose, Pad.	.237	29	67	59	3	14	16	2	0	0	7	1	0	1	6	0	5	0	0	3	.271	.318
Perez, Radhame, Ath.	.299	40	163	144	34	43	54	5	3	0	22	2	1	0	16	0	33	3	2	2	.375	.366
Pilkington, Ross, Rock.	.280	29	119	107	19	30	48	5	5	1	18	0	1	1	10	0	35	5	1	0	.449	.345
Pina, Enmanuel, Cubs	.320	9	26	25	4	8	8	0	0	0	5	0	0	0	1	0	4	0	0	0	.320	.346
Pinango, Ever, Gia.†	.238	47	151	130	23	31	35	4	0	0	11	3	0	4	14	0	17	13	7	5	.269	.331
Pines, Gregory, Mar.	.263	42	179	156	32	41	65	12	0	4	19	0	2	4	17	0	29	1	1	2	.417	.346
Presichi, Christian, Mex.	.326	49	203	172	38	56	107	14	5	9	34	0	0	1	30	1	27	20	0	4	.622	.429
Puccinelli, John, Pad.	.188	8	32	32	5	6	12	4	1	0	3	0	0	0	0	0	5	0	0	1	.375	.188
Quintero, Humberto, W.S.	.393	15	58	56	13	22	28	2	2	0	8	0	0	2	0	0	3	1	0	2	.500	.414
Rafael, Alberto, W.S.	.239	39	139	117	18	28	40	9	0	1	20	2	1	3	16	0	33	0	6	2	.342	.343
Ramirez, Alexander, Gia.	.157	40	75	70	15	11	16	1	2	0	4	0	1	0	4	0	26	5	5	1	.229	.200
Ramirez, Allan, Mex.	.224	50	223	201	30	45	55	6	2	0	17	2	4	2	14	0	43	1	1	9	.274	.276
Ramirez, Domingo, Gia.	.268	19	45	41	2	11	13	2	0	0	4	0	1	1	2	0	4	1	1	2	.317	.311
Ramirez, Wagner, Cubs†	.241	39	126	112	15	27	30	3	0	0	6	2	2	2	8	0	22	5	2	2	.268	.298
Ramsey, Brad, Cubs	.333	5	20	15	5	5	12	2	1	1	3	0	0	0	5	0	2	0	0	0	.800	.500
Reyes, Henry, Gia.†	.245	47	186	151	30	37	49	5	2	1	15	4	1	4	26	0	39	14	7	1	.325	.368
Reynoso, Paulino, W.S.*	.240	42	153	129	19	31	42	6	1	1	13	0	3	0	21	0	44	1	0	0	.326	.340
Roenicke, Jarett, Pad.*	.269	49	197	171	22	46	58	9	0	1	21	1	1	4	20	3	28	2	2	3	.339	.357
Romero, Flavio, Mex.	.343	51	235	178	40	61	77	8	4	0	26	0	3	1	52	0	27	8	7	2	.433	.487
Romero, Nicholas, Pad.	.275	29	122	102	19	28	39	2	3	1	12	1	0	3	16	1	30	9	5	1	.382	.388
Rosa, Ivan, Ath.*	.260	36	138	123	19	32	50	3	3	3	23	1	2	2	10	0	27	2	1	1	.407	.321
Rosa, Wally, W.S.	.344	17	70	61	11	21	28	4	0	1	10	0	1	0	8	0	11	1	1	1	.459	.414
Rosario, Vicente, Mar.	.343	34	162	143	33	49	65	2	4	2	16	1	4	2	12	0	27	10	2	1	.455	.391
Rossellini, William, Dia.	.000	4	1	0	0	0	0	0	0	0	0	0	0	0	1	0	0	0	0	0	.000	1.000
Saba, Cesar, Pad.†	.200	2	5	5	0	1	1	0	0	0	0	0	0	0	0	0	0	0	0	0	.200	.200
Sadler, Raymond, Cubs	.339	42	185	165	32	56	74	5	5	1	27	0	3	1	16	1	27	4	3	1	.448	.395
Sanchez, Braulio, Dia.*	.206	14	42	34	7	7	12	1	2	0	4	0	0	0	8	0	9	1	0	0	.353	.357
Sandoval, Jhensy, Dia.	.286	7	25	21	2	6	8	2	0	0	5	0	2	0	2	0	2	0	0	1	.381	.320
Santana, Jorge, Cubs	.115	11	29	26	3	3	6	0	0	1	3	0	0	0	3	0	10	1	0	0	.231	.207
Santana, Mayobanex, W.S.	.403	18	84	72	16	29	43	12	1	0	23	1	1	0	10	0	6	1	0	2	.597	.470
Santos, Deivis, Gia.*	.372	12	50	43	13	16	26	2	1	2	10	0	0	0	7	0	6	4	1	0	.605	.460
Santos, Sneideer, Dia.*	.342	43	167	152	28	52	76	6	6	2	23	0	2	3	10	0	32	4	3	3	.500	.389
Serrano, Eddie, Pad.	.159	29	74	63	7	10	10	0	0	0	3	0	1	1	9	0	16	4	4	1	.159	.270
Sherlock, Jon, Dia.	.205	26	58	44	5	9	11	2	0	0	3	3	0	1	10	0	16	0	1	1	.250	.364
Spidale, Mike, W.S.	.318	21	87	66	21	21	25	2	1	0	7	1	0	2	18	0	10	16	4	2	.379	.477
Stone, Jon, Pad.	.133	13	38	30	2	4	6	2	0	0	5	0	1	2	5	0	9	2	0	1	.200	.289
Storey, Eric, Rock.	.328	47	222	180	40	59	107	13	4	9	40	0	3	3	36	0	56	10	3	2	.594	.441
Stottlemyre, Todd, Dia.*	.000	2	2	1	0	0	0	0	0	0	0	0	0	0	1	0	1	0	0	0	.000	.500
Suomi, Richard, Ath.*	.264	31	106	87	19	23	27	2	1	0	14	2	2	1	14	0	10	1	1	2	.310	.365
Tapia, Roman, W.S.	.280	27	104	93	14	26	37	7	2	0	13	0	0	1	10	0	26	1	1	5	.398	.356
Tejada, Michael, Rock.†	.235	5	21	17	4	4	8	1	0	1	3	0	0	1	3	0	3	0	0	2	.471	.381
Testa, Chris, Rock.*	.345	44	197	177	43	61	83	10	3	2	30	0	2	2	16	0	24	8	4	0	.469	.401
Thornton-Murray, Jandin, Cubs†	.279	50	200	179	30	50	84	10	9	2	35	2	3	1	14	0	32	3	2	2	.469	.330
Toledo, Eduardo, Mar.	.245	36	154	139	19	34	39	3	1	0	22	2	1	1	11	1	22	3	2	6	.281	.303
Tress, Jose, Mex.	.186	29	113	102	9	19	29	8	1	0	13	1	0	4	6	0	46	0	0	2	.284	.259
Tritle, Chris, Ath.	.233	44	172	150	30	35	56	10	1	3	21	1	0	1	20	0	39	8	1	2	.373	.327
Trumble, Dan, Gia.	.366	42	185	161	40	59	106	15	4	8	36	0	3	6	15	0	53	9	3	3	.658	.432
Uruata, Luis, Dia.†	.235	54	219	183	31	43	71	15	2	3	27	1	2	3	30	0	56	6	1	1	.388	.349

SUMMER CLASS A Arizona League

Player, Team	Avg.	G	TPA	AB	R	H	TB	2B	3B	HR	RBI	SH	SF	HP	BB	IBB	SO	SB	CS	GDP	Slg.	OBP
Valdez, Tommy, Ath.	.093	25	68	54	8	5	8	1	1	0	5	1	1	1	11	0	20	0	1	2	.148	.254
Vasquez, Jose, Rock.*	.311	46	209	177	37	55	92	12	5	5	38	0	1	4	27	0	73	10	2	1	.520	.411
Villilo, Miguel, Mar.†	.347	44	192	167	30	58	87	14	3	3	37	0	1	1	23	1	37	2	0	2	.521	.427
Virgen, Constancio, Mex.	.231	39	146	130	12	30	39	6	0	1	18	1	1	2	12	0	22	0	1	4	.300	.303
Vizcaino, Maximo, Dia...........	.246	53	234	211	27	52	61	3	3	0	27	2	2	2	16	0	48	1	3	3	.289	.303
Walkill, Juance, Rock.	.242	28	135	120	26	29	38	3	3	0	18	0	3	3	9	0	24	9	3	3	.317	.304
Warrior, Joseph, Mar.............	.143	7	15	14	0	2	2	0	0	0	2	0	0	0	1	0	4	0	0	0	.143	.200
White, Walt, Dia.	.500	3	7	6	1	3	3	0	0	0	1	0	0	1	0	0	0	0	0	0	.500	.571
Williams, Jason, Dia.	.200	2	5	5	1	1	1	0	0	0	0	0	0	0	0	0	1	0	0	0	.200	.200
Williams, Peanut, Mar.	.353	4	21	17	6	6	8	2	0	0	3	0	0	0	4	1	6	0	0	0	.471	.476

GRAND SLAMS: Bird, Chavez, F. Gomez, Mulqueen, Storey, Uruata, Vasquez, 1 each.

AWARDED FIRST BASE ON CATCHER'S INTERFERENCE: Amador (O. Martinez), F. Romero (Montilla), Thornton-Murray (Oliveros), Vizcaino (Oliveros).

2000 PITCHING

TEAM

Team	W	L	Pct.	ERA	G	CG	ShO	Sv.	IP	H	TBF	R	ER	HR	SH	SF	HB	BB	IBB	SO	WP	Bk.
Rockies	35	19	.648	3.83	54	0	2	7	461.0	447	2054	271	196	12	10	25	21	215	2	332	37	13
Mariners	39	16	.709	4.10	55	0	6	16	481.0	457	2087	276	219	17	7	16	29	197	1	478	49	4
Athletics	29	25	.537	4.67	54	0	1	14	474.0	567	2143	336	246	29	20	29	36	140	4	334	38	7
Cubs	32	24	.571	4.92	56	0	2	13	495.1	558	2304	344	271	15	22	26	54	237	3	394	54	8
Diamondbacks ..	27	27	.500	4.95	54	0	3	9	472.2	507	2196	358	260	13	4	16	35	278	2	394	48	20
Giants	22	32	.407	5.46	54	1	1	13	463.0	531	2146	354	281	19	24	21	50	187	12	364	46	11
Padres	17	38	.309	5.59	55	0	2	10	479.2	571	2247	383	298	21	23	27	23	232	4	397	47	10
White Sox	22	33	.400	5.90	55	0	2	10	476.0	573	2279	419	312	30	14	21	33	284	4	419	64	10
Mexico	23	32	.418	6.62	55	8	2	7	467.1	598	2220	383	344	22	8	23	41	243	0	419	59	12

INDIVIDUAL

TOP QUALIFIERS FOR EARNED-RUN AVERAGE TITLE

Minimum 45 innings.*Lefthanded pitcher.

Pitcher, Team	W	L	Pct.	ERA	G	GS	CG	ShO	GF	Sv.	IP	H	TBF	R	ER	HR	SH	SF	HB	BB	IBB	SO	WP	Bk.
Villacis, Eduardo, Rock.	4	2	.667	1.86	13	9	0	0	1	1	48.1	39	202	17	10	0	3	2	2	19	1	37	3	1
Hollifield, Alec, W.S.	4	3	.571	2.05	8	8	0	0	0	0	52.2	58	220	26	12	1	2	1	4	12	0	34	4	0
Nageotte, Clint, Mar.	4	1	.800	2.16	12	7	0	0	1	1	50.0	29	207	15	12	0	0	2	3	28	0	59	2	0
Buret, Jorge, Rock.	5	1	.833	2.39	14	9	0	0	0	0	52.2	50	224	21	14	2	2	3	4	14	0	29	2	2
Matos, Jesus, Rock.	5	1	.833	2.54	15	4	0	0	6	0	46.0	40	186	20	13	2	0	3	1	8	0	41	2	0
Merricks, Charles, Rock.*	2	1	.667	2.72	13	10	0	0	0	0	49.2	47	216	27	15	0	0	4	4	24	0	37	1	1
Diaz, Alex, Ath.	3	1	.750	3.26	13	9	0	0	2	0	60.2	71	255	27	22	0	3	4	1	4	0	39	2	1
Huerta, Edgar, Mex.*	4	2	.667	3.33	9	8	3	1	1	0	54.0	54	241	23	20	0	3	0	8	25	0	78	10	1
Earley, Andrew, Cubs.............	2	0	1.000	3.97	12	6	0	0	4	0	45.1	37	211	22	20	0	2	2	8	33	0	29	4	0
Davies, Michael, Rock.*	4	1	.800	4.05	15	7	0	0	2	1	46.2	51	208	26	21	3	0	2	1	19	0	38	1	2
McCall, Derell, Ath.	5	3	.625	4.10	13	8	0	0	1	0	48.1	56	217	27	22	1	0	4	2	16	0	32	3	3
Smith, Joseph, Gia.	1	4	.200	4.12	12	11	0	0	0	0	63.1	69	270	40	29	1	1	3	6	9	0	55	4	3
Vazquez, William, Rock.	3	3	.500	4.13	13	11	0	0	0	0	52.1	52	236	36	24	4	1	1	1	21	0	38	7	1
Diaz, Felix, Gia.	3	4	.429	4.16	11	11	0	0	0	0	62.2	56	270	35	29	0	4	4	5	16	0	58	3	3
Medina, Franklin, Dia.	3	3	.500	4.34	13	8	0	0	1	1	56.0	43	248	36	27	2	0	2	4	37	0	53	4	9

DEPARTMENTAL LEADERS: W—Van Dusen, G. Martinez, 6 each; L—Dominquez, 8; Pct.—Van Dusen, 1.000; G—Madril, 24; GS—Patten, 14; CG—Huerta, Dominquez, 3 each; ShO—Huerta, Mora, 1 each; GF—H. Ramirez, Wiles, 15 each; Sv.—H. Ramirez, 10; IP—Patten, 73; H—Dominquez, Hernandez, 90 each; TBF—Patten, 344; R—Hernandez, 61; ER—Dominquez, 54; HR—C. Gonzalez, Rojas, 5 each; SF—Patten, 8; HB—Clark, Encarnacion, 9 each; BB—A. Jones, Patten, 41; IBB—Whiteaker, 4; SO—Huerta, 78; WP—A. Jones, 17; BK—Medina, 9.

ALL PITCHERS

*Lefthanded pitcher.

Pitcher, Team	W	L	Pct.	ERA	G	GS	CG	ShO	GF	Sv.	IP	H	TBF	R	ER	HR	SH	SF	HB	BB	IBB	SO	WP	Bk.
Abreu, Jonathan, Gia.*	0	1	.000	5.79	8	0	0	0	1	0	14.0	21	71	16	9	0	2	0	2	7	1	12	1	0
Adames, Martin, Gia.	3	0	1.000	4.08	10	0	0	0	5	0	17.2	22	86	11	8	2	0	0	1	11	1	11	0	2
Adkins, Jon, Ath.	1	1	.500	3.00	4	2	0	0	1	0	15.0	15	68	6	5	1	0	0	1	3	0	17	0	0
Aguilar, Mario, Mex.*	0	1	.000	6.84	5	5	0	0	0	0	25.0	33	118	20	19	2	0	1	1	11	0	16	0	1
Alvarez, Junior, Mex.	5	1	.833	6.45	13	7	0	0	5	0	60.0	77	283	50	43	3	2	1	23	0	58	6	0	
Amancio, Jose, Ath.	3	3	.500	6.88	14	6	0	0	3	0	34.0	53	173	46	26	4	2	4	5	12	0	20	2	1
Arellano, Salvador, Pad.	0	5	.000	7.07	14	6	0	0	1	0	42.0	69	216	41	33	2	1	2	5	16	0	34	6	1
Askew, William, Pad.	0	1	.000	4.96	14	0	0	0	3	0	16.1	16	79	13	9	2	0	0	13	0	17	2	0	
Atencio, Donald, Ath.	1	3	.250	7.53	11	5	0	0	1	1	34.2	46	177	40	29	2	0	7	6	26	0	23	10	0
Barber, Scott, Dia.	0	0	.000	3.00	2	1	0	0	0	0	3.0	0	11	1	1	0	0	0	2	0	4	0	0	
Bastardo, Jose, Gia.*	0	0	.000	18.47	6	0	0	0	4	0	6.1	6	41	14	13	0	0	2	14	0	7	1	0	
Batista, Javier, Mar.	3	1	.750	5.54	12	0	0	0	2	0	39.0	54	188	33	24	2	2	0	3	21	0	14	10	2
Berryman, Brian, Pad.	1	0	1.000	11.37	9	0	0	0	6	1	12.2	23	74	21	16	2	0	0	2	9	0	2	1	0
Bierbrodt, Nick, Dia.*	0	0	.000	4.50	4	3	0	0	0	0	8.0	4	34	4	4	0	0	1	5	0	10	1	0	
Bingler, Travis, W.S.*	2	2	.500	6.65	19	0	0	0	12	3	21.2	30	103	25	16	2	1	1	0	11	1	15	0	0
Blanco, Jimmy, Pad.	1	1	.500	4.35	13	0	0	0	6	1	20.2	23	84	10	10	0	3	2	1	0	0	10	2	0
Blood, Darin, Gia.	0	1	.000	9.82	2	0	0	0	1	0	3.2	3	19	4	4	0	0	2	3	0	3	2	0	
Brohawn, Troy, Dia.*	0	0	.000	0.00	3	3	0	0	0	0	4.0	5	16	1	0	0	0	1	0	6	0	0	
Bruney, Brian, Dia.	4	1	.800	6.48	20	2	0	0	11	2	25.0	21	131	23	18	2	0	1	6	29	0	24	5	1
Buret, Jorge, Rock	5	1	.833	2.39	14	9	0	0	0	0	52.2	50	224	21	14	2	2	3	4	14	0	29	2	2
Burnau, Ryan, Cubs	2	2	.500	5.35	10	5	0	0	3	0	37.0	46	175	27	22	1	0	3	5	14	0	33	4	1
Calandriello, Donato, Ath.*......	0	0	.000	5.40	2	2	0	0	0	0	1.2	3	9	1	1	0	0	0	1	0	1	0	0
Chavarria, Hector, Mex.	0	3	.000	11.68	11	1	0	0	7	1	24.2	45	138	38	32	0	0	1	6	13	0	13	3	4

Pitcher, Team	W	L	Pct.	ERA	G	GS	CG	ShO	GF	Sv.	IP	H	TBF	R	ER	HR	SH	SF	HB	BB	IBB	SO	WP	Bk.
Christensen, Deryck, Rock.	3	1	.750	4.88	17	0	0	0	3	0	24.0	22	112	17	13	0	0	2	2	17	1	14	4	0
Clark, Jeffrey, Gia.	2	5	.286	5.56	11	11	0	0	0	0	56.2	66	247	41	35	2	2	2	9	10	0	35	0	0
Collado, Jerry, Rock.	0	1	.000	6.86	16	0	0	0	3	0	19.2	19	99	18	15	0	1	1	4	20	0	9	5	1
Corbin, John, Cubs	3	0	1.000	4.88	17	0	0	0	11	3	24.0	24	113	18	13	1	0	3	3	11	1	31	1	0
Crespo, Jorge, Mex.	2	4	.333	7.31	11	3	0	0	6	1	44.1	58	211	38	36	3	1	3	3	24	0	37	6	0
Cyr, Eric, Pad.	0	0	.000	3.00	2	1	0	0	1	0	3.0	4	14	1	1	0	0	0	0	2	0	4	0	0
Davies, Michael, Rock.*	4	1	.800	4.05	15	7	0	0	2	1	46.2	51	208	26	21	3	0	2	1	19	0	38	1	2
Davis, Mikael, Dia.	0	1	.000	7.36	17	0	0	0	8	0	25.2	34	138	32	21	0	0	2	2	31	0	14	8	0
De Jesus, Hanki, Dia.	3	2	.600	8.26	20	0	0	0	8	1	28.1	44	152	36	26	1	0	0	3	19	0	19	2	0
Delgadillo, Julian, Mex.	1	1	.500	8.91	14	1	0	0	9	1	33.1	55	179	37	33	5	0	2	5	28	0	18	9	0
DePaula, Freddy, Ath.*	1	1	.500	0.79	5	0	0	0	1	0	11.1	7	44	2	1	0	2	0	1	3	0	9	0	0
Diaz, Alex, Ath.	3	1	.750	3.26	13	9	0	0	2	0	60.2	71	255	27	22	0	3	4	1	4	0	39	2	1
Diaz, Eddy, Cubs	1	0	1.000	4.84	5	3	0	0	0	0	22.1	27	102	16	12	0	2	1	2	10	1	14	4	0
Diaz, Felix, Gia.	3	4	.429	4.16	11	11	0	0	0	0	62.2	56	270	35	29	0	4	4	5	16	0	58	3	3
Diaz, Franklin, Ath.	0	0	.000	15.43	1	0	0	0	0	0	2.1	5	13	4	4	1	0	0	0	1	0	0	1	0
Dominquez, Carlos, Mex.*	2	8	.200	7.18	13	11	3	0	2	1	67.2	90	315	56	54	4	2	4	2	31	0	54	9	1
Drain, Bradley, Mar.	2	2	.500	2.84	4	1	0	0	0	0	19.0	18	74	6	6	2	0	1	0	1	0	15	0	0
Dulkowski, Marc, Pad.	0	0	.000	2.45	4	0	0	0	2	0	3.2	4	20	4	1	0	0	1	0	6	0	3	0	0
Dunphy, Micah, Ath.*	2	0	1.000	1.54	7	0	0	0	1	0	11.2	9	57	6	2	1	1	0	4	9	0	11	0	0
Earley, Andrew, Cubs	2	0	1.000	3.97	12	6	0	0	4	0	45.1	37	211	22	20	0	2	2	8	33	0	29	4	0
Elguezabal, Octavio, Mex.*	0	0	.000	5.40	3	0	0	0	2	1	5.0	11	26	5	3	0	0	0	0	2	0	3	2	1
Encarnacion, Luis, Mar.	1	2	.333	12.33	13	4	0	0	5	0	27.0	43	147	39	37	4	0	6	9	16	0	20	10	0
Featherstone, Deron, Gia.	0	0	.000	13.50	1	0	0	0	1	0	1.1	2	8	2	2	1	0	0	0	2	0	2	1	0
Ferrand, Julian, Rock.	0	0	.000	2.05	16	0	0	0	4	1	22.0	18	96	5	5	0	0	1	0	12	0	12	1	1
Flanagan, Jeremy, Cubs	0	1	.000	5.81	9	6	0	0	1	1	26.1	33	120	19	17	2	1	1	1	15	0	20	4	0
Gentile, Mark, W.S.	0	0	.000	63.00	3	0	0	0	0	0	1.0	4	12	7	7	0	0	0	1	5	0	0	5	0
Germano, Justin, Pad.	5	5	.500	4.59	17	8	0	0	4	1	66.2	65	277	36	34	4	3	1	3	9	0	67	5	1
Glascock, John-paul, Cubs	2	5	.286	7.63	15	1	0	0	7	0	30.2	38	157	33	26	0	3	3	8	25	0	20	6	0
Gonzalez, Cristian, Ath.	3	1	.750	5.27	14	6	0	0	3	1	54.2	78	249	45	32	6	5	2	6	8	1	36	0	0
Gonzalez, Enrique, Dia.	1	0	1.000	1.53	11	0	0	0	8	1	17.2	16	80	13	3	0	0	0	1	12	0	17	3	0
Gonzalez, Jeremi, Cubs	0	1	.000	2.70	4	4	0	0	0	0	10.0	8	40	3	3	0	0	0	0	2	0	15	0	0
Gonzalez, Miguel, Rock.	2	2	.500	4.79	15	0	0	0	6	0	20.2	19	91	13	11	0	1	1	1	15	0	17	1	1
Granados, Bernie, Rock.	1	1	.500	4.50	12	0	0	0	10	2	12.0	17	61	11	6	0	1	0	0	7	0	12	2	1
Haase, Frank, Rock.*	1	2	.333	9.50	14	1	0	0	1	0	18.0	16	88	21	19	0	1	1	1	16	0	9	2	0
Hammons, Matt, Cubs	0	0	.000	0.00	1	1	0	0	0	0	1.2	1	6	0	0	0	0	0	0	0	0	4	0	0
Hannaman, Ryan, Gia.	0	1	.000	21.60	5	0	0	0	2	0	3.1	4	26	8	8	0	0	2	1	11	0	6	4	0
Harvey, Victor, W.S.	0	2	.000	12.68	16	2	0	0	4	0	22.0	43	129	35	31	3	0	0	2	20	0	25	3	1
Hernandez, Juan, W.S.	2	3	.400	7.11	13	9	0	0	0	0	57.0	90	285	61	45	4	3	3	2	26	0	43	2	1
Hoane, Wes, Mar.	1	0	1.000	2.49	15	0	0	0	10	5	25.1	17	93	8	7	0	1	1	0	4	0	24	2	0
Hoffman, Matt, Rock.	3	0	1.000	8.31	4	0	0	0	1	0	4.1	7	24	4	4	0	0	0	0	4	0	6	2	0
Hoffpauir, Josh, Ath.	0	0	.000	9.00	1	0	0	0	1	0	1.0	2	5	1	1	1	0	0	0	0	0	2	1	0
Hollifield, Alec, W.S.	4	3	.571	2.05	8	8	0	0	0	0	52.2	58	220	26	12	1	2	1	4	12	0	34	4	0
Huber, Jon, Pad.	1	4	.200	6.60	14	10	0	0	0	0	45.0	54	223	49	33	1	3	3	1	32	0	39	6	0
Huerta, Edgar, Mex.*	4	2	.667	3.33	9	8	3	1	1	0	54.0	54	241	23	20	0	3	0	8	25	0	78	10	1
Jacob, Russell, Dia.	0	0	.000	0.00	3	2	0	0	0	0	4.0	2	14	1	0	0	0	0	0	0	0	2	0	0
Johnston, Sean, Cubs*	0	0	.000	0.00	1	1	0	0	0	0	2.0	1	6	0	0	0	0	0	0	0	0	2	0	0
Johnstone, John, Gia.	0	0	.000	0.00	1	1	0	0	0	0	1.0	0	3	0	0	0	0	0	0	0	0	1	0	0
Jones, Alvin, W.S.	1	3	.250	7.51	14	6	0	0	3	1	44.1	48	225	49	37	4	2	3	5	41	0	45	17	0
Jones, Geoffrey, Pad.*	0	3	.000	7.94	20	0	0	0	3	0	28.1	45	149	30	25	2	3	1	0	18	1	35	1	1
Kesten, Michael, Mar.*	5	0	1.000	4.78	16	0	0	0	5	0	26.1	29	120	16	14	0	0	1	1	13	0	23	1	0
Ketchner, Ryan, Mar.*	1	2	.333	4.21	9	1	0	0	2	0	25.2	22	104	14	12	0	0	3	1	3	0	27	2	1
Kinnie, Gary, Mar.	3	3	.500	5.64	12	10	0	0	0	0	52.2	55	238	44	33	3	2	0	2	29	0	44	10	1
Laureano, Edgardo, Pad.	0	1	.000	5.73	12	0	0	0	7	2	11.0	12	57	12	7	0	1	1	0	7	1	10	1	0
Lavery, Tim, Cubs	0	2	.000	4.80	5	5	0	0	0	0	15.0	17	69	11	8	1	0	1	2	3	0	13	0	0
Lawton, Charles, Pad.	1	4	.200	5.65	12	6	0	0	0	0	36.2	37	165	28	23	2	1	5	3	18	0	25	4	1
Lee, Jonathan, Dia.	0	1	.000	3.33	9	0	0	0	2	1	24.1	30	106	15	9	0	1	1	0	8	1	19	4	1
Leon, Brigmer, Ath.	1	0	1.000	3.34	12	1	0	0	1	1	32.1	28	136	15	12	3	0	1	4	5	1	15	1	0
Lewis, Peyton, Cubs	1	0	1.000	0.00	5	0	0	0	5	3	7.0	6	28	0	0	0	1	0	0	1	0	8	1	0
Lopez, Arturo, Mar.	2	0	1.000	4.91	10	3	0	0	1	0	22.0	23	96	15	12	1	0	0	2	11	0	20	1	0
Madril, Steve, W.S.*	3	2	.600	3.92	24	1	0	0	13	4	43.2	44	185	25	19	1	2	2	1	7	0	51	6	3
Mapes, Jake, Gia.	1	1	.500	10.24	8	1	0	0	3	0	9.2	13	53	16	11	1	1	1	3	7	1	4	3	1
Marquez, Jose, Dia.	2	5	.286	5.56	13	8	0	0	0	0	68.0	71	305	48	42	2	1	3	4	30	0	33	6	2
Marte, Damaso, Mar.	0	0	.000	0.00	2	2	0	0	0	0	5.0	1	17	0	0	0	0	0	1	0	0	6	0	0
Martinez, Gustavo, Mar.	6	3	.667	3.59	17	1	0	0	4	1	42.2	42	197	27	17	0	0	0	3	25	0	53	3	0
Martinez, Javier, Pad.	0	0	.000	0.00	3	0	0	0	2	1	3.1	0	13	0	0	0	0	0	0	3	0	2	0	0
Matos, Jesus, Rock.	5	1	.833	2.54	15	4	0	0	6	0	46.0	40	186	20	13	2	0	3	1	8	0	41	2	0
Matos, Raymond, Gia.*	0	1	.000	6.04	10	3	0	0	2	0	25.1	33	128	23	17	2	2	2	3	19	0	16	4	0
Maurer, Mike, Ath.	1	0	1.000	3.48	11	1	0	0	8	1	10.1	5	38	5	4	1	0	0	0	1	0	5	1	1
McCall, Derell, Ath.	5	3	.625	4.10	13	8	0	0	1	0	48.1	56	217	27	22	1	0	4	2	16	0	32	3	3
McKinley, Ryan, Cubs	1	3	.250	7.62	15	0	0	0	11	2	26.0	36	130	27	22	1	4	1	1	13	0	17	4	0
Medina, Franklin, Dia.	3	3	.500	4.34	13	8	0	0	1	1	56.0	43	248	36	27	2	0	2	4	37	0	53	4	9
Merricks, Charles, Rock.*	2	1	.667	2.72	13	10	0	0	0	0	49.2	47	216	27	15	0	0	4	4	24	0	37	1	1
Meyer, Jake, Mar.	0	0	.000	4.50	3	3	0	0	0	0	4.0	4	19	2	2	0	0	0	0	3	0	6	0	0
Montgomery, Greg, W.S.	0	0	.000	12.27	2	0	0	0	1	1	3.2	4	18	5	5	0	0	0	0	3	0	4	1	0
Montoya, Saul, Dia.	1	2	.333	9.53	3	1	0	0	0	0	11.1	15	61	13	12	0	0	0	2	8	0	5	1	4
Mora, Sergio, Mex.	5	3	.625	5.20	10	9	2	1	0	0	55.1	60	247	35	32	2	0	3	8	28	0	47	10	0
Morgan, Russ, Mar.*	1	0	1.000	2.70	12	0	0	0	8	1	20.0	17	81	10	6	2	1	0	1	3	0	29	0	0
Nacar, Yimmy, Gia.	0	1	.000	9.74	12	0	0	0	6	0	20.1	25	107	22	22	1	0	2	2	20	0	17	6	0
Nageotte, Clint, Mar.	4	1	.800	2.16	12	7	0	0	1	1	50.0	29	207	15	12	0	0	2	3	28	0	59	2	0
Negron, Alex, Cubs	2	0	1.000	3.77	9	0	0	0	7	2	14.1	11	62	7	6	0	0	1	1	8	0	15	1	0
Olivero, Pedro, Cubs	3	1	.750	6.15	7	4	0	0	1	0	26.1	29	129	21	18	3	0	3	2	16	0	16	5	0
Patten, Scott, W.S.	4	4	.500	5.05	14	14	0	0	0	0	73.0	80	344	55	41	1	0	8	8	41	0	58	12	1
Perez, Amauris, Gia.	1	2	.333	4.82	10	0	0	0	4	0	18.2	25	91	12	10	0	1	1	2	6	1	13	2	0
Perez, Armando, W.S.*	0	3	.000	6.07	15	8	0	0	2	0	43.0	51	204	38	29	4	2	1	2	26	0	37	3	1

Pitcher, Team	W	L	Pct.	ERA	G	GS	CG	ShO	GF	Sv.	IP	H	TBF	R	ER	HR	SH	SF	HB	BB	IBB	SO	WP	Bk.
Perez, Beltran, Dia.	5	1	.833	5.81	11	4	0	0	0	0	48.0	61	221	37	31	1	2	2	2	25	1	47	0	1
Perez, Henry, Pad.	2	5	.286	4.53	13	10	0	0	2	0	47.2	40	215	32	24	3	2	1	1	36	0	39	5	3
Perkins, Gregory, Dia.	0	0	.000	0.00	2	0	0	0	1	0	3.0	3	12	0	0	0	0	0	0	0	0	2	0	0
Pignatiello, Carmen, Cubs*	4	1	.800	4.46	9	3	0	0	1	0	36.1	48	169	26	18	1	1	1	1	13	0	32	1	2
Pillier, Santo, Ath.	2	3	.400	2.10	17	0	0	0	10	1	25.2	22	110	13	6	2	3	1	0	9	2	22	3	0
Pimentel, Gregorio, Gia.	1	1	.500	1.02	9	1	0	0	3	0	17.2	14	67	3	2	0	1	0	1	5	0	10	0	0
Pinto, Renyel, Cubs*	0	2	.000	6.30	9	4	0	0	0	0	30.0	42	152	29	21	3	2	0	5	16	0	23	6	3
Pulsipher, Bill, Dia.*	0	0	.000	4.50	3	3	0	0	0	0	6.0	8	24	3	3	0	0	0	1	0	0	4	1	0
Ramirez, Hector, Dia.	1	2	.333	5.40	16	0	0	0	15	10	16.2	24	78	12	10	0	1	0	1	6	1	10	2	0
Ramirez, Joslin, Dia.	4	5	.444	6.44	15	4	0	0	2	0	50.1	70	245	50	36	2	0	1	1	28	0	47	3	1
Revenig, Todd, Dia.	0	0	.000	0.00	2	0	0	0	2	0	2.0	2	9	0	0	0	0	0	0	0	0	1	1	0
Reyes, Junior, Cubs	4	2	.667	5.44	13	3	0	0	3	2	41.1	57	206	35	25	2	3	4	6	24	0	39	5	1
Rivera, Jimmy, Mar.	0	2	.000	9.82	7	1	0	0	0	0	11.0	12	56	13	12	0	0	0	0	17	0	7	5	0
Rodriguez, Orlando, W.S.*	2	5	.286	4.20	16	5	0	0	4	0	40.2	36	190	30	19	3	1	1	2	32	0	53	3	1
Rojas, Ramon, Gia.	3	4	.571	6.37	18	2	0	0	3	1	35.1	55	181	38	25	1	5	2	3	15	3	20	2	0
Romero, Garvis, Rock.	2	2	.500	5.06	20	0	0	0	9	0	21.1	29	104	18	12	1	0	2	0	8	0	15	1	2
Romo, Noe, Mex.*	0	2	.000	7.71	7	1	0	0	4	1	18.2	21	95	20	16	0	0	3	3	16	0	13	1	4
Rosario, Dionis, W.S.*	0	0	.000	8.10	2	2	0	0	0	0	3.1	2	18	4	3	0	0	0	0	6	0	3	0	0
Rosario, Hipolito, Pad.	3	2	.600	6.87	19	0	0	0	7	2	36.2	50	173	29	28	0	0	6	4	16	2	24	1	1
Rossellini, William, Dia.	0	1	.000	0.00	4	1	0	0	0	0	8.0	2	30	2	0	0	0	0	1	6	0	8	1	0
Ruelas, Heriberto, Mex.*	0	3	.000	8.06	6	4	0	0	2	0	22.1	33	108	23	20	2	0	2	1	14	0	24	3	0
Sandoval,, Mex.	1	3	.250	6.75	7	1	0	0	0	5	16.0	25	82	14	12	1	0	2	5	16	0	16	0	0
Schultz, Michael, Dia.	0	1	.000	6.75	2	0	0	0	0	0	2.2	7	17	7	2	1	0	1	1	1	0	2	0	0
Scott, John, Pad.	1	3	.250	6.33	15	5	0	0	6	2	27.0	39	140	28	19	1	1	2	1	20	0	21	6	0
Serrano, Alex, Rock.	0	0	.000	0.00	6	0	0	0	4	1	6.1	2	23	0	0	0	0	0	0	1	0	5	0	0
Simpson, Joe, Rock.	0	0	.000	4.63	11	0	0	0	4	1	11.2	11	55	9	6	0	0	1	0	6	0	6	2	0
Slaten, Douglas, Dia.	0	0	.000	0.96	9	4	0	0	3	0	9.1	7	40	1	1	0	0	0	2	3	0	7	0	0
Smith, Joseph, Gia.	1	4	.200	4.12	12	11	0	0	0	0	63.1	69	270	40	29	1	1	3	6	9	0	55	4	3
Smith, Justin, Mar.	0	0	.000	1.80	3	3	0	0	0	0	5.0	5	24	1	1	0	0	0	2	5	0	5	0	0
Snider, John, Ath.	2	2	.500	2.48	9	3	0	0	2	1	29.0	30	116	8	8	0	1	0	2	2	0	30	1	0
Sobchuk, Justin, Ath.	1	4	.200	6.91	14	8	0	0	1	0	43.0	60	214	44	33	3	1	4	4	26	0	23	8	0
Soto, Darwin, Pad.	2	2	.500	4.53	17	2	0	0	5	0	45.2	64	219	34	23	1	2	1	0	18	0	28	4	1
Stockman, Phil, Dia.	3	2	.600	2.59	14	2	0	0	5	1	41.2	40	194	22	12	2	0	0	2	23	0	40	3	1
Stottlemyre, Todd, Dia.	1	1	.500	3.60	2	2	0	0	0	0	10.0	10	40	4	4	0	0	2	1	1	0	10	2	0
Szuminski, Jason, Cubs	2	1	.667	2.43	10	4	0	0	0	0	40.2	39	171	15	11	0	1	0	3	13	0	31	2	0
Thomson, John, Dia.	0	1	.000	13.50	3	3	0	0	0	0	5.1	8	29	8	8	0	0	1	0	4	0	7	1	0
Trosper, Tanner, Ath.	0	1	.000	1.57	17	0	0	0	14	6	23.0	17	95	7	4	0	1	1	1	7	0	24	3	0
Urrutia, Carlos, Dia.	0	2	.000	4.94	7	5	0	0	1	0	31.0	32	140	20	17	0	1	0	5	12	0	16	6	1
Van Dusen, Derrick, Mar.*	6	2	01.000	2.63	10	2	0	0	0	0	41.0	38	166	14	12	1	0	1	0	6	0	58	2	0
Vazquez, William, Rock.	3	3	.500	4.13	13	11	0	0	0	0	52.1	52	236	36	24	4	1	1	1	21	0	38	7	1
Velazquez, Elih, Ath.*	3	2	.600	8.92	15	3	0	0	4	2	35.1	46	167	39	35	3	1	1	1	7	0	25	2	1
Villacis, Eduardo, Rock.	4	2	.667	1.86	13	9	0	0	1	1	48.1	39	202	17	10	0	3	2	2	19	1	37	3	1
Villarreal, Oscar, Dia.	0	0	.000	9.00	1	0	0	0	0	0	1.0	2	5	1	1	0	0	0	0	0	0	1	0	0
Villatoro, Wilmer, Pad.	0	0	.000	15.43	2	0	0	0	0	0	2.1	3	11	4	4	0	0	1	2	0	5	0	0
Walk, Mitch, Gia.*	4	4	.500	4.43	12	12	1	0	0	0	63.0	63	280	37	31	5	2	1	6	17	0	68	7	2
Ward, Jeremy, Dia.	0	0	.000	0.00	2	0	0	0	0	0	2.0	0	6	0	0	0	0	0	0	0	0	2	0	0
Webb, Brandon, Dia.	0	0	.000	9.00	1	1	0	0	0	0	1.0	2	5	1	1	0	0	0	0	0	0	3	0	0
Westfall, Allan, Mar.	0	0	.000	0.00	1	1	0	0	0	0	3.0	2	12	0	0	0	0	0	0	2	0	3	0	0
White, Bill, Dia.*	0	1	.000	6.00	4	1	0	0	0	0	6.0	3	25	4	4	0	0	1	0	5	0	9	3	0
Whiteaker, Gregg, Gia.	1	1	.500	5.47	12	1	0	0	3	2	26.1	30	120	20	16	3	2	1	1	9	4	16	4	0
Wiles, Chad, Mar.	3	0	1.000	1.35	17	0	0	0	15	7	33.1	25	133	7	5	0	1	0	1	8	1	36	0	0
Wiley, Skip, Mar.	1	0	1.000	3.71	7	3	0	0	2	0	17.0	14	69	9	7	2	0	1	4	0	13	1	0
Willis, Dontrelle, Cubs*	3	1	.750	3.86	9	1	0	0	3	0	28.0	26	118	15	12	0	1	2	1	8	1	22	0	0
Wood, Brandon, Dia.	0	0	.000	2.84	5	0	0	0	5	2	6.1	5	27	3	2	0	0	0	1	4	0	5	0	0
Yoshida, Nobuaki, Pad.*	0	2	.000	2.32	7	7	0	0	0	0	31.0	23	118	11	8	1	1	1	1	7	0	32	3	1
Zaug, Kevin, W.S.	3	6	.333	5.98	22	0	0	0	10	1	46.2	58	227	41	31	4	1	1	6	26	3	29	1	2
Zimmerman, Jordan, Mar.*	0	0	.000	0.00	10	10	0	0	0	0	12.0	7	46	3	0	0	0	1	3	0	14	0	0
Zorrilla, Reinaldo, W.S.	1	0	1.000	6.56	20	0	0	0	6	0	23.1	25	119	18	17	3	0	0	0	28	0	22	7	0

COMBINATION SHUTOUTS: **Athletics (1)**—McCall-Amancio. **Cubs (2)**—Olivero-Willis-Negron, Earley-Reyes. **Diamondbacks (3)**—White-Perez-Davis-Wood, Medina-Lee-Wood, Revening-Bierbrodt-Perez-Bruney. **Giants (1)**—Walk-Ramirez. **Mariners (6)**—Nageotte-Van Dusen-Kesten-Hoane, Westfall-Kesten-Morgan-Hoane, Smith-Kinnie-Wiles, Ketchner-Lopez, Marte-Ketchner-Martinez, Lopez-Van Dusen-Morgan. **Mexico (0)**—None. **Padres (2)**—Germano-Askew-Rosario, Perez-Soto. **Rockies (2)**—Villacis-Collado-Haase-Simpson. **White Sox (2)**—Hollifield-Bingler-Zorrilla, Hernandez-Madril.

NO-HIT GAMES: None.

2000 FIELDING

TEAM

Team	Pct.	G	PO	A	E	TC	DP	TP	PB
Giants	.954	54	1389	549	93	2031	35	0	12
Mariners	.952	55	1443	562	101	2106	51	0	14
Mexico	.952	55	1402	438	93	1933	30	0	9
Diamondbacks ..	.947	54	1418	563	111	2092	45	0	18
Athletics	.947	54	1422	635	116	2173	45	0	10
Cubs	.945	56	1486	582	120	2188	44	0	12
Padres	.944	55	1439	545	118	2102	39	1	27
Rockies	.942	54	1383	554	120	2057	38	0	14
White Sox	.941	55	1428	540	124	2092	39	0	16

INDIVIDUAL

FIRST BASEMEN

NOTE: All caps denotes fielding-percentage leader based on 28 games for catchers, 37 for all other non-pitchers and 45 innings for pitchers. *Throws lefthanded.

Player, Team	Pct.	G	PO	A	E	TC	DP
Baez, Carlos, Mex.	.982	50	361	29	7	397	30
Brack, Josh, Ath.	1.000	1	7	0	0	7	2
Chiarini, Mario, Mar.	.800	1	2	2	1	5	0
Coats, Buck, Cubs	.973	11	70	3	2	75	7
Collins, Kevin, Cubs*	.971	31	261	11	8	280	22
Corporan, Roberto, Dia.	1.000	2	2	0	0	2	0
Cruz, Israel, Mar.	1.000	2	19	3	0	22	1

Player, Team	Pct.	G	PO	A	E	TC	DP
Davis, Ryan, Gia.*	.957	20	151	6	7	164	6
Dean, Mike, Gia.	1.000	2	5	0	0	5	1
D'Jesus, Francisco, Gia.	.955	9	39	3	2	44	2
Durazo, Erubiel, Dia.*	1.000	1	6	2	0	8	0
Ellis, Alvyn, Ath.	.980	40	370	16	8	394	24
Figueroa, Eduardo, Mar.	.000	1	0	0	0	0	0
Garrido, Tomas, Gia.	1.000	3	22	1	0	23	1
Golden, Bryan, Cubs	1.000	4	35	2	0	37	3
Gomez, Andre, Pad.	.889	4	8	0	1	9	1
Gomez, Francis, Ath.	.000	1	0	0	0	0	0
Gonzalez, Carlos, Mar.	1.000	1	4	0	0	4	0
Jackson, Steve, Ath.	.994	17	146	19	1	166	14
Johnson, Jonathan, Cubs	.959	7	43	4	2	49	2
Jung, Young-jin, Pad.	.983	32	279	9	5	293	17
Liriano, Pedro, Mar.	1.000	4	30	3	0	33	2
Mapes, Jake, Gia.	.875	2	7	0	1	8	0
Matos, Cesar, Ath.	1.000	1	6	0	0	6	0
McKnight, Lukas, Cubs	.986	13	70	2	1	73	7
Melton, John, Dia.	1.000	1	4	0	0	4	0
Montilla, Samuel, Dia.	.909	1	9	1	1	11	0
Mulqueen, Dave, Rock.	.978	37	363	33	9	405	23
Oliveros, Luis, Mar.	1.000	1	3	0	0	3	1
OLKOWSKI, Kevin, Mar.	.989	41	339	32	4	375	33
Ortiz, Luis, Dia.	1.000	1	5	0	0	5	0
Paulino, Miguel, Cubs	.000	1	0	0	2	0	0
Pinango, Ever, Gia.	.979	17	84	11	2	97	10
Pines, Gregory, Mar.	1.000	9	77	1	0	78	8
Puccinelli, John, Pad.	1.000	7	63	3	0	66	3
Ramirez, Domingo, Gia.	1.000	1	6	0	0	6	0
Ramirez, Wagner, Cubs	.000	1	0	0	0	0	0
Reynoso, Paulino, W.S.*	.983	26	203	24	4	231	15
Roenicke, Jarett, Pad.*	.969	19	147	10	5	162	17
Sanchez, Braulio, Dia.*	.000	1	0	0	1	1	0
Santana, Mayobanex, W.S.	.982	18	151	9	3	163	11
Santos, Deivis, Gia.*	1.000	12	103	8	0	111	9
Suomi, Richard, Ath.	1.000	1	9	0	0	9	1
Tapia, Roman, W.S.	.976	14	115	6	3	124	9
Trumble, Dan, Gia.	.952	6	56	3	3	62	4
Uruata, Luis, Dia.	.984	54	484	18	8	510	39
Vasquez, Jose, Rock.*	.939	17	146	7	10	163	11
Virgen, Constancio, Mex.	1.000	1	12	0	0	12	0
Williams, Peanut, Mar.	1.000	1	11	0	0	11	2

TRIPLE PLAY: Jung.

SECOND BASEMEN

Player, Team	Pct.	G	PO	A	E	TC	DP
Alexander, Kevin, Gia.	.978	12	21	24	1	46	6
AMADOR, Christopher, W.S.	.943	42	59	106	10	175	16
Brack, Josh, Ath.	.929	14	21	31	4	56	8
Cabrera, Leonel, Gia.	.942	19	24	41	4	69	6
Cameron, Antoine, Cubs*	1.000	2	1	0	0	1	0
Cano, Octavio, Mex.	.909	9	12	18	3	33	3
Castro, Julio, W.S.	.980	12	27	23	1	51	7
Chilsom, Tawan, Dia.	.789	11	8	7	4	19	0
Coats, Buck, Cubs	.938	4	6	9	1	16	3
Corporan, Roberto, Dia.	.969	33	50	76	4	130	19
Cruz, Israel, Mar.	.966	19	34	51	3	88	15
Delanuez, Orlando, Dia.	.957	26	32	58	4	94	14
Figueroa, Carlos, Rock.	.907	20	27	51	8	86	10
Floyd, Daniel, Mar.	.889	4	1	7	1	9	2
Frazier, Carlos, Gia.	1.000	1	1	2	0	3	1
Garcia, Isaac, Ath.	.957	12	27	40	3	70	4
Garrido, Tomas, Gia.	1.000	1	0	1	0	1	0
Hoffpauir, Josh, Ath.	.935	34	67	92	11	170	14
Infantes, Juan, Pad.	.978	13	12	32	1	45	5
Liriano, Pedro, Mar.	.924	38	60	111	14	185	23
Lopez, Oliver, Pad.	.000	1	0	0	0	0	0
Martinez, Orlando, Mex.	1.000	1	0	2	0	2	0
Nulton, Kevin, Pad.	.941	31	49	63	7	119	11
Olson, David, Pad.	.818	4	3	6	2	11	3
Ortiz, Jorge, Ath.	1.000	1	1	0	0	1	0
Paulino, Miguel, Cubs	.941	3	9	7	1	17	2
Pinango, Ever, Gia.	.929	7	7	6	1	14	0
Ramirez, Alexander, Gia.	.941	11	21	11	2	34	0
Ramirez, Allan, Mex.	.946	33	62	61	7	130	13
Ramirez, Domingo, Gia.	.000	1	0	0	0	0	0
Ramirez, Wagner, Cubs	.938	32	75	76	10	161	14
Reyes, Henry, Gia.	.922	24	34	37	6	77	6
Romero, Flavio, Mex.	.933	10	11	17	2	30	2
Serrano, Eddie, Pad.	.939	19	23	39	4	66	8
Spidale, Mike, W.S.	.923	4	5	7	1	13	0
Storey, Eric, Rock.	.929	8	10	16	2	28	3
Tapia, Roman, W.S.	1.000	1	1	1	0	2	0
Thornton-Murray, Jandin, Cubs	.960	23	55	64	5	124	19

THIRD BASEMEN

Player, Team	Pct.	G	PO	A	E	TC	DP
Allegra, Matthew, Ath.	.500	1	0	1	1	2	0
Barrera, Reinaldo, Dia.	.909	37	32	78	11	121	8
Biercan,, Mex.	1.000	1	0	2	0	2	0
Brack, Josh, Ath.	.908	31	18	71	9	98	3
Cabrera, Leonel, Gia.	.821	10	7	16	5	28	1
Canales, Joel, Mex.	1.000	1	3	1	0	4	0
Castro, Julio, W.S.	.813	22	10	29	9	48	5
Chiarini, Mario, Mar.	.806	17	12	17	7	36	2
Corporan, Roberto, Dia.	.667	6	1	1	1	3	0
Cruz, Israel, Mar.	.857	7	6	6	2	14	1
Delanuez, Orlando, Dia.	.936	15	13	31	3	47	2
Falcon, Omar, Pad.	.000	1	0	0	0	0	0
Floyd, Daniel, Mar.	.889	3	2	6	1	9	1
Garcia, Isaac, Ath.	.000	1	0	0	0	0	0
GARRIDO, Tomas, Gia.	.917	37	17	60	7	84	7
Golden, Bryan, Cubs	.800	2	0	4	1	5	0
Gomez, Francis, Ath.	.000	1	0	0	0	0	0
Hoffpauir, Josh, Ath.	.800	2	0	4	1	5	0
Johnson, Jonathan, Cubs	.840	35	27	57	16	100	2
Klatt, Joel, Pad.	.897	49	38	92	15	145	6
Martinez, Orlando, Mex.	.000	1	0	0	0	0	0
Materano, Oscar, Rock.	.833	29	25	50	15	90	5
Mejia, Anderson, Cubs	.750	2	1	2	1	4	0
Molina, Gustavo, W.S.	1.000	2	2	2	0	4	0
Montero, Esteban, Rock.	1.000	2	0	1	0	1	1
Nulton, Kevin, Pad.	.880	9	8	14	3	25	1
Ortiz, Jorge, Ath.	.857	28	16	38	9	63	2
Pena, Amaury, W.S.	.951	17	20	38	3	61	2
Pinango, Ever, Gia.	.500	1	1	0	1	2	0
Presichi, Christian, Mex.	.911	36	24	58	8	90	9
Puccinelli, John, Pad.	.500	2	0	1	1	2	0
Ramirez, Alexander, Gia.	.778	9	5	9	4	18	0
Ramirez, Allan, Mex.	.914	13	11	21	3	35	0
Ramirez, Domingo, Gia.	.500	1	1	0	1	2	0
Reyes, Henry, Gia.	.882	6	3	12	2	17	2
Spidale, Mike, W.S.	.824	7	4	10	3	17	0
Storey, Eric, Rock.	.929	26	18	61	6	85	4
Tapia, Roman, W.S.	.850	10	6	11	3	20	1
Thornton-Murray, Jandin, Cubs	.946	21	11	42	3	56	2
Villilo, Miguel, Mar.	.870	36	27	53	12	92	5
Virgen, Constancio, Mex.	.800	2	3	1	1	5	0

SHORTSTOPS

Player, Team	Pct.	G	PO	A	E	TC	DP
Alexander, Kevin, Gia.	.846	4	1	10	2	13	1
Amador, Christopher, W.S.	.878	8	17	19	5	41	6
Brack, Josh, Ath.	.958	8	9	14	1	24	2
Castro, Julio, W.S.	.933	6	6	8	1	15	4
Chavez, Angel, Gia.	1.000	7	13	16	0	29	2
Corporan, Roberto, Dia.	.778	3	3	4	2	9	1
Cruz, Israel, Mar.	.933	22	35	48	6	89	12
Delanuez, Orlando, Dia.	.750	5	1	8	3	12	0
Figueroa, Carlos, Rock.	.667	2	1	1	1	3	1
Garcia, Isaac, Ath.	.909	39	59	140	20	219	17
Garrido, Tomas, Gia.	.957	13	16	29	2	47	3
Gomez, Francis, Ath.	.825	11	16	31	10	57	6
Infantes, Juan, Pad.	.833	10	10	25	7	42	4
Lopez, Oliver, Pad.	.887	17	18	29	6	53	7
Martinez, Orlando, Mex.	1.000	1	1	1	0	2	1
Materano, Oscar, Rock.	.950	3	10	9	1	20	2
Mendoza, Carlos, Gia.	1.000	4	3	17	0	20	1
Montanez, Luis, Cubs	.893	47	59	141	24	224	30
Montero, Esteban, Rock.	.894	47	80	140	26	246	24
Morse, Michael, W.S.	.897	45	60	97	18	175	14
Nulton, Kevin, Pad.	.840	9	9	12	4	25	3
Paulino, Miguel, Cubs	.882	5	8	7	2	17	2
Pinango, Ever, Gia.	.965	15	25	30	2	57	2
Presichi, Christian, Mex.	.912	13	33	29	6	68	3
Ramirez, Alexander, Gia.	1.000	3	0	1	0	1	0
Ramirez, Wagner, Cubs	.857	2	1	5	1	7	1
Reyes, Henry, Gia.	.852	24	16	59	13	88	7
Romero, Flavio, Mex.	.916	39	77	76	14	167	18
Romero, Nicholas, Pad.	.902	28	49	70	13	132	12
Saba, Cesar, Gia.	1.000	1	1	6	0	7	0
Storey, Eric, Rock.	.818	3	1	8	2	11	2
Thornton-Murray, Jandin, Cubs	1.000	9	10	17	0	27	3
Toledo, Eduardo, Mar.	.937	36	57	91	10	158	28

Continuation (top right):

Player, Team	Pct.	G	PO	A	E	TC	DP
Vizcaino, Maximo, Dia.	1.000	2	7	6	0	13	2
Walkill, Juance, Rock.	.905	28	40	65	11	116	13
White, Walt, Dia.	1.000	2	5	2	0	7	0

Player, Team	Pct.	G	PO	A	E	TC	DP
Virgen, Constancio, Mex.	.000	1	0	0	0	0	0
VIZCAINO, Maximo, Dia.	.941	53	81	144	14	239	22
White, Walt, Dia.	.667	1	2	0	1	3	0

TRIPLE PLAY: N. Romero.

OUTFIELDERS

Player, Team	Pct.	G	PO	A	E	TC	DP
Abate, Mike, Mar.	1.000	6	10	0	0	10	0
Allegra, Matthew, Ath.	.976	39	79	4	2	85	1
Anderson, Syketo, Cubs	.978	24	41	3	1	45	2
Avila, Carlos, Mex.	.973	50	107	2	3	112	0
Banks, Gary, Cubs	.939	15	31	0	2	33	0
Bird, T.J., Rock.*	.968	45	58	2	2	62	0
Bojorquez, Jose, Mex.	.956	43	75	12	4	91	0
Borchard, Joe, W.S.	1.000	1	2	0	0	2	0
Brown, Larry, Mar.*	.929	18	22	4	2	28	0
Cabrera, Alex, Dia.	1.000	1	1	0	0	1	0
Cabrera, Leonel, Dia.	1.000	9	25	0	0	25	0
Cameron, Antoine, Cubs*	.972	43	68	2	2	72	1
Canales, Joel, Mex.	.962	21	23	2	1	26	0
Carrera, Franklin, Pad.	.842	13	13	3	3	19	0
Castro, Juan, Cubs	1.000	17	30	1	0	31	0
Cavin, Jonathan, W.S.	.950	39	53	4	3	60	0
Chiarini, Mario, Mar.	.000	2	0	0	0	0	0
Chilsom, Marques, Dia.	.989	53	85	4	1	90	0
Chilsom, Tawan, Dia.	1.000	8	1	0	0	1	0
Ciraco, Darren, W.S.	1.000	8	12	1	0	13	0
Coats, Buck, Cubs	1.000	13	14	4	0	18	0
Conyer, Darryl, Dia.*	1.000	2	3	0	0	3	0
Daniels, Claiborne, Pad.	.897	29	51	1	6	58	0
Davis, Ryan, Gia.*	.980	32	50	0	1	51	0
Dean, Mike, Gia.	1.000	8	3	0	0	3	0
Dellucci, David, Dia.*	.000	1	0	0	0	0	0
Elguezabal, Octavio, Mex.*	1.000	1	1	0	0	1	0
Encarnacion, Julio, W.S.	.918	43	66	1	6	73	0
Esqueda, Jonathan, Mex.	1.000	10	18	0	0	18	0
Esterlin, Ivan, Cubs*	.936	24	38	6	3	47	1
Figueroa, Eduardo, Mar.	.929	46	69	10	6	85	0
Floyd, Daniel, Mar.	.974	38	34	3	1	38	0
Frazier, Carlos, Gia.	.954	34	58	4	3	65	1
Gann, Jamie, Dia.	1.000	6	13	1	0	14	0
Gearlds, Aaron, Rock.	.899	37	69	2	8	79	0
Giorgis, David, Pad.	.962	48	73	2	3	78	0
Gustafson, Troy, Gia.	.948	47	87	5	5	97	2
Hoffpauir, Josh, Ath.	1.000	5	8	0	0	8	0
Ivy, Bjorn, W.S.	.949	36	71	4	4	79	0
Jones, Jared, Mar.	1.000	2	1	1	0	2	0
Koreger, Joshua, Dia.*	.905	54	80	6	9	95	0
Martinez, Greg, Ath.	1.000	5	11	1	0	12	1
Martinez, Orlando, Mex.	.750	4	3	0	1	4	0
Matos, Cesar, Ath.	.600	4	3	0	2	5	0
Mora, Ruben, Pad.	1.000	29	46	1	0	47	0
Nunez, Argelis, Dia.	.962	18	24	1	1	26	0
O'Donnell, Ryan, Pad.	.942	37	76	5	5	86	0
Olson, David, Pad.	.941	8	16	0	1	17	0
Perez, Radhame, Ath.	.979	37	40	6	1	47	0
Pilkington, Ross, Rock.	.951	24	39	0	2	41	0
Pinango, Ever, Gia.	1.000	19	24	0	0	24	0
Pines, Gregory, Mar.	.926	25	24	1	2	27	0
Quintero, Humberto, W.S.	.000	1	0	0	0	0	0
Rafael, Alberto, W.S.	.897	38	64	6	8	78	1
Ramirez, Wagner, Cubs	.500	1	1	0	1	2	0
Reynoso, Paulino, W.S.*	.947	10	18	0	1	19	0
Roenicke, Jarett, Pad.*	.923	23	23	1	2	26	1
Rosa, Ivan, Ath.*	.941	34	43	5	3	51	1
Rosa, Wally, W.S.	.000	1	0	0	0	0	0
Rosario, Vicente, Mar.	.942	34	49	0	3	52	0
Sadler, Raymond, Cubs	.988	40	76	3	1	80	0
Sanchez, Braulio, Dia.*	.867	12	13	0	2	15	0
Sandoval, Jhensy, Dia.	1.000	3	3	1	0	4	0
Santana, Jorge, Cubs	.800	6	8	0	2	10	0
Santos, Sneideer, Dia.	.979	24	40	7	1	48	3
Serrano, Eddie, Pad.	.000	1	0	0	0	0	0
Spidale, Mike, W.S.	1.000	6	7	1	0	8	0
Storey, Eric, Rock.	1.000	5	10	2	0	12	0
TESTA, Chris, Rock.*	.991	44	103	6	1	110	2
Tress, Jose, Mex.	.962	28	49	2	2	53	0
Tritle, Chris, Ath.	.947	43	68	3	4	75	1
Trumble, Dan, Gia.	.985	37	60	5	1	66	0
Valdez, Tommy, Ath.	.938	15	14	1	1	16	0
Vasquez, Jose, Rock.*	.929	12	13	0	1	14	0
Virgen, Constancio, Mex.	1.000	4	1	0	0	1	0
Warrior, Joseph, Mar.	1.000	7	3	0	0	3	0

CATCHERS

Player, Team	Pct.	G	PO	A	E	TC	DP	PB
Alvarado, Damien, Mar.	.981	7	41	11	1	53	0	0
Anderson, Syketo, Cubs	.000	1	0	0	0	0	0	0
Bullard, Kevin, Dia.	.800	2	4	0	1	5	0	1
Cadena, Alejandro, Mar.	.975	18	140	13	4	157	0	3
Cerda, Jose, Gia.	1.000	5	24	4	0	28	1	0
Colina, Alvin, Rock.	.984	28	162	26	3	191	3	5
Dean, Mike, Gia.	.971	11	32	1	1	34	0	1
Delgado, Jorge, Dia.	1.000	1	9	0	0	9	0	0
D'JESUS, Francisco, Gia.	.991	37	182	33	2	217	2	7
Esqueda, Jonathan, Mex.	.982	12	99	8	2	109	0	4
Essery, Frederick, Rock.	.983	18	55	4	1	60	0	3
Falcon, Omar, Pad.	.981	34	234	27	5	266	1	21
Golden, Bryan, Cubs	.949	10	68	7	4	79	1	4
Goldfield, Josh, Dia.	.968	5	25	5	1	31	0	0
Gomez, Andre, Pad.	.960	18	103	17	5	125	1	5
Gonzalez, Carlos, Mar.	1.000	9	35	4	0	39	0	1
Gonzalez, Jose, Gia.	1.000	2	5	0	0	5	0	0
Laird, Gerald, Ath.	1.000	9	43	12	0	55	1	2
Madera, Sandy, Ath.	.942	17	120	10	8	138	0	3
Mapes, Jake, Gia.	1.000	9	42	3	0	45	0	0
Martinez, Orlando, Mex.	.929	15	94	10	8	112	0	0
Matos, Cesar, Ath.	.980	17	89	10	2	101	1	3
McKnight, Lukas, Cubs	.993	21	127	14	1	142	1	3
Mejia, Anderson, Cubs	.943	27	132	18	9	159	0	4
Melton, John, Dia.	.914	12	71	14	8	93	0	3
Molina, Gustavo, W.S.	.959	27	208	23	10	241	3	12
Montilla, Samuel, Dia.	.984	42	230	23	4	257	1	11
Oliveros, Luis, Mar.	.973	26	199	17	6	222	0	7
Ortega, Sixto, Rock.	1.000	20	115	12	0	127	0	6
Perez-Bermudez, Jose, Pad.	1.000	14	39	9	0	48	0	0
Pina, Enmanuel, Cubs	.983	9	54	4	1	59	0	1
Pines, Gregory, Mar.	.966	6	53	4	2	59	0	3
Quintero, Humberto, W.S.	.976	13	104	20	3	127	1	1
Ramirez, Alexander, Gia.	1.000	2	5	1	0	6	0	0
Ramirez, Domingo, Gia.	.975	15	67	11	2	80	0	4
Ramsey, Brad, Cubs	1.000	4	31	3	0	34	0	0
Rosa, Wally, W.S.	.962	16	106	22	5	133	3	3
Sherlock, Jon, Dia.	.970	19	58	7	2	67	0	3
Stone, Jon, Pad.	.943	6	26	7	2	35	0	1
Suomi, Richard, Ath.	.983	21	104	9	2	115	2	2
Tejada, Michael, Rock.	1.000	1	5	0	0	5	0	0
Virgen, Constancio, Mex.	.967	26	182	25	7	214	0	5

PITCHERS

Player, Team	Pct.	G	PO	A	E	TC	DP
Abreu, Jonathan, Gia.*	.500	8	1	0	1	2	0
Adames, Martin, Gia.	1.000	10	1	3	0	4	0
Adkins, Jon, Ath.	1.000	4	1	0	0	1	0
Aguilar, Mario, Mex.*	1.000	5	0	4	0	4	0
Alvarez, Junior, Mex.	.583	13	1	6	5	12	1
Amancio, Jose, Ath.	.625	14	2	3	3	8	0
Arellano, Salvador, Pad.	1.000	14	3	5	0	8	0
Askew, William, Pad.*	.000	14	0	0	1	1	0
Atencio, Donald, Ath.	.875	11	2	5	1	8	1
Barber, Scott, Gia.	.000	2	0	0	0	0	0
Bastardo, Jose, Gia.*	1.000	6	1	1	0	2	0
Batista, Javier, Mar.	.923	12	4	8	1	13	1
Berryman, Brian, Pad.	.800	9	2	2	1	5	1
Bierbrodt, Nick, Dia.*	.000	4	0	0	0	0	0
Bingler, Travis, W.S.*	.833	19	1	4	1	6	0
Blanco, Tommy, Pad.	.800	13	1	3	1	5	0
Blood, Darin, Gia.	.000	2	0	0	0	0	0
Brohawn, Troy, Dia.*	.667	3	0	2	1	3	0
Bruney, Brian, Dia.	.333	20	1	1	4	6	0
Buret, Jorge, Rock.	.889	14	2	6	1	9	1
Burnau, Ryan, Cubs	.800	10	2	2	1	5	1
Calandriello, Donato, Ath.*	.000	2	0	0	0	0	0
Chavarria, Hector, Mex.	.800	11	2	6	2	10	1
Christensen, Deryck, Rock.	.800	17	2	2	1	5	1
Clark, Jeffrey, Gia.	.846	11	4	7	2	13	0
Collado, Jerry, Rock.	.750	16	0	3	1	4	0
Corbin, John, Cubs	.500	17	1	2	3	6	0
Crespo, Jorge, Mex.	.917	11	8	14	2	24	0
Cyr, Eric, Pad.*	.000	2	0	0	0	0	0
Davies, Michael, Rock.*	.933	15	5	9	1	15	0
Davis, Mikael, Dia.	.750	17	0	3	1	4	0
De Jesus, Hanki, Dia.	.857	20	1	5	1	7	0
Delgadillo, Julian, Mex.	1.000	14	1	5	0	6	0
DePaula, Freddy, Ath.*	1.000	5	0	3	0	3	0
DIAZ, Alex, Ath.	1.000	13	4	18	0	22	1
Diaz, Eddy, Cubs	1.000	5	0	2	0	2	0

Player, Team	Pct.	G	PO	A	E	TC	DP	Player, Team	Pct.	G	PO	A	E	TC	DP
Diaz, Felix, Gia.	.846	11	6	5	2	13	0	Negron, Alex, Cubs	1.000	9	0	3	0	3	0
Diaz, Franklin, Ath.	.000	1	0	0	0	0	0	Olivero, Pedro, Cubs	.500	7	0	1	1	2	0
Dominguez, Carlos, Mex.*	.625	13	0	5	3	8	0	Patten, Scott, W.S.	.769	14	5	5	3	13	0
Drain, Bradley, Mar.	.800	4	2	2	1	5	0	Perez, Amauris, Gia.	1.000	10	2	2	0	4	0
Dulkowski, Marc, Pad.	.000	4	0	0	0	0	0	Perez, Armando, W.S.*	.923	15	3	9	1	13	0
Dunphy, Micah, Ath.*	1.000	7	0	2	0	2	1	Perez, Beltran, Pad.	.778	11	0	7	2	9	0
Earley, Andrew, Cubs	.875	12	5	2	1	8	0	Perez, Henry, Pad.	.571	13	1	3	3	7	0
Elguezabal, Octavio, Mex.*	1.000	3	0	1	0	1	1	Perkins, Gregory, Dia.	.000	2	0	0	0	0	0
Encarnacion, Luis, Mar.	.333	13	2	0	4	6	0	Pignatiello, Carmen, Cubs*	1.000	9	4	5	0	9	0
Featherstone, Deron, Gia.	.000	1	0	0	0	0	0	Pillier, Santo, Ath.	.333	17	0	1	2	3	0
Ferrand, Julian, Rock.	1.000	16	0	1	0	1	0	Pimentel, Gregorio, Gia.	1.000	9	1	4	0	5	0
Flanagan, Jeremy, Cubs	1.000	9	1	1	0	2	0	Pinto, Renyel, Cubs*	.923	9	1	11	1	13	0
Gentile, Mark, W.S.*	1.000	3	0	1	0	1	0	Pulsipher, Bill, Dia.*	.500	3	0	1	1	2	0
Germano, Justin, Pad.	.938	17	4	11	1	16	0	Ramirez, Hector, Gia.	.800	16	2	2	1	5	0
Glascock, John-paul, Cubs	.636	15	2	5	4	11	0	Ramirez, Joslin, Dia.	.538	15	2	5	6	13	0
Gonzalez, Cristian, Ath.	.950	14	5	14	1	20	2	Revenig, Todd, Dia.	.000	2	0	0	0	0	0
Gonzalez, Enrique, Dia.	.750	11	0	3	1	4	0	Reyes, Junior, Cubs	.900	13	2	7	1	10	1
Gonzalez, Jeremi, Cubs	1.000	4	3	0	0	3	0	Rivera, Jimmy, Mar.	1.000	7	0	2	0	2	0
Gonzalez, Miguel, Rock.	1.000	15	4	1	0	5	1	Rodriguez, Orlando, W.S.*	1.000	16	0	6	0	6	0
Granados, Bernie, Rock.	1.000	12	2	1	0	3	0	Rojas, Ramon, Gia.	1.000	18	2	7	0	9	1
Haase, Frank, Rock.*	.800	14	1	3	1	5	0	Romero, Garvis, Rock.	.000	20	0	0	0	0	0
Hammons, Matt, Cubs	.000	1	0	0	0	0	0	Romo, Noe, Mex.*	.000	7	0	0	0	0	0
Hannaman, Ryan, Gia.*	1.000	5	1	0	0	1	0	Rosario, Dionis, W.S.*	1.000	2	1	0	0	1	0
Harvey, Victor, W.S.	1.000	16	2	1	0	3	0	Rosario, Hipolito, Pad.	1.000	19	0	7	0	7	0
Hernandez, Juan, W.S.	.895	13	3	14	2	19	0	Rossellini, William, Dia.	.000	4	0	0	0	0	0
Hoane, Wes, Mar.	1.000	16	1	8	0	9	1	Ruelas, Heriberto, Mex.*	1.000	6	1	3	0	4	0
Hoffman, Matt, Rock.	1.000	4	0	1	0	1	0	Sandoval,, Mex.	1.000	7	1	1	0	2	0
Hoffpauir, Josh, Ath.	.000	1	0	0	0	0	0	Schultz, Michael, Dia.	.000	2	0	0	0	0	0
Hollifield, Alec, W.S.	.897	8	8	18	3	29	2	Scott, John, Pad.	1.000	15	2	3	0	5	0
Huber, Jon, Pad.	.750	14	3	6	3	12	0	Serrano, Alex, Rock.	.000	7	0	0	0	0	0
Huerta, Edgar, Mex.*	.875	9	1	6	1	8	0	Simpson, Joe, Rock.	1.000	11	1	0	0	1	0
Jacob, Russell, Dia.	1.000	3	0	1	0	1	0	Slaten, Douglas, Dia.*	1.000	9	0	4	0	4	0
Johnston, Sean, Cubs*	1.000	1	0	2	0	2	0	Smith, Joseph, Mar.	1.000	12	5	10	0	15	0
Johnstone, John, Gia.	.000	1	0	0	0	0	0	Smith, Justin, Mar.*	1.000	3	1	1	0	2	0
Jones, Alvin, W.S.	.571	14	3	1	3	7	0	Snider, John, Ath.	.875	9	2	5	1	8	0
Jones, Geoffrey, Pad.*	1.000	20	0	7	0	7	0	Sobchuk, Justin, Ath.	.909	14	3	7	1	11	0
Kesten, Michael, Mar.*	1.000	16	0	2	0	2	0	Soto, Darwin, Pad.	.889	17	3	5	1	9	0
Ketchner, Ryan, Mar.*	1.000	9	2	4	0	6	1	Stockman, Phil, Dia.	1.000	14	1	0	0	1	0
Kinnie, Gary, Mar.	.818	12	5	13	4	22	0	Stottlemyre, Todd, Dia.	1.000	2	0	4	0	4	0
Laureano, Edgardo, Pad.	.667	12	1	1	1	3	0	Szuminski, Jason, Cubs	1.000	10	1	8	0	9	0
Lavery, Tim, Cubs*	.000	5	0	0	0	0	0	Thomson, John, Rock.	1.000	3	0	1	0	1	0
Lawton, Charles, Pad.	1.000	12	1	4	0	5	0	Trosper, Tanner, Ath.	.750	17	0	3	1	4	0
Lee, Jonathan, Dia.	.750	9	1	2	1	4	0	Urrutia, Carlos, Cubs	.000	7	0	0	0	0	0
Leon, Brigmer, Ath.	.800	12	2	2	1	5	0	Van Dusen, Derrick, Mar.*	1.000	10	2	2	0	4	1
Lewis, Peyton, Cubs	1.000	5	0	2	0	2	0	Vazquez, William, Rock.	1.000	14	5	4	0	9	0
Lopez, Arturo, Mar.	1.000	10	4	0	0	4	0	Velazquez, Elih, Ath.*	.917	15	3	8	1	12	0
Madril, Steve, W.S.*	.750	24	3	3	2	8	1	Villacis, Eduardo, Rock.	.900	13	3	6	1	10	1
Mapes, Jake, Gia.	1.000	8	1	2	0	3	0	Villarreal, Oscar, Dia.	.000	1	0	0	0	0	0
Marquez, Jose, Dia.	.917	13	3	8	1	12	0	Villatoro, Wilmer, Pad.	.000	2	0	0	0	0	0
Marte, Damaso, Mar.*	1.000	2	0	1	0	1	0	Walk, Mitch, Gia.*	1.000	12	5	15	0	20	0
Martinez, Gustavo, Mar.	.889	16	3	5	1	9	0	Ward, Jeremy, Dia.	1.000	2	1	0	0	1	0
Martinez, Javier, Pad.	1.000	3	0	1	0	1	0	Webb, Brandon, Dia.	.000	1	0	0	0	0	0
Matos, Jesus, Rock.	.917	15	3	8	1	12	0	Westfall, Allan, Mar.	1.000	1	1	0	0	1	0
Matos, Raymond, Gia.*	.571	10	1	3	3	7	0	White, Bill, Dia.*	1.000	4	1	0	0	1	0
Maurer, Mike, Ath.	1.000	11	1	3	0	4	0	Whiteaker, Gregg, Gia.	1.000	12	3	5	0	8	0
McCall, Derell, Ath.	.857	13	3	3	1	7	0	Wiles, Chad, Mar.	1.000	17	2	1	0	3	0
McKinley, Ryan, Cubs	.667	15	1	3	2	6	0	Wiley, Skip, Mar.	1.000	7	3	2	0	5	0
Medina, Franklin, Dia.	.643	14	1	8	5	14	0	Willis, Dontrelle, Cubs*	.909	9	2	8	1	11	0
Merricks, Charles, Rock.*	.810	13	5	12	4	21	0	Wood, Brandon, Gia.	.000	5	0	0	0	0	0
Meyer, Jake, Mar.	.000	3	0	0	0	0	0	Yoshida, Nobuaki, Pad.*	1.000	7	1	3	0	4	0
Montgomery, Greg, W.S.	.000	2	0	0	0	0	0	Zaug, Kevin, W.S.	.500	22	1	3	4	8	0
Montoya, Saul, Dia.	1.000	3	1	4	0	5	0	Zimmerman, Jordan, Mar.*	1.000	10	3	4	0	7	0
Mora, Sergio, Mex.	.923	10	2	10	1	13	1	Zorrilla, Reinaldo, W.S.	.800	20	1	3	1	5	1
Morgan, Russ, Mar.*	.833	12	3	2	1	6	0								
Nacar, Yimmy, Gia.	.750	12	0	3	1	4	0								
Nageotte, Clint, Mar.	.923	12	6	6	1	13	0								

The following players appeared only as designated hitter, pinch-hitter or pinch runner: Essian, ph; J. Williams, dh.

LEAGUE CHAMPIONS

Year	Team	Pct.	Year	Team	Pct.	Year	Team	Pct.
1988—	Peoria Brewers	.690	1993—	Scottsdale A's	.636	1998—	Rockies	.750
1989—	Peoria Brewers	.732	1994—	Chandler Cardinals	.607	1999—	Athletics	.696
1990—	Peoria Brewers	.679	1995—	Scottsdale A's	.661	2000—	Mariners	.709
1991—	Scottsdale A's	.650	1996—	Padres	.643			
1992—	Scottsdale A's	.607	1997—	Cubs	.618			

GULF COAST LEAGUE

LEAGUE OFFICE

President
Tom Saffell
Address
1503 Clower Creek Dr., H-262
Sarasota, FL 34231
Phone
941-966-6407

Teams*
Braves
Dodgers
Expos
Marlins
Orioles
Phillies
Pirates
Rangers
Reds
Red Sox

Royals
Tigers
Twins
Yankees

*Teams play their games in Bradenton,
Clearwater, Fort Myers, Haines City,
Jupiter, Lakeland, Melbourne,
Orlando, Port Charlotte, Sarasota,
Tampa and Vero Beach.

2000 FINAL STANDINGS

EASTERN DIVISION

Team	W	L	T	Pct.	GB
Marlins	40	20	0	.667	...
Tigers	34	26	0	.567	6.0
Braves	26	34	0	.433	14.0
Royals	20	40	0	.333	20.0

NORTHERN DIVISION

Team	W	L	T	Pct.	GB
Yankees	38	22	0	.633	...
Pirates	34	26	0	.567	4.0
Phillies	31	29	0	.517	7.0
Expos	17	43	0	.283	21.0

WESTERN DIVISION

Team	W	L	T	Pct.	GB
Rangers	38	18	0	.679	...
Twins	33	23	0	.589	5.0
Red Sox	29	26	0	.527	8.5
Orioles	25	31	0	.446	13.0
Reds	14	41	0	.255	23.5

COMPOSITE

Team	Rang.	Mar.	Yank.	Twins	Tig.	Pir.	R.S.	Phi.	Ori.	Brav.	Roy.	Exp.	Reds	W	L	T	Pct.	GB
Rangers	...	0	0	6	0	0	10	0	10	0	0	0	12	38	18	0	.679	...
Marlins	0	...	0	0	13	0	0	0	0	13	14	0	0	40	20	0	.667	...
Yankees	0	0	...	0	0	11	0	13	0	0	0	14	0	38	22	0	.633	2.0
Twins	8	0	0	...	0	0	7	0	7	0	0	0	11	33	23	0	.589	5.0
Tigers	0	7	0	0	...	0	0	0	0	11	16	0	0	34	26	0	.567	6.0
Pirates	0	0	9	0	0	...	0	9	0	0	0	16	0	34	26	0	.567	6.0
Red Sox	4	0	0	7	0	0	...	0	6	0	0	0	12	29	26	0	.527	8.5
Phillies	0	0	7	0	0	11	0	...	0	0	0	13	0	31	29	0	.517	9.0
Orioles	4	0	0	7	0	0	8	0	...	0	0	0	6	25	31	0	.446	13.0
Braves	0	7	0	0	9	0	0	0	0	...	10	0	0	26	34	0	.433	14.0
Royals	0	6	0	0	4	0	0	0	0	10	...	0	0	20	40	0	.333	20.0
Expos	0	0	6	0	0	4	0	7	0	0	0	...	0	17	43	0	.283	23.0
Reds	2	0	0	3	0	0	1	0	8	0	0	0	...	14	41	0	.255	23.5

Games played in Bradenton, Dunedin, Fort Myers, Melbourne, Osceola, Port Charlotte, St. Lucie County, Sarasota, Tampa and West Palm Beach, Fla.

FORFEIT: Orioles forfeited to Rangers, August 21 (Rangers won 9-0).

Club names are major league affiliations.

PLAYOFFS: Yankees defeated Marlins one game to none; Rangers defeated Yankees two games to one to win league championship.

REGULAR-SEASON ATTENDANCE: No total official attendance figures reported.

MANAGERS: Braves, Rick Albert; Expos, Steve Phillips; Marlins, Kevin Boles; Orioles, Jesus Alfaro; Phillies, Ramon Aviles; Pirates, Woody Huyke; Rangers, Darryl Kennedy; Red Sox, John Sanders; Reds, Luis Quinones; Royals, Ron Karkovice (Through July 31), Andre David (August 1 through end of season); Tigers, Kevin Bradshaw; Twins, Al Newman; Yankees, Derek Shelton.

ALL-STAR TEAM: 1B—Justin Morneau, Twins; 2B—Hector De Los Santos, Red Sox; 3B—Tony Blanco, Red Sox; SS—Deivi Mendez, Yankees; OF—Humberto Aliendo, Pirates; Yhency Brazoban, Yankees; William Smith, Marlins; C—Bryan Barnowski, Red Sox; Starting pitcher—Yoel Hernandez, Phillies; Relief pitcher—Reggie Laplante, Yankees; Manager of the Year—Darryl Kennedy, Rangers.

2000 BATTING

TEAM

Team	Avg.	G	TPA	AB	R	H	TB	2B	3B	HR	RBI	SH	SF	HP	BB	IBB	SO	SB	CS	GDP	LOB	ShO	Slg.	OBP
Red Sox	.276	55	2087	1832	297	505	752	84	8	49	252	1	15	41	198	7	371	90	27	45	408	0	.410	.357
Twins	.276	56	2181	1796	345	495	654	91	10	16	273	29	19	40	297	13	320	77	32	46	439	3	.364	.387
Yankees	.265	60	2246	1925	311	510	768	115	19	35	278	7	28	44	242	1	399	43	18	34	476	2	.399	.356
Marlins	.265	60	2306	1987	316	526	739	114	18	21	262	4	21	40	254	6	502	55	17	44	471	2	.372	.356
Orioles	.262	56	2114	1810	266	474	653	77	18	22	214	33	23	41	207	11	392	92	34	39	404	4	.361	.347
Rangers	.260	56	2230	1856	318	483	662	100	11	19	266	29	20	45	280	14	370	51	23	28	467	0	.357	.367
Phillies	.257	60	2196	1953	269	502	697	93	12	26	229	20	17	43	163	2	353	72	26	43	421	4	.357	.325
Pirates	.253	60	2198	1951	295	494	719	104	17	29	250	11	16	36	184	1	428	83	25	33	409	1	.369	.326
Expos	.236	60	2186	1961	210	462	590	60	16	12	170	18	9	42	156	0	420	37	22	45	420	10	.301	.304
Tigers	.233	60	2168	1852	265	432	583	58	15	21	213	10	19	43	244	3	529	90	25	29	452	5	.315	.333

Team	Avg.	G	TPA	AB	R	H	TB	2B	3B	HR	RBI	SH	SF	HP	BB	IBB	SO	SB	CS	GDP	LOB	ShO	Slg.	OBP
Braves	.226	60	2153	1890	251	428	592	85	11	19	204	5	13	47	198	2	458	36	25	21	417	9	.313	.313
Reds	.223	55	1982	1736	188	387	504	67	16	6	156	15	5	25	201	8	470	59	43	29	379	6	.290	.312
Royals	.210	60	2080	1778	195	374	468	47	10	9	158	27	14	34	227	6	365	50	23	43	421	8	.263	.309

INDIVIDUAL

TOP QUALIFIERS FOR BATTING CHAMPIONSHIP

Minimum 162 plate appearances. *Lefthanded batter. †Switch-hitter.

Player, Team	Avg.	G	TPA	AB	R	H	TB	2B	3B	HR	RBI	SH	SF	HP	BB	IBB	SO	SB	CS	GDP	Slg.	OBP
Morneau, Justin, Twi.*	.402	52	226	194	47	78	129	21	0	10	58	0	2	0	30	7	18	3	1	5	.665	.478
Blanco, Tony, R.S.	.384	52	215	190	32	73	127	13	1	13	50	0	3	4	18	2	38	6	4	3	.668	.442
Smith, William, Mar.*	.368	54	233	204	37	75	106	21	2	2	34	0	1	1	26	1	24	7	3	3	.520	.440
Griggs, Reginald, Phi.*	.340	57	230	206	35	70	110	18	2	6	42	2	2	3	17	1	38	0	1	8	.534	.395
Tomlin, James, Twi.	.338	42	168	145	24	49	61	12	0	0	18	1	3	4	15	0	11	12	3	2	.421	.407
Botts, Jason, Rang.†	.319	48	200	163	36	52	82	12	0	6	34	0	1	10	26	4	29	4	1	5	.503	.440
Turner, Jason, Yan.*	.314	58	242	207	35	65	96	9	2	6	42	0	3	4	28	0	34	2	2	3	.464	.401
Encarnacion, Edwin, Rang.	.311	51	205	177	31	55	67	6	3	0	36	3	3	1	21	1	27	3	1	7	.379	.381
Campos, Julio, Phi.	.310	54	224	203	37	63	79	9	2	1	16	7	3	0	11	0	17	22	3	3	.389	.341
Seiber, Antron, R.S.	.306	49	221	196	36	60	81	7	1	4	21	0	2	7	16	0	31	21	5	4	.413	.376
Johnson, Nelson, Ori.	.306	48	205	180	22	55	72	5	3	2	33	2	6	4	13	0	38	7	5	2	.400	.355
Brazoban, Yhency, Yan.	.303	54	218	201	36	61	98	14	4	5	28	0	2	4	11	0	28	2	3	7	.488	.349
Camacho, Juan, Yan.†	.302	46	185	162	21	49	75	10	2	4	27	1	1	2	19	1	24	1	0	5	.463	.380
Barnowski, Bryan, R.S.	.301	50	194	166	40	50	98	9	0	13	33	0	1	4	23	0	46	1	0	2	.590	.397
Mendez, Deivi, Yan.	.300	56	244	210	37	63	91	20	1	2	25	3	2	3	26	0	39	4	0	4	.433	.382

DEPARTMENTAL LEADERS: G—Turner, 58; AB—M. Cabrera, 219; R—Morneau, 47; H—Morneau, 78; TB—Morneau, 129; 2B—Morneau, W. Smith, 21 each; 3B—Morban, 8; HR—Blanco, Barnowski, 13; RBI—Morneau, 58; SH—Merchan, 8; SF—Bocaranda, N. Johnson, 6 each; HP—Botts, 10; BB—Tamburrino, 49; IBB—Morneau, 7; SO—Acevedo, 71; SB—Chourio, Francia, 23 each; CS—Solano, 8; GIDP—Griggs, 8; Slg.—Blanco, .668; OBP—Morneau, .478.

ALL PLAYERS

*Lefthanded batter. †Switch-hitter.

Player, Team	Avg.	G	TPA	AB	R	H	TB	2B	3B	HR	RBI	SH	SF	HP	BB	IBB	SO	SB	CS	GDP	Slg.	OBP
Abad, Juan, Exp.	.149	29	107	101	9	15	16	1	0	0	4	0	0	2	3	0	32	1	0	4	.158	.189
Abreu, Cesar, Reds	.128	13	45	39	4	5	6	1	0	0	2	0	0	1	5	0	11	0	1	1	.154	.244
Abreu, Nielsen, Phi.	.242	24	72	66	6	16	18	2	0	0	4	2	0	1	3	0	7	5	2	5	.273	.286
Acevedo, Juan, Reds†	.180	49	195	172	23	31	46	5	2	2	13	0	0	3	20	1	71	8	6	2	.267	.277
Acosta, Johe, Pir.	.159	31	117	107	7	17	18	1	0	0	8	1	1	1	7	0	28	1	0	1	.168	.216
Agar, Cory, Twi.	.299	48	191	157	27	47	70	17	0	2	30	0	2	3	29	1	20	0	3	7	.446	.414
Alexander, Lawrence, Phi.	.238	53	222	193	28	46	57	5	0	2	12	1	1	1	26	0	32	15	5	4	.295	.330
Aliendo, Humberto, Pir.	.271	54	222	203	33	55	90	15	1	6	38	0	1	1	17	0	41	6	3	8	.443	.329
Alley, Charles, Ori.	.333	6	21	15	3	5	7	2	0	0	3	0	1	1	4	1	4	0	1	0	.467	.476
Almeida, Brian, Brav.*	.000	11	0	0	0	0	0	0	0	0	0	0	0	0	0	0	0	2	0	0	.000	.000
Alvarez, Aaron, Mar.	.258	31	116	97	15	25	37	5	2	1	9	2	0	4	13	0	25	2	0	2	.381	.368
Ambrosini, Dominick, Exp.*	.302	27	98	86	10	26	33	3	2	0	9	0	1	0	9	0	16	1	0	6	.384	.365
Anderson, Melvin, Phi.	.183	36	136	120	7	22	34	6	0	2	16	1	1	2	12	0	25	0	2	5	.283	.267
Anderson, Nat, Tig.*	.196	30	116	92	5	18	18	0	0	0	8	0	1	4	19	0	28	0	1	2	.196	.353
Arko, Thomas, Ori.	.205	37	153	127	12	26	39	6	2	1	11	2	4	2	18	0	42	0	0	6	.307	.305
Asadoorian, Rick, R.S.	.264	54	232	197	43	52	82	9	3	5	31	0	3	6	26	1	56	22	2	2	.416	.362
Ayala, Odannys, Roy.	.267	37	136	101	20	27	35	2	3	0	9	1	2	5	27	0	20	4	1	2	.347	.437
Baker, Casey, Yan.	.156	33	80	64	9	10	13	3	0	0	5	1	1	6	8	0	20	4	1	0	.203	.304
Barnowski, Bryan, R.S.	.301	50	194	166	40	50	98	9	0	13	33	0	1	4	23	0	46	1	0	2	.590	.397
Bartee, Khareta, Roy.	.221	45	156	140	10	31	36	5	0	0	7	2	0	4	10	0	33	9	1	2	.257	.292
Bass, Christopher, Pir.	.294	47	193	163	32	48	71	11	3	2	26	0	0	7	23	0	28	10	0	0	.436	.404
Bautista, Augusto, Reds	.200	21	70	65	8	13	17	4	0	0	2	0	0	2	3	0	21	0	0	0	.262	.257
Beltran, Carlos, Roy.†	.500	1	5	4	3	2	6	1	0	0	1	0	0	1	0	0	0	0	0	0	1.500	.600
Bera, Roberto, Ori.	.233	43	167	159	18	37	51	9	1	1	21	2	1	3	2	1	27	3	1	5	.321	.255
Bergolla, William, Reds	.182	8	26	22	2	4	4	0	0	0	0	0	0	0	4	0	2	3	1	0	.182	.308
Bernard, Miguel, Brav.	.241	42	149	137	20	33	41	5	0	1	10	0	0	3	9	0	18	0	0	5	.299	.302
Bessa, Laumin, Brav.	.293	27	103	92	17	27	40	8	1	1	11	1	0	4	6	0	22	4	0	1	.435	.363
Birkett, Matthew, Tig.†	.175	42	128	114	16	20	21	1	0	0	11	1	0	5	8	0	42	5	2	3	.184	.260
Blanco, Tony, R.S.	.384	52	215	190	32	73	127	13	1	13	50	0	3	4	18	2	38	6	4	3	.668	.442
Bludau, Frank, Reds	.000	10	1	0	1	0	0	0	0	0	0	0	0	0	1	0	0	0	0	0	.000	1.000
Bocaranda, Nestor, Tig.	.248	43	165	149	22	37	50	7	0	2	33	0	6	5	9	0	30	4	2	2	.336	.285
Borges, Luis, Roy.*	.229	43	160	144	12	33	38	3	1	0	14	2	2	0	12	1	11	1	3	4	.264	.285
Borjas, Henry, R.S.†	.311	15	54	45	7	14	19	2	0	1	9	0	1	1	7	0	3	2	0	1	.422	.407
Botts, Jason, Rang.†	.319	48	200	163	36	52	82	12	0	6	34	0	1	10	26	4	29	4	1	5	.503	.440
Bouie, Aaron, Ori.	.000	3	2	1	0	0	0	0	0	0	0	0	0	0	1	0	0	0	0	0	.000	.500
Bourgeois, Jason, Rang.	.239	24	106	88	18	21	25	4	0	0	6	2	0	2	14	0	15	9	2	0	.284	.356
Brazoban, Yhency, Yan.	.303	54	218	201	36	61	98	14	4	5	28	0	2	4	11	0	28	2	3	7	.488	.349
Brewer, Anthony, Mar.	.215	47	212	181	35	39	63	9	3	3	18	0	1	5	25	0	54	13	1	1	.348	.325
Bronowicz, Scott, Brav.*	.000	4	10	8	1	0	0	0	0	0	0	0	0	0	2	0	2	0	0	0	.000	.200
Brown, Matthew, Exp.	.211	43	172	152	14	32	41	3	0	2	14	0	0	0	20	0	46	3	1	1	.270	.302
Bryan, Jason, Rang.	.249	54	237	181	35	45	73	14	1	4	35	0	3	8	45	2	49	3	2	5	.403	.414
Buttler, Victor, Pir.	.133	4	16	15	1	2	2	0	0	0	1	0	0	0	1	0	0	0	1	0	.133	.188
Cabrera, Miguel, Mar.	.260	57	250	219	38	57	77	10	2	2	22	0	2	6	23	0	46	1	0	7	.352	.344
Cabrera, Yoelmis, Pir.	.270	40	162	141	32	38	56	6	3	2	19	0	2	1	18	0	23	12	3	1	.397	.352
Camacho, Juan, Yan.†	.302	46	185	162	21	49	75	10	2	4	27	1	1	2	19	1	24	1	0	5	.463	.380
Camilli, Jason, Exp.	.267	5	20	15	1	4	5	1	0	0	2	1	2	0	3	1	0	0	0	0	.333	.316
Campos, Julio, Phi.	.310	54	224	203	37	63	79	9	2	1	16	7	3	0	11	0	17	22	3	3	.389	.341
Campos, Tiago, Reds	.198	30	108	101	6	20	28	4	2	0	7	0	1	1	5	0	26	10	4	2	.277	.241
Cancio, Antonio, Phi.	.232	18	76	69	8	16	23	2	1	0	8	0	0	2	5	0	19	0	0	3	.333	.303

SUMMER CLASS A *Gulf Coast League*

Player, Team	Avg.	G	TPA	AB	R	H	TB	2B	3B	HR	RBI	SH	SF	HP	BB	IBB	SO	SB	CS	GDP	Slg.	OBP
Candelaria, Tito, Yan.*	.056	7	21	18	0	1	1	0	0	0	1	0	0	0	3	0	4	0	0	0	.056	.190
Caraballo, Carlos, R.S.	.254	34	66	59	10	15	22	2	1	1	2	0	0	3	4	0	18	2	2	0	.373	.333
Caridi, Tony, R.S.†	.077	18	52	39	7	3	3	0	0	0	2	0	1	0	12	0	10	1	0	1	.077	.288
Castro, Bernabel, Yan.†	.441	9	40	34	7	15	21	4	1	0	6	0	0	0	6	0	4	3	1	1	.618	.525
Castro, Javier, Roy.	.229	44	154	140	18	32	36	2	1	0	8	3	0	3	8	0	40	5	2	4	.257	.285
Chapman, Travis, Phi.	.188	9	39	32	3	6	11	3	1	0	5	0	1	2	4	0	4	0	1	0	.344	.308
Chauncey, Clinton, Yan.	.240	11	30	25	1	6	6	0	0	0	5	0	2	0	3	0	6	0	0	0	.240	.300
Chourio, Jorjanis, Pir.	.291	51	210	182	37	53	70	13	2	0	23	2	3	2	21	0	46	23	5	3	.385	.365
Cline, Shawn, Twi.	.000	2	7	7	0	0	0	0	0	0	0	0	0	0	0	0	2	0	0	2	.000	.000
Colameco, Joe, Yan.*	.111	11	34	27	1	3	4	1	0	0	4	1	0	0	6	0	6	1	0	0	.148	.273
Colon, Roberto, Tig.	.237	15	47	38	4	9	14	2	0	1	5	0	1	0	8	0	10	0	0	1	.368	.362
Cooper, Matthew, R.S.	.270	26	94	74	10	20	28	5	0	1	6	0	0	4	16	1	18	0	1	2	.378	.426
Cotto, Luis, Roy.	.180	46	164	133	17	24	26	2	0	0	6	3	1	4	23	0	25	5	1	0	.195	.317
Cruz, Alex, Pir.	.211	45	179	166	20	35	45	5	1	1	12	2	0	3	8	0	26	5	0	2	.271	.260
Cruz, Orlando, Rang.	.167	9	31	24	5	4	7	1	1	0	1	2	0	0	5	0	9	0	0	0	.292	.310
Cuevas, Alvin, Roy.	.115	21	61	52	5	6	8	0	1	0	4	1	0	0	8	0	18	0	0	3	.154	.233
Davis, Daniel, Tig.*	.184	46	169	141	13	26	36	4	0	2	16	0	1	5	22	0	56	4	2	1	.255	.314
De La Cruz, Miguel, R.S.	.245	16	53	49	7	12	16	1	0	1	5	0	0	0	4	0	9	3	1	0	.327	.302
De Los Santos, Hector, R.S.	.295	46	156	149	28	44	58	7	2	1	11	0	0	2	5	0	13	19	2	5	.389	.327
Demarco, Matt, Mar.*	.000	1	4	3	0	0	0	0	0	0	0	0	0	0	1	0	1	0	0	2	.000	.250
Diaz , Jorge, Rang.	.333	3	11	9	1	3	3	0	0	0	0	0	0	1	1	0	2	1	0	0	.333	.455
Dohrman, Bruce, Twi.*	.133	5	19	15	3	2	2	0	0	0	3	0	1	0	3	0	2	0	0	1	.133	.263
Dolton, Odis, Reds	.202	35	126	114	9	23	30	5	1	0	8	1	0	3	8	0	44	4	4	1	.263	.272
Domero, William, Tig.	.299	43	174	154	28	46	71	6	5	3	28	0	1	5	14	1	33	5	2	4	.461	.374
Dorsey, Ryan, Pir.	.242	38	138	120	14	29	54	11	1	4	28	1	3	1	13	0	46	1	1	2	.450	.314
Driggers Jr, Richard, Phi.	.263	36	126	118	14	31	34	3	0	0	8	2	0	1	5	0	26	7	3	1	.288	.298
Duran, Deudis, Phi.†	.281	34	137	121	19	34	47	7	0	2	11	3	0	3	10	0	18	6	2	1	.388	.351
Durand, Jose, Roy.	.152	37	119	99	8	15	20	5	0	0	3	0	1	1	18	1	29	1	1	4	.202	.286
Durham, Robert, Tig.*	.286	3	14	14	1	4	6	2	0	0	0	0	0	0	0	0	4	1	0	0	.429	.286
Eiguren, Chaz, Reds	.500	1	5	2	3	1	1	0	0	0	0	0	0	0	3	0	0	0	0	1	.500	.800
Emmerick, Joshua, Exp.	.223	34	126	112	13	25	25	0	0	0	7	0	0	4	10	0	19	4	2	7	.223	.310
Encarnacion, Edwin, Rang.	.311	51	205	177	31	55	67	6	3	0	36	3	3	1	21	1	27	3	1	7	.379	.381
Encarnacion, Henry, Exp.	.192	24	80	73	8	14	16	0	1	0	2	0	0	0	7	0	12	1	2	1	.219	.263
Escobar, Luis, Roy.*	.116	20	55	43	9	5	7	2	0	0	2	1	0	1	10	0	10	0	0	0	.163	.296
Espino, Damaso, Reds†	.269	48	180	167	15	45	52	5	1	0	19	1	0	1	11	0	27	1	5	3	.311	.318
Evans, Mitch, Yan.	.186	16	50	43	3	8	9	1	0	0	1	0	1	1	5	0	4	0	1	0	.209	.280
Everett, Rob, Twi.	.225	21	46	40	5	9	9	0	0	0	5	2	0	0	4	0	12	0	0	0	.225	.295
Farris, Brant, Roy.	.218	45	164	133	13	29	34	5	0	0	14	5	1	4	21	0	19	0	1	6	.256	.340
Fears, Christopher, Roy.	.208	44	163	144	19	30	32	2	0	0	10	2	1	2	14	0	22	13	4	1	.222	.286
Febles, Carlos, Roy.	.333	1	4	3	0	1	2	1	0	0	0	0	0	0	1	0	0	1	0	0	.667	.500
Fernandez, Alejandro, Yan.	.313	46	156	115	20	36	52	7	0	3	23	0	2	8	30	0	31	2	0	1	.452	.477
Foster, Gregg, Phi.	.281	50	201	178	36	50	67	7	2	2	31	0	4	6	13	0	24	8	0	1	.376	.343
Foster, Quincy, Mar.*	.250	5	18	16	2	4	5	1	0	0	1	0	0	1	1	0	0	0	1	0	.313	.333
Francia, Juan, Tig.†	.268	53	219	194	34	52	63	5	3	0	14	5	0	1	19	0	43	23	4	0	.325	.336
Francisco, Ruben, Ori.*	.205	44	176	151	32	31	45	4	2	2	17	7	2	2	14	0	22	7	2	4	.298	.278
Frazier, Charles, Mar.	.291	48	193	172	23	50	70	10	2	2	23	0	0	2	19	0	46	6	1	2	.407	.368
Freeman, Miguel, Exp.	.246	49	200	183	18	45	76	11	4	4	21	1	0	3	13	0	58	0	1	3	.415	.307
Freeman, Terrence, Tig.†	.333	1	4	3	0	1	2	1	0	0	1	0	0	0	1	0	0	0	0	0	.667	.500
Galarraga, Luis, R.S.	.216	19	47	37	6	8	11	3	0	0	5	0	2	2	6	0	12	2	0	3	.297	.340
Gambino, Michael, R.S.	.214	5	16	14	2	3	3	0	0	0	2	0	0	0	2	0	2	1	1	2	.214	.313
Garcia, Cristian, Mar.	.167	25	82	66	10	11	17	1	1	1	8	0	0	3	13	0	29	1	0	3	.258	.329
Garcia, Juan-Carlos, Mar.†	.233	34	141	116	24	27	41	9	1	1	15	0	2	0	23	1	45	3	2	1	.353	.355
Garcia, Nicolas, Ori.	.250	6	25	24	0	6	6	0	0	0	3	0	0	1	0	0	3	0	1	1	.250	.280
Garcia, Sandy, Yan.	.296	54	209	186	36	55	93	12	4	6	29	0	1	2	20	0	54	5	2	5	.500	.368
Garland, Ross, Tig.	.252	39	148	127	20	32	46	6	1	2	12	0	1	4	16	0	47	0	0	2	.362	.351
Gibbs, Mark, Ori.	.259	44	176	143	23	37	48	8	0	1	12	1	2	7	23	1	33	13	2	1	.336	.383
Gonzalez, Adrian, Mar.*	.295	53	229	193	24	57	69	10	1	0	30	0	2	2	32	3	35	0	0	6	.358	.397
Gonzalez, Jose, Rang.†	.241	33	101	87	13	21	26	3	1	0	7	2	1	0	11	2	27	4	3	0	.299	.323
Gonzalez, Reggie, Yan.*	.211	21	86	71	13	15	23	3	1	1	8	1	2	5	7	0	9	1	1	3	.324	.313
Gray, Jason, Rang.*	.274	52	222	186	31	51	70	10	3	1	32	3	4	6	23	0	31	2	2	1	.376	.365
Gredvig, Doug, Ori.	.444	2	9	9	0	4	4	0	0	0	1	0	0	0	0	0	1	0	0	0	.444	.444
Griffin, Daniel, Exp.	.245	13	51	49	3	12	17	1	2	0	7	0	0	0	2	0	7	0	0	2	.347	.275
Griggs, Reginald, Phi.*	.340	57	230	206	35	70	110	18	2	6	42	2	2	3	17	1	38	0	1	8	.534	.395
Guante, Domingo, Twi.	.302	37	147	129	28	39	47	8	0	0	12	0	1	0	17	0	21	13	4	1	.364	.381
Guerrero, Jorge, Mar.	.232	35	130	112	18	26	38	9	0	1	11	0	3	1	14	0	25	4	1	2	.339	.315
Guilliams, Earl, Brav.	.286	23	65	63	9	18	20	2	0	0	4	0	0	0	2	0	7	0	0	1	.317	.308
Guzman, Carlos, Brav.	.219	38	131	114	14	25	34	4	1	1	20	0	2	3	12	0	45	3	1	1	.298	.305
Hairston, Jerry, Ori.	.300	4	16	10	3	3	5	2	0	0	3	0	1	2	3	0	2	4	0	0	.500	.500
Harper, Brandon, Mar.	.296	8	34	27	8	8	9	1	0	0	2	0	0	0	7	0	4	0	0	0	.333	.441
Harris, Karl, Exp.	.266	44	183	158	16	42	54	6	0	2	24	1	4	9	11	0	21	3	3	4	.342	.341
Heard, Scott, Rang.*	.351	31	137	111	21	39	61	16	0	2	16	2	0	4	20	0	17	1	0	1	.550	.467
Hernandez, Yorky, Pir.	.218	16	61	55	7	12	21	4	1	1	7	0	0	1	5	0	10	0	0	0	.382	.295
Herr, Aaron, Brav.	.223	49	195	175	27	39	59	11	0	3	19	0	3	4	13	0	37	3	1	1	.337	.287
Huguet, J.C., Reds	.240	33	129	104	11	25	30	5	0	0	17	3	1	0	21	1	16	3	0	4	.288	.365
Ide, Antoine, Ori.	.345	8	37	29	4	10	10	0	0	0	1	2	0	1	5	0	6	7	2	1	.345	.457
Infante, Franklin, Brav.	.191	41	141	131	16	25	35	4	0	2	13	0	0	1	9	0	39	2	2	2	.267	.248
Infante, Juan, Exp.†	.238	42	165	143	26	34	38	2	1	0	12	3	1	4	14	0	21	2	4	2	.266	.321
Jackson, Wilbur, Reds	.324	9	36	34	3	11	15	4	0	0	3	0	0	0	2	0	13	1	1	1	.441	.361
Jaile, Chris, Rang.	.193	35	139	114	14	22	33	5	0	2	16	2	3	2	18	1	23	1	0	3	.289	.307
Jansen, Ardley, Brav.	.267	46	181	150	22	40	50	6	2	0	16	2	0	1	28	1	36	3	3	2	.333	.385
Jenkins, Darryl, Exp.*	.147	11	39	34	2	5	6	1	0	0	1	0	0	0	5	0	16	1	0	0	.176	.256
Jimenez, D'Angelo, Yan.†	.100	4	15	10	2	1	1	0	0	0	0	0	0	0	5	0	1	0	0	0	.100	.400
Johnson Iii, Nelson, Ori.	.306	48	205	180	22	55	72	5	3	2	33	2	6	4	13	0	38	7	5	2	.400	.355

Player, Team	Avg.	G	TPA	AB	R	H	TB	2B	3B	HR	RBI	SH	SF	HP	BB	IBB	SO	SB	CS	GDP	Slg.	OBP
Johnson, Kelly, Brav.	.269	53	219	193	27	52	82	12	3	4	29	1	1	0	24	0	45	6	1	4	.425	.349
Johnson, Patrick, R.S.*	.214	8	30	28	2	6	11	2	0	1	4	0	0	0	2	0	5	1	0	3	.393	.267
Johnson, Seth, Exp.	.299	47	198	187	22	56	68	9	0	1	18	1	0	1	9	0	21	1	2	5	.364	.335
Johnson, Tristan, Pir.	.057	11	37	35	1	2	2	0	0	0	0	0	0	0	2	0	22	0	0	1	.057	.108
Jones, Dwayne, Pir.*	.103	15	42	39	3	4	5	1	0	0	3	0	0	1	2	0	23	0	0	1	.128	.167
Joyce Jr., Thomas, Ori.*	.209	44	153	129	13	27	37	6	2	0	9	6	0	1	17	1	28	2	3	3	.287	.306
Kingsale, Eugene, Ori.*	.313	5	21	16	7	5	5	0	0	0	4	0	1	0	4	0	0	2	0	0	.313	.429
Knox, Matthew, Exp.	.194	23	69	62	1	12	13	1	0	0	4	2	0	2	3	0	15	2	1	1	.210	.254
Kropf, Andrew, Tig.†	.176	12	38	34	3	6	11	2	0	1	3	0	1	0	3	0	3	1	1	0	.324	.237
Kubel, Jason, Twi.*	.282	23	91	78	17	22	29	3	2	0	13	1	1	1	10	0	9	0	0	1	.372	.367
Laidlaw, Jacob, Mar.	.250	23	92	76	13	19	32	5	1	2	14	0	3	3	10	0	14	2	0	0	.421	.348
Lambert, Shawn, Tig.	.246	37	142	118	15	29	48	4	0	5	16	0	0	0	24	0	48	2	3	3	.407	.373
Laureano, Wilfredo, Roy.	.211	46	164	147	9	31	44	4	0	3	24	1	3	2	11	1	28	2	0	6	.299	.270
Lebron, Edgardo, Twi.	.244	32	129	119	13	29	36	3	2	0	9	1	0	1	8	0	31	2	3	5	.303	.297
Leon, Donny, Yan.†	.167	5	21	18	3	3	9	0	0	2	4	0	2	1	0	0	6	0	0	0	.500	.190
Leon, Omar, Mar.	.298	22	63	57	4	17	21	2	1	0	10	0	2	2	2	0	6	0	1	5	.368	.323
Leonardo, Santos, Tig.	.169	26	101	89	17	15	27	1	1	3	12	0	0	5	7	0	18	12	1	1	.303	.267
Lewis, Darren, R.S.	.167	2	7	6	0	1	1	0	0	0	1	0	0	0	1	0	0	1	0	0	.167	.286
Llamas, Juan, Reds.	.299	24	93	87	10	26	32	1	1	1	11	0	0	2	4	0	15	1	1	1	.368	.344
Logan, Exavier, Tig.	.279	43	171	136	29	38	44	2	2	0	14	1	2	1	31	0	36	20	3	1	.324	.412
Lomasney, Steve, R.S.	.267	6	19	15	2	4	6	2	0	0	1	0	0	0	4	0	6	0	1	0	.400	.421
Lopez, Youanny, R.S.	.242	41	145	124	10	30	37	1	0	2	15	0	0	1	20	1	27	8	5	4	.298	.352
Louisa, Lorvin, Exp.	.136	38	131	118	7	16	22	4	1	0	6	0	0	2	11	0	49	1	0	2	.186	.221
Love, Marc, Pir.*	.241	33	119	108	11	26	30	4	0	0	11	2	0	3	6	0	28	5	1	2	.278	.299
Malloy, Marty, Tig.	1.000	2	3	1	0	1	1	0	0	0	1	0	0	0	2	0	0	0	0	0	1.000	1.000
Manning, Ricky, Twi.*	.275	26	92	69	20	19	19	0	0	0	10	3	1	3	16	1	13	6	3	1	.275	.427
Markray, Thad, Reds	.200	10	5	5	0	1	1	0	0	0	1	0	0	0	0	0	1	0	0	0	.200	.200
Marquie, Craig, Yan.	.167	5	13	12	3	2	2	0	0	0	1	0	0	0	1	0	4	1	0	0	.167	.231
Martinez, Edgar, R.S.	.168	35	129	119	12	20	32	3	0	3	14	0	1	4	5	0	23	0	2	4	.269	.225
Martinez, Peter, Twi.†	.237	39	166	131	24	31	37	6	0	0	20	4	5	3	22	0	23	4	4	2	.282	.348
Martinez, William, Ori.	.273	38	145	132	16	36	47	6	1	1	8	3	0	3	7	1	27	6	3	3	.356	.324
Masino, Adam, Twi.	.177	30	117	96	12	17	27	4	0	2	14	0	0	3	18	1	33	2	0	2	.281	.325
Matthews, Michael, Roy.*	.242	35	131	120	11	29	35	4	1	0	21	2	1	1	7	1	24	1	0	2	.292	.287
McDonald, Jason, Rang.*	.200	3	12	10	0	2	2	0	0	0	0	1	0	0	1	0	2	0	0	0	.200	.273
McRoberts, Mark, Phi.	.188	6	18	16	2	3	4	1	0	0	1	0	0	1	1	0	11	0	0	0	.250	.278
Mejia, Manuel, Pir.	.342	34	130	114	18	39	57	8	2	2	9	0	1	2	13	0	23	1	3	3	.500	.423
Melo, Hanlet, Brav.	.265	44	174	155	18	41	50	4	1	1	10	1	1	2	15	0	28	6	7	2	.323	.335
Mendez, Deivi, Yan.	.300	56	244	210	37	63	91	20	1	2	25	3	2	3	26	0	39	4	0	4	.433	.382
Mercado, Onix, Reds.	.229	45	177	157	10	36	47	11	0	0	20	1	2	3	14	3	39	0	3	1	.299	.301
Merchan, Jesus, Twi.	.314	36	143	118	22	37	42	5	0	0	16	8	1	5	11	0	15	1	2	5	.356	.393
Minor, Ryan, Ori.	.154	3	14	13	2	2	6	1	0	1	4	0	0	0	1	0	6	0	0	0	.462	.214
Molina, Angel, Mar.	.148	10	33	27	3	4	5	1	0	0	3	0	0	1	5	0	11	1	0	1	.185	.303
Morban, Dany, Reds*	.231	53	216	182	23	42	68	7	8	1	22	1	0	3	30	3	59	11	2	2	.374	.349
Morneau, Justin, Twi.*	.402	52	226	194	47	78	129	21	0	10	58	0	2	0	30	7	18	3	1	5	.665	.478
Motooka, Rafael, Reds	.250	7	12	12	0	3	3	0	0	0	0	0	0	0	0	0	3	0	0	1	.250	.250
Moya, Wilson, Rang.	.219	35	110	96	16	21	25	2	1	0	7	1	0	3	10	0	26	2	1	0	.260	.312
Nix, Laynce, Rang.*	.226	51	230	199	34	45	60	7	1	2	25	2	4	2	23	1	37	4	2	3	.302	.307
Nixon, Trot, R.S.*	.400	3	13	10	3	4	7	0	0	1	5	0	0	1	2	1	0	0	0	0	.700	.538
Nunn, Jason, Yan.	.232	47	167	151	19	35	54	9	2	2	24	0	0	2	14	0	43	7	2	0	.358	.305
Oetting, Todd, Phi.	.250	20	68	60	8	15	19	4	0	0	6	1	0	1	6	0	5	0	2	1	.317	.328
Oh, Chul, R.S.*	.286	24	74	70	8	20	32	6	0	2	9	0	0	0	4	0	16	0	0	3	.457	.324
O'Leary, Troy, R.S.*	.750	3	11	8	3	6	7	1	0	0	1	0	0	0	3	0	1	0	0	0	.875	.818
Ortega, Felix, Phi.	.180	19	60	50	6	9	12	0	0	1	4	0	0	0	10	0	19	0	0	0	.240	.317
Padilla, Juan, Rang.	.254	41	149	142	16	36	53	7	2	2	17	0	1	3	3	0	35	0	2	3	.373	.282
Pagana, Mike, Rang.	.250	4	19	16	5	4	4	0	0	0	2	1	0	0	2	0	2	1	0	1	.250	.333
Parrott, Tom, Brav.	.250	9	28	24	0	6	8	2	0	0	3	0	1	1	2	0	6	0	1	0	.333	.321
Patchett, Gary, Reds	.292	19	76	65	9	19	22	3	0	0	5	1	0	2	8	0	11	1	3	3	.338	.387
Patterson, Sean, Reds.	.143	17	57	49	2	7	8	1	0	0	3	0	0	0	8	0	22	0	0	0	.163	.263
Peguero, Miguel, Tig.†	.250	41	163	148	22	37	44	5	1	0	13	2	0	2	11	0	34	9	2	3	.297	.311
Pena, Onesimo, Rang.	.182	7	28	22	3	4	4	0	0	0	2	2	0	1	3	0	3	0	0	0	.182	.308
Perez, Kenny, R.S.†	.285	43	173	158	28	45	55	7	0	1	23	1	1	1	12	1	12	3	2	3	.348	.337
Perkins, Robert, Brav.	.214	38	131	112	12	24	35	5	0	2	8	0	0	5	14	0	27	0	1	0	.313	.328
Pfister, Billy, Tig.	.250	15	52	44	6	11	11	0	0	0	4	0	0	0	8	0	7	0	0	1	.250	.365
Pickering, Kelvin, Ori.	.210	27	90	81	11	17	25	2	0	2	6	0	0	1	8	1	25	3	0	2	.309	.289
Quintin, Luis, Rang.	.225	22	77	71	6	16	23	4	0	1	10	2	0	0	4	0	27	1	1	0	.324	.267
Ramirez, Jordy, Reds†	.172	40	160	128	21	22	29	2	1	1	6	6	1	0	25	0	37	4	3	1	.227	.305
Ramos, Victor, Pir.*	.209	27	97	91	4	19	21	2	0	0	14	1	0	0	5	0	15	1	1	3	.231	.250
Reed, Matthew, Twi.	.256	33	113	86	21	22	23	1	0	0	12	2	0	6	19	0	17	7	4	3	.267	.423
Reed, Robert, R.S.	.111	17	29	27	1	3	4	1	0	0	0	0	0	0	2	0	4	0	0	0	.148	.172
Remekie, Collin, Brav.	.037	13	32	27	2	1	1	0	0	0	0	0	0	0	5	0	17	0	1	0	.037	.188
Reyes, Ivan, Yan.	.182	54	229	192	37	35	56	13	1	2	27	0	4	3	30	0	52	4	2	4	.292	.297
Riek, Cliff, Pir.	.156	10	41	32	5	5	8	3	0	0	2	0	1	2	6	0	12	1	0	1	.250	.317
Rivas, Norberto, Exp.	.000	1	4	4	0	0	0	0	0	0	0	0	0	0	0	0	1	0	0	0	.000	.000
Rivera, Carlos, Phi.	.194	26	82	72	5	14	19	2	0	1	4	0	0	2	8	0	28	0	0	0	.264	.293
Rivera, Carlos, Pir.*	.292	6	25	24	2	7	7	0	0	0	0	0	0	0	1	0	2	0	0	1	.292	.320
Rivera, Erick, Phi.	.167	43	148	126	17	21	31	2	1	2	14	0	2	9	11	0	34	2	0	0	.246	.277
Roberts, Brian, Ori.	.310	9	38	29	8	9	17	1	2	1	3	0	1	0	7	0	4	7	1	0	.586	.432
Rodgers, Mackeel, Roy.†	.209	26	106	91	14	19	27	3	1	1	6	0	0	3	12	0	18	2	5	1	.297	.321
Rodriguez , Ricardo, Brav.	.209	20	81	67	11	14	19	2	0	1	2	0	1	7	6	1	10	2	2	1	.284	.333
Rodriguez, Jose, Ori.†	.400	1	5	5	2	2	2	0	0	0	1	0	0	0	0	0	1	1	0	1	.400	.400
Rodriguez, Ronny, R.S.	.250	20	58	52	3	13	15	2	0	0	6	1	0	1	5	0	17	0	0	1	.288	.328
Roger, Omar, Ori.	.218	31	91	78	16	17	25	2	0	2	9	3	0	1	9	1	22	4	2	0	.321	.307
Rogers, Brian, Mar.*	.389	5	20	18	3	7	10	0	0	1	3	0	0	0	2	1	4	0	1	0	.556	.450

Player, Team	Avg.	G	TPA	AB	R	H	TB	2B	3B	HR	RBI	SH	SF	HP	BB	IBB	SO	SB	CS	GDP	Slg.	OBP
Romero, Gabriel, Brav............	.198	36	126	116	12	23	28	5	0	0	9	0	1	4	5	0	16	3	4	0	.241	.254
Rosas, Luis, Exp.	.191	33	103	94	8	18	20	2	0	0	5	1	0	2	6	0	21	0	1	3	.213	.255
Ruiz, Carlos, Phi.	.277	38	143	130	11	36	48	7	1	1	22	0	2	2	9	0	9	3	0	5	.369	.329
Rush, Travis, Pir...................	.200	4	11	10	0	2	2	0	0	0	0	0	0	1	0	0	0	2	0	0	.200	.273
Russell, Byron, Roy.*...........	.200	47	162	140	12	28	41	4	0	3	19	3	0	1	18	1	35	3	0	6	.293	.296
Russell, Michael, Ori............	.284	24	87	74	9	21	28	4	0	1	9	1	1	1	10	0	14	1	4	1	.378	.372
Saba, Cesar, R.S.†...............	.167	2	7	6	0	1	1	0	0	0	1	0	0	0	1	0	3	0	0	0	.167	.286
Sandoval, Michael, Twi..........	.302	17	77	63	13	19	27	1	2	1	10	0	0	0	14	0	8	2	2	3	.429	.429
Santoro, Pat, R.S.	.233	12	45	43	4	10	12	2	0	0	4	0	0	0	2	0	10	0	0	2	.279	.267
Saucke, Casey, Ori.	.294	48	206	187	29	55	81	6	1	6	26	2	1	4	12	1	46	12	3	4	.433	.348
Schalick, Jr, George, Ori.*	.286	22	81	63	11	18	26	5	0	1	11	0	0	1	17	2	8	1	1	2	.413	.444
Schnabel, Nicholas, Exp.......	.233	13	56	43	5	10	10	0	0	0	4	4	0	4	5	0	3	0	1	1	.233	.365
Segar, Jeff, Yan....................	.253	23	96	83	11	21	22	1	0	0	6	0	3	2	8	0	12	4	0	0	.265	.323
Seiber, Antron, R.S.	.306	49	221	196	36	60	81	7	1	4	21	0	2	7	16	0	31	21	5	4	.413	.376
Sena, Sonel, Ori.	.357	9	32	28	3	10	11	1	0	0	4	0	0	2	2	0	5	0	0	0	.393	.438
Severino, Cleris, Reds*.........	1.000	13	1	1	0	1	1	0	0	0	0	0	0	0	0	0	0	0	0	0	1.000	1.000
Shier, Peter, Ori.	.471	6	31	17	5	8	11	3	0	0	3	0	1	2	11	0	3	2	0	2	.647	.677
Silvera, Andres, Phi..............	.259	53	214	193	27	50	84	15	2	5	24	1	1	7	12	0	37	4	5	4	.435	.324
Sizemore, Grady, Exp.*	.293	55	237	205	31	60	77	8	3	1	14	2	0	6	23	0	24	16	2	1	.376	.380
Smiley, Jermaine, Roy.*.........	.471	6	27	17	5	8	9	1	0	0	3	0	0	1	9	0	3	3	1	0	.529	.667
Smith, Marcus, Brav..............	.125	8	19	16	1	2	2	0	0	0	3	0	0	2	1	0	8	0	0	0	.125	.263
Smith, Nate, Brav..................	.000	1	3	3	0	0	0	0	0	0	0	0	0	0	0	0	3	0	0	0	.000	.000
Smith, Sean, Pir...................	.254	21	76	63	12	16	20	2	1	0	6	2	1	1	9	0	8	3	0	0	.317	.351
Smith, Toebius, Brav.............	.000	1	3	3	0	0	0	0	0	0	0	0	0	0	0	0	0	0	0	0	.000	.000
Smith, William, Mar.*	.368	54	233	204	37	75	106	21	2	2	34	0	1	1	26	1	24	7	3	3	.520	.440
Solano, Francisco, Reds†.......	.259	33	140	116	20	30	36	6	0	0	6	1	0	2	21	0	31	11	8	2	.310	.381
Soriano, Jairo, Ori.†..............	.300	36	134	110	17	33	45	4	4	0	12	2	1	2	19	1	25	10	3	1	.409	.409
Soto, Jose, Mar.†..................	.218	42	184	165	24	36	58	9	2	3	19	2	1	4	12	0	62	8	4	3	.352	.286
Stankiewicz, Andy, Yan.	.000	1	5	3	0	0	0	0	0	0	0	0	0	0	2	0	1	0	0	0	.000	.400
Suarez, Victor, Roy.†.............	.189	47	149	127	10	24	32	1	2	1	7	1	2	2	17	1	30	0	3	2	.252	.291
Sulbaran, Orlando, Rang........	.222	17	53	36	9	8	10	2	0	0	1	1	0	3	13	0	6	0	0	0	.278	.462
Svihlik, D.J., Yan.*	.333	9	20	18	4	6	7	1	0	0	3	0	1	0	0	0	3	0	0	0	.389	.316
Swenson, Leland, Rang..........	.257	28	92	70	8	18	20	2	0	0	5	2	0	0	20	1	10	4	1	0	.286	.422
Tamburrino, Brett, Twi.†	.244	52	230	172	43	42	53	7	2	0	25	3	1	5	49	2	27	18	2	3	.308	.423
Taveras, Frank, Mar.	.275	53	210	182	25	50	63	7	0	2	30	0	3	5	20	0	45	7	2	5	.346	.357
Tejero, Armando, Brav.*	.161	33	118	93	9	15	20	2	0	1	12	0	0	2	23	0	39	0	0	0	.215	.339
Tellis, Antoine, Tig................	.153	21	68	59	6	9	9	0	0	0	1	1	0	0	8	0	32	1	1	2	.153	.254
Thomman, John, Twi.	.150	35	131	107	15	16	21	1	2	0	8	3	1	4	16	0	38	4	1	3	.196	.281
Thompson, Kevin, Twi.*	.267	20	87	75	13	20	35	7	1	2	9	0	1	1	10	0	14	2	3	1	.467	.356
Thorman, Scott, Brav.*	.227	29	115	97	15	22	34	7	1	1	19	0	2	4	12	0	23	0	1	1	.351	.330
Timaure, Jesus, Mar..............	.250	20	63	56	10	14	18	4	0	0	10	0	1	0	6	0	26	0	0	1	.321	.317
Tomlin, James, Twi.	.338	42	168	145	24	49	61	12	0	0	18	1	3	4	15	0	11	12	3	2	.421	.407
Tope, Stephen, Twi................	.243	24	89	70	11	17	22	2	0	1	10	1	0	2	16	1	20	3	0	0	.314	.398
Turner, Jason, Yan.*	.314	58	242	207	35	65	96	9	2	6	42	0	3	4	28	0	34	2	2	3	.464	.401
Valera, Luis, Red..................	.193	33	124	114	8	22	28	3	0	1	11	0	0	2	8	0	21	1	1	3	.246	.258
Villalobos, Carlos, Tig.	.429	2	7	7	1	3	3	0	0	0	0	0	0	0	0	0	1	0	0	1	.429	.429
Volquez, Julio, Rang.†	.293	42	185	164	31	48	61	10	0	1	25	1	1	2	17	2	22	10	7	2	.372	.364
Ware, Anthony, Tig................	.211	50	190	147	21	31	50	9	2	2	20	0	4	6	33	0	48	3	1	2	.340	.368
Warriax, Brandon, Rang.........	.125	7	35	32	1	4	6	2	0	0	6	0	0	0	3	0	6	1	0	0	.188	.200
Woods, Ahmad, Brav.	.184	38	129	114	18	21	34	6	2	1	16	0	1	4	10	0	30	2	0	0	.298	.271
Yan, Edwin, Pir.†..................	.357	12	54	42	10	15	17	0	1	0	1	0	0	0	12	0	8	5	4	1	.405	.500
Yingling, Joe, Tig..................	.163	16	49	43	2	7	8	1	0	0	1	0	1	0	5	0	9	0	0	0	.186	.245
Young, Walter, Pir.*	.296	45	182	162	32	48	91	11	1	10	34	0	3	9	8	1	29	3	2	2	.562	.357
Zosky, Eddie, Pir..................	.333	8	33	30	7	10	16	6	0	0	3	0	0	0	3	0	1	1	0	1	.533	.394

GRAND SLAMS: Aliendo 2; Blanco, Borjas, Brewer, Infante, Laureano, Masino, Morneau, Nixon, Oh, Russell, Valera, 1 each.

AWARDED FIRST BASE ON CATCHER'S INTERFERENCE: Abad (Candelaria), Fernandez (Mejia), C. Martinez (Sulbaran), Roberts (Sulbaran), Sizemore (Ruiz), W. Smith (Bernard), Svihlik (Ruiz).

2000 PITCHING
TEAM

Team	W	L	Pct.	ERA	G	CG	ShO	Sv.	IP	H	TBF	R	ER	HR	SH	SF	HB	BB	IBB	SO	WP	Bk.
Yankees............	38	22	.633	3.25	60	0	8	18	493.2	465	2129	227	178	13	9	16	28	180	1	429	31	7
Marlins.............	40	20	.667	3.25	60	2	6	16	514.1	440	2226	232	186	20	11	18	57	209	7	450	49	12
Braves.............	26	34	.433	3.33	60	1	5	12	491.1	443	2179	263	182	16	15	10	23	234	2	507	58	9
Phillies	31	29	.517	3.35	60	3	6	15	503.0	487	2186	252	187	29	13	10	28	167	2	442	44	8
Pirates	34	26	.567	3.38	60	1	3	12	500.1	504	2194	255	188	23	15	23	56	150	1	365	44	7
Twins..............	33	23	.589	3.43	56	5	3	9	470.0	439	2040	236	179	18	24	14	41	195	5	423	42	2
Tigers	34	26	.567	3.70	60	4	7	23	488.1	429	2125	245	201	19	12	18	33	224	5	460	49	6
Red Sox	29	26	.527	3.75	55	1	3	15	462.2	482	2090	268	193	22	21	17	34	224	10	367	34	9
Rangers............	38	18	.679	3.77	56	0	4	24	492.0	476	2138	253	206	23	14	18	34	205	7	363	19	3
Royals.............	20	40	.333	4.28	60	0	6	14	479.1	448	2178	287	228	15	8	21	51	256	3	437	56	7
Orioles............	25	31	.446	4.44	56	0	0	9	476.1	479	2174	307	235	22	19	15	38	284	23	377	42	7
Expos	17	43	.283	4.58	60	3	0	11	509.1	512	2321	351	259	37	19	21	53	248	0	364	53	7
Reds...............	14	41	.255	5.04	55	0	3	5	460.2	468	2154	350	258	27	29	18	45	275	8	393	71	6

TOP QUALIFIERS FOR EARNED-RUN AVERAGE TITLE

Minimum 48 innings. *Lefthanded pitcher.

Pitcher, Team	W	L	Pct.	ERA	G	GS	CG	ShO	GF	Sv.	IP	H	TBF	R	ER	HR	SH	SF	HB	BB	IBB	SO	WP	Bk.
Hernandez, Yoel, Phi.	4	1	.800	1.35	10	9	2	1	0	0	60.0	39	237	10	9	2	0	0	7	17	0	46	4	1
Graham, Thomas, Rang.	5	0	1.000	2.29	18	4	0	0	3	2	59.0	57	236	17	15	1	0	2	4	8	1	53	1	0
Bautista, Denny, Mar.	6	2	.750	2.43	11	11	2	0	0	0	63.0	49	260	24	17	1	1	0	8	17	1	58	3	1
Miyamoto, Eij, Exp.	0	2	.000	2.52	9	8	1	0	0	0	50.0	37	198	16	14	4	1	2	1	16	0	40	5	0
Brito, Eude, Phi.*	3	5	.375	2.54	9	7	0	0	1	0	49.2	38	205	20	14	1	0	1	3	19	0	42	10	0
Esquivia, Manuel, Mar.	6	1	.857	2.78	12	11	0	0	0	0	64.2	42	263	20	20	4	1	5	3	24	0	77	5	0
Miller, Colby, Twi.	3	2	.600	3.09	14	10	0	0	0	0	55.1	44	231	26	19	2	5	0	3	21	0	55	3	0
Severino, Cleris, Reds*	1	3	.250	3.12	13	5	0	0	1	0	52.0	46	224	25	18	3	1	1	4	23	0	36	2	0
Randazzo, Jeffrey, Twi.*	7	2	.778	3.15	13	12	3	1	0	0	68.2	70	283	35	24	2	3	2	6	19	0	58	4	1
Guerrero, Julio, Pir.	5	3	.625	3.16	11	9	0	0	1	0	57.0	56	242	28	20	2	1	2	4	9	0	25	2	2
Smith, Jason, Yan.	6	2	.750	3.45	10	10	0	0	0	0	57.1	57	249	26	22	2	0	1	4	13	0	54	2	0
Acosta, Manuel, Yan.	4	2	.667	3.47	12	10	0	0	1	0	62.1	64	270	28	24	3	4	0	0	21	0	46	1	0
Delossantos, Carlos, Pir.	3	5	.375	3.48	11	7	0	0	3	1	51.2	45	227	24	20	4	0	0	10	23	0	53	5	2
Beltre, Omar, Rang.	5	4	.556	3.54	13	13	0	0	0	0	61.0	54	251	30	24	2	1	2	6	15	0	44	2	2
Thompson, Matthew, R.S.	4	2	.667	3.65	12	11	0	0	0	0	56.2	65	258	33	23	5	1	3	4	18	0	54	6	0

DEPARTMENTAL LEADERS: W—Randazzo, 7; L—Sauer, Ewin, Almeida, Marrero, Rice, 6 each; Pct.—Esquivia, .857; G—F. Hernandez, 27; GS—Rice, Beltre, 13 each; CG—Randazzo, 3; ShO—Mims, Tejeda, Y. Hernandez, Randazzo, 1 each; GF—F. Hernandez, 25; Sv.—F. Hernandez, 17; IP—Randazzo, 68.2; H—Randazzo, 70; TBF—Randazzo, 283; R—Rice, 46; ER—Marrero, Rejean, 35 each; HR—Dubuc, Mitchell, Rejean, Messenger, 6 each; SH—several tied, 5 each; SF—A. Jones, 7; HB—Marrero, 12; BB—Rice, 48; IBB—Cotton, 4; SO—Esquivia, 77; WP—Anez, 15; BK—Gutierrez, 5.

ALL PITCHERS

*Lefthanded pitcher.

Pitcher, Team	W	L	Pct.	ERA	G	GS	CG	ShO	GF	Sv.	IP	H	TBF	R	ER	HR	SH	SF	HB	BB	IBB	SO	WP	Bk.
Abreu, Winston, Brav.	0	0	.000	3.00	2	2	0	0	0	0	3.0	2	14	1	1	0	0	1	2	0	2	0	0
Acosta, Manuel, Yan.	4	2	.667	3.47	12	10	0	0	1	0	62.1	64	270	28	24	3	4	0	0	21	0	46	1	0
Akens, Phil, Mar.	4	0	1.000	4.79	18	0	0	0	7	3	35.2	33	162	21	19	2	0	0	9	15	0	35	5	0
Albertus, Roberto, Brav.*	3	3	.500	4.54	9	8	0	0	0	0	35.2	52	163	22	18	1	0	1	1	11	0	27	5	1
Alcantara, Over, Mar.	2	4	.333	3.98	14	10	0	0	4	2	54.1	66	244	33	24	1	0	2	4	9	0	32	3	3
Almeida, Brian, Brav.	2	6	.250	3.30	11	9	0	0	0	0	43.2	40	193	22	16	1	0	2	2	20	0	35	4	1
Almonte, Hector, Mar.	0	0	.000	4.50	1	1	0	0	0	0	2.0	3	8	1	1	0	0	0	0	1	0	2	0	0
Andujar, Jesse, Phi.	0	0	.000	3.60	2	1	0	0	0	0	5.0	3	21	3	2	0	0	1	4	0	4	1	0
Anez, Omar, Ori.	3	3	.500	4.76	15	8	0	0	3	0	51.0	55	235	38	27	5	2	2	1	31	2	45	15	1
Arias, Miguel, Roy.	1	3	.250	3.95	18	1	0	0	7	2	27.1	26	128	20	12	0	0	2	3	17	1	17	7	0
Armitage, Barry, Roy.	0	1	.000	1.80	5	3	0	0	0	0	10.0	9	40	3	2	0	0	0	1	0	10	0	0
Artiles, Carlos, Yan.*	1	2	.333	2.45	17	0	0	0	7	0	25.2	26	119	11	7	0	2	0	0	13	0	33	5	0
Baker, Brett, Mar.	0	0	.000	0.00	1	0	0	0	0	0	0.0	0	0	0	0	0	0	0	0	0	0	0	0	0
Barkley, Brian, R.S.*	0	0	.000	0.00	1	0	0	0	0	0	2.0	2	8	0	0	0	0	0	1	0	1	0	0
Bartlett, Richard, Ori.	0	0	.000	4.31	10	0	0	0	0	0	39.2	46	181	25	19	2	1	0	6	21	2	32	1	0
Bass, Brian, Roy.	3	5	.375	3.89	12	9	0	0	0	0	44.0	36	200	27	19	0	1	1	9	18	0	40	10	0
Baum, David, Pir.*	0	0	.000	0.00	2	0	0	0	1	0	4.1	2	17	0	0	0	0	0	0	4	0	4	0	0
Bautista, Denny, Mar.	6	2	.750	2.43	11	11	2	0	0	0	63.0	49	260	24	17	1	1	0	8	17	1	58	3	1
Beigh, David, Pir.	1	1	.500	3.68	7	4	0	0	0	0	22.0	24	89	15	9	2	0	1	4	0	13	3	0
Bell, Tom, Mar.	1	0	1.000	1.84	7	0	0	0	5	2	14.2	11	60	4	3	0	1	0	1	8	1	3	0	0
Beltre, Omar, Rang.	5	4	.556	3.54	13	13	0	0	0	0	61.0	54	251	30	24	2	1	2	6	15	0	44	2	2
Benitez, Fabricio, R.S.	0	1	.000	18.00	1	1	0	0	0	0	1.0	4	8	3	2	0	0	0	0	1	0	0	0	0
Berry, Casey, Rang.	1	2	.333	4.05	12	12	0	0	0	0	46.2	48	196	26	21	3	0	2	1	13	0	38	0	0
Berube, Martin, Ori.	2	1	.667	3.04	9	9	0	0	0	0	47.1	43	199	21	16	4	1	1	1	13	0	39	1	0
Blair, David, Ori.*	1	3	.250	3.95	14	0	0	0	3	0	13.2	17	75	17	6	1	1	2	4	18	2	4	3	0
Blankenship, John, Yan.*	2	0	1.000	1.09	6	2	0	0	2	0	24.2	17	97	4	3	1	0	1	1	4	0	19	0	0
Bludau, Frank, Reds	2	4	.333	1.59	10	3	0	0	5	1	28.1	22	112	9	5	0	3	2	0	6	0	23	2	0
Borkowski, Dave, Tig.	0	0	.000	2.25	3	3	0	0	0	0	8.0	7	32	3	2	0	0	0	0	6	0	6	0	0
Borrell, Danny, Yan.*	0	1	.000	0.00	1	1	0	0	0	0	3.0	2	11	1	0	0	0	0	0	0	0	2	1	0
Boughey, William, Phi.	2	2	.500	2.35	15	2	0	0	2	0	38.1	46	172	19	10	1	2	1	0	6	0	33	1	1
Bouie, Aaron, Ori.	0	0	.000	7.36	2	0	0	0	0	0	3.2	6	19	4	3	0	0	0	3	0	5	1	0
Bowers, Robert, Rang.	2	3	.400	4.63	20	0	0	0	14	5	35.0	35	157	26	18	2	2	0	3	14	2	24	1	0
Bowyer, Travis, Twi.	3	5	.375	4.07	12	12	1	0	0	0	55.1	55	250	31	25	2	2	2	8	22	0	36	5	0
Boyer, Blaine, Brav.	1	3	.250	2.51	11	5	0	0	2	1	32.1	24	142	16	9	0	0	3	3	19	0	27	3	2
Brito, Eude, Phi.*	3	5	.375	2.54	9	7	0	0	1	0	49.2	38	205	20	14	1	0	1	3	19	0	42	10	0
Brito, Jose, Reds	1	0	1.000	10.80	4	0	0	0	0	0	10.0	16	53	13	12	3	1	1	1	5	0	8	3	0
Brito, Juan, Exp.*	1	0	1.000	3.60	2	0	0	0	0	0	5.0	3	21	2	2	1	0	0	0	2	0	3	0	1
Buchholz, Taylor, Phi.	2	3	.400	2.25	12	7	0	0	2	0	44.0	46	188	22	11	2	0	1	2	14	0	41	3	1
Bucktrot, Keith, Phi.	3	2	.600	4.78	11	7	0	0	0	0	37.2	39	166	21	20	5	0	0	1	19	0	40	3	2
Bullinger, Kirk, Phi.	0	0	.000	0.00	1	1	0	0	0	0	1.0	0	3	0	0	0	0	0	0	0	0	1	0	0
Burnett, Sean, Pir.*	2	1	.667	4.06	8	6	0	0	1	0	31.0	31	128	17	14	0	0	1	0	3	0	24	2	1
Bynum, Matthew, Reds	1	1	.500	3.38	8	0	0	0	6	0	13.1	11	67	5	5	0	2	0	3	14	0	9	4	0
Camelia, Aron, Yan.	0	0	.000	0.00	2	0	0	0	1	0	1.1	1	8	1	0	0	0	0	0	3	0	1	0	0
Campbell, Dayle, Tig.	1	3	.250	3.74	11	8	0	0	0	0	45.2	39	205	21	19	0	1	8	25	0	32	11	1
Castillo, Carlos, R.S.	1	0	1.000	2.35	2	1	0	0	0	0	7.2	11	40	8	2	0	0	1	5	0	5	1	1
Castillo, Jose, Tig.	0	0	.000	18.00	1	0	0	0	0	0	1.0	4	7	2	2	0	0	0	1	0	1	0	0
Chacon, Ernesto, Yan.	0	1	.000	1.93	18	0	0	0	7	1	18.2	15	77	7	4	0	0	1	7	0	13	3	0
Cheek, Andrew, R.S.*	1	1	.500	2.70	7	0	0	0	5	0	10.0	11	47	4	3	0	1	0	5	1	5	1	0
Collazo, Rafael, Tig.*	0	0	.000	1.59	6	0	0	0	0	0	5.2	4	24	1	1	0	0	0	2	0	7	0	0
Colon, Roberto, Yan.	0	0	.000	63.00	1	0	0	0	1	0	1.0	8	12	7	7	1	0	0	1	0	1	0	0
Connolly, Michael, Pir.*	1	2	.333	2.29	11	0	0	0	7	2	19.2	20	84	6	5	0	2	0	1	6	0	25	2	0
Cooke, Andrew, Twi.*	2	1	.667	4.78	11	5	0	0	1	0	26.1	36	128	17	14	1	0	1	0	16	1	26	2	0
Cotton, Nathan, Reds	1	3	.250	3.51	14	0	0	0	11	3	25.2	19	106	10	10	1	4	1	1	11	4	24	0	0

Pitcher, Team	W	L	Pct.	ERA	G	GS	CG	ShO	GF	Sv.	IP	H	TBF	R	ER	HR	SH	SF	HB	BB	IBB	SO	WP	Bk.
Crawford, Tristan, Twi.	0	0	.000	9.95	8	0	0	0	6	0	6.1	12	34	9	7	0	0	0	0	2	0	3	2	0
Cristobal, Luis, Rang.	2	0	1.000	4.74	8	3	0	0	1	0	19.0	24	93	13	10	1	0	1	3	10	0	13	0	0
Crump, Joel, Ori.*	2	1	.667	8.10	12	0	0	0	3	0	20.0	32	97	20	18	1	1	2	0	11	3	7	3	0
Cuello, Manolin, Tig.	6	0	1.000	2.27	11	5	0	0	0	0	47.2	37	201	14	12	0	1	2	7	22	2	41	5	0
Cummings, Frank, Brav.	0	0	.000	0.00	3	0	0	0	2	1	4.0	3	15	0	0	0	0	0	0	0	0	5	0	0
DeLaCruz, Juan, Pir.	0	1	.000	7.71	3	0	0	0	3	2	2.1	1	12	2	2	0	0	0	0	4	0	5	0	0
Delgado, Joseph, Roy.	0	1	.000	11.57	1	1	0	0	0	0	2.1	4	15	3	3	0	0	0	0	4	0	2	0	0
Delossantos, Carlos, Pir.	3	5	.375	3.48	11	7	0	0	3	1	51.2	45	227	24	20	4	0	0	10	23	0	53	5	2
De Los Santos, Luis, Yan.	2	0	1.000	3.00	4	3	0	0	0	0	15.0	15	64	5	5	0	0	0	0	6	0	19	0	1
Detillion, Jamie, Tig.*	5	3	.625	2.60	16	1	0	0	4	2	34.2	23	136	11	10	2	3	2	1	10	1	29	3	0
Diaz, Elisandy, Exp.	1	1	.500	4.27	13	9	0	0	1	0	52.2	58	234	35	25	4	0	1	7	12	0	38	2	1
Digby, Bryan, Brav.	1	3	.250	7.33	10	3	0	0	0	0	27.0	28	133	28	22	3	1	0	2	21	0	34	10	1
Dishman, Richard, Brav.	0	1	.000	6.30	5	5	0	0	0	0	10.0	18	48	8	7	1	0	1	1	0	0	12	3	0
Douglas, Rod, Brav.	1	3	.250	5.32	13	0	0	0	4	0	23.2	25	123	20	14	0	1	0	2	19	0	24	4	2
Dubuc, Charles, Exp.*	1	4	.200	6.14	12	3	0	0	2	0	44.0	46	212	38	30	6	1	4	7	24	0	44	6	1
Dumatrait, Phillip, R.S.*	0	1	.000	1.65	6	6	0	0	0	0	16.1	10	73	6	3	0	1	0	2	12	0	12	0	0
Durbin, Joseph, Twi.	0	0	.000	0.00	2	0	0	0	0	0	2.0	2	9	0	0	0	0	0	0	0	0	4	0	0
Edwards, Bryan, Reds	0	0	.000	3.72	9	0	0	0	4	0	9.2	10	55	7	4	0	2	0	4	9	0	7	3	0
Elskamp, Andrew, Phi.	5	1	.833	3.67	11	0	0	0	2	0	27.0	23	118	14	11	1	1	0	1	12	0	20	3	0
Eshelman, Vaughn, Reds*	0	1	.000	1.86	2	2	0	0	0	0	9.2	1	35	2	2	0	1	0	0	4	0	6	0	0
Espaillat, Ezequiel, Mar.	3	0	1.000	1.74	11	1	0	0	5	2	31.0	23	127	6	6	1	1	2	1	14	3	19	3	1
Esquivia, Manuel, Mar.	6	1	.857	2.78	12	11	0	0	0	0	64.2	42	263	20	20	4	1	5	3	24	0	77	5	0
Ewin, Ryan, Brav.	0	6	.000	2.70	10	8	0	0	0	0	43.1	31	185	23	13	1	3	0	0	22	0	51	5	0
Feleciano, Ruben, Rang.*	6	2	.750	3.65	19	0	0	0	8	3	37.0	38	166	17	15	1	2	1	3	21	2	23	7	1
Forystek, Brian, Ori.*	4	0	1.000	3.72	11	0	0	0	3	1	19.1	18	86	10	8	1	2	0	1	8	2	28	3	0
Francisco, Franklin, R.S.	0	0	.000	18.00	1	0	0	0	0	0	1.0	2	7	3	2	0	0	0	0	2	0	1	1	0
Freeman, Miguel, Exp.	0	1	.000	9.00	2	0	0	0	2	0	2.0	3	11	2	2	0	1	0	0	2	0	0	0	0
Fuell, Jerrod, Tig.	1	2	.333	8.31	13	0	0	0	6	0	21.2	30	114	23	20	4	0	1	0	19	0	25	2	0
Fussell, Chris, Roy.	0	1	.000	2.45	2	2	0	0	0	0	3.2	6	23	5	1	0	0	0	2	2	0	6	0	0
Galarraga, Luis, R.S.	0	0	.000	2.70	2	0	0	0	2	0	3.1	3	14	1	1	1	0	0	0	1	0	2	1	0
Galvez, Willy, R.S.	2	1	.667	3.07	3	2	0	0	0	0	14.2	11	57	6	5	0	0	0	1	7	0	11	0	0
Garcia, Cristian, Mar.	0	1	.000	18.00	1	0	0	0	1	0	1.0	3	7	2	2	0	0	0	0	1	0	1	0	1
Garcia, Rafael, Roy.	4	4	.500	3.25	13	6	0	0	2	0	44.1	34	189	22	16	1	1	1	3	24	0	55	4	1
Gardner, Hayden, Rang.	0	3	.000	2.25	17	1	0	0	10	3	28.0	28	128	11	7	1	2	3	0	16	1	23	0	0
Geigel, Rolando, Mar.	1	2	.333	6.43	8	0	0	0	5	1	14.0	18	72	16	10	2	1	1	6	4	0	18	3	0
Generelli, Daniel, R.S.	1	1	.500	3.63	7	1	0	0	1	1	17.1	12	80	10	7	1	0	0	1	16	0	17	5	3
George, Nelson, Reds	1	0	1.000	9.45	10	0	0	0	4	0	20.0	21	113	26	21	1	1	1	5	25	1	15	11	0
Gerlach, Brian, Twi.	3	1	.750	0.91	25	0	0	0	14	4	29.2	15	110	5	3	1	1	0	0	12	3	35	0	0
Gilbert, Richard, Rang.*	0	0	.000	13.50	1	1	0	0	0	0	4.0	7	22	6	6	0	0	2	1	4	0	0	0	0
Gill, Ryan, Yan.	2	0	1.000	0.00	10	0	0	0	5	3	16.1	6	60	1	0	0	0	0	1	5	0	10	1	1
Gleason, Michael, Rang.	2	0	1.000	3.68	10	0	0	0	4	2	14.2	12	71	9	6	0	1	0	2	14	1	9	0	0
Gonzalez, Giovanni, Pir.	1	0	1.000	4.00	7	0	0	0	4	0	9.0	8	42	7	4	0	0	3	2	5	0	5	0	0
Gonzalez, Jose, R.S.	1	0	1.000	3.46	6	6	0	0	0	0	26.0	24	114	12	10	1	0	0	8	13	0	14	1	0
Gonzalez, Mike, Pir.*	1	0	1.000	4.50	2	1	0	0	1	0	6.0	8	35	6	3	1	0	0	1	4	0	7	3	0
Gooden, Dwight, Yan.	0	0	.000	0.00	2	2	0	0	0	0	8.0	3	29	0	0	0	0	0	0	1	0	12	0	0
Grace, Bryan, Yan.	1	1	.500	3.50	5	3	0	0	1	0	18.0	15	79	10	7	1	0	1	1	6	0	22	2	0
Graham, Thomas, Rang.	5	0	1.000	2.29	18	4	0	0	3	2	59.0	57	236	17	15	1	0	2	4	8	1	53	1	0
Grahe, Joe, Phi.	0	0	.000	4.50	3	3	0	0	0	0	6.0	7	28	4	3	0	0	1	2	1	0	2	0	0
Granado, Jan, Reds*	0	0	.000	0.87	6	0	0	0	2	0	10.1	11	44	1	1	0	0	0	0	4	0	8	0	0
Griswold, Jordan, Exp.*	1	1	.500	3.62	14	4	0	0	5	1	32.1	22	146	13	13	0	1	1	0	33	0	30	2	0
Guerrero, Julio, Pir.	5	3	.625	3.16	11	9	0	0	1	0	57.0	56	242	28	20	2	1	2	4	9	0	25	2	2
Gutierrez, Fernando, Ori.	3	2	.600	5.25	17	0	0	0	13	1	24.0	22	116	15	14	1	3	1	1	20	3	28	2	5
Hall, Josh, Reds	0	5	.000	10.57	6	6	0	0	0	0	15.1	26	84	25	18	2	0	1	0	13	0	20	3	0
Hall, Kevin, Pir.	1	2	.333	1.59	13	0	0	0	11	4	17.0	21	79	4	3	0	2	2	1	7	0	20	1	0
Hall, Shane, R.S.	4	2	.667	4.14	15	3	0	0	2	0	45.2	47	216	27	21	2	2	1	3	28	1	31	1	1
Hamilton, Charles, Roy.	0	1	.000	5.63	3	2	0	0	0	0	8.0	10	35	5	5	1	0	1	1	2	0	7	1	0
Harris, Karl, Exp.	0	0	.000	0.00	1	0	0	0	0	0	2.0	2	8	0	0	0	0	0	0	0	0	3	0	0
Hassler, Drew, Ori.	1	0	1.000	10.95	7	0	0	0	1	0	12.1	17	64	16	15	0	0	0	0	10	0	10	1	0
Haynes, Brad, Mar.	4	1	.800	2.91	10	8	0	0	0	0	46.1	25	199	19	15	1	1	0	5	34	0	51	7	1
Heredia, Nixon, Reds	0	0	.000	3.38	5	0	0	0	4	0	5.1	8	27	4	2	0	0	1	0	2	0	3	0	1
Hernandez, Fausto, Tig.	1	1	.500	2.23	27	0	0	0	25	17	32.1	20	129	10	8	2	1	1	1	13	1	31	1	0
Hernandez, Yoel, Phi.	4	1	.800	1.35	10	9	2	1	0	0	60.0	39	237	10	9	2	0	0	7	17	0	46	4	1
Hill, Jamie, Yan.*	0	0	.000	7.71	2	0	0	0	0	0	4.2	5	23	4	4	0	0	0	1	3	0	4	2	0
Hill, Shawn, Exp.	1	3	.250	4.81	7	7	0	0	0	0	24.1	25	117	17	13	0	0	1	6	10	0	20	3	1
Hopper, Kevin, Brav.	0	0	.000	2.45	2	0	0	0	1	0	3.2	3	18	3	1	0	0	0	0	2	0	2	1	0
Janek, John, Reds	0	0	.000	0.00	1	0	0	0	0	0	0.0	0	3	3	3	0	0	0	2	1	0	0	0	0
Jimenez, Ronal, Phi.	2	2	.500	2.39	20	0	0	0	17	6	26.1	19	115	10	7	3	2	1	0	14	1	23	3	0
Johnson, Jeremy, Tig.	3	1	.750	4.15	12	7	0	0	1	0	39.0	37	176	24	18	1	0	2	2	19	0	41	3	0
Johnston, Dave, Mar.	1	1	.500	3.20	14	0	0	0	8	3	25.1	21	110	12	9	0	1	1	4	11	0	19	1	0
Jones, Andrew, Pir.	1	3	.250	3.89	11	1	0	0	5	0	44.0	45	201	28	19	5	1	7	10	14	1	20	2	0
Joseph, Glen, Reds	0	1	.000	16.88	7	1	0	0	2	1	8.0	12	55	20	15	1	0	0	3	16	0	4	3	0
Kaanoi, Jason, Roy.	2	1	.667	0.56	4	4	0	0	0	0	16.0	13	62	2	1	0	0	0	0	2	0	20	2	1
Keefer, Ryan, Ori.	1	2	.333	4.43	13	1	0	0	4	0	22.1	26	102	13	11	0	1	0	3	6	3	21	1	0
Kemp, Bo, Twi.	0	1	.000	3.12	7	0	0	0	2	1	8.2	6	37	5	3	0	0	1	1	3	0	10	3	0
Keyser, Timothy, Pir.	0	0	.000	5.14	4	0	0	0	1	1	7.0	8	31	4	4	0	1	0	1	2	0	7	0	0
Kimball, Cody, Twi.	2	0	1.000	1.35	18	3	0	0	1	0	33.1	30	138	8	5	0	0	0	1	12	1	26	2	0
King, Jeremy, Yan.	2	4	.333	4.39	11	11	0	0	0	0	55.1	65	252	35	27	2	0	5	3	24	0	46	6	1
Lajara, Eudy, Mar.*	4	1	.800	0.94	11	1	0	0	5	1	28.2	22	122	6	3	1	1	1	1	7	1	35	1	0
Laplante, Reggie, Yan.	6	0	1.000	1.04	24	0	0	0	22	13	26.0	9	97	4	3	1	0	1	3	9	1	27	1	0
Lee, Kevin, Pir.	4	0	1.000	1.80	9	0	0	0	4	0	15.0	16	69	5	3	1	2	0	3	4	0	7	0	0
Legette, Richard, Phi.	0	1	.000	5.30	12	2	0	0	5	0	18.2	14	85	12	11	2	0	0	2	12	0	20	3	1
Leon, Omar, Mar.	0	0	.000	0.00	2	0	0	0	2	0	1.1	0	6	0	0	0	0	0	0	2	0	0	0	0
Lewis, Jeremy, Tig.*	2	5	.286	4.68	12	10	1	0	0	0	57.2	52	252	38	30	1	1	3	2	28	0	57	8	1

Pitcher, Team	W	L	Pct.	ERA	G	GS	CG	ShO	GF	Sv.	IP	H	TBF	R	ER	HR	SH	SF	HB	BB	IBB	SO	WP	Bk.
Lima, Juan, Exp.	2	1	.667	2.60	8	3	0	0	1	0	27.2	21	112	13	8	1	1	0	1	9	0	15	1	0
Lindsey, Bart, Phi.*	1	1	.500	3.98	13	0	0	0	1	1	20.1	23	85	11	9	1	1	2	0	6	0	17	2	0
Loiselle, Rich, Pir.	0	0	.000	0.00	1	1	0	0	0	0	1.0	0	3	0	0	0	0	0	0	0	0	2	0	0
Lombardi, Justin, Mar.*	2	1	.667	1.13	6	0	0	0	3	0	8.0	4	35	4	1	0	0	1	0	6	0	15	1	0
Lopez, Omar, Reds	1	1	.500	4.13	8	5	0	0	1	0	32.2	30	136	18	15	0	1	0	5	12	0	24	2	1
Lopez, Samuel, Roy.	1	1	.500	3.29	23	0	0	0	21	11	27.1	23	123	12	10	1	1	1	7	13	0	25	2	0
Love, Brandon, Reds	0	1	.000	0.00	2	2	0	0	0	0	6.2	4	31	4	0	0	0	1	6	0	8	0	0	0
Lundgren, Wayne, R.S.	2	2	.500	3.41	11	2	0	0	1	1	29.0	39	135	20	11	1	0	2	1	8	0	12	1	0
Mabry, Barry, Brav.	0	1	.000	2.04	8	0	0	0	5	1	17.2	13	68	4	4	2	0	0	4	4	0	13	0	0
Machen, Mike, Brav.	2	1	.667	2.97	12	1	0	0	2	0	30.1	22	147	15	10	1	1	2	7	26	1	28	7	0
Madritsch, Robert, Reds*	1	1	.500	2.01	6	4	0	0	0	0	22.1	15	90	5	5	0	1	0	2	9	0	27	0	0
Manon, Julio, Exp.	2	0	1.000	0.87	4	0	0	0	1	0	10.1	4	36	1	1	0	2	0	1	2	0	10	0	0
Marceau, Pierre-luc, Exp.*	0	4	.000	6.97	6	3	0	0	1	0	10.1	9	62	18	8	0	1	1	4	17	0	9	6	0
Markray, Thad, Reds	1	1	.500	6.08	9	0	0	0	2	0	13.1	18	63	12	9	1	1	0	0	6	0	11	1	0
Marrero, Darwin, Exp.	1	6	.143	6.34	11	7	1	0	0	0	49.2	60	231	42	35	3	0	1	12	15	0	36	4	2
Martinez, Anastacio, R.S.	0	1	.000	9.45	2	1	0	0	0	0	6.2	15	38	9	7	0	0	1	0	3	0	1	0	0
Martinez, Jesus, Yan.	0	1	.000	9.00	3	0	0	0	2	0	3.0	4	16	3	3	0	0	0	0	2	0	3	0	1
Mayfield, James, Phi.	4	3	.571	4.93	11	8	0	0	2	1	42.0	48	184	28	23	2	2	0	0	10	1	25	0	0
McCasland, Ralph, Exp.*	3	0	.000	3.07	7	4	1	0	1	0	29.1	32	127	13	10	2	1	4	3	0	18	3	0
McGlinchy, Kevin, Brav.	0	0	.000	9.00	4	2	0	0	0	0	5.0	12	29	8	5	0	0	0	1	0	6	0	0
McKay, John, Mar.	0	0	.000	0.00	1	0	0	0	1	0	1.0	1	4	0	0	0	0	0	0	0	0	2	0	0
McNatt, Josh, Ori.*	0	0	.000	8.59	9	0	0	0	2	0	14.2	19	78	19	14	1	0	0	0	17	0	10	3	0
Meisenheimer, Matthew, Rang.	0	1	.000	2.30	6	5	0	0	0	0	15.2	15	69	5	4	0	0	1	7	0	13	1	0
Melendez, Dave, Tig.	1	1	.500	2.12	5	2	1	0	2	1	17.0	12	68	7	4	2	0	1	3	9	0	9	0	0
Mendible, Franklin, Twi.	2	2	.500	2.70	17	0	0	0	2	0	20.0	16	87	6	6	0	1	2	1	14	0	23	3	0
Merrell, Phil, Reds	0	2	.000	2.92	3	3	0	0	0	0	12.1	11	58	9	4	1	0	0	2	4	0	17	0	0
Merricks, Matt, Brav.*	1	0	1.000	2.53	9	0	0	0	6	1	21.1	21	96	15	6	0	0	1	1	11	0	28	2	0
Messenger, Randall, Mar.	2	2	.500	4.83	12	12	0	0	0	0	59.2	66	263	37	32	6	1	1	3	22	0	29	7	2
Miceli, Danny, Mar.	0	0	.000	0.00	2	2	0	0	0	0	3.0	0	10	0	0	0	0	0	0	1	0	3	0	0
Middleton, Kyle, Roy.	0	2	.000	14.85	15	1	0	0	2	0	20.0	32	109	34	33	2	0	1	0	17	0	14	6	0
Miller, Colby, Twi.	3	2	.600	3.09	14	10	0	0	0	0	55.1	44	231	26	19	2	5	0	3	21	0	55	3	0
Miller, Jason, Twi.*	0	0	.000	0.00	2	1	0	0	0	0	4.0	2	15	1	0	0	1	0	0	0	0	3	0	0
Miller, Matt, Rang.	0	0	.000	4.50	1	0	0	0	0	0	2.0	2	9	1	1	0	0	1	0	4	0	4	0	0
Miller, Matt, Brav.*	0	0	.000	3.60	3	0	0	0	2	0	5.0	5	23	2	2	0	0	0	3	0	7	0	0
Mims, Brandon, R.S.*	1	1	.500	1.38	4	2	1	1	0	0	13.0	10	54	3	2	1	1	2	1	8	0	15	2	1
Minaya, Pedro, Reds	1	3	.250	7.71	6	4	0	0	0	0	16.1	28	80	17	14	0	2	0	8	0	14	1	0
Miniel, Rene, R.S.	2	4	.333	4.00	21	1	0	0	17	5	36.0	37	162	21	16	1	5	1	0	21	3	31	3	0
Mitchell, Thomas, Exp.	2	3	.400	3.72	10	9	0	0	1	0	46.0	43	201	29	19	6	1	1	3	18	0	26	0	0
Miyamoto, Eij, Exp.	0	2	.000	2.52	9	8	1	0	0	0	50.0	37	198	16	14	4	1	2	1	16	0	40	5	0
Montalbano, Greg, R.S.*	0	2	.000	3.75	4	4	0	0	0	0	12.0	13	51	6	5	1	0	0	3	0	14	1	0
Montgomery, Steve, R.S.	0	1	.000	13.50	2	0	0	0	0	0	4.0	7	25	10	6	0	0	0	1	4	0	4	2	0
Montilla, Elvis, Ori.	3	2	.600	3.48	16	2	0	0	4	0	31.0	24	129	14	12	3	0	1	3	10	1	15	0	0
Moore, Chris, Mar.	1	0	1.000	2.13	6	0	0	0	4	1	12.2	9	55	3	3	0	0	1	4	4	0	13	1	0
Morel, Jesus, Twi.	0	1	.000	1.86	8	0	0	0	1	0	9.2	6	36	4	2	1	0	0	1	3	0	11	0	0
Moreno, Darwin, Brav.	4	3	.571	5.34	14	1	0	0	7	0	30.1	35	150	23	18	2	0	1	0	18	0	25	1	1
Moreno, Julio, Ori.	0	0	.000	0.00	3	0	0	0	0	0	6.0	6	27	3	0	0	0	0	3	0	6	0	0
Mosley, Eric, Yan.	0	0	.000	15.75	5	0	0	0	1	0	4.0	11	24	7	7	0	0	0	1	2	0	2	0	1
Negrette, Richard, Ori.	0	2	.000	7.30	7	0	0	0	3	0	12.1	13	61	10	10	0	0	0	2	12	2	8	1	0
Nelson, Bubba, Brav.	3	2	.600	4.23	12	6	1	0	4	0	44.2	40	190	24	21	2	3	1	1	13	0	54	6	0
Nelson, Joe, Brav.	1	0	1.000	2.25	4	0	0	0	1	1	4.0	3	18	1	1	0	0	0	3	0	7	0	0
Neubauer, Marc, Mar.*	0	0	.000	0.00	2	0	0	0	0	0	2.1	0	9	0	0	0	0	0	2	1	0	3	0	0
Nunez, Maximo, R.S.	0	0	.000	3.00	2	0	0	0	1	0	6.0	12	29	3	2	0	0	0	0	8	0	8	0	0
Nye, Ryan, Phi.	0	0	.000	1.93	2	2	0	0	0	0	4.2	6	21	1	1	1	0	0	1	0	7	0	0
O'Brien, Patrick, Pir.	3	1	.750	4.96	10	10	1	0	0	0	49.0	66	235	32	27	1	1	3	9	19	0	31	2	0
Olive, Jesse, R.S.	3	1	.750	6.97	13	0	0	0	3	1	31.0	45	153	26	24	0	2	1	1	18	3	16	1	0
Ortega, Orlando, Roy.	1	4	.200	5.34	20	0	0	0	9	1	32.0	33	153	23	19	0	1	1	22	2	41	1	2
Ortiz, Javier, Yan.	0	0	.000	7.71	1	0	0	0	0	0	2.1	3	11	2	2	0	0	0	1	0	2	0	0
Parker, Dwayne, Roy.*	0	2	.000	4.22	12	0	0	0	3	0	21.1	22	103	10	10	0	1	2	19	0	31	4	0
Parris, Matt, Tig.	3	0	1.000	2.14	9	6	0	0	1	0	33.2	29	148	11	8	0	5	0	2	17	1	29	1	1
Paz, Jackson, Brav.	2	0	1.000	1.29	8	0	0	0	5	1	14.0	12	56	4	2	0	0	0	2	0	11	0	0
Peeples, Jim, Yan.*	0	1	.000	10.38	5	0	0	0	2	0	4.1	9	29	7	5	0	0	4	5	0	4	0	0
Pena, Domingo, Pir.	0	0	.000	1.93	2	2	0	0	0	0	4.2	4	17	1	1	0	0	0	1	0	4	0	0
Peres, Luis, R.S.*	3	1	.750	2.36	9	5	0	0	2	1	34.1	24	139	12	9	2	0	0	1	13	0	43	0	0
Perez, Franklin, Tig.	1	2	.333	3.63	6	3	1	0	2	1	22.1	21	90	9	9	1	0	1	0	4	0	25	3	0
Petty, Chad, Tig.*	2	3	.400	3.00	9	7	1	0	1	0	39.0	31	165	18	13	0	0	2	1	20	0	38	1	1
Pfalzgraf, Christopher, Rang.	3	0	1.000	4.50	20	0	0	0	10	5	30.0	23	129	17	15	2	2	0	1	17	0	30	2	0
Pike, Matthew, Reds	0	1	.000	3.69	11	3	0	0	2	0	31.2	26	138	18	13	2	2	1	1	17	1	42	2	0
Pineda, Isauro, R.S.	0	1	.000	4.20	4	3	0	0	0	0	15.0	13	65	8	7	0	1	0	1	7	0	11	2	0
Powell, Maurice, Twi.	1	1	.500	4.61	11	0	0	0	2	0	13.2	14	68	12	7	0	3	1	6	5	0	11	3	0
Puello, Ignacio, Exp.	1	1	.500	6.06	4	3	0	0	0	0	16.1	20	82	13	11	0	0	0	12	0	13	4	0
Rada, Gerald, Yan.	2	1	.667	1.35	8	7	0	0	0	0	33.1	25	128	8	5	0	0	1	0	4	0	27	0	2
Ramirez, Eucebio, Mar.	1	1	.500	1.47	3	3	0	0	0	0	18.1	14	71	3	3	1	0	0	0	4	0	16	1	3
Ramos, Victor, Pir.	0	0	.000	0.00	1	0	0	0	1	0	0.1	1	1	0	0	0	0	0	0	0	0	0	0	0
Randazzo, Jeffrey, Twi.*	7	2	.778	3.15	13	12	3	1	0	0	68.2	70	283	35	24	2	3	2	6	19	0	58	4	1
Rejean, Rhett, Rang.*	3	2	.600	5.73	15	11	0	0	1	0	55.0	58	249	41	35	6	2	3	2	29	0	34	3	0
Rengifo, Nohemar, Exp.	1	3	.250	9.30	11	0	0	0	10	1	20.1	27	103	27	21	2	3	2	3	17	0	10	8	0
Reyes, Hipolito, Roy.	2	1	.667	2.19	9	8	0	0	1	0	37.0	28	162	14	9	1	1	0	8	22	0	23	3	0
Reynolds, Eric, Yan.*	2	3	.400	3.86	9	9	0	0	0	0	39.2	37	166	20	17	1	1	1	8	18	0	33	3	0
Rice, Scott, Ori.*	1	6	.143	5.21	13	13	0	0	0	0	57.0	61	273	46	33	0	2	3	8	48	1	34	3	1
Richardson, Jason, Twi.	1	1	.500	1.46	6	0	0	0	1	0	12.1	10	60	6	2	0	1	1	4	9	0	10	4	1
Rijo, Hector, Exp.*	0	2	.000	4.76	18	0	0	0	15	6	34.0	39	151	23	18	3	0	1	1	12	0	21	0	0
Rivera, Luis, Brav.	0	0	.000	0.00	3	3	0	0	0	0	4.0	2	16	0	0	0	1	0	1	0	2	1	0
Rodriguez, Ricardo, Brav.	0	0	.000	0.00	1	0	0	0	0	0	1.0	0	4	0	0	0	0	0	0	1	0	3	0	0

Pitcher, Team	W	L	Pct.	ERA	G	GS	CG	ShO	GF	Sv.	IP	H	TBF	R	ER	HR	SH	SF	HB	BB	IBB	SO	WP	Bk.
Rodriguez, Alejandro, Phi.	1	0	1.000	2.81	3	1	0	0	0	0	16.0	15	68	6	5	1	0	1	4	0	21	1	0
Rodriguez, Eddy, Ori.	2	1	.667	2.00	18	0	0	0	14	6	27.0	17	116	8	6	0	3	0	2	19	1	31	0	0
Rodriguez, George, Phi.	0	0	.000	1.61	19	0	0	0	14	7	22.1	17	91	6	4	0	3	0	1	6	0	30	0	0
Rodriguez, Juan, Pir.	1	2	.333	3.71	12	3	0	0	4	0	34.0	39	154	24	14	1	1	2	2	8	0	24	5	1
Rodriguez, Luis, Rang.	2	0	1.000	3.16	6	6	0	0	0	0	25.2	23	109	11	9	0	0	1	0	13	0	19	2	0
Rodriguez, Marino, Mar.*	1	0	1.000	4.15	7	0	0	0	5	1	8.2	10	40	4	4	0	2	1	1	5	0	4	2	0
Rogers, Bradley, Ori.	2	2	.500	2.86	9	9	0	0	0	0	44.0	34	183	16	14	2	1	1	5	16	0	24	2	0
Rogers, Jon, Brav.	1	0	1.000	0.53	8	0	0	0	5	2	17.0	13	69	1	1	0	1	1	1	8	1	10	1	0
Romero, Cesar, Yan.	3	2	.600	5.03	14	0	0	0	6	0	19.2	16	94	14	11	1	0	3	3	14	0	13	2	0
Rosa, Elias, Roy.*	1	0	1.000	4.91	6	1	0	0	0	0	11.0	15	60	8	6	0	0	2	9	0	4	1	0
Rosado, Hector, Roy.*	1	3	.250	2.88	14	1	0	0	4	0	25.0	15	98	12	8	2	0	2	0	8	0	18	0	0
Ross, Christian, Reds	0	3	.000	4.29	6	3	0	0	0	0	21.0	18	87	14	10	1	0	1	0	7	1	21	1	0
Rundles, Richard, R.S.*	3	1	.750	2.45	9	6	0	0	0	0	40.1	31	158	15	11	3	2	0	4	10	0	32	0	1
St. Amant, John, Phi.	0	2	.000	5.50	11	1	0	0	7	0	18.0	25	95	17	11	1	0	0	3	6	0	18	3	0
Sak, Jim, Pir.	0	0	.000	0.00	2	0	0	0	0	0	3.0	0	11	0	0	0	0	0	0	2	0	5	3	0
Salazar, Luis, Mar.	0	0	.000	0.00	1	0	0	0	0	0	2.0	0	7	0	0	0	0	0	0	1	0	3	0	0
Salinas, Sean, Reds	0	0	.000	21.60	2	0	0	0	1	0	1.2	2	10	4	4	1	1	0	0	3	0	3	0	0
Sanchez, Elby, Roy.	2	2	.500	5.00	19	2	0	0	7	0	28.2	25	137	17	16	2	1	2	2	23	0	25	3	0
Sanchez, Pedro, Twi.*	0	0	.000	5.54	19	0	0	0	6	0	13.0	13	66	8	8	0	0	2	2	11	0	11	0	0
Santana, Eddy, Yan.	4	0	1.000	3.62	17	0	0	0	4	0	32.1	40	143	16	13	0	2	2	1	12	0	17	1	0
Santos, Victor, Tig.	0	0	.000	0.00	1	1	0	0	0	0	3.0	2	13	1	0	0	0	0	0	2	0	5	0	0
Sauer, Danny, Exp.	1	6	.143	4.85	14	0	0	0	8	2	29.2	28	151	27	16	2	2	3	3	34	0	17	9	1
Saye, Thomas, Roy.	0	1	.000	6.94	8	0	0	0	4	0	11.2	10	57	10	9	0	1	3	7	0	11	6	0
Schachleiter, Jeff, Reds.	1	2	.333	2.45	6	4	0	0	0	0	22.0	17	103	13	6	2	1	0	4	13	0	16	6	3
Schmidt, Jason, Pir.	0	0	.000	2.25	1	1	0	0	0	0	4.0	4	16	2	1	0	0	0	0	0	0	1	1	0
Schoening, Brent, Twi.	0	0	.000	1.29	2	2	0	0	0	0	7.0	2	25	1	1	1	0	0	3	0	8	0	0
Searles, Jonathan, Phi.	2	2	.500	3.65	7	6	0	0	0	0	37.0	41	170	23	15	2	1	1	3	10	0	19	7	0
Severino, Cleris, Reds*	1	3	.250	3.12	13	5	0	0	1	0	52.0	46	224	25	18	3	1	1	4	23	0	36	2	0
Severino, Jose, Tig.	2	0	1.000	5.40	2	2	0	0	0	0	13.1	15	56	8	8	2	0	1	2	3	0	11	1	0
Shafer, Kurt, Phi.	2	1	.667	2.77	8	1	0	0	6	1	13.0	15	54	4	4	0	1	0	3	0	5	2	0
Shortslef, Josh, Pir.*	3	2	.600	3.73	11	3	0	0	3	0	31.1	26	132	15	13	1	0	4	11	0	19	2	1
Sierra, Jr., Auvin, Tig.*	3	1	.750	1.35	13	0	0	0	5	1	20.0	15	77	5	3	0	0	2	4	0	23	4	1
Simon, Janewrys, Twi.	0	0	.000	6.35	9	1	0	0	4	1	11.1	8	57	8	8	1	0	0	4	11	0	16	3	0
Simpson, Cory, Brav.	0	0	.000	0.00	4	1	0	0	0	0	6.2	6	28	6	0	1	0	0	1	5	0	4	0	0
Smith, Brian, Pir.	0	0	.000	0.00	5	2	0	0	1	0	6.0	2	19	0	0	0	0	0	1	0	5	0	0
Smith, Jason, Yan.	6	2	.750	3.45	10	10	0	0	0	0	57.1	57	249	26	22	2	1	0	4	13	0	54	2	0
Snell, Ian, Pir.	1	0	1.000	2.35	4	0	0	0	1	0	7.2	5	28	2	2	1	1	0	1	8	0	0	0	0
Snyder, Kyle, Roy.	0	0	.000	0.00	1	1	0	0	0	0	2.0	1	7	0	0	0	0	0	0	0	0	5	0	0
Spear, Russell, Tig.	0	0	.000	2.45	3	0	0	0	1	0	3.2	2	18	1	1	0	0	0	0	5	0	5	0	1
Sperring, Jayme, Ori.	0	0	.000	0.00	3	0	0	0	1	0	5.0	2	18	0	0	0	0	0	1	5	0	4	0	0
Spillers, Larry, Ori.	0	0	.000	0.90	3	3	0	0	0	0	10.0	5	40	1	1	0	1	1	2	6	0	8	0	0
Steele, Bradley, Phi.	2	1	.667	4.00	13	3	0	0	3	0	27.0	35	126	18	12	3	1	1	2	4	0	30	2	1
Sterett, Adam, Mar.	1	3	.250	6.75	11	0	0	0	2	0	16.0	19	86	15	12	0	0	2	7	14	0	13	6	0
Stodolka, Michael, Roy.*	0	3	.000	2.68	9	6	0	0	1	0	37.0	31	157	18	11	1	0	1	2	16	0	32	3	1
Story, Aaron, Pir.*	2	0	1.000	1.57	5	3	0	0	1	1	23.0	16	94	5	4	2	0	3	7	0	27	2	0
Tate, Matthew, Ori.	1	0	1.000	6.19	9	2	0	0	2	1	16.0	16	75	11	11	1	0	1	11	1	13	2	0
Tejada, Sandy, Twi.	6	2	.750	4.53	15	10	1	0	0	0	57.2	57	243	30	29	3	2	1	20	0	49	4	0
Tejada, Robinson, Phi.	2	5	.286	5.54	10	6	1	1	1	0	39.0	44	178	30	24	3	1	2	2	12	0	22	5	1
Thigpen, Joshua, R.S.	1	0	1.000	15.00	2	0	0	0	0	0	3.0	3	17	5	5	1	0	1	0	6	0	2	1	0
Thompson, Jesse, Reds	0	2	.000	5.14	7	1	0	0	3	0	14.0	16	67	12	8	2	1	1	6	0	18	2	0
Thompson, Matthew, R.S.	4	2	.667	3.65	12	11	0	0	0	0	56.2	65	258	33	23	5	1	3	4	18	0	54	6	0
Timaure, Jesus, Mar.	0	0	.000	27.00	1	0	0	0	1	0	0.2	1	6	2	2	0	0	0	3	0	1	0	0
Timm, Dan, Reds	0	1	.000	81.00	1	1	0	0	0	0	0.2	4	9	6	6	0	0	0	2	0	0	1	0
Torres, Alex, Tig.*	0	1	.000	6.19	3	3	0	0	2	0	4.2	4	29	6	2	0	0	0	8	0	7	1	0
Torres, Carlos, Reds	2	3	.400	5.19	11	7	0	0	1	0	43.1	56	217	42	25	3	3	4	5	26	0	17	13	1
Tremont, Harold, Rang.	5	0	1.000	2.76	16	0	0	0	4	4	45.2	38	191	15	14	3	1	1	6	0	26	0	0
Trevino, Chris, Brav.*	0	0	.000	4.09	4	1	0	0	1	0	11.0	10	46	7	5	1	0	1	0	5	0	10	2	0
Troilo, Joseph, R.S.	1	1	.500	2.64	24	0	0	0	19	4	30.2	31	142	17	9	2	5	4	4	14	2	25	4	2
Truselo, Randy, Rang.	1	1	.500	3.95	8	0	0	0	1	0	13.2	14	62	8	6	1	1	0	8	0	10	0	0
Turner, Jess, Twi.	1	1	.500	6.94	16	0	0	0	8	2	11.2	14	59	12	9	1	4	0	2	7	0	15	2	0
Valdez, Jose, Reds	0	0	.000	0.00	1	1	0	0	0	0	2.0	0	10	1	0	0	0	0	3	0	1	0	0
Valentin, Emmanuel, Tig.	1	2	.333	12.06	9	1	0	0	2	0	15.2	23	89	21	21	2	0	1	18	0	16	3	0
Valenzuela, Ramon, Twi.	2	2	.500	3.75	18	0	0	0	5	1	24.0	27	104	12	10	3	1	0	5	0	13	2	0
Valle, Yoiset, Yan.*	1	1	.500	6.75	5	1	0	0	0	0	12.0	15	60	13	9	1	0	3	7	0	13	1	0
Velasquez, Reinaldo, Roy.	1	0	1.000	5.63	6	2	0	0	0	0	16.0	15	70	11	10	0	0	2	8	0	15	0	0
Wahlbrink, Steven, Pir.	0	0	.000	27.00	1	0	0	0	1	0	0.1	3	4	1	1	0	0	0	0	0	0	1	0
Wainwright, Adam, Brav.	4	0	1.000	1.13	7	5	0	0	1	0	32.0	15	120	5	4	1	0	0	10	0	42	1	1
Watson, Allen, Yan.*	0	0	.000	0.00	1	1	0	0	0	0	1.0	1	4	0	0	0	0	0	0	0	1	0	0
Weber, Brett, Yan.	0	0	.000	0.00	4	0	0	0	3	0	5.2	4	19	0	0	0	0	1	0	8	0	7	1	0
Wheatland, Matthew, Tig.	2	1	.667	1.25	5	4	0	0	0	0	21.2	14	84	4	3	1	0	1	1	5	0	21	2	0
Williams, Marcus, Reds	0	2	.000	11.45	9	0	0	0	5	0	11.0	14	56	15	14	3	2	1	0	9	1	8	4	0
Wise, Eric, Exp.	2	2	.500	5.01	12	0	0	0	7	1	23.1	33	118	22	13	3	4	3	0	10	0	18	1	0
Wright, Matt, Brav.	0	2	.000	0.86	12	0	0	0	10	4	21.0	8	85	5	2	0	1	1	0	11	0	30	2	0
Wright, Raymond, Reds	0	0	.000	40.50	3	0	0	0	1	0	2.0	4	21	10	9	1	0	0	1	10	0	3	7	0
Wrightsman, Dustin, Roy.	1	3	.250	7.64	8	4	0	0	0	0	22.1	25	104	14	14	3	2	2	0	12	0	15	1	2
Zurita, Thomas, Roy.	0	1	.000	3.90	11	5	0	0	0	0	32.1	35	146	17	14	1	1	1	6	10	0	18	2	0

COMBINATION SHUTOUTS: **Braves (5)**—Abreu-Wainwright, Digby-Rogers, Dishman-Simpson-Nelson-Douglas-Rogers-Mabry, Almeida-McGlinchy-Paz, Nelson-Digby-Marricks-Wright. **Expos (0)**—None. **Marlins (6)**—Haynes-Ohada, Miceli-Esquivia-Moore, Haynes-Lajara, Bautista-Lombardi, Messenger-Sterrett, Esquivia-Espaillat. **Orioles (0)**—None. **Phillies (4)**—Hernandez-Buchholz-Rodriguez, Nye-Brito, Hernandez-Mayfield, Grahe-Bucktrot-Elskamp-Jimenez. **Pirates (3)**—Story-Keyser, Shortslef-Lee-Hall, Delossantos-Guerrero. **Rangers (4)**—Beltre-Bowers, Rivard-Graham-Tremont, Graham-Feliciano, Beltre-Gardner-Pfalzgraf. **Red Sox (2)**—Gonzalez-Generelli, Peres-Miniel. **Reds (3)**—Torres-Severino, Schachlei-Bludau, Severino-Cotton-Bludau. **Royals (6)**—Garcia-Ortega, Wrightsman-Sanchez-Lopez, Kaanoi-Arias-Sanchez-Lopez, Bass-Middleton-Arias, Kaanoi-Arias, Reyes-Armitage-Ortega-Lopez. **Tigers (7)**—Cuello-Collazo-Hernandez, Johnson-Detillion-Parris,

Cuello-Johnson, Johnson-Detillion, Wheatland-Perez, Lewis-Johnson-Sierra, Borkowski-Parris-Hernandez. **Twins (2)**—Miller-Kimball-Sanchez-Simon, Miller-Durbin-Gerlach. **Yankees (8)**—De Los Santos-Artiles, De Los Santos-Artiles-Laplante, Rada-Gill-Artiles-Laplante, Smith-Santana, Acosta-Chacon-Laplante, Blankenship-Romero, Acosta-Chacon-Laplante, Smith-Gill.

NO-HIT GAMES: None.

2000 FIELDING

TEAM

Team	Pct.	G	PO	A	E	TC	DP	TP	PB
Marlins	.966	60	1543	623	76	2242	40	0	17
Twins	.962	56	1410	545	77	2032	42	0	16
Rangers	.962	56	1476	630	83	2189	49	0	11
Yankees	.961	60	1481	613	84	2178	41	0	4
Royals	.958	60	1438	505	86	2029	37	0	26
Tigers	.957	60	1465	564	91	2120	45	0	19
Red Sox	.953	55	1388	606	99	2093	53	0	31
Phillies	.952	60	1509	616	106	2231	40	0	10
Reds	.952	55	1382	583	99	2064	37	0	19
Orioles	.951	56	1429	613	106	2148	66	0	20
Pirates	.950	60	1501	591	111	2203	60	0	15
Expos	.944	60	1528	633	128	2289	67	0	12
Braves	.943	60	1474	514	121	2109	40	0	28

INDIVIDUAL

FIRST BASEMEN

NOTE: All caps denotes fielding-percentage leader based on 30 games for catchers, 40 for all other non-pitchers and 48 innings for pitchers. *Throws lefthanded.

Player, Team	Pct.	G	PO	A	E	TC	DP
Abreu, Cesar, Reds	.955	9	79	5	4	88	6
Alvarez, Aaron, Mar.	.000	1	0	0	0	0	0
Ambrosini, Dominick, Exp.*	1.000	8	48	0	0	48	5
Anderson, Nat, Tig.	.981	24	193	10	4	207	17
Arko, Thomas, Ori.	.933	3	27	1	2	30	4
Borjas, Henry, R.S.	.897	3	24	2	3	29	4
BOTTS, Jason, Rang.	.991	44	426	12	4	442	34
Bouie, Aaron, Ori.	.000	1	0	0	1	1	0
Brown, Matthew, Exp.	.987	11	74	4	1	79	14
Cancio, Antonio, Phi.	.988	10	75	5	1	81	6
Caridi, Tony, R.S.	.990	15	87	11	1	99	8
Colameco, Joe, Yan.	.000	1	0	0	0	0	0
Cooper, Matthew, R.S.	.986	26	197	10	3	210	17
Eiguren, Chaz, Reds	1.000	1	16	1	0	17	2
Foster, Gregg, Phi.	1.000	1	1	0	0	1	0
Galarraga, Luis, R.S.	.947	17	119	6	7	132	18
Garcia, Juan-Carlos, Mar.	.000	1	0	0	0	0	0
Gibbs, Mark, Ori.	1.000	10	66	6	0	72	7
Gonzalez, Adrian, Mar.*	.986	53	450	31	7	488	31
Gonzalez, Reggie, Yan.*	.984	19	176	5	3	184	12
Gredvig, Doug, Ori.	.957	2	21	1	1	23	2
Griggs, Reginald, Phi.*	.989	41	345	18	4	367	29
Harris, Karl, Exp.	.966	39	326	20	12	358	31
Huguet, J.C., Reds	.980	29	232	16	5	253	15
Jaile, Chris, Rang.	.963	5	50	2	2	54	4
Johnson iii, Nelson, Ori.	1.000	1	9	3	0	12	1
Johnson, Seth, Exp.	.985	9	58	8	1	67	6
Johnson, Tristan, Pir.*	.949	8	53	3	3	59	6
Joyce Jr., Thomas, Ori.*	1.000	8	66	1	0	67	7
Laidlaw, Jacob, Mar.	.983	6	57	1	1	59	4
Lambert, Shawn, Tig.	.959	26	203	8	9	220	15
Laureano, Wilfredo, Roy.	.939	12	43	3	3	49	3
Marquie, Craig, Yan.	.000	1	0	0	0	0	0
Martinez, William, Ori.	1.000	1	1	0	0	1	0
Masino, Adam, Twi.	.972	20	129	9	4	142	10
Matthews, Michael, Roy.	.982	16	105	3	2	110	11
Mercado, Onix, Reds	.976	8	82	1	2	85	2
Morneau, Justin, Twi.	.996	27	217	15	1	233	20
Moya, Wilson, Rang.	1.000	2	8	0	0	8	1
Nunn, Jason, Yan.	.000	1	0	0	0	0	0
Patchett, Gary, Reds	1.000	2	7	2	0	9	1
Patterson, Sean, Reds	.958	8	69	0	3	72	4
Pickering, Kelvin, Ori.	.961	13	95	4	4	103	15
Reed, Robert, R.S.	.975	6	37	2	1	40	1
Riek, Cliff, Pir.	.979	10	93	1	2	96	13
Rivera, Carlos, Phi.	.953	11	77	5	4	86	2
Rivera, Carlos, Pir.*	1.000	3	16	2	0	18	2
Rivera, Erick, Phi.	1.000	1	4	0	0	4	0
Romero, Gabriel, Brav.	.978	29	215	8	5	228	12
Russell, Byron, Roy.*	.986	38	265	25	4	294	18
Sandoval, Michael, Twi.	1.000	1	9	1	0	10	1

Player, Team	Pct.	G	PO	A	E	TC	DP
Saucke, Casey, Ori.	.958	11	65	3	3	71	7
Schalick, Jr, George, Ori.	.992	17	124	3	1	128	15
Segar, Jeff, Yan.	1.000	2	18	0	0	18	0
Sizemore, Grady, Exp.*	.000	1	0	0	0	0	0
Smith, William, Mar.	1.000	1	11	0	0	11	0
Swenson, Leland, Rang.	.962	9	72	4	3	79	2
Tamburrino, Brett, Twi.	1.000	13	86	6	0	92	6
Taveras, Frank, Mar.	1.000	1	5	0	0	5	1
Tejero, Armando, Brav.*	.969	33	238	12	8	258	25
Tope, Stephen, Twi.	1.000	1	5	0	0	5	0
Turner, Jason, Yan.*	.989	40	344	18	4	366	23
Yingling, Joe, Tig.	.989	13	87	3	1	91	3
Young, Walter, Pir.	.975	41	325	27	9	361	31

SECOND BASEMEN

Player, Team	Pct.	G	PO	A	E	TC	DP
Abreu, Nielsen, Phi.	.984	15	25	35	1	61	3
Baker, Casey, Yan.	1.000	17	15	24	0	39	3
Bautista, Augusto, Reds	1.000	2	1	3	0	4	0
Bera, Roberto, Ori.	.000	1	0	0	0	0	0
Bergolla, William, Reds	.952	3	7	13	1	21	3
Bocaranda, Nestor, Tig.	.889	2	5	3	1	9	1
Borges, Luis, Roy.	.950	41	76	76	8	160	18
Borjas, Henry, R.S.	.966	7	12	16	1	29	4
Bourgeois, Jason, Rang.	.971	23	36	66	3	105	16
Cabrera, Yoelmis, Ori.	.954	16	41	42	4	87	12
Camacho, Juan, Yan.	.000	1	0	0	0	0	0
Camilli, Jason, Exp.	1.000	1	1	2	0	3	1
Campos, Tiago, Reds	.953	9	15	26	2	43	4
Castro, Bernabel, Yan.	.867	3	6	7	2	15	2
Castro, Javier, Roy.	1.000	3	5	4	0	9	0
Cotto, Luis, Roy.	.789	5	8	7	4	19	2
Cruz, Alex, Pir.	1.000	13	25	32	0	57	6
De Los Santos, Hector, R.S.	.976	32	75	87	4	166	20
Demarco, Matt, Mar.	1.000	1	2	4	0	6	1
Diaz , Jorge, Rang.	.933	3	5	9	1	15	2
Dorsey, Ryan, Pir.	.978	24	44	43	2	89	15
Duran, Deudis, Phi.	.966	21	47	65	4	116	13
Farris, Brant, Roy.	.962	13	26	25	2	53	2
Febles, Carlos, Roy.	1.000	1	0	1	0	1	0
FRANCIA, Juan, Tig.	.971	53	101	136	7	244	31
Freeman, Terrence, Tig.	1.000	1	2	2	0	4	0
Gambino, Michael, R.S.	.889	5	8	16	3	27	5
Garcia, Juan-Carlos, Mar.	.901	29	51	77	14	142	13
Garcia, Nicolas, Ori.	.857	2	4	8	2	14	2
Gibbs, Mark, Ori.	.918	18	39	51	8	98	18
Gonzalez, Jose, Rang.	1.000	1	2	1	0	3	1
Guerrero, Jorge, Mar.	.955	32	57	71	6	134	10
Hairston, Jerry, Ori.	1.000	2	5	5	0	10	0
Herr, Aaron, Brav.	.938	46	72	108	12	192	24
Infante, Franklin, Brav.	.909	7	10	10	2	22	0
Infante, Juan, Exp.	.986	31	62	77	2	141	19
Jackson, Wilbur, Reds	.889	2	2	6	1	9	0
Jimenez, D'Angelo, Yan.	.917	2	5	6	1	12	0
Knox, Matthew, Exp.	.987	19	37	40	1	78	14
Laidlaw, Jacob, Mar.	1.000	3	1	2	0	3	0
Martinez, Peter, Twi.	.973	16	33	40	2	75	5
Merchan, Jesus, Twi.	1.000	2	2	0	0	2	0
Moya, Wilson, Rang.	.972	20	28	41	2	71	9
Patchett, Gary, Reds	1.000	3	5	5	0	10	0
Pfister, Billy, Tig.	.970	10	14	18	1	33	3
Ramirez, Jordy, Reds	.966	37	65	107	6	178	16
Reed, Matthew, Twi.	.958	18	18	28	2	48	5
Reyes, Ivan, Yan.	.970	37	71	92	5	168	14
Rodriguez , Ricardo, Brav.	.892	10	19	14	4	37	5
Rodriguez, Jose, Ori.	1.000	1	3	5	0	8	1
Rodriguez, Ronny, R.S.	.903	7	10	18	3	31	4
Roger, Omar, Ori.	.964	26	51	57	4	112	12
Romero, Gabriel, Brav.	.700	3	4	3	3	10	2
Rosas, Luis, Exp.	1.000	1	0	1	0	1	0
Santoro, Pat, R.S.	.939	12	27	19	3	49	4
Saucke, Casey, Ori.	.953	13	11	30	2	43	6
Schnabel, Nicholas, Exp.	.903	13	31	34	7	72	14
Silvera, Andres, Phi.	.938	24	41	49	6	96	10
Smith, Sean, Pir.	.935	10	13	16	2	31	3

Player, Team	Pct.	G	PO	A	E	TC	DP
Soriano, Jairo, Ori.	.750	1	2	1	1	4	1
Stankiewicz, Andy, Yan.	1.000	1	2	6	0	8	1
Svihlik, D.J., Yan.	.000	2	0	0	1	1	0
Swenson, Leland, Rang.	.944	4	5	12	1	18	2
Tamburrino, Brett, Twi.	.958	28	54	60	5	119	18
Thompson, Kevin, Yan.	.970	7	15	17	1	33	4
Volquez, Julio, Rang.	.957	12	16	29	2	47	3
Warriax, Brandon, Rang.	.000	1	0	0	0	0	0
Yan, Edwin, Pir.	1.000	1	1	4	0	5	1

THIRD BASEMEN

Player, Team	Pct.	G	PO	A	E	TC	DP
Abreu, Cesar, Reds	.800	3	3	1	1	5	0
Anderson, Melvin, Phi.	.820	19	15	35	11	61	2
Baker, Casey, Yan.	1.000	2	0	1	0	1	0
Bass, Christopher, Pir.	.870	26	18	49	10	77	9
Bergolla, William, Reds	1.000	3	1	6	0	7	0
Bessa, Laumin, Brav.	.600	2	2	1	2	5	0
Blanco, Tony, R.S.	.864	47	33	94	20	147	8
Borjas, Henry, R.S.	1.000	1	1	0	0	1	0
Brown, Matthew, Exp.	.757	25	15	41	18	74	6
CAMACHO, Juan, Yan.	.947	45	26	117	8	151	5
Camilli, Jason, Exp.	1.000	1	1	2	0	3	0
Campos, Tiago, Reds	.727	5	5	3	3	11	0
Chapman, Travis, Phi.	.967	9	5	24	1	30	0
Colon, Roberto, Tig.	.950	12	6	13	1	20	1
Cotto, Luis, Roy.	1.000	5	5	8	0	13	2
De La Cruz, Miguel, Pir.	.962	15	12	39	2	53	2
De Los Santos, Hector, R.S.	1.000	5	6	17	0	23	0
Domero, William, Tig.	.867	19	11	28	6	45	1
Dorsey, Ryan, Pir.	.864	15	7	31	6	44	2
Duran, Deudis, Phi.	.800	13	8	20	7	35	1
Encarnacion, Edwin, Rang.	.927	48	35	105	11	151	6
Encarnacion, Henry, Exp.	.000	1	0	0	0	0	0
Espino, Damaso, Reds	.906	19	5	24	3	32	2
Farris, Brant, Roy.	.971	25	18	50	2	70	4
Garcia, Juan-Carlos, Mar.	.833	2	1	4	1	6	0
Garcia, Nicolas, Ori.	1.000	1	0	5	0	5	2
Garcia, Sandy, Yan.	.821	9	6	17	5	28	2
Gibbs, Mark, Ori.	1.000	2	0	3	0	3	0
Gonzalez, Jose, Rang.	.000	1	0	0	1	1	0
Guerrero, Jorge, Mar.	.000	3	0	0	0	0	0
Infante, Franklin, Brav.	.872	14	12	22	5	39	2
Jackson, Wilbur, Reds	1.000	2	0	5	0	5	0
Jenkins, Darryl, Exp.	.714	10	5	20	10	35	3
Johnson, Nelson, Ori.	.883	43	30	61	12	103	7
Johnson, Kelly, Brav.	.733	4	3	8	4	15	1
Johnson, Seth, Exp.	.838	23	11	46	11	68	5
Knox, Matthew, Exp.	1.000	2	2	4	0	6	0
Laidlaw, Jacob, Mar.	.857	12	11	19	5	35	3
Lebron, Edgardo, Twi.	.906	27	21	37	6	64	3
Llamas, Juan, Reds	.919	18	12	45	5	62	4
Marquie, Craig, Yan.	1.000	4	3	4	0	7	1
Martinez, Peter, Twi.	1.000	1	1	0	0	1	0
Martinez, William, Ori.	.000	1	0	0	0	0	0
Minor, Ryan, Ori.	.750	2	2	1	1	4	0
Moya, Wilson, Rang.	.000	2	0	0	1	1	0
Nunn, Jason, Yan.	1.000	1	1	1	0	2	0
Pagana, Mike, Rang.	1.000	2	0	6	0	6	1
Parrott, Tom, Brav.	.926	8	10	15	2	27	1
Patchett, Gary, Reds	.972	10	9	26	1	36	2
Peguero, Miguel, Tig.	.905	28	17	59	8	84	8
Pfister, Billy, Tig.	1.000	1	1	3	0	4	1
Reed, Robert, R.S.	.000	2	0	0	2	2	0
Rodgers, Mackeel, Roy.	.786	15	13	20	9	42	3
Rodriguez , Ricardo, Brav.	.750	3	1	2	1	4	0
Rodriguez, Ronny, R.S.	.889	9	9	7	2	18	4
Romero, Gabriel, Brav.	.750	3	1	2	1	4	0
Sandoval, Michael, Twi.	.900	15	9	27	4	40	1
Saucke, Casey, Ori.	.833	5	5	15	4	24	2
Schalick, Jr George, Ori.	1.000	4	0	7	0	7	0
Segar, Jeff, Yan.	.750	2	2	1	1	4	1
Silvera, Andres, Phi.	.871	21	16	58	11	85	5
Smith, Sean, Pir.	.806	7	12	17	7	36	1
Suarez, Victor, Roy.	.857	20	11	31	7	49	4
Svihlik, D.J., Yan.	1.000	3	2	2	0	4	0
Swenson, Leland, Rang.	1.000	11	3	14	0	17	0
Tamburrino, Brett, Twi.	.919	13	12	22	3	37	2
Taveras, Frank, Mar.	.927	48	41	98	11	150	5
Thorman, Scott, Brav.	.889	29	22	42	8	72	4
Tope, Stephen, Twi.	.667	5	2	2	2	6	0
Villalobos, Carlos, Tig.	1.000	1	0	1	0	1	0
Ware, Anthony, Tig.	.800	3	1	3	1	5	0

SHORTSTOPS

Player, Team	Pct.	G	PO	A	E	TC	DP
Abreu, Nielsen, Phi.	.818	4	1	8	2	11	1
Baker, Casey, Yan.	1.000	1	1	1	0	2	1
Bass, Christopher, Pir.	.976	12	17	23	1	41	4
Bautista, Augusto, Reds	.905	19	30	56	9	95	11
Bergolla, William, Reds	.000	1	0	0	0	0	0
Borjas, Henry, R.S.	.900	4	10	17	3	30	6
CABRERA, Miguel, Mar.	.950	56	90	156	13	259	27
Camacho, Juan, Yan.	1.000	1	1	1	0	2	0
Camilli, Jason, Exp.	1.000	3	6	8	0	14	2
Campos, Julio, Phi.	.925	54	81	155	19	255	23
Cotto, Luis, Roy.	.915	35	61	89	14	164	14
Cruz, Alex, Pir.	.847	32	32	84	21	137	21
De Los Santos, Hector, R.S.	.960	6	11	13	1	25	1
Domero, William, Tig.	.800	2	3	5	2	10	1
Dorsey, Ryan, Pir.	1.000	1	1	3	0	4	1
Encarnacion, Henry, Exp.	.953	23	36	66	5	107	16
Espino, Damaso, Reds	.908	30	40	78	12	130	10
Farris, Brant, Roy.	1.000	3	3	9	0	12	2
Garcia, Juan-Carlos, Mar.	.929	3	6	7	1	14	0
Garcia, Nicolas, Ori.	1.000	3	3	19	0	22	6
Gibbs, Mark, Ori.	.909	15	30	50	8	88	10
Gonzalez, Jose, Rang.	.944	28	39	79	7	125	13
Infante, Franklin, Brav.	.908	18	28	41	7	76	2
Infante, Juan, Exp.	.963	10	20	32	2	54	4
Jackson, Wilbur, Reds	.929	4	7	6	1	14	1
Jimenez, D'Angelo, Yan.	.875	2	2	5	1	8	0
Johnson, Kelly, Brav.	.913	36	41	95	13	149	21
Knox, Matthew, Exp.	.800	2	1	3	1	5	1
Lebron, Edgardo, Twi.	1.000	5	3	6	0	9	0
Logan, Exavier, Tig.	.887	43	57	108	21	186	18
Malloy, Marty, Tig.	1.000	1	0	1	0	1	1
Martinez, Peter, Twi.	.904	23	37	67	11	115	16
Mendez, Deivi, Yan.	.917	49	62	136	18	216	23
Merchan, Jesus, Twi.	.937	33	36	68	7	111	8
Patchett, Gary, Reds	.909	5	7	13	2	22	2
Peguero, Miguel, Tig.	.957	13	12	32	2	46	4
Perez, Kenny, R.S.	.944	43	55	114	10	179	17
Pfister, Billy, Tig.	.944	4	6	11	1	18	2
Ramirez, Jordy, Reds	.000	1	0	0	0	0	0
Reed, Robert, R.S.	.000	1	0	0	0	0	0
Reyes, Ivan, Yan.	.929	13	11	28	3	42	3
Roberts, Brian, Ori.	.905	4	8	11	2	21	4
Rodgers, Mackeel, Roy.	1.000	2	4	3	0	7	0
Rodriguez , Ricardo, Brav.	.958	8	6	17	1	24	1
Rodriguez, Ronny, R.S.	.889	5	9	15	3	27	3
Rosas, Luis, Exp.	.884	28	42	72	15	129	19
Saba, Cesar, R.S.	1.000	2	1	2	0	3	0
Saucke, Casey, Ori.	1.000	1	3	3	0	6	1
Shier, Peter, Ori.	.970	6	7	25	1	33	4
Silvera, Andres, Phi.	.778	5	2	5	2	9	1
Smith, Sean, Pir.	.000	1	0	0	0	0	0
Soriano, Jairo, Ori.	.888	33	54	81	17	152	21
Suarez, Victor, Roy.	.882	22	28	39	9	76	4
Swenson, Leland, Rang.	1.000	3	5	10	0	15	1
Taveras, Frank, Mar.	.800	1	0	4	1	5	0
Volquez, Julio, Rang.	.912	23	32	71	10	113	13
Warriax, Brandon, Rang.	.947	7	9	27	2	38	5
Yan, Edwin, Pir.	.920	11	15	31	4	50	5
Zosky, Eddie, Pir.	.955	8	17	25	2	44	5

OUTFIELDERS

Player, Team	Pct.	G	PO	A	E	TC	DP
Acevedo, Juan, Reds	.913	49	60	3	6	69	1
Acosta, Johe, Pir.	.804	24	34	3	9	46	0
Alexander, Lawrence, Phi.	.991	53	106	4	1	111	0
Aliendo, Humberto, Pir.	.964	49	101	6	4	111	1
Ambrosini, Dominick, Exp.*	.971	20	31	2	1	34	0
Anderson, Melvin, Phi.	.880	15	21	1	3	25	0
Anderson, Nat, Tig.	1.000	2	3	0	0	3	0
Asadoorian, Rick, R.S.	.983	50	113	6	2	121	1
Ayala, Odannys, Roy.	1.000	35	37	3	0	40	0
Baker, Casey, Yan.	1.000	4	4	0	0	4	0
Bartee, Khareta, Roy.	.957	31	43	2	2	47	1
Bera, Roberto, Ori.	.975	42	72	6	2	80	2
Bessa, Laumin, Brav.	.943	23	32	1	2	35	0
Birkett, Matthew, Tig.	.961	39	68	5	3	76	1
Bocaranda, Nestor, Tig.	.000	1	0	0	0	0	0
Brazoban, Yhency, Yan.	.980	54	96	3	2	101	1
Brewer, Anthony, Mar.	.989	47	85	1	1	87	0
Bryan, Jason, Rang.	.978	53	82	5	2	89	3
Buttler, Victor, Pir.	1.000	2	3	1	0	4	0

Player, Team	Pct.	G	PO	A	E	TC	DP
Cabrera, Yoelmis, Pir.	.927	21	35	3	3	41	1
Campos, Tiago, Reds.	1.000	14	28	0	0	28	0
Cancio, Antonio, Phi.	1.000	1	5	0	0	5	0
Candelaria, Tito, Yan.	.000	1	0	0	0	0	0
Caraballo, Carlos, R.S.	.957	25	22	0	1	23	0
Castro, Javier, Roy.	.987	41	71	6	1	78	1
CHOURIO, Jorjanis, Pir.	1.000	45	117	2	0	119	2
Colameco, Joe, Yan.	.867	10	13	0	2	15	0
Davis, Daniel, Tig.*	.971	46	65	2	2	69	0
Dohrman, Bruce, Twi.	.000	3	0	0	0	0	0
Dolton, Odis, Reds	.952	30	39	1	2	42	0
Domero, William, Tig.	.964	18	25	2	1	28	0
Driggers Jr, Richard, Phi.	.970	36	57	8	2	67	1
Evans, Mitch, Yan.	.000	1	0	0	0	0	0
Fears, Christopher, Roy.	1.000	43	77	1	0	78	0
Foster, Gregg, Phi.	1.000	44	60	7	0	67	0
Foster, Quincy, Mar.	1.000	3	3	0	0	3	0
Francisco, Ruben, Ori.*	.976	45	78	4	2	84	1
Frazier, Charles, Mar.	.976	48	81	0	2	83	0
Freeman, Miguel, Exp.	.943	40	80	3	5	88	0
Garcia, Cristian, Mar.	1.000	16	27	0	0	27	0
Garcia, Sandy, Yan.	.944	41	32	2	2	36	1
Gibbs, Mark, Ori.	1.000	3	2	0	0	2	0
Gray, Jason, Rang.	.980	46	88	9	2	99	1
Griffin, Daniel, Exp.	.952	12	20	0	1	21	0
Guante, Domingo, Twi.	.945	35	65	4	4	73	0
Guzman, Carlos, Brav.	.938	33	41	4	3	48	0
Hernandez, Yorky, Pir.	.909	14	20	0	2	22	0
Ide, Antoine, Ori.	.957	8	20	2	1	23	2
Jansen, Ardley, Brav.	.975	46	73	4	2	79	1
Johnson, Patrick, R.S.*	.909	8	10	0	1	11	0
Joyce Jr., Thomas, Ori.*	1.000	34	44	3	0	47	0
Kingsale, Eugene, Ori.	1.000	1	2	0	0	2	0
Kubel, Jason, Twi.	1.000	22	35	1	0	36	0
Laureano, Wilfredo, Roy.	1.000	28	34	1	0	35	1
Lebron, Edgardo, Twi.	1.000	2	2	0	0	2	0
Leonardo, Santos, Tig.	1.000	26	39	3	0	42	1
Lewis, Darren, R.S.	1.000	2	2	0	0	2	0
Lopez, Youanny, R.S.	.927	40	47	4	4	55	0
Louisa, Lorvin, Exp.	.947	37	50	4	3	57	1
Love, Marc, Pir.*	1.000	29	45	1	0	46	1
Manning, Ricky, Twi.*	.949	24	34	3	2	39	0
Marquie, Craig, Yan.	.000	1	0	0	0	0	0
Martinez, William, Ori.	.945	33	49	3	3	55	1
Matthews, Michael, Roy.	1.000	5	4	1	0	5	0
McDonald, Jason, Rang.	1.000	1	2	0	0	2	0
Melo, Hanlet, Brav.	.969	39	60	2	2	64	1
Mercado, Onix, Reds	1.000	7	7	0	0	7	0
Morban, Dany, Reds*	.961	41	70	3	3	76	0
Morneau, Justin, Twi.	1.000	7	16	0	0	16	0
Moya, Wilson, Rang.	1.000	6	8	0	0	8	0
Nix, Laynce, Rang.	.991	48	104	4	1	109	1
Nixon, Trot, R.S.*	1.000	2	3	0	0	3	0
Nunn, Jason, Yan.	.983	43	56	2	1	59	0
Oh, Chul, R.S.	1.000	13	9	2	0	11	0
Padilla, Juan, Exp.	.986	34	72	1	1	74	0
Pena, Onesimo, Rang.	.941	7	16	0	1	17	0
Pickering, Kelvin, Ori.	.000	1	0	0	0	0	0
Quintin, Luis, Rang.	.867	16	12	1	2	15	0
Reed, Matthew, Twi.	.952	15	17	3	1	21	1
Reed, Robert, R.S.	1.000	1	1	0	0	1	0
Remekie, Collin, Brav.	.917	9	11	0	1	12	0
Rivera, Carlos, Phi.	.000	1	0	0	0	0	0
Rivera, Erick, Phi.	.953	37	57	4	3	64	0
Russell, Byron, Roy.*	.000	1	0	0	0	0	0
Saucke, Casey, Ori.	1.000	14	26	4	0	30	2
Segar, Jeff, Yan.	.930	20	37	3	3	43	0
Seiber, Antron, R.S.	.949	48	73	2	4	79	1
Sizemore, Grady, Exp.*	.975	49	114	3	3	120	2
Smiley, Jermaine, Roy.*	1.000	6	6	1	0	7	0
Smith, Marcus, Brav.	1.000	5	5	1	0	6	0
Smith, Toebius, Brav.	1.000	1	3	0	0	3	0
Smith, William, Mar.	1.000	52	70	4	0	74	0
Solano, Francisco, Reds	.966	31	57	0	2	59	0
Soto, Jose, Mar.	.750	6	6	0	2	8	0
Tellis, Antoine, Tig.	1.000	11	23	0	0	23	0
Thomman, John, Twi.	.980	35	47	3	1	51	1
Timaure, Jesus, Mar.	1.000	15	13	3	0	16	1
Tomlin, James, Twi.	1.000	41	61	1	0	62	0
Turner, Jason, Yan.*	1.000	20	34	2	0	36	0
Ware, Anthony, Tig.	1.000	48	42	0	0	42	0
Woods, Ahmad, Brav.	.929	33	37	2	3	42	0

CATCHERS

Player, Team	Pct.	G	PO	A	E	TC	DP	PB
Abad, Juan, Exp.	.982	29	184	37	4	225	8	10
Agar, Cory, Twi.	.982	30	189	25	4	218	1	7
Alley, Charles, Ori.	1.000	3	14	4	0	18	0	5
ALVAREZ, Aaron, Mar.	.996	30	213	28	1	242	1	9
Arko, Thomas, Ori.	.973	27	202	16	6	224	0	11
Barnowski, Bryan, R.S.	.970	28	167	26	6	199	1	12
Bernard, Miguel, Brav.	.970	37	288	30	10	328	2	12
Bocaranda, Nestor, Tig.	.982	31	200	19	4	223	1	13
Bronowicz, Scott, Brav.	1.000	2	13	1	0	14	0	0
Candelaria, Tito, Yan.	.933	2	12	2	1	15	0	0
Caridi, Tony, R.S.	1.000	3	2	0	0	2	0	2
Chauncey, Clinton, Yan.	.984	11	53	8	1	62	1	2
Cline, Shawn, Twi.	1.000	1	8	1	0	9	0	0
Cuevas, Alvin, Roy.	.969	16	87	6	3	96	0	8
Domero, William, Tig.	1.000	1	2	0	0	2	0	1
Durand, Jose, Roy.	.986	37	261	21	4	286	3	10
Emmerick, Joshua, Exp.	.980	33	173	27	4	204	0	2
Escobar, Luis, Roy.	.992	18	109	8	1	118	1	8
Evans, Mitch, Yan.	.980	14	94	6	2	102	0	2
Everett, Rob, Twi.	.992	21	108	10	1	119	1	6
Fernandez, Alejandro, Yan.	.980	40	255	35	6	296	0	0
Garland, Ross, Tig.	.985	23	182	15	3	200	1	4
Guilliams, Earl, Brav.	.989	17	82	6	1	89	0	5
Harper, Brandon, Mar.	1.000	5	35	2	0	37	0	1
Heard, Scott, Rang.	.982	23	146	15	3	164	2	4
Huguet, J.C., Reds.	.958	2	21	2	1	24	0	0
Jaile, Chris, Rang.	.984	27	158	25	3	186	1	5
Jones, Dwayne, Pir.	1.000	2	8	2	0	10	0	1
Kropf, Andrew, Tig.	.987	10	72	6	1	79	0	1
Leon, Omar, Mar.	.986	20	131	13	2	146	0	5
Lomasney, Steve, R.S.	.956	6	37	6	2	45	1	4
Martinez, Edgar, R.S.	.983	26	138	31	3	172	1	10
Masino, Adam, Twi.	1.000	1	4	0	0	4	0	0
McRoberts, Mark, Phi.	.500	2	0	1	1	2	0	1
Mejia, Manuel, Pir.	.978	32	201	23	5	229	3	11
Mercado, Onix, Reds	.971	30	202	33	7	242	3	8
Molina, Angel, Mar.	1.000	8	54	9	0	63	0	2
Morneau, Justin, Twi.	.986	17	122	22	2	146	2	3
Motooka, Rafael, Reds	.976	7	38	2	1	41	0	1
Oetting, Todd, Pir.	1.000	19	113	8	0	121	0	2
Ortega, Felix, Phi.	.969	13	87	7	3	97	0	4
Perkins, Robert, Brav.	.970	18	122	9	4	135	1	11
Pickering, Kelvin, Ori.	1.000	2	5	0	0	5	1	0
Ramos, Victor, Pir.	.972	26	158	18	5	181	3	3
Reed, Robert, R.S.	1.000	5	11	0	0	11	0	3
Rogers, Brian, Mar.	.833	2	13	2	3	18	0	0
Ruiz, Carlos, Phi.	.971	34	236	29	8	273	0	3
Rush, Travis, Pir.	.917	3	9	2	1	12	0	0
Russell, Michael, Ori.	.978	22	116	19	3	138	3	4
Sena, Sonel, Ori.	.964	8	48	5	2	55	1	5
Sulbaran, Orlando, Rang.	.924	15	72	13	7	92	1	2
Valera, Luis, Reds	.987	22	139	16	2	157	2	10

PITCHERS

Player, Team	Pct.	G	PO	A	E	TC	DP
Abreu, Winston, Brav.	1.000	2	1	0	0	1	0
Acosta, Manuel, Yan.	.783	12	1	17	5	23	0
Akens, Phil, Mar.	1.000	18	1	3	0	4	0
Albertus, Roberto, Brav.*	.625	9	1	4	3	8	1
Alcantara, Over, Mar.	1.000	14	0	6	0	6	0
Almeida, Brian, Brav.	.778	11	1	6	2	9	0
Almonte, Hector, Mar.	1.000	1	0	2	0	2	2
Andujar, Jesse, Phi.	1.000	2	0	2	0	2	0
Anez, Omar, Phi.	.833	15	2	8	2	12	1
Arias, Miguel, Roy.	1.000	18	0	2	0	2	0
Armitage, Barry, Roy.	1.000	5	0	1	0	1	0
Artiles, Carlos, Yan.*	1.000	17	1	2	0	3	0
Baker, Brett, Mar.	.000	1	0	0	0	0	0
Barkley, Brian, R.S.*	.000	1	0	0	0	0	0
Bartlett, Richard, Ori.	.818	10	1	8	2	11	2
Bass, Brian, Roy.	.813	12	7	6	3	16	1
Baum, David, Pir.*	1.000	2	1	1	0	2	0
Bautista, Denny, Mar.	.929	11	3	10	1	14	0
Beigh, David, Pir.	.857	7	0	6	1	7	0
Bell, Tom, Mar.	1.000	7	0	3	0	3	0
Beltre, Omar, Rang.	.818	13	2	7	2	11	0
Benitez, Fabricio, R.S.	1.000	1	1	0	0	1	0
Berry, Casey, Rang.	1.000	12	5	7	0	12	0
Berube, Martin, Ori.	1.000	9	3	1	0	4	0
Blair, David, Ori.*	1.000	13	0	6	0	6	0
Blankenship, John, Yan.*	1.000	6	2	4	0	6	0

Player, Team	Pct.	G	PO	A	E	TC	DP
Bludau, Frank, Reds	1.000	10	1	10	0	11	0
Borkowski, Dave, Tig.	.667	3	1	1	1	3	0
Borrell, Danny, Yan.*	1.000	1	0	1	0	1	0
Boughey, William, Phi.	.667	15	1	3	2	6	1
Bouie, Aaron, Ori.	1.000	2	1	1	0	2	0
Bowers, Robert, Rang.	.875	20	1	13	2	16	0
Bowyer, Travis, Twi.	.917	12	6	5	1	12	0
Boyer, Blaine, Brav.	1.000	11	2	3	0	5	2
Brito, Eude, Phi.*	1.000	9	4	11	0	15	1
Brito, Jose, Reds	1.000	4	0	1	0	1	0
Brito, Juan, Exp.*	1.000	2	0	1	0	1	0
Buchholz, Taylor, Phi.	.600	12	2	1	2	5	0
Bucktrot, Keith, Phi.	.667	11	0	2	1	3	0
Bullinger, Kirk, Phi.	.000	1	0	0	0	0	0
Burnett, Sean, Pir.*	1.000	8	1	2	0	3	0
Bynum, Matthew, Reds	1.000	8	1	1	0	2	0
Camelia, Aron, Yan.	.000	2	0	0	0	0	0
Campbell, Dayle, Tig.	1.000	11	2	5	0	7	0
Castillo, Carlos, R.S.	.667	2	0	2	1	3	0
Castillo, Jose, Tig.	.000	1	0	0	0	0	0
Chacon, Ernesto, Yan.	1.000	18	1	1	0	2	0
Cheek, Andrew, R.S.*	1.000	7	0	4	0	4	0
Collazo, Rafael, Tig.*	.000	6	0	0	0	0	0
Colon, Roberto, Tig.	.000	1	0	0	0	0	0
Connolly, Michael, Pir.*	1.000	11	0	5	0	5	1
Cooke, Andrew, Twi.*	1.000	11	1	12	0	13	0
Cotton, Nathan, Reds	.800	14	0	4	1	5	0
Crawford, Tristan, Twi.	.000	8	0	0	2	2	0
Cristobal, Luis, Rang.	1.000	8	0	1	0	1	0
Crump, Joel, Ori.*	.778	12	1	6	2	9	0
Cuello, Manolin, Tig.	.875	11	0	7	1	8	0
Cummings, Frank, Brav.	.000	3	0	0	0	0	0
DeLaCruz, Juan, Pir.	.000	3	0	0	0	0	0
Delgado, Joseph, Roy.	.000	1	0	0	0	0	0
Delossantos, Carlos, Pir.	1.000	11	3	9	0	12	0
De Los Santos, Luis, Yan.	1.000	4	1	2	0	3	0
Detillion, Jamie, Tig.*	1.000	16	1	4	0	5	0
Diaz, Elisandy, Exp.	.786	13	5	6	3	14	1
Digby, Bryan, Brav.	1.000	10	0	2	0	2	0
Dishman, Richard, Brav.	1.000	5	2	1	0	3	0
Douglas, Rod, Brav.	.800	13	1	3	1	5	0
Dubuc, Charles, Exp.*	.714	12	1	4	2	7	1
Dumatrait, Phillip, R.S.*	1.000	6	0	2	0	2	0
Durbin, Joseph, Twi.	.000	2	0	0	0	0	0
Edwards, Bryan, Reds	1.000	9	0	2	0	2	0
Elskamp, Andrew, Phi.	1.000	11	2	7	0	9	0
Eshelman, Vaughn, Reds*	1.000	2	1	1	0	2	0
Espaillat, Ezequiel, Mar.	1.000	11	3	4	0	7	0
Esquivia, Manuel, Mar.	1.000	12	4	7	0	11	1
Ewin, Ryan, Brav.	.556	11	0	5	4	9	0
Feliciano, Ruben, Rang.*	.600	19	0	3	2	5	0
Forystek, Brian, Ori.*	.800	12	2	2	1	5	1
Francisco, Franklin, R.S.	1.000	1	0	1	0	1	0
Freeman, Miguel, Exp.	.000	2	0	0	0	0	0
Fuell, Jerrod, Tig.	1.000	13	1	2	0	3	1
Fussell, Chris, Roy.	.000	2	0	0	0	0	0
Galarraga, Luis, R.S.	.000	2	0	0	0	0	0
Galvez, Willy, R.S.	.833	3	3	2	1	6	2
Garcia, Cristian, Mar.	1.000	1	0	1	0	1	0
Garcia, Rafael, Roy.	.938	13	5	10	1	16	0
Gardner, Hayden, Rang.	1.000	17	2	7	0	9	1
Geigel, Rolando, Mar.	.750	8	0	3	1	4	0
Generelli, Daniel, R.S.	.667	7	1	1	1	3	0
George, Nelson, Reds	.600	10	1	2	2	5	1
Gerlach, Brian, Twi.	.833	25	0	5	1	6	0
Gilbert, Richard, Rang.*	.000	1	0	0	0	0	0
Gill, Ryan, Yan.	1.000	10	3	2	0	5	0
Gleason, Michael, Rang.	1.000	10	1	3	0	4	1
Gonzalez, Giovanni, Pir.	1.000	7	0	1	0	1	0
Gonzalez, Jose, R.S.	1.000	6	2	0	0	2	0
Gonzalez, Mike, Pir.*	.000	2	0	0	1	1	0
Gooden, Dwight, Yan.	.000	2	0	0	0	0	0
Grace, Bryan, Yan.	.600	5	1	2	2	5	0
Graham, Thomas, Rang.	.917	18	1	10	1	12	1
Grahe, Joe, Phi.	.000	3	0	0	0	0	0
Granado, Jan, Reds*	1.000	6	0	1	0	1	0
Griswold, Jordan, Exp.*	1.000	14	1	4	0	5	0
Guerrero, Julio, Pir.	1.000	11	1	3	0	4	0
Gutierrez, Fernando, Ori.	.833	17	0	5	1	6	0
Hall, Josh, Reds	.500	6	0	1	1	2	0
Hall, Kevin, Pir.	1.000	13	0	2	0	2	0
Hall, Shane, R.S.	1.000	15	0	4	0	4	0
Hamilton, Charles, Roy.	1.000	3	1	2	0	3	0
Harris, Karl, Exp.	.000	1	0	0	0	0	0

Player, Team	Pct.	G	PO	A	E	TC	DP
Hassler, Drew, Ori.	1.000	7	2	2	0	4	0
Haynes, Brad, Mar.	1.000	10	6	9	0	15	1
Heredia, Nixon, Reds	.000	5	0	0	0	0	0
Hernandez, Fausto, Tig.	1.000	27	1	1	0	2	0
Hernandez, Yoel, Phi.	1.000	10	2	7	0	9	0
Hill, Jamie, Yan.*	1.000	2	1	1	0	2	0
Hill, Shawn, Exp.	.800	7	1	7	2	10	0
Hopper, Kevin, Brav.	.800	2	1	3	1	5	0
Janek, John, Reds	.000	1	0	0	0	0	0
Jimenez, Ronal, Phi.	1.000	20	1	6	0	7	0
Johnson, Jeremy, Tig.	1.000	12	1	5	0	6	0
Johnston, Dave, Mar.	1.000	14	2	4	0	6	0
Jones, Andrew, Pir.	1.000	11	1	1	0	2	0
Joseph, Glen, Reds	1.000	7	1	1	0	2	0
Kaanoi, Jason, Roy.	1.000	4	2	3	0	5	0
Keefer, Ryan, Ori.	1.000	13	1	3	0	4	0
Kemp, Bo, Twi.	1.000	7	2	1	0	3	0
Keyser, Timothy, Pir.	.000	4	0	0	0	0	0
Kimball, Cody, Twi.	1.000	18	1	1	0	2	1
King, Jeremy, Yan.	.800	11	2	6	2	10	0
Lajara, Eudy, Mar.*	.667	11	0	2	1	3	0
Laplante, Reggie, Yan.	1.000	24	1	2	0	3	0
Lee, Kevin, Pir.	1.000	9	1	1	0	2	0
Legette, Richard, Phi.	1.000	12	2	2	0	4	0
Leon, Omar, Mar.	1.000	2	0	1	0	1	0
Lewis, Jeremy, Tig.*	.824	12	5	9	3	17	1
Lima, Juan, Exp.	1.000	7	1	8	0	9	0
Lindsey, Bart, Phi.*	.667	13	0	2	1	3	0
Loiselle, Rich, Pir.	.000	1	0	0	0	0	0
Lombardi, Justin, Mar.*	.000	6	0	0	1	1	0
Lopez, Omar, Reds	1.000	8	0	2	0	2	0
Lopez, Samuel, Roy.	1.000	23	1	0	0	1	0
Love, Brandon, Reds	.800	2	3	1	1	5	1
Lundgren, Wayne, R.S.	.667	11	0	2	1	3	1
Mabry, Barry, Brav.	1.000	8	0	2	0	2	0
Machen, Mike, Brav.	1.000	12	1	3	0	4	0
Madritsch, Robert, Reds*	1.000	6	0	3	0	3	1
Manon, Julio, Exp.	1.000	4	0	2	0	2	0
Marceau, Pierre-luc, Exp.*	.833	6	2	3	1	6	0
Markray, Thad, Reds	.800	9	1	3	1	5	0
Marrero, Darwin, Exp.	.769	11	3	7	3	13	0
Martinez, Anastacio, R.S.	1.000	2	2	0	0	2	0
Martinez, Jesus, Yan.	.000	3	0	0	0	0	0
Mayfield, James, Phi.	1.000	11	2	9	0	11	0
McCasland, Ralph, Exp.*	1.000	7	2	5	0	7	0
McGlinchy, Kevin, Brav.	1.000	4	1	0	0	1	0
McKay, John, Mar.	1.000	2	1	1	0	2	0
McNatt, Josh, Ori.*	.833	9	0	5	1	6	1
Meisenheimer, Matthew, Rang.	.000	6	0	0	2	2	0
Melendez, Dave, Tig.	1.000	5	1	3	0	4	0
Mendible, Franklin, Twi.	1.000	17	1	1	0	2	1
Merrell, Phil, Reds	1.000	3	1	1	0	2	0
Merricks, Matt, Brav.*	.000	9	0	0	1	1	0
MESSENGER, Randall, Mar.	1.000	12	7	20	0	27	1
Miceli, Danny, Mar.	1.000	2	0	2	0	2	0
Middleton, Kyle, Roy.	1.000	15	2	5	0	7	0
Miller, Colby, Twi.	.909	14	3	7	1	11	0
Miller, Jason, Twi.*	1.000	2	1	1	0	2	0
Miller, Matt, Brav.*	1.000	3	0	0	0	0	0
Miller, Matt, Rang.	.000	1	0	0	0	0	0
Mims, Brandon, R.S.*	1.000	4	0	1	0	1	0
Minaya, Pedro, Reds	1.000	6	1	1	0	2	0
Miniel, Rene, R.S.	1.000	22	2	8	0	10	0
Mitchell, Thomas, Exp.	1.000	10	3	7	0	10	0
Miyamoto, Eij, Exp.	1.000	9	4	2	0	6	0
Montalbano, Greg, R.S.*	1.000	4	0	1	0	1	0
Montgomery, Steve, R.S.	1.000	2	1	0	0	1	0
Montilla, Elvis, Ori.	1.000	16	0	4	0	4	0
Moore, Chris, Mar.	.500	6	0	1	1	2	1
Morel, Jesus, Twi.	1.000	8	0	0	0	0	0
Moreno, Darwin, Brav.	.833	14	2	3	1	6	0
Moreno, Julio, Ori.	1.000	3	1	0	0	1	0
Mosley, Eric, Yan.	.000	5	0	0	0	0	0
Negrette, Richard, Ori.	1.000	7	1	2	0	3	0
Nelson, Bubba, Brav.	.800	12	0	4	1	5	0
Nelson, Joe, Brav.	1.000	4	1	1	0	2	0
Neubauer, Marc, Mar.*	1.000	2	1	0	0	1	0
Nunez, Maximo, R.S.	1.000	2	0	1	0	1	0
Nye, Ryan, Phi.	1.000	2	0	1	0	1	0
O'Brien, Patrick, Pir.	1.000	10	4	9	0	13	1
Olive, Jesse, R.S.	1.000	13	3	3	0	6	1
Ortega, Orlando, Roy.	.800	20	0	4	1	5	0
Ortiz, Javier, Yan.	1.000	1	1	1	0	2	0
Parker, Dwayne, Roy.*	1.000	12	3	0	0	3	1

Player, Team	Pct.	G	PO	A	E	TC	DP
Parris, Matt, Tig.	.917	9	5	6	1	12	1
Paz, Jackson, Brav.	1.000	8	1	2	0	3	0
Peeples, Jim, Yan.*	.000	5	0	0	0	0	0
Pena, Domingo, Pir.	1.000	2	0	1	0	1	0
Peres, Luis, R.S.*	1.000	9	1	4	0	5	0
Perez, Franklin, Tig.	.700	6	1	6	3	10	1
Petty, Chad, Tig.*	.909	9	1	9	1	11	0
Pfalzgraf, Christopher, Rang.	1.000	20	0	4	0	4	0
Pike, Matthew, Reds	.750	11	2	1	1	4	0
Pineda, Isauro, R.S.	1.000	4	2	5	0	7	1
Powell, Maurice, Twi.	.778	11	3	4	2	9	0
Puello, Ignacio, Exp.	.667	4	1	3	2	6	0
Rada, Gerald, Yan.	1.000	8	2	3	0	5	0
Ramirez, Eucebio, Mar.	1.000	3	1	4	0	5	0
Ramos, Victor, Pir.	.000	1	0	0	0	0	0
Randazzo, Jeffrey, Twi.*	.950	13	3	16	1	20	0
Rejean, Rhett, Rang.*	.923	15	5	7	1	13	1
Rengifo, Nohemar, Exp.	1.000	12	0	5	0	5	0
Reyes, Hipolito, Roy.	.700	9	2	5	3	10	0
Reynolds, Eric, Yan.*	1.000	9	2	4	0	6	0
Rice, Scott, Ori.*	.833	13	3	17	4	24	2
Richardson, Jason, Twi.	.600	6	1	2	2	5	1
Rijo, Hector, Exp.*	.714	18	0	5	2	7	0
Rivera, Luis, Brav.	1.000	3	1	1	0	2	0
Rodriguez , Ricardo, Brav.	.000	1	0	0	0	0	0
Rodriguez, Alejandro, Phi.	1.000	3	1	3	0	4	0
Rodriguez, Eddy, Ori.	1.000	18	0	4	0	4	0
Rodriguez, George, Phi.	.800	19	0	4	1	5	0
Rodriguez, Juan, Pir.	.875	12	2	5	1	8	0
Rodriguez, Luis, Rang.	.000	6	0	0	1	1	0
Rodriguez, Marino, Mar.*	1.000	7	0	3	0	3	0
Rogers, Bradley, Ori.	1.000	9	1	7	0	8	0
Rogers, Jon, Brav.	1.000	8	3	3	0	6	0
Romero, Cesar, Yan.	1.000	14	3	0	0	3	0
Rosa, Elias, Roy.*	.500	6	0	2	2	4	0
Rosado, Hector, Roy.*	1.000	14	1	2	0	3	0
Ross, Christian, Reds	1.000	6	1	5	0	6	0
Rundles, Richard, R.S.*	1.000	9	2	11	0	13	1
Sak, Jim, Pir.	.000	2	0	0	0	0	0
Salazar, Luis, Mar.	.000	1	0	0	0	0	0
Salinas, Sean, Reds	1.000	2	1	0	0	1	0
Sanchez, Elby, Roy.	1.000	19	3	5	0	8	0
Sanchez, Pedro, Twi.*	.750	19	1	2	1	4	0
Santana, Eddy, Yan.	1.000	17	2	7	0	9	1
Santos, Victor, Tig.	.000	1	0	0	0	0	0
Sauer, Danny, Exp.	.800	15	2	2	1	5	0
Saye, Thomas, Roy.	1.000	8	0	1	0	1	0
Schachleiter, Jeff, Reds	.500	6	0	3	3	6	0
Schmidt, Jason, Pir.	.000	1	0	0	0	0	0
Schoening, Brent, Twi.	1.000	2	0	3	0	3	0
Searles, Jonathan, Pir.	.889	7	7	1	1	9	1
Severino, Cleris, Reds*	.895	13	4	13	2	19	2
Severino, Jose, Tig.	1.000	2	0	3	0	3	0
Shafer, Kurt, Pir.	.667	8	1	1	1	3	0
Shortslef, Josh, Pir.*	1.000	11	4	6	0	10	2
Sierra, Jr., Auvin, Tig.*	.833	13	1	4	1	6	0
Simon, Janewrys, Twi.	.000	9	0	0	0	0	0
Simpson, Cory, Brav.	1.000	4	1	4	0	5	0
Smith, Brian, Pir.	1.000	5	1	0	0	1	0
Smith, Jason, Yan.	.800	10	0	4	1	5	0
Snell, Ian, Pir.	1.000	4	0	2	0	2	0
Snyder, Kyle, Roy.	.000	1	0	0	0	0	0
Spear, Russell, Tig.	.000	3	0	0	0	0	0
Sperring, Jayme, Ori.	1.000	3	0	1	0	1	0
Spillers, Larry, Ori.	1.000	3	0	3	0	3	0
St. Amant, John, Phi.	.750	11	2	1	1	4	0
Steele, Bradley, Phi.	1.000	13	3	1	0	4	0
Sterett, Adam, Mar.	1.000	11	0	2	0	2	0
Stodolka, Michael, Roy.*	.900	9	4	5	1	10	0
Story, Aaron, Pir.*	.600	5	1	2	2	5	1
Tate, Matthew, Ori.	1.000	9	1	2	0	3	0
Tejada, Sandy, Twi.	.882	15	3	12	2	17	0
Tejeda, Robinson, Phi.	.556	10	2	3	4	9	0
Thigpen, Joshua, R.S.	1.000	2	0	1	0	1	0
Thompson, Jesse, Reds	1.000	7	1	1	0	2	0
Thompson, Matthew, R.S.	1.000	12	1	7	0	8	0
Timaure, Jesus, Mar.	.000	1	0	0	0	0	0
Timm, Dan, Reds	.000	1	0	0	0	0	0
Torres, Alex, Tig.*	1.000	3	1	1	0	2	0
Torres, Carlos, Reds	.938	11	1	14	1	16	1
Tremont, Harold, Rang.	.833	16	0	5	1	6	0
Trevino, Chris, Brav.*	1.000	4	1	0	0	1	0
Troilo, Joseph, R.S.	.667	24	1	3	2	6	0
Truselo, Randy, Rang.	1.000	8	0	3	0	3	0
Turner, Jess, Twi.	.917	16	2	9	1	12	0
Valdez, Jose, Reds	.000	1	0	0	0	0	0
Valentin, Emmanuel, Tig.	.667	9	2	0	1	3	0
Valenzuela, Ramon, Twi.	.750	18	0	3	1	4	0
Valle, Yoiset, Yan.*	.667	5	1	1	1	3	0
Velasquez, Reinaldo, Roy.	1.000	6	0	3	0	3	0
Wahlbrink, Steven, Pir.	.000	1	0	0	0	0	0
Wainwright, Adam, Brav.	1.000	7	1	2	0	3	0
Watson, Allen, Yan.*	1.000	1	0	0	0	0	0
Weber, Brett, Yan.	1.000	4	1	1	0	2	0
Wheatland, Matthew, Tig.	1.000	5	1	2	0	3	0
Williams, Marcus, Reds	.800	9	1	3	1	5	0
Wise, Eric, Exp.	.636	12	2	5	4	11	0
Wright, Matt, Brav.	.750	12	1	2	1	4	0
Wright, Raymond, Reds	.000	3	0	0	0	0	0
Wrightsman, Dustin, Roy.	1.000	8	3	0	0	3	0
Zurita, Thomas, Roy.	1.000	11	4	6	0	10	0

The following players appeared only as designated hitter, pinch-hitter or pinch runner: Beltran, dh; O. Cruz, dh-ph; Durham, dh; D. Leon, dh; O'Leary, dh-ph; Rivas, dh; N. Smith, dh.

LEAGUE CHAMPIONS

Year	Team	Pct.	Year	Team	Pct.	Year	Team	Pct.
1964—	Sarasota Braves	.610	1981—	Kansas City-Gold	.688	1991—	Orioles	.593
1965—	Bradenton Astros	.632	1982—	New York AL	.667		Expos∞	.533
1966—	New York AL	.667	1983—	Texas	.645	1992—	Royals∞	.695
1967—	Kansas City	.614		Los Angeles†	.617		Expos	.593
1968—	Oakland	.650	1984—	White Sox	.651	1993—	Rangers▲	.667
1969—	Montreal	.585		Rangers†	.571		Astros	.593
1970—	Chicago AL	.600	1985—	Yankees§	.705	1994—	Royals◆	.797
1971—	Kansas City	.755		Rangers	.532		Astros	.695
1972—	Chicago NL*	.651	1986—	Reds	.548	1995—	Royals■	.649
	Kansas City*	.651		Dodgers†	.541		Tigers	.579
1973—	Texas	.732	1987—	Dodgers†	.683	1996—	Yankees◆	.638
1974—	Chicago NL	.702		Royals	.635		Rangers	.617
1975—	Texas	.774	1988—	Yankees†	.714	1997—	Mets▼	.700
1976—	Texas	.704		Royals	.619		Rangers	.567
1977—	Chicago AL	.731	1989—	Yankees‡	.651	1998—	Marlins	.633
1978—	Texas	.600		Dodgers	.635		Rangers◆	.567
1979—	Houston	.635	1990—	Expos	.635	1999—	Mets◆	.650
1980—	Kansas City-Blue	.635		Dodgers‡	.603	2000—	Rangers◆	.679

*Declared co-champions; no playoff. †League divided into Northern and Southern divisions; won one-game playoff for league championship. ‡League divided into Northern and Southern divisions; won best-of-three playoff for league championship. §Yankees declared champion based on winning percentage when one-game play-off against Rangers was rained out. ∞League divided into Northern, Southern and Central divisions; won best-of-three playoff for league championship. ▲League divided into Eastern, Central and Western divisions; won three-team playoff. ◆League divided into Eastern, Northern and Western divisions; won three-team playoff. ■League divided into Eastern, Northern, Northwest and Southwest divisions; won four-team playoff. ▼League divided into Eastern, Western and Northwest divisions; won four-club playoff. (Note—Known as Sarasota Rookie League in 1964 and Florida Rookie League in 1965.)

PIONEER LEAGUE

LEAGUE OFFICE

President
Jim McCurdy
Address
P.O. Box 2564
Spokane, WA 99220
Phone
509-456-7615

Teams (affiliation)
Billings Mustangs (Reds)
Casper Pro Baseball Club (Rockies)
Great Falls Dodgers (Dodgers)
Idaho Falls Padres (Padres)

Medicine Hat Blue Jays (Blue Jays)
Missoula Osprey (Diamondbacks)
Ogden Raptors (Brewers)
Provo Pro Baseball Club (Angels)

2000 FINAL STANDINGS
FIRST HALF

NORTH DIVISION

Team	W	L	T	Pct.	GB
Medicine Hat (Blue Jays)	23	15	0	.605	...
Missoula (Diamondbacks)	22	16	0	.579	1.0
Great Falls (Dodgers)	18	20	0	.474	5.0
Helena (Brewers)	12	26	0	.316	11.0

SOUTH DIVISION

Team	W	L	T	Pct.	GB
Idaho Falls (Padres)	23	15	0	.605	...
Ogden (Brewers)	20	18	0	.526	3.0
Billings (Reds)	20	18	0	.526	3.0
Butte (Angels)	14	24	0	.368	9.0

SECOND HALF

NORTH DIVISION

Team	W	L	T	Pct.	GB
Great Falls (Dodgers)	24	14	0	.632	...
Missoula (Diamondbacks)	22	16	0	.579	2.0
Helena (Brewers)	14	24	0	.368	10.0
Medicine Hat (Blue Jays)	13	25	0	.342	11.0

SOUTH DIVISION

Team	W	L	T	Pct.	GB
Idaho Falls (Padres)	22	14	0	.611	...
Ogden (Brewers)	21	16	0	.568	1.5
Billings (Reds)	19	18	0	.514	3.5
Butte (Angels)	15	23	0	.395	8.0

COMPOSITE

Team	I.F.	Miss.	G.F.	Ogd.	Bil.	M.H.	But.	Hel.	W	L	T	Pct.	GB
Idaho Falls (Padres)	...	4	5	10	13	4	6	3	45	29	0	.608	...
Missoula (Diamondbacks)	2	...	9	3	4	10	4	12	44	32	0	.579	2.0
Great Falls (Dodgers)	1	9	...	2	4	9	5	12	42	34	0	.553	4.0
Ogden (Brewers)	7	3	4	...	6	3	12	6	41	34	0	.547	4.5
Billings (Reds)	4	2	2	10	...	4	13	4	39	36	0	.520	6.5
Medicine Hat (Blue Jays)	2	6	9	3	2	...	4	10	36	40	0	.474	10.0
Butte (Angels)	10	2	1	6	5	2	...	3	29	47	0	.382	17.0
Helena (Brewers)	3	6	4	0	2	8	3	...	26	50	0	.342	20.0

Club names are major league affiliations.

PLAYOFFS: Idaho Falls defeated Ogden two games to one; Great Falls defeated Medicine Hat two games to one; Idaho Falls defeated Great Falls two games to none to win league championship.

REGULAR-SEASON ATTENDANCE: Billings, 92,669; Butte, 21,975; Great Falls, 81,266; Helena, 25,979; Idaho Falls, 64,697; Medicine Hat, 27,143; Missoula, 53,173; Ogden, 95,213. Total—462,115. Playoffs (8 games)—6,184.

MANAGERS: Billings, Russ Nixon; Butte, Joe Urso; Great Falls, Juan Bustabad; Helena, Dan Norman; Idaho Falls, Don Werner; Medicine Hat, Paul Elliot; Missoula, Chip Hale; Ogden, Ed Sedar.

ALL-STAR TEAM: 1B—J.P. Woodward, Idaho Falls; 2B—Wandel Campana, Billings; 3B—Daryl Clard, Ogden; SS—J.J. Furmaniak, Idaho Falls; OF—Jeremy Johnson, Medicine Hat; Luis Terrero, Missoula; David Krynzel, Ogden; RHP—Ricardo Rodriguez, Great Falls; LHP—Justin Gordon, Ogden; RP—Andrew McCulloch, Medicine Hat; Most Valuable Player—Jeremy Johnson, Medicine Hat; Manager of the Year—Don Werner, Idaho Falls.

2000 BATTING
TEAM

Team	Avg.	G	TPA	AB	R	H	TB	2B	3B	HR	RBI	SH	SF	HP	BB	IBB	SO	SB	CS	GDP	LOB	ShO	Slg.	OBP
Idaho Falls	.317	74	3155	2684	585	850	1293	170	24	75	497	5	33	38	395	11	569	78	39	74	626	1	.482	.407
Ogden	.292	75	3126	2696	531	788	1168	151	26	59	454	23	24	61	322	12	460	115	42	50	602	0	.433	.377
Billings	.282	75	3064	2652	513	749	1119	120	23	68	443	14	23	67	308	7	564	93	32	57	584	2	.422	.369
Butte	.282	76	3096	2655	486	749	1111	137	33	53	413	26	29	46	340	4	551	73	32	57	619	0	.418	.370
Medicine Hat	.264	74	3114	2660	457	703	1044	125	21	58	378	20	9	43	382	12	563	50	20	52	645	2	.392	.365
Missoula	.258	76	2987	2567	429	663	985	125	34	43	348	11	29	53	327	6	583	132	49	50	569	2	.384	.350
Great Falls	.250	76	2908	2513	394	629	866	86	26	33	341	37	21	41	296	5	598	129	44	41	542	3	.345	.336
Helena	.250	76	2919	2545	377	635	906	127	18	36	298	21	18	46	289	2	644	105	51	41	523	5	.356	.335

INDIVIDUAL

TOP QUALIFIERS FOR BATTING CHAMPIONSHIP

Minimum 205 plate appearances. *Lefthanded batter. †Switch-hitter.

Player, Team	Avg.	G	TPA	AB	R	H	TB	2B	3B	HR	RBI	SH	SF	HP	BB	IBB	SO	SB	CS	GDP	Slg.	OBP
Ruiz, Randy, Bil.	.381	61	273	231	55	88	135	15	1	10	55	1	2	10	29	0	56	1	2	6	.584	.467
Johnson, Jeremy, M.H.*	.376	67	308	245	66	92	149	24	3	9	58	1	1	6	55	3	29	5	3	8	.608	.498
Reese, Kevin, I.F.*	.358	53	249	201	51	72	100	14	4	2	36	0	2	3	43	2	30	12	3	5	.498	.474
Campo, Michael, But.*	.358	48	211	176	44	63	97	13	3	5	37	1	0	8	26	0	17	4	2	4	.551	.462
Thompson, Craig, I.F.	.358	58	281	218	52	78	124	14	1	10	62	2	7	2	52	3	23	5	2	0	.569	.473
Davenport, Ron, M.H.	.345	59	255	229	37	79	111	16	2	4	46	0	2	3	21	0	28	5	2	7	.485	.404
Furmaniak, Jason, I.F.	.343	62	298	245	72	84	121	18	2	5	38	0	4	5	44	1	48	10	3	8	.494	.446
Guerrero, Cris, Og.	.341	66	297	255	56	87	145	14	4	12	54	0	1	4	37	1	42	24	6	8	.569	.431
Clark, Daryl, Og.*	.339	64	290	218	54	74	139	12	4	15	64	1	2	2	67	3	53	5	4	1	.638	.495
Ayala, Elio, Og.	.338	59	271	237	57	80	111	16	3	3	21	2	5	2	25	0	18	14	4	4	.468	.409
Woodward, John, I.F.*	.317	68	333	281	67	89	175	26	0	20	92	0	4	5	43	0	76	9	4	5	.623	.411
Smitherman, Stephen, Bil.	.316	70	332	301	61	95	166	16	5	15	65	0	2	6	23	2	67	14	1	10	.551	.373
Hake, Travis, Og.	.310	50	240	210	53	65	96	17	4	2	33	1	2	5	22	0	32	19	2	2	.457	.385
McCool, Lee, I.F.	.309	56	279	236	62	73	114	17	3	6	30	1	0	6	36	0	46	10	4	2	.483	.414
Johnson, Chris, Bil.	.308	51	254	208	53	64	75	8	0	1	22	1	3	4	38	1	16	15	4	3	.361	.419

DEPARTMENTAL LEADERS: G—Myers, 75; AB—Smitherman, 301; R—Furmaniak, 72; H—Smitherman, 95; TB—Woodward, 175; 2B—Woodward, 26; 3B—V. Hall, 9; HR—Woodward, 20; RBI—Woodward, 92; SH—West, 8; SF—C. Thompson, 7; HP—Callen, Delgado, 12 each; BB—V. Hall, 77; IBB—several tied, 3 each; SO—Mayo, 84; SB—V. Hall, 47; CS—V. Hall, 14; GIDP—Smitherman, 10; Slg.—Clark, .638; OBP—J. Johnson, .498.

ALL PLAYERS

*Lefthanded batter. †Switch-hitter.

Player, Team	Avg.	G	TPA	AB	R	H	TB	2B	3B	HR	RBI	SH	SF	HP	BB	IBB	SO	SB	CS	GDP	Slg.	OBP
Abercrombie, Reginald, G.F.	.273	54	253	220	40	60	75	7	1	2	29	3	0	8	22	0	66	32	8	1	.341	.360
Abruzzo, Jared, But.†	.255	62	274	208	46	53	88	11	0	8	45	0	3	2	61	1	58	1	0	3	.423	.423
Anderson, Bryan, Bil.	.257	58	269	218	51	56	75	4	3	3	24	4	0	5	42	0	38	7	2	5	.344	.389
Ansman, Craig, Miss.	.284	28	83	67	7	19	24	5	0	0	7	0	2	2	12	0	21	0	0	1	.358	.394
Aracena, Sandy, G.F.	.316	5	20	19	1	6	7	1	0	0	3	0	0	0	1	0	1	1	0	1	.368	.350
Arroyo, Abner, I.F.*	.394	25	114	109	26	43	63	11	0	3	28	0	2	0	3	0	13	2	2	4	.578	.404
Ayala, Elio, Og.	.338	59	271	237	57	80	111	16	3	3	21	2	5	2	25	0	18	14	4	4	.468	.409
Aybar, Willy, G.F.†	.263	70	310	266	39	70	99	15	1	4	49	6	2	0	36	2	45	5	5	3	.372	.349
Baderdeen, Kevin, Bil.	.263	19	86	80	9	21	29	3	1	1	13	0	0	1	5	0	19	0	1	4	.363	.314
Banks, Almonzo, But.	.211	20	22	19	6	4	5	1	0	0	1	0	0	0	3	0	6	0	0	1	.263	.318
Barrow, Corey, Bil.	.233	45	185	163	29	38	55	3	4	2	21	1	1	5	15	0	43	5	4	1	.337	.315
Belcher, Jason, Hel.*	.333	46	188	162	30	54	88	18	2	4	36	1	3	1	20	1	25	3	1	3	.543	.403
Bell, Paul, Hel.	.229	39	149	140	14	32	35	3	0	0	4	0	0	3	6	0	24	3	3	2	.250	.275
Bitter, Jarrod, I.F.	.425	11	53	40	12	17	26	7	1	0	12	0	2	2	9	0	6	0	0	1	.650	.528
Blackburn, John, M.H.	.193	18	69	57	5	11	19	3	1	1	8	1	1	0	10	0	9	0	0	0	.333	.309
Buelna, Lorenzo, But.	.262	59	228	202	44	53	78	10	3	3	25	3	6	14	0	31	17	6	7	.386	.324
Burns, Kevan, Miss.*	.533	4	18	15	6	8	12	0	2	0	4	0	0	3	0	1	3	1	0	.800	.611
Calitri, Mike, Bil.	.542	7	33	24	11	13	20	2	1	1	11	0	0	1	8	0	5	1	0	0	.833	.667
Callen, Thomas, M.H.	.258	50	237	182	44	47	59	4	1	2	25	4	0	12	39	0	39	5	3	3	.324	.421
Campana, Wandel, Bil.	.278	66	270	248	42	69	87	6	3	2	34	4	2	6	10	0	28	22	9	7	.351	.320
Campo, Michael, But.*	.358	48	211	176	44	63	97	13	3	5	37	1	0	8	26	0	17	4	2	4	.551	.462
Candelaria, Scott, Og.	.288	66	301	281	41	81	120	16	1	7	42	3	3	5	9	2	39	4	2	4	.427	.319
Castillo, David, I.F.†	.274	53	230	190	51	52	69	8	3	1	17	1	1	0	38	0	56	8	5	6	.363	.393
Clark, Daryl, Og.*	.339	64	290	218	54	74	139	12	4	15	64	1	2	2	67	3	53	5	4	1	.638	.495
Contrera, Albino, But.*	.298	39	150	131	24	39	62	7	2	4	27	1	5	0	13	0	18	4	2	3	.473	.349
Contreras, Sergio, But.*	.399	45	201	173	44	69	104	10	8	3	28	2	2	5	19	1	25	8	4	2	.601	.467
Conyer, Darryl, Miss.*	.228	17	70	57	7	13	21	3	1	1	14	0	2	0	11	1	25	2	0	2	.368	.343
Cordova, Ricardo, G.F.†	.316	41	160	133	29	42	45	3	0	0	14	5	1	1	20	0	25	9	1	6	.338	.406
Culwell, Nathan, Bil.†	.299	48	204	177	31	53	69	7	0	3	29	0	2	5	20	0	38	3	1	3	.390	.382
Davenport, Ron, M.H.	.345	59	255	229	37	79	111	16	2	4	46	0	2	3	21	0	28	5	2	7	.485	.404
Davis, James, But.	.269	41	169	130	21	35	40	3	1	0	13	3	0	6	30	0	22	3	1	2	.308	.428
Davis, Morrin, M.H.	.222	40	174	162	17	36	61	6	2	5	16	0	0	1	11	0	59	2	1	3	.377	.276
Davison, Ashanti, Hel.	.220	10	44	41	3	9	12	3	0	0	2	1	0	2	0	0	10	1	2	0	.293	.256
Day, Nick, I.F.	.444	9	44	36	13	16	25	1	1	2	7	0	0	2	6	1	3	3	1	0	.694	.545
De La Paz, Camilo, Hel.	.189	40	142	122	15	23	35	9	0	1	16	1	2	1	16	0	33	5	2	2	.287	.284
Delgado, Jorge, Miss.	.312	43	181	138	26	43	64	6	0	5	31	0	3	12	28	0	17	5	1	5	.464	.459
De Los Santos, Nelson, Hel.†	.302	47	193	169	27	51	77	12	4	2	31	2	3	2	17	0	32	9	4	1	.456	.366
Detienne, Dave, G.F.	.241	64	271	241	41	58	90	10	2	6	34	2	2	4	22	1	60	18	5	3	.373	.312
Diaz, Jose, G.F.	.219	57	236	210	29	46	78	9	1	7	31	3	1	4	18	0	52	2	4	3	.371	.292
Duenas, Manuel, I.F.	.287	46	194	174	24	50	74	11	2	3	20	0	1	0	19	0	58	2	0	8	.425	.356
Duplissea, William, G.F.	.154	5	16	13	1	2	2	0	0	0	1	0	1	0	2	0	3	0	0	0	.154	.250
Egly, John, Miss.†	.254	59	239	205	43	52	91	8	2	9	30	0	1	3	29	0	65	9	5	3	.444	.353
Encarnacion, Santos, I.F.	.278	47	169	158	24	44	61	8	3	1	27	0	0	0	11	0	34	7	3	5	.386	.325
Epstein, Jake, But.	.336	39	162	143	16	48	79	14	1	5	33	0	2	4	13	0	32	1	0	5	.552	.401
Escalante, Jose, G.F.	.262	55	243	221	29	58	83	6	5	3	43	1	4	5	12	0	25	7	5	4	.376	.310
Forelli, Anthony, Hel.	.254	18	69	63	9	16	29	1	0	4	11	0	0	1	5	0	20	2	0	1	.460	.319
Foster, Brian, Og.	.216	45	162	134	27	29	42	7	0	2	15	4	2	5	17	0	29	2	4	4	.313	.323
Furmaniak, Jason, I.F.	.343	62	298	245	72	84	121	18	2	5	38	0	4	5	44	1	48	10	3	8	.494	.446
Garabito, Vianney, Bil.	.268	39	168	157	26	42	80	6	1	10	42	0	3	3	5	0	15	1	0	5	.510	.298
Garcia, Jose, G.F.	.211	6	22	19	2	4	4	0	0	0	3	0	0	2	1	0	4	2	1	0	.211	.318
Geraldo, Anulfo, Hel.	.280	70	305	268	41	75	102	17	2	2	32	4	2	0	31	0	50	11	4	1	.381	.352
Gil, Jerry, Miss.	.225	58	241	227	24	51	65	10	2	0	20	0	1	2	11	1	63	7	3	5	.286	.266
Godbolt, Keith, G.F.	.283	65	254	230	31	65	81	7	3	1	25	2	0	0	22	0	49	7	3	8	.352	.345
Gomez, Andre, I.F.	.250	9	37	32	5	8	16	2	0	2	5	0	0	1	4	0	6	1	0	1	.500	.351
Gragg, Shaun, Og.*	.254	50	192	177	25	45	66	13	1	2	35	0	2	0	13	0	43	1	2	3	.373	.302

Player, Team	Avg.	G	TPA	AB	R	H	TB	2B	3B	HR	RBI	SH	SF	HP	BB	IBB	SO	SB	CS	GDP	Slg.	OBP
Gray, Joshua, But.	.327	40	170	147	31	48	89	11	3	8	36	0	1	3	19	1	41	1	0	1	.605	.412
Green, Andy, Miss.	.229	23	103	83	10	19	23	2	1	0	16	1	5	2	12	0	9	8	3	1	.277	.324
Guerrero, Cris, Og.	.341	66	297	255	56	87	145	14	4	12	54	0	1	4	37	1	42	24	6	8	.569	.431
Guerrero, Hector, G.F.*	.313	8	34	32	3	10	16	4	1	0	5	0	1	0	1	0	9	0	0	1	.500	.324
Gutierrez, Said, I.F.	.220	17	61	50	4	11	12	1	0	0	5	0	2	0	9	0	10	1	0	3	.240	.328
Hake, Travis, Og.	.310	50	240	210	53	65	96	17	4	2	33	1	2	5	22	0	32	19	2	2	.457	.385
Hall, Victor, Miss.*	.307	70	329	241	70	74	108	7	9	3	26	3	3	5	77	0	38	47	14	0	.448	.479
Hart, Jon, Og.	.287	57	233	216	32	62	79	9	1	2	30	1	1	2	13	0	27	6	0	6	.366	.332
Hawes, Bobby, Bil.	.231	4	14	13	2	3	3	0	0	0	1	0	1	0	0	0	3	0	0	0	.231	.214
Hicks, Brian, Hel.*	.221	60	244	213	41	47	63	8	1	2	23	2	2	3	24	0	65	10	6	2	.296	.306
Janek, John, Bil.*	.000	2	7	6	1	0	0	0	0	0	0	0	0	0	1	0	2	0	0	0	.000	.143
January, Javerro, Og.	.208	43	120	101	19	21	27	4	1	0	12	1	1	5	12	0	29	9	5	0	.267	.319
Jaramillo, Milko, G.F.†	.250	41	179	144	25	36	41	3	1	0	16	6	1	2	26	0	23	13	4	3	.285	.370
Jenkins, Kevin, But.*	.196	48	164	143	26	28	39	5	0	2	15	1	0	1	19	0	47	6	3	2	.273	.294
Johnson, Chris, Bil.	.308	51	254	208	53	64	75	8	0	1	22	1	3	4	38	1	16	15	4	3	.361	.419
Johnson, Jeremy, M.H.*	.376	67	308	245	66	92	149	24	3	9	58	1	1	6	55	3	29	5	3	8	.608	.498
Johnson, Kade, Og.	.316	28	117	98	16	31	68	7	0	10	35	0	1	4	14	2	20	2	1	1	.694	.419
Kail, Tom, Miss.	.246	42	154	134	20	33	42	7	1	0	9	0	3	0	17	0	23	1	2	7	.313	.325
Kenney, Jeff, Og.	.306	9	45	36	10	11	12	1	0	0	9	0	2	2	5	1	6	0	0	1	.333	.400
Kimberley, Glynn, M.H.	.229	26	96	83	13	19	26	4	0	1	13	0	1	3	9	0	32	0	0	2	.313	.323
Krynzel, Dave, Og.*	.359	34	155	131	25	47	64	8	3	1	29	1	2	5	16	3	23	8	4	0	.489	.442
Lagana, Shawn, Miss.	.288	68	262	226	40	65	87	12	2	2	20	1	0	2	33	0	33	10	1	3	.385	.383
Lake, Josh, Hel.-Og.	.167	8	23	18	1	3	3	0	0	0	1	1	0	1	3	0	8	0	0	0	.167	.318
Leflore, Alex, Bil.	.224	17	67	58	11	13	20	4	0	1	5	1	0	2	6	0	10	5	0	0	.345	.318
Lipowicz, Nathan, G.F.	.241	43	155	145	22	35	55	5	3	3	12	0	2	1	7	0	36	2	2	2	.379	.277
Little, James, But.	.261	51	207	184	33	48	72	9	3	3	25	3	2	3	14	0	29	5	2	5	.391	.320
Llamas, Juan, Bil.	.316	4	20	19	1	6	7	1	0	0	1	1	0	0	0	0	3	0	0	1	.368	.316
Loeb, Bryan, Miss.	.330	32	106	88	16	29	43	9	1	1	10	1	0	6	11	0	21	0	0	2	.489	.438
Martinez, Casey, M.H.	.280	9	32	25	5	7	13	3	0	1	3	0	0	1	6	0	7	0	0	1	.520	.438
Matthews, Delvon, Hel.	.170	38	123	100	10	17	20	3	0	0	4	0	1	3	19	0	30	4	3	5	.200	.317
Mayo, Terry, Hel.	.239	58	215	184	22	44	72	13	0	5	21	0	1	6	24	0	84	10	3	1	.391	.344
Mayorson, Manuel, M.H.	.220	56	254	218	39	48	52	2	1	0	12	2	0	1	33	0	27	3	2	6	.239	.325
McCarty, Brock, Miss.	.239	46	128	117	18	28	42	1	5	1	13	2	0	2	7	1	25	4	4	3	.359	.294
McClanahan, Jonah, Og.	.248	37	141	117	20	29	39	6	2	0	17	1	0	4	19	0	16	0	1	1	.333	.371
McCool, Lee, I.F.	.309	56	279	236	62	73	114	17	3	6	30	1	0	6	36	0	46	10	4	2	.483	.414
Melton, John, Miss.	.200	2	8	5	2	1	1	0	0	0	0	0	0	0	3	0	3	0	0	0	.200	.500
Mendez, Mario, Hel.	.429	5	16	14	2	6	7	1	0	0	3	0	0	0	2	0	3	2	0	0	.500	.500
Mendez, Pastor, Hel.	.333	3	3	3	0	1	2	1	0	0	2	0	0	0	0	0	1	0	0	1	.667	.333
Mendoza, Adrian, G.F.	.221	45	165	140	17	31	42	6	1	1	12	2	1	2	20	2	45	5	2	3	.300	.325
Myers, Corey, Miss.	.217	75	312	272	40	59	97	16	2	6	49	1	5	3	30	2	62	5	2	5	.357	.297
Napoli, Michael, But.	.231	10	36	26	3	6	8	2	0	0	3	1	1	0	8	1	8	1	0	2	.308	.400
Negron, Miguel, M.H.*	.232	53	218	190	26	44	49	5	0	0	13	2	0	3	23	3	39	5	3	2	.258	.324
Noboa, Joel, Miss.	.213	53	209	202	18	43	83	16	3	6	34	0	2	2	3	0	67	0	1	4	.411	.230
Nohr, Ryan, Og.	.252	44	172	147	27	37	50	7	0	2	18	2	1	4	18	0	21	2	2	4	.340	.347
Nunez, Manuel, G.F.	.229	59	267	210	43	48	61	4	3	1	24	6	3	3	45	0	70	15	3	1	.290	.368
O'Donnell, Ryan, I.F.*	.365	14	59	52	14	19	25	0	0	2	13	0	1	1	5	0	5	1	3	5	.481	.424
Pagan, Andres, I.F.	.312	41	170	154	25	48	68	8	0	4	24	1	2	0	13	0	41	3	3	4	.442	.361
Palomares, Luis, Hel.	.192	8	29	26	2	5	5	0	0	0	2	0	0	1	2	0	7	0	0	0	.192	.276
Paulino, Armando, M.H.	.259	62	248	224	30	58	99	14	6	5	25	0	0	4	20	0	51	6	4	2	.442	.331
Pichardo, Maximo, But.	.280	28	112	100	14	28	34	4	1	0	13	1	0	1	10	0	8	0	4	4	.340	.351
Pregnalato, Bob, Og.	.278	59	232	205	49	57	73	9	2	1	25	5	0	2	20	0	37	15	5	2	.356	.348
Price, Jared, G.F.	.191	27	109	89	13	17	25	3	1	1	10	0	1	6	13	0	30	2	2	0	.281	.330
Puccinelli, John, I.F.	.270	46	190	163	25	44	65	9	0	4	11	0	1	5	21	1	38	0	0	2	.399	.368
Ramos, Ebaldo, M.H.	.233	26	101	90	13	21	29	8	0	0	11	1	0	0	10	0	24	0	0	2	.322	.310
Reese, Kevin, I.F.*	.358	53	249	201	51	72	100	14	4	2	36	0	2	3	43	2	30	12	3	5	.498	.474
Ridley, Jeremy, M.H.†	.286	3	10	7	3	2	3	1	0	0	1	0	0	0	3	0	2	0	0	0	.429	.500
Rikert, Wade, M.H.	.247	24	117	97	27	24	40	4	0	4	15	1	1	3	15	2	19	6	1	0	.412	.362
Riley, Brett, But.	.250	12	19	16	4	4	6	0	1	0	1	0	0	1	2	0	9	0	0	0	.375	.368
Rivera, William, M.H.*	.274	39	152	124	22	34	39	3	1	0	8	4	0	0	24	0	29	0	0	2	.315	.392
Rogers, Brandon, But.	.316	11	48	38	5	12	20	2	0	2	5	0	1	0	9	0	8	0	0	1	.526	.438
Romero, Nicholas, I.F.	.111	5	18	18	1	2	2	0	0	0	2	0	0	0	0	0	4	0	0	2	.111	.111
Rowan, Chris, Og.	.267	4	17	15	0	4	4	0	0	0	1	0	1	0	1	0	5	1	0	0	.267	.294
Ruiz, Randy, Bil.	.381	61	273	231	55	88	135	15	1	10	55	1	2	10	29	0	56	1	2	6	.584	.467
Santiago, Daniel, Bil.†	.258	18	78	66	11	17	21	4	0	0	6	0	1	1	10	1	15	1	0	1	.318	.359
Santos, Luis, Miss.	.286	2	7	7	0	2	2	0	0	0	1	0	0	0	0	0	4	0	0	1	.286	.286
Schilling, Chris, Og.-Hel.	.119	18	48	42	2	5	7	2	0	0	1	1	0	2	3	0	17	0	0	1	.167	.213
Sein, Javier, Bil.*	.284	57	233	215	33	61	90	11	0	6	36	0	3	1	13	0	59	1	0	6	.419	.323
Siriveaw, Nom, M.H.†	.243	63	270	235	40	57	93	8	2	8	40	0	0	0	35	1	64	7	0	2	.396	.341
Sisk, Aaron, M.H.	.257	59	257	218	32	56	109	10	2	13	50	0	2	3	34	1	56	4	0	7	.500	.362
Small, Chris, M.H.	.221	38	153	131	13	29	29	0	0	0	6	4	1	3	14	0	23	2	1	2	.221	.309
Smith, Ryan, Bil.	.209	48	214	172	28	36	56	9	1	3	23	0	0	6	36	0	41	13	3	2	.326	.364
Smitherman, Stephen, Bil.	.316	70	332	301	61	95	166	16	5	15	65	0	2	6	23	2	67	14	1	10	.551	.373
Sobet, Renato, I.F.	.290	41	170	155	20	45	63	7	1	3	33	0	3	2	10	1	32	0	4	6	.406	.335
Soriano, Carlos, Hel.	.171	37	130	123	16	21	33	4	1	2	12	0	1	1	5	0	43	7	2	3	.268	.208
Spadt, Eric, Bil.	.000	3	13	12	1	0	0	0	0	0	1	0	0	0	1	0	4	0	0	0	.000	.077
Sparks, Eddie, Bil.	.227	6	25	22	2	5	6	1	0	0	2	0	0	0	3	1	7	0	0	1	.273	.320
Stockton, Jeffrey, But.	.249	51	207	185	32	46	69	11	0	4	23	3	1	2	16	0	60	3	4	3	.373	.314
Stone, Todd, Bil.	.170	18	73	47	8	8	14	0	0	2	5	1	0	8	17	0	21	1	1	0	.298	.458
Story-Harden, Thomari, G.F.	.232	55	207	177	27	41	62	3	3	4	30	1	1	3	25	0	55	9	1	1	.350	.335
Templeton, Garry, But.	.250	21	93	80	19	20	27	3	2	0	9	1	0	1	11	0	22	6	1	0	.338	.348
Terrero, Luis, Miss.	.261	68	296	276	48	72	106	10	0	8	44	1	1	8	10	0	75	23	11	5	.384	.305
Thompson, Craig, I.F.	.358	58	281	218	52	78	124	14	1	10	62	2	7	2	52	3	23	5	2	0	.569	.473
Thompson, Zachary, Hel.*	.165	43	126	103	11	17	24	3	2	0	7	0	0	6	17	0	44	1	5	1	.233	.317
Thulin, Thomas, But.	.125	7	22	16	5	2	5	0	0	1	4	0	0	0	6	0	3	1	0	2	.313	.364

Player, Team	Avg.	G	TPA	AB	R	H	TB	2B	3B	HR	RBI	SH	SF	HP	BB	IBB	SO	SB	CS	GDP	Slg.	OBP
Tindell, Matt, Hel.	.200	44	145	135	9	27	31	4	0	0	7	0	0	1	9	0	35	3	6	4	.230	.255
Trout, Casey, Og.	.203	21	83	69	13	14	15	1	0	0	10	0	1	4	9	0	10	2	1	9	.217	.325
Trzesniak, Nick, I.F.	.341	36	159	132	32	45	76	6	2	7	30	0	0	4	23	2	30	4	2	6	.576	.453
Umbria, Jose, M.H.	.345	14	66	55	11	19	30	2	0	3	14	0	0	0	11	0	10	0	0	0	.545	.455
Valdez, Ramon, But.	.316	30	136	117	33	37	62	7	3	4	17	1	2	1	15	0	15	11	1	3	.530	.393
Valenzuela, Christian, But.	.299	56	217	194	25	58	70	7	1	1	26	3	5	1	14	0	31	1	0	4	.361	.341
Vandemore, Tony, I.F.*	.250	12	47	40	5	10	14	2	1	0	5	0	1	0	6	0	10	0	0	1	.350	.340
Varner, Gary, Bil.	.257	11	37	35	4	9	12	1	1	0	3	0	0	0	2	0	10	0	0	1	.343	.297
Vega, Jesus, But.	.187	28	98	91	0	17	19	2	0	0	10	1	1	0	5	0	25	0	1	1	.209	.227
Villero, Armando, Hel.*	.306	54	224	196	32	60	74	8	0	2	18	0	0	6	22	0	26	16	1	8	.378	.393
Voltz, Robert, Hel.*	.285	67	285	242	47	69	129	12	6	12	53	0	3	1	39	1	66	11	3	4	.533	.382
Wallace, Kellen, But.*	.240	34	131	121	9	29	36	5	1	0	16	1	0	1	8	0	27	0	1	2	.298	.292
Ward, Corey, Hel.	.263	25	85	80	13	21	39	9	0	3	11	0	0	3	2	0	32	1	3	0	.488	.306
Warren, Tom, Hel.	.333	1	4	3	1	1	1	0	0	0	0	0	1	0	0	0	2	0	0	0	.333	.333
West, Todd, Hel.-Og.	.291	62	273	227	49	66	75	9	0	0	16	8	0	8	30	0	29	8	7	1	.330	.392
Williamson, Chris, Bil.*	.310	25	125	100	30	31	60	10	2	5	33	0	3	0	22	2	32	2	1	1	.600	.424
Williford, Dan, Miss.*	.232	20	73	69	11	16	24	4	2	0	2	0	0	1	3	1	16	2	0	2	.348	.274
Wilson, Jacob, But.*	.133	8	20	15	2	2	2	0	0	0	1	0	0	0	5	0	5	0	0	0	.133	.350
Wood, Stephen, M.H.	.227	21	97	88	14	20	34	8	0	2	14	0	0	0	9	2	16	0	0	3	.386	.299
Woodward, John, I.F.*	.317	68	333	281	67	89	175	26	0	20	92	0	4	5	43	0	76	9	4	5	.623	.411
Wright, Nate, G.F.	.000	4	7	4	2	0	0	0	0	0	0	0	0	0	0	0	3	0	0	0	.000	.429
Yakopich, Joseph, Miss.*	.261	48	170	138	23	36	50	9	1	1	20	1	1	3	27	0	15	6	1	1	.362	.391

GRAND SLAMS: Clark, Woodward, 2 each; Abruzzo, Anderson, Campo, Candelaria, Contreras, DeLaPaz, J. Johnson, K. Johnson, Krynzel, McCool, Noboa, Pagan, Reese, Rikert, Ruiz, Siriveaw, Smitherman, Umbria, Voltz, 1 each.

AWARDED FIRST BASE ON CATCHER'S INTERFERENCE: Belcher (Delgado), Egly (Culwell), Little (Culwell), Myers (Culwell), Sein (Trzesniak).

PLAYERS WITH TWO OR MORE TEAMS

Player, Team	Avg.	G	TPA	AB	R	H	TB	2B	3B	HR	RBI	SH	SF	HP	BB	IBB	SO	SB	CS	GDP	Slg.	OBP
Lake, Josh, Hel.	.200	4	13	10	0	2	2	0	0	0	1	1	0	1	1	0	6	0	0	0	.200	.333
Lake, Josh, Og.	.125	4	10	8	1	1	1	0	0	0	0	0	0	0	2	0	2	0	0	0	.125	.300
Schilling, Chris, Og.	.143	10	25	21	1	3	4	1	0	0	1	0	0	2	1	0	8	0	0	0	.190	.250
Schilling, Chris, Hel.	.095	8	23	21	1	2	3	1	0	0	1	0	0	0	2	0	9	0	1	0	.143	.174
West, Todd, Hel.	.271	57	250	207	44	56	62	6	0	0	12	8	0	7	28	0	29	7	6	1	.300	.376
West, Todd, Og.	.500	5	23	20	5	10	13	3	0	0	4	0	0	1	2	0	0	1	1	0	.650	.565

2000 PITCHING

TEAM

Team	W	L	Pct.	ERA	G	CG	ShO	Sv.	IP	H	TBF	R	ER	HR	SH	SF	HB	BB	IBB	SO	WP	Bk.
Missoula	44	32	.579	3.92	76	1	4	16	668.1	640	2969	396	291	28	20	11	56	303	4	618	65	10
Great Falls	42	34	.553	4.51	76	2	3	18	658.2	670	2983	416	330	42	14	18	48	333	3	618	77	4
Medicine Hat	36	40	.474	4.56	76	0	1	17	669.1	711	2995	443	339	57	29	29	38	273	4	574	83	5
Ogden	41	34	.547	4.87	75	1	5	25	667.1	736	3048	456	361	73	17	35	42	309	7	588	63	9
Idaho Falls	45	29	.608	5.02	74	0	1	16	655.0	742	2988	453	365	56	19	19	50	288	5	561	71	8
Helena	26	50	.342	5.44	76	0	0	14	663.0	734	3109	513	401	57	24	26	55	378	22	515	102	14
Billings	39	36	.520	5.76	75	0	0	18	659.1	702	3101	504	422	59	18	22	53	441	7	557	96	9
Butte	29	47	.382	5.84	76	2	1	13	656.1	831	3181	591	426	53	16	26	53	334	7	501	98	11

INDIVIDUAL

TOP QUALIFIERS FOR EARNED-RUN AVERAGE TITLE

Minimum 61 innings.*Lefthanded pitcher.

Pitcher, Team	W	L	Pct.	ERA	G	GS	CG	ShO	GF	Sv.	IP	H	TBF	R	ER	HR	SH	SF	HB	BB	IBB	SO	WP	Bk.
Rodriguez, Ricardo, G.F.	10	3	.769	1.88	15	15	2	0	0	0	95.2	66	374	32	20	2	3	3	1	23	0	129	4	0
Miniel, Roberto, Og.	9	3	.750	2.70	16	14	0	0	0	0	83.1	84	355	41	25	7	0	3	4	22	0	80	5	0
Bevis, P.J., Miss.	3	6	.333	3.33	14	14	0	0	0	0	83.2	92	354	50	31	4	1	2	2	22	1	63	8	1
Lugo, Ruddy, Og.	5	5	.500	3.44	16	16	1	0	0	0	91.2	82	397	48	35	7	3	6	12	52	1	88	7	0
Miller, Ryan, Og.	7	3	.700	3.64	15	10	0	0	2	0	76.2	62	318	35	31	8	1	7	8	27	0	66	1	3
Chulk, Charles, M.H.	2	4	.333	3.80	14	13	0	0	0	0	68.2	75	295	36	29	5	0	2	2	20	0	51	3	0
Sheefel, Adam, Bil.*	9	1	.900	4.14	16	16	0	0	0	0	91.1	111	412	53	42	4	2	1	6	27	0	83	5	0
Maysonet, Roberto, Hel.	3	6	.333	4.23	15	15	0	0	0	0	78.2	78	358	52	37	5	0	1	7	39	1	84	13	0
Gordon, Justin, Og.*	5	5	.500	4.26	16	15	0	0	0	0	76.0	69	337	45	36	7	1	2	1	42	0	53	10	0
McMillan, Joshua, M.H.*	3	3	.500	4.34	15	15	0	0	0	0	64.1	72	293	47	31	5	3	1	2	29	0	56	5	0
Hosford, Clinton, G.F.	2	7	.222	4.35	17	5	0	0	0	0	68.1	76	313	50	33	5	2	3	7	25	2	56	7	0
Daigle, Casey, Miss.	3	5	.375	4.90	15	15	0	0	0	0	82.2	88	390	57	45	4	2	0	9	54	0	56	10	3
Vitek, Josh, I.F.	5	4	.556	5.05	15	15	0	0	0	0	73.0	92	343	48	41	4	1	5	6	40	0	42	5	1
Earey, Ryan, I.F.	4	3	.571	5.04	15	14	0	0	0	0	69.1	93	306	47	39	8	3	2	4	14	0	45	1	0
Ozuna, Benigno, Hel.	2	5	.286	5.54	21	8	0	0	5	0	66.2	82	317	51	41	5	3	3	3	36	2	27	9	0

DEPARTMENTAL LEADERS: W—Rodriguez, 10; L—Guzman, 8; Pct.—Sheefel, .900; G—Belanger, 31; GS—Lugo, 16; CG—Rodriguez, 2; ShO—Perkins, 1; GF—Belanger, 26; Sv.—McCulloch, 15; IP—Rodriguez, 95.2; H—Sheefel, 111; TBF—Sheefel, 412; R—Wallace, 73; ER—Castillo, 52; HR—Wallace, 10; SH—several tied, 4 each; SF—Miller, 7; HB—Lugo, 12; BB—Daigle, 54; IBB—several tied, 3 each; SO—Rodriguez, 129; WP—Jenks, 19; BK—Gomez, 4.

ALL PITCHERS

*Lefthanded pitcher.

Pitcher, Team	W	L	Pct.	ERA	G	GS	CG	ShO	GF	Sv.	IP	H	TBF	R	ER	HR	SH	SF	HB	BB	IBB	SO	WP	Bk.
Abbott, James, M.H.	2	1	.667	1.99	8	4	0	0	0	0	22.2	19	95	11	5	0	1	3	1	6	0	18	1	0
Andrews, Aron, G.F.	5	0	1.000	2.16	19	0	0	0	14	4	25.0	19	105	6	6	0	0	0	3	7	0	25	2	0
Arellan, Felix, G.F.*	0	1	.000	6.11	13	0	0	0	3	0	17.2	25	115	21	12	0	0	0	2	30	0	24	12	0

Pitcher, Team	W	L	Pct.	ERA	G	GS	CG	ShO	GF	Sv.	IP	H	TBF	R	ER	HR	SH	SF	HB	BB	IBB	SO	WP	Bk.
Artman, Dane, Og.	1	0	1.000	5.33	7	7	0	0	0	0	25.1	35	123	18	15	2	0	1	1	11	0	19	1	1
Baldassano, Joseph, But.	1	5	.167	10.22	25	0	0	0	12	0	37.0	58	212	50	42	5	0	3	8	34	1	28	15	0
Banks, Almonzo, But.	1	0	1.000	10.80	3	0	0	0	3	0	3.1	8	18	4	4	1	0	0	0	0	0	1	0	0
Batson, Byron, Og.	0	3	.000	4.88	20	0	0	0	7	3	51.2	54	240	38	28	3	4	0	5	29	2	45	3	0
Belanger, Brandon, I.F.	3	1	.750	4.76	31	0	0	0	26	12	34.0	35	148	19	18	5	2	0	1	8	0	27	1	1
Belicic, Adam, But.*	1	2	.333	3.23	17	0	0	0	5	3	30.2	38	144	24	11	1	0	1	4	12	0	29	3	0
Bell, Casey, But.	1	1	.500	9.00	3	1	0	0	0	0	6.0	11	31	8	6	1	0	0	0	2	0	4	2	0
Belson, Gregory, Miss.	1	0	1.000	1.80	3	0	0	0	3	1	5.0	4	18	2	1	1	0	0	0	4	0	4	0	0
Bevis, P.J., Miss.	3	6	.333	3.33	14	14	0	0	0	0	83.2	92	354	50	31	4	1	2	2	22	1	63	8	1
Bimeal, Matt, M.H.	1	0	1.000	6.02	21	0	0	0	8	0	43.1	55	199	40	29	8	1	3	1	13	0	50	8	2
Bonilla, Ben, Miss.*	0	0	.000	6.23	2	0	0	0	0	0	4.1	4	18	4	3	0	0	0	3	0	3	1	0
Boutwell, Andy, Bil.	4	1	.800	5.10	23	0	0	0	11	4	30.0	22	143	21	17	3	1	0	1	33	0	24	3	2
Brazoban, Jose, Hel.	2	1	.667	7.76	24	0	0	0	13	2	31.1	42	166	30	27	3	1	0	5	32	2	25	6	2
Brown, Paul, Bil.*	1	2	.333	7.16	5	5	0	0	0	0	27.2	35	126	23	22	4	2	4	2	12	1	17	1	0
Brown, Tighe, Bil.	3	1	.750	3.13	7	5	0	0	0	0	37.1	29	156	16	13	4	0	1	2	16	0	30	4	0
Bussard, Jesse, I.F.	0	0	.000	6.38	20	0	0	0	8	1	24.0	27	118	24	17	3	0	1	4	13	0	18	7	0
Bynum, Matthew, Bil.	0	2	.000	7.85	8	2	0	0	3	1	18.1	24	100	23	16	3	1	2	1	18	1	18	2	0
Cassel, Jack, I.F.	0	0	.000	1.42	7	0	0	0	2	0	12.2	10	52	8	2	1	0	1	0	3	1	13	0	1
Castillo, Geraldo, Hel.	4	5	.444	6.69	17	10	0	0	1	0	70.0	81	323	58	52	6	2	4	10	31	2	55	7	2
Chapman, Dennis, I.F.	1	2	.333	9.59	21	0	0	0	8	0	25.1	30	131	31	27	4	1	3	3	20	1	33	8	1
Chulk, Charles, M.H.	2	4	.333	3.80	14	13	0	0	0	0	68.2	75	295	36	29	5	0	2	2	20	0	51	3	0
Cimorelli, Brett, But.	1	0	1.000	5.84	7	4	0	0	0	0	24.2	23	113	19	16	3	0	0	6	12	0	11	1	0
Collins, Clint, Bil.	2	5	.286	4.20	22	0	0	0	17	4	40.2	32	179	24	19	6	1	1	4	25	1	46	6	0
Cooper, Eric, Bil.	1	0	1.000	10.29	3	3	0	0	0	0	7.0	8	35	9	8	1	0	0	1	6	0	4	3	0
Cordero, Jesus, G.F.	1	1	.500	2.37	18	1	0	0	6	1	30.1	30	143	15	8	1	0	1	1	21	0	27	6	0
Cordero, Victor, Hel.	1	2	.333	3.86	8	0	0	0	4	0	18.2	19	96	12	8	1	1	0	5	12	2	29	3	0
Cramblitt, Joey, Miss.	2	0	1.000	1.59	5	0	0	0	0	0	11.1	8	44	3	2	2	0	0	0	0	0	11	1	1
Culp, Brandon, Bil.	1	0	1.000	6.61	7	0	0	0	2	0	16.1	19	78	12	12	0	0	0	2	6	0	19	1	0
Curtis, Bill, But.	1	0	1.000	3.97	7	0	0	0	4	0	11.1	11	46	5	5	1	0	0	1	3	1	11	0	0
Daigle, Casey, Miss.	3	5	.375	4.90	15	15	0	0	0	0	82.2	88	390	57	45	4	2	0	9	54	0	56	10	3
D'Amico, Leonardo, But.	0	3	.000	5.40	7	4	0	0	0	0	30.0	40	147	32	18	5	0	1	4	12	0	19	3	1
De La Cruz, Pedro, Hel.	0	1	.000	4.74	8	4	0	0	0	0	19.0	18	89	15	10	1	1	0	3	13	0	14	2	0
Durkee, Jeremy, Hel.*	0	3	.000	7.34	18	4	0	0	4	0	38.0	67	194	41	31	4	4	4	3	13	2	24	7	1
Duverge, Alcides, But.	0	1	.000	11.88	8	0	0	0	4	0	8.1	13	50	13	11	2	0	0	2	10	0	7	6	0
Earey, Ryan, I.F.	4	3	.571	5.06	14	13	0	0	0	0	69.1	93	306	47	39	8	3	2	4	14	0	45	1	0
Edwards, Bryan, Bil.	0	2	.000	12.00	4	2	0	0	1	0	6.0	5	39	9	8	0	0	1	1	18	0	4	4	1
Eppolito, Vince, Miss.	4	0	1.000	7.24	20	0	0	0	8	0	32.1	30	153	28	26	1	0	1	8	25	0	35	9	0
Fawcett, Mike, Bil.	2	1	.667	6.61	14	0	0	0	4	1	16.1	28	81	15	12	1	1	1	0	4	0	7	0	0
Fischer, Richard, But.	3	5	.375	5.91	18	13	1	0	2	1	70.0	103	335	63	46	8	0	1	3	26	0	45	6	0
Flading, Cameron, But.	0	0	.000	1.93	4	0	0	0	2	0	4.2	4	22	2	1	0	0	2	0	4	1	3	0	0
Fletcher, Daniel, Bil.	0	2	.000	12.00	8	4	0	0	0	0	18.0	25	100	31	30	5	0	0	3	22	0	14	4	0
Flores, Neomar, M.H.	0	0	.000	12.00	1	1	0	0	0	0	3.0	6	14	4	4	0	0	0	1	0	2	0	0
Gardea, Mario, Bil.	0	3	.000	5.29	23	0	0	0	12	2	32.1	32	166	27	19	0	0	1	2	40	1	35	13	0
George, Bradley, Bil.	2	0	1.000	4.72	11	8	0	0	1	1	47.2	51	215	28	25	2	0	1	6	21	0	55	9	0
Gilmore, Travis, But.*	1	1	.500	7.57	14	1	0	0	3	0	27.1	32	143	28	23	2	1	3	0	27	1	24	1	0
Glidewell, Clifton, G.F.*	1	1	.500	0.84	6	0	0	0	1	0	10.2	8	43	4	1	1	0	0	1	5	0	10	0	0
Gomez, Hunter, Hel.	1	3	.250	6.30	12	0	0	0	9	2	20.0	25	96	16	14	2	0	0	3	9	1	25	1	4
Gordon, Justin, Og.*	5	5	.500	4.26	16	15	0	0	0	0	76.0	69	337	45	36	7	1	2	1	42	0	53	10	0
Gracesqui, Franklyn, M.H.*	0	1	.000	2.63	8	4	0	0	0	0	24.0	15	105	11	7	1	1	0	2	21	0	20	5	0
Gray, Rusty, Og.	2	0	1.000	3.00	8	0	0	0	2	1	15.0	18	68	9	5	0	1	2	0	4	1	11	2	0
Gruban, Jarret, But.	1	1	.500	4.11	8	7	0	0	0	0	35.0	31	162	26	16	1	1	1	2	23	0	26	11	0
Guzman, Alexis, M.H.	6	8	.429	2.38	27	1	0	0	6	0	53.0	49	226	25	14	3	4	2	6	11	0	35	2	0
Hall, Dan, Og.	1	3	.250	3.81	23	0	0	0	21	11	26.0	27	119	13	11	5	2	1	1	12	0	36	0	2
Hanrahan, Joel, G.F.	3	1	.750	4.75	12	11	0	0	0	0	55.0	49	240	32	29	4	0	0	5	23	0	40	4	0
Hanson, David, M.H.	7	3	.700	5.81	15	15	0	0	0	0	79.0	82	352	55	51	6	3	2	5	29	0	79	12	1
Hebert, Cedric, Bil.	5	2	.714	3.43	8	7	0	0	0	0	39.1	31	161	17	15	4	0	1	5	18	0	33	2	3
Heck, Christopher, I.F.*	1	1	.500	4.02	19	0	0	0	3	0	31.1	42	145	19	14	3	2	0	0	9	0	25	2	0
Henderson, Eric, Og.*	0	0	.000	0.00	1	1	0	0	0	0	1.2	1	5	0	0	0	0	0	0	1	0	2	0	0
Hendrickson, Benjamin, Og.	4	3	.571	5.68	13	7	0	0	2	1	50.2	50	237	37	32	7	1	2	1	29	0	48	12	0
Hensley, Matthew, But.	1	2	.333	2.57	8	5	0	0	0	0	28.0	29	132	21	8	0	0	2	10	0	22	3	3
Herbert, John, I.F.	2	2	.500	4.57	17	0	0	0	7	0	21.2	17	91	14	11	2	2	0	0	6	0	24	5	0
Hickman, Jason, G.F.	3	3	.500	4.88	12	9	0	0	0	0	55.1	65	250	32	30	6	1	1	3	25	0	52	5	1
Hosford, Clinton, G.F.	2	7	.222	4.35	17	5	0	0	5	0	68.1	76	313	50	33	5	2	3	7	25	2	56	7	0
Hoyt, Michael, I.F.	1	1	.500	6.12	16	1	0	0	3	0	25.0	27	125	20	17	2	2	0	4	17	1	20	4	0
Hussman, Darrell, Bil.	0	0	.000	1.54	3	3	0	0	0	0	11.2	5	42	2	2	0	0	0	1	3	0	9	0	0
Jenks, Robert, But.	1	7	.125	7.86	14	12	0	0	0	0	52.2	61	265	57	46	2	2	4	5	44	0	42	19	2
Joseph, Glen, Bil.	0	1	.000	8.03	8	0	0	0	3	0	12.1	15	69	13	11	1	1	3	0	17	1	10	8	0
Keirstead, Michael, G.F.	4	3	.571	4.81	18	7	0	0	2	0	58.0	68	262	38	31	3	1	3	4	23	0	36	2	0
Laesch, Michael, Bil.	5	2	.714	5.95	24	3	0	0	7	3	56.0	69	259	47	37	6	0	2	6	21	1	49	6	0
Landkamer, Michael, Bil.	0	0	.000	6.75	6	0	0	0	2	0	8.0	9	36	6	6	0	0	1	0	6	0	3	3	1
Lansford, Dustin, Hel.*	1	3	.250	4.86	11	6	0	0	2	0	37.0	30	162	20	20	4	1	0	2	32	1	36	5	0
Larman, Jayson, Bil.	0	1	.000	11.45	7	2	0	0	0	0	11.0	13	72	16	14	1	0	0	3	27	0	9	4	0
Lasose, Enrique, Og.	1	0	1.000	11.40	13	0	0	0	12	0	15.0	23	83	23	19	3	0	1	2	12	0	10	2	0
Lesieur, Christopher, Miss.	1	0	1.000	4.68	23	0	0	0	6	2	25.0	27	128	24	13	2	1	0	3	19	0	26	5	0
Lizarraga, Edgar, G.F.	2	1	.667	5.40	24	0	0	0	20	7	30.0	32	138	20	18	3	1	0	4	11	0	51	5	1
Lorenzen, Jonathan, G.F.	2	3	.400	5.33	14	7	0	0	0	0	49.0	46	217	32	29	2	0	3	3	28	0	39	6	0
Lowe, Matt, Og.	0	0	.000	9.00	2	0	0	0	1	0	3.0	2	18	5	3	0	0	0	1	4	0	6	3	0
Lugo, Ruddy, Og.	5	5	.500	3.44	16	16	1	0	0	0	91.2	82	397	48	35	7	3	6	12	52	1	88	7	0
Lutz, Kenneth, G.F.	2	3	.600	6.11	7	7	0	0	0	0	35.1	44	158	26	24	3	1	1	3	11	0	16	2	0
Martinez, Ramon, G.F.	0	0	.000	7.20	6	0	0	0	5	3	5.0	8	28	6	4	0	0	2	4	0	7	2	0
Maysonet, Roberto, Hel.	3	6	.333	4.23	15	13	0	0	0	0	78.2	78	358	52	37	5	0	1	7	39	1	84	13	0
McAdoo, Duncan, I.F.	4	1	.800	3.40	9	7	0	0	1	0	42.1	42	173	17	16	1	2	0	3	6	0	37	1	1
McCullem, Ryan, M.H.*	2	2	.500	3.95	16	6	0	0	1	0	54.2	64	254	34	24	5	3	2	2	27	0	53	5	0
McCulloch, Andrew, M.H.	0	0	.000	2.67	27	0	0	0	24	15	27.0	24	112	9	8	3	0	0	0	7	0	26	2	0

Pitcher, Team	W	L	Pct.	ERA	G	GS	CG	ShO	GF	Sv.	IP	H	TBF	R	ER	HR	SH	SF	HB	BB	IBB	SO	WP	Bk.
McGowan, Dustin, M.H.	0	3	.000	6.48	8	8	0	0	0	0	25.0	26	129	21	18	2	1	5	3	25	0	19	8	0
McMillan, Joshua, M.H.*	3	3	.500	4.34	15	15	0	0	0	0	64.1	72	293	47	31	5	3	1	2	29	0	56	5	0
McMurray, Heath, Og.	3	2	.600	4.50	12	0	0	0	6	3	26.0	31	116	13	13	6	1	1	7	0	26	0	2
Mendez, Pastor, Hel.	1	1	.500	9.00	2	1	0	0	0	0	6.0	10	33	12	6	0	1	1	4	0	3	1	1
Meyer, John, I.F.	0	1	.000	8.10	17	0	0	0	0	0	20.0	19	108	21	18	1	0	0	4	27	0	15	4	0
Miller, Ryan, Og.	7	3	.700	3.64	15	10	0	0	2	0	76.2	62	318	35	31	8	1	7	8	27	0	66	1	3
Milo, Anthony, But.*	1	3	.250	4.54	12	2	0	0	3	2	35.2	44	166	25	18	2	1	2	2	10	0	44	2	0
Miniel, Roberto, Og.	9	3	.750	2.70	16	14	0	0	0	0	83.1	84	355	41	25	7	0	3	4	22	0	80	5	0
Montero, Agustin, G.F.	2	1	.667	3.93	11	0	0	0	3	0	18.1	16	85	10	8	1	0	0	2	12	0	21	3	0
Montoya, Saul, Miss.	2	2	.500	2.37	8	8	0	0	0	0	49.1	36	197	15	13	0	3	0	2	16	0	39	2	1
Moore, Greg, But.	3	1	.750	5.29	7	5	1	0	0	0	34.0	44	152	23	20	3	1	2	0	6	0	19	1	0
Morris, William, M.H.	3	4	.429	5.52	24	0	0	0	8	0	44.0	46	192	33	27	4	3	3	1	17	1	29	3	0
Neary, Andrew, Hel.-Og.	4	3	.571	4.25	22	0	0	0	9	1	48.2	43	203	25	23	7	2	2	1	14	3	29	2	0
Nielsen, Brian, Og.*	1	3	.250	6.43	10	2	0	0	2	1	28.0	39	127	23	20	6	0	1	0	6	0	25	2	0
Nohr, Ryan, Og.	0	0	.000	0.00	1	0	0	0	1	0	1.0	2	5	0	0	0	0	0	0	0	0	1	0	0
Nunez, Severino, Hel.*	2	1	.667	3.99	16	10	0	0	0	0	58.2	52	262	33	26	2	1	2	0	32	2	40	12	1
Nunley, Derrek, M.H.	1	0	1.000	2.63	8	0	0	0	2	0	13.2	10	57	4	4	0	0	0	2	6	0	11	5	0
O'Gara, Dan, Hel.	0	3	.000	4.74	10	0	0	0	6	0	24.2	28	115	13	13	1	0	1	1	16	2	17	4	0
Ovalles, Juan, Miss.	4	2	.667	2.17	8	7	0	0	0	0	45.2	46	192	21	11	1	1	0	2	7	0	40	0	0
Ozuna, Benigno, Hel.	2	5	.286	5.54	21	8	0	0	5	0	66.2	82	317	51	41	5	3	3	3	36	2	27	9	0
Padilla, Edgar, But.	1	0	1.000	10.80	4	0	0	0	3	0	5.0	6	26	6	6	1	1	0	1	4	0	1	0	0
Pape, Stace, Bil.	0	0	.000	7.71	4	0	0	0	0	0	4.2	5	27	5	4	0	0	1	1	5	0	1	0	0
Patten, Lanny, M.H.	2	3	.400	3.71	17	3	0	0	5	0	43.2	57	196	31	18	5	0	1	5	11	0	38	8	0
Peralta, Joel, But.	2	1	.667	6.63	10	1	0	0	8	1	19.0	24	87	15	14	2	1	2	2	10	1	17	2	1
Perez, Oliver, I.F.*	3	1	.750	4.07	5	5	0	0	0	0	24.1	24	100	14	11	1	0	1	1	9	0	27	3	0
Perkins, Gregory, Miss.	2	1	.667	3.56	6	6	1	1	0	0	30.1	29	127	13	12	2	0	1	4	10	0	28	3	2
Phillips, Mark, I.F.*	1	1	.500	5.35	10	10	0	0	0	0	37.0	35	164	30	22	2	1	1	0	24	0	37	4	2
Pike, Matthew, Bil.	0	1	.000	14.73	2	1	0	0	0	0	3.2	6	24	6	6	1	0	0	0	8	0	2	1	0
Reynoso, Roberto, But.	1	4	.200	5.66	11	8	0	0	1	1	41.1	59	200	40	26	1	2	2	0	12	0	37	3	1
Ricciardi, Joseph, Miss.	2	1	.667	4.88	25	1	0	0	14	2	31.1	30	149	21	17	0	1	1	7	22	0	36	4	1
Rivera, Ramon, But.*	0	3	.000	4.82	15	1	0	0	7	4	28.0	33	134	22	15	3	1	0	0	15	0	16	1	1
Rodriguez, Ricardo, G.F.	10	3	.769	1.88	15	15	2	0	0	0	95.2	66	374	32	20	2	3	3	1	23	0	129	4	0
Rojas, Chris, I.F.	1	0	1.000	5.00	2	2	0	0	0	0	9.0	8	43	5	5	0	0	3	4	0	13	4	0
Rosario, Andres, G.F.	1	1	.500	6.28	19	1	0	0	5	1	28.2	39	153	27	20	1	0	0	2	26	1	29	8	1
Ross, Brian, Bil.*	0	1	.000	4.80	14	0	0	0	3	2	15.0	14	70	10	8	2	0	0	0	8	0	12	2	0
Ross, Lew, Miss.*	2	4	.333	3.93	23	0	0	0	14	6	34.1	27	148	16	15	4	1	4	11	2	46	3	0
Rossellini, William, Miss.	0	4	.000	12.34	5	4	0	0	0	0	11.2	15	75	23	16	1	2	1	7	19	0	7	3	0
Schachleiter, Jeff, Bil.	0	1	.000	17.74	7	2	0	0	1	0	11.2	20	70	23	23	3	1	0	2	18	0	13	5	1
Shabansky, Rob, Miss.	3	1	.750	3.92	11	7	0	0	1	0	39.0	35	175	26	17	1	1	3	0	18	0	40	0	0
Sheefel, Adam, Bil.*	9	1	.900	4.14	16	15	0	0	0	0	91.1	111	412	53	42	4	2	1	6	27	0	83	5	0
Shorey, Jeremy, Og.	2	1	.667	9.10	15	0	0	0	5	2	29.2	56	157	37	30	2	1	3	1	12	0	16	4	0
Shrout, Kevin, Og.	1	1	.500	7.63	14	2	0	0	5	3	46.0	73	228	46	39	6	2	4	2	18	0	39	5	1
Shwam, Mike, Hel.	1	3	.250	3.95	23	0	0	0	21	9	27.1	26	123	12	12	2	1	0	2	12	0	34	5	0
Silverio, Marcelino, I.F.	1	3	.250	4.33	25	0	0	0	8	2	27.0	33	121	17	13	3	1	1	1	9	0	22	3	0
Smith, Ryan, Bil.	0	0	.000	0.00	1	0	0	0	1	0	1.0	2	6	2	0	0	0	0	0	0	0	0	0	0
Spillman, Jeromie, M.H.*	4	3	.571	4.15	22	0	0	0	7	1	39.0	34	169	22	18	4	4	1	0	18	3	36	2	2
Steele, Matt, Miss.	2	0	1.000	3.08	16	1	0	0	3	0	26.1	17	120	14	9	1	1	0	4	21	0	32	5	0
Steffek, Brian, G.F.	1	1	.500	4.91	21	0	0	0	10	2	29.1	25	132	19	16	4	1	2	1	18	0	28	3	0
Stephenson, Eric, M.H.	1	1	.500	8.33	19	0	0	0	8	0	27.0	41	134	28	25	2	1	2	2	13	0	21	9	0
Stockman, Phil, Miss.	2	0	1.000	2.45	2	2	0	0	0	0	11.0	10	46	3	3	0	0	0	3	0	4	0	0
Takach, Ryan, Miss.*	3	2	.600	3.10	24	1	0	0	6	0	40.2	39	183	16	14	0	2	0	1	19	0	37	3	1
Thomas, Adam, But.	0	2	.000	4.50	6	6	0	0	0	0	34.0	44	159	26	17	3	1	0	4	10	0	22	3	2
Thompson, Jesse, Bil.	1	0	1.000	4.19	9	0	0	0	4	0	19.1	18	85	10	9	2	3	0	0	14	1	18	3	0
Thompson, Mike, I.F.	6	4	.600	5.94	14	14	0	0	0	0	72.2	99	339	56	48	8	1	1	8	30	0	52	8	0
Thorpe, Tracy, M.H.	0	4	.000	8.54	11	6	0	0	0	0	26.1	28	126	28	25	3	3	1	3	17	0	15	3	0
Tibbs, Jeffrey, G.F.	2	5	.286	7.85	14	13	0	0	0	0	47.0	54	227	46	41	6	4	1	4	41	0	28	6	1
Tisdale, Marlyn, Bil.	2	1	.667	0.52	8	1	0	0	3	0	17.1	9	74	6	1	0	2	1	2	11	0	17	1	0
Tomsu, Joshua, Bil.	2	5	.286	6.52	12	12	0	0	0	0	59.1	65	276	50	43	6	3	2	2	37	0	25	6	1
Trejo, Francisco, Miss.*	3	3	.500	4.08	10	10	0	0	0	0	46.1	53	209	29	21	2	2	0	2	17	0	48	3	0
Valenzuela, Christian, But.	0	0	.000	0.00	2	0	0	0	0	0	2.0	2	9	1	0	0	0	0	0	0	0	1	0	0
Valverde, Jose, Miss.	1	0	1.000	0.00	12	0	0	0	11	4	11.0	3	44	0	0	0	0	0	0	4	0	24	2	0
Vega, Vigri, M.H.	2	0	1.000	1.64	10	0	0	0	7	1	11.0	8	47	4	2	0	1	1	2	0	15	2	0
Velazquez, Ernesto, I.F.	3	0	1.000	3.52	6	1	0	0	1	0	15.1	19	68	9	6	1	0	0	2	0	15	1	1
Vitek, Josh, I.F.	5	4	.556	5.05	15	15	0	0	0	0	73.0	92	343	48	41	4	1	5	6	40	0	42	5	1
Wagner, Frank, Hel.*	1	1	.500	10.24	6	4	0	0	0	0	19.1	28	102	28	22	2	1	1	5	14	0	12	6	0
Wallace, Ben, Hel.*	3	7	.300	5.94	16	14	0	0	0	0	69.2	78	332	73	46	10	4	3	3	46	0	44	17	1
Wallace, Kellen, But.	0	0	.000	0.00	1	0	0	0	1	0	1.2	1	5	0	0	0	0	0	0	0	0	0	0	0
Wardle, Sean, Hel.-Og.	0	3	.000	5.35	20	1	0	0	8	0	37.0	41	184	31	22	5	1	3	1	31	3	29	7	2
Warren, Joshua, But.	3	5	.375	8.10	23	4	0	0	10	0	46.2	78	252	62	42	5	2	1	2	31	2	29	11	0
Webster, Jeremy, I.F.*	5	4	.556	4.50	21	0	0	0	7	3	30.0	31	145	23	15	3	0	1	4	24	1	28	3	0
Wells, Carlton, Miss.*	6	2	.750	3.50	24	0	0	0	8	1	43.2	42	184	26	17	2	1	0	12	0	39	3	0
Werner, Kelly, Og.-Hel.*	0	1	.000	6.92	8	2	0	0	1	0	13.0	14	69	16	10	1	0	3	2	14	0	5	1	0
Williams, Justin, I.F.	3	0	1.000	3.98	25	2	0	0	5	0	43.0	43	192	23	19	2	1	1	3	20	1	47	6	0
Williamson, Charles, Miss.	0	0	.000	27.00	1	0	0	0	0	0	0.2	1	5	2	2	0	1	0	1	1	0	0	0	0
Williford, Dan, Miss.*	0	0	.000	13.50	1	0	0	0	1	0	2.0	4	10	3	3	0	0	0	0	3	0	0	0	0
Wilson, Jacob, But.	0	0	.000	0.00	1	0	0	0	0	0	0.0	1	4	4	0	0	0	0	3	0	0	0	0	0
Wright, Shayne, But.	5	0	1.000	2.70	15	5	0	0	4	1	40.0	33	167	15	12	1	2	1	5	14	0	43	5	0
Yoshida, Nobuaki, I.F.*	3	0	1.000	3.00	4	4	0	0	0	0	18.0	16	76	8	6	2	0	0	1	3	0	21	1	0

COMBINATION SHUTOUTS: **Billings (0)**—None. **Butte (1)**—Wright-Warren-Reynoso. **Great Falls (3)**—Rodriguez-Steffek, Tibbs-Glidewell-Keirstad, Hickman-Steffek-Andrews. **Helena (0)**—None. **Idaho Falls (1)**—Velazquez-Meyer-Williams-Belanger. **Medicine Hat (1)**—Hanson-Spillman. **Missoula (3)**—Montoya-Eppolito-Steele-Valverde, Montoya-Steele-Valverde, Stockman-Takach-Ricciardi. **Ogden (5)**—Lugo-Shrout, Gordon-Shorey-Hall, Hendrickson-Nielsen-Batson-Hall, Miniel-McMurray-Hall, Gordon-Batson.

NO-HIT GAMES: None.

Pitcher, Team	W	L	Pct.	ERA	G	GS	CG	ShO	GF	Sv.	IP	H	TBF	R	ER	HR	SH	SF	HB	BB	IBB	SO	WP	Bk.
Neary, Andrew, Hel.	4	3	.571	4.34	21	0	0	0	8	1	47.2	43	199	25	23	7	2	2	1	14	3	27	2	0
Neary, Andrew, Og.	0	0	.000	0.00	1	0	0	0	1	0	1.0	0	4	0	0	0	0	0	0	0	0	2	0	0
Wardle, Sean, Hel.	0	1	.000	4.12	9	1	0	0	1	0	19.2	17	89	12	9	2	1	2	0	14	2	14	1	2
Wardle, Sean, Og.	0	2	.000	6.75	11	0	0	0	7	0	17.1	24	95	19	13	3	0	1	1	17	1	15	6	0
Werner, Kelly, Og.*	0	0	.000	23.14	1	1	0	0	0	0	2.1	4	16	6	6	1	0	1	1	5	0	0	0	0
Werner, Kelly, Hel.*	0	1	.000	3.38	7	1	0	0	1	0	10.2	10	53	10	4	0	0	2	1	9	0	5	1	0

2000 FIELDING

TEAM

Team	Pct.	G	PO	A	E	TC	DP	TP	PB
Idaho Falls	.957	74	1965	833	125	2923	63	0	16
Billings	.957	75	1980	832	127	2939	91	0	19
Ogden	.953	75	2002	751	135	2888	54	0	19
Helena	.952	76	1989	900	147	3036	74	0	29
Missoula	.949	76	2005	898	155	3058	57	0	15
Medicine Hat	.946	76	2008	835	162	3005	65	0	15
Great Falls	.946	76	1976	806	160	2942	67	0	21
Butte	.926	76	1969	828	224	3021	70	0	33

INDIVIDUAL

FIRST BASEMEN

NOTE: All caps denotes fielding-percentage leader based on 38 games for catchers, 51 for all other non-pitchers and 61 innings for pitchers. *Throws lefthanded.

Player, Team	Pct.	G	PO	A	E	TC	DP
Abruzzo, Jared, But.	.978	6	39	5	1	45	5
Anderson, Bryan, Bil.	1.000	1	2	0	0	2	0
Ansman, Craig, Miss.	1.000	2	3	0	0	3	0
Bitter, Jarrod, I.F.	1.000	1	11	0	0	11	1
Calitri, Mike, Bil.	.983	7	54	5	1	60	5
Clark, Daryl, Og.	.971	21	162	7	5	174	6
Contreras, Sergio, But.*	.989	36	335	20	4	359	35
Davenport, Ron, M.H.	.976	42	374	29	10	413	28
De Los Santos, Nelson, Hel.	.971	6	59	9	2	70	4
Detienne, Dave, G.F.	.948	7	49	6	3	58	6
Egly, John, Miss.	.985	57	563	28	9	600	34
Encarnacion, Santos, I.F.	.980	15	138	9	3	150	14
Epstein, Jake, But.	.976	27	226	15	6	247	20
Forelli, Anthony, Hel.	1.000	4	26	4	0	30	0
Geraldo, Anulfo, Hel.	1.000	1	9	0	0	9	2
Hart, Jon, Og.	.978	55	439	40	11	490	39
Jenkins, Kevin, But.*	.906	7	29	0	3	32	6
Kenney, Jeff, Og.	.968	4	26	4	1	31	2
Llamas, Juan, Bil.	.000	1	0	0	0	0	0
Mendoza, Adrian, G.F.	.978	26	208	13	5	226	15
Myers, Corey, Miss.	.974	8	69	6	2	77	7
Napoli, Michael, But.	.962	6	47	3	2	52	0
Noboa, Joel, Miss.	.967	8	84	3	3	90	3
Ramos, Ebaldo, M.H.	.994	19	168	12	1	181	16
Rogers, Brandon, But.	1.000	1	6	1	0	7	0
Ruiz, Randy, Bil.	.984	20	184	3	3	190	22
Sein, Javier, Bil.	.992	48	458	18	4	480	51
Smitherman, Stephen, Bil.	1.000	1	8	0	0	8	1
Story-Harden, Thomari, G.F.	.984	48	413	26	7	446	36
Thompson, Craig, I.F.	1.000	6	66	0	0	66	4
VOLTZ, Robert, Hel.*	.994	64	637	42	4	683	64
Warren, Tom, Hel.	1.000	1	5	0	0	5	0
Williamson, Chris, Bil.*	1.000	3	27	1	0	28	3
Williford, Dan, Miss.*	1.000	4	38	6	0	44	2
Wood, Stephen, M.H.	.993	17	133	8	1	142	10
Woodward, John, I.F.*	.992	52	500	22	4	526	40

SECOND BASEMEN

Player, Team	Pct.	G	PO	A	E	TC	DP
Anderson, Bryan, Bil.	.923	9	21	27	4	52	11
Ayala, Elio, Og.	.989	34	81	93	2	176	22
Bell, Paul, Hel.	.968	5	12	18	1	31	6
Callen, Thomas, M.H.	.965	46	81	111	7	199	27
Campana, Wandel, Bil.	.973	43	78	137	6	221	39
Cordova, Ricardo, G.F.	.933	33	70	96	12	178	20
Davis, James, But.	.919	35	66	71	12	149	17
De La Paz, Camilo, Hel.	.985	19	32	32	1	65	2
Detienne, Dave, G.F.	.898	24	37	60	11	108	10
Duenas, Manuel, I.F.	.939	23	48	60	7	115	16
Furmaniak, Jason, I.F.	.964	11	25	28	2	55	5
GERALDO, Anulfo, Hel.	.951	61	135	178	16	329	34
Green, Andy, Miss.	.963	14	30	47	3	80	11

Player, Team	Pct.	G	PO	A	E	TC	DP
Hake, Travis, Og.	.951	44	84	128	11	223	24
Jaramillo, Milko, G.F.	.945	16	25	44	4	73	13
Johnson, Chris, Bil.	.952	21	52	48	5	105	18
Lagana, Shawn, Miss.	.922	36	48	71	10	129	15
Mayorson, Manuel, M.H.	1.000	1	1	2	0	3	1
McCool, Lee, I.F.	.930	43	87	113	15	215	26
Nunez, Manuel, G.F.	.909	7	7	23	3	33	5
Pichardo, Maximo, But.	.917	25	54	68	11	133	15
Pregnalato, Bob, Og.	1.000	1	1	2	0	3	0
Rivera, William, M.H.	.933	35	66	86	11	163	20
Santos, Luis, Miss.	1.000	1	1	6	0	7	0
Spadt, Eric, Bil.	1.000	3	6	4	0	10	1
Stockton, Jeffrey, But.	.889	7	13	11	3	27	1
Templeton, Garry, But.	.969	8	14	17	1	32	6
Trout, Casey, Og.	.000	1	0	0	0	0	0
Valenzuela, Christian, But.	.868	9	16	17	5	38	8
Varner, Gary, Bil.	.600	1	2	1	2	5	0
Wright, Nate, G.F.	.917	4	5	6	1	12	3
Yakopich, Joseph, Miss.	.917	36	50	82	12	144	12

THIRD BASEMEN

Player, Team	Pct.	G	PO	A	E	TC	DP
Ayala, Elio, Og.	.948	27	20	53	4	77	2
AYBAR, Willy, G.F.	.908	66	51	127	18	196	14
Baderdeen, Kevin, Bil.	.897	17	12	40	6	58	7
Bell, Paul, Hel.	.907	27	18	50	7	75	5
Buelna, Lorenzo, But.	.619	7	5	8	8	21	3
Campo, Michael, But.	1.000	1	2	0	0	2	0
Candelaria, Scott, Og.	.950	5	5	14	1	20	2
Clark, Daryl, Og.	.804	36	22	60	20	102	2
Contrera, Albino, But.*	.692	5	1	8	4	13	0
Davenport, Ron, M.H.	.600	1	0	3	2	5	0
De La Paz, Camilo, Hel.	.846	19	17	38	10	65	3
Detienne, Dave, G.F.	.893	10	6	19	3	28	1
Diaz, Jose, G.F.	1.000	2	1	3	0	4	0
Duenas, Manuel, I.F.	.789	12	9	21	8	38	1
Duplissea, William, G.F.	1.000	1	1	1	0	2	0
Encarnacion, Santos, I.F.	.833	22	8	22	6	36	0
Epstein, Jake, But.	.733	6	4	7	4	15	0
Forelli, Anthony, Hel.	.875	9	6	15	3	24	1
Furmaniak, Jason, I.F.	.667	1	0	2	1	3	0
Garabito, Vianney, Bil.	.921	39	22	83	9	114	4
Geraldo, Anulfo, Hel.	.000	1	0	0	0	0	0
Gray, Joshua, But.	.000	1	0	0	0	0	0
Green, Andy, Miss.	.889	3	2	14	2	18	0
Johnson, Chris, Bil.	.900	11	7	20	3	30	3
Kenney, Jeff, Og.	1.000	4	1	7	0	8	0
Lagana, Shawn, Miss.	.927	20	11	40	4	55	5
Llamas, Juan, Bil.	1.000	4	4	8	0	12	0
Matthews, Delvon, Hel.	.830	36	29	59	18	106	3
McCool, Lee, I.F.	.000	1	0	0	0	0	0
Myers, Corey, Miss.	.880	62	37	109	20	166	5
Noboa, Joel, Miss.	.000	1	0	0	0	0	0
Puccinelli, John, I.F.	.943	46	26	106	8	140	6
Siriveaw, Nom, M.H.	.874	51	39	114	22	175	15
Sisk, Aaron, M.H.	.920	26	20	61	7	88	8
Stockton, Jeffrey, But.	.917	6	2	9	1	12	0
Stone, Todd, Bil.	.833	1	3	2	1	6	2
Story-Harden, Thomari, G.F.	1.000	1	5	0	0	5	1
Templeton, Garry, But.	.846	13	12	21	6	39	2
Trout, Casey, Og.	.933	10	6	8	1	15	0
Valdez, Ramon, But.	1.000	1	1	2	0	3	0
Valenzuela, Christian, But.	.841	44	37	79	22	138	7
Varner, Gary, Bil.	.818	7	4	5	2	11	0
Wilson, Jacob, But.	.833	7	2	8	2	12	0
Yakopich, Joseph, Miss.	.000	1	0	0	0	0	0

SHORTSTOPS

Player, Team	Pct.	G	PO	A	E	TC	DP
Anderson, Bryan, Bil.	.935	48	103	154	18	275	36
Baderdeen, Kevin, Bil.	1.000	2	4	8	0	12	0

SUMMER CLASS A *Pioneer League*

Player, Team	Pct.	G	PO	A	E	TC	DP
Bell, Paul, Hel.	.867	8	10	16	4	30	3
Campana, Wandel, Bil.	.900	24	44	64	12	120	19
Candelaria, Scott, Og.	.892	58	68	146	26	240	27
Cordova, Ricardo, G.F.	.889	2	1	7	1	9	1
Davis, James, But.	.730	8	6	21	10	37	7
De La Paz, Camilo, Hel.	1.000	2	1	1	0	2	0
Detienne, Dave, G.F.	.854	13	20	21	7	48	3
Duenas, Manuel, I.F.	.923	10	9	27	3	39	7
Encarnacion, Santos, I.F.	.952	7	6	14	1	21	2
Furmaniak, Jason, I.F.	.951	47	72	179	13	264	33
Geraldo, Anulfo, Hel.	.900	10	13	23	4	40	1
Gil, Jerry, Miss.	.891	58	98	189	35	322	27
Hake, Travis, Og.	.879	7	10	19	4	33	2
Hawes, Bobby, Bil.	.786	4	0	11	3	14	3
Jaramillo, Milko, G.F.	.935	11	16	27	3	46	5
Lagana, Shawn, Miss.	.955	20	29	55	4	88	11
Mayorson, Manuel, M.H.	.927	53	86	157	19	262	30
McCool, Lee, I.F.	.789	9	6	24	8	38	5
Mendez, Mario, Hel.	.667	5	6	12	9	27	1
Mendez, Pastor, Hel.	1.000	1	1	1	0	2	0
Nunez, Manuel, G.F.	.906	50	76	156	24	256	25
Pichardo, Maximo, But.	.688	4	6	5	5	16	0
Ridley, Jeremy, M.H.	.000	1	0	0	1	1	0
Rivera, William, M.H.	.800	3	4	4	2	10	0
Romero, Nicholas, I.F.	.905	5	6	13	2	21	2
Rowan, Chris, Og.	.818	2	3	6	2	11	1
Santos, Luis, Miss.	1.000	2	0	3	0	3	0
Siriveaw, Nom, M.H.	1.000	1	1	2	0	3	0
Sisk, Aaron, M.H.	.885	21	34	51	11	96	9
Stockton, Jeffrey, But.	.866	40	60	147	32	239	33
Templeton, Garry, But.	.000	2	0	0	1	1	0
Trout, Casey, Og.	.867	5	4	9	2	15	2
Valdez, Ramon, But.	.868	28	37	75	17	129	15
Valenzuela, Christian, But.	.714	2	1	4	2	7	0
WEST, Todd, Hel.-Og.	.943	62	93	221	19	333	52
Wilson, Jacob, But.	1.000	1	2	0	0	2	0
Yakopich, Joseph, Miss.	1.000	1	3	0	0	3	0

SHORTSTOPS WITH TWO OR MORE TEAMS

Player, Team	Pct.	G	PO	A	E	TC	DP
West, Todd, Hel.	.945	57	85	208	17	310	48
West, Todd, Og.	.913	5	8	13	2	23	4

OUTFIELDERS

Player, Team	Pct.	G	PO	A	E	TC	DP
Abercrombie, Reginald, G.F.	.914	52	92	4	9	105	0
Arroyo, Abner, I.F.*	.976	22	39	1	1	41	0
Banks, Almonzo, But.	.500	8	2	0	2	4	0
Barrow, Corey, Bil.	.875	44	36	6	6	48	1
Buelna, Lorenzo, But.	.960	52	114	7	5	126	1
Burns, Kevan, Miss.*	.667	2	2	0	1	3	0
Campo, Michael, But.	.863	34	42	2	7	51	0
Castillo, David, I.F.*	1.000	49	97	7	0	104	0
Contrera, Albino, But.*	.946	33	51	2	3	56	0
Contreras, Sergio, But.*	1.000	11	9	0	0	9	0
Conyer, Darryl, Miss.*	.882	12	15	0	2	17	0
Culwell, Nathan, Bil.	.000	1	0	0	0	0	0
Davenport, Ron, M.H.	1.000	2	1	0	0	1	0
Davis, Morrin, Miss.	.864	34	51	0	8	59	0
Davison, Ashanti, Hel.	1.000	9	11	3	0	14	0
Day, Nick, I.F.	.857	9	10	2	2	14	0
Escalera, Jose, G.F.	.928	51	64	0	5	69	0
Garcia, Jose, G.F.	1.000	3	1	0	0	1	0
Godbolt, Keith, G.F.	.937	47	58	1	4	63	1
Gray, Joshua, But.	.667	1	2	0	1	3	0
GUERRERO, Cris, Og.	.981	63	97	9	2	108	0
Guerrero, Hector, G.F.*	.857	8	12	0	2	14	0
Hall, Victor, Miss.*	.974	70	104	7	3	114	3
Hicks, Brian, Hel.*	.938	59	103	2	7	112	0
Janek, John, Bil.	1.000	2	1	0	0	1	0
January, Javerro, Og.	.974	42	68	6	2	76	0
Jaramillo, Milko, G.F.	1.000	14	18	3	0	21	0
Jenkins, Kevin, But.*	.860	40	46	3	8	57	0
Johnson, Chris, Bil.	1.000	19	38	0	0	38	0
Johnson, Jeremy, M.H.*	.960	48	93	2	4	99	1
Kail, Tom, Miss.	.909	27	28	2	3	33	0
Kimberley, Glynn, M.H.	.935	25	42	1	3	46	1
Krynzel, Dave, Og.*	.955	34	61	3	3	67	1
Leflore, Alex, Bil.	.926	17	24	1	2	27	1
Lipowicz, Nathan, G.F.	.932	43	66	3	5	74	0
Little, James, But.	.973	49	104	4	3	111	1
Mayo, Terry, Hel.	.941	57	91	4	6	101	1
McCarty, Brock, Miss.	.971	41	32	1	1	34	0

Player, Team	Pct.	G	PO	A	E	TC	DP
McClanahan, Jonah, Og.	.917	28	43	1	4	48	0
Mendoza, Adrian, G.F.	.944	16	16	1	1	18	0
Negron, Miguel, M.H.*	.941	52	92	4	6	102	0
Noboa, Joel, Miss.	.875	25	26	2	4	32	0
Nohr, Ryan, Og.	1.000	22	18	2	0	20	0
O'Donnell, Ryan, I.F.	.938	13	28	2	2	32	1
Palomares, Luis, Hel.	1.000	3	5	0	0	5	0
Paulino, Armando, M.H.	.922	62	98	9	9	116	3
Pregnalato, Bob, Og.	.946	58	114	8	7	129	0
Reese, Kevin, I.F.*	.925	44	59	3	5	67	1
Rikert, Wade, M.H.	.852	17	22	1	4	27	0
Smith, Ryan, Bil.	1.000	46	79	5	0	84	0
Smitherman, Stephen, Bil.	.965	60	76	6	3	85	0
Sobet, Renato, I.F.	.879	33	45	6	7	58	0
Soriano, Carlos, Hel.	.884	33	34	4	5	43	0
Terrero, Luis, Miss.	.949	68	80	14	5	99	0
Thompson, Craig, I.F.	.985	49	63	4	1	68	0
Thompson, Zachary, Hel.*	.923	36	45	3	4	52	0
Thulin, Thomas, But.	1.000	6	9	2	0	11	0
Trout, Casey, Og.	1.000	6	7	0	0	7	0
Vandemore, Tony, I.F.	1.000	10	8	2	0	10	0
Villero, Armando, Hel.	.941	50	48	0	3	51	0
Wallace, Colin, But.	.950	25	35	3	2	40	1
Ward, Corey, Bil.	.967	24	26	3	1	30	1
Williamson, Chris, Bil.*	.929	21	37	2	3	42	0
Williford, Dan, Miss.*	1.000	1	1	0	0	1	0

CATCHERS

Player, Team	Pct.	G	PO	A	E	TC	DP	PB
Abruzzo, Jared, But.	.970	47	280	39	10	329	0	24
Ansman, Craig, Miss.	.979	17	120	18	3	141	1	2
Aracena, Sandy, G.F.	1.000	6	46	3	0	49	1	4
Belcher, Jason, Hel.	.983	26	152	22	3	177	1	7
Bitter, Jarrod, I.F.	1.000	3	17	3	0	20	1	1
Blackburn, John, M.H.	.956	18	124	7	6	137	1	7
CULWELL, Nathan, Bil.	.988	39	284	46	4	334	4	12
Delgado, Jorge, Miss.	.982	37	290	42	6	338	3	6
De Los Santos, Nelson, Hel.	.966	11	74	10	3	87	0	2
Diaz, Jose, G.F.	.973	54	479	62	15	556	4	9
Duplissea, William, G.F.	.909	2	9	1	1	11	0	0
Foster, Brian, Og.	.976	44	306	19	8	333	1	9
Gomez, Andre, I.F.	.986	9	62	8	1	71	2	0
Gragg, Shaun, Og.	.985	34	234	25	4	263	0	8
Gutierrez, Said, I.F.	.917	6	39	5	4	48	0	1
Johnson, Kade, Og.	1.000	2	9	0	0	9	0	0
Lake, Josh, Hel.-Og.	.938	3	13	2	1	16	0	4
Loeb, Bryan, Miss.	.980	31	178	22	4	204	0	6
Martinez, Casey, M.H.	.987	9	68	7	1	76	0	4
Melton, John, Miss.	1.000	2	15	2	0	17	0	1
Napoli, Michael, But.	.933	3	10	4	1	15	0	1
Pagan, Andres, I.F.	.985	40	294	25	5	324	0	10
Price, Jared, G.F.	.980	16	88	8	2	98	0	8
Riley, Brett, But.	1.000	1	1	0	0	1	0	0
Rogers, Brandon, But.	1.000	6	43	4	0	47	0	3
Santiago, Daniel, Bil.	.979	18	125	12	3	140	1	2
Schilling, Chris, Og.-Hel.	.990	18	80	17	1	98	0	6
Small, Chris, M.H.	.984	38	264	35	5	304	0	3
Sparks, Eddie, Bil.	1.000	6	36	6	0	42	0	2
Stone, Todd, Bil.	.933	16	97	15	8	120	0	3
Tindell, Matt, Hel.	.975	40	243	34	7	284	2	12
Trzesniak, Nick, I.F.	.984	24	163	20	3	186	0	4
Umbria, Jose, M.H.	.985	14	114	17	2	133	0	1
Vega, Jesus, But.	.980	26	162	30	4	196	1	5

CATCHERS WITH TWO OR MORE TEAMS

Player, Team	Pct.	G	PO	A	E	TC	DP	PB
Lake, Josh, Hel.	.929	2	11	2	1	14	0	4
Lake, Josh, Og.	1.000	1	2	0	0	2	0	0
Schilling, Chris, Og.	1.000	10	47	6	0	53	0	2
Schilling, Chris, Hel.	.978	8	33	11	1	45	0	4

PITCHERS

Player, Team	Pct.	G	PO	A	E	TC	DP
Abbott, James, M.H.	1.000	2	1	4	0	5	0
Andrews, Aron, G.F.	1.000	19	1	4	0	5	0
Arellan, Felix, G.F.*	.000	13	0	0	1	1	0
Artman, Dane, Og.*	1.000	7	3	3	0	6	1
Baldassano, Joseph, But.	.875	25	3	4	1	8	0
Banks, Almonzo, But.	.000	3	0	0	0	0	0
Batson, Byron, Og.	1.000	20	6	4	0	10	0
Belanger, Brandon, I.F.	.917	31	4	7	1	12	0
Belicic, Adam, But.*	1.000	17	2	5	0	7	1
Bell, Casey, But.	1.000	3	0	1	0	1	0

Player, Team	Pct.	G	PO	A	E	TC	DP
Belson, Gregory, Miss.	1.000	3	1	1	0	2	0
Bevis, P.J., Miss.	.914	14	6	26	3	35	1
Bimeal, Matt, M.H.	1.000	21	1	4	0	5	0
Bonilla, Ben, Miss.*	1.000	2	1	1	0	2	0
Boutwell, Andy, Bil.	.625	23	0	5	3	8	0
Brazoban, Jose, Hel.	1.000	24	1	1	0	2	0
Brown, Paul, Bil.*	.800	5	2	6	2	10	0
Brown, Tighe, Bil.	1.000	7	0	5	0	5	1
Bussard, Jesse, I.F.	1.000	20	0	5	0	5	0
Bynum, Matthew, Bil.	.429	8	1	2	4	7	0
Cassel, Jack, I.F.	1.000	7	0	1	0	1	0
Castillo, Geraldo, Hel.	.875	17	3	11	2	16	3
Chapman, Dennis, I.F.	1.000	21	1	2	0	3	0
Chulk, Charles, M.H.	.950	14	7	12	1	20	0
Cimorelli, Brett, But.	1.000	7	1	3	0	4	0
Collins, Clint, Bil.	1.000	22	1	5	0	6	1
Cooper, Eric, Bil.	.000	3	0	0	0	0	0
Cordero, Jesus, G.F.	.875	18	2	5	1	8	1
Cordero, Victor, Hel.	1.000	8	2	5	0	7	1
Cramblitt, Joey, Miss.	.333	5	0	1	2	3	0
Culp, Brandon, Bil.	1.000	7	1	0	0	1	0
Curtis, Bill, But.	1.000	7	1	4	0	5	2
Daigle, Casey, Miss.	.826	15	7	12	4	23	0
D'Amico, Leonardo, But.	1.000	7	2	2	0	4	0
De La Cruz, Pedro, Hel.	1.000	8	1	1	0	2	0
Durkee, Jeremy, Hel.*	1.000	18	2	7	0	9	0
Duverge, Alcides, But.	.000	8	0	0	0	0	0
Earey, Ryan, I.F.	.923	14	0	12	1	13	0
Edwards, Bryan, Bil.	1.000	4	0	1	0	1	0
Eppolito, Vince, Miss.	.833	20	2	8	2	12	2
Fawcett, Mike, Bil.	.800	14	0	4	1	5	1
Fischer, Richard, But.	.833	18	3	17	4	24	4
Flading, Cameron, But.	.000	4	0	0	0	0	0
Fletcher, Daniel, Bil.	.667	8	1	1	1	3	0
Flores, Neomar, M.H.	.000	1	0	0	0	0	0
Gardea, Mario, Bil.	1.000	23	2	2	0	4	1
George, Bradley, Bil.	1.000	11	4	2	0	6	1
Gilmore, Travis, But.*	.800	14	2	2	1	5	0
Glidewell, Clifton, G.F.*	.857	6	0	6	1	7	0
Gomez, Hunter, Hel.	1.000	12	0	3	0	3	0
Gordon, Justin, Og.*	.889	16	5	11	2	18	0
Gracesqui, Franklyn, M.H.*	.818	8	0	9	2	11	1
Gray, Rusty, Og.	1.000	8	2	4	0	6	0
Gruban, Jarret, But.	.900	8	2	7	1	10	0
Guzman, Alexis, M.H.	.875	27	2	12	2	16	2
Hall, Dan, Og.	1.000	23	4	1	0	5	0
Hanrahan, Joel, G.F.	.867	12	3	10	2	15	0
Hanson, David, M.H.	.889	15	7	9	2	18	1
Hebert, Cedric, Bil.	.917	8	2	9	1	12	0
Heck, Christopher, I.F.*	1.000	19	1	2	0	3	0
Henderson, Eric, Og.	.000	1	0	0	0	0	0
Hendrickson, Benjamin, Og.	1.000	13	3	5	0	8	0
Hensley, Matthew, But.	.846	8	1	10	2	13	0
Herbert, John, I.F.	1.000	17	2	5	0	7	0
Hickman, Jason, G.F.	.889	12	1	7	1	9	2
Hosford, Clinton, G.F.	1.000	17	3	11	0	14	0
Hoyt, Michael, I.F.	1.000	16	1	2	0	3	0
Hussman, Darrell, Bil.	1.000	3	0	2	0	2	0
Jenks, Robert, But.	.929	14	3	10	1	14	0
Joseph, Glen, Bil.	1.000	8	0	3	0	3	0
Keirstead, Michael, G.F.	.933	18	8	6	1	15	2
Laesch, Michael, Bil.	1.000	24	3	6	0	9	1
Landkamer, Michael, Bil.	1.000	6	0	2	0	2	0
Lansford, Dustin, Hel.*	1.000	11	2	3	0	5	2
Larman, Jayson, Bil.	1.000	7	1	0	0	1	0
Lasose, Enrique, Og.	1.000	13	2	0	0	2	0
Lesieur, Christopher, Miss.	1.000	23	2	0	0	2	0
Lizarraga, Edgar, G.F.	.833	24	2	3	1	6	0
Lorenzen, Jonathan, G.F.	1.000	14	3	5	0	8	0
Lowe, Matt, Og.	.000	2	0	0	0	0	0
Lugo, Ruddy, Og.	.737	16	7	7	5	19	1
Lutz, Kenneth, G.F.	.600	7	0	3	2	5	0
Martinez, Ramon, G.F.	1.000	6	0	1	0	1	0
Maysonet, Roberto, Hel.	.857	15	4	8	2	14	0
McAdoo, Duncan, I.F.	1.000	9	2	15	0	17	0
McCullem, Ryan, M.H.*	.900	16	2	7	1	10	0
McCulloch, Andrew, M.H.	1.000	27	1	1	0	2	0
McGowan, Dustin, M.H.	.875	8	1	6	1	8	0
McMillan, Joshua, M.H.*	.850	15	2	15	3	20	0
McMurray, Heath, Og.	1.000	12	4	5	0	9	0
Mendez, Pastor, Hel.	.000	2	0	0	0	0	0
Meyer, John, I.F.	.800	17	2	6	2	10	1
MILLER, Ryan, Og.	1.000	15	8	12	0	20	1
Milo, Anthony, But.*	1.000	12	2	5	0	7	0
Miniel, Roberto, Og.	.900	16	3	6	1	10	0
Montero, Agustin, G.F.	.750	11	0	3	1	4	0
Montoya, Saul, Miss.	1.000	8	4	9	0	13	1
Moore, Greg, But.	1.000	7	0	7	0	7	1
Morris, William, M.H.	1.000	24	1	5	0	6	0
Neary, Andrew, Hel.-Og.	1.000	22	3	10	0	13	0
Nielsen, Brian, Og.*	1.000	10	0	1	0	1	0
Nohr, Ryan, Og.	.000	1	0	0	0	0	0
Nunez, Severino, Hel.*	1.000	16	3	8	0	11	1
Nunley, Derrek, M.H.	1.000	8	0	2	0	2	0
O'Gara, Dan, Hel.	.833	10	2	3	1	6	0
Ovalles, Juan, Miss.	.917	8	6	5	1	12	0
Ozuna, Benigno, Hel.	.938	21	9	6	1	16	0
Padilla, Edgar, But.	1.000	4	0	2	0	2	0
Pape, Stace, Bil.	.000	4	0	0	0	0	0
Patten, Lanny, M.H.	.769	17	2	8	3	13	0
Peralta, Joel, But.	.500	10	0	1	1	2	0
Perez, Oliver, I.F.*	1.000	5	1	10	0	11	1
Perkins, Gregory, Miss.	.889	6	0	8	1	9	0
Phillips, Mark, I.F.*	.714	10	0	5	2	7	0
Pike, Matthew, Bil.	1.000	2	0	1	0	1	0
Reynoso, Roberto, But.	.786	11	4	7	3	14	0
Ricciardi, Joseph, Miss.	1.000	25	2	6	0	8	0
Rivera, Ramon, But.	1.000	15	1	5	0	6	0
Rodriguez, Ricardo, G.F.	.875	15	7	7	2	16	1
Rojas, Chris, I.F.	1.000	2	1	0	0	1	0
Rosario, Andres, G.F.	.800	19	2	2	1	5	0
Ross, Brian, Bil.*	.500	14	0	1	1	2	0
Ross, Lew, Miss.*	1.000	23	3	3	0	6	0
Rossellini, William, Miss.	.750	5	0	3	1	4	0
Schachleiter, Jeff, Bil.	.333	7	1	0	2	3	0
Shabansky, Rob, Miss.*	.917	11	3	8	1	12	0
Sheefel, Adam, Bil.*	.950	16	0	19	1	20	2
Shorey, Jeremy, Og.	.750	15	3	0	1	4	0
Shrout, Kevin, Og.	.818	14	6	3	2	11	0
Shwam, Mike, Hel.	.857	23	0	6	1	7	1
Silverio, Marcelino, I.F.	.833	25	2	3	1	6	0
Smith, Ryan, Bil.	1.000	1	0	2	0	2	0
Spillman, Jeromie, M.H.*	.786	22	1	10	3	14	1
Steele, Matt, Miss.	.800	16	1	3	1	5	0
Steffek, Brian, G.F.	1.000	21	3	3	0	6	0
Stephenson, Eric, M.H.	1.000	19	3	4	0	7	0
Stockman, Phil, Miss.	1.000	2	1	0	0	1	0
Takach, Ryan, Miss.*	1.000	24	3	10	0	13	0
Thomas, Adam, But.	1.000	6	1	3	0	4	1
Thompson, Jesse, Bil.	.833	9	1	4	1	6	1
Thompson, Mike, I.F.	1.000	14	2	10	0	12	0
Thorpe, Tracy, M.H.	.800	11	1	3	1	5	0
Tibbs, Jeffrey, G.F.	1.000	14	1	9	0	10	1
Tisdale, Marlyn, Bil.	1.000	8	1	4	0	5	0
Tomsu, Joshua, Bil.	.889	12	3	5	1	9	0
Trejo, Francisco, Miss.*	.786	10	2	9	3	14	1
Valenzuela, Christian, But.	.000	2	0	0	0	0	0
Valverde, Jose, Miss.	1.000	12	2	1	0	3	0
Vega, Vigri, M.H.	.500	10	0	1	1	2	0
Velazquez, Ernesto, I.F.	.833	6	0	5	1	6	0
Vitek, Josh, I.F.	1.000	15	3	8	0	11	2
Wagner, Frank, Hel.*	.667	6	0	4	2	6	0
Wallace, Ben, Hel.*	.905	16	3	16	2	21	0
Wallace, Kellen, But.	.000	1	0	0	0	0	0
Wardle, Sean, Hel.-Og.	.750	20	0	6	2	8	0
Warren, Joshua, But.	.923	23	5	7	1	13	1
Webster, Jeremy, I.F.*	.500	21	2	2	4	8	0
Wells, Carlton, Miss.*	1.000	24	2	14	0	16	0
Werner, Kelly, Og.-Hel.*	1.000	8	3	2	0	5	0
Williams, Justin, I.F.	.800	25	0	4	1	5	0
Williamson, Charles, Miss.	.000	1	0	0	0	0	0
Williford, Dan, Miss.*	1.000	1	0	1	0	1	0
Wilson, Jacob, But.	.000	1	0	0	0	0	0
Wright, Shayne, But.	.889	15	3	5	1	9	0
Yoshida, Nobuaki, I.F.*	1.000	4	0	1	0	1	0

PITCHERS WITH TWO OR MORE TEAMS

Player, Team	Pct.	G	PO	A	E	TC	DP
Neary, Andrew, Hel.	1.000	21	3	10	0	13	0
Neary, Andrew, Og.	.000	1	0	0	0	0	0
Wardle, Sean, Hel.	1.000	9	0	6	0	6	0
Wardle, Sean, Og.	.000	11	0	0	2	2	0
Werner, Kelly, Og.*	1.000	1	0	1	0	1	0
Werner, Kelly, Hel.*	1.000	7	3	1	0	4	0

LEAGUE CHAMPIONS

Year	Team	Pct.	Year	Team	Pct.	Year	Team	Pct.
1939—	Twin Falls*	.581		Billings (2nd)*	.523	1984—	Billings	.691
1940—	Salt Lake City	.608	1960—	Boise†	.686		Helena▲	.647
	Ogden (4th)*	.492		Idaho Falls	.650	1985—	Great Falls	.771
1941—	Boise	.623	1961—	Boise	.638		Salt Lake City▲	.657
	Ogden (2nd)*	.598		Great Falls*	.571	1986—	Salt Lake City◆	.643
1942—	Pocatello†	.690	1962—	Boise§	.565		Great Falls	.571
	Boise	.683		Billings†	.706	1987—	Salt Lake City◆	.700
1943-44-45—Did not operate.			1963—	Idaho Falls	.702		Helena	.657
1946—	Twin Falls‡	.585		Magic Valley†	.643	1988—	Great Falls◆	.754
	Salt Lake City†	.585	1964—	Treasure Valley	.615		Butte	.629
1947—	Salt Lake City	.618	1965—	Treasure Valley	.530	1989—	Great Falls◆	.791
	Twin Falls†	.600	1966—	Ogden	.591		Butte	.621
1948—	Pocatello	.611	1967—	Ogden	.621	1990—	Great Falls◆	.706
	Twin Falls (2nd)*	.595	1968—	Ogden	.609		Salt Lake	.618
1949—	Twin Falls	.624	1969—	Ogden	.620	1991—	Salt Lake City◆	.700
	Pocatello (3rd)*	.595	1970—	Idaho Falls	.629		Great Falls	.657
1950—	Pocatello	.635	1971—	Great Falls	.643	1992—	Salt Lake	.697
	Billings (3rd)*	.571	1972—	Billings	.694		Billings◆	.697
1951—	Salt Lake City	.618	1973—	Billings	.629	1993—	Billings◆	.653
	Great Falls (3rd)*	.559	1974—	Idaho Falls	.569		Helena	.589
1952—	Pocatello	.595	1975—	Great Falls	.577	1994—	Billings◆	.694
	Idaho Falls (2nd)*	.573	1976—	Great Falls	.577		Helena	.611
1953—	Ogden	.679	1977—	Lethbridge	.629	1995—	Billings	.710
	Salt Lake City (4th)*	.527	1978—	Billings∞	.735		Helena■	.690
1954—	Salt Lake City	.595	1979—	Helena	.623	1996—	Helena■	.597
	Great Falls (4th)*	.530		Lethbridge	.559		Ogden	.583
1955—	Boise	.588	1980—	Lethbridge▲	.743	1997—	Great Falls	.556
	Magic Valley (4th)*	.489		Billings	.629		Billings■	.549
1956—	Boise	.561	1981—	Calgary	.657	1998—	Medicine Hat	.622
1957—	Salt Lake City	.650		Butte▲	.557		Idaho Falls■	.618
	Billings†	.582	1982—	Medicine Hat▲	.629	1999—	Idaho Falls	.640
1958—	Great Falls	.582		Idaho Falls	.600		Missoula■	.592
	Boise†	.615	1983—	Billings▲	.614	2000—	Idaho Falls■	.608
1959—	Boise	.633		Calgary	.600			

*Won four-club playoff. †Won split-season playoff. ‡Ended first half in tie with Salt Lake City and won one-game playoff. §Ended first half in tie with Billings and Great Falls and won playoff. ∞Billings (first place) defeated Idaho Falls (second place) in first place-second place playoff. ▲League divided into Northern and Southern divisions; won two-club playoff. ◆Won two-club playoff. ■League divided into Northern and Southern divisions; won four-club playoff.

MINOR LEAGUE INDEX

TEAMS AND CITIES

MINOR LEAGUE INDEX